To Phil,

Divided by a common language
(and you can't spell either!)

Jane

May 1995.

COLLINS
TODAY'S
ENGLISH
DICTIONARY

THE UNIVERSITY OF BIRMINGHAM

COLLINS COBUILD

HarperCollins*Publishers*

HarperCollins Publishers
77-85 Fulham Palace Road
London W6 8JB

COBUILD is a trademark of William Collins & Sons Ltd

This edition, first published in Great Britain 1995
© HarperCollins Publishers Ltd. 1995

10 9 8 7 6 5 4 3 2 1

ISBN 0 00 370949 3

Computer Typeset by
Morton Word Processing, Scarborough, England
Printed in Great Britain by
HarperCollinsManufacturing, Glasgow

Corpus Acknowledgements

We would like to acknowledge the assistance of the many
hundreds of individuals and companies who have kindly given
permission for copyright material to be used in The Bank of
English. The written sources include many national and regional
newspapers in Britain and overseas; magazine and periodical
publishers; and book publishers in Britain, the United States and
Australia. Extensive spoken data has been provided by radio
and television broadcasting companies; research workers at
many universities and other institutions; and individual
numerous contributors. We are grateful to them all.

Note

Entered words that we have reason to believe constitute
trademarks have been designated as such. However, neither the
presence nor absence of such designation should be regarded
as affecting the legal status of any trademark.

Editorial Team

Editor in Chief
John Sinclair

Editorial Director
Gwyneth Fox

Editor
John Todd

Compilers

Catherine Brown	Isabel Griffiths	Sean Lynch
Helen Bruce	Hazel Harrison	David Morrow
Sheila Ferguson	Ann Hewings	Heather Raybould

Researcher	**Computer Staff**	**Production and Design**
Rita Todd	Zoe James	Jill McNair
	Tim Lane	Ted Carden
		Greg Whyte

**Managing Director,
Collins Dictionaries**
Richard Thomas

The publishers and editorial team would like to thank Diana Adams and
Sheila Ferguson from Collins English Dictionaries for editorial
assistance; and Julie Till for additional research.

Preface

The editors of this dictionary have made use of today's ideas and technology to create a dictionary which is as simple and straightforward to use as possible. There are two essential stages in the dictionary-making process. First, the evidence for the meanings of words in present-day English is gathered and processed by computer; and then the definitions are written in plain, everyday English.

This represents a revolution in the way dictionaries are made. Since the early eighties computers have made it possible for us to store more and more documents, and read them automatically and at speeds well beyond human powers. Behind this dictionary there is a huge store of over 200 million words of very recent English, and all the statements we make about the language arise from and agree with this store, which is called The Bank of English.

Many kinds of English are found in the Bank. The language of newspapers, books, magazines, official documents, and correspondence is there in large quantities. A quarter or so consists of transcriptions from the spoken language, including 15 million words recorded and transcribed from ordinary conversation. Around a quarter of it is from America, and there are smaller amounts from other English-speaking countries.

When we came to write the dictionary in the light of this evidence, we turned our backs on centuries of dictionary-making, and worked out a style of presentation that is very close to the way ordinary people talk about words. We give top priority to a straightforward explanation of meaning, using full English sentences, not notes and abbreviations. We write informally when we are defining a word that is used informally, and we use quite colloquial English. If a word is really restricted in use, we say so, but only sparingly.

We pay most attention to the words and phrases that are commonly in use, rather than load the book with technical terms or words found only in crossword puzzles. So this is a dictionary for a *user* of English, not a mere observer or critic.

We do not draw attention to the spelling or pronunciation of a word unless there is a possible difficulty – a rare word with an unusual pronunciation or an irregular past tense of a verb. In particular, we do not include any grammatical parts of speech, because our full-sentence definitions make it clear whether a word is a noun or a verb, an adjective or an adverb, and so on.

Why should you turn to a dictionary of your own language? Perhaps to check a meaning that you are not quite sure of, or to settle an argument, or to look up a new word. This dictionary is as up-to-date as modern methods can make it, and all the examples are quotations from recent texts. It should help you keep abreast of how the language is changing and how words are being used today.

We hope that you will find this new style of dictionary genuinely helpful. However, our work continues, and we would be grateful to hear from any users who have suggestions for further improvements.

John Sinclair
Editor in Chief
Professor of Modern English Language
University of Birmingham

A a

a (an) ❏ A and **an** are called the 'indefinite article'. You use them when you are mentioning someone or something for the first time. *A motorist escaped injury when her car overturned on the M25... Ludwig used the $5,000 to buy an old paddle steamer.* ◇ You also use **a** or **an** when you are making a general statement about a kind of person or thing. *A nurse must follow the doctor's orders... It is virtually impossible to force an aircraft to change course.* ❏ A and **an** are sometimes used instead of the number one. *The meeting was all over in less than an hour.* ◇ A and **an** are used to talk about rates, prices, and measurements. For example, if someone charges £10 an hour for their work, they charge £10 for each hour. *A patterned floor costs between £35 and £100 a square metre... ...a following wind of 3.9 metres a second.*

A-bomb See atomic bomb.

à la in front of a name means 'in the style of'. *...a peace camp à la Greenham Common... Bradshaw made Southall scramble with a shot from wide on the right à la Peter Beardsley.*

à la carte If you eat à la carte in a restaurant, you choose individual dishes from the menu, rather than paying a fixed price for a complete meal. ◇ À la carte is used to talk about other situations where people can make their own selection of what they want. For example, a travel firm might offer à la carte holidays, in which customers plan a holiday from available units, rather than having to have a complete package.

A-Level A-levels are the exams English, Welsh, and Northern Irish teenagers usually take if they stay on at school until they are 18. 'A-level' stands for 'Advanced Level'.

a priori (*pron:* ch pry or rye) If you work something out a priori, you do it using reason alone, rather than by experiment or finding out facts.

AA The AA is a British organization which helps members with advice on motoring and when their cars break down. AA stands for 'Automobile Association'. ◇ AA is also an organization which helps people suffering from alcoholism. AA stands for 'Alcoholics Anonymous'.

aback See take.

abacus (*pron:* ab-a-cuss) (abacuses) An **abacus** is a device for counting. It consists of horizontal metal rods mounted on a frame; on the rods are coloured beads, which you slide to left or right.

abandon (abandoning, abandoned; abandonment) ❏ If people **abandon** a place, they leave it empty with nobody to look after it. *...an abandoned Catholic church... Abandonment of the area looks inevitable.* Similarly, a vehicle can be **abandoned**. ◇ When people **abandon ship**, they leave it because it is sinking.

❏ If someone **abandons** a member of their family, they leave them for good, because they do not love them or cannot look after them.

❏ If you **abandon** something you are doing, you stop doing it without finishing it. *He abandoned his studies after two years... Israel had to abandon plans to build its own*

fighter-bomber. ◇ If you **abandon** hope, you give up hope of something happening. ◇ If you **abandon** something like a religion or a political theory, you give it up, because you no longer believe in it.

❏ If you do something **with abandon**, you do it in an unrestrained way, without worrying about the consequences.

abase (abasing, abased) If you **abase** yourself, you say how unimportant or useless you are, or draw attention to all your faults.

abate (abating, abated; abatement) If something unpleasant **abates**, it becomes less severe. *The violence seems unlikely to abate in the near future.* When people reduce the effects of something unpleasant, this is called **abatement**. *...pollution abatement... ...the Noise Abatement Society.*

abattoir (*pron:* ab-a-twahr) An **abattoir** is a place where animals are taken to be killed for their meat.

abbess (abbesses) An **abbess** is a nun in charge of other nuns, especially in an abbey.

abbey An **abbey** is a church with buildings attached for monks or nuns to live in, or a church which originally had buildings like these.

abbot An **abbot** is a monk in charge of other monks in a monastery or abbey.

abbreviate (abbreviating, abbreviated; abbreviation) If something is **abbreviated**, it is made shorter. *...an abbreviated schedule.* ◇ If a word or phrase is **abbreviated**, it is made shorter by leaving out some of the letters, or by using only the first letters of each word. A shortened form of a word or phrase is called an **abbreviation**.

ABC ❏ When children learn their ABC, they learn to recognize, write, or say the alphabet.

❏ ABC often appears in the titles of books which claim to tell you the basic, most important things about a subject. *'The ABC of Communism'... 'ABC of Herbs and Plants and their Growing Requirements'.*

abdicate (abdicating, abdicated; abdication) ❏ If a monarch **abdicates** or **abdicates** the throne, he or she formally gives up their position of monarch. *...the abdication of Edward VIII.*

❏ If you **abdicate** a right, you give it up. ◇ If you **abdicate** an opportunity, you fail to take advantage of it. *Mrs Thatcher abdicated the chance for Britain to influence Europe in the next decade.* ◇ If you **abdicate** responsibility for something, you say you will not be responsible for it any more.

abdomen (abdominal) The **abdomen** is the part of the body below the chest where the stomach and intestines are. **Abdominal** is used to talk about things to do with the abdomen. *...the abdominal cavity... ...abdominal pain.*

abduct (abduction, abductor) If someone **abducts** another person, they take them away illegally, usually by force; you say they are the person's **abductor**. *A woman posing as a social worker tried to abduct a two-year-old boy... ...the abduction and harassment of anti-apartheid activists.*

aberrant (*pron:* ab-ber-ant) (aberration) If you say something is **aberrant** or an **aberration**, you mean it is not normal or not part of the natural order of things. *...aberrant behaviour... Violations of human rights were not aberrations but part of official policy.*

abet (abetting, abetted) If you **abet** someone, you help or encourage them to do something wrong or illegal. *Milken pleaded guilty to aiding and abetting tax crimes.*

abeyance If something is in **abeyance**, it will not be carried out for the time being. *The threat is likely to remain in abeyance... The plan has been put in abeyance.*

abhor (*pron:* ab-**hor** *or* ab-**bor**) (abhorring, abhorred; abhorrence, abhorrent) If you **abhor** something or find it **abhorrent**, you feel it is extremely unpleasant or evil. You can talk about your **abhorrence** of something. *He abhorred violence... This practice is abhorrent to the Asian-American community... The world community has marked its abhorrence of what happened last year.*

abide (abiding, abided) ❑ If you say you cannot **abide** someone or something, you mean you dislike them very much.
❑ If you **abide by** a law, agreement, or decision, you do what it says. ◇ See also **law-abiding**.
❑ An **abiding** feeling, impression, or quality lasts for a long time. *His abiding passion was ocean racing... ...an image which will be my abiding memory of the Games.*

ability (abilities) If you have the **ability** to do something, you have the skills or qualities needed for it. *No one doubts his ability to make sound judgments... I did not trust my swimming abilities and stayed on the beach.*

abject (abjectly) **Abject** is used to emphasize how shameful or depressing something is. *Most of them live in abject poverty... ...a policy that ended in abject failure... High street sales were abjectly weak.* ◇ If someone's behaviour is **abject**, they show no self-respect, courage, or pride.

abjure (abjuring, abjured) If you **abjure** something like a belief or way of behaving, (a) you announce you are giving it up. *It's the signal for them to abjure their responsibilities.* (b) you avoid it, or say you are against it. *The Pope is likely to abjure any triumphalist tone... He does not abjure violence.*

ablaze If something is **ablaze**, it is on fire. *New Age travellers set a County Council building ablaze yesterday.* ◇ If something is **ablaze** with bright colours or lights, it is full of them, and they are very noticeable. *The churchyard is ablaze with crimson lobelia.*

able (abler, ablest; ably) ❑ If you are **able** to do something, you have the skill, qualities, knowledge, means, or opportunity to do it.
❑ An **able** person can be relied on to do something well. If you do something **ably**, you do it well. *...one of the brightest and ablest members of the government... He will be ably assisted by the new deputy Prime Minister.*

able-bodied people are strong, healthy, and capable of working.

ablutions If you perform your **ablutions**, you wash yourself.

ably See **able**.

abnegate (abnegating, abnegated) If you **abnegate** something like a duty or responsibility, you do not do what you are supposed to.

abnormal (abnormally; abnormality, abnormalities) You say something is **abnormal** when it happens or develops in an unusual way. *...abnormal behaviour... The cells divide*

and grow abnormally. You call something like this an **abnormality**. *...bone abnormalities.*

aboard If you are **aboard** a ship or plane, you are on it or in it.

abode Your **abode** is the place where you live. ◇ If you have the **right of abode** in a country, you are legally entitled to live there.

abolish (abolishes, abolishing, abolished) If something like a system is **abolished**, it is officially ended.

abolition (abolitionist) The ending of something like a system is called its **abolition**. *He argued for the abolition of the monarchy.* **Abolitionists** are people who want something to be ended.

abominable (abominably) If you say something is **abominable**, you mean it is extremely unpleasant and evil. *...an abominable crime... He treated her abominably.* ◇ **Abominable Snowman:** see **yeti**.

abominate (abominating, abominated; abomination) If you **abominate** something or regard it as an **abomination**, you dislike it intensely, because you think it is wrong or evil.

aboriginal An **Aboriginal** is a member of one of the tribes who were already living in Australia when Europeans arrived. **Aboriginal** is used to talk about things connected with these people. *...Aboriginal leaders... ...Aboriginal art.* ◇ The **aboriginal** people of a place are the ones who lived there first, before others arrived. *...India's aboriginal tribes.*

Aborigine (*pron:* ab-or-**rij**-in-ee) An **Aborigine** is the same as an Aboriginal. Some people think 'Aborigine' is a racist word.

abort (abortion) ❑ If a woman has an **abortion**, her pregnancy is deliberately ended before the foetus has formed properly and the foetus dies. When this happens, you can say the foetus is **aborted**. ◇ In medical terms, if a pregnant woman **aborts**, she has a miscarriage.
❑ If something which had been planned is **aborted**, it does not take place, because something is wrong. *The plane had to abort its takeoff... ...an aborted attack.*

abortive If an attempt to do something is **abortive**, it fails. *...an abortive coup.*

abound If things **abound** in a place or it **abounds** with them, there are a lot of them there. *Clubs and societies abound... San Francisco abounds with lawyers and consultants... Stories abound about how difficult it is to get in touch with the landlords.*

about is used to mention the subject of something like a book or speech. *...a book about the monarchy.* **About** is also used to mention the subject of someone's thoughts or feelings. *...rising public concern about unemployment.*
❑ **About** is used when mentioning characteristics. For example, if you say there is something strange **about** someone, you mean they are strange in some way.
❑ If you **do** something **about** an unsatisfactory situation, you do something to change it.
❑ **About** is used to say a number or amount is not exact. *...a population of about ten million.*
❑ If you are **about** to do something, you are just going to do it. Similarly, something can be **about** to happen. *Britain's most popular soap opera is about to celebrate its thirtieth birthday.*

about-turn When someone completely changes their attitude, opinion, or plans, you call this an **about-turn** or **about-face**. ...*a dramatic about-turn in policy.*

above ❑ If something is **above** something else, it is in a higher position, or directly over it.

   ❑ **Above** is used to say something is more than a particular amount, rate, or level. *The inflation rate has risen above 15% a year.*

   ❑ If someone is **above** you at your workplace, they are in a higher position than you.

   ❑ If you say someone is **above** something, you mean they would not become involved with it, because they would regard it as undignified, or think they were too important or intelligent for it. ◇ If someone thinks they are **above the law,** they think they are so important they do not have to obey the law like other people.

   ❑ If you say someone is **above** criticism, you mean people are not supposed to criticize them, because of their special position. ◇ If you say someone is **above** suspicion, you mean they are too honest to be suspected of something.

   ❑ In a piece of writing, **above** is used to refer to something which has appeared earlier in the text. *I hope the above will reassure the reader.*

   ❑ If you hear something **above** other noise, you hear it in spite of it.

abrasion An **abrasion** is an area of something, especially a person's skin, which has been damaged by scraping. *12 police officers were treated for shock, cuts and abrasions.*

abrasive (abrasiveness) An **abrasive** person is rude and unkind. *The staff resented what they saw as unwarranted abrasiveness.* ◇ An **abrasive** substance is rough and can be used to clean hard surfaces.

abreast ❑ When a group of people or vehicles are moving along in rows, you use **abreast** to say how many there are in each row. *Thousands of cars, seven abreast, queued at the frontier.*

   ❑ If you **keep abreast of** something, you make sure you have all the latest information about it.

abridged (abridgement) An **abridged** version of a book or article has had parts removed, to make it shorter. A short version like this is called an **abridgement.** ◇ **Abridged** is also used to describe other things which have been reduced in this way. *...an abridged education.*

abroad If you are **abroad,** you are in a country which is not the one you usually live in. *He was engaged in political activities abroad... The money would be used to send medical staff abroad for training.*

abrogate (abrogating, abrogated; abrogation) If something like a law or agreement is **abrogated,** it is cancelled or withdrawn. *Mr Pehoua criticised the abrogation of political and trade union rights by the government.*

abrupt (abruptly, abruptness) **Abrupt** is used to talk about things ending suddenly, usually with unfortunate consequences for someone. *Hodkinson brought the contest to an abrupt end with a devastating left hook... The programme was abruptly halted... ...the unseemly abruptness of the cancellation.*

abscess (*pron:* ab-sess) (abscesses) An **abscess** is a painful swelling on the skin or in the body, containing a thick pale liquid called pus. Abscesses are usually caused by bacterial infection.

abscond If someone **absconds,** (a) they escape from somewhere like a prison. (b) they walk out on someone who depends on them. *He got his girlfriend pregnant and absconded to London.*

abseil (*pron:* ab-sale) (abseiling, abseiled) When people abseil, they walk backwards down something like a wall or cliff face, using a rope which is attached to the top. They usually wear a special belt with a ring attached, through which they feed the rope.

absent (absently, absence) ❑ If someone is **absent** from a place, they are not there. Their **absence** is the fact that they are not there. ◇ If people **absent themselves** (*pron:* ab-**sent**), they are not in the place where they are supposed to be. *He pleaded guilty to absenting himself without leave.*

   ❑ You also say someone is **absent** when they are not paying attention, because they are thinking about something else. *He was looking rather absently at a large white cloth held before him.*

absent-minded (absent-mindedly, absent-mindedness) **Absent-minded** people are forgetful and often make mistakes. *Her absent-mindedness caused her considerable anxiety.* ◇ You also say someone is **absent-minded** when they are not paying attention to what they are doing, because they are thinking about something else. *He munched absent-mindedly on a sausage.*

absentee An **absentee** is someone who is not in the place where they should be.

absenteeism is regularly being away from work or school without a good reason.

absentia See in absentia.

absolute (absolutely) ❑ **Absolute** is used to say something is total and complete. *...absolute adherence to principle... He is absolutely right.* ◇ **Absolute** rulers have complete authority over their people. *...an absolute monarch.*

   ❑ **Absolute** principles are believed to be true or appropriate in all situations. Principles like these are sometimes called **absolutes.**

   ❑ If a political party wins an **absolute majority,** they win more seats or votes than all the other parties put together.

   ❑ **Absolute** and **absolutely** are used to talk about amounts when they are considered independently of other amounts. For example, if defence spending this year has risen **absolutely,** the actual amount has gone up, although as a proportion of government expenditure it may have gone down. *We can expect a substantial reduction in inflation over the coming year, both in absolute terms and in relation to inflation in other European countries.*

   ❑ People sometimes use **absolute** and **absolutely** to emphasize what they are saying. *Britain has described their reports as an absolute disgrace... It's absolutely amazing.*

absolute zero is the coldest possible temperature (about -273° Centigrade).

absolution In some Christian Churches, if someone is given **absolution,** they are forgiven for some sin they have committed, because they have repented.

absolutism (absolutist) When one person has all the political power in a country, this is called **absolutism.** Absolutist is used to describe systems like this, and things connected with them. *...Asia's absolutist traditions.*

absolve (absolving, absolved) If someone is **absolved** of blame or responsibility for something, they are declared or shown not to be responsible for it. ...*a report absolving the police of any responsibility... ...an effort to absolve himself from the charge of mismanaging the crisis... That does not absolve the authorities of their share of the guilt.*

absorb (absorption) ❑ If a substance is **absorbed**, it is soaked up by something. This process is called **absorption**. ◇ If something **absorbs** a form of energy like heat or light, it takes it in, rather than reflecting it. ...*the heat-absorbing capacity of the clouds... ...the absorption and emission of photons.*

❑ If you **absorb** something you read or hear, you remember it well.

❑ If something **absorbs** time, money, or effort, it uses it up. *Income taxes absorb 32% of the pay of a British executive... The task absorbs the energies of the two men.*

❑ If a group is **absorbed** by a larger group, it becomes part of it.

❑ If something **absorbs** a shock or force, it reduces its effect. *Car bumpers are designed to absorb some of the impact... ...a shock-absorbing shoe insert.* ◇ If people **absorb** changes to their way of life, they cope with them without being too badly affected.

❑ If something **absorbs** you or you become **absorbed** with it, you are greatly interested by it and give it all your attention. You say something like this is **absorbing**. *Bandsmen were so absorbed by their performance that they failed to notice the water around their ankles... It was an absorbing contest.*

absorbent materials soak up liquid easily. ...*absorbent paper... ...an absorbent pad.*

absorption See absorb.

abstain (abstaining, abstained; abstention) If you **abstain** from something, you do without it, or do not involve yourself with it. You can talk about someone's **abstention** from something. *Patients were supposed to abstain from alcohol... The armed forces would in future abstain from politics... ...his abstention from sexual relations.* ◇ If you **abstain** in a vote or election, you do not vote. When a vote is taken, the **abstentions** are the number of people who do not vote.

abstemious An **abstemious** person avoids doing too much of something enjoyable like eating or drinking.

abstinence is denying yourself pleasures like alcohol, tobacco, or sex.

abstract (abstraction) ❑ **Abstract** is used to describe very general ideas and theories, which can seem a long way from people's everyday concerns. Ideas and theories like these can be called **abstractions**. ...*abstract disputes about European unity... The budget deficit was something of an abstraction for most Americans.* ◇ If you talk **in the abstract** about something, you talk about it generally, without mentioning specific examples or experiences.

❑ **Abstract** paintings and sculptures are created using shapes and bold colours, rather than showing people or things as they actually look. Paintings and sculptures like these are sometimes called **abstracts**.

❑ An **abstract** of an article or speech is a short piece of writing summarizing its main points.

❑ If a person is **abstracted**, they are deep in thought and do not notice things going on around them.

abstruse If what a person says or writes is **abstruse**, it is complicated and difficult to understand.

absurd (absurdly; absurdity, absurdities) If you say something is **absurd**, you mean it does not make sense. You can talk about the **absurdity** of something or say it is an **absurdity**. ...*prices that are absurdly low... ...the absurdity of supporting a treaty which has been rendered null and void... This allows the viewer to laugh at life's absurdities.*

absurdum See reductio ad absurdum.

abundant (abundantly, abundance) If something is **abundant** or if there is an **abundance** of it, there is a lot of it. *Mongolia has abundant wildlife... Dead wood is abundantly available... ...an abundance of ideas.* You can also say something is present **in abundance**. *The property market was booming and jobs were in abundance.* ◇ If something is **abundantly clear**, it is very clear and obvious.

abuse (abusing, abused) ❑ If someone is **abused** (*pron:* ab-**yoozd**) or suffers **abuse** (*pron:* ab-**yoos**), they are ill-treated in some way, often by someone who should be taking care of them. *He had been sexually abused as a child... ...a victim of child abuse.* ◇ You also say someone is **abused** when people say rude insulting things to them. You call what they say **abuse**. *He was punched, kicked and verbally abused... ...the torrent of abuse hurled at the Prime Minister... The word 'Communist' has become a term of abuse.*

❑ If people's rights are **abused** or subjected to **abuse**, they are ignored, and the people are treated badly or unfairly. *They accused the government of abusing civil liberties... ...military officers convicted of human rights abuses.*

❑ If someone **abuses** something, they use it in a wrong way or for a bad purpose. *A medicine designed to treat anaemia was being abused by athletes... Few words are more abused by politicians than 'fairness'.* Wrong use of something is called **abuse**. *He was found guilty of abuse of power.*

abuser People who abuse things or other people are sometimes called **abusers**. ...*a convicted child abuser... ...drug and alcohol abusers.*

abusive (abusively) If someone is **abusive**, they say rude insulting things. ...*abusive letters... The term 'kaffir' was used to refer abusively to blacks.*

abut (abutting, abutted) If land or a building **abuts** something, it is right next to it. *The Duke's estates abut the Mar Forest.*

abuzz If a place or group of people is **abuzz**, there is an atmosphere of excitement. *The place was abuzz with scientists and reporters.*

abysmal (abysmally) If you say something is **abysmal**, you mean it is very bad or of very poor quality. *Prison conditions are abysmal... ...an abysmal performance... ...an abysmally low turn-out.*

abyss (abysses) An **abyss** is a very deep hole in the ground. ◇ If someone is heading for an **abyss**, they are in danger of getting into a disastrous situation. ...*an institution which has been allowed to slip towards the abyss... The world trading community is on the edge of an abyss.*

AC is used to describe an electric current which continually changes direction as it flows. AC stands for 'alternating current'. See also DC.

acacia (*pron:* a-kay-sha) The **acacia** is a tree with small, usually yellow flowers, which grows in warm countries. It is also called 'mimosa'.

academia or **academe** is used to talk about universities and the people who work and study in them. *Many of* *these students now occupy senior positions in academia... As a civil servant, he had hankerings after academe.*

academic (academically) ❏ An **academic** is a person who teaches or does research at a university or college. ◇ **Academic** is used to talk about study or research in schools or colleges, as opposed to work in places like factories or offices. *...academic activities... ...his academic background.* ◇ If a young person is **academic** or has good **academic** skills, they are good at studying and passing exams. *The system is failing among less academic children... New pupils are selected from across the academic ability range... ...an academically gifted girl.* ❏ If you say something like the solution to a problem is **academic**, you mean a solution can be found, but it cannot make any difference to anything else, so it is hardly worth bothering with. *....an academic question.*

academy (academies; academician) Schools and colleges, especially those specializing in particular subjects or skills, sometimes have **Academy** as part of their name. *...the Royal Scottish Academy of Music and Drama.* ◇ **Academy** also appears in the names of some societies formed to promote and maintain standards in a particular field. *...the British Academy of Film and Television Arts.* Members of some academies are called **academicians**.

accede (*pron:* ak-seed) (acceding, acceded) ❏ If you **accede** to someone's request or demand, you agree to what they want. ◇ If a country **accedes** to a treaty, it signs it. ❏ If someone **accedes** to a position of importance, especially the position of a ruler, they take it up. *King Ludwig III acceded to the throne of Bavaria in 1913.* ❏ If one country **accedes** to another, it becomes part of it. ◇ If a country **accedes** to independence, it is declared an independent country.

accelerate (accelerating, accelerated; acceleration) ❏ If something which is growing or developing **accelerates**, it does it at an increasing rate. *Job losses were expected to accelerate to 9,000 a month... ...the accelerating crisis... ...an acceleration in sales.* ◇ When people **accelerate** something, they make it happen more quickly. *The two leaders considered how to accelerate European integration.* ❏ When a vehicle or other moving thing **accelerates**, its speed increases. Its **acceleration** is the rate at which its speed increases.

accelerator The **accelerator** in a vehicle is the pedal you push to make it go faster. ◇ Some other devices used to speed up the movement of things are also called **accelerators**. *...a particle-accelerator.*

accent ❏ A person's **accent** is the way they pronounce the words of a language, especially when this shows where they come from or their social class. **Accented** is used to describe someone's accent. *...the heavily accented Brazilian voice.* ❏ An **accent** is also a mark written above or below certain letters in some languages, to indicate a change in pronunciation. See **acute, grave, circumflex, cedilla, tilde, umlaut.** ❏ If a musical note is **accented**, it is emphasized. ❏ If you say the **accent** is on something, you mean that is what is regarded as most important in the situation you are talking about. *The accent is on youth in this new government.*

accentuate (accentuating, accentuated) If an aspect of something is **accentuated**, it is emphasized. *The humour serves to accentuate the author's sense of the hopelessness of human endeavour.* ◇ If something **accentuates** people's feelings, it makes them more intense. *The speed of the rhinos' decline has accentuated fears for a growing number of African species.*

accept (acceptance) ❏ If you **accept** something someone offers you, you take it. ◇ If you **accept** an invitation, you say you will come. ❏ If you **accept** a suggestion or plan, you agree to it. ◇ If you **accept** a decision, you agree to what has been decided. ◇ If you **accept** a story or statement, you believe it. *Mr Carville refused to accept White House denials of complicity.* ❏ If you **accept** that something is true, you admit it. *Maybe he accepts that he is going to lose.* You can also **accept** that something needs to be done. *There is a widespread acceptance of the need to prolong the talks beyond the original deadline.* ◇ If you **accept** the blame or responsibility for something, you admit it is your fault. ❏ If you **accept** a difficult or unpleasant situation, you recognize it cannot be changed and put up with it. ❏ When an institution or organization **accepts** someone, they let them join, or give them a job. ◇ If a group of people **accept** you, they start treating you as one of their group. ❏ If people **accept** something like a new idea, they do not resist it or object to it. *It has taken a long time for hypnotherapy to be accepted by the medical profession.* ◇ **Accepted** ideas are generally thought to be correct.

acceptable (acceptably, acceptability) If something is **acceptable** to people, they do not object to it. *They feared the victory would make discrimination against immigrants more acceptable... This assumption played a considerable part in increasing the social acceptability of divorce.* ◇ **Acceptable** is also used to say something is good enough for a particular purpose. *The Plus 8 rides acceptably well on roads that are reasonably smooth.*

access (accesses, accessing, accessed) ❏ **Access** is used to talk about getting into a place. If you gain **access** to a building, you succeed in getting into it. If there is **access** to a place from a road, there is a way into it from the road. ❏ If you have **access** to something, you have the right or opportunity to use it or look at it. *They had access to a radio... Lawyers were denied access to official documents.* ◇ If you have **access** to a person, you have the right or opportunity to see them. *They can have access to a lawyer.* ❏ If you **access** information stored on a computer, you get the computer to show it on a screen or print it out, so you can read it.

accessible (accessibility) ❏ If a place is **accessible**, people can get to it. *East Midlands Airport makes much of central England easily accessible... Their headquarters is accessible only by boat... Property prices vary, depending upon location and accessibility to the ski-slopes.* ◇ If an object is **accessible**, you can get at it. *It is a good idea to pack a red warning triangle and keep it readily accessible.* ❏ You also say something is **accessible** when it is available for people to see or use. *...the accessibility of information.* ❏ An **accessible** person is easy to approach and talk to.

❑ If something like a piece of writing is **accessible**, it is not too difficult for people to understand and appreciate.

accession ❑ When someone takes up the position of ruler of a country, this is called their **accession**.

❑ When a country accepts the terms of a treaty or other international agreement, this is called the country's **accession** to the treaty or agreement. *...Britain's accession to the European exchange rate mechanism.*

accessory (accessories) ❑ **Accessories** are extra parts added to a machine, tool, or vehicle to make it more useful, efficient, or pleasant to use.

❑ **Accessories** are things like shoes, a scarf, jewellery, or a bag which a woman wears in addition to her main outfit.

❑ An **accessory** to a crime is someone who helps the person who commits it either before or after it is committed. *...an accessory to murder.*

accident (accidental, accidentally) If something is an **accident** or happens **by accident**, it happens by chance, rather than because of someone's deliberate intention. You say something like this is **accidental**. *...accidental finds of Roman coins... Diplomats believe he accidentally drove over the border.* ◇ An **accident** is also an unintended happening which causes damage, injury, or death. If someone has a lot of accidents, you say they are **accident-prone**.

acclaim (acclaiming, acclaimed) If someone or something is **acclaimed** or wins **acclaim**, they are praised enthusiastically. *...a widely acclaimed British film... Lisa Alther won international acclaim for her first novel, 'Kinflicks'.*

acclamation is loud or enthusiastic praise or applause. ◇ At a meeting, if a decision is made by **acclamation**, it is made by people showing overwhelming general approval, rather than by taking a vote.

acclimatize (acclimatizing, acclimatized; acclimatization) (*can be spelled with an 's' instead of a 'z'*) If you **acclimatize** to something or **acclimatize** yourself to it, you get used to it. *I became acclimatized to the realities of rural life... A couple of days acclimatization is essential.*

accolade You say someone receives an **accolade** (a) when they are awarded something like a title. *He was delighted when the accolade of Young Engineer of the Year went to one of his pupils.* (b) when they are mentioned publicly in a way which shows approval or admiration.

accommodate (accommodating, accommodated; accommodation) ❑ If someone is **accommodated**, they are provided with a place to stay or live. *They'll be accommodated in camps... ...the accommodation of staff.* **Accommodation** is places where people can stay or live. *...rented accommodation.*

❑ If something is **accommodated**, space is found for it. *I can never understand why BR finds it so difficult to accommodate bicycles on trains.* ◇ If a place can **accommodate** a certain number of people or things, it has room for that number. *Strangeways Prison was designed to accommodate around 900 prisoners.*

❑ If you **accommodate** something in a schedule, you find time for it.

❑ If you **accommodate** someone's wishes when planning or deciding something, you make sure your plan or decision fits in with what they want. ◇ An **accommodating** person takes other people's needs and wants into account.

accompanist An **accompanist** is a musician who plays one part of a piece of music while someone else sings or plays the main part.

accompany (accompanies, accompanying, accompanied; accompaniment) ❑ If you **accompany** someone, you go somewhere with them.

❑ If one thing **accompanies** another, it happens immediately it begins, and as a result of it. *...the violent pressure changes that accompany a bomb explosion... His appearance is accompanied by whooping and hollering.* ◇ You also say something **accompanies** something else when it is sent somewhere with it, or when it appears with it in a newspaper or magazine. *He sent back impassioned reports accompanied by heart-rending film of children suffering.* ◇ If one food **accompanies** another or is an **accompaniment** to it, it is served with it. *I liked the idea of the maize sauce to accompany courgettes stuffed with brown rice.*

❑ If you **accompany** a singer or musician, you play one part of a piece of music while they sing or play the main part. Your part is called the **accompaniment**.

accomplice An **accomplice** is someone who helps someone else commit a crime.

accomplish (accomplishes, accomplishing, accomplished; accomplishment) ❑ If you **accomplish** something, you succeed in doing it. *West Germany's famous economic miracle took six years to accomplish... General Jaruzelski wished Mr Walesa success in the accomplishment of his mission.* An **accomplishment** is something difficult someone has managed to do. *He counts the treaty as the greatest accomplishment of his administration.*

❑ **Accomplished** is used to describe (a) someone who is very good at something. *Townsend is a most accomplished writer.* (b) something which is very well done. *It was Lewis's most accomplished performance.*

accord ❑ An **accord** is an agreement between countries or organizations. ◇ If people are **in accord**, they agree about something.

❑ If something is done **in accord with** a requirement, it is done the way the requirement says. *Everything is happening in accord with the orders given by the head of the military district.*

❑ The treatment **accorded** to someone or something is the treatment they get. *Mr Kintanar has been accorded respect and affection... Sometimes inaccurate surveys are accorded an importance they do not deserve.*

❑ If you do something **of your own accord**, you do it freely, without being asked, persuaded, or forced to do it. *He is leaving the company of his own accord.*

accordance If something is done **in accordance with** a rule or law, it is done in the way the rule or law says it should be done. You can also say something is done **in accordance with** someone's wishes.

according **According to** is used to say where some information is obtained from. *According to a friend, McCaughey was always determined to fight to the bitter end... Most leading companies do not expect the economy to recover until the second half of next year, according to a Sunday Times survey.* ◇ If something is done **according to** a principle or plan, it follows that principle or plan. *Children are grouped according to age... The money was distributed according to the rules of the compensation scheme.*

accordingly is used to say something is done in a way which fits in with what you have just described. *People in public life have to recognise their behaviour is of public interest, and should act accordingly... Any soldier failing to report would be considered absent without leave and punished accordingly.*

accordion The **accordion** is a box-shaped musical instrument which you hold between your hands. You play it by pressing keys on one side and buttons on the other, and moving the two sides together and apart.

accost If someone **accosts** you, they stop you and insist on speaking to you when you do not want to speak to them.

account ❑ An **account** is a written or spoken record of something which has happened. *Donaldson provides an absorbing account of her wartime farming experiences.*
❑ **Accounts** are detailed records of the money a person or organization receives, spends, owes, and is owed. **Accounting** is the same as accountancy. ◇ **creative accounting**: see **creative**.
❑ If you have a **bank account**, you keep an amount of money in a bank. You can add to the amount, or take some of it out when you need it. See also **current account**, **deposit account**. ◇ If you have an **account** with a shop or other organization, you can buy goods or services there and pay later, or pay in instalments.
❑ If you **take account of** something or **take it into account**, you consider it or allow for it when you are working something out or deciding what to do. *The tax is unfair because it does not take account of a person's ability to pay... Animals' suffering should be taken into account whenever a decision about their treatment is made.* ◇ If you do something **on account of** something else, you do it because of it. *The book was burnt by a bishop on account of its allegedly blasphemous content.*
❑ If you say something should **on no account** be done, you mean it should not be done under any circumstances.
❑ If something **accounts for** something else, it explains it. *The bomb had detonated when only a few members of staff were present – a fact which accounted for the low casualty figure.* ◇ If people or things **account for** a certain part of something, they are what it consists of, or what it is used for. *The Italians and French now account for one third of all foreign visitors to Argyll... Nationalised industries account for more than a quarter of the country's non-housing investment.* ◇ If you **account for** people after something like an accident, you find out where everyone is and what has happened to them.

accountable (accountability) If you are **accountable** for things you do, you can be held responsible if they go wrong. *Schools will be held accountable for their performance.* ◇ If you are **accountable** to someone else, they have authority over you and you must explain and justify to them the things you do. *The system has produced autocratic decision-making without public accountability.*

accountant (accountancy) **Accountants** are people whose job it is to keep or check financial accounts. The work they do is called **accountancy.**

accoutrements (*pron:* ak-**koo**-tra-ments) are the things you have with you when you take part in something.

accredit (accrediting, accredited; accreditation) ❑ **Accredited** is used to say a person or organization is officially recognized as being a particular thing. *...an accredited teacher of theology... ...fully accredited diplomats... ...producers who do not belong to an accredited association.* This recognition is called **accreditation.** *Only the college can give accreditation.*
❑ If diplomats or journalists are **accredited** somewhere, they are sent to work there and officially accepted as representatives of their country or organization. *About half a dozen Polish and Hungarian journalists are now accredited to the State Department... Iraq has withdrawn diplomatic accreditation from eight British diplomatic personnel.*

accretion (*pron:* ak-**kree**-shun) An **accretion** is a layer of material which gradually forms on top of something. *...an accretion of sand and shells.* The process by which layers like this are formed is also called **accretion.** *Soon ice accretion would cause the engine to stop.* ◇ **Accretion** is also used to talk about other things building up gradually. *...the accretion of more presidential powers.*

accrue (accruing, accrued) ❑ **Accrue** is used to talk about an amount of money gradually increasing. For example, when money earns interest, you say the interest **accrues.**
❑ You can say other things **accrue** when they build up over a period of time. *...accrued leave... ...the fuss that has accrued since the archbishop refused his patronage.*

accumulate (accumulating, accumulated; accumulation) When things **accumulate**, they build up over a period of time. An **accumulation** is something which has built up like this. *...a six-foot accumulation of soil and rubbish.* ◇ If you **accumulate** things, you gradually add to the number you have. *The winner will be the first player to accumulate 10 victories.* Similarly, you can **accumulate** money. *...the accumulation of great wealth.*

accurate (accurately, accuracy) ❑ An **accurate** account or description gives a true idea of what someone or something is like. *Travel agents have been told to ensure that their advertising is fair and accurate... New cases are being reported more accurately.* You talk about the **accuracy** of an account or description like this. ◇ An **accurate** prediction or forecast turns out to be correct.
❑ An **accurate** machine or other device performs a task without making mistakes. You can also say the work a person does or a method of doing something is **accurate.** *...the accurate analysis of minerals, rocks and meteorites.*
❑ You say a gun or some other weapon is **accurate** when you can rely on it to hit a target. Similarly, you say someone's aim is **accurate** when they throw, kick, or hit a ball to exactly the right place. *He bowled with accuracy and pace.*

accusatory If someone's behaviour or something they say or write is **accusatory**, it gives the impression they are blaming or criticizing someone. *When he looked back, his gaze seemed to have become accusatory.*

accuse (accusing, accused; accusation, accuser) If you **accuse** someone of doing something wrong, you say they did it. You can also **accuse** someone of a fault, such as laziness. An **accusation** is a statement in which you accuse someone. **Accusing** is used to describe actions which suggest someone is being accused of something. *...an accusing gesture.* A person's **accusers** are people who accuse them of something. *The former first lady says she is ready to face her accusers.* ◇ If someone is **accused** of a crime, they have been charged with it and are on trial. In court, they are called the **accused**. *The accused is the first Westerner to go on trial for a drug-related offence in recent years.*

accustom (accustoming, accustomed) If you **accustom** yourself to something or become **accustomed** to it, you get used to it and become familiar with it. *Most hospitals had to accustom themselves to new ways of working... Both sides have become accustomed to a state of permanent hostility.* ◇ **Accustomed** is used to talk about people behaving in their usual way. *...their accustomed brutality.*

ace ❑ In a pack of cards, an **ace** is a card with a single symbol on it. It is usually the highest ranking card, although in some games it can be the lowest ranking. ◇ In an argument or discussion, if someone **plays their ace**, they say something which gives them a strong advantage, and which they had previously been keeping back. ❑ **Ace** is used to describe things which are extremely good, or people who are extremely good at something. *...ace striker Jean-Pierre Papin.* ❑ If you come **within an ace** of doing something, you very nearly do it. ❑ In tennis, an **ace** is a serve which is so fast and accurate that the other player fails to hit it at all.

acerbic (*pron:* ass-sir-bik) If something someone says is **acerbic**, it is clever and witty, but in a bitter or cruel way. Talking like this is called **acerbity**. *She replied with characteristic acerbity.*

acetate (*pron:* ass-it-tate) is a man-made fabric used for making clothes.

acetic acid (*pron:* ass-see-tik) is a colourless acid which is the main ingredient of vinegar.

acetylene (*pron:* ass-set-ill-een) is a colourless gas. When mixed with oxygen, it produces a very powerful flame, which is used in cutting and welding metal.

ache (aching, ached; achingly) ❑ If you **ache** or a part of your body **aches**, you feel a constant dull pain. An **ache** is a pain like this. ❑ **Aching** is used to describe strong feelings, especially of sadness. *...an aching regret... ...achingly beautiful ballads.* ◇ If you **ache** for something, you want it very much.

achieve (achieving, achieved; achievement) If you **achieve** something, especially something difficult, you succeed in getting it or bringing it about. An **achievement** is a success of this kind.

achiever is used to talk about how successful people are. For example, an **under-achiever** is someone who does not do as well as most other people, especially in their career. A **young achiever** is someone who has had a lot of success despite being quite young.

Achilles heel (*pron:* ak-kill-eez) If a powerful person has an **Achilles heel**, they have a weak point which their opponents can use to attack them. *Former colleagues would say that Clark's Achilles heel is that he is too nice.*

Achilles tendon (*pron:* ak-kill-eez) Your **Achilles tendon** is the cord of tissue which connects your heel bone to your calf muscle.

acid (acidic, acidity; acidly) ❑ **Acids** are a group of liquids with certain chemical characteristics such as the ability to dissolve metals to form salts. Strong acids are used in industrial processes, and in some household products like strong cleaning fluids. Weaker acids exist in many foods – for example, fruit contains citric acid and milk contains lactic acid. If something is **acidic**, it has acid in it. This property is called **acidity**. ◇ If someone suffers from stomach **acidity**, they feel uncomfortable, because they have too much acid in their stomach. ◇ An **acid** taste is sour or sharp.
❑ **Acid** is also LSD.
❑ **Acid** is used to describe things people say or write which are harsh or unkind. *Mr Gummer acidly remarked that subsidised farming was not unique to the EU.*
❑ An **acid test** is a sure way of proving whether something works properly or is of good quality. *The acid test for most companies was whether they could sell in the American market.*

acid house is a style of dance music with a repetitive hypnotic beat produced by modern technology rather than traditional instruments. An **acid house party** is an event in a large building such as a nightclub or warehouse where people dance all night to acid house music. Acid house parties are also called 'raves'.

acid rain is rain which has been made acidic by fumes and gases. Rain polluted in this way is believed to destroy crops, trees, and fish, as well as causing damage to buildings.

acknowledge (acknowledging, acknowledged; acknowledgement) ❑ If you **acknowledge** a situation, you accept or admit it exists. If you **acknowledge** that something is true, you accept or admit it is true. *He acknowledged that Germany had played better during the tournament.*
❑ If someone or something is **acknowledged** as a certain thing, they are recognized as being that thing. *Rauh was acknowledged as the leading civil liberties lawyer in the US... AT&T's Bell Labs are an acknowledged seat of engineering excellence... Norman Heatley received full public acknowledgement of his remarkable achievements at a ceremony in Oxford yesterday.*
❑ If you **acknowledge** applause, you show your gratitude or appreciation in some way. *Mr Thorpe waved acknowledgment to a large crowd as he left the Old Bailey.* ◇ In a book, the **acknowledgements** are notes, usually at the beginning, in which the author thanks people for their help while the book was being written, or for permission to include copyright material.

acne (*pron:* ak-nee) If someone has **acne**, they have blackheads and spots on their face, neck, and sometimes their upper body, caused by blockage and inflammation of the oil glands. Acne is most common among teenagers.

acolyte (*pron:* ak-o-lite) An important person's **acolytes** are people who support them uncritically and agree with everything they say. ◇ An **acolyte** is also a person who assists a priest at certain church ceremonies.

acorn Acorns are brown or green egg-shaped nuts which grow on oak trees in woody cup-like cases.

acoustic (acoustically) **Acoustic** is used to talk about things to do with sound and hearing. *The torpedo transmits acoustic pulses into the water.* ◇ When people talk about the **acoustic** or **acoustics** of a building, they mean the physical features which determine how well an audience can hear music or speech. *The church is fully air-conditioned and acoustically perfect.* ◇ An **acoustic** guitar is any guitar which is not an electric one.

acquaint If you are **acquainted** with someone, you know them. If you are **acquainted** with something, you are familiar with it or used to it. ◇ If you **acquaint yourself** with something, you get to know it. *Hopkins recently returned to Snowdonia to acquaint himself with the terrain.* ◇ If you **acquaint** someone else with something, you tell them about it. *Britain and Czechoslovakia were at the stage of acquainting each other with their views.*

acquaintance An **acquaintance** is someone you have met but do not know well. ◇ If you **make** someone's **acquaintance**, you are introduced to them, or you meet them for the first time. ◇ Your **acquaintance** with a subject is your knowledge or experience of it. *Vir's acquaintance with the styles he was trying to absorb was relatively slight.* ◇ If you have a **nodding** or **passing acquaintance** with someone, you know them, but not well. Similarly, you can have a **nodding** or **passing acquaintance** with a subject.

acquiesce (*pron:* ak-wee-**ess**) (acquiescing, acquiesced; acquiescent, acquiescence) If you **acquiesce** in something or **acquiesce** to it, you agree to accept it. *Mr Shamir says he will not acquiesce in any move to appease Iraq.* When someone agrees to accept something, you can say they are **acquiescent** or talk about their **acquiescence**. *The unification of Germany would have been impossible without Soviet acquiescence.*

acquire (acquiring, acquired; acquisition) ❑ If you **acquire** something, you get it, for example by buying it. *The Tate Gallery has acquired a portrait by William Dobson.* When you acquire something, you can talk about your **acquisition** of it; your **acquisitions** are things you have acquired.
   ❑ If you **acquire** a certain reputation, you get it as a result of your behaviour. *He had acquired a well-earned reputation as a schemer.* ◇ If you **acquire** a skill, you obtain it through experience.
   ❑ If you say something is an **acquired taste**, you mean it has to be experienced several times before it can be enjoyed. Calling something an **acquired taste** is often just a humorous way of saying it is rather unpleasant.

acquisitive people like to keep getting new possessions.

acquit (acquitting, acquitted; acquittal) If someone is **acquitted** of a crime, they are found not guilty. You call this their **acquittal**. ◇ If you **acquit yourself** well on a particular occasion, you do something well, or deal with a situation well.

acre Area is sometimes expressed in **acres**. An acre is 4840 square yards (about 4047 square metres). ◇ **Acres** of something means a lot of it. *...acres of newsprint.*

acreage The **acreage** of a piece of land is its area, expressed in acres.

acrid An **acrid** smell or taste is strong, sharp, and unpleasant.

acrimonious (*pron:* ak-ri-**moan**-ee-uss) (acrimoniously) You say discussions are **acrimonious** when the people taking part say angry and bitter things. *The meeting began acrimoniously... Acrimonious exchanges went on for a long time.*

acrimony (*pron:* ak-ri-mon-ee) is bitterness and anger. *There are reports of considerable acrimony amongst the top leadership.*

acrobat An **acrobat** is an entertainer who performs gymnastic feats like jumps, somersaults, and balancing acts.

acrobatic (acrobatically) **Acrobatic** movements involve fitness and skill and include doing things like jumps or somersaults. *...acrobatic dance routines... Olhovskiy leapt acrobatically to deliver an overhead volley beyond Courier's reach.*

acronym (*pron:* ak-ro-nim) An **acronym** is a series of letters which stand for the name of an organization and which can be pronounced as though they were a single word. For example, NATO (*pron:* **nay**-toe) is an acronym for 'North Atlantic Treaty Organization'.

across ❑ If you go **across** something, you go from one side to the other. ◇ If something stands **across** something else, it stretches from one side to the other. *...the bridge across the River Jordan.* ◇ You also say something is **across** something else when it is resting on it and partly covering it. *...rifles slung across their shoulders.*
   ❑ **Across** is also used to say something is on the other side of something like a street, river, or border. *Just across the Thames is the Department of Education and Science.* ◇ If you are on one side of something and look **across** it, you look at things on the other side.
   ❑ **Across** is used when giving the width of something. *Each satellite will measure one metre across and two metres high.*
   ❑ If something exists **across** a wide area, it exists all over it. ◇ **Across** is also used to say something involves a wide range of people. *The about-turn follows a wave of protests across the political spectrum.*
   ❑ If you **put across** an idea or **get** it **across,** you get people to understand it.
   ❑ If you **come across** someone or something, you meet them or find them by accident.

acrylic fibres are man-made fibres resembling wool. ◇ **Acrylic** paints are durable quick-drying paints used by artists and decorators.

act ❑ When you **act,** you do something, especially something positive. **Acts** are things people do. *The government wants the police to act quickly in cases of violence within the home... The public would not tolerate such acts of terrorism.* ◇ If something happens to you while you are **in the act** of doing something, it happens while you are doing it. ◇ If someone is **caught in the act,** they are discovered committing a crime or doing something else wrong.
   ❑ If you **act** as a particular thing, that is your role. *He acted as a go-between for Roberto Calvi in some of his financial deals.* ◇ **Acting** in front of a title means someone is holding a post temporarily. *...the acting President.*
   ❑ If you **act on** someone's demands or advice, you do what they ask or suggest. ◇ If you **act on** information you receive, you do something which makes use of it. *Detectives, acting on a tip-off, lay in wait for the gang.*
   ❑ If someone like a lawyer **acts** for you or **acts** on your behalf, he or she is employed by you to deal with a particular matter.
   ❑ You can describe someone's behaviour by saying they **act** in a particular way. *Police have appealed for witnesses to come forward if they saw anyone acting suspiciously.*
   ❑ If you talk about the way an object or substance **acts,** you are talking about what happens to it in particular circumstances, or about its effects on other things. *Cocaine acts on the central nervous system to induce sensations of intense euphoria.* You can also say something **acts** as a par-

ticular thing. *The belt of ash acts as a barrier to the loss of heat from the Earth.*

❏ If someone **acts** in a play or film, they have a part in it. **Acting** is doing this regularly, especially for a living. ◇ If you **act out** a story, you perform it like a play. You can also **act out** other things. *Many patients become experts in diseases and past masters in acting out the symptoms.* ◇ If you say someone's behaviour is an **act**, you mean it does not show their true feelings.

❏ An **act** in a play, opera, or ballet is one of the sections it is divided into. ◇ The **acts** in a cabaret or circus are the separate performances in it. An **act** is also a person or group specializing in a type of performance. *...the famous Ganjou Brothers dancing act.*

❏ If you talk about someone performing a **balancing act** or a **juggling act**, you mean they are managing to control a difficult situation; often this involves keeping several different people or groups satisfied.

❏ If you **get in on the act**, you take advantage of something started by someone else and start doing it yourself.

❏ If you say someone should **get their act together**, you mean they should organize their activities properly so they can deal with something in an effective way.

❏ An **Act** or **Act of Parliament** is a law passed by Parliament. *...the Financial Services Act.*

act of God (acts of God) If people say something serious which has happened is an **act of God**, they mean it was beyond human control and nobody is to blame.

Act of Parliament See act.

action is doing something, especially something with a definite purpose. *Urgent action was needed.* An **action** is something someone does. *The shelling appeared to be a deliberate action.* See also **direct action**.

❏ In sport, a person's **action** is the way they do something, for example the way someone bowls in cricket. *He still has his lovely, fluent sideways-on action.*

❏ The **action** of something is the way it works, or the effects it has. *This drug will inhibit the action of an enzyme.*

❏ **Action** is used to talk about important or exciting things happening. *Watching the action was David Mercer... ...two hours of non-stop action.* ◇ The **action** in a film or play is the way the story develops. *The action centres on the identity crisis of a young business couple.*

❏ Military **action** is fighting between armed forces. If soldiers **go into action**, they start fighting. If they are killed **in action**, they are killed during fighting.

❏ You can say other people **go into action** when they tackle something which needs doing. *The transport department swung into action to investigate these incidents.* ◇ If someone puts an idea or a policy **into action**, they start applying it.

❏ If something is **out of action**, it is not working. ◇ If someone is **out of action**, they cannot take part in something, because they are ill or injured.

❏ A legal **action** is a process in which someone tries to get a court to force someone else to do something, for example pay compensation. *...a libel action.*

action replay On TV, if viewers are shown an **action re-play** of something, they are shown it again in slow motion.

actionable If you say what someone has done is **action-able**, you mean a legal case could be brought against

them because of it.

activate (activating, activated; activation) ❏ If a device or system is **activated**, something makes it start working. *...the sudden activation of the radar system.* ◇ If a plan or scheme is **activated**, people go ahead with it.

❏ If someone is **activated** by a feeling or emotion, that is what makes them behave the way they do. *The three councillors denied that they were activated by malice.*

active (actively) ❏ An **active** person is energetic and always busy or moving about. ◇ If someone is **active** in an organization or cause, they do a lot to help it. ◇ **Active** is also used to say someone does something in a positive or determined way. *His mother actively discouraged him.*

❏ If something is **active**, it is moving, working, or having an effect. *The virus is still active.* ◇ An **active** volcano has erupted recently or may erupt soon.

active service People on **active service** or **active duty** are fighting as members of the armed forces.

activist (activism) An **activist** is someone who tries to bring about political or social change by doing things like organizing campaigns and taking part in demonstrations. *...anti-apartheid activists... ...animal rights activists.* Attempting to bring about change like this is called **activism**.

activity (activities) An **activity** is something someone does. *...leisure activities... They will be asked to stop their illegal activities.* ◇ If you say there is **activity** in a place, you mean things are happening or being done there. *There were few signs of activity.*

actor An **actor** is a person whose job is acting in films or plays.

actress (actresses) An **actress** is a woman whose job is acting in films or plays.

actual (actually) ❏ **Actual** is used to emphasize that you are talking about a particular thing, and not just something like it or connected with it. *...the actual working platform where the tunnelling is taking place.* ◇ **Actual** and **actually** are used with words like 'no' and 'not' to say something is not a particular thing, although it may be like it. *The UN inspectors saw no actual weapons... The document was not actually a press release, but a report... Nobody is actually rioting... He was charged with attempted rather than actual murder.*

❏ You use **actually** when you are saying what you claim is the truth about something, as distinct from what has just been said or mentioned. *They claim they work to promote the family, but actually they are involved in separating families.* ◇ **in actual fact**: see fact. ◇ **Actual** is used to say what a figure or amount really is, rather than what it is claimed or forecast to be. *More than 500 executions have been reported this year and the actual number is probably higher.*

actual bodily harm If someone is charged with causing **actual bodily harm**, they are charged with injuring someone deliberately. This is a more serious charge than assault, but it is less serious than causing grievous bodily harm.

actuality is things which really exist, rather than imaginary things. *For him it's image that matters, not actuality.*

actually See actual.

actuary (actuaries; actuarial) An **actuary** is a person whose job is to calculate insurance risks and work out how much insurance companies should charge their clients. **Actuarial** is used to talk about things to do with actuaries and their work. *...actuarial calculations.*

acuity (*pron:* ak-kew-it-ee) is (a) sharpness of vision or hearing. *...visual acuity.* (b) quickness and clarity of thought. *...a man of great acuity.*

acumen (*pron:* ak-yew-men) is the ability to make good decisions and judgements. *...business acumen... He prides himself on his political acumen.*

acupuncture is a traditional Chinese treatment of illness or pain, now used to some extent in the West. It involves putting fine needles into the skin in different parts of the body.

acute (acutely, acuteness) ❑ **Acute** is used to emphasize how bad a situation is. *...the country's acute economic crisis... Tower Hamlets is facing an acute teacher shortage.* ◇ An **acute** illness is a very severe one. *...acute appendicitis.* ◇ If you are **acutely** aware of something, especially something unpleasant, you are strongly aware of it. ◇ **Acute** is also used to describe strong feelings about something unpleasant. *...acute concern... The situation is acutely embarrassing.*

❑ If your sight, hearing, or sense of smell is **acute,** it is unusually sensitive and powerful. ◇ **Acute** is used to describe other abilities which are well-developed and powerful. *President Najibullah has an acute sense of survival... Her memory remained acute... ...the acuteness of his intelligence.*

❑ An **acute** angle is any angle of less than 90 degrees. See also **obtuse, reflex.**

❑ The **acute** accent is a symbol sometimes written over 'e' in French and over other letters in some other languages. It indicates a change in the pronunciation of the letter. *...the film director René Clair.*

ad An **ad** is an advertisement. *...a Pepsi ad.*

AD is used in dates to say something happened a certain number of years or centuries after Christ is believed to have been born. **AD** stands for 'anno Domini', which is Latin for 'in the year of our Lord'. *The town was founded at the end of the first century AD... The Temple was destroyed by the Romans in 70 AD.*

ad hoc is used to say something is not done as part of a regular arrangement or system. *Large projects are put out to agencies on an ad-hoc basis... ...an ad hoc meeting.*

ad-lib (ad-libbing, ad-libbed) If someone **ad-libs** in a play or speech, they say something which has not been prepared beforehand, often because they have forgotten what they were supposed to say.

ad nauseum (*pron:* ad naw-zee-am) If someone does something **ad nauseum,** they keep doing it and it gets boring or annoying.

adage (*pron:* ad-ij) An **adage** is a saying which expresses a general truth. *...the old adage that one player does not make a team.*

Adam's apple Your **Adam's apple** is the lump sticking out at the front of your throat, where the thyroid cartilage of your larynx is.

adamant (adamantly) If you are **adamant** about something, you are not prepared to change your mind about it. *They are adamantly opposed to any deal with Argentina.* ◇ If you are **adamant** that something is true, you insist it is true. *The group is adamant that the painting is theirs.*

adapt (adaptation) ❑ If you **adapt** to a new situation or **adapt** yourself to it, you make some changes in your life, to be able to deal with it. You can talk about a person's **adaptation** to a new situation.

❑ If you **adapt** something, you alter it to make it suitable for a new purpose or situation. *...adaptation of equipment... The design has been adapted to make it fit the new mortar.* ◇ If someone **adapts** a story or novel, they write a version which can be performed as a play or made into a film. This new version is called an **adaptation** of the story or novel.

adaptable (adaptability) If someone or something is **adaptable,** they can change or be changed to deal with different situations. *The flu virus is amazingly adaptable... ...his adaptability to virtually any role.*

adaptation See **adapt.**

adaptive is used to talk about ways of adapting to new situations. *...adaptive strategies... ...the adaptive capacity of living systems.*

adaptor ❑ An **adaptor** is (a) a device which two or more plugs can be fitted into, so they can be used from the same wall socket. (b) a device which a single plug can fit into, allowing it to be used from a socket which it would not fit into directly. ◇ A mains **adaptor** is an electrical lead with a plug on the end which allows you to power a device from the mains rather than by battery. ◇ Various other devices which link things together or allow them to be used in different ways are called **adaptors.**

❑ The **adaptor** of a story or novel is the person who has adapted it for the theatre, cinema, TV, or radio.

add ❑ If you **add** something to something else, you attach it to it, or include it with it. *The Romans added a second set of walls to those built by the Etruscans.* ◇ If something **adds to** a feeling, it makes it greater. *It all adds to the fun... This can only have added to his frustration.* ◇ If you say someone **adds** a certain quality to something, you mean it gains that quality because of them. *The new governor will add a little stability to Arizona's politics.*

❑ If you **add** numbers or amounts or **add** them **up,** you calculate their total. You can say numbers or amounts **add up** to a certain total.

❑ **Add up** is also used to talk about the result of putting several things together. *Skills without arts and culture do not add up to a good education... It all adds up to a disturbing picture from Israel's point of view.* ◇ If you say something like a statement **adds up,** you mean it is believable or makes sense.

❑ If you **add** something when you are speaking, you say something extra. *The spokesman added that the incident would be discussed with Egypt.*

add-on is used to describe things which are not essential but can be added to something to make it more useful or effective. *...a home computer with add-on memory.*

addendum (*plural:* addenda) An **addendum** is a section at the end of a book or document, containing extra information.

adder The **adder** is a small poisonous snake with a black zig-zag pattern on its back. Adders are the only poisonous snakes in the wild in Britain.

addict (addicted, addiction) If someone is **addicted** to a harmful drug, they cannot stop taking it. You call someone like this an **addict**; you talk about their **addiction** to the drug. ◇ You also say someone is **addicted** to something when they enjoy it very much and spend as much time on it as they can. Someone like this can also be called an **addict**. *She is addicted to golf... ...sci-fi addicts.*

addictive If a drug is **addictive**, people find they need to keep on taking it. ◇ You can say other things are **addictive** when people find it hard to give them up.

addition (additional, additionally) ❏ **Addition** is calculating totals. ◇ When something is added to something which already exists, you talk about the **addition** of this extra thing. *The final five wickets fell for the addition of just 25 runs.* Something added like this can be called an **addition**. *An airlift would be a welcome addition to our contribution.* ◇ **Additional** is used to describe things which are extra to something which already exists. *An additional 400 job losses have been announced.*

❏ People say **in addition** or **additionally** when they are giving extra information or mentioning an extra requirement. *In addition, other companies organise excursions from riverside towns... The ceasefire required all fighting to stop by 0400 hours and additionally stipulated that forces should withdraw from their forward positions by 1600 hours.*

additive Additives are substances added to products by manufacturers, especially chemicals added to food to preserve it, colour it, or flavour it.

addled is used to describe people who are confused and unable to think properly, for example because they have taken drugs. *...Ecstasy-addled ravers.*

address (addresses, addressing, addressed) ❏ Your **address** is the number of your house, the name of the street, the name of the town, and the postcode. If a letter is **addressed** to you, it has your name and address on it.

❏ If you **address** a group of people, you make a speech to them. A speech can be called an **address**. *...a televised address to the nation.* ◇ If you are **addressing** someone, you are speaking to them.

❏ If you **address** a problem or **address yourself** to it, (a) you start dealing with it. *Mr Patten addressed himself to five tasks.* (b) you talk about it when you are making a speech. *Mr Lee addressed the future of Hong Kong by saying that no political argument would move the basic position of the Chinese government.*

addressee The **addressee** of a letter or parcel is the person it is addressed to.

adduce (adducing, adduced) If you **adduce** a fact, a reason, or evidence, you bring it forward to support a claim or argument. *Two reasons were adduced to explain her decision... The plaintiff could not adduce evidence of actual loss.*

adenoids are two soft lumps of flesh at the back of a child's nose, just above its tonsils. In most children, they get smaller from about the age of five and disappear at puberty.

adept (adeptly) If someone is **adept** at something, they do it very skilfully. *He became an adept public speaker... Mrs Marcos' lawyer adeptly exploited the prosecution's weakness.*

adequate (adequately, adequacy) If something is **adequate**, it is good enough, or there is enough of it. You can talk about the **adequacy** of something. *They will look at whether existing penalties are adequate... The Festival has never been adequately funded... ...the adequacy of security measures.*

adhere (adhering, adhered; adherence) ❏ If something **adheres** to a surface or object, it sticks to it.

❏ If you **adhere** to a rule, agreement, or principle, you keep to it. You can talk about someone's **adherence** to one of these things. *...a strict adherence to a fundamentalist Islamic way of life.*

adherent The followers of a religion or other set of beliefs can be called its **adherents**. *...adherents of Christianity.*

adhesion is used to talk about things sticking together. *...the adhesion of the fibre to its matrix.* ◇ A car's or train's **adhesion** is the ability of its wheels to grip the road or track.

adhesive An **adhesive** is a substance used to stick things together. ◇ If something is **adhesive**, it sticks firmly to something else. *...the first adhesive postage stamp.*

adieu (pron: a-dew) if you bid someone **adieu**, you say goodbye.

adjacent If one thing is **adjacent** to another or if two things are **adjacent**, they are next to each other.

adjective Adjectives are words used to describe things. For example, in 'The night was dark', 'dark' is an adjective.

adjoin (adjoining, adjoined) If one thing **adjoins** another or if two things are **adjoining**, they are next to each other.

adjourn (adjournment) If a meeting or trial **adjourns** or is **adjourned**, it is stopped temporarily. A stoppage like this is called an **adjournment**.

adjudge (adjudging, adjudged) If you are **adjudged** to be something, it is officially decided that you are that thing. *Mr Flint was adjudged bankrupt.* You can also be **adjudged** to have done something. *She was disqualified when adjudged to have hampered another runner at the start.*

adjudicate (adjudicating, adjudicated; adjudication, adjudicator) If someone **adjudicates** on a dispute or problem, they make an official decision about it. The decision is called an **adjudication**; the official making it is sometimes called an **adjudicator**.

adjunct Something used in connection with a larger or more important thing can be called an **adjunct** to it. *Psychological warfare has long been a valuable adjunct to technology and weaponry.*

adjust (adjustment) ❏ If you **adjust** to a new situation, you get used to it by changing your behaviour or ideas. This process is called **adjustment**. *After the war, Miller found it hard to adjust to peace... British companies face a painful adjustment process.* ◇ If someone is well **adjusted**, they get on well with other people and are good at coping with everyday problems.

❏ If you **adjust** something or make an **adjustment** to it, you make slight changes, to make it more effective or appropriate. *An adjustment of prices and tariffs is inevitable.* ◇ If you **adjust** a TV or radio, you change its setting to get a clearer picture or sound. ◇ If you **adjust** something you are wearing, you change its position to get it looking the way you want it to.

adjustable If something is **adjustable**, you can change its position or setting. *...an adjustable spanner.*

adjutant (pron: aj-oo-tant) An **adjutant** is an army officer who deals with administrative work.

adman (admen) An **adman** is someone who works in advertising, especially one of the people who write or design the adverts.

administer (administering, administered) ❏ The people who administer a country, organization, or event are the ones responsible for controlling and supervising it.

❏ If you **administer** a medicine or drug, you give it to someone, for example by injecting it or giving it to them to swallow.

administrate (administrating, administrated) To **administrate** a country or organization means the same as to administer it.

administration (administrative, administratively; administrator) ❏ The **administration** of a country or area is its government. ◇ **Administration** is the work of organizing and controlling something. ...*the administration of justice.* **Administrative** is used to talk about things connected with this work. ...*administrative costs... ...an administratively simple way to raise revenue.* People responsible for administration are called **administrators**.

❏ If a company with financial problems is in **administration**, a representative of creditors or shareholders has been chosen to take over its management. This person is called an **administrator**; it is his or her job to try to improve the company or sell it, so people get their money back.

admirable (admirably) If you say something is **admirable**, you mean it deserves to be praised and admired. ...*his admirable qualities... The boldness of the undertaking is admirable... The book is admirably free of bitterness.*

admiral An **admiral** is a high-ranking naval officer. In the Royal Navy, the highest rank is **admiral of the fleet**, followed by **admiral**, **vice admiral**, and **rear admiral**.

Admiralty The **Admiralty** is the former name of the Royal Navy Department of the Ministry of Defence.

admire (admiring, admired; admiringly, admiration, admirer) ❏ If you **admire** someone, you like and respect them, because you think they have special qualities or talents. You can also **admire** what they do. You can talk about your **admiration** for a person, or for what they do. ...*admiring letters... Singers would speak admiringly of working with Reggie.* You can also describe yourself as an **admirer** of a person or their work. ...*admirers of Lynch's films... The Secretary has his admirers among MPs hostile to European union.*

❏ If you **admire** something like a view, you look at it with pleasure.

admissible If evidence is **admissible**, it can be considered in court.

admit (admitting, admitted; admission; admittance) ❏ If you **admit** something is true, you reluctantly say or agree it is true. What you say is called an **admission**. ...*his admission that he was having an affair.* ◇ If you **admit** responsibility or liability for something, you say you are responsible or liable for it. *The IRA admitted responsibility for two bombs last month... Hospital authorities admitted liability for mistakes during her birth.* ◇ If you **admit** defeat, you accept you have lost, or cannot achieve what you wanted to.

❏ If you are **admitted** to a place or gain **admission** or **admittance**, you are allowed in. *He tried to get into a Los Angeles nightclub but was refused admission.* ◇ If you are **admitted** to hospital, you are taken in as a patient. People admitted to a hospital are called **admissions**.

❏ If someone is **admitted** to a group or organization or gains **admission** or **admittance** to it, they are allowed to join. ...*Namibia's admission to the United Nations.* ◇ **Admissions** is the process of deciding which students will go to which university. ...*admissions interviews.*

admittedly You say **admittedly** when you are mentioning something which weakens the main point you are making. *Production has risen significantly, though admittedly it's still short of target levels... Although the risk is admittedly small, it's a definite one.*

admonish (admonishes, admonishing, admonished; admonishment) If you **admonish** someone, you tell them off or warn them not to do something. What you say is called an **admonishment**.

admonition An **admonition** is something you say or do to warn someone not to do something.

ado (*pron:* a-doo) If something is done **without further ado** or **without more ado**, it is done immediately. *He ordered the men to be released without further ado.*

adolescent (adolescence) An **adolescent** is a young person at an age between childhood and adulthood. This stage of your life is called **adolescence**. **Adolescent** is used to talk about things connected with people of this age, especially behaviour which shows they are not yet fully grown up. ...*a typically adolescent joke.*

adopt (adoption, adoptive) ❏ If you **adopt** an attitude or way of doing things, you start thinking or behaving like that. *Smith has adopted a quieter, understated approach... He suggested that his government would adopt a flexible policy.* ◇ If people **adopt** something like a plan, they decide to put it into action. *The Security Council has adopted a resolution to relax the sanctions... ...the adoption of new laws.*

❏ If a child is **adopted**, a couple take it into their own family and make it legally their own. This process is called **adoption**. The couple are called the child's **adoptive** parents.

❏ If you **adopt** a country you have gone to live in, you regard it as your home; you can call a country your **adopted** home or **adoptive** home. ◇ If you **adopt** a name, you start using it as your own name.

adorable Some people use **adorable** to describe animals or other people they find delightful, lovable, and attractive.

adore (adoring, adored; adoringly, adoration) If you **adore** someone, you love and admire them, and tend to ignore their faults. This feeling is called **adoration**. ...*a charming woman adored by her family... He raised his arms to the adoring public... She gazed adoringly at her husband.* ◇ If you **adore** something, you enjoy it very much or are very keen on it. *He adores music... I adore cooking home-made pastas.*

adorn If something is **adorned** with things or if they **adorn** it, it is decorated with them.

adornments are things worn for decoration, such as jewellery.

adrenal glands The **adrenal glands** are glands on top of each of your kidneys. They secrete several substances including adrenalin.

adrenalin (or **adrenaline**) is a substance produced by your body in stressful situations, for example when you are angry, frightened, or excited. It has many effects, including making your heart beat faster and giving you more energy.

adrift If a boat is **adrift**, it is not tied up or under control and is being carried along by the wind or tide. ◇ In sport, if a competitor is a number of points **adrift**, they are that number of points behind the competitor who is winning.

adroit (adroitly) If someone is **adroit**, they are quick and skilful in their thoughts or actions. *Fashanu controlled Earle's pass adroitly off his chest to put Wimbledon ahead.*

adulation (adulatory) **Adulation** is enthusiastic admiration and praise. You say people who behave like this are **adulatory**. *...the President's adulatory reception... He is constantly followed by adulatory hangers-on.*

adult An **adult** is a mature fully-developed person or animal. *In rural Bihar, 90% of adult women are illiterate.* ◇ **Adult** is used to describe things intended or suitable for adults. *...adult prisons... ...adult entertainment.*

adult education is for people who are no longer at school or college and wish to learn a new skill. Adult education classes are usually run by local authorities.

adulterate (adulterating, adulterated) If food, drink, or a drug is **adulterated**, something is added which weakens or contaminates it.

adultery (adulterer, adulteress; adulterous) If a married person commits **adultery**, they have sex with someone they are not married to. An **adulterer** is someone who commits adultery; a woman who commits adultery can also be called an **adulteress**. **Adulterous** is used to describe people who commit adultery, and relationships involving adultery. *...an adulterous affair.*

adulthood is the part of your life when you are an adult.

advance (advancing, advanced; advancement) ❑ When troops **advance**, they move forward towards the enemy. You also say they **advance** or make an **advance** when they capture territory, driving the enemy back. ◇ You can talk about other people or things **advancing** when they move towards someone or something. *In some places the water has advanced nearly two kilometres inland.* ◇ An **advance party** is a group of people sent to a place before the main group, to make preparations or find out what conditions are like.

❑ If you **advance** in your career, you get a higher position or become more successful. You can talk about an **advancement** in someone's career. *This is a society with no chance of advancement.*

❑ **Advance** is used in front of words like 'booking', 'warning', and 'notice' to talk about something being done a certain length of time before an event takes place. *...advance warning of earthquakes... They would have to give ten days' advance notice of a strike.* ◇ If something is done **in advance** of something else, it is done before it. *They are staking out their claim in advance of a political settlement.*

❑ If something like a meeting is **advanced**, it is brought forward to an earlier time.

❑ If a subject **advances**, progress is made in it, with knowledge increasing and problems being solved. You can talk about **advances** being made in a subject. *Medical research continually produces new advances.* ◇ Other kinds of progress can also be called **advances**. *Although Albania made some advances under Hoxha's rule, rigid central control created a stagnant backward economy.* Progress can be called

advancement. *...economic advancement.*

❑ Countries which have reached a high level of industrial and technological development are sometimes called **advanced** countries. ◇ **Advanced** designs and methods involve modern technology and have been developed from earlier versions of the same thing. *...Britain's most advanced fighter plane.* ◇ **Advanced** is used to describe people who have been studying or learning something for some time and have reached a high level of knowledge or skill. *...advanced students... ...advanced skiers.* ◇ If something is at an **advanced** stage, it has been proceeding or developing for some time. *Negotiations are at an advanced stage... The old system is in an advanced state of decay and cannot survive.*

❑ If you **advance** something like a cause, you do something to improve its chances of success. Similarly, you can **advance** your claim to be something or have something. ◇ If you **advance** a theory or point of view, you put it forward and argue in favour of it.

❑ If you are given an **advance**, you are given some money before it is due. Authors are often given advances by publishers, so they have money to live on while they are writing a book.

❑ If an amount **advances**, it increases. *Sales advanced by a fifth to £179.9m.*

❑ If someone is of an **advanced age**, they are very old.

❑ If someone makes **advances** to you, (a) they try to start a friendly relationship with you. *The President had shunned any advances from Libya.* (b) they try to get you to take part in sexual activities with them.

Advanced Level See A-Level.

advantage (advantaged) ❑ An **advantage** is something which puts you in a better position than someone else. *The carbon-fibre design gave Boardman an advantage of half a second per lap.* ◇ **Advantaged** people have more money and a higher standard of living than most other people.

❑ If something is **to your advantage**, it benefits you in some way. ◇ If you use something **to good advantage**, you use it in a way which brings real benefits to you or someone else. *Taxpayers may wonder whether their money is being spent to best advantage.* ◇ If you **take advantage** of an opportunity, you use it to do something you want.

❑ The **advantages** of something are the good things about it, which make it more desirable than other things. ◇ When something is better than something else, you can say it **has the advantage** over it.

❑ In tennis, **advantage** is the first point scored after deuce. If the same player wins the next point, he or she wins the game.

advantageous If something is **advantageous** to you, it benefits you or puts you in a better position than other people.

advent When something new is introduced which brings significant changes to people's lives, you call this its **advent**. *...the advent of the personal computer... ...the advent of democracy in eastern Europe.* ◇ **Advent** is the period just before Christmas, including the four Sundays before Christmas Day, when Christian worship concentrates on the coming of Jesus.

adventure (adventurer) **Adventure** is doing unusual exciting things. *Sevareid always had a taste for adventure.* An

adventurer is someone who likes doing things like this. ◇ An **adventure** is a series of exciting things someone is involved in.

adventure playground An **adventure playground** is an area of land with special equipment for children to play on, such as climbing frames, ropes, nets, and tyres.

adventurism (adventurist) **Adventurism** is behaving in a reckless way, to try and get some advantage for yourself. When someone behaves like this, you say their behaviour is **adventurist** or you call them an **adventurist**.

adventurous (adventurousness) An **adventurous** person is willing to take risks and eager to have new experiences. ◇ You say something someone does is **adventurous** when it shows a willingness to try out new things. *Aston Villa made an adventurous choice of manager... ...the adventurousness of his style.*

adverb An **adverb** is a word which says where, when, or how something is done. In 'They went outside', 'She arrived late', and 'He stood up quickly', 'outside', 'late', and 'quickly' are adverbs.

adversarial (*pron:* ad-ver-**sair**-ree-al) An **adversarial** system is based on the idea of two people or groups being opposed to each other, with one of them eventually beating the other. *Sir Peter criticised the adversarial nature of criminal trials... ...Mrs. Thatcher's adversarial approach to the European Community.*

adversary (*pron:* **ad**-ver-ser-ree) (adversaries) Your **adversary** is someone you are competing or arguing with, or fighting against.

adverse (adversely) **Adverse** is used to describe things which make it difficult for you to achieve what you want. *...adverse weather conditions... ...adverse publicity.* You can also talk about the **adverse** effects of something. *The team has not been too adversely affected by the news.*

adversity is used to talk about times when you experience misfortune and hardship. *He showed courage in adversity... ...the will to triumph against adversity.*

advert An **advert** is an advertisement.

advertise (advertising, advertised; advertisement, advertiser) ❑ When a product is **advertised**, people are told it is available, for example by an item on TV or in a newspaper. Items like these are called **advertisements**; they also try to persuade people to buy the product. Jobs and events can also be **advertised**. ◇ **Advertising** is the job of designing and producing advertisements. Companies who advertise products are called **advertisers**. ◇ An **advertising feature** is the same as an advertorial.
❑ If you **advertise** something about yourself, you make people aware of it. *They do not wish to advertise the fact that they need such aids.*

advertorial An **advertorial** is an item in a magazine or newspaper which is made to look like an article, but is actually an advertisement.

advice If you give someone **advice**, you tell them what you think they should do. ◇ **Advice** is also help and information. *Building societies can give advice on mortgages and savings schemes.*

advisable (advisability) If you say something is **advisable**, you mean it is a good idea to do it or have it. *It is advisable to avoid mountain roads... A packed lunch is advisable.* The **advisability** of something is whether it is a good

idea or not. *The ministers discussed the advisability of resuming full diplomatic relations with China.*

advise (advising, advised; adviser) ❑ If you **advise** someone, you tell them what you think they should do. *American citizens have been advised to leave the country as soon as possible... He advised against over-optimism.* ◇ If you say someone would be **well advised** to do something, you mean they ought to do it, for their own sake. *The White House would be better advised to concentrate on reducing America's budget deficit.* ◇ See also **ill-advised**.
❑ If someone **advises** on a subject, they give people help and information about it. *He has lately been advising on privatisations in Eastern Europe.* Someone who gives help like this is called an **adviser**. *...financial advisers.* ◇ If you are **advised** of something, you are told about it. *Consultants advised them that the building lacked historical or architectural merit.*

advisedly If you say you use a word or phrase **advisedly**, you mean you have chosen it deliberately, because it is the right word or phrase for what you want to say. *Young boys will degenerate into barbarism without adult supervision. I say 'boys' advisedly because we are talking almost entirely about male behaviour.*

adviser See **advise**.

advisory An **advisory** group gives suggestions, help, or information, without having the power to make decisions themselves. *...the Government's advisory committee on social security.*

advocate (advocating, advocated; advocacy) If you **advocate** something, you say publicly you think it should be done, used, or introduced. *...the constitutional changes advocated by the Labour Party.* You can talk about someone's **advocacy** of something, or say they are an **advocate** (*pron:* **ad**-vo-kut) of it. *...his advocacy of the use of 'necessary' violence... I am not an advocate of the death penalty.* ◇ An **advocate** is also a lawyer who puts someone's case in court. Putting a case in court is called **advocacy**. *...an impressive feat of advocacy by Louis Blom-Cooper, QC.*

aegis (*pron:* **ee**-jiss) If something is done **under the aegis** of an organization, it is done with their support and backing. *...the joint international response under the aegis of the United Nations.*

aeon (*or* eon) (*both pron:* **ee**-on) An **aeon** is an extremely long period of time. *The Hindu fundamentalists believe that aeons ago Lord Rama was born on this very site.*

aerate (aerating, aerated; aeration) If something is **aerated**, air is introduced into it. *The hoofs of cattle break the crust on the soil, permitting aeration and water absorption.*

aerial is used to describe things happening in or from the air, especially things to do with aircraft. *...aerial bombing.* ◇ **Aerial** photographs are of things on the ground, taken from the air.
❑ An **aerial** is a long thin piece of metal for sending or picking up TV or radio signals.

aerobatics are skilful and spectacular movements made by planes, usually to entertain people watching from the ground.

aerobics is a type of vigorous exercise, often to music, which increases the amount of oxygen in your blood and strengthens your heart and lungs.

aerodrome is an old word for an airfield.

aerodynamic (aerodynamics) **Aerodynamic** is used to talk about the movement of objects through air, especially planes and cars. *The plane has long slender wings to minimise aerodynamic drag.* **Aerodynamics** is the study of movement like this. The **aerodynamics** of an object are the things about it, especially its shape, which affect the ease with which it moves through the air. *Modifications have resulted in improved aerodynamics.* If something is **aerodynamic**, its shape is designed to stop it being slowed down by air resistance. *...the aerodynamic Lotus Sport bike.*

aeronautics (aeronautical) **Aeronautics** is the design and construction of aircraft. **Aeronautical** is used to talk about things to do with aeronautics. *...aeronautical principles... ...aeronautical engineering.*

aeroplane An **aeroplane** is a powered aircraft with wings.

aerosol An **aerosol** is a pressurized container with liquid inside. The liquid is forced out as a fine spray when a button is pressed on the top. Things like furniture polish, deodorant, and hairspray often come in aerosols.

aerospace is used to talk about the developing and making of rockets, missiles, and spacecraft. *...the aerospace industry.*

aesthete (*pron:* eess-theet) An **aesthete** is a person who loves and appreciates beautiful things, especially works of art.

aesthetic (*pron:* iss-thet-ik) (aesthetically) **Aesthetic** is used to talk about things involving beauty or art, and people's appreciation of these things. *...aesthetic responses... ...work that is aesthetically attractive.* ◇ **Aesthetics** is the study of beauty in art, literature, and music.

afar If something is seen or done from **afar**, it is seen or done from a long way off.

affable (affably) An **affable** person is good-natured and friendly. *He smiled affably.*

affair ❑ An **affair** is a series of happenings which attracts a lot of attention, especially one which involves dishonest or careless behaviour. *The Labour Party has called for a judicial inquiry into the whole affair.* ◇ You can describe something which takes place by saying it is an **affair** of a particular kind. *An experiment run by Dr Ting is not a casual affair... The European conquest of the Americas was a brutal affair.* Similarly, you can call something like a building or machine an **affair** of a particular kind. *Pham took me to Ho Chi Minh's home, a simple, open, tile-roofed affair.*

❑ Things which people are concerned with can be called **affairs** of different kinds. For example, you can talk about 'economic affairs' or 'affairs of state'. **Affairs** is often used when mentioning someone's area of responsibility or interest. *...the Iranian Minister for Religious Affairs... ...a writer on East European affairs.* ◇ Your **affairs** are the things you are involved in, especially things to do with money and business. *He resigned because of the police investigation into his affairs.* ◇ If you say something is someone's **affair**, you mean it is their business and nobody else's.

❑ An **affair** is a sexual relationship between two people who are not married to each other, especially when one or both of them is married to someone else.

❑ See also **state of affairs**, **current affairs**.

affect (affectation) ❑ If something **affects** something else,

it influences it or causes it to change, often in a harmful or damaging way. *He was asked if today's failure would affect his future chances... ...people affected by cystic fibrosis... The storms are now easing in the worst-affected areas.*

❑ If someone **affects** a characteristic or style of behaviour, they adopt it and pretend it is natural to them. *She affected a lisp... He affected to despise every Briton he met.* You call a pretence like this an **affectation**. ◇ **Affected** people behave in a false unnatural way intended to impress other people. You call their behaviour **affectation**.

affection is a feeling of fondness for someone. *His son can still write about him with affection.* Feelings of this kind are called **affections**. *...his loss of his wife's affections.*

affectionate (affectionately) If your behaviour is **affectionate**, you show fondness for someone. *They were treated warmly and affectionately.*

affidavit (*pron:* af-fid-**dave**-it) An **affidavit** is a written statement which you swear is true and which may be used as evidence in court.

affiliate (affiliating, affiliated; affiliation) If an organization **affiliates** itself to another organization, it becomes a part of it or forms a close official link with it; this makes it an **affiliate** of the other organization. *...the affiliation of unions to the Congress of Trade Unions.* ◇ Your political **affiliation** is the party you regularly support. Your religious **affiliation** is the church you belong to.

affinity (affinities) If you have an **affinity** with someone or something, you feel you understand them, belong with them, or are like them in some way. *Liszt was a composer with whom Bolet always had special affinity.*

affirm (affirmation) If you **affirm** something like an intention, you say you definitely have it. *He affirmed France's willingness to use force if necessary... The ministers issued a robust affirmation of their faith in the European Monetary System.*

affirmative If you give an **affirmative** response, you say 'yes', or something which means yes.

affix (affixes, affixing, affixed) If you **affix** something somewhere, you stick, fasten, or attach it there.

afflict (affliction) If someone is **afflicted** by a serious illness, they have it. An illness can be called an **affliction**. *...one of the most tragic afflictions facing modern medicine.* People can also be **afflicted** by other things, such as war or famine. *...the pollution problems afflicting the East... ...Ethiopia's drought-afflicted highlands.*

affluent (affluence) **Affluent** people have a lot of money and a high standard of living. You talk about the **affluence** of people like these.

afford ❑ If you can **afford** something, you have enough money to buy it or pay for it.

❑ If you say someone cannot **afford** to do something or let something happen, you mean they must avoid it, because of the trouble it would bring. *The president cannot afford to upset his farmers any further.* Similarly, you can say someone can **ill afford** to do something or let something happen. *Japan feels it can ill afford to jeopardise its economic links with its huge neighbour.*

❑ If you are **afforded** something, you are provided with it. *His business interests afforded him the chance for extensive travel... The crossing takes around 30 minutes and affords great views of the Golden Gate Bridge.* ◇ If something **affords** you a pleasant feeling, it gives you it. *The prospect afforded him* *the liveliest satisfaction.*

affordable You say something is affordable when people can afford to buy it or pay for it. *...affordable housing.*

afforestation is the planting of large numbers of trees on bare land.

affray An affray is a noisy and violent fight, especially in a public place. Affray is the criminal offence of using or threatening to use violence in a public place.

affront If you are affronted by something or regard it as an affront, you feel insulted by it.

aficianado (*pron:* af-fish-yo-**nah**-do) (aficianados) If someone is an aficianado of something, they are knowledgeable and enthusiastic about it. *...whisky aficianados.*

afield Far afield is used to emphasize how far away something is. *The championships have attracted competitors from as far afield as Alaska and Australia.* ◇ Further afield is used to say something is further away than the place just mentioned. *Artillery shells have landed further afield, in residential areas of Sidon itself.*

afloat If you say a ship or boat is afloat, you mean it is floating rather than resting on something solid. If you say a damaged ship is still afloat, you mean it has not sunk. ◇ If a business or a country's economy is kept afloat, there is just enough money to keep it going.

afoot If you say something is afoot, you mean people are planning or organizing something. *Moves are afoot to establish a new company.*

aforementioned is used to talk about someone or something that has already been mentioned. *The audience included all of the aforementioned... All of the aforementioned moves are being introduced elsewhere in Eastern Europe.*

afraid If you are afraid of someone or something, you feel fear because of them. ◇ If you are afraid for someone, you are worried something bad will happen to them. ◇ If you are afraid something unpleasant will happen, you are worried it will happen. *The farmers are afraid their sheep will have to be sold at a loss.* ◇ You say 'I'm afraid' when you are mentioning something which might upset or displease people. *I'm afraid England were out for 194.*

afresh If you do something afresh, you start doing it again, as if you were doing it for the first time. *The government says it will look afresh at the legislation.*

African-American An African-American is a black American whose ancestors came from Africa.

afro hair is a hairstyle in which a black person's hair is allowed to grow in a frizzy mass.

aft See fore.

after ❑ If something happens after a certain time or event, it happens at a later time. ◇ After is used to say how much time passes before something happens. *The fight ended after 51 seconds of the third round... A retrial several years after the original crime would carry obvious risks.*

❑ If one thing comes after another, it follows it. You can say several things happen one after another. ◇ If something happens day after day or year after year, it keeps happening every day or every year.

❑ After is used to talk about the period following something, when its effects are still being felt. *Alan Little has been assessing the reaction and the mood after Mr Heath's visit... Mr Major's hand-wringing seemed odd after a decade of Thatcherism.*

❑ If you go after someone, you follow them or chase them. ◇ If the police are after someone, they are trying to catch them.

❑ The thing you are after is the thing you are trying to find or achieve.

❑ If you are named after someone, you were given their name when you were a baby. Similarly, something can be named after a well-known person, as a sign of respect. *The Ramon Magsaysay Award is named after a Philippine president who died in a plane crash in 1960.*

after-effects The after-effects of something are the bad or harmful effects which continue after it is over. *...the after-effects of the Chernobyl disaster... He is still suffering the after-effects of a bout of glandular fever.*

afterbirth The afterbirth is the material which comes out of a woman's or female animal's womb after she has given birth.

afterglow The afterglow of an enjoyable experience is a pleasant feeling which remains after the experience is over. *...the afterglow of victory.*

afterlife The afterlife is a life some people believe begins after you die, for example a life in heaven or as another person or animal.

aftermath The aftermath of a major event is the period just after it, and the situation it leaves when it is over. *The Council had been set up in the aftermath of the Iranian revolution.*

afternoon The afternoon is the part of each day which begins at lunchtime and ends at about 5 or 6 o'clock.

aftershave is a scented liquid men sometimes put on their faces, especially after they have shaved.

aftershocks The aftershocks of an earthquake are a series of lesser tremors which come after it. ◇ The aftershocks of an important and dramatic event are a series of smaller events which follow it and are a result of it. *...the aftershocks of last week's failed coup.*

aftertaste An aftertaste is a taste, especially an unpleasant one, which remains in your mouth after you have finished eating or drinking something. ◇ If something leaves an aftertaste, it creates an impression which is still there when it is finished. *Mr Major's speech left an odd aftertaste.*

afterthought If you say or do something as an afterthought, you say or do an extra thing which you had not planned beforehand.

afterwards is used to say something happens at a later stage, after something else has finished. *He launched an anti-litter campaign but was spotted shortly afterwards tossing away the wrappings of a cigarette pack.*

afterword An afterword is a brief extra chapter or section at the end of a book.

again is used to talk about things being repeated. *Stockton won the PGA championship in 1970 and again six years later.* ◇ If something happens again and again, it keeps happening.

❑ Again is used to talk about things going back to the way they were. *The laundry was working again.*

❑ As much again means an additional amount equal to the one just mentioned. *The Red Cross has spent $100 million in Somalia over the past year and intends to spend as much again.* ◇ If an amount is half as much again as another amount, it is 50 per cent larger.

against is used to talk about something being in contact with something else. *She leant against the despatch box... She cleaned the edge of her knife against the plate.*

❑ If you are **against** something, you are opposed to it or disapprove of it. ◇ **Against** is used to talk about resisting something or showing opposition to it. *...the tendency of children to rebel against their parents' ideas... More women are taking measures to protect themselves against being attacked.*

❑ **Against** is used to say someone attacks someone else, or tries to harm them in some other way. *The security forces moved against the students this morning... General Nimely accused the joint West African force of plotting against him.* ◇ **Against** is used to talk about fighting someone, or trying to beat them in a game. *...Norwich City's glorious efforts against Liverpool.*

❑ If you **have something against** someone or something, you have a reason to dislike them.

❑ If something is **against** the law, it is not allowed by law. Similarly, you can say something is **against** a rule or a person's principles. ◇ If something is **against** someone's wishes or orders, they have said it should not be done.

❑ If you decide **against** doing something, you decide not to do it.

❑ If you are moving **against** a current, tide, or wind, you are moving in the opposite direction to it. ◇ If something goes **against** a trend, it is the opposite of what has generally been happening.

❑ **Against** is used to mention the circumstances in which something happens. *The congress comes against a background of new fighting between the rebels and government forces.*

❑ The odds **against** something happening are the odds that it will not happen.

❑ Evidence **against** an idea or claim is evidence which suggests it is wrong. Evidence **against** a person suggests they have done something wrong or committed a crime.

❑ If something is measured or valued **against** something else, it is measured or valued by comparing it with that thing. *The pound has risen against the franc.* ◇ **As against** is used to compare something with something else, or to distinguish between things. *The party now has 119 seats in India's parliament, as against two in 1985... It is not clear yet to what extent the climatic changes are the result of natural variations, as against human factors.*

agape If you say people are **agape**, you mean they are amazed at something which is happening. *...a bitter feud that has left New York agape.* ◇ You can also say someone is **agape** when their mouth is wide open, especially with shock or surprise.

agar is a jelly-like substance made from seaweed. It is used for growing cultures in biological experiments.

agate is a type of striped quartz. An **agate** is a piece of polished agate used in jewellery.

age (ageing *or* aging, aged) ❑ Your **age** is how old you are. **Aged** is used to say how old someone is. *...youngsters aged 11 to 13.* ◇ If someone is in your **age group**, they are about the same age as you.

❑ **Age** is being old. *The organisation is rusty with age... Barrett must hope that age has blunted the reflexes of the champion.* ◇ When someone **ages**, they get older, or seem to get older. *She aged about 20 years in 2 weeks.* ◇ If something happens **with age**, it happens as someone or something

gets older. *The wood develops an attractive patina with age.* ◇ **Ageing** is used to describe people or things that are getting old. *...the ageing chairman... ...London's ageing transport system.* ◇ An **aged** person (*pron:* **age**-id) is very old. Old people in general are sometimes called the **aged**. *...housing for the aged.*

❑ If someone is **under age**, they are not old enough to do something, for example to buy alcohol. ◇ When someone **comes of age**, they legally become an adult. In Britain, people come of age at 18. The day when they reach this age is called their **coming of age**. ◇ You say something **comes of age** when it reaches the stage where it is fully developed. You call this its **coming of age**. *By the turn of the century the bicycle had come of age.*

❑ An **age** is a period in history. *...the age of television... It could be the beginning of a new age of friendship between the two countries.* ◇ If something takes an **age** or **ages**, it takes a long time.

age limit The **age limit** for something is the oldest or youngest age at which you are allowed to do it or be it.

age of consent The **age of consent** is the age at which a person can legally marry or have a sexual relationship.

age-old If something is **age-old**, it has been around for a very long time. *...the age-old conflict between fathers and sons.*

aged See **age**.

ageism (ageist) **Ageism** is discriminating against people because they are middle-aged or old. Rules or behaviour which discriminate in this way are called **ageist**. People who discriminate against older people are called **ageists**.

ageless If you call someone **ageless**, you mean (a) they never seem to get any older. (b) it is impossible to tell how old they are. ◇ If you call something **ageless**, you mean it does not seem to belong to any particular period in history. *...ageless ceremonies.*

agency (agencies) An **agency** is a business which provides a particular service. *...an advertising agency... ...adoption agencies.* ◇ In the US, an **agency** is also an administrative organization run by the government. *...the Central Intelligence Agency.*

agenda An **agenda** is a list of subjects, points, or questions to be discussed at a meeting. ◇ An **agenda** is also a list of things which need to be done. *The Foreign Secretary set out his agenda for a fourth Conservative term.* ◇ If you say something is **high on the agenda**, you mean it is one of the first things you intend to deal with. ◇ **hidden agenda**: see **hidden**.

agent ❑ An **agent** is someone who arranges work or business for other people, especially people like actors and musicians. ◇ An **agent** is also someone who works for a country's secret service.

❑ An **agent** of something is a cause of it. *Will the American military presence be an agent of change for women in Saudi Arabia?*

agent provocateur (agents provocateurs) (*both pron:* azh-on prov-vok-at-**tur**; *the 'zh' sounds like 's' in 'pleasure'*) An **agent provocateur** is a person employed by a police force or government to encourage people to cause trouble or break the law, so they can then be arrested or public opinion can be turned against them.

agglomeration An **agglomeration** of things is a group of them gathered together in no particular order or arrangement. *The album is a bizarre agglomeration of styles.*

aggrandizement (aggrandizing) (*can be spelled with an 's' instead of a 'z'*) If someone does something for their own **aggrandizement** or **self-aggrandizement**, they do it so people will think they are powerful and important. You say what they do is **self-aggrandizing**. *....self-aggrandizing propaganda.*

aggravate (aggravating, aggravated; aggravation) ❑ If something **aggravates** a problem, it makes it worse.
❑ If something **aggravates** people, it upsets them and makes them angry. *The police are doing nothing for fear of aggravating the demonstrators... ...the daily aggravation caused by the congestion.*

aggregate (aggregating, aggregated; aggregation) ❑ An **aggregate** is a total of several amounts added together. *MISYS is buying SCSS and SCPM for an aggregate £2.87 million.* You can say several amounts **aggregate** a total. *RWC's commercial director anticipated eight prime sponsorships aggregating around £16m.* ◇ In football, if one team beats another **on aggregate**, it wins because it has scored more goals in the two matches played between the teams.
❑ If things are **aggregated,** they are added or grouped together, although they may have no connection with each other. An **aggregation** is a group of things brought together like this. *Society is more than an aggregation of individuals.*

aggressive (aggressively, aggressiveness, aggression) ❑ If people are **aggressive**, they behave in an angry threatening way. *...beggars aggressively accosting shoppers.* You call behaviour like this **aggressiveness**. If actual violence is used, you call it **aggression**. ◇ When one country attacks another, this is called **aggression**. *He said that any military aggression by India would cost it very heavily.* Repeated attacks can be called **aggressions**.
❑ You also say people are **aggressive** when they behave in a forceful and determined way because they are eager to succeed.

aggressor When there is a fight or battle, the **aggressor** is the person or country that started it.

aggrieved If you feel **aggrieved**, you feel upset and angry because of the way you have been treated.

aggro is aggressive and violent behaviour.

aghast If you are **aghast** at something, you are surprised, shocked, and horrified. *Shoppers looked on aghast.*

agile (agility) An **agile** person can move very quickly and easily. You talk about the **agility** of someone like this. ◇ If someone can think quickly and cleverly, you can say they have an **agile** brain or talk about their mental **agility**.

aging See **age**.

agitate (agitating, agitated; agitation) ❑ If you **agitate** for something like a political cause, you campaign or demonstrate in support of it. *This has encouraged many Africans to agitate for multi-party democracy... Students have been at the forefront of the violent agitation that has swept north India.*
❑ If you are **agitated**, you are worried and cannot relax or think clearly.

agitator An **agitator** is someone who campaigns to bring about political or social change, often in a way which causes trouble.

agitprop is stories, plays, and art which try to promote political views, especially left-wing ones, and do it in a crude and obvious way.

AGM An AGM is a meeting held by a company or other organization once a year to discuss business such as the accounts for the previous year. AGM stands for 'Annual General Meeting'.

agnostic (agnosticism) An **agnostic** is someone who is unsure whether God exists or not. Some agnostics also say that nobody can ever know this; this view is called **agnosticism**. ◇ You also say someone is **agnostic** or an **agnostic** when they are unsure about something else. *As for whether Israel was wise to build nuclear weapons at all, Mr Hersh is agnostic.*

ago is used to say how long it is since something happened. For example, you say something happened five years ago.

agog If you are **agog**, you are surprised and excited by something, and eager to know more about it.

agonize (agonizing, agonized; agonizingly) (*can be spelled with an 's' instead of a 'z'*) ❑ If you **agonize** over something, you spend a lot of time worrying about it. You can call a long troubled discussion **agonized**.
❑ If something is **agonizing**, it causes great pain, worry, or frustration. *...slow, agonizing deaths... ...one of the most agonizing decisions of her life... ...the agonizingly slow rate of progress.* ◇ You call someone's expression **agonized** when it shows they are suffering great pain or misery.

agony (agonies) **Agony** is severe physical or mental pain. Mental suffering can also be called **agonies**. *...the agonies that writing caused him.*

agony aunt (agony uncle) An **agony aunt** or **agony uncle** is someone who writes a newspaper or magazine column or has a slot on TV or radio in which they reply to people who have written to them for advice on their personal problems.

agoraphobia (agoraphobic) Agoraphobia is a fear of open spaces, public places, or of going outside your own home. An **agoraphobic** is someone who has this fear.

agrarian is used to talk about things to do with the ownership and use of land, especially farmland. *...agrarian reforms.*

agree (agreeing, agreed; agreement) ❑ If you **agree** with someone or are **in agreement** with them, you have the same opinion about something. ◇ If you **agree** with something, you approve of it. *The federal government does not agree with the proposals.* ◇ If something **agrees** with you, you find it pleasant and it does not upset you or make you ill. *I asked if prison life agreed with him.* ◇ If you **agree** to do something, you say you will do it.
❑ If something like a deal is **agreed**, the people involved reach a joint decision on it. What they decide is called an **agreement**; the document setting out their decision, which they sign, is also called an **agreement**.
❑ If two accounts of an event **agree**, they are the same, and so are probably both correct. Similarly, you can say two sets of figures **agree**.

agreeable (agreeably) ❑ If something is **agreeable**, it is pleasant. *The sun was agreeably warm.* ◇ If someone is **agreeable**, they are pleasant and friendly.
❑ If you are **agreeable** to something, you are willing to do it or allow it.

agribusiness (agribusinesses) **Agribusiness** is the commercial side of farming. An **agribusiness** is a large company involved in the production, processing, distribution, and selling of farm products.

agriculturalist An **agriculturalist** or **agriculturist** is an expert on agriculture.

agriculture (agricultural, agriculturally) **Agriculture** is farming. **Agricultural** is used to talk about things to do with farming. *...Europe's common agricultural policy... ...the agriculturally important north-west of India.*

agriculturist See agriculturalist.

agro-chemicals (*or* agrochemicals) are chemicals used in farming, for example fertilizers.

agronomy (*pron*: ag-ron-om-mee) (agronomist) **Agronomy** is the study of the scientific and economic issues involved in the cultivation of land and crop production. An **agronomist** is an expert on this.

aground If a ship runs **aground**, it becomes stuck on rocks or a sandbank, or the bottom of a shallow river or lake.

ahead ❑ If something is **ahead**, it is in front of you. *Now I could see Denver looming ahead of me.*
❑ If you get somewhere **ahead** of someone else, you get there first.
❑ If you are **ahead** of someone in your work or achievements, you have made better progress than them. *His inventiveness keeps him ahead of the field.* ◇ If a person or team is **ahead** in a game or competition, they are winning.
❑ **Ahead** is used to talk about the future. *There are difficult times ahead... Staff are trying to plan ahead.* ◇ If one thing happens **ahead** of another, it happens before it. *The meeting took place ahead of the annual discussions of the IMF and the World Bank.*
❑ **go ahead: see go.**

AI See artificial insemination.

aid (aiding, aided) ❑ **Aid** is money, food, equipment, or services provided for people in need.
❑ If an event is **in aid of** something like a charity, it is organized to raise money for it. *The concert was in aid of an international fund for disaster relief.* ◇ If you say what something is **in aid of**, you are saying what it is for, or what its purpose is. *Supposedly this is all in aid of widening the audience for classical music.*
❑ If you **aid** someone, you help or assist them. ◇ If you do something **with the aid of** someone or something, they help you do it. *With the aid of the binoculars he could see into the room.* ◇ An **aid** is a device which helps you to do something. *...navigational aids... ...children's swimming aids.* ◇ If you **come to** someone's **aid**, you help them when they are having problems. ◇ If one thing **aids** another, it makes it easier or more likely to happen. *The planting of huge tracts of conifers has aided the catastrophic depopulation of hills and glens.*

aide An **aide** is an assistant to someone with an important job, especially in the government or armed forces.

aide-de-camp (*pron*: aid-de-kom) (*plural*: aides-de-camp) An **aide-de-camp** is an officer in the armed forces who serves as a personal assistant to an officer of higher rank.

AIDS (*or* Aids *or* aids) is a condition which results from infection by the human immunodeficiency virus (HIV). In people with AIDS, this virus destroys the body's natural system of protection against disease, leaving the body vulnerable to a wide range of infections and other disorders, such as pneumonia and cancer, which then often cause death.

ail (ailing, ailed) ❑ An **ailing** person is ill. If you ask what **ails** someone, you are asking what their illness is.
❑ If something **ails** a country or an organization, it is a serious problem for it. *Banks sometimes pretend that recession is all that ails their industry.* If something is **ailing**, it is having serious problems. *...a package to revive the ailing economy... ...an ailing marriage.*

ailment An **ailment** is an illness.

aim (aiming, aimed) ❑ If you **aim** a gun at someone or something, you point it towards them, intending to fire it. ◇ If you **aim** a stone or some other object at someone, you throw it at them. ◇ If you **aim** a kick or punch at someone, you try to kick or punch them.
❑ If an action is **aimed** at particular people, they are the ones it is intended to affect. *The army operation is not aimed against the civilian population.* ◇ If a product is **aimed** at a group of people, they are the ones who are meant to buy it. *Hamlet cigars are aimed at the popular end of the market.* ◇ If a remark or joke is **aimed** at someone, it is about them, although it may not mention them directly. *His comments were aimed at critics of the nomination of Mr Rowland.*
❑ If you **aim** at something or **aim** to do it, you try to achieve it. *He is aiming at a compromise... We will aim to sell to the highest bidder.* You can also say an action or policy is **aimed** at achieving something. *...a draft law aimed mainly at regulating television advertising.* Your **aim** or **aims** are what you are trying to achieve. *His aim was to take education out of local politics.*

aimless (aimlessly) If someone is **aimless**, they have no clear purpose or plan. *She was wandering around aimlessly.* You can also call an activity **aimless**. *These annual meetings seem an aimless shambles.*

air (airing, aired) ❑ **Air** is the mixture of gases which forms the earth's atmosphere and which we breathe. ◇ If you **air** a room, you let fresh air into it. ◇ If you **air** clothes, you hang them up in a warm place, to get them completely dry.
❑ **Air** is used to talk generally about the space above the ground. *The balloon was about 20ft in the air.* ◇ If an aircraft **takes to the air**, it takes off.
❑ **Air** is used to talk about travel by aircraft, and military activity involving aircraft. *...an air crash... ...an air and sea search... ...an air attack.*
❑ If you **air** your feelings or opinions, you express them publicly. *These are just some of the criticisms that were aired in Washington yesterday.* ◇ If a subject is **aired** or given an **airing**, it is discussed. *Details of his private life were aired in public... Both these notions got an airing during the campaign.*
❑ When a TV or radio programme is **aired**, it is broadcast. When it is being broadcast, you can say it is **on air** or **on the air**. You can also say the people in it are **on air** or **on the air**. *The army commander went on air to say that the military had seized power.*
❑ If you say someone or something has a particular **air**, you are describing the general impression they give. *There's been an air of desperation in many of the pronouncements... The capital has taken on the air of a city at war.*
❑ If you say something is **in the air**, you mean it is likely

to happen soon. *Change is in the air.*

❏ If a question or decision is **hanging in the air**, nothing has been done about it and it is waiting to be dealt with. *Various possibilities are still hanging in the air... His resignation leaves a number of important decisions hanging in the air.*

❏ If you do something to **clear the air**, you try to sort out misunderstandings and get rid of resentment.

❏ If someone puts on **airs**, they behave in an exaggerated unnatural way, intended to impress people.

❏ An **air** is a simple tune.

air base (*or* **airbase**) An **air base** is a place where military aircraft take off, land, and are serviced.

air brakes are brakes operated by compressed air, typically used on larger vehicles like buses and trains.

air commodore An **air commodore** is a high-ranking officer in the RAF.

air-conditioned (air-conditioner, air-conditioning) If a building or vehicle is **air-conditioned**, it has a machine in it called an **air-conditioner** which keeps the air inside cool and dry. This method of regulating temperature is called **air-conditioning**.

air force (*or* **airforce**) A country's **air force** is the part of its armed forces which is involved in making attacks from the air and fighting air battles.

air gun See airgun.

air hostess The women who look after the passengers on a plane used to be called **air hostesses**.

air raid An **air raid** is an attack by military aircraft on a ground target using bombs or rockets.

air rifle An **air rifle** is a rifle which fires pellets by means of compressed air.

air-sea rescue is the use of helicopters, other aircraft, and boats to rescue people who are in danger of drowning in the sea.

air show (*or* **airshow**) An **air show** is an event held for entertainment or publicity in which people on the ground watch aircraft flying past or performing stunts.

air strike An **air strike** is the same as an air raid.

air terminal An **air terminal** is a building in a city from which passengers are taken by road or rail to an airport.

air time is broadcasting time on TV or radio.

air-to-air missiles are fired by one aircraft at another.

air traffic control (air traffic controller) **Air traffic control** is the organizing of air flights from the ground. It includes constant checking of the position of aircraft, and giving instructions to pilots over the radio. The people who do this work are called **air traffic controllers**.

airbag An **airbag** is a safety device sometimes fitted to cars. It is folded flat in a compartment in the steering wheel; if the car crashes, the device inflates automatically, forming a cushion between the driver and the steering wheel.

airbase See air base.

airborne is used to describe (a) things or people being taken somewhere by plane. *...airborne troops.* (b) things carried by the wind. *...airborne bacteria.*

airbrick An **airbrick** is a brick with holes in it which is put into the wall of a building so air can get in.

airbrush (airbrushes, airbrushing, airbrushed) An **airbrush** is a tool which uses compressed air to spray paint onto a surface. It is used in modern art, and for customizing

cars. If a photograph is **airbrushed**, it is altered using an **airbrush**. Alterations made in this way are difficult to detect.

aircraft (*plural:* aircraft) An **aircraft** is any vehicle which can fly, for example a plane or helicopter.

aircraft carrier An **aircraft carrier** is a warship which can carry several planes and has a deck for them to land and take off.

aircraftsman (aircraftsmen; aircraftswoman, aircraftswomen) **Aircraftsman** (or **aircraftswoman**) is the lowest rank in the RAF. The ranks above it are **leading aircraftsman** (or **aircraftswoman**) and **senior aircraftsman** (or **aircraftswoman**).

aircrew The **aircrew** on a passenger plane are the pilot and the other people on board who help to fly it and look after the passengers. The **aircrew** of a military aircraft are the personnel who fly it and operate it.

airfield An **airfield** is an area of land where aircraft can land and take off.

airflow The **airflow** in something like a wind tunnel is the movement of air in it.

airforce See air force.

airframe A plane's **airframe** is its body and wings, not including the engines.

airgun (*or* **air gun**) An **airgun** is a pistol or rifle which fires pellets or darts by means of compressed air.

airily See airy.

airing cupboard An **airing cupboard** is a warm cupboard, especially one with a water heater in it, where you put things like clothes, sheets, and towels after they have been washed and partly dried, to get them completely dry.

airless If a place is **airless**, no fresh air gets into it.

airlift If people, troops, or goods are **airlifted**, they are moved by air, especially during wartime or when land routes are closed. An operation like this is called an **airlift**.

airline An **airline** is a company or other organization which provides regular plane services carrying people or goods.

airliner An **airliner** is a large passenger plane.

airlock An **airlock** is a compartment between places which do not have the same air pressure, for example in a spacecraft or submarine. Airlocks are used to prevent the air pressure in one place from being altered when someone enters from the other place. ◇ An **airlock** is also a blockage in a pipe caused by a bubble of air.

airmail is the system of sending mail by air.

airman (airmen) An **airman** is a man who serves in his country's air force.

airplane In the US, planes are sometimes called **airplanes**.

airport An **airport** is a place where passenger-carrying planes regularly land and take off.

airpower is the military power exerted by a country's air force. *American airpower should be used if necessary.*

airship An **airship** is a powered aircraft with no wings which is held up in the air by a large long gas-filled balloon. Passengers sit in a compartment underneath the balloon. Airships were tried out as an alternative to passenger planes in the 1920s and 1930s.

airshow See air show.

airspace A country's **airspace** is the sky above it, which is considered to belong to it. *Iraq says two aircraft violated its airspace yesterday.*

airstream An **airstream** is a current of moving air.

airstrip An **airstrip** is a stretch of land which has been cleared so planes can land and take off.

airtight If a container is **airtight**, no air can get into it or out of it.

airwaves If something is sent out **over the airwaves**, it is broadcast on TV or radio. *Policy experts took to the airwaves to explain the West's new intervention in the Gulf.*

airway ❑ An **airway** is a route for aircraft between major cities, mapped out to prevent collisions and monitored by air traffic control systems. ◇ **Airways** is used in the names of some airlines. *...British Airways.*
  ❑ Your **airway** is the passage which connects your mouth and nose to your lungs, through which air travels in and out of your body.

airworthy If an aircraft is **airworthy**, it is safe to fly.

airy (airily) ❑ An **airy** room is large and has plenty of fresh air.
  ❑ **Airy** is also used to describe a light-hearted or casual response to something which ought to be taken seriously. *...his airy musings... The Government is airily dismissing the complaints.*

airy-fairy ideas are vague, idealistic, and inappropriate in the real world.

aisle (*rhymes with 'mile'*) An **aisle** is a narrow gap separating blocks of seats, for example in a church, cinema, or plane.

ajar If a door is **ajar**, it is slightly open. ◇ If you say the door on something is **ajar**, you mean there is still an opportunity for someone to do something or take part in something.

aka (*pronounce each letter separately*) **aka** is used when mentioning someone's false or alternative name. It stands for 'also known as'. *...Mark Little aka Joe Mangel from Neighbours... ...Muhammad Ali (aka Cassius Clay).*

akin If something is **akin** to something else, it is similar to it. *English club sides tend to regard playing Australia as somewhat akin to being attacked by an angry boar.*

alabaster is a white stone used for making statues, vases, and other ornaments.

alacrity If you do something with **alacrity**, you do it quickly and eagerly.

alarm (alarming, alarmingly) ❑ If something **alarms** people, it makes them worried or anxious. You say something like this is **alarming**; the feeling it gives people is called **alarm**. *...the alarming increase in crime... ...the alarmingly high rate of heart disease... Israel has watched these developments with alarm.*
  ❑ An **alarm** is an automatic device which wakes you up or warns you of something, usually by making a loud noise. ◇ If you **sound the alarm** or **raise the alarm**, you warn people about something. *...a woman who raised the alarm after finding a bomb in a suitcase.* ◇ If something **sets** or **starts the alarm bells ringing**, people recognize it as a sign of trouble.

alarm clock An **alarm clock** is a clock you can set to wake you at a particular time. It does it by making a ringing or buzzing noise, or playing a tune.

alarmist If you accuse someone of being **alarmist** or an **alarmist**, you mean they are causing unnecessary worry and anxiety. *The change is not as dramatic as some alarmist reports would have us believe.*

alas is used to express regret or sadness about what you are saying. *Belize is beautiful but, alas, also extremely expensive... Alas, cumulative stress and disappointment had proved too overwhelming.*

albatross (albatrosses) The **albatross** is a very large white and black sea bird with a hooked beak and long narrow wings. ◇ You can say something is an **albatross** when it is a burden and causes serious problems. *This will be an albatross around the neck of Scottish industry.*

albeit You use **albeit** when you are adding a comment which takes something away from what you have just said. *Their pretty dream turned into an industrial success story, albeit on a smaller scale than expected.*

albino (albinos) An **albino** is a person or animal with very white skin, white hair, and pink eyes, caused by lack of pigment.

album An **album** is (a) a book for putting photographs or stamps in. (b) an LP containing several short items.

albumen is (a) another name for egg white. (b) another name for albumin.

albumin is a protein in substances like blood plasma and egg white.

alchemy (*pron: al-kem-ee*) (alchemist) In the Middle Ages, **alchemy** was a combination of chemistry and magic by which people called **alchemists** tried to discover how to change ordinary metals into gold. ◇ Nowadays, people use **alchemy** to talk about things being achieved by secret and mysterious means. *Top appointments tend to reflect the complex alchemy of party politics.*

alcohol is drinks like beer, wine, and whisky which can make people drunk. ◇ **Alcohol** is also the chemical in these drinks which produces this effect. It is made by fermenting sugars, and is also used as a solvent.

alcoholic (alcoholism) An **alcoholic** is someone who is addicted to alcohol. This addiction is called **alcoholism**. ◇ **Alcoholic** drinks are drinks like beer, wine, and whisky which can make people drunk.

alcove An **alcove** is a small area of a room where part of a wall has been built farther back than the rest.

alder The **alder** is a small tree with toothed rounded leaves, woody cones, and catkins. It is related to the birch, and grows near rivers.

ale is an alcoholic drink similar to beer except that it is not flavoured with hops. ◇ **Ale** is also another word for beer.

alert (alertness) ❑ If you are **alert**, you are paying full attention to what is happening and are ready to deal with it. *A doctor's alertness saved her son.* ◇ If you are **alert** to something, you are fully aware of it or quick to notice it. *The public is alert to environmental abuse and quick to demand action.* ◇ If something **alerts** you to something, it draws your attention to it. *Users are alerted to an incoming message by a flashing light or a tone.*
  ❑ If people are **on the alert**, they have been warned of a danger or problem and are ready to deal with it. *Coastal districts are on the alert in case the oil comes ashore.* If people are **on red alert**, they are ready to deal with a serious situation which is likely to happen at any moment. *The*

government has put security forces on red alert, fearing sabotage by militants. ◇ If you **alert** someone, you warn them of danger or trouble.

alfalfa or **lucerne** is a green plant with tiny three-pointed leaves and clusters of purple flowers. It is usually grown to feed farm animals.

alfresco If something such as a meal or a performance is alfresco, it is held in the open air.

algae are primitive plants without stems or leaves which grow in water or on damp surfaces. Seaweed and the green slime in ponds are types of algae.

algebra (algebraic) Algebra is a branch of maths in which letters are used to represent unknown amounts, and calculations are made to work out these amounts. Algebraic is used to talk about things to do with algebra. *...an algebraic formula.*

algorithm An **algorithm** is a series of mathematical instructions or procedures which, when carried out in sequence, lead to the solution of a problem.

alia See inter alia.

alias (aliases) An **alias** is a false or alternative name. *...funds held by an individual with several aliases.* Alias is used when mentioning someone's false or alternative name. *...David Taylor, alias the Silver Fox.*

alibi (*pron:* al-i-bye) (alibis) If you have an **alibi**, you can prove you were somewhere else when a crime was committed. ◇ You can also say someone has an **alibi** when they can prove something was not their fault.

alien ❏ If something is **alien** to you, you have never experienced it before and are not familiar with it. *After seventy years of Communist rule, a stock market was an alien concept in the Soviet Union.*
❏ Foreigners are sometimes called **aliens**, especially when they are illegally living in a country where they are not citizens. ◇ In science fiction, an **alien** is a creature from another planet.

alienate (alienating, alienated; alienation) If you **alienate** someone, you make them unfriendly or unsympathetic towards you. *Potential supporters may be alienated by headline-grabbing tactics... ...customer alienation.* ◇ If you are **alienated** from something, it seems strange, unpleasant, or hostile and you feel emotionally separated from it. *Young people in Britain feel alienated from adult society.*

alight ❏ If something is **alight**, it is on fire. *A car was set alight.*
❏ When you **alight** from a bus, train, or plane, you get out of it at the end of a journey.

align (alignment) ❏ If you are **aligned** with a group of people, you support them and have similar aims. You can talk about your **alignment** with a group. *Dr Geagea firmly aligned himself with the government of Lebanon... India continued to profess non-alignment.* ◇ If you **align** something with something else, you make it agree with it or conform to it. *We must aim to keep managers' behaviour aligned with shareholders' interests.* ◇ If countries **align** their economies or currencies, they agree to keep the value of their currencies as stable as possible in relation to each others' and to work together when deciding financial policies.
❏ You say two objects are **aligned** when they are in the position you want in relation to each other. *The opportunity to send a spacecraft to the planet comes only when Mars*

and the Earth are correctly aligned... They will cease drilling to allow for any readjustment in the alignment of the two tunnel-boring machines.

alike If people or things are **alike** in some way, they are similar. ◇ If people are treated **alike**, they are treated the same way. ◇ **Alike** is used to emphasize that something applies equally to two people, things, or groups. *The Mars bar is chewed by children and adults alike... ...a world trade war affecting rich and poor countries alike.*

alimentary canal Your **alimentary canal** is the passage in your body through which food travels from your mouth to your anus.

alimony is money a court decides someone must pay to their former husband or wife after they have been separated or divorced. 'Alimony' is a US legal word. In the UK, this money is called 'maintenance'.

alive ❏ If a person or animal is **alive**, they are not dead. ◇ If you say something is still **alive**, you mean it is still functioning or still around. *The company is being kept alive by hard-nosed financial management... Tribal politics is still alive.* If you say something is **alive and kicking** or **alive and well**, you mean it still exists and is thriving. *Racism is alive and well in Europe.*
❏ If you say a place is **alive** with people or animals, you mean it is full of them and they are very active. *The surrounding reef is alive with fish.* You can also say a place is **alive** with activity or noise. *Budapest was alive with demonstrations... The air was alive with the hum of aeroplane engines.* ◇ When a lot of stories are being passed around, you can say a place is **alive** with them. *Westminster was alive with rumours.*
❏ If an event or performance **comes alive**, it suddenly gets lively and interesting. You can also say a subject **comes alive** when something makes it more interesting for you.
❏ If you are **alive** to something, you are aware of it. *The Bank of England should have been alive to the legal risks.*

alkali (alkaline) **Alkalis** are a group of substances with certain chemical characteristics, such as the ability to form a salt when combined with an acid. An **alkaline** substance either is an alkali or contains one.

all is used to show you are talking about the whole of something or every one of a group of people or things. *...sitting in his room all day... They are calling on all their staff to ignore the strike call.* **All of** is used in a similar way. *All of the building is above ground level.*
❏ **All** is used to mean 'the only thing'. *All that is missing from the show is a self-portrait.*
❏ **all-** is added to words to say something consists of just one type of thing or person. *...an all-star cast... Pan Ding won the men's singles in an all-Chinese final.* ◇ **all-** is added to words ending in '-ing' to say something includes or affects everyone or everything. *...the all-conquering Neath side... ...all-embracing legislation.*
❏ **all-** is added to words like 'important' and 'powerful'. If you say someone is **all-important**, you mean they are extremely important. ◇ **all-** is added to words like 'purpose' and 'weather'. **All-purpose** things can be used for any purpose. ◇ **all-too-** is added to words to express regret. For example, if you say something is **all-too-familiar**, you mean it is very familiar and you wish it was not.

❑ **Above all** is used to say what is most important in a situation. *What prisoners need above all is somebody to talk to.* ◇ **After all** means 'in spite of all the things that have happened'. *Maybe the new government will after all prove to be clear-minded, bold and sturdily united.* ◇ **After all** is also used to mention a well-known fact which supports what you have been saying. *Animal physiology is after all significantly different from our own.*

❑ **For all** is used to mention something someone has said which has since been contradicted by their actions. *For all their sympathetic words, Western governments have not rushed to help.*

❑ **In all** means 'in total'. *The gang numbered seven in all.*

❑ You use **in all** in front of words like 'honesty' and 'seriousness', to say you are being completely honest or serious. *In all honesty, I find myself unable to share your view.* ◇ **In all probability** and **in all likelihood** are used to say something is very likely. *...eleventh century pillars which in all likelihood were part of a temple.*

❑ **At all** is used in sentences with 'not' in them, for emphasis. *A lot of the girls didn't play tennis at all before they came... But this was not bad at all.* ◇ **All that** is used in sentences with 'not' in them to say something is not as good, bad, etc as was expected. *It wasn't all that wonderful living in a thatched house... There wasn't all that much opposition.*

❑ You say **all the same** when you are mentioning something which happened or is true in spite of what you have just said. *It wasn't the white Christmas many had been hoping for, but the weather has been spectacular all the same.*

❑ You say **all in all** when you are summarizing a situation. *All in all, this was a surprisingly mild response.*

❑ If you are **all alone**, you are completely alone.

❑ If you say something is **all the better** for something else, you mean it is better because of it, although this may be a surprising claim to make. *The book has no pretensions whatsoever, and is all the better for it.* ◇ **All the more** is used in front of words like 'surprising' and 'important'. You say something is **all the more surprising** when you are mentioning an additional reason why it is surprising. *The allegations are all the more surprising because they have come from a former senior Communist official.*

❑ If something is done **once and for all**, it is done in such a way that it will not need to be done again. *Chemical weapons should be destroyed once and for all.*

❑ **All or nothing** is used to say you must either be totally committed to doing something or not do it at all. *In this area, it is all or nothing if you want to enforce regulations properly.* ◇ **All or nothing** is also used to talk about a situation where you either get everything you want or nothing.

❑ In some sports, **all** is used to say two teams or competitors have an equal score. *The overall score is tied at six games all.*

all-clear The **all-clear** is a signal that some danger is over. ◇ If you are given the **all-clear** to do something, you are given official permission to do it.

all-comers If someone competes against **all-comers**, they compete against anyone who is willing to face them, regardless of age, nationality, or experience.

all-in is used to say a price or charge covers everything. *Weekend courses start from £56 all-in.*

all-out is used to say people use all their efforts to achieve something, and commit themselves totally to it.

...an all-out effort to clean up the sea... ...an all-out attack.

all right (*or* **alright**) If you say something is **all right**, you mean it is satisfactory or acceptable. ◇ **All right** is also used to emphasize that something is true. *They gave the Angolans a hard time all right.*

all-round is used to say someone or something is able to do many different things. *...the world's finest all-round sports car... ...a talented all-round family entertainer.*

all-rounder In cricket, an **all-rounder** is a player who does not specialize in batting or bowling but is good at both.

all-time If you say something is at an **all-time** high or low, you mean it is higher or lower than it has ever been. ◇ **All-time** is also used to say someone is one of the best people ever at a sport. *...one of golf's all-time great players.*

Allah is the Muslim name for God.

allay If you **allay** someone's fears or doubts, you do or say something to reassure them.

allege (*alleging, alleged; allegedly, allegation*) If you **allege** that someone has done something wrong, you claim they have done it, although you cannot prove it. *...officers removed from power because of alleged corruption... ...people allegedly involved in the plot.* An **allegation** is a statement like this.

allegiance If you swear **allegiance** to someone or something, you swear to be loyal to them and support them. ◇ If you talk about a person's political **allegiance**, you mean the political group they support.

allegory (*allegories; allegorical*) An **allegory** is a story or painting in which characters and events represent something more general. You say a story or painting like this is **allegorical**.

allergic (*allergy, allergies; allergen*) If you are **allergic** (*pron:* al-ler-jik) to something, you become ill or get a rash when you eat it, touch it, or breathe it in. Being allergic to something is called having an **allergy** (*pron:* al-ler-jee). A substance people can be allergic to is called an **allergen** (*pron:* al-ler-jen).

alleviate (*alleviating, alleviated; alleviation*) If you **alleviate** something which causes problems or distress, you make it less severe. *...the alleviation of poverty.*

alley An **alley** or **alleyway** is a narrow path or street between two groups of buildings. See also **blind alley**.

alliance An **alliance** is a group of countries or organizations which have formally agreed to work together to achieve the same aims. You say countries or organizations like these are **in alliance**.

allied See **ally**.

alligator **Alligators** are large meat-eating reptiles with long bodies and tails. They live in rivers in China and the south-eastern US. They are similar to crocodiles, but their snouts are shorter and broader.

alliteration (*alliterative*) **Alliteration** is getting words which are close together in a sentence to begin with the same sound, as in 'Age with his stealing steps hath clawed me in his clutch'. You say speech or writing like this is **alliterative**.

allocate (*allocating, allocated; allocation*) If something is **allocated** to you, it is decided you shall have it. Similarly, something can be **allocated** for a particular purpose. *The official would allocate responsibilities and work between vari-*

ous UN agencies... ...the allocation of tickets.

allot (allotting, allotted) If something is **allotted** to you, it is decided you shall have it as your share.

allotment ❏ **Allotments** are small areas of land which people rent, usually from the council, to grow vegetables on.

❏ An **allotment** of something is an amount given to someone as their share.

allow ❏ If you are **allowed** to do something, you are given permission to do it, or are not prevented from doing it. *They were allowed to smoke... Most detainees have now been allowed to go home.* Similarly, if you are **allowed** something, you are given permission to have it, or are not prevented from having it. *They were demanding that the public be allowed unlimited access to personal files.*

❏ If you **allow** something to happen, you do not prevent it. ◇ If circumstances **allow** something to happen, they make it possible. *The lull in the fighting has allowed thousands of residents to leave their underground shelters.*

❏ If you **allow** a certain amount of time or money for something, you make sure you have that amount available. *Allow ten hours for the drive from Calais.* ◇ If you **allow** for something, you take it into consideration in your plans or calculations. *There's been a very steady change, once you've allowed for the seasonal effects.*

allowable If something is **allowable,** you can have it or do it without breaking a law or rule. ◇ If something is **allowable** for tax purposes, its cost can be deducted from your income when calculating how much tax you must pay.

allowance ❏ An **allowance** is an amount of money given regularly to someone to pay for the things they need. ◇ An **allowance** for tax purposes is an amount of money which is deducted from your income when calculating how much tax you must pay.

❏ If you **make allowances** for something, you take it into consideration when making plans or deciding how to behave.

alloy An **alloy** is a metal made by mixing two or more metals together. For example, brass is an **alloy** of copper and zinc.

allude (alluding, alluded; allusion) If you **allude** to something or make an **allusion** to it, you do not mention it directly, but say things intended to make people realize you are talking about it. *This last point was understood to be an allusion to the long standing hostility between Syria and Iraq.*

allure (alluring) The **allure** of something is the pleasing or exciting qualities it has, which attract people to it. If something is **alluring,** it has qualities like these.

allusion See allude.

allusive If a piece of writing such as a novel or poem is **allusive,** it is full of allusions, for example to older stories, myths, or things which have happened in the past.

ally (allies, allying, allied) ❏ If you **ally** yourself with someone, you agree to help and support each other. When this happens, you can say you become **allies.** Similarly, countries or organizations can become **allies.**

❏ If two qualities are **allied,** they are combined in an effective way. *He had a childlike simplicity allied to a determination to go his own way.*

❏ If something is **allied** to something else, it is similar to it or related to it. *...an eating disorder allied to anorexia.*

alma mater (*usual pron:* al-ma **mah**-ter) Your **alma mater** is the school, college, or university where you were educated.

almanac An **almanac** is a book published every year containing facts, figures, and other information about a subject. *...Wisden Cricketers' Almanac.*

almighty The **Almighty** is another name for God. ◇ **Almighty** is also used in a sarcastic way to talk about very powerful things or people. *...enticing the almighty dollar to our shores.* ◇ **Almighty** is used with some words to say something is very extreme. For example, an angry quarrel can be called an 'almighty row'. Similarly, you can say there is an 'almighty fuss' about something or call a loud explosion an 'almighty bang'.

almond **Almonds** are long flattish nuts. They are used in cooking and baking. Almond trees grow mainly in Asia and Africa, but they are also grown in Britain for their blossom.

almost means the same as 'nearly', but is not used after 'not', 'very', or 'so'.

alms are gifts of money, clothes, or food to poor people.

almshouse **Almshouses** are groups of small houses built and run by charities for local poor or old people to live in, sometimes without paying rent. Many almshouses are very old.

aloe **Aloes** are African plants with long thorny leaves and bright red flowers. They are used in medicines and cosmetics.

aloft means up in the air. *After the result was announced, Mr Peres was raised aloft by his supporters.*

alone ❏ If you are **alone,** there is nobody else with you. If you are **alone** with someone else, there are just the two of you. ◇ You can also say someone is **alone** when they live on their own and have no close friends or relatives.

❏ If you do something **alone,** you do it without help from anyone else. *She has brought up her two children alone.* When someone deals with a difficult situation without help from anyone else, you can say they **go it alone.** ◇ If you **leave** someone **alone,** you let them do what they want, and do not bother, annoy, or interfere with them.

❏ **Alone** is used to talk about something being true of only one person or thing, or being restricted to just one person or thing. *She alone will have her hallowed name in the history books... Financial criteria alone must not be allowed to dictate policy.* ◇ If you say there are a certain number of things in one place **alone,** you mean there are a lot of them just in that one place, so the total number must be very great indeed. *A million copies have been sold in the United Kingdom alone.*

along is used to talk about movement on something like a road, following its direction. *I walked along the street.* ◇ **Along** is used to talk about going to a place or event. *A lot of anarchist groups seemed to come along intent on causing trouble.* ◇ **Along** is also used to talk about any kind of continuous movement. *He was just a bloke walking along on his own.* ◇ If you take someone **along** when you go somewhere, you take them with you.

❏ If things are situated **along** something like a road, they are at various places on its sides or edges. *...the population living along the coast.*

❏ **Along** is used to talk about things advancing or progressing. *Trade officials see no good reason to hurry things along.*

❑ **Along with** means 'together with' or 'as well as'. *ICI, along with the rest of the drugs industry, is trying to find ways to cut costs.*

❑ **All along** is used to say something has been going on throughout a period of time. *This is what Iraq has been calling for all along.*

❑ **go along with:** See **go.**

alongside ❑ If something is **alongside** something else, it is next to it. ◇ If you work **alongside** other people, you work in the same place and co-operate with them.

❑ **Alongside** is also used to talk about things existing together. *Vocational qualifications should be introduced alongside A-levels.*

aloof (aloofness) If you say someone is **aloof** or talk about their **aloofness**, you mean they are not friendly or open with people. ◇ If you remain **aloof** from something, you do not get involved with it.

aloud If you read **aloud**, you say the words you read, so people can hear them. If you think **aloud**, you speak your thoughts as they come to you. *Frustrated negotiators have wondered aloud whether it is worth carrying on.*

alpaca The **alpaca** is a South American animal related to the llama. **Alpaca** is the wool from this animal.

alpha is α, the first letter of the Greek alphabet.

alphabet (alphabetical) The **alphabet** is the letters of a language in a fixed order. A number of words can be arranged so their first letters are in this order; you then say the words are in **alphabetical** order.

alpine is used to talk about things connected with high mountains, especially the Alps. *...alpine villages... ...alpine weather.* **Alpines** are plants from areas like these.

already is used to say something has happened earlier than expected. *The manoeuvring for these elections has already begun... Most people appear to have made up their minds already.*

alright See **all right.**

Alsatian **Alsatians** are large dogs with thick brownish coats, upright pointed ears, and long snouts. They are used as police dogs and guard dogs. **Alsatians** are also called 'German Shepherd Dogs'.

also You use **also** when you are adding an extra piece of information. *We've got a big table and also some stools and benches.* ◇ You use **also** to say something applies to other people or things, besides the ones you have just mentioned. *The appointment will also be welcomed by the Government.*

also-ran In horse-racing, an **also-ran** is a horse which is not listed among the winners. ◇ You say someone or something is an **also-ran** when they have not been successful compared to other people or things of their kind. *This helped to boost Italy from economic also-ran to one of Europe's front-runners in the 1980s.*

altar An **altar** is a table or raised platform used for religious purposes, especially in a Christian church. ◇ If you say something has been **sacrificed on the altar of** something else, you mean it has been made to suffer because of efforts to make the other thing succeed.

altarpiece An **altarpiece** is a painting, tapestry, or carving mounted above and behind the altar in a church.

alter (altering, altered; alteration) If something **alters** or is

altered, it changes; the change is called an **alteration.** ◇ **Alterations** are also building works which change the appearance of a building or make it more convenient or suitable for a particular use.

alter ego Your **alter ego** is a real or fictional person who can be regarded as another version of yourself. For example, if an actor regularly plays the same character on TV, you can say the character is the actor's **alter ego.** If a novelist creates a character who is very like himself or herself, you can say this character is the novelist's **alter ego.**

altercation (*pron:* ol-ter-**kay**-shun) An **altercation** is a noisy argument.

alternate (alternating, alternated; alternately, alternation) ❑ If you **alternate** (*pron:* **all**-ter-nate) between two things, you repeatedly have, use, or do each in turn. *He alternated between powder-pink and powder-blue jackets.* You can also say things **alternate** when they happen in turn. *Hope of economic rescue has alternated with fear of humiliation... ...the alternation of civilian and military governments.* **Alternate** (*pron:* **alt**-ter-nat) things keep happening one after another in turn. *The Soviet leader was pulled in alternate directions between the advocates of reform and the conservatives... Carson alternately slowed and quickened the tempo.*

❑ If something happens on **alternate** days, it happens every other day. Similarly something can happen on alternate weeks, months, etc.

alternating current See **AC.**

alternative (alternatively) ❑ If something is an **alternative** to something else, it can exist, be used, or be done instead of it. *He was concerned at the cost of new drugs, claiming more could be done to use cheaper alternatives... He has to sign the declaration or alternatively register a protest.*

❑ **Alternative** is also used to talk about things being done in a different way from the traditional or established way. *...alternative medicine... ...alternative comedians.*

alternator An **alternator** is an electric generator which produces alternating current, especially in a car.

although is used to mention something which contrasts with the rest of what you are saying. *Although bikes were a hindrance on certain stretches, the trip would have been impossible without them.*

altimeter An **altimeter** is an instrument which measures height above sea level, or above the ground.

altitude The **altitude** of something is its height above sea level.

alto (altos) An **alto** is a male singer whose voice has a similar quality and range to a female contralto. In four-part choral music, the second highest part is often called the **alto** part, whether it is sung by a man or a woman. ◇ Some musical instruments have **alto** as part of their name. They are smaller and have a higher pitch than tenor versions of the same instrument. *...an alto saxophone.*

altogether means 'completely'. For example, if something has stopped **altogether**, it has stopped completely. ◇ **Not altogether** means 'not absolutely'. *It was not altogether good advice.*

❑ **Altogether** is also used to emphasize that something is better or more satisfactory than something else. *His reception was altogether more cordial than the one that greeted* *his predecessor 11 years ago.* ◇ **Altogether** is also used to show an amount is a total. *Altogether £187m is to be spent on improving old jails.*

altruism (altruistic) **Altruism** is helping other people without having any selfish motive for what you do. When someone behaves like this, you say they are being **altruistic**.

aluminium is a light silvery-white metal which is easily worked. It does not corrode easily, and is used more than any other metal except iron and steel. In the US, aluminium is called **aluminum** (*pron:* al-**loom**-in-um).

alumnus (*plural:* alumni) An **alumnus** of a college or university, especially in the US, is a person who has studied at it or graduated from it. A woman graduate is sometimes called an **alumna** (*plural:* alumnae).

always is used to say something is constantly happening or is true all the time. *It was always a delight to visit him.* ◇ **Always** is also used to say a situation will not change in the future. *There will always be business travellers who want to fly in comfort.*

❑ If you say someone can **always** do something, you mean that option will continue to be open to them. *If necessary, the journalist can always obtain and add the more technical details.*

am See be.

a.m. is used when stating a time between midnight and noon. For example, 7 a.m. means 7 o'clock in the morning. **a.m.** stands for 'ante meridiem', which is Latin for 'before noon'.

amalgam An **amalgam** of two or more things is a mixture of them. ◇ **Amalgam** is the substance dentists sometimes use to make fillings. It is an alloy of mercury and other metals.

amalgamate (amalgamating, amalgamated; amalgamation) When two or more organizations **amalgamate**, they join together to become one organization. *The amalgamation of famous regiments has provoked a storm of protest.*

amanuensis (*plural:* amanuenses) (*prons:* am-man-yew-en-siss, am-man-yew-en-seez) An **amanuensis** is a person employed to take dictation or copy manuscripts.

amass (amasses, amassing, amassed) If you **amass** something, you gradually get more of it.

amateur (amateurism, amateurish) ❑ An **amateur** is someone who does something like acting or playing sport for pleasure and is not paid for it. Taking part in sport for pleasure rather than money is called **amateurism**.

❑ **Amateur** and **amateurish** are used to describe things which are not done skilfully. *The coup attempt was amateurish and poorly thought out.*

amaze (amazing, amazed; amazement, amazingly) If something **amazes** you, you are extremely surprised by it. When this happens, you say you are **amazed**. The feeling you get is called **amazement**. ◇ If you say something is **amazing**, you mean it is very remarkable or impressive. *The flu virus is amazingly adaptable.*

ambassador (ambassadorial) ❑ An **ambassador** is someone who is the official representative of their own country in a foreign country. **Ambassadorial** is used to talk about things to do with ambassadors. *Diplomatic ties have been restored to the ambassadorial level.*

❑ You can say someone is an **ambassador** for some-

thing like a sport or a cause when they act as a representative of it, or behave in a way which is good for its public image.

amber is a yellowish-brown fossilized resin, often used to make jewellery and other ornaments. ◇ **Amber** is also a gold or yellowish-brown colour.

ambiance See ambience.

ambidextrous An **ambidextrous** person can do the same things with either their right or left hand.

ambience (*or* **ambiance**) The **ambience** of a place is its character and atmosphere. *.....a hotel with a 1940s ambience.*

ambient music is produced using computers and consists of electronic sound intended to create background atmosphere rather than to be danced to or listened to.

❑ The **ambient** temperature of an object is the temperature of the air surrounding it.

ambiguous (ambiguously; ambiguity, ambiguities) If something is **ambiguous**, it can be understood in different ways, or could have more than one meaning. You talk about the **ambiguity** of something like this. The aspects of something which are unclear because they can be understood in different ways are called **ambiguities**. *...an ambiguously-worded statement... ...the ambiguities of contemporary Italian history.*

ambit The **ambit** of something like a law is the range of people or things it applies to.

ambition (ambitious, ambitiously) An **ambition** is something you want to achieve. *He fulfilled a lifelong ambition by becoming a fully qualified football referee.* ◇ **Ambition** is a strong desire to be successful or powerful. You say people who have this desire are **ambitious**. ◇ An **ambitious** plan or programme is on a large scale. *More ambitiously, plans have been mooted for a 450,000-strong Ukrainian army.*

ambivalent (*pron:* am-biv-a-lent) (ambivalence) If you are **ambivalent** about something, you are not sure what you think about it. This feeling of uncertainty is called **ambivalence**. *These mixed reactions reflect Latin America's ambivalence about relations with the United States.*

amble (ambling, ambled) If you **amble** somewhere, you walk slowly and in a relaxed manner. An **amble** is a walk like this.

ambulance An **ambulance** is a vehicle for taking people to and from hospital.

ambulanceman (ambulancemen) **Ambulancemen** are people whose job is to drive ambulances or take care of patients in ambulances until they get to hospital.

ambush (ambushes, ambushing, ambushed) If you are **ambushed**, people hide and wait for you, then attack you when you come past. An attack like this is called an **ambush**.

ameba See amoeba.

ameliorate (*pron:* a-meal-yor-ate) (ameliorating, ameliorated) If you **ameliorate** a bad situation, you do something to improve it.

amen is said or sung at the end of a prayer. 'Amen' is a Hebrew word meaning 'certainly'.

amenable (*pron:* a-mean-a-bl) If you are **amenable** to something, you are willing to do it or accept it.

amend (amendment) If you **amend** something which has been written or said, you alter it. An alteration like this is called an **amendment**. ◇ If you **make amends** for a mistake or some harm you have done, you do something to make up for it.

amenity (*pron:* a-**mean**-i-tee) (**amenities**) **Amenities** are facilities provided for people's convenience or enjoyment.

American is used to talk about (a) people and things in or from the US. *...an American cartoon series.* (b) things to do with the continent of America. ◇ An **American** is someone who comes from the US.

American football is a team game similar to rugby, except that the ball can be thrown forward. The players usually wear bulky protective equipment.

American Indian American Indians are people descended from the tribes who lived in North America before Europeans arrived. They are called by a variety of other names, including Amerindians, Indians, Red Indians, and Native Americans.

Americanise See Americanize.

Americanism An Americanism is a word or way of describing something which was first used in the US. *We have even ceased to call them chips, accepting the Americanism 'fries'.*

Americanize (Americanizing, Americanized; Americanization) (*can be spelled with an 's' instead of a 'z'*) If a country is Americanized, its way of life becomes similar to that of the US. *Many will rue the further Americanization of our cities.*

Amerindian See American Indian.

amethyst (*pron:* am-**myth**-ist) is a purple semiprecious stone, used in making jewellery. An **amethyst** is a jewel made from amethyst.

amiable (amiably, amiability) If someone is **amiable**, they are friendly, pleasant, and likeable. This quality is called **amiability**. *We chatted amiably about old friends.*

amicable (amicably) An **amicable** agreement or relationship does not involve disagreement or unpleasantness. *Last year Mr Black divorced amicably from his wife.*

amid (amidst) If something happens **amid** or **amidst** other things, it happens while they are happening. *The Chinese Foreign Minister has gone to Saudi Arabia, amidst speculation that the two countries are about to establish full diplomatic relations.* ◇ If something is **amid** or **amidst** other things, it is in the middle of them. *The body was found amid a mass of wreckage.*

amidships is used to talk about the middle part of a ship or boat.

amidst See amid.

amino acid (*pron:* am-**mean**-oh) **Amino acids** are molecules used by the body to make proteins. Some amino acids are produced by the body itself and others are obtained from food.

amir See emir.

amiss If you say there is something **amiss**, you mean something is wrong. ◇ If you say something would **not come amiss**, you mean it would be welcome or a good idea.

amity You say there is **amity** between people or countries when they have a friendly peaceful relationship.

ammeter An **ammeter** is a device for measuring electric current.

ammonia is a colourless liquid or gas with a strong sharp smell. It is used for making cleaning substances, explosives, and fertilizer.

ammonite Ammonites are the fossilized coiled shells of prehistoric shellfish, often found in rocks.

ammunition is bullets, missiles, or anything which can be fired from a gun. ◇ **Ammunition** is also information or other things which can be used against someone. *He used the better-than-expected inflation figures as ammunition against his critics.*

amnesia is loss of memory.

amnesty (amnesties) An **amnesty** is (a) a period during which people can confess to a crime, come out of hiding, or give up weapons without being punished. (b) an official pardon granted to a group of people by the state.

amniocentesis is the insertion of a hollow needle into a woman's womb to remove some of the amniotic fluid for testing.

amniotic fluid is the liquid surrounding a foetus in the womb.

amoeba (*pron:* am-**mee**-ba) (*plural:* amoebas *or* amoebae) (*American spelling:* ameba) Amoebas are microscopic animals, each consisting of a single cell. They keep changing shape, and reproduce by dividing themselves in two.

amok (*pron:* a-**muck**) If people or animals **run amok**, they behave in a violent uncontrolled way.

among (*or* amongst) ❑ Among and amongst are used to say something is one of several things. *The report notes, among other things, that real competition is long overdue in the domestic electric-power industry... Temporary buildings are amongst the most urgent needs for the people made homeless by the earthquake.*

❑ Among and amongst are also used to talk about several people having the same experience. *The news has caused considerable alarm amongst finance ministers.*

❑ If something is divided **among** a group of people, they all get some of it.

❑ If people talk, argue, or fight **among themselves**, they do it without involving anyone else.

amoral (*pron:* aim-**mor**-ral) (amorality) If you say someone is **amoral** or talk about their **amorality**, you mean they have no sense of right and wrong.

amorous is used to talk about things to do with sexual love. An **amorous** person is always falling in love or wanting sex, or both.

amorphous If something is **amorphous**, it has no clear shape or structure.

amount ❑ An **amount** of something is a quantity of it.

❑ You say numbers **amount to** a total when they add up to it. *The potential saving for the taxpayer amounts to £2 million.* ◇ **Amount to** is also used to say what something really means, or what its significance is. *Such a change amounts to an economic and social revolution... Moving people into special areas of their own lands amounts to an admission that they do not really belong there.*

amour is the French word for love. It is often used to talk about love in a humorous way.

amp Electric current is measured in **amps**. 'amp' is short for 'ampère'.

ampersand An **ampersand** is the symbol & which means 'and'.

amphetamine (*pron:* am-**fet**-am-mean) **Amphetamines** are addictive drugs like methedrine which make people energetic and excited. Most amphetamines are illegal in Britain. They are sometimes called 'speed'.

amphibian Amphibians are a group of animals which breathe air as adults, but lay their eggs in rivers or ponds and have gills for the first part of their lives. Frogs, toads, newts, and salamanders are amphibians.

amphibious creatures live both in water and on land. ◇ An **amphibious** vehicle can operate both in water and on land. ◇ In war, an **amphibious** attack is made from the direction of the sea and can include landing troops, air attacks, or firing missiles from ships.

amphitheatre An **amphitheatre** is a large bowl-shaped area, used for theatrical performances. The performances take place in the centre and the audience look down from the sides.

amphora (*plural:* amphoras *or* amphorae) An **amphora** was an ancient Greek or Roman narrow-necked jar with two handles. It was used for storing things like oil and wine.

ample (amply) **Ample** is used to say there is plenty of something. *There is ample evidence that this right can be exercised... His quality is amply demonstrated in a work like 'The Last Enchantments'.* ◇ **Ample** is also used to say something is on the large side. *...her ample bosom.*

amplifier An **amplifier** is a device for increasing electrical power. Amplifiers are used in radios and stereo systems, and are connected to some musical instruments to make them sound louder.

amplify (amplifies, amplifying, amplified; amplification) ❑ If you **amplify** a sound, you make it louder, especially by using electrical equipment. **Amplification** is making a sound louder; the equipment you use is also called **amplification**. ◇ You can also use **amplify** to talk about increasing the intensity of something. *There will be an amplification of warming in the polar regions.*
  ❑ If you **amplify** an idea, you say more about it. *The democratic theme of this visit was amplified by the President.*

amplitude The width of a radio or sound wave is called its **amplitude**.

ampoule An **ampoule** is a small glass or plastic container, in which a liquid for use in an injection is kept sealed so no air can get in or out.

amputate (amputating, amputated; amputation, amputee) If a surgeon has to **amputate** a part of someone's body, he or she has to cut it off, because it is diseased or badly injured. The operation is called an **amputation**. Someone who has had a limb amputated is called an **amputee**.

amulet An **amulet** is a piece of jewellery worn to give protection from evil or injury.

amuse (amusing, amused; amusingly, amusement) ❑ If something **amuses** you or you find it **amusing**, it makes you feel like laughing or smiling. When this happens, you say you are **amused**. *I find this amusingly apt.* Being amused is called **amusement**. *She looked back at all the fuss with some amusement.*
  ❑ If you **amuse** yourself or keep yourself **amused**, you do things to pass the time pleasantly and avoid getting bored. **Amusements** are things which keep people amused. *People had very few amusements to choose from.* ◇ **Amusements** are also slot machines like video games and fruit machines.

amusement arcade An **amusement arcade** is a large room full of things like video games and fruit machines.

amusement park An **amusement park** is a large outdoor area with fairground rides, amusement arcades, and other forms of entertainment.

an See a.

anabolic steroid Anabolic steroids are substances which speed up muscle growth. They are sometimes used by sports people to improve performance, although they are banned by most sporting organizations.

anachronistic (*pron:* an-nak-kron-**niss**-tik) (anachronism) If you say someone or something is **anachronistic** or an **anachronism**, you mean they belong to an earlier period in history and do not fit in with the modern world. *...anachronistic theories about class struggle.*

anaemia (anaemic) (*or* anemia, anemic) If you have **anaemia** or are **anaemic**, you do not have enough red cells in your blood, and you look pale and feel tired as a result.

anaerobic (*or* anerobic) Anaerobic things do not contain or use oxygen. *...anaerobic organisms.* ◇ **Anaerobic** exercise is any exercise performed at a rate which makes you out of breath.

anaesthesia (*or* anesthesia) (*both pron:* an-niss-**theez**-ee-a) is the use of anaesthetics in surgery.

anaesthetic (*or* anesthetic) (*both pron:* an-niss-**thet**-ik) An anaesthetic is a drug which stops you feeling pain. Anaesthetics are commonly used in surgical operations. See also general anaesthetic, local anaesthetic.

anaesthetise See anaesthetize.

anaesthetist (*or* anesthetist) (*both pron:* an-neess-**thet**-ist) An **anaesthetist** is a doctor who specializes in giving anaesthetics.

anaesthetize (*or* anesthetize) (*pron:* an-**neess**-thet-ize) (anaesthetizing, anaesthetized) (*can be spelled with an 's' instead of a 'z'*) If someone is **anaesthetized**, they are given an anaesthetic to make them unconscious or stop them feeling pain. A part of someone's body can also be **anaesthetized**. ◇ You also say people are **anaesthetized** when they have become so accustomed to something unpleasant they no longer react to it the way other people do. *...a society anaesthetized by a daily murder toll of 44 and an assault rate running into hundreds.*

anagram An **anagram** is a word, phrase, or jumble of letters formed by rearranging the letters of another word or phrase. For example, 'integral' is an anagram of 'triangle'.

anal See anus.

analgesic (*pron:* an-nal-**jeez**-ik) An **analgesic** is a drug which reduces or stops pain.

analog See analogue.

analogous (*pron:* an-**nal**-o-guss) If something is **analogous** to something else, there are similarities in their structures or the way they operate.

analogue (*or* analog) ❑ If something is an **analogue** of something else, it is equivalent to it. *They see the Antarctic base as the terrestrial analogue of a space station.*
  ❑ An **analogue** device measures information using variable rather than fixed voltage. *...analogue cassettes.* ◇ An **analogue** watch or clock has rotating hands on a dial, rather than a digital display.

analogy (*pron:* an-**nal**-lo-jee) (analogies) If you make or draw an **analogy** between two things, you show a way in which they are similar to each other. Analogies are often used to explain complicated things by means of simple everyday ones.

analyse (analysing, analysed; analysis) (*American spelling:* analyze, analyzing, analyzed) ❑ If you **analyse** something, you consider it in detail or examine and test it, to understand it or find out what it is made of. An **analysis** is a procedure like this. ◇ You say **in the final analysis** when you are stating a basic truth about a situation. *Consumer demand will in the final analysis continue to determine the overall rate of oil output.*

❑ When a psychiatrist or psychologist **analyses** a patient, he or she asks them questions and talks to them about their feelings and experiences, to try and discover what is causing their psychological problems. This procedure is called **analysis.** See also **psychoanalyse.**

analyst An **analyst** is an expert who can explain and interpret the latest developments in his or her field of interest. *...political analysts... ...City analysts.* ◇ An **analyst** is also a psychiatrist who analyses patients, to try and discover what is causing their psychological problems.

analytic means the same as 'analytical'.

analytical (analytically) **Analytical** is used to talk about people's ability to reason logically. *The system challenges candidates' practical, analytical and critical skills... You can be analytically intelligent but uncreative.* ◇ **Analytical** is also used to describe people and procedures involved in analyzing things. *...an analytical chemist.*

anarchic (*pron:* a-nar-kik) behaviour shows no respect for laws, rules, or customs. *...the naturally anarchic selfishness of unsupervised children... ...anarchic humour.*

anarchism (*pron:* an-ar-kizm) (anarchist) **Anarchism** is the theory or belief that people should not be controlled by laws or governments, but should work together freely. **Anarchists** are people who support this view. Some anarchists also believe that governments should be overthrown.

anarchy (*pron:* an-ark-ee) is a situation where nobody is in control in an area, and there is general disorder, violence, and lawbreaking.

anathema (*pron:* an-nath-im-a) If something is **anathema** to you, you dislike it strongly and are totally against it.

anatomy (anatomies; anatomical, anatomically; anatomist) ❑ **Anatomy** is the study of the structure of human or animal bodies. **Anatomical** is used to talk about things to do with anatomy. *...anatomical descriptions... Anatomically correct in every known detail, the dinosaurs appear terrifyingly real on screen.* An **anatomist** is an expert on anatomy. ◇ A person's body can be humorously referred to as their **anatomy.** *...dislodging a drawing pin from the more sensitive portion of his anatomy.*

❑ The **anatomy** of something is what it consists of and the way it works. *...the anatomy of the English class system.* ◇ A book can be called an **anatomy** of a subject when it gives a good general description of it.

ancestor Your **ancestors** are the people you are descended from. ◇ An **ancestor** of something modern is an earlier thing which it has developed from. *The immediate ancestor of rock 'n' roll is rhythm-and-blues.*

ancestral is used to describe things which have belonged to or have been associated with a family for many generations. *...the Duke's ancestral home.*

ancestry If you talk about a person's **ancestry,** you mean the people they are descended from, especially what

kind of people they were and where they came from. *...Americans of Japanese ancestry... She could trace her ancestry back to the famous 19th century trainer John Day.*

anchor (anchoring, anchored; anchorman, anchorwoman) ❑ An **anchor** is a heavy hooked object attached to a long chain, which is dropped from a ship so that it catches on the seabed or riverbed, and stops the ship drifting. When this happens, you say the ship is **anchored** or has **dropped anchor.** When the anchor is pulled in ready for the ship to leave, you say the ship **weighs anchor.**

❑ Anything used to keep something still or stable can be called an **anchor.** *ERM economies could use the German mark as a counter-inflation anchor.*

❑ In a relay race, the person who **anchors** a team is the one who runs the final leg.

❑ When someone **anchors** a TV or radio programme, especially a news programme, they present the programme and act as a link between film footage, live interviews, and reports inside and outside the studio. The person who does this is called an **anchorman** or **anchorwoman.**

anchorage An **anchorage** is a place where ships can anchor.

anchovy (*pron:* an-chov-ee) (anchovies) **Anchovies** are very small herring-like sea fish with a strong salty taste.

ancien régime (*pron:* ons-yan ray-zheem; *the 'zh' sounds like 's' in 'pleasure'*) The **ancien régime** was the political and social system in France before the Revolution. Nowadays, people use this term to talk about other systems which are old and outdated.

ancient is used to describe things which existed a long time ago, or which have been around for a very long time. *...ancient Greece... The ceremony was steeped in ancient tradition.* ◇ People who lived a long time ago, for example the Greeks and the Celts, are sometimes called the **ancients.**

❑ **Ancient history** is the study of civilizations which existed from earliest times until the collapse of the Western Roman Empire in A.D. 476. ◇ If you say something is **ancient history,** you mean it is outdated and no longer relevant. *By this time next year today's winner will be ancient history.*

ancillary (ancillaries) ❑ **Ancillary** workers support the people who do the main work of an organization. For example, the people working in a hospital canteen are ancillary staff.

❑ **Ancillary** things are additional things which are not used for something's main purpose. Things like these can also be called **ancillaries.** *...ancillary equipment... The Sainsbury Wing gave the gallery badly needed space, both for hanging pictures and for ancillaries such as lecture theatres.*

and is used to link words or groups of words. *...fish and chips... He asked me out for a drink and I went.*

androgynous (*pron:* an-droj-in-us) In science, **androgynous** is used to describe people, animals, and plants that have characteristics of both sexes. ◇ In fashion, the **androgynous** look consists of typical features of male dress appearing in women's clothes, and features of female dress appearing in men's clothes.

android In science fiction, an **android** is a man-made creature which is part robot, part human.

anecdote (anecdotal) An **anecdote** is a short entertaining account of something which has happened. If something spoken or written is **anecdotal,** it is full of anecdotes. ◇ **Anecdotal** evidence is based on what someone has heard from someone else, rather than on something they have witnessed personally.

anemia (anemic) See **anaemia.**

anemone (*pron:* an-nem-on-ee) **Anemones** are plants with large red, purple, yellow, or white cup-shaped flowers and feathery leaves.

anerobic See anaerobic.

anesthetic See anaesthetic.

aneurysm (*pron:* an-yer-iz-um) An **aneurysm** is a blood-filled sac caused by the swelling of a weakened blood-vessel wall.

anew If something happens **anew,** it happens again. *The guerrilla war has flared up anew.*

angel (angelic) **Angels** are spiritual beings some people believe are God's messengers and servants in heaven. **Angelic** is used to talk about things to do with angels. *...bright angelic wings.* ◇ If you say someone is an **angel,** you mean they have been very kind or helpful. ◇ **Angelic** is used to describe people who behave in a very good righteous way, or pretend to. *As always when evading a question, he treats me to his most angelic smile.*

angelica is a sweet-scented herb. Its stem is crystallized and used for decorating cakes and puddings.

anger (angering, angered) **Anger** is the strong emotion you feel when you think someone has behaved badly or stupidly, and you feel like expressing your feelings in a forceful or violent way. When someone or something **angers** you, they make you feel like this.

angina (*pron:* an-jine-a) is pain in a person's chest and left arm, usually caused by heart disease.

angle (angling, angled; angler) ❑ An **angle** is the difference in direction between two lines or surfaces. Angles are measured in degrees.
 ❑ If something is **angled** or **at an angle,** it is not straight, horizontal, or vertical. ◇ If you look at something from an **angle,** you are not directly in front of it when you look at it. Similarly you can aim at something from an **angle.** If a footballer makes an **angled** shot at goal, he is not directly in front of the goal when he shoots.
 ❑ If you consider something from a particular **angle,** you look at it from that point of view.
 ❑ **Angling** is fishing with a rod as a hobby. A person who does this is called an **angler.** ◇ If someone is **angling** for something, they are trying to get people to offer it to them without having to ask for it.

Anglican (Anglicanism) An **Anglican** is a member of one of the churches belonging to the Anglican Communion, a group of Protestant churches which includes the Church of England, the Church of Ireland, the Scottish Episcopal Church, and the Church in Wales. **Anglicanism** is the beliefs and practices of Anglicans.

anglicize (anglicizing, anglicized) (*can be spelled with an 's' instead of a 'z'*) If something is **anglicized,** it is adapted to make it seem English or to fit in with English custom and practice.

angling See angle.

Anglo- is added to other nationality words to describe something which involves England or Britain and another country. *...the Anglo-Irish Agreement.*

Anglo-Saxon The **Anglo-Saxons** were the people from Germanic tribes who settled in Britain from the 5th century A.D. ◇ **Anglo-Saxon** is now used to describe English-speaking people descended from white British people, especially in Britain itself, the US, Australia, and New Zealand.

Anglophile (*pron:* ang-glo-file) (Anglophilia) An **Anglophile** is someone from another country who admires England or the English. This admiration is called **Anglophilia** (*pron:* ang-glo-fill-ee-a).

Anglophobe An **Anglophobe** is someone from another country who dislikes England or the English.

angora An **angora** is a breed of rabbit with long silky hair. **Angora** is soft yarn made from this hair. Some long-haired breeds of goats and cats are also called **angoras.**

angry (angrier, angriest; angrily) If you are **angry,** you think someone has behaved in a bad or stupid way, and you feel like expressing your feelings about it forcefully or violently. *Drivers hooted angrily at me as I ran across the streets.*

angst is a feeling of anxiety, especially one about the general state of things rather than anything specific.

angstrom An **angstrom** is a very small measurement, equal to one ten-millionth of a millimetre. The wavelengths of electromagnetic radiation are measured in angstroms. 'Angstroms' is usually written 'A' or 'Å'.

anguish (anguished) **Anguish** is being extremely upset about something. **Anguished** is used to describe people who are in this state, and the things they do and say. *...anguished protests.*

angular If something is **angular,** its shape has a lot of straight lines or sharp points. ◇ An **angular** person is thin and bony.

animal ❑ In science, an **animal** is any living creature which is not a plant. However, when people talk about **animals,** they usually mean non-human mammals like dogs, horses, and mice, rather than people, insects, or birds.
 ❑ **Animal** is used to describe people's behaviour when it is related to their physical needs, rather than to rational thought or consideration for other people. *...a look at man's more animal instincts.*
 ❑ You can describe a person by calling them a particular kind of **animal.** *Taylor was a passionate and highly articulate political animal.*

animate (animating, animated; animatedly, animation, animator) ❑ **Animate** is used to talk about things which are alive, in contrast to things like stones or machines which are not.
 ❑ If something **animates** people, it gets them excited, or gets them to show an interest in something. When people are excited, you can say they are **animated.** *My companion was talking animatedly to his girlfriend.*
 ❑ An **animated** film is a cartoon, or a film made using computer graphics. Another type of animated film is made by photographing puppets while constantly adjusting their position to make it look as if they are moving. Making films in any of these ways is called **animation;** a person who does it is called an **animator.**

animism (animist, animistic) **Animism** is any religion based on the idea that things, especially animals, trees, or rivers, have spirits. **Animist** and **animistic** are used to describe people who believe in animism, and beliefs and practices which conform to the ideas of animism. ...*animist tribesmen*... ...*the old animistic world view.*

animosity (animosities) **Animosity** is a strong feeling of dislike and hostility. When a feeling like this is common somewhere, you can talk about the **animosities** there. ...*age-old ethnic animosities.*

animus An **animus** is a feeling of strong dislike. *In London young artists felt the same animus against the pretensions of high culture.*

aniseed is a flavouring made from the seeds of the anise plant. It tastes of liquorice, and is used in sweets, drinks, and medicines.

ankle A person's **ankle** is the joint where their foot meets their leg.

anklet An **anklet** is an ornamental chain or band worn around the ankle.

annals If you say something will be written in the **annals** of a subject, you mean it will be remembered for a long time by people interested in that subject. ...*an occasion writ large in the annals of world rugby... This letter deserves a special place in the annals of modern Arab history.*

annex (annexes, annexing, annexed; annexation) If a country **annexes** another country or area of land, it seizes it and takes control of it. *The Baltic States argued that their annexation by the Soviet Union was illegal.* ◇ In the US, an annex is what we call an annexe.

annexe An **annexe** is a building joined to or next to a larger main building.

annihilate (*pron:* an-nye-ill-ate) (annihilating, annihilated; annihilation) If a group of people are **annihilated,** they are all killed. ...*the threat of nuclear annihilation.* ◇ If a sports team **annihilates** another team, they beat them by a large score.

anniversary (anniversaries) An **anniversary** is a date which is remembered or celebrated because something special happened on that date in a previous year.

annotate (annotating, annotated; annotation) If a piece of writing is **annotated,** notes are added to it by hand. Notes like these are called **annotations.**

announce (announcing, announced; announcement) If you **announce** something, you tell people about it publicly or officially. An **announcement** is a public statement.

announcer An **announcer** is someone you see on TV or hear on radio between programmes, introducing the next programme and giving information about future programmes.

annoy (annoying, annoyed; annoyingly, annoyance) If someone or something **annoys** you, they make you rather angry and impatient. When this happens, you say you are **annoyed;** the feeling is called **annoyance.** Annoyances are things which annoy you. *Alex looked annoyingly cheerful... These petty annoyances exhausted Haig's patience.*

annual (annually) **Annual** is used to describe things which happen every year. ...*the annual meeting of the Delta Council... A contest for the leadership takes place annually.* ◇ **Annual** is also used to talk about amounts received or spent each year. ...*annual income... The museum is expected to attract 400,000 visitors annually.* ◇ An **annual** is (a) a book or magazine published every year. (b) a plant

which grows, flowers, produces seeds, and dies, all within the same year.

annuity (annuities) An **annuity** is (a) a fixed sum of money paid every year to someone. (b) an agreement by which you pay a company a large fixed sum and they then pay you regular amounts for the rest of your life.

annul (annulling, annulled; annulment) If a contract is **annulled,** it is cancelled and no longer applies. ◇ If a marriage is **annulled,** it is officially declared invalid, so that legally it is considered never to have existed. *Nasreen Akmal is seeking the annulment of her arranged marriage.*

annum See per annum.

Annunciation The **Annunciation** is the event described in the Bible when Mary is told by an angel that she will give birth to the Son of God.

anode In an electric cell, the **anode** is the positive electrode. See also **cathode.**

anodyne is used to describe things which are safe and unremarkable rather than risky and exciting.

anoint If someone is **anointed,** they have holy oil or other liquids poured or dabbed on them as part of a religious ceremony. ◇ You can also describe someone as **anointed** when they have been chosen by someone in authority to do an important job. *Anthony Eden was Churchill's anointed successor as prime minister.*

anomalous (anomaly, anomalies) If you say something is **anomalous** or an **anomaly,** you mean it does not fit in, or does not conform to what is usual. ...*Britain's anomalous Sunday trading restrictions.*

anomie (*pron:* an-oh-mee) is a lack of conviction, purpose, or moral standards. *Central to the anomie of the present generation is the belief that politics of any sort is automatically corrupting.*

anon. is sometimes written where you would expect to see a name, to show that nobody knows who wrote a poem or piece of music. It stands for 'anonymous'.

anonymous (anonymously, anonymity) ❑ If you remain **anonymous** when you do something, you do not let people know you are the person doing it. **Anonymity** is not having your name or identity known. ...*an anonymous telephone warning... A copy of the letter was sent anonymously to The Sunday Times... The companies declined to name the source, who had been promised anonymity.* ◇ If a way of doing things is **anonymous,** it does not involve people meeting each other. This characteristic is called **anonymity.** *Computers are impersonal, and their transactions more anonymous than the old paper-based financial systems... He preferred the anonymity of the phone.* ◇ **Anonymous** is used in the names of organizations which help people with personal problems without asking about their identities. ...*Alcoholics Anonymous.*

❑ You can also call something **anonymous** when there is nothing striking or interesting about it to distinguish it from other things of the same type. *His office is modern, anonymous and tasteless.*

anorak An **anorak** is a warm waterproof hip-length jacket, usually with a hood.

anorexia (anorexic) **Anorexia** or **anorexia nervosa** is a mental illness in which people develop a strong fear of getting fat, so they refuse to eat, making themselves thin and ill. You say someone suffering from this illness is **anorexic** or an **anorexic.** See also **bulimia.**

another means in addition to the people or things you have just mentioned. *The prison has room for another 820 prisoners.* ◇ **Another** also means different to the person or thing you have just mentioned. *I like to think of it in another way.*

❏ If people or organizations do something to **one another**, each of them does it to some or all of the others. *Charities have to compete with one another for donations.* ◇ **One after another** is used to say several people or things do something in turn, or something happens to several of them in turn. *One East European country after another ditched Communist ideologies.*

answer (answering, answered) ❏ If you **answer** someone when they speak or write to you, you say or write something back. What you say or write is called an **answer**. ◇ If you **answer** a question in an exam, you write down what you think is required. What you write is called your **answer**. ◇ If you **answer** something like a small ad in a newspaper, you contact the person who placed it there. ◇ If you **answer** an appeal for help, you do something to help the person in trouble.

❏ When you **answer** the phone, you pick it up when it rings and speak into it. When you **answer** the door, you open it when someone knocks or rings the bell.

❏ An **answer** to a problem is a possible solution to it.

❏ If you **answer** a criticism or accusation made against you, you say or write something in your defence.

❏ If someone you have authority over **answers back**, they speak disrespectfully to you when you say something to them.

❏ If someone has to **answer for** something they have done wrong, (a) they are made to explain it. *In the debate he had to answer for the disastrous campaign in Norway.* (b) they are punished for it. *He must be made to answer for his terrible crimes.* ◇ If you say someone has **a lot to answer for**, you mean they have caused a lot of trouble.

answerable If you are **answerable** to someone, you have to report to them and explain the things you do. ◇ If you are **answerable** for your own or someone else's actions, you are held responsible for them.

answering machine An **answering machine** is a device you connect to your telephone to record messages from people who phone when you are out.

answerphone An **answerphone** is a telephone which can record messages from people who phone when you are out.

ant **Ants** are small crawling insects which live in large colonies.

ant hill An **ant hill** is a mound of earth formed by ants making a nest.

antacid An **antacid** is a substance used to treat stomach acidity.

antagonise See antagonize.

antagonism See antagonistic.

antagonist In a fight or game, your **antagonist** is your enemy or opponent. ◇ An **antagonist** is also a drug which counteracts or neutralizes the effects of other drugs or of substances produced in excess by the body.

antagonistic (antagonism) If people are **antagonistic**, they are hostile and suspicious. You call their behaviour **antagonism**. ◇ If you are **antagonistic** to something, you are bitterly opposed to it. *...Conservatives antagonistic to*

the European Union.

antagonize (antagonizing, antagonized) (*can be spelled with an 's' instead of a 'z'*) If you **antagonize** someone, you make them angry.

ante-natal See antenatal.

ante-room (*or* anteroom) An **ante-room** is a small room where you wait before going into a larger one.

anteater The **anteater** is a South American animal with a long snout and no teeth. It has a long sticky tongue which it uses to catch ants and termites.

antecedent Your **antecedents** are your ancestors. ◇ An **antecedent** of something is a similar thing which happened or existed in an earlier time, and from which it developed. *The Scottish law system proudly traces its antecedents back to the judicial codes of ancient Rome.*

antechamber An **antechamber** is the same as an ante-room.

antediluvian (*pron:* an-ti-dil-**loo**-vee-ann) is used to describe things which are extremely old or old-fashioned. *...eastern Germany's antediluvian communications system.*

antelope (*plural:* antelopes *or* antelope) **Antelopes** are long-legged horned animals in Africa and Asia. Gazelles and springbok are types of antelopes.

antenatal (*or* ante-natal) care is given to pregnant women and their unborn children.

antenna (*plural:* antennae *or* antennas) The **antennae** of an insect are the two long thin parts attached to its head which it feels things with. ◇ An **antenna** is also an aerial.

anterior In medicine, **anterior** is used to describe the front parts of things. *...the anterior margin of the limb.*

anteroom See ante-room.

anthem An **anthem** is (a) a sacred choral work, sung as part of the service in some Protestant Churches. (b) a song written or chosen to represent a country or organization.

anthology (anthologies; anthologist) An **anthology** is a collection of writings by different authors, collected together in one book. An **anthologist** is a person who has compiled an anthology.

anthracite is a type of high-quality coal. It is hard and shiny and burns slowly with a small flame and little smoke, giving off a lot of heat.

anthrax is a serious, highly infectious disease, causing fever, a swollen throat, and painful boils. It is most common in cattle, but can be caught by humans.

anthropology (anthropologist, anthropological) **Anthropology** is the study of the human race and its social systems and cultures. An **anthropologist** is an expert on this. **Anthropological** is used to talk about things to do with anthropology. *...anthropological research.*

anthropomorphism (anthropomorphic) **Anthropomorphism** is talking about animals or non-living objects as if they had human thoughts and feelings. When people do this, you say they are being **anthropomorphic**.

anti- is added to words to form other words. Words formed like this are used to talk about (a) people's opposition to something. *...anti-abortion protesters... ...anti-establishment views.* (b) things intended to prevent or destroy other things. *...anti-pollution laws... ...anti-theft devices... ...anti-malarial drugs.*

❏ Some words beginning with 'anti' can be spelled with

a hyphen after the 'i'. For example, 'antifreeze' is sometimes spelled 'anti-freeze'. See **Antichrist, anticlockwise, antifreeze, antihistamine, antimatter, antisemitism, antisocial**.

anti-aircraft weapons and systems are designed to destroy enemy aircraft.

anti-hero The main male character of a play or novel is called its **anti-hero** when he is the opposite of what is traditionally expected of a hero; for example, he may be rude, dishonest, or cowardly.

anti-tank weapons and defences are designed to destroy or halt enemy tanks.

antibiotic Antibiotics are medicines developed to kill bacteria and fight infections. Penicillin is an antibiotic.

antibody (antibodies) Antibodies are proteins produced in your blood. They destroy harmful bacteria.

Antichrist (or anti-Christ) The Antichrist is the enemy of Christ, who some Christians believe will rule the world before being overthrown when Christ returns.

anticipate (anticipating, anticipated; anticipation) ❑ If you **anticipate** something, (a) you expect it to happen. *We do not anticipate too much trouble.* (b) you foresee it is going to happen and take some action to be ready for it. *They anticipated the slow-down in the economy by downgrading share prices.*

❑ You also say someone **anticipates** something when they produce something of a similar kind before it. *He argues that he and his organisation anticipated the Charter by several years.*

❑ You also say you **anticipate** something when you look forward to it with pleasure and excitement. Looking forward to something is called **anticipation**.

anticlimax (anticlimaxes) If something is an **anticlimax**, it is disappointing because it is not as exciting as you had expected.

anticlockwise (or anti-clockwise) If something moves in an **anticlockwise** direction, it moves in the opposite direction to the hands of a clock.

antics When you talk about someone's **antics,** you mean the funny, silly, or unusual things they do.

anticyclone An anticyclone is an area of high atmospheric pressure. It causes settled weather conditions and, in summer, clear skies and high temperatures.

antidote ❑ An **antidote** is a chemical substance which stops or controls the effect of a poison.

❑ An **antidote** to a problem is something which solves it or makes it less severe. ◇ An **antidote** to something is also something different, which makes a pleasant change. *Warshawski's courage, obstinacy and wit are a welcome antidote to the negative portrayal of women by writers like Raymond Chandler.*

antifreeze (or anti-freeze) is a liquid you add to water to stop it freezing, especially the water in your car radiator in winter.

antigen (pron: an-tee-jen) An **antigen** is anything harmful which causes antibodies to be produced when it enters your body, for example a substance which brings on an allergic reaction.

antihistamine (or anti-histamine) Antihistamines are medicines used to treat allergies, such as hay fever.

antimacassar An antimacassar is a decorative cloth for protecting the back of a chair.

antimatter (or anti-matter) is a form of matter which has properties and characteristics opposite to those of ordinary matter.

antipathy (pron: an-tip-a-thee) (antipathetic) Antipathy is a feeling of strong dislike or hostility. If you are **antipathetic** (pron: an-tip-a-thet-ik) to someone or something, you feel like that about them.

antiperspirant (pron: an-tee-pers-per-ant) An **antiperspirant** is a substance you spray or wipe on your skin to reduce sweating.

Antipodes (pron: an-tip-oh-deez) Australia and New Zealand are sometimes jokily called the **Antipodes**.

antiquarian is used to talk about old and rare things. *...an antiquarian book.*

antiquary (antiquaries) An **antiquary** is a person who collects, deals in, or is an expert on antiquities.

antiquated things are old and out-of-date.

antique Antiques are old objects which are valuable because of their beauty or rarity.

antiquity (antiquities) Antiquity is used to talk about the distant past, especially the ancient Egyptian, Greek, and Roman periods. *...one of the most crucial battles of antiquity.* ◇ **Antiquities** are objects from earlier times, for example statues or coins.

antisemitism (antisemitic, antisemite) (or anti-Semitism, anti-Semite, *etc*) Antisemitism is racism directed against Jewish people. People with racist beliefs of this kind are called **antisemites**. You say their beliefs and behaviour are **antisemitic**.

antiseptic If something has **antiseptic** properties, it kills harmful bacteria. An **antiseptic** is a substance which does this.

antisocial (or anti-social) Antisocial behaviour is doing things like being noisy in a public place or leaving litter, which is annoying or upsetting to other people. ◇ You say a person is being **antisocial** when they are unwilling to meet and mix with other people.

antithesis (pron: an-tith-iss-iss) The **antithesis** of something is its exact opposite.

antler A deer's **antlers** are its branched horns. In most species, only the male has antlers.

antonym The **antonym** of a word is another word which means the opposite. For example, the antonym of 'good' is 'bad'.

anus (pron: ain-uss) (anuses; anal) A person's or animal's **anus** is the hole through which they get rid of faeces from their body. **Anal** is used to talk about things which involve the anus. *...anal intercourse.*

anvil An anvil is a heavy iron block on which hot metals are beaten into shape.

anxious (anxiously; anxiety, anxieties) ❑ If you are **anxious,** you feel nervous or worried about something. This feeling is called **anxiety**. *Candidates are anxiously awaiting the results of today's voting... The trouble will heighten anxieties about the behaviour of English fans.* An **anxious** time is one when people are anxious.

❑ If you are **anxious** to do something, you are very eager to do it, to avoid an unpleasant situation or bring an end to one. *Firms are anxious to avoid a reputation for callous behaviour.* Similarly, you can be anxious for something to happen. *India is very anxious for the fighting to end.*

any ❑ You use **any** to say something is true about each thing or person of a certain type, each member of a group, or each part of something. *The Lensman can be mounted onto any 35mm camera.*

❑ You use **any** in questions to ask if something exists. *Does it have any basis in fact?* ◇ You use **any** with words like 'not' and 'never' to say something of a particular kind does not exist. *There has never been any doubt about Gower's keenness.*

anybody See anyone.

anyhow means the same as 'anyway'. *The United States and Western Europe have restrictive policies, but illegal immigrants get in anyhow.*

anymore means the same as 'any more'. See **more**.

anyone (*or* anybody) ❑ You use **anyone** to say something is true about every person, or each person of a certain kind. *The remaining space is available to anyone able to pay for their stay... If anyone lets him down, they hear about it.*

❑ You use **anyone** in questions to ask if there are people about whom something is true. *Can anyone keep a secret for a lifetime?* ◇ You use **anyone** with words like 'not' and 'never' to say there is nobody about whom something is true. *I don't think I've met anyone with a good word to say about him.*

anything ❑ You use **anything** to say something is true about every thing of a certain kind. *Seaside audiences will laugh at almost anything.*

❑ You use **anything** in questions to ask if something of a certain kind exists. *Can you see anything?* ◇ You use **anything** with words like 'not' to say there is nothing of a certain kind. *The student had not stolen anything.*

❑ You use **anything like** with words like 'not' to emphasize that there is not enough of something. *The city does not have anything like the funds needed for such large-scale redevelopment.*

anyway ❑ You say **anyway** when you are saying something extra which supports the main point you are making. *By then he was bored with the subject, and anyway there was not enough time to get the project through before the election.*

❑ You say **anyway** when you are making a slight correction to what you have just said. *The well-paid should have the longest faces after the budget – or some of them, anyway.*

❑ **Anyway** is also used to say something is true or will happen in spite of other things. *The anxiety in his voice increased as he realised I was going to write about this anyway.*

anywhere ❑ You use **anywhere** to say something is true about every place, or every part of a place. *...a portable phone which will work anywhere.*

❑ You use **anywhere** in questions to ask if there is a place where something exists or is true. *Is there anywhere that people can get this information?* ◇ You use **anywhere** with words like 'not' to say there is no place where something exists or is true. *Motorists cannot find anywhere to fill up.*

aorta The **aorta** is the body's main artery. It conveys oxygen-rich blood from the heart to all other parts of the body except the lungs.

apace is used to say something happens at a steady rate. *The military build-up continues apace.*

apart ❑ If people or things are **apart**, they are not together. ◇ If things are a certain distance **apart**, they are that distance away from each other. ◇ If things move **apart**,

they move away from each other.

❑ If you **take** something **apart**, you separate it into its parts. If it **comes** or **falls apart**, it comes or falls to pieces. ◇ If an organization or arrangement **falls apart**, it comes to an end, because of problems or disagreements.

❑ If people who want to fight are **kept apart**, they are prevented from fighting each other.

❑ If you cannot **tell** two people or things **apart**, they seem the same to you. ◇ If you say someone's abilities or achievements **set** them **apart** from other people, you mean their abilities or achievements show they are a very special or talented person.

❑ If things happen a certain length of time **apart**, there is that amount of time between them. *...two photographs taken 80 years apart.*

❑ You say **apart from** when you are mentioning an exception to the thing you have just described. *Arsenal were disjointed and directionless apart from 10 minutes of brilliance by Paul Merson.* ◇ You also say **apart from** when you are mentioning one aspect of something before going on to talk about a different one. *Apart from losing its market share at home, the company has also been having a fight with its distributor in Britain.*

apartheid was a system which existed in South Africa until recently, in which people of different races were kept apart by law.

apartment is the usual American word for a flat. ◇ **Apartments** are a set of large rooms used by an important person like a king, queen, or president.

apathetic (apathy) You say people are **apathetic** when they are not interested in something important that is going on and do not care what happens. You call this feeling **apathy**.

ape (aping, aped) **Apes** are animals like chimpanzees and gorillas which look similar to monkeys but do not have tails. ◇ If you **ape** someone's speech or behaviour, you imitate it.

apéritif (*pron:* ap per rit-tccf) An **apéritif** is any alcoholic drink you have just before a meal.

aperture An **aperture** is a hole, gap, or other opening.

apex (apexes) ❑ The **apex** of a triangle or pyramid is the point at the top. ◇ The **apex** of an organization is the highest level of its management. *At the apex of the party was its central committee.*

❑ An **Apex** ticket is a plane ticket which costs less than the standard fare but which must be booked a specified time in advance.

aphasia is a mental condition which makes people forget words and fail to recognize them.

aphid (*pron:* eh-fid) **Aphids** are small soft-bodied insects which suck sap from plants. Greenflies and blackflies are aphids.

aphorism An **aphorism** is a short saying which expresses something people think is generally true.

aphrodisiac (*pron:* af-roh-diz-zee-ak) An **aphrodisiac** is a food, drink, or drug which creates or increases sexual desire.

apiary (*pron:* ape-yar-ee) (apiaries; apiarist) An **apiary** is a place where bees are kept, usually in hives. An **apiarist** is someone who keeps or studies bees.

apiece If people have a number of things **apiece**, they each have that number. ◇ If things cost a certain amount **apiece**, they cost that much each.

aplenty is used to say there is a lot of something. *There were chances aplenty to win the game.*

aplomb (*pron:* ap-**plom**) If you do something with **aplomb**, you do it with confidence and in a calm steady way.

apocalypse (*pron:* a-**pok**-ka-lips) When Christians talk about the **apocalypse**, they mean the end of the world, which may come about as a result of war, a natural disaster, or some action by God. The possible end of life on Earth resulting from a nuclear war is sometimes called the **nuclear apocalypse**. ◇ People sometimes call a less serious disaster an **apocalypse**. *Beckman warned of financial apocalypse and falling house prices.*

apocalyptic (*pron:* a-**pok**-ka-lip-tik) is used to describe beliefs that the world is going to end, and happenings which might bring it about. *...medieval apocalyptic thought... ...an apocalyptic battle.*

apocryphal (*pron:* ap-**pok**-rif-fal) If a story told about someone is **apocryphal**, it is probably not true.

apogee (*pron:* ap-oh-jee) The **apogee** of something is its best or most successful time. *The apogee of his political life was his six months as Under-Secretary for War.*

apolitical If someone is **apolitical**, they are not interested in politics or do not have any political allegiances.

apologetic (apologetically) If you are **apologetic**, you say or show you are sorry for something you are responsible for. *...an apologetic telephone call... 'I'm afraid some of the shirts are a little mouldy,' said the auctioneer apologetically.*

apologia (*pron:* a-pol-**loje**-ee-a) An **apologia** is a statement or piece of writing in which someone defends something they believe in.

apologise See **apologize**.

apologist An **apologist** for an idea, belief, or cause is someone who writes or speaks in defence of it.

apologize (apologizing, apologized; apology, apologies) (*can be spelled with an 's' instead of a 'z'*) If you **apologize** for something you have done, you say you are sorry. What you say is called an **apology**.

apoplexy (*pron:* ap-**pop**-plex-ee) (apoplectic) If someone has **apoplexy** or an **apoplectic** attack (*pron:* ap-pop-**plek**-tik), they suffer a stroke. ◇ You also say someone is **apoplectic** when they get very excited and angry, especially if this makes their face go red.

apostate (*pron:* ap-**poss**-tate) (apostasy, apostasies) An **apostate** is someone who has abandoned their religious faith or some other strongly-held belief. Abandoning a faith or belief is called **apostasy**.

apostle (*pron:* ap-**poss**-l) The **Apostles** were the twelve disciples chosen by Christ to preach the gospel. ◇ An **apostle** of an idea or cause is someone who strongly believes in it and works hard to promote it.

apostolic (*pron:* ap-**poss**-toll-ik) **Apostolic** is used to talk about things connected with the Pope. *He was appointed Apostolic Administrator of Minsk by Pope John Paul II.* ◇ **Apostolic** is also used to talk about traditions believed to date back to the Apostles.

apostrophe (*pron:* ap-**poss**-trof-fee) An **apostrophe** is the punctuation mark ' used to show a letter has been missed out, for example when 'do not' is shortened to 'don't'. It is also used to show something belongs to someone or something. *...Japan's aircraft makers.*

apothecary (*pron:* ap-**poth**-ik-ar-ee) (apothecaries) In the past, an **apothecary** was someone who prepared medicines and drugs.

apotheosis (*pron:* ap-**poth**-ee-oh-siss) The **apotheosis** of something is the best example of it, or the time when it is at its best. *Murray Walker's whimsical comedy surely marks the apotheosis of the American small-town play.*

appal (*usual American spelling:* **appall**) (appalling, appalled; appallingly) If something **appals** you or you are **appalled** by it, it shocks and disgusts you. You say something like this is **appalling**. *Many people are living in appalling conditions... ...the appallingly wasteful attitude to grain and bread.*

apparatus (apparatuses) The **apparatus** for a task or activity is the equipment needed for it. *...breathing apparatus... ...weight-lifting apparatus.* ◇ The **apparatus** of an organization is its structure, methods, and other things which enable it to operate.

apparel (*pron:* ap-**par**-rel) Someone's clothing can be referred to humorously as their **apparel**.

apparent (apparently) **Apparent** is used to describe something which seems to be a certain thing. *...an apparent attempt to smuggle a bomb into Belfast airport.* ◇ **Apparent** is also used to say something seems to be true. *It became apparent that it was going to be an extremely good year for rainfall... Apparently a deal is in the offing to broadcast live opera from major houses around the world.*

apparition An **apparition** is a supernatural figure which someone claims to have seen, for example a ghost.

appeal (appealing, appealed; appealingly) ❑ If you **appeal** for something, you make an urgent request for it. A request like this is called an **appeal**. *The authorities have appealed for calm.*

❑ If you **appeal** against a decision, for example one made by a court, you make a formal request for it to be changed. This request is called an **appeal**.

❑ If something **appeals** to you, you find it attractive or interesting. You can say something like this is **appealing** or has **appeal**. *There is something appealingly whimsical about it... ...books which have wide public appeal.*

appear (appearing, appeared) ❑ If something **appears**, it becomes visible. *The sun appeared from behind the clouds.* ◇ When a person **appears**, they turn up somewhere unexpectedly. ◇ When something like a new product **appears**, it becomes available.

❑ If you **appear** in a play or show, you have a part in it. ◇ If you **appear** in court, you go there to answer charges or give information.

❑ If something **appears** to be true, it seems to be true. Similarly, if something **appears** to be a particular thing, it seems to be that thing.

appearance ❑ When someone turns up at a place, you can call this their **appearance**. *The atmosphere has been exacerbated by the appearance of squads of riot police.*

❑ If someone makes an **appearance** in a film, play, or show, they have a part in it. Similarly, you can say a sportsperson makes an **appearance** when they take part in a competition.

❑ If someone famous makes a **public appearance**, they are seen in public, for example at a large party or the theatre. If they make a **personal appearance**, they do something like making a speech or opening a shop, and usually receive payment for it. The money they receive is called **appearance money**. ◇ If someone makes an **appearance** in court, they go to court to answer charges or give information.

❑ When something new comes into existence or becomes available, you call this its **appearance**.

❑ Your **appearance** is what you look like.

❑ **Appearance** is also used to talk about the impression created by someone's behaviour. *At least they give the appearance of trying to do something.* ◇ **By all appearances** or **from all appearances** means something seems to be true. *From all appearances, business is booming.*

appease (appeasing, appeased; appeasement, appeaser) If you appease someone who is demanding something, you offer them something or give in to some of their demands. A person who does this is called an **appeaser**. *...Britain's disastrous policy of appeasement towards Hitler.*

appellant An appellant is someone who has lodged an appeal against an official decision.

appellation An appellation is a name or title.

appellation contrôlée on a wine bottle label means the wine genuinely comes from a particular region of France, and is not a mixture of wines from different regions. It also shows the wine has fulfilled certain quality requirements.

append If you append something to something else, especially a note to a document, you add it to it.

appendage If you say something is an appendage of something else, you mean it is joined to it or controlled by it, and is regarded as an unimportant extra part of it. *The central bank was little more than an administrative appendage of the government.*

appendectomy (appendectomies) An appendectomy is a surgical operation to remove a person's appendix.

appendices See appendix.

appendicitis is a painful illness caused by an infected appendix. It is usually treated by removing the appendix.

appendix ❑ The appendix (*plural:* appendixes) is a small tube hanging from one end of the large intestine. In animals like cows, the appendix is used to digest grass, but it has no function in humans.

❑ An appendix to a book (*plural:* appendices) is extra information added at the end of it.

appetiser See appetizer.

appetising See appetizing.

appetite Your appetite is your desire to eat. ◇ If you have an appetite for something, you enjoy it and try to get a lot of it. *...his appetite for gossip.*

appetizer (*or* appetiser) An appetizer is a small amount of food you eat before a meal, which is intended to give you an appetite.

appetizing (appetizingly) (*can be spelled with an 's' instead of a 'z'*) If food is appetizing, it looks and smells good and makes you want to eat it. *The fish was appetizingly cooked and served.*

applaud (applauding, applauded; applause) When people applaud, they clap their hands to show they have enjoyed something, or to show they approve of what someone has said in a speech. This clapping is called **applause**. ◇ You also say people applaud something when they are pleased with it and praise it. *The Euro-sceptic wing will applaud the rate cut, for which it has been pressing for months.*

apple Apples are round fruit with smooth green, red, or yellow skins and firm white flesh.

applecart If you upset the applecart, you do something which causes a plan or system to go wrong when it was working well.

appliance An appliance or domestic appliance is a machine for doing a job in the home, for example a washing machine or a vacuum cleaner.

applicable (applicability) If something is applicable to a person, thing, or situation, it concerns or affects them. You talk about the applicability of something to a person, thing, or situation. *Piaget himself wrote relatively little about the applicability of his theories to education.*

applicant See apply.

application See apply.

applicator An applicator is a device for applying a substance to a surface.

applied See apply.

appliqué (*pron:* ap-plee-kay) is a type of decoration in which pieces of one fabric are sewn onto another.

apply (applies, applying, applied; application; applicant) ❑ If you apply for something like a job, a place on a course, or a loan, you formally ask to be given it, usually in writing. An application is a request like this; a person making it is called an **applicant**.

❑ If something applies to certain people or things, it concerns or affects them. *The current sanctions do not apply to food or medicine.*

❑ If a term is applied to someone or something, it is used to describe them or refer to them. *'Liberal' is a term I don't think we can apply to the present government.*

❑ If you apply yourself to something, you work hard at it. ◇ If you apply a technique or branch of knowledge to something, you use it. *...the application of genetic engineering to brewing.* ◇ The applied form of a subject deals with practical ways in which it can be used. *...applied mathematics... ...applied economics.*

❑ If you apply a substance to a surface, you paint it on or spread it on.

❑ If something like a law or policy is applied, it is put into operation.

appoint (appointment, appointee) ❑ If someone is appointed to a job, they are officially chosen to do it. The person chosen is sometimes called the **appointee**; the job itself is called an **appointment**.

❑ The appointed time for something is the time chosen for it to take place. Similarly, there can be an appointed place for something. ◇ If you have an appointment with someone, you have arranged to meet or visit them at a certain time and place.

apportion (apportioning, apportioned; apportionment) If something is apportioned among a group of people, it is decided how much each of them will get. *...the apportionment of resources.*

apposite If you say something like a comment is apposite, you mean it fits a situation or sums it up nicely.

appraise (appraising, appraised; appraisal) If you appraise something or make an appraisal of it, you consider it carefully and make a judgement about it.

appreciable (appreciably) An appreciable amount of

something is quite a large amount. *In the last few months his authority has grown appreciably.* Similarly, you can say something has an **appreciable** effect.

appreciate (appreciating, appreciated; appreciation) ❏ If you **appreciate** a situation or problem, you are aware of it. *As a new company, we appreciate how tough it is in business.*

❏ If you **appreciate** something like music or good food, you enjoy it because you recognize its good qualities. You can also have an **appreciation** of something like this. ◇ An **appreciation** of someone like a writer or an artist is a discussion and evaluation of their work.

❏ If you say you **appreciate** what someone has done, you mean you are grateful for it.

❏ If something **appreciates** in value, its value increases over a period of time.

appreciative An appreciative reaction shows pleasure or gratitude. If people are **appreciative**, they react like this.

apprehend (apprehension, apprehensive, apprehensively) ❏ If the police **apprehend** someone who is suspected of a crime, they catch them and arrest them; this is called the **apprehension** of the person.

❏ **Apprehension** is also a feeling of fear, worry, or anxiety. If you are **apprehensive** about something, you feel like this about it. *People listened apprehensively to the boom and thud of artillery.*

apprentice (apprenticed, apprenticeship) An **apprentice** is a young person who works with someone for a number of years on quite low pay, in order to learn a skill. You say someone like this is **apprenticed** to the person they work with; the period they spend as an apprentice is called their **apprenticeship**. ◇ Any period spent gaining experience which afterwards helps you in your career can be called an **apprenticeship**. *Pendry has served a long apprenticeship on Labour's sports committee and the all-party football committee.*

approach (approaches, approaching, approached) ❏ When someone or something **approaches** you, they get nearer to you; you call this their **approach**.

❏ An **approach** to a place is a road or path leading to it.

❏ If you **approach** someone about something, you mention it to them in the hope that they will become involved in it. This can be called making an **approach**.

❏ If a time or situation is **approaching**, it will happen soon. You talk about the **approach** of a time or situation. ◇ If something is **approaching** a level or state, it has almost reached it. *Inflation is approaching 30 per cent.*

❏ The way you **approach** a situation, problem, or task is the way you look at it or deal with it; this is called your **approach**.

approachable If someone is **approachable**, they are friendly and ready to listen to people's problems and questions.

approbation is approval of something or agreement to it.

appropriate (appropriately, appropriateness; appropriating, appropriated, appropriation) ❏ If something is **appropriate** to a situation, it is right or suitable. *Drizzle and overcast skies lent an appropriately dreary air to the post-lunch play... ...doubts about the appropriateness of government policy.*

❏ If you **appropriate** (*pron:* a-pro-pree-ate) something which belongs to someone else, you take it for your own use without getting their permission. *...the appropriation of*

property. ◇ If words or ideas are **appropriated** by a group of people, they begin using them in a new way for their own purposes.

approve (approving, approved; approvingly, approval) ❏ If someone in authority **approves** a plan or request or gives it their **approval**, they officially agree to it.

❏ If you **approve of** what someone has said or done, you have a good opinion of it. *He has spoken approvingly of China's contribution.* You can also show your **approval** of something, for example by cheering or applauding. ◇ If you **approve of** something being done, you think it is a good idea. You can also say it has your **approval**.

approx is short for 'approximately'.

approximate (approximately; approximating, approximated; approximation) ❏ **Approximate** and **approximately** are used to show that a figure or number is not exact. *...an approximate price of £125 per person... ...approximately three hours later.*

❏ If something **approximates** (*pron:* ap-**prox**-i-mates) to something else or is an **approximation** of it, it is similar to it but not quite the same.

après ski (*pron:* ap-ray **skee**) is evening entertainment and social activities in skiing resorts.

apricot Apricots are small soft round fruit with yellowish-orange flesh and a stone in the middle.

apron ❏ An **apron** is a piece of clothing worn over the front of other clothes, to stop them getting dirty.

❏ The **apron** at an airport is the area near the runways where aircraft are parked.

apropos (*pron:* ap-prop-**poh**) You use **apropos** to give an indication of what you are going to talk about. *Apropos your obituary of Viscount Muirshiel, allow me to add a small footnote.*

apt (aptly, aptness) ❏ If a way of describing something is **apt**, it sums it up nicely. *The Committee on Energy and Commerce would be more aptly named the Committee on Everything... The aptness of Eisenman's anecdote was brought home again and again.*

❏ If someone is **apt** to do something, they often do it or tend to do it.

aptitude If you have an **aptitude** for something, you are able to learn it quickly and do it well.

aquaculture is fish farming and underwater plant farming.

aqualung An **aqualung** is a piece of equipment which enables divers to breathe underwater. It consists of a large container full of compressed air which is carried on the diver's back and connected to his or her mouth by a tube.

aquamarine is a greenish-blue colour.

aquarium (*plural:* aquariums *or* aquaria) An **aquarium** is a water-filled glass tank for keeping fish in. ◇ An **aquarium** is also a building, often in a zoo, where fish and other underwater animals are kept.

aquatic is used to describe (a) animals and plants which live in water. (b) things which take place in water. *...aquatic cinematography.*

aqueduct An **aqueduct** is a bridge carrying water across a valley or river.

aquifer An **aquifer** is a layer or area of rock containing water which can be used to supply wells.

Arab Arabs are people whose first language is Arabic, especially people from North Africa and the Middle East.

arabesque (*pron:* ar-ab-esk) An **arabesque** is a design made up of complex patterns of intertwining lines and shapes, sometimes including pictures of flowers, leaves, and animals.

Arabia (Arabian) **Arabia** is the area of land between the Red Sea and the Persian Gulf which includes the present-day countries of Saudi Arabia, Yemen, Oman, Bahrain, Qatar, Kuwait, and the United Arab Emirates. **Arabian** is used to talk about things to do with Arabia. ...*the Arabian peninsula... ...an Arabian prince.*

Arabic is a language spoken in a variety of dialects by about 75 million people, mainly in the Middle East and north Africa. It is the official language of several countries including Egypt and Iraq.

arable land is used for growing crops.

arbiter An **arbiter** is a person or organization appointed to judge and settle a dispute between two people or groups. ◇ If someone or something is regarded as an **arbiter**, people always accept what they say as right. *Mao's writings were the sole arbiter of political right and wrong.*

arbitrary (arbitrarily, arbitrariness) You say something is **arbitrary** when it involves a choice or decision for which there is no good reason. ...*arbitrary arrests... No country will be arbitrarily excluded from the currency union... ...the apparent arbitrariness by which she sets the prices.*

arbitrate (arbitrating, arbitrated; arbitration, arbitrator) If someone **arbitrates** in a dispute between two people or groups, they consider all the facts and try to settle the dispute fairly. A person who does this is called an **arbitrator**; settling disputes in this way is called **arbitration**.

arboreal (*pron:* ahr-bore-ee-al) is used to describe things to do with trees. **Arboreal** animals live in trees.

arboretum (*pron:* ahr-bore-ree-tum) An **arboretum** is a place where trees are grown, especially exotic and unusual trees which can be studied.

arbour (*American spelling:* arbor) An **arbour** is a shelter in a garden formed by leaves and stems of plants growing together over a light framework.

arc An **arc** is a smoothly curving line. If something **arcs** or moves in an **arc**, it moves in a line like this. ◇ In maths, an **arc** is part of the circumference of a circle.

arcade An **arcade** is a covered passageway with shops on each side, leading off a street.

arcane If something is **arcane**, it is mysterious, or you need special knowledge to understand it.

arch (arches, arching, arched; archly, archness) ❑ An **arch** is a structure consisting of two pillars or walls which curve towards each other at the top and meet. An **arched** doorway or window has a top like this.

❑ If you **arch** your back, you make it into a curved shape. ◇ If you **arch** an eyebrow, you raise it.

❑ You say someone is being **arch** when they say things in a clever knowing way, to make fun of someone; this kind of talk is called **archness**. *Lord Lambton suggested archly that Cyril Bence should be declared 'Director of Conservative Shipping Policy'.*

arch- is added to words like 'rivals' and 'enemies' to describe people who are great long-standing rivals or enemies. ...*Dr Mahathir's arch-foe, Tengku Razaleigh.* ◇ **Arch-** is also used to describe people who have extreme and inflexible views. ...*an arch-traditionalist.*

archaeology (archaeological, archaeologist) (*can be spelled with an 'e' instead of 'ae'*) **Archaeology** is the study of the past by examining the remains of buildings and other things which are found buried in the ground. An **archaeologist** is an expert on this. **Archaeological** is used to describe things to do with archaeology. ...*one of England's most important archaeological sites.*

archaic (*pron:* ark-kay-ik) (archaism) If something is **archaic**, it is extremely old-fashioned and out-of-date. You call something like this an **archaism** (*pron:* ark-kay-iz-zum).

archangel (*pron:* ark-ain-jel) An **archangel** is a high-ranking angel.

archbishop An **archbishop** is a bishop of the highest rank.

archdeacon An **archdeacon** is an Anglican clergyman ranking just below a bishop. He looks after a sub-division of a bishop's diocese.

archdiocese (*pron:* arch-die-a-siss) (archdioceses) An **archdiocese** is the area over which an archbishop has control.

archeology See **archaeology**.

archer (archery) In former times, an **archer** was someone who shot arrows from a bow in war. Today an **archer** is someone who shoots arrows as a sport; the sport is called **archery**.

archetypal (*pron:* ark-ee-**type**-al) (archetype) You say something is **archetypal** or an **archetype** when it is a perfect example of its kind, because it has all the features associated with that kind of thing.

archipelago (*pron:* ark-ee-pel-a-go) (archipelagos) An **archipelago** is a group of small islands.

architect An **architect** is a person whose job is designing buildings. ◇ The **architect** of a plan or policy is the person who invented it.

architectural (architecturally) **Architectural** is used to talk about things to do with the design and construction of buildings. ...*one of the architectural masterpieces of Europe... ...sites which are architecturally interesting.*

architecture is the art of designing and constructing buildings. ◇ The **architecture** of a building is the style it is constructed in.

archive (*pron:* ark-ive) (archivist) **Archives** are collections of documents and records relating to past events. These documents and records are also called **archive** material. An **archivist** (*pron:* ark-iv-ist) is someone whose job is to collect, sort, and preserve archives.

archway An **archway** is a passage or entrance with a curved roof.

arctic weather is extremely cold.

ardent (ardently) **Ardent** is used to describe people who strongly support or oppose something. ...*the most ardent opponents of abortion... The Liberal Democrats have always been the most ardently pro-European of the political parties.*

ardour is passion or great enthusiasm.

arduous If something you do is **arduous**, it is very hard work.

are See **be**.

area ❑ An **area** of a city or region is a part of it.

❑ The **area** of a room or piece of land is a measurement of the space it covers, expressed, for example, in square metres or hectares.

❑ An **area** is also a subject or field of interest. *These mol-*

ecules could be of interest in the area of laser photochemistry.

arena ❑ An arena is a place where sports or other public performances take place. It has seats for spectators around the outside.

❑ The field of competition or public life in which someone operates can also be called an **arena**. *The South Africans were banned from competing in the international arena in most sports.*

argot (*pron:* ahr-go) An **argot** is the slang or specialist words used by a group of people. *...drug-users' argot.*

arguable (arguably) If a claim or belief is **arguable**, you can make a good case for it. *The battle was arguably a tactical defeat for the Americans.* ◇ You can also describe an idea or comment as **arguable** when it is rather doubtful whether it is true. *It is arguable whether he ever had much control over the army.*

argue (arguing, argued; argument) ❑ When people **argue** or have an **argument**, they say things which show they disagree, and sometimes speak angrily or shout.

❑ If you **argue** for something or put up an **argument** for it, you say it is a good idea and give reasons why. *Britain has always argued for political control over central banks.* You can also **argue** against something. ◇ If you **argue** that something is true, you say it is true and give reasons why.

argumentative people are always arguing.

aria (*pron:* ah-ree-a) An **aria** is an elaborate song for a solo singer, especially in an opera or oratorio.

arid (aridity) ❑ If a place is **arid**, it is extremely dry and very few plants grow there. You talk about the **aridity** of a place like this.

❑ If you call what someone says or writes **arid**, you mean it is uninteresting, because it is concerned with abstract principles, rather than people and their feelings.

arise (arising, arose, have arisen) When something like a problem, an opportunity, or a new state of affairs **arises**, it comes into existence.

aristocracy (aristocrat, aristocratic) The **aristocracy** are people of high social rank, especially people with titles like 'duke' or 'earl'. Individual members of the aristocracy are called **aristocrats**. **Aristocratic** is used to describe things relating to or typical of the aristocracy. *Table tennis was a fashionable aristocratic sport in the late nineteenth century.*

arithmetic (arithmetical) **Arithmetic** is the part of maths which deals with addition, subtraction, multiplication, and division. **Arithmetical** is used to describe things involving arithmetic. *...basic arithmetical skills.*

arm ❑ A person's **arms** are the parts of their body between their hands and their shoulders. ◇ If you are **arm in arm** with someone, your arm is linked through theirs.

❑ If you hold something **at arm's length**, you hold it as far away from you as possible. ◇ If you **keep** someone **at arm's length**, you avoid a close relationship with them.

❑ If you welcome someone **with open arms**, you are delighted to see them, and show it. You can also welcome something new **with open arms**. *Far from welcoming the Ecu with open arms, many leading European companies would shun it.*

❑ If someone is **up in arms** about something, they are angry about it and are strongly voicing their objections.

❑ An **arm** of an organization is a section of it. *...the mer-chant banking arm of National Westminster Bank.*

❑ The **arms** of a chair are the raised parts on each side where you rest your arms.

❑ **Arms** are weapons of war like tanks, missiles, and guns. ◇ The **arms race** was a situation which existed from the end of the Second World War to the collapse of the USSR, during which the US and the USSR constantly tried to get more powerful weapons than each other.

❑ If someone is **armed**, they are carrying a weapon, especially a gun. ◇ If someone **arms** a group of people, they give them weapons. ◇ A country's **armed forces** are its army, navy, and air force. ◇ An **armed** attack or conflict involves the use of weapons.

❑ If you go somewhere **armed** with something like equipment or information, you have it with you ready for use.

armada An **armada** is a large fleet of warships, sent to invade or attack a place. ◇ Any other large group of ships or boats heading for a place can be called an **armada**. *...an armada of pleasure boats.*

armadillo (armadillos) The **armadillo** is a Central and South American animal which is covered with hard bony plates for protection.

Armageddon is the final battle between good and evil which some Christians believe will come at the end of the world.

armament A country's or army's **armaments** are its weapons. The **armament** in a place is the weapons there.

armband An **armband** is a band of fabric someone wears around their arm, usually to indicate their official position. A black armband indicates that someone is in mourning.

armchair An **armchair** is a comfortable chair with a support on each side for your arms.

armful An **armful** of something is the amount you can carry in one or both of your arms.

armhole The **armholes** of a piece of clothing are the openings you put your arms through and where the sleeves are attached, if it has them.

armistice An **armistice** is an agreement between countries at war to stop fighting for a time, often to discuss ways of reaching a peaceful settlement.

armlock If you have someone in an **armlock**, you have twisted their arm behind their back so they cannot escape and are under your control. ◇ If you have something in an **armlock**, you have the power to restrain or control it. *His aim is to break the Likud armlock on Israeli politics.*

armour (armoured) (*American spelling:* armor, armored) ❑ An **armoured** vehicle has a hard metal covering to protect it from attack. This covering is called its **armour**. ◇ **Armour** is also groups of armoured vehicles, especially tanks. *Britain is ready to send more troops, armour and aircraft.*

❑ **Armour** is also protective clothing worn by people to protect them from attack. When battles were fought with swords and arrows, the metal suits worn by soldiers were called **armour**. In modern times, people like the police sometimes wear clothing called **body armour** over places like the chest, to protect it from gunfire.

armour-plated If something like a vehicle is armour-plated, it has a hard metal covering to protect it from attack.

armoury (armouries) (*American spelling:* armory, armories) ❑ An **armoury** is a place where weapons are stored. ◇ A country's **armoury** is its total collection of weapons and other military equipment.

❑ Any large collection of useful things for dealing with something can be called an **armoury**. *Drugs derived from the immune systems of insects could be formidable additions to the pharmaceutical armoury.*

armpit A person's **armpits** are the areas under their arms where their arms join their shoulders.

armrest The armrests on something like a chair are the raised parts where you rest your arms.

army (armies) An **army** is a large organized group of people who are armed and trained to fight, especially one controlled by a government. ◇ An **army** of people, animals, or things is a large number of them together. *He fought his way through the army of television cameras.*

aroma An **aroma** is a strong pleasant smell.

aromatherapy (aromatherapist) **Aromatherapy** is a treatment, used especially to relieve tension, which involves massaging the body with special fragrant plant oils. An aromatherapist is someone trained to give treatment like this.

aromatic things have a strong pleasant smell. *...aromatic herbs.*

arose See arise.

around can be used instead of 'round' for some of its meanings. See round.

❑ If you talk about someone being **around**, you mean they are present, or not far away. ◇ If you say something has been **around** for a certain length of time, you mean it has existed or been available for that time.

❑ **Around** is also used to say a number is not exact. *In 1960 around 30% of women with children worked.*

arouse (arousing, aroused; arousal) If something **arouses** certain feelings or reactions, it makes people have them. You talk about the **arousal** of feelings or reactions. *...the part of the brain known to have a role in sexual arousal.*

arraign (*pron:* ar-rain) (arraignment) If someone is **arraigned**, they are brought before a court to answer charges against them. *On arraignment, the appellant pleaded not guilty.*

arrange (arranging, arranged; arrangement, arranger) ❑ If you **arrange** something, you make the necessary preparations for it to take place. These preparations are called **arrangements**. ◇ If people **arrange** to do something at a certain time, they agree they will do it at that time. ◇ In an **arranged** marriage, the parents choose the person their son or daughter will marry.

❑ If things are **arranged** in a certain way, they are positioned or ordered that way. The way they are positioned or ordered is called an **arrangement**. *The roof is supported by tubular steel columns arranged in clusters of four.*

❑ If someone **arranges** a piece of music, they adapt it to be performed in a different way, usually on different instruments. An adaptation like this is called an **arrangement**. A person who arranges music is called an **arranger**.

arrant is used to mean 'utter' or 'total' when you are criticizing something strongly. *They dismissed the claims as arrant nonsense.*

array (arrayed) An **array** of things is a large number of them collected or positioned together. You say things like these are **arrayed**. *...a vast array of switches... He didn't realise the tremendous forces arrayed against him.*

arrears If you are in **arrears** with something like your mortgage or rent, you are behind with your payments. ◇ If you are paid in **arrears**, your wages are paid at the end of each period in which you earn them.

arrest (arresting, arrestingly) ❑ If the police **arrest** someone or make an **arrest**, they catch them and take them somewhere, usually to a police station, to question them and decide whether to charge them. You say people in this situation are **under arrest**.

❑ If you **arrest** something, you stop it happening. *Only swift government action will arrest the acceleration of small retail business failures.*

❑ If something is **arresting**, it attracts your attention, because it is surprising, interesting, or beautiful. *...that perfect face, so arrestingly lovely that you couldn't believe it was flesh and blood.*

arrhythmia (*pron:* a-rith-mee-a) is any variation in the normal rhythm of a person's heartbeat.

arrive (arriving, arrived; arrival) ❑ When you **arrive** at a place, you get there after a journey. You talk about your **arrival** at a place. People who have just arrived at a place can be called **arrivals**. *Most of the new arrivals have fled from heavy fighting around Ganta.* ◇ If something like a letter **arrives**, it is delivered to you.

❑ When something new is introduced to a place, you can say it **arrives** there or talk about its **arrival**. *...the arrival of multichannel television.* ◇ When an expected event **arrives**, it happens. *The summer sales arrived.*

❑ When people **arrive** at a decision or conclusion, they reach it. ◇ If you **arrive** at the answer to a problem, you eventually work it out.

❑ When a new baby **arrives**, it is born.

arriviste (*pron:* a-reeve-ist) An **arriviste** is a person who is extremely ambitious and does not mind whether what they do is right or wrong, so long as they get what they want.

arrogant (arrogantly, arrogance) If someone is **arrogant**, they behave in a proud unpleasant way, because they think they are more important than other people. Behaviour like this is called **arrogance**. *He arrogantly displayed his utter contempt for our community.*

arrow An **arrow** is (a) a pointed weapon fired from a bow. (b) a pointed symbol showing which direction something is.

arrowhead An **arrowhead** is the sharp pointed end of an arrow, especially a stone one fitted to a very early kind of arrow.

arrowroot is starch from a West Indian plant. It is used in cooking, for example in biscuits and for thickening sauces.

arsenal ❑ A country's **arsenal** is all its weapons and other military equipment. ◇ An **arsenal** is also a building where weapons and other pieces of military equipment are made and stored.

❑ An **arsenal** of things is a large collection of them ready for use. *Swiss-born director Carl Schenkel lets loose an arsenal of flashy effects.*

arsenic is a poisonous substance which has some of the

qualities of metal. It is used in transistors, lead-based alloys, and some brasses. It is also used in rat poison and insecticides.

arson (arsonist) **Arson** is the crime of deliberately setting fire to a building. An **arsonist** is someone who does this.

art is painting, drawing, and sculpture. ◇ When people talk about the **arts**, they mean things like drama, music, and poetry, as well as painting and sculpture. ◇ At a school or college, **arts** subjects are subjects like literature, languages, and history, rather than science or engineering.
  ❏ If you have learned the **art** of doing something, you have learned how to do it. *He has never mastered the art of dealing with the press.*

Art Deco was a style of art, decoration, and architecture popular in the 1920s and 1930s. It involved the use of simple, bold, and often geometrical designs and man-made materials.

Art Nouveau was a style of decoration and design common at the end of the 19th century. Its typical features were flowing lines and many leaves and flowers.

artefact (*or* artifact) An **artefact** is an ornament, tool, or other man-made object, especially an old one which is of historical interest.

arteriosclerosis is a serious condition in which the walls of a person's arteries thicken and lose their elasticity. This condition is also called 'hardening of the arteries'.

artery (arteries; arterial) ❏ Your **arteries** are tubes which carry blood from your heart to the rest of your body. **Arterial** is used to talk about things to do with a person's arteries. *...the arterial wall.*
  ❏ An important road or railway can also be called an **artery**. Main roads are sometimes called **arterial** roads.

artesian well (*pron:* art-teez-yan) An **artesian well** is a type of well in which the water is continually forced up out of the ground by pressure from water flowing in from a higher level.

artful (artfully) An **artful** person is clever and cunning. ◇ If something has been made in an **artful** way, it has been made with great skill. *...products that were well-made and artfully designed.*

arthritis (arthritic) **Arthritis** is a condition in which the joints in someone's body become swollen and painful. If someone is **arthritic**, they suffer from arthritis.

artichoke The **artichoke** or **globe artichoke** is a round green vegetable with fleshy leaves. ◇ The **artichoke** or **Jerusalem artichoke** is a small yellowish-white vegetable which grows underground and looks like a knobbly potato.

article (articled) ❏ An **article** is a piece of writing in a newspaper or magazine.
  ❏ An **article** is also a clause or section of something like a treaty or Act of Parliament.
  ❏ If you say something is an **article of faith** with someone, you mean they believe in it strongly and are prepared to disregard any evidence against it.
  ❏ An **article** is any object, especially a small man-made one.
  ❏ 'A', 'an', and 'the' are called **articles**. 'A' and 'an' are called the **indefinite article** and 'the' is called the **definite article**.
  ❏ A person who is **articled,** for example to a firm of so-

licitors, is employed by the firm and is training to become qualified. **Articles** is the two-year period of training and work experience which all new solicitors must complete before qualifying. Trainee solicitors are sometimes called **articled clerks.**

articulate (articulating, articulated; articulacy, articulation) ❏ If you are **articulate** (*pron:* ar-tik-yoo-let), you are able to express yourself well. This ability is called **articulacy.** ◇ When you **articulate** (*pron:* ar-tik-yoo-late) your ideas or feelings, you say in words what you think or feel. ◇ If you talk about an actor's or singer's **articulation,** you are talking about how precisely and clearly they pronounce their words.
  ❏ An **articulated** vehicle is made in two sections, so it can bend in the middle and go round corners more easily.

artifact See artefact.

artifice is deceiving people in a clever way. An **artifice** is a clever trick or piece of deception.

artificial (artificially, artificiality) ❏ **Artificial** things have been made by man, rather than being produced by nature. *...artificial limbs... ...an artificial lake.* ◇ An **artificial** situation is one which has been created, rather than arising of its own accord. *Financial regulation kept interest rates artificially low.*
  ❏ If someone's behaviour is **artificial,** they pretend to have attitudes and feelings they do not really have. ◇ You can say other things are **artificial** when they seem unnatural, contrived, or false. This characteristic is called **artificiality.**

artificial insemination or **AI** is the placing of sperm into a woman or female animal, to make her pregnant without direct contact with a male.

artificial intelligence is the study of how to make computers behave in a similar way to humans, especially in the areas of reasoning, language, and vision.

artificial respiration When someone who has stopped breathing is given **artificial respiration,** air is forced into their lungs, to keep them alive and help them start breathing again.

artillery consists of large powerful guns like cannons, howitzers, and missile launchers.

artisan In the past, people like carpenters and stonemasons whose jobs involve skill with their hands used to be called **artisans.**

artist An **artist** is someone who draws, paints, or produces other works of art. ◇ Musicians, actors, dancers, or other performers can also be called **artists.**

artiste (*pron:* ar-teest) An **artiste** is a professional entertainer, for example a singer or dancer.

artistic (artistically) ❏ **Artistic** is used to talk about things involving art or artists. *...the campaign for artistic freedom.* ◇ If someone is **artistic,** they are good at drawing and painting or at creating things which look attractive. *...those who are artistically gifted.*
  ❏ artistic licence: see licence.

artistry is great skill, especially the skill of a musician or of a sportsman or sportswoman.

artless You say people are **artless** when they say things in a blunt straightforward way and do not try to deceive people.

artwork The **artwork** in a book or advertisement is the drawings or photographs in it.

arty is used to talk, especially in a disapproving way, about people who are artistic or seem preoccupied with fashionable intellectual ideas.

Aryan (*pron:* **air-ree-an**) is used to describe people with racial characteristics associated with Northern Europeans, especially fair skin and hair and blue eyes. The Nazis considered Aryan people to be superior to other races.

as is used to say one thing happens while something else is happening. *As he waited to speak, a member of Mr Smith's staff handed Mr Gould his reply.* ◇ If you say something will happen **as from** or **as of** a certain time, you mean it will happen from that time onwards.
❑ As is used to talk about someone's job, role, or function. *Jaroszewicz was forced to step down as prime minister.* ◇ As is used to say what something is used for. *The composted material was then used as fertiliser.* ◇ As is used to say why someone does something. *Soldiers are expected to shoot in the air as a warning.* ◇ As is used to talk about a result of something. *As a result, only the armed have access to food.*
❑ As is used when mentioning someone's description or opinion of something. *Current-affairs programmes are dismissed as being soft on criminals and terrorists.*
❑ As is used when making comparisons. *At Wimbledon, as at other sporting events, flash photography is a nuisance... The problem is not nearly as bad as Labour claims.* ◇ As if and as though are used to say how something appears. *He looked as if his mind was elsewhere.*
❑ As is used to talk about people having the freedom to do what they want. *This gave them carte blanche to behave as they liked.*
❑ As is sometimes used to mean 'because'. *I am livid, particularly as they seem to have details of my income.*
❑ As to is used to say what something like a statement or question is about. *The packaging doesn't give any indication as to what the products contain.* ◇ You say as for... when you are going on to a different aspect of a subject. ◇ You say as you know... when you are reminding someone of something.

asbestos is a grey mineral which does not burn and is used in making some fireproof materials. It used to be used in buildings until it was found that asbestos dust caused lung problems.

asbestosis is a disease of the lungs caused by breathing in asbestos dust over a long period of time.

ascend ❑ If something **ascends**, it moves upwards. ◇ If you ascend something like a staircase, you go up it.
❑ If a group of things is arranged in **ascending** order, the smallest is put first, followed by the next smallest, and so on.
❑ You can also use ascend to talk about someone progressing to a position of power or success. *Natalie Wood plays a girl who ascends to Hollywood stardom.*
❑ When someone like a queen or emperor **ascends** the throne, they are crowned queen or emperor.

ascendancy (ascendant) If someone or something is **in the ascendancy** or **in the ascendant,** they are becoming more powerful, influential, or popular. *Democratic trends are now in the ascendant in many African countries.* ◇ If something has **ascendancy** over other things, it is in favour and they are not. *If Thatcherite policies regain the ascendancy, he will become a marked man.*

ascent (ascension) An **ascent** is a movement from a lower to a higher level. *...a balloon ascent.* An ascent of something like a mountain is a climb to the top. ◇ When someone or something reaches a position of power or success, you can talk about their **ascent** or **ascension** to that position.

ascertain (ascertaining, ascertained) If you **ascertain** something, you find it out, by questioning or investigation. *They were unable to ascertain the extent of the damage.*

ascetic (*pron:* **ass-set-tik**) (asceticism) If someone is **ascetic** or an **ascetic**, they have a simple and strict lifestyle, for example because of their religious beliefs. Behaviour like this is called **asceticism.**

ascribe (ascribing, ascribed) If you **ascribe** something to a particular thing, you say that thing caused it. *The increase in the divorce rate could largely be ascribed to an increase in the confidence of working-class women.* ◇ If you **ascribe** a quality or characteristic to someone, you say they have it. *Ethiopian ancestry was ascribed to Pushkin.*

asexual (*pron:* **eh-sex-yew-al**) (asexually) If an animal or plant is **asexual**, it has no sex organs and so cannot be called a male or a female. **Asexual** reproduction is done without sexual activity. *These parasites reproduce asexually.* ◇ You can describe a person as **asexual** when there is little or nothing about their clothes, physical characteristics, or behaviour which identifies them as a man or a woman.

ash (ashes) ❑ Ash or ashes is the black or grey powdery substance left after something has burned. ◇ If something **rises from the ashes** of something which has ended or been destroyed, it appears in its place.
❑ The **ash** is a tree which produces black buds and winged seeds. Wood from this tree is called ash.

ashamed If you feel **ashamed**, you feel embarrassed and guilty about something you have done. ◇ If you are **ashamed** to do something, you are reluctant to do it because you would feel embarrassed and guilty about it. ◇ If you are **ashamed** of someone, you disapprove of them or of something they have done, and feel embarrassed to be connected with them.

ashen If someone is **ashen** or **ashen-faced**, they are pale with shock or fear.

ashore If you are **ashore**, you are on land, rather than in a boat at sea. If you step onto the land from a boat, you say you come **ashore**. Similarly, you can say a piece of driftwood is washed **ashore**.

ashram An **ashram** is a Hindu hermitage or religious retreat.

ashtray An **ashtray** is a small dish which smokers flick ash into and use to put out their cigarettes or cigars.

Asian is used to talk about people and things in or from the continent of Asia. *...Asian forests.* ◇ An **Asian** is someone who comes from Asia, especially someone from India, Pakistan, Bangladesh, or Sri Lanka.

aside ❑ If you **move aside**, (a) you get out of someone's way. (b) you give up a position or post so someone else can take your place.
❑ You use aside to say you are ignoring one aspect of something for the moment. *Politics aside, American unemployment insurance deserves another look... Leaving aside for a moment controversies about populism, there is much to welcome in the plans.* ◇ **Aside from** means the same as 'apart

from'. *Aside from these pleasantries, the only material outcome appears to be an economic cooperation treaty.*

❏ If people **put** or **set aside** something like a problem or a feeling, they reject it or ignore it so they can concentrate on more important things.

❏ If money is **set aside** for a certain purpose, it is kept for that purpose and not used for anything else.

❏ If you **take** someone **aside**, you lead them away from other people, so you can talk to them in private.

❏ An **aside** is a brief casual comment you make in the middle of saying something else.

ask ❏ If you **ask** someone something, you put a question to them. ◇ If you **ask** someone to do something, you say you would like them to do it. ◇ If you **ask** for something, you say you would like it to be given or brought to you. ◇ If you **ask** someone to something like a party or a meal, you invite them to it.

❏ If you say someone is **asking for trouble**, you mean they are behaving in a way which will probably lead to something unpleasant happening to them.

❏ The **asking price** for something is the price the person selling it says they want for it.

askance (*pron:* ass-**kanss**) If you talk about someone **looking askance** at something, you mean they disapprove of it.

askew If something is **askew**, it is not straight or level.

asleep If someone is **asleep**, they are sleeping.

asp Asps are small poisonous snakes in southern Europe. They have brown skins with black stripes.

asparagus is a vegetable which consists of long thin green shoots with pointed ends.

aspect An **aspect** of something is a part of its character or nature. *...the radical change which is affecting every aspect of Algerian life... Perhaps the most interesting aspect of the proposals is the language employed by the Khmer Rouge.*

aspen The **aspen** is a type of poplar. Its leaves are attached by long flat stalks, and quiver in the breeze.

aspersions If you **cast aspersions** on someone or something, you make critical remarks about them.

asphalt is a mixture of bitumen, oil, and small stones. It is used to make surfaces for roads.

asphyxiate (*pron:* ass-**fix**-ee-ate) (asphyxiating, asphyxiated; asphyxia, asphyxiation) If someone is **asphyxiated**, they become unconscious through lack of oxygen, and may die as a result. You can say someone dies of **asphyxia** or **asphyxiation**.

aspic is a clear jelly made from meat or fish juices. ◇ If you say a place or way of life is preserved or held **in aspic**, you mean it has remained unchanged for a long time.

aspirant An **aspirant** to something is a person who wants to achieve it. *...gold medal aspirants.* ◇ **Aspirant** is also used to describe someone who wants to be a particular thing. For example, an **aspirant** writer is someone who wants to be a writer.

aspiration People's **aspirations** are the things they hope to achieve.

aspire (aspiring, aspired) If you **aspire** to something like an important job, you have an ambition to have it.

aspirin is a drug which reduces pain and fever. It is often sold as tablets called **aspirins**.

ass (asses) The **ass** is an animal like a horse but smaller and with longer ears. A wild ass is always called an ass; a domesticated ass is usually called a donkey. ◇ If you call someone an **ass**, you mean they are stupid.

assail (assailing, assailed; assailant) If you are **assailed** by doubts, fears, or problems, you are greatly troubled by them. ◇ If you are **assailed** by a person, you are threatened or attacked by them. You call the person who does this your **assailant**. ◇ You also say someone is **assailed** when they are strongly criticized.

assassinate (assassinating, assassinated; assassination, assassin) If an important person is **assassinated**, they are murdered, usually for political reasons. A murder like this is called an **assassination**. The murderer is called an assassin.

assault ❏ An **assault** by an army is a strong attack.

❏ If someone is **assaulted**, they are physically attacked. An attack like this is called an **assault**. ◇ In law, **assault** is the criminal offence of threatening to attack someone. **Assault and battery** is the crime of threatening to attack someone and then actually doing it.

❏ An **assault** on something is a strong criticism of it, or an attempt to damage or weaken it. *His book is a radical assault on feminism... He continued his assault on local councils by launching a green paper on local-government reform.*

assault course An **assault course** is an area of land covered with obstacles such as rope nets and water-filled ditches. People like soldiers have to make their way round it as an exercise.

assay An **assay** is an analysis to see how much metal there is in an ore, or to what extent a precious metal consists of impurities.

assemblage An **assemblage** of people or things is a collection of them of different kinds.

assemble (assembling, assembled; assembly, assemblies) ❏ When people **assemble**, they gather together in order to do something. **Assembly** is the gathering together of people, especially for political meetings. *The freedoms of association, assembly and speech are fundamental rights.* ◇ An **assembly** is a group of people gathered together, especially a group who meet regularly to take important decisions.

❏ If you **assemble** a number of people, objects, or facts, you get them together.

❏ When something like a machine is **assembled**, its parts are fitted together. *Final assembly of the engine will take place in Germany.*

assembler An **assembler** is a person who works on an assembly line. ◇ An **assembler** is also a firm which assembles products like cars or computers from components supplied by other firms.

assembly line An **assembly line** is an arrangement of workers and machines in a factory where each product passes from one worker to another until it is finished.

assent If someone in authority **assents** to something or gives their **assent** to it, they agree to it.

assert (assertion) ❏ If you **assert** something, you state it firmly. A statement like this is called an **assertion**.

❏ If you **assert** yourself, you speak and act in a forceful way, so people take notice of you. Similarly, if you **assert** your authority or control, you speak or act forcefully, so people see you are in control. *This assertion of authority has alienated moderates.*

assertive (assertively, assertiveness) You say someone is being **assertive** when they speak and act in a forceful way, so people take notice of them. *They find it difficult to act assertively... ...the new-found assertiveness of Japanese foreign policy.*

assess (assesses, assessing, assessed; assessment) When you **assess** someone or something, you consider them carefully and make a judgement about them. This judgement is called an **assessment**.

assessable Your **assessable** income is the part of your income which you must pay tax on.

assessor An **assessor** is an expert whose job is to assess something, usually the cost of something.

asset An **asset** is something like a quality or skill which is useful to the person who has it. *His greatest asset is the courage and competitiveness which impels him to take risks.* ◇ A person's or organization's **assets** are the valuable things they own, including their money and investments.

asset-stripping (asset-stripper) **Asset-stripping** is buying a company in difficulties, then selling off its assets at a profit. The company is then either closed down or rebuilt from scratch. An **asset-stripper** is someone who makes money this way.

assiduous (assiduously) If someone is **assiduous**, they work hard and diligently. You talk about the **assiduity** of someone like this. *This will encourage them to study a little more assiduously.*

assign (assignment) If you are **assigned** a task, it is given to you to deal with. An **assignment** is a task given to someone. ◇ If you are **assigned** to a place, you are sent to work there. You can also be **assigned** to an organization or group.

assignation (pron: ass-sig-**nay**-shun) An **assignation** is a secret meeting.

assimilate (assimilating, assimilated; assimilation) ❑ If something is **assimilated** by something else, it is absorbed by it and becomes a part of it.
❑ If immigrants or ethnic groups are **assimilated** into the population of a country, they adopt the way of life there, either freely or because they are made to. *...the campaign of national assimilation waged against the country's Moslems.*
❑ If a group of people **assimilates** the customs or beliefs of another group, it adopts them as additions to its own system of customs or beliefs.
❑ If you **assimilate** facts or ideas, you learn them and make use of them.

assist (assistance) If you **assist** someone or give them **assistance,** you help them. If something **assists** something else, it helps it. *...a chemical that assists in the manufacture of proteins.*

assistant Someone's **assistant** is a person who helps them in their work. ◇ **Assistant** is used in front of job titles to indicate a slightly lower rank. For example, an assistant director is one rank lower than a director. ◇ A **shop assistant** helps customers in a shop, or sells things to them.

assizes were regular court sessions held by an important travelling judge in county towns in England and Wales until 1971.

associate (associating, associated; association) ❑ If you asso-ciate something with something else, you connect the two things in your mind. ◇ If you say something has particular **associations,** you mean it reminds you of something you have experienced in the past. *Revolutions have unhappy associations for most Afghans.* ◇ If something is **associated** with a particular thing, you tend to get it where you get that thing. *...the problems associated with inner-city housing.*
❑ If someone is **associated** with an organization or cause, they are involved with it, or publicly support it.
❑ If you **associate** with a group of people, you spend time with them. ◇ If you do something **in association with** someone else, you do it together. ◇ Your **associates** are your work or business colleagues.
❑ An **association** is a group of people who have joined together because they have a common occupation, aim, or interest. *...the British Medical Association.* ◇ **Associated** appears in the name of some organizations made up of smaller organizations. *...Associated British Ports.*
❑ **Associate** in front of a word like 'member' means someone does not have full membership of an organization, or is of slightly lower rank than others with the same title. *...the Sun's associate editor.*

assorted (assortment) **Assorted** is used to describe a collection of things which are in a variety of sizes or colours, or different from each other in some other way. A collection like this can also be called an **assortment**. *...assorted chocolates... ...an assortment of motorbikes.* Similarly, you can talk about an **assorted** group of people or call them an **assortment**. *...the oddly assorted coalition against Maastricht.*

assuage (pron: ass-**wage**) (assuaging, assuaged) If you **assuage** someone's feelings of fear, worry, anger, or guilt, you say or do something to calm them.

assume (assuming, assumed; assumption) ❑ If you **assume** something is true, you suppose it is true or behave as if it were true, although you cannot be sure of it. This is called making an **assumption**. ◇ You say **assuming...** when you are mentioning something which might happen or might be true; you then go on to talk about the possible consequences. *But assuming that the talks make progress, won't they do too little, too late?*
❑ When a person or group **assumes** power, they become the new ruler or government of a country. Similarly, you can talk about someone **assuming** control or **assuming** responsibility for something. You can also talk about someone's **assumption** of power, control, or responsibility. *...his assumption of the office of Prime Minister.*
❑ If something **assumes** a particular characteristic, it takes it on. *Mrs Zuckerman's face assumed a contemptuous expression... The dispute has assumed an increasingly bitter and personal character.*

assurance ❑ If you give someone an **assurance** about something, you tell them it is definitely true or will definitely happen.
❑ If you do something with **assurance,** you do it with confidence and certainty.
❑ **Assurance** or life **assurance** is insurance on someone's life.

assure (assuring, assured) ❑ If you **assure** someone that something is true or will happen, you tell them it is definitely true or will definitely happen. ◇ If you are assured of something, you will definitely get it. *The communists are assured of retaining at least some of their power.* ❑ If someone is **assured**, they are confident and at ease.

assuredly If you say something is **assuredly** true, you mean it is definitely true. *Those headlines will assuredly hurt Labour.*

asterisk An **asterisk** is the symbol * which is used in a piece of writing to indicate that there is more information at the bottom of the page.

astern If something is **astern** of a ship, it is behind it.

asteroid Asteroids are large lumps of rock, between one and several hundred miles across, which orbit the sun, especially between Mars and Jupiter.

asthma (*pron:* ass-ma) (asthmatic) **Asthma** is an illness, often brought on by allergies. People who suffer from asthma are called **asthmatics**; they have sudden sharp attacks when they cough and gasp for breath. **Asthmatic** is used to talk about things relating to asthma.

astonish (astonishes, astonishing, astonished; astonishingly, astonishment) If something **astonishes** you, you are extremely surprised by it. *I was astonished to see these reports... ...an astonishing statement... ...an astonishingly short period... His request will be viewed with astonishment and outrage.*

astound (astounding, astoundingly) If something **astounds** you, you are absolutely amazed by it. *...one of the most astounding discoveries of the 20th century... ...an astoundingly brilliant win.*

astray ❑ If someone is **led astray**, they do things which are foolish, wrong, or against the law, as a result of the bad influence of other people.
❑ If something **goes astray**, it gets lost or goes missing.

astride If you are **astride** something, you are sitting or standing with one leg on each side of it. ◇ If a place is **astride** something like a road or river, it is situated on both sides of it.

astringent An **astringent** is a substance for drying greasy skin. ◇ **Astringent** comments are sharp and sarcastic.

astrology (astrologer, astrological) **Astrology** is the study of the movements of the planets, sun, moon, and stars in the belief that they influence people's lives. An **astrologer** is someone who studies this subject, and predicts what will happen to people. **Astrological** is used to talk about things to do with astrology. *...astrological predictions.*

astronaut An **astronaut** is a person who travels in a spacecraft.

astronomy (astronomical, astronomer; astronomic, astronomically) ❑ **Astronomy** is the scientific study of the planets, stars, and other natural objects in space. An **astronomer** is a scientist who studies astronomy. **Astronomical** is used to talk about things to do with astronomy. *...an astronomical telescope.*
❑ If you call a cost, value, or amount **astronomical** or **astronomic**, you mean it is extremely high. *...astronomic rents... Docklands house prices had risen astronomically.*

astrophysics (astrophysicist) **Astrophysics** is the study of the physical and chemical structure of the planets, stars, and other natural objects in space. An **astrophysicist** is a scientist who studies this subject.

AstroTurf is artificial grass used as a playing surface for sports. 'AstroTurf' is a trademark.

astute (astutely, astuteness) If someone is **astute**, they are good at interpreting situations and at making the right judgements and decisions. *The ruling family read the American mood pretty astutely... They were known for their reliability and astuteness.*

asunder If something is torn, split, or ripped **asunder**, it is forcefully separated into two parts.

asylum See political asylum, lunatic asylum.

asymmetric (asymmetrical, asymmetry) If something is **asymmetric** or **asymmetrical**, its two parts or halves are different, for example in size, shape, or colour. You talk about the **asymmetry** of something like this.

asymptomatic If someone who has an illness is **asymptomatic**, they are not yet showing any of its usual symptoms.

at is used to say where something happens, or where it is. *...a meeting held at the Central Science Laboratory.* ◇ **At** is used to say where someone looks or points. *I glanced at my watch.* ◇ **At** is also used to say where something is fired or thrown. *The holidaymakers tossed missiles at Mr Tjolle.*
❑ **At** is used to say when something happens. *...at eight o'clock this evening... His death comes at a time when the overall level of violence has declined.* ◇ **At** is used to say how quickly something happens, or how often. *He was driving at over 100 miles per hour... Elections have been held at regular intervals since independence.*
❑ **At** is used to talk about amounts and levels. *...glossy cookery books published at £25 to £35... The television was left on at full volume.*
❑ **At** is used to talk about someone's reaction to something. *She was surprised at the news.* ◇ **At** is used to say something happens as a result of a request or order. *The festival was cancelled at the request of the police.*
❑ If you are good **at** something, you do it well.

atavistic is used to describe instinctive feelings and behaviour which are inherited from our primitive ancestors. *...an atavistic fear of spiders.*

ate See eat.

atelier (*pron:* at-tell-yay) An **atelier** is an artist's or designer's studio or workshop.

atheism (*pron:* aith-ee-iz-zum) (atheistic, atheist) **Atheism** is the belief that there is no god. An **atheist** is someone who believes this. **Atheist** and **atheistic** are used to describe things connected with this belief. *...atheist propaganda... ...an atheistic Communist state.*

athlete An **athlete** is a person who takes part in athletics competitions.

athletic (athletics, athletically, athleticism) ❑ **Athletics** consists of sports like running, the high jump, and the javelin. **Athletic** is used to talk about things to do with athletics and athletes. *...my athletic career.*
❑ If someone is **athletic**, they are fit, active, and agile. You talk about the **athleticism** of someone like this. *Marshall dived athletically to take a fine catch left-handed.*

atlas (atlases) An **atlas** is a book of maps.

atmosphere (atmospheric) ❑ An **atmosphere** is a layer of gases round a planet. The **atmosphere** is the layer of air round the earth. **Atmospheric** is used to talk about things to do with the atmosphere. *...atmospheric pollution.*
❑ The **atmosphere** of a place is the air you breathe

there. ...*the smoky atmosphere of the gaming room.* ◇ The atmosphere of a place is also its special character. *Durrell had lived in Alexandria and had absorbed its unique atmosphere.* ◇ The **atmosphere** in a place can also mean the mood of the people there. *There is a nasty, tense atmosphere... The change of venue was intended to bring a more informal and relaxed atmosphere.*

atoll An **atoll** is a ring-shaped coral reef or coral island which partially or completely encloses a lagoon.

atom An **atom** is the smallest amount of a substance which can take part in a chemical reaction. It consists of a central nucleus, containing protons and neutrons, with electrons orbiting around it.

atom bomb See atomic bomb.

atomic is used to talk about (a) things to do with atoms. *...the structure at the atomic level of these molecules.* (b) things to do with the power produced by splitting atoms. *...the peaceful uses of atomic energy... ...the world's biggest atomic explosion.*

atomic bomb The **atomic bomb** or **atom bomb** was the earliest kind of nuclear bomb. It used nuclear fission to produce a powerful explosion. Atomic bombs were dropped on Hiroshima and Nagasaki in 1945.

atomizer An **atomizer** is a device which turns a liquid into a fine spray. Atomizers are used to spray on perfume.

atone (atoning, atoned; atonement) If you **atone** for something wrong you have done, you do something to show you are sorry. *General Chun has been living in a remote Buddhist temple as a gesture of atonement after admitting that abuses of power took place during his years in office.*

atop If something is **atop** something else, it is on top of it. *...the stone statue atop the mountain... ...Mr Cheney's position atop the bureaucratic hierarchy.*

atrium (*pron:* ate-ree-um) An **atrium** is a cavity or chamber in the body, especially the two upper chambers of the heart. ◇ In a building like a hotel or shopping mall, an **atrium** is a central hall which often has a glass roof and extends through several storeys.

atrocious (atrociously) If you say something is **atrocious**, you mean it is extremely bad. *Service in the dining-room was atrocious... The place stank atrociously.* ◇ An **atrocious** act is shocking and cruel. *...atrocious crimes.*

atrocity (atrocities) An **atrocity** is a shocking cruel act. *Both sides accused each other of committing atrocities against prisoners.*

atrophy (*pron:* at-trof-fee) (atrophies, atrophying, atrophied) **Atrophy** is the wasting away of an organ or some other part of the body, as a result of disease or a poor diet. *...spinal muscular atrophy.* ◇ **Atrophy** is also the disappearance or reduction in size or importance of something, because it is no longer needed or used. When this happens to something, you say it **atrophies**. *...job-sharing, a policy she admits has atrophied in recession.*

attach (attaches, attaching, attached; attachment) ❑ If you **attach** something to something else, you join or fix it to it. ◇ An **attachment** is a device fixed to something like a machine to enable it to do different jobs.

❑ If conditions are **attached** to an agreement, they are included as part of it.

❑ If someone is **attached** to an organization, they are working for it on a temporary basis. A period of time spent working with an organization is sometimes called an **attachment**.

❑ If you **attach** importance or significance to something, you consider it to be important or significant. ◇ If you **attach** blame to someone, you say they are to blame for something.

❑ If you are **attached** to someone or something, you are fond of them and would not like to be without them; you can talk about your **attachment** to them.

attaché (*pron:* at-tash-shay) ❑ An **attaché** is a member of an embassy's staff or a representative of an organization, especially one with a particular area of responsibility. *...the senior defence attaché at the Iraqi embassy... ...the cultural attaché of the ANC.*

❑ An **attaché case** is a reinforced briefcase with a handle, for carrying documents and other papers.

attack (attacker) ❑ If a person is **attacked** or is the victim of an **attack**, someone tries to hurt or kill them. The person who attacks them is called their **attacker**. ◇ If soldiers are **attacked** or an **attack** is launched against them, enemy forces open fire on them. When this happens, you say the soldiers come **under attack**. A place can also be **attacked** or come **under attack**.

❑ You also say someone **attacks** someone else when they criticize them strongly. You can also talk about ideas or policies being **attacked**. *China has bitterly attacked the proposal.* When people criticize someone or something, you can say they are **on the attack**. *The report goes on the attack over subsidised loans to eastern Germany.* You can also say ideas or policies come **under attack**.

❑ If you **attack** a problem or launch an **attack** on it, you start dealing with it in a determined way.

❑ When a sports team **attacks** or goes **on the attack**, the players make an effort to score points or goals, rather than just trying to stop the other side scoring.

❑ An **attack** of an illness is a short period in which you suffer badly from it. *...an asthma attack.*

attain (attaining, attained; attainment) If you **attain** something you are aiming for, you succeed in achieving it. Your **attainments** are things you have achieved.

attainable If something is **attainable**, it is possible to achieve it, although it might be difficult. *Reaching the final is an attainable goal.*

attempt If you **attempt** to do something or make an **attempt** to do it, you try to do it. ◇ **Attempted** is used to describe an unsuccessful attempt to do something, especially something criminal. *...attempted rape... ...an attempted coup.*

attend (attendance) ❑ If you **attend** something like a meeting or a ceremony, you are present at it. ◇ The **attendance** at a meeting or ceremony is the total number of people present. *Church attendance in England is much lower than in Wales or Scotland.*

❑ If someone is present when something is taking place, you can say they are in **attendance**. *With the army in attendance, two tractors began levelling a sand dune overlooking the village.*

❑ If you **attend** something like a school or college, you are taught there regularly.

❑ If you **attend** to something, you deal with it.

attendant ❑ An **attendant** is a person whose job is to serve or help people. *...a deckchair attendant.*

❑ If you talk about something being **attendant** on something else, you mean you get the first thing as a result of the second one. *...the advantages attendant on the possession of such a vehicle... Economic restructuring would mean more unemployment with the attendant risk of social instability.*

attender An **attender** at some kind of event or meeting is someone who goes to it regularly. *Henry was an assiduous attender at branch reunions of the Old Bridlingtonian Club.*

attention ❑ If you give something your **attention** or turn your **attention** to it, you look at it, listen to it, or start to deal with it. ◇ If you **pay attention** to something, you listen to it or show interest in it. ◇ If something gets a lot of **attention**, people are interested in it and it gets reported and discussed a lot.

❑ If someone **brings** something **to your attention** or **draws your attention** to it, they point it out to you. ◇ If something **attracts** or **catches your attention**, you notice it.

❑ If something needs **attention**, it needs to be dealt with. ◇ If someone needs medical **attention**, they need medical treatment.

❑ Unwelcome sexual advances are sometimes called **attentions**. *To escape the attentions of a horrible stepfather, she married a rich young banker.*

❑ When soldiers **stand to attention**, they stand up straight with their feet together and arms by their sides.

attentive (attentively) If you are **attentive**, you are paying close attention to what is being said or done. *He listened attentively.* ◇ You also say someone is **attentive** when they are helpful and polite.

attenuate (attenuating, attenuated) If something is **attenuated**, it is reduced or weakened.

attest If someone **attests** to something, they say it is true or exists. *The people who know her attest to her strength of character and intelligence.* ◇ If something **attests** to something else, it shows or proves it exists. *The very ambitiousness of Mr Yeltsin's demands attests to his political strength.*

attic An **attic** is a room at the top of a house, just below the roof.

attire (attired) A person's **attire** is the clothes they are wearing, especially clothes worn for a special occasion or activity. *...people in funeral attire.* The way you are **attired** is the way you are dressed. *Her Majesty was attired in black satin.*

attitude Your **attitude** to someone or something is the way you think and feel about them, which shows in the things you say and the way you behave.

attitudinizing (*or* attitudinising) is pretending to have certain attitudes or opinions, for the sake of effect.

attorney is the usual American word for a lawyer.

Attorney General A country's **Attorney General** is its chief law officer, who advises its government or monarch.

attract ❑ If something **attracts** people, it has features which make them come to it. *The four-day show is expected to attract 50,000 visitors.* Similarly, you can talk about something **attracting** animals. *The trap uses light to attract insects.*

❑ If someone or something **attracts** you, they have qualities which make you interested in them, like them, or want them. *The structure of the detective story is what has always attracted me.*

❑ If something like a political movement **attracts** support, it has features which appeal to people, and they support it. ◇ If something **attracts** publicity, it is interesting enough to make the media report on it and discuss it.

❑ If something magnetic **attracts** an object, its magnetic force pulls the object towards it.

attraction ❑ If you have a feeling of **attraction** for someone, you enjoy their company or you desire them sexually.

❑ The **attractions** of something are the things which make it interesting or desirable. ◇ The **attractions** in an area are the buildings and other things which people visit for interest or enjoyment.

attractive (attractively, attractiveness) ❑ An **attractive** person is pretty or handsome. ◇ If you call an object or place **attractive**, you mean it has a pleasant appearance. *...an attractively designed restaurant.*

❑ You also say something is **attractive** when it seems desirable. *The amount of cash to be won should make Japan an attractive place for foreign-owned horses to race in... ERM entry was likely to enhance the attractiveness of the pound to international investors.*

attributable If something is **attributable** to a particular thing, that thing is the most likely cause of it. *She believes the party's lack of electoral success is attributable to its lack of 'professionalism'... ...personal injury directly attributable to a crime of violence.*

attribute (attributing, attributed; attribution) ❑ If you **attribute** (*pron:* at-trib-byoot) something to a particular thing, you decide it was caused by that thing. *This success was largely attributed to the diplomatic efforts of Prince Sihanouk.*

❑ If something like a comment is **attributed** to someone, they are supposed to have said it. ◇ If a painting is **attributed** to someone, they are thought to have painted it. *He is questioning the attribution of two items due to be sold at Sotheby's.*

❑ If you **attribute** a quality or feature to someone or something, you think they have it, or you say they have it. *Radiance, vivacity, courage, a certain magic – these were the qualities attributed to the Queen Mother on all sides of the House.* ◇ An **attribute** (*pron:* at-trib-byoot) is a quality or feature.

attrition is a process in which people or things are gradually weakened or worn out. *There is likely to be further attrition of older industries.* A **war of attrition** is a war or some other kind of activity in which people gradually weaken their opponents by continual attack.

attuned If you are **attuned** to something like people's wishes, you understand them and can respond to them in an appropriate way.

atypical (*pron:* eh-tip-ik-al) If something is **atypical**, it does not have the usual features of things of its kind.

au fait (*pron:* oh fay) If you are **au fait** with a subject, you are familiar with it and know quite a lot about it.

au pair An **au pair** is a person, usually a young woman, who lives for a time with a family in a foreign country, to gain experience of that country and learn the language. Au pairs help with housework and the care of small children and receive a small wage.

aubergine Aubergines are pear-shaped vegetables with smooth purple skins. In the US, they are called 'eggplants'.

auburn hair is reddish-brown.

auction (auctioning, auctioned) An **auction** is a public sale at which goods are sold to the person who offers the highest price. When goods are sold like this, you say they are **auctioned** or **auctioned off**.

auctioneer An **auctioneer** is a person who organizes an auction or is in charge of it, and calls out the amounts people bid for goods being sold.

audacious (audacity) If something you do is **audacious**, it is daring and risky. **Audacity** is doing daring or risky things. ◇ **Audacity** is also cheeky behaviour. *On 25 July 1909 a foreigner had the audacity to fly across the Channel and land beside Dover Castle.*

audible (audibly, audibility) If a sound is **audible**, it can be heard. The **audibility** of something is how well it can be heard. *Aubrey sighed audibly... ...improvements in the BBC's audibility.*

audience ❑ The **audience** in a theatre, cinema, or concert hall is the people watching or listening to a performance. Similarly, the **audience** for a TV or radio programme is the people watching or listening to it. ◇ You can also call people who read someone's books or hear about their ideas their **audience**. *The Dalai Lama's words are now reaching a wider audience.*

❑ If you have an **audience** with a very important person, you have a formal meeting with them.

audio is used to talk about things to do with recording and reproducing sound. *...digital audio tape... ...video and audio equipment.*

audio book An **audio book** is a book recorded on cassettes.

audio-typist An **audio-typist** types letters and reports which have been dictated into a recording machine.

audio-visual is used to describe teaching aids which involve listening to things other than the teacher's voice and looking at things other than books. Typical audio-visual aids are projectors, tape recorders, TV, charts, and models.

audit (auditing, audited) When an accountant **audits** an organization's accounts, he or she checks them to make sure they give an accurate statement of the organization's financial affairs. This check is called an **audit**. The job of carrying out audits is called **auditing**. ◇ Checks on other aspects of an organization can also be called **audits**. For example, a **safety audit** checks that safety regulations are being observed.

audition (auditioning, auditioned) If you **audition** for a part in a play or film or are **auditioned** for it, you do a short performance so people can see if you are suitable for it. This performance is called an **audition**.

auditor An **auditor** is an accountant or firm of accountants that checks organizations' accounts to make sure they give an accurate picture of their financial affairs.

auditorium (*plural:* auditoriums *or* auditoria) In a building like a theatre or concert hall, the **auditorium** is the place where the audience sits.

auditory is used to talk about things to do with hearing. *...auditory nerves... ...auditory data.*

augment If you **augment** something, you make it larger by adding something else to it. *His wife augmented the family income by growing food crops for sale.*

augur (auguring, augured) If something **augurs** well, it suggests things will go well. If it **augurs** badly, it suggests things will go badly. *His capriciousness and populist style do not augur well for Poland's future development.*

augury (auguries) An **augury** is a sign of what is likely to happen in the future. A good **augury** suggests things will go well; a bad **augury** suggests they will go badly.

august (*pron:* aw-**gust**) An **august** person is dignified and impressive.

auk Auks are a group of sea-birds including razorbills, puffins, and little auks. They have black and white feathers, a heavy body, and a short tail. Auks dive into the sea to catch fish.

aunt Your **aunt** is the sister of your mother or father, or the wife of your mother's or father's brother.

auntie (*or* aunty) (aunties) A person's **auntie** is their aunt. ◇ **Auntie** is also a jokey name for the BBC.

aura If you say someone or something has a certain **aura**, you are talking about the general impression created by their reputation, behaviour, or appearance. *There is now such an aura of invincibility about Faldo that his mere presence appears to intimidate his rivals.*

aural (aurally) **Aural** is used to talk about things to do with the hearing process and things people hear. *...the aural nerves... The film is visually and aurally audacious.*

aurora borealis (*pron:* aw-**raw**-ra bor-ee-**ay**-liss) The **aurora borealis** or **Northern Lights** is a natural phenomenon consisting of moving bands of coloured lights seen in the sky in Arctic regions. It is thought to be caused by charged particles caught in the Earth's magnetic field. A similar phenomenon in Antarctic regions is called the **aurora australis**.

auspices (*pron:* aw-**spiss**-siz) If something is done **under the auspices** of a person or organization, it is done with their approval and support. *...arms control negotiations under United Nations auspices.*

auspicious If something is **auspicious**, it gives hope of future success. *His government got off to an auspicious start with the announcement of the latest economic growth figures... The circumstances did not look auspicious.*

Aussie means 'Australian'. An **Aussie** is an Australian.

austere (austerity) If something like a building or room is **austere**, it is plain and undecorated, and therefore not very cheerful. ◇ An **austere** way of life is simple and has no luxuries. **Austerity** is a situation in which people have to live like this. ◇ An **austere** person is serious, strict, and severe.

Australasia (Australasian) **Australasia** is a name given to the south-west Pacific area, including Australia, New Zealand, New Guinea, and sometimes other islands. **Australasian** is used to talk about things connected with this area.

autarky (*pron:* aw-**tar**-kee) is a system or policy in which a country tries to be economically self-sufficient, without importing anything from other countries.

authentic (authentically, authenticity) ❑ If something is **authentic**, it is genuine rather than an imitation or forgery. You talk about the **authenticity** of something like this. *...the most authentically Hawaiian hotel in the area...*

Nobody doubts the authenticity of the diaries.
❑ **Authentic** is also used to describe things which are based on correct information. You talk about the **authenticity** of things like these. *...authentic reports... They should closely examine the authenticity of the players' claims.*

authenticate (authenticating, authenticated; authentication) If something is **authenticated**, it is shown or officially stated to be genuine. *They were authenticated as pages from Goebbels's diaries... ...certificates of authentication.*

author (authorial) ❑ An **author** is a person who writes books, especially novels. **Authorial** is used to talk about things to do with a novel's author. *In Barchester Towers, the authorial voice breaks into a description of the bishop's throne.* ◇ The person responsible for any piece of writing can be called its **author**. For example, you can talk about the **author** of a report.
❑ The person responsible for bringing any situation into existence can be called its **author**. *The real author of the idea of progress was Adam Smith... Britain is the author of its own misfortunes.*

authorise See authorize.

authoritarian (authoritarianism) An **authoritarian** person or government keeps firm control of the people under them and does not allow them much freedom. You can also say behaviour or policies are **authoritarian**. *...authoritarian rule... ...an increasingly authoritarian approach.* An authoritarian style of government is called **authoritarianism**.

authoritative (authoritatively) If something spoken or written is **authoritative**, it is based on sound knowledge, and can therefore be relied on. *He longed for someone to tell him authoritatively that the tumour was not malignant.* ◇ If someone is **authoritative** on a subject, they know a great deal about it.

authority (authorities) ❑ An **authority** is an official organization with the power to make decisions. *...the National Rivers Authority.* ◇ The **authorities** in a place are the people officially in control there. ◇ The **local authority** in an area is the local council.
❑ If someone has **authority** over a group of people, they have the legal right or power to tell them what to do. *The ruling party's authority is crumbling.*
❑ **Authority** is also official permission. *The bank changed my current account to a business account without obtaining my authority.*
❑ If someone is an **authority** on a subject, they know a great deal about it.

authorize (authorizing, authorized; authorization) (*can be spelled with an 's' instead of a 'z'*) If someone **authorizes** something or **authorizes** someone to do something, they give official permission for it. This permission is called **authorization**.

authorship If you talk about the **authorship** of a piece of writing, you are talking about the identity of the person who wrote it. *His claims to sole authorship were being challenged... This is not proof of authorship.* ◇ **Authorship** is also writing books or articles for a living. *In due course his job led to acting, though not before he had considered authorship.*

autistic (autism) If someone is **autistic**, they are suffering from a serious mental disorder called **autism** which makes them unable to respond to other people. Autism usually begins in early childhood. Some autistic children do not learn to speak.

auto is used in the US to talk about things to do with cars. *...the American auto industry... ...the production of auto parts.*

auto-immune An **auto-immune** disease or reaction involves antibodies attacking normal tissues in the body rather than the harmful bacteria which they are meant to attack.

auto-pilot See automatic pilot.

autobahn (*plural:* autobahns *or* autobahnen) In places where German is spoken, motorways are called **autobahns**.

autobiography (autobiographies; autobiographer, autobiographical) If someone writes their **autobiography**, they write the story of their own life. Anyone who has done this can be called an **autobiographer**. If a book or film is **autobiographical**, it is based on things which really happened to the author or director.

autocracy (autocracies; autocrat) **Autocracy** is government or management by one person who has complete power. An **autocracy** is a country or organization ruled or controlled like this. The person who rules or controls it is called an **autocrat**.

autocratic (autocratically) If someone is **autocratic**, they have complete power and make decisions without consulting other people. *...a ruthless businessman who rules his companies autocratically.*

autocue (*or* Autocue) The **autocue** is a device used by people speaking on TV. It displays words for them to read in such a way that they can look straight at the camera when they are speaking. 'Autocue' is a trademark.

autograph If you ask a famous person for their **autograph**, you ask them to sign their name on something for you. If they **autograph** something like a book or record, they sign their name on it.

automate (automating, automated; automation) If something like a factory, office, or industrial process is **automated**, machines are brought in to do jobs formerly done by people. *...fully automated assembly plants... ...the ambitious automation strategy pursued by General Motors.*

automatic (automatically) ❑ **Automatic** is used to describe machines which do things without needing someone to control them. *...an automatic four-speed gear box... Baggage tags are automatically printed as the passenger's details are put into the computer.* ◇ An **automatic** weapon is one which continues to fire shells without the trigger needing to be pressed each time. A weapon like this is sometimes called an **automatic**.
❑ An **automatic** right or requirement is one which always applies in particular circumstances. *Israel offers automatic citizenship to all Jews who want it... Any product will automatically be immune from prosecution if it complies with a European Directive.* Similarly, an **automatic** punishment is one which is always given for a particular crime. *The penalty for murder must be an automatic life sentence.*
❑ If something you do is **automatic**, you do it without thinking about it. *Ordinarily I would have said yes automatically.*

automatic pilot (*or* auto-pilot *or* autopilot) If a plane is being flown on **automatic pilot**, its speed and direction are being controlled by computers or other automatic devices. ◇ If you say you are **on automatic pilot**, you mean you are doing something without thinking about it, usually because you have done it so many times before.

automaton (*pron:* aw-tom-mat-ton) (*plural:* automatons *or* automata) An **automaton** is a robot or machine which operates by itself rather than being controlled by a human being. ◇ If you say someone is an **automaton**, you mean they do things without thinking about them, like a machine.

automobile An automobile is a car.

automotive is used to talk about things to do with cars, lorries, and other motor vehicles. *...the automotive components industry.*

autonomous (*pron:* aw-tonn-nom-muss) (autonomously, autonomy.) An **autonomous** region has a large degree of self-government but does not have the full status of a country. Having this degree of self-government is called **autonomy**. ◇ Similarly, when part of a company has a large degree of independence, you can talk about it being **autonomous**. *Perrier had prided itself on being a highly decentralised company, with each of its subsidiaries operating autonomously.*

autopilot See automatic pilot.

autopsy (autopsies) An **autopsy** is an examination of a dead body by a doctor who cuts it open to try to discover the cause of death. An examination like this is also called a 'post-mortem'.

autoroute In places where French is spoken, motorways are called **autoroutes**.

autostrada (*plural:* autostradas *or* autostrade) In Italy, motorways are called **autostradas**.

autumn is the season between summer and winter. In the northern hemisphere, this is between September and December. In Canada and the US, it is called the fall, because it is the season when the leaves fall.

autumnal is used to describe things which are characteristic of autumn or take place in autumn. *...autumnal bronzes and coppers... ...a chilly autumnal evening.*

auxiliary (auxiliaries) **Auxiliary** is used to describe people employed to provide assistance and back-up. *...an auxiliary coastguard.* People like these are sometimes called **auxiliaries**. *...police auxiliaries.* ◇ **Auxiliary** equipment is extra equipment which is there for use when necessary, for example in emergencies or when the usual equipment fails. *...an auxiliary power unit.*

auxiliary verb 'Do' is called an **auxiliary verb** when it is used in questions, as in 'Do you want an apple?' or in negative sentences like 'I do not want to go out'. 'Have' and 'be' are auxiliary verbs when they are used to form tenses, as in 'I have eaten my lunch' or 'I am eating my lunch'.

avail (availing, availed) ❏ If something you do is to **no avail**, it does not achieve what you want.

❏ If you **avail** yourself of something, you make use of it.

available (availability) ❏ If something is **available**, it is there for you to use, or you can obtain it. *£10,000 was available to refurbish the kitchen.* **Availability** is used to talk about the extent to which something is available. *...the easy availability of guns in the US.*

❏ You say a person is **available** when they are free to talk to you, or free to take part in something. *Nobody from Nike was available to comment... He will be available for the Five Nations Championship.*

avalanche An **avalanche** is a large mass of snow or rock falling down the side of a mountain. ◇ An **avalanche** of things is a large amount of them arriving, happening, or coming into existence at the same time. *...an avalanche of applications.*

avant-garde (*pron:* av-ong-gard) art, music, and theatre are concerned with trying out new ideas and new techniques.

avarice (*pron:* av-a-riss) (avaricious) **Avarice** is a greedy desire for money. If someone is **avaricious**, they have this desire.

avenge (avenging, avenged; avenger) If you **avenge** something wrong which has been done to someone, you make the person who did it suffer in return. Someone who avenges a wrong is called an **avenger**.

avenue An **avenue** is a wide road with trees on either side. ◇ An **avenue** is also a way of getting something done. *China wanted every avenue for a peaceful solution explored.*

aver (*pron:* av-vur) (averring, averred) If you **aver** something, you state it as a definite fact. *His wife averred that no woman over thirty could ever look really smart in pink.*

average (averaging, averaged; averagely) ❏ An **average** is the result you get when you add several amounts together and divide the total by the number of amounts. For example, the average of 10, 5, 3, and 2 is 5. You say something **averages** a certain amount when the amount is calculated in this way. *Production averaged 14,412 barrels a day.* You can also say something is a certain amount **on average**. *Every tonne of coal contains on average 30 kilograms of nitrogen.*

❏ **Average** is also used to say someone or something is standard or normal, rather than extreme or exceptional. *...an average schoolboy... ...an averagely fit person.*

averse If you say someone is not **averse** to doing something, you mean they see nothing wrong in it and do it fairly often. *She is not averse to dishing out rough treatment.* ◇ If you say someone would not be **averse** to doing something, you mean they would be quite happy to do it.

aversion If you have an **aversion** to someone or something, you dislike them.

avert ❏ If something undesirable is **averted**, it is prevented from happening.

❏ If you **avert your eyes**, you avoid looking at something, because you are embarrassed or find it unpleasant. You also say someone **averts their eyes** when they ignore something bad which is happening. *Mr Bush said the holocaust occurred because good men and women averted their eyes from unprecedented evil.*

aviary (aviaries) An **aviary** is a large cage or covered area in which birds are kept.

aviation is used to talk about the operation and manufacture of aircraft. *...America's aviation industry... ...the most famous names in British aviation history.*

aviator In the early days of flying, pilots who flew small planes were called **aviators**.

avid (avidly) **Avid** is used to say someone is keen and enthusiastic about something. *He is an avid basketball player... Wartime naval service offered occasional opportunities for conducting orchestras, which he avidly seized.*

avionics is electronics technology applied to aircraft, missiles, and spacecraft.

avocado (avocados) The **avocado** or **avocado pear** is a dark green tropical fruit with a large stone and smooth oily flesh.

avoid (avoiding, avoided; avoidance) ❑ If you **avoid** something bad which looks like happening, you succeed in preventing it. *...the prospects for avoiding a war... ...the avoidance of scandal.* ◇ If you **avoid** doing something, you deliberately do not do it. *Both sides are avoiding direct comment on each other's internal politics.* ◇ If you **avoid** doing something you do not want to do, you find a way out of it. *...his avoidance of military service.*
❑ If you **avoid** someone or something, you deliberately keep away from them. *Drivers now have a better route down the eastern side of France, avoiding Paris.* ◇ If you **avoid** a subject, you deliberately do not talk about it.
❑ **Tax avoidance** is finding ways of paying as little tax as possible without breaking the law.

avoidable If you say something bad which has happened was **avoidable**, you mean it could have been prevented.

avoidance See **avoid**.

avow (avowal; avowed, avowedly) If you **avow** something, you admit it or declare it. What you say is called an **avowal**. ◇ **Avowed** is used to describe intentions and beliefs which people openly admit they have. *...Ted Kennedy's avowed aim to seek re-election... ...avowed nationalists... ...the avowedly Stalinist Albanian Party of Labour.*

avuncular You say an older man is **avuncular** when he is kind and helpful to younger people.

await (awaiting, awaited) If you are **awaiting** someone or something, you are waiting for them. ◇ If something **awaits** you, it is going to happen to you in the future. *A worse fate awaited the visiting fans... Jail awaits anybody who publishes a document classified as secret.*

awake (awaking, awoke, have awoken) ❑ If someone is **awake**, they are not asleep. ◇ If you **awake**, you wake up. *Gilbert awoke feeling nauseous and dizzy.* If something **awakes** you, it wakes you up. *Mr Didier was awoken by a bang on his front door.*
❑ If people **awake to** a danger, they become aware of it. You then say they are **awake to** it.

awaken (awakening, awakened) ❑ If feelings are **awakened** in people, they start having them. *...the fears and anxieties awakened by unification... The politicians have been struggling to awaken people's interest in local issues.* The beginning of certain kinds of feelings and beliefs can be called an **awakening**. *...her intense sexual awakening... ...the story of a young boy's moral awakening.*
❑ If you **awaken** or are **awakened** to problems, ideas, or facts, you become aware of them. ◇ If you have a **rude awakening**, you are suddenly made aware of an unpleasant fact.
❑ When you **awaken** or are **awakened**, you wake up.

award ❑ If you are **awarded** something like a prize, you are given it for doing something well. What you are given is called an **award**. *...an award-winning film.*
❑ If someone is **awarded** a salary, pay rise, or bonus, they are given it. ◇ If you are **awarded** money by a court, you are given it as compensation. The money is called an **award**. ◇ If the government or some other organization **awards** money, it gives it to people for a special purpose.

The English Badminton Association has been awarded a grant of £60,000 by the Sports Council.

aware (awareness) ❑ If you are **aware** of a fact or situation, you know about it.
❑ If you say someone is **aware**, you mean they are alert and notice what is going on around them. ◇ You also say someone is **aware** when they are knowledgeable about a subject and quick to notice new developments in it. *They are becoming more politically aware every day... ...the ecological awareness of Brazil's new president.*

awash If a place is **awash**, there is water all over it. ◇ If you say a place is **awash** with certain people or things, you mean there are a lot of them there. *...a nation awash with guns.*

away ❑ If you move **away** from a person or object, you move so you are no longer close to them. You are then a certain distance **away** from them. ◇ If you move **away** from a place, you go somewhere else. *My education drew me away from home.*
❑ You say someone is **away** when they are not in their usual place, for example at work or at home. ◇ In sport, an **away** game is played on an opponent's ground, rather than on a team's own ground.
❑ If something is a certain length of time **away**, that time will pass before it happens.
❑ People say **away from...** when they are mentioning one aspect of something before going on to talk about a different one. *Away from the developments over South Africa, the main sporting news of the day has involved cycling and cricket.*
❑ **Away** is used to say something goes on continuously. *...working away on his word processor... ...with the engine humming away.*

awe (awed) **Awe** is a feeling of great admiration and respect. If you are **in awe** of something or someone, you feel like that about them. *The British are in awe of Italy's artistic achievements.* If someone is **awed** by something, they are overcome with admiration for it, and may feel inferior because of it. *Thomson, clearly awed by her first Olympics, needed to have her confidence boosted.*

awe-inspiring You say something is **awe-inspiring** when it makes a great impression on you, because it is very beautiful or outstanding in some other way. *...an awe-inspiring glimpse of an ancient culture... ...an awe-inspiring canyon in the Rockies.*

awesome (awesomely) If you say something is **awesome**, you mean it is extremely impressive. *Their batting strength is awesome... ...this awesomely talented young Welshman.* ◇ If you call a problem or task **awesome**, you mean it will be very difficult to deal with.

awestruck If you are **awestruck** by something, it fills you with amazement and admiration.

awful (awfully, awfulness) **Awful** is used to describe things which are very bad or unpleasant. *...overcrowding and awful conditions... They've been treated so awfully... ...the awfulness of Britain's economic plight.* ◇ People also use **awful** to express their dislike of someone or something. *...an awful child... ...awful jokes... ...an awful French restaurant.* ◇ People also use **awful** and **awfully** in front of other words to emphasize them. *An awful lot of people have no insurance... It's an awfully simple thing to do.*

awhile means for a short time. *They must wait awhile be-*

fore they find out who their next landlord is to be.

awkward (awkwardly; awkwardness, awkwardnesses) ❑ Awkward situations and problems are difficult to deal with. *She posed some awkward questions about NATO's future... Awkwardly for the government, the most sensible measures are the gloomiest.* An **awkwardness** is a situation or problem like this.
❑ If someone is **awkward**, they are unreasonable and difficult to deal with. ◇ You also say someone is **awkward** when they do not behave in a confident way, because they are shy and embarrassed. *He displayed all the awkwardness of adolescence.* ◇ If someone's movements are **awkward**, they are clumsy and inelegant.

awning An awning is a piece of canvas or other material attached to something like a caravan or the front of a shop to provide shelter from the rain or sun.

awoke (awoken) See **awake**.

awry (*pron:* a-rye) If something goes **awry**, it goes wrong. ◇ If something is **awry**, it is not in its normal or proper position. *...men with shirts open to the waist and ties awry.*

axe (*American spelling:* ax) (axes, axed, axing *or* axeing) ❑ An **axe** is a tool for cutting wood. It has a heavy metal blade and a long handle.
❑ If a project is **axed**, it is scrapped. You can also talk about people's jobs being **axed**. ◇ If the **axe** falls on something, it is brought to an end.
❑ If you **take an axe** to something, you drastically reduce it. *Lloyds has discovered that it cannot take an axe to its costs without suffering a slump in business.*
❑ If you say someone **has an axe to grind**, you mean they have strong feelings about something, and use every opportunity to express them or to try to get something done.

❑ 'Axes' is also the plural of 'axis'.

axiom An **axiom** is a saying or idea which people accept as true. *It's an axiom of mountaineering that the good climber knows when to turn back.*

axiomatic If you say something is **axiomatic**, you mean it is a basic truth which cannot be questioned.

axis (*plural:* axes, *pron:* ak-seez) ❑ An **axis** is an imaginary line through the centre of something, around which it seems to turn. *...a shift in the earth's axis.*
❑ An **axis** is also one of the lines on a graph on which the scales of measurement are marked. Most graphs have two axes: one horizontal and one vertical.
❑ An **axis** is also a friendly relationship between two countries. *...the Franco-German axis.*

axle An **axle** is a bar or shaft on which a wheel or wheels rotate.

ayatollah (*pron:* aye-a-toll-ah) An **ayatollah** is a Shi-ite Muslim religious leader.

aye (*rhymes with 'lie'*) **Aye** is an old word for 'yes'. It is still used in some parts of Britain, especially Northern England and Scotland. ◇ In Parliament, the **ayes** are the people who vote in favour of a motion. The people who vote against it are called the 'noes'. *The ayes to the right are 313; the noes to the left 216. So the ayes have it.*

azalea (*pron:* a-zayl-ya) The **azalea** is a garden shrub, related to the rhododendron, with brightly coloured sweet-smelling flowers.

AZT is a medicine which has been tried as a treatment for people who are HIV positive and for AIDS sufferers. AZT is short for 'azidothymidine'.

azure is a bright blue colour.

B b

b. and b. A **b. and b.** is a house providing people with a bed and breakfast at a reasonably low cost.

B.A. A **B.A.** is a university degree in a subject such as languages, literature, history, or social science. B.A. stands for 'Bachelor of Arts'.

babble (babbling, babbled) If you say someone is **babbling**, you mean they are talking in a confused or excited way. ◇ You can call the sound of a lot of people talking at once a **babble**. *...a babble of foreign tongues.*

babe is an old-fashioned word for a baby.

baboon Baboons are a type of African monkey with pointed faces, large teeth, and long tails.

baby (babies) A **baby** is a very young child who cannot walk or talk. ◇ **Baby** is also used to talk about young animals and plants. *...a baby alligator... ...baby sweetcorn.* ◇ People sometimes call a plan or project they are involved with their **baby**, often because they first thought of it. ◇ If someone tries to get rid of the bad parts of a system, and in doing so also gets rid of something important, you can say they have **thrown the baby out**

with the bathwater.

baby-boom (baby-boomer) When people talk about the **baby-boom**, they mean a period just after the Second World War when there was a big increase in the number of babies being born. A **baby-boomer** is someone born at that time.

baby buggy A **baby buggy** is a type of lightweight folding pushchair.

baby-sit (baby-sitter) If you **baby-sit** for someone, you look after their children while they go out somewhere. Someone who does this is called a **baby-sitter**.

baccarat (*pron:* back-a-rah) is a card game often played in casinos.

bachelor A **bachelor** is a man who has never married. ◇ A **bachelor's degree** is the lowest kind of university degree, for example Bachelor of Arts (B.A.) or Bachelor of Science (B.Sc.).

Bachelor of Arts See **B.A.**

Bachelor of Science See **B.Sc.**

back (backing) ❑ If you move **back**, you move away from something, or move in the opposite direction to the one you are facing. ◇ If you move **back and forth**, you keep moving first one way then the other. ◇ If a vehicle **backs** or is **backed**, it moves backwards.

❑ **Back** is used to say someone returns to where they were before, or to what they were doing before. *I would prefer to go back to work... I couldn't get back to sleep.*

❑ If you get something **back**, you get it again after you have been without it for a while. ◇ If you get money **back** from an investment, you get interest from it.

❑ If you do something **back** to someone, you do what they have done to you. *She said she would call back... He just smiled back at me.*

❑ You use **back** when you are talking about the past. *The treasure dates back to the sixth century BC... There's no going back to the old days.* ◇ A **back** copy of a newspaper or magazine is an edition published before the most recent one. It can also be called a **back issue** or **back number.** ◇ **Back** is used to talk about money owing from the past. *They may face large claims for back tax.*

❑ A person's **back** is the part of their body below their shoulders and neck and above their buttocks. ◇ If you do something **behind someone's back**, you do it without telling them. ◇ If you **turn your back** on someone, you ignore them or refuse to help them. If you **turn your back** on something, you decide to have nothing more to do with it. ◇ An animal's **back** is the top of its body.

❑ The **back** of something is the part furthest from the front. *...the back of the house... The jacket was found in the back of a wardrobe.* ◇ You add **-backed** to say what kind of back something has. *...silver-backed brushes.* ◇ If something is **back to front**, its back is where its front should be. ◇ The **back** of a car is the part behind the driver. ◇ The **back** of something like a chair is the part you lean against.

❑ **Backing** is a layer of material put on the back of something, to protect it or make it stronger.

❑ The area a building **backs onto** is the area just behind it.

❑ A **back** road is small and narrow with very little traffic. See also **back street.**

❑ In games like football and hockey, a **back** is a player whose main job is to stop the other team from scoring.

❑ If you **back** someone or something or give them **backing**, you support or help them, often by giving them money. A **backer** is someone who does this. You add **-backed** to a word to show who someone or something is backed by. *...an American-backed film.*

❑ If you **back** someone **up**, you support them. ◇ If you **back up** something with something else, you use it to make the other thing succeed. *...action by workers to back up demands for pay increases.*

❑ If musicians or singers **back** a rock or pop singer or provide the **backing** for them, they accompany them. Musicians or singers who do this are called a **backing** group.

❑ If you **back** a horse in a race, you place a bet on it.

❑ If someone **backs off** or **backs away**, they decide not to go ahead with something. ◇ If someone **backs down** after making something like a demand, claim, or threat, they withdraw it. ◇ If someone **backs out** of something they had agreed to do, they break the agreement.

❑ If something **backs up** a claim, argument, or story, it supports it. *There is no reliable data available to back up these*

observations.

❑ **the back of beyond:** see **beyond.**

back bench (backbencher) In the House of Commons, the **back benches** are all MPs who are not leading members of the government or opposition. These MPs are also called **backbench** MPs or **backbenchers.**

back-breaking work is very hard physical work.

back-burner See **burner.**

back door (*or* backdoor) If something is done by or through the **back door**, it is done secretly and avoiding the usual procedures.

back-handed See **backhanded.**

back-pack See **backpack.**

back-pedal If someone **back-pedals**, they go back on something they have said. ◇ You can also say someone **back-pedals** when they do something more slowly than before.

back-seat driver A **back-seat driver** is a car passenger who keeps telling the driver what to do. ◇ You also say someone is a **back-seat driver** when they give unwanted advice or want to take charge of things.

back-slapping behaviour is friendly in a rather hearty way.

back street (*or* backstreet) The **back streets** of a town or city are the parts with smaller and poorer houses, away from the main streets. ◇ **Back-street** is used to talk about things done in back streets, especially things which are secret, unofficial, or illegal. *...a back-street abortion.*

back-track See **backtrack.**

back-up is used to talk about extra help or support which is available if it is needed. *There is a demand for better back-up facilities.* ◇ A **back-up** is something like an extra plan or system, which is there in case the main one goes wrong. ◇ See also **back.**

back yard See **backyard.**

backache is an ache or pain in your back.

backbencher See **back bench.**

backbiting is saying unpleasant things about someone when they are not there.

backbone The **backbone** of a person or animal is the column of small linked bones down the middle of their back. ◇ If you say something is the **backbone** of an organization or system, you mean it makes it work, or holds it together. *The regimental system is the backbone of the British army.* ◇ If you say someone has **backbone**, you mean they have the courage to do things in spite of risks or danger.

backcloth See **backdrop.**

backdate (backdating, backdated) If something like an agreement or law is **backdated**, it is made to operate from an earlier date than when it is settled or approved.

backdoor See **back door.**

backdrop (backcloth) A **backdrop** or **backcloth** is a large piece of cloth, often with scenery painted on it, hung at the back of a stage when a play is being performed. ◇ If you say something happens against a particular **backdrop** or **backcloth**, you are talking about the general situation at the time it happened, or about other things happening then. *This is a love story, played out against a backdrop of revolution and civil war.*

backer See back.

backfire (backfiring, backfired) If a motor vehicle **backfires**, unburnt exhaust gases explode in the exhaust pipe, making a loud bang. ◇ If something like a plan or project **backfires**, it has the opposite effect from what is intended.

backgammon is a game for two people who throw dice and move counters around a board marked with long triangles.

background ❑ Someone's **background** is the kind of family they come from and the education and experience they have had. ...*a self-educated man from a working class background*.
❑ The **background** to a situation is what has led up to it and caused it. *Our reporter looks at the background to this week's conference*.
❑ **Background** is used to talk about things you can hear or see at the same time as the thing you are paying attention to. *You could hear the little children in the background*.

backhand In games like tennis, a **backhand** is a stroke made with the back of the player's hand facing the direction they are hitting the ball. See also **forehand**.

backhanded (or **back-handed**) A **backhanded** compliment contains a criticism as well as praise.

backhander A **backhander** is a bribe.

backing See back.

backlash You say there is a **backlash** when people react strongly to something.

backlog A **backlog** is a build-up of things waiting to be dealt with. ...*a backlog of unpaid bills*.

backpack (or **back-pack**) (backpacker, backpacking) A **backpack** is a rucksack. People who travel around with their belongings in a backpack are called **backpackers**. You say people like this are **backpacking**.

backroom People who do important work but are never seen by the public are sometimes called **backroom boys**. ◇ **Backroom** is also used to talk about things which are arranged or decided in secret. ...*a backroom deal*.

backside A person's **backside** is their bottom. If someone gets off their **backside**, they start doing something, instead of waiting for something to happen.

backsliding is going back on something which has been agreed or promised. ◇ **Backsliding** is also a return to something bad after a period of reform. *One of the main tasks will be to halt any backsliding towards totalitarianism*.

backstage is the part of a theatre behind the stage, where the dressing rooms are. ◇ **Backstage** is also used to talk about things which are decided or arranged in secret. *He played a significant backstage role in the creation of Pakistan*.

backstreet See back street.

backstroke is a swimming stroke. When you do the backstroke, you lie on your back, kick your legs, and move your arms back over your head.

backtrack (or **back-track**) If someone **backtracks** on a decision or something they have said, they change their mind and no longer stand by it.

backward (backwards; backwardness) ❑ If you move **backwards** or make a **backward** movement, you move in the direction your back is facing. ◇ If you go **backwards and forwards**, you keep going from one place to another then back again.

❑ If you say someone leaves without a **backward** glance, you mean they go without thinking any more about the person or place they are leaving. ◇ If you **bend** or **fall over backwards** to do what someone wants, you do everything you can to achieve it.
❑ If you do something **backwards**, you do it the opposite way to the way it is usually done. *He is telling the story backwards*. ◇ If you say someone **knows** something **backwards**, you mean they know it very well.
❑ A country is called **backward** when its people still live in a fairly primitive way with a low standard of living and poor communications. ...*the country's ability to overcome its economic backwardness*. ◇ People with learning difficulties are sometimes called **backward**. This is an offensive use.
❑ People who are **backward-looking** are not interested in new ideas and methods, and prefer things to be done the way they have always been done.

backwash The **backwash** of a moving boat is the wave spreading out behind it. ◇ **Backwash** is also used to talk about the effects something has on other things. *The Treasury had been blaming the pound's weakness on the backwash from the falling dollar*.

backwater You call a place a **backwater** when it is cut off from modern ideas or influences and from important things happening in the world.

backwoods When people talk about the **backwoods**, they mean the parts of a country or region which are a long way from large towns and are cut off from modern ideas and ways of life.

backwoodsman (backwoodsmen) People described as **backwoodsmen** are satisfied with simple old-fashioned ways of doing things and do not want any changes.

backyard (or **back-yard**) A **backyard** is a small area behind a house, usually paved and with no grass or plants. ◇ In America, a **backyard** is a small garden behind a house. ◇ When people talk about things happening in **their own backyard**, they mean things happening close to their country, rather than in other parts of the world. *The government should be paying attention to what is going on in their own backyard*.

bacon is salted meat from the sides or back of a pig.

bacteria See bacterium.

bacteriology (bacteriologist; bacteriological) **Bacteriology** is the study of bacteria. A **bacteriologist** is an expert on this. **Bacteriological** is used to talk about things connected with bacteriology.

bacterium (plural: bacteria) **Bacteria** are very small organisms, many of which cause disease.

bad (badly, badness) ❑ **Bad** is used to describe something unpleasant, undesirable, or of poor quality. ...*bad weather*... ...*bad news*... ...*bad housing*... *The duplicate key was so badly made it failed to open the door*. ◇ If a situation keeps deteriorating, you can say it goes from **bad to worse**.
❑ When people say something is **not bad**, they mean they approve of it or are impressed by it.
❑ A **bad** person is wicked or evil. *Who can deny a thrill in the badness of Iago?* ◇ **Bad** behaviour is rude or inconsiderate. *Some people's children are so badly behaved that they make conversation impossible*. ◇ If someone uses **bad** language, they use offensive swear words. ◇ If someone is in a **bad** mood or **bad** temper, they are cross and irritable.
❑ If you feel **bad** about something, you feel guilty or

uncomfortable. ◇ Some people say they feel **bad** when they feel ill.

❏ If you are **bad** at something, you are not skilful at it.

❏ If someone says they have, for example, a **bad** leg, they mean there is something wrong with it.

❏ When food has gone **bad**, it is no longer fit to eat, because it has decayed.

❏ A **bad** debt is unlikely to be repaid.

❏ See also **badly**.

bad-mouth If you **bad-mouth** someone or something, you say critical or unpleasant things about them.

baddy (or **baddie**) (**baddies**) The bad characters in a story or film are sometimes humorously called the **baddies**.

bade See **bid**.

badge A **badge** is a small piece of metal, plastic, or cloth worn on someone's clothes to show their rank, to show they belong to an organization, or just for decoration. ◇ When something is regarded as standing for a particular quality, you can say it is a **badge** of that quality. *When he began work, being a Communist was a badge of honour for trade union activists.*

badger (badgering, badgered) ❏ The **badger** is a wild animal which lives underground in a sett and is active mainly at night. It has a white head with two broad black stripes from its nose to the back of its neck.

❏ If someone **badgers** you, they keep trying to get you to do something, or asking you questions.

badly is used to emphasize the harmful effects of something. *Some people have suffered badly... Things had gone rather badly wrong.*

❏ If someone is **badly** off, they have very little money and few possessions.

❏ If you say something reflects **badly** on someone, you mean it gives a bad impression of them. You can also say they come out of it **badly**. ◇ If you think **badly** of someone, you have a poor opinion of them.

❏ If someone wants or needs something **badly**, they want or need it very much.

❏ See also **bad**.

badminton is a game in which players with racquets hit a small feathered object called a shuttlecock over a high net.

baffle (baffling, baffled; bafflement) If something **baffles** you or you are **baffled** by it, you cannot understand it or solve it. You say something like this is **baffling**. *Their Lordships sat in apparent bafflement as he attempted to explain the distinction between rock and pop music.*

bag (bagging, bagged) ❏ A **bag** is a container made of something like leather, plastic, or paper and used for carrying things. ◇ When something is **bagged**, it is put into a bag or bags. *Compost was bagged and sold at the other end of the building.*

❏ **Bags** of something means a lot of it. *The house has bags of character.* ◇ If you say something is **in the bag**, you mean you are certain to get it or achieve it. *Planning permission seems to be in the bag.* ◇ If someone **lets the cat out of the bag**, they give away a secret.

❏ A person's **bags** are their luggage. ◇ If someone **packs their bags**, they leave the place where they have been living.

❏ If you **bag** something, you get it for yourself before anyone else has a chance to. *I arrived early enough to bag the*

corner table. ◇ If someone **bags** an animal or bird, they shoot it or catch it while hunting. The **bag** is the number of animals or birds killed at a particular time or place.

bagel (*pron:* bay-gl) **Bagels** are hard ring-shaped bread rolls traditional in Jewish baking.

baggage ❏ A person's **baggage** is all their cases, bags, and other things packed for a journey.

❏ You can call ideas, attitudes, or policies **baggage** when they are unnecessary and are getting in the way of progress. *The new councils could start life with a clean sheet, free from their predecessors' baggage.*

baggy clothing hangs loosely on a person's body, because it is too big or has stretched.

bagpipes are a musical instrument on which you can play long continuous stretches of melody by means of reed pipes supplied with air from a bag. In Irish and Scottish bagpipes, the bag is inflated by the player blowing air into it; in other bagpipes, the player pumps air into the bag using an arm-operated bellows.

baguette (*pron:* bag-get) A **baguette** is a small narrow loaf.

Baha'ism (Baha'i) **Baha'ism** is a religious system which emphasizes the value of all religions and tries to bring about world peace through religious unity. Followers of this system are called **Baha'is**.

bail (bailing, bailed) ❏ In Britain, someone held in custody awaiting trial or appeal can be released on **bail**. This means they are set free until they are due to appear in court, usually provided someone agrees to pay a sum of money if they fail to do so. When someone is released on bail, you can say they are **bailed**. ◇ If someone **jumps bail**, they fail to appear in court when they should. ◇ When someone takes responsibility for someone else's bail, you can say they **stand bail** for them.

❏ If you **bail** someone **out**, you help them out of a difficult situation, often by providing money. When bail has this meaning, it can also be spelled **bale**.

❏ When someone **bails out** (or **bales out**) a boat, they remove water from it, either by scooping it with something like a bucket, or by using a pump.

❏ In cricket, the **bails** are the two wooden bars across the stumps. If one or both bails are knocked off, the batsman is out.

❏ See also **bale**.

bailiff A **bailiff** is an officer of the law courts who sees that decisions of the court are obeyed, often by taking someone's property as payment for money which is owed.

bait (baiting, baited) ❏ **Bait** is a small piece of food on a hook for catching a fish. It is also food in a trap for catching an animal. When someone **baits** a hook or trap, they put food on it or in it. ◇ If someone or something is used as **bait**, they are used to tempt or encourage someone to do something. ◇ If someone **rises to the bait** or **takes the bait**, they react to something in the way they are meant to.

❏ **Baiting** is a pastime in which people deliberately get dogs to attack an animal like a bear or badger. ◇ If someone **baits** a person, they deliberately try to make them angry by teasing them.

baize is a smooth thick woollen material, usually green, used for covering things like snooker and card tables.

bake (baking, baked) ❑ If you **bake** something, you cook it in an oven without extra fat or liquid.

❑ When the climate is very hot and dry, you can say it is **baking**. You can also describe hot dry places as **baking**. *...the baking Jordanian desert.* ◇ You can describe the ground as **baked** when the sun has made it very dry and hard.

baker (bakery, bakeries) A **baker** is a person or firm that makes things like bread, cakes, and pastry. A **bakery** is a place where things like these are made. ◇ A **bakery** or **baker's** is also a shop where things like bread and cakes are sold.

balaclava A **balaclava** is a close-fitting woollen hood which covers all your head and neck except your face.

balalaika A **balalaika** is a guitar-like instrument from Russia. It has a triangular body and three strings.

balance (balancing, balanced) ❑ If you **balance** on something, you remain there without falling. Similarly, you can say an object **balances** somewhere or is **balanced** there. *He balanced a full glass of port on his head.* ◇ If someone or something is **off balance**, they are unsteady and likely to fall. ◇ When someone becomes unsteady and falls, you can say they **lose their balance**.

❑ A **balance** is a pair of scales.

❑ **Balance** is used to talk about situations in which everything is in the right proportion to everything else. *They were intent on keeping Antarctica's fragile ecological balance untouched.* ◇ The **balance of power** is a situation in which two opposing groups of countries have equal military power. ◇ If a political party holds the **balance of power**, they are in a position to influence things one way or the other, depending on which of the other parties they support.

❑ If you **balance** one thing with another, you treat them as equally important. *...programmes trying to balance information with entertainment.* ◇ If something like a fault is **balanced** by something else, the other thing makes up for it.

❑ When someone **balances** their finances, they make sure the amount spent is not more than the amount received. If they succeed, you say the two amounts **balance** or the books **balance**. ◇ The **balance** in something like a bank account is the amount of money in it. ◇ A **balance sheet** is a statement showing the financial position of a business.

❑ A country's **balance of payments** is the difference between the amount paid for its imports and the amount paid for its exports. Its **balance of trade** or **trade balance** is the difference in value between its imports and exports.

❑ If something like a game or contest is finely **balanced**, the result could go either way. ◇ If something is **in the balance**, or **hangs in the balance**, it is uncertain what will happen to it. *The outcome of the match was in the balance until the very end.*

❑ If something like a report is **balanced** or **well-balanced**, it is fair and reasonable, giving all points of view. *...a well-balanced summary of the case.* ◇ If you say a person is **well-balanced**, you mean they are calm and reasonable.

❑ **Balanced** is also used to describe something which is arranged well or has the correct proportions. *...a balanced education... ...a balanced diet.*

❑ You say someone is doing a **balancing act** when they try to satisfy people who have conflicting views or ideas.

❑ People say **on balance** to show that, although there are factors against the opinion they are expressing, the factors supporting it are stronger. *The deal was not very good but, on balance, preferable to no deal at all.*

balcony (balconies) A **balcony** is a platform on the outside wall of a building, with a wall or railing along its outer edge. Usually you get to it from a door or window inside the building. ◇ In a theatre or cinema, the **balcony** is an upstairs seating area.

bald (balding; baldness; baldly) ❑ If someone is **bald**, they have little or no hair on top of their head. *Scientists don't know the cause of baldness.* ◇ When someone is beginning to lose their hair, you say they are **balding**. ◇ When tyres are **bald** or **balding**, they have worn smooth and do not grip the road properly.

❑ A **bald** statement or question is made plainly, with no attempt to be polite or hide anything. *Asked whether doctors would willingly be monitored by outsiders, a leader of the Association baldly said no.*

balderdash When people say something is **balderdash**, they mean it is very silly or untrue.

bale (baling, baled; baler) ❑ A **bale** is a large amount of something like hay, straw, paper, or cloth tied into a bundle. When something is tied up into bundles like this, you say it is **baled**. A **baler** is a machine which forms things into bales. **Baling** twine or wire is used to tie bales.

❑ When someone **bales out** of an aircraft, they make an emergency parachute jump.

❑ See also **bail**.

baleful (balefully) **Baleful** people are full of hatred. A person's expression can also be **baleful**. *He gazed balefully at Sunflower House.* ◇ If something has a **baleful** effect or influence, it causes harm.

balk (or **baulk**) If someone **balks** at something, they are unwilling to do it. ◇ If someone is **balked**, they are prevented from doing something, or from getting what they want.

ball ❑ A **ball** is a round object used in games like tennis, cricket, and football. Games like these are called **ball games**. See also **ball game**. ◇ In sport, people use **ball** to talk about the way a ball has been struck or thrown, or the distance it travels. They talk, for example, about a 'good ball', a 'long ball', or a 'difficult ball'.

❑ In other situations, if someone **keeps their eye on the ball**, they pay careful attention to what is going on. If they **take their eye off the ball**, they lose concentration for a time. ◇ If someone **sets** or **starts the ball rolling**, they start something happening. ◇ If someone **plays ball**, they co-operate.

❑ Anything with a round shape can be called a **ball**. *Roll the dough into a ball... The huge ball of the sun sank to the west.*

❑ A **ball** is also a formal event where people dance.

ball bearing Ball bearings are small metal balls used to make the moving parts of a machine run smoothly.

ball game When Americans talk about the **ball game**, they mean baseball. ◇ If you say something is **a different ball game** or **a whole new ball game**, you mean a new situation has arisen and things have to be looked at in a different way.

ball gown See ballgown.

ballad A ballad is a long song or poem which tells a story. It often has lines which are repeated at the end of each verse. ◇ A ballad is also a slow romantic popular song.

ballast is a material carried by ships when they are not carrying cargo, to make them more stable. Some balloons also carry ballast; it is released to make the balloon go upwards. ◇ Ballast is also the small stones or rocks used as a foundation for railways or roads.

ballcock A ballcock is a device which controls the flow of water into a tank or cistern. It consists of a floating ball attached to a hinged rod which has a valve at the other end. When the water level drops, the ball sinks and the valve opens to let more water in.

ballerina A ballerina is a female ballet dancer.

ballet (balletic) ❏ Ballet is a style of graceful and athletic dancing, with set steps and movements. ◇ A ballet is a work for the theatre in which ballet and mime are used to tell a story. ◇ Groups of ballet dancers often have Ballet as part of their name. ...the New York City Ballet.
❏ Balletic (pron: bal-let-tik) is used to talk about things to do with ballet. ...a balletic entertainment. ◇ Balletic is also used to describe movements which remind you of ballet. The penguin is at its balletic best underwater.

ballgown (or ball gown) A ballgown is an elegant long dress, usually made of silk, satin, or velvet, and worn at a ball or other formal evening occasion.

ballistic Ballistics is the study of the movement of things shot or thrown through the air, for example bullets fired from a gun. Ballistic is used to talk about things to do with ballistics. ...ballistic tests. ◇ A ballistic missile is one which is guided automatically in the first part of its flight, then falls freely near the target.

balloon (ballooning, ballooned; balloonist) ❏ A balloon is a small bag made of thin rubber which expands when you blow air into it. Balloons are used as toys or decorations.
❏ A balloon is also a large strong bag filled with gas or hot air, which can rise up into the atmosphere carrying passengers in a basket or compartment underneath. Travelling in a balloon like this is called ballooning; the people who do it are called balloonists.
❏ If an object balloons, it gets bigger and rounder. My knee ballooned again with fluid. ◇ If something like an amount balloons, it suddenly gets bigger. The cost of health has ballooned... ...the country's ballooning energy needs.

ballot (balloting, balloted) A ballot is a system of voting secretly. Each voter has a ballot paper, which they mark their vote on. In a postal ballot, people send their votes in by post. ◇ When balloting takes place, a ballot is held. ◇ When people are balloted, a ballot is used to find out their views about what action should be taken.

ballot box A ballot box is a strong sealed box with a slot in the top for people to put their ballot papers in when they vote. ◇ When people talk about the ballot box, they mean the system of democratic elections, as distinct from other ways of deciding who rules a country. The party has the opportunity of trying to win power through the ballot box.

ballot-rigging is interfering with the way a ballot is carried out, to make the result go in favour of a particular party or person.

ballpoint A ballpoint or ballpoint pen is a pen with a small metal ball at the end. Ink from inside the pen flows over the point and is transferred onto the paper when you write.

ballroom A ballroom is a large room, often in a building like a hotel or palace, used for dancing or formal balls. ◇ Ballroom dancing is a style of dancing in which a man and woman dance together following a set routine of steps. Typical dances are the waltz, the quickstep, and the tango.

ballyhoo The publicity surrounding a planned event is sometimes called ballyhoo.

balm is sweet-smelling soothing ointment. ◇ If you say a piece of news is balm to someone, you mean it comforts them or cheers them up.

balmy (balmier, balmiest) When the weather is balmy, it is mild and pleasant.

balsa or balsa wood is a very light wood used for making things like rafts and model aeroplanes.

balsam is a sweet-smelling resin from various trees and shrubs. It is used in medicines and ointments. ◇ Balsam is also a type of flowering plant.

balti is a type of cooking which is very common in restaurants in the Birmingham area. It came originally from Baltistan in north Pakistan. Balti dishes are cooked and served in wok-like vessels called 'karahi'.

Baltic The Baltic States are Lithuania, Latvia, and Estonia.

balustrade A balustrade is a rail or wall along the edge of something like a balcony or staircase.

bamboo is a kind of tall fast-growing tropical grass. The stems are woody and hollow and are used to make things like furniture. The young shoots can be eaten.

bamboozle (bamboozling, bamboozled) If someone bamboozles you, they deliberately trick or confuse you.

ban (banning, banned) If someone in authority bans something, they forbid it to be done, shown, or used. ◇ If someone is banned from doing something, they are officially forbidden to do it. If they are banned from a place, they are forbidden to go there. ◇ An order forbidding something is called a ban. ...a trade ban.

banal (banality, banalities) If something is banal (pron: ban-nahl), it is not at all original or interesting. You can talk about the banality (pron: ban-nal-i-ty) of something like this. Banalities are ordinary uninteresting remarks and happenings.

banana ❏ Bananas are long curved fruit with cream-coloured flesh and bright yellow skins. ◇ A banana skin is something which causes someone to make a mistake and look silly. The government was slithering from one banana skin to another. ◇ Poor countries with unstable governments are sometimes called banana republics. This is an offensive use.
❏ If someone goes bananas, (a) they behave in a silly or excitable way. (b) they become very angry.

band ❏ A band is a group of musicians who play together. They can play, for example, jazz, rock, or pop. Musicians who play brass instruments together are called a brass band. A military band is a group of wind and percussion musicians in the armed forces; often they play music for ceremonial occasions.

❑ A group of people who share the same interests or beliefs can also be called a **band.** *...a band of enthusiastic supporters.* ◇ When people **band together,** they join together to try and get something done.

❑ A **band** is a flat narrow strip of something like cloth, worn around a person's head or wrist. ◇ A **band** is also a strip of colour or light. *Some viewers prefer to see all of the picture, even if it means having a black band at top and bottom of the screen.*

❑ A **band** is also a range of numbers or values in a system of measurement. When something is divided into bands, this is called **banding.** *...a basic-rate tax band of up to £20,000... ...the banding system for valuing houses.*

Band-Aid A **Band-Aid** is a sticky plaster for covering small cuts. It has a patch of gauze in the middle. 'Band-Aid' is a trademark.

bandage (bandaging, bandaged) A **bandage** is a strip of cloth wrapped round a wound or an injured part of the body. When someone wraps a bandage round a part of someone's body, you say they **bandage** it.

bandanna A **bandanna** is a large brightly-coloured handkerchief worn around the neck or head.

bandit (banditry) A **bandit** is an armed robber, usually belonging to a gang. **Banditry** is armed robbery.

bandolier (*pron:* ban-dol-leer) A **bandolier** is a broad shoulder belt with small loops or pockets for holding things like gun cartridges.

bandsman (bandsmen) Musicians who play in brass or military bands are called **bandsmen.**

bandstand A **bandstand** is a platform with a roof and open sides where a brass or military band can play in the open air.

bandwagon If you talk about someone jumping or climbing on the **bandwagon,** you mean they are joining or supporting a party or movement because they think it is certain to succeed, or because it has become popular. ◇ If someone starts a **bandwagon** rolling, they start a movement or group which they hope will attract a lot of support. *Seven weeks before voting day, the rival bandwagons are beginning to roll.* ◇ When a leading politician is accompanied everywhere by advisers and staff, these people are often called his or her **bandwagon.**

bandwidth A **bandwidth** is the range of frequencies within a particular waveband used for a radio transmission.

bandy (bandies, bandying, bandied) ❑ When people **bandy** ideas or arguments, they discuss them in a casual way. You can also say ideas are **bandied about** or **bandied around.** ◇ When words are **bandied around,** people use them a lot without paying much attention to their meaning. *The catch phrase bandied about by the company's chairman is 'global localization'.* ◇ If you **bandy** words with someone, you argue with them.

❑ If someone has **bandy** legs or is **bandy-legged,** their legs curve outwards at the knees.

bane If something is the **bane** of someone or something, it causes them a lot of annoyance or distress.

bang ❑ A **bang** is a short loud noise. ◇ If you **bang** something, you hit or knock it with a lot of noise or force. ◇ If you **bang** a door or window, you shut it quickly and noisily. ◇ If you **bang** into something or go **bang** into it, you collide with it.

❑ If something happens **with a bang,** it happens in a dramatic or noticeable way. *The Christmas increase in sales was slow in coming, but arrived with a bang in mid-December.*

❑ When someone talks about **banging** people's **heads together,** they are talking about getting them to stop quarrelling or arguing.

❑ If you say someone is **banging on** about something, you mean they keep talking about it. *He's been banging on about education reform for years.* ◇ If you **bang the drum** for someone or something, you try to get people to support them.

❑ When people talk about the **big bang,** they mean (a) the enormous explosion which, according to many scientists, caused the beginning of the universe. (b) what happened to the London Stock Exchange in October 1986, when its internal organization was radically changed.

❑ **Bang** is used to emphasize that something is exactly in a particular place, or happens at exactly a particular time. *...bang in the middle of Whitehaven town centre... He arrived bang on time.*

banger A **banger** is (a) an old car in a bad condition. (b) a type of small firework which goes off with a loud bang. (c) a sausage.

bangle A **bangle** is a band of something like metal, glass, or plastic worn for decoration round a person's wrist, or sometimes round their ankle.

banian See banyan.

banish (banishes, banishing, banished; banishment) If someone is **banished,** they are sent away from the country or area where they live and not allowed to return. You call this their **banishment.** ◇ If you **banish** something, you get rid of it. *The international community has failed to banish hunger.*

banister (*can be spelled with double 'n'*) A **banister** is a rail supported by posts along the side of a staircase.

banjo (banjos *or* banjoes) The **banjo** is a guitar-like instrument with a long fingerboard, a flat circular body, and usually five strings.

bank ❑ A **bank** is an institution where people or businesses can keep their money. Banks also offer services such as lending, exchanging, or transferring money. When people pay money into a bank, you say they **bank** it. *By this time officials had banked the £3,407 cheque.* The business carried on by banks is called **banking.** ◇ The building where a bank carries on its business is also called a **bank.**

❑ A store of something kept ready for use can also be called a **bank.** For example, data is often stored in a **data bank** and blood is kept in a **blood bank.**

❑ The **bank** of a river or lake is the ground along its edge. ◇ A **bank** is also an area of raised ground, usually with sloping sides and a flat top. Its sides are also called **banks.**

❑ Rows of things can be called **banks.** *There is a vast bank of instruments on one side of the stage... ...banks of empty seats.*

❑ When an aircraft **banks,** one of its wings rises higher than the other, usually because it is turning.

❑ If you **bank on** something, you expect it to happen or be available, and plan things accordingly. *The Prime Minister was warned he should not bank on their support.*

bank holiday A **bank holiday** is a public holiday when banks and public offices are closed by law and many shops and other businesses are also closed.

bank loan A bank loan is a sum of money which a bank lends for a period of time and which has to be paid back with interest.

bank note (*or* banknote) A bank note is a piece of paper money.

banker A banker is someone involved in banking at a senior level.

banker's order A banker's order is the same as a standing order.

banknote See bank note.

bankrupt (bankruptcy, bankruptcies) ❏ If someone is bankrupt, they do not have enough money to pay their debts. If they are declared bankrupt in a court of law, they have to hand over the running of their affairs to a trustee or the Official Receiver, and their property can be sold to repay their debts. Someone in this situation is called a bankrupt; their situation is called bankruptcy.

❏ If something bankrupts someone, it makes them go bankrupt or lose a lot of money.

❏ Bankrupt is also used to say someone is completely without a particular quality. For example, if you say a person is morally bankrupt, you mean they are completely immoral.

banner ❏ A banner is a long strip of material, often cloth, with a message or slogan on it. Banners are stretched between two points high above the ground, for example across a street, or attached to poles and carried in processions. ◇ If you say something is done under the banner of a particular belief or principle, you mean that is the reason given for doing it. *This dictatorship was introduced under the banner of economic efficiency.*

❏ A banner headline in a newspaper is a very large one extending right across the front page.

bannister See banister.

banns The banns are a spoken or printed declaration of an intended marriage in church. In Anglican churches, they are usually published on three successive Sundays in the parish churches of the people who are about to be married.

banquet (banqueting) A banquet is a grand formal dinner, usually with many courses and followed by speeches. A banqueting hall or room is a place where banquets are held.

bantam A bantam is a small-sized breed of chicken.

banter (bantering, bantered) Banter is friendly joking or teasing among a group of people. When people behave like this, you can say they are bantering.

banyan (*or* banian) The banyan is a tree in India and the East Indies. Its branches grow down into the soil, forming new roots.

bap A bap is a soft bread roll.

baptise See baptize.

baptism is a Christian religious ceremony in which a person is sprinkled with water, or immersed in water, as a sign they have become a Christian.

❏ If you say someone has had a baptism of fire, you mean they have had a particularly difficult or dangerous first experience of something.

Baptist Baptists are members of the Baptist Church, a branch of the Protestant church. They believe people should not be baptized until they are old enough to

understand what they are doing. In this Church, baptism usually involves total immersion.

baptize (baptizing, baptized) (*can be spelled with an 's' instead of a 'z'*) When someone is baptized, water is sprinkled on them or they are immersed in water, as a sign they have become a member of a Christian Church.

bar (barring, barred) ❏ A bar is a place where alcoholic drinks are sold and drunk. The counter where the drinks are served is also called a bar. ◇ Some kinds of cafes are called bars, and so are some stalls and small shops offering a limited range of items or services. *...a burger bar... ...a heel bar.*

❏ A bar is also a strong straight narrow piece of wood or metal. ◇ A barred window has metal bars across it. ◇ If someone is behind bars, they are in prison. ◇ In sports like football, the bar is the piece of wood across the top of the goal.

❏ Some small rectangular objects are called bars. *...a bar of soap... ...a chocolate bar.*

❏ In Britain, when a lawyer is accepted as a barrister, you say he or she is called to the Bar. ◇ The Bar is also used to talk about barristers as a group. *The Bar has campaigned very strongly for a reduction in the retirement age of judges.* In some countries, the Bar includes all members of the legal profession, not just barristers.

❏ If someone is barred from doing something, they are officially prevented from doing it. An order or rule preventing them is called a bar. *She told the Swiss that their neutrality was not a bar to membership.* ◇ If someone bars your way, they stop you going somewhere by standing in front of you.

❏ A bar is one of several short equal parts which a piece of music is divided into.

❏ Bar is sometimes used to mean 'except for'. *He won every match, bar one.* ◇ Bar none is used to emphasize that someone or something is the best of their kind. *His description is the best in the English language, bar none.* ◇ If you say something will happen barring something else, you mean it will happen provided the other thing does not happen. *Barring illness or accident, he will win the race.*

❏ no holds barred: see hold.

bar code (bar-coded) A bar code is a rectangular area of thick and thin vertical lines printed on something. When it is fed into a computer or passed over a scanner, the computer 'reads' the information in the code. Goods sold in shops often have bar codes with information on them such as the price, the quantity sold, and the amount left in stock. Objects with bar codes on them are said to be bar-coded.

Bar Council The Bar Council is the professional organization responsible for the training, appointment, and professional conduct of barristers.

bar mitzvah A Jewish boy's bar mitzvah is a ceremony and celebration marking his 13th birthday, after which he takes on the status, religious duties, and responsibilities of an adult. See also bat mitzvah.

barb (barbed) ❏ A barb is a sharp curved point on the end of something like an arrow or fish-hook. You say something with a point like this is barbed.

❏ A barb is also an unkind or unpleasant remark. Barbed is used to describe remarks like these. *He is preparing a few choice barbs in reply... They can shrug off the occa-*

sional barbed comment from fellow golfers.

barbarian The **barbarians** were violent uncivilized tribes like the Huns, Goths, and Vandals, who lived in Europe in earlier times. ◇ Nowadays, people sometimes get called **barbarians** when they behave in a rough or violent way.

barbaric People use **barbaric** to express their disgust at behaviour they think is cruel or uncivilized. *Prisoners are kept in barbaric and overcrowded conditions... ...the barbaric practice of kidnapping.*

barbarism is cruel or uncivilized behaviour.

barbarity (barbarities) **Barbarity** is extremely cruel behaviour. **Barbarities** are cruel and shocking acts.

barbarous (barbarously) People use **barbarous** to express their disgust at behaviour they think is cruel or uncivilized. *...the barbarous attacks of the enemy.... She was gunned down barbarously.*

barbecue (barbecuing, barbecued) If you **barbecue** food, you cook it on a grill over hot charcoal, usually out of doors. An outdoor occasion when food is cooked like this is called a **barbecue**. The grill the food is cooked on is also called a **barbecue**.

barbed wire is twisted strands of strong wire with sharp points sticking out, used for fences and in military defences.

barbell A **barbell** is a metal bar to which disc-shaped weights can be added at each end. It is used in weight-lifting.

barber A **barber** is a man who cuts men's hair and shaves or trims their beards. The place where a barber works is sometimes called a **barber's** or **barber's shop**.

barbershop is a type of close harmony singing usually performed by four men and especially popular in the US.

barbiturate **Barbiturates** are drugs which people take to calm them or help them sleep.

bard is an old-fashioned word for a poet. People sometimes call William Shakespeare **the Bard**.

bare (barer, barest; baring, bared; barely) ❑ If someone is **bare**, they are not wearing any clothes. You can also say, for example, that someone has **bare** arms or **bare** legs. ◇ If someone **bares** part of their body, they uncover it. ◇ If you do something **with your bare hands**, you do it without weapons or tools.

❑ **Bare** is used to describe something like a hillside or field where nothing is growing. *Where there used to be bare chalk, now there's a flourishing plantlife.* ◇ If an area of countryside does not have a particular feature, you can say it is **bare** of it. *The farm was quite bare of trees.*

❑ A **bare** floor or wall does not have any covering or decoration.

❑ If a room or cupboard is **bare**, there is little or nothing in it. ◇ If a place is **stripped bare**, all the contents are taken away. *Shops have been stripped bare in panic buying.*

❑ If unpleasant facts are **laid bare**, the public is told about them. ◇ If someone **lays bare** their feelings or thoughts, they tell someone else about them. If they **bare their soul**, they talk about their most secret thoughts or feelings.

❑ **Bare** and **barely** are used to say that a number or amount is only just that number or amount. *There was a bare 15 seconds of applause... The Lake District is barely 30 mi-*

les across in any direction.

❑ **Barely** is used to mean 'only just'. For example, if something is **barely** possible, it is only just possible. *They can barely look after themselves.* ◇ The **bare minimum** is the smallest number or amount required for something to be possible. *Two weekends a month and three weeks each summer would be a bare minimum for training reserve troops.* ◇ The **bare essentials** or **bare necessities** are the things you must have in order to survive.

❑ If you give someone the **bare** facts about something, you tell them the facts without adding anything extra, such as your own opinions. ◇ **Bare** is also used to describe something like a statement which gives only the most essential facts, without any additional information. *There are no further details beyond the bare announcement that he has been chosen as the new deputy Chairman.* ◇ **bare bones**: see **bone**.

bare-faced (*or* barefaced) You use **bare-faced** to describe someone's behaviour when they show they are not ashamed of something they have done. *The book was a barefaced chronicle of giving aid to a spy.*

barefoot (barefooted) If someone is **barefoot** or **barefooted**, they are not wearing anything on their feet. ◇ In some developing countries, a person trained in the basic health care and treatment of people or animals is called a **barefoot** doctor or **barefoot** vet.

bargain (bargaining, bargained) ❑ A **bargain** is a business agreement in which two people or groups agree what each of them will do, pay, or receive. When people or groups try to reach an agreement like this, you say they **bargain** with each other. When they reach agreement, you can say they **make** or **strike a bargain**. ◇ In a discussion, if someone has a **bargaining chip** or **bargaining counter**, they have something of value to the other side which they can use to get what they want. When someone has an advantage like this, you can say they have **bargaining power**.

❑ When people like politicians are at the **bargaining table**, they are having serious discussions to try and reach agreement on something.

❑ If you say someone **drives** or **strikes a hard bargain**, you mean they are only satisfied with an agreement which is particularly favourable to them.

❑ A **bargain** is something sold at a lower price than usual, which is good value for money. ◇ A **bargain basement** is part of a large department store, where you can buy goods very cheaply. **Bargain-basement** is used to describe anything which costs very little to buy or operate. *...a bargain-basement rock musical.*

❑ If something unexpected happens which interferes with your plans, you can say you had not **bargained for** it.

❑ You say **into the bargain** when you are mentioning something extra about the person or thing you have just been talking about. *...a machine that not only uses a simpler recording method but which can also play ordinary cassettes into the bargain.*

barge (barging, barged) ❑ A **barge** is (a) a large flat-bottomed boat carrying goods or people, usually on a canal or river. (b) a large motorboat used by a high ranking naval officer.

❑ If you **barge** someone or **barge into** them, you bump into them clumsily or roughly. ◇ If you **barge into** a place, you rush in without taking any notice of what might be in the way. ◇ If you say you would not touch someone or something **with a barge pole,** you mean you do not want to have anything to do with them.

baritone A **baritone** is a man with a fairly deep singing voice. ◇ The **baritone** saxophone is a large saxophone with a range of notes lower than a tenor saxophone.

barium is a soft silvery-white metal. ◇ A **barium meal** is a preparation of a chemical called barium sulphate, which a patient swallows before having X-rays of the upper part of the alimentary canal. When the X-rays are developed, the barium sulphate can be seen and this helps the doctor see if anything is wrong.

bark ❑ A **bark** is the short loud noise made by dogs and some other animals, for example foxes. When an animal makes this noise, you say it **barks.** ◇ When a person **barks** something like an order, they shout it at someone. *...sitting on the sidelines barking instructions to the players.* ◇ You can talk about the **bark** of other things when they make short loud noises. *...the bark of automatic rifles.*

❑ If you say someone's **bark is worse than their bite,** you mean they are not as unpleasant as their manner suggests. ◇ If you say someone is **barking up the wrong tree,** you mean they have got the wrong idea about something, or are setting about something the wrong way.

❑ The **bark** of a tree is its tough outer skin.

barley is a cereal grown for food. It is also used in the making of beer and whisky.

barley sugar is a hard sweet made from boiled sugar.

barley water is a non-alcoholic drink made from barley and water, often flavoured with lemon or orange.

barmaid A **barmaid** is a woman who serves drinks in a bar or pub.

barman (barmen) A **barman** is a man who serves drinks in a bar or pub.

barmy (barmier, barmiest) If you say an idea or action is **barmy,** you mean it is very silly. ◇ If someone goes **barmy,** (a) they go mad. (b) they get very angry. *If the club has to sell Gazza, the fans will go barmy.*

barn A **barn** is a large building on a farm for storing grain, other crops, or equipment.

barn dance A **barn dance** is an informal event at which people take part in country dancing.

barn owl The **barn owl** is a type of owl with pale brown and white feathers and a heart-shaped face. Barn owls hunt at night for small animals, and often nest in old barns and other farm buildings.

barnacle Barnacles are small shellfish which fix themselves tightly to rocks and the bottoms of boats.

barnstorming is used to describe a campaign or tour made by a politician when he or she travels round a country making speeches. *Mr Clinton resumed his barnstorming bus tour.* ◇ **Barnstorming** is also used to describe other things done in an energetic or forceful way. *...a barnstorming performance from Gerard Depardieu.*

barometer (barometric) A **barometer** is an instrument which measures air pressure and shows when the weather is changing. The pressure measured by a barometer is called **barometric** pressure. ◇ Something which gives a hint of how a situation is likely to develop can also be called a **barometer.** *The survey should be a*

useful barometer of UK small business performance.

baron (barony, baronies) A **baron** is a nobleman. In Britain, a baron is a member of the lowest rank of the nobility. A **barony** is the rank or position of being a baron. Some barons inherit an area of land called a **barony.** ◇ Powerful people at the head of large organizations are sometimes called **barons.** *...drug barons.*

baroness (baronesses) A **baroness** is the wife or widow of a baron, or a woman holding the rank of baron. She ranks below a viscountess.

baronet (baronetcy, baronetcies) A **baronet** is a commoner who holds a hereditary title of honour ranking below that of a baron. A baronet puts 'Bart.' or 'Bt.' after his name. ◇ A **baronetcy** is the rank or position of being a baronet.

baronial is used to describe castle-like houses with large high rooms. *...baronial halls.*

baroque (*pron:* bar-rock) **Baroque** was a European style of architecture and art from the late 16th to the early 18th century. Baroque buildings, paintings, and other objects are elaborate and heavily decorated. *...baroque churches... ...a baroque gilded cherub.* ◇ **Baroque** music was a style of music from about 1600 to 1750. Bach, Handel, and Vivaldi wrote music in this style.

barrack ❑ A **barracks** (*plural:* barracks) is a building or group of buildings where members of the armed forces work and live. A **barrack block** is one of the buildings in a barracks. **Barrack** is used to talk about other things connected with a barracks. *...a barrack room.* ◇ Large ugly blocks of flats are sometimes called **barracks.**

❑ If people **barrack** someone who is making a speech, they shout things out because they disagree with them, often interrupting what they are saying.

barracuda (*pron:* ba-rak-kew-da) The **barracuda** is a large tropical fish with sharp teeth and a lower jaw which sticks out.

barrage (*pron:* bar-rahzh; *the 'zh' sounds like 's' in 'pleasure'*) ❑ A **barrage** of something like questions or complaints is a lot of them coming one after another. ◇ A **barrage** is also (a) a rapid series of shells or rockets being fired at something. (b) a shower of stones or other missiles being thrown at someone.

❑ A **barrage** is also an artificial barrier built across a river to control the water level.

barrage balloon Barrage balloons are large balloons which float above the ground at the end of long steel cables. In wartime, they were used to protect cities and other important places; the idea was that low-flying enemy aircraft would fly into the cables and crash.

barred See **bar.**

barrel (barrels; -barrelled) (*usual American spelling:* -barreled) ❑ A **barrel** is a round container, usually for liquids, which is wider in the middle than at the top and bottom. Barrels used to be made of wood held together by bands of metal, but are now mostly made of metal or plastic. ◇ The volume of large quantities of oil is expressed in **barrels.** A barrel is usually taken as 35 gallons (about 159 litres).

❑ If someone is in a difficult situation and forced to agree to someone else's demands, you can say they are **over a barrel.** ◇ You say someone is **scraping the barrel** when they produce something of very low quality. *The*

game designers were scraping the bottom of the barrel for ideas when they came up with this one.
❑ The **barrel** of a gun is the tube which the bullets or missiles come out of. **-barrelled** is added to words to describe a gun's barrel or to say how many barrels it has. *...short-barrelled weapons... ...double-barrelled shotguns.*

barrel organ A **barrel organ** is a machine on wheels which plays music when you turn a handle on the side. Barrel organs used to be played in the street to entertain passers-by.

barren (barrenness) **Barren** is used to describe places where nothing can grow. *...countryside of vast but beautiful barrenness.* ◇ If a woman is **barren,** she cannot have babies. You can also say a female animal is **barren.** ◇ When trees or plants fail to produce fruit, you say they are **barren.** ◇ A **barren** period for someone is one when they do not achieve very much.

barricade (barricading, barricaded) A **barricade** is a line of things placed across a road to stop people getting past. When people **barricade** a road, they put a barricade across it. ◇ If you **barricade** yourself inside a room or building, you block up the doors and windows so no one can get in.

barrier A **barrier** is something like a fence or wall which stops people or things moving from one place to another. ◇ Something which makes something difficult or impossible to achieve can also be called a **barrier.** *The lack of cheap child care is the main barrier to women having choice.* ◇ In sport, a particular level of achievement is sometimes called a **barrier.** When someone reaches this level, you say they have **broken the barrier.** *The European champion shattered the ten-second barrier for the first time in his home country.*

barrier cream is a cream used to protect the skin, especially the hands, against things like dirt or water.

barrier reef A **barrier reef** is a long narrow coral reef running parallel to the shore and separated from it by water.

barring See **bar.**

barrister A **barrister** is a lawyer in England, Wales, or Northern Ireland who speaks in court for the defence or prosecution. Unlike solicitors, barristers can speak in the higher courts, such as the crown courts.

barrow A **barrow** is (a) a wheelbarrow. (b) a small cart or movable stall used by a street or market trader. ◇ A **barrow** is also a mound of earth containing the graves of prehistoric people.

Bart. See **baronet.**

bartender In the US, a person who serves drinks in a bar is called a **bartender.**

barter (bartering, bartered) **Barter** is a system of trading by exchanging goods for other goods, instead of selling them for money. When people operate a system like this, you say they **barter.**

bas-relief (*pron:* bah-relief *or* bass-relief) is a method of sculpture in which shapes are carved so they stand out from a flat surface. A sculpture done in this way is called a **bas-relief.**

basalt is a type of black rock produced by volcanoes.

base (basing, based; baser, basest) ❑ A military **base** is a place where part of an army, air force, or navy is stationed and which it operates from. ◇ The place which

any organization operates from can be called its **base;** you say the organization is **based** there. *The Australian Chamber Orchestra is based at the Sydney Opera House.* ◇ You can add **-based** to the name of a place or nationality, to show where someone or something operates from. *...a London-based firm of chartered surveyors... ...ground-based missiles.*
❑ The **base camp** of something like an expedition is the place where supplies are kept and where the expedition is controlled from.
❑ A **base** is something which is already established and from which it is possible to develop or achieve other things. *One of his main aims now is to expand his political base.*
❑ When you are preparing food or a drink, the **base** is the part you start with, before adding other things. ◇ You can add **-based** to a word to talk about the main ingredient of something. *...oil-based products.*
❑ The **base** of a standing object is its lowest part. *...the base of a small tree.*
❑ You say a statement is **based** on something when you are mentioning where the information came from. *He said he was basing his remarks on a conversation with an official of ministerial rank.* You can also say a decision is **based** on some information. *The ban was not based on any scientific evidence.* ◇ If a story, play, or film is **based** on something else, it is developed from it, keeping the main characters but changing many details. *...a play based on Henry James's novel The Turn of the Screw.*
❑ **Base** is used to describe feelings and behaviour which are not honourable or moral. *Love has the power to overcome the baser emotions.* ◇ **Base** metals are common metals like copper, lead, tin, and zinc, as distinct from precious metals like gold.

base rate The **base rate** is the rate of interest banks use when they are calculating the rates they charge on loans.

baseball is a game played by two teams of nine players using a wooden bat and a hard ball. The playing area has four bases laid out in the shape of a diamond. The teams take it in turns to bat and field, and the player who is batting has to run from base to base in order to score. When a player gets all the way round to the fourth base before the opposing team has returned the ball, he scores a 'home run'. Baseball is the national game in the US, where it is often just called 'the ball game'.

baseless If you say a story or belief is **baseless,** you mean there is no truth in it and it is not supported by facts.

baseline The **baselines** of a tennis or badminton court are the lines at each end of the court which mark the limits of play. ◇ A **baseline** is also a standard by which things can be measured or compared. *The organization wants to establish baselines for monitoring their future progress.*

basement The **basement** of a building is a room or rooms partly or completely below ground level.

bases See **base.** ◇ See **basis.**

bash (bashes, bashing, bashed) ❑ If you **bash** someone or something, you hit them. ◇ A **bash** is a blow, especially to the head or face. ◇ If you **bash** into something, you bump into it accidentally.

❑ If someone **bashes** a person or group, they criticize them continually or make things difficult for them. -**bashing** is added to a word to say someone is being criticized or treated in this way. ...*a decade of remorseless teacher-bashing in the press.*

❑ A **bash** is also a party.

bashful (bashfully) **Bashful** people are shy and easily embarrassed. If you are **bashful** about doing something, you are reluctant to do it, because you find it embarrassing. *He was a bit bashful about bringing up the subject.*

basic is used to describe the simplest and most essential things of a particular kind. ...*basic human rights... ...the basic needs of day-to-day living.* You call things like these the **basics**. ◇ **Basic** is also used to describe things which are at a very elementary level. *Their basic reading skills would also be tested.* These things can also be called the **basics**. *We place great emphasis on making sure our students understand the basics.* ◇ The **basic** rate of something like a tax is the level of payment which applies to most people, without any extra allowances or payments. ◇ If something is very plain, with only the essential features and no luxuries, you can say it is **basic**. *The accommodation at the camp was basic but clean.* ◇ See also **basically**.

BASIC is a simple computer language which uses English words. BASIC stands for 'Beginners' All-purpose Symbolic Instruction Code'.

basically is used to mention the most important feature of something, or to explain something in a simple or general way. *This was basically a political row... Basically they want to make politicians accountable to constituencies.* ◇ **Basically** is also used to say something is generally true, though not entirely so. *He is basically healthy.*

basil is a sweet-scented herb used to add flavour to food, especially tomatoes.

basilica A **basilica** is a church built in the shape of an oblong with a rounded end called an apse and two side aisles. ◇ In the Roman Catholic church, a **basilica** is a church or cathedral which has special ceremonial rights.

basin ❑ A **basin** is a deep bowl for mixing, cooking, or storing food. ❑ The **basin** of a large river or lake is the area around it, from which water and streams run into it. ◇ A **basin** is also a sheltered area of water where ships or boats can be moored.

basis (plural: bases, pron: bay-seez) ❑ The **basis** of something is the essential part of it, from which the rest is developed. ...*a document which would become the basis of a treaty.* ❑ If a particular thing is done **on the basis** of something, it is done as a result of it. *We were all selected on the basis of outstanding ability in maths and science.* ❑ The **basis** for a decision is the reason for making it. ◇ The **basis** for an improvement of some kind is the thing which makes it possible. *A lower exchange rate and lower interest rates should provide a sound basis for recovery.* ❑ If you talk about the **basis** on which something is done, you are talking about the general way it is organized. *We have been able to send out help on an emergency basis... ...the chance to save on a regular basis.*

bask If you **bask** in sunshine or some other kind of warmth, you lie in it and enjoy it. ◇ If someone has become very famous or popular, you can say they are basking in their fame or popularity.

basket ❑ A **basket** is a container traditionally made of thin strips of wood or cane woven together and usually having one or two handles. Baskets can also be made of wire or plastic. ◇ **Basket** is used to describe things which look as if they have been woven like a basket. ...*a basket chair.* ❑ A **basket** is also a group or collection of things. *The survey is based on a basket of 151 products ranging from food to transportation.* ◇ A **basket** of currencies is a group of currencies from different countries used as a measure of the value of another country's currency. ❑ **put all your eggs in one basket**: see **egg**. ❑ See also **basketball**.

basket-case When people call someone or something a **basket-case**, they mean they are worn-out, useless, or unable to do anything.

basketball is a game played on a court between two teams of five players. At opposite ends of the court are two circular nets called 'baskets' hanging from metal rings. Each team tries to score points by throwing a large ball so it drops through their opponents' basket. A point scored like this is also called a 'basket'.

basque A **basque** is a tight-fitting bodice for women, usually worn as underwear.

bass (basses) ❑ A **bass** (*pron:* base) is a man with a deep rich singing voice, who can sing a slightly lower range of notes than a baritone. ◇ Several musical instruments have **bass** as part of their name. They are usually the largest of a particular type of instrument, and have the lowest range of notes. ...*a bass trombone.* ◇ In popular music, a **bass** guitar or double bass is often called a **bass**. ❑ The **bass** (*rhymes with 'gas'; usual plural:* bass) is a fish which people catch in rivers or the sea. There are several types of bass.

basset hound The **basset hound** is a smooth-haired dog with a long body, short legs, and long ears.

bassoon (bassoonist) The **bassoon** is a large woodwind instrument which can produce some very low notes. It is shaped like a long wooden pipe with keys, and has a metal mouthpiece. A person who plays the bassoon is sometimes called a **bassoonist**.

bastard A **bastard** is someone who was born to parents who were not married at the time. 'Bastard' is an offensive word.

bastardized (*or* bastardised) A **bastardized** version of something has something else mixed with it, and so is not as good as the pure form. *Scots is a separate language, not a bastardized or inferior version of something else.*

baste (basting, basted) If you **baste** food, you spoon hot fat or other liquids over it while it is cooking. ◇ If you **baste** pieces of material together, you sew them with large temporary stitches to hold them in place, before sewing them together permanently. See also **tack**.

bastion A **bastion** is part of the wall of something like a castle or fortress. It sticks out from the main part of the wall. ◇ Something is called a **bastion** when it is seen as important and effective in defending a way of life or protecting people from something unpleasant. ...*one of the last remaining male bastions – the pavilion at Lords... Quite a lot of people regard the Church as a bastion of decency and spiritual freedom.*

bat (batting, batted; batsman, batsmen) ❑ A **bat** is a specially shaped piece of wood used to hit the ball in a game like cricket, table tennis, or baseball. ◇ When a person or team is **batting** in a game like cricket or baseball, it is their turn to try to hit the ball with the bat. A player whose turn it is to bat, or who specializes in batting, is called a **batsman** in cricket and a **batter** in baseball.
❑ **Bats** are small mouse-like flying animals with leathery wings. They are usually active at night.
❑ If someone does something **off their own bat**, they do it without anyone else suggesting it.
❑ **bat an eyelid**: see **eyelid**.

bat mitzvah A Jewish girl's **bat mitzvah** is a ceremony and celebration marking her 12th birthday, after which she takes on the status, religious duties, and responsibilities of an adult. See also **bar mitzvah**.

batch (batches) A **batch** of things or people is a group of them of the same kind. *Yesterday another batch of prisoners gave up their protest... ...the latest batch of EU statistics.*

bated If you say someone is waiting **with bated breath**, you mean they are waiting very anxiously to see what happens. ◇ If people talk about something **with bated breath**, they talk about it with great respect and admiration.

bath A **bath** is a large rectangular container which you fill with water and sit in to wash your body. ◇ If you wash yourself in a bath, you say you **have a bath**. If you wash someone else in a bath, you **bath** them, or **give** them a **bath**. Americans say someone **takes a bath** or **bathes**. ◇ A public swimming pool is often called the **baths** (plural: **baths**).

bath oil is a thick perfumed liquid used in the bath to make the water smell nice and soothe the skin.

bath salts are mineral salts which dissolve in water. They are sprinkled in the bath to soften the water and make it smell nice.

bathe (bathing, bathed) ❑ When you **bathe** or go for a **bathe**, you swim in the sea or in some other natural area of water. ◇ See also **bath**. ◇ If you **bathe** something like a wound, you wash it gently.
❑ If something is **bathed** in light, light is shining all over it. You can also say something is **bathed** in sunshine. ◇ If someone is enjoying having a lot of attention or admiration, you can say they are **bathing** in it.

bathmat A **bathmat** is (a) a soft mat which you stand on while you dry yourself after a bath. (b) a rubber mat placed on the bottom of a bath to stop you slipping when you get in and out.

bathos (*pron:* bay-thoss) is a sudden change in speech or writing from a serious or important subject to a silly or very ordinary one.

bathrobe A **bathrobe** is a loose coat-like garment, usually made of towelling and worn before or after a bath or swim. ◇ In the US, a dressing-gown is usually called a **bathrobe**.

bathroom The **bathroom** in a house is a room with a bath or shower, washbasin, and often a toilet.

bathtub A **bathtub** is a bath. In Britain, a bathtub is usually something movable, like a tin bath. In the US, a bathtub is a bath of any kind.

batik (*pron:* bat-teek) is a method of printing designs on cloth. The areas of cloth which are not meant to be col-oured are coated with wax, and then the cloth is put into a dye. A **batik** is a cloth printed in this way. Batiks are often used as wall hangings.

batman A serviceman who acted as a personal servant to an army officer used to be called a **batman.**

baton A **baton** is (a) a light thin stick used by a conductor to direct an orchestra or choir. (b) a short metal or wooden stick passed from one runner to another in a relay race. ◇ A **baton** is also a short heavy stick used as a weapon by a policeman. When there is a **baton charge,** a group of policemen carrying batons move forward in an attack.

batsman See **bat**.

battalion A **battalion** is a large group of soldiers, made up of three or more companies and forming part of a brigade.

batten (battening, battened) A **batten** is a long strip of wood fixed to something to strengthen it or hold it firm. ◇ If you **batten** something **down**, you make it secure, either by fixing battens to it or by closing it firmly. ◇ When people **batten down the hatches**, they try to reduce the bad effects of some trouble which is on the way. ◇ If someone **battens on** something, they make use of it for their own purposes. *...the growth of extremist parties, battening on fears about mass immigration and unemployment.*

batter (battering, battered) ❑ If someone **batters** a person or thing, they repeatedly hit them hard. You use **battered** to describe someone who has been repeatedly hit like this; you also say they have taken a **battering**. ◇ If something like the rain or a storm **batters** something, it keeps striking or beating against it.
❑ **Battered** is also used to describe something which is old, worn, and damaged. *...a battered old suitcase.*
❑ You say something like an organization has been **battered** or has taken a **battering** when it has suffered a lot of problems or setbacks.
❑ If someone **batters down** something like a door or gate, they hit it so hard and often that it breaks and falls down. ◇ A **battering ram** was a long heavy piece of wood, possibly the size of a tree trunk, which was used in the past to batter down the doors of a castle or fortified building.
❑ **Batter** is a liquid mixture, usually of milk, eggs, and flour, used to make pancakes or Yorkshire pudding, or to coat other foods before cooking them.
❑ See also **bat**.

battery (batteries) ❑ A **battery** is a device which produces electricity and is used to provide the power for something.
❑ A **battery** of things like large guns or missile launchers is a large group of them operating in one place. ◇ A lot of things which have to be dealt with together can be called a **battery**. *This battery of tests covers literally hundreds of drug types.*
❑ A **battery** farm is one where a lot of hens are kept in rows of small cages to produce large amounts of eggs as cheaply as possible. The hens are called **battery** hens; the eggs they produce are called **battery** eggs.

battle (battling, battled) ❑ A **battle** is a fight between armies, or between groups of ships or planes. ◇ When people fight, you can say they **battle**. *Police and angry de-*

monstrators battled for several hours.

❑ A **battle** is also a struggle between people, or groups of people, competing for power or to achieve opposite things. *...a takeover battle... ...the battle for the leadership of the Conservative Party.* ◇ An attempt to achieve something difficult can also be called a **battle**. You can say people **battle** to achieve something. *...the battle against inflation... His company is battling for survival.* ◇ When people **battle it out**, they compete or fight very hard with each other.

❑ If you say someone is **fighting a losing battle**, you mean they are trying to achieve something but will not succeed. ◇ If you say something is **half the battle**, you mean it the most important step towards achieving something.

battle cry A **battle cry** is (a) a shout which soldiers used to make as they went into battle. (b) a phrase or speech used to encourage people to support a cause or campaign.

battledress is the ordinary uniform worn by a soldier, rather than a uniform used for ceremonial occasions.

battlefield A **battlefield** is the place where a battle is being fought or has been fought. **Battlefield** is also used to talk about things to do with fighting battles. *...lack of battlefield experience.*

battleground A **battleground** is the same as a battlefield. ◇ Something which people disagree, fight, or compete over is also called a **battleground**. *Education will be a major battleground at the next election.*

battlements The **battlements** of a castle or fortress are the wall round the top. There are gaps for guns or arrows to be fired through, and a ledge round the inside for soldiers to stand on.

battleship A **battleship** is a very large, heavily armoured warship.

batty (battier, battiest) If you say someone is **batty**, you mean they are slightly mad. You can also say something like a plan or policy is **batty**.

bauble A **bauble** is a small cheap ornament, usually with a rich shiny appearance. ◇ If you call a piece of jewellery or a trophy a **bauble**, you mean it is not worth much, although it looks expensive.

baulk See **balk**.

bauxite is an ore which aluminium is obtained from.

bawdy A **bawdy** story, song, or joke contains humorous references to sex.

bawl If someone **bawls**, they shout or sing very noisily. ◇ When a child cries very loudly, you can say it **bawls**.

bay ❑ A **bay** is a part of a coastline where the land curves inwards.

❑ A **bay** is also a space or area used for a particular purpose, for example a loading bay or parking bay.

❑ In a room, a **bay** is an alcove or recess formed where part of the room is set back from the rest. ◇ A **bay window** is a window which sticks out from the main wall of a building and so forms a bay inside the building.

❑ When a dog or wolf **bays**, it howls loudly. ◇ When people call loudly and angrily for something to be done or for someone to be punished, you can say they **bay** for it. *The referee ignored voices baying for a penalty.*

❑ The **bay** is a type of laurel tree. Its leaves can be dried and used as a herb in cooking. ◇ A **bay** horse is a reddish-brown colour, usually with darker legs, mane, and tail.

❑ If you **keep** someone or something **at bay**, you stop them reaching you. *The President's security men keep autograph-hunters at bay.* ◇ If an animal or person is **at bay**, they have been forced into a place where they cannot escape from whatever is attacking or chasing them.

bayonet (bayonetting, bayonetted) (*usual American spelling:* bayoneting, bayoneted) A **bayonet** is a long sharp blade fixed to the end of a rifle and used as a weapon. If someone is **bayonetted**, they are stabbed with a bayonet.

bazaar A **bazaar** is an area with a lot of small shops and stalls, especially in the Middle East or India. ◇ A **bazaar** is also a sale held to raise funds for something like a school, voluntary organization, or charity. ◇ An arms **bazaar** is any place where military weapons can be bought easily.

bazooka A **bazooka** is a long tube-shaped gun, held on the shoulder. It fires small armour-piercing rockets.

BBC The **BBC** is an organization which broadcasts television and radio programmes. BBC stands for 'British Broadcasting Corporation'.

BC is used to say something happened a certain number of years or centuries before Christ is believed to have been born. BC stands for 'before Christ'. *Timoleon lived between 411 and 337 BC... Trade began as early as the second century BC.*

BCG is a vaccine against tuberculosis. BCG stands for 'Bacillus Calmette-Guérin'.

be The words **be, being, been, am, are, is, was,** and **were** are used in the following ways:

❑ They are used in front of words ending in '-ing' to talk about something continuing to happen. *The government is considering the introduction of student loans... Everyone was begging the captain to surrender.*

❑ They are used in front of 'to' to talk about something which is going to happen. *She is to appeal against the decision... Sara Murchison was to leave for New York the following morning.*

❑ They are used after mentioning a person or thing to talk about something happening to that person or thing. *Mr Harris was elected by the Council last month... Both of these books can be obtained from the public library.*

❑ They are used to describe someone or something, or give information about them. *I thought the photographs were deeply offensive... The head of the Corporation is Mr Paul Simpson.*

❑ **Be** is used when telling someone to behave in a particular way. *Be precise and accurate... Be aware of your posture as you walk.*

❑ See also **been, being**.

be-all and end-all If someone regards something as the **be-all and end-all** of doing something, they think it is the only good reason for doing it. *Results are not the be-all and end-all of education.*

beach (beaches, beaching, beached) A **beach** is an area of sand or pebbles beside the sea. ◇ If you **beach** a boat, you pull it out of the water onto the land. ◇ If something like a whale is **beached**, it has been washed up on land and is stranded and helpless.

beachhead A **beachhead** is a beach where an attacking army has taken control and is preparing to advance further.

beacon ❑ A **beacon** is a light or fire on top of a hill or tower, which acts as a signal or warning. Some hills which once had beacons on them now have **Beacon** as part of their name. *...Firle Beacon... ...Beacon Hill.* ◇ A **beacon** is also a radio station or transmitter which sends out signals as a guide or warning to ships or aircraft.

❑ Someone or something that acts as an inspiration to people can also be called a **beacon.** *He used to speak of the regime as if it were a beacon of democracy.*

bead (beaded) ❑ **Beads** are small pieces of a hard material like glass or wood, each with a hole through the middle. They can be threaded onto a piece of string or wire to make something like a necklace or bracelet. They can also be sewn onto a dress or cushion as a decoration; you can talk about a **beaded** dress or cushion.

❑ A **bead** of moisture is a small drop of it. If something is **beaded** with moisture, it is covered with small drops.

beading is a narrow strip of wood for decorating or edging things like doors and furniture.

beady eyes are small, round, and bright. ◇ If you say someone has a **beady eye** on something, you mean they are paying close attention to it.

beagle The **beagle** is a short-haired black and brown hunting dog with long droopy ears and short legs.

beak A bird's **beak** is the hard curved or pointed part of its mouth. Different birds have different shaped beaks, depending on what they feed on.

beaker A **beaker** is (a) a large drinking cup without a handle. (b) a glass or plastic jar with a pouring lip, used in chemistry.

beam (beaming, beamed) ❑ If someone **beams,** they smile broadly because they are happy or pleased.

❑ A **beam** of light is a ray of it shining from something like a torch or the sun. You can also talk about a **beam** of something like electric waves or particles. ◇ If you **beam** a signal or information somewhere, you send it by radio waves.

❑ A **beam** is also a long thick bar of wood, metal, or concrete, especially one used to support the roof of a building. **Beamed** is used to describe the parts of a building where wooden beams can be seen. *...beamed ceilings.*

bean Beans are the pods of certain tall climbing plants, or the seeds inside the pods, which are eaten as vegetables. ◇ Some other seeds are also called **beans,** for example the seeds which coffee, cocoa, and some kinds of oil are made from.

beansprout Beansprouts are small shoots growing from beans, which you can eat raw or cooked. They are often used in Chinese food.

bear (bearing, bore, have borne) ❑ **Bears** are large wild animals with thick fur and sharp claws.

❑ If you **bear** something somewhere, you carry it there. You can also say a vehicle **bears** something or someone somewhere. ◇ If someone is **bearing** news or information, they are taking it somewhere. ◇ People who have the right to **bear arms** have the right to carry a gun.

❑ If something **bears** someone **out,** or **bears out** what they are saying, it supports what they are saying.

❑ **Bear** can be used instead of 'have' to say someone or something has a particular mark or feature. *He was still bearing the marks of an eye injury.* ◇ If something **bears** a resemblance to something else, it is like it. ◇ If someone or something **bears** a title or name, they have it. ◇ If a no-

tice **bears** particular words, those words are on it. *...a placard bearing the words 'Safety Helmet Area'.*

❑ If something **bears** a heavy weight, it supports it.

❑ If you **bear** pain or difficulty, you put up with it. *He bore his illness with remarkable courage.* ◇ If you **bear up** when you are having problems or suffering pain, you stay cheerful and brave.

❑ If you **bear** the cost of something, you have to pay for it. *Families with children are bearing a bigger share of the tax burden.*

❑ If someone is responsible for something bad which has happened, you can say they **bear** the responsibility for it.

❑ When a woman **bears** a baby, she gives birth to it. ◇ When a tree or plant **bears** flowers, fruit, or leaves, it produces them.

❑ If you **bear** someone a grudge, you are resentful towards them because of something they have done. Similarly, you can talk about **bearing** ill will towards someone.

❑ If someone **brings** pressure or influence **to bear** on you, they use it to try and persuade you to do something.

❑ If you are driving somewhere and you **bear** left or **bear** right, you turn slightly in that direction. ◇ If someone or something is **bearing down** on you, they are moving towards you in a threatening way.

❑ If someone asks you to **bear with** them, they are asking you to be patient with them.

❑ **bear in mind:** see mind. ◇ **bear witness:** see witness.

❑ See also **bearing.**

bearable If something is **bearable,** you can put up with it, although it is not pleasant.

beard (bearded) A man's **beard** is the hair on his chin and cheeks. If a man has a beard, you can describe him as **bearded.** *...a bearded clergyman.*

bearer Some kinds of people who carry things are called **bearers.** *...a stretcher bearer... ...pall bearers.* ◇ The **bearer** of something like news is the person bringing it. ◇ The **bearer** of something like a passport is the person entitled to have it in their possession. ◇ The **bearer** of a name or title is the person who has it.

bearing ❑ If something has a **bearing** on a situation, it has a connection with it or an effect on it. *The level of aid would have a bearing on the speed at which reform would go forward.*

❑ A person's **bearing** is the way they move or stand. *He is straight-backed with an imposing military bearing.*

❑ A **bearing** is part of a machine which supports another part, especially a part which reduces friction.

❑ If you **get** or **find your bearings,** you find out where you are or what to do next. If you **lose your bearings,** you are not sure where you are or what you should be doing.

bearskin A **bearskin** is a tall fur hat worn by soldiers of some British regiments on ceremonial occasions.

beast ❑ A **beast** is an animal, especially a large fierce one. ◇ A man who behaves with great cruelty is sometimes called a **beast.**

❑ When people talk about **the nature of the beast,** they are talking about a characteristic someone or something has which is part of what they are and is unlikely to change. *Man needs enemies; that is the nature of the beast.*

beastly behaviour is very unpleasant.

beat (beating, beat *not* 'beated', have beaten) ❑ If you **beat**

someone in a game or competition, you win. You say the person who has lost is **beaten**; if they lose badly, you say they take a **beating**.

❏ If you **beat** a record, you improve on it and set a new one. ◇ If you **beat** a problem or difficulty, you solve it or deal with it successfully. If you are **beaten** by a problem, you fail to solve it or deal with it. ◇ If you say something **beats** something else, you mean it is better. *Being happy and fit beats being depressed or in pain.*

❏ If someone **beats** another person or **beats them up**, they hit them hard and repeatedly. When this happens to someone, you say they have been **beaten** or have suffered a **beating**. ◇ **Beat** is used with 'against', 'at', or 'on' to say someone hits something repeatedly and forcibly. *...a man beating his head against the wall.* ◇ If you **beat** something like a piece of metal or a metal object, you hit or hammer it to flatten it. ◇ If you **beat** something like a drum, you hit it repeatedly. You can talk about the **beat** or **beating** of a drum, or say someone **beats out** a rhythm on it.

❏ If someone **beats a path to your door**, they make a determined effort to see you. *He hand-crafts bats of such quality that many of the world's top batsmen beat a path to his door in Somerset.*

❏ If you **beat off** someone who is attacking you, you successfully defend yourself. You can also say you **beat off** something such as competition or a challenge. ◇ If you **beat** someone **down** when they are trying to sell you something, you persuade them to accept a lower price. You can also say you **beat** their price **down.**

❏ You say the sun is **beating down** when it is very bright and hot. If you say the rain is **beating down,** you mean it is raining very hard.

❏ If you **beat** something like an egg or cake mixture, you mix it thoroughly with a fork or whisk.

❏ When a bird **beats** its wings, it moves them up and down.

❏ The **beat** of a person's heart or pulse is its regular rhythm. You talk about someone's heart or pulse **beating**. ◇ The **beat** of a piece of music is its regular rhythm. You can describe the rhythm of a piece of music by saying it has a certain number of **beats** to the bar. ◇ If you **beat time** to a piece of music, you move your foot or hand in time with the rhythm. A conductor **beats** time with a baton to show how fast music should be played or sung.

❏ The **beat** of someone like a police officer is the area they are responsible for and which they patrol regularly. If you say someone like this is **on the beat,** you mean they are on duty walking round their area.

❏ **beat about the bush**: see bush. ◇ **beat a retreat**: see retreat.

beater A **beater** is a person employed to flush out game birds or animals and drive them from cover. ◇ **Beater** is also used to talk about (a) someone who hits another person. *...a wife beater.* (b) a device for beating something. *...a carpet beater.* (c) someone or something that successfully deals with a problem or difficulty. *...an inflation beater.*

beatific (*pron:* bee-at-tif-ic) is used to describe someone's expression when it shows great calm and happiness.

beatify (*pron:* bee-at-if-fie) (beatifies, beatifying, beatified; beatification) In the Roman Catholic church, when a dead person is **beatified**, the Pope formally declares them to

be a blessed or holy person; this is usually the first step towards making them a saint. You talk about the **beatification** of someone like this.

beatitude (*pron:* bee-at-it-tude) is extreme blessedness or happiness.

beatnik Beatniks were young people in the late 1950s and early 1960s who showed their rebellion against society by dressing and behaving in an unconventional way.

beau (*pron:* boh) (*plural:* beaus *or* beaux, *both pron:* boze) A woman's **beau** is her boyfriend or admirer. ◇ In the 17th and 18th centuries, a man who wore very fashionable clothes was called a **beau.**

beautician A **beautician** is a person whose job is giving people beauty treatments.

beautiful (beautifully) **Beautiful** is used to describe someone or something that is extremely attractive. *...beautiful countryside... ...a beautifully illustrated book.* ◇ You also use **beautiful** to describe something which is done in a very skilful way. *...a beautiful display of bowling... ...a beautifully taken goal.*

beautify (beautifies, beautifying, beautified) If you **beautify** something, you make it look attractive.

beauty (beauties) ❏ If you think something or someone is beautiful, you can talk about their **beauty**. *...the sheer beauty of the music.* ◇ A beautiful woman is sometimes called a **beauty**. *She was still a beauty in her early 50s.* ◇ The **beauties** of something are its beautiful qualities or features. *...the beauties of the countryside.*

❏ **Beauty** is used to talk about things to do with make-up and treatments intended to make women look beautiful. *...beauty treatments.*

❏ You can show admiration for something by calling it a **beauty**. *His second goal was a beauty.* ◇ The **beauty** of something is what makes it so good or special. *The beauty of this job is that you are constantly learning.*

beauty contest A **beauty contest** is a competition for young women in which a panel of judges decides which of the entrants is the most beautiful.

beauty queen A **beauty queen** is a woman who has won a beauty contest.

beauty spot A **beauty spot** is a place famous for its beautiful countryside or views.

beaver (beavering, beavered) ❏ The **beaver** is a furry animal like a very large rat with a big flat tail. Beavers live partly on land and partly in the water. Their back feet are webbed and they have large front teeth for gnawing bark and felling trees to build dams.

❏ If someone **beavers** or **beavers away** at something, they work very hard at it.

becalmed If a sailing ship is **becalmed**, it cannot move because there is no wind. You say something like a process or system is **becalmed** when it has got stuck because conditions are not right for it to make progress. *...Britain's becalmed manufacturing industry.*

became See become.

because is used to show the reason for something. *There's been no play at Old Trafford because of rain.*

beck If you are at someone's **beck and call,** you have to be constantly available and ready to do what they ask.

beckon (beckoning, beckoned) If you **beckon** to someone, you indicate with your hand or finger that you want them to come towards you. ◇ If something **beckons**

you, it appears so interesting or attractive that you want to become involved with it. *...mountains where the dramatic slopes beckon walkers and horse riders.*

become (becoming, became, have become) ❑ If someone or something **becomes** a particular thing, they start to be that thing, or they change or develop into it. *The crowd became angry... The seaside is fast becoming a vast caravan park.*

❑ If you wonder **what has become of** someone or something, you wonder what has happened to them. You can also wonder **what will become of** someone or something.

❑ If something **becomes** you, it suits you, or seems right for you. You say something like this is **becoming**. *I have to say that the uniform is most becoming.*

becquerel (*pron:* be-ke-rel) Radioactive activity is measured in **becquerels**. 'Becquerels' is usually written 'Bq'.

B.Ed. A **B.Ed.** is a university degree in education. B.Ed. stands for 'Bachelor of Education'.

bed (bedding, bedded) ❑ A **bed** is a piece of furniture for sleeping on. ◇ When people talk about the number of **beds** in a place like a hospital or hotel, they mean the number of people it can accommodate overnight.

❑ When a person or animal **beds down**, they settle down to sleep. ◇ When a system or organization is **bedded down**, it becomes established and starts working. *He believed more time should be allowed to bed down the existing reforms.*

❑ **Bed** is used to talk about something which something else rests on. For example, you can say food is served on a bed of rice or lettuce.

❑ A flower **bed** is a part of a garden or park where flowers are grown.

❑ The **bed** of the sea, a river, or a lake is its bottom.

❑ bed of roses: see rose. ◇ bed of nails: see nail.

bed and breakfast is a system in which you pay for a room for the night with breakfast the following morning. A **bed and breakfast** is a house providing low-cost accommodation like this.

bed linen is sheets and pillowcases.

bedclothes are the sheets and covers you have over you in bed.

bedding is sheets, blankets, and other covers used on beds.

❑ **Bedding plants** are flowering plants which have been grown from seed in pots or seed-trays and planted out into flower beds when they are big enough. They are removed when they have finished flowering.

bedeck (*pron:* bid-dek) If something is **bedecked** with flags or flowers, it is decorated with them.

bedevil (*pron:* bid-dev-ill) (bedevilling, bedevilled) If you are **bedevilled** by someone or something, they keep causing you problems or difficulties.

bedlam If you say a place or situation is **bedlam**, you mean it is very noisy and confused.

bedpan A **bedpan** is a shallow bowl which people use as a toilet when they are too ill to get out of bed.

bedraggled is used to describe someone or something that is untidy, wet, or dirty.

bedridden is used to describe someone who is so ill or disabled they cannot get out of bed.

bedrock is the solid rock underneath soil or loose rocks.

◇ The **bedrock** of something like a belief or system is the principles, ideas, or facts it is based on. You also use **bedrock** to describe people or things that form the foundation of something. *Education is the bedrock of civilized society.*

bedroom A **bedroom** is a room for sleeping in.

bedside ❑ If you are at a sick person's **bedside**, you are standing or sitting next to the bed they are lying in. ◇ A **bedside** table is a small table next to someone's bed. ◇ **Bedside** reading consists of books and other things suitable for reading in bed before you go to sleep.

❑ A doctor's **bedside manner** is their behaviour towards their patients.

bedsit (bedsitter) A **bedsit** or **bedsitter** is a rented room, furnished as a combined living-room and bedroom.

bedspread A **bedspread** is a decorative cover put on top of other covers on a bed.

bedstead A **bedstead** is the metal or wooden frame of an old-fashioned bed which the mattress rests on.

bedtime A person's **bedtime** is the time they usually go to bed. ◇ **Bedtime** is used to talk about things to do with going to bed, for example bedtime drinks or bedtime stories.

bee Bees are four-winged insects which make a loud buzzing noise when they fly. They usually live in large groups and make honey and wax. They can sting if provoked.

bee-keeper A **bee-keeper** is a person who keeps bees and collects their honey.

Beeb People sometimes call the BBC the **Beeb**.

beech (beeches) The **beech** is a large tree with a smooth grey trunk.

beef (beefing, beefed) Beef is the meat of a cow, bull, or ox. ◇ If you **beef** something **up**, you make it stronger, more effective, or more interesting. *Most governments have confined themselves to beefing up security at airports... Coverage of news and current affairs had to be beefed up.*

beefburger Beefburgers are flat round cakes of minced beef, mixed with flavourings. They are grilled or fried and often served in a bap.

Beefeater The Beefeaters are the guards at the Tower of London, who wear a uniform in the style of the 16th century. They are also called **Yeoman Warders**. The Yeomen of the Guard, who wear a similar uniform, are also sometimes called **Beefeaters**.

beefy (beefier, beefiest) Beefy is used to describe a person, usually a man, who is strong and muscular. ◇ Beefy is also used to describe things which are strong and forceful. *...a beefy speech from the top table.*

beehive A **beehive** is a man-made structure to keep bees in, so their honey can be collected by the person who looks after them.

been ❑ See be.

❑ If you have **been** to a place, you have visited it.

beep (beeping, beeped) If a device **beeps** or makes a **beep**, it makes a short high-pitched sound.

beer (beery) ❑ Beer is an alcoholic drink brewed from hops and malt. ◇ Beery people drink a lot of beer. Their behaviour and lifestyle can also be called **beery**.

❑ If you say something is **small beer**, you mean it is small or unimportant compared to other things of the same kind.

beeswax is wax produced by bees. It is used to make candles and furniture polish.

beet is a root vegetable used for cattle food. ◇ In the US, **beet** is the usual word for beetroot. ◇ See also **sugar beet**.

beetle Beetles are insects whose front wings form a hard covering over their rear wings when they are not flying.

beetroot is a dark red root vegetable which is often eaten in salads.

befall (befalling, befell, have befallen) If something bad or unlucky **befalls** someone, it happens to them.

befit (befitting, befitted) If you say something **befits** a person or thing, you mean it is suitable for them. *She never offered him a post befitting his seniority and experience.*

before ❑ If something happens **before** a certain time or event, it happens at an earlier time.

❑ **Before** is used to say something has happened on an earlier occasion. *The president has made such appeals many times before.* ◇ **Before** is used with 'not' or 'never' to say something is happening for the first time. *Many had never set foot on a yacht before.*

❑ **Before** is used to say what must be done or provided to make something possible. *You need £3,000 before you can move.* ◇ **Before** is used to warn someone who is intending to do something that they should do something else first. *Think carefully before you invest your time and money.* ◇ **Before** is used to say how long something takes. *It was several minutes before police were able to restore order.*

❑ If something is **before** you, it is in front of you. *The medicine was placed before me.* Similarly, you say an event takes place **before** a crowd of people. ◇ If you stand **before** something like a building, you stand in front of it. ◇ When an accused person appears in court, you say they are brought **before** the judge or magistrate. ◇ When something is considered by a committee, you can say it goes **before** them.

beforehand is used to say something has been prepared or arranged in advance, or someone has been told about something in advance. *The pieces they performed had been thoroughly learned beforehand... His department had been warned beforehand of a planned breakout.*

befriend If you **befriend** someone, you make friends with them.

befuddle (befuddling, befuddled) If something **befuddles** someone, it makes them confused and muddled.

beg (begging, begged) ❑ If you **beg** someone to do something, you ask them to do it in an anxious or eager way.

❑ When people **beg**, they ask other people to give them money or food, because they are poor. ◇ A **begging bowl** is a container people collect money in when they are begging. If you say a country or organization is holding out a **begging bowl,** you mean they are asking other people or countries for money or some other kind of aid.

❑ If you say something is **going begging,** you mean it is available for anyone who wants it. *Prices remain at 1990 levels and with marina berths going begging, boat ownership will never be cheaper.*

❑ beg the question: see **question**.

began See **begin**.

beggar (beggaring, beggared) A person who begs is called a **beggar**. ◇ If you say something **beggars** belief or **beggars** description, you mean it is impossible to believe it

or describe it.

begin (beginning, began, have begun) ❑ If you **begin** to do something, you start doing it. If you **begin** something, you start doing it, saying it, or dealing with it. If you **begin with** a particular thing, it is the first thing you say, do, or deal with. *We begin with this announcement by the Home Secretary.*

❑ When something **begins**, it starts to happen. The **beginning** of something is the time it starts, or its earliest part. *...the beginning of the epidemic... ...the beginning of the 17th century.* ◇ If something **begins** as a particular thing, it is like that at first, before it changes to something else. *What began as a pastime quickly became an obsession.*

❑ You use **to begin with** to talk about the earliest part of something, before it changes. *He will be employed on a part-time basis to begin with.* ◇ You also say **to begin with** when you are mentioning the first of a series of things. *To begin with, I know nothing about sailing.*

beginner A **beginner** is someone who has just started learning how to do something, and is not yet very good at it.

begonia Begonias are tropical flowering plants with ornamental leaves and waxy flowers. In this country, they are grown as bedding plants or pot plants.

begrudge (begrudging, begrudged) If you **begrudge** doing something, you are unwilling to do it. *People begrudge spending £15 to £20 on oil to protect their engine.* ◇ If someone **begrudges** you something you have, they are resentful or envious because of it. *Nobody could begrudge the Sussex girl her victory.*

beguile *(pron: big-ile)* (beguiling, beguiled; beguilingly) If you are **beguiled** by something or find it **beguiling**, you are delighted by it. *...beguiling singing... At times he can be beguilingly charming.* ◇ You can also say someone is **beguiled** by something when they are misled by it, because it seems pleasing or attractive. *The idea of victory through air power alone has long beguiled military planners.*

begum *(pron: bay-gum)* is a title used by a Muslim woman of high rank, especially in India. *...Mirza Begum... ...Begum Khaleda Zia.*

begun See **begin**.

behalf If you do something on someone's **behalf**, you do it for them. *The award was received on his behalf by his son... He is speaking on behalf of a very large proportion of the parliamentary group.*

behave (behaving, behaved) ❑ **Behave** is used to describe the way someone acts on a particular occasion. For example, you say someone behaves sensibly or behaves like a coward. ◇ If you **behave** or **behave yourself,** you act in a way people think is correct. If someone acts like this, you say they are **well-behaved;** if they act in a way you do not approve of, you say they are **badly behaved**.

❑ If you say an object or substance **behaves** in a particular way, you mean it acts or functions that way. *...the ways in which electrons behave within atoms.*

behaviour *(American spelling:* **behavior**) A person's **behaviour** is the way they behave. ◇ The **behaviour** of an object or substance is the way it acts, functions, or changes.

behead (beheading, beheaded) If someone is **beheaded,** their head is cut off.

beheld See **behold**.

behemoth (*pron:* bi-hee-moth) In the Old Testament, the behemoth was a huge beast, probably a hippopotamus. ◇ Other things which seem extremely large can be called **behemoths**. *The city is a sprawling behemoth... IBM, another behemoth, is splitting itself into smaller operating units.*

behest If you do something at someone's **behest**, you do it because they order you to, or request you to.

behind ❑ If one thing is **behind** another, it is at the back of it, or on the other side of it. ◇ If you are **behind** someone, you are facing their back, or following them.

   ❑ If you are **behind** with something, you are failing to keep up with it. ◇ In a sport or competition, you say a person or team is **behind** when they are losing. If at the finish they come **close behind** someone, they are only just beaten.

   ❑ If you leave someone or something **behind,** you do not take them with you. ◇ If you stay **behind,** you do not go somewhere with other people.

   ❑ If you want to know what is **behind** someone's actions, you want to know the reasons for them. ◇ You use **behind** to say who is responsible for something. *...the company behind the alleged sale of the chemical.* ◇ You use **behind** to mention the way someone appears, before you say what they are really like. *Behind her grandmotherly appearance, she is a shrewd political operator.*

   ❑ If you say you are **behind** a person or idea, you mean you support them.

   ❑ If a part of someone's life is **behind** them, it is over. If an experience is **behind** you, it is over, and you do not need to worry about it any more.

   ❑ A person's **behind** is the part of their body they sit on.

behold (beholding, beheld; beholder) If you **behold** something, you see it, notice it, or look at it. *Beauty is often said to be in the eye of the beholder.*

beholden If you are **beholden** to someone, you are under an obligation to them.

behoves If it **behoves** you to do something, it is necessary or fitting for you to do it.

beige (*pron:* bayzh; *the 'zh' sounds like 's' in 'pleasure'*) Beige is a pale creamy-brown colour.

being ❑ See be.

   ❑ A **being** is a living person or creature.

   ❑ When something comes **into being**, it starts to exist. *Channel Four came into being in 1982.*

bejewelled (*American spelling:* bejeweled) A **bejewelled** person is wearing a lot of jewellery. ◇ A **bejewelled** object is decorated with jewels.

belabour (belabouring, belaboured) (*American spelling:* belabor, *etc*) If you **belabour** someone, (a) you hit them hard and repeatedly. *She belaboured them with her handbag.* (b) you criticize them severely. *He belaboured the Government for allowing academic salaries to fall.*

belated (belatedly) **Belated** is used to talk about things happening later than they should. *...a belated Christmas present... I've just enjoyed reading – very belatedly – an article in last September's issue.*

belch (belches, belching, belched) When someone **belches** or lets out a **belch**, wind from their stomach comes out noisily through their mouth. ◇ If something **belches** smoke or steam, it sends out large amounts of it.

beleaguered (*pron:* bil-leeg-ed) You say a person or or-ganization is **beleaguered** when they are having a lot of difficulties, or being criticized by a lot of people. ◇ A **beleaguered** place is surrounded by enemies.

belfry (belfries) The **belfry** of a church is the tower or steeple where the bells are.

Belgian is used to talk about people and things in or from Belgium. *...Belgian beers.* ◇ A **Belgian** is someone who comes from Belgium.

belie (belying, belied) If one thing **belies** another, it makes it seem surprising. *Her fragile looks belie her determination.* ◇ You also say something **belies** something else when it shows it is not true or correct. *The economy has taken a turn for the worse, belying government forecasts.*

belief (beliefs) If you have a particular **belief,** you think something is true. *Contrary to popular belief, the police have almost no powers over noise.* ◇ A person's **belief** or **beliefs** are their religious faith, or the principles they try to live by. *She had strong feminist beliefs.*

believable If what someone says is **believable,** you can accept that it might be true. ◇ If you say something in a book or film is **believable,** you mean something like that could happen or exist in real life.

believe (believing, believed; believer) ❑ If you **believe** something, you think it is true. *There are still some people who believe that the earth is flat.* ◇ If you **believe** someone, you feel sure they are telling the truth.

   ❑ If you **believe in** God, you feel sure he exists. People who believe in God are often called **believers**. ◇ If you **believe in** something like ghosts or miracles, you are sure they exist or can happen.

   ❑ If you **believe in** something like a principle, you think it is right. You can say someone is a **believer** in something like this. *...believers in human rights.* ◇ If you **believe in** a person or a project, you think they will be successful.

Belisha beacon (*pron:* bel-lee-sha) A **Belisha beacon** is a post with a round orange light on top which flashes on and off. Belisha beacons are used at zebra crossings to warn motorists that people may be crossing the road.

belittle (belittling, belittled) If you **belittle** someone or something, you make them out to be unimportant or of little value.

bell ❑ A **bell** is a small device which makes a ringing sound to attract people's attention, for example a doorbell or a bicycle bell.

   ❑ A **bell** is also a cup-shaped metal object with a loose piece inside called a clapper which hits the sides and makes a loud sound. Bells of this kind can be quite small or they can be very large, for example the bells in a church tower. The people who ring church bells are called **bell ringers;** what they do is called **bell ringing.**

bell-bottomed (bell-bottoms) **Bell-bottomed** trousers or **bell-bottoms** are trousers which flare out from below the knee and become very wide round the ankles.

belladonna or **deadly nightshade** is a bushy plant from which several important drugs are obtained. Its leaves are poisonous.

belle A beautiful woman used to be called a **belle.** For example, people used to call the most beautiful woman at a dance 'the belle of the ball'.

bellicose (bellicosity) **Bellicose** behaviour is aggressive and threatening. You can call someone who behaves like this **bellicose** or talk about their **bellicosity.**

belligerent (belligerently; belligerence, belligerency) Belligerent behaviour is hostile and aggressive. *'Why not?' he asked, belligerently.* You can call a person or country belligerent or talk about their **belligerence** or **belligerency**. ◇ The countries or armies that start a war can be called the **belligerents**.

bellow ❑ If someone **bellows** or lets out a **bellow**, they call out in a deep loud voice. ◇ When an animal like a bull **bellows**, it makes a deep loud sound.

❑ A **bellows** (*plural:* bellows) is (a) a device for blowing air into a fire to make it burn more fiercely. (b) part of an instrument like an accordion or organ, which blows air into the reeds or pipes to produce the sound.

belly (bellies, bellied) A person's **belly** is their stomach. ◇ The **belly** of an animal like a cow or horse is the underneath part of its body. ◇ The **belly** of a ship or plane is its underneath part. ◇ **-bellied** is added to other words to describe the belly of a person, animal, or thing. *...the yellow-bellied sea-snake... ...a wide-bellied US cargo plane.*

belly dance A belly dance is a type of Middle Eastern dance performed by a woman making movements of her belly and hips. A woman who does this kind of dance is called a **belly dancer**; what she does is called belly dancing.

belong ❑ If something **belongs** to you, you own it, or it is yours.

❑ If you **belong** to an organization, you are a member of it. Similarly, you can say someone or something **belongs** to a group of people or things. *He belongs to a new generation of politicians... Cauliflowers, cabbages, sprouts and kale all belong to the same class of plants.*

❑ If something **belongs** in a place, that is where it is usually kept. ◇ You also say someone or something **belongs** somewhere when you are expressing an opinion about where they should be. *The Queen Mary should come back to Southampton where she belongs.* ◇ If you say you **belong** to a place, you mean you feel happy and comfortable there. Similarly, you can say you **belong** with a group of people. You can also say you have a sense of **belonging** to a place or with a group of people.

❑ If something like a building **belongs** to a period in the past, that is when it was built. ◇ You also say something **belongs** to an earlier period when it is typical of that period and now seems out-of-date. *They appeared still to hold attitudes which belonged to the 1970s.*

belongings Someone's **belongings** are their personal possessions.

beloved (*pron:* bi-luv-id) is used to describe someone or something a person loves. *...his beloved wife... A few years ago he left his beloved London.* ◇ A person's **beloved** is the person they love. ◇ If someone or something is loved by a group of people, you can say they are **beloved** (*pron:* bi-luvd) by them. *These books are still beloved by me and my children.*

below ❑ If something is **below** something else, it is in a lower position, or underneath it.

❑ **Below** is also used to say something is less than an amount, rate, or level. *The temperature dropped below freezing point.*

❑ In a piece of writing, **below** is used to say something will come later in the text. *Most good libraries will have some of the books listed below.*

belt ❑ A **belt** is a strip of leather or cloth you fasten round your waist.

❑ If you say remarks or actions are **below the belt**, you mean they are unkind or unfair. ◇ If you say someone has something like knowledge **under their belt**, you mean they have acquired it. *... with a decade of experience under our belts.* ◇ If you have to **tighten your belt**, you have to cut back on what you spend or use, because you cannot afford as much as before. When you do this, you say you are **belt-tightening**.

❑ A **belt** is a circular strip of rubber used to drive a moving part in a machine.

❑ A **belt** of something is a long narrow strip of it. For example, you can talk about a belt of land, sea, or trees.

❑ If you **belt** somewhere, you move or travel very fast. You can also say someone **belts** through something when they deal with it very quickly.

❑ If you **belt** someone or something, you hit them hard. ◇ If someone **belts out** a song or tune, they sing or play it very loudly.

bemoan (bemoaning, bemoaned) If you **bemoan** something, you grumble about it. *She was bemoaning the shortage of qualified staff.*

bemused (bemusement) If you are **bemused** by something, you are puzzled or confused by it. *A look of bemusement spread on their faces.*

bench (benches) ❑ A **bench** is a long seat for two or more people, usually made of wood or metal. ◇ In Parliament, the seats used by MPs are called **benches**. You talk, for example, about the government benches or opposition benches. *His remark brought angry reaction from the Labour benches.* See also **back bench, front bench**.

❑ In court, the judge or magistrates are sometimes called the **bench**. *The chairman of the bench imposed a fine.*

❑ A **bench** is also a long narrow table in a factory, laboratory, or workshop.

benchmark A **benchmark** is a mark on a fixed object such as a stone post, showing the height above sea level. ◇ You say something is a **benchmark** when its quality, quantity, or capability is known and can be used as a standard by which to judge other things. *Their pay deals are regarded as a benchmark for the rest of the industry.*

bend (bending, bent) ❑ When you **bend** or **bend down**, you lean forwards and downwards. ◇ If you **bend** your knee or elbow, you move it so the joint forms an angle; you then say the knee or elbow is **bent**. See also **bended**. ◇ If you **bend** something which is flat or straight, you force it into a curved or angled shape.

❑ When a road or river changes direction, you say it **bends**. The place where it does this is called a **bend**.

❑ When someone is persuaded or forced to change their opinion or attitude, you can say they **bend**. *Do you think she's likely to bend on her attitude to Europe?*

❑ If someone **bends the rules**, they interpret them in a way which allows them to do things the rules were meant to forbid.

❑ **bend over backwards**: see **backward**. ◇ **the bends**: see **decompression**. ◇ See also **bent**.

bended If someone asks for something **on bended knee**, they do it in a very humble way.

beneath ❑ If something is **beneath** something else, it is in a lower position, or underneath it.

❑ If you say something is **beneath** someone, you mean they would object to doing it, because they would regard it as undignified, or think they were too important or intelligent for it.

❑ If at work you have a certain number of people beneath you, you are in charge of them.

benediction A **benediction** is a prayer asking for God's blessing, especially at the end of a religious service. ◇ A **benediction** is also a gesture in which you ask God to bless someone. *He lifted a hand in benediction.*

benefactor A person's or organization's **benefactor** is someone who helps them out by giving them money.

beneficial is used to describe things which do good or are helpful. *The new agreement is extremely beneficial to the country... The treatment appears to have had beneficial results.*

beneficiary (beneficiaries) A **beneficiary** of something is someone who benefits from it. ◇ A person who is left money or property in someone's will is also called a **beneficiary.**

benefit (benefiting, benefited) ❑ If something **benefits** you or you **benefit** from it, you are better off as a result of it. You call something like this a **benefit.** *...the benefits of fresh air.* You can also say something is to your **benefit** or of **benefit** to you.

❑ If you have the **benefit** of something, it gives you an advantage. *...the benefit of a good education.*

❑ If you do something for someone's **benefit**, you do it especially for them. *This information was broadcast from the public address system for the benefit of the spectators.* ◇ If you give someone the **benefit of the doubt**, you accept what they say as true, because you cannot prove otherwise.

❑ **Benefit** is money paid out by the DSS, for example child benefit or housing benefit.

Benelux The **Benelux** countries are Holland, Belgium, and Luxembourg.

benevolent (benevolence) **Benevolent** people are kind, helpful, and tolerant. You talk about the **benevolence** of people like these.

benevolent fund A **benevolent fund** is money kept to help members of a group of people when they are in need.

benighted is sometimes used to describe people who are thought to be unfortunate or ignorant.

benign (*pron:* bin-**nine**) (benignly) **Benign** people are kind, gentle, and harmless. *She smiled benignly.* ◇ A **benign** tumour or disease is one which will not cause death or serious harm.

bent ❑ See bend.

❑ If something is **bent**, it is not straight.

❑ If you are **bent** on doing something, you are determined to do it. ◇ If you have a **bent** for something, you like doing it or are naturally good at it.

benzene is a colourless flammable liquid obtained from petroleum. It is used to make a wide variety of chemical products including detergents, dyes, and insecticides.

benzine (*pron:* benz-**een**) is a mixture of hydrocarbons obtained by distilling petroleum. It is used for dry-cleaning and as a cleaning fluid.

bequeath If someone **bequeaths** money or property to you, they leave it to you in their will. You can also say a

dead person **bequeaths** other things, for example their beliefs or ideas. *His aunt had bequeathed him a deep interest in medicine.* ◇ If someone dies or goes away leaving a situation for someone else to deal with, you can say they **bequeath** them the situation.

bequest A **bequest** is money or property which someone leaves you in their will.

berate (berating, berated) If you **berate** someone, you tell them off angrily.

bereaved (bereavement) A **bereaved** person has had a relative or close friend who has recently died. You say someone like this has suffered a **bereavement.** Bereaved people are sometimes called **the bereaved.**

bereft If you say someone or something is **bereft** of something, you mean they are completely without it. *Its government seems bereft of ideas... The novel is bereft of vitality.* You can also say a place or organization is **bereft** of things which are needed or important. *...houses bereft of electricity.*

beret (*pron:* ber-ray) A **beret** is a round flat hat with no brim, made of soft material.

Bermuda shorts are close-fitting shorts which come down to the knees.

berry (berries) **Berries** are small round soft fruit.

berserk If people go **berserk**, they lose control of themselves and become violent and destructive.

berth A **berth** is a space in a harbour where a ship can be tied up and stay for a period of time. When a ship moves into a space like this, you say it **berths** or is **berthed.** ◇ A **berth** is also a bed in a boat, train, or caravan. ◇ If you **give** someone or something **a wide berth,** you avoid them.

beseech (beseeches, beseeching, beseeched *or* besought; beseechingly) If you **beseech** someone to do something, you appeal to them to do it, in an anxious and urgent way.

beset (besetting, beset *not* 'besetted') If you are **beset** by problems, there are a lot of them and you keep coming up against them.

beside (besides) ❑ If someone or something is **beside** another person or thing, they are at their side, or next to them. ◇ You use **beside** when you are saying how something seems when compared to something else. *By the 1970s, zoos seemed drab beside theme parks and other new entertainments.*

❑ You say people are **beside themselves** with anger or fear when they feel it so strongly they have lost control over what they are saying and doing.

❑ You use **beside** or **besides** (a) when saying an additional thing about someone or something. *Beside being the guardians of our frontiers, they will be the guardians of our Amazon rainforest.* (b) when mentioning an additional person or thing something applies to. *He did, however, blame others beside himself... There are other risks besides.* ◇ **Besides** is also used to introduce an additional point. *Besides, breast-milk is naturally clean and wholesome.*

besiege (besieging, besieged) If armed forces **besiege** a place, they surround it and try to capture it. ◇ You say other people **besiege** a place when they gather there and try to get in, because they want something, or want to see someone who is there. *He agreed to make a statement to the press, who were besieging his hotel.*

besmirch (besmirches, besmirching, besmirched) If something besmirches a person's reputation, it damages it.

besotted If you are besotted with someone, you are in love with them and constantly thinking about them. Similarly, you can say someone is besotted with something like an idea, meaning they are very excited and enthusiastic about it.

besought See beseech.

bespectacled A bespectacled person wears glasses.

bespoke is used to describe clothes made specially to suit someone's requirements. A bespoke tailor makes or sells clothes like these. ◇ Bespoke is used to describe other things which are made or arranged to suit a particular person's needs. ...a bespoke holiday service.

best ❑ You use best to describe things which are of the highest quality of their kind. He scored the best try of the match. ◇ Your best friends are your closest friends. ◇ You use best when you are talking about the person most likely to succeed at something, or the method most likely to be effective. ...the person who has the best chance of winning the next election... A transplant operation is the best form of treatment available.
❑ The person or thing that does something best is the one that achieves the highest standard or most successful results. ◇ The thing you do best is the one you are most skilful at.
❑ Best is also used to talk about the most effective or satisfactory way of doing something. ...areas that are best explored on foot... Educationalists are divided about how best to teach reading. ◇ The thing you like best is the one which gives you most pleasure or satisfaction. ◇ The thing someone is best known for is the one people usually associate them with. He is best known for his campaigning on behalf of the disabled.
❑ If you do your best at something or do it as best you can, you try as hard as you can to do it successfully. ◇ If you make the best of an unfavourable situation, you accept it and try to enjoy it or use it to your advantage; you can also say you make the best of a bad job.
❑ A person's best is the highest standard they are capable of. In the final set Edberg showed only glimpses of his best. In sport, best is often used to talk about someone's personal record in an event. He is 126 not out, a career-best... She ran a personal best of 13.01sec for the 100m hurdles. ◇ The best of something is its most impressive or effective parts or features. This is athletics at its best... She was willing to pay for the best that medical science could offer.
❑ If you say something is for the best, you mean it will eventually have good results, and is therefore worthwhile. ◇ You use at best to show you are putting the most favourable interpretation on something which is not good. The outlook for the economy was gloomy at best.
❑ If you are bested by someone, they do something more successfully than you, or beat you in a game or competition.
❑ know best: see know.

best man At a wedding, the best man is the bridegroom's attendant and helper.

best-seller (or bestseller) (best-selling) A best-seller is a book which sells a very large number of copies. A best-selling author writes books like these. ◇ Other things besides books are sometimes called best-sellers. The sur-

prise best-sellers are scooters for very young children.

bestial (bestiality) Bestial behaviour is very unpleasant or disgusting. Behaviour like this is called bestiality.

bestiary (bestiaries) A bestiary is a medieval book containing pictures of real and imaginary animals. Each picture is accompanied by a story with a moral.

bestow (bestowal) If someone bestows a gift or honour on you, they give it to you. You call this the bestowal of a gift or honour.

bestride (bestriding, bestrode) If someone bestrides something, they stand with one leg on each side of it. ◇ When someone was the outstanding figure in an activity over a period of time, you can say they bestrode it. Piggott and Shoemaker were the two jockeys who bestrode international racing after Sir Gordon Richards retired.

bestseller See best-seller.

bet (betting, bet or betted) ❑ If you bet or put a bet on something, you gamble with money on something happening a particular way. He bet his father he could open a vineyard in Utah.
❑ If you are betting on something happening, you are expecting it to happen, and relying on it. Most economists are betting on output starting to rise this year. ◇ If you say the betting is something will happen, you mean it is very likely to happen. You can also say something is a fair bet or a good bet. The betting is the resolution will be passed by the bishops and the clergy... It is a fair bet there will be another cut in interest rates.
❑ If someone is about to make a choice, you use bet to comment on what they might choose. For example, you say something would be 'a good bet' or 'a safe bet'. These companies were always going to be a safe bet for investors.

beta (pron: bee-ta) Beta is β, the second letter of the Greek alphabet. ◇ Beta is used to describe things involving or relating to electrons. For example, a beta particle is an electron sent out from a radioactive nucleus; a beta ray is a stream of beta particles.

beta blocker A beta blocker is a drug which slows down the action of the heart by blocking the action of nerve endings. Beta blockers are used in the treatment of angina and high blood pressure.

bête noire (plural: bêtes noires) (both pron: bet nwahr) If you say a person or thing is your bête noire, you mean you especially dislike them.

betel (pron: bee-tl) The betel is a climbing plant in Asia. The betel nut is the red nut of a kind of palm-tree. Some people chew the nut wrapped in the leaf of the betel plant, as a kind of drug.

betide If you say woe betide the person who does something, you mean something nasty will happen to them if they do it. Woe betide them if they vote against the government.

betoken (betokening, betokened) If something betokens something else, it is a sign of it. His expression betokened embarrassment.

betray (betrayal) If someone you love or trust betrays you, they do something disloyal or treacherous. You call their behaviour a betrayal. ◇ If someone betrays a secret or a confidence, they tell it to other people. ◇ If someone betrays something like an ideal or promise, they go back on it. He is guilty of the fastest betrayal of election promises in history. ◇ If someone betrays their feelings or thoughts, they show them without meaning to. *His parting words betrayed a sense of injustice.*

betrothed (betrothal) If you are **betrothed**, you are engaged to be married. Your **betrothed** is the person you are engaged to. A **betrothal** is an engagement.

better (bettering, bettered; betterment) ❑ **Better** is used to describe things which are of higher quality than other things of the same kind. *They swear their produce tastes better than anything bought in the shops.* ◇ **Better** is also used to describe things which have been improved in some way. *He looks a better, more mature cricketer now.* When something has been improved, you can talk about its **betterment**. *...the betterment of Russian-Japanese relations.*

❑ If you do something **better** than someone else, you are more successful or skilful at it. You can also do one thing **better** than another, or do something **better** than you did it before. ◇ You use **better** when mentioning a more effective or satisfactory way of doing something. *They would have done better to put their money in National Savings.* ◇ If something is **better** known than something else, more people know it than the other thing. Similarly, you can say something is **better** known than it was before, or **better** known in one place than another. ◇ If you like something **better** than something else, it gives you more pleasure or satisfaction.

❑ If you say a sick or injured person is **better**, you mean (a) they are less ill. (b) they are completely recovered.

❑ If you are **better off** than you were before, you have more money or are in a more pleasant situation. Similarly, you can say someone is **better off** than someone else.

❑ If you **get the better** of someone in a contest or argument, you defeat them. ◇ If you **better** what someone else has done, you improve on it.

❑ If something changes **for the better**, it improves. ◇ If you say someone will **be the better for** something, you mean they will benefit from it. ◇ If you say something has happened **for better or worse**, you mean you are not sure whether it is a good thing or a bad thing.

❑ If you say someone **had better** do something, you mean they ought to do it. *Investors who want to secure the best buys had better act fast.* ◇ You say **the sooner the better** to emphasize that you want something to happen as soon as possible. *I want a move for the sake of my career – and the sooner the better... The sooner we reach the decision, the better for all concerned.*

❑ **know better: see** know. ◇ **think better of: see** think.

betting shop A **betting shop** is a place where you go to bet on something like a horse race.

between ❑ If someone or something is **between** two people or things, they are in the middle, with one person or thing on each side. ◇ If something is **between** or **in between** two numbers or points on a scale, it is higher than one and lower than the other.

❑ If you travel **between** two places, you go regularly from one to the other and back again. ◇ **Between** is also used to say an event is held first in one place, then another. *These meetings alternated between Paris and New York.* ◇ The distance **between** two places is the distance from one to the other.

❑ If something happens **between** two times, (a) it begins at one and ends at the other. *He was Prime Minister be-*

tween 1970 and 1974. (b) it happens after the first one but before the second one. *...sometime between May and October next year.*

❑ **Between** is used to talk about two people or groups being involved in some way with each other. *Fighting has continued between government troops and rebels... ...the relationship between the unions and the Labour Party.*

❑ If people have an amount of something **between** them, that is the total amount they have. ◇ When something is divided **between** two people or groups, they each have a share of it.

❑ You talk about a gap **between** two things. *...the widening rift between the poor and the prosperous.*

❑ If something comes or stands **between** you and something you want, it stops you having it.

beverage A **beverage** is a drink.

bevy (bevies) A **bevy** of people or things is a large number of them in one place together. *The ship has recently completed a voyage with a bevy of scientists on board.*

bewail (bewailing, bewailed) If you **bewail** something, you express sorrow or regret about it. *British scientists bewail cuts in the money the government pays for their work.*

beware If you tell someone to **beware** of something, you are warning them to be on their guard against danger or deception. *Beware of schemes promising lots of money without much effort.*

bewilder (bewildering, bewildered; bewilderment) If someone is **bewildered** or in a state of **bewilderment**, they are confused and unable to understand what is going on.

bewitch (bewitches, bewitching, bewitched) If you are **bewitched** by something, it has a strong effect on you, as if you were under a spell. You say something like this is **bewitching**. *North Sligo is bewitching country.* ◇ If a woman **bewitches** a man, he finds her so attractive she can make him do anything she wants.

beyond ❑ If something is **beyond** a wall or river, it is on the far side of it. ◇ If something extends **beyond** a place, it extends to other places. *The conflict has shown signs of spreading beyond the area.* Similarly, you can talk about something extending **beyond** a time, level, or limit.

❑ If a task is **beyond** you, it is too difficult for you. ◇ If you cannot understand something, you can say it is **beyond** you. *Why these books have not been banned is beyond me.* ◇ **Beyond** is used to talk about other things which cannot be done. For example, if you say something is 'beyond belief', you mean nobody could believe it. *In the last few years their world has changed beyond recognition.*

❑ If you say a place is at **the back of beyond**, you mean it is lonely and isolated, and a long way from towns and cities.

bi- Some words beginning with **bi-** can be spelled with a hyphen after the 'i'. For example, 'bicentenary' can be spelled 'bi-centenary'. See entries at **biannual**, **bicentenary**, **bifocals**, **bilateral**, **bilingual**, **bipartisan**.

bi-monthly is used in two ways. Some people use it to say something happens every two months; others use it to say something happens twice a month.

biannual (*or* **bi-annual**) (biannually) **Biannual** and **biannually** are used to describe things which happen twice a year. *...their biannual conference... The honours list is published bi-annually.* See also **biennial**.

bias (biases; biased) ❏ If someone shows a **bias** towards something or someone, they prefer them to other things or people, often unfairly. Similarly, if they show a **bias** against someone or something, they are prejudiced against them. When someone shows a bias in either of these ways, you can say they are **biased**.

❏ A **bias** is also a tendency for things to happen in one way rather than another. *Female chimpanzees show the same left side bias for cradling as human mothers.*

❏ If a piece of cloth is cut on the **bias**, it is cut at an angle to the weave of the cloth. **Bias binding** is a strip of material cut on the bias for extra stretch. It is used to bind the hems or seams of articles of clothing.

bib A **bib** is a small apron tied under the chin. Cloth or plastic bibs are worn by very young children to protect their clothes while they are eating.

bible (biblical) ❏ The **Bible** is the sacred book of the Christian religion. The first part of it, the Old Testament, is also a sacred book for Jews. ◇ **Biblical** is used to talk about things in or relating to the Bible. ...*the biblical account of the creation of man.*

❏ The best or most important book on a subject can be called the **bible** of that subject. *Ramblers say that Wainwright's 50 hand-drawn guide books are the walker's bible.*

bibliography (bibliographies; bibliographical) ❏ A **bibliography** is a list of books on a subject or by a particular author. ◇ The **bibliography** at the end of a book or article is a list of the books and articles used by the author when writing it, or suggested for study.

❏ **Bibliography** is the study of different editions of books. ◇ **Bibliographical** information is information about a book, such as the publisher and date of publication.

bibliophile A **bibliophile** is (a) a person who loves books. (b) a book collector.

bibulous If someone is **bibulous**, they are very fond of alcohol.

bicarbonate of soda or **bicarb** is a white powder used to make cakes rise. It is also used as a medicine to relieve indigestion.

bicentenary (or bi-centenary) (bicentenaries) A **bicentenary** is a year when you celebrate something important which happened exactly 200 years earlier.

bicentennial is the usual American word for a bicentenary.

biceps (plural: biceps) Your **biceps** are the large muscles at the front of your upper arms.

bicker (bickering, bickered) When people **bicker**, they argue or quarrel about unimportant things.

bicycle (bicycling, bicycled) A **bicycle** is a two-wheeled vehicle propelled by pedals. If you **bicycle** somewhere, you go there on a bicycle.

bid (bidding; bid or bade; have bid or have bidden; *if you are talking about the past, you say someone* bid *for something, but that they* bade *someone good morning or* bade *someone to do something*) ❏ If someone **bids** for something or makes a **bid** for it, they try to get it or do it. *Wigan are bidding to win the trophy for a third successive year... ...Northamptonshire's late bid for the championship.*

❏ If you **bid** for something which is being sold or make a **bid** for it, you offer an amount of money for it.

❏ **Bid** is used to talk about greetings. For example, if you **bid** someone good morning, you say good morning to them.

❏ If you **bid** someone to do something, you ask, order, or invite them to do it. If you do someone's **bidding**, you do what they ask, order, or invite you to do. You can also be **bidden** to do something. *He was bidden to lunch on board the flagship.*

biddable A **biddable** person is willing to do what they are told. *At school she had been a most biddable child.*

bidder Someone who makes a bid for something which is being sold is called a **bidder**. If something is sold to the **highest bidder**, it is sold to the person who offers most for it.

bide (biding, bided) If you **bide** your **time**, you wait for a good opportunity before doing something.

bidet (pron: bee-day) A **bidet** is a low basin fitted in a bathroom, for washing your bottom.

biennial is used to describe something which happens once every two years. *The biennial event takes place this year at Farnborough.* See also **biannual**. ◇ **Biennial** plants or **biennials** live for two years; they flower, seed, and die in their second year.

bier (pron: beer) A **bier** is a movable stand or frame on which a corpse or coffin is placed or carried at a funeral.

bifocals (or bi-focals) are spectacles with special lenses. The top part of each lens is for looking at distant things, and the bottom part is for reading and looking at things nearby.

big (bigger, biggest) ❏ **Big** is used to describe things which are of a greater size than normal. ...*big crowds... The figure of £70 million was twice as big as expected.*

❏ **Big** is also used to describe things which are very significant, and people who are powerful and important. *Boredom is a big problem... The government has attracted some big foreign firms into the market* ◇ If you say someone is **big** in something, you mean they are important in it. *The company is big in marine and catastrophe insurance.* ◇ If someone is a **big name**, they are successful and famous. ◇ The **big time** is the highest level of success, fame, or importance in an activity or career. *One way for a young performer to break into the big time is as an 11th-hour substitute.*

❏ **Big business** involves very large companies and very large sums of money. If you say something is **big business**, you mean people spend a lot of money on it and it has become an important commercial activity. *The trade in illegal immigrants has become big business.*

❏ A person's **big** brother or sister is their older brother or sister.

big game Large wild animals like lions and elephants are often called **big game** from the days when people hunted them for sport.

big-hearted If someone is **big-hearted**, they are kind and generous.

big toe A person's **big toe** is the fat one on the inside of their foot.

big top The **big top** is the large round tent which a circus uses for its performances. **Big top** is used to talk about things to do with circuses. ...*traditional big top skills.*

bigamy (bigamist; bigamous) If a person who is already married gets married to someone else, this is called **bigamy**. Someone who does this is called a **bigamist**; you say their second marriage is **bigamous**.

biggish is used to describe people or things which are fairly big.

bigot (bigoted; bigotry) A **bigot** is a person with strong unreasonable attitudes and opinions which they refuse to change. **Bigoted** is used to describe someone like this; their behaviour and attitudes are called **bigotry**.

bigwig Important people are sometimes humorously called **bigwigs**.

bijou (pron: bee-zhoo; the 'zh' sounds like 's' in 'pleasure') Bijou is used to describe places or buildings which are small but very fashionable or elegant. ...a bijou French villa.

bike A bike is a bicycle or motorcycle.

bikini A bikini is a brief two-piece swimming costume worn by women.

bilateral (or bi-lateral) is used to describe things which involve two people, groups, or countries. ...bilateral negotiations... ...a series of bilateral agreements.

bilberry (bilberries) Bilberries are bluish-black berries. They grow on small bushes.

bile is a bitter liquid produced by the liver, stored in the gall bladder, and passed into the bowels to help the digestion of fat. ◇ Bile is also irritable behaviour. He has reserved his bile for investigative journalists.

bilingual (or bi-lingual) If someone is bilingual, they can speak two languages fluently. A bilingual book or document is written in two langauges.

bilious comments show extreme irritation and dislike. ◇ A bilious colour looks revolting. ◇ If you feel bilious, you feel sick and have a headache.

bill ❑ A bill is a written statement of how much money needs to be paid for something. If someone bills you for something, they give or send you the bill. ◇ foot the bill: see foot.

❑ In the US, banknotes are called bills. ◇ In a restaurant, the bill of fare is the menu.

❑ A bill is a poster advertising an event, especially a small poster stuck on an outside wall. ◇ In entertainment, the bill is the performers or acts due to appear in a show. You say someone or something is billed to appear in a show. ◇ If a performer has top billing or is top of the bill, they are the most important person in a show. In other situations, you say something has top billing when it is the most important thing being discussed or dealt with. Trade had top billing at last year's Houston summit. ◇ If someone is given a particular billing, people are told in advance what they are like. The hooligans were living up to their advance billing. ◇ When it has been announced that an event is going to happen, you can say it is billed to happen. ◇ If something is billed as a particular thing, it is advertised as being that thing. The film is billed as a political comedy.

❑ If someone or something fits the bill, they are just what is needed.

❑ In parliament, a bill is a proposed new law which is discussed and then voted on. If it is approved, it becomes an Act. ◇ A bill of rights is a written list of citizens' rights, usually part of the constitution of a country.

❑ If a person is given a clean bill of health, they are declared to be fit and to have nothing physically wrong with them. Similarly, if something like a system or institution is given a clean bill of health, it is officially decided there is

nothing wrong with it.

❑ A bird's bill is its beak.

billboard A billboard is a large board used for displaying posters.

billet (billeting, billeted) When servicemen or women are billeted somewhere, they live in non-military accommodation; this accommodation is called their billets. ◇ You can say other large groups of people are billeted somewhere when accommodation is found for them at short notice. One hundred male students have been billeted in a sports hall.

billet-doux (plural: billets-doux) (both pron: bill-ee-doo) A billet-doux is a love-letter.

billhook A billhook is a cutting tool with a wooden handle and a curved blade ending in a hook, used for pruning or chopping back branches.

billiards is an indoor game for two people, played on a large cloth-covered table with three balls. Players use a cue to hit one of the balls; the aim is to hit a second ball so that either a third ball is hit or a ball goes into one of six pockets at the edges of the table.

billion (billionth) A billion is the number 1,000,000,000.

billionaire A billionaire is a person whose wealth is equal to at least a billion pounds or dollars.

billow When something like a sail or flag billows, it swells out and flaps slowly in the wind. ...washing billowing from a clothes-line. ◇ When something like smoke or cloud billows, large amounts of it roll slowly along and upwards.

billy goat A billy goat is a male goat.

bimbo (bimbos) Young women who are thought to be empty-headed but sexually attractive are sometimes called bimbos.

bimonthly See bi-monthly.

bin (binning, binned) A bin is a container for putting rubbish in. If you bin something, you throw it away because you do not want it. ◇ A bin is also a container, usually with a lid, for keeping things in.

binary (pron: bine-a-ree) The binary system is a way of writing down numbers using only two digits, 0 and 1, in various combinations. It is used especially in computing. ◇ Binary is also used to describe things which are made up of two different parts. Pluto and its moon together orbit the sun as a binary planet.

bind (binding, bound not 'binded') ❑ If you bind something like a parcel or bundle, you tie something round it to hold it together. Similarly, you can bind someone's wrists and ankles. When this is done to someone, you say they are bound. The van crew were left bound and gagged. ◇ If you bind something like a carpet or a piece of cloth, you cover the edges with stitching or a strip of material, to stop it fraying or to decorate it. Material used for this purpose is called binding. ◇ When a book is bound, the pages are joined together and the covers put on. The binding of a book is its cover.

❑ If something binds people together, it unites them because they have the same feelings about it. You can also say people are bound by things like family connections. ◇ If two or more things are bound together, they are closely linked so that each affects the other. Economic and political reform are inextricably bound together.

❑ If you bind a mixture of food, you mix it with a liquid

so all the ingredients stick together. Other things can be **bound** in a similar way. *The plastic melts and, on cooling, binds the aluminium together as a thin, light fabric.*

❏ If something like a legal order **binds** you to do something, it forces you to do it. A **binding** promise or agreement must be obeyed or carried out. ◇ If someone is **bound over** in court, they are given a legal order and can be fined or imprisoned if they do not obey it.

❏ If you say something you have to do is a **bind**, you mean it is a nuisance and you wish you did not have to do it. ◇ If someone is **in a bind**, they are in a difficult situation.

❏ You say someone **binds their wounds** when they try to put things right after they have suffered a defeat or difficulty.

binder A **binder** is a hard cover, usually of card or plastic, for holding loose papers or things like back numbers of magazines.

bindweed is a climbing plant with pink or white trumpet-shaped flowers. It twists round other plants as it grows.

binge (binging *or* bingeing, binged) If someone goes on a **binge**, they drink a lot of alcohol. ◇ When people do something intensively for a short time, such as spending a lot of money, you can call this a **binge**. *...a consumer spending binge.* ◇ If someone **binges** on something, they over-indulge in it. *Most people binge on things like ice-cream, chocolate and sweets.*

Bingo is a game played for money or prizes. Players have cards with a selection of numbers printed on them and randomly-chosen numbers are read out to them by a **Bingo caller**. The players mark off any matching numbers on their own card and the first person to mark off all their numbers wins the game.

binoculars are a device like two small telescopes joined side by side, for seeing things at a distance.

biochemistry (biochemist; biochemical) **Biochemistry** is the study of the chemical processes in living things. **Biochemical** is used to talk about things to do with these processes. *...the biochemical basis of the disease.* A **biochemist** is a scientist who works in this field.

biodegradable If something is **biodegradable**, it breaks down or decomposes naturally without any special scientific treatment, and so does not cause pollution.

biography (biographies; biographer, biographical) A **biography** is an account of a person's life written by someone else. Someone who writes a biography is called a **biographer**. **Biographical** is used to describe something which gives information about a person's life. *...a biographical film.*

biological (biologically) **Biological** is used to talk about things connected with the natural processes in plants, animals, and other living things. *...using biological methods to control pests... Madagascar is biologically one of the richest places on earth.* ◇ **Biological** sciences are concerned with the study of living things. ◇ **Biological** warfare and weapons involve the use of chemicals or living organisms which harm people, animals, and plants. ◇ Someone's **biological clock** is their body's way of telling them it is time for something. For example, your biological clock might tell you it is time to wake up or have a meal. ◇ A person's **biological parent**

is their real father or mother, rather than someone who has adopted them.

biology (biologist) **Biology** is the study of living things. An expert in this field is called a **biologist**. The **biology** of a living thing is the way it works. *...the biology of marine life... The biology of these diseases is terribly complicated.*

bionic **Bionics** is the study of certain biological functions, especially those of the brain, which can be applied to the development of electronic equipment to make it operate in the same way. **Bionic** is used to describe things developed in this way. *An Australian invention, a so-called bionic ear, helps deaf people hear.* ◇ If you call a person **bionic**, you mean they seem to have superhuman powers, such as exceptional strength or very good eyesight, as if parts of their body had been replaced by machinery.

biophysics (biophysicist) **Biophysics** is a science which tries to explain how living things work using the laws of physics. A scientist who specializes in this is called a **biophysicist**.

biopic (*pron:* bi-oh-pick) A **biopic** is a film based on the life of a real person.

biopsy (biopsies) If someone has a **biopsy**, a small sample is taken from part of their body and examined medically to find out the cause of a disease or see how far it has spread.

biosphere The **biosphere** is the part of the earth's surface and atmosphere which is inhabited by living things.

biotechnology (biotechnological; biotechnologist) is the use of living organisms to improve medical, agricultural, and industrial processes. Someone specializing in this is called a **biotechnologist**. **Biotechnological** is used to talk about things connected with biotechnology. *...finding a biotechnological solution to world hunger.*

bipartisan If something is **bipartisan**, it involves two different political parties or groups. *Continued bipartisan support for the President's policies is far from guaranteed.*

biped (*pron:* bye-ped) A **biped** is any creature with two feet.

biplane A **biplane** is an old-fashioned plane with two sets of wings, one above the other.

birch (birches, birching, birched) The **birch** is a tree which has thin peeling bark and long catkins. There are several kinds of birch. ◇ The **birch** was a cane or bunch of twigs, used in the past to flog people. If someone was **birched**, they were flogged with a birch.

bird **Birds** are two-legged creatures with feathers and wings. Female birds lay eggs which their young hatch from. Most birds can fly, although a few species cannot, for example the kiwi and the emu. ◇ If you have a **bird's eye view** of something, you see it from far above, for example from a plane or high up in a building.

bird of prey (birds of prey) **Birds of prey** are birds like eagles, hawks, and owls which kill and eat other birds and animals.

bird-watcher (*or* birdwatcher) **Bird-watchers** are people whose hobby is observing wild birds in their natural surroundings.

birdie In golf, a **birdie** is a score of one below par on any hole. See also **bogey**, **eagle**.

birdwatcher See **bird-watcher**.

Biro (Biros) A **Biro** is a ballpoint pen. 'Biro' is a trademark.

birth ❏ The **birth** of a person or animal is the time when they are born. ◇ When a woman **gives birth,** she has a baby. ◇ The place of someone's **birth** is the place where they were born. If someone has a particular nationality **by birth,** they have that nationality because they or their parents were born in that country. You can also say someone has a particular status or rank **by birth.** *He is a prince by birth.*

❏ The **birth** of something like an organization is its beginning. ◇ If something like a type of music started in a place, you can say the place **gave birth** to it. *The south side of the city gave birth to the music known as the Chicago blues.*

birth control is the same as contraception.

birth rate The **birth rate** in a place is the number of babies born live for every 1000 people during a certain period of time.

birthday A person's **birthday** is the anniversary of the date they were born.

birthmark A **birthmark** is a mark on the skin formed before birth. Birthmarks are usually brown or dark red.

birthplace A person's **birthplace** is the place where they were born.

birthright A person's **birthright** is something they are entitled to have or enjoy because of the place where they were born or the family they were born into. If you say something is everyone's **birthright,** you mean everyone is entitled to it.

biscuit A **biscuit** is a small flat crisp cake, usually sweet.

bisect In maths, if you **bisect** something like a line or angle, you draw a line exactly through the middle of it. ◇ If a road cuts across an area dividing it in two, you say it **bisects** the area.

bisexual (bisexuality) If someone is **bisexual** or a **bisexual,** they are sexually attracted to both men and women. You can talk about the **bisexuality** of someone like this. ◇ **Bisexual** is also used to describe plants or animals which contain both male and female characteristics in one individual.

bishop In many Christian churches, a **bishop** is the head of a diocese or group of parishes. ◇ The **bishop** is also a piece in chess. Each player has two bishops.

bison (*plural:* bison) The **bison** is a large animal of the cattle family, with a dark-brown coat, a shaggy mane, and short curved horns. Bison are native to North America where there used to be large numbers of them living in the wild.

bistro (bistros) A **bistro** is a small restaurant or bar.

bit ❏ A **bit** of something is an amount or piece of it, especially a small amount or piece. ◇ A **bit** of something is also an example or instance of it. *...a lovely bit of bowling.* ◇ If you know a **bit** about something, you have some knowledge of it. *I've learned a bit about mechanics.*

❏ A **bit** is also a passage in a piece of writing. *There is a very amusing bit in one of his books.* ◇ A **bit part** is a small unimportant part for an actor in a film or play.

❏ A **bit** means to a small extent or degree. *Sometimes the moon's a bit closer to Earth... Lower the flame a bit and cook the steak for two minutes on each side.* ◇ **For a bit** means for a short time. *I was sad for a bit.* ◇ **Quite a bit** of something means rather a lot of it. *They made quite a bit of money.*

❏ If something happens **bit by bit,** it happens gradually. ❏ If you **do your bit,** you help to achieve something. ❏ You use **every bit** to emphasize that something has as much of a quality as something else. *The 1990s will be every bit as exciting as the 1980s.*

❏ The **bit** on a tool is the cutting or drilling part. ◇ A horse's **bit** is the piece of metal held in its mouth by the bridle and reins. It is used to control the horse.

❏ In computing, a **bit** is the smallest unit of information held in a computer's memory. 'Bit' is short for 'binary digit'. See also **byte.**

❏ **Bits and pieces** are small objects of different kinds. ◇ A person's **bits and pieces** are their personal belongings, or things they have with them on a particular occasion.

❏ **Bits** is used to say something is broken into small pieces. You say, for example something is 'smashed to bits'.

❏ See also **bite.**

bitch (bitches, bitching, bitched; bitchy, bitchiness) ❏ A **bitch** is a female dog.

❏ If someone calls a woman a **bitch,** they mean she behaves in an unpleasant way and causes trouble. ◇ If someone is **bitchy,** they say nasty things about people. *The bitchiness and jealousy starts in the locker room.* ◇ If someone **bitches,** they complain about something.

bite (biting, bit, have bitten) ❏ When a person or animal **bites** something, they use their teeth to cut through it or into it. ◇ If an insect or snake **bites** you, it pierces your skin and leaves a poisonous substance there. ◇ A **bite** is the injury you get if a person, animal, or insect bites you.

❏ If you have a **bite** to eat, you have a small meal or snack.

❏ If something like an action or policy **bites,** it has a noticeable effect. *The blockade is beginning to bite.*

❏ If you say **once bitten twice shy,** you mean someone will not do something again, because of what happened the first time. ◇ If someone **bites the bullet,** they do something they do not want to, because it seems the only way out of a difficulty. ◇ If someone **bites off more than they can chew,** they try to do something which is too difficult for them.

biting cold or a **biting** wind is extremely cold and piercing. ◇ If someone makes a **biting** remark, they are sarcastic or cruel. ◇ See also **bite.**

bitten See **bite.**

bitter (bitterly, bitterness) ❏ If someone is **bitter,** they are angry and resentful because they feel they have been unfairly treated. *There's a great deal of bitterness within the party.* ◇ If someone has had a **bitter** disappointment, they are very unhappy and disappointed about something. *His supporters are bitterly disappointed that he has broken his campaign promise.* ◇ If you know something **from bitter experience,** you know it because of unpleasant things which have happened to you in the past.

❏ In a **bitter** war, struggle, or argument, people fight or argue fiercely and angrily.

❏ **Bitter** is used to describe very cold weather. *...the bitter winter months... ...a bitterly cold December night.*

❏ If something tastes **bitter,** it has a sour unpleasant flavour. ◇ **Bitter** is a type of beer made with more hops than other beers.

❏ **bitter end:** see **end.** ◇ **bitter pill:** see **pill.**

bitter-sweet (*or* bittersweet) If something tastes or

smells **bitter-sweet**, it seems both bitter and sweet at once. ◇ A **bitter-sweet** experience or memory is both sad and happy.

bittern The **bittern** is a long-legged wading bird related to the heron. It has a loud booming cry.

bittersweet See **bitter-sweet**.

bitumen (*pron:* bit-yoo-min) is a black sticky substance obtained from petroleum. It is used for surfacing roads and waterproofing roofs.

bivouac (*pron:* biv-oo-ak) (bivouacking, bivouacked) A **bivouac** is a temporary camp made by soldiers or mountaineers. When they **bivouac**, they set up a camp like this.

bizarre is used to describe things or people that are very odd or strange.

black (blackness) ❑ **Black** is the colour of coal.
❑ Someone who is **black** belongs to a race of people with dark skins. ...*the town's black community*.
❑ If someone is **black and blue**, they are badly bruised, because they have had an accident or been beaten. If they have a **black eye**, they have a dark coloured bruise around their eye, usually because they have been hit.
❑ **Black** coffee or tea is drunk without milk or cream.
❑ **Black** humour involves dealing humorously with something like death or violence which is not usually thought to be funny. ...*a black joke... ...a black comedy*.
❑ If someone **blacks** out or has a **blackout**, they lose consciousness for a short time. ◇ If a place is **blacked out** or there is a **blackout**, there are no lights, because the power supply has been cut off. During a war, a **blackout** is a time when buildings and streets are kept as dark as possible, to avoid being seen by enemy aircraft. ◇ If someone **blacks out** a TV or radio programme, they stop it being broadcast. You say there is a news **blackout** when no news is allowed to be broadcast or published.
❑ If something like a bank account is **in the black**, it has money in it and is not overdrawn. You say a person or organization is **in the black** when they are not in debt.
❑ If you give someone a **black mark**, you notice something they do which you do not approve of, and you view them less favourably because of it. ◇ If you say someone is the **black sheep** of a family, you mean they are the one bad person in it.
❑ **Black** is used to talk about feelings of great unhappiness or misery. *People sank into black despair*.

black and white In a **black and white** film or photograph, the picture is in shades of black, white, and grey. A **black and white** TV set shows these colours only. ◇ If you say you have something **in black and white**, you mean you have it written down or printed, and so there can be no doubt about it. *The results are here in black and white... He'd seen the proof in black and white*. ◇ If you say something like a problem or situation is **black and white**, you mean it is simple and straightforward, and not difficult to sort out.

black belt If someone is a **black belt** in judo or karate, they have achieved a particular high standard. The black sash they are entitled to wear is also called a **black belt**.

black box See **flight recorder**.

black economy A country's **black economy** is money earned without the government being informed, so no income tax is paid on it.

black hole **Black holes** are areas which scientists believe exist in space and where gravity is so strong that nothing, not even light, can escape from them. They are thought to be formed by collapsed stars.

black ice is a thin transparent layer of ice on a road or path which is particularly dangerous because it is difficult to see.

black magic is magic used for evil purposes.

black market (black marketeer; black marketeering) Illegal trade in goods or currency is called the **black market** or **black marketeering**. A person who trades in this way is called a **black marketeer**.

black pudding is a thick sausage with black skin. It is made from pork fat and pig's blood.

black spot A **black spot** is a place where road accidents often happen. ◇ A **black spot** is also a part of the country where a problem is especially bad. ...*an unemployment black spot*.

black tie At a **black tie** event, for example a dinner or ball, the men wear formal clothes including dinner jackets and black bow ties.

blackball If someone is **blackballed**, they are excluded from a group or club, because its members vote against them.

blackberry (blackberries; blackberrying) **Blackberries** are small soft black or dark purple fruit which grow on prickly bushes, often in the wild. Each berry is made up of very small round sections. When you pick blackberries, you say you are **blackberrying**.

blackbird **Blackbirds** are common European birds belonging to the thrush family. Male blackbirds have black feathers and a bright yellow beak; female blackbirds have brown feathers.

blackboard A **blackboard** is a board with a hard black surface suitable for writing on with chalk.

blackcurrant **Blackcurrants** are very small dark purple fruit which grow in bunches on a bush. They are usually cooked before eating.

blacken (blackening, blackened) If something is **blackened**, its colour changes to black. ◇ If someone **blackens** your name or reputation, they make people believe bad things about you. You can also say people's behaviour **blackens** the name of a sport or organization. *Hooliganism and commercialization have blackened the name of football*.

blackhead **Blackheads** are small black spots on a person's skin, caused by a pore in the skin being blocked by grease.

blackjack is another name for the card game pontoon.

blackleg is an insulting word used to describe either a person who keeps working when other people are on strike, or someone brought in from outside to do the work of a person who is on strike.

blacklist (blacklisted) A **blacklist** is a list of people or organizations that it is thought cannot be trusted, or that have done something wrong. When someone is put on a blacklist, you say they are **blacklisted**.

blackmail (blackmailing, blackmailed; blackmailer) If someone **blackmails** you, they threaten to do something like revealing a secret unless you give them money or do what they want. Someone who does this is called a **blackmailer**; what they do is called **blackmail**.

blackout See black.

blacksmith A blacksmith is someone who makes and mends metal items, for example tools, farm implements, and wrought iron gates and fences. A person who makes and fits horseshoes is sometimes called a blacksmith, but is more correctly called a farrier.

bladder A person's bladder is the bag-like organ in their body which holds urine. See also gall bladder.

blade The blade of a knife or other tool is the part with a sharp edge. ◇ The blades of something like a propeller, fan, or engine are the parts which turn. ◇ The blade of an oar is the thin flat part which is pushed against the water to propel the boat. ◇ A blade of grass is a single leaf of it.

blame (blaming, blamed) If a person is blamed for something bad or gets the blame for it, they are held responsible for it. Things can also be blamed. *Overcrowding and staff shortages are now being blamed for yesterday's riot.* ◇ If you say you do not blame someone for doing something, you mean their action was reasonable in the circumstances.

blameless If you say someone is blameless, you mean they have done nothing wrong.

blanch (blanches, blanching, blanched) If someone blanches, they turn pale. ◇ If you say someone blanches at the thought of something, you mean they are shocked or alarmed at it.

blancmange (*pron:* blam-**monj**) is a flavoured milk pudding like thick custard. It is left to set and eaten cold.

bland (blandly, blandness) If someone makes a bland statement, they deliberately avoid saying or doing anything which might cause excitement or trouble. *He blandly said the government had done no more than bring the economy to normality.* ◇ Bland things are dull and unremarkable, and do not create much interest or excitement. ...*a bland performance... ...the blandness of our daily diet.*

blandishments are attempts to persuade someone to do something by flattering or coaxing them.

blank (blankly) ❑ If something like a wall or piece of paper is blank, there is nothing on it. ◇ If someone looks blank, their face shows no feeling, understanding, or interest. *I was just staring blankly out to sea.* ◇ If your mind goes blank, you cannot think of anything. ◇ If you draw a blank, you fail to find what you are looking for. *A search for signs of intelligent life in outer space has so far drawn a blank.*

❑ If you blank something out, you wipe it out or cover it up, so it can no longer be seen. ◇ If you blank out something which has happened to you in the past, you avoid thinking about it.

❑ If you give someone a blank cheque, you sign it but leave the amount for them to fill in. ◇ You also say you give someone a blank cheque when you give them the freedom to do what they want, or to spend as much money as they want.

❑ A blank cartridge has explosive in it but no bullet, so when it is fired you get a loud bang but nothing else happens. Blank cartridges are often called blanks.

blank verse If a poem is written in blank verse, the lines do not rhyme.

blanket (blanketing, blanketed) ❑ A blanket is a large bed cover, often made of wool.

❑ If something blankets an area or forms a blanket over it, it covers it. *Two days later a blanket of snow settled.* ◇ Blanket is also used to describe something which affects or includes every person or thing in a group. *It's impossible to impose a blanket ban on all supporters travelling to away matches... It would be wrong to give a blanket condemnation of the health service.*

blare (blaring, blared) When something like a radio, siren, or musical instrument blares, it makes a loud harsh noise. You can talk about the blare of something like this. ...*the continual blare of pop music.*

blarney is saying a lot of pleasant things which may not be true, to make someone like you or to persuade them to do something.

blasé (*pron:* blah-zay) If you are blasé about something which other people think is interesting or exciting, you are bored by it or treat it carelessly, because you have experienced it before.

blaspheme (blaspheming, blasphemed; blasphemy, blasphemous) If someone blasphemes, they say or write something disrespectful about God, or use God's name as a swear word. This kind of behaviour is called blasphemy; you can say someone is being blasphemous, or describe what they say or write as blasphemous.

blast ❑ A blast is a big violent explosion, especially one made by a bomb. You can say a place is blasted by an explosion or gunfire. ◇ When people blast through rock or blast a tunnel, they force a way through using explosives.

❑ A blast is also a short loud noise on something like a whistle or horn. ◇ When music or noise blasts from something like a radio, it comes out very loudly. If it is at full blast or going full blast, it is producing noise at its loudest possible volume.

❑ A blast is also a sudden strong rush of something like liquid or gas.

❑ When a space rocket blasts off, it is launched into the air. Blast-off is the moment it leaves the ground.

❑ If a person severely criticizes someone or something, you can say they blast them. You can also talk about a blast of criticism.

blast-furnace A blast-furnace is a large structure for making iron. Iron ore and solid fuel are fed into the top and a blast of preheated air is forced through the bottom of the furnace. As the heated metal melts, the pure iron separates and can be collected. Blast furnaces are also used to produce lead, copper, and tin.

blatant (*pron:* blay-tant) (blatantly) Blatant is used to describe something bad or wrong which is done in a very obvious way. ...*blatant disregard for international law... ... a blatantly unfair trial.*

blather (blathering, blathered) If someone blathers, they go on talking in a silly or pointless way. Talk like this is called blather.

blaze (blazing, blazed) ❑ When a fire blazes, it burns very fiercely and brightly. ◇ A blaze is a large fierce fire which causes a lot of damage and destruction.

❑ Blazing is used to talk about very hot weather. ...*the blazing sun... ...a blazing Saturday afternoon.*

❑ A blaze is a very bright light, or an area of very bright colour. *The parks have come out in a blaze of colour.* ◇ A blaze is also a broad light-coloured mark down the front of a horse's face.

❏ **Blaze** is used to say a lot of attention is paid to something. You say, for example, something is done in a **blaze** of publicity. *She went out in a spectacular blaze of scandal.*

❏ **Blazing** is used to describe extremely strong feelings of anger or excitement. *...a blazing row... Their eyes were blazing with fury.*

❏ If someone **blazes a trail**, they lead the way to something new and exciting.

blazer A **blazer** is a kind of jacket, especially one worn by schoolchildren or members of a sports team.

bleach (bleaches, bleaching, bleached) **Bleach** is a chemical used to whiten things like clothes or sheets, or to clean and disinfect things. ◇ If something is **bleached**, it is made white or paler in colour, either by bleach or by something like strong sunlight. *...bleached blond hair.*

bleak (bleaker, bleakest; bleakly, bleakness) ❏ A **bleak** situation is bad, and seems unlikely to improve. ◇ If a person looks or sounds **bleak**, they seem depressed or hopeless. *He spoke bleakly of the choices his party now faced.*

❏ If a place is **bleak**, it seems cold and bare. *...the loneliness and bleakness of Exmoor.* ◇ **Bleak** weather is cold and miserable.

bleary If someone's eyes are **bleary**, they are red and watery from tiredness. You say someone with eyes like this is **bleary-eyed**.

bleat (bleating, bleated) When a sheep or goat **bleats**, it makes a high-pitched quavery sound in its throat. ◇ If a person **bleats**, they complain about things in a weak and ineffective way. *It's no good the Prime Minister bleating on about it, he ought to do something.*

bleed (bleeding, bled) ❏ When someone **bleeds**, they lose blood from part of their body, as a result of an injury or illness.

❏ You say a coloured piece of cloth **bleeds** if the colour runs when it is washed. ◇ If you **bleed** something like a radiator or brake system, you release the seal for a short time, to let out a small amount of liquid or gas.

❏ If someone **bleeds** a person or organization **dry**, they take all their money over a period of time.

bleep (bleeping, bleeped; bleeper) When an electronic device **bleeps**, it makes a short high-pitched sound. A **bleeper** is a small device carried or worn by someone like a doctor. It bleeps when someone wants to contact them. When this happens, you say someone **bleeps** them.

blemish (blemishes, blemished) If something is **blemished** or has a **blemish**, it has a small mark or stain on it. ◇ A **blemish** is also a failing or shortcoming. *Another blemish on British justice was revealed this week.*

blench (blenches, blenching, blenched) If you **blench** at something, you back away in fear or horror. If you say something would make someone **blench**, you mean they would be horrified by it.

blend (blender) ❏ If you **blend** two or more substances together, you mix them together to make a single smooth substance. A **blender** is a kitchen appliance which mixes liquids and soft foods together. ◇ A **blend** of something like tea or whisky is a combination of different types, with its own special flavour. You say a product like this is **blended**. *...blended cider.*

❏ When things are combined together in a pleasant or satisfactory way, you say they are **blended**. *The Senate plan must be blended with a version agreed earlier this week.* You can talk about a **blend** of things like these. *The building is a pleasing blend of stained wood and glass... ...a blend of youth and experience.*

❏ If something **blends in** with its surroundings, it fits in with them, and does not stand out in any way.

bless (blesses, blessing, blessed) ❏ When a priest **blesses** someone or something, he asks for God's favour and protection for them.

❏ If you say something like a plan or project is **blessed** by someone, you mean it has their support. *The deal has been blessed by the Monopolies and Mergers Commission.* You can also say something is done with someone's **blessing**.

❏ If you say someone is **blessed with** a quality or skill, you mean they have it.

❏ A good feature of your life can be called a **blessing**. *That strength of relationship with a partner is the greatest blessing in life.* ◇ If you say something is a **blessing in disguise**, you mean it seemed to be a problem but has turned out to be an advantage. ◇ If something is a **mixed blessing**, it has advantages and disadvantages.

blessed (*pron:* **bless**-id) (blessedly) People use **blessed** to describe things they are especially thankful for or relieved about. *Rainy weather brings blessed relief to hay fever victims... Most British election campaigns are blessedly brief.* ◇ **Blessed** is also used to describe holy people or things. *...blessed Thomas Becket.*

blew See **blow**.

blight is any disease which makes plants wither, especially one caused by fungi or viruses. ◇ A **blight** is the harmful effects of something over a long period of time. You can talk about things being **blighted** by something. *...a local economy blighted by high unemployment.*

blind (blindly, blindness, blindingly) ❏ If someone is **blind**, they cannot see. **Blindness** is being unable to see. If something **blinds** you, it makes you unable to see, either for a short time or permanently. ◇ If something like light or a colour is **blinding**, it is extremely bright and dazzling.

❏ If something is **blindingly** obvious, it is very obvious.

❏ If someone is **blind** to something which is going on, they have failed to notice it. ◇ If you **turn a blind eye** to something, you pretend not to notice it. ◇ If something prevents someone from noticing something, you say it **blinds** them to it. *His determination to win the war is blinding him to other dangers.*

❏ **Blind** is also used to describe people's behaviour when they do something without thinking. *We blindly follow their lead.*

❏ A **blind** corner curves sharply, so you cannot see what is coming towards you.

❏ A **blind** is a roll of cloth which can be pulled down over a window to keep out the light. See also **Venetian blind**.

blind alley A **blind alley** is a narrow street blocked at one end so there is no way out. ◇ If you go up a **blind alley** when you are trying to achieve something, you get to a situation where no further progress is possible, and you have to go back several stages.

blind date A **blind date** is an arranged social meeting between a man and woman who have not met each other before.

blind man's buff is a party game in which a blindfold person tries to catch one of the other players.

blind spot A blind spot is a part of an area which you cannot see, because it is hidden behind something. ◇ You say you have a blind spot when there is something you keep failing to understand or appreciate. *I have a blind spot to the genius of Picasso.*

blindfold A blindfold is a strip of cloth tied round someone's eyes so they cannot see. When someone is prevented from seeing like this, you say they are blindfold or blindfolded.

blink ❏ When you blink, you close and open your eyes quickly. A movement of the eyes like this is called a blink. ◇ A blink is also a very short period of time. People sometimes say something happens in the blink of an eye. *The intercity 125s cross in the blink of an eye.*
❏ You can also say people blink when they are very surprised at something. *Shoppers on Warsaw's Franzuska Street blinked in disbelief.*
❏ When something like a light blinks, it flashes on and off.
❏ If something is on the blink, it is not working.

blinkers (blinkered) Blinkers are two leather flaps attached to a horse's bridle, so it can only see straight ahead. ◇ If you say a person is wearing blinkers or has blinkered views or attitudes, you mean they have a narrow point of view and do not take other people's opinions into consideration.

blip A blip is a small spot of light flashing on and off regularly. ◇ A blip is also a sudden brief change or interruption in something which is proceeding in a regular way. *A Government spokesman dismissed the rise as a temporary blip in the drive for zero inflation.*

bliss (blissful, blissfully) Bliss is a state of extreme happiness. A blissful time or state is a very happy one. *I was blissfully happy.*

blister (blistering, blistered) ❏ If you get a blister or your skin blisters, you get a painful, bubble-like swelling on the surface of your skin. ◇ If something like paint blisters, small bumps appear on its surface.
❏ Blistering weather is extremely hot. ◇ Angry or sarcastic remarks can be called blistering. *...a blistering attack.*

blithe (blithely) Blithe is used to say something is done without serious or careful thought. *They talk blithely of promoting forests as tourist centres.*

blitz (blitzes, blitzing, blitzed) ❏ When a town or city is blitzed, it is bombed by enemy aircraft and destroyed or damaged. An attack like this is called a blitz. The bombing of British cities during World War II is often called the Blitz.
❏ A blitz is also (a) a determined effort to get something done or to deal with something. *...a 10-day blitz on illegal parking.* (b) a concentrated campaign or series of events. *...a blitz of television interviews.*

blizzard A blizzard is a heavy snowstorm with strong winds.

bloated If something is bloated, it is much larger than usual, because it has a lot of liquid, food, or gas inside. ◇ You say things like costs are bloated when they have become unreasonably large. *...bloated house prices.*

bloater A bloater is a herring which has been salted and smoked.

blob A blob is a small amount of thick or sticky liquid. ◇ Something which appears unclear or shapeless can also be called a blob. *The bacteria appear under the electron microscope as a dark, fuzzy blob.*

bloc A bloc is a group of people or countries with similar aims and interests acting together. See also en bloc.

block ❏ A block of flats or offices is a large building containing flats or offices. ◇ A building or group of buildings bounded on four sides by streets can also be called a block. *The hotel is two blocks back from the beach.*
❏ A block of a substance is a large rectangular piece of it. *...a block of marble.* ◇ A block of something like tickets, seats, or shares is a large number of them, grouped together or numbered consecutively.
❏ If people block something like a road or pipe, they put something across it, so nothing can get through. ◇ If you are blocked in, you cannot get out of a place because something is in your way.
❏ If something blocks out what you are trying to see, it gets in the way and stops you seeing it; you can also say it blocks your view.
❏ If something like a deal or payment is blocked, it is prevented from going ahead.
❏ chip off the old block: see chip.

block and tackle A block and tackle is a device for lifting heavy objects. It consists of a rope or chain passed round blocks containing pulleys.

block-book (block-booking) If someone reserves a block of seats in a theatre or stadium, you say they block-book them. A reservation like this is called a block-booking.

block capitals or block letters are simple capital letters.

block vote A block vote is a large number of votes all cast in the same way by one person on behalf of a group of people.

blockade (blockading, blockaded) When a place is blockaded or there is a blockade, no people or goods are allowed in.

blockage If there is a blockage in something like a pipe or tube, it is blocked by something.

blockbuster A blockbuster is a film or book which is very popular and makes a lot of money.

blonde (blond) Blonde hair is pale yellow. The spelling blond is sometimes used when talking about men and boys. *...a girl with long blonde hair... ...a blond boy dressed in white.* ◇ A blonde is a woman with blonde hair.

blood is the red fluid which the heart pumps around the body. If you give blood, you allow blood to be taken from your body so it can be stored and used in an operation or blood transfusion. A person who does this is called a blood donor.
❏ Blood is sometimes used to talk about the race or social class of someone's parents or ancestors. *The heir to the throne must marry a woman of royal blood.* ◇ If someone is a blood relation, they are part of your family by birth, rather than by marriage. ◇ If something like a talent or ability is in your blood, it is part of your nature, and other members of your family may have it too.
❏ If there is bad blood between people, they have feelings of hatred and resentment towards each other. ◇ If a cruel act is done in cold blood, it is done deliberately and

without emotion.

❑ New people introduced into an organization are sometimes called **new blood**, especially when it is thought their ideas might improve things.

blood bank See bank.

blood cell Blood cells are the red and white cells in the blood.

blood count A blood count is a check on the number of red and white blood cells in a sample of blood. It shows how healthy a person is.

blood donor See blood.

blood group A person's **blood group** or **blood type** is the type of blood they have. There are several different blood groups, the most common being O and A.

blood-letting (or bloodletting) is the killing and injuring of people during an outbreak of violence. ◇ You also say there is **blood-letting** when there is anger and quarrelling among a group of people.

blood poisoning is a serious illness resulting from an infection in the blood.

blood pressure A person's **blood pressure** is the force with which their blood is being pumped round their body.

blood sport A **blood sport** is an activity like hunting which involves killing animals.

blood transfusion A blood transfusion is a process in which blood is injected into the body of someone who has lost a lot of blood.

blood type See blood group.

blood vessel Blood vessels are the tubes which blood flows through. Arteries, veins, and capillaries are all blood vessels.

bloodbath You say there is a **bloodbath** when a lot of people are violently killed.

bloodcurdling noises are frightening and horrible. ...a bloodcurdling shriek.

bloodhound The bloodhound is a large dog with a smooth coat, droopy ears, and sagging jowls. Bloodhounds have a good sense of smell, and in the past were used to follow people, or to find them when they were lost.

bloodless If you say someone's face or skin is **bloodless**, you mean they look very pale. ◇ In a **bloodless** coup or revolution, nobody is killed.

bloodletting See blood-letting.

bloodshed You say there is **bloodshed** when quarrelling turns to violence, and people get killed or injured.

bloodshot If someone's eyes are **bloodshot**, the parts which are usually white have turned red or pink.

bloodstain (bloodstained) Bloodstains are marks left by blood on something like clothing. When something is marked or covered with blood, you say it is **bloodstained**.

bloodstock Thoroughbred horses bred for racing are called **bloodstock**.

bloodstream A person's **bloodstream** is the flow of blood round their body.

bloodthirsty people are cruel and violent. ◇ You also say people are **bloodthirsty** when they enjoy watching or hearing about violence.

bloody (bloodier, bloodiest) You say something is **bloody** when it involves a lot of people being killed and injured. ...a bloody civil war. ◇ You say an object is **bloody** when it has blood on it. ◇ If someone gets a **bloody nose**, they come off worse in a quarrel or fight which they started.

bloody-minded (bloody-mindedness) If someone is **bloody-minded**, they are deliberately awkward and unhelpful. Stubbornness can easily become bloody-mindedness.

bloom (blooming, bloomed) ❑ A **bloom** is a flower on a plant. When flowers **bloom**, their buds open and the petals appear. ◇ When a tree **blooms**, it produces flowers; you then say it is **in bloom**.

❑ If a person **blooms**, they seem to take on new attractive qualities. ◇ If you talk about a young person's **bloom**, you mean their fresh healthy appearance. If you say someone is **blooming**, you mean they are attractively healthy and full of energy.

bloomers are large baggy knickers.

blossom (blossoming, blossomed) ❑ Blossom is the flowers on fruit trees before the fruit grows. When a fruit tree **blossoms**, blossom appears on it; you then say it is **in blossom**. ◇ When a flower **blossoms**, the flower bud opens.

❑ If a person **blossoms**, they develop new qualities or abilities and become more interesting or attractive. ◇ You can say other things **blossom** when they develop successfully. Trade relationships abroad have blossomed.

blot (blotting, blotted) ❑ A **blot** is a drop of liquid, especially ink, which has been spilled and has left a mark on a surface. ◇ If you **blot** something which is wet, you soak up the liquid on it with soft paper or cloth.

❑ If something damages someone's reputation, you can say it is a **blot** on it. ◇ **blot your copybook**: see copybook. ◇ If something is ugly and spoils the look of a place, you can say it is a **blot** on the landscape.

❑ If one thing **blots out** another, it is in front of it and prevents it being seen. A black cloud blotted out the sun. ◇ If you **blot out** something like a memory or a thought, you avoid thinking about it.

blotch (blotches; blotched, blotchy) A **blotch** is a discoloured area or a stain, for example on a person's skin. When something has marks like this, you can say it is **blotched** or **blotchy**.

blotting paper is soft absorbent paper for soaking up ink.

blouse A blouse is a kind of shirt worn by a girl or a woman.

blow (blowing, blew, have blown) ❑ You say a wind **blows**. If something is carried somewhere by a wind, you say it is **blown** there.

❑ When you **blow**, you send out a stream of air from your mouth. If you **blow out** something like a candle, you make it go out by blowing on it. If you **blow** bubbles, you produce them by blowing air into a liquid. ◇ If you **blow** something like a whistle or a trumpet, you make a sound by blowing into it.

❑ When you **blow** your nose, you force air out through your nostrils, to clear it.

❑ If something makes you very disappointed or unhappy, you can say it is a **blow**. ◇ A **blow** is also something which causes harm or damage. For example, you can say something is a **blow** to someone's hopes, or their reputation. ◇ If someone or something **softens the blow**, they reduce the harmful effects of something.

❏ If you get a **blow** on the head, someone or something hits you there. ◇ If people **come to blows**, they get angry and start hitting each other.

❏ If you strike a **blow** for a cause or principle, you do something to help it succeed. *He urged them to strike a blow for equality.* You can also strike a **blow** against something.

❏ If you **blow** your money, you spend a lot of it quickly on things you do not really need. ◇ If you get a chance to do something and then do it badly, you can say you **blew** the chance. ◇ If something like a secret is **blown**, people find out about it.

❏ When a fuse **blows**, it burns and is destroyed because too much electricity has been sent through it.

❏ When trouble **blows over**, it comes to an end.

❏ If something is **blown up**, it is destroyed by an explosion. **Blow** is used in other ways to describe the effects of an explosion. *Windows were blown out... Roofs have been blown off... Engineers blew a large hole in a dam.*

❏ If something like a photograph is **blown up**, it is made larger; an enlarged photograph is called a **blow-up**. ◇ If you **blow up** something like a tyre or balloon, you fill it with air.

blow-by-blow A **blow-by-blow** account of something describes every stage in detail.

blow-dry If someone has their hair **blow-dried**, they have it styled by drying with a hand-held hairdryer.

blow-out A **blow-out** is a sudden uncontrolled rush of oil or gas from a well. ◇ If there is a **blow-out** on a vehicle, a tyre bursts suddenly. ◇ A **blow-out** is also a very large meal.

blow-up See **blow**.

blowlamp A **blowlamp** is the same as a blowtorch.

blown See **blow**.

blowpipe A **blowpipe** is a long tube which arrows are blown from.

blowtorch (blowtorches) A **blowtorch** is a hand-held device which uses gas to produce a hot flame. It is used for removing old paint.

blubber is the thick layer of fat beneath the skin of animals like whales and seals.

bludgeon (*pron:* **bluj**-jon) (bludgeoning, bludgeoned) ❏ A **bludgeon** is a thick heavy stick used as a weapon. ◇ If someone is **bludgeoned**, they are badly beaten with a heavy object.

❏ If someone is **bludgeoned** into doing something, they are threatened or bullied into doing it.

blue is the colour of the sky on a clear sunny day.

❏ If you feel **blue** or have **the blues**, you feel sad and depressed. ◇ **Blues** or **the blues** is a type of slow sad jazz originally sung and played by black Americans at the beginning of the 20th century.

❏ **Blue** jokes and films are indecent or pornographic.

❏ If something happens **out of the blue**, it happens suddenly and unexpectedly.

❏ If you say someone can do something until they are **blue in the face**, you mean they can keep doing it but it will not have any effect.

blue blood (blue-blooded) If you say someone has **blue blood**, you mean they belong to a royal or noble family. **Blue-blooded** is used to talk about things connected with people like these.

blue-chip A **blue-chip** investment or company is one which people think is safe and profitable to invest in.

blue-collar workers do physical work in industry, rather than office work. See also **white-collar**.

blue tit The **blue tit** is a small European bird with a blue head, wings, and tail, and a yellow breast.

bluebell **Bluebells** are woodland plants with tall thin stems and blue bell-like flowers. They flower in early summer.

blueberry (blueberries) In the US, bilberries are called **blueberries**.

bluebottle The **bluebottle** is a large fly with a shiny dark-blue body. It makes a loud buzzing noise as it flies.

blueish See **bluish**.

blueprint A **blueprint** is a photographic print of an architect's or engineer's plan. It consists of white lines on a blue background. ◇ A **blueprint** for something is a plan of how it is expected to work. *...a detailed blueprint for agricultural reform.*

bluff ❏ A **bluff** is an attempt to make someone believe you will do something when you do not really intend to do it. If you think someone is behaving like this, you can say they are **bluffing**. If you **call someone's bluff**, you tell them to do what they are threatening to do, because you think they will not really do it. See also **double bluff**. ◇ If you **bluff** your way through a difficult situation, you get through it by pretending to know more than you really do.

❏ If someone has a **bluff** manner, they are hearty, down-to-earth, and frank.

bluish (*or* **blueish**) If something is **bluish**, it is slightly blue.

blunder (blundering, blundered) If you **blunder** or make a **blunder**, you make a silly mistake. ◇ If someone **blunders** about, they move about in a clumsy way.

blunderbuss (blunderbusses) A **blunderbuss** is an old-fashioned gun with a short wide barrel which scatters shot at close range. ◇ **Blunderbuss** is used to talk about things being done in a clumsy forceful way. *...his blunderbuss strategy... ...a blunderbuss of a speech.*

blunt (bluntly) ❏ If someone is **blunt**, they talk in a very direct way, without trying to be polite.

❏ A **blunt** object has a rounded or flat end, rather than a pointed one. ◇ A **blunt** knife has lost its sharpness.

blur (blurring, blurred; blurry) ❏ A **blur** is a shape or area which you cannot see clearly because it has no distinct outline, or because it is far away or moving very fast. ◇ If something is **blurred** or **blurry**, you cannot see it clearly because it is indistinct.

❏ If you cannot remember something well, you can say it is a **blur**. ◇ If the difference between two things becomes **blurred**, they are no longer obviously different from each other.

blurb The **blurb** on a book is a note on the cover giving information about the book and encouraging people to buy it. ◇ A **blurb** is also a leaflet or advertisement promoting goods or services for sale.

blurt If you **blurt** something **out**, you say it suddenly and without stopping to think about the consequences.

blush (blushes, blushing, blushed) If you **blush**, your face goes red, because you are embarrassed or ashamed.

blusher is a cosmetic used to add colour to a woman's

cheeks.

bluster (blustering, blustered) If someone **blusters,** they talk in an angry or boastful way, to hide the fact that they are afraid or embarrassed. You call this behaviour **bluster.**

blustery weather is rough and windy.

BMA The BMA is an organization which represents doctors' interests and regulates their professional conduct. BMA stands for 'British Medical Association'.

boa Boas are large snakes which coil around their prey and squeeze it to death. The boa constrictor is a type of boa, and so is the python. ◇ A **boa** is also a long fluffy scarf made of something like fur or feathers.

boar (plural: boar or boars) An uncastrated male pig is called a **boar.** ◇ The **boar** or **wild boar** is a wild pig with tusks.

board (boarder) ❑ A **board** is a long flat piece of wood. ◇ Flat pieces of wood or other material used for a special purpose often have **board** as part of their name. ...a drawing board... ...a notice board. ◇ If a door or window is **boarded up,** pieces of wood are fixed over it, for security reasons. When an empty building is **boarded up,** the doors and windows are covered like this.

❑ The **board** of a company or organization is the group of people who control or direct it. A **board meeting** is a meeting for all the people on the board of a company or organization.

❑ When you **board** a boat, train, or plane, you get on it; you then say you are **on board.** When officials **board** a ship, they get on it to carry out an investigation or take control of it. ◇ If you **take on board** something like an idea or suggestion, you understand it and accept it.

❑ Your **board** is the food you pay for when you stay somewhere. See also **board and lodging, full board, half board.** ◇ If you **board** somewhere, you stay there for a short time, and pay for your accommodation. If you are **boarded out** with someone, you are sent to stay with them. ◇ You say a pupil who lives at school during the term **boards** there or is a **boarder.**

❑ If you say something is **above board,** you mean it is open, fair, and honest. ◇ If something like a policy applies **across the board,** it affects everyone. He would reduce taxes across the board... ...across-the-board spending cuts. ◇ If someone **sweeps the board** in a competition or election, they win everything, or nearly everything.

board and lodging is food and a place to sleep, usually provided in a boarding house or sometimes offered as part of the conditions of a job.

board game Board games are games like chess or snakes and ladders, which people play by moving small pieces around on a board.

boarding card A **boarding card** is a card which each passenger must have before being allowed to board a plane or boat for a journey.

boarding house A **boarding house** is a private house which provides meals and accommodation for paying guests.

boarding party A **boarding party** is a group of people sent on board a ship to carry out an official investigation or to take over the ship.

boarding pass A **boarding pass** is the same as a boarding card.

boarding school A **boarding school** is one where pupils live during the term. See also **day school.**

boardroom The **boardroom** of a company or organization is the room where board meetings are held. Boardroom is also used to talk about people at the highest level of management in a company or organization. ...a boardroom reshuffle.

boardwalk In the US, a **boardwalk** is a raised footpath made of boards, usually beside the sea.

boast (boastful) If someone **boasts** or is **boastful,** they talk too proudly about something they own or have done. You call what they say a **boast.** ◇ If someone or something **boasts** a feature, they have it. The town boasts a 12th-century domed church.

boat (boating) ❑ A **boat** is a small vessel for travelling across water. If you go **boating,** you go on a lake or river in a boat for pleasure. ◇ A passenger ship can also be called a **boat.** As he hates flying he always goes by boat.

❑ If you say someone has **missed the boat,** you mean they have missed the chance of doing or having something, because they did not act quickly enough. ◇ If someone **rocks the boat,** they upset a calm situation and cause trouble for other people. ◇ If you say people are **in the same boat,** you mean they are in the same bad situation.

boat-hook A **boat-hook** is a long pole with a hook at the end. It is used to pull a boat to the bank, or to push it away from other boats.

boat people are refugees who have escaped from their country in small boats, especially refugees who left Vietnam in the 1970s and 1980s.

boat train A **boat train** is a train which takes you to or from a port.

boater A **boater** is a hard straw hat with a flat top and a brim.

boathouse A **boathouse** is a building near a lake or river where boats are stored.

boatswain See bosun.

bob (bobbing, bobbed) ❑ When something **bobs,** it moves up and down repeatedly. Yachts bobbed up and down in the bay. ◇ If you **bob,** you briefly lower your body. She bobbed down to tug the creases from the bride's crinoline.

❑ A **bob** is a hairstyle with the hair cut to about chin length all round. When a woman's hair is cut like this, you say it is **bobbed.**

❑ In the past **bob** was often used to mean 'shillings'. For example, people would say something cost 'five bob' (25p) or 'ten bob' (50p).

bobbin A **bobbin** is a reel or spool for holding thread.

bobble Bobbles are small fluffy balls, used to decorate clothes or furnishings like lampshades or curtains.

bobby (bobbies) A **bobby** is a policeman.

bobsleigh (pron: bob-slay) A **bobsleigh** is a large metal sledge, used for racing. It has a cockpit, usually for two people.

bode (boding, boded) If something **bodes well,** it shows something good is likely to happen. If it **bodes ill,** it shows you can expect something bad. Continued cuts in investment boded very ill for Britain's competitiveness.

bodice The **bodice** of a dress is the upper part, above the waist.

bodice-ripper A **bodice-ripper** is a sensational romantic novel or film, often with a historical setting.

bodily is used to describe things relating to a person's body. ...*bodily pain...* ...*bodily processes.* ◇ **Bodily** is also used to say something happens to the whole of someone's body. ...*lifting him bodily into the air.*

bodkin A **bodkin** is a blunt large-eyed needle used to thread elastic or cord through the waistband of a garment.

body (bodies) ❑ The **body** of a person or animal is (a) the whole of their physical shape, including their head, arms, and legs. (b) the main part of this shape, not including their head, arms, or legs. ◇ A **body** is the body of a dead person.

❑ A **body** of people is an organized group. ...*the governing body of football.* ◇ The main **body** of something is its largest or most important part. *They had broken away from the main body of the crowd.* ◇ A **body** of something like information or opinion is a large amount of it.

❑ The **body** of a car is the main part, not including the engine.

❑ **Body** is used after words like 'heavenly' to talk about planets, stars, and other natural objects in space. ...*celestial bodies.*

❑ If you receive a **body blow**, something happens which causes you great disappointment and difficulty.

body-builder (body-building) A **body-builder** is a person who regularly does special exercises to develop their muscles. Exercises like these are called **body-building.**

body language is the way you show your thoughts or feelings using the movements or position of your body.

body politic The **body politic** in a country is the people who operate the political system there.

bodyguard Someone's **bodyguard** is a person or group of people employed to protect them.

bodywork The **bodywork** of a motor vehicle is its outside part.

boffin is a humorous word for a scientist or some other kind of technical expert.

bog (bogged) A **bog** is an area of wet spongy ground. ◇ If a vehicle is **bogged down,** it is stuck in something like mud and cannot move. ◇ If you get **bogged down** by something, it prevents you from making progress. *Negotiations have become bogged down by a number of problems.*

bogey (or **bogy**) (bogeys, bogies) ❑ A **bogey** is something which causes problems for people. ...*the twin bogeys of soaring budget deficits and hyper-inflation.*

❑ In golf, a **bogey** is a score of one above par on any hole. See also **birdie, eagle.**

❑ See also **bogeyman.**

bogeyman (bogeymen) A **bogeyman** or **bogey** is a frightening evil spirit. ◇ Someone who is thought to be evil or wicked can be called a **bogeyman.** ...*that bogeyman of the communists known as a capitalist.*

boggle (boggling, boggled) If your mind **boggles** at something, you find it difficult to imagine or understand.

bogus (*pron:* **boh-guss**) **Bogus** is used to describe people who pretend to be something they are not. ...*a series of incidents involving bogus health visitors.* ◇ **Bogus** is also used to describe things which are not genuine. *They issued bogus receipts to their suppliers.*

bogy See **bogey.**

bohemian Artistic people with an unconventional life-

style used to be called **bohemians.** Their lifestyle was called **bohemian,** and so were the places where they lived and worked. ...*the bohemian cafes of pre-war Paris.*

boil (boiling, boiled) ❑ When a heated liquid **boils** or comes to the **boil,** bubbles appear in it and it starts to change into steam or vapour. If a liquid like milk **boils over,** it rises and spills out of a container. ◇ When you **boil** a kettle, you heat the water in it until it boils. ◇ When you **boil** food, you cook it in boiling water.

❑ If someone is **boiling** with anger, they are very angry indeed. ◇ If people's anger **boils over,** they become so angry they behave in an uncontrolled way.

❑ If you say something **boils down** to a particular thing, you mean that is what it amounts to, in its simplest terms.

❑ A **boil** is a painful red swelling on a person's skin.

boiler A **boiler** is a piece of equipment which burns fuel to provide hot water, for example a central heating boiler. Steam-driven vehicles and machinery are powered by steam from boilers.

boiler suit A **boiler suit** is a piece of clothing consisting of trousers and a top joined together in one piece, often made of strong cotton material. People wear boiler suits to protect their ordinary clothes when they are doing dirty or messy jobs.

boiling point The **boiling point** of a liquid is the temperature at which it starts to change into steam or vapour. Different liquids have different boiling points, and the same liquid has different boiling points at different pressures. ◇ If a situation has reached **boiling point,** people have become so agitated or angry that they are about to lose control of themselves.

boisterous people are rough, noisy, and lively. Their behaviour and activities can also be called **boisterous.**

bold (boldly; boldness) ❑ **Bold** people behave in a confident fearless way. The things they do, say, or write can also be called **bold.** ...*a bold plan of economic reform...* ...*a boldly outspoken document... Without an element of boldness, few Himalayan climbs would be completed.*

❑ **Bold** writing stands out clearly and distinctly.

bolero (boleros) A **bolero** (*pron:* bol-er-o) is a very short jacket, usually sleeveless and without buttons, worn over a woman's blouse or dress. ◇ The **bolero** (*pron:* bol-air-o) is a traditional Spanish dance.

bollard Bollards are (a) strong thick posts, usually made of concrete, used to mark off an area and stop vehicles getting past. (b) fixed or movable posts, often with a light inside, used to mark road junctions.

bolster (bolstering, bolstered) ❑ If you **bolster** something which is declining or getting weak, you do something which improves it, or stops it getting worse. For example, you can **bolster** someone's confidence or reputation. You can also **bolster** something like a system or an organization.

❑ A **bolster** is a long firm pillow or cushion.

bolt ❑ A **bolt** is a metal pin with a flat end which screws into a nut to fasten two things together. When you **bolt** things together, you fasten them together using nuts and bolts. ◇ If you **bolt** a door, gate, or window, you fasten it with a sliding metal device called a **bolt.**

❑ If a horse **bolts,** it suddenly runs away, because it has been frightened. Similarly, you can say a person **bolts** when they get away from a place as quickly as they can.

When a prisoner or captured animal **bolts**, they escape.
❑ A **bolt** of lightning is a flash of it, especially one which hits the ground. ◇ If a piece of news comes as **a bolt from the blue**, it comes as a complete surprise.

bolt hole A bolt hole is a place where you can go to get away from people.

bomb (bombing) ❑ A **bomb** is a weapon which explodes and damages or destroys a large area. Bombs are either placed somewhere where they are meant to explode or dropped from aircraft. ◇ If a place is **bombed**, it is attacked by bombs. A **bombing** is a bomb attack. If you say people have been **bombed out**, you mean the place they live in has been destroyed by bombs.
❑ If there is a **bomb scare** or a **bomb threat**, a warning, usually by phone, is received claiming a bomb has been placed somewhere. ◇ A **bomb factory** is a place where bombs are made illegally. ◇ **Bomb disposal** is the job of removing unexploded bombs safely.
❑ When people talk about **the bomb**, they mean nuclear weapons. *Other countries want the bomb.*

bombard (bombardment) ❑ If a place is **bombarded**, it is attacked with continuous heavy gunfire or bombing. You talk about the **bombardment** of a place. ◇ You say people are **bombarded** when a lot of things are thrown at them. *...a bombardment of stones.* ◇ You say an object is **bombarded** when it is hit by many smaller objects. *Objects in orbit are constantly bombarded by space dust.*
❑ If you are **bombarded** with questions or criticisms, you have to deal with a lot of them, one after the other. If you are **bombarded** with things like advertisements, you are continually seeing them or hearing them.

bombardier A bombardier is an NCO in an artillery regiment.

bombast (bombastic) If you call what someone says **bombast**, you mean they are just trying to impress people, by using long words or behaving in a pompous way. You say a person who behaves like this is **bombastic**.

bomber A bomber is (a) an aircraft which drops bombs. (b) a person who places a bomb somewhere.

bomber jacket A bomber jacket is a short jacket gathered into a band at the waist or hips.

bombshell A bombshell is a shocking or unwelcome surprise. When someone gives people a surprise like this, you can say they **drop a bombshell**.

bona fide (*pron:* bone-a fide-ee) (bona fides) Bona fide means genuine or real. *It was a bona fide mistake... They obviously were not bona fide students.* A **bona fide** action is done in good faith. *He was acting bona fide in the interests of another person.* ◇ Someone's **bona fides** are their good or sincere intentions. *This form allows lawyers to withhold a client's identity provided they vouch for his bona fides.*

bonanza A bonanza is something which makes people suddenly rich.

bond ❑ A **bond** between people is a strong feeling which unites them, for example a feeling of friendship or love. ◇ When someone develops a close relationship with another person or people, you can say they **bond** with each other. For example you can talk about a mother **bonding** with her baby. ◇ **Male bonding** is the development of close friendships between men, often based on their shared experience of all-male activities.
❑ When a person is tied up, you can call the rope or

string they are tied up with their **bonds**. *Someone loosed my bonds and poured water over my face.*
❑ When two things are **bonded** together, they are closely joined or fastened, for example with an adhesive substance. *The building has walls bonded with clay.* ◇ If a substance acts as a **bond** in a mixture of different things, it holds them together. You say the mixture is **bonded** by the substance. *The compound is bonded with polymers.*
❑ A **bond** is a certificate of debt issued by a government or corporation to raise funds. It carries a fixed rate of interest and is repayable with or without security at a specified future date.
❑ A **bond** is also a written or spoken agreement, especially a promise. If someone says **their word is their bond**, they mean they will definitely do what they have promised.
❑ A **bonded** travel company belongs to an association of travel agents which provide a guarantee that a person will not forfeit their holiday if the company they book it with goes out of business.

bondage is slavery. ◇ Bondage is also the practice of being tied up to get sexual pleasure.

bonded labour is a system in which people are forced to repay a debt by working unpaid for the person who lent them the money.

bone (boning, boned; bony, boneless) ❑ The **bones** of a person or animal are the hard parts which form their skeleton. **Bony** people or animals are thin, with not much flesh covering their bones. ◇ If you **bone** a piece of meat or fish, you take out the bones before cooking it. **Boned** or **boneless** meat has had the bones removed from it.
❑ The **bare bones** of something are the most important parts, which the other parts are constructed around. *The bare bones of representative democracy are there.*
❑ A **bone of contention** is something people argue or quarrel over. ◇ If you say someone **makes no bones about** something, you mean they have no hesitation in saying or doing it.
❑ If something is **bone dry**, it is very dry indeed.
❑ If you cut something like costs or services **to the bone**, you reduce them to the lowest possible amount.
❑ If you **bone up** on a subject, you learn as much as you can as quickly as possible.

bone china is very fine porcelain containing the ash of burned animal bones.

bone marrow See marrow.

bone meal (or bonemeal) is a substance made from dried and ground animal bones. It is used as a fertilizer or to feed animals.

bonfire A bonfire is a large fire out of doors, usually to burn garden rubbish. ◇ **Bonfire Night** is the night of November 5, when people have bonfire parties and let off fireworks to commemorate the arrest of Guy Fawkes in 1605 for trying to blow up the Houses of Parliament.

bongo (bongos) Bongo drums or bongos are small drums, usually in pairs, played by tapping with the fingers.

bonhomie (*pron:* bon-om-ee) is happy jolly friendliness.

bonkers If you say someone is **bonkers**, you mean they are mad.

bonnet The bonnet of a car is the metal cover over the

engine. ◇ A **bonnet** is also a woman's or baby's hat which ties under the chin.

bonny (bonnier, bonniest) is used to describe someone or something that is attractive or beautiful. ...*a bonny face*... ...*the bonny banks of Loch Lomond.*

bonsai (*pron:* bon-sigh) A **bonsai** (*plural:* bonsai *or* bonsais) is a dwarf tree which is kept small by growing it in a little pot and trimming it in a special way. The art of growing trees in this way, which originated in Japan, is called **bonsai**.

bonus (bonuses) A **bonus** is an amount of money you get on top of your usual pay or income. ◇ A **bonus** is also something good you get in addition to something else. *No one expects the weather to be good, and any sunshine is treated as a bonus.*

boo (booing, booed) If you **boo** someone who is giving a performance or speech, you shout 'boo' or make a similar loud noise. You do this to show you do not like what they are doing, or disagree strongly with what they are saying. A **boo** is a noise like this.

boob (boobing, boobed) ❑ If you **boob** or make a **boob**, you make a silly mistake.

❑ A woman's **boobs** are her breasts.

booby trap (booby-trapped) A **booby trap** is something like a bomb which is hidden or disguised and explodes when it is touched or moved. If something has a booby trap in it, you say it is **booby-trapped**.

boogie (boogying, boogied) If you **boogie**, you dance to pop music.

book (booking, booked) ❑ A **book** consists of sheets of paper, printed or blank, bound together inside a cover. ◇ A **book** is also one of the large sections which a long work like the Bible is divided into.

❑ The **books** of a company or organization are its written records of money spent and earned. ◇ If you say someone or something is **on the books** of a company or organization, you mean they belong to it or have their name listed in its records. ◇ If you say something like a law is **on the books**, you mean it is currently in force.

❑ When you **book** something like a hotel room or a ticket, or make a **booking**, you arrange to have it or use it. When you **book** an appointment with someone, you arrange to see them. ◇ If somewhere is **booked up** or **fully booked**, there are no rooms or tickets left for a particular time or date. ◇ When someone **books** an entertainer, they arrange for them to perform somewhere.

❑ When you **book into** a hotel, you inform the receptionist you have arrived and sign your name in the hotel register.

❑ When a police officer **books** someone, he or she officially records their name and the offence they may be charged with. Similarly, when a football referee **books** someone who has broken a rule, he officially records the player's name. A player who is booked twice in the same game is sent off. ◇ If someone is **brought to book**, they are punished for an offence or are made to explain their actions.

❑ If you say something is a **closed book** to you, you mean you know nothing about it.

book-keeping (book-keeper) **Book-keeping** is the work of keeping an accurate record of money spent and received by a business or other organization. A person who does this work is called a **book-keeper**.

bookable is used to describe things which can be booked in advance. ◇ In football, a **bookable** offence is one a player can be booked for.

bookbinding is the work of fastening the pages of a book together and putting the covers on.

bookcase A **bookcase** is a piece of furniture with shelves for books.

bookends are a pair of supports for keeping a row of books upright by placing one at each end.

bookie A **bookie** is the same as a bookmaker.

booking office A **booking office** is a place where tickets are booked and sold, especially in a railway station.

bookish If you say someone is **bookish**, you mean they are quiet and serious, and enjoy studying and reading. You can call an environment **bookish** when reading and studying are considered important there.

booklet A **booklet** is a book with a small number of pages and often a paper cover. Booklets give information, or instructions on how to use something.

bookmaker A **bookmaker** is someone who takes your money when you bet on something like a horse race, and pays you if you win. A betting shop is sometimes called a **bookmaker's**.

bookseller A **bookseller** is (a) a person who owns or manages an independent bookshop. (b) a bookshop, or a company which controls a chain of bookshops.

bookshelf (bookshelves) A **bookshelf** is a shelf for books.

bookshop A **bookshop** is a shop which specializes in selling books.

bookstall A **bookstall** is (a) a table or stall where books are sold, for example at a market or jumble sale. (b) a small shop with an open front where books, magazines, and papers are sold, for example at a railway station.

bookstore is the usual American word for a bookshop.

bookworm Bookworms are types of small insect which damage books by eating the binding. ◇ If you call a person a **bookworm**, you mean they read and study a lot.

boom (booming, boomed) ❑ If there is a **boom** in something, it increases or develops rapidly. When this happens, you say it is **booming**. ...*a boom in tourism*... *The economy was booming.* A **boom** time is one when there is a boom. ...*the boom years of yuppie extravagance.* A **boom** town is one which grows rapidly as a result of a boom.

❑ When something like a drum **booms**, it makes a loud deep echoing sound.

❑ A **boom** is a floating barrier used on a river or in the sea to soak up or enclose large quantities of spilt oil or some other liquid.

❑ On a sailing boat, the **boom** is the horizontal pole which the bottom of the main sail is attached to. One end of the boom is fixed to the mainmast. ◇ A **boom** is also a long pole with a microphone on the end, used in a film or TV studio.

boomerang A **boomerang** is a curved piece of wood, originally thrown by native Australians as a weapon. Some boomerangs can be made to come back to the person who throws them. ◇ If something you are trying to do **boomerangs**, it has bad effects for you which you are not expecting.

boon If something is a **boon**, it makes life better or easier for you.

boor (boorish) If you say someone is **boorish** or a **boor**, you mean they behave in a rude and clumsy way.

boost (booster) ❑ If something **boosts** something else or gives it a **boost**, it makes it grow. ...*a boost to inflation.* Something which has this effect can be called a **booster**.
❑ If you have a **booster** injection, you have a small additional injection some months or years after the original one, to make sure the original one still has its effect.
❑ A **booster** is also a rocket used to launch a missile or space vehicle.

boot (booting, booted) ❑ **Boots** are strong shoes which cover the ankle and sometimes the lower leg. ◇ If you **boot** a ball, you kick it hard. ◇ If someone kicks a person who has already been knocked to the ground, you say they **put the boot in**. You also say someone **puts the boot in** when they say or do something unkind to a person who is already unhappy or upset.
❑ If someone is **booted out** of a job, organization, or place, they are forced to leave.
❑ The **boot** of a car is a covered space, usually at the back, for carrying things like luggage, shopping, or tools.
❑ People sometimes say **to boot** when they are making an extra point or mentioning an additional thing. *The organization faces all of its old problems – and a few new ones to boot.*

booth A **booth** is (a) a small compartment screened off from a larger area. ...*a telephone booth.* (b) a small tent or stall where you can buy something or watch some kind of entertainment. ...*fairground booths.*

bootleg (bootlegging, bootlegged; bootlegger) **Bootleg** is used to describe things which have been illegally made, recorded, copied, or transported. ...*bootleg liquor...* ...*bootleg videos.* When something is produced or transported in this way, you say it is **bootlegged**. A person involved in bootlegging is called a **bootlegger**.

bootstraps If you **pull yourself up by your bootstraps**, you work hard to get yourself into a better situation, without help from anyone else.

booty is valuable things taken by a thief, or by the winning side in a battle.

booze (boozing, boozed; boozy, boozer) **Booze** is alcoholic drink. When someone **boozes**, they drink alcohol. If they do it a lot, you say they are **boozy** or a **boozer**. A **boozy** occasion is one when a lot of alcohol is drunk. ◇ People sometimes call a pub the **boozer**.

bop (bopping, bopped) When you **bop** or have a **bop**, you dance to pop music. ◇ **Bop** is a style of jazz.

borax is a mineral in the form of white crystals. It is used in making glass and as a cleaning agent.

bordello (bordellos) A **bordello** is a brothel.

border (bordering, bordered) ❑ The **border** between two countries or regions is the dividing line between them, or land close to this line. When two countries or regions share a border, you say one country **borders** the other or **borders on** it. You can also say a country or area of land **borders** something like a river, or is **bordered by** it.
❑ In a garden, a **border** is a long narrow flowerbed, often at the edge of a lawn or path.
❑ A **border** is also a strip or band around the edge of something. Borders are often there for decoration.
❑ If you say someone's behaviour **borders on** something, you mean it is almost that thing. ...*actions which border on the reckless... His confidence borders on arrogance.*

borderline is used to talk about situations in which it is difficult to decide whether something fits into one category or another. *So many umpiring decisions are borderline... They would all be borderline cases for getting housing benefit.*

bore (boring, bored) ❑ If you say someone or something is **boring**, you mean they are dull and uninteresting. You can also say you are **bored** by them or with them. *He soon became bored with politics.* You can call something dull and uninteresting a **bore**. ◇ If you call a person a **bore**, you mean they talk a lot about things nobody is interested in. ◇ If you are **bored**, you have lost interest in something, or you have nothing interesting to do.
❑ If you **bore** a hole in something, you make a hole using something like a drill.
❑ The **bore** of a gun is the inside diameter of its barrel.
❑ See also **bear**.

boredom is the feeling you have when you are bored.

borehole A **borehole** is a deep hole drilled in the ground to search for water, oil, or mineral ores, or to extract water from an underground source.

born ❑ When a baby is **born**, it comes out of its mother's womb. ◇ **-born** is added to words to show where someone was born. ...*Austrian-born muscleman Arnold Schwarzenegger.* ◇ If you say someone is **born of** particular parents, you are saying who their parents were.
❑ You use **born** to say someone has a natural ability to do something well. *She was a born storyteller.* If you say someone was **born to** do something, you mean they have great natural ability for it. *He was born to be a soldier.*
❑ You also use **born** to say when or where something started or was created. *The movement was born 12 years ago... Hatfield is where the wartime Mosquito fighter was born.*
❑ If you say one thing was **born of** another, you mean it happened because of it. *This is fear born of ignorance.*

born-again A **born-again** Christian is a person who has experienced a spiritual conversion and become a devout and often evangelizing Christian. ◇ **Born-again** is also used to describe someone who has become an enthusiastic convert to a new idea or way of life, or has renewed an interest in something they had neglected. ...*a born-again rock fan... ...born-again Communists.*

borne See **bear**.

borough (*pron:* **bur-ruh**) In the past, a **borough** was an English or Welsh town which had its own local council and mayor. Since 1974, the only official boroughs have been the districts which make up Greater London; however, some district councils have been allowed to call themselves 'boroughs' as a courtesy title and to elect a mayor. In the US and New Zealand there are towns called 'boroughs'; the city of New York is divided into five boroughs.

borrow (borrower) ❑ If you **borrow** something which belongs to someone else, you take it, with or without their permission, intending to return it. ◇ If you **borrow** money from a person or organization, they give it to you and you agree to pay it back at some future time, usually with interest. A person who borrows money is called a **borrower**. *Borrowers can choose endowment, repayment or pension mortgages.*
❑ If you **borrow** something like an idea from someone,

you make use of it for your own purposes.

borscht (*or* **borsch**) is a Russian or Polish soup which has beetroot as its main ingredient. It can be served either hot or cold, sometimes with sour cream.

borstal Prisons for young criminals used to be called borstals, but are now known as 'young offenders' institutions'.

bosom (*pron:* **buz-um**) ❑ A woman's **bosom** is her breasts.

❑ A **bosom** friend is a very close friend. ◇ If someone is living in the **bosom** of their family or community, they are among people who love and protect them.

boss (**bosses**, **bossing**, **bossed**) Someone's **boss** is the person in charge of the organization where they work. ◇ If someone **bosses** you **about**, they keep telling you what to do.

bossy (**bossiness**) A **bossy** person enjoys telling other people what to do. You can talk about the **bossiness** of someone like this.

bosun A ship's **bosun** or **boatswain** (*both pron:* **boh-sn**) is the person on board who is officially responsible for the ship's maintenance and equipment.

botany (**botanic**, **botanical**; **botanist**) **Botany** is the scientific study of plants. **Botanic** and **botanical** are used to talk about things to do with botany; a person who specializes in studying plants is called a **botanist**. ◇ **Botanic** or **botanical gardens** are gardens where plants are grown for public display and scientific study.

botch (**botches**, **botching**, **botched**) If you **botch** something or make a **botch** of it, you do it badly and clumsily. *Building repairs were sometimes botched.*

both When you mention two people or things, you use **both** to make it clear you are including each of them in what you say. *Both her parents had died... My sister and I both chose pasta... After the meeting, both the French and the Germans claimed success.*

bother (**bothering**, **bothered**; **bothersome**) ❑ **Bother** is trouble, fuss, or difficulty. ◇ If you do not **bother** to do something or cannot be **bothered** to do it, you do not do it because you think it is unnecessary or too much trouble. *Only a tiny proportion of its members bothered to vote.* ◇ If you think it is pointless to do something, you can say **why bother** to do it? *Why bother with dealers at all?* ◇ If you are not **bothered** about something or it does not **bother** you, you do not mind whether it happens or is done.

❑ If something **bothers** you, it worries or irritates you. You can say something like this is **bothersome**. ◇ If people **bother** you, they make nuisances of themselves, for example by trying to get some information out of you.

bottle (**bottling**, **bottled**) ❑ A **bottle** is a glass or plastic container, especially one for liquids. ◇ A baby's **bottle** is a drinking container with a rubber teat on the end through which the baby sucks. You say a baby is **bottle-fed** when it drinks milk from a bottle rather than its mother's breast.

❑ If you **bottle** something like wine, beer, or jam, you put it into bottles to store it. ◇ **Bottled** gas is kept under pressure in special metal cylinders.

❑ If you **bottle up** strong feelings, you do not show them or say how you feel. ◇ If a group of people are **bottled up** somewhere, they are kept there by force and cannot get out.

bottle bank A **bottle bank** is a large container in a public place for people to dispose of used glass bottles and containers, so the glass can be collected and recycled.

bottleneck A **bottleneck** is a narrow part of a road where traffic has to slow down or stop, often causing a jam. You can also have a **bottleneck** on a river or canal. ◇ Something which slows progress can be called a **bottleneck**. *More investment is going towards transport and agriculture where supply bottlenecks have been serious.*

bottom (**bottoming**, **bottomed**) ❑ A person's **bottom** is the part of their body they sit on.

❑ The **bottom** of something is its lowest part. ◇ The **bottom** thing in a series is the lowest one, the last to be added, or the least important. *...the bottom shelf... New motorway building was placed at the bottom of a list of priorities.* ◇ The **bottom** of a street is its end, where it meets another street. The **bottom** of a garden is the end furthest from the house.

❑ If someone comes **bottom** in a test or exam, they have the lowest marks. Similarly, if a person or team comes **bottom** in a game or competition, all the other competitors do better than they do. If they are **bottom** of a league or table, they have the lowest number of points.

❑ If you say someone is **at the bottom of the pile** or **heap**, you mean they are poorer or lower in status than everyone else.

❑ If you **get to the bottom of** something, you discover the truth about it or its real cause.

❑ When something **bottoms out**, it stops falling or getting worse, and stays at the level it has reached. *House prices appear to have bottomed out.*

bottom line In business, the last line of a financial statement summarizing the net profit or loss of a company is called the **bottom line**. When you talk about a company's **bottom line**, you mean its profit or loss. *...businessmen whose only measure of success is the bottom line.* ◇ The **bottom line** is also the thing which counts most in a situation. *The bottom line is value for money.*

bottomless If you talk about someone's purse or pocket being **bottomless**, you mean they have an unlimited supply of money. ◇ If you talk about money or resources disappearing into a **bottomless** pit, you mean someone's requirements or demands are never satisfied, no matter how much help they receive.

botulism is a serious form of food poisoning usually caused by eating food which has not been tinned properly.

boudoir (*pron:* **boo-dwahr**) A **boudoir** is a woman's bedroom or private sitting room.

bouffant (*pron:* **boof-fon**) When a woman has a **bouffant** hairstyle, her hair has a raised or puffed-out appearance. This is often achieved by combing the hair down towards the scalp.

bougainvillea (*pron:* **boo-gan-vill-ee-a**) is a tropical climbing plant with vivid mauve flowers.

bough (*rhymes with* '**now**') A large branch of a tree is called a **bough**.

bought See **buy**.

boulder **Boulders** are large round rocks.

boulevard (*pron:* **boo-le-vard**) A **boulevard** is a wide street in a city, often with trees on either side.

bounce (bouncing, bounced; bouncy) ❑ When an object bounces, it springs back from something after hitting it. If you **bounce** something like a ball, you throw it against a surface to make it do this. ◇ When a person **bounces**, they jump up and down, often on something springy like a trampoline. ◇ You say a vehicle **bounces** when it is driven on an uneven surface and jolts up and down.

❑ If something like light or sound **bounces off** a surface, it reaches the surface and is reflected back.

❑ If something like hair has **bounce** or is **bouncy**, it is springy and will not flatten easily.

❑ If a person is **bouncy** or full of **bounce**, they have a lot of energy and confidence. ◇ If someone **bounces** somewhere, they move with a lot of energy, often because they are happy and confident. ◇ A **bouncing** baby is attractively fit and healthy.

❑ When someone or something **bounces back** after a setback, they quickly get back to their previous state or level.

❑ A **bounce** is also a noticeable rise in the success or popularity of something. *The company enjoyed a strong bounce in its share price this week.*

❑ If someone is **bounced** into doing something, they are hurried into doing it against their wishes or before they are ready for it.

❑ If a cheque you write **bounces**, your bank will not pay any money to the person you make it out to, because you do not have enough money in your account. The bank sends the cheque back to you.

bouncer ❑ A **bouncer** is a man whose job is to stop undesirable people getting into a place like a pub or nightclub, and to throw people out if they cause trouble.

❑ In cricket, a **bouncer** is a ball which bounces very high after it has been bowled.

bound (bounding, bounded; boundless) ❑ If you say something is **bound** to happen, you mean it is certain to happen. *An increase in oil prices is bound to increase inflationary pressures.*

❑ If you are **bound** by something like an agreement or law, you have a duty or responsibility to obey it. ◇ If you feel **bound** to do something, you feel morally obliged to do it.

❑ If one thing is **bound up** with another, the two things are closely linked. *The future of this country is inextricably bound up with Europe.*

❑ See also **bind**.

❑ If you are **bound** for a place, you are on your way there. You add **-bound** to a word to say where someone is going. *...homeward-bound commuters.*

❑ The **bounds** of something are its limits. *Optical astronomy is extending the bounds of some already intensely explored territory.* You add **-bound** to a word to show what someone or something is limited or restricted to. *Some sufferers of ME become wheelchair-bound.* ◇ If you say something **knows no bounds** or is **boundless**, you mean it does not seem to have any limits. *...Strachan's boundless enthusiasm.*

❑ **Bounds** is used to say whether something is possible or can be believed. You say, for example, that something is within the **bounds** of possibility. *It's not beyond the bounds of possibility that a decision might be taken... His ex-*planation stretched the bounds of belief.

❑ If an area or place is **out of bounds**, you are forbidden to go there.

❑ If an area is **bounded** by something, it is bordered by it. *...rolling fields bounded by dry-stone walls.*

❑ When someone **bounds** somewhere, they move there quickly and energetically. *He bounded up the stairs.* ◇ If something **bounds** ahead, it increases or progresses rapidly. If it increases by **leaps and bounds**, it increases quickly, by large amounts at a time.

boundary (boundaries) ❑ The **boundary** of an area of land is its outer edge, which separates it from other areas. ◇ In cricket, the **boundary** is the line marking the edge of the pitch. When a batsman hits the ball beyond this line, he scores a **boundary**.

❑ The **boundary** between two similar kinds of thing is the point at which something ceases to be one thing and becomes the other. *The boundary between public and private health care is being blurred.*

boundless See **bound**.

bounty (bountiful) ❑ If someone is very generous, you can talk about their **bounty** or say they are **bountiful**. ◇ If there is a **bountiful** supply of something, there is a lot of it.

❑ **Bounty** is also a reward or payment for something. In the past, a person could be paid **bounty** for capturing or killing a dangerous criminal; someone who made a living from this was called a **bounty hunter**. Nowadays, when people talk about a **bounty hunter**, they usually mean someone who tries to make money by offering their services to people involved in serious accidents. *...bounty-hunting lawyers.*

bouquet (*pron:* boo-**kay**) ❑ A **bouquet** is an attractively arranged bunch of flowers, especially one given as a present. ◇ If you give someone praise or a compliment, you can say you give them a **bouquet**. *A bouquet to the Treasury, by the way, for taking our criticisms seriously.*

❑ The characteristic smell of wine and some spirits is called its **bouquet**.

bouquet garni (*plural:* bouquets garni) (*both pron:* boo-**kay** gah-**nee**) A **bouquet garni** is a small bunch of herbs tied together and used for flavouring when making soups and stews.

bourbon (*pron:* **bur**-bon) is a type of American whisky. Its main ingredient is maize.

bourgeois (bourgeoisie) (*pron:* **boorzh**-wah, boorzh-wah-**zee**; *the 'zh' sounds like 's' in 'pleasure'*) **Bourgeois** means middle-class. The **bourgeoisie** are middle-class people. If you say someone has **bourgeois** attitudes, you mean they are materialistic and narrow-minded.

bout ❑ If you have a **bout** of some illness, you have it badly for a short time. You can also have a **bout** of nerves or anxiety. ◇ A concentrated burst of activity can be called a **bout**. *Shops remained open for a final bout of trading.*

❑ A **bout** is also a boxing or wrestling match.

boutique (*pron:* boo-**teek**) A **boutique** is a small shop which sells fashionable clothes, shoes, or jewellery.

bouzouki (*pron:* boo-**zoo**-kee) The **bouzouki** is a Greek stringed instrument, which sounds a bit like a mandolin.

bovine is used to talk about things connected with cattle. *...bovine growth hormone.*

bow (bowing, bowed) ❏ If you **bow** (*pron like 'now'*) or make a **bow**, you briefly bend forward as a formal greeting, or to show respect. ◇ If you **take a bow**, you acknowledge applause or praise, by bowing or in some other way.

❏ If a person is **bowed**, their body is bent forward, usually because they are very old. ◇ If you say someone is **bowed down by** something, you mean it seems too much for them to bear. *He put his head in his hands as though suddenly bowed down with grief.*

❏ If you **bow** your head, you bend it downwards as a mark of respect, or because you are ashamed.

❏ If you **bow to** someone's wishes, you agree to do what they want. ◇ If you **bow out** of something, you stop taking part in it.

❏ The front part of a ship is called the **bow** or **bows**. If someone **fires a shot across your bows**, they give you a warning.

❏ A **bow** (*pron like 'low'*) is a knot with two loops and two loose ends, for tying things like shoelaces or ribbons.

❏ A **bow** is also a weapon for shooting arrows. It consists of a long piece of wood bent into a curve by a string attached to both ends.

❏ The **bow** of a violin or other stringed instrument is a long thin piece of wood with horsehair stretched along it, which you move across the strings to play the instrument.

bow tie A **bow tie** is a man's tie in the form of a bow, worn especially on formal occasions.

bow window A **bow window** is a curved window sticking out from a wall.

bowdlerized (bowdlerization) (*can be spelled with an 's' instead of a 'z'*) A **bowdlerized** version of a book has had words or sections removed or changed, because they are thought to be indecent or offensive. *...a bowdlerization of A Midsummer Night's Dream.*

bowel ❏ A person's **bowels** or **bowel** are the tubes in the lower part of their body through which waste matter passes on its way to their anus.

❏ You can say the parts deep inside something are its **bowels**. *I found myself in the bowels of the theatre, underneath the stage.*

bowl ❏ A **bowl** is a circular container with a wide uncovered top, used especially in cooking or for serving food. ◇ A **bowl** is also the hollow rounded part of something. *... a lavatory bowl.*

❏ **Bowls** is a game in which the players try to roll heavy wooden balls called **bowls** as near as possible to a small white ball called the jack.

❏ When someone **bowls** in cricket, they throw the ball down the pitch towards the batsman. If they hit the batsman's wicket, you say he is **bowled** or **bowled out**.

❏ If you are **bowled over** by something, it makes a great impression on you.

bowler ❏ In a cricket match, the **bowler** is the person who is bowling. A **bowler** is a cricketer who specializes in bowling.

❏ A **bowler** or **bowler hat** is a stiff round black hat with a narrow curved brim, worn by some British businessmen.

bowling is a game in which you roll a heavy ball down a long narrow track to try to knock down ten objects called pins standing at the other end. The track you roll the ball along is called a **bowling alley**. A **bowling alley** is also a building containing several tracks.

bowling green A **bowling green** is an area of very smooth short grass on which the game of bowls is played.

bowls See bowl.

box (boxes, boxing, boxed; boxer) ❏ A **box** is a container with a firm base, sides, and usually a lid. **Boxed** things are packed or sold in boxes.

❏ On a form, a **box** is a rectangular space to write something in.

❏ In a theatre, a **box** is a separate area like a little room where a small number of people can sit to watch the performance. When an area like this is occupied by the Queen or other members of the royal family, it is called the **royal box**. ◇ At a football ground, the **directors' box** is an enclosed area, sometimes a small glass-sided room, where members of the club's management sit to watch the game.

❏ If you are **boxed in**, you are unable to move your car, because it is surrounded by other vehicles. ◇ If someone is **boxed in** during a race, they are surrounded by other competitors, and cannot get clear of them.

❏ **Boxing** is a sport in which two men called **boxers**, wearing large padded gloves, try to knock each other out or score points by hitting each other.

❏ **Boxers** are also smooth-haired dogs with flat faces.

❏ **Box** is a slow-growing evergreen shrub with shiny leaves, often used for hedges.

box office The **box office** in a theatre, cinema, or concert hall is the place where the tickets are sold. **Box office** is often used to say how successful a production or performer is in terms of the number of tickets sold. *...one of the greatest box-office hits of all time.*

boxer See box.

boxer shorts are men's underpants shaped like shorts but with a front opening.

Boxing Day is the first weekday after Christmas, observed as a public holiday.

boy A **boy** is a male child.

Boy Scout See Scout.

boycott If people **boycott** a product, they refuse to buy it. If they **boycott** an organization or event, they refuse to have anything to do with it. When any of these things happen, you say there is a **boycott**.

boyfriend A person's **boyfriend** is the man they are having a romantic or sexual relationship with.

boyhood A man's **boyhood** is the period of his life when he is a boy.

boyish If you say someone is **boyish**, you mean they look or behave like a boy.

bra A **bra** is a piece of underwear worn by a woman to support her breasts.

brace (bracing, braced; braces) ❏ If you **brace** yourself for something unpleasant or difficult, you prepare to face it or deal with it. You can also say you are **braced** for something like this.

❏ A **brace** is an object fastened to something to straighten or support it. *...a knee brace.*

❏ **Braces** are elasticated straps worn over the shoulders and attached to the front and back of a pair of trousers to hold them up.

❏ A **brace** of things is two of the same kind. ...*a brace of artichokes*. The plural of 'brace' is **brace**. ...*a few brace of grouse*.

❏ If something is **bracing**, it is refreshing and stimulating. ...*bracing draughts of air*... ...*a bracing game of squash*.

brace and bit A **brace and bit** is a hand-operated tool for boring holes in wood.

bracelet A **bracelet** is a chain or band worn around the wrist.

bracken is a plant like a large fern which grows on hills and in woods.

bracket (bracketing, bracketed) ❏ A **bracket** is a piece of metal or wood fastened to a wall to support something like a shelf.

❏ **Brackets** are a pair of written marks, such as ( ), placed round a word or several words, to separate them from the words surrounding them.

❏ A **bracket** is also a range of things, for example ages or prices. ...*the lower income bracket*... ...*the 35-54 age bracket*. ◇ If you **bracket** two or more things together, you treat them as if they belong together. *She objected to pregnant women being bracketed with the sick.*

brackish water is slightly salty.

bradawl A **bradawl** is a small hand-operated tool for piercing holes, especially in wood or leather.

brag (bragging, bragged) If someone **brags** about something they own or have done, they boast about it.

Brahmin (*or* Brahman) A **Brahmin** is a Hindu of the highest caste.

braid (braiding, braided) **Braid** is a strip of contrasting cloth or twisted threads used to decorate clothes or soft furnishings. ◇ If you **braid** hair or thread, you plait it. A **braid** is a length of hair which has been plaited and tied.

Braille is a system of printing for the blind, in which letters are represented by raised dots which can be felt with the fingers.

brain ❏ The **brain** of a person or animal is the mass of nerve tissue inside their skull which controls their body and enables them to think and feel.

❏ A person's **brain** is also their mind and the way they think. *She is more articulate and has a faster brain.* ◇ If you say someone has **brains** or a good **brain**, you mean they are able to learn and understand things quickly, solve problems, and make good decisions.

❏ If you **pick** someone's **brains**, you ask for their help on a subject they know a lot about.

❏ The **brains** behind something is the person or people organizing it. ◇ When people talk about the **brain drain**, they mean the movement of large numbers of highly qualified people away from their own country to countries where conditions and salaries are better.

brain death (brain dead) **Brain death** is a condition in which someone's brain has permanently stopped working, though their heart and lungs may be kept going by a machine. When someone is in this condition, you say they are **brain dead.**

brain power (*or* brainpower) is the ability to think intelligently and logically.

brainchild Someone's **brainchild** is something they have invented or created.

brainstorm (brainstorming) ❏ If someone has a **brainstorm**, they suddenly become unable to think sensibly, and do things they would not normally do.

❏ **Brainstorming** is intensive discussion to solve problems or develop ideas.

brainwash (brainwashes, brainwashing, brainwashed) If someone is **brainwashed**, they are made to believe something they would not normally believe, often by forcing them to listen to it repeated over and over again while they are kept in isolation or deprived of sleep.

brainwave If you have a **brainwave**, you suddenly have a good idea.

brainy A **brainy** person is clever or intelligent.

braise (braising, braised) When you **braise** food, you brown it lightly by frying, then cook it slowly in a small amount of liquid.

brake (braking, braked) ❏ A **brake** is a device for making a vehicle slow down or stop. When you **brake,** you apply the brakes on a vehicle. A road vehicle's **brake lights** are lights at the back which light up when the brakes are applied.

❏ A **brake** is also something which has the effect of slowing something down. *The skills shortage in Britain is still a brake on economic recovery.*

bramble **Brambles** are thorny bushes which produce blackberries. Blackberries are themselves sometimes called **brambles.** ◇ Other types of thorny bushes growing in the wild can also be called **brambles.**

bran is the small brown flakes left over when wheat grains have been made into white flour. Wholemeal bread and some cereals contain bran. People are recommended to have it in their diet, because of its fibre content.

branch (branches, branching, branched) ❏ The **branches** of a tree are the parts growing out of its trunk.

❏ A **branch** of a business or other organization is one of its offices, shops, or local groups. ◇ A **branch** of a subject is one of its areas of study or interest. *Electricity in those days was seen as a branch of chemistry.*

❏ If you **branch out**, you start doing a greater variety of work, or take up new interests.

❏ If a road **branches off**, it goes off at an angle from another one.

❏ A **branch line** is a railway built to serve small towns, as distinct from a main line between cities.

brand (branded) ❏ A **brand** of something is a kind or variety of it. ...*his own brand of socialism*.

❏ A **brand** of a product is the version made by one manufacturer. The **brand name** of a product is the name of the company which makes it, or its trademark. ◇ A **branded** product is made by a well-known manufacturer and has the manufacturer's name on the label. ◇ **Own-brand** products are made and sold by a supermarket or chain store, and have the store's name on them.

❏ When an animal is **branded**, a permanent mark is made on its skin, either by burning or freezing, to show who owns it. A **branding iron** is a long-handled metal tool used for this purpose. ◇ If someone is **branded** as something bad, they are given a reputation for being that thing.

❏ If something is **brand new**, it is completely new and has never been used before.

brandish (brandishes, brandishing, brandished) If you **brandish** something like a weapon, you wave it in the air in a threatening way. You can also **brandish** an object to draw attention to it. *Demonstrators brandished placards.*

brandy is a strong alcoholic spirit distilled from wine or fermented fruit juice.

brash (brashness) If you say someone is **brash,** you mean their behaviour is tasteless or unpleasantly loud and over-confident. *They were amused by his youthful brashness.*

brass is an alloy made from copper and zinc. ◇ In an orchestra, the **brass** or **brass section** consists of the brass wind instruments, such as the trumpets and trombones. ❑ The **top brass** of an organization are its most senior members.

brasserie A brasserie is (a) a bar where food is sold. (b) a kind of small restaurant.

brassiere (*pron:* bra-zee-er) A **brassiere** is the same as a bra.

brassy A brassy woman dresses or behaves in a showy and rather tasteless way. ◇ **Brassy** music is played on brass instruments and is harsh and loud.

brat People sometimes call a badly-behaved child a **brat.** ◇ A group of successful and influential young people is sometimes called a **brat pack.**

bravado (*pron:* bra-vah-doh) is an appearance of courage or self-confidence, put on to impress people.

brave (braver, bravest; braving, braved; bravely, bravery) You say people are **brave** when they put themselves in danger in order to achieve something; you also talk about their **bravery.** *They fought bravely.* ◇ If you **brave** an uncomfortable or dangerous situation, you put up with it in order to do something. *About 150,000 people braved the downpour to listen to the concert... ...a reporter who has braved bullets and bombs.*

bravura (*pron:* brav-yoor-a) When someone puts on a **bravura** performance, they show off their skill at something.

brawl A brawl is a fight or struggle, especially one where people hit each other with their fists. When people fight like this, you say they are **brawling.**

brawn (brawny) ❑ Someone who has **brawn** or is **brawny** is strong and muscular. Brawn is often used to talk about physical strength in contrast to intelligence. *He has proved his brains match his brawn.* ❑ Brawn is also meat taken from a cooked pig's head, set in jelly and eaten cold.

bray When a donkey **brays,** it makes a loud 'hee-haw' sound. ◇ If a person **brays,** they speak or laugh with a loud harsh sound, a bit like a donkey.

brazen (brazenly) You say someone is **brazen** when they do something bad or shocking without caring what people think. *The children were brazenly stripping off and leaping into the sea.* ◇ If someone who has done something wrong **brazens** it **out,** they do not show any shame about what they have done.

brazier A brazier is a metal container in which coal or charcoal is burned to keep people warm out of doors.

brazil nut Brazil nuts are large three-sided nuts from a South American tree.

breach (breaches, breaching, breached) ❑ If there is a **breach** of something like a law, promise, or agreement, or if it is **breached,** it is broken. ◇ If a person or company is **in breach of contract,** they have failed to carry out the terms of a legal agreement. ◇ If someone is charged with a **breach of the peace,** they are charged with behaving threateningly in a public place, in a way which frightens other people. ❑ A **breach** in a relationship is a quarrel or serious disagreement. ❑ When someone **breaches** a barrier, they make a gap in it. *...the breaching of the Berlin Wall.* You can also say a river **breaches** its banks. You can talk about a **breach** in a barrier or a river's banks. ❑ If someone **steps into the breach,** they help out in a difficult situation by taking over someone else's duties or responsibilities.

bread is a food made from flour, water, and often yeast, which is made into a soft dough and baked in an oven. ❑ The business or work which provides someone's main income can be called their **bread and butter.** ◇ **Bread and butter** is also used to talk about the basic or routine part of something. *It's the bread and butter of police work, checking if anybody had seen anything suspicious.*

bread-bin A bread-bin is a container for bread.

bread-board A bread-board is a board for cutting bread on.

breadcrumbs are tiny pieces of bread, which are often used in cooking.

breadline If you say someone is living on or near the **breadline,** you mean they are very poor.

breadth The breadth of something is the distance between its sides. ◇ If you talk about the **breadth** of something like a person's knowledge, you mean it covers a wide range of things.

breadwinner The breadwinner of a family is the person who earns the money to pay for its needs.

break (breaking, broke, have broken) ❑ When an object **breaks,** it separates or splits into smaller pieces. ◇ If you **break** a part of something **off,** you separate it from the main part. ◇ If you **break** a bone in your body, the bone cracks or splits. ❑ If something is **broken down,** it is split into smaller parts or sections. *...the assumption that work can be broken down into a collection of small tasks.* ◇ If statistical information is **broken down,** it is divided up in a way which makes it easier to understand. You call this a **breakdown** of the information. ❑ When a ship which has run aground **breaks up,** it splits into two or more parts. Similarly, you can say a country or organization **breaks up;** you can also talk about its **break-up.** ❑ If something like a system **breaks down,** it no longer works. When talks **break down,** they stop because the people involved cannot reach agreement. You can talk about a **breakdown** in things like these. *...the temporary breakdown in law and order.* ❑ When someone **breaks** something like a promise or agreement, they do not do what they promised or agreed to do. ◇ If someone **breaks** a rule or a law, they do something which goes against it. ❑ If someone **breaks** a record, especially in sport, they improve on the previous best performance. You also say a record is **broken** when something is bigger, lasts longer, or reaches a higher level than ever before. ❑ If someone **breaks** a code, they work out what it means, so coded messages can be interpreted.

❏ When people **break** a strike, they make it ineffective, by doing the work of the people on strike. ◇ If the police **break up** a demonstration or a fight, they put a stop to it, often using force.

❏ If there is a **break** in something like a deadlock or stalemate or if it is **broken**, it is brought to an end.

❏ When something like a meeting **breaks up**, it finishes. ◇ When a school **breaks up**, it finishes for the holidays.

❏ If you **break off** in the middle of doing something, you suddenly stop doing it. ◇ If you **break in** when something is happening, you interrupt it. ◇ If you say or do something which interrupts a period of silence or monotony, you can say you **break** the silence or monotony. ◇ **break the ice: see ice.**

❏ If you **break** a habit, you succeed in giving it up. ◇ If people **break with** something like a tradition, they no longer observe it. You can talk about a **break** with a tradition or with the past. ◇ If someone **breaks the mould**, they start a new way of doing things, when things had been unchanged for a long time.

❏ If someone **breaks** another person, they deliberately ruin their success or career. ◇ If you **break** someone's resistance or patience, you wear it down. ◇ If you **break** someone's grip or hold on something, you end their control over it. ◇ **break** someone's **heart: see heart.**

❏ When someone **breaks** a piece of news, they tell it to other people. ◇ If someone **breaks** their silence, they speak out about something they had earlier been refusing to discuss.

❏ When something like a crisis or storm **breaks**, it suddenly happens. ◇ When something like a fight, argument, or disease **breaks out**, it begins suddenly.

❏ When a boy's voice **breaks**, it becomes permanently deeper and sounds like a man's.

❏ If people **break away** from a group or organization, they leave, often to form a new group or organization. An organization formed like this is called a **breakaway** organization. ◇ If you **break free** from someone or something, you get away from them. ◇ **break ranks: see rank.**

❏ If a tool or machine is **broken**, it is damaged and does not work. ◇ If a machine or vehicle **breaks down**, it stops and cannot be restarted. When this happens, you say there is a **breakdown. Broken-down** machines and vehicles no longer work.

❏ If you **break down** something like a wall or barrier, you destroy it by knocking it down. ◇ If you **break through** a barrier, you find or force a way through it. ◇ If someone **breaks into** a car or building, they get into it illegally, using force. When this happens, you say there is a **break-in.** ◇ If someone **breaks into** a computer system, they gain access to the information stored in it without permission. ◇ If someone **breaks out** of jail, they escape. A **breakout** is an escape.

❏ If a person **breaks down**, they start crying uncontrollably. ◇ If someone has a **breakdown**, they become very depressed and ill. ◇ If something is at **breaking point**, it has reached the limits of what it can cope with. *The city's public services are at breaking point.*

❏ If a business **breaks even**, it makes enough money to cover its costs, so it has no losses but does not make a profit either.

❏ A **break** is an interruption or pause in something.

◇ When people take a **break**, they stop work for a short time. You can also say they **break** for a meal or coffee. ◇ You also say people take a **break** when they have a short holiday.

❏ **Break into** is used to say someone starts to do something. For example, you can say someone 'breaks into song' or 'breaks into a run'. ◇ If you **break into** a new business or career, you start to become involved in it, or to get power or influence in it. ◇ **break new ground: see ground.**

❏ If someone gets a **break**, they have an unexpected lucky opportunity which helps them to be successful or famous.

❏ If you **break** your ties or links with someone or something, you cut yourself off from them. ◇ If you **break off** a relationship or contact, you end it. ◇ If people in a relationship **break up**, they separate, and the relationship ends. When this happens, you say there is a **break-up.** Similarly, you can say a group or organization **breaks up** or talk about its **break-up.**

break-in See break.

break-up See break.

breakage When something is broken, you say there is a **breakage.** *Any business needs insurance against risks such as breakage of plate glass.*

breakaway See break.

breakdown See break.

breaker ❏ **-breaker** is added to words to say someone has broken something. For example you can call someone a 'law-breaker', a 'record-breaker', or a 'strike-breaker'.

❏ **Breakers** are large waves in the sea.

breakfast is the first meal of the day.

breakfast television consists of TV programmes broadcast when most people are having breakfast.

breakneck If something is happening at **breakneck** speed, it is happening very fast.

breakthrough When someone makes an important scientific discovery, you can say they have made a **breakthrough.**

breakwater A **breakwater** is a wooden or stone wall extending from the shore into the sea. It is built to protect a harbour or beach from the force of the waves.

breast ❏ A woman's **breasts** are the two soft rounded fleshy parts on her chest which can produce milk to feed a baby. When a woman feeds her baby with milk from her breasts, you say she **breast-feeds** the baby. ◇ A person's chest can also be called their **breast.** *We saw a little man on the footpath with his arms folded over his breast.*

❏ If you say someone is **beating their breast,** you mean they are making a big show of their guilt or regret about something. ◇ If you **make a clean breast** of something, you tell someone the truth about yourself or about something wrong you have done.

❏ A bird's **breast** is the front part of its body.

breastbone See sternum.

breastplate A **breastplate** was the part of a suit of armour which covered and protected a soldier's chest.

breaststroke is a swimming stroke. When you do the breaststroke, you lie on your front, moving your arms horizontally through the water and kicking both legs in a frog-like way.

breath ❏ Your **breath** is the air you take in and let out when you breathe. If you take a **breath**, you breathe in deeply. ◇ If you are **out of breath**, you are breathing quickly and with difficulty, usually because you have been doing something energetic. ◇ If you are **short of breath** or **gasping for breath**, you are having difficulty breathing, for example because you are ill.

❏ If you **hold your breath**, you stop breathing for a short time. ◇ You also say someone is **holding their breath** when they are anxiously waiting for something.

❏ If you **catch your breath**, you have a short rest in the middle of doing something. ◇ If you do something without **drawing breath** or without **pausing for breath**, you keep doing it without stopping.

❏ If you say someone **takes a deep breath**, you mean they pause for a moment before doing something difficult or dangerous.

❏ If something **takes your breath away**, it is so beautiful or surprising you are moved or amazed by it.

❏ If you say something **under your breath**, you say it very quietly so nobody can hear. ◇ If you say someone says something **in the next breath**, you mean they seem to be contradicting what they have just said. *The same officials who stress the possibility of a breakdown say in the next breath that ministers are keen to see Maastricht succeed.* ◇ If you say something can be mentioned **in the same breath** as something else, you mean it is of a similar standard. *Glasgow likes to think it is a sophisticated cosmopolitan centre, deserving to be mentioned in the same breath as Munich and Milan.*

❏ If you say something is **a waste of breath**, you mean there is no point in saying it, because the person you say it to will not take any notice.

❏ If you say something is like **a breath of fresh air**, you mean it comes as a refreshing change.

breath test If someone in charge of a vehicle is given a **breath test**, they are breathalyzed by the police.

breathable materials are used to make clothing which is rainproof yet does not develop condensation on the inside.

breathalyze (breathalyzing, breathalyzed; breathalyzer) (*can be spelled with an 's' instead of a 'z'*) If the driver of a vehicle is **breathalyzed**, they are asked by the police to breathe into a machine called a 'breathalyzer', which measures the amount of alcohol they have drunk. 'Breathalyzer' is a trademark.

breathe (breathing, breathed) ❏ When a person or animal **breathes**, they take air into their lungs and let it out again.

❏ If you **breathe a sigh of relief** or **breathe more easily**, you are very glad something is over or has been avoided. ◇ If you are given a **breathing space**, you have a short time in which to recover from one thing and prepare for something else.

❏ If someone is **breathing down your neck**, they are following very close behind you. You also say someone is **breathing down your neck** when they are closely and impatiently watching everything you do.

❏ If you **breathe new life** into something, you revive interest in it, or make it more likely to succeed.

breather If you take a **breather**, you stop what you are doing and have a short rest.

breathless (breathlessly; breathlessness) If you are **breathless**, you are having difficulty breathing properly. *He hurried breathlessly towards the lifts... ...a lung condition that causes chronic breathlessness.* ◇ **Breathless** is also used to describe someone's behaviour when they are very excited. *...a breathless phone call.*

breathtaking A **breathtaking** view is outstandingly beautiful. ◇ You can also call an amazing fact **breathtaking**.

bred See **breed**.

breech ❏ In a **breech** birth or delivery, the baby is born with its feet or buttocks appearing first.

❏ The **breech** of a firearm is the part behind the barrel.

breeches (*pron:* **brit**-chiz) are trousers which come down to the knees, worn especially for riding.

breed (breeding, bred; breeder) ❏ A **breed** of an animal is one particular kind of it. For example, terriers are a breed of dog. ◇ **Breed** is also used to talk about a kind of person. *He was that rare breed – a politician without political ambition.* ◇ If you say someone is one of a **dying breed**, you mean there are not many people like that nowadays.

❏ A new or improved version of something can be called a **new breed** of it. *...a new breed of portable computers.*

❏ When animals **breed**, they mate and produce offspring. ◇ When people **breed** animals, they select pairs for mating, to try and produce the best example of a breed, or improve its suitability for a particular purpose. *The pit-bull has been bred as a fighting dog.* Similarly, when people **breed** plants, they use special methods to produce the types they want. People who breed animals or plants are called **breeders**. *...a pig breeder.*

❏ If one thing **breeds** another, it causes it to exist or happen. *Research breeds new products, which generate profits and growth... Success has bred complacency and self-satisfaction.*

❏ If you say someone was **born and bred** somewhere, you mean they were born and spent their childhood there.

❏ If you say someone has **breeding**, you mean they belong to the upper classes and are very well-mannered. See also **well-bred**.

breeding ground An animal's **breeding ground** is the place where it goes to breed. ◇ You also say something is a **breeding ground** when a type of feeling or behaviour is likely to develop there. *Harsh economic conditions are a breeding ground for political extremism.*

breeze (breezing, breezed; breezy) ❏ A **breeze** is a gentle wind. ◇ If the weather is **breezy**, it is rather windy.

❏ You say someone **breezes into** a place when they come in in an unconcerned way, although they have arrived late or have no right to be there. ◇ If someone's behaviour is **breezy**, they behave in a bright lively way. ◇ If you **breeze through** something, you get it done quickly and easily.

breeze block Breeze blocks are light building blocks made from the ashes of coal or coke bonded together with cement.

Bren gun A Bren gun is a type of light machine gun.

brethren is an old word for brothers. People who belong to the same religion are sometimes called **brethren**. *In a chamber far below the abbey, a group of brethren sat.* Brethren is used in a jokey way to talk about other people with something in common. *Larger banks will be goaded to take their weaker brethren over.*

breviary (breviaries) A **breviary** is a book of prayers, hymns, and bible readings for each day of the year, to be recited by Roman Catholic clergy.

brevity When you talk about the **brevity** of something, you mean it does not last long.

brew ❑ When you **brew** a drink like tea or coffee, you make it by pouring hot water over tea leaves or coffee grounds, then letting it stand while the water absorbs the flavour. A pot of tea or coffee can be called a **brew**.

❑ **Brewing** is the process by which beer is made. It involves boiling malt and other ingredients, then allowing the mixture to ferment.

❑ A bad mixture of things can be called a **brew**. *Sport and money can often provide a nasty brew.* ◇ If something unpleasant is developing, you can say it is **brewing**. *The violence has been brewing for the last two years.*

brewer A **brewer** is a person or company that makes beer.

brewery (breweries) A **brewery** is (a) a company which makes beer. (b) a place where beer is made.

briar Briars are wild roses with long thorny stems.

bribe (bribing, bribed; bribery) If someone offers you a **bribe** or tries to **bribe** you, they offer you money or something else, to try to get you to do something wrong or illegal. Bribing people is called **bribery**.

bric-a-brac consists of assorted small ornamental objects, which are not of very much value, such as odd pieces of furniture and china.

brick Bricks are rectangular blocks used for building. They are made from clay mixed with water and baked hard. A **brick** building or wall is made of bricks. ◇ If something like a doorway is **bricked up**, it is filled in with a wall of bricks.

brickbats are blunt criticisms of someone or something.

bricklayer A **bricklayer** is a person trained or skilled in building with bricks.

brickwork The **brickwork** of a building is the parts made from bricks.

bride (bridal) A **bride** is a woman who is getting married or who has just got married. **Bridal** is used to talk about things to do with a bride or a wedding. *...bridal gowns.*

bridegroom A **bridegroom** is a man who is getting married or who has just got married.

bridesmaid At a wedding, a **bridesmaid** is the bride's attendant.

bridge (bridging, bridged) ❑ A **bridge** is a structure built over a river, road, or railway so people or vehicles can cross from one side to the other.

❑ If you act as a **bridge** between two groups of people, you make it possible for them to communicate with each other. Establishing links between people is often called **bridge building**. *The Pope hoped his visit would build bridges to unite the nations of Central Europe.* ◇ When something which keeps people apart is reduced or done away with, this can be called **bridging the gap**. *The two leaders talked informally for hours, bridging a rift created by 16 years of war... This gulf of misunderstanding must be bridged.*

❑ The **bridge** of a ship is the platform or area it is controlled from. It is positioned above the main deck.

❑ **Bridge** is a card game for four players, based on whist.

bridgehead A **bridgehead** is an area of captured ground, from which an army can advance or attack. ◇ A **bridgehead** is also a secure position from which someone can advance or improve their prospects. *British Airways has never hidden its desire to secure a bridgehead in the American domestic market.*

bridging loan A **bridging loan** is a loan from a bank or other institution to provide money for a short period between two transactions, for example when you are buying a new house before the sale of the old one is completed.

bridle (bridling, bridled) ❑ A **bridle** is a harness fitted round a horse's head to enable its rider to control it.

❑ If someone **bridles** at something, they are angry about it or take offence.

bridleway A **bridleway** is a public path or track which can be used by people on horses.

brief (briefing, briefed; briefly) ❑ **Brief** is used to describe something which lasts only a short time. *...a brief visit... The President spoke briefly to the press.*

❑ If you **brief** someone, you give them information or instructions. *Lobby journalists assemble regularly to be briefed about government policy... He briefed his assistant on how the operation should be completed.* See also **briefing**. ◇ A person's **brief** is what they have officially been instructed to do. *His brief is to prepare the ground for the November visit.*

❑ A **brief** is a set of documents containing all the facts about a legal case. It is prepared by a solicitor and given to the barrister representing someone in the case.

❑ **Briefs** are pants or knickers.

briefcase A **briefcase** is a small case for carrying things like documents and books.

briefing When someone holds a **briefing**, they give journalists the latest information on something. ◇ A **briefing** is also a meeting at which people who are going to do something are given information and instructions.

brigade A **brigade** is an army unit consisting of three battalions. ◇ Some groups of people organized for a particular task are called **brigades**, for example the fire brigade. ◇ Some people use **brigade** to talk about groups of people they do not like. *...the anti-zoo brigade... ...the muesli and brown rice brigade.*

brigadier A **brigadier** is a high-ranking officer in the British army and the Royal Marines.

brigand A **brigand** is a highway robber, especially a member of a gang operating in remote or mountainous country.

bright (brightly, brightness) ❑ A **bright** colour is strong and noticeable, and not dark. ◇ A **bright** day is very sunny. ◇ A **bright** light shines strongly. *...bright sunshine... ...the flame burned brightly... ...the brightness of the stars on a winter's night.* ◇ When people talk about the **bright lights**, they mean the attractions of a big city.

❑ A **bright** idea is clever and original. ◇ **Bright** people are clever and quick at learning things. ◇ The most successful members of a talented group of people are sometimes called its **brightest stars**.

❑ If someone looks or sounds **bright**, they seem cheerful. *She smiled at me brightly.* ◇ If the future looks **bright**, things are likely to go well. ◇ A **bright spot** is a hopeful feature in an otherwise bad situation. *The only economic bright spot was the better-than-expected September trade figures.* You say **on the bright side** when you are mentioning a good feature like this. *On the bright side is the fact that some African countries now have grain surpluses.* ◇ If you **look on the bright side,** you find something to be cheerful about in a bad situation.

brighten (brightening, brightened) ❏ When something **brightens** or is **brightened,** it becomes lighter or brighter. ◇ When a place is **brightened up,** it is made more attractive and colourful.

❏ When a situation **brightens,** it becomes more pleasant or hopeful. ◇ When a person **brightens,** they become more cheerful.

brilliant (brilliantly; brilliance) ❏ If you call a person **brilliant** or talk about their **brilliance,** you mean they are extremely clever. You can also say an idea or plan is **brilliant.** *...a brilliant diplomatic manoeuvre.*

❏ **Brilliant** is also used to say someone does something extremely well. *My husband is a brilliant cook... He ran brilliantly in all the heats.* ◇ If someone has a **brilliant** career, they are very successful.

❏ A **brilliant** light or colour is extremely bright.

brim (brimming, brimmed; brimful) ❏ The **brim** of a hat is the wide sticking-out part round the bottom.

❏ If a container is filled **to the brim,** it is filled right to the top. ◇ If something is **brimming** with things or **brimful** of them, it is very full of them. ◇ If someone is **brimming** with a feeling or **brimming over** with it, they are full of it. *Both sides are brimming with confidence.*

brimstone is an old word for sulphur. ◇ When evangelical preachers talk about **fire and brimstone,** they mean hell and the punishment awaiting people there. ◇ **Fire and brimstone** is also used to talk about fierce threatening behaviour. *The editor is breathing fire and brimstone down the phone.*

brine is salt water, especially when it is used for preserving food.

bring (bringing, brought) ❏ If you **bring** someone or something to a place, you take them with you. ◇ If you **bring** something to someone, you fetch it for them or carry it to them.

❏ If something new is **brought** to a place, it is introduced there. *He was looking at ways of bringing new employment to the area.* ◇ If something **brings** people to a place, it makes them come. *The conference may bring 10,000 people to the town.* ◇ If something **brings** people **together,** it gives them the chance to get to know each other.

❏ If something has a certain effect, you can say it **brings** that effect. ◇ If something **brings** another thing **with** it, the second thing happens as a result of the first. *Greater prosperity is bringing with it a more cultured approach.* You can also say something is **brought on** by something else. *...a heart attack brought on by overwork.* ◇ If something produces a change, you can say it **brings** it **about.**

❏ If someone **brings** shame or disgrace on the group they belong to, they damage its reputation by behaving badly. Similarly, someone can **bring** honour or credit to a group. ◇ If you have **brought** trouble on yourself, it is your own fault you are in trouble. ◇ If you say someone **brings** a certain ability or attitude to what they are doing, you mean they have it and their work benefits from it. *She*

brought a touch of class to every part she played.

❏ If an amount or rate is **brought** to a certain level, it is made to reach that level. *The chairman received an increase of about 30%, bringing his salary to £150,000.* Similarly, an amount or rate can be **brought up** or **down.**

❏ If something **brings** a certain price, that is how much it is sold for. ◇ The amount of money something **brings in** is the amount it raises or earns.

❏ When something like a TV or radio programme is **brought** to people, it is presented for them to watch or listen to.

❏ If something from the past is **brought back,** it is reintroduced. *The government has refused to bring back free eye tests and dental checks.* ◇ If something **brings back** a memory, it reminds you of something in the past. ◇ If something is **brought** to an end, it is finished.

❏ If you cannot **bring** yourself to do something, you cannot make yourself do it, because it is so unpleasant or humiliating.

❏ If a legal action is **brought** against someone, they are officially accused of doing something unlawful.

❏ If someone or something **brings down** a government, they make it lose power.

❏ If you **bring forward** something like a meeting or an appointment, you arrange for it to take place at an earlier time than had been planned.

❏ If you **bring up** a subject, you introduce it into a discussion or argument. ◇ If someone **brings forward** a proposal, they make it known, so people can consider or discuss it. ◇ When a government or organization **brings in** a new law or system, they introduce it.

❏ When someone is **brought in** to deal with a task or problem, they are employed specially for it.

❏ If someone succeeds in doing something difficult, you can say they **bring it off.**

❏ When a new product is **brought out,** it is made available for people to buy.

❏ If something **brings out** a type of behaviour in someone, it makes them behave like that.

❏ If you **bring** someone **round** to your way of thinking, you get them to change their opinion and agree with you.

❏ When someone **brings up** a child, they care for it while it is growing up, and teach it how to behave.

brink If you are on the **brink** of something, it could happen to you at any moment. *The company had been on the brink of bankruptcy for almost three years.*

brinkmanship is the tactic of deliberately taking a difficult or dangerous situation to the limit, to try to get an advantage.

briquette Briquettes are blocks of compressed coal dust or charcoal, used for fuel.

brisk (briskly) ❏ People say trade or business is **brisk** when things are being sold quickly and a lot of money is being made. ◇ If something happens at a **brisk** pace, it happens quite quickly.

❏ You call someone's behaviour **brisk** when they deal with things in a quick efficient way, without wasting time. *She briskly set about negotiating a price.* ◇ A **brisk** action is done quickly and energetically. *Take a brisk walk round the block.*

❏ If the weather is **brisk,** it is cold but pleasant. *...a brisk autumn morning.*

brisket is a cut of beef taken from the breast of the animal.

bristle (bristling, bristled) ❑ Bristles are short stiff animal hairs, often used to make brushes. Short tufts of manmade fibres, for example nylon or plastic, are also called bristles. ◇ A bristling moustache has thick rough hairs.

❑ When an animal bristles, the hair or fur on its back stands up, because it is afraid or angry. ◇ You say a person bristles when they get angry at something someone says.

❑ When there are a lot of people or things in a place, you can say it bristles with them. ...a cultural centre bristling with foreign scholars.

Brit British people are sometimes called Brits.

Britannia is a mythical female warrior, used as a symbol of Great Britain.

British is used to talk about people and things in or from the United Kingdom. ...the British countryside. ◇ The British are the British people.

British Summer Time See BST.

Briton A Briton is someone who comes from the United Kingdom.

brittle (brittleness) ❑ Brittle things are hard but easily broken. ◇ Brittle is also used to describe things like relationships when they are not firmly established and could easily break down.

❑ If you call a person brittle, you mean they behave in a hard unfeeling way.

broach (broaches, broaching, broached) If you broach a subject, you introduce it into a discussion or conversation.

broad (broader, broadest; broadly) ❑ Broad is used to say the sides of something are unusually far apart. He was tall, with very broad shoulders... The decks were broad enough to walk right round. ◇ Broad is also used to talk about measurements. For example, if a river is 1000 metres broad, it is 1000 metres from side to side.

❑ If someone has a broad smile, their smile seems wider than usual, because they are pleased or happy. The mayor was smiling broadly.

❑ You use broad to describe things which include or involve a wide variety of things or people. ...a broad and balanced education... ...a broad coalition of workers, peasants, and middle-class professionals. You can also say something like this is broad-based or broadly-based.

❑ Broad and broadly are also used to talk about the general idea of something, rather than its details. The Chancellor spelled out the broad outline of his new economic strategy... Party officials say the report is broadly accurate. ◇ You say broadly or broadly speaking when you are making a general statement about something, which may not be true about every aspect of it.

❑ A broad accent is strong and noticeable.

❑ If you give a broad hint, you indicate your attitude or reveal information in an indirect but obvious way.

❑ If a crime is done in broad daylight, it is done during the day, rather than when it is dark.

broad bean Broad beans are light-green beans with thick flat edible seeds.

broad-minded If you say someone is broad-minded, you mean they are tolerant of different kinds of behaviour and opinions.

broadcast (broadcasting, broadcast not 'broadcasted'; broad-caster) When a TV or radio programme is broadcast, it is transmitted for people to see or hear. A person who gives talks or interviews on TV or radio is called a broadcaster. A programme can be called a broadcast. ◇ You can also say an announcement is broadcast over something like a loudspeaker system.

broaden (broadening, broadened) When something broadens, it becomes wider. Here the Nile broadens out between yellow sands and huge granite boulders. ◇ You talk about things being broadened when they are extended to include a wider variety of people or things. She has broadened the scope of her research.

broadsheet A broadsheet is a newspaper printed on large sheets of paper, measuring about 38cm by 61cm. Broadsheets are usually more serious than other newspapers. See also tabloid.

broadside ❑ A broadside is a strong written or spoken attack on someone or something. Officials launched a fierce public broadside against EU farm subsidies.

❑ If a vehicle is moving broadside on, it is moving with its side to the front.

brocade is a thick expensive fabric, woven with a raised pattern, often using gold and silver threads.

broccoli is a vegetable with green stalks and green or purple flower heads.

brochure (pron: broh-sher) A brochure is a booklet containing information about a product or service.

brogue (pron: broag) ❑ Brogues are sturdy walking shoes.

❑ A brogue is a broad accent, especially an Irish one.

broil (broiling, broiled) When Americans grill food, they say they broil it.

broiler Broilers are young tender chickens, suitable for roasting or grilling. They are reared in large sheds called broiler houses.

broke ❑ See break.

❑ If you are broke, you have no money. You say a company goes broke when it loses money and cannot continue in business.

❑ If you go for broke, you take a risky course of action in the hope of achieving a great success.

broken See break.

broker (brokering, brokered) ❑ A broker is a person or firm that buys and sells things like shares, foreign money, or goods on behalf of other people and is paid a commission for doing the work. ...a mortgage broker... ...an insurance broker. See also stockbroker.

❑ A broker is also someone who acts as a negotiator between people or organizations. ...a marriage broker. ◇ If someone brokers a deal or agreement, they negotiate something which is acceptable to everyone involved.

brokerage A brokerage is a broker's business or office. ◇ Brokerage is the commission charged by a broker.

brolly (brollies) A brolly is an umbrella.

bromide is a chemical used to make bromide paper, which is used in photographic processes. It is also used as a sedative. ◇ Bland or meaningless remarks can be called bromides.

bronchial (pron: bronk-ee-al) A person's bronchial tubes are the tubes which connect their windpipe to their lungs. Bronchial is used to talk about things to do with these tubes. ...a bronchial infection.

bronchitis (pron: bronk-eye-tiss) is an illness in which the bronchial tubes become inflamed.

brontosaurus (brontosauruses) The **brontosaurus** was a type of large four-legged plant-eating dinosaur, with a long neck and a long tail.

bronze (bronzed) ❑ **Bronze** is a hard yellowish-brown alloy made mainly of copper and small amounts of tin. It is used to make statues and sculptures because it is highly water-resistant. ◇ **Bronze** statues and sculptures are often called **bronzes**. ◇ A **bronze medal** is awarded as third prize in a race or competition.
❑ **Bronze** is a yellowish-brown colour. ◇ **Bronzed** people are attractively sun-tanned.

Bronze Age The **Bronze Age** was the phase of human cultural development between the Stone Age and the Iron Age. It began in the Middle East about 4000BC, lasting in Britain from about 2000BC to 500BC.

brooch (*rhymes with 'coach'*) (brooches) A **brooch** is a piece of jewellery with a pin at the back for attaching to a dress or coat.

brood (brooding, brooded; broody) ❑ A **brood** is a group of baby birds hatched from the same batch of eggs. ◇ A **broody** hen is ready to sit on eggs to hatch them.
❑ When there are a lot of small children in a family, they are sometimes called a **brood**.
❑ If someone **broods** about something, they think about it a lot, seriously and often unhappily. ◇ **Brooding** is used to describe something disturbing and threatening. *...a dark, brooding sky... ...a brooding silence.*

brook (brooking, brooked) ❑ A **brook** is a small stream.
❑ If you say someone will not **brook** something, you mean they will not allow it or accept it.

broom ❑ A **broom** is a long-handled brush. ◇ When someone who has just started a new job intends to make a lot of changes, you can call them a **new broom**.
❑ **Broom** is a thorny shrub with yellow flowers.

broomstick A **broomstick** is (a) the long handle of a broom. (b) a broom which witches are supposed to fly on, with a bundle of twigs at the end.

broth is soup, usually with meat or vegetables in it.

brothel A **brothel** is a house where men pay to have sex with prostitutes.

brother Your **brother** is a boy or man who has the same parents as you. ◇ You can use **brother** to describe someone who belongs to the same group or organization as yourself. *...his brother architects.* ◇ **Brother** is a title given to a man who belongs to a religious institution like a monastery. *...Brother Cadfael.*

brother-in-law (brothers-in-law) Your **brother-in-law** is the brother of your husband or wife, or your sister's husband.

brotherhood is affection and loyalty between groups of people who have something in common. ◇ A **brotherhood** is a group or organization of men with common interests, jobs, or beliefs.

brotherly is used to describe the feelings brothers have for each other, and the ways they typically behave towards each other. *They may squabble in public but underneath there is a bond of brotherly affection.* **Brotherly** can also be used to describe a man's feelings towards anyone, when these feelings are affectionate and friendly, like those of a brother.

brought See bring.

brouhaha (*pron:* brew-hah-hah) is a lot of fuss about something.

brow Your **brow** is your forehead. ◇ Your **brows** are your eyebrows. ◇ The **brow** of a hill is its top.

browbeat (browbeating, browbeat *not 'browbeated',* have browbeaten) (*or* brow-beat, *etc.*) If someone **browbeats** you, they bully you and try to force you to do what they want. ◇ **Browbeaten** people have been bullied so much they have become quiet, obedient, and depressed.

brown is the colour of earth or wood. ◇ If something is **browned**, it becomes brown. For example, you can say a person's skin is **browned** by the sun. ◇ If you **brown** food, you cook it till it turns brown.

brownie A **Brownie Guide** or **Brownie** is a girl aged 7 to 10 who belongs to the junior branch of the Girl Guides. ◇ In fairy stories, a **brownie** is a kind of elf, especially one who does household chores during the night.

brownish If something is **brownish**, it is slightly brown.

browse (browsing, browsed; browser) ❑ If you **browse** through a book or magazine or have a **browse** through it, you look through it in a casual way. ◇ If you **browse** in a shop, you look at things in a casual unhurried way, often without intending to buy anything. People who do this are called **browsers**.
❑ When animals **browse**, they continually nibble at grass or leaves.

bruise (bruising, bruised) ❑ A **bruise** is a purple mark on your skin caused by an injury. If a part of your body is **bruised**, it has several marks like this; the marks are called **bruising**. ◇ If fruit or grain is **bruised**, it has been crushed and damaged.
❑ If a person's feelings are **bruised**, they are hurt or upset by something someone has said. ◇ You can say other things are **bruised** when they are affected badly by something which has happened. *The incident has left the government's policy initiatives badly bruised.* ◇ **Bruising** is used to describe things which cause harm or distress. *...a bitter and bruising leadership contest.*

bruiser A **bruiser** is a strong tough person, for example a boxer or a bully.

brunch is a meal which combines breakfast and lunch, usually eaten in the late morning.

brunette A **brunette** is a girl or woman with dark brown hair.

brunt If someone **bears the brunt** of something unpleasant, they suffer most of the effects of it.

brush (brushes, brushing, brushed) ❑ A **brush** is an object consisting of bristles fixed into a firm back or handle. Brushes come in many different shapes and sizes; they are used for cleaning, tidying, sweeping, and painting. If you **brush** something, you clean or tidy it with a brush.
❑ You also say you **brush** something when you touch against it lightly and briefly. *His cat brushed against his legs.*
❑ If you have a **brush** with someone, you have a brief unfriendly argument or disagreement with them. ◇ **Brush** is used to talk about other unpleasant experiences. *...a brush with death.*
❑ If you **brush** something **aside** or **brush** it **off**, you refuse to consider it, because you think it is unimportant. ◇ If someone **brushes** you **off** or gives you the **brush-off**, they refuse to have anything to do with you.
❑ If you **brush up** on a subject, you renew or improve

your knowledge of it.

❏ **Brush** is shrubs and small trees growing thickly together.

❏ A fox's tail is called its **brush**.

❏ **Brushed** fabrics have been treated in a special way to make them soft and furry.

brushwood is (a) cut or broken-off branches or twigs. (b) shrubs and small trees growing thickly together.

brushwork The **brushwork** in a painting is the skilful way the paint has been applied with a brush or brushes.

brusque (*pron: broosk*) (brusquely) If someone is **brusque**, their manner is blunt or abrupt. *He brusquely demanded that they get to business.*

Brussels sprouts See sprout.

brutal (brutally; brutality, brutalities) ❏ **Brutal** behaviour is cruel and vicious. Behaviour like this is also called **brutality**; cruel acts can be called **brutalities**. *Resistance was brutally crushed.*

❏ If you say something like the truth is **brutal**, you mean it is unpleasant or hurtful. Similarly, you can say someone is **brutally** honest. *The brutal truth is that a depressing number of Glaswegians will die prematurely because of their unhealthy lifestyle.*

brutalize (brutalizing, brutalized) (*can be spelled with an 's' instead of a 'z'*) If people are **brutalized** by their experiences, they become cruel and heartless.

brute (brutish) ❏ You call a man a **brute** when he behaves in rough or violent way, showing no regard for other people's feelings. Behaviour like this is called **brutish**.

❏ If you use **brute** force to do something, you use physical strength rather than reason.

B.Sc. A B.Sc. is a university degree in a science subject. B.Sc. stands for 'Bachelor of Science'.

BSE See mad cow disease.

BSI The BSI or **British Standards Institution** is an association which lays down standards of quality for things like manufacturing processes, building works, and household products. Products which have reached BSI standards often have a symbol called a 'kite mark' on them.

BST or **British Summer Time** is the system of telling the time used in Britain from late March to late October. During this time, clocks are set one hour ahead of Greenwich Mean Time. See also **GMT**.

Bt. See baronet.

BTEC courses are work-related courses available to people aged 16 and over, usually at a college of further education. They are courses leading to the BTEC First and BTEC National Certificates, and to the HNC and HND. BTEC stands for 'Business and Technology Education Council'. See also **GNVQ**.

bubble (bubbling, bubbled) ❏ A **bubble** is a ball of air in a liquid, or on its surface. When a liquid **bubbles**, bubbles form in it. ◇ A soap **bubble** is a hollow delicate ball of soapy liquid on the surface of a liquid or in the air.

❏ When something like a feeling **bubbles up**, it gradually increases or becomes more obvious. *...a bubbling up of enthusiasm... The violence has bubbled up alarmingly.* ◇ If someone is **bubbling** with a feeling, they are full of it.

❏ When something which has been going well suddenly collapses, you can say the **bubble has burst**. *...the bursting of the house price bubble in August 1988.*

bubble and squeak is leftover cooked cabbage, potato, and sometimes meat, mashed together and fried.

bubble-bath is pleasant-smelling liquid soap which you pour into running bathwater to make a lot of foam.

bubble gum is chewing gum which you can blow into bubbles.

bubbly people are lively and cheerful. ◇ Champagne is sometimes called **bubbly**.

buccaneer (buccaneering) ❏ **Buccaneers** were pirates, especially the ones who attacked ships in the Caribbean during the 17th and 18th centuries.

❏ People who are adventurous, especially in their business dealings, are sometimes called **buccaneers** or described as **buccaneering**. *...buccaneering capitalists.*

buck ❏ The males of various animals, including the goat, hare, kangaroo, rabbit, and reindeer, are called **bucks**.

❏ A US or Australian dollar is often called a **buck**. If someone makes **big bucks**, they make a lot of money. If they **make a fast buck**, they make a lot of money quickly, usually by doing something dishonest.

❏ If you **pass the buck**, you pass responsibility for something to someone else. If, on the other hand, you say **the buck stops here**, you mean there is nobody to pass things on to, and you have to deal with them yourself.

❏ If a business **bucks the trend** or **bucks the market**, it is successful when other businesses are in difficulty.

❏ When a horse **bucks**, it jumps about wildly, to try and unseat its rider.

bucket A **bucket** is an open-topped metal or plastic container with a handle.

bucket shop A **bucket shop** is a travel agency which sells airline tickets at a discount to fill seats which would otherwise be empty.

buckle (buckling, buckled) ❏ A **buckle** is a fastening on one end of a belt or strap. It has a prong which hooks into a hole on the other end of the belt or strap when it is slotted through the buckle. When you **buckle** a belt, you fasten it like this.

❏ When something **buckles**, it becomes twisted or bent as a result of severe heat or force. ◇ If your legs **buckle**, they suddenly bend because you are weak or exhausted. ◇ If someone **buckles** under pressure, they are overcome by it. *He refused to buckle under the weight of criticism.*

❏ If you **buckle down** to something, you start working hard at it.

buckwheat is a type of small black grain used for feeding animals and making flour.

bucolic (*pron: bew-kol-ik*) is used to talk about things to do with the countryside or country people. *...bucolic peace... ...a bucolic sense of humour.*

bud (budding, budded) ❏ A **bud** is a small pointed lump which appears on a tree or plant and develops into a leaf or flower. When this happens, you say the tree or plant **buds**.

❏ **Budding** is used to describe someone who is just starting to be a success at something. *...a budding writer.* You can talk about the **budding** career of someone like this.

❏ If you **nip something in the bud**, you put a stop to it before it has a chance to develop.

Buddha or the Buddha is the title given to Siddhartha Gautama, a religious teacher and the founder of Buddhism. ◇ A **Buddha** is a statue or picture of the Buddha.

Buddhism (Buddhist) **Buddhism** is an Eastern religion which teaches that the way to end suffering is by overcoming your desires. Followers of this religion are called **Buddhists.**

buddleia (pron: bud-lee-a) The **buddleia** is a bush with spikes of scented mauve or white flowers, which attract butterflies.

buddy (buddies) Your **buddy** is a close friend, usually someone of the same sex as yourself.

budge (budging, budged) If someone will not **budge** from something like a point of view, they refuse to change their mind or compromise. ◇ If someone will not **budge** from a place, they will not move from it. ◇ If you cannot **budge** something, you cannot get it to move.

budgerigar Budgerigars are small brightly-coloured birds belonging to the parakeet family. They are wild birds in Australia, and are bred and kept as pets in other countries.

budget (budgeting, budgeted; budgetary) ❑ A **budget** is a plan showing how much money an organization has available for a certain period, and how it will be spent. ◇ The **Budget** is the financial plan announced by the government, showing how much money it intends to raise through taxation and how it is going to spend it. ◇ **Budgetary** is used to talk about things to do with a budget. ...budgetary control... ...budgetary policies. ◇ **budget deficit:** see **deficit.**
❑ If you **budget,** you plan carefully how you will spend your money. If you **budget for** something, you allow enough money for it in your plan. ...parents budgeting for school fees. ◇ **Budgeted** is used to talk about the amount of money allocated for something. ...a modestly budgeted courtroom comedy. -**budget** is used in a similar way after 'high' and 'low'. ...low-budget films.

budgie A **budgie** is the same as a budgerigar.

buff ❑ You call a person a **buff** when they know a lot about a subject. For example, a film buff is a person who knows a lot about films.
❑ If you **buff** something, you clean or polish it with a soft cloth or brush.
❑ **Buff** is a pale yellow or yellowish-brown colour.

buffalo (plural: buffaloes or buffalo) **Buffaloes** are a type of cattle in southern and eastern Africa with large upward-curving horns. ◇ American bison are sometimes called **buffaloes.** ◇ See also **water buffalo.**

buffer ❑ The **buffers** on a train are two metal discs on springs at the ends of each carriage. They lessen the impact when carriages bump against each other. Similarly, there are buffers at the end of a railway track.
❑ If something acts as a **buffer,** it is placed between two areas or groups of people, to keep them apart and prevent trouble. The federal army has been called in to act as a buffer in areas of high tension. A **buffer zone** is an area of land between two rival countries or areas, which is meant to keep them apart. ◇ A **buffer state** is a small, usually neutral, country between two rival countries.

buffet (buffeting, buffeted) ❑ A **buffet** (pron: boof-ay) is a meal of cold food at a party or public occasion. Guests usually help themselves to the food. ◇ On a railway station, a **buffet** is a cafe selling snacks and drinks. On a

train, the **buffet car** is a carriage where you can buy snacks and drinks.
❑ If the wind or sea **buffets** something (pron: buff-its), it keeps striking it or beating against it. ◇ When someone is upset or shaken by a bad experience, you can say they are **buffeted** by the experience. Similarly, you can talk about firms being **buffeted** by things which harm trade.

buffoon (buffoonery) If you say someone is a **buffoon,** you mean they are extremely silly. You can call their behaviour **buffoonery.**

bug (bugging, bugged) ❑ A **bug** is a tiny insect, especially one which causes damage. ◇ When someone has a minor illness, you can say they have a **bug.** ...a stomach bug. ◇ A **bug** in a computer program is a small error which stops the program working properly.
❑ If a place is **bugged,** tiny microphones called **bugs** are hidden there to pick up what people are saying. A bug can also be hidden in a telephone.
❑ When someone suddenly becomes very enthusiastic about something like a hobby or an idea, you can say they have been **bitten by** a **bug.** We got bitten by the sight-seeing bug in Italy.
❑ If something **bugs** you, it annoys you.

bugbear A **bugbear** is something which worries or annoys people. Stress is one of the bugbears of modern life.

buggy (buggies) A **buggy** is (a) a small cart or truck. (b) a pushchair.

bugle (bugler) A **bugle** is a brass instrument like a cornet but usually without valves. A **bugler** is a person who plays the bugle.

build (building, built) ❑ When something like a house or road is **built,** it is put together from its separate parts.
❑ When someone **builds** an organization or system or **builds** it **up,** they establish it and develop it. ◇ If something is **built into** a policy, product, or system, it is included as an essential part. They were satisfied with the safeguards built into the treaty.
❑ When someone gradually acquires a good reputation, you can say they **build** it. He has built a reputation for personal honesty... He has built a name as a solo performer.
❑ If something **builds up,** it gradually increases, because more is being added to it. You can talk about a **build-up** of something. ...a military build-up... ...a big build-up of 'greenhouse gases' in the atmosphere. ◇ If you **build up** something such as someone's morale, you gradually improve it. ◇ If you **build up** your strength, you eat nourishing food and take exercise to improve your health, especially after an illness.
❑ If you **build up** a picture of something, you gradually form a complete impression by putting together separate items of information.
❑ When an event moves towards an exciting stage, you can say it **builds** to it or **builds up** to it. ◇ The **build-up** to an event is everything connected with it which happens just before it starts, especially the preparations and publicity.
❑ If you **build on** a previous success or achievement, you take advantage of it in order to make further progress.
❑ A person's **build** is the shape their bones and muscles give to their body. You can say someone is **built** in a certain way. He is built like a sturdy Welsh bull.

builder A builder is a person or firm whose job is to build and alter houses and other buildings. ◇ Some other people and firms who construct things are also called builders. ...*aircraft builders... ...boat builders.*

building A building is a structure with walls and a roof.

building block The building blocks of an object or structure are the basic parts it is made up of. *Transistors are the building-blocks of computers... Physicists believe that they have now found the basic building blocks of matter.*

building site A building site is an area of land where a building or group of buildings is being built.

building society A building society is an organization which lends money to people to buy houses, and pays interest to people who invest money in it. Since 1986, building societies have also been able to offer banking services.

built See build.

built-in cupboards and wardrobes are constructed in the room where they are to be used. They are fitted against a wall and cannot usually be moved. ◇ A built-in feature of something is included as an essential part of it. *The device is powered by a built-in battery.*

built-up A built-up area is one where there are a lot of buildings.

bulb A bulb is an onion-shaped root which a plant grows out of. Flowers grown from bulbs, for example daffodils or hyacinths, are sometimes called bulbs. ◇ A light bulb is an object consisting of a filament surrounded by glass, which lights up when a current of electricity is passed through it.

bulbous things look unattractively fat or swollen. ...*a bulbous nose.*

bulge (bulging, bulged) ❑ A bulge is a swelling or outward curve. When something swells outwards, you say it bulges. ...*a creature with bulging black eyes.* ◇ If a room or container is bulging with things, it is full of them.
❑ A bulge is also a sudden increase in something like an amount of money. ...*a big bulge in debt repayments.*

bulimia (bulimic) Bulimia or bulimia nervosa is an eating disorder. People who have it go in for compulsive overeating, after which they make themselves sick or use laxatives. A bulimic is someone who suffers from bulimia. See also anorexia.

bulk (bulky, bulkier, bulkiest) ❑ If an object is very large, you can talk about its bulk, meaning its large size. A bulky object is large and heavy.
❑ If goods or products are handled, bought, or sold in bulk, they are dealt with in large quantities. Bulk is used to describe things dealt with in this way. ...*bulk orders.*
❑ When you talk about the bulk of something, you mean most of it. Similarly, the bulk of a group of people or things means most of them. *The great bulk of India's poor live in the countryside.*

bulk carrier Bulk carriers are large ships designed to carry cargoes like coal, grain, timber, or oil.

bulkhead On a ship or aircraft, the bulkheads are strong partition walls which divide the inside into separate compartments. Bulkheads help prevent the spread of leakages or fire.

bull Bulls are adult male cattle. ◇ The males of some other species are also called bulls, for example male elephants, seals, and whales.

bull terrier The bull terrier is a dog with a muscular body, a thick neck, and a short smooth whitish-coloured coat. Bull terriers were developed by crossing the bulldog with various terriers. See also pit bull terrier.

bull's-eye The bull's-eye is the small circular area at the centre of a dartboard or target. When someone hits this area with a dart, arrow, or bullet, you say they score a bull's-eye.

bulldog The bulldog is a short-haired dog with a broad head, strong square jaws, and a stocky body.

bulldog clip A bulldog clip is a strong spring-operated metal clip for holding papers together.

bulldoze (bulldozing, bulldozed; bulldozer) ❑ A bulldozer is a large powerful tractor with a broad blade in front, used for moving earth or knocking things down. You say something is bulldozed when a bulldozer is used to push it aside or demolish it.
❑ When someone gets something done using force and determination and often ignoring the wishes of others, you can say they bulldoze it through. *The government bulldozed the amendment through parliament.* When someone is bulldozed into doing something, they are forced into it, often without having time to think about it.

bullet A bullet is a small piece of metal fired from a gun. If something is bullet-proof, it is made especially strong so bullets cannot pass through it. ◇ bite the bullet: see bite.

bulletin A bulletin is (a) a short news report on TV or radio. (b) a short official report about something, saying what the latest situation is. *A medical bulletin on his health is expected soon.* (c) a regular newspaper or leaflet produced by an organization. ...*The Bank of England Quarterly Bulletin.*

bulletin board A bulletin board is a facility which people can access by computer to send or receive information on topics which interest them. ◇ Americans call a notice board a bulletin board.

bullfight (bullfighting; bullfighter) A bullfight is a traditional Spanish, Portuguese, or Latin American entertainment in which a man called a bullfighter taunts, and usually kills, a fierce bull. These entertainments are called bullfighting.

bullfinch (bullfinches) The bullfinch is a small bird with a short thick bill. The male has a black head, wings, and tail, and a grey and white back, with a red breast; the female is similar but with a brown breast. Bullfinches often damage fruit trees by eating the buds.

bullfrog Bullfrogs are large frogs which make a loud deep croaking noise.

bullion is gold or silver in the form of bars.

bullish You say people are bullish, when they are optimistic or confident. *Negotiators are reported to be in a bullish mood.*

bullock A bullock is a castrated bull.

bullring A bullring is a circular arena where bullfights are held.

bully (bullies, bullying, bullied) Bullies are people who use their strength or power to hurt or frighten other people weaker than themselves. When they do this, you say they bully the other people. ◇ A bully-boy is a tough aggressive man, especially one hired to frighten or hurt other people. ◇ If someone bullies you into doing something, they make you do it, using force or threats.

bulrush (bulrushes) Bulrushes are tall stiff reeds on the edges of ponds and rivers.

bulwark A bulwark against an unpleasant or dangerous situation is something which protects you from it. *The security forces remain the ultimate bulwark against the breakdown of society.*

bum A person's bum is their bottom. ◇ Bum is the usual American word for a tramp.

bum-bag A bum-bag is a small zip-top bag attached to a belt worn around the waist. You use it to carry things like money and keys.

bumble (bumbling, bumbled) When someone speaks or behaves in a confused or disorganized way, you can say they bumble. Bumbling is used to describe people who speak or behave like this. *He was seen as a clumsy, bumbling, inarticulate figure.*

bumblebee Bumblebees are large fuzzy bees.

bumf (*or* bumph) Things like pamphlets, forms, and official documents can be called bumf.

bump (bumpy) ❑ If you bump into someone or something, you accidentally knock against them. A bump is a collision between two things or people.
  ❑ A bump on a surface is a raised uneven part. A bumpy surface has a lot of bumps. ◇ When a vehicle bumps over a surface, it travels in a rough bouncing way, because the surface is uneven. When you travel over a surface like this, you can say you have a bumpy journey.
  ❑ Bumpy is also used to describe things people are involved in which do not go smoothly. *The talks got off to a bumpy start.*
  ❑ If you bump into someone, you meet them by chance.
  ❑ If something is increased by a large amount in a short time, you can say it is bumped up.

bumper ❑ Bumpers are the bars at the front and back of a vehicle which protect it if it bumps into something.
  ❑ Bumper is used to talk about things being much larger than usual. *...a bumper crop of rice.*

bumph See bumf.

bumpkin A bumpkin is a country person who is thought to be simple or stupid.

bumptious If you say someone is bumptious, you mean they are unpleasantly full of their own importance.

bun A bun is a small round cake or bread roll, often containing fruit or spices. ◇ If a woman has her hair in a bun, it is fastened in a round shape at the back of her head.

bunch (bunches, bunching, bunched) ❑ A bunch of flowers is a number of them held or tied together. ◇ A bunch of fruit is several of them growing on the same stem. *...a bunch of grapes.* ◇ A bunch of keys is several of them on one ring. ◇ A bunch of people is a group of them.
  ❑ When people or things are bunched together, they are grouped closely together.

bundle (bundling, bundled) ❑ A bundle is a number of things tied together or wrapped in a cloth, so they can be carried or stored. When you gather things into a bundle, you can say you bundle them up.
  ❑ If you are bundled somewhere, you are pushed there in a rough hurried way. *She was bundled off for questioning.*

bung ❑ A bung is a round piece of wood, cork, or rubber

for closing the hole in a barrel or flask.
  ❑ If you bung something somewhere, you put it there quickly and carelessly.

bungalow A bungalow is a single-storey house.

bungee-jumping or bungy-jumping consists of jumping off a high place, usually a bridge or crane, with an elastic rope attached to you, the other end of which is secured to the thing you jump off.

bungle (bungling, bungled; bungler) If someone bungles something, they do not do it properly because they are clumsy or make mistakes. You say someone like this is bungling or a bungler.

bungy-jumping See bungee-jumping.

bunion A bunion is a large painful lump at the base of the big toe.

bunk ❑ A bunk is a narrow bed fixed to a wall, especially in a ship or caravan. ◇ Bunk beds are beds constructed one above the other.
  ❑ If someone does a bunk, they suddenly leave a place without telling anyone.
  ❑ If you say something is bunk, you mean it is nonsense or not true.

bunker ❑ A bunker is a shelter, usually underground, with very strong walls to protect it from gunfire and bombing. ◇ A bunker is also a container for storing coal or some other fuel.
  ❑ On a golf course, a bunker is a large hollow filled with sand, placed there as an obstacle.

bunkum If you say something like an idea or theory is bunkum, you mean it is nonsense.

bunny (bunnies) Small children sometimes call a rabbit a bunny.

bunsen burner A bunsen burner is a small gas burner used in laboratories.

bunting is rows of small coloured flags used to decorate streets and buildings on special occasions.

buoy (*pron:* boy) ❑ A buoy is a floating object anchored to the bottom of the sea, marking the route a ship should take, or warning of dangers like rocks.
  ❑ If something is buoyed or buoyed up by something else, it stays at a fairly high level because of it. *The trade had been buoyed up by demand for expensive finished products.* ◇ If you are buoyed up by something, it keeps you cheerful and optimistic.

buoyant (*pron:* boy-ant) (buoyancy) ❑ If something is buoyant, it floats easily. Buoyancy is the ability to float.
  ❑ If you feel buoyant, you feel lively and cheerful.
  ❑ Buoyant is also used to describe something like the economy when it is doing well and seems unlikely to be affected by any crisis. *Some dealers report buoyant sales... There has been more buoyancy on the stock markets.*

burble (burbling, burbled) You say someone is burbling when they are talking continuously and not making much sense. ◇ If something like a stream burbles, it makes a continuous low bubbling sound; you can call this sound a burble.

burden (burdening, burdened; burdensome) ❑ A burden is a heavy load which is difficult to carry.
  ❑ If you are burdened with something, you are unable to be happy or make progress because of it. You say something like this is burdensome or a burden. *...burdened with family cares... The cost can be burdensome... These rules will*

add an extra burden on already overworked officials.

□ If you say the **burden of proof** is on someone, you mean it is up to them to prove what they say is true.

□ The **burden** of what someone says is the main point they are trying to make.

bureau (*pron:* byoo-roh) (*plural:* bureaux *or* bureaus, *both pron:* byoo-rose) □ A **bureau** is a desk with drawers, pigeonholes, and a lid which folds down to make a writing surface.

□ A **bureau** is also an office, organization, or government department which collects and distributes information. *...the Citizens Advice Bureau.*

bureaucracy (*pron:* byoo-rok-rass-ee) (bureaucracies) A **bureaucracy** is an administrative system run by a large number of officials. ◇ The civil servants who run the administration of a country are often called the **bureaucracy**. ◇ **Bureaucracy** is all the rules and procedures followed by government departments and similar organizations.

bureaucrat (*pron:* byoo-roh-crat) (bureaucratic) A **bureaucrat** is an official who works in a large administrative system, especially one who seems to follow rules and procedures too strictly. ◇ **Bureaucratic** is used to describe rules and procedures which seem unnecessarily complicated and slow things up.

burgeon (burgeoning, burgeoned) When something **burgeons,** it develops or grows quickly.

burger A **burger** is a flat round cake of minced food, which is grilled or fried.

burgh (*pron:* bur-ruh) In Scotland, a **burgh** is a town, especially an old one which had its own local government until 1975.

burgher (*pron:* burg-er) In the past, the important citizens of a town or city were called its **burghers.**

burglary (burglaries; burglar) **Burglary** is the crime of breaking into a building and stealing things. A **burglar** is someone who does this. A **burglar alarm** is a device which makes a bell ring loudly if someone tries to break into a building.

burgle (burgling, burgled) If a house is **burgled,** someone breaks in and steals things.

burgundy is (a) any wine from the Burgundy region of France. (b) any heavy red table wine.

□ **Burgundy** is also a dark purplish-red colour.

burial or a **burial** is the burying of a dead body. A **burial ground** is a place where bodies have been buried, usually a long time ago.

burlesque (*pron:* burl-lesk) **Burlesque** is used to describe something which makes fun of a type of thing by imitating it in an exaggerated way. *...a burlesque gothic melodrama.* ◇ **Burlesque** was a type of comedy show popular in the US in the late 19th and early 20th centuries.

burly A **burly** man has a broad body and strong muscles.

burn (burning, burnt *or* burned) □ You say a fire **burns.** If you **burn** something, you destroy it by setting fire to it. If something is **burning,** it is on fire. ◇ If something is **burnt up,** it is destroyed by fire or strong heat. ◇ **Burnt-out** buildings or vehicles have been badly damaged by fire. If a building is **burnt down,** it is completely destroyed by fire.

□ If you **burn** yourself, you are injured by fire or something hot. You can also be **burnt** by chemicals, electricity,

radiation, or the sun. Injuries caused in any of these ways are called **burns.**

□ When something stings or feels hot, you can say it **burns.** *The brandy burned her throat.* ◇ **Burning** is used to describe things which are extremely hot. *...the burning midday sun.*

□ You can say a light is **burning** when it is on.

□ If an engine **burns up** fuel, it uses a lot of it. You can also say a person **burns up** energy. ◇ If you **burn yourself out,** you make yourself exhausted or ill by working too hard. Someone who does this is said to suffer **burn-out.**

□ **Burning** is also used to describe strong feelings. *She was burning with rage... They have a burning desire to succeed.*

burner A **burner** is a device which produces heat or a flame, especially as part of a cooker or heater. ◇ If something is put **on the back burner,** it is not dealt with immediately but left until later, because it is not considered urgent or important.

burnish (burnishes, burnishing, burnished) If you **burnish** something like metal or leather, you polish it until it shines.

burp When someone **burps,** they make a noise because air from their stomach has been forced up through their throat. A noise like this is called a **burp.**

burr □ **Burrs** are the rough prickly husks or seed pods of some plants, for example the chestnut or the burdock, which stick to people's clothes and animals' fur.

□ You say someone has a **burr** when they pronounce their 'r's in a noticeable way.

burrow A **burrow** is a tunnel or hole in the ground, dug by a rabbit or other small animal. When the animal digs a burrow, you say it **burrows.**

bursar The **bursar** of a school or college is the person in charge of its finances or administration.

bursary (bursaries) A **bursary** is a sum of money awarded to someone to enable them to study at a college or university.

burst (bursting, burst *not* 'bursted') □ When something **bursts,** it splits open and air or some other substance comes out. You use **burst** to describe something which has split open like this. *...a burst pipe.* ◇ If a river **bursts** its banks, the water rises over them, causing a flood.

□ If a place is **bursting** or **bursting at the seams,** it is very full of people or things.

□ If you are **bursting** with a feeling, you are very full of it. If you are **bursting** to do something, you are very eager to do it. ◇ If you **burst into** tears, laughter, or song, you suddenly start crying, laughing, or singing. You can also **burst out** crying, laughing, or singing.

□ If you **burst** into or out of a place, you suddenly go into it or out of it. If you **burst through** something, you force your way through it.

□ If someone **bursts onto the scene,** they suddenly come to people's notice. *The Rolling Stones burst onto the scene in 1963.*

□ A **burst** of something is a sudden short period of it. *...bursts of gunfire... ...a sudden burst of activity.*

□ **burst into flames: see flame.**

bury (buries, burying, buried) □ When a dead person is **buried,** their body is put into a grave and covered with earth. ◇ If you **bury** an object, you put it in a hole in the ground and cover it with earth. ◇ If someone or something is **buried** in or under something, they are covered by it.

❑ If you **bury** your face or **bury** your head, you cover your face with your hands so nobody can see it. ◇ If you **bury your head in the sand**, you refuse to recognize there is a danger or a serious problem to be dealt with.

❑ If you **bury** a feeling of dislike or suspicion, you decide you will no longer feel like that about someone or something. Similarly, you can **bury** a memory.

❑ If you **bury yourself** in your work or a book, you concentrate hard on it and do not think about anything else.

bus (bussing, bussed) (*usual American spelling: busing, bused*) A **bus** (*plural: buses*) is a large motor vehicle for taking passengers from one place to another. ◇ You say people are **bussed** to a place when arrangements are made for them to travel there by bus.

bus shelter A **bus shelter** is a shelter at a bus stop, for people waiting for a bus.

bus stop A **bus stop** is a place where buses stop to let people get on and off.

busby (busbies) A **busby** is the same as a bearskin.

bush (bushes; bushy) ❑ A **bush** is a woody plant like a very small tree. ◇ The **bush** is large areas of land, especially in Africa and Australia, where nothing grows but trees or shrubs, and few people live.

❑ If you tell someone to stop **beating about the bush**, you mean they should get to the point of what they are saying.

bushel ❑ The volume of a quantity of grain can be expressed in **bushels**. A British bushel is 8 gallons (about 0.036 cubic metres). A US bushel is slightly smaller (about 0.035 cubic metres).

❑ If you say someone is **hiding their light under a bushel**, you mean they are being very modest about their abilities or good qualities.

bushy hair or fur grows extremely thickly.

busily If you do something **busily**, you do it in an energetic way.

business (businesses) ❑ A **business** is an organization which produces or sells goods or provides a service, and operates for profit. ◇ **Business** is buying and selling goods and services. You say someone involved in this work is **in business**. When people or companies **do business**, one of them sells goods or provides a service to the other.

❑ If a shop or company is **in business**, it is continuing to trade, often in spite of difficulties. If it goes **out of business**, it stops trading because it is not making enough money.

❑ **Business as usual** means something is carrying on as normal, despite an emergency or crisis.

❑ Any activity, situation, or series of events can be called a **business**. *Divorce can be a dreadful business... The whole business of present-giving has got hopelessly out of hand.*

❑ If you **get down to business**, you start dealing with something in a serious way. If you say someone **means business**, you mean they are serious and determined about what they are doing.

❑ If you are **minding your own business**, you are paying attention to your own concerns and not involving yourself in what other people are doing. ◇ If you tell someone to **mind their own business**, you mean they

should not ask about things which do not concern them. Similarly, you can tell someone something is **none of their business**. ◇ If you say someone **has no business** doing something, you mean they have no right to do it.

business school A **business school** is a college where people go to learn about various aspects of managing a business, for example finance, marketing, and law.

businesslike If someone is **businesslike**, they deal with things in an efficient way, without wasting time.

businessman (businessmen; businesswoman, businesswomen) A **businessman** or **businesswoman** is a person who works in a commercial or industrial business, especially as an owner or executive.

busker (busking) A **busker** is a person who plays music or sings in city streets or other public places, hoping to get money from passers-by. You say someone who does this is **busking**.

busman's holiday When someone spends their holiday doing something similar to their usual work, you call this a **busman's holiday**.

bust (busting, busted) ❑ If something is **bust**, it is broken.

❑ If a business **goes bust**, it loses so much money it is forced to close down.

❑ **Busting** is used to talk about ways of overcoming rules or restrictions. *...sanctions-busting.*

❑ If someone is **busted**, they are arrested by the police. *He was busted on a drugs charge.* You say a place is **busted** when the police raid it to arrest people. A raid or arrest can be called a **bust**.

❑ A **bust** is a statue of someone's head and shoulders.

❑ A woman's **bust** is her breasts.

bustle (bustling, bustled) If someone **bustles** somewhere, they move in a busy hurried way. ◇ **Bustle** is busy noisy activity. You say a place is **bustling** when there is a lot of noise and activity there.

busy (busier, busiest; busies, busying, busied) ❑ If you are **busy**, you are working hard at something, and do not have much time for other things. A **busy** time is one when you have a lot of things to do. ◇ A **busy** place is full of people or traffic.

❑ If you **busy** yourself with something, you occupy yourself by doing it.

❑ See also **busily**.

busybody (busybodies) If you call someone a **busybody**, you mean they are always interfering in other people's affairs.

but is used when two things are being contrasted. *The rooms are small but spacious... This is a bad time to be selling property. But it is a great time to be a buyer.*

❑ **But** is used after words like 'everything', 'anyone', or 'nobody' to mean 'except'. *They refused to eat anything but steak... At supper we talk of nothing but the game.*

❑ **But for** is used to say what prevents something happening or being true. *Seven players would be in contention for places but for injuries.*

❑ **All but** means 'almost'. *The town is all but deserted.*

butane is a type of gas used for fuel.

butch is used to describe a man or woman with a strong masculine appearance. Many people find this word offensive.

butcher (butchering, butchered; butchery) ❑ A **butcher** is a shopkeeper who sells meat. A shop where meat is sold is called a **butcher** or **butcher's.**

❏ When people are killed in a particularly brutal way, you can say they are **butchered.** Someone who kills people like this can be called a **butcher. Butchery** is the brutal and random killing of a lot of people.

butler A **butler** is the chief male servant in a rich household.

butt ❏ The **butt** of a handgun is the thick end of its handle. ◇ The **butt** of a cigar or cigarette is the small part left when someone has finished smoking it.

❏ A **butt** is also a large barrel for collecting or storing liquid.

❏ If someone is the **butt** of teasing or criticism, they are singled out to be teased or criticized.

❏ If you **butt** someone, you drive your head into part of their body. Similarly, animals can **butt** someone or something with their head or horns.

❏ If someone **butts in,** they interrupt when someone else is speaking.

butter (buttering, buttered) **Butter** is a fatty substance made from cream, which you spread on bread or use in cooking. If you **butter** bread, you spread butter on it.

buttercup Buttercups are small wild plants with bright yellow flowers.

butterfly (butterflies) ❏ **Butterflies** are insects with large colourful wings and thin bodies.

❏ The **butterfly stroke** is a swimming stroke. When you do it, you lie on your front and bring both arms together over your head in a large circular movement.

butterscotch is a hard sticky sweet made by boiling sugar, butter, and water. These ingredients are also used in a sauce called **butterscotch sauce.**

buttery (butteries) ❏ **Buttery** things taste of butter or contain a lot of butter.

❏ A **buttery** is a room where you can buy meals and drinks, especially at a college or university.

buttocks A person's **buttocks** are the part of their body they sit on.

button (buttoning, buttoned) **Buttons** are small hard objects used as fastenings on clothes. If you **button** a piece of clothing or **button** it **up,** you fasten it with its buttons. ◇ A **button** is also a small switch or knob which you press to operate a machine.

buttonhole (buttonholing, buttonholed) **Buttonholes** are the holes buttons fit through. ◇ If you **buttonhole** someone, you stop them and ask them something or get them to listen to you.

buttress (buttresses, buttressing, buttressed) **Buttresses** are stone or brick supports for a wall. ◇ If something **buttresses** something else, it helps to support or strengthen it. *He has apparently opted to buttress his position through an alliance with the army.*

buxom A **buxom** woman is attractively plump and full-bosomed.

buy (buying, bought) ❏ When you **buy** something, you obtain it by paying money for it. ◇ If you say something is a **good buy,** you mean it is good value for money.

❏ If someone **buys up** something like land or goods, they buy large amounts, or all that is available.

❏ If someone **buys into** a business or organization, they buy part of it, often to try and get some control of it. If they **buy** it **up** or **buy** it **out,** they buy enough shares to get

complete control; this is called a **buyout.** ◇ When the senior staff of a subsidiary buy it to run it themselves, this is called a **management buyout.**

❏ If you **buy** someone **off,** you offer them money or something else so they will stop opposing you or give up a claim against you. ◇ If you do something to **buy** time, you do it to gain time in which to think what to do next.

buyer A **buyer** is (a) someone who buys something. *He found a buyer for his Ford Escort.* (b) someone who works for a large store or organization, and whose job is to decide what to buy for sale in the store or for use by the organization. *...a fashion buyer.*

buyout See buy.

buzz (buzzes, buzzing, buzzed) ❏ A **buzz** is a continuous low humming sound, like the sound a bee makes when it is flying. When something makes this sound, you say it **buzzes.** ◇ The sound of a lot of people talking can be called a **buzz.** *...the buzz of conversation.*

❏ If you say a place is **buzzing,** you mean there is a lot of noise, excitement, or activity there. *The city has been buzzing with rumours.*

❏ If you get a **buzz** from something, it gives you a feeling of excitement or pleasure.

buzz word (*or* **buzzword**) A **buzz word** is a word which is widely used, because the thing it describes is thought to be very important. *Openness and flexibility have been the buzz words of the three-day gathering.* You can also have **buzz phrases.** *'The low maintenance garden' has become the latest buzz phrase in garden design circles.*

buzzard The **buzzard** is a large brown and white bird of prey, with broad wings and tail.

buzzer A **buzzer** is a device which makes a buzzing sound, for example on an alarm clock or telephone.

buzzword See buzz word.

by is used to say who or what does something. *The turtle was discovered by a local fisherman... ...small fields separated by thick hedges.* ◇ If a book, painting, or piece of music is **by** someone, they wrote it or created it.

❏ **By** is used to talk about the means used to do something. *The refund would be paid by cheque... He travelled south by train.* ◇ **By** is also used to mention the circumstances in which something happens or is done. *The research team made the discovery almost by accident.*

❏ **By** is used to say which way someone goes into or out of a building or other place. *She always entered by the front door.*

❏ If you are **by** someone or something, you are beside them or near to them. *...standing by the willow tree... ...a warehouse by Tower Bridge.* ◇ If someone or something goes **by,** they go past without stopping.

❏ **By** is used to talk about time passing. *The morning dragged by.* ◇ If something happens **by** a certain time, it happens at or before that time.

❏ If you are required to do something **by** a law or rule, that law or rule says you must do it.

❏ **By** particular standards means according to those standards. *The gift is generous by any standards.*

❏ If you are **by yourself,** you are on your own. If you do something **by yourself,** you do it without help from anyone else.

❏ In calculations, you multiply or divide one figure **by** another.

❑ **By** is used when giving measurements which show the size or extent of something. *...an office measuring 15 feet by 6.*

❑ **By** is used to show the quantities or sizes in which things are made or sold. *You can buy sheeting by the metre to make your own bedlinen.*

❑ **By** is used when mentioning an increase or decrease. *Exports of cars rose by 5.5 per cent... The original deadline has been extended by two days.* ◇ **By** is used when mentioning the difference between amounts or numbers. *Middlesex beat Leicestershire by 103 runs.*

❑ **By** can be used when describing someone's job or character. *He was a carpenter by trade... By temperament I'm always nervous and dissatisfied.*

❑ **By** is used to say what time of day something happens. *The owl hunts by night.*

❑ **by and large:** see large.

by-election A **by-election** is an election to choose a new MP for a constituency whose previous MP has resigned or died during a parliamentary term.

by-law (*or* **bye-law**) A **by-law** is a law made by a local authority which applies only in that authority's area.

by-pass See bypass.

by-product ❑ A **by-product** is something made or produced during manufacture or processing, which is not as important as the main product.

❑ The **by-product** of an event or situation is an unexpected or unplanned result of it.

bye In sport, you say there is a **bye** when a player or team automatically goes through to the next round of a competition because they do not have an opponent.

bye-law See by-law.

bygone is used to talk about things in the past. *The streets still retain much of the flavour of a bygone Elizabethan England.* ◇ If you say people should let **bygones** be bygones, you mean they should agree to forget their quarrels.

byline A **byline** under the title of a newspaper or magazine article says who the article is by.

bypass (bypasses, bypassing, bypassed) (*or* **by-pass,** *etc*) ❑ A **bypass** is a main road which takes traffic round the edge of a town rather than through its centre. ◇ If you **bypass** a place, you avoid going through it.

❑ If you **bypass** a person or part of a system, you miss them out when you are dealing with something, usually to save time.

❑ In a **bypass** operation, doctors redirect the flow of blood to avoid the heart, often because the heart is diseased or weak.

bystander A **bystander** is a person who is present when something happens, but is not involved in it.

byte In computing, a **byte** is a unit of storage equal to eight bits. See also bit.

byway **Byways** are quiet roads which are not used by many cars or people. ◇ Things which are interesting but not the main part of a subject can also be called **byways.** *...the byways of children's literature.*

byword If you say someone or something is a **byword** for a certain quality, you mean they are well know for having it. *At the end of the Seventies this country was a byword for inefficiency and inadequacy.*

Byzantine is used to describe methods and systems which are extremely complicated. *...the byzantine ramifications of the European common agricultural policy.*

C c

C stands for 'Centigrade' or 'Celsius'.

❑ **C** is used before or after a number to talk about a particular century. *...education and culture in the early 19th C.*

❑ **C** is also the name of a widely-used computer programming language.

c. See circa.

C of E See Church of England.

C.A.B. See Citizens' Advice Bureau.

cab A **cab** is a taxi. ◇ The **cab** of a lorry is the part where the driver sits.

cabal (*pron:* kab-**bal**) A **cabal** is a small group of powerful people who secretly arrange or influence things.

cabaret (*pron:* kab-a-**ray**) A **cabaret** is a show at a nightclub or restaurant, with singing, dancing, or other light entertainment.

cabbage **Cabbages** are large leafy vegetables which can be green, white, or purple.

cabbie (*or* **cabby**) A **cabbie** is a taxi-driver.

caber Tossing the **caber** is a traditional sport in the Highlands of Scotland. Competitors try to throw a tree-trunk (the **caber**) as far as possible.

cabin A **cabin** is a small room in a ship, boat, or plane. ◇ A **cabin** is also a small wooden building, especially one used for living in.

cabin crew The **cabin crew** on a plane are the people who look after the passengers.

cabin cruiser A **cabin cruiser** is a motorboat with a cabin for people to live or sleep in.

cabinet ❑ The **cabinet** is a group of the most senior ministers in a government.

❑ A **cabinet** is a cupboard for things like medicines or alcoholic drinks.

cabinet maker A **cabinet maker** is a person who makes high-quality wooden furniture.

cable (cabling, cabled) ❑ A **cable** is a thick strong rope. ◇ A **cable** is also one or more electrical wires in a rubber or plastic covering.

❑ **Cable** or **cable television** is a television system in which signals are sent along wires, rather than by radio waves.

❑ A **cable** is a telegram. If you **cable** someone, you send them a message by telegram.

cable car A **cable car** is a cabin suspended from a moving cable which takes people up a mountain.

cacao (*pron:* kak-kah-oh) The **cacao** is a tropical tree. Cocoa and chocolate are made from its seeds.

cache (*pron:* kash) A **cache** is a hidden store of things. *Police discovered an arms cache at his home.*

cachet (*pron:* kash-shay) If something you possess has **cachet**, people admire it and think it is a smart thing to have. If someone has **cachet**, people admire them and want to be like them.

cackle (cackling, cackled) If someone **cackles** or gives a **cackle**, they laugh in a loud unpleasant way.

cacophony (*pron:* kak-koff-on-nee) (cacophonous) A **cacophony** is a mixture of loud unpleasant noises. You can say a lot of noises together are **cacophonous**.

cactus (*plural:* cactuses *or* cacti) **Cactuses** are thick fleshy plants which grow in the desert and often have spines.

CAD is the use of computer technology to help people like engineers design their products. **CAD** stands for 'computer-aided design'.

cad Upper-class people used to say a man was a **cad** if he treated someone badly or deceived them.

cadaver (*pron:* kad-dav-ver) is the usual American word for a corpse.

caddie (*or* **caddy**) (caddies, caddying, caddied) If you **caddie** for someone or act as their **caddie**, you carry their clubs and equipment while they play golf.

cadence (*pron:* kade-enss) When people talk about someone's **cadences**, they mean the way their voice goes up and down, especially when they are making a speech. ◇ In music, a **cadence** is the end of a phrase.

cadet A **cadet** is a young person training for the police force, or to be an officer in one of the armed forces.

cadge (cadging, cadged) If someone **cadges** something like a cigarette from you, they ask you for one and you give it to them.

cadmium is a bluish-white metal used in making alloys and in electroplating.

cadre (*pron:* kah-der) A **cadre** is a person or a small group of people specially chosen and trained for a particular purpose within an organization.

Caesarean (*pron:* see-zair-ee-an) A **Caesarean** or **Caesarean section** is an operation in which a woman's body is cut open and her baby is lifted out, particularly if the birth is difficult or she cannot give birth normally.

cafe (*or* **café**) A **cafe** is a small restaurant where you can buy light meals or refreshments.

cafeteria A **cafeteria** is a self-service restaurant in a place like a factory or hospital.

caffeine (*or* **caffein**) is a substance in coffee and tea which makes you feel more alert. Some people avoid drinks with caffeine in them because they think it is harmful.

caftan (*or* **kaftan**) A **caftan** is a long loose robe with long sleeves, worn in Arab countries. ◇ A **caftan** is also a similar garment worn by Western women.

cage (caging, caged) A **cage** is a container with bars to keep animals or birds in, to stop them escaping. If you **cage** something, you put it in a cage. A **caged** animal or bird is inside a cage.

cagey If someone is being **cagey** about something, they are being careful not to say very much about it.

cagoule (*pron:* kag-gool) A **cagoule** is a lightweight waterproof jacket with a hood.

cahoots If you say someone is **in cahoots** with someone else, you mean they are working together and planning something which may harm other people.

cairn A **cairn** is a pile of stones placed somewhere as a monument or to help people find their way across wild country.

cajole (*pron:* ka-jole) (cajoling, cajoled) If you **cajole** someone into doing something they do not want to do, you get them to do it by flattering them.

cake (caked) ❑ A **cake** is a sweet food, usually made by baking flour, sugar, eggs, and fat together into a solid shape. ◇ Some savoury foods made in a solid shape are also called **cakes**. ...*potato cakes.*

❑ If you say something is a **piece of cake**, you mean it is very easy to do. ◇ If someone says you cannot **have your cake and eat it**, they mean you have a choice of two things but you cannot have both.

❑ **Cake** is used to talk about something like an amount of money which is shared out among different groups of people. ...*the battle over who gets the biggest share of the cake.*

❑ A **cake** of soap is a small block of it.

❑ If something is **caked** with a thick liquid, the liquid has got onto it and dried there.

calamity (calamities; calamitous) You call something a **calamity** when it is very serious and causes a lot of distress. You also say something like this is **calamitous**.

calcium is a soft silvery-white chemical element found in teeth and bones, and in limestone, chalk, and marble.

calculate (calculating, calculated; calculation, calculable) ❑ If you **calculate** a number or amount, you work it out; this is called making a **calculation**. ◇ If you say an amount is **calculable**, you mean it is possible to work it out.

❑ You also say someone **calculates** something when they come to a conclusion based on all the available facts. *Many might calculate that a new leader offers their only chance of survival.*

❑ A **calculating** person gets what they want by controlling people and arranging things for their own benefit; you call behaviour like this **calculation**. *The government believes that he acted out of calculation, and not humanity, in freeing the hostages.* ◇ If someone does something in a **calculated** way, they do it deliberately, having decided to do it beforehand. ...*a brutal calculated killing.*

❑ If something is **calculated** to have an effect, it is intended to have that effect.

❑ A **calculated** risk is one you think worth taking because of the advantages if you are successful.

calculator A **calculator** is an electronic device for doing calculations.

calculus is a type of maths which deals with such things as variable quantities. It can be used, for example, to calculate rates of change.

caldron See **cauldron**.

calendar ❑ A **calendar** is a system of dividing time into fixed periods of years, months, and days. ◇ A **calendar** is also a chart showing the days, weeks, and months of one or more years.

❑ A **calendar year** begins on January 1st and ends on

December 31st. See also **financial year**. ◇ A **calendar month** is one of the twelve months in a year, for example March or April, as distinct from fixed 28 or 30 day periods, also called 'months', which are used for some purposes.

❏ A **calendar** is also a list of important dates for an organization or type of activity. ...*a big event in the city's calendar*.

calf (calves) ❏ A **calf** is a young cow or bull. ◇ The young of some other animals are also called **calves**, for example young elephants, giraffes, whales, and seals.

❏ A person's **calves** are the backs of their legs between their knees and their ankles. ◇ If something like a coat is **calf-length**, it reaches to your calves. ...*a calf-length robe*.

caliber See **calibre**.

calibrate (calibrating, calibrated; calibration) If a tool or instrument is **calibrated**, marks are put on it so it can be used to measure things accurately. A scale of marks like this is called a **calibration**.

calibre (*American spelling:* **caliber**) ❏ The **calibre** of a gun is the width of the inside of its barrel. You also talk about the **calibre** of the bullets or shells it fires.

❏ **Calibre** is used to talk about someone's intelligence and ability, especially when these are of a high standard. *Many employees have not been of the right calibre.* ◇ You say things like organizations and events have **calibre** when they are associated with high standards. *For an event of this calibre, the performances were, on the whole, disappointing.* ◇ **High-calibre** people or things are of a very high standard. ...*a high-calibre politician... ...high-calibre productions*.

calico is a type of plain cream or white cotton cloth.

caliper See **calliper**.

call (called) ❏ You use **called** when you are mentioning the name of a person, place, or thing. ...*a district of old Cairo called Gamaliyya*. ◇ If you **call** someone or something a name, you give them that name. *His Scottish mother wanted to call him Hamish.*

❏ If you **call** a person something, you use a word or phrase to describe them. *Some people are calling them irresponsible scaremongers.* ◇ If you **call** yourself something, you claim that is what you are, though it might not be true. ...*the store that likes to call itself the most famous in the world*. ◇ **Call** is used with 'own' to emphasize that something really belongs to someone. For example, if you have a home you can **call your own**, it is really yours, and you are not renting it or sharing it with other people.

❏ If you **call** someone or give them a **call**, you phone them. ◇ If you **call** someone **back**, you phone them again or return their call. ◇ If you **call in**, you phone somewhere like your workplace, to report where you are or what you are doing. You can also **call in** to a radio or television station.

❏ If you **call** someone like a doctor or **call** them **out**, you ask them to come to you, especially in an emergency. ◇ If someone like a doctor is **on call**, they are ready to go out to work when someone asks them to, especially in an emergency. ◇ If you **call** someone **in**, you ask them to come to your home or workplace, because you need help. ◇ If you **call** someone **back**, you ask them to return. *The agriculture minister has been called back from holiday.* Ships and planes can also be **called back**. *Congress may yet decide that the warships should be called back from the Gulf.*

❏ If someone **calls for** an action, they ask for it to be done. If several people want something done, you can say there is a **call** for it. *There's been a call for improvements to international air safety procedures.* ◇ If you **call on** someone to do something, you ask them to do it. *A wildlife rescue centre is calling on people to put out bowls of water to save hedgehogs wilting in the heat.* ◇ If something **calls for** qualities or action of a particular kind, they are needed for it. *The economics of construction calls for even faster building programmes.*

❏ If someone is **called** before a court of law or committee, they have to go there, for example to give evidence. ◇ If someone is **called to order** by the person in charge of a meeting, they are asked to behave themselves and keep the rules.

❏ If someone is **called up**, or gets their **call-up**, they are ordered to join one of the armed forces. ◇ If workers are **called out** on strike, they are ordered to go on strike.

❏ If you **call** something like a meeting, you announce that it will take place. ◇ If something is **called off**, it is cancelled or stopped.

❏ If you can **call on** something, it is there to be used if you need it. *They can call on my experience if they have a problem.*

❏ If something is **called in**, you are asked to repay it or return it. ...*borrowers whose loans are called in by the receivers*.

❏ When you get a computer to display information on a screen, you say you **call** the information **up**.

❏ If you **call** or make a **call** somewhere, you make a short visit. ◇ If you **call on** someone, you visit them. ◇ When a ship, bus, or train **calls** at a place, it stops there for a short time.

❏ If you **call** something **out**, you shout it.

❏ Some sounds made by birds or animals are known as **calls**. ...*the calls of song-birds... ...a whale distress call*.

❏ **call** someone's **bluff**: see **bluff**. ◇ **call it a day**: see **day**. ◇ **call** something **to mind**: see **mind**. ◇ **call** something **into question**: see **question**. ◇ **call the tune**: see **tune**.

call box A **call box** is the same as a telephone box.

call girl A **call girl** is a prostitute who makes appointments by phone.

call sign The **call sign** of a person, organization, or vehicle is a series of letters and numbers used to identify them when radio messages are sent or received.

caller A **caller** is (a) someone who phones you. (b) someone who comes to see you for a short visit.

calligraphy (*pron:* kal-lig-ra-fee) (calligrapher) **Calligraphy** is the art of doing beautiful handwriting, often using a special brush or pen. A **calligrapher** is someone who does beautiful handwriting.

calliper (*American spelling:* **caliper**) **Callipers** are instruments used to measure the size of things. They are made of two long pieces of metal joined at one end by a hinge. ◇ **Callipers** are also devices for supporting a person's leg if they cannot walk properly. They are made of metal rods held together by straps.

callous (callously; callousness) **Callous** behaviour is cruel or heartless. *Rations are callously reduced... ...the callousness of the fighters.*

callow If you say a young person is **callow**, you mean they are immature and do not have much experience of life.

callus (callused) A **callus** is an area of thick hard skin caused by rubbing, usually on someone's palms or the soles of their feet. You can say someone's hands or feet are **callused**.

calm (calmly; calmness) ❑ You say someone is **calm** when they do not panic or get excited in a difficult or dangerous situation. *The man acted calmly throughout the hijacking... Drivers who had been stranded had shown patience and calmness.* ◇ If you **calm** someone or **calm** their worries or fears, you do something to make them less upset, worried, or excited. ◇ If someone **calms down**, they become less upset, excited, or angry.

❑ If a place or situation is **calm**, there is no fighting or trouble. When things are like this, you say there is **calm**. *Many inmates were wounded before calm was restored.* ◇ When fighting or an argument gets less intense, you can say things **calm down**.

❑ **Calm** weather is very still, with no wind. ◇ If the sea is **calm**, there are no big waves.

Calor Gas is gas sold in portable metal containers. It is used by campers, and by people who live in a place with no gas supply. 'Calor Gas' is a trademark.

calorie The **calorie** is a unit of measurement for the energy value of food. On packets of food it is often written as 'cal'.

calorific is used to talk about things to do with calories. *...calorific intake.*

calumny (calumnies) If you say something is **calumny** or a **calumny**, you mean it is untrue and is meant to get people to lose respect for someone or no longer admire them. *The mayor alleged that he was the victim of calumny and dirty tricks.*

Calvinism (Calvinist) **Calvinism** is a type of Protestantism based on the religious theories of John Calvin, a sixteenth-century French religious reformer. His followers have a strict set of moral rules and believe, among other things, that people have no control over what happens to them because God has already decided this. A **Calvinist** is a follower of Calvinism.

calypso (calypsos) A **calypso** is a type of song from the West Indies. The words are usually improvised and are a comment on things happening at the time.

cam A **cam** is a device or part of an engine which changes circular motion into up-and-down or side-to-side motion.

camaraderie (*pron:* kam-mer-**rard**-er-ree) is a feeling of trust and friendship among a group of people.

camber The **camber** of a road is the slight downward slope towards each side, which allows water to flow off.

camcorder A **camcorder** is a combined video camera and recorder which is small enough to be held in one hand.

came See come.

camel The **camel** is a large animal which is used for crossing the desert. It has a long neck and either one or two humps.

camellia (*pron:* kam-**meal**-ya) The **camellia** is a tall shrub with shiny leaves and large rose-like flowers which can be white, pink, or red.

cameo (cameos) ❑ When a small part in a play or film is played by a well-known actor or actress, it can be called a **cameo** or **cameo role**. ◇ A **cameo** is also a short piece of writing or acting that cleverly describes something

like a place or a person's character.

❑ A **cameo** is also a piece of jewellery, usually oval, with a raised stone design on a different coloured flat stone.

camera ❑ A **camera** is a device for taking photos or making films. ◇ A television **camera** is a piece of equipment for changing images into electrical signals, so live pictures can be shown on television. ◇ If something is done **on camera**, it is televised.

❑ If a trial or hearing is held **in camera**, the public and the press are not allowed in.

cameraman (cameramen) A **cameraman** is a person who operates a television or film camera.

camisole A **camisole** is a short sleeveless top worn by women as underwear.

camomile (*or* chamomile) is a type of scented plant with daisy-like flowers. It is used to make herbal tea.

camouflage (*pron:* kam-moo-**flahj**) (camouflaging, camouflaged) ❑ **Camouflage** is things like leaves, paint, and special clothes worn by soldiers to make them blend in with their surroundings, so the enemy will not see them. Camouflage is also used on ships, planes, lorries, and buildings. ◇ If a soldier **camouflages** himself or his equipment, he uses camouflage.

❑ When an animal's skin markings or shape help it blend with its surroundings, this is also called **camouflage**.

❑ If a fact or feeling is **camouflaged**, it is hidden or made to look different. *He has never camouflaged his desire to better himself.*

camp (camping) ❑ A **camp** is a group of buildings specially built for people like prisoners or refugees to live in. ◇ A **camp** is also a group of huts and other buildings built for members of the armed forces to live in temporarily. ◇ A **camp** is also a group of tents, caravans, or buildings which people like travellers or gypsies live in. ◇ When people **set up camp** somewhere, they make a camp there.

❑ A **camp** is a group of tents for people on holiday to live in. ◇ If you **camp** somewhere, you stay there in a tent. ◇ If you go **camping**, you go somewhere on holiday and stay in a tent. ◇ If you **camp out** somewhere, you sleep outdoors or in an uncomfortable place.

❑ A **camp** is also a group of people who support an idea, person, or belief. *...the Clinton camp... ...the anti-Maastricht camp.*

❑ People say something like a show is **camp** when it is done in an exaggerated way which makes it absurd and funny. ◇ If someone **camps it up**, they deliberately behave in an exaggerated and artificial way. ◇ If you say a man is **camp**, you mean he behaves or dresses in a way usually associated with homosexual men.

camp bed A **camp bed** is a small portable folding bed.

camp fire A **camp fire** is a fire you make outdoors when you are camping.

camp follower A **camp follower** is someone who does not officially belong to a group or organization but is interested in it and supports it, often because it makes them feel important. ◇ Originally, a **camp follower** was someone who travelled with an army and earned money by doing jobs for them.

camp site A **camp site** is a place where holiday-makers can put their tents or caravans.

campaign (campaigner) ❑ A **campaign** is a series of planned activities aimed at achieving a particular result, such as a social or political change. A person who organizes something like this is called a **campaigner**; you say they **campaign** for something. *The RSPCA has campaigned strongly for compulsory registration of dogs.*

❑ In a war, a **campaign** is a series of planned movements or actions aimed at achieving a particular result.

campanile (*pron:* camp-an-nee-lee) A **campanile** is a bell tower, especially one which stands on its own and is not attached to another building.

camper A **camper** is (a) someone who goes camping. (b) a van with beds and cooking equipment.

camphor is a whitish substance, usually in the form of crystals. It has a strong smell and is used, among other things, in medicines and mothballs.

campion Campions are a kind of red, pink, or white wild flower.

campus (campuses) A university or college **campus** is the area where its main buildings are. If someone is **on campus**, they are somewhere in this area.

camshaft A **camshaft** is a part of an engine consisting of a rod with one or more cams attached to it.

can (canned) ❑ If you **can** do something, it is possible for you to do it. If something **can** happen, it is possible for it to happen. Instead of 'can not', you write **cannot** or **can't**. ◇ **Can** is also used to talk about people being allowed to do things. *A child can apply for a residence order away from home.*

❑ **Cannot** is used to express a strong belief that something is not true or will not happen. *Such a tragic situation cannot continue any longer.* ◇ **Cannot** is also used to say someone should not do something, or something should not happen. *The current situation cannot be allowed to continue indefinitely.*

❑ A **can** is a sealed metal container for food, drink, or paint. When food or drink is **canned**, it is put in a can. **Canned** food or drink comes in a can.

❑ **Canned** music is recorded music played as a background in places like supermarkets. ◇ **Canned** laughter or applause has been pre-recorded and is added to a television or radio programme to make it sound as if there is a live audience.

❑ The person who **carries the can** for something is the one who takes the blame.

can-opener A **can-opener** is the same as a tin opener.

Canada goose The **Canada goose** is a very common wild goose, often seen in parks, waterways, and fields. It is grey, with a black head and neck and a white face-patch.

canal ❑ A **canal** is a long man-made strip of water, for boats to travel along. ◇ An irrigation **canal** is a similar strip, built to bring water to an area.

❑ Some tubes inside the body are called **canals**. They are there to carry food, air, or other substances. *...the alimentary canal.*

canapé (*pron:* kan-nap-pay) A **canapé** is a small piece of biscuit or bread with meat, cheese, or other savoury food on top. Canapés are often served with drinks at parties.

canard (*pron:* kan-nahd) A **canard** is a wrong idea or piece of false information which circulates among peo-

ple, and is sometimes spread deliberately.

canary (canaries) Canaries are small yellow birds with a pleasant song. They are often kept as pets.

canasta is a card game similar to rummy, played with two packs of cards.

cancan The **cancan** is a dance in which women kick up their legs and shake their skirts to fast music.

cancel (cancelling, cancelled; cancellation) (*usual American spelling:* canceling, canceled, cancellation) ❑ If you **cancel** something which has been arranged, you stop the arrangement and it does not take place. *...the cancellation of the prime minister's visit.* ◇ If you **cancel** something you have reserved like a hotel room or a theatre seat, you tell the management you no longer want it.

❑ If you **cancel** something like a cheque, you make it invalid.

❑ If two things **cancel** each other **out**, they have opposite effects, producing no real effect at all. You can also say one thing **cancels** another **out**. *A Steve Bruce penalty was cancelled out by a Gary Pallister own goal.*

cancer (cancerous) **Cancer** is a serious disease caused by cells in part of the body dividing quickly in an uncontrolled way. This produces a growth or tumour called a **cancer**. You call a growth of this kind **cancerous**.

candelabra (*pron:* kan-del-lah-bra) (*plural:* candelabra *or* candelabras) A **candelabra** is a large ornamental candle holder with several arms.

candid (candidly) If you are **candid** with someone, you speak to them honestly and do not try to hide anything, even if it might shock or upset them. *He gave remarkably candid interviews to journalists... The two sides are said to have talked candidly into the night.* ◇ A **candid** photo of someone is one they have not posed for.

candidate (candidacy, candidacies; candidature) ❑ A **candidate** is someone being considered for a position, for example one of the people standing in an election or applying for a job. ◇ If a person is a candidate in an election, you can talk about their **candidacy** or **candidature**. *There were calls for him to withdraw his candidature.*

❑ A **candidate** is also a person taking an exam.

❑ You say someone or something is a **candidate** for something when they are likely to be chosen for it or affected by it. *The most obvious candidate for privatization within the Post Office is its Parcel Force business.*

candied fruit or other food has a covering of sugar, or has been cooked in sugar syrup to preserve it.

candle A **candle** is a stick or block of hard wax with a wick through the middle which is lit to provide light. ◇ If you say something is not **worth the candle**, you mean it is not worth the effort or trouble needed to do it or get it.

candlelight (candlelit) **Candlelight** is the light from a candle or candles. A **candlelit** room or table is lit by candles.

candlestick A **candlestick** is a holder for a candle.

candlewick is a type of tufted cloth used for things like bedspreads and dressing gowns.

candour (*American spelling:* candor) If you speak or write with **candour** about something, you are honest and open about it.

candy (candies) **Candy** is the usual American word for sweets. A **candy** is a sweet.

candy floss (*or* **candyfloss**) is a large fluffy mass of sugar threads wrapped round a stick for someone to eat. It is often sold at fairs or by the seaside.

cane (caning, caned) ❑ **Cane** is the long hollow stems of plants like bamboo. ◇ **Cane** furniture is made from strips of cane woven together. ◇ See also **sugar cane**.
❑ A **cane** is a walking stick, particularly an ornamental one. The white sticks blind people carry are sometimes called **canes**. ◇ A **cane** is also a long thin flexible stick for hitting people as a punishment, especially at school. If someone is **caned** or given the **cane**, they are hit with a cane. ◇ A **cane** is also a narrow stick, usually bamboo, for supporting plants.
❑ The woody stems of plants like blackberries and raspberries are also called **canes**.

canine (*pron:* kay-nine) ❑ **Canine** is used to talk about dogs. *...the canine star, Lassie... ...a canine population of 7.3 million.* ◇ A **canine** is (a) a dog. *Woolly has beaten a score of other canines to land a role with the Royal Shakespeare Company.* (b) any member of the dog family, which includes wolves, foxes, and jackals.
❑ A person's or animal's **canines** or **canine teeth** are pointed teeth near the front of their mouth. They are also called their **eye teeth**.

canister A **canister** is a metal container, often used for storing gas or other chemicals under pressure.

canker A **canker** is something evil which spreads and affects other things or people. *The canker of anti-Semitism is growing again in America.*

cannabis is a drug made from the hemp plant. Some people smoke or eat it to make them feel relaxed. Cannabis is illegal in many countries.

canned See **can**.

cannery (canneries) A **cannery** is a factory where food is canned.

cannibal (cannibalism) A **cannibal** is a person who eats human flesh. ◇ Animals which eat their own species are also called **cannibals**. ◇ When people or animals eat their own species, this is called **cannibalism**.

cannibalize (cannibalizing, cannibalized) (*can be spelled with an 's' instead of a 'z'*) If you **cannibalize** something like a machine or vehicle, you take parts from it to repair another one.

cannon (*plural:* cannons *or* cannon) (cannoning, cannoned) ❑ In the past, a **cannon** was a large gun on wheels which fired heavy metal balls. ◇ Nowadays, a **cannon** is a heavy automatic gun, especially one fired from an aircraft. ◇ See also **water cannon**.
❑ If a moving object **cannons** off something, it hits it and moves off in a different direction.
❑ If you say someone who is on your side in a dispute or contest is a **loose cannon**, you mean they could cause you problems, as they are liable to do unpredictable things.

cannon ball See **cannonball**.

cannon fodder You say soldiers are **cannon fodder** when their leaders regard them as unimportant because, if they are killed, there are plenty of others to take their place.

cannonball (*or* **cannon ball**) Cannonballs were heavy metal balls fired from a cannon.

cannot See **can**.

canny (cannier, canniest; cannily, canniness) You say someone is **canny** when they are clever in their judgement of things, or in the way they handle their affairs, especially where money is concerned. *He is cannily avoiding the continuing fall in prices by renting... He gained a reputation for canniness.*

canoe (*pron:* kan-noo) (canoeist; canoeing) A **canoe** is a small narrow boat which you propel through the water using a paddle. Someone who does this is called a **canoeist**; what they do is called **canoeing**.

canon ❑ A **canon** is a priest on the staff of a cathedral.
❑ A **canon** is also a rule or principle.
❑ **Canon** is used to talk about an entire range of literary or musical compositions of a particular kind. For example, the **canon** of a writer's works is everything he or she has ever written.
❑ A **canon** is a piece of music in several parts. The parts are identical, but begin and end at different times.

canon law is a set of rules for running the affairs of a Christian church, for example the Roman Catholic Church or the Anglican Church.

canonize (canonizing, canonized; canonization) (*can be spelled with an 's' instead of a 'z'*) If a dead person is **canonized**, they are officially recognized as a saint, especially in the Catholic Church. *The campaign for his canonization has little popular following.*

canoodle (canoodling, canoodled) If a couple are **canoodling**, they are kissing and cuddling.

canopy (canopies) ❑ A **canopy** is a cover suspended above something, for decoration or shelter. ◇ The branches and leaves of trees can be called a **canopy** when they spread out, covering a wide area.
❑ The **canopy** of a parachute is the large circle of nylon or silk connected to the harness.

cant When someone makes a moral statement to justify a bad or selfish action, you can call this **cant**. *It is time to end the cant about how and why these honours are awarded.*

cantankerous A **cantankerous** person keeps finding things to argue or complain about.

cantata (*pron:* kan-tah-ta) A **cantata** is a musical work for singers and instruments, usually based on a religious text.

canteen A **canteen** is part of a place like a factory or office where the workers go to eat.

canter (cantering, cantered) When a horse **canters**, it moves at a speed slower than a gallop, but faster than a trot. You call this way of moving a **canter**.

cantilever A **cantilever** is a long horizontal structure fixed in only one place with the rest overhanging. A **cantilever** bridge is made of two or more connecting cantilevers. The Forth railway bridge is a cantilever bridge.

canton A **canton** is a political or administrative region in some countries, for example Switzerland.

cantor A **cantor** is a singer, usually a man, employed to lead the services in a synagogue.

canvas (canvases) **Canvas** is strong heavy cloth used for making tents, sails, and bags. ◇ If you sleep **under canvas**, you sleep in a tent. ◇ A **canvas** is a piece of canvas on which an oil painting is done. The painting itself can also be called a **canvas**. If an artist puts something **on canvas**, he or she paints it.

canvass (canvasses, canvassing, canvassed; canvasser) If you **canvass** or do a **canvass** for a person or a party, you go round an area and try to persuade people to vote for them. A person who does this is a called a **canvasser**. ◇ If you **canvass** people's opinions, you find out how they feel about something by asking them.

canyon A **canyon** is a long narrow valley with very steep sides, often with a river at the bottom.

cap (caps, capping, capped) ❑ Several kinds of hats are called **caps**, including hats worn as part of a uniform. You can add **-capped** to a word to say what kind of cap someone is wearing. ...*white-capped traffic policemen.*

❑ If you go to someone **cap in hand**, you go to them humbly, to ask for something.

❑ If someone is **capped** or awarded a **cap**, they are chosen to represent their country or school in a game like rugby or cricket.

❑ The **cap** of a bottle is its lid. ◇ A **cap** is also a protective covering. ...*a lens cap*... ...*hub caps.* See also **diaphragm**.

❑ **Caps** are very small explosives used in toy guns.

❑ You use **capped** to say something is on top of something else. ...*snow-capped mountains.*

❑ If the government **caps** a local authority, it limits the amount of money the authority can spend. A restriction like this is called a **cap**. Other things like prices and rates can also be **capped**.

❑ If someone **caps** a joke told by someone else, they follow it with a better one. Similarly, you can say a story or film **caps** an earlier one.

❑ **Cap** is also used to talk about the last thing which adds the finishing touch to a series of things. *An epic victory for the coxed pairs capped a wonderful weekend for Britain at the Olympic Games.*

CAP The **CAP** or **Common Agricultural Policy** is the system used by the European Union to protect farm incomes by keeping agricultural prices at agreed levels.

capability (capabilities) ❑ **Capability** is the ability to take a particular kind of military action. *Some nations are working on a biological weapons capability.*

❑ If you have the **capability** to do something, you are able to do it. A person's **capabilities** are the things they are able to do.

capable (capably) If someone or something is **capable** of doing something, they have the ability to do it. ◇ If you say someone is **capable** of a kind of behaviour, you mean they could easily behave like that. *Someone who'd killed twice would be capable of killing a third time.* ◇ A **capable** person can be relied on to do something well. *They are capably led by Mark Benson.* Military aircraft and equipment can also be described as **capable**. *Canada requires very capable helicopters for its surface ships.*

capacious If something is **capacious**, there is a lot of room in it.

capacitor A **capacitor** is a device for storing electric charge. It used to be called a 'condenser'.

capacity (capacities) ❑ The **capacity** of something is the largest amount it can hold, produce, or carry. ◇ If something is filled **to capacity**, it is as full as possible. ◇ If there is a **capacity** crowd at a stadium, the stadium is completely full. Similarly, you can talk about a **capacity** audience in a theatre or cinema. ◇ If a factory or industry is working to **capacity**, it is producing as much as

it is able to.

❑ If you have the **capacity** to do something, you are able to do it. *What Hicks lacks is the capacity to handle the business.* ◇ If someone does something in a particular **capacity**, they do it as part of the duties which go with that job or position. *Fred Titmus was present in his capacity as an England committee observer.*

cape A **cape** is a large piece of land that sticks out into the sea. ◇ A **cape** is also a short cloak.

caper (capering, capered) ❑ **Capers** are the flower buds of a Mediterranean bush. They are pickled and used to season food.

❑ A **caper** is (a) a practical joke or trick. (b) a crime or other illegal activity.

❑ If someone **capers** around, they dance or jump around energetically.

capillary (capillaries) **Capillaries** are tiny blood vessels.

capital ❑ The **capital** of a country is the city or town where its government meets. The **capital** of a region is its main town. ◇ A town which is famous for something is sometimes called the **capital** of that thing. ...*Nashville, the capital of country music.*

❑ **Capital** is a large amount of money used to start or expand a business, or invested to make more money. ◇ **Capital** is also money you invest or save instead of spending, so you can get regular payments or interest. ◇ In industry, **capital** investment or expenditure is money spent on things like buildings and machinery. ◇ **Capital** is also used to talk about any useful resource which a country or industry has. *Money spent on education is investment in human capital.*

❑ If you **make capital** out of a situation, you use it to your advantage. *The Conservatives have consistently made political capital out of the close links between the Labour Party and the trade unions.*

❑ A **capital** or **capital** letter is the large form of a letter used, for example, at the beginning of a sentence or name.

❑ A **capital** offence is one which, according to the law, can be punished by death.

capital gains are the profits you make when you buy something then sell it again.

capital punishment is the legal killing of someone convicted of a serious crime like murder.

capitalise See **capitalize**.

capitalism (capitalist) ❑ **Capitalism** is an economic and political system where property, business, and industry are owned by individuals and not by the state. In this system, companies compete with each other to make a profit. A **capitalist** system or economy is based on capitalism. A **capitalist** country has a capitalist economy.

❑ People who own capital or businesses are sometimes called **capitalists**. **Capitalist** is used to describe things thought to be typical of capitalists. ...*a life of capitalist luxury.*

capitalistic A **capitalistic** system or economy is the same as a capitalist one. See **capitalism**.

capitalize (capitalizing, capitalized; capitalization) (*can be spelled with an 's' instead of a 'z'*) ❑ If you **capitalize** on a situation, you use it to your own advantage.

❑ **Capitalized** is used to say how much capital a business or other organization has. ...*an under-capitalized tourist trade.* ◇ If a business **capitalizes** something like its costs, it treats them as assets, instead of expenses. This sort of accounting is called **capitalization**. ◇ A company's **market capitalization** is the total value of its shares.

capitation A **capitation** fee or payment is set at a fixed amount per person.

Capitol In the US, the **Capitol** is the main building in Washington where Congress meets. The media often talk about things happening on **Capitol Hill**, the hill where the Capitol is. **Capitol Hill** is also used to talk about Congress itself. *The President felt he already had full authority to order American troops into battle – if necessary without consulting Capitol Hill.*

capitulate (capitulating, capitulated; capitulation) If an army **capitulates**, it surrenders. ◇ If you **capitulate** to someone, you give in to them and agree to what they want. *...the government's capitulation on the poll tax.*

cappuccino (*pron:* kap-poo-**cheen**-oh) (cappuccinos) **Cappuccino** is a type of coffee made with frothy steamed milk. Chocolate is often sprinkled on top of it.

caprice (*pron:* kap-**reess**) A **caprice** is an unexpected action or decision which has no real purpose.

capricious (capriciously; capriciousness) A **capricious** person often changes their mind unexpectedly. ◇ **Capricious** is also used to describe things which change unexpectedly and cannot be relied on. *He had spent half an hour trying to board the capriciously tossing and turning vessel... ...the capriciousness of the American legal system.*

capsicum Capsicums are large mild-tasting peppers.

capsize (capsizing, capsized) If a ship or boat **capsizes** or is **capsized**, it turns upside down or tips over on its side. You can talk about the **capsize** of a ship or boat.

capsule ❏ A **capsule** is a small container with powdered medicine inside which you swallow like a pill.

❏ A **time capsule** is a container with objects and documents in it, each of which is supposed to stand for some aspect of present-day life. The capsule is buried in the earth or the foundations of a building, so it can be discovered at some future time.

❏ The **capsule** on a manned spacecraft is the part where the crew are, which returns to earth after the voyage.

captain (captaining, captained; captaincy, captaincies) ❏ The **captain** of a plane or ship is the officer in charge. ◇ A **captain** is a middle-ranking officer in the British army and in some other armed forces, also a high-ranking officer in the British and US navies.

❏ The **captain** of a sports team is its leader. You can say someone **captains** a sports team, or talk about their **captaincy** of it.

❏ A person in charge of a large company or group of companies is sometimes called a **captain of industry**.

caption (captioning, captioned) A **caption** is the title or other words next to a picture, explaining what it is about. When a picture is **captioned**, words are added to it like this. ◇ A **caption** is also the headline of an article.

captivate (captivating, captivated) If you are **captivated** by someone or something, you find them fascinating and attractive. *...his captivating smile.*

captive (captivity) ❏ A **captive** is a prisoner. When someone is **taken captive**, they are taken prisoner. If they are **held captive**, they are kept as a prisoner. ◇ A **captive** person or animal is kept somewhere and not allowed to go free. You say a person or animal in this situation is in

captivity.

❏ If you have a **captive audience**, a group of people have to watch or listen to you because they are unable to leave. ◇ A **captive market** is a group of consumers who have to buy or use something because no-one else produces or provides the same thing.

captor Someone's **captor** is the person who has captured them.

capture (capturing, captured) ❏ If someone is **captured**, they are taken prisoner, especially in a war or after a struggle. ◇ If an animal is **captured**, it is caught or trapped. ◇ If military forces **capture** a place, they take control of it by force. Things like arms or installations can also be **captured**. ◇ When someone or something is captured, you can talk about their **capture**.

❏ If you **capture** something like a prize, you win it. Similarly, you can say a politician **captures** a certain number of votes.

❏ If someone **captures** the atmosphere or quality of something, they represent it successfully in pictures, music, or words. *Today's newspapers capture the mood of the nation in reporting England's exit from the World Cup.* ◇ If something **captures** your imagination, you find it very exciting or interesting.

car A **car** is a motor vehicle, usually with four wheels, which can carry a small number of people. ◇ Car is also the usual American word for a railway carriage. ◇ In Britain, railway carriages used for a particular purpose used to be called **cars**. *...a dining car.*

car bomb A **car bomb** is a bomb placed inside or under a car, to kill the driver or passers-by.

car boot sale A **car boot sale** is a sale where people sell things from the boots of their cars on a car park or field hired for the occasion.

car maker A **car maker** is a firm which manufactures cars.

car park (*or* carpark) A **car park** is an area or building where people are allowed to leave their cars.

car phone (*or* carphone) A **car phone** is a telephone in a car.

car port (*or* carport) A **car port** is a shelter for one or two cars, consisting of a flat roof supported on pillars.

carafe (*pron:* kar-**raff**) A **carafe** is a glass container for water or wine.

caramel A **caramel** is a kind of toffee. ◇ **Caramel** is burnt sugar used for colouring and flavouring food.

caramelize (caramelizing, caramelized) (*can be spelled with an 's' instead of a 'z'*) When sugar **caramelizes** or is **caramelized**, it turns into caramel.

carapace The **carapace** of a creature like a tortoise, crab, or lobster is its thick hard upper shell.

carat (*usual American spelling:* karat) The weight of diamonds and other precious stones is expressed in **carats**. A carat is 0.20 grams (about 0.007 ounces). ◇ The purity of gold is also measured in **carats**. The purest gold is 24-carat.

caravan (caravanning) ❏ A **caravan** is a vehicle without an engine in which people live or spend their holidays. Caravans can be towed by cars or they can be parked in one place permanently. Having a holiday in a caravan is called **caravanning**. ◇ A **caravan site** or **caravan park** is a place where caravans are parked, either temporarily or permanently.

❏ A **caravan** is also a group of people and animals travelling together for safety in places like the desert.

caraway is a plant with finely-divided leaves and clusters of small whitish flowers. Its seeds are used in cooking and in medicine.

carbine A carbine is a light automatic rifle.

carbohydrate is a substance in foods like sugar and bread which gives you energy. Foods with a lot of carbohydrate in them are called **carbohydrates**.

carbolic acid is a liquid used as a disinfectant and antiseptic. It is also called 'phenol'.

carbon is a chemical element which diamonds, graphite, and coal are made of.

❏ A **carbon** is the same as a carbon copy.

carbon copy A carbon copy is a copy made using carbon paper. ◇ If you say a person or thing is a **carbon copy** of an earlier person or thing, you mean they are identical or very similar. *Yesterday's coup bid appeared to be a carbon copy of a similar attempt on July 24 last.*

carbon dating is a method of calculating the age of something very old like a fossil by measuring the amount of radioactive carbon in it. 'Carbon dating' is short for 'radiocarbon dating'.

carbon dioxide is a gas breathed out by people and animals. It is also produced by certain chemical reactions. It has no smell. It is used in fizzy drinks and fire extinguishers.

carbon monoxide is a poisonous gas produced when carbon is burnt in a very small amount of air. It has no smell.

carbon paper is thin paper with a dark substance on one side, used for making copies. Carbon paper is put between two sheets of paper so that, when you write or type on the top piece, the writing also appears on the bottom piece.

carbonate (carbonating, carbonated) A **carbonate** is a chemical compound containing carbon, oxygen, and another chemical element. *...calcium carbonate.* ◇ When a liquid is **carbonated**, carbon dioxide is added to make it fizzy.

carbuncle A carbuncle is a large swelling under the skin like a group of boils.

carburettor (*American spelling:* **carburetor**) The **carburettor** is the part of an engine where air and petrol are mixed together.

carcass (*or* carcase) (carcasses, carcases) An animal's carcass is its dead body.

carcinogen (carcinogenic) A **carcinogen** is a substance which can cause cancer. If something is **carcinogenic**, it is likely to cause cancer.

carcinoma A carcinoma is a cancerous growth.

card is strong stiff paper or thin cardboard. ◇ A card is a piece of card with information on it. *...his report card.* ◇ Cards are also small pieces of cardboard, paper, or plastic which you carry around with you. They are for such things as showing your identity or membership of an organization. *...a credit card... ...a library card.* ◇ A person's **card** is a small piece of card with their name, address, phone number, and occupation on it, which they give to other people, usually for business purposes.

❏ Greetings cards are often simply called **cards**. Post-

cards are also called **cards**.

❏ **Cards** or **playing cards** are pieces of card with numbers or pictures on them, for playing games. If you play **cards**, you play a game using cards like these. ◇ You can call something which gives someone an advantage a **card**. *East Germany's sporting prowess was the strongest card in the hand of their leader Erich Honecker.*

❏ If you say something is **on the cards**, you mean it is very likely to happen. ◇ If someone **puts their cards on the table**, they talk openly about something, and do not try to hide anything.

❏ See also red card, smart card, wild card, yellow card.

card-carrying Official fully-committed members of a political organization are sometimes called **card-carrying** members.

card index A card index is a set of cards with information on them arranged in a particular order, usually alphabetically.

card vote A card vote is a way of voting used especially at trade union conferences, where one delegate votes on behalf of all the members of the organization he or she represents.

cardboard is thick stiff paper used to make things like boxes. ◇ Areas where homeless people live in cardboard boxes are sometimes called **cardboard cities**.

❏ **Cardboard** is used to describe characters in books or plays who are unconvincing because the author makes them talk or behave in a mechanical rather than a realistic way.

cardiac is used to talk about things to do with the heart. *...cardiac surgery.* ◇ A **cardiac arrest** is a heart attack.

cardigan A cardigan is a knitted garment like a sweater but with buttons or a zip down the front.

cardinal ❏ A **cardinal** is a senior archbishop of the Roman Catholic church. Cardinals are personally chosen by the Pope, and rank next to him in importance.

❏ A **cardinal** rule or principle is one which is extremely important because other things are based on it or depend on it. ◇ The **cardinal sins** are the seven deadly sins. People also jokingly call something a **cardinal sin** when it breaks a rule which other people think is very important. *By raising a hand to an opponent, he had committed one of football's cardinal sins.*

cardinal number The cardinal numbers are the numbers used for counting, like 1, 7, or 23, as distinct from numbers like 1st, 7th, and 23rd. See also ordinal number.

cardiogram A cardiogram is the same as an electrocardiogram.

cardiology (cardiologist) Cardiology is the study of the heart and heart disease. A **cardiologist** is an expert on these things.

cardiomyopathy is a disease of the heart muscle.

cardiopulmonary is used to talk about things to do with the heart and lungs. *...cardiopulmonary arrest.*

cardiovascular is used to talk about things to do with the heart and the blood vessels. *...cardiovascular treatments.*

care (caring, cared) ❏ If you **care** about something, you are concerned about it or interested in it. ◇ If someone does not **care** about some harm they do, it does not matter to them. You can also say someone does not **care** about something which is happening. *Nobody really cares whether the vote is yes or no.* You can also say someone **could not care less** about things like these.

❑ If you **care for** someone or **take care of** them, you look after them. ◇ **Care** is providing what people need to keep them healthy, or to make them well after they have been ill, and making sure nothing happens to them. *It would be far better to give priority to the care of mothers and babies.* ◇ Children who are **in care** or have been taken **into care** are being looked after by the state instead of by their parents.

❑ If you **care for** someone or **care about** them, you are concerned about their happiness. ◇ A **caring** person is affectionate, helpful, and sympathetic. Organizations and countries can also be called **caring.** *...caring banks.* ◇ **Caring** is affectionate or helpful behaviour. *He felt passionately that modern humanity was lacking older values of caring and support.*

❑ If you do not **care for** something, you do not like it or enjoy it. ◇ If someone asks you if you would **care to** do something, they are suggesting politely that you do it. *Congress might care to note that trade imbalances are declining everywhere.*

❑ If you **take care** to do something, you make sure you do it. ◇ If you do something with **care**, you pay attention to what you are doing, so you do not make any mistakes or damage anything.

❑ If you **take care** of something like a problem, you deal with it. ◇ If you say something will **take care** of itself, you mean it will sort itself out.

❑ **Cares** are worries. *...without a care in the world.*

career (careering, careered) ❑ A **career** is the sort of work you decide to do after leaving school, especially if you are trained for it and there are opportunities for promotion. *...a career in the media.* ◇ **Career** politicians or soldiers are people who work in the same type of work for all or most of their lives. ◇ A **career** woman is one with a career who wants to work and do well in her job until she retires. ◇ **Careers** advisers or offices give people advice and information about jobs and professions. ◇ The time you spend doing a particular thing or type of work is also called a **career.** *Her career as Prime Minister may be at an end.*

❑ You say a vehicle **careers** somewhere when it is moving fast and out of control.

careerist A **careerist** is someone who thinks their career is more important than anything else and will do anything to succeed in it.

carefree A **carefree** person has no worries, troubles, or responsibilities. A **carefree** time is one when you do not have such things. *...her carefree childhood.*

careful (carefully) If you are **careful,** you try to avoid having an accident, making a mistake, or upsetting someone. *...a careful driver... The politicians have so far been careful not to offend the bankers... The wording and conditions of the clause were being carefully checked.*

careless (carelessly; carelessness) If you are **careless,** you do not pay enough attention to what you are doing, so that you make mistakes or have an accident. *...carelessly applied make-up... The major cause of car theft is carelessness.* ◇ If someone is **careless** with something like money, they waste it or do not use it sensibly.

carer A **carer** is someone who looks after an ill, disabled, or elderly person, usually a relative living with them.

caress (pron: ka-ress) (caresses, caressing, caressed) If you **caress** a person or give them a **caress**, you gently stroke them, often to show affection.

caretaker A **caretaker** is someone who looks after a large building like a school or block of flats. ◇ **Caretaker** is also used to talk about someone who is doing an important job temporarily. *...a caretaker administration.* You can also say someone does something in a **caretaker** capacity.

careworn If someone looks **careworn,** they look worried, tired, and unhappy.

cargo (cargoes) A ship's, plane's, or lorry's **cargo** is the goods it is carrying.

caribou (plural: caribou or caribous) The **caribou** is a North American deer which is the same species as the European reindeer.

caricature (caricaturing, caricatured; caricaturist) A **caricature** is a comical drawing or description of someone, which exaggerates some part of their appearance or personality. **Caricature** is drawing or describing someone like this. *...an effective piece of caricature.* You can say someone is **caricatured** in a drawing or piece of writing. A person who draws or writes caricatures is called a **caricaturist.** ◇ If information is presented in a distorted way, you can call it a **caricature** of the facts or the truth.

caries (pron: care-reez) is tooth decay.

carjacking (carjacker) **Carjacking** is stealing cars by threatening the driver with a weapon. A **carjacker** is someone who does this.

carload A **carload** of people or things is a number of them being taken somewhere in a car and filling it completely.

carmine is a deep bright red colour.

carnage You say there is **carnage** when many people are killed, especially in a war.

carnal is used to talk about bodily feelings and activities, especially sexual ones. *...the restriction of carnal relations to marriage.*

carnation Carnations are many-petalled red, pink, white, or yellow flowers, usually scented.

carnival A **carnival** is a public festival with music, processions, and dancing. ◇ If there is a **carnival** atmosphere or people are in a **carnival** mood, everyone is happy and light-hearted.

carnivorous (carnivore) A **carnivorous** animal eats meat; meat-eating animals are also called **carnivores.** ◇ A **carnivorous** plant catches and eats insects.

carob is the powdered pods of a Mediterranean tree. It is used instead of cocoa or chocolate in some health foods.

carol A **carol** is a religious song, especially one sung at Christmas.

carotid The **carotid** arteries are the two arteries in the neck which supply blood to the head.

carouse (pron: ka-rowz) (carousing, caroused) When people **carouse,** they enjoy themselves by drinking a lot of alcohol and making a lot of noise.

carousel At an airport, a **carousel** is a rotating conveyor belt which passengers collect their luggage from. ◇ In the US, a **carousel** is also a merry-go-round.

carp (plural: carp) ❑ The **carp** is a large freshwater fish.

❑ If someone **carps,** they keep complaining, especially about things which are not important. *He had had enough* *of his deputy's carping.*

carpal is used to talk about any of the bones forming the human wrist.

carpenter (carpentry) A **carpenter** is a person who makes and repairs wooden objects. A carpenter's work is called carpentry. See also **joiner**.

carpet (carpeting, carpeted) ❑ A **carpet** is a thick covering for a floor, made of wool or a similar material. ◇ **Carpeting** is (a) the carpets fitted in a room or building. ...*wall-to-wall carpeting.* (b) material used for carpets. ...*tufted or woven carpeting.* ◇ If you **carpet** a room, you lay a carpet in it. ...*a thickly carpeted flight of stairs.* ❑ If you sweep a problem **under the carpet**, you try to hide it, rather than dealing with it. ❑ A **carpet** is also a layer of something covering the ground or another surface. ...*a carpet of volcanic ash.*

carriage ❑ A **carriage** is (a) one of the sections of a passenger train. (b) a four-wheeled horse-drawn vehicle for carrying passengers. ◇ **Carriage** is used to talk about carrying, transporting, or delivering things. ...*the carriage of unfit animals...* ...*the carriage of letters by air.* ❑ A **carriage** is a part of a machine that moves and supports another part. ...*a typewriter carriage.*

carriageway A dual **carriageway** is a road divided in the middle to separate traffic going in opposite directions. Each half of the road can be called a **carriageway**. ...*the westbound carriageway.*

carrier ❑ In the armed services, vehicles for transporting troops, weapons, or other things are called **carriers**. ◇ Aircraft carriers are sometimes called **carriers**. ◇ Some other vehicles and devices for carrying things are also called **carriers**. *The carcass was placed on an iron carrier and run into the furnace.* ❑ Carrier bags are sometimes called **carriers**. ◇ A **carrier** is also (a) an airline. ...*a major American carrier, Delta Airlines.* (b) a person employed to carry things. *He became a hod carrier on a building site.* ❑ A **carrier** of a germ or disease is a person or animal infected with it and capable of giving it to other people or animals.

carrier bag A **carrier bag** is a plastic or paper bag with handles used especially for carrying shopping.

carrier pigeon Carrier pigeons are pigeons trained to fly back to a place, carrying messages attached to their leg.

carrion is the decaying flesh of dead animals.

carrot ❑ Carrots are thin orangey-red root vegetables. ❑ A **carrot** is something offered to someone, to persuade them to do something. *This incentive scheme is a little carrot to bribe farmers to restore the vanishing hedgerows.* ◇ If you talk about a **carrot and stick** approach to something, you mean people are being offered a reward for doing something and at the same time threatened with some harm if they do not do it.

carry (carries, carrying, carried) ❑ If you **carry** something, you move it somewhere, holding it so it does not touch the ground. ◇ If you **carry** something like an identity card or **carry** it with you, you have it with you wherever you go. ❑ When a vehicle **carries** people or goods, it travels somewhere taking them there. ◇ If something is **carried** somewhere by a river or the wind, it is taken there by it. ❑ If a woman is **carrying** a child, she is pregnant. ◇ If a

person, animal, or thing is **carrying** something like a disease, they are infected with it and can infect someone else. ❑ If a newspaper or poster **carries** a picture or piece of writing, it contains it or displays it. Similarly, if a radio or TV station **carries** a programme, it broadcasts it. ❑ If you **carry** something like an idea or a message, you spread it, or take it from one place to another. *Mr Mandela, in his address, carried a message of hope that those oppressed by apartheid would eventually see it done away with.* ❑ The person who **carries** the cost of something is the person who pays for it. ◇ If something or someone **carries weight**, they are respected by people and can influence them. *As a former President he still carries weight in the White House.* ❑ If you **carry out** something like a task, you do it. ◇ If you **carry through** something like a plan, you succeed in putting it into practice. ◇ If you **carry on** doing something, you continue doing it. *Everyone just carried on eating.* ❑ If you **carry on** a kind of work, you do it. ◇ If you **carry out** an order, you do what you are told. ❑ If a feeling, practice, or idea is **carried** to a particular point or extent, it is developed that far. ...*love carried to the point of adoration... Nowhere is manufacture carried to such perfection.* ❑ In a meeting or debate, if a proposal or motion is **carried**, a majority of people vote for it. *The motion was carried by 115 votes to 105.* ◇ If someone receives the support of most of the people at a meeting, you can say they **carry** the meeting. ◇ If you **carry the day**, you are the winner in something like a battle, debate, or competition. ❑ If you **carry off** something, you succeed in doing it. *'Look Who's Talking' has the simplest of ideas, but carries it off with great panache.* ◇ If you **carry off** a prize or reward, you win it. ◇ If someone **carries all before** them, they keep being successful at something. ❑ If something you do **carries** a risk, there is a risk involved in doing it. You can also say something **carries** an advantage. *The normalization of relations between China and Japan carries with it enormous economic benefits for China.* ◇ If an action like breaking the law **carries** a punishment, anyone caught doing it gets that punishment. ...*an offence which carries the death penalty.* ❑ If something **carries over** from one situation to another, it continues in the new situation. *The effect of the privatization campaign has not carried over to other companies.* ◇ If something **carries you through** a particular time, it makes it possible for you to put up with something unpleasant or difficult during that time. *The extra capacity will enable Kingston to generate the finance necessary to carry them through the next four months.* ❑ If a sound **carries**, it can be heard a long way away. ❑ If you get **carried away** by something, you are so eager and enthusiastic that you behave in a silly way.

carrycot A carrycot is a light portable cot for a baby.

cart ❑ A **cart** is (a) a wooden vehicle pulled by an animal. (b) a two-wheeled wooden vehicle pulled or pushed by hand. ❑ If you **cart** things or people somewhere, you transport them, using whatever means are available. ◇ If someone is **carted off** or **carted away**, they are removed from a place, often against their will. ❑ If you say someone is **putting the cart before the**

horse, you mean that they are doing things in the wrong order.

carte blanche (*pron: kart blahnsh*) If someone gives you carte blanche, they give you the authority to do whatever you want.

cartel (cartelize, cartelizing, cartelized; cartelization) (*can be spelled with an 's' instead of a 'z'*) If a group of companies operate as a **cartel** (*pron: kar-***tell**), they work together to stop other companies from competing with them, and to keep prices high. ◇ If an industry is **cartelized** (*pron: kar-***tell**-ized), it is turned into a cartel. *...an end to cartelization.*

carthorse A carthorse is a big powerful horse used to pull things like carts and wagons.

cartilage (*pron: kar-***till**-ij) is a strong flexible substance in the body, for example round the joints.

cartography (cartographer, cartographic) Cartography is the art of drawing or designing maps. A **cartographer** is someone who does this. **Cartographic** is used to talk about thing to do with drawing or designing maps. *...the Cuban Cartographic Institute.*

carton A carton is (a) a plastic or cardboard container in which food or drink is sold. (b) a large strong cardboard box.

cartoon (cartoonist) A cartoon is (a) a drawing in a newspaper or magazine which is there to make people laugh or to make a political point. (b) a series of drawings in a newspaper or magazine which tells part of a story or shows an amusing incident involving a familiar character. ◇ A **cartoonist** is a person who draws cartoons for newspapers and magazines.
❏ A cartoon is also a film in which the characters and scenery are drawn, instead of being real people or objects.

cartridge A cartridge is a tube containing a bullet and an explosive substance, which is inserted into a gun. ◇ The **cartridge** on a record player is the part of the arm which holds the needle. ◇ A **data cartridge** or **cartridge tape** is a tape used for storing or transferring computer data.

cartridge paper is a type of thick paper used for drawing.

cartridge pen A cartridge pen is a type of fountain pen. It has a removable tube filled with ink inside which you replace when it runs out.

cartwheel (cartwheeling, cartwheeled) ❏ If you do a **cartwheel**, you do a circular movement, throwing yourself sideways on to one hand and then on to the other, ending up back on your feet. ◇ If a vehicle **cartwheels** when it is out of control, it turns over several times.
❏ Cartwheels are large wheels with wooden spokes and metal tyres fitted to horse-drawn carts.

carve (carving, carved; carver) ❏ If you **carve** an object, you make it out of a piece of wood, stone, or some other substance, by cutting pieces away. An object like this is called a **carving**; the person making it is sometimes called a **carver**. ◇ If you **carve** a design on something, you cut it into the surface. The design is also called a **carving**. ◇ **Carving** is the art of cutting objects, patterns, and designs out of substances like wood and stone.
❏ When you **carve** meat, you cut slices from it. ◇ If someone **carves up** another person, they cut them badly with a knife.
❏ If something is **carved up**, it is divided into smaller

pieces or areas and shared out among two or more groups or people. Something like this can be called a **carve-up**.
◇ If you **carve out** something for yourself, you get hold of it or establish it. *The company is carving out a huge slice of the electronics market.* ◇ If a country or state is **carved out** of a larger area, it is created from a part of that area.

carvery (carveries) A carvery is a restaurant where roast meat is carved and served in the room where you eat.

carving knife A carving knife is a large knife for cutting cooked meat.

Casanova (*pron: kass-a-***noh**-va) A man who has a lot of love affairs is sometimes called a **Casanova**.

casbah See kasbah.

cascade (cascading, cascaded) A cascade is a waterfall or series of waterfalls flowing over rocks. ◇ When water **cascades**, it pours down over something. Similarly, you can talk about a lot of objects **cascading** over something. ◇ A **cascade** of things is a lot of them coming one after the other. *...a cascade of words.*

case ❏ A case is a container specially designed to hold or protect something. *...a camera case... ...a glass case.* ◇ Suitcases are often called **cases**. ◇ A **case** of something like wine, whisky, or sherry is a box containing twelve bottles.
❏ A case is an instance of something. *In cases like this you have to move very fast... ...thousands of cases of torture and internment.*
❏ **Case** is used to say how often something happens or is true. You say, for example, that something happens in many cases or in most cases. *In most cases rivers were the source of more than half of the pollutants reaching the sea.* ◇ If you say something is a **case in point**, you mean it is a typical example of the thing you have just mentioned.
❏ You say **in that case** or **in which case** when you are making a comment about something which has just been mentioned. *TSA members are concerned that a merger might mean higher costs, in which case they would oppose it.* ◇ If you say something **is the case**, you mean it is true. *If England do win the bid, the competition will run throughout August, as was the case on previous occasions.*
❏ You say **as the case may be** when it is not certain which of two or more alternatives might happen or be true. *The country is preparing itself, with satisfaction or resignation, as the case may be, for the return to power of the Christian Democrats.* ◇ You say **in case** to show something is done because a certain thing might happen. *An emergency helicopter stood by in case evacuation was needed... Take an umbrella, just in case.* ◇ You say **in any case** when you are giving another reason for something you have said or done. *The administrators said the agreement had been struck when the property market was in better shape than now, and in any case, had never been signed.*
❏ In law, a case is (a) a trial or other legal inquiry to settle a lawsuit or decide if a person is guilty or not. (b) the evidence presented for or against a person or issue. ◇ If there is a **case** for having or doing something, there are good reasons for having or doing it. If you **make a case** for something, you provide good reasons for it. *There is a strong case for higher taxes to reduce the government's massive spending deficit... I want to make a case for the speedy sale of the company to get us out of the hands of the banks.*
❏ A case is a crime or mystery being investigated by the

police or a detective. ◇ A **case** is also a person or problem being dealt with by someone like a doctor, solicitor, or social worker. ◇ A **case** of an illness or disease is a person who has got it. ...*HIV-positive cases*. ◇ If you say someone is a sad **case** or a hopeless **case**, you mean they are in a sad or hopeless situation.

case history Someone's **case history** is a record of their background and the problems affecting them. Doctors and social workers study the case histories of their patients and clients.

case law is law established by decisions made by judges in earlier cases.

case load See caseload.

case study A **case study** is an account giving detailed information about a person, group, or thing and their development over a period of time.

casebook If you talk about the **casebook** of someone like a social worker, you are talking about the cases they have dealt with.

casein is a protein found mainly in milk and cheese.

caseload (*or* case load) A doctor's or social worker's **caseload** is the number of cases he or she has to deal with.

casement A **casement** is a window hinged on one side.

casework is social work involving actually dealing or working with people who need help.

cash (cashes, cashing, cashed) **Cash** is money in the form of notes and coins, rather than cheques. ◇ **Cash** is also used to talk about money in general. *They can't even feed their families properly, never mind having enough cash to buy seeds and fertilizer.* ◇ If you **cash** a cheque, you exchange it at a bank for the amount it is worth. Similarly, you can **cash in** something like an insurance policy or shares. ◇ If someone **cashes in** on a situation, they use it to their advantage, especially by doing something slightly unfair or dishonest.

cash-and-carry (cash-and-carries) A **cash-and-carry** is a shop or warehouse where goods are sold at wholesale prices. Originally cash-and-carries were used by shopkeepers only, but now many of them also allow members of the public to come and buy their goods.

cash book A **cash book** is a book kept as a record of payments made and money received by an organization or person.

cash card A **cash card** is a plastic card for withdrawing money from a cash dispenser.

cash crop A **cash crop** is a crop grown to be sold. See also subsistence.

cash desk A **cash desk** is the place in a large shop where you pay.

cash dispenser A **cash dispenser** is a machine inside a bank or on its outside wall where you can withdraw money from your account using a card and a special code. Many building societies also have cash dispensers.

cash flow The **cash flow** of a firm or business is the movement of money into and out of it.

cash register A **cash register** is a machine in a place like a shop for adding up how much people have to pay and for keeping the money in.

cashew Cashews or **cashew nuts** are curved nuts which you eat roasted.

cashier (cashiering, cashiered) ❏ In some large shops, a **cashier** is a person who you give your money to when you buy something. ◇ In a bank, a **cashier** is a person who does things like receiving customers' deposits and cashing cheques.
  ❏ If a member of the armed forces is **cashiered**, they are forced to leave, because they have done something wrong.

cashmere is a kind of very fine soft wool.

Cashpoint A **Cashpoint** is the same as a cash dispenser. 'Cashpoint' is a trademark.

casing A **casing** is something surrounding or covering something else, usually to protect it. ...*engine casings*.

casino (casinos) A **casino** is a place where people play gambling games like roulette.

cask A **cask** is a wooden barrel for storing alcoholic drink.

casket A **casket** is a small box, often beautifully decorated, for keeping valuable things in, such as jewellery. ◇ In the US and Canada, a **casket** is also a coffin.

cassava (*pron:* ka-sah-va) is a plant grown in some tropical countries for its thick roots, from which a kind of flour is made. This flour, also called **cassava**, is used to make other foods, including tapioca.

casserole A **casserole** is a dish made by cooking meat or fish with vegetables in liquid at a low temperature in an oven. ◇ A **casserole** is also a large deep container with a lid, for cooking food in an oven, and also for serving it.

cassette A **cassette** or **cassette tape** is a rectangular plastic container with a reel of magnetic tape inside. Cassettes are used for recording and playing sound. ◇ A **cassette player** is a machine for playing cassettes. A cassette player which can also record sound is called a **cassette recorder**. ◇ A **cassette deck** is part of a hi-fi system for playing cassettes.

cassock A **cassock** is a long robe worn by some priests. Church officials and choir members also wear cassocks during services in some churches.

cassowary (cassowaries) The **cassowary** is a long-legged bird, rather like an emu, in Australia and New Guinea. It has a bony projection on top of its head. Cassowaries cannot fly.

cast (casting, cast *not 'casted'*) ❏ The **cast** of a play or film is all the people acting in it. When a play or film is **cast**, people are chosen to play the parts in it. ◇ When an actor or actress is given a part in a play or film, you say they are **cast** in that part.
  ❏ If you say someone is **cast** in a particular way, you mean they are represented as that sort of person. *She claims the article cast her as a 'social outcast and leper'.*
  ❏ If you **cast** doubt or **cast doubts** on something, you make people less sure about it.
  ❏ If something **casts** a light or shadow onto a place or thing, it makes it appear there. ◇ You say bad news **casts** a shadow or cloud over a place or event when people keep thinking about it and so cannot enjoy themselves or are less hopeful about the future. *News of the murder cast a shadow over the village.* ◇ If someone or something **casts** a long shadow, they have a lot of influence on people or on the way things turn out. ◇ **cast new light on:** see light.
  ❏ If you **cast** a vote, you vote. ◇ At a meeting, when

there are an equal number of votes for and against a proposal, the chairman or chairwoman is sometimes allowed to vote, so a decision can be reached. Their vote is called a **casting vote.**

❏ If you **cast your mind back** to a time in the past, you think about it. ◇ If you **cast** your eyes or **cast a glance** in a particular direction, you look in that direction. ◇ **cast an eye over**: see **eye.**

❏ If you **cast** something like a stone, you throw it. ◇ If you **cast** a fishing line, you throw one end into the water. ◇ **cast the net wider**: see **net.** ◇ **the die is cast**: see **die.**

❏ If you **cast** someone or something **aside**, you get rid of them because you no longer like them or approve of them. You can also say you **cast** them **out.** ◇ If you **cast** something **off**, you get rid of it. **Cast-offs** are things, especially clothes, which you give to someone else because you no longer want them.

❏ In children's stories, when someone **casts** a spell, they use magic to put someone or something into a particular state. ◇ If a person, place, or thing **casts their spell** on you, you are delighted and fascinated by them.

❏ If you **cast around** for something, you look for it.

❏ When someone **casts** an object, they make it by pouring a liquid like plaster, molten metal, or molten glass into a mould called a **cast** and letting it set. An object made like this is also called a **cast**; if it is metal, it is called a **casting.**

❏ When someone **casts on**, they make stitches on a needle to start a piece of knitting. When they **cast off**, they get rid of the stitches at the end of the knitting.

❏ If you are in a boat and you **cast off**, you untie the rope fastening it to its mooring.

❏ The **cast** of someone's mind is the sort of mind they have. ...*an authoritarian cast of mind.*

cast iron is iron with a small amount of carbon in it. Cast-iron objects are made of this iron. ◇ A **cast-iron** guarantee, assurance, or excuse is certain to be effective, real, or true.

castanets are a Spanish musical instrument made of two small round pieces of wood which you click together in your hand.

castaway A castaway is a person who has survived a shipwreck and has managed to reach an isolated island or shore.

caste (*pron:* **kahst**) A Hindu's caste is the social class he or she is born into. The four main groups of castes are Brahmin, Kshatriya, Vaisya, and Sudra. There is also a fifth group called panchamas (untouchables). ◇ In other cultures where social class is regarded as important, you can talk about someone belonging to a particular **caste.** ...*the old German governing caste.*

castellated A castellated wall or building has turrets and battlements like a castle.

caster See **castor.**

caster sugar is finely ground white sugar.

castigate (castigating, castigated; castigation) If you **castigate** someone or something, you scold them or criticize them severely. ...*her castigation of collectivism.*

castle ❏ A castle is a large building or group of buildings with thick high walls for protection against attack. ◇ If someone is building **castles in the air**, they are making plans which they know are unlikely to be fulfilled.

❏ A **castle** is also a piece in chess. Each player has two castles. They are sometimes called **rooks.**

castor (*or* caster) Castors are small wheels on furniture.

castor oil is a thick yellow oil which comes from the seeds of the castor oil plant. In the past, it was used as a laxative.

castrate (castrating, castrated; castration) If a man, boy, or male animal is **castrated,** their testicles are removed. This is called **castration.**

casual (casually; casualness) If someone is **casual,** they are calm and do not seem worried or concerned about what is happening or what they are doing. *Some thieves walk into galleries and casually make off with pictures.* ◇ **Casual** is also used (a) to talk about things being done carelessly through lack of attention or interest. ...*a certain casualness with details.* (b) to describe something said or done which was not planned beforehand. *Anyone casually tuning in to Radio 3 will have switched off well before the interval.* ◇ **Casual** work is done occasionally for short periods of time, and not on a permanent or regular basis. A **casual** worker or labourer is someone who does work like this. ◇ **Casual** clothes are for wearing at home or on holiday, rather than on formal occasions.

casualty (casualties) ❏ A casualty is a person who has been killed or injured in a war or accident. The **casualties** in a war or accident are the number of people killed or injured. ◇ The **casualty department** in a hospital is the place where you are taken if you have had an accident or need emergency treatment. Officially, these departments are now usually called 'Accident and Emergency Departments'.

❏ A **casualty** of something which has happened is a person or thing that has suffered badly because of it. *The most spectacular casualty of the property collapse is Olympia and York.*

casuistry is the use of clever arguments to persuade people that something is true or right, often when it is not.

cat ❏ The cat family includes lions, tigers, leopards, and lynxes, as well as the ordinary domestic **cat** which people keep as a pet.

❏ If you play **cat and mouse** with someone, you provoke them by letting them think they have an advantage, then taking it away from them. ◇ If someone **sets the cat among the pigeons,** they do or say something which causes a lot of arguments or makes people angry. ◇ If you say someone does not have **a cat in hell's chance** of doing something, you mean there is absolutely no chance of them doing it.

cat flap A cat flap is a small hole in a door with a flap so a cat can get in and out.

cat litter is absorbent material put in a box for a cat to urinate and defecate on indoors.

cat's eyes are reflective pieces of glass fixed in the middle of a road or on the edges, so motorists can see where they are going at night. 'Cat's eyes' is a trademark.

cataclysm (*pron:* **kat-a-kliz-zum**) (cataclysmic) A **cataclysm** is a major happening which affects many people, changing their way of life or the social system they live in. **Cataclysmic** (*pron:* **kat-a-kliz-mik**) is used to describe something like this, or its effects. *If Labour turned its back on European union, the consequences would be cataclysmic.*

catacomb (*pron:* **kat-a-koom**) Catacombs are underground passages and rooms where bodies used to be buried, especially in ancient Rome.

catalogue (cataloguing, catalogued) (*American spelling:* catalog, cataloging, cataloged) ❑ A **catalogue** is a book containing a list and sometimes pictures of goods you can buy from a company, either by mail order or from their shop. ◇ A **catalogue** is also (a) a list of objects in an exhibition, museum, or art gallery. (b) a list of books and other documents in a library.

❑ If someone **catalogues** a collection of books, paintings, or other objects, they make a list of them. Similarly, you can say someone **catalogues** something like a series of happenings. *The complaints catalogued by regional watchdogs reveal widespread dissatisfaction with BR.* ◇ A **catalogue** of unpleasant things is several of them happening one after another. *...a catalogue of disasters.*

catalyse (catalysing, catalysed) (*American spelling:* catalyze, etc) If you **catalyse** something, you help it come into existence. *Holst can be suspected of having catalysed vital aspects of Britten's development.* ◇ If a chemical reaction is **catalysed**, it is speeded up by a catalyst.

catalyst (catalysis) A **catalyst** is someone or something that makes something happen or change. ◇ In chemistry, a **catalyst** is a substance which speeds up a chemical reaction, without changing itself. This speeding-up process is called **catalysis**.

catalytic converter A catalytic **converter** is a device fitted to a car's exhaust system to reduce the amount of poisonous gases coming from its engine.

catalyze See **catalyse**.

catamaran A catamaran is a boat with two parallel hulls held in place by a single deck.

catapult A **catapult** is a device for shooting small objects like stones. It is made of a Y-shaped stick with a piece of elastic tied to the two top parts. ◇ A **catapult** is also a device for launching aircraft from an aircraft carrier. ◇ If something **catapults** or is **catapulted** somewhere, it is sent very suddenly, quickly, and violently through the air. ◇ If something **catapults** you into a situation, you find yourself suddenly and unexpectedly in it. *He was a valley miner's son catapulted into sporting greatness.*

cataract If you have a **cataract**, part of the lens of your eye has become cloudy, and you cannot see well because of it. ◇ A **cataract** is also a large waterfall, especially one with a sheer drop or rapids.

catarrh (*pron:* kat-**tar**) If you have **catarrh**, you have a lot of mucus in your nose and throat.

catastrophe (*pron:* kat-**tass**-trof-fee) (catastrophic) A **catastrophe** is an unexpected happening which causes a lot of suffering or damage. You say a happening like this is **catastrophic** (*pron:* kat-ass-**strof**-ik).

catcall Catcalls are loud noises and shouting people make to show they disapprove of something.

catch (catches, catching, caught; catcher) ❑ If you **catch** an animal or bird, you capture it. If an animal or bird **catches** another creature, it seizes it, in order to eat it. If you **catch** a fish, you pull it out of the water, usually so it can be eaten. People who catch animals for a living are sometimes called **catchers**. *...a rat-catcher.* ◇ In fishing, the **catch** is the number of fish caught on a single fishing trip.

❑ If you **catch** a ball moving through the air, you take

hold of it when it comes near you; in a game, this is called a **catch**. ◇ In cricket, if the batsman is **caught**, a fielder catches the ball he has hit before it touches the ground, and the batsman is out. ◇ In baseball, a **catcher** is a player who stands behind the batter and catches the ball when the batter does not hit it.

❑ If the police **catch** the person who has committed a crime, they find out who they are and take them into custody. If they **catch** someone who has escaped, they recapture them.

❑ If you **catch** a bus or train, you get on it to travel somewhere. ◇ If you **catch** the post, you manage to put a letter or parcel in the post-box before it is emptied. ◇ If you **catch** something like a television programme or a concert, you manage to see it.

❑ If you **catch** an illness, disease, or virus, you get it or become infected with it. If an illness is **catching**, it is infectious.

❑ If you see someone doing something they should not, you can say you **catch** them doing it. ◇ If you **catch** yourself doing something, you notice you are doing it. ◇ If you **catch** someone **out**, you get them to make a mistake, which shows they are not telling the truth or are doing something wrong. ◇ If you are **caught out** by something which happens, you find yourself in a bad situation or weak position. *Firms have been caught out by the fall in sales.* ◇ If you are **caught** in the rain or a storm, it happens suddenly before you can shelter from it. ◇ If you are **caught** in something which is happening or get **caught up** in it, you become involved in it, without meaning to. *Several foreigners have been caught up in the fighting.*

❑ If a moving object **catches** something, it hits it. *That massive wave had caught the trawler on the port bow.* ◇ If a moving object **catches on** something, it becomes attached to it. *Their nets apparently caught on a submarine and their boat was sunk.* ◇ If you **catch** something like your finger, you get it trapped between two objects. ◇ A **catch** is a device like a hook for fastening or locking something like a door or window.

❑ If something **catches the light**, it reflects the light and looks bright and shiny. ◇ **catch fire:** see **fire**.

❑ If you **catch** someone's mood, it affects you and you begin to feel the same way. ◇ If a feeling is **catching**, it spreads quickly among a group of people. ◇ If something **catches** your imagination, you find it very interesting or exciting. ◇ If something **catches on**, it becomes popular. ◇ If an artist, writer, or composer **catches** a mood, atmosphere, or personality, they successfully represent it in pictures, words, or music.

❑ If you **catch sight** of someone or something, you suddenly see them or notice them. If you **catch a glimpse** of them, you see them briefly. ◇ **catch your eye:** see **eye**. ◇ **catch your breath:** see **breath**.

❑ If you **catch up** with someone in front of you, you reach them by moving faster than they do. In a race, you can say one runner **catches** another. ◇ You also say someone **catches up** with someone else when they reach the same standard or level. ◇ If something unpleasant **catches up with** you, you can no longer avoid it and have to deal with it or accept it. *Age has caught up with her at last.* ◇ If you **catch up on** something you were unable to do earlier, you spend some time doing it.

❑ If you **catch on** to something, you understand it

quickly.

❏ A **catch** is a problem or difficulty which makes something less attractive. *The catch is that as part of the deal the contractor will also have to build a brand new library for the university.*

Catch-22 A **Catch-22** situation is one where you cannot do one thing until you do another thing, but you cannot do the second thing until you have done the first. It is therefore impossible for you to do anything.

catch-all is used to describe things designed to cover all types of situations or possibilities. *...catch-all regulations.*

catch-phrase A **catch-phrase** is a sentence or phrase which becomes well-known for a time, usually because a famous person uses it.

catchment area The **catchment area** of something like a school or hospital is the area it serves.

catchy (catchier, catchiest) A **catchy** tune is very easy to remember.

catechism (*pron:* kat-ti-kiz-zum) A **catechism** is a book of questions and answers about the Christian religion, used in the Anglican and Roman Catholic churches. Children are expected to study their catechism before they are confirmed.

categoric means the same as 'categorical'.

categorical (categorically) A **categorical** statement is firm and definite. *They categorically denied any involvement in illegal acts.*

categorize (categorizing, categorized; categorization) (*can be spelled with an 's' instead of a 'z'*) If you **categorize** someone or something, you decide what group of people or things they belong to. *Michael Moorcock defies categorization as a writer.*

category (categories) If people or things are divided into **categories**, they are divided into groups according to their qualities and characteristics.

cater (caterer; catering) If you **cater** for a person or group, you provide them with the things they need or want. ◇ When someone **caters** for an event like a wedding or party, they provide the food and drink. A person or firm that does this is called a **caterer**; what they do is called **catering**.

caterpillar **Caterpillars** are small worm-like animals which feed on plants and develop into butterflies or moths. ◇ The **caterpillar tracks** on a vehicle like a tank or bulldozer are the ridged belts round its wheels which allow it to travel over different kinds of terrain.

catfish (*plural:* catfish) The **catfish** is a freshwater fish which has spines round its mouth like a cat's whiskers.

catgut is strong cord made from the intestines of sheep or other animals. The strings of some musical instruments are made from it, and surgeons use it for sewing. In the past, sports rackets were strung with catgut.

catharsis (*pron:* kath-thar-siss) (cathartic) **Catharsis** is getting rid of strong emotions, fears, or unhappy memories, by expressing them or living through them in some way. You say something which allows you to do this is **cathartic** or has a **cathartic** effect. *Being able to laugh at the old oppressor had a cathartic effect on the audience.*

cathedral A **cathedral** is a large church which is the main church in a diocese.

catheter (*pron:* kath-it-er) A **catheter** is a tube put into a person's body to collect fluid, especially urine, or some-

times to insert fluid.

cathode In an electric cell, the **cathode** is the negative electrode. See also **anode**.

cathode ray tube A **cathode ray tube** is the device in a television or computer which sends an image on to the screen.

Catholic (Catholicism) ❏ A **Catholic** is someone who belongs to the Roman Catholic Church, a branch of the Christian church which accepts the Pope as its leader. **Catholicism** (*pron:* ka-tholl-iss-izz-um) is the set of beliefs held by Catholics. **Catholic** is used to talk about things to do with Catholics and their beliefs. *...the Catholic community.*

❏ If a person has **catholic** tastes, they enjoy or are interested in a wide range of things.

catkin **Catkins** are small thin bunches of tiny flowers hanging from trees like the birch and hazel.

catsuit A **catsuit** is a tight-fitting female garment made in one piece and covering the body, arms, and legs.

catsup See **ketchup**.

cattery (catteries) A **cattery** is a place where cats are bred, or where they are looked after while their owners are away.

cattle are cows and bulls kept for farming or for carrying loads.

cattle-grid A **cattle-grid** is a metal grid in a road. It allows vehicles to pass along the road, while stopping animals from doing so.

catty (cattily) A **catty** remark is spiteful and unpleasant. *She remarked cattily that you only got to the top because you look good in a short skirt.*

catwalk In a fashion show, the **catwalk** is the narrow platform the models walk along to display clothes. ◇ A **catwalk** is also a narrow bridge high in the air between two parts of a tall building or on the outside of a large structure.

Caucasian is sometimes used to describe people with white skins, as distinct from people with black, brown, or yellow skins.

caucus (caucuses) A **caucus** is a small group of people within a political party or other organization who meet to discuss important things and have a lot of influence within the organization. ◇ A **caucus** is also a meeting of a group like this.

caught See **catch**.

cauldron (*American spelling:* caldron) A **cauldron** is a very large round metal pot for cooking over a fire. ◇ You call a situation a **cauldron** when it involves strong feelings such as hatred or anger, with violence likely to break out. You can also call the place where this is happening a **cauldron**. *Azerbaijan is a cauldron of ethnic unrest.*

cauliflower **Cauliflowers** are cabbage-like vegetables which have green leaves around a large white ball of flower buds.

causal (causation, causality) If there is a **causal** relationship between two things, one thing makes the other happen. The relationship is called **causation** or **causality**. *...the causal link between smoking and ill health.*

cause (causing, caused) ❏ If someone or something **causes** a situation, they make it happen. ◇ A **cause** is something which makes something else happen. *Doctors have* *carried out a lung biopsy to try to determine the cause of her illness.* ◇ If you say someone has **cause** for a type of feeling or behaviour, you mean they have good reasons for feeling or behaving like that. *The league champions were given cause for concern when Tony Dorigo limped off.*

❑ A **cause** is also something a group of people are fighting for or trying to achieve, because they believe it is right or desirable. ◇ If you say something is **in a good cause** or **for a good cause**, you mean it is worth doing or contributing to, because it will help people who need help.

cause célèbre (*plural:* causes célèbres) (*both pron:* kaws sill-leb-ra) A **cause célèbre** is a controversial issue or criminal trial which attracts a lot of public attention. When an issue of this kind is centred round one person, he or she can also be called a **cause célèbre**.

causeway A **causeway** is a raised path or road crossing water or marshland.

caustic (caustically) **Caustic** chemicals can dissolve other substances. ◇ A **caustic** comment is very critical or bitter. *His new book is knowledgeable, caustically funny and sometimes alarming.*

caustic soda is a powerful chemical substance used to make cleaning materials like strong soaps and drain cleaners.

cauterize (cauterizing, cauterized) (*can be spelled with an 's' instead of a 'z'*) When a wound is **cauterized**, it is treated with heat, electricity, or a chemical, to close it up and stop it getting infected.

caution (cautioning, cautioned; cautionary) ❑ **Caution** is care taken to avoid possible danger or something going wrong. *Investigators are moving with extreme caution after following a number of false trails.* ◇ If someone **cautions** you, they warn you of possible problems or danger. ◇ If someone **cautions** you **against** doing something, they advise you not to do it. ◇ A **cautionary** tale or piece of advice is intended to warn people about something.

❑ If you are **cautioned** or get a **caution** when you have done something wrong or broken a rule, you are warned you will be punished if you do it again. ◇ When the police **caution** someone, they warn them that anything they say may be used as evidence in a trial.

cautious (cautiously; cautiousness) A **cautious** person does things very carefully to avoid possible danger or making mistakes. *Britain is behaving cautiously about how the EU should act on Yugoslavia... A little cautiousness seems in order.*

cavalcade A **cavalcade** is a procession of people on horses or in cars or carriages.

cavalier If someone acts in a **cavalier** way, they behave arrogantly and without thinking about other people.

cavalry In the past, the **cavalry** was part of an army which consisted of soldiers on horses. ◇ Nowadays, the **cavalry** is the part of an army which uses armoured vehicles.

cave (caving, caved) ❑ A **cave** is a large hole in the side of a cliff or hill, or under the ground.

❑ If a roof or wall **caves in**, it collapses inwards. ◇ If a person or government **caves in** to someone who is putting pressure on them, they give in to them. When this happens, you say there is a **cave-in**. *Labour's agriculture spokesman called the settlement a cave-in.*

caveat (*pron:* kav-vee-at) If someone adds a **caveat** to what they have just said, they mention something like a snag, a disadvantage, or an exception to a general rule. A snag or disadvantage can itself be called a **caveat**. ◇ A **caveat** is also a legal clause restricting what someone is allowed to do.

caveman (cavemen) **Cavemen** were people in prehistoric times who lived in caves.

cavern A **cavern** is a large deep cave.

cavernous A **cavernous** building is very large inside.

caviar (*or* caviare) is a food consisting of the salted eggs of a fish called the sturgeon. In most countries, caviar is a luxury.

cavil (cavilling, cavilled) (*American spelling:* caviling, caviled) If someone **cavils**, they complain about a minor aspect of something. A complaint like this is called a **cavil**.

cavity (cavities) A **cavity** is a hollow area or gap in something solid. Some parts of the human body are called **cavities**. *...the resonant cavities of the mouth.* ◇ A **cavity** is also a small hole or soft area in a person's tooth, caused by decay.

cavity wall A **cavity wall** consists of two parallel walls with a narrow space between them. Cavity walls help keep in warmth and keep out damp and noise.

cavort (cavorting) If people **cavort**, they dance around. ◇ Sexual activities are also sometimes called **cavorting**. *Cavorting between crew members is strictly forbidden.*

cawing is the noise made by crows and rooks.

cay A **cay** is a low island or bank made of fragments of sand and coral.

cayenne or **cayenne pepper** is a hot-tasting red powder made from dried chillies. It is used to flavour food.

CB is the range of radio waves which members of the public are allowed to use to send messages to one another. CB stands for 'citizens' band'.

CBE The **CBE** is an honour given by the British monarch for an outstanding service or achievement. CBE stands for 'Commander of the Order of the British Empire'.

CBI The **CBI** is an organization which a large number of companies belong to and which is concerned with all aspects of business and industry. CBI stands for 'Confederation of British Industry'.

cc See cubic centimetre.

CD A **CD** is a compact disc.

CD-ROM A **CD-ROM** is a compact disc containing large amounts of information for use with a computer system. CD-ROM stands for 'compact disc read-only memory'.

cease (ceasing, ceased) If something **ceases,** it stops happening or existing. ◇ If you **cease** to do something, you stop doing it.

ceasefire (*or* cease-fire) A **ceasefire** is an agreement between countries or groups who are at war to stop fighting for a time.

ceaseless (ceaselessly) **Ceaseless** is used to talk about things which go on without stopping. *He lobbied the government ceaselessly for an increase in the funding of facilities.*

cedar The **cedar** is a large evergreen tree. It has needle-like leaves and brown cones. Its wood is also called cedar.

cede (ceding, ceded) If one country **cedes** territory to another, it gives it away, usually because it is forced to. Similarly, you can talk about people **ceding** power or control.

cedilla The **cedilla** is a symbol sometimes written under 'c' in French and Portuguese. It shows that the 'c' is pronounced like 's' rather than 'k'. ...*Françoise Sagan*... ...*Lourenço Marques.*

Ceefax is the BBC's teletext system. 'Ceefax' is a trademark.

ceilidh (*pron:* **kay-lee**) A **ceilidh** is an organized entertainment in Scotland or Ireland with folk music, singing, and dancing. Originally, ceilidhs were informal events in people's houses.

ceiling In a room, the **ceiling** is the surface above your head. ◇ A **ceiling** is also an official upper limit on something like prices or wages.

celeb (*pron:* **sil-leb**) Celebrities are sometimes called **celebs.**

celebrant The person who performs a religious ceremony can be called a **celebrant.** The people taking part can also be called **celebrants.**

celebrate (celebrating, celebrated; celebration, celebratory)
❑ If you **celebrate** something like a wedding or an anniversary, you do something enjoyable like having a party, to show it is a special occasion. An event like this is called a **celebration.** ◇ **Celebratory** is used to talk about things to do with celebrating. *The Germans were clearly in a celebratory mood.*
❑ A **celebrated** person or thing is famous. If someone or something is **celebrated** for a particular thing, they are famous for it.
❑ When a priest **celebrates** Mass, he performs the actions and ceremonies involved in it.

celebrity (celebrities) A **celebrity** is someone who is famous, especially in show business. ◇ **Celebrity** is used to talk about things involving celebrities. ...*celebrity interviews.* ◇ A person's **celebrity** is the fact that they are famous. *James Dean's celebrity exists because he died in a car wreck.*

celery is a vegetable with long, pale green stalks.

celeste A **celeste** is a keyboard instrument which looks like a miniature piano. The notes are produced by a set of steel plates hit by hammers.

celestial is used to talk about things to do with the sky or space. A **celestial** object or body is something seen in the sky, like a star. ◇ **Celestial** is also used to talk about things to do with heaven. ...*angels running up and down celestial ladders.*

celibate (celibacy) Someone who is **celibate** does not marry or have sex. A person like this is called a **celibate.** **Celibacy** is not marrying or having sex.

cell (celled) ❑ **Cells** are the tiny basic units which all living things are made of. Each cell is enclosed by a membrane and is controlled by a nucleus. A **single-celled** or **one-celled** creature consists of just one cell.
❑ A **cell** is a small room where prisoners are locked up, or a similar room where a monk or nun lives. ◇ A **cell** is also a small group of people specially trained to work together as part of a larger organization.
❑ A **cell** is also a device which uses energy from chemicals, heat, or light to produce electricity.

cell-mate See cellmate.

cell-phone (*or* cellphone) A **cell-phone** is a cordless telephone which uses radio signals and a network of transmitters to send and receive messages.

cellar A **cellar** is a room underneath a building, often used for storing things like wine. ◇ A person's **cellar** is the wines stored in their cellar. *He keeps a modest cellar.*

cellist See cello.

cellmate (*or* cell-mate) People sharing the same prison cell can be called **cellmates.**

cello (*pron:* **chell**-oh) (cellos; cellist) A **cello** is a low-pitched instrument from the violin family. It is played in an upright position between the player's knees. 'Cello' is short for 'violoncello'. A person who plays the cello is called a **cellist.**

Cellophane is a thin transparent material for wrapping things like food. 'Cellophane' is a trademark.

cellphone See cell-phone.

cellular is used to talk about things to do with animal and plant cells. ...*cellular protein.* ◇ **Cellular** is also used to talk about things to do with cell-phones. ...*the cellular market.* A **cellular** telephone is a cell-phone. ◇ **Cellular** fabrics are loosely woven and keep you warm.

cellulite is a layer of fat in places like the thighs, which is supposed to be different from ordinary fat, and harder to get rid of. Some people think there is no difference between cellulite and ordinary fat.

celluloid is a plastic material used for making things like children's toys. 'Celluloid' is a trademark. ◇ **Celluloid** is also used to talk about films and the cinema. ...*a celluloid fantasy.* If something is **on celluloid,** it appears on film.

cellulose is a substance found in the cell walls of plants. It is used to make paper, plastic, and various textiles and fibres.

Celsius is a scale for measuring temperature, in which water freezes at 0° and boils at 100°. When you write down a temperature using this scale, you put 'C' after the number of degrees. 'Celsius' is also called 'centigrade'.

Celt (*pron:* **kelt**) (Celtic) In ancient times, the **Celts** were a race of people who lived in Britain, Ireland, and other parts of Europe, but were driven to remoter areas by other invading races. Nowadays, if you call someone a **Celt,** you mean they come from somewhere like Scotland, Wales, Cornwall, or Ireland. **Celtic** is used to talk about things to do with the Celts. ...*the Celtic languages.*

cement is a grey powder made from clay and either limestone or chalk. It is mixed with sand and water to make concrete. The mixture can also be used to fix something firmly in place; you say something is **cemented** in a particular place.
❑ Some types of glue are called **cement.** If you **cement** things together, you stick them together using glue or something similar.
❑ If something **cements** a relationship or agreement, it makes is stronger or firmer.

cement mixer A **cement mixer** is a machine with a large revolving container for mixing cement, sand, and water to make concrete.

cemetery (cemeteries) A **cemetery** is a place where dead people are buried, especially one which is not immediately next to a church.

cenotaph A **cenotaph** is a monument built in honour of soldiers killed in a war.

censer A **censer** is a container for burning incense, especially at religious ceremonies.

censor (censoring, censored; censorship) If someone **censors** a piece of writing which is intended to be published or broadcast, they officially examine it and cut out any parts they think are unacceptable. A person who does this is called a **censor**; making cuts like this is called **censorship**.

censorious If someone is **censorious**, they strongly criticize someone else's behaviour.

censure (censuring, censured) If you are **censured** for something you have done, you are told by someone in authority that they strongly disapprove of it. What they say is called **censure**. *He could not expect to escape censure.*

census (censuses) A **census** is an official survey of a country's population.

cent In many countries, a **cent** is a small coin or unit of money worth one hundredth of the country's main currency unit. For example, there are 100 cents in a US dollar, a Dutch guilder, or a Kenyan shilling.

centaur In Greek myths, a **centaur** was a creature with the head, arms, and upper body of a man, and the body, legs, and tail of a horse.

centenarian A **centenarian** is a person who is a hundred years old or older.

centenary (*pron:* sen-teen-a-ree) (centenaries) A **centenary** is a year when people celebrate something which happened a hundred years earlier.

centennial is the usual American word for a centenary.

center See **centre**.

centi- at the beginning of a word indicates that a unit of measurement is one-hundredth of a larger unit. For example, a centigram is one-hundredth of a gram.

Centigrade is the same as Celsius.

centime (*pron:* son-teem) In France and many other countries, a **centime** is a hundredth of a franc. In some countries, it is a hundredth of some other unit of money; for example, in Algeria it is a hundredth of a dinar.

centimetre (*American spelling:* **centimeter**) A **centimetre** is a hundredth of a metre, or about 0.3937 inches. 'Centimetres' is usually written 'cm'.

centipede A **centipede** is an insect with a long thin body divided into many segments, each with a pair of legs.

central (centrally, centrality) ❑ The **central** part of something is the part in the middle. ◇ If something is in a **central** position, it is in the middle of something. *The cellos were grouped centrally behind the soloist.* ◇ In a city, a **central** place or building is easy to reach because it is in the city centre. *...a centrally located warehouse.*

❑ **Central** is used to distinguish the main government of a country from regional governments or local authorities. *...central government... The three special hospitals are funded centrally.*

❑ **Central** is used to say something is very important in something like a process. You can talk about the **centrality** of something to a process. *...the centrality of education to economic performance.*

central heating (centrally heated) **Central heating** is a system in which water or air is heated and passed round a building through pipes and radiators. When a building has this system, you say it is **centrally heated.**

central processing unit The **central processing unit** or **central processor** of a computer is the part which interprets and carries out the instructions of a program. 'Central processing unit' is often shortened to CPU.

centralise See **centralize**.

centralism (centralist) **Centralism** is the idea that the affairs of a country or group of countries should be controlled by one central government, rather than by several governments. **Centralist** is used to talk about people and things connected with this idea.

centrality See **central**.

centralize (centralizing, centralized; centralization) (*can be spelled with an 's' instead of a 'z'*) When power in a country or organization is **centralized**, it is concentrated in one place, or in the hands of one person or group. *...the centralization of the steel industry.*

centre (centring, centred) (*American spelling:* center, centering, centered) ❑ The **centre** of something is the part furthest from its sides, edges, boundaries, or outer surface. ◇ The **centre** of a town or city is the part where the largest number of shops, cinemas, etc are.

❑ If something **centres** on a place, it is positioned around it. *...formal gardens centring on a lake.* ◇ If something like a battle is **centred** somewhere, most of it is happening there. ◇ If a discussion **centres** on something, that is what it is mainly about.

❑ If someone or something is the **centre** of attention, people are particularly interested in them.

❑ **-centred** is added to words to describe a system in which one group of people is given special importance. *...a patient-centred health service.* ◇ **-centred** is also used to say where someone or something is based. *...Westminster-centred business.*

❑ If a place is a **centre** for an industry or activity, that industry or activity is particularly important there. ◇ A **centre** is a place where people go to have meetings, get help, or take part in an activity. *...a leisure centre.* ◇ A **centre** is also a place where research is carried out. *...the National Centre for Health Statistics.*

❑ In politics, groups who are neither left-wing nor right-wing can be called the **centre**.

❑ The **centre** of something like a chocolate is its filling.

❑ In games like rugby and netball, a **centre** is someone who plays most of the time in a middle position, rather than on the wing.

centre of gravity (centres of gravity) The **centre of gravity** of an object is the one point on it where it would balance perfectly.

centre stage You say someone or something takes **centre stage** when a lot of attention is paid to them.

centreboard On a yacht or windsurfing board, a **centreboard** is a keel which can be lowered and raised.

centrepiece The **centrepiece** of an organized event is the most important part of it. ◇ The **centrepiece** in a display of objects is the most important one.

centrifugal A **centrifugal** force is one which makes objects tend to move outwards when they are spinning around or moving in a curve. See also **centripetal**.

centripetal (*pron:* sen-tri-peet-al) A **centripetal** force is one which acts against a centrifugal force and prevents an object from moving outwards when it is spinning or moving in a curve.

centrist In politics, a **centrist** is someone with moderate political views who is neither strongly left-wing nor right-wing.

centurion A **centurion** was a non-commissioned officer in the Roman army, in charge of a unit of about 100 men.

century (centuries) ❑ A **century** is a 100-year period beginning with a year ending in '00'. For example, the 19th century was the period from 1800 to 1899. ◇ A **century** is also any period of 100 years. *...a century or so of close friendship.*

❑ In cricket, a **century** is a total of 100 runs scored by a batsman in one innings.

ceramic (*pron:* si-**ram**-ik) (ceramicist) **Ceramic** objects are made of clay which has been heated to a very high temperature. **Ceramics** are ceramic objects. A person who makes ceramics is sometimes called a **ceramicist** (*pron:* si-**ram**-iss-ist).

cereal A **cereal** is a plant like wheat, maize, or rice which produces grain. ◇ **Cereal** is a food made from grain, which people eat for breakfast.

cerebellum (*pron:* serr-rib-**bell**-um) (*plural:* cerebellums *or* cerebella) The **cerebellum** is a part of the brain, situated towards the back. It is responsible for co-ordinating muscle movements and for the sense of balance.

cerebral (*pron:* ser-**rib**-ral) **Cerebral** is used to talk about things to do with thinking and reasoning, rather than emotions. *...cerebral work.* ◇ **Cerebral** is also used to talk about things to do with the brain. *...cerebral arteries.*

cerebral palsy If someone has **cerebral palsy**, their limbs and muscles are permanently weak, usually because their brain was damaged during or before birth. People with cerebral palsy used to be called 'spastics'.

cerebrum (*plural:* cerebrums *or* cerebra) The **cerebrum** is the front part of the brain. It is concerned with thought and perception.

ceremonial (ceremonially) **Ceremonial** is used to talk about things to do with ceremonies. *...a ceremonial drinking cup... The warship has been ceremonially handed over to the Trust.* ◇ The **ceremonial** at something like a royal occasion is all the formal and traditional aspects of it, including things like fanfares and officials in costume.

ceremony (ceremonies) ❑ A **ceremony** is the formal part of an event like a wedding or coronation, when certain traditional things are done and said. ◇ **Ceremony** is used to talk about all the special things said and done on formal occasions. *The first session of the new assembly was held amidst much ceremony.*

❑ **Ceremony** is very formal and polite behaviour. ◇ If you say someone **does not stand on ceremony**, you mean they behave in a natural, rather than formal, way.

cerise (*pron:* ser-**reess**) is a cherry-red colour.

certain (certainly) ❑ If you are **certain** about something or know something **for certain**, you have no doubt about it. ◇ If you say something is **certain** to happen, you mean it will definitely happen. *They would almost certainly face persecution.* ◇ If you **make certain** something happens or is done, you take action to make sure of it. ◇ **Certain** is also used to say something will definitely have a particular effect. *...a certain cure.*

❑ If something is **certain**, it has been established as being true or correct. *There's no certain evidence that he will try to get rid of her.*

❑ You use **certainly** to emphasize that you feel strongly about what you are saying. *It is certainly disappointing.*

❑ **Certain** is used to talk about a particular person, group, or thing, without naming them. *...certain ambitious cabinet members... Making certain noises will help a baby get to sleep.* ◇ **Certain** is used to talk about a special quality which something has. *The city has a certain magic.* ◇ If something is true **to a certain extent**, it is only partly true.

certainty (certainties) ❑ If there is **certainty** about something, there is no doubt about it. *The hormone still cannot be identified with certainty.* ◇ A **certainty** is something which is not doubted or questioned. *It is a certainty that if yesterday's scenes are repeated in Sardinia, the European ban will be extended.*

❑ **Certainty** is also used to talk about things being certain to happen. *The best deterrent is the certainty of detection.* ◇ If you call someone like a sportsman or woman a **certainty**, you mean they will definitely win.

certifiable If you call a kind of behaviour **certifiable**, you mean it is extremely risky or foolish.

certificate A **certificate** is an official document stating particular facts, for example giving details of someone's birth or death. ◇ A **certificate** is also an exam or qualification. *...the General Certificate of Education.* ◇ A film's **certificate** is one of five categories it is put into by the censors, depending on who they think it is suitable for. In Britain, the certificates are: U, PG, 12, 15, and 18.

certify (certifies, certifying, certified; certification) ❑ If something is **certified** as being a particular thing, it is formally declared to be that thing. *One of the men was certified dead upon arrival at the hospital... ...reliable birth certification.* ◇ **Certified** is used to say someone has a certificate saying they have successfully completed their professional training. *...a certified accountant.* ◇ If something is **certified**, a certificate is issued saying it has reached a particular standard. *The aeroplane would be certified to American standards.*

❑ If someone is **certified**, they are officially declared insane.

certitude is the same as certainty.

cervix (*pron:* ser-**viks**) (*plural:* cervixes *or* cervices) (cervical) The **cervix** is the entrance to the womb. **Cervical** is used to talk about things to do with the cervix. *...cervical screening.* ◇ **Cervical** is also used to talk about things to do with the neck. *...cervical vertebrae.*

cessation When something stops happening, you can talk about its **cessation**.

cesspit A **cesspit** is a hole or tank in the ground which waste water and sewage flow into.

cesspool A **cesspool** is the same as cesspit.

cetacean (*pron:* sit-**tay**-shun) **Cetaceans** are members of the whale family, for example dolphins and porpoises.

cf. In a piece of writing, **cf.** is used to mention something else which can be compared with the thing being discussed. *The remark pinpoints the artistic dilemma Yeats faced (cf. A Garden of Pomegranates, p 140).*

CFC **CFCs** are chemicals used in aerosols, fridges, and air-cooling systems. They are thought to harm the ozone layer. CFC stands for 'chlorofluorocarbon'.

CH after a person's name means they have been awarded the Order of Companions of Honour, an honour which is awarded to British and Commonwealth citizens.

chafe (chafing, chafed) If you **chafe** at something like a restriction, you feel annoyed and impatient about it. ◇ If your skin **chafes** or something **chafes** it, it becomes sore as a result of being rubbed.

chaff is the outer parts of a grain like wheat, which are removed before the grain is used to make food. ◇ If you **separate the wheat from the chaff,** you decide which things or people in a group are good or important, so they can be given special treatment.

❑ **Chaff** is also thin strips of metallic foil released by a plane to confuse radar signals.

chaffinch (chaffinches) The **chaffinch** is a small European songbird. The male bird has an orange chest and face; the top of its head is grey.

chagrin (*pron:* shag-grin) (chagrined) **Chagrin** is a feeling of annoyance and disappointment. When someone has this feeling, you say they are **chagrined.**

chain (chaining, chained) ❑ A **chain** is a set of metal rings linked together. If you **chain** one thing to another, you fasten the first thing to the second with a chain.

❑ In chemistry, a **chain** is two or more atoms or chemical groups bonded together in a chain-like way.

❑ Things like duties or responsibilities can be called **chains** when they prevent people from leading a free life and doing what they want to.

❑ A **chain** of things is a group of them arranged in a line. ...*the small chain of islands.* ◇ A **chain** of shops or hotels is several of them owned by the same company.

❑ A **chain** is a series of things or events in which each one is affected by the one before it. ...*the first event in the chain of destruction.*

chain gang In the US, a **chain gang** is a group of prisoners chained together, usually while doing hard labour,

chain letter If someone sends a **chain letter,** they send several copies to different people, asking them to send copies to other people. Chain letters usually ask for money.

chain mail is flexible armour made from small metal rings joined together.

chain reaction In chemistry, a **chain reaction** is a series of processes in which each individual process starts the next one off. Any series of processes in which this happens can be called a **chain reaction.** *They are watching each other's sales figures from day to day, knowing that the first to cut prices could start a chain reaction.*

chain saw A **chain saw** is a large motorized saw.

chain-smoke (chain-smoker) If someone **chain-smokes,** they keep smoking one cigarette straight after another. You call someone like this a **chain-smoker.**

chain store A **chain store** is one of many similar shops owned by the same company.

chair (chairing, chaired) ❑ A **chair** is a piece of furniture for one person to sit on.

❑ At a university, a **chair** is the post of professor. ...*the chair of Medieval History at Birmingham.*

❑ If you **chair** a meeting or are the **chair,** you are the chairperson; you can also say you are **in the chair** or **take the chair.**

chairlift A **chairlift** is a line of chairs attached to a moving cable for carrying people up a mountain.

chairman (chairmen; chairmanship) ❑ The **chairman** of a meeting or debate is the person in charge, who decides when each person will speak. A chairman can be a man or a woman, but some people prefer the neutral words 'chairperson' or 'chair'.

❑ The **chairman** of a company, organization, or committee is its head. ◇ **Chairmanship** is used to talk about the position of being chairman, or the period when a particular person is chairman. *It is the first time that the chairmanship has been contested... Under his chairmanship everything has come to fruition.*

chairperson The **chairperson** of a meeting or debate is the person in charge.

chairwoman (chairwomen) The **chairwoman** of a meeting or debate is the woman in charge.

chaise longue (chaises longues) (*both pron:* shaze long) A **chaise longue** is a couch with only one arm and usually a back along half its length.

chalet (*pron:* shal-lay) A **chalet** is a small wooden house, especially in a mountain area or holiday camp.

chalice (*pron:* chal-liss) A **chalice** is a large metal cup with a thin stem, used, for example, in the Christian service of Holy Communion.

chalk (chalky) ❑ **Chalk** is a kind of soft white rock. If something is **chalky,** it contains chalk or is covered with chalk. ◇ **Chalks** or sticks of **chalk** are small rods of white or coloured chalk for writing or drawing with. ◇ If you say two people or things are as different as **chalk and cheese,** you mean they are completely different from each other.

❑ If you **chalk up** a success, you achieve it. Similarly, if you **chalk up** a number of points in a game, you win them.

challenge (challenging, challenged; challengingly, challenger) ❑ If you say something you are doing is **challenging** or a **challenge,** you mean it is new and exciting and will need great effort and determination. *The expedition was a serious challenge... ...a challenging match... ...a challengingly inventive show.*

❑ If you **challenge** someone to do something, you invite them to do it, believing they will not dare to do it, or not be able to. *They challenged him to prove his claim.* An invitation like this is called a **challenge.** ◇ If one person **challenges** another for something like the leadership of a party, they try to become leader instead of them. When this happens, you say there is a leadership **challenge.** A **challenger** for the leadership of a party is someone who is trying to take over as leader.

❑ If you **challenge** a statement or belief, you question whether it is true or valid. Similarly, you can **challenge** someone's authority or do or say something which is a **challenge** to it. *The move is seen as a direct challenge to the prime minister's authority.*

❑ If someone like a sentry **challenges** you, they order you to stop, and ask you who you are and what you are doing.

chamber ❑ A **chamber** is a large room for formal meetings. The room where a parliament meets is often called a **chamber,** and **chamber** is often used to talk about the parliament itself. *The President himself will address the chamber.* ◇ A **chamber** is also a room designed and equipped for a particular purpose. ...*a burial chamber.* ◇ The **chambers** of a group of barristers are a set of offices where they talk to their clients.

❏ Some hollow places inside a person's or animal's body are called **chambers**. ...*the chambers of the heart.*

chamber music is classical music written for a small number of instruments.

Chamber of Commerce A Chamber of Commerce is a group of business people who work together to improve business and industry in their area.

Chamber of Trade A Chamber of Trade is a group of local shopkeepers who work together to protect their interests.

chamber orchestra A chamber orchestra is a small orchestra.

chamber pot A chamber pot is a round china bowl for urinating in during the night.

chamberlain A chamberlain is the person in charge of the household affairs of a monarch or noble.

chambermaid A chambermaid is a woman who cleans and tidies the bedrooms in a hotel.

chameleon (*pron:* kam-**meal**-yon) A chameleon is a small lizard which changes colour according to its surroundings. People are often compared to chameleons when they are good at changing their opinions to fit in with other people.

chamois (*plural:* **chamois**) The chamois (*pron:* sham-wah) is a small antelope which lives in the mountains of Europe and South West Asia. ◇ A chamois (*pron:* sham-ee) or chamois leather is a soft leather cloth made from the skin of a chamois, or more usually a sheep, and used for cleaning and polishing.

chamomile See camomile.

champ People sometimes call a champion the **champ**.

champagne is an expensive sparkling white French wine.

champion (championing, championed; championship) ❏ A champion is someone who has won first prize in a competition, or who has beaten everyone else in a contest or fight. ◇ A **championship** is a competition to find the best player or team of a particular sport. ❏ If you **champion** something like a cause or principle, you support it in an active way. You can say someone is a champion of a cause or principle. *He was a formidable champion of justice.*

chance (chancing, chanced; chancy) ❏ If there is a **chance** of something happening or being true, it could possibly happen or be true. ◇ If you talk about someone **standing a chance** of doing something, you are talking about the possibility that they will be able to do it. *The party had to decide who stood the best chance of leading it to victory.* If you say someone does not **stand a chance** of doing something, you mean there is no possibility they will be able to do it. ❏ A **chance** is an opportunity for someone or something to do something. *The aircraft had a chance to show off its firepower.* ❏ If you **take a chance**, you do something even though there is a risk of danger or failure. You can also say you **chance** something. *He was run out chancing a single to mid-off.* ◇ Something which is **chancy** is risky. ◇ If you are in a risky situation and **take your chances**, you make the most of opportunities which come along and hope things will work out. ❏ **Chance** is used to talk about things which happen for

no special reason and in a way which cannot be predicted. ...*a chance discovery.* You say things like these happen **by chance**. ◇ If someone **leaves nothing to chance**, they take all possible precautions to make sure something is a success.

❏ If you **chance on** or **chance upon** someone or something, you meet or discover them unexpectedly.

chancel In a church, the **chancel** is the part where the altar is and the priest and choir usually sit.

chancellery (chancelleries) A **chancellery** is (a) the residence or office of a chancellor. (b) an office in an embassy or consulate.

chancellor (chancellorship) The **Chancellor** is the head of government in Germany and Austria. ◇ In Britain, the Chancellor is the Chancellor of the Exchequer. ◇ The Chancellor of a British university is its official head. ◇ **Chancellorship** is the position of chancellor. ...*the Social Democratic candidate for the chancellorship.*

Chancellor of the Exchequer In Britain, the **Chancellor of the Exchequer** is the minister who makes decisions about finance and taxes.

chancer If you say someone is a **chancer**, you mean they exploit situations to their own advantage, often dishonestly.

Chancery The **Chancery Division** is a department of the British High Court of Justice. It often deals with problems which cannot be solved by applying the law in the normal way.

chancy See chance.

chandelier (*pron:* shan-dill-**eer**) A **chandelier** is an ornamental light fitting decorated with a lot of hanging pieces of glass.

chandler A **chandler** is someone who sells ships' supplies and equipment.

change (changing, changed) ❏ If there is a **change** in something or if it **changes**, it becomes different in some way. If you **change** something, you make it different. ◇ **change your mind**: see mind. ◇ **ring the changes**: see ring. ◇ **change of heart**: see heart.

❏ If you say something is a **change** or **makes a change**, you mean it is different, in a pleasant or interesting way, from the usual thing. *Derbyshire's spirit was a welcome change from the boredom of recent matches... The Bundesbank had no comment, which made a nice change.* ◇ You say **for a change** when you are describing something surprising and unusual which is happening. *Sweden, for a change, is having a bad time economically.*

❏ When the wind **changes**, it blows from a different direction. ◇ When traffic lights **change**, they show a different colour.

❏ **Change** is used to talk about getting rid of something and getting something else of the same kind in its place. For example, you say someone **changes** their car or has a **change** of car. *The engine had been serviced, brakes tightened, oil changed.* ◇ **change the subject**: see subject. ◇ If you **change over** from one thing to another, you stop doing or using the first thing and start doing or using the second. See also changeover.

❏ If you **change** or **change** your clothes, you take off some or all of them and put on different ones. If you take a **change** of clothes with you somewhere, you take a spare set to change into. ◇ If you **change** a baby or **change** its nappy, you take off its dirty nappy and put a clean one on. ◇ If you **change** a bed, you take off the dirty sheets and put clean ones on.

❑ If you **change** trains or buses, you get off one and onto another.

❑ **change hands**: see hand.

❑ If you **change** gear, you move the gear lever on a vehicle to get into a different gear. If you **change down**, you move into a lower gear; if you **change up**, you move into a higher gear. Moving from one gear to another is called a gear change.

❑ **Change** is (a) the money you get back when you pay for something with more money than it costs. (b) coins rather than notes. ◇ If someone asks you if you can **change** some money or if you have **change**, they want you to exchange some money they have for the same amount in smaller notes or coins. ◇ You also say you **change** money when you are given an amount of one country's money in exchange for an equivalent amount of another's.

change of life The change of life is the same as the menopause.

changeable If something like the weather is **changeable**, it is likely to change.

changeling In stories, a **changeling** is a baby who has been substituted for another baby by fairies.

changeover A **changeover** is a change from one activity or system to another. *...a phased changeover to metric measurements.*

channel (channelling, channelled) (*American spelling:* channelling, channeled) ❑ A **channel** is (a) a wavelength on which TV programmes are broadcast. (b) a wavelength for sending and receiving radio messages.

❑ A **channel** is also (a) a passage along which water or some other liquid flows. *...irrigation channels.* (b) a route used by boats to cross an area of water. ◇ The English Channel is often called the **Channel**.

❑ If you **channel** something like money, you control and direct it so it is used in a particular way or for a particular purpose. *More resources should be channelled into new technology.* ◇ If you talk about something being done through particular **channels**, you are talking about the people who arrange it. *All those seeking asylum would be granted passports if they applied through the official channels.*

chant If you **chant**, you repeat a word or group of words over and over again. A **chant** is a word or group of words repeated like this. ◇ A **chant** is also a religious song or prayer sung or spoken on only a few notes. *...Gregorian chant.*

chaos (chaotic, chaotically) **Chaos** is complete disorder and confusion. If a something like a situation is **chaotic**, it is disordered and confused. *Over the past decade professional sport has expanded chaotically.*

chap (chapping, chapped) You can use **chap** to talk about a man or boy. ◇ If your skin **chaps**, it becomes raw and cracked by exposure to the cold.

chapati (*or* chapatti) In Indian cookery, a **chapati** is a flat piece of unleavened bread.

chapel A **chapel** is (a) a building used for worship by some Protestant churches. *...a Baptist chapel.* (b) part of a church with its own altar for private prayer. (c) a small church in a school, hospital, or prison.

chaperone (*or* chaperon) (*pron:* **shap**-per-rone) (chaperon-

ing, chaperoned) If you **chaperone** someone or are their **chaperone**, you go with them to make sure they behave or do not come to any harm. ◇ Originally, a **chaperone** was an older or married woman who used to accompany a young unmarried woman on social occasions.

chaplain (chaplaincy, chaplaincies) A **chaplain** is a member of the clergy who works in the armed forces, a hospital, school, prison, or for an important person like a monarch. **Chaplaincy** is used to talk about the job and work of a chaplain. *...his industrial chaplaincy work.*

chapter ❑ A **chapter** is one of the parts of a book. ◇ If you give someone **chapter and verse**, you tell them precisely where you got something like a piece of information. *A senior manager was happy to recite the appropriate law chapter and verse.*

❑ A **chapter** is a period in history, or in someone's life. *...a momentous chapter in British history.*

❑ The **chapter** of a cathedral is the clergy who work in it or are connected with it. ◇ In the US, a **chapter** is a local branch of an organization.

char (charring, charred) If something **chars**, it turns black after being burned. *...the charred remains of a tank.*

charabanc (*pron:* shar-rab-bang) A **charabanc** was a large old-fashioned coach for taking people on holiday.

character ❑ A person's **character** is all the qualities they have which make up their personality. Similarly, the **character** of a place is the qualities which make up its atmosphere. *...the distinctive character of Catalonia.* ◇ If someone behaves **in character**, they do what you would expect them to do. If they behave **out of character**, they do something you would not expect them to do. ◇ If you talk about, say, the British **character** or the German **character**, you mean the qualities which people from these countries are supposed to have.

❑ A person's **character** is also how honest and reliable they are. *The electorate still has doubts about his character.* If you say someone is of good **character**, you mean they are respected by other people and have a good reputation. ◇ If someone tries to destroy another person's reputation by criticizing them in an unfair and dishonest way, you call this **character assassination**. ◇ If someone has **character**, they are able to deal effectively with difficult, unpleasant, or dangerous situations. *John McCarthy said that whatever strength of character he had displayed he owed to the other hostages.*

❑ If you talk about the **character** of something, you mean the special features which make it what it is, or make it work the way it does. ◇ If you say something has **character**, you mean it has a special, interesting, or unusual quality. *Marsh's batting, arguably, had the most character about it.*

❑ The **characters** in a film, book, or play are the people in it. ◇ If you call someone a **character**, you mean they are interesting, unusual, or amusing. ◇ A **character actor** or **character actress** is an actor who specializes in playing unusual or eccentric people.

❑ A **character** is a letter, number, or other symbol written, printed, or displayed on a VDU.

characterise See characterize.

characteristic (characteristically) A **characteristic** is a quality or feature which is typical of someone or something. *She believes that it is possible to identify 'criminal character-*

istics' in handwriting. ◇ If something is **characteristic** of a person, thing, or place, it is typical of them. *The owners refrained from interfering with the shop's characteristic image... His defence of the deal has been characteristically negative.*

characterize (characterizing, characterized; characterization) (*can be spelled with an 's' instead of a 'z'*) If you say something **characterizes** a thing, you mean it is a typical feature of it. *...the cruelty and piety which characterize life in the Middle Ages.* ◇ If you **characterize** someone or something in a particular way, you describe them by saying they have particular characteristics. *We have made what I would characterize as outstanding progress.* ◇ If you talk about the **characterization** in a story or film, you mean the extent to which the characters are made interesting or believable.

characterless A **characterless** person or thing is dull and uninteresting.

charade (*pron:* shar-**rahd**) If you call something that is happening a **charade**, you mean it is not what it is supposed to be and nobody is really deceived by it. ◇ **Charades** is a party game in which two teams act a word or phrase for the other team to guess.

charcoal is a black substance made by burning wood without much air. Charcoal can be used as a fuel. ◇ **Charcoals** are small sticks of charcoal used for drawing with.

charge (charging, charged) ❑ The money you are **charged** for something is the amount you have to pay for it; this money is called a **charge**. ◇ If something is **free of charge**, it does not cost anything. ◇ If goods or services are **charged** to a person or organization, the bill is sent to them.

❑ When the police **charge** someone, they formally accuse them of having committed a crime. An accusation like this is called a **charge**.

❑ If you are **in charge** of someone or something, they are under your control and you are responsible for them. You can also say you **have charge** of them or they are **in your charge**. If you **take charge** of someone or something, you become responsible for them. ◇ If someone is your **charge**, they have been given to you to look after and you are responsible for them.

❑ If you **charge** somewhere, you dash there in a clumsy way. ◇ If a group of soldiers or police **charge**, they move forward quickly, to attack people or disperse them.

❑ An electrical **charge** is an amount of electricity stored in something. If you **charge** something, you give it an electrical charge by passing electricity through it. ◇ The **charge** in a cartridge or shell is the explosive in it.

❑ **Charged** is used to describe situations in which there is a lot of tension because the people present have very strong feelings about something. *...a highly-charged debate.*

❑ If someone is **charged** with doing something, it is their responsibility. *...a bank charged with maintaining the value of its currency.*

charge card A **charge card** is a card provided by a shop allowing you to buy goods on credit which you pay for later.

chargé d'affaires (chargés d'affaires) (*both pron:* shar-zhay daf-fair; *the 'zh' sounds like 's' in 'pleasure'*) A chargé d'affaires is (a) a person appointed to act as the head of a diplomatic mission in a foreign country while the ambassador is away. (b) the head of a small or not very important diplomatic mission.

charge hand A **charge hand** is a worker of slightly less importance than a foreman.

charge nurse A **charge nurse** is a senior male nurse in a hospital, equivalent to a sister.

charge sheet A **charge sheet** is the official form on which the police write down legal charges against a person.

chargeable If something is **chargeable**, (a) you have to pay money for it. *...fees chargeable by the solicitor.* (b) you have to pay tax on it.

charger A **charger** is a device for charging or recharging batteries. ◇ In the Middle Ages, a **charger** was a strong horse ridden by a knight in battle.

chariot (charioteer) A **chariot** was a horse-drawn vehicle with two wheels used in ancient times. Chariots were used for racing and fighting. A **charioteer** was a chariot driver.

charisma (*pron:* kar-**rizz**-ma) (charismatic) ❑ If someone has **charisma**, they can attract, influence, and inspire people by their personal qualities. You say someone like this is **charismatic** (*pron:* kar-rizz-**mat**-ik).

❑ The **charismatic** church is part of the Christian Church which believes people can receive special supernatural gifts from God like prophecy and speaking in tongues.

charitable (charitably) ❑ A **charitable** person is kind and tolerant. ◇ If you say you are being **charitable**, you mean you are describing someone or something in a more favourable way than they really deserve. *There was what might charitably be called a lack of integrity in the British cabinet.*

❑ A **charitable** organization or activity helps and supports people or animals in need. *...charitable donations.* ◇ **charitable trust:** see **trust**.

charity (charities) ❑ A **charity** is an organization which raises money for a particular cause. **Charity** is used to talk about the work of organizations like this. *Over 15 million pounds had been raised for charity.* ◇ **Charity** is also money or gifts given to poor people. *His country did not want to depend on charity.* ◇ If you say **charity begins at home**, you mean people should start helping their own family or people near to them before they think about the needs of others.

❑ **Charity** is also a kind and sympathetic attitude towards other people.

charlady (charladies) A **charlady** is the same as a **charwoman**.

charlatan (*pron:* shar-lat-tan) A **charlatan** is someone who pretends to have skills or knowledge they do not really have.

charleston The **charleston** was a lively dance popular in the 1920s.

charm (charming, charmed; charmingly) ❑ **Charm** is the quality of being attractive and pleasant. *...the unique charm and character of this historic town.* You say someone or something that has this quality is **charming**. *The waiters are all young and charmingly laid-back.* ◇ If you are **charmed** by someone or something, you are delighted by them. ◇ If someone **charms** you, they use their

charmer

cheap

charm to please you, often to get you to do something.
□ A **charm** is also an action, saying, or object believed to be lucky or to have magic powers. ◇ If you say someone leads a **charmed life**, you mean they keep narrowly escaping danger. ◇ A **charmed circle** is a group of people who have advantages other people do not have.
□ A **charm** is a small ornament fixed to a bracelet or necklace.

charmer If you call someone a **charmer**, you mean they appear to be very charming but in fact they are rather insincere.

charnel house A **charnel house** is a building or vault for the bones of the dead.

chart □ A **chart** is something like a diagram or graph which makes information easy to understand. ◇ A **chart** is also a map of part of the sea, or of the stars. ◇ When an area of land or water is **charted**, it is surveyed and a map is made of it.
□ When something like progress is **charted**, it is studied and recorded carefully. ◇ If you **chart** a course of action, you plan it.
□ The **charts** are weekly lists showing which pop records have sold most copies.

charter (chartering, chartered; charterer) □ A **charter** is (a) a document showing the rights of a group of people, or demanding rights for them. ...*a customers' charter.* (b) a document issued by the government or ruler of a country allowing an organization to be founded and listing its rights and functions. ...*the BBC's royal charter.* (c) a list of the aims and principles of an organization. ...*Article 50 of the United Nations Charter.*
□ **Chartered** is used in front of words like 'accountant' and 'surveyor' to show someone is fully qualified in their profession. ...*a chartered physiotherapist.*
□ If you **charter** a plane or ship, you hire it for your private use. The **charterer** of a ship is a person or firm hiring it. ◇ A **charter** plane or boat is hired by a person or organization and is not part of a regular service.

charwoman (charwomen) A **charwoman** is a woman employed as a cleaner.

chary (*pron:* chair-ee) If you are **chary** of doing something, you are not at all keen to do it.

chase (chasing, chased) □ If you **chase** someone, you run after them or follow them quickly in a vehicle, to try to catch them. Following someone like this is called a **chase**; when people chase someone, you can say they **give chase**.
□ If you **chase** something you want, you spend a lot of time and effort trying to get it. Trying to get something like this can be called a **chase**. ...*the chase for memorabilia.* ◇ If you **chase** someone or something **up**, you try to find them.
□ If you **chase** someone from a place, you force them to leave.

chaser A **chaser** is an alcoholic drink drunk straight after a different kind of alcoholic drink.

chasm (*pron:* kaz-zum) A **chasm** is a very deep crack in rock or ice. ◇ A **chasm** is also a great difference between two things, ideas, or groups of people. ...*the chasm between rich and poor... There is a growing chasm between Britain and Germany on a whole range of issues.*

chassis (*pron:* shass-ee) (*plural:* chassis) A vehicle's chas-

sis is the framework it is built on.

chaste (chastity) A **chaste** person does not have sex, or only has sex with their husband or wife. You call their behaviour **chastity**. ◇ **Chaste** things are very simple in style. ...*a chaste diamond.*

chasten (chastening, chastened) If you are **chastened** by something, it makes you regret your behaviour. *He has clearly not been chastened by his thirteen days in detention... ...the chastening memory of the final game of last season.*

chastise (chastising, chastised; chastisement) If someone is **chastised**, they are told off or punished; you call this their **chastisement**.

chastity See **chaste**.

chat (chatting, chatted) When people **chat** or have a **chat**, they talk in a friendly way, often about unimportant things. ◇ A **chat show** is a TV or radio programme in which people talk like this. ◇ If you **chat** someone **up**, you talk to them in a friendly way because you are sexually attracted to them.

chateau (*plural:* chateaux) (*both pron:* shat-toe) A **chateau** is a large country house or castle in France.

chatline A **chatline** is a commercial telephone service allowing you to have a conversation with more than one person at the same time.

chattel Your **chattels** are the things you own.

chatter (chattering, chattered; chatterer; chatterbox, chatterboxes) □ If someone **chatters**, they talk quickly and continuously, often about unimportant things. This kind of talk is called **chatter**; someone who does it a lot is called a **chatterer** or a **chatterbox**. ◇ The **chattering classes** are trendy left-wing professional people, often involved in the media, who talk a lot about things like politics.
□ If a small animal or bird **chatters**, it makes quick short high-pitched noises. ◇ If your teeth **chatter**, they rattle together because you are cold.

chatty A **chatty** person is friendly and informal. **Chatty** writing reminds you of someone like this.

chauffeur (chauffeuring, chauffeured) A **chauffeur** is someone employed to drive and look after someone else's car. ◇ If you **chauffeur** someone somewhere, you drive them there as if you were their chauffeur.

chauvinism (*pron:* show-vin-iz-zum) (chauvinist; chauvinistic) **Chauvinism** is a strong unreasonable belief that your own country or race is the best and most important one. Someone who has this belief is called **chauvinistic** or a **chauvinist**. ...*the notoriously chauvinistic French press.* ◇ A **chauvinist** or **male chauvinist** is a man who believes men are better or more important than women. This belief and the kind of behaviour it leads to are also called **chauvinism**.

cheap (cheaper, cheapest; cheaply, cheapness, cheapish) □ **Cheap** goods or services do not cost much. *Booksellers are battling to sell new books more cheaply... ...the cheapness of the interrail ticket.* **Cheapish** things are fairly cheap. ◇ You also say things are **cheap** when they cost less money than average because they are of poor quality. ...*scruffy youths guzzling cheap wine.* ◇ If something is done **on the cheap**, not enough money is spent on it, and it is not done properly as a result.
□ If you say life is **cheap** somewhere, you mean little value is put on people and what happens to them.
□ You say behaviour and remarks are cheap when they

are unkind and unnecessary. ....*cheap jokes*.

cheapen (cheapening, cheapened) If something **cheapens** you, it lowers your reputation or dignity. ◇ If you **cheapen** something, you reduce its price to sell it more easily.

cheapskate A cheapskate is someone who does not like spending money. ◇ **Cheapskate** things are done or produced as cheaply as possible. ....*cheapskate winemaking*.

cheat (cheating, cheated) ❑ If someone **cheats**, they lie or behave dishonestly to get what they want. You call someone who does this a **cheat**. ◇ If someone **cheats** you out of something, they get it from you by behaving dishonestly. ◇ If you feel **cheated**, you feel bitter, because you have not got something you were expecting to get.

❑ If you **cheat on** someone you are having a sexual relationship with, you deceive them by secretly having a relationship with someone else.

check (checker) ❑ If you **check** something or **check on** it, you make sure it is satisfactory, safe, or correct. An inspection or examination like this is called a **check**; someone who checks things as their job is called a **checker**.

❑ If you **check** something **out**, you look into it thoroughly, to make sure nothing is wrong. Similarly, if you **check** someone **out**, you find out more about them. ◇ If you **check** one thing **against** another, you compare them, looking for differences or mistakes.

❑ If something harmful or dangerous is **checked**, it is prevented from continuing or spreading. *The dollar's rise was checked, at least for a time.* ◇ If you keep or hold something **in check**, you keep it under control.

❑ If you **check into** a hotel or **check in**, you arrive and fill in the necessary forms. Similarly, if you **check out**, you pay the bill and leave. ◇ When you **check in** at an airport, you arrive and show your ticket before going on a flight. The place where you do this is called the **check-in**.

❑ **Check** or **checked** fabric has a pattern made up of squares.

❑ In a restaurant in the US, the **check** is the bill. ◇ **Check** is also the American spelling of 'cheque'.

❑ In chess, you say 'check' when you have moved one of your pieces into a position where it could take your opponent's king. If you are **in check**, your own king is being attacked.

check-in See check.

check-up A check-up is a routine examination by a doctor or dentist.

checkered See chequered.

checkers is the usual American word for draughts.

checklist A checklist is a list of things to be checked.

checkmate In chess, checkmate is a situation in which you cannot stop your king being captured and so you lose the game.

checkout In a supermarket, a checkout is a counter where you pay for the goods you are buying.

checkpoint A checkpoint is a place where traffic is stopped and checked.

cheek (-cheeked) ❑ A person's **cheeks** are the soft parts of their face on either side of their nose. You can add -cheeked to a word to describe someone's cheeks. ....*a rosy-cheeked woman*. ◇ If you **turn the other cheek**, you decide not to get angry or violent when someone has

treated you badly. ◇ If things are **cheek by jowl**, they are very close together.

❑ If you say someone has a **cheek**, you mean they are doing something they have no real right to do.

cheekbone A person's **cheekbones** are the two bones in their face just below their eyes.

cheeky (cheekier, cheekiest; cheekily) A **cheeky** person is rude or disrespectful. A **cheeky** action shows no respect for someone. *His error allowed Degryse to run at goal and cheekily put the ball between Southall's legs.*

cheer (cheering, cheered) ❑ When people **cheer**, they shout something like 'hooray', to show approval or encouragement. A shout like this is called a **cheer**. ◇ If you **cheer** someone **on**, you cheer loudly to encourage them.

❑ If a piece of news brings people **cheer**, it makes them pleased or relieved. *The immediate cause for cheer is the deal for a new airport.* You can also say something like this **raises a cheer**. ◇ If you are **cheered** by something, it makes you happier or less worried. ◇ If you **cheer up** or someone **cheers** you **up**, you stop feeling depressed and become more cheerful.

cheerful (cheerfully; cheerfulness) A **cheerful** person is happy and joyful; you can also say their behaviour is **cheerful**. *They cheerfully admitted it... His constant cheerfulness kept us all determined not to let him down.* ◇ **Cheerful** things make you feel cheerful. ....*cheerful music*.

cheerleader In the US, cheerleaders are people who lead the crowd in cheering at a large public event like a football match. ◇ A **cheerleader** is also someone who actively supports an organization or cause. *He is among the cheerleaders for constitutional change.*

cheerless You say something is **cheerless** when it is gloomy and depressing.

cheery (cheerier, cheeriest; cheerily) Cheery behaviour is bright and cheerful. *The children welcomed me cheerily.* ◇ **Cheery** things make you feel cheerful. ....*cheery news*.

cheese (cheesy; cheesed) Cheese is a solid food made from milk. There are many kinds of cheese. ◇ A **cheese** is (a) a kind of cheese. *We use only British cheeses.* (b) a block of cheese before it is cut up for selling or eating. ◇ **Cheesy** things contain cheese or look, taste, or smell like cheese. ....*an aubergine bake with a crisp cheesy top*.

cheeseboard A cheeseboard is a board on which you put different types of cheese so people can choose which ones they want, usually as the last course of a meal. This course can itself be called the **cheeseboard**.

cheeseburger A cheeseburger is a burger with a slice of cheese served in a bread roll.

cheesecake A cheesecake is a cake with a soft sweet topping made of cream cheese on a biscuit base.

cheetah The cheetah is a large wild cat with spots, found mainly in Africa. Cheetahs are the fastest land mammals over a short distance.

chef (*pron:* sheff) A chef is a cook in a restaurant or hotel.

chef-d'oeuvre (*plural:* chefs-d'oeuvre) (*both pron:* shay-durv) A writer's, artist's, or composer's **chef-d'oeuvre** is the best and most impressive piece of work they have produced.

chemical (chemically) ❑ **Chemical** is used to talk about things to do with chemistry or made by a process in chemistry. ....*a chemical reaction... ...chemically treated* *water*. ◇ A **chemical** is a substance used in or made by a chemical process.

❏ **Chemical** weapons are weapons with chemicals in them, which are used, for example, to burn, poison, or choke people. **Chemical** warfare is the use of chemical weapons in war.

chemist A **chemist** or **chemist's** is a shop selling medicine, cosmetics, and some household goods. ◇ A **chemist** is a person qualified to sell medicines prescribed by a doctor. ◇ A **chemist** is also a scientist who does research in chemistry.

chemistry is the scientific study of the characteristics and composition of substances. ◇ The **chemistry** of a substance is its characteristics and composition, and the way it reacts with other substances.

❏ **Chemistry** is used to talk about how two people react to each other, for example when they work together or have a sexual relationship. *The personal chemistry between the two leaders has improved a lot.*

chemotherapy (*pron:* kee-mo-theh-rap-ee) is the treatment of infections using antibiotics, or the treatment of cancer using special anti-cancer drugs.

cheque (*American spelling:* check) A **cheque** is a printed form on which you write an amount of money and say who it is to be paid to. Your bank then pays them the money from your account. ◇ blank cheque: see **blank**.

cheque card A **cheque card** is a small plastic card given to you by your bank, which you show when paying for something by cheque.

chequebook (*American spelling:* checkbook) A **cheque-book** is a book of cheques.

chequered (*American spelling:* checkered) If a person or organization has had a **chequered** career or history, they have had a varied past with good and bad parts. ◇ **Chequered** fabric has a pattern of squares of two or more colours. ◇ In motor racing, the **chequered flag** is the black and white checked flag waved as each contestant passes the finishing line.

cherish (cherishes, cherishing, cherished) If you **cherish** a hope or memory, you keep it in your mind so that it continues to give you happy feelings. ◇ If you **cherish** someone, you care for them in a loving way. ◇ You also say you **cherish** someone or something when you are very pleased with them and glad to have them. *...a cherished colleague.* ◇ If people **cherish** a right or privilege, they believe it is important and try hard to keep it.

cheroot A **cheroot** is a cigar with both ends cut flat.

cherry (cherries) **Cherries** are small round fruit with red or black skins and a hard stone in the middle. The tree they grow on is called a **cherry** or a **cherry tree**. ◇ If you have a **second bite at the cherry** or **another bite at the cherry**, you have another chance to do something when you did not succeed the first time. ◇ **Cherry red** is a deep red colour.

cherub (*plural:* cherubs *or* cherubim) (cherubic) A **cherub** is an angel represented in art as a plump naked child with wings. ◇ If you say someone looks **cherubic** (*pron:* cher-rew-bic), you mean they look sweet and innocent like a cherub.

chess is a game for two people, played on a chessboard. Each player has sixteen pieces of various kinds. You try to move your pieces so your opponent's king cannot

escape being taken.

chessboard A **chessboard** is a square board for playing chess. It is divided into sixty-four squares of two colours, usually black and white.

chessman (chessmen) A **chessman** is a playing piece used in chess, usually coloured black or white. Each player starts the game with sixteen chessmen.

chest (-chested) ❏ A person's **chest** is the front of their body between the neck and the waist. You can add **-chested** to a word to describe someone's chest. *...hairy-chested men.* ◇ If you **get** something **off your chest**, you tell people what you have been thinking or worrying about. ◇ If you **keep** or **hold your cards close to your chest**, you do not tell people your plans.

❏ A **chest** is a large heavy box, usually made of wood, for storing things or moving personal possessions from one place to another.

chest of drawers (chests of drawers) A **chest of drawers** is a piece of furniture with drawers.

chestnut Chestnuts are shiny reddish-brown nuts with a prickly green outer casing. The tree they grow on is called a **chestnut** or a **chestnut tree**. See also **horse chestnut**. ◇ **Chestnut** is a reddish-brown colour. ◇ An **old chestnut** is a joke or story which is so well-known it is no longer funny.

chesty If you have a **chesty** cough, you have a lot of catarrh in your lungs.

chevron (*pron:* shev-ron) A **chevron** is a V shape. ◇ A **chevron** is also one of the V shapes on the sleeve of a person in the armed forces or the police force, which shows their rank.

chew (chewy) ❏ When you **chew** food, you break it up with your teeth to make it easier to swallow. **Chewy** food needs to be chewed a lot before you can swallow it. ◇ If you **chew** something like gum, you keep biting it, to taste the flavour without eating it. ◇ If an animal **chews** a hole in something, it makes a hole by biting.

❏ If you **chew over** something like a problem or an idea, you think carefully about it. ◇ If you say someone has **bitten off more than they can chew**, you mean they are trying to do something too difficult for them.

chewing gum is a kind of sweet you chew but do not swallow.

chic (*pron:* sheek) people or things are fashionable and sophisticated. You can also say people or things have **chic**. *Currently, tennis fashion defies all notions of chic.*

chicanery (*pron:* shi-kane-er-ee) is deceitful and dishonest behaviour.

chick A **chick** is a baby bird.

chicken A **chicken** is a bird kept for its meat or eggs. Chicken is the meat from a chicken. ◇ If you say someone is **counting their chickens**, you mean they are making plans based on the idea that something will happen, when it may not happen at all. ◇ If you talk about a **chicken-and-egg** situation, you mean it is impossible to decide which of two things caused the other.

chickenpox is a disease which gives you a high temperature and itchy red spots. It is caught mainly by children.

chickpea Chickpeas are the hard round edible seeds of a plant grown in the Mediterranean area, Africa, and Asia.

chickweed is a common garden weed with small white flowers.

chicory is a plant with crunchy sharp-tasting leaves which people put in salads. The root of this plant is also called chicory; it is roasted and used in some types of coffee.

chide (chiding, chided) If you **chide** someone, you tell them off.

chief (chiefs; chiefly) ❑ The **chief** of an organization is the person in charge. ...*the Army chief*. The main person in an organization often has **chief** in the name of their job. ...*the chief fire officer*. ◇ The **chief** of a tribe is its leader.

❑ The **chief** person or thing in a group is the most important one. ...*the chief guest of honour*. You can say one person or thing is **chief** among others. *Chief among their demands was the establishment of an independent television station.* ◇ The **chief** cause of something is the main one. *Djibouti has survived as a state chiefly because of long-standing French support.*

❑ If something is done **chiefly** in a particular way, it is done mainly that way. You can also say something is done **chiefly** in a particular place. *The numbers of grouse shot, chiefly in northern England and Scotland, had fallen by about 40 per cent.*

Chief Constable The **Chief Constable** of a county or area is the officer in charge of the police force.

Chief Justice A **Chief Justice** is the head judge of a court, especially a supreme court.

Chief of Staff (Chiefs of Staff) The **Chiefs of Staff** are the highest-ranking officers of each service of the armed forces.

chieftain A **chieftain** is the leader of a tribe.

chiffon (*pron:* **shif-fon**) is a kind of very thin silk or man-made fabric which you can see through.

chignon (*pron:* **sheen-yon**) A **chignon** is a knot of hair worn at the back of the head.

chihuahua (*pron:* **chee-wah-wah**) The **chihuahua** is a tiny short-haired dog with large pointed ears, originally from Mexico.

chilblain **Chilblains** are painful or itchy red swellings people get on their fingers and toes in cold weather.

child (children) ❑ A **child** is (a) a human being who is not yet an adult. (b) a newborn or unborn baby. ◇ If you say something is **child's play**, you mean it is very easy to do.

❑ Someone's **children** are their sons and daughters of any age. ◇ If you say someone is the **child** of a particular time, you mean they were strongly influenced by what was going on then. ...*a child of the Swinging Sixties*.

child abuse is physical, sexual, or emotional ill-treatment of children.

child-care See childcare.

child-minder (child-minding) (*or* childminder, childminding) A **child-minder** is someone who is paid to use their own home to look after children. **Child-minding** is the supervision and care given by a childminder.

child prodigy A **child prodigy** is a child who is very talented in some way.

childbearing is the process of giving birth to babies. ◇ A woman of **childbearing age** is of an age when women are usually able to give birth to children.

childbirth is the act of giving birth to a child.

childcare (*or* child-care) is the care provided by people like child-minders or local authorities who look after children while their parents are at work.

childhood A person's **childhood** is the time when they were a child.

childish (childishly; childishness) A **childish** person behaves in a silly or immature way. *Her leg was propped up childishly on the table... You have to ignore the male jokes and childishness.*

childless (childlessness) Someone who is **childless** has no children. **Childlessness** is having no children.

childlike A **childlike** person is like a child in appearance, character, or behaviour.

childminder (childminding) See child-minder.

childproof If something is **childproof**, it is specially designed so children cannot harm it or be harmed by it.

children's home A **children's home** is a place where children live when their parents cannot look after them properly.

chili See chilli.

chill (chilling, chillingly; chilly, chillier, chilliest) ❑ If you **chill** something, you lower its temperature without freezing it. ...*a chilled beer*. ◇ If something like the weather is **chill** or **chilly**, it is cold and unpleasant. When it is cold in a place, you can talk about the **chill** there.

❑ If something like a piece of news **chills** you or gives you a **chill**, it makes you frightened or anxious. ...*a chilling thought... ...a chillingly cold-blooded plan.*

❑ If the relationship between two countries or people **chills** or becomes **chilly**, it becomes less friendly. You can talk about a **chill** developing in a relationship. ◇ If the response to something you do is **chilly**, it is not friendly, welcoming, or enthusiastic. You can also say someone who behaves like this is **chilly**.

❑ A **chill** is a mild illness which can give you a slight fever and headache.

chilli (chillies) (*or* chili, chilies) **Chillies** are the small red or green seed pods of a pepper plant. They have a hot spicy taste and are used for flavouring food.

chime (chiming, chimed) ❑ When bells or clocks **chime**, they make a series of deep ringing sounds. You can talk about the **chime** of a bell or clock.

❑ If something new **chimes with** something which already exists, it fits in well with it.

chimera (*pron:* **kime-meer-a**) A **chimera** is an unrealistic idea, or a hope which is unlikely to be fulfilled. ◇ In Greek mythology, a **chimera** was a fire-breathing monster with the head of a lion, the body of a goat, and the tail of a serpent.

chimney A **chimney** is a hollow structure above a fireplace or furnace, for letting the smoke out.

chimney breast In a room, a **chimney breast** is a projecting part of a wall, built round a chimney.

chimney pot A **chimney pot** is a short pipe on top of a chimney stack, for letting the smoke out.

chimney stack A **chimney stack** is the brick or stone part of a chimney on the roof of a building.

chimney sweep A **chimney sweep** is someone whose job it is to clean the soot out of chimneys.

chimp Chimpanzees are sometimes called **chimps**.

chimpanzee Chimpanzees are small intelligent African apes with black or brown fur and large ears.

chin A person's **chin** is the part of their face below their mouth and above their neck. ◇ If something unpleasant happens to you and you **take it on the chin**, you accept it bravely and without complaining.

china China clay is a soft white clay used to make things like cups and plates. Cups and plates made of china clay are called **china.**

chinchilla The **chinchilla** is a South American rodent with soft grey fur.

Chinese is used to talk about things to do with China or its people. *...the Chinese authorities.* ◇ **Chinese** is any of the main languages spoken in China, for example Mandarin or Cantonese. ◇ The **Chinese** are the people who live in or come from China.

chink A **chink** is a very narrow opening. ◇ A **chink** of light is a thin ray of light. ◇ If someone has a **chink in their armour,** they have a small but dangerous weakness which makes it easy for people to attack or hurt them, especially emotionally.

chinless If you call someone **chinless,** you mean they are weak and rather cowardly.

chino (*pron:* chee-noh) (chinos) **Chino** is a hardwearing cotton twill fabric. ◇ **Chinos** are trousers made out of chino.

chintz (chintzy) **Chintz** is a shiny cotton fabric with bright patterns on it. It is used for making curtains or covering chairs and cushions. **Chintzy** things are covered in chintz, or look like chintz.

chip (chipping, chipped) ❑ **Chips** are thin pieces of deep-fried potato. ◇ In the US and Canada, **chips** are potato crisps.

❑ A **chip** or **silicone chip** is a very small piece of silicone with electric circuits on it. Chips are used in computers. They can hold large quantities of information or perform mathematical or logical operations.

❑ If something **chips** or is **chipped,** a small piece of it is broken off. **Chips** or **chippings** are small pieces broken off something. ◇ If someone **chips away** at something like a system, they keep removing small parts of it, gradually making it weaker.

❑ If someone has a **chip on their shoulder,** they behave rudely and aggressively, because they feel they have been treated unfairly. ◇ If you say someone is a **chip off the old block,** you mean they are like one of their parents in their character or behaviour.

❑ **Chips** are counters used in gambling to represent a certain amount of money. ◇ You say **when the chips are down** when you are discussing how people will behave in a serious situation when there is a lot at stake, which may be very different from the way they behave normally. *The heats gave little indication of what will happen when the chips are down in the final.* ◇ **bargaining chip:** see **bargain.**

❑ When people **chip in,** they contribute money towards something. ◇ If someone **chips in** during a conversation, they interrupt it.

❑ In sports like golf or football, if a player **chips** the ball, he or she makes it go high in the air and land a short distance away. A shot like this is called a **chip.**

chipboard is a hard material made out of wood chips pressed together. It is used as a cheap substitute for wood in making doors and furniture.

chipmunk The **chipmunk** is a small North American animal which looks like a squirrel with a striped back.

chipolata A **chipolata** is a small sausage.

chiropody (chiropodist) **Chiropody** (*pron:* kir-rop-pod-y) is the professional care and treatment of people's feet by a qualified person called a **chiropodist.**

chiropractic (chiropractor) **Chiropractic** (*pron:* kire-oh-prak-tik) is a system of treating things like back injuries by manipulating the spine with short fast jerks. A person who does this is called a **chiropractor.**

chirp When a bird or insect **chirps** or **chirrups,** it makes short high-pitched sounds.

chirpy A **chirpy** person is cheerful and lively.

chirrup See chirp.

chisel (chiselling, chiselled) (*American spelling:* chiseling, chiseled) ❑ A **chisel** is a tool for cutting and shaping wood or stone. It has a long metal blade with a sharp straight edge at the tip. ◇ If you **chisel** wood or stone, you cut and shape it with a chisel.

❑ If you say someone has **chiselled** features, you mean their features are sharply defined.

chit A **chit** is a short official note such as a receipt, order, or memo, usually signed by someone in authority.

chit-chat is informal talk about things which are not very important.

chitty (chitties) A **chitty** is the same as a chit.

chivalrous (*pron:* shiv-val-russ) (chivalry) **Chivalrous** people are polite, kind, and unselfish. You call behaviour like this **chivalry,** especially when you are talking about a man's behaviour to a woman.

chives is a herb with long thin hollow leaves tasting of onions.

chivvy (chivvies, chivvying, chivvied) If you **chivvy** someone, you keep urging them to do something they do not want to do.

chlorine (chlorinated) **Chlorine** is a strong-smelling gas used to disinfect water and make cleaning products. ◇ **Chlorinated** water has had chlorine added to it, to disinfect it.

chloroform is a colourless liquid with a strong sweet smell. You can become unconscious if you breathe its vapour.

chlorophyll is a green substance in plants which lets them use the energy from sunlight to grow. See also **photosynthesize.**

choc-ice A **choc-ice** is a small block of ice cream covered in chocolate.

chock ❑ A **chock** is a block or wedge used to stop a heavy object moving.

❑ If a place is **chock-a-block,** it is very full. ◇ If something is **chock-full** of things, it is very full of them.

chocolate is a sweet hard food made from cocoa beans. ◇ **Chocolates** are sweets or nuts covered with chocolate. ◇ **Hot chocolate** or **drinking chocolate** is a hot drink made from a powder containing chocolate.

❑ **Chocolate** or **chocolate brown** is a dark brown colour.

chocolate-box is used to describe scenery or pictures which are pretty in a rather conventional way. *...chocolate-box timbered houses.*

choice (choicest) ❑ You say there is a **choice** when there are at least two people or things you can choose from. Your **choice** is the person or thing you choose. ◇ The place or thing **of your choice** is one you choose for yourself, rather than having it chosen for you. ◇ If you have **no choice** but to do something, you cannot avoid doing it. You can also say someone has **little choice** but to do something.

❑ **Choice** things are of specially high quality. ...*the choicest pubs*.

choir A **choir** is a group of people who sing together. ◇ In a church or cathedral, the **choir** is the area in front of the altar where the choir sits.

choirboy A **choirboy** is a boy who sings in a church choir.

choirgirl A **choirgirl** is a girl who sings in a church choir.

choirmaster A **choirmaster** is a person whose job is to train a choir.

choirstall In a church, the **choirstalls** are the benches where the choir sits.

choke (choking, choked) ❑ If you **choke** or something **chokes** you, you cannot breathe properly because something is blocking your windpipe. ◇ If someone **chokes** someone else, they squeeze their neck until they are dead.

❑ If something like a system **chokes** on something or is **choked** by it, it is prevented from working properly because of it. *Financial systems, especially in America, are choking on bad debts*. ◇ If something **chokes** something else **off**, it stops it happening.

❑ If a place is **choked** with people or things, it is full of them and nothing can move.

❑ If you are **choked** about something, you are angry, upset, or disappointed.

❑ The **choke** in a car or other vehicle is a device which reduces the amount of air going into the engine, making it easier to start.

choker A **choker** is a necklace which fits very closely round a woman's neck.

cholera (*pron:* kol-ler-a) is a serious and often fatal disease affecting the small intestine. It is usually caught by drinking infected water. The symptoms are severe diarrhoea and often vomiting.

choleric (*pron:* kol-ler-rik) A **choleric** person is angry or bad-tempered.

cholesterol (*pron:* kol-lest-er-oll) is a substance in the tissues and blood of all animals. Too much cholesterol in your blood can cause heart disease.

chomp If a person or animal **chomps** their food, they chew it noisily.

choose (choosing, chose, have chosen) ❑ If you **choose** something or someone, you decide which one you want from a range of things or people. ...*their chosen profession*. ◇ If there is **little to choose between** things or **not much to choose between** them, it is difficult to decide which is best.

❑ If you talk about the **chosen few**, you mean a group of people who are special or important in some way.

❑ If you **choose** to do something, you do it because you want to or feel it is right.

choosy A **choosy** person will only accept something if it is exactly right or of very high quality.

chop (chopping, chopped) ❑ If you **chop** something, you cut it by hitting it with a sharp tool like an axe. ◇ If you **chop** food, you cut it into small pieces. Similarly, if you **chop** something **up**, you cut or divide it into small pieces. ◇ If you **chop down** a tree, you cut through its trunk with an axe and it falls to the ground.

❑ If something is **for the chop**, it is going to be stopped or closed down. ◇ If a person gets **the chop**, they lose their job.

❑ If people **chop and change**, they keep changing their minds about what to do or how to act.

❑ A **chop** is a small piece of meat cut from the ribs of a sheep or pig.

chopper A **chopper** is (a) an axe. (b) a helicopter.

chopping block If someone has their **head on the chopping block**, they are at risk in some way, for example in danger of losing their job.

chopping board A **chopping board** is a board you cut meat and vegetables on.

choppy When water is **choppy**, there are a lot of small waves on it.

chopsticks are a pair of thin sticks used by people in the Far East for eating their food.

choral music is written to be sung by a choir.

chorale (*pron:* kor-rahl) A **chorale** is a slow stately hymn tune.

chord (*pron:* kord) A **chord** is three or more different musical notes played or sung at the same time, producing a pleasing or satisfying effect. ◇ If something **strikes a chord** with you, you respond to it with feelings of sympathy and understanding.

chore A **chore** is a boring or unpleasant task which has to be done.

choreograph (choreography, choreographer, choreographic) ❑ If someone **choreographs** (*pron:* kor-ee-o-grafs) a ballet or other dance, they invent the steps and movements and tell the dancers how to perform them. Inventing dance movements like this is called **choreography** (*pron:* kor-ee-og-raf-ee); a person who does it is called a **choreographer**. **Choreographic** (*pron:* kor-ee-o-graf-ik) is used to talk about things to do with choreography. ...*her choreographic work*.

❑ When something looks spontaneous but has actually been carefully planned, you can say it is **choreographed**.

chorister (*rhymes with 'forester'*) A **chorister** is a singer in a church choir.

chortle (chortling, chortled) If you **chortle**, you laugh with pleasure or amusement.

chorus (choruses, chorusing, chorused) ❑ A **chorus** is a large group of people who sing together. ...*the City of Birmingham Symphony Orchestra and Chorus*. ◇ In a show, the **chorus** are the people who sing or dance in a group, rather than the soloists. ...*members of the show's chorus line*.

❑ A **chorus** is also a piece of music written to be sung by a large group of people. ...*the Hallelujah Chorus*. ◇ The **chorus** of a song is the part repeated after each verse.

❑ **Chorus** is used to talk about something expressed by a lot of people at the same time. For example, you can talk about a **chorus** of agreement or disapproval. ...*a chorus of boos, jeers and laughter*. ◇ A **chorus** of people is a group of them all demanding a particular thing. ◇ If a group of people **chorus** something, they all say it at the same time.

chorus girl A **chorus girl** is a young woman who sings and dances in the chorus of a show or film.

chose (chosen) See **choose**.

chow The **chow** is a thick-coated dog with a curled tail, originally from China.

Christ See **Jesus**.

christen (christening, christened) When a baby is **christened**, it is given Christian names during the Christian ceremony of baptism. The ceremony is called a **christening**. ◇ If you **christen** a place or thing, you choose a name for it and start calling it by that name.

Christendom is all the Christian people and countries in the world.

Christian (Christianity) A **Christian** is someone who believes in Jesus Christ and follows his teachings. The religion based on Jesus and his teachings is called **Christianity**. ◇ **Christian** is used to describe things connected with Christianity. ...*a Christian tradition*.

Christian name A person's **Christian names** are the names they are given when they are born or when they are christened. See also **first name**.

Christian Science (Christian Scientist) **Christian Science** is a church and religious system which emphasizes religious healing. People who belong to this church are called **Christian Scientists**.

Christmas (Christmases) **Christmas** is the Christian festival celebrating the birth of Jesus Christ.

Christmas Day is December 25th, when Christmas is celebrated.

Christmas Eve is December 24th.

Christmas pudding A **Christmas pudding** is a special round pudding eaten at Christmas, made of dried fruit, spices, and suet.

Christmas tree A **Christmas tree** is a fir tree, or an artificial tree which looks like a fir tree. People have Christmas trees in their houses at Christmas, and put decorations on them.

chrome is metal plated with chromium.

chromium is a hard shiny metallic element used to make steel alloys and to coat other metals.

chromosome A **chromosome** is part of an animal or plant cell containing genes which determine what the animal or plant will look like.

chronic (chronically) A **chronic** illness lasts for a very long time. Someone who is **chronically** ill has been ill for a long time. ◇ You call someone's bad habits or behaviour **chronic** when they have behaved like that for a long time and do not seem able to stop. ...*a chronic worrier*. ◇ A **chronic** situation is very severe and unpleasant. ...*a chronically weak export sector*.

chronicle (chronicling, chronicled; chronicler) A **chronicle** is a formal account or record of a series of happenings. ◇ If you **chronicle** things, you write about them in the order in which they happen; you say you are the **chronicler** of these things.

chronological (chronologically; chronology) If you describe a series of events in **chronological** order, you describe them in the order in which they happen. You also say you describe them **chronologically**. A **chronology** of past events is a list of them in the order in which they happened, giving their times or dates.

chrysalis (chrysalises) A **chrysalis** is a butterfly or moth in the stage between a larva and a fully grown adult. A chrysalis has a hard protective covering, and does not move.

chrysanthemum Chrysanthemums are flowers with a lot of long thin petals.

chub The **chub** is a freshwater fish of the carp family.

chubby (chubbier, chubbiest) A **chubby** person is rather fat.

chuck If you **chuck** something somewhere, you throw it there. ◇ If you **chuck** something **away** or **chuck** it **out**, you throw it away. ◇ If you **chuck** a person **out** of a job or place, you force them to leave. ◇ If you **chuck in** your job or some other activity, you stop doing it.

chuckle (chuckling, chuckled) If you **chuckle** or give a **chuckle**, you laugh quietly.

chuff (chuffed) If smoke **chuffs** from somewhere like a chimney, it comes out with a puffing sound. ◇ If you are **chuffed** about something, you are very pleased about it.

chug (chugging, chugged) If a vehicle **chugs** somewhere, it moves along slowly, with its engine making short thudding sounds. ◇ If an activity **chugs along**, it takes place quietly, without anything dramatic happening.

chum (chummy; chumminess) Someone's **chums** are their friends. If someone is **chummy**, they are friendly. **Chumminess** is friendship.

chunk (chunky) A **chunk** of something solid is a large piece of it. ◇ A **chunk** is also a large amount or part of something. ...*a big chunk of my mortgage*. ◇ A **chunky** person or thing is large and heavy.

Chunnel The **Chunnel** is the Channel Tunnel.

chunter (chuntering, chuntered) You can say someone is **chuntering** when they are grumbling about something. ◇ If a vehicle or machine **chunters**, it makes a regular throbbing sound. *Police helicopters chuntered overhead*.

church (churches) A **church** is a building where Christians worship. **Church** is used to talk about the services held in a church. *Going to church was often the only way people could show their opposition to Communism*. ◇ A **Church** is one of the groups of people within the Christian religion, for example Catholics or Methodists, who have their own beliefs, clergy, and form of worship. ◇ The **Church** is the people who have authority in a Church and who decide what its doctrines are. ...*the Church's drive to re-establish its influence in public life*.

Church of England The **Church of England** is the main church in England. It is a Protestant church, and belongs to the Anglican Communion. Its head is the king or queen. 'Church of England' is often shortened to 'C of E'.

churchgoer A **churchgoer** is someone who goes to church regularly.

churchman (churchmen) A **churchman** is the same as a clergyman.

churchwarden A **churchwarden** is someone chosen by a church congregation to help the priest with administration and other duties.

churchyard A **churchyard** is an area of land around a church, where dead people are buried.

churlish people are unfriendly, bad-tempered, and rude.

churn ❑ A **churn** is a container for milk, or one in which milk or cream is made into butter.
  ❑ If something **churns** mud or water or **churns** it **up**, it moves it about violently. ◇ If your stomach **churns**, you feel sick, because you are frightened or have seen something unpleasant. ...*stomach-churning atrocities*.
  ❑ If something like a factory **churns** things **out**, it produces them in large numbers.

chute A **chute** is a steep narrow slope for people or

things to slide down. ◇ A **chute** is also a parachute.

chutney is a relish made from fruit, vinegar, sugar, and spices.

chutzpah If someone behaves with **chutzpah**, they do things in a cheerful confident way, showing no respect for anyone.

CIA The **CIA** is a US government agency which tries to get secret information about the political and military activities of individuals or governments in other countries. CIA is short for 'Central Intelligence Agency'.

cicada (*pron*: sik-kah-da) **Cicadas** are large insects which live in hot countries. They make a loud high-pitched noise.

CID The **CID** is the detective branch of the British police force. CID is short for 'Criminal Investigation Department'.

cider is an alcoholic drink made from fermented apples.

cigar **Cigars** are rolls of dried tobacco leaves which people smoke.

cigarette **Cigarettes** are small tubes of paper with tobacco inside which people smoke.

cigarette end A **cigarette end** is what is left of a cigarette after it has been smoked.

cigarette holder A **cigarette holder** is a narrow tube for smoking a cigarette through.

cigarette lighter A **cigarette lighter** is a device which produces a small flame for lighting a cigarette or cigar.

cigarette paper A **cigarette paper** is a thin piece of paper which you put tobacco on and roll into a tube to make a cigarette.

cinch (*pron*: sinch) If you say something is **a cinch**, you mean it is very easy to do.

cinder **Cinders** are the powdery material left after wood or coal has burned. ◇ A **cinder track** is a running track covered with cinders.

Cinderella If you say something is a **Cinderella**, you mean it is neglected and does not receive any attention. *The Chiltern line, once the Cinderella of London commuting lines, now glides along in super turbos.*

cine camera (*pron*: sin-ee) A **cine camera** is a camera which takes moving film rather than still photographs.

cine film is the film which is wound on a spool for use in a cine camera.

cinema (cinematic) A **cinema** is a place where people go to watch films. ◇ **Cinema** is the business and art of making films. **Cinematic** is used to talk about things to do with films made for the cinema. *...India's highest cinematic award.*

cinemagoer A **cinemagoer** is someone who goes to the cinema regularly.

cinematography (cinematographer) **Cinematography** is the technique of photographing films. A **cinematographer** is the person in charge of the photography and lighting when a film is being made.

cinnamon is a spice taken from the bark of a tree. It is used for flavouring sweet food.

cipher (*or* cypher) A **cipher** is a secret system of writing, used for sending messages which can only be understood by someone who knows the system. ◇ If you say a person is a **cipher**, you mean they have no real power, and are used by other people for their own purposes.

circa is used in front of a number representing a year to give an approximate date. 'Circa' is often shortened to 'c.' *...an emerald and diamond ring circa 1910.*

circle (circling, circled) ❑ A **circle** is a two-dimensional, perfectly symmetrical round shape. Every part of its edge is the same distance from its centre. ◇ A **circle** of people or things is a group of them arranged in the shape of a ring or circle. ◇ If one thing is **circled** by another, the second thing is arranged in a circle around the first. *The Westfalen Stadion is circled by a running track.*
❑ If a bird or aircraft **circles**, it flies in a circle. ◇ If you **circle** something on a piece of paper, you draw a circle round it.
❑ If you are **going around in circles**, you are not achieving anything because you keep coming back to the same point or problem. ◇ **full circle**: see **full**.
❑ A **circle** of people or friends is a group of them who meet regularly.
❑ In a theatre or cinema, the **circle** is an area of seats on an upper floor.

circlet A **circlet** is a decorated band of precious metal worn around a person's head, especially in the past.

circuit (circuitry) ❑ An electrical **circuit** is a complete route which an electric current can flow around. **Circuitry** is a system of electronic circuits.
❑ A **circuit** is also a series of places visited regularly by a person or group for a particular purpose, for example to play a sport. *...the most promising young players on the international circuit.* ◇ A **circuit** is also a journey all the way around a place or area. *He is near the end of a 500-mile circuit of the Ulster Way.* ◇ A racing **circuit** is a track on which cars or motorbikes race.

circuit breaker A **circuit breaker** is a device which can stop the flow of electricity around a circuit by switching itself off if anything goes wrong.

circuitous (*pron*: sir-kew-it-uss) If you go somewhere by a **circuitous** route, you go by a long indirect route rather than the direct one.

circular (circularity) ❑ **Circular** things are shaped like a circle. ◇ If you make a **circular** journey, you go somewhere and return by a different route.
❑ A **circular** argument is not valid because it uses a statement to prove the conclusion and the conclusion to prove the statement. You talk about the **circularity** of an argument like this.
❑ A **circular** is a letter or advertisement sent to a large number of people at the same time.

circulate (circulating, circulated; circulation, circulatory) ❑ If a piece of writing **circulates** or is **circulated**, copies are passed round among a group of people. ◇ If a joke or rumour **circulates** or is **circulated**, people tell it to each other. ◇ The **circulation** of a newspaper or magazine is the number of copies sold each time it is produced.
❑ If a substance **circulates**, it moves around within a closed place or system. *...immune cells circulating in the blood.* ◇ A person's **circulation** is the movement of blood around their body. **Circulatory** (*pron*: sir-kew-late-torree) is used to talk about things to do with the circulation of the blood. *...the body's circulatory system.*
❑ When money **circulates** or is in **circulation**, it is in use by the public.

circumcise (circumcising, circumcised; circumcision) If a man is **circumcised,** the loose skin is cut off the end of his penis for religious or medical reasons. If a woman is **circumcised,** part or all of her clitoris is removed; the entrance to her vagina may also be sewn together. Circumcision is an operation in which someone's genitals are cut in one of these ways.

circumference The **circumference** of a circle, place, or round object is its outer edge, or the distance around this edge.

circumflex The **circumflex** is a symbol sometimes written over 'a', 'e', 'i', 'o', or 'u' in French and some other languages. If a letter has a circumflex over it, it is usually pronounced as a longer sound than usual. *He voted in his home town of Château Chinon.*

circumlocution A **circumlocution** is a way of saying or writing something which uses more words than are necessary.

circumnavigate (circumnavigating, circumnavigated; circumnavigation) If you **circumnavigate** something, you sail right round it. Sailing round something once is called a **circumnavigation.**

circumscribe (circumscribing, circumscribed) If something like a person's power is **circumscribed,** it is limited.

circumspect (circumspection) If someone is **circumspect,** they are cautious and avoid taking risks. **Circumspection** is cautious behaviour.

circumstance ❑ **Circumstances** are the conditions in which something happens or is done. *The referee did a reasonable job in difficult circumstances.* When it is not clear how something happened, people talk about the **circumstances** in which it happened. *Some detainees have died in mysterious circumstances.*

❑ You say **in the circumstances** or **under the circumstances** to show you have considered everything affecting a situation. *In the circumstances, Rolls-Royce might have been forgiven for postponing the launch of its new model.* ◇ You can emphasize that something will not take place by saying it will not take place **under any circumstances.** Similarly, you can warn someone not to do something **under any circumstances.**

❑ A person's **circumstances** are the conditions of their life, for example the amount of money they have or the sort of home they live in. *She had been brought up in hard circumstances.*

❑ **Circumstance** is things which happen which have not been planned and cannot be controlled. *This looks like a government driven by circumstance rather than design.*

circumstantial evidence suggests strongly that something happened, but does not prove it.

circumvent (circumvention) If someone **circumvents** a rule or restriction, they get round it in a clever and perhaps dishonest way. *America won't countenance any circumvention of the sanctions.*

circus (circuses) A **circus** is a travelling show performed in a large tent, with clowns, acrobats, and animals. ◇ If you call something like a meeting a **circus,** you mean it is put on to attract attention or impress people, rather than to achieve anything.

cirrhosis (*pron:* sir-roh-siss) is a serious disease which affects the liver. It is often caused by drinking too much alcohol.

cirrus is a type of thin cloud very high in the sky.

cissy (cissies) See **sissy.**

cistern A **cistern** is a container which holds water, for example to flush a toilet or to store a building's water supply.

citadel A **citadel** is a strongly fortified building in a city.

cite (citing, cited; citation) ❑ If you **cite** something, you quote or mention it as an example or proof of what you are saying. *Every family can cite a tragedy caused by drink.* ◇ A **citation** from a book or piece of writing is a quotation from it.

❑ If someone is **cited** in a legal case, they are officially required to appear in court.

❑ A **citation** is an official document or speech praising a person for something brave or special they have done.

citizen (citizenship; citizenry) If someone is a **citizen** of a country or has **citizenship** of it, they are legally accepted as belonging to it. ◇ The **citizens** of a town are the people who live there; they can also be called its **citizenry.** ◇ **Citizenship** is regarding yourself as belonging to a community and being prepared to contribute something towards it, for example by helping other people who belong to it.

Citizens Advice Bureau The Citizens Advice Bureau or C.A.B. is a voluntary organization which gives people free advice, often on legal or financial problems.

Citizens' Band See **CB.**

citric acid is a weak acid found in many kinds of fruit, especially citrus fruits like oranges and lemons.

citrus fruits are juicy sharp-tasting fruit like oranges, lemons, limes, and grapefruit.

city (cities) A **city** is a large town. In Britain, a city usually has a bishop and a cathedral. ◇ The **City** is the part of London where many banks and other financial institutions have their main offices. The **City** is often used to talk about the views and reactions of people who work in the City. *The City is expecting disappointing profits next month.*

civic (civics) **Civic** is used to talk about people or things with an official or important status in a town or city. *...civic and business leaders.* ◇ **Civic** is also used to describe people's duties, rights, or feelings as members of a community. *...civic pride.* ◇ **Civics** is the study of the way central and local government works, and of the rights and duties of citizens.

civil (civility) ❑ **Civil** is used to talk about the ordinary people of a country as distinct from the armed forces, and about non-military organizations and activities. *...a fast developing civil airline business.*

❑ If someone is **civil,** they are polite, but not very friendly; you call their behaviour **civility.**

civil defence is the organization and training of ordinary people so they can help the armed forces, fire service, and police force if their country is attacked by an enemy.

civil disobedience If there is a campaign of **civil disobedience,** a group of people refuse to obey some of their country's laws, as a way of getting a law changed which they think is wrong or discriminatory.

civil engineering (civil engineer) **Civil engineering** is the planning, design, and construction of roads, bridges, harbours, and public buildings. A qualified person who does this kind of work is called a **civil engineer**.

civil law is the part of a country's set of laws concerned with the private affairs of citizens. It deals with things like marriage and property ownership. See also **criminal law**.

civil liberties are the rights people have in many countries to do and say what they like, provided they do not interfere with other people's rights.

civil list The civil list is the money voted by parliament for the support of the royal household and certain members of the royal family.

civil marriage A civil marriage is a non-religious marriage ceremony performed by a government official.

civil rights are rights to such things as equal treatment and equal opportunities, regardless of a person's race, sex, or religion.

Civil Service (civil servant) A country's Civil Service is its government departments and the people who work in them. A person who works in the Civil Service is called a civil servant.

civil war A civil war is fought between groups of people living in the same country.

civilian A civilian is anyone who is not a member of the armed forces.

civilize (civilizing, civilized; civilization) (*can be spelled with an 's' instead of a 'z'*) ❏ A **civilized** country or society is one with a highly developed culture and social system. Having a culture and social system like this is called **civilization**; places which have these things are called **civilizations**. When a place is **civilized**, it acquires a culture and social system.

❏ **Civilized** behaviour is polite and reasonable. ◇ You say a way of doing things is **civilized** when it is well-arranged for people's comfort or convenience. *Lunch at Hockney's is a civilized affair.*

civvies are ordinary clothes which are not part of a uniform.

clack If something **clacks**, it makes a short loud sound, like the sound of two flat pieces of wood being struck together. A sound like this is called a **clack**.

clad (cladding, clad *not 'cladded'*) ❏ If you are **clad** in particular clothes, you are wearing them. You can add **-clad** to a word to describe what someone is wearing. *...denim-clad plainclothes policemen.*

❏ When people **clad** a building, they cover the exterior with tiles, wooden boards, or other materials, to protect it against bad weather or to make it look more attractive. This covering is called **cladding**. You can say a building is **clad** with particular materials.

❏ If an area is **clad** with trees, it is covered with them.

claim (claiming, claimed; claimant) ❏ If someone **claims** something, they say it is true or a fact, although they might not be able to prove it and other people might not believe them. A statement like this is called a **claim**. ◇ If someone **claims** responsibility or credit for an action or achievement, they say they were responsible or deserve the credit, even though they might not be able to prove it.

❏ If you **claim** something of value like property, land, or money or **lay claim** to it, you say it legally belongs to you. You can **claim** other things you think you have a right to. *The republics are claiming the right to run their own*

affairs. ◇ If you **claim** money from someone like the government or an insurance company, you officially apply for it, because you think you are entitled to it; your application is called a **claim**. ◇ If you **claim** something like money from your employers, you officially ask for it because you think you deserve it. Demanding money like this is called a **claim**. *...pay claims.* ◇ A **claimant** is a person who asks to be given something they think they are entitled to.

❏ If you have a **claim** on someone, you have the right to demand things from them.

❏ If something like a war **claims** someone's life, they are killed by it or in it.

clairvoyance (clairvoyant) **Clairvoyance** is the ability some people claim to have to see into the future or communicate with dead people. A **clairvoyant** is someone who claims to have this ability.

clam (clamming, clammed) **Clams** are a kind of shellfish. They have soft edible bodies and a shell in two parts which can close very tightly. ◇ If someone **clams up**, they refuse to talk about something.

clamber (clambering, clambered) If you **clamber** somewhere, you climb there with difficulty.

clammy things are unpleasantly damp and sticky.

clamour (clamouring, clamoured; clamorous) (*American spelling:* clamor, clamoring, clamored) If people **clamour** for something, they demand it noisily or angrily. You can talk about people's **clamour** for something. ◇ If people are talking or shouting together loudly, you can say they are making a **clamour**. **Clamorous** people or voices are very noisy.

clamp ❏ A **clamp** is a device for holding two things together firmly. If you **clamp** one thing to another, you fasten them together with a clamp. ◇ If your car is **clamped**, a device is fitted to one of its wheels to stop you driving away until you have paid a fee to have it removed. ◇ If you **clamp** something somewhere, you put or hold it there firmly. *The animal clamped its jaws on his left hand.*

❏ When people in power **clamp down** on something, they stop it or restrict it. You call their action a **clampdown** or **clamp-down**. ◇ If a restriction is **clamped** on a place, it is imposed on it.

clampdown See **clamp**.

clan A **clan** is a group of families, especially in Scotland, related to each other because they are all descended from the same person.

clandestine (clandestinely) **Clandestine** things are hidden or secret. *Others arrive clandestinely by boat.*

clang When large metal objects **clang**, they make a loud deep noise by banging against each other or something else. A noise like this is called a **clang**.

clanger If you **drop a clanger**, you do or say something embarrassing which you regret afterwards.

clank When metal objects **clank**, they make a loud noise by banging against each other or something else.

clap (clapping, clapped) ❏ When you **clap**, you hit your hands together to show appreciation of someone or something. ◇ If you **clap** someone on the back or shoulder, you hit them with your hand in a friendly way. ◇ If you **clap** an object somewhere, you put it there quickly and firmly.

❏ A **clap** of thunder is a sudden loud burst of it.

clapboard consists of long narrow pieces of wood fixed onto the roof or outside walls of a house to protect it from the weather. Clapboard is used especially in the US.

clapped-out If you say a vehicle or machine is **clapped-out**, you mean it is old and no longer works properly. Businesses and factories are also sometimes called **clapped-out**.

clapper The **clapper** on a bell is the small piece of loose metal which beats against the side, making the bell sound.

clapperboard A **clapperboard** is a device used by people making films to help them match the pictures and sound. It is made of two pieces of wood connected by a hinge with the scene number written on it. The clapperboard is banged together just before a scene.

claptrap If you call what someone says **claptrap**, you mean it is stupid or silly.

claque A **claque** is a group of people who all admire, support, and flatter someone in a position of power.

claret is a French dry red wine.

clarify (clarifies, clarifying, clarified; clarification) ❑ If you **clarify** something, you make it easier to understand. *What we are asking for is a clarification of the current laws.*
    ❑ **Clarified** butter has been heated to remove impurities from it.

clarinet (clarinettist) A **clarinet** is a woodwind instrument with a single reed in its mouthpiece. A person who plays the clarinet is called a **clarinettist**.

clarion A **clarion** call is a strong emotional appeal to people to do something.

clarity If you talk about the **clarity** of something like a statement, you mean it is easy to understand. ◇ **Clarity** of thought is the ability to think clearly. *Matisse's clarity of mind was such that he could lucidly explain even his maddest notions.* ◇ **Clarity** is also used to talk about things being easy to see or hear. *The telescope will show us our Universe as we've never seen it before, with wonderful sharpness and clarity.*

clash (clashes, clashing, clashed) ❑ If there is a **clash** between people or if they **clash**, they fight, argue, or disagree with each other. ◇ In sport, when people who are equally matched compete against each other, you can say they **clash**; you can also talk about a **clash** between them. ◇ If there is a **clash** of beliefs, ideas, or systems or if they **clash**, they contradict each other. *...clashing legal systems.*
    ❑ If two events **clash**, they happen at the same time, so you cannot go to both. You can talk about a **clash** of events. ◇ If colours or styles **clash**, they do not look good together.
    ❑ A **clash** is a loud noise made by metal objects being hit together.

clasp If you **clasp** someone or something, you hold them tightly in your hands or arms. ◇ A **clasp** is a small device for fastening something or holding it shut. *...a belt clasp.*

class (classes, classing, classed) ❑ A **class** is a group of pupils being taught together. If something is done **in class**, it is done during lessons. ◇ A **class** is also a short period of teaching given regularly in a subject. *...an aerobics class.* ◇ The students of a school or university who start

or finish their course in a the same year are often called the **class** of that year. *...the class of 1990.*
    ❑ **Class** is used to talk about the division of people in society according to their social status. *...the professional classes... The elections have shown up the deep divisions of class and outlook.*
    ❑ A **class** of things is a group of them with similar characteristics. *...a class of molecules known as prostaglandins.* If someone or something is **classed** as a particular thing, they are considered as belonging to that group of things.
    ❑ **-class** is added to words like 'first' and 'second' to talk about things of a particular standard. *...first- and business-class fares.* ◇ In Britain, university degrees are graded into classes. *...a first class honours degree.* ◇ If you say someone or something is **in a class of their own,** you mean they are much better than other people or things of their kind.

classic (classicist) ❑ A **classic** example of something has all the features you expect that kind of thing to have. *It was a classic case of turning a hobby into a business.*
    ❑ A **classic** is a well-known book or play of a high literary standard. Well-known pieces of classical music are also called **classics**. ◇ A **classic** film or piece of writing is of high quality and has become a standard against which similar things are judged. *...his classic book on economic management.*
    ❑ **Classic** clothes are simple but elegant, and never go out of fashion. ◇ **Classic** cars are cars which are no longer made, but are still admired and collected.
    ❑ **Classics** is the study of ancient Greek and Roman civilizations, especially their languages, literature, and philosophy. Someone who studies these things is called a **classicist** (*pron:* **klass**-iss-sist).

classical (classically) ❑ **Classical** is used to describe things which are traditional in form, style, or content. *...classical ballet.*
    ❑ **Classical** music is music written by composers like Bach, Schubert, Verdi, and Sibelius. *...a classically trained pianist.*
    ❑ **Classical** is also used to talk about (a) things connected with ancient Greek and Roman civilization. *...classical Greek sculptures.* (b) architecture which imitates Greek or Roman buildings.

classicism (*pron:* **klass**-iss-iz-um) is a style of art and architecture which has simple regular forms and in which the artist does not try to express strong emotions. It is associated especially with the 18th century in Europe.

classify (classifies, classifying, classified; classification) ❑ If you **classify** people and things, you divide them into groups so that those with similar characteristics are in the same group. *A thick rule book governs classification.* A **classification** is a system of dividing people or things into groups.
    ❑ **Classified** advertisements are small advertisements placed in newspapers and magazines by people wanting to buy or sell things.
    ❑ **Classified** information is kept secret by a government and only a few people are allowed to see it.

classless (classlessness) When people talk about a **classless** society, they mean one where everyone has the same social and economic status. *...a move towards classlessness.* ◇ A **classless** person is one who does not belong to any particular social class.

classmate The **classmates** of someone attending a school are other students in the same class.

classroom A **classroom** is a room in a school where lessons take place. **In the classroom** is used to talk about things to do with teaching and lessons. *...the increase of pupil violence in the classroom.* ◇ A **classroom teacher** is one who spends most of his or her time teaching, rather than doing administrative duties like a head teacher.

classy (classier, classiest) **Classy** people or things are stylish and sophisticated.

clatter (clattering, clattered) If something **clatters** or makes a **clatter**, it makes a series of short loud noises.

clause A **clause** is a section of a legal document. ◇ In grammar, a **clause** is a group of words containing a verb. For example, in the sentence 'When he saw me, he smiled' 'saw' and 'smiled' are verbs, and 'when he saw me' and 'he smiled' are clauses. 'He smiled' is called a **main clause**.

claustrophobia (claustrophobic) **Claustrophobia** is a fear of being in small or enclosed places. Someone who has this fear is called a **claustrophobic**. ◇ If you call a place or situation **claustrophobic**, you mean it makes you feel restricted, unhappy, or nervous.

clavichord (*pron*: klav-vi-kord) A **clavichord** is an instrument similar to a small piano, in which wires are hit by pieces of metal when the keys are pressed. Clavichords were especially popular before the piano was invented.

clavicle The **clavicle** is the same as the collarbone.

claw ❑ The **claws** of a bird or animal are the thin curved nails on its feet. ◇ The **claws** of a lobster, crab, or scorpion are the two pointed parts at the end of its legs, which it uses for grasping things. ◇ If an animal **claws** something, it scratches or damages it with its claws.

❑ If you **claw back** money which you have given away or which has been taken from you, you get it back using whatever methods are available. Getting back money like this is called a **clawback**. ◇ If you **claw yourself back** or **claw your way back**, you get back into a favourable position after being in great difficulties.

clawback See **claw**.

clay is a substance found in the ground which is soft when wet and hard when dry. It is used to make things like pots. ◇ **feet of clay**: see **foot**.

clay pigeon A **clay pigeon** is a baked clay disc used as a shooting target. It is thrown into the air by a machine.

clean (cleaner, cleanest; cleaning, cleaned; cleanly) ❑ If something is **clean**, it is free from dirt and unwanted marks. If you **clean** something, you make it clean, for example by washing it. ◇ If you **clean up** something which has become dirty, you make it clean again. An operation like this can be called a **clean-up**. ◇ If you **clean up** something which has been spilled, you get rid of it. ◇ If you **clean out** something like an animal's cage, you clean it thoroughly.

❑ You say people or animals are **clean** when they keep themselves or their surroundings clean. ◇ If something like air or water is **clean**, it is free from germs, impurities, or other harmful substances. *...a clean environment.* You also say products or processes are **clean** when they do not produce harmful substances. *Rape seed oil may provide a clean fuel... Alternative ways to burn coal more cleanly are*

being developed.

❑ If a game or contest is **clean**, it is played fairly and according to the rules. ◇ If someone has a **clean** record or reputation, they are not known to have committed a crime or to have done anything dishonest. Similarly, you can say someone's hands are **clean**. ◇ If the police or other authorities **clean up** a place or activity, they make it free from crime or other unacceptable activities. ◇ If you **come clean** about something you have been keeping secret, you admit it or tell people about it.

❑ **Clean** is used to say something happens completely or thoroughly. *Australia blasted South Africa clean out of the match.* ◇ If you make a **clean** break with something, you end your connection with it completely.

❑ If a place like a shop is **cleaned out**, everything of value is bought or stolen. Similarly, you can say a person is **cleaned out** if they lose all their money or possessions.

❑ A **clean** movement is skilful and accurate. *...clean and elegant strokes... He jumped neatly and cleanly.*

clean-cut A **clean-cut** man looks neat and tidy.

clean-shaven A **clean-shaven** man has no beard or moustache.

cleaner A **cleaner** is someone paid to clean the inside of a building. Other people who clean things for a living have **cleaner** as part of the name of their job. *...street cleaners.* ◇ A **cleaner** is also (a) a substance for cleaning things. *...household cleaners.* (b) a machine or device for cleaning. *...a vacuum cleaner.* ◇ If someone is **taken to the cleaners**, they end up losing all their money or possessions. *They know that, if they get it wrong, they can be taken to the cleaners in the courts.*

cleanliness (*pron*: klen-lee-ness) **Cleanliness** is the habit of keeping yourself and your surroundings clean. ◇ **Cleanliness** is also used to talk about how clean things are. *Many of Britain's beaches fail to meet minimum standards of cleanliness.*

cleanse (cleansing, cleansed; cleanser) If you **cleanse** something, you make it clean. A **cleanser** is a liquid for cleaning something, for example a person's face. ◇ If someone **cleanses** something like an organization, they get rid of the bad or corrupt elements in it. You can also say people **cleanse themselves** of evil things in their lives.

clear (clearing, cleared; clearly) ❑ If something is **clear**, it is easy to understand. If you make something **clear**, you express yourself in a way which leaves no doubt about what you mean. *We've set out clearly what we think they ought to do.* ◇ If you understand something **clearly**, you understand it properly, and are not muddled or confused about it. *...a clearer understanding of the issue.* ◇ If you **clear up** a problem, disagreement, or misunderstanding, you settle it or resolve it. ◇ **clear the air**: see **air**.

❑ If you say it is **clear** that something is true, you mean it is obviously true. *Much of the attraction is clearly due to the low prices of goods.* ◇ If you are **clear** about something, you are convinced of it. ◇ **Clear** is used to describe things which leave people in no doubt about something. *...a clear choice... We had no clear evidence on which we could act.*

❑ **Clear** is used to say something is easy to see or hear. *The company's logo was clearly visible.* ◇ If your view of something is **clear**, it is not blocked or obstructed. ◇ If the weather is **clear**, there is no rain, mist, or cloud. ◇ If bad weather or smoke **clears,** it gradually disappears. ◇ **Clear** water or air is clean and free from impurities.

❑ A **clear** substance is one you can see through. ◇ A **clear** voice or sound has a pure quality, with no roughness or harshness.

❑ If your mind is **clear,** you are able to think sensibly and logically. *He was not thinking clearly at the time.* ◇ If your conscience is **clear,** you have nothing to feel guilty about.

❑ If you **clear** a surface or area, you remove the things or people blocking it; you then say it is **clear.** ◇ If you **clear** something **away,** you remove it. ◇ If people are **cleared out** of a place or building, they are forced to leave. ◇ If a building is **cleared,** it is evacuated. ◇ **clear the way:** see **way.**

❑ If an illness **clears up,** it gets better and finally disappears.

❑ If you **clear up,** you tidy things or put them away in their correct places. ◇ If you **clear out** a cupboard, room, or house, you clean it, tidy it, and throw away things you do not want; you call this having a **clear-out.** Similarly, you can talk about someone **clearing** people out of an organization or having a **clear-out.** *There needs to be a general clear-out of the old guard.*

❑ If you **clear** something like an amount of work, you deal with it and get it out of the way. ◇ **clear the decks:** see **deck.**

❑ If someone or something **clears** a fence, wall, or hedge, they jump or pass over it without touching it. ◇ In show jumping, if a competitor has a **clear** round, he or she jumps over all the fences without knocking any down.

❑ If something is **clear** of something else, no part of it is on it or touching it. *The tractor towed a truck clear of the highway.* ◇ In sport, if one competitor is **clear** of another, they are well ahead. *Purvis won in 23min 05sec, 22 seconds clear of the former champion.* ◇ If you **steer clear** or **stay clear** of something, you avoid it.

❑ If someone in authority **clears** something like a plan or course of action, they say it can go ahead. ◇ When a cheque is **cleared,** it goes through the banking system and is accepted for payment.

❑ If a crime is **cleared up,** it is solved. ◇ If someone is **cleared** of a crime or mistake, they are proved to be not guilty of it. ◇ If you **clear your name,** you establish that you are not guilty of something, and your good reputation is restored.

❑ If you **clear** your throat, you make a sound like a quiet cough, usually because you are preparing to speak or trying to attract someone's attention.

clear-cut things are straightforward and easy to understand.

clear-headed A **clear-headed** person is sensible and thinks clearly in difficult situations.

clear-out See **clear.**

clear-sighted A **clear-sighted** person is good at weighing up people and situations, and can make sensible judgements and decisions.

clearance is used to talk about the removal of old or unwanted buildings, trees, or other things from an area. *The job of mine detection and clearance is a massive one.* ◇ If a shop holds a **clearance sale,** its goods are sold at reduced prices, because the shopkeeper wants to make room for new stock.

❑ If you are given **clearance** to do something, you get official permission. If a plane, ship, or person is given **clearance,** they are given official permission to enter or leave an airport, harbour, or country.

❑ In games like football and hockey, if a defender makes a **clearance,** he or she sends the ball to a position where there is no danger of the other team scoring a goal.

clearing See **clear.** ◇ A **clearing** is a small area of grass or bare ground in a wood.

clearing house A **clearing house** is an organization which collects, sorts, and distributes information used by a number of similar organizations. ◇ A **clearing house** is also a central bank which deals with all the transactions between the banks which use its services, for example exchanging cheques.

clearway A **clearway** is a road on which vehicles are not allowed to stop or park.

cleavage ❑ A woman's **cleavage** is the space between her breasts, especially the top part you see when she is wearing a low-cut dress.

❑ A **cleavage** between people is a division or disagreement between them.

cleave (cleaving, cleaved) (*'clove' is sometimes used instead of 'cleaved' and ' have cleft' instead of 'have cleaved'*) If you **cleave** something, you split it in two.

cleaver A **cleaver** is a knife with a large square blade for chopping meat or vegetables.

clef A **clef** is a symbol at the beginning of a line of music showing the range of notes. There are several clefs, the most common being the treble clef for high notes, and the bass clef for low notes.

cleft See **cleave.** ◇ If someone has a **cleft palate,** they were born with a narrow opening along the roof of their mouth, making it difficult for them to speak properly. ◇ A **cleft lip** is the same as a harelip.

clematis (*pron:* **klem**-mat-tiss *or* klem-**mate**-iss) is a climbing plant with purple, pink, or white flowers.

clemency If someone is shown **clemency,** they receive kind and merciful treatment from a person who has the authority to punish them.

clementine A **clementine** is a small citrus fruit similar to a tangerine.

clench (clenches, clenching, clenched) If you **clench** your fist, you curl your fingers up tightly. ◇ If you **clench** your teeth, you squeeze them together firmly.

clergy The **clergy** are the religious leaders of a Christian church. ◇ Leaders of other churches are sometimes called **clergy.** *...Buddhist clergy.*

clergyman (clergymen) A **clergyman** is a male member of the clergy.

clergywoman (clergywomen) A **clergywoman** is a female member of the clergy.

cleric A **cleric** is a member of the clergy.

clerical is used to talk about things to do with the clergy. *...Mexico's strict anti-clerical laws.* ◇ **Clerical** is also used to talk about routine office jobs and the people who do them. *...clerical staff.*

clerk A **clerk** is someone who works in an office, bank, or law court and looks after things like records or accounts. ◇ In the US, a **clerk** is also a sales assistant in a shop or large store.

clever (cleverer, cleverest; cleverly, cleverness) A **clever** person is intelligent, and can learn and understand things easily. *He has a high reputation for cleverness and honesty.* ◇ If someone is **clever** at something which requires skill or expertise, they are good at it. *...clever accountants... ...a cleverly judged performance.* ◇ You also say someone is **clever** when they are good at handling people and situations, especially to their own advantage. A person like this is sometimes said to be **too clever by half.** ◇ If you say something is **clever,** you mean it is skilfully done or made, and very effective. *...a clever compromise... The exhibition is cleverly lit.*

cliché (*pron:* klee-shay) (clichéd) A **cliché** is a phrase or idea which has been used so much it no longer has any real effect. You can say something like a novel which is full of clichés is **clichéd.**

click If something **clicks,** it makes a short sharp sound. A sound like this is called a **click.**

client A **client** of a professional person or organization is someone they are providing a service for.

clientele (*pron:* klee-on-tell) The **clientele** of a place or business are its customers or clients.

cliff A **cliff** is a place where the land falls away suddenly and very steeply, often down to the sea. The steep part is called the **cliff face.**

cliff-hanger (cliff-hanging) (*or* cliffhanger, cliffhanging) If you call a situation a **cliffhanger,** you mean it is very exciting, because you are left for a long time not knowing what is going to happen. **Cliff-hanging** is used to describe situations like this.

clifftop A **clifftop** is the top part of a cliff.

climactic is used to describe a very exciting or important moment in something like an event or piece of music. *...the climactic chorale of Mahler's Fifth Symphony.* You can also describe a situation or work which includes a moment like this as **climactic.** *...a climactic championship.*

climate (climatic) ❏ The **climate** of a place is the weather conditions there over a long period. **Climatic** is used to talk about things to do with a place's climate. *...climatic changes.*
❏ **Climate** is used to talk about some aspect of the general situation in a place. You can talk, for example, about the political climate there.

climatologist A **climatologist** is someone who studies climates.

climax (climaxes) The **climax** of an experience or series of happenings is the most exciting or important part, usually near the end. You can say something **climaxes** with a particular happening. *...a tightly organised event, climaxing with a sit-down meal for the entire neighbourhood.* You can also talk about the **climax** of a book, play, or piece of music. ◇ A **climax** is also an orgasm.

climb (climber) ❏ If you **climb** something like a tree, ladder, or mountain, you move towards the top, often with some effort or difficulty. If you **climb down** something, you move towards the bottom. Climbing something can be called a **climb.** *Another cottage was noticed during the climb back up the lane.* ◇ **Climbing** is the sport of climbing mountains; a person who does it is called a **climber.** A **climb** is a route up a mountain. *...two demanding climbs of Holme Moss.* ◇ If you **climb** over or through something, you get over or through it with

difficulty.
❏ If something like a road **climbs,** it moves gradually towards a higher position. ◇ A **climber** or **climbing** plant is one which grows upwards, attaching itself to other plants or objects.
❏ If something like the cost of living **climbs,** it rises; you call this rise a **climb.**
❏ If you **climb down** in an argument or dispute, you admit you are wrong, or agree to accept less than you were insisting on. Doing this is called a **climbdown.**

climbing frame A **climbing frame** is a structure of metal or wooden bars for children to play on.

clime is used to talk about a place with a particular type of climate. *...the sunnier climes of Southern France.*

clinch (clinches, clinching; clincher) If you **clinch** something like a victory or business deal, you succeed in getting it. ◇ If something uncertain or doubtful is **clinched,** it is settled in a definite way. *...the clinching evidence.* ◇ A **clincher** is something which finally settles a disagreement or argument, or decides something which had been uncertain.

cling (clinging, clung, have clung) ❏ If you **cling** to someone or something, you hold onto them tightly. ◇ If a building or village is built on the side of a mountain, you can say it **clings** to it. ◇ **Clinging** clothes fit tightly around the body.
❏ If you **cling** to something which is very important to you, you are very unwilling to give it up. ◇ If you **cling** to a belief, you go on thinking it is correct, though there are good reasons for thinking it might be wrong. ◇ If someone **clings on** in a race or contest, they just succeed in preventing someone else beating them.

clingfilm (*or* cling film) is a thin transparent plastic material for wrapping things in.

clinic A **clinic** is a place where people go to get medical treatment or advice.

clinical (clinically, clinician) ❏ **Clinical** is used to talk about the direct medical treatment of patients, as opposed to research done in a laboratory. *The company has completed some clinical trials of the product... The next stage is to test it clinically.* ◇ **Clinical** is also used to describe a doctor, psychologist, or psychiatrist who deals with patients, as opposed to doing theoretical research. *...a clinical neurologist.* A person like this can also be called a **clinician.**
❏ **Clinical** thought or behaviour is very logical and unemotional. ◇ If you call something like a room or building **clinical,** you mean it is very plain, or too neat and clean, so people do not enjoy being in it.

clink If glass or metal objects **clink,** they touch each other and make a short light sound. ◇ If you **clink** glasses with someone, you touch their glass with yours before drinking.

clip (clipping, clipped) ❏ A **clip** of a film or TV programme is a short piece shown by itself.
❏ If you **clip** something like hair, you cut small pieces from it. **Clipped** hair is neatly trimmed. ◇ A **clipping** is an advertisement, article, or picture cut from a newspaper or magazine.
❏ If you **clip** a small amount off something, you reduce it by that amount. *She clipped seven-hundredths of a second of her previous best time.*
❏ If you **clip** someone's **wings,** you restrict their free-

dom to do what they want.

❏ A **clip** is a small metal or plastic device for holding things together. If you **clip** one thing to another, you fasten it with a clip.

❏ If you **clip** someone or give them a **clip**, you hit them lightly with your hand or fist. You can also **clip** an object with part of your body, especially accidentally. *He was denied the silver medal when he clipped the bar with his heels.*

❏ If someone has a **clipped** way of speaking, their speech comes out as a series of short quick sounds.

clipboard A **clipboard** is a board with a clip at the top for holding together pieces of paper and providing a firm base to write on.

clipper **Clippers** are a tool for cutting small amounts from something, for example someone's hair or nails, or a hedge. ◇ In the past, a **clipper** was a fast sailing ship.

clique (*pron:* kleek) A **clique** is a small group of people in a place or organization who spend a lot of time together and seem unfriendly towards other people.

clitoris (clitoral) A woman's **clitoris** is the small sensitive sexual organ above her vagina which, when touched, causes pleasant feelings that can lead to an orgasm. **Clitoral** is used to talk about things relating to the clitoris. *...clitoral enlargement.*

Cllr. in front of a person's name means 'Councillor'.

cloak (cloaking, cloaked) ❏ A **cloak** is a wide loose coat which fastens at the throat and does not have sleeves.

❏ If one thing **cloaks** another, it hides it. Something which is intended to hide the truth can be called a **cloak**. *Secrecy must not be used as a cloak for anything a security service does.* ◇ If something is **cloaked** with something else, it is covered with it.

cloak-and-dagger A **cloak-and-dagger** situation or activity involves a lot of mystery and secrecy.

cloakroom The **cloakroom** in a public building is a place where you can leave your coat. ◇ The toilets in a public building are also sometimes called the **cloakrooms**.

clobber (clobbering, clobbered) If you are **clobbered** by something, you come off badly as a result of it. *Owners clobbered by compulsory purchase orders can expect extra compensation.*

cloche (*pron:* klosh) A **cloche** is a long low plastic or glass cover, put over young plants to protect them from the cold. ◇ The **cloche** hat was a close-fitting woman's hat worn in the 1920s and 1930s.

clock ❏ A **clock** is an instrument which tells you the time. ◇ The **24-hour clock** is a system of telling the time, used especially in timetables. Each hour of the day is given as a number between 00 and 23, and the minutes are given as numbers after the hour. For example, 5.15am in this system is 0515, and 7.30pm is 1930.

❏ If something is done **round the clock**, it goes on all day and night, without stopping. ◇ If you do something **against the clock**, you do it very quickly, to meet a deadline. ◇ If you say someone wants to **turn the clock back**, you mean they want to return to ideas or situations of the past and ignore the changes that have taken place since.

❏ In athletics, if someone **clocks** a particular time, they are recorded as having run a race in that time. Similarly, a racing driver can be **clocked** at a particular speed.

❏ A **clock** or **time clock** is a device which makes things happen automatically at particular times. ◇ The **clock** in a vehicle is an instrument which shows the distance it has travelled.

❏ When workers **clock in** or **clock on** at a factory or office, they record the time they arrive, by putting a special card into a machine. Similarly, when they finish work, they **clock out**.

❏ If you **clock up** a number or total, you reach it. *Japanese motorists clock up an average of 8,000 kilometres a year.*

clock tower A **clock tower** is a tower with a clock, either part of a building or standing on its own.

clock-watcher If you say someone is a **clock-watcher**, you mean they are always looking at the clock while they are at work, because they are waiting for a break or the end of the day.

clockwise If something moves in a **clockwise** direction, it moves in a circle in the same direction as the hands on a clock.

clockwork is machinery in some toys or models which makes them move or work when they are wound up with a key. ◇ If something happens **like clockwork**, it happens without problems or delays.

clod A **clod** is large lump of earth.

clog (clogging, clogged) ❏ If something **clogs** something else or **clogs** it **up**, it blocks it up, so it no longer works properly. *...clogged arteries.*

❏ **Clogs** are leather or wooden shoes with thick wooden soles and heels.

cloister (cloistered) A **cloister** is a covered paved area around an open square, usually in a monastery or next to a cathedral. The side of the cloister facing the square is open, and the roof there is supported by pillars. ◇ If someone leads a **cloistered** life, they live quietly and have little contact with other people or the outside world.

clone (cloning, cloned) If an animal, plant, or substance has been **cloned**, it has been produced naturally or artificially from the cells of another animal, plant, or substance, and is identical to the original one. Something produced like this is called a **clone**. ◇ If you call a person or thing a **clone**, you mean they look or behave like a well-known person or thing. *...an Elizabeth Taylor clone.*

close (closing, closed; closer, closest; closely, closeness) ❏ If you **close** (*pron:* klohz) a door, window, or lid, you move it so it fills or covers the opening it is designed to fit.

❏ When something like a shop or public building **closes**, work or business stops for a short time, or until the next working day.

❏ If someone in authority **closes** something like a road, border, or airport, they block it off so nobody can use it. ◇ If an area is **closed off**, people are prevented from getting in and out.

❏ If a factory, business, or public building **closes** or **closes down**, all work stops there, usually forever. When this happens, you say there is a **closedown**.

❏ If you **close** a bank account, you take all the money out and say you will not be using the account any more.

❏ A **closed** group of people is one which other people are not normally admitted to. *Recently Polish-American society has become less closed.*

❏ If an activity **closes** or comes to a **close**, it finishes. *...the closing ceremony... ...the close of the party conference.*

◇ If something finishes gradually, you can say it **draws to a close**. *The Uruguay round of trade talks is struggling to an unpredictable close.* ◇ When something like a share **closes** at a particular value, it has that value at the end of the day's trading.

❏ If the police **close** a case, they stop investigating it. ◇ If you **close** a deal with someone, you agree on the form it will take.

❏ If something is done **behind closed doors**, it is done in secret. *...closed-door meetings.*

❏ If people **close in** on someone or something, they gradually come nearer to them and surround them.

❏ When the nights **close in**, it gets dark earlier at night.

❏ If you say something is a **closed book** to you, you mean you know nothing about it. ◇ **close your eyes to** something: see **eye**. ◇ **close the door to** something: see **door**.

❏ If something is **close** (*pron:* klohss) to something else, it is only a short distance from it. If something is only a short distance from where you are, you can say it is **close by** or **close at hand**. ◇ If you see something from **close quarters**, you are near to it when you see it. ◇ If you look at something **close up**, you get very near to it to look at it. ◇ If soldiers fire at something from **close range**, they are quite near to it when they fire. Similarly, you can say a footballer scores a goal from **close range**.

❏ People who are **close** to each other are fond of each other and understand each other's feelings. *...one of her closest friends.* ◇ Your **close** relatives are the members of your family most directly related to you, for example your mother or sister. ◇ **Closely** related animals or plants belong to the same family of animals or plants and are similar to one another.

❏ **Close** is used to emphasize the extent to which people are involved in something together. *...a close adviser... The two men had worked together closely.* ◇ If you are in **close** contact with someone, you see them, speak to them, or write to them often.

❏ If one thing is **closely** connected with another, there are many connections between them.

❏ **Close** inspection or observation of something is careful, thorough, and often detailed. ◇ If you keep **a close eye** or **close watch** on something, you make sure you know how it is developing or progressing. If you keep a **close eye** or a **close watch** on a person, you make sure you know what they are doing. ◇ If someone or something is **closely** guarded, they are guarded very carefully.

❏ A **close** or **close-run** game or contest is won by only a small margin.

❏ If something people want or expect is **close**, it will happen soon. You can also say people are **close to** something. *We are very close to peace.*

❏ If you say there has been a **close shave**, you mean an accident or disaster very nearly happened.

❏ If there is a **close** resemblance between two things or people, they are very like each other. ◇ If you say something is the **closest thing** to a particular type of thing, you mean it is the thing most like it. *...Gyles Brandreth, the closest thing the House has to a stand-up comedian.* ◇ If something **comes close** to something else, it is very like it. ◇ **Close to** an amount means nearly that amount.

❏ If the atmosphere or weather is **close**, it is uncomfortably warm, and there is not enough fresh air.

close-cropped hair or grass has been cut very short.

close-fitting clothes fit tightly and show the shape of the body.

close-knit (*or* closely-knit) A **close-knit** group of people are closely linked and share similar beliefs or interests.

close season (*pron:* klohss) In hunting, fishing, and shooting, the **close season** is the time of the year when you are not allowed to kill certain birds, animals, or fish. ◇ In football and some other sports, the **close season** is the time of the year when the sport is not played by professional clubs.

close-up A **close-up** is a photograph or film taken very near to a subject and showing a lot of detail.

closed circuit A **closed circuit** is a complete electrical circuit, which electricity can flow right round. ◇ **Closed-circuit television** is a TV system used inside buildings, for example to film customers in a shop so thieves can be identified. The cameras used are called **closed-circuit cameras**.

closed-door See **close**.

closed shop If you say a place of employment is a **closed shop**, you mean the employees have to belong to a particular trade union.

closedown See **close**.

closely-knit See **close-knit**.

closet (closeted) ❏ **Closet** is the usual American word for a cupboard. ◇ **Closet** is used to describe people who have beliefs, habits, or feelings which they keep private and secret, often because they are embarrassed about them. *...closet homosexuals.* If someone decides to tell people about their beliefs, habits, or feelings, you can say they **come out of the closet**.

❏ If you are **closeted** somewhere, you are away from other people, because you want to be alone or to talk privately to someone.

closing time is the time when places like pubs and banks shut, and people have to leave.

closure When a business is permanently shut down, this is called a **closure**. *...large-scale pit closures.* ◇ If something causes the **closure** of something like a road or airport, it causes it to be closed, usually temporarily.

clot (clotting, clotted) When blood or another liquid **clots**, it dries and becomes thick, forming a lump. The lump is called a **clot**.

cloth is fabric made by weaving, knitting, or some similar process. A **cloth** is a piece of cloth used for a particular purpose, like cleaning. ◇ If you say someone is **cutting their coat according to their cloth**, you mean they are trying not to do more than they have the money, power, or ability to do.

❏ People sometimes use **the cloth** to talk about the Christian clergy. *...a man of the cloth.*

clothe (clothing, clothed) If you are **clothed** in something, you are dressed in it. You can add **-clothed** to a word to say what sort of clothes someone is wearing. *...poorly-clothed guards.* ◇ If you **clothe** someone, you provide them with clothes.

clothes are the things people wear.

clothes horse A **clothes horse** is a folding framework for hanging wet washing on inside a house.

clothes line A **clothes line** is a rope hung between two places for hanging washing on.

clothes peg A **clothes peg** is a wooden or plastic clip for attaching washing to a clothes line.

clothing is the clothes people wear. ...*protective clothing.*

clotted cream is very thick cream made by heating milk gently, cooling it, then taking the cream from the top. It is made and eaten mainly in South West England.

cloud (clouding, clouded; cloudy, cloudier) ❑ A **cloud** is a mass of water vapour floating in the sky. ◇ If the sky **clouds over**, it becomes covered with clouds. If there are a lot of clouds, you say it is **cloudy**. ◇ A **cloud** of smoke or dust is a mass of it floating in the air.
   ❑ If a liquid is **cloudy**, it is less clear than it should be.
   ❑ If one thing **clouds** another, it makes it difficult to understand. ◇ **Cloudy** is sometimes used to describe things which are confused or uncertain. *However cloudy the future of the TUC, the modernization of trade unionism may yet restore the movement's fortunes.*
   ❑ If something **clouds** a situation or event, it makes it less successful or enjoyable. ◇ If you talk about something being under a **cloud**, you mean something unpleasant is likely to happen. *The issue cast a cloud of tension over the summit.*

cloud-cuckoo-land If you say someone is living in **cloud-cuckoo-land**, you mean they have an unrealistic idea of what life is like, and think everything will happen exactly as they want.

cloudburst A **cloudburst** is a sudden heavy fall of rain.

cloudless A **cloudless** sky has no clouds in it.

clout (clouting, clouted) ❑ If someone has **clout**, they have influence and power.
   ❑ If you **clout** someone or something, you hit them.

clove ❑ **Cloves** are small strong-smelling dried flower buds from a tropical tree. They are used as a spice. ◇ A **clove** of garlic is one of the small sections of a garlic bulb.
   ❑ See also **cleave**.

clover is a small plant with pink or white ball-shaped flowers and three leaves at the end of each stem. ◇ If you say someone is **in clover**, you mean they are living a luxurious comfortable life.

clown (clowning) A **clown** is a performer who wears funny clothes and bright make-up, and does silly things to make people laugh. ◇ If you **clown around**, you do silly things. This sort of behaviour is called **clowning**. ◇ If you call someone a **clown**, you mean they behave in a silly way and you cannot take them seriously.

cloying (cloyingly) If something is **cloying**, it is unpleasant because it is too sweet or sickly, or too sentimental. *The Republicans will be at least as cloyingly patriotic as the Democrats.*

club (clubbing, clubbed; clubber) ❑ A **club** is (a) an organization for people with the same hobby or interest. ...*a vintage car club.* (b) an organization with its own premises where elected members go to drink, eat, or read. ◇ A sports **club** is an organization of people, including players and coaches, who form teams to compete against other clubs. ◇ A **club** is also a place where members of a club meet.
   ❑ A nightclub can be called a **club**. **Clubbing** is used to talk about going to nightclubs; someone who does this regularly is called a **clubber**.
   ❑ If people **club together**, they all give money to share

the cost of something.
   ❑ A **club** is a thick heavy stick used as a weapon. ◇ If you **club** someone, you hit them with something blunt and heavy. ◇ A **club** or **golf club** is a long thin stick with a curved end for hitting a golf ball.
   ❑ **Clubs** is one of the four suits in a pack of playing cards. All cards in this suit have the symbol ♣ on them.

clubhouse A **clubhouse** is the place where members of a sports club meet.

clubland is used to talk about the nightclubs in an area, and the people who go to them. ...*the latest music style to hit clubland.*

cluck When a hen **clucks**, it makes a short repeated sound in its throat. ◇ If a person **clucks**, they say things in an anxious or excited way.

clue A **clue** is a piece of information or something you notice which helps you solve a problem. ◇ When the police are investigating a crime, a **clue** is an object or piece of information which helps them discover who did it. ◇ A **clue** is also a short piece of writing in a puzzle or game which tells you what you need to know to work out the answer. ◇ If someone **hasn't got a clue**, they have no idea what the answer to a question is, or no idea how to do something.

clued-up If you say someone is **clued-up**, you mean they have a lot of detailed knowledge and information about something.

clueless If you say someone is **clueless**, you mean they are stupid and incapable of doing anything properly.

clump ❑ A **clump** of things like plants is a small group of them. ...*clumps of white tulips.*
   ❑ If someone **clumps** about, they walk with heavy clumsy footsteps.

clumsy (clumsier, clumsiest; clumsily, clumsiness) A **clumsy** person moves or handles things in an awkward way. ◇ **Clumsy** things are badly designed or made, and awkward to use. ◇ If something is done in a **clumsy** way, it is done carelessly, tactlessly, or with little thought for the best way of doing it. *The company reacted clumsily to union resistance... A certain amount of slackness and clumsiness has permeated the security provisions at Brixton.*

clung See **cling**.

clunk A **clunk** is the sort of sound you get when two heavy objects hit against each other.

cluster (clustering, clustered) A **cluster** of people or things is a small group of them close together. ◇ If people or things **cluster** somewhere or **cluster** together, they gather together or are found together in small groups.

cluster bomb A **cluster bomb** is a type of bomb dropped from an aircraft which scatters a lot of smaller bombs as it falls.

clutch (clutches, clutching, clutched) ❑ If you **clutch** something, you hold it tightly. If you **clutch at** something, you move your hand quickly to take hold of it. ◇ If you are in someone's **clutches**, they have power or control over you. ◇ **clutch at straws**: see **straw**.
   ❑ A **clutch** of people or things is a small group of them.
   ❑ The **clutch** in a car or other vehicle is the mechanism which disconnects the power from the engine when you change gear. The pedal you press to control the mechanism is also called the **clutch**.

clutch bag A **clutch bag** is a handbag without a handle.

clutter (cluttering, cluttered) If things **clutter** a place or clutter it up, they fill it in an untidy way. ◇ **Clutter** is a lot of things arranged in an untidy way, especially things which are not useful or necessary.

cm See centimetre.

CND is a British organization which opposes the development and use of nuclear weapons. CND is short for 'Campaign for Nuclear Disarmament'.

Co is short for 'company' in the names of companies. *...European Credit Co Ltd.*

co- is used to form words which say someone does something jointly with someone else, rather than on their own. *...the co-chairman of the Geneva conference.*

co-author When people write a book together, you say they are its **co-authors**.

co-defendant A **co-defendant** in a court case is one of two or more people accused of the same crime.

co-ed A **co-ed** school is the same as a co-educational one.

co-education (co-educational) **Co-education** is teaching girls and boys together in the same school. **Co-educational** is used to talk about things to do with this type of education. *...a co-educational environment.* A co-educational school is one attended by both sexes.

co-exist (co-existence) (or coexist, coexistence) If two or more things **co-exist**, they exist at the same time or in the same place. ◇ If countries with different political systems **co-exist**, they avoid quarrelling or interfering with each other. This kind of relationship is called **co-existence**.

co-habit See cohabit.

co-incide See coincide.

co-op A **co-op** is (a) a co-operative. (b) a co-operative society.

co-operate (co-operating, co-operated; co-operation) (or co-operate, etc) When people **co-operate**, they work together to try to achieve something. *He called for closer co-operation between the republics.* ◇ If you **co-operate** with someone who is trying to do something, you help them and do not make difficulties for them.

co-operative (or cooperative) (co-operatively) A **co-operative** is a business or organization owned by the people who run it; they also share its benefits and profits. ◇ **Co-operative** activities involve people working together. *They agreed to work co-operatively to ease tensions wherever possible.* ◇ You say someone is being **co-operative** when they are helpful and do not make difficulties for you.

co-operative society A **co-operative society** is a commercial organization which passes on its profits in some way to its customers.

co-opt If the members of a committee or other organization **co-opt** you, they vote to make you a member of their committee or organization. ◇ If you **co-opt** someone, you persuade them to help you or support you in what you are doing.

co-ordinate (co-ordinating, co-ordinated; co-ordination, co-ordinator) (or coordinate, etc) ❏ If you **co-ordinate** a project or activity, you organize the people taking part and make sure they work together properly. A person who does this is called a **co-ordinator**.
❏ If you cannot **co-ordinate** the movements of your body, you cannot get them to work together properly.

Cerebral palsy left him with little physical co-ordination.
❏ A **co-ordinate** is one of a pair of numbers or letters which give the location of a point on a map or graph.

co-pilot The **co-pilot** of a plane helps the chief pilot and sometimes flies the plane.

co-produce (co-producer) If two or more people **co-produce** something like a film, they organize it jointly and decide how it should be made; they are called the **co-producers**.

co-star (co-starring, co-starred) If an actor or actress **co-stars** in a film or play, they star in it with someone else; you say they are the other person's **co-star**.

co-write (co-writer) If two or more people **co-write** something like a book or piece of music, they create it together; they are called its **co-writers**.

coach (coaches, coaching, coached) ❏ A **coach** is a bus which carries passengers on long journeys. A **coach station** is a building or area where coaches arrive and leave on regular journeys. ◇ A **coach** is also an enclosed four-wheeled vehicle pulled by horses. ◇ A **coach** on a train is one of the separate sections for passengers.
❏ If you **coach** someone, you help them to be better at a sport or subject. Someone who does this is called a **coach**.

coachload A **coachload** of people is a group of them who have just arrived somewhere by coach.

coachman (coachmen) In the past, a **coachman** was a man who drove a horse-drawn coach or carriage.

coachwork The **coachwork** of a car is its exterior.

coagulate (pron: koh-ag-yew-late) (coagulating, coagulated; coagulation) When a liquid like blood or paint **coagulates**, it becomes thick. This process is called **coagulation**.

coal is a hard black substance taken from under the ground and burned as fuel. Pieces of coal for burning on a fire are sometimes called **coals**.

coal-face (or coalface) The **coal-face** is the part of a mine where the coal is being cut.

coal gas is gas produced from coal. It is used especially for heating and cooking in people's homes. See also natural gas.

coal scuttle A **coal scuttle** is a kind of bucket for keeping coal in.

coal tar is a thick black liquid made from coal. It is used to make drugs and chemical products.

coalesce (pron: koh-a-less) (coalescing, coalesced) If things or people **coalesce**, they join together to form a larger system or group.

coalface See coal-face.

coalfield A **coalfield** is a region where there is coal under the ground.

coalition (pron: koh-a-lish-un) A **coalition** is a government made up of people from two or more political parties. ◇ A **coalition** is also a temporary alliance between two or more groups of people trying to achieve something together.

coalmining (coalmine, coalminer) **Coalmining** is the mining of coal. A place where coal is removed from under the ground is called a **coalmine**; the people who do the physical work are called **coalminers**.

coarse (coarser; coarsely, coarseness) You say something is coarse when it has a rough texture. ◇ A **coarse** person talks or behaves in a rude offensive way. You can also call the things they say **coarse.**

coarse fishing is the sport of catching freshwater fish other than trout or salmon. See also **fly-fishing.**

coarsen (coarsening, coarsened) If something **coarsens**, it becomes rougher in texture.

coast (coastal) ❑ A **coast** is a place where an area of land meets the sea. *...the east coast of Malaysia.* If something is **off the coast**, it is in the sea near to a coast. ◇ **Coastal** is used to describe things which are on or next to a coast, or connected in some way with a coast. *...coastal waters... ...coastal erosion.* ◇ If something happens **from coast to coast**, it happens in every part of a large country bordered by sea.

❑ If a vehicle is **coasting**, it is moving without being driven by its motor, or without being pushed or pedalled. ◇ If you are **coasting**, you are doing something without difficulty, worry, or effort.

coaster A **coaster** is a ship which sails along a coast, taking goods to the ports there. ◇ A **coaster** is also a mat you put underneath a glass or mug to protect the surface of a table.

coastguard The **coastguard** is an organization which gets out help to swimmers, sailors, and ships. The members of the coastguard are called **coastguards.**

coastline The **coastline** is the outline of a coast, especially as seen from the sea or the air.

coat (coating, coated) ❑ A **coat** is a piece of clothing with long sleeves worn over other clothes to keep you warm or protect you from bad weather. You can add -coated to a word to say what kind of coat someone is wearing. *...a duffle-coated train spotter.* ◇ **cut your coat according to your cloth**: see **cloth.** ◇ An animal's **coat** is its fur or hair.

❑ If you **coat** something with a substance, you cover it with a thin layer of it; the layer is called a **coat** or **coating.**

coat hanger A **coat hanger** is a curved piece of wood, metal, or plastic for hanging clothes on.

coat of arms (coats of arms) A **coat of arms** is a design in the form of a shield used as an emblem by a family, town, or organization.

coat-tails A man's **coat-tails** are the two long parts at the back of his dress coat. ◇ If someone **rides on your coat-tails** or **hangs onto your coat-tails**, they take advantage of something you have done, without making any real effort of their own.

coax (coaxes, coaxing, coaxed) If you **coax** someone, you gently try to persuade them to do something. ◇ If you **coax** information out of someone, you get it from them by being gentle and pleasant. ◇ If you **coax** a machine or device into doing something, you make it work by operating it slowly, gently, or carefully.

cob A **cob** is a small round loaf of bread.

cobalt is a hard silvery-white metal used in hardening steel and for producing a blue dye. ◇ **Cobalt** or **cobalt blue** is a deep greenish-blue.

cobble (cobbling, cobbled) **Cobbles** are cobblestones. A **cobbled** street has a surface made of cobblestones. ◇ If you **cobble** something **together**, you put it together quickly and roughly.

cobbler A **cobbler** is a person who mends or makes shoes for a living.

cobblestone **Cobblestones** are stones with a rounded upper surface. They used to be used for making roads.

COBOL is a computer language designed for general commercial use. COBOL stands for 'Common Business Oriented Language'.

cobra (*pron:* koh-bra) The **cobra** is a large poisonous snake in Africa and Asia. It makes the skin at the back of its head into a large hood when it is alarmed.

cobweb (cobwebbed) A **cobweb** is a spider's web, especially a dust-covered one in a house. **Cobwebbed** things are covered in cobwebs. ◇ If something **blows the cobwebs away**, it makes you feel alert and lively when you had previously been feeling tired. ◇ If something has been left unchanged for a long time, you can talk about the **cobwebs** on it. If someone then comes and changes things, you can say they **sweep away the cobwebs.**

Coca-Cola is a sweet brown non-alcoholic fizzy drink. 'Coca-Cola' is a trademark.

cocaine is a powerful addictive drug which some people take for pleasure and which can have dangerous side-effects. In most countries, it is illegal to take cocaine, but it is sometimes used by doctors as an anaesthetic.

coccyx (*pron:* kok-six) The **coccyx** is the small triangular bone at the lower end of the spine in humans and some apes.

cochineal is a red substance used for colouring food. It is obtained from a Mexican insect.

cochlea (*pron:* kok-lee-a) (*plural:* cochleae) The **cochlea** is a spiral tube in the inner ear, shaped like a snail's shell. It converts sound vibrations into nerve impulses.

cock ❑ A **cock** is an adult male chicken. ◇ A **cock** is also a male bird of any species. *...a cock pheasant.*

❑ If you **cock** an eyebrow, you raise it. ◇ If you **cock** your head, you lean it to one side. ◇ If you say someone's ear is **cocked**, you mean they are listening for something. ◇ **cock a snook**: see **snook.**

❑ If you **cock** a gun, you set the hammer so it is ready to fire.

cock-a-hoop If you are **cock-a-hoop**, you are very pleased about something you have done.

cock-and-bull A **cock-and-bull** story is an improbable or unbelievable one, especially one given as an excuse.

cock-eyed A **cock-eyed** idea is stupid and unlikely to succeed.

cock-up A **cock-up** is something which has been done very badly because of mistakes or stupidity.

cockatoo (cockatoos) The **cockatoo** is a parrot with a crest. It comes from Australia and New Guinea.

cockerel A **cockerel** is a young cock.

cockfight (cockfighting) A **cockfight** is a fight between two cocks with sharp pieces of metal fixed to their claws. People watch the fight for entertainment and to bet on it. Making cocks fight like this is called **cockfighting.** It is illegal in Britain.

cockle **Cockles** are small edible shellfish.

cockney (cockneys) A **cockney** is a person born in the East End of London. **Cockney** is the dialect and accent of this area. *...cockney rhyming slang.*

cockpit The **cockpit** of a racing car or small plane is the part where the driver or pilot sits.

cockroach (cockroaches) Cockroaches are large brown beetle-like insects. They are found especially in dirty rooms and in places where food is kept.

cocksure If you say someone is cocksure, you mean they are too confident and sure of their own abilities.

cocktail ❑ A cocktail is an alcoholic drink containing several ingredients, including a spirit. ◇ An unusual mixture of substances is sometimes called a cocktail. *Unless this toxic cocktail of chemicals, oils and metals is cleaned up, it will blight any development prospects.*

❑ Some kinds of food eaten as the first course of a meal are called cocktails, for example a shrimp cocktail or a grapefruit cocktail.

cocktail dress A cocktail dress is a woman's dress suitable for formal occasions. Cocktail dresses are usually short, rather than full-length.

cocky (cockily, cockiness) A cocky person is conceited and very self-confident. You can talk about the cockiness of someone like this. *He could not resist smiling cockily at the police as he left the court.*

cocoa is a brown powder made from the seeds of the cacao tree. It is used in making chocolate. ◇ Cocoa is also a hot drink made with cocoa powder and milk.

coconut ❑ A coconut is a large nut with a hard hairy shell; it has milky juice inside and white flesh. This flesh is called coconut; it is chopped into tiny pieces and used to flavour cakes and other food. ◇ A coconut shy is a stall at a fair where you throw balls at coconuts on stands. If you knock one off, you win a prize.

❑ Coconut matting is a kind of coarse straw-coloured matting made from the fibre on the outside of coconuts.

cocoon (cocooning, cocooned) A cocoon is a covering of silky threads made by the larvae of moths and other insects before they grow into adults. ◇ If someone is cocooned, they are protected from everyday life, or from something unpleasant. Something which protects someone like this can be called a cocoon.

cod (*plural:* cod) Cod are large edible sea fish found especially in the North Atlantic.

cod-liver oil is a thick yellow oil used as a medicine, because it is full of vitamins A and D.

coda (*pron:* kode-a) A coda is a small extra section added at the end of fairly long piece of music, to finish it off. A similar section at the end of a book or speech can be called a coda.

coddle (coddling, coddled) If you coddle someone, you treat them too kindly or generously, and protect them too much.

code (coding, coded) ❑ A code is a set of rules about how people should behave.

❑ If you code a message, you change it by replacing the letters and symbols with different ones, so people who do not know the code cannot understand it. A system like this is called a code.

❑ A code is also a group of numbers or letters which enable you to identify something. If you code something, you identify it using numbers or letters like these. *The cheque is sent to the bank's clearing centre where it is coded, sorted and credited to the customer's account.*

❑ Coded is used to talk about things said in a rather indirect way, often because it would be dangerous or embarrassing to express them more plainly.

code name (code-named) See codename.

code of practice (codes of practice) A code of practice is a set of written rules which explain how people in a particular profession should behave.

code word A code word is a word or phrase which has a special meaning for people who have agreed to use it that way.

codebreaker A codebreaker is someone who works out what codes mean, so that coded information can be understood.

codeine (*pron:* kode-een) is a drug used to relieve pain, especially headaches and cold symptoms.

codename (codenamed) (*or* code name, code-named) A codename is a name given to someone or something to keep their identity secret. If a police or military operation is codenamed in a particular way, it is known by a special name to the people involved in it.

codger Old men who have lost some of their physical and mental powers are sometimes called old codgers.

codicil (*pron:* kode-iss-ill) A codicil is an instruction added to a will after the main part has been written.

codify (codifies, codifying, codified; codification) If something like a group of laws is codified, it is organized into a proper system. *...a new codification of pension law.*

coerce (*pron:* koh-urss) (coercing, coerced; coercion, coercive) If people are coerced into doing something, they are made to do it. Forcing people to do something like this is called coercion. Coercive laws or powers are used to force people to do things they do not want to.

coeval (*pron:* koh-eev-al) Someone who is your coeval is the same age as you.

coexist (coexistence) See co-exist.

coffee is a substance made by roasting and grinding the beans of a tropical shrub; the shrub is also called coffee. ◇ Coffee is also a hot drink made by pouring boiling water onto ground coffee beans or instant coffee powder.

coffee bar A coffee bar is a small cafe where drinks and snacks are sold.

coffee break A coffee break is a short time, usually in the morning or afternoon, when people stop work and have a cup of coffee or tea.

coffee cup A coffee cup is a small cup you drink coffee from.

coffee grinder A coffee grinder is a machine you have in your house for grinding coffee beans.

coffee house A coffee house is a place where coffee and light meals are served, especially one which is a fashionable meeting place. Coffee houses are common in Central Europe, and were popular in 18th-century London.

coffee morning A coffee morning is a social event which takes place in the morning at someone's house. It is usually held to raise money for charity.

coffee pot A coffee pot is a tall narrow jug for making and serving coffee.

coffee shop A coffee shop is (a) a restaurant which sells tea, coffee, and light meals and snacks. (b) a shop which sells different kinds of ground coffee and coffee beans.

coffee table A coffee table is a small low table. ◇ A coffee-table book is a large expensive book with a lot of pictures. It is usually put where people can see it easily, and is designed to be looked at rather than read.

coffer A coffer is a large strong chest for storing valuable objects. ◇ When people talk about an organization's coffers, they mean the money it has to spend. *His critics say the money was syphoned from state coffers.*

coffin A coffin is a box in which the body of a dead person is buried or cremated. ◇ If you say that one thing is a nail in another thing's coffin, you mean it will help bring about its end or failure.

cog A cog is a small wheel with teeth around the edge, which connects with other wheels in a machine. ◇ If you say someone is a cog in the machine, you mean they have no importance or power, and are just a small part of a large organization.

cogent (*pron:* koh-jent) (cogently, cogency) A cogent reason, argument, or example is strong and convincing. You can talk about the cogency of something like this. *He spoke cogently and movingly against war.*

cognac (*pron:* kon-yak) is a kind of brandy made in south-western France.

cognisance See cognizance.

cognitive is used to talk about things to do with the process of learning. *...cognitive skills.*

cognizance (*or* cognisance) If you take cognizance of something, you take account of it when you are making decisions about what to do. *Policing is best tackled by professionals who take cognizance of public opinion and wishes.*

cognoscenti (*pron:* kon-yo-shen-ti) The cognoscenti are the people who know a lot about a subject. *...the football cognoscenti.*

cohabit (cohabiting, cohabited; cohabitation) (*or* co-habit, *etc*) If a man and a woman are cohabiting, they are living together and have a sexual relationship, but are not married. *...the trend towards cohabitation.* ◇ When politicians from different parties cohabit, they share power. ◇ When groups of people from different backgrounds cohabit, they live in the same area.

coherence If something someone says or does has coherence, it makes sense or is satisfying because all its parts fit together well and logically. ◇ If you talk about the coherence of a system, you are talking about the fact that it holds together, rather than falling apart. *Allowing children to sue their parents for divorce will further damage the coherence of the American family.*

coherent (coherently) If something is coherent, it is clear and easy to understand. *The World Bank did not respond coherently to the third world's debt burden.*

cohesion (cohesive) If something has cohesion, its parts fit together well and form a united whole. You say something like this is cohesive. *...a cohesive leadership.*

cohort A cohort is a group of people with something in common. *He faces a growing cohort of doubters at home.* ◇ In the Roman army, a cohort was a military unit. There were ten cohorts in a legion.

coiffed (coiffure) Coiffed (*pron:* kwaft) is used to talk about someone's hair, especially when it has been carefully styled. *...his neatly coiffed hair.* A person's coiffure (*pron:* kwa-fyoor) is their hairstyle.

coil (coiling, coiled) ❑ A coil of rope or wire is a length of it wound into a series of loops. ◇ If you coil something or coil it up, you wind it into a series of loops. ❑ A coil is a thick spiral of wire through which an electric current is passed, for example to make a magnetic field. ◇ In a petrol engine, the coil is the part which sends electricity to the spark plugs.
❑ See also IUD.

coin (coining, coined) ❑ A coin is a small piece of metal used as money. ◇ If you say things are two sides of the same coin, you mean they are two different aspects of the same thing. ◇ When you are introducing a new aspect of something which contrasts with what you have just said, you can say it is the other side of the coin. *Sales turnover has risen 11% in the past year. The other side of the coin is that the number of jobs has fallen.*
❑ If you coin a word or phrase, you invent it, or use it for the first time.

coin box A coin box is a public phone where you pay with coins rather than a card.

coinage The coinage in a country is the coins used there.

coincide (coinciding, coincided) (*or* co-incide, *etc*) When things happen at the same time by chance, you can say they coincide. *The kick-off had coincided with a cloudburst, leaving the pitch perfect for sliding tackles.* ◇ If things like people's opinions coincide, they are the same. *The interests of the politician and the citizen do not always coincide.*

coincidence (coincidental, coincidentally) You say there is a coincidence when by accident two things are very similar, or happen at the same time, or appear to be closely connected. You say things like these are coincidental. *The similarities are entirely coincidental... The number of share owners has gone up while the number of trade unionists, coincidentally, has declined.*

coir is a rough material made from the hairy outer shell of coconuts. It is used to make ropes and mats.

coitus (*pron:* koh-it-uss) (coital) Coitus is sexual intercourse. Coital is used to talk about things to do with sexual intercourse. *...the post-coital pill.*

coke (coking) ❑ Coke is a grey-black substance produced from coal and burned as a fuel. Coking is used to talk about things to do with making coke. *...a coking plant.* ❑ Cocaine is sometimes called coke. ◇ Coke is also short for Coca-Cola. 'Coke' is a trademark.

cola is a sweet brown non-alcoholic fizzy drink.

colander A colander is a bowl-shaped container with holes in it for washing or draining food.

cold (coldly, coldness) ❑ If something is cold, it has a very low temperature. ◇ Cold food is not intended to be eaten hot. *...cold lobster.*
❑ If you say it is cold, you mean the temperature is very low outside, or in the place where you are. The cold is the weather outside when the temperature is low. ◇ If you are cold, your body is at an unpleasantly low temperature.
❑ A cold is a mild common illness (also called the common cold) which makes you sneeze and gives you a sore throat or cough. If you catch cold, you become ill with a cold.
❑ A cold person does not show much emotion, especially affection. *His arrogance and coldness have earned him few friends.* A person like this is sometimes called a cold fish. ◇ Cold behaviour is not friendly or welcoming. *She was coldly received.*
❑ If you get cold feet about doing something, you become nervous or frightened of doing it.

❑ If you **come in from the cold**, you become involved with a group of people in doing something, when you had previously avoided them. ◇ If you are **left out in the cold**, you are ignored by a group of people, rather than being invited to take part in something.

❑ If something **leaves you cold**, it does not excite or interest you.

❑ **pour cold water on** something: see **water**. ◇ **give** someone **the cold shoulder**: see **cold-shoulder**. ◇ **cold comfort**: see **comfort**. ◇ **in cold blood**: see **blood**.

cold-blooded (cold-bloodedly) You say someone is **cold-blooded** when they do something cruel without showing any emotion or pity; you also call their actions **cold-blooded**. *...a new generation of terrorists more cold-bloodedly sophisticated than the last.* ◇ A **cold-blooded** creature has a body temperature which changes according to the surrounding temperature. Reptiles, fish, frogs, and toads are cold-blooded. See also **warm-blooded**.

cold frame A **cold frame** is a wooden box-like structure with a glass or plastic top for protecting small plants in cold weather.

cold front See **front**.

cold-shoulder (cold-shouldering, cold-shouldered) If you **cold-shoulder** someone or **give** them **the cold shoulder**, you ignore them or behave in an unfriendly way towards them.

cold sore Cold sores are small sore spots which can appear on or near someone's lips and nose when they have a cold or are not well.

cold storage If something like food is put in **cold storage**, it is kept in an artificially cooled place to preserve it. ◇ If you put something like an idea or plan into **cold storage**, you postpone doing anything about it.

cold store A **cold store** is an artificially cooled building or room where frozen food is kept to preserve it.

cold sweat A **cold sweat** is a reaction of your body to fear and nervousness which makes you sweat and feel cold.

cold turkey is the unpleasant physical reaction someone gets when they suddenly stop taking a drug they are addicted to.

Cold War When people talk about the **Cold War**, they mean the threatening and hostile behaviour which took place until recently between the US and its allies and the former Soviet bloc. This included the build-up of nuclear arms on both sides, but no actual fighting.

coleslaw is a salad of chopped cabbage, often with carrot and onions in mayonnaise.

colic is a sudden pain in the stomach and bowels. It mainly affects babies.

colitis (pron: ko-lie-tiss) is an illness in which a person's colon becomes inflamed.

collaborate (collaborating, collaborated; collaboration, collaborator, collaborative, collaborationist) ❑ When people **collaborate**, they work together to achieve something. You can talk about their **collaboration** or say they are **collaborators**. You can also say people do something **in collaboration**, or call their work **collaborative**.

❑ If someone **collaborates** with an enemy which has taken control of their country, they help them or cooperate with them. You call a person who does this a **collaborator** or describe them as **collaborationist**.

collage (pron: kol-lahzh; the 'zh' sounds like 's' in 'pleasure') **Collage** is a method of making pictures by arranging and glueing things like newspaper cuttings, cloth, and photographs onto a flat backing. A picture created like this is called a **collage**. ◇ A **collage** of things is a number of them brought together to create a special effect. *The film includes a collage of recent events.*

collapse (collapsing, collapsed; collapsible) ❑ If something like a building **collapses**, it falls down. You can talk about the **collapse** of a building. ◇ If a person **collapses**, they fall down, because they are ill or exhausted. ◇ If something like a system **collapses**, it fails completely and suddenly. You can talk about the **collapse** of a system.

❑ A **collapsible** object is designed to be folded flat when it is not being used.

collar (collared) The **collar** of a shirt or coat is the part which fits round the neck and is usually folded over. You use **collared** to say a garment has a collar, or to describe its collar. *...collared polo shirts... ...a panther skin collared coat.* ◇ A **collar** is also a leather band or chain put around the neck of an animal like a cat or dog.

collarbone The **collarbone** is one of two long bones which run from the base of your neck to your shoulder. It is also called the **clavicle**.

collate (collating, collated; collation) If you **collate** pieces of information, you gather them together, examine them carefully, and identify any similarities or differences. *His collation of the papers was now complete.*

collateral is money or property used as a guarantee that someone will repay a loan. ◇ **Collateral damage** is accidental injury to civilians, or damage to non-military buildings during a military operation.

colleague A professional person's **colleagues** are the people they work with.

collect (collection, collector, collectable) ❑ If you **collect** things you need, you obtain them from several places.

❑ If you **collect** things like stamps or coins, you acquire different kinds, because you are interested in them. A person who does this is called a **collector**; the things they have obtained are called their **collection**. If you say a type of thing is **collectable**, you mean it is worth collecting, because it is interesting or valuable. If something is a **collector's item**, it is highly valued by collectors, because it is rare or beautiful.

❑ Any group of similar things gathered together can be called a **collection**. *...a collection of short stories.* ◇ Someone's **collected** works are all their writings published together.

❑ If you **collect** someone or something, you get them from somewhere. *Motorists will start collecting their ration cards tomorrow.*

❑ If you **collect** for something like a charity, you ask people to give you money for it. A **collecting** tin or box is used to collect money for charity. ◇ If you **collect** money from someone who owes it, you get it from them. A **collector** is someone whose job is to take money or tickets from people. *...a debt collector.*

❑ If a sportsman or woman **collects** a title or prize, they win it.

❑ A fashion designer's **collection** is the clothes they have designed for a particular season.

collected If someone is **collected**, they are calm and self-controlled.

collective (collectively) ❑ **Collective** is used to talk about things shared by or involving every member of a group of people. ...*a collective decision... The cabinet shall be collectively responsible to the parliament.* ◇ A **collective** is a group of people who share the running of something like a farm or business.

❑ **Collective bargaining** is the talks a trade union has with an employer to settle what the workers' pay or conditions should be.

❑ If a word is used as a name for a whole group of people or things, you can say they are known **collectively** by that name. ...*a whole network of telescopes collectively called MERLIN.*

collectivise See **collectivize**.

collectivism (collectivist) **Collectivism** is the belief that the needs of the state are more important than the needs of the individual. **Collectivist** systems are systems like communism and fascism, based on this belief.

collectivize (collectivizing, collectivized; collectivization) (*can be spelled with an 's' instead of a 'z'*) In the former USSR, when farms or factories were **collectivized**, they were brought under state ownership and control, usually by combining a number of small farms or factories into one large one. ...*the forced collectivization of agriculture.*

college A **college** is a place where people study after they have left school. ◇ Some universities are divided into separate institutions called **Colleges**. ...*King's College, Cambridge.* ◇ See also **electoral college**.

collegiate (*pron:* col-**leej**-yit) is used to talk about things to do with a college. ...*the former collegiate football player.*

collide (colliding, collided) If you **collide** with something, you bump into it. People or objects can also **collide** with each other. ◇ You can also say people **collide** when they have different ideas about how something should be done. *He was colliding continually with the government.* You can also say people's ideas **collide**.

collie A **collie** is a type of sheepdog with long hair and a long muzzle.

colliery (collieries; collier) A **colliery** is the same as a coalmine. A **collier** is a coalminer.

collision You say there is a **collision** when a moving object hits something, or two objects hit each other. ◇ You say there is a **collision** of cultures or ideas when people with different cultures or ideas come into contact and this leads to problems. ◇ If people are on a **collision course**, there is likely to be a sudden and violent disagreement between them.

colloquial (colloquially, colloquialism) **Colloquial** language is the kind of language people use in ordinary conversation, rather than in formal writing. *The people who write parking tickets in New York are known colloquially as 'brownies'.* A word or phrase which is only used in conversation is called a **colloquialism**.

collude (colluding, colluded; collusion) If you **collude** with someone, you co-operate with them secretly or illegally. Secret or illegal co-operation is called **collusion**.

collywobbles If you have the **collywobbles**, you are very nervous or worried.

cologne (*pron:* kol-**lone**) is a kind of weak perfume.

colon ❑ The **colon** is the part of the intestine above the rectum.

❑ A **colon** is the mark : often used in front of a list, or to link two sentences which are closely related. *The result of the voting is as follows: 12 votes in favour, 2 against.*

colonel (*pron:* **ker**-nel) A **colonel** is a high-ranking officer in the British army and in some other armed forces. The rank below colonel is **lieutenant colonel**.

colonialism (colonial, colonialist) **Colonialism** is a system in which a powerful country controls less powerful countries or territories and uses their resources to increase its own power and wealth. **Colonial** and **colonialist** are used to talk about colonialism. ...*colonial rule...* ...*colonialist oppression.* ◇ A **colonial** is someone who comes from a colony.

colonize (colonizing, colonized; colonization) (*can be spelled with an 's' instead of a 'z'*) If a place is **colonized**, it is made into a colony. *This treaty between Britain and the Maori people started the process of colonization.* ◇ If animals **colonize** a place, they move there and make it their home.

colonnade (colonnaded) A **colonnade** is a row of evenly spaced columns. If something is **colonnaded**, it has a colonnade or colonnades.

colony (colonies; colonist) A **colony** is a country controlled by a more powerful country, which uses the colony's resources to increase its own power and wealth. A **colonist** is someone who founds a colony, or one of the first people to live in a colony. ◇ A **colony** is also a place where a particular group of people lives. ...*a leper colony.* ◇ A **colony** of animals or insects is a group of them living together. ...*seal colonies.*

color See **colour**.

coloration The **coloration** of something is its colours.

coloratura is ornamental and complicated music for a solo singer, for example in an opera or oratorio.

colossal is used to describe things which are very large in size, amount, or degree.

colossus (colossuses) A **colossus** is an enormous statue. ◇ An extremely large country or institution can be called a **colossus**. ◇ A person is sometimes called a **colossus** when they have been enormously successful in their particular field, and are greatly admired for it.

colour (colouring, coloured) (*American spelling:* color, coloring, colored) ❑ The **colour** of something is the way it appears as a result of reflecting light. **Coloured** is used to say something has a definite colour or colours, or to describe its colour. ...*a coloured illustration...* ...*red-coloured substances.* ◇ The **colouring** of something is the colours it has. ◇ **Colour** is the effect of different colours together. *The Royal Albert Hall was a riot of colour.*

❑ **Colours** are substances used to give things a particular colour. ...*a range of nail colours.* ◇ **Colouring** is a substance added to food to give it a particular colour.

❑ If a child **colours in** a drawing or picture, it gives it different colours using paints or crayons. A **colouring book** is a book of pictures for a child to colour in.

❑ A person's **colour** is the normal colour of their skin, for example whether they are white, brown, or black. Their **colouring** is the colour of their hair, skin, and eyes. ◇ A **coloured** person belongs to a race of people who do not have white or pale skins.

❑ A **colour** TV, film, or photograph shows things in all

their colours and not just in black and white. Similarly, if something like a film is **in colour** or **full-colour**, it has been produced in all colours.

❑ The **colours** of a sports team are the ones they wear when competing, and which are associated with them. ◇ A country's **colours** are the colours of its flag.

❑ If you pass a test with **flying colours**, you do it easily. ◇ If someone reveals **their true colours**, they show they are not as nice as people thought. ◇ **nail your colours to the mast**: see nail.

❑ **Colour** is a quality which makes something enjoyable and exciting. *The audiences liked the romance and colour of 'The Lady's Not for Burning'.*

❑ If something **colours** your opinion, it affects the way you think about something.

colour bar If there is a **colour bar** in a place, non-white people are not allowed to mix freely with white people. You also say there is a **colour bar** when non-white people are not allowed to join an organization, or do a certain kind of work.

colour-blind people cannot distinguish clearly between certain colours.

colour-coded things have different colours on them to show what they contain, what group they belong to, or what their function is.

colour fast If a fabric is **colour fast**, its colours do not run or fade when it is washed or worn.

colour scheme A **colour scheme** is the colours chosen for a group of things which will be seen together, such as the walls, curtains, and carpet in a room.

colour supplement A **colour supplement** is a magazine you get free with a newspaper.

colourful (colourfully) **Colourful** things are brightly coloured. *...colourfully decorated arches.* ◇ **Colourful** is also used to describe things which are interesting and exciting. *They have a colourful and rather romantic history.* ◇ If you call a person **colourful,** you mean they behave in an interesting, amusing, or eccentric way. ◇ If someone's language is **colourful,** they use a lot of rude words.

colourless things have no colour at all. ◇ If you say something like an entertainment is **colourless,** you mean it is unexciting.

colt A **colt** is a young male horse.

column (columnist) ❑ A **column** is a stone or wooden cylinder standing on its end, especially one supporting part of a building. ◇ Other things with a tall narrow shape can be called **columns.** *...columns of smoke.*

❑ A **column** of people or vehicles is a group of them moving in a line.

❑ In a newspaper, magazine, or dictionary, a **column** is a vertical section of writing. ◇ A **column** is also a regular section or article in a newspaper or magazine. *...a gardening column.* A journalist who writes a section or article like this is called a **columnist.**

coma (comatose) If someone is in a **coma,** they are deeply unconscious. You can also say they are **comatose.**

comb A **comb** is a metal or plastic object with a row of needle-like teeth for tidying your hair. When you **comb** your hair, you tidy it with a comb. ◇ If you **comb** a place for something, you search for it thoroughly.

combat (combating, combated) **Combat** is fighting in a war.

◇ If people in authority **combat** something, they try to stop it happening.

combatant (*pron:* kom-bat-ant) The **combatants** in a fight or war are the people taking part.

combative (*pron:* kom-bat-tiv) (combatively, combativeness) A **combative** person is aggressive and eager to fight or argue. *Then, a little more combatively, he added: 'We cannot jeopardize the course on which Poland is set.'... The Swiss are not renowned for their combativeness.*

combination ❑ A **combination** of things is two or more of them together. ◇ The **combination** of a lock is the series of letters or numbers used to open it. A **combination lock** is one which can only be opened this way.

❑ **Combinations** are an old-fashioned undergarment which covers the body and has long legs.

combine (combining, combined) ❑ If you **combine** two or more things, you get them to exist or operate together. *The issue is how to combine low inflation and sustainable growth.* ◇ If something **combines** several features, it has all of them. Similarly, a person can **combine** qualities or abilities. ◇ If you **combine** two or more activities, you do them at the same time.

❑ If people **combine,** they join together to achieve something. ◇ A **combined** effort is made by people acting together. ◇ A **combine** (*pron:* kom-bine) is a group of people or organizations working together.

❑ A **combine** or **combine harvester** is a large machine used on a farm to cut, sort, and clean grain.

combo (combos) A **combo** is a small group of jazz musicians.

combustible If something is **combustible,** it catches fire and burns easily. ◇ If you call a situation **combustible,** you mean the people involved could easily start fighting or arguing. A place where this might happen can also be called **combustible.**

combustion is the burning of something *...the combustion of fuel for energy.*

come (coming, came, have come) ❑ **Come** is used to talk about movement to the place where you are, or to the place you are talking about. *A demonstrator came over... The first boat came into the harbour about an hour late.* ◇ If you **come** to a place, you reach it. ◇ If something moving through the air **comes down** somewhere, it lands there.

❑ If you can **come and go,** you are allowed to move freely between different places. ◇ The **comings and goings** in a place are the arrivals and departures of people or vehicles.

❑ The place you **come from** is the one where you were born, or the one you regard as your home. You can also say someone **comes from** a particular family or background. ◇ If an object **comes from** a particular place, it was made or produced there. You can talk about other things **coming from** a place, for example ideas or fashions.

❑ If an advantage **comes from** a particular thing, you have it because of that thing. *Much of this power and wealth has come from drugs.* ◇ If something **comes of** something else or **comes out of** it, it is the result of it. *The main thing is to see what comes out of our proposed action.* You can also say something **comes about** as a result of something else.

❑ In a story or account, **came** is used to say something happened. *Then came his triumph.* ◇ If something **comes** at a particular time, it happens at that time. ◇ When a regular event happens, you say it comes round or comes around. ◇ If something is coming up, it is going to happen soon. Coming is used to describe things which are going to happen soon. ...*the coming elections.* ◇ To come is used to talk about the future. *Babies born with the disease may well be saved in the years to come... I think there is still more improvement to come.* ◇ If you say you will do something come what may, you mean you will do it whatever happens.

❑ When a period of time comes, it starts. *The switching-on of the tree's lights signals the coming of Christmas.* If you say the time has come for something, you mean it should now happen.

❑ If something like a problem comes up, it appears and you have to deal with it. You can also say you come up against a problem. ◇ If something like an opportunity comes along or comes your way, it is there for you to take advantage of.

❑ Come to is used to talk about a gradual change in someone's feelings or understanding. *People are coming to regard him with sympathy.*

❑ If something you are making comes out in a certain way, that is what it is like when you have finished. ◇ If something does not come up to a standard, it does not reach it. ◇ If something comes off, it succeeds. *The gamble came off.* ◇ If a person comes off well or badly, they are in a good or bad position at the end of something.

❑ Come is used to talk about the order things happen in. *A ceasefire must come first and the rebels must surrender their arms.* ◇ Come is used to say how people finish in a race or competition. *Canada came second.* ◇ Come is also used to talk about the order of importance of things. *Safe sex comes high on our agenda.*

❑ When something comes up for discussion by a committee, it is the next thing for them to discuss, and they begin discussing it. Similarly, you say a case comes before a court.

❑ When information comes out, it is revealed or made public. When it reaches the place where you are, you say it comes in or comes through. *Final results won't come through for at least another 24 hours.*

❑ Come is used with words like 'surprise' and 'shock' to show a person's reaction to something. *The completion of the financing for the Tunnel will come as a huge relief to Eurotunnel.*

❑ If you come round to someone's way of thinking, you change your mind and agree with them.

❑ Come is used with 'into' to say something starts to exist, operate, or be seen. *The new law comes into force immediately... You cross the pass and the plain comes into view.*

❑ If you come under attack or fire, people start attacking you or firing at you. Similarly, you can come under pressure or suspicion. You can also say someone comes in for something like criticism.

❑ If something comes under a particular authority, it is managed by that authority. *Both forces will come under the control of the new Ministry.*

❑ Come is used to say what category something belongs in. *Uranium atoms come in two types.*

❑ If a product comes in a particular style or colour, or with particular features, it is available like that for you to buy.

❑ If you come across or come upon someone or something, you meet or find them by accident. ◇ If you come by something you want, you find it or get it.

❑ If someone comes across or comes over in a particular way, that is the impression you get of them. ◇ If something comes across or comes through in a talk or piece of writing, people are able to understand or appreciate it. ◇ If someone comes out of something well, people get a good impression of the way they have behaved.

❑ If you come down in favour of something, you support it. If you come down against it, you oppose it. You can also come out for or against something. Come out is used in other ways to talk about people openly declaring their opinions. *The governing party came out with a statement of their own.*

❑ If you come up with something like a plan, you think of it and suggest it. ◇ If you come forward with a plan or information, you offer it to someone. ◇ If you come up with a sum of money, you produce it when it is needed.

❑ If something comes up in a conversation or meeting, it is mentioned or discussed.

❑ If someone in authority comes down on something, they take action to stop it.

❑ If something comes to a particular amount, it adds up to it. ◇ If the cost, level, or amount of something comes down, it becomes less.

❑ When something like a book or record comes out, it is published or becomes available to the public.

❑ If something comes into fashion, it becomes fashionable. If it comes back, it becomes fashionable again. If you say things like fashions come and go, you mean they keep changing.

❑ If something like a wall or barrier comes down, it is removed. ◇ If something comes apart, it splits or breaks into two or more parts. ◇ If a part of something comes off, it becomes unfastened or unstuck.

❑ If you come down with an illness, you catch it. ◇ If you come out in spots or a rash, they appear on your skin.

❑ If you come round, you recover consciousness. ◇ If you come through a dangerous or difficult situation, you survive it.

❑ If something comes back to you, you remember it.

❑ When something like electricity comes on, it starts to function.

❑ If workers come out, they go on strike.

❑ If something comes between people, it causes trouble between them.

❑ If you say something like a problem comes down to a particular thing, you mean that is what it is really about. ◇ If you say something does not come into it, you mean it is not an important aspect of the thing you are talking about. ◇ If you say this is where something comes in, you mean this is how it is involved in the thing you are talking about. *As rock becomes increasingly threadbare and dreary, the vacuum has to be filled, which is where world music comes in.*

❑ You say 'When it comes to...' to introduce a new subject. ◇ You say 'Come to think of it...' when you suddenly remember something.

❑ You add as they come for emphasis when you are describing someone. For example, if you say someone is as stupid as they come, you mean they are very stupid.

come-back See comeback.

come-on A come-on is something designed to make you want to do something or buy something.

come-uppance (*or* comeuppance) If you say a person gets their **come-uppance**, you mean something unpleasant happens to them and they deserve it.

comeback (*or* come-back) If someone or something makes a **comeback**, they become popular or successful again.

comedian A comedian is an entertainer whose job it is to make people laugh by telling jokes and funny stories.

comedienne A comedienne is a female comedian.

comedown If you say something is a **comedown**, you mean it is not as good as the thing you had before.

comedy (comedies) Comedy is entertainment which makes people laugh or amuses them. ◇ A comedy is an amusing play or film.

comely (*pron:* kum-ly) In the past, an attractive woman was sometimes described as **comely**.

comet (cometary) A comet is an object similar to a star which orbits the sun and has a long bright tail of gas and dust. Cometary is used to talk about things to do with comets. *...cometary orbits.*

comeuppance See come-uppance.

comfort (comforting, comfortingly) ❏ Comfort is a feeling of being physically relaxed, because of such things as the clothes you wear, or the chair or bed you are sitting or lying on. *Business travellers want to fly in comfort.* ◇ Comfort is also a pleasant lifestyle in which you have everything you need and enough money to live on without financial worries. *She lived in comfort.* ◇ Comforts are things which are not necessary but make your life more pleasant.

❏ If you **comfort** someone, you make them less anxious or distressed. Something which has this effect can be called **comforting**. *It was all comfortingly familiar.* You can also say something is a **comfort** or gives you **comfort**. ◇ If you say something is **cold comfort**, you mean it is no real comfort at all.

❏ If you say something is **too close for comfort**, you mean it is very close, and you are worried about it. You can use other words with 'comfort' like this; for example, you can say things are happening too fast for comfort.

comfortable (comfortably) ❏ If you are **comfortable**, you have a feeling of being physically relaxed, because of things like the clothes you are wearing or the chair you are sitting on. You call things which make you feel like this **comfortable**. *My room was comfortably furnished.* ◇ You also say you are **comfortable** when you feel confident and are not worried, afraid, or embarrassed.

❏ You also say someone is **comfortable** when they are able to live pleasantly without financial problems. *...a comfortable existence.*

❏ If a sick or injured person is **comfortable**, they are in a stable condition and not getting any worse.

❏ A **comfortable** belief is easy to accept because it helps you forget about the difficult or unpleasant side of something.

❏ **Comfortable** is used to say something is done or achieved without much difficulty. *The pipeline is sixteen miles long, and a van could drive through it comfortably.*

comfy (comfier, comfiest) Comfy means comfortable.

comic people and things are amusing and make you want to laugh. ◇ Comic is used to talk about things to do with comedy. *...a comic actress.* ◇ A comic is a person who tells jokes and stories to make people laugh.

❏ A **comic** or **comic book** is a magazine, usually for children, which tells stories in rows of small pictures.

comic strip A comic strip is a series of small pictures which tell a story.

comical (comically) Comical people or things are odd and amusing. *...comically big boots.*

coming of age See age.

comma A comma is the punctuation mark , used to separate parts of a sentence or items on a list.

command (commanding) ❏ If someone in authority commands someone to do something, they order them to do it. An order like this is called a **command**. ◇ A command is also an instruction given to a computer.

❏ An officer who **commands** part of one of the armed forces is in charge of it. You talk about someone being in **command** of forces, or the forces being under their **command**. ◇ If someone is **second-in-command** of a group or organization, they are the second most important person in it.

❏ In the armed forces, a **command** is (a) a group of officers in charge of part of an army. *...the French high command.* (b) a part of an army or air force with a particular function. *...Strike Command.*

❏ If you **command** something, you have it in your control. *Up to then GM had commanded about half the American car market.* ◇ If you are **in command** of a situation, you have control of it. ◇ If a sports team is in a **commanding** position, they are well ahead of the team they are playing.

❏ If someone has a **commanding** voice or manner, they seem powerful or confident. ◇ If someone **commands** respect, they get it because of their personal qualities. Similarly, you can say something **commands** interest or attention. ◇ If something **commands** a particular price, that is what you have to pay for it.

❏ A person's **command** of a language is their knowledge of it and their ability to use it.

❏ If there is a good view from a place, you can say the place **commands** a view.

command post A command post is a place from which an army commander controls and organizes his forces.

commandant (*pron:* kom-man-dant) A senior army officer in charge of a place or group of people is sometimes called the **commandant**.

commandeer (commandeering, commandeered) If the armed forces or police **commandeer** something, they officially take it for their own use.

commander A commander is an officer in charge of a military operation. ◇ A commander is also a middle-ranking naval officer. The rank below commander is lieutenant commander. ◇ See also wing commander.

commander-in-chief (commanders-in-chief) The **commander-in-chief** is the officer in charge of all the armed forces fighting on one side in an area or military operation. 'Commander-in chief' is often shortened to 'C-in-C'.

commanding officer A commanding officer is an officer in charge of a military unit. 'Commanding officer' is often shortened to 'CO'.

commandment The Ten Commandments are the rules of behaviour which, according to the Old Testament, everyone should obey. Other rules of behaviour are sometimes called **commandments**. *...the first commandment of showbiz: 'The show must go on'.*

commando (commandos) A **commando** is a small group of soldiers specially trained to attack targets which are difficult to reach. A member of this group is also called a **commando**.

commemorate (commemorating, commemorated; commemoration, commemorative) If an object **commemorates** a person or event, it is intended to remind people of them. **Commemorative** is used to describe objects like this. *...commemorative mugs.* ◇ If people **commemorate** something, they do something special to show they remember it. What they do can be called **commemoration** or a **commemoration**. *...a commemorative service.*

commence (commencing, commenced; commencement) ❑ When something **commences**, it begins. *...the week commencing August 17.* The **commencement** of something is its beginning. ◇ If you **commence** doing something, you start doing it.
❑ In the US, **Commencement** is a ceremony in which university or college graduates formally receive their degrees or diplomas.

commend (commendation; commendable, commendably) If you **commend** someone or **commend** what they do, you praise them to other people. *The Lithuanians deserve commendation for courage.* **Commendable** behaviour is behaviour you think should be admired or praised. *Herr Kohl was commendably forthright.* ◇ A **commendation** is official praise and recognition of something someone has done. ◇ If you **commend** something to someone, you tell them it is very good. *His book is to be commended on three counts.* ◇ If a course of action commends itself to you, you think it is a good idea.

commensurate (*pron*: kom-men-sur-ret) (commensurately) If one thing is **commensurate** with another, it is in proportion to it. *The smaller the groups are, the easier it is to measure their output, and then to charge commensurately for it.*

comment If you **comment** on something or make a **comment** about it, you say something about it. ◇ **Comment** is criticism or discussion. *Much media comment has been critical of this unexpected step.*

commentary (commentaries) On TV or radio, a **commentary** is a description of something while it is taking place. ◇ A **commentary** is also a book or article explaining or discussing something.

commentate (commentating, commentated; commentator) When a broadcaster **commentates**, he or she gives a TV or radio commentary. A broadcaster who does this is called a **commentator**.

commerce is the buying and selling of things on a large scale.

commercial (commercially) ❑ **Commercial** is used to talk about things to do with commerce and business. *...the country's commercial and political leaders.* ◇ A **commercial** activity involves producing goods to make a profit. *Japan, Norway and Iceland want to start whaling commercially again.* **Commercial** can be used to say something makes a profit. *Disney's new animated feature had been a huge commercial success.* ◇ **Commercial** products or services are available to the public. *Of the three cars, only the Fiat is available commercially.*
❑ **Commercial** TV and radio are paid for by broadcasting advertisements. A **commercial** is an advertisement broadcast on TV or radio.

commercial art (commercial artist) **Commercial art** is the designing and drawing of advertisements and the designing of the way products look. A person who does this kind of work is called a **commercial artist**.

commercial bank **Commercial banks** are the large 'high street' banks which operate current and deposit accounts and make short-term loans.

commercial traveller (*American spelling*: **commercial traveler**) A **commercial traveller** is a salesperson who travels to different places to sell goods or take orders.

commercial vehicle **Commercial vehicles** are vehicles like lorries and vans which are used for carrying goods or passengers along roads, as distinct from private cars and public transport.

commercialise See **commercialize**.

commercialism is emphasis on making a profit, rather than on things like providing a service.

commercialize (commercializing, commercialized; commercialization) (*can be spelled with an 's' instead of a 'z'*) If something is **commercialized**, it is used as a means of making money, rather than providing a service or giving pleasure or satisfaction. *Hooliganism and commercialization have blackened the name of football.*

commie Communists or people with left-wing views are sometimes called **commies** by people who do not like them or do not agree with their views.

commis chef A **commis chef** is a trainee or assistant chef.

commiserate (commiserating, commiserated) If you **commiserate** with someone, you show pity or sympathy for them when they are unhappy or when something unpleasant has happened to them.

commissar A **commissar** was an official responsible for political education in the former USSR.

commission (commissioning, commissioned) ❑ If someone **commissions** a piece of work, they arrange to pay someone to make it or do it; you can also say they **commission** the person. A **commission** is a piece of work an artist, designer, or other person is asked to do and is paid for.
❑ A **commission** is also a group of people appointed to find out about something, or to control something. *...the Monopolies and Mergers Commission.*
❑ **Commission** is money paid to a salesperson for each sale they make. ◇ A **commission** is a sum of money paid to an organization for carrying out a service.
❑ See also **commissioned officer**.

commissionaire A **commissionaire** is a person employed somewhere like a hotel or theatre to open doors and help customers.

commissioned officer A **commissioned officer** is an officer in the armed forces who has a **commission**. Commissioned officers have authority over other ranks, including non-commissioned officers like sergeants. They are usually recruited and specially trained as officers, rather than being promoted through the ranks.

commissioner A **commissioner** is an important official in a government department or some other organization.

commit (committing, committed; committal) ❑ If someone **commits** a crime or some other wrong act, they do it. You can also say someone **commits** a mistake. ◇ If someone **commits** suicide, they take their own life.

❑ If an organization **commits** money or resources to something, it makes them available for that purpose. ◇ If you **commit** yourself to something, you say you will definitely do it. ◇ If you are **committed** to a cause or belief, you believe in it strongly. *...a committed Catholic.*

❑ If someone is **committed** to hospital or prison, they are sent there. You can talk about a person's **committal** to prison.

commitment is a strong belief in something, shown in the way a person behaves. ◇ A **commitment** is a regular task which takes up some of your time. *A lot of women are unable to come because of family commitments.* ◇ If you give a **commitment** to something, you make a firm promise to do it.

committal See commit.

committee A committee is a group of people who represent a larger organization and make decisions or plans on its behalf.

commode A commode is a piece of furniture shaped like a chair or stool which contains a large pot. It is used as a toilet, especially by people who are ill.

commodity (commodities) Anything sold commercially on a large scale can be called a **commodity,** for example foodstuffs or raw materials.

commodore A commodore is a high-ranking naval officer.

common (commoner, commonest; commonly) ❑ If something is **common,** it is found in large numbers, or it happens often. *Light trucks are commonly used for passenger transport.* ◇ **Common** appears in the names of some plants and animals, especially when they exist in greater numbers than other similar species. *...the common dormouse.*

❑ **Common** is used to talk about things possessed, done, or used by two or more people or groups. *...a common ancestor of humans and apes.* ◇ If things have something **in common,** they have the same characteristic or feature. ◇ If people have something **in common,** they share the same interests or experiences. ◇ When people who are in disagreement find **common ground,** they find something they can agree about. ◇ If something is done for the **common good,** it is done for the benefit of everyone.

❑ The **common people** in a place are the ordinary people there. If someone rich or famous has the **common touch,** they have the ability to get on with ordinary people. ◇ **Common-or-garden** is used to describe things which are not special in any way.

❑ If something is **common knowledge,** people in general know about it.

❑ A **common** is a public area of grassy land near a village.

❑ The **Commons** is the House of Commons.

Common Agricultural Policy See CAP.

common cold See cold.

common denominator A common denominator is a characteristic shared by all the members of a group of people or things. See also lowest common denominator.

common land is land everyone is allowed to go on.

common law is the system of law, especially in England, which is based on judges' decisions and custom, rather than Acts of Parliament. ◇ When an unmarried couple have lived together a long time, their relationship is sometimes called a **common-law** marriage. *...his common-law wife.*

Common Market The Common Market is the same as the European Union.

common room A common room is a room in a place like a university or school where people can sit, talk, and relax.

common sense is the natural ability to make good judgements and behave practically and sensibly.

commoner A commoner is anyone who is not a member of the peerage.

commonplace If something is **commonplace** or a **commonplace,** it happens often, and is not surprising or worth commenting on.

Commonwealth The **Commonwealth** or **British Commonwealth** is an association of countries which were once part of the British Empire and still have political and other links with each other.

commotion A commotion is a lot of noise and confusion.

communal (communally; communalism) ❑ **Communal** things are used by a group of people, rather than by one person or family. ◇ **Communal** is also used to describe a way of life in which a group live and do things together. *They lived communally with their road crew.*

❑ **Communal** is also used to talk about things taking place between the different racial or religious groups in a place. *...communal violence.* **Communalism** is loyalty to the interests of your own racial or religious group, rather than to the social system as a whole.

commune (communing, communed) ❑ A **commune** (*pron:* kom-mune) is a group of people who live together and share everything.

❑ If you **commune** (*pron:* kom-mune) with nature or some other power, you spend time thinking about it, feeling you are in close contact with it in some way.

communicable A communicable disease can be passed easily from one person to another.

communicant A communicant is a member of a Christian Church who receives Communion.

communicate (communicating, communicated; communication) ❑ If you **communicate** with someone, you exchange information with them, by speaking, writing, or radio signals. ◇ **Communications** are the systems and processes used to communicate or broadcast information. *Communications between Togo and the outside world appear to have been cut off.* ◇ A **communication** is a letter or phone call.

❑ If you **communicate** an idea or feeling, you make people aware of it. ◇ If people who live or work together can **communicate,** they can understand each other's feelings or attitudes.

❑ **Communicating** doors link one room directly with another.

communication cord The communication cord on a train is a chain passengers can pull to stop the train in an emergency.

communicative A communicative person is willing to

talk to other people.

communicator If you say someone is a good communicator, you mean they are good at communicating ideas to people.

communion or **Holy Communion** is the Christian ceremony in which the priest and congregation eat bread and drink wine in remembrance of Christ's death and resurrection. Communion is also called the Eucharist.

communiqué (*pron:* kom-**mune**-ik-kay) A communiqué is an official statement or announcement.

communism (communist) **Communism** is the doctrine that the state should control all means of producing things, and that there should be no private property; attempts to put this into practice are also called communism. **Communist** is used to talk about things to do with communism. *...a communist regime.* A person who believes in communism is called a **communist**.

community (communities) ❑ The **community** is all the people living in an area. If you say people have a sense of **community**, you mean they are proud of the place they live in, and feel they have something in common with the other people there. ◇ A **community** is a group of people with something in common, living among other people. *...the black community.*

❑ A **community** is also a group of countries who have agreed to work together or help each other. *...the West African Economic Community.*

community centre A community centre is a place where the people, groups, and organizations in an area can hold meetings and run courses or other social activities.

community charge The community charge was a local tax introduced by the government in Scotland in 1989 and in England and Wales in 1990. It was based on the principle that all adults should pay the same for their local services. The community charge was commonly known as the Poll Tax. It was very unpopular, and was replaced by the Council Tax in 1993.

community policing is a system in which policemen and women work only in one area, so everyone gets to know them.

community service is unpaid work done to help other people. People who have been convicted of minor crimes are sometimes ordered to do community service for a certain number of hours.

commute (commuting, commuted; commuter) ❑ If you **commute**, you travel a fairly long distance regularly between your home and your workplace. A person who does this is called a **commuter**.

❑ If the authorities **commute** a death sentence, prison sentence, or some other punishment, they change it to a less severe punishment.

compact ❑ If something is **compact** (*pron:* kom-**pakt**), it takes up little space. *...compact camcorders.* ◇ If you **compact** something, you press it to make it more dense.

❑ A **compact** person is small and short.

❑ A **compact** (*pron:* kom-**pakt**) is a small flat round case containing a mirror and face powder.

❑ A **compact** is also an official agreement.

compact disc A compact disc or CD is a small circular piece of hard plastic on which recorded sound or large quantities of information can be stored. Compact discs have high-quality sound reproduction and are played

using a laser on a **compact disc player**.

companion (companionship) A **companion** is someone you travel or spend time with. **Companionship** is having a friend or companion, rather than being on your own. ◇ A **companion** is also a woman employed to live or travel with an older woman.

companionable A companionable person is friendly and pleasant to be with.

companionway A companionway is a stairway or ladder between the decks of a ship.

company (companies) ❑ A **company** is a business organization which makes money by selling goods or services. ◇ A theatre or dance **company** is a group of performers who work together. ◇ A **company** is also a group of soldiers, usually part of a battalion or regiment. A company is divided into two or more platoons.

❑ **Company** is having someone with you, rather than being on your own. *While he was working, he avoided company.* ◇ If you **keep** someone **company**, you spend time with them and stop them feeling lonely or bored. If you **keep company with** someone, you spend a lot of time with them. ◇ If you **part company** with someone, you end a friendship or association, often as a result of an argument.

❑ If you talk about someone's behaviour **in company**, you mean the way they behave when they are with a group of people, for example on a social occasion. ◇ If someone is good **company**, they are pleasant to be with.

❑ **In company with** means 'as well as'. *Saudi Arabia, in company with some other Gulf oil states, is concerned to avoid any repetition of the oil price shocks of the 1970s.*

company car A company car is one loaned to an employee by the company he or she works for.

comparable (*pron:* kom-**pra**-bl) (comparably; comparability) If two things are **comparable**, they are similar in size or quality, or correspond to each other in some way. *...comparably sized companies... ...comparability of standards.*

comparative (comparatively) You use **comparative** or **comparatively** to show that your description of something is accurate only when it is compared to something else, or to what is usual. *...a player who spent most of his formative years in comparative obscurity... The city remained comparatively calm.* ◇ A **comparative** study involves the comparison of similar things.

compare (comparing, compared; comparison) ❑ If you **compare** two or more things or make a **comparison**, you consider them together and discover or point out their differences or similarities.

❑ If you **compare** one person or thing to another or make a **comparison**, you say they are similar. ◇ If you say something can **stand comparison** with something else, you mean it is good enough to be compared with it. If something **compares favourably** with something else, it is better. You can also say something **compares unfavourably** with something else.

compartment A **compartment** is (a) one of the separate sections of an old-fashioned railway carriage. (b) one of the separate parts of a container. (c) a small cupboard in a boat, plane, or road vehicle.

compartmentalize (compartmentalizing, compartmentalized) (*can be spelled with an 's' instead of a 'z'*) If something is

compartmentalized, it is divided into separate sections.

compass (compasses) ❑ A **compass** is an instrument for finding directions. It has a magnetic needle which always points north. ◇ **Compasses** are a hinged V-shaped instrument for drawing circles.

❑ The **compass** of something is its range. *It soon became clear that within the compass of a normal-sized book such a survey was not practicable.*

compass point A **compass point** is is one of the 32 marks on the dial of a compass, for example north, south-east, or north-north-west.

compassion (compassionate, compassionately) **Compassion** is a strong feeling of pity and sympathy for someone who is suffering. A **compassionate** person has feelings of this kind. If they do something to help someone who is suffering, you say they act **compassionately** or for **compassionate** reasons. ◇ If you are granted **compassionate leave**, you are allowed time away from work for personal reasons, usually because a member of your family is seriously ill or has died.

compatible (compatibility) If things or ideas are **compatible**, they can exist together, or be used together. *...IBM-compatible computers... National courts can freeze any law while its compatibility with EU legislation is being tested.* ◇ If people are **compatible**, they are suited to each other, and can live or work together successfully.

compatriot Your **compatriots** are people from your own country.

compel (compelling, compelled) If something **compels** you to do something, it forces you to do it. ◇ If you say something **compels** an attitude or feeling, you mean you cannot help responding to it like that. *There was enough good playing in the Symphony to compel admiration.* ◇ A **compelling** reason for doing something is very strong. ◇ A **compelling** argument is very convincing. ◇ If you call something like a book or film **compelling**, you mean you have to keep reading or watching it, because it is so interesting.

compendium (*plural:* compendiums *or* compendia) A **compendium** is a book containing short but detailed information about something.

compensate (compensating, compensated; compensation, compensatory) ❑ If someone is **compensated** for something unpleasant which has happened to them, they are given money to make up for it. **Compensatory** is used to talk about money being given like this. *...a package of compensatory measures for farmers hit by the cuts.* ◇ **Compensation** is money you claim from a person or organization responsible for something unpleasant which has happened to you.

❑ If something **compensates** for an unpleasant experience or is a **compensation** for it, it helps to cancel out its bad effects.

compere (*pron:* kom-pare) (compering, compered) A **compere** is a person who introduces a TV, radio, or stage show. You can also say they **compere** the show.

compete (competing, competed; competition, competitor) ❑ If one firm **competes** with another, it tries to get people to buy its goods in preference to the other firm's. When this happens, you say there is **competition** between the firms. Firms which sell the same kind of goods are called **competitors**. ◇ If you **compete** with someone for something you both want, you both try to get it. When several people are trying to get the same thing, you can say there is **competition** for it.

❑ If a person or team **competes** in a contest or game, they take part and try to win. ◇ A **competition** is an event held to find out who is best at something. The people taking part are called **competitors**.

❑ **Competing** accounts of something which has happened are different, and cannot both be right. Similarly, **competing** proposals conflict with each other, and cannot both be carried out.

competent (competently, competence, competency, competencies) ❑ If you are **competent** at something, you are able to do it efficiently and effectively. **Competence** is having this ability. *Women can fulfil those requirements as competently as men.*

❑ The **competence** of a court is its ability to deal with particular matters. ◇ **Competences** or **competencies** are areas of responsibility.

competitive (competitively, competitiveness) A **competitive** situation or event is one where people or firms are competing with each other. ◇ A **competitive** person is eager to be more successful than other people. ◇ You say goods are **competitive** when they are cheaper than similar goods sold elsewhere. You also say goods like these are sold at **competitive** prices. *Only a few publishers have responded by pricing books more competitively.*

compile (compiling, compiled; compiler, compilation) If you **compile** something like a book or report, you produce it by collecting and putting together different pieces of information. *...the compilation of data.* A person who does this kind of work is called a **compiler**. ◇ A **compilation** is something like a book or record containing a lot of different things. *...a compilation of scientific findings.*

complacent (*pron:* kom-play-sent) (complacently, complacency) If someone is **complacent** about something like a threat or danger, they behave as if nothing is wrong. You call their attitude **complacency**. *MPs cannot sit back complacently as they have during other recessions.*

complain (complaining, complained; complaint, complainer) If you **complain** or make a **complaint**, you say you are not satisfied with something. People who make complaints are sometimes called **complainers**. ◇ If you **complain** of a pain or illness, you say you have it. A **complaint** is an illness.

complainant A **complainant** is a person who starts a case in a court of law.

complaisant If you are **complaisant**, you are willing to accept what other people want without complaining.

complement (complementary) ❑ If two people or things **complement** each other, they make a good combination, because their qualities go well together. You say people or things like these are **complementary**.

❑ A **complement** or **full complement** of things is a complete set of them.

complementary medicine is the same as alternative medicine.

complete (completing, completed; completely, completeness, completion) ❑ If something is **complete**, it contains all the parts it should have. *...a work which set new standards of completeness.* ◇ If something **completes** a group or set, it is the last item needed to make it complete.

❏ If you **complete** something, you finish doing, making, or producing it. You then say it is **complete**.

❏ **Complete** and **completely** are used to say something is true to its fullest extent. For example, you can say a man is 'completely bald' or talk about his 'complete baldness'.

❏ If something comes **complete with** something else, it has it as one of its parts.

❏ **Completion** is the finishing of the legal and financial formalities involved in buying or selling a house or land.

complex (complexes; complexity, complexities) ❏ **Complex** things are made up of many different parts. ◇ You also say something is **complex** when it is difficult to understand, because of the way its different parts or details connect up. You can talk about the **complexity** of something like this; its different parts or details can be called **complexities**. ◇ A **complex** is a group of things connected with each other in a complicated way. ...*the whole complex of issues to do with birth control.*

❏ A **complex** is also a group of buildings used for a particular purpose. ...*a leisure complex.*

❏ If someone has a **complex** about something, they are worried or obsessed about it. ◇ In psychoanalysis, a **complex** is a repressed group of ideas or beliefs which influences someone's behaviour.

complexion ❏ Your **complexion** is the natural colour and appearance of the skin on your face.

❏ The **complexion** of something is its general nature or character.

compliance See comply.

compliant You say people or organizations are **compliant** when they do what they are asked to.

complicate (complicating, complicated; complication) ❏ If something **complicates** a situation, it makes it more difficult to understand or deal with. ◇ A **complication** is a problem or detail which makes a situation harder to deal with. ◇ If something is **complicated**, it has many parts or details.

❏ In medicine, a **complication** is an additional problem which makes the treatment of an illness more difficult.

complicity (complicit) **Complicity** in something wrong or illegal is being involved in it. You can say someone is **complicit** in something like this. ...*a body set up to investigate alleged police complicity in serious crimes... He is himself complicit in mass murder.*

compliment (complimentary) ❏ If you **compliment** someone or pay them a **compliment**, you praise them or say you admire something they own. If you are **complimentary** about something, you express admiration for it. ◇ If you **return the compliment** when someone has said something nice or been helpful to you, you behave in a similar way to them. You can also call this **repaying the compliment**.

❏ If you send your **compliments** to someone, you express good wishes or respect.

❏ If something is **complimentary**, you get it free.

comply (complies, complying, complied; compliance) If you **comply** with a request, order, or rule, you do what you are required to. *The document calls for full compliance with the ceasefire.*

component The **components** of a machine are its parts. You can also talk about the **components** of something like a system or policy.

comport The way you **comport** yourself is the way you behave.

compose (composing, composed; composer) ❏ If something is **composed** of certain people or things, they are what it consists of. You can also say people or things **compose** something, or **compose** a part or proportion of it. *Before long, Scots will compose little more than 8% of the population of the United Kingdom.*

❏ If someone **composes** a piece of music, they write it. A person who writes music is called a **composer**. ◇ If you **compose** a letter, poem, or speech, you write it, taking some trouble over it.

❏ A **composed** person is calm and able to control their feelings.

composite (*pron:* **kom**-poz-it) things are made up of several different things or parts. A **composite** is something made up of different things.

composition (compositional) ❏ The **composition** of something is the things it consists of and the way they are arranged. *Venus is similar in size and composition to the Earth.*

❏ **Composition** is composing music. **Compositional** is used to talk about things to do with composing. ...*a study of Olivier Messiaen's compositional style.* A **composition** is a piece of music.

❏ A **composition** is also a painting, photograph, or sculpture, seen as an arrangement of shapes, rather than as representing something. ...*abstract compositions in deep, dark colours.*

❏ A **composition** is also a piece of writing written as part of school work.

compositor A **compositor** is a person whose job is setting up the text and illustrations for a book, magazine, or newspaper before it is printed.

compost is a mixture of dead leaves, lawn cuttings, and kitchen waste which are left to rot, then dug into garden soil. If you **compost** things, you make them into compost.

composure is the ability to stay calm and unworried.

compound ❏ A **compound** is an enclosed area of land.

❏ In chemistry, a **compound** is a substance consisting of two or more elements. For example, water is a compound of hydrogen and oxygen. ◇ If something is a **compound** of different things or is **compounded** of them (*pron:* kom-**pownd**-id), it consists of them.

❏ If something **compounds** (*pron:* kom-**pownds**) a problem or a difficult situation, it makes it worse.

compound fracture A **compound fracture** is a broken bone which has cut through the flesh or skin near it.

compound interest is interest calculated not only on the original amount of money invested, but also on the interest earned, which is added to the original amount. See also simple interest.

comprehend If you cannot **comprehend** something, you cannot fully understand or appreciate it.

comprehensible (comprehension) If something is **comprehensible**, it can be understood. **Comprehension** is the ability to understand or appreciate something. ◇ A **comprehension** is an exercise to find out how well you understand a piece of text.

comprehensive (comprehensively) If something is **comprehensive**, it includes everything possible. ...*a comprehen-*

sive training programme... The board has comprehensively reviewed its requirements. ◇ In sport, if someone has a **comprehensive** win or defeat, they win or lose by a large margin. ◇ In a **comprehensive** system of education, children of different abilities are taught in the same school. Schools like these are called **comprehensive schools.**

compress (compresses, compressing, compressed; compression, compressor) If you **compress** something, you press or squeeze it so it takes up less space. *...the compression of molecules.* Similarly, you can talk about a lot of information being **compressed** into a short book, lecture, or broadcast. You can also talk about something being **compressed** into a short period of time. ◇ A **compressor** is a machine or part of a machine which compresses gas or air.

comprise (comprising, comprised) If an organization or group **comprises** a number of people or things or is **comprised** of them, it has them as its members or parts. *The delegation will comprise 40 people from the United States and other countries.* You can also say people or things **comprise** a group or organization. *...the many nationalities that comprise Ethiopia.*

compromise (compromising, compromised) A **compromise** is an agreement in which someone agrees to accept less than they originally wanted. When people **compromise,** they come to an agreement like this. ◇ If someone **compromises** their beliefs or principles, they depart from them in a way which makes people doubt their sincerity or honesty. When people behave like this, you can also say they **compromise** themselves.

comptroller A **comptroller** is a person responsible for financial planning and control in an organization.

compulsion A **compulsion** is a strong desire to do something, which is difficult to control. ◇ **Compulsion** is the use of threats or violence to make people do something they do not want to.

compulsive (compulsively) **Compulsive** is used to describe people's behaviour when they keep doing something, and seem unable to stop themselves. *She brushes her teeth compulsively throughout the day.* ◇ If a book or TV programme is **compulsive,** you do not want to stop reading it or watching it.

compulsory (compulsorily) If something is **compulsory,** people have to do it because of a rule or law, or because someone in authority insists on it. *Five senior managers have been made compulsorily redundant.*

compunction If you do something without **compunction,** you do not feel ashamed or guilty about doing it.

computation (computational) **Computation** is mathematical calculation, especially using a computer. A **computation** is a calculation. **Computational** is used to talk about things to do with calculations, or with computers. *...computational techniques.*

compute (computing, computed) ❑ If you **compute** a quantity or number, you calculate it.
❑ **Computing** is using a computer and writing programs for it.

computer A **computer** is an electronic machine which can rapidly make calculations, store, rearrange, and retrieve information, or control another machine.

computerize (computerizing, computerized; computerization)

(can be spelled with an 's' instead of a 'z') If a system, process, or type of work is **computerized,** the work is transferred to computers. *The computerization of the benefits system has brought a significant increase in accuracy.* ◇ A **computerized** piece of equipment uses a computer or is controlled by one. ◇ If information is **computerized,** it is stored or processed in a computer.

comrade (comradely, comradeship) Old-fashioned communists and socialists sometimes call each other **comrade.** ◇ In a war or battle, a soldier's **comrades** are other people fighting on the same side. ◇ **Comradely** behaviour is friendly behaviour between soldiers or other people closely involved in something together. Behaviour like this can also be called **comradeship.**

comrade-in-arms (comrades-in-arms) You say people are **comrades-in-arms** when they are working for the same cause or purpose, and sharing the same difficulties or dangers. ◇ A soldier's **comrades-in-arms** are other people fighting on the same side.

con (conning, conned) ❑ If someone **cons** you, they trick you into doing something or believing something, by telling you things which are not true. You call a trick like this a **con** or a **con trick.** ◇ A **con man** or **con artist** makes a living by persuading people to give him money or property in return for something which turns out to be worthless.
❑ A **con** is also a convict.

concave A **concave** lens or mirror curves inwards towards its centre. See also **convex.**

conceal (concealing, concealed; concealment) If you **conceal** an object, you put it somewhere where it cannot be seen or found. *The policy was introduced to prevent the concealment of weapons.* ◇ If you **conceal** information, you do not let other people have it. ◇ If you **conceal** a feeling, you do not let people know you are experiencing it.

concede (conceding, conceded) If you **concede** something, you admit it is true or correct. ◇ If a country **concedes** something like territory to another country, it agrees to let it have it. ◇ In a contest, if someone **concedes** defeat, they accept that they have lost. ◇ When a sports team **concedes** goals or points, it fails to stop the other side scoring them.

conceit (conceited) ❑ **Conceited** people have an absurdly high opinion of themselves or their achievements. You can talk about the **conceit** of people like these.
❑ A **conceit** is a clever or unusual way of presenting things in a book, play, or film. *The conceit that the whole play is set in a music hall does become rather tiresome.*

conceivable (conceivably) If something is **conceivable,** you can imagine it happening, existing, or being true. *The world could conceivably divide into three giant trading blocs.*

conceive (conceiving, conceived) ❑ If a woman or female animal **conceives,** she becomes pregnant.
❑ If you **conceive** something like a plan or idea, you think of it and work out how it can be put into practice. ◇ If you **conceive** something in a particular way, that is how you see it. *These things are conceived as beneficial to the nation as a whole.* ◇ If you cannot **conceive** of something, you cannot imagine it happening, existing, or being true.

concentrate (concentrating, concentrated; concentration) ❑ If you **concentrate,** you give something all your attention.

It is difficult to maintain concentration when victory is a foregone conclusion. ◇ If a serious situation **concentrates your mind,** it forces you to think more clearly and carefully than usual.

❑ If you **concentrate** on something, you give it more attention than other things.

❑ If something is **concentrated** in one place, it is nearly all there, rather than being distributed over a wider area. *Governments should concentrate medical services on really poor districts.* Similarly, you can talk about power being **concentrated** in a few people's hands. ◇ A **concentration** of things is a lot of them together. ◇ A **concentrated** activity involves a lot of things being done in a short time. *...a week of concentrated political activity.*

❑ A **concentrated** liquid has had substances like water removed from it, to increase its strength. Liquids like these are sometimes called **concentrates.** ◇ The **concentration** of a substance in a liquid is the proportion of the substance in it. *...drinking water with aluminium concentrations above the authorised level.*

concentration camp A concentration camp is a prison where a large number of people are kept in very bad conditions, especially during a war.

concentric circles have the same centre.

concept A concept is an idea or abstract principle.

conception is the forming of an idea in someone's mind. Your **conception** of something is your idea of what it is.

❑ **Conception** is also the process in which an egg in a woman's or female animal's womb is fertilized by a sperm, and she becomes pregnant.

conceptual (conceptually) **Conceptual** is used to talk about things to do with ideas and the mind. *...a conceptual breakthrough... The history of the world can be divided into three conceptually manageable periods.*

concern ❑ If something **concerns** you or causes you concern, it worries you. *With tighter credit has come a new concern about cash flow.* If you are **concerned** about something, you are worried about it.

❑ If you are **concerned** with something or **concern** yourself with it, you give attention to it, because you think it is important. Your **concerns** are things which are important to you. *The main concern of the Japanese is the terms on which their vehicles will enter the single European market.* ◇ If something is not your **concern,** it is not your job to deal with it.

❑ If you feel **concern** for someone, you want them to be happy, safe, and well. *I was impressed with his loving concern for abandoned children.*

❑ **Concern** is used to say what something is about. *The plot concerns a young married couple who have started a country hotel... The strikes were mainly concerned with job security... Some official material concerning the raid is still too sensitive to be made public.* ◇ You use 'as far as' or 'where' with **concerned** to say what aspect of something you are talking about. *As far as food is concerned, the criterion which drives almost all research is safety and hygiene... They have tried to improve their image where human rights are concerned.* ◇ If you talk about the people **concerned,** you mean the people involved in something.

❑ You say **as far as I am concerned** when you are giving your opinion about something.

❑ A **concern** is a company or business.

concert (concerted) ❑ A **concert** is a performance by one or more musicians. **In concert** is used to say someone is giving a live performance. *...José Carreras in concert.*

❑ If people do something **in concert,** they do it together. A **concerted** action (*pron:* con-**ser**-tid) is done by several people together.

concert-goer A concert-goer is someone who goes regularly to concerts.

concertina (concertinaing, concertinaed) A **concertina** is a musical instrument like a small accordion. It has no keyboard, just buttons which you press to produce the notes. ◇ If something is **concertinaed,** it is squeezed or concentrated into a smaller shape or area.

concerto (*pron:* kon-**cher**-toe) (*plural:* concertos *or* concerti) A **concerto** is a piece of music for one or more solo instruments and an orchestra.

concession (concessionary, concessional; concessionaire) ❑ If you make a **concession,** you agree to let someone do or have something, often in order to end a conflict or argument. ◇ A **concession** is also something given to someone as a special right or privilege. **Concessionary** and **concessional** are used to describe things given like this. *...concessionary fares... ...concessional loans.*

❑ A **concession** is also a business run on another business's property, for example within a department store. A person who owns or runs a concession is called a **concessionaire.**

concierge (*pron:* kon-see-**airzh**; *the 'zh' sounds like 's' in 'pleasure'*) A **concierge** is a person, especially in France, who looks after a block of flats and checks people entering and leaving the building.

conciliate (conciliating, conciliated; conciliatory, conciliator, conciliation) If you do something to **conciliate** someone, you do it to try to end a disagreement with them. When someone behaves like this, you say they are being **conciliatory.** ◇ If someone **conciliates,** they try to end a disagreement between other people; a person who does this is called a **conciliator.** ◇ The process of trying to end a disagreement is called **conciliation.**

concise (*pron:* kon-**sice**) (concisely) If something you say or write is **concise,** it gives a lot of information in a few words. *...an ability to present cases precisely and concisely.*

conclave A conclave is a meeting whose proceedings are kept secret, for example the meeting of cardinals which elects a new Pope. The people at the meeting are also called a **conclave.**

conclude (concluding, concluded) ❑ If you **conclude** that something is true, you decide it is true on the basis of other things you know.

❑ When something **concludes,** it finishes. The **concluding** part of something is the last part. ◇ If you **conclude** something, you finish it. ◇ If you **conclude,** you say the last thing you are going to say.

❑ When people **conclude** something like a treaty or a business deal, they agree on the final version of it.

conclusion ❑ If you come to a **conclusion,** you decide something is true. ◇ If you **jump to conclusions,** you decide too quickly that something is true, without knowing all the facts. ◇ **foregone conclusion:** see foregone.

❑ The **conclusion** of something is its end. ◇ People say **in conclusion...** when they are beginning the last part of a report or speech.

❑ The final settling of a treaty or business deal can be called its **conclusion**.

conclusive (conclusively) If something like evidence or proof is **conclusive**, it shows with certainty that something is true. *It is hard to predict whether the trial will succeed in proving conclusively that a deal was made.*

concoct (concoction) If you **concoct** an excuse or explanation, you invent one. ◇ If you **concoct** something like an unusual drink, you make it by mixing several things together. What you make is called a **concoction**.

concomitant If something is **concomitant** with something else, you always get it when you get the other thing. You can say it is the other thing's **concomitant**. *Low wages are the inevitable concomitant of low skills.*

concord If there is **concord** in a place, there is widespread agreement about the way things should be organized.

concordance A **concordance** is an alphabetical list of the words in a book or set of books. It says where each word can be found and how often it is used.

concourse A **concourse** is a wide hall in a building, where people can walk about.

concrete is a building material made from cement, sand, small stones, and water.

❑ **Concrete** is used to describe things which are specific and definite, rather than vague. *So far there is little concrete evidence to back up their words.*

concubine (*pron:* **kon-kew-bine**) In some parts of the world, mostly in the past, a **concubine** was a woman who lived in the house of a man she was not married to and was kept by him for his sexual pleasure.

concur (concurring, concurred; concurrence) If you **concur** with someone, you agree with them. You can also **concur** with what they say. ◇ If something is done with someone's **concurrence**, they have agreed to it.

concurrent (concurrently) If two things are **concurrent**, they happen at the same time. *The General had held the two posts concurrently.*

concussed (concussion) If you are **concussed** by a blow to the head or suffer **concussion**, you lose consciousness for a short time and may feel sick or confused when you come round.

condemn (condemnation, condemnatory) ❑ If you **condemn** something which is happening or **condemn** the people doing it, you say it is bad or wrong. *The occupation has led to sharp international condemnation.* **Condemnatory** is used to describe statements which condemn something.

❑ If someone is **condemned** to a certain punishment, they are sentenced to be punished that way. ◇ A **condemned** prisoner has been sentenced to death. The cell where condemned prisoners are kept until their execution is called the **condemned cell**.

❑ If you are **condemned** to something unpleasant, you have to suffer it.

❑ If a building has been **condemned**, the authorities have decided it is not safe and must be pulled down.

condensation consists of tiny drops of water on a cool surface, formed when steam or moist air touches the surface.

condense (condensing, condensed) If a piece of writing or speech is **condensed**, it is made shorter, by taking parts of it out. ◇ When a gas or vapour **condenses**, it changes into a liquid.

condensed milk is milk thickened by having some of the water removed from it, and sugar added.

condenser A **condenser** is (a) a device for changing a vapour into a liquid. (b) a device for storing electric charge.

condescend (condescending; condescension) You say someone is **condescending** when they behave as if they think they are superior to other people. You call this sort of behaviour **condescension**. ◇ If you talk about someone **condescending** to do something, you are suggesting they would not normally do it, because they would consider it beneath them.

condiment **Condiments** are things like salt, pepper, and mustard, which you add to food which has already been served, to give it more flavour.

condition (conditioning, conditioned) ❑ The **condition** of someone or something is the state they are in. *...a large house in good condition.* ◇ The **condition** of a group of people is their situation in life. *...the rapidly deteriorating condition of America's black underclass.* ◇ The **condition** of a sick or injured person is their state of health. ◇ A **condition** is an illness or other medical problem.

❑ The **conditions** in which you live or work are the things around you which affect your comfort, health, and safety. *...a protest over pay and conditions.* ◇ The **conditions** in which something is done are all the factors and circumstances affecting it. *This year, the three-man team had tried to simulate the conditions of an Olympic final.*

❑ A **condition** is something which must happen for something else to be possible. *Sanctions could not be dropped until five conditions had been met.* If you agree to do something **on condition that** something else happens, you say you will do it only if that thing happens.

❑ If you are **conditioned** to do something or to think in a particular way, you do it as a result of your upbringing or training. The influence of your upbringing or training is called **conditioning**.

❑ If you **condition** your hair, you put conditioner on it to keep it healthy.

conditional (conditionally) If something is **conditional** on something else happening, it will happen only if the other thing happens. *The Pope accepted only conditionally.* ◇ If someone who has committed a minor crime is given a **conditional** discharge by a court, they are not punished, provided they do not re-offend within a certain period. *They were conditionally discharged for a year.*

conditioner is (a) a cosmetic put on hair, usually when washing it, to make it smoother and more manageable. (b) a thick liquid used when washing clothes to make them softer. (c) a substance designed to improve the condition of something. *...a soil conditioner.*

condo (condos) A **condo** is the same as a condominium.

condolence If you express your **condolences**, you tell someone in a formal way that you are sorry a relative or friend of theirs has died. Expressing sympathy like this is called **condolence**.

condom A **condom** is a thin rubber covering which a man wears on his penis during sexual intercourse. A similar device called a **female condom** can be worn inside a woman's vagina. Condoms are worn as a contraceptive or as a protection against catching sexually transmitted diseases.

condominium In the US, a **condominium** is a block of flats in which each flat is owned by the occupier. The individual flats are also sometimes called **condominiums**.

condone (condoning, condoned) When people **condone** wrong behaviour, they accept it and allow it to happen.

conducive If something is **conducive** to something else, it has qualities which make the other thing likely to happen. ...*a business climate conducive to foreign investment*.

conduct (conductivity, conduction) ❑ If someone **conducts** something like an inquiry or survey, they carry it out. The **conduct** (*pron:* kon-dukt) of something like this is the way it is carried out.

❑ The way you **conduct** yourself is the way you behave. A person's way of behaving is also called their **conduct**.

❑ If you **conduct** someone somewhere, you go with them, to show them the way. ◇ A **conducted tour** is the same as a guided tour. See **guide**.

❑ When someone **conducts** an orchestra or choir, they stand in front of it and direct its performance.

❑ If heat or electricity can pass through a substance, you say the substance **conducts** heat or electricity. The extent to which it is allowed through is called the substance's **conductivity**. The passing of heat or electricity through substances is called **conduction**.

conductor ❑ The **conductor** of an orchestra or choir is the person who conducts it.

❑ The **conductor** on a train is the official who checks people's tickets and sometimes issues them. Some buses also have conductors who issue tickets.

❑ If a substance is a **conductor** of heat or electricity, it allows heat or electricity to pass through it. ◇ See also **lightning conductor**.

conduit ❑ You say a person or organization is a **conduit** when they are used as a means of communication between other people or organizations. ◇ You say a place is a **conduit** when things are allowed to pass through it, often illegally. *The country has become a conduit for drugs to the West*.

❑ A **conduit** is a small tunnel, pipe, or channel which water or electricity cables pass through.

cone ❑ A **cone** is a three-dimensional shape with a circular base and a pointed top. ◇ **Cones** are cone-shaped objects made of plastic, used for temporarily closing off roads or guiding traffic into lanes. ◇ Ice-cream cornets are sometimes called **cones**.

❑ The **cones** on a tree such as a pine or fir are its fruit. Each cone consists of a cluster of woody scales containing seeds.

confection A **confection** is an elaborately decorated cake or other sweet food. ◇ Other things which are elaborately put together can be called **confections**. ...*an extraordinary architectural confection*.

confectionery (confectioner) **Confectionery** is sweets, chocolates, and fancy cakes. A **confectioner** is a person or company that makes or sells confectionery.

confederacy (confederacies) A **confederacy** is an alliance of states or people trying to achieve the same thing.

confederate A person's **confederates** are other people involved with them in a secret activity.

confederation (confederated, confederative) A **confederation** is a group of states allied for political purposes, and often considered as a single country. ...*the Swiss Confederation*. A **confederated** group of states operates as a confederation. **Confederative** is used to talk about things to do with a confederation. ...*a new confederative system*. ◇ Some organizations representing the interests of a group of people have **Confederation** as part of their name. ...*the Building Employers' Confederation*.

confer (conferring, conferred; conferment) ❑ If something like an honour is **conferred** on someone, it is given to them. ...*the conferment of a special title*.

❑ If you **confer** with someone, you discuss something with them, before deciding what to do.

conference A **conference** is a meeting, often lasting several days, where people discuss a subject or a shared interest. ◇ If people are **in conference**, they are having a formal meeting.

confess (confesses, confessing, confessed; confession) If you **confess** something or make a **confession**, you admit you have done something wrong. ◇ When Christians **confess** or **confess** their sins, they tell God or a priest about their sins so they will be forgiven. **Confession** is the act of doing this.

confessional In a Catholic church, a **confessional** is a small structure which people go into to confess their sins to a priest, who is separated from them by a partition.

confessor A **confessor** is a priest who hears people's confessions. ◇ A **confessor** is also someone who confesses to something.

confetti is small pieces of coloured paper thrown over the bride and groom at a wedding.

confidant (confidante) (*both pron:* kon-fid-ant) A male friend who you discuss your private problems with can be called your **confidant**. If the friend is a woman, you call her your **confidante**.

confide (confiding, confided) If you **confide in** someone, you tell them about a private problem or some other secret matter. ◇ If you **confide** a secret to someone, you tell it to them and trust them not to tell it to anyone else.

confidence ❑ If you have **confidence** in someone or something, you feel you can trust them to do what they are supposed to, and they will not disappoint you or let you down. See also **vote of confidence**. ◇ Someone who has **confidence** is sure of their own abilities.

❑ If you tell someone something **in confidence**, you do not want them to repeat it to anyone else. This is called **taking someone into your confidence**. A **confidence** is something you tell someone which you do not want them to repeat to other people.

confidence trick A **confidence trick** is a crime in which someone persuades you to give them money or property in return for something which turns out to be worthless.

confident (confidently) If you are **confident** about something, you are certain things will happen in a particular way. *It is confidently predicted that these rates will continue until the end of the century*. ◇ Someone who is **confident** is sure of their own abilities.

confidential (confidentially, confidentiality) If something is confidential, it is meant to be kept secret. *The Prime Minister treated the matter confidentially.* You can talk about the **confidentiality** of something like this.

configuration A **configuration** is a group of things arranged in a particular way. ...*an ancient configuration of giant stones.* ◇ The political **configuration** in a place is the political groups or parties there and the way power is distributed among them.

confine (confining, confined; confinement) ❏ If something is **confined** to one place, it exists there and nowhere else. Similarly, if something is **confined** to one group of people, they are the only ones involved in it or affected by it. ◇ If you **confine** yourself to something, you do not deal with anything except that thing. ◇ The **confines** (*pron:* kon-fines) of a subject or system are the limits of what it can deal with. You say, for example, that something is 'within' or 'outside' the confines of a subject or system.

❏ If someone is **confined** to a place, they cannot leave it. *The boredom of confinement may increase experimenting with drugs.* ◇ If people **confine** something to a place or area, they stop it spreading beyond it. ◇ The **confines** of an area are its boundaries.

❏ A **confined** space is enclosed and very small, so movement inside it is difficult.

confirm (confirmed; confirmation) ❏ If someone **confirms** something like a report or rumour, they say it is true. *There has been no confirmation from the White House.* ◇ If something **confirms** what you believe, suspect, or fear, it shows you were right.

❏ If you **confirm** an appointment or arrangement, you say it is definite.

❏ If someone **confirms** their position, role, or power, they do something to make it stronger or more definite.

❏ If someone is **confirmed**, they are formally accepted as a member of a Christian church at a ceremony in which they say they believe in the church's teachings. This ceremony is called **confirmation**.

❏ **Confirmed** is used to describe someone who has a habit, attitude, or belief which they are unlikely to change. ...*a confirmed hypochondriac.*

confiscate (confiscating, confiscated; confiscation) If someone in authority **confiscates** something, they take it away from someone, often as a punishment. ...*the confiscation of assets.*

conflagration A **conflagration** is a sudden outburst of violence involving a large number of people. ◇ A **conflagration** is also a large fire.

conflate (conflating, conflated; conflation) If you **conflate** two or more accounts, ideas, or pieces of writing, you combine them to make one. A combination of things like this is called a **conflation**.

conflict (conflicting) ❏ **Conflict** (*pron:* kon-flikt) is disagreement and argument. When people are disagreeing or arguing, you say they are **in conflict**. *Governors are coming into conflict with head teachers.*

❏ **Conflict** is also war. *Two decades of conflict have devastated Chad.* A **conflict** is a war or battle.

❏ If ideas **conflict** (*pron:* kon-flikt), they are different in a way which would make it impossible for them to be held by the same person at the same time. You can talk about a **conflict** of ideas. Similarly, if laws or rules con-

flict, they say opposite things and cannot all be observed. ◇ If people's interests **conflict**, some people want things to happen which others do not want. When this happens, you say there is a **conflict** of interests. ◇ If descriptions of the same event **conflict**, they are different and therefore cannot all be correct. *Magistrates heard conflicting views from several witnesses.*

confluence The **confluence** of two rivers is the place where they join and become one large river. ◇ When other things mingle together to form one thing, you can call this a **confluence**.

conform (conformist, conformity, conformism) ❏ If you **conform**, you behave the way you are expected to behave, or the way most people behave. When someone does this, you talk about their **conformity** or **conformism**. You can say a person like this is **conformist** or a **conformist**.

❏ If something **conforms** to a law or regulation or is in **conformity** with it, it meets its requirements. Similarly, something can **conform** to someone's wishes or be in **conformity** with them.

confound If someone **confounds** their critics, they prove them wrong, by succeeding in something they were expected to fail in. ◇ If something **confounds** you, you are unable to explain it or account for it.

confrere (*or* confrère) (*pron:* kon-frare) A person's **confreres** are people who have similar views or interests to them, or do the same kind of work.

confront ❏ If a problem or task **confronts** you, you have to deal with it. You can also say you are **confronted** with a task or problem. You can also say someone **confronts** a task or problem, especially when they make a determined effort to deal with it.

❏ If you are **confronted** by an object or a group of people, they are there in front of you. ◇ If you **confront** a person, you meet them face to face, because you are going to fight, argue, or compete with them.

confrontation (confrontational) A **confrontation** is a fight, battle, or war. ◇ A **confrontation** is also a serious dispute between two groups of people who have opposing ideas or policies. ◇ If someone's behaviour is **confrontational**, they are ready to fight or argue, rather than solve things in a peaceful way.

confuse (confusing, confused; confusion) ❏ If you **confuse** two things, you get them mixed up and think one of them is the other. *The name will be phased out to avoid confusion.*

❏ If something **confuses** you, it makes it difficult for you to understand something. You say something like this is **confusing**. In a situation like this, you talk about your **confusion** or say you are **confused**. ◇ If something **confuses** a situation or **throws it into confusion**, it makes it complicated and difficult to resolve or understand. You say a situation like this is **confused**.

❏ A **confused** person is forgetful and does not really understand what is happening around them. Very old people are often confused.

conga The **conga** is a Latin American dance performed by a number of people in single file.

congeal (congealing, congealed) If a liquid **congeals**, it becomes thick and sticky.

congenial (*pron:* kon-jeen-ee-al) If you call your surroundings **congenial**, you mean they are pleasant and they suit you. Similarly, you can call people **congenial** when you like them and get on well with them.

congenital (congenitally) Congenital illnesses or disorders are ones which people have from birth. ◇ **Congenital** faults seem to be part of a person's character and you cannot imagine them ever losing them. *He is congenitally incapable of giving an honest opinion.*

conger The **conger** or **conger eel** is a type of large seawater eel.

congestion (congested) If there is **congestion** in a place or it is **congested**, it is so crowded with traffic or people that normal movement is impossible.

conglomerate A **conglomerate** is a large business made up of several companies, often ones dealing in different types of products.

conglomeration A **conglomeration** is a group of many things, especially things you would not expect to find together.

congratulate (congratulating, congratulated; congratulation, congratulatory) If you **congratulate** someone or offer them your **congratulations**, you express pleasure for something good which has happened to them, or praise them for something they have achieved. **Congratulatory** is used describe things which express congratulations. *...a congratulatory speech.* ◇ If you **congratulate** yourself, you tell yourself you have done something well, or that you have some special quality which has just proved useful.

congregate (congregating, congregated) When people congregate, they gather together.

congregation The **congregation** are the people attending a church service, other than the person taking the service, church officials, and the choir.

congress (congresses; congressional) ❑ A **congress** is a large meeting held by a national or international organization to discuss ideas and policies.
❑ **Congress** is the elected group of politicians responsible for making the law in the US. It is made up of two parts: the House of Representatives and the Senate. **Congressional** is used to talk about things to do with Congress. *...a congressional committee.*

congressman (congresswoman) A **congressman** or **congresswoman** is a member of the US Congress, especially in the House of Representatives.

congruence If there is **congruence** between things, they correspond closely to each other in the way they are formed or the way they operate.

conical objects are cone-shaped.

conifer (coniferous) A **conifer** is a tree which produces cones, for example the pine or the fir. Most conifers are evergreen, with needle-like leaves. **Coniferous** woodland is made up of conifers.

conjecture (conjecturing, conjectured) If you **conjecture**, you make a guess, basing it on incomplete or doubtful information. Guessing like this is called **conjecture**; a **conjecture** is a guess.

conjugal (*pron:* kon-jew-gal) is used to talk about things to do with marriage and the relationship between a husband and wife, especially their sexual relationship. *...her conjugal rights.*

conjunction A **conjunction** of things is (a) a combination of them. *...a conjunction of new transport projects.* (b) two or more of them happening at the same time. *...the conjunction of so many anniversaries.* ◇ If someone does something in **conjunction** with someone else, they do it together. Similarly, if something is done in **conjunction** with another thing, both things are done together.

conjunctivitis (*pron:* kon-junk-tiv-vie-tiss) is a painful inflammation of the membrane covering the eyeball.

conjure (conjuring, conjured) If you **conjure** something into existence or **conjure** it **up**, you make it appear, as if by magic. *Under its restructuring plan, the bank is seeking to conjure up some $4 billion of capital.* ◇ If you **conjure up** a memory, picture, or idea, you create it in your mind.

conjurer See conjuror.

conjuring trick A **conjuring trick** is a trick in which an object is made to appear or disappear, as if by magic.

conjuror (*or* conjurer) A **conjuror** is an entertainer who does magic tricks.

conk out If a machine or vehicle **conks out**, it stops working or breaks down.

conker Conkers are large brown nuts from the horse chestnut tree. ◇ **Conkers** is a children's game. You tie your conker to a piece of string and try to break your opponent's conker by hitting it with your own.

connect (connection) ❑ If you **connect** something to something else, you join it to it. A **connection** is something put between two things to join them. ◇ When a building is **connected** to the electricity, gas, or water supply, wires or pipes are put in so the supply can reach the building. Similarly, you can say a machine or device is **connected** to a power supply.
❑ If a road or railway **connects** two places, it runs between them. You can also say a ferry, bus, or air service **connects** two places. ◇ If a train, plane, or boat **connects** with another one, it arrives in time to allow passengers to change to the other one. When this happens, you say the passengers make a **connection**.
❑ If one thing is **connected** with another or if there is a **connection** between them, they are related or linked in some way. ◇ If you **connect** a person or thing with something or make a **connection** between them, you realize there is a link between them. *They fail to connect getting a good job with finishing high school.*
❑ If something is done in **connection** with something else, it is done for a purpose related to it. *The equipment was purchased for use in connection with the study of body tissues.* ◇ If the police arrest or charge someone in **connection** with a crime, they do it because they think the person was involved in it.
❑ **In this connection** and **in that connection** are used to say something relates to the thing you have just mentioned. *It was for his work in this connection that he was awarded the OBE.*
❑ A person's **connections** are people they know in the business or social world, especially people who can help them in their business or career. Similarly, someone's family **connections** are people they are related to who can help them.

connecting rod In a machine, a **connecting rod** is part of a system for converting the back-and-forward motion of a piston into circular motion. The connecting rod connects the piston to a crankshaft.

connection See connect.

conning tower A submarine's **conning tower** is the raised part containing the periscope.

connive (conniving, connived; connivance) If someone **connives** at something, they allow it to happen, although they know it is wrong and they ought to prevent it; you can also say it is done with their **connivance**. ◇ When people **connive**, they secretly plan to do something together, especially something wrong or illegal.

connoisseur (pron: kon-noss-sir) A **connoisseur** is someone who knows a lot about the arts, food, or drink.

connotation The **connotations** of a word are the ideas or qualities it suggests to you.

conquer (conquering, conquered; conquest, conqueror) ❑ If one country or group of people **conquers** another, they defeat them in battle and take control of them or their land. You call this the **conquest** of the defeated people or their land. The people who win the battle are called **conquerors**; the territories they capture are called their **conquests**. ◇ If a sports team **conquers** another team, especially a higher-placed one, they beat them.

❑ If someone **conquers** something which is causing unhappiness or hardship, they succeed in getting rid of it. *They dream of conquering poverty.* ◇ If people **conquer** a mountain, they are the first ones to climb it. You talk about the **conquest** of a mountain.

❑ A person's **conquests** are the people who have fallen in love with them, or the people they have succeeded in seducing.

conscience Your **conscience** is the part of your mind which tells you whether what you are doing is right or wrong. ◇ If you have a **guilty conscience** or a **bad conscience**, you feel guilty because you have done something wrong. If you say your **conscience is clear**, you mean you have done nothing wrong. ◇ If you say you cannot **in conscience** do something, you mean you cannot do it because you believe it is wrong. ◇ See also **prisoner of conscience**.

conscientious (conscientiously) If someone is **conscientious**, they always do their work properly and thoroughly. *They carry out their duties conscientiously and cheerfully.*

conscientious objector A **conscientious objector** is someone who refuses to take part in fighting in the armed forces, because they think it is morally wrong.

conscious (consciously) ❑ If you are **conscious** of something, you notice it or are aware of it.

❑ **-conscious** is added to some words to describe people who are very concerned about their health or appearance. *...fashion-conscious women... ...the health-conscious 1980s.* ◇ **Conscious** is used after words like 'politically' and 'socially' to describe people who are particularly concerned about some aspect of life or their surroundings. *The hope is that electric cars will appeal to environmentally conscious drivers.*

❑ A **conscious** action is done deliberately. *Beethoven was the first great composer consciously to write 'for a future age'.*

❑ If someone is **conscious**, they are awake rather than asleep or unconscious.

consciousness ❑ Your **consciousness** is your mind and thoughts. ◇ The **consciousness** of a group of people is the ideas, beliefs, and attitudes they share. *...a growth in national consciousness.* ◇ **Consciousness** is also used to talk about interest in a particular subject or idea. *...consciousness of women's issues.*

❑ If you lose **consciousness**, you become unconscious. If you regain **consciousness**, you become conscious again.

conscript (conscription) If someone is **conscripted** (pron: kon-skrip-tid), they are officially made to join the armed forces. People who have been made to do this are called **conscripts** (pron: kon-skripts). *...a concerted campaign against conscription.*

consecrate (consecrating, consecrated; consecration) If a building, place, or object is **consecrated**, it is officially declared to be holy, and can therefore be used for religious purposes. *His final engagement was the consecration of a huge Roman Catholic basilica.*

consecutive (consecutively) **Consecutive** periods of time come one after the other. *He was sentenced to two years on each of the charges, to be served consecutively.* ◇ **Consecutive** things of the same kind come one after the other, with nothing of a different kind in between. *...his third consecutive victory.*

consensus (consensuses) If there is a **consensus** about something, there is general agreement about it.

consent (consenting) If someone **consents** to something, they allow it or agree to it. You can also say they give their **consent**. ◇ When there is **consent**, people agree about something. ◇ **Consenting** is used to say someone takes part in sexual activities willingly, rather than being made to. *...homosexual acts between consenting males.* See also **age of consent**.

consequence ❑ A **consequence** of something is a result or effect of it. ◇ If something happens **in consequence** of something else, it happens as a result of it. ◇ If someone says you must do something or face the **consequences**, they mean something very unpleasant will happen to you if you do not do it.

❑ If you talk about something **of consequence**, you are talking about something which is very important or valuable. ◇ If you say someone or something is **of little consequence** or **of no consequence**, you mean they are not considered to be important.

consequent (consequently) **Consequent** and **consequently** are used to say something happens or is true as a result of something you have just mentioned. *...the Gulf crisis and the consequent rise in oil prices... Constant repetition can cause damage to the tendons and consequently pain.*

consequential things are important or significant.

❑ **Consequential** is also sometimes used to mean 'consequent'. *...the risk of British companies going to the wall and the consequential loss to the national wellbeing.*

conservation (conservationist) ❑ **Conservation** is the preservation and protection of the environment and the natural things in it. A **conservationist** is someone who cares about these things. ◇ The **conservation** of old buildings or works of art is care taken of them, to make sure they do not deteriorate or become damaged.

❑ The **conservation** of a supply of something is careful use of it, to make sure it is not wasted.

conservatism is unwillingness to accept changes and new ideas. ◇ **Conservatism** is also the political philosophy of the Conservative Party.

conservative (conservatively) ❏ **Conservative** is used to talk about a country's Conservative Party. *...Conservative policies... ...the Conservatives' fourth electoral victory.* ◇ Right-wing politicians are sometimes called **conservatives**, although they may belong to parties with a different name. In Communist countries, **conservatives** are usually Party members who do not want to see any changes in the existing system and resist reform.
❏ You say people are **conservative** when they are unwilling to accept changes or new ideas. *Most of the companies are conservatively run.*
❏ A **conservative** guess or estimate puts a figure at a lower level than it is likely to be.

Conservative Party The **Conservative Party** is the main right-of-centre party in the United Kingdom. It believes especially in a capitalist economy with private ownership rather than state control.

conservatoire (*pron:* kon-serv-a-twahr) A **conservatoire** is a school where musicians are trained.

conservator A **conservator** is someone whose job is to prevent deterioration and decay in the objects and works of art in a museum.

conservatory (conservatories) A **conservatory** is a glass room attached to a house, where plants are kept and people sit in summer. ◇ A conservatoire is sometimes called a **conservatory.**

conserve (conserving, conserved) If you **conserve** a supply of something, you use it carefully, so it lasts as long as possible. ◇ When people try to **conserve** something like their environment, they try to keep it in its original form, protecting it from harm, loss, or change.

consider (considering, considered) ❏ If you **consider** a person or thing to be something, that is your opinion of them, or how you see them. *Some of them consider women as fit only to be secretaries.*
❏ If you **consider** something, you think about it carefully. A **considered** opinion or action is the result of careful thought. ◇ If a group of people **consider** something like a report or case, they discuss it before coming to a conclusion or decision about it.
❏ If you **consider** a person's needs, wishes, or feelings, you pay attention to them.
❏ You use **considering** to say you are taking something into account in what you are saying. *The casualty figures appear to be small, considering the size of the earthquake.*

considerable (considerably) A **considerable** amount is very large. Similarly, you can talk about a **considerable** change or say something has a **considerable** effect. *The road should relieve city centre congestion considerably.*

considerate A **considerate** person pays attention to the needs and feelings of other people.

consideration is careful thought about something. If you give **consideration** to something, you think about it carefully. ◇ If something is **under consideration**, it is being discussed or thought about.
❏ If you **take** something **into consideration**, you think about it when you are planning or deciding something. Things which affect plans and decisions are called **considerations**. *Sport is increasingly dominated by commercial considerations.*
❏ If someone shows **consideration**, they pay attention to the needs and feelings of other people.

consign If you **consign** something somewhere, you put it there, to get rid of it. *Previous treaties have provided for medium-range nuclear missiles to be consigned to the scrapheap.* ◇ If someone or something is **consigned** to an undesirable situation, they are placed in it as a result of other people's actions.

consignment A **consignment** of goods is a load of them being delivered somewhere.

consist If something **consists of** certain things, it is made up of them or formed from them. ◇ If something **consists in** a particular thing, it is just that thing and nothing else. *Economic reform has so far consisted only in transferring 'socially owned' companies into state-owned ones.*

consistent (consistently; consistency, consistencies) ❏ **Consistent** is used to describe things which stay the same. *...Labour's consistent lead in the opinion polls.* ◇ If someone's behaviour is **consistent**, they keep doing things the same way, or saying the same thing. *Jordan has consistently argued it is entitled to full compensation.* You can talk about the **consistency** of someone's behaviour. ◇ **Consistent** is often used to say someone continues to do something well. *...Somerset's most consistent bowler.*
❏ If reports, statements, or ideas are **consistent**, they do not contradict each other. You can talk about the **consistency** of things like these. ◇ If something is **consistent** with a type of thing, it has many of its features and could therefore be that thing. *The injuries were consistent with injuries sustained from missiles.*
❏ The **consistency** of a substance is its thickness and texture.

consolation ❏ See console.
❏ A **consolation prize** is (a) a small prize given to one of the losers in a competition. (b) something given to someone who has failed to get what they really wanted. *Her appointment was seen as a consolation prize after she had failed to win a seat in the Senate.*

console (consoling, consoled; consolation, consolatory) ❏ If something **consoles** you (*pron:* kon-**soles**) when you have had a loss or disappointment, it makes you feel less sad. *He finds consolation in the financial success of the season so far.* **Consolatory** is used to talk about things which console someone. *...consolatory words.*
❏ A **console** (*pron:* kon-**sole**) is a panel with switches or knobs for operating a machine.

consolidate (consolidating, consolidated; consolidation) If you **consolidate** something you have, you strengthen it, to make it more effective or secure. *Women are consolidating their place in the workforce... The 1990s were meant to be a period of consolidation for the Community.* ◇ When small firms or organizations are **consolidated**, they are formed into one large one.

consommé (*pron:* kon-som-may) is a thin clear soup, usually made from meat juices.

consonant ❏ A **consonant** is a sound like 'p', 'f', 'n', or 't', which you pronounce by stopping the air flowing freely through your mouth. All speech sounds are either consonants or vowels.
❏ If one thing is **consonant** with another, it fits in with it or agrees with it.

consort ❏ If someone is spending time with someone you do not like, you can say they are **consorting** (*pron:*

kon-sort-ing) with them.

❑ The **consort** (*pron:* kon-sort) of a reigning monarch is their husband or wife.

❑ A **consort** is also a small group of musicians who perform old music on old-fashioned instruments like viols.

consortium (*plural:* consortiums *or* consortia) A **consortium** is a group of firms who have agreed to work together on a project or contract.

conspicuous (conspicuously) If something is **conspicuous**, it is easily seen or noticed. *There was some conspicuously bad bowling.* ◇ If you say someone or something is **conspicuous by their absence**, you mean they are not where they should be, or where they are expected to be.

conspiracy (conspiracies; conspirator, conspiratorial) You say there is a **conspiracy** when a group of people secretly plan to overthrow a government, or to do something else wrong or illegal. The people involved in a conspiracy are called **conspirators**. **Conspiratorial** is used to describe things connected with a conspiracy. ◇ If you say someone is being **conspiratorial**, you mean they are behaving as if they are sharing a secret with you. ◇ A **conspiracy of silence** is an agreement by a group of people not to talk publicly about something.

conspire (conspiring, conspired) If people **conspire**, they secretly plan to commit treason, or to do something else wrong or illegal. ◇ When everything that happens seems to make a particular result more likely, you can say things **conspire** to produce this result. *Everything from the weather to the calendar seemed to conspire in Faldo's favour.*

constable A **constable** is a police officer of the lowest rank.

constabulary (constabularies) The **constabulary** is the local police force in an area.

constant (constantly, constancy) ❑ If something is **constant**, it happens all the time or is always there. *...his constant companion... ...a constantly growing population.* ◇ A **constant** level or amount stays the same. *...a constant calorie intake.*

❑ A **constant** is something which does not change. *...one of the few constants in his ideology.* When something does not change, you can talk about its **constancy**. ◇ **Constancy** is also faithfulness and loyalty to a person or belief.

constellation A **constellation** is a group of stars which has been given a name.

consternation is alarm and anxiety.

constipated (constipation) If someone is **constipated** or suffering from **constipation**, they are having difficulty emptying their bowels.

constituency (constituencies, constituent) ❑ An MP's **constituency** is the town or area he or she represents. The people who live there are called the MP's **constituents**. ◇ A **constituent** assembly is a group of people who have the power to frame a country's constitution or to decide who will be its government.

❑ The **constituents** of something are the parts it consists of. You can also talk about the **constituent** parts of something. *Eventually the substance degrades grease down to its constituent components of water and carbon dioxide.*

constitute (constituting, constituted) ❑ You use **constitute** to say what something consists of. For example, if something consists of a number of parts, you can say the parts **constitute** the whole. *...a commodity which constitutes over 90% of the country's exports.* ◇ If something has all the features which together make a particular thing, you can say it **constitutes** that thing. *Health education has made young people more aware of what constitutes a healthy diet.*

❑ When something is **constituted**, it is put together from different parts or elements. *...the newly-constituted parliament.*

constitution (constitutional, constitutionally) ❑ A country's **constitution** is usually a written statement of the way its government is organized and the rights and duties of its citizens. The British constitution, however, consists of various traditions and customs which have never been written down in a single document. **Constitutional** is used to talk about things to do with a country's constitution. *...a constitutional amendment... Constitutionally the women have equal rights.* ◇ A **constitutional monarchy** is a country which has a king or queen but is governed by a democratically elected government; the king or queen is called a **constitutional monarch**.

❑ Your **constitution** is your general health, especially your ability to resist illness or recover from it quickly. You say, for example, that someone has a good constitution.

constrain (constraining, constrained; constraint) If something **constrains** something else or acts as a **constraint** on it, it prevents it developing freely. ◇ If something **constrains** you, it limits your freedom of action. ◇ If you feel **constrained** to do something, you feel forced to do it although you might prefer not to. ◇ If you exercise **constraint**, you control your behaviour and resist doing some of the things you want to.

constrict (constricted; constriction) If something **constricts** an object, it squeezes it tightly. *...the dilation and constriction of blood vessels.* ◇ If something **constricts** you, it limits your actions and stops you doing what you would like to; you call something like this a **constriction**.

construct (construction, constructor) ❑ When something like a building or vehicle is **constructed**, it is built or put together. Some firms which build or assemble things are called **constructors**. If something is **under construction**, it is being built or made.

❑ If someone **constructs** something like an idea, a story, or a system, they create it. ◇ A **construct** (*pron:* kon-struct) is a complex idea. ◇ The **construction** you place on something is the way you interpret it. *He rejected the construction put on his remarks.*

constructive (constructively) If what someone says or does is **constructive**, it is helpful to people who are trying to achieve something. *...their willingness to work closely and constructively with other members of the Security Council.*

construe (construing, construed) If something is **construed** as a particular thing, people see it as being that thing. *Such actions may be construed as significant by foreign observers.*

consul (consular, consulate) A **consul** is a government official who lives in a foreign city and looks after the interests of people and businesses there from his or her own country. **Consular** is used to talk about things to do with a consul or a consul's work. A **consulate** is the place where a consul works.

consult (consulting; consultation) ❏ If you **consult** someone, you ask for their opinion or advice. *The proposals will be put forward for public consultation.* ◇ **Consulting** is used to describe some people who give professional advice. *...a firm of consulting actuaries.* ◇ A **consultation** document is produced for people to read and make comments on. ◇ When people **consult**, they talk and exchange ideas and opinions.

❏ If you **consult** a book or map, you refer to it for information.

consultancy (consultancies) A **consultancy** is a group of people who give professional advice on something. *...a management consultancy.*

consultant A **consultant** is (a) a senior doctor specializing in one area of medicine. *...a consultant anaesthetist.* (b) someone who gives expert advice to people who need professional help. *...a design consultant.*

consultation See **consult**.

consultative A **consultative** committee or assembly is set up to give advice or make suggestions. ◇ A **consultative** document is the same as a consultation document. See **consult**.

consulting room A **consulting room** is a room where a doctor sees his or her patients.

consumables are consumer goods, especially goods like food, which are quickly used up.

consume (consuming, consumed) ❏ If something **consumes** fuel, energy, or time, it uses it up. ◇ If you **consume** something, you eat or drink it. ◇ If something is consumed by a fire, it is destroyed in it.

❏ If someone is **consumed** with a feeling or desire, it affects them so strongly they cannot think of anything else. **Consuming** is used to describe feelings like this. *The stage was his single most consuming interest.*

consumer A **consumer** is anyone who buys goods or pays for a service. ◇ **Consumer goods** are things like food, clothes, and domestic appliances, which are bought for people's personal needs. ◇ **Consumer durables** are things like cars and TV sets which last a long time and so are not bought very often, in contrast to things like clothes and food.

consumerism (consumerist) **Consumerism** is the belief that the more goods people buy, the better it is for the economy. **Consumerist** is used to talk about things connected with this belief.

consummate (consummating, consummated; consummation) ❏ **Consummate** (*pron:* kon-syoo-mat) is used to describe people who are very skilful at something. *...a consummate professional.*

❏ If two people **consummate** (*pron:* kon-syoo-mate) their marriage or relationship, they make it complete by having sex. *...the consummation of their marriage.* ◇ If something like an agreement or business deal is **consummated,** it is completed.

consumption is used to talk about fuel or energy being used, or the amount of it which is used. *...the consumption of fossil fuels... Consumption is being reduced by 25 per cent.* ◇ **Consumption** is used to talk about eating and drinking, or the amount of something which is eaten or drunk. *The meat is safe for human consumption... Statistics have established that alcohol consumption rises in line with increases in income.*

❏ If something is for a particular person's or group's **consumption,** it is meant to be seen or heard by them. *The film should be available for public consumption.*

contact involves meeting or communicating with someone, especially on a regular basis. *Radio contact with the vessel was lost.* If you are **in contact** with someone, you are meeting them or communicating with them. ◇ If you **contact** someone, you get in touch with them, usually by phoning or writing. ◇ If you **make contact** with someone you have been trying to find or speak to, you manage to speak to them or get a letter to them. ◇ If you **come into contact with** someone or something, you meet them in the course of your work or other activities.

❏ A **contact** is someone you know in an organization or profession who is able to give you special help or information.

❏ If something comes into **contact** with something else, it touches it.

contact lens Contact lenses are small plastic lenses which people wear directly on the surface of their eyes instead of glasses.

contagion People use **contagion** to describe the spreading of ideas and opinions they do not like. *The President was determined to insulate his country from the contagion of foreign ideas.*

contagious A **contagious** disease can be caught by contact with people who have it. ◇ A **contagious** feeling or attitude spreads quickly among people or countries.

contain (containing, contained; containable) ❏ If something like a box or room **contains** certain things, those things are inside it. Similarly, you can say a book or document **contains** information or ideas. ◇ If something **contains** a substance, that substance is one of its ingredients. ◇ If something **contains** a quality or feature, it has it. *Not one of these reports contained any truth.*

❏ If people **contain** something like an activity or problem, they stop it spreading or getting worse. If a problem is **containable,** it can be prevented from getting worse.

❏ If you cannot **contain** a feeling, you cannot help showing it. A **contained** person keeps their feelings under control and does not show them to other people.

container A **container** is a very large sealed metal box for transporting goods by road, rail, or ship. A **container** vehicle is designed to carry containers. *...container ships.* ◇ Anything like a box or bottle which is used to hold, carry, or store things can be called a **container.**

containment is used to talk about actions taken to keep a country's power or influence within acceptable limits. ◇ The **containment** of something dangerous or unpleasant is keeping it within a particular area.

contaminate (contaminating, contaminated; contamination, contaminant) If something is **contaminated** by dirt, chemicals, or other substances, they get into it and it becomes impure or harmful. Substances which contaminate are called **contaminants.** ◇ You can say other things are **contaminated** when they are harmed by coming into contact with something else. *...criminal contamination of younger people by older teenagers.*

contd. at the bottom of a page means 'continued'; it shows that an article or story is continued on another page.

contemplate (contemplating, contemplated; contemplation) ❑ If you **contemplate** doing something, you think about it and try to decide whether to do it or not. ◇ If someone will not **contemplate** something, they will not consider it as a possibility. *He refuses to contemplate failure.* ◇ If something which might happen would be extremely unpleasant, you can say it is too unpleasant to **contemplate**.

❑ If you **contemplate**, you spend a long time thinking deeply about something, especially something of a spiritual nature. *The Dalai Lama spent his time largely in prayer and contemplation.*

❑ If you **contemplate** something like a view, you look at it for a long time.

contemplative is used to describe someone's behaviour when they spend a long time thinking deeply about something. *I went for long contemplative walks.*

contemporaneous (contemporaneously) If two things are **contemporaneous**, they happen or exist at the same time. *Forensic tests showed that the record of the interview may not have been made contemporaneously.*

contemporary (contemporaries) **Contemporary** is used to describe things which exist or are happening now, rather than in the past. *...one of Australia's finest contemporary writers.* ◇ If you are talking about the past, you can use **contemporary** to describe things which existed or happened at the same time as the thing you are talking about. *The huge palace contained many of the trappings of contemporary Bronze Age power.* ◇ Your **contemporaries** are people about the same age as yourself, or people who were at your school or university at the same time as you.

contempt ❑ If someone feels **contempt** for a person or holds them in **contempt**, they dislike them, because they think they are inferior in some way, or because they disapprove of the way they behave.

❑ **Contempt of court** is the criminal offence of disobeying an instruction from a judge or court, or behaving disrespectfully in court. Someone who commits this offence is said to be in **contempt**.

contemptible If you call what someone does **contemptible**, you mean it is so mean or selfish you find it shocking or disgusting.

contemptuous (contemptuously) If someone is **contemptuous** of a person, or of what they say or do, they show no respect for them at all. *The report was contemptuously dismissed by Peking.*

contend (contender) ❑ If you have to **contend** with a problem or difficulty, you have to deal with it or overcome it. ◇ When people **contend** for something, they compete with each other for it. You call the people competing for something the **contenders**.

❑ If you **contend** that something is true, you state or argue that it is true.

content (contents; contented, contentedly, contentment) ❑ The **contents** (*pron:* kon-tents) of something are the things inside it. ◇ The **contents** of a piece of writing are the things written in it. ◇ The **content** of a piece of writing, speech, or TV programme is its subject matter and the ideas expressed in it. ◇ **Content** is used to talk about the amount or proportion of one substance contained in another. *...the carbon content of fossil fuels.*

❑ If you are **content** (*pron:* kon-tent) with something, you are satisfied with it. You can also be **content** to do something. ◇ If you **content** yourself with something, you satisfy yourself with it, although it is not what you originally wanted. *Having missed a tour, I contented myself with a visit to nearby Mount Diablo.* ◇ If you are **content** or **contented**, you are happy and satisfied with your way of life. This feeling is called **contentment**. *She sighed contentedly.*

contention (contentious) ❑ If someone keeps saying something is true, you can say it is their **contention** that it is true. ◇ If something is **contentious** or a source of **contention**, there is disagreement or argument about it. ◇ **bone of contention:** see **bone**.

❑ If you are **in contention** in a competition, you have a chance of winning. If you are **out of contention**, you have no chance.

contentment See **content**.

contest (contestant) ❑ A **contest** is a competition or game. The people taking part are called the **contestants**. ◇ When people compete for power, this is also called a **contest**. *...a contest for the leadership.* ◇ If a political party **contests** (*pron:* kon-tests) an election, they put up a candidate or candidates. You can also say they **contest** a particular seat.

❑ If someone **contests** something like a statement or decision, they disagree with it and make a formal objection to it.

context ❑ If you talk about the **context** in which something happens, you mean the circumstances surrounding it, and everything which leads up to it and follows it. *This conflict needs to be placed in its historical context.*

❑ The **context** of a word or sentence is the words or sentences before it and after it, which help make its meaning clear. ◇ If a statement or remark is taken or quoted **out of context**, the rest of what is said is left out, giving a misleading impression.

contiguous If things are **contiguous**, they are next to each other, or touching each other.

continent (continental) ❑ A **continent** is one of the world's large land masses, for example Europe or Africa. **Continental** is used to talk about things to do with a continent. *...continental Asia.*

❑ In Britain and Ireland, the mainland of Europe is sometimes called the **Continent**, especially central and southern Europe. **Continental** is used to talk about things to do with this area; the people who live there are sometimes called **continentals**.

continental breakfast A **continental breakfast** is a light breakfast, usually consisting of bread, butter, jam, and coffee or tea, without any cooked food.

continental quilt A **continental quilt** is the same as a duvet.

contingency (*pron:* kon-tin-jen-see) (contingencies) A **contingency** is something which might happen in the future. *The force would be large enough to deal with any contingency... ...contingency plans.*

contingent ❑ A **contingent** is a group of people representing a country or organization. *The Scottish contingent will form the bulk of the staff for a 600-bed field hospital.* ◇ A **contingent** of police or soldiers is a group of them.

❑ If one thing is **contingent** on another, it can only happen if the other thing happens or exists.

continual (continually) Continual is used to describe (a) something which goes on without stopping. ...*continual torrential rain*... ...*an occupation force continually at risk.* (b) something which is repeated again and again. ...*his continual efforts*... *New moves could be made to stop oil companies continually increasing prices.*

continuance The continuance of something is the same as its continuation.

continuation The continuation of something is the fact that it continues to happen or exist. *The continuation of general economic weakness will put pressure on profit margins.* ◇ If one thing is a continuation of another, it follows on from it and forms an extra part of it. *The election of John Major as Prime Minister is a continuation of the Conservative Party's recent practice of choosing leaders from relatively humble backgrounds.*

continue (continuing, continued) ❑ If someone or something continues to do something, they keep doing it. ◇ If you continue with something, you keep doing it or using it. *If they continue with their planned agitation, the president will have to make additional concessions.*
❑ If something continues, it does not stop. ...*the continuing row over British exports to Iraq*... *They have won the continued support of the US.* ◇ You also say something continues or is continued when it starts again after stopping for a period of time. ◇ You say someone continues when they begin speaking again after stopping or being interrupted.
❑ If someone or something continues in a particular direction, they keep going in that direction.

continuing education consists of courses for adults in subjects which interest them. These courses do not usually lead to a qualification.

continuity (continuities) You say there is continuity when something stays the same although other things are being changed. *The President has stressed that he wants to maintain continuity between the old government and the new.* ◇ Continuity is also the smooth arrangement of the scenes in a film or TV programme so there are no gaps between them.

continuous (continuously) If something is continuous, it goes on without stopping or being interrupted. *The Conservatives had been in power for the longest continuous period in post-war Britain*... *The civil war has raged almost continuously since 1976.* ◇ A continuous line or surface has no gaps or holes in it.

continuum (pron: kon-tin-yu-um) A continuum is a series or progression of things in which each thing is slightly different from the next one to it in the series.

contorted (contortion) If something is contorted, it is twisted into an unnatural and unattractive shape. Twisted shapes can be called contortions. ◇ You can say other things are contorted when they are used in an unnatural and unattractive way. ...*contorted language.* ◇ You can describe people's actions as contortions when they are forced to do something difficult or complicated to achieve what they want. *The BBC has lately gone through contortions to let outsiders sponsor its weather programmes.*

contortionist A contortionist is an entertainer who twists his or her body into strange and unnatural posi-

tions.

contour If you talk about the contours of something, you mean its shape or outline. ◇ On a map, a contour is a line joining points of equal height.

contraband is goods brought into a country or taken out illegally, to avoid taxation.

contraception (contraceptive) Contraception is preventing pregnancy, especially by using a device or pill. Contraceptive is used to talk about things connected with contraception. ...*contraceptive methods.* ◇ A contraceptive is a device or pill for preventing pregnancy.

contract (contraction) ❑ A contract (pron: kon-trakt) is a written legal agreement, usually to do with the sale of something or with work done for money. If you contract (pron: kon-trakt) with someone to do something, you promise to do it by signing an agreement like this. ◇ If you are under contract to someone, you have signed a contract agreeing to work for them and nobody else during a fixed period of time.
❑ If something contracts, it gets smaller or shorter. *The weapons industry in the West is facing severe contraction.* ◇ A contraction is a shortened form of a word or words. For example, 'Ltd' is a contraction of 'Limited'.
❑ Contractions are the painful tightening of a woman's muscles during the birth of her baby.
❑ If you contract an illness, you get it.

contractor A contractor is a person or company that does work for other people or companies.

contractual (contractually) Contractual is used to talk about something to do with a legal contract. *The defendant was contractually bound to contribute to the fund.*

contradict (contradiction, contradictory) If you contradict someone, you say the opposite of what they have said. ◇ If two statements contradict each other or are contradictory, they cannot both be correct. When you get statements like these, you say there is a contradiction. ◇ If you say something is a contradiction in terms, you mean it cannot exist, because nothing can have the combination of qualities it is described as having.

contraflow On a motorway or other main road, a contraflow is a line of traffic using a lane normally used by traffic going in the opposite direction.

contralto A contralto is a female singer with a low singing voice.

contraption People sometimes call a strange-looking device or machine a contraption.

contrary opinions or views are opposing ones which cannot be held by the same person at the same time. ◇ If something is contrary to accepted rules or practices, it goes against them.
❑ You say contrary to... when mentioning a wrong statement or mistaken belief, before going on to say what the truth is. *Contrary to reports, no one had been executed.* ◇ You say on the contrary when you are contradicting what has just been said. *The rebels argue that the scheme will on the contrary be divisive and counter-productive.* ◇ If you talk about a statement to the contrary, you mean a statement which says the opposite of what has just been said. *He denounced statements to the contrary as slanderous and untrue.*

contrast (contrasting, contrastingly) ❑ If one thing contrasts (pron: kon-**trasts**) with another or there is a **contrast** (pron: kon-**trast**) between them, they appear very different when you compare them. You can also say one thing is a **contrast** to the other. ...*players of different generations and contrasting styles.* ◇ If you **contrast** two or more things, you compare them to show the differences between them.

❏ You say **by contrast** or **in contrast** when you are mentioning something which has opposite features from the thing you have just described.

contravene (contravening, contravened; contravention) If someone **contravenes** a rule or a law, they do something which is forbidden by it. You call this a **contravention** of the rule or law.

contretemps (pron: kon-tra-ton) (plural: contretemps) A **contretemps** is a small but embarrassing disagreement.

contribute (contributing, contributed; contribution; contributor, contributory) ❏ When people **contribute** to something, they each do something to help it succeed. What each person does is called their **contribution**. ◇ When people **contribute** money to a cause, they each give something. You say each person is a **contributor**; what they give is called their **contribution**.

❏ If something **contributes** to a situation, it is one of the factors responsible for it. You call something like this a **contributor** to a situation or a **contributory** factor. *High blood pressure is known to be a major contributory factor in heart attacks.*

❏ If you **contribute** to a book or magazine, you write a piece which is printed in it. Each piece like this is called a **contribution**; the people who write the pieces are called **contributors**.

contrite (contrition) If you are **contrite**, you are ashamed and sorry about something you have done wrong. This feeling is called **contrition**.

contrivance is getting something done using unorthodox or slightly dishonest methods. A **contrivance** is an unorthodox or dishonest way of achieving something.

❏ People sometimes call an unusual device or machine a **contrivance**.

contrive (contriving, contrived) ❏ If you **contrive** to do something difficult, you succeed in doing it.

❏ If you **contrive** an event or situation, you get it to happen, often by dishonest means.

❏ If you say the plot of a novel or film is **contrived**, you mean it is forced and unconvincing.

control (controlling, controlled) ❏ The people who **control** a country or organization are the ones who decide how it is run. *The two controlling bodies plan further talks aimed at creating a single organization.* You can say someone has **control** of a country or organization, or that it is **under** their **control**. You can also say they are **in control**.

❏ If something is **controlled** by an automatic system, the system makes it do whatever is required. *...computerised systems for controlling glasshouses.* ◇ A **control** on a machine is a switch or device used to operate it.

❏ **Controls** are methods a government uses to restrict certain things, like wage increases.

❏ If you **control** yourself or **keep control** of yourself, you act calmly and do not give way to your feelings. A **controlled** person is like this all the time. ◇ If you **lose control** of yourself, you give way to your feelings.

❏ If people **control** something unpleasant or dangerous, they stop it spreading or getting worse; when they succeed, you say it is **under control**. ◇ If something has got **out of control**, nobody has the power to stop it causing damage or harm.

❏ If something is **outside your control** or **beyond your control**, you have no power to do anything about it.

control tower A **control tower** is a building at an airport from which instructions are given to aircraft, especially when they are taking off and landing.

controllable If something is **controllable**, it can be managed or limited.

controller A **controller** in an organization is someone with responsibility for a part of its work. *...the BBC's controller of editorial policy.*

controversial (controversially; controversy, controversies) If something is **controversial** or causes **controversy**, it causes a lot of discussion and disagreement, because many people disapprove of it. *He has been campaigning controversially for the building of a Hindu temple on the site of a mosque.*

contusion A **contusion** is a bruise.

conundrum A **conundrum** is a baffling or puzzling problem.

conurbation A **conurbation** is a large urban area formed when several towns have grown and joined together.

convalesce (convalescing, convalesced; convalescent, convalescence) If you are **convalescing**, you are resting and getting your health back after an illness or operation. **Convalescence** is the period during which you do this. **Convalescent** is used to talk about things connected with this period. *...convalescent weakness.*

convection is the process by which heat travels through gases and liquids.

convector A **convector** or **convector heater** is a heater which heats a room by circulating hot air.

convene (convening, convened) When a meeting or conference is **convened**, someone arranges for it to take place, according to an established procedure. ◇ When a group of people **convene**, they come together for a meeting.

convener (or convenor) A **convener** is (a) someone who arranges for a meeting to take place. (b) a trade union official responsible for organizing shop stewards.

convenience ❏ The **convenience** of something is the fact that it fits in well with what you want. *The convenience of the arrangement pleased Paulette.* ◇ If something is done for your **convenience**, it is done to make things easy for you. **Conveniences** are things which are there to make things easy for you. *...luxury tents containing every convenience.*

❏ See also **public convenience**, **flag of convenience**, **marriage of convenience**.

convenience food Convenience foods are frozen, dried, or tinned foods which require no preparation except heating.

convenience store Convenience stores are shops which stay open long hours.

convenient (conveniently) You say something is **convenient** when it fits in well with what someone wants. *Macnamara's kick had ricocheted conveniently from a defender.* ◇ If something like a shop or station is **convenient**, it is nearby and can easily be reached.

convenor See convener.

convent A convent is (a) a building where nuns live. (b) a school run by nuns.

convention ❑ Conventions are accepted ways of behaving or doing things.
❑ A convention is also (a) a large meeting of an organization or political group. (b) an international agreement, especially one concerned with people's rights. ...*the Geneva Convention.*

conventional (conventionally) ❑ Conventional opinions and behaviour are accepted by most people as normal and right. ◇ The conventional wisdom about something is the generally accepted view of it. ◇ If you say a person is conventional, you mean there is nothing unusual about them or their way of life. ◇ The conventional way of doing something is the way it is normally done. ...*conventionally produced British wines.*
❑ Conventional forces, weapons, or wars are non-nuclear ones.

converge (converging, converged; convergence, convergent) ❑ When people converge on a place, they reach it from different directions. ◇ When roads or rivers converge, they meet or join together.
❑ If things like ideas or systems converge, they become more and more alike until there is no difference between them. You can talk about a convergence of ideas or systems. If different people's ideas are convergent, they are the same. *France and Germany had convergent views about supporting the initiative.*

conversant If you are conversant with something, you are familiar with it.

conversation (conversational, conversationally; conversationalist) When people have a conversation, they talk to each other. If you make conversation, you talk to someone to be polite, rather than because you want to. Conversational is used to talk about things to do with conversations. *She finds his friends elderly, stuffy, and conversationally very heavy going.* If someone is a good conversationalist, they are good at keeping a conversation going.

converse (conversing, conversed; conversely) ❑ When people converse (*pron:* kon-**verse**), they talk to each other.
❑ Converse (*pron:* kon-verse) is used to talk about something working or applying in opposite ways. For example, if John admires Rita, the converse would be that Rita admires John. *Some people mistake politeness for weakness, and conversely, they think that rudeness is a sign of strength.*

convert (conversion) ❑ If something is converted into something else, it is turned into it. You talk about the conversion of one thing to another.
❑ If you convert to a different set of religious or political beliefs or are converted to them, you adopt them in place of the ones you had before. You can talk about someone's conversion to a different set of beliefs. A convert (*pron:* kon-vert) is someone who has changed their religious or political beliefs.
❑ In rugby, if a player converts a try, he scores extra points by kicking the ball over the crossbar. This is called a conversion.

converter See catalytic converter.

convertible ❑ If something is convertible, it can be changed from one thing into another. ◇ A convertible currency is one which can easily be exchanged for another currency.
❑ A convertible is a car with a soft roof which can be folded down or taken off.

convex A convex lens or mirror curves outwards towards its centre. See also concave.

convey ❑ If you convey an idea or piece of information, you succeed in making it understood.
❑ If a vehicle conveys you somewhere, it takes you there.

conveyancing is the process of transferring legal ownership of property.

conveyor belt A conveyor belt is a moving strip or series of rollers used in factories to move items from one place to another.

convict (conviction) ❑ If someone is convicted (*pron:* kon-vikt-id) of a crime, they are found guilty of it. If this has happened to them several times, you can say they have had several convictions. ◇ A convict (*pron:* kon-vikt) is someone serving a prison sentence.
❑ A person's convictions are their strongly held beliefs. Conviction is believing strongly in something. *He talks quickly, voicing his opinions with conviction and persuasiveness.* If someone has the courage of their convictions, they are prepared to stick up for the things they believe in. ◇ If you say something carries conviction, you mean it is likely to be true or likely to be believed.

convince (convincing, convinced; convincingly) ❑ If you convince someone of something, you persuade them it is true. ◇ If you are convinced of something, you are sure it is true. ◇ If you say something is convincing, you mean it makes you believe something is true. *The statistical proof convincingly identified smoking as the commonest cause of premature death in the Western world.*
❑ Convinced is used to describe someone who believes strongly in something. For example, if someone is a convinced Marxist, they believe strongly in the theories of Karl Marx.

convivial (conviviality) A convivial occasion is friendly and enjoyable. You talk about the conviviality of an occasion like this. ◇ A convivial person is friendly and cheerful.

convocation A convocation is a large meeting, especially a meeting of clergy or politicians.

convoluted You say something is convoluted when it is complicated and difficult to follow.

convoy A convoy is a group of ships or other vehicles travelling together.

convulse (convulsing, convulsed; convulsion) ❑ If something like a disaster convulses an area, it stops it functioning in its normal way.
❑ If someone convulses or has convulsions, their body muscles jerk violently and uncontrollably.

convulsive (convulsively) Convulsive body movements are violent and cannot be controlled. *A middle-aged woman shaking convulsively was rushed in for treatment.*

coo When pigeons or doves coo, they make soft low sounds. ◇ If a person coos something, they say it in a soft low voice.

cook (cooking, cooked) ❑ If you cook some food, you heat it, to make it ready to eat. Cooking is preparing food like this. Cooking is also used to talk about a particular style of preparing and cooking food. *Italian seafood cooking has only recently come to the fore.* ◇ A **cook** is someone who prepares food, especially as their job.

❏ If you say someone is **cooking the books**, you mean they are changing figures or a written record, to deceive people. ◇ If someone **cooks up** a dishonest scheme, they plan it.

cookbook A **cookbook** is the same as a cookery book. See **cookery**.

cooker A **cooker** is a piece of equipment for heating food. It is powered by gas or electricity, and is usually a large box-shaped object with an oven, grill, and a top called a hob on which there are gas burners or electric rings.

cookery is preparing and cooking food. ◇ A **cookery book** is a book which suggests different dishes and tells you how to prepare them.

cookie is the usual American word for a biscuit.

cooking oil is oil for frying food.

cool (cooler, coolest; coolness; cooling, cooled; coolly) ❏ If something is **cool**, it has a low temperature but is not cold. ◇ If you **cool** something, you make it less warm. ◇ If you let something **cool down**, you wait for it to become less warm. ◇ If you **cool off**, you make yourself cooler after being too hot.

❏ If someone is **cool** towards another person, they are unfriendly to them. You can talk about someone's **coolness** towards someone else. ◇ If someone is **cool** towards an idea or suggestion, they are not enthusiastic about it. *His programme for economic reform has been coolly received.*

❏ If you remain **cool** in a difficult situation, you stay calm. ◇ If you **keep your cool** or **keep a cool head**, you keep calm and do not panic or lose your temper. ◇ If you **lose your cool**, you are unable to control your temper. ◇ If you **cool down**, you gradually stop being angry. ◇ If an emotion **cools off**, it becomes less strong.

coolant A **coolant** is a liquid or gas used for cooling in various industrial processes.

cooler A **cooler** is a container for making something cool or keeping something cool.

coolie Unskilled workers in China, India, and other parts of Asia used to be called **coolies**.

cooling-off A **cooling-off period** is time taken by both sides during a dispute to rethink their position before further action.

cooling tower A **cooling tower** is a building for cooling water, for example for cooling the water in a factory or power station.

coop (cooped) A **coop** is a cage for a small number of hens. ◇ You say someone is **cooped up** in a place when the place is too small for them, or they are unable to leave it.

cooperate See **co-operate**.

cooperative See **co-operative**.

coordinate See **co-ordinate**.

coot **Coots** are small water birds with black feathers and a white patch above their beaks.

cop (copping, copped) ❏ A **cop** is a police officer.

❏ If you say someone is **copping out** of something, you mean they are avoiding doing it or will not take responsibility for it, and you think they ought to. A **cop-out** is a way of avoiding doing something or taking responsibility.

cope (coping, coped) If you **cope** with a problem or a difficult situation, you manage to deal with it.

copier A **copier** is a machine which can make an exact copy of a piece of writing or a picture.

coping is a rounded, sloping, or roof-shaped layer of bricks, stones, or concrete along the top of a wall.

copious (copiously) A **copious** amount of something is very large. *They drink copiously.*

copper is a soft reddish-brown metal. It is used as an electrical and thermal conductor and in alloys like brass and bronze. ◇ **Copper** is also a reddish-brown colour. ◇ **Coppers** are brown coins of low value. ❏ A **copper** is a police officer.

copper beech The **copper beech** is a type of beech tree with purple or copper-coloured leaves.

copper-bottomed is used to describe things which are financially reliable. *It sounded exactly the copper-bottomed sort of crop a beginner ought to grow.*

copperplate is a style of very neat and regular handwriting.

coppice A **coppice** is a group of trees which are regularly cut low so the shoots which then appear can be used as posts or poles.

copse A **copse** is a small wood.

copulate (copulating, copulated; copulation) When a man and a woman **copulate**, they have sex. You can also say animals **copulate**. **Copulation** is having sex.

copy (copies, copying, copied) ❏ A **copy** is something made to look exactly like something else. ◇ If you **copy** a document, you make a copy of it on a machine such as a photocopier. ◇ If you **copy** what someone has written, you write it down. You can also say you **copy** it **down** or **copy** it **out**.

❏ If you **copy** another person, you do what they do or try to be like them, for example by dressing like them. You can also say you **copy** their behaviour or clothes.

❏ A **copy** of a book, newspaper, or record is one of many identical ones produced at the same time.

copybook If someone **blots their copybook**, they spoil their record of good behaviour or success by doing something wrong. *This is the one blot on his copybook.*

copycat A **copycat** act or crime imitates one that has been done earlier by someone else.

copyright If someone has the **copyright** on something like a piece of writing or music, it is illegal to print it or perform it without their permission.

copywriter A **copywriter** is someone who writes words for advertisements.

coquettish You say a woman is being **coquettish** when she behaves in a playful way, to make herself attractive to men.

cor anglais (*plural:* cors anglais) The **cor anglais** is a woodwind instrument with a double reed. It has a slightly lower pitch than the oboe.

coracle A **coracle** is a simple rounded rowing boat made of woven sticks covered with skins or canvas.

coral is a hard substance found on the seabed of some warm oceans. It is made up of skeletons of very small sea animals.

corbel A **corbel** is a piece of stone or wood sticking out of a wall and supporting an arch, pillar, or beam.

cord is a type of strong string or thin rope.

cordial (cordially, cordiality) ❏ A **cordial** relationship between countries or political leaders is a friendly one. You say a meeting or discussion is **cordial** when the people get on well together; you can also say things take place in a **cordial** atmosphere. *The meetings ended cordially... An official said this year's meeting was remarkable for the cordiality shown by both sides.*
❏ **Cordial** is a sweet non-alcoholic fruit drink. ◇ In the US, **cordial** is a sweet liqueur.

cordite is an explosive substance formerly used in guns and bombs.

cordon (cordoning, cordoned) A **cordon** is a line of police, soldiers, or vehicles formed to stop people entering or leaving an area. If police or soldiers **cordon off** an area, they form a line around it to stop people entering or leaving.

cordon bleu (*pron:* bluh) **Cordon bleu** cookery is of the highest standard.

corduroy is a thick velvety ridged cotton fabric.

core (coring, cored) ❏ The **core** of a fruit is the hard part through its centre where the seeds are. If you **core** an apple or pear, you remove its core. ◇ The **core** of some other object is its central part. *...the sun's core.*
❏ The **core** of something like a problem or proposal is its most important part.
❏ If you say someone is a type of person **to the core**, you mean they are like that and their behaviour or views are never likely to change. *The villagers are royalist to the core.* ◇ If you say a government or political system is **rotten to the core**, you mean it is hopelessly corrupt.

corgi Corgis are a type of dog with short legs and sturdy bodies.

coriander is a plant with parsley-like leaves. Its seeds are used as a spice and its leaves as a herb.

cork is the soft light spongy bark of a Mediterranean tree. A **cork** is a stopper for a bottle, made from cork.

corkscrew A **corkscrew** is a device with a metal spiral-shaped part, for removing the corks from bottles.

cormorant Cormorants are large dark-coloured sea birds with long necks.

corn ❏ Various cereal crops are called **corn**. The word tends to be used for whatever cereal crop is mainly grown in a region or country. It is used for wheat or barley in England, oats in Scotland and Ireland, and maize in the US, Canada, Australia, and New Zealand. ◇ **Corn on the cob** is the long round part of the maize plant with sweetcorn on it. It is eaten as a vegetable.
❏ A **corn** is a small painful area of hard skin which can form on your foot.

cornea (*pron:* korn-ee-a) (corneal) The **cornea** is the curved transparent layer of skin covering the front of your eyeball. **Corneal** is used to talk about things to do with the cornea. *...corneal grafts.*

corned beef is beef which has been cooked, preserved in salt water, then tinned.

corner (cornering, cornered) ❏ A **corner** is a place where two sides or edges of something meet.
❏ A **corner** is also a place where a road bends sharply. ◇ The **corner** of a street is the place where one of its sides comes to an end as it meets another street.
❏ If you say something happens **in every corner** of a place, you mean it happens in all parts of it.
❏ If you **corner** a person or animal, you trap them in a place or situation they cannot escape from. ◇ If you are **in a corner**, you are in a difficult situation from which there seems to be no escape.
❏ If someone **corners the market** in a commodity, they gain control of the trade in it, so that nobody else can succeed in buying or selling it.
❏ If you say something is **around the corner**, you mean it will happen soon. ◇ If you say someone or something has **turned the corner**, you mean they have got through the most difficult part of a problem or crisis.
❏ If you **fight your corner**, you stick up for your own interests in a determined way.
❏ If you **cut corners** when you do something, you do it quickly by being less thorough than you should.
❏ In football, a team is awarded a **corner** when one of the other side sends the ball over their own goal line. The player who takes the corner is allowed a kick from one of the corners at the other side's end of the pitch.

corner shop A **corner shop** is a small shop, usually on a street corner, which sells food and household goods.

cornerstone The **cornerstone** of something is the basis of its existence or success. *He saw European union as a cornerstone of peace and prosperity in the world.*

cornet The **cornet** is a brass band instrument which looks like a short fat trumpet. ◇ An ice-cream **cornet** is a cone-shaped wafer filled with ice cream.

cornfield A **cornfield** is a field where corn is being grown.

cornflakes are a breakfast cereal of flakes made from maize.

cornflour is a very fine white flour made from maize. It is used to make sauces thicker.

cornflower Cornflowers are small flowers with deep blue petals.

cornice (*pron:* korn-iss) A **cornice** is a decorative strip of plaster, wood, or stone along the top of a wall.

Cornish pasty A **Cornish pasty** is a long flat pie with pointed ends and meat and vegetables inside.

cornucopia (*pron:* korn-yew-kope-ee-a) A **cornucopia** of good things is a large number of them.

corny (cornier, corniest) **Corny** jokes, stories, and entertainments are too simple and obvious, or not at all original.

corollary (*pron:* kor-roll-a-ree) (corollaries) A **corollary** of something is something else which follows or results directly from it.

corona (*pron:* kor-rone-a) (*plural:* coronas or coronae) The moon's **corona** is a circle of light surrounding it. ◇ The sun's **corona** is the outermost part of its atmosphere, visible as a faint halo during an eclipse.

coronary (coronaries) **Coronary** is used to talk about things relating to the arteries around the heart. *...coronary disease.* ◇ A **coronary** is a coronary thrombosis.

coronary thrombosis See **thrombosis**.

coronation A king's or queen's **coronation** is the ceremony during which they are crowned.

coroner A **coroner** is an official responsible for investigating sudden, violent, or suspicious deaths.

coronet A **coronet** is a small crown. Coronets are worn by peers and peeresses on formal occasions.

corpora See **corpus**.

corporal A corporal is a junior NCO in the British army, the RAF, and some other armed forces.

corporal punishment is punishing people by hitting or beating them.

corporate is used to talk about something owned by or relating to one or more large businesses or companies. *The company was the subject of several corporate takeovers.* ◇ Corporate is also used to talk about something owned or shared by all the members of a group or organization. *We are a company which places tremendous emphasis on corporate identity.*

corporation A corporation is a large business or company. ◇ The corporation of a town or city is the local authority responsible for running it.

corporation tax is a tax companies have to pay on their profits.

corporatism is a system in which large self-interest groups such as employers' associations and trade unions co-operate with the government in return for a large say in how the country is governed.

corporeal (*pron:* kor-pore-ee-al) is used to talk about things relating to the human body, rather than the mind or spirit. *His temptations lie in the corporeal realm: food, drink, women.*

corps (*pron:* **kore**) (*plural:* corps) A corps is a part of the army which has special duties. *...the catering corps.* ◇ A corps is also a small group of people who do a special job. *...the New Zealand press corps.*

corpse A corpse is a dead body.

corpulent (corpulence) If someone is corpulent, they are fat. Corpulence is being fat.

corpus (*plural:* corpora) The corpus of an author's work is all his or her writings which have been collected or identified. Similarly, you can talk about the corpus of writing on a subject.

corpuscle Corpuscles are red or white blood cells.

corral (*pron:* kor-**rahl**) (corralling, corralled) In the US and Canada, a corral is a fenced-off area where cattle or horses are kept. When horses or cattle are corralled, they are driven into a corral. ◇ You say people are corralled when a lot of them are forced into a confined place.

correct (correctly, correctness, correction) ❏ If something is correct, there are no mistakes in it. *I have to make sure the boxes are all labelled correctly.* ◇ If you correct a mistake, problem, or fault, you put it right. ◇ If you correct a piece of writing or make corrections to it, you indicate the mistakes, or alter them to put them right.

❏ If you say someone is correct, you mean what they have said is true. ◇ If you correct a person, you point out that what they have said is wrong, and tell them what they should have said.

❏ The correct thing is the right or most suitable one. *Beekeepers have to be dressed correctly to cope with the bees... ...the correctness of the umpire's decision.* ◇ Correct behaviour is doing what is thought to be the right thing in a particular situation. ◇ political correctness: see politically correct.

corrective actions are intended to put something right. An action or piece of writing which puts something right can be called a corrective. ◇ Corrective treatment of offenders is intended to stop them offending again.

correlate (correlating, correlated; correlation) If one thing correlates with another, there is a definite connection between them, so that a change in the second thing tends to produce a change in the first. When this happens, you say there is a correlation between the two things.

correspond (corresponding, correspondingly; correspondence) ❏ If something corresponds to something else, the two things are closely related. You can say there is a correspondence between two things. *The government's measure corresponds to the demands of radical economists... Local loans are easier to monitor and are correspondingly less risky.* ◇ You also say something corresponds to something else when it is like it, but affects different people or things, or happens in a different place. *There was no corresponding thaw in the Antarctic during the same period.*

❏ If numbers or amounts correspond, they are the same. *The amount to be borrowed corresponds to about a third of Britain's official reserves.* ◇ Corresponding is used when comparing the same period in different years. For example, if you are talking about June 16th to July 15th 1995, the corresponding period in 1994 was June 16th to July 15th 1994.

❏ If people correspond or carry on a correspondence, they write letters to each other. ◇ A person's correspondence is the letters they receive.

correspondence course A correspondence course is one where you study at home and your work is sent to you by post.

correspondent A TV, radio, or newspaper correspondent is a reporter who covers a special subject or a particular country.

corridor ❏ A corridor is a passage between rooms in a building. ◇ When people talk about the corridors of power, they mean the places where the most important government decisions are made.

❏ The corridor of an old-fashioned railway carriage was a passage down one side, with doors leading into separate compartments.

❏ A corridor is also a strip of land or air space across a country or between two parts of a country along which planes, trains, or road vehicles from another country are allowed to travel.

corroborate (corroborating, corroborated; corroboration, corroborative) If you corroborate what someone says, you provide facts which support it and make it more likely to be true or correct. You call these facts corroboration or describe them as corroborative.

corrode (corroding, corroded; corrosive, corrosion) When a metal corrodes or is corroded, it rusts or is eaten away by chemical action. A corrosive substance is one which has this effect. Damage caused in this way is called corrosion.

corrugated (corrugation) Corrugated metal or cardboard has parallel grooves and ridges in it to make it stronger. These folds are called corrugations.

corrupt (corrupting, corrupted; corruptly, corruption) ❏ A corrupt person behaves dishonestly or illegally in exchange for money or power. *...accusations that he acted corruptly.* ◇ If a system is corrupt, it is run dishonestly and is open to bribery. You can say there is corruption in a system like this.

❏ If someone is **corrupted** by another person, they are made dishonest or immoral. ...*an outcry about the corruption of children's morals.*

corruptible If someone is **corruptible,** they are easily corrupted.

corsair A **corsair** was a pirate, or a pirate ship.

corset A **corset** is a stiff tight piece of underwear worn by some women to make them look slimmer.

cortege (*pron:* kor-**tayzh;** *the 'zh' sounds like 's' in 'pleasure'*) A **cortege** is a procession of cars and people at a funeral.

cortex (cortices) The **cortex** of the brain, or of another organ, is its outer layer.

cortisone is a hormone used to treat arthritis, allergies, and some skin diseases.

corvette A **corvette** is a lightly armed warship.

cosh (coshes, coshing, coshed) A **cosh** is a heavy blunt weapon for hitting people. If someone **coshes** you, they hit you on the head with a cosh or something like it.

cosily (cosiness) See **cosy.**

cosmetic ❏ **Cosmetics** are things like creams and lipsticks which people use on their face or body, to make it look better. ◇ **Cosmetic surgery** is an operation carried out to improve someone's appearance, rather than to treat an illness.

❏ **Cosmetic** measures or changes alter the appearance of something without actually improving its basic nature.

cosmic is used to talk about things belonging to or connected with the universe. ...*cosmic radiation... ...cosmic dust.* ◇ **Cosmic rays** are rays of radiation which reach the earth from outer space.

❏ **Cosmic** is also used to describe things which are to do with everyone, rather than just a few people. ...*themes of cosmic significance.*

cosmology (cosmological, cosmologist) **Cosmology** is the study of the origin and nature of the universe. **Cosmological** is used to talk about things connected with this study. *These first observations raise great cosmological questions.* A **cosmologist** is an expert in this field.

cosmonaut is a Russian name for an astronaut.

cosmopolitan (cosmopolitanism) You say a place is **cosmopolitan** when the people there come from many different countries or cultures. ◇ You say a person is **cosmopolitan** or a **cosmopolitan** when they have lived in several countries and feel equally at home in any of them. You talk about the **cosmopolitanism** of someone like this.

cosmos The **cosmos** is the universe.

cosset (cosseting, cosseted) If you **cosset** someone, you spoil them by doing too much for them and protecting them too much.

cost ❏ The **cost** of something or what it **costs** is how much you need to spend to buy it, make it, or do it. ◇ If you **cost** something, you work out how much it will cost to do it or make it. ◇ If something is sold at **cost price,** it is sold for what it cost the manufacturer to make it or the seller to buy it.

❏ The **cost of living** is the average amount people need to pay for things like food, clothing, housing, and power.

❏ The **cost** of achieving something is the loss, damage, or injury involved in achieving it. ...*their pursuit of profits, made at the cost of much misery to tens of thousands of people.*

◇ If you **count the cost** of something you have done, you try to decide whether you are better off or worse off as a result of it. ◇ If you say something must be done **at all costs,** you mean it must be done even if it means making sacrifices. ◇ If a mistake **costs** you something, you fail to get it as a result of the mistake. *It was his uncharacteristic error that cost the team its first victory in the Premier League.*

cost-effective If something is **cost-effective,** it saves or makes more money than it costs to do or make.

costly (costlier, costliest) If something is **costly,** you have to pay a lot of money for it. ◇ You can also say something people do is **costly** when it causes great loss or damage.

costume is used to talk about the style of clothing traditional to a place or worn during a certain time in history. ...*revellers in medieval costume.* ◇ An actor's **costume** is the set of clothes he or she wears on stage.

❏ A **costume drama** is a play or film set in the past, with the actors wearing the style of clothing from that period.

costume jewellery is jewellery which is not made from real stones or precious metals.

costumier A **costumier** is a person or firm that makes or supplies theatrical or fancy dress costumes.

cosy (cosier, cosiest; cosily, cosiness) (*American spelling:* cozy, cozier *etc*) **Cosy** buildings and rooms are small, warm, and comfortable. ...*sitting cosily around the fire... ...the cosiness of the tearooms.* ◇ If people are on friendly terms, you can call their relationship **cosy.**

cot ❏ A **cot** is a bed with high sides for a very young child. ◇ A **cot death** is the sudden death of a young baby in its sleep, which doctors cannot explain. This phenomenon is sometimes known as SIDS or 'sudden infant death syndrome'.

❏ Americans call a camp bed a **cot.**

coterie (*pron:* kote-er-ee) A **coterie** is a small group of people who work together or are close friends and do not want other people to join them.

cottage A **cottage** is a small house in the country.

cottage cheese is a soft mild white cheese made from sour milk.

cottage industry A **cottage industry** is a small business run from someone's home.

cottage loaf A **cottage loaf** is a loaf consisting of a large round base with a smaller round part on top.

cottage pie is a dish of minced meat with a layer of mashed potato on top.

cotton (cottoning, cottoned) ❏ **Cotton** is cloth made from the soft white fibres of a plant called the **cotton plant.** ◇ **Cotton** is also thread used for sewing.

❏ If you **cotton on** to something, you realize it or understand it.

cotton wool is a white fluffy substance made from the fibres of the cotton plant. It is used for things like applying creams or lotions to the skin.

couch (couches, couching, couched) ❏ A **couch** is a long cushioned piece of furniture for sitting or lying on.

❏ If something like a statement is **couched** in a certain style, it is expressed in that way. *Although couched in the diplomatic language one would expect, the report's contents are devastating.*

couch grass (*pron:* couch *or* cooch) **Couch grass** is a type of grassy weed. It has long roots which help it to spread quickly.

couch potato A couch potato is a lazy person who spends all their spare time watching TV or videos.

couchette (*pron:* koo-**shet**) A couchette is a bed in a railway carriage or ferry boat, which is either folded against the wall or used as an ordinary seat during the day.

cougar (*pron:* koo-gar) A cougar is the same as a puma.

cough ❑ When you cough, you force the air out of your throat with a sudden harsh noise. ◇ If you have a cough, you have an illness which makes you cough a lot. ◇ If you cough blood or phlegm or cough it up, it comes out of your throat when you cough.

❑ If you have to cough up money, you have to give it to someone when you do not want to.

could ❑ When you are talking about the past, you use could to say someone was able to do something, or was allowed to do something. *I was thankful I could walk again... The Olympic Committee said that South Africa could come back.* ◇ If you are talking about the present, you use could to say someone is able to do something, but is not actually doing it. *A fifth of Europe's chemical producers could easily do such deals.* You use could have in a similar way when you are talking about the past. *The soldiers could have used tear gas or rubber bullets; instead they had mown people down with live ammunition.*

❑ You use could when you are describing someone's reactions to something. *Firemen said they were amazed that one truck of liquid gas could cause such a fire.* ◇ You also use could when you are mentioning someone else's use of 'can'. For example, if a man says 'I can speak Gaelic', you report this as 'He said he could speak Gaelic'.

❑ You use could to talk about a possibility in the present or the future. *Don't eat it. It could be a toadstool.*

❑ You use could when you are asking for something politely. *Could I take the car to meet him, please?*

council ❑ A council is the organization responsible for local government in a town or county. A council has elected members called councillors and paid officials. ◇ A council house or flat is one owned by the local council and rented out to people; a person living in one of these houses or flats is called a council tenant.

❑ A council is a panel of people who give advice or run an organization. *...the Arts Council.* ◇ A council is also a specially organized meeting. *The union hopes that a successor will be appointed at its December council.*

Council of Europe The Council of Europe is an organization set up in 1949 to try to get a greater degree of unity between European countries. The Council, which has its headquarters in Strasbourg, has over 30 members.

Council Tax The Council Tax is a local government tax based on the value of people's houses. It replaced the Community Charge in 1993.

councillor A councillor is an elected member of a council.

counsel (counselling, counselled; counsellor) (*American spelling:* counseling, counseled, *etc*) ❑ Counsel is advice or guidance. *I value her counsel.* If you counsel a course of action, you advise someone to take it.

❑ If you counsel someone, you give them advice on how to deal with their problems. Giving advice like this is called counselling; a person who does it is called a coun-

sellor. *...debt counselling.*

❑ A counsel is a barrister who gives advice on a legal case and fights the case in court.

count ❑ When you count, you say all the numbers in order, up to a certain number.

❑ If you count a number of things, you add them up, to see how many there are. A figure worked out like this is called a count. *No wholly reliable count has yet been given.* ◇ If you keep count of a number of things, you keep a record of how many there have been. ◇ If you lose count of a number of things, you cannot remember how many there have been, because there have been so many.

❑ count the cost: see cost.

❑ If something counts, it matters. *It's the small victories that count.* ◇ If something counts against you, it puts you at a disadvantage. *His inexperience might count against him.*

❑ If you count someone or something when you are making a statement, you include them in what you are saying. *Fishing is still the single most popular sport unless you count rambling.* ◇ If you count someone or something as a particular thing, you regard them as that thing. *This will count as a victory.*

❑ If you say you can count on someone or something, you mean you can rely on them.

❑ A count is a legal charge brought against someone. *He was convicted on three counts of fraud.* ◇ If you say something is wrong on a number of counts, you mean it is wrong for that number of reasons.

❑ A count is a European nobleman with the same rank as a British earl.

countdown When there is a countdown before an event such as the launch of a spacecraft, the last remaining hours, minutes, and finally seconds are counted aloud, down to zero. ◇ The period of time leading up to any keenly awaited event can be called a countdown. *The countdown to next month's Games is now well-advanced.*

countenance (countenancing, countenanced) If you say someone will not countenance something, you mean they will never agree to it. ◇ A person's countenance is their face and the expression on it.

counter (countering, countered) ❑ A counter is a long flat surface in a shop where goods are laid out or sold. A counter in a bank or post office is a similar surface where you carry out your business. ◇ If you buy something under the counter, you buy it secretly and illegally.

❑ A counter is also a small flat disc used in board games. ◇ bargaining counter: see bargain.

❑ If you counter something that someone does, you take action to limit its effects. ◇ If you counter what someone says, you put forward a different point of view.

counter- is added to a word (a) to talk about actions aimed against the thing described by the word. *...counter-corruption measures.* (b) to talk about something similar to the thing described by the word and done in response to it. *There's been a flurry of accusations and counter-accusations.*

counter-attack When an army counter-attacks or launches a counter-attack, they attack an enemy which has just attacked them. Similarly, you can talk about a sports team counter-attacking.

counter-espionage is the actions a country takes to limit the effects of another country spying on it.

counter-measure A counter-measure is (a) an action taken to reduce the effects of something harmful. *...counter-measures against the epidemic.* (b) an action taken by a government in response to an unfriendly act by another government.

counter-productive If something is counter-productive, it has the opposite effect from what is intended.

counter-revolution (counter-revolutionary, counter-revolutionaries) A counter-revolution is a revolution aimed at undoing changes brought about in a previous revolution. ◇ In a Communist country, if someone is accused of being a counter-revolutionary or of taking part in counter-revolutionary activities, it is claimed they are trying to undo the good work of the Party and restore features of the pre-Communist regime.

counteract If you counteract something, you do something which reduces its effects. *...an inhaler to counteract asthma.*

counterbalance (counterbalancing, counterbalanced) If something counterbalances something else, it makes up for it with something which has an equal but opposite effect.

counterclockwise is the usual American word for 'anticlockwise'.

counterfeit (counterfeiting, counterfeited; counterfeiter) If someone counterfeits money or a document, they illegally make something which looks like the real thing. You say the thing they make is counterfeit or a counterfeit. *...counterfeit currency.* A person who counterfeits things is called a counterfeiter.

counterfoil A counterfoil is part of a cheque or ticket which you keep as proof of payment.

countermand If someone countermands an order, they cancel it, usually by giving a different order.

counterpane A counterpane is a fancy cover for a bed.

counterpart A counterpart of someone or something is a person or thing with a similar role in a different place. *London Zoo now has fewer visitors than its counterpart in Chester.*

counterpoint In music, counterpoint is two or more tunes being played together to produce a pleasing or satisfying effect.

countersign If you countersign a document, you sign it after someone else has signed it, to confirm that the signature is theirs.

countertenor A countertenor is a male singer with a special kind of high singing voice, closer in quality to a woman's or boy's voice than an ordinary tenor's.

counterweight If something acts as a counterweight to something else, it acts in an opposite way, and prevents it having any extreme effects. *The party promoted several more pragmatic men as a counterweight to the impassioned anti-communists.*

countess (countesses) In Britain, a countess is the wife or widow of an earl, or a peeress in her own right. She ranks below a marchioness, but above a viscountess. ◇ In some other countries, a countess is the wife or widow of a count, or a woman with the same rank as a count.

countless things means a great many of them, too many to be counted. *It was a routine maintenance operation that has been carried out countless times in the past.*

country (countries) ❏ A country is one of the political units the world is divided into. Countries have distinct boundaries and usually their own government, flag, and official language or languages. ◇ The people who live in a country are sometimes referred to as the country. *The announcements immediately alienated half the country.* ◇ When a prime minister goes to the country, he or she holds a general election.
❏ The country is all land which is away from towns and cities. ◇ Country music is the same as country-and-western music.

country-and-western is a style of popular music based on the folk songs of white people in country areas of the southern and western US. It consists mainly of sad and sentimental ballads with guitar accompaniment.

country club A country club is a club in the country where members can play sports or attend social events.

country dancing is traditional folk dancing which several couples perform in rows, circles, or squares.

country house A country house is a large house in the country owned by a rich or titled family.

country seat The country seat of a rich or titled person is their large house in the country, as distinct from their house in town.

countryman (countrymen) ❏ Your countrymen are people who belong to the same country as you.
❏ A countryman is a person brought up in the country who prefers living there, rather than in the town.

countryside The countryside is land away from towns and cities.

countrywide is used to describe things which happen or exist across an entire country. *...countrywide demonstrations.*

countrywoman (countrywomen) Your countrywomen are women who belong to the same country as you.

county (counties) A county is one of the administrative areas which England, Wales, Ireland, and some other English-speaking countries are divided into.

county council A county council is the organization responsible for local government in an English, Welsh, or Irish county.

county town A county town is the most important town in a county, from which the county is run.

coup (*pron:* koo) ❏ A coup is the same as a coup d'état.
❏ A coup is also an unlikely achievement which someone manages to pull off.

coup d'état (coups d'état) (*both pron:* koo day-tah) If someone stages a coup d'état, they violently seize power from the government of a country.

coup de grâce (*pron:* koo de grahss) If you give something the coup de grâce, you destroy its last remaining chance of success.

coupé (*pron:* koo-pay) A coupé is a car with a sloping back, two doors, and seats for two or four people.

couple (coupling, coupled) ❏ A couple is two people who are married, living together, or having a sexual or romantic relationship.
❏ A couple of people or things usually means two of them. Sometimes people use it in a vague way to mean a small number, not necessarily two.
❏ If you talk about something coupled with something else, you mean the two things together, especially when

you are talking about the effects they produce together. *Economic mismanagement coupled with the absence of Western aid have reduced it to the status of one of the world's poorest countries.*

couplet A couplet is two lines of poetry, one coming after the other. They usually rhyme with each other and have the same rhythm.

coupon A coupon is a slip of paper printed by the maker or supplier of a product. If you present the coupon in a shop, you pay less for the product. ◇ A coupon is also a small form you fill in and send off to ask for information about something. ◇ A football coupon is an entry form for the football pools.

courage (courageous, courageously) You talk about a person's courage or say they are courageous when they do something difficult or dangerous in spite of being afraid. *He courageously voiced his political convictions.* ◇ courage of your convictions: see convict.

courgette (*pron:* koo-er-zhet; *the 'zh' sounds like 's' in 'pleasure'*) Courgettes are a type of small green marrow.

courier A courier is (a) someone paid to carry a letter or special goods from one place to another. (b) someone whose job is looking after holidaymakers.

course (coursing, coursed) ❑ You add of course to a statement to suggest that what you are saying is obviously true. *There is of course an element of truth in this argument.*

❑ A course or course of action is a possible way of dealing with a problem or issue.

❑ A course is (a) a series of lessons or lectures on a subject. (b) a series of things you have done to you as part of medical treatment. *...a course of chemotherapy.*

❑ A course is one part of a meal.

❑ A golf course or racecourse is often called a course.

❑ The course taken by a ship or plane is the direction it goes in. When this direction alters, you say the ship or plane changes course. Similarly, when a government alters its policy on something, you can say it changes course. ◇ If something is on course, it is progressing in the right way at the expected rate. If something happens to spoil this, you can say it has been sent off course. *The Chancellor said the government was on course for its goal of permanently low inflation.*

❑ The course of something is the way it develops or progresses. *In the course of her career she has sung around 48 different operatic roles.* When something runs or takes its course, it progresses naturally and comes to a natural end. ◇ If something is done as a matter of course, it is done as part of a regular routine. *All prison phone calls are recorded legally as a matter of course.* ◇ in due course: see due.

❑ If water or some other liquid courses somewhere, it flows quickly.

court ❑ A court or court of law is a place where legal matters are decided by a judge and jury or by a magistrate. The judge and jury in a case are sometimes called the court. *The court was told that some of the attacks lasted for two hours.* ◇ When people settle a dispute or disagreement out of court, they settle it amongst themselves, without going to a court. *...out-of-court damages.*

❑ If an idea or suggestion is laughed out of court, it is dismissed as being too silly to be worth thinking about.

❑ A court is an area marked out for playing a game like tennis, badminton, or squash. ◇ If you say the ball is in

someone's court, you mean it is now up to them to take some action.

❑ The court of a king or queen is the household where they live and work, and the people who work for them.

❑ If one person or organization courts another, they try to win them over to their way of thinking or gain their support. ◇ If someone courts popularity, they do things which they hope will make them popular.

❑ If a man courts a woman, he tries to win her affection. ◇ If a man and woman are courting, they are going out with each other regularly.

❑ If you say someone is courting danger or disaster, you mean they are doing something very risky, which could have serious consequences if things go wrong.

court martial (court martialling, court martialled) (*American spelling:* court martialing, court martialed) If someone in the armed forces is court martialled, they are tried by a military court called a court martial for something wrong they have done. The trial is also called a court martial. The plural of 'court martial' is court martials or courts martial.

court of appeal (courts of appeal) A court of appeal is a court which deals with appeals against legal decisions.

court of inquiry (courts of inquiry) In the armed forces, a court of inquiry is an official investigation into a serious incident. The people who carry out the investigation are also called a court of inquiry.

court of law (courts of law) See court.

courteous (courteously) A courteous person is well-mannered and considerate. *Mr Coleridge answered questions courteously and directly.*

courtesan (*pron:* kor-tiz-zan) In the past, a courtesan was a woman who was looked after financially by a wealthy man she had sexual relations with.

courtesy (courtesies) ❑ Courtesy is polite and considerate behaviour. Courtesies are polite or considerate words or actions.

❑ If you say something happens courtesy of someone or something, you mean they made it possible. ◇ If something is done courtesy of someone, they have given their permission for it. *The extracts appear courtesy of Jonathan Cape.*

courthouse In the US and some other countries, a courthouse is a building containing one or more law courts.

courtier In the past, courtiers were people who spent a lot of time at the court of a king or queen.

courtly behaviour is dignified and polite.

courtroom A courtroom is a room where a law court meets.

courtship A couple's courtship is the time they spend getting to know each other, before deciding to make their relationship permanent. ◇ Displays by birds and animals to attract a mate are also called courtship.

courtyard A courtyard is a small area surrounded by buildings or walls.

cousin ❑ Your cousins or first cousins are the children of your aunts and uncles. See also second cousin.

❑ People or animals that have something in common with other people or animals are sometimes called their cousins. *A whole series of cold-water marine animals have been displaced in the past decade by their warm-water cousins.*

couture (*pron:* koo-tyoor) (couturier) Couture is high fashion designing and dressmaking. A **couturier** is someone who designs, makes, and sells expensive fashion clothes for women. See also **haute couture**.

cove A cove is a small bay.

coven (*pron:* kuv-ven) A coven is a meeting of witches.

covenant (*pron:* kuv-ven-ant) A covenant is a legal written agreement between two people or groups. ◇ If you covenant money to a charity or a trust, you make a formal written promise to pay that sum each year for a fixed period. The promise is called a covenant or deed of covenant.

cover (covering, covered) ❑ If you cover something or cover it up, you put something over it to hide or protect it. ◇ A cover is something put over an object to hide or protect it. ◇ The cover of a book or magazine is its outside part. ◇ Bed covers are things like sheets, blankets, and duvets which go on top of a bed.

❑ You say something covers something else when it forms a layer over it.

❑ If you do something under cover of darkness, you take advantage of the dark in order to do it. You can also do things under cover of other situations. *Soldiers were ransacking shops under cover of a curfew.*

❑ If you take cover, you shelter from the weather or gunfire. Cover is used to talk about places where you can shelter or hide. *People ran for cover to air raid shelters.*

❑ If you cover a certain distance, for example when you are driving or running, that is how far you go. ◇ If something covers a certain area, it extends over it. *Some of the warrens cover almost one acre.*

❑ If something covers a certain topic, it deals with it or includes it. ◇ If something like a law covers a particular set of people or things, it applies to them.

❑ If a journalist covers an event, he or she reports on it.

❑ If a sum of money covers something, it is enough to pay for it. ◇ A cover charge is a set sum you have to pay in some clubs and restaurants, in addition to the money you spend on food and drinks.

❑ If an insurance policy covers someone or something, it guarantees that money will be paid if they come to some harm.

❑ A cover is something used to hide or disguise what is really going on. *He accused the government of using the relationship as a cover for drug activities.* ◇ If someone covers up something they do not want other people to know about, they hide it from them. Hiding something like this is called a cover-up.

❑ A cover of a song is another version made by a different performer from the original one.

cover girl A cover girl is a woman whose photograph appears on the front of a magazine.

cover-up See cover.

coverage The coverage of something which is happening is the reporting of it in the newspapers or the showing of it on TV.

covering A covering of something is a layer of it on top of something else.

covering letter A covering letter is a letter sent with another document or a parcel, to give more information or explain why it is being sent.

coverlet A coverlet is a fancy cover for a bed.

covert (*usual pron:* koe-vert) (covertly) Covert is used to describe things which are done secretly. *His screenplay reveals the dirty tricks carried out covertly at that time.*

covet (coveting, coveted) If you covet something belonging to someone else, you want very much to have it for yourself.

covetous (covetousness) Covetous behaviour shows a longing to have something belonging to someone else. *...objects which are likely to arouse covetousness.*

cow (cowed) ❑ Cows are adult female cattle. When people talk about cows, they often mean cattle generally, and not just the adult females. ◇ The females of some other species are also called cows, for example female elephants, seals, and whales.

❑ If someone is cowed, they are frightened into behaving a certain way.

coward (cowardly, cowardice) A coward is someone who lacks courage and is unable to face difficult or dangerous situations. You say someone like this is cowardly or talk about their cowardice. ◇ People call a violent act cowardly when it involves little risk to the person who commits it.

cowboy ❑ In the US, a cowboy is a man whose job is to look after cattle. In films about the Wild West, male characters are often called cowboys, whether they have anything to do with cows or not; these films are sometimes called cowboy films.

❑ If you call contractors or tradesmen cowboys, you mean they do their job badly or sell shoddy goods.

cower (cowering, cowered) If people are cowering somewhere, they are hiding and afraid to come out. ◇ You also say someone cowers when they shrink away from someone, because they are afraid of them.

cowhide is leather made from the skin of a cow.

cowl ❑ A cowl is a large loose hood, especially one worn by a monk.

❑ A cowl is also a metal cover on a chimney which helps the smoke get out and stops the wind coming down.

cowman (cowmen) A cowman is a man whose job is looking after cattle on a farm.

cowpat A cowpat is a pool of cow's dung, which gradually becomes solid.

cowrie A cowrie is an oval shell with bright markings on it. The shellfish which lives in it is also called a cowrie.

cowshed A cowshed is a building where cows are kept or milked.

cowslip Cowslips are small wild plants with sweet-smelling yellow flowers.

cox (coxes) The cox of a rowing boat is its coxswain.

coxswain (*pron:* kok-sn) The coxswain of a rowing boat is the person who steers it.

coy (coyly, coyness) If a woman is being coy, she is pretending to be shy and modest. *She bowed her head coyly... There was no need for this coyness.* ◇ If someone is coy about something, they are unwilling to give information about it.

coyote (*pron:* koy-ote-ee) Coyotes are wolf-like wild dogs in North America.

cozy See cosy.

crab Crabs are sea creatures which people eat. They have a flat oval body covered by a shell, and five pairs of legs with claws on the front pair.

crab apple A crab apple is a kind of small sour apple.

crabbed handwriting is squashed up and difficult to read. ◇ Crabbed also means the same as 'crabby'.

crabby A crabby person is bad-tempered and unpleasant.

crack ❏ If something cracks, it gets slightly damaged and lines called cracks appear in it. You say objects with cracks in them are cracked. ◇ Cracks are also narrow gaps formed naturally in the ground or in rock.
❏ A crack is a loud sharp sound, as if something is breaking.
❏ If a relationship cracks, it begins to weaken, because of quarrels or disagreements. You can talk about cracks in a relationship. ...the first signs of the cracks in the coalition.
❏ If a person cracks or cracks up, they become mentally ill, because of stress. ◇ If you say someone is cracked, you mean they are mentally ill.
❏ If you have a crack at something, you make an attempt at it. ◇ If you crack a problem or code, you succeed in working it out.
❏ If you crack a joke, you make a witty remark. ◇ Crack is amusing and enjoyable banter, especially in Ireland. ◇ A crack is a humorous comment, especially a slightly rude or insulting one.
❏ Crack is a crystalline form of the drug cocaine which some people smoke. Overdosing with crack can be fatal.
❏ Crack is used to describe someone who is excellent at what they do. ...crack troops.
❏ If you do something at the crack of dawn, you do it very early in the morning.
❏ If people in authority crack down on someone or something, they apply rules or laws strictly against them. A crackdown is strong official action taken against a group of people.
❏ If you get cracking with something, you get down to it, without wasting time. ◇ If something is done at a cracking pace, it is done very briskly.
❏ If you say something is not all it's cracked up to be, you mean it is not as good as people say.

crackdown See crack.

cracker ❏ A cracker is a thin crisp biscuit, usually eaten with cheese.
❏ A cracker is also a cardboard tube wrapped in fancy paper, which is pulled apart with a bang to get the small gift and paper hat inside.
❏ You can praise something highly by saying it is a cracker. It is a cracker of a book.
❏ If you say someone is crackers, you mean they are crazy.

crackle (crackling, crackled) If something crackles, it makes a series of short harsh noises. You talk about the crackle of something like this. ◇ If you say something like a show crackles, you mean it is lively and exciting.

crackling is a series of short harsh noises.
❏ Crackling is also the crunchy brown skin of roasted meat, especially pork.

crackpot ideas are strange or crazy. You say someone who has ideas like these is a crackpot.

cradle (cradling, cradled) ❏ A cradle is a small bed with sides for a baby. Some cradles can be rocked from side to side. ◇ If something happens to you from the cradle to the grave, it carries on throughout your lifetime.
❏ If you cradle something, you hold it very carefully in your hands or arms.
❏ The cradle of something is the place where it began. ...Pittsburgh, the cradle of that industrial revolution.

craft ❏ A boat or spacecraft can be called a craft (plural: craft).
❏ A craft (plural: crafts) is an activity like weaving, carving, or pottery which involves making things skilfully by hand. ◇ Craft is used to talk about things connected with crafts. ...craft fairs. ◇ Other activities which involve skill can also be called crafts. He learned his craft in provincial theatre. ◇ If someone makes something in a skilful way, you can say they craft it. People often say something is well crafted.

craftsman (craftsmen; craftsmanship) Craftsmen are people who make things skilfully with their hands. Their skill is called craftsmanship. You also talk about the craftsmanship of something which is beautiful and skilfully made. The silver is superb in its craftsmanship and design.

crafty (craftily) A crafty person gets what they want by using clever and often deceitful methods. You can also call their ideas or methods crafty. ...a craftily designed referendum.

crag (craggy) A crag is the rocky top of a mountain, or a steep rocky cliff. A craggy mountain or cliff is steep and rocky. ◇ A craggy face has strong features and deep lines.

cram (cramming, crammed) If people or things cram a place or are crammed into it, it is very full of them. You can also say a place is crammed with people or things.

cramp ❏ If you have cramp or cramps, you feel a severe pain caused by a muscle suddenly contracting.
❏ If you say a person or a thing cramps something, you mean they limit or restrict it. The trouble is that the system cramps productivity gains.
❏ If a place is cramped, there is not enough room there.

crampon Crampons are spikes which climbers attach to their boots so they can climb rocks covered with ice or snow.

cranberry (cranberries) Cranberries are sour-tasting red berries. They are used to make a sauce which is eaten with turkey.

crane (craning, craned) ❏ A crane is a large machine which moves heavy things by lifting them in the air.
❏ Cranes are long-legged wading birds with long necks and long bills. They live in marshes and other flat areas.
❏ If you crane your neck, you stretch it so you can see better.

crane fly See daddy-long-legs.

cranial is used to talk about things to do with the cranium. ...cranial cavity.

cranium (plural: craniums or crania) The cranium is the round part of the skull which contains the brain.

crank (cranky) ❏ If you call someone a crank, you mean they have odd ideas or behave in a strange way. You can say someone like this is cranky, or call their ideas cranky.
❏ If you crank a device or machine, you turn a handle to make it work. The handle is called a crank. ◇ If you crank up a machine of any kind, you get it started. ◇ If someone cranks up something like a system or organization, they get it to operate more effectively. ◇ If a person or firm cranks something out, they produce it in large

numbers.

crankshaft In an internal combustion engine, the crankshaft is the main shaft, which the connecting rods are attached to.

cranny (crannies) The crannies of something are the parts which are most secret or most difficult to reach. *Background music is creeping into just about every cranny of urban life.* ◇ nook and cranny: see nook.

crap is used to say (a) something is useless or of poor quality. *He described one of the group's products as 'total crap'.* (b) someone is no good at something. *I'm a crap swimmer.* ◇ If you say someone is talking crap, you mean they are talking nonsense.

crash (crashes, crashing, crashed) ❑ If a vehicle crashes, it runs into something and gets damaged. An accident like this is called a crash. ◇ If someone or something crashes to the ground, they fall noisily. ◇ A crash is a sudden loud noise.
❑ If a business or system crashes, it fails suddenly, due to money problems. ◇ If a computer or computer program crashes, it breaks down suddenly.
❑ Some people use crashing to emphasize how bad something is. *I thought Napoleon's birthplace a crashing bore.*

crash barrier A crash barrier is a safety fence to stop vehicles going off the road or crossing over to the wrong side.

crash course A crash course is a very short course in which you learn the basics of a subject.

crash helmet A crash helmet is a helmet worn by cyclists and motor cyclists to protect their heads if they have an accident. Crash helmets are also worn in some sports.

crash-land (crash-landing) If a plane crash-lands or makes a crash-landing, it makes an emergency landing and is damaged. You can also say the pilot crash-lands the plane.

crass If you call something a person does or says crass, you mean it is particularly stupid.

crate A crate is a large box for storing or transporting things.

crater A crater is a very large hole in the ground, caused by something crashing into it, or by an explosion. ◇ The crater of a volcano is the bowl-shaped area surrounding its mouth.

cravat (*pron:* cra-vat) A cravat is a scarf made of silk or a similar material, which a man wears tucked inside the open collar of his shirt.

crave (craving, craved) If you crave something or have a craving for it, you desperately want to have it.

craven If you say someone is craven, you mean they are afraid of people who are putting pressure on them, and give in to them too easily. You can also talk about craven attitudes or behaviour. *...a craven anxiety to please.*

crawl (crawler; crawling) ❑ If you crawl, you move forward on your hands and knees. When insects, worms, or snakes crawl, they creep along with their bodies close to the ground. ◇ If something crawls or moves at a crawl, it moves very slowly. You can also say something takes place at a crawl.
❑ The crawl is a swimming stroke. When you do the crawl, you lie on your front and kick your feet like paddles, at the same time bringing your arms over your head

one after the other.
❑ If someone crawls to someone else, they try to win their favour by flattering them and playing up to them. You call someone like this a crawler.
❑ If a place is crawling with people or things, it seems to be full of them.

crayfish (*plural:* crayfish *or* crayfishes) Crayfish are shellfish like small lobsters which live in rivers and ponds.

crayon A crayon is a coloured pencil, or a stick of coloured wax or clay.

craze A craze is something which is very popular for a short time.

crazed If you say someone or their behaviour is crazed, you mean they are wild and out of control.

crazy (crazier, craziest; crazily, craziness) ❑ If you say someone is crazy, you mean they behave oddly, because they are mentally ill. ◇ You also say someone is crazy when they do or say something very silly. An action or idea can also be called crazy. ◇ Crazy is also used to describe things which seem very strange or extreme. *The ball ricocheted crazily... ...the craziness of the situation.*
❑ If someone is crazy about something, they are very keen on it.

crazy paving is a ground covering made up of differently sized and shaped pieces of stone fitted together.

creak (creaking, creaked; creaky) If something creaks, it makes a harsh squeaking sound; you can say something like this is creaky or creaking. ◇ You can also say something is creaky or creaking if it is likely to break down or collapse.

cream (creaming, creamed) ❑ Cream is a fatty substance made from milk which can be used in cooking or added to desserts to improve flavour. ◇ Other substances with a similar texture are also called cream. *...moisturizing cream.* ◇ If you cream two or more substances, you mix them together until they are smooth.
❑ You can call the best people or things in a group the cream. *They draw their men from the cream of the Party's youth trainees.* ◇ If someone creams off the best people or things in a group, they separate them from the others, so they can be given special treatment.
❑ Cream is a yellowish-white colour.

cream cheese is a rich soft white cheese.

cream cracker A cream cracker is a crisp unsweetened biscuit which is often eaten with cheese.

cream tea A cream tea is an afternoon snack of a pot of tea and scones with jam and clotted cream.

creamy food has cream in it. ◇ Creamy things are a yellowish-white colour.

crease (creasing, creased) If you crease a material, you crush it and cause lines or folds called creases to appear in it. ◇ If your face creases or is creased, lines appear there, because you are laughing or frowning. ◇ The creases in someone's trousers are the folds at the front and back. ◇ In cricket, the crease is a line near the wicket where the batsman stands.

create (creating, created; creator, creation) If someone creates something, they make it happen or exist. When this happens, you say they are the thing's creator; you also talk about the creation of the thing. *...the creation of a multi-party state.* ◇ You also say a writer creates the characters in a book. The writer is the creator of the characters; each of them is his or her **creation**. ◇ In the Bible, the making of the universe by God is called the **Creation**. God is often called **the Creator**.

creative (creativity) ❏ If you say someone is **creative**, you mean they are able to think up and develop original ideas, especially in art. You call this ability **creativity**. Creative is also used to describe activities in which people are encouraged to develop original ideas. ...*a creative writing course.*

❏ **Creative accounting** is the practice of setting out accounts or balance sheets in such a way that they give a misleading impression; this is sometimes done to cover up irregularities or make things look better than they really are.

creature A **creature** is any living thing which can move about. ◇ A person who is strange or remarkable in some way is sometimes called a **creature**. *James Stirling was that rare creature, a British architect of world renown.* ◇ **Creature comforts** are the things you need to live a comfortable life.

crèche (*pron:* kresh) A **crèche** is a place where parents can leave their children to be looked after while they are at work.

credence (*pron:* creed-dens) If something gives **credence** to a statement or idea, it makes it easier to believe.

credentials If you talk about someone's **credentials**, you mean their experience and qualifications, which make them suitable for a particular task or job. You can also use **credentials** to talk about a letter or certificate which proves they have these things.

credible (credibly, credibility) ❏ If you say something is **credible**, you mean you can believe it might be true. You talk about the **credibility** of something like this.

❏ You use **credible** to say someone or something could be successful in the future; for example, if you say someone is a **credible** leader, you mean they could succeed as a leader. *He was the only figure who could credibly run the country... This will damage Labour's credibility as an alternative government.* ◇ You say there is a **credibility gap** when there is a difference between what someone says and what they actually do.

credit (crediting, credited) ❏ **Credit** is a system by which goods or services can be obtained before they have been paid for. You say goods and services like these are bought **on credit**. ◇ If a bank account is **in credit**, it has some money in it and is not overdrawn.

❏ If you get the **credit** for something or are **credited** with it, people believe you are responsible for it and praise you. ◇ The **credits** are a list of people who helped to make a film or TV programme. The list appears at the beginning or end of the film or programme.

❏ If you say you cannot **credit** something, you mean you cannot believe it.

credit account If a customer has a **credit account** with a shop, they do not have to pay for goods until some time after they get them.

credit card A **credit card** is a plastic card with which you can buy goods on credit.

credit note A **credit note** is a slip of paper given to someone who returns goods to a shop; it allows them to buy other goods of the same value without paying for them.

credit transfer A **credit transfer** is a direct payment of money from one bank account to another.

creditable (creditably) If you say something is **creditable**, you mean it deserves credit or praise. *The magazine performed creditably, increasing its circulation by 4.8%.*

creditor Someone's **creditors** are the people or businesses they owe money to.

creditworthy (creditworthiness) If you say someone is **creditworthy** or talk about their **creditworthiness**, you mean you can safely lend them money, because everything you can find out about them suggests they would pay it back.

credo (*pron:* kree-doh *or* kray-doh) (credos) Someone's **credo** is a set of beliefs, principles, or opinions which strongly influences the way they behave.

credulous (credulity) You say someone is **credulous** when they are too ready to believe what they are told. You can talk about the **credulity** (*pron:* cred-yool-it-y) of someone like this.

creed A **creed** is a set of beliefs, principles, or opinions which strongly influences the way people live their lives. ◇ You can also call a religion a **creed**.

creek A **creek** is an arm of the sea which stretches a long way into the land. ◇ In America and Australia, a **creek** is a small stream or river.

creel A **creel** is a basket for putting fish in.

creep (creeping, crept *not* 'creeped') ❏ If someone or something **creeps** somewhere, they move there very quietly and slowly. ◇ If someone **creeps up on** you, they approach you very slowly, without you noticing.

❏ If something like an amount or rate **creeps up**, it gradually gets bigger or higher. ◇ If something **creeps in**, it gradually begins to appear. *You can't allow complacency to creep in.*

creeper Creepers are plants with long stems which wrap themselves around things.

creepy If something is **creepy**, it makes you frightened and uneasy.

creepy-crawly (creepy-crawlies) A **creepy-crawly** is any small insect which gives you feelings of fear or disgust.

cremate (cremating, cremated; cremation) When someone is **cremated**, their dead body is burned. The burning of a dead body is called a **cremation**.

crematorium (*plural:* crematoria *or* crematoriums) A **crematorium** is a building where cremations take place.

crème de la crème (*pron:* crem de la crem) If you talk about the **crème de la crème**, you mean the very best people or things of their kind.

creole ❏ A **creole** is a language developed from a mixture of different languages, which has become the main language in a place. See also **pidgin**.

❏ A **Creole** is a person descended from the Europeans who first colonized the West Indies or the southern US. You can also call someone a **Creole** if they are of mixed African and European race and live in the West Indies.

creosote (creosoting, creosoted) **Creosote** is a thick dark liquid made from coal tar which is used to protect wood from the weather. If you **creosote** something wooden, you coat it with creosote.

crepe is a thin fabric with an uneven wrinkled surface.

crepe paper is a brightly coloured paper with an uneven ridged surface, often used for making decorations.

crept See **creep**.

crescendo (*pron:* kre-shen-doh) (*plural:* crescendos *or* crescendi) A **crescendo** is a gradual increase in loudness, particularly in music. ◇ You can also use **crescendo** to talk about an increase in intensity of behaviour or feelings. ...*a crescendo of discontent.*

crescent A **crescent** is a curved shape which is wide in the centre with narrow pointed ends, like the moon in its first and last quarters. ◇ A **crescent** is also a curved row of buildings, or a curved street.

cress is a plant with small strong-tasting green leaves, which are used in salads or as a garnish.

crest (crested) ❑ The **crest** of a hill or wave is the highest part. If you **crest** a height, you reach its highest point. ◇ You say someone is **on the crest of a wave** when things are going very well for them.
❑ A **crest** is a design used as a symbol by a family, town, or organization. If something has a crest on it, you can say it is **crested**.
❑ Some birds have a tuft of feathers on their head called a **crest**. Birds with a crest sometimes have **crested** as part of their name. ...*the crested tit.*

crestfallen If someone looks **crestfallen**, they look sad and disappointed.

cretin If you call someone a **cretin**, you mean they are very stupid.

crevasse (*pron:* kriv-vass) A **crevasse** is a deep crack in thick ice.

crevice (*pron:* krev-iss) A **crevice** is a narrow crack in a rock.

crew (crewed) The **crew** of a ship, plane, or spacecraft are the people on it who operate it. You can say a ship, plane, or spacecraft is **crewed** by particular people. ◇ A **crew** is also a group of people with special technical skills who work together. ...*the camera crew.*

crew cut A **crew cut** is a short cropped hairstyle for men.

crewman (crewmen) A **crewman** is a member of a ship's or boat's crew.

crib (cribbing, cribbed) If you **crib**, you copy something written by someone else. ◇ A **crib** is a translation or list of answers used by students, often to cheat. ◇ Americans call a baby's cot a **crib**.

cribbage is a card game in which you keep the score by putting pegs in a wooden board.

crick If you have a **crick** in your neck, you have a pain there caused by a sore muscle.

cricket (cricketer) ❑ **Cricket** is an outdoor game played between two teams who try to score points, called runs, by hitting a ball with a wooden bat. Someone who plays cricket is called a **cricketer**.
❑ **Crickets** are small jumping insects which produce a chirping sound by rubbing their wings together.

crime A **crime** is an illegal action for which someone can be punished by law. ◇ You can also call something which is morally wrong a **crime**. *For that generation, dipping into capital was as heinous a crime as getting into debt.*

criminal (criminally) A **criminal** is someone who has committed a crime. ◇ You use **criminal** to talk about things connected with crime. *These people are criminally insane.*

criminal law is the part of country's set of laws concerned with what counts as a crime, and with the punishment of people who commit one. See also **civil law**.

criminology (criminologist) **Criminology** is the scientific study of crime and criminals. A **criminologist** is an expert on this.

crimp If something **crimps** something else, it restricts it. A **crimp** is a restriction. ◇ If you **crimp** a piece of pastry or fabric, you make small folds along its edges. ◇ If you **crimp** your hair, you make tight waves in it, usually with heated tongs.

crimson is a dark purplish-red colour.

cringe (cringing, cringed) If something makes you **cringe**, it makes you feel very embarrassed. ◇ If you **cringe** from someone or something, you back away because you are afraid.

crinkle (crinkling, crinkled; crinkly) If something **crinkles** or is **crinkled**, it gets creased or slightly folded. **Crinkles** are small creases or folds. ◇ If something has a lot of crinkles, you can say it is **crinkly**.

crinoline (*pron:* krin-o-lin) **Crinolines** were full stiff petticoats worn by women in the nineteenth century to make their skirts stick out.

cripple (crippling, crippled) ❑ If someone is **crippled** or a **cripple**, they cannot move their body properly because of illness or injury. Using 'cripple' like this can be offensive. ◇ You can call an illness or injury **crippling**. *Rheumatoid arthritis and multiple sclerosis are both crippling diseases.*
❑ You can say something **cripples** an organization or system if it stops it working properly.

crisis (*plural:* crises, *pron:* cry-seez) A **crisis** is a very serious situation. You can say there is a **crisis** when relations between countries have become very bad and war seems likely. You can also talk about an **economic crisis**, or say there is a **political crisis** somewhere. If a person faces serious problems in their life, you can say they are going through a **personal crisis**.

crisp (crisply, crispness) ❑ If something is **crisp**, it feels pleasantly stiff and fresh. ...*crisp new banknotes.* ◇ If the air or weather is **crisp**, it is pleasantly fresh, cold, and dry. ◇ If a speech or piece of writing is **crisp**, it does not go into any unnecessary details. *He put his views over crisply and clearly...* ...*the crispness of Borges's work.*
❑ **Crisps** are thin slices of potato fried until they are hard and crunchy.

crispbread is a thin dry biscuit made from rye or wheat.

crispy You say food is **crispy** when it has been cooked until it is pleasantly hard and crunchy.

criss-cross A **criss-cross** pattern is one with lots of lines crossing each other. If things **criss-cross** an area, they create a pattern like this. ◇ If people **criss-cross** an area, they move backwards and forwards across it.

criterion (*plural:* criteria) A **criterion** is a standard by which you judge or decide something. *The criteria for participation at the Olympics have changed dramatically.*

critic A **critic** is someone who is paid to give their opinions on books, films, music, or art. ◇ A **critic** of a person or system is someone who condemns them in public.

critical (critically) ❑ You say a situation or time is **critical** when what happens is extremely important, because it will determine which way things go in the future. *The peace process is entering a critically sensitive stage.* ◇ If someone is **critically** ill, they are very seriously ill.

❏ If you are **critical** of someone or something, you show you disapprove of them or are dissatisfied with them. *People talk about the government more critically than they did before.* ◇ A **critical** approach to something involves a careful study and judgement about it. *Schools have started to look very critically at their expenditure.*

criticise See criticize.

criticism ❏ If there is **criticism** of someone or something, people show they disapprove of them, or are dissatisfied with them. If you make a **criticism** of someone, you point out a fault you think they have.

❏ **Criticism** is also the serious examination and judgement of books, films, plays, or other works of art.

criticize (criticizing, criticized) (*can be spelled with an 's' instead of a 'z'*) If you **criticize** someone or something, you say what you think is wrong with them. ◇ If you **criticize** a book, film, play, or other work of art, you study it closely and give your opinion of it.

critique (*pron:* krit-**teek**) A **critique** is a study and judgement of something, usually in written form.

croak (croaking, croaked) If a frog or bird **croaks**, it makes a low hoarse cry. ◇ If a person **croaks** something, they say it in a rough hoarse voice. You can also say someone speaks in a **croak**.

crochet (*pron:* **kroh**-shay) (crocheting, crocheted) **Crochet** is a craft like knitting but done with only one needle, with a special hook at the end. When someone **crochets**, they do this kind of work.

crock is an old word for an earthenware pot or jar.

crockery is plates, cups, and saucers.

crocodile **Crocodiles** are large scaly reptiles with long bodies and short legs. They eat meat and live in tropical rivers. ◇ If you say someone sheds **crocodile tears**, you mean their display of grief is not genuine.

crocus (crocuses) **Crocuses** are small yellow, white, or purple flowers which come out in the winter and early spring.

croft (crofter) A **croft** is a small piece of land attached to a house and farmed by one family, especially in Scotland. The owner or tenant of a croft is called a **crofter**.

croissant (*pron:* **krwah**-son) A **croissant** is a light flaky crescent-shaped roll.

crone In stories, a **crone** is an unpleasant old woman.

crony (cronies) An unpleasant person's **cronies** are their friends and hangers-on.

crook (crooking, crooked) ❏ A **crook** is a dishonest person or criminal.

❏ If you **crook** your arm or finger, you bend it. ◇ The **crook** of someone's elbow is the inside of their arm at the point where it bends.

crooked (*pron:* **kruk**-id) A **crooked** person is dishonest or a criminal. ◇ If something is **crooked**, it is twisted or bent.

croon (crooning, crooned; crooner) If someone **croons** something, they sing or say it softly and quietly. ◇ **Crooning** was a kind of soft-voiced sentimental singing which was popular in the 1930s and 1940s. People who sang in this style were called **crooners**.

crop (cropping, cropped) ❏ **Crops** are plants like potatoes and wheat which are grown in large quantities for food. ◇ The plants gathered at a particular time are called a **crop**. *This will enable them to survive until the first crop is*

harvested. ◇ A lot of people or things appearing together can be called a **crop**, and so can a series of similar happenings coming one after the other. *Every summer appears to produce its crop of manic crimes.*

❏ If you **crop** someone's hair, you cut it very short; you then say their hair is **cropped**.

❏ If something **crops up**, it happens or appears without warning.

cropper You say someone **comes a cropper** when they try something out and it fails badly.

croquet (*pron:* **kroh**-kay) is a game in which the players use long-handled wooden hammers to hit balls through metal arches stuck in a lawn.

croquette (*pron:* **kroh**-kett) A **croquette** is a savoury cake of minced food coated in breadcrumbs and fried.

cross (crosses, crossing, crossed; crossly) ❏ If you **cross** an area of land or water, you go over to the other side. ◇ If lines or roads **cross**, they meet and go across each other. ◇ If you **cross** your legs, arms, or fingers, you put one on top of the other.

❏ If an expression **crosses** someone's face, it appears there briefly. ◇ If a thought **crosses** your mind, it suddenly occurs to you.

❏ A **cross** is a written mark in the shape of an X.

❏ In the ancient world, people were sometimes executed by being tied or nailed to an object called a **cross** and left to die. The cross consisted of an upright post with a horizontal bar to which the victim's hands were tied or nailed. When Christians talk about the **Cross**, they mean a cross like this on which Jesus Christ died.

❏ If someone is **cross**, they are angry. *She spoke to me very crossly.* ◇ If you **cross** someone, you make them angry by opposing them in some way, especially by interfering with their plans or wishes.

❏ If something is a **cross** between two things, it is neither one thing nor the other but a mixture of both.

❏ If you **cross off** items on a list, you draw a line through them, one by one, to show they have been dealt with. ◇ If you **cross out** words on a page, you put a line through them, because they are incorrect, or because you want to reduce the amount of writing.

cross-check If you **cross-check** something, you make sure it is correct by checking it in different ways or with different sources.

cross-country is a long race run across open countryside. ◇ If you go somewhere **cross-country**, you go across land rather than following roads.

cross-cultural is used to talk about anything involving two or more cultures. *...cross-cultural issues.*

cross-examine (cross-examination) If someone is **cross-examined** in court, they are questioned about information or evidence they have given. You call this process **cross-examination**. ◇ In other situations, you can say someone is being **cross-examined** when they are being questioned very thoroughly.

cross-eyed If someone is **cross-eyed**, their eyes seem to look towards their nose.

cross-legged If someone sits **cross-legged**, they are on the floor with their feet pulled up close to their body, their calves crossing, and their knees pointing outwards.

cross-purposes If people are **at cross-purposes**, they cannot understand each other, because they are talking about different subjects without realizing it.

cross-question If someone is **cross-questioned**, they are questioned very thoroughly.

cross-reference (cross-referencing) A **cross-reference** is a note in a book which tells you where in the book you will find more information on the same subject. Putting in notes like these is called **cross-referencing**.

cross-section A **cross-section** of a group of people is a random selection which is thought to be a typical sample. ◇ A **cross-section** of an object is what you would see if you cut through the middle of it.

crossbar In games like football, the **crossbar** is the horizontal piece of wood across the top of the goal.

crossbones See **skull**.

crossbow The **crossbow** was a weapon consisting of a small bow at the end of a long piece of wood called a stock. The bow was drawn back using a handle or lever, and the arrows were released with great force.

crossfire is gunfire from different directions which meets and crosses at the same point. ◇ If you get **caught in the crossfire**, you get involved against your will in a disagreement or conflict.

crossing A **crossing** is a boat journey across a stretch of water. ◇ A **crossing** is also a place with markings or traffic lights where you cross a street.

crossing point A **crossing point** is a point on the border between two countries where people and vehicles are allowed through.

crossroads A **crossroads** is a place where two or more roads meet and cross each other. ◇ If you say someone is **at a crossroads**, you mean that they are at a stage when they need to make an important decision.

crosswind A **crosswind** is a strong wind blowing across the direction a plane or boat is travelling in, making it difficult for it to keep steady.

crossword A **crossword** or **crossword puzzle** is a printed word game where you work out answers to clues, then write them in the white squares of a black and white grid.

crotch (crotches) A person's **crotch** is the angle made by the tops of their legs. You can also talk about the **crotch** of a pair of trousers.

crotchet A **crotchet** is a musical note with the same time value as two quavers or half a minim. It is often used to represent a beat.

crouch (crouches, crouching, crouched) If you **crouch**, you bend your legs under you so you are near the ground and leaning forward slightly.

croup (pron: kroop) is a disease in which the throat swells, making breathing difficult and causing coughing. It particularly affects children.

croupier (pron: kroop-ee-ay) A **croupier** is someone who works in a casino, taking bets and dealing cards at a gambling table.

crouton (pron: kroot-on) **Croutons** are small pieces of toasted or fried bread which are added to soup just before it is served.

crow ❑ **Crows** are large black birds with a loud harsh cry. ◇ If you say something is a certain distance away **as the crow flies**, you mean it is that distance measured in a straight line.
  ❑ When a cock **crows**, it makes a loud harsh sound,

usually early in the morning. ◇ If someone is **crowing** about something, they are telling other people about it in a boastful way.

crow's feet are the little lines that appear at the outside corners of the eyes as people get older.

crowbar A **crowbar** is a heavy iron bar for levering things open.

crowd A **crowd** is a large number of people gathered together in one place. ◇ If people **crowd** a place or **crowd** into it, they gather in large numbers and completely fill it. You then say the place is **crowded**. ◇ If people **crowd** round someone or something, they gather closely in a group around them. ◇ You can say problems are **crowding in on** someone if they suddenly have to deal with a lot of them at the same time.

crown ❑ A **crown** is a round gold ornament with jewels, worn on the head of a king or queen as a sign of their position. The **Crown** is whoever happens to be king or queen at the time. *He advised the Crown on appointments.* ◇ When someone is **crowned**, a crown is put on their head at a special ceremony to show they have become king or queen. ◇ Kings and queens are sometimes called **crowned heads**.
  ❑ If one thing **crowns** another, it is on the top of it. ◇ If you say something **crowns** an event or series of events, you mean it is the best part of it. *The summit meeting was crowned by the signing of the historic treaty.* ◇ A **crown** is also a title or championship in sport. *Tom Collins has retained his European light-heavyweight crown.*

crown court In England and Wales, a **crown court** is a court where crimes are tried by a judge and jury, rather than a magistrate.

crown jewels A country's **crown jewels** are the crown, sceptre, and other jewels used by the king or queen on state occasions.

Crown Prince A **Crown Prince** is a prince who will become king of his country when the present king or queen dies.

Crown Princess A **Crown Princess** is (a) the wife of a Crown Prince. (b) a princess who will become queen of her country when the present king or queen dies.

crucial (crucially) **Crucial** is used to describe things which are vitally important. *Tropical forests are a crucially important source of plant and animal life.*

crucible A **crucible** is a pot in which metals can be melted or heated to very high temperatures. ◇ You say a situation or place is a **crucible** when a lot of different people, things, or ideas are brought together and something interesting or worthwhile comes out of it. *Perugia was to become the crucible of painting in Umbria.*

crucifix (crucifixes) A **crucifix** is a model of the Cross with a figure of Christ on it.

crucifixion was a way of executing people in the ancient world. The victim was tied or nailed to a cross and left to die. When people talk about the **Crucifixion**, they mean the death of Christ on a cross like this.

crucify (crucifies, crucifying, crucified) If someone is **crucified**, they are killed by being tied or nailed to a cross and left to die. ◇ You can also say someone is **crucified** when they are humiliated or made to suffer in public.

crude (cruder, crudest; crudely, crudity) ❑ You say something like a system or idea is **crude** when it is very basic and unsophisticated; you can also talk about its **crudity**. *Such pension or insurance funds as do exist are crudely run.* ◇ You can say an object is **crude** or **crudely** made when it has been roughly made and is very basic in style.

❏ If someone's behaviour or language is **crude**, it is vulgar and offensive. You can talk about a person's **crudity**.

crude oil is oil in its natural state before it has been processed.

crudity See crude.

cruel (crueller, cruellest; cruelly) (*usual American spelling:* crueler, cruelest) If someone is **cruel** or behaves **cruelly**, they deliberately cause pain or distress to other people or to animals.

cruelty (cruelties) Cruelty is cruel behaviour. **Cruelties** are cruel acts.

cruet A **cruet** is a frame for holding small pots of salt, pepper, and mustard.

cruise (cruising, cruised) ❏ If you **cruise** or go on a **cruise**, you spend a holiday on a large ship which visits a lot of different places. ◇ If a car, ship, or plane **cruises**, it travels at a steady speed.

❏ If you **cruise** through something like a competition, you win without any effort.

cruise missile A **cruise missile** is a type of missile which carries a warhead and is guided towards its target by a computer.

cruiser A **cruiser** is (a) a motor boat with a cabin for people to sleep in. (b) a large fast warship.

crumb Crumbs are tiny pieces which have broken off bread, cakes, or biscuits. ◇ A **crumb** is also a very small amount of something good or useful. For example, you can talk about a **crumb** of comfort or information.

crumble (crumbling, crumbled; crumbly) If something **crumbles**, it breaks up into small pieces. If this happens easily to something, you say it is **crumbly**. ◇ If you say something like a system or organization is **crumbling**, you mean it is beginning to break down.

crummy is used to say something is poor or unsatisfactory. *Half of his own party say he is doing a crummy job.*

crumpet Crumpets are round flat bread-like cakes which are toasted and eaten with butter.

crumple (crumpling, crumpled) If you **crumple** something like paper or material, you crush it until it becomes creased and out of shape. ◇ If something **crumples**, it collapses suddenly. *Profits have crumpled by more than a third.*

crunch (crunches, crunching, crunched) ❏ If you **crunch** something between your teeth or under your feet, you crush it noisily.

❏ **The crunch** is used to talk about a critical situation when a decision must be made or some action must be taken. *If it came to the crunch, I would have to stay.*

crunchy (crunchier, crunchiest) If food is **crunchy**, it is crisp or brittle and makes a noise when you eat it.

crusade (crusading; crusader) A **crusade** is a long determined attempt to win support for a cause, or to put an end to something wrong. A **crusading** person is someone who tries to do this; you also call them a **crusader**. *...a crusade against poverty.*

crush (crushes, crushing, crushed) ❏ If something is **crushed**, it is squeezed until it loses its shape or is broken into pieces. ◇ **Crushed** material is deliberately made with

creases in it. *...crushed velvet.*

❏ If people are **crushed** or caught in a **crush**, they are pressed against something or against each other, as a result of the movement of a large crowd. ◇ **Crush barriers** are safety fences used to split up large crowds and prevent people being **crushed**. They are used at events like football matches and pop concerts.

❏ If something like a revolt is **crushed**, it is defeated completely. Similarly, you can say a political movement is **crushed**. You can also say a sports team is **crushed** by another team. If someone suffers a **crushing** defeat, they are defeated completely.

crust (crusted) The **crust** on a loaf is the crisp dark outer edge. ◇ If other things have a **crust** or are **crusted**, they have a hard layer surrounding them or on top of them. *The water was crusted over with ice.* ◇ The earth's **crust** is its hard outer layer.

crustacean (*pron:* cruss-taysh-an) Crustaceans are creatures with hard outer shells and several pairs of legs. Most crustaceans live in water. Crabs, lobsters, and shrimps are crustaceans.

crusty (crustier, crustiest) If something is **crusty**, it has a hard outer layer. *...crusty bread.* ◇ **Crusty** people are impatient and short-tempered.

crutch (crutches) ❏ A **crutch** is a stick-like object which fits under your armpit to support you if you have an injured foot or leg. ◇ Someone or something you depend on for help or support can also be called a **crutch**.

❏ A person's **crutch** is the same as their crotch.

crux The **crux** of a problem or dispute is the most important or difficult part which is central to everything else.

cry (cries, crying, cried) ❏ If you **cry** or have a **cry**, tears come from your eyes, because you are upset.

❏ If you **cry** something or **cry** it **out**, you shout it or say it loudly. ◇ A **cry** is (a) a loud call made by a person. (b) a call made by a large bird.

❏ If you **cry off**, you decide not to do something you had arranged to do.

❏ If you say something is **crying out for** a particular thing, you mean it needs it badly. You can also say there is a **crying** need for something. ◇ If you say something is a **crying shame**, you mean it is very regrettable or unfortunate.

❏ If you say something is **a far cry** from something else, you mean the two things are very different.

❏ **cry wolf:** see wolf.

crypt The **crypt** of a church is an underground room, often used as a burial place.

cryptic (cryptically) A **cryptic** remark or message has a hidden meaning. *He has said cryptically he will unmask a number of spectacular cases if arrested.*

crystal ❏ A **crystal** is a piece of mineral which has formed naturally into a regular shape. ◇ **Crystal** is a type of transparent rock used in jewellery. ◇ **Crystal** is also high quality glassware with patterns cut into its surface.

❏ If you say something is **crystal clear**, you mean it is very easy to understand.

crystal ball A **crystal ball** is a clear glass globe in which fortune-tellers claim they can see what will happen in the future.

crystalline If something is **crystalline**, it contains or is made up of crystals.

crystallize (crystallizing, crystallized) (*can be spelled with an 's' instead of a 'z'*) If a substance **crystallizes**, it turns into crystals. ◇ If a thought **crystallizes**, it becomes clear in your mind.

CS gas is a gas used to control mobs in riots. It makes breathing difficult and causes crying.

cub ❑ Cubs are the young of certain animals, for example lions, bears, and seals.
    ❑ A **cub** is also a boy aged 8 to 10½ who belongs to the Cub Scouts, a junior branch of the Scout Association.

cub reporter A **cub reporter** is a young newspaper reporter who is being trained for the job.

cubby-hole A **cubby-hole** is a small closed-in space.

cube (cubing, cubed) ❑ A **cube** is a three-dimensional shape, with six square surfaces of equal size. ◇ If you **cube** something like food, you cut it into cubes.
    ❑ The **cube** of a number is another number obtained by multiplying the first number by itself twice. For example, the cube of 2 is 8. In maths, this is expressed as $2^3 = 8$.

cube root The **cube root** of a number is another number which when multiplied by itself twice produces the first number. For example the cube root of 27 is 3. In maths, this is expressed as $\sqrt[3]{9} = 3$.

cubic is used in front of units of length to change them to units of volume. *...cubic metres.*

cubic centimetre Volume is often expressed in **cubic centimetres**. There are 1,000 cubic centimetres in a litre. 'Cubic centimetres' is usually written 'cc'.

cubicle A **cubicle** is a small enclosed area in a public building which is there for a particular purpose, such as changing your clothes or talking to someone in private.

cubism (cubist) **Cubism** was an early 20th century style of art, in which objects were drawn or painted as if they could be seen from several positions at once. People who drew or painted in this style were called **cubists**.

cuckold In the past, a man whose wife was unfaithful to him was called a **cuckold**. The wife was said to have **cuckolded** her husband.

cuckoo The **cuckoo** is a grey bird with a loud call consisting of one note quickly followed by another lower one. Cuckoos lay their eggs in other birds' nests.

cuckoo clock A **cuckoo clock** is a wooden clock in the shape of a small house. When the hour strikes, a toy bird springs out of a small door and makes a sound like a cuckoo.

cucumber Cucumbers are long vegetables with dark green skin and white flesh. They are usually eaten uncooked in salads.

cud is the partly digested food which a cow brings back up to chew again.

cuddle (cuddling, cuddled) If you **cuddle** someone or give them a **cuddle**, you put your arms round them and hold them close. ◇ If you **cuddle up** to someone who is sitting or lying next to you, you press your body against theirs.

cuddly If you say a person is **cuddly**, you mean they appeal to you and you would like to cuddle them. You can also say a small animal or toy is **cuddly**.

cudgel A **cudgel** is a short thick stick used as a weapon. ◇ If you **take up the cudgels** for someone, you speak or fight on their behalf.

cue ❑ A **cue** is a word or action from one performer which is a signal for another performer to say or do something. ◇ In other situations, a **cue** is a signal for something to begin. ◇ If you **take** your **cue** from someone, you use their behaviour as an indication of what you should do. ◇ If something happens **on cue**, it happens just at the time it is expected to.
    ❑ A **cue** is also a long narrow stick used to hit the ball in snooker, billiards, or pool.

cuff ❑ **Cuffs** are the ends of sleeves on a piece of clothing. ◇ If you speak **off the cuff**, you have not prepared what you are saying.
    ❑ If you **cuff** someone, you hit them lightly with your hand.

cufflinks are small decorative objects for holding shirt cuffs together.

cuisine (*pron*: quiz-**zeen**) is used to talk about styles of cooking. *...the great dishes of European cuisine.*

cul-de-sac A **cul-de-sac** is a road which does not lead to other roads.

culinary is used to talk about things to do with meals and cooking. *...his culinary skills.*

cull When a group of animals is **culled**, the weaker ones are killed, to reduce the numbers. You call an action like this a **cull**. ◇ If you **cull** things, you take the ones you want from a large number of things. *The selection has been culled from over 100,000 photographs.*

culminate (culminating, culminated; culmination) When something **culminates** in something else, it finally develops into it. *The demonstration was the culmination of three weeks of protests by the union.*

culottes are women's wide trousers or shorts, cut to look like a skirt.

culpable (culpability) If you say someone is **culpable**, you mean they are to blame for what has happened; you can also talk about their **culpability**.

culprit The **culprit** is the person or thing responsible for something bad or harmful.

cult A **cult** is a religious group with its own special rituals, especially one which is seen as dangerous or harmful by other people. ◇ **Cult** is also used to talk about situations in which a section of the public greatly admires a person or thing. *...a cult sixties TV series.*

cultivate (cultivating, cultivated) If land is **cultivated**, crops are grown on it. *Farmers need to clear wooded areas for cultivation.* ◇ If you **cultivate** an appearance or attitude, you try to develop it. ◇ If you **cultivate** someone, you try to make them your friend.

cultivated You say someone is **cultivated** when they are well-educated and good-mannered, and appreciate things like music and art. ◇ **Cultivated** plants have been developed specially to be grown in gardens or on a farm.

cultural (culturally) **Cultural** is used to talk about things to do with the arts. *...a culturally thriving city.* ◇ **Cultural** is also used to talk about things to do with social systems and ways of life. *...the cultural identity of the Kuwaiti people... Europe is culturally different from America.*

culture ❑ A **culture** consists of the ideas, customs, and art created and shared by the people of a country, region, or ethnic group. *...western culture.* ◇ **Culture shock** is the feeling of confusion and anxiety you get when you first arrive in a country with very different traditions from your own. ◇ **Culture** is also used to talk about a way of life shared by many people which seems to be based on a particular idea or represented by a particular thing. For example, you can talk about 'the consumer culture' or 'the drug culture'.

❑ **Culture** is also used to talk about the arts generally. *Some cities are starved of any sort of culture.*

❑ A **culture** is a group of bacteria or cells grown in a laboratory.

cultured A **cultured** person is well-educated and interested in the arts. ◇ A **cultured** pearl is created by putting sand or grit in an oyster's shell.

culvert A **culvert** is a water pipe or sewer which crosses under a road or railway.

-cum- is placed between two words to talk about something which is a mixture of two different things. *...a new personal computer-cum-video telephone.*

cumbersome If something is **cumbersome**, it is heavy and awkward to carry. ◇ If something like a system is **cumbersome**, it is complicated and inefficient.

cummerbund A **cummerbund** is a wide sash round the waist, especially one worn by a man as part of evening dress.

cumulative (cumulatively) The **cumulative** effect of several things happening is the effect they produce together. *His administration was plagued by one petty scandal after another, which was cumulatively very damaging.*

cumulus (*pron:* kyoo-myoo-luss) is a type of thick fluffy white cloud formed when hot air rises quickly.

cunning (cunningly) A **cunning** person is clever and deceitful. *They cunningly deceive their victims and each other.* You can talk about the **cunning** of someone like this.

cup (cupping, cupped) A **cup** is a small container with a handle, for drinking out of. ◇ Some other round hollow things are also called **cups**. *...egg cups... ...bra cups.* ◇ A **cup** is also a metal container, often with two handles, given as a prize. ◇ If your hands **cup** something, they make a cup-like shape around it.

cupboard A **cupboard** is a piece of furniture or a recess with a door, often with shelves inside it. It is used for storing things. ◇ **Cupboard love** is a show of affection used by someone to get what they want.

cupful A **cupful** of something is the amount one cup can hold.

cupidity is a greedy desire for money and possessions.

cupola (*pron:* kyoo-po-la) A **cupola** is a domed roof, often with a spire rising from the middle of it.

cuppa A **cuppa** is a cup of tea.

curable If an illness or disease is **curable**, it can be cured.

curate (curacy, curacies) A **curate** is a clergyman who helps a vicar or priest. A **curacy** is the position held by a curate, or the work he has to do.

curative If something is **curative**, it can cure illnesses.

curator A **curator** is someone in charge of the contents of a museum or gallery.

curb If you **curb** something or put a **curb** on it, you keep it within certain limits. *...measures to curb industrial pollution.* ◇ See also **kerb**.

curd is the thick white substance formed when milk goes sour.

curdle (curdling, curdled) When something like milk cur-

dles, it turns sour.

cure (curing, cured) ❑ If an illness is **cured**, it is ended by treatment or medicine; you also say the person who has been ill is **cured**. A successful treatment or medicine is called a **cure**.

❑ If you **cure** a habit, you successfully break it. ◇ If you **cure** a problem or find a **cure** for it, you manage to solve it.

❑ If food is **cured**, it is salted or smoked, to preserve it.

cure-all A **cure-all** is something people believe will solve all their problems.

curfew A **curfew** is a law requiring people to stay inside their homes between certain hours, usually at night.

curio (curios) A **curio** is a small unusual ornament.

curiosity (curiosities) **Curiosity** is a desire to find out about things. ◇ A **curiosity** is an unusual and interesting thing.

curious (curiously) If you say something is **curious**, you mean it is strange or unusual. *The papers have curiously vanished from the Public Record Office.* ◇ If you are **curious** about something, you want to find out more about it.

curl (curly) ❑ **Curls** are strands of hair shaped in curves and circles. When hair grows like this, you describe it as curly or say it **curls**.

❑ If something **curls**, it moves in a curve or spiral.

❑ When you **curl up**, you sit or lie with your arms, legs, and head pulled in towards your stomach.

curler **Curlers** are plastic or metal tubes which strands of hair are rolled around to make curls.

curlew **Curlews** are brownish wading birds with long bills which curve downwards.

curling is a game like bowls, only played on ice with large stones.

curly See curl.

curmudgeon (curmudgeonly) If you say someone is **curmudgeonly** or a **curmudgeon**, you mean they are bad-tempered or mean.

currant **Currants** are small dried grapes used in cooking.

currency (currencies) A country's **currency** is (a) its money system. *...European countries whose currencies are linked to Germany's.* (b) the coins and notes used there. ◇ If an idea or story has **currency**, people get to hear about it and accept it.

current (currently) ❑ **Current** is used to talk about things which are taking place now, or are being done or used now. *Young jobless currently account for a third of the unemployed population.* ◇ **Current** is also used to talk about the people who have a particular position now, which they may lose later. *...the current leadership.*

❑ A **current** of air or water is a continuous steady flow of it. ◇ An electric **current** is a flow of electricity through a wire or circuit.

current account A **current account** is a bank account which you can take money out of at any time, using your cheque book or cheque card.

current affairs are political and social events happening at the present time.

curriculum (*plural:* curricula *or* curriculums) ❑ The **curriculum** at a school or university is the choice of different courses there. ◇ The **National Curriculum** is a feature introduced into the educational system in England and

Wales in 1988. It established that children aged 5 to 16 in state schools should all study the same group of subjects. ◇ **Curriculum** can also be used to talk about a particular course of study. ...*the content of the history curriculum.*

❑ **curriculum vitae:** see **CV**.

curry (curries, currying, curried) ❑ A **curry** is a hot spicy Asian dish. If you **curry** food, you make it into a curry. **Curry powder** is a mixture of spices which you add to food to make a curry.

❑ If you **curry favour** with someone, you try to win their goodwill by doing things to please them.

curse ❑ If someone **curses**, they swear because they are angry. ◇ If you **curse** someone or something, you say rude things about them because you are angry with them. ◇ People sometimes use **cursed** (*pron:* kerss-id) to describe someone or something they are angry with or greatly dislike. ...*the cursed tax.*

❑ If people say there is a **curse** on someone, they mean something supernatural is causing unpleasant things to happen to them.

❑ When something causes a lot of trouble or distress, you can say people are **cursed** by it or call it a **curse**. ...*the curse of unemployment.*

cursor A **cursor** is a moving mark on a computer screen which shows you where anything you type will appear.

cursory is used to describe things done in a hasty and superficial way. *The doctor made a cursory examination of the body.*

curt (curtly) If someone is **curt** or speaks **curtly**, what they say is very brief and abrupt. Something like a letter can also be **curt**.

curtail (curtailing, curtailed; curtailment) If you **curtail** something, you restrict it or reduce it. *They will be furious at any curtailment of their activities.*

curtain (curtained) ❑ **Curtains** are large pieces of material hung at a window or other opening as a screen. A **curtained** window or room is one which has curtains.

❑ In a theatre, the **curtain** is a hanging which conceals the stage until the performance starts. You say there is a **curtain call** when the artists come on stage at the end of a performance to receive applause.

curtain-raiser A **curtain-raiser** is a small event which takes place before a larger one.

curtsy (curtsies, curtsying, curtsied) (*or* curtsey, curtseys, curtseying, curtseyed) If a woman **curtsies** or drops a **curtsy**, she puts one foot in front of the other and briefly lowers her body by bending her knees. Women sometimes do this to show respect for someone like a member of the royal family.

curvaceous is used to describe a woman's body when it has noticeable curves which make her sexually attractive.

curvature If you talk about the **curvature** of something, you mean the extent to which it curves.

curve (curving, curved; curvy) A **curve** is a line which bends gradually and smoothly. ◇ If something **curves**, it moves in a curve, or has the shape of a curve. *The ball curved strangely in the air... The unpaved alley curves sharply behind the shops.* ◇ If something is **curved**, it has the shape of a curve. If it is **curvy**, it has several curves.

cushion (cushioning, cushioned) A **cushion** is a soft object

put on a seat to make it more comfortable. ◇ If something is **cushioned** from something harmful, it is prevented from receiving its full effects.

cushy (cushier, cushiest) A **cushy** job or task is very easy.

cusp The **cusp** is the point in a process where something ceases to be one thing and becomes something else.

cussed (*pron:* kuss-id) A **cussed** person is very stubborn.

custard is a sweet yellow sauce made from milk and eggs or milk and a powder.

custodial is used to talk about imprisonment. A **custodial** sentence is one in which someone is sentenced to prison, rather than being put on probation or given some other punishment.

custodian The **custodian** of something like a building is the person in charge. ◇ If someone has the responsibility of looking after something important, you can say they are its **custodian**. *The Italians are the custodians of one of the world's richest historical and artistic legacies.*

custody If someone has **custody** of a child, they have the legal right to keep it and look after it. ◇ If someone is in **custody**, they are being kept in prison until they can be tried.

custom ❑ A **custom** is an activity which has been taking place somewhere on special occasions for a very long time. *Easter eggs are perhaps the most widespread custom associated with this time of year.* ◇ If it is the **custom** to do something in a particular situation, that is what is usually done.

❑ **Customs** is the place where people arriving from another country must declare goods they have brought with them.

❑ If a shop or business has your **custom**, you regularly buy things from them.

custom-made (custom-built) If something is **custom-made** or **custom-built**, it is made or built to someone's special requirements.

customary (customarily) You use **customary** to describe what normally happens in particular circumstances. *The customary standing ovation went on for ten minutes... Science is customarily associated with the pursuit of knowledge.*

customer A firm's or shop's **customers** are people who buy things from them. ◇ British Rail calls the people who travel on its trains **customers**.

customize (customizing, customized) (*can be spelled with an 's' instead of a 'z'*) If something is **customized**, it has been specially made to someone's requirements.

cut (cutting) ❑ If you **cut** something, you use a knife or scissors to mark it, damage it, or remove part of it. Each action with the knife or scissors is called a **cut**. ◇ If you **cut** something **up**, you cut it into several pieces. ◇ If you **cut** something **out** or **cut** it **off**, you remove it using scissors or a knife. ◇ If you **cut down** a tree, you saw through its trunk so it falls down. ◇ If you **cut** yourself or get a **cut**, you suffer an injury which makes you bleed. ◇ If you get your hair **cut**, someone shortens it using scissors.

❑ If something like an amount or a public service is **cut**, it is reduced; the reduction is called a **cut**. You can also say someone **cuts back** an amount or service or **cuts back on** it. People talk about a **cutback** in an amount or service. ...*the cutback in consumer spending.* ◇ If a supply of something is **cut off**, you no longer get it.

❑ If you **cut down** on an activity, you do less of it. If you **cut down** on something you use, you use less of it. ◇ If you **cut** something **out**, you stop doing or using it altogether.

❑ If a piece of writing is **cut**, parts of it are not printed or broadcast.

❑ If an engine or piece of machinery **cuts out**, it suddenly stops working.

❑ If you say someone is **cut out** for something, you mean they have the right qualities for it. ◇ If you say someone **cuts** a particular type of figure, you mean that is the impression people have of them. *He's trying hard to cut a more moderate figure.*

❑ If you talk about the **cut** of someone's clothes, you are describing the way they have been made or designed.

❑ A **cut** of meat is a large piece of it, ready for cooking.

❑ If something is a **cut above** other things of the same kind, it is better than them.

❑ If you are **cut up** about something, you are very upset by it.

❑ If you **cut through** a place or **cut across** it, you go that way because it is shorter. ◇ If a place or person becomes **cut off**, they are separated from things they are usually connected with. *Snow cut off many parts of the country.*

❑ If you say something **cuts across** the division between two or more groups, you mean it affects everyone. *There are issues that cut across the economic quarrel between have-nots and haves.*

❑ If someone **cuts in,** they interrupt other people when they are speaking.

cut-and-dried If you say something is **cut-and-dried,** you mean its outcome is obvious.

cut glass is glass with patterns cut into its surface.

cut-off The **cut-off** or **cut-off point** is the level or limit at which something will be stopped.

cut-price A **cut-price** item is on sale at a reduced price.

cut-throat is used to describe situations where people compete for something without caring if they harm each other. *...the cut-throat world of modern politics.*

cutback See cut.

cute means 'pretty'. It is usually used to describe things which try to be attractive or appealing in a rather obvious way. Toys are often called **cute,** and so are drawings of animals and children.

cuticle Cuticles are the strips of skin at the base of fingernails and toenails.

cutlass (cutlasses) A **cutlass** is a curved sword with one sharp edge. Cutlasses were used by sailors.

cutlery is knives, forks, and spoons.

cutlet A **cutlet** is (a) a small chop, with or without the bone. (b) a mixture of nuts and vegetables, pressed into a flat shape. Both sorts of cutlets are usually grilled or fried.

cutter A **cutter** is (a) a person whose job involves cutting something. *...a glass cutter.* (b) a tool or machine for cutting something. *...a brush cutter.* ◇ A **cutter** is also a small fast boat.

cutting ❑ A **cutting** is a piece cut from a plant, used to grow a new plant. ◇ A **cutting** is also a piece of writing or a photograph cut from a newspaper or magazine. ◇ A railway **cutting** is a narrow valley cut through a hill for a railway line to pass through.

❑ If you say something like a remark is **cutting,** you mean it is unkind and hurtful.

❑ If someone is the **cutting edge** of something new which is happening, they are mainly responsible for bringing it about. ◇ If you are **at the cutting edge** of something, you are involved in its most recent developments.

cuttlefish (*plural:* cuttlefish *or* cuttlefishes) Cuttlefish are animals with hard internal shells. They live close to the seabed near the coast. A **cuttlefish** is also the shell of a cuttlefish, which people give to pet birds to eat.

CV Someone's **CV** is a short written account of their education, work experience, and personal details, which they send when they apply for a job. CV stands for 'curriculum vitae'.

cwt See hundredweight.

cyanide is an extremely poisonous chemical.

cybernetics is the study of communication and control systems in machines, animals, and organizations.

cyclamen (*pron:* sik-lam-men) Cyclamens are plants with white, pink, or red flowers whose petals turn back.

cycle (cycling, cycled) ❑ If you **cycle,** you ride a bicycle. You call this activity **cycling.** ◇ A **cycle** is another name for a bicycle.

❑ A **cycle** is also a series of events repeated over and over in the same order. *...the cycle of famine and disease.* ◇ A **cycle** of songs or poems is a series of them, intended to be performed or read one after the other.

❑ A **cycle** in an electrical, electronic, mechanical, or organic process is one complete series of movements or events.

cyclic (cyclical) If something is **cyclic** or **cyclical,** it happens again and again in cycles.

cyclist A **cyclist** is someone who rides a bicycle.

cyclone A **cyclone** is a violent storm, especially one in the Indian Ocean, in which the wind moves in a circular direction.

cygnet A **cygnet** is a young swan.

cylinder (cylindrical) A **cylinder** is a three-dimensional shape with straight sides and circular ends. You say something with this shape is **cylindrical.** ◇ The **cylinder** in an engine is the part in which the piston moves backwards and forwards.

cymbal A **cymbal** is a brass plate used as a musical instrument. You hit it with a stick or another cymbal to produce a crashing or hissing sound.

cynic (cynical, cynically) A **cynic** is someone who always believes the worst of people or their actions. You say someone like this is **cynical.** *The postman eyed him cynically.*

cynicism is the belief that people always behave selfishly or dishonestly.

cypher See cipher.

cypress (*pron:* sigh-pruss) (cypresses) Cypresses are evergreen trees with dark green leaves and rounded cones. The wood from these trees is also called **cypress.**

cyst (*pron:* sist) A **cyst** is a lump containing liquid which grows inside your body or on your skin.

cystic fibrosis is a hereditary disease which affects children from birth and is sometimes fatal before they reach adulthood. It causes poor digestion, difficulty in breathing, and excessive mucus.

cystitis (*pron:* siss-tite-iss) is an inflammation of the bladder, usually caused by an infection.

D d

D.A. See district attorney.

dab (dabbing, dabbed) If you **dab** a substance onto a surface, you put it there with quick light strokes. You can also say you **dab** the surface with the substance. ◇ If you are a **dab hand** at something, you are very good at it.

dabble (dabbling, dabbled) If you **dabble** in something, you take part in it in a not very serious way.

dace (*plural:* dace) The **dace** is a small freshwater fish.

dacha A **dacha** is a cottage or country house in Russia, usually a second home for people who live in the city.

dachshund (*pron:* daks-und) The **dachshund** is a small dog with very short legs, a long body, and long ears.

daddy-long-legs (*plural:* daddy-long-legs) The **daddy-long-legs** is a harmless flying insect with very long legs. It is also called the 'crane fly'.

daffodil Daffodils are yellow bell-shaped flowers which bloom in early spring.

daft If you say an idea or statement is **daft**, you mean it is not sensible. You say a person is **daft** when they do a lot of silly things.

dagger A **dagger** is a short pointed weapon with sharp edges, used for stabbing.

dahlia (*pron:* day-lya) Dahlias are brightly-coloured garden flowers with many petals.

Dáil (*pron:* doil) The **Dáil** is the lower house of parliament in the Irish Republic.

daily (dailies) If something happens **daily**, it happens every day. ...*Margaret's daily visits.* ◇ **Daily** is also used to say how much of something is used, paid, or received each day. *Daily wage rates were around two dollars.* ◇ A **daily** is a newspaper published every day except Sunday.

dainty (daintier, daintiest; daintily) You call a woman or girl **dainty** when she is attractive in a delicate way with, for example, a slim waist and small hands and feet. You can also call a part of her body **dainty**. You say she does something in a **dainty** way when she does it with small attractive delicate movements. *Amanda stepped daintily across the lawn.* ◇ A **dainty** object is pretty and delicate.

dairy (dairies) A **dairy** is a company which sells milk and also things made from milk like butter and cheese. ◇ A **dairy** is also a building where milk is processed or kept, or foods like butter and cheese are made. ◇ **Dairy products** are foods like butter and cheese. ◇ **Dairy cattle** are cows kept for their milk. ◇ A **dairy farm** is one where dairy cattle are kept.

dais (*pron:* day-iss) (*plural:* dais) A **dais** is a raised platform used by a person speaking to a group of people.

daisy (daisies) Daisies are small wild flowers with yellow centres and white petals. ◇ A **daisy chain** is a string of daisies joined by their stems to make a necklace.

czar See tsar.
czarist See tsarist.

daisywheel A daisywheel on an electric typewriter or word processor is a small flat disc with letters round the edge which prints what you type. Typewriters and printers with a daisywheel can themselves be called daisywheels.

dale A **dale** is a valley in Scotland or Northern England.

dally (dallies, dallying, dallied) If someone **dallies**, they waste a lot of time before deciding to do something. ◇ If you **dally** with the idea of doing something, you consider doing it, but not very seriously. ◇ If someone **dallies** with you, they flirt with you.

dalmatian Dalmatians are large white short-haired dogs with black or brown spots.

dam (damming, dammed) ❑ A **dam** is a wall built across a river to hold back the water and make a lake. When a wall like this is built, you say the river is **dammed** or **dammed up**.

❑ The **dam** of a farm animal, for example a horse or sheep, is its mother.

damage (damages, damaging, damaged) If you **damage** something, you harm it so that it does not work properly or its appearance is spoiled. The harm you do is called **damage**. ◇ When a law court awards **damages** to someone, it orders a person who has harmed them to pay them an amount of money.

Damascus (Damascene) When a new idea becomes very important to someone and takes the place of what they had previously believed, you can say they have found their road to **Damascus** or had a **Damascene** conversion (*pron:* dam-a-seen).

damask is a heavy cloth, usually silk or linen, used to make tablecloths and curtains.

Dame is an official title given to a woman in recognition of something she has achieved. ...*Dame Peggy Ashcroft.*

damn (damnation) ❑ According to some religions, if someone is **damned** or condemned to **damnation**, they are sent to Hell for ever when they die because of the evil they have done. The **damned** are the people in Hell.

❑ If you call something like a report **damning**, you mean it suggests strongly that someone is guilty of a crime or serious error.

damp (dampness) ❑ If something is **damp**, it is slightly wet. ...*the dampness in the air.* ◇ If there is **damp** somewhere, surfaces are wet and the air is moist. ◇ A **damp course** or **damp-proof course** is a layer of waterproof material put into the bottom of a wall to prevent damp from rising.

❑ If you **damp down** a situation where people are angry or quarrelling, you calm them.

dampen (dampening, dampened; dampener) ❑ If something **dampens** a feeling like hope, it makes people feel it less strongly. Something which has this effect can be called a **dampener**.

❑ If you **dampen** a surface, you make it slightly wet.

damper ❑ If something **puts a damper** on things, it spoils people's enjoyment of them.

❑ A **damper** is a metal plate on a fire, boiler, or furnace which you move to control the amount of air getting in.

damsel A young unmarried woman used to be called a **damsel**.

damson Damsons are small sour purple plums.

dance (dancing, danced) ❑ When you **dance**, you move your body in time to music. The steps and other movements you make are called a **dance**. ◇ A **dance** is also a social event where people dance with each other. ◇ A **dance-floor** is part of a restaurant or nightclub where there is space for people to dance.

❑ **Dance** is the art of performing dances in front of an audience. *They are supreme artists of dance and theatre.* ◇ A **dance studio** is a place where people practice dancing or learn to dance.

❑ If a person **dances** about or **dances** from one place to another, they move lightly and quickly, because they are happy.

dancer A **dancer** is a person who earns money by dancing. ◇ **Dancer** is also used to talk about anyone who dances. For example, you say someone is a 'good dancer' or a 'keen dancer'. The **dancers** in a place like a ballroom are the people dancing there.

dandelion Dandelions are bright yellow wild flowers with many thin petals. When the petals drop off, they leave fluffy balls of seeds.

dandruff is tiny flakes of dry skin from a person's scalp, sometimes seen in their hair or on their shoulders.

dandy (dandies) A **dandy** is a man who is concerned about the way he looks and wears smart fashionable clothes.

Dane A **Dane** is someone who comes from Denmark.

danger You say there is **danger** when there is a risk of someone being hurt. A **danger** is something which can hurt people. ◇ If you say there is a **danger** of something bad happening, you mean there is a chance it will happen. ◇ A **danger sign** or **danger signal** is something which warns you of possible trouble or danger. ◇ **Danger money** is extra money paid to someone for doing a dangerous job.

dangerous (dangerously) If something is **dangerous**, it could lead to people being physically hurt or harmed in some other way. ◇ A **dangerous** person or animal is capable of killing or injuring people. You can also say a person's behaviour is **dangerous**. *Many motorists acted dangerously through frustration or ignorance.*

dangle (dangling, dangled) If something **dangles** or is **dangled**, it hangs or swings loosely. ◇ If you **dangle** something attractive in front of someone, you suggest they might get it if they do what you want.

Danish is used to talk about people and things in or from Denmark. *...the Danish national anthem.* ◇ **Danish** is the main language spoken in Denmark.

Danish pastry A Danish pastry is a cake made of rich pastry with a sweet filling like apple or almond paste.

dank A dank place is uncomfortably damp and cold.

dapper A dapper man is slim and neatly dressed.

dappled If something is **dappled**, it has light and dark patches.

dare (daring, dared) ❑ If you **dare** to do something, you are brave enough to do it. ◇ If you **dare** someone else to do something, you challenge them to prove they are not frightened of doing it. A challenge like this is called a **dare**.

❑ **Daring** is used to describe (a) actions which involve danger. *...a daring helicopter rescue.* (b) things which are likely to shock people. *...daring new ideas.* ◇ **Daring** is also used to describe someone who does dangerous things or behaves in a way likely to shock people. *...a daring reformer.* **Daring** is the courage shown by someone like this.

❑ You say 'I **dare** say...' to show you think something is probably true. *If he was locked away for years, I dare say he would survive, but it would be bound to change him.*

❑ People say '**dare** I say it' when they are going to say something which might be regarded as shocking or indiscreet. *I can see he's got, dare I say it, baggier eyes.*

daredevil is used to describe people who enjoy doing dangerous things.

dark (darkly, darkness) ❑ When it is **dark**, there is not enough light to see clearly. You can talk about the **dark** or **darkness** in a place.

❑ When **darkness** falls, it gets dark because the sun is setting. ◇ If you do something **before dark**, you do it before the sun sets. If you do it **after dark**, you do it at night. If you do it **under cover of darkness**, you do it at night when you cannot be seen.

❑ If you are kept **in the dark** about something, you are not told anything about it.

❑ **Dark** colours are like the colours things seem to have when they are seen in shadow. *...a dark blue suit.* ◇ If someone is **dark** or has **dark** hair, their hair is dark brown or black. ◇ If someone has **dark** skin, their skin is naturally brown. ◇ **Dark** eyes are a deep brown colour.

❑ **Dark** is used to talk about things to do with evil. *...the dark side of human nature.*

❑ When someone suggests that something unpleasant is happening or going to happen, you can say they say it **darkly**. *One man hinted darkly that there would be violence.*

❑ A **dark** period of time is one when there is great suffering or danger. *...the dark days of July 1940.*

❑ You say someone is a **dark horse** when they have been involved in something unusual or exciting and have not told anyone about it.

dark age The **Dark Ages** were the period of European history between about 500 and 1000 A.D.

dark glasses are glasses with dark lenses to protect your eyes in bright sunlight.

darken (darkening, darkened) If something **darkens** or is **darkened**, it becomes darker. ◇ A **darkened** building, room, or street has no lights on. ◇ If something **darkens** a situation, it makes it less hopeful or enjoyable.

darkroom A **darkroom** is a room without daylight where photographs are developed.

darling People who are very fond of each other sometimes call each other **darling**. ◇ **Darling** is used to talk about a person someone is very fond of. *...her darling baby brother.* ◇ The **darling** of a group of people is their favourite. *Strachan was once the darling of the Manchester crowd.*

darn If you **darn** something made of wool or cloth, you mend a hole in it by sewing stitches across the hole, then weaving stitches in and out of them. A repair like this is called a **darn**.

dart ❏ If a person or animal **darts** somewhere, they move there suddenly and quickly. ◇ If you **dart** a glance at something, you look at it quickly, then look away.

❏ **Darts** are small pointed objects which you throw at a numbered board in a game called **darts**. ◇ **Darts** are also pointed objects fired from something like a blowpipe.

Darwinism (Darwinian) **Darwinism** is Charles Darwin's theory of the development of plants and animals by natural selection. **Darwinian** is used to talk about things connected with this theory. ◇ **Darwinian** is also used to talk about the idea that, in any situation, it is the strongest or cleverest people who come off best.

dash (dashes, dashing, dashed) ❏ If you **dash** somewhere, you go there quickly. ◇ If you **make a dash** for a place, you suddenly hurry towards it. ◇ If you **dash off**, you leave a place in a hurry.

❏ If you **dash off** something you are writing, you write it quickly, without thinking much about it.

❏ If you **dash** something against a surface, you throw it there violently. ◇ If your hopes are **dashed**, something spoils your chances of getting what you want.

❏ If you add a **dash** of something, you add a small amount of it. *The costumes gave the production a much-needed dash of glamour.*

❏ If you do something with **dash**, you do it in a stylish way. ◇ If someone **cuts a dash**, they look stylish and impressive. ◇ A **dashing** person is stylish and attractive.

❏ A **dash** is the short straight horizontal line – . It is used, for example, in the middle of a sentence when you are making a comment on what you are saying. *Number seventeen was – of all things – underground.*

dashboard A car's **dashboard** is the panel facing the driver, where most of the instruments and switches are.

dastardly A **dastardly** person is cunning and evil. You can also call their plans or behaviour **dastardly**.

data is information, usually in the form of facts or statistics. ◇ A **data bank** is a collection of data stored on computer. ◇ **Data processing** is a series of operations carried out on data, especially by computers, to obtain, interpret, or present information. ◇ **data cartridge**: see cartridge.

database A **database** is a collection of data stored on computer in such a way that it can be retrieved quickly and efficiently.

date (dating, dated) ❏ A **date** is a particular year or day, for example 1066 or 23rd November 1994. ◇ When you **date** a letter or a cheque, you write the day's date on it.

❏ If something **dates back to** a particular time or **dates from** it, it started or was made then. *The treasure dates back to the sixth century B.C.*

❏ You use **to date** when you are saying what has happened so far, although the situation may change. *200 vampire movies have been made to date.*

❏ If you want to say something will happen in the future, without saying exactly when, you can say it will happen at a later **date**.

❏ If something is **out of date**, it no longer applies, or is no longer useful or relevant. ◇ **Dated** things seem old-fashioned, although they were once fashionable.

❏ A **date** is also an appointment to meet someone or go out with them. You call the person you meet your **date**. ◇ If you are **dating** someone, they are your girlfriend or boyfriend.

❏ **Dates** are small sticky brown fruit. The trees they grow on are called **date palms**.

daub (daubing, daubed) If you **daub** something like paint onto a surface, you put it on with a brush in a quick careless way. You can also **daub** a message using paint like this. *They had daubed slogans on the walls.*

daughter A person's **daughter** is their female child.

daughter-in-law (daughters-in-law) A person's **daughter-in-law** is the wife of their son.

daunt If you are **daunted** by something, you are worried or alarmed at having to deal with it. You say something like this is **daunting**. *...a daunting task.*

dawdle (dawdling, dawdled) If you **dawdle**, you spend more time than necessary doing something or going somewhere.

dawn is the beginning of the day, just before sunrise, when light first appears. When a day **dawns**, the sky grows light after the night. ◇ The **dawn chorus** is the sound of large numbers of birds singing at dawn.

❏ When a period of time **dawns**, it begins. You can talk about the **dawn** of a period of time. *...the dawn of the 20th century.*

❏ If the truth about something **dawns on** you, you realize it.

day ❏ A **day** is one of the seven twenty-four hour periods in a week. ◇ **Day** is the part of a day when it is light.

❏ If it is a year **to the day** since something happened, it happened exactly a year ago. ◇ If you say something happens or is true **to this day**, you are emphasizing that it still happens or is true. ◇ If something happens **day and night**, it goes on all the time without stopping. ◇ If something happens **day in, day out**, it happens all day, every day. ◇ If you say something has been true from **day one**, you mean it has been true from the very beginning of something. ◇ If you say something will happen **one day** or **some day**, you mean it will happen at some future time. ◇ If you say something will happen **one of these days**, you mean it could happen at any time. ◇ **Day-to-day** is used to describe things which happen as part of ordinary life. *...the day-to-day running of schools.*

❏ **Day** is used to talk about a particular time in history. *...in Shakespeare's day... Are students interested in religion these days?* ◇ If you talk about the **day** of a person or thing, you mean the time when they were successful or important. *The day of the yuppie is gone.* ◇ When people talk about **the good old days**, they mean a time in the past when they think things were better than they are now. ◇ When people say **in this day and age**, they mean in modern times.

❏ If you decide to **call it a day**, you give up what you are doing altogether, or leave it to be finished another day. ◇ If something **makes your day**, it makes you very happy or pleased. ◇ If something **wins the day**, it is the strongest force in a situation, and determines what happens. *The views of the moderates seem to have won the day.* ◇ If a person **wins the day**, they get the better of their opponents in a struggle or contest. ◇ If something **saves the day** for someone, it prevents them from being defeated in a game or contest.

day care is a system in which sick or handicapped people get treatment at home instead of having to go into hospital. Day care also includes the provision of day centres for people such as the old.

day centre Day centres are places where people like the old or the homeless can spend time during the day. They often provide meals.

day nursery A day nursery is a place where children too young to go to school can be left while their parents are at work.

day return A day return is a ticket which allows you to go somewhere and come back the same day for a lower price than an ordinary return ticket.

day school A day school is one which pupils go to each day from their own homes.

day trip A day trip is a journey to a place and back the same day, made for pleasure.

daybreak is the beginning of the morning, when light first appears.

daydream (daydreaming, daydreamed) If you daydream, your attention wanders and you think about pleasant things; these thoughts are called daydreams. ◇ A daydream is also a hope or ambition you are unlikely to achieve.

daylight is (a) the light during the day. (b) the part of the day when it is light. ◇ in broad daylight: see broad.

daytime is the part of the day when it is light. ◇ Daytime is used to describe things which are used or operate during the day, when most people are at work. ...your daytime telephone number.

dazed (daze) If someone is dazed after an accident or an unpleasant experience, they are shocked or confused and unable to think clearly. You say someone like this is in a daze.

dazzle (dazzling, dazzled) ❑ If you are dazzled by something, you are amazed and impressed by its quality or beauty. You say something like this is dazzling. ❑ If you are dazzled by a bright light, you cannot see properly because of it. You talk about the dazzle of a light like this.

dB See decibel.

DC is used to describe an electric current which always flows in the same direction. DC stands for 'direct current'. See also AC.

DDT is a poisonous chemical used to kill insects. DDT stands for 'dichlorodiphenyltrichloroethane'.

de facto (pron: day fac-to) is used in front of an expression to say something operates as the thing described by the expression, although it is not legally recognized as that thing. ...thirty years of de facto single party rule.

de jure (pron: day jew-ray) is used to talk about things which are recognized by law, as distinct from things which operate without being recognized by law. See also de facto. Full de jure independence was accorded to the new state on 4 October 1932.

de luxe is used to describe things which are better and more expensive than other things of the same kind.

de rigueur (pron: de rig-gur) If you say something is de rigueur, you mean you must have it or do it if you do not want to seem old-fashioned or out-of-place.

deacon In some churches, including the Church of England, a deacon is a member of the clergy who is lower in rank than a priest. In other churches, a deacon is a non-ordained person who assists the minister.

deaconess (deaconesses) In some Protestant churches, a deaconess is a woman who helps look after the congregation.

deactivate (deactivating, deactivated) If someone deactivates something like a bomb or missile, they make it incapable of exploding.

dead ❑ A dead person, animal, or plant is no longer living. The dead are people who have died, especially people who have been killed. People gathered in the city centre to mourn the dead. ◇ If a victim of an attack or accident is left for dead, they may still be alive but are assumed to be dead and are not attacked any more or given any help. ◇ If you say someone is half-dead, you mean they are very tired or ill and very weak. ❑ If a phone or radio goes dead, you can no longer hear anything from it and it seems to have stopped working. ❑ A dead language is one which is no longer generally used, although people may still study it. Latin and Ancient Greek are dead languages. ❑ If you say an idea, theory, or belief is dead, you mean most people no longer think it is appropriate or important. Socialism is dead. ◇ If you say something like an organization is dead, you mean it no longer exists or is no longer useful or important. The Warsaw Pact is dead. ◇ If you talk about someone or something coming back from the dead, you mean they suddenly reappear or become important again, after people had forgotten about them. ❑ The dead centre of something is its exact centre. ◇ If there is dead silence, there is total silence. ◇ If something comes to a dead stop, it stops completely. ❑ The dead of night is the middle of the night, when it is darkest. ❑ If you are dead against something, you are totally opposed to it. ❑ If you say you would not be seen dead or caught dead doing something, you mean you would never do it because you think it is unfashionable or embarrassing. ❑ dead wood: see wood.

dead end If a street is a dead end, there is no way out at one end. ◇ Dead end is used to talk about things which will not lead to anything interesting or successful. ...a dead end job.

dead heat If a race ends in a dead heat, two or more competitors reach the finishing line first at exactly the same time. Similarly, you say a competition is a dead heat when two or more competitors beat everyone else but have the same number of points each.

dead weight You say something or someone is a dead weight when they are heavy and difficult to lift. ◇ You also use dead weight to describe something which makes change or progress difficult. ...a dead weight of tradition.

deaden (deadening, deadened) If something deadens a feeling, it makes it less strong. ◇ If something deadens a sound, it makes it less loud.

deadline A deadline is a time or date by which something must be finished.

deadlock (deadlocked) If a discussion or argument reaches deadlock or is **deadlocked**, neither side is willing to give in, so no agreement can be reached.

deadly (deadlier, deadliest) If something is **deadly**, it is capable of killing people. ◇ **Deadly** is used in front of some words to mean 'extremely', and in front of others to mean 'extreme'. *They told him they were deadly serious about their plans... Agassi served with deadly accuracy.*

deadpan is used to describe someone's behaviour or expression when they hide the fact that they are joking or teasing and pretend to be serious.

deaf A deaf person cannot hear very well, or cannot hear at all. **The deaf** are people who are deaf. ◇ If you are **deaf** to what someone says or **turn a deaf ear** to it, you ignore it.

deaf-mute A deaf-mute is a person who cannot hear or speak.

deafen (deafening, deafened) If a person is **deafened**, they are made deaf. ◇ If you are **deafened** by a noise, it is so loud you cannot hear anything else. You say a noise like this is **deafening**.

deal (dealing, dealt) ❑ A **deal** is an agreement or arrangement, especially a business one.
❑ If a person or business **deals in** a type of goods, they buy and sell them.
❑ When you **deal with** a situation or a problem, you do what needs to be done to get the result you want.
❑ A **great deal** or **good deal** of something is a lot of it.
❑ If you **deal** someone a blow, you hit them. ◇ If something **deals** you a blow, it harms you in some way. *The reforms could deal a serious blow to their living standards.*
❑ In a game of cards, when someone **deals** the cards, they give them out to the players. If it is your **deal**, it is your turn to deal.
❑ If you say someone has had a **bad deal**, you mean they have been unlucky or have been treated unfairly.

dealer (dealership) ❑ A **dealer** is a person who makes money by buying and selling things for a profit. *...an antiques dealer.* A **dealership** is a business which makes money in this way.
❑ In a game of cards, the **dealer** is the person who gives out cards to the other players.

dealings If you have **dealings** with someone, you are involved with them in some way, for example having discussions or arranging a business deal.

dean A **dean** at a university or college is the chief administrator of a faculty. ◇ In the Church of England, a **dean** is a high-ranking priest who is in charge of a group of priests and is the administrator of a cathedral. See also **rural dean**.

deanery (deaneries) A **deanery** is an area for which a rural dean has responsibility. It consists of several parishes.

dear (dearer, dearest) ❑ You can use **dear** to describe someone you are fond of. *He is a dear friend of mine.* ◇ If something is **dear** to you, you care deeply about it. ◇ When people say something is their **dearest wish**, they mean they want it more than anything else.
❑ If something is **dear**, it costs a lot of money.

dearly If you love someone **dearly**, you love them very much. ◇ If you would **dearly** like to have or do something, you want to have or do it very much. ◇ If you **pay dearly** for something you have done, you suffer a lot because of it.

dearth If there is a **dearth** of something, there is not enough of it.

death is the end of a person's or animal's life. ◇ If someone has a **death wish**, they are attracted by the idea of dying and are likely to do very dangerous things. ◇ The **death toll** of an accident, disaster, or war is the number of people killed. ◇ A fight **to the death** is one which does not end until the winner kills the loser.
❑ If someone is **put to death**, they are killed as a punishment. ◇ A **death warrant** is an official document ordering someone to be killed. ◇ If someone **signs the death warrant** of something like an organization, they do something which makes it impossible for it to continue.
❑ The **death penalty** is the punishment of death. ◇ If a person is given the **death sentence**, a court decides they will be punished by death. ◇ **Death row** is the part of a prison where prisoners sentenced to death are kept.
❑ A **death camp** is a prison camp where all the prisoners are intended to be killed. ◇ **Death squads** are groups of people in some countries who go around killing their political enemies.
❑ If you are **scared to death**, you are extremely frightened. ◇ If you are **sick to death** of something, you have become very bored with it or irritated by it, and do not want it to continue.
❑ The **death** of something like an organization or way of life is its end. *...the death of the Communist Party.* ◇ If you say the **death knell** of something has sounded, you mean it will soon end. ◇ The thing which causes the end of something can be called its **death knell**. *A United States veto could be the death knell for the fragile coalition.*
❑ Dying people sometimes make violent uncontrolled movements called their **death throes**. ◇ The **death throes** of something like a system or organization are its final stages, just before it fails completely or ends.
❑ You say a place or vehicle is a **death trap** when it is in such a dangerous condition that it is likely to cause someone's death.

death certificate A death certificate is an official statement signed by a doctor which gives the cause of a person's death.

death duties are a tax paid by people who inherit property from someone who has died.

death-watch beetle The death-watch beetle is an insect which burrows into wood, for example in old houses, and makes a clicking noise by hitting its head against the wood.

deathbed If someone is on their **deathbed**, they are in bed and about to die.

deathly is used to describe things which remind you of a dead person. *Her feet were deathly cold.* ◇ When people stop talking suddenly and are completely quiet, you can say there is a **deathly** silence.

debacle (*pron:* day-bah-kl) A **debacle** is a complete and embarrassing failure.

debag (debagging, debagged) If someone is **debagged**, they have their trousers pulled off by people as a joke.

debar (debarring, debarred) If you are **debarred** from something, you are legally prevented from doing it or taking part in it.

debase (debasing, debased) If something has been **debased**, it is not of such good quality or of such a high standard as it once was.

debate (debating, debated; debater, debatable) ❏ When people **debate** something, they discuss it formally, putting forward different opinions. A **debate** is a discussion like this. People taking part in a debate are called **debaters**.

❏ If you say something is **debatable** or **open to debate**, you mean there is no certainty about it. *How much a good bathroom adds to the value of a house is debatable.*

❏ If you **debate** what to do, you think about possible alternatives before making up your mind.

debauched (*pron:* dib-**bawcht**) (debauchery) If you call someone **debauched**, you mean they indulge too much in physical pleasures, for example by drinking too much or visiting prostitutes. This kind of behaviour is called **debauchery**.

debenture Debentures are portions of a long-term loan made to a company. They are often bought and sold by investors who receive regular interest payments of an agreed percentage.

debilitated (debilitating, debility) If a person is **debilitated**, they are made weak. **Debilitating** is used to describe things like diseases or severe weather conditions which make people weak. *The humidity is debilitating.* Weakness caused like this is called **debility**. ◇ **Debilitated** and **debilitating** are also used to talk about other things being weakened, such as a country's economy. *...debilitating subsidies.*

debit (debiting, debited) ❏ If your bank account is **debited**, money is taken from it by your bank and paid to someone else. ◇ A **debit card** is a card which acts like a cheque. When you use it to pay someone, the money is transferred automatically from your bank account to theirs. ◇ If you pay bills by **direct debit**, you arrange for regular payments to be made from your bank account.

❏ People say **on the debit side** when they are mentioning a disadvantage of something. *On the debit side, researchers listed five ways that nutrients were being lost from the soil.*

debonair (*pron:* de-bon-**air**) A **debonair** man is handsome, well-dressed, and confident.

debrief (debriefing, debriefed) If someone is **debriefed**, they are interrogated about something they have just done or experienced. An interrogation like this is called a **debriefing** or a **debriefing session**.

debris (*pron:* **deb**-ree) is broken pieces of something which has recently been destroyed, such as a plane or a building.

debt (debtor) ❏ A **debt** is an amount of money you owe someone. If you are **in debt**, you owe someone money. ◇ People who owe someone money are called that person's **debtors**. ◇ **bad debt:** see **bad**.

❏ If you say you are **in someone's debt**, you mean you are grateful for something they have done for you.

debug (debugging, debugged) If someone **debugs** a computer program, they find the faults in it and put them right so the program will work properly.

debunk If you **debunk** an idea or belief, you show it is false or unimportant.

debut (*pron:* **day**-byoo) The **debut** of an actor or musician is their first public performance. ◇ **Debut** is also used in sport. For example, a footballer's **debut** with a team is his first game with them.

debutante (*pron:* **day**-byoo-tont) A **debutante** is a young

upper-class woman who has just started going to dances and parties.

decade A **decade** is a period of ten years, especially one beginning with a year ending in 0.

decadence (*pron:* dek-a-**denss**) (decadent) **Decadence** is a way of living or behaving which shows lower standards, especially moral standards, than in a previous time. People behaving like this are called **decadent**, and so is their behaviour.

decaffeinated coffee has had most of the caffeine removed from it.

decamp If someone suddenly leaves a place and goes to live somewhere else, you can say they **decamp** there.

decant If you **decant** wine, you pour some of it carefully from one container to another, making sure any sediment is left behind.

decanter A **decanter** is a glass bottle or jug used for serving drinks like sherry or whisky.

decapitate (decapitating, decapitated; decapitation) If a person is **decapitated**, their head is cut off. *The sentence was to be carried out by means of decapitation.*

decathlon (decathlete) The **decathlon** is a competition in which athletes called **decathletes** take part in ten different sporting events.

decay ❏ If something **decays**, it rots and starts to fall apart. This process is called **decay**. ◇ If buildings **decay**, their condition becomes worse because they have not been looked after and repaired. ◇ Parts of a town or city are described as **decaying** when many of the buildings are empty and everything is badly looked after.

❏ If something like an organization or country **decays**, it gradually becomes weak or corrupt.

deceased A **deceased** person has recently died. People sometimes call someone who has just died **the deceased**. *...an engraved likeness of the deceased's face and clothing.*

deceit (deceitful) **Deceit** is behaviour intended to make people believe things which are not true. You say people who behave like this are **deceitful**; their behaviour can also be called **deceitful**.

deceive (deceiving, deceived) If you **deceive** someone, you deliberately make them believe something which is not true.

decelerate (decelerating, decelerated; deceleration) If something **decelerates**, it slows down. *The parachute opens and deceleration begins.*

decency (decencies) **Decency** is used to talk about behaviour which is considered to be correct or acceptable. *He should have the decency to resign.* ◇ **Decencies** are accepted standards of behaviour.

decent (decently) **Decent** is used to say something is of an acceptable standard or quality. *In those days a three-bedroomed house might be decently furnished for about £100.* ◇ **Decent** behaviour is honest and respectable. *We are striving to treat each other more decently.*

decentralize (decentralizing, decentralized; decentralization) (*can be spelled with an 's' instead of a 'z'*) If a large organization **decentralizes**, it transfers some of its functions from its main office to smaller offices in other areas. This process is called **decentralization**.

deception is deceiving people. A **deception** is something you say or do to deceive someone.

deceptive (deceptively) If you say something is **deceptive**, you mean it might make people believe something which is not true. *It all looks deceptively simple.*

decibel The intensity of sound is measured in **decibels**. 'Decibels' is often written 'dB'.

decide (deciding, decided; decidedly, decider) ❑ If you **decide** to do something, you make up your mind to do it. ◇ If you **decide on** a plan or course of action, you choose it from two or more alternatives. ◇ When something like a court case is **decided**, the evidence is considered and a verdict is reached.

❑ If what happens is **decided** by a particular thing, it depends on that thing. *The team's World Cup fate was decided by a penalty shoot-out.* ◇ If something is a **deciding factor**, it is one of the things which affect what happens. ◇ In a competition, a **decider** is the game or part of a game which determines who wins the competition.

❑ If you **decide** something is true, you form that opinion on the basis of what you know. *He decided it was safe to come home.*

❑ **Decided** and **decidedly** are used in front of some words and expressions to say something is definitely a particular thing. For example, if you say something is a 'decided drawback', you mean it is definitely a drawback. *His control of the company seems decidedly less secure.*

deciduous trees lose their leaves in the autumn.

decimal A **decimal** system involves counting in units of ten. ◇ A **decimal** is a fraction written as a dot followed by one or more numbers representing tenths, hundredths, and so on. For example, three-eighths can be written .375. The dot in a fraction like this is called the **decimal point**.

decimalization (*or* decimalisation) was the change made to the money system in February 1971 when the old system of pounds, shillings, and pence was replaced by the present decimal system.

decimate (decimating, decimated; decimation) If a group of people, animals, or things is **decimated**, most of them are killed or destroyed. *A huge storm had decimated the Kirkwall fishing fleet.* ◇ People also talk about things being **decimated** when they are reduced to a fraction of their former strength or importance. *...the decimation of the British aircraft industry.* ◇ Originally, to **decimate** something meant to reduce it by a tenth.

decipher (deciphering, deciphered) If you **decipher** a piece of writing, speech, or coded information, you work out what it says.

decision When you make a **decision**, you make up your mind about something.

decisive (decisively, decisiveness) ❑ If something is **decisive**, it determines which way things will go in the future. *...a decisive battle.* ◇ In sport, if a person or team gets a **decisive** victory, they win by a large margin. A person or team can also suffer a **decisive** defeat.

❑ A **decisive** person makes quick firm decisions. *The real problem is lack of decisiveness.* ◇ If you do something **decisively**, you do it in a firm deliberate way.

deck ❑ The **deck** of a ship is the level part you stand on. A large ship can have several **decks**. ◇ A **deck hand** is a person who does the cleaning and other work on a ship's deck.

❑ If you **clear the decks**, you finish off the things you

are dealing with at present, so you can concentrate on something else which is about to start.

❑ The **decks** of a bus are its upper and lower floors.

❑ In the US, a patio is called a **deck**.

❑ A pack of playing cards can be called a **deck**.

❑ If something is **decked** with attractive things, it is decorated with them. *...lorries and buses decked with flags.* ◇ If someone is **decked out** in something bright and attractive, they are wearing it.

deckchair **Deckchairs** are adjustable folding chairs used in the open air.

declaim (declaiming, declaimed; declamatory; declamation) If you **declaim** something, you say it dramatically, as if you were on a stage. Speaking like this can be called **declamation**. Anything which reminds you of a dramatic speech can be called **declamatory** (*pron:* dik-klam-ator-y). *The poem was delivered in Eldritch's usual declamatory voice.*

declaration A **declaration** is an official announcement, especially one made by a government. *...a declaration of war.* ◇ If you tell someone that you love them, this is called a **declaration** of love.

declare (declaring, declared) ❑ If you **declare** something, you say it in a firm clear way. ◇ If you **declare** your feelings or intentions, you tell people about them. *...the declared aims of the Security Council.* ◇ When a country or government **declares** something, it announces it officially and formally. *Hungary declared itself a democracy.*

❑ If you **declare** something you have obtained, you tell someone in authority about it, as required by a law or rule. *Ministers have a rule book whereby they have to declare any form of gift.*

❑ If a cricket team **declares**, they decide to stop batting and let the other team in, though some of their own players are not yet out. This is usually because they believe they have enough runs to win, and want to give themselves time to get the other team out.

declassify (declassifies, declassifying, declassified) When official documents are **declassified**, the government declares they are no longer secret. You can also say the information they contain is **declassified**.

decline (declining, declined) ❑ If something is **declining**, it is becoming poorer or weaker. *Living standards are declining.* You can talk about a **decline** in something like this; you can also say it is **in decline** or **on the decline**. *...a decline in the value of investments... The economy is on the decline.*

❑ If you **decline** something which is offered to you, you do not accept it. ◇ If you **decline** a request, you turn it down. ◇ If you **decline** to do something, you do not do it.

decode (decoding, decoded) When information is **decoded**, it is changed into ordinary language or into a form which can be easily understood.

decoder A **decoder** is something used to decode information. ◇ A **decoder** is also a device you need to attach to your TV set to watch some satellite and cable TV programmes.

décolleté (décolletage) If a woman is **décolleté** (*pron:* day-kol-tay), she is wearing a dress or blouse with a very low neckline which does not cover the top of her breasts. You can also say her dress or blouse is **décolleté**. The neckline of a dress or blouse like this is called its

décolletage (*pron*: day-kol-tazh; *the 'zh' sounds like 's' in 'pleasure'*).

decolonization (*or* **decolonisation**) When **decolonization** takes place, a powerful country gives up control of a weaker country, which then has political independence.

decommission (decommissioning, decommissioned) If something like a ship or power station is **decommissioned**, it is taken out of use.

decompose (decomposing, decomposed; decomposition) When something **decomposes**, it changes chemically and begins to rot. This process is called **decomposition**.

decompression If something undergoes **decompression**, the air pressure on it is reduced. ◇ **Decompression** is also the process by which divers are brought back to normal air pressure after they have been at great pressure underwater. This usually takes place in a **decompression chamber**. ◇ **Decompression sickness** is what happens to divers when they rise to the surface of the water too quickly. The rapid change in the water pressure makes the air in their blood expand to form bubbles; this causes pain in the joints, cramps, paralysis, and sometimes death. Decompression sickness is sometimes called the 'bends'.

decongestant A **decongestant** is a medicine which helps someone with a cold to breathe more easily.

decontaminate (decontaminating, decontaminated; decontamination) If something is **decontaminated**, radioactivity, germs, or other dangerous substances are removed from it. This process is called **decontamination**.

decontrol (decontrolling, decontrolled) If prices or rents are **decontrolled**, they are no longer set by the government.

decor The **decor** of a house or room is the style it is furnished and decorated in.

decorate (decorating, decorated; decoration) ❏ If you **decorate** something, you add something attractive to it to brighten it up. Things added like this are called **decorations**. ◇ If you **decorate** a building or room, you paint or wallpaper it. The **decoration** of a building is its paintwork, wallpaper, and ornaments.
   ❏ If a person is **decorated**, they are given a medal as an official honour. Medals like these are called **decorations**.

decorative things are intended to look attractive rather than be useful. ◇ When people talk about the **decorative arts**, they mean arts and crafts like pottery and cabinet-making, which involve making things to be used for decoration or furnishing.

decorator A **decorator** is a person who paints and wallpapers houses and other buildings for a living.

decorous (decorously; decorum) Someone's behaviour is called **decorous** (*pron*: dek-a-russ) when it is polite, dignified, and correct. People like this are also said to behave with **decorum** (*pron*: dik-core-um). *She disrobed as decorously as possible.*

decouple (decoupling, decoupled) If something is **decoupled** from something else, it is separated from it. *...the desire to decouple economic decision-making from politics.*

decoy A **decoy** is something intended to attract someone's attention, either to catch them or to stop them noticing something.

decrease (decreasing, decreased; decreasingly) If something **decreases** or is **decreased**, it gets smaller. ◇ A **decrease** is a reduction in size or number. ◇ You use **decreasingly** to say something has less and less of a quality. *The parliamentary forum becomes a decreasingly effective democratic institution.*

decree (decreeing, decreed) A **decree** is an official order, especially one made by the ruler of a country. If someone in authority **decrees** something, they officially order that it shall be done.

decree absolute A **decree absolute** is the final order which ends a marriage, made by a court in a divorce case.

decree nisi (*pron*: nice-sigh) A **decree nisi** is an order issued by a court saying a divorce will take place at a certain time unless a good reason is produced to prevent it.

decrepit (decrepitude) If something is **decrepit**, it is very old and in bad condition. You can talk about the **decrepitude** of something like this.

decriminalize (decriminalizing, decriminalized; decriminalization) (*can be spelled with an 's' instead of a 'z'*) If something is **decriminalized**, it is no longer a crime to have it or do it. *...the decriminalization of homosexuality.*

decry (decries, decrying, decried) If you **decry** someone or something, you say publicly they are bad or worthless.

dedicate (dedicating, dedicated; dedication, dedicatee) ❏ If you **dedicate** yourself to something, you make it the most important thing in your life. You say you are **dedicated** to something like this; you can also talk about your **dedication** to it.
   ❏ If a writer or composer **dedicates** a book or piece of music to someone, they say they want them to be associated with it, because they are fond of them or respect them. They announce this at the beginning of the book or piece of music in a statement called a **dedication**. ◇ The **dedicatee** of a book or piece of music is the person it is dedicated to. ◇ When a monument, building, or church is **dedicated** to someone, a formal ceremony is held to show it will always be associated with that person. The ceremony is called a **dedication** ceremony.

deduce (deducing, deduced) If you **deduce** something, you work it out from what you already know.

deduct When you **deduct** an amount from a total, you reduce it by that amount.

deductible If something is **deductible** or **tax-deductible**, the cost of it can be deducted from your income before your income tax is calculated.

deduction ❏ A **deduction** is an amount taken off a total. **Deduction** is taking an amount off a total. *...national insurance deductions.*
   ❏ A **deduction** is also something you work out from what you already know. *What scientific deductions can you make from an observation of this eclipse?*

deed A **deed** is something which is done, especially something very good or very bad. *...his latest good deed... ...a dirty deed... He said that what mattered were deeds not words.* ◇ A **deed** is also a legal document containing an agreement or contract.

deed poll If you change your name by **deed poll**, you do it officially and legally.

deem (deeming, deemed) If something is **deemed** to be a particular thing, it is believed or declared to be that thing.

deep (deeper, deepest; deeply) ❏ If something is **deep**, it extends a long way down from its surface. ◇ **Deep** is also used to talk about measurements. For example, if something is two metres **deep**, it measures two metres from top to bottom or from front to back. ◇ If you go **deep** into an area, you go a long way inside it. *...deep inside British territory.* ◇ If something happens **deep** into a period of time, it happens a long way into that period. *...a season that extends deep into July.*

❑ **Deep** feelings are strongly felt. *...my deepest fear... Voters are deeply distrustful of all politicians.* ◇ **Deep** is used to emphasize the seriousness of something. *...in deep trouble.* ◇ If you say something **runs deep**, you mean it is well-established and difficult to change. *The causes of the violence run deep.* ◇ **Deep down** and **deep inside** are used to talk about strong feelings and beliefs which someone has without showing them. *Deep down he is longing to conform.*

❑ If you say someone is **deep** or a **deep** thinker, you mean they have great intellectual understanding. You can also say their thoughts or ideas are **deep**.

❑ If someone is **deep in debt**, they owe a lot of money.

❑ If you **jump in at the deep end**, you choose to do the most difficult part of a job first. ◇ If you are **thrown in at the deep end**, you are put in a completely new situation or given something difficult to do without any training or preparation.

❑ **Deep breathing** is taking in long slow breaths which fill your lungs. ◇ If you say you **took a deep breath** before doing something, you mean you tried to prepare yourself, knowing it was going to be difficult or dangerous.

❑ If someone is in a **deep sleep**, they are sleeping peacefully and it is difficult to wake them.

❑ **Deep** colours are strong and rather dark. ◇ A **deep** sound is low in pitch. *She has a deep, sexy voice.*

deep freeze A **deep freeze** is the same as a freezer. ◇ If something is kept **in deep freeze**, it is stored at an extremely low temperature.

deep-fried food has been fried by being submerged in deep fat or oil.

deep-rooted feelings or ideas are firmly fixed and difficult to change.

deep-sea activities take place in parts of the sea a long way from the coast. *...deep-sea fishing.*

deep-seated A **deep-seated** feeling or belief is strongly held and difficult to change. ◇ A **deep-seated** problem is caused by conditions which are difficult to change.

deepen (deepening, deepened) ❑ If a river or the sea **deepens** somewhere, it gets deeper. ◇ If you **deepen** something, you make it deeper. *The authority wants to widen and deepen the River Soar.*

❑ If a situation or feeling **deepens** or is **deepened**, it becomes more serious or intense. *...the deepening crisis.* ◇ If your knowledge or understanding of something is **deepened**, you learn more about it.

❑ When a sound **deepens**, it becomes lower in pitch.

deer (plural: deer) **Deer** are agile wild animals which eat grassy food and chew the cud like cows. In most species, the male deer has large branching horns called antlers.

deerstalker A **deerstalker** is a soft cloth hat, with peaks at the front and back and earflaps that can be folded upwards and tied on top.

deface (defacing, defaced) If someone **defaces** something

like a wall or a notice, they spoil it by writing or drawing on it.

defame (defaming, defamed; defamatory, defamation) If you say you have been **defamed**, you mean someone has said or written untrue things about you which may damage your reputation; you call what they have said or written **defamatory** (pron: dif-**fam**-a-tree). You can take legal action against someone for this; this is called an action for **defamation** (pron: def-fam-**may**-shun).

default (defaulter) ❑ If you **default** on something you are legally supposed to do, such as make a payment, you do not do it. You are then said to be **in default**. An individual case of someone doing this is called a **default**; the person or firm doing it is called a **defaulter**.

❑ If something happens **by default**, it happens only because something else has not happened. *He kept the title by default because no one else wanted to compete for it.*

defeat (defeating, defeated) ❑ If you **defeat** someone in a game or contest, you beat them. If you suffer a **defeat**, you lose. **Defeat** is being beaten in a game or contest. *If we don't change the leadership, we stand to face defeat at the elections.* ◇ If a country or army is **defeated**, they lose a war or battle. Losing a battle is called a **defeat**.

❑ If a proposal or motion in a debate is **defeated**, more people vote against it than for it. You say this is a **defeat** for the person proposing it.

❑ If you **defeat** a problem or difficulty, you solve it or deal with it successfully. If it **defeats** you, you fail to solve it or deal with it. ◇ If someone's efforts are **defeated**, they fail to achieve what they want.

defeatist (defeatism) A **defeatist** is someone who thinks and talks in a way which shows they expect to be unsuccessful. You call their behaviour **defeatist**; you can also talk about their **defeatism**.

defecate (pron: **def**-fe-cate) (defecating, defecated) When animals or people **defecate**, they get rid of solid waste from their bodies.

defect (defection, defector) ❑ A **defect** (pron: **dee**-fect) is a fault in a person or thing. *...a character defect... Several of the planes had wiring defects.*

❑ If someone **defects** (pron: dif-**fects**), they secretly leave their country, political party, or other group and join an opposing one. Someone doing this is called a **defector**; you talk about their **defection** to the other country, party, or group.

defective If something is **defective**, there is something wrong with it and it is not working properly.

defector See **defect**.

defence (American spelling: **defense**) ❑ **Defence** is action taken to protect someone or something from attack. *He said the new missiles were purely for defence... ...the defence of civil liberties.* ◇ A **defence** is something people or animals use or do to protect themselves. *...the body's defences against disease... Successful comedians have often developed their art as a defence against being bullied.* ◇ A **defence mechanism** is an instinctive reaction to something, which may protect you from a possible danger.

❑ **Defence** is used to talk about a country's armed forces and weapons. *...defence spending... ...the Ministry of Defence.* ◇ The **defences** of a country, town, or building are its armed forces, weapons, and other things used to protect it, such as fortifications.

❏ If someone puts up a **defence** of something which is being criticized, they say things in support of it. You can say they are speaking **in defence of** the thing being criticized. Someone can also speak **in defence of** a person.

❏ In court, a person's **defence** consists of all the things they say to support their claim that they are innocent. The accused person and any lawyers representing them are also called the **defence**.

❏ The **defence** in a game like football or hockey is the group of players whose main job is to stop the opposing team scoring. ◇ In games and sports, when someone makes a **defence** of their title, they compete with other people to decide whether they remain champion or a new champion takes over.

defenceless If someone or something is **defenceless**, they are unable to protect themselves.

defend ❏ If you **defend** someone or something when they are being attacked, you try to protect them. ◇ If you **defend** someone or something when they are being criticized, you argue in support of them. ◇ When a lawyer **defends** someone in court, he or she tries to show they are innocent.

❏ In games or sports, when a champion **defends** their title, they compete with other people to decide whether they remain champion or a new champion takes over.

defendant The **defendant** in a court case involving a crime is the accused person. Similarly, in a civil case, the **defendant** is the person who has had an action brought against them.

defender When someone supports ideas or values which are being criticized or threatened, you say they are a **defender** of those ideas or values. ...a defender of law and order. Similarly, you can say someone is a **defender** of a person who is being criticized or in danger. ◇ A **defender** in a game like football or hockey is a player whose main job is to stop the other side scoring.

defense See **defence**.

defensible ❏ If you say something like a point of view is **defensible**, you mean there are good reasons for having it, though you may not agree with it. ◇ If you say someone's behaviour is **defensible**, you mean they can be excused for what they have done.

❏ A **defensible** place is capable of being defended against attack.

defensive (defensively) ❏ You use **defensive** to describe things intended to protect someone or something from attack. ...a defensive wall... ...a defensive strategy. ◇ If people are **on the defensive**, they are ready to protect themselves or their interests because they feel threatened.

❏ If someone is **defensive**, they talk as if they think they are being accused of something. He insists defensively that he got the job for his administrative abilities, not for political reasons.

defer (deferring, deferred; deferment, deferral) ❏ If you **defer** something, you arrange for it to take place at a later date than was planned. An arrangement like this is called a **deferment** or a **deferral**.

❏ If you **defer** to someone, you accept their opinion or do what they want, because you respect them.

deference (deferential) If you treat someone with **deference**, you behave politely towards them because you re-

spect or admire them, or because they have authority over you. **Deferential** is used to describe behaviour like this. She was talking in quiet, deferential tones about her admiration for Gertrude Stein. ◇ If you do something **in deference** or **out of deference** to someone, you do it to show politeness and respect for them, though you may not want to do it.

defiant (defiantly, defiance) If someone is **defiant**, they show they are not willing to obey someone or are not worried about someone's disapproval. Behaviour like this is called **defiance**. The prisoners are still on the roof shouting defiantly at officers below.

deficiency (deficiencies) A **deficiency** in something, especially something your body needs, is a shortage of it. ...vitamin deficiency. ◇ A **deficiency** is also a weakness or a fault. They have complained of deficiencies in the electoral system.

deficient If someone or something is **deficient** in something, they do not have as much of it as they need. ...a magnesium deficient diet. ◇ **Deficient** is also used to say something is not good enough. ...deficient standards of hygiene and sanitation.

deficit (pron: def-fiss-it) ❏ A **deficit** is the amount by which the money received by a country or organization falls short of the amount it has spent. ◇ A country's **budget deficit** is the amount by which the money received in one year from taxes and other sources falls short of the amount spent on things like education and defence. A country's **trade deficit** is the amount by which money received from exports falls short of money paid for imports.

❏ In sport, a **deficit** is the amount by which the number of goals or points scored by one side is less than those scored by the other. Germany retrieved a two-goal deficit to win 3-2.

❏ If there is a **deficit** in something, there is not enough of it.

defile (defiling, defiled) If someone **defiles** something holy or something which is precious to people, they treat it disrespectfully, or spoil or damage it.

definable If something is **definable**, it can be described clearly and distinguished from other similar things.

define (defining, defined) ❏ If you **define** something like a policy or plan, you say what it is. ...a new treaty to define the relationship between Moscow and the republics. ◇ If you **define** a word or expression, you say what it means.

❏ If you talk about the way an area is **defined**, you are talking about how far it extends and what its boundaries are. This area is almost 50 per cent larger than the forest defined by the medieval boundary.

definite (definitely) ❏ If something like an arrangement is **definite**, it is fixed and not likely to be changed. ◇ If you are **definite** about something, you are sure about it.

❏ **Definite** is used to emphasize that something really exists or really happened. There has been a definite increase in Army activity. ◇ **Definitely** is used to emphasize that something is true. This kid is definitely a future champion.

definite article The definite article is the word 'the'.

definition ❏ A **definition** of a word or expression is a statement giving its meaning. ◇ If you say something has a quality **by definition**, you mean it has that quality simply by being what it is.

❏ If something has **definition**, it has a clear and distinct outline. ◇ **Definition** is also used to describe how clear and distinct a picture or sound is. For example, you can talk about **high-definition** television.

definitive (definitively) If something is the **definitive** thing of its kind, it is the best example of it. *Transplants can be considered as a definitive solution to kidney disease.* ◇ **Definitive** and **definitively** are used to say something is stated or established clearly and without any doubt. *No evidence has yet been produced definitively linking his campaign contributions with politicians' efforts on his behalf.*

deflate (deflating, deflated) If something **deflates** your hopes or feelings, it makes them suddenly less certain or less strong. ◇ When a tyre or balloon **deflates** or is **deflated**, the air is let out of it.

deflation (deflationary) **Deflation** is a reduction in the rate of inflation, especially as a result of government policies. When there is deflation, prices stop rising or go down, and wages do not rise so quickly. A **deflationary** policy or measure is meant to cause deflation; you can also say something has a **deflationary** effect. See also **disinflation**.

deflect (deflection) If you **deflect** something like attention or criticism from something, you get people to turn their attention to something else. ◇ If a moving object is **deflected**, it hits something and changes direction slightly. *Richard Jones's corner shot took a deflection off the goalkeeper for the third goal.*

defoliate (defoliating, defoliated; defoliation, defoliant) If something **defoliates** trees or plants, it makes their leaves fall off. *Trees in Britain are suffering from a high rate of defoliation.* ◇ A **defoliant** is a chemical sprayed or dusted onto trees to make their leaves fall off. It is used in wartime to prevent an enemy using forest or woodland as cover.

deforest (deforestation) If a tree-covered area is **deforested**, all the trees are cut down or destroyed. This process is called **deforestation**.

deform (deformity, deformities) If something **deforms** a person's body, its shape changes and it looks unnatural. You can talk about a part of someone's body being **deformed** or say they have a **deformity**. However, this is not usually considered polite. *Richard's only deformity is a paralysed left arm.* You can also talk about things such as trees being **deformed**.

deformation in something like rock is a change in its shape caused by powerful forces such as an earthquake.

defraud (defrauding, defrauded) If someone **defrauds** you of something which belongs to you, they illegally use deceit to take it away from you or stop you getting it.

defray If someone **defrays** your costs or expenses, they give you money to make up for an amount you have spent, for example when you have done something for them.

defrost When you **defrost** a fridge or freezer, you switch it off so the ice inside can melt. When this happens, you say the fridge or freezer **defrosts**. ◇ If you allow frozen food to **defrost**, you allow its temperature to increase until it is no longer frozen and is ready to be cooked or eaten.

deft (deftly, deftness) A **deft** action is quick, neat, and skilful. *This piece is deftly written and performed... ...his consid-*

erable political deftness.

defunct If something is **defunct**, it no longer exists or is no longer used. *They bought all their equipment from a defunct brewery.*

defuse (defusing, defused) If someone **defuses** an argument or a tense situation, they calm it down. ◇ If someone **defuses** a bomb, they make it incapable of exploding.

defy (defies, defying, defied) ❏ If you **defy** a law or restriction, you break it in order to do something you believe is morally right. Similarly, you can **defy** a person who is trying to stop you doing something.
❏ If you **defy** someone to do something difficult or impossible, you challenge them to do it. *I defy anyone to look at the evidence for ghosts and say there are no such things.*
❏ If you say something **defies** belief, you mean it is almost too strange to believe. Similarly, you can say something **defies** explanation or the imagination.

degenerate (degenerating, degenerated; degeneration, degeneracy) ❏ If things or people **degenerate** (*pron:* di-jen-er-ait), they get worse in some way. *Cows affected by this disease suffer degeneration of the brain.*
❏ If someone is **degenerate** (*pron:* di-jen-er-et) or a **degenerate**, they behave in a way people find immoral or disgusting. Behaviour like this is called **degeneracy**.

degenerative A **degenerative** illness or condition is one which gets slowly worse.

degrade (degrading, degraded; degradation) ❏ If someone is **degraded** by an experience, they feel less human and less respectable as a result of it. Something which has this effect is called **degrading**; the effect itself is called **degradation** (*pron:* de-gra-day-shun). *Criminals are kept in degrading circumstances... A drug like crack has a potential of tremendous human degradation.*
❏ If a substance is **degraded**, it is broken down into its simplest chemical elements, usually by a natural process like the action of bacteria. ◇ If rock is **degraded**, it is worn down by something such as the action of water or wind. ◇ If soil is **degraded**, it is made poorer as a result of substances being washed out of it.

degree is used to say how much there is of something. For example, you can say there is a high or low degree of something. *There were varying degrees of enthusiasm for military action.* ◇ If you say there is a degree of something, you mean there is some of it, but not a lot. *Most pension policies provide a degree of choice.* ◇ If something happens by **degrees**, it happens gradually.
❏ Temperature is expressed in **degrees**. See **Celsius** and **Fahrenheit**. Angles are usually expressed in **degrees**, and so are longitude and latitude. 'Degrees' is usually represented by the symbol °; for example 30 degrees is written 30°.
❏ A **degree** is a qualification you get after completing a university course.

degustation is wine tasting.

dehumanize (dehumanizing, dehumanized) (*can be spelled with an 's' instead of a 'z'*) If something **dehumanizes** people, it takes away from them the qualities thought to be most typically human, such as kindness and individuality.

dehydrate (dehydrating, dehydrated; dehydration, dehydrator) **Dehydrated** food has had all the water removed from it, usually to preserve it. A **dehydrator** is a machine which does this. ◇ If someone is **dehydrated** or suffering from **dehydration**, they are ill because of a lack of water in their body.

deify (*pron:* **day**-if-fie) (deifies, deifying, deified; deification) If someone or something is **deified**, they are treated with great awe and respect, as if they were a god. *...the deification of science.*

deign (*pron:* **dane**) If you talk about someone **deigning** to do something, you are suggesting they might think it is beneath their dignity to do it.

deity (*pron:* **dee**-it-ee) (deities) A **deity** is a god or goddess.

déjà vu (*pron:* **day**-zhah **voo**; *the 'zh' sounds like 's' in 'pleasure'*) Déjà vu is the feeling you get that something you are experiencing has happened to you before.

dejected (dejection) If you are **dejected**, you are unhappy and disappointed. You call this feeling **dejection**.

delay (delaying, delayed) If you **delay** doing something, you put it off until a later date. ◇ If someone or something is **delayed**, they are slowed down or made late. *His flight to London was delayed.* ◇ If there is **delay** or a **delay**, something does not happen until later than planned or expected.

delectable is used to describe things, especially foods, which are extremely pleasant and enjoyable.

delectation If something is done for your **delectation**, it is done to give you pleasure and enjoyment.

delegate (delegating, delegated; delegation) ❑ A **delegate** (*pron:* **del**-i-get) is someone chosen to make decisions on behalf of other people, especially at a meeting. A **delegation** is a group of people chosen to represent a larger group.
❑ If you **delegate** (*pron:* **del**-i-gait) someone to do something, you formally ask them to do it on your behalf. ◇ If you **delegate** duties or responsibilities, you give them to someone else so they can act on your behalf. *...the delegation of authority.*

delete (deleting, deleted; deletion) If you **delete** information which is written down or stored on a computer, you remove it. *...the deletion of entire chapters.*

deleterious (*pron:* del-lit-**eer**-ee-uss) If something is **deleterious** or has **deleterious** effects, it is harmful or damaging.

deli A **deli** is a delicatessen.

deliberate (deliberating, deliberated; deliberately, deliberation) ❑ If something you do is **deliberate**, you intend to do it. *The fire was started deliberately.* ◇ **Deliberate** is also used to describe things being done or said in a slow careful way. *...his dry, precise, deliberate speech.*
❑ If you **deliberate** (*pron:* di-**lib**-er-ait), you think about something carefully before making a decision. ◇ **Deliberations** are formal discussions to decide something. *The Royal Commission is now about midway through its deliberations on the criminal justice system.*

delicacy (delicacies) ❑ **Delicacy** is gracefulness and attractiveness. ◇ **Delicacy** is also careful and tactful behaviour in a situation where people might easily be offended. If you talk about the **delicacy** of a situation, you mean it requires this sort of behaviour.
❑ A **delicacy** is a scarce and expensive food which is considered to be particularly good.

delicate (delicately) ❑ You say things made up of small parts are **delicate** when they are graceful and attractive.

...delicately embroidered tablecloths. ◇ **Delicate** is also used to describe things which are easily broken or damaged. *Even a mild frost can harm the delicate flowers.*
❑ A **delicate** colour, taste, or smell is pleasant and not strong or intense. *...delicate pastel shades... ...the delicate flavour of the salmon.* ◇ A **delicate** movement is gentle and controlled.
❑ A **delicate** situation or problem needs to be handled carefully and tactfully. You can talk about someone's **delicate** handling of a situation like this. ◇ If a situation is **delicately** poised or **delicately** balanced, it is unstable, and a small change in circumstances may have a large effect.

delicatessen A **delicatessen** is a shop which sells high quality foods such as cheeses and cold meats imported from other countries.

delicious (deliciously) You say food is **delicious** when it tastes extremely good. ◇ A **delicious** feeling is extremely pleasant. *The air was deliciously cool.* ◇ People sometimes use **delicious** to describe things they find particularly enjoyable or attractive. *...delicious decorative plasterwork.*

delight is a feeling of great pleasure. If someone or something **delights** you, they give you this feeling. ◇ If you say something is a **delight**, you mean it gives you great pleasure. ◇ The **delights** of a place or event are the things about it you like or enjoy.
❑ If you **delight** in something, you enjoy it. If you take **delight** in doing something, you enjoy doing it.

delighted (delightedly) If you are **delighted**, you are very pleased about something. *The newspapers delightedly repeated the scandal.*

delightful (delightfully) If you say something is **delightful**, you mean it is very pleasant and enjoyable. *...a delightfully simple little story.*

delimit (delimiting, delimited; delimitation) If the borders of a country or region are **delimited**, their exact positions are formally decided. *...the final delimitation of the border.*

delineate (*pron:* dill-lin-**ee**-ate) (delineating, delineated; delineation) If something like an idea or theory is **delineated**, it is defined or described in detail. *...a detailed delineation of the principles of force reductions.* ◇ If the borders of a country or region are **delineated**, their exact positions are formally decided.

delinquent (delinquency) A **delinquent** is someone, especially a child or young person, who behaves in a criminal or antisocial way. Behaviour like this is called **delinquency**. ◇ **Delinquent** is sometimes used to describe people who disobey a rule of some kind or do not behave in an expected way. *...delinquent Conservatives.*

delirious (deliriously; delirium) If someone is **delirious** or in a **delirium**, they are unable to speak or think in a rational way, usually because they have a fever. *He rambled deliriously from time to time.* ◇ You can also say someone is **delirious** when they are extremely excited and happy. *She was delirious with joy.*

delirium tremens See **DTs**.

delist If a stock exchange **delists** a company, the company's shares can no longer be bought and sold there, usually because the company is in a poor financial condition or has behaved badly in some way.

deliver (delivering, delivered; deliverance) ❑ If you **deliver** something, you take it somewhere, for example to someone's house or office.

❑ When someone **delivers** something like a speech or lecture, they give it. You can also say someone **delivers** something like a formal statement. *The court is expected to deliver its verdict later this month.*

❑ When someone **delivers** a baby, they help the woman who is giving birth.

❑ If you **deliver** something you have promised to do or something which is expected of you, you do it. You can also say you **deliver the goods.** *We were promised a patient-centred health service, but the government has not delivered.*

❑ If someone is **delivered** from something unpleasant, they are saved from it. You can talk about someone's **deliverance** from something unpleasant; you can also say the thing which saves them is a **deliverance.**

delivery (deliveries) ❑ **Delivery** is the bringing of things like letters, parcels, or goods to somewhere like a house or office. A **delivery** of something is an amount which is delivered. *...a delivery of frozen cod.* When someone makes a **delivery**, they deliver something; the person who receives it **takes delivery** of it.

❑ **Delivery** is used to describe the way someone gives a speech or sings a song. *He has a nasal delivery that takes some getting used to.*

❑ **Delivery** is also the process of giving birth to a baby. *If a mother has a traumatic delivery, it can be difficult for a man to watch.*

dell A **dell** is a small valley with trees in it.

Delphic When people call a remark or statement **Delphic**, they mean it is not at all clear what it means. *The Lisbon summit produced a Delphic utterance about not excluding the use of force.*

delphinium **Delphiniums** are large garden plants. They have tall stems with blue flowers growing along them.

delta is Δ or δ, the fourth letter of the Greek alphabet.

❑ A **delta** is an area of flat muddy land where a river branches out into several smaller rivers before it enters the sea.

delude (deluding, deluded) If you are **deluding yourself,** you are letting yourself believe something which is not true. ◇ If you **delude** someone else, you deliberately make them believe something which is not true.

deluge (*pron:* del-lyooj) (deluging, deluged) A **deluge** is a sudden heavy fall of rain. You can say rain **deluges** a place. ◇ A **deluge** of things is a very large number of them arriving at the same time. You can say someone is **deluged** by something. *...a deluge of criticism... The Prime Minister has been deluged by messages of goodwill.*

delusion A **delusion** is a false belief. ◇ **delusions of grandeur:** see **grandeur.**

delve (delving, delved) If you **delve** into a subject, you try to find out more about it. ◇ If you **delve** inside something like a bag, you put your hand inside it, to try to find something.

demagogue (*pron:* dem-a-gog) (demagogic, demagogy, demagoguery) A **demagogue** is a political leader who tries to win people's support by appealing to their emotions rather than using reasoned arguments. You say a person like this is **demagogic**; you can also call what they say **demagogic.** *He accused the Democrats of making misleading and demagogic claims.* The behaviour of a demagogue is

called **demagogy** or **demagoguery.**

demand ❑ If you **demand** something or make a **demand,** you ask for something forcefully. ◇ If someone asks a question in a forceful way, you can say they **demand** it. *'Where is your luggage?' he demanded.*

❑ If a job or a situation **demands** something, it needs it so it can be performed or resolved successfully. *Skilled political leadership demands balanced judgement.* ◇ The **demands** of something are the things which have to be done or provided for it. *No one could cope with the demands of the job for more than ten years.*

❑ If there is a **demand** for something, people want it. *There is a demand for British brandy.* You say something like this is **in demand.** You can also say a person is **in demand.** *He was in demand as a commentator around the world.* ◇ If something is available **on demand,** people can get it whenever they want it.

demanding A **demanding** job or task requires a lot of time, energy, or attention. ◇ A **demanding** person is always wanting something and is not easily satisfied.

demarcate (demarcating, demarcated; demarcation) If something is **demarcated,** its limits are clearly established, to distinguish it from other similar things. ◇ If the border between two countries or regions is **demarcated,** its position is established. *...a border demarcation agreement.*

demarche (or **démarche**) (*pron:* dem-marsh) A **demarche** is a formal statement made to a foreign government. *There's to be an EU demarche to President Iliescu about the situation.* ◇ A **demarche** is also a move or manoeuvre made by a country in its dealings with other countries.

demean (demeaning, demeaned) If something **demeans** someone, it makes people lose respect for them. You say something like this is **demeaning.**

demeanour A person's **demeanour** is the way they behave, which gives people an impression of their character and feelings.

demented If someone is **demented,** they behave in an uncontrolled, irrational, and often violent way, because they are mentally ill.

dementia (*pron:* dim-men-sha) is an illness in which a person's mind deteriorates. It is common among very old people.

demerara sugar is a type of light brown, unrefined sugar from the West Indies.

demerge (demerging, demerged; demerger) If a company is **demerged** from another company or group of companies, it separates from them. When this happens, you say there is a **demerger.**

demijohn A **demijohn** is a very large wine bottle, often in a wicker case.

demilitarize (demilitarizing, demilitarized; demilitarization) (*can be spelled with an 's' instead of a 'z'*) When an area is **demilitarized,** all armed forces are taken out of it. *It will be some time before large-scale demilitarization becomes the rule in Central America.*

demise (*pron:* di-mize) A person's **demise** is their death. ◇ The **demise** of something like a system is its end. *...the demise of communism in Eastern Europe.*

demister The **demister** on a car is a mechanism which removes condensation from the windscreen, usually by blowing warm air over it.

demo (demos) A **demo** is a demonstration.

demob (demobbing, demobbed) When someone is de-mobbed, they are demobilized.

demobilize (demobilizing, demobilized; demobilization) (*can be spelled with an 's' instead of a 'z'*) When a member of the armed forces is **demobilized**, he or she is released from military service. ...*the demobilization of 150,000 troops.*

democracy (democracies) **Democracy** is a system of government or way of running an organization in which people choose their leaders or make other important decisions by voting. A **democracy** is a country where the people choose their government in this way.

democrat A **democrat** is a person who believes in democracy. ◇ A **Democrat** is a supporter of a political party which has 'Democrat' or 'Democratic' in its name.

democratic (democratically) In a **democratic** system, leaders are chosen or decisions are made by voting. ...*a democratically elected parliament.* ◇ **Democratic** is used in the titles of some political parties. ...*the Social Democratic party.*

democratize (democratizing, democratized; democratization) (*can be spelled with an 's' instead of a 'z'*) If a country, organization, or system is **democratized**, it is made democratic. ...*the democratization of the political processes.*

demography (demographics, demographic, demographer) The **demography** or **demographics** of a group of people are statistics about them, including things like numbers of births and deaths and numbers in different income groups. **Demographic** is used to talk about things connected with these statistics; a **demographer** is a person who studies and analyzes them.

demolish (demolishes, demolishing, demolished; demolition) When a building is **demolished**, it is knocked down. When this happens, you talk about the **demolition** of the building. ◇ If you **demolish** an idea, argument, or belief, you prove it is completely wrong.

demon A **demon** is an evil spirit.

demonic (*pron:* di-**mon**-ik) If something is **demonic**, it is evil. ...*the demonic influence of Rasputin.*

demonize (demonizing, demonized) (*can be spelled with an 's' instead of a 'z'*) If someone is **demonized**, they are made to seem evil. *Feuding neighbours have a tendency to demon-ize each other.*

demonology (demonologies) The **demonology** of a group of people is the people or things it considers to be evil or its enemies. ...*that bogeyman of communist demonology known as a capitalist.*

demonstrable (demonstrably) If something is **demon-strable**, it is obvious, or it can be shown to be true or exist. *The attack has been weakened demonstrably.*

demonstrate (demonstrating, demonstrated; demonstration, demonstrator) ❑ If something is **demonstrated**, people are made aware of it. *It was an unforgettable demonstration of the power of reason.* ◇ If you **demonstrate** something to someone, you show them how to do it, or how it works.
   ❑ If you **demonstrate** a skill, quality, or feeling, you show you have it.
   ❑ When people **demonstrate**, they take part in a march or a meeting to show they oppose or support something. A march or meeting like this is called a **demonstration**; the people taking part are called **demonstrators**.

demonstrative A **demonstrative** person shows their feelings freely and openly.

demonstrator See **demonstrate**.

demoralize (demoralizing, demoralized; demoralization) (*can be spelled with an 's' instead of a 'z'*) If something **demoralizes** people, it makes them lose confidence and feel depressed. *The level of demoralization was increasing.*

demote (demoting, demoted; demotion) If someone is **demoted**, they are reduced in rank or status, often as a punishment. *The demotion was imposed as a punishment for infringement of rules.*

demotic (*pron:* di-**mot**-tik) is used to describe things which are typical of or used by ordinary people. ...*television's demotic style of language.*

demotivate (demotivating, demotivated) If you are **demotivated**, you lose your determination to do something. *Many local government officers are demoralized and demotivated by constant criticism.*

demur (demurring, demurred) If you **demur**, you say you do not agree with something, or do not want to do something.

demure (demurely) A **demure** woman is quiet, modest, and rather shy. *She smiled demurely.*

demystify (demystifies, demystifying, demystified; demystification) If something which seems complicated or strange is **demystified**, it is made easier to understand or made to seem more ordinary. ...*an effort to demystify information technology... The personality cult which once enveloped him has been replaced by a process of demystification.*

demythologize (demythologizing, demythologized) If you **demythologize** something, you disprove what people have come to believe about it and show what it is really like.

den A lion's **den** is its home. Foxes and some other wild animals also have dens. ◇ A **den** is also a secret place where people meet, usually to do something illegal or immoral. ...*a gambling den... ...this den of iniquity.*

denationalize (denationalizing, denationalized; denationalization) (*can be spelled with an 's' instead of a 'z'*) If a government-owned industry is **denationalized**, its ownership is transferred to private hands. ...*the government's policy of denationalization.*

dengue (*pron:* **deng**-ee) is a dangerous tropical illness spread by mosquitos. It causes severe headache, pains in the joints, skin rash, and sometimes death.

deniable If something a public figure says or does is **deniable**, they can claim afterwards they did not say it or do it.

denial A **denial** of something like an accusation is a claim that it is not true. ◇ If there is **denial** of something people want or have a right to, they are not allowed to have it. ...*denials of human rights.*

denier (*pron:* **den**-yer) The thickness of nylon or silk thread is often measured in **denier**. ...*a pair of 15 denier stockings.*

denigrate (denigrating, denigrated; denigration) If you **denigrate** someone, you say things about them which damage their reputation. ...*a campaign of denigration against his government.*

denim is a thick, hard-wearing cotton cloth used to make clothes. **Denims** are clothes made of denim, such as jeans.

denizen The **denizens** of a place are people or animals who live there or spend most of their time there.

denominate (denominating, denominated) When an amount of money is **denominated** in a currency, it is expressed in that currency. *...claims and liabilities denominated in Canadian dollars.*

denomination (denominational) ❏ The **denomination** of a bank note is the amount of money printed on it, which shows what it is worth.

❏ A **denomination** is a division of Christianity, such as the Church of England or the Baptist Church. If something like a school is **denominational**, it is connected with a particular denomination. If something is **non-denominational**, it is not connected with any particular denomination; if it is **multi-denominational**, it involves several denominations.

denominator The **denominator** is the number under the line in a fraction. For example, in the fraction $\frac{1}{5}$, the denominator is 5. See also **common denominator** and **lowest common denominator**.

denote (denoting, denoted) If you say something **denotes** something else, you mean it is a sign or indication of it. *The agreement seems to denote a virtual surrender.* ◇ If a word or expression **denotes** something, that is what it means or refers to.

denouement (*or* dénouement) (*pron:* day-**noo**-mon) The **denouement** of a story is the final sorting-out of the plot, which brings the story to an end. In real life, when a situation is brought to an end in a similar way, you can call this a denouement. *A denouement of sorts was reached on October 14th.*

denounce (denouncing, denounced; denunciation) If you **denounce** someone or something, you accuse them of being something bad or wrong. A **denunciation** is an accusation like this. *Today's court hearing was denounced by the protesters as anti-democratic... The statements are certain to provoke angry denunciations.*

dense (denser, densest; densely) ❏ If something is **dense**, it contains a lot of people or things in proportion to its size. *...dense undergrowth... ...the most densely populated country in Africa.* ◇ **Dense** fog or smoke is thick and difficult to see through. ◇ A **dense** substance is very heavy.

❏ If you say someone is **dense**, you mean they are stupid and take a long time to understand things.

density (densities) **Density** is used to talk about the extent to which something is filled with people or things. *...high population density... ...the density of traffic.* ◇ The **density** of a substance is how heavy it is. Densities are usually given as **relative densities**; the relative density of a solid or liquid is how much heavier it is than water. For example, copper has a relative density of 8.96, which means it is 8.96 times heavier than water.

dent ❏ If you **dent** something, you damage its surface by hitting it and making a hollow in it. The hollow is called a **dent**.

❏ If something like your confidence or pride is **dented**, it is weakened by something happening. *The fighting has dented hopes for a sustained ceasefire.* ◇ If something makes a **dent** in an amount, it reduces it. *Price cutting does not make too big a dent in their profit margins.*

dental is used to describe things to do with teeth or dentists. *...dental treatment.*

dental floss See **floss**.

dental surgeon A **dental surgeon** is the same as a dentist.

dentist A **dentist** is a person qualified to treat people's teeth.

dentistry is the treatment of teeth.

dentures are false teeth.

denude (denuding, denuded) If something is **denuded** of things which cover it or belong to it, they are taken away from it. *The Embassy is now denuded of all foreign and local staff.*

denunciation See **denounce**.

deny (denies, denying, denied) ❏ If you **deny** something, you say it is not true. ◇ If you **deny all knowledge** of something, you claim to know nothing about it.

❏ If you are **denied** something you want or something you are entitled to, you are prevented from having it. *The system denied them the chance of a fair trial.*

deodorant is a substance people spray or wipe on their bodies to reduce the smell of sweat.

depart (departure) ❏ If you **depart** from a place, you leave. When someone or something leaves a place, you call this their **departure**.

❏ **Departed** friends or relatives are people who have died.

❏ If you **depart** from the normal way of doing something, you do it a different way. *...a departure from traditional practice.*

department (departmental) A **department** is one of the sections of a large shop or organization. **Departmental** is used to talk about things connected with a department. *...a departmental committee.*

department store A **department store** is a large shop divided into sections, each selling a particular type of goods.

departure See **depart**.

departure lounge The **departure lounge** at an airport is the place where passengers spend time waiting to board an aircraft. It usually has shops and places to eat and drink.

depend If you **depend** on someone or something, you need them. *People depend on gas for heating.* ◇ If you say you can **depend** on someone or something, you mean you can rely on them. ◇ If one thing **depends** on another, the first thing will be affected or decided by the second. *The outcome of the election could depend on the extent to which the government succeeds in getting to grips with inflation.*

dependable (dependability) If someone or something is **dependable**, they can be relied on to do what is needed, or to behave the way you expect. *He had a reputation for toughness and dependability.*

dependant (*or* dependent) A person's **dependants** are their children or other members of their family who they support by the money they earn.

dependence See **dependent**.

dependency (dependencies) ❏ A **dependency** is a country controlled by another country.

❏ If you have a **dependency** on something, you need it or rely on it. *...drug dependency.* ◇ When people talk about a **dependency culture**, they mean a situation where many people do not work or do things for themselves, because they know they can rely on the government for things like housing, unemployment money, and free health care.

dependent (dependence) If you are **dependent** on someone or something, you need them. *...the increasing dependence of schools upon parental generosity.* ◇ If one thing is **dependent** on another, the first thing will be affected or decided by the second. *The type of bacon used is largely dependent on what can be afforded.* ◇ See also **dependant**.

depict (depiction) If an artist **depicts** someone in a particular way, he or she shows them that way in a picture. *Cartoonists often depicted her as a boxer or a wrestler.* Similarly, you can say a writer or speaker **depicts** someone or something in a particular way. *The plot is uncompromising in its depiction of a ruthless, lethal underworld.*

deplete (depleting, depleted; depletion) If something is **depleted**, the amount of it is reduced. *...the depletion of Brazil's forests.*

deplore (deploring, deplored; deplorable, deplorably) If you **deplore** something, you think it is extremely bad or wrong. You say something like this is **deplorable**. *The spokesman said reporters had behaved deplorably.*

deploy (deployment) When troops or resources are **deployed**, they are organized and moved into position, ready for immediate action. *The Iranians have strongly criticized the military deployment.*

depoliticize (depoliticizing, depoliticized; depoliticization) (*can be spelled with an 's' instead of a 'z'*) If an organization is **depoliticized**, it no longer serves the interests of a particular political group. *...the depoliticization of the army.*

depopulate (depopulating, depopulated; depopulation) If an area is **depopulated**, nobody lives there any more, or the number of people living there is greatly reduced. **Depopulation** is a reduction in the population of an area.

deport (deportation, deportee) If someone is **deported**, they are made to leave a country, because they have committed a crime or are not officially allowed to be there. *...people facing deportation.* A person who is being deported is called a **deportee**.

deportment A person's **deportment** is the way they behave in company, especially the way they walk and move.

depose (deposing, deposed) If a ruler or leader is **deposed**, they are removed from their position by force.

deposit (depositing, deposited) ❏ If you **deposit** something somewhere, you put it there. *He deposited a small case in one of the lockers.*

❏ A **deposit** is an amount of money you put in a bank account or other savings account. ◇ A **deposit** is also money given in part payment for something, usually to ensure it is not sold to someone else. If you decide not to buy it, you do not get the deposit back. ◇ A **deposit** is also an amount of money you give someone when you rent or hire something. They give you the money back if the thing you rent or hire is not damaged when you return it.

❏ If a substance is **deposited** somewhere, it is left there as a result of a chemical or geological process. A **deposit** is an amount of a substance left like this. *Fats are deposited in the walls of blood vessels... The Nile waters spread over the flat lowlands, leaving a deposit of fertile silt.*

deposit account A **deposit account** is a type of bank account in which money earns interest.

depositary (depositaries) A **depositary** is a person or organization you can leave money or valuables with for safekeeping. See also **depository**.

deposition A **deposition** is a formal statement, made on oath by a witness to a crime. It is taken down in writing, and can be used in court if the witness cannot be present.

depositor Depositors are people who have an account with a bank or building society.

depository (depositories) A **depository** is a place where things are stored. *...the Texas School Book Depository.* See also **depositary**.

depot A **depot** is a place where goods or vehicles are kept when they are not being used. ◇ In the US and Canada, a railway station is sometimes called a **depot**.

deprave (depraving, depraved; depravity) If someone says a book or film is likely to **deprave** people, they mean it is likely to make them behave immorally. ◇ A **depraved** person is morally bad. **Depravity** (*pron:* dip-**prav**-i-ty) is immoral behaviour.

deprecate (*pron:* **dep**-re-kate) (deprecating, deprecated) If you **deprecate** something, you say you strongly disapprove of it. See also **self-deprecating**.

depreciate (depreciating, depreciated; depreciation) If something **depreciates**, it loses some of its value. *...currency depreciation.*

depredations are attacks aimed at destroying something. *The Olympic spirit has survived the depredations of terrorists, politicians and commercialism.*

depress (depresses, depressing, depressed; depressingly) ❏ If something **depresses** you or makes you **depressed**, it makes you sad and disappointed. You say something like this is **depressing**. *Attempts to improve motorways have made roadworks a depressingly familiar sight.*

❏ If something **depresses** things like wages or prices, it causes them to fall in value. ◇ If the economy or an industry is **depressed**, business is bad and not much money is being made. ◇ If an area is **depressed**, there is a lack of business and jobs and the people are poor.

❏ You can also say something is **depressed** when it is lowered or pushed down. *Ice is heavy enough to depress the surface of the Earth.*

depression ❏ A **depression** is a time when economic activity is very low and there is a lot of unemployment. When people talk about the **Depression** or the **Great Depression**, they mean the severe depression which occurred in most industrialized countries during the 1930s.

❏ **Depression** is a form of mental illness in which someone feels unhappy and has no energy or enthusiasm.

❏ A **depression** in a surface is a part which is lower than the rest. *...a depression in the ground.*

depressive A **depressive** is someone who often suffers from depression. ◇ A **depressive** illness is one which includes periods of depression.

depressurize (depressurizing, depressurized) (*can be spelled with an 's' instead of a 'z'*) When divers are **depressurized**, the air pressure inside them is reduced artificially as they come to the surface. This stops them suffering illness caused by a sudden change from high to low pressure. See also **decompression**. ◇ If an aircraft or spacecraft **depressurizes,** the air pressure inside is reduced because air is escaping.

deprive (depriving, deprived; deprivation) If someone is **deprived** of something they want, need, or are entitled to, they do not get it or are not allowed to have it. *They faced deprivation of their civil rights.* ◇ You say people are **deprived** when they do not have the things most people have, such as a pleasant home and new clothes.

dept is short for 'department'.

depth ❑ The **depth** of something like a river is the distance between its surface and its bottom. If something happens at a particular **depth,** it happens at that distance below the surface. ◇ The **depths** of an ocean are the parts a long way down. ◇ If someone who is learning to swim gets **out of their depth,** they get into water they can no longer stand up in. ◇ You also say someone is **out of their depth** when they are trying to do something which is too difficult for them.
 ❑ The **depth** of something like a cupboard is the distance from its front to its back.
 ❑ If you deal with a subject **in depth,** you deal with it in detail.
 ❑ If someone has strong feelings of anger or unhappiness, you can talk about the **depth** of their feelings. *The depth of feeling within the fishing communities forced him to withdraw the remark.*
 ❑ The **depths** of winter is the time in the middle of winter when it is coldest.

depth charge A **depth charge** is a type of bomb which explodes underwater. Depth charges are used mainly against submarines.

deputation A **deputation** is a small group of people sent to speak or act on behalf of a larger group.

depute (deputing, deputed) If someone is **deputed** to do something, they are chosen to do it as the representative of a group.

deputize (deputizing, deputized) (*can be spelled with an 's' instead of a 'z'*) If you **deputize** for someone, you do something on their behalf, such as attend a meeting or give a speech.

deputy (deputies) The second most important person in an organization is often called the **deputy,** or has **deputy** as part of the name of their job. This person stands in for the head of the organization when they are not there.

derail (derailing, derailed; derailment) If a train is **derailed,** it comes off the track. This is called a **derailment.** ◇ If discussions or negotiations are **derailed,** something stops them from progressing. *...the derailment of the peace process.*

deranged A **deranged** person behaves in a wild or strange way, because they are mentally ill.

derby (*pron:* dar-bee) (derbies) ❑ The **Derby** is a famous English horse race which takes place at Epsom. Some other countries also have horse races with 'Derby' in their names. *...the Irish Derby.* ◇ A **derby** or local **derby** is a sporting event between teams from the same city or area.
 ❑ In the US, a **derby** (*pron:* der-bee) is a bowler hat.

derecognize (derecognizing, derecognized) (*can be spelled with a hyphen after 'de'; also with an 's' instead of 'z'*) If a company **derecognizes** a trade union, they refuse to accept that the union represents their employees.

deregister (deregistering, deregistered; deregistration) If someone is **deregistered,** their name is taken off an official list of some kind, for example the list of people entitled to vote.

deregulate (deregulating, deregulated; deregulation, deregulatory) If something like an industry or a country's economy is **deregulated,** it is no longer required to conform to government controls. You call this the **deregulation** of the industry or economy. A **deregulatory** policy or measure is one which brings about deregulation.

derelict (dereliction) ❑ A **derelict** building or area of land has not been used for a long time and is in a bad state. You can also say it is in a state of **dereliction.**
 ❑ A **derelict** is a person who has no permanent home, no job, and no money.
 ❑ If someone is guilty of a **dereliction of duty,** they have deliberately or accidentally failed to do something they should have done as part of their job.

deride (deriding, derided; derision) If you **deride** someone or treat them with **derision,** you make fun of them because you think they are stupid or worthless. You can also **deride** something a person says or does.

derisive (derisively) A **derisive** noise, expression, or remark shows amusement and contempt. *Brian looked at the two men derisively.*

derisory If something is **derisory,** it is so small or inadequate it seems insulting or not worth considering. *...a derisory pay offer.*

derivation The **derivation** of a word is another word or words which it gets its form or meaning from. *...words of Anglo-Saxon derivation.*

derivative A **derivative** is something which has been developed from something else. *...the highly addictive cocaine derivative, crack.* ◇ If you say a piece of writing is **derivative,** you mean it is not original but copies the style or ideas of other writing.

derive (deriving, derived) ❑ If something is **derived** from another thing, it comes from it or is developed from it. *A third of all medicines are derived from plants.*
 ❑ If you **derive** feelings like comfort or pleasure from something, it gives you those feelings. ◇ If you **derive** benefit from something, it does you some good.

dermatitis is a disease which makes your skin red and sore.

dermatology (dermatologist) **Dermatology** is the study of the skin and the treatment of its diseases. A **dermatologist** is a doctor who specializes in this.

derogate (derogating, derogated) If part of a law or agreement **derogates** from the law or agreement as a whole, it weakens it or makes it less effective.

derogatory A **derogatory** remark is one which shows your low opinion of someone or something.

derrick A **derrick** is a tower over an oil well from which the drill is raised and lowered. ◇ A **derrick** is also a simple crane used to move cargo on a ship.

derring-do is a humorous word for heroic and brave deeds.

derv See diesel.

dervish (dervishes) **Dervishes** are a Muslim religious group whose worship includes a lively dance in which they spin round and round.

desalinate (desalinating, desalinated; desalination) When sea water is **desalinated,** the salt is taken out of it. This process is called **desalination.**

descend ❑ When something like a plane **descends,** it moves downwards. ◇ If you **descend** something like a mountain, you go down it. ◇ If people **descend** on a place, a lot of them arrive suddenly.

❑ If a group of things is arranged in **descending** order, the largest or most important is put first, followed by the next largest or most important, and so on.

❑ The people you are **descended** from are your relatives who lived a long time ago.

❑ If someone **descends** into a kind of bad behaviour, they start behaving like that. *City currency dealing rooms descended into madness.* ◇ If someone does something which would normally be considered beneath them, you can say they **descend** to it. *Towards the end of the story the high-born lass descends to chicken-plucking.* ◇ **Descend** is also used to describe a sudden change in the behaviour or mood of a group of people. For example, if silence **descends,** everyone becomes silent.

descendant The **descendants** of people who lived in the past are their relatives who are living now.

descent is used to say what country or race a person's family originally came from. For example, you can say someone is of African descent.

❑ When someone or something moves to a lower level, you can talk about their **descent.** *The plane began its descent into Sarajevo airport.*

❑ You can also talk about a person's **descent** into bad behaviour or madness.

describe (describing, described) If you **describe** someone or something, you say what they are like, or what they look like. ◇ If you **describe** a sequence of events, you say what happened.

description ❑ If you give a **description** of someone or something, you say what they are like.

❑ **Description** is used to mean 'type' in phrases like 'of every description' and 'of any description'. *...ships of every description... Events of this description occurred daily.*

descriptive writing contains a lot of detailed descriptions of places and things.

desecrate (desecrating, desecrated; desecration) If someone **desecrates** something people regard as special or sacred, they treat it disrespectfully, or spoil or damage it. *...the desecration of Muslim shrines.*

desegregate (desegregating, desegregated; desegregation) If something like a place or public service is **desegregated,** the different races using it are no longer kept separate from each other. *...the desegregation of schools.*

deselect (deselecting, deselected; deselection) (*or* de-select, etc) If an MP is **deselected,** their local constituency party decides not to support them in the next election and chooses someone else.

desert (desertion) A **desert** (*pron:* dez-ert) is an area of land with very little water or rainfall and very few trees or plants. ◇ If a place is **deserted** (*pron:* diz-zert-id), there is nobody there. ◇ If someone **deserts** a person or an organization, they leave them and no longer help or support them. ◇ If someone **deserts** from the armed forces, they leave without permission. *There were a growing number of desertions from the federal army.*

desert island A **desert island** is an island where nobody lives. When people talk about a desert island, they usually imagine it as small and tropical.

deserter A **deserter** is someone who runs away from the armed forces.

desertification (*pron:* dez-ert-if-i-**kay**-shun) is the gradual transformation of fertile land into desert.

deserve (deserving, deserved; deservedly) If you say someone **deserves** something, you mean they ought to have it. ◇ If you say something which someone has is **deserved** or **well-deserved,** you mean it is right they should have it. *...a well-deserved reputation... ...this deservedly popular hotel.* ◇ A **deserving** cause is one you think should be helped. Similarly, you can talk about **deserving** people.

desiccated If something is **desiccated,** all the water has been taken out of it. ◇ If you call a person **dessicated,** you mean they have no enthusiasm or interest in anything.

design ❑ When someone **designs** something, they draw it and plan what it will be like. The activity of designing things is called **design.** ◇ The **design** of something is the form or style in which it is made. *...the decision to improve the design of the plastic bullet.* ◇ A **design** is a drawing of something which is going to be made, which shows its form or style.

❑ A **design** is also a pattern of lines, flowers, or other shapes which decorates something.

❑ If something is **designed** to achieve a particular result, that is what it is intended for. *The Ministry said the measure was designed to avoid a last-minute panic.*

❑ If someone has **designs** on something, they want it and are planning to get it.

designate (designating, designated; designation) ❑ If someone or something is **designated** a particular thing, they are officially declared to be that thing. *The surrounding area is designated a nature reserve.* ◇ A **designation** is a name given to something, which describes what it is. *They are entitled to use the designation 'Chartered Chemist'.* ◇ If something is **designated** for a particular purpose, it is officially chosen for that purpose.

❑ If someone is **designated** to do a job, they are officially chosen to do it. *...the designation of new judges.* ◇ **Designate** is used after a word like 'ambassador' or 'chairman' to say someone has been officially chosen to do a job but has not yet started doing it. *The author is editor designate of Country Life.*

designer ❑ A **designer** is someone whose job involves planning the forms or styles of new things.

❑ **Designer** clothes are expensive and fashionable and made by a famous designer or fashion house. ◇ **Designer** drugs are made in a laboratory and are intended to have a similar effect to illegal drugs like cocaine and heroin, but are not themselves illegal.

desirable (desirability) If something is **desirable,** it is worth having or doing. You can talk about the **desirability** of something like this.

desire (desiring, desired) ❑ If you **desire** something, you want it. You can talk about someone's **desire** for something. *...his desire for revenge.* ◇ **Desire** or **sexual desire** is a feeling of wanting to make love to someone.

❑ If you say something **leaves a lot to be desired,** you mean it is not as good as it should be.

desist If you **desist** from doing something, you stop doing it.

desk A **desk** is a table, often with drawers, where you write or work. ◇ **Desk** is used in connection with the media to talk about a team of people concerned with one aspect of the news. *...our foreign news desk.* ◇ A **desk** is also part of a shop, station, or airport where you go for a particular service. *...the information desk.*

desktop (*or* **desk-top**) computers or other machines are the right size for using on a desk or table.

desolate (desolation) A **desolate** area is wild and empty of people. ◇ If someone feels **desolate**, they feel lonely and depressed. *...a sense of desolation.*

despair (despairing, despaired; despairingly) **Despair** is a feeling of hopelessness. If you **despair**, you lose hope. *The pharmacist shook her head despairingly.* ◇ If you **despair** of something, you feel there is no hope it will happen or improve. *Some fat people despair of ever losing weight... I despair of some journalists.*

despatch (despatches, despatching, despatched) (*can be spelled 'di-' instead of 'de-'*) If you **despatch** someone or something somewhere, you send them there. ◇ A **despatch** is a report sent to a person or organization from one of their representatives in another country or place.

desperate (desperately, desperation) ❑ If you are **desperate**, you are in such a bad situation you will do anything to get out of it. **Desperation** is the feeling you have in a situation like this. ◇ A **desperate** situation is so difficult or dangerous there is almost no hope of getting out of it. If you do something **desperate** in a situation like this, you take an extreme action because it seems the only thing left to do.
❑ If you are **desperate** for something, you want it or need it urgently. *We desperately need new tanks and equipment.* ◇ **Desperately** is used to emphasize how anxious someone is about something. *Environmentalists are desperately concerned about the situation.* ◇ **Desperately** is also used to emphasize that something is of very poor quality. *...desperately bad television.*

despicable If you say someone or something is **despicable**, you mean they are extremely nasty or evil.

despise (despising, despised) If you **despise** someone or something, you have a very low opinion of them.

despite If you say one thing happened **despite** another, you mean it happened though the second thing might have prevented it. *Despite the force of the wind, he was keeping the boat on a straight course.*

despoil (despoiling, despoiled) If countryside is **despoiled**, it is ruined, for example by pollution.

despondent (despondently, despondency) If you are **despondent**, you are unhappy because of difficulties which seem hard to overcome. This feeling is called **despondency**. *...out-of-work actors who trudge despondently from audition room to audition room.*

despot (despotic, despotism) A **despot** is someone like a political ruler who has a lot of power and uses it cruelly or unfairly. You say a ruler like this is **despotic**. You say someone's behaviour is **despotic** when they behave like a despot. *...a despotic attack on their liberty.* **Despotism** is rule by a despot.

dessert (*pron:* diz-**zert**) is something sweet you eat at the end of a meal, like fruit or a pudding.

dessertspoon A **dessertspoon** is a spoon which is in between a teaspoon and a tablespoon in size and is the type of spoon you would eat a pudding with.

destabilize (destabilizing, destabilized; destabilization) (*can be spelled with an 's' instead of a 'z'*) If something **destabilizes** a government or economy, it makes it function less efficiently and makes a sudden change likely. *This could lead to a serious destabilization in the Balkans.*

destination Your **destination** is the place you are going to.

destined If someone or something is **destined** for a place, they are going there, or will be sent there. ◇ If something is **destined** to happen to someone or something, it is going to happen and nothing can prevent it. *The ploy was destined to fail.*

destiny (destinies) A **person's** destiny is what will happen to them in the future. *He has long seen it as his destiny to become Conservative Prime Minister.* ◇ **Destiny** is the force some people believe controls the things which happen to us.

destitute (destitution) If someone is **destitute**, they have no money or possessions. *They slipped into unemployment and destitution.*

destroy If something is **destroyed**, it is damaged so badly it is completely ruined or brought to an end.

destroyer A **destroyer** is a small fast warship armed with guns, torpedoes, depth charges, and sometimes guided missiles. ◇ The **destroyer** of something is the person or thing that destroys it. *They loathed him as a destroyer of free enterprise in America.*

destruction When something is destroyed, you can talk about its **destruction**. *They ordered the destruction of the forest.*

destructive (destructively, destructiveness) If something is **destructive**, it causes a lot of damage or harm. *Inflation is still destructively high... ...the destructiveness of modern weapons.*

desultory is used to describe things which are done in a half-hearted or disorganized way. *Only a few desultory efforts were made to attract Western oil companies.*

detach (detaches, detaching, detached; detachment) ❑ If you **detach** something, you remove it from the thing it is attached to. ◇ A **detached** house is not joined to any other house.
❑ If you **detach** yourself from something, you stop being involved with it. *...the pressures upon the US to detach themselves from PLO contacts.* ◇ If you stay **detached** from something you are dealing with, you do not get personally involved in it. ◇ If you take a **detached** view of something, you are not emotionally affected by it. *He views events with a certain cynical detachment.*
❑ A **detachment** of soldiers or military vehicles is a group of them sent away from the main group to do a particular task.

detachable If something is **detachable**, it has been made so it can be removed from the larger thing it is attached to.

detachment See detach.

detail (detailing, detailed) ❑ The **details** of something are the small parts it is composed of. If you are concerned with **detail**, you are concerned with these small parts. ◇ If you examine, explain, or discuss something in detail, you do it thoroughly and carefully, taking account of all the small points which need to be considered. You say an examination, explanation, or discussion like this is **detailed**.

❑ **Details** about someone or something are items of information about them. ◇ If you **detail** things, you list them or give full information about them.

detain (detaining, detained) When people like the police **detain** someone, they keep them in a certain place and do not let them go. ◇ If something **detains** you, it delays you.

detainee Detainees are people held prisoner by a government because of their political beliefs or activities.

detect (detection) If you **detect** something, you notice it or discover it. *...an advertising campaign to promote early detection of the disease.*

detectable If something is **detectable**, it can be noticed or discovered. *Low doses of radiation have no detectable effect in the first years after an accident.*

detective A **detective** is someone, usually a police officer, whose job is to discover the facts about something like a crime.

detector A **detector** is a machine for discovering whether something exists or is taking place. *...a metal detector... ...a lie-detector.*

detente (or **détente**) (*pron:* day-tont) is a friendly relationship between countries where there had previously been disagreement and mistrust.

detention is the arrest or imprisonment of someone. *Several people are in detention awaiting trial.* ◇ A **detention centre** or **detention camp** is a place where prisoners or refugees are kept on a temporary basis. In Britain, prisons for young people used to be called **detention centres**.

deter (deterring, deterred) If something **deters** you, it stops you doing something. *I was worried that his article would deter potential buyers.*

detergent Detergents are chemicals for washing things like clothes and dishes.

deteriorate (deteriorating, deteriorated; deterioration) If something like a situation or a person's condition **deteriorates**, it gets worse. *...a sharp deterioration in Anglo-Irish relations.*

determinant A **determinant** of something is one of the things which decides what form it will take. *Along with interest rates, inflation is the main determinant of people's sense of economic well-being.*

determinate A **determinate** period is fixed at a particular length. *...the possession of land for some determinate period.*

determine (determining, determined; determination, determinedly) ❑ If you are **determined** to do something, you have made a firm decision to do it and will not let anything stop you. *...his determination to do things his way.*

❑ If you **determine** the cause of something or the truth about something, you find it out. *...experiments to determine the cause of cancer.*

❑ If what happens depends on a particular thing, you can say that thing **determines** what happens. *Community rules will determine who needs a visa to get into the EU.* ◇ When something is **determined**, it is decided or settled. *The amount of government money has yet to be determined.*

determinism (deterministic, determinist) **Determinism** is the belief that everything that happens is the result of things which have already happened, and so we are powerless to change things or stop them happening. Ideas which conform to this belief are called **deterministic**. A **determinist** is someone who believes in determinism.

deterrence (deterrent) **Deterrence** is preventing people from doing something by making them afraid of the consequences for themselves. So, for example, having nuclear weapons to stop your country being attacked is called **nuclear deterrence**. Something which stops people doing something is called a **deterrent**.

detest (detestable) If you **detest** someone or something or find them **detestable**, you hate them.

dethrone (dethroning, dethroned; dethronement) If someone in a powerful position is **dethroned**, they are removed from power. You can call this their **dethronement**.

detonate (detonating, detonated; detonation) If something like a bomb **detonates** or is **detonated**, it explodes. *...the accidental detonation of a shell.*

detonator A **detonator** is a small amount of explosive or an electronic device which causes something like a bomb to explode.

detour If you make a **detour** on a journey, you take a longer route than would normally be necessary, because the usual way is blocked, because you want to avoid something, or because you want to call somewhere on the way.

detoxify (detoxifies, detoxifying, detoxified; detoxification) If something is **detoxified**, poisonous substances are removed from it. ◇ If a person is **detoxified**, they are gradually cured of alcoholism, usually at a place called a **detoxification centre**.

detract If one thing **detracts** from another, it makes it seem less good or impressive.

detractor A person's or thing's **detractors** are people who find fault with them.

detriment (detrimental) If something is to the **detriment** of something else, it has a harmful effect on it. You can also say something is **detrimental** to something else.

detritus (*pron:* dit-trite-uss) is broken and damaged things left as a result of something violent happening. *All around lay the detritus of war: smashed buildings, gutted shops, houses with curtains flapping in broken windows.*

deuce (*pron:* dyewss) If the score is **deuce** in a game of tennis, each player has a score of forty. If you win two points in a row immediately after deuce, you win the game.

deus ex machina (*pron:* day-us eks mak-a-na) People call someone or something a **deus ex machina** when they suddenly appear and resolve a difficulty which had seemed incapable of being resolved. 'Deus ex machina' is Latin for 'god out of a machine'.

Deutschmark (*pron:* doytch-mark) The **Deutschmark** is the unit of currency in Germany. 'Deutschmarks' is often shortened to 'DM'.

devalue (devaluing, devalued; devaluation) If a country's **currency** is devalued, its value is reduced in relation to other currencies. For example, if the pound is devalued against the Deutschmark, fewer Deutschmarks can be bought with one pound. *...a devaluation of 11.5 per cent.*

◇ When you talk about other things being **devalued**, you mean they are made to seem less important or less worthy of respect. *We have to ensure standards are maintained, otherwise qualifications will be devalued.*

devastate (devastating, devastated; devastation, devastatingly) ❏ If something **devastates** a place or thing, it damages it very badly or destroys it completely. *...a devastating blow to the Prime Minister's hopes... ...the devastation caused by Hurricane Andrew.* ◇ If you are **devastated** by something, you are very shocked and upset by it. If something is **devastating**, it has this effect on people.

❏ **Devastating** is also used to say something or someone is very effective or very funny. *...a stylish and devastatingly witty character.*

develop (developing, developed) ❏ When something **develops**, it grows or changes over a period of time into a better, more advanced, more serious, or more complete form. ◇ When people **develop** something like a new product, they produce it by a process of experimenting, testing, and improving earlier ideas or designs.

❏ If you **develop** a skill, you acquire it or improve it by working hard at it. ◇ If you **develop** an illness, fault, or characteristic, you begin to have it.

❏ If an area of land is **developed**, houses, offices, or other buildings are built there.

❏ The **developed** countries are the rich industrialized countries like those of Europe and North America. ◇ The **developing** countries are the poorer, less industrialized countries like those of Africa and South America.

❏ When a photographic film is **developed**, the pictures recorded on it are made visible by treating it with chemicals.

developer ❏ A **developer** is a person or company that buys land in order to build houses, offices, or other buildings. ◇ The **developer** of a product is a person or firm responsible for producing it, especially by improving on earlier ideas or designs.

❏ If you call someone a **late developer**, you mean they were older than usual when they acquired a skill or started doing something.

❏ **Developer** is a chemical used for developing photographs or films.

development (developmental) ❏ The **development** of something is its growth or progress into a more advanced form. *...the mental development of children.* ◇ **Development** is also the process of improving a basic design. *NATO's plans still include development of an air-launched nuclear missile.* **Developmental** is used to talk about things connected with processes like these. *...developmental engineering.*

❏ A **development** is an estate of houses, offices, or other buildings built by a developer. **Development** is the process of preparing land for this purpose and building on it.

❏ **Development** projects and aid are intended to help poorer, less industrialized countries produce more of the things their people need.

❏ If you say there have been **developments** in a situation, you mean further things have happened which may affect the way the situation turns out.

deviant (deviance) People are called **deviants** when they behave in ways which are not considered socially or politically acceptable. **Deviance** is behaviour like this.

deviate (deviating, deviated; deviation) If you **deviate** from a belief or an accepted way of doing something, you do something which does not fit in with it. *Pyongyang has derided the reforms as deviations from the socialist path.*

device ❏ A **device** is a thing made for a particular purpose, for example for recording or measuring something. ◇ A **device** is also a way of getting a result you want. *...a device for bringing down inflation.*

❏ If you say someone is **left to their own devices**, you mean they are allowed to do whatever they want.

devil ❏ In Christianity, the **Devil** is the most powerful evil spirit, formerly an angel. He is also called 'Satan' and 'Lucifer'. ◇ A **devil** is an evil spirit.

❏ If you say someone has a **devil-may-care** attitude, you mean they are reckless and not worried about anything.

❏ If you play **devil's advocate** in an argument or discussion, you argue in favour of an alternative or unpopular point of view, to make the argument more interesting.

devilish is used to describe things which are cruel or wicked. *...a devilish dictatorship.*

devious (deviousness) A **devious** person gets what they want by doing things in a clever complicated secretive way. You talk about the **deviousness** of someone like this.

devise (devising, devised) If you **devise** something like a plan, a product, or an entertainment, you design it, think of it, or work it out.

devoid If someone or something is **devoid** of a certain thing, they are completely without it. *...an area devoid of wildlife.*

devolve (devolving, devolved; devolution) If power is **devolved**, it is transferred from a central government or other organization to regional governments or organizations. This process is called **devolution**.

devote (devoting, devoted; devotion) ❏ If you **devote** yourself to something, you spend most of your time and energy on it. *At the age of 20 he gave up the City to devote himself to painting.* ◇ If you are **devoted** to someone or something, you love them and will do all you can for them. *...her display of loyalty and devotion.*

❏ If you **devote** money, time, or space to something, you use it on that thing. *At that time Westminster devoted precisely two hours a year to the business of Northern Ireland.* ◇ If something is **devoted** to a subject, it deals only with that subject. *...the only major festival in France devoted exclusively to British cinema.*

❏ **Devotion** is strong religious feeling. ◇ A person's **devotions** are their prayers.

devotee (*pron:* dev-vote-tee) A **devotee** of a subject is someone who is very interested in it and enthusiastic about it. *...a passionate devotee of socialism.*

devotion See devote.

devotional is used to describe things which are dedicated to a religious faith. *...devotional music.*

devour (devouring, devoured) If you **devour** food, you eat it quickly and eagerly. ◇ If you **devour** something like a book, you read it enthusiastically.

devout (devoutly) **Devout** people have strong religious beliefs. People like these are sometimes called the **devout**. ◇ You can call other kinds of belief **devout**. *He was devoutly committed to a unified Germany.*

dew is small drops of water which form on the ground during the night.

dewlap A dewlap is a loose fold of skin which hangs under the throat of an animal like a dog or cow.

dewy-eyed If you say someone is **dewy-eyed**, you mean they are innocent and inexperienced.

dexterity (dextrous) **Dexterity** is the ability to do things quickly and skilfully, especially with your body or hands. If someone is **dextrous**, they have this ability.

dhoti (pron: doe-tee) A dhoti is a long loose covering for the lower part of the body, worn by some Hindu men.

DHSS The DHSS (Department of Health and Social Security) was the British government department responsible for the National Health Service and all social security services until 1988, when it was split into the DoH (Department of Health) and DSS (Department of Social Security).

DI is a way of trying to make a woman pregnant by artificially putting sperm in her womb from an anonymous man. DI stands for 'donor insemination'.

diabetes (pron: die-a-beet-eez) (diabetic) Diabetes is a name given to several illnesses, all of which make the sufferer thirsty and want to pass urine. The most common kind, **diabetes mellitus** ('sugar diabetes'), occurs mostly in older people and results in an insulin deficiency and an excess of sugar in the blood. Sufferers from this kind of diabetes are called **diabetics** (pron: die-a-bet-iks).

diabolic means relating to the devil. ...diabolic powers.

diabolical (diabolically) Very wicked acts are sometimes described as diabolical. ...diabolical crimes. ◇ Diabolical and diabolically are also used to say something is very badly made or very badly done. Their forecasting record has been diabolical... He governed the country diabolically in his eleven months in power.

diadem A diadem is a crown, especially a small jewelled one.

diagnose (diagnosing, diagnosed) When a doctor diagnoses an illness in someone, he or she identifies what is wrong. You can also say the doctor diagnoses the person. Doctors have diagnosed him as suffering from paranoid psychosis.

diagnosis (plural: diagnoses) Diagnosis is identifying what is wrong with people who are ill. A diagnosis is the opinion a doctor forms about what is wrong with someone.

diagnostic (diagnostics) Diagnostic equipment, drugs, and methods are used to find out what is wrong with people who are ill. ◇ Diagnostics is the study of things connected with the making of diagnoses.

diagonal (diagonally) A diagonal is a line which joins opposite corners of a four-sided shape or area. Diagonal is used to say something moves or is placed between opposite corners of an area like this. Screens are placed diagonally across the table.

diagram A diagram is a drawing used to explain something.

dial (dialling, dialled) (usual American spelling: dialing, dialed) ❑ The dial of a clock is the part which shows the time. The dial of a meter or other measuring device is the part where you read a measurement. ◇ On a radio, the dial is the part you move to tune in to a station.

❑ The dial on an old-fashioned telephone is a circle with holes in it which you turn to dial a number. If you dial a number, you turn the dial or press the buttons on a telephone to phone someone.

dialect A dialect is a form of a language spoken in a particular area. It includes words and expressions not used in the standard form of the language.

dialling code A dialling code is a number you dial before someone's personal number to connect you with the right area.

dialogue You say there is dialogue or a dialogue when discussions are taking place between groups of people, especially governments or political groups. ◇ Dialogue is also the things people say in a play, film, or book.

dialysis (pron: die-al-iss-iss) is a process in which particles are separated from liquids. It is used in purifying the blood of people whose kidneys do not work properly.

diamanté (pron: die-a-man-tee) is a material decorated with sequins or artificial jewels.

diameter The diameter of a circle or sphere is its width measured by a straight line passing through its centre.

diametrically If things like opinions are diametrically opposed, they are exactly opposite to each other.

diamond ❑ A diamond is a hard bright colourless precious stone.

❑ The shape ♦ is called a diamond. ◇ Diamonds is one of the four suits in a pack of playing cards. All cards in this suit have the symbol ♦ on them.

❑ If you celebrate the diamond jubilee of something, you celebrate the fact that it has been going for 60 years. ◇ A diamond wedding is a 60th wedding anniversary.

diaphanous (pron: die-af-fan-ous) material is thin and transparent.

diaphragm (pron: die-a-fram) Your diaphragm is a muscle between your lungs and your stomach. ◇ A diaphragm is a flexible disc, which a woman puts inside her vagina, covering the opening of her womb, to prevent her getting pregnant during sex. The diaphragm is also known as the 'cap'.

diarist A diarist is a person who records things in a diary.

diarrhoea (or diarrhea) (pron: die-a-ree-a) When someone who is ill has diarrhoea, they produce frequent and watery excrement.

diary (diaries) A diary is a book with a separate space for each day of the year. You use it to write down things you plan to do or to record what happens in your life.

diaspora (pron: die-ass-spor-a) A diaspora is a spreading of people from the country of their origin to other countries. The spreading of Jews from ancient Palestine to other places is often called the Diaspora. Jewish communities living outside Israel are also sometimes called the Diaspora.

diatribe (pron: die-a-tribe) A diatribe is an angry speech or piece of writing attacking someone or something.

dice (plural: dice) (dicing, diced) A dice is a small six-sided block of wood or plastic. Each side has a number of dots on it from one to six. You throw dice in games to decide things by chance. A single dice is sometimes called a 'die'. ◇ When you dice food, you cut it into small square pieces.

dichotomy (pron: die-kot-a-mee) You say there is a dichotomy between things when they do not go together, because they are very different or contradict each other. *...the widely-accepted dichotomy between science and art... One of the odd things about Hardy was the dichotomy between his sympathetic treatment of women in his fiction and his attitude towards them in his own life.*

Dickensian is used to describe people or things similar to those described in the novels of Charles Dickens. **Dickensian** is especially used to describe dirty or cramped working and living conditions like those described in Dickens' novels.

dictaphone A **dictaphone** is a machine into which you dictate something like a letter. The dictation can be played back later for someone to type. 'Dictaphone' is a trademark.

dictate (dictation) ❑ If you **dictate** something like a letter, you speak it into a machine or say it aloud for someone else to write down. *...secretaries taking dictation.*
❑ If someone in power **dictates** something, they say it shall be done, or say what form it shall take. **Dictates** (*pron:* dik-tates) are orders issued by someone in power. *They have to abide by the dictates of the new government.*
❑ If the form something takes is determined by something else, you can say it is **dictated** by that thing. *The president's approach was partly dictated by election considerations.* ◇ If one thing **dictates** another, it makes it necessary. *The local climate dictates a certain kind of costume.*

dictator (dictatorial, dictatorially) A **dictator** is a ruler who has complete power in a country or organization. You call people or governments who have this power **dictatorial** (*pron:* dik-ta-**tor**-1-al). You also say someone is being **dictatorial** when they behave like a dictator. *The government is acting dictatorially.*

dictatorship is government by a dictator. A **dictatorship** is a country ruled by a dictator.

diction A person's **diction** is how clearly they pronounce words when they speak or sing.

dictionary (dictionaries) A **dictionary** is a book which lists words in alphabetical order and gives their meanings either in the same language or in a different language.

dictum (*plural:* dictums *or* dicta) A **dictum** is a saying which describes an aspect of life in an interesting or wise way. *...Lord Acton's dictum that power tends to corrupt and absolute power corrupts absolutely.*

did see **do.**

didactic (*usual pron:* die-**dak**-tik) If you say something like a novel or film is **didactic**, you mean it is trying to teach people something and is therefore less entertaining than it might be. Similarly, if a person is being **didactic**, they are talking to you like a teacher talking to a class.

didgeridoo A **didgeridoo** is a musical instrument used by Australian Aborigines. It is a long wooden tube which you blow down to produce a deep wavering note.

die (dying, died) ❑ When a living thing **dies**, it stops living. ◇ A **dying** person or animal is very ill and likely to die soon. People in this condition are sometimes called the **dying.** ◇ When people **die off**, they die one by one, until there are none left. ◇ If a type of animal **dies out**, its numbers get smaller until the last ones die without reproducing. ◇ **dying breed:** see **breed.**
❑ If something **dies out**, it becomes less and less common and finally comes to an end. ◇ If something like an industry is **dying**, it is becoming less important and is un-

likely to continue.
❑ If a sound **dies away**, it fades until it can no longer be heard. ◇ If something like an emotion **dies down**, it loses its intensity. ◇ **Dying** is used to say something happens very close to the end of an event or period of time. For example, you can say a goal is scored in the 'dying moments' or 'dying seconds' of a football match.
❑ When people say something like a custom or a habit **dies hard,** they mean it is difficult to change.
❑ If you are **dying** to do something, you are very eager to do it.
❑ A **die** is a specially shaped or patterned tool, used to press, cast, or cut metal or some other material into a particular shape. ◇ If you say the **die is cast,** you mean something is going to happen and nothing can stop it.
❑ See also **dice.**

diehard You call someone a **diehard** when they have fixed ideas or beliefs which are not likely to change.

diesel or **diesel oil** is the fuel commonly used to power trains, buses, and lorries. It is also used in some cars. Diesel is also called 'derv'. ◇ A **diesel** engine is powered by diesel. A **diesel** is a vehicle with a diesel engine.

diet (dieting, dieted; dieter) Your **diet** is the kind of food you usually eat. *...a high fibre diet.* ◇ If you are **dieting** or on a **diet,** you are eating less fattening foods, because you want to lose weight. People who do this are sometimes called **dieters.**

dietary is used to talk about things connected with the kinds of foods people eat. *...their dietary habits*

dietician A **dietician** is someone whose job is to advise people what to eat to be healthy.

differ (differing, differed) If two things **differ** or one of them **differs** from the other, they are unlike in some way. ◇ If people **differ** about something, they disagree about it.

difference ❑ A **difference** between things is a way in which they are unlike each other. ◇ **With a difference** is used to say something has a feature which makes it different to, and better than, other things of the same kind. *...a holiday with a difference.* ◇ If you say something **makes a difference,** you mean it changes a situation. *Coleridge says the vote makes no difference to his decision to leave.*
❑ The **difference** between two amounts is the amount by which one is greater than the other. For example, the difference between 8 and 5 is 3.
❑ People's **differences** are the things they disagree over.

different (differently) You say two things are **different** when they do not have the same set of features or characteristics. If two people do something **differently,** they do not do it the same way. ◇ You also use **different** to emphasize that the things you are talking about are distinct from each other. *The injured are being treated in hospitals in four different towns.*

differential A **differential** is a difference between two rates. *In 1979-85 the differential between the unemployment rates of the south-east and north-west grew from 3 to 6.3 percentage points.*

differentiate (differentiating, differentiated; differentiation) If you **differentiate** between things, you recognize or show the differences between them. *...the lack of a clear* *differentiation between 'urban' and 'rural' land-use.* ◇ If two things are the same except for one feature, you can say the feature **differentiates** one from the other.

difficult If something is **difficult**, it is hard to do, solve, or understand. *...a difficult problem... It's a very difficult subject to come to grips with.* ◇ A **difficult** situation needs to be handled carefully. ◇ If someone is being **difficult**, they are behaving in an unreasonable and unhelpful way.

difficulty (difficulties) **Difficulties** are problems. If you are **in difficulty** or **in difficulties**, you are having problems. ◇ If you have **difficulty** doing something, you find it hard to do.

diffident (diffidently, diffidence) If you say someone is **diffident** or talk about their **diffidence**, you mean they are rather shy and modest. *I approached Clyde diffidently and he agreed to explain the system to me.*

diffuse (diffusing, diffused; diffusion) ❑ If something like light is **diffuse** (*pron:* dif-**fyooss**), it is not concentrated in one place but spread over a large area and is therefore less bright. ◇ If you say something written or spoken is **diffuse**, you mean it is vague and difficult to understand or explain.
   ❑ If a liquid or a gas **diffuses** (*pron:* dif-**fyooz**-iz), it spreads over a wider area. This process is called **diffusion**. ◇ If things like ideas are **diffused**, they spread over a wider area or to more people.

dig (digging, dug) ❑ If you **dig**, you make a hole in the ground or move the earth, with something like a spade. ◇ If you **dig** something **up**, you get it out of the ground by digging. ◇ A **dig** is an archaeological excavation.
   ❑ If you **dig** one thing into another, you press the first thing hard into the second. *I dug my nails into her hand.*
   ❑ If you **dig** someone **out** when they are trapped or buried, you get them out by removing the things trapping them. ◇ If you **dig up** something like information, you discover it through careful searching.
   ❑ If you say someone has to **dig deep**, you mean they are forced to spend a lot of money on something.
   ❑ If you have a **dig** at someone, you make a humorous and rather unkind comment about some aspect of their behaviour or character.

digest (digestion, digestible) ❑ If you **digest** something you have heard or read, you think about it and work out what it means. If something like this is easily **digestible**, it is easy to understand.
   ❑ When you **digest** food, your body breaks it down, absorbs all it can, and gets rid of what is left. This process is called **digestion**. **Digestible** food is easy to digest.

digestive is used to talk about things connected with the digestion of food. *...digestive juices.*

digger A **digger** is a vehicle with a powerful mechanical arm for scooping up large amounts of earth.

digit **Digits** are written single-figure numbers like 0, 3, or 8. You use **digit** to say how many figures a number has; for example, you say 527 is a three-digit number. ◇ Your **digits** are your fingers, thumbs, and toes.

digital (digitally) **Digital** systems record or transmit information, especially sounds and pictures, in the form of many very small electrical signals. *...a digital sound system... ...digitally recorded music.* ◇ **Digital** instruments such as watches or clocks give information by displaying

numbers rather than by a pointer moving round a dial.

digitalize (digitalizing, digitalized; digitalization) (*can be spelled with an 's' instead of a 'z'*) If a system is **digitalized**, it is converted into a digital one. *...digitalization of telephone systems.*

dignify (dignifies, dignifying, dignified) **Dignified** behaviour is calm and impressive. A **dignified** occasion is one when people behave like this. ◇ If you **dignify** something, you make it seem more impressive or respectable than it really is.

dignitary (dignitaries) **Dignitaries** are high-ranking people in the government or the church.

dignity ❑ If someone behaves with **dignity**, their behaviour is calm and impressive.
   ❑ If you talk about human **dignity**, you are talking about people's right to be treated with respect. ◇ A person's **dignity** is their sense of self-respect. *He said the Palestinian people had their dignity and would not surrender.* ◇ If people regard something as **beneath their dignity**, they consider themselves too important to do it.

digress (*pron:* die-**gress**) (digresses, digressing, digressed; digression) If you **digress**, you stop talking about your main subject and talk about something else for a while; what you say is called a **digression**.

dike See dyke.

diktat A **diktat** is an order, especially a harsh one made without considering the opinions of the people expected to obey it. If a person or government rules by **diktat**, they do it by giving orders like this.

dilapidated (dilapidation) A **dilapidated** building or vehicle is old and in bad condition. *...churches in advanced stages of dilapidation.*

dilate (dilating, dilated; dilation) When the pupils of your eyes **dilate**, they become wider. Similarly, you can talk about blood vessels and other parts of the body **dilating**. *...the full dilation of the uterus.*

dilatory (*pron:* dill-a-tree) (dilatoriness) If you say someone is being **dilatory**, you mean they are taking too long over something. *They are often accused of dilatoriness.*

dilemma A **dilemma** is a difficult situation where you have to choose between two or more alternatives, none of which is entirely satisfactory.

dilettante (*pron:* dill-it-**tan**-tee) A **dilettante** is someone who is involved in something like politics or the arts, but not in a serious or committed way.

diligent (diligently, diligence) A **diligent** person works hard and carefully and does everything which is expected of them. You talk about the **diligence** of someone like this. *We worked diligently on our assignments.*

dill is a herb with yellow flowers and a strong sweet smell.

dilute (diluting, diluted; dilution) If someone's power or control over something is **diluted**, it is weakened. You call this a **dilution** of power or control. Similarly, if something like a proposed law is **diluted**, it is made less effective. ◇ If you **dilute** a liquid, you make it weaker by adding water or another liquid.

dim (dimmer, dimmest; dimming, dimmed; dimly, dimness) ❑ A **dim** light is not bright. If a light **dims** or is **dimmed**, it becomes less bright. If there are few lights on in a place or if they are not bright, you say the place is **dimly** lit. If you can only just see something, you can say it is **dimly**

visible.

❏ If your memory of something is **dim,** you can hardly remember it. ◇ If you **dimly** understand something, your ideas about it are very unclear. Similarly, you can say you are **dimly** aware of something. ◇ If you say someone is **dim** or **dim-witted,** you mean they are of low intelligence.

❏ If your hopes or prospects are **dim,** they are not very good. ◇ If you take a **dim view** of something, you disapprove of it.

dime A **dime** is a US coin worth ten cents.

dimension ❏ A **dimension** of a subject is an aspect of it. *MPs are convinced that cameras have added a new dimension to their role as public watchdogs.* ◇ When people talk about the **dimensions** of something that is happening, they mean its seriousness or importance. *The affair is beginning to take on national dimensions.*

❏ The **dimensions** of an object are its length, width, and other measurements.

diminish (diminishes, diminishing, diminished) ❏ If something **diminishes** or is **diminished,** it becomes smaller. *...the diminishing role played by Britain in international affairs... His personal prestige had already diminished.*

❏ If a court accepts **diminished responsibility** as a defence for an accused person, it agrees that the person was mentally ill when they committed a crime and so their punishment should be less severe.

diminution A **diminution** of something is a reduction in its size or importance. *Britain consistently opposes any diminution of national powers.*

diminutive A **diminutive** person or thing is very small.

dimmer A **dimmer** is a control or switch which allows you to alter the brightness of an electric light.

dimple (dimpled) **Dimples** are small hollows like the ones on a golf ball. Some people have dimples on their chin or cheeks. If something is **dimpled,** it has dimples on it.

din A **din** is a loud unpleasant noise.

dinar (*pron:* **dee-nahr**) The **dinar** is the unit of currency in some north African and Middle Eastern countries, and also in the republics which were parts of Yugoslavia.

dine (dining, dined) When you **dine,** you have dinner.

diner People eating dinner, especially in a restaurant, can be called **diners.** ◇ In the US, a **diner** is also a small cheap restaurant.

ding-dong A **ding-dong** is an argument or fight.

dinghy (dinghies) A **dinghy** is a small boat which you can sail, row, or power by outboard motor.

dingo (dingoes) **Dingoes** are wild dogs in Australia. They look like wolves with yellowish-brown coats.

dingy A **dingy** place is dark and gloomy or dirty.

dining car The **dining car** on a train is a carriage where passengers are served meals. British trains no longer have dining cars.

dining room The **dining room** in a house or hotel is the room where people have their meals.

dining table A **dining table** is a table you sit at to eat your meals.

dinner is the main meal of the day. Some people call their evening meal **dinner;** for others, **dinner** is a mid-day meal. ◇ A **dinner** is a formal evening meal.

dinner dance A **dinner dance** is a social occasion, usually at a hotel or large restaurant, where guests have a formal meal after which they dance.

dinner jacket A **dinner jacket** is a black jacket a man wears with a bow tie on formal social occasions in the evening.

dinner lady A **dinner lady** is a woman employed in a school, especially a state primary school, to serve dinners or look after children during their lunch break.

dinner party If you have a **dinner party,** you invite a small group of people to your house to spend the evening with you and have dinner.

dinner service A **dinner service** is a set of matching plates and dishes for eating meals.

dinosaur **Dinosaurs** were large reptiles which lived millions of years ago. ◇ If you call a large organization a **dinosaur,** you mean it is left over from the past and is clumsy and inefficient.

dint If you achieve a result **by dint** of something, you achieve it by means of that thing. *By dint of hard work, Senator Specter reached university and eventually went to Yale law school.*

diocese (*pron:* **die-a-siss**) (dioceses, diocesan) A **diocese** is the area over which a bishop has control. **Diocesan** is used to talk about things to do with a diocese. *...diocesan problems.*

diode A **diode** is an electrical device with two terminals which allows electrical current to flow in only one direction. It is used in circuits for converting alternating current to direct current.

dioxide appears in the names of chemical compounds which have two oxygen atoms in each molecule. See **carbon dioxide** and **sulphur dioxide.**

dioxin is a highly poisonous substance produced during the manufacture of certain herbicides. It can cause cancer.

dip (dipping, dipped) ❏ If you **dip** something into a liquid, you put it in the liquid then take it out again straight away. ◇ A **dip** is a thick creamy mixture which you eat by scooping it up with something like a biscuit or raw vegetable.

❏ When farmers **dip** sheep, they herd them through a trough filled with liquid disinfectant which kills parasites in their wool.

❏ If you take a **dip,** you have a quick swim.

❏ If something **dips,** it makes a sudden downward movement. ◇ If something like a road **dips,** it goes down steeply to a lower level. ◇ A **dip** in a surface is a part which is lower than the rest. *...a dip in the ground.*

❏ If there is a **dip** in an amount of something, it decreases briefly before returning to its original level. *Holiday companies must expect a dip in profits.*

❏ If you **dip into** an amount of money, you use some of it. ◇ If you **dip into** a book, you have a quick look at it.

diphtheria (*pron:* **dif-theer-ya**) is a dangerous infectious disease which causes fever, weakness, and difficulty in breathing.

diphthong (*pron:* **dif-thong**) A **diphthong** is a combination of two vowel sounds. For example, the sound 'ow' in 'cow' is a diphthong consisting of an 'a' sound followed by a short 'oo' sound.

diploma A **diploma** is a qualification from a college or university which has a lower status than a degree.

diplomacy is the management of relations between countries. ◇ Diplomacy is also saying or doing the right thing in difficult situations and avoiding offending people.

diplomat A diplomat is a government official, usually in an embassy in a foreign country, who helps manage relations between that country and his own.

diplomatic (diplomatically) ❑ Diplomatic is used to describe things connected with diplomacy and diplomats. *...diplomatic staff... He did not want to see China diplomatically isolated.* ◇ The **Diplomatic Service** is the part of the Civil Service which provides diplomats to work abroad. ◇ The **diplomatic corps** is the group of all the diplomats from different countries working in one city or country. ◇ **Diplomatic immunity** is a legal privilege diplomats have which entitles them not to pay taxes and not to be taken to court in the foreign country they are working in.
❑ A **diplomatic** person is good at avoiding offending people in difficult situations.

dipsomania (dipsomaniac) Dipsomania is an uncontrollable craving for alcohol. A **dipsomaniac** is someone who suffers from dipsomania.

dipstick A dipstick is a metal rod with notches in the end which you dip into a container to measure how much liquid is in it. Dipsticks are most commonly used to measure the amount of oil in a car engine.

dire (direr, direst) ❑ Dire is used to emphasize the seriousness of something. For example, you can give a **dire** warning of trouble. *He warned of dire consequences if the refugees were not quickly moved into Jordan.* You can say something like a country's economy is in a **dire** state. If someone or something is in **dire straits**, they are in serious trouble. ◇ If you are in **dire need** of something, you need it urgently.
❑ Dire is also used to say something is of very poor quality. *The standard of presentation and newswriting is dire.*

direct (directness) ❑ Direct is used to say someone is involved in the main part of something, rather than in other things connected with it. *Djibouti's government had avoided any direct involvement in the conflict.* ◇ Direct is also used to say something is done in a clear and straightforward way. *The move is seen as a direct challenge to the King's power.* ◇ If political leaders have **direct** talks, they meet each other face-to-face, rather than communicating through other people.
❑ You say people are **direct** when they are honest and say what they think. *His outgoing personality and directness ensured good relations with ministers.*
❑ Direct is used to say you can make a journey using just one plane, train, or bus, without having to change. *...direct flights from Glasgow to Florida.*
❑ If something like gunfire is **directed** at a place, it is aimed at it. ◇ If something you say is **directed** at a person or group, it is intended for them to hear or take notice of.
❑ If you **direct** someone somewhere, you tell them how to get there.
❑ If you **direct** something like a project, you are in charge of it. ◇ When someone **directs** a film, play, or TV programme, they control the making or performance of it.

direct action is action by a group of people aimed at forcing people in authority to do something, or at stopping them from doing something. Direct action can include such things as obstructing roads and occupying property.

direct current See DC.

direct debit See debit.

direct hit If something suffers a **direct hit**, a bomb or missile lands exactly on it.

direct mail is advertising material sent by post to people's homes without them asking for it. It is sometimes called 'junk mail'.

direct rule is a system in which a central government takes charge of the affairs of a province which had previously had its own government or law-making organization.

direct speech is a way of repeating things people have said using their exact words. When direct speech is written down, it is usually enclosed in quotation marks. Here are some examples of direct speech. *'Is it a nice house?' I asked... 'My interpretation was quite different,' muttered Sir Robert.* See also reported speech.

direction ❑ You can describe the way something is developing or progressing by saying it is moving in a particular **direction**. *Health authorities are moving in the right direction.*
❑ If you say what **direction** something is, you are saying, for example, that it is to the north or south-west. Similarly, you can say something is moving or pointing in a particular **direction**.
❑ **Directions** are instructions which tell you how to get to a place, or how to do something.
❑ The person responsible for the **direction** of a film, play, or piece of music is the one who controls the way it is made or performed. ◇ If you do something under someone's **direction**, they tell you what to do.

directional is used to talk about transmitting sound in one direction only, or receiving it from just one direction. *...highly directional transmitting aerials.*

directionless You say an activity is **directionless** when it is not operating to any real plan.

directive A directive is an official instruction. When an EU **directive** is issued, member countries are required to carry it out by introducing their own laws to produce the desired result.

directly ❑ If you do something **directly**, you do it in a clear and straightforward way. *He denied bidding directly for the leadership.* ◇ If a subject is spoken about **directly**, it is spoken about in an open and straightforward way, and not just implied or hinted at.
❑ If you are **directly** involved in something, you are involved in the thing itself, rather than other things connected with it. *...countries directly concerned with the problem of refugees.* ◇ If someone is **directly** accountable to someone else, they must explain and justify what they do to that person rather than to other people representing them.
❑ If something happens as an immediate result of something else, you say it is **directly** attributable to that thing. *...personal injury directly attributable to a crime of violence.*
❑ If something points **directly** at something else, it points straight towards it. *They aimed directly at the legs of the rioters.* ◇ If one thing is **directly** above, below, or in

front of another, it is exactly in that position.

❏ If a political leader is **directly** elected, he or she is chosen by a vote of all the people rather than by their representatives.

director (directorial) A **director** is a person who controls the way something like a film, play, or piece of music is made or performed. **Directorial** is used to talk about things to do with directors and their work. *...directorial freedom of invention.* ◇ A **director** is also someone on the board of a company or in charge of a group, institution, or project.

director general The person in charge of a large institution or organization is sometimes called the **director general.**

Director of Public Prosecutions The Director of Public Prosecutions or DPP is the person in charge of the Crown Prosecution Service, who takes responsibility for all prosecutions made by the police.

directorate The board of directors of a company is sometimes called the **directorate.** ◇ A **directorate** is also a branch of government with a particular responsibility. *...the Road and Vehicle Safety Directorate.*

directorship A **directorship** is the job or position of a company director.

directory (directories) A **directory** is a book which lists things like names, addresses, and phone numbers, usually in alphabetical order.

directory enquiries is a service you can phone to find out someone's phone number.

dirge A **dirge** is a slow sad song or piece of music, for performing at a funeral. Any piece of music which sounds like this can also be called a **dirge.**

dirk A **dirk** is a short sword which used to be worn by Scottish Highlanders.

dirt ❏ If there is **dirt** on something, there is dust, mud, or a stain on it. ◇ **Dirt** is also earth. A **dirt** road or track consists of earth, with no gravel or tarmac surface.

❏ **Dirt** is also information about people's private lives, when it is used by other people to try to embarrass them.

❏ If something is **dirt cheap**, it costs very little, often because it is of poor quality. ◇ If an area is **dirt-poor**, there is extreme poverty there, often with people living in dirty overcrowded conditions.

dirty (dirtier, dirtiest; dirties, dirtying, dirtied) ❏ If something is **dirty**, it has dust, mud, or stains on it. If you **dirty** something, you make it dirty.

❏ **Dirty** is used to talk about dishonest or unfair ways of gaining an advantage over someone. *...the dirtiest leadership contest the party has seen.*

❏ **Dirty** jokes, books, and language deal with sex in a way many people find vulgar or offensive. ◇ A person whose sexual behaviour offends people can also be called **dirty**. *...a dirty old man.*

disability (disabilities) A person with a **disability** has a serious problem with their body or mind which restricts their way of life.

disable (disabling, disabled; disablement) If something **disables** you, it affects you physically or mentally and restricts your way of life. *...a disabling illness.* People whose lives are affected in this way are sometimes called the **disabled;** their condition is called a **disablement.** ◇ If a machine is **disabled**, it is damaged so badly

it no longer works.

disabuse (*pron:* dis-a-**byooz**) (disabusing, disabused) If you **disabuse** someone of something they think is true, you show them it is not true.

disadvantage (disadvantaged) ❏ A **disadvantage** is a factor which makes something less acceptable or less desirable. ◇ If you are **at a disadvantage,** you have a problem which other people do not have.

❏ **Disadvantaged** people live in bad conditions and do not have the means to improve their situation. People like these are sometimes called the **disadvantaged.**

disadvantageous If something is **disadvantageous** to you, it puts you in a bad position compared to other people.

disaffected (disaffection) You say people are **disaffected** when they no longer believe in something and have stopped supporting it. *Rising prices and rising crime have led to public disaffection with the government.*

disagree (disagreed, disagreeing) If you **disagree** with someone about something, you have a different opinion from them about it. ◇ If you **disagree** with what someone does, you disapprove of it.

disagreeable (disagreeably) If something is **disagreeable,** it is unpleasant or annoying. *The music became disagreeably harsh and noisy.* ◇ A **disagreeable** person is unpleasant or unfriendly.

disagreement If there is **disagreement** or a **disagreement,** people have different views about something, especially how something should be dealt with. When this happens, you say the people concerned are **in disagreement.**

disallow If someone in authority **disallows** something, they do not allow it to take place. ◇ If a goal is **disallowed** in football, it is not allowed to count, because a rule has been broken.

disappear (disappearing, disappeared; disappearance) If someone or something **disappears,** they are not where they should be, and cannot be found. When this happens, you talk about their **disappearance.** ◇ You also say someone **disappears** when they go somewhere where they cannot be seen. *He disappeared into the trees.* ◇ If something like a feeling **disappears,** it ceases to exist. *The general discontent will not disappear.*

disappoint (disappointing, disappointed; disappointingly, disappointment) If something **disappoints** you, it is not as good as you expected, or does not do what you wanted it to. You say something like this is **disappointing.** *The limitations of this process became disappointingly clear.* When something disappoints you, you say you feel **disappointed** or talk about your **disappointment.**

disapprove (disapproving, disapproved; disapprovingly, disapproval) If you **disapprove** of something, you do not like it, or you think it is morally wrong. *My neighbours stared disapprovingly into my windows.* When people express **disapproval,** they show they disapprove of something.

disarm (disarmament, disarmer) ❏ If someone is **disarmed,** they have their weapons taken away. ◇ If a country or organization **disarms,** it gets rid of some or all of its weapons. This process is called **disarmament.** People who try to persuade governments to get rid of their nuclear weapons are called nuclear **disarmers.**

❏ If something like a bomb is **disarmed,** its detonator is removed so it cannot explode.

disarming (disarmingly) If someone is **disarming**, they are so pleasant it is difficult to have any critical or hostile feelings towards them. *The people were disarmingly friendly.*

disarray If people are in **disarray**, they are confused and disorganized. ◇ If something is in **disarray**, it is in an untidy state.

disassociate (disassociating, disassociated) If you **disassociate** yourself from someone or something, you say you are not involved with them.

disaster (disastrous, disastrously) ❑ A **disaster** is something which happens unexpectedly and causes a lot of damage or suffering. You say something like this is **disastrous** or talk about its **disastrous** effects. *...a disastrous earthquake.*
  ❑ If you say something someone does is **disastrous** or a **disaster**, you mean it is very unsuccessful. *Their scheme went disastrously wrong... A spokesman described the party's performance as a disaster.*

disavow (disavowal) If you **disavow** something, you say you are not responsible for it or do not agree with it. What you say is called a **disavowal.**

disband (disbandment) If an organized group **disbands** or is **disbanded**, it breaks up and no longer exists as a unit. You call this its **disbandment.**

disbelieve (disbelieving, disbelieved; disbelief) If you **disbelieve** what someone tells you, you do not believe it. **Disbelief** is unwillingness to accept that something is true.

disburse (disbursing, disbursed; disbursement) When an amount of money is **disbursed**, it is paid out, usually from a special fund. **Disbursement** is paying out money like this; a **disbursement** is a payment.

disc (*usual American spelling:* **disk**) ❑ A **disc** is a flat circular object. ◇ **Discs** are also pieces of cartilage between the bones in your spine. If a piece gets displaced, you say you have **slipped a disc.**
  ❑ Gramophone records are often called **discs.**
  ❑ See also **disk.**

disc jockey A **disc jockey** or **DJ** is someone who introduces or mixes records on radio programmes or at discos or nightclubs.

discard If you **discard** something, you get rid of it.

discern (discernible) If you can **discern** something, you can see it, or see that it exists. You say something like this is **discernible.** *...a discernible shift in public opinion.*

discerning (discernment) A **discerning** person is good at judging the quality of something; this ability is called **discernment.**

discharge (discharging, discharged) ❑ When someone is **discharged** from hospital, prison, or the armed forces, they are allowed to leave.
  ❑ When a substance is **discharged**, it is released somewhere. This is called the **discharge** of the substance. *...the discharge of sewage effluent into the River Avon.* A quantity of a substance released like this is called a **discharge.**
  ❑ If someone **discharges** their duties or responsibilities, they carry them out.

disciple The **disciples** of a teacher or leader are his or her followers. Christ's **disciples** were his twelve closest followers during his life on Earth.

disciplinarian If you describe someone in authority as a

disciplinarian, you mean they insist on people obeying a set of rules and punish them if they do not.

discipline (disciplining, disciplined; disciplinary) ❑ **Discipline** is insisting on people obeying rules and punishing them when they do not. **Disciplinary** is used to talk about enforcing discipline. *Two players face disciplinary action.* ◇ If someone is **disciplined**, they are punished for breaking rules or behaving badly.
  ❑ **Discipline** or **self-discipline** is the ability to control your behaviour and finish the things you set out to do. A **disciplined** or **self-disciplined** person has this ability.
  ❑ In some sports competitions, each competitor does several different events called **disciplines**. For example, the three disciplines of world cup skiing are downhill, slalom, and giant slalom.
  ❑ A **discipline** is also a subject which people study.

disclaim (disclaiming, disclaimed; disclaimer) If you **disclaim** something like a feeling or desire, you say you do not have it. ◇ If you **disclaim** knowledge of something, you say you know nothing about it. ◇ If you **disclaim** responsibility for something, you say you are not responsible for it. A statement in which someone disclaims responsibility for something is called a **disclaimer.**

disclose (disclosing, disclosed; disclosure) If someone **discloses** new or secret information, they tell people about it. You call this the **disclosure** of information or say there have been **disclosures.**

disco (discos) A **disco** is an event at which people dance to pop records. There are usually lights which flash in time with the music, and a disc jockey who plays the records. ◇ A **disco** is also (a) a building or room where discos take place. (b) a set of equipment for putting on a disco, including things like record players, records, and lights. ◇ **Disco** is a type of music with a regular beat, suitable for dancing to in discos.

discolour (discolouring, discoloured; discolouration) (*American spelling:* **discolor,** *etc*) If something **discolours** or is **discoloured**, its original colour changes in an unattractive way. *.....a brown discolouration caused by residual iron salts.*

discomfit (discomfiting, discomfited; discomfiture) If something **discomfits** you, it makes you embarrassed or confused. This feeling is called **discomfiture.**

discomfort is an unpleasant or slightly painful feeling in part of your body. ◇ **Discomforts** are conditions which make you physically uncomfortable. *...the discomforts of camping.* ◇ **Discomfort** is also a feeling of worry or embarrassment. If something **discomforts** you or is **discomforting**, it makes you feel like this.

disconcert (disconcertingly) If something **disconcerts** you or makes you feel **disconcerted**, it makes you less sure of something and has a worrying effect. You say things like this are **disconcerting**. *Disconcertingly, the Hebridean Dance instructor comes from Stockholm.*

disconnect If you **disconnect** things which are joined together, you separate them. ◇ If you **disconnect** a piece of equipment, you detach it from its source of power. ◇ If a gas, electricity, water, or telephone company **disconnects** someone, it turns off the supply to their house.

disconsolate (disconsolately) If someone is **disconsolate**, they are deeply unhappy or disappointed. *Prost walked off disconsolately while Senna waved to his fans.*

discontent (discontented, discontentedly) If you are **discontented**, you are not happy with your situation. This feeling is called **discontent**. You can also be **discontented** with a particular thing. *The protest highlighted a deep discontent about falling living standards.* People's **discontents** are the things they are not satisfied with.

discontinue (discontinuing, discontinued) If you **discontinue** something, you stop doing it.

discontinuous (discontinuity, discontinuities) A **discontinuous** process happens in stages, with breaks between each stage. You say there is **discontinuity** in a process like this. A **discontinuity** is a break or pause in something.

discord You say there is **discord** when people argue or disagree about something.

discordant If things like colours are **discordant**, they do not go well together. ◇ **Discordant** music is harsh and unpleasant.

discotheque A discotheque is the same as a disco.

discount ❑ A **discount** is a reduction in the price of something. If a product is **discounted**, it is sold at a cheaper price. ◇ **Discount** things are cheap and usually of poor quality. *...discount clothing.*
❑ If you **discount** something (*pron: diss-***count**), you reject it or ignore it. *You cannot discount the deeply held convictions of one third of the population.*

discourage (discouraging, discouraged; discouragement) If something **discourages** you, it makes you lose hope or enthusiasm. ◇ If someone **discourages** you from doing something, they try to persuade you not to do it. Their attempts at persuading you are called **discouragement**. ◇ If something **discourages** you from doing something, it makes you less keen to do it.

discourse A **discourse** is a talk or piece of writing which is intended to teach or explain something. ◇ **Discourse** is spoken or written communication between people.

discourtesy (discourteous) **Discourtesy** is behaviour which is not polite and shows bad manners. You say people who behave like this are **discourteous**.

discover (discovering, discovered; discovery, discoveries) If you **discover** something, you find it or find out about it. You talk about a person's **discovery** of something. *...her discovery of an Elizabethan cookbook.* A **discovery** is something which has been discovered. *These diaries are a discovery of great importance.* ◇ You say something like a place or process is **discovered** when someone finds it, or finds out about it, for the first time. ◇ When a person with talent is **discovered**, someone realizes how talented they are and helps them to become famous.

discoverer The **discoverer** of something is the first person to find out about it. *...Sir Alexander Fleming, discoverer of penicillin.*

discredit (discrediting, discredited) If someone is **discredited**, people stop trusting them or respecting them. *...a deliberate attempt to discredit the police.* ◇ If something like an idea or belief is **discredited**, it is shown to be false. ◇ **Discredit** is shame and disapproval. *This will serve only to bring discredit on him.*

discreditable behaviour is considered to be shameful and wrong.

discreet (discreetly) If you are **discreet**, you avoid causing embarrassment when dealing with secret or private matters. *British officials are remaining discreetly silent.* ◇ You say things are **discreet** when they have been designed not to draw attention to themselves. *...discreet lighting.*

discrepancy (discrepancies) A **discrepancy** is a small difference between two things which ought to be the same.

discrete things are separate from each other. *The development unit aims to cut up the work into discrete stages.*

discretion (discretionary) ❑ If you behave with **discretion**, you avoid causing embarrassment when dealing with secret or private matters.
❑ **Discretion** is also the ability to judge a situation and make the right sort of decisions. ◇ If a decision is at the **discretion** of someone in authority, it depends on what they think is best, rather than on a fixed rule. When someone uses this power, you say they are **exercising their discretion**. **Discretionary** is used to describe things connected with decisions like this. *...discretionary grants... The attorney general had exceeded his discretionary powers.*

discriminate (discriminating, discriminated; discrimination, discriminatory) ❑ If someone **discriminates** against you, they do not treat you as well as they treat other people. *It is unlawful to discriminate against a woman because she is pregnant.* If someone **discriminates** in favour of you, they unfairly treat you better than other people. When some people are unfairly treated differently from others, this is called **discrimination**; a law or rule which treats people differently is called **discriminatory**. *...discriminatory employment policies.*
❑ If you can **discriminate** between two things, you can recognize the difference between them. ◇ A **discriminating** person recognizes and appreciates things of good quality.

discursive speech or writing expresses things in a long roundabout way.

discus (discuses) The **discus** is a field event in athletics. Competitors throw a heavy disc-shaped object called a **discus** as far as they can.

discuss (discusses, discussing, discussed; discussion) When people **discuss** things, they talk about them seriously. Talking seriously about things is called **discussion**; a **discussion** is a serious conversation. If something is **under discussion**, it is being talked about and no decision has yet been made. ◇ A **discussion** is also a serious piece of writing in which the writer examines a subject in detail and expresses opinions about it.

disdain (disdaining, disdained; disdainful, disdainfully) If someone behaves with **disdain**, they show they dislike someone and treat them as inferior or unimportant. You call behaviour like this **disdainful**. *The idea was dismissed disdainfully.* ◇ If someone **disdains** something, they reject it because they do not think it is good enough for them. *Steel-shafted golf clubs are on the whole disdained by collectors.* ◇ If someone **disdains** to do something, they do not do it because they think it is beneath them.

disease (diseased) A **disease** is an illness caused by an infection or by a part of the body not working properly. Infections affecting animals and plants are also called **diseases**. ◇ A type of bad behaviour can be called a **disease** when it is very common. *...the disease of idleness.*

disembark (disembarkation) When you **disembark** from a ship or plane, you get off it at the end of a journey. ...*the point of disembarkation.*

disembodied A **disembodied** head has been separated from someone's body. ◇ A **disembodied** voice seems to come from a place where you cannot see anyone.

disembowel (disembowelling, disembowelled) If a person or animal is **disembowelled**, their intestines are removed or ripped out.

disenchanted (disenchantment) If you are **disenchanted** with something, you are disappointed by it and no longer think it is good or worthwhile. *The elections were marked by a mood of disenchantment among the voters.*

disenfranchize (disenfranchizing, disenfranchized) *(can be spelled with an 's' instead of a 'z')* If someone is **disenfranchized**, they lose their right to vote.

disengage (disengaging, disengaged; disengagement) If people fighting a battle **disengage**, they stop fighting. ...*the disengagement of the warring sides.* ◇ If you **disengage** something which is fastened or trapped, you free it.

disentangle (disentangling, disentangled; disentanglement) If you **disentangle** something, you separate it from other things it has become attached to. ◇ If you **disentangle** a complicated issue or situation, you sort out the different things involved, so it can be better understood.

disequilibrium If something is in **disequilibrium**, it is uncertain, unstable, and likely to change.

disestablish (disestablishes, disestablishing, disestablished; disestablishment) When people talk about the Church of England being **disestablished,** they are talking about a change which would make it no longer the official religion of the United Kingdom. *The Liberal Democrats voted overwhelmingly in favour of disestablishment.*

disfavour is dislike or disapproval. If someone is **in disfavour,** they are not liked by someone in authority.

disfigure (disfiguring, disfigured; disfigurement) If something is **disfigured**, its appearance is spoiled. ◇ If a person is **disfigured**, they have a scar or mark on their face or some other part of their body, and this spoils their appearance. You can call a scar or mark like this a **disfigurement.**

disgorge (disgorging, disgorged) When a lot of people get out of a vehicle, you can say it **disgorges** them. ◇ If a substance is **disgorged** into the atmosphere, or into a river or the sea, it is released into it. ◇ If someone **disgorges** information, they release it.

disgrace (disgracing, disgraced; disgraceful, disgracefully) If someone is **disgraced** or **in disgrace**, they have done something shocking which has made people lose respect for them. ◇ If someone **disgraces** an organization they belong to, they do something which harms its reputation. You can also say they are a **disgrace** to the organization. ◇ If you **disgrace yourself**, you behave badly in public. ◇ If you say something is a **disgrace** or **disgraceful**, you mean it is shocking and unacceptable. *The prisons are disgracefully overcrowded.*

disgruntled If you are **disgruntled**, you are cross and dissatisfied about something.

disguise (disguising, disguised) If someone or something is **disguised** or **in disguise**, their appearance has been changed to prevent people recognizing them. A **disguise** is something like a set of clothes which is used to change someone's appearance. ◇ If something **disguises**

what is happening, it prevents people noticing it. *Until recently this weakness was disguised by steady profits.*

disgust (disgusting) **Disgust** is a strong feeling of dislike or disapproval. If something **disgusts** you or you are **disgusted** by it, it makes you feel like this. If you say something is **disgusting**, you mean you dislike it or disapprove of it strongly.

dish (dishes, dishing, dished) ❑ A **dish** is a round shallow container which food is served or cooked in. ◇ A **dish** is also food prepared in a particular style. ...*my favourite pasta dish.* ◇ When food is **dished up**, it is served.
  ❑ A **dish** is also a dish-shaped TV aerial for picking up signals from satellites.
  ❑ If money is **dished out** to people, it is given to them. You can also talk about punishment being **dished out**. *They then dish out heavy fines.*

disharmony You say there is **disharmony** among a group of people when they fail to get on with each other.

dishcloth A **dishcloth** is a cloth for washing up.

dishearten (disheartening, disheartened) If something **disheartens** you, it makes you less hopeful or confident. You say something like this is **disheartening**; when it happens to you, you say you are **disheartened**.

dishevelled *(American spelling: disheveled)* A **dishevelled** person looks very untidy.

dishonest (dishonestly, dishonesty) You say someone is **dishonest** when they lie, cheat, or break the law. *He dishonestly concealed information from another businessman.* You talk about the **dishonesty** of someone like this.

dishonour (dishonouring, dishonoured) ❑ If you **dishonour** someone or something or bring **dishonour** on them, you behave in a way which damages their reputation.
  ❑ If a cheque is **dishonoured**, the bank refuses to pay up to the person who has received it, because the person who wrote it does not have enough money in their account.

dishonourable behaviour is dishonest or morally unacceptable.

dishwasher A **dishwasher** is a machine for washing crockery and cutlery.

dishwater is water which has been used for washing up.

disillusion (disillusioning, disillusioned; disillusionment) If you are **disillusioned**, you are disappointed because someone or something is not as good as you thought they were. This feeling is called **disillusion** or **disillusionment**. A **disillusioning** experience is one which makes you feel like this.

disincentive A **disincentive** is something which discourages people from doing something.

disinclined (disinclination) If you are **disinclined** to do something, you are unwilling to do it, or you do not feel like doing it. ...*the government's disinclination to interfere with market forces.*

disinfect (disinfectant) If you **disinfect** something, you clean it using a liquid called a **disinfectant** which kills germs.

disinflation (disinflationary) **Disinflation** is a reduction in the rate of inflation, especially as a result of government policies. When there is disinflation, prices stop rising or go down, but without the usual problems associated with price decreases like unemployment and lack of investment. A **disinflationary** policy or measure is meant to cause disinflation; you can also say something has a **disinflationary** effect. See also **deflation**.

disinformation is false or misleading information, especially information spread by a government which is trying to damage the reputation of its enemies.

disingenuous (disingenuously) If someone is being **disingenuous**, they are being insincere and slightly dishonest. *The ministry claims disingenuously that it did not know this was going on.*

disintegrate (disintegrating, disintegrated; disintegration) If an object **disintegrates**, it breaks into many small pieces. ◇ If something like a relationship or organization **disintegrates**, it breaks up, or the people involved separate into smaller groups. *This was the only way of saving the country from disintegration and collapse.*

disinter (*pron:* diss-in-ter) (disinterring, disinterred) If someone **disinters** something, they start using it again after it has not been used for a long time. *The government plans to disinter an anti-subversive law dating from 1952.* ◇ When a dead body is **disinterred**, it is dug up out of the ground.

disinterested (disinterest) ❑ You say someone is **disinterested** when they are not personally involved in something and so can make unbiased judgements or decisions about it.

❑ If people are **disinterested** in something, they are not interested in it, or not enthusiastic about it. This feeling is called **disinterest**. *Registration figures indicate a general disinterest towards the elections.* Some people think this use of 'disinterested' is wrong, and say there is no such word as 'disinterest'. Instead of 'disinterested', they say you should say 'uninterested'; instead of 'disinterest', you should say 'lack of interest'.

disinvestment If there is **disinvestment** in a country, other countries withdraw money they have invested there.

disjointed If something is **disjointed**, it has sudden gaps or changes, and does not proceed in a smooth flowing way. *...a scrappy, disjointed game.*

disk A **disk** is a part of a computer which stores information. See also **hard disk, floppy disk**. ◇ **Disk** is also the usual American spelling of 'disc'.

disk drive A **disk drive** is a device attached to a small computer which allows you to read from and write to floppy disks.

dislike (disliking, disliked) If you **dislike** someone or something, you find them unpleasant. This feeling is called **dislike**. Your **dislikes** are things you do not like.

dislocate (dislocating, dislocated; dislocation) If you **dislocate** a part of your body, a bone is forced away from another bone it is normally connected to. *...a suspected dislocation of the right big toe.* ◇ If something like a way of life is **dislocated**, other things interfere with it and it cannot function in its usual way.

dislodge (dislodging, dislodged) If you **dislodge** someone or something, you cause them to move from the place where they are.

disloyal (disloyalty) If someone is **disloyal** to their friends, family, or country, they do things which harm them, or they fail to support them. Behaviour like this is called **disloyalty**.

dismal (dismally) If you call a person's attempt at doing something **dismal**, you mean it is very unsuccessful. *They failed dismally.* ◇ **Dismal** is also used to say something is unattractive and depressing.

dismantle (dismantling, dismantled; dismantlement) If you **dismantle** something like a machine, you take it apart. ◇ If an organization or political system is **dismantled**, it is brought to an end by taking away its parts or functions, one at a time. *...the virtual dismantlement of the country's armed forces.*

dismay If something **dismays** you, it makes you sad or alarmed. This feeling is called **dismay**.

dismember (dismembering, dismembered; dismemberment) If a body is **dismembered**, its arms and legs are removed. ◇ If a country is **dismembered**, it is split into separate parts. *The country was plunged into a civil war that led to its dismemberment.*

dismiss (dismisses, dismissing, dismissed; dismissal) ❑ If you **dismiss** something like a person's ideas, you say they are incorrect or unimportant, and therefore not worth bothering about. You call this a **dismissal** of a person's ideas.

❑ When a judge **dismisses** an action in court, he or she says it cannot proceed any further. ◇ If an appeal is **dismissed**, it is turned down.

❑ If someone is **dismissed** by their employer, they lose their job. Losing your job like this is called a **dismissal**. *The authorities threatened mass dismissals.*

❑ If the people in a room are **dismissed**, they are given permission to leave. ◇ In cricket, when a batsman is **dismissed**, the opposing team gets him or her out.

dismissive (dismissively) If you are **dismissive** of something, you show you are unwilling to accept it or take it seriously. *'It's only rock and roll,' he mutters dismissively.*

dismount If you **dismount** from a horse or bicycle, you get off it.

disobedient (disobedience) If someone is **disobedient**, they do not do what they are told to. **Disobedience** is behaviour like this.

disobey If you **disobey** an order or **disobey** the person giving it, you do not do what they tell you to.

disorder (disordered; disorderly) ❑ **Disorder** is a situation in which people behave in an uncontrolled way and break the law. You say people who behave like this are **disorderly**. *The country is in the grip of widespread urban disorder... He was arrested for being drunk and disorderly.*

❑ If something is **disordered**, **disorderly**, or **in disorder**, it is very untidy or disorganized. *The refugees were shepherded into a disorderly queue.*

❑ A **disorder** is an illness of the mind or body. *...a blood disorder.*

disorganized (disorganization) (*can be spelled with an 's' instead of 'z'*) If something is **disorganized**, it is in a confused and badly prepared state. *The army is suffering from low morale, disorganization and indiscipline.* ◇ A **disorganized** person is no good at planning or arranging things.

disorientate (disorientating, disorientated) If something **disorientates** you, it makes you confused or unsure where you are; if you are in this state, you say you are **disorientated** or **disoriented**. Something which has this effect can be called **disorientating** or **disorienting**.

disoriented (disorienting) See **disorientate**.

disown If you **disown** something or someone, you claim you have no connection with them, or say you no longer wish to be connected with them.

disparage (disparaging, disparaged; disparagingly, disparagement) If you **disparage** someone or something, you talk about them in a way which shows you have a low opinion of them. *...his disparaging comments about the European Union... They are disparagingly referred to as 'Seventies' playwrights... ...his crude disparagement of the ethical message of Jesus.*

disparate (*pron:* diss-par-et) If things are **disparate**, they are very different from each other. *Members voiced a range of views on issues as disparate as education and foreign investment.*

disparity (disparities) A **disparity** between things is a difference between them. *...the growing disparity between male and female suicide rates.*

dispassionate (dispassionately) If you give a **dispassionate** account of something, you state the facts without showing your feelings. Similarly, if you make a **dispassionate** judgement, you do not let your feelings interfere with what you decide. *...dealing with the topic dispassionately.*

dispatch See **despatch**.

dispel (dispelling, dispelled) If something **dispels** an idea or feeling, it makes people no longer have it. *His re-election has dispelled speculation that he is ready to give up power.*

dispensable If someone or something is **dispensable**, you can do without them.

dispensary (dispensaries) A **dispensary** is a place, for example in a hospital or prison, where medicines are stored and given out.

dispensation If someone is given a **dispensation**, they are given official permission to do something which is not normally allowed.

dispense (dispensing, dispensed) ❏ If you **dispense** something, you hand it out. *He dispensed advice on how to sterilize needles.* ◇ A machine which **dispenses** something provides it when you put money in it or a card. ◇ When a pharmacist **dispenses** medicine, he or she gives it to people, making sure the doctor's instructions are carried out correctly.

❏ If you **dispense with** something, you get rid of it, or do without it.

dispenser A **dispenser** is a machine or container you can obtain things from, for example a cash dispenser or a soft drinks dispenser.

dispensing optician See **optician**.

dispersant **Dispersants** are chemicals sprayed on oil slicks to break them up so they do not pollute the coastline.

disperse (dispersing, dispersed; dispersal, dispersion) When a group of people **disperse** or are **dispersed**, they move away in different directions. *Police used teargas to disperse demonstrators outside the state parliament.* You can talk about the **dispersal** of a group of people. ◇ When things **disperse** or are **dispersed**, they spread out and affect a large area or a large number of people. You talk about the **dispersal** of substances. *...the dispersal of radioactive material.* You usually talk about the **dispersion** of other things, such as ideas.

dispirit (dispiriting, dispirited; dispiritingly) If you are **dispirited**, you are disappointed and have lost your enthusi-asm or determination to do something. If something is **dispiriting**, it has this effect on you. *The gap between the two sides remains dispiritingly large.*

displace (displacing, displaced; displacement) ❏ If one thing **displaces** another, it forces it out and takes its place. Similarly, you can talk about one political leader **displacing** another one. ◇ If people are **displaced**, they are forced to move away from the area where they live, usually because of a war. *...the displacement of two million people.*

❏ The **displacement** of a ship or boat is the weight of water it displaces when it is afloat.

display ❏ If you **display** something, you put it somewhere where people can see it; you then say it is **on display**. ◇ A **display** is an attractive arrangement of things. *...a window display... ...a summer flower display.* ◇ A **display** is also a show, especially an outdoor one, put on to impress and entertain people. *...a firework display.*

❏ The **display** of something like a computer is the electronic representation of information on the screen.

❏ If you **display** a quality, you show you have it. You can also **display** an emotion, or a skill. When several people show the same feeling about something, you can talk about a **display** of that feeling. *...a display of enthusiasm.*

displease (displeasing, displeased; displeasure) If something **displeases** you, it makes you dissatisfied or annoyed. When this happens, you say you are **displeased**; you call this feeling **displeasure**.

disposable things are designed to be thrown away after they have been used once. *...disposable nappies... ...disposable syringes.*

❏ Your **disposable income** is the money you have left to spend after you have paid your taxes. **Disposable income** is also sometimes used to talk about the money someone has left to spend on luxuries, after they have paid for essentials like food.

disposal ❏ If something is at your **disposal**, you can use it whenever you want to.

❏ **Disposal** is getting rid of something. *...the disposal of hazardous waste.*

dispose (disposing, disposed) ❏ If you **dispose of** something you no longer want or need, you get rid of it. ◇ If a business or organization **disposes** of some of its property, it sells it off.

❏ If you say someone is **disposed** to do something, you mean they want to do it, or are willing to do it. ◇ If you are **well disposed** towards something like a proposal, you are in favour of it. ◇ If you are **well disposed** to a person, you feel friendly towards them.

disposition If you talk about a person's **disposition**, you are describing the way they tend to behave and respond to things. *...not recommended for those of a nervous disposition.* ◇ A **disposition** to do something is a willingness to do it. *This has given him a disposition to consider our traditions critically.*

dispossess (dispossesses, dispossessing; dispossession) If you are **dispossessed** of something which belongs to you, especially your home, it is taken away from you. *...the dispossession of peasants and smallholders.* People who have lost their homes are often called the **dispossessed**.

disproportion (disproportionate, disproportionately) If there is a **disproportion** of something, there is an unusually large amount of it compared to other things. You say something like this is **disproportionate**. *A huge disproportion of those who died in Vietnam were black... ...the disproportionate amount of time devoted to sport... There is a disproportionately high suicide rate among prisoners facing very long sentences.*

disprove (disproving, disproved) If you **disprove** a statement or belief, you show it is not true or not correct.

disputable If you say something is **disputable**, you mean it is not necessarily true or correct.

disputatious people tend to argue about things.

dispute (disputing, disputed) A **dispute** is a disagreement or quarrel. ◇ If people are **in dispute**, they are having a serious disagreement about something. ◇ If something is **in dispute**, people disagree about it. ◇ If you **dispute** something, you say it is not true. ◇ When people **dispute** the ownership of something, they all claim it is theirs.

disqualify (disqualifies, disqualifying, disqualified; disqualification) If someone is **disqualified** from a competition, they are no longer allowed to compete, because they have broken a rule. If they are disqualified after the competition is over, they lose any position or prize they may have gained. ◇ If someone is **disqualified** from doing something, they are not allowed to do it, usually because they have broken the law. *...disqualification from driving.*

disquiet (disquieting, disquieted) **Disquiet** is a feeling of anxiety or worry. If someone has this feeling, you say they are **disquieted**. If something is **disquieting**, it makes you anxious or worried.

disregard If you **disregard** something, you ignore it, or do not take it seriously. You can talk about someone's **disregard** for something. *...the regime's total disregard for human rights.*

disrepair If something like a building is **in disrepair** or has **fallen into disrepair**, it is in bad condition because it has not been maintained properly.

disreputable A **disreputable** person is not respectable or trustworthy.

disrepute If something is brought into **disrepute**, it loses its good reputation.

disrespect (disrespectful) If you show **disrespect** for someone or something, you behave in a way which shows you do not care about them, or do not think they are important. When people behave like this, you say they are being **disrespectful**.

disrobe (disrobing, disrobed) When someone **disrobes**, they take their clothes off.

disrupt (disruption) If you **disrupt** something, you interfere with it and stop it proceeding in its normal way. *...widespread disruption caused by transport strikes.*

disruptive A **disruptive** person causes problems and prevents things proceeding smoothly.

dissatisfied (dissatisfaction) If you are **dissatisfied** with something, you are not happy about it and are not prepared to accept it. This feeling is called **dissatisfaction**.

dissect (dissection) If someone **dissects** a dead animal or person, they cut up their body so they can examine it. This is called a **dissection**. ◇ If someone examines something carefully and in great detail, you can say they **dissect** it. *...the dissection of the mind under psychoanalysis.*

dissemble (dissembling, dissembled) If someone **dissembles**, they hide their real motives or feelings by pretending to have different ones.

disseminate (disseminating, disseminated; dissemination) If information is **disseminated**, it is distributed to many people. *...the dissemination of anti-communist literature.*

dissent (dissenter, dissension) When people **dissent**, they express disagreement with established ideas. People who do this are called **dissenters**; their disagreement is called **dissent** or **dissension**.

dissertation A **dissertation** is a long formal piece of writing, especially one written for a university degree.

disservice If you do someone a **disservice**, you unintentionally harm them or make things difficult for them.

dissident (dissidence) A **dissident** is someone who criticizes their government or the organization they belong to, especially when such behaviour is not normal or not allowed. **Dissidence** is behaviour like this.

dissimilar (dissimilarity, dissimilarities) If two things are **dissimilar**, they are not like each other. **Dissimilarities** are differences between things.

dissipate (dissipating, dissipated; dissipation) If something **dissipates** or is **dissipated**, it gradually gets less and disappears. *...the dissipation of her wealth.* ◇ You call a person **dissipated** when they have harmed their health by too much drinking and other physical pleasures. You can say a person like this has lived a life of **dissipation**.

dissociate (dissociating, dissociated; dissociation) If you **dissociate** yourself from someone or something, you say you are not involved with them, or you refuse to have anything to do with them. *...his dissociation from the crimes of the past.* ◇ If you **dissociate** one thing from another, you regard them as two separate things.

dissolute A **dissolute** person lives in a way considered to be immoral or wicked.

dissolve (dissolving, dissolved; dissolution) ❑ If something solid **dissolves** in a liquid, it becomes absorbed in it.

❑ If an organization is **dissolved**, it is officially ended. You call this its **dissolution**. ◇ When parliament is **dissolved**, it breaks up just before a general election. You call this the **dissolution** of parliament.

❑ If something **dissolves into** a particular state, it deteriorates or breaks down into that state. *He warned that the country would dissolve into chaos.*

dissonant (dissonance) If music is **dissonant**, groups of notes are played together which do not harmonize. The effect produced is called **dissonance**.

dissuade (dissuading, dissuaded) If you **dissuade** someone from doing something, you persuade them not to do it.

distaff The **distaff side** means women generally, or the female members of a particular group.

distance (distancing, distanced) ❑ The **distance** between two places or things is how far it is between them. ◇ If something is **in the distance** or **at a distance**, it is a long way away. If you do something **from a distance**, you do it from a long way away.

❑ **Distance** is also used to say how different one thing is from each other. For example, you can talk about the **distance** between two points of view. ◇ If you **distance** yourself from a person or situation, you claim not to be involved with them.

❑ If a boxing match **goes the distance**, it lasts its full number of rounds, and is not stopped because of an injury or knockout.

distant (distantly) ❏ **Distant** is used to describe things which are a long way away. ...*the rumble of distant artillery.* ◇ **Distant** is sometimes used to say how far away something is. *Wimereux is four-and-a-half miles distant.*

❏ If you talk about the **distant past**, you mean a very long time ago. Similarly, you can talk about the **distant future**. If you say something will happen in the **not too distant future**, you mean it will happen quite soon. ◇ **Distant** memories are of things which happened a long time ago. ◇ **Distant** is sometimes used to say how long it will be before something happens. *A general election is four years distant.*

❏ A **distant** relative is one you are not closely related to. *His father is distantly related to the royal family.*

❏ **Distant** people are cold and unemotional. ◇ **Distant** is also used to say someone is not paying attention, because they are thinking about something else. *His eyes took on a glazed, distant look.*

distaste (distasteful) **Distaste** is a strong feeling of dislike. If you find something **distasteful**, you strongly dislike it.

distemper is a dangerous infectious disease which affects animals, especially dogs. ◇ In the past, **distemper** was a type of paint used for decorating.

distended If a part of someone's body is **distended**, it is swollen.

distil (distilling, distilled; distillation) When a liquid is **distilled**, it is heated until it becomes a vapour, then cooled until it is a liquid again; this is a way of removing substances from it, for example salt from sea water. The process is called **distillation**. ◇ You also say something is **distilled** when it is concentrated or condensed into something relatively small and simple. *First transmitted in 1964, 'The Great War' distilled a conflict lasting 1,551 days into 17 hours of television.*

distiller A **distiller** is a person or company that makes whisky or some other spirit by distillation.

distillery (distilleries) A **distillery** is a place where whisky or some other spirit is made.

distinct (distinctly, distinctness) ❏ If one thing is **distinct** from another, it has features the other thing does not have, and is therefore not the same thing. You say several things are **distinct** when each has features the others do not have. *Scientists will identify six distinct areas in the forest.* If something is unlike anything else, you can talk about its **distinctness**. ◇ You use **as distinct from** to show you are talking about one thing rather than another. *He is said to be defending the benefits paid to the disabled as distinct from the long-term sick.*

❏ **Distinct** and **distinctly** are also used to say something is noticeable or significant. *I gained the distinct impression that they are ready for a compromise... ...a distinctly cool response.*

distinction ❏ A **distinction** is a difference between two similar things. ◇ **draw a distinction: see draw.**

❏ If you do something with **distinction**, you do it extremely well. ◇ A **distinction** is (a) an honour. *The Order of Merit was created in 1902 as a special distinction for eminent men and women.* (b) something which makes someone special or unique. *The goal gave him the distinction of being Northern Ireland's all-time leading scorer.*

distinctive (distinctively, distinctiveness) If something is **distinctive**, there is something about it which distinguishes it from other similar things. ...*his distinctively exotic style... Channel 4's distinctiveness is its unique selling point.*

distinguish (distinguishes, distinguishing, distinguished) ❏ If you can **distinguish** one thing from another, you can see or understand the difference between them. ◇ If a feature **distinguishes** one thing from another, it makes them recognizable as different things.

❏ If you can **distinguish** something, you can just see it, hear it, or taste it.

❏ If you **distinguish** yourself, you do something which makes you famous, important, or admired. A **distinguished** person is very successful, famous, or important.

distinguishable If something is **distinguishable** from other things, it can be recognized as different from them. ◇ You also say something is **distinguishable** when it can just be seen or heard.

distort (distortion) If a fact or idea is **distorted**, it is represented wrongly. A wrong representation of something is called a **distortion**. *Jana said the charges were a distortion of what had actually happened.* ◇ If an object is **distorted**, it is changed in an unusual way or forced into an unnatural or strange shape. ...*blackened skeletons of trees and shrubs distorted by fire.*

distract (distraction) ❏ If something **distracts** you or **distracts** your attention, it makes you take notice of it, so you cannot concentrate on what you are trying to do. You say something like this is **distracting** or a **distraction**. ◇ If someone is **distracted**, they are not concentrating on what they are doing, because they have something on their mind. ◇ If something is done to **distract attention** from something unpleasant or embarrassing, it is done to draw people's attention away from it.

❏ **Distractions** are things which are there for you to enjoy, and which take your mind off your problems or work. ...*a city with many distractions.*

distraught If someone is **distraught**, they are extremely worried or upset.

distress (distresses, distressing, distressed; distressingly) ❏ **Distress** is extreme anxiety, sorrow, or pain. *The Prime Minister has expressed deep distress at recent incidents... Gascoigne collapsed in obvious distress.* If you are **distressed** or something **distresses** you, it gives you these feelings. If something is **distressing**, it makes you feel like this. *He had a distressingly sad start in life.*

❏ **Distress** is also used to talk about dangerous situations in which people urgently need help. *The vessel sent out a distress call.*

distribute (distributing, distributed; distribution) ❏ If you **distribute** things like leaflets, you hand them out to people or send them by post. ◇ When goods are **distributed**, they are supplied to the shops or businesses which sell them or use them.

❏ If you talk about the way things are **distributed**, you are talking about the numbers of them in different places. *The provision of help for children with mental problems was unevenly distributed through the country... ...changes in the distribution of animals and plants.*

distributor ❏ A **distributor** is a person, company, or organization that supplies goods to shops, businesses, or countries. ◇ Shops are sometimes called **distributors**.

❏ In the ignition system of a petrol engine, the **distributor** is a device which sends electric current to the spark plugs in the correct sequence.

district A **district** is an area of town or country without definite boundaries but with features which distinguish it from other areas. ◇ A **District** is an area which has official boundaries for administration purposes. *...North Cornwall District.*

district attorney (*pron:* a-ter-nee) In the US, a **district attorney** or **D.A.** is a lawyer who prosecutes criminal cases on behalf of the State or Federal government.

district nurse A **district nurse** is a nurse who goes to people's homes to give them medical treatment.

distrust (distrustful) If you **distrust** someone or something or are **distrustful** of them, you do not think they are honest or reliable; you can also talk about your **distrust** of them.

disturb (disturbingly) ❏ If you **disturb** someone, you interrupt them while they are doing something. ◇ If someone or something **disturbs** a situation, they make it less peaceful, organized, or stable. *Anyone disturbing public order will be treated with the full rigour of the law.*

❏ If something **disturbs** people, it makes them upset or worried. You say something which has this effect is **disturbing**. *Human rights abuses are disturbingly frequent.* You talk about people being **disturbed** by things like this.

❏ A **disturbed** person has serious psychological problems.

❏ If you **disturb** something, you move it away from its usual position.

disturbance If there is a **disturbance** somewhere, people start behaving violently. ◇ If there is a **disturbance** of something, it is made less peaceful or stable. *...a disturbance of the heart's rhythm.* ◇ **Disturbance** is also extreme unhappiness or mental illness. *The impact on children often involved high levels of disturbance and traumatization.*

disunity (disunited) **Disunity** is a lack of agreement between people, which prevents them working together effectively. You say people like this are **disunited**.

disuse (disused) If something falls into **disuse** (*pron:* dis-yooss) or is **disused** (*pron:* dis-yoozd), it is no longer used. *...a disused quarry.*

ditch (ditches, ditching, ditched) ❏ A **ditch** is a long narrow channel cut into the ground at the side of a road or field, usually for water to drain into.

❏ If you **ditch** something, you get rid of it.

❏ If you make a **last ditch** attempt to achieve something, you make a final attempt to achieve it, knowing you will not get another chance.

dither (dithering, dithered; ditherer) If someone **dithers**, they hesitate because they cannot decide what to do. Someone who does this is called a **ditherer**.

ditto You use **ditto** to represent a word or phrase you have just used, to avoid repeating it. *Sinatra's fee was so huge the show was not a great earner. Ditto the George Foreman fight.* In written lists, 'ditto' can be represented by the symbol " underneath the word or phrase you want to avoid repeating.

ditty (ditties) A **ditty** is a short simple song or poem.

diuretic (*pron:* die-yoo-ret-ik) **Diuretics** are medicines or

drinks which increase the amount of urine produced by the body.

diva (*pron:* dee-va) A **diva** is a famous female opera singer.

divan (*pron:* di-van) A **divan** or **divan bed** is a bed with a thick padded base rather than a frame.

dive (diving, dived; diver) ❏ If you **dive**, you jump head-first into water. A jump like this is called a **dive**. When people do this in a skilful way, it is called **diving**; the people who do it are called **divers**.

❏ You also say someone **dives** when they fling their body in a particular direction. *Dr Mogoba had to dive for cover as the bullets flew.* ◇ If an aircraft **dives** or goes into a **dive**, it falls rapidly with its nose towards the ground.

❏ **Diving** is also used to talk about people going underwater for long periods, with or without breathing equipment. A person who does this is called a **diver**.

❏ When things like prices **dive** or **take a dive**, they drop suddenly by a large amount.

diverge (diverging, diverged) ❏ If things **diverge**, they are different, or become different. *...diverging interests... No wonder fact and forecast diverge so often and by so much.* ◇ When someone **diverges** from something like a rule, they do not follow it.

❏ If a road **diverges**, it splits into two or more roads.

divergent (divergence) If things are **divergent**, they are opposing or different. *...widely divergent economies... ...the wide divergence between opinion polls.*

diverse (diversity) **Diverse** people, places, ideas, or objects are different and distinct from each other. *The world of politics relies on persuasion and co-operation to reconcile diverse interests.* ◇ If something is **diverse**, it is made up of a wide variety of things. You talk about the **diversity** of something like this. *...the diversity of British broadcasting.*

diversify (diversifies, diversifying, diversified; diversification) When a business **diversifies**, it makes or does types of things it did not previously do. *...a programme of growth and diversification.*

diversion ❏ A **diversion** is something which distracts your attention and makes you think about something else. ◇ **Diversion** is enjoyment. *They meet together for merriment and diversion.*

❏ A **diversion** is also a special route for traffic when the usual route cannot be used. ◇ The **diversion** of something is the changing of its route or destination. *The diversion of the rivers began twenty years ago.* ◇ If you talk about the **diversion** of something like money, you mean its use for a purpose it was not intended for.

diversionary activities are intended to draw people's attention away from something.

diversity See **diverse**.

divert If something is **diverted**, its route or destination is changed. ◇ If something like money is **diverted**, it is used for a purpose it was not intended for. ◇ If you **divert** someone's attention, you stop them thinking about something by making them think about something else.

divest If you **divest** yourself of something, you get rid of it. If you **divest** someone else of something, you take it away from them. *The young man was divested of his briefcase and shirt.*

divide (dividing, divided) ❏ When something **divides** or is **divided**, it separates into two or more parts. ◇ If you divide something among a group of people or **divide it up**, you give some of it to each of them. ◇ If something **divides** two areas, it forms a barrier or boundary between them. *...the river that divides Chad from Cameroon.*

❏ If you **divide** one number by another, you work out how many times the second one will go into the first.

❏ If people are **divided** about something or it **divides** them, they disagree about it. ◇ If someone has **divided loyalties,** they feel they have a duty towards two or more people and cannot choose between them.

❏ A **divide** is a significant difference between people or things. *...the big divide between classical music and jazz.* ◇ A **dividing line** is something which distinguishes one group of people or things from another. *The 80-metre mark is the dividing line between throwers of true class and the rest.*

dividend A **dividend** is a part of a company's profits which is paid to its shareholders in proportion to the number of shares they own.

dividers are an instrument for measuring and marking points along lines. They are made of two pointed arms joined together at one end.

divination is the supernatural ability some people claim to have to predict the future or find out other unknown information.

divine (divining, divined; divinely) ❏ **Divine** is used to talk about things connected with God, or with some other god or goddess. *...the divinely inspired word of the Bible.* If people say something has happened as a result of **divine intervention,** they mean God made it happen. ◇ If someone claims to have a **divine right** to something, they mean their right to it is decreed by God.

❏ If you **divine** something, you sense it or find it out intuitively. *He will have to divine his enemies' motives carefully.*

diving bell A **diving bell** is a chamber where people can work deep underwater. It has a roof and walls, but it is open to the water underneath and is supplied with pressurized air from tubes connecting it to the surface.

diving board A **diving board** is a board above a swimming pool which people can dive from.

divinity (divinities) **Divinity** is the study of the Christian religion. ◇ **Divinity** is also the quality of being divine. *...the divinity of Christ.* ◇ A **divinity** is a god or goddess.

division ❏ When the **division** of something takes place, it is separated into two or more parts. ◇ **Division** is also used to talk about the sharing of power. *...the division of authority between federal and republican governments.* ◇ When there is a **division of labour** in a community or organization, each member has a special task which contributes to the running of the whole.

❏ **Division** is disagreement within a group of people, or between groups.

❏ In sports and other competitions, league tables are often separated into **divisions.** In each season, a team plays all the other teams in its division twice, and at the end of the season it moves up or down a division or stays where it is, depending on its results.

❏ A **division** is also (a) a group of military units fighting as a single unit. (b) a section of a large organization dealing with one part of its business.

❏ **Division** is the mathematical process of dividing one number by another.

divisional is used to talk about (a) things connected with

a military division. *...a divisional commander.* (b) things connected with one of the divisions of a business. *...the store's divisional manager for fashion.*

divisive (divisiveness) If something is **divisive,** it makes people split into groups with opposite points of view. *...the divisiveness of party politics.*

divorce (divorcing, divorced; divorcee) ❏ When someone **divorces** their husband or wife or gets a **divorce,** their marriage is legally ended. A **divorced** person or **divorcee** is someone whose marriage has ended in this way.

❏ If one thing is **divorced** from another, it is separated from it.

divot A **divot** is a small piece of grass and earth which is dug out accidentally, especially by a golf club.

divulge (divulging, divulged) If you **divulge** information, especially secret or private information, you tell it to people.

Diwali (*pron:* di-wah-lee) is the major Hindu festival honouring Lakshmi, the goddess of wealth. It takes place in the Autumn. People give each other presents, and there is feasting and the lighting of lamps.

dixieland is a traditional type of jazz which developed in New Orleans. It is played by a small group of instruments, usually including a trombone, clarinet, and trumpet.

DIY See **do-it-yourself.**

dizzy (dizziness, dizzying) If you feel **dizzy,** you have a feeling of loss of balance or confusion. This feeling is called **dizziness.** You say something is **dizzying** when it makes you feel like this. ◇ If someone rises to **dizzy** or **dizzying heights,** they become very successful and famous.

DJ See **disc jockey.**

DM See **Deutschmark.**

DMs See **Doc Martens.**

DNA is an acid in the cells of living things. It contains a biological code which determines the characteristics of a person or other living thing, and is the means by which these characteristics are passed on from parents to children. DNA stands for 'deoxyribonucleic acid'.

do (does, doing, did, have done) ❏ **Do** is used with 'not' to form negative statements. 'Do not', 'does not', and 'did not' are often shortened to 'don't', 'doesn't', and 'didn't'. ◇ **Do** is also used with 'not' to tell someone not to behave in a certain way. *Do not let the water boil... Don't worry.*

❏ **Do** is used in questions. *When did they actually happen?... Why don't you go home?*

❏ **Do** is used instead of repeating a word. *She knew more about Dorothy than I did.*

❏ **Do** is used to give emphasis. *You really do deserve the award.*

❏ When you **do** something, you perform an action, activity, or task. **Do** is often used to talk about common actions, or ones you perform regularly. For example, if you **do** the dishes, you wash them. ◇ **Do** is used to say what someone's job is. *What do you want to do when you leave school?*

❏ **Do** is used to say something has a particular result or effect. *Sulphur does far less damage to forests than car exhausts.*

❏ **Do** is used to talk about how fast something is going or how fast it can go. *The vehicle had been doing 65mph.*

❏ **To do with** is used to say what something is related to or concerned with. *The attacks had nothing to do with drugs-related terrorism.*

❏ If you say you **could do with** something, you mean you need it or it would be helpful. ◇ If you **do without** something, you manage or survive in spite of not having it. ◇ **make do with**: see **make**. ◇ If you say something will **do**, you mean it is satisfactory.

❏ If you have **done** with something, you have finished with it. ◇ If you **do away** with something, you get rid of it. *...the proposal to do away with nuclear weapons.* ◇ If someone **does away** with someone else, they kill them.

❏ If you ask how someone or something is **doing**, you are asking how they are getting on. ◇ When someone is performing a task and you say they **know what they are doing**, you mean they are competent and capable of doing the task well.

❏ If someone **does you out** of something you are entitled to, they cheat you out of it.

❏ If you say something is **the done thing**, you mean it is respectable, fashionable, or usual to do it.

❏ If food, especially meat, is **well done**, it has been cooked very thoroughly.

do-gooder If you call someone a **do-gooder**, you mean they think they are helping people, but in fact they are just interfering or being a nuisance.

do-it-yourself or **DIY** is making or repairing things in your own home. **Do-it-yourself** and **DIY** are also used to talk about unqualified people doing things which are usually done by experts. *...do-it-yourself cholesterol tests... ...a little legal DIY.*

Doc Martens or **DMs** are heavy-duty lace-up shoes or boots with thick resistant soles and strong yellow stitching. They were originally designed for workmen, but have been incorporated into various fashion trends since the late 1960s. 'Doc Martens' is a trademark.

docile (docility) A **docile** person or animal is quiet and easily controlled. You can talk about a person's or animal's **docility**.

dock ❏ A **dock** is an enclosed area of water where ships are loaded, unloaded, and repaired. When a ship **docks**, it comes into a dock. ◇ When spaceships **dock**, they move together and connect; a spaceship can also **dock** with a space station.

❏ In a law court, the **dock** is the place where the accused person stands or sits.

❏ If your pay is **docked**, some of it is kept by your employer, for example because you have been absent from work. ◇ If an animal's tail is **docked**, it is cut off.

docker Dockers or dock workers are people who work at the docks, loading and unloading ships.

dockland The **dockland** of a large port is the area around its docks.

dockside The **dockside** area of a large port is the area next to its docks. *...dockside slums.*

dockyard A **dockyard** is a place where ships are built, maintained, and repaired.

doctor (doctorate, doctoral; doctoring, doctored) ❏ A **doctor** is a person qualified in medicine who treats sick or injured people. In front of a person's name, 'Doctor' is usually shortened to 'Dr'.

❏ **Doctor** is also a title given to someone who has been awarded the highest kind of academic degree. This degree is called a **doctorate**. A **doctoral** thesis or piece of research is completed to achieve this degree.

❏ If something is **doctored**, it is deliberately changed, to deceive people. *...a doctored photograph.*

doctrinaire When people behave in a **doctrinaire** way, they put theories or principles into practice regardless of the practical difficulties.

doctrine (doctrinal) A **doctrine** is a principle or belief, or a set of principles or beliefs. **Doctrinal** is used to talk about things to do with doctrines. *Religious groups are free to air their doctrinal differences.*

docudrama A **docudrama** is a film based on actual events, with actors playing the parts of real people. The dialogue is invented, but is intended to represent the sort of conversations which probably took place.

document A **document** is an official piece of paper containing written information. ◇ If you **document** something, you make a detailed record of it.

documentary (documentaries) A **documentary** is a TV or radio programme or film which gives information rather than telling a story. ◇ **Documentary** evidence is written information in support of something like a legal case.

documentation is written permission, evidence, or proof.

doddering (doddery) Old people are sometimes called **doddering** or **doddery**, especially when they are thought to be too old to do something properly.

doddle If you say something is a **doddle**, you mean it is extremely easy.

dodge (dodging, dodged; dodger) ❏ If you **dodge** something, you avoid doing it, dealing with it, or paying it. *Mr Baker dodged the question... ...their tax-dodging friends.* A **dodge** is a way of avoiding something. *...a legal dodge.* People who try to avoid doing things or paying for things are called **dodgers**. *...fare dodgers.*

❏ If you **dodge** a moving object, you get out of its way quickly. ◇ If you **dodge** somewhere, you move there quickly, to avoid being seen.

dodgem A **dodgem** or **dodgem car** is a small electric car with a thick rubber bumper all round its outside. Dodgems are driven for fun in special enclosures at fairgrounds.

dodgy If you call something someone does **dodgy**, you mean it seems dishonest or not respectable. ◇ You can also call something **dodgy** when it is unreliable or of poor quality.

dodo (dodos) The **dodo** was a large flightless bird on the island of Mauritius, which became extinct in the 17th century. If you say something is **dead as a dodo**, you mean it no longer exists. If you call something a **dodo**, you mean it is out-of-date.

doe The females of various animals, including deer, rabbits, and hares, are called **does**.

doer If you call someone a **doer**, you mean they do things, rather than just talking or writing about them. ◇ **Evil doers** or **wrong doers** are people who do bad or wicked things.

dog (dogging, dogged) ❏ **Dogs** are four-legged animals, kept as pets or for guarding or hunting. There are many different breeds. ◇ The **dog** family includes wild animals like foxes, wolves, and hyenas, besides the dog kept by man. The male of any of these species is called a dog, to distinguish it from the female.

❑ If someone is **in the dog house**, they are in disgrace.

❑ If something **dogs** you, it continually causes you trouble. *His international career has been dogged by controversy and injury.*

❑ See also **dogged**.

dog-collar A **dog-collar** is a white collar worn back-to-front by Christian priests and ministers.

dog-eared A **dog-eared** book or piece of paper has been used so much the corners of the pages are folded or crumpled.

dogfight (dogfighting) ❑ A **dogfight** is a mid-air battle between two fighter aircraft. ◇ When there is fierce competition for something, you can call this a **dogfight**.

❑ **Dogfighting** is an illegal blood sport in which two specially trained dogs are allowed to fight to the death, usually with spectators betting on the result.

dogged (*pron:* dog-gid) (doggedly) If you do something in a **dogged** way, you keep doing it in spite of all difficulties. *He is still doggedly pursuing a diplomatic solution.*

doggerel You call poetry **doggerel** when it is of very poor quality. *...greetings-card doggerel.*

dogma A **dogma** is a rigid belief or system of beliefs, especially one held by a religious or political group.

dogmatic (dogmatically, dogmatist, dogmatism) If someone is being **dogmatic**, they are following a set of rules or principles rigidly, regardless of practical difficulties and other people's opinions or suggestions. Someone who behaves like this is called a **dogmatist**; their behaviour is called **dogmatism**.

doily (doilies) A **doily** is a decorative mat made from paper or cloth with a pattern of small holes in it. You put a doily on a plate under something like a cake.

doings You can call someone's activities their **doings**, especially when they are reported in the media. *...the mundane doings of the royal family.*

dojo (dojos) A **dojo** is a place where people practise martial arts like judo or karate.

Dolby is a technique or system which uses electronic processing to reduce the amount of background noise on a sound recording. 'Dolby' is a trademark.

doldrums If something is **in the doldrums**, it is in a depressed state with not much happening to it.

dole (doling, doled) ❑ The **dole** is money given regularly by the government to some unemployed people. Its proper name is 'unemployment benefit'. If someone is **on the dole**, they are receiving dole.

❑ If you **dole** something **out**, you give amounts of it to several people or groups.

doleful (dolefully) If someone is **doleful**, they are sad and depressed. *Keeler glanced back dolefully.*

doll (dolled) ❑ A **doll** is a small model of a person or baby, especially one used as a child's toy. ◇ A **doll's house** is a model house used as a toy.

❑ If a woman is **dolled up**, she is wearing expensive or eye-catching clothes.

dollar The **dollar** is the unit of currency in the US, Canada, Australia, New Zealand, and many other countries. One dollar is divided into 100 cents. Dollars are usually represented by the symbol $.

dollop A **dollop** of something is a largish amount of it.

The film contains a good dollop of witty lines. ◇ A **dollop** of soft or sticky food is an amount served in a lump.

dolphin Dolphins are small whales with long snouts. They live in the sea and usually swim in groups. They are thought to be unusually intelligent.

dolphinarium A **dolphinarium** is a large pool, often in a zoo, where trained dolphins and killer whales perform.

domain Someone's **domain** is the area they have control or influence over. ◇ If you say something is the **domain** of a group of people, you mean it is regarded as something they deal with, rather than anyone else.

dome (domed) A **dome** is a round roof shaped like half a ball. If a building is **domed**, it has a roof like this.

domestic (domestically) ❑ **Domestic** is used to talk about things happening within a country, rather than between that country and other countries. *...Canada's domestic air traffic... The objective is to make Indian industry more competitive domestically.*

❑ **Domestic** is also used to talk about (a) things to do with the home and the family. *...domestic violence.* (b) objects for use in the home rather than in factories, shops, or offices. *...domestic electric appliances.* ◇ A **domestic** is a person employed to do work like cooking and cleaning in someone's home.

❑ **Domestic** animals are kept in people's homes or on farms, and are there as pets or to do work or provide food.

domestic science is the same as home economics.

domesticate (domesticating, domesticated) When wild animals are **domesticated**, they are brought under human control and kept as pets or to do work or provide food. ◇ If you say a person is **domesticated**, you mean they are able to do household tasks like cooking and cleaning, and do not mind doing them.

domesticity is being at home with your family.

domicile (domiciled) Your **domicile** is the place where you live. You can say someone is **domiciled** in a place. *...the Surrey-domiciled New Zealander.* Officially, your **domicile** is the country where you have a permanent home. ◇ The **domicile** of an organization is its location for tax and legal purposes. You say an organization is **domiciled** in a particular location.

dominant (dominance) ❑ You say someone is **dominant** when they have a lot of power over other people. *Morgan Phillips was a dominant figure in the Labour Party.* You can talk about someone's **dominance** over other people. ◇ You also say someone is **dominant** or talk about their **dominance** when they are more successful at something than other people. *...Wigan's dominance of the game.*

❑ The **dominant** feature of something is the most noticeable thing about it.

dominate (dominating, dominated; domination) ❑ If a system or organization is **dominated** by a group of people, they are the ones with most power in it. ◇ If one country **dominates** another one, it has power and control over it. *The republics see themselves as breaking free from Russian domination.* ◇ If someone **dominates** something like a sport, they are better at it than anyone else.

❑ If a feature **dominates** a place or a view, it is so large it draws your attention more than anything else. *Manningham Mills dominates Bradford's skyline.*

domineering A **domineering** person likes telling other people what to do.

dominion If someone has **dominion** over a group of people, they have control or authority over them.

domino (dominoes) ❑ A **domino** is a small flat rectangular block divided in two, with a number of spots in each half. A set of these blocks is used to play **dominoes**, a game in which players try to get rid of all their dominoes by matching up halves of dominoes which have the same number of spots.

❑ When people talk about the **domino** effect, they are describing a series of happenings in which each thing sets off the next one. The happenings are being compared to a line of dominoes standing on their ends; when you knock the first one down, the others all go down in turn.

don (donning, donned) ❑ A **don** is a lecturer at Oxford or Cambridge University.

❑ If you **don** a piece of clothing, you put it on.

donate (donating, donated; donation) If you **donate** something, for example to a charity, you give it; your gift is called a **donation**.

done See **do**.

doner kebab See **kebab**.

donkey The **donkey** is an animal related to the horse but smaller and with longer ears. ◇ The **donkey work** is the part of a job which is particularly boring and does not require much skill, intelligence, or imagination.

donkey jacket A **donkey jacket** is a thick warm jacket with a waterproof panel across the shoulders, often worn by workmen.

donnish A **donnish** person is clever and rather serious.

donor A **donor** is someone who allows organs to be removed from their body, either before or after their death, for use in transplants. ◇ **blood donor**: see **blood**. ◇ A **donor** is also someone who gives money or something else to a charity.

doodle (doodling, doodled) If you **doodle**, for example at a meeting, you draw a pattern or picture on the paper in front of you, often because you are bored. Drawings like these are called **doodles** or **doodlings**.

doom (dooming, doomed) **Doom** is used to talk about death or some other terrible and final situation which cannot be avoided. *The fish are lured to their doom... ...forecasts of environmental doom.* You can say someone or something is **doomed** to something like this. ◇ If you say something like a project was **doomed**, you mean it was certain to fail. *The whole affair was doomed from the start.*

doomsayers are people who expect the worst to happen and depress people by continually talking about it.

doomsday is the end of the world.

door ❑ A **door** is a swinging or sliding piece of wood, glass, or metal which is used to open and close the entrance to a building, room, cupboard, or vehicle. ◇ If you **show** someone **the door**, you ask them to leave.

❑ When you are **out of doors**, you are in the open air, rather than in a building.

❑ If something is a certain number of **doors** up or down from you, it is that number of houses further along the road.

❑ If something **opens the door** to something else, it makes it possible. If it **closes the door**, it rules out all possibility of it happening. *A deal with Japan could open the door to economic co-operation with East Asia.* ◇ If you have **the door shut** or **slammed in your face**, you are told firmly

you will not be allowed to do something.

❑ If you **lay** something **at** someone's **door**, you blame them for it.

❑ **next door**: see **next**. ◇ See also **back door**.

door-to-door activities involve people calling at one house after another along a street, to sell things or get information.

doorbell A **doorbell** is a bell on or near an outside door, which you ring to get the people inside to open the door.

doorknob A **doorknob** is a round handle on a door, for opening it.

doorman (doormen) A **doorman** is a man whose job it is to stand at the entrance of a place like a hotel or club, and to maintain security and help visitors.

doormat A **doormat** is a mat by a door for people to wipe their feet on. ◇ If you say a person is a **doormat**, you mean people make use of them without showing any interest in their feelings.

doorstep (doorstepping, doorstepped) ❑ A **doorstep** is a step on the outside of a building, in front of a door. ◇ When reporters and photographers **doorstep** someone, they wait outside their house or workplace, asking them questions or trying to photograph them when they go in or out.

❑ If something is **on the doorstep** of a place, it is very near to it. *Italy and Austria are worried about instability on their doorstep.*

doorstop A **doorstop** is an object used to hold a door open.

doorway A **doorway** is the space left in a wall when a door is open.

dopamine (*pron:* dop-a-min) is a chemical in the brain. It helps nerve impulses to travel from one nerve to another, or from a nerve to a muscle. Lack of dopamine can cause Parkinson's disease.

dope (doping, doped) ❑ **Dope** is drugs taken illegally by sportspeople to improve their performance. Racehorses can also be given dope, either to make them go faster or to slow them down. All these practices are called **doping**. When a horse is given drugs, you say it is **doped**. ◇ You also say someone **dopes** a person or animal when they put a drug in their food or drink to make them drowsy or unconscious.

❑ **Dope** is also cannabis.

dopey If you say someone is **dopey**, you mean (a) they are half-asleep. (b) they are slow and rather stupid.

doppelgänger In myth and fairytale, a person's **doppelgänger** is a ghostly creature who looks exactly like them. If you see someone who looks exactly like someone else, you can say they are their **doppelgänger**.

dorm A **dorm** at a boarding school is a dormitory.

dormant If something is **dormant**, it is not active at present but might become so in the future. *...a dormant volcano... The bacterium remains dormant when in contact with the air.*

dormer window A **dormer window** or **dormer** is an upright window projecting from a sloping roof.

dormitory (dormitories) A **dormitory** is a large room where a number of people sleep, for example in a boarding school or hostel.

dormouse (dormice) **Dormice** are small animals similar to mice. They sleep for several months each winter.

dorsal fin A fish's **dorsal fin** is the fin sticking up on top of its back.

dosage A **dosage** of a medicine or drug is an amount taken at one time.

dose (dosing, dosed) A **dose** of a vitamin, medicine, or drug is an amount taken at one time. ◇ If you **dose** someone with drugs or medicine, you administer them to them.

dosh is money.

doss (dosses, dossing, dossed) If you **doss down** somewhere, especially in an uncomfortable place, you settle down to sleep there.

doss-house A **doss-house** is a cheap unpleasant city hotel for people with no home and very little money.

dossier A **dossier** is a collection of papers containing information on a subject.

dot (dotting, dotted) A **dot** is a very small round mark. ◇ If things are **dotted** around an area, they are in many different parts, and in no particular pattern. ...*refugee camps dotted around Italy*. You can also say an area is **dotted** with things. *The shoreline was dotted with lights*.

dotage If someone is **in their dotage**, they are very old and have lost some of their mental powers.

dote (doting, doted) If someone **dotes on** you, they are obsessively fond of you and keep showing you love and affection. **Doting** is used to describe people who behave like this. ...*a young woman with a doting father*.

doth is an old word for 'does'. *Conscience doth make cowards of us all*.

dotty If you say an idea or action is **dotty**, you mean it is silly. ◇ If you say a person is **dotty**, you mean they are slightly mad.

double (doubling, doubled) ❑ **Double** is used to talk about pairs of similar things. ...*double yellow lines*. ◇ **Double** is also used to talk about things intended for two people. ...*a double bed*. ◇ **Doubles** is a game of tennis or badminton played by two people against two other people.
    ❑ If something is **double** the size of something else, it is twice as big. ◇ **Double** the amount of something is twice as much. ◇ If something **doubles** or is **doubled**, it becomes twice as large, or there is twice as much of it. *The number of cases is doubling every 12 to 18 months*. ◇ **Double** is also used to describe a portion of food or drink which is twice as big as a normal portion. ...*a double whisky*.
    ❑ A person's **double** is someone who looks just like them. ◇ If something **doubles** as something else, it is used as that thing, in addition to its main use.
    ❑ If someone is **bent double**, they are bending right over. If they are forced into this position by pain, you say they **double up** with pain. ◇ If something makes you **double up** with laughter, it makes you laugh a lot.

double-act A **double-act** is a team of two people, especially comedians, who work together.

double agent A **double agent** is a spy who works for two opposing countries at the same time.

double-barrelled (*American spelling:* **double-barreled**) A **double-barrelled** shotgun has two barrels. Only one can be fired at a time. ◇ A **double-barrelled** surname has two parts joined by a hyphen, for example 'Miss J. Hunter-Dunne'.

double bass The **double bass** is a large stringed musical instrument shaped like a violin. You play it standing up.

double bill A **double bill** is a theatre or cinema performance or a sporting event in which there are two main items.

double bluff A **double bluff** is an attempt to deceive people by telling them the truth when you know they will assume you are lying.

double-book If a theatre or hotel **double-books**, it accidentally books the same seats or rooms to two sets of people.

double-breasted A **double-breasted** suit has buttons on each of the overlapping sections of the jacket.

double-check If you **double-check** something, you check it again, in case you missed something the first time.

double chin If someone has a **double chin**, they have a fold of loose skin under their chin.

double-cross If someone **double-crosses** you, they betray you instead of doing what you had planned to do together.

double-dealing is deceitful or treacherous behaviour.

double-decker A **double-decker** is a bus with two floors. ◇ **Double-decker** is used to describe other things with two levels. ...*a double-decker conservatory*.

double-digit A **double-digit** rate is a rate of 10% or more.

double-edged If you say a remark is **double-edged**, you mean it could be taken two ways, one of which is not very pleasant. ◇ If you say something is **double-edged** or a **double-edged sword**, you mean it has disadvantages as well as advantages.

double entendre (*pron:* doob-bl on-tond-ra) A **double entendre** is something someone says which has two meanings, and this makes it funny because one of the meanings is rude.

double-glaze (double-glazing, double-glazed) If you **double-glaze** windows, you fit them with a second layer of glass to keep the inside of a house warm or quiet. This second layer is called **double-glazing**.

double life If you say someone is leading a **double life**, you mean they have a secret private life which is very different from their public one.

double-quick If something happens **double-quick** or in **double-quick time**, it happens very quickly indeed.

double standards If you say someone is applying **double standards**, you mean they are unfairly treating one group of people differently from another.

double-take If you do a **double-take**, you are very surprised at something, and have to think twice about it or look at it again.

double talk If you accuse someone of **double talk**, you mean they are deliberately trying to deceive or confuse people, by saying things which can be taken two ways.

double-think is the ability to hold contradictory beliefs, and to ignore the fact that they cannot both be true.

double vision If you have **double vision**, you see two images of everything you look at, for example because of an illness or a blow to the head.

double whammy (double whammies) A **double whammy** is two problems or mistakes, one coming straight after the other.

doublet A **doublet** was a short tight-fitting man's jacket in the 15th, 16th, and 17th centuries. See also **hose**.

doubly means 'twice as', and usually indicates that there are two reasons for something. *Trying to block them now would be doubly difficult.*

doubt is a feeling of uncertainty. If you have **doubts** about something or are **in doubt** about it, you are unsure about it. ◇ If you **doubt** whether something is true or possible, you think it is probably not true or possible. ◇ If you **doubt** something, you think it might not be true or might not exist. *No-one can doubt the seriousness of Nicaragua's economic crisis.*

❏ If you say something is **in doubt**, you mean it is uncertain. ◇ If you say something is **open to doubt**, you mean it may not be correct. ◇ If you say something is **beyond doubt** or there is **no doubt about** it, you mean it is definitely true.

❏ You say **no doubt** when you are assuming something is true. *Their competitors are no doubt hard at work on ways to be faster and smarter still.* ◇ You say **without doubt** to emphasize that something is definitely true. *This choir is without doubt the best cathedral choir in the country.*

❏ **benefit of the doubt**: see **benefit**.

doubter You call people **doubters** when they are unwilling to believe something. *The government has yet to convince many doubters that its plans match the country's needs.*

doubtful (doubtfully) If something is **doubtful**, it seems unlikely or uncertain. ◇ If you are **doubtful** about something, you are unsure about it. *Ben looked at him doubtfully.*

doubtless (doubtlessly) You say **doubtless** or **doubtlessly** when you are assuming something is true. *Such sentiments would doubtlessly appal Alan Milburn.*

dough is a mixture, mainly of flour and water, which is cooked to make bread, pastry, or biscuits.

doughnut A **doughnut** is a lump or ring of sweet dough cooked in hot fat.

doughty (*pron:* dowt-ee) people are brave and determined.

dour (*pron:* doo-er) (dourly, dourness) **Dour** people are stern and unfriendly. *...her dourly conventional employers... ...the dourness with which he is associated.*

douse (dousing, doused) If you **douse** something with liquid, you throw it over it. ◇ If you **douse** a fire, you stop it burning.

dove **Doves** are birds of the pigeon family. They are smaller than most pigeons and are often white. The dove is a symbol of peace. ◇ In politics, a **dove** is someone who believes a problem should be solved by peaceful means, rather than by war or threats. See also **hawk**.

dovecote (*or* dovecot) A **dovecote** is a box, shelter, or part of a house built for doves or pigeons to live in.

dovetail (dovetailing, dovetailed) If you **dovetail** things, you get them to work together. *It is important that we dovetail our respective interests.* ◇ In carpentry, a **dovetail** or **dovetail joint** is a wedge-shaped joint for fitting pieces of wood tightly together.

dowager When a duke or some other nobleman dies and his title is passed on to someone else, his widow keeps her own title but adds **Dowager** to it. *...the Dowager Viscountess Hambleden.*

dowdy If you call someone **dowdy**, you mean they are wearing dull and unfashionable clothes. ◇ A **dowdy**

place is poorly decorated in dull colours.

down is used to talk about movement towards a lower place or position. *John came briskly down the steps... She fell down and hit her head.*

❏ If you **down** an alcoholic drink, you drink it. ◇ If workers **down tools**, they stop working as a protest or to persuade employers to give in to their demands.

❏ If an aircraft is **downed**, it is shot down.

❏ If you go **down** a road, you go along it. If you go **down** a river, you go along it in the direction it flows.

❏ If an amount or level goes **down**, it gets smaller or lower.

❏ **Down to** is used to emphasize that something is done very completely, with every detail being considered. *We place tremendous emphasis on corporate identity, even down to the type of tile for the showrooms.*

❏ If a computer is **down**, it is not working.

❏ If you are feeling **down**, you are unhappy and depressed.

❏ **Down** is the small soft feathers on young birds. It is often used as stuffing in pillows and quilts.

down-and-out A **down-and-out** is a person with no job or home and not much hope of getting either.

down-at-heel people wear old shabby clothes, because they cannot afford new ones. Similarly, a **down-at-heel** place has a shabby look, because no money has been spent on it.

down-market products are cheap, of poor quality, and aimed mainly at people who are unable to appreciate anything better.

down payment A **down payment** is money you pay at the start when you buy something using a credit arrangement or pay by instalments. The down payment is usually a set percentage of the cost of the thing.

down-to-earth people are concerned with ordinary sensible practical things.

down under is used to talk about Australia and New Zealand. *A squad of netballers arrived from down under.*

Down's syndrome is a medical condition caused by abnormal chromosomes. Down's syndrome children develop a flattish face and narrow sloping eyes, and have learning difficulties.

downbeat behaviour is deliberately casual and restrained. *He was in a curiously downbeat mood.*

downcast If someone is **downcast**, they are sad, disappointed, and pessimistic.

downer Downers are drugs which make you feel sleepy or very calm, for example barbiturates. ◇ If you are **on a downer**, you feel depressed and pessimistic.

downfall The **downfall** of a person or institution is their failure or loss of power. The cause of this can also be called their **downfall**. *His pride may still be his downfall.*

downgrade (downgrading, downgraded) If you **downgrade** something, you regard it as less important, or not as good as it once was.

downhearted If you are **downhearted**, you feel sad and discouraged.

downhill If something is moving **downhill**, it is moving down a slope. ◇ If you say something is going **downhill**, you mean it is getting worse. *The property market was heading downhill fast.*

Downing Street is the London street where the Prime

Minister and the Chancellor of the Exchequer live. Downing Street is sometimes used to talk about the Prime Minister and his or her officials. *Downing Street said last night that the position remained unchanged.*

download (downloading, downloaded) In computing, if you download information or a program from a central source, you transfer it to your own computer.

downplay If you downplay something, you try to make it seem less important.

downpour A downpour is a heavy fall of rain.

downright is used to emphasize that something is very bad or unpleasant. *Such attitudes are not only complacent, they are downright dangerous.*

downs are low rounded grassy hills, especially the chalk hills of south-east England.

downside The downside of something is its bad side. *The downside of a childhood at sea is that you cannot make any friends.*

downstairs If something is downstairs, it is on the ground floor of a building, or on a lower floor than you. If you go downstairs, you go down to a lower floor. ◇ A downstairs room or window is on the ground floor of a building.

downstream If you go downstream, you go along a river in the direction of its flow. If something is downstream of you, it is further along the river in this direction.

downswing If there is a downswing in a country's economy, it suddenly becomes less successful.

downtown is used to talk about the area around the centre of a city. *...downtown Chicago.*

downtrodden is used to describe groups of people who are treated badly and without respect.

downturn If there is a downturn in something like a country's economy, it becomes less successful.

downward (downwards) If you move or look downward or downwards, you move or look towards the ground or a lower level. ◇ If an amount or rate moves downward or downwards, it decreases.

downwind If you are downwind of something, the wind is blowing past it or through it towards you.

dowry (dowries) A woman's dowry is money or goods given by her family to the man she marries.

dowsing (dowsers) Dowsing is a procedure by which people called dowsers claim to be able to locate water or mineral deposits underground. They hold a pendulum over a place and claim to be able to detect what is underground by changes in the way the pendulum swings.

doyen (doyenne) The doyen of a group or profession is the most senior and respected person in it. Doyenne is used if this person is a woman. *Ernest Stahl was the doyen of German studies at Oxford.*

doze (dozing, dozed) If you doze or have a doze, you sleep lightly, or for a short period. ◇ If you doze off, you fall asleep.

dozen A dozen is twelve. ◇ Dozens is used to mean 'very many'. *At least four people were killed and dozens injured.* If things come by the dozen, they come in large numbers.

dozy If someone is dozy, they are not alert and may fail to notice things.

DPP See Director of Public Prosecutions.

Dr See doctor.

drab (drabness) If you say something is drab, you mean it is dull and not attractive or exciting. *...the drabness of the nearby villages.*

drachma The drachma is the unit of currency in Greece.

draconian laws or measures are extremely harsh.

draft (drafter) ❑ If you draft a book, speech, or letter, you prepare an early version called a draft, which may then need altering before a satisfactory version is produced. ◇ When people draft a plan or agreement, they draw it up; these people are called the plan's or agreement's drafters.

❑ In the US, if you are drafted, you are ordered to serve in one of the armed forces. When people talk about the draft, they usually mean the orders issued to young American men to join the armed forces and fight in the Vietnam War in the 1960s and 1970s.

❑ If people are drafted in to do something, they are brought in from somewhere else to do it.

❑ See also draught.

draftsman See draughtsman.

drag (dragging, dragged) ❑ If you drag something somewhere, you pull it along the ground. ◇ If you drag someone or something out of a building or vehicle, you pull them out quickly and roughly.

❑ If you drag someone to a place they do not want to go to, you make them go there. ◇ If you drag yourself somewhere, (a) you go there unwillingly. (b) you go slowly and with difficulty, because you are tired or ill. ◇ If someone is dragged into an unpleasant situation, they become involved in it against their will.

❑ If you say something is a drag, you mean it is boring. ◇ If something drags, it seems to last a long time, because it is boring. *The play drags a little here and there.* ◇ If something drags on, it lasts longer than is necessary or was expected. ◇ If you drag something out, you make it last longer than necessary. ◇ If you say someone is dragging their feet or dragging their heels, you mean they are deliberately taking a long time over something.

❑ If something which is not succeeding drags something else down, it makes it unsuccessful too. *Sterling has been dragged down by the weak dollar.* ◇ If something is a drag on something else, it slows it down.

❑ If a man is in drag, he is dressed as a woman.

drag racing is a sport in which people try to achieve fast times driving specially built cars or motor bikes over very short distances.

dragnet A police dragnet is an intense search of an area using extra forces, to try to capture a suspect.

dragon A dragon is a mythical monster. It is usually portrayed as breathing fire, having a scaly body, wings, claws, and a long barbed tail.

dragonfly (dragonflies) Dragonflies are large brightly-coloured insects with long bodies and two pairs of wings.

dragoon (dragooning, dragooned) From the 16th century to the 19th century, various kinds of soldiers were called dragoons. ◇ If you are dragooned into something, you are made to do it.

drain (draining, drained) ❑ When wet land is drained, the water is made to flow away from it. Similarly, a pond can be **drained**. ◇ If you **drain** a wet object, you stand it somewhere so the water runs off. ◇ When liquid **drains** somewhere, it flows there gradually.

❑ A **drain** is (a) a pipe which carries water or sewage away from a place. (b) a metal grid in a road through which rainwater flows away. ◇ If you say something has gone **down the drain**, you mean it has been wasted or ruined.

❑ If you **drain** a glass, you drink all the liquid in it.

❑ If you are **drained**, you feel tired and weak. Similarly, something can **drain** your strength. ◇ If something is a **drain** on resources, it uses them up. ◇ If something like a feeling **drains away**, it decreases until there is none left. *Popular support for the government has drained away.*

drainage is the system or process by which water or other liquids are drained away from a place.

draining board A **draining board** is a sloping area next to a sink where you put things like plates and cutlery to drain when you have washed them.

drainpipe A **drainpipe** is a pipe down the outside of a building, through which water flows from the roof into a drain.

drake A **drake** is a male duck.

dram A **dram** is a small amount of whisky or some other spirit.

drama ❑ A **drama** is a serious play for the theatre, TV, or radio. **Drama** is used to talk about plays in general. *He was studying drama at Bristol University.*

❑ **Drama** is also used to talk about exciting aspects of real situations. *If the hostage is released, it could mark the end of a long and painful drama.*

dramatic (dramatically) ❑ A **dramatic** change is sudden and striking. *The mood has changed dramatically.* ◇ **Dramatic** events are exciting or alarming. News can also be **dramatic**.

❑ **Dramatic** is also used to talk about things to do with the writing and performance of plays. *...the American Musical and Dramatic Academy.*

dramatise See **dramatize**.

dramatist A **dramatist** is someone who writes plays.

dramatize (dramatizing, dramatized; dramatization) (*can be spelled with an 's' instead of a 'z'*) ❑ If a book or story is **dramatized**, it is rewritten as a play or film. *...Robin Brooks's dramatization of Virginia Woolf's novel.*

❑ If someone **dramatizes** a situation, they try to make it seem more serious or exciting than it really is.

drank See **drink**.

drape (draping, draped) If something like a piece of cloth is **draped** somewhere, it is placed there so it hangs down. ◇ If something is **draped** with a piece of cloth, it is covered with it and the edges of the cloth hang down around it. ◇ **Drapes** are curtains made of heavy material or hanging in folds. In the US, curtains of any kind are usually called **drapes**.

draper A **draper** or **draper's** is a shop which sells cloth and household linen.

drapery In art, **drapery** is used to talk about cloth or clothing hanging in folds. *...a figure whose head is obscured by drapery.* ◇ The **drapery** trade is concerned with buying and selling fabrics and household linen.

drastic (drastically) If you take **drastic** action, you do something extreme, usually because you have to. *Many*

countries are drastically curtailing the funds they are making available. ◇ If something **drastic** happens to you, you suffer badly because of it. *He warned them to give themselves up or suffer drastic consequences.* ◇ A **drastic** change is a sudden and striking, and usually for the worse. *The loss of the old buildings would drastically alter the character of that part of London.*

draught (draughty) (*American spelling:* draft, drafty) ❑ A **draught** is a cold current of air coming into a room. If a place is **draughty**, it has a lot of currents like this.

❑ **Draught** beer and cider are served from casks or barrels. You say drinks served like this are **on draught**.

❑ **Draught** animals are large animals like horses and oxen which are used to pull heavy loads.

❑ **Draughts** is a game for two people played on a chequered board. To win the game, you have to capture all your opponent's pieces.

draughtboard A **draughtboard** is a square chequered board on which the game of draughts is played. It is the same as a chessboard.

draughtsman (draughtsmen; draughtsmanship) (*American spelling:* draftsman, *etc*) A **draughtsman** is a person whose job is to prepare technical drawings. ◇ **Draughtsmanship** is the ability to draw well.

draw (drawing, drew, have drawn) ❑ If you **draw** a picture, pattern, or diagram, you create it using a pencil, pen, or crayon. A **drawing** is a picture created like this.

❑ When a vehicle **draws up**, it comes to a place and stops. ◇ If people or vehicles **draw near** to a place, they get close to it. If they **draw away**, they move away from it.

❑ You say something is **drawing** near when it will happen soon. ◇ When something **draws to an end** or **draws to a close**, it finishes.

❑ If something like a cart or a plough is **drawn** by an animal, the animal is pulling it.

❑ If you **draw** a curtain or blind, you pull it across a window to cover or uncover it.

❑ If someone **draws** a gun, sword, or knife, they pull it out, ready for use.

❑ If you **draw** a breath, you take air into your lungs. ◇ If you **draw on** a cigarette, you suck it and breathe in the smoke.

❑ If something like a blow **draws blood**, it causes bleeding. A person who kills or injures someone can be said to have **drawn blood**. ◇ You also say someone **draws blood** or **draws first blood** when they have an early victory in a contest or competition.

❑ If you **draw** money out of a bank, you take it out of your account.

❑ If people or things are **drawn** from a place or group, they are obtained from it. *...the increasing number of finance directors drawn from business school graduates.* ◇ If something you write is **drawn** from something else, it is based on it. *...short stories drawn from daily life.* ◇ If you **draw on** something, you make use of it. *...a needlework designer who draws on Victorian patterns for her inspiration.*

❑ If you **draw** a conclusion, you come to it after considering the facts. ◇ If you **draw** a comparison, you say two things are similar. *She drew a parallel between the uprising and the Falklands War.* ◇ If you **draw** a distinction between two things, you say or show they are different.

❑ If you **draw comfort** from something, you are less

worried because of it.

❏ If something you do **draws** a particular reaction, that is how people react to it. *The plan drew prolonged applause.* ◇ **draw attention to:** see **attention**. ◇ If people are **drawn** by something, they are attracted by it, or go to see it because it interests them.

❏ If you are **drawn into** something, you become involved in it. ◇ If you are **drawn into** saying something, someone gets you to say it, although you were not intending to.

❏ If you **draw up** a document, list, or plan, you prepare it and write it out.

❏ In a game or competition, if two people or teams **draw**, they get the same number of points, runs, or goals, and nobody wins or loses. You can also say the game or competition ends in a **draw**.

❏ If someone looks **drawn**, they look very tired and worried.

❏ **draw a blank:** see **blank**. ◇ **draw the line:** see **line**.

drawback A **drawback** is a snag or difficulty in adopting a particular course of action.

drawbridge A **drawbridge** is a bridge which can be pulled up or lowered. Castles used to have drawbridges which could be pulled up to prevent attackers from getting in.

drawer A **drawer** is a box-like part of a desk or other piece of furniture which slides in and out.

drawing board A **drawing board** is a large flat board, often on a metal frame. You fix paper on it when you are drawing or designing something. ◇ If you have to go **back to the drawing board**, something you have done has not succeeded and you have to think of another way of going about it.

drawing pin A **drawing pin** is a small thin nail with a broad circular head, used for such things as pinning notices to walls.

drawing room A **drawing room** is a room in a large house where people sit and relax or entertain guests.

drawl If someone **drawls** or speaks with a **drawl**, they speak slowly in a low voice, slurring their words.

drawn-out If something is **drawn-out**, it lasts a long time.

drawstring A **drawstring** is a cord which goes through a seam round an opening, for example at the top of a bag or round the waist of a pair of trousers. When the cord is pulled tighter, the opening gets smaller.

dray A **dray** is a low cart for carrying heavy loads.

dread (dreading, dreaded) If you **dread** something which is going to happen or likely to happen, you are worried and frightened about it. This feeling is called **dread**. Dread and **dreaded** are used to describe things which make people feel like this. *...dread diseases... ...as the dreaded brown envelopes land on the nation's doormats.*

dreadful (dreadfully, dreadfulness) If you say something is **dreadful**, you mean it is extremely unpleasant or evil. *Those responsible had committed a dreadful act.* ◇ You also say something is **dreadful** when it is of very poor quality. *...the dreadfulness of English disc jockeys.* ◇ **Dreadfully** is used to emphasize a bad quality. *It seems dreadfully expensive over here.*

dreadlocks If someone has **dreadlocks**, they have their hair long and in tight ringlets.

dream (dreaming, dreamed *or* dreamt) ❏ If you **dream** or have a **dream**, you have experiences in your mind while you are asleep.

❏ A **dream** is also something you often think about and would love to happen. *Navratilova achieved her dream of winning a record ninth women's singles title.* You can say you **dream** about something like this. ◇ If you say a combination of two people is a **dream ticket**, you mean they should be extremely successful at doing something together.

❏ If you call a place a **dream world**, you mean it seems very strange and unreal, like a dream.

❏ If you say you **would not dream** of doing something, you mean you would never do it.

❏ If you think a new invention or idea is strange or silly, you can say someone has **dreamed** it **up**.

dreamer You say someone is a **dreamer** when they are always looking forward to pleasant things which might never happen.

dreamily See **dreamy**.

dreamlike See **dreamy**.

dreamt See **dream**.

dreamy (dreamily, dreamlike) If someone's behaviour is **dreamy**, they look as though they are thinking about something pleasant. *'You know,' she said dreamily, 'I'd like to get into the movies.'* ◇ If something is **dreamy** or **dreamlike**, it seems strange and unreal, like a dream. *Jawahirilal's paintings have a naive, dreamlike quality.*

dreary (dreariest; drearily, dreariness) You say something is **dreary** when it is dull and makes you feel bored or depressed. *...one of the dreariest things I have seen on the box this year... The cricket was drearily uncompetitive... ...the uninspired dreariness of 'Give Peace a Chance'.*

dredge (dredging, dredged; dredger) ❏ When a river, harbour, or other water is **dredged**, mud and other unwanted material is removed from the bottom. A **dredger** is a boat fitted with machinery for doing this. You say something is **dredged** from water when it is found there by dredging.

❏ If you **dredge up** something from your memory, you recall it when you have not thought about it for a long time. You can also **dredge up** ideas, stories, or other things from the past.

dregs The **dregs** are what is left at the bottom of a bottle or other container when all the liquid has been poured out. ◇ If you call someone or something the **dregs**, you mean they are the worst examples of their kind of person or thing. *...the dregs of society.*

drench (drenches, drenching, drenched) If you are **drenched** by something like rain, you get very wet. ◇ If you have been exposed to a lot of something, you can say you are **drenched** in it. *...a country drenched in propaganda.* ◇ A sun-drenched place has a lot of sunshine.

dress (dresses, dressing, dressed) ❏ When you **dress** or get **dressed**, you put on your clothes. You can also **dress** someone else, for example a child. ◇ If you are **dressed**, you are wearing clothes. You can also be **dressed in** a particular way. *He is always elegantly dressed.* ◇ If you are **dressed as** a person or thing, you are wearing clothes intended to make you look like them. ◇ If you **dress up**, you put on different clothes, to look like someone else or to look smarter. **Dressing-up** is a game played by children in which they put on clothes they do not normally wear.

❏ If you dress something **up,** you change small details or present it differently, to make it more acceptable.

❏ A **dress** is a piece of clothing worn by a woman or girl which covers her body and extends down over her legs.

❏ If you **dress** someone's wounds, you clean them and put protective coverings called **dressings** on them.

❏ A salad **dressing** is a mixture including oil and vinegar which you pour over a salad.

dress circle The **dress circle** is the first level of seats above the ground floor in a theatre.

dress rehearsal A **dress rehearsal** of a play, opera, or show is a rehearsal held not long before performances begin, in which the performers wear their costumes and lights and scenery are used. ◇ You can say something is a **dress rehearsal** for a later event when it has similar features but is less important or on a smaller scale. *Leeds meet VFB Stuttgart tomorrow in a full dress-rehearsal for their clash in the European Cup.*

dress shirt A **dress shirt** is a smart shirt, usually white, worn by a man with a dinner jacket and bow tie on special occasions.

dressage (*pron:* dress-ahzh; *the 'zh' sounds like 's' in 'pleasure'*) In horse-riding competitions, **dressage** is an event in which riders make their horse perform controlled movements like trotting, cantering, or changing direction, in response to signals.

dresser ❏ A **dresser** is a piece of furniture with cupboards or drawers in the lower part and shelves in the top part.

❏ You can use **dresser** to talk about the kind of clothes someone wears. For example, you can say someone is a 'neat dresser'. ◇ A **dresser** is also someone who works in a theatre, helping actors or actresses to dress.

dressing-down If you give someone a **dressing-down,** you tell them off.

dressing gown A **dressing gown** is a long loose-fitting jacket worn over pyjamas or a nightdress when you are not in bed.

dressing room A **dressing room** is a room in a theatre where actors get themselves ready for a performance.

dressing table A **dressing table** is a small bedroom table with drawers and a mirror.

dressmaker (dressmaking) A **dressmaker** is a person who is paid to make clothes for women or children. This work is called **dressmaking.**

drew See **draw.**

dribble (dribbling, dribbled) ❏ When a liquid **dribbles** down a surface, it moves down it in a thin stream. ◇ When a person or animal **dribbles,** saliva trickles from their mouth. ◇ A **dribble** is a very small flow of something. *The debt problem and collapsing economy have slowed the flow of funds to a dribble.*

❏ When footballers **dribble,** they move with the ball, keeping it under close control. A movement like this is called a **dribble.**

dribs and drabs If people or things arrive or leave in **dribs and drabs,** they come and go in small numbers over a period of time.

dried See **dry.**

drier (driest) See **dry.**

drift ❏ When something **drifts** somewhere, it is carried there by the movement of wind or water. *The vessel is drifting in gale-force winds.* ◇ A **drift** is a snowdrift, or a similar pile of material created by the wind. *...great drifts of leaves.*

❏ When people **drift** somewhere, they move there slowly and without a sense of purpose. ◇ If people are **drifting** towards a bad situation, they are slowly getting into it. You can talk about a **drift** towards a bad situation. *...a drift towards political instability.* ◇ If something **drifts** away from you, you gradually lose it. *There is a danger that control will drift away from shareholders.*

❏ If you **drift off,** you fall asleep.

drift net See **drifter.**

drifter ❏ A **drifter** is a person who does not stay in one place or job for long.

❏ A **drifter** is also a kind of fishing boat for catching herring. It uses a very long net called a **drift net.**

driftwood is wood floating on the sea or a river, or washed up onto the shore.

drill ❏ When you **drill** a hole in something, you make it using a revolving tool called a **drill.** ◇ When people **drill** for oil or water, they search for it by drilling deep holes in the ground or the sea bed.

❏ When people carry out a **drill,** they practise doing the things they are supposed to do in an emergency. *...a fire drill... ...gas mask drill.* ◇ If people are **well-drilled,** they have practised and know exactly what to do in a certain situation. ◇ When people in the armed forces **drill,** they march and move together in response to commands.

drily See **dry.**

drink (drinking, drank, have drunk) ❏ When you **drink** a liquid, you take it into your mouth and swallow it. ◇ A **drink** is an amount of liquid in a cup or glass for someone to drink.

❏ **Drinking** is used to talk about drinking alcohol. For example, if you say someone drinks a lot, you mean they drink a lot of alcohol. *A generation ago, mothers-to-be smoked and drank and no-one took any notice.* ◇ **Drink** is any alcoholic drink like whisky, wine, or beer. *...a lawyer with a drink problem.* ◇ See also **drunk.**

drink-driving is breaking the law by driving a vehicle with more than a certain level of alcohol in your blood-stream.

drinkable water is clean and safe to drink. ◇ If you say some other drink is **drinkable,** you mean it is not especially good, but at least it is not too unpleasant to drink.

drinker A **drinker** is someone who drinks alcohol, especially a lot of it. ◇ The **drinkers** in a place are the people having a drink there. ◇ **Drinker** is also used to talk about the kind of drink someone regularly drinks. *...beer drinkers... ...coffee drinkers.*

drinking fountain A **drinking fountain** is a device, usually in a public place, which supplies water for people to drink.

drinking water is water which is safe to drink.

drip (dripping, dripped) ❏ When liquid **drips,** it falls in small drops. You also say something like a tap **drips** when small drops of liquid fall from it. ◇ If something is **dripping** wet, it is very wet indeed.

❏ A **drip** is a machine which supplies the body through tubes with things essential for its survival, like blood plasma, salt, and sugar. People are put on drips when they are unconscious or too weak to feed themselves.

❑ **Dripping** is the fat which comes out of meat when it is fried or roasted. It can be eaten or used to fry other foods.

drive (driving, drove, have driven) ❑ If you **drive** a vehicle, you ride in it and control it. ◇ If you **drive** someone somewhere, you take them there by car. A **drive** is a journey by car. ◇ The car you **drive** is the type of car you own or have the use of.

❑ A **drive** is the same as a driveway.

❑ You say something **drives** a machine when it supplies or transmits the power which makes it work. ◇ You say something **drives** a system when it keeps it going. *It is conflict that drives the arms trade.*

❑ If something **drives** you to do something, it makes you do it. *Financial necessity drove him to break a promise to his wife.* ◇ If something **drives** you into a bad state, it puts you into that state. *...as recession drives more borrowers out of business.* ◇ When people are **driven** out of a place, they are forced to leave.

❑ If you **drive** something like a post or nail into something, you force it in, usually by hitting it with a hammer. ◇ If you **drive** a ball in a game like cricket or golf, you hit it straight and hard. A shot like this is called a **drive**.

❑ **Drive** is energy and determination. *Too much stress can exhaust staff and ruin their creativity and drive.* ◇ A **drive** is a special effort by a group of people to achieve something. *...recruiting drives.* ◇ The **driving force** behind something is the person or group mainly responsible for it, who also provide the enthusiasm and initiative to keep it going.

❑ drive home: see home.

drive-in places offer a service which people can use without getting out of their cars. *...a drive-in cinema.*

drive shaft In a motor vehicle, the **drive shaft** is a rotating rod which turns the wheels and is connected to the gearbox.

drivel If you call what someone says **drivel**, you mean it is silly and tedious.

driven See drive.

driver A **driver** is someone who drives a vehicle.

driveway A **driveway** is a private road, usually a short one, leading from a public road to someone's house or garage.

driving seat The **driving seat** in a car or other vehicle is the seat where the driver sits. ◇ In other situations, when you talk about the person **in the driving seat**, you mean the one who is in charge.

drizzle (drizzling, drizzled; drizzly) **Drizzle** is light rain falling in tiny drops. When it is raining like this, you say it is drizzling or drizzly.

droll (pron: drole) is used to describe people and things that are amusing in a calm restrained way.

dromedary (usual pron: drum-e-dery) A **dromedary** is a one-humped camel.

drone (droning, droned) ❑ If something **drones**, it makes a low continuous humming noise. A **drone** is a noise like this. ◇ If someone **drones on** about something, they talk about it at length in a boring way.

❑ A **drone** is a male bee which does not work. ◇ People who work hard year after year at dull routine jobs are sometimes called **drones**.

drool (drooling, drooled) If someone **drools**, saliva falls from their lips. ◇ You also say someone **drools** when they show their delight at something in a very obvious way. *Politicians began drooling with expectation.*

droop (drooping, drooped; droopy) If something **droops** or is droopy, it hangs or leans downwards with no strength or firmness. *...a droopy moustache.*

drop (dropping, dropped) ❑ A **drop** of liquid is a very small amount, shaped like a tiny ball.

❑ If something **drops** or is **dropped**, it falls straight down. ◇ A **drop** is a vertical distance downwards, for example from the top of a cliff to the bottom.

❑ If a level or amount **drops**, it suddenly gets lower or less. A **drop** is a reduction like this. *...the drop in reading standards.* ◇ If your voice **drops** or you **drop** it, you start speaking more quietly.

❑ If you **drop** something you are doing, you stop doing it. ◇ If you **drop out** of something, you give it up before completing it. ◇ If someone is **dropped**, they are left out of something. *He was dropped for the first championship game.* ◇ If charges against someone are **dropped**, they are not proceeded with.

❑ In a competition, if you **drop** a game or point, you lose it.

❑ If you **drop** a hint, you give it in a casual way. ◇ If you **drop** someone **a line**, you send them a letter.

❑ If a vehicle **drops** you somewhere or **drops** you **off**, it stops so you can get out. ◇ If someone **drops by** or **drops in**, they call on you, usually without arranging it beforehand.

❑ If you **drop off**, you fall asleep.

❑ If you do something **at the drop of a hat**, you do it suddenly without warning.

drop-out (or dropout) **Drop-outs** are people who reject the accepted ways of the society they live in, especially by choosing not to have a regular job. ◇ People who have left school or university without completing their studies are also called **drop-outs**.

droplet A **droplet** is a very small drop of liquid.

dropout See drop-out.

dropper A **dropper** is a small tube with a rubber bulb on one end. It is used to suck up and release small amounts of liquid.

droppings are the faeces of birds and small animals.

dropsy is a medical problem in which parts of the body become swollen with fluid. It can be caused by various illnesses.

dross If you call something **dross**, you mean it is of very poor quality. ◇ **Dross** is also the waste material left floating on the surface when a metal like gold has been melted.

drought or a **drought** is a long period when there is no rain.

drove ❑ See drive.

❑ If you say people are doing something **in droves**, you mean very large numbers of them are doing it.

drown ❑ When someone **drowns**, they die underwater because they cannot breathe.

❑ If a sound **drowns** another sound or **drowns** it **out**, it is so much louder that you cannot hear the other sound.

drowsy If you are **drowsy**, you feel sleepy and cannot think clearly.

drubbing If someone is given a **drubbing** in a competition or contest, they are humiliatingly beaten.

drudgery (drudge) Drudgery is boring repetitive work. A drudge is someone who does work like this.

drug (drugging, drugged) A drug is a chemical given to people to treat or prevent illness or disease. ◇ Drugs are also substances, especially illegal ones, which people smoke, inject, swallow, or inhale to enjoy their effects. ◇ If someone is drugged, they are given a drug which makes them sleepy or unconscious.

drugstore In the US, a drugstore is a shop rather like a chemist's, where you buy things like medicine, cosmetics, and newspapers. Drugstores also provide simple meals and snacks.

druid Druids were priests of a pre-Christian religion in Britain, Ireland, and France. People who follow this religion in modern times also call themselves druids.

drum (drumming, drummed; drummer) ❑ A drum is a musical instrument consisting of a skin stretched tightly over a round frame. You play it by beating it with sticks or with your hands. A drummer is someone who plays a drum or drums. ◇ If you drum on a surface, you hit it regularly, making a continuous beating sound.
  ❑ If you drum something into someone, you keep saying it, to make them understand or remember it. ◇ If you drum up support for something, you go round getting people to support it. Similarly, you can drum up business.

drum majorette See majorette.

drum roll A drum roll is a series of drumbeats following each other rapidly to make a continuous sound.

drumbeat A drumbeat is the sound of a beat on a drum.

drummer See drum.

drumstick A drumstick is (a) a thin rod for beating a drum. (b) the lower part of the leg of a cooked bird like a chicken.

drunk ❑ See drink.
  ❑ If someone is drunk, they cannot behave sensibly because they have drunk too much alcohol. A drunk is someone who is drunk or often gets drunk.

drunkard A drunkard is someone who often gets drunk.

drunken (drunkenly, drunkenness) Drunken is used to describe people who are drunk, and their behaviour. *She giggled drunkenly... A group of fans have appeared in court charged with drunkenness.*

dry (dryer *or* drier, driest; dryly *or* drily; dryness; dries, drying, dried) ❑ If something is dry, it has no liquid in it or on it. *...disintegration of the subsoil through excessive dryness.* ◇ When something dries or dries out, it becomes dry. ◇ If a lake or river dries up, it loses all its water. ◇ If the weather is dry, there is no rain.
  ❑ If you dry up, you wipe the water off cutlery and crockery which has just been washed. ◇ A dryer is a machine which dries things.
  ❑ When a supply or series of things dries up, it stops.
  ❑ Dry is used to describe less sweet varieties of some alcoholic drinks. *...dry gin... ...a good dry cider.*
  ❑ Dry humour is subtle and sarcastic. ◇ If you call a piece of writing dry, you mean it is rather dull. *His style is scholarly without sounding too dryly academic.*
  ❑ When someone who has been in danger at sea gets ashore, you can say they reach dry land.

dry-clean (dry cleaner) When clothes are dry-cleaned, they are cleaned using a liquid chemical rather than wa-

ter, because water would damage them. A dry cleaner or dry cleaner's is a shop where things like clothes are taken for dry-cleaning.

dry dock A dry dock is a dock from which water can be removed after a ship has entered it, so the ship can be repaired.

dry ice is carbon dioxide preserved in a solid state by keeping it at a very low temperature. It is used to keep food cold.

dry rot is a rapid-spreading disease caused by a fungus. It affects the wooden parts of buildings, making them turn brittle and powdery.

dry-run A dry-run of something is a trial or practice to see if it works properly.

dry-stone wall A dry-stone wall is built by fitting loose stones together rather than joining them with mortar.

D.Sc. A D.Sc. is the highest degree awarded by a university in the sciences. D.Sc. stands for 'Doctor of Science'.

DSS The DSS or Department of Social Security is the government department responsible for benefit payments, for example for the sick, old, and people on low incomes.

DTs If alcoholics get the DTs, they shake uncontrollably and may see things which do not exist. DT stands for 'delirium tremens'.

dual is used to talk about things which have two parts, functions, or aspects. *...America's dual commitment to promoting peace while being resolute in countering terrorism.*

dual carriageway A dual carriageway is a road with a strip of grass or concrete down the middle to separate traffic going in opposite directions.

dualism and duality are used to talk about something having two parts or aspects. *...the traditional Christian dualism between body and soul.*

dub (dubbing, dubbed) If you dub someone something, you give them that name. ◇ If a film is dubbed, the voices of the actors are replaced with the voices of other actors speaking a different language.

dubious (dubiously) You say something is dubious when you think it is not completely honest, respectable, or reliable. *Some of their wins have been dubiously gained.* ◇ If you say something is a dubious pleasure, you mean you are not sure it is really a pleasure at all. Similarly, you can talk about something being a dubious distinction or honour. ◇ If you are dubious about a proposal or suggestion, you are not sure it is a good idea.

ducal (*pron:* duke-al) is used to talk about things belonging to or connected with a duke. *...a ducal country house.*

duchess (duchesses) A duchess is the wife of a duke, or a woman with an equivalent title in her own right.

duchy (duchies) A duchy is an area of land owned or ruled by a duke or duchess.

duck ❑ A duck is a common water bird with short legs, webbed feet, and a large flat beak. There are many different species of duck. Duck is the meat of a duck.
  ❑ If you duck, you move your head downwards quickly, to avoid being seen or to avoid being hit by something. ◇ If you duck somewhere, you move there suddenly and quickly, to avoid danger.
  ❑ If someone ducks a responsibility or duty, they avoid it. ◇ If someone ducks an issue, they avoid talking about it. ◇ If someone ducks out of something which they

are supposed to do, they avoid doing it.
❑ In cricket, if a batsman is out for a **duck**, he or she is out without scoring any runs.
❑ **lame duck**: see **lame**. ◇ **sitting duck**: see **sit**.

duckling A **duckling** is a young duck.

duct (ducting) A **duct** is a pipe, tube, or channel for a liquid or gas to pass through. **Ducting** is a system of ducts. ◇ A **duct** is also a tube in your body which a liquid passes through. ...*the sperm duct*.

dud If you say something is a **dud**, you mean it is no good or does not work properly. ...*a dud bullet*. ◇ A **dud** loan is one which will not be repaid.

dude A **dude** is a cool trendy man.

dudgeon If someone is in **high dudgeon**, they are angry or resentful, because of something someone has said or done.

due ❑ If something is **due** to something else, it exists or happens as a result of it.
❑ If something is **due** at a certain time, it is expected to happen or arrive then.
❑ Some amounts of money which people are required to pay are called **dues**. ...*trade union dues*. ◇ If some money is **due** to you, you have a right to it.
❑ **Due** is used with words like 'respect' and 'consideration' to mean 'an appropriate amount of'. *After due consideration, she decided that the name sounded right for him*. ◇ If you say something will happen **in due course**, you mean it will happen eventually, when the time is right.
❑ **Due** is used to talk about exact compass directions. For example, 'due north' means exactly to the north.

due process In the US, **due process** or **due process of law** means the procedures set out in the Constitution which are there for the protection of the rights and freedom of individuals. ◇ **Due process** is also used more generally to talk about things being done in accordance with rules and regulations. *All democratic leaders can be removed from office by due process and without bloodshed*.

duel (duelling, duelled) (*usual American spelling:* dueling, dueled) A **duel** is a fight in which two people use guns or swords to settle an argument or quarrel. When people **duel**, they fight like this. ◇ You can refer to any conflict or competition between two people or groups as a **duel**. *In 1980, Coe and Ovett duelled in the middle distance events*.

duet A **duet** is a piece of music sung or played by two people.

duff If something is **duff**, it is useless or not working properly.

duffel bag A **duffel bag** is a strong tube-shaped cloth bag with a drawstring around the top which is also attached to the bottom. You carry it over your shoulder.

duffel coat A **duffel coat** is a short heavy coat with toggles down the front and a hood.

duffer If you call someone a **duffer**, you mean they are a very slow learner, or not very bright generally.

dug See **dig**.

dug-out (*or* dugout) The **dug-out** at a football ground is a shelter at the side of the pitch where people like team managers, trainers, and substitutes sit during games. ◇ A **dug-out** is also a shelter made by tunnelling or digging a hole in the ground and covering it with a roof. Dug-outs are usually made by soldiers. ◇ A **dug-out** canoe is made by hollowing out a log.

duke A **duke** is a male aristocrat. In Britain, a duke ranks just below a prince.

dull (dullness) ❑ If you say something is **dull**, you mean it is not interesting or exciting. *They try to defend the dullness of their trade*. You can also say people are **dull**. ◇ People who are not very intelligent are sometimes called **dull** or **dull-witted**.
❑ A **dull** sound is not loud or clear. ...*a dull thud*. ◇ A **dull** colour is not bright. ◇ When the weather is **dull**, it is grey and cloudy.
❑ **Dull** feelings are not strong or intense. *Relations between staff and students have deteriorated to dull hostility*. If something **dulls** a feeling, it makes it less intense. *Time had dulled the pain*.

duly is used to say something is done according to the correct procedure, or at the right or appropriate time. *The treasures were duly sent to Cairo for museum display*.

dumb people do not have the ability to speak. ◇ You also say someone is **dumb** when they cannot say anything on a particular occasion, for example because they are shocked or angry.
❑ If you call someone **dumb**, you mean they are stupid. You can also say something like a decision is **dumb**.

dumb waiter A **dumb waiter** is a lift for carrying things like food from one floor of a building to another.

dumbbell A **dumbbell** is a short bar with weights at each end. Dumbbells are used in pairs to strengthen arm and shoulder muscles.

dumbfound (dumbfounded) If something **dumbfounds** you or leaves you **dumbfounded**, you are so shocked and surprised by it that you cannot say anything.

dummy (dummies, dummying, dummied) ❑ A **dummy** is a rubber or plastic object given to a baby to suck, to comfort it. ◇ A **dummy** is also a model of a person in a clothes shop, used to display clothes.
❑ **Dummy** is used to describe things made to look like a particular object, often in order to deceive someone. ...*a dummy hand grenade*. ◇ When a footballer **dummies** the ball or **dummies** an opposing player, he pretends to play the ball but allows it to run past him or stay where it is.

dump ❑ When something is **dumped**, it is put somewhere and left there for good or for a very long time, because it is not wanted. *Britain is now committed to stop dumping raw sewage in the sea*. A **dump** is a place where unwanted material is dumped. ◇ An ammunition or arms **dump** is a place where weapons are stored.
❑ If you **dump** something somewhere, you put it there quickly and carelessly.
❑ You can say a person is **dumped** when they are dismissed from their job, because they are no longer needed. ◇ If someone **dumps** their boyfriend or girlfriend, they leave them.

dumper truck A **dumper truck** is a truck with a carrying part which can tip backwards so the load falls out.

dumping ground A **dumping ground** is a place where waste material is left. ◇ You can call any place a **dumping ground** when things are left there in large quantities, because they are unwanted and there is nowhere else to put them. *These places cannot just be used as a dumping ground for unwanted youngsters*.

dumpling Dumplings are small balls of suet dough, usually cooked in a stew.

dumpy A dumpy person is short and fat.

dunce A dunce is a very slow learner. ◇ A dunce's cap or dunce's hat was a tall cone-shaped hat which slow-learning or lazy schoolchildren used to be made to wear. Nowadays, if you say someone is wearing the dunce's cap, you mean they have been made to look foolish.

dune Dunes or sand dunes are hills of sand formed by the wind in a desert or near the sea.

dung is the faeces of large animals.

dungarees are a one-piece garment consisting of trousers and a front part covering your chest which is held up by straps over your shoulders.

dungeon A dungeon is a dark underground prison, especially one in a castle.

dunk If you dunk something in a liquid, you hold it there briefly, then take it out again.

duo A duo is two people who do something together, for example two entertainers.

duodenum (duodenal) Your duodenum is the part of your intestine just below your stomach. Duodenal is used to talk about things to do with the duodenum. ...*duodenal ulcers.*

duopoly (duopolies) If there is a duopoly in an area of business, everything is controlled by two companies or organizations.

dupe (duping, duped) If someone dupes you, they trick you. A dupe is someone who has been tricked.

duplex (duplexes) In the US, a duplex is a building divided into two living units. It can be either a pair of semi-detached houses or two flats, one above the other.

duplicate (duplicating, duplicated; duplication) If you dupli-cate something (*pron:* dyoo-pli-kate), you make an exact copy of it. The copy is called a duplicate (*pron:* dyoo-pli-ket). ◇ If work is being duplicated, two people or groups are doing the same thing. *The job losses will end duplication in administration.*

duplicity (duplicitous) If you accuse someone of duplicity or say they are being duplicitous, you mean they are behaving in a deceitful way.

durable (durably, durability) ❑ If a product is durable, it is strongly made and should last a long time. *Because of their durability, CDs are now replacing floppy discs.* ◇ A durable arrangement is likely to last. *It will take several years to bring inflation durably down.*
❑ See also consumer durables.

duration The duration of something is (a) how long it lasts. ...*a general strike of two or three weeks' duration.* (b) the period of time when it is happening. ...*free accommo-dation for the duration of the Games.*

duress If you do something under duress, you are fright-ened or forced into doing it.

Durex (*plural:* Durex) A Durex is a condom. 'Durex' is a trademark.

during is used to talk about something happening con-tinuously or repeatedly over a period of time. *In England you would have to heat your glasshouses to grow these plants during the winter.* ◇ During is also used to talk about something happening at some point in a period of time. *Six prison staff were injured during the protest.*

dusk is the time just after sunset when the light is dim but it is not completely dark.

dusky If something is dusky, it is dark or dark-coloured.

dust (dusty) ❑ Dust is a powder-like substance made up of fragments of earth, dirt, and pollen. If something is dusty, it is covered in dust. ◇ When you dust or do the dusting, you remove dust from things like furniture using a duster.
❑ If you dust a surface with a powder, you cover it lightly with it. A dusting is a light covering like this.
❑ If you say something is being dusted down or dusted off, you mean it is being prepared for use again, after it has not been used for a long time. ◇ If something bites the dust, it fails, finishes, or is rejected.
❑ If you talk about the dust settling, you mean things are calming down after a period of excitement or change.

dust jacket The dust jacket or dust cover of a book is a loose paper cover put on to protect it. It often contains information about the book and its author.

dustbin A dustbin is a large round container with a lid which people put their rubbish in ready for collection.

dustcart A dustcart is a lorry for taking away rubbish from people's dustbins.

duster A duster is a cloth for cleaning the dust off things like furniture.

dustman (dustmen) A dustman is a person whose job is to collect the rubbish from people's dustbins and take it away to be disposed of.

dustpan A dustpan is a small flat container with an open-ing at the front and a handle on top. You hold it flat on the floor and sweep dirt and dust into it.

dustsheet A dustsheet is a large piece of cloth put over furniture to protect it from dust, especially when it is not in use.

Dutch is used to talk about people and things in or from Holland (the Netherlands). ...*Dutch beer.* ◇ The Dutch are the Dutch people. ◇ Dutch is the main language spoken in Holland.

Dutchman (Dutchwoman) A Dutchman or Dutchwoman is a person who comes from Holland (the Netherlands).

dutiful (dutifully) A dutiful person does everything they should do or are expected to do. *She answers with dutiful politeness... The journalists all laughed dutifully.*

duty (duties) ❑ A person's duties are the things they have to do as their job. ◇ When people like doctors, nurses, and police are on duty, they are working. When they are off duty, they are not working.
❑ If something is your duty, you have a moral or legal responsibility to do it. If you are duty bound to do some-thing, you have to do it, because it is your duty.
❑ Duties are taxes you pay on things you buy, especial-ly when you bring them into the country.

duty-free goods can be bought at airports or on planes or ships at a cheaper price than usual, because no tax is paid on them. A duty-free area is one where you can buy duty-free goods.

duvet (*pron:* doo-vay *or* dyoo-vay) A duvet is a large flat bag filled with feathers or a similar material, which you use to cover yourself in bed.

dwarf (dwarfs, dwarfing, dwarfed) ❑ If one thing dwarfs an-other, it is so large it makes the other thing look small. *The citadel of Calvi is dwarfed by the mountains.* ◇ Dwarf plants and animals are much smaller than other plants and animals of the same kind. ...*dwarf chrysanthemums.*

❏ A **dwarf** (*plural:* dwarfs *or* dwarves) is a person who is much shorter than most people. This use of 'dwarf' is offensive. ◇ In children's stories, a **dwarf** is a very small ugly man with magical powers.

dwell (dwelling, dwelt *not* 'dwelled'; dweller) ❏ If you **dwell** somewhere, you live there. *...our cave-dwelling ancestors.* **Dweller** is used after words like 'town' to say where someone lives. *...city dwellers... ...slum dwellers.*

❏ If you **dwell on** something, you keep thinking, speaking, or writing about it.

dwelling A **dwelling** is a building or part of a building where people live together.

dwelt See dwell.

dwindle (dwindling, dwindled) If something **dwindles**, it becomes smaller or weaker.

dye (dyeing, dyed) If you **dye** hair or cloth, you change its colour by soaking it in a coloured liquid called a **dye**.

dyed-in-the-wool is used to describe people who have very strong opinions, attitudes, or habits which they refuse to change.

dying See die.

dyke (*or* dike) A **dyke** is a thick wall which stops water flooding onto land from a river or the sea. ◇ **Dyke** is also an offensive word for a lesbian.

dynamic (dynamically, dynamism) A **dynamic** person is full of energy and purpose. This quality is called **dynamism**. **Dynamic** is used to describe energetic behaviour. *Steinberg conducted the delicious score vigorously and dy-*namically. ◇ The **dynamics** of a situation are the forces which cause it to change.

dynamite (dynamiting, dynamited) **Dynamite** is an explosive made by soaking a substance like sawdust with nitroglycerin. If you **dynamite** something, you blow it up with dynamite. ◇ If you say something like a piece of news is **dynamite**, you mean it could have a powerful effect on people's thoughts or behaviour.

dynamo (dynamos) A **dynamo** is a device for converting mechanical energy into electrical energy.

dynasty (dynasties; dynastic) A **dynasty** is a series of rulers of a country who all belong to the same family. **Dynastic** is used to talk about things connected with dynasties. *...China's dynastic history.* ◇ Families are also called **dynasties** when they have been successful in politics, business, or entertainment through several generations. *...the Sainsbury supermarket dynasty.*

dysentery is an infection of the lower intestine which causes pain, fever, and severe diarrhoea.

dysfunction If there is **dysfunction** or a **dysfunction** in a part of your body, the part is not working properly.

dyslexic (dyslexia) **Dyslexic** people or **dyslexics** are people of normal intelligence who have difficulty with reading. This problem is called **dyslexia**.

dyspepsia (dyspeptic) **Dyspepsia** is the same as indigestion. If someone is **dyspeptic**, they have indigestion.

dystrophy See muscular dystrophy.

E e

E number E numbers are numbers with the letter 'E' in front of them, which appear on food labels, to indicate which additives the product contains. Additives themselves are often called E **numbers**.

each is used to talk about all the people or things in a group, considered as individuals. *Each country can enter two swimmers per event... Each of the elephants costs £15,000 a year to feed... The guests paid two hundred pounds each.*

❏ **Each other** is used to say two people or groups do the same thing: the first person or group does it to the second, and the second one does it to the first. *They glared at each other.*

❏ If you bet on a horse **each way**, you bet on it to come first, second, or third.

eager (eagerly, eagerness) If you are **eager** for something, you want it very much. If you are **eager** to do something, you are very keen or willing to do it. *Other publishing companies will be eager to take up this challenge... The results are eagerly awaited... He spoke with an eagerness I'd never seen in him before.*

eagle ❏ Eagles are large birds of prey with hooked bills, long broad wings, and powerful eyesight. ◇ If someone is **eagle-eyed**, they have very good eyesight, or are quick to spot small details or irregularities. *Three cannabis plants were found by eagle-eyed police officers.*

❏ In golf, an **eagle** is a score of two below par on any hole. See also birdie, bogey.

ear ❏ A person's or animal's **ears** are the organs which enable them to hear.

❏ An **ear-splitting** noise is extremely loud. An **ear-piercing** noise is very loud and shrill.

❏ If you **give ear** to someone, you pay attention to what they are saying. ◇ If you **have the ear** of someone in authority, they listen to you and are influenced by what you say. ◇ If someone **turns a deaf ear** to a request, claim, or piece of advice, they ignore it. When this happens, you say it **falls on deaf ears**.

❏ If you have an **ear** for music, you have the ability to listen to it and then reproduce its tunes and harmonies accurately.

❏ If someone is grinning **from ear to ear**, they are smiling broadly.

❏ An **ear** of a cereal plant like wheat or barley is the part at the top of the stalk which contains the seeds, grains, or kernels.

ear-bashing If someone is given an **ear-bashing**, they are given a telling-off or made to listen to a lot of talking.

ear-plug See earplug.

eardrum A person's **eardrums** are the thin pieces of skin, stretched across the inside of their ears, which help them to hear sounds.

earful If you give someone an **earful**, you speak angrily to them for quite a long time.

earl An **earl** is a British nobleman, ranking below a marquess but above a viscount.

earlobe A person's **earlobes** are the soft fleshy parts at the bottom of their ears.

early (earlier, earliest) ❑ **Early** means soon after the beginning of something. *...early in the morning... ...in the early 1980's... He was killed early on in the invasion.*

❑ **Early** is used to talk about people and things connected with the first stage in the development of something. *...early Christians... ...early cinema... ...his early poems.* ◇ The period when something was first developed can be called its **early days**. *In its early days, the motor car was known as the 'horseless carriage'.*

❑ If you say it is **early days**, you mean something has only just started, and nobody can tell how things will eventually turn out.

❑ **Early** is used to talk about something happening soon. For example, if people are hoping for an **early** solution to a problem, they are hoping it will be solved soon.

❑ If something happens **early**, it happens before the usual or expected time. *We got up early... Most shops will close early.* ◇ If you say someone is an **early bird**, you mean they rise early, or do things earlier than other people. ◇ You use **as early as** to say something happened or will happen earlier than might be expected. *It could take place as early as next year.*

❑ You use **at the earliest** to say something will not happen before a certain time, and it will probably be later still. *The tests won't be completed until next April at the earliest.*

early warning An **early-warning** device or system is designed to give advance warning of something like a flood or hurricane. ◇ An **early-warning system** is also a network of radar stations and satellites, designed to give advance warning of an air or missile attack.

earmark If something, especially money, is **earmarked** for a certain purpose, it is set aside for that purpose.

earn (earning, earned *or* earnt; earnings) ❑ The amount of money a person **earns** is the amount they are paid for the work they do; you call this money their **earnings**.

❑ The amount a business or investment **earns** is the profit it makes or returns; this profit is called its **earnings**. *BP's earnings nearly quadrupled to £822 million.* You can also talk about a country's **earnings** or the amount it **earns**. *Last year, Britain earned £11 million from apple exports.*

❑ If something you do **earns** you something, you get it as a result of doing it. *His next foul earned him a booking.* ◇ If you say something is **well-earned** or **hard-earned**, you mean it is thoroughly deserved. *...a well-earned holiday... ...a hard-earned victory.*

earner An **earner** is (a) a person who earns money. (b) something which makes money for someone. *Shipping is the country's greatest earner.*

earnest (earnestly, earnestness) ❑ If someone is **earnest**, they are very serious and sincere. *They talked earnestly to each other... ...speaking with great earnestness.* ◇ If someone is **in earnest**, they mean what they say. ◇ If something starts **in earnest**, it gets going properly. *Negotiations began in earnest.*

❑ An **earnest** is a foretaste or indication of what will happen. *They took it as an earnest of even bigger changes to come.*

earnings See **earn**.

earphone An **earphone** is a small receiver which fits inside a person's ear, so they can listen to a radio or tape without anyone else hearing. See also **headphones**.

earpiece The **earpiece** is the part of a telephone receiver you hold next to your ear. ◇ An **earpiece** is also a small receiver, which TV presenters wear in their ear, so they can receive instructions from the director without anyone else hearing. ◇ The **earpieces** of a pair of glasses are the parts which fit over a person's ears.

earplug (*or* ear-plug) **Earplugs** are small pieces of soft material which fit inside the ears and keep out noise or water.

earring **Earrings** are pieces of jewellery which people attach to their ears.

earshot If you are **within earshot** of something, you are close enough to hear it. You can also say the thing you hear is **within earshot**. If you are **out of earshot**, you are too far away to hear something.

earth ❑ The **Earth** is the planet we live on. ◇ The ground can also be called the **earth**. *The earth shook.* ◇ **Earth** is also another name for clay or soil. *...rich black earth.*

❑ An **earth** is a wire fitted to a plug or electrical appliance, through which electricity can pass into the ground, so the plug or appliance is safe to use. If you **earth** a plug or electrical appliance, you fit it with an earth.

❑ People use **on earth** after words like 'how', 'why', 'what', and 'who' to make a point more strongly. *How on earth does everyone cope?... What on earth gave him that idea?*

❑ If a person or group of people is brought **down to earth**, they are forced to be more realistic about what they can achieve. See also **down-to-earth**.

earthbound If an object in space is **earthbound**, it is heading towards the Earth. ◇ You also say someone or something is **earthbound** when they are confined or attached to the Earth. *...earthbound telescopes.*

earthen structures are made of compacted earth.

earthenware pottery is made of baked clay.

earthly things exist on Earth, as opposed to Heaven. *...earthly pleasures.*

❑ **Earthly** is often used to mean 'possible'. For example, if you say there is no **earthly** reason to do something, you mean there is no possible reason to do it.

earthquake An **earthquake** is a series of vibrations along the Earth's surface, which make the ground shake. Earthquakes are caused by movements along cracks in the Earth's surface.

earthwork **Earthworks** are large banks of earth put up at an early time in history, usually for defensive purposes. More recent excavations, where earth has been piled up in banks, are also sometimes called **earthworks**.

earthworm See **worm**.

earthy (earthier, earthiest; earthiness) If you call someone **earthy**, you mean they are unrefined or coarse. You can also call their behaviour **earthy**. *...earthy language... ...their natural earthiness.* ◇ You can also use **earthy** to describe something which reminds you of earth or soil. *...an earthy aroma... ...the earthy taste of wild mushrooms.*

earwig **Earwigs** are small brown insects, with a pair of pincers at the rear end of their bodies.

ease (easing, eased) ❑ If you do something with **ease**, you do it with little or no difficulty. ◇ A life of **ease** is free from worry or hard work. ◇ If you are at **ease**, you are comfortable and relaxed. If you are ill at **ease**, you are anxious or awkward.
❑ If a situation **eases** or is **eased**, it becomes less tense or difficult. ◇ If a restriction on something is **eased**, it is made less harsh or severe. ◇ If pain or a worry **eases** or is **eased**, it becomes less severe.
❑ If you **ease** something somewhere, you move it slowly and gently. *He eased the door open... He eased himself into his chair.* ◇ If you **ease up**, you take things more slowly or gently. *He eased up on training.* If you **ease up** on someone else, you treat them more leniently. ◇ If something **eases off**, there is less of it. *The rain has now eased off.*

easel An **easel** is a wooden stand on which a blackboard or artist's canvas is placed.

easily See **easy**.

east is one of the four main points of the compass. ◇ The **east** is the direction where the sun rises. If you go in that direction, you go **east**; a place in that direction is **east** of the place where you are now. ◇ The **east** part of a place is the part east of its centre. *...the east of the country... ...East Africa.*
❑ An **east** wind blows from the east.
❑ The **East** is used to talk about (a) Russia and the other former Communist countries in Eastern Europe. (b) China, Japan, and other Asian countries, taken as a whole.

eastbound traffic is heading towards the east.

Easter is a religious festival held in March or April, in which Christians celebrate Jesus Christ's resurrection. The period of time around Easter is also called **Easter**.

Easter egg Easter eggs are eggs, especially large chocolate eggs, given as gifts at Easter.

easterly ❑ An **easterly** wind blows from the east. ◇ If you travel in an **easterly** direction, you travel towards the east. Similarly, if you face in an **easterly** direction, you face towards the east.
❑ The most **easterly** part of a place is the part furthest to the east. *...the most easterly tip of Papua New Guinea.* Similarly, the most **easterly** place of a group of places is the one furthest to the east.

eastern ❑ The **eastern** part of a place is the part east of its centre. *...eastern Australia.* ◇ **Eastern** also means to the east of a country or region. *...Iraq's eastern neighbour, Iran.*
❑ **Eastern** is also used to talk about things which come from Asia. *...Eastern philosophy... ...Eastern religions.*

easterner An **easterner** is a person who was born in or lives in the eastern part of a country or region.

easternmost The **easternmost** part of a place is the part furthest to the east. Similarly, the **easternmost** place of a group of places is the one furthest to the east. *...the country's easternmost island.*

eastward (eastwards) If you go **eastward** or **eastwards**, you go towards the east. You can also say you go in an **eastward** direction. *The disease is spreading eastwards... ...an eastward flight.*

easy (easier, easiest; easily) ❑ If something is **easy** to do, it can be done without much effort or difficulty. *It is easy to reach any of these places... He won easily.* ◇ **Easy** is used

with words like 'no' and 'not' to say how difficult something is. *Tracking him down was no easy task... The job is far from easy.* ◇ If something does not come easily to you, you find it difficult to do or achieve.
❑ If someone suggests doing something, you can point out how difficult it is by saying it is **easier said than done**.
❑ An **easy** life or time is free from pain, worry, or hard work. ◇ **Easy** money is money you do not have to work hard to get. ◇ If you **take it easy** or **take things easy**, you relax and do very little.
❑ If someone has an **easy** manner, they are relaxed and friendly.
❑ You use **easily** after 'could', 'can', or 'might' to say something is quite likely to happen. *The events of 1987 could easily be repeated... Such a situation might easily arise again.* ◇ You also use **easily** to emphasize that something is beyond a doubt. *It is easily the fastest boat in the regatta.*

easy chair An **easy chair** is a large comfortable chair.

easy-going An **easy-going** person is relaxed and tolerant.

easy listening is gentle music with light melodies, aimed at older people.

eat (eating, ate, have eaten) ❑ When you **eat** something, you put it in your mouth, chew it, and swallow it. ◇ If you **eat** at a certain time, that is when you normally have a meal. If you **eat** at a particular place, you have meals there regularly. ◇ If you **eat in**, you have a meal at home, rather than in a restaurant. If you **eat out**, you do the opposite.
❑ If something **eats up** resources, it uses them in large amounts. *Old properties need a lot of maintaining and seem to eat up money.* ◇ If something **eats away** at something else, it slowly reduces it. *New development will rapidly eat away what green countryside remains.* ◇ If a disease **eats away** at something, it spreads and grows, destroying it. *Dry rot ate away ship's timbers from the inside.*
❑ **eat your words:** see **word**.

eater is used to describe how a person eats, or what they eat. *...a fast eater... ...a meat eater.*

eatery (eateries) Restaurants are sometimes called **eateries**.

eau de cologne (*pron:* oh de kol-lone) is a lightly scented perfume, originally made in Cologne.

eaves The overhanging edges of a roof are called the **eaves**.

eavesdrop (eavesdropping, eavesdropped: eavesdropper) If you **eavesdrop** on someone, you secretly listen to what they are saying. This is called **eavesdropping**; someone doing it is called an **eavesdropper**.

ebb (ebbing, ebbed) ❑ When something like a feeling or a person's strength **ebbs**, it gets weaker. If it **ebbs away**, it gets weaker, then disappears altogether. ◇ If something is at a low **ebb**, it has become very weak or unsuccessful. *Confidence is at a very low ebb.*
❑ When the tide **ebbs**, it goes out. When it is going out, you can talk about its **ebb** or call it an **ebb tide**. ◇ The **ebb and flow** of something is the way its pace picks up then slows down again. *...the ebb and flow of the match.*

ebony is (a) a dark black colour. (b) a hard black wood, used for making high-quality furniture.

ebullient (ebullience) An **ebullient** person is overflowing with enthusiasm and excitement. You can talk about the **ebullience** of someone like this.

EC See European Community.

eccentric (eccentricity, eccentricities: eccentrically) Eccentric behaviour is odd and unconventional. A person who behaves like this is called an **eccentric**. You call their behaviour **eccentricity**; you can also talk about a person's **eccentricities**. *He wore, eccentrically, a Wolf Cub's cap.*

ecclesiastical (ecclesiastic) **Ecclesiastical** is used to talk about things to do with the Church. *...ecclesiastical history.* ◇ An **ecclesiastic** is a member of the clergy.

ECG See electrocardiograph.

echelon (*pron*: esh-e-lon) ❑ An **echelon** is a level of power or responsibility within an organization or group of people. *...the lower echelons of the police.*
❑ An **echelon** is also a military formation in which each of the vehicles, ships, or soldiers in a group is behind and slightly to the left or right of the one in front.

echo (echoes, echoing, echoed) ❑ An **echo** is a repetition of a sound, caused by the sound bouncing off a surface such as a wall or cliff. If a sound **echoes**, it creates an echo. If a place **echoes**, it is filled with echoes.
❑ The signal reflected by a radar target is also called an **echo.**
❑ An **echo** is also an expression of a view which has already been expressed. If you **echo** someone's views, you repeat them, or say something very similar. ◇ If something like an attitude or opinion **finds an echo** in another place or situation, people there have it too. *The mutiny is the first sign that the unrest has found an echo in the army.*
❑ If you say something **echoes** something else, you mean it resembles it in some way.
❑ If you cheer someone **to the echo**, you cheer them very loudly.

echo-location is a way of locating an obstacle by measuring the time it takes for an echo to return from it. Echo-location is used by creatures like bats and dolphins.

éclair An **éclair** is a finger-shaped cake made of choux pastry filled with cream and covered with chocolate.

eclectic (eclecticism) An **eclectic** mixture of people, ideas, or things comes from a wide range of sources, rather than just one. Mixing people, ideas, or things in this way is called **eclecticism**. *The station's greatest asset is its eclecticism.* ◇ If you have **eclectic** tastes, you enjoy a wide range of things.

eclipse (eclipsing, eclipsed) ❑ When there is an **eclipse** of the sun, the moon passes between it and the Earth, hiding the sun partly or completely from view and briefly blocking out the sunlight. An eclipse of the sun is called a **solar eclipse**. When there is an **eclipse** of the moon, the earth passes between the sun and the moon, casting a shadow on the moon. This is called a **lunar eclipse**.
❑ If something suffers an **eclipse**, it goes into decline. *...the eclipse of the influence of the Republican party.*
❑ If a person or thing is **eclipsed** by someone or something else, they are overshadowed or surpassed by them.

eco- (*pron*: eek-oh) is short for 'ecology' or 'ecological'. It is added to words to create new words describing things connected with the environment. *...an eco-labelling scheme to highlight environmentally friendly products... ...eco-friendly packaging.*

ecology (ecologies; ecological, ecologically; ecologist) Ecology is the study of the relationship between living things and their environment. An expert on this is called an ecologist. ◇ When people talk about the **ecology** of an area, they mean the balance between living things and their environment. ◇ **Ecological** is used to talk about things to do with ecology. *...an ecologically unique area of heath and woodland.* ◇ **Ecological** groups or movements campaign to protect the environment.

economic (economics; economically, economist) ❑ Economic is used to talk about things to do with a country's or region's economy. *...the government's economic policies... ...the economically important Firestone rubber plantation.* ◇ If a business or venture is **economic**, it has reasonable running costs, and makes a profit.
❑ **Economics** is the study of the production of goods and services, and of their consumption or use. An expert in economics is called an **economist**. ◇ Economics is also used to talk about methods of organizing money, production, and trade. *...old-fashioned Marxist economics.* ◇ When people talk about the **economics** of a business or venture, they mean the cost of setting it up and running it, and the profit it makes.

Economic and Monetary Union (*or* European Monetary Union *or* EMU) is the proposed setting up of a European central bank, and the introduction of a single European currency.

economic refugee An **economic refugee** is a person who moves from a poor country to a rich one, in the hope of finding a higher standard of living.

economical (economically) ❑ If something is **economical**, it does not cost much to run. *This way the boat's engines will run more economically.* ◇ If a person is **economical**, they are careful with their money.
❑ You also use **economical** to talk about something being done with the minimum of effort or waste. *His gestures were economical.* ◇ If you say someone has been **economical with the truth**, you mean they have not told the whole truth about something.

economize (economizing, economized) (*can be spelled with an 's' instead of a 'z'*) If you **economize**, you cut down on your spending, to save money.

economy (economies) ❑ The **economy** of a country or region is the system it uses to organize and manage its money, industry, and trade. ◇ The wealth a country or region obtains from business and industry is also called its **economy**. *The monarchy pulls in millions of pounds in tourism for the British economy.*
❑ **Economy** is careful spending, or the careful use of things to avoid waste or save money. A way of avoiding waste or saving money is called an **economy**. *There is a need to make every possible economy.* ◇ Economy is also used to talk about using no more of something than is necessary. For example, you can do something with economy of effort. *...economy of movement... ...economy of language.*
❑ **Economy class** travel is cheaper than other kinds, with no luxuries or extras.

ecosystem When people talk about the **ecosystem** in a place like a forest or lake, they are supposing that all the living things there are part of one large system, and that any change, such as the destruction of a species, would affect the whole system.

ecstasy (ecstasies; ecstatic, ecstatically) ❑ Ecstasy is a feeling of overwhelming happiness. If someone has this feeling, you say they are **ecstatic**. *...a man ecstatically in love.* ◇ You also say people are **ecstatic** when they are thoroughly delighted with something.

❏ **Ecstasy** is also an illegal drug which acts as a stimulant and can cause hallucinations.

ecu (*or* Ecu *or* ECU) (*pron:* ay-kew) (*plural:* ecu *or* ecus) The **ecu** is a unit of money used for accounting purposes by the European Union's financial institutions, though it is not a currency in its own right. Some people want the ecu to be the single European currency, replacing the individual currencies of member states. 'ecu' stands for 'European Currency Unit'. ◇ The **hard ecu** was an alternative to the ecu, proposed by the British government in 1990. It would be legal tender in every country in the EU, but would not replace individual currencies.

ecumenical (*pron:* ee-kew-**men**-ik-al *or* ek-kew-**men**-ik-al) (ecumenism, ecumenist) **Ecumenical** is used to talk about places or events which cater for Christians of all sects, or for Christians and people of other religions. *...ecumenical prayer meetings.* ◇ The **ecumenical** movement is a movement which seeks to unite all Christian sects. This movement is also called **ecumenism** (*pron:* ee-kew-min-ism *or* ek-kew-min-ism); the people involved are called **ecumenists**.

eczema (*pron:* ek-sim-a) is a skin condition which causes parts of the skin to become red and itchy.

eddy (eddies, eddying, eddied) If water, wind, fog, or snow **eddies**, it swirls round and round. The swirling patches it forms are called **eddies**.

edema See oedema.

edge (edging, edged) ❏ The **edge** of something is its boundary, border, or rim, or the place where it begins or ends. *...the edge of the city... ...the sea's edge.* ◇ The **edge** of something like a cliff is the place where the level land ends and the steep drop begins.

❏ If you **edge** a lawn, you trim its edges.

❏ If an area or object is **edged** with something, it has it around its edges or borders. *...a vast fenland region, edged with poplar trees.* ◇ An **edging** is a decorative border round something. *...windows decorated with brick edging.*

❏ The **edge** of an object like a ruler is the narrow ridge where the two flat sides meet. ◇ The **edge** of a blade is the sharp part.

❏ If you **edge** towards something, you move towards it slowly and cautiously. Similarly, you can **edge** along something, or away from something. *Rebels have edged closer to the centre of the capital.* ◇ If you **edge** through a crowd, you gradually push your way through it.

❏ If a figure **edges up** or **down**, it increases or decreases slightly. *Pre-tax profits edged up by 1.7% last year.*

❏ If you have an **edge** over someone, you have an advantage over them.

❏ If you **edge towards** doing or achieving something, you get gradually closer to it. ◇ If a country, community, or organization is **on the edge** of something unpleasant, it is likely to happen to it soon. *The country is hovering on the edge of civil war.*

❏ If you are **on edge**, you are tense and irritable. ◇ If something **sets your teeth on edge**, it makes you extremely irritated. ◇ If a person's voice has an **edge** to it, it

shows their feelings of bitterness, anger, or strain.

❏ If a book or film has you **on the edge of your seat**, you become very involved in the action, and are eager to know what happens next.

❏ If something **takes the edge off** an achievement or enjoyable experience, it makes it less impressive or enjoyable. You can also say something **takes the edge off** a bad experience. *It is to be hoped this will take the edge off their disappointment.*

edgy (edginess) You say someone is **edgy** when they are tense, nervous, and likely to lose control of their feelings. *This may be a sign of increasing edginess in the Iraqi capital.*

edible If something is **edible**, it is not poisonous and can be eaten. *...edible fungi.*

edict (*pron:* ee-dict) An **edict** is an official order or instruction, issued by a ruler or some other very high authority.

edifice People sometimes call a large impressive building an **edifice**. ◇ A very large organization or institution can also be called an **edifice**. *...the crumbling edifice of Communist rule.*

edify (*pron:* ed-if-fie) (edifies, edifying, edified) If something **edifies** you, it adds to your knowledge and understanding. You say something like this is **edifying**.

edit (editing, edited) ❏ When someone **edits** written material, they check it and correct it, to make sure it is suitable for publication. ◇ When someone **edits** a collection of essays, letters, stories, or poems, they choose which ones to include, and often write an introduction or notes.

❏ When someone **edits** a film or a TV or radio programme, they choose which material to use, and arrange it in a particular order. ◇ If material is **edited out** of a manuscript, film, or broadcast, it is removed, for reasons of space or time, or because people might find it offensive. An **edited** version of something is one which has had material removed like this.

❏ If someone **edits** a newspaper or magazine, they are its editor.

edition An **edition** of a book or newspaper is a particular version of it. ◇ An **edition** of a TV or radio programme is a single programme which is part of a series.

editor (editorship) ❏ The **editor** of a newspaper or magazine is the person in charge, who decides which news stories or articles will go into it. The position of editor is called the **editorship**. ◇ The person in charge of a section of a newspaper or magazine is also called an **editor**. *...the fashion editor of Harpers & Queen.*

❏ In book publishing, an **editor** is a person whose job is to edit written material before it is published. ◇ A person who puts together a collection of essays, letters, stories, or poems for publication is also called an **editor**.

❏ In films and broadcasting, an **editor** is a person whose job is to edit a film or programme before it is released or broadcast. ◇ An **editor** is also a senior TV or radio journalist who reports on a particular type of news. *...BBC Television's Foreign Affairs editor, John Simpson.*

editorial (editorially) ❏ An **editorial** is a newspaper article which gives the opinions of the editor or publisher on a topic. **Editorial** comments appear in an editorial. *Many papers comment editorially that the proposals could damage* *press freedom.*

❑ The people involved in planning the contents of a newspaper, magazine, or book series are called the **editorial staff.** ◇ **Editorial** is used to talk about things like the attitudes, opinions, and choice of contents of a newspaper or TV programme. *...editorial policy.*

educate (educating, educated) ❑ When someone is **educated,** they are taught a variety of subjects at a school or college. ◇ If you say someone is **educated** or **well-educated,** you mean they have had a good education.

❑ If people are **educated** in something like health care or protecting the environment, they are given information about it and made aware of its importance.

❑ An **educated** guess is based on previous experience, and therefore more likely to be correct.

education (educational, educationally) ❑ **Education** is the process by which a person gains knowledge and understanding through study or experience. ◇ A country's **education** system is the system it uses for teaching people in schools and colleges. If someone is **in education,** they are attending a school or college. *More young people are remaining in education.* **Educational** is used to talk about things to do with education. *...educational reforms... Educationally the pre-primary school years are very important.*

❑ If you say something is an **education,** you mean you can learn a lot from it. *The book is not only a pleasure to read, but an education.* ◇ An **educational** toy helps a child to learn something.

educationalist (educationist) An **educationalist** or **educationist** is a specialist in the theories and methods of education.

educative is used to talk about things which increase people's knowledge. For example, you can say something has an **educative** purpose, or talk about its **educative** value.

educator An **educator** is a person who contributes something to education, for example by teaching at a school or university, or by writing educational books.

Edwardian The **Edwardian** period was from 1901 to 1910, the reign of King Edward VII. **Edwardian** is used to describe people or things from that time. *...an Edwardian country house.* People associated with the Edwardian period are sometimes called **Edwardians.**

EEC See **European Economic Community.**

eel Eels are long thin snake-like fish.

eerie (eerily) If something is **eerie,** it is strange and unsettling. *...an eerie silence... The click of footsteps echoed eerily along the High Street.*

efface (effacing, effaced) If a piece of writing is **effaced,** it is rubbed away. ◇ If something **effaces** a bad memory or impression, it creates a new one and the old one is forgotten. ◇ See also **self-effacing.**

effect ❑ An **effect** of something is a change or result which it produces on something else. ◇ Some scientific phenomena which involve changes or results have **effect** as part of their name. *...the Doppler effect.*

❑ The **effect** something creates is the impression it gives. *The effect was of an indoor garden.* ◇ If someone does something **for effect,** they do it to impress people.

❑ If you **effect** a change, you bring it about.

❑ If something **takes effect** from a certain time, it starts

to operate or apply then. You can also say something **comes into effect** at a particular time. *The ceasefire was due to come into effect next month... The ban on her return to the country would remain in effect.* ◇ If you say something is beginning to **take effect,** you mean it is beginning to produce the results it was intended to.

❑ **In effect** is used to say something is true for all practical purposes, though it is not officially true. *He has in effect declared martial law.*

❑ **To this effect** and **to that effect** are used to say a statement expresses or summarizes something which has just been mentioned. For example, if you say 'Sir George was opposed to the treaty, and made a statement to that effect', you mean Sir George made a statement that he was opposed to the treaty. ◇ You say **to the effect that** when you are reporting what someone has said or written, without using their actual words. *He said something to the effect that he had retreated from politics.* Similarly, you say **or words to that effect** to indicate that you are not quoting someone's exact words. *He told the traffic warden to go away, or words to that effect.*

❑ A person's belongings are sometimes called their **effects.** ◇ The **effects** in a film or play, or in a TV or radio programme, are things like the sound and lighting, which are used to create a mood or setting.

effective (effectively, effectiveness) ❑ If something is **effective,** it produces the result that is wanted. *There are many doubts as to the effectiveness of the boycott.*

❑ If something like a law, treaty, or policy becomes **effective** from a particular date, it starts to apply then.

❑ **Effective** and **effectively** are used to say something is true in practice, though not officially. For example, you can say something has **effectively** ended or talk about its **effective** end. *The area is effectively closed to foreigners... He has been the effective leader of the party since the revolution.*

effectual If something is **effectual,** it produces the result you want.

effeminate If you say a man is **effeminate,** you mean he looks, sounds, or behaves like a woman.

effervescent (effervescence) An **effervescent** liquid is full of fizzy bubbles of gas. This fizziness is called **effervescence.** ◇ An **effervescent** person is lively and energetic. *Her mood swung from effervescence to black despair.*

effete is used to describe people who are weak and powerless, especially people who have grown soft or lazy as a result of too much good living.

efficacious (pron: eff-i-kay-shus) (efficacy) If something, particularly a treatment or remedy, is **efficacious,** it is very good at producing the result you want. You can talk about the **efficacy** (pron: ef-ik-ass-ee) of something like this. *They are testing the efficacy of an ancient herbal remedy for malaria.*

efficient (efficiently, efficiency) If someone is **efficient,** they do their job well. **Efficiency** is used to talk about people's ability to do their job. *...managerial efficiency.* ◇ If something like a machine is **efficient,** it does its work using a minimum amount of power. *...fuel that will burn more efficiently... This helps increase the power of the engine and enhance its efficiency.*

effigy (effigies) An **effigy** is a roughly made figure, made to look like a well-known person. Effigies are sometimes publicly burned or hanged as a demonstration of hatred for the person they represent. ◇ An **effigy** is also a statue or carving of someone, especially one from an earlier period of history.

effluent is liquid waste, especially waste from factories and sewage works, when it is discharged into rivers or the sea.

effort is hard work. ◇ An **effort** is an attempt to do something. *...an effort to combat drug trafficking.* ◇ If you do something with an **effort**, you do it with difficulty. *With an effort, she contained her irritation.*

effortless (effortlessly) If something is **effortless**, it does not require any effort. *Tulu and Meyer broke effortlessly away from McColgan after 15 laps.*

effrontery is bold, rude, or cheeky behaviour.

effusion An **effusion** of a liquid is a quantity of it pouring from somewhere. ◇ When someone expresses a strong feeling by talking or writing a lot, you can call what they say an **effusion** of the feeling. *His employer greeted him with an effusion of relief.*

effusive (effusively) If someone is **effusive**, they are full of praise or enthusiasm for someone or something. *...the event which she had effusively welcomed.*

e.g. means 'for example'. *He could have spent some of the extra revenue on e.g. higher child benefit.*

egalitarian (egalitarianism) In an **egalitarian** system, everyone is treated equally. The principle of treating people equally is called **egalitarianism**; someone who accepts this principle and tries to follow it is called an **egalitarian.**

egg ❑ **Eggs** are round or oval objects, laid by female birds, reptiles, fish, and insects. The young of all these creatures develop in an egg before they hatch. ◇ An **egg** is a hen's egg, eaten as food or used in cooking.
❑ An **egg** or **egg cell** is a cell produced in the body of a woman or female animal, which can develop into a baby if it is fertilized by sperm.
❑ If someone is **egged on** into doing something, especially something foolish or aggressive, they are encouraged to do it. ◇ If something leaves you **with egg on your face**, it leaves you looking foolish.
❑ If you **put all your eggs in one basket**, you pin all your hopes on on the success of one person or thing, without giving yourself someone or something else to fall back on.

egg cup An **egg cup** is a small cup-shaped container for putting a boiled egg in while you eat it.

egg timer An **egg timer** is a device for telling you when an egg has boiled.

egg white is the transparent liquid surrounding the yolk of a hen's egg. It is also called 'albumen'.

egghead is a humorous word for a person who is very clever or intelligent.

eggplant In the US, aubergines are called **eggplants**.

eggshell An **eggshell** is the hard outer part of an egg.

ego (pron: ee-go or egg-go) ❑ A person's **ego** is their own high opinion of their abilities and importance. *He had a massive ego and would never admit he was wrong.* ◇ If you say someone is on an **ego trip,** you mean they are doing something just to satisfy their feeling of being cleverer or more important than other people.
❑ In psychoanalysis, a person's **ego** is their conscious mind.

❑ See also **alter ego.**

egocentric You say people are **egocentric** when they think only of themselves, and do not consider the wishes of other people.

egoism is the same as egotism.

egoist (egoistic, egoistical) An **egoist** is the same as an egotist.

egomaniac (egomania) An **egomaniac** is someone who thinks only of their own interests and does not worry about harming other people. This sort of behaviour is called **egomania.**

egotist (egotism; egotistical, egotistic) An **egotist** is someone who acts selfishly and believes they are more important than other people. You can talk about a person's **egotism** or say they are **egotistical** or **egotistic.**

egregious (*pron:* ig-greej-uss) (egregiously) **Egregious** is used to describe things which are really badly done. An **egregious** person is always doing things badly or saying silly things. *...egregious errors... ...the egregious mayor of Chicago... Their economic policies had been egregiously ill-managed.* ◇ **Egregious** is also used to describe wrong or harmful actions carried out in an open way. *...his egregious use of government aeroplanes and cars.*

Egyptology (Egyptologist) **Egyptology** is the study of ancient Egypt. An expert on this subject is called an **Egyptologist.**

eiderdown An **eiderdown** is a quilt filled with feathers or some other warm material.

eight is the number 8.

eighteen (eighteenth) **Eighteen** is the number 18.

eighth The **eighth** item in a series is the one counted as number 8. ◇ An **eighth** or **one eighth** is the fraction $\frac{1}{8}$.

eighty (eightieth, eighties) **Eighty** is the number 80. ◇ The **eighties** was the period from 1980 to 1989. ◇ If someone is in their **eighties,** they are aged 80 to 89.

Eire is another name for the Republic of Ireland.

Eisteddfod (*pron:* ice-sted-fod) An **Eisteddfod** is a Welsh festival in which competitions are held; they can be in music, poetry, dance, or drama.

either means one or the other. *If either side deserved a goal, United did... The government no longer listens to either of them.*
❑ If something is on **either** side of something, it is on each of its sides. *...giant video screens on either side of the stage.*
❑ **Either** is used with 'or' to show there are two, or sometimes more, possibilities or alternatives. *You'll either love it or loathe it... China must either go along or be isolated.* ◇ An **either / or** situation is one where someone only has two alternatives.
❑ If you make two statements with a word like 'no' or 'not' in them, you can put **either** at the end of the second one. *Saddam Hussein has shown no signs of backing down. The message from San Francisco is that Mr Bush has no intention of backing down either.* Similarly, you use **either** when you have made a statement with 'no' or 'not' in it and you want to show it applies to another person or thing. *It would not be in the interests of France, or of Israel either.*

ejaculate (ejaculating, ejaculated; ejaculation) When a man **ejaculates,** he discharges semen from his penis.

eject (ejecting, ejected; ejection) When something is **eject**ed by or from something else, it is pushed or sent out with considerable force. ◇ If someone is **ejected** from a place, they are made to leave, often by physical force. ◇ If someone is **ejected** from a position of power, they are sacked or forced to resign. *This led to his ejection from office.* ◇ When a pilot **ejects** from a plane which is about to crash, he escapes using his ejector seat.

ejector seat An **ejector seat** is a special seat fitted in some aircraft. It is used in an emergency to eject the person sitting in it out of the plane, so they can parachute to safety.

eke (eking, eked) If someone **ekes out** a living, they earn just enough money to buy the things they need. ◇ If you **eke out** a supply of something, you make it last by using it sparingly. ◇ If something is **eked out** with something else, it is supplemented with it, to make it go further. *Their diet consisted almost entirely of rice, eked out by the occasional piece of meat.*

elaborate (elaborating, elaborated; elaborately, elaboration) ❑ If something is **elaborate**, it is complicated or has many parts. ◇ If something decorative is **elaborate**, it is full of small details. *...elaborately carved thrones.*
  ❑ If you **elaborate** (*pron:* i-**lab**-er-ate) on something, you give more details about it. *NASA is not giving any further elaboration.* If you **elaborate** something like a line of thought or a plan of action, you develop it.

élan (*pron:* ale-an) If something is done with **élan**, it is done with style and flair.

elapse (elapsing, elapsed) **Elapse** is used to talk about time passing. For example, if you say four years have **elapsed** since something happened, you mean it happened four years ago.

elastic (elasticated, elasticity) ❑ **Elastic** is a kind of flexible tape, usually made of rubber. If part of a piece of clothing is **elasticated**, it has elastic threaded through it, to make it fit more closely. ◇ An **elastic band** is a thin loop of elastic which you put around things to hold them together.
  ❑ If a material is **elastic**, it stretches and returns to its original shape like elastic. You can talk about the **elasticity** (*pron:* el-ass-tiss-it-ee) of an object or material. ◇ If a way of doing things is **elastic**, it can be adapted to meet new circumstances.

elated (elation) If someone is **elated**, they are extremely happy. This feeling is called **elation.**

elbow ❑ A person's **elbow** is the joint between their upper arm and forearm, which allows their arm to bend. ◇ If you **elbow** someone, you give them a sharp dig with your elbow. If you **elbow** them **aside**, you push them aside with your elbow. ◇ You also say someone **elbows** someone else **aside** when they force them out of a position of power or advantage, and take their place.
  ❑ **Elbow grease** is physical effort. *It took a lot of elbow grease to crank the apparatus.* ◇ **Elbow room** is space to move in, or freedom to do what you want. *There was not much elbow room in the cockpit... His speech was designed to give himself more political elbow room.*

elder ❑ The **elder** of two people is the one who was born first. You can call people who are older than you your **elders.** If you have an **elder** brother or sister, he or she is older than you.
  ❑ An **elder** is a senior member of a tribe or community,

with influence or authority in it. ◇ An **elder** is also a lay member of the Presbyterian church, who plays a part in all its courts and assemblies. Elders are sometimes called 'presbyters'.
  ❑ An **elder** or **elderberry** is a small tree or shrub, with clusters of tiny white flowers and red, purple, or black berries. The berries, which are used to make wine, are called **elderberries.**

elder statesman An **elder statesman** is an old and respected politician, either retired or still in parliament, whose opinion is valued because of their long experience.

elderberry (elderberries) See **elder.**

elderly An **elderly** person is old. **The elderly** are old people in general.

eldest The **eldest** of a group of people is the one who was born first.

elect ❑ When people **elect** someone, they choose them to lead or represent them, by voting for them. ◇ If someone is **elected** to a prestigious body, they are voted in by its members.
  ❑ **-elect** is used after a person's title, to show that, although they have been appointed to a position, they have not yet formally taken office. *He is president-elect of the American Association of the Advancement of Science.*
  ❑ If you **elect** to do something, you choose to do it. *Most companies elect to use fax transmission so that reports can be sent back to them on the same day.*

electable If you say a politician or political party is **electable**, you mean they stand a real chance of being elected.

election An **election** is a process in which people vote to choose a person or group to lead or represent them. ◇ The **election** of a person or political party is their success in winning an election.

electioneering is the things politicians and their supporters do to persuade people to vote for them in an election, such as making speeches and visiting voters in their homes. Governments are sometimes accused of **electioneering** when they do something just to win votes in a forthcoming election, rather than because it is for the good of the country.

elective ❑ An **elective** system of government is one in which people elect their leaders. ◇ An **elective** post is one someone is elected to, rather than just being appointed.
  ❑ **Elective** surgery is planned in advance.

elector (electorate) An **elector** is someone who has the right to vote in an election. All the electors in a place are called the **electorate.**

electoral (electorally) **Electoral** is used to talk about things to do with elections or being elected. *...electoral reform... ...the electoral process... This could be electorally disastrous.*

electoral college In the US, the **Electoral College** is a body of electors chosen by voters in each State, who formally elect the country's President and Vice-President. Any similar body of electors can be called an **electoral college.**

electoral register The **electoral register** or **electoral roll** is an official list of all the people in an area who have a right to vote in an election. It is also called the 'voters' list'.

electorate See elector.

electric (electrics) ❏ Electric is used to describe things which produce or carry electricity, or are powered by electricity. ...*an electric generator... ...electric cables.* ◇ An electric guitar or other instrument is amplified electrically. ◇ The electrical wiring in a house or vehicle is sometimes called the **electrics**.
   ❏ If you say the atmosphere in a place is **electric,** you mean the people there are very excited about something which is happening.

electric blanket An electric blanket is a blanket with wires inside which can be heated electrically to warm up a bed.

electric-blue is a very bright blue colour.

electric chair An electric chair is a special chair used in some states in the US to execute criminals. The condemned person is killed by a powerful electric current being sent through their body.

electric shock An electric shock is a shock caused by electricity passing through a person's body.

electrical (electrically) Electrical is used to describe things which produce or carry electricity, or are powered by electricity. ...*an electrical charge... ...electrically powered cars.* ◇ Electrical is also used to describe people or companies involved in developing, maintaining, manufacturing, or selling electrical goods or equipment. ...*the German electrical group Siemens.*

electrical engineering (electrical engineer) Electrical engineering is a branch of engineering concerned with the practical applications of electricity and electronics. An **electrical engineer** is an expert in this field.

electrician An electrician is a person whose job is to install, service, and repair electrical equipment.

electricity is a form of energy used for heating and lighting, and to power machines. An **electricity company** produces electricity and supplies it to homes and businesses.

electrify (electrifies, electrifying, electrified; electrification) ❏ If a system is **electrified**, it is converted to run on electricity. ...*the electrification of the East Coast main line.* ◇ An **electrified** fence has an electric charge running through it, which gives a shock to anyone or anything touching it. Electrified fences are used to stop people or animals getting into or out of a place.
   ❏ If something **electrifies** you, you find it very exciting.

electrocardiograph (*or* electro-cardiograph) An electrocardiograph is a machine used to measure the electrical activity of a person's heart, which it records on a tracing called an **electrocardiogram** or **ECG**. Electrocardiographs are sometimes called 'ECG machines'.

electrocute (electrocuting, electrocuted; electrocution) If someone is **electrocuted**, they are accidentally killed or injured by electricity. *One man died of electrocution.* ◇ You also say someone is **electrocuted** when they are tortured or killed by having electricity deliberately passed through their body.

electrode An electrode is a piece of metal which carries an electric current to or from a source of power such as a battery.

electrolysis (*pron:* ill-lek-troll-iss-iss) is (a) a process in which an electric current is passed through a substance or solution to break it down into its chemical elements.
(b) a process for removing unwanted facial or body hair, by killing it with an electric current and plucking it out.

electrolyte An electrolyte is a liquid which conducts electricity.

electromagnet An electromagnet is a magnet consisting of an iron or steel core with a coil of wire around it. An electric current is passed through the coil, and this magnetizes the core.

electromagnetic (*or* electro-magnetic) is used to describe magnetic forces and effects produced by an electric current. ...*electromagnetic waves.*

electron An electron is a tiny particle of matter with a negative electrical charge, which orbits round the nucleus of an atom. ◇ An **electron microscope** uses a beam of electrons, rather than light, to magnify objects.

electronic (electronically; electronics) ❏ An **electronic** device, such as a TV or computer, contains transistors, silicon chips, or valves which control the electric current flowing through it. The electronic parts of something are often called its **electronics**. ◇ Electronic processes involve or are controlled by electronic equipment. ...*electronic tagging of offenders... ...electronically controlled doors.* ◇ An **electronics** company manufactures electronic equipment or components.
   ❏ **Electronics** is a science concerned with the study and development of electronic equipment and components.
   ❏ **Electronic** is also used to talk about things connected with electrons. ...*a stream of electronic pulses.*

electrostatic is used to talk about things connected with static electricity. ...*an electrostatic charge.*

elegant (elegantly; elegance) ❏ If you say someone or something is **elegant,** you mean they are attractive in a graceful or stylish way. You call this quality **elegance**. ...*an elegantly dressed Englishwoman.*
   ❏ An **elegant** idea or plan is clever and simple. *He devised a cheaper and more elegant solution.*

elegy (elegies; elegiac) An elegy is a sad poem, written in memory of someone who has died. ◇ A story or piece of music can be called an elegy when it expresses regret at the loss of someone or something. You say a story or piece of music like this is **elegiac** (*pron:* el-li-jie-ik).

element ❏ An element of something is one of the parts which make up the whole thing. ◇ An element is also a group within an organization or community. ...*the hooligan element... He accused elements in the security forces of orchestrating the violence.*
   ❏ The **elements** of a subject are its basic points. *He attempted to teach the elements of biology.*
   ❏ If you are **in your element,** you are doing something you are good at and enjoy doing.
   ❏ If a statement contains an **element** of truth, it contains a certain degree of truth. You can talk about other things having an **element** of something in them. *His victory had an element of luck about it.*
   ❏ When people talk about **the elements,** they mean the weather, especially when it is wet and windy. *They were forced back after weeks of futile struggle against the elements.*
   ❏ The **element** in something like an electric fire or kettle is the part which gets hot when electricity passes through it.
   ❏ The chemical **elements** are the basic substances, for example oxygen or carbon, which all matter consists of.

elemental is used to describe the basic forces of nature, and things which remind you of those forces. *The paintings on display are powerful, energetic, and elemental... The plays come across with a rousing, elemental force.*

elementary is used to describe the simplest or most basic things of a particular kind. *They are being deprived of elementary human rights.* ◇ Elementary is also used to describe things which are very easy to do or understand. *...an elementary duet.*

elementary school Primary schools in Britain used to be called **elementary schools.** In the US, an **elementary school** is a school for children aged between about 5 and 13.

elephant Elephants are very large animals, with thick skin, trunks, tusks, and large ears. They live in Africa and India. ◇ If you say something, for example a new building, is a **white elephant,** you mean it is a waste of money because it is completely useless.

elephantiasis (*pron:* el-lee-fan-tie-a-siss) is a disease which causes a person's legs or other parts to swell to an enormous size.

elephantine is used to describe something which reminds you of an elephant, for example because it is very large or slow-moving.

elevate (elevating, elevated; elevation) ❑ If a person is el-evated, they are raised to a higher rank or status. *...Tony Blair's elevation to the Labour leadership.* Similarly, something like an activity can be elevated when its status is raised. *John Ford elevated the western into an art form.* ◇ If someone elevates a discussion, they raise it to a higher intellectual or moral level.
  ❑ Elevated is used to describe things which are higher than their surroundings. *...an elevated expressway.* ◇ The elevation of a place is its height above sea level. *The city of Bogota sits at an elevation of nearly 8,700 feet.*
  ❑ An elevation is a plan or drawing showing one side of a building or other structure.

elevator In the US, a lift is called an **elevator.** ◇ Some other machines which raise and lower things are called **elevators.**

eleven (eleventh) ❑ Eleven is the number 11.
  ❑ If something is done at the **eleventh hour,** it is done at the last possible moment. *...an eleventh-hour reprieve.*

elf (elves) In folklore, an **elf** is a small mischievous fairy.

elfin If someone has an **elfin** face, their features are small and delicate.

elicit (eliciting, elicited) If something **elicits** a certain reaction, that is how people react to it. *The mere mention of her name elicits scorn.* ◇ If you **elicit** something you want from someone, for example support or information, you succeed in getting it.

elide (eliding, elided; elision) In a description or account, if something unpleasant or embarrassing is **elided,** it is glossed over or missed out. *Other difficult issues are elided... ...the sort of chores familiar to most women but invariably elided on the screen.* Something like this can be called an **elision.** ◇ Elision is also the missing out of the beginning or end of a word, so that it merges with another word. This feature is very common in Italian.

eligible (eligibility) ❑ If you are **eligible** for something, you are entitled to have it. *She was eligible for Income Support.* You can also be **eligible** to join or do some-

thing. You can talk about someone's **eligibility** to receive, join, or do something.
  ❑ An **eligible** bachelor is an unmarried man who people think would be a good catch as a husband.

eliminate (eliminating, eliminated; elimination) ❑ If you **eliminate** something, you get rid of it completely. *It should be possible to eliminate all these diseases... ...calls for the elimination of all nuclear weapons from Europe.* ◇ If someone **eliminates** a rival or enemy or has them **eliminated,** they kill them or have them killed.
  ❑ When a person or team is **eliminated** from a contest or competition, they can take no further part in it, because another person or team has beaten them. ◇ When someone is **eliminated** from a police inquiry into a crime, they are no longer considered to be a suspect. ◇ If you choose something by a **process of elimination,** you get there by going through all the possibilities and rejecting the unsuitable ones.

elision See elide.

elite (*or* élite) ❑ An **elite** is a group of rich, talented, or upper-class people who have special rights or privileges. Elite things are available only to an elite. *...elite schools.*
  ❑ Elite is also used to describe people who are the best of their kind. *...elite athletes... ...elite troops.*

elitism (elitist) Elitism is treating one group of people better than others, for example because of their social background. Something which discriminates in this way can be called **elitist.** *They claim the measure is elitist, offering British passports only to a privileged minority.*

elixir (*pron:* ill-ix-ir) An **elixir** is a magic potion.

Elizabethan The Elizabethan period was from 1558-1603, the reign of Queen Elizabeth I. **Elizabethan** is used to describe people and things from that time. *...Elizabethan drama.* People who lived during that period are called **Elizabethans.**

elk (*plural:* elk *or* elks) Elk are large deer with broad flat antlers. They live in parts of northern Europe and Asia, and also in North America, where they are called moose.

ellipse An ellipse is an oval shape, like a flattened circle.

elliptical ❑ If something is **elliptical,** it is shaped like an ellipse. *...elliptical leaves... ...an elliptical orbit.*
  ❑ If someone's language is **elliptical,** it is condensed into very few words, which makes it difficult to understand.

elm Elms are tall trees with broad leaves, which they shed in winter. The wood from an elm tree, which is used as timber and to make furniture, is also called **elm.**

elocution is the art of speaking clearly in public, with a standard accent.

elongated If a shape or object is **elongated,** it is long and thin, and looks as if it has been stretched out of its natural shape. ◇ You can also say something is **elongated** when it goes on longer than usual. *...an elongated lunch hour.*

elope (eloping, eloped; elopement) When a couple **elope,** they run away in secret to get married. This is called an **elopement.**

eloquent (eloquently; eloquence) You say people are **eloquent** when they express themselves in a clear and persuasive way. You can talk about the **eloquence** of people like these, or describe what they say as **eloquent.** *He* *wrote very eloquently... ...an eloquent plea.* ◇ You can say other things about a person are **eloquent** when they tell you something about their character or feelings. *His eyes pleaded with anguished eloquence.*

else is used after words like 'someone', 'somewhere', and 'anything' to talk about another person, place, or thing, without saying which. *Better still, get someone else to do it... A Lewis man never thinks of anywhere else as home.*

❑ **Else** is used after words like 'everyone' and 'everything' to talk about all the other people, places, or things except the one you have just mentioned. *...wearing a tie when everyone else is in jeans.*

❑ **Else** is used after words like 'nobody', 'nowhere', and 'anything' to mean 'besides' or 'in addition'. *Nobody else had his detailed knowledge of the council's finances... He has to sleep in a church hall because there's nowhere else to go... There's no time for anything else... There was little else he could say.* **Else** is also used like this after words like 'who' and 'what'. *Who else was there?... What else do I need to do?*

❑ You say **if nothing else** when you are mentioning the one good thing about someone or something. *If nothing else, he is decisive.*

❑ **Or else** means 'otherwise'. *Junk mail must work, or else the advertisers wouldn't keep sending it.* ◇ **Or else** is also used as a warning or threat. *He received a single black glove, a Mafia warning to pay up, or else.*

elsewhere You use **elsewhere** to say something happens in another place or places, without saying exactly where. *Demonstrations took place elsewhere throughout Europe.* ◇ You also use **elsewhere** to talk about going to another place, without saying where. *The majority would prefer to go elsewhere.*

elucidate (elucidating, elucidated; elucidation) If you **elucidate** something, you explain it or make it clearer. *They waited for further elucidation.*

elude (eluding, eluded) ❑ If something you want **eludes** you, you fail to get it or achieve it. *Outright victory just eluded her.* ◇ If something like an idea **eludes** you, you fail to grasp it. *The distinction between anthropology and sociology has always eluded me.* ◇ If something you are trying to remember **eludes** you, you fail to remember it.

❑ If you **elude** someone, they fail to capture you.

elusive (elusiveness) If a person or animal is **elusive**, they are difficult to find or catch. ◇ You also say something is **elusive** when it is difficult to obtain. *...the elusiveness of happiness.*

elves See **elf**.

emaciated An **emaciated** person or animal is extremely thin, usually through illness or lack of food.

emanate (emanating, emanated; emanation) ❑ You use **emanate** to say where something comes from. *A lot of junk mail emanates from abroad... A series of penetrating blasts emanated from the tower.* ◇ You also use **emanate** to say what caused something. *The party is not an emanation of the revolution, as it claims to be.*

❑ If someone **emanates** a quality, they show it in the way they behave. *Field was one of nature's gentlemen, emanating kindness, courtesy and humour.*

emancipate (emancipating, emancipated; emancipation) If something **emancipates** people, it frees them from oppression or slavery, or from some other kind of constraint or restriction. *...the emancipation of the South Afri-*

can people. ◇ **Emancipated** is used to describe people who reject social conventions, especially when they live somewhere where conventions are very strict. *...an emancipated woman.*

emasculate (emasculating, emasculated) If someone or something is **emasculated**, they are deprived of their power or strength. *It is their best hope of emasculating the bill... Left-wing dissidents have been emasculated and marginalized.*

embalm When a dead person is **embalmed**, their body is treated with chemicals to stop it decaying.

embankment An **embankment** is a mound of earth or stone, built to carry a road or railway over an area of low ground, or to hold back water.

embargo (embargoes, embargoing, embargoed) ❑ An **embargo** is a ban on trade with a country, or a ban on supplying certain goods to it. If something is not allowed to be sold because of a ban, you say it is **embargoed**.

❑ An **embargo** is also an order prohibiting the release of information before a certain time. When this happens, you say the information is **embargoed**.

embark (embarkation) When you **embark** on a ship or plane, you board it. *...the embarkation point for the islands.* ◇ If you **embark on** something or **embark upon** it, you begin it. *He embarked upon a career in surgery.*

embarrass (embarrasses, embarrassing; embarrassingly, embarrassment) ❑ If something **embarrasses** you, it makes you feel self-conscious, awkward, or ashamed. This feeling is called **embarrassment**. ◇ You also say something is **embarrassing** when people do not know what to do or say about it, because it so rude or of such poor quality. *...embarrassingly awful versions of the latest hit records.*

❑ If something **embarrasses** a country's government, it puts it in an awkward position.

❑ Someone or something which **embarrasses** people can be called an **embarrassment**. *Her name had been an embarrassment to her since her early school days.*

❑ If you have a wide range of attractive things to choose from, and do not know which to go for, you can say there is an **embarrassment of riches**.

embassy (embassies) An **embassy** is a group of officials, headed by an ambassador, who represent their government in a foreign country. The building they work in is also called an **embassy**.

embattled An **embattled** person, group, or organization is facing a lot of problems or difficulties. ◇ An **embattled** area or country is fighting a war, or under siege.

embed (embedding, embedded) If an object is **embedded** somewhere, it is fixed there, firmly and deeply. *There is a small granite plaque embedded in the grass.* ◇ If something like an attitude or feeling is **embedded** among a group of people, it is fixed and not likely to change.

embellish (embellishes, embellishing, embellished; embellishment) If you **embellish** something, you add things to it for decoration. You call this process **embellishment**; the things you add are called **embellishments**. *The dress is made of fabric spun with gold and embellished with diamonds.* ◇ If you **embellish** a story, you add things to it for effect. This is also called **embellishment**.

ember Embers are the glowing pieces of wood or coal in a dying fire. ◇ The **dying embers** of something are its last remains.

embezzle (embezzling, embezzled; embezzlement, embezzler) If someone **embezzles** money which has been entrusted to them, they steal it, usually over a period of time. A person who does this is called an **embezzler**. *He was charged with embezzlement of public funds.*

embitter (embittering, embittered) If something **embitters** someone, it makes them bitter.

emblazon (emblazoning, emblazoned) If something is **emblazoned** somewhere, it is displayed in a very noticeable way. *His name is emblazoned in giant letters on the front of the building.*

emblem (emblematic) ❏ An **emblem** is a design representing a country or organization.
❏ Something which seems to sum up an event, situation, or period in history can be called an **emblem**. You say something like this is **emblematic**. *Blazing oil wells and a huge oil slick are emblems of the destruction that is a part of war... The Vatican tends to see Mexico as an emblematic country, reflecting the troubles of the continent at large.*

embody (embodies, embodying, embodied; embodiment) If someone **embodies** something like a quality, or is an **embodiment** of it, they are a perfect example of it. *He was the embodiment of excellence.* ◇ If something **embodies** certain features, it has them. *The new draft constitution embodies reforms first called for several weeks ago.*

embolden (emboldening, emboldened) If something **emboldens** you, it gives you the courage to do something.

embolism An **embolism** is a blockage in a vein or artery, caused by a blood clot or air bubble.

embossed If something is **embossed** with a design or letters, the design or letters stand up slightly from its surface.

embrace (embracing, embraced) ❏ If you **embrace** someone or give them an **embrace**, you hug them.
❏ If you **embrace** something which other people are doing, you start doing it yourself. *Britain has been reluctant to embrace full-blooded economic sanctions.*
❏ If something **embraces** certain things, they are covered by it or included in it. *The championship embraces 35 events and 16 countries.*

embroider (embroidering, embroidered; embroidery) If you **embroider** fabric, you sew a design on it. Doing work like this is called **embroidery**; the work produced is also called **embroidery**. ◇ If someone **embroiders** a story, they add things to it for effect.

embroil (embroiling, embroiled) If you are **embroiled** in a fight or argument, you become involved in it.

embryo (pron: em-bree-oh) (embryos; embryonic, embryology) ❏ An **embryo** is an unborn human being or animal at an early stage of development. **Embryonic** is used to talk about things to do with embryos. *...embryonic development.* The scientific study of embryos is called **embryology**.
❏ If something exists in **embryo**, it exists, but has not yet developed into its full form. You say something like this is **embryonic**. *The idea was at an embryonic stage.*

emerald is a bright green colour. ◇ An **emerald** is a bright green precious stone.

emerge (emerging, emerged; emergence) ❏ If you **emerge** from something, you come out of it. *They emerged from their meeting describing their talks as frank, friendly, and constructive.* ◇ You also say someone **emerges** when they suddenly become well-known, because of something they have achieved. *The 1992 Games saw the emergence of African women runners.*
❏ If you **emerge** from an experience in a particular state, that is what you are like at the end of it. *He emerged from that traumatic year a stronger and wiser young man.*
❏ When information **emerges**, it becomes known. *Following the emergence of new facts, the conviction was quashed.*
❏ When something like a political movement or a new country **emerges**, it comes into existence. *...the emerging countries of eastern Europe.*

emergency (emergencies) An **emergency** is a serious situation which has suddenly arisen and which must be dealt with quickly. **Emergency** is used to describe things which are available for use in a situation like this. *...emergency stocks... ...an emergency exit.* ◇ **Emergency** is also used to describe things done or supplied quickly in response to an emergency. *...an emergency debate... ...emergency repairs... Emergency supplies of medicines and blankets are arriving at the airport.* ◇ The **emergency services** are the police, fire brigade, and ambulance service.

emergent An **emergent** country, political group, or movement is coming into existence, or starting to become powerful or influential. *...emergent democracies in Eastern Europe... ...the emergent folk club scene of the late 1950s.*

emeritus (pron: im-mer-rit-uss) is used before or after a person's title to show they have retired, but have kept their title as an honour. *...Professor Emeritus L.C. Green.*

emery is a hard grey mineral, which is ground into a powder and used to make various articles for smoothing or polishing things. An **emery board** is a strip of wood or card coated with this powder; people use it to file their nails. **Emery paper** is paper coated with emery powder; it is used for polishing and smoothing surfaces.

emetic (pron: im-met-ik) An **emetic** is a medicine which causes vomiting. If something is **emetic**, it makes people vomit.

emigrate (emigrating, emigrated; emigration, emigrant) If you **emigrate**, you leave your own country, to live in another country. Someone who does this is called an **emigrant**. *Trinidad's middle class, thinned by emigration, is small.* See also **immigrant**.

émigré (pron: em-mig-gray) An **émigré** is someone living in a country which is not their own, especially someone who has had to leave their own country for political reasons.

éminence grise (plural: éminences grises) (both pron: em-mi-nons greez) An **éminence grise** is a person who wields power behind the scenes, using their influence over someone in power.

eminent (eminently, eminence) ❏ **Eminent** people are very well-known and respected in their field. *...an eminent scientist... He has already achieved eminence in the world of cookery.*
❏ **Eminent** and **eminently** are used to say someone or something has a quality in a very obvious way. For example, you can say someone is 'eminently honest' or talk about their 'eminent honesty'. *Her contribution was one of eminent common sense... ...an eminently likeable man.*
❏ Roman Catholic cardinals are called **His Eminence** and addressed as **Your Eminence**.

emir (*pron:* em-**meer**) (*or* amir) (emirate) An **emir** is a Muslim ruler, prince, or chieftain in the Middle East and parts of Africa. Some countries ruled by emirs or other Muslim rulers are called **emirates**.

emissary (emissaries) An **emissary** is a representative of a government, leader, or organization, sent to deliver a message or act on their behalf.

emit (emitting, emitted; emission) ❑ If something **emits** a gas, it sends it out into its surroundings, or into the atmosphere. You talk about the **emission** of a gas; a quantity of gas sent out is called an **emission**. ...*car exhaust emissions.*

❑ If someone or something **emits** a sound, they produce it. *He emitted a long, soft whistle.* You can also say something **emits** light.

Emmy (Emmys *or* Emmies) An **Emmy** is an award given by the American TV industry for an outstanding programme or performance.

emollient ❑ An **emollient** is a substance, especially a cream or oil, which soothes or softens the skin.

❑ If someone is being **emollient,** they are trying to calm things down or smooth them over.

emolument (*pron:* im-**moll**-yoo-ment) An **emolument** is a payment, especially one made on top of a person's basic salary.

emotion is strong feeling, such as joy, anger, or sorrow. Feelings like these are called **emotions**.

emotional (emotionally) ❑ **Emotional** is used to talk about things connected with a person's feelings. ...*emotional turmoil*... ...*emotional support*... *It was difficult not to get emotionally involved.*

❑ If something a person says or does is **emotional**, it is full of strong feeling. ...*an emotional homecoming.* ◇ An **emotional** issue arouses strong feelings.

❑ If you call someone **emotional**, you mean they give way to their emotions very easily. ◇ If you say someone is **emotional** on a particular occasion, you mean they are overcome by emotion, and close to tears.

emotionalism is a display of emotion, or an attempt to rouse people's emotions.

emotive An **emotive** issue arouses strong feelings.

empathize (empathizing, empathized; empathy) (*can be spelled with an 's' instead of a 'z'*) If you **empathize** with someone, you feel sympathy for them, because you can imagine what it would be like to be in their position. *He instantly empathized with our distress.* This ability to put yourself in someone else's position is called **empathy**.

emperor An **emperor** is the male ruler of an empire.

emphasis (emphases) **Emphasis** is special importance given to one part or aspect of something. *There should be less emphasis in schools on academic results.* ◇ If you put **emphasis** on a word or syllable, you say it with extra force.

emphasize (emphasizing, emphasized) (*can be spelled with an 's' instead of a 'z'*) If a speaker or writer **emphasizes** something, they give particular importance to it. *His campaign for the leadership emphasized his own humble origins.* ◇ If someone **emphasizes** a point, they make it in a forceful way. *They emphasized that there was no quick solution in sight.* ◇ If you **emphasize** a word or syllable, you say it with extra force.

emphatic (emphatically) ❑ An **emphatic** statement is firm and forceful. *He was emphatic that he wanted to stay... He emphatically denied he had any part in last week's failed coup.*

❑ An **emphatic** victory is complete and decisive. *Durie overwhelmed her opponent, winning emphatically 6-0, 6-1.*

❑ You say **emphatically** to emphasize that something is not the case. *It is emphatically not a wine to be gulped.*

emphysema (*pron:* em-**fiss**-see-ma) is a lung disease. People who have it get short of breath very easily.

empire An **empire** is (a) a group of countries under the control of one country or ruler. (b) a large group of companies built up or controlled by one person. *His business empire includes property, construction and hotel companies.*

empirical (empirically) **Empirical** knowledge is based on observation, experiment, or experience, rather than theory. ...*empirical evidence*... *Scientific knowledge is empirically based.*

emplacement An **emplacement** is a prepared position for a large gun.

employ (employment) ❑ If someone **employs** you, they pay you to work for them as your job. You can say you are in someone's **employ**. *He is in the employ of the Sunday Times.* ◇ If someone is **employed** or in **employment**, they have a job. ...*employed mothers*... *He did not find it easy to find employment.*

❑ If you **employ** something like a method, tactic, or device, you use it.

employable If someone is **employable**, they have the sort of qualities or experience which would make an employer choose them to do a job.

employee An **employee** is a person who works for another person, a company, or an organization, in return for a wage.

employer Your **employer** is the person, company, or organization you work for.

employment See employ.

employment agency An **employment agency** is an agency which places people in work.

emporium (*plural:* emporiums *or* emporia) In the past, a large store selling a lot of different things was sometimes called an **emporium**.

empower (empowering, empowered; empowerment) If someone has been **empowered** to do something, they have been given the authority to do it. *Police have been empowered to track down and seize the assets of suspected drug traffickers.* ◇ If a group of people are **empowered,** they are given some control over their own lives. ...*the empowerment of the poor.*

empress (empresses) An **empress** is (a) the female ruler of an empire. (b) the wife of an emperor.

empty (emptier, emptiest; emptiness; empties, emptying, emptied) ❑ If a container is **empty**, there is nothing inside. If you **empty** a container, you remove its contents, or pour or tip them out. You can also say you **empty** the contents. *Empty the noodles and liquid into a serving bowl.* ◇ Empty bottles are often called **empties**.

❑ If a building, room, or vehicle is **empty**, there is nobody inside. If a building, room, or vehicle **empties**, everyone gets out. You can also say a town **empties** when a large proportion of its inhabitants leave. *Every major city and town empties for the August holidays.* ◇ If you talk about the **emptiness** of a place, you mean there are very few people there.

❑ If a seat is **empty**, nobody is sitting there.

❑ If a liquid is **emptied** into a river or lake, or into the sea, it is discharged into it.

❑ If you call something like a threat or promise **empty**, you mean it is meaningless, because there is no way it can be carried out. ◇ If your life is **empty**, it lacks meaning or purpose.

empty-handed If you come away from a place **empty-handed**, you have not got what you went for. ◇ You can also say someone is **empty-handed** when they have nothing in their hands.

empty-headed If you say someone is **empty-headed**, you mean they behave in a silly way, because they are not very bright.

EMS See European Monetary System.

emu Emus are large greyish-brown Australian birds with long legs. They can run very fast but cannot fly.

EMU See Economic and Monetary Union.

emulate (emulating, emulated; emulation, emulator) If you try to **emulate** someone you admire, or **emulate** their achievements, you try to copy them, or do as well as them. *The band are well known for their emulation of the Beatles.* People who try to copy other people's achievements are called their **emulators**.

emulsifier An **emulsifier** is a substance which binds molecules together. In the manufacture of food and other products, emulsifiers bind oil and water molecules together, and keep them from separating.

emulsify (emulsifies, emulsifying, emulsified) When oil or fat and another liquid **emulsify**, they combine to form an emulsion.

emulsion (emulsioning, emulsioned) An **emulsion** is a milky liquid, in which particles of oil or fat are evenly distributed. ◇ **Emulsion** or **emulsion paint** is a water-based paint. If you **emulsion** something, you paint it with emulsion. ◇ **Emulsion** is also a substance used to coat photographic film, to make it sensitive to light.

en bloc (*pron:* on **block**) is used talk about something happening to, or being done by, a whole group of people or things together. *The radicals may leave the Party en bloc... They could sell their holding en bloc to a single buyer.*

en masse (*pron:* on **mass**) If a group of people do something **en masse**, they do it all together at the same time.

en passant (*pron:* on **pass-on**) If you say something **en passant**, you say it in the middle of saying something else.

en route (*pron:* on **root**) If you are **en route** somewhere, you are on your way there.

en suite (*pron:* on **sweet**) If a bedroom has a bathroom **en suite**, it has its own bathroom leading directly off it.

enable (enabling, enabled) If someone or something **enables** you to do something, they make it possible for you to do it.

enact (enactment) When a government **enacts** a piece of legislation, it passes it and makes it law. *Since enactment of the law, thousands of people have been detained.* ◇ When people **enact** a story or play, they perform it.

enamel (enamelled) (*American spelling:* enameled) Enamel is a glass-like substance, used as a protective or decorative coating, especially on metal. An **enamel** or **enamelled**

object is coated with enamel. *...an enamel bowl... ...enamelled cast-iron pans.* ◇ **Enamel** is also the hard white substance which coats and protects the surface of teeth.

enamoured (*American spelling:* enamored) If someone is **enamoured** of an idea or system, they are very keen on it, and want to see it implemented or used. ◇ If someone is **enamoured** of another person, they are in love with them. ◇ If you say someone is not **enamoured** of something, you mean they are not at all keen on it. *The Americans are less than enamoured of the regimes they are being asked to support.*

encamp When people **encamp** somewhere, they establish themselves there and show no signs of leaving. *The press were encamped outside his home.*

encampment An **encampment** is a place where a camp has been set up, especially a soldiers' camp.

encapsulate (encapsulating, encapsulated) If a remark or piece of writing **encapsulates** something, it sums it up in a concise way. ◇ If an object or substance is **encapsulated**, it is enclosed in a capsule.

encase (encasing, encased) If something is **encased** in a container or material, it is completely enclosed within it. *...a gold and jewelled coffin, encased in a sarcophagus of gilded wood... His leg was encased in plaster.*

encash (encashes, encashing, encashed; encashment) If you **encash** something like shares, you cash them in. *The company charges investors for early encashment.*

encephalitis (*pron:* en-sef-a-lite-iss) is an inflammation of the brain, usually caused by an infection.

enchant (enchanting, enchanted; enchantingly, enchantment) If something **enchants** you, it charms and delights you. You can talk about the **enchantment** of something like this or say it is **enchanting**. *...an enchantingly pretty girl.* ◇ In fairy tales, when someone with magical powers **enchants** someone or something, they place them under a spell.

enchantress (enchantresses) In fairy tales, myths, and legends, an **enchantress** is a woman with magical powers, which she uses to cast spells. ◇ A woman whose beauty captivates men is sometimes called an **enchantress**.

encircle (encircling, encircled; encirclement) If one thing **encircles** another, it forms a circle round it. *The M25 motorway encircles outer London.* ◇ If people **encircle** something, they surround it. *A swarm of people encircled the hotel... The Red Army completed its encirclement of Berlin.*

enclave An **enclave** is (a) a small territory belonging to one country but lying within another country's borders. (b) an area where an ethnic or religious group lives surrounded by a much larger group. *...the Christian enclave in Beirut.*

enclose (enclosing, enclosed; enclosure) ❑ If an object or area is **enclosed** by something, it is completely surrounded by it or sealed within it. *...an enclosed courtyard.* ◇ An **enclosure** is an area of land surrounded by a wall or fence, and used for a special purpose. *...the unsaddling enclosure... The zoo has a new tiger enclosure.*

❑ An **enclosed** community is very self-contained, and has little to do with the outside world. ◇ An **enclosed** order is a Christian religious order whose members are not allowed to go into the outside world or meet outsiders without special permission.

❑ If you **enclose** something with a letter, you put it in

the same envelope. You call this extra thing an **enclosure**.

encode (encoding, encoded) When information is **encoded**, it is put into code.

encomium An **encomium** is a formal expression of praise.

encompass (encompasses, encompassing, encompassed) If something **encompasses** a wide range of things, it includes them all. ...*a remarkable display, encompassing architecture, painting, jewellery, and furniture... His repertoire encompassed everything from traditional jazz to sea shanties and ballads.*

encore An **encore** is a short extra item added by a singer, musician, or entertainer at the end of a show, because their performance has been well received.

encounter (encountering, encountered) ❏ If you **encounter** someone, you meet them unexpectedly. A meeting like this is called an **encounter**.
❏ If you **encounter** something, you experience it. You can talk about your **encounter** with something. *It was his first encounter with sophisticated food.* People often talk about **encountering** problems, difficulties, or setbacks.
❏ An **encounter** is also a battle or contest. *He was killed in an encounter with the security forces... New Zealand beat Italy in the opening encounter of the competition.*

encourage (encouraging, encouraged; encouragingly) ❏ If you **encourage** someone to do something, you urge them to do it, because you think they will benefit from it. *He encouraged her to study in Vienna.* ◇ If you **encourage** an activity, you give it your backing and support. ...*allegations that the CIA encouraged a wave of terrorist attacks.*
❏ If something **encourages** you to do something, it gives you the courage or confidence to do it. *Her success encouraged her to leave the shop and become a professional film actress.* ◇ If news or a development **encourages** you, it gives you hope or confidence for the future. *He said that he had been encouraged by their discussions... The theatre reopened to encouragingly large audiences.* ◇ If something **encourages** an attitude or kind of behaviour, it makes it more likely to happen. *It has long been a principle that paying ransoms encourages further criminal acts.*

encouragement If you give someone **encouragement**, you tell them they are doing something well, and should keep doing it. ◇ If something gives you **encouragement**, it gives you courage, confidence, or hope.

encroach (encroaches, encroaching, encroached; encroachment) ❏ If a country **encroaches** on another country's territory, it moves onto part of it and takes it over. An action like this is called an **encroachment**. ◇ If something **encroaches** on your time, it takes up more of it than you would like. ◇ If something **encroaches** on people's rights, it takes some of them away. *Gun lovers argue that any form of gun control is an encroachment on civil liberties.*
❏ If something **encroaches** on an area of land or water, it gradually eats away at it. *Sand dunes began encroaching on agricultural land in the mid-seventies.*

encrusted If a surface is **encrusted** with something, it is thickly covered with it. ...*a gold bracelet encrusted with diamonds... ...snow-encrusted pavements.*

encrypt When a TV signal is **encrypted**, it is deliberately distorted so that it cannot be picked up without special equipment.

encumber (encumbering, encumbered; encumbrance) ❏ If you are **encumbered** by something you are wearing or carrying, it makes it difficult for you to move around. You can say something like this is an **encumbrance**. Similarly, you can say you are **encumbered** by something when it makes it difficult for you to carry on with something successfully. ...*a debt-encumbered property company.*
❏ In law, an **encumbrance** is a charge upon land, such as a mortgage.

encyclical (*pron:* en-sik-lik-kl) An **encyclical** is a religious letter, especially one written by the Pope, stating a Church's official position on something.

encyclopaedia (encyclopaedic) (*or* encyclopedia, encyclopedic) An **encyclopaedia** is a book or set of books, giving information on a single subject or a range of subjects. ◇ If something is **encyclopaedic**, the information contained in it is very full and complete. ...*an encyclopaedic survey... He had an encyclopaedic knowledge of medals.*

end (ending) ❏ The **ends** of a long object are its two furthest points or edges. Similarly, you talk about the **ends** of a street or a long piece of land. ◇ The place where a road or path **ends** is the point where it does not go any further.
❏ When people talk about the top **end** of a range of things, they mean the best or most expensive things in the range. *House prices collapsed at the top end of the market.* Similarly, you can talk about the bottom **end** of a range of things.
❏ When something **ends** or **comes to an end**, it does not continue. You call this its **end**. If you **end** something, you stop it continuing. *He begged me not to end our relationship.* ◇ The **ending** of a story is the way it ends. ...*a happy ending.*
❏ The last part of an event or period of time is called its **end**. *The two sides will meet again at the end of next month.* You can say an event **ends** in a particular way. *The evening ended with a display of fireworks.* ◇ You say **in the end** when you are mentioning the last thing which happened in a series of events. *In the end, the family moved to another town twenty miles away.*
❏ People say **at the end of the day** when they are making a basic and important point about a situation. *At the end of the day we have the same problems that affect everyone else.* Sometimes **at the end of the day** is used in a rather meaningless way.
❏ If you are at the **end** of something, you have none of it left, because you have used it all up. *I was at the end of my strength.* ◇ If something is **at an end**, it is over.
❏ If something goes on for a long time, you can say it goes on for hours, days, months, or years **on end**.
❏ If you **end up** in a place, that is where you are at the end of a series of events. Similarly, you can **end up** in a good or bad situation or **end up** with something. *Wright ended up with a dislocated finger.* You can also **end up** doing something. *Initially, he sold rugs, but he ended up selling lighting.* ◇ Someone's **end** is their death. *No-one knows exactly how or where he met his end.*
❏ If you say you will do something to the **bitter end**, you mean you will keep doing it until it is impossible to continue any longer.
❏ An **end** is an aim, goal, or purpose. *Terrorists often resort to violence to accomplish their ends.* ◇ If you regard something as **an end in itself**, you do it for its own sake,

rather than because it will help you to achieve something. ◇ The **end result** or **end product** of something is what is finally achieved or produced at the end of it.

❑ If you manage to **make ends meet**, you make just enough money to live on.

❑ **No end** means a lot. *This has caused no end of trouble.*

❑ **loose end:** see **loose.** ◇ See also **dead end.**

endanger (endangering, endangered) ❑ If something **endangers** something else, it puts it at risk. *Some people are so overweight that they endanger their health... Banks have to be rescued if their collapse endangers the financial system.*

❑ An **endangered** people or species is in danger of becoming extinct. *...the endangered Siberian tiger.* You say other things are **endangered** when they are in danger of being destroyed. *...the endangered Amazon rain forest.*

endear (endearing, endeared; endearingly) If something about a person **endears** them to you, it makes you fond of them. *His antics endeared him to those he worked with.* People, animals, and places can **endear** themselves to you. You say their attractive characteristics are **endearing**. *Wolf puppies are playful creatures, rolling around endearingly, and offering no threats.*

endearment Endearments are words like 'dear' and 'darling' which people use to show affection.

endeavour (endeavouring, endeavoured) (*American spelling:* endeavor, endeavoring, endeavored) If you **endeavour** to do something, you try to do it. An **endeavour** is an attempt at something. *The Guinness Book of Records refuses to accept endeavours which might put people in danger.*

endemic It something bad is **endemic** in a country or region, it occurs everywhere there. *Cholera is endemic in many African countries... ...endemic poverty.*

ending See **end.**

endless (endlessly) You say something is **endless** when it seems to go on forever. *...an endless round of meetings... An issue may be talked about endlessly at economic summits.*

endocrine The **endocrine** glands produce the hormones which control many of the processes going on inside the body. The system by which these hormones are produced and secreted into the bloodstream is called the **endocrine** system. **Endocrine** is also used to talk about other things connected with the endocrine glands. *...endocrine disease.*

endorphin Endorphins are chemical substances produced in the brain and other parts of the body, which relieve pain.

endorse (endorsing, endorsed; endorsement, endorser) ❑ If an important person **endorses** you or **endorses** what you are doing, they give you their public backing or approval; you call this their **endorsement.** ◇ When a celebrity **endorses** a product, they allow their name to be associated with it, in return for a fee. Fees received this way are called **endorsements.** The person who endorses a product is called its **endorser.**

❑ When someone's driving licence is **endorsed,** details are recorded on it of a motoring offence they have committed. Each entry on their licence is called an **endorsement.**

endow (endowment) ❑ If someone is **endowed** with a desirable quality or ability, they have it. *He was endowed with good looks.* A person's qualities and abilities can be called their **endowments.** ◇ If you **endow** someone with a quality or ability, you talk about them as if they have it. *She endows babies with more complicated emotions than evidence can support.* ◇ When people say a woman is **well-endowed,** they mean she has large breasts.

❑ When someone **endows** an institution or organization, they provide it with land, property, or a large sum of money for its use. A gift like this is called an **endowment.**

endowment mortgage An endowment mortgage is a mortgage linked to an endowment policy. The borrower pays interest on the loan plus the premiums on the policy. By the time the policy matures, it should provide the borrower with enough cash to repay the loan, with some left over.

endowment policy An endowment policy is a life insurance policy which provides you with a lump sum after a number of years, or pays out the lump sum if you die first.

endure (enduring, endured; enduringly, endurance) ❑ If you **endure** something unpleasant, you suffer it or put up with it. *She was to endure two more spells of mental illness.* ◇ If you say someone can **endure** something, you mean they can survive it without breaking down physically or mentally. Their ability to do this is called their **endurance.** *He had reached the limits of his endurance.*

❑ If something has **endured,** it has lasted. *The friendship they struck up then has endured.* **Enduring** is used to describe things which last or continue. *...an enduring problem... Brass has a warm, nostalgic appeal that makes it an enduringly popular choice for bedrooms.*

enema (*pron:* en-im-a) If someone is given an **enema,** liquid is injected into their bowels by way of their rectum, to clear the bowels.

enemy (enemies) Your **enemies** are people you are fighting against in a war. Often a country or army you are fighting against is just called **the enemy.** *The enemy suffered heavy losses.* **Enemy** is used to describe things belonging to an enemy. *...enemy aircraft.* ◇ You can call other people who are trying to harm you your **enemies.** *He has more than his share of enemies.* ◇ Something which does harm can also be called an **enemy.** *Inflation was the real enemy.* ◇ If you are an **enemy** of something, you are opposed to it. *She was an enemy of all forms of racialism.*

energetic (energetically) An **energetic** person is full of energy. When someone shows a lot of energy, you can call their behaviour or movements **energetic.** *The dancers perform energetically on an empty stage.*

energize (energizing, energized) (*can be spelled with an 's' instead of a 'z'*) If something **energizes** you, it fills you with energy. ◇ If something like an electrical circuit is **energized,** an electric current is passed through it.

energy (energies) ❑ **Energy** is the ability and strength a person has to do active physical things. ◇ If you put all your **energy** or **energies** into something, you give it all your time, effort, and attention. *In recent years she has devoted her energies to helping the world's starving children.*

❑ **Energy** is also the power obtained from things like oil, electricity, and water, which is needed to make machines work and to provide heating and lighting. ◇ In physics, **energy** is the capacity of an object or system to do work. It is measured in joules.

enervate (enervating, enervated) If something **enervates**

you, it leaves you weak and drained of energy. ...*a hot and enervating climate.*

enfant terrible (enfants terribles) (*both pron:* on-**fon** ter-**reeb**-la) An **enfant terrible** is a talented person whose behaviour or attitude shocks or upsets other members of their profession.

enfeeble (enfeebling, enfeebled) If something **enfeebles** you, it makes you very weak. ...*an enfeebling illness.* Similarly, something can **enfeeble** an organization or system.

enfold If you **enfold** something in your hand or arms, you clasp it there tightly. ◇ If you say something **enfolds** a place or person, you mean it is all around them. *The hills enfold the little North Wales town... Silence enfolded us.*

enforce (enforcing, enforced; enforcement, enforcer, enforceable) ❑ If people in authority **enforce** something like a law or ban, they make sure it is obeyed. *The army has been posted on the streets to enforce the curfew.* People like the police who are employed to make sure the law is obeyed are sometimes called law **enforcers**. If a law is **enforceable**, it is possible to enforce it.
❑ **Enforced** is used to describe a situation which has been forced on someone who did not want it. ...*enforced retirement.*

enfranchise (enfranchising, enfranchised; enfranchisement) When people are **enfranchised**, they are given the right to vote in elections. ...*the enfranchisement of women.*

engage (engaging, engaged; engagement) ❑ If you **engage** in an activity, you take part in it. *He told his supporters they should not engage in acts of revenge.*
❑ If something **engages** you, it takes up all your attention. You can also say something **engages** your attention or interest.
❑ When a military force **engages** an enemy, it attacks it and starts a battle. A battle can be called an **engagement**.
❑ An **engagement** is also an arrangement made to meet someone or attend something. *He has cancelled all engagements for the coming week.* ◇ If someone is **engaged**, they are dealing with a visitor and therefore cannot see anyone else. ◇ If you are unable to attend something because you are doing something else, you can say you are **otherwise engaged**.
❑ If someone's telephone is **engaged**, you cannot get through to them because there is someone else on the line. ◇ If a public toilet is **engaged**, it is already in use.
❑ If two people are **engaged**, they have formally agreed to marry each other. *Friends say the couple are to announce their engagement soon.*
❑ If you **engage** someone in conversation, you start a conversation with them.
❑ If you **engage** someone or **engage** their services, you employ them to do something for you. *He advised me to engage a solicitor.* ◇ When an entertainer is booked to perform somewhere, this is called an **engagement**.
❑ When a part of a machine **engages** with another part, it locks into it as the machine begins to operate.

engaging (engagingly) An **engaging** person is pleasant and charming. ...*his many engagingly English characteristics.*

engender (engendering, engendered) If something **engenders** a feeling, it gives it to people. *The vote has engendered disappointment as well as joy... He engenders an extraordinary affection in his followers.*

engine (-engined) ❑ An **engine** is a machine which converts heat or some other kind of energy into power, especially the power to make a vehicle move. **-engined** is used to describe the type of engine or number of engines a vehicle has. ...*a petrol-engined Ford Transit... ...a four-engined aircraft.* ◇ An **engine** is also a railway locomotive.
❑ If you say something is the **engine** of something like progress, you mean it is the means of achieving it. *Exports, which used to be the engine of growth, are down.*

engineer (engineering, engineered) ❑ An **engineer** is a person who designs and supervises the construction of machinery, engines, or electrical devices, or things like roads and bridges. The construction of these things is called **engineering**. ◇ A person who repairs and services mechanical or electrical devices is also called an **engineer**. ...*a television engineer... ...a maintenance engineer.* ◇ In the US, the driver of a railway engine is called the **engineer**.
❑ If you **engineer** something, you plan it and bring it about. *He engineered the overthrow of the country's hard-line Communists.*

English (Englishness) ❑ **English** is used to talk about people and things in or from England. ...*English villages.* If someone or something is typically English, you can talk about their **Englishness**. ◇ The **English** are the English people.
❑ **English** is the main language spoken in the British Isles, the US, Canada, Australia, and many other countries.
❑ If you are served an **English breakfast** in a hotel or guest house, you get a cooked breakfast, typically consisting of bacon, eggs, tomatoes, and fried bread.

Englishman (Englishwoman) An **Englishman** or **Englishwoman** is a person who comes from England.

engorged If an organ is **engorged**, it is swollen with blood. ...*an engorged liver.*

engrained see ingrained.

engrave (engraving, engraved; engraver) ❑ If you **engrave** something with a design or inscription, you cut, carve, or etch it into the surface. When work like this is done in an artistic way, it is called **engraving**. An **engraving** is an engraved picture or design, or a print made from an engraved metal sheet. An **engraver** is a person who produces engravings.
❑ If you say something is **engraved** on your heart, mind, or memory, you mean it has made such a deep impression on you that you will never be able to forget it.

engross (engrossing, engrossed) If something **engrosses** you, it completely absorbs your attention. ...*an engrossing novel.*

engulf If something like war or fire **engulfs** a place, it quickly spreads over every part of it. *The conflict threatens to engulf the tiny state... Within minutes one of the prison buildings was engulfed in flames.* ◇ If a feeling **engulfs** you, it overwhelms you. *A terrible fear engulfed her.*

enhance (enhancing, enhanced; enhancement) If something **enhances** something else, it improves it or makes it more attractive. ...*athletes who take drugs to enhance performance... Flowers or plants will enhance any room... We can now look forward to a considerable enhancement of our* *quality of life.*

enigma (enigmatic, enigmatically) An **enigma** is something very puzzling which you cannot explain. *The cause of his death was another enigma.* ◇ If you call a person an **enigma**, you mean you do not understand their behaviour or the way their mind works. You can say someone like this is **enigmatic**. *He is in many ways an enigmatic figure... She smiled at him enigmatically.*

enjoin (enjoining, enjoined) If someone is **enjoined** to do something, they are urged to do it. *Iraq was enjoined to accept humanitarian aid agencies on its territory.*

enjoy (enjoyment) ❑ If you **enjoy** something or get **enjoyment** from it, it gives you satisfaction and pleasure. ◇ If you **enjoy** yourself, you have a good time.
❑ If someone **enjoys** an advantage, right, or privilege, they have it.

enjoyable (enjoyably) If something is **enjoyable**, it gives you pleasure. *Take along some light reading so you can pass the time enjoyably.*

enlarge (enlarging, enlarged; enlargement) ❑ If you **enlarge** something, you make it bigger. If something **enlarges**, it gets bigger. *...an enlarged liver... ...the enlargement of the European Union.* ◇ If you **enlarge** a photograph, you produce a bigger version, showing everything to a larger scale. The bigger version is called an **enlargement**.
❑ If you **enlarge on** a subject, you give more details about it.

enlighten (enlightening, enlightened) ❑ If someone **enlightens** you, they make something clearer to you by giving you more information. A book or talk can also **enlighten** you; if it does, you say it is **enlightening**. *The book provides some enlightenment.*
❑ You call people **enlightened** when they have sensible modern attitudes and ways of dealing with things.
❑ In Buddhism, **enlightenment** is a final blessed state in which everything is understood and there is no desire or suffering.

enlist (enlistment) ❑ If someone **enlists**, they join one of the armed forces. *...the enlistment of new recruits.*
❑ If you **enlist** someone or **enlist** their help, support, or services, you get them to help you with something.

enliven (enlivening, enlivened) If someone or something **enlivens** an event or situation, they make it more lively or cheerful.

enmeshed If you become **enmeshed** in a complicated process, you become involved in it. *He is now enmeshed in a long legal battle to retrieve his house.*

enmity (enmities) **Enmity** is a feeling of ill-will or hatred towards someone. When this feeling is widespread in a place, you can talk about the **enmities** there.

ennoble (ennobling, ennobled) If someone is **ennobled**, they are elevated to the ranks of the nobility. ◇ If something **ennobles** you, it makes you more noble or dignified.

ennui (*pron:* on-nwee) is a feeling of listlessness, boredom, and dissatisfaction.

enormity (enormities) The **enormity** of something is its sheer size or scale. *...the enormity of the problems they face.* ◇ When someone has done something very wicked, you can talk about the **enormity** of what they have done. **Enormities** are acts of great wickedness.

enormous (enormously) **Enormous** is used to describe things which are very large in size or scale. *The research shows enormous variations in pay... Reactions varied enormously.*

enough of something is as much as is needed. *She hasn't secured enough votes to win the contest outright... He does not believe enough is being done.* ◇ **Enough** is also used to say someone or something is able to do something, because they have reached a certain age or standard, or have a quality or ability to the right extent. *She is legally old enough to refuse medical treatment.*
❑ If you say you have had **enough** of someone or something, you mean you find them unpleasant and do not want to have any more to do with them. ◇ If you say **enough is enough**, you mean you are not prepared to put up with a situation any longer.
❑ **Enough** is used after words like 'pleasant' to indicate reasonable satisfaction with something. *Tottenham were happy enough with their evening's work.*
❑ You use **enough** with words like 'curiously' when you are saying something which might seem strange or surprising. *Oddly enough, I found them quite tasty.*

enquire (enquiry, enquirer) See inquire.

enrage (enraging, enraged) If something **enrages** you, it makes you very angry.

enrapture (enrapturing, enraptured) If something **enraptures** you, it fills you with delight.

enrich (enriches, enriching, enriched; enrichment) ❑ If something is **enriched**, something else is added to it which improves its quality. *Buildings, he says, must enrich the towns in which they stand... ...job enrichment.* ◇ If you feel **enriched** by something, you feel it has made your life better in some way. *...an enriching experience.*
❑ If you **enrich** yourself, you take advantage of a situation to make yourself richer. *They are accused of corruption and self-enrichment.*
❑ If a substance like uranium is **enriched**, the proportion of one of its components or isotopes is increased in relation to the others.

enrol (enrolling, enrolled; enrolment) (*American spelling:* enroll, enrollment) If someone **enrols** at a school or college, they sign on to be a student there. Similarly, you can **enrol** for a particular course. *...applications for enrolment.* The **enrolment** for a school, college, or course is the number of people who have enrolled for it. *Schools are financed according to their enrolment.*

ensconce (ensconcing, ensconced) If you are **ensconced** somewhere, you are firmly or comfortably settled there. *She was soon ensconced in a sumptuous, wood-panelled apartment on East 47th Street.*

ensemble (*pron:* on-som-bl) ❑ An **ensemble** is a group of musicians who play or sing together. ◇ An **ensemble** is also a company of actors or dancers. ◇ **Ensemble** is used to say how well musicians or dancers keep together during a performance. For example, you can say they have 'good ensemble' or 'bad ensemble'. *Some acute problems of ensemble marred the performance.*
❑ An **ensemble** is also a woman's matching set of clothes.

enshrine (enshrining, enshrined) If a right or principle is **enshrined** in something like a country's constitution, it is specifically mentioned in it, and therefore cannot be disregarded. *Their rights are enshrined in the 1975 agreement.*

ensign ❑ An **ensign** is a flag, especially a flag flown on a ship to show what country it belongs to.

❑ An **ensign** is also an officer of the lowest rank in the US Navy.

enslave (enslaving, enslaved; enslavement) If people are enslaved, they are made into slaves. *...the enslavement of up to thirty million Africans.*

ensnare (ensnaring, ensnared) If you become **ensnared** in something bad, you become involved in it and have great difficulty escaping from it. *...a poverty trap that ensnares women.* ◇ If someone **ensnares** you, they trap you into something.

ensue (ensuing, ensued) If something happens immediately after something else, you can say it **ensues**, especially when it is a result of it. *The police were met with gunfire and a battle ensued... The ensuing publicity actually did the group more good than harm.*

ensure (ensuring, ensured) If you **ensure** that something happens, you make sure of it.

entail (entailing, entailed) If one thing **entails** another, it necessarily involves or causes it. *This will almost certainly entail a sharp rise in unemployment.*

entangle (entangling, entangled; entanglement) ❑ If something becomes **entangled** in a rope or net, it gets caught up in it and cannot easily be freed. *...measures to avoid entanglement in drift nets.*

❑ If issues or problems become **entangled**, they get mixed up, and it becomes difficult to deal with them separately. ◇ If you become **entangled** in a process of some kind, you become involved in it and look like being so for some time. *She was entangled in a bitter court case with a former assistant.* ◇ If you become **entangled** with a person, you start a relationship with them without intending to, and cannot get out of it easily.

entente (*pron:* on-**tont**) An **entente** or **entente cordiale** (*pron:* cor-dee-**al**) is a friendly agreement between two or more countries.

enter (entering, entered) ❑ When you **enter** a place, you go into it. ◇ If you **enter** a profession or institution, you become a member of it. *She entered Parliament in 1959.*

❑ When something **enters** a new period in its development or history, this period begins. *The motor industry has entered a period of radical restructuring.*

❑ If you **enter** for a competition or contest, you apply to take part in it and are accepted. You can also be **entered** by someone else.

❑ When people **enter** into something like discussions, they take part in them.

❑ If something **enters** into a decision, it is one of the factors influencing it. *The fact that she is a woman did not even enter into it.*

❑ If you **enter** something in a book such as a log book, you write it in. Similarly, if you **enter** something into a computer, you type it in.

enterprise (enterprising) ❑ An **enterprise** is a business or company. ◇ See **free enterprise**, **private enterprise**.

❑ If someone is **enterprising**, they show boldness and initiative. You can talk about the **enterprise** of someone like this. ◇ An **enterprise** is an undertaking or venture, especially one involving a certain amount of risk.

entertain (entertaining, entertained; entertainingly) ❑ When comedians, singers, or dancers **entertain** people, they perform to them. ◇ If you say someone or something is **entertaining**, you mean they are interesting and amusing. *He writes well and entertainingly.*

❑ If you **entertain** guests, you receive them in your house and offer them food and hospitality; this is called **entertaining**. ◇ When a sports team **entertains** another team, they play at home against them.

❑ If you say someone will not **entertain** something, you mean they will not consider it.

entertainer An **entertainer** is someone whose job is to entertain audiences, for example by telling jokes, singing, or dancing.

entertainment is films, plays, and shows in the cinema or theatre or on TV or radio.

enthral (*usual American spelling:* **enthrall**) (enthralling, enthralled) If something **enthrals** you, you find it so interesting and enjoyable that it holds your attention completely. *...an enthralling biography... I sat enthralled.*

enthrone (enthroning, enthroned; enthronement) When a new king, queen, or religious leader is **enthroned**, they officially take up their position in a ceremony during which they sit on a throne. *World leaders gathered for the enthronement of Emperor Akihito.*

enthuse (enthusing, enthused) If you **enthuse** over something, you speak excitedly about it, saying how wonderful or pleasing it is. ◇ If something **enthuses** you, it fills you with enthusiasm.

enthusiasm is eagerness to do something or to be involved in something. *We are looking for people with drive, enthusiasm, and ability.* ◇ **Enthusiasm** is also a passionate interest in something. *...his enthusiasm for motor sport... Racing was one of his many enthusiasms.*

enthusiast An **enthusiast** is someone with a special interest or hobby. *...classic car enthusiasts.* ◇ An **enthusiast** for something is someone who is very keen on it. *He is an enthusiast for closer European integration.*

enthusiastic (enthusiastically) If someone is **enthusiastic** about something, they are very keen on it. *The railway is mainly staffed by enthusiastic amateurs... The plan has been enthusiastically received.*

entice (enticing, enticed; enticement, enticingly) If you **entice** someone, you try to get them to do something or go somewhere, by offering them something. The thing you offer is called an **enticement**. *Shoppers are being enticed with a wide range of 'extra value' goods.* ◇ If something is **enticing**, it is extremely tempting. *Estimates are enticingly low.*

entire is used to talk about the whole of something. *The prisoners took over the entire prison.*

entirely means 'wholly' or 'completely'. *I entirely agree with him... The plans haven't been abandoned entirely.*

entirety If something is done **in its entirety**, all of it is done. *He has not yet met those conditions in their entirety.*

entitle (entitling, entitled; entitlement) ❑ If you are **entitled** to receive or do something, you have a right to it. *Sixty million Germans were entitled to vote.* Your **entitlement** to something is your right to receive it or do it. *...his entitlement to unemployment benefit.* **Entitlements** are things you are entitled to. *...holiday entitlements.*

❑ If a book or record is **entitled** something, that is its name. *Prince's first album, entitled 'For You', appeared in 1978.*

entity (entities) An **entity** is something which exists separately from other things and has its own distinct identity. *...the establishment of an independent Palestinian entity.*

entomb When a body is **entombed,** it is placed in a grave or tomb. ◇ If an object is **entombed,** it is encased in something, or buried underground.

entomology (entomologist) **Entomology** is the study of insects. An **entomologist** is an expert on insects.

entourage (*pron: on-toor-ahzh; the 'zh' sounds like 's' in 'pleasure'*) An important person's **entourage** is the group of assistants or other people travelling with them.

entrails A person's or animal's **entrails** are their intestines.

entrance (entrancing, entranced) ❑ **Entrance** is (a) getting into a place. *They had been refused entrance.* (b) the money you pay to get in *...entrance: £6 adults, £4 children.* ◇ The **entrance** to a place is the way in.

❑ When someone comes into a room, you can say they **make their entrance,** especially if they do it in a noticeable way. ◇ In the theatre, an actor's arrival on stage is called his or her **entrance.**

❑ **Entrance** to a school or university is getting a place there.

❑ If something **entrances** you (*pron: en-tran-siz*), it fills you with delight and wonder. *Her singing has entranced opera-lovers the world over... ...the entrancing Arizona landscape.*

entrant An **entrant** is (a) someone who has entered for something like a competition. (b) someone who has just started working for a firm or other organization.

entrap (entrapping, entrapped; entrapment) ❑ If the police **entrap** someone, they trick them into committing an offence, in order to arrest them. *...an entrapment operation.*

❑ If someone or something is **entrapped** somewhere, they cannot get out. *...entrapped gases.*

entreat (entreating, entreated; entreaty, entreaties) If you **entreat** someone to do something, you beg them to do it. Similarly, you can **entreat** someone not to do something. The things you say are called your **entreaties.**

entrée (*pron: on-tray*) ❑ An **entrée** is a savoury course served as part of a meal in a restaurant, or as part of a formal meal.

❑ When someone is first accepted as belonging to a group of people, you can call this their **entrée** into the group. *He gave her her entrée into the New York literary establishment.*

entrench (entrenches, entrenching, entrenched; entrenchment) ❑ If something is **entrenched,** it is firmly established, and difficult to remove or change. *...an entrenched managerial system... ...the legal entrenchment of civil rights.*

❑ If an army is **entrenched,** it is firmly established in a well-defended position. ◇ An **entrenchment** is a deep trench, dug for defence.

entrepôt (*pron: on-tr-poh*) An **entrepôt** is a warehouse at a port or airport, where exported and imported goods are stored temporarily.

entrepreneur (*pron: on-tr-pren-ur*) (entrepreneurial, entrepreneurialism, entrepreneurship) An **entrepreneur** is someone who arranges business deals in order to make a profit. **Entrepreneurial** is used to talk about things to do with entrepreneurs and their deals. *...entrepreneurial skills.* Arranging business deals like these is called **entrepreneurialism** or **entrepreneurship.**

entropy has various meanings in science. In one meaning, it is a measure of the efficiency of a system, in another it is the amount of disorder in a system. It is also a measure in thermodynamics.

entrust (entrusting, entrusted) If you **entrust** something important to someone or **entrust** them with it, you place it in their care or charge.

entry (entries) ❑ **Entry** is getting into to a place. *Some bailiffs pose as council officials to gain entry... Some fans may be refused entry... Entry costs £6.* ◇ An **entry** is a way into a place, for example a door or gate.

❑ When someone comes into a room, you can say they **make their entry,** especially when they do it in a very noticeable way. *She made her entry in a shiny black vinyl catsuit.*

❑ When a country joins an existing organization, you call this their **entry** into it. Similarly, you can talk about a country's **entry** into a war.

❑ The **entries** for a competition are the items entered for it. ◇ The **entry** for a competition or contest is the total number of items or people entered. *The entry was enormous.*

❑ The separate items in a diary, ledger, dictionary, or encyclopaedia are called **entries.**

entwine (entwining, entwined) If two objects are **entwined,** they are threaded through each other or wrapped round each other. ◇ You say other things are **entwined** when there are strong connections between them. *His career was closely entwined with Mitchell's... World population growth and the greenhouse effect are inextricably entwined.*

enumerate (enumerating, enumerated) If you **enumerate** a list of things, you name each one in turn.

enunciate (enunciating, enunciated; enunciation) ❑ If you **enunciate** a word, you pronounce it clearly and distinctly. If you say someone has good **enunciation,** you mean they pronounce words like this.

❑ If something like a principle or policy is **enunciated,** it is set out clearly in a speech or document. *...the clearest enunciation of government policy so far.*

envelop (*pron: in-vel-up*) (enveloping, enveloped) If something **envelops** a person or place, it completely covers or surrounds them. *He was enveloped in a hooded white robe... ...the smoke that enveloped the area.*

envelope An **envelope** is a flat rectangular paper container with a gummed flap, for sending letters through the post.

enviable (enviably) If you describe something someone has as **enviable,** you mean a lot of people would be glad to have it. *The club is now in an enviable position... The region is enviably prosperous.*

envious (enviously) If you are **envious** of someone, you wish you had something they have. *Others can only stand and look on enviously.*

environment (environmental, environmentally) ❑ A person's **environment** is their surroundings, especially the conditions in which they grow up, live, or work. *From the beginning, he was at odds with his environment... They have seen their working environment decline sharply.* Similarly, an animal's or plant's **environment** is the conditions in which it lives, which affect its chances of survival.

❑ The **environment** is the natural world: the land, the

sea, the air, and all creatures and plants. **Environmental** is used to describe things to do with the environment. *...environmental issues... ...environmentally friendly cars.*

environmentalism (environmentalist) **Environmentalism** is a concern to protect and preserve the environment. People who have this concern are called **environmentalists.**

environs A place's **environs** are the areas surrounding it.

envisage (envisaging, envisaged) If you **envisage** something, (a) you form a mental picture of it. *Mention the word 'pump' and most people envisage a bicycle pump.* (b) you foresee it as likely to happen in the future. *He envisages peace talks within the next few weeks.*

envision (envisioning, envisioned) To **envision** something means the same as to envisage it.

envoy ❑ An **envoy** is a representative of a government, leader, or organization, sent to another country to deliver a message, or to represent them at talks.
❑ An **envoy** is also a diplomat in an embassy, ranked just below the ambassador.

envy (envies, envying, envied) If you **envy** someone, you wish you had something they have. This feeling is called **envy.** ◇ If something you have is **the envy of** other people, they wish they had it too. *Taiwan's economy is the envy of the developing world.*

enzyme **Enzymes** are proteins produced by animal and plant cells, which speed up natural chemical processes such as the digestion of food. They can be extracted from animal and plant materials, or they can be manufactured. Enzymes are used in certain products such as biological washing powders.

EOC See **Equal Opportunities Commission.**

eon See **aeon.**

EP An **EP** is a gramophone record. It is the same size as a single, but has extra tracks.

epaulette (*or* **epaulet**) (*both pron:* ep-pol-et) **Epaulettes** are pieces of decorative material worn on the shoulders of certain uniforms, especially military ones.

épée (*pron:* ep-pay) An **épée** is a thin light sword, used in fencing.

ephedrine (*pron:* eff-fid-dreen) is a drug used in the treatment of various complaints, including asthma and other allergies.

ephemeral (*pron:* if-fem-er-al) (ephemera) If something is **ephemeral,** it lasts only a short time. *History can teach us how ephemeral many ideas are... Companies invested in ephemeral goods like computers, with an average life of five years.* Things which last for a short time can be called **ephemera.**

epic Originally, an **epic** was a long poem about the deeds of a legendary hero. ◇ **Epic** is now used to describe real-life happenings which are like those in an epic. *...an epic voyage... ...an epic battle.* ◇ Any book, film, or play which is very long or involves a great number of events or people can be called an **epic.** *...Kevin Costner's western epic 'Dances With Wolves'.*

epicene (*pron:* ep-i-seen) An **epicene** man is rather effeminate in his looks or behaviour.

epicentre (*American spelling:* **epicenter**) The **epicentre** of an earthquake is the point on the ground immediately above the place where it starts.

epicure (epicurean) An **epicure** is a person who enjoys

good food and drink. **Epicurean** is used to describe people like this. *...an epicurean elite.*

epidemic An **epidemic** is a widespread occurrence of a disease. ◇ If something else unpleasant becomes widespread, you can call it an **epidemic.** *...an epidemic of theft, burglary and vandalism.*

epidemiology (epidemiological, epidemiologist) **Epidemiology** is the study of disease as it affects groups of people rather than individuals. **Epidemiological** is used to talk about things connected with this study. *...epidemiological research.* An expert in this field is called an **epidemiologist.**

epidermis (epidermises, epidermal) The **epidermis** is the thin protective outer layer of your skin. **Epidermal** is used to talk about things relating to the epidermis. *...epidermal cells.*

epidural (*pron:* ep-pid-dure-al) An **epidural** is an injection of anaesthetic into a patient's spine to relieve pain, especially one given to a woman during childbirth.

epiglottis (epiglottises) Your **epiglottis** is a thin flap at the back of your tongue, which closes when you swallow food, to stop the food going down your windpipe.

epigram (epigrammatic) An **epigram** is a short poem or remark which expresses an idea in a clever and amusing way. You call a remark like this **epigrammatic.** If a play or speech is **epigrammatic,** it is full of epigrams.

epigraph An **epigraph** is a quotation at the start of a book or chapter.

epilepsy (epileptic) **Epilepsy** is a brain disorder which can cause people to have convulsions and lose consciousness. **Epileptic** is used to talk about things connected with this disorder. *...epileptic children... ...an epileptic fit.* People who suffer from epilepsy are called **epileptics.**

epilogue An **epilogue** is a short poem or passage at the end of a play or book.

epiphany (epiphanies) **Epiphany** is a Christian festival held on January 6th. It commemorates the visit of the Three Wise Men, who came to see Jesus soon after he was born. ◇ An **epiphany** is a moment when you suddenly understand something which has been puzzling you.

episcopal (*pron:* ip-piss-kop-al) means relating to or governed by bishops. *...episcopal duties... ...the creation of three episcopal areas.*

Episcopal Church In Scotland, the **Episcopal Church** is a Protestant church which has bishops and is similar to the Church of England. **Episcopal Churches** also exist in the US and several other countries.

Episcopalian If someone is **Episcopalian** or an **Episcopalian,** they are a member of an Episcopal Church.

episode An **episode** is an incident, usually one in a series of incidents. ◇ An **episode** of a TV serial, soap, or sitcom is one of its separately broadcast parts.

episodic If a novel is **episodic,** its plot consists of a series of separate incidents, rather than developing smoothly. You say other things are **episodic** when they happen at irregular and infrequent intervals.

epistle The **Epistles** are the letters written by the Apostles to early Christians, collected in the New Testament. ◇ Any letter can jokily be called an **epistle.** *I wrote a lengthy epistle describing the family.*

epistolary An **epistolary** novel consists of imaginary letters written by one or more of the characters.

epitaph An **epitaph** is an inscription on a gravestone, or a short poem or passage commemorating a dead person. ◇ If you say something will be someone's **epitaph**, you mean it is what they will be remembered for. *Mr Kinnock described the 1980s as a wasted decade which would be Mrs Thatcher's political epitaph.*

epithet An **epithet** is a word or phrase used to describe someone or something. *He attracted epithets such as 'scruffy', 'ugly' and 'dirty'.*

epitome (*pron:* ip-**pit**-a-mee) If someone or something is the **epitome** of a quality, they are a perfect example of it. *He was the epitome of calm.*

epitomize (epitomizing, epitomized) (*can be spelled with an 's' instead of a 'z'*) If someone or something **epitomizes** a particular thing, they are a perfect example of it. *The house epitomizes the classic country farmhouse... Fair play, epitomized by cricket, is dying out.*

epoch (*pron:* ee-pok) (epochal) An **epoch** is a period of history. When an important change takes place in the history of a country or region, people talk about the **end of an epoch** or the **beginning of a new epoch**. An important change or development can be called **epochal** or **epoch-making**.

eponymous (*pron:* ip-**pon**-im-uss) is used to describe a fictional character whose name is the same as the name of the book, play, or film in which he or she appears. For example, the eponymous hero of the novel 'Tom Jones' is Tom Jones. *In the Dirty Harry movies, the eponymous cop cleaned up the streets of San Francisco using his .44 Magnum.*

epoxy (epoxies) An **epoxy** or **epoxy resin** is a tough synthetic resin, used in plastics and also in paints and adhesives.

equable (equably) **Equable** behaviour is fair and reasonable. *...an equable share-out... In the end, they accepted it all quite equably.*

equal (equalling, equalled; equally) (*American spelling:* equaling, equaled) ❑ **Equal** and **equally** are used to talk about things being the same in some way, for example having the same size, effect, or importance. *EU legislation guarantees equal pay for men and women... He left his children £20,000, to be divided equally between them... Equally important, solar energy can be significantly cheaper than other forms of power.* ◇ If something **equals** an amount, it comes to that amount. *2 plus 2 equals 4.*

❑ If people are **equal**, they have the same rights or status. You can also talk about people having **equal** rights, status, or opportunities.

❑ If someone is your **equal**, they are as good as you at something. If you say someone has **no equal**, you mean they are better at something than anyone else. *As a historian he has no equal.* ◇ If you treat someone as an **equal**, you regard them as having the same status as yourself. ◇ If people do something **on equal terms**, neither person has an advantage over the other.

❑ If you **equal** something someone else has done, you do as well as them. ◇ If you are **equal to** something, you have the ability, strength, or courage to deal with it. *He is determined to show that his government is equal to the problems facing his country.*

❑ **Equally** is used to emphasize that the statement you are about to make is as true as the one which has just been made. *There is no excuse for criminality and offenders have to be caught. Equally, there are underlying reasons for crime such as the high level of unemployment.*

Equal Opportunities Commission The **Equal Opportunities Commission** or **EOC** is an organization set up by the government in 1975 to promote sexual equality and make sure the law on equal pay for men and women and the laws against sexual discrimination are not broken.

equal sign See equals sign.

equalise See equalize.

equality If there is **equality** in a place or organization, everyone has the same rights and opportunities as everyone else. *...racial equality... Women soldiers are calling for equality with their male colleagues.*

equalize (equalizing, equalized; equalization, equalizer) (*can be spelled with an 's' instead of a 'z'*) ❑ If two things are **equalized**, they are made equal. *...equalization of the ages at which men and women receive state pensions.*

❑ If a football team **equalizes**, they score a goal which brings their score level with that of the other side. The goal they score is called an **equalizer**.

equals sign (*or* equal sign) An **equals sign** is the sign = .

equanimity is calmness of mind.

equate (equating, equated) ❑ If you **equate** one thing with another, you regard them as being the same. *It is not correct to equate currency union with political union.*

❑ If one thing **equates** to another, it is equivalent to it. *In many primary schools, the amount available for books and equipment equates to the cost of three Mars bars per child per week.*

equation ❑ In mathematics, an **equation** is a statement that two amounts or values are equal, for example $x^2 - y^2 = (x + y)(x - y)$. ◇ In chemistry, an **equation** is a representation of a chemical reaction using the symbols of the elements.

❑ All the factors which have to be taken account of in a situation can be called an **equation**. *The variability of rainfall is a crucial element in the whole equation.*

❑ You can talk about the **equation** of two things when one is linked to the other. *...the equation of salaries with responsibility.*

equatorial is used to describe places and conditions on or near the Equator. *...equatorial Africa... ...equatorial winds.*

equerry (*pron:* ek-**kwer**-ee) (equerries) An **equerry** is an officer of the royal household, who acts as a personal assistant to a member of the royal family.

equestrian is used to talk about things connected with horse-riding. *...equestrian events.*

equestrianism is the art of horse riding.

equidistant If something is **equidistant** from two or more places, it is the same distance from each.

equilateral An **equilateral** triangle has all its sides the same length.

equilibrium You say there is **equilibrium** in a situation when things are in a balanced state, with no particular thing having too strong an influence. *A flood of new goods may threaten the equilibrium of the market.* ◇ A person's **equilibrium** is their calm state of mind, which can be upset when things go wrong.

equine is used to talk about things to do with horses. *...the equine herpes virus.*

equinox (equinoxes) The **equinoxes** are the two days each year – one in March and one in September – when the hours of daylight and darkness are of equal length.

equip (equipping, equipped) ❏ If you **equip** yourself with something you need for an activity, you obtain it. ◇ If people, especially soldiers, are **equipped** with something, they have it with them. ◇ If something is **equipped** with a particular feature, it has it. *...a helicopter equipped with powerful searchlights.*

❏ If something **equips** you for a task or experience, it prepares you for it. *...the skills that equipped him so well for international diplomacy.*

equipment is the things needed for a particular activity. *...medical equipment.*

equitable (equitably) If a system or arrangement is **equitable**, it is fair to all the people concerned. *...an equitable settlement... ...the policy of seeking to distribute the country's wealth more equitably.*

equity (equities) ❏ **Equity** is fairness. ◇ In law, **equity** is the principle which allows a fair judgement to be made where the existing law does not provide a reasonable answer to a problem.

❏ **Equities** are shares which do not have a fixed rate of interest. They are also called 'ordinary shares'. ◇ A company's **equity** is the value of its equities.

equivalent (equivalence) If one thing is **equivalent** to another or is the **equivalent** of it, it is the same or similar in size, amount, value, or function. *The sugar in a single can is equivalent to the daily maximum amount recommended by government guidelines... There are no East Asian equivalents of NATO, the Council of Europe or the European Union.* If there is an **equivalence** between two things, they are equivalent.

equivocal (equivocally) If something is **equivocal**, it is open to different interpretations. *...an equivocal statement... He smiled at me equivocally.*

equivocate (equivocating, equivocated; equivocation) If someone **equivocates**, they deliberately say things which can be interpreted in different ways. When someone behaves like this, you can accuse them of **equivocation** or describe their statements as **equivocations**.

era An **era** is a period of time, especially one dominated by a particular person or feature. *...the Thatcher era... ...the era of political correctness.*

eradicate (eradicating, eradicated; eradication) If you **eradicate** something, you destroy it, or remove all traces of it. *...the eradication of poverty.*

erase (erasing, erased) ❏ If you **erase** a piece of writing, you rub it out or wipe it out. Similarly, you can **erase** a recording on tape.

❏ You say a bad memory is **erased** when something good happens which makes you forget about it.

eraser An **eraser** is a rubber.

ere is an old word meaning 'before'.

erect (erection) ❏ When a building or wall is **erected**, it is put up. ◇ When something like a tent or flagpole is **erected**, it is raised to an upright position. ◇ If you say someone is **erect**, you mean they are straight and upright. *...the erect figure of a Second World War veteran.*

❏ When a system is **erected**, it is set up. *...the erection of the welfare state.*

❏ If a man has an **erection**, his penis becomes firm and

rises, because he is sexually aroused.

ergo is sometimes used to mean 'therefore' when the conclusion of an argument is being presented. *Communism claimed to fill all earthly needs. Ergo, charities along Western lines were superfluous.*

ergonomics (ergonomic) **Ergonomics** is the study of how people's working environments can be designed to ensure maximum comfort and convenience. **Ergonomic** is used to describe things which have been devised with this in mind. *...ergonomic designs.*

ERM See Exchange Rate Mechanism.

ermine (plural: ermine or ermines) The **ermine** is a stoat when it has its white winter coat. **Ermine** is the white fur taken from the dead animal. *...ermine robes.*

Ernie is the computer which selects winning Premium Bond numbers. 'Ernie' stands for 'Electronic Random Number Indicator Equipment'.

erode (eroding, eroded; erosion) If rock or soil **erodes** or is **eroded**, it is gradually worn down or worn away. You talk about the **erosion** of rock or soil. ◇ You can talk about other things being **eroded** when they are gradually reduced or taken away. *...the erosion of educational standards.*

erogenous (pron: ir-roj-i-nuss) The **erogenous** zones are the parts of the body which respond to sexual stimulation.

erosion See erode.

erotic (erotically, eroticism) If something is **erotic**, it is sexually stimulating. *...erotic literature... Breaking taboos is always erotically exciting.* You can talk about the **eroticism** (pron: i-rot-iss-iz-um) of something like this.

erotica is sexually stimulating art or literature.

err If you **err**, you make a mistake or a wrong decision. ◇ If you **err on the side of** something, you show a bias in that direction. *The plan appears to err on the side of caution.*

errand If you go on an **errand**, you go somewhere to do something for someone. ◇ If you **run errands** for someone, you go to various places taking or collecting things for them.

errant is used to describe people who behave badly, for example by drinking too much, losing money through gambling, or being unfaithful to their partners. *...her errant husband.*

errata An **errata slip** is a slip of paper inserted into a book after printing, listing errors and corrections.

erratic (erratically) **Erratic** behaviour is not consistent. *Police claimed he had been driving erratically.* ◇ You say other things are **erratic** when they are irregular or unpredictable. *...erratic weather.*

erroneous (pron: ir-rone-ee-uss) (erroneously) If information is **erroneous**, it is incorrect. Similarly, a statement or belief can be **erroneous**. *...the erroneous assumption that 'any teacher can teach English'.* ◇ If something someone does is **erroneous**, it is a mistake and they should not have done it. *...banks who erroneously refuse to honour cheques.*

error An **error** is a mistake. **Error** is making mistakes. *There is no room for error.* If something is done **in error**, it is done by mistake.

ersatz (pron: air-zats) is used to describe things which are an imitation, especially a poor imitation, of something else. ...*ersatz soul music... ...ersatz Louis XIV plastic chairs.*

erstwhile means 'former'. It is used especially about someone who used to have a job, position, or role, but no longer has it. *He was critical of his erstwhile friend.*

erudite (*pron:* air-rude-ite) (erudition) An **erudite** person is very well-read, and has a wide knowledge of academic things. You can talk about the **erudition** of someone like this. You can also say their conversation or writing is **erudite**.

erupt (eruption) ❑ When a volcano **erupts**, it throws out lava and ash. When this happens, you say there is an **eruption**. ◇ If something suddenly begins to burn fiercely, you can say it **erupts** in flames.

❑ When fighting **erupts**, it suddenly breaks out or becomes more widespread.

❑ If a person **erupts**, they suddenly get angry.

escalate (escalating, escalated; escalation) ❑ When prices or costs **escalate**, they increase considerably. You can talk about an **escalation** in costs or prices.

❑ When fighting or a dispute **escalates**, it becomes fiercer or more widespread.

escalator An **escalator** is a moving staircase which takes people from one level of a building to another.

escalope (*pron:* ess-kal-lop) An **escalope** is a thin boneless slice of meat, especially veal.

escapade (*pron:* ess-kap-paid) An **escapade** is a reckless adventure.

escape (escaping, escaped; escaper, escapee) ❑ If someone escapes from a place where they are held prisoner, they get away. You can also say someone **escapes** from a place where they are in danger. *He managed to escape from Poland on the outbreak of war.* You can also say someone **escapes** an unpleasant situation. *Thousands of Mexicans seek to escape poverty by migrating to the United States.* You can talk about someone's **escape** from a place or situation. *There was no hope of escape.* Someone who has escaped from prison can be called an **escaper** or **escapee**. ◇ If you **escape** something unpleasant which seems likely to happen to you, you manage to avoid it. *They narrowly escaped arrest.*

❑ If what someone is saying **escapes** you, you fail to understand it. ◇ If something you used to know **escapes** you, you cannot remember it. *Their names escaped him.* ◇ If something **escapes** your attention or notice, you fail to notice it.

❑ Something which provides a temporary relief or distraction can be called an **escape**. *For many, alcohol is an escape from pain, depression, grief or sheer boredom.*

❑ If a gas or liquid **escapes**, it leaks out.

escapist (escapism) You say a book or film is **escapist** when it deals with things far removed from everyday life and problems, and can therefore provide a relief from them. Finding relief like this is called **escapism**.

escapologist (escapology) An **escapologist** is an entertainer whose act involves getting free of chains and handcuffs, often while in a confined space. Performing acts like this is called **escapology**.

escarpment An **escarpment** is a steep slope on one side of a hill or line of hills, which has a much gentler slope on the other side.

eschew (eschewal) If you **eschew** something, you do not indulge in it, or do not make use of it. *He eschewed*

alcohol... *She eschewed publicity.* You can talk about someone's **eschewal** of something.

escort ❑ If a person or group of people **escorts** you somewhere, they go with you, to make sure you get there all right. The person or group is called your **escort**. ◇ If someone is taken somewhere **under escort,** they are taken under armed guard.

❑ A man who accompanies a woman to a social occasion can be called her **escort**.

Eskimo (Eskimos) **Eskimos** are a group of people who live in various parts of the Arctic, and have their own customs and language. Although the name 'Eskimo' is very common, the people themselves prefer to be known as 'Inuits'.

esophagus See oesophagus.

esoteric (*pron:* ee-so-ter-rik) is used to describe things which can only be understood by a small number of people with special knowledge of a subject.

ESP is the ability to send or receive telepathic messages. ESP stands for 'extra-sensory perception'.

espadrille Espadrilles are light canvas shoes with braided cord soles.

especial is used to say (a) someone likes or enjoys something more than other things. *...their especial fondness for animals.* (b) more attention is paid to something than other things. *Friday's press conference was of especial interest.*

especially is used to say something applies more to one situation, person, or thing than others. *Some countries, Germany especially, believe urgent aid is now required.* ◇ **Especially** also means more than usually. *This year's negotiations will be especially difficult.*

Esperanto is an invented language, based on words common to several European languages. It was designed to help people from different countries communicate with each other.

espionage (*pron:* ess-pyon-ahzh; *the 'zh' sounds like 's' in 'pleasure'*) **Espionage** is spying.

esplanade An **esplanade** is a wide open road where people walk for pleasure, especially by the sea in a seaside town.

espouse (espousing, espoused; espousal) If you **espouse** a cause, you support it. You talk about someone's **espousal** of a cause. *...his espousal of democracy.*

espresso is strong black coffee made by forcing steam or boiling water through ground coffee beans.

esprit de corps (*pron:* ess-pree de **kore**) is a feeling of loyalty and pride in belonging to a particular group.

espy (espies, espying, espied) If you **espy** something, you catch sight of it.

Esq. (*or* Esquire) is sometimes written after a man's name, especially when addressing a letter. *...Chris Green Esq.*

essay (essayist) ❑ An **essay** is a piece of writing on a subject, either written by a student as part of a course, or by a writer for publication. A writer whose essays are well-known is called an **essayist**.

❑ If you **essay** something, you attempt it. An **essay** is an attempt at something. *It was his one essay in postmodernism.*

essence ❑ The **essence** of something is the most important thing about it. *The essence of a good government is that it is prepared to take difficult decisions.* ◇ When people say time or speed is **of the essence,** they mean it is of the greatest importance. ◇ **In essence** means basically or fundamentally. *In essence, all computers are the same.*

❏ **Essences** are concentrated liquids extracted from plants or sometimes from meat or fish; they can also be produced artificially. Essences are used in cooking to flavour food. Some essences are used as an ingredient in perfume.

essential (essentials) ❏ If something is **essential,** you must have it, do it, or show it. *Shorthand is an essential qualification for a good secretary... Caution is essential.* ◇ Things people must have are called **essentials.**

❏ The **essential** aspects of something are its most basic or important aspects; they can also be called its **essentials.** *Amendments are possible if they do not alter the essentials of the plan.*

❏ **Essential oils** are concentrated aromatic oils extracted from plants and used in aromatherapy.

essentially You use **essentially** when you are mentioning the main characteristic that someone or something has. *He was essentially a patient and modest man... Her nature is essentially cheerful.* ◇ You use **essentially** to say something is generally true. *The rules remain essentially unchanged.* ◇ You also use **essentially** when you are saying what a situation really amounts to. *Essentially, the opposition wants to curb the President's powers.*

establish (establishes, establishing, established; establishment) ❏ When people **establish** something like a system or organization, they set it up and get it going. *...the establishment of a multi-party system.* **Established** is used to describe systems and organizations which have been successfully set up like this. *We are not trying to rival the established system.* See also **well-established.** ◇ The **established church** of a country is the one recognized as the country's official church. This term is particularly used to talk about the Church of England.

❏ If something **establishes** a principle or precedent, it causes it to be recognised and accepted. *The Act established the principles of freedom of association, movement and ideas.*

❏ If you **establish** contact with someone, you succeed in getting in touch with them.

❏ If you **establish** the cause of something, you find out for certain what caused it. If you **establish** someone's innocence or guilt, you find out for certain that they are innocent or guilty.

❏ If you **establish** yourself somewhere, you secure a place there. *He is desperately keen to establish himself in the England cricket team.* ◇ If you **establish** yourself as something, or **establish** your reputation as something, you get a reputation for being that thing. *With her first three novels Jeanette Winterson established herself as the most original voice of her generation.* ◇ **Established** is used to describe people who have been successful in their careers. *...established stars.*

❏ The people in positions of power and authority in a country are sometimes called the **Establishment.** You can also talk, for example, about the 'scientific establishment' or the 'medical establishment'.

❏ A shop, restaurant, or other business premises is sometimes called an **establishment.** *He has now opened another establishment in Soho.*

estate ❏ An **estate** is a large area of land in the country,

owned by one person or organization. ◇ A housing or factory development is also called an **estate.** *...an industrial estate.*

❏ Someone's **estate** is the money and property they leave when they die.

❏ An **estate** or **estate car** is a car with a long body, a rear door, and luggage space behind the back seats.

estate agent An **estate agent** is a person or company that arranges the sale of property.

esteem (esteemed) **Esteem** is admiration and respect. If someone is **esteemed,** they are greatly admired and respected.

ester **Esters** are a class of chemical compounds produced by the reaction between an alcohol and an acid.

estimable You use **estimable** to describe people who you think deserve to be praised and admired. *...the estimable conductor Sir Edward Downes.*

estimate (estimating, estimated; estimation) ❏ If you **estimate** something, you calculate it approximately. *An estimated 30 million people will watch the game on television... Sotheby's were left with 13 paintings, worth on their own estimation $23.5m.* An approximate calculation is called an **estimate.** ◇ An **estimate** is also a statement from someone like a builder or plumber of how much a job is likely to cost.

❏ Your **estimation** of someone or something is your opinion of them. *He was the best player on the pitch in his manager's estimation.*

estrange (estranging, estranged; estrangement) If you **estrange** friends or people who have been supporting you, you do something which makes them turn away from you. ◇ If people are **estranged,** they no longer live together, or no longer communicate with each other. *...an estranged couple... ...his estranged wife... The trip will bring to an end more than twenty years of estrangement.*

estrogen See **oestrogen.**

estuary (estuaries) An **estuary** is the wide part of a river where it joins the sea.

et al means 'and others'. It is used after a name or list of names to show there are others that you have not mentioned. *A company will be formed to run the airports in Johannesburg, Cape Town, Durban et al.*

etc (or **etcetera**) (*both pron:* it-set-ra) means 'and so on' or 'and other things'. It is used after a list to show there are other things or people you have not mentioned. *...tape decks, compact disc systems, amplifiers, etc.*

etch (etches, etching, etched) ❏ If you **etch** a design or pattern on a surface, you cut it into the surface with acid or a sharp tool. This process is called **etching.** ◇ An **etching** is a picture printed from a metal plate which has had a design cut into it like this.

❏ If something is **etched** on your mind or memory, it has made such a deep impression on you that you are unlikely ever to forget it.

eternal (eternally) ❏ If something is **eternal,** it will never end. *...the eternal struggle between good and evil... She is eternally grateful to her family for their support.* ◇ **Eternal** truths and values never change, and are thought to be true in all situations.

❏ When people talk about the **eternal triangle,** they mean a situation where a husband or wife has to choose between their partner and someone else.

eternity is time without end, or a state of existence outside time, especially the state some people believe they will pass into when they die. ◇ If a period of time seems **like an eternity**, it seems as if it will never end, because you are waiting anxiously for something.

eternity ring An eternity ring is a ring given to someone as a token of lasting affection. It usually has tiny stones in a row all the way, or halfway, round it.

ether is a colourless sweet-smelling liquid, used in industry as a solvent. In the past, it was also used as an anaesthetic. ◇ The **ether** is the air or the sky. *Gases and smoke disperse into the ether.*

ethereal (*pron:* ith-eer-ee-al) is used to describe things which are very light and delicate, and seem to have a supernatural quality. *...the ethereal song of the lark.*

ethic (ethics) Ethics are moral beliefs about right and wrong. ◇ The **ethics** of a decision or course of action are the rights and wrongs of it. ◇ Ethics is also a branch of philosophy which deals with moral questions.

ethical (ethically) Ethical is used to talk about things to do with questions of right and wrong. *The case raises important ethical issues.* ◇ If what you do is **ethical**, it conforms to accepted principles of correct behaviour. *He tried to run his business as ethically as possible.*

ethnic (ethnically) Ethnic is used to describe (a) things based on racial or cultural differences. *...an ethnic conflict.* (b) things relating to minority racial or cultural groups. *...ethnic Chinese Cambodians... 90% of the population are ethnically Albanian... ...ethnic food.*

ethnic cleansing is the forcible removal of an ethnic group from an area where they live, so that everyone in the area has the same ethnic origins.

ethnicity Someone's **ethnicity** is their racial or cultural origins. ◇ Ethnicity is also deliberately stressing your racial or cultural origins. *Ethnicity is fashionable in the United States.*

ethnography (ethnographic, ethnographer) Ethnography is the detailed study of groups of people, mainly through interviews and observation. **Ethnographic** is used to describe studies of this kind. A person who carries them out is called an **ethnographer.**

ethnology (ethnologist, ethnological) Ethnology is the comparative study of different cultures. An **ethnologist** is an expert on this. **Ethnological** is used to talk about things relating to ethnology. ◇ Ethnology is also another name for ethnography. An **ethnologist** can be the same as an ethnographer, and **ethnological** can have the same meaning as ethnographic.

ethos (*pron:* eeth-oss) The **ethos** of a group of people is the ideas and attitudes they share.

ethylene is a colourless gas. It has many industrial uses, for example in the manufacture of polythene.

etiolated (*pron:* ee-tee-oh-late-id) If a plant becomes etiolated, it turns pale through lack of sunlight. ◇ If someone or something is **etiolated**, they lack colour, strength, or vigour. *...a small etiolated blonde.*

etiquette (*pron:* et-ik-ket) is the polite behaviour expected on a particular occasion or among members of a group or profession. *...golfing etiquette... ...business etiquette.*

etymology (*pron:* et-tim-ol-loj-ee) (etymologies; etymological, etymologist) Etymology is the study of the origins and historical development of words. **Etymological** is used to talk about things connected with etymology. An expert in this field is called an **etymologist.** ◇ The **etymology** of a word is a description of how it is derived from other words.

EU See European Union.

eucalyptus trees are evergreen trees found mainly in Australia. They are grown for their timber, and for the strong-smelling oil produced by their leaves, which has a number of medical uses. The oil and timber from eucalyptus trees is also called **eucalyptus.**

Eucharist (*pron:* yew-kar-ist) See communion.

eugenics (*pron:* yew-jen-iks) is selective breeding, especially a policy of only allowing certain people to have children.

eulogize (eulogizing, eulogized) (*can be spelled with an 's' instead of a 'z'*) If you **eulogize** someone, you praise them highly.

eulogy (eulogies) A eulogy is a speech or piece of writing praising someone or something, especially someone who has recently died.

eunuch (*pron:* yoo-nuk) A eunuch is a man who has had his testicles removed.

euphemism (euphemistic, euphemistically) A euphemism is an inoffensive word or phrase people use instead of one they think is upsetting, embarrassing, offensive, or too blunt. **Euphemistic** is used to describe words and phrases like these. *...mobile brothels, euphemistically named 'comfort stations'.*

euphonious is used to describe things which are pleasant to listen to. *...euphonious verse.*

euphonium The euphonium is a large brass instrument of the tuba family.

euphoria (euphoric) Euphoria is a feeling of great happiness. If you are **euphoric,** you are extremely happy.

Eurasian people are of mixed European and Asian descent.

Euro- at the beginning of a word shows it has something to do with either Europe or the European Union. *...a Euro-American alliance... ...the Lisbon Euro-summit.*

Eurocentric (Eurocentrism) You say people or things are Eurocentric when you think they are biased towards Western Europe and neglect the rest of the world. Having a bias like this is called **Eurocentrism.**

Eurocrat Civil servants who work for the European Commission in Brussels are sometimes called **Eurocrats.**

Eurocurrency (Eurocurrencies) Eurocurrencies are currencies held in banks outside their countries of origin and used in international trade, for example the Eurodollar and the Euroyen.

Eurofed The Eurofed is the European central bank proposed under European Monetary Union.

European is used to talk about people or things in or from Europe. *...European aid.* ◇ A European is someone who comes from Europe.

European Commission The European Commission is the executive body of the European Union, based in Brussels. It can propose legislation, and implements it when it is passed.

European Community The European Union was formerly called the **European Community** or EC.

European Economic Community The European Union was originally called the European Economic Community or EEC.

European Monetary System The European Monetary System or EMS is a system which exists to harmonize the finances of EU member countries. It regulates the exchange rates of member currencies.

European Monetary Union See Economic and Monetary Union.

European Parliament The European Parliament is the assembly of the European Union, based in Luxembourg. Most of its sessions are held in Strasbourg and some in Brussels. It has over 600 members, directly elected by voters in member states. Its role is largely advisory, although there are moves to increase its powers.

European Union The European Union, formerly called the European Community and before that the European Economic Community, is an association of European countries, founded by the Treaty of Rome in 1957. It was created so that goods, services, people, and capital could move freely between the member states. The current members are Austria, Belgium, Finland, France, Denmark, Germany, Greece, Italy, Luxembourg, the Netherlands, Portugal, the Republic of Ireland, Spain, Sweden, and the United Kingdom. 'European Union' is often shortened to 'EU'.

Europeanise See Europeanize.

Europeanism is support for closer European integration.

Europeanize (Europeanizing, Europeanized; Europeanization) *(can be spelled with an 's' instead of a 'z')* If a country is Europeanized, its people become typically European in such things as their dress and way of life.

Europhile Europhiles are people who are generally in favour of the European Union, and support closer European integration.

Europhobe Europhobes are people who are generally hostile to the European Union.

Eurosceptic Eurosceptics are people who are against closer European integration.

euthanasia is painlessly killing people who are very ill or seriously injured, to end their suffering when there is no chance of them being cured or recovering.

evacuate (evacuating, evacuated; evacuation, evacuee) If you evacuate a place or are evacuated from it, you leave it, because it has become dangerous. *Foreigners have been taken to a military base to await evacuation.* People who have evacuated a place or been evacuated from it are called evacuees.

evade (evading, evaded; evader) ❑ If you evade doing something or evade something happening to you, you avoid it. *The bomber is designed to evade detection by radar.*
  ❑ If you evade someone, (a) you avoid meeting them. (b) you avoid being caught by them. You can also say someone evades capture.
  ❑ If you evade a question, you avoid answering it.
  ❑ People who avoid paying tax are called tax evaders.

evaluate (evaluating, evaluated; evaluation) If you evaluate something, (a) you decide how good it is. *They do not use western criteria when evaluating art.* (b) you decide how much it is worth. *...the evaluation of assets.*

evanescent is used to describe things which fade away and disappear. *...to capture on film something as evanescent*

as a steam cloud... ...the evanescent notions of economists.

evangelical is used to describe Protestant Christian beliefs which stress the importance of the Bible and of a personal conversion to Jesus Christ. Christians with these beliefs are sometimes called evangelicals.

evangelise See evangelize.

evangelism (evangelist, evangelistic) Evangelism is the preaching and spreading of the gospel, especially to non-Christians. A person who travels around doing this is called an evangelist. Evangelistic is used to talk about things to do with evangelism. *...evangelistic campaigns.* ◇ The Evangelists were Matthew, Mark, Luke, and John, the writers of the four New Testament Gospels.

evangelize (evangelizing, evangelized; evangelization) *(can be spelled with an 's' instead of a 'z')* If the people in a place are evangelized, attempts are made to convert them to Christianity. *The Pope is contemplating a new evangelization of Europe.*

evaporate (evaporating, evaporated; evaporation) When a liquid evaporates, it changes to a vapour. *...the evaporation of lake and ground water.* ◇ You say other things evaporate when they disappear. *Hopes for a diplomatic solution have all but evaporated... With the evaporation of the threat that called it into existence, NATO is falling apart.*

evaporated milk is tinned creamy milk with over half the water removed.

evasion (evasive, evasiveness) ❑ If someone deliberately avoids paying something or doing something, you can talk about their evasion of it. *...tax evasion.*
  ❑ Evasion is deliberately not telling someone what they want to know when you are talking to them. When someone behaves like this, you say they are being evasive; you can also talk about their evasiveness. The things they say to avoid telling you what you want to know are called evasions.
  ❑ If the driver of a vehicle takes evasive action, he or she does something to avoid a collision.

eve The eve of an event is the period just before it. *On the eve of the war interest rates went up by 4 per cent.*

even (evening, evened; evenly, evenness) ❑ You use even when you are mentioning something unexpected or surprising. *Even the most popular First Division clubs are lucky to fill two-thirds of their stands.*
  ❑ You use even to say something is better, larger, etc than something else which is itself very good or very large. *This year the prize is even bigger.*
  ❑ Even as is used to say something happens at exactly the same time as something else. *Even as he was speaking, shots were being fired less than two kilometres away.*
  ❑ Even so is used to say something happened or is true in spite of what you have just said. *The treaty fixed the number of warheads that missiles were allowed to carry. Even so, the number of warheads continued to rise.* ◇ Even if is used to say something is true, whether something else is true or not. *Even if the World Bank pulls out, the project will still go ahead.* ◇ Even though is used to say something is true in spite of something else. *I was glad he mentioned the subject, even though I disagreed with most of his observations.*
  ❑ Even surfaces are flat and level. ◇ If a measurement or rate is even, it stays at about the same level. *...an even pulse.* ◇ If something evens out, it stops rising or falling and becomes level.

❏ If there is an **even** distribution or division of something, each person, group, or area gets an equal amount. *Ability is not evenly distributed.* ◇ If you **even** something or **even** it up, you make it even. *He beat arch-rival Chris Law to even the score at nine wins apiece.*

❏ If there is an **even chance** of something happening, it is equally likely to happen or not happen.

❏ An **even** number can be divided exactly by two.

even-handed (even-handedly, even-handedness) You say someone is **even-handed** when they treat all sides equally fairly. *The president insists that the police are acting even-handedly... He was respected by all for his even-handedness.*

even-tempered people are calm and not easily provoked.

evening The **evening** is the part of the day between the end of the afternoon and bedtime.

evening class An **evening class** is a course of study for adults, taught in the evening.

evening dress is the kind of clothing people wear on formal occasions in the evening. An **evening dress** is a woman's long dress for wearing on occasions like these.

evensong is a Church of England service held in the late afternoon or early evening.

event ❏ An **event** is something which happens, especially something important. *The news has been dominated by events in Russia.* ◇ An **event** is also an organized social occasion. *The event is in aid of Cancer Research.* ◇ In sport, an **event** is one of the competitions in a sporting programme. *Britain won the first event, the 100 metres.*

❏ You say **in the event** when you are describing what actually happened, as distinct from what people were expecting to happen or were afraid might happen. *In the event, she needn't have bothered.* ◇ You say **in any event** when you are mentioning something which is true regardless of what you have just said. *In any event, the matter is now in the hands of the Director of Public Prosecutions.* ◇ **In the event of**, **in the event that**, and **in that event** are used to say what action will be taken if something happens. *In the event of a tie, the team with the highest goal average takes the gold... In the event that any part of the deal may be blocked, the remainder would go ahead... In that event, lower interest rates might not help.*

eventful An **eventful** time is full of exciting or important happenings.

eventing is taking part in a horse-riding competition which includes dressage, cross-country, and show jumping.

eventual The **eventual** result of a process or series of events is what happens at the end of it.

eventuality (eventualities) An **eventuality** is a possible future event. *We are fully prepared to deal with such an eventuality.*

eventually is used to say (a) something happens after a lot of delays. *Eventually, she told me what had happened.* (b) something happens at the end of a series of events, or as a final result of it. *Muggeridge returned to journalism and eventually became editor of Punch.*

ever means at any time. *It is unlikely that his performance will ever be equalled... Living alone is more common now than it has ever been.*

❏ **Ever** is used to say someone or something continues to have a certain quality or continues to behave in a certain way. *Ever optimistic, airlines betted on a recovery and piled on extra flights.* ◇ **Ever-** is used to say something continues to get larger or smaller, or to have more or less of a quality. *...the ever-swelling numbers of the homeless... ...evermore sophisticated missiles.*

❏ You use **ever since** to emphasize that something has continued to happen or be true from a time you have just mentioned, and is still happening or true now. *In ancient Egypt, gold was no more valuable than silver. Ever since then, gold has had the edge.*

❏ You use **ever** after words like 'how' and 'where' to express surprise. *How ever did you find me?... Why ever did you do that?*

evergreen An **evergreen** tree or shrub has green leaves all the year round. Trees and shrubs like these are also called **evergreens**. ◇ If you call a person **evergreen**, you mean they never seem to lose the attractive qualities for which they are famous. *...the evergreen Cliff Richard.*

everlasting (everlastingly) **Everlasting** is used to say something will never end, or seems as if it will never end. *...everlasting revelations about his private life... He was everlastingly optimistic.*

evermore For **evermore** means the same as 'forever'. *He thought there'd be a socialist state here for evermore.*

every is used to say something about all people or things of a particular kind. *The two things every young person needs are love and success... Climate and weather affect every aspect of our lives.*

❏ **Every** is used to say what proportion of a group something applies to. For example, if you say 'Every third applicant was a graduate', you mean one-third of the applicants were graduates. ◇ **Every** is used to say things are positioned at regular intervals. *There are military checkpoints every 500 yards along the road.*

❏ **Every** is used to say something happens at regular intervals. *Intensive cleaning takes place once every five months.* ◇ **Every** is also used in phrases like 'every now and then' and 'every so often' to say something happens occasionally or fairly often. *Every so often the telephone rang.*

❏ **Every** is used with words like 'chance', 'intention', and 'reason' to emphasize a point. For example, if you say there is every chance something will happen, you mean there is a very good chance it will happen. If you say someone has every intention of doing something, you mean they fully intend doing it. *Ambassador Connolly says he has every reason to believe that there will be a hostage release... Poland was making bold economic reforms and showed every sign of continuing to do so.*

everybody means the same as 'everyone'.

everyday is used to talk about things which are happening all the time and are not unusual in any way. *Torture, says Amnesty, is an everyday occurrence... Millions of adults are incapable of using simple maths in everyday situations.*

everyone means all the people in a group, or people in general. *They have been asking £1 admission from everyone who visits... Everyone knows that lunch in London can cost an arm and a leg.*

everything means all the things in a group or place, or things in general. *Everything in the museum has to be cleaned... He said everything was under control.*

everywhere means all parts of a place or area, or all places in general. *Dow's waste reduction policy is evident* *everywhere in its Kings Lynn plant... The prehistoric ammonites left their fossils almost everywhere.*

evict (eviction) If people are **evicted**, they are forced to move out of the house they are living in, usually by a court order. This is called an **eviction**.

evidence (evidencing, evidenced) ❑ **Evidence** is anything you see, hear, or experience which suggests something is true or something exists. *The report found no evidence of fraud.* If something is **evidenced** by something else, the second thing shows the first thing is true or exists. *The outlook for corporate earnings has turned gloomy again, as evidenced by IBM's slow recovery from its losses last year.*
  ❑ If you **give evidence**, you appear in court to say what you know about something.
  ❑ If you say people or things are **in evidence**, you mean they are present and can be clearly seen.

evident If something is **evident**, it can easily be seen to exist or be a fact. *Deep discontent has been evident there for some time.*

evidently You use **evidently** when you are mentioning something which seems to be true. *He had evidently made up his mind to attack Poland whatever happened.*

evil is a wicked power which some people believe exists and which is supposed to be opposed to God and all that is good. ◇ If you call someone or something **evil**, you mean they are totally wicked.
  ❑ The **evils** of something are all the bad or harmful things about it. *...the evils of drugs... ...the evils of capitalism.*
  ❑ If you choose the **lesser of two evils** or the **lesser evil**, you have to choose between two bad options and you choose the one which is less bad. ◇ **necessary evil**: see **necessary**.

evince (evincing, evinced) If someone **evinces** a quality, feeling, or ability, they show they have it. *Early in life, he evinced an interest in landscaping.*

eviscerate (eviscerating, eviscerated; evisceration) If something is **eviscerated**, it loses its strength or importance, or the main part of it is destroyed. *...the evisceration of French socialism.* ◇ When a dead bird, animal, or fish is **eviscerated**, its intestines are removed.

evocation If you describe something as an **evocation** of a place or something in the past, you mean it gives a vivid impression of it. *The film is a wonderful, gritty evocation of the style and music of the Weimar era.*

evocative (evocatively) If something like a description is **evocative**, it strongly reminds you of something or gives you a powerful impression of what it is like. *...the evocative smell of linseed oil and turpentine... ...the collection of islands evocatively known as the South Seas.*

evoke (evoking, evoked) If something **evokes** a sensation or impression, it makes you think of something you have experienced in the past. Similarly, you can talk about something **evoking** a memory.

evolution (evolutionary) **Evolution** is a process of gradual change, often over millions of years, by which scientists believe animals and plants adapt to their environments, usually becoming more complex and sophisticated, and sometimes forming new species. **Evolutionary** is used to talk about things to do with this process. *...evolutionary theory... ...evolutionary change.* ◇ Evolution and evolutionary are also used to talk about other processes in which something gradually develops or changes. *...the*

evolution of musical tastes... He argued for a peaceful evolution towards social democracy.

evolve (evolving, evolved) ❑ When animals or plants **evolve**, they gradually change by evolution. You talk about one species **evolving** into another one, or about a species **evolving** certain features. *To eat rock, the snails have evolved a tongue, studded with lots of little, sharp teeth.*
  ❑ If something like an organization or system **evolves**, it gradually develops or changes.

ewe A **ewe** is an adult female sheep.

ewer A **ewer** is a large wide-mouthed pitcher or jug.

ex- is used with words like 'president', 'member', and 'husband' to say someone is no longer the thing described by the word. *...ex-Communists... ...ex-servicemen.*

ex-directory If you are **ex-directory**, you have arranged for your phone number not to be in the phone book, to prevent certain people from ringing you. When you do this, the phone company will also refuse to give your number to people who ask for it.

ex gratia (*pron:* eks gray-sha) If someone is given an **ex gratia** payment, they are given money as a favour or a gift, rather than because it is legally owed to them.

ex-pat See **expat**.

ex-patriate See **expatriate**.

exacerbate (*pron:* ig-zass-er-bate) (exacerbating, exacerbated; exacerbation) If something **exacerbates** a bad situation, it makes it worse. *...the exacerbation of hostilities.*

exact (exactly, exactness; exacting) ❑ An **exact** figure or number is precise and correct, rather than an approximation. Similarly, you can talk about an **exact** location or an **exact** time. *We reached the summit at exactly 3pm.* ◇ An **exact** description of something represents it correctly, with nothing added or left out. *Cook writes with a stomach-churning exactness about murder and mutilation.*
  ❑ **Exactly** is used to emphasize that something is just like something else, or just what is needed. *Its screams were exactly like a baby's... Arguably, a slower recovery than normal is exactly what America needs.* ◇ You say '**to be exact**' when you are improving on what you have just said, by describing something more precisely. *Birds are supposed to have evolved from reptiles – dinosaurs to be exact.* ◇ If you say something is **not exactly** a particular thing, you mean it would be exaggerating to describe it like that; you then use a more appropriate word to describe it. *The former deadly rivals were becoming – if not exactly allies – at least partners in some recognisable sense.*
  ❑ If you **exact** something from someone, you make them give it to you. For example, you can **exact** an apology, or you can talk about a country **exacting** reparations from another country. ◇ If you **exact** your revenge on someone, you get it.
  ❑ **Exacting** is used to describe things which are difficult to achieve, because they involve high standards. *The material did not meet their current exacting standards.* Similarly, an employer who demands high standards from his or her workers can be called **exacting**.

exactitude If something is done with **exactitude**, it is done with great accuracy and care.

exactly See **exact**.

exaggerate (exaggerating, exaggerated; exaggeration, exaggeratedly) ❑ If you **exaggerate**, you make what you are talking about seem larger, better, worse, or more important than it really is. An **exaggeration** is a claim of this sort.

❑ **Exaggerated** behaviour is extreme, and is usually put on to create an impression. *She grimaced in exaggerated surprise... ...an exaggeratedly casual gesture.*

exalt (exalted, exaltation) ❑ If people **exalt** something, they keep saying how wonderful it is. ◇ **Exalted** is used, usually humorously, to talk about people who have very high rank or a very important position. *...the more exalted members of the British government.*

❑ **Exaltation** is a powerful feeling of joy and happiness.

exam See examine.

examine (examining, examined; examination) ❑ If you **examine** something, you look at it closely and carefully.

❑ When people **examine** something like a plan or a problem, they investigate it and consider or discuss it in detail. An investigation like this is called an **examination**. *...a wide ranging examination of adolescents' rights.*

❑ When students are **examined**, they are set questions, usually on paper, to test their knowledge. This test is called an **exam** or an **examination**.

❑ If you are **examined** by a doctor, he or she checks your body to find out whether there is anything wrong with you. This check is called an **examination**.

examinee An **examinee** is a person who is taking an examination.

examiner An **examiner** is a person who sets or marks a test or examination.

example ❑ If you give an **example** of something, you mention one thing which is typical of that kind of thing. ◇ You say **for example** when you are giving an example of something. *Other historians, for example Charles Maier, have advanced similar arguments.*

❑ If you say someone is an **example** to other people, you mean they behave in a way which other people would do well to copy. You can also say someone like this **sets an example**. ◇ If you **follow** someone's **example**, you do what they have done.

❑ If people in authority **make an example** of someone who has done something wrong, they punish them severely, to discourage other people from behaving the same way.

exasperate (exasperating, exasperated; exasperatingly, exasperation) If something **exasperates** you, it makes you annoyed or frustrated, because you do not understand it or do not know how to deal with it. You say something like this is **exasperating**; the feeling it gives you is called **exasperation**. *...an exasperatingly inconsistent genius.*

excavate (excavating, excavated; excavation) When archaeologists **excavate** a piece of land, they remove earth from it, to search for things buried there and find out more about the past. A search like this is called an **excavation**. ◇ You also say people **excavate** when they remove earth while digging something like a hole or a tunnel.

excavator An **excavator** is a large machine with a mechanical arm used for digging, for example on a building site.

exceed (exceeding, exceeded) If something **exceeds** an amount, it is more than that amount. *Debts are believed to exceed £500,000.* ◇ If you **exceed** a limit, you go beyond it. *Exceeding the stated dose can be harmful.*

exceedingly means the same as 'extremely'. *Progress is exceedingly slow.*

excel (excelling, excelled) If you **excel** at something, you are extremely good at it.

excellence See excellent.

Excellency (Excellencies) Some officials of extremely high rank, for example ambassadors and governors, are given the title **His Excellency** or **Her Excellency**. *...Her Excellency Dame Catherine Tizard.*

excellent (excellently, excellence) If something is **excellent**, it is extremely good. *...excellent news... ...excellently maintained roads... ...academic excellence.*

except (excepting, excepted) ❑ You use **except**, **except for**, or **excepting** when you are mentioning the only person, thing, or group something does not apply to. *Over the last three years all except one of London's 21 casinos have changed hands... Except for some senior officers, no other person has reported for work today... We are self-supporting for every kind of food excepting tea, coffee, sugar and salt.* ◇ You use **excepted** after the name of a person or thing to say they are not included in the group of people or things you are talking about. *Very few pre-war managers, Herbert Chapman excepted, had much in the way of prestige and authority.*

❑ If someone or something is **excepted** from a requirement or restriction, it does not apply to them. *Two social groups had been excepted from the regulations on asylum.*

exception ❑ An **exception** to what you are saying is someone or something it does not apply to. *With the exception of Romania, all the Kremlin's former allies had refused to agree to this provision.* ◇ If you **make an exception**, you do something which goes against a general rule or principle.

❑ If you **take exception** to something, you feel annoyed or offended by it.

exceptional (exceptionally) **Exceptional** is used to describe situations which are very unusual. *Buddhism forbids the taking of life – save in exceptional circumstances.* ◇ **Exceptional** and **exceptionally** are used to say someone or something has a quality to an unusual degree. *Thompson was an exceptional athlete... The climate along this part of the coast is exceptionally mild.*

excerpt An **excerpt** is a short piece of writing, film, or music taken from a longer piece.

excess (excesses) ❑ If there is an **excess** of something, there is more than is necessary or appropriate.

❑ **In excess of** an amount means more than that amount. *Sir James is estimated to be worth in excess of $5 billion.*

❑ **Excesses** are examples of extreme behaviour, for example extreme cruelty, wastefulness, or silliness. *...protests against violent excesses by the security forces... Westminster managed to avoid the worst excesses of schoolboy humour.*

excessive (excessively) If something is **excessive**, it goes beyond what is appropriate or reasonable. *The police had used excessive force... ...excessively high interest rates.*

exchange (exchanging, exchanged) ❑ When people **exchange** things, they give them to each other at the same time. For example, people can **exchange** gifts, or they can **exchange** things like addresses. People can also **exchange** things like compliments. You can talk about an **exchange** of any of these things. *...an exchange of insults.* ◇ If you **exchange** one thing for another, you replace the first thing with the second.

❑ If you agree to do something **in exchange for** something else, you say you will do it if the other thing is done.

❑ An **exchange** is a brief conversation, especially an angry one. *...heated exchanges.*

❑ If there is an **exchange** of fire between two groups of soldiers, they fire at each other for a short time.

❑ An **exchange** is also an arrangement by which people go to live in each other's houses or do each other's jobs for an agreed time. When this happens, you say the people **exchange** houses or jobs.

❑ **Exchange** is used to talk about things connected with trading one currency for another. *...exchange controls... ...the foreign-exchange markets.*

exchange rate An **exchange rate** is the number of units of one country's currency you get for each unit of another country's currency.

Exchange Rate Mechanism The **Exchange Rate Mechanism** or **ERM** is an agreement involving some EU countries, under which governments must take action to stop the exchange rate values of their currencies going above or below certain limits. This is to keep exchange rates stable, making trade easier.

exchangeable If something is **exchangeable** for something else, it can be given up in return for the other thing. *...a privatisation coupon exchangeable for free shares in a company of your choice.*

Exchequer The **Exchequer** is the government department responsible for collecting taxes and paying out public money.

excise (excising, excised; excision) ❑ **Excise** is tax on certain goods which are produced in the country they are sold in, rather than imported.

❑ If a diseased part of a person's body is **excised**, it is removed by surgery. The operation is called an **excision**. ◇ If something is **excised** from a piece of writing, it is removed, because someone disapproves of it.

excitable (excitability) An **excitable** person gets excited very easily. *She had a look about her of nervous excitability.*

excite (exciting, excited; excitement, excitedly, excitingly) If something **excites** you, it gives you strong feelings of interest, enthusiasm, or anticipation, so you cannot keep calm or relax. *He was so excited he could hardly speak... He excitedly unwraps a toy rifle... He was trembling with excitement.* You say something which has an effect like this is **exciting**. *He is an excitingly original writer.* ◇ If something **excites** a feeling like anger or envy, it makes a lot of people have it.

exclaim (exclaiming, exclaimed; exclamation) If you **exclaim** something, you say it in a way which shows you are surprised, angry, or excited. You call what you say an **exclamation**.

exclamation mark An **exclamation mark** is the punctuation mark ! written after the actual words of an exclamation, as in 'Oh no!'

exclude (excluding, excluded; exclusion) If you are **excluded** from something, you are not allowed to join it or take part in it. You talk about someone's **exclusion** from something. *...Shelford's exclusion from the touring party.* ◇ If you are **excluded** from a place, you are not allowed to go there. ◇ If you **exclude** something, you leave it out. *The underlying inflation rate, excluding mortgage*

interest payments, was heading for zero.

exclusion zone An **exclusion zone** is an area where certain people, planes, or ships are forbidden to go.

exclusive (exclusiveness, exclusivity) ❑ You call something **exclusive** when it is only available to a certain type of people, for example rich people or people of a high social class. You talk about the **exclusiveness** or **exclusivity** of something like this. *...an exclusive club... The ruling National Party abandoned its racial exclusivity.*

❑ If someone has **exclusive** ownership of something, they own it completely, rather than being a joint owner with someone else. Similarly, you can say someone has **exclusive** use of something. *BSKYB has exclusive rights to broadcast live Premier League soccer... The paper passed into the exclusive control of the Russian Communist Party.* ◇ When a newspaper calls one of its stories an **exclusive**, it means no other paper has it.

❑ If two things are **mutually exclusive**, they contradict each other. So, for example, if two options are **mutually exclusive**, you can choose one or the other, but not both.

❑ **Exclusive of** is used to say something is not included in what you are talking about. *They earn up to £100 a week, exclusive of board.*

exclusively If something is **exclusively** a particular thing, it is that thing and nothing else. *The congregation is almost exclusively white and middle-class.* You can also say something is done **exclusively** in a particular way. *...making judgments exclusively on the basis of cost.*

excommunicate (excommunicating, excommunicated; excommunication) If someone, especially a Roman Catholic, is **excommunicated**, they are proclaimed no longer a member of their Church, as a punishment for doing something wrong.

excoriate (excoriating, excoriated) If someone is **excoriated**, they are strongly criticized for something they have done. ◇ If part of your body is **excoriated**, the skin comes off it, because of something like chafing or the action of a chemical.

excrement (*pron:* eks-krim-ment) is the solid waste matter which passes out of the body through the bowels.

excresence (*pron:* iks-kress-ens) An **excresence** is a lump or growth on an animal's body, or on a plant.

excreta (*pron:* iks-kree-ta) is human or animal waste matter, for example faeces, urine, or sweat.

excrete (excreting, excreted; excretion) When you **excrete** waste matter from your body, you get rid of it through your anus, your bladder, or your skin. This process is called **excretion**.

excruciating (excruciatingly) An **excruciating** pain is very severe and difficult to bear. *...an excruciatingly painful headache.* ◇ **Excruciating** is also used to describe things which are frustrating or embarrassing. *Currency reform moves with excruciating slowness.*

exculpate (exculpating, exculpated; exculpatory) If someone is **exculpated**, they are shown to be free from guilt or blame. **Exculpatory** is used to describe things which have this effect. *Evidently, the government hopes a few exculpatory resignations will defuse international criticism.*

excursion An **excursion** is a short journey, especially one taken for pleasure. ◇ If you make an **excursion** into a subject or new activity, you try it out. *...Radio 3's latest excursion into ethnic music, dance and literature.*

excusable If you say a mistake or inappropriate remark is **excusable**, you mean it is understandable in the circumstances and can be excused.

excuse (excusing, excused) ❑ An **excuse** is a reason why someone should not be blamed or punished for doing something wrong. ◇ If you **excuse** (*pron: ex-kyooz*) yourself or **excuse** what you have done, you say why you should not be blamed or punished. *He excused himself by saying he was forced to rob to maintain his wife and children.* ◇ If you **excuse** someone else for something they have done, you forgive them.
❑ If someone **excuses** you from a duty or responsibility, they let you off it. ◇ You also say someone is **excused** when they are given permission to leave.

exec An **exec** is an executive.

execrable When people say something is **execrable**, they mean it is of extremely poor quality.

execrate (execrating, execrated) If you **execrate** someone or something, you dislike them intensely.

execute (executing, executed; execution) ❑ If someone is **executed**, they are put to death for committing a crime. Killing someone like this is called an **execution**.
❑ The way you **execute** something is the way you carry it out. *This spectacular move is now executed with comparative ease by top gymnasts everywhere.*

executioner An **executioner** is someone whose job is executing criminals.

executive ❑ An **executive** is someone employed by a company at a senior level. ◇ **Executive** is also used to describe luxurious things intended for rich or important people. *...his plush executive suite... ...executive class fares.*
❑ The **executive** or **executive committee** of an organization is a group of people who make important decisions on its behalf.

executor (*pron: ik-zek-yoo-tor*) Your **executor** is the person you appoint in your will to deal with your affairs after your death, especially the implementing of the will. ◇ The **executor** of an order, wish, or policy is the person who carries it out.

exemplar If you say someone or something is the **exemplar** of a type of thing, you mean they are the perfect example of it.

exemplary is used to describe things which are done extremely well. *Ian Ross has done an exemplary job... He performed his duties with exemplary thoroughness.* **Exemplary** is also used to describe people who do something extremely well. *...an exemplary host.* ◇ An **exemplary** punishment is a severe one intended to discourage other people from committing the same crime.

exemplify (exemplifies, exemplifying, exemplified) If something **exemplifies** the situation you are talking about, it is a typical example of it. Similarly, a person can **exemplify** a good quality. *They exemplified the team spirit and physical zest that are the company's hallmarks.* ◇ If you **exemplify** something, you provide an example of it.

exempt (exemption) If you are **exempt** or **exempted** from something like a rule or a duty, it does not apply to you. *Pensioners should be exempted from paying the licence fee... He could have gained exemption from conscription.*

exercise (exercising, exercised) ❑ When you **exercise** or take **exercise**, you do something energetic to keep yourself fit and healthy. **Exercises** are special ways of keeping fit, usually involving repeated movements of parts of the body. ◇ If you **exercise** a dog, you take it out and let it run around, to keep it healthy. Other animals can be **exercised** in similar ways.
❑ If something like a problem **exercises** you or **exercises** your mind, it puzzles you and you think about it a lot.
❑ An **exercise** is a short piece of work you do to see if you have learned something properly, especially at school. ◇ **Exercises** are things you do repeatedly to practise something and acquire the ability to do it easily, for example when you are learning a musical instrument. ◇ **Exercises** are also practice operations or manoeuvres performed by the armed forces.
❑ You can explain the purpose of something by saying it is an **exercise** of a particular kind. *...a public relations exercise... The object of the exercise is to raise money for charity.*
❑ When people **exercise** their power or authority, they use it. You can talk about the **exercise** of power. You can also talk about people **exercising** their rights. ◇ If you **exercise** something like restraint, you show it in the way you behave.

exercise bike An **exercise bike** is a stationary fitness machine which you pedal like a bicycle to get fit.

exercise book An **exercise book** is a book with lined pages, for doing school work.

exert (exertion) If you **exert** something like influence or pressure, you use it to get what you want. ◇ If you **exert** yourself, you make a physical or mental effort to achieve something. Efforts made to achieve something are called **exertions**.

exhale (exhaling, exhaled; exhalation) When you **exhale**, you breathe out. *...an exhalation of breath.*

exhaust (exhausted, exhaustion) ❑ If something **exhausts** you or leaves you **exhausted**, it uses up all your energy and makes you extremely tired. This state of tiredness is called **exhaustion**.
❑ If you **exhaust** something, you use it all up. *...the need to exhaust all peaceful ways of solving the crisis.*
❑ **Exhaust** is waste gases produced by the engine of a motor vehicle. It is released through a pipe called the **exhaust** or **exhaust pipe**.

exhaustive (exhaustively) If something like a search or investigation is **exhaustive**, it is complete and thorough. *...exhaustive inquiries by police... All means to resolve the crisis should be exhaustively pursued.*

exhibit (exhibiting, exhibited) ❑ If something is **exhibited**, it is put on public display, for example in a museum. Items displayed like this are called **exhibits**. ◇ An **exhibit** is also an object shown in court as evidence. For example, in a murder trial the murder weapon might be shown as an **exhibit**. ◇ In the US, an **exhibition** is sometimes called an **exhibit**.
❑ If you **exhibit** something like a skill or characteristic, you show you have it.

exhibition ❑ An **exhibition** is a collection of things like pictures or new products which are put on display somewhere.
❑ If a sportsperson's skills are very obvious during a game, you can say they give an **exhibition** of their skills. *Hodgkinson gave an almost flawless exhibition of kicking with 10 successes from 11 attempts.*

exhibitionist (exhibitionism) You say someone is an exhibitionist when they keep doing very noticeable things, to make people notice them. You call their behaviour exhibitionism.

exhibitor An exhibitor is someone who has provided things for display at an exhibition.

exhilarate (exhilarating, exhilarated; exhilaration) If you are exhilarated by something, it gives you a feeling of pleasure and excitement. You call this feeling exhilaration.

exhort (exhortation) If you exhort someone to do something, you urge them to do it as persuasively as you can. The things you say are called exhortations. *All Cubans are being exhorted to conserve electricity.*

exhume (exhuming, exhumed; exhumation) When a dead body is exhumed, it is taken out of its grave. This is called an exhumation of the body. ◇ You can talk about other things being exhumed when they are used again after they have been forgotten or ignored for a very long time. *Commonweal Theatre Company has exhumed a Jacobean tragi-comedy by Middleton.*

exigencies The exigencies of a situation or a job are the difficulties you have to deal with as part of it.

exile (exiling, exiled) If someone is exiled or sent into exile, they are sent away from their home country and not allowed to return. When this has happened to someone, you call them an exile or describe them as exiled. *...the exiled King Michael of Romania.* ◇ People who have left their country voluntarily to live somewhere else can also be called exiles. *Welsh exiles come to the ceremony from all over the world.*

exist (existence) ❑ If something exists, it is really there, and not just something in someone's imagination. *No one doubts the existence of a lucrative market.* If something exists for a particular purpose, that is why it is there. *The arch exists to commemorate a victory.* If something still exists, it has not yet come to an end. *The death penalty still exists in England and Wales for treason.* ◇ Existing is used to describe things which are there now, as distinct from things which may replace them in the future.

❑ You call someone's way of life an existence when you think they get very little enjoyment from it, because they are very poor or very lonely. *...his bachelor existence.*

existentialism (existentialist, existential) Existentialism is a philosophy associated with writers like Kierkegaard and Sartre. It upholds the importance of the individual person, expresses distrust for political idealism, and is often characterized by feelings of disillusion. An existentialist is someone who believes in this philosophy. Existential is used to describe behaviour and feelings typical of an existentialist. *...existential doubts.*

exit ❑ An exit is a way out of a building or other place. ◇ An exit is also a place where traffic can leave a motorway.

❑ When someone leaves something like a place or an organization, you can call their leaving an exit. *...Mr Lenihan's exit from the cabinet.* ◇ Exit is used to describe official documents which give people permission to leave their country. *...exit visas.*

❑ When a sportsperson makes an exit from a competition, they are knocked out of it. *...Chang's early exit from the German Open.* ◇ When an actor makes an exit, he or she leaves the stage.

❑ An exit or exit route is also a way out of an undesirable situation. *He is desperately trying to find an exit from the crisis.*

exit poll In an election, an exit poll is a survey carried out as people leave the polling stations, in which they are asked who they voted for.

exodus In the Bible, the Exodus was the journey of the Jews, led by Moses, out of their slavery in Egypt. The term exodus is now used to talk about any large group of people leaving a place or organization. *...a huge exodus of refugees.*

exonerate (exonerating, exonerated; exoneration) If someone is exonerated, they are shown not to be to blame for something. *...the Commission's exoneration of the police.*

exorbitant (exorbitantly) If you say the price of something is exorbitant, you mean it is much higher than it should be. *...exorbitantly priced jewels and watches.*

exorcize (exorcizing, exorcized; exorcism, exorcist) (can be spelled with an 's' instead of a 'z') People who believe a place or person can be possessed by evil spirits often think these spirits can be exorcized; this means driving them out in a special ceremony called an exorcism. The person who conducts the ceremony is called an exorcist. ◇ If you exorcize something like a bad memory or a run of bad luck, you succeed in getting rid of it or putting an end to it.

exotic (exotically; exoticism, exotica) If something is exotic, it is unusual and interesting, because it is connected with a faraway country. *...exotic species... ...the exotically designed restaurant.* You can talk about the exoticism of something like this or call it an exoticism. *The Canada goose was once a beloved exoticism.* Exotic things generally can be called exotica.

expand (expansion) ❑ If something expands or is expanded, it gets larger. When this happens, you talk about its expansion. *...a rapidly expanding market.*

❑ If you expand on something you have already mentioned, you talk about it in greater detail.

expanse An expanse of something is a very large area of it. *...wide expanses of forest.*

expansionary is used to describe policies and conditions which lead to an increase in a country's economic activity. *...an expansionary fiscal policy.*

expansionism (expansionist) If a country has a policy of expansionism, it aims to increase its size by taking land from other countries. Expansionist is used to describe a country or policy like this.

expansive (expansively, expansiveness) ❑ If an area is expansive, it is unusually large. *...the expansiveness of the courtyard.*

❑ If someone is expansive or in an expansive mood, they are relaxed, happy, friendly, and able to express their feelings freely. *Mansell beamed and expansively clapped the Brazilian on the back.*

expat (or ex-pat) An expat is the same as an expatriate.

expatriate (or ex-patriate) (pron: eks-pat-ree-it) An expatriate is someone who lives in a country which is not their own.

expect ❑ If you expect something to happen, you think it will happen. ◇ If you are expecting something like a letter, you believe it will arrive soon.

❑ If you say someone can expect a certain kind of treatment, you mean that is the way they are likely to be treated. *A member of the royal family can never expect the privacy of a commoner.* ◇ If you say you **expect** someone to do something, you mean they ought to do it, as their duty. *We expect our governments and employers to protect us.*

❑ People say I **expect...** when they are saying something which they think is probably true. *I expect you're right.*

❑ If a woman is **expecting** a baby, she is pregnant.

expectant (expectantly, expectancy) ❑ If people are **expectant**, they are excited, because they think something interesting is going to happen. This feeling is called **expectancy**. *The media assembled expectantly outside the Treasury building.*

❑ An **expectant** mother or father is someone whose baby is going to be born soon.

❑ See also **life expectancy**.

expectation Your **expectations** are your beliefs about what is going to happen. *Contrary to our expectations, he did not try to take over the running of the home.* ◇ People's **expectations** are also their beliefs about what they are entitled to, for example a good standard of living. *...the rising expectations of workers.*

expedient (expediency) If you do something because it is **expedient**, you do it because it is easy and convenient, rather than because it is morally right or the best thing to do. Behaviour like this is called **expediency**. ◇ An **expedient** is something you do which gets you out of an immediate problem, though it may not be the right thing to do in the long run.

expedite (expediting, expedited) If you **expedite** something like a plan or an arrangement, you hurry it up.

expedition An **expedition** is an organized journey made for a special purpose, for example exploration. A group of people who make a journey like this can also be called an **expedition**.

expeditionary is used to talk about groups of soldiers sent to fight in a foreign country. *...an expeditionary force.*

expeditious (expeditiously) **Expeditious** is used to describe things which are done quickly and efficiently. *The matter has been handled expeditiously by the Canadian authorities.*

expel (expelling, expelled; expulsion) ❑ If someone is **expelled** from school, they are thrown out for bad behaviour. People can also be **expelled** from other organizations. *...the underwriter expelled from Lloyd's for discreditable conduct.* Expelling someone is called **expulsion**. ◇ When people are **expelled** from a place, they are forced to leave. *...the brutal expulsion of Bulgarian Turks.*

❑ If something like a liquid or gas is **expelled** from a place, it is forced out of it.

expend If you **expend** time, energy, or money on something, you spend or use it that way. *Little effort has been expended on finding an alternative.*

expendable If you say someone or something is **expendable**, you mean they are not important and can be sacrificed if necessary.

expenditure is the amount spent on something. *The programme would involve total expenditure of £1,000 million a year.* Similarly, an **expenditure** of time or energy is an amount of it spent in a particular way.

expense ❑ The **expense** of doing something is what it

costs. *The move is aimed at saving the expense of bringing witnesses to Britain.* An **expense** is something you have to spend money on. ◇ **Expenses** are amounts of money you spend in connection with your job, which you can claim back from your employer.

❑ If someone provides the money for something, you can say it is done at their **expense**. *...a government that bailed out banks at local taxpayers' expense... Many Japanese parents supplement good state provision with private teaching at their own expense.* ◇ You can also say something is done at someone's **expense** when they are worse off as a result of it. *Serbia was looking to expand its territory at Croatia's expense.* ◇ If you make a joke at someone's **expense**, they are the subject of it and it can make them seem foolish.

expense account An **expense account** is an arrangement made by the company you work for which allows you to spend its money on things which are part of your job, for example travelling or entertaining clients.

expensive (expensively) If something is **expensive**, it costs a lot of money. *...expensively-produced Broadway shows.*

experience (experiencing, experienced) ❑ If you have had **experience** of something, you have seen it, done it, or felt it. ◇ An **experience** is something which happens to you or something you do. ◇ If you **experience** a situation or feeling, it happens to you or you are affected by it. *Budapest is experiencing serious flooding.*

❑ Your **experience** is all the things which have happened to you, especially things which have increased your knowledge or understanding. *Kiet has further broadened his experience by travelling abroad.* ◇ If someone is **experienced** at something, they have been doing it for a long time and know a lot about it. *...experienced lawyers.*

experiment (experimentation, experimenter, experimentalist) ❑ An **experiment** is a scientific test to prove or discover something. When a scientist **experiments** with something, he or she does a test like this. This method of gaining knowledge is called **experimentation**.

❑ If you do something new to see how it works out, you can say you are **experimenting** or call it an **experiment**. *More than 20% of young people have experimented with drugs by the age of 16.* People who try out new things can be called **experimenters** or **experimentalists**. Trying out new things is called **experimentation**.

experimental (experimentally) ❑ If something is **experimental**, it involves new ideas and is being tried out to see if it works. *...an experimental regulation... The scheme was run experimentally in Scotland in 1988.* ◇ You call something like a novel or play **experimental** when it involves new ways of telling a story or new ways of presenting things in the theatre.

❑ **Experimental** is also used to talk about things to do with scientific experiments. *...experimental evidence... Species can be studied experimentally under controlled conditions.*

experimentalist See **experiment**.

expert (expertly) An **expert** on a subject is someone who is extremely knowledgeable about it. ◇ If someone is **expert** at doing something or an **expert** at it, they are extremely good at it. *The French are expert at providing attractive camp sites... ...three expertly-taken goals.*

expertise (*pron:* eks-per-teez) is special skill or knowledge.

expiate (expiating, expiated; expiation) If you **expiate** some wrong you have done, you do something which makes up for it. This is called an **expiation** of the wrong.

expire (expiring, expired; expiration, expiry) ❑ When a period of time **expires**, it comes to an end. You talk about the **expiration** of a period of time. *There was no procedure to allow a return to the crown court after the expiration of 28 days.* ◇ When a document **expires**, the period for which it is valid comes to an end. Similarly, you can say an agreement **expires**. You talk about the **expiry** of a document or agreement.

❑ When a person **expires**, they die.

explain (explaining, explained; explanation) ❑ If you **explain** something or give an **explanation** of it, you go into details about it, to help people understand it.

❑ If someone asks you to **explain yourself**, they want you to say why you have behaved in what seems a bad way. ◇ If you **explain** something you have done, you give reasons for it. *Miss Zettner demanded an explanation for these changes.* ◇ If you **explain away** a problem or a mistake, you try to show it is not really your fault or it is not important.

explanatory is used to describe something like a diagram or piece of writing which is provided to help people understand something. *...an explanatory video.*

expletive (*pron:* iks-plee-tiv) An **expletive** is a swear word, for example 'shit' or 'fuck'.

explicable If something is **explicable**, it can be explained.

explicit (explicitly, explicitness) If you are **explicit**, you say clearly and openly what you mean. *Europe's leaders are quite explicit about their hopes... This is not explicitly called for in the resolution.* ◇ If a book or film is sexually **explicit**, it deals with sex in a frank and open way, which some people might find shocking. *...toning down the explicitness of his love scenes.*

explode (exploding, exploded) ❑ When a bomb **explodes**, it goes off.

❑ You also say something **explodes** when it increases suddenly and rapidly. *The sports market has exploded in the past 20 years.*

❑ If someone **explodes**, they lose their temper.

❑ If a situation **explodes**, violence or war suddenly breaks out. *This latest unrest could explode into conflict between the two republics.*

❑ If you **explode** a theory or a belief, you prove it is wrong.

exploit (exploiting, exploited; exploitation, exploiter) ❑ If someone **exploits** you, they treat you unfairly by using your work or ideas and giving you little in return. Behaviour like this is called **exploitation**; a person who exploits people is called an **exploiter**.

❑ If you **exploit** something, you make use of it, to make money or get some other advantage. *...the commercial exploitation of fast-growing trees... ...his considerable skill as an exploiter of the British media.*

❑ When you talk about a person's **exploits** (*pron:* ex-ploits), you mean the exciting or interesting things they have done.

exploitable If something is **exploitable**, you can use it to make money or get something else you want. *...deposits of oil in exploitable quantities.*

exploitative If a person or organization is **exploitative**, they treat people unfairly by using their work or ideas

and giving them little in return.

exploratory is used to describe something like a preliminary meeting which is held to find out what the situation is before going ahead with the main meeting. *...exploratory talks... This project has gone no further than the exploratory stage.*

explore (exploring, explored; exploration) ❑ If you **explore** a place or area, you go to different parts of it, seeing what it is like and finding out things about it. *Further exploration of the cave has already begun.* ◇ Oil or gas **exploration** is searching for oil or gas.

❑ If you **explore** an idea, you think about it and try to decide what would happen if it were carried out. *The two governments are exploring the possibility of improving diplomatic ties.*

explorer An **explorer** is a person who travels to places about which little is known, to discover what is there. ◇ An oil or gas **explorer** is a person or organization whose business involves searching for oil or gas.

explosion ❑ An **explosion** is a sudden violent release of energy, for example one caused by a bomb.

❑ You can say there is an **explosion** of something when there is a sudden rapid increase in it. *...an explosion of evangelical Protestantism.*

❑ When people suddenly become very angry, you can say there is an **explosion** of anger.

explosive (explosively) ❑ An **explosive** substance is one which can cause an explosion. ◇ An **explosive** is a substance manufactured for the purpose of causing explosions.

❑ An **explosive** issue is capable of causing a lot of argument and controversy. ◇ An **explosive** situation could easily turn to violence.

❑ An **explosive** increase is sudden and rapid. *Sales all round the world have grown explosively.*

exponent An **exponent** of something like a theory or idea is someone who argues in favour of it or explains it to people. *...an exponent of free enterprise... ...the leading exponent of human ethology.* ◇ An **exponent** of something which involves skill is someone who is good at it. *...the greatest serve-and-volley exponent we have seen.*

exponential (exponentially) If there is **exponential** growth in something, it grows at an increasing rate. *The number of these animals grows exponentially.*

export If materials or goods are **exported**, they are sent out of the country and sold to people or firms in other countries. You talk about the **export** of goods or materials; the goods and materials are called **exports**. ◇ If a country's ideas or values are **exported**, they are introduced to other countries and adopted by the people there. You can talk about the **export** of ideas or values.

exportable If you say something is **exportable**, you mean people in other countries would be willing to buy it.

exporter An **exporter** is a person or firm that sells goods to people or firms in other countries. A country can also be an **exporter**. *The Ivory Coast became the world's fourth-largest coffee exporter.*

expose (exposing, exposed) ❑ If you **expose** something which is normally covered, you uncover it and make it visible. *Steroids can cause a thinning of the skin, exposing the blood vessels underneath.*

❑ If an undesirable situation is **exposed**, the public are made aware of it. *The incident exposed the conflict between traditional fishing and fish-farming.* ◇ If a well-known person is **exposed,** they are shown to have been behaving in a shocking or dishonest way. You can also say someone's wrongdoings are **exposed.**

❏ If you are **exposed** to something dangerous or unpleasant, you are in a situation where you can be affected by it. *Redecorating had exposed him to high levels of asbestos.*

❏ An **exposed** place is one where you get little protection from bad weather.

❏ If a man **exposes** himself, he deliberately shows his genitals in a public place.

exposé (*pron:* iks-pose-ay) An **exposé** is a newspaper article or TV programme which reveals the truth about something shocking or dishonest.

exposition (expository) An **exposition** of an idea or theory is a detailed explanation of it. **Expository** is used to talk about explaining things. *For expository purposes the distinctions have to be presented as clear-cut and absolute.*

expostulate (expostulating, expostulated) If you **expostulate,** you protest at something someone has just said. '*I didn't say that,' he expostulated.*

exposure to something unpleasant or harmful is being in a situation where you can be affected by it. *...a possible link between aluminium exposure and brain damage.* ◇ If someone is suffering from **exposure,** their body temperature has become dangerously low as a result of being out in cold weather with not enough clothing to protect them. People sometimes die from exposure.

❏ Exposure is publicity. *...the instant success that national television exposure can offer.*

❏ If you talk about the **exposure** of some wrongdoing, you mean it is discovered and made public. You can also talk about the **exposure** of the people responsible. *...sensational exposures of officials in high places.* ◇ indecent exposure: see **indecent.**

❏ In photography, an **exposure** is a single photograph.

expound If you **expound** an idea or opinion, you go into details about it. *Schmidt continued to expound his views on economics and politics.*

express (expresses, expressing, expressed; expressly) ❏ The way you **express** yourself is the way you use language to say what you mean. ◇ If you **express** an idea or feeling, you put it into words. *He expressed his anger at what had happened.* ◇ If you **express** your feelings by doing something, you show your feelings that way. *Truck drivers expressed their anger by blocking major roads.* ◇ If an idea or feeling **expresses** itself in a certain way, you can see it in the things people do.

❏ If an amount is **expressed** as a fraction or percentage of another amount, it is given in that form.

❏ An **express** order or instruction is stated very clearly, without any possibility of misunderstanding. *We were expressly forbidden to join in any singing.* ◇ The **express** purpose of something is the whole reason for doing it. *The express purpose of the flights was to get Americans out.*

❏ An **express** service gets things done quicker than usual. *...express mail.* ◇ An **express** is a fast train or coach which makes fewer stops than other trains or coaches.

expression ❏ When ideas or feelings are put into words, you call this the **expression** of those ideas or feelings. ◇ An action can also be described as an **expression** of

someone's feelings, or of their intentions. *The 1976 Constitution was an expression of the state's attempts to acquire complete control over its citizens' lives.*

❏ Your **expression** is the look on your face, which shows what you are thinking or feeling.

❏ An **expression** is also a word or phrase. *Alfred Sauvy coined the expression 'the Third World'.*

expressionism (expressionist, expressionistic) **Expressionism** was an early 20th century movement in art, literature, and film which aimed to express the state of mind of the artist, writer, or director, rather than to show objects and events realistically. Expressionism is characterized by distortion, exaggeration, and symbolism. People involved in this movement were called **expressionists. Expressionist** and **expressionistic** are used to talk about things connected with this movement.

expressionless If someone is **expressionless,** their face does not show any emotion.

expressive (expressively, expressiveness) If something is **expressive,** it clearly shows someone's feelings. *The endings of his last two letters are as expressive as he ever allowed himself to be.* ◇ If a musical performance is **expressive,** it succeeds in bringing out the emotional qualities in the music. *Joanna Cole sings expressively and vividly... Her performance showed exceptional maturity and expressiveness.*

expressway An **expressway** is a road with several lanes designed for a lot of traffic to move along quickly, especially in a city.

expropriate (expropriating, expropriated; expropriation) If something is **expropriated,** it is taken away from its owner, especially by a government. *There should be no expropriation of land without proper compensation.*

expulsion See **expel.**

expunge (expunging, expunged) If something unpleasant is **expunged** from your memory, you succeed in forgetting about it. ◇ If something is **expunged** from written records, it is removed from them.

expurgate (*pron:* eks-per-gate) (expurgating, expurgated) If something like a film or article is **expurgated,** parts of it are removed to avoid shocking or offending people. *...the expurgated version.*

exquisite (exquisitely) **Exquisite** is used to describe things which are extremely beautiful, especially things done or made with great skill and artistry. *...exquisitely crafted dolls' houses.* ◇ **Exquisite** pleasure, pain, or embarrassment is very intense.

extant is used to describe things from the past which have survived, rather than being lost or destroyed. *The one extant Holbein portrait of Henry is awesome and unforgettable... Extant correspondence shows that Michelangelo begged Pope Julius II not to give him the Sistine commission.*

extempore (*pron:* eks-tem-por-ree) An **extempore** talk or speech has not been prepared in advance.

extend ❏ If you **extend** something, you make it bigger, make it include more, or make it last longer. *Mongolia has plans to extend its airport... There will be extended highlights of two of the afternoon's Premier League games.*

❏ If something **extends** for a certain distance, that is how long it is. *The line of cars extended for over 12 miles.* ◇ If something **extends** over a certain area, it covers all of that area. *The Turkish empire extended over much of the Middle East.* ◇ If something **extends** over a period of time, it continues for that period.

❏ If you **extend** a part of your body, you straighten it or stretch it out. *Karpov was seen to extend his arm.*

❏ If you **extend** an invitation to someone, you invite them to do something or come to something.

❏ If you say something **extends** to certain things or people, you mean they are covered by it or included in it.

❏ Your **extended** family includes people like your aunts, uncles, and cousins, as well as your father, mother, sisters, and brothers.

extension ❏ An **extension** is something added to something else, making it larger. *...a £5 million runway extension.* ◇ An **extension** is also an added amount of time, making something last longer. *...a six-month extension to his visa.* ◇ An **extension** of something like a law is an alteration which makes it apply to more people or things. *He says an extension of tax relief would be welcome.*

❏ A telephone **extension** is one of several phones in a building or group of buildings connected to a central phone or switchboard.

extensive (extensively) If something is **extensive**, there is a lot of it or it covers a large area. *The blast caused extensive damage... He travelled extensively.*

extent ❏ The **extent** of something is its size or scale. *The full extent of the damage is not yet known.*

❏ Phrases like **to some extent**, **to a certain extent**, and **to a large extent** are used to say something is partly but not entirely true. *Germany's slowdown has, to a large extent, been deliberately induced by the Bundesbank.* ◇ Phrases like **to what extent**, **to the extent that**, and **to that extent** are used when talking about the degree to which something is true. *Stephen Dalziel considers to what extent Lenin has fallen out of favour... He is professional only to the extent that the Sports Aid Foundation and Minet have sponsored him.*

❏ Phrases like **to the extent of** and **to such an extent that** are used to say how far someone goes in the way they behave. *America had for years supported Iraq even to the extent of taking part in joint military action against Iran... He bullied his staff to such an extent that their health declined.*

extenuating If you say there are **extenuating circumstances**, you mean someone's mistake or crime can be considered less serious because of the situation they were in at the time.

exterior ❏ The **exterior** of something is its outside. *The house has a handsome stone exterior.* **Exterior** is used to describe things which are on the outside of something. *...exterior warning lights.*

❏ When you talk about a person's **exterior**, you mean their appearance and the kind of impression they create, which may be different from their real character.

exterminate (exterminating, exterminated; extermination) When a group of people are **exterminated**, they are all killed. You can also talk about animals or plants being **exterminated**. *The threat from rabies was largely eradicated by the extermination of wild dogs.*

exterminator An **exterminator** is (a) someone who has caused the deaths of a large number of people. (b) a substance for destroying plants or animals. *...a weed exterminator.*

external (externally) **External** is used to talk about the dealings a country or organization has with other countries or organizations. *...Argentina's minister of external*

affairs. ◇ **External** is also used to talk about things on the outside of a building or other object. *...an external staircase... ...externally mounted cameras.*

extinct (extinction) ❏ If a species of animal becomes **extinct**, the whole species dies out.

❏ If a volcano is **extinct**, it is not expected to erupt again.

❏ You can say things like beliefs or types of people are **extinct** when they no longer exist. *...an ethical principle that now looks threatened with extinction.*

extinguish (extinguishes, extinguishing, extinguished) ❏ If you **extinguish** a fire or a light, you put it out.

❏ If someone's hopes or fears are **extinguished**, something puts an end to them. You can also talk about a danger being **extinguished**.

extirpate (*pron*: eks-tir-pate) (extirpating, extirpated) If you **extirpate** something, you get rid of it completely.

extol (extolling, extolled) If you **extol** something, you praise it highly and talk about it enthusiastically.

extort (extortion) If someone **extorts** money from you, they get it by using force or threats. **Extortion** is the crime of getting money from people in this way. ◇ If someone **extorts** a confession from you, they get you to confess to something by using force or threats.

extortionate If you say the price of something is **extortionate**, you mean it costs far more than is fair or reasonable.

extra is used to talk about something being added to other things of the same kind. *Hospitals will receive extra money... He was asked to stay an extra day.* ◇ **Extras** are things which are not standard or essential but which make something more comfortable, useful, or enjoyable. *...optional extras.* ◇ **Extras** are also additional amounts of money added to the basic price of something. *Diana Wallace is disgusted by big hotels adding so many extras to the bill.*

❏ An **extra** is someone who plays an unimportant part in a film, especially a non-speaking part.

❏ In cricket, **extras** are runs added to a team's score but not to the batsman's individual score, for example wides and leg-byes.

❏ If you take **extra** care when you do something, you are more careful than usual. ◇ If something is **extra-large**, it is larger than usual. Similarly, something can be **extra-wide** or **extra-long**.

extra-curricular activities are things like sports and drama, which a school or college provides for its students, and which are not part of their regular timetable.

extra-judicial (extra-judicially) **Extra-judicial** killings are carried out on behalf of a government without a trial or any other legal procedure. *Hundreds of suspected government opponents were executed extra-judicially by police.*

extra-marital (or extramarital) An **extra-marital** relationship is between a married person and someone who is not their husband or wife.

extra-parliamentary political activity is aimed at producing changes to society without involving parliament.

extra-sensory perception See ESP.

extra-terrestrial See extraterrestrial.

extra time In knock-out competitions like the FA Cup, **extra time** is an additional period of playing time which is added on when the result is still a draw after normal playing time.

extract ❏ If something is **extracted**, it is taken out or pulled out. *I had three wisdom teeth extracted.* ◇ When coal or other raw materials are **extracted**, they are taken from the ground. ◇ You also say a substance is **extracted** when it is obtained by separating it from other substances. An **extract** is a substance obtained in this way. *...vegetable extract.*

❏ If you **extract** something from someone, you get it from them although they do not want to give it to you. *Moscow seemed to be using the occasion to extract every possible concession from Bonn.*

❏ An **extract** from a piece of writing or music is a small part printed or played separately.

extraction ❏ If you say someone is of a particular **extraction**, you mean their family originally came from a different country. *...an American of German extraction.*

❏ **Extraction** is the removal of something, especially the removal of things like minerals from the ground.

extractor An **extractor** or **extractor fan** is a device in a window or wall which draws steam, hot air, or smoke out of a room.

extradite (extraditing, extradited; extradition) If someone is **extradited**, they are officially sent back to their own country to stand trial for a crime they are accused of. An **extradition warrant** is a legal document issued by one country and sent to another country, asking them to hand over someone they want to put on trial. An **extradition treaty** is an official arrangement between two countries under which each agrees to send back any of the other's citizens if they are wanted for trial in their home country.

extramarital See extra-marital.

extraneous is used to describe matters which are brought into something like a discussion and which are not relevant to it.

extraordinaire (*pron:* iks-tra-ord-in-air) is used to say someone is outstandingly successful at something. *...Michael Jackson, pop star extraordinaire... He is considered a party-giver extraordinaire.*

extraordinary (extraordinarily) ❏ **Extraordinary** is used to say someone or something has a quality or characteristic to a very high degree. *...the extraordinary beauty of the setting... ...extraordinarily high tax rates.* ◇ If you say someone or something is **extraordinary**, you mean they are very remarkable or unusual. *...this extraordinary actress... ...extraordinary events.*

❏ An **extraordinary meeting** of a committee or group is arranged specially to deal with a particular problem. ◇ An **extraordinary general meeting** of a company is an official meeting of the directors and shareholders which is not an annual general meeting.

extrapolate (*pron:* iks-trap-a-late) (extrapolating, extrapolated; extrapolation) In maths or statistics, if you **extrapolate** a result which cannot be calculated exactly or measured directly, you estimate it from figures which you know are correct. A result obtained like this is called an **extrapolation**. Similarly, you can **extrapolate** a piece of information from known facts.

extrasensory perception See ESP.

extraterrestrial (*or* extra-terrestrial) Extraterrestial is used to describe things which happen, exist, or come from somewhere beyond the planet Earth. *...extraterrestrial rocks.* ◇ In science fiction, an **extraterrestrial** is a creature from another planet.

extravagant (extravagantly, extravagance) ❏ If someone is **extravagant**, they keep spending money on things which are not really necessary. You talk about the **extravagance** of someone like this. You say the things they buy are **extravagances**.

❏ **Extravagant** is also used to describe things people say or do which are exaggerated or overdone. *...extravagantly dramatic gestures.* ◇ **Extravagant** ideas or claims are unrealistic and impractical. *...extravagant promises... ...the extravagance of these demands.*

❏ **Extravagant** entertainments or designs are colourful or spectacular and meant to impress people. *...an extravagant display of colourful lights.*

extravaganza An **extravaganza** is an elaborate and impressive performance or public event.

extreme (extremely) ❏ **Extreme, extremely,** and **in the extreme** are all used to say something has a characteristic to a very great degree. For example, you can talk about **extreme** danger, or say something is **extremely** dangerous or dangerous **in the extreme**.

❏ **Extremes** are the highest and lowest points on a scale. *Fescue species are more adaptable to climatic extremes than ryegrasses.* ◇ The **extreme** points or edges of something are the ones furthest from its centre. *...the extreme north-east of the country.*

❏ **Extreme** opinions go beyond what most people believe is sensible or reasonable. Similarly, you can talk about **extreme** methods or **extreme** political movements. *...extreme socialism... ...extreme nationalists.*

❏ If you say someone is going to **extremes** or taking something to **extremes**, you mean they are behaving in a foolish or unacceptable way by taking something too far. You can also say they are taking something to its **extreme**.

extremis See in extremis.

extremist (extremism) An **extremist** is a person who wants to bring about social or political change using extreme methods which most people find unacceptable. You talk about the **extremism** of someone like this.

extremity (extremities) ❏ The **extremities** of something are its farthest points or edges. *...the northwest extremity of Europe.* ◇ A person's **extremities** are the parts of their body which are at the ends of their arms and legs, i.e. their fingers and toes.

❏ When people go too far in their behaviour and do things which are foolish or unacceptable, you can talk about the **extremity** of their actions. ◇ An **extremity** is also a very serious situation. *Never has the public been reduced to such an extremity of helplessness as by this recent strike.*

extricate (extricating, extricated) If you **extricate** someone from a difficult situation, you get them out of it.

extrovert An **extrovert** is an outgoing person who enjoys being the centre of attention.

extrude (extruding, extruded) If something **extrudes** or is **extruded**, it is squeezed out through a small opening.

exuberant (exuberantly, exuberance) **Exuberant** behaviour is energetic and high-spirited. *Many students are exuberantly hospitable and friendly... ...a display of modern dance performed with youthful exuberance.*

exude (exuding, exuded) ❑ If you say someone **exudes** a characteristic or feeling, you mean they give the impression of having a lot of it. *The chief minister exudes confidence.* ❑ If something **exudes** a substance, the substance comes out through its surface. *...fatty acids exuded from the human skin.* ◇ If something **exudes** a smell, it gives it off.

exult (exultant, exultation) If you **exult** at something or **exult** in it, you feel or show triumphant pleasure about it. You say someone who feels or behaves like this is **exultant**; you call their feelings or behaviour **exultation**.

eye (eyeing, eyed) ❑ A person's or animal's **eyes** are the organs they use for seeing. ◇ If you **eye** something, you look at it. ◇ You also say someone **eyes** something when they show great interest in it or concern about it. ◇ If you say **all eyes** are on something, you mean everyone is looking at it or is very interested in it. *All eyes are now on the European Community, to see if it will follow the US's example and lift its sanctions.* ❑ The first time you **set eyes** on something is the first time you see it. If you have never **set eyes** on something, you have never seen it. ◇ If you **cast your eye over** something like a document, you look at it quickly to see what it says. ❑ A person's **eye** for something is their ability to spot it or make good judgements about it. *Honda has a keen eye for market opportunities.* ◇ Someone's **eye** for something can also be their attitude towards it. For example, if you look at something with a **critical eye**, you have a critical attitude towards it and are looking out for faults. ❑ If something **catches your eye**, you suddenly notice it, or it attracts your attention. ◇ If you try to **catch** someone's **eye**, you try to attract their attention. ◇ If you make **eye contact** with someone, you look at each other at the same time and your eyes meet. ❑ If you **keep an eye out** for something, you watch out for it. ◇ If you **keep your eye on** someone or something, you watch them, to see what happens to them. ◇ If you **keep your eye on** a situation, you pay attention to it, to see how it develops. ◇ If you have **got your eye on** something, you want to get it. *Who will be the next dictator with his eye on a slice of his neighbour's territory?* ❑ **With an eye to** is used to say why something is done. *They have travelled around Europe with an eye to expansion.* ❑ You say **in the eyes of...** when you are describing someone's interpretation of events. *The chief culprit in the eyes of the Stradey Park faithful was Colin Stephens at fly-half.* ❑ If there is **more to** something **than meets the eye**, it is more complicated or significant than it seems at first. You can also say there is **less to** something **than meets the eye**. ❑ If you do something **with your eyes open**, you are fully aware of what you are doing and of what the consequences might be. ❑ If something **opens your eyes**, it makes you aware of things you did not know about. ◇ If you **shut** or **close your eyes to** something, you ignore it. *The statement accused the human rights group of closing its eyes to the hundreds of children who had died as a result of the sanctions.* ❑ If you do not **see eye to eye** with someone, you disagree with them. ❑ If you are **up to your eyes**, you are very busy. ❑ If someone or something is **in the public eye**, they

are often mentioned in the papers and seen on TV. ❑ The **eye** of a needle is the hole at the blunt end which you pass the thread through. ❑ On a potato, the **eyes** are the tiny buds on its surface from which shoots grow if it is left for long enough. ❑ The **eye** of a storm or hurricane is the small area of low pressure and calm at its centre. ◇ If you say someone is at the **eye of the storm**, you mean they are at the centre of a row or crisis. ❑ **mind's eye**: see mind.

eye-catching things are very noticeable.

eye-opener If something is an **eye-opener**, it makes you aware of things you knew nothing about before.

eye-shadow is make-up put on the eyelids to colour them.

eye socket A person's **eye sockets** are the two bony holes on either side of their face which hold their eyeballs.

eye strain is pain you feel around your eyes or at the back of your eyes, caused by tiredness or not wearing glasses when you need them.

eye tooth See canine.

eye-witness See eyewitness.

eyeball A person's **eyeballs** are the white ball-shaped parts of their eyes, which have a coloured centre containing the retina and pupil. ◇ If people are **eyeball to eyeball**, they are facing each other at close range, often in a confrontational way.

eyebrow A person's **eyebrows** are the curved lines of hair on the ridges above their eye-sockets. ◇ If you say **eyebrows are raised**, you mean people are rather surprised at something.

eyelash (eyelashes) A person's **eyelashes** are the hairs on the edges of their eyelids.

eyelet An **eyelet** is a small hole with a metal or leather ring round it, for example in a tent or a sail, through which cord or rope is threaded.

eyelid A person's **eyelids** are the flaps of skin which cover their eyes when they are shut. ◇ If you say nobody **bats an eyelid** when something happens, you mean nobody is shocked or surprised. If someone does something shocking **without batting an eyelid**, they do it completely calmly, without any feeling of shame or embarrassment.

eyeliner is make-up used to draw an outline round the eyes.

eyepiece The **eyepiece** of a telescope or microscope is the glass at one end you put your eye to.

eyesight Your **eyesight** is your ability to see.

eyesore If you call something like a building an **eyesore**, you mean it is ugly and spoils the view.

eyewitness (eyewitnesses) (*or* eye-witness, eye-witnesses) If someone is an **eyewitness** to something like a crime or accident, they saw it happen.

eyrie (*pron:* **ear-ree**) An **eyrie** is the nest of an eagle, falcon, or similar bird, usually built high up on the side of a cliff or mountain. ◇ A house in a very high place or a room high up in a tower block can also be called an **eyrie**. *A telephone call to Lonrho's eyrie near St Paul's yesterday indicated that everyone was out on business.*

F f

F See Fahrenheit.

fable A **fable** is a story with a moral.

fabled people, things, and places are well-known because of the stories told about them.

fabric is cloth, or a stiffer material like cloth. A **fabric** is a type of fabric. ◇ The **fabric** of a building is its walls, roof, and other parts. ◇ When people talk about the **fabric** of a social system, they are talking about the way it holds together. *After a bloody revolution and 40 years of abuse, the fabric of Hungarian society is distinctly fragile.*

fabricate (fabricating, fabricated; fabrication) If someone **fabricates** news or information, they invent it. A **fabrication** is a bit of news or information someone has invented.

fabulous (fabulously) **Fabulous** people and things are very famous, often because people connect them with great wealth. *...the fabulous Del Monte hotel... The villagers maintain that she is fabulously wealthy.* ◇ **Fabulous** creatures and places exist only in stories and legends. *...the towers and turrets of some fabulous city.* ◇ Some people use **fabulous** to show how pleased or impressed they are with something. *Wendy looked fabulous... I feel absolutely fabulous.*

facade (or **façade**) (*pron:* fas-**sahd**) The **facade** of a large building is the outside of its front wall. ◇ You call people's behaviour a **facade** when it hides the real truth about something. *...the grim facts behind the facade of gaiety.*

face (facing, faced) ❑ A person's **face** is the front of their head from their chin to their forehead. ◇ If you **make** or **pull a face**, you put on an ugly expression. ◇ You can add **-faced** to a word to describe someone's face or expression. *...a chubby-faced teenager.*

❑ If two people are **face to face**, they are looking directly at each other. If they are **facing** each other, they are standing in front of each other, looking at each other.

❑ If you **lose face**, something happens which makes people lose respect for you. If you do something to **save face**, you do it to avoid losing people's respect. ◇ If you **put on a brave face**, you pretend things are not as bad as they really are. ◇ If you **set your face against** something, you decide to oppose it.

❑ A clock's **face** is the part which shows the time.

❑ A **face** of a mountain is a very steep side. ◇ A cliff **face** is the vertical part of a cliff. ◇ The coal **face** is the part of a mine where coal is dug.

❑ You use **face** to talk about a person who is seen a lot because of their job. *It was felt that a new face was needed to head the department.* ◇ You also use **face** to talk about the impression people have of a political party or other organization. *NATO must come up with a new face.* ◇ You use **face** to talk about the general appearance of a place. *...the transformation of the face of London.* ◇ You say **on the face of it** when you are mentioning how something seems, although you are not sure it is really like that. *On the face of it, it sounds like a good idea.* ◇ **face value:** see **value.**

❑ If something is **face down**, it is lying with its front pointing downwards. If it is **face up**, its front is pointing upwards. ◇ If you say part of a building **faces** a particular direction, you are saying on which side of the building it is. *I rarely use this room as it faces north.*

❑ If someone **faces** a difficulty, challenge, or choice or is **faced** with one, they have got to deal with it. ◇ If someone **faces up to** a difficult situation, they accept it and deal with it. ◇ **In the face of** is used to say how someone behaves or feels in a difficult or dangerous situation. *They showed the most awesome courage in the face of horrifying penalties... ...a feeling of helplessness in the face of insurmountable odds.* ◇ **fly in the face of:** see **fly.**

face-saving (face-saver) A **face-saving** arrangement or agreement is intended to prevent someone losing other people's respect. An arrangement or agreement like this can be called a **face-saver.**

faceless You use **faceless** to talk about the people belonging to an organization you are dealing with, who you never meet or get to know as individuals. *...faceless bureaucrats.*

facelift A **facelift** is an operation to tighten the skin on someone's face, to make them look younger. ◇ When a building or district is given a **facelift**, work is done to improve its appearance. ◇ You can also say something is given a **facelift** when people try to improve its image.

facet (*pron:* **fas**-it) A **facet** of something is a part or aspect of it. *...an interesting facet of his character.* ◇ The **facets** of a jewel are its flat regularly-shaped sides.

facetious (*pron:* fas-see-**shuss**) If someone makes a humorous remark in the middle of a serious discussion, you can say they are being **facetious.**

facia See fascia.

facial (*pron:* **fay**-shal) is used to talk about something to do with a person's face. *...facial hair... ...facial surgery.*

facile (*pron:* **fas**-sile) is used to say that something such as an explanation is too simple and obvious. *It would be facile to call this a conspiracy.*

facilitate (facilitating, facilitated) If something **facilitates** a process, it makes it easier.

facility (facilities) **Facilities** are buildings or equipment which are there for a particular purpose. *...play facilities for young children.* ◇ You can call a useful feature a **facility.** *...a computer with a message-swapping facility.* ◇ If you have a **facility** for something, you are good at it. *...his facility for languages.*

facsimile (*pron:* fak-**sim**-ill-lee) A **facsimile** of something is an exact copy of it. *The Financial Times carries a facsimile of the four-page issue it published a hundred years ago.*

fact ❑ **Facts** are correct pieces of information. You can call the truth about something **the facts.** *He'll be asking ministers to reveal what they know of the facts of the affair.* If you say something is a **fact**, you mean it is true. ◇ You use **the fact that** or **the fact of** when you are mentioning something which happens to be true. *The situation is complicated by the fact that a conflict has occurred... ...the fact of belonging to a certain race.*

❑ You say **in fact** (a) to emphasize that something actually happened or is actually true. *We were asked to look into this, and we did in fact do so.* (b) when you are improving on what you have just said, by being more frank or giving a better description. *This isn't very interesting – in fact, I think it's remarkably dull... It was terribly cold weather – a blizzard, in fact.* ◇ You use **in fact, in actual fact, in point of fact,** or **as a matter of fact** when you are correcting what has just been said. *In point of fact, they arrived early.*

❑ If you say something is **a fact of life,** you mean people have to put up with it, because there is nothing they can do about it. *Hunger is already a fact of life in some areas.* ◇ If you tell a child **the facts of life,** you tell him or her about sex and how babies are born.

fact-finding If someone goes on a **fact-finding** mission or trip, they try to find out what is going on in a place, usually on behalf of an official organization or group.

faction (factional, factionalism) A **faction** is an organized group of people inside a larger group, with their own ideas and beliefs. When there is **factionalism,** a group splits up into factions. **Factional** fighting or arguments occur between factions.

factor A **factor** is one of the things affecting a decision or something that happens. *There are other important factors to be considered.*

factory (factories) A **factory** is a large building or group of buildings where goods are made using machinery.

factory farming is a type of farming in which animals or poultry are kept indoors in a confined space and sometimes given special food to make them grow more quickly or produce more eggs.

factory floor is used to talk about the activities or opinions of the workers in a factory, as distinct from those of the management. *Concern has also come from the factory floor itself.*

factory ship A **factory ship** is a ship with equipment for processing fish at sea.

factual (factually) If something like a report is **factual,** it consists of facts, rather than theories or opinions. ◇ **Factual** knowledge or ignorance is knowledge or ignorance of facts. ◇ **Factually** is used to say that the information in something is correct or incorrect. *...a factually accurate pamphlet.*

faculty (faculties) A person's **faculties** are their physical and mental abilities. *...the faculty of hearing... He is in full control of his faculties.* ◇ In a university or college, a **faculty** is a group of departments.

fad A **fad** is something people do which is popular for a short time. *...the skateboard fad.*

fade (fading, faded) If something **fades,** it becomes less bright, loud, or strong. *The afternoon light was fading... Interest in the story will fade.* ◇ If something coloured **fades,** its colour becomes paler. *...an old man in a faded blue suit.* ◇ If something **fades away,** it gradually gets weaker until it stops or disappears altogether. *Your enthusiasm for running will soon fade away.*

faecal (*American spelling:* fecal) (*pron:* fee-kal) **Faecal** is used to talk about things connected with faeces. *...faecal bacteria.*

faeces (*American spelling:* feces) (*both pron:* fee-seez) **Faeces** is the solid waste people and animals get rid of from their bodies.

fag A **fag** is a cigarette. ◇ In the US, **fag** is an offensive word for a homosexual man.

faggot A **faggot** is a bundle of sticks for firewood. ◇ **Faggots** are balls of minced pork mixed with herbs and breadcrumbs. ◇ In the US, **faggot** is an offensive word for a homosexual man.

Fahrenheit (*pron:* far-ren-hite) is a scale for measuring temperature, in which water freezes at 32° and boils at 212°. When you write down a temperature using this scale, you put 'F' after the number of degrees, for example 65°F.

fail (failing, failed) ❑ If you **fail** to do something you are trying to do, you do not succeed. ◇ If something you do **fails,** it does not have the effect you want. *Should military force be used if sanctions fail?* ◇ If you **fail** a test or exam, you do not pass. ◇ You use **failed** to describe (a) an attempt which has not succeeded. *...a failed coup attempt.* (b) a person who has not been a success at something. *...a failed novelist.*

❑ If you **fail** to do something you are supposed to do, you do not do it. ◇ If something mechanical **fails,** it does not work. ◇ If someone **fails** you, they let you down.

❑ If you say something happens **without fail,** you mean it always happens. *He attended every meeting without fail.*

fail-safe A **fail-safe** device or system is part of a larger system and is there to stop anything dangerous happening if something goes wrong.

failing ❑ A person's **failings** are small faults in their behaviour. ◇ The **failings** of a system or organization are the ways in which it does not work.

❑ You use **failing that, failing this,** or **failing which** (a) to suggest an alternative, in case the thing you have just mentioned is not possible. *Wear your national dress, or, failing that, a suit.* (b) to say what will happen if something is not done. *I had five days in which to seek both informants' permission, failing which the police would take action against me.*

failure is lack of success. If something is a **failure,** it does not produce the results you want. ◇ If someone is a **failure,** they have not succeeded in the things they set out to do.

❑ If someone has not done something they were supposed to, you can talk about their **failure** to do it. *...his failure to appear at the party.* ◇ You use **failure** to talk about what happens when something stops working or does not do what it is supposed to. *...kidney failure... ...engine failure.*

faint (faintly) ❑ You use **faint** to describe things which can only just be seen, heard, smelled, or tasted. *There was a faint smell of gas... The tea tasted faintly of bitter almonds.* ◇ If there is a **faint** hope or chance of something happening, it might just happen. ◇ **Faintly** is used to say something is only just true. *They were faintly amused.*

❑ If you **faint,** you lose consciousness for a short time. If you **feel faint,** you feel as if you are going to faint.

faint-hearted people do not have much courage.

fair (fairer, fairest; fairly, fairness) ❑ **Fair** behaviour is reasonable and just. *She won't get a fair trial... You haven't played the game fairly... There is no such thing as fairness in business.* ◇ If you want **fair play,** you want people to be treated in a reasonable and just way. ◇ You say **in fairness** or **in all fairness** when you have mentioned a criticism of someone and you want to defend or excuse them. *In fairness, Britain would otherwise not have been self-sufficient until the mid-1980s.* ◇ If people think someone is **fair game**, they think it is all right to criticize or attack them.

❑ A **fair** number or size is quite large. *...a fair-sized bedroom.* ◇ If you have a **fair** idea of something, you know reasonably well what it is like. ◇ If there is a **fair** chance of something happening, it is quite likely to happen.

❑ If the weather is **fair**, it is quite sunny and not raining.

❑ Someone who is **fair** has gold- or straw-coloured hair. You can also say they have **fair** hair. ◇ **Fair** skin is pale-coloured.

❑ A **fair** is (a) an event in a park or field where people ride on machines for fun, or try to win prizes in games. (b) an event where people or firms display or sell goods. *...the Leipzig Trade Fair.*

fairground A **fairground** is the piece of ground where a fair is held.

fairly means to quite a large degree. *The information was fairly accurate.* ◇ See also **fair**.

fairway The **fairway** on each hole of a golf course is the strip of short grass between the tee and the green.

fairy (fairies) In children's stories, **fairies** are tiny people with wings and magical powers.

fairy tale (fairy story) A **fairy tale** or **fairy story** is a children's story about magical happenings and imaginary creatures. ◇ **Fairy-tale** is used to describe places which look like the pictures in children's storybooks. *...the fairy-tale villages of Lake Constance.* ◇ If you do not believe someone's account of something, you can say it is a **fairy tale** or a **fairy story**.

fait accompli (*pron:* fate ak-**kom**-plee) You say an action is a **fait accompli** when it has already been done and it is too late to do anything about it.

faith ❑ If you have **faith** in something or someone, you believe you can trust them or rely on them. ◇ If you **break faith** with someone who trusts you, you let them down. If you **keep faith** with them, you do not let them down. ◇ If you do something **in good faith**, you believe at the time it is right, honest, or legal.

❑ A **faith** is a religion, such as Christianity or Buddhism. ◇ **Faith** is strong religious belief.

faith healing (faith healer) **Faith healing** is the treatment of a sick person by someone who believes they can cure people by praying and by the power of their religious faith. Someone who treats people like this is called a **faith healer.**

faithful (faithfully) ❑ If you stay **faithful** to a person or organization, you go on supporting them. ◇ If you stay **faithful** to an idea or belief, you go on believing in it. ◇ Someone who is **faithful** to their husband, wife, or lover does not get involved sexually with anyone else.

❑ A **faithful** account of something describes accurately what happened. *Their activities were faithfully described in the newspapers.* ◇ A **faithful** translation or adaptation of a book sticks closely to the original.

fake (faking, faked) A **fake** is an object made to look like something useful or valuable, so people will believe it is the real thing. ◇ If you **fake** something, you make or do something which looks like the real thing. *They faked antiques of all kinds... Fourteen years ago he faked suicide.*

falcon **Falcons** are birds of prey, some of which can be trained to hunt other birds and animals. The commonest British **falcon** is the kestrel.

fall (falling, fell, have fallen) ❑ If something **falls**, it drops towards the ground. ◇ If someone **falls**, **falls down**, **falls over**, or has a **fall**, they lose their balance and end up lying or kneeling on the ground. A tall object can also **fall**, **fall down**, or **fall over**. ◇ If a roof or ceiling **falls in**, it collapses. ◇ If a person's hair or teeth **fall out**, they work loose and come away from the person's scalp or gums. ◇ If something **falls apart**, it breaks into pieces because it is old or badly made.

❑ When people in a position of power **fall**, they lose that position. You call this their **fall**. ◇ If a place **falls** in a war, an army captures it and it changes hands. You call this the **fall** of the place. *...the fall of Saigon.*

❑ If something like a rate or amount **falls**, it decreases. *There's been a sharp fall in the price of oil.* ◇ If a number or amount **falls off**, it gets smaller. *We knew that the numbers of overseas students would fall off drastically.*

❑ When a shadow **falls** on something, it reaches it and makes it darker. ◇ When night or darkness **falls**, it gets dark.

❑ **Fall** is used in some expressions to say someone or something changes to a different state. *I fell asleep... They both fell silent... Their ideas had fallen into disuse.*

❑ When you are classifying things, you can say they **fall** into a number of groups or categories. *North Wales pubs fall into three broad groups.* You can also say something **falls** into a particular group or category. ◇ If something **falls** on a particular day, that is when it happens. *The first of May fell on a Sunday this year.* ◇ If it **falls** to you to do something, you are the one who has to do it.

❑ If you **fall behind**, you fail to keep up with someone or something. *They fell behind with their mortgage repayments.* ◇ If you **fall back on** something, you do it or use it when other things fail. ◇ If something planned **falls through**, it does not go ahead.

❑ If you **fall for** a lie or trick, you are taken in by it. ◇ If you **fall for** a person or **fall in love** with them, you are suddenly in love with them. ◇ If you **fall out** with someone, you quarrel.

❑ A large waterfall is sometimes called the **falls.**

❑ Americans call autumn the **fall.**

❑ **fall flat:** see **flat.** ◇ **fall short:** see **short.**

fall-back is used to describe something like a plan which is kept in reserve in case something else fails. *As a fall-back position, Pena is proposing a deal with another airline.*

fallacious (fallacy, fallacies) If you say an argument or idea is **fallacious** (*pron:* fal-**lay**-shus) or a **fallacy** (*pron:* fal-**lass**-ee), you mean it is based on wrong information or bad reasoning.

fallen is used to describe (a) an object lying on the ground which has dropped from a high place. *...fallen leaves... ...a fallen rock.* (b) a tall object which has collapsed onto the ground. *...a fallen tree.* ◇ See also **fall.**

fallible (fallibility) If you say someone is **fallible** or talk about their **fallibility**, you mean they are capable of making mistakes.

fallopian tube A woman's **fallopian tubes** are the two tubes which eggs pass along from her ovaries to her womb.

fallout Nuclear **fallout** is the radioactive material which settles over a large area after a nuclear explosion. ◇ **Fallout** is also used to talk about the unpleasant side-effects of other things. *The economic fallout of international sanctions could well go beyond a cut-back in luxuries.*

fallow If land is lying **fallow**, no crops have been planted there, and the soil is being allowed to rest and improve.

false (falsely) ❏ **False** information is not true. A false statement or report contains untrue information. ◇ A false conclusion or impression is wrong or mistaken. ◇ If you call someone's hopes or expectations **false**, you mean things will not work out the way they hope they will. ◇ If someone makes a **false** promise, they do not mean to carry it out. ◇ If someone is the victim of a **false** arrest or **false** imprisonment, they are arrested or imprisoned for something they did not do. *He claimed that he was falsely imprisoned.*

❏ You use **false** to describe (a) something made to look like a particular thing, to deceive people. *...a false beard.* (b) behaviour which is not sincere. *...false modesty.*

false alarm If there seems to be a danger and then nothing happens, you can say there was a **false alarm**.

false start A **false start** is an unsuccessful attempt to start something. ◇ When there is a **false start** at the beginning of a race, the competitors are called back to the start line, because one of them moved before the signal was given.

false teeth are a set of removable artificial teeth, worn by someone who has lost their own teeth.

falsehood is telling lies. A **falsehood** is a lie. ◇ If you try to establish the truth or **falsehood** of something, you try to work out whether it is true or false.

falsetto If a man speaks or sings in a **falsetto**, he uses a voice more like a woman's or boy's.

falsify (falsifies, falsifying, falsified; falsification) If someone **falsifies** a written record, they put wrong information into it. *...falsification of accounts.*

falter (faltering, faltered) If something **falters**, it gets weaker and is likely to stop or break down. *The economy is faltering.* ◇ If someone **falters**, they hesitate, because they are not sure what to do or say. ◇ If you make a **faltering** attempt at something, you do it in a hesitant way, because you are nervous or not really sure what you are doing.

fame If **fame** comes to someone, they become famous.

famed If someone or something is **famed** for something, they are famous because of it.

familial (*pron:* fam-mil-ee-al) is used to talk about something to do with families or a particular family. *...familial needs... ...familial activities.*

familiar (familiarity) If someone or something is **familiar** to you, you recognize them or know them well. *...the familiarity of the surroundings.* ◇ If you are **familiar** with something, you know it well. *I am of course familiar with your work.* ◇ You say someone is being **familiar** when they speak or behave in an intimate way to someone they do not know well. *She disliked intensely the man's familiar tone.*

familiarize (familiarizing, familiarized; familiarization) (*can be spelled with an 's' instead of a 'z'*) If you **familiarize** yourself with something, you learn about it or get to know it. *...an intensive familiarization programme.*

family (families) ❏ A **family** is a group of people who are related to each other. When people talk about a **family**, they usually mean a couple and their children. ◇ **Family** is used to talk about (a) something belonging to a particular family. *...the family business.* (b) something which can be used or enjoyed by all the members of a family, including the children. *...family entertainment.* ◇ If you say a man is a **family man**, you mean he likes to spend a lot of time with his wife and children.

❏ **Family** is also used to talk about a group of related species of animals or plants. *The weaver bird is a member of the sparrow family.*

family doctor A **family doctor** is a GP.

family name Your **family name** is your surname.

family planning is the use of contraception to control the number of children in a family.

family tree A **family tree** is a chart showing all the people in a family over several generations and the way they are related to each other.

famine When there is **famine** or a **famine**, there is a serious shortage of food in a country or region, which can lead to many deaths.

famished If you say you are **famished**, you mean you are very hungry.

famous (famously) If someone or something is **famous**, they are very well-known. ◇ If you get on **famously** with someone, you enjoy each other's company.

fan (fanning, fanned) ❏ If you are a **fan** of a sport, you enjoy watching it. If you are a **fan** of a well-known person or group of people, you admire them and enjoy watching them, listening to them, or reading their books.

❏ A **fan** is a flat object which you wave in front of you to cool yourself down. If you **fan** yourself, you try to cool yourself by waving a fan or some other object in front of you. ◇ A **fan** is also a piece of electrical equipment with revolving blades which keeps a room or machine cool, or gets rid of smells.

❏ If something **fans** a fire, it creates a current of air which makes it burn better. ◇ If something **fans** a feeling like fear or hatred, it makes people feel it more strongly.

❏ If people **fan out**, they move forward in the same general direction, getting further apart from each other.

fan belt See fanbelt.

fan club A **fan club** is an organized group of people who take part in various activities together because they admire the same person or support the same sports team.

fan heater A **fan heater** is an electric heater with revolving blades for spreading warm air round a room.

fanatic (fanaticism) A **fanatic** is someone with strong political or religious views who behaves in an extreme or violent way. Behaviour like this is called **fanaticism** (*pron:* fa-nat-is-iz-um). ◇ You also say someone is a **fanatic** when they are very keen on something and spend a lot of time on it. *...a fitness fanatic.*

fanatical (fanatically) **Fanatical** people feel very strongly about something and behave in an extreme way because of it. *They are fanatically devoted to their cause.*

fanaticism See fanatic.

fanbelt (*or* fan belt) A car's **fanbelt** is the belt that drives the fan which keeps the engine cool.

fancier A **fancier** of something is someone with a special interest or hobby. *...flower fanciers.* ◇ See also **fancy**.

fanciful (fancifully) You use **fanciful** to describe something someone makes or does which is unusual and imaginative. *He employs some fanciful devices to get his ideas* *across... The presents were fancifully wrapped.* ◇ If you say an idea or description is **fanciful**, you mean it is based on someone's imagination, rather than reality.

fancy (fancies, fancying, fancied; fancier, fanciest) ❏ If you **fancy** something, you want it. ◇ If you **fancy** someone, you are attracted to them sexually. ◇ If you **take a fancy** to someone or something, you start liking them, for no special reason. ◇ If something you see **takes your fancy**, you want it.

❏ You say people **fancy** themselves when they think they are clever, attractive, or good at something. If they **fancy** themselves as a particular thing, that is how they see themselves. *He fancies himself as the great white hunter.*

❏ If you **fancy** you can see or hear something, you think you can see or hear it. You can also **fancy** something is happening to you, or is true about you.

❏ **Fancy** is used to talk about ideas created by someone's imagination. *It is difficult to separate fact from fancy.* Ideas like these are called **fancies**.

❏ **Fancy** things are not simple or plain.

fancy dress When people wear **fancy dress** for a party or dance, they dress up as something like a famous person.

fandango (fandangos) The **fandango** is a Spanish dance in which a couple dance close together accompanied by a guitar, castanets, and sometimes a singer.

fanfare A **fanfare** is a short loud tune played on trumpets to announce a special event. ◇ **Fanfare** is also used to talk about a lot of attention being drawn to something which is happening or about to happen. *The three hostages were released amid a fanfare of publicity.*

fang The **fangs** of something like a snake or wolf are its long sharp teeth.

fanlight A **fanlight** is a small window over a door.

fantasize (fantasizing, fantasized) (*can be spelled with an 's' instead of a 'z'*) If someone **fantasizes**, they get pleasure from thinking about something improbable they would like to happen.

fantastic (fantastically) People say something is **fantastic** when they like or admire it very much. ◇ **Fantastic** is also used to emphasize how big something is, or how much of it there is. *The equipment is of a fantastic size... The divorce rate is fantastically high here.* ◇ You can also say something is **fantastic** when it seems strange and wonderful, or highly improbable.

fantasy (fantasies) ❏ **Fantasy** is what goes on in someone's imagination. *To a child, fantasy and reality are very close to each other.* ◇ A **fantasy** is something someone enjoys imagining. *...three men playing out a sexual fantasy.* ◇ If you say a statement or claim is **fantasy**, you mean it is something someone has dreamed up, rather than the truth.

❏ A **fantasy** is also a book or play written or presented in an unusual and imaginative way.

fanzine (*pron: fan-zeen*) A **fanzine** is a magazine for people who admire the same well-known person or support the same sports team.

far (farther *or* further, farthest *or* furthest) ❏ **Far** is used to talk about distance. *How far is Amity from here?... Vita went as far as Bologna... The furthest I have ever fallen was from the 10-metre board.* ◇ If something is **far** away, it is a long way away. ◇ The **far** north, south, east, and west of a country are the parts which are the greatest dis-

tance from its centre. ◇ The **far** end or side of something is the one which is the greatest distance from you. ◇ If something happens **far and wide**, it happens in a lot of places over a large area.

❏ **Far** is used to talk about things happening a long time ahead, or a long time ago. *The Fourth of July isn't far off... ...as far back as the twelfth century.* ◇ You use **so far** to talk about a period of time leading up to the present. *What do you think of the town so far?*

❏ **Far** is used to talk about extent or degree. *How far have you got in developing this?... The government will be able to cut interest rates further... ...using her methods as far as possible.* ◇ If you think someone's behaviour is becoming extreme or embarrassing, you can say they are going **too far**.

❏ You use **far** to say something is much bigger, better, etc than something else. *...a far greater problem... The firm had far outstripped its rivals.* ◇ You use **by far** or **far and away** to say someone or something has much more of an ability or quality than anyone or anything else. *She was by far the camp's best swimmer.* ◇ You use **far from** to say that the opposite of something is true. *His hands were far from clean... Far from speeding up, the tank slithered to a halt.* ◇ If you say an answer or idea is **not far wrong**, **not far out**, or **not far off**, you mean it is nearly correct.

❏ **Far right** and **far left** are used to talk about people with extreme right- or left-wing views. *...far right voters... The far left has been keeping a low profile.*

❏ See also **further**.

Far East The countries of eastern Asia, including China and Japan, are sometimes called the **Far East**.

far-fetched If you say a story sounds **far-fetched**, you mean it is very unlikely to be true.

far-flung is used to talk about the parts of a place which are a very long way from its centre. *...a far-flung corner of the Empire.*

far-off A **far-off** place is a long way away. ◇ A **far-off** time was a long time ago.

far-reaching A **far-reaching** decision or action affects many things, in many different ways. You can also say a decision or action has **far-reaching** effects.

far-sighted people are good at guessing what will happen in the future and at making decisions which turn out to be the right ones.

faraway places or sounds are a long way away. ◇ If someone has a **faraway** look, they are thinking about something else and not paying much attention.

farce A **farce** is a comic play in which the characters get involved in unlikely and complicated situations. ◇ If you say something is a **farce**, you mean it is done so badly it cannot be taken seriously. *The elections have been reduced to a farce.*

farcical If you say a situation or something that happens is **farcical**, you mean things turn out in a ridiculous way. ◇ You also use **farcical** to say something has been organized very badly. *The catering arrangements were completely farcical.*

fare (faring, fared) ❏ The **fare** is the money you pay for a journey by bus, taxi, train, boat, or plane.

❏ **Fare** is used to talk about a particular kind of food. *Rice, beans, and corn are the basic fare of the Nicaraguans.*

❏ If someone **fares** badly in a situation, they do not get on well. You can also say, for example, someone fares better or worse than someone else.

farewell 'Farewell' is an old-fashioned way of saying goodbye. A farewell is what someone says or does when they say goodbye. *He smiled a farewell.* ◇ Farewell is used to talk about something done by or for someone who is leaving their job or career. *...a farewell dinner.*

farm A farm is an area of land where crops are grown or animals are raised. If someone **farms** an area of land, they grow crops or raise animals there.

farmer A farmer is someone who owns or manages a farm.

farmhouse On a farm, the farmhouse is the house where the farmer lives.

farmland is land used for farming or suitable for farming.

farmworker A farmworker is someone employed to work on a farm.

farmyard A farmyard is a small area on a farm surrounded by buildings and walls or fences.

farrago (*pron: far-rah-go*) A farrago is a confused mixture of things. *I consider this statement to be a farrago of insolent nonsense.*

farrier A farrier is someone who fits horseshoes.

farther (farthest) See **far**.

farthing The farthing was a small British coin worth a quarter of a penny.

fascia (*or* facia) (*pron: fay-shya*) In a car, the fascia is the dashboard. ◇ A shop fascia is the flat surface above a shop window, where the name of the shop is.

fascinate (fascinating, fascinated) If something fascinates you, you find it very interesting. You can also say you are fascinated by something, or find it fascinating.

fascination If someone is very interested in something, you can talk about their fascination with it. ◇ The fascination of something is a feature it has which makes it very interesting.

fascism (*pron: fash-iz-zum*) (fascist) Fascism is a right-wing political philosophy or movement which stands for centralized government under a dictator, with no political opposition or individual freedom. Fascist is used to talk about things connected with fascism. *...fascist regimes.* A fascist is someone who believes in fascism or supports a fascist regime. ◇ People in authority who behave in a bullying way sometimes get called fascists.

fashion (fashioning, fashioned) ❏ Fashion is used to talk about things like styles of clothing and hairstyles, which keep changing as people's tastes change. ◇ A fashion is a style of clothing or hairstyle which is popular for a time. ◇ If something is in fashion, it is popular at the moment. If it is out of fashion, it is no longer popular.
  ❏ If you do something in a particular fashion, that is how you do it. *He greeted us in his usual friendly fashion.* ◇ If you say something is done after a fashion, you mean it is done, but not very well. You can also say something works after a fashion. *Their system worked after a fashion, although no one was sure how.*
  ❏ If you fashion something, you make it, using whatever materials and tools are available.

fashionable (fashionably) If something is fashionable, a lot of people do it, have it, or wear it, because they think it is the right thing to do, have, or wear. *...fashionably dressed ladies.*

fast is used to describe things which move or happen quickly. *...a fast car... It'll only take an hour if you move fast... Resources are consumed at an increasingly fast rate.* ◇ Fast is also used in questions and statements about speed. *How fast does it lay the surface?... ...looking out of the windows to see how fast we were going.* ◇ Fast is also used to say something is done without delay. *Treat stains as fast as possible.*
  ❏ If a clock is fast, it is showing a time later than the real time.
  ❏ If something is held or stuck fast, it is held or stuck firmly. ◇ If you hold fast to something you believe, you go on believing it. ◇ If someone is fast asleep, they are completely asleep.
  ❏ When people fast or go on a fast, they go without food for a time, usually for religious reasons.

fast breeder reactor A fast breeder reactor is a kind of nuclear reactor which produces more plutonium than it uses.

fast food is food you buy such as hamburgers which can be produced and served very quickly.

fast track is used to talk about methods and schemes for getting something done as quickly as possible. *...fast-track methods of building... This programme has, in theory, put Romania on the fast track to the free market.*

fasten (fastening, fastened) ❏ If you fasten something, you fix it in a closed position with something like a button or strap. ◇ If you fasten one thing to another, you attach it to it. ◇ If you fasten your hands round something, you grip it firmly.
  ❏ If you fasten on to something, you concentrate your attention or efforts on it.

fastener A fastener is a device like a button, zip, or safety pin.

fastening A fastening is a device which keeps something fixed or closed.

fastidious (fastidiously) A fastidious person is fussy and likes things to be clean, tidy, and properly done. *The process was fastidiously checked.*

fat (fatter, fattest; fatness) ❏ A fat person has a lot of flesh on their body and weighs too much. *He was embarrassed to hear her discussing his fatness.* ◇ The fat in your body is the layer of flesh which stores energy and keeps you warm.
  ❏ Fat is also (a) a substance in food which gives you energy. (b) a substance used in cooking which comes from vegetables or meat.
  ❏ A fat object is very thick or wide. ◇ Fat is also used to talk about things which involve large sums of money. *...fat profits... ...a fat cheque.*

fatal (fatally) A fatal accident, injury, or illness causes someone's death. *Four men were fatally stabbed.* ◇ You use fatal when you are mentioning an action which has had unfortunate results. *Gorbachov's second fatal mistake was to delay seeking popular support.* ◇ If something like a system or policy is fatally flawed, it is wrong and cannot be put right without being completely changed.

fatalism (fatalistic, fatalist) Fatalism is the belief that people have no control over what happens. If someone believes this, you say they are fatalistic or a fatalist.

fatality (fatalities) When someone is killed in an accident or some other violent incident, you can say there has been a **fatality**.

fate is a power which some people believe controls everything that happens. ◇ Someone's **fate** is what happens to them. *Other companies suffered a similar fate.*

fated If you say someone is **fated** to do something, you mean they will end up doing it, whatever happens. See also **ill-fated**.

fateful You use **fateful** when you are mentioning something which has had serious consequences. *...Vorster's fateful decision.* ◇ You also use **fateful** when you are mentioning a time when something serious happened. *One man described his impressions of that fateful Thursday.*

father (fathering, fathered) ❑ Your **father** is your male parent. If a man has **fathered** a child, he is its father. ◇ If a man is a **father figure** for you, he gives you the kind of support and advice a father might give.

❑ Christians often call God **Father** in their prayers. ◇ In some Christian churches, priests are called **Father**. ◇ Catholics often call the Pope **the Holy Father**.

❑ If you say a man is the **father** of something, you mean he started or invented it. *...the father of English poetry.*

father-in-law (fathers-in-law) Your **father-in-law** is the father of your husband or wife.

fatherhood is the state of being a father.

fatherland When people talk about their **fatherland**, they mean the country where they or their ancestors were born.

fatherless Children are described as **fatherless** when their father has died or does not live with them.

fatherly If someone behaves in a **fatherly** way, they behave like a kind father.

fathom (fathomed, fathoming) ❑ If you cannot **fathom** something or **fathom** it **out**, you cannot understand it, in spite of thinking about it.

❑ The depth of the sea used to be measured in **fathoms**. One fathom was 6 feet or about 1.8 metres.

fatigue (fatiguing, fatigued) **Fatigue** is extreme tiredness. If someone is in this state, you say they are **fatigued**. If something **fatigues** someone, it tires them out. ◇ See also **metal fatigue**.

fatten (fattening, fattened) If you **fatten** an animal or **fatten** it **up**, you feed it till it gets to a particular weight. ◇ **Fattening** food tends to make you fat.

fatty foods have a lot of fat in them. *...fatty meat.*

fatuous If you call something someone says or does **fatuous**, you mean it is very silly.

fatwa (*or* fatwah) A **fatwa** is an order issued by a Muslim leader saying something must be done.

faucet is the usual American word for a tap.

fault ❑ If something bad is your **fault**, you are responsible for it. ◇ If you are **at fault**, you have done something wrong or made a mistake. ◇ If you **find fault** with someone or something, you criticize them. ◇ If you say something **cannot be faulted**, you mean there is nothing wrong with it at all.

❑ If you say, for example, someone is generous **to a fault**, you mean they are almost too generous.

❑ If there is something wrong with a machine, you say it has a **fault**. ◇ A person's **faults** are weaknesses in their character which make them do wrong or silly things.

❑ In tennis, a **fault** is a service which is wrong according to the rules.

❑ A **fault** is also a large crack in the Earth's surface.

faultless (faultlessly) If you say something is **faultless**, you mean there is nothing wrong with it at all. *They behaved faultlessly.*

faulty A **faulty** machine or piece of equipment does not work properly.

fauna The **fauna** in a place are the animals, birds, fish, and insects there. See also **flora**.

faux pas (*plural:* faux pas) (*both pron:* foe **pah**) If someone commits a **faux pas**, they make a socially embarrassing mistake.

favour (favouring, favoured) (*American spelling:* favor, favoring, *etc*) ❑ If you regard someone or something with **favour**, you like or support them. ◇ If you are **in favour** of something, you think it is a good thing. ◇ If you **favour** something, you prefer it to the other choices available. ◇ If you **favour** someone, you treat them better than other people. ◇ If you do someone a **favour**, you do something to help them, though you do not have to.

❑ If something is **in favour**, people like it or support it. If it is **out of favour**, they no longer like or support it. ◇ If something is **in your favour**, it gives you an advantage. *The system is biased in favour of young people.* ◇ If someone makes a judgement **in your favour**, they decide you are right, or give something to you rather than someone else. ◇ If something is rejected **in favour of** something else, the second thing is done or chosen instead of the first one.

❑ See also **most-favoured-nation**.

favourable (favourably) (*American spelling:* favorable, favorably) ❑ If someone is **favourable** to something, they agree with it or approve of it. You can also say there is a **favourable** reaction to something. *Many reacted favourably to the plan.*

❑ If someone or something makes a **favourable** impression on you, you like them or approve of them. *I could see she was favourably impressed by Jeremy.* ◇ If someone gives a **favourable** account of something or presents it **in a favourable light**, they try to get other people to like it or approve of it. ◇ If something compares **favourably** with something else, it is at least as good as the other thing.

❑ **Favourable** conditions make something more likely to succeed.

favourite (*American spelling:* favorite) Your **favourite** thing of a particular type is the one you like best. ◇ The **favourite** in a contest or race is the person or animal most likely to win.

favouritism (*American spelling:* favoritism) You say there is **favouritism** when one person or group unfairly gets treated better than others.

fawn is a pale yellowish-brown colour.

❑ A **fawn** is a very young deer.

❑ People who **fawn** on powerful or rich people flatter them, to try to get something out of them.

fax (faxes, faxing, faxed) **Fax** is a system by which an exact copy of a document can be made in a different place by sending information electronically along a telephone line. When someone uses this system, you say they **fax** something. The machine they send the information from is called a **fax** or a **fax machine**. The copy produced is also called a **fax**.

faze (fazing, fazed) If something **fazes** you, it puts you off what you are doing, because it is confusing, surprising, or upsetting.

FBI The FBI is a government organization in the US which investigates crimes in which a national law is broken or the country's security is threatened. FBI stands for 'Federal Bureau of Investigation'.

fear (fearing, feared) ❑ Fear is the unpleasant feeling you get when you think you are in danger. ◇ A fear is a worry that something very unpleasant might happen to you or to someone else. ◇ If you do not do something for fear of something happening, you do not do it because it might cause that thing.

❑ If you fear someone or something, you are afraid of them. ◇ If you fear something unpleasant will happen, you are worried because you think it might happen. ◇ If you fear for something, you are worried it might be in danger. *Morris began to fear for the life of Mrs Reilly.*

❑ People say I fear... when they are mentioning something they are sorry about. *I fear some people will be disappointed.*

fearful (fearfully) ❑ If someone is fearful of something or fearful it will happen, they think it might happen, and are worried about it. *Japan is particularly fearful of instability in China.* ◇ If someone is fearful of doing something, they are afraid to do it, because of what might happen. *...old people who are fearful of venturing out of doors.* ◇ If someone does something fearfully, they do it in a frightened way. *The boys looked at each other fearfully.*

❑ Fearful is also used to say something is particularly unpleasant or bad. *...a fearful attack... The leg was fearfully gashed.*

fearless (fearlessly) You say someone is fearless when they are not afraid of doing something. *A successor is needed who will preach the Gospel fearlessly.*

fearsome is used to describe something which is terrible or frightening. *The dog had a fearsome set of teeth.*

feasible (feasibility) If something is feasible, it can be done or made. *The electric car is technically feasible.* When people look into the feasibility of something, they try to decide whether it can be done, made, or achieved.

feast ❑ A feast is a very large meal, usually prepared for a special occasion. When people feast, they have a feast. ◇ If you feast off some kind of food, you take advantage of the fact that it is there and eat a lot of it.

❑ A feast of enjoyable things is a lot of them in one place. *...that annual feast of the arts, the Edinburgh Festival.*

feat A feat is an impressive and difficult act or achievement.

feather (feathering, feathered) A bird's feathers are the light waterproof objects covering its body. ◇ A feathered object is covered with feathers. *...feathered headdresses.* ◇ If you say someone is feathering their nest, you mean they are getting a lot of money out of something, so they can lead a comfortable life.

feather boa A feather boa is a long thin scarf made of soft feathers.

feathery objects remind you of feathers, because of their shape or softness. *...feathery palm trees.*

feature (featuring, featured) ❑ A feature of something is a part of it, or something about it, which is interesting or important. *Every car will have built-in safety features.* ◇ A person's features are their eyes, nose, mouth, and other parts of their face.

❑ If someone or something features in a book, an incident, or something someone says, they come into it in an important way. *This is not the first time he has featured in allegations of violence.*

❑ A feature is also (a) a special programme on TV or radio. (b) a special article in a newspaper or magazine. ◇ If something is featured in a newspaper or magazine, it is given special treatment in it.

❑ A feature or feature film is a full-length film in the cinema. ◇ If a film features someone, he or she is one of the main actors in it.

featureless is used to say something has no interesting features. *...a featureless block of flats.*

febrile (*pron:* fee-brile) is used to describe someone's behaviour when they keep doing something in a nervous way. *She kept up a febrile chatter.* ◇ A febrile illness is one in which you get a fever.

fecal See faecal.

feces See faeces.

feckless You say someone is feckless when they do not have much strength of character, and cannot run their life properly.

fecund (*pron:* fek-und *or* feek-und) If a living thing is fecund, it produces a lot of offspring.

fed ❑ See feed.

❑ If you are fed up with someone or something, they have made you annoyed or angry and you do not want to put up with them any longer.

federal In a federal country or system, a group of states come under a central government, besides having governments of their own. ◇ Federal is used to talk about things connected with the central government in a federal country, rather than one of the state governments. *...the Federal Department of the Environment.*

federalism (federalist) Federalism is belief in or support for a federal system. A federalist is someone who wants a federal system. Federalist is used to talk about things connected with federalism. *She will continue to oppose what she sees as Brussels' federalist ambitions.*

federate (federating, federated) When countries or territories federate, they join together to form a federation. A country with Federated in its name has been formed in this way. *...the Federated States of Micronesia.*

federation A federation consists of territories which have been formed into a federal country. ◇ A federation is also an organization which deals with general matters of policy in a particular field, and which several smaller organizations belong to. *...the International Judo Federation.*

fee A fee is (a) a fixed sum you pay to have something, belong to something, or do something. *...the £10 membership fee.* (b) a fixed sum charged by someone for a job or service. ◇ A transfer fee is the money a sports team pays when they buy a player from another team.

fee-paying A fee-paying school is a private school which charges fees.

feeble (feebler, feeblest; feebly, feebleness) You say people or things are feeble when they do not have much power, strength, or energy. *He waved his hands feebly.* ◇ If you call what someone says feeble, you mean it is not very good, convincing, or effective. *...a feeble joke... If anything, his remarks about the railways exceeded in feeble-*

ness what he had to say about roads.

feed (feeding, fed) ❑ When you **feed** an animal or baby, you give it food. ◇ When a person or organization **feeds** a group of people, they supply them with the food they need to stay alive. ◇ When an animal **feeds** on something, it eats it. ◇ You call each occasion when a baby is given food a **feed**. *What time is his next feed?* ◇ **Feed** is food given to farm animals.

❑ If you **feed** something into a container or other object, you gradually put it in.

❑ If something **feeds** on something else or is **fed** by it, it gets stronger because of it. *Anger feeds on disappointment.*

feedback When you get **feedback** on something you have done or made, you get comments on how good or bad it is.

feeder ❑ A **feeder** road, railway, or air service is a minor one which connects up with a major network.

❑ A **feeder** is a device for feeding animals or sick people. ◇ You can use **feeder** to talk about an animal's or baby's eating habits. *Sharks can sometimes be finicky feeders.*

feedstock A **feedstock** is a raw material from which something is made by a chemical or industrial process.

feedstuff A **feedstuff** is a food given to farm animals.

feel (feeling, felt) ❑ If you **feel** a sensation or emotion, you experience it. *Mrs Oliver felt a sudden desire to burst out crying.* ◇ If you **feel like** doing or having something, you want to do it or have it. ◇ If you **feel like** a type of person or thing, you think you have some of their characteristics. *I felt like a murderer.* ◇ If you say how an experience **feels**, you are describing the emotions and sensations connected with it. *What does it feel like to watch yourself on TV?* ◇ If you **feel** something is true or should be done, you believe it. *He felt I was making a terrible mistake.* ◇ If you ask someone how they **feel** about something, you want to know their opinion of it.

❑ If you can **feel** something, you are aware of it touching or happening to your body. *He could feel himself blushing.* ◇ If you **feel** something, you touch it deliberately, to find out what it is like. ◇ If you **feel for** an object, you try to find it using your hands, because you cannot see it. ◇ The **feel** of an object, or the way it **feels**, is the way it seems when you touch it or hold it.

❑ The **feel** of something you are experiencing is the general impression you have of it. *The whole feel of the project is now different.* ◇ If you say something has the **feel** of a particular thing, you mean it makes you think of it. *Mr Yeltsin's visit to Siberia had the unmistakable feel of a Western-style election campaign tour.* ◇ If you have a **feel** for something, you understand it well and know how to deal with it. *The band's feel for funk makes this track an exhilarating experience.* ◇ If you **feel for** someone, you have a lot of sympathy for them.

feeler An insect's **feelers** are the two thin stalks on its head which it uses to touch and sense things with. ◇ If you put out **feelers**, you make enquiries to see how people would react to something you are thinking of doing.

feeling ❑ A **feeling** is an emotion, such as anger or happiness. ◇ Your **feelings** about something are what you think and feel about it. ◇ If you **hurt** someone's **feelings**, you upset them. ◇ If there is **ill feeling** or **bad feeling** among a group of people, they are angry or bitter about something. ◇ If you say there are **no hard feelings**, you mean someone does not feel angry or bitter about something that has happened. ◇ **Feeling for** someone is affection or sympathy for them.

❑ A **feeling** is also a physical sensation. ◇ If you have no **feeling** in a part of your body, you cannot feel anything when something touches you there.

❑ If you have a **feeling** something is true or will happen, you think it is probably true or will probably happen.

feet See **foot**.

feign (*pron:* **fane**) is used to talk about pretending. For example, if you **feign** illness, you pretend you are ill.

feint (*pron:* **faint**) If someone **feints** in a sport like football or boxing, they make a move intended to mislead someone. A move like this is called a **feint**.

feisty (*pron:* **fice-ty**) people are lively and energetic.

feline (*pron:* **fee-line**) is used to talk about something to do with cats. *...the feline leukaemia virus.* ◇ You can use **feline** to describe someone whose movements or behaviour make you think of a cat. *The two women scowled with feline fury at each other.*

fell ❑ See **fall**.

❑ If someone **fells** a tree, they cut it down. ◇ If someone is **felled** in football or a fight, they are tripped or hit, and fall to the ground.

❑ In the north of England, a **fell** is a mountain, hill, or moor.

fellow A **fellow** is a man. ◇ You also use **fellow** to describe someone who has something in common with you. *...a fellow passenger.* ◇ **Fellow feeling** is sympathy and friendship between people who have had similar experiences or difficulties. ◇ A **fellow** of a society or academic institution is a senior member.

fellowship A **fellowship** is a university post involving research and sometimes teaching. ◇ **Fellowship** is a feeling of friendship between people involved in something together. ◇ **Fellowship** appears in the names of some organizations for people who have a shared aim or interest. *...the Industrial Christian Fellowship.*

felony (felonies; felon) In the US and some other countries, a **felony** is a serious crime. A **felon** is someone who has committed a felony.

felt ❑ See **feel**.

❑ **Felt** is a type of thick smooth cloth made by pressing fibres together.

felt-tip A **felt-tip** pen has a nib made from fibres pressed together.

female A **female** is a person or animal belonging to the sex which can have babies or lay eggs. *...a female toad.* ◇ **Female** is used to talk about (a) things to do with women. *...female emancipation.* (b) women of a particular kind. *...female members of parliament.*

feminine is used to talk about (a) something thought to be typical of women. *...feminine handwriting.* (b) a woman thought to have attractive features which are typical of women. *...a good, calm, deeply feminine woman.*

femininity If you talk about a woman's **femininity**, you mean the attractive qualities she has which are thought to be typical of women.

feminism (feminist) **Feminism** is the belief that women should have the same rights, power, and opportunities as men. A **feminist** is someone who believes this, and tries to bring it about. **Feminist** is used to talk about things produced or done by feminists. ...*feminist literature*.

femur (femoral) The **femur** (*pron:* fee-mer) is the thigh bone. **Femoral** (*pron:* fem-er-al) is used to talk about things to do with the femur. ...*the femoral artery*.

fen (fenland) **Fens** are areas of low-lying flat land which are marshy or artificially drained. They are also called **fenland** or **fenlands**.

fence (fencing, fenced; fencer) ❑ A **fence** is a wood, metal, or wire barrier, supported by posts. ◇ **Fencing** is a fence or fences. ...*spending his money on fencing to keep off the sheep*. ◇ If an area is **fenced** or **fenced off**, it has a fence round it. ...*a fenced enclosure*. ◇ In horseracing, the jumps are usually called the **fences**.
  ❑ If someone is **sitting on the fence**, they are avoiding taking sides in a discussion or argument.
  ❑ **Fencing** is a sport in which two people called **fencers** fight each other with thin swords called foils.

fend ❑ If you **fend off** something difficult or embarrassing, you avoid having to deal with it. ◇ If you **fend off** someone who is close behind you in a contest or race, you do not let them beat you. ◇ If you **fend off** something which is aimed or thrown at you, you hold up your arms or something else to stop it hitting you.
  ❑ If you have to **fend for yourself**, you have to look after yourself without help from anyone else.

fender A **fender** is (a) a low metal wall round a fireplace. (b) a fireguard. ◇ On a boat, a **fender** is an object hanging over the side to protect the boat if it bumps into something. ◇ **Fender** is the usual American word for the wing of a car.

fenland See fen.

fennel is a plant with a strong aniseed-like smell. Its seeds and leaves are used to flavour food.

feral (*pron:* ferr-al *or* feer-al) is used to describe birds and animals born in the wild whose ancestors were at one time kept by people as pets or as a food supply. ...*feral pigeons... ...a feral cat*.

ferment (fermentation) ❑ When wine, beer, or fruit **ferments** (*pron:* fer-ments) or is **fermented**, a chemical change takes place in it, producing alcohol. This process is called **fermentation**.
  ❑ **Ferment** (*pron:* fer-ment) is excitement or unrest caused by change or uncertainty. ...*the nationalist ferment in Central Europe... The Muslim world was in ferment*.

fern Ferns are plants with long stems, feathery leaves, and no flowers.

ferocious (ferociously, ferocity) **Ferocious** behaviour is fierce and violent. *They tackled ferociously*. You can talk about the **ferocity** of an action. *Seles often caught Graf by surprise with the ferocity of her forehand*.

ferret (ferreting, ferreted) **Ferrets** are small fierce animals used for hunting rabbits and rats. ◇ If you **ferret around** for something, you make a thorough search for it. If you **ferret** it **out**, you find it.

ferrous metals contain iron.

ferry (ferries, ferrying, ferried) A **ferry** is a ship or boat which takes people or vehicles across a river or narrow strip of sea. ◇ You say a plane, ship, or other vehicle **ferries** goods or people somewhere when it makes several journeys to take them all there.

fertile (fertility) ❑ If land or soil is **fertile**, plants grow easily in it. You can talk about the **fertility** of land or soil. ◇ If people or animals are **fertile**, they can produce babies. A person's or animal's **fertility** is their ability to have babies. ◇ A **fertility drug** helps a woman to become pregnant.
  ❑ If someone has a **fertile** mind or imagination, they keep having clever or unusual ideas.
  ❑ If strong feelings about something are likely to break out in a place, you can say it is **fertile ground** for those feelings.

fertilize (fertilizing, fertilized; fertilization) (*can be spelled with an 's' instead of a 'z'*) When an egg or plant is **fertilized**, sperm joins with the egg, or pollen gets to the reproductive part of the plant, and the process of reproduction begins. ◇ When people **fertilize** land, they spread manure or chemicals on it, to help the plants grow. This process is called **fertilization**.

fertilizer (*or* fertiliser) is a substance used to help plants grow. Fertilizers are dug into the ground, spread on it, or sprayed onto the plants themselves.

fervent (fervently) **Fervent** is used to describe (a) very strong beliefs or wishes. ...*his fervent Christian beliefs*. (b) people who strongly support or oppose something. *The vast majority of North Africans fervently supported Iraq*.

fervid (fervidly) **Fervid** is used to describe strong or agitated feelings or behaviour. *In 1922 the Mirror was fervidly anti-Socialist*.

fervour (*American spelling:* fervor) is a very strong feeling in favour of something. ...*revolutionary fervour*.

fester (festering, festered) If a bad situation or feeling **festers**, it gets worse. ...*festering resentment*. ◇ If a wound festers, it becomes infected and produces pus.

festival A **festival** is (a) an organized series of events and performances, often held in the same place each year. ...*the London Film Festival*. (b) an annual holiday in which people celebrate a religious event. ...*a traditional Muslim festival*.

festive If people are in a **festive** mood, they are ready to enjoy themselves, because they think they have something to celebrate. When this happens, you can say there is a **festive** air or atmosphere. ◇ Christmas is often called the **festive season**.

festivity (festivities) **Festivity** is the celebrating of something in a happy way. **Festivities** are things people do to celebrate something.

festoon (festooning, festooned) If something is **festooned** with objects, there are a lot of them draped over it or hanging above it.

fetal See foetal.

fetch (fetches, fetching, fetched) ❑ If you **fetch** something, you go and get it. ◇ If something **fetches** a particular price, that is what someone pays for it.
  ❑ If you **fetch up** somewhere, you arrive there without really intending to.
  ❑ **Fetching** is used, often in a rather insincere way, to say someone or something is pretty or attractive. *Pamphlets show Signora Mussolini looking fetching in a short brown dress with a plunging neckline*.

fete (feting, feted) (*or* fête, fêting, *etc*) A **fete** is an outdoor event, usually to raise money for charity, with entertainments, competitions, and home-made goods for sale.

◇ If someone is **feted**, they are given an enthusiastic public welcome.

fetid (*pron:* **fet**-id *or* **feet**-id) A **fetid** place has a foul smell.

fetish (fetishes; fetishism, fetishist) If someone has a **fetish** for something, they like to have it or do it, because it excites them sexually. You can talk about **fetishism** or **fetishists** of a particular kind. *...a shoe fetishist.*

fetlock A horse's **fetlock** is the back part of its leg, just above the hoof.

fetter (fettering, fettered) If something **fetters** your powers or rights, it stops you exercising them. Something like this can be called a **fetter**.

fettle If someone or something is **in good fettle** or **in fine fettle**, they are healthy or performing well.

fetus See **foetus**.

feud (feuding) A **feud** is a long-lasting series of fights or arguments between two people or groups. When people carry on a **feud**, you say they are **feuding**.

feudal (feudalism) The **feudal** system was a system in the past in which people were given land or protection by people of higher rank; in return, they worked and sometimes fought for them. This system is called **feudalism**.

fever is excitement in a place caused by something happening there. *India is in the grip of election fever.* ◇ When people are extremely excited about something, you can say their feelings are at **fever pitch**.

❑ If someone has a **fever**, their temperature is higher than usual, because they are ill. ◇ **Fever** appears in the names of several illnesses. *...rheumatic fever... ...glandular fever.*

feverish (feverishly) You call people's behaviour **feverish** when they do something in a very busy or agitated way. *Most of the guests were crumbling bread feverishly.* ◇ If someone is **feverish**, they have a fever.

few ❑ You use **a few** to talk about a small number of things or people. *The window opened a few inches... A few were smoking.* ◇ You use **quite a few** or **a good few** to talk about a fairly large number of things or people. *We had quite a few friendly arguments.*

❑ You use **few** or **very few** to say something is true of only a small number of things or people. *Very few people survived.* ◇ If you say certain things are **few and far between**, you mean there are not many of them, or they do not happen often.

❑ You use **fewer** to say a number of things or people is smaller than something else, or smaller than before. *There are fewer trains at night.* ◇ You use **fewer than** to say a number is below a certain level. *Fewer than 20 pages of his book deal with the leadership fight itself.* ◇ You use **no fewer than** to emphasize how large a number is. *No fewer than five cameramen lost their lives.*

fey is used to describe behaviour which is strange and rather embarrassing.

fez (fezzes) A **fez** is a round flat-topped hat without a brim, worn by a Muslim man.

fiancé (fiancée) If a man and a woman are engaged, you say he is her **fiancé** and she is his **fiancée**.

fiasco (fiascos) You say something is a **fiasco** when it fails completely and makes the people involved look rather silly.

fiat (*pron:* **fee**-at) When someone in power issues an official order which must be carried out, you can call this order a **fiat**. You can say someone gets something done **by fiat**. *He denied he would attempt to control the level of private sector pay by fiat.*

fib (fibbing, fibbed) If you say someone is **fibbing** or telling a **fib**, you mean they are not telling the truth.

fiber See **fibre**.

fibre (*American spelling:* **fiber**) ❑ A **fibre** is a thin thread of a natural or artificial substance. ◇ You use **fibre** to talk about a type of cloth or other material made from fibres. *...coconut fibre... ...synthetic fibres.* ◇ The **fibres** in your body are thread-like pieces of tissue. Nerve-cells are connected by fibres, and muscles consist of fibres.

❑ **Fibre** is the parts of fruit and vegetables which the body cannot digest, and which help food to pass through more quickly.

❑ If you say someone has **fibre** or **moral fibre**, you mean they are capable of showing courage and determination.

fibre optics is a way of sending information in the form of light, using long thin threads of glass.

fibreglass (*American spelling:* **fiberglass**) is (a) a plastic strengthened with glass fibres, used to make lightweight boats and car bodies. (b) an insulating material made from glass fibres.

fibrillate (fibrillating, fibrillated) If a person's heart **fibrillates**, the muscles in it twitch in an irregular way, and the working of the heart may be affected.

fibrosis See **cystic fibrosis**.

fibrous (*pron:* **fie**-brus) things contain a lot of fibres or fibre.

fibula (*pron:* **fib**-yew-la) The **fibula** is the outer and thinner of the two bones in your lower leg.

fickle (fickleness) If you say someone is **fickle**, you mean they keep changing their mind about what they like or want. *...the fickleness of the electorate.*

fiction is novels and other stories about imaginary people and events. ◇ If you say what someone says is **fiction**, you mean they made it up. ◇ A **fiction** is something someone pretends is true, although it is not true. *Moscow persisted for years in the fiction that the Baltic states asked to join the Soviet Union in 1940.*

fictional people, places, and things exist only in books, plays, or films. ◇ **Fictional** is also used to talk about things connected with the writing of fiction. *...fictional technique.*

fictionalize (fictionalizing, fictionalized) (*can be spelled with an 's' instead of a 'z'*) If someone **fictionalizes** something which actually happened, they write a story or play based on it. *...a fictionalized account of the assassination in Dallas.*

fictitious is used to describe things or people that do not exist and have been invented to deceive someone. *...acting as buyers for a fictitious Arab businessman.*

fiddle (fiddling, fiddled; fiddler) ❑ If you **fiddle** with something, you keep moving it or touching it with your fingers.

❑ If someone **fiddles** something connected with money, they do something dishonest to get money they are not entitled to. *He was sacked for fiddling expenses.*

❑ You use **fiddling** to describe things you have to deal with which seem unimportant and unnecessary. *...the sheer range of fiddling bureaucratic Euro-issues.*

❑ A violin is sometimes called a **fiddle**. Violinists are sometimes called **fiddlers**. ◇ If you talk about someone **playing second fiddle** to someone else, you mean they are less important than them and have to accept their decisions and do what they say. ◇ If you say someone is **fiddling while Rome burns,** you mean they are doing unimportant things, instead of dealing with a serious situation.

fidelity to something like a promise or belief means sticking to it. ◇ **Fidelity** to your husband, wife, or lover means not having a sexual relationship with anyone else.

fidget (fidgeting, fidgeted; fidgety) If someone **fidgets** or is **fidgety**, they keep moving their hands or feet or changing position slightly, because they are nervous or bored.

fiefdom (*pron:* feef-dom) If someone has complete control over a place or organization, you can call it their **fiefdom.**

field ❑ A **field** is an enclosed area of land where crops are grown or animals are kept.

❑ The area where a game like cricket or football is played is sometimes called the **field**. When a game is taking place, the area within the boundaries is called the **field of play**. ◇ In athletics, a **field** event is one which is not a race. The javelin and high jump are field events. ◇ **Field sports** are country activities like hunting and shooting birds.

❑ The people or horses in a race are often called the **field**. ◇ The players **fielded** by a sports club are the ones chosen to play in a particular game. ◇ In cricket or baseball, the team which is **fielding** is the one which is trying to get the other one out. ◇ When a cricketer **fields** the ball, he or she gets a hand to it and stops it going any further after the batsman has hit it.

❑ You say a political party **fields** someone when they put them up for election. ◇ You say someone **fields** a criticism or question when they deal with it skilfully.

❑ **Field** is used to talk about a subject or area of interest. *...those working in the field of child abuse.* ◇ **Field** is also used to talk about research and tests done in a natural environment, rather than, for example, in a laboratory. *...field studies... ...experience in the field.* See also **fieldwork**.

❑ If you say someone is having a **field day,** you mean they have been given an opportunity to do something they enjoy doing, and are making the most of it. *The lawyers will have a field day trying to determine who owns what.*

❑ **Field** is used to talk about things used in a battlefield. *...field guns... ...a field hospital.*

❑ Your **field of vision** is the area you can see without turning your head.

field marshal A **field marshal** is an officer of the highest rank in the British army.

field mouse The **field mouse** is a long-tailed mouse which lives in fields and woods.

fielder In cricket, the **fielders** are the players trying to get the batsmen out, other than the bowler and the wicket-keeper.

fieldwork (fieldworker) (*or* field work, field worker) **Fieldwork** is the part of a course or job which involves going to a place to gather information or to do some kind of practical work. A **fieldworker** is someone doing fieldwork.

fiend (*pron:* feend) (fiendish, fiendishly) ❑ Newspapers often call someone who behaves in a very cruel way a **fiend**.

Sex fiend strangles boy. ◇ **Fiendish** is used to describe very cruel people, their behaviour, or their weapons.

❑ **Fiendish** is also used to describe things which are very difficult to deal with. *...fiendish obstacles... This must be fiendishly difficult to sing.*

fierce (fiercely) A **fierce** battle or argument is carried on in an intense and determined way. *They were arguing fiercely.* ◇ **Fierce** feelings are very strong. *They are torn between fear of bloodshed and fierce loyalty to their republic.* ◇ A **fierce** kick or blow is very powerful. ◇ A **fierce** wind blows very strongly. ◇ **Fierce** people and animals easily become angry or aggressive.

fiery ❑ A **fiery** person tends to behave or speak in an angry way. You can say someone like this makes a **fiery** speech or gets involved in a **fiery** argument.

❑ **Fiery** is also used to describe things which are burning, or very hot. *Hysen looked flustered in the fiery heat.*

fiesta A **fiesta** is a time of public entertainment and parties, especially in Spain and Latin America.

fife A **fife** is a kind of small flute.

fifteen (fifteenth) **Fifteen** is the number 15.

fifth The **fifth** item in a series is the one counted as number 5. ◇ A **fifth** or **one fifth** is the fraction $\frac{1}{5}$.

fifty (fiftieth, fifties) ❑ **Fifty** is the number 50. ◇ The **fifties** was the period from 1950 to 1959. ◇ If someone is in their **fifties,** they are aged 50 to 59.

❑ When something is divided **fifty-fifty** between two people or groups, each gets half. ◇ If there is a **fifty-fifty** chance of something happening, it is equally likely to happen or not happen.

fig. is short for 'figure'. *The piston moves into a horizontal position (see fig. 3).*

fig Figs are soft sweet tropical fruit, full of tiny seeds. The tree they grow on is called a **fig** or a **fig tree**. ◇ If someone does not **give a fig** or **care a fig** about something, they are not concerned about it at all.

fig leaf A **fig leaf** is a large leaf from a fig tree. In paintings and sculpture, you sometimes see a fig leaf covering the genitals of a nude figure. ◇ If something is used to stop people noticing something unpleasant or embarrassing, you can call it a **fig leaf.**

fight (fighting, fought) ❑ If you **fight** something, you try hard to stop it. You can talk about a **fight** against something. *...the fight against illegal drugs.* ◇ If you **fight** for something, you try hard to get it or keep it. You can talk about a **fight** for something. *...the fight for equality.*

❑ When two countries or armies **fight,** they have a war or battle. ◇ When a battle is taking place, you can call it the **fighting**. *We were only metres away from the fighting.* ◇ If you **fight** in a war or battle, you take part in it. ◇ If an army **fights off** an attack, it deals with it successfully.

❑ When people **fight** or have a **fight,** they try to hurt each other using their fists or weapons. ◇ You can also say people **fight** when they quarrel. ◇ When a political leader **fights** an election, he or she tries to win it.

❑ When you **fight** an emotion or desire, you try not to feel it, show it, or act on it. You can also say someone **fights back** an emotion.

❑ If someone **puts up a fight,** they do not give in easily to an opponent who is stronger. ◇ If you **fight back** when someone does something to harm you, you defend yourself by taking some action against them. ◇ If you **fight off** something, you succeed in getting rid of it. *We can fight off most minor ailments.* ◇ If people **fight out** something like a game or battle, they go on with it in a determined way until it finishes, or until one side wins. ◇ **fight shy: see shy.**

fighter ❑ A **fighter** is a fast military aircraft used for destroying other aircraft.

❑ People who do not belong to an official army but who are fighting an enemy are often called **fighters.** *...a resistance fighter.* ◇ Boxers are sometimes called **fighters.** ◇ You say someone is a **fighter** when they keep on trying to achieve something, and are not put off by difficulties or opposition.

figment If you say something is a **figment** of someone's imagination, you mean they are imagining it and it does not really exist.

figurative (figuratively) You use **figurative** or **figuratively** to show you are not using a word or expression with its most obvious meaning. *...his attempts to offer a figurative olive branch to the gay community... He should be able to, at least figuratively, pat them on the head and say 'Well done.'*

figure (figuring, figured) ❑ A **figure** is an amount expressed as a number. *...unemployment figures.* ◇ A **figure** is also a symbol representing a number, like 3 or 8.

❑ Your **figure** is the shape of your body. You can call a person a **figure** of a certain kind when you are mentioning the shape of their body. *...the small but bulky figure of Yasser Arafat.* You can also call an unknown person a **figure** when you cannot see them clearly. *I could see a small female figure advancing towards us.* ◇ **Figure** is often used to talk about a well known or important person. *He was a key figure in the independence struggle.*

❑ In a book, a **figure** is a drawing or diagram. *The original design was modified (see Figure 4).*

❑ If someone or something **figures** in a report or discussion, they are mentioned in it. ◇ If someone or something **figures** in a story or event, they come into it.

❑ If you **figure** something is true, you reckon it is true. *Lamb figured he needed three wickets in an hour to have a chance.* ◇ If you **figure** something **out**, you work it out.

figure skating is skating in an attractive pattern, often with spins and jumps.

figurehead If you talk about the **figurehead** of a group or organization, you mean the person thought of as its leader. Sometimes **figurehead** is used to say someone does not have any real power. *He is now simply a figurehead president.* ◇ Originally, a **figurehead** was a large wooden model of a person under the prow of a sailing ship.

figurine (*pron:* fig-yoo-**reen**) A **figurine** is a small ornamental model of a person.

filament **Filaments** are very thin pieces or threads of something. *...carbon filaments.*

filch (filches, filching, filched) If someone **filches** something, they steal it.

file (filing, filed) ❑ A **file** on someone or something is a collection of information about them. ◇ A **file** is also a box or folder for keeping documents in. If you **file** a document, you put it in the file where it belongs. ◇ A computer **file** is a set of data with its own name. ◇ If information is **on file**, it is in a written file or computer file.

❑ If you **file** a lawsuit, you begin legal proceedings against someone. If you **file for** something, you apply for it legally. *The firm filed for bankruptcy shortly after the crash.* ◇ If you **file** a complaint, you make it officially. ◇ When a reporter **files** a report or news story, he or she sends it or hands it in.

❑ When people **file** somewhere, they walk one behind the other in a long line. When people or vehicles move in a line, one behind the other, you say they are **in single file.**

❑ A **file** is a tool with rough surfaces, used for smoothing and shaping. If you **file** an object, you smooth or shape it with a file.

filial is used to talk about some aspect of a person's relationship with their parents. For example, 'filial respect' means respect for one or both of your parents.

filibuster (filibustering, filibustered) A **filibuster** is a way of stopping a law being passed. A long speech or series of speeches is made, so that time runs out before a vote can be taken. When politicians do this, you say they are **filibustering.**

filigree is delicate ornamental designs made with gold or silver wire.

fill ❑ If you **fill** an object or **fill** it **up**, you keep putting something into it until it is full. You can also say an object **fills** with something. *Their boat filled with water.* ◇ You say people or things **fill** a space when they leave very little room for anything else. You can also say a space **fills** or **fills up** with people or things. *His office began to fill up with people.*

❑ If you **fill in** a form or **fill** it **out**, you write information in the spaces.

❑ If someone **fills in** for someone who is not there, they take their place. When someone does this, you can say they **fill** a gap. ◇ If someone is elected or appointed to a vacant post, you say they **fill** it.

❑ If something **fills** people with an emotion, they feel it strongly. *The release of Brian Keenan filled them with hope.*

❑ If you have **had your fill** of something, you do not want any more of it.

❑ See also **filling.**

filler ❑ A **filler** is (a) an item added to a CD, tape, or record to make up the required length of playing time. (b) a short item on TV or radio put in to fill a period of time between other pieces.

❑ **Filler** is a substance used for filling cracks or holes.

fillet (filleting, filleted) When fish or meat is **filleted,** the bones are taken out. A **fillet** is a piece of fish or meat with the bones taken out.

filling A **filling** is a piece of metal or plastic in a hole in a tooth. ◇ The **filling** in a pie, chocolate, sandwich, or cake is the mixture inside. ◇ If you say food is **filling,** you mean it makes you feel full.

filling station A **filling station** is the same as a petrol station.

fillip If something gives you a **fillip,** it encourages you in what you are doing.

filly (fillies) A **filly** is a young female horse.

film ❑ A **film** is a motion picture shown in the cinema or on TV. If someone is **filming,** they are making a film. ◇ If you **film** something which is happening, you record it using a cine camera or video camera.

❑ A **film** is also a roll of thin plastic used in a camera to take photographs.

❏ A **film** of powder or liquid is a very thin layer of it.

film maker A **film maker** is someone who produces or directs films.

film star A **film** star is an actor or actress famous for appearing in films.

filmgoer A **filmgoer** is someone who goes to the cinema regularly.

Filofax (Filofaxes) A **Filofax** is a personal filing system in the form of a small ring-bound book. 'Filofax' is a trademark.

filter (filtering, filtered; filtration) If you **filter** a substance, you pass it through a device called a **filter**, which removes particles from it. You say you **filter out** the particles. The process is called **filtration.** ◇ When news or information **filters** through to people, it gradually reaches them.

filthy (filthier, filthiest; filth) If something is **filthy**, it is very dirty. **Filth** is a lot of dirt. ◇ When people call a book, picture, or film **filth** or say it is **filthy**, they mean it is shocking and disgusting, because it is full of sex.

filtration See filter.

fin A fish's **fins** are the wing-like parts sticking out of its body which it uses for swimming.

final ❏ The **final** one of a series of events, things, or people is the last one. ◇ The **final** of a competition is the last game or contest, which decides who is the overall winner. Sometimes the last few games or contests are called the **finals.** ◇ **Finals** are the last and most important exams in a university course.

❏ If a decision is **final**, it cannot be changed or questioned.

finale (*pron:* fin-nah-lee) The **finale** of a show or piece of music is the last part.

finalise See finalize.

finalist A **finalist** is one of the people taking part in the final of a competition.

finality If you say something with **finality**, you make it clear you are not prepared to discuss things any further.

finalize (finalizing, finalized; finalization) (*can be spelled with an 's' instead of a 'z'*) When something like a deal is **finalized**, it is completed. *...the finalization of contracts.*

finally ❏ If you say something **finally** happened, you mean (a) it happened after a long time. *House prices have finally started to fall.* (b) it was the last of a series of things to happen. *He finally chose music for his career.*

❏ People say **finally** when they are introducing a final point, question, or topic. *Finally, I would add that Dover District Council has invested heavily in the area.*

finance (financing, financed; financier) When someone **finances** something, they put up the money for it. Someone who does this is called a **financier.** The money is called **finance.** ◇ **Finance** is also the management of money. *...local government finance.* ◇ Your **finances** are how much money you have.

financial (financially) **Financial** is used to talk about things connected with money. *...financial advisers... They find they are in difficulties financially.*

financial year The **financial year** is a twelve-month period which businesses and other organizations operate by. For most businesses, the **financial year** begins on 1st April, but for income tax purposes it starts on 6th April.

financier See finance.

finch (finches) **Finches** are small seed-eating birds with short strong beaks. Chaffinches, bullfinches, and canaries are all finches.

find (finding, found) ❏ If you **find** something you are looking for, you see it or discover where it is. ◇ If you **find** something somewhere, you notice it. If it turns out to be interesting or useful, you call it a **find.** *She found a drawing on her bed... Among the finds so far are pottery and jewellery.*

❏ If you **find** something you need or want, you succeed in getting it. *He cannot find work.* ◇ If you **find your way** somewhere, you succeed in getting there. ◇ If you **find** time to do something, you do it in spite of being busy.

❏ You use **find** to say someone realizes something, or becomes aware of it. *I found that the reading lamp would not work.* ◇ You use **find out** to say someone gets to know the truth about something. *We found out that she was wrong.*

❏ You can use **find** to describe impressions and experiences. *I don't find that funny at all... He found it hard to make friends.* ◇ If you **find** yourself in a situation, you are in it without intending to be. *Senna found himself chasing a gap of 37 seconds.*

❏ When someone is discovered doing something dishonest, you can say they are **found out.**

❏ When a court or jury reaches a verdict, you say they **find** someone innocent or guilty.

❏ If you say particular things are **found** somewhere, you mean that is where they are. *Four different species of lungfish are found in Africa.*

❏ **find fault:** see fault.

findings Someone's **findings** are the information they get as a result of research or an investigation.

fine (finer, finest; fining, fined; finely) ❏ **Fine** is used to say something is very good, or someone is very good at something. *...fine walking country... Wilson is a fine rugby player.* ◇ In conversation, if you say something is **fine**, you mean it is satisfactory. ◇ When the weather is **fine**, it is sunny and not raining.

❏ **Fine** is used to say something is very narrow, or consists of very small or narrow parts. *...fine hair... ...finely chopped meat.* ◇ **Fine** is also used to say something is very small, and therefore hard to see or distinguish. *...fine detail... ...a fine distinction.* ◇ **the fine print:** see print. ◇ If you say a situation is **finely** balanced, you mean the two people, groups, or forces involved are equally powerful, and things could go one way or the other.

❏ If you are **fined**, you are punished by being ordered to pay a sum of money called a **fine.**

fine art When people talk about **fine art** or the **fine arts**, they mean painting, sculpture, or the making of any objects meant to be beautiful rather than useful. The objects are also called **fine art.**

fine tune If you **fine tune** something which is already operating, you make small adjustments to it, to make it work better.

finesse (*pron:* fin-ness) If something is done with **finesse**, it is done in a skilful and elegant way.

finger (fingering, fingered) ❏ A person's **fingers** are the four long jointed parts at the end of each hand. Sometimes thumbs are also counted as fingers. ◇ If you **finger** something, you touch it with one of your fingers.

❑ If you **point the finger** at someone, you say they are to blame for something. ◇ If you **put your finger** on something like a problem, you identify it. ◇ If you are **keeping your fingers crossed**, you are anxiously hoping something will happen or not happen. ◇ If you **burn your fingers** or **get your fingers burned**, you come off badly when something you are involved in fails. ◇ If something **slips through your fingers**, you have it for a time but cannot hold on to it. *Millions of pounds slipped through his fingers.* ◇ **green fingers**: see **green**.

fingernail A person's **fingernails** are the hard areas at the end of their fingers.

fingerprint A **fingerprint** is a mark made by the tip of someone's finger, showing the pattern of lines there. When the police **fingerprint** someone or **take their fingerprints**, they get a record of their fingerprints by making them press their fingers on an inky pad, then onto paper. See also **genetic fingerprinting**.

fingertip Your **fingertips** are the ends of your fingers. ◇ If you have information **at your fingertips**, you know it, or know where you can get it straight away.

finish (finishes, finishing, finished; finisher) ❑ When you **finish** something, you get to the end of it, or complete it. When you put the **finishing touches** to something, you do the last small things needed to complete it. You can also say someone **finishes** something **off**, especially something started by someone else. ◇ If you have **finished** with something, you no longer want it.
❑ When something **finishes**, it ends. ◇ The **finish** of something like a race is the last part. When people or horses **finish** a race, they get to the end. You call them the **finishers**. *The top British finisher was Richard Dean, of Leeds.*
❑ You use **finish up** to say what happens to someone or something at the end of a series of events. *He finished up as a fashionable doctor in Berlin.*
❑ If you say someone or something is **finished**, you mean they have lost their power or importance and will not get it back. ◇ If someone **finishes off** an injured person or animal, they kill them.
❑ The **finish** on a product is the treatment given to its outside or surface, which gives it its appearance or texture.

finishing school A **finishing school** is a private school where upper-class young women are taught manners and other social skills.

finite If something is **finite**, there is only a limited amount of it. ◇ A **finite** period of time is fixed at a particular length.

Finn A **Finn** is someone who comes from Finland.

Finnish is used to talk about people and things in or from Finland. *...a Finnish farmhouse.* ◇ **Finnish** is the main language spoken in Finland.

fiord See **fjord**.

fir **Firs** or **fir trees** are tall pointed evergreen trees with needle-like leaves.

fire (firing, fired) ❑ **Fire** is the flames produced by something burning. When something like a house is burning, you say there is a **fire**. ◇ When something starts to burn, you say it **catches fire**. When it is burning, you say it is **on fire**. ◇ If you **set fire** to something, you start it burning.
❑ A **fire** is also a burning pile of coal or logs in a fireplace

or in the open, lit to keep people warm. ◇ Gas and electric **fires** are appliances which give out direct heat from an element.
❑ When a gun is **fired**, it sends out a bullet or shell. Shots fired from guns are called **fire**. *We climbed up the hill under fire.*
❑ In a battle, if you are **in the firing line**, you are in a dangerous place where you might be killed. ◇ You also say someone is **in the firing line** when they are being criticized or blamed for something.
❑ If someone **fires** questions at you, they ask several of them quickly, one after the other.
❑ If your employer **fires** you, he or she dismisses you from your job.

fire alarm A **fire alarm** is a device which makes a loud noise to warn people of a fire.

fire brigade The **fire brigade** in an area is the organization responsible for putting out fires.

fire crew A **fire crew** is a team of firemen.

fire door A **fire door** is a door which is supposed to be kept closed when not in use, to stop a fire spreading.

fire engine A **fire engine** is a large vehicle for carrying a fire crew and their equipment.

fire escape A **fire escape** is a staircase on the outside of a building, to help people get away if there is a fire.

fire extinguisher A **fire extinguisher** is a metal cylinder with water or a chemical inside, used to put out a fire.

fire hydrant A **fire hydrant** is a pipe in the street which firemen can get water from

fire officer A **fire officer** is an officer in the fire service, for example one in charge of a fire brigade.

fire sale A **fire sale** is a sale of goods damaged in a fire. ◇ When a company has to sell some of its assets for less than they are worth, this is also called a **fire sale**.

fire service The **fire service** in an area is its fire brigade. ◇ The **fire service** is also fire brigades in general. *Britain's fire service is highly disciplined, with clear objectives.*

fire station A **fire station** is a building where fire engines are kept.

firearm A **firearm** is a gun, especially one you can carry.

fireball A **fireball** is a ball of fire, like the one at the centre of a nuclear explosion.

firebomb A **firebomb** is a bomb designed to start a fire. When a place is **firebombed**, firebombs are thrown into it or dropped on it.

firebrand You call someone a **firebrand** when they keep calling for some strong action to be taken.

firecracker A **firecracker** is a firework which makes a series of loud bangs.

firefighting (firefighter) **Firefighting** is putting out fires. A **firefighter** is a member of a fire brigade, or someone else helping to put out a fire.

firefly (fireflies) **Fireflies** are beetles which glow in the dark.

fireguard A **fireguard** is a wire mesh screen put in front of a fire to stop people burning themselves.

firelight is the light coming from a fire.

fireman (firemen) A **fireman** is a man who is a member of a fire brigade.

fireplace A **fireplace** is a space in the wall of a room where you can light a fire.

firepower An army's **firepower** is the number and effectiveness of its weapons.

fireproof (fireproofing) **Fireproof** things and materials do not melt or catch fire and are used to stop fire getting to something. **Fireproofing** is used to talk about methods and materials for stopping fire getting to things. ...*the move towards better fireproofing.*

fireside If you sit by the **fireside** in a room, you are close to the fire.

firewood is wood for burning on a fire.

firework **Fireworks** are small objects with chemicals inside, which burn, bang, or sparkle colourfully when you light them. ◇ You can say there are **fireworks** when there is an angry argument. ◇ In sport or entertainment, a fast skilful performance which is exciting to watch or listen to can be called **fireworks**. ...*vocal fireworks from one of Germany's most distinguished tenors.*

firing line See fire.

firing squad A **firing squad** is a group of soldiers chosen to shoot someone who has been found guilty of a serious offence.

firm (firmly, firmness) ❑ A **firm** is a business.

❑ A **firm** object keeps its shape when you press something against it. ◇ If the ground is **firm**, it is not soft or muddy.

❑ If you give something a **firm** hit, you hit it hard but in a controlled way.

❑ If you have a **firm** grip on an object, you are holding it tightly. ◇ If someone has a **firm** grip on something such as power, they have it and are not likely to lose it. You can also say they are **firmly** in control.

❑ **Firm** is used to say something is clear and definite. You can talk about a **firm** plan or proposal. You can also say there is **firm** evidence of something. You can also talk about someone having a **firm** impression, or coming to a **firm** conclusion.

❑ **Firm** opinions and beliefs are strongly held, and not likely to change. ◇ If people **stand firm**, they do not give in to a threat or attack. ◇ If you **stand firm** on something like a decision, you stick to it.

❑ You use **firmly** to say someone strongly supports or opposes something. *She said the United States was firmly opposed to the use of force.* If someone **firmly** denies something, they say emphatically it is not true.

❑ If you are **firm** with someone, you do not let them do something they are not supposed to. ◇ If someone in authority takes **firm** action, they make sure bad behaviour is stopped or punished. *The firmness of the judge was widely applauded.*

firmament The **firmament** is the sky. ◇ People who are successful or famous are sometimes described as stars in a particular **firmament**. *They are a busy couple, giving dinner parties for the stars of the literary, theatrical and left-wing firmaments.*

first (firstly) ❑ The **first** thing of a particular kind happens or exists before all the others. ◇ The **first** person to do something does it before anyone else. ◇ You can talk about the **first** time something happened, or say it **first** happened at a particular time. *Vita and Harold first met in the summer of 1910.* ◇ You use **first** to say someone does something before they do anything else. *First I went to*

see the editor of the Dispatch. ◇ You use **at first** when you are talking about the early stages of something, compared to what happened later. *At first I was reluctant.*

❑ If you do something **first thing**, you do it at the beginning of the day. If you do it at **first light**, you do it when it is getting light.

❑ You say **first** or **firstly** when you are mentioning the first in a series of items. *The main protagonists had agreed to a three-point plan. Firstly, there would be a ceasefire in Slovenia.*

❑ The **first** person or vehicle in a line or queue is the one at the front.

❑ **First** is used to talk about the best or most important thing of a particular kind. *She won first prize... The first duty of the state is to ensure that law and order prevail.* ◇ If you put someone or something **first**, you treat them as more important than anything else.

first aid is medical treatment given immediately to someone who has had an accident or become suddenly ill.

first-class is used to describe people or things of the highest quality. ...*a first-class administrator.* ◇ If you travel **first class**, you do it in greater comfort and pay more for it. ◇ If you send a letter **first class**, you pay more and the letter gets there more quickly.

first cousin Your **first cousins** are the children of your aunts and uncles.

first-degree burns are the least serious kind, in which only the surface of the skin is burned. ◇ In the US, **first-degree** murder is the crime of actually killing someone, rather than, for example, helping the killer.

first-ever is used to say someone or something is the first of their kind. ...*the first-ever Piccadilly Festival.*

first floor In Britain, the **first floor** of a building is the one above the ground floor. In the US, the **first floor** is the ground floor.

first-hand You get **first-hand** knowledge when you experience something directly. Afterwards, you can give a **first-hand** account of it. You can also say you experience something **first hand** or **at first hand**.

first name A person's **first name** is the first of the names before their surname. Sometimes all the names before someone's surname are called their **first names**.

first officer The **first officer** of a plane or merchant ship is second-in-command to the captain.

first-past-the-post The **first-past-the-post** system is a way of electing a parliament. A country is divided into constituencies and the voters have just one vote each. The candidate who gets most votes in each constituency becomes its MP. See also **proportional representation**.

first person (first-person) If a story is told in the **first person**, it is told by one of the characters, using 'I'. You call this a **first-person** account or narrative.

first-rate is used to describe people or things of the highest quality. ...*a first-rate golfer.*

first refusal See refuse.

first school A **first school** is a school for young children, usually aged 5 to 9.

First Secretary The **First Secretary** of a communist party is its leader. ◇ The **First Secretary** at an embassy is second-in-command to the ambassador.

first-time (first-timer) **First-time** is used to talk about someone doing something for the first time. *Fiona*

McIntosh, of Scotland, emerged a first-time winner. A **first-timer** is someone doing something for the first time. *Nearly a third of the runners were first-timers.* A **first-time buyer** is someone buying a house for the first time.

firstly See first.

firth In Scotland, a **firth** is a long strip of water stretching inland from the sea.

fiscal is used to talk about things connected with government-controlled finances. *...fiscal controls.* ◇ In the US, the **fiscal year** is similar to the British financial year.

fish (fishes, fishing) (*usual plural:* fish) ❑ **Fish** are creatures with fins which live in water and breathe using gills which take in oxygen from the water. ◇ When people **fish**, they try to catch fish in the sea or a river, lake, or canal. You can say ships **fish** a particular area of sea. *It was the first trawler ever to fish those waters.*

❑ If you **fish** something out of a liquid or container, you take it out.

❑ You say someone is **fishing** for something when they try to get you to say something they would like to hear. *...fishing for a compliment.*

❑ **a cold fish:** see cold.

fish cake A **fish cake** is a mixture of fish and mashed potato made in a flat round shape and coated in breadcrumbs.

fish farm (fish farming) A **fish farm** is an enclosed area of water where fish are bred for food. Breeding fish like this is called **fish farming.**

fish finger Fish fingers are small oblong pieces of fish coated in breadcrumbs and sold frozen.

fisherman (fishermen) A **fisherman** is a man who catches fish as his job, or for pleasure.

fishery (fisheries) **Fisheries** are areas of sea where fish are caught.

fishing grounds are the same as fisheries.

fishing net A **fishing net** is (a) a large net for fishing from a ship or boat. (b) a small net on a pole used by children for fishing.

fishing rod A **fishing rod** is a pole with a line and hook, used for fishing.

fishmonger A **fishmonger** is a shopkeeper who sells fish.

fishnet is a net-like material used for making stockings and tights.

fishy (fishier, fishiest) If something has a **fishy** smell or taste, it smells or tastes like fish. ◇ You say something is **fishy** when it makes you suspicious.

fissile material contains atoms which can be split in the process of nuclear fission. See nuclear.

fission See nuclear.

fissure A **fissure** is a deep crack in rock or in the ground.

fist A person's **fist** is their hand with the fingers bent tightly.

fistful A **fistful** of things is several of them held in someone's fist.

fisticuffs If there are **fisticuffs,** people start hitting each other.

fit (fitting, fitted; fitter, fittest; fitness) ❑ You say something **fits** when it is the right size and shape for what you want. If it fits well, you say it is a good **fit.** ◇ If something **fits** into something else, it is small enough to go into it.

❑ If you **fit** something somewhere, you attach it there. ◇ A **fitted** cupboard or wardrobe has been made to fit into a particular space, and is fixed in place. ◇ A **fitted** carpet has been cut to fit a particular room. ◇ **Fitted** clothes follow the line of a person's body.

❑ If someone or something is like certain other people or things, you can say they **fit** into a type or pattern. *Malcolm fits into none of the traditional categories.* ◇ If a description **fits** someone or something, they could be the person or thing described. You also say someone or something **fits** a particular description. *The car fitted the description of one they had been seeking.*

❑ If someone is **fit,** they are strong and healthy as a result of taking exercise. *They were trained to a peak of physical fitness.* ◇ If something is **fit** for a particular purpose, it is good enough for that purpose. *The houses are now fit for human habitation.* ◇ If someone is **fitted** to do something, they have the right qualities for it.

❑ If you deal with something **as you see fit,** you deal with it in whatever way you think is best. ◇ If you say someone has **seen fit** to do something, you mean they have done it and you do not approve of it.

❑ If someone has a **fit,** they lose consciousness and their body makes violent movements. ◇ If someone does something in a **fit** of anger, they do it because they are very angry. You can also say, for example, that someone does something in a **fit** of enthusiasm.

❑ If something happens in **fits and starts,** it keeps starting and stopping.

❑ See also fitter, fitting.

fitful (fitfully) **Fitful** is used to describe things which keep starting and stopping. *...fitful sunshine... Babies dozed fitfully in their cots.*

fitment A **fitment** is something fixed to the wall of a room or the inside of a car, which can be removed fairly easily. *...bathroom fitments.*

fitted See fit.

fitter A **fitter** is a person whose job is to put together or install machinery or equipment.

fitting (fittingly) ❑ If you say something is **fitting,** you mean it is right or suitable. *Alex Moore looked the livelier of the two and fittingly scored his side's only try.*

❑ A **fitting** is a small object or device fitted to the outside of something. Taps and handles are fittings. ◇ The **fittings** in a house are things like cookers and gas fires, which are fixed but can be taken away when you move. See also fixture.

five is the number 5.

fiver A **fiver** is (a) five pounds. (b) a five-pound note.

fix (fixes, fixing, fixed) ❑ If you **fix** something somewhere, you attach it firmly and securely. ◇ If you **fix** something which is broken or not working, you mend it.

❑ If you **fix** something **up,** you arrange it. *It was here that the firm fixed up its deals.* If you **fix** someone **up** with something, you arrange for them to have it. ◇ When an amount or rate is **fixed,** someone decides what it will be. When a date is **fixed** for something, someone decides when it will happen.

❑ If someone's eyes are **fixed** on something, they are looking at it attentively. You also say people's eyes or attention are **fixed** on a part of the world when people are paying a lot of attention to what is going on there.

❏ If someone **fixes** a race or competition, they make unfair or illegal arrangements to get the result they want.

❏ If you **fix** a drink or food for someone, you prepare it.

❏ A **fix** is an injection of a drug like heroin.

❏ See also **fixed, fixer, fixing.**

fixated (fixation) If someone is **fixated** on something, they are interested in it, or concerned about it, to an absurd extent. You can also say someone has a **fixation** with something.

fixative is (a) a substance for preserving the surface of something like a drawing. (b) a substance for preserving scientific or medical specimens. (c) a glue-like substance for holding something in place.

fixed is used to talk about (a) things which do not change. ...*fixed rates of interest.* (b) things which have a definite form, length, or position. ...*a fixed agenda... ...a fixed period of time.*

fixed-wing is used to describe aircraft which have rigid wings which do not move, as distinct from helicopters or planes with swing or folding wings.

fixer A **fixer** is someone who is good at arranging for things to happen, often by knowing the right people.

fixing Fixings are small objects for holding something in place.

fixture ❏ A **fixture** is a sporting event arranged for a particular date.

❏ The **fixtures** in a house are things like power points and fitted cupboards which cannot be taken away when you move. See also **fitting.** ◇ You say someone or something has become a **fixture** when you always expect to see them in a particular place. ...*the Checker Board Lounge where Dixon was a fixture for years.*

fizz (fizzes, fizzing, fizzed) ❏ If a drink **fizzes**, it produces little bubbles of gas. ◇ **Fizz** is champagne, or some other fizzy white wine.

❏ You can say something **fizzes** when it is exciting. You can also talk about its **fizz.** *Politics has lost its fizz.*

fizzle (fizzling, fizzled) If something **fizzles out**, it ends in a weak or disappointing way.

fizzy A fizzy drink is full of little bubbles of gas.

fjord (or **fiord**) (pron: fee-ord) A **fjord** is a strip of sea which comes into the land between high cliffs, especially in Norway.

fl.oz. See **fluid ounce.**

flab See **flabby.**

flabbergasted If you are **flabbergasted** by something, you are extremely surprised.

flabby (flab) Flabby people are fat, and have loose flesh on their bodies. You call this loose flesh **flab.**

flaccid (pron: flas-sid or flak-sid) If an object is **flaccid**, it is loose or limp, rather than firm. ◇ If you call a performance or piece of writing **flaccid**, you mean it is weak or careless, and ineffective.

flag (flagging, flagged) ❏ A **flag** is a piece of coloured cloth used as a symbol of a country or organization. Flags are also used as signals or markers.

❏ If you think people are showing patriotic feelings in an unnecessary or exaggerated way, you can say they are **flag-waving** or call them **flag-wavers.** ◇ If you call someone the **flag bearer** of a group, you mean they are helping its reputation by doing something extremely well. ◇ A

country's **flag carrier** is its national airline.

❏ You say something is **flagged** as a particular thing when people regard it as important in some way. *The Earth Summit had been flagged as the moment when world leaders would attempt to solve the environmental crisis.*

❏ If you **flag down** a vehicle, you signal the driver to stop.

❏ If you are **flagging**, you are getting tired, and losing your ability to do something. ◇ You also use **flagging** to describe things which have become weaker or are no longer successful. *Volvo hopes to revive its flagging fortunes with its new model.*

❏ Flags or **flagstones** are large flat square pieces of stone used for paving. A **flagged** path, area, or floor is paved with flags.

flag of convenience (flags of convenience) If a ship sails under a **flag of convenience**, it has been registered in a country with lower safety standards and lower taxation than its country of origin.

flagellate (pron: flaj-i-late) (flagellating, flagellated; flagellation) When people with certain religious beliefs **flagellate** themselves, they beat themselves, as a penance. Sometimes they **flagellate** each other. Some people **flagellate** each other for sexual pleasure. These practices are called **flagellation.**

flagon A **flagon** is a large wide bottle or jug for cider or wine.

flagpole A **flagpole** or **flagstaff** is a tall pole for displaying a flag.

flagrant (flagrantly) Flagrant is used to describe wrong or harmful actions carried out in an open and unashamed way. ...*a flagrant violation of the law... The bank appears to have been flagrantly negligent.*

flagrante See **in flagrante delicto.**

flagship The **flagship** of a fleet is its most important ship. It carries the commander of the fleet. ◇ **Flagship** is used to talk about the most important thing owned or produced by an organization. *David Wilson Homes is building its flagship development at Kenilworth.*

flagstaff See **flagpole.**

flagstone See **flag.**

flail (flailing, flailed) If you **flail** your hands, arms, or legs, you wave them about. ◇ You use **flailing** to describe a clumsy and not very successful attempt to do something. ...*a flailing, dislocated performance.*

flair If you have **flair**, you do things in an original and stylish way. ◇ If you have a **flair** for something, you are naturally good at it.

flak If you get **flak**, you get a lot of criticism. ◇ **Flak** is also explosive shells or missiles fired in large numbers at aircraft from the ground. ◇ A **flak jacket** is a thick sleeveless jacket worn by soldiers and policemen for protection against bullets.

flake (flaking, flaked) A **flake** of something is a small thin piece, broken off a larger piece. ◇ When something like paint **flakes**, pieces of it come loose.

flambé (flambéing, flambéed) When food is **flambéed**, it is served in flaming brandy or some other spirit.

flamboyant (flamboyantly, flamboyance) Flamboyant people behave in a confident, unconventional, and very noticeable way. You talk about the **flamboyance** of people like these. *Some critics are behaving as flamboyantly as any-*

thing they have to write about.

flame (flaming) ❏ A **flame** is a pointed stream of burning gas coming from something which is on fire. ◇ If something **bursts into flames,** it suddenly starts burning. If it is **in flames,** it is burning. ◇ If something **goes up in flames,** all of it burns and it is destroyed. ◇ **Flaming** is used to describe things which are burning and sending out flames. *...flaming torches.*

❏ If someone is **fanning the flames** of a nasty situation, they are making it worse.

❏ An **old flame** is someone you once had a romantic relationship with.

❏ If something is **flame-coloured,** it is bright orangey-red. ◇ If someone is **flame-haired,** their hair is a vivid red colour.

flame-thrower A **flame-thrower** is a gun which sends out a stream of burning liquid. It can be used as a weapon, or for clearing away plants.

flamenco is a rhythmic Spanish dance accompanied by guitar playing and sometimes a singer.

flamingo (flamingos *or* flamingoes) **Flamingos** are pink birds with long thin legs and curved beaks.

flammable objects and materials catch fire easily.

flan A **flan** is a kind of tart, made of pastry and filled with fruit or something savoury.

flank A **flank** of something is one side of it. When an army is fighting a battle, you talk, for example, about its western **flank.** In football, you talk about a team's left or right **flank.** ◇ If you are **flanked** by people or things, you have them on each side of you. ◇ An animal's **flanks** are its sides.

flanker In rugby, a **flanker** is a player who plays on the outside of his team's front line.

flannel is a lightweight cloth used for making clothes. ◇ A **flannel** is a small cloth you wash yourself with. ◇ If someone talks a lot but does not tell you what you want to know, you call what they say **flannel.**

flap (flapped, flapping) When a bird **flaps** its wings, it moves them quickly up and down. Similarly, a person can **flap** a piece of cloth or paper. ◇ A **flap** is a piece of material or a flat object attached loosely to something by one edge. ◇ If someone is **in a flap,** they are anxious and excited about something.

flare (flaring, flared) ❏ A **flare** is a small device which produces a bright flame. Flares are used as signals.

❏ If violence **flares** or **flares up,** it starts suddenly. You can say there is a **flare-up** of violence. ◇ If tempers **flare,** people become angry.

❏ **Flared** skirts or trousers become wider towards the hem or the bottom of the legs. Trousers like these are called **flares.**

flare-up See flare.

flash (flashes, flashing, flashed) ❏ When a light **flashes,** it shines brightly, once or several times. You can talk about a **flash** of light. ◇ You say bright objects **flash** when they reflect light.

❏ If something **flashes** past, it passes you very quickly. ◇ If news **flashes** somewhere, it gets there very quickly.

❏ If you have a **flash** of intuition or inspiration, you suddenly realize something. ◇ If someone shows a **flash** of temper, they lose their temper briefly.

❏ If you call an achievement a **flash in the pan,** you

mean it is not likely to be repeated.

flashback A **flashback** is a scene in a film, play, or book where the story suddenly goes back to events in the past.

flashbulb A **flashbulb** is a small bulb which you fix to a camera. It makes a flash so you can take photos indoors.

flashlight A **flashlight** is a portable lamp powered by batteries.

flashpoint The **flashpoint** in a situation of hatred or resentment is the moment when something causes violence to break out. ◇ You call a place a **flashpoint** when fighting breaks out there and spreads to other places.

flashy (flashier, flashiest; flashily, flashiness) If you say something is **flashy,** you mean it is bold, bright, and expensive-looking. *...flashy ski outfits... Flashily put together, the film seems sure of success... ...the flashiness of outsize headlights and gleaming chrome.*

flask A **flask** is the same as a Thermos flask.

flat (flatter, flattest; flatly, flatness) ❏ A **flat** is a set of rooms for living in, on one floor of a building.

❏ A **flat** surface is level and does not have any bumps or holes. ◇ **Flat** countryside does not have hills. *...the flatness of Norfolk.* ◇ **Flat** racing is horseracing without jumps. You say this kind of racing is run on the **Flat.** ◇ If someone is lying **flat** on the ground, they are lying with as much of their body touching the ground as possible. You can also say they are lying **flat on their back** or **flat on their face.**

❏ A **flat** charge or fee is the same for everyone. You can also talk about a **flat rate** charge, fee, or tax. ◇ **Flat** is used to say an amount of money is not getting bigger or smaller. *Underlying profits are expected to be flat.* ◇ If there is no increase in demand for a product, you say there is a **flat** market.

❏ If you do something **flat out,** you do it as fast or as hard as you can. ◇ If something is done in a number of seconds, minutes, or hours **flat,** it is done in exactly that time.

❏ A **flat** denial, rejection, or refusal is firm and absolute. You can also say someone turns something down **flat.** *His party has flatly rejected the new constitution.*

❏ In music, **flat** is used to talk about a note a semitone lower than another note. For example, E flat is a semitone lower than E. 'Flat' is usually written ♭. ◇ If a note is played or sung **flat,** it is slightly lower than it should be.

❏ If a plan or attempt to do something **falls flat,** it fails. ◇ If you call something like a performance or piece of writing **flat,** you mean it is not exciting or interesting.

❏ A **flat** battery has lost its power. ◇ A **flat** tyre does not have enough air in it. ◇ If a drink is **flat,** it no longer has bubbles of gas in it.

flat cap A **flat cap** or **flat hat** is a man's cloth cap with a stiff peak.

flat-footed A **flat-footed** person has feet whose arches are too low. ◇ A sportsman who is left or caught **flat-footed** is made to seem slow or clumsy because of someone else's speed or skill.

flat hat See flat cap.

flat screen computer consoles and TV sets use a liquid crystal display instead of a cathode ray tube. They are smaller and flatter than the older kind, and give a sharper image.

flatfish (*usual plural:* flatfish) Flatfish are sea fish with wide flat bodies, like plaice or sole.

flatly See flat.

flatmate Someone's **flatmate** is the person they share a flat with.

flatten (flattening, flattened) ❑ If you **flatten** something, you make it flat. A **flattened** object has been made flat, or has a flatter shape than usual. ◇ If a village or building is **flattened**, it is destroyed by bombing or shelling. ◇ If you **flatten** someone, you hit them hard or collide with them and knock them down.

❑ If a road or curve **flattens** or **flattens out**, it stops climbing or falling and becomes horizontal. ◇ If something which has been increasing **flattens out**, it stops increasing and stays at the same level. *Consumerism has also flattened out.*

flatter (flattering, flattered; flattery) ❑ If someone **flatters** you, they praise you in an exaggerated way. You call their praise **flattery**. You can also say a writer gives a **flattering** description of someone, or an artist paints a **flattering** portrait.

❑ If something **flatters** someone, it makes them seem more attractive or better at something than they really are. *...denims which flatter the fuller figure... This gave the United States a slightly flattering 4-1 win.*

❑ If someone is **flattered** by something, they are pleased because it makes them feel important.

flatulent (flatulence) If someone is **flatulent** or suffers from **flatulence**, they have too much gas in their stomach or bowels, and feel uncomfortable.

flaunt If someone **flaunts** something they have, they display it in an obvious way. *They drove around in Rolls Royces, openly flaunting their wealth.*

flautist A **flautist** is someone who plays the flute.

flavour (flavouring, flavoured; flavourless) (*American spelling:* **flavor**, *etc*) ❑ The **flavour** of food or drink is its taste. If food has no taste, you say it is **flavourless**. ◇ If you **flavour** food or drink, you add something to it to give it a special taste. What you add is called **flavouring** or a **flavouring**.

❑ You can call a special quality which something has its **flavour**. *The pianist understood perfectly the flavour of the work.* You can also say something has a particular **flavour**. *The women's race had an international flavour to it.*

flaw (flawed, flawless, flawlessly) ❑ A **flaw** in something is a fault or mistake which spoils it or makes it unsatisfactory. If something is **flawed**, it has a flaw. ◇ **fatally flawed:** see fatal.

❑ If you say something is **flawless**, you mean it is perfect. *The docking manoeuvre was carried out flawlessly.*

❑ A **flaw** in someone's character is a fault. Famous people with serious faults in their character are sometimes described as **flawed**.

flax is a plant used for making rope and linen.

flaxen hair is pale yellow.

flay If someone **flays** a dead animal, they cut off its skin. ◇ If you **flay** someone, you criticize them severely.

flea A **flea** is a small jumping insect which sucks human or animal blood.

flea market A **flea market** is an outdoor market selling cheap second-hand goods.

fleapit A **fleapit** is an old shabby cinema or theatre.

fleck (flecked) Flecks are small spots of something on a surface. If there are a lot of them, you say the surface is **flecked** with them.

fled See flee.

fledgling (*or* fledgeling) A **fledgling** is a young bird. ◇ A **fledgling** system or organization is new and has not yet developed properly. *...Hungary's fledgling democracy.* ◇ **Fledgling** is used to describe someone who is just starting out in an occupation. *...a fledgling choreographer.*

flee (fleeing, fled) If someone **flees**, they run away.

fleece (fleecing, fleeced; fleecy) ❑ A sheep's **fleece** is its wool. When this wool is cut off in one piece, it is called a **fleece**. ◇ You use **fleecy** to describe something which looks or feels like a fleece. *...fleecy clouds... ...a tracksuit with a fleecy lining.*

❑ If you are **fleeced** by someone, they get a lot of money out of you in a dishonest way.

fleet A **fleet** is a large group of ships operating together. You can also talk about a **fleet** of aircraft or road vehicles.

fleet-footed (fleetness of foot) If you call someone **fleet-footed**, you mean they are capable of running or moving around very quickly. When someone is like this, you can talk about their **fleetness of foot**.

Fleet Street is used to talk about British national newspapers and the people who write for them.

fleeting (fleetingly) **Fleeting** is used to describe things which last only a short time. *...fleeting glimpses... ...a way to assert power, however fleetingly.*

fleetness of foot See fleet-footed.

Flemish is one of the two main languages spoken in Belgium. It is very similar to Dutch.

flesh (fleshes, fleshing, fleshed) ❑ Your **flesh** is the soft part of your body between your bones and your skin. ◇ When a politician **presses the flesh,** he or she shakes hands with a lot of people. ◇ When a part of someone's body is exposed, you can say you see their **flesh**.

❑ If you are in the same place as someone famous and you see them, you can say you saw them **in the flesh**.

❑ You use **flesh and blood** to emphasize that you are talking about something real and alive, in contrast to something imaginary or artificial. ◇ **Flesh** is used to talk about the human body, as distinct from the mind or spirit. *...the pleasures of the flesh.*

❑ If someone demands their **pound of flesh**, they insist on having something they are entitled to, though it may hurt other people.

❑ The **flesh** of a fruit or vegetable is the soft inner part.

❑ If you **flesh** something **out** or **put flesh on** it, you add details to it. *He is expected to flesh out the agreement.*

fleshy (fleshier, fleshiest) **Fleshy** people have a lot of fat on their bodies. ◇ The **fleshy** part of something like a fruit is the soft part inside.

fleur-de-lis (*or* fleur-de-lys) (*both pron:* flur-de-lee) A **fleur-de-lis** is a design of a lily with three petals, often on something like a flag or coat of arms.

flew See fly.

flex (flexes, flexing, flexed) ❑ A **flex** is a length of plastic tube with electric wires inside.

❑ If you **flex** part of your body, you bend or stretch it. ◇ If a group or country **flexes its muscles,** it threatens to use its power against someone else.

flexible (flexibly; flexibility) Flexible objects bend easily without breaking. You talk about the **flexibility** of objects like these. ◇ Flexible is also used to describe things which can be varied to suit different circumstances. *...flexible working hours... Junior doctors' time should be used more flexibly.* ◇ If you are **flexible** about something, you are willing to change it if necessary.

flexitime is a system which allows employees to vary the time they start or finish work, provided they work an agreed number of hours over a certain period.

flick If something **flicks** or is **flicked**, it makes a short sudden movement. A movement like this is called a **flick**. *Fried scored with a brilliant flick into the net.* ◇ If you **flick through** a book or magazine, you turn the pages quickly, without reading anything carefully.

flick knife A flick knife has a hidden blade which springs out when a button is pressed.

flicker (flickering, flickered) When a flame or light **flickers**, it shines unsteadily. ◇ A **flicker** of feeling lasts only a short time.

flier see flyer.

flight ❑ A **flight** is (a) a journey made by flying. *The flight will take 17 hours.* (b) a scheduled plane journey. *...Flight DA 1392 from Gatwick.* ◇ **Flight** is used to talk about the action of flying. *...30 years of manned space flight.*
　❑ Running away from something is called **flight** or a **flight**. *Some families have reclaimed the cars they abandoned in their original flight.*
　❑ A person or animal **in full flight** is running very fast.
　❑ A **flight** of steps or stairs is a row of them leading to another level.

flight deck The **flight deck** of a plane is the crew area where the controls are. ◇ The **flight deck** of an aircraft carrier is the long flat deck where aircraft take off and land.

flight lieutenant A flight lieutenant is a middle-ranking officer in the RAF.

flight recorder A plane's **flight recorder** or **black box** is an instrument on the plane which records all information about a flight. If there is a crash, the information can help investigators find out what went wrong.

flightless A flightless bird or insect cannot fly.

flighty (flightier, flightiest) **Flighty** is used to describe people, especially women, who are not serious or reliable.

flimsy (flimsier, flimsiest) **Flimsy** things are badly made, or not very strong. ◇ Flimsy cloth or clothing is very thin. ◇ Flimsy is also used to describe something like a reason or a story which is not very good or convincing. *Their lawyers described the evidence as flimsy... ...a flimsy plot.*

flinch (flinches, flinching, flinched) If you **flinch** when you are startled or hurt, you make a small sudden movement without meaning to. ◇ If you say someone does not **flinch** from doing something, you mean they are not afraid to do it.

fling (flinging, flung) ❑ If you **fling** something somewhere, you throw it. ◇ If you **fling** up an arm or hand, you move it upwards suddenly. ◇ If you **fling** open a door or gate, you push it open violently. ◇ If you **fling** yourself somewhere, you move suddenly and quickly. *Becker flung himself across the court to produce a winning volley.*
　❑ If someone **has a fling**, they have a brief sexual or ro-

mantic relationship. ◇ A **last fling** or **final fling** is a final opportunity to do or achieve something.

flint is a type of very hard grey stone. It is sometimes used for building, and in prehistoric times pieces of it were made into tools. When these tools are found now, they are called **flints**.
　❑ The **flint** in a cigarette lighter is a small piece of an iron alloy, used to produce the flame.

flip (flipping, flipped) ❑ If a small object **flips** or is **flipped**, it makes a sudden rapid movement. ◇ If you **flip** a coin, you toss it. ◇ If you **flip** a page of a book, you turn it quickly. If you **flip through** a book, you turn the pages quickly, without reading anything properly. ◇ If you **flip** a switch, you turn it on or off.
　❑ If someone **flips**, they suddenly become angry.
　❑ The **flip side** of a record is the less important side. ◇ You can call the less familiar aspects of something the **flip side**, especially when they are unpleasant. *...the flip side of their country's brand of socialism.*

flip-flops are sandals held on by a strap between the big toe and the one next to it.

flippant (flippantly, flippancy) You say someone is being **flippant** when their remarks show they are not taking something seriously. *The prince said flippantly, 'We go into the red next year. We may have to move into smaller premises.'* Making remarks like this is called **flippancy**.

flipper The flippers of an animal like a seal are the flat limbs it uses for swimming. ◇ Flippers are also flat pieces of rubber which swimmers wear on their feet to help them swim faster.

flirt (flirtation, flirtatious) ❑ If you **flirt** with someone or have a **flirtation** with them, you behave as if you are sexually attracted to them, in a not very serious way. ◇ If someone flirts with a lot of people, you say they are **flirtatious** or a **flirt**.
　❑ If you **flirt** with an activity of some kind, you go in for it in a not very serious way. If you **flirt** with an idea, you consider acting on it, but do not actually do anything.

flit (flitting, flitted) ❑ If someone **flits** somewhere, they move quickly and lightly. *She flits athletically about the stage.* You can also say birds and small animals **flit**. ◇ You say someone flits around when they keep visiting different places or doing different things. *He flits effortlessly between politics and industry.*
　❑ If an idea **flits** across your mind, it is only there for a moment. Similarly, you can talk about a look **flitting** across someone's face.
　❑ If someone does a **flit**, they secretly leave the place where they have been living.

float (floating, floated) ❑ If something is **floating**, it is lying on the surface of a liquid. ◇ A **float** is a light buoyant object which helps keep someone or something afloat.
　❑ If something like a plan or idea is **floated**, it is suggested as a possible course of action.
　❑ If a company is **floated**, shares in it are offered to the public. ◇ If a government **floats** its country's currency, it lets it find its own value. Similarly, things like prices and interest rates can be allowed to **float**.
　❑ A **float** is a decorated lorry in a procession or carnival, often carrying people in costume. ◇ Electric vehicles which deliver milk are also called **floats**.
　❑ A **float** is also a small amount of money kept some-

where, for buying small items or for use as change.

❑ If you say a place has a **floating population**, you mean people keep arriving and leaving. ◇ Someone who votes in elections but is not a firm supporter of any party is called a **floating voter**.

flock ❑ A group of birds, sheep, or goats is called a **flock**. ◇ A clergyman's **flock** are the people attending his church. ◇ When a lot of people go to a place or event, you can say they **flock** there.

❑ **Flock** is used to describe wallpaper with a raised pattern of wool or some other fibre. ◇ A **flock** mattress is stuffed with small pieces of wool or cloth.

flog (flogging, flogged) If someone **flogs** a person or animal, they beat them with a whip or stick. ◇ If you **flog** something to someone, you sell it to them.

flood (flooding, flooded) ❑ If a river or lake **floods**, the water flows onto areas which are usually dry. When this happens, you say the areas are **flooded**; you also say there is a **flood** or **flooding**.

❑ **Flood** is used to talk about large numbers of things being received. For example, you can say someone gets a **flood** of requests, or is **flooded** with requests. ◇ **Flood** is also used to talk about the movement of large numbers of people. ...*a flood of refugees... Investors flooded in from abroad.*

floodgates If you say the **floodgates** are open, you mean something has suddenly become possible for a large number of people, and they are taking advantage of it.

floodlight (floodlighting; floodlit) **Floodlights** are powerful lamps used to light sports grounds or the outside of large buildings. This kind of lighting is called **floodlighting**. Places lit like this are described as **floodlit**.

floodwater is the water covering flooded land.

floor (flooring, floored) ❑ The **floor** of a room is the flat part you walk on. ◇ **Flooring** is hard material used to cover a floor.

❑ A **floor** of a building is all the rooms on one level. ◇ The **floor** of a stock exchange is a large open area where trading takes place. ◇ People also talk about official debates taking place on a **floor**. *Labour's allegations prompted furious exchanges on the floor of the Commons.*

❑ The seabed is sometimes called the sea **floor** or the ocean **floor**.

❑ If you **floor** someone, you knock them down. ◇ If you are **floored** by a question or remark, you cannot think of an answer to it.

flop (flopping, flopped) If something **flops** or is a **flop**, it fails. ◇ If you **flop** somewhere, you sit down as though your body were very heavy, because you are tired.

floppy (floppier, floppiest; floppies) You say something is **floppy** when it hangs down loosely. ...*a floppy bow tie.* ◇ A **floppy** is a floppy disk.

floppy disk A **floppy disk** is a small flexible magnetic disk used for storing computer data.

flora The **flora** in a place are all the plants there. See also fauna.

floral is used to describe (a) something made of flowers or consisting of flowers. ...*a floral clock.* (b) something with a pattern of flowers on it. ...*a floral carpet.*

floret A **floret** is a small flower forming part of a large flower head. The head of a cauliflower is made up of white florets.

florid ❑ You say someone's writing or speech is **florid** when they use unusual expressions or long complicated sentences to express something fairly simple.

❑ You can call a red-faced person **florid** or say their face is **florid**.

florin The **florin** was a British coin worth two shillings. It was replaced by the 10p piece.

florist A **florist** or **florist's** is a shop where you can buy flowers and indoor plants. Someone who runs a shop like this is also called a **florist**.

floss (flosses, flossing, flossed) When you **floss** your teeth, you clean between them using a thread called dental floss.

flotation When a new company is launched, this is called its **flotation**. ◇ When shares in a company are offered to the public, this is called a **flotation** of shares.

flotilla A **flotilla** is (a) a small fleet of naval ships. (b) a group of small ships of any kind.

flotsam is odds and ends of rubbish floating in the sea or washed up on the shore. See also jetsam.

flounce (flouncing, flounced) ❑ If someone **flounces** somewhere, they walk with exaggerated movements, drawing attention to the fact that they are angry.

❑ A **flounce** is a frill or ruffle on something like a dress or curtain.

flounder (floundering, floundered) ❑ You talk about people **floundering** through mud or water when they are getting through it with difficulty, trying not to slip or sink. ◇ You also say someone is **floundering** when they do not know what to do or say, or are struggling to cope with something.

❑ **Flounders** are a type of flatfish.

flour (floury) **Flour** is the powder made by grinding grain, which is used to make bread, cakes, and pastry. You say something is **floury** when it is covered in flour.

flourish (flourishes, flourishing, flourished) ❑ If something like a business is **flourishing**, it is doing well. ◇ When plants or animals **flourish**, they grow well or are healthy, because they are in conditions which suit them.

❑ If you **flourish** something, you hold it up and wave it about. ◇ If you do something with a **flourish,** you do it with a bold movement intended to attract attention.

❑ A **flourish** is also an ornamental curly line in handwriting.

flout (flouting, flouted) If someone **flouts** a law, order, or rule of behaviour, they deliberately disobey it.

flow ❑ You talk about a river **flowing**. For example, you say it **flows** through a particular area. ◇ You say liquid or gas **flows** when it moves continuously along something like a pipeline. You also say electricity **flows** along a wire. You talk about a **flow** of liquid, gas, or electricity. *The oil flow was falling.*

❑ You talk about people or things **flowing** when a steady stream of them is passing a place, or arriving somewhere. You can talk about a **flow** of people or things. *There is a steady flow of applications for the courses.* ◇ **Cash flow** is the movement of money in and out of a business.

❑ You say an event is **in full flow** when it is at its busiest stage. ◇ You say someone is **in full flow** when they are in the middle of a long speech. ◇ You say a performer, sportsman, or sports team is **in full flow** when they are performing in an impressive way.

❑ You use **flowing** to describe long hair or clothing which hangs down loosely. *...horses with flowing manes.*

❑ You can say results or consequences **flow** from something. *She was convinced that the benefits that would flow from her reforms would win her further support.*

flow chart A **flow chart** is a diagram which shows a sequence of operations, including alternatives, and how they follow from each other.

flower (flowering, flowered) ❑ **Flowers** are small plants, often with brightly-coloured petals. ◇ The **flowers** on a plant or tree are the parts which produce seeds. ◇ When a plant or tree **flowers**, it produces flowers or blossom. You then say it is **in flower**. ◇ **Flowered** cloth, paper, or china has a pattern of flowers on it.

❑ If something **flowers**, it develops fully and is successful. *A planned career as a film actor had flowered, briefly, in 1954.* ◇ Young people, especially soldiers, are sometimes called the **flower** of their country, meaning they are the best of their country's young people.

flowerbed A **flowerbed** is an area in a garden or park where flowers are grown.

flowery things have a pattern of flowers. *...flowery wallpaper.* ◇ **Flowery** speech or writing uses long complicated words and expressions.

flown See fly.

flu is an illness like a bad cold which makes you feel weak, and makes your muscles ache. 'Flu' is short for 'influenza'.

fluctuate (fluctuating, fluctuated; fluctuation) If something fluctuates, its level keeps going up and down. *...temporary fluctuations in the exchange rate.*

flue A **flue** is a chimney, or a pipe acting as a chimney.

fluent (fluently, fluency) ❑ **Fluent** is used to say someone can speak a foreign language easily and correctly. You say, for example, someone is **fluent** in French, speaks **fluent** French, or speaks French **fluently**. You can also talk about someone's **fluency** in a language. ◇ **Fluent** and **fluency** are also used to talk about (a) children's ability to read and write their own language. *Fluent, efficient word recognition is not the only reading lesson children need to learn.* (b) the ability of adults to express themselves in their own language unusually well. *The fluency of his writing ensured he was much in demand.*

❑ **Fluent** is also used to describe easy flowing movements. *The cast now dance far more fluently than they did.*

fluff is bits of wool-like material on clothes or in dusty corners of a room.

❑ If you **fluff** something or make a **fluff**, you make a small mistake. *The City full back fluffed his clearance.*

fluffy (fluffier, fluffiest) You say a small animal is **fluffy** when its fur is thick and soft. ◇ You say other things are **fluffy** when they are soft like an animal's thick fur. *...fluffy white towels.* ◇ In cooking, you say food is **fluffy** when it has been whipped up to make it soft and light.

fluid (fluidity) ❑ A **fluid** is a substance which can flow and change shape. Liquids are fluids, and so are thicker substances like oil and mercury. In science, gases are also considered to be fluids.

❑ If a situation is **fluid**, things are likely to change. *Ministers, aware of the fluidity of the situation, discouraged talk of an immediate settlement.* ◇ If an arrangement is **fluid**, it can be changed if necessary.

❑ In sport, you call moves or actions **fluid** when they are smooth and efficient.

fluid ounce The volume of a fairly small amount of liquid can be expressed in **fluid ounces**. There are 20 fluid ounces in an imperial pint and 16 in an American pint. 'Fluid ounces' is usually shortened to 'fl.oz'.

fluke ❑ If you say something was a **fluke**, you mean it happened by accident.

❑ **Flukes** are a type of parasitic worm.

flummox (flummoxes, flummoxing, flummoxed) If you are **flummoxed** by something, it catches you by surprise, and you do not know what to do or say.

flung See fling.

fluorescent objects shine brightly when light falls on them in the dark. ◇ A **fluorescent** light consists of a tube with a gas like neon inside. Electricity is passed through the tube, producing a hard bright light. ◇ **Fluorescent** clothes are very brightly coloured.

fluoridate (fluoridating, fluoridated; fluoridation) When drinking water is **fluoridated**, fluoride is added to it. This process is called **fluoridation**.

fluoride is a mixture of chemicals sometimes added to drinking water or toothpaste, because it is good for people's teeth.

fluorine is a pale yellow poisonous gas.

flurry (flurries) A **flurry** of things is several of them, happening one after the other. *...a flurry of meetings.* ◇ When a lot of things are happening together, you can say there is a **flurry** of activity. ◇ A **flurry** of snow is a sudden light shower of it.

flush (flushes, flushing, flushed) ❑ If someone **flushes**, their face goes red, because they are embarrassed, hot, or ill. When this happens, you say they are **flushed** or there is a **flush** in their cheeks. ◇ If someone is **flushed** with success, they are pleased and excited because something they are involved in has turned out well. ◇ If you talk about the **first flush** of something, you mean the start of it, when it seems exciting and new.

❑ When a toilet is **flushed**, water is released which washes it out. A **flush** toilet has a handle for making this happen. ◇ If you **flush** something out of a tube or container, you get it out by passing water or some other liquid through. ◇ When people in hiding are **flushed out**, they are forced to come out.

❑ If you are **flush** with money, you have plenty of it.

❑ If something is **flush** with a surface, it is level with it and does not stick up. *...a flush-fitting metal cover.*

❑ In card games, a **flush** is a hand consisting of all the same suit.

flustered If someone is **flustered**, they are confused or nervous, because they are having difficulty coping with something.

flute The **flute** is a musical instrument like a long tube with holes and keys. You play it by holding it sideways and blowing over a hole near one end. In Britain, a flute player is called a 'flautist'. In the US, he or she is called a 'flutist'.

fluted If something is **fluted**, it has long grooves cut or shaped into it.

flutist See flute.

flutter (fluttering, fluttered) ❑ When something like a flag **flutters**, it makes a small rapid movement in the wind.

◇ When a butterfly or small bird **flutters** somewhere, it flies there. ◇ If someone's heart **flutters**, it beats faster then usual, for no apparent reason. When the heartbeat is dangerously fast, you say the person has a heart **flutter**.

❑ If there is a **flutter** of excitement, people become mildly excited about something.

❑ If you have a **flutter**, you have a small bet on something.

flux If a situation is in a state of **flux**, it keeps changing.

fly (flies, flying, flew, have flown) ❑ When a bird, insect, or aircraft **flies**, it moves through the air. ◇ If you **fly** somewhere, you travel by aircraft. You also say the pilot **flies** the aircraft. ◇ If you **fly** something somewhere, you send it by aircraft.

❑ When a flag is **flying**, it is displayed on a pole. ◇ When someone represents their country in a competition, you can say they are **flying the flag** for their country. ◇ **flying colours**: see **colour**.

❑ If you want to emphasize how fast something moves, you can say it **flies**. *A stunning volley flew past the goalkeeper.* ◇ If someone loses control of their footing and falls, you can say they **go flying**. If they fall because of a blow or push, you can say they are **sent flying**.

❑ When people say time **flies**, they mean it seems to pass very quickly. ◇ A **flying visit** is a very short one. ◇ If something gets off to a **flying start**, it begins very well. You can also say the people involved get off to a **flying start**.

❑ If someone **lets fly**, they suddenly attack someone with their fists, or start criticizing them fiercely. ◇ If someone **flies at** another person, they suddenly attack them. ◇ If someone **flies into** a rage, they get very angry.

❑ If something **flies in the face of** what has previously been believed, it contradicts it. Similarly, you can say something **flies in the face of** a decision or principle.

❑ **Flies** are small two-winged insects. ◇ If you say someone **wouldn't hurt a fly**, you mean they are gentle and harmless. ◇ If you say people are **dropping like flies**, you mean they are dying, or falling ill, in large numbers.

❑ The front fastening on a pair of trousers is called the **fly** or **flies**.

fly-fishing is a kind of fishing using an imitation fly as bait. See also **coarse fishing**.

flyer (*or* **flier**) ❑ A **flyer** is a leaflet or pamphlet advertising something.

❑ Pilots are sometimes called **flyers**.

flying boat In the past, **flying boats** were large aeroplanes fitted with floats so they could operate from water. They were mainly used for luxury air travel.

flying doctor A **flying doctor** is a doctor who travels by air to visit patients in isolated parts of countries like Australia and Canada.

flying fish are fish which can jump out of the water and move through the air using their large fins.

flying officer A **flying officer** is a junior officer in the RAF.

flying picket A **flying picket** is a group of striking trade unionists who travel to a different workplace to try to get other people to join their strike.

flying saucer Flying saucers are saucer-shaped flying objects which are reported to have been seen and which some people think come from outer space.

flyleaf (flyleaves) The **flyleaf** of a book is the blank page at the beginning or end.

flyover A **flyover** is (a) a road which crosses another road by a bridge. (b) a railway line which crosses another line before joining it.

flypast When there is a **flypast** at a ceremony or air display, a group of aircraft fly over in formation.

flywheel A **flywheel** is a heavy wheel which regulates the speed of a machine.

FM is a broadcasting system in which a signal is transmitted by varying the frequency of the radio wave. FM is short for 'frequency modulation'.

foal (foaling, foaled) A **foal** is a very young animal of the horse family. When a mare **foals**, she has a foal.

foam (foaming, foamed) ❑ Foam is a mass of small bubbles. When a liquid **foams**, it has small bubbles on its surface. *...foaming waterfalls.* ◇ Some substances made up of small bubbles are called **foam**, for example shaving foam. ◇ Foam or **foam rubber** is a light sponge-like material used for packing and insulating.

❑ When someone is very angry, you can say they are **foaming** or **foaming at the mouth**.

fob (fobbing, fobbed) If you are **fobbed off** when you want to talk to someone, you are prevented from doing so by being told lies or excuses. ◇ If someone is **fobbed off** with something, they are persuaded to have it instead of what they really want.

focal point The **focal point** of something is its most important feature, or the one which arouses most interest. ◇ The **focal point** of something which is happening is the place where most of it is taking place. *The war memorial became a focal point of the protests.* ◇ The **focal point** of a lens is the point on its axis where parallel rays of light passing through it meet.

focus (focuses, focusing, focused) (*or* focusses, focussing, focussed) ❑ If you **focus** on one part of something, you pay particular attention to it. *The new course focuses on management skills.* ◇ A plan or policy which concentrates on a particular aspect of something is said to be **focused**. ◇ If people are paying a lot of attention to something, you can say it is the **focus** of attention or interest.

❑ If you **focus** a telescope on an object, you adjust it so you can see the object clearly. The object is then **in focus**. If you cannot see it clearly, it is **out of focus**. Similarly, you can focus a camera on something, and talk about photographs being **in focus** or **out of focus**. ◇ If you **focus** your eyes on something, you adjust them to see it more clearly. ◇ When a beam of light is **focused** on something, it is directed towards it.

fodder is food given to animals like cows and horses. ◇ If you say someone is being used as **fodder**, you mean they are being used or exploited for a particular purpose. *The psychologist seemed interested in him only as fodder for her research.* See also **cannon fodder**.

foe In a war, the **foe** is the enemy. ◇ In sport or politics, someone's **foes** are their opponents.

foetal (*or* **fetal**) (*both pron:* fee-tal) **Foetal** is used to talk about things to do with a foetus. *...an early stage of foetal development.* ◇ If someone is in the **foetal** position, they are hunched or crouched like a human foetus in the womb.

foetus (*or* fetus) (*both pron:* fee-tuss) (foetuses, fetuses) A foetus is an unborn human being or animal in the womb.

fog (fogging, fogged) When there is **fog** or a **fog**, tiny drops of water in the air form a thick cloud and make it difficult to see. ◇ If something like a window is **fogged**, it is steamed up and hard to see through. ◇ If a photograph is **fogged**, it is blurred or cloudy. ◇ You say someone is in a **fog** when they are muddled or confused.

fog-bound If you are **fog-bound**, you cannot make a journey because of fog. Similarly, you can say a plane or ship is **fog-bound**. If an airport is **fog-bound**, no planes can fly from it.

fogey (*or* fogy) (fogeys, fogies) If you call someone a **fogey** or an **old fogey**, you mean they are boring and old-fashioned. Young people who have old-fashioned attitudes and wear old-fashioned clothes are sometimes called **young fogeys**.

foggy (foggier, foggiest) When there is a fog, you say it is **foggy**. ◇ If someone's thoughts are **foggy**, they are muddled. ◇ If you do not have the **foggiest** idea about something, you do not understand it or know anything about it.

foghorn A **foghorn** is a loud horn sounded to warn ships when it is foggy.

fogy See **fogey**.

foible **Foibles** are odd habits, or strange ways of doing things.

foil (foiling, foiled) ❑ **Foil** is metal in the form of a thin sheet. ◇ A **foil** is a thin flexible sword with a button on the end, used in fencing.
❑ If a plan or attempt is **foiled**, it is prevented from succeeding.
❑ If something acts as a **foil**, it contrasts with something else, and shows off the other thing's good qualities. Similarly, if you act as a **foil** for another person, you behave in a way which helps them make the most of their talents or abilities.

foist If something is **foisted** on people, they are forced to accept it.

fold ❑ If you **fold** something like paper or cloth, you bend it, so one part covers another. If you **fold** it **up**, you make it into a small neat shape by folding it several times. ◇ **Folding** objects are designed to fold up, to make them easier to store or carry. ...*folding chairs.* ◇ A **fold** is a crease made in paper or cloth when it is bent. ◇ The **folds** in a piece of cloth are the curved shapes you get when it is not extended or lying flat.
❑ If you **fold** your arms, you link them across your chest. ◇ If you **fold** your hands, you put them together with the fingers intertwined.
❑ In cooking, if you **fold** something like flour into a mixture, you mix it in by gently turning one part over the other with a spoon.
❑ If a business, organization, or system **folds**, it fails and comes to an end.
❑ A **fold** is a small fenced-off area where sheep are kept. ◇ If someone re-joins a group or organization, you can say they **return to the fold**.
❑ **-fold** is used to talk about rates of increase. For example, if something is four times as big as it was, you say there has been a **four-fold** increase. *Profits rose six-fold.*

◇ **-fold** is also used to say how many parts something has. *The purpose of the meeting was two-fold: to explain the position of the Palestinians, and to discover what movement there was on the peace process.*

folder A **folder** is a thin piece of cardboard, plastic, or leather folded to make a container for papers.

foliage is the leaves of plants and trees. ◇ **Foliage plants** are grown because of their attractive or unusual leaves.

folio (folios) A **folio** is a book made from large-size paper folded in two, especially one made in the early days of printing.

folk is used to talk about traditional music, art, and customs. ...*English folk tales.* ◇ A **folk hero** is a well-known and popular figure from a nation's history, for example Robin Hood. A more recent figure can be called a **folk hero** when he is admired by the general public for something he has done. *A New York man who shot dead a subway train robber has earned instant status as a folk hero.*
❑ **Folk** means the same as 'people'. It is usually used to talk about people of a particular kind, or from a particular place. ...*the good folk of Lanark.* ◇ When Americans talk about their **folks**, they mean their close relatives.

folklore The traditional stories and customs of a nation are called its **folklore**. ◇ When stories are often told about an unusual person or event, you can say they become part of a particular **folklore**. *The game earned a place in cricket folklore.*

folksy things are intended to appeal to people because they are simple and ordinary in the traditional way of a country or region. ...*folksy clothes*... ...*his folksy manner.*

follicle The **follicles** in a person's skin are the small hollows which hairs grow out of.

follow (follower) ❑ If something **follows** something else, it happens after it. ...*the firework display that followed the dance.* **Follow** is often used to say something happens as a result of something else. *The decision follows negotiations with the trades unions.*
❑ If you **follow** something by doing something else, you do the second thing straight after the first. If you **follow up** something with something else, you continue what you started in the first thing. *Colonel Love followed up his report with another one.* **Follow-up** is used to talk about things which continue something started earlier. ...*a follow-up conference*... ...*a follow-up to the Paris summit.*
❑ If you **follow** someone in doing something, you do the same thing. You can also say you **follow** their example or lead.
❑ If something **follows** from something else, it is true because the other thing is true.
❑ You say **as follows** before giving a list of things, or before describing the way something is done. *The leading characters are as follows... The proof is as follows.*
❑ If you **follow** someone somewhere, (a) you go behind them. (b) you go to the same place at a later time. ◇ If you **follow** something like a path or river, you keep on it or close beside it.
❑ If you **follow** instructions or advice, you do what you are told or advised to do. ◇ If you **follow** a plan or policy, you carry it out.
❑ People who **follow** a religion accept its teachings and base their way of life on it. You say they are **followers** of the religion. ◇ When people support a political leader,

you call them his or her **followers**. ◇ People who follow something like a sport take a keen interest in it. If you follow a sports team, you support the team. Supporters are sometimes called **followers**.

❏ If you are **following** something like a TV serial or a series of events, you are taking an interest in it and making sure you know what happens.

❏ If you can **follow** what someone or something says, you can understand it. ◇ If you **follow up** something you hear, you try to get more information about it.

following ❏ You use **following** to talk about the next period of time of a particular kind. *The monthly payments are set in February and run from the following April.*

❏ You also use **following** when you are introducing some information. *The following checklist of important dates may be helpful.*

❏ A person's or organization's **following** is the people who support them.

❏ If there is a **following wind**, it is behind you and can help you move faster. ◇ You can also say someone has a **following wind** when everything is going right for them.

folly (follies) ❏ **Folly** is foolish behaviour. If you say a course of action is **folly**, you mean it is foolish. A person's **follies** are foolish things they have done.

❏ A **folly** is a building put up in the 18th or early 19th century and made to look like something like a castle or ruin, to create a picturesque effect.

foment (*pron:* foam-**ment**) If someone **foments** trouble, they stir it up.

fond (fondly, fondness) ❏ If you are **fond** of someone, you feel affection for them. ◇ If you have **fond** memories of someone or something, you remember them with affection. *She recalled fondly the weekly dances with American troops.* ◇ When people say goodbye in an affectionate way, you can call this a **fond** farewell.

❏ If you are **fond** of something like music or reading, you enjoy it. ◇ You can say someone is **fond** of doing something when they keep doing it. *United's fondness for the offside trap had them in trouble.*

❏ You use **fond** to describe beliefs and hopes which you think are mistaken. *...executives who fondly think they can produce their own colour brochures.*

fondant Fondants are soft sugary sweets which melt in your mouth. **Fondant** icing is made of a similar substance.

fondle (fondling, fondled) If you **fondle** someone, you touch or stroke them gently. You can also **fondle** a small animal.

fondue is a traditional Swiss dish. It is a hot sauce, often made with melted cheese, which you dip pieces of bread, meat, or vegetables into.

font The **font** in a church is the bowl which holds the water for baptisms.

fontanel (*or* fontanelle) The **fontanel** is the soft membrane between the gaps in a baby's skull. As the baby develops, the gaps gradually close until the skull is fully formed.

food is what people and animals eat. ◇ If something gives **food for thought**, it makes people think about possibilities they had not thought of before.

food chain A **food chain** is a series of living things. Each thing feeds off the one below it in the series.

food poisoning is an illness caused by eating food which has gone bad. It results in sickness and diarrhoea.

food processor A **food processor** is an electrical kitchen gadget for preparing food in various ways, for example mixing, chopping, and mincing.

foodie People who like cooking and eating good food are sometimes called **foodies**.

foodstuff Any substance used as food can be called a **foodstuff**.

fool (fooling, fooled) ❏ If you call someone a **fool**, you mean they are silly, or have done something silly. ◇ If you **make a fool of** someone, you make them look silly. If you **make a fool of** yourself, you do something which makes you look silly.

❏ If someone **fools** you, they trick you. If they **fool** you into thinking something, they make you believe it is true, when it is not. ◇ If you say someone is living in a **fool's paradise**, you mean they think their happy way of life is secure, when in fact it is not likely to last.

❏ When people **fool about**, **fool around**, or **play the fool**, they behave in a playful or silly way.

foolhardy If someone is **foolhardy**, they behave in a reckless way or take unnecessary risks.

foolish (foolishly, foolishness) You say behaviour or a decision is **foolish** when it is not sensible. *The West foolishly puts its faith in the unelected central government... The market was destabilised by government foolishness.* ◇ If someone is made to look **foolish**, they are put in an absurd or embarrassing position.

foolproof If something like a machine, system, or plan is **foolproof**, it cannot go wrong or be used wrongly.

foolscap is a size of writing or printing paper, measuring about 34 by 43 centimetres (13.5 by 17 inches).

foot (feet; foots, footing, footed) ❏ A person's **feet** are the parts of their body they stand on. ◇ When someone **gets to their feet**, they stand up. When they are **on their feet**, they are standing up. ◇ If someone is **back on their feet**, they are up and about again, after being ill. ◇ If something like an organization is **back on its feet**, someone has got it going again, after it had failed or collapsed. ◇ If someone can **stand on** their own **feet**, they can manage without help from anyone else.

❏ If you go somewhere **on foot**, you walk. ◇ When someone visits a place, especially for the first time, you can say they **set foot** there. *She became the first British sovereign to set foot on Spanish soil.*

❏ If you **put your feet up**, you sit or lie back with your feet on something like a stool. ◇ You also say someone **puts their feet up** when they do nothing for a time after being busy.

❏ If you are doing something and **do not put a foot wrong**, you do not make any mistakes. If, on the other hand, you **shoot yourself in the foot**, you make a careless mistake and spoil your chances of success. ◇ If you **put your foot in it**, you do or say something which causes embarrassment.

❏ If someone in authority **puts their foot down**, they say firmly that something must be done, or something must stop.

❏ If someone who you have long admired and respected turns out to have **feet of clay**, you discover that they have a serious fault or weakness which spoils your good opinion of them.

❑ The person who **foots the bill** for something is the one who pays for it.

❑ The **foot** of something is the bottom or lower end of it. ...*the foot of the cliff*... ...*the foot of the bed*.

❑ Length is often expressed in **feet**. A foot is about 30.48 centimetres. There are 12 inches in a foot. 'Feet' is usually written 'ft'.

foot-and-mouth disease is a serious disease of cattle, sheep, pigs, and goats. The animals get blisters in their mouths and around their hooves and have to be slaughtered.

footage of something is a film, or part of a film, showing it happening.

football (footballer; footballing) The game usually called football is played by two teams of eleven players kicking and heading a ball called a **football** in an attempt to score goals. People who play this game are called **footballers**. ◇ **Footballing** is used to talk about things to do with football. *Gascoigne's footballing future remains uncertain.* ◇ **football pools**: see **pool**.

footbridge A footbridge is a bridge for people to walk across.

foothills are low hills at the base of a mountain or at the edge of a mountain range.

foothold Footholds are small ledges or hollows where climbers can put their feet. ◇ If someone gets a **foothold**, for example in their career, they get established in a position from which they can make further progress.

footing is used to talk about the basis on which something is able to proceed. *The company still needs a breakthrough to put it on a firm financial footing.* ❑ When you are walking or climbing, your **footing** is the grip your feet have on the ground. If you lose your footing, you slip or stumble.

footlights In a theatre, the footlights are the row of lights along the front of the stage.

footloose If you say someone is **footloose**, you mean they have no responsibilities or commitments and can do what they like.

footman (footmen) A footman is a male servant who does things like opening doors and serving food. Footmen often wear a special uniform.

footnote A footnote is a note at the bottom of a page giving more information about something on the page. ◇ If you say you want to add a **footnote** to something that has happened or been said, you mean you want to make a comment on it. ◇ If you say something will make a **footnote in history**, you mean it will be remembered, but not thought of as important.

footpath A footpath is a path for people to walk on. It can be paved, for example alongside a road or street, or it can be just a narrow track across land.

footprint A person's or animal's **footprints** are the marks their feet leave on the ground.

footsore If you are footsore, your feet are sore and tired.

footstep Footsteps are the sound of someone walking or running. ◇ If you **follow in** someone's **footsteps**, you do what they did earlier.

footstool A footstool is a low stool for someone to rest their feet on while sitting down.

footwear Boots, shoes, sandals, and slippers are sometimes called **footwear**.

footwork In sport or dancing, someone's **footwork** is the way they move their feet. ◇ **Footwork** is also used to talk about clever ways of dealing with difficult situations. *He demonstrated his mastery of political footwork.*

fop (foppish) In the 17th, 18th, and 19th centuries, a fop was a vain man who wore fancy clothes. Men like this were called **foppish**.

for is used to say who or what a statement applies to. *For the Baltic governments this was a final hurdle before complete statehood... UK manufacturing output for August is down.* ◇ **For** is used to say who will benefit from something. *Special arrangements will be made for blind people.* ◇ **For** is used to say something would suit a type of person or thing. *It's a good life for a young man.* ◇ **For** is used to talk about the use or function of something. *The process released valuable floor space for production.*

❑ **For** is used to say someone represents a person, group, or country. ...*a spokesman for the District Council.* ◇ If you work **for** a person or organization, they employ you.

❑ **For** is used to say how long something lasts. *The area remained cordoned off for five hours.* ◇ **For** is used with 'time' to say how often something has happened before. *Last week the council rejected the application for the second time.* ◇ If something is planned or arranged **for** a particular time, it is meant to happen then.

❑ **For** is used to talk about distances. ...*a traffic jam that stretched for several miles.* ◇ **For** is used to say where someone is going. ...*fifteen trucks bound for Phnom Penh.*

❑ **For** is used to talk about someone's feelings about someone or something. *I'm very happy for Peter... Mr Hurd spoke of their hopes for the UN.* ◇ If you are **for** something, you are in favour of it. If you are **all for** it, you are strongly in favour of it.

❑ **For** is used to say how much something costs. *For 44p a minute you can listen to a recorded message giving advice about your problem.* ◇ **For** is used to talk about ratios. *You can take one bonus share for every ten shares allocated.*

❑ **For** is sometimes used to mean 'because'. *This is where he spent most of his time, for he had nowhere else to go.*

forage (*pron:* for-ridge) (foraging, foraged) When animals **forage**, they look for food. ◇ **Forage** is food for horses or cattle, especially hay or straw. ◇ When people **forage** for something, they try to find it by looking among other things.

foray When soldiers make a **foray** into an area, they make a quick raid or attack. ◇ If someone makes a **foray** into something new, they make an attempt at it.

forbade See **forbid**.

forbearance is patience and self-control.

forbears See **forebears**.

forbid (forbidding, forbade, have forbidden) If a rule or law **forbids** people to do something, it says they must not do it. You say something like this is **forbidden**, or people are **forbidden** to do it. ◇ A **forbidden** place is one people are not allowed to visit. ◇ A **forbidden** subject is one which must not be mentioned. ◇ **Forbidden fruit** or **forbidden fruits** are things which seem particularly attractive because people know they are not supposed to have them or do them.

forbidding is used to describe places, people, and things that look grim and unfriendly.

force (forcing, forced) ❑ A **force** is a group of people trained and organized for a special purpose, often a military one. *...an international peace-keeping force... ...a skilled labour force.* ◇ When people talk about the **forces** or the **armed forces**, they mean the army, navy, and air force.

❑ If people or circumstances **force** you to do something, they make you do it. You can also say people or circumstances **force** someone into a state or situation. *By dumping food the EU depresses prices and forces poorer farmers out of business.* ◇ Circumstances which affect people's behaviour and decisions are sometimes called **forces**. *Market forces have made people act, for purely selfish reasons, in socially desirable ways.*

❑ When people use **force** to get or achieve something, they use physical strength or violence. ◇ If you **force** something or **force** it open, you use your physical strength or something like a lever to open it. ◇ If you **force** your **way** into a place, you get there in spite of someone trying to stop you. ◇ If someone **forces** you into a place, they make you go there.

❑ You talk about a person or group being a **force** when they exert a strong influence in a particular field. *For over thirty years, Foster was a political force in the city.* ◇ **driving force**: see **drive**.

❑ When people **join forces**, they work together to achieve something. ◇ If people do something **in force**, they do it in large numbers. *Police were out in force.*

❑ When a law or system **comes into force**, it starts to apply. After that, it is **in force**. *Drought orders are already in force in three counties.*

❑ **Force** is used to talk about the power exerted by things like gravity and magnetism. *...the increased gravitational force as the plane turns.* ◇ **Force** is also used to show the speed and strength of a wind. *...a force nine gale.*

❑ **Forced** flowers and vegetables are made to grow faster or earlier than they normally would.

forceful (forcefully) ❑ You use **forceful** to say someone expresses their views or wishes in a strong and effective way. *He was a forceful and spirited debater... Mr Chowdhry has made a forceful statement in defence of his sport.*

❑ **Forceful** actions (a) are strong and effective. *...the forceful programme now being implemented by the government.* (b) involve the use of force. *Deane was brought down forcefully on the edge of the penalty area.*

forceps are an instrument with two pincer-like arms which a doctor, surgeon, or nurse uses for holding things.

forcible (forcibly) **Forcible** actions involve physical force or violence. *The Community would not accept any forcible change of borders... A small group of demonstrators were forcibly hustled off the Square.* ◇ If you express yourself in a **forcible** way, you make it clear how strongly you feel. *He is expected to put this position very forcibly.* ◇ **Forcible** and **forcibly** are also used to say something is brought firmly to someone's attention. *These latest figures are a forcible reminder of what is happening.*

ford If you **ford** a river or stream, you walk or drive through it at a shallow place. A place where people regularly do this is called a **ford**.

fore ❑ If something comes **to the fore** or is brought **to the fore**, it is given more attention than other things.

The issue of human rights has come to the fore during the last two days.

❑ **Fore** and aft are the front and back parts of a ship or boat.

forearm Your **forearm** is the part of your arm between your wrist and elbow.

forebears (*or* forbears) A person's **forebears** are their ancestors, or people who lived in the same place as them in earlier times. *The location and composition of our hedgerows have much to tell us about the lives of our forebears.*

foreboding is a feeling that something bad is going to happen.

forecast (forecaster) If you **forecast** something or make a **forecast**, you say what is going to happen. *He forecast that the party would split over the issue... Forecasters said last night that the hot weather is temporarily over.*

foreclose (foreclosing, foreclosed; foreclosure) If a person or organization **forecloses** on someone they have lent money to, they take ownership of property bought with the money, usually because repayments have not been made. This process is called **foreclosure**.

forecourt The **forecourt** of a large building is an open area at the front. ◇ A garage **forecourt** is the area where the petrol pumps are.

forefather A person's **forefathers** are their ancestors.

forefinger Your **forefinger** is the one next to your thumb.

forefront If someone is at the **forefront** of something, they are playing an important part in it. *Vivienne Westwood has been at the forefront of British fashion for 20 years.* ◇ If something is at the **forefront** of your mind, you are thinking about it continually and mean to act upon it or do something about it.

forego See **forgo**.

foregoing (*or* forgoing) is used to talk about something which has just been mentioned. *No order shall be made under any of the foregoing rules.*

foregone (*or* forgone) If you say something is a **foregone conclusion**, you mean there can be no doubt about what will happen.

foreground The **foreground** of a picture is the part which seems nearest to you.

forehand In games like tennis, a **forehand** is a stroke made with the palm of the player's hand facing the direction they are hitting the ball. See also **backhand**.

forehead A person's **forehead** is the front of their face above their eyebrows.

foreign ❑ You use **foreign** to talk about things connected with other countries. ◇ A **foreign national** is a person staying in a country they are not a citizen of. ◇ A country's **foreign affairs** are its dealings with other countries. The government department handling these affairs is usually called the **Foreign Ministry** and is headed by the **Foreign Minister**. In Britain, the department is called the **Foreign Office** and is headed by the **Foreign Secretary**.

❑ **Foreign exchange** is (a) the foreign currency held in a country. (b) the system by which one country's currency can be converted to another's, so things can be bought and sold internationally without gold having to change hands.

❑ A **foreign** object is one that has got into something,

usually by accident, and should not be there. An object like this is sometimes called a **foreign body**.

❏ If you say something is **foreign** to you, you mean you know nothing about it or are unfamiliar with it.

foreigner A **foreigner** is someone from another country.

foreknowledge If you have **foreknowledge** of something, you know about it in advance.

foreleg An animal's **forelegs** are its front legs.

forelock When people behave with exaggerated respect towards someone they regard as their social superior, you can call this **forelock touching** or **forelock tugging**.

foreman (foremen) A **foreman** is the person in charge of a group of workers. ◇ The **foreman** of a jury is its leader.

foremost People say **first** and **foremost** when mentioning the most important thing about someone or something. *He wants, first and foremost, international recognition.* ◇ The **foremost** of a group of things or people is the best or most important one. *Scudamore has been the foremost National Hunt rider since John Francome retired.*

forename Your **forenames** are the names in front of your surname.

forensic is used to describe things connected with the scientific examination of the evidence when a crime is being investigated. *...forensic scientists... ...forensic data.*

foreplay is kissing and caressing before sex.

forerunner The **forerunner** of something like a machine is something similar which existed at an earlier period in history.

foresee (foreseeing, foresaw, have foreseen) If you **foresee** something, you think or say it is going to happen.

foreseeable is used to talk about things which could reasonably be regarded as possible in the future. *Industry has enough excess capacity to meet any foreseeable upturn in demand.* ◇ When people talk about the **foreseeable future**, they mean the time for which it is possible to make reasonable predictions about what will happen. *There's no opportunity in the foreseeable future to make any money out of property dealing.* ◇ If you say something will happen **for the foreseeable future**, you mean it will go on for some time and no one knows when it will end.

foreshadow If something **foreshadows** something else, it shows or suggests it is going to happen. *The change was foreshadowed in the Chancellor's March Budget.*

foreshortened You say something is **foreshortened** when it is drawn or seen from a sharp angle so that its two ends appear closer to each other than they really are.

foresight You say someone has **foresight** when they see what is likely to happen in the future and take the right sort of action.

foreskin A man's **foreskin** is the loose skin covering the end of his penis.

forest (forestry, forester, forested) ❏ A **forest** is a very large area of woodland. Someone who manages an area like this is called a **forester**. The work he or she does is called **forestry**. ◇ A **forested** area is covered in trees.

❏ A **forest** of objects is a large group of them clustered together. *...a forest of chairs and tables.*

forestall If something is **forestalled**, it is prevented from happening. *He warned that only a united opposition could forestall a new dictatorship.*

forester (forestry) See **forest**.

foretaste A **foretaste** of something is a small part or early stage, which gives people some idea what the rest might be like.

foretell (foretelling, foretold) If someone **foretells** things in the future, they say what will happen. *Many prophets have foretold the end of the world.*

forethought If a crime is committed with **forethought**, it is planned in advance. ◇ **Forethought** is also thinking carefully about something before doing it. *A little forethought can avoid a lot of problems.*

foretold See **foretell**.

forever (or **for ever**) ❏ If you say something will go on **forever**, you mean it will never end.

❏ If you say something has gone **forever**, you mean it has gone and will not come back. You can also say something is lost **forever** or has changed **forever**.

❏ If you say someone is **forever** doing something, you mean they keep doing it.

forewarn (forewarning) If you are **forewarned** of something or receive **forewarning** of it, you are told in advance it is going to happen.

foreword The **foreword** of a book is its introduction, written by the author or someone else.

forfeit (forfeiting, forfeited; forfeiture) ❏ If someone **forfeits** something they own, they have to give it up, because of something they have done. People can also **forfeit** things like rights and privileges. You can talk about the **forfeiture** of any of these things.

❏ If you have to pay a **forfeit** as part of a game, you have to give something up, or do something silly.

forgave See **forgive**.

forge (forging, forged; forger; forgery, forgeries) ❏ When people **forge** an agreement or an alliance, they succeed in creating it.

❏ If someone **forges** a signature, document, or painting, they produce something that looks like the real thing, to deceive people. Someone who does this regularly is called a **forger**; what they do is called **forgery**. You call a forged banknote, document, or painting a **forgery**.

❏ **Forged** metal objects are made by shaping heated metal, usually in a place called a **forge**.

❏ If someone **forges ahead**, they make a lot of progress, or they do better than other people.

forget (forgetting, forgot, have forgotten) ❏ If you **forget** something you used to know, you cannot remember it. ◇ If you **forget** something like an appointment or birthday, or **forget** to do something, you do not remember it at the right time. ◇ If you **forget** something you meant to bring, you do not remember to bring it.

❏ If someone does something to **forget** something else, they do it to stop themselves thinking about it. *For many people a football match is a chance to forget the worries of work.* ◇ **Forgotten** is used to describe places and people that are ignored by the rest of the world. *...this forgotten corner of Ethiopia.*

forget-me-not Forget-me-nots are small plants with tiny blue flowers.

forgetful (forgetfulness) People who are **forgetful** often forget things. *People affected by ME can suffer mental problems such as forgetfulness.*

forgettable If you say something is **forgettable**, you mean it has nothing special or memorable about it.

forgivable (forgivably) If you say what someone has done is **forgivable**, you mean they should not be blamed for it, because of the circumstances in which they did it. *It was a blunder, but a forgivable one... Its president could forgivably feel that he quit just in time.*

forgive (forgiving, forgave, have forgiven) ❑ If you **forgive** someone for something they have done, you stop blaming them or being angry with them. ◇ If a person or organization **forgives** a debt, they say they no longer expect it to be repaid.

❑ If you say people **could be forgiven** for thinking something, you mean they could easily get a wrong impression. *Viewers of medical television dramas might be forgiven for thinking all doctors and nurses possess emergency life-saving skills.*

forgiveness If you ask someone for **forgiveness**, you ask them to forgive you for something wrong you have done.

forgo (forgoes, forgoing, have forgone) (*can be spelled with an 'e' after the 'r'*) If you **forgo** something, you go without it or give it up. ◇ See also **foregoing, foregone**.

forgot (forgotten) See **forget**.

fork (forked) ❑ A **fork** is an object with prongs, used for eating. ◇ A **fork** is also a large tool with prongs, used in gardening and farming. ◇ If you **fork** something somewhere, you move it using a fork.

❑ If a road or river **forks**, it divides into two. You call the place where it divides a **fork.** You also use **fork** to say which direction someone takes when they reach a fork. *Fork right at the church.*

❑ A **forked** object divides into two at one end. ◇ **Forked** lightning divides into two or more parts near the ground.

❑ If you say someone is speaking with a **forked tongue**, you mean they are not telling the truth.

❑ If you **fork out** for something, you spend a lot of money on it.

fork-lift truck A **fork-lift truck** is a small vehicle with two movable arms at the front, for lifting heavy loads.

forlorn (forlornly) A **forlorn** person looks sad and lonely. *A small group of protestors stood forlornly in St John's Wood Road.* ◇ **Forlorn** is also used to describe places which look deserted. *...the forlorn looking cottages by the harbour.* ◇ A **forlorn** hope or attempt has little or no chance of success.

form ❑ When something **forms** or is **formed**, it comes into existence. *Queues formed outside many stores.* ◇ When people **form** an organization, they start it. ◇ When someone **forms** a government, they get enough people to agree to serve under them as prime minister, so they can begin governing their country.

❑ You use **form** when you are saying what something consists of. For example, if something consists of a number of parts, you say the parts **form** the whole. *The two pieces of metal together form a complete tube... They form only nine per cent of the population.*

❑ A **form** of something is a type or kind of it. *...cheaper forms of energy.* ◇ You can say what kind of thing something is by saying it exists in a particular **form.** *The book is in the form of a travel diary.*

❑ You also say something is in a particular **form** when you are talking about its shape. *They placed candles in the form of a cross.* ◇ If a group of things together **form** a shape, they have that shape. ◇ **Form** is used to talk about the shape of the human body. *Nothing about the designs enhanced the female form.*

❑ In sport, someone's **form** is their level of fitness and ability. You say, for example, someone is in good **form.** *Edberg was in stunning form.* ◇ You say musicians or entertainers are in good **form** or on good **form** when they give an impressive or enjoyable performance. ◇ You use **true to form** to say someone is behaving in their normal way. *True to form she kept her guests waiting for 90 minutes.*

❑ A **form** is one or more sheets of paper with printed questions and space for people to write the answers.

❑ At a school, a **form** is a class, or all the classes for children of a similar age.

formal (formally; formality, formalities) ❑ **Formal** is used to talk about the official part of an event, as distinct from unofficial things which may happen before or afterwards. *The formal opening of the conference is due in a few hours time... The ceasefire has been formally agreed after several hours of talks.* ◇ The **formal** part of your education is the part you get officially, for example at school or college, as distinct from things you may learn at other times.

❑ **Formalities** are things which have to be done for official or legal reasons on a particular occasion. *They would be free to leave as soon as passport formalities had been completed.* ◇ If you say something is a **formality,** you mean it has to be done, but will not make much difference to anything. *The decision is seen as a formality... The second leg of this tie is little more than an annoying formality.*

❑ **Formal** is used to describe people's behaviour when they are being very correct, rather than relaxed or casual. Behaviour like this is called **formality.** ◇ On **formal** occasions, people wear smart clothes and behave according to accepted rules. **Formal** clothes are suitable for occasions like these.

❑ A **formal** garden is laid out in a neat and regular way, like the flower-beds in a park.

formaldehyde (*pron:* for-mal-de-hide) is a strong-smelling gas which is dissolved in water to make formalin.

formalin is a liquid which is used to preserve specimens in biology.

formalise See **formalize**.

formality See **formal**.

formalize (formalizing, formalized; formalization) (*can be spelled with an 's' instead of a 'z'*) When a plan or agreement is **formalized**, it is made official. *...the formalization of co-operation between the republics.*

format The **format** of something is the way it is arranged or presented. *The film is now available in a wide-screen format... They have agreed on a format for the December elections.*

formation ❑ When something is brought into existence, you call this its **formation.** *The Prime Minister has announced the formation of a special commission.*

❑ You can say people or things are in a particular **formation** when they are arranged in a pattern. *The troops had regrouped into a battle formation.* ◇ A rock or cloud **formation** is the shape of a group or mass of rocks or clouds.

formative A **formative** period in someone's life is a time when their character and attitudes are being shaped by things happening around them. You can also talk about **formative** influences on someone or on their life. ◇ The **formative** stage of something is the time when it is beginning to take shape or develop.

former (formerly) ❑ **Former** and **formerly** are used to say what someone or something used to be. *...the former world champion... The territory was formerly used as a training site.* ◇ When people talk about **former** times, they are talking about the way things used to be in the past. *In former times shortages were shrugged off.*

❑ When you have mentioned two things or people, you can call the first one the **former**. *His books include The General of the Dead Army and his masterpiece Doruntine. The former began to make his reputation here after it was published in 1986.*

Formica is a stiff hard plastic used for covering surfaces like kitchen worktops. 'Formica' is a trademark.

formidable (formidably) **Formidable** is used to say someone or something is very difficult to deal with. *...a formidable opponent... ...a formidably difficult task.* ◇ **Formidable** is also used to say something is very impressive. *...a formidable display of dishes, receivers and accessories... The company remains formidably strong financially.*

formula (*plural:* formulae *or* formulas) ❑ A **formula** is a group of letters, numbers, or other symbols which stand for a scientific or mathematical rule. ◇ The **formula** for a substance is the set of instructions for making it from other substances. ◇ The chemical **formula** of a substance is a group of letters and numbers representing the proportion of elements in each molecule of the substance.

❑ A plan for dealing with a problem can be called a **formula**. ◇ When a book, film, or TV series has a plot which follows a familiar pattern, you can say it is written to a **formula**.

❑ In motor racing, **formula** is used to talk about particular categories of car. *...the winner of the British Formula Three championship.*

❑ Baby or infant **formula** is specially prepared milk powder which you mix with water to make baby food.

formulate (formulating, formulated; formulation) ❑ When people **formulate** something like a plan, they work it out. *...the formulation of national economic programmes.* ◇ If you **formulate** an opinion or thought, you put it into words.

❑ When something like a cream or drug is **formulated**, it is prepared according to a formula. This kind of formula is sometimes called a **formulation**.

fornicate (fornicating, fornicated; fornication, fornicator) Religious people who do not approve of sex outside marriage sometimes call it **fornication**. They say the people who do it are **fornicating**. They may also call people who do it **fornicators**.

forsake (forsaking, forsook, have forsaken) If you **forsake** something, you give it up. *The government is not willing to forsake its status as a nuclear power.* ◇ If you **forsake** a person, you stop helping them or looking after them. ◇ **Forsaken** is used to describe someone or something that is forgotten or neglected. *...a forsaken church.*

forsythia is a bush with yellow flowers which appear in the early spring before its leaves.

fort A **fort** is a strong building used as a base for soldiers defending a place. ◇ If you say someone is **holding the fort,** you mean they are looking after something while someone else is away.

forte (*pron:* for-tay) Someone's **forte** is the thing they are particularly good at.

forth ❑ When someone leaves a place, you can say they go **forth** or set **forth.** ◇ **Forth** is also used to talk about sounds coming out of a place. *Loud music blared forth.*

❑ If someone sets **forth** something like a proposal or plan, they give details of it. ◇ If something is brought **forth,** it is made to appear or happen. *My letters have failed to bring forth information.*

❑ **hold forth:** see **hold.** ◇ **and so forth:** see **so.** ◇ **back and forth:** see **back.**

forthcoming ❑ A **forthcoming** event will happen soon. *...the forthcoming elections.*

❑ If something like help or information is **forthcoming,** it is provided or made available. *Foreign financial help has not yet been forthcoming.* ◇ If someone is **forthcoming,** they are willing to talk freely about something.

forthright If you are **forthright,** you say what you think clearly and directly. *The churches issued a forthright rejection of racial separateness.*

forthwith If you do something **forthwith,** you do it straight away. *These methods should be abandoned forthwith.*

fortify (fortifies, fortifying, fortified; fortification) ❑ When people **fortify** a place, they make it stronger and less easy to attack by putting up buildings, walls, or ditches. This process is called **fortification.** The buildings, walls, or ditches are called **fortifications.**

❑ If you are **fortified** by something, it makes you feel stronger, or better able to deal with something. *...huddled in warm coats and fortified by a tot of brandy... ...fortified by a crash course in management techniques.* ◇ If something **fortifies** a feeling or belief, it makes it stronger. *A recent incident fortifies that suspicion.*

❑ **Fortified** is used to describe food which has something added to it to make it healthier. *...fortified breakfast cereals.* ◇ **Fortified** wines are made by mixing wine with a small amount of brandy or some other spirit.

fortitude You say someone shows **fortitude** when they cope with pain or difficulty in a brave and determined way.

fortnight (fortnightly) A **fortnight** is a period of two weeks. If an event happens **fortnightly,** it happens once a fortnight. A **fortnightly** magazine or bulletin comes out once a fortnight.

fortress (fortresses) A **fortress** is a large fort or a fortified town. ◇ **Fortress** is sometimes used in front of the name of a geographical area when talking about laws which would make it difficult for people outside to come to live in it or trade with it. *...Fortress Europe.*

fortuitous (fortuitously) You say something is **fortuitous** when it is lucky for someone. *...a fortuitous discovery... The ball fell fortuitously to Ardley, who scored with a left-foot shot.*

fortunate (fortunately) You say people are **fortunate** when they have some special advantage in life, or when things turn out well for them on a particular occasion. ◇ You can express pleasure or relief at something by saying it is **fortunate**, or by adding **fortunately** to what you are saying. *It was fortunate that there were no other casualties... Fortunately, the inspector is a football fan.*

fortune ❑ A **fortune** is a very large amount of money. *That dress must have cost a fortune.* ◇ A **fortune** is also all the money and valuable possessions owned by a very rich person. *...a personal fortune estimated at more than 6 billion pounds.*

❑ **Fortune** or good **fortune** is good luck. **Ill fortune** is bad luck. *It has been my good fortune to work with many great players... Ill fortune again dogged him.* ◇ If you talk about the **fortunes** of a person or organization, you are talking about all the good and bad things that have happened to them. *The fortunes of the party have gone from bad to worse.*

❑ If someone **tells your fortune**, they tell you what will happen to you in the future, for example by looking at playing cards or your palm. Someone who does this for money is called a **fortune teller.**

forty (fortieth, forties) **Forty** is the number 40. ◇ The **forties** was the period from 1940 to 1949. ◇ If someone is in their **forties**, they are aged 40 to 49.

forum A **forum** is a meeting where people exchange ideas and discuss things, especially public issues.

forward (forwards) ❑ If someone or something moves **forward** or **forwards**, they move in the direction they are facing. ◇ If you are in a **forward** position, you are near the front of something. You can also say someone is **forward** of something or someone else.

❑ In football and hockey, a **forward** is a player whose job is to try and score goals rather than defend.

❑ **Forward** and **forwards** are used to talk about things progressing or becoming more modern. When people talk about the way **forward**, they mean the way to make progress. *Independent taxation is a great step forward... Reform is the only way forward.* ◇ People who are **forward-looking** are interested in new ideas and methods, rather than the way things have been done in the past.

❑ If you are **looking forward to** something, you are pleased it is going to happen and are expecting to enjoy it.

❑ If you **forward** a document you have received, you send it on to someone else. ◇ If you **forward** a letter to someone who has moved away, you send it on to their new address. The address they leave for this purpose is called a **forwarding address.**

fossil A **fossil** is the hardened remains of a prehistoric plant or animal, sometimes in the form of a print left inside a rock.

fossil fuel Fossil fuels are fuels like coal, oil, and natural gas, which have been formed from the decayed remains of plants and animals.

fossilize (fossilizing, fossilized; fossilization) (*can be spelled with an 's' instead of a 'z'*) When the remains of a plant or animal **fossilize** or are **fossilized**, they become hard and form a fossil. ◇ If you say an organization or its methods have become **fossilized**, you mean they have not changed at all for a long time.

foster (fostering, fostered) ❑ If a couple **foster** a child, they officially look after it for a time as part of their family, without becoming its legal parents. A single person can also **foster** a child. A person who fosters a child is called its **foster mother, foster father,** or **foster parent.**

❑ If something **fosters** a feeling, activity, or idea, it

helps it develop. *GATT has been enormously successful in helping foster the expansion of world trade.*

fought See **fight.**

foul (fouler, foulest; fouling, fouled) ❑ You use **foul** to describe things which are dirty or smell nasty. ◇ If something **fouls** a place, it makes it dirty. *...the problems caused by dogs fouling the streets.*

❑ If you dislike something very much, you can say it is **foul.** *...this foul place.* ◇ You can describe very bad weather as **foul.** ◇ **Foul** language is swear words or other rude words. ◇ If someone is in a **foul** mood or temper, they are angry about something and behave in an irritable way.

❑ In a game or sport, a **foul** is an action which is against the rules. If someone **fouls** someone else, they do something which breaks a rule.

❑ If you **fall foul** of someone, you do something which gets you into trouble with them. If you **fall foul** of something like a law, you break it and are in trouble because of it.

❑ You say there has been **foul play** when it turns out that something happened as the result of a crime. *She died as a result of foul play by a person or persons unknown.* ◇ You can call any unfair or dishonest way of achieving something **foul play.** *He would be willing to use any amount of foul play to get what he wanted.*

❑ If you **foul** something **up**, you spoil it by doing something wrong or stupid. You can call what you have done a **foul-up.**

found ❑ See **find.**

❑ If someone **founds** an organization or town, they are responsible for starting it. ◇ If something is **founded** on a particular thing, it is based on it. *Corish's success was founded on his ability to counter-attack.* ◇ If you say an idea, opinion, or feeling is **well-founded,** you mean there are good reasons for having it.

foundation ❑ The **foundation** of something like a belief or way of life is the idea, attitude, or experience it is based on. *Respect for the law is the foundation of civilised living.* ◇ If you say a story or idea has no **foundation,** you mean it is not based on anything which is really true or really happened.

❑ The **foundations** of a building are the layers of bricks or concrete below the ground which support it.

❑ If you talk about the **foundation** of a group or organization, you are talking about the time when it was first started. *...the ANC's biggest rally since its foundation.* ◇ A **foundation** is also an organization which provides money for a special purpose. *...the National Foundation for Educational Research.*

foundation course A **foundation course** is a university or college course which prepares students for a longer or more advanced course.

foundation stone A **foundation stone** is a block of stone built into a public building. It is usually set in place at a public ceremony, and unveiled when the building is complete. Foundation stones often have words cut into them to record these events.

founder (foundering, foundered) ❑ The **founder** of an organization or town is the person who created it. ◇ A **founder member** of a group or organization is one of the members who started it.

❑ If something **founders,** it fails. ◇ If a ship or boat

founders, it fills with water and sinks.

foundry (foundries) A **foundry** is a place where metal or glass is melted down and poured into moulds to form a variety of objects.

fount The **fount** of something is the person or place it comes from. *...London's days as the fount of all things fashionable.*

fountain A **fountain** is an ornamental feature in a pool or lake. It consists of a jet of water forced up into the air by a pump.

fountain pen A **fountain pen** is a pen with a nib and its own supply of ink.

four is the number 4. ◇ If someone is **on all fours**, they are on their hands and knees.

four-letter word **Four-letter words** are short words which people think are rude or offensive, because they are connected with sex or other body functions.

four-wheel drive A **four-wheel drive** vehicle has all its four wheels connected directly to the engine.

foursome A **foursome** is a group of four people who go around together, or do something together.

fourteen (fourteenth) **Fourteen** is the number 14.

fourth The **fourth** item in a series is the one counted as number 4. ◇ In the US, a **fourth** is a quarter.

Fourth of July In the US, the **Fourth of July** is a national holiday when people celebrate the Declaration of Independence in 1776.

fowl Birds are sometimes called **fowls** or **fowl**.

fox (foxes, foxing, foxed) ❑ **Foxes** are dog-like animals with reddish-brown fur and bushy tails.
❑ If something **foxes** you, you cannot understand it or solve it. ◇ If a person **foxes** you, they trick you or confuse you in some way.

fox-hunting is a pastime in which people on horseback accompanied by hounds chase a fox across the countryside, and the hounds kill it.

foxhole A **foxhole** is a small hole which soldiers dig to shelter in and shoot from.

foxhound The **foxhound** is a type of dog bred and trained for fox-hunting.

foyer (*pron:* foy-ay *or* foy-er) The **foyer** of a theatre or hotel is the area just inside the main doors, where people can wait for each other.

Fr. Fr. is short for 'franc'. *Profits were around Fr.550 million in 1989.* ◇ Fr. in front of a priest's name means 'Father'. *...Fr. Newman.*

fracas (*pron:* frak-ah) (*plural:* fracas) A **fracas** is a rough noisy quarrel or fight.

fraction (fractional, fractionally) A **fraction** of something is a very small part of it. *They cannot win more than a fraction of popular support.* A **fractional** amount is very small. *They're only fractionally different.* ◇ In maths, a **fraction** is an exact part of a number. ¼ and ⅝ are fractions.

fractious You say someone is being **fractious** when they get upset or angry about things which do not matter, often because they are tired.

fracture (fracturing, fractured) If something **fractures** or is **fractured**, it cracks or breaks. You call the crack or break a **fracture**. ◇ If something like a system or relationship **fractures**, it becomes disorganized or confused, and so it stops working properly. You can talk about a

fracture in something like this. *This could widen the ethnic fractures in the republic.* ◇ If you say someone's speech is **fractured**, you mean they keep making mistakes because they are speaking a language which is not their own.

fragile (fragility) **Fragile** things are easily broken, damaged, or destroyed. You can talk about the **fragility** of things like these. *The continued fighting points to the fragility of the peace plan.*

fragment (fragmentation) A **fragment** of something is a small piece or part of it. ◇ If something **fragments** (*pron:* frag-ments) or is **fragmented**, it breaks up into smaller parts. *...the fragmentation of the country into small nations.* ◇ You say a speech or piece of writing is **fragmented** when it is made up of parts which seem unconnected with each other.

fragmentary You say something is **fragmentary** when it is incomplete and the parts you have do not fit together. *...the fragmentary evidence for this story.*

fragrant (fragrance) You say something is **fragrant** when it has a sweet or pleasant smell. You call this smell its **fragrance**.

frail people are not strong or healthy. ◇ If an object is **frail**, it is easily broken or damaged.

frailty (frailties) People's **frailties** are their small faults and weaknesses. The tendency to have faults and weaknesses is sometimes called **frailty**. ◇ **Frailty** is also used to talk about physical weakness brought on by age or ill health. *Despite failing sight and frailty, he still maintained a lively interest in the company's affairs.*

frame (framing, framed) ❑ A **frame** is a structure for fitting something into, for example a door frame or a picture frame. ◇ If you **frame** a picture or photograph, you put it in a frame. *...a framed photograph of her mother.* ◇ A **frame** is also a structure, for example of bars or posts, which gives an object its shape and strength. ◇ The **frames** of a pair of glasses are the wire or plastic parts which hold the lenses in place. ◇ If you say someone has a small **frame** or a large **frame**, you mean they have the bone structure of a small or large person.
❑ Your **frame of mind** is the mood you are in at a particular time. ◇ Your **frame of reference** is the set of beliefs, ideas, or observations on which you base your judgement of things.
❑ If someone **frames** something like a plan or system, they decide on its form and details. *He was sure the government would be able to frame a new, acceptable electoral law.*
❑ If something is **framed** in particular language, that is how it is expressed.
❑ If someone **frames** you, they make it look as though you have committed a crime, although you have not.
❑ In snooker, a **frame** is part of a match. The player who wins most frames wins the match.
❑ If you are **in the frame** for something, you have a good chance of winning, achieving, or getting it. If you are **out of the frame**, you have no chance.

framework A **framework** for something is a set of rules or guidelines by which it can be done or achieved. *The Communist Party must operate within the framework of the constitution.* ◇ The **framework** of an object is its basic structure, around which the rest of it is built.

franc The franc is the unit of currency in France. Some

other countries, for example Switzerland and Belgium, also have a unit of currency called a **franc**.

franchise ❏ If people have the **franchise**, they have the right to vote in an election which elects their country's government.

❏ A **franchise** is an authority granted by a company to someone, allowing them to use the company's name or methods in exchange for a sum of money or a share of the profits.

frank (frankly, frankness) ❏ If you are **frank**, you talk in an open and honest way. ...*a frank admission of failure... He asked me to tell him frankly what I wished to do... He seemed to be speaking with complete frankness.* ◇ People add **frankly** to what they are saying when they are admitting the truth about something. *Frankly, this has all come as a bit of a shock.*

❏ If you **frank** a letter or parcel, you put a mark on it, to show the postage has been paid or no stamp is needed.

frankfurter A **frankfurter** is a type of smoked sausage.

frantic (frantically) You say someone is **frantic** when they behave in a wild and desperate way, because they are frightened or worried. ◇ If there is **frantic** activity, people are very busy doing a lot of things. *They worked frantically throughout the day.*

fraternal is used to describe links of friendship which are officially supposed to exist between certain countries or groups of people. ...*the former regime's fraternal bond with the Soviet Union.*

fraternity (fraternities) ❏ People belonging to the same profession or having the same interest are sometimes called a particular **fraternity**. ...*the banking fraternity... ...the yachting fraternity.* ◇ In the US, a **fraternity** is a society of male students formed for social reasons.

❏ **Fraternity** is used to talk about friendly feelings which are officially supposed to exist between certain countries or groups of people.

fratricide If someone commits **fratricide**, they kill their brother. ◇ When people kill other people from the same country or community, for example during a civil war, this is often called **fratricide**.

fraud is the crime of obtaining money by deceit or trickery. A **fraud** is a scheme for obtaining money in this way. ◇ If you say someone is a **fraud**, you mean they are pretending to be something they are not.

fraudulent statements and claims are deliberately deceitful, dishonest, or untrue.

fraught If something is **fraught** with problems or difficulties, it is full of them. *The Secretary General's task is fraught with obstacles and frustration... This is a fraught and busy week for the country's top women golfers.* ◇ When people are **fraught**, they are worried and anxious.

fray ❏ When a material like cloth or rope **frays**, its threads or strands become worn and it is likely to tear or break. ◇ When people's nerves or tempers **fray**, they get irritable and behave in a bad-tempered way.

❏ If you say someone enters the **fray**, you mean they get involved in something like a conflict, disagreement, or competition.

freak (freakish) People who behave or dress in an unusual way sometimes get called **freaks**. ◇ Other people get called **freaks** when they have particular interests or hobbies. ...*a fitness freak... ...an Elvis freak.* ◇ If you call

something that has happened a **freak**, you mean it was the result of unusual circumstances, and is not likely to be repeated. You say things like this are **freakish**. ...*a freak accident... There was something slightly freakish about Britain's last win in Sydney.* ◇ If someone **freaks out**, they get very emotional and excited, either because they are very happy or because they are upset and cannot cope with something.

freckles are light-brown spots on a person's skin, especially their face.

free (freer, freest; freeing, freed) ❏ You say people are **free** when their way of life is not restricted by unjust laws, or they are not ruled by people who they have not chosen as their leaders. Similarly, you say institutions are **free** when they are allowed to operate without interference. *Algeria already possesses one of the freest presses in the Arab world.* ◇ If people **free** themselves from rulers they do not want, they get rid of them.

❏ When prisoners are **freed** or **set free**, they are released. You can say a released prisoner is a **free** man or woman.

❏ If you are **free** from something unpleasant, you can live your life without being affected by it. ...*a life free from terror.* ◇ If you are in a situation where you can do something on your own without being responsible to anyone else, you say you are a **free agent**. ◇ If you say someone is a **free spirit**, you mean they are independent and live the way they want, rather than in a conventional way.

❏ If you believe in **free will**, you believe people choose what they do, rather than having their actions controlled by God or some other power. ◇ If you do something **of your own free will**, you do it because you want to and not because you are made to.

❏ **-free** is added to words to say something does not have the thing described by the word. *Each submarine reported a trouble-free launch... ...error-free computer programs.* ◇ If a place is **free** of something unpleasant, it does not have it. *The area will be free of pollution by the year 2000.*

❏ If you **free** something which is fixed or trapped, you release it. You can also cut or pull something **free**. *I shook my jacket free and hurried off.*

❏ You say something is **free** when people can get it or use it without having to pay for it. ◇ If something like a seat is **free**, it is not occupied or not being used. ◇ If you have a **free** period of time or are **free** at a particular time, you are not busy then.

❏ When a government **frees** something like money or resources, it makes them available for a particular use.

❏ If you say someone is **free** with something, you mean they give it or use it a lot. *He is not known for being free with his money.*

❏ **a free hand: see hand.** ◇ See also **freely**.

free enterprise is an economic system in which businesses compete for profit with little government control or interference.

free fall In parachuting, **free fall** is the part of the jump before the parachute opens. ◇ If things like prices go into **free fall**, they begin to drop uncontrollably.

free-for-all A **free-for-all** is a fight or argument which everyone joins in. ◇ You call a situation a **free-for-all** when several people or groups are trying to get something and there are no controls on how they do it.

free kick When there is a **free kick** in football, a player is allowed to kick the ball once without interference, because a member of the other side has broken a rule. If the kick is a **indirect free kick**, the player cannot score from it directly; if it is a **direct free kick**, he can.

free market In a country with a **free market** economy, people decide what prices to sell their goods at, rather than having them determined by the government.

free-range poultry and pigs are allowed to move freely on an area of open ground. The eggs of free-range poultry are called **free-range** eggs.

free-standing A **free-standing** building or other object is standing on its own and is not joined or attached to anything else. ◇ You can say an organization is **free-standing** when it is independent of other organizations.

free trade is trade between countries without restrictions or taxes on what is bought or sold.

freedom If there is **freedom** in a country, people are allowed to do what they want, provided they do not harm anyone else. If there is **freedom** of speech, they can say what they want; if there is **freedom** of movement, they can go where they want. Similarly, you can talk about political **freedom** or religious **freedom**. All these things together are called **freedoms**. *Poles and Hungarians could find their new freedoms threatened by economic disorders.* ◇ If there is **freedom** from something unpleasant, people do not have it or are not affected by it. *...freedom from hunger and starvation.* ◇ When prisoners gain their **freedom**, they escape or are released.

freedom fighter If you support or admire a group of people who are fighting against an occupying army or against the army of their own country, you can call them **freedom fighters**.

freehand A **freehand** drawing is done without using any implements such as a ruler or compasses.

freehold (freeholder) If you own the **freehold** of a building or piece of land, you own it for life, rather than leasing it from someone else. People who own buildings or land like this are called **freeholders**. If a building or piece of land is for sale **freehold**, you can buy its freehold. See also **leasehold**.

freelance A **freelance** journalist or photographer is self-employed and usually works for several organizations rather than one. **Freelance** is also used to describe self-employed people in some other occupations. *...freelance accountants... He ran the orchestra for five years before deciding to go freelance.*

freeloader If you call a group of people **freeloaders**, you mean they are getting advantages or benefits without contributing anything towards them.

freely If you can do something **freely**, you can do it without being restricted in any way. ◇ If you can talk **freely**, you do not need to be careful what you say. ◇ If something is **freely** available, you can get hold of it easily. ◇ **Freely** is also used to say something is done, used, or produced in large quantities. *During a recession consumers do not spend so freely.*

Freemason (Freemasonry) A **Freemason** is a man who belongs to a secret society whose members promise to help each other. Freemasons recognize each other using a system of secret signs. Their beliefs and practices are called **Freemasonry**.

Freepost is a system by which an organization pays the postage when someone writes to them. 'Freepost' is written on the envelope as part of the address. 'Freepost' is a trademark.

freesia Freesias are a kind of plant with white, yellow, pink, or mauve tube-shaped flowers which give out a pleasant smell.

freestyle is used to talk about sports competitions, especially swimming and wrestling, in which competitors can use any style or method they want.

freeway In the US, a **freeway** is similar to a motorway.

freewheeling is used to describe events or arrangements which are not limited by rules or fixed ideas about the way things should be done. *He said the meetings should be informal to allow freewheeling discussions.*

freeze (freezing, froze, have frozen) ❑ When a liquid **freezes**, it becomes solid because the temperature has dropped below a certain level. When water **freezes**, it turns to ice. ◇ If an area of water **freezes over**, it becomes completely covered by a layer of ice. ◇ If something like a pipe **freezes up**, it becomes completely blocked with ice. ◇ If it is **freezing** outside, the temperature is below freezing point. ◇ In conversation, people also say it is **freezing** when it is very cold. Similarly, they say very cold water is **freezing**, or they themselves are **freezing** or **frozen**.

❑ If you **freeze** food, you store it at a temperature below freezing point, so it will keep longer.

❑ If someone **freezes to death**, they become so cold in freezing temperatures that they die.

❑ You also say someone **freezes** when they suddenly become completely still.

❑ If something such as prices are **frozen**, they are prevented from rising. ◇ If money held somewhere is **frozen**, a legal order is made preventing anyone, including the owner, from using it.

freeze-dried food has been frozen then dried very quickly, to make it keep longer.

freezer A **freezer** is a metal container whose inside temperature is kept below freezing point, so frozen food can be kept in it for long periods.

freezing point or freezing is 0° Celsius, the temperature at which water freezes. ◇ The **freezing point** of any liquid is the temperature at which it becomes solid.

freight is the movement of goods by lorries, trains, ships, or planes. Goods moved like this are also called **freight**. *37 percent of the nation's freight moves by rail.* You can say goods are **freighted** from one place to another.

freight train A **freight train** carries goods rather than passengers.

freighter A **freighter** is a ship or plane designed to carry goods rather than people.

French is used to talk about people and things in or from France. *...the French coast.* ◇ The **French** are the French people. ◇ **French** is the main language spoken in France. It is also spoken in some other countries, including Belgium, Canada, and Switzerland.

French beans are long thin green beans.

French bread is bread baked in long thin crusty loaves.

French doors are the same as French windows.

French dressing is a thin sauce for putting on salads. It is made of oil, vinegar, and spices.

French fries See **fry**.

French horn See **horn**.

French loaf A **French loaf** or **French stick** is a long thin crusty loaf.

French polish is a type of varnish painted onto wood to give it a hard shiny surface.

French windows are glass doors which lead onto a garden or balcony.

Frenchman (Frenchwoman) A **Frenchman** or **Frenchwoman** is a person who comes from France.

frenetic (*pron:* frin-net-ik) (frenetically) **Frenetic** behaviour is fast, energetic, and rather uncontrolled. *The visit was preceded by two weeks of frenetic cleaning-up... Byrne lurched frenetically around the stage.*

frenzied (frenzy) If people are **frenzied** or in a **frenzy**, they have lost control of themselves and are behaving in an excited or violent way. *...a frenzied mob of students.*

frequency (frequencies) The **frequency** of something is how often it happens. *He fired his assistants with startling frequency.* ◇ The **frequency** of a sound or radio wave is the rate at which it vibrates.

frequent (frequently) **Frequent** is used to describe things which happen often. *...frequent abuses of privilege... She frequently accompanied him to concerts.* ◇ If you **frequent** (*pron:* free-**kwent**) a place, you go there often. *They stay at home rather than frequenting clubs and restaurants.*

fresco (frescoes) A **fresco** is a picture painted onto a plastered wall while the plaster is still wet.

fresh (freshness) ❑ You use **fresh** to describe new things which come after other things of the same kind. *Rose had given him fresh instructions... He poured himself a fresh drink.* ◇ You also use **fresh** to describe things done in a new way which you find interesting or attractive. *This gives the novel freshness and charm.*

❑ If something is **fresh in your mind**, you remember it clearly, because it is very recent or because it made a strong impression on you.

❑ If you are **fresh** from a place, you have just been there. You can also say someone is **fresh** from an experience or activity. *...Nigel Mansell, fresh from wins in the last three Grand Prixs.*

❑ **Fresh** food has been made, killed, or gathered recently, and so has not been preserved in any way.

❑ You use **fresh** to describe things which feel, taste, or smell pleasant and refreshing. *Grated lemon peel gives a fresh flavour to almost anything.* ◇ **Fresh** air is the air you get outside, compared to the air inside a building. ◇ **Fresh** water is water you can drink, because it is not polluted or salty. See also **freshwater**.

❑ If someone looks **fresh**, they do not look at all tired.

fresh-faced people are young and innocent-looking.

freshen (freshening, freshened) If you **freshen** something or **freshen** it **up**, you try to improve it by making it more interesting or attractive. *They freshened the party's image with a new leader and manifesto.* ◇ If a wind **freshens**, it gets stronger.

fresher A **fresher** is a student who has just started at university or college.

freshly is used to say something has been made or done recently. *...the scent of freshly ground coffee.*

freshman (freshmen) A **freshman** is a first-year student at a university or college.

freshwater A **freshwater** river, lake, or pool is one where the water is not salty. **Freshwater** fish and other creatures live in water like this.

fret (fretting, fretted) If you **fret** about something, you worry about it.

fretful people behave in a way which shows they are worried or uncomfortable.

fretwork is thin wood or metal with bits cut out to make a pattern.

Freudian (*pron:* froy-dee-an) is used to talk about the ideas and methods of the psychiatrist Sigmund Freud, especially his ideas about people's hidden fears and sexual feelings.

friar A **friar** is a member of a Catholic religious order. There are a number of orders whose members are called **friars**.

friction (frictional) ❑ You say there is **friction** when one thing rubs against another. You talk about the **frictional** effects of something like this. ◇ In science, **friction** is the force that stops things moving freely when they are touching each other.

❑ **Friction** is also quarrelling and disagreement. *The Macedonian question had long been a source of friction between Yugoslavia and its neighbours.*

fridge A **fridge** is a large metal container for storing food at low temperatures, to keep it fresh. 'Fridge' is short for 'refrigerator'.

friend ❑ A **friend** is someone you like and know well and can talk to about personal things. ◇ If you are **friends** with someone, you like each other and enjoy spending time together. ◇ If you **make friends** with someone, you start a friendship with them.

❑ People who help and support a country are sometimes called its **friends**. *One might have expected all friends of Cambodia to have welcomed these developments.* ◇ **Friends** comes in the names of several organizations which support a cause or institution. *...Friends of the Earth... ...the Friends of Norwich Museum.*

friendless A **friendless** person has no friends.

friendly (friendlier, friendliest; friendliness; friendlies) ❑ **Friendly** people are pleasant, helpful, and kind. *He had been received with friendliness and warmth.* ◇ If you are **friendly** with someone, you like each other and enjoy spending time together.

❑ In wartime, a **friendly** country is one fighting on the same side as your own. Its forces, ships, and seaports can also be called **friendly**. *Some friendly ships have been stopped.* ◇ When people are hit by **friendly fire**, they are hit by bombs or missiles fired from their own side.

❑ A **friendly** fight or argument is not serious. *We have a little friendly competition with New York.* ◇ A **friendly** is a sports match which is not part of a competition.

❑ You use **friendly** to describe a place or object which makes you feel comfortable and safe. *...a small room lit by friendly lamps... ...the friendly clang of the cable cars.*

❑ **-friendly** is often added to words to say something is designed to suit a particular group of people or to fit in with a particular policy. *Edinburgh claims to be Britain's most child-friendly city... ...an environment-friendly weedkiller.*

friendly society A **friendly society** is an organization people regularly pay small amounts of money to; the society then gives them money if they are ill or when they retire. It also gives money to their family if they die.

friendship is the relationship between people who like each other and enjoy spending time together. A friendship is a particular relationship like this. ◇ Friendship is also used to talk about the relationship between countries who help and support each other. ...*a treaty of friendship and co-operation.*

frieze A frieze is a decorative strip or border along an inside or outside wall of a building.

frigate A frigate is a small fast ship used by the navy to protect other ships.

fright is a feeling of fear. If something gives you a fright, it frightens or alarms you. ◇ If someone takes fright at something, they become alarmed and often change their mind about something they were intending to do. *The local council took fright at the use of the word 'rave' and refused a licence.*

frighten (frightening, frightened) If something frightens you, it makes you afraid, nervous, or worried. ◇ If something frightens you off or frightens you away, it makes you decide not to become involved in something, because you are worried about what might happen. ◇ If something frightens you into doing something, it makes you do it because you are worried about what might happen otherwise.

frightened You say people are frightened when they feel fear. If this fear prevents them from doing something, you say they are frightened to do it.

frightening (frighteningly) You say something is frightening when it alarms you or makes you afraid. *Secondhand rifles are frighteningly cheap.*

frightful (frightfully) Frightful is used to describe something very bad or unpleasant. ...*the frightful nature of modern weapons.* ◇ Some people use frightful to express their dislike for something or someone. *He has this frightful lodger.* ◇ Some people use frightfully in front of other words to emphasize them. *I remember being frightfully anxious to get pregnant.*

frigid Women who are not easily sexually aroused are sometimes called frigid. This word can be offensive.

frill (frilly) A frill is a strip of cloth with many folds, attached to something as a decoration. Frilly clothes or other things have many frills.

fringe (fringed) ❑ If someone has a fringe, the front of their hair has been cut so it hangs straight down over their forehead. ◇ A fringe is also a row of hanging threads attached to something as a decoration. Fringed things have a fringe or fringes. ...*a suede fringed jacket.* ◇ If a place is fringed with things, it has them along its edges. ...*a bay of blue water fringed by palm trees.* ◇ The fringes of a place are the parts furthest from its centre.

❑ If someone is on the fringe of something, they are only loosely connected with it. *She hung about on the fringe of the group.* ◇ Fringe is used to talk about the more unusual parts of an activity or organization. ...*fringe theatre...* ...*the radical fringe of the Labour party.*

❑ Fringe benefits are extra things which you get with some jobs, like a house or car.

Frisbee A Frisbee is a very light plastic disc which people throw at each other as a game. 'Frisbee' is a trademark.

frisk If someone frisks you, they search you quickly with their hands, to see if you are hiding something like a weapon. ◇ When animals frisk, they run around in a happy way. You can also say people frisk.

frisky (friskier, friskiest) A frisky horse is restless and difficult to handle.

frisson (*pron:* frees-sonn) If something gives you a frisson, you get a feeling of excitement because of it.

fritter (frittering, frittered) ❑ Fritters are fruit or vegetables dipped in batter and fried.

❑ If you fritter something or fritter it away, you waste it. ...*the country's mistake of frittering away its oil wealth.*

frivolous (frivolously, frivolity) If you say someone is being frivolous, you mean they are being silly and not taking things seriously. *These comments are not meant frivolously.* ◇ If you do something frivolous, you do it for fun, rather than for any practical reason. Behaviour like this is called frivolity.

frizzy hair has stiff wiry curls.

fro If someone or something moves to and fro, they move repeatedly from one place to another. *Couriers run to and fro with messages and documents to be signed.* Behaviour like this is called to-ing and fro-ing.

frock A frock is the same as a dress.

frock coat Frock coats were long coats worn by men in the 19th century.

frog Frogs are small smooth-skinned creatures with long back legs which they use for jumping. Frogs eat insects and usually live near water.

frog-march If you are frog-marched somewhere, you are forced to walk there by two people, each holding one of your arms.

frogman (frogmen) A frogman is a person who works underwater wearing a rubber suit and flippers and using breathing equipment.

frolic (frolicking, frolicked) When animals or people frolic, they enjoy themselves in a lively energetic way. ...*dolphins frolicking with the boats.* When newspapers talk about people frolicking, they are usually talking about sexual behaviour. They also talk about people's frolics. ...*poolside frolics.*

from is used to say where something starts or originates. ...*wisps of smoke from a small fire.* ◇ From is used to say where someone's home or birthplace is. *She came from Ilford.*

❑ From is used to mention a place of departure. *They drove down from Leeds.* ◇ From is used to talk about a route between two places. ...*the main road from Paris to Marseilles.* ◇ From is used to say how far it is between two things or places. *From our back door to their back door was just a few yards.* ◇ From is used to say where someone is when they see or hear something. *From a distance it looks like an obelisk or a pillar.*

❑ From is used when talking about objects which are projecting or hanging, to say where they are fixed or attached. *She has the keys to the house dangling from her apron.*

❑ From is used to talk about removing something. *We went around clearing rubbish from the fields.*

❑ From is used to talk about a reduction in something. *This amount will be deducted from your pension.*

❑ From is used to talk about a change in something. ...*translating from one language to another.*

❑ **From** is used to say when something begins. *She was deaf from birth... We had no rain from March to October.*

❑ **From** is used to mention the cause of something. *My eyes hurt from the wind.* ◇ **From** is used to say why someone thinks or believes something. *I could see from her face that she felt disappointed.*

❑ If someone returns **from** doing something, they return after doing it. *The men had not yet come back from fishing.*

❑ **From** is used to talk about a range of possibilities. *The process takes from two to five weeks... The flowers may be anything from pink to crimson.*

frond The leaves of a fern or palm tree are called **fronds**.

front ❑ The **front** of something is the part which is nearest to you when it is facing you. ◇ The **front** of a house is the main outside wall, usually facing the street. **Front** rooms and **front** windows are on this side of the house. The **front** door is the main door on this side. The **front** garden is between the front of the house and the street.

❑ The **front** page of a newspaper is the outside part where the first words or pictures are. The **front** cover of a book is the outside part at the beginning of the book.

❑ If something is **in front of** you, it is in the direction you are looking when you are facing forward. ◇ If you are **in front of** a building, you are close to its front part.

❑ You say someone is **in front** when they are ahead of other people going the same way. ◇ You also say someone is **in front** when they are winning in a competition.

❑ During a war, the **front** or **front line** is the place where two armies are fighting each other. ◇ You can also say someone is in the **front line** when they are playing an important part in something and may be criticized for what they say or do. *Blake has placed himself in the front line in the argument over medical experiments.*

❑ In weather forecasting, a **front** is a place where a mass of cold air meets a mass of warm air. If the cold air is replacing the warm air, you say there is a **cold front**; if the warm air is replacing the cold air, you say there is a **warm front**.

❑ **Front** is used to talk about an area of activity. You say something is happening on a particular **front**. *On the intellectual front, little advance has been made.*

❑ If someone puts on a **front**, they try to give a particular impression, usually a misleading one. *The Americans and Europeans are anxious to present a solid front.* ◇ If an organization or activity is a **front** for something illegal, it is there to stop people finding out what is going on. ◇ If you say a pop group is **fronted** by someone, you are saying who its lead singer is. If he is a man, you call him the group's **front man**. ◇ A **front man** is also a man who acts as a firm's representative, dealing with other people or firms.

❑ **Front** appears in the names of some political organizations. *...the National Liberation Front.*

front bench (frontbencher) When people talk about the government **front bench** or **front benches**, they mean the leading members of the government in the House of Commons. Similarly, people talk about the opposition **front bench** or **front benches**. Leading politicians on both sides are also called **frontbenchers**.

front runner The **front runner** in a competition or contest is the person most likely to win or succeed.

frontage A **frontage** of a building is a side facing a street.

frontal ❑ A **frontal** or **full-frontal** attack is made directly at the main part of something. *...a frontal attack on the camp.* ◇ **Full-frontal** is also used to describe the front view of a nude person. *...the first full-frontal male nude to appear in a play here.*

❑ In biology, **frontal** is used to talk about things to do with the forehead. *...the frontal cortex.*

frontbencher See front bench.

frontier The border between two countries is sometimes called a **frontier**, especially when the countries have different types of government or are in dispute about something. ◇ The **frontiers** of a branch of knowledge or activity are its normally recognized limits. People sometimes talk about 'extending' or 'pushing back' these frontiers. *...the frontiers of technology... ...extending the frontiers of broadcasting.*

frontispiece The **frontispiece** of a book is a picture at the beginning, opposite the title page.

frost When there is a **frost**, the ground is covered with powdery white ice crystals because the temperature has fallen below freezing.

frostbite (frostbitten) **Frostbite** is a painful condition caused by severe cold. It can damage a person's fingers, toes, nose, or ears. When this happens, you say the affected part is **frostbitten**.

frosted glass has an uneven and slightly rough surface on one side, to stop people seeing through it.

frosty (frostily) If the weather is **frosty**, the temperature has fallen below freezing. ◇ If you call someone's behaviour **frosty**, you mean they are being unfriendly. *The organization has reacted frostily to such moves.*

froth (frothy, frothing) **Froth** is a mass of small bubbles on the surface of a liquid. A **frothy** liquid has bubbles on its surface. A **frothing** liquid has bubbles appearing there. ◇ **Frothy** is also used to describe light-hearted entertainment with nothing serious in it. *...frothy musicals.*

frown When someone **frowns**, they move their eyebrows close together and wrinkle their forehead, because they are worried, annoyed, or deep in thought. You call their expression a **frown**. ◇ If people **frown on** something, they disapprove of it.

froze (frozen) See freeze.

fructose is a kind of sugar which you get in honey and some fruit.

frugal (frugally, frugality) You say people are **frugal** when they are careful how they spend their money, and do not spend much on themselves. When people are like this, you can talk about their **frugality** or say they lead **frugal** lives. *...three years of living frugally.* ◇ A **frugal** meal is small and does not cost much.

fruit (*usual plural:* fruit) ❑ A **fruit** is something you can eat which grows on a tree or bush. A fruit has soft or firm flesh and often contains seeds or a stone.

❑ The **fruit** or **fruits** of someone's work or efforts are the results, especially the good ones. *Mansell is enjoying the fruits of his labour.* ◇ If something you do **bears fruit**, it produces good or useful results.

fruit cake is a type of cake made with dried fruit.

fruit cocktail A **fruit cocktail** is a mixture of pieces of different kinds of fruit, usually eaten as a first course.

fruit fly Fruit flies are small fast-breeding flies which lay their eggs on fruit.

fruit machine A fruit machine is a machine for gambling. You put a coin in a slot, and the machine pays out money if a particular pattern of symbols appears on its screen.

fruit salad is a mixture of pieces of different kinds of fruit in fruit juice, usually eaten as a dessert.

fruitful (fruitfully) Fruitful actions have good or useful results. ...*fruitful discussions*... *They have taken their skills where they can be applied most fruitfully.*

fruition (pron: froo-ish-on) If something you have done or planned **comes to fruition**, things turn out the way you want.

fruitless (fruitlessly) You say something is fruitless when it does not achieve what you want. ...*their fruitless search for the plane*... *We have frequently but fruitlessly drawn attention to the fact that he is still a trustee.*

fruity (fruitiness) Fruity things taste or smell of fruit. *This wine has an appealing fruitiness.*

frustrate (frustrating, frustrated; frustration) ❑ If something frustrates you, it makes you angry or upset, because it stops you doing what you want. You say something like this is **frustrating**. You call your feelings **frustration**. ◇ If you **frustrate** someone's hopes or plans, you stop them being fulfilled.

❑ You use **frustrated** to describe someone who has not succeeded in being what they wanted to be. For example, a frustrated actor is someone who wanted to be an actor, but has never become one.

fry (fries, frying, fried) ❑ When you fry food, you cook it in a pan with hot fat. A **fry-up** is a meal of fried food. ◇ Fries or French fries are chips cut very thin.

❑ **small fry**: see **small**.

frying pan A frying pan is a shallow metal pan with a long handle, for frying food. ◇ If you say someone has got **out of the frying pan into the fire**, you mean they have left a bad situation and got into a worse one.

ft See **foot**.

FTSE Index The FTSE Index or FTSE (pron: foot-sie) is an indicator of share values. It gives the average price of 100 leading shares on the stock market during each day of trading. 'FTSE Index' stands for 'Financial Times Stock Exchange 100 Index'.

fuchsia (pron: fyew-sha) ❑ Fuchsias are a kind of shrub with pink, purple, or white flowers. The flowers hang downwards and their outer petals curve backwards. ❑ Fuchsia is a bright pinky-purple colour.

fuddled If someone is fuddled, they cannot think clearly, often because they have been drinking.

fudge (fudging, fudged) ❑ Fudge is a soft brown sweet made from butter, milk, and sugar. ❑ When people avoid making clear or definite decisions, you can say they are **fudging** things. You can also call their behaviour a **fudge**.

fuel (fuelling, fuelled) (American spelling: fueling, fueled) ❑ Fuel is a substance like wood, coal, or petrol which is burned to give heat or power. ◇ If a machine or vehicle is fuelled by a particular substance, it uses it as a fuel. ❑ If something is fuelled by something else, it gets stronger or more intense because of it. *Hugh's anger was fuelled by resentment.*

fuel injection is a system for introducing liquid fuel under pressure directly into a vehicle's engine without the use of a carburettor.

fuel pump In a car engine, the fuel pump is a device which pumps the petrol from the tank through a narrow pipe to the carburettor.

fugitive A fugitive is someone who has run away or is trying to avoid their enemies.

fugue (pron: fyoog) A fugue is a complex piece of music in several parts. The parts begin at different times, each one starting with the same tune. The tune keeps coming back throughout the piece.

fulcrum The fulcrum of something is its most important part, which everything else depends on. *The Politburo has been replaced by the Presidential Council as the fulcrum of the system.* ◇ In physics, a **fulcrum** is a point where something balances or pivots.

fulfil (fulfils, fulfilling, fulfilled; fulfilment) (American spelling: fulfill, fulfills; fulfillment) ❑ If you fulfil a promise or duty, you do what you have promised to do, or are expected to do. ◇ If you fulfil an ambition, you succeed in doing something you have tried or wanted to do for a long time. ◇ If your expectations or hopes are fulfilled, what you expect or hope for happens.

❑ If someone or something fulfils a role or function, they do whatever is required. ◇ If something you do fulfils you, it makes you happy and satisfied. ...*fulfilling jobs*... *People find fulfilment in working for a common goal.*

full ❑ If something is full or full up, there is no room inside it for anything or anyone else. ◇ You also say a place is full of things or people when there are a lot of them there. *His office was full of policemen.*

❑ If you are affected very strongly by a feeling, you can say you are full of it. *I was full of confidence.*

❑ Full is used to talk about the whole of something. *I paused to allow the full impact of this to strike home.* ◇ When there is a full moon, you can see the whole face of the moon looking like a bright circle.

❑ Full is used to mean 'complete'. ...*my last full day in Warsaw*... *I haven't got his full name.* If something has been done in full, it has been done completely. *The bill has been paid in full.* ◇ If something is used to the full, it is used to the greatest extent possible. Similarly, something can be tested to the full. *How can we be sure we exploit this opportunity to the full?* ◇ If you enjoy something to the full, you get the maximum enjoyment out of it.

❑ If someone leads a full life, they do a lot of different things, and are always busy. ◇ If there is full employment, there is work for everyone who wants to work and is able to.

❑ If you get full marks in a test or exam, you are given the maximum number of marks. You can also say someone gets full marks when they have done something particularly well. *The event got full marks for atmosphere.*

❑ You use full with 'dress' to say someone is wearing all the right clothes for a type of activity or occasion. ...*full evening dress*... *The troops were in full battle dress.*

❑ If you say something has gone full circle, you mean that after many events or changes things are the same as they were at the beginning.

❑ If machinery or equipment is full on or at full capacity, it is working at its greatest power.

❑ See also **fully**, **fullness**.

full back A full back is a defending player in football, rugby or hockey.

full-blooded You use full-blooded in front of another word to emphasize that you are talking about the complete form of the thing described by the word. ...*a full-blooded privatization programme.* ◇ Full-blooded is also used to describe things done with great intensity or enthusiasm. *The performance was admirably full-blooded.*

full-blown You use full-blown in front of another word to emphasize that you are talking about the complete form of the thing described by the word. ...*a full-blown military operation.*

full board If a hotel or guest house provides full board, you can get all your meals there.

full-fledged See fully-fledged.

full-frontal See frontal.

full-grown See fully-grown.

full-length things are the normal length, as distinct from shorter things of the same kind. *'The Birthday Party' was Harold Pinter's first full-length play.* ◇ If someone falls full-length, they fall flat with their arms outstretched.

full-page A full-page advertisement, picture, or article takes up a whole page in a newspaper or magazine.

full-scale You use full-scale in front of another word to say something has all the features of the thing described by the word. ...*a full-scale war.*

full-size (full-sized) Full-size or full-sized things are the normal size, as distinct from smaller things of the same kind. ...*a full-size grand piano.* ◇ A full-size model or replica is the same size as the original.

full stop A full stop is the punctuation mark . used at the end of a sentence.

full-time work or study takes up the whole of a normal working week. ◇ In games like football, full time is the end of the match.

fullness If you say something will happen in the fullness of time, you mean it might take a long time but it will happen eventually.

fully is used to mean 'completely'. For example, if you are fully awake, you are completely awake. ◇ If something is done fully, it is done to the greatest possible extent. ...*a willingness to participate fully in such activities.*
  ❑ Fully is used in front of numbers or measurements for emphasis. For example, if you say it is fully ten miles to the nearest town, you are emphasizing that it really is as far as that.

fully-fledged (*Americans say* full-fledged) You use fully-fledged in front of another word to describe people or things that have developed completely into the thing described by the word. ...*his first film as a fully-fledged producer.*

fully-grown or full-grown animals and plants have reached their natural size and stopped growing.

fulsome (fulsomely) When someone praises something in an exaggerated way, you can call their praise fulsome. *The IMF has, rather fulsomely, praised Vietnam's economic policies.* You can also say that a welcome or apology is fulsome.

fumble (fumbling, fumbled) If you fumble with something, you handle it in a clumsy way. ◇ If you fumble for something you cannot see, you feel for it in a clumsy way. ◇ If you fumble what you are trying to do or say,

you make mistakes and do it badly.

fume (fuming, fumed) ❑ Fumes are smoke, gases, or unpleasant smells given off by chemicals or something burning.
  ❑ If you say someone is fuming, you mean they are very angry.

fun ❑ You use fun to talk about something pleasant and enjoyable. *It's fun working for him... Thousands of people have come down here to join in the fun.* ◇ If you do something for fun or for the fun of it, you do it because you enjoy it, and not for any other reason. ◇ If you say someone is fun, you mean they are interesting or amusing and you enjoy being with them.
  ❑ If you make fun of someone, you tease them or make jokes about them. If you poke fun at them, you make jokes about them in an unkind way.

function (functioning, functioned) ❑ The function of a person or thing is their purpose or role. *The essential function of trade unions is to bargain with employers.* ◇ If something functions as a particular thing, that is what it is used for. *The room had previously functioned as a playroom.* If someone functions as a particular thing, that is their role or job. *Six former ministers are known to be functioning as a government-in-exile.*
  ❑ The way something functions is the way it works. ...*an idea of how the civil service functions.* ◇ If something like a machine is functioning, it is working.
  ❑ If something is a function of something else, its size or form depends on the size or form of the other thing. *The supply of money was a function of the amount of gold discovered.* ◇ In computing, function is used to talk about a sequence of operations performed by a computer when a single key is pressed. ...*the memory function.*
  ❑ A function is also a formal social event like a dinner or dance.

functional (functionally) ❑ Functional things are useful and practical rather than attractive. ◇ When something like a machine or system is functional, it is working and ready to be used. ◇ If you give a functional description of something, you describe how it works.
  ❑ Functionally is used to talk about the ability or usefulness of a thing or person in actual situations. *One in four of the population is functionally illiterate.*

functionary (functionaries) A functionary is an official who does administrative work, especially for a government or political party.

fund ❑ Funds are money available for spending. *The Home Office would be forced to seek extra funds.* ◇ A fund is money being collected for a particular purpose. *He made a generous donation to our campaign fund.* ◇ If a person or organization funds something or provides funding for it, they provide the money for it.
  ❑ If someone has a fund of stories or jokes, they know a lot of them. You can also say someone has a fund of knowledge, information, or experience.

fund-raising (fund-raiser) Fund-raising is raising money for a particular purpose, often by organizing events like street collections. People who obtain money like this are called fund-raisers.

fundamental (fundamentally) ❑ Fundamental is used to describe something which other things are based on. ...*the fundamental cause of the crisis... Our criminal code is* *based fundamentally on fear.*

❏ **Fundamental** and **fundamentally** are used to describe things of the most basic and important kind. For example, you talk about a **fundamental** difference between two things or say they are **fundamentally** different. *The project is fundamentally flawed.* ◇ The **fundamentals** of something are its most basic or important parts. *...the fundamentals of police work.*

fundamentalism (fundamentalist) **Fundamentalism** is the name given to various religious movements in which people adopt what they believe is the original form of a religion, and reject all later forms. **Fundamentalist** is used to describe these people and their beliefs. *...Hindu fundamentalists... ...a fundamentalist preacher.*

funeral A **funeral** is a ceremony for the burial or cremation of a dead person.

funereal (*pron:* fyoo-**neer**-ee-al) You use **funereal** to describe things which remind you of funerals. For example, you talk about a **funereal** silence or say someone is dressed in **funereal** black.

funfair A **funfair** is a place, for example at a holiday resort, where people can ride on machines for fun or try to win prizes in games.

fungal is used to talk about something to do with fungus.

fungi See **fungus**.

fungicide (*pron:* fun-ji-side) is a chemical used to kill fungus or stop it growing.

fungus (*plural:* fungi) **Fungi** are non-green plants like mushrooms and toadstools which have no leaves, flowers, or roots, and grow on living or dead animal or plant matter. ◇ **Fungus** is a soft furry or powdery growth on dead or diseased animals or plants.

funk is a type of music based on jazz and blues. It has a strong repeated bass.

funnel (funnelling, funnelled) (*American spelling:* funneling, funneled) ❏ A **funnel** is a device for pouring substances through small openings. It has a wide open top which narrows to a tube at the bottom. ◇ If people or things are **funnelled** somewhere, they are made to pass through a narrow space. *Visitors are funnelled in to see the painting.* ◇ If money is **funnelled** into a place or organization, it is directed there from several different places.

❏ A **funnel** on a ship or railway engine is an upright cylinder like a chimney, for getting rid of smoke or exhaust gases.

funnily You say **funnily enough** when you are mentioning something which is surprising but true. *I started here about the same time as you, funnily enough.*

funny (funnier, funniest) You say people or things are **funny** when they make you smile or laugh. ◇ You also say something is **funny** when it is strange, surprising, or puzzling. *Shock does funny things to people.*

fur An animal's **fur** is its thick hair. ◇ **Fur** is the fur-covered skins of animals which is used to make clothes and rugs. Some artificial materials are also called **fur**. ◇ A **fur** is a coat or stole made from real or artificial fur.

furious (furiously) If someone is **furious**, they are extremely angry. ◇ **Furious** is also used to say something is done with a lot of energy, speed, or violence. *...a weekend of furious diplomatic activity... Its hard-pressed suppliers are working furiously to cut costs.*

furlong A **furlong** is 220 yards (about 201.2 metres).

Nowadays, this measurement is used only for giving the distance of a horse race.

furnace A **furnace** is an enclosed space for a very hot fire, in which metal is heated for forging or rubbish is burned.

furnish (furnishes, furnishing, furnished) ❏ If you **furnish** a room or house, you put furniture in it. ◇ **Furnished** is used to describe the furniture in a room or house. *...his elegantly furnished house in Wimborne.* ◇ **Furnished** accommodation is let with furniture already in it.

❏ If you **furnish** someone with something, you give it them or make it available to them.

furnishings The **furnishings** in a room are the furniture and fittings.

furniture is objects like tables and chairs.

furore (*pron:* fyoo-**ror**-ee) (*American spelling:* furor) If there is a **furore** about something, people get excited and angry about it.

furrier A **furrier** is a person or firm that makes clothes from fur, or sells clothes made from fur.

furrow A **furrow** is a long groove made in the earth, for planting seeds. ◇ If someone's brow is **furrowed**, they are frowning.

furry A **furry** animal has thick soft hair. ◇ A **furry** object is covered with fur, or something like fur.

further (furthering, furthered; furtherance) ❏ See **far**.

❏ A **further** thing, person, or amount is an additional one. *...the release of further American hostages.*

❏ If you **further** something, you help it make progress or succeed. *Hall helped to further the careers of several future stars... £5,000 is to be spent on the furtherance of the winning project.* ◇ If you go **further** with something or take it **further**, you take it to a more advanced or detailed stage.

❏ You say **further** when you are adding information to what you have just said, or are making an additional point. *Further, commission members were booked to leave Trinidad.*

further education is education after leaving school, at a college rather than a university.

furthermore You say **furthermore** when you are adding information to what you have just said, or are making an additional point. *This is a place to soak up the sun and the silence of the hills. Furthermore, it's only 40 minutes from Bulawayo airport.*

furthest See **far**.

furtive (furtively) If you do something in a **furtive** way, you try not to be noticed doing it. *...a furtive glance... ...a couple sitting holding hands furtively.*

fury If someone is very angry, you can talk about their **fury**. *...an outburst of fury.*

fuse (fusing, fused; fusion) ❏ A **fuse** is a wire which acts as a safety device in an electrical circuit. If an appliance develops a fault, the wire melts, breaking the circuit. When this happens, you say the appliance has **fused**.

❏ A **fuse** is also part of a firework, bomb, or other explosive device which delays the explosion, so people can move to a safe distance. ◇ If you say someone has a **short fuse**, you mean they lose their temper easily.

❏ If objects **fuse** or are **fused**, they are joined together by heat or a biological process. ◇ If people **fuse** things like ideas or methods, they combine them successfully. You can talk about a **fusion** of ideas or methods.

fuse box A fuse box is a box, usually on an inside wall of a building, with fuses in it for all the electrical circuits in the building.

fuselage (*pron:* fyoo-zil-lahzh; *the 'zh' sounds like 's' in 'pleasure'*) The fuselage of a plane is the main part, which the wings and the tail are attached to.

fusillade (*pron:* fyoo-zil-laid) A fusillade of shots is a lot of them fired at the same time.

fusion See fuse, nuclear.

fuss (fusses, fussing, fussed) If you say someone is fussing about something, you mean they are behaving in an unnecessarily anxious way. You call behaviour like this fuss. ◇ If someone fusses over you or makes a fuss of you, they keep showing concern for things like your comfort or health. ◇ If someone makes a fuss or kicks up a fuss, they object strongly to something.

fussy (fussier, fussiest; fussiness) ❏ You say someone is being fussy when they are too concerned with unimportant details. *...bureaucratic fussiness.* ◇ You also say someone is fussy when they are difficult to please.

❏ You can say something like a building is fussy when it is too full of decoration.

fusty (fustier, fustiest) You say people are fusty when they are old-fashioned in their ideas and attitudes. You can also call their ideas fusty. ◇ If something smells fusty, it has an unpleasantly stale smell because it is old or neglected.

futile (futility) You say something is futile when it does not achieve anything. *...the futility of their attempts.*

futon (*pron:* foo-tonn) A futon is a type of padded quilt which can be laid on the floor as a bed, or folded up and used as a sofa.

future ❏ The future is the time which has not yet happened. ◇ Future is used to talk about a time in the future, or about something that will happen in the future. *Let's meet again at some future date... ...the future development of the company.* ◇ Future is also used to talk about things or people that are expected to have a different status in the future. *...Nigeria's future capital... Herr Ruhe sees himself as a future chancellor.* ◇ A person's future is what will happen to them in the rest of their life or career. *I decided that my future lay in medicine.*

❏ You say in future when you are saying what will happen from now on. *The two clubs will play each other in future on a regular basis.*

❏ If you say something has a future, you mean it is likely to be successful.

❏ Futures are goods or shares bought or sold on the stock market at an agreed price and paid for at a later date.

futuristic is used to describe unusual-looking things which seem to belong to some time in the future. *...a futuristic office development.*

fuzzy (fuzzier, fuzziest) A fuzzy picture or sound is blurred or indistinct. ◇ Fuzzy hair sticks up in a soft curly mass.

G g

g See gram.

G-7 The G-7 is a group of seven major industrial countries which has been meeting since 1976 to try to reach agreement on economic matters. The seven countries are Canada, France, Germany, Italy, Japan, Great Britain, and the USA. G-7 stands for 'Group of Seven'.

G-string A G-string is a narrow piece of cloth worn by strippers to cover their genitals.

gab People who have the gift of the gab can speak easily, confidently, and in a persuasive way.

gabardine (*or* gaberdine) is a thick cloth used for making coats.

gabble (gabbling, gabbled) If someone gabbles, they talk so fast it is difficult to make out what they are saying.

gaberdine See gabardine.

gable (gabled) A gable is the pointed top of an outside wall of a building, made by two sloping sides of a roof. ◇ A gabled house has a noticeable gable or gables, especially at the front.

gadfly (gadflies) Gadflies are flies which bite and annoy horses and cattle. ◇ Someone who annoys people by criticizing them publicly can also be called a gadfly.

gadget (gadgetry) A gadget is a small machine or device which does a useful job. When you are talking about several gadgets, you can call them gadgetry.

Gaelic (*pron:* gay-lic *or* gal-lic) is a language spoken in parts of Scotland. A similar language spoken in parts of Ireland is called Irish or Irish Gaelic.

gaff If you blow the gaff, you reveal something which someone had been trying to keep secret.

gaffe If someone commits a gaffe, they cause embarrassment by saying or doing the wrong thing in public.

gag (gagging, gagged) ❏ If someone gags you, they tie a piece of cloth round your mouth to stop you speaking or crying out. The cloth is called a gag. ◇ You say someone is being gagged when someone in authority stops them speaking out about something. Newspapers call an action like this a gag. *Hanoi tightens press gag.*

❏ A gag is also something said or done to make people laugh.

gaggle A gaggle of people is a bunch of them doing something together.

gaiety is liveliness and fun.

gaily Something which is gaily decorated has been decorated in a bright pretty way. ◇ If you do or say something gaily, you do it in a lively happy way. ◇ You also use gaily to say someone does something without being aware how silly or inappropriate it is. *The Commission has been gaily telling everyone what hours to work, how to manage their identity card systems, even in southern France whether or not to shoot woodcock.*

gain (gaining, gained; gainer) ❏ Gain is used to say someone gradually gets something which will benefit them. For example, someone can **gain** experience or confidence. ◇ Gain is also used to say someone gets control of something. *Labour gained control of the council in 1988.* ◇ If you **gain** access to a place, you get into it.

❏ If someone **gains from** something, they get a benefit from it. The person who gets the benefit can be called the **gainer**.

❏ **Gain** is used to say something gets a favourable reaction. For example, something can **gain** approval, support, or popularity.

❏ If you **gain** something like a medal, you are awarded it. ◇ If a sports team **gains** a victory, they win.

❏ If you **gain on** someone, you gradually catch them up. ◇ If a clock or watch **gains**, the hands move round slightly too fast, and it shows the wrong time.

❏ A **gain** in something is an improvement or increase. *...further gains in productivity.* ◇ If you do something for **gain**, you do it to get some profit for yourself.

❏ **gain ground:** see **ground**.

gait Your gait is the way you walk. *...his ambling gait.*

gaiter Gaiters are coverings for a person's lower legs. These days, gaiters are mainly worn by climbers and skiers, for protection.

gala (*usual pron:* gah-la) A **gala** is a public celebration. ◇ Gala is used to talk about events or entertainments put on to celebrate something. *...a gala dinner.*

galactic is used to talk about things connected with a galaxy or galaxies. *...galactic dust.*

galaxy (galaxies) A **galaxy** is a huge group of stars and planets. The group the Earth and solar system belong to is called **the Galaxy**. ◇ You also use **galaxy** to talk about a group of famous people with the same occupation, when they are together in one place. *...a galaxy of sports stars.*

gale A **gale** is a very strong wind. ◇ If people are laughing noisily, you can say there are **gales** of laughter.

gall (*pron:* gawl) (galling) If something **galls** you, it makes you angry or annoyed. You say something like this is **galling**. ◇ If someone does something which is obviously unfair or dishonest, you can say they have the **gall** to do it. *Few institutions would have the gall to charge £15 for a sandwich.*

gall bladder The gall bladder is the organ next to the liver which stores bile.

gallant (gallantly) Gallant is used to describe people who act bravely in a dangerous situation. Soldiers are often called **gallant**, and so are sportsmen and women who do well against more powerful or skilled opponents. *Both sides fought gallantly.*

gallantry is brave behaviour in a dangerous situation. ◇ When a man is very polite and considerate towards a woman, this is also called **gallantry**.

galleon A galleon was a type of three-masted sailing ship, in use from the 15th to the 18th century.

gallery (galleries; galleried) ❏ A **gallery** or **art gallery** is a large building in which there are permanent exhibitions of works of art. The rooms in an art gallery or museum are sometimes called **galleries**. ◇ A place where works of art are sold is sometimes called a **gallery**.

❏ A **gallery** in a room, hall, or church is a raised area like a long balcony at the back or sides. A **galleried** room or hall has an area like this. ◇ The **gallery** in a theatre is an upper floor at the back, where the cheapest seats are. ◇ If you say someone is **playing to the gallery,** you mean they are trying to impress the public, rather than dealing with something seriously.

galley The galley in a ship or plane is the part where food is prepared. ◇ A **galley** kitchen is very small. ◇ Originally, a galley was a ship with sails and many oars, rowed by slaves.

Gallic is used to talk about things to do with French people. *...our Gallic neighbours.*

gallon The volume of an amount of liquid can be expressed in **gallons**. A British gallon is about 4.5 litres, and an American gallon is about 3.79 litres.

gallop (galloping, galloped) ❏ When a horse **gallops**, it moves very fast, so that all its legs are off the ground at the same time. You call this way of moving a **gallop**. You can also say the horse's rider **gallops**. *The first time he got on a horse he could gallop without falling off.* ◇ You also say someone **gallops** when they run somewhere quickly.

❏ **Gallop** is also used to talk about something being dealt with quickly. *Parliament had galloped through the remaining business.* ◇ **Galloping** is used to describe something which is increasing or developing so fast it is difficult to control. *...galloping inflation.*

gallows A gallows was a wooden frame which criminals were hanged from. ◇ **Gallows humour** consists of finding something humorous in grim situations.

gallstone A gallstone is a lump of hard material which can develop in the gall bladder and sometimes causes pain and sickness.

Gallup poll A Gallup poll is a kind of opinion poll.

galore is used to talk about a large number of things. For example, 'carrots galore' means a lot of carrots.

galvanize (galvanizing, galvanized) (*can be spelled with an 's' instead of a 'z'*) If something **galvanizes** you into taking some action, it makes you suddenly go ahead and do it. ◇ **Galvanized** metal has been covered with zinc to protect it from rust.

gambit A **gambit** is something someone says or does to get an advantage. *...a gambit to impress voters before the election.* ◇ A conversational **gambit** is a way of starting a conversation.

gamble (gambling, gambled; gambler) ❏ A **gamble** is something risky someone does in the hope of getting an advantage. When they do this, you say they **gamble**. ◇ If you **gamble** on something happening, you take action as if you expect it to happen, although you cannot be sure it will. *The City gambled on an early cut in base rates.*

❏ If you **gamble**, you bet money in a game, or on the result of a race or competition. Someone who does this a lot is called a **gambler**. The activity is called **gambling**.

gambol (gambolling, gambolled) (*American spelling:* gamboling, gamboled) When lambs **gambol**, they run and jump around. ◇ When people **gambol**, they run or dance around and do silly things.

game (gamey, gamely) ❏ A **game** is a sport or other activity with rules, which people play for enjoyment or to entertain other people. ◇ A **game** is also a match. *Mackay was having a good game.* ◇ In some sports, a **game** is part of a match. In tennis, a **game** is one of the parts of a set.

◇ **Games** are sports played at school. *I was hopeless at games.* ◇ International athletics and equestrian meetings are also called **games**. *...the World Student Games.* ◇ A **game** is also the bits and pieces, usually bought together, which you need for playing a game at home.

❏ If you **beat someone at their own game**, you use their own methods to gain an advantage over them. ◇ If you say **the game is up**, you mean someone's secret plans or activities have been discovered. ◇ **give the game away**: see **give away**. ◇ **the name of the game**: see **name**.

❏ **Game** is wild animals or birds hunted for sport or food. **Game birds** are birds hunted in this way. If something smells or tastes **gamey**, it reminds you of game which has been hung. See also **big game**. ◇ In Africa, a **game reserve** is an area where wild animals are given limited protection, so they can later be caught or shot. A **game warden** is someone whose job is to look after them. See also **game park**. ◇ **fair game**: see **fair**.

❏ If you say someone is **game**, you mean they are willing to try something new, unusual, or risky. ◇ If you say someone does something **gamely**, you mean they keep doing it in spite of difficulties or hardship.

game park In Africa, a **game park** is a large area of public land where wild animals are officially protected.

game show A **game show** is a TV show in which people play a specially devised game.

gamekeeper (gamekeeping) A **gamekeeper** is a person employed to look after the game on someone's land. What he or she does is called **gamekeeping**.

gamesmanship consists of defeating your opponent in a game by using unfair methods which are not actually against the rules.

gamey See **game**.

gamine (*pron:* gam-een) is used to describe a woman or girl whose looks or behaviour are attractive in a boyish way.

gaming is the same as gambling.

gamma is Γ or γ, the third letter of the Greek alphabet.
❏ **Gamma rays** are a form of electromagnetic radiation. They are similar to X-rays, but have a shorter wavelength.

gammon is smoked or salted meat from a pig.

gammy A **gammy** leg is crippled or injured.

gamut (*pron:* gam-ut) You use **gamut** to emphasize that you are talking about the entire range of something. *The Kilroy programme has run the full gamut of problems from baby-battering to compulsive sandwich-eating.*

gander A **gander** is a male goose.

gang ❏ A **gang** is (a) a group of criminals who work together. (b) a group of people who go around together and cause trouble or commit violent acts. *...a gang of soccer hooligans.* ◇ When rival gangs keep fighting each other, you say there is a **gang war** or **gang warfare**.

❏ A **gang** of workmen is a group who work together.

❏ If people **gang up** on you, they get together to prevent you succeeding in something.

gangland is used to talk about organized crime and the people involved in it. *...a gangland boss.*

ganglia See **ganglion**.

gangling (*or* gangly) is used to describe someone, especially a young person, who is tall, thin, and clumsy.

ganglion (*plural:* ganglia) A **ganglion** is (a) a group of nerve cells. (b) a small harmless tumour.

gangly See **gangling**.

gangplank A **gangplank** is a short bridge or platform between a ship and the quay, for people to get on and off.

gangrene (gangrenous) **Gangrene** is decay in a part of a person's body, caused by not enough blood getting there. You say the affected part is **gangrenous** (*pron:* gan-grin-uss).

gangster A **gangster** is a member of a violent criminal gang.

gangway A **gangway** is (a) a passage left between two rows of seats, for people to get through. (b) a narrow bridge or platform, for people to walk along.

ganja is a form of cannabis which people smoke.

gannet **Gannets** are large white seabirds. They nest in colonies on cliffs. ◇ If you call someone a **gannet**, you mean they are greedy and always eating.

gantry (gantries) A **gantry** is a high metal structure supporting something like a crane or a set of road signs or railway signals.

gaol (gaoler) See **jail**.

gap ❏ A **gap** is a space between two things, or a hole through something. ◇ A **gap** is also a period of time when something is not happening. *After a gap of two years, she went back to college.*

❏ If someone or something leaves a **gap** when they go or cease to exist, it is not easy to replace them. ◇ If a new person or thing fills a **gap**, they are what is needed to make something satisfactory or complete.

❏ A **gap** is a great difference between two things, ideas, or groups. *The gap between rich and poor nations is widening.* ◇ **credibility gap**: see **credible**. ◇ **generation gap**: see **generation**.

gape (gaping, gaped) If you **gape** at someone or something, you look at them with an amazed expression. ◇ **Gaping** is used to emphasize how wide a hole or opening is. *...a gaping wound.*

garage A **garage** is (a) a building you keep a car in. (b) a place where you get your car repaired, buy a car, or buy petrol.

garb (garbed) Someone's **garb** is the clothes they are wearing. You can say someone is **garbed** in particular clothes.

garbage is rubbish. In the US, you put rubbish, especially kitchen waste, in a **garbage can**; it is taken away in a **garbage truck**. ◇ If you call what someone says **garbage**, you mean it is nonsense. ◇ You can also call very poor quality entertainment **garbage**.

garbled If something written or spoken is **garbled**, the details are confused or wrong.

garda The **Garda** is the Irish police force. A member of the force is called a **garda** (*plural:* gardai).

garden (gardening, gardened) A **garden** is an area next to a house, with a lawn and plants. If someone is attending to the plants, you say they are **gardening**. ◇ Large parks with plants and trees are sometimes called **gardens**.

garden centre A **garden centre** is a place where you buy plants and other things for a garden.

garden city A **garden city** is a planned town with a lot of open spaces, trees, and grass.

garden party A **garden party** is a formal party held in a large private garden, usually in the afternoon.

gardener A gardener is someone whose job is to look after a garden or gardens. ◇ If you say someone is a keen gardener, you mean they enjoy looking after their own garden.

gardenia (*pron*: gar-deen-ya) Gardenias are large white or yellow flowers with a pleasant smell. The bush they grow on is also called a gardenia.

gargantuan (*pron*: gar-gan-tyoo-an) is used to talk about people eating very large amounts of food. *...his gargantuan appetites.* ◇ Gargantuan is also used to talk about other things which are extremely large. *...a gargantuan 405 ft long swimming pool.*

gargle (gargling, gargled) When you gargle, you wash your throat by filling your mouth with liquid, tilting your head back, and making a bubbling noise.

gargoyle A gargoyle is a stone carving of an ugly creature on the outside of an old building. Water drains through it from the roof of the building.

garish (*pron*: gair-ish) (garishly) You say something is garish when its colours are very bright and stand out in an unpleasant way. You can also say the colours are garish. *They gazed across the garishly lit no man's land.*

garland (garlanded) A garland is a circle of flowers and leaves, worn round someone's neck or head. When someone is wearing a garland, you can say that they are garlanded.

garlic (garlicky) Garlic is the small white bulb of an onion-like plant. It is used to flavour food, and has a strong smell and taste. You use garlicky to describe something flavoured with garlic.

garment A garment is a piece of clothing.

garner (garnering, garnered) If you garner something you need, you succeed in getting it. You say, for example, that a politician garners support or votes.

garnet A garnet is a hard shiny stone used in jewellery. It is usually red.

garnish (garnishes, garnishing, garnished) If food is garnished, it is decorated with small amounts of a different food. You call these small amounts garnish or a garnish.

garotte See garrotte.

garret A garret is a very small room at the top of a house.

garrison (garrisoned) A garrison is a group of soldiers stationed in a town or building, to guard it. You say the town or building is garrisoned by the soldiers, or they are garrisoned there.

garrotte (*pron*: ga-rot) (garrotting, garrotted) (*can be spelled with one 'r'*) If someone is garrotted, a piece of wire or a metal collar is used to strangle them or break their neck. The wire or collar is called a garrotte.

garrulous A garrulous person is very talkative.

garter A garter is a piece of material worn round the top of a stocking or sock, to stop it slipping down. ◇ Garter is the American word for a suspender.

gas (*plural*: gases) (gasses, gassing, gassed) ❑ Gas is the inflammable air-like substance used for cooking and heating. In Britain, the gas most commonly used is called natural gas and consists mainly of methane. ◇ Gas fires and cookers use gas as fuel. ◇ A gas is any air-like substance, for example oxygen or hydrogen. ◇ When a person or animal is gassed, they are killed by poisonous gas.

❑ Gas is also the usual American word for petrol.

gas chamber A gas chamber is a room designed to be filled with poisonous gas, to kill people or animals.

gas field A gas field is an area of land or part of the seabed from which natural gas is taken.

gas-fired power or heating uses gas as its fuel.

gas lamp A gas lamp produces light by burning gas. Street lighting used to be by gas lamps, and people used to have them in their homes.

gas-lit See gaslight.

gas mask A gas mask is a device you wear over your face to avoid breathing in poisonous gas.

gas meter A gas meter is a device which measures and records the amount of gas going through it.

gas rig A gas rig is a structure on land or sea used as a base for obtaining natural gas.

gas ring A gas ring is a circular device, for example on a cooker, which gives out jets of gas.

gas station Americans call a petrol station a gas station.

gaseous (*pron*: gas-yus *or* gay-shus) is used to talk about things which contain or consist of a gas. *...gaseous material.*

gash (gashes, gashing, gashed) A gash is a long deep cut. If you gash a part of your body, you get a gash there.

gasket A gasket is a flat piece of material placed between two joined surfaces in a pipe or engine, to stop gas or liquid escaping. ◇ If someone blows a gasket, they break out in a violent temper.

gaslight (gas-lit) Gaslight is the light given off by gas lamps. When a room or street is lit this way, you say it is gas-lit.

gasoline (*or* gasolene) is an American word for petrol. See also gas.

gasometer (*pron*: gas-som-it-er) A gasometer is a very large metal cylinder used for storing gas before it is piped to people's homes.

gasp If you gasp, you take in breath quickly, because you are surprised or in pain. You call this intake of breath a gasp. ◇ Last gasp is used to describe things done at the last possible moment. *Their 12 men beat Widnes with a last gasp try from Ward.*

gassy A gassy drink has a lot of bubbles in it.

gastric is used to talk about things to do with the stomach. *...a gastric complaint.*

gastritis is an illness in which the stomach becomes inflamed.

gastroenteritis is an illness in which the stomach and intestines become swollen and painful, causing diarrhoea and sickness.

gastroenterology (gastroenterologist) Gastroenterology is the study of diseases of the stomach and intestines. A gastroenterologist is a specialist in this field.

gastronome See gastronomy.

gastronomic (gastronomical) Gastronomic and gastronomical are used to talk about things connected with good food. *...the gastronomic centre of the region.*

gastronomy (gastronome) Gastronomy (*pron*: gas-tron-o-my) is the preparation and enjoyment of good food. A gastronome (*pron*: gas-tron-ome) is someone who enjoys good food.

gasworks (*plural*: gasworks) A gasworks is a place where gas, especially coal gas, is made.

gate (gated) ❏ A **gate** is a door-like structure at the entrance to an area of land. ◇ A **gated** road has a gate or gates across it. ◇ At an airport, a **gate** is one of the exits you go through to get to your plane.

❏ The **gate** at a sporting event is the total number of spectators. *Their average gate is 23,000 this season.* The **gate money** is the total amount the spectators pay to watch.

❏ When there is a scandal involving politicians or royalty, people sometimes invent a new word to talk about it. The word is formed by adding -**gate** to the name of a place or person. *...Irangate.*

gate-crash (gate-crasher) See **gatecrash**.

gateau (*pron:* gat-toe) (*plural:* gateaux) A **gateau** is a rich cake, usually with cream in it.

gatecrash (gatecrashes, gatecrashing, gatecrashed; gatecrasher) (*or* gate-crash, *etc*) If you **gatecrash** a party, you go without being invited. You call someone who does this a **gatecrasher**.

gated See **gate**.

gatehouse A **gatehouse** is a building next to a large entrance gate, where someone like a porter lives.

gatepost A **gatepost** is one of the posts on either side of a gate.

gateway A **gateway** is an entrance with a gate. ◇ A place is called the **gateway** to a country or region when people often enter the country or region there. ◇ If someone or something helps you get something you want or need, you can say they are a **gateway** to it. *He views Saturday's FA Cup third round as a gateway to better things.*

gather (gathering, gathered; gatherer) ❏ If people **gather** somewhere, they arrive from different places. You can also say someone **gathers** people together. *When he left, he gathered the staff around to say goodbye.* ◇ A **gathering** is a group of people meeting for a special purpose.

❏ If you **gather** objects, you collect them, or bring them together in one place. ◇ If you **gather** information, you collect it. *...an IRA intelligence gatherer.*

❏ You use **gather** to talk about an increase in something. For example, if something **gathers** speed, it gets faster. *The reform movement gathered strength.* ◇ You use **gathering** to describe a bad situation which is getting worse. *...the gathering crisis.* ◇ When clouds **gather**, they appear in increasing numbers, and there is likely to be a storm. ◇ When darkness or dusk **gathers**, it gets darker.

❏ If you say something is **gathering dust**, you mean it is not being used.

❏ You use **gather** to say someone gets to hear a bit of information. *I gather Lee is now keeping quiet about his research plans.*

❏ If you **gather** material, you make small folds or pleats in it by sewing a thread through it and pulling the thread tight.

GATT (*often pron:* gat) is an international treaty signed in 1947 to promote trade. GATT stands for 'General Agreement on Tariffs and Trade'.

gauche (*pron:* gohsh) people are awkward or uncomfortable in company.

gaucho (*pron:* gow-choh) (gauchos) A **gaucho** is a South American cowboy.

gaudy (gaudily) If you call something **gaudy**, you mean it is brightly coloured and rather vulgar. *The package was*

tatty, cheap and gaudily ribboned.

gauge (*pron:* gayj) (gauging, gauged) If you **gauge** something, you work out what it is, using tests, instruments, or your own judgement. *...tests to gauge a child's abilities... The long term damage is hard to gauge.* ◇ A **gauge** is a device which shows the amount of something. *...a fuel gauge.* ◇ A **gauge** is also something like a set of statistics which people use to judge whether something is succeeding. *...waiting lists, the most politically sensitive gauge of NHS performance.* ◇ The **gauge** of a railway is the distance between the rails.

gaunt A **gaunt** person looks thin and unhealthy. ◇ **Gaunt** buildings look bare and unattractive.

gauntlet **Gauntlets** are long thick protective gloves. ◇ If someone **throws down the gauntlet,** they do something which is seen as a challenge. ◇ If someone **picks up the gauntlet,** they show they are prepared to fight, compete, or argue with someone. ◇ If you **run the gauntlet,** you risk physical or verbal attack by going somewhere or doing something.

gauze is (a) light soft cloth with tiny holes in it. (b) fine wire mesh.

gave See **give**.

gavel (*pron:* gav-el) A **gavel** is small hammer which the chairman of a meeting bangs on the table to get attention.

gawky A **gawky** person stands and moves awkwardly and clumsily.

gawp If people **gawp** at something, they stare at it in a rather stupid way.

gay (gayness) ❏ If someone is **gay** or a **gay**, they are homosexual. You can talk about a person's **gayness**. ◇ Attempts to improve the rights of homosexuals are called **gay action**. People involved in these attempts are called **gay activists**.

❏ In the past, **gay** was used to describe things which looked or sounded bright and cheerful.

gaze (gazing, gazed) If you **gaze** at something, you look at it for a long time. When someone does this, you can talk about their **gaze**. ◇ If you do something under someone's **gaze**, they watch you while you do it.

gazebo (*pron:* gaz-zee-boh) (gazebos) A **gazebo** is a small open-sided building, put up so people can enjoy the view from it.

gazelle **Gazelles** are a kind of small antelope.

gazette (gazetting, gazetted) **Gazette** appears in the names of many newspapers and journals. *...Antiques Trade Gazette.* ◇ A **gazette** is an official journal in which honours and public appointments are announced. When an honour or appointment is **gazetted,** it appears in a journal like this.

gazetteer A **gazetteer** is a book or part of a book which lists and describes places.

gazump If you are **gazumped,** someone agrees to sell you their house, then sells it to someone else who offers a higher price.

GBH See **grievous bodily harm**.

GCE **GCE** 'A' level exams are usually taken by young people in England, Wales, and Northern Ireland at the age of 17 or 18. GCE 'O' level exams for 15- and 16-year-olds were replaced by GCSEs in 1988. GCE stands for 'General Certificate of Education'.

GCSE exams are usually taken by English, Welsh, and Northern Irish school students at the age of 15 or 16. GCSE stands for 'General Certificate of Secondary Education'.

gear (gearing, geared) ❑ The **gear** or **gears** on a machine or vehicle are a device for changing the rate at which energy is converted to motion. When this rate is at a particular level, you say the machine or vehicle is in a particular **gear**. *The first corner is taken flat out in top gear.* ◇ **Gear** is also used to describe the level of effort someone puts into something. *Stich is moving into top gear a month before he defends his Wimbledon title.*

❑ The **gear** for an activity is the clothes or equipment needed for it. *...the latest American sports gear.*

❑ If something is **geared** to a type of person, it has been designed or organized specially for them. You can also say something is **geared** for a particular purpose. *...developments geared to the foreign investor.* ◇ If someone **gears up** for something, they get ready to deal with it. When they are **geared up,** they are ready.

gear box See gearbox.

gear lever The **gear lever** in a vehicle is the lever you use to change gear.

gearbox (*or* gear box) The **gearbox** is the system of gears in an engine or vehicle.

gearshift is the American word for a gear lever.

gecko (geckos) **Geckos** are small insect-eating lizards, famous for being able to walk on smooth vertical or overhanging surfaces.

geese See goose.

Geiger counter (*pron:* guy-ger) A **Geiger counter** is a device for detecting and measuring radioactivity.

geisha (*pron:* gay-sha) A **geisha** or **geisha girl** is a Japanese woman specially trained in music, dancing, and the art of conversation, whose job is to entertain men.

gel (*pron:* jell) (gelling, gelled) ❑ A **gel** is a smooth soft jelly-like substance. Some people use a type of gel to keep their hair in a particular style.

❑ If things **gel,** they go together in a satisfactory way. ◇ You say people **gel** when they do something well and efficiently together. *London Monarchs have yet to gel as a team this season.*

gelatine (*pron:* jel-at-teen) (*or* gelatin) (*pron:* jel-at-tin) is a clear tasteless substance, usually in the form of a powder. It is used, especially in cooking, to make liquids set, for example when making jellies.

gelatinous (*pron:* jel-at-in-uss) **Gelatinous** substances have the consistency of jelly.

geld If a male animal is **gelded,** it is castrated.

gelding A **gelding** is a male horse which has been castrated to make it easier to control.

gelignite is a type of dynamite.

gem **Gems** are jewels. ◇ If you call something a **gem,** you mean it is especially pleasing or good. *The castle's undoubted gem is a tiny 12th century chapel.*

gemstone A **gemstone** is a precious stone which can be cut and polished to make a jewel.

gendarme (*pron:* zharn-darm; *the 'zh' sounds like 's' in 'pleasure'*) (gendarmerie) A **gendarme** is a member of a military-type police force in France and some other countries. The members of a force like this can be called the **gendarmerie** (*pron:* zharn-darm-er-ee).

gender If you talk about a person's **gender,** you are talking about the fact that they are male or female.

gene (*pron:* jean) **Genes** are parts of a cell, each gene consisting of DNA in a fixed pattern. Genes are inherited, and determine a living thing's physical characteristics, growth, and development. ◇ When a group of living things breed among themselves, the total set of genes they share is called a **gene pool.**

genealogy (genealogies; genealogical, genealogist) **Genealogy** (*pron:* jean-ee-al-a-gee) is the study of the history of families. **Genealogical** (*pron:* jean-ee-a-lodge-i-cal) is used to talk about things connected with this study. *...genealogical history.* A **genealogist** (*pron:* jean-ee-al-a-jist) is an expert at genealogy. ◇ A person's **genealogy** is the history of their family.

genera See genus.

general (generally) ❑ **General** is used to talk about something as a whole, ignoring any parts which are different. *His account was generally accurate.* ◇ **General** is also used to talk about people as a whole, or most of the people in a group. *There was a general movement to leave the table... When will this material become generally available?*

❑ **General** is used to talk about something like a statement or rule which applies to most situations. *Generally speaking, there are union instructions about such situations.* ◇ People say **in general** when they are making a statement which sums up a situation, without being true about all aspects of it. *In general, the policies we are putting to the conference will receive overwhelming agreement.* ◇ **In general** is also used to talk about the whole of something, as distinct from one part of it. *Neither Italy in general nor Cervinia in particular is cheap.*

❑ **General** is used to talk about something which covers a wide range of things. *...a general grocery store.* ◇ **General** is also used to describe people who do a variety of jobs. *...unskilled general labourers.*

❑ A **general** is a high-ranking officer in the British army and in some other armed forces. The rank below general is **lieutenant general,** followed by **major general.**

general anaesthetic A **general anaesthetic** is one which affects the whole of your body, and makes you unconscious. See also local anaesthetic.

general election A **general election** is one to elect a new parliament, in which every parliamentary seat is contested.

general hospital A **general hospital** treats injuries and all common illnesses, and takes in male and female patients of all ages.

general practice (general practitioner) **General practice** is the work of a non-specialist doctor who treats people at a local surgery or in their own homes. A doctor who does this is called a **general practitioner** or **GP.** The organization he or she runs, usually with other doctors, is called a **general practice.**

general public The **general public** consists of people in general, rather than experts or specialists.

general-purpose things have a wide range of uses, rather than one particular use.

general staff A country's **general staff** are a group of senior military officers who advise about the planning and execution of military operations.

general strike When there is a **general strike,** a large part of a country's workforce go on strike together.

generalise (generalisation) See **generalize**.

generalist A generalist is someone with a wide range of skills or knowledge.

generality (generalities) Generalities are statements which are so general they do not tell you anything interesting or useful. ◇ The generality of something is most of it.

generalize (generalizing, generalized; generalization) *(can be spelled with an 's' instead of a 'z')* ❑ If you generalize or make a generalization, you say something which is true in most cases.

    ❑ Generalized is used to talk about something involving a wide range of people or things. *...generalized research.*

generally See **general**.

generate (generating, generated; generation) ❑ If something generates a feeling or kind of behaviour, people react to it in that way. *...the confidence that has been generated by winning.* ◇ If something generates money, it earns it. *...the generation of wealth.* ◇ If something generates jobs, it causes them to be created.

    ❑ When heat, electricity, or some other form of energy is generated, it is produced.

generation (generational) ❑ You use generation to talk about the people in a country or group who were born about the same time. *Few actresses of her generation could play the part well.* ◇ Generational, cross-generational, and inter-generational are used to talk about relations between older and younger people. *...inter-generational squabbles.* ◇ When people talk about the generation gap, they mean the differences in attitudes and behaviour between older and younger people.

    ❑ When a new stage is reached in the development of a type of product, people talk about a new generation of products of that kind. *...a new generation of microprocessors.*

    ❑ A generation is also an approximate period of time, roughly the time it takes for a child to grow up and have children of its own.

    ❑ See also **generate**.

generator A generator is a device used for producing electricity.

generic *(pron:* jin-ner-ik) (generically) Generic is used to say something has the typical features of a particular kind of thing. *The music is generic heavy metal... ...a generically 1930's style.* ◇ A generic word is used to talk about a group of similar things. *Computers have become as much a generic term for pc's as Hoovers are for vacuum cleaners.* ◇ A generic drug is sold under a name which is not a trademark.

generous (generously, generosity) You say people are generous when they give more money, or more of something else, than is usual or expected. You can also call their gift generous. *He gave generously to charity.* When people behave like this, you talk about their generosity. ◇ You also say people are generous when they are helpful and obliging, or willing to see good qualities in other people or things. ◇ A generous amount of something is rather a lot of it. *...a generous portion of fish.*

genesis If you talk about the genesis of something, you are talking about what started it or brought it into existence. *It is difficult to pinpoint the genesis of any idea.*

genetic *(pron:* jin-net-tik) (genetically; genetics, geneticist)

Genetic and genetically are used to talk about something to do with genes. *...genetic tests... Thousands of illnesses are genetically determined.* ◇ Genetics is the study of how characteristics are passed on by genes. A geneticist *(pron:* jin-net-tiss-ist) is an expert on this.

genetic code A living thing's genetic code is its own particular arrangement of genes, which determines how it will develop.

genetic engineering (genetic engineer) Genetic engineering consists of changing the genetic structure of a living thing, to correct something which is wrong or to make the thing develop in a different way. People who do this are called genetic engineers.

genetic fingerprinting (genetic fingerprint) Genetic fingerprinting is a way of identifying someone by the DNA molecules in their blood, saliva, hair, or skin tissue. Everyone has their own particular genetic fingerprint.

genial *(pron:* jean-ee-al) (genially, geniality) Genial people are good-humoured and friendly. *He began to smile genially... An appearance of geniality is most important.*

genie *(pron:* jean-ee) In fairy stories, a genie is a magical being which obeys the orders of the person who has control over it.

genitals (genitalia, genital) A person's or animal's genitals or genitalia are their external sexual organs. Genital is used to talk about things relating to the genitals. *...genital diseases.*

genius (geniuses) A genius is an exceptionally intelligent, creative, or talented person. You call their talents or abilities genius. ◇ If someone has a genius for something, they are unusually good at it.

genocide *(pron:* jen-no-side) (genocidal) Genocide is the murder of a whole community or race. Genocidal is used to describe people or things involved in something like this. *...the genocidal SS guard known to everyone as Ivan the Terrible.*

genre *(pron:* zhahn-ra; *the 'zh' sounds like 's' in 'pleasure')* A genre is a type of literature, art, music, or film.

gent (gents) A gent is a gentleman. ◇ A gents is a men's public toilet.

genteel people are quiet, respectable, and refined. Their way of life and the places they live in can also be called genteel.

gentian *(pron:* jen-shun) Gentians are small plants with trumpet-shaped flowers which are usually blue. Gentians grow mainly in mountainous areas.

Gentile Non-Jewish people are sometimes referred to as Gentiles.

gentility is (a) the social status and way of life of upper-class people. *...an atmosphere of faded gentility.* (b) well-mannered behaviour associated with some members of the upper class. *...the soft gentility of her manner.*

gentle (gentler, gentlest; gently, gentleness) ❑ Gentle people are mild, sensitive, and kind. You can call someone's behaviour, voice, or expression gentle. *There is a strain of gentleness running through everything he does.* ◇ Gentle is used to describe tactful ways of getting someone to do something. *...a gentle hint.*

    ❑ A gentle action is done carefully and not forcefully, so as not to harm something. *I gently lifted it off the ground.* ◇ Gentle is used to describe activities which are not strenuous or difficult. ...*a gentle stroll.* ◇ If you cook something over a **gentle** heat or cook it **gently**, you cook it with the electricity or gas turned very low.

❏ You can call small movements of air or water **gentle**. ...*gentle air currents.* ◇ **Gentle** scenery has soft shapes and colours which are pleasant and relaxing.

gentlefolk is an old-fashioned word for upper-class people.

gentleman (gentlemen; gentlemanly) **Gentleman** is a polite word for a man. ◇ A **gentleman** is an upper-class man. ◇ If you say a man is a **gentleman**, you mean he is polite and considerate in a way associated with some British upper-class men. You can call his behaviour **gentlemanly**. ◇ A **gentleman's agreement** is an unwritten one in which it is accepted that someone will do what they have promised to do.

gentleness See gentle.

gentlewoman (gentlewomen) A **gentlewoman** is an upper-class woman.

gently See gentle.

gentrify (gentrifies, gentrifying, gentrified; gentrification) When a street or area is **gentrified**, houses previously occupied by poor people are taken over by well-off people and become much more expensive as a result. This process is called **gentrification**.

gentry Upper-class people just below the level of the aristocracy used to be called the **gentry.**

genuflect (genuflection) In church, when people **genuflect**, they bend one or both knees, to show respect. An action like this is called a **genuflection.**

genuine (genuinely, genuineness) You use **genuine** and **genuinely** to describe things which are what they appear to be, and are not fakes or imitations. ...*genuine visas...* ...*genuinely democratic countries.* ◇ You say feelings or beliefs are **genuine** when they are real and not put on to impress or deceive people. You can also talk about a **genuine** offer or a **genuine** attempt to do something. *We genuinely want to raise standards... The board accepted the genuineness of his desire to live independently.* ◇ If you say someone is **genuine**, you mean they are honest, truthful, and sincere.

genus (*pron:* jean-uss) (*plural:* genera) (*pron:* jen-er-a) A **genus** is a group of animals or plants. A **genus** consists of one or more species.

geography (geographer; geographical, geographic, geographically) ❏ **Geography** is the study of different countries and the natural features of the earth's surface. A **geographer** is an expert on this. **Geographical** and **geographic** are used to talk about things to do with geography. ...*the Royal Geographical Society.*

❏ The **geography** of a place is the location of its physical and man-made features. **Geographical, geographic,** and **geographically** are used to talk about things connected with the geography of a place. *Ethiopia is geographically suited to training long-distance athletes.* ◇ **Geographical** and **geographic** are also used to talk about the position of a place in relation to other places. ...*the country's geographical remoteness.*

geology (geologist; geological) **Geology** is the study of the Earth's structure, surface, and origins. A **geologist** is an expert on this. **Geological** is used to talk about things to do with geology. ...*geological data.*

geometry (geometric, geometrical; geometrics) **Geometry** is the branch of maths dealing with lines, angles, curves, and shapes. **Geometric** and **geometrical** are used to talk about things to do with geometry. ...*geometric principles.* ◇ **Geometric** or **geometrical** designs are made up of regular shapes and lines, often with sharp angles. These shapes and lines are sometimes called **geometrics.**

geophysics (geophysicist; geophysical) **Geophysics** is the branch of geology which uses physics to examine the Earth's structure, climate, and oceans. A **geophysicist** is an expert on geophysics. **Geophysical** is used to talk about things to do with geophysics.

geopolitics (geopolitical) **Geopolitics** is the study of politics on a worldwide scale, especially as it affects the relations between countries. **Geopolitical** is used to talk about things to do with international relations on a worldwide scale. ...*decisions of geopolitical importance.*

Geordie A **Geordie** is someone from Tyneside. ◇ **Geordie** is a Tyneside dialect.

George Cross The **George Cross** is a medal awarded for acts of great heroism and courage in circumstances of extreme danger. It was first awarded by George VI in 1940 and was intended primarily for civilians. 'George Cross' is shortened to 'GC' after a person's name.

Georgian is used to talk about 18th century Britain, its architecture, and other things which were in fashion then.

geranium **Geraniums** are plants with small red, pink, or white flowers, often grown indoors or as summer bedding plants. They are also called 'pelargoniums'.

gerbil **Gerbils** are small furry rodents, often kept as pets.

geriatric is used to talk about things to do with very old people and their illnesses. ...*geriatric medicine.*

germ ❏ **Germs** are very small organisms which cause disease. ◇ **Germ warfare** is the deliberate spreading of harmful germs to cause disease among enemy troops or destroy their food supply.

❏ If the **germ** of an idea comes to you, you think of something which may later develop into something important. ◇ The **germ** of a poem or book is the idea or experience it grew from.

German is used to talk about people and things in or from Germany. ...*German newspapers.* ◇ A **German** is someone who comes from Germany. ◇ **German** is the main language spoken in Germany and Austria. It is also spoken in Switzerland and in parts of some other countries.

German measles is a disease similar to measles which gives you a cough, a sore throat, and spots. Its medical name is **rubella.**

German shepherd dog A **German shepherd dog** is the same as an alsatian.

germane (*pron:* ger-mane) If something is **germane** to what is being done or considered, it is relevant or important to it.

Germanic was a northern European language from which many modern languages including English and German were derived. **Germanic** is used to talk about the people who spoke this language and about their culture. ...*Germanic migrations in the fourth to seventh centuries.*

germinate (germinating, germinated; germination) When seeds **germinate**, they start to grow. If you **germinate**

them, you get them to grow, for example by planting them in the right conditions. *Germination takes place over a wide temperature range.* ◇ If an idea **germinates,** it starts to grow in someone's mind.

gerontology is the study of the ageing process and problems faced by old people.

gerrymander (gerrymandering, gerrymandered) **Gerrymandering** is the changing of political boundaries, to give an unfair advantage to one party in an election. When this happens, you talk about a place or system being **gerrymandered.**

gestation is the development of a baby inside its mother's body. ◇ **Gestation** is also used to talk about the slow development of something like an idea or plan. *These ideas, eight years in gestation, are strong enough to stand the test of public debate.*

gesticulate (gesticulating, gesticulated; gesticulation) If you **gesticulate,** you make movements with your hands and arms, often while you are talking, to try to express or explain something. Movements like these are called **gesticulations.**

gesture (gesturing, gestured) ❏ If you describe something someone does as a **gesture,** you mean it is done mainly to impress or please people.

❏ If someone makes a **gesture,** they use their fingers, hands, or head to show their feelings about something. *He spread his hands in a gesture of despair.* ◇ If you **gesture** towards something, you draw someone's attention to it by pointing or nodding towards it. ◇ If you **gesture** to someone to do something, you tell them to do it by moving your hands or head, rather than speaking.

get (getting, got) ❏ If you **get** something, you obtain or receive it. If you **get** something for someone else, you obtain it for them. *Get advice from your local health department... He was with us when we got the news... He got her a job with the telephone company.* ◇ If you **get at** something, you manage to reach or obtain it. *...a determination to get at the facts.* ◇ If you **get** an idea or feeling, you have it or experience it. ◇ If you **get** an illness or disease, you become ill.

❏ If you **get** a train or bus, you catch it.

❏ **Get** is used to mean 'become'. *As women get older, the risk increases... Finding food is getting difficult.* ◇ **Get** is used to say someone changes the state they are in, or their status. *He needed one or two more bouts to get into shape... We decided to get married.* ◇ You say someone **gets into** a state or situation. *I have got into debt... He got into such a muddle.*

❏ **Get** is used to say something is done to someone or something. *...people who get shot accidentally.* ◇ If you **get** someone to do something, you ask or tell them to do it, and they do it. *We got John to stand on the bottom step.* You can also **get** something done. *I got safety belts fitted.*

❏ **Get** is used to talk about going to a place, arriving there, or leaving. *Consider getting there slowly, and coming back fast... They eventually got home exhausted... What time does the coach get in?* ◇ **Get** is used to say someone goes into something like a building or vehicle, or comes out of it. *He got in by breaking a window... I got off the plane around midday.* ◇ **Get** is used to say someone or something goes past or through something. *...a lorry too big to get through the arch.* ◇ **Get** is used to say news, information, or rumour travels somewhere. *The news got around very quick-*

ly... *The word got out that he would go ahead.* ◇ **Get** is used to talk about visiting other places and meeting people. *I can't get about as much as I used to... You've got to get out and make friends.*

❏ If a person or animal **gets away,** they escape. ◇ When criminals make a **getaway** after a robbery or other crime, they leave the scene as quickly as possible. If they use a vehicle, you call it a **getaway** vehicle.

❏ When people **get together,** they meet to discuss something or to spend time together. You call a meeting like this a **get-together.**

❏ **Get** is used to say someone moves to a different position, or an object is moved to a different place or position. *Raymond got down on his hands and knees... They can't get a helicopter down there.* ◇ **Get** is used to talk about removing and putting on clothes. *Get your shirt off.*

❏ **Get** is used to talk about joining something or becoming involved in something. *He was determined to get into politics.*

❏ **Get** is used to talk about dealing with people, problems, difficult situations, and things generally. *He was easy to get along with... Irving got round the problem in a novel way... It's possible to get by in an interview by just talking about your interests.*

❏ If you **get to hear** of something, you eventually hear about it. You can also **get to know** someone or something, or **get to like** them. ◇ If you **get to do** something, you have the opportunity to do it, and you do it. *Men get to run things more often than women.*

❏ If you **get round to** doing something, you eventually do it. *It took her two years to get around to buying a car.* ◇ If you **get down to** something, you start doing it seriously. If you **get on with** it, you keep doing it, or start doing it again after an interruption. If you **get through** it, you finish it. ◇ If you **get out of** doing something, you manage to avoid doing it.

❏ If something **gets off** to a good start, it begins well.

❏ **Get** is used to say what stage someone has reached in something. *Policy makers have not got very far in working out how this might be done.*

❏ If you say someone is **getting on,** you mean they are old.

❏ If you **get on** in your career, you are successful at it.

❏ If you **get** something right, you produce a correct answer, description, or forecast. Similarly, you can **get** something wrong.

❏ **Get** is used to talk about ideas or arguments being expressed or communicated. *This is the only way I know of getting my message over... ...words which will somehow get through to the child.* ◇ If you **get onto** a topic, you start talking about it, after talking about something else. ◇ If you ask what someone is **getting at,** you want to know what they mean.

❏ **Get** is used to talk about using the phone. *Get on to Central Records... I told him to get off the phone... I've been trying for a whole hour to get through to you.*

❏ If an experience **gets to** you, it affects you strongly. *Will the pressure get to him?* ◇ If something **gets you down,** it makes you unhappy. ◇ If you **get over** an illness or unpleasant experience, you recover from it.

❏ If you **get back at** someone, you criticize them when they have been criticizing you.

❏ If you **get away with** something you are not supposed to do, you do it and are not criticized or punished. ◇ If someone is given a surprisingly small punishment, you say they **get off** with the punishment. *He got off with a £50 fine.*

    ❑ If a law or proposal **gets through**, it is approved.

    ❑ If a political party or a politician **gets in**, they are elected.

    ❑ When you **get up**, you get out of bed.

    ❑ If a wind **gets up**, it starts to blow.

    ❑ People sometimes say **'you get'** instead of 'there is' or 'there are'. *You get some rather curious effects.*

    ❑ **Getting on for** in front of a number means 'nearly'. *We have getting on for six weeks before the first arrivals.*

    ❑ **get going**: see **going.** ◇ See also **got, gotten.**

get-up If someone is wearing unusual clothes, you can call these clothes their **get-up.**

getaway See **get.**

gewgaw (*pron:* gyoo-gaw) **Gewgaws** are cheap brightly-coloured ornaments and jewellery.

geyser (*pron:* geez-er) A **geyser** is a hole in the Earth's surface which hot water and steam are forced out of.

ghastly (ghastlier, ghastliest; ghastliness) People use **ghastly** to describe (a) things which are extremely unpleasant. *...ghastly scenes of battle and death.* (b) people or things they dislike very much. *His paintings must rival contemporary architecture for sheer ghastliness.* ◇ If someone looks **ghastly,** they look very pale and ill.

ghee is clarified butter used in Indian cookery.

gherkin Gherkins are small cucumbers pickled in vinegar.

ghetto (ghettos *or* ghettoes) A **ghetto** is part of a city, often a poor area, inhabited by large numbers of people of the same nationality, religion, or ethnic group.

ghetto-blaster Large portable stereo cassette players with built-in speakers are often called **ghetto-blasters.**

ghost People who believe in **ghosts** believe dead people's spirits are still around on earth. ◇ **Ghost** is also used to talk about something from the past which keeps cropping up, though some people want to forget it. *...the ghost of Margaret Thatcher's poll tax.* ◇ If you **lay the ghost** of something which has gone wrong in the past, you do something which makes up for it. ◇ If something like a machine **gives up the ghost,** it breaks down completely.

ghost town You call a town a **ghost town** when it used to be busy and prosperous but is now full of empty shops and houses.

ghost-write (ghost-writer *or* ghostwriter) If a book or article is **ghost-written,** it is supposed to be by someone famous but is actually written by a professional writer called a **ghost-writer.**

ghostly You use **ghostly** to describe things to do with ghosts, or things which seem unnatural or unreal and make you think of ghosts. *As you approach the front doors, they swing open in ghostly fashion.*

ghostwriter See **ghost-write.**

ghoul (*pron:* gool) (ghoulish) A **ghoul** is an imaginary evil spirit, especially one which eats dead bodies. ◇ If you call someone a **ghoul,** you mean they are interested in things like torture, death, and dead bodies. You say people like this are **ghoulish.**

GHQ is a place which military operations are organized

from. GHQ stands for 'General Headquarters'.

GI A **GI** is a soldier in the US Army. GI originally stood for 'government issue'.

giant In children's stories, a **giant** is an impossibly big person. ◇ A very tall person is sometimes called a **giant.** ◇ People thought to be better than anyone else in their field can also be called **giants.** *At the time Camus and Sartre were the two literary giants.* ◇ Very large firms are called **giants.** *...the car giants.* ◇ **Giant** is used to describe unusually large objects. *...a giant Christmas pudding.*

giant-killer (giant-killing) In sport, lowly-rated teams who beat famous ones are called **giant-killers.** Their victories are described as **giant-killing.** *...such giant killing acts as Swindon's overpowering of Arsenal.*

giant panda See **panda.**

giantess (giantesses) A **giantess** is a female giant.

gibber (*pron:* jib-ber) (gibbering, gibbered) If someone **gibbers,** they talk very fast in a confused way.

gibberish If you say someone is talking **gibberish,** you mean what they say does not make sense.

gibbet (*pron:* jib-bit) A **gibbet** was a wooden structure which the bodies of executed criminals used to be left hanging from so people could see them.

gibbon Gibbons are a kind of ape with very long arms. They live in forests in southern Asia.

gibe See **jibe.**

giblets The **giblets** of a chicken or other bird are parts like the heart and liver which are taken out before the bird is cooked.

giddy (giddiness) If you feel **giddy,** you feel you are about to fall over, usually because you are ill. *...complaining of chest pains and bouts of giddiness.* ◇ You can use **giddy** to describe happy excited behaviour. *He worked the crowd to a giddy high with songs like 'Beautiful Noise'.*

gift (gifted) ❑ A **gift** is something you give someone.

    ❑ **Gift** and **gifted** are used to say someone is naturally very good at something. For example, you can say someone has a **gift** for comedy or is a **gifted** athlete. A **gifted** child is naturally good at several things.

gift-wrapped If you buy something **gift-wrapped,** it is attractively packaged so you can give it to someone without having to wrap it yourself.

giftware is objects made specially to be sold as gifts.

gig A **gig** is a live performance by a pop musician. ◇ A **gig** used to be a kind of open two-wheeled carriage, pulled by a single horse.

giga- (*pron:* gig-a) is added to words to talk about very large amounts of something. **Giga-** usually means 1000 million. For example, a **gigawatt** is 1000 million watts. However, in computing, **giga-** means 2^{30} (about 1074 million). A **gigabyte** is 2^{30} bytes.

gigantic things are extremely large.

gigawatt See **giga-.**

giggle (giggling, giggled; giggly) If someone **giggles,** they laugh in a silly or nervous way. If they do it often, you say they are **giggly.**

gigolo (*pron:* jig-a-lo) (gigolos) A **gigolo** is a man paid to be the lover and companion of a rich older woman.

gild (gilding, gilded; gilt) When someone **gilds** an object, they cover it with a thin layer of gold paint. **Gilded**

objects have been painted like this. The paint on them is called **gilding** or **gilt**. ◇ **Gilded** is used to describe people who are rich and have opportunities other people do not have. *...the gilded elite who get into the top schools.* ◇ If someone **gilds the lily**, they try to improve something which is good enough already.

gill ❏ A fish's **gills** (*pron:* **gills**) are the organs at the sides of its body which it breathes through.

    ❏ A **gill** (*pron:* **jill**) is a quarter of a pint.

gilt See **gild, gilt-edged**.

gilt-edged stocks and securities (also called **gilts**) are issued by the government for people to invest in for a fixed time at a fixed rate of interest. With stocks and securities like these, there is little risk of losing money.

gimcrack (*pron:* **jim-krak**) things look attractive but are badly made and are not of much use or value.

gimlet (*pron:* **gim-let**) A **gimlet** is a small sharp tool for making holes in wood. ◇ When people talk about someone's **gimlet** eyes or **gimlet** stare, they mean they are looking at things very intently, because they are determined to find out the truth about something.

gimmick (gimmicky, gimmickry) If you call something a **gimmick**, you mean it has no real value and is just done to attract interest or publicity. You say things like this are **gimmicky**. *...a sales gimmick.* A lot of gimmicks can be called **gimmickry**. *This is no time for gimmickry or the pursuit of short cuts.*

gin is a colourless alcoholic drink distilled from grain and flavoured with juniper berries.

ginger (gingery) ❏ **Ginger** is a tropical plant grown for its root. This root, also called **ginger**, has a spicy hot flavour and is used in cooking. **Ginger wine** and **ginger beer** are mildly alcoholic drinks made partly from fermented ginger. **Ginger ale** is a sweet non-alcoholic drink flavoured with ginger.

    ❏ A **ginger group** is a group of people within an organization who have strong ideas which they try to get other people in the organization to accept.

    ❏ **Ginger** is a bright orange-brown colour. If something has this colour to some extent, you say it is **gingery**.

gingerbread is a kind of sweet biscuit flavoured with ginger, often made in the shape of a person or animal.

gingerly If you do something **gingerly**, you do it cautiously and rather nervously.

gingham (*pron:* **ging-am**) is checked or striped cotton cloth.

gingivitis (*pron:* **jin-jiv-vite-iss**) is an inflammation of the gums.

ginseng (*pron:* **jin**-seng) is a plant from China and Korea, or a similar one from North America. Its root is also called **ginseng**, and is thought by some people to be good for your health.

gipsy See **gypsy**.

giraffe The **giraffe** is a central African animal with very long legs and a long neck.

gird If people **gird themselves** or **gird their loins**, they prepare to tackle something difficult.

girder A **girder** is a long thick piece of steel or iron used in the frameworks of buildings and bridges.

girdle (girdling, girdled) If one thing **girdles** another, it is all the way round it. *The town centre is girdled by a boulevard lined with plane trees.* You can say something has a

girdle of things round it. ◇ A **girdle** is a piece of women's underwear which fits tightly round the stomach and hips.

girl A **girl** is a young woman up to the age of about 30. This use of 'girl' is very common, but some people object to it. ◇ A **girl** or **little girl** is a female child.

girl friend See **girlfriend**.

girl guide A **girl guide** or **guide** is a girl aged 10 to 15 who belongs to the Girl Guides Association. Girl guides are encouraged to be disciplined and to learn practical skills.

girl scout In the US, a **girl scout** is a young girl who belongs to the Girl Scouts Association, which is similar to the Girl Guides Association.

girlfriend (*or* **girl friend**) A man's or boy's **girlfriend** is the woman he is having a romantic or sexual relationship with. ◇ A woman's **girlfriends** are her female friends.

girlhood A woman's **girlhood** is the time when she was a girl.

girlie magazines and calendars have photos of naked or almost naked women, to titillate men.

girlish is used to describe things which are typical of a young girl. *...her girlish excitement.*

giro (giros) **Giro** is a system for paying money to people who might not have a bank account. If you receive a **giro cheque**, you can cash it at a post office. A giro cheque for unemployment money is often called a **giro**.

girth The **girth** of an object is the distance round it. *With a height of 85ft and a girth of 19ft 2in, the tree is said to be the biggest in Britain.* You can also talk about the **girth** of a person, especially a fat person.

gist (*pron:* **jist**) The **gist** of what someone says is its general meaning.

give (giving, gave, have given) ❏ **Give** is used to describe something someone does. For example, if you **give** something a push, you push it. *She gave a smile... Any aircraft carrying the Prime Minister is given a thorough check.*

    ❏ **Give** is used to talk about doing something for someone. *He gave her a lift back to London... ...a tutor who came to give lessons to my son.* ◇ **Give** is used to talk about providing someone with something. *The authorities have given him a flat in Istanbul.* ◇ **Give** is used to say someone is allowed time or the opportunity to do something. *The Parliament gave him two weeks to come up with a solution.* ◇ In sport, **give** is used to mention the thing which makes someone win, or puts them in a winning position. *A last-minute penalty gave Ireland victory against Argentina... Connolly gave St Helens the lead after ten minutes.*

    ❏ **Give** is used to say someone gets a present or award. *...soldiers who have been given medals.* ◇ **Give** is used to talk about something being handed over. *She gave them the keys and told them to get on with it.*

    ❏ If you **give** something **away**, you give it to someone rather than selling it. A **give-away** is something you are given free, for example when you buy something. ◇ **Give-away** prices are much lower than usual.

    ❏ **Give** is used to talk about greeting or welcoming someone. *The students gave him a rapturous welcome.* ◇ **Give** is used to talk about telling someone to do something. *He gave orders to the military to fire on the protestors*

◇ **Give** is used to talk about punishing someone. *He was given an eighteen-month sentence.*

❑ **Give** is used to talk about passing on information or news. *They gave details of several operations they had carried out.* ◇ **Give** is used to talk about providing an explanation or example. *Let me give you two examples of what I mean.*

❑ If you **give away** something someone is trying to keep secret, you tell people about it. When someone does this, you can say they **give the game away.** ◇ A **giveaway** is something which makes you realize the truth about something. *The only giveaway was the look of amusement in her eyes.*

❑ **Give** is used to talk about speaking to people or entertaining them. *She gave a speech to the company's lawyers... The orchestra gave its first performance in 1932.*

❑ If you **give** attention or thought to something, you deal with it or think about it.

❑ If you **give up** something you stop doing it or having it. *The prisoners gave up their protest... He almost gave up hope.* ◇ If you **give up** your job, you resign. ◇ When people who have committed a crime **give themselves up,** they surrender to the police.

❑ If you **give in** or **give way** to something like a demand, you agree to do something you do not want to. ◇ When one thing is replaced or followed by another, you can say the first thing **gives way** to the second. *The rain gave way to sunshine.*

❑ If something you see or hear **gives** you a feeling or idea, you have it because of what you have seen or heard. *The Irish victory gave me particular pleasure.*

❑ **Give** is used to say someone or something is made to have a particular appearance. *...a bri-nylon anorak which gave him the look of a warehouse foreman... The substance is suspended in the liquid, giving it the colour of red wine.*

❑ If something **gives off** or **gives out** heat, gas, or a smell, it sends it out into the air.

❑ If a door **gives onto** something like a garden, it leads to it.

❑ If something **gives way,** it collapses because of the weight pressing on it.

❑ If someone **gives as good as they get** in an argument or fight, they argue or fight as well as their opponent.

❑ You use **give or take** to say how exact an amount is. *They moved onto land 414 million years ago – give or take a million years.* ◇ **Give and take** is willingness to listen to other people's opinions and make compromises.

❑ **give birth:** see birth. ◇ **give evidence:** see evidence. ◇ **give ground:** see ground. ◇ **give rise to:** see rise.

❑ See also **given.**

giveaway See give.

given ❑ See give.

❑ **Given** and **given that** are used to say something is being taken into account. *Given the number of rules, a solicitor setting up on his own is likely to get into a muddle... This may seem an odd view to take, given that I am strongly in favour of the treaty.*

❑ If someone is **given to** doing something, they keep doing it. *Darvell was given to making false confessions.*

❑ If a place is **given over** to something, that is what it is used for. ◇ If a book, talk, or meeting is **given over** to something, that is what is discussed in it.

❑ A **given** date or time is one fixed for something to happen. *Each company is required to finish cabling its area by a given date.* ◇ You use **any given** to say something is true about each thing of a particular kind. *It's impossible to make precise predictions about the extent of any given disease.*

given name Your **given names** are all your names except your surname.

gizzard A bird's **gizzard** is a part of its digestive system where hard food is broken up.

glacé (*pron:* glass-ay) **Glacé** fruits have been preserved in a thick sugary syrup.

glacial (*pron:* glay-shal) (glacially) ❑ **Glacial** is used to talk about things to do with glaciers. ◇ A **glacial** period was a time in the past when large parts of the earth were covered with ice.

❑ You call people's behaviour **glacial** when they show no signs of warmth or friendliness.

❑ **Glacial** is also used to say something moves or happens very slowly. *...a glacially slow way to improve the skills of a country's workforce.*

glaciation (glaciated) **Glaciation** is the process by which a glacier slowly moves across land, creating a new landscape. **Glaciated** land has been formed like this.

glacier A **glacier** is a huge mass of ice which moves very slowly, often down a mountain valley.

glad (gladly) If you are **glad** about something, you are pleased, thankful, or relieved because of it. *I was glad to get inside... I gladly accepted the offer of a lift.* ◇ If you are **glad** of something, you are pleased you have it. *Party officials are glad of the chance to speak out.* ◇ If you say someone would be **glad** to do something, you mean they are willing to do it. *We will gladly assist in any enquiry that the BOA may hold.*

glad-handing You say a politician is **glad-handing** when he or she mingles with people and chats to them in a friendly way.

gladden (gladdening, gladdened) If you say something will **gladden** someone or **gladden** their heart, you mean they will be pleased or delighted with it.

glade A **glade** is an open area in a wood or forest.

gladiator (gladiatorial) In ancient Rome, a **gladiator** was a man trained to fight with weapons in an arena, to entertain people. ◇ People use **gladiatorial** to describe things which remind them of gladiators fighting. *...a gladiatorial contest.*

gladiolus (*plural:* gladioli) The **gladiolus** is a plant with sword-shaped leaves and spikes of brightly-coloured flowers.

glamor See glamour.

glamorize (glamorizing, glamorized) (*can be spelled with an 's' instead of a 'z'*) If a book or film **glamorizes** something dull or unpleasant, it makes it seem attractive.

glamorous A **glamorous** woman is very attractive in a stylish way. Men can also be called **glamorous.** ◇ A **glamorous** job or way of life is one which many people find attractive and exciting, because it involves things like meeting rich and famous people.

glamour (*American spelling:* glamor) You say a place or way of life has **glamour** when people find it attractive and exciting. ◇ A person's sexual attractiveness can also be called **glamour.**

glance (glancing, glanced) ❑ If you **glance** at something or cast a **glance** at it, you look at it quickly, then look away. ◇ If you **glance** through something like a magazine, you look at it quickly without reading it properly. ◇ If you can see or tell something **at a glance**, you can see or recognize it immediately.

❏ You say **at first glance** when you are talking about a first impression of someone or something. *At first glance she seems soft and feminine.*

❏ If one object **glances off** another, or strikes it a **glancing** blow, it hits it at an angle and bounces away in another direction.

gland Glands are cells or organs which produce substances the body needs in order to function.

glandular fever is an infectious disease which causes fever, a sore throat, and a painful swelling of the lymph glands.

glare (glaring, glared; glaringly) ❏ If you **glare** at someone, you look at them angrily. This way of looking at someone is called a **glare**.

❏ When a light shines very brightly, making it difficult to see, you can talk about its **glare**.

❏ When someone's actions are constantly being watched and reported by the media, you can say they are in the **glare** of publicity.

❏ If you call a fault **glaring**, you mean it is very obvious. You can also say someone makes a **glaring** mistake. ◇ If something is **glaringly** obvious, it is very obvious indeed.

glasnost is a policy introduced by President Gorbachev in the former Soviet Union. It involved greater openness and accountability by the Soviet government, and an improvement in relations with other countries. ◇ **Glasnost** is now used to talk about the behaviour of other governments and organizations when they start revealing things they had previously kept secret.

glass (glasses) Glass is the hard transparent substance windows are made from. ◇ A **glass** is a glass container for drinking from. ◇ A person's **glasses** are two lenses in a frame which they wear in front of their eyes, to see better.

glass-blower (glass-blowing) A **glass-blower** is someone whose job is to make round glass objects by blowing air into molten glass and shaping it. This work is called **glass-blowing.**

glass fibre is the same as fibreglass.

glass house See glasshouse.

glass-maker (glass-making) A **glass-maker** is a firm or person that makes sheets of glass or glass objects. These processes are both called **glass-making.**

glasshouse (*or* glass house) A **glasshouse** is a large greenhouse.

glassware is objects made of glass, such as glasses for drinking or glass ornaments.

glassworks (*plural:* glassworks) A **glassworks** is a factory where glass is made.

glassy objects are hard, smooth, and shiny, like glass. ◇ If you say someone is **glassy-eyed,** you mean their eyes do not show any feeling or understanding, because they have been through a very unpleasant experience. You can also say their eyes are **glassy.**

glaucoma (*pron:* glaw-koh-ma) is a serious eye disease which can lead to blindness.

glaze (glazing, glazed) ❏ The **glaze** on a piece of pottery is a thin layer of a hard shiny substance on its surface. You

say pottery like this is **glazed.** ◇ If you **glaze** food like pastry, you spread a layer of beaten egg, milk, or other liquid on it before you cook it, to give it a shiny surface. This layer is called a **glaze.**

❏ When windows are **glazed,** glass is put into them.

❏ If someone's eyes **glaze** or **glaze over,** they become dull and expressionless, often because the person is bored. You say someone like this has a **glazed** look.

glazier A **glazier** is someone whose job is fitting glass into windows and doors.

gleam (gleaming, gleamed) ❏ If a light **gleams,** it shines brightly. If an object or surface **gleams,** it shines because it is reflecting light. You can talk about the **gleam** of a light, object, or surface. ...*the first gleam of dawn.*

❏ If you say there is a **gleam** in someone's eye, you mean their eyes seem to shine because they feel very strongly about something. ◇ If you say something is no more than a **gleam** in someone's eye, you mean it is just an idea they have, and has not yet been properly designed or planned.

glean (gleaning, gleaned) If you **glean** information about something, you obtain it with difficulty. Similarly, you can say someone **gleans** an education or a living. You can say someone **gleans** a small amount of money, or a sports team **gleans** points or runs.

glee (gleeful, gleefully) You talk about a person's **glee** when they show their delight at something which has happened, especially some misfortune happening to a rival, opponent, or enemy. You say someone like this is **gleeful** or talk about their **gleeful** behaviour. *These remarks have been gleefully seized on by the opposition.*

glen A **glen** is a deep narrow valley, especially in Scotland or Ireland.

glib (glibly, glibness) You say someone is being **glib** when they try to mislead people by making something out to be simpler or more straightforward than it really is. ...*glib promises... The authorities talk glibly about wanting to ease relations with China... ...the glibness of the prime minister's response.*

glide (gliding, glided; glider) If a vehicle **glides** somewhere, it moves smoothly and quietly. ◇ When birds **glide,** they float on air currents. ◇ When a plane **glides,** it floats towards the ground, with its engine off. ◇ **Gliding** is the sport of flying in a plane called a **glider,** which has no engine and floats on air currents.

glimmer (glimmering, glimmered) A **glimmer** of something is a faint sign of it. ...*a glimmer of hope.* ◇ When a light **glimmers,** it shines in a faint unsteady way. You can talk about a **glimmer** of light.

glimpse (glimpsing, glimpsed) If you **glimpse** something or catch a **glimpse** of it, you see it briefly and not very well. ◇ You can also say you **glimpse** something or are given a **glimpse** of it when you experience it briefly. *The trip will give the orphans a glimpse of a world they have barely encountered.*

glint If an object or surface **glints,** it gives out little flashes of reflected light. Each flash is called a **glint.** ◇ You say someone's eyes **glint** when they seem to shine because of eagerness, expectation, or pleasure. You can talk about a **glint** in someone's eyes. *There was always a wicked glint in his eyes as he exploited politicians.*

glisten (glistening, glistened) If something **glistens,** it shines, because it is smooth, wet, or oily.

glitch (glitches) A **glitch** is a small problem which stops something working properly or being successful. ◇ A glitch is also a false electronic signal caused by a sudden increase in power.

glitter (glittering, glittered; glittery) ❏ If something **glitters**, it shines and sparkles. ◇ A **glittering** occasion is attended by rich people wearing expensive clothes and jewellery.
  ❏ A **glittering** career is very successful. ◇ When people talk about the **glittering prizes**, they mean things like well-paid jobs which are available to certain people because of their education or social status.
  ❏ If something is attractive in a superficial way, you can talk about its **glitter** or call it **glittery**. *I found his books very unsatisfactory beneath their surface glitter.*

glitterati (*pron:* glit-ter-**ah**-tee) The fashionable celebrities in a place are sometimes called its **glitterati**.

glitzy (glitzier, glitziest; glitz) **Glitzy** is used to describe things which are attractive in a showy and rather superficial way. When something is like this, you can talk about its **glitz**. *...the glitz of the US entertainment industry.*

gloaming Twilight is sometimes called the **gloaming**.

gloat (gloating, gloated; gloatingly) If someone **gloats** over something, they show pleasure at their own success or someone else's failure. You can say someone does something **gloatingly**. *He gloatingly went back to his old school in a Rolls Royce.*

global (globally) **Global** is used to talk about things involving the whole world. *...helping British industries to be more globally competitive.* ◇ People sometimes call the world **the global village**. This is a way of emphasizing how closely linked the parts of the modern world are, so that things happening in one place can have effects everywhere else. ◇ **Global warming** is the gradual rise in temperature thought to be taking place in the Earth's atmosphere. It happens because of the 'greenhouse effect', in which heat absorbed from the sun cannot escape from the atmosphere, due to a build-up of carbon dioxide and other gases.

globalize (globalizing, globalized; globalization) (*can be spelled with an 's' instead of a 'z'*) If something is **globalized**, it is changed so that it involves or affects the whole world. *...the globalization of financial markets.*

globe People sometimes call the world the **globe**. *Airlines throughout the globe are losing money.* ◇ A **globe** is a ball-shaped object with a map of the world on it.

globetrotter (globetrotting) You say someone is a **globetrotter** when they are always visiting different parts of the world. When they do this, you say they are **globetrotting**.

globular A **globular** object is round like a ball.

globule A **globule** of liquid is a tiny round drop.

glockenspiel The **glockenspiel** is a musical instrument consisting of a row of tuned metal plates which the player hits with a pair of small hammers.

gloom is a feeling of unhappiness, especially one shared by a lot of people. ◇ **Gloom** is also a state of semi-darkness. *A strange man emerged from the gloom.*

gloomy (gloomier, gloomiest; gloomily) You say someone is **gloomy** when they are unhappy and pessimistic. You can talk about someone's **gloomy** remarks or behav-

iour. *The umpires gloomily trod the outfield looking for puddles.* ◇ You say news or a situation is **gloomy** when it is likely to make people disappointed and unhappy. ◇ A **gloomy** place is dark and depressing.

glorify (glorifies, glorifying, glorified; glorification) When something is **glorified**, attempts are made to convince people that it is wonderful or desirable. *...the glorification of speed in car ads.* ◇ **Glorified** is used to say something is not as big or important as it is reckoned to be. For example, if you say a lake is no more than a glorified pond, you mean it is really no bigger than a pond.

glorious (gloriously) ❏ You call something you see or hear **glorious** when it is very beautiful and impressive. *...a gloriously picturesque village.* ◇ **Glorious** weather is very sunny.
  ❏ A **glorious** time in someone's life is one when they have many successes. ◇ You call something someone does **glorious** when they do it exceptionally well. *He struck a glorious third shot over the water.*
  ❏ People sometimes use **gloriously** to say something is so bad or absurd that they find it amusing or delightful. *The Panthermal Therapy Bath is a gloriously absurd contraption.*

glory (glories, glorying, gloried) ❏ **Glory** is the fame and admiration someone gets when they have done something remarkable. *...the pursuit of sporting glory.* ◇ If you say someone is bathing or basking in someone else's **reflected glory**, you mean they are enjoying the attention they are getting as a result of being connected with someone famous.
  ❏ If you talk about the **glories** of a person or group, you mean the occasions in the past when they did something remarkable. Similarly, you can talk about someone's **glory days**.
  ❏ The **glories** of a culture or place are the things people find most attractive or impressive about it. *The royal parks are among the glories of London.*
  ❏ You talk about the **glory** of something when you are mentioning a feature it has which makes it particularly satisfactory. *The glory of the Times crossword is that the answers can usually be arrived at by two routes.*
  ❏ If you **glory in** something, you thoroughly enjoy it.

gloss (glosses, glossing, glossed) ❏ **Gloss** is a bright shine on a surface. ◇ **Gloss** paint looks shiny when it is dry.
  ❏ **Gloss** is used to talk about the superficially attractive features of something. *The book is all gloss and no substance.* ◇ If someone puts a **gloss** on something, they make it seem better than it is. ◇ If someone **glosses over** a problem or mistake, they try to make it seem less serious. ◇ If something **takes the gloss off** an event or achievement, it makes it seem less satisfactory.

glossary (glossaries) A **glossary** in a book is an alphabetical list of special or technical words used in the book, with explanations of their meanings.

glossy (glossier, glossiest; glossies) If something is **glossy**, it is smooth and shiny. ◇ **Glossy** photographs and booklets are produced on expensive shiny paper. ◇ **Glossy magazines** or **glossies** are printed on shiny paper and typically have pictures of fashionable clothes, famous people, and expensive houses.

glove (gloved) ❏ **Gloves** are items of clothing worn over a person's hands and wrists with separate sections for each finger. **Gloved** is used to say someone is wearing gloves. *...a gloved lady... ...grey-gloved hands.*

❏ If something **fits like a glove**, it fits exactly.

❏ You say people are **hand in glove** when they are closely involved in something together. *He accused Mr de Klerk of being hand in glove with communists and terrorists.* ◇ You say the **gloves are off** when people start attacking or criticizing each other openly. *The gloves came off yesterday between the two leaders.*

glove compartment A car's glove **compartment** is a small cupboard or shelf just below the windscreen.

glow (glowing, glowingly) ❏ If something **glows**, it produces a gentle steady light, or looks bright because of reflected light. You call this effect a **glow**. *In the distance, the Andes glowed pink.* ◇ If someone **glows**, their face is pink as a result of exercise, excitement, or pleasure. ◇ A **glow** is a strong feeling of pleasure or satisfaction. *...a song to send everyone home with a warm glow in their hearts.*

❏ If you give a **glowing** description of someone or something, you praise them highly. *His obituary notice glowingly describes him as 'a great Englishman'.*

glow-worm Glow-worms are a kind of beetle. They produce a greenish light from their bodies.

glower (*rhymes with 'power'*) (glowering, glowered) If someone **glowers** at you, they look at you in an angry or hostile way. You call their expression a **glower**.

glucose is a type of sugar produced by a natural process in the bodies of people and animals, and in plants. It is an important source of energy. ◇ **Glucose** is also a yellowish syrup made from starch. It is used in confectionery and the fermentation of alcohol.

glue (glueing *or* gluing, glued) ❏ **Glue** is a sticky substance used for joining things together. If you **glue** one thing to another, you stick them together using glue. ◇ You say objects are **glued** together when they are stuck firmly together, as if by glue.

❏ If you say someone is **glued** to their TV or computer screen, you mean they are watching it very closely and are not interested in anything else.

glue sniffing is the dangerous practice of inhaling the vapour from glue, to experience pleasant sensations.

glum (glummer, glummest; glumly) You say someone is **glum** when they are sad because they have had a disappointment. *...glumly contemplating a wasted afternoon.*

glut (glutted) If there is a **glut** of something like a raw material or type of goods, there is more than can be sold or used. When this happens, people talk about a **glutted** market.

gluten is a protein which occurs in cereal grains, especially wheat.

glutinous A glutinous substance has the same texture as glue.

glutton (gluttonous, gluttony) ❏ A **glutton** is a greedy person who eats too much. You say someone like this is **gluttonous** or talk about their **gluttony**.

❏ If someone is a **glutton** for something, they like to have a lot of it. *...a glutton for detail.*

glycerine (*or* glycerin) is a thick colourless liquid, used in medicines and explosives.

gm See gram.

GMT is the standard time in Britain, and is used to calculate the time in the rest of the world. GMT stands for 'Greenwich Mean Time'. See also **BST**.

gnarled A gnarled tree has a twisted shape. ◇ A **gnarled** person has a twisted body, as a result of age or hard work. ◇ If a person's hands are **gnarled**, they have bent fingers and swollen joints.

gnash (gnashes, gnashing, gnashed) When people get very angry and frustrated about something, you can say they **gnash their teeth**.

gnat Gnats are small flying insects which bite.

gnaw If an animal or person **gnaws** something or **gnaws** at it, they bite into it repeatedly. ◇ If something gradually reduces something else, you can say it **gnaws at it**. *The recession is going to gnaw away at all segments of the economy.* ◇ If something like a feeling **gnaws at you**, it keeps troubling you.

gnome In children's stories, a **gnome** is a little old man with a beard and a pointed hat. Some people have statues of gnomes in their gardens.

gnomic is used to describe things which are difficult to understand, because they are expressed in a peculiar way. *...John Wheeler's gnomic utterance 'A black hole has no hair'.*

GNP A country's GNP or **gross national product** is the total value of all the goods it has produced and services it has provided, plus its income from abroad, during one year.

gnu (*pron:* noo) The **gnu** or **wildebeest** is a large African antelope.

GNVQ GNVQs or **General National Vocational Qualifications** are qualifications related to the world of work.

go (goes, going, went, have gone) ❏ Go is used to talk about movement or travel from one place or level to another. *She went into the sitting-room... We can go up in the elevator.* ◇ Go is used to talk about leaving a place. *Our train went at 2.25... They went away empty-handed.* ◇ Go is used to talk about leaving a place temporarily in order to do something. *Let's go fishing.* ◇ Go is used to talk about attending a place regularly. *She went to London University.* ◇ Go is used to say where a road or path leads to. *It gets you to the N137, which goes to Nantes via Rennes.*

❏ Go is used with words like 'far' and 'way' to comment on the extent to which something is done or achieved. *The government is not going far enough... The investigation still had a long way to go.*

❏ Go is used with 'up' or 'down' to say an amount rises or falls. *Interest rates went up by 4 per cent.*

❏ Go is used with words beginning with 'un-' to say something is not noticed or mentioned. *His appointment went unnoticed... Nationalisation went almost unmentioned... The ceremony went unreported.*

❏ Go is used with some words to describe the state a person is in. *Foreign workers are being allowed to go hungry... Nobody has yet been arrested for going naked.* ◇ Go is used with 'into' to say someone enters a particular state. *Its leader has gone into hiding... The others went into retirement.*

❏ If you talk about what is **going on**, you are talking about what is happening. *She decided to enter the flat to see what was going on.* ◇ If something **goes on** happening, it does not stop. *Prices go on rising.*

❏ If you **go into** a type of work, you start doing it. *Have you ever thought of going into journalism?* ◇ If you **go on to** do something, you do it after doing something else. *She went on to head Conran Design Group.* ◇ If you **go back** to something, you start doing it again, after doing something else. ◇ If you **go through** with something you have been planning to do, you do it. ◇ The way you **go about** something is your method of dealing with it. ◇ When people talk about someone **going around** doing something, they are showing disapproval of what the person does. *What kind of nutcase goes around spreading germs?*

❑ **Go** is used to say how successful something is. *Sales are going well... Voting went off peacefully.* ◇ If something like a speech or performance **goes down** well, people like it.

❑ When people say a political leader or minister should **go** or may have to **go,** they are talking about them resigning or being removed from power. ◇ When people say a certain number of jobs will **go,** they are talking about people being made redundant. ◇ If you say someone's eyesight or hearing is **going,** you mean they are becoming blind or deaf.

❑ If you say a problem **will not go away,** you mean it will continue until something is done about it.

❑ If something **goes** to someone, they are given it or awarded it. *The rights went to an American-Japanese consortium... Victory went to Zimbabwe's Mark McNulty.*

❑ **Go** is used to talk about money or resources being used to support or finance something. *More than three quarters of council spending goes on salaries.* ◇ **Go** is used with 'round' or 'around' to say whether there is enough of something for everyone. *There is not enough food to go round.*

❑ **Go** is used with some words to mean 'become'. *The phone went dead... My brain went blank.*

❑ **Go** is used with 'by' to talk about time passing. *It got worse as the months went by.* ◇ **Go** is used with 'back' to talk about a period of time measured back from the present. *He has been accused of widespread fraud going back a number of years.*

❑ If you **go ahead** with something you have been planning to do, you do it. ◇ If someone is given the **go-ahead,** they are told they can start doing something. ◇ If a planned event **goes ahead,** it takes place.

❑ If you **go for** something, you choose it. *We both went for the same turquoise jumper.* ◇ If you **go in for** something, you make use of it. *Students are not going to go in for elaborate recipes... He decided not to go in for what he called 'tit for tat' action.*

❑ If you **go by** something, you use it as a basis for a judgement or action. *I go by my own eyes... If the London to Aberdeen service is anything to go by, there are still teething problems.*

❑ If you **go along with** a decision or idea, you accept it and obey it. If you **go against** it, you do something which conflicts with it. ◇ If you **go back on** a promise, you do not do what you promised.

❑ If a business deal **goes through,** it is successfully completed. ◇ If a law or official decision **goes through,** it is officially approved. ◇ If a decision **goes against** you, you lose.

❑ If you **go through** a difficult time, you experience it. ◇ If you **go without** something for a time, you do not have it. *I have known what it is like to go without food.*

❑ You say a machine or device is **going** when it is oper-

ating. ◇ You say a building is **going up** when it is being built. ◇ When a bell or alarm **goes** or **goes off,** it sounds. ◇ When a bomb **goes off,** it explodes. ◇ When a light **goes out** or **goes off,** it stops shining. ◇ When a fire **goes out,** it stops burning.

❑ **Go** is used to talk about examining something or describing it in detail. *I went through the booklet of instructions... The more you go into it, the more complicated it seems.* ◇ If you talk about the information you have **to go on,** you mean the information which is available.

❑ If news, information, or a story is **going around,** it is being told by many people.

❑ You use **goes** when you are mentioning that something is part of a story, theory, or idea. *As soon as he delivered his news, the story goes, he fell dead... After the impact, the theory goes, the climate was cooled by dust and debris.* ◇ When you have mentioned part of what someone has said, you use **went on** when mentioning the rest of it. *He went on: 'We have been successful in getting inflation down to under 4 per cent.'*

❑ If you talk about something **going** with something else, you mean you get it when you get the other thing. *...the house that goes with the job... ...the way of life that goes with mechanical engineering.* ◇ If you say two things can **go together,** you mean they can exist or operate together successfully.

❑ If you say a statement about one person or thing **goes for** another person or thing, you mean it applies also to the second person or thing. *It is illegal to dishonour bookings; that goes for restaurants as well as customers.*

❑ You use **go** with 'as' when making a statement about something, to show you are comparing it to other things of the same kind. *As comets go, Chiron is enormous.*

❑ When people say something **goes to** show something else or **goes to** prove it, they mean it shows or proves it. *It just goes to show you can't believe all you read in the papers.*

❑ If you have a **go** at someone, you criticize them. ◇ If you have a **go** at something or give it a **go,** you try it out. ◇ If you **make a go** of something, you succeed. ◇ If it is your **go,** it is your turn to do something.

❑ You use **to go** when you are saying (a) how many things are remaining to be dealt with, or how much distance remains to be covered. *...one match down with only three to go... She ran into breathing difficulties with six laps to go.* (b) how long it is before something will happen. *There's still a year to go.*

❑ If something has been true from the very beginning of a situation, you can say it was true **from the word go.** *Oil was at the centre of the crisis right from the word go.*

❑ When the sun **goes down,** it sets.

❑ If you **go down** with an illness, you catch it.

❑ If you are **going out** with someone, you are spending time with them and having a sexual or romantic relationship with them.

❑ **goes without saying:** see **say.** ◇ **let go:** see **let.**

❑ See also **going, gone.**

go-ahead ❑ See **go.**

❑ A **go-ahead** person or organization deals with things in an enterprising way, often trying out new methods.

go-between A **go-between** is someone who takes messages between people who are not able or willing to

meet each other.

go-getter You say someone is a **go-getter** when they are ambitious and enterprising.

go-go dancing is a kind of entertainment in some pubs and clubs. Young women called **go-go** dancers perform a dance to pop music, wearing very few clothes.

go-kart A **go-kart** is very small racing car with a low-powered engine.

go-slow A **go-slow** is a kind of industrial action in which workers deliberately work slowly.

goad (goading, goaded) If someone is **goaded** into doing something, they do it as a result of being made angry.

goal ❑ In games like football, the winning team is the one which scores the most **goals**. A goal is scored when someone succeeds in getting the ball between two posts in a way which is acceptable according to the rules. In football and some other games, the area the ball enters when a goal is scored is called the **goal**.
  ❑ A person's **goal** is what they are hoping to achieve.

goalie A **goalie** is a goalkeeper.

goalkeeper In a sports team, the **goalkeeper** is the person who stays near the goal and tries to stop the ball going in.

goalmouth In games like football and hockey, the **goalmouth** is the area in front of the goal.

goalpost In games like football and hockey, the **goalposts** are the two upright posts the ball passes between when a goal is scored. ◇ In other situations, if you accuse someone of **moving the goalposts**, you mean they have changed an objective from what it was originally, making it easier for them to achieve it, or harder for someone else.

goat Goats are sheep-like animals with long horns and often a beard.

goatee A **goatee** is a short pointed beard which covers a man's chin only.

goatskin is leather made from a goat's skin.

gobbet Gobbets of information are interesting or amusing pieces of it.

gobble (gobbling, gobbled) ❑ When a country **gobbles up** land or a neighbouring country, it seizes it. Similarly, you can talk about a large company **gobbling up** smaller ones. ◇ You say something **gobbles up** money when it is expensive to operate. Similarly, you can talk about a car **gobbling up** petrol.
  ❑ If a person or animal **gobbles** their food or **gobbles** it up, they eat it quickly and greedily.

gobbledegook (or **gobbledygook** or **gobbledigook**) When something official is expressed in language no one can understand, people say it is written in **gobbledegook**.

goblet A **goblet** is a long-stemmed cup without handles.

goblin A **goblin** is a small ugly creature in fairy stories.

gobsmacked If you are **gobsmacked** by something, you are amazed by it.

god In religions such as Christianity, Judaism, and Islam, God is the being worshipped as the creator and ruler of the universe. ◇ In some religions, there are many **gods**. They are spiritual beings believed to have power over an aspect of life. ...*the pagan god Vaval, symbol of evil.*

god-fearing is used to describe people who believe in God and apply the principles of their religion to their everyday lives. ...*a god-fearing community.*

godchild (godchildren; goddaughter, godson) A person's **godchild** is a child they have promised to help bring up as a Christian. They make this promise at the child's baptism, and the child then becomes their **goddaughter** or **godson**.

goddaughter See godchild.

goddess (goddesses) A **goddess** is a female god.

godfather See godparent.

godless People who do not have any religion are sometimes called **godless**.

godly (godliness) **Godly** is used to describe people who believe in God and lead a good life. You call their behaviour **godliness**.

godmother See godparent.

godparent (godfather, godmother) A child's **godparents** are people who attend its baptism and promise to help bring it up as a Christian. A man is known as a child's **godfather** and a woman as its **godmother**.

godsend If something good comes your way unexpectedly when things are not going well, you can call it a **godsend**.

godson See godchild.

goggle (goggling, goggled) If you **goggle** at something, you stare at it because you are amazed or fascinated. You use **goggle-eyed** to describe someone who stares like this.

goggles are large close-fitting protective glasses.

going ❑ See go.
  ❑ **Going to** is used to make statements about what will happen in the future. *She is going to vote for him.*
  ❑ In horseracing, the **going** is the condition of the ground. ◇ If you want to describe the conditions in which someone does something, you can say, for example, the **going** is good. *Unigate is finding the going difficult in its traditional areas of transport and dairy products.*
  ❑ If you call a business a **going** concern, you mean it is making a profit, and not likely to fail. ◇ The **going** rate for something is the usual and expected rate.
  ❑ When someone **gets going**, they start doing something, often after a delay. You can also say what they are doing **gets going**, or they **get it going**.

goings-on A person's **goings-on** are the things they do, which some people find shocking.

goitre (American spelling: **goiter**) (pron: goy-ter) **Goitre** is a swelling of the thyroid gland in the neck.

gold is a valuable yellow metal used in jewellery and as an international currency. ◇ **Gold** is also a bright yellow colour. ◇ The winner of a race or competition often gets a **gold** medal, made either of gold or a gold-coloured metal. *The Italians won the gold.*

gold leaf is paper-thin gold sheet used for gilding statues and woodwork.

gold-plated objects are covered with a very thin layer of gold.

gold rush A **gold rush** is a large-scale migration of people to an area where gold has been found.

golden things are gold-coloured. ◇ Objects made of gold used to be called **golden**. ...*a golden casket.*
  ❑ A **golden** opportunity is an unusually good one. You

use **golden** to describe other things which come your way which are very special. ...*a golden chance*... ...*a golden asset*. ◇ If you say someone or something has a **golden future**, you mean they will be very successful.

❑ A **golden rule** is a principle which must be stuck to. *Her one golden rule was that she never spoke to the press.*

❑ If you say someone has the **golden touch**, you mean they are good at making money. ◇ If a senior employee gets a **golden handshake**, he or she is given a large sum of money and told they are no longer needed.

❑ The **golden age** of something is the time when it was at its best. You can also talk about the **golden era** or **golden days** of something.

❑ If you celebrate the **golden jubilee** of something, you are celebrating the fact that it has been going for 50 years. ◇ A **golden wedding** is a 50th wedding anniversary.

golden eagle The **golden eagle** is a very large bird of prey which lives in mountains in northern Europe.

goldfinch (goldfinches) The **goldfinch** is a common European seed-eating bird. The adult bird has a red and black face. The rest of its plumage is black, yellow, white, and brown.

goldfish (*usual plural*: goldfish) **Goldfish** are small orange-coloured ornamental fish.

goldmine A **goldmine** is a place where gold ore is dug out of the ground. ◇ If you say something is a **goldmine**, you mean a lot of money is being made out of it.

golf (golfer, golfing) **Golf** is an outdoor game in which a player tries to hit a ball into a series of small holes in the ground. A person doing this is called a **golfer**; the activity is called **golfing**.

golf club A **golf club** is an organization for people who play golf, with its own golf course and clubhouse. The clubhouse and course can also be called a **golf club**. ◇ A **golf club** is also a stick for hitting the ball in golf.

golf course A **golf course** is an area of land where golf is played.

golliwog (*or* gollywog) A **golliwog** is a kind of black male doll, made from fabric.

gonad (*pron*: goh-nad) **Gonads** are reproductive organs, such as the testicles or ovaries.

gondola (gondolier) A **gondola** (*pron*: gon-do-lah) is a long narrow canal boat in Venice. It is propelled by a man called a **gondolier** (*pron*: gon-do-leer), using a pole. ◇ A **gondola** is also a type of large cable car.

gone ❑ See go.

❑ If you say something is **gone**, you mean it is no longer there. *This opportunity is gone... That world, of course, is gone for ever.*

❑ If it is **gone** a certain time, it is later than that time. *I didn't get off till gone four.*

gong A **gong** is a flat metal disc, suspended vertically, which can make a loud noise when hit. ◇ Some people call a medal a **gong**.

gonorrhoea (*or* gonorrhea) (*pron*: gon-or-ree-a) is a type of venereal disease.

good (goodness) ❑ **Good** is used to describe things which are pleasing, acceptable, or of high quality. ...*good food*... ...*a good idea*. If you say something is **no good**, you mean it is unacceptable or unsatisfactory. ◇ The **goodness** of a food is its nutritional value.

❑ If you are **good** at something, you are skilful and successful at it. If you are **no good** at something, you have no skill at it and cannot do it successfully. ◇ If you say someone has **done a good job**, you mean they have done something well.

❑ A **good** person is kind and considerate. *They believed in the fundamental goodness of all human beings.* ◇ You say animals or children are **good** when they are well-behaved. ◇ **Good** is moral or religious correctness. ...*a struggle between the forces of good and evil.*

❑ If something is done for the **good** of a person or organization, it is done to benefit them. ◇ Something that is **good for you** or **does you good** benefits you in some way.

❑ **Good** is used in greetings like 'Good afternoon' and 'Good evening'.

❑ **Good** is used to add emphasis. ...*a good while ago.* ◇ If something has gone **for good**, it has gone permanently.

❑ **Goods** are things to be sold. ...*high tariffs on Chinese goods.* ◇ Someone's **goods** are their possessions. ◇ If someone **delivers** or **comes up with the goods**, they do what is expected of them, or what they promised to do.

❑ You use **as good** as to say something is practically true. *The game was as good as over.*

❑ If someone **makes good** some damage or a loss, they repair or replace the damaged or lost thing.

❑ **in good time**: see time. ◇ **as good as your word**: see word.

good-bye See goodbye.

Good Friday is the Friday before Easter, when Jesus Christ's crucifixion is commemorated.

good-humoured people are happy and cheerful.

good-looking (good looks) You say someone is **good-looking** or talk about their **good looks** when they have regular attractive features.

good-natured people are kind and even-tempered.

good night See goodnight.

Good Samaritan In the Bible, the **Good Samaritan** was a man who helped someone who had been beaten and robbed. You say someone is a **good samaritan** when they help someone in trouble, rather than ignoring them.

goodbye (*or* good-bye) People say 'Goodbye' to each other when parting. You call what they say a **goodbye**. *We made our way back to the car, murmuring goodbyes.*

goodie See goody.

goodness See good.

goodnight (*or* good night) People say 'Goodnight' late in the evening before parting or going to bed.

goods See good.

goods train A **goods train** is the same as a freight train.

goodwill When people show **goodwill**, they are friendly and helpful. *Mr Clarke needs the goodwill of the opposition parties to get the legislation on the statute book.* ◇ A firm's **goodwill** consists of things like its reputation and the regular customers it has, as distinct from other assets like buildings and machinery.

goody (*or* goodie) (goodies) **Goodies** are things for people to enjoy, especially food. ...*a Christmas hamper packed with goodies.* ◇ The **goodies** in a book or film are the good characters, as distinct from the bad ones.

goody-goody (goody-goodies) A **goody-goody** is someone who always seems to be on their best behaviour, which other people may find annoying.

gooey substances are soft and sticky.

goof (goofed, goofing) If someone goofs, they make a mistake. A goof is a mistake.

goofy (goofier, goofiest) If you say someone is goofy, you mean they are rather stupid. You can also talk about actions or plans being goofy.

goose (geese) Geese are large duck-like birds with long necks. They are usually seen in flocks.

goose-pimples (goose-flesh) If someone gets goose-pimples or goose-flesh, their skin comes out in tiny bumps, because they are cold or frightened.

goose-step When soldiers goose-step, they march slowly with stiff legs, kicking their feet high.

gooseberry (gooseberries) Gooseberries are small round green fruit which grow on bushes.

gopher (pron: go-fer) The gopher is a kind of burrowing animal in North and Central America. It has short legs and cheek pouches.

gore (goring; gored; gory) If an animal gores someone, it wounds them badly with its horns. ◇ Gore is a lot of blood from a wound. ◇ You describe something as gory when it involves a lot of bloodshed.

gorge (gorging, gorged) ❏ A gorge is a narrow steep-sided valley.
   ❏ If you gorge on something or gorge yourself on it, you eat a lot of it greedily.

gorgeous (gorgeously) If you say someone or something is gorgeous, you mean they are strikingly beautiful or attractive. ...a wide choice of gorgeously sited hotels.

Gorgonzola is a sharp-flavoured blue-veined Italian cheese.

gorilla Gorillas are the largest members of the ape family. They live in forests in central West Africa.

gormless If you say someone is gormless, you mean they look or behave as if they were stupid.

gorse is a spiny-leaved yellow-flowered evergreen shrub. It is also called 'whin' or 'furze'.

gory See gore.

gosling A gosling is a young goose.

gospel The Gospels are the first four books of the New Testament, which describe the life of Jesus. ◇ Gospel is black religious music which originated in the churches of the southern United States. ◇ If you say someone preaches a particular gospel, you mean they urge other people to adopt their standards, or follow their beliefs. ...the Thatcherite gospel of individualism. ◇ If something is taken as gospel, it is accepted as unquestionably true.

gossamer consists of streams of cobwebs floating in the air, or spread over plants or the ground. ◇ Gossamer is also a type of fine delicate material.

gossip (gossiping, gossiped; gossipy) Gossip is casual or malicious talk about people's private lives. When someone talks like this, you say they are gossiping. If they do it a lot, you call them a gossip. ◇ You say books or articles are gossipy when they give details of people's private lives.

gossip column (gossip columnist) The gossip column in a newspaper or magazine is the part dealing with the social activities of famous people. The person who writes it is called a gossip columnist.

got ❏ See get.
   ❏ If you have got something, you have it with you, or you own it. ◇ You use got to talk about a feature that someone or something has. He's got a lovely smile. ◇ You also use got to talk about illnesses. Sam's got measles. ◇ You use got to say what relatives someone has. She's got two sisters. ◇ You use got to talk about the availability of something. Come in and have a chat when you've got time. ◇ You use got to talk about a future event you are involved in. I've got a date.
   ❏ If something has got to be done, it must be done.
   ❏ If you ask what has got into someone, you want to know why they are behaving in an unusual way.

Goth The Goths were an East Germanic people who invaded the Roman Empire. ◇ Nowadays, goths are young people who wear black clothes and heavy black eye make-up. They listen to a gloomy kind of rock music called goth.

gothic was a style of architecture common in Western Europe from the 12th to the 16th centuries, and imitated in some 19th century buildings. Gothic buildings have tall pillars, high vaulted ceilings, and pointed arches.
   ❏ Gothic stories were popular in the late 18th century. They are full of gloom and the supernatural. ◇ Gothic is a kind of heavy ornate lettering.

gotten Americans often say have gotten (rather than 'have got') to mean 'have obtained', 'have received', or 'have become'. He could have gotten his boots without anyone seeing him... His leg may have gotten tangled in a harpoon line.

gouache (pron: goo-ash) is a painting technique using thick non-transparent watercolours; the watercolours are also called gouache. Originally, gouache was made by mixing ordinary watercolours with glue. A gouache is a painting done using gouache.

Gouda (pron: gow-dah) is a flat round Dutch cheese with a mild flavour.

gouge (pron: gowj) (gouging, gouged) If someone's eyes are gouged out, they are cut or pulled out violently. ◇ If a hole is gouged out, it is made in a rough or violent way. ◇ If you gouge something, you make a groove in it.

gourd (pron: goord) A gourd is a large marrow-like fruit. Gourds are sometimes dried and used as containers.

gourmand (pron: goor-mand) A gourmand is someone who enjoys eating and drinking, especially in large quantities.

gourmet (pron: goor-may) A gourmet is someone who knows a lot about good food and wine. ◇ Gourmet is used to talk about things intended for gourmets. ...a six-course gourmet dinner.

gout is a disease which causes painful swollen joints, especially in a person's foot.

govern ❏ The people who govern a country are the ones who make its laws and look after its affairs. ◇ If something is governed by a set of laws or regulations, it is controlled or regulated by them. ◇ Governing is used to describe a group of people officially responsible for making and enforcing laws or regulations. ...the zoo's governing council.
   ❏ If something governs an event or situation, it controls or influences it. The family's lives are governed by his

sporting demands.

governable You say a country is **governable** when the people are willing to accept and obey laws introduced by its government.

governance The **governance** of an industry or institution is the way it is managed. *...the CBI's conference on corporate governance.* ◇ The **governance** of a country is the way it is administered.

governess (governesses) A **governess** is a woman who lives with a family and teaches its children.

government The **government** of a country or state is the group of people responsible for governing it. ◇ **Government** is the organization and administration involved in governing a country, state, or smaller area. *Having intellectuals in high places does not guarantee good government... ...the reorganization of local government.* ◇ **Government** is used after other words to talk about different political systems. *...parliamentary government.*

governmental is used to talk about things to do with government or governments. *He sees no governmental solution to the problems... ...inter-governmental exchanges.*

governor A **governor** is the person in charge of the political administration of an area. American states have governors. ◇ In British colonies, the **governor** is the representative of the monarch. ◇ In Britain, the heads of prisons and some other large institutions are called **governors**. *...the Governor of the Bank of England.* ◇ The members of the committees which control schools and some other organizations are called **governors**.

governor general (governor generals *or* governors general) Some former British colonies have a **governor general**, who is the chief representative of the British monarch.

governorship If someone is appointed or elected to the **governorship** of an area or institution, they become its governor.

gown A **gown** is a long expensive dress worn on formal occasions. ◇ A **gown** is also a long loose coat worn by judges, lawyers, and academics. ◇ The protective outer garment worn by nurses and doctors in an operating theatre is called a surgical **gown**.

goy (*plural:* goyim *or* goys) **Goy** is an offensive Jewish word for a non-Jew.

GP A **GP** is a doctor who treats people at a local surgery or in their own homes. GP stands for 'general practitioner'.

GPO The **GPO** or **General Post Office** was the organization which used to be in charge of all mail and telephone services in Britain.

grab (grabbing, grabbed) ❏ If you **grab** something, you take hold of it quickly. If you **grab** at something or make a **grab** for it, you try to get hold of it. ◇ If you **grab** an opportunity, you take it eagerly. ◇ If someone **grabs** power or territory, they seize it. ◇ In sport, if someone **grabs** a victory, they win at the last moment.
❏ If someone is **grabbed,** they are kidnapped.
❏ If something **grabs** people's attention, they become very interested in it. ◇ If something is **up for grabs**, it is available to anyone who wants it.

grace (gracing, graced) ❏ **Grace** is used to talk about something being done in a smooth and elegant way. *They glide with superhuman grace across the floor.*
❏ **Grace** is also used to talk about polite and considerate behaviour. *The Queen received it with customary grace.* ◇ If what someone does **graces** an event, it makes it more attractive and enjoyable. *...Frank Worthington, whose talents graced the Wembley turf in 1974.*
❏ If someone does something with **good grace,** they do it willingly or cheerfully. If they do it with **bad grace,** they do it unwillingly or grudgingly.
❏ If you say someone has **fallen from grace,** you mean they are no longer in favour with the public, or with whoever is in power. *He was tipped as presidential candidate before his spectacular fall from grace.*
❏ **Grace** is used to say how much time someone has in which to do something. For example, if you are given ten days' **grace,** you must do something in the next ten days.
❏ In Christianity, **grace** is the special goodwill of God towards man. *Holiness was only possible by the grace of God.* A person who has received **grace** from God, is said to be in a **state of grace.** ◇ **Grace** is also a short prayer said before or after a meal.
❏ You say **Your Grace** when talking to a duke, duchess, or archbishop.
❏ A **grace and favour** house is let rent-free to someone by the monarch, the government, or an institution, as a special privilege. A **grace and favour** appointment is one which relies on the goodwill of whoever is in charge.
❏ **saving grace:** see **saving**.

graceful (gracefully, gracefulness) ❏ **Graceful** movements are pleasant to watch, because they are smooth and elegant. You call people and animals **graceful** when they move like this. *It has taught my daughters to move more gracefully... Her solo dance was a breath-stopping moment of gracefulness.* ◇ You say something like a building is **graceful** when it has a delicate kind of beauty.
❏ **Graceful** behaviour is polite and dignified. *...a graceful apology.*

graceless You say something is **graceless** when it is unattractive and has no interest or charm. ◇ You say someone's behaviour is **graceless** when they are rude or thoughtless, especially to someone who has been kind to them.

gracious (graciously, graciousness) You say someone is being **gracious** when they behave in a polite and unselfish way. *He was gracious in defeat... ...the graciousness of his manners.* ◇ **Gracious** and **graciously** are used on ceremonial occasions and in formal writing to describe things done by the monarch. *The Queen was graciously pleased to address the Regiment.* ◇ **Gracious** is used to describe the leisured lifestyle of rich upper-class people, especially in the past. *...a monument to 1930s gracious living.*

gradation is used when talking about the extent to which people or things can have something like a quality. For example, instead of talking about a range of income groups, you can talk about **gradations** of wealth.

grade (grading, graded) ❏ When a group of things or people is divided into **grades**, it is split into smaller groups, based on things like size, quality, or rank, with each group being given a name, number, or letter. *...the executive grade of the diplomatic service.* When a group is divided up like this, you say the people or things are **graded** or given a **grading**. *The hotel has been awarded a deluxe grading by the Tourist Board.* **Graded** is also used to talk about systems in which things are divided into grades.

...graded reading schemes.

❑ In schools in the USA and Canada, a **grade** is a group of similar age children being taught together.

❑ If you say someone **makes the grade,** you mean they succeed in something, or reach a required standard. *Staff who failed to make the grade were demoted.*

gradient A **gradient** is a slope, or the angle of a slope. *The railway climbs up a 1 in 100 gradient.*

gradual (gradually) A **gradual** change happens slowly or by small stages. *The forest is gradually disappearing.*

gradualism When people in power try to change a situation in small stages rather than all at once, this is called **gradualism.**

graduate (graduating, graduated) ❑ When someone **graduates,** they successfully complete a first degree at a university or college. Someone who has done this is called a **graduate.** A **graduate student** is someone who already has a degree and is studying for another one. ◇ In the United States and Canada, young people also **graduate** from high school. When they do this, they are called **high school graduates.**

❑ When someone goes from doing something easy to something harder, you can say they **graduate** to the second thing. You can also say someone **graduates** to a more important job.

❑ **Graduated** is used to describe something that increases by regular amounts or grades. *...graduated physical exercises.* ◇ If an object is **graduated,** it is marked with lines and numbers so that something can be accurately measured.

graduation is (a) the successful completion of a course at a university, college, or North American high school. (b) the ceremony at which students receive their certificates.

graffiti is words or drawings scribbled or sprayed on walls.

graft ❑ When doctors **graft** a piece of healthy tissue or an organ onto someone's body, they surgically attach it, to replace or repair a damaged part. Tissue or organs attached like this are called **grafts** or **transplants.**

❑ When one plant is **grafted** onto another, a shoot from one is joined to the stem and root system of the other, so they grow as one plant. ◇ If something new is **grafted** onto something which already exists, the two things are combined successfully. *Local customs were grafted on to traditional Iberian ways.*

❑ **Graft** is hard unglamorous work. If a person **grafts,** they work hard. *His career has been one of hard graft.*

❑ **Graft** is also obtaining money dishonestly by misusing a position of authority.

grain is a cereal crop like wheat or rice. The **grains** from a cereal crop are its seeds.

❑ A **grain** of something like sand or pollen is a very small particle. ◇ If you say there is a **grain** of truth in what someone says, you mean a small part of it is true and it should not be regarded as completely wrong or silly.

❑ The **grain** in wood is the pattern and direction of lines on its surface. ◇ You say something **goes against the grain** when it conflicts with someone's natural inclinations. You also say something **goes against the grain** when it conflicts with other things, such as people's beliefs or customs.

grainy You say something is **grainy** when it has a rough surface or texture as if it were made up of a lot of small grains. ◇ A **grainy** photograph or film is of poor quality and looks as if it is composed of grains of colour.

gram (or **gramme**) The weight of something can be expressed in **grams.** There are 1000 grams in a kilogram. A gram is about 0.035 of an ounce. **Grams** is usually written 'g' or 'gm'.

grammar The **grammar** of a language consists of rules which say how sentences should be formed. ◇ A **grammar** is a book which describes the rules of a language. ◇ A person's **grammar** is the way they apply or misapply the rules of a language. *Bad grammar is a sign of carelessness.*

grammar school A **grammar school** is a school for children who have shown high academic ability at age 11. Grammar schools now exist only in certain areas.

grammarian A **grammarian** is someone who studies and writes about grammar.

grammatical (grammatically) **Grammatical** is used to talk about things connected with grammar. *...grammatical errors... ...grammatically complete sentences.* ◇ If what someone says is **grammatical,** it follows the accepted rules of a language. *...a test to determine whether students can write grammatical English.*

gramme See gram.

gramophone A **gramophone** is a record player.

granary (granaries) A **granary** is a building for storing grain. ◇ **Granary** bread contains whole grains of malted wheat. 'Granary' is a trademark. ◇ The **granary** of a country or region is the place where most of its grain is produced. *Ukraine once prided itself on being the granary of Europe.*

grand (grandly) ❑ You use **grand** to describe things which are splendid and impressive. *Boulevards and avenues sweep grandly through the woods.* ◇ A **grand** event is large and expensive, and is often attended by important or famous people. ◇ If something is on a **grand** scale, it is much larger than usual. ◇ **Grand** plans and actions are intended to achieve important results.

❑ **Grand** is used in some titles to indicate high rank. *...the Grand Duke of Luxembourg.* ◇ When a man has been well-known for his work over a long period of time, he is sometimes called the **grand old man** of the thing he produces or does. *...Anthony Powell, the Grand Old Man of the English novel.*

❑ If you say a building or organization is **grandly** named, you mean its name makes it sound more important or interesting than it really is. *...my bank, or business centre as it is grandly called these days.*

❑ When you add together a series of totals, you get a **grand** total.

grand jury In the US and Canada, a **grand jury** is a group of people summoned to decide whether there is enough evidence to bring a criminal case to trial.

grand piano A **grand piano** is a large harp-shaped piano with the strings running horizontally.

Grand Prix (pron: gron pree) (plural: Grands Prix or Grand Prix) A **Grand Prix** is one of a series of international motor races for powerful racing cars.

grand slam If a sports team achieves a **grand slam,** it wins all its major matches or competitions in a season.

◇ In tennis, a **grand slam** tournament is one of a series of top international championships.

grandad (*or* **granddad**) Your **grandad** is your grandfather.

grandchild (**grandchildren**) A person's **grandchild** is the child of their son or daughter.

granddaughter A person's **granddaughter** is the daughter of their son or daughter.

grandee People who have power or influence, especially in politics, are sometimes called **grandees**. ...*the greatest Tory grandee of them all.* ◇ In Spain and Portugal, a **grandee** is a nobleman of the highest rank.

grandeur When something is splendid or magnificent, you can talk about its **grandeur**. ...*the grandeur of the mountains.* ◇ You can also talk about an important person's **grandeur**. If someone has **delusions of grandeur**, they are not as important as they think they are.

grandfather A person's **grandfather** is the father of their mother or father.

grandfather clock A **grandfather clock** is a clock with a pendulum in a very tall wooden case. It is also called a 'longcase clock'.

grandiloquent (**grandiloquence**) If someone is **grandiloquent**, they try to impress people by speaking in a pompous or unnecessarily complicated way. *He dismisses these criticisms with characteristic grandiloquence.*

grandiose is used to describe something which is very large, and meant to be impressive. ...*a grandiose 190-foot statue.* ◇ If someone is planning to do something on an unnecessarily large scale, you can say they have **grandiose plans or ideas**.

grandma Your **grandma** is your grandmother.

grandmaster is the title awarded to people who reach the highest international standard in chess.

grandmother A person's **grandmother** is the mother of their father or mother.

grandpa Your **grandpa** is your grandfather.

grandparent A person's **grandparents** are the parents of their mother or father.

grandson A person's **grandson** is the son of their daughter or son.

grandstand A **grandstand** is a terraced block of seats, usually with a roof, which give the best view of a sporting event. ◇ If a sporting event has a **grandstand finish**, it finishes in an exciting way, often with the result being decided at the very end. ◇ If you have a **grandstand view** of something which is happening, you can see it all very clearly.

granite is a very hard rock used for building.

granny (*or* **grannie**) (**grannies**) Your **granny** is your grandmother. ◇ A **granny flat** is an extension to a house, or part of a house which has been converted, to provide a flat for an elderly person.

grant ❑ When the government or a public body gives money for a particular purpose, you say it **grants** the money or makes a **grant**. ◇ If someone in authority **grants** an application or request, they agree to what is wanted. ◇ When someone receives something like an honour, you say they have been **granted** it.

  ❑ If you **take** what someone says **for granted**, you accept it as true. ◇ If something like a right or freedom is **taken for granted**, the people who have it accept it and do not think about it. ◇ If a person is **taken for granted**, the

things they do are not appreciated.

  ❑ People sometimes say **granted** when admitting something is true; they then go on to say something else. *Granted, summits are not the usual stuff of Community work. But at times they seem a disturbing symbol of the EU's elitism.*

granulated sugar is coarsely ground white sugar, often used to sweeten hot drinks.

granule (**granular**) A **granule** is a small grain of something. A **granular** substance is made up of granules.

grape **Grapes** are the green or purple berries of a cultivated plant called a grapevine. Grapes are used to make wine. They can also be eaten raw, or dried to make raisins, currants, or sultanas.

grapefruit (*usual plural:* **grapefruit**) **Grapefruit** are large round yellow citrus fruit with a sharp taste.

grapevine A **grapevine** is the plant grapes grow on. ◇ If you hear something on the **grapevine**, you hear it as a result of news or gossip being passed around.

graph A **graph** is a way of showing how numbers and quantities increase or decrease in relation to each other. It usually consists of two lines called 'axes' drawn at right angles. Further lines are drawn between the axes, and these show the relationship between the different numbers and quantities. ◇ When people are discussing an increase or decrease in something, they often talk about the **graph** going up or coming down. *Next year won't be brilliant but at least the graph will start to go up.*

graph paper is paper printed with small squares to make graph drawing easier.

graphic (**graphically**) ❑ If someone gives a **graphic** description or account of something, they describe it in a detailed and vivid way. *Miss Martin graphically described the injuries she had suffered.*

  ❑ **Graphics** are the drawings, photographs, and general art work associated with the production of books, magazines, and TV programmes. **Graphic** is used to talk about people and things connected with this kind of work. ...*a graphic designer.* ◇ Computer **graphics** are pictures, graphs, and diagrams produced on a computer.

graphite is a soft black form of carbon, used to make pencil leads.

graphology (**graphologist**) **Graphology** is the study of the way people's handwriting relates to their character. A **graphologist** is an expert on this.

grapple (**grappling**, **grappled**) If you **grapple** with a problem, you try hard to solve it. ◇ If two people **grapple**, they take hold of one another and struggle or fight.

grasp ❑ If you **grasp** something, you grip it firmly. When someone is gripping something, you can talk about their **grasp** of it. ◇ If you **grasp** something difficult or complicated, you understand it. *They had failed to grasp the need for economic reform.* You can talk about someone's **grasp** of something like this.

  ❑ If you **grasp** an opportunity, you take it. ◇ If something is **within your grasp**, it is likely you will get it or achieve it.

  ❑ If you describe someone as **grasping**, you mean they are selfish and want to get as much money for themselves as possible.

grass (**grasses**, **grassing**, **grassed**; **grassy**) ❑ **Grass** is the green narrow-leaved plant which grows naturally over large areas and is used to create lawns. Bamboo and cereals like wheat and rice are also types of grass. ◇ A **grassy** area is covered with grass. *The path picks its way over grassy banks.* ◇ A **grassed** area is one like a lawn where grass has been introduced and made to grow.

❏ If a person is **put out to grass,** they are made to retire, because they are no longer needed. Similarly, you can talk about an organization being **put out to grass** when it is disbanded.

❏ If someone **grasses** on a criminal, they tell people in authority what he or she has done or is planning to do. Someone who does this is called a **grass.**

❏ Grass is another name for marijuana.

grass roots (*or* grassroots) The **grass roots** of an organization are its ordinary members, as opposed to its leaders.

grass snake The **grass snake** is a brownish-green non-poisonous European snake.

grasshopper The **grasshopper** is a jumping insect which makes a ticking sound by rubbing its legs and wings together.

grassland is land covered with wild grass.

grassroots See grass roots.

grate (grating, grated; grater) ❏ If you **grate** food, you shred it into small pieces by rubbing it on the rough metal surface of a device called a **grater.**

❏ If things **grate,** they rub against each other, producing a harsh unpleasant sound. ◇ A **grating** sound is harsh and unpleasant. ◇ If something **grates** on you or **grates** on your nerves, you find it very irritating.

❏ A **grate** is a metal framework for holding coal or logs in a fireplace. ◇ A **grating** is a framework of wire or metal covering a hole.

grateful (gratefully) If you are **grateful** to someone for their help or kindness, you appreciate what they have done. *All donations will be gratefully received.*

gratify (gratifies, gratifying, gratified; gratifyingly, gratification) If you are **gratified** by something or find it **gratifying,** it gives you pleasure and satisfaction. *Davies has waited a long time to be so gratifyingly sought after... Eventually they recognised him, much to his gratification.* ◇ If someone's desire for something is **gratified,** it is satisfied.

grating See grate.

gratis If something is done or provided **gratis,** you do not have to pay for it.

gratitude is the feeling of being grateful for someone's kindness or help.

gratuitous (gratuitously) **Gratuitous** is used to describe something harmful or upsetting which is done without any justification. *...a gratuitous attack on the homosexual community... Surely drama has some function other than to shock gratuitously?*

gratuity (gratuities) Money given as a tip is sometimes called a **gratuity.** ◇ A **gratuity** is also a fairly large amount of money given to a member of the armed forces when he or she leaves after many years of service.

grave (gravely) ❏ **Grave** is used to describe things which are very serious. *...a grave crisis... There is something gravely wrong with the law.*

❏ **Grave** is used to describe people's feelings when they are very worried about something. *The government expressed its grave concern at the escalation of violence.* ◇ **Grave**

behaviour is quiet and serious. *Many Indians will tell you gravely that caste is the basis of their civilisation's survival.*

❏ A **grave** is a place where a dead person is buried. ◇ If you say someone who is dead would **turn in their grave,** you mean they would be very shocked or upset by something happening now.

❏ The **grave** accent (*pron:* grahv) is a symbol sometimes written over 'a' or 'e' in French. It indicates a change in the pronunciation of the letter. *...Sèvres porcelain.*

gravedigger A **gravedigger** is someone whose job is digging graves.

gravel is a mixture of small rock fragments and pebbles.

gravelly A **gravelly** voice is low and rough.

graveside If you are at someone's **graveside,** you are standing next to their grave at their funeral.

gravestone A **gravestone** is a large stone marking a grave, usually with some information on it about the person buried there.

graveyard A **graveyard** is a burial ground, especially one next to a church.

gravitas (*pron:* grav-it-ass) Someone who has **gravitas** is respected for their seriousness and intelligence.

gravitate (gravitating, gravitated) If you **gravitate** towards something, you are drawn towards it. *Newly released central European states gravitated towards the EU.*

gravitational The effect gravity has on something is called the **gravitational** force or pull.

gravity is the force which pulls things towards the centre of a planet, star, or moon. It is because of the Earth's gravity that things fall when you drop them. See also **centre of gravity.**

❏ If you talk about the **gravity** of a situation, you mean it is very serious.

gravy is a thin hot savoury brown sauce, served with meat. ◇ If you call an organization a **gravy train,** you mean people who join it get a lot of money for very little effort.

gray is the usual American spelling of 'grey'.

graze (grazing, grazed) ❏ When an animal **grazes,** it eats grass. ◇ When farmers **graze** their animals somewhere, they leave them there to eat grass. The land or grass they graze on is called **grazing.**

❏ If a bullet **grazes** you, it touches you as it passes, taking off some of your skin. ◇ If you **graze** yourself, you injure your skin by scraping it against something. You call an injury like this a **graze.**

grease (greasing, greased) **Grease** is soft or melted animal fat. ◇ If you **grease** something like a pan, you put oil or grease on it, to stop food sticking to it. ◇ **Grease** is also the thick oil used to lubricate machinery. If you **grease** machinery, you lubricate it with grease.

greasepaint is the oily make-up worn by actors in the theatre.

greaseproof paper does not absorb grease. It is often used to line baking tins.

greasy things contain grease or are covered in grease.

great (greater, greatest; greatly, greatness) ❏ **Great** is used to say something is very large. *Butterflies are out in great numbers... The scope for such reforms is great.*

❏ **Great** is used to say something is very important or significant. *The greatest threat is the onset of winter... The*

Middle East crisis has raised questions about America's greatness in the world.

❑ **Great** is used to say someone is outstandingly good at something. *...one of the world's greatest operatic sopranos.*

❑ **Great** and **greatly** are used to emphasize other words. *Movie stars go to great lengths to protect their privacy... He has benefited greatly from the breaching of the Berlin Wall.*

❑ You can show enjoyment or approval by saying something is **great**. *It's great to be back.*

❑ **Great-** is added to words like 'uncle', 'niece', and 'grandmother' to talk about relatives a generation further away than uncles, nieces, or grandparents. For example, your **great-aunt** is your mother's or father's aunt, and someone's **great-grandson** is a son of one of their grandchildren.

❑ **Greater** is used in front of the name of a city to talk about the city and its suburbs. *...Greater Manchester.* ◇ **Greater** is also used in front of the name of a country to talk about an area beyond the country's present borders, which some of its citizens feel should be part of the country. *...a Greater Albania.*

Great Britain is the island consisting of England, Scotland, and Wales, which together with Northern Ireland make up the United Kingdom.

Great Dane Great Danes are very large dogs with short hair.

greatcoat A greatcoat is a thick overcoat, especially one worn by people in the armed forces.

grebe Grebes are diving birds which live in lakes and ponds. The most common British grebes are the great crested grebe and the little grebe.

Grecian is used to talk about (a) things to do with Ancient Greece. *...a Grecian urn.* (b) things copied from the style of Ancient Greece. *...the club's elegant Grecian columns.*

greed is the desire for more money or possessions than you really need.

greedy (greedily) You say someone is being **greedy** when they try to get more of something than they really need. ◇ You also say someone is **greedy** when they eat more food than they really need. *...lunching greedily on steak and chips.*

Greek is used to talk about people and things in or from Greece. *...Greek voters.* ◇ A **Greek** is a person from Greece. ◇ The inhabitants of ancient Greece are sometimes called the **Greeks**. *The art was first introduced to the region by the Greeks.* ◇ The languages of modern Greece and ancient Greece are both called **Greek**.

green (greener, greenest) ❑ Green is the colour of grass.

❑ **Green** issues are concerned with protecting the environment. *...a green energy strategy.* ◇ **Green** often appears in the names of political parties or groups concerned with protecting the environment. The people in these parties and groups are sometimes called **greens**. *...the power of the Green movement in West Germany.*

❑ The **green revolution** is the increase in agricultural production in developing countries following the introduction of new crop types and farming methods.

❑ **Green** places are covered with grass or trees and shrubs. ◇ A **green** is a public area of grass in a town or village. ◇ The **greens** on a golf course are the areas of close-cut grass around each hole.

❑ **Greens** are the cooked leaves of vegetables like cabbage and spinach. ◇ A **green salad** is made mainly with lettuce and other green vegetables.

❑ If you say someone is **green**, you mean they are inexperienced or naive. ◇ If someone has **green fingers**, they are good at growing plants. ◇ If someone is **green with envy**, they are very envious of something someone else has.

❑ If you get the **green light** to do something, you get permission to go ahead with it.

green belt A green belt is a large area of countryside surrounding a city, where new building is limited by law.

Green Beret British and American commandos are sometimes called **Green Berets**.

green card If you have a green card, your motor insurance covers accidents abroad. ◇ A **green card** is also a document giving immigrants the right to live and work temporarily in the United States.

green paper A green paper is a document, usually prepared by the Government, which contains policy proposals to be discussed by Parliament and other groups.

greenback A greenback is a US dollar bill.

greenery ❑ Greenery is used to talk about green plants when they produce an attractive effect, for example in the countryside or a garden, or when used as a decoration inside a building. *...archways draped with greenery.*

❑ Policies aimed at protecting the environment are sometimes called **greenery**. *Economics and greenery are, on this occasion, on the same side.*

greenfly (plural: greenfly or greenflies) Greenfly are tiny green creatures which damage plants.

greengrocer A greengrocer or greengrocer's is a fruit and vegetable shop. The person who runs it is also called a **greengrocer**.

greenhouse A greenhouse is a transparent building, usually of glass, for growing plants in controlled conditions. ◇ The **greenhouse effect** is what happens when heat absorbed from the sun cannot escape from the atmosphere, due to a build-up of carbon dioxide and other gases. This produces 'global warming', in which the temperature of the atmosphere gradually rises. ◇ **Greenhouse** is used to talk about things to do with the greenhouse effect. *...the main greenhouse gas.*

greenish If something is greenish, it is slightly green.

Greenwich Mean Time See GMT.

greet (greeting, greeted) ❑ When you greet someone who has just arrived, you welcome them by saying pleasant or polite things. The things you say are called **greetings**. ◇ When a crowd greets someone, they welcome them with applause or cheers.

❑ You can describe people's reaction to something by saying it is **greeted** in a particular way. *His stubborn loyalty was greeted with irritation and even incredulity.*

❑ If you arrive somewhere and see something surprising or impressive, you can say you are **greeted** by the sight of it.

greetings card (or greeting card) Greetings cards are cards like birthday and Christmas cards which are sent on special days.

gregarious people like being with other people.

gremlin Gremlins are imaginary beings which people pretend are responsible for problems in machines.

grenade A **grenade** is a small bomb which can be thrown by hand or fired from a rifle.

grew See **grow**.

grey (greying; greyness) (*American spelling:* **gray**, *etc*) ❑ Any colour between black and white can be called **grey**. ◇ If you say someone is **grey**, you mean they have grey hair. If they are **greying**, their hair is going grey. ◇ A **grey** is a grey or white horse.

❑ If the weather is **grey**, the sky is covered with cloud and it is very dull. ...*the greyness of late September.*

❑ You use **grey** to describe things which are boring and unattractive. ...*Britain's grey political establishments.*

❑ You say there is a **grey area** when there is no clear dividing line between two things. *Whether feminists like it or not, there is a grey area between rape and persuasion.*

greyhound **Greyhounds** are thin fast-moving dogs bred for racing.

greyish If something is **greyish**, it is slightly grey.

grid ❑ A **grid** is a pattern of straight lines crossing each other to form squares. **Grid** is used to talk about various things which have this pattern, for example metal objects or the layout of a city's streets. *He is separated by a wire grid from his brothers and sister.* ◇ A **grid** reference is a series of numbers which help pinpoint a place on a map. It is based on the National Grid, a system in which the whole country is divided into squares.

❑ An electricity **grid** is a large number of power lines which are interconnected to make sure electricity is available throughout an area. ◇ A currency **grid** is a system involving several currencies in which the exchange rates between all the currencies remains fixed.

❑ In a car or motorcycle race, the starting **grid** is the place where the vehicles are positioned ready to begin.

griddle A **griddle** is a flat heavy piece of metal with a handle over the top, which is placed on a stove and used for cooking, especially baking scones.

grief is extreme sadness, often caused by someone's death. When someone is strongly affected by this feeling, you say they are **grief-stricken**. ◇ If something **comes to grief**, it ends unsuccessfully or disastrously.

grievance If you have a **grievance**, you feel resentful because you think you have been unfairly treated.

grieve (grieving, grieved) When people **grieve**, they feel very sad about something, especially someone's death. ◇ If something **grieves** you, you are annoyed or upset by it. *It grieves me to see some of the prices being charged.*

grievous (grievously) A **grievous** mistake or injury is a very serious one. *He became a national hero after being grievously burned during the Falklands conflict.*

grievous bodily harm If someone is charged with **grievous bodily harm** or **GBH**, they are charged with seriously injuring someone deliberately. This is a more serious charge than actual bodily harm.

griffin The **griffin** or **gryphon** was a mythological creature with the head and wings of an eagle, the body of a lion, and sometimes the tail of a serpent.

grill ❑ If you **grill** food, you cook it over or under a strong heat. The part of a cooker where you do this is called a **grill**, and so is the metal grid the food is placed on. ◇ A **grill** is also food cooked on a grill. *The cooking is mostly grills.* ◇ Some restaurants serving grilled food are also called **grills**. ...*the Savoy Grill.* ◇ See also **grille**.

❑ If someone is **grilled** or given a **grilling**, they are questioned intensively about something.

grille (*or* **grill**) A **grille** is a protective framework of wire or metal bars in front of a window or machine.

grim (grimmer, grimmest; grimly, grimness) ❑ A **grim** situation is harsh, unpleasant, or depressing. You can also say news or a description of something is **grim**. ...*the grimness of his first feature film.* ◇ A **grim** place is unattractive and depressing.

❑ If someone looks **grim**, they look serious or stern. You can also say someone is in a **grim** mood or does something **grimly**.

❑ **Grim** humour consists of finding something to laugh at in serious or sad situations. *There are haunting set-pieces, grimly funny, horrifying, or just bizarre.*

❑ If you **hang on grimly**, you continue with a course of action despite all difficulties.

grimace (*pron:* grim-uss) (grimacing, grimaced) If someone **grimaces**, their face twists into an ugly expression because they are in pain or annoyed. You call their expression a **grimace**.

grime (grimy, grimier, grimiest) **Grime** is dirt which has built up over a long time. If something is **grimy**, it is covered in dirt.

grin (grinning, grinned) If you **grin**, you smile broadly, usually showing your teeth. A smile like this is called a **grin**. ◇ If you say someone will have to **grin and bear** something, you mean they have no choice but to put up with it.

grind (grinding, ground) ❑ If you **grind** something or **grind** it **up**, you crush it to a powder. ...*freshly ground black pepper.* ◇ If someone tries to **grind down** an opponent, they try to break their resistance by continually putting pressure on them.

❑ If two hard things **grind** against each other, they rub together, often making a harsh noise. ◇ If a vehicle is **grinding** along, it is moving slowly and noisily because the engine is working hard. ◇ If something **grinds on**, it carries on slowly. If it **grinds to a halt**, it slows down and eventually stops. *The political process grinds on.*

❑ Hard dull routine work is sometimes called **the daily grind**. ◇ A **grinding** situation is one which never seems to get better and leaves people unhappy, tired, or bored.

gringo (gringos) Latin Americans sometimes call people from English-speaking countries **gringos**.

grip (gripping, gripped; grippingly) ❑ If you have a **grip** on something, it is under your control. *Rebel forces continued to tighten their grip around the capital.* ◇ If you have a **grip** on a subject, you understand it.

❑ If people are in the **grip** of something unpleasant, they are seriously affected by it. *The grip of sanctions tightened.* ◇ If people are **gripped** by a strong feeling, they experience it. ◇ If a story or performance **grips** you, it holds your attention. You say a story or event like this is **gripping**. ...*the most grippingly dramatic music around.*

❑ If you **grip** something, you take hold of it firmly. Your hold is called your **grip**. ◇ In sport, your **grip** is the way you hold something like a bat, golf club, or tennis racquet. *Marshall says he could adjust to a one-handed grip.*

❑ If tyres **grip** a road well, they do not skid easily. You say tyres like this have a good **grip**.

❑ If you **get to grips** with something like a problem or

come to **grips** with it, you begin to understand it and to deal with it in an effective way.

gripe (griping, griped) If someone keeps protesting or complaining about something, you can say they have a **gripe** or are **griping**.

grisly (*or* **grizzly**) A **grisly** murder is a particularly horrible one. A **grisly** story is about people dying in a horrible way.

grist If you say something is **grist to the mill** or **grist to your mill**, you mean you can make use of it in what you are trying to do or achieve. *The pound's difficulties remained grist to the mill for Tory Euro-sceptics.*

gristle is tough strands of cartilage in meat.

grit (gritting, gritted) ❑ If you say someone has **grit**, you mean they have a lot of courage.
  ❑ When people prepare to carry on in a difficult situation, you can say they **grit their teeth**.
  ❑ **Grit** is tiny pieces of stone. ◇ When lorries **grit** roads during very cold weather, they sprinkle them with grit to make them less slippery.

gritty (grittier, grittiest) ❑ A **gritty** person is courageous and determined. ◇ A **gritty** description of something is harsh and unsentimental.
  ❑ If something is **gritty**, it is covered in grit, or has a texture like grit.

grizzle (grizzling, grizzled) If a baby or child **grizzles**, it keeps crying and whining. ◇ You say an adult **grizzles** when they complain about something in an irritating way.

grizzled people have grey or grey-streaked hair.

grizzly (grizzlies) ❑ **Grizzlies** or **grizzly bears** are large fierce greyish-brown bears in North America.
  ❑ See also **grisly**.

groan (groaned, groaning) ❑ If you **groan**, you make a long low sound, because you are in pain, or to express disappointment or disapproval. A sound like this is called a **groan**. ◇ When people complain about something, you can say they **groan** about it.
  ❑ If wood **groans**, it makes a deep straining sound as it moves. ◇ You can say something is **groaning** when it is very heavily loaded. *...groaning shelves of books.*

grocer A **grocer** or **grocer's** is a small local shop which sells food and other household goods. The person who runs it is also called a **grocer**.

grocery (groceries) A **grocery** shop or **grocery** is the same as a grocer's. ◇ **Groceries** are things like flour, tea, and tinned foods.

grog is a drink made by diluting a spirit such as rum with water.

groggy (grogginess) If you feel **groggy**, you feel weak and dizzy. *The grogginess continued for a few days.*

groin A person's **groin** is the area around the fold where their legs join their body.

grommet A **grommet** is a plastic tube put into the eardrum of someone who has sticky fluid in their ear as a result of an infection. The grommet allows air to enter and dry out the ear.

groom (grooming, groomed) ❑ If a person is **groomed** for a possible future job, they are given special training or experience which will help them.
  ❑ At a wedding, the **groom** is the bridegroom.
  ❑ If a person is **well-groomed**, their appearance is very neat and tidy. You can talk about the **grooming** of someone like this.
  ❑ If you **groom** a horse, you clean and brush it. A person whose job is to clean, brush, and look after horses is called a **groom**. ◇ When animals **groom** each other, they clean each other's fur.

groove ❑ A **groove** is a narrow channel cut into a surface.
  ❑ The **groove** of pop music is its rhythm.

groovy Some people say things are **groovy** when they think they are attractive, exciting, or fashionable.

grope (groping, groped) If you **grope** for a solution to a problem, you try hard to think of one. ◇ If you **grope** for something, you feel about for it, to try to find it. ◇ If a woman is **groped**, she is touched and felt by someone for their sexual pleasure.

gross (grosses, grossing, grossed; grossly) ❑ A **gross** amount is a total amount before any deductions have been made. *The bond will pay 8.2% net, 10.93% gross.* See also **net**. ◇ If a person or business **grosses** an amount of money, they earn that amount before deductions are made for tax or expenses.
  ❑ The **gross** weight of something is its weight including the weight of its container or wrapping. See also **net**.
  ❑ You use **gross** or **grossly** when you are talking about something wrong, bad, or illegal to say it is particularly bad. *...a gross miscarriage of justice... Many public services are still grossly inefficient.*
  ❑ **Gross** speech or behaviour shows a lack of taste, or is very rude.
  ❑ A **gross** (*plural:* gross) is a dozen dozen, or 144. Some articles used to be sold by the gross.

gross national product See **GNP**.

grotesque (*pron:* grow-tesk) (grotesquely) You use **grotesque** to describe things which are ugly because they have exaggerated features. *...his grotesque makeup.* ◇ You also use **grotesque** when you are talking about something like a lie to say it is so far from the truth that it is absurd. *...information which is grotesquely misleading.*

grotto (grottoes) A **grotto** is a small pretty cave.

grotty is used to describe things and places which are unpleasant and of poor quality.

grouch (grouches; grouchy) A **grouch** is something you complain about. *One of the biggest grouches is the new system of payment.* ◇ A **grouchy** person is bad-tempered and always complaining.

ground ❑ The **ground** is the surface of the Earth. *We were airborne, all wheels off the ground.*
  ❑ **Ground** is used to talk about things connected with the land rather than the sea or air. *...ground troops.* ◇ If aircraft or pilots are **grounded**, they are not allowed to fly. *...the grounding of the 14 Indian Airbuses.*
  ❑ **Ground** is an area of open land. *...derelict ground.* ◇ **Ground** is used to talk about land used for a particular purpose. *...a camping ground.* ◇ The **grounds** of a large building are the land surrounding it and belonging to it.
  ❑ **Grounds** for doing something are reasons for doing it. *He has called for their release on humanitarian grounds.* ◇ **Grounds** for a feeling are reasons for having it. *There are grounds for optimism.* If a feeling is **well-grounded**, there are strong reasons for having it. ◇ If something is **grounded** in something else, it is based on it. *His cuisine is grounded in the rustic traditions of his homeland.*

❑ If someone **gains ground** in something like a competition or election, they improve their position. If they **lose ground**, their position becomes weaker. *This is his best chance to win back lost ground.* ◇ If something like an idea **gains ground**, it becomes more widely accepted. ◇ If you **stand your ground**, you stick to what you have said or decided, and do not let people make you change your mind. If you **give ground**, you take a less firm position, and agree to compromise.

❑ When people take the **high ground** or the **moral high ground**, they try to make people believe they are morally superior to their opponents. Similarly, you can say someone takes the intellectual **high ground**. *She's already seized the high ground, accusing her opponents of cheating... The President must seek to regain the high ground in the intellectual debate.* ◇ People who occupy the **middle ground** in a party or political system are not on its right or left wings.

❑ The **ground** you cover when you are discussing something is the range of things you talk about. ◇ If you **break new ground**, you make a discovery or start a new activity. ◇ If you get something **off the ground**, you get it started.

❑ **Ground** is used to talk about a place or situation where particular ideas or attitudes can develop. *Depression may make the village a fertile ground for ethnic hatred.*

❑ You use **on the ground** to emphasize that you are talking about the actual place where something is happening. *The UN has far too few troops on the ground to monitor the silencing of heavy guns.* ◇ **thin on the ground:** see thin.

❑ If you **go to ground**, you hide somewhere for a time.

❑ **Grounds** are the bits of coffee beans left at the bottom of a cup or jug when the coffee is finished.

❑ See also **grind**.

ground floor The **ground floor** of a building is the one which is level with the ground.

ground level If something is at **ground level**, it is at the same level as the ground.

ground plan A **ground plan** is a plan of the ground floor of a building. ◇ A **ground plan** is also a plan outlining how something is to develop.

ground rent is rent paid by the owner of a house or flat to the owner of the land on which it is built.

ground rules The **ground rules** for something people take part in are the basic principles on which it is supposed to operate.

ground staff are (a) people employed to look after and maintain sports grounds. (b) people whose job is to help maintain aircraft and runways, and to deal with passengers at airports.

ground-to-air missiles are fired from the ground at aircraft or other missiles in the air.

grounding If you are given a **grounding** in a subject, you are taught the basic facts or principles.

groundless If you say a fear or suspicion is **groundless**, you mean it is based on a mistake or misunderstanding.

groundnut **Groundnuts** are peanuts.

groundsman (groundsmen) A **groundsman** is someone whose job is to look after a sports ground or park.

groundswell If you say there is a **groundswell** of feeling or opinion about something, you mean a particular view of things is growing among people.

groundwork If you do the **groundwork** for something,

you do the early work which later work is based on.

group ❑ A **group** of people or things is (a) a number of them with something in common. *The scheme will be directed at the 13-17 age group.* (b) a number of them standing close together. *...an interesting group of trees.*

❑ When people or things are **grouped**, they are divided into groups. ◇ You also say things are **grouped** when they are put together in groups rather than scattered over an area. *These old houses were traditionally grouped into small hamlets.*

❑ If people **group together**, they join together to achieve a particular aim. If they **group around** someone, they support that person as their leader.

❑ A **group** is also (a) a small number of singers and musicians who perform pop songs together. (b) a number of associated companies owned and controlled by one person or organization. *...William Penn, the New York insurance group.*

group captain A **group captain** is a high-ranking officer in the RAF.

group practice A **group practice** is a small number of GPs working together in the same building to provide general health care in an area.

group therapy is a form of psychological counselling in which people discuss their problems with others in a group.

groupie A **groupie** is someone who admires a pop group or star, and follows them round and tries to meet them. ◇ People who behave in a similar way towards other famous people are also called **groupies**. *...literary groupies who haunt book launches.*

grouping A **grouping** is a set of people with the same interests or objectives, who organize themselves to work or act together. *...a grouping of fifteen developing countries.*

grouse (grousing, groused) ❑ The **grouse** (*plural:* grouse) is a small fat bird. Grouse are often reared for shooting and are afterwards eaten.

❑ If you **grouse**, you keep complaining about something. This kind of complaint is called a **grouse**.

grout is a thin mortar or cement for filling the joins between tiles and bricks.

grove A **grove** is (a) a plantation of olives, bananas, or citrus fruits. *...an orange grove.* (b) a group of trees growing close together, without undergrowth.

grovel (grovelling, grovelled) (*usual American spelling:* groveling, groveled) You say someone **grovels** when they act in a very humble way towards someone and try to please them. *She was not satisfied with this grovelling apology.*

grow (growing, grew, have grown) ❑ **Grow** is used to talk about an increase of some kind. For example, if the number of people out of work **grows**, it gets bigger. If a feeling **grows**, it gets stronger.

❑ When people or animals **grow**, their bodies mature and get bigger. ◇ A **grown** man or woman is fully developed and mature. ◇ **-grown** is added to words like 'full' and 'half' to say what stage an animal has reached in its development. *Golden plovers up on the mountains now have fully-grown young.*

❑ When someone **grows up**, they gradually change from a child to an adult. When they become an adult, you say they are **grown-up**. Children sometimes call adults **grown-ups**.

❑ When someone's hair **grows,** it gets longer. Similarly, you talk about nails **growing.** When a man **grows** a beard, he allows it to grow, instead of shaving.

❑ If a plant or tree is **growing** somewhere, it is coming out of the ground there. ◇ If you **grow** plants, you put them in the soil and look after them as they develop. Similarly, scientists **grow** cells or bacteria in laboratories by creating the conditions for them to develop and increase.

❑ **Grow** is used with some words to mean 'become'. *She grew distraught.* ◇ When people or things **grow** into something else, they develop and change into that thing. *This row threatens to grow into a full-blown crisis.*

❑ When young people give up a childish interest or hobby, you say they **grow out of** it. Similarly, someone can **grow out of** a childish way of behaviour.

❑ You say something **grows up** when it comes into existence somewhere and gradually becomes larger or more important. *Closer links between the centre and local authorities have grown up in many service areas.*

grower A **grower** is someone who grows and sells large quantities of a plant or crop.

growing pains are (a) pains children get in their muscles and joints, which some people think are the result of growing. (b) the temporary difficulties new organizations experience when they start to develop.

growl (growling, growled) When an animal **growls,** it makes a low noise in its throat, usually because it is angry. This noise is called a **growl.** ◇ If someone **growls** something, they say it in a low rough angry voice.

grown See grow.

grown-up See grow.

growth ❑ When economists talk about **growth,** they mean the increase in the amount of things a country or industry produces and sells at a profit. *...a slowing-down in economic growth.*

❑ A **growth** in something is an increase in it. *...the growth of public expenditure.* ◇ The **growth** of an attitude or feeling is its beginning and development. *...the growth of anti-Semitism in Eastern Europe.*

❑ When you talk about a person's **growth,** you are talking about the way their body grows as they develop from a baby to an adult. *Too little fat can stunt a child's growth.*

❑ A **growth** is an abnormal lump which grows on or inside a person, animal, or plant.

grub (grubbing, grubbed) ❑ **Grub** is food.

❑ A **grub** is the worm-like young of an insect.

❑ If you **grub** something up or **grub** it out, you dig it out of the ground.

grubby (grubbiness) **Grubby** things are dirty or dingy. ◇ **Grubby** is also used to describe behaviour of a very low standard. *...the grubbiness of illicit affairs.*

grudge (grudging, grudgingly) ❑ If you have a **grudge,** you go on feeling bitter towards someone who has harmed you in the past.

❑ A **grudging** feeling is one you have in spite of other feelings. For example, you might dislike someone, but have a **grudging** admiration for them. ◇ **Grudging** and **grudgingly** are used to describe things people do or say unwillingly. *His athletic status is somewhat grudgingly acknowledged.*

❑ If you say you do not **grudge** someone something, you mean you do not mind them having it. *In an editorial*

The Times says that nobody grudges her the birthday honour.

gruel is a simple cheap food made by boiling oats or another cereal with milk or water.

gruelling (*American spelling:* **grueling**) If something you take part in is **gruelling,** it is extremely difficult and tiring.

gruesome (gruesomely) A **gruesome** death is a particularly horrible one. A **gruesome** story is about people dying like this. A **gruesome** picture is of dead bodies, or people dying. *...gruesomely realistic depictions of death, punishment and plague.*

gruff (gruffly) A **gruff** voice is low, rough, and unfriendly. *He gruffly dismissed the criticism.*

grumble (grumbling, grumbled) When people **grumble,** they complain about something. A **grumble** is a complaint. You can also talk about people's **grumblings.**

grumpy (grumpily) A **grumpy** person is bad-tempered and miserable. *He drove off grumpily into the village.*

grunge is a type of guitar-based rock music which started in Seattle. The fashion associated with this type of music is also called **grunge;** followers of this fashion wear lumberjack-style shirts and heavy boots, and have unkempt hair.

grunt If someone **grunts,** they make a short low noise. You call this noise a **grunt.** ◇ If someone **grunts** something, they say it in a low rough voice, because they are not paying attention, or in a bad mood.

Gruyère (*pron:* **grew**-yair) is a hard yellow Swiss cheese with holes.

guano (*pron:* **gwah**-no) is dried sea-bird droppings. It is used as a fertilizer.

guarantee (guaranteeing, guaranteed) ❑ If one thing **guarantees** another or is a **guarantee** of it, it is certain to make it happen. *Independence from the ex-Soviet Union is no guarantee of democracy.*

❑ If you **guarantee** something, you promise it will definitely happen, or that you will do it or provide it. A promise like this is called a **guarantee.** *Funding is guaranteed for a trial period of three years.*

❑ If a company **guarantees** their work, they give a written promise that any faults occurring within a certain time will be repaired or the goods replaced free of charge. This written promise is called a **guarantee.**

guarantor A **guarantor** of a plan or policy is someone who guarantees to see it is carried out. ◇ A **guarantor** of a loan is someone who promises to repay it if the borrower fails to do so.

guard ❑ If someone **guards** a place or object, they watch over it, to protect it. Similarly, someone can **guard** a person. When soldiers are protecting a place or person, you can say they are **on guard.** ◇ If someone **guards** a person who is being held prisoner, they watch over them, to make sure they do not escape. ◇ If someone **stands guard** over something, they stand next to it, guarding it. ◇ If someone is **under guard,** they are being watched over or accompanied somewhere by soldiers or police, to protect them or make sure they do not escape. A building can also be **under guard.**

❑ If something is a carefully **guarded** or closely **guarded** secret, great care is taken to make sure only a few people know about it.

❑ A **guard** is someone who protects something or

someone, or prevents someone from escaping. *...border guards... ...prison guards.* ◇ **Guards** is used in the names of some military units. *...the Coldstream Guards.*

❑ When people talk about the **old guard,** they mean a group who have been powerful within a political party or organization for some time, but whose ideas now seem out of date.

❑ A **guard** is a railway official on a train. The part of the train where he or she travels and where things like bicycles are carried is called the **guard's van.**

❑ A **guard** on a piece of machinery is a cover over a dangerous part.

❑ If you **guard against** something happening, you take precautions to prevent it. ◇ If you are **on your guard,** you are being careful because a situation might become difficult or dangerous. ◇ If you catch someone **off guard,** you surprise them by doing something unexpected, which puts them at a disadvantage. ◇ See also **guarded.**

guard dog A **guard dog** is a large dog which has been trained to protect a place.

guarded (guardedly) You say people's behaviour is **guarded** when they are careful about what they say, because they are unsure about something or do not want to give away information. *They expressed guarded optimism about a peaceful outcome... Until last autumn most energy lobbyists were guardedly positive.*

guardian (guardianship) If you say someone is a **guardian** of something, you mean they are a protector or defender of it. ◇ If something is under someone's **guardianship,** they are responsible for looking after it. ◇ A **guardian** is someone who is named by the courts to look after a child. ◇ A person's **guardian angel** is someone who helps to guide and protect them.

guardsman (guardsmen) Soldiers belonging to some regiments are called **guardsmen.**

guava (*pron:* gwah-va) **Guavas** are round yellow tropical fruit with pink or white flesh.

gubernatorial (*pron:* gyoo-ber-nat-tor-i-al) is used to talk about things connected with the post of governor. *The Republican gubernatorial candidates appear to be just ahead in Illinois and Ohio.*

guerrilla (*or* guerilla) A **guerrilla** is a person who fights for a political cause with an unofficial army, usually against regular forces.

guess (guesses, guessing, guessed) ❑ If you **guess** something or make a **guess,** you give an answer or opinion without certainty, because you do not have all the facts. ◇ You also say someone **guesses** something when they give a correct answer or make a correct assumption without having all the facts. *The army had guessed that this was in the rebels' minds.*

❑ If you say something is **anybody's guess,** you mean nobody really knows what the true situation is. ◇ If you **keep someone guessing,** you do not tell them what they want to know.

guesstimate A **guesstimate** is an estimate based partly on guesswork.

guesswork is working something out by guessing, because you do not have all the facts.

guest ❑ A **guest** is someone you have invited to your home to stay, or to something like a party or dinner.

❑ You use **guest** to talk about someone being specially invited to appear or perform somewhere. *...a guest team from the Czech Republic.*

❑ A **guest** at a hotel is someone staying there. Some hotels and restaurants also refer to people who have a meal there as **guests.**

guest house (*or* guesthouse) A **guest house** is a private house where paying guests can stay. Guests are given rooms, breakfast, and sometimes evening meals.

guest of honour (guests of honour) The **guest of honour** is the most important guest at a dinner or other occasion.

guest room The **guest room** in a house is a room for visitors to sleep in.

guest worker Guest workers are people from poorer countries who are allowed into a developed country for a limited time to work at unskilled jobs.

guesthouse See **guest house.**

guff is used to talk about statements which are meant to sound impressive or important, but in fact have very little meaning. *Much guff is talked about Victorian values.*

guffaw If you **guffaw,** you laugh loudly and heartily. This type of laugh is called a **guffaw.**

guidance is help and advice from someone who knows more about a subject than you do. *...parents who want more guidance in choosing a school.*

❑ The **guidance** system on an aircraft or missile helps to control its course.

guide (guiding, guided) ❑ A **guide** is someone who shows people round buildings like museums and stately homes, or round historic cities. You can say someone **guides** people round places like these, or takes them on a **guided tour.**

❑ A **guide** or **guidebook** is a book which gives information about places like museums, cities, or countries. ◇ A **guide** is also (a) a book which tells you where to find things like the best hotels and restaurants. (b) a book which gives you information or instructions to help you do or understand something. *...a guide on how to sell a story to a national paper.*

❑ If you **guide** something, you control or strongly influence what happens to it. *He became the guiding force behind the reforms.* ◇ If you are **guided** by something, it controls or influences what you do. *...Lenin's guiding principles.*

❑ If something acts as a **guide,** it helps you understand something or predict what will happen. *If previous recoveries are any guide, unemployment may rise for two years after output touches bottom.*

❑ When something like a missile is **guided** towards a place, its route there is controlled from somewhere else.

❑ Girl guides are sometimes called **guides.**

guide dog A **guide dog** is a dog which is specially trained to help a blind person get about.

guidebook See **guide.**

guided missile A **guided missile** is one whose course can be controlled while it is in the air.

guideline Guidelines are official advice about how something should be done.

guild A **guild** is an organization of people who do the same job or share an interest. *...the Townswomen's Guild.*

guilder The **guilder** is the unit of currency in Holland. There are 100 cents in a guilder.

guile is crafty behaviour.

guileless Someone who is **guileless** behaves in an innocent and trusting way.

guillemot (*pron:* gil-lee-mot) The **guillemot** is a black and white seabird which catches fish by diving into the sea. Guillemots do not build nests, but lay their eggs on bare rock.

guillotine (*pron:* gil-o-teen) (guillotining, guillotined) ❑ The **guillotine** was an apparatus used in the past for executing people. It released a sharp blade which cut off the person's head. If someone was **guillotined**, they were executed in this way.

❑ In parliament, if the government **guillotines** a debate, it officially limits the amount of time for discussion before a vote must be taken. A limit of this kind is called a **guillotine.**

❑ A **guillotine** is also a device for cutting and trimming paper.

guilty (guiltily, guilt) ❑ If you feel **guilty** about something, you realize you have done something wrong and are sorry about it. You call this feeling **guilt.** *I would drop a book guiltily if anyone came into the room.* ◇ You use **guilty** with words like 'memory' and 'secret' to say that thinking about certain things brings on feelings of guilt. *...guilty memories from previous love affairs.*

❑ If someone has committed a crime, you say they are **guilty** of it.

guinea A **guinea** is an old British unit of money worth 21 shillings, or £1.05.

guinea fowl (*plural:* guinea fowl) **Guinea fowl** are plump grey birds, related to the pheasant and originally from Africa. They are kept on farms for their meat.

guinea pig Guinea pigs are small furry animals, originally from South America and often kept as pets. ◇ People used in experiments are sometimes called **guinea pigs.**

guise (*rhymes with 'size'*) **Guise** is used to say something is made to look like something else. *Under the guise of 'scientific whaling' the Japanese have continued to hunt.*

guitar (guitarist) A **guitar** is a six-stringed instrument played by plucking or strumming. A guitar player is called a **guitarist.**

gulag A **gulag** was a prison or labour camp in the former Soviet Union, often used for political prisoners. If you talk about **the gulag,** you mean all prisons of this type. *Most of the priests perished in the gulag.*

gulf A **gulf** is a very large bay. *...the Gulf of Mexico.* ◇ A **gulf** is also a large gap or difference between things, especially between people's understanding or opinions. *The gulf between the moderates and the fundamentalists is as wide as ever.*

Gulf States The **Gulf States** are the oil-producing states around the Persian Gulf. They are Iran, Iraq, Kuwait, Saudi Arabia, Bahrain, Qatar, the United Arab Emirates, and Oman.

Gulf Stream The **Gulf Stream** is a warm ocean current flowing from the Gulf of Mexico towards north-west Europe.

gull ❑ Gulls are common long-winged sea birds with piercing cries. There are many kinds of gulls; the most common British species is the herring gull.

❑ If you **gull** someone, you get them to believe something which is not true. Someone who is deceived like this is called a **gull.**

gullet The **gullet** is the muscular tube connecting the mouth to the stomach. ◇ If you say something **sticks in your gullet,** you mean you find it completely unacceptable.

gulley (*or* gully) A **gulley** is a long narrow valley with steep sides.

gullible (gullibility) A **gullible** person is easily tricked. You talk about the **gullibility** of someone like this.

gully (gullies) See **gulley.**

gulp If you **gulp** food or drink, you eat or drink it quickly, swallowing large quantities at a time. Each swallow can be called a **gulp.** ◇ If you **gulp,** you swallow air, often because you are surprised or nervous.

gum (gumming, gummed) ❑ **Gum** is a type of glue for sticking paper. If you **gum** things together, you stick them together using gum.

❑ Chewing gum is often called **gum.**

❑ A person's **gums** are the firm pink flesh which their teeth grow out of.

gun (gunning, gunned) ❑ A **gun** is a weapon which fires bullets, shells, or missiles. ◇ If someone is **gunned down,** they are shot and fall to the ground, either injured or dead.

❑ If someone is **gunning for** you, they are trying to harm you or make trouble for you.

❑ If you say someone has **jumped the gun,** you mean they have done something before they were supposed to. ◇ If you **stick to your guns,** you continue to have your own opinions or behave in the same way, in spite of pressure from other people.

gun dog A **gun dog** is a dog trained to find and bring back birds or animals after they have been shot.

gun-running (gun-runner *or* gunrunner) **Gun-running** is smuggling weapons and ammunition between countries. Someone who does this is called a **gun-runner.**

gunboat A **gunboat** is a small warship with several large guns.

gunfire is the repeated shooting of guns.

gung-ho If someone has a **gung-ho** attitude to getting involved in a war, they are very keen on it, often without considering the consequences. You can say people are **gung-ho** about getting involved in other things. *The west is gung-ho for free trade.*

gunman (gunmen) A **gunman** is an armed criminal.

gunner A **gunner** is an ordinary soldier in an artillery regiment. ◇ A **gunner** is also a member of the crew of a ship, plane, or helicopter who is responsible for firing a gun from it.

gunpoint If someone is forced to do something at **gunpoint,** they are threatened with a gun and told to do it.

gunpowder is an explosive mixture of potassium nitrate, sulphur, and charcoal.

gunrunner See **gun-running.**

gunship See **helicopter.**

gunshot A **gunshot** is a single shot fired from a gun.

gurgle (gurgling, gurgled) When liquids **gurgle,** they make a bubbling sound. ◇ When a baby **gurgles** or produces **gurgles,** it makes happy bubbling noises in its throat.

Gurkha A Gurkha is a person from a Hindu group in Nepal. Gurkha men are often soldiers in the British Army.

guru A **guru** is a Hindu or Sikh spiritual leader or teacher. ◇ The chief thinker behind an intellectual or political movement can be called its **guru**. ◇ An expert on a subject is also sometimes called a **guru**.

gush (gushes, gushing, gushed) When liquid **gushes** out of something, if flows out quickly and in large quantities. You can talk about a **gush** of liquid coming out of something. ◇ If someone **gushes**, they express admiration or pleasure by speaking in an exaggerated way. ...*gushing television commentators.*

gusset A **gusset** is a piece of material sewn into clothes to make them stronger, wider, or more comfortable.

gust (gusty) A **gust** of wind is a sudden strong burst of it. You can talk about winds being **gusty** or say they **gust**. ...*violent winds, which at times gusted up to 138 mph.*

gusto If you do something with **gusto**, you do it with energy and enthusiasm.

gut (gutting, gutted) ❑ The **gut** is the tube inside the body which food passes through as it is being digested. ◇ If you talk about a person's or animal's **guts**, you mean their intestines, or all their internal organs. ◇ If you **gut** an animal or fish, you take out its internal organs.

❑ A **gut** feeling is one based on instinct or emotion rather than reason. ◇ If you say someone has **guts**, you mean they are brave and determined.

❑ If a building or vehicle is **gutted**, the inside is destroyed by fire.

gutless A **gutless** person has a weak character and lacks courage and determination.

gutsy A **gutsy** person is brave and determined.

gutter ❑ A **gutter** is (a) a channel at the side of a road for carrying away rainwater. (b) a long trough along the edge of a roof for taking rainwater to a drainpipe.

❑ If you say someone is in the **gutter**, you mean they are forced to live in a very poor and dirty environment, especially in a city. *The hero eventually struggles out of the gutter to become a film director.* ◇ The **gutter press** are newspapers which rely on sensational stories rather than serious news about politics or international affairs.

guy Some people call a man a **guy**. ◇ A **guy** is also a model of Guy Fawkes, burned on November 5th. ◇ If you **guy** someone, you make fun of them.

guzzle (guzzling, guzzled; guzzler) If you **guzzle** something, you eat or drink it quickly and greedily. Someone who eats or drinks like this can be called a **guzzler**.

gym A **gym** is the same as a gymnasium.

gymkhana (*pron:* jim-kah-na) A **gymkhana** is an event consisting of horse riding and jumping competitions.

gymnasium A **gymnasium** is a large room with exercise equipment.

gymnastics (gymnast; gymnastic) **Gymnastics** (*pron:* jim-nas-tiks) are physical exercises involving things like ropes and wooden bars, which develop your agility and strength. People who are very good at these exercises and compete against each other are called **gymnasts** (*pron:* jim-nasts). ◇ **Gymnastic** is used to talk about things to do with gymnastics. ...*gymnastic ability.*

gymslip A **gymslip** is a sleeveless dress which schoolgirls used to wear over a blouse or jumper as part of their school uniform.

gynaecology (*pron:* guy-nee-kol-la-jee) (gynaecologist; gynaecological) (*can be spelled with an 'e' instead of 'ae'*) **Gynaecology** is the branch of medicine dealing with diseases and illnesses suffered only by women, particularly those affecting the reproductive system. A doctor who specializes in this is called a **gynaecologist**. **Gynaecological** is used to talk about things to do with gynaecology. ...*gynaecological investigations.*

gypsum is a chalk-like mineral used for making plaster of paris.

gypsy (gypsies) (*or* gipsy, gipsies) **Gypsies** are a race of travelling people found throughout Europe.

gyrate (gyrating, gyrated; gyration) If something **gyrates**, it turns round and round in a circle, usually very fast. A movement like this is called a **gyration**. ◇ When people who are dancing **gyrate**, they make circular movements with their hips. Movements like these can be called **gyrations**.

H h

H-bomb See hydrogen bomb.

ha See hectare.

habeas corpus (*pron:* hay-bee-ass kor-puss) A writ of **habeas corpus** is a legal document ordering an arrested person to be brought before a judge or court, who must then decide whether it is lawful to keep them in prison.

haberdasher (haberdashery) A **haberdasher** or **haberdasher's** is a shop selling small things for sewing like buttons and zips. The **haberdashery** department of a large store is the part where you can buy things like this.

habit ❑ A **habit** is something you do often or regularly. *He got into the habit of visiting her every morning.* ◇ A **habit** is also something which is bad for you but which it is difficult to stop doing. ...*helping smokers give up the habit.*

❑ A monk's or nun's **habit** is their clothing, which is often long and loose-fitting.

habitable If a building is **habitable**, it is in a fit state for people to live in.

habitat The **habitat** of an animal or plant is its natural environment.

habitation If a place is used for **habitation** or for **human habitation**, people live there. If you say a building is unfit for **habitation**, you mean it is not in a fit state for people to live in.

habitual (habitually) **Habitual** and **habitually** are used to talk about things a person often does. For example, you can say someone **habitually** tells lies or is a **habitual** liar. Similarly, you can say someone is **habitually** cheerful, or talk about their **habitual** cheerfulness.

habituated If you are **habituated** to something, you are used to it. *He wiped out enemies at a rate spectacular even for a man habituated to mass murder.*

habitué (*pron:* hab-it-yew-ay) A **habitué** of a place is someone who goes there regularly.

hacienda (*pron:* hass-ee-end-a) A **hacienda** is a ranch or large estate in Latin America.

hack (hacker, hacking) ❑ If you **hack** at something, you cut it with a sharp tool, using strong strokes.

❑ If you call a journalist or writer a **hack**, you mean they work quickly without worrying about the quality of their work.

❑ If someone **hacks** into a computer, they get unauthorized access to it, usually from a different place, to see the information stored there or to interfere with it in some way. Someone who does this is called a **hacker**; what they do is called **hacking**.

hackles are the hairs on the back of a dog's neck, which stick up when the dog gets angry or frightened. If you say a person's **hackles** are raised, you mean they are angry about something.

hackneyed A **hackneyed** word or phrase has lost a lot of its meaning or impact because it has been overused. You can also say something like the plot of a play or film is **hackneyed**.

hacksaw A **hacksaw** is a small saw for cutting metal.

had See **have**.

haddock (*plural:* haddock) **Haddock** are large fish caught in the North Atlantic. They are similar to cod, but smaller.

Hades In Greek mythology, **Hades** is the home of the dead.

haematology (*pron:* hee-ma-tol-o-jee) (haematologist) (*can be spelled with an 'e' instead of 'ae'*) **Haematology** is the branch of medicine concerned with diseases of the blood. A person who specializes in this is called a **haematologist**.

haemoglobin (*or* hemoglobin) (*pron:* hee-moh-globe-in) **Haemoglobin** is a protein in red blood cells which carries oxygen from the lungs.

haemophilia (*pron:* hee-moh-fill-lee-a) (haemophiliac) (*can be spelled with an 'e' instead of 'ae'*) **Haemophilia** is a hereditary disease in which the blood does not clot properly, so the sufferer bleeds for a long time. Someone who has this disease is called a **haemophiliac**.

haemorrhage (*pron:* hem-or-ij) (haemorrhaging, haemorrhaged) (*can be spelled with an 'e' instead of 'ae'*) ❑ A **haemorrhage** is serious heavy bleeding in part of someone's body. If someone is bleeding like this, you say they are **haemorrhaging**.

❑ If a place or institution is losing people or resources at a rapid rate, you can say it is **haemorrhaging**. You can talk about a **haemorrhage** of people or resources. *...the haemorrhage of BBC-trained talent into the private sector.*

haemorrhoids (*or* hemorrhoids) (*pron:* hem-or-oydz) are painful swollen veins in and around the anus. They are also called 'piles'.

hag When people dislike a woman very much, they sometimes call her a **hag**.

haggard If someone is **haggard**, they look worried and tired, or thin and ill.

haggis (haggises) A **haggis** is a Scottish dish made from oatmeal, onion, and offal, boiled in a bag made from a sheep's stomach lining.

haggle (haggling, haggled) If someone **haggles**, they argue about the cost of something they are buying.

hail (hailing, hailed) ❑ You say something is **hailed** as a particular thing when it receives a lot of praise. For example, you can say a new book is **hailed** as a masterpiece. *The agreement was hailed as a breakthrough.*

❑ When it **hails**, tiny balls of ice called hailstones fall from the sky. A shower of these hailstones is called **hail**. ◇ A **hail** of objects is a large number of them falling on you or around you.

❑ If you **hail** from a place, that is where you come from.

❑ If you **hail** a taxi, you signal to the driver to stop so you can get in.

hailstone Hailstones are the tiny balls of ice which fall to the ground when it hails.

hailstorm A **hailstorm** is a storm in which hailstones fall.

hair (-haired) ❑ **Hair** on a person or animal is the mass of fine strands which grow out of the skin, especially on the head, and help keep heat in the body. Individual strands are called **hairs**. -**haired** is used to say what kind of hair a person or animal has. *...a long-haired poet.*

❑ If something comes within a **hair's breadth** of happening, it nearly happens.

hair-grip A **hair-grip** is a metal clip for holding hair back from the face.

hair-raising A **hair-raising** experience is frightening, because of the danger involved. You can also call a description of something **hair-raising**.

hair-shirt If you are wearing a **hair-shirt**, you are making yourself suffer, often so things will improve in the future. *For the last 10 years he has lived a life of almost hair-shirt austerity.* ◇ Originally, a **hair-shirt** was a shirt made of rough horsehair cloth worn by some Christians to show they were sorry for their sins.

hair slide A **hair slide** is a decorative clip which women and girls put in their hair to hold it in place.

hairbrush (hairbrushes) A **hairbrush** is a brush for your hair.

haircut A person's **haircut** is the style in which their hair has been cut. ◇ If you have a **haircut**, someone cuts your hair for you.

hairdo (hairdos) Someone's **hairdo** is the way their hair has been cut and styled.

hairdressing (hairdresser) **Hairdressing** is cutting and styling hair. A person who does this for a living is called a **hairdresser**. A place where people go to get their hair cut and styled is called a **hairdresser's**.

hairdryer (*or* hairdrier) A **hairdryer** is a machine for drying hair.

hairless If a part of someone's body is **hairless**, there is little or no hair there.

hairline Your **hairline** is the edge of your hair next to areas of smooth skin.

hairpiece A **hairpiece** is a piece of false hair used to make natural hair look thicker or longer.

hairpin bend A **hairpin bend** is a sharp U-shaped bend in a road.

hairstyle Someone's **hairstyle** is the way their hair has been cut and styled.

hairy (hairier, hairiest) A **hairy** person or animal is covered with hair. ◇ If you call a situation **hairy**, you mean it is dangerous and frightening.

hake (plural: hake) **Hake** are large fish similar to cod.

halal (pron: hal-lahl) If something is **halal**, it is approved by the laws of the Muslim religion. **Halal** meat is from animals slaughtered according to Muslim law.

halcyon (pron: hal-see-on) A **halcyon** time is a peaceful or happy one. *The halcyon days are over in South-East Asia.*

half (halves) ❑ A **half** is one of two equal parts of something. If something is divided in **half**, it is divided into two equal parts. ◇ A **half** or **one half** is also the fraction written as ½.
  ❑ In games like football, the playing time is divided into two parts called **halves**.
  ❑ **Half past** means thirty minutes after the hour.
  ❑ **Half** is used to mean 'not completely'. For example, if something is half empty, it is only partially empty. *I think that NATO half expected this to happen... ...from behind half-closed blinds.* ◇ **Half-** is added to words like 'English', 'German', and 'American' to say someone has one parent from one country and one from another country.
  ❑ If something is increased **by half**, half the original amount is added to it. If you decrease it **by half**, half the original amount is taken away. ◇ If you say someone does not do things **by halves**, you mean they do them very thoroughly.

half-baked ideas or plans are poorly thought out, and so are usually foolish or impractical.

half board is used to talk about hotel accommodation which includes breakfast and an evening meal but not lunch.

half-brother If someone is your **half-brother**, he has the same father as you or the same mother, but not both.

half-caste is an offensive word for someone who has parents of different races.

half-cock A **half-cock** plan or scheme has not been planned properly, and goes wrong.

half-hearted (half-heartedly) If someone is **half-hearted** about something, they do not show any real enthusiasm for it. *Poland has half-heartedly offered us a solution.*

half-life The **half-life** of something radioactive is the time it takes to lose half its radioactivity.

half-mast If a flag is at **half-mast**, it is flying half-way down the pole, as a sign of mourning.

half-moon A **half-moon** shape is a semi-circle.

half-price If something is **half-price**, it is being sold for half its usual price.

half-sister If someone is your **half-sister**, she has the same father as you or the same mother, but not both.

half-term is a short holiday in the middle of a school term.

half-timbered A **half-timbered** building has a framework of wooden beams which can be seen from the outside.

half-time is the short break when players have a rest between the two halves of a sports match.

half-yearly events happen every six months.

halfpenny (pron: hape-nee) The **halfpenny** was a British coin worth half an old penny (about 0.2p).

halfway ❑ The **halfway** point in an event is the time when half of it is over. You can also say something happens **halfway** through an event.
  ❑ If something is **halfway** between two places, it lies between them and is the same distance from each of them. ◇ If you **meet someone halfway**, you compromise on some points to reach an agreement. A compromise position can be called a **halfway house.**

halibut (plural: halibut) The **halibut** is a large fish caught in the North Atlantic. It is the largest flatfish.

halite is a rock deposit which is an important source of the mineral salt known as 'rock salt'.

hall A **hall** is a large room or building used for public events like concerts and meetings. ◇ A **hall** is also an entrance area just inside the front door of a house.

hall of residence Halls of residence are blocks of rooms or flats owned by universities or colleges, for students to live in.

hallmark If you say something is the **hallmark** of a type of person, you mean it is their most typical quality or feature. *Believing in greater equality is the traditional hallmark of the socialist.* ◇ A **hallmark** is an official mark on a gold or silver object which indicates its origin and quality.

hallo See hello.

hallowed things are greatly respected.

Halloween (or Hallowe'en) is October 31st, the night when witches and ghosts are supposed to be about.

hallucinate (hallucinating, hallucinated; hallucination) If someone **hallucinates**, they see things which are not really there, because they are ill or on drugs. The things they see are called **hallucinations.**

hallucinatory If someone is in a **hallucinatory** state, they are likely to have hallucinations. **Hallucinatory** drugs can have this effect on people.

hallucinogenic drugs can make people hallucinate.

hallway The **hallway** of a building is its entrance hall.

halo (haloes or halos) A **halo** is a ring of light round a star or planet. ◇ In pictures of Jesus, a circle of light called a **halo** is often drawn round his head. Haloes are also drawn round the heads of saints and angels. ◇ A glow of light surrounding anything can be called a **halo.**

halogen (pron: hal-oh-jen) is a name given to any of the nonmetallic chemical elements fluorine, chlorine, bromine, iodine, and astatine.

halt ❑ If growth, development, or an activity **halts** or is **halted**, it stops completely. You can also say it **comes to a halt** or **grinds to a halt.** ◇ If someone **calls a halt** to something, they decide not to continue with it.
  ❑ If people or vehicles **halt** or are **halted**, they stop moving. You can also say they **come to a halt.**

halter A **halter** is a strap round an animal's head with a lead attached to it.

halting (haltingly) **Halting** speech has many pauses and hesitations. *Mr Delors recently made a speech, haltingly, in German.*

halve (halving, halved) If something **halves** or is **halved**, it is reduced to half its original size. ◇ When you **halve** something like an orange, you cut it into two equal parts.

ham (hamming, hammed) ❑ **Ham** is smoked or salted meat from a pig's thigh. A **ham** is a joint of this meat.
  ❑ A **ham** is also an amateur radio operator, especially

ham-fisted

359

hand-picked

one who uses radio equipment at home.

❑ If you say actors are **hamming it up**, you mean they are overacting, either deliberately or because they are bad actors.

ham-fisted If you say someone is **ham-fisted**, you mean they are clumsy and awkward with their hands.

hamburger A **hamburger** is a flat round piece of fried or grilled minced beef, often served in a bread roll.

hamlet A **hamlet** is a small village.

hammer (hammering, hammered) ❑ A **hammer** is a tool with a heavy head for hitting things. If you **hammer** something somewhere, you force it there by hitting it with a hammer. ◇ If you **hammer** on a surface, you keep hitting it with your fists.

❑ If someone is **hammered** or takes a **hammering**, they are heavily defeated in something like a game or debate.

❑ If someone **hammers away** at a point or **hammers** it **home**, they keep mentioning it, to get people to think about it. ◇ When people **hammer out** something like an agreement, they reach it after long and difficult discussions.

❑ If something is **under the hammer**, it is being sold by auction.

❑ The **hammer** is a field event in athletics. Competitors throw a metal ball on the end of a wire (the **hammer**) as far as they can.

hammock A **hammock** is a hanging bed made of string or canvas.

hamper (hampering, hampered) ❑ If something **hampers** you, it makes it difficult for you to move. If something **hampers** what you are doing, it makes progress difficult.

❑ A **hamper** is a large basket with a lid for taking food on picnics. A hamper packed with food can also be given as a present.

hamster A **hamster** is a small mouse-like animal with a short tail and cheek pouches. It is often kept as pet.

hamstring (hamstringing, hamstrung) A person's **hamstrings** are the tendons at the back of their knees. ◇ If someone is **hamstrung**, the actions they can take in a situation are very limited.

hand ❑ A person's **hands** are the parts of their body attached to their arms at the wrists. Monkeys and apes also have hands. ◇ If you do something **by hand**, you do it using your hands rather than a machine. ◇ **Hand** is used in front of words like 'mirror', 'bell', and 'drill' to talk about a small version of an object, designed to be held in a person's hand.

❑ If you **hand** something to someone, you give it to them. ◇ If you **hand out** a set of things, you give one to each person. See also **handout**.

❑ If you **hand in** something, you give it to someone in authority. *Lobbyists will hand in a 50,000-signature petition.* ◇ If you **hand** something **over**, you give it to someone else, and it becomes theirs instead of yours. ◇ If you **hand over** to someone, you give them responsibility for something you were previously in charge of.

❑ If you **hand** something **on** to someone, you give it or leave it to them. *They generate ideas which are then handed on for civil servants to turn into plans.* ◇ If possessions are **handed down**, they are given or left to younger people in the same family. ◇ If something **changes hands**, it goes from one person to another. ◇ If something dangerous or

secret gets into the **wrong hands**, it is obtained by people who will use it for illegal or harmful purposes.

❑ If you **have a hand** in something, you are actively involved in it. ◇ If you talk about someone's **hand** being in something, you mean they are secretly involved in it. *Do you see the hand of the military in this?*

❑ If you **give** someone **a hand**, you help them in some way. ◇ If you give someone a **free hand**, you let them deal with something exactly as they want.

❑ If you have your **hands full**, you are very busy and cannot take on anything else. ◇ If you have a responsibility or problem **on your hands**, you have to deal with it. When it is **off your hands** or **out of your hands**, it is no longer your responsibility. ◇ If you **wash your hands** of a problem, you refuse to take any more responsibility for it.

❑ If someone's **hands are tied**, they are unable to act as they would like, because of something like a law or rule. ◇ If you **take the law into your own hands**, you break the law by punishing someone yourself when they have done something wrong.

❑ The job or problem **in hand** is the one you are dealing with now. ◇ If a sports team has games **in hand**, they have played fewer games than their opponents.

❑ If you have something **to hand**, you have it ready to use when needed. ◇ Something which is **at hand** is close by. ◇ You also say something is **at hand** when it is going to happen soon. ◇ If someone is **on hand**, they are near and ready to help. *Waiters serving chilled champagne will be on hand.*

❑ If you reject an idea **out of hand**, you reject it immediately and completely. ◇ If a situation **gets out of hand**, it is no longer controllable.

❑ If two things **go hand in hand**, you tend to get one where you get the other. ◇ **hand in glove**: see **glove**.

❑ A **hand** of cards is all the cards dealt to a player in a game. You say, for example, that someone has 'a good hand'. Similarly, the strength of someone's position in an argument or conflict can be called their **hand**. *The ruling has strengthened the hand of those who back Mr Powell's bill.* If someone is in a strong position and does not let people know about it, you can say they do not **show their hand**.

❑ When people in authority **hand out** advice or punishment, they give it. ◇ When a judge **hands down** a sentence, he or she announces what it will be.

❑ People employed to do manual work on a farm or at a factory are sometimes called **hands**.

❑ An **old hand** is someone who has had a lot of experience of something.

❑ You say **on the one hand** and **on the other hand** when mentioning contrasting aspects of a problem or situation. *France were unable to create scoring chances. The All Blacks, on the other hand, scored two tries.*

hand baggage See hand luggage.

hand gun See handgun.

hand-held A **hand-held** machine is small enough to use or carry in your hand.

hand luggage or **hand baggage** is the bags or cases you keep with you during a coach or plane journey.

hand-me-downs are clothes passed from one person to another when the first person has finished with them.

hand-picked If someone is **hand-picked**, they are carefully chosen for a particular job.

hand-to-hand fighting is between people confronting each other directly and using their hands, knives, or swords.

hand-to-mouth If you live **hand-to-mouth,** you are very poor and have barely enough money or food to live on.

handbag A handbag is a small bag a woman uses for carrying things like keys and money.

handball is a game played by two teams in which a ball is hit with the palm of the hand. ◇ In football, if anyone except the goalkeeper handles the ball, this is an offence and it is called **handball.**

handbook A handbook is a book giving advice or instructions on something.

handbrake In a car, the **handbrake** is a brake operated by hand.

handcart A handcart is a small two-wheeled goods cart which is pushed or pulled along.

handcuff If someone is **handcuffed,** they have two metal rings linked by a short chain locked round their wrists, to prevent them escaping; these rings are called **handcuffs.**

handful A handful of people or things is a small number of them. ◇ A **handful** is also a small amount, or the amount you can hold in one hand. ...*a handful of cherries.*

handgun (*or* hand gun) A **handgun** is a gun you can hold and fire using only one hand.

handicap (handicapping, handicapped) ❑ If someone is **handicapped** or has a **handicap,** they have a physical or mental disability. People who are handicapped are sometimes called the **handicapped.**

   ❑ If something makes things difficult for you, you can say you are **handicapped** by it or call it a **handicap.** *Japanese car makers were handicapped by a dramatic rise in the yen.*

   ❑ A **handicap** is a disadvantage given to someone who is good at a sport, to make the competition between them and others more equal. A game or race in which some of the competitors have a disadvantage like this is called a **handicap.**

handicraft Handicrafts are objects made skilfully by hand. Handicraft is used to talk about things connected with handicrafts. ...*handicraft material.*

handiwork A person's **handiwork** is something they have made or created. ◇ If you say something bad is someone's **handiwork,** you mean they did it.

handkerchief (handkerchiefs) A **handkerchief** is a small square of material or paper for blowing your nose into.

handle (handling, handled) ❑ If you **handle** something like a task or problem, you deal with it.

   ❑ If you **handle** people well, you avoid upsetting them and make the best use of their abilities. ◇ If you **handle** a piece of equipment well, you use it or control it effectively. Equipment which **handles** well is easy to use. *The car handles very neatly.*

   ❑ When you **handle** something, you hold, touch, or move it about with your hands.

   ❑ An object's **handle** is the part you hold when you are carrying it or using it.

handlebar The **handlebars** on a bicycle are the curved metal bars used to steer it.

handler A handler is someone who controls an animal. ...*dog handlers.* ◇ A handler is also someone who han-

dles particular objects as their job. ...*baggage handlers.*

handmade If something is **handmade,** it is made by hand without using machines. ◇ Other things which are not mass-produced are also called **handmade.** *I have my suits handmade.*

handmaiden is an old word for a woman servant. ◇ If something is a **handmaiden** to something else, it is there to help or support it. *He disliked the idea that science should be a handmaiden to commerce.*

handout ❑ A handout is money, clothing, or food given free to poor people.

   ❑ A **handout** is also a copy of a document given to a number of people in a class or at a meeting.

handrail A handrail is a rail next to a stairway.

hands-off If you have a **hands-off** approach to a problem, you let it develop or resolve itself, and intervene as little as possible.

hands-on instruction is practical rather than theoretical. *There are hands-on cookery courses where the guests prepare dinner under guidance from the chefs.* ◇ If you have a **hands-on** approach to a problem, you involve yourself directly in trying to solve it.

handset The handset of a telephone is the part you listen to and speak into.

handshake When people shake hands, you call their action a **handshake.** ◇ **golden handshake: see golden.**

handsome (handsomely) A **handsome** person is attractive to look at. ◇ A **handsome** amount of money is fairly large. ...*a handsomely paid job.*

handwriting (handwritten) Your **handwriting** is your style of writing with a pen or pencil. If something is **handwritten,** it is written with a pen or pencil rather than typed.

handy (handier, handiest; handily) **Handy** things are useful and easy to use. If something **comes in handy,** it is useful. ◇ You also say something is **handy** when it is nearby or conveniently placed. ...*jumping off the train at a handy station... Our table was very handily placed in front of flight timetable screens.* ◇ Someone who is **handy** with something is skilful at using it.

handyman (handymen) A **handyman** is someone who is good at making and repairing things.

hang (hanging, hung *or* hanged; *you say an object is 'hung' but a person is 'hanged'*) ❑ If you **hang** something somewhere, you place it so the highest part is supported and the rest is not. *The sacks were hung from the roof.* ◇ If you **hang up** clothing, you put it on a hanger or over a hook. ◇ If you **hang out** washing, you leave it hanging in the open air, so it will dry. Similarly, you can **hang out** something like a banner, so it will be seen. ◇ If you **hang** a picture, you attach it to the wall.

   ❑ If someone is **hanged,** they are killed by having a rope tied round their neck which tightens when a support is moved from under their feet. Killing someone in this way is called a **hanging.**

   ❑ If you **hang on to** something you own or have obtained, you do not get rid of it, or do not give it up. ◇ If you **hang on,** you wait for a situation to improve.

   ❑ If one thing **hangs on** another, it depends on it. *Some people believe that the future of Europe should not hang on a referendum by the French or Danes.* ◇ If you have something like a problem or a danger **hanging over** you, it is there all the time and your life is seriously affected by it.

❑ If someone **hangs on your every word**, they pay careful attention to everything you say.

❑ If you **hang around** or **hang about** somewhere, you wait there, doing very little. ◇ If you **hang out** in a place or use it as a **hang-out**, you spend a lot of time there.

❑ If you **hang up** when you are on the phone, you end the call by putting the receiver back.

❑ If you say you have **hung up** something to do with your work or a hobby, you mean you have given up the work or hobby. *She feels she should never have hung up her backpack.*

hang-glider (hang-gliding) A **hang-glider** is a lightweight kite-shaped glider. The pilot hangs underneath it in a harness. Flying a hang-glider is called **hang-gliding**.

hang-up If you have a **hang-up** about something, you feel anxious or embarrassed about it.

hangar A **hangar** is a large building for storing aircraft.

hangdog If you say someone has a **hangdog** expression, you mean they look miserable or guilty.

hanger A **hanger** is a curved piece of metal or wood for hanging clothes on.

hanger-on Hangers-on are people who try to be friendly with the rich and famous, to get some advantage for themselves.

hangman (hangmen) A **hangman** is a person who executes people by hanging.

hangover ❑ A **hangover** is a headache and feeling of sickness caused by drinking too much alcohol.

❑ If you say ideas or attitudes are a **hangover** from the past, you mean they have continued into the present even though they are no longer useful.

hanker (hankering, hankered) If you **hanker** after something or have a **hankering** for it, you want it a lot.

hankie (*or* **hanky**) (hankies) A **hankie** is the same as a handkerchief.

hanky-panky If you say there is **hanky-panky**, you mean something suspicious or illegal is going on. ◇ Sexual activity between unmarried couples is sometimes humorously called **hanky-panky**.

haphazard (haphazardly) If something is **haphazard**, it is not organized according to a plan. *Hundreds of suitcases lay around, piled haphazardly.*

hapless is used to describe someone who is unlucky. *...hapless motorists trapped in the blockade.*

happen (happening, happened) ❑ When something unplanned takes place, you say it **happens**. *The explosion happened at nine thirty in the morning.* Something unplanned like this is called a **happening**. ◇ If you **happen** to do something, you do it by chance. You can also **happen** to be somewhere at a particular time.

❑ When something **happens** to you, it takes place and affects you.

❑ You say **as it happens** when you are mentioning a new or surprising piece of information. *As it happens, the judge has already said he will not impose a prison term today.*

happy (happier, happiest; happily, happiness) ❑ If you are **happy**, you have feelings of joy or contentment. *...an Englishman who has lived most happily for 12 years in the Hebrides... They want to find happiness in life.* A **happy** time is one when you feel happy. *...a historic day for Europe and a happy one for Germany.* ◇ If you say some-

one is **happy-go-lucky**, you mean they enjoy life and do not worry about the future.

❑ If you are **happy** about a situation or arrangement, you are satisfied with it.

❑ If you say you are **happy** to do something, you mean you are willing to do it.

❑ A **happy** chance or coincidence is a lucky one for someone.

harangue (haranguing, harangued) If you **harangue** someone, you speak to them in an angry or forceful way, often because you are trying to get them to do something or to come round to your way of thinking. You call this way of speaking a **harangue**.

harass (harasses, harassing, harassed; harassment) If someone **harasses** you, they are a nuisance or keep interfering with you in an unpleasant way. This kind of behaviour is called **harassment**. *Sexual harassment in schools is becoming a serious problem.* ◇ You say someone is **harassed** when they are upset or worried because they have more work or problems than they can handle.

harbinger (*pron:* har-bin-jer) A **harbinger** of something is a sign that it is going to happen. *The industrial action could be a harbinger of further troubles.*

harbour (harbouring, harboured) (*American spelling:* **harbor**, *etc*) ❑ A **harbour** is a sheltered area of water used as a safe mooring for ships and boats. ◇ If you **harbour** someone, you give them shelter and protection.

❑ If someone **harbours** certain feelings, they have them but do not talk about them.

hard (hardness) ❑ If you work **hard**, you put a lot of effort into your work. *...a system of bonus points earned for hard work or good behaviour.* You can also work **hard** or try **hard** to achieve something.

❑ If something is **hard** to do, it cannot be done easily.

❑ **hard of hearing**: see **hearing**.

❑ If an object or surface is **hard**, it is firm, rather than soft or yielding. *...pencils colour-coded according to their hardness.*

❑ **Hard** water is water obtained through the water supply in some parts of the country. It contains fairly large amounts of iron, calcium, and magnesium, and does not produce a lather easily when soap is added. See also **soft**.

❑ **Hard** is used to say something is done with a lot of force. *...a student who was clubbed hard with a baseball bat.*

❑ If someone is **hard hit** by something, they are badly affected by it. ◇ A **hard-hitting** speech is tough or critical.

❑ If you say someone is **hard**, you mean they show little kindness or pity. If you are **hard on** someone, you treat them unkindly or unfairly.

❑ If a period of your life is **hard**, it is unpleasant and difficult.

❑ If you say someone is on the **hard** left or **hard** right of a political grouping, you mean they are extremely left-wing or extremely right-wing.

❑ A **hard** winter or frost is very cold or severe.

❑ **Hard** drugs are strong illegal drugs like heroin and cocaine. ◇ **Hard** drink is strong alcoholic drink like whisky or gin. ◇ A **hard-drinking** person drinks heavily and often.

❑ **Hard** porn or pornography shows sex in a very explicit, violent, or unpleasant way. See also **soft porn**.

❑ **Hard** facts are definitely true. ◇ **Hard and fast** is used to describe things which are definite or fixed. *There are no hard and fast answers.*

❑ If you are **hard up,** you have very little money. ◇ If you feel **hard done by,** you feel you have been unfairly treated.

❑ **hard ecu:** see **ecu.** ◇ **hard on the heels of:** see **heel.**

hard-bitten people are tough and unsentimental.

hard-boiled A hard-boiled egg has been boiled until both the white and the yolk are firm. ◇ If you say a person is hard-boiled, you mean they are unusually tough and unemotional.

hard cash is (a) real money, rather than promises of money or credit. (b) notes and coins, as opposed to cheques or credit cards.

hard copy is computer output printed on paper.

hard core (*or* hardcore) ❑ The **hard core** of a group of people are the ones most involved in its activities. ◇ Hard-core pornography is the same as hard porn: see hard.

❑ Hardcore is pieces of broken stone used as a base on which to build something like a road.

hard currency A **hard currency** is one which can be bought and sold on the international money markets, and for which demand is high because it is unlikely to lose its value.

hard disk A **hard disk** is a piece of stiff plastic coated with a magnetic substance on which computer information can be stored. A hard disk can store much more information than a floppy disk.

hard-headed people are determined, practical, and capable of being tough.

hard-hearted people are unfeeling or unkind.

hard-hitting See hard.

hard labour is hard physical work which is part of a punishment for a crime.

hard line (hardline, hardliner) If you take a **hard line** on something, you have a firm policy which you refuse to change. ◇ A **hardline** approach is strict and often extreme. Someone with an approach like this is called a hardliner.

hard-nosed people are tough and realistic and take decisions on practical grounds.

hard-pressed If you are **hard-pressed,** you are under a great deal of strain and worry. ◇ If you are hard-pressed to do something, you have great difficulty doing it, and may not succeed.

hard sell When people give something the **hard sell,** they try to sell it using high pressure sales techniques.

hard shoulder The **hard shoulder** of a motorway is the strip of road along the edge where you can stop in an emergency.

hard-wearing things are tough and long-lasting.

hard-won A **hard-won** victory or success is one which was difficult to achieve.

hardback A hardback is a book with a stiff cover.

hardboard is a thin stiff board made from compressed sawdust and woodchips.

hardcore See hard core.

harden (hardening, hardened) ❑ If ideas or attitudes **harden,** they become fixed, or they change in a way which makes them tougher and less sympathetic. You can talk about a **hardening** of ideas or attitudes. *The factions appear to have hardened their positions during peace talks.*

❑ If people are **hardened** by things which happen to them, they become tougher and less sympathetic. *...battle-hardened troops.* ◇ If people have become hardened to something unpleasant, it no longer affects them, because they have experienced it so much. *...a world hardened to political injustice and cynicism.*

❑ If a substance **hardens,** it becomes stiff or firm.

❑ When the prices of stocks and shares **harden,** they stop going up and down and remain at a steady price.

hardline (hardliner) See **hard line.**

hardly is used to say something is only just true, or someone is only just able to do something. *He has hardly allowed himself a day off since his release from prison... The police and courts can hardly cope.*

❑ **Hardly** is used with 'without' to emphasize how often something happens. *Hardly an hour goes by without state-owned radio and television blasting out the campaign song.* ◇ If something **hardly ever** happens, it almost never happens. ◇ **Hardly** is used to say one thing happened immediately after another. *Baklanov had hardly begun speaking when he was again interrupted by the president.*

❑ **Hardly** is sometimes used in a joking way. If you say something is **hardly** a surprise, you mean it is not a surprise at all. *With little cheer in the American economy, the dollar was hardly going to prosper.*

hardship If someone suffers **hardship** or **hardships,** they have difficulties and problems, often because they do not have enough money.

hardware ❑ Military **hardware** is the weapons and equipment used in war. ◇ Computer **hardware** is the machinery of a computer as opposed to the programs written for it.

❑ A **hardware** shop sells tools and equipment for the home and garden.

hardwood Hardwoods are trees like oak or mahogany which produce strong hard timber. Timber of this type is called **hardwood.**

hardy (hardier, hardiest; hardiness) **Hardy** things are strong and able to survive in difficult conditions. *...a shrub thoroughly recommends for its hardiness.*

hare A **hare** is a wild animal like a rabbit but with longer ears and legs.

hare-brained If you say something like a scheme or plan is **hare-brained,** you mean it is not very sensible or well thought out.

hare-coursing is a sport in which two greyhounds are matched against each other to chase and kill a hare by sight rather than scent.

Hare Krishna (*pron:* har-ee krish-na) The **Hare Krishna** movement is a Hindu religious sect devoted to the worship of the god Krishna.

harebell Harebells are blue bell-shaped wild flowers.

harelip If someone has a **harelip,** they are born with a split in their upper lip.

harem (*pron:* har-eem *or* har-eem) In former times, a **harem** was the women's section of a house in many Muslim countries. The women who lived there were also called a **harem.**

haricot bean (*pron:* har-rik-oh) Haricot beans are small, pale, usually dried beans often used in dishes such as casseroles.

hark If you **hark back** to a topic, you keep returning to it.

harlot A **harlot** is a prostitute.

harm ❑ If you **harm** someone or something or cause them **harm**, you injure or damage them.

❑ If you are **in harm's way**, you are in danger. If you are **out of harm's way**, you are safe and not at risk.

harmful Something **harmful** has a bad effect on people or things.

harmless (harmlessly) Something **harmless** is safe and does not harm anyone or anything. *The shots went off harmlessly in the air.*

harmonic is used to talk about things connected with harmony. *...the music's harmonic structure.* ◇ A **harmonic** is an additional higher sound produced when a note is played on a musical instrument. A sound like this can be produced as a separate note on some instruments.

harmonica A **harmonica** is a small hand-held musical instrument played by blowing and sucking air through it.

harmonious (harmoniously) A **harmonious** relationship or discussion is friendly and peaceful. ◇ **Harmonious** is also used to describe things which go well together. *The finest gardens to my mind fit harmoniously within a wider landscape.*

harmonise See harmonize.

harmonium A **harmonium** is a keyboard instrument like a small organ. The sound is produced when air from pedal-operated bellows causes reeds to vibrate.

harmonize (harmonizing, harmonized; harmonization) (*can be spelled with an 's' instead of a 'z'*) If two or more things **harmonize**, they fit in well with each other. When things are **harmonized**, they are made to fit in with each other or operate smoothly together. *...harmonization of regulations and standards.*

harmony ❑ If people are living in **harmony**, they are living peacefully together.

❑ **Harmony** can also be used to talk about a pleasant and satisfying arrangement of things, especially buildings. *Oxford can't challenge the architectural harmony of Cambridge's Backs.*

❑ In music, **harmony** is a pleasant effect produced by different notes being played at the same time.

harness (harnesses, harnessing, harnessed) ❑ If you **harness** something, you bring it under your control to use its energy. *...Turkey's plans to harness the waters of the Tigris and Euphrates.*

❑ A **harness** is a set of straps for attaching an animal to a plough, cart, or carriage. If you **harness** an animal, you attach it to one of these vehicles with a harness. ◇ A **harness** is also a set of straps fastened around your body to hold something like a backpack on, or to keep you safely attached to something like a rope or seat.

harp (harpist) ❑ A **harp** is a large triangular musical instrument with vertical strings which are plucked by hand. Someone who plays the harp is called a **harpist**.

❑ If someone keeps **harping on** about something, they keep talking about it.

harpoon (harpooning, harpooned) A **harpoon** is a barbed spear attached to a rope, used for catching whales or fish. If you **harpoon** a whale or fish, you fire or throw a harpoon into it.

harpsichord A **harpsichord** is an instrument which looks like a small piano. When you press the keys, the strings inside are plucked rather than hit.

harrow A **harrow** is an implement used for breaking up big clods of earth after land has been ploughed.

harrowing A **harrowing** experience or situation is very upsetting or disturbing.

harry (harries, harrying, harried) If you **harry** someone, you keep asking them to do something.

harsh (harshly; harshness) ❑ **Harsh** behaviour or actions are cruel or severe and show no sympathy or understanding. *No drug addict has ever been so harshly punished... ...the harshness of some of the language.* ◇ If you live in **harsh** conditions, they are difficult or extreme.

❑ A **harsh** light or sound is unpleasantly bright or loud.

harvest A **harvest** is a crop of grain or fruit when it is gathered at the end of the growing season. **Harvest** or the **harvest** is the gathering of this crop. When it is gathered, you say it is **harvested**.

harvest festival A **harvest festival** is a Christian service of thanksgiving for the harvest.

harvester A **harvester** is a machine for gathering crops. ◇ A person who helps with the harvest can also be called a **harvester**.

has See have.

has-been If you say someone is a **has-been**, you mean they used to be important or successful but are not any longer.

hash ❑ If you say someone has **made a hash** of a job, you mean they have done it very badly.

❑ **Hash** is a dish of cooked meat and vegetables mixed together and fried or baked.

hashish (*pron:* hash-eesh) is a resin made from the flowers of the cannabis plant and smoked by some people for its intoxicating effects. Hashish is an illegal drug in Britain.

hassle (hassling, hassled) **Hassle** or a **hassle** is something which causes trouble or difficulty. *...all the hassles of car driving.* ◇ If someone **hassles** you, they pester you to do something.

hassock A **hassock** is a cushion for kneeling on in church.

haste If you do something in **haste**, you do it quickly and hurriedly. *Mr Yeltsin warned against undue haste in preparing a new treaty.* ◇ If you **make haste**, you get on with something as quickly as you can and do not waste time.

hasten (hastening, hastened) If you **hasten** something, you make it happen sooner or faster. ◇ If you **hasten to do** something, you do it as quickly as you can. ◇ If you **hasten** somewhere, you hurry there.

hasty (hastily) **Hasty** is used to talk about things being done or arranged in a hurry. *Tory MPs will do some hasty sums and discover that they stand to lose their seats unless something is done.* Sometimes, **hasty** is used to describe things which have been done too quickly, without proper thought being given to them. *His mother complained that police had acted hastily.*

hat ❑ A **hat** is a covering for a person's head.

❑ If you say you **take your hat off** to someone, you mean you admire them for something they have done. ◇ If you **pass the hat around**, you collect money from people in order to buy something or pay for something.

◇ If you **throw your hat into the ring**, you enter a contest or show you are willing to be considered for a vacant post. ◇ If you say something is **old hat**, you mean it is no longer interesting, or has become unfashionable. ◇ **at the drop of a hat**: see **drop**.

hat-trick In sport, a **hat-trick** is a series of three achievements, for example three goals scored by the same person in a football match.

hatch (hatches, hatching, hatched) ❑ When an egg **hatches** or is **hatched**, it breaks open and a baby creature comes out.

❑ If you **hatch** a plot or scheme, you think it up and plan it.

❑ A **hatch** is an opening in a ship or spacecraft which people or things can get in and out through. ◇ A **hatch** is also a small opening in a wall or door through which things can be passed.

hatchback A **hatchback** is a car with an extra door at the back which opens upwards.

hatchery (hatcheries) A **hatchery** is a place where eggs are hatched under artificial conditions.

hatchet ❑ A **hatchet** is a small axe.

❑ If people **bury the hatchet**, they become friendly again after a quarrel or disagreement.

❑ If someone does a **hatchet job** on a person or their work, they make a violent written or spoken attack on them. ◇ A **hatchet man** is someone employed to do unpleasant tasks which cause harm or suffering.

hate (hating, hated) If you **hate** someone, you dislike them intensely. This feeling is sometimes called **hate**, especially when it is whipped up by other people. *...a campaign of hate, slander and abuse.*

hateful is used to describe things which are extremely unpleasant.

hatred is an extremely strong feeling of dislike.

hatstand A **hatstand** is an upright pole with hooks for hanging coats and hats on.

haughty (haughtily, haughtiness) You say someone is **haughty** when they behave as if they are superior to other people. *He was seen stalking haughtily through the corridors of the Pentagon... He had a reputation for haughtiness and arrogance.*

haul (hauling, hauled) ❑ If you **haul** something somewhere, you pull or drag it there. ◇ If a person is **hauled** somewhere, they are made to go there unwillingly. *He was hauled back from his holiday.*

❑ A **haul** is the quantity of fish caught in a net. ◇ A **haul** of drugs or stolen goods is the amount recovered by police or stolen by criminals.

❑ **Long-haul** flights are long journeys by air, usually between continents. **Short-haul** flights are journeys covering shorter distances. ◇ If a journey or struggle is a **long haul**, it takes a long time and needs a lot of effort.

haulage A **haulage** company transports goods by road.

haulier A **haulier** is a haulage company or a person who runs one.

haunches Your **haunches** are your buttocks and the tops of your thighs.

haunt (haunting, hauntingly) ❑ When people talk about a ghost **haunting** a place, they mean it appears there from time to time and frightens people.

❑ If unpleasant memories or thoughts **haunt** you, they keep coming back to you. ◇ You can also say something **haunts** you when it keeps making difficulties for you and you do not seem to be able to get away from it. *Labour has been haunted by the reputation of being the party of devaluation and financial mismanagement.* ◇ You call something **haunting** when it stays in your thoughts because it is very beautiful or sad. *...the hauntingly beautiful 'Smokehouse Blues'.*

❑ Your **haunts** are places you visit regularly.

haute couture (*pron:* **oat** koo-**ture**) is used to talk about expensive fashionable clothes which are made by exclusive designers.

hauteur (*pron:* oat-**ur**) If someone behaves with **hauteur**, they behave as if they are superior to other people.

have (has, having, had) ❑ **Have, has, having,** and **had** are most commonly used in front of words like 'been' and 'done' and words ending in '-ed'. You use them when you are mentioning something which happened recently and which affects the present situation. *A convoy of fifteen trucks carrying food and medicines has left the capital... 5,000 workers have lost their jobs.* ◇ **Have** is used after 'would' to say what might have happened if someone had behaved differently. *If self-restraint had not been exercised, we would have got into conflict.*

❑ If someone **has to** do something, it is necessary for them to do it. *He will have to consult his family.* You can also say someone **has to** have something or **has to** be something. *We have to have troops on the ground... To win a place in the athletics team you have to be a serious medal contender.*

❑ If you **have** something, you own it or it is in your possession. *He had a tiny mews house full of antiques.* ◇ You can also say someone or something **has** a quality or characteristic. *Weld had a remarkable ability to remember things... The walled city has the largest concentration of Muslim population in Delhi.* ◇ You can say someone **has** a feeling or desire. *Home buyers have a deep longing to own historic buildings.* ◇ You can say someone **has** power, responsibility, or the support of a group of people. *He now has the firm backing of 150 of the 372 Conservative MPs.* ◇ You can say someone **has** an opportunity or choice. *Moscow may feel it has no choice.* You can also say someone **has** an advantage, or a problem or difficulty. ◇ If you **have** an illness or disability, you suffer from it.

❑ If you **have** an experience, it happens to you. *More than half had had at least one exploratory operation.* ◇ If you **have** a discussion or conversation, you take part in it. *Mr Hurd said he'd had a constructive meeting.* Similarly, someone involved in sport can **have** a game or match. ◇ If you **have** a meal, you eat it. ◇ If a woman **has** a baby, she gives birth to it.

❑ If you **have** a question, you want to ask it. ◇ If you **have** a certain amount of time to do something in, you must do it before that time finishes.

❑ If someone **has it in for** you, they are determined to make life difficult for you because they dislike you or are angry with you.

❑ People sometimes talk about the **haves** and the **have-nots** when they are comparing people who have a lot of possessions with those who have very few. *...the growing gap between the haves and the have-nots.*

haven A **haven** is a place where a person or animal is safe from trouble or danger. *...old fruit orchards, valuable ha-*

vens for wildlife. ◇ A **tax haven** is a place with a low rate of taxation, where people and companies go to avoid paying higher tax in their own countries.

haversack A **haversack** is a canvas bag worn on your back or shoulder and used for carrying things when out walking.

havoc is disorder or destruction. *Rioters caused havoc in the centre of the town.* You can say something **plays** or **wreaks havoc** with something else. *Violent storms wreaked havoc on the French Riviera.*

haw See **hawthorn**.

hawk (hawkish, hawker) ❏ **Hawks** are birds of prey with strong claws, short rounded wings, and long tails. The commonest British hawk is the sparrowhawk. ◇ Politicians who favour war or aggressive policies are sometimes called **hawks**; their behaviour is described as **hawkish**. See also **dove**.
❏ If you **hawk** something, you try hard to sell it, often by taking it from place to place. People who sell things on the street or door-to-door are called **hawkers**.

hawser A **hawser** is a large rope used on a ship.

hawthorn The **hawthorn** is a small thorny tree or bush with white or pink flowers in spring and red berries in autumn. The flowers are called **may** and the berries are called **haws**.

hay is dried grass used to feed animals. ◇ If you **make hay while the sun shines**, you make the most of an opportunity because it is not likely to last.

hayfever is an allergy to pollen, especially grass pollen, which causes sneezing and runny eyes.

haystack A **haystack** is a large pile of stored hay. ◇ If trying to find something is like looking for **a needle in a haystack**, it is almost impossible, because there are so many places where it could be.

haywire If something goes **haywire**, it goes badly wrong or gets out of control.

hazard (hazardous) ❏ If something is a **hazard**, it can cause disease, injury, or death. You say something like this is **hazardous**. *...hazardous waste.* ◇ A **hazardous** activity is one where things can easily go wrong.
❏ If you **hazard** a guess, you make one.

haze (hazy) A **haze** is a mist caused by heat or by dust in the air. When there is a haze, you say the sky or view is **hazy**. ◇ If you are in a **haze**, your thoughts are unclear or confused. ◇ If a memory of something is **hazy**, it is not at all clear.

hazel (hazelnut) The **hazel** is a small tree or bush with edible nuts called **hazelnuts**. ◇ **Hazel** eyes are greenish-brown.

he You use **he** to talk about a man or boy you have already mentioned. *He was known to all as Eddie.* ◇ People also use **he** to talk about someone whose sex is unknown. *A doctor who prescribed drugs only because he was paid by the drug company would deserve to be struck off.*

he-man (he-men) A **he-man** is a strong muscular man.

head (heading, headed; header) ❏ A person's **head** is the part of their body above their neck. An animal's **head** is the part at the front or top of its body containing its brain and sense organs.
❏ If a horse or greyhound wins a race by a **head**, it beats the next animal by the length of its own head. ◇ If you fall **head first**, your head is furthest forward as you fall. ◇ If

you are covered from **head to toe** in something, it is all over your body. ◇ If a footballer **heads** a ball, he knocks it somewhere with his head. Knocking a ball like this is called a **header**.
❏ If you have a **head start** on other people, you have an advantage over them in a competition or race. ◇ If you **keep your head down**, you avoid doing things which would make you noticeable. ◇ If you **give** someone **their head**, you let them do something the way they want to, without trying to stop or advise them. ◇ If two people or groups compete **head-to-head**, they compete very fiercely to win or obtain something.
❏ If something costs a certain amount **a head** or **per head**, it costs that amount for each person. ◇ If you do a **head count**, you count the number of people in a place, or the number supporting a person.
❏ If you toss a coin and it comes down **heads**, the side uppermost has a person's head on it.
❏ A person's **head** is also their mind. *His head was clear.* ◇ If you have some information **in your head**, you know it without looking it up. ◇ If you have something like an idea **in your head**, you have not yet written it down. *Her third book, already written in her head, is to be committed to paper this summer.* ◇ If someone **keeps their head** or **keeps a cool head**, they do not panic.
❏ The **head** of an organization, school, or department is the person in charge. You can say someone **heads** an organization. *The team is headed by the deputy prime minister.*
❏ The **head** of something is the top, start, or most important part of it. *He continued to increase his lead at the head of the table... ...the mast-head.* If you **head** a queue or list, you are the first person in it.
❏ If you **head** in a particular direction, you go in that direction. ◇ **Heading for** can be used to say what is going to happen to someone or something. *Foreign exchange markets were heading for turmoil this morning.* ◇ If a situation **comes to a head**, it reaches a state where something has to be done urgently. ◇ If you **head off** something unpleasant, you stop it happening.
❏ If a newspaper article is **headed** by certain words, those words are at the top and give information about what is in the article. See also **heading**. ◇ **Headed** notepaper has the name and address of the sender printed at the top.

head boy (head girl) The **head boy** or **head girl** of a school is the leader of the prefects and often represents the school on public occasions.

head-dress See **headdress**.

head girl See **head boy**.

head-hunt (head-hunter) If an executive is **head-hunted**, he or she is offered better pay and more status to leave their job and come and work for someone else. A person who tries to tempt an executive like this is called a **head-hunter**. ◇ Originally, **head-hunting** meant cutting off the heads of dead enemies and preserving them as trophies. People who did this were called **head-hunters**.

head of state (heads of state) The **head of state** is the leader of a country, for example its president, king, or queen.

head office The **head office** of a company is its main office where major decisions are taken.

head-on You say there is a **head-on** conflict or argument when two people or groups confront each other directly over something they strongly disagree about. ◇ If two vehicles hit each other **head-on**, their front parts collide.

head teacher A **head teacher** is the teacher in charge of a school.

headache If you have a **headache**, you have a pain in your head. ◇ If you say something is a **headache**, you mean it causes worry or difficulty.

headband A **headband** is a narrow strip of material worn round a person's head and across their forehead, usually to keep hair or sweat out of their eyes or to show they belong to a particular group.

headboard The **headboard** of a bed is an upright board fixed at the top end, next to where the pillows are.

headdress (headdresses) (or head-dress, head-dresses) A **headdress** is something worn on a person's head for decoration or as a protection against the sun.

header See **head**.

headgear You can call a hat or anything worn on a person's head their **headgear**.

heading A **heading** is the title of a piece of writing, written or printed at the top.

headlamp A **headlamp** is the same as a headlight.

headland A **headland** is a narrow piece of land sticking out into the sea.

headless A **headless** body has no head. ◇ If an organization is **headless**, there is no one in charge.

headlight A car's **headlights** are the two bright lights at the front.

headline A **headline** is the title of a newspaper story, printed in large letters at the top. You can say a story is **headlined** in a particular way. *...an editorial headlined 'Way Off Target'.* ◇ The **headlines** are the main points of the news given on the TV or radio. ◇ If a person **hits the headlines**, they suddenly becomes famous, because they have done something which attracts a lot of media attention.

headlong If you rush **headlong** into something, you do it quickly and without thinking about the consequences. ◇ If you move **headlong** in a particular direction, you move there quickly and in an uncontrolled way.

headman (headmen) A **headman** is a chief or tribal leader in a village.

headmaster (headmistress) A **headmaster** or **headmistress** is a person who is the head teacher of a school and is in charge of it.

headphones are small speakers connected by a headband and worn over or in someone's ears, so they can listen to music or other things without other people hearing.

headquarters (headquartered) The **headquarters** of an organization are its main offices. Military **headquarters** are decision-making centres. You can say an organization or military group is **headquartered** in a certain place. 'Headquarters' is often shortened to 'HQ'.

headrest A **headrest** is a support for a person's head on the back of a chair or seat.

headroom is the amount of space below a ceiling, arch, or bridge.

headscarf (headscarves) A **headscarf** is a scarf of thin material worn by a woman on her head.

headset A **headset** is a pair of headphones, often with a microphone attached. Virtual reality **headsets** are helmets which include earphones and a video screen.

headship The **headship** of a school is the job of being headteacher.

headstand If you do a **headstand**, you balance upside down on your head and hands with your legs up in the air.

headstone A **headstone** is a large stone at one end of a grave, showing the name of the dead person.

headstrong If you say someone, especially a child or young person, is **headstrong**, you mean they are very determined to do what they want.

headway If you **make headway**, you make progress towards achieving something.

headwind A **headwind** is a wind blowing straight towards you when you are going somewhere.

heady (headier, headiest) A **heady** atmosphere or experience strongly affects people's feelings, for example by making them very excited.

heal (healing, healed; healer) ❏ If a rift between friends is **healed**, the damage to their friendship is repaired, and they become friends again.
  ❏ When an injury **heals** or is **healed**, the injured part becomes healthy again.
  ❏ If someone **heals** you when you are ill, they make you well again, without using medicine. Someone who does this is called a **healer**. See also **faith healing**.

health Your **health** is the condition of your body. ◇ **Health** or **good health** is being fit and well. **Ill health** is being ill. ◇ The **health** of an organization or system is how well it is working.

health care is the arrangements a public authority makes to keep people healthy, or to make them better when they are ill.

health centre A **health centre** is a building where local GPs and other NHS professionals work together.

health food **Health foods** are foods made or grown using few artificial chemicals or ingredients, or none at all. People eat health foods because they think they are better for them than other foods.

Health Service The **Health Service** is the same as the NHS.

health visitor A **health visitor** is a trained nurse employed to visit people in their homes and give help and advice. Health visitors deal especially with families with young children, and with the elderly.

healthy (healthier, healthiest; healthily) ❏ A **healthy** person is not suffering from any illness. ◇ **Healthy** things are good for you and likely to make you fit and strong. *...a campaign to persuade people to eat more healthily.* ◇ You say someone has **healthy** skin or a **healthy** appetite when these things show they are fit and well.
  ❏ A **healthy** organization or system is working well. *The telecommunications industry is healthily competitive.* ◇ **Healthy** is sometimes used to talk about large numbers of goods being sold, or large amounts of money being made from something. *...healthy profits.*
  ❏ If you call someone's attitude to something **healthy**, you mean it shows good sense. *The head of the CIA had a healthy suspicion that Philby was a double agent.*

heap (heaping, heaped) ❏ A **heap** of things is a pile of them lying one on top of the other, in a disordered way.

When someone makes a pile like this, you say they **heap** things together or **heap** them **up**.

❑ If you **heap** praise or criticism on someone, you praise or criticize them a lot.

❑ **Heaps** of something means a lot of it.

hear (hearing, heard) ❑ When you **hear** sounds, you are aware of them because your ears respond to them and send a message to your brain. ◇ If you **hear** something like a piece of music or a radio broadcast, you listen to it. ...*the kind of short story you might hear on a Friday night.*

❑ If you **hear** some news or information, you are made aware of it, because someone tells you about it or because it is on TV or the radio. ◇ If you **hear** from someone, you receive a letter or phone call from them.

❑ When a court or judge **hears** a case or **hears** evidence, they listen to it, in order to make a decision about it.

hearing ❑ A **hearing** is a meeting where people put their case or their evidence to a judge or other official. ◇ If someone gives you a **hearing**, they listen to your point of view.

❑ **Hearing** is one of the five senses. It makes it possible for you to be aware of sounds. ◇ If someone is **hard of hearing**, they cannot hear well, but are not completely deaf.

hearing aid A **hearing aid** is a device worn in the ear by people with hearing problems, to help them hear better.

hearsay If something someone tells you is **hearsay**, they have heard it from someone else, and this makes it less likely to be true than if it was based on their own experience.

hearse A **hearse** is a funeral car used to carry a coffin.

heart ❑ A person's **heart** is the organ in their chest which pumps blood around their body.

❑ People sometimes mention their **heart** when they are talking about their feelings. *I cannot find it in my heart to think harshly of her.* ◇ If something is **close** or **dear to your heart**, you care deeply about it. ◇ If you say something **from the heart** or **from the bottom of your heart**, you are saying what you truly feel or believe.

❑ If you have a **change of heart**, your feelings about something change.

❑ If you believe something **in your heart of hearts**, you know it is true though you may be reluctant to admit it.

❑ If you have **set your heart** on something, you want it very much and will be disappointed if you cannot have it.

❑ If something **gives you heart** or you **take heart** from it, it makes you feel encouraged and optimistic.

❑ If your **heart leaps**, you suddenly feel very excited and happy. If your **heart sinks**, you feel disappointed and unhappy. ◇ If someone or something **breaks your heart**, they make you very unhappy.

❑ If you **take** some advice **to heart**, you take it seriously and act on it. ◇ If you **take** an unpleasant experience **to heart**, you are deeply affected and upset by it.

❑ If you have someone's interests **at heart**, you are acting in a way which is intended to help them.

❑ If you say someone is a particular kind of person **at heart**, you mean that is what they are really like, though they may give a different impression.

❑ If you know a poem **by heart**, you can remember all the words.

❑ The **heart** of a place is its centre. ...*Magdalen Chapel, in the heart of Edinburgh's Old Town.* ◇ If you say something is **at the heart of** a system or way of doing things, you mean it is the most important part of it.

❑ The shape ♥ is called a **heart** and is often used as a symbol of love. ◇ **Hearts** is one of the four suits in a pack of playing cards. All cards in this suit have the symbol ♥ on them.

heart attack If someone has a **heart attack**, blood fails to reach a part of their heart, usually because of the blockage of an artery. This causes damage to the heart, and can be fatal.

heart failure is a serious medical condition in which the heart fails to pump enough blood round the body, resulting in symptoms like swollen ankles and breathlessness.

heart-rending If something is **heart-rending**, it makes you feel great sadness and pity.

heart-throb A **heart-throb** is a male actor or singer who is physically attractive to women.

heart-to-heart A **heart-to-heart** talk is a conversation, usually between close friends, in which feelings and problems are discussed openly.

heart-warming things make people pleased and happy.

heartache is very great sadness and emotional suffering.

heartbeat Your **heartbeat** is the regular movement of your heart as it pumps blood around your body. Each movement of the heart is called a **heartbeat**.

heartbreak (heartbroken, heartbreaking) **Heartbreak** is very great sadness or disappointment. If someone has this feeling, you say they are **heartbroken**. ◇ If you say something is **heartbreaking**, you mean it is extremely sad and upsetting.

heartburn is a painful burning sensation in the chest, caused by indigestion.

hearten (heartening, heartened) If you are **heartened** by something, it makes you more cheerful and optimistic. You call something which has this effect **heartening**.

heartfelt emotions are sincerely and deeply felt.

hearth (*pron:* harth) A **hearth** is the floor of a fireplace. **Hearth** is often used to talk about the home and the warmth and comfort found there. ...*a man who leaves his hearth and home to labour as a miner in the inhospitable north.*

heartland is used to talk about the part of a place where something important is based. For example, the industrial heartland of a country is the area where most of its industry is.

heartless (heartlessly) You say something done to someone is **heartless** when it is cruel and shows no pity for them. *Western citizens have been heartlessly used as hostages.* You call people who behave like this **heartless**.

heartstrings If sights or sounds tug or pull at your **heartstrings**, they make you feel very emotional.

hearty (heartier, heartiest; heartily) ❑ **Hearty** people are loud, cheerful, and enthusiastic.

❑ If you dislike something very much, you can say you **heartily** dislike it. You can also can say you **heartily** approve of something.

❑ A **hearty** meal is large and satisfying.

heat (heating, heated; heatedly) ❑ When you **heat** something, you raise its temperature. ◇ When something

heats up or is **heated up**, it gradually becomes hotter. ◇ **Heat** is used to talk about high temperatures and their effects. *...buildings severely damaged and twisted by the explosions and heat.* ◇ The **heat** is hot weather.

❑ Your **heating** is the system and equipment you use for warming your house. See also **central heating**.

❑ If you **turn up the heat** on someone, you try to make life difficult for them.

❑ You use **heat** to talk about strong feelings, especially anger or excitement. *The political heat generated will be intense... The meeting is said to have taken some of the heat out of the confrontation.* ◇ If people are having a **heated** discussion, they are getting excited and rather angry. *The Crown Prince spoke heatedly in defence of Jordan's position.* ◇ When a situation or crisis **heats up**, people's feelings are roused and things may get out of control. ◇ **Heat** is used to talk about situations where people are very excited and not thinking clearly. For example, you say someone does something 'in the heat of battle' or 'in the heat of the moment'.

❑ A **heat** is an early round in a competition. The winners of each heat go on to compete in the next round. See also **dead heat**.

heat-seeking equipment is used to find sources of heat which cannot easily be seen, for example people buried under buildings after an earthquake. ◇ **Heat-seeking** missiles are used to destroy fighter planes. They are attracted towards their targets by the heat from the planes' engines.

heat-stroke is an illness caused by the body getting very hot. It can lead to unconsciousness and eventually death.

heater A **heater** is a piece of equipment for warming a room or heating water.

heath A **heath** is an area of open land covered with rough grass or heather.

heathen Christians used to call anyone who was not a Christian a **heathen**.

heather is a low spreading plant with small purple, pink, or white flowers. It grows wild on hills and moorland.

heatwave A **heatwave** is a fairly long period of time during which the weather is much hotter than usual.

heave (heaving, heaved) ❑ If you **heave** something or give it a **heave**, you pull, push, or lift it using a lot of effort. ◇ If someone throws something heavy, you can say they **heave** it.

❑ If you say someone **heaves a sigh of relief**, you mean they are very relieved that something is over or has been avoided.

❑ If someone **heaves**, they vomit or feel sick.

❑ When someone or something **heaves into view** or **heaves into sight**, they appear round a corner or in the distance and you can see them. If you are talking about the past, you say someone or something **hove into view** or **hove into sight**.

heaven is the place where God is believed to be and where the souls of the dead are believed to live in everlasting happiness.

❑ When people talk about **the heavens**, they mean the sky. ◇ If you say **the heavens opened**, you mean it started to rain very heavily.

❑ If you say an experience is **heaven** or like **heaven**, you

mean it is wonderful. ◇ If you are in **heaven** or in **seventh heaven**, you are extremely happy or pleased. ◇ A **heaven-sent** opportunity is very welcome because it comes just at the right time.

❑ You say **heaven knows** to emphasize that you do not know something. *Heaven knows how this happened.* **Heaven knows** is also used to emphasize how true something is. *I don't mind criticism – heaven knows I wouldn't still be here if I did.*

❑ If you say **heaven help** the person who does something, you mean anyone who does it will be in great trouble. *Heaven help any foreign investor who needs to go to court to uphold his rights under any such lease.* ◇ You say **heaven help us** when you are mentioning something you find shocking or regrettable. *There are those and, heaven help us, they include women, who think political and foreign news is only of interest to men.* ◇ You say **heaven forbid** when you are mentioning something someone would be strongly opposed to. *Most Japanese do not want to see their sport turned into an entertainment on the lines of athletics or, heaven forbid, professional wrestling.*

heavenly ❑ If you say something is **heavenly**, you mean it is very pleasant and enjoyable.

❑ You use **heavenly** to talk about things connected with heaven. *Being a Christian is no longer about mere heavenly rewards.*

❑ A **heavenly body** is a planet, star, moon, or other natural object in space.

heavenwards (heavenward) If you look **heavenwards** or **heavenward**, you look up towards the sky or heaven.

heavy (heavier, heaviest; heavily, heaviness; heavies) ❑ **Heavy** things weigh a lot, or more than usual. *Always test the heaviness of a load before you lift it.* ◇ **Heavy** work needs a lot of physical effort.

❑ **Heavy** is used to say something is done in a very intensive way. *...heavy drinking... ...heavily advertised brands.* ◇ **Heavy** is also used to say there is a lot of something. *...heavy traffic.* ◇ **Heavy** is used to talk about things which involve a lot of money. *...heavy fines... The group continued to invest heavily.*

❑ A **heavy** responsibility has to be taken very seriously, because of the serious consequences if anything goes wrong.

❑ If a tree is **heavy** with fruit, there is a lot of fruit on it.

❑ You also use **heavy** to say something has a solid thick appearance or texture. *...a heavy black outline.*

❑ **Heavy** weapons or machines are large and powerful.

❑ **Heavy** seas are rough with big waves. ◇ If you say someone is **making heavy weather** of a task, you mean they are making it more difficult by not doing it in the most efficient way.

❑ If a sports team suffers a **heavy** defeat, it loses a game by a large number of goals or points. If a political party suffers a **heavy** defeat, they lose a debate or an election by a large number of votes.

❑ A **heavy** is a strong man whose job is to protect a person or place, using violence if necessary.

❑ If you say someone's build is **heavy**, you mean their body is large, solid, and strong. ◇ If someone moves in a **heavy** way, they move as if their body weighs a lot.

❑ If your heart is **heavy**, you feel sad about something.

❑ If you say a piece of writing or a speech is **heavy**, you mean you need to concentrate to understand it.

heavy-duty machines and equipment are strong and made to last a long time.

heavy-handed actions are done in a clumsy, forceful, and thoughtless way.

heavy industry is concerned with processing large amounts of raw materials, for example turning iron into steel, or with producing large machines. See also **light industry**.

heavy metal is a type of loud rock music with a strong beat.

heavyweight If you say someone is a **heavyweight**, you mean they are important and have a lot of experience and influence.

Hebrew was the language spoken by the Israelites. A modern form of Hebrew is now spoken in Israel.

heckle (heckling, heckled; heckler) When people **heckle** a public speaker, they interrupt them by shouting out questions, comments, or rude remarks. Someone who does this is called a **heckler**.

hectare (*pron:* hek-tair) Area is often expressed in hectares. A hectare is 10,000 square metres (about 2.5 acres). 'Hectares' is usually written 'ha'.

hectic activities are very busy and involve a lot of rushing around.

hector (hectoring, hectored) If someone **hectors** you, they talk to you in a bullying and critical way.

hedge (hedging, hedged) ❏ A **hedge** is a row of bushes along the edge of a garden, field, or road.
❏ If you **hedge** against something unpleasant happening, you try to protect yourself from its effects. The protection you give yourself is called a **hedge**. ...*people hoarding dollars as a hedge against inflation.* ◇ If you **hedge your bets**, you try to avoid losing by backing more than one thing or person.
❏ If you **hedge**, you avoid answering a question or committing yourself to something. ◇ If an agreement is **hedged about** with conditions, the conditions make the agreement less effective or more difficult to operate.

hedgehog Hedgehogs are small brown mammals with sharp spines on their backs.

hedgerow A **hedgerow** is a row of bushes, trees, and plants, usually growing along a country lane or between fields.

hedonism (hedonist, hedonistic) **Hedonism** is the belief that pleasure is the most important thing in life. Someone who believes this, or acts as though they do, is called a **hedonist**. Their behaviour can be called **hedonistic**. ...*the hedonistic pleasures of partying until dawn.*

heed (heeding, heeded) If you **heed** what someone says, you do what they advise or suggest. You can also **take heed** of what someone says or **pay heed to** it.

heedless If you are **heedless** of advice or of a situation, you ignore it.

heel ❏ A person's **heel** is the back part of their foot, just below their ankle. ◇ The **heel** of a sock or shoe is the part covering the heel, or below it.
❏ If one situation follows hard, hot, or close **on the heels** of another, it happens very soon after it. ◇ If you say a rival is **at your heels** or **snapping at your heels**, you mean they are close to overtaking you. ◇ You can also say that someone who is being a nuisance and forcing you

to do things is **snapping at your heels**.
❏ If you **bring** someone **to heel** or if they **come to heel**, you bring them under your control. ◇ If you **dig in your heels**, you refuse to be persuaded to do something.
❏ **drag your heels:** see **drag**. ◇ See also **down-at-heel**, **well-heeled**.

hefty amounts of money are very large. You can call other things which are large **hefty**. ...*a hefty Labour majority.*
❏ Hefty people are large and well-built.
❏ If someone gives you a **hefty** kick or shove, they kick or shove you with a lot of force.

hegemony (*pron:* hig-em-on-ee) If one country or organization has **hegemony** over another one, it dominates or controls it.

Hegira (*pron:* hej-ira) was Mohammed's flight from Mecca to Medina in 622 AD. The Muslim calendar dates from this event.

heifer (*pron:* hef-fer) A **heifer** is a young cow which has not yet had a calf.

height ❏ The **height** of a person or thing is the measurement from their lowest part to their highest. ◇ If something is at a particular **height**, it is that distance above the ground or above sea level. *The cell has one small window, which is above head height.* ◇ The top of a hill or cliff is sometimes called the **heights**. ...*the Golan Heights.* ◇ If you say something is at a **height**, you mean it is a long way above the ground. *They fish by diving from a height.*
❏ If something is at its **height**, it is at its most successful, powerful, or intense. *Sheets of metal sailed down the streets at the height of the hurricane.* ◇ If something reaches great **heights**, it becomes very good or very extreme. *Recently the speculation has reached new heights.*
❏ Height is used to talk about the greatest extreme of something. For example, if you say something is the **height** of luxury, you mean it is as luxurious as possible.

heighten (*pron:* high-ten) (heightening, heightened) If a feeling **heightens** or is **heightened**, it becomes stronger and more intense.

heinous (*pron:* hee-nuss *or* hay-nuss) A **heinous** crime is very evil.

heir (*pron:* air) Someone's **heir** is the person who will inherit their money, property, or title when they die. ◇ You can also say a person is someone's **heir** when they seem to have taken their place, by doing the same things they did when they were alive or in power. *John Major is being portrayed as the true heir to Mrs Thatcher.* ◇ Someone's **heir apparent** is the person who is expected to take their place, for example as leader of a political party.

heiress (heiresses) An **heiress** is a woman who has inherited, or will inherit, property, money, or a title.

heirloom An **heirloom** is an object which has been handed down within the same family over several generations.

heist (*rhymes with 'sliced'*) A **heist** is a robbery, often of large amounts of money or valuables.

held See **hold**.

helicopter A **helicopter** is an aircraft with overhead propellers which rotate horizontally. ◇ A **helicopter gunship** is a military helicopter fitted with several large guns.

heliport A heliport is a place where helicopters land and take off.

helium (*pron:* heel-ee-um) is a colourless gas which is lighter than air. It is used to fill balloons and to maintain pressure in rockets.

helix (*pron:* heel-iks) (*plural:* helixes *or* helices) A helix is a spiral shape.

hell (hellish) ❏ Hell is the place where Christians believe the souls of wicked people go to be punished when they die. ◇ If you describe something as hell or hellish, you mean it is very unpleasant. *Their life is made hell by muggers, pimps and drug dealers.*
    ❏ Some people use hell to add emphasis to what they are saying. *He's been spending a hell of a lot of money.*
    ❏ If you do something for the hell of it, you do it for fun, or for no particular reason.
    ❏ If you go for something hell for leather, you press ahead with it in a determined way. ◇ If you are hell-bent on doing something, you are determined to do it, whatever the consequences.

Hellenic is used to describe things to do with Ancient Greece. *...the greatest funeral monument of the Hellenic world.*

hello (*or* hallo *or* hullo) People say 'Hello' to each other when they meet. ◇ If you say hello to someone, you greet them and have a brief friendly conversation with them. ◇ Hello is used to describe other ways of greeting someone. *...couples kissing each other hello.*

helm The helm of a boat is the place where the tiller or wheel is. ◇ You say someone is at the helm when they are in control or in a position or leadership.

helmet (helmeted) Helmets are hard hats worn to protect the head. A helmeted person is wearing a helmet.

helmsman (helmsmen) The helmsman of a boat is the person steering it.

help ❏ If you help someone, you make things easier for them, for example by doing some of their work or giving them advice or money. You can also say you help someone out or give them help. When someone is in difficulties, you can talk about giving them a helping hand. ◇ Help is also assistance given to someone in danger or difficulty.
    ❏ If something helps or is a help, it makes something easier to deal with. *Facilities like piped water would be a big help.* You also say something helps when it contributes towards achieving something. *Mrs Thatcher said radical policies had helped to win three general elections.*
    ❏ If you cannot help the way you feel or behave, you cannot change or stop it.
    ❏ If you help yourself, you serve yourself with food or drink.

helper A helper is someone who helps another person or group with what they are doing.

helpful (helpfully, helpfulness) If someone is helpful, they help you by doing something for you or giving you advice, information, or support. *Mr Dornan helpfully delivered a letter to the Emir... ...the helpfulness of local officials.* ◇ If something is helpful, it makes a situation more pleasant or easier to deal with.

helping ❏ See help.
    ❏ A helping of food is the amount you get in a single serving.

helpless (helplessly; helplessness) If you are helpless, you cannot do anything for yourself or cannot protect yourself. *The yacht drifted helplessly for more than a month... Feelings of helplessness are commonly experienced by people when they are first diagnosed with cancer.*

helpline A helpline is a telephone line for contacting counsellors or specialists to talk about problems and get advice.

helter-skelter ❏ If something happens helter-skelter, it happens very quickly and is difficult to control.
    ❏ A helter-skelter is a tower with a spiral-shaped slide around the outside for people to slide down on a mat for fun.

hem (hemming, hemmed) ❏ The hem of a garment or piece of material is the part at the edge which is turned under and sewn down.
    ❏ If you are hemmed in, you are surrounded and cannot move.

hematology See haematology.

hemisphere (hemispherical) A hemisphere is a shape like half a sphere. Something shaped like this is called hemispherical. The Earth is often considered as two hemispheres, usually the northern and southern hemispheres separated by the equator. ◇ The two halves of the brain are called the left and right hemispheres.

hemline The hemline of a skirt or dress is the bottom edge.

hemlock is a plant with small white flowers, a spotted stem, and finely divided leaves. A poison derived from this plant is also called hemlock.

hemoglobin See haemoglobin.

hemophilia See haemophilia.

hemorrhage See haemorrhage.

hemorrhoids See haemorrhoids.

hemp is an Asian plant used for making rope and in the production of cannabis.

hen ❏ A hen is a female chicken. ◇ A hen is also a female bird of any species.
    ❏ All-women parties and social evenings are sometimes called hen parties or hen nights. A woman often has a hen party just before she gets married.

hence means for the reason just mentioned. *The United States is a much larger and hence more self-reliant economy.* ◇ If something is going to happen a certain length of time hence, it will happen that length of time from now. *The government would aim to ensure that we were emitting no more carbon-dioxide fifteen years hence than we did today.*

henceforth or henceforward means from this time on. *It was decided that henceforth the event would be called the Nations Cup.*

henchman (henchmen) The henchmen of a powerful and unpleasant person are his or her supporters or assistants.

henna (hennaing, hennaed) Henna is a reddish-brown dye used for colouring hair or skin. It is made from the leaves of an Asian or North African shrub. When someone hennas their hair or skin, they dye it with henna.

henpecked If you say a man is henpecked, you mean he is dominated and controlled by his wife.

hepatitis (*pron:* hepa-tie-tis) is a serious liver disease which often leads to fever, weakness, and jaundice.

heptagon (heptagonal) A heptagon is a geometric shape

with seven straight sides. Something with this shape is called **heptagonal**.

heptathlon The **heptathlon** is an athletics competition in which each competitor has to take part in seven different events.

her You use **her** to talk about a girl or woman you have already mentioned. *I was at school with her.* ◇ You also use **her** when you are talking about something belonging to or connected with a girl or woman you have mentioned. *She accused the police of illegally arresting her son.* ◇ You use **Her** when you are talking in a formal way about a royal or titled woman. *...Her Ladyship.*

herald ❑ If something **heralds** something else or is a **herald** of it, it is a sign it has started to happen, or will happen soon. *These sales heralded a reawakening of interest in stained glass.* ◇ If something new is **heralded** as a particular thing, people say it is that thing. *America's common market agreement has been heralded as a rival to the EU.*

❑ In the past, a **herald** was a man who delivered and announced important messages and news.

heraldic jewellery and flags have coats of arms on them.

heraldry is the study of coats of arms, and of the history of the families who have them.

herb (herbal) A **herb** is a plant used to flavour food, or as a medicine. **Herbal** teas and medicines are made from herbs, or based on the use of herbs.

herbaceous (*pron:* her-**bay**-shus) **Herbaceous** is commonly used to describe plants which die down in winter and reappear in spring. In botany, **herbaceous** is used to describe plants which are soft and fleshy rather than hard and woody. ◇ A **herbaceous border** is a strip of ground containing a mixture of herbaceous plants.

herbalist A **herbalist** is a person who grows or sells medicinal herbs or makes herbal medicines.

herbicide A **herbicide** is a chemical which destroys plants. Herbicides are used in farming to kill weeds.

herbivore (herbivorous) A **herbivore** is an animal which only eats plants. You say an animal like this is **herbivorous** (*pron:* herb-**biv**-or-uss).

herculean (*pron:* her-kew-lee-an) A **herculean** task is on a very large scale and needs a lot of effort and determination.

herd A **herd** of animals is a large group of them living and feeding together. ◇ If you **herd** people or animals, you group them together and make them go where you want them to.

herdsman (herdsmen) A **herdsman** is a person who looks after a herd of animals kept for food or breeding.

here ❑ You use **here** to talk about the place where you are. *I think the people here will take it calmly.* ◇ You also use **here** to say you have something with you. *I have here a very important message that has just arrived.*

❑ **Here** is used to mean 'in this situation' or 'in this case'. *The problem here is that the government has been trying to curb consumer spending.* ◇ **Here** is also used to introduce a person or subject, especially on TV or radio. *Here's our Moscow correspondent, Bridget Kendall.*

❑ **Here and there** is used to say something happens or exists in several places. *The Bundesbank may be unpopular here and there but its analysis of the pound's problems commands respect.* ◇ If someone goes **here and there**, they go to several places.

❑ If you say something should be done **here and now**, you mean it should be done right away. ◇ When people talk about **the here and now**, they mean life on this Earth, as distinct from life after death.

hereabouts If you talk about something being **hereabouts**, you mean it is not far away.

hereafter ❑ The **hereafter** is life after death.

❑ **Hereafter** means 'from now on'. In legal documents, **hereafter** is used to say a word, phrase, or abbreviation will be used with a particular meaning from that point on in the document. *...the South China Morning Post (referred to hereafter as SCMP).*

hereby If you use **hereby** in a statement, you are indicating that by making the statement you are doing the thing mentioned. For example, you can resign by saying 'I hereby resign'.

hereditary (*pron:* hir-red-it-tree) A **hereditary** disease or characteristic is passed on to a child from its parents before it is born. ◇ A **hereditary** title or position in society is passed on from parent to child.

heredity (*pron:* hir-red-it-ee) is the biological process by which characteristics are passed on from parents to their children before the children are born.

herein You use **herein** when you are drawing attention to a feature or consequence of the thing you have just been talking about. *They will also have to accept future EU legislation concerning the single market. Herein lies the big problem for EFTA.* ◇ **Herein** also means 'in this place' or 'in this document'. *This book is dedicated to my parents who, they'd like it to be known, are not portrayed herein.*

heresy (heresies; heretic, heretical) ❑ You call what someone says **heresy** when it goes against generally accepted beliefs, or against the beliefs of the people in authority. A person who says something like this can be called a **heretic**; what they say can be described as **heretical**.

❑ If a religious person commits **heresy**, they say or do something which goes against an accepted principle of their religion. A person like this is called a **heretic**; what they say or do is called **heretical**.

herewith is used in letters to say something is enclosed. *A schedule of the event is appended herewith.*

heritage A country's **heritage** is things from its past which are still valued, such as its buildings, monuments, and traditions. ◇ Anything left over from an earlier time can be called a **heritage**. *The present legal system, a heritage of the Ceausescu regime, is badly suited to the task.*

hermaphrodite (*pron:* her-maf-roe-dite) A **hermaphrodite** is an animal, plant, or person that has both male and female reproductive organs.

hermetic (hermetically) If a container is **hermetic** or **hermetically sealed**, no air can get in or out. ◇ If you say a place or culture is **hermetically sealed**, you mean no outside influences are allowed into it.

hermit In early Christian times, a **hermit** was a person who lived alone in an isolated place in order to pray and meditate.

hermit crab A **hermit crab** is a small crab which lives in the empty shells of other shellfish.

hernia A **hernia** is a medical condition in which an inner organ pushes out through a weak point in the surrounding muscle. When people talk about a hernia, they usually mean an **abdominal hernia**, in which part of the bowel pushes out through the wall of the abdomen. With a **hiatus hernia**, part of the stomach pushes out through the diaphragm muscle. Hernias are often called 'ruptures'.

hero (heroes) ❏ A **hero** is someone brave or good who is admired by a lot of people. If you say a man is your hero, you mean he is the person you most admire.
  ❏ The **hero** of a book, play, or film is its main male character.

heroic (heroically; heroics) You talk about a person being **heroic** when they show great courage or determination. *A friend tried heroically to drag the dogs off.* ◇ **Heroics** are brave actions.

heroin is a highly addictive drug made from morphine.

heroine ❏ The **heroine** of a book, play, or film is its main female character.
  ❏ A **heroine** is a brave or good woman who is admired by many people. If you say a woman is your **heroine**, you mean she is the person you most admire.

heroism (*pron:* herr-oh-izz-um) is courageous behaviour in a dangerous situation.

heron The **heron** is a large wading bird with a long neck and legs, a thin body, and a long beak.

herpes (*pron:* her-peez) is the name given to several inflammatory skin diseases. When people talk about **herpes**, they usually mean **herpes simplex**, a disease that affects the lips, nostrils, and genitals. It can be sexually transmitted. Shingles and cold sores are other kinds of herpes.

herring (*plural:* herring *or* herrings) **Herring** are fish with silvery bodies. They live in shoals in northern seas. ◇ **red herring**: see **red**.

herringbone is a pattern in things like fabrics and brickwork; it consists of rows of V shapes.

hers You use **hers** to say something belongs to a girl or woman you have just mentioned. *She says her husband's belongings are now hers.*

herself You use **herself** to say something done by a woman or girl affects that same woman or girl. *She killed herself by inhaling carbon monoxide.* ◇ You also use **herself** to emphasize that your statement really does apply to the woman or girl you are talking about. *The Order of Merit is awarded by the Queen herself at her own discretion.*

hertz (*plural:* hertz) Frequency is sometimes expressed in **hertz**. A hertz is equal to one cycle per second. 'Hertz' is usually written 'Hz'.

hesitate (hesitating, hesitated; hesitation; hesitant, hesitantly; hesitancy) ❏ If someone does not **hesitate** to do something, they do it and are not at all worried or unsure about it. You can also say someone does something without **hesitation**. *The soldiers haven't hesitated to burn villages and shoot suspected collaborators.*
  ❏ If you **hesitate**, you pause while you are doing something or just before you do it, because you are uncertain or worried. You say someone who pauses like this is **hesitant**; you also talk about their **hesitancy**. Each occasion when someone pauses is called a **hesitation**. *They have acted too hesitantly in tackling Hungary's economic mess.*

hessian is a thick rough cloth, used for making sacks.

heterodox beliefs are different from the ones people usually have.

heterogeneous (*pron:* het-er-oh-jean-ee-us) You say something is **heterogeneous** when it consists of many different types of things or people. *...modern societies with heterogeneous populations.* See also **homogeneous**.

heterosexual (heterosexuality) A **heterosexual** is someone who is sexually attracted to people of the opposite sex, rather than their own sex. This kind of attraction is called **heterosexuality**. A **heterosexual** relationship is one between a man and a woman.

heuristic (*pron:* hew-rist-ik) is used to talk about ways of learning and understanding which involve reasoning and experiments rather than rules or formulae.

hew If someone **hews** wood or stone, they chop or carve it roughly.

hexagon (hexagonal) A **hexagon** is a geometric shape with six straight sides. Something with this shape is called **hexagonal**.

hey presto People say **hey presto** or just **presto** when they are talking about something producing an instant result, as if by magic. *It was believed that if industry's exports exceeded its imports then, hey presto, balance of payments problems would disappear.*

heyday If you talk about the **heyday** of someone or something, you mean the time when they were most successful, powerful, or popular.

HGV Someone who has an **HGV** licence is authorized to drive lorries. HGV stands for 'Heavy Goods Vehicle'.

hi-fi A **hi-fi** is a set of stereo equipment on which you can play records, tapes, and often CDs.

hi-tech see **high technology**.

hiatus (*pron:* hie-ay-tuss) (*usual plural:* hiatuses) A **hiatus** is a pause in which nothing happens. *There was a 24-hour hiatus before a message came back from Iran.* ◇ **hiatus hernia**: see **hernia**.

hibernate (hibernating, hibernated; hibernation) Animals which **hibernate** spend the winter in a resting state, in which their temperature, heartbeat, and breathing rate become very low. When an animal starts to hibernate, you say it goes into **hibernation**.

hibiscus (hibiscuses) The **hibiscus** is garden or pot plant with large bell-shaped flowers and long stamens.

hiccup (*or* hiccough) (*both pron:* hik-kup) (hiccupping, hiccupped) ❏ A **hiccup** is a minor problem or difficulty.
  ❏ If you **hiccup** or have **hiccups**, you keep making a sound like 'hup', usually because you have been eating or drinking too quickly.

hickory is a kind of wood from the North American hickory tree. It is used in barbecuing and smoking food to add flavour.

hid See **hide**.

hidden ❏ See **hide**.
  ❏ Hidden things are not easily noticed. ◇ **Hidden** places are difficult to find. ◇ If you say someone has a **hidden agenda**, you mean they are keeping some of their intentions secret.

hide (hiding, hid, have hidden) ❏ If you **hide** something, you cover it up or put it somewhere where it cannot be seen. ◇ If you **hide**, you go somewhere where you cannot easily be seen or found.
  ❏ If you **hide** what you feel or know, you keep it a secret.

❏ A **hide** is a skin taken from the dead body of a large animal.

❏ A **hide** is also a place built to look like its surroundings, from which people watch or photograph animals or birds.

hide-and-seek is a children's game in which one child tries to find others who are hiding.

hideaway A **hideaway** is a place where you go to avoid other people.

hidebound You say people are **hidebound** when they are unwilling to change or to accept new ideas.

hideous (hideously) If you say something is **hideous**, you mean it is extremely unpleasant or ugly. *He has been left hideously disfigured.*

hideout A **hideout** is a hiding place for someone who is trying to avoid being caught by the police or soldiers.

hiding ❏ If someone is **in hiding**, they have gone somewhere where they hope they cannot be found. ◇ A **hiding place** is a place where people or things are hidden.

❏ If a child is given a **hiding**, it is smacked or hit repeatedly as a punishment. ◇ If a sports team takes a **hiding**, it is easily beaten by another team.

hierarchy (*pron:* hire-ark-ee) (hierarchies; hierarchical, hierarchically) A **hierarchy** is a system in which people have different ranks or positions depending on how important they are. A system like this is called **hierarchical**. *Most newspapers are run hierarchically.*

hieroglyphics (*pron:* hire-oh-**gliff**-iks) are pictures or symbols used in some writing systems, for example in ancient Egypt.

higgledy-piggledy If you say something is **higgledy-piggledy**, you mean it is untidy or disordered.

high is used to say something contains or involves a lot of something. *...high-nicotine cigarettes... Yachting is a high risk sport.*

❏ If something is **high**, it extends a long way upwards. *...high mountains.* ◇ **High** is also used to say something is a long way up in the air. *The arrow streaked across the stadium, high above the city of Barcelona.* ◇ **High** is also used to talk about measurements. For example, if something is 10 metres **high**, it is 10 metres from bottom to top.

❏ A **high** temperature is above what is normal. **High** can be used to talk about other things which are towards the top of a scale. *...high pressure.* ◇ A **high** note in music is close to the top of a singer's or instrument's range.

❏ A **high** is the greatest level or amount that something reaches. *Wall Street rose to an all-time high.*

❏ In meteorology, a **high** is an area of high atmospheric pressure.

❏ The **high point** or **high spot** of an occasion is the most exciting or enjoyable part.

❏ If something is of **high** quality, it is extremely good. ◇ **High-class** things are of very good quality.

❏ A **high** position at work or in society is an important one. *...a highly-placed government source.* ◇ **High-level** talks or discussions involve very senior politicians, officials, or business executives.

❏ If you talk about the **high and mighty**, you mean people who are important, famous, or rich. ◇ If you say someone's behaviour is **high and mighty**, you mean they are too confident and full of their own importance.

❏ If someone has **high** standards, (a) they like things to

be done well. (b) they try to behave in a very moral way. ◇ If you have a **high** opinion of someone, you admire them or respect them. ◇ If something receives **high** praise, people praise it enthusiastically.

❏ If someone is **high** on a drug, they are under its influence. You can also say someone is **high** on something else, when it affects them like a drug. ◇ If someone enjoys the **high life**, they enjoy good food and wine and a luxurious lifestyle.

❏ **High summer** is the middle of summer. ◇ **High season** is the time of year when holiday resorts and attractions are most busy. ◇ **High noon** is a time when a conflict or crisis will come to a head and a dispute will be settled, one way or another.

❏ **high time:** see time.

high chair A **high chair** is a chair for young children. It has extra long legs and a tray at the front.

High Church The **High Church** group within the Church of England is concerned to keep the authority of bishops and the ceremony and ritual which come from the Catholic tradition.

high command The **high command** of a country's armed forces is its commander-in-chief and senior officers.

High Commissioner (High Commission) Members of the Commonwealth have **High Commissioners** in each other's countries instead of ambassadors. The building where a High Commissioner and his or her staff work is called a **High Commission**.

High Court The **High Court** is a law court which deals mainly with important civil cases.

high explosive is an extremely powerful explosive substance such as gelignite or TNT.

high-flier See high-flying.

high-flown is used to describe grand or literary language when it is used on an inappropriate occasion. *In war-weary Phnom Penh, cash, not high-flown rhetoric, is what counts.*

high-flying (high-flyer or high-flier) **High-flying** people are very talented, and are likely to succeed in their careers. People like these are also called **high-flyers**.

high-handed (high-handedness) A **high-handed** person uses their authority in an unnecessarily forceful way without considering other people's ideas or feelings. *...the bullying and high-handedness he has displayed.*

high heels (high-heeled) **High heels** or **high-heeled** shoes are women's shoes with high narrow heels.

high jinks See jinks.

high jump The **high jump** is an athletics event which involves jumping over a raised bar.

high-minded people have strong moral principles. You can also say their ideas are **high-minded**.

high-pitched A **high-pitched** sound is high and shrill.

high-powered ❏ A **high-powered** person has a career in which they are powerful and successful. You can also say their job is **high-powered**.

❏ A **high-powered** machine or piece of equipment is powerful and performs well.

high priest (high priestess) If you call someone the **high priest** or **high priestess** of something, you mean they are recognized as being the person who knows most about it.

high-rise buildings are many storeys high. A **high-rise**

flat is near the top of a building like this.

high school In Britain, some schools for older students have High School as part of their name. ◇ In the US, a high school is a school for students aged 15 to 18.

high-sounding statements seem very grand and important but do not actually mean very much.

high-spirited people are very lively.

high street shops and banks are the branches of major companies in main shopping areas.

high tea is a meal eaten in the early evening, often with tea to drink.

high technology equipment uses advanced electronics and computers or is developed using such techniques. 'High technology' is sometimes shortened to 'high-tech' or 'hi-tech'.

high tide is the time when the sea is at its highest level on the coast. This usually occurs twice a day.

high treason See **treason**.

high water High water is the same as high tide. A high-water mark is the level reached by the sea at high tide or by a river in a flood. ◇ The **high-water mark** of something like a person's career is the point at which it is most successful, after which there is a decline.

highbrow is used to describe books and music which are thought to be serious and intellectual.

higher ❑ A **higher** plant or animal is one with a complex or advanced biological form.
❑ A **higher** exam or qualification is of an advanced standard or level. ...*the Higher National Certificate*. ◇ In Scotland, **highers** are the advanced level of the Certificate of Education. They are taken at 17 or 18. Their proper name is 'SCE Higher Grade'.

higher education is degree courses and other courses of a higher standard than 'A' levels or highers.

highlands (highland; Highlander) ❑ **Highlands** are mountainous areas. **Highland** is used to talk about things connected with these areas, and people who come from them. ...*the central highland city of Huambo*.
❑ A **Highlander** is someone who comes from the Highlands of Scotland.

highlight ❑ If you **highlight** a problem or point, you draw attention to it.
❑ The **highlight** of an occasion is the most interesting or exciting part of it.
❑ **Highlights** are light-coloured streaks is someone's hair.

highly is used in front of some words to mean 'very'. *The Australian coach was highly critical of the referee*.
❑ If something is **highly** praised, it receives a lot of praise. You can also say a person is **highly** praised for something they have done.

highly-strung people are nervous and easily upset. Horses can also be **highly-strung**.

Highness (Highnesses) **Highness** is used when talking to a royal person who is not a king or queen, or when talking about them in a formal way. *Her Majesty and His Royal Highness toured the Flower Show*.

highway A **highway** is a public road, especially a main road connecting towns and cities.

Highway Code The **Highway Code** is an official booklet containing the rules relating to driving and public safety on the roads.

highwayman (highwaymen) A **highwayman** was a robber, usually on horseback, who held up travellers in the past.

hijack (hijacker) If someone **hijacks** a plane or other vehicle, they illegally take control of it by force and make the pilot or driver follow their instructions. This is called a **hijack** or **hijacking**. A person who hijacks a plane or vehicle is called a **hijacker**.

hike (hiking, hiked; hiker) ❑ A **hike** in prices, wages, or interest rates is a large increase. If things like these are **hiked**, they are increased.
❑ A **hike** is a long walk in the countryside for pleasure. If you **hike** or go **hiking**, you go for a walk of this kind. People who do this are called **hikers**.

hilarious (hilariously) If something is **hilarious**, it is extremely funny. *The production is hilariously funny*.

hilarity If something causes **hilarity**, people think it is very funny.

hill (hilly) A **hill** is a rounded area of land higher than its surroundings. A **hilly** area has many hills.

hillbilly (hillbillies) In the US, a **hillbilly** is someone from a remote mountain area who is thought by townspeople to be uneducated and not very bright.

hillock A **hillock** is a small hill.

hillside A **hillside** is the side of a hill.

hilltop is used to talk about things at or near the top of a hill. ...*hilltop villages*.

hilly See **hill**.

hilt ❑ If you support someone **to the hilt**, you give them all the support you can.
❑ The **hilt** of a sword or knife is its handle.

him You use **him** to talk about a boy or man you have already mentioned. *Dr Ames's one-time admirers now accuse him of being a turncoat*.

himself You use **himself** to say something done by a man or boy affects that same man or boy. *Jan Palach set himself alight in 1969 to protest against the Soviet army's occupation*. ◇ You also use **himself** to emphasize that your statement really does apply to the man or boy you are talking about. *The president himself addressed the nation from the Oval Office*.

hind ❑ An animal's **hind** legs are the ones at the back of its body.
❑ A **hind** is a female deer.

hinder (hindering, hindered) If something **hinders** you, it makes it difficult for you to do what you are trying to do. ◇ If people **hinder** something, they get in the way and delay it.

hindquarters The **hindquarters** of a four-legged animal are its back parts and its back legs.

hindrance If something is a **hindrance**, it makes it difficult for something to succeed. ◇ If someone is a **hindrance**, they get in the way and delay things. ◇ If you do something **without hindrance**, you do it freely and without anyone stopping or delaying you.

hindsight If you say with **hindsight** you would have acted differently, you mean you would not have acted the way you did if you had known what would happen.

Hinduism (Hindu) **Hinduism** is an Indian religion, which has many gods and teaches that people have another life on earth after they die. **Hindu** is used to talk about things connected with this religion ...*Hindu temples*. Someone who practises Hinduism is called a **Hindu**.

hinge (hinging, hinged) ❏ If something **hinges on** something else, it depends on it. *Victory or defeat hinged on her final putt at the 18th.*

❏ A **hinge** is a device for joining things like doors and windows to their frames while allowing them to be opened and closed.

hint ❏ If you **hint** something or give a **hint**, you indicate your attitude or reveal information in an indirect way. If you **take a hint**, you act on something which has been communicated to you in an indirect way. ◇ If something **hints** that something may happen or **hints at** it, it suggests it may happen. *Opinion polls hinted he was becoming as much of a vote-winner as Mr Heseltine.*

❏ If you give **hints** on something, you give helpful advice.

❏ A **hint** of something is a very small amount of it.

hinterland The **hinterland** of a coast is the inland area close to it. ◇ You can also describe any remote or underdeveloped area as a **hinterland**.

hip ❏ A person's **hips** are the sides of their body between their waist and the tops of their legs.

❏ If you say someone or something is **hip**, you mean they are very modern and fashionable.

❏ If you say someone **shoots from the hip**, you mean they make quick replies or decisions without careful thought.

hip flask A **hip flask** is a small metal bottle for spirits like whisky. You carry it in your jacket or trouser pocket.

hippie See hippy.

hippo (hippos) A **hippo** is a **hippopotamus**.

Hippocratic oath The **Hippocratic oath** is a solemn promise made by new doctors to try to save life and uphold the standards of their profession.

hippopotamus (hippopotamuses) The **hippopotamus** is large fat tropical African animal with short legs and thick wrinkled skin which lives near rivers and lakes.

hippy (*or* **hippie**) (hippies) In the 1960s and 1970s, **hippies** were people who rejected conventional society and tried to live a life based on peace and love. They wore colourful clothes and the men often had long hair. ◇ These days, groups of unemployed young people who travel about in old cars and vans are sometimes called **hippies**.

hire (hiring, hired) ❏ If you **hire** a vehicle or piece of equipment, you pay to use it for a period of time. When an owner makes something available for use like this in return for money, you say they **hire** it **out**. Hiring things out can be called, for example, **car hire** or **plant hire**. If something is **for hire**, you can hire it.

❏ If you **hire** a person, you employ them to do a job.

hire purchase is a way of buying something by making small regular payments rather than paying the full cost straight away. 'Hire purchase' is often shortened to 'HP'.

hireling A **hireling** is someone who is hired to do something, especially someone who does not care too much what they do as long as they are paid.

hirsute (*pron:* her-suit) A **hirsute** person is very hairy.

his You use **his** when you are talking about something belonging to or connected with the boy or man you have just mentioned. *Mansell, using a new engine in his car, broke his own qualifying record.* ◇ You use **His** when you are talking in a formal way about a royal or titled man. *His Royal Highness later attended a reception.*

Hispanic people or things come from Spain or a Spanish-speaking country.

hiss (hisses, hissing, hissed) If something **hisses**, it makes a long 'sss' sound. The sound is called a **hiss**. ◇ If a crowd **hisses**, they make long 'sss' sounds to show disapproval. ◇ If you **hiss** something, you say it in a strong whisper.

histamine is a substance produced by the body and released during allergic reactions, causing irritation.

historian See history.

historic If you call an occasion or meeting **historic**, you mean it will continue to be regarded as important for a very long time. ◇ **Historic** buildings or places are ones where important things happened in the past.

historical (historically) ❏ **Historical** is used to talk about things known to have existed or taken place in the past. *Frank McLynn places these adventures in their historical context.* ◇ If you say someone who appears in stories is a **historical** figure, you mean they really existed.

❏ If the feelings shared by a group of people are **historical**, they have existed for a very long time. *...the historical animosity between Japan and South Korea.* ◇ You say **historically** when you are making a statement about a long period of history, rather than just recent times. *Historically, most women have been working women.*

❏ **Historical** is used to talk about things to do with the study of history. *The discovery of the diaries is a historical find of great significance.* ◇ **Historical** places and objects are associated with important events in the past.

❏ **Historical** novels are set in the past. **Historical** pictures show events from the past.

history (histories; historian) ❏ **History** is the study of the past. A **history** is an account of things which happened in the past over a period of time. Someone who studies the past and writes about it is called a **historian**.

❏ If you say someone or something will **go down in history**, you mean they are so remarkable they will be remembered in the future. ◇ If someone **makes history**, they do something remarkable which will be remembered for a long time, often because it is the first time it has been done.

❏ When you talk about a place's **history**, you mean all the things which have happened there. ◇ If you say there is a **history** of something happening in a place, you mean things of that kind have happened there. *...the recent history of civil disturbance in England.* ◇ A person's **history** is the facts known about their past which may be of relevance now or in the future. *He was said to have a history of sex offences from the age of 11.*

histrionic (histrionics) **Histrionic** behaviour is dramatic and over-emotional. Behaviour like this can be called **histrionics**. ◇ **Histrionic** is also used to talk about a person's ability and achievements as an actor. *...the histrionic talents of Kenneth Branagh and Daniel Day-Lewis.*

hit (hitting, hit) ❏ If places and businesses are **hit** by things like bad weather, strikes, or economic recession, they are badly affected by them. ◇ If a person is **hit** by some news, they are badly affected by it.

❏ If a bomb or other missile **hits** something, it lands on it or goes into it, causing damage. When this happens, you say there has been a **hit**.

❑ If you **hit** someone, you punch or slap them. If you **hit** someone or something with a weapon or other object, you strike them with it. ◇ If a moving vehicle **hits** something, it runs into it.

❑ If you **hit out** at someone, you criticize them strongly. ◇ If you **hit back** at someone, you criticize or attack them in response to their attack on you.

❑ If you **hit on** something like a solution to a problem, you suddenly think of it.

❑ If something **hits** a high or low point on a scale, it reaches it. ◇ A **hit** is a record, play, or film which is very successful.

❑ If two people **hit it off** when they meet, they immediately get on well together.

❑ If something you do is **hit and miss**, it involves a lot of guesswork, because you do not have the information or equipment you need to do it properly. ◇ If someone or something **hits the headlines**, they get a lot of publicity, particularly in the media.

❑ A **hit man** is a person hired to kill someone. A **hit squad** is a group of people formed to carry out murder and intimidation for an organization. ◇ A **hit list** is a list which terrorists or gangsters have of people they intend to kill. ◇ A **hit list** is also a list of countries or organizations a government means to take action against.

hit-and-run ❑ In warfare, a **hit-and-run** attack is a surprise raid on an enemy position, after which the attackers escape quickly back to their own strongholds.

❑ A **hit-and-run** car accident is one where the driver responsible does not stop.

hitch (hitches, hitching, hitched) ❑ A **hitch** is a slight problem or difficulty.

❑ If you **hitch** a lift, you hitch-hike.

❑ If you **hitch up** a trailer to a vehicle or **hitch** them together, you connect them so the vehicle can tow the trailer. ◇ If you **hitch up** a piece of clothing, you pull it up to a higher level.

hitch-hike (hitch-hiking, hitch-hiker) (or **hitchhike**, etc) If you **hitch-hike**, you travel around by getting free lifts from passing vehicles. Travelling like this is called **hitch-hiking**; someone who does it is called a **hitch-hiker**.

hither means towards the place where you are. ◇ If something moves **hither and thither**, it moves in all directions.

hitherto If something has been happening **hitherto**, it has been happening up until now. ...*a biography of a writer hitherto neglected in his own country.*

HIV is a virus which reduces people's resistance to illness and can cause AIDS. If someone is **HIV positive**, they have the virus and may develop AIDS. HIV stands for 'human immunodeficiency virus'.

hive (hiving, hived) ❑ A **hive** is the same as a beehive. ◇ If you say a place is a **hive** of activity, you mean there is a lot of activity there. *The cities are hives of crime and drugs.*

❑ If part of a business in **hived off**, it is separated from the rest by being sold or put under new ownership.

HM is short for 'Her Majesty's' or 'His Majesty's' in the names of organizations.

HMS is used in the names of ships in the Royal Navy. It stands for 'Her Majesty's Ship'.

HNC An HNC is a qualification in technical and practical subjects. HNC stands for 'Higher National Certificate'.

HND An HND is a higher qualification in technical and practical subjects. It is equivalent to an ordinary degree. HND stands for 'Higher National Diploma'.

hoard (hoarder) If you **hoard** things, you save or store them, often secretly, for future use or because they are valuable. Things saved and stored like this are called a **hoard**. Someone who hoards things is called a **hoarder**.

hoarding A **hoarding** is a large advertising board, usually at the side of a road.

hoarse (hoarsely) If you are **hoarse**, your voice sounds rough and unclear. ...*a hoarsely pleading voice.*

hoary is used to describe things like jokes which are old and familiar.

hoax (hoaxes; hoaxer) A **hoax** is an attempt to deceive people, as a joke. ...*hoax bomb calls.* The person responsible is called a **hoaxer**.

hob A **hob** is the top part of a cooker with gas or electric cooking rings.

hobble (hobbling, hobbled) ❑ If you **hobble**, you walk in an awkward way, because you are injured or in pain.

❑ If you **hobble** an animal, you tie its legs together, to stop it running away. ◇ If a person or organization is **hobbled**, their freedom to do as they want is limited.

hobby (hobbies) A **hobby** is something you enjoy doing in your spare time.

hobby-horse ❑ Your **hobby-horse** is a topic you have strong feelings on and like talking about.

❑ A **hobby-horse** is a toy consisting of a horse's head on a stick, which a child can pretend to ride.

hobnail boot (or **hobnailed boot**) **Hobnail boots** are heavy boots with short large-headed nails in the soles to make them wear out less quickly.

hobnob (hobnobbing, hobnobbed) If someone **hobnobs** with rich or famous people, they talk to them and are friendly with them.

hobo (hobos or hoboes) In the US, a **hobo** is someone who has no home or work and often travels from town to town.

Hobson's choice You describe a situation as **Hobson's choice** when there appear to be alternatives but really there is only one thing you can do.

hock ❑ If you are **in hock** to a bank or institution, you owe them money.

❑ An animal's **hock** is the angled joint in its back leg.

❑ **Hock** is a type of white wine from the Rhineland.

hockey is an outdoor game for two teams of 11 players. They use long sticks with curved ends to try and hit a small hard ball into their opponents' goal.

hocus-pocus is something said or done in an elaborate or mysterious way, to trick people or make things difficult to understand.

hod A **hod** is a box-like container on a stick used by workmen to carry bricks on a building site.

hodge-podge A **hodge-podge** is a confused or disorderly mixture of different types of things.

hoe (hoeing, hoed) A **hoe** is a long-handled gardening tool, used to remove small weeds and break up the soil. When you use a hoe, you say you are **hoeing**.

hog (hogging, hogged) ❑ If you **hog** something, you take more than your fair share, or keep it for too long. ◇ If

you **go the whole hog**, you do something thoroughly or completely.
❑ In the US, a **hog** is a pig. ◇ In the UK, a **hog** is a castrated male pig.

Hogmanay is New Year's Eve in Scotland.

hogwash If you say an idea is **hogwash**, you mean it is nonsense.

hoi polloi (*pron:* hoy pol-**loy**) **Hoi-polloi** or the **hoi-polloi** are ordinary people as opposed to rich or upper-class people.

hoist ❑ If you **hoist** something into position, you lift or pull it up. A machine for lifting heavy things is called a **hoist**. ◇ If you **hoist** something like a sail or flag, you pull it into position using ropes.
❑ **hoist with their own petard**: see **petard**.

hokum If you call a film or show **hokum**, you mean it tries to appeal to audiences in an obvious way, and is actually rather shallow and silly. ◇ When Americans say someone is talking **hokum**, they mean they are talking nonsense.

hold (holding, held) ❑ If someone **holds** something like a meeting or an election, they organize it and it takes place. ◇ If a group of people **hold** talks with another group, they meet them and talk to them.
❑ If someone is **held** somewhere, they are kept there as a prisoner. ◇ If a place is **held** by an army, it is under their control.
❑ If someone **holds** an important post, they have it. ◇ In sport, if someone **holds** a title, they are the person who currently has it. If they **hold** a record, they were the last person to break it.
❑ If you have a **hold** over someone, you have power or control over them. ◇ **Hold** is used to talk about people having political power. For example, you can say a party **holds** a majority of seats or **holds** the balance of power.
❑ When you **hold** something, you carry, support, or grasp it. If you **hold onto** something, you grasp it tightly. ◇ If you **hold on** to something you have, you keep it in your possession. *The financial community wants the Conservatives to hold on to power.*
❑ If a container **holds** a certain amount, that is how much is in it, or how much you can get into it. ◇ If a building **holds** a certain number of people, that is how many people it can legally contain, or how many are actually in it. *It was designed to accommodate a maximum of about 1000 prisoners. It now holds 1600.* ◇ If something **holds** an object, the object is in it or on it. If it **holds** the object in position, it keeps it in that position. *...the locks that held his mooring ropes in place.* ◇ If something **holds** a system or country together, it stops it falling apart. ◇ If something is **held** at a certain level, it is kept there and not allowed to rise or fall. *The interim dividend is held at 3.3p a share.*
❑ The **hold** of a ship or plane is the part where the cargo is stored.
❑ When a court or other body makes a legal judgement, you say they **hold** that something is the case. *The Supreme Court held that Congress could insist on the inspection of steamships.*
❑ If you **hold** an attitude or opinion, you have it. *...strongly held loyalties.* ◇ If you **hold** a qualification, licence, or other official document, you have it. ◇ If you **hold** some shares, you own them. If you have a **holding** in

a company, you own shares in it.
❑ If you say someone can **hold their head up**, you mean they can feel proud of their achievements.
❑ **Hold** can be used to talk about your feelings about someone or something. For example, if you **hold** someone in respect or affection, you respect them or are fond of them.
❑ If an idea or belief **holds good**, it remains useful or true despite changing circumstances.
❑ If you **hold off** from doing something, you delay doing it. ◇ If you put something **on hold**, you stop it temporarily, or delay its start. ◇ If you **hold back**, you do not do something you had planned to do. ◇ If troops **hold their fire**, they do not shoot. You can also say someone **holds their fire** when they delay taking some other action.
❑ If something **holds** you **up**, it delays you. A **hold-up** is a delay. ◇ A **hold-up** is also an armed robbery, usually of a bank or shop.
❑ If people are **held back**, they are physically prevented from getting somewhere. ◇ If things like prices are **held back** or **held down**, they are prevented from rising.
❑ If you **hold off** a challenge, you manage to prevent someone beating you. ◇ If you **hold your own**, you do as well as other people around you.
❑ If someone **holds forth** about something, they speak at length about it. ◇ If you **hold** someone's interest or attention, you keep them interested in what you are saying or doing.
❑ When something **takes hold**, it starts to have an effect.
❑ If you **get hold of** someone or something, you manage to get them or find them.
❑ If you **hold down** a job, you manage to keep it.
❑ If you **hold out** for something, you keep insisting you are given it. ◇ If you **hold out** against something, you resist it.
❑ If there are **no holds barred** when people are fighting, competing, or arguing, there is no limit to what they will do or say.

hold-up See **hold**.

holdall A **holdall** is a large bag for carrying clothes and other belongings on a journey.

holder ❑ The **holder** of something like a share or a bank account is the person who owns it. ◇ The **holder** of a title is the person who currently has it. The **holder** of a record is the last person to break it.
❑ A **holder** is a container for putting something in, or for keeping it in position.

holding ❑ See **hold**.
❑ A **holding** operation is a temporary measure designed to make a difficult situation easier. ◇ A **holding** area is a place where people or things are kept temporarily. ◇ A **holding** is an area of farmland rented or owned by the person who farms it.

hole (holing, holed) ❑ A **hole** is an opening or hollow area in something solid. ◇ If a ship or building is **holed**, holes are made in it, for example by gunfire.
❑ If someone is **holed up** somewhere, they are hiding there to avoid trouble.
❑ If you call a place a **hole**, you mean it is an unpleasant place to be in. ◇ If you say someone is **picking holes** in something, you mean they are looking for weaknesses or

faults in it, when there is really very little wrong with it.

holiday A **holiday** is time spent enjoying yourself away from home, or a period of time when you are not working or studying.

holiday camp A **holiday camp** is a place which provides accommodation and entertainment for large numbers of holidaymakers.

holidaymaker A **holidaymaker** is a person who is away from home on holiday.

holiness See holy.

holistic A **holistic** approach to something treats it as a whole, rather than as a number of different parts. For example, holistic medicine treats the whole person, not just different parts of the body.

holler (hollering, hollered) If you **holler** something, you shout it loudly.

hollow (hollowness) ❏ If something is **hollow**, it has a hole or space inside it. If it has been **hollowed out**, a hole or space has been made in it. ◇ A **hollow** is an area of ground lower than the ground surrounding it.

❏ If you call what someone says **hollow**, you mean it is unconvincing, because it is contradicted by what you know. ...*the hollowness behind his rhetoric.* ◇ If someone has a **hollow** victory, they get the better of someone else, but are no better off as a result of it.

❏ A **hollow** sound is dull and echoing.

❏ If someone is **hollow-eyed**, they look very tired.

holly is an evergreen shrub with spiky leaves and, in winter, red berries.

hollyhock Hollyhocks are plants with tall spikes of colourful flowers.

Hollywood is used to talk about the American film industry, especially the part centred on the Hollywood area of Los Angeles.

holocaust The **Holocaust** was the mass murder of Jews by the Nazis between 1933 and 1945. ◇ Any loss of life on a huge scale can be called a **holocaust**. ...*the nuclear holocaust.*

hologram (holography) A **hologram** is a three-dimensional photographic image created by laser beams. The science of producing holograms is called **holography** (*pron:* hol-log-gra-fee).

hols Some people call their holidays their **hols**.

holster A **holster** is a holder for a gun, worn at the waist or under the arm.

holy (holier, holiest; holiness) ❏ A **holy** place or thing has special significance for the followers of a particular religion. ...*the Sikh holy city of Amritsar.* ◇ A **holy** person is religious and leads a good and pure life. *Holiness was only possible by the grace of God.* ◇ If a person takes **holy orders**, they become an ordained Christian minister.

❏ **Holiness** is used when talking to some religious leaders, such as the Pope or the Dalai Lama, or when talking about them in a formal way. *His Holiness fled Lhasa in 1959.*

❏ If someone has a **holier-than-thou** attitude, they think and act as if their views and behaviour are more correct than other people's.

❏ If you jokingly call a place a **holy of holies**, you mean only certain people are allowed into it.

Holy Communion See communion.

Holy Father Roman Catholics often call the Pope the Holy Father.

Holy Ghost The **Holy Ghost** is the same as the Holy Spirit.

Holy Grail In medieval legend, the **Holy Grail** was the cup used by Jesus at the Last Supper. Many people, including some of King Arthur's knights, tried to find it. ◇ Nowadays, when people talk about a **holy grail**, they mean the solution to a problem, which people search for and which is very difficult to find. *The holy grail for malaria researchers is likely to be a vaccine.*

Holy Spirit In Christianity, the **Holy Spirit** is the third aspect of God, the other two being God the Father and God the Son.

Holy Week is the week before Easter when Christians remember the events leading up to the crucifixion of Christ.

Holy Writ Followers of a religion sometimes call their sacred books **Holy Writ**. ◇ If you say a person regards something as **Holy Writ**, you mean they think it is unquestionably true.

homage (*pron:* hom-ij) If you pay **homage** to someone, you show your respect or admiration for them.

home (homing, homed) ❏ Your **home** is the building, place, or country where you live or come from. Your **home** town or village is the one you come from. ◇ **Home** is used to talk about things relating to your own country, rather than other countries. *The growth of competition at home leaves them little choice but to expand overseas.*

❏ In sport, a **home** game is played on a team's own ground.

❏ A **home** is a place where people who cannot care for themselves are looked after. ...*a children's home.*

❏ If you **home in** on something, you focus your attention on it. ◇ If a missile **homes in** on a target, it goes towards it. Missiles and other moving objects can be guided to their targets by **homing** devices. ◇ If an animal has a **homing** instinct, it can make its way home from any direction.

❏ If you drive **home** a message, you emphasize it, to make sure people understand it. ◇ If something is brought **home** to you, you are made to realize it. ◇ A **home truth** is an unpleasant fact about yourself which you are told about by someone else.

❏ If you call a place the **home** of something, you mean that is where it started or where most of it comes from.

❏ If you say someone is **home and dry**, you mean they have completed something successfully.

home economics is a school subject dealing with how to cook and run a home efficiently.

home-grown If something is **home-grown**, it develops in your own country or area. *They will have to rely more on their home-grown talent.* ◇ **Home-grown** fruit and vegetables come from your own garden and were not bought from a shop.

home help A **home help** is a person employed by a local authority to help elderly or disabled people look after themselves in their own homes.

home-made If something is **home-made**, it has been made at someone's own home, shop, or restaurant, rather than in a factory.

Home Office The **Home Office** is the government department responsible for law and order and immigration.

Home Secretary The Home Secretary is the government minister in charge of the Home Office.

homecoming Someone's **homecoming** is their return to their home or country after they have been away a long time.

homeland Your **homeland** is your native country. ◇ When people are fighting to establish a new state for their own ethnic group, they often call it their **homeland**. ...*an independent Kurdish homeland.* ◇ In South Africa, **homelands** were regions allocated under the apartheid system to the black population.

homeless (homelessness) If someone is **homeless**, they have nowhere to live. People in this situation are often referred to as the **homeless**. *The only way to solve homelessness is to provide more homes.*

homely (homeliness) ❑ If something is **homely**, it is simple, ordinary, and comfortable. ...*a hotel that seeks to combine luxury with homeliness.*

❑ When Americans say a person is **homely**, they mean they are not attractive to look at.

homeopathy (*pron:* home-ee-op-ath-ee) (homeopathic, homeopath) (*or* homoeopathy, *etc*) **Homeopathy** is a way of treating illness using minute amounts of a substance which would in large doses cause symptoms similar to the illness. **Homeopathic** medicine (*pron:* home-ee-oh-path-ic) follows these principles. A person who practises **homeopathy** is called a **homeopath** (*pron:* home-ee-oh-path).

homeowner A **homeowner** is someone who owns or is buying their own home.

homesick (homesickness) If you are **homesick**, you feel lonely and unhappy because you are away from home and miss your family and friends. *Homesickness usually wears off with time.*

homespun is used to describe remarks and ideas which are simple and unsophisticated. ...*homespun advice.*

homestead In America, a **homestead** is a family-run farmhouse and its surrounding land.

homeward (homewards) If you travel **homeward** or **homewards**, or make a **homeward** journey, you travel towards your home. You can also say you are **homeward bound**.

homework is work given to pupils to do at home. ◇ If you say someone has done their **homework**, you mean they have researched something thoroughly.

homicide (homicidal) In the US, the killing of one person by another is called **homicide**. Someone who is likely to commit murder can be described as **homicidal**.

homily (homilies) A **homily** is a speech or sermon telling someone how to behave.

homing pigeon Homing pigeons are pigeons trained to return to a place. They are used either as messengers or in racing.

hominid Man and his extinct ancestors are sometimes called **hominids**.

homo sapiens (*pron:* hoe-moh sap-ee-enz) is the scientific name for human beings.

homoeopathy See homeopathy.

homogeneous (*pron:* hom(e)-oh-jean-ee-uss) (*or* homogenous) (*pron:* hom-moj-in-uss) (homogeneity) If you say something is **homogeneous**, you mean it consists of things or people that are very similar to each other. You can talk about the **homogeneity** (*pron:* hom-moj-in-ay-ity) of something like this. *Romania is not an ethnically homogenous state.* See also **heterogeneous**.

homogenize (*pron:* hom-moj-in-ize) (homogenizing, homogenized) (*can also be spelled with an 's' instead of a 'z'*) If you say something is **homogenized**, you mean all its parts are very similar and there are no interesting differences. ◇ **Homogenized** milk has been treated to distribute the cream evenly through the milk.

homogenous See homogeneous.

homophobia (homophobic) **Homophobia** is hatred or fear of homosexuals. People who have these feelings are described as **homophobic**.

homosexual (homosexuality) If someone is **homosexual** or a **homosexual**, they are sexually attracted to people of their own sex. This kind of attraction is called **homosexuality**. **Homosexual** behaviour is sexual behaviour between people of the same sex.

Hon is short for 'honourable' or 'honorary' in people's titles.

hone (honing, honed) If you **hone** something, you carefully develop it for a special purpose.

honest (honestly; honesty) ❑ You say people are **honest** when they do not try to cheat or deceive other people. You talk about the **honesty** of people like these. ◇ You say someone is being **honest** when they are telling the truth and not concealing anything. ◇ If someone makes an **honest** attempt at something, they genuinely try to do it, rather than just pretending. Similarly, if someone **honestly** believes something, they genuinely believe it.

❑ If someone acts as **honest broker**, they negotiate with both sides in a conflict to try and bring peace.

honey is an edible sweet sticky substance made by bees.

honey-pot A **honey-pot** is something which attracts a lot of people. *York is a honey-pot for tourists from all over the world.*

honeycomb (honeycombed) A **honeycomb** is a wax structure made by bees, consisting of hundreds of cells for storing honey and eggs. ◇ Other structures with a lot of holes or spaces in them can be called **honeycombs**. You can also say something is **honeycombed** with holes or spaces.

honeyed If you talk about someone using **honeyed** words, you mean what they say is soothing and pleasant but they are probably trying to deceive you or get something out of you.

honeymoon A **honeymoon** is a holiday taken by a newly-married couple. ◇ A **honeymoon** period is a time when someone is treated kindly because they are beginning something like a new job.

honeysuckle is a climbing plant with sweet-smelling cream or pink flowers.

honk If a car horn **honks**, it makes a short loud sound. You can talk about the **honking** of car horns.

honky-tonk A **honky-tonk** is a disreputable nightclub or bar. ◇ **Honky-tonk** is a style of ragtime piano-playing using a tinny-sounding piano called a **honky-tonk** piano.

honor See honour.

honorable See honourable.

honorary An **honorary** title is given as a mark of respect to someone who does not qualify for it in the normal way. *He was made an honorary citizen of his parents' home* *town.* ◇ **Honorary** is also used to describe a job or position which is not paid. *He was honorary secretary of the Burma Star Association.*

honorific An **honorific** title is given to someone as a mark of respect.

honour (honouring, honoured) (*American spelling:* honor, *etc*) ❑ Your **honour** is your good reputation and the respect people have for you.

❑ If someone is **honoured**, they are given special attention, public praise, or an award for something they have done. An award like this is called an **honour**. ◇ If something is held in someone's **honour**, it is arranged specially for them. ◇ If someone says something is an **honour** or that they feel **honoured** by it, they mean they are pleased and proud it has happened to them.

❑ If you **honour** an agreement or promise, you keep it.

❑ **Honours** is a class of university degree which is higher than an ordinary or pass degree. 'Honours' is usually written 'Hons' after the name of a degree.

❑ **Honour** is used in the titles of judges as a sign of respect. *...His Honour Judge Patrick Medd, QC.*

honourable (honourably) (*American spelling:* honorable, honorably) ❑ If you call an action **honourable**, you mean it deserves to be respected and admired. *He was widely praised for acting honourably and decisively.* An **honourable** person is someone whose behaviour you respect and admire.

❑ If you get an **honourable mention** in a competition, you are praised but do not win one of the prizes.

❑ **Honourable** is used as a title in front of the names of government ministers, High Court judges, and some members of the nobility. In writing, it is usually shortened to 'Hon'. ◇ In Parliament, MPs use **Honourable** when talking about each other. *I was not referring to the Honourable Member.*

honours list The **honours list** is a list of people who are to receive official honours from the Queen.

Hons See honour.

hoo-ha A **hoo-ha** is a fuss or commotion.

hood (hooded) ❑ A **hood** is a loose covering for the head, usually part of a jacket or coat. **Hooded** clothing has a hood. ◇ A **hooded** person is wearing a hood which also covers most of their face, to hide their identity.

❑ Someone with **hooded** eyes has large eyelids which are partly closed.

❑ In US, the bonnet of a car is called the **hood**.

hoodlum A **hoodlum** is a gangster or a young violent criminal.

hoodwink If someone is **hoodwinked**, they are deliberately deceived or tricked.

hoof (*plural:* hooves *or* hoofs) An animal's **hooves** are the hard horny parts of its feet. ◇ If you make decisions on **the hoof**, you make them quickly without having time to think about them.

hook (hooking, hooked) ❑ A **hook** is a curved piece of metal or plastic for holding things or hanging things on. If you **hook** things together, you attach them to each other using hooks. If you **hook** a fish, you catch it using a hook.

❑ If someone is **hooked** on drugs, they are addicted to them. You can also say people are **hooked** on other things. *He is hooked on railways.* ◇ If someone gets **off the**

hook, they manage to get out of a difficult situation.

❑ If you **hook up** a computer or other electronic machine, you connect it to other similar machines or to a central power supply.

❑ If you are batting in cricket and you **hook** the ball, you hit it with the middle of the bat and make it go in a direction somewhere behind you.

hook and eye A **hook and eye** is a small metal hook and a bar which it hooks into. It is used as a fastening on clothes.

hooker ❑ In a rugby team, the **hooker** is the central forward in the front row of the scrum. He has the job of kicking the ball backwards out of the scrum.

❑ In the US, a **hooker** is a prostitute.

hooligan (hooliganism) **Hooligans** are young people who behave in a noisy and destructive way. Their behaviour is called **hooliganism**.

hoop A **hoop** is a large ring. Children use hoops as toys, and animals are sometimes trained to jump through them. ◇ If someone is made to **jump through hoops**, they are made to go through a lot of unnecessary procedures.

hoopla (*or* hoop-la) is a traditional fairground game in which you try to throw small hoops over objects in order to win them.

Hooray Henry (Hooray Henries) **Hooray Henries** are empty-headed upper-class young men with loud voices who behave in a hearty or arrogant way.

hoot (hooting, hooted) ❑ If you **hoot** the horn of a car, you get it to make a short loud sound. You can talk about the **hoot** of a horn or say the horn itself **hoots**.

❑ If someone **hoots**, they laugh in a noisy way. Noisy laughter can be called **hoots** of laughter. ◇ You can say something very funny is a **hoot**.

❑ If you say someone does **not give a hoot** about something, you mean they do not care about it at all.

hooter A **hooter** is a device which makes a loud noise as a warning or signal. Hooters are sometimes used to mark the beginning or end of a sports event.

hoover (hoovering, hoovered) A **hoover** is a vacuum cleaner. If you **hoover** a carpet you vacuum it. 'Hoover' is a trademark.

hooves See hoof.

hop (hopping, hopped) ❑ If you **hop**, you jump along on one foot. ◇ When birds **hop**, they make a series of small jumps with both feet together.

❑ If you **hop** somewhere, you get there quickly. *The president hopped from one airport rally to another.* ◇ If you catch someone **on the hop**, you take them by surprise.

❑ **Hops** are the dried flowers of the hop plant, used to give beer a bitter flavour.

hope (hoping, hoped) ❑ If you **hope** something is true, you want it to be true. If you **hope** something will happen, you want it to happen. Your **hopes** are all the things you want to happen in the future. ◇ **Hope** is a feeling that something good will happen in the future.

❑ If you do something **in the hope** that something will happen, you do it because it might lead to that thing happening. *Equipment is being sent to them in the hope that their damaged spaceship can be repaired.* ◇ If you are **pinning your hopes** on something happening, you want it to happen, because you think it will solve a difficulty for you.

◇ If something raises your **hopes**, it makes you more confident that something you are hoping for will happen.

❑ If there is a **hope** of something you want happening, there is a chance it might happen. If there is **no hope** of it happening, there is no chance of it. If you give up **hope** of something happening, you decide there is no point in hoping for it any more, because it will not happen.

hopeful ❑ If you are **hopeful** about something, you think there is a good chance things will turn out the way you want. A **hopeful** sign is something which encourages you to think like this.

❑ People who are hoping to achieve something are sometimes called **hopefuls**. ...*Olympic medal hopefuls.*

hopefully ❑ People say **hopefully** to indicate they are hoping things will turn out the way they are describing them. *This, hopefully, will go towards finding a solution.*

❑ If you do something **hopefully**, you do it hoping that something you want will happen.

hopeless (hopelessly, hopelessness) ❑ If a situation is **hopeless**, there is no chance of things turning out the way you want. ◇ If an attempt to achieve something is **hopeless**, there is no chance of it succeeding. ◇ If someone is **hopelessly** in love, there is no chance of them being loved in return. ◇ If people are **hopeless**, they see no hope of their situation improving. *The centre of each city becomes a hive of deprivation, crime and hopelessness.*

❑ If you say something is **hopeless**, you mean it is no good at all. *The distribution system is hopelessly outdated and inefficient.* ◇ If you are **hopeless** at something, you are no good at it.

hopper A **hopper** is a large funnel-shaped device for temporarily storing things like grain, coal, sand, or cement before directing them into containers below.

horde A **horde** is a very large crowd. **Hordes** of people means a lot of them.

horizon The **horizon** is the distant line where the sky seems to meet the land or the sea. ◇ If you talk about things being **on the horizon**, you mean they are likely to happen soon. ◇ Your **horizons** are the limits of your ambitions. *His horizons had begun to broaden.*

horizontal (horizontally) If something is **horizontal**, it is parallel to the ground, rather than at an angle to it. *The plane crashed horizontally into a classroom.*

hormone (hormonal) **Hormones** are chemicals produced by glands to stimulate certain organs in the body. Artificial hormones are produced synthetically outside the body. **Hormonal** is used to talk about things to do with hormones. ...*the hormonal systems of the body.* ◇ **hormone replacement therapy**: see HRT.

horn (-horned) ❑ **Horns** are the hard pointed growths on the heads of animals like cows and goats. **-horned** is used to describe an animal's horns, or to say how many horns it has. ...*a big-horned wild sheep...* ...*a two-horned rhinoceros.* The substance horns are made of is called **horn**. ◇ If you **lock horns** with someone, you have a dispute with them, or compete with them for something.

❑ A **horn** or **French horn** is a fairly large valved brass instrument played in orchestras and bands. Some other brass instruments have **horn** as part of their name. In jazz, any brass instrument can be called a **horn**.

❑ A car **horn** is a device which makes a loud noise as a signal or warning.

hornet **Hornets** are very large wasps with a painful sting. ◇ If you stir up a **hornets' nest**, you do or say something which causes controversy.

horny If someone feels **horny**, they feel like having sex.

horny-handed people have rough hard-skinned hands through doing hard manual work.

horoscope Your **horoscope** is a prediction about what is going to happen to you, based on the position of the stars and planets when you were born.

horrendous (horrendously) **Horrendous** is used to describe things which are extremely unpleasant and shocking. ◇ People also use **horrendous** to describe things which they find worrying or alarming. ...*horrendously high interest rates.*

horrible (horribly) People use **horrible** to describe things which they find unpleasant, frightening, or disgusting. ◇ **Horribly** is used to stress how bad something is. *The agreement could still go horribly wrong.*

horrid is used in the same way as 'horrible'. ...*a horrid smell.* ◇ If someone is **horrid** to someone else, they behave in an unpleasant way to them. If they are **horrid** about them, they say unpleasant things about them.

horrific (horrifically) **Horrific** is used to describe things which are extremely unpleasant, especially things involving violence. *Marcelo was horrifically tortured to death.*

horrify (horrifies, horrifying, horrified; horrifyingly) If you are **horrified** by something, you are very shocked and upset by it. You say something is **horrifying** when it makes people feel like this. ...*horrifyingly high levels of infant mortality.*

horror is a strong feeling of alarm, dismay, and disgust. You can talk about the **horror** of something when it makes you feel like this. ...*the sheer horror of the Bosnian massacres.* Incidents which give you this feeling can be called **horrors**. *The report recalls the horrors of the last war.* ◇ If you have a **horror** of something, it frightens or disgusts you and you do not want to have anything to do with it. ◇ A **horror** film is meant to frighten people and usually involves a monster and a lot of violence.

hors d'oeuvre (hors d'oeuvres) (*both pron:* ore **durv**) **Hors d'oeuvres** are a variety of foods, usually cold, served before the main course of a meal.

horse **Horses** are four-legged animals with manes, which people ride. ◇ In gymnastics, a **horse** is a piece of equipment with four legs or a solid base, for jumping over.

horse-box See horsebox.

horse chestnut The **horse chestnut** is a large tree. It has tall sticky buds and white flowers in spring and large nuts called conkers in the autumn. See also **chestnut**.

horse-drawn A **horse-drawn** vehicle is pulled by one or more horses.

horse-trading is unofficial bargaining to try to reach an agreement about something.

horseback If someone is **on horseback**, they are riding a horse.

horsebox (horseboxes) (*or* horse-box, horse-boxes) A **horsebox** is a van or trailer for transporting horses.

horseflesh is used to talk about (a) horses as a group. ...*Ascot's annual parade of fashion and horseflesh.* (b) meat from horses.

horseman (horsewoman) A **horseman** is a man riding a horse. If he does it well, you say he is a good **horseman**. A woman rider is called a **horsewoman**.

horsemanship is the skill of riding horses well.

horseplay If there is **horseplay** among a group of people, they push each other around and perhaps hit each other, but all in fun and without really intending to hurt each other.

horsepower The power of an engine can be expressed in **horsepower**. One horsepower is about 746 watts. 'Horsepower' is sometimes written 'hp'.

horseracing is a sport in which horses ridden by jockeys run in races.

horseradish is the sharp-tasting root of a plant called the horseradish. A sauce made from it is often served with roast beef.

horseshoe A **horseshoe** is a U-shaped piece of metal fixed to a horse's hoof to strengthen it.

horsey (or **horsy**) people are keen on horses and riding.

horticulture (horticultural, horticulturalist or horticulturist) Horticulture is growing flowers, fruit, or vegetables or doing landscape gardening for a living. An expert on this is called a **horticulturalist** or **horticulturist**. **Horticultural** is used to talk about things connected with horticulture. ...*horticultural products.*

hose (hosing, hosed) ❑ A **hose** is a long flexible pipe made of rubber or plastic. ◇ When firemen **hose** a fire, they spray water on it through a hose, to put it out. ◇ If you **hose** something **down**, you spray water on it through a hose, to clean it.
❑ In the past, **hose** were men's skin-tight trousers worn with a close-fitting jacket called a doublet.

hosepipe A **hosepipe** is the same as a hose.

hosiery firms make and sell tights and stockings.

hospice A **hospice** is a special nursing home for people who are dying.

hospitable You say people are **hospitable** when they are friendly and welcoming towards guests and strangers.

hospital A **hospital** is a place where sick and injured people are treated and cared for by doctors and nurses.

hospitalise See hospitalize.

hospitality is (a) friendly welcoming behaviour towards guests or strangers. (b) food and drink provided by companies for their guests or clients.

hospitalize (hospitalizing, hospitalized; hospitalization) (*can be spelled with an 's' instead of a 'z'*) If someone is **hospitalized**, they are admitted to a hospital and kept there for treatment. *The children needed hospitalization.*

host ❑ The **host** at a dinner or other gathering is the person who invited the guests and looks after them while they are there. ◇ The **host** of a TV or radio show introduces it and talks to the people taking part.
❑ If a town or country **hosts** something like a conference or sports meeting, it provides the facilities for it. The town or country that does this is called the **host** town or country. ◇ A country where refugees or migrant workers live is also called a **host** country.
❑ A **host** is also any living thing which has other things living and feeding on it.
❑ A **host** of things or people is a lot of them.
❑ The **Host** is the consecrated bread used in Holy Communion.

hostage ❑ A **hostage** is a person who is illegally held prisoner and threatened with injury or death unless certain demands are met by other people. When someone is captured for this purpose, you say they are **taken hostage**; you then say they are being **held hostage**.
❑ If you are a **hostage** to something, your freedom to do things is limited by arrangements or promises you made earlier, or by things you cannot control. *Future growth will clearly be hostage to improvements in the country's physical condition.*

hostel A **hostel** is a building providing cheap temporary accommodation. ...*a hostel for homeless young families.*

hostelry (hostelries) **Hostelry** is an old or jokey name for a pub.

hostess (hostesses) The **hostess** at a dinner or other gathering is the woman who invited the guests and looks after them while they are there. ◇ The **hostess** of a TV or radio show is a woman who introduces it and talks to the people taking part. ◇ See also **air hostess**.

hostile (hostility, hostilities) ❑ **Hostile** people are unfriendly and aggressive. You call their behaviour **hostility**. ◇ If you are **hostile** towards something or feel **hostility** towards it, you oppose it or mistrust it.
❑ In a war, **hostile** is used to describe things to do with the enemy. ...*hostile forces.* ◇ Fighting between countries is often called **hostilities**.
❑ A **hostile** environment is one where it is difficult to achieve something, for example because the terrain is difficult or the weather is almost always bad.
❑ A **hostile** takeover bid is one where a larger company tries to buy a smaller company against its wishes.

hot (hotter, hottest; hotly) ❑ If something is **hot**, it has a high temperature. If you are **hot**, your body temperature is unpleasantly high. ◇ **Hot** food is spicy and seems to burn your mouth.
❑ If something is **hot news**, people have just got to know about it and are very excited about it. Other things which people get excited about can also be called **hot**. *Any nuclear-related issue in Russia is now a hot political issue.*
❑ In a horse race, the **hot** favourite is a horse which is much more likely to win than any of the others. Similarly, a person can be the **hot** favourite in a race or contest.
❑ If one thing comes **hot on the heels** of another, it happens very soon after it. ◇ If you are **hot on the trail** of something, you are close to catching or finding it. ◇ If you are in **hot pursuit** of something, you are trying hard to catch it. ...*a pig, hotly pursued by its owner.* ◇ If a country has the right of **hot pursuit**, it is allowed to try to catch criminals who have crossed into a neighbouring country.
❑ If you say someone is **hot** on something, you mean they use it a lot, or talk about it a lot.
❑ **Hotly** is used to say someone expresses strong disagreement with something. *The allegation has been hotly denied by the opposition.*
❑ If you say someone is in the **hot seat**, you mean they are in a position of responsibility and have to make important decisions. ◇ If you call a place a **hot spot**, you mean there is fighting or unrest there.
❑ If you describe a speech or statement as **hot air**, you mean it is meant to impress and does not really say very much.
❑ **hot potato**: see potato.

hot-air balloon A hot-air balloon is large gas-filled balloon with a basket hanging from it for people to travel in.

hot-blooded If someone is hot-blooded, they easily become angry or lustful.

hot dog A hot dog is a sausage served hot in a long roll.

hot flush A hot flush is a sudden hot feeling in the skin, often experienced by women during the menopause.

hot-headed (hothead) A hot-headed person tends to act first, often in anger, then think of the consequences later. You call someone like this a hothead.

hot line A hot line is (a) a direct telephone link between governments. (b) a similar link for the public to contact emergency or information services.

hot-tempered people get angry very easily.

hot-water bottle A hot-water bottle is a rubber container which is filled with hot water and used to warm a bed.

hot-wire If thieves hot-wire a car, they start the engine without using the key.

hotbed If you call a place a hotbed of some illegal or undesirable activity, you mean a lot of it goes on there.

hotchpotch (hotchpotches) A hotchpotch is a jumbled mixture of things.

hotel A hotel is a place which provides overnight accommodation and food in return for payment.

hotelier A hotelier is a person or company that owns or runs a hotel or several hotels.

hotfoot (hotfooting, hotfooted) If you hotfoot it somewhere, you go there in a hurry.

hothead See hot-headed.

hothouse A hothouse is a large heated greenhouse for growing plants which originally came from hot countries. ◇ You call a place a hothouse when there is a lot of intensive activity there, aimed at achieving a result in a short time. *He insisted that his school was not an academic hothouse.*

hotplate A hotplate is a heated surface on an electric cooker for frying or boiling food.

hound A hound is a dog, especially one used in hunting or racing. ◇ If someone hounds you, they keep criticizing you or troubling you.

hour (hourly) ❏ An hour is a period of sixty minutes. 'Hours' is often shortened to 'hrs' when saying how long something lasts or takes. ◇ If something happens hourly, it happens every hour. If it happens on the hour, it happens every hour at exactly one o'clock, two o'clock, and so on. ◇ A person's hourly pay is what they earn each hour they work.

❏ Hour is used to talk about a particular time of day. *Fewer private cars were going south at that hour.* ◇ If something happens in the early hours or the small hours, it happens early in the morning. ◇ See also rush hour.

❏ Hour is used to talk about a very special time for someone. *...their hour of triumph.* ◇ Hours is used to talk about periods during which something regularly happens. For example, 'school hours' is the time when children are at school. *The cuts will involve shorter opening hours.*

❏ eleventh hour: see eleven. ◇ hour of need: see need.

house (housing, housed) ❏ A house is a building where a family or small group of people live. ◇ If people are housed, they are given a place to live.

❏ If something is housed in a building, it is kept there.

❏ A country's parliament is often divided into separate assemblies called Houses. *...the legislation was approved by the Lower House.* ◇ House also appears in the names of some large buildings. *...the Royal Opera House.*

❏ In many schools, pupils belong to different houses. Houses compete against each other in sports and other activities.

house arrest If someone is under house arrest, they are forbidden to leave their home.

house guest A house guest is a person staying at someone's house.

house martin House martins are small black and white birds with slightly forked tails. They gather mud and use it to make nests, often under the eaves of houses. In the winter, they migrate to Africa.

House of Commons The House of Commons is the more powerful of the two parts of Parliament. It is elected by the public.

House of Lords The House of Lords is the less powerful of the two parts of Parliament. Its members have the right to belong because they come from noble families or are appointed by the government.

House of Representatives The House of Representatives is one of the two parts of the US Congress. The New Zealand parliament is also called the House of Representatives, and so is one of the two parts of the Australian parliament.

house party When the owner of a big country house has a house party, he or she invites several people to stay for a few days, for sport or entertainment. The guests are also called a house party.

house-to-house If the police carry out a house-to-house search, they search all the houses in an area. Similarly, they can make house-to-house enquiries.

house-trained If a dog or cat is house-trained, it has learned not to urinate or defecate on the floor.

house-warming A house-warming is a party you give for friends when you first move into a new home.

houseboat A houseboat is a stationary boat on a river, canal, or lake which people live in or rent for a holiday.

housebound If someone is housebound, they cannot leave their home because they are too ill or old.

housebreaking (housebreaker) Housebreaking is entering another person's house to steal things. Someone who does this is called a housebreaker.

household A household is all the people living in a house or flat. *The average household would save £140 a year.* ◇ Household is used to talk about things connected with the home. *...household appliances.* ◇ If someone or something is a household name, they are well-known to the public.

householder A householder is the legal owner or tenant of a house or flat.

housekeeper Someone's housekeeper is a person employed to cook, clean, and look after their house.

housekeeping is (a) the work and organization involved in running a home. (b) money set aside each week to buy food and other household necessities.

housemaid In a large house, a housemaid is a female servant who does the housework.

houseman (housemen) A **houseman** is a junior doctor in a hospital.

housemaster (housemistress) A **housemaster** or **house-mistress** is a teacher, usually in a boarding school, who is in charge of one of the school's houses and the welfare of its pupils.

houseplant A **houseplant** is a plant which grows in a pot indoors.

Houses of Parliament The **Houses of Parliament** are the buildings in London where MPs and Lords do their work. See **House of Commons, House of Lords.**

housewife (housewives) A **housewife** is a married woman who runs her own home and does not usually have a full-time job.

housework is work like cleaning and cooking, done in the home.

housing is buildings for people to live in. ◇ A **housing association** is an organization which builds and owns low-cost homes for people to rent or buy.

hove See **heave.**

hovel You call someone's house a **hovel** when it is small, dirty, and cramped.

hover (hovering, hovered) ❏ When a bird or insect **hovers,** it stays in the same position in the air. Similarly, a helicopter can **hover.** ◇ If someone **hovers** somewhere, they wait there, because they are not sure what to do.
❏ If something **hovers** at a particular level on a scale, it stays roughly at that level. *The unemployment rate hovered around 2%.*

hovercraft (*plural:* hovercraft *or* hovercrafts) A **hovercraft** is a vehicle which can travel across land or water on a cushion of air.

how is used to talk or ask about the way something is done. *...a series of investigations into how BCCI operated.* ◇ **How** is also used to talk or ask about the effects of something. *How did that affect you?* ◇ **How** is used to talk or ask about the state of something, especially a person's health. *How is she this morning?*
❏ **How** is used with words like 'long' or 'far' to talk or ask about a measurement or quantity. *They are still unsure how far they want to go... How distant is that in terms of light years?... There is disagreement over how much power the President should have.* ◇ **How** is used with many other words to talk or ask about the extent to which something has a quality, especially a good one. *We're used to hearing how clever computers are... How useful were these lessons?*

however You say **however** when you are adding a comment which contrasts with what has just been said. *A group of thirteen Canadian men were refused exit visas. However, about twenty men holding dual nationality were freed.* ◇ You also use **however** to say something makes no difference to the main point you are making. *No machine is infallible, however advanced the technology may be.*

howitzer A **howitzer** is a large gun which fires shells upwards at a steep angle, so they will fall towards a target which cannot be aimed at directly.

howl ❏ If an animal like a dog **howls,** it makes a long loud wailing sound. A sound like this is called a **howl.** ◇ If a person **howls** or lets out a **howl,** they make a loud noise, because they are in pain, angry, or distressed. ◇ If a speaker is **howled down,** people deliberately make so much noise he or she has to stop. ◇ If

you **howl** with laughter, you laugh very loudly.
❏ When the wind **howls,** it blows hard and makes a loud wailing noise.

howler A **howler** is a stupid, but often funny, mistake.

hp See **horsepower.**

HP See **hire purchase.**

HQ See **headquarters.**

hr (hrs) See **hour.**

HRH is a short way of writing 'His Royal Highness' or 'Her Royal Highness'.

HRT is a treatment for symptoms of the menopause and for the brittleness of bones common in older women. HRT stands for 'hormone replacement therapy'.

hub The **hub** of an organization is the place where its most important activities are based. ◇ The **hub** of a wheel is the part at the centre.

hubbub A **hubbub** is great noise, fuss, or confusion.

hubcap A **hubcap** is a metal or plastic disc which covers and protects the hub of a car wheel.

hubris (*pron:* hew-briss) is arrogant pride which leads to someone's downfall.

huddle (huddling, huddled) If you **huddle** somewhere, you crouch or curl up with your arms and legs close to your body for warmth or through fear. ◇ A **huddle** of people or things is a small group of them close together.

hue ❏ A **hue** is a colour, or a shade of a colour. ◇ When people talk about politicians of all **hues,** they mean politicians with views ranging from extreme left to extreme right.
❏ If people make a **hue and cry** about something, they make a lot of fuss and protest, because they think it is wrong or unjust.

huff (huffy, huffily) ❏ If someone **huffs and puffs** about something which goes against their wishes, they say a lot of angry things but do not actually do anything.
❏ If someone is **huffy** or **in a huff,** they are bad-tempered because they have been annoyed or offended. *When she failed to write, he would complain huffily.*

hug (hugging, hugged) If you **hug** someone or give them a **hug,** you put your arms round them and hold them close. ◇ If a road **hugs** something, it stays close to it. ◇ If clothes **hug** a person's body, they fit closely to it.

huge (hugely) **Huge** is used to describe objects or amounts which are very large. *...a huge gun... The patterns of unemployment vary hugely from country to country.*

hula-hoop A **hula-hoop** is a large ring which children spin round their waists.

hulk (hulking) You can call something like a large building or ship a **hulk,** especially when it is in a ruined state. ◇ You can call a person a **hulk** when they are unusually large and heavy. You can also say they are **hulking.**

hull ❏ The **hull** of a boat or ship is the main curved part which rests in the water.
❏ If you **hull** strawberries, you pull out the central core and top leaves.

hullo See **hello.**

hum (humming, hummed) If you **hum,** you sing a tune with your lips closed. ◇ If something like a motor **hums,** it makes a continuous low noise. You call this noise a **hum.** ◇ If a place **hums** with activity or talk, there is a lot of it there.

human ❑ A **human** or **human being** is a man, woman, or child. **Human** is used to describe things which relate to human beings. ...*the human body.* ◇ The **human race** is the whole of mankind.

❑ If you say it is **human nature** to behave in a certain way, you mean it is a normal to behave like that. Similarly, you can say it is **only human** to behave in a certain way, especially when you are making an excuse for what someone has done. ◇ **Human error** is mistakes made by people, as distinct from faults in a machine or system.

❑ **Human rights** are the rights which it is widely believed everyone should have, such as the rights to freedom and justice.

humane (humanely) If you treat people or animals in a **humane** way, you avoid causing them unnecessary suffering. *The Vietcong told the ICRC that it was treating prisoners humanely.*

humanise See humanize.

humanism (humanist, humanistic) **Humanism** is the belief that people can achieve happiness and fulfilment without religion. **Humanist** and **humanistic** are used to talk about things connected with this belief; a person who believes in humanism is called a **humanist**.

humanitarian (humanitarianism) **Humanitarian** is used to describe concern for people's sufferings, and attempts to help them. ...*humanitarian aid.* Concern for people's sufferings is sometimes called **humanitarianism**.

humanities The **humanities** are subjects like literature, history, languages, and philosophy, as opposed to scientific subjects.

humanity is people in general. ...*research that could benefit humanity.* ◇ Your **humanity** is the fact that you are a human, rather than an animal or a thing.

❑ If someone behaves with **humanity**, they show kindness to people in distress, rather than ignoring them or ill-treating them.

humanize (humanizing, humanized) (*can be spelled with an 's' instead of a 'z'*) If you **humanize** something people are involved in, you make it less harsh and unfeeling. ...*programmes to humanize the prison system.*

humankind is the same as mankind.

humanly If you do what is **humanly** possible, you do everything which can possibly be done.

humble (humbler, humblest; humbly; humbling, humbled) ❑ If someone behaves in a **humble** way, they behave as if they are very unimportant, or they show they are ashamed of something they have done. *'We are novices in this world of private business,' a diplomat humbly explains.* ◇ If someone is **humbled**, they are humiliated or made to feel unimportant. *The experience was a humbling one.* ◇ If someone has to eat **humble pie**, they have to behave humbly and admit they have made a mistake.

❑ People with low social status are sometimes called **humble**. ...*a career that saw him rise from a humble milk-bar owner to become chairman of an international catering giant.* ◇ **Humble** is also used to describe places and things which are not special in any way. ...*the humble, tree-lined Dequetteville Terrace.*

humbug ❑ If you accuse someone of **humbug**, you mean they say things which sound impressive but are actually dishonest or meaningless. *She exposed the humbug of his campaign against Congress.*

❑ **Humbugs** are hard striped sweets which taste of peppermint.

humdrum things are ordinary and dull.

humerus (*pron:* hew-mer-uss) The **humerus** or upper arm bone is the bone which extends from the shoulder to the elbow.

humid If it is **humid**, the atmosphere feels damp, heavy, and warm.

humidifier A **humidifier** is a device for putting moisture into the atmosphere of a room or building.

humidity The **humidity** in a place is the amount of moisture in the atmosphere.

humiliate (humiliating, humiliated; humiliatingly, humiliation) If you are **humiliated** by something which happens, you are made to feel stupid or ashamed. You say something like this is **humiliating** or a **humiliation**. *The scheme was humiliatingly refused planning permission.*

humility is humble behaviour.

hummingbird The **hummingbird** is a tiny brightly-coloured bird which lives mainly in Mexico and some parts of the southern United States. Its wings beat very rapidly, making a humming sound.

humor See humour.

humorist A **humorist** is a writer or entertainer who makes jokes and tells funny stories.

humorless See humourless.

humour (humorous, humorously; humouring, humoured) (*American spelling:* humor, *etc*) ❑ If you have a sense of **humour**, you can see the funny side of things and say amusing things yourself. People like this can be called **humorous**. You can also say something is done in a **humorous** way. ...*Mr Bush and Mr Gorbachev posing humorously for a photo-session.* ◇ If something is **humorous**, it is amusing and makes you want to laugh. You can talk about the **humour** of something like this.

❑ If you are in a good **humour**, you are happy and cheerful. ◇ If you **humour** someone, you try to please them in order to avoid trouble.

humourless (*American spelling:* humorless) If you say someone is **humourless**, you mean they do not have a sense of humour.

hump ❑ A **hump** is a small rounded lump or mound. ◇ An animal's **hump** is a rounded lump on its back. Some animals have **hump-backed** as part of their name. ...*hump-backed dolphins.*

❑ If you **hump** something heavy somewhere, you carry it there.

humus is decaying plant and animal matter in the soil.

hunch (hunches) ❑ A **hunch** is a feeling or suspicion about something, not based on facts or evidence.

❑ If you are **hunched** over something or **hunched** in front of it, you are sitting close to it with your shoulders drawn forward and your back curved.

hunchback A **hunchback** is someone with a deformity of the spine which causes a hump on their back. 'Hunchback' is an offensive word.

hundred A **hundred** is the number 100. ◇ **Hundreds** of things means very large numbers of them.

hundredth The **hundredth** item in a series is the one counted as number 100. ◇ A **hundredth** or **one hundredth** is the fraction $\frac{1}{100}$.

hundredweight (*plural:* hundredweight *or* hundredweights) Weight is sometimes expressed in **hundredweights**. In Britain, a hundredweight is 112 pounds (about 50.8 kilograms); in the US, it is 100 pounds (about 45.4 kilograms). 'Hundredweights' is usually written 'cwt'.

hung ❑ See hang.
❑ A **hung** parliament or council is one in which none of the parties has a clear majority.
❑ If someone is **hung over**, they have a headache and feel ill as a result of drinking too much.

hunger (hungering, hungered) ❑ **Hunger** is a serious lack of food which can lead to illness or death. ◇ **Hunger** is also the feeling you get when you are hungry.
❑ If you **hunger** for something or have a **hunger** for it, you want it very much.

hunger strike (hunger striker) If someone goes on **hunger strike**, they refuse to eat as a protest, or to try to persuade someone in authority to do something. A person who does this is called a **hunger striker**.

hungry (hungrier, hungriest; hungrily) ❑ If you are **hungry**, your stomach feels empty and you want food. ◇ If you eat something **hungrily**, you eat it eagerly because you are very hungry. ◇ If people **go hungry**, they suffer from hunger because there is no food for them to eat.
❑ If you are **hungry** for something, you want it very much.

hunk A **hunk** of something like bread or cheese is a large piece of it. ◇ Some people call a big strong man a **hunk** when they find him sexually attractive.

hunker (hunkering, hunkered) If you **hunker** down, you squat or crouch.

hunt (hunting, hunter; huntsman, huntsmen) ❑ When people or animals **hunt**, they chase animals and kill them for food. A person who does this is called a **hunter**. ◇ In Britain and Ireland, when people **hunt**, they ride horses across countryside, following hounds which are chasing a fox. This activity is called **hunting**. A group of people who do it regularly in a particular area are called a Hunt. A **huntsman** is a man who is a member of a Hunt. A **hunter** is a fast strong horse used for hunting. ◇ In the US, **hunting** is the killing of wild animals or birds for sport or food, usually by shooting them. A **hunter** is someone who does this.
❑ If you **hunt** for someone or something, you try to find them. You can call your search a **hunt**. People who search for things of a particular kind are called **hunters**. ...*a souvenir hunter.* A **hunting ground** is a place where you are likely to find what you are looking for. ◇ If the police **hunt** someone **down**, they try to find and catch them.

hurdle (hurdling, hurdler) ❑ The **hurdles** is an athletics event, usually run over 110 metres or 400 metres. Runners have to jump over a series of fences called **hurdles**. People who specialize in this event are called **hurdlers**.
❑ A **hurdle** is also a difficulty which has to be overcome if something is to be achieved.

hurl If you **hurl** something somewhere, you throw it with a lot of force. ◇ If people **hurl** abuse or insults at someone, they shout these things at them repeatedly. People can also **hurl** questions at someone.

hurling is an Irish outdoor game resembling hockey.

hurly-burly The **hurly-burly** of a place is all the noise and activity there.

hurricane A **hurricane** is a very fierce tropical storm, with winds of force 12 or more which move round in a circle.

hurry (hurries, hurrying, hurried; hurriedly) ❑ If you **hurry** somewhere, you go there quickly.
❑ If you are in a **hurry**, you need to do something quickly. If you do something in a **hurry** or in a **hurried** way, you do it quickly, usually because you do not have much time. ...*the Pope's hurriedly arranged schedule.*
❑ If you **hurry** to do something, you do it as soon as possible. ◇ If you say someone should **hurry up**, you mean they should do something more quickly, or as soon as possible. ◇ If you **hurry** something **up**, you make it happen more quickly.
❑ If something like a new law is **hurried through**, it is approved as quickly as possible, often without proper consideration being given to it.

hurt (hurtful) ❑ If someone **hurts** you, they do something which makes you feel pain. If you **hurt** yourself, you injure yourself. If you have been injured, you can say you are **hurt**. ◇ If a part of your body **hurts**, you feel pain there.
❑ You also say someone **hurts** you when they upset you by being unkind or inconsiderate. When this happens, you can say you feel **hurt**; you can also call a person's behaviour **hurtful**.
❑ If countries or organizations are **hurt** by something, they are badly affected by it.

hurtle (hurtling, hurtled) If something **hurtles** along, it moves very fast, in an uncontrolled way.

husband A woman's **husband** is the man she is married to. ◇ If people **husband** resources, they manage them carefully, especially by holding some of them back for later use.

husbandry is (a) farming. (b) careful management of land or other resources.

hush (hushes, hushing, hushed) ❑ If there is a **hush**, everything is quiet. **Hushed** is used to describe a quiet sound or a quiet place. ...*his hushed tones...* ...*the hushed dining room of a small hotel.*
❑ If something is **hush-hush**, it is secret and not to be discussed with other people. ◇ If some wrongdoing is **hushed up**, people in authority deliberately keep it secret.

husk The **husk** of a grain or seed is its outer covering.

husky (huskies) ❑ If someone's voice is **husky**, it sounds a little hoarse, often in an attractive way.
❑ **Huskies** are strong furry dogs, used to pull sledges.

hustings When a politician is on the **hustings**, he or she is campaigning and making speeches before an election.

hustle (hustling, hustled; hustler) ❑ If someone is **hustled** into doing something, they are hurried into doing it by persuasive and perhaps dishonest talk. In the US, someone who gets people to do things like this is called a **hustler**. ◇ If someone is **hustled** somewhere, they are made to move there quickly.
❑ **Hustle and bustle** is a lot of noise and activity.

hut A **hut** is a small simple building, especially one made of wood, mud, or grass.

hutch (hutches) A **hutch** is a box made from wire mesh and wood, for keeping pets like rabbits and guinea pigs in.

hyacinth Hyacinths are plants which grow from bulbs.

hybrid

hypochondriac

They have a lot of small sweet-smelling flowers on a single stem.

hybrid A hybrid is an animal or plant bred from two different types of animal or plant. ◇ Anything which is an unusual mixture of different things can be called a hybrid.

hybridize (hybridizing, hybridized) (can be spelled with an 's' instead of a 'z') If animals or plants of different kinds hybridize, they breed and produce a hybrid. Wild boar readily hybridize with the domestic pig.

hydra ❏ The Hydra was a mythical many-headed water serpent which grew two new heads for each one cut off. ◇ You can call any persistent problem a hydra. Killing the hydra of drug production is impossible.

❏ A hydra is also a very small freshwater creature with a slender tubular body and tentacles round its mouth.

hydrangea (pron: high-drain-ja) Hydrangeas are garden shrubs with large clusters of blue or pink flowers.

hydrant A hydrant is a pipe in a street which supplies water for use in emergencies.

hydraulic (hydraulically) A hydraulic machine or device is operated by oil, water, or some other fluid under pressure. ...a hydraulically powered cargo lift.

hydro-electric (hydro-electricity) (or hydroelectric, etc) Hydro-electric power or hydro-electricity is electrical power created from the energy of running water.

hydrocarbon A hydrocarbon is a chemical compound of hydrogen and carbon.

hydrocephalus is a condition in which there is an accumulation of fluid in the brain. In children, this leads to an enlarged head.

hydrochloric acid is a very strong acid used in chemical processes and in industry.

hydroelectric See hydro-electric.

hydrofoil A hydrofoil is a boat which has fins like skis which raise the hull above the water when it is moving at speed.

hydrogen is a chemical element. It is the most abundant element in the universe. It exists on its own as a colourless gas, and also in many compounds.

hydrogen bomb A hydrogen bomb or H-bomb is a nuclear bomb in which energy is released by fusion of hydrogen nuclei to give helium nuclei.

hydrogen peroxide is a colourless liquid used to bleach hair and as an antiseptic.

hydrology (hydrological) Hydrology is the study of the earth's water resources and their management. Hydrological is used to talk about things to do with hydrology. ...hydrological studies.

hydroponics is a way of growing plants without soil, either in water or in something like sand or gravel.

hydropower is the same as hydro-electric power.

hydrotherapy is a way of treating people with certain illnesses or injuries by getting them to swim and exercise in water.

hyena Hyenas are dog-like animals in Africa and Asia. They hunt in packs and make a loud noise like high-pitched laughter.

hygiene (hygienic, hygienically) Hygiene is keeping yourself and your surroundings clean, especially to prevent the spread of disease. Hygienic things are clean and un-

likely to cause disease. The process was hygienically supervised.

hymen (pron: high-men) A woman's hymen is the piece of skin which partly covers her vagina. It is broken when she first has sex, if not earlier.

hymn A hymn is a Christian song sung in praise of God.

hymnal A hymnal is a book of hymns.

hype (hyping, hyped) ❏ Hype is the advertising of someone or something using intensive or extravagant methods of publicity. If someone or something is hyped or hyped up, they are promoted in this way.

❏ You can also say a person is hyped up when they are very excited or nervous.

hyper- is added in front of words to talk about an extreme form of something. ...hyper-inflation... ...one of those lean, hyper-fit people.

hyperactive (hyperactivity) (or hyper-active, etc) A hyperactive person is unable to relax and is always in a state of restless activity. You say someone like this suffers from hyperactivity.

hyperbole (pron: hie-per-bol-ee) is using deliberate exaggeration in speech or writing.

hypermarket A hypermarket is a very large supermarket, usually built on the edge of a town or city.

hypersensitive If you say someone is hypersensitive, you mean they are easily annoyed or offended. ◇ You can also say someone is hypersensitive when they are extremely sensitive to something like drugs, chemicals, or weather conditions.

hypersonic is used to talk about things travelling at five times the speed of sound, or faster.

hypertension is abnormally high blood pressure.

hyperventilate (hyperventilation) If you hyperventilate, your breathing rate increases, usually because of stress. This can cause cramp and dizziness. An increase in someone's breathing is called hyperventilation.

hyphen (hyphenated) A hyphen is a punctuation mark used to link words or parts of words and make new words, as for example in 'left-handed'. Words like 'left-handed' are called hyphenated words.

hypnosis is the technique of hypnotizing people.

hypnotic (hypnotically) If you call something hypnotic, you mean it is so fascinating you cannot stop watching it or listening to it. Fassbinder has the gift of making the most mundane subjects hypnotically watchable.

hypnotise See hypnotize.

hypnotism (hypnotist) Hypnotism is the same as hypnosis. A hypnotist is someone who hypnotizes people.

hypnotize (hypnotizing, hypnotized) (can be spelled with an 's' instead of a 'z') ❏ If someone hypnotizes you, they use a special technique to put you into a trance, during which you are very receptive to suggestions.

❏ If you are hypnotized by something, you are so fascinated by it you have to keep watching it or listening to it.

hypoallergenic jewellery and cosmetics are made from materials which are not likely to cause an allergic reaction.

hypochondriac (hypochondria) A hypochondriac is someone who continually worries about their health, often thinking something is wrong when they are perfectly healthy. Behaviour like this is called hypochondria.

hypocrisy (*pron:* hip-**pok**-rass-ee) (hypocritical, hypocritically; hypocrite) If you accuse someone of **hypocrisy**, you mean they pretend to have certain beliefs or principles, while behaving in a way which goes against those beliefs or principles. You say someone like this is being **hypocritical**; you can also call them a **hypocrite**. *Governments are hypocritically condemning some abuses but ignoring others.*

hypodermic A **hypodermic** needle or syringe is used for giving injections.

hypotension is abnormally low blood pressure.

hypotenuse (*pron:* hie-**pot**-a-news) The **hypotenuse** of a right-angled triangle is its longest side.

hypothermia is a condition in which a person's body temperature is very low as a result of being in cold conditions for a long time. Severe hypothermia can cause death.

hypothesis (*pron:* high-**poth**-iss-iss) (*plural:* hypotheses) A **hypothesis** is an explanation or theory which has not yet been proved to be correct.

hypothesize (hypothesizing, hypothesized) (*can be spelled with an 's' instead of a 'z'*) If you **hypothesize** about something, you put forward an explanation or theory.

hypothetical (hypothetically) A **hypothetical** situation is a possible one, which you think about to consider the possible consequences. *We work out in some detail – although hypothetically, of course – what a House of Representatives would be like if it was drawn from the people by random lot.*

hysterectomy A **hysterectomy** is an operation to remove a woman's womb.

hysteria (hysterical, hysterically; hysterics) **Hysteria** is uncontrolled excitement, anger, or panic among a group of people. ◇ If an individual person is **hysterical** or suffering from **hysteria**, they are in an uncontrolled emotional state as a result of shock. *A young mother began shrieking hysterically.* You can also say someone in this state is in **hysterics** or having **hysterics**.

I i

I A speaker or writer uses **I** to refer to himself or herself.

IBA The **IBA** was an organization which controlled all the broadcasting companies in the UK except the BBC until 1992. It was replaced by the Independent Television Commission. IBA is short for 'Independent Broadcasting Authority'.

ice (icing, iced) ❑ **Ice** is frozen water. ◇ If something **ices up**, it becomes so cold that ice forms around it or inside it. ◇ **Ice** is pieces of ice used to keep food or drink cool. ◇ An **iced** drink has been made very cold.

❑ If you are **on thin ice**, you are in a tricky situation and need to be careful. ◇ If a project or plan is put **on ice**, it is decided that no action will be taken on it for a while. ◇ If you **break the ice**, you do something to make people feel relaxed and comfortable. ◇ If something **cuts no ice** with someone, it does not impress or influence them.

❑ An **ice** is an ice cream.

❑ If you **ice** a cake, you cover it with icing. An **iced** cake is covered with icing.

ice age When people talk about the **ice age**, they mean one of the periods when a large part of the earth's surface was covered with ice.

ice axe An **ice axe** is an axe-like tool which is used by mountaineers.

ice-breaker An **ice-breaker** is a ship designed to break a channel through ice.

ice-cap An **ice-cap** is a layer of thick ice and snow which permanently covers an area of land.

ice-cold things are very cold.

ice cream is a food made from frozen milk, fats, and sugar. An **ice cream** is a portion of ice cream, usually bought in a wrapper or container.

ice-cream soda is a sweet thick drink made from ice cream, fruit-flavoured syrup, and soda water.

ice cube An **ice cube** is a small block of ice put into a drink to make it cold.

ice floe An **ice floe** is a large area of ice floating in the sea.

ice hockey is a game like hockey played on ice.

ice lolly An **ice lolly** is a piece of flavoured ice or ice cream on a stick.

ice rink An **ice rink** is a level area of ice for skating on, usually inside a building.

ice-skate Ice-skates are boots with metal blades, for skating on ice.

ice-skating (ice-skater) **Ice-skating** is skating on ice, for amusement or as a sport. People who do it are called **ice-skaters**.

iceberg An **iceberg** is a large tall mass of ice floating in the sea. ◇ If you say something is the **tip of the iceberg**, you mean it is only a small part of a problem which is actually much more serious and widespread.

icicle An **icicle** is a long pointed piece of ice hanging from a surface.

icily See icy.

icing is a sweet substance used to cover and decorate cakes. ◇ If you say something is the **icing on the cake**, you mean it is an attractive but unnecessary addition to something which is already satisfactory.

icing sugar is finely-ground white sugar for making icing and sweets.

icon (*pron:* **eye**-kon) (iconic) ❑ An **icon** or ikon is a picture of Christ or some other religious figure painted on a wooden panel. In Orthodox churches, icons are regarded as holy. ◇ An **icon** is also someone or something that is greatly admired, often because they are seen as a perfect example of something. You say someone or something like this is **iconic**.

❑ An **icon** is also a small sign on a computer screen, representing a function. You activate the function by moving the cursor onto the icon.

iconoclast (iconoclastic, iconoclasm) An **iconoclast** is someone who criticizes generally accepted beliefs. You describe what they say or write as **iconoclastic** or call it **iconoclasm**.

icy (icier, iciest; icily) ❑ **Icy** air or water is extremely cold. ◇ An **icy** road has ice on it.
❑ You say someone's behaviour is **icy** when they show dislike or anger in a quiet controlled way. *She smiled icily.*

ID cards or badges show a person's identity. ID is short for 'identity' or 'identification'.

idea ❑ An **idea** is something such as a possible course of action which comes into your mind and which you can then describe to other people. *Further ideas will be put forward at the summit next month.* ◇ The **idea** of an action or activity is its aim or purpose. *The idea is to build confidence and reduce suspicion.*
❑ If you have an **idea** what something is, you think you know what it is, but you are not sure. Your **idea** of something is your belief about what it is like, or what it should be like. *People have these very peculiar ideas about bats being a bit like lizards or perhaps even laying eggs.* Similarly, you can have an **idea** where something is, or how something is done. ◇ If you have an **idea** something is true, you think it might be true, but you are not sure. *I have an idea that he left for Australia.* ◇ If you have **no idea** about something, you do not know anything about it.

ideal ❑ An **ideal** is a principle, idea, or standard which you believe in and try to achieve.
❑ You say someone or something is **ideal** when they are just what is wanted for a particular job or purpose. *...the ideal candidate... This area is ideal for excursions.* ◇ You say **in an ideal world** when you are talking about something which would be very desirable but which is never likely to happen, because conditions will never be right for it. *In an ideal world all parents would find places for their children in the schools of their first choice.*

idealise See idealize.

idealism (idealist, idealistic) **Idealism** is having ideals. A person who has ideals and tries to achieve them is called an **idealist**. You call their ideas and behaviour **idealistic**.

idealize (idealizing, idealized; idealization) *(can be spelled with an 's' instead of a 'z')* If you **idealize** someone or something, you think of them as perfect, or much better than they really are. *...his romantic idealization of the Russian past.*

ideally If you say **ideally** something should happen, you mean it would be the best thing that could happen, although it is not really likely or possible. *Ideally, the amounts of money raised and spent by the town halls would be the same.* ◇ If someone or something is **ideally** suited for something, they are just right for it. Similarly, you can say a place is **ideally** situated for something.

identical (identically) If things are **identical**, they are exactly the same. *They were dressed identically.* ◇ **Identical twins** are two people or animals who were conceived from a single egg. They are the same sex and look very much alike.

identifiable If someone or something is **identifiable**, you can tell who or what they are.

identify (identifies, identifying, identified; identification) ❑ If you **identify** someone or something, (a) you establish who or what they are. *This is the first time DNA analysis has been used to identify a human skeleton... The positive identification was made from dental records.* (b) you reveal who or what they are to other people. *...a state organisation which he refused to identify.* ◇ Your **identification** is a document like your driving licence or passport which proves who you are. ◇ An **identification parade** is the same as an identity parade.
❑ If you **identify** the people or places particularly affected by something, you establish who or what they are and make this information public. *The report identifies a number of developing countries badly hit by the increase.*
❑ If something is **identified** with a particular thing, (a) people associate it with that thing. *The area is now identified with quality wines.* (b) people see them as amounting to the same thing. *The need to identify nationhood with language is just as strong today as it was in the last century.*
❑ If you can **identify** with someone, you can understand their feelings or imagine yourself in their situation.

identikit is a collection of pictures of facial features, from which pictures of complete faces can be constructed. The police use identikit to construct faces like those of people who have committed a crime, in the hope that someone will recognize them. 'Identikit' is a trade mark. **Identikit** is also used to describe someone or something that gives the impression of having been put together in this way. *...an identikit Nazi, complete with leather coat and Himmler glasses.*

identity (identities) Your **identity** is who you are. *Her accomplice has still not revealed his identity.* ◇ The **identity** of a group of people is all the things about them which are special to them and distinguish them from other groups. ◇ If you say there is an **identity** of interests or aims, you mean two groups of people have the same interests or aims.

identity card An **identity card** is a card with your name and other information on it, which you carry with you to prove who you are.

identity parade When the police hold an **identity parade**, they get together a line of people, to see if a victim or witness of a crime recognizes anyone in the line as the person who committed it.

ideologist (ideological) See ideology.

ideologue *(pron:* eye-dee-a-log*)* An **ideologue** is the same as an ideologist.

ideology (ideologies; ideologist, ideological, ideologically) An **ideology** is a set of beliefs on which a political party or government bases its policies. An **ideologist** is someone who believes in an ideology, and works out how it can be turned into action. **Ideological** is used to talk about things to do with ideologies. *The two sides are economically and ideologically compatible.*

idiocy See idiotic.

idiom An **idiom** is a group of words whose meaning cannot be worked out from the words taken separately. For example, 'let the cat out of the bag' is an idiom. ◇ An **idiom** is also a style of speech, writing, or music. *He skilfully fused the jazz idiom with classical music.*

idiomatic language is the kind of language you use in conversation, rather than in a report or formal letter.

idiosyncrasy (*pron:* id-ee-o-sin-krass-ee) (idiosyncrasies; idiosyncratic) A person's **idiosyncrasies** are their special habits and ways of doing things, especially when these are a little unusual; you can say someone's habits and ways are **idiosyncratic**. You can also say someone's opinions and tastes are **idiosyncratic**.

idiot If you call someone an **idiot**, you mean they are very stupid, or have done something stupid. ◇ In the past, a person with a severe mental handicap was often referred to as an **idiot**.

idiotic (idiocy, idiocies) If you say something is **idiotic**, you mean it is very stupid. You can talk about the **idiocy** of something like this. **Idiocies** are stupid actions.

idle (idling, idled; idly, idleness, idler) ❑ Someone who is **idle** is not doing any work, because they are prevented from doing it. *Doctors are forced into idleness through lack of drugs.* ◇ If things like machines or factories are **idle**, they are not being used.
❑ If a car engine is **idling**, it is running slowly and is not in gear.
❑ You also say someone is **idle** when they are too lazy to do any work. A lazy person who spends their time doing nothing is called an **idler**. ◇ **Idle** is used to describe things people feel or do for no special reason, often because they have nothing else to occupy them. *The first reaction was idle curiosity... I inquired idly after the time.*
❑ If you call what people are saying **idle** talk, you mean it is not based on any real facts or intentions and should not be taken seriously. *...idle rumours... The threat to cut aid is not an idle one.* ◇ If you say it would be **idle** to do something, you mean nothing useful would come of it.
❑ If you say you will not **stand idly by** if something happens, you mean you will take some positive action.

idol (idolatry) (*pron:* ide-ol-a-tree) An **idol** is someone like a pop star who is greatly admired and loved by many people. ◇ An **idol** is also a statue worshipped by people who believe it is a god. Worshipping statues is called **idolatry**. ◇ Obsessive admiration for a person can also be called **idolatry**.

idolize (idolizing, idolized; idolization) (*can be spelled with an 's' instead of a 'z'*) If you **idolize** someone like a pop star, you admire them very much. *...the idolization of the Kray brothers.*

idyll (*pron:* id-ill) (idyllic) An **idyll** is a simple life of peace and happiness, often in the country. **Idyllic** (*pron:* id-dill-ik) is used to describe a life like this. *...an idyllic childhood.*

i.e. You write **i.e.** when you are putting something you have just mentioned in a different way, to make it clearer what you mean. *Britain has the second lowest minimum wage in the EU, ranking alongside the Community's poorest members, i.e. Greece, Portugal and Spain.*

if is used to mention something which might happen. *If convicted, the elder girl could be sentenced to death.* If is also used to mention something which might have happened, but did not happen. *If we had chosen last weekend, people would have said we were seeking to wreck the conference.* ◇ You say **if only...** when you are mentioning something you would like to happen, although it is unlikely to happen.
❑ If is used to say one thing must happen before something else can happen. *Yet more subsidies must end if Zimbabwe is to get the hard-currency loans it needs.*
❑ If **anything** is used to say something is not true, and in fact the opposite may be true. *He said citizens should gather outside their parliament – but, if anything, the crowd has thinned out since this morning.*
❑ If is used when mentioning a question someone has asked. *He asked if we were still interested.*
❑ If **not** is used to suggest something might be larger, earlier, etc than you have just said. *I will be ready in a couple of weeks, if not sooner.* ◇ If **only** is used when mentioning a reason for something, to suggest there may be other reasons. *We felt obliged to accept the holiday, if only to give us time to re-think our decision.*
❑ If is used to say something has a second quality which contrasts with the one you have just mentioned. *The strike produced a dramatic, if temporary, worsening of Britain's overseas trade position.*
❑ If a statement is full of **ifs and buts**, it shows a lot of doubts about whether something is possible.

iffy things are full of uncertainties. *It sounds a risky time to buy shares in such an iffy sector.*

igloo An **igloo** is a house shaped like half a ball, made from blocks of snow.

igneous rock is very hard rock, originally formed by molten material hardening. Granite and basalt are types of igneous rock.

ignite (igniting, ignited; ignition) ❑ If something **ignites** or is **ignited**, it starts burning. *The blast was caused by the ignition of methane gas.* ◇ A car's **ignition** is the part of the engine which ignites the fuel and starts the car. The **ignition** is also the keyhole which is used to turn on the ignition.
❑ If something **ignites** an argument or conflict, it starts it off.

ignoble (ignobly) **Ignoble** is used to describe behaviour, experiences, and feelings which are thought to be shameful. *...an ignoble episode from their country's past... The Prime Minister has gone in a noble way instead of being ignobly beaten.*

ignominious (*pron:* ig-no-min-ee-uss) (ignominiously; ignominy) **Ignominious** is used to describe things which are shameful or embarrassing. *...an ignominious defeat... The law was ignominiously withdrawn.* **Ignominy** (*pron:* ig-nom-in-ee) is shame or public disgrace.

ignorant (ignorantly, ignorance) If you are **ignorant** of something, you do not know about it. *Many people are ignorant of the facts... Rosé wines are ignorantly looked down on as wine for wimps... The public is kept in ignorance about potential disasters.* ◇ If you say someone is **ignorant**, you mean they are impolite or inconsiderate.

ignore (ignoring, ignored) If you **ignore** someone or something, you deliberately take no notice of them. *The DTI is ignoring the advice of the Bank of England.* ◇ If something **ignores** an important aspect of a situation, it fails to take it into account. *The agreement also ignores the fact that Europe's skies and airports are already full.*

ikon See icon.

ilk is used in some phrases to mean 'kind' or 'type'. For example, 'a man of his ilk' means 'a man of that kind'.

ill (illness, illnesses) ❑ If you are **ill** or have an **illness**, you are suffering from a disease or health problem. If you fall ill or are **taken ill**, you become ill suddenly. **Illness**

is being ill.

❏ Ill is evil or harm. *Information can be used for ill as well as for good.* ◇ Ill luck is bad luck. *Ferrari bore the brunt of the ill fortune.* ◇ Ills are difficulties and problems. *...the nation's economic ills.*

❏ The ill effects of something are its bad or harmful effects. If something happens for good or ill, its effects may be good or bad. *For good or ill, national sovereignty would remain.* ◇ 'It's an ill wind that blows nobody any good' means a bad situation usually has some good effects. People often talk about 'an ill wind blowing some good'. *The fire was an ill wind that blew the company some good.*

❏ If you speak ill of someone, you criticize them. ◇ Ill will or ill feeling is a feeling of hostility towards someone.

❏ Ill- is added to words to say something is done badly or inadequately. *...an ill-cut suit... ...ill-considered plans.*

❏ ill at ease: see ease. ◇ ill afford: see afford.

ill-advised An ill-advised action is not sensible or wise.

ill-equipped If you are ill-equipped for something, you do not have the right ability, qualities, or equipment for it.

ill-fated is used to describe things which end in a tragic or unfortunate way. *...his ill-fated attempt on the world water speed record.*

ill-founded You say a belief or feeling is ill-founded when there is no good reason to have it.

ill-gotten things have been obtained or achieved illegally. *...ill-gotten wealth.* Things like these are often called ill-gotten gains.

ill health See health.

ill-mannered people are rude and inconsiderate.

ill-starred means the same as ill-fated.

ill-tempered An ill-tempered occasion is one when people are hostile and aggressive towards each other. ◇ An ill-tempered person has a bad temper.

ill-timed If something is ill-timed, it is done at the wrong time.

ill-treat (ill-treatment) If someone is ill-treated, they are treated badly or cruelly. *...the ill-treatment of political detainees.*

illegal (illegally; illegality, illegalities) If something is illegal, it is against the law to have it or do it. Illegality is having or doing something which is forbidden by law. Illegalities are illegal acts. *...foreigners working in the country illegally... The government has denied any illegalities took place.* ◇ An illegal organization is forbidden by law. ◇ An illegal immigrant is someone who has entered a country without official permission.

illegible writing is so bad or unclear that you cannot read it.

illegitimate (illegitimacy) ❏ An illegitimate person's parents were not married to each other at the time he or she was born. Illegitimacy is being born to parents who were not married to each other.

❏ Illegitimate activities are against the law.

illiberal If you call a law or system of government illiberal, you mean it restricts people's freedom in an unnecessary or unjust way.

illicit (illicitly) An illicit activity or substance is not allowed by law. *...illicit drugs... ...illicitly acquired material.* ◇ Illicit is also used to describe activities which are not acceptable according to the social customs of a country.

...illicit sex.

illiterate (illiteracy) An illiterate person cannot read or write. Illiteracy is not being able to read or write. Illiterate people are sometimes called illiterates.

illness See ill.

illogical (illogically, illogicality) If something is illogical, it is not reasonable or sensible. *This means gun control, which urban blacks want, but many whites illogically hate.* You talk about the illogicality of something like this.

illuminate (illuminating, illuminated; illumination) ❏ If a light illuminates something, it shines on it, so that it stands out or can be seen in the dark. If something is illuminated, it has lights shining on it, or lights placed on it. The illumination in a place is the lighting there. ◇ Illuminations are coloured lights put up in a town for decoration, especially at Christmas.

❏ If you illuminate something which is difficult to understand, you make it clearer by explaining it or giving examples. If you say something is illuminating, you mean it helps you to understand something better. *...an illuminating book.*

❏ Illuminated medieval books and manuscripts have intricate brightly-coloured drawings and designs, often in gold paint, which decorate the writing.

illusion ❏ An illusion is something someone believes is true, though it is in fact false. You say someone is under an illusion about something. ◇ If you have no illusions about something or are under no illusion about it, you are fully aware of the truth about it. *China's drug smugglers can have few illusions about the risks they run.*

❏ An illusion or optical illusion is something which looks like one thing, but is really something else or not there at all.

illusionist An illusionist is a conjuror who tries to make people believe they have seen things which have not really happened.

illusive means the same as illusory.

illusory things seem to exist but do not really exist at all. *The much-heralded recovery is still illusory.*

illustrate (illustrating, illustrated; illustration, illustrator) ❏ If something illustrates a situation or is an illustration of it, it is an example of it, and therefore proves it exists. *The study's findings illustrate the growing insecurity among teenagers.* ◇ If you illustrate a point you are making, you provide an example which shows the kind of thing you mean.

❏ If someone illustrates a book, they draw the pictures or diagrams which go into it. An illustration is a picture or diagram in a book. An illustrator is an artist who draws pictures for books.

illustrative is used to describe things which provide an example of something. *The budget package was illustrative of what the final budget would look like.*

illustrator See illustrate.

illustrious If someone is illustrious or has had an illustrious career, they are famous and their work is greatly admired.

image (imagery; imaging, imaged) ❏ If you have an image of someone or something, you have a picture or idea of them in your mind. ◇ An image in a film or book is something which catches your attention and is meant to stand for something important or significant. *A handful* *of recent films capture raw and contemporary images of Latin America.* The images in a film or book can also be called its **imagery**.

❏ Your **image** is the way you appear to other people. *Birmingham has had an image problem in selling itself as a desirable international city.* ◇ Your **image** is also your reflection in something like a mirror. See also **mirror image**.

❏ An **image** of an object, especially one which you cannot see with the naked eye, is a picture of it produced by photography or radar. ◇ When a piece of equipment **images** something, it produces a picture of it. *...a thermal imaging camera.*

❏ If you create something **in your own image**, you give it the qualities you possess yourself. *She has moulded British politics in her own image.*

imaginable is used to describe the most extreme example of something you can think of. *Migraine is the worst form of headache imaginable.*

imaginary See imagine.

imagination (imaginative, imaginatively) Your **imagination** is your ability to form new ideas and think about things which do not exist. If someone has this ability, you say they are **imaginative**. **Imaginative** is also used to describe things created by such people. *...imaginative schemes... Architects can work imaginatively with older streets and buildings.*

imagine (imagining, imagined; imaginary) ❏ If you **imagine** a situation which does not exist, you form a picture of it in your mind. *Who in 1988 would have imagined the fall of the Berlin wall in 1989?* ◇ **Imagined** or **imaginary** things exist only in people's minds; such things can also be called **imaginings**. *...the imaginings of young children.*

❏ If you **imagine** something is true, you suppose it is true. *I imagine this happens a lot in television.*

imam (*pron:* im-**mahm**) An **imam** is a Muslim prayer-leader at a mosque.

imbalance (imbalanced) If there is an **imbalance** in a situation, things are not evenly or fairly arranged. *...the imbalance in trade between the two countries.* You say a situation like this is **imbalanced**.

imbecile (imbecility) If you call someone an **imbecile**, you mean they are stupid, or have done something stupid. You can talk about a person's **imbecility** or about the **imbecility** of something they have done.

imbibe (imbibing, imbibed) If you **imbibe** alcohol, you drink it. ◇ When people **imbibe** ideas or arguments, they listen to them and accept them as right or true.

imbroglio (*pron:* imb-**role-lee-oh**) (imbroglios) An **imbroglio** is a confusing or complicated situation.

imbue (imbuing, imbued) If something is **imbued** with a quality, it is filled with it. *The organization allowed itself to become imbued with an air of hopelessness.*

IMF The **IMF** is an international agency which is part of the United Nations. It exists to promote trade and to improve economic conditions in the countries belonging to it. It also lends money to its members. **IMF** is short for 'International Monetary Fund'.

imitate (imitating, imitated; imitative, imitator) If you **imitate** someone or **imitate** what they do, you copy them. Behaviour like this is called **imitative** behaviour. People who copy what a well-known person does are called that person's **imitators**.

imitation is copying what someone else does. ◇ If you give an **imitation** of someone, you copy the way they speak or behave, to amuse or entertain people.

❏ **Imitation** things are made to look like other things, especially things of better quality. An object made to look like something else is called an **imitation**.

immaculate (immaculately) You say someone or something is **immaculate** when they have an exceptionally clean and tidy appearance. ◇ **Immaculate** is also used to describe things which are done perfectly, without any mistakes. *The orchestra plays immaculately.*

immaterial If you say something is **immaterial**, you mean it makes no difference to a situation, or to the thing you are talking about. *Who is elected is immaterial to us.*

immature (immaturity) **Immature** is used to describe things which are not yet fully developed. *...ovary tissue containing immature eggs.* ◇ If you call a person **immature** or talk about their **immaturity**, you mean they do not behave in a sensible and adult way.

immeasurable (immeasurably) **Immeasurable** is used to say something is so great that it cannot be measured, or cannot be appreciated. *...the immeasurable suffering of the Second World War... The strength of the reserve players has grown immeasurably.*

immediacy If you talk about the **immediacy** of something, you mean it gives you a strong impression of things happening now, and makes you feel very close to them. *...the immediacy of television news reporting.*

immediate (immediately) ❏ **Immediate** and **immediately** are used to talk about something happening straight away. *Officials called for an immediate ceasefire... The news immediately pushed up share values.* ◇ **Immediately** is also used to talk about something being understood straight away. *It is not immediately clear what happened.* ◇ If something is **immediately** available, you can get hold of it straight away.

❏ **Immediately** is used to say something happens or is done as soon as something else has happened. *They would fly out immediately the President gave the order.* ◇ If something happens **immediately** before or after something else, it happens just before or after it.

❏ **Immediate** needs or concerns must be attended to straight away.

❏ The **immediate** future is the period which lies just ahead. Similarly, you can talk about the **immediate** past.

❏ **Immediate** is used to say something is just next to something else. *Argentina was creating a free trade area with its immediate neighbours... The floating power stations would be based immediately over the oil or gas wells.* ◇ Your **immediate** family are close relatives like your parents, brothers, and sisters.

immemorial If you say something has been happening **since time immemorial**, you mean it has been happening for longer than anyone can remember.

immense (immensely, immensity) If something is **immense**, it is extremely large. For example, you can talk about an immense object or an immense amount of something. You can also talk about immense difficulties or achievements. *It was an issue of immense concern... ...an immensely successful record.* When something is extremely large, you can talk about its **immensity**.

immerse (immersing, immersed; immersion) ❏ If you im-merse yourself in something, you become completely involved in it. *She immersed herself in music and dance.*
❏ If you **immerse** something in a liquid, you put it in the liquid so that it is completely covered. *The process involves immersion first in dry salt or brine, and then in vinegar.*

immersion heater An **immersion heater** is an electric heater which provides hot water in a home. The heater is immersed in water inside a hot-water tank.

immigrant (immigration; immigrate, immigrating, immigrated) **Immigrants** are people who come to live and work in a country. Coming to live and work in a country is called **immigration**. People sometimes say someone **immi-grates** into a country, but this use is not common. ◇ At a port, airport, or border, **immigration** is the place where the passports of people entering the country are checked. ◇ See also **emigrate**.

imminent (imminently, imminence) If something is **immi-nent**, it will happen very soon. *A further round of talks is due to begin imminently... ...the imminence of the election.*

immobile (immobility) ❏ If someone or something is im-mobile, they are not moving.
❏ You also say someone is **immobile** when they are un-able to move, for example because of a serious injury. *Muscle weakness and consequent falls and fractures are a major cause of immobility among the extremely old.*

immobilize (immobilizing, immobilized; immobilization) *(can be spelled with an 's' instead of a 'z')* If something is im-mobilized, it is prevented from working or moving. *The stroke immobilized the left side of his body... ...temporary im-mobilization of mechanical parts.*

immoderate (immoderately) **Immoderate** behaviour is ex-treme or overdone. *He was seen to laugh immoderately.*

immodest (immodesty) ❏ **Immodest** behaviour shocks or embarrasses people, because they think it is rude.
❏ An **immodest** person is boastful. **Immodesty** is boast-ful behaviour.

immolation is killing someone as a sacrifice, especially by burning them alive. If people die by **self-immolation**, they burn themselves alive, usually for religious or po-litical reasons.

immoral (immorality) If you say someone's behaviour is **immoral**, you mean it is morally wrong. You can also talk about its **immorality**. *...the immorality of drink driv-ing.* ◇ People sometimes call a person **immoral** when they do not approve of their sexual behaviour.

immortal (immortality) You say someone or something is **immortal** when they are famous and will be remem-bered for a long time. You can talk about the **immortal-ity** of someone or something like this. An **immortal** is a famous person who will be remembered for a long time. *Harrison Ford has joined the ranks of the movie im-mortals.* ◇ When a religious person talks about some-one being **immortal**, they mean they will live forever in Heaven.

immortalize (immortalizing, immortalized) *(can be spelled with an 's' instead of a 'z')* If someone or something is immortalized, they are made famous, for example in a book or film, and will continue to be remembered be-cause of it.

immovable (immovably) An **immovable** object cannot be moved. *The rudder remained immovably jammed.* ◇ You

say a person is **immovable** when they will not change their mind about something.

immune (immunity) ❏ If you are **immune** to a disease or have **immunity** to it, you cannot be made ill by it. ◇ The body's **immune system** is the way it fights infec-tion, especially by producing antibodies to destroy disease-carrying substances. **Immune** is used to talk about things to do with this system. *...immune cells.*
❏ If you are **immune** to things happening around you, you are not affected by them. *People in both communities had become immune to violent death.* ◇ **Immune** is also used to say some action cannot be taken against someone. For example, if you are **immune** from prosecution, you can-not be prosecuted. *He has been demanding immunity from prosecution for himself and his followers.* ◇ diplomatic im-munity: see **diplomatic**.

immunize (immunizing, immunized; immunization) *(can be spelled with an 's' instead of a 'z')* If you are **immunized** against a disease, you are made immune to it, usually by an injection. *...immunization for whooping cough.*

immunodeficiency (immunodeficiencies) An **immunodefi-ciency** is a breakdown in the body's immune system, or a serious weakness in it. See also **AIDS, HIV.**

immunology (immunologist, immunological) **Immunology** is the study of immunity to disease. An expert on this is called an **immunologist**. **Immunological** is used to talk about things to do with immunity to disease.

immutable (immutably) If something is **immutable**, it can-not be changed. *He stated categorically that Poland's bor-ders were immutable Intelligence is not immutably fixed, but can be improved by the right sort of teaching.*

imp In fairy tales, an **imp** is a small mischievous creature with magical powers.

impact ❏ If something has an **impact** on a person or situation, it has a strong effect on them. You can also say something **impacts** (*pron:* im-**pakts**) on a person or situation. *...decisions which have so clearly impacted on the company.*
❏ The **impact** of one object on another is the force with which it hits it. *A number of cars caught fire on impact.* If an object **impacts** with something, it collides with it.

impair (impairing, impaired; impairment) If something is im-paired, it is damaged or weakened, and this stops it be-ing effective or working properly. *These developments would not impair future relations... ...visually impaired peo-ple... ...hearing impairment.*

impale (impaling, impaled) If you **impale** something, you stick a sharp pointed object through it.

impart If you **impart** information or knowledge to some-one, you give it to them. ◇ If something **imparts** a qual-ity to something else, it gives it to it. *His clothes seem to impart an arrogant self-confidence to anybody who wears them.*

impartial (impartially, impartiality) If you are **impartial**, you act fairly and do not take sides in a situation or argu-ment. When someone behaves like this, you talk about their **impartiality**. *...an open and impartial investigation... The army wants to be seen to be acting impartially.*

impassable If a road is **impassable**, you cannot get along it, because it is blocked or in a bad condition.

impasse (*pron:* am-**pass**) An **impasse** is a difficult situation where no progress can be made.

impassioned If someone speaks in an **impassioned** way, they show strong emotion, because they feel very strongly about something.

impassive (impassively) If you are **impassive**, you do not show any emotion. *The General sat impassively as the evidence was given.*

impatient (impatiently, impatience) ❑ If you are **impatient**, you are annoyed because you have to wait for something. *He repeated his question impatiently.* ◇ If you are **impatient** to do something, you are eager to do it. Similarly, if you are **impatient** for something to happen, you are eager for it to happen. *The demonstration reflected public impatience for change.*
  ❑ **Impatient** people have very little patience.

impeach (impeaches, impeaching, impeached; impeachment) If a politician or government official is **impeached**, they are charged with committing a serious crime in connection with their job. *...a petition calling for the President's impeachment.*

impeccable (impeccably) If you call someone's behaviour or dress **impeccable**, you mean it is perfect in every detail. *Impeccably dressed, he was often seen browsing in the most expensive boutiques.*

impecunious If someone is **impecunious**, they have very little money.

impede (impeding, impeded; impediment) If you are **impeded** by something, it hinders you and makes it difficult for you to move or make progress. Something which has this effect is called an **impediment**. *Their work was being impeded by shortages of essential supplies.* ◇ A speech **impediment** is a disability like a stammer which makes speaking difficult.

impel (impelling, impelled) If something **impels** you to do something, it forces you to do it.

impending is used to describe things which are going to happen soon. *...the impending elections.*

impenetrable (impenetrability, impenetrably) If an area is **impenetrable**, it is impossible to get through it or into it. *...impenetrable forests and swamps.* ◇ If something written or spoken is **impenetrable**, it is impossible to understand it. *...impenetrably detailed reports... ...the impenetrability of his speeches.*

imperative If you say it is **imperative** that something is done, you mean it must be done. ◇ If there is an **imperative** need for something, it is needed urgently. ◇ An **imperative** is something you must do or have. *...the strategic imperative for the US to have military bases in South East Asia.*

imperceptible (imperceptibly) If something is **imperceptible**, it is so small or slight you do not notice it. *The land slopes upwards imperceptibly for 800 miles.*

imperfect (imperfection, imperfectly) If a system is **imperfect**, it has faults or weaknesses. You call these faults or weaknesses **imperfections**. ◇ If an object is **imperfect**, it has been made with a slight fault, or has been damaged. You call the fault or damage an **imperfection**. ◇ If something has been done **imperfectly**, it has not been done correctly.

imperial is used to talk about things to do with an emperor, empress, or empire. *...Imperial Russia... ...the first ever imperial visit to South Korea.*
  ❑ The **imperial** system of measurement uses miles, feet and inches, pounds and ounces, gallons and pints.

imperialism (imperialist, imperialistic) **Imperialism** is a system in which a rich and powerful country controls other countries. **Imperialist** and **imperialistic** are used to talk about things to do with imperialism.

imperil (imperilling, imperilled) (*American spelling*: imperiling, imperiled) If something **imperils** something else, it puts it in danger. *The violence imperils the programme of reform which the world has been demanding.*

imperious (imperiously) An **imperious** person is proud and expects to be obeyed. *He held up his hand imperiously.*

imperishable If something is **imperishable**, it cannot be removed or destroyed. *...an imperishable memory.*

impermeable If a substance or layer of something is **impermeable**, liquid cannot get through it.

impermissible If something is **impermissible**, it is not allowed.

impersonal is used to describe treatment of people in which they are made to feel they are unimportant, and that their personality, feelings, and opinions do not matter. A place where people are treated like this can also be called **impersonal**. *...impersonal hospitals.* ◇ **Impersonal** is also used to describe things which cannot be identified with any particular person. *...impersonal market forces.*

impersonate (impersonating, impersonated; impersonation, impersonator) If you **impersonate** someone or do an **impersonation** of them, you pretend to be them, either to deceive people or to entertain them. An **impersonator** is an entertainer who impersonates famous people.

impertinent (impertinence) If you say someone's behaviour is **impertinent**, you mean it is rude and disrespectful. *He was taken aback by their sheer impertinence.*

imperturbable If someone is **imperturbable**, they remain calm and untroubled in a disturbing situation.

impervious (imperviousness) If you are **impervious** to what people say or do, you do not let it affect you. *...the state's imperviousness to ordinary Peruvians.* ◇ If something is **impervious** to liquids or heat, it does not let them pass through it.

impetuous (impetuosity) You say someone is **impetuous** when they act quickly and suddenly without thinking. Behaviour like this is called **impetuosity**.

impetus ❑ If something is given **impetus**, it is made more powerful or effective. *The government is to open a dialogue with all parties to give new impetus to democracy... The armed struggle has lost its impetus over recent months.*
  ❑ The **impetus** of a moving object is the force it exerts when it hits something.

impinge (impinging, impinged) If something **impinges** on you or on your life, it makes a difference to the way you live. ◇ If something **impinges** on your rights, it has a serious effect on them. Similarly, something can **impinge** on something you are trying to achieve.

impish An **impish** person is cheeky and mischievous. You can also call someone's expression **impish** or say they have an **impish** sense of humour.

implacable (implacably) You say someone is **implacable** when their attitude to something is firm and shows no sign of changing. *...their implacable hostility to the treaty... The Socialist Party is implacably opposed to any constitutional change.*

implant (implantation) If something is **implanted** in a person's or animal's body, it is put there, usually by an operation. The process is called **implantation**; the thing placed in the body is called an **implant**. ...*orthopaedic implants*. ◇ If something like a belief is **implanted** in a place, it is introduced from outside and becomes widely accepted.

implausible (implausibly, implausibility) If something is **implausible**, it is difficult to believe and therefore unlikely to be true. *A poll suggested, implausibly, that nearly half the people in the city had met the mayor... The case for the soldiers rests on the implausibility of the Crown version of events.*

implement (implementation) ❑ When a plan or decision is **implemented**, it is put into practice. *The government has postponed implementation of its decision to raise food prices.*
❑ An **implement** is a tool or other piece of equipment.

implicate (implicating, implicated) If someone is **implicated** in something like a crime, they are shown to have been involved in it. ◇ If something is **implicated** in something that happens, it is one of the causes of it. *Cholesterol is implicated in gallstone formation.*

implication The **implications** of something are its indirect effects. *The social and economic implications of AIDS are very serious.* ◇ If something is true **by implication**, it follows indirectly from what has just been said. *The trial provided the first opportunity to convict her – and by implication her dead husband – of corruption.*

implicit (implicitly) ❑ An **implicit** criticism is made in an indirect way. *The Pope implicitly criticised the handling of the crisis.* Similarly, you can talk about an **implicit** challenge, warning, or threat. ◇ If something is **implicit** in a statement or attitude, it is there but not stated openly. *The desire to maintain a nuclear policy seems implicit in official remarks.*
❑ If you have **implicit** faith in someone or something, you believe in them completely. *The newspaper trusted him implicitly.*

implode (imploding, imploded; implosion) If an object **implodes**, it collapses inwards because the pressure inside is less than the pressure outside. This is called **implosion**. ◇ If a system or organization **implodes**, it collapses as a result of internal faults.

implore (imploring, implored) If you **implore** someone to do something, you beg them to do it.

implosion See implode.

imply (implies, implying, implied) ❑ If you **imply** that something is true, you suggest it is true without actually saying so. ◇ If what someone says **implies** an attitude or opinion, it suggests they have it. *His hostility to capital punishment in no way implies a soft approach to law and order... ...an implied criticism.*
❑ If one thing **implies** another, you always get the second thing when you get the first. *It is a gross exaggeration to say that a single currency implies a single government.*

impolite behaviour is rude and offends people.

impolitic An **impolitic** action is unwise and likely to cause difficulty or embarrassment.

imponderable things are impossible to assess or estimate. Things like these can be called **imponderables**.

import (importation, importer) ❑ If a person, country, or business **imports** goods, they buy them from another country and bring them into their own country. You talk about the **import** or **importation** of goods. A person, country, or business that does this is called an **importer**; the goods imported are called **imports**. ◇ If ideas or values are **imported** into a place, they are introduced from outside.
❑ The **import** of something is its importance. ...*a matter of such life-changing import.*

important (importantly, importance) If something is **important**, it has special significance, or is very useful or valuable. ...*his first important book... Very importantly, the coup leaders failed to bring the media under control... ...the island's strategic importance.* ◇ An **important** person has a lot of influence or power.

importation (importer) See import.

importunate An **importunate** person is persistent in trying to get something they want.

importune (pron: im-por-**tune**) (importuning, importuned) If you **importune** someone, you pester them for something or urge them to do something.

impose (imposing, imposed; imposition) If something like a rule is **imposed** on people, it is introduced and they have to obey it. ...*the strict imposition of the Islamic dress code.* ◇ If you **impose** your opinions or beliefs on people, you force them to accept them. ◇ If someone **imposes** on you, they unreasonably expect you to do something for them.

imposing (imposingly) You say someone or something is **imposing** when they have an impressive appearance or manner. ...*an imposing building... ...an imposingly tall and good-looking military figure.*

imposition See impose.

impossible (impossibly; impossibility, impossibilities) ❑ If something is **impossible**, it cannot be done, cannot happen, or cannot be true. You say something like this is an **impossibility**. *The standards she set herself were impossibly high... All parties agreed that the plan was a practical impossibility.* ◇ If you say someone is asking for **the impossible**, you mean they are asking for something which cannot possibly be done. ◇ If you say someone has done **the impossible**, you mean they have done something which people thought could not be done.
❑ An **impossible** situation is one which cannot be dealt with satisfactorily. *Hospital managers are being placed in the impossible position of implementing and then justifying these drastic cuts in services... She is faced with an impossible choice.* ◇ If you say someone is **impossible**, you mean they are very difficult to deal with.

impostor (or imposter) An **impostor** is someone who tricks people by pretending to be someone else.

impotent (impotently, impotence) ❑ You say someone is **impotent** when they have no control over what is going on. *He has been forced to fret impotently in the shadows.*
❑ If a man is **impotent**, he is unable to have or keep an erection during sex. This condition is called **impotence**.

impound If someone in authority **impounds** something, they legally take possession of it, because it is connected in some way with breaking the law.

impoverish (impoverishes, impoverishing, impoverished; impoverishment) ❑ **Impoverished** people are poor. If something **impoverishes** people, it makes them poor.
❑ If something becomes **impoverished**, it suffers a loss

in quality. *An obsession with material progress has led to spiritual impoverishment.*

impracticable If a course of action is **impracticable**, it cannot be carried out.

impractical (impracticality, impracticalities) If an idea or course of action is **impractical**, it is not realistic or practical. You can talk about the **impracticality** of something like this. The parts of something which are not practical can be called its **impracticalities**.

imprecise (imprecision) If something is **imprecise**, it is too general or vague. *...imprecise information... Imprecision on policy helps them attract support from a broad cross-section of voters.*

impregnable If a place is **impregnable**, it cannot be broken into. ◇ If a ruler is **impregnable** or in an **impregnable** position, he or she cannot be removed from power. If a sportsperson is in an **impregnable** position, he or she cannot be beaten.

impregnate (impregnating, impregnated) If something is **impregnated** with a substance, the substance is made to spread through it. ◇ If a man **impregnates** a woman, he makes her pregnant.

impresario (*pron:* im-pris-**sar**-ee-oh) (impresarios) An **impresario** is someone who arranges for plays, concerts, and other entertainments to be performed.

impress (impresses, impressing, impressed; impressive, impressively) ❑ If something **impresses** you, you are struck by how good or admirable it is. You can say you are **impressed** by something like this or describe it as **impressive**. *...an impressive performance... ...an impressively long career.* ◇ If you try to **impress** someone, you try to get them to admire you.
   ❑ If you **impress** something on someone, you get them to see how important it is.

impression ❑ Your **impression** of someone or something is the way they look or seem to you. *My impression is that the country is terribly run-down.* You can say someone or something creates a certain **impression**. *The new Prime Minister has created a favourable impression.* ◇ If you **make an impression**, people notice you and remember you.
   ❑ If you are **under the impression** that something is true, you believe it is true.
   ❑ An artist's **impression** is a drawing showing what someone is thought to look like. ◇ An **impression** is also an amusing imitation of a well-known person.
   ❑ An **impression** of an object is a mark or outline left on a surface after the object has been pressed against it.

impressionable people are easy to influence.

Impressionism (impressionist) **Impressionism** is a style of painting developed in France between 1870 and 1900. Artists concentrated on the effects of outdoor light on their subjects, and painted shapes with blurred edges, rather than showing things in realistic detail. **Impressionist** is used to talk about things to do with Impressionism. *...impressionist landscapes.* Artists who painted in this style are called **impressionists**.

impressionistic is used to describe any kind of music, painting, or writing which gives pleasing or interesting impressions, rather than being concerned with form or accurate representation.

impressive See impress.

imprimatur (*pron:* imp-rim-**ah**-ter) If you have an important person's **imprimatur** to do something, you have their approval.

imprint ❑ If something is **imprinted** on your mind or memory, you cannot forget it. You can also say something leaves an **imprint** on your mind or memory.
   ❑ If an object is **imprinted** onto a surface, it is pressed hard onto it, leaving a mark or outline. The mark or outline is called an **imprint**.
   ❑ An **imprint** is also the name of a publisher printed in a book.

imprison (imprisoning, imprisoned; imprisonment) If someone is **imprisoned**, they are sent to prison. **Imprisonment** is a period spent in prison. *They were sentenced to life imprisonment.* ◇ You also say someone is **imprisoned** when they are trapped in a room or some other enclosed space, and cannot get out. *Sniper fire had kept people imprisoned in their basements.*

improbable (improbably; improbability, improbabilities) If something is **improbable**, it is unlikely to be true or to happen. *...the improbability of suffering from chickenpox again.* ◇ **Improbable** and **improbably** are also used to talk about things happening which you would not expect to happen. *Squat and balding, he was an improbable hero... The Chancellor was having an improbably good week.*

impromptu things are not planned or organized in advance. *...an impromptu news conference.*

improper (improperly) **Improper** is used to describe things which are illegal, dishonest, or unacceptable. *...improper share dealing... ...the improper use of medicine... There were claims that some delegates were appointed improperly.* ◇ **Improper** is also used to describe rude or shocking behaviour. *He accused me of making improper suggestions to his wife.*

impropriety (*pron:* imp-roe-**pry**-a-tee) (improprieties) **Impropriety** is improper behaviour. **Improprieties** are improper acts. *...allegations of financial improprieties.*

improve (improving, improved; improvement) If something **improves** or there is an **improvement** in it, it gets better. An **improvement** is also a change which makes something better. *...home improvements.* ◇ If a sick or injured person **improves**, their health gets better. ◇ If you **improve** on an achievement, you do better than it. *She was ready to improve on the bronze medal she won at the Olympics.*

improvident If someone is **improvident**, they are wasteful and do not think about what they might need in the future.

improvisation (improvisational, improvisatory) **Improvisation** is making up music while playing it on an instrument. **Improvisational** and **improvisatory** are used to talk about things to do with improvising. *...improvisational jazz... ...improvisatory techniques.*

improvise (improvising, improvised) If you **improvise**, you make or do something without planning it in advance, using whatever materials are available. *As a boy he experimented with vaulting, improvising with his mother's clothes prop and washing line... ...an improvised press conference.* ◇ If you **improvise** when you are playing an instrument, you make up the music as you go along. Similarly, an actor can **improvise** with words.

imprudent (imprudently, imprudence) **Imprudent** behaviour is not sensible or careful. *The authorities imprudently cut interest rates... 60 farmers lost their livelihoods because of a minister's imprudence.*

impudent (impudence) If someone is **impudent**, they behave in a rude and disrespectful way. You call behaviour like this **impudence**.

impugn (*pron:* imp-**yoon**) If you **impugn** someone, you criticize them, especially by saying they are not all they pretend to be. You can also **impugn** someone's reputation or character.

impulse (impulsive, impulsively) ❑ An **impulse** is a sudden desire to do something. If you do something **on impulse**, you do it suddenly, without planning to. You call behaviour like this **impulsive**. *Do you buy unneeded items impulsively?* You say a person is **impulsive** when they keep behaving like this. ◇ An **impulse buy** is something you buy because you notice it and like it, rather than because you had planned to.
❑ If you talk about a person's **impulses**, you mean their tendency to behave in certain ways. *...his criminal impulses.*
❑ An **impulse** is also a short electrical signal sent along a wire, a nerve, or through the air.

impunity If you do something wrong with **impunity**, you get away with it.

impure (impurity, impurities) If a substance is **impure**, it is of inferior quality because it has small amounts of other substances in it. You call these other substances **impurities**.

impute (imputing, imputed; imputation) If you **impute** a kind of bad behaviour to someone, you say they have behaved like that. *We apologise unreservedly for any imputation of incorrect behaviour by His Lordship.*

in is used to say where something is, or where it happens. *His aircraft crashed in Mongolia.*
❑ If something is **in** something else, it is enclosed or surrounded by it. *There are all the usual drinks in the cupboard.* ◇ If something is **in** a window, it is just behind the window so you can see it from outside. ◇ When you see something **in** a mirror, you see its reflection.
❑ If you are **in**, you are at your home or place of work. ◇ When someone comes **in**, they enter a room or a building.
❑ When a train, boat, or plane comes **in**, it arrives. ◇ When the sea or tide comes **in**, the sea gradually moves further towards the shore.
❑ **In** is used to say what someone is wearing. *...people in rags, with no shoes.*
❑ If something is **in** a book, film, play, or speech, you can read, see, or hear it there.
❑ If something happens **in** a particular century, year, or month, it happens then. ◇ **In** is used to say something will happen after a certain length of time. *The meeting is to be held in three weeks' time.*
❑ If you are **in** a play, race, or other activity, you are one of the people taking part. ◇ If you are **in** an organization, you are a member of it. ◇ **In** is used to say what kind of work you do. *...a distinguished career in journalism.*
❑ **In** is used to say what general subject or field of activity you are talking about. *...advances in computer technology.* ◇ **In** is used to say what aspect of something you are talking about. *The whales grow to about ten metres in length.*

◇ **In that** is used to say in what way something is true. *We are no different from other manufacturers in that we offer discounts to our employees and their families.*
❑ **In** is used to talk about something happening to a rate or commodity. *There was no sign of any real pick-up in consumer spending.*
❑ You talk about something being **in** a particular state or situation. *The ship was never in any danger of sinking... Local government finance is in a state of chaos.* ◇ If something happens **in** a particular situation, it happens during it and as a result of it. *Eight people have been killed in unrest in the townships.*
❑ **In** is used to say how many people or things do something. *The recent elections show that people vote in greater numbers if they feel their vote is going to count.*
❑ **In** is used to say how something is communicated. *The opera was sung in English.*
❑ **In** is used to show approximate ages or temperatures. *...a couple in their seventies... Britain was roasting in the nineties.* ◇ **In** is used to express a ratio, proportion, or probability. *Doctors gave him a one in ten chance of survival.*
❑ **In** is used to talk about strong reactions to something. *The country recoiled in horror at the bombing campaign.* ◇ If you say someone is **in** for a shock or a surprise, you mean they are going to experience it. You can also say someone is **in** for some other kind of unwelcome experience. *The President is in for a rough ride.*
❑ If you are **in on** something, you are involved in it. *He was in on the crucial planning stages of the restaurant.*
❑ If something is **in**, it is fashionable.
❑ If you discuss the **ins and outs** of something, you discuss all its detailed points.

in. is short for 'inches'.

in- is added to some words to form a word with the opposite meaning. For example, 'incorrect' means 'not correct'.

in absentia If something concerning a person is done **in absentia**, it is done when they are not there. *He was sentenced to death in absentia.*

in as much (*or* inasmuch) **In as much as** means 'seeing that' or 'because'. *The dissidents will not be charged with any crime in as much as they left the embassy under their own free will.*

in-depth An **in-depth** investigation or report is very thorough and detailed.

in extremis is used to talk about someone being in a very difficult situation in which they have to use extreme methods to solve their problems. *In France, house surveyors are used only in extremis, and at great expense.*

in-fighting (*or* infighting) is rivalry or quarrelling between members of the same organization.

in flagrante delicto (*pron:* in fla-**grant**-eh de-**lict**-toh) If a couple are caught **in flagrante delicto**, they are caught having sex.

in-flight is used to describe things which are used or provided on a plane when it is in the air. *...in-flight entertainment.*

in-house is used to talk about things being done within a company or organization, rather than being subcontracted to someone else. *...in-house caterers... Training is normally provided in-house.*

in-laws Your **in-laws** are your husband's or wife's close relatives, especially their parents.

in loco parentis If you are **in loco parentis** you are, for a time, acting as a parent towards someone else's child. Teachers are often regarded as being in loco parentis.

in-patient An **in-patient** is someone who stays in hospital while they receive treatment.

in situ If something stays **in situ**, it stays where it is. *The owners are willing to give the house free to the nation, provided somebody pays for the contents to be left in situ.*

in-tray An **in-tray** is a tray or shallow basket used in an office to put letters and documents in when they arrive, or when they are waiting to be dealt with.

in vitro See IVF.

inability If someone is unable to do something, you talk about their **inability** to do it.

inaccessible (inaccessibility) An **inaccessible** place is impossible or very difficult to reach. *Poor roads and inaccessibility make food distribution very difficult.* ◇ If something like music or art is **inaccessible**, it is hard for people to understand or appreciate.

inaccurate (inaccurately; inaccuracy, inaccuracies) If something is **inaccurate**, it is not correct. *The distance travelled was inaccurately registered.* When something is not correct, you talk about its **inaccuracy**; its incorrect parts can be called **inaccuracies**. *Critics of the report say it is riddled with inaccuracies.*

inaction If you accuse someone of **inaction**, you mean they are failing to do something they should be doing.

inactivate (inactivating, inactivated) If something like a virus is **inactivated**, it is made harmless.

inactive If something is **inactive**, it is not operating. *They expect the province to come to a standstill, with most shops and public transport inactive.*

inadequate (inadequately, inadequacy, inadequacies) ❑ If something is **inadequate**, there is not enough of it, or it is not good enough. You talk about the **inadequacy** of something like this. *...inadequately supervised junior doctors... They denied any inadequacy of safety standards.* **Inadequacies** are aspects of something which are wrong or not good enough. *...the inadequacies of security measures.*
   ❑ If you say a person is **inadequate** or talk about their **inadequacy,** you mean they do not have the qualities necessary to do something or to cope with life.

inadmissible If something is **inadmissible**, it is not allowed. *The use of force would be inadmissible.* ◇ In a court case, **inadmissible** evidence is evidence which cannot be used.

inadvertent (inadvertently) **Inadvertent** is used to describe something you do without intending to. *...competitors who have inadvertently taken medicines containing substances on the banned list.*

inadvisable If you say it would be **inadvisable** to do something, you mean it would not be a good idea.

inalienable An **inalienable** right is one which cannot be taken away from you.

inane (inanely; inanity, inanities) An **inane** remark or action is a particularly silly one. *All the delegates seemed to be gibbering inanely about tax cuts and anti-abortion laws.* An **inanity** (*pron:* in-an-it-ee) is a remark or action like this.

inanimate can be used to describe anything which is not a living thing.

inanity See inane.

inapplicable If something is **inapplicable** to the thing you are considering, it does not apply to it.

inappropriate (inappropriately, inappropriateness) If something is **inappropriate**, it is not the right thing to do, say, or use. *The West has so far responded inappropriately to the crisis... He spoke about the 'inappropriateness' of the block vote.*

inarticulate If you are **inarticulate**, you cannot express yourself easily.

inasmuch See in as much.

inattentive (inattention) If you are **inattentive**, you are not paying attention to what is being said or done. **Inattention** is lack of attention.

inaudible If a sound is **inaudible**, it is not loud enough to be heard.

inaugural An **inaugural** meeting is the first meeting of a new organization. An **inaugural** speech is a speech given on an occasion like this, or the first speech given by a new leader.

inaugurate (inaugurating, inaugurated; inauguration) When a new leader is **inaugurated**, he or she officially takes up their new position at a special ceremony. *...the presidential inauguration.* Similarly, when a new organization is **inaugurated**, it is officially opened and begins to operate. ◇ If something like a system is **inaugurated**, it is introduced and put into action.

inauspicious (inauspiciously) You say something has an **inauspicious** beginning when something goes wrong and this suggests things are not going to turn out well. *The special summit began inauspiciously, with five leaders absent for various reasons.*

inborn qualities are ones you are born with.

inbred (inbreeding) ❑ **Inbred** ways of behaving come naturally to you, because you have inherited them from your parents.
   ❑ **Inbreeding** is the repeated breeding of closely related people or animals. People or animals born as a result of inbreeding are described as **inbred;** they are more liable to hereditary defects or weaknesses.

inbuilt ❑ An **inbuilt** attitude is well-established and not likely to change. ◇ If a group has an **inbuilt** advantage, they are always likely to be in a better position than other groups. *This would give the coalition an inbuilt majority.*
   ❑ **Inbuilt** is also used to describe things which are included as part of a device or machine, rather than obtained separately. *...the only answering machine with inbuilt fax and printer.*

Inc. See incorporate.

incalculable You say something is **incalculable** when it is too great to be counted or estimated. *...a place where Americans spend incalculable millions of dollars... This fly is capable of inflicting incalculable damage.*

incandescent things give out a lot of light when heated. ◇ If someone is **incandescent** with fury or rage, they are extremely angry.

incantation An **incantation** is a magic spell which is chanted or sung.

incapable If someone is **incapable** of doing something, they are unable to do it. *A surprising number of executives are incapable of writing a CV.* ◇ An **incapable** person is unable to do anything satisfactorily.

incapacitate (incapacitating, incapacitated) If an illness or injury **incapacitates** you, it prevents you from doing certain things.

incapacity Someone's **incapacity** to do something is their inability to do it. ◇ If someone suffers from **mental incapacity**, they are mentally handicapped in some way.

incarcerate (incarcerating, incarcerated; incarceration) If someone is **incarcerated,** they are put in prison. *Journalists are facing incarceration, torture and even execution.*

incarnate (incarnating, incarnated) You say a character from fiction or legend is **incarnated** when you are able to see them as a human being, for example because an actor plays them in a film. ◇ If you say someone is a thing **incarnate,** you mean they represent that thing in human form. *The Rolling Stones were thought to be devils incarnate.*

incarnation An **incarnation** is one of the lives a person has, according to some religions. ◇ When someone or something has appeared in several different forms or roles, you can refer to each of them as an **incarnation.** *...Michael Heseltine, in his first incarnation as Environment Secretary.*

incautious (incautiously) An **incautious** action is done without considering the possible consequences. *...the deadlines they had incautiously promised would be met.*

incendiary weapons and devices are used to set fire to something. An attack using incendiary weapons is called an **incendiary** attack.

incense (incensing, incensed) ❏ **Incense** (*pron:* in-sense) is a substance burned for its sweet smell, often during religious ceremonies.
  ❏ If you are **incensed** (*pron:* in-**senst**) by something, it makes you extremely angry. *...an approach which will incense environmentalists.*

incentive An **incentive** is something which encourages you to do something.

inception The **inception** of an organization or activity is its start. *A review of the plan has just appeared, one year on from its inception.*

incessant (incessantly) **Incessant** is used to describe things which go on without stopping. *...incessant rain... She talks incessantly.*

incest (incestuous) ❏ If someone commits **incest,** they have sex with someone they are closely related to, such as their sister or daughter. **Incestuous** is used to talk about things to do with incest. *...incestuous feelings.*
  ❏ An **incestuous** group of people is a small group who do everything together and tend not to bother with anyone outside their group.

inch (inches, inching, inched) ❏ Length is often expressed in **inches.** An inch is about 2.54 centimetres. There are 12 inches in a foot. 'Inches' can be written 'in.' or 'ins.'
  ❏ If you **inch** somewhere, you get there a bit at a time. *...commuters inching along a motorway during the rush-hour... They are slowly inching towards agreement.*

inchoate (*pron:* in-koe-ate) ideas or attitudes are newly formed and not yet properly developed or organized. *...inchoate Russian nationalism.*

incidence An **incidence** of something, especially something unpleasant, is a case of it, or an occasion when it happens. *...incidences of leukaemia.* The **incidence** of something is how often it happens. *Safety experts are per-* plexed by the rising incidence of car fires.

incident An **incident** is something which happens, especially something undesirable. *...a shooting incident.* If something takes place **without incident,** it takes place without anything troublesome happening.

incident room An **incident room** is a room set up in a police station or near the scene of a serious crime, from which the police carry out their investigation into the crime.

incidental is used to describe things which happen in connection with something more important. *Sporadic incidental violence continued in different parts of the country.*
  ❏ **Incidental music** is background music for a play or film.

incidentally You say **incidentally** when you are adding an extra piece of information. *Attendance at mosques has dropped sharply (so, incidentally, has worship in churches).*

incinerate (incinerating, incinerated; incineration, incinerator) If you **incinerate** something, you get rid of it by burning it. *...the incineration of chemical weapons.* An **incinerator** is a furnace for burning things, especially rubbish.

incipient is used to talk about things which are just starting to happen or appear. *...incipient middle age.*

incise (incising, incised; incision) If something is **incised** into a surface, it is cut into it. If you make an **incision** in something, you make a cut in it.

incisive speech or writing is clear and forceful.

incisor Your **incisors** are the teeth at the front of your mouth. They have a sharp edge for biting into food.

incite (inciting, incited; incitement) If you **incite** someone to do something wrong, you encourage them to do it by getting them angry or excited. *...incitement to murder.* You can also **incite** strong feelings. *...a new law banning incitement to religious hatred.*

inclement weather is unpleasantly cold or stormy.

incline (inclining, inclined; inclination) ❏ If someone is **inclined** to behave in a certain way, they tend to behave like that. You can also say someone has an **inclination** to behave in a certain way. *He is inclined to drink too much... Japan's traditional inclination to take a back seat in international diplomacy.*
  ❏ If you feel **inclined** to do something, you feel an urge to do it, and probably will do it. *They may feel inclined to start work late... She was inclined to accept the lawyer's advice.* You can also say you **incline** to do something, or have an **inclination** to do it. *He had neither the time nor the inclination to think of other things.*
  ❏ **Inclined** is used after words ending in '-ly' to describe someone's character, opinions, or natural abilities. *...a venue for the romantically inclined... His grandfather had been artistically inclined.*
  ❏ If a line is **inclined** at a certain angle, it is sloping at that angle. ◇ If you **incline** your head, you move it downwards and forwards. ◇ An **incline** (*pron:* in-kline) is a slope.

include (including, included; inclusion) ❏ If something **includes** something else, it has it as one of its parts. If you **include** one thing in another, you make it part of it. *The demonstrators want their demands included in the country's new constitution... He was almost certain of inclusion in the England squad.*
  ❏ When you mention a group of things or people, you

can use **including** to say who some of them are. *Reports say about 100 people were injured, including 45 policemen.* **Included** is used in a similar way. *Many African countries, Nigeria included, broke off diplomatic ties in protest.*

inclusive is used to say everything is included in the price you pay for something, and no extra payments are necessary. *...a fully inclusive holiday.* ◇ You also use **inclusive** when you are talking about a range of things, to show it includes the first and last one you mention. *...August 17-20 inclusive.*

incognito (*pron:* in-kog-nee-toe) If someone famous is travelling **incognito**, they are travelling in disguise or using another name, so they will not be recognized.

incoherent (*pron:* in-koe-**heer**-rent) (incoherently, incoherence) If something is **incoherent**, it is unclear and difficult to understand. *...the incoherence of government policies.* ◇ If someone is **incoherent**, they are talking in an unclear way. *He was mumbling incoherently.*

income A person's **income** is the money they earn or receive regularly. You can also talk about the **income** of an organization or a country. *Half the national income comes from agriculture.*

income support is a state benefit paid to people with a very low income or no income.

income tax is a tax paid regularly to the government. It consists of a certain percentage of your income.

incoming is used to talk about things coming into a place. *...an incoming flight... ...incoming calls... ...the incoming tide.* ◇ An **incoming** government or official has just been elected or appointed.

incommunicado If you are being held **incommunicado**, you are not allowed to talk to anyone from outside the place where you are.

incomparable (incomparably) If you say something is **incomparable**, you mean it is so good nothing else can be compared with it. *...an area of incomparable beauty.* ◇ **Incomparably** is used to say something has much more of a quality than anything else. *South Africa seems incomparably richer than the rest of Africa.*

incompatible (incompatibility) If two things are **incompatible**, they cannot exist or be used together, because of the differences between them. *...problems of incompatibility between the two railway systems.* ◇ If a couple are **incompatible**, they cannot have a satisfactory relationship, because of differences in their character or outlook.

incompetent (incompetently, incompetence) You say someone is **incompetent** when they keep doing things badly. *The secret service had behaved almost as incompetently as the men they were after... ...bureaucratic incompetence.* Someone who is incompetent can be called an **incompetent**.

incomplete If something is **incomplete**, it does not have all the parts it should have, or it is not finished. *...an incomplete account of what happened.*

incomprehensible (incomprehension) If something is **incomprehensible**, it is impossible to understand. **Incomprehension** is being unable to understand something. *...the child's incomprehension of what happened to his father.*

inconceivable If you say something is **inconceivable**, you mean you cannot believe it could possibly happen or be true.

inconclusive (inconclusively) If something like a discussion is **inconclusive**, it fails to settle something. *...an inconclu-*

sive first round ballot... The war shows every sign of dragging on inconclusively. ◇ If evidence or an experiment is **inconclusive**, it fails to prove anything.

incongruous (incongruously; incongruity, incongruities) If something is **incongruous**, it seems strange because it does not fit in with the things around it, or with things happening at the same time. You talk about the **incongruity** of something like this. Incongruous things can be called **incongruities**. *...a marble and stained-glass building which towers incongruously over the mud huts.*

inconsequential If something is **inconsequential**, it is not very important.

inconsiderable A not **inconsiderable** amount of something is a rather large amount.

inconsiderate people do not care how their behaviour affects other people.

inconsistent (inconsistency, inconsistencies) ❑ If someone is **inconsistent**, they behave differently in similar situations at different times. Behaviour like this is called **inconsistency**. You can also call people's work or methods **inconsistent**.
   ❑ If two or more statements are **inconsistent** or there is an **inconsistency** between them, they contradict each other. ◇ If something is **inconsistent** with a set of ideas, values, or requirements, it is not in accordance with them.

inconsolable If you are **inconsolable**, you are very sad about something, and cannot be comforted.

inconspicuous (inconspicuously) If something is **inconspicuous**, it does not stand out, or is not noticeable at all. *The owl perched inconspicuously on one of the lower branches.*

incontestable (incontestably) If something is **incontestable**, it is obviously true and cannot be denied. *McGuire, who seemed a likely suspect, had been, incontestably, at a prayer meeting.*

incontinent (incontinence) If someone is **incontinent**, they have no control over their bladder or their bowels, or both. This condition is called **incontinence**.

incontrovertible (incontrovertibly) **Incontrovertible** evidence or proof shows something is definitely true. *He was the first person to show incontrovertibly that people can be allergic to foods.*

inconvenient (inconveniently; inconvenience, inconveniencing, inconvenienced) If something is **inconvenient** or causes **inconvenience**, it causes problems or difficulties. You can also say something **inconveniences** someone or is an **inconvenience**. *...an elegant hotel, but rather inconveniently situated.* ◇ You also say something is **inconvenient** when it causes someone embarrassment. *Some inconvenient results have emerged... There are, obviously, some inconvenient questions lurking here.*

incorporate (incorporating, incorporated; incorporation) ❑ If something **incorporates** certain things, they are included in it. *A bill incorporating most of the recommendations is already progressing through Congress.* ◇ If something is **incorporated** into something else, it becomes a part of it. *...the incorporation of women into the priesthood.*
   ❑ In the US, **Incorporated** after the name of a company means it has been legally formed into a corporation. '**Incorporated**' is often shortened to 'Inc.' *...Harley-Davidson Inc.*

incorrect (incorrectly) If a statement is **incorrect**, it is not true. If something like a name is **incorrect**, it is wrong. *A picture with the report was incorrectly captioned.*

incorrigible (incorrigibly) If you say someone is **incorrigible**, you mean they have faults which will never change. *He was an incorrigible noser into other people's business... The colonists are incorrigibly racist.*

incorruptible (incorruptibility) If someone is **incorruptible**, they cannot be bribed or persuaded to do things they should not do. *His incorruptibility makes him a possible winner.*

increase (increasing, increased) If something **increases** or you **increase** it, it gets bigger. If something is getting bigger, you can say it is **on the increase**. If it has got bigger, you say there has been an **increase** in it.

increasingly If something is becoming **increasingly** difficult, it is becoming more and more difficult. **Increasingly** can be used with many other words like this. *Investors have become increasingly jittery... Economists are increasingly concerned at the rising public borrowing requirement.* ◇ **Increasingly** is also used to say something is happening more and more often. *Agriculture in Japan is increasingly becoming a part-time profession for elderly people.*

incredible (incredibly) ❑ If something is **incredible**, it is hard to believe. *Because of a fault in the telescope's mirror (which incredibly had not been tested before take-off), the images beamed to earth are fuzzy.*
    ❑ **Incredible** is also used to say how big something is, or what a lot of it there is. *There was an incredible bang... The electoral system is incredibly complicated.* ◇ People also use **incredible** to express great delight or admiration at something. *The view was incredible.*

incredulous (incredulously, incredulity) If you are **incredulous**, you have difficulty believing what you have just heard and seen, because it is very surprising or shocking. You can also say you react to something with **incredulity**. *I stared at him incredulously... His stubborn loyalty was greeted with incredulity.*

increment (incremental, incrementally) An **increment** in something is an increase, especially one in a series of increases. **Incremental** and **incrementally** are used to talk about things which increase like this. *...the ability of Japanese engineers to improve incrementally on other people's ideas.* ◇ An **increment** is also an automatic regular rise in someone's salary.

incriminate (incriminating, incriminated) If something **incriminates** someone, it suggests they are the person responsible for a crime. *...incriminating evidence.*

incubate (incubating, incubated; incubation) When eggs **incubate** or are **incubated**, they are kept warm until they are ready to hatch. ◇ The **incubation** period for a disease is the period from the time when the infection enters your body to the time when symptoms first appear.

incubator An **incubator** is a device in which premature babies are kept until they are strong enough to survive in normal conditions.

incubus (*pron:* in-cube-uss) (*plural:* incubuses or incubi) An **incubus** is something which brings you problems and which you would like to get rid of. *The pound still has some way to fall to a competitive level – we cannot put all our resources back to work until we shed that incubus.*

inculcate (inculcating, inculcated) If you **inculcate** an idea in someone, you teach it to them so it becomes fixed in

their minds.

incumbent (incumbency, incumbencies) The person who holds a post at a particular time can be called the **incumbent**. You call the period when they hold the post their **incumbency**. ◇ If it is **incumbent** on you to do something, it is your duty to do it.

incur (incurring, incurred) If you **incur** something undesirable, it happens to you because of what you do. *This decision is likely to risk incurring the wrath of animal rights activists... The package includes writing off debts incurred by state companies.*

incurable (incurably) ❑ An **incurable** disease cannot be cured. *Some of the children are incurably ill.*
    ❑ **Incurable** is also used to describe people or animals with fixed attitudes or habits. *He was an incurable romantic... Calves are incurably curious.*

incursion An **incursion** is a sudden invasion, attack, or raid.

indebted (indebtedness) ❑ **Indebted** is used to describe people who owe money. *...heavily indebted countries... It is in the south-east that costs are highest and indebtedness is greatest.*
    ❑ If you say you are **indebted** to someone, you mean you are grateful to them for something they have given you or done for you.

indecent (indecently, indecency) ❑ **Indecent** is used to describe things involving sex or nakedness which people find shocking. **Indecency** is sexually offensive behaviour. *He denied touching the women indecently... Police in Toronto want to arrest her for public indecency.* ◇ **Indecent assault** is a sexual attack which does not include rape. *He denied indecently assaulting four young women.* ◇ If someone is charged with **indecent exposure**, they are charged with exposing their genitals in public.
    ❑ **Indecent** is also used to describe things which break rules of good behaviour or morality. *...the indecent haste of the leadership election.*

indecipherable If writing is **indecipherable**, you cannot read it.

indecisive (indecision, indecisiveness) If you are **indecisive**, you cannot decide what to do. Uncertainty about what to do is called **indecision** or **indecisiveness**. ◇ If a vote is **indecisive**, there is no definite result one way or the other.

indeed You use **indeed** when you are confirming that something is true. *He admitted that there is indeed a 'territorial dispute' between the two countries.* ◇ You also use **indeed** when you are adding information which strengthens the point you are making. *Most households feel, and indeed are, less wealthy than they were... In private schools corporal punishment is still legal – indeed, some of the most prestigious schools in Britain have a long tradition of flogging and caning.* ◇ You use **indeed** with 'very' for extra emphasis. *...a very big iceberg indeed.* ◇ You use **indeed** after other words to emphasize them. *The country's prospects for resolving its oil problems look grim indeed.*

indefatigable (indefatigably) If someone is **indefatigable**, they keep on with something and never get tired. *He worked indefatigably to interest the young in music.*

indefensible If a wrong action is **indefensible**, it cannot be justified.

indefinable An **indefinable** quality or feeling is impossible to describe. *...that indefinable magical appeal of Paris at the beginning of the century.*

indefinite (indefinitely) If something is **indefinite** or will go on for an **indefinite** time, no decision has been taken about when it will end. *The trial was adjourned for an indefinite period... ...an indefinite general strike... Industrial action began this week when staff walked out indefinitely.*

indefinite article The **indefinite article** is 'a' or 'an'.

indelible (indelibly) **Indelible** dye or ink cannot be removed or washed out. *The names are indelibly recorded on my Visa statement.* ◇ **Indelible** is also used to say the bad effects of something are permanent. *The experience left an indelible mark on him... Passing retrospective legislation would impose an indelible blot on British law and justice.*

indelicate behaviour is rude or offensive.

indemnify (indemnifies, indemnifying, indemnified) If you are **indemnified** for some loss or damage, you receive compensation for it.

indemnity (indemnities) If something provides **indemnity**, it provides insurance or protection against damage or loss, especially in the form of financial compensation. An **indemnity** is an amount of money or goods received by someone as compensation for loss or damage.

indent ❏ In a piece of writing, if you **indent** a line, you set it back further from the margin than other lines, for example at the beginning of a paragraph.
❏ If you **indent** for goods, you order them by filling in a special form.

indentation An **indentation** is a dent in the surface or edge of something.

independent (independently, independence) ❏ **Independent** is used to describe things you do on your own, rather than jointly with other people. *France was pursuing an independent foreign policy... The Regional Crime Squad had acted independently of the local force.*
❏ If someone is **independent**, they look after their own affairs, without help from anyone else. You talk about the **independence** of someone like this. ◇ An **independent** company is not controlled by a larger one. ◇ An **independent** hospital, school, broadcasting company, or other organization does not receive money from the government or a local authority, and is not controlled by them.
❏ If a country or state becomes **independent** or gains its **independence**, it gets its own government and is no longer ruled by another country.
❏ An **independent** inquiry is held by people who are not involved in a situation and so are able to make a fair judgement. Similarly, you can say someone gives an **independent** opinion about something. *...independent legal advice... The figures have not been independently confirmed.*
❏ If someone stands in an election as an **Independent**, they do not represent any political party.

indescribable (indescribably) If you say something is **indescribable**, you mean it is so bad or unpleasant no words can properly describe it. *...indescribably filthy conditions.*

indestructible If something is **indestructible**, it cannot be destroyed.

indeterminate An **indeterminate** period of time has not been fixed. *...prisoners serving indeterminate sentences.* ◇ **Indeterminate** is also used to describe things which cannot be decided or worked out. For example, if you say someone is of **indeterminate** age, you mean it is im-

possible to tell how old they are.

index (indexes, indexing, indexed; indices) ❏ An **index** is an alphabetical list at the back of a book saying where you can find things in the book.
❏ An **index card** is a small card on which you write information for future reference. See also **card index**.
❏ If something is used as an **index** of something else, it is used as a way of measuring it. (For this and the following meanings, the usual plural of 'index' is 'indices', pron: in-disseez.) ◇ An **index** is also a system by which changes in the value of something can be compared or measured. *...the cost of living index... Rumours of war sent stock market indices into decline.* ◇ If something is **indexed** to something else, things are arranged so that when the second thing increases or decreases, the first one does too. *...a price indexed to inflation.*
❏ In maths, **indices** are the little numbers showing how many times a number is to be multiplied by itself. For example, in the equation $3^2 = 9$, 2 is an index.

index finger Your **index finger** is the one next to your thumb.

index-linked (index-linking) **Index-linked** wages, pensions, and interest rates are linked to an index measuring inflation or the cost of living. This system is called **index-linking**.

indexation is the same as index-linking.

Indian is used to talk about people and things in or from India. *...the Indian Civil Service.* An **Indian** is someone who comes from India.
❏ An **Indian** is also someone descended from the earliest inhabitants of North, South, and Central America. **Indian** is used to talk about things connected with these people. *...Indian reservations.*

Indian summer An **Indian summer** is a period of warm weather during the autumn. ◇ If someone has an **Indian summer,** they have a period of success towards the end of their life or career.

indicate (indicating, indicated) ❏ If something **indicates** that a certain thing is the case, it shows it. *Research indicates that dolphins live just as long in captivity as they do in the wild.* ◇ If you **indicate** something, you mention it in an indirect way. *Some American airlines have already indicated they are interested in flying to Vietnam.*
❏ If you **indicate** something to someone, you show them where it is, usually by pointing to it.
❏ If a device or instrument **indicates** something, it gives information or a reading.
❏ If you **indicate** when you are driving, you show which way you are going to turn.

indication An **indication** is a sign giving an idea of what someone feels, what is happening, or what might happen. *There is no clear indication of when those arrested will be brought to trial.*

indicative (pron: in-dik-a-tiv) If something is **indicative** of something else, it is a sign of it.

indicator ❏ An **indicator** is something which acts as a sign, telling you how people feel, or what the situation is. *New car sales are taken to be one of the best indicators to the economic health of the nation.*
❏ A car's **indicators** are the lights which show whether it is turning left or right. ◇ An **indicator** is also an instrument or device giving a measurement or warning, for

example telling you if a vehicle's fuel is low.

indices See **index**.

indict (*pron: in-dite*) (indictment, indictable) ❏ If someone is **indicted** for a crime, they are officially charged with it. An **indictment** is a criminal charge. An **indictable** offence is one you can be charged with.

❏ An **indictment** of someone is a strong verbal attack on them for their behaviour or policies. ◇ When something goes badly wrong, you can say it is an **indictment** of the person responsible, or of their methods.

indie music is music produced by a small independent record company, especially guitar-based rock music.

indifferent (indifferently, indifference) You say people are **indifferent** to something when they show no interest in it. **Indifference** is lack of interest. *Most French people greeted the new law with indifference.* ◇ If you say something is **indifferent**, you mean it is of a rather low standard. *...indifferent cooking... Fauré's Pavane had been indifferently sung.*

indigence See **indigent**.

indigenous (*pron: in-dij-in-uss*) The **indigenous** inhabitants of a country are the ones who have been there from earliest times, rather than people who arrived later. ◇ If a type of plant or animal is **indigenous** to a place, it grows or lives there naturally, rather than being introduced from outside.

indigent (*pron: in-dij-ent*) (indigence) If someone is **indigent**, they are very poor. **Indigence** is poverty.

indigestible food is difficult to digest. ◇ **Indigestible** facts or ideas are difficult to understand because they are very complicated.

indigestion is pain caused by difficulty in digesting food.

indignant (indignantly, indignation) If you are **indignant**, you are shocked and angry at the way someone has behaved. You call this feeling **indignation**. *The offer was indignantly rejected.*

indignity (indignities) If you suffer an **indignity**, you are made to feel embarrassed or humiliated.

indigo is a dark violet-blue colour.

indirect (indirectly) If something has **indirect** effects, it has effects which themselves produce more effects. *Alcohol consumption has serious indirect consequences, causing children to be malnourished and productivity to fall.* ◇ If people have **indirect** contact, they deal with each other through someone else. *He was allegedly paid indirectly by the Mafia.* ◇ If you say something in an **indirect** way, you do not mention it directly, but say other things which make your meaning clear. *...an indirect threat of force... Mr Delors indirectly challenged Britain to come clean on its attitude to Europe.* ◇ An **indirect** route or journey does not use the shortest way between two places.

indirect speech is the same as reported speech.

indirect tax (indirect taxation) **Indirect taxes** are taxes on goods and services which are added to their price. VAT and import duty are indirect taxes. **Indirect taxation** is the raising of money through indirect taxes.

indiscipline (indisciplined) **Indiscipline** is a lack of discipline. *There are growing reports of indiscipline among the troops.* If people are **indisciplined**, they behave badly, because they are not used to obeying rules.

indiscreet (indiscretion) If you are **indiscreet**, you do things openly, or talk about things openly, which you

ought to keep secret. Behaviour like this is called **indiscretion**. **Indiscretions** are indiscreet acts.

indiscriminate (indiscriminately) You say an action is **indiscriminate** when it does not involve any kind of selection, and can affect anyone or anything. *...indiscriminate arrests... Environmentalists have opposed this practice, which kills marine life indiscriminately.*

indispensable If something is **indispensable**, you cannot do without it.

indisposed If someone is **indisposed**, they are ill, and therefore not available to do something.

indisputable (indisputably) If you say something is **indisputable**, you mean there is no question that it is true. *...Anna Pavlova, indisputably the greatest dancer of her time.*

indissoluble (indissolubly) An **indissoluble** connection or relationship is so strong it can never be broken. *His life and work are indissolubly bound up with the Unity Movement.*

indistinct If something is **indistinct**, it is difficult to see, hear, or recognize, because it is very faint or unclear.

indistinguishable If two or more things are **indistinguishable**, they are so similar it is impossible to tell them apart.

individual (individually) ❏ **Individual** is used to talk about things which involve one person or thing, rather than a group. *The President said he would see the opposition leaders only on an individual basis... Implementing measures will be taken by member states individually.* ◇ **Individual** is also used to say something applies to each member of a group separately. *The terms of each deal vary with individual governments' performance... Sponsors have backed each individual yacht... ...individually wrapped candies.*

❏ When people talk about **the individual**, they mean every human being, considered as something special and different from every other human being. *In China the state always takes precedence over the individual.*

❏ **Individual** is also used to say something has a special character which makes it different from other things of the same type. *...strongly individual buildings.*

individualise See **individualize**.

individualist (individualistic, individualism) ❏ An **individualist** is someone who likes to do things their own way. You talk about the **individualism** of someone like this, or say they are **individualistic**.

❏ **Individualism** is also the belief that it is in everyone's best interest that people should be given as much freedom as possible and be allowed to use their own initiative without interference from the state.

❏ **Individualist** and **individualistic** are also used to say something has a special character which makes it different from other things of the same type. *...individualist design.*

individuality A person's or thing's **individuality** is all the things about them which make them different from other people or things.

individualize (individualizing, individualized) (*can be spelled with an 's' instead of a 'z'*) If you **individualize** something, you make it recognizably different from other things of the same kind.

indivisible If something is **indivisible**, it cannot be split up into separate parts. ◇ If something is **indivisible** from something else, the two things cannot be regarded as separate. *Her image was indivisible from her physical* *appearance: frail, pale and interesting.*

Indo- is joined to another word to talk about something which involves India and another country. *...the Indo-Pakistan border... ...Indo-Nepalese relations.*

indoctrinate (indoctrinating, indoctrinated; indoctrination) When people are **indoctrinated** with a belief, they are made to accept it without questioning it. This process is called **indoctrination.**

indolent (indolence) If someone is **indolent,** they are lazy. **Indolence** is laziness.

indomitable (indomitably) If you say someone is **indomitable,** you mean they carry on trying to achieve something, and never give up. ◇ **Indomitable** is also used to describe qualities in someone or something which never change or disappear. *...his indomitable courage... Much of Star Trek's attraction came from its indomitably optimistic view of the future.*

indoor (indoors) **Indoor** is used to describe things inside a building. *...an indoor swimming pool.* ◇ If something happens **indoors,** it happens inside a building.

indubitable (indubitably) **Indubitable** is used to say there is no doubt that something exists or is true. *His generosity is indubitable... These 20 tracks are indubitably the best of Ewan MacColl.*

induce (inducing, induced; inducement) ❑ If something **induces** a situation, it brings it on. *...an economic crisis induced by high oil prices.* ◇ If doctors **induce** labour or birth, they give a pregnant woman drugs to make the birth begin.

❑ If you are **induced** to do something, you are persuaded to do it. An **inducement** is something like a gift or bribe, which is offered to someone to persuade them to do something.

induct (induction) ❑ When someone is **inducted,** they are officially placed in an important job, rank, or position. ◇ You also say someone is **inducted** when they are given training at the beginning of a new job. *Only a fifth of trustees receive proper induction to charity work.*

❑ **Induction** is the process by which electricity or magnetism is passed between two objects or circuits without them touching each other.

induction coil An **induction coil** is a transformer used to produce a high voltage from a low voltage.

indulge (indulging, indulged; indulgence, indulgent, indulgently) ❑ If you **indulge** in something you enjoy doing, you do it. The thing you do can be called an **indulgence;** you can also talk about your **indulgence** in it. *...indulgence in alcohol.* You can also say someone **indulges** something like a craving. *He still indulges one of his great passions, motor-mechanics.* See also **self-indulgent.**

❑ If you **indulge** someone else, you treat them with special kindness and let them have or do whatever they want, even if it is not good for them. An **indulgent** person behaves like this to other people. *...indulgent parents.* ◇ If you are **indulgent,** you are kind to people and do not criticize their weaknesses. *He smiled indulgently... The staff treated him with amused indulgence.*

industrial (industrially) ❑ **Industrial** is used to talk about things to do with industry. *...industrial jobs... ...industrial espionage.* ◇ An **industrial** city, country, or area is one where industry is important or highly developed. *...one of the most industrially developed parts of the republic.* ◇ An

industrial estate is an area, often on the edge of a town, specially designed for industry and business.

❑ **Industrial relations** are the relations between employers and workers. ◇ If workers take **industrial action,** they go on strike or take some other action, to protest about pay or working conditions.

industrial revolution The **Industrial Revolution** was the period from about 1750 to 1850 when Britain became an industrial nation. Any similar period in a country's history can be called an **industrial revolution.**

industrialise See **industrialize.**

industrialist An **industrialist** is a person who owns or controls large amounts of money or property in industry.

industrialize (industrializing, industrialized; industrialization) *(can be spelled with an 's' instead of a 'z')* When a country **industrializes** or is **industrialized,** industry is introduced there on a large scale. *He called for rapid industrialization.*

industrious If you are **industrious,** you work very hard.

industry (industries) ❑ **Industry** is the work and processes involved in making things in factories. ◇ An **industry** consists of all the people and processes involved in manufacturing or producing a particular type of product. *...the computer industry.*

❑ **Industry** is also working very hard. *He was well known locally for his industry in raising funds for charity.*

inebriated *(pron: in-nee-bree-ate-ed)* If someone is **inebriated,** they are drunk.

inedible (inedibility) If something is **inedible,** it is poisonous, or it is too unpleasant to eat. *...the inedibility of the pastry.*

ineffable (ineffably) **Ineffable** and **ineffably** are used to say something has more of a quality than can be expressed in words. For example, you can say something is **ineffably** sad or talk about its **ineffable** sadness.

ineffective (ineffectively, ineffectiveness) If something you do is **ineffective,** it does not produce the effect you want. *Lenin tried ineffectively to persuade his fellow-leaders to drop Stalin as secretary-general... ...the ineffectiveness of the sanctions against Serbia.*

ineffectual (ineffectually) If something you do is **ineffectual,** it does not produce the results you want. *They were nabbed outside his house, ineffectually trying to spy on it.* ◇ An **ineffectual** person does not get satisfactory results, or fails to get things done.

inefficient (inefficiency, inefficiencies) If a person or organization is **inefficient,** they are badly organized and do not use their resources, equipment, or time in the best way. You can also say their methods are **inefficient.** You talk about the **inefficiency** of someone or their methods. The inefficient parts of something can be called **inefficiencies.** *...inefficiencies in the education system.* ◇ If a machine or piece of equipment is **inefficient,** it does not work properly and is wasteful.

inelastic If you say something like the demand for a product is **inelastic,** you mean it never varies.

inelegant (inelegance) If you say something is **inelegant** or talk about its **inelegance,** you mean it is not attractive or graceful.

ineligible (ineligibility) If you are **ineligible** for something, you are not qualified for it or not entitled to have it. *Homeless people were ineligible for any extra help... ...his* *ineligibility for an American visa.*

ineluctable If something is **ineluctable**, there is no escape from it.

inept (ineptly, ineptitude) You say someone is **inept** when they do something in a clumsy and unskilful way. You talk about the **ineptitude** of someone like this. *...the government's inept handling of the communal violence... The coup was ineptly organised... Financial and managerial ineptitude is threatening many law firms.*

inequality (inequalities) If there is **inequality** somewhere, there are differences in wealth and opportunity between different social or racial groups. An **inequality** is a difference like this. *The survey shows that regional inequalities of income in the UK are greater than in France or Spain.*

inequitable (inequity, inequities) If something is **inequitable**, it is unfair or unjust. You talk about the **inequity** of something like this. **Inequities** are things which are unfair or unjust. *...the fundamental inequity of Britain's electoral system... ...glaring inequities between the black and white communities.*

ineradicable If something is **ineradicable**, it cannot be removed or destroyed.

inert If someone or something is **inert**, they are not moving. ◇ **Inert** is also used to describe substances, especially gases, which do not react chemically with other substances.

inertia (*pron:* in-ner-sha) ❑ If you have a feeling of **inertia**, you feel very lazy and unwilling to do anything. ◇ **Inertia** is also used to talk about an organization's lack of energy or initiative in dealing with a problem. *Congressional inertia will ensure that change will be slow.* ❑ In physics, **inertia** is the tendency of an object to remain still, or to continue moving if it is already moving, unless a force is applied to it.

inertia reel An **inertia reel** seat belt is designed to unwind freely from a metal drum at all times except when your body is thrown forward; when this happens, the drum locks.

inertia selling is sending goods to people who have not ordered them, then sending a bill if the goods are not returned.

inescapable (inescapably) If something is **inescapable**, it cannot be avoided. *Mass tourism is an inescapable fact of modern life... Britain's future is inescapably in Europe.*

inessential If something is **inessential**, it is not needed.

inestimable If you say something is of **inestimable** value, you mean its value is very great indeed. *The festival and the opera house are inestimable assets.*

inevitable (inevitably, inevitability) If something is **inevitable**, it cannot be prevented or avoided. *This will inevitably lead to disillusionment... ...the inevitability of a single currency.* ◇ **The inevitable** is something which cannot be avoided. *He was forced to bow to the inevitable.*

inexact If something is **inexact**, it is not precise or accurate.

inexcusable (inexcusably) If you say something is **inexcusable**, you mean it is so bad that it cannot be justified or tolerated. *...inexcusable incompetence... Some of his public relations has been inexcusably dreadful.*

inexhaustible If something is **inexhaustible**, there is so much of it that it can never be used up. *...an inexhaustible supply of cheap labour.* ◇ If a person is **inexhaustible**,

they have the ability to keep on doing something without getting tired.

inexorable (inexorably) If a process is **inexorable**, nothing can be done to stop it. *We are moving inexorably towards a sterling crisis.*

inexpedient (*pron:* in-iks-pee-dee-ant) If you say it would be **inexpedient** to do something, you mean it would not be a good idea, as it might produce undesirable results.

inexpensive (inexpensively) **Inexpensive** things do not cost much. *This technology is simple and can be applied inexpensively.*

inexperienced (inexperience) If you are **inexperienced** at something, you have little knowledge or experience of it. **Inexperience** is lack of experience.

inexpert If you are **inexpert** at something, you have very little skill at it.

inexplicable (inexplicably) If something is **inexplicable**, there seems to be no explanation for it. *Some country towns look inexplicably healthier and brighter than others.*

inextricable (inextricably) If there is an **inextricable** connection between things, they cannot be separated or considered separately. *Economic and political reform are inextricably bound together.*

infallible (infallibility) If you claim something like a system is **infallible** or talk about its **infallibility**, you mean it cannot go wrong. ◇ If you say someone or something is **not infallible**, you mean they are capable of making mistakes.

infamous (*pron:* in-fam-uss) (infamously, infamy) **Infamous** people and things are well-known for bad reasons. *...the infamous poll tax... ...an infamously treacherous coast.* You can talk about the **infamy** of a wicked person or their deeds. *...an act of the most terrible infamy.*

infant (infancy) An **infant** is a very young child or baby. **Infancy** is the period of someone's life when they are a very young child. ◇ An **infant** organization or movement is new and has not yet developed properly. *...Poland's infant stock exchange.... ...Jordan's infant democracy.* You say something like this is **in its infancy**.

infant school An **infant school** is one for children aged about 4 to 7.

infanticide is the killing of a baby, especially by its own mother.

infantile is used to talk about things to do with very young children. *Much infantile unhappiness is attributed to teething.* ◇ If you say someone is being **infantile**, you mean they are behaving in a silly childish way.

infantry (infantryman, infantrymen) The **infantry** are soldiers who fight on foot rather than in tanks. An **infantryman** is a soldier in an infantry regiment.

infatuated (infatuation) If you are **infatuated** with someone, you are so much in love with them that you cannot think sensibly about the relationship. Being in this state is called **infatuation**. ◇ If someone is passionately interested in something, you can talk about their **infatuation** with it. *...his infatuation with cinema.*

infect (infected, infection) ❑ If someone or something **infects** you, they give you a disease. An **infection** is a disease you catch, especially by breathing in germs. ◇ An **infected** district is one where an infection is present and spreading. ◇ When food or some other substance is **infected**, it becomes contaminated by germs or dirt. ◇ An infected wound is unable to heal properly because of germs.

❏ If something bad **infects** people, places, or things, it spreads to them and affects them as if it were a disease. *The ills of the banking sector are no longer as likely to infect the rest of the economy as in the 1930s.*

infectious If you have an **infectious** disease, other people can catch it from you, especially by breathing in the germs. ◇ If something like a feeling is **infectious**, it spreads easily to other people.

infective is used to describe things like viruses which can cause an infection. *...the infective organism that caused BSE.*

infer (inferring, inferred; inference) If you **infer** something, you decide it is true on the basis of the information you have. *From the distance his car was thrown, it can be inferred that he was travelling at less than 55mph.* An **inference** (pron: in-fer-renss) is a conclusion you draw about something.

inferior (inferiority) If you feel **inferior**, you feel other people are better in some way than yourself. Someone who feels like this is said to have a sense of **inferiority**. People can also regard other people as **inferior** or treat them as their **inferiors.** ◇ If something is **inferior** to something else, it is not of such good quality.

inferiority complex If someone has an **inferiority complex**, they tend to feel they are less important or less worthwhile than other people.

inferno (infernos) An **inferno** is a large dangerous fire.

infertile (infertility) If people or animals are **infertile**, they cannot produce babies. *...infections which can lead to infertility.* ◇ If land or soil is **infertile**, very few plants can grow there.

infest (infestation) If a place is **infested** with insects, rats, or other unwelcome animals, they are there in large numbers. When this happens, you say there is an **infestation** of insects or animals. ◇ You can also talk about a place being **infested** with other harmful things. *...drug-infested ghettos.*

infidel Some people with strong religious beliefs call other people **infidels** when they belong to a different religion or have no religion at all.

infidelity (infidelities) **Infidelity** is being unfaithful to a husband, wife, or lover. A person's **infidelities** are the occasions when they are unfaithful.

infighting See in-fighting.

infill (infilling) **Infill** is material used to fill a gap or hole, especially a large hole in the ground. ◇ **Infill** or **infilling** is houses built in gaps between existing houses.

infiltrate (infiltrating, infiltrated; infiltration, infiltrator) If one organization **infiltrates** another, it gets some of its members to join the other organization secretly, to spy on it or influence it in some way. The people it gets into the other organization are called **infiltrators.** *...attempts to prevent the infiltration of the political system by organised crime networks.* ◇ If soldiers **infiltrate** enemy territory, they get into it without being seen.

infinite (infinitely) **Infinite** is used to describe things which have no end or limit. ◇ If you talk about an **infinite** number of things, you mean the number seems endless. *She wore an infinite variety of black clothes.* ◇ If you say something is **infinitely** better than something

else, you mean it is very much better.

infinitesimal (pron: in-fin-i-tess-i-mal) (infinitesimally) If something is **infinitesimal**, it is extremely small. *The danger of blood clotting is infinitesimally small for healthy women.*

infinitive In grammar, the **infinitive** is the base form of a verb, usually with 'to' in front of it. For example, 'to make' is the infinitive, and so is 'make' in 'They might make a mistake'. When people talk about **splitting the infinitive** or a **split infinitive**, they mean putting another word between 'to' and the verb, as in 'to boldly go'. This is thought by some people to be bad grammar.

infinity In maths, **infinity** is the number which is larger than any other number. It is represented by the symbol ∞. ◇ You say there is an **infinity** of things when there seems to be an endless number of them. *The desert stretches away in an infinity of identical brown ridges.*

infirm (infirmity, infirmities) If someone is **infirm**, they are weak or ill, usually because they are old. **The infirm** are people like this. An **infirmity** is a weakness or illness. *She would spend as much time at her piano as her infirmities allowed.*

infirmary (infirmaries) Some older hospitals are called **infirmaries.**

infirmity See infirm.

inflame (inflaming, inflamed; inflammation) ❏ If something **inflames** a difficult situation or a bad feeling, it makes it worse. *The shooting has only inflamed passions further.* ◇ If something **inflames** you, it makes you angry.

❏ If part of your body is **inflamed**, it is red or swollen because of an infection or injury. When this happens, you say there is **inflammation** or an **inflammation.**

inflammable An **inflammable** material or chemical catches fire and burns easily. ◇ An **inflammable** situation could easily become violent.

inflammation See inflame.

inflammatory comments are likely to make people angry or hostile. ◇ **Inflammatory** diseases make parts of the body become inflamed.

inflatable objects are objects like tyres and balloons which are filled with air or some other gas to get them to their full size. ◇ An **inflatable** is (a) an inflatable dinghy. (b) a large air-filled plastic or rubber object for children to jump about on, for example at a fair or carnival.

inflate (inflating, inflated) If you **inflate** something like a tyre or balloon, you fill it with air or some other gas, to get it to its full size. ◇ If something **inflates** prices or costs, it sends them up to a very high level. ◇ You also say someone **inflates** something when they make it out to be bigger or more important than it really is. *She has an inflated sense of her own worth.*

inflation (inflationary) **Inflation** is a general increase in the prices of goods and services in a country. **Inflationary** is used to talk about things to do with inflation, or things which cause inflation. *We are still living with the inflationary consequences of the boom of 1988.*

inflection (or inflexion) The **inflection** of your voice is the way it sounds, for example the way you emphasize certain words.

inflexible (inflexibly, inflexibility) If someone is **inflexible**, they are unwilling to change their attitude or opinions. *Observers are alarmed by the President's inflexibility on this* *issue.* ◇ If something like a rule or system is **inflexible**, it cannot be departed from. A rule can also be applied in an **inflexible** way. *The attempts to reduce the deficit will not be applied inflexibly.*

inflexion See inflection.

inflict If you **inflict** something unpleasant on someone, you make them suffer it.

inflow The **inflow** of people or things into a place is the numbers arriving there. *...a fast-growing inflow of asylum-seekers.*

influence (influencing, influenced) ❑ If someone has **influence**, they have the power to affect other people's actions. ◇ If you are **under** someone's **influence**, they are able to affect what you say or do.

❑ If something **influences** something else or has an **influence** on it, it affects it in some way. *Wages may be only one factor influencing investment.* Similarly, a person can be **influenced** by another person, or by something like a book or an experience. ◇ You can describe the effect someone has on other people by saying they are a particular kind of **influence**. *He accused them of being a disruptive influence.* ◇ In music or art, an **influence** is a style used or adapted by a musician or artist in their own work. *The band's fusion of reggae and jazz influences worked well.*

❑ If you say someone is **under the influence**, you mean they are drunk.

influential people and things have a lot of influence over people.

influenza is the same as flu.

influx (influxes) If there is an **influx** of people or things into a place, they arrive in large numbers.

info is the same as information.

inform (informed) ❑ If you **inform** someone of something, you tell them about it.

❑ If you are well **informed**, you know a lot about a subject or situation. If you are badly **informed**, you know very little about it. **Informed** people are well informed. *Informed sources say there must have been many casualties.* ◇ An **informed** decision or guess is based on good knowledge of a subject or situation.

❑ If you **inform** on someone, you tell the police or someone else in authority about something wrong they have done.

informal (informally, informality) ❑ **Informal** behaviour is relaxed and casual, rather than correct, official, or serious. *A lot of business is done informally on the golf course... His cheerful informality made for excellent relations with successive British and American commanders.* ◇ An **informal** occasion is a relaxed friendly one, where you do not have to dress up or follow some accepted procedure. ◇ **Informal** clothes are suitable for wearing when you are relaxing.

❑ An **informal** arrangement is not officially established, and works on a casual basis. *...informal agreements... Switzerland has been informally involved with IMF activities since the 1970s.*

informant An **informant** is (a) someone who provides you with information. (b) an informer.

information is facts or news which you obtain from someone or something.

information technology or IT is the theory and practice of using computers to transmit information.

informative If something is **informative**, it gives you useful information.

informer An **informer** is someone who gives information about a crime to the police, sometimes in exchange for money.

infra-red light is below the colour red in the spectrum and cannot be seen.

infrastructure The **infrastructure** of a country or region is the structure which enables it to function effectively, for example its public services and communications.

infrequent (infrequently) If something is **infrequent**, it does not happen very often. *This kind of bee swarms infrequently.*

infringe (infringing, infringed; infringement) If a law or agreement is **infringed**, someone breaks it. You call this an **infringement** of the law or agreement. *The company has issued a writ alleging infringement of copyright.* ◇ If something **infringes** people's rights or is an **infringement** of them, it takes part of them away.

infuriate (infuriating, infuriated; infuriatingly) If something **infuriates** you, it makes you angry or frustrated. *Hall infuriatingly let slip a big lead for the second time in four days.*

infuse (infusing, infused; infusion) ❑ If something is **infused** with a quality, it is full of it. *The summit continues to be infused with goodwill.* ◇ If you **infuse** people with something like hope or enthusiasm, you fill them with it.

❑ If a lot of money is **infused** into something, it is spent on it, to try to make it work.

❑ If a patient is given an **infusion** of a fluid, they are given it slowly from a drip.

❑ If you **infuse** a drink such as tea or a medicine, you make it by pouring hot water onto herbs or leaves, letting it stand, and straining it. An **infusion** is a drink or medicine prepared in this way.

ingenious (*pron:* in-jeen-ee-uss) (ingeniously, ingenuity) If you call something like a device or plan **ingenious**, you mean it has been cleverly designed or thought out. *The roof has been ingeniously designed to provide solar heating.* ◇ If you call a person **ingenious**, you mean they are able to invent things, or think of clever ways of doing things. You talk about the **ingenuity** (*pron:* in-jen-new-it-ee) of someone like this.

ingenue (ingenu) (*both pron:* an-zhay-new; *the 'zh' sounds like 's' in 'pleasure'*) In a play or film, an **ingenue** role is that of an innocent young woman. An **ingenu** role is a similar one for a man.

ingenuity See ingenious.

ingenuous (*pron:* in-jen-new-uss) (ingenuousness) An **ingenuous** person is innocent, trusting, and honest. You talk about the **ingenuousness** of someone like this.

ingest (ingestion) If you **ingest** a substance, you eat it or drink it. *Chronic high levels of alcohol ingestion frequently lead to addiction and to liver diseases.*

inglenook An **inglenook** is a corner by a large open fireplace.

inglorious (ingloriously) **Inglorious** behaviour is shameful and disgraceful. *...the inglorious exploits of the hooligan element among English football supporters... If the fighting worsens, the troops might have to be ingloriously withdrawn.*

ingot An **ingot** is a lump of metal, usually shaped like a brick.

ingrained (*or* engrained) habits and beliefs are difficult to change.

ingratiate (*pron:* in-**gray**-shee-ate) (ingratiating, ingratiated) If you **ingratiate** yourself with people, you try to make yourself popular with them.

ingratitude is a lack of gratitude, shown in the way someone behaves to a person who has helped them.

ingredient The **ingredients** of something like a cake are the things it is made from. ◇ The factors which lead to something happening can also be called **ingredients**. *Economists believe that the housing market is a key ingredient in economic recovery.*

ingrowing An **ingrowing** toenail is growing into the toe, and can be painful.

inhabit (inhabiting, inhabited; inhabitant) The people or animals that **inhabit** a place are the ones that live there; you can also call them its **inhabitants** or say the place is **inhabited** by them. ◇ If a place or house is **inhabited**, there are people living in it.

inhale (inhaling, inhaled; inhalation) When you **inhale**, you breathe in. If you **inhale** something like smoke, you breathe it in. *30 passengers suffering from smoke inhalation have been taken to hospital.*

inhaler An **inhaler** is a device for inhaling vaporized medicines, especially ones which make breathing easier.

inherent (inherently) If a characteristic is **inherent** in something, it is built into it, or part of its nature. *This strategy has inherent dangers for the army... ...an inherently unstable government.*

inherit (inheriting, inherited; inheritance, inheritor) ❑ If you **inherit** money or property, you get it from someone when they die. The money or property is called an **inheritance**; you are called the **inheritor**.

❑ You can say people **inherit** things like customs or traditions when these things are handed down to them from other people who have gone before them. Things like these can also be called an **inheritance**. *Mosques have been reminding people of their Sunni Islamic inheritance.*

❑ If you **inherit** a characteristic or disease, you are born with it because your parents or ancestors had it.

inhibit (inhibiting, inhibited; inhibition) If something **inhibits** a process, it stops it or slows it down. *...chemicals which inhibit normal cell division.* ◇ If you **inhibit** someone from doing something, you make it difficult for them to do it. ◇ If you are **inhibited** or have **inhibitions**, you find it difficult to behave naturally and show your real feelings, because you worry too much about what people might think.

inhibitor An **inhibitor** is a substance which stops or slows down a chemical reaction.

inhospitable An **inhospitable** place is unpleasant to be in, for example because of bad weather conditions or lack of shelter. ◇ You say a person is **inhospitable** when they do not make visitors feel welcome.

inhuman behaviour is extremely cruel.

inhumane (inhumanity) You say treatment of people or animals is **inhumane** when it involves cruelty of some kind. *He criticised the inhumane way in which whales were killed... The Red Cross said all factions were guilty of inhumanity.*

inimical If conditions are **inimical** to something, they are not favourable to it.

inimitable (inimitably) **Inimitable** is used to describe something special about a person which cannot be copied by anyone else. *...his inimitable culinary skills... He replied in his inimitably gruff fashion.*

iniquitous (iniquity, iniquities) If you say something is **iniquitous** or an **iniquity,** you mean it is very bad and unfair. *...an iniquitous law.*

initial (initially; initialling, initialled) (*American spelling:* initialing, initialed) ❑ **Initial** is used to say what happens at the beginning of something, in contrast to what happens later. *...the initial response of the markets... His criticism initially went unheeded.*

❑ An **initial** or **initial letter** is the first letter of a word or name. Your **initials** are the capital letters representing each of your names. If you **initial** a document, you write your initials on it as a signature.

initiate (initiating, initiated; initiation, initiator) ❑ If you **initiate** something, you start it, or cause it to happen. *...the initiation of negotiations with the United States and Canada.* Someone who initiates something can be called its **initiator.**

❑ If you **initiate** someone into something, you introduce them to it and teach them about it. *His elder brother initiated him into books at the age of three.* ◇ If someone is **initiated** into a group or society, a ceremony is held to make them a member or to teach them secrets or skills. The ceremony is called an **initiation** ceremony; the person being initiated is called an **initiate.**

initiative ❑ An **initiative** is something positive someone does in an attempt to resolve a problem or crisis. ◇ If you **take the initiative** or **seize the initiative** in a situation, you do not wait to see what other people do, but take some action yourself. ◇ If you have the **initiative,** you are in a stronger position than your opponents. *The goal gave the Belgians the initiative for just five minutes.*

❑ Someone who has **initiative** has the ability to take action without being told what to do. If you do something **on your own initiative,** you do it without being told to.

initiator See initiate.

inject (injecting; injection, injectable) ❑ If you are **injected** with a medicine or have an **injection,** the medicine is put into your body with a syringe. **Injectable** medicines are ones which can be injected into someone. People can also **inject** themselves with harmful drugs.

❑ If you **inject** a quality like excitement into a situation, you do something which adds this quality to it.

❑ If money is **injected** into a business or organization, an additional amount is provided to keep it going. You can say an organization receives an **injection** of money.

injudicious (injudiciously) **Injudicious** behaviour is unwise and shows poor judgement. *It would be unwise to alienate the President with such injudiciously aggressive tactics.*

injunction An **injunction** is a court order issued to make someone do something, or to stop someone doing something. ◇ An **injunction** is also a command or instruction to behave in a certain way.

injure (injuring, injured; injury, injuries) ❑ If you are **injured** or receive an **injury,** a part of your body is damaged in a battle or accident. **Injury** is being injured. *Injury threatened his career.* In a battle or accident, **the injured** are the people who have been injured. *A number of Spanish tourists are reported to be amongst the injured.* ◇ **Injury time** is extra playing time at the end of a football match to make up for time lost during the match when players were injured.

❑ If your feelings are **injured,** you are upset or offended about something. ◇ In a dispute, if you claim you are the **injured party,** you say you are the one who has been treated wrongly or unfairly.

injurious If something is **injurious,** it is harmful or damaging.

injury See injure.

injustice is a lack of fairness or justice in a situation, or in something someone does. If someone commits an **injustice,** they treat someone wrongly or unfairly. ◇ If you say you do not want **to do** someone **an injustice,** you mean you do not want to say something critical about them which might not be true. *I may be doing him an injustice, but he didn't seem awfully interested.*

ink is black or coloured liquid for writing, drawing, or printing. If you **ink in** something which has been written in pencil, you go over the letters in ink.

❑ If you say the **ink was hardly dry** on something like an agreement before a certain thing happened, you mean the thing happened very soon after the agreement was drawn up. *Almost before the ink had dried on the unification treaty, the trickle of inquiries about property in the east became a torrent.*

inkling If you **have an inkling** of something, you have a vague idea or suspicion about it. *It was the first inkling the minister had of what was about to hit him... He has no inkling of what administration is about.*

inky things are covered in ink, or very dark like ink.

inlaid (inlay) An **inlaid** object has a flat surface with a design on it made by putting thin pieces of a substance into grooves made to hold them. A design like this is called an **inlay.**

inland If you go **inland,** you go away from the coast. If something takes place **inland,** it takes place away from the coast. **Inland** areas are not on the coast.

Inland Revenue The **Inland Revenue** is the government authority which collects income tax and some other taxes.

inlay See inlaid.

inlet An **inlet** is a narrow strip of water stretching from the sea into the land or lying between two islands.

inmate The **inmates** of a prison or psychiatric hospital are the people being kept there.

inmost See innermost.

inn An **inn** is a pub or small hotel.

innards When people talk about the **innards** of a person or animal, they mean the organs inside their body. People also talk about the **innards** of a machine, meaning its inside parts.

innate (innately) An **innate** quality or ability is one you seem to have naturally, as if you had been born with it. *...an innately courteous man.*

inner ❑ The **inner** one of two things is the one which is inside the other. *The prisoners were caught as they tried to scale the inner perimeter fence.*

❑ **Inner** is used to talk about the central part of a large city. *...Inner London.* ◇ **Inner city** areas are areas of housing close to the centre of a city, where there are often social and economic problems.

❑ **Inner** is used to talk about a person's thoughts and feelings, as distinct from their outward behaviour. *...her inner turmoil.*

❑ **Inner** is also used to talk about people and things close to the centre of power and influence in an organization. *...the prime minister's inner circle of advisers.*

inner ear The **inner ear** is a part inside the head which is essential for hearing and balance.

inner tube An **inner tube** is the rubber tube containing air inside a tyre.

innermost Your **innermost** or **inmost** feelings are your most personal and private ones. ◇ **Innermost** is also used to talk about people and things closest to the centre of power and influence in an organization. *...the innermost group of politicians.*

inning (innings) In a cricket match, an **innings** is a period during which one or other team is batting. The time each batsman spends on the field is also called his or her **innings.** ◇ In a baseball game, an **inning** is a period during which both teams have a turn at bat. Each team's turn is called a **half-inning.**

innkeeper is an old word for someone who looks after an inn.

innocent (innocently, innocence) If an accused person is **innocent,** they are not guilty of the crime they are accused of. *All the accused vigorously maintained their innocence.* ◇ You also say people are **innocent** when they suffer in a crime or conflict they are not involved in. *...an innocent bystander... ...tourists innocently caught in the fighting.* ◇ You also say someone is **innocent** when they are inexperienced and ignorant about the more unpleasant side of people's behaviour. ◇ An **innocent** remark or action is not meant to offend or upset anyone.

innocuous (innocuously) If you say something is **innocuous,** you mean it is harmless or inoffensive, or appears to be. *Perched innocuously between Eccles Funerals and Eccles Thrift and Fancy stands the Adam and Eve Sauna Club.*

innovate (innovating, innovated; innovation, innovator, innovative, innovatory) If someone **innovates,** they introduce changes and new ideas to the way something is done or made. The changes are called **innovations.** A person who introduces something new is called an **innovator;** you also say they are being **innovative.** *In their haste to innovate, many firms botched their investment in technology... Manchester has a strong tradition for innovation, dating back to the industrial revolution.* **Innovative** or **innovatory** things are new and original. *...innovative advertising... ...innovatory educational methods.*

innuendo (innuendoes *or* innuendos) **Innuendo** is indirect reference to something rude or unpleasant. An **innuendo** is a remark like this. *Both companies have engaged in a phony war of hints, nudges and sly innuendo.*

innumerable is used to say a number of things is very large. *We have held innumerable meetings, seminars and discussions.*

innumerate If someone is **innumerate,** they cannot understand basic arithmetic or do simple calculations.

inoculate (inoculating, inoculated; inoculation) If you are **inoculated** against a disease or are given an **inoculation,** you are injected with a weak form of the disease, to protect you against it.

inoffensive If something you say or do is **inoffensive,** it is not likely to offend or upset anyone. An **inoffensive**

person is never likely to offend anyone.

inoperable If a medical condition like a tumour or cancer is **inoperable,** it cannot be removed or cured by an operation. ◇ If something like a piece of equipment is **inoperable,** it cannot be made to work.

inoperative If something like a system is **inoperative,** it does not work any more or cannot be made to work.

inopportune If something happens at an **inopportune** time, it happens at an unsuitable time and causes trouble or embarrassment.

inordinate (inordinately) You use **inordinate** to talk about extreme feelings and behaviour. *He had an inordinate interest in people... ...inordinately demanding parents.* ◇ An **inordinate** amount of something is much greater than you would normally expect. *They wield an inordinate amount of power... ...inordinately high costs.*

inorganic matter has never at any time been part of a living thing. So, for example, metal is inorganic, whereas coal is not.

input (inputting, inputted) **Input** is money and other resources put into a project to make it work. ◇ Your **input** into a discussion or activity is your contribution to it. ◇ If you **input** information into a computer, you feed it in, for example by typing it on a keyboard. This information is called **input.** See also **output.**

inquest An **inquest** is an official inquiry to investigate something in detail, especially one held by a coroner to investigate a death which may not be from natural causes.

inquire (inquiring, inquired; inquiry, inquiries; inquirer) (or **enquire,** *etc*) ❏ If you **inquire** about something, you ask for information about it. **Inquiry** is asking about something. *This is the line of inquiry being taken.* An **inquiry** is a question you ask to get information. If you **make inquiries** about something, you ask about it. *One foreign company made inquiries about buying the land.* A person who is asking for information can be called an **inquirer.** *...the procession of inquirers seeking news at the Embassy.* ◇ If you **inquire into** something, you investigate it thoroughly. An **inquiry** is an official investigation. *Police in Essex have launched a murder inquiry.*

❏ If you have an **inquiring** mind, you are always interested in learning new things.

inquisition (inquisitorial, inquisitor) People sometimes call an official investigation an **inquisition** when it is very thorough and uses harsh methods of questioning. The person asking the questions can be called an **inquisitor.** **Inquisitorial** is used to describe harsh methods of questioning. ◇ An **inquisitorial** system of justice is one which involves an accused person being questioned directly by a judge or magistrate.

inquisitive (inquisitiveness) If you are **inquisitive,** you are always wanting to find out about things. *...his insatiable inquisitiveness.*

inquisitor (inquisitorial) See **inquisition.**

inquorate (*pron:* in-kwor-it) If something like a committee meeting is **inquorate,** there are not enough members present to meet the minimum number officially required before any decisions can be made.

inroads If you **make inroads** into an area of activity, you start to be successful in it, often at the expense of someone else. *Evangelical groups have made great inroads into*

traditionally Catholic Guatemala. ◇ If something harmful makes inroads into something, it spreads into it, causing damage. *Dry rot had made serious inroads into the joists... The forest has suffered from the inroads of mining.*

insane (insanely, insanity) ❏ If someone is **insane,** their mind does not work in a normal way, and this makes their behaviour very strange. This condition is called **insanity.** People who are insane are sometimes called the **insane.**

❏ If you call someone's plans or actions **insane,** you mean they are extremely silly. You can talk about the **insanity** of plans or actions like these. *She was insanely cheerful... Some journalists deserve special praise for their ability to communicate the insanity of the war.*

insanitary If something is **insanitary,** it is so dirty it is likely to have a bad effect on people's health.

insanity See **insane.**

insatiable (*pron:* in-saysh-a-bl) If someone's desire for something is **insatiable,** it can never be satisfied.

inscribe (inscribing, inscribed; inscription) If words are inscribed on an object or if the object is **inscribed** with them, they are written or carved on it. An **inscription** is words written or carved on something.

inscrutable (inscrutably) If you say someone is **inscrutable,** you mean you cannot tell what they are thinking. *He remained inscrutably silent during the news conference.*

insect An **insect** is a small creature with six legs. Most insects have wings. Ants, flies, and butterflies are all insects.

insecticide An **insecticide** is a chemical used to kill insects.

insecure (insecurity, insecurities) ❏ If you feel **insecure** or have feelings of **insecurity,** you lack confidence and do not think other people like you or respect you. Worries about things like these are called **insecurities.** ◇ If your job is **insecure,** it could come to an end at any time. *Research staff were particularly concerned about job insecurity.*

❏ If an object is **insecure,** it is unsafe and likely to fall or come apart.

inseminate (inseminating, inseminated; insemination) If a woman or female animal is **inseminated,** sperm is put inside her to make her pregnant. *...children conceived by donor insemination.* See also **artificial insemination.**

insensitive (insensitively, insensitivity) If someone is **insensitive,** they behave in a way which shows they are unaware of other people's feelings, or do not care about them. Behaviour like this is called **insensitivity.** *They felt that he had behaved insensitively.* ◇ If you are **insensitive** to something, you are not aware of it, or not interested in it. *They became insensitive to the demands of rank-and-file members of the party.*

inseparable (inseparably) ❏ If two things are **inseparable,** they are so closely connected they cannot be separated. *He believes liberty is inseparable from social justice... The British economy will become inseparably interwoven with the growing market-place of the European Union.*

❏ **Inseparable** friends are always together.

insert (insertion) ❏ If you **insert** an object into something, you put it inside it. *...the insertion of acupuncture needles.* ◇ An **insert** (*pron:* in-sert) is something inserted somewhere, especially a piece of paper with an advert on it placed inside a magazine or newspaper.

❏ If something is **inserted** into a speech or piece of writing, it is put in at a late stage.

inset If an object is **inset** with something like jewels, they are fixed into its surface.

inshore waters are the parts of the sea which are close to land.

inside (insider) ❏ **Inside** is used to talk about things being in an enclosed space or area. *The officer asked him to open his car boot and found golf clubs inside... ...a house inside the embassy compound... Frost formed on the inside of the window panes.* ◇ The **inside** of a building is the part enclosed by the walls and roof. ◇ If something happens inside a country, it happens within its borders.

❏ The **inside** pages of a newspaper are the ones you have to open the paper to see. ◇ If something like a piece of clothing is **inside out**, the inside part has been turned so it faces outwards. ◇ If you know someone or something **inside out**, you know them extremely well.

❏ When people talk about their **insides**, they mean their internal organs, especially their stomach. ◇ **Inside** is used to talk about feelings someone has without showing them. *I was furious inside.*

❏ If something happens **inside** an organization, it involves members of the organization and nobody else. ◇ If you have **inside** information about something, you know more about it than other people, because you are involved in it or have been told about it by someone who is. Someone who is involved in a situation and knows more about it than other people can be called an **insider**. See also **insider dealing.**

❏ On a road with more than one lane, the **inside** lane is the left-hand lane in countries where you drive on the left, and the right-hand one in countries where you drive on the right. ◇ On a racetrack, the **inside** is the lane nearest the centre, which is shorter than the other lanes. If you say someone is on the **inside track,** you mean they have the advantage in a competitive situation.

❏ If you do something **inside** a particular time, you do it before that time is finished. *They were a goal up inside four minutes.*

insider dealing or **insider trading** is illegally buying or selling shares by someone with special knowledge of the companies concerned. People who do this are called **insider dealers.**

insidious (insidiously) **Insidious** is used to describe harmful things which develop gradually without being noticed. *...an insidiously destructive influence.*

insight (insightful) If something gives you an **insight** into a situation, it helps you to understand it better. If you call something like a book or article **insightful,** you mean it makes you realize things you had not thought of before.

insignia (*plural:* insignia) An **insignia** is an official badge or sign showing that a person, vehicle, etc belongs to a particular organization. *...the Red Cross insignia.*

insignificant (insignificance) If something is **insignificant,** it is so small or unimportant it is not worth bothering about. *The party committee has been reduced to insignificance.* ◇ If something **pales** or **fades into insignificance,** it becomes unimportant when compared with something else. *She makes a few trifling slips, but these fade into insignificance in the warm glow she brings to her subject.*

insincere (insincerity) If someone is **insincere,** they pretend to have feelings they do not have. Behaviour like this is called **insincerity.**

insinuate (insinuating, insinuated; insinuation) If someone **insinuates** that something is true, they hint at it in an unpleasant way. This is called making an **insinuation.** ◇ When people **insinuate** themselves into positions of power or influence, they manage to get there using patience and cunning.

insipid If you call someone or something **insipid,** you mean they are dull and boring. ◇ **Insipid** food or drink has very little taste.

insist If you **insist** that something must happen, you say very firmly it must happen. *The government is insisting that the farmers leave the building.* You can also **insist** on doing something. *Shop staff insisted on inspecting people's residence permits.* You can also **insist** that something is true. *He insists he is innocent.*

insistent (insistently, insistence) If you are **insistent,** you say very firmly that something must be done. *The calls for realignment grow increasingly insistent... This question has been raised most insistently in the courts... The soldiers are there at the insistence of officials brought in to restore essential services.* ◇ If a noise is **insistent,** it continues for a long time and you cannot help being aware of it.

insofar Insofar as is used to say in what way something is true. *This decision is welcome insofar as it expresses the commitment of all parties to refrain from the use of force.*

insole The **insole** of a shoe is the soft layer of material which the sole of your foot rests on.

insolent (insolence) An **insolent** person is rude and disrespectful. **Insolence** is behaviour like this.

insoluble An **insoluble** problem cannot be solved. ◇ An **insoluble** substance cannot be dissolved.

insolvent (insolvency, insolvencies) If a person or organization is **insolvent,** they do not have enough money to pay their debts. Being in this position is called **insolvency;** individual cases of people or firms being insolvent are called **insolvencies.**

insomnia (insomniac) If someone suffers from **insomnia,** they find it difficult to get to sleep. You say someone like this is **insomniac** or an **insomniac.**

insouciant (*pron:* in-soo-si-ant) (insouciantly, insouciance) **Insouciant** behaviour shows a lack of concern. *Dictators should no longer be able to stamp insouciantly on their people's rights... The UN treats the kidnappings with apparent insouciance.*

inspect (inspection; inspector, inspectorate) ❏ If you **inspect** something, you examine it carefully, to find out about it or to check that it is all right. An **inspection** is an examination like this. ◇ If an official **inspects** a place or carries out an **inspection,** he or she visits the place and looks at it carefully, to find out if regulations are being obeyed. Someone who does this is called an **inspector.** A group of inspectors with a particular responsibility is sometimes called an **inspectorate.** ◇ An **inspector of taxes** is employed by the government to calculate the amount of tax people or companies should pay.

❏ An **inspector** is also an officer in the police force, ranked above a sergeant and below a superintendent.

inspire (inspiring, inspired; inspiration, inspirational) ❏ If someone or something **inspires** you or is an **inspiration**

to you, they make you want to do something by giving you new ideas and enthusiasm. You say people and things that have this effect are **inspiring** or **inspirational**. ...*programmes inspiring millions of volunteers to give their time to aid organisations.* ◇ If you say something someone does is **inspired**, you mean they do it especially well, as if something was inspiring them. *India played inspired hockey.*

❑ If you have an **inspiration**, you suddenly have a good idea. **Inspiration** is having a good idea.

❑ If something **inspires** an emotion in you, it makes you feel it. *The agency inspires an almost cult-like devotion among its staff.*

instability (instabilities) **Instability** is a lack of stability in a place, situation, or person. The unstable aspects of something can be called its **instabilities**. *On Thursday the Group of Seven met and discussed the markets' instabilities.*

install (installation) ❑ When a machine or piece of equipment is **installed** in a place, it is placed or fitted there, ready for use. ...*the installation of smoke alarms.* ◇ An **installation** is a place containing equipment and machinery for a particular purpose. ...*oil installations.*

❑ When a new government is **installed**, it is chosen to govern and begins its work. You can also say someone like a dictator **installs** himself as a country's leader.

instalment (*American spelling:* **installment**) If you pay for something in **instalments**, you pay small sums at regular intervals over a period of time. ◇ If a story comes out in **instalments**, it appears in parts published or broadcast at regular intervals. Similarly, a plan or scheme can be carried out in **instalments**.

instance ❑ You say **for instance** when giving an example. *Subsidies for the arts, for instance, will be slashed.* ◇ An **instance** is a case of something happening. *The report details instances where journalists have been detained, tortured and harassed.*

❑ **In this instance** means in this particular case. *Even with a limited technology package (in this instance seeds and fertiliser) excellent results can be achieved.* ◇ You say **in the first instance** when you are mentioning the first in a series of steps or actions. *The two men then agreed to meet privately for, in the first instance, fifteen minutes.*

❑ If you do something **at someone's instance**, you do it because they have asked or ordered you to.

instant (instantly) ❑ **Instant** is used to talk about things having an immediate effect. *They were instantly obeyed.* ◇ **Instant** food can be prepared very quickly and easily, for example by just adding boiling water.

❑ An **instant** is an extremely short period of time. ◇ If something happens at a particular **instant**, that is the actual moment when it happens. *At one and the same instant the audience burst into a thundering shout.* ◇ If you do something **the instant** something happens, you do it straight after it. *Shareholders had a tendency to sell their shares the instant a firm hit trouble.*

instantaneous (instantaneously) If something is **instantaneous**, it happens immediately or is over very quickly. *Jennifer's acute pain was relieved instantaneously.*

instead is used to say one thing happens or is done rather than another. *Last year, the bank actually gained customers instead of seeing numbers fall.*

instep Your **instep** is the middle part of your foot. The

part of a shoe which covers this area is called the shoe's **instep**.

instigate (instigating, instigated; instigator, instigation) If someone **instigates** trouble of some kind, they are responsible for starting it. You say the people responsible for causing trouble are its **instigators**. ...*the instigators of the plot.* ◇ If something is done at someone's **instigation**, they are responsible for bringing it about.

instil (instilling, instilled) (*American spelling:* **instill**) If an idea is **instilled** into someone, strong measures are taken to make sure that they accept it completely. *Military training is seen as an effective way of instilling loyalty to the government.*

instinct (instinctive, instinctively) **Instinct** or an **instinct** is a natural tendency in people or animals to behave or react in a certain way, without thinking about it or planning it. Animals' instincts are mostly inherited; whereas what we call an instinct in humans is usually the result of earlier experience. You call feelings or actions **instinctive** when people have them or do them without necessarily being able to explain or justify them. *I have an instinctive horror of signing anything... ...MPs who are instinctively opposed to any extension of censorship.* ◇ If it is your **instinct** to do something in a particular situation, it seems the natural thing to do.

institute (instituting, instituted; institution) An **institute** is an organization set up to do a particular type of work, especially research or teaching. ◇ If someone **institutes** something like a system, rule, or course of action, they introduce it. *The government has instituted an inquiry... ...demands for the institution of multi-party democracy.*

institution (institutional) ❑ You call something an **institution** when it is a well-established feature somewhere. ...*that great British institution, the pub... ...the institution of marriage.* **Institutional** is used to describe things like this. *Regular afternoon siestas haven't yet become institutional in Britain.*

❑ An **institution** is also (a) a large organization like a university or a bank. (b) a building where people of a certain kind are kept or looked after. ...*mental institutions... ...institutional care.*

❑ See also **institute**.

institutionalize (institutionalizing, institutionalized; institutionalization) (*can be spelled with an 's' instead of a 'z'*) ❑ If something is **institutionalized**, it becomes an accepted part of a social system. *The External Affairs Minister said the proposed constitution would mean the institutionalization of racial discrimination.*

❑ If a person is **institutionalized**, they are put in an institution like a mental hospital. If they become **institutionalized**, they get so used to living in an institution they can no longer cope on their own.

instruct (instruction, instructional, instructor) ❑ If you **instruct** someone to do something, you tell them to do it. What you say is called an **instruction**. ◇ An **instruction** is also a command given to a computer to carry out a particular function.

❑ If you **instruct** someone in a subject or skill, you teach it to them. An **instructor** is someone who does this as their job. **Instructional** things teach you how to do something. ...*an instructional video.* **Instructions** are information, often written, on how to do something.

instructive If you say an experience is **instructive**, you mean you can learn something from it.

instructor See **instruct**.

instrument (instrumental, instrumentalist) ❑ An **instrument** is (a) a tool or device designed to do a particular task, especially precise or delicate work. *...surgical instruments.* (b) a device for taking measurements, for example of speed or height. *...navigational instruments.* ◇ The **instrument panel** on a vehicle or machine is the part where all the dials and switches are.

❑ A musical **instrument** is something like a piano, guitar, or flute, which has been skilfully made so that music can be played on it. **Instrumental** music is written to be played on instruments, rather than sung. Musicians who play instruments are sometimes called **instrumentalists**.

❑ Anything which is used to achieve a particular aim can be called an **instrument**. *Devaluation is an overrated economic instrument.* ◇ If you are **instrumental** in getting something done, you play an important part in it.

instrumentation The **instrumentation** in a place, for example in the cabin of a plane, is all the instruments there. ◇ The **instrumentation** of a piece of music is the instruments needed to perform it, and the way the music has been written or adapted for them to play it.

insubordinate (insubordination) **Insubordinate** people disobey orders from people who have authority over them. Behaviour like this is called **insubordination**.

insubstantial You say something is **insubstantial** when it is not large, solid, or strong. ◇ **Insubstantial** is also used to describe something like a policy or action which is weak and has no effect.

insufferable (insufferably) If you call someone or something **insufferable**, you mean they are very unpleasant or annoying. *...an insufferably bossy mother.*

insufficient (insufficiently, insufficiency) If something is in-**sufficient** or there is an **insufficiency** of it, there is not enough of it. *The general workforce is insufficiently educated to do the jobs available... ...insufficiency of funds.*

insular (insularity) If you say a group of people are **insular** or have an **insular** outlook, you mean they tend to think of things in terms of their own country or community, and are suspicious of anything that comes from outside. You talk about the **insularity** of people like these.

insulate (insulating, insulated; insulation, insulator) ❑ If something **insulates** you from some harm, it protects you from it. *Farmers cannot insulate themselves from the rest of the economy... They live in a cosy, insulated world.*

❑ If something is **insulated**, it is covered with a thick layer of a substance or material, to stop heat escaping. *...roof insulation.* A substance or material used for this purpose is called an **insulator**.

❑ If an electrical device is **insulated**, parts of it are covered with rubber, glass, or porcelain to stop people touching them and getting a shock. ◇ **Insulating tape** is a special adhesive tape used to cover electrical wires which might become exposed.

insulin is a substance in the body which controls the level of sugar in the blood. People with diabetes cannot produce sufficient insulin, and may have to have it injected into their body.

insult (insulting, insultingly) If you **insult** someone, you speak to them in a rude way, saying unpleasant things about them. What you say is called an **insult**. *Tottenham's supporters had behaved insultingly.* ◇ If someone is **insulted**, they are offended at something someone has said to them, or at something someone has done. ◇ If you **add insult to injury**, you annoy or upset someone by adding to some harm you have already done them.

insuperable If you say a problem is **insuperable**, you mean there is no way it can be dealt with successfully.

insupportable If you find something **insupportable**, it is so unpleasant you cannot tolerate it or accept it.

insure (insuring, insured; insurance) ❑ If you **insure** yourself or your property or take out **insurance**, you have an agreement with a company to pay a certain amount of money regularly as protection against something like ill health, loss, or damage. If you become ill, or if your property is damaged or stolen, the company pays you a sum of money. The written agreement you sign to insure yourself or your property is called an **insurance policy**.

❑ If you do something to **insure** against something undesirable, you do it to protect yourself in case it happens. You can also do something as an **insurance** against something undesirable. *The oil reserves were stockpiled in disused mines as an insurance against sanctions and oil embargoes.*

❑ Americans sometimes use **insure** to mean 'ensure'.

insurer An **insurer** is a company which sells insurance.

insurgent (insurgency, insurgencies) **Insurgents** are people rebelling against the government or army in their own country. A rebellion of this sort is called an **insurgency**.

insurmountable If you say a task or problem is **insurmountable**, you mean there is no way it can be dealt with successfully.

insurrection An **insurrection** is violent action taken by a group of people against the rulers of their own country.

intact If something is **intact**, it has not broken up into smaller pieces and none of it is missing. *The team that reached the finals in 1984 was virtually intact four years later.* ◇ If someone's reputation is **intact**, it has not been harmed by something which has happened.

intake Your **intake** of food, drink, or air is the amount you eat, drink, or breathe. ◇ If you say something like an announcement is followed by an **intake of breath**, you mean people are very shocked by it. ◇ The **intake** of an institution or organization is the number of people or things accepted into it at a particular time.

intangible If something is **intangible**, it exists but cannot be seen, touched, or easily explained. *...the intangible benefits of improved confidence and 'image'.* ◇ A company's **intangible** assets are things like customer goodwill which cannot be seen or given an exact value, but are nevertheless important for the company's financial success. Things like these can be called **intangibles**.

integer (*pron:* in-ti-jer) An **integer** is a whole number like 5 or 23, as opposed to a fraction or a minus number.

integral If something is an **integral** part of something else, it is an essential part of it.

integrate (integrating, integrated; integration) ❑ If people **integrate** into a social group, they become a part of it. *...the integration of black people within British society.* ◇ If something like an institution or activity is **integrated**, it

is open to people of all races and groups. *He said he was confident that South African cricket was now fully integrated.*
❑ If you **integrate** things, you combine them to form one thing. *We integrate contemporary dance with acrobatics... ...moves towards closer economic integration.*
❑ An **integrated circuit** is a very small electric circuit on a silicon chip.

integrity If you talk about someone's **integrity**, you mean they are honest and firm in their moral principles. ◇ If you talk about the **integrity** of a group of people, you mean they are united and form a whole.

intellect A person's **intellect** is their ability to think intelligently, understand ideas and information, and be logical. *Books satisfy a part of the intellect that needs to be stimulated... ...a man of limited intellect.*

intellectual (intellectually, intellectualism) **Intellectual** activities involve the use of a person's intellect. *...intellectual pursuits... ...intellectually demanding work.* If people enjoy intellectual activities, you can talk about their **intellectualism**. *...a country that prides itself on its intellectualism.* ◇ You say someone is **intellectual** or an **intellectual** when they are interested in ideas and theories and have a good understanding of them.

intelligent (intelligently, intelligence) ❑ An **intelligent** person has the ability to understand, learn, and think things out quickly and well. A person's **intelligence** is the extent to which they have this ability. **Intelligent** behaviour shows a high level of intelligence. *She talks intelligently about everything.* ◇ **intelligence quotient**: see **IQ**.
❑ If you say an animal is **intelligent**, you mean it is able to learn things and work things out to a greater extent than most animals. ◇ People sometimes call a machine **intelligent** when it is programmed to respond to a wide range of situations, so it almost seems able to think for itself.
❑ **Intelligence** is information gathered by a government about its country's enemies. The people responsible for gathering this information are also called **intelligence**. *Western intelligence were spending several times more than the KGB on their spying operations.*

intelligentsia The **intelligentsia** in a country or community are the most educated people there, especially those interested in the arts, philosophy, and politics.

intelligible (intelligibly) If something is **intelligible**, it can be understood. *Banks need to present complex financial information more intelligibly to their customers.*

intend If you **intend** to do something, you have decided or planned to do it. ◇ If you **intend** something to happen or to have a particular effect or function, that is what you have planned. *...moves intended to stop the violence.* ◇ **Intended** is used to describe things which are meant to happen or be created. *Sanctions will take time to have their full intended effect... ...the intended high-speed rail link.* ◇ If something is **intended** for a particular person, they are meant to have it. ◇ If something is **intended** for a particular use, that is what is supposed to happen to it. *...seed stocks intended for next season's planting.*

intense (intensely, intensity) ❑ **Intense** is used to describe things which are very powerful or extreme. *Media interest was intense... ...intense heat... ...an intensely competitive market.* You can talk about the **intensity** of things like these. *...rains of monsoon intensity.* ◇ An **intense** light is

extremely bright.
❑ If you call a person **intense**, you mean they are very serious and do not show much sense of humour.

intensify (intensifies, intensifying, intensified; intensification) If something is **intensified**, the level of activity in it is increased. *...efforts to intensify agriculture... ...intensified fighting... Any intensification of sanctions could bring serious hardship.*

intensity See **intense**.

intensive (intensively) ❑ An **intensive** activity involves a great concentration of energy, resources, or people on one task. *...an intensive advertising campaign... He has been lobbied intensively by various factions.*
❑ **Intensive care** is extremely thorough care provided for seriously ill people in hospital.

intent (intently) ❑ **Intent** is used with a similar meaning to 'intention'. *It was our intent to provide a general-purpose research facility.* ◇ In law, **intent** is the intention to commit a crime. *A man will appear in court on charges of possessing illegal firearms with the intent to endanger life... He admitted communicating false information with intent.*
❑ If you are **intent** on doing something, you are determined to do it. ◇ If you are **intent** on what someone is saying, you are paying close attention to it. *She listened intently.*
❑ **To all intents and purposes** means something is not exactly true, but is true in all important respects.

intention If it is your **intention** to do something, you are planning to do it. ◇ If you say you have **no intention** of doing something, you mean you definitely will not do it.

intentional (intentionally) If something you do is **intentional**, you do it deliberately. *She said her family was being intentionally victimised.*

inter (interring, interred) When a dead body is **interred**, it is buried.

inter- is used to form words which describe something as existing or happening between similar things or groups of people. For example, inter-governmental relations are relations between governments. Some words beginning with 'inter' can also be spelled without a hyphen after the 'r'. For example, 'inter-governmental' can be spelled 'intergovernmental'. *...intercontinental flights... ...intercommunal tension... ...inter-party talks... ...the inter-war years.*

inter alia (*pron:* ay-lee-a) means 'among other things'. *The company has filed a complaint against its American distributor, alleging, inter alia, breach of contract, copyright infringement and negligence.*

inter-city trains are fast trains travelling between major towns and cities.

interact (interaction) If people **interact** or there is **interaction** between them, they co-operate or exchange ideas. ◇ If one thing **interacts** with another, the two things react together and affect each other.

interactive You say a computer program is **interactive** when it involves communication between the computer and the user, with, for example, the computer asking questions and not just obeying instructions. **Interactive** is used to talk about other machines or systems which the user can communicate with in this way. *...interactive television.*

interbreed (interbreeding, interbred) When plants or animals of different groups **interbreed**, they produce offspring combining the characteristics of both groups; this is called **interbreeding**. Similarly, you can talk about people from different societies **interbreeding**. *Farmers spreading across Europe would have interbred with the people they were overrunning.* ◇ **Interbreeding** is sometimes used to mean inbreeding.

intercede (interceding, interceded; intercession) If someone **intercedes** in a dispute, they try to settle it, by talking to both sides. Trying to settle a dispute like this is called **intercession**. ◇ If someone **intercedes** on behalf of someone in trouble, they try to help them by talking to someone in authority.

intercept (interception, interceptor) If you are **intercepted**, you are stopped when you are on your way somewhere. Similarly, a ship or road vehicle can be **intercepted**. *The authorities have strongly denounced the interception of the vessel.* ◇ When a plane **intercepts** another plane, it closes in on it and tries to destroy it. An attempt to destroy another plane like this is called an **interception**. An **interceptor** is a fighter aircraft designed to intercept and attack enemy planes.

intercession See **intercede**.

interchange (interchanging, interchanged; interchangeable, interchangeably) ❑ If there is an **interchange** of ideas or information between groups, they pass these things on to each other. ◇ If things can be **interchanged**, one can be substituted for the other without making any real difference. You say things like these are **interchangeable**. *In Kiev Ukrainian and Russian are often spoken interchangeably.*
❑ An **interchange** is a junction of interconnecting roads and bridges where a motorway meets another road.

intercom An **intercom** is a device consisting of a microphone and a loudspeaker, for talking to people in another room.

interconnect (interconnection) If things **interconnect** or are **interconnected**, they are joined together, so people or things can get from one to the other. **Interconnections** are links between things. *...interconnecting rooms... ...a maze of interconnected pipes, seals and valves.* ◇ If things which are happening are **interconnected**, they are related or linked in some way. *...interconnected economic and social problems... ...the interconnection of drug abuse and AIDS infection.*

intercourse If people have **intercourse** or sexual **intercourse**, they have sex. ◇ Social **intercourse** is meeting other people and having conversations with them.

intercut (intercutting, intercut) In a film, if one sequence or shot is **intercut** with another, the film keeps going backwards and forwards between them, suggesting that they are taking place at the same time.

interdependent (interdependence) If people or things are **interdependent**, they depend on each other. *...the heavy interdependence of the East European economies.*

interdiction is preventing a supply of something, especially illegal drugs, from reaching a place.

interdisciplinary is used to talk about things involving more than one academic subject. *...the Interdisciplinary Research Centre.*

interest (interesting, interestingly; interested) ❑ If something **interests** you or you are **interested** in it, you want to know more about it; you can also talk about your **interest** in it.

❑ You say something is **interesting** when it is unusual or exciting and attracts people's attention. *They had the ability to present complex matters lucidly and interestingly.* You can also say something is **of interest**. *As a warship, the Mary Rose was of extraordinary historical interest... The shift in American policy has added new interest to the talks.* ◇ You say **interestingly** when you are introducing a piece of information which you think is interesting and significant. *But interestingly, although the overwhelming majority felt that people should complain when they consider an advert offensive, most said that they themselves were unlikely to complain.*

❑ Your **interests** are the things you concern yourself with or enjoy doing. *Her varied interests range from horse-racing and farming to humanitarian causes.*

❑ If you are **interested** in doing something, you are keen to do it. If you **interest** someone else in something, you persuade them to do it or buy it. *...the CBI's attempt to interest the public in wider share ownership.*

❑ If you have an **interest** in something, you want it because you will benefit from it. *The United States and Israel have a long-term strategic interest in maintaining friendly regimes on the Red Sea coast.* A group of people who have an interest in something is called an **interest group**. ◇ If something is **in your interest** or **in your interests**, it is a good thing from your point of view. *He was satisfied it was in the child's best interests to remain in Britain.* If something is harmful to your **interests**, it could have bad effects for you in the future.

❑ If something is done **in the interests** of a particular objective, it is done to try and achieve that objective. *They were not afraid to try economic experiments, even elements of a market economy, in the interests of greater efficiency.*

❑ If a person or large organization has **interests** in a type of business, they own shares or companies in it. *The company may float off its leisure and hotel interests.*

❑ An **interested** party or group of people is affected by or involved in the situation you are talking about. *He is due to hold meetings with other interested bodies.*

❑ **Interest** is a sum of money paid as a percentage of a larger sum which has been borrowed or invested. You receive interest on money you invest and pay interest on money you borrow. An **interest-free** loan has no interest charged on it. See also **compound interest**, **simple interest**.

interface The **interface** between two groups or systems is the area in which they affect each other or have links with each other. *The centres will serve as an interface between businesses and the experts employed by universities... ...the interface between computers and camcorders.*

interfere (interfering, interfered; interference) ❑ If you say someone is **interfering** in something, you mean they have become involved in it and it has nothing to do with them. You call people like this **interfering**; you say their behaviour is **interference** or an **interference**.

❑ If someone **interferes** with a process or system, they damage it or stop it working properly; you call this an **interference** with the process or system.

❑ If you get **interference** when you are listening to the radio, you cannot hear a programme properly because you can hear another station broadcasting at the same time.

interferon An **interferon** is one of various types of protein produced by cells which stop a virus invading the body. Some interferons can stop cell growth and have been tested for use against cancer.

interim is used to describe (a) something established on a temporary basis. *...the interim government.* (b) the first part of something which will be given in full later. *...an interim payment.* ◇ **In the interim** means in the period between two events. *Almost a fifth of Americans who are released pending trial are re-arrested for crimes they commit in the interim.*

interior ❑ The **interior** of something is its inside part. *...the interior of the eye... ...the interior of the Earth.* ◇ The **interior** of a country is its central area, especially when this is a wild area away from its main centres of population.
❑ An **interior** minister or ministry deals with things within their own country, rather than things involving other countries.

interior decorator An **interior decorator** is a person or firm that decorates the insides of buildings.

interior designer An **interior designer** is a person who gives advice on the way the inside of a building can be decorated and furnished, and sometimes arranges for the work to be done.

interject (interjection) If you **interject**, you say something when someone else is speaking. What you say is called an **interjection**.

interlace (interlacing, interlaced) If two things are **interlaced**, they are joined together closely as if they are woven. *He sat with his fingers interlaced.*

interlink (interlinked) If things are **interlinked**, they are connected up to each other. *...a system of interlinked databases.*

interlock (interlocking, interlocked) If objects **interlock**, they fit together and are firmly joined to each other. ◇ If systems or plans **interlock**, they operate in conjunction with each other.

interlocutor (*pron:* in-ter-lok-yew-ter) Your **interlocutor** is the person you are having a conversation with.

interloper (*pron:* in-ter-lope-er) An **interloper** is a person who interferes in something, or is in a place where they are not supposed to be.

interlude An **interlude** is a short period of time when an activity or event stops for a while.

intermarry (intermarries, intermarrying, intermarried; intermarriage) If two social, racial, or religious groups **intermarry**, people from one group marry people from the other. When this happens, you say there is **intermarriage** between the groups.

intermediary (intermediaries) An **intermediary** is someone who tries to get two groups to come to an agreement, by negotiating with both sides.

intermediate An **intermediate** stage or level comes between two others. ◇ An **intermediate** course is for students who are no longer beginners at their subject but have not yet reached an advanced level.

interminable (interminably) If you say something is **interminable**, you mean it has been going on for a long time and it seems as if it will never end. *The negotiation drags interminably on.*

intermingle (intermingling, intermingled) If people or things **intermingle**, they move around among each other.

intermission An **intermission** is an interval between two parts of something like a film or play.

intermittent (intermittently) If something is **intermittent**, it happens occasionally rather than all the time. *Talks have been held intermittently over the years.*

intern (internment; internee) ❑ If someone is **interned**, they are put in prison or confined somewhere, because they are thought to be a danger to the country they are living in. This is usually because they are citizens of an enemy country, or because they are associated with a terrorist or revolutionary organization. Interning people is called **internment**; a person who is interned is called an **internee**.
❑ In the US, an **intern** (*pron:* in-tern) is a senior student or graduate doing supervised work, especially a medical student working in a hospital as a junior doctor.

internal (internally) **Internal** is used to talk about things inside a building, an object, or a person's body. *...an internal wall... This condition makes you more liable to bleed internally.* ◇ **Internal** is also used to talk about things happening inside a country or organization, which do not involve other countries or organizations. *The two countries had pledged not to interfere in each other's internal affairs... This fragmentation has begun to affect the parties internally.*

internal combustion engine An **internal combustion engine** is an engine with one or more cylinders which creates energy by burning fuel inside the cylinders. Most road vehicles have an engine like this.

internalize (internalizing, internalized) (*can be spelled with an 's' instead of a 'z'*) If you **internalize** something like a belief or set of values, it becomes a part of your attitude or way of thinking.

international (internationally) **International** is used to talk about things involving more than one country. *...an international conference... ...internationally recognised boundaries.* **International relations** are the relationships between countries. ◇ In sport, an **international** is a match between teams from different countries. A player who plays in one of these matches is also called an **international**.

internationalise See internationalize.

internationalism is the belief that countries should co-operate with one another and try to understand each other better.

internationalize (internationalizing, internationalized) (*can be spelled with an 's' instead of a 'z'*) If something to do with a country is **internationalized**, other countries become involved in it. *Internationalizing the conflict could spread the war beyond Yugoslav borders.*

internecine (*pron:* in-ter-nee-sine) An **internecine** conflict is one which causes suffering and destruction to both sides.

internment (internee) See intern.

interpersonal is used to talk about people's ability to communicate with other people. *...interpersonal skills.*

interplay The **interplay** between things is the way they affect or influence each other.

Interpol is an international police organization which co-ordinates national police forces in their fight against international crime.

interpose (interposing, interposed) If you **interpose** something between two people or things, you place it between them.

interpret (interpreting, interpreted; interpretation, interpreter) ❑ If you **interpret** what someone says or does in a particular way, you decide that is its meaning or significance. *The protest may be interpreted as a strong challenge to the authority of the government... There are two distinct interpretations of the purpose of his visit.* ◇ If you **interpret** something like a set of figures or the result of an experiment, you say what it shows or proves. Similarly, people can **interpret** things like dreams or religious writings. *...an interpretation of the Koran.*
   ❑ When an actor **interprets** a part or a musician **interprets** a piece of music, he or she performs it in a particular way. When an actor is famous for playing certain roles, you can call him or her an **interpreter** of those roles. Similarly, a musician can be called an **interpreter** of a type of music. *...one of the greatest interpreters of Wagner.*
   ❑ If you **interpret** what someone is saying, you immediately translate it into another language, for the benefit of someone who does not speak the first language. An **interpreter** is someone who does this as their job.

interpretative is used to talk about things which provide an interpretation of something. *...interpretative notes.*

interpreter See interpret.

interpretive means the same as 'interpretative'.

interregnum (plural: interregnums or interregna) An **interregnum** is a period of time between the end of one ruler's reign and the beginning of the next one's.

interrelate (interrelating, interrelated; interrelation) If two things are **interrelated** or there is an **interrelation** between them, there are connections between them or they have an effect on each other. *...the interrelation between law and morality.*

interrogate (interrogating, interrogated; interrogation, interrogator) If someone **interrogates** you, they question you thoroughly, to get information from you. Questioning someone like this is called **interrogation**; the person doing it is called an **interrogator**.

interrupt (interruption) If someone **interrupts** you, they say or shout something while you are speaking. *He was subjected to a stream of interruptions.* ◇ If something **interrupts** something else, it stops it for a time. *His study of French and German was interrupted by the Second World War... The game continued without further interruption.*

intersect (intersection) If lines **intersect**, they cross each other. Similarly, roads can **intersect**. An **intersection** is a place where roads cross.

intersperse (interspersing, interspersed) If something is **interspersed** with other things, these things occur in it here and there. *...bouts of imprisonment interspersed with moments of freedom.* Similarly, you can **intersperse** one thing with another. *He has interspersed negotiations with his legal advisers with media interviews.*

interstate In the US, an **interstate** is a main road running through several states. ◇ **Interstate** is also used to talk about things which happen between states. *...interstate banking.*

interstellar is used to talk about things which exist or happen between stars. *...interstellar travel.*

intertwine (intertwining, intertwined) If two things are **intertwined**, they are threaded through each other or wrapped around each other. ◇ If things like systems are **intertwined**, there are many connections between them.

interval ❑ An **interval** is a period of time between two events or dates. *...a short interval of industrial peace... ...an interval of 25 years.* ◇ If something happens **at intervals**, it happens from time to time. ◇ An **interval** is also a short break during a play, film, or concert.
   ❑ If things are placed **at intervals**, they are placed along something with gaps between them. *To ensure that the footpaths are not washed away in winter storms, water gullies are built at regular intervals.*
   ❑ In music, an **interval** is the difference in pitch between two notes.

intervene (intervening, intervened; intervention) ❑ If someone **intervenes** in a situation, they become involved in it and try to change it, usually to help someone else. Becoming involved in a situation like this is called **intervention** or an **intervention**. *Perhaps a personal intervention by the President might prevent bloodshed.* ◇ If an event **intervenes**, it happens unexpectedly and stops something happening.
   ❑ The **intervening** period between two events is the time between them. *Great progress had been made during the intervening fifteen months.*

interventionism (interventionist) **Interventionism** is a government's policy when it intervenes either in the affairs of other countries or in the economic affairs of its own country. A policy like this is called **interventionist**.

interview (interviewer, interviewee) ❑ When a journalist or broadcaster **interviews** someone, he or she asks them questions about their work, their achievements, or their opinions. The conversation they have is called an **interview**. A person who interviews people on TV or radio is called an **interviewer**.
   ❑ If an employer **interviews** you for a job or gives you an **interview**, he or she asks you questions, to see if you are suitable for the job. People being interviewed for a job are called **interviewees**. ◇ If the police **interview** someone, they question them about a crime.

interweave (interweaving, interwove, have interwoven) If two things **interweave** or are **interwoven**, they are threaded through each other or wrapped round each other. ◇ If you say things like systems are **interwoven**, you mean there are many connections between them.

intestate If someone dies **intestate**, they die without having made a will.

intestine (intestinal) Your **intestines** or **intestine** is the tube which carries food from your stomach to your bowels. **Intestinal** is used to talk about things to do with the intestines. *...an intestinal tumour.*

intimacy (intimacies) When there is **intimacy** between people, they have a very close relationship. **Intimacies** are things people do together and say to each other when they have a close relationship.

intimate (intimately; intimating, intimated, intimation) ❑ If two people are **intimate** or have an **intimate** relationship, they are very good friends. You can call someone's close friends their **intimates**. ◇ You also say people are **intimate** when they have a sexual relationship with each other.

❑ **Intimate** is used to describe things which are very personal and private. ...*the most intimate aspects of her personal life.* ◇ If you call a place like a restaurant **intimate**, you mean it is small and cosy.

❑ If you have an **intimate** knowledge of something, you know it in great detail. *As a boy, I knew Palermo intimately.* ◇ An **intimate** link or connection between things is a very close one. *There is an intimate connection between a healthy economy and a healthy environment.*

❑ If you **intimate** (*pron:* in-ti-mate) something, you suggest it is true without actually saying so. Suggestions made like this are called **intimations**. ◇ If you have an **intimation** or **intimations** of something, you become aware that it is happening, or will happen in the future. *The actuaries said they had no intimation of any irregularities in the schemes' assets.*

intimidate (intimidating, intimidated; intimidation, intimidatingly) If someone **intimidates** you, they frighten you by making threats, often to get you to do what they want. *Journalists have complained of police harassment and intimidation.* ◇ If you find someone or something **intimidating**, they make you nervous and lose confidence in yourself; you can also say you are **intimidated** by them. *These products can appear intimidatingly complex.*

intimidatory behaviour is meant to intimidate people.

into is used to say something is put inside something else. ◇ If something gets **into** a substance, it enters it and becomes part of it. *The substances get into drinking water in a variety of ways.*

❑ If you put money **into** a bank, you leave it there for safekeeping.

❑ If you go **into** a building, you go inside. Similarly, you can get **into** a vehicle. ◇ If you fly or sail **into** a place, you arrive there by plane or ship.

❑ If you get **into** a piece of clothing, you put it on.

❑ If you bump or crash **into** something, you collide with it.

❑ If someone or something gets **into** a state or situation, they are affected that way. *The whole city was plunged into darkness... Britain should avoid getting sucked into military involvement.* ◇ If something is changed **into** something else, it becomes that thing. *Cinemas were turned into bingo halls.*

❑ An investigation **into** a subject or event is concerned with it. ...*research into fish farming.*

❑ **Into** is used to say how long something goes on for. *Officials argued into the small hours over the draft final declaration.* ◇ **Into** is also used to say how much of a period of time has passed. *A month into the financial year, the £3.5 billion fund is already half gone.*

❑ **Into** is used to say how many parts are created when something is divided or split up. *The estate has been split into five areas.*

❑ If you are **into** something, you are very interested in it or involved with it.

intolerable (intolerably) If something is **intolerable**, it is so bad people cannot tolerate or accept it. *The tunnel became intolerably hot.*

intolerant (intolerance) **Intolerant** people disapprove of behaviour and opinions which are different from their own. ...*intolerant attitudes... ...religious intolerance.*

intonation Your **intonation** is the way your voice rises and falls in pitch when you speak. ◇ When music is being performed, the **intonation** of the singers or players is how well they keep to the correct pitch.

intone (intoning, intoned) If you **intone** something, you speak or recite it slowly and clearly, without changing the pitch of your voice very much.

intoxicant An **intoxicant** is a substance like alcohol which affects your behaviour and judgement. ◇ In medicine, an **intoxicant** is a substance like a poison which has a harmful effect on your body processes.

intoxicated (intoxicating; intoxication) If someone is **intoxicated**, they are drunk or under the influence of drugs. **Intoxication** is being in this state. **Intoxicating** drinks are capable of making people drunk; you can also say they have an **intoxicating** effect. ◇ If you are **intoxicated** by something, it makes you so excited that you behave in an uncontrolled or silly way. If something has this effect on you, you can say it is **intoxicating**. ...*a young climber intoxicated with danger... ...the intoxication of power.*

intra- is used to form words which describe something within or inside something else. For example, intra-European trade is trade carried on inside Europe. Some words beginning with 'intra' can be spelled without a hyphen after the 'a'. ...*intramuscular fat.*

intra-uterine device See IUD.

intracranial is used to talk about things inside the skull. ...*an intracranial tumour.*

intractable (intractability) An **intractable** problem or situation is hard to solve or deal with. ...*the intractability of the present political crisis.* ◇ An **intractable** illness is hard to cure. ◇ An **intractable** person is stubborn and hard to influence or control.

intransigent (intransigence) If someone is **intransigent**, they refuse to change their behaviour or opinions. *The Australian Trade Minister is blaming EU intransigence for the present stalemate.*

intravenous (*pron:* in-tra-vee-nuss) (intravenously) **Intravenous** treatment involves giving blood, food, or medicine to sick people through their veins by a drip. *She is being treated intravenously with antibiotics.* ◇ An **intravenous** drug user is someone who injects addictive drugs into their veins.

intrepid An **intrepid** person is brave and daring.

intricate (intricately; intricacy, intricacies) If something like a design is **intricate**, it has many small parts or details, often as a result of skilful artistic work. ...*intricately quilted satin.* ◇ If a system is **intricate**, it works in a complicated way. You can talk about the **intricacies** of a system like this.

intrigue (intriguer; intriguing, intrigued; intriguingly) ❑ **Intrigue** (*pron:* in-treeg) is making secret plans, often aimed against other people. An **intrigue** is a plan like this; the person making it can be called an **intriguer**.

❑ If something **intrigues** you (*pron:* in-treegs) or you are **intrigued** by it, you are fascinated by it and curious about it. You can say something like this is **intriguing**. You say **intriguingly** when you are mentioning a piece of information which you think is curious and interesting. *Intriguingly, malaria probably began to flourish when Africa's population started to grow 5,000 or so years ago.*

intrinsic (intrinsically) The **intrinsic** qualities of something are the ones it has because of what it is. *Science is intrinsically sceptical.* ◇ If something has **intrinsic** value, it is valuable because of what it is, rather than because of its connection with something else.

introduce (introducing, introduced; introduction) ❏ If you **introduce** someone to someone else, you tell them each other's name, so they can get to know each other. This is called making an **introduction.** ◇ If you **introduce** someone to something, you tell them about it or get them involved in it for the first time. The first time someone becomes involved in something can be called their **introduction** to it. *60% of all sailing enthusiasts were first introduced to the sport by family or friends.*
❏ When something is **introduced** in a place, it is done or used there for the first time. *...the introduction of 20mph zones in residential areas.* ◇ When the government **introduces** a bill in the House of Commons, they present it formally so it can be discussed and voted on.
❏ The **introduction** to a book is a part at the beginning which tells you what the book is all about.

introductory remarks are made at the beginning of a talk or speech, to give some idea of what is to follow. ◇ An **introductory** book or course gives you a general idea of a subject, which you can then study in more detail if you wish.

introspective (introspection) **Introspective** people spend a lot of time examining their own thoughts, ideas, and feelings. Behaviour like this is called **introspection.**

introvert (introverted; introversion) If you say someone is **introverted** or an **introvert,** you mean they spend more time thinking about their own feelings than about the world around them, and often find it difficult to talk to people or make friends. Similarly, you can say countries or institutions are **introverted** when they are wrapped up in their own affairs and do not show much interest in anything else. Being wrapped up in your own affairs is called **introversion.**

intrude (intruding, intruded; intrusion) If something **intrudes** on your way of life, it has an unwelcome or unpleasant effect on it. You say something which has this effect is an **intrusion.** ◇ If someone **intrudes** on you, they disturb you when you are in a private place. You call this an **intrusion.**

intruder An **intruder** is someone who goes into a place where they are not supposed to be, often to steal things.

intrusion See intrude.

intrusive (intrusiveness) You say something is **intrusive** when it has an unwelcome or unpleasant effect on your way of life. *...press intrusiveness.*

intuition (intuitive, intuitively) An **intuition** is a feeling you have about something, which is not backed up by any evidence or proof. The part of your mind which gives you feelings like this is called your **intuition.** You say feelings of this kind are **intuitive.** *He intuitively understood that his party had had enough of the ERM.*

Inuit (pron: in-yoo-it) **Inuits** are Eskimos from North America or Greenland. They themselves prefer the name 'Inuit' to 'Eskimo', which they find offensive.

inundate (inundating, inundated; inundation) If you are **inundated** with things, you receive so many you cannot deal with them all. *The programme has been inundated*

with calls since its telephone lines were opened yesterday morning. ◇ If an area of land is **inundated,** it becomes covered with water, for example when a river bursts its banks. *...a rise of sea-levels which would lead to the inundation of many major centres of population.*

inure (pron: in-yoor) (inuring, inured) If you become **inured** to something unpleasant, you become used to it, so that it no longer shocks or upsets you. *Doctors become inured to death.*

invade (invading, invaded; invasion, invader) ❏ If an army **invades** a country, it enters it by force. *...the 1968 Soviet invasion of Czechoslovakia.* The soldiers invading a country can be called **invaders.** An invading army is sometimes called an **invader.** *The territorial defence forces would mobilise the population to wage an all-out partisan war against an invader.*
❏ When people or animals arrive in large numbers in a place, you can say they **invade** it, especially when their arrival is unwelcome. *The craze for mountain bikes has meant that parks are invaded by hordes of bikers... The locals were on the look-out for a hippie invasion.* ◇ If someone **invades** your privacy, they disturb you when you want to be alone. You call this an **invasion** of your privacy.

invalid (invaliding, invalided; invalidity) ❏ An **invalid** is someone who is very ill or disabled and needs to be cared for by someone else. ◇ If someone is **invalided** out of the armed forces, they have to leave because of wounds or ill-health.
❏ If something like an agreement is declared **invalid** (pron: in-val-id), it is decided that it is illegal because it has not been made in the correct way. Similarly, a marriage can be declared **invalid.** An election can be declared **invalid** if it is found it has not been carried out properly. You can talk about the **invalidity** of any of these things. ◇ If something like a pass or type of currency becomes **invalid,** it can no longer be used. ◇ If a result or argument is **invalid,** it is not acceptable because it is based on a mistake.

invalidate (invalidating, invalidated) If a fault in an agreement **invalidates** the agreement, it prevents it being legal. Similarly, a mistake in an experiment or line of reasoning can **invalidate** the result.

invalidity See invalid.

invalidity benefit is a weekly benefit which you can apply for if you have been off work through illness for more than six months. It is proposed to replace this with a new 'incapacity benefit' in April 1995.

invaluable If you say someone or something is **invaluable,** you are emphasizing how useful they are.

invariable (invariably) If something is **invariable,** it never changes. **Invariable** is also used to describe people who do not change in their views or habits. *...an invariable supporter of government philosophy.* ◇ If something **invariably** happens, it always happens in particular circumstances. *Economic liberalisation invariably leads to demands for political reform.*

invasion See invade.

invasive surgery or medicine involves entering the body in some way, for example by cutting it open or inserting something into it. *...invasive methods of diagnosis.*
❏ **Invasive** is also used to describe things which keep getting into a place where you do not want them. *...invasive weed roots.*

invective is unpleasant and sarcastic things said about someone.

inveigh (*pron:* in-**vay**) If you **inveigh** against something, you criticize it strongly.

inveigle (*pron:* in-**vay**-gl *or* in-**vee**-gl) (inveigling, inveigled) If you **inveigle** someone into doing something, you cleverly persuade them to do it when they do not really want to.

invent (invention, inventor) ❑ If you **invent** something, you are the first person to think of it or make it. The thing you invent is called an **invention**; you are called its in**ventor**. ◇ **Invention** is the ability to invent things or to have clever and original ideas. *...the richness of Purcell's musical invention.*

❑ If you **invent** a story or excuse, you make it up, hoping people will believe it is true. A story or excuse like this is called an **invention**.

inventive (inventively, inventiveness) An **inventive** person is good at inventing things, or has clever and original ideas. *This freedom allows us to express ourselves inventively... ...her unflagging energy and inventiveness.* You can also call someone's ideas or creations **inventive**.

inventor See invent.

inventory (*pron:* **in**-ven-tree) (inventories) An **inventory** is a written list of the things an organization owns, or of the things in a room or building.

inverse (inversely) If there is an **inverse** relationship between two things, one of them decreases as the other increases. *Stress is inversely related to job satisfaction.*

inversion If there is an **inversion** of something, it is changed so it is the opposite way round to the usual way. *...a curious inversion whereby the outlaws came to represent something more national than the state they defied.*

invert (inverted) ❑ If you **invert** something, you turn it upside down or back to front.

❑ An **inverted snob** is an upper-class or well-educated person who pretends to like the things working class or uneducated people are supposed to like. Behaviour like this is called **inverted snobbery**.

invertebrate An **invertebrate** is a creature without a spine, for example an insect, a worm, or an octopus. Some invertebrates, for example crabs, have an external skeleton.

inverted commas are the punctuation marks ' ' or " ". They are used to show where speech or a quotation begins and ends.

invest (investment, investor) ❑ If you **invest** in a company, you buy shares in it, because you think you will make a profit from it. A person who does this is called an **investor**. You can also **invest** in things like government securities and national savings. The money you invest in something is called an **investment**. If you say something is an **investment** or a good **investment**, you mean it is likely to make a profit.

❑ If a government **invests** in something, it spends money on it because it will eventually benefit the country's economy. *We must invest in new and improved roads to ensure efficient access to key markets.*

❑ If you spend a lot of time trying to make something successful, you can say you **invest** time in it. *This type of course demands a considerable investment of GPs' time.*

❑ If someone is **invested** with certain rights or respon-

sibilities, they are given them legally or officially. *France and Germany want to invest all the Community bodies with considerably more authority.* ◇ If someone is **invested** with a title or honour, they are given it at a special ceremony.

investigate (investigating, investigated; investigation, investigator) If someone **investigates** something or conducts an **investigation** into it, they find out all the facts about it, to try get at the truth. *Police said they were investigating the incident.* A person who investigates something is sometimes called an **investigator**.

investigative activities involve finding out the facts about something. *...investigative journalism.*

investigator See investigate.

investigatory means the same as 'investigative'.

investiture An **investiture** is a ceremony in which someone is given an official title or position. *...Edward VIII's investiture as Prince of Wales.*

investment (investor) See invest.

inveterate is used to say someone has been doing something for a long time, and is unlikely to get out of the habit of doing it. *...an inveterate gambler.*

invidious If you are in an **invidious** position, whatever you do will be judged to be wrong. *Channel 4 has been placed in the invidious position of having to choose between breaking the law and putting individuals' lives in danger.* ◇ An **invidious** comparison or choice is unfair or pointless, because the things in question cannot really be compared, or because they are equally bad or good.

invigilate (invigilating, invigilated; invigilator) If someone **invigilates** an exam, they supervise the people taking it, make sure it starts and finishes on time, and try to prevent cheating. A person who does this is called an in**vigilator**.

invigorate (invigorating, invigorated) If something **invigorates** you, it makes you feel more energetic. *...the invigorating northern air.* ◇ If a system or activity is **invigorated**, it is made more lively or successful.

invincible (invincibility) If someone or something is **invincible**, they cannot be beaten. *Furtado demonstrated her seeming invincibility by winning yet another race.*

inviolable (inviolability) If you say something like a right is **inviolable**, you mean it cannot or must not be taken away. *...the inviolability of human life.*

inviolate If something is **inviolate**, it has not been harmed, or cannot be harmed. *He still believes his organization to be inviolate.*

invisible (invisibly, invisibility) ❑ If something is **invisible**, you cannot see it, because it is hidden or because it is too small to be seen with the naked eye. *A piano played invisibly behind the scenes... Our safety depended on my invisibility.* ◇ In stories, **invisible** people or things are present but cannot be seen by anyone.

❑ **Invisible** earnings are the money a country makes from services like banking or tourism, rather than by producing goods. *...invisible exports.*

invite (inviting, invited; invitation, invitingly) ❑ If you **invite** someone to something like a party or a meal, you ask them to come. This is called making an **invitation**. If you ask someone in writing, the letter or note you send is also called an **invitation**. ◇ If you **invite** someone to do something, you formally ask them to do it. *He has accepted an invitation to become honorary president.*

❑ If you say something could **invite** a particular reaction, you mean people might react to it in that way. *It was out of the question for them to indulge in transactions which could invite suspicion.* ◇ If you say something **invites** comparison with something else, you mean it is good enough to be compared to it. *Glasgow now invites favourable comparisons with London and Edinburgh.*

❑ If something **invites** danger or trouble or is an **invitation** to it, it makes it more likely. ◇ If you say a careless or silly action is an **open invitation** to a criminal, you mean it makes it easy for them to commit a crime.

❑ If you say something is **inviting,** you mean it is attractive and desirable. *The democratic future beckoned invitingly.*

invocation See invoke.

invoice (invoicing, invoiced) An **invoice** is a document listing goods or services you have received, and saying how much you owe for them. If someone **invoices** you, they send you an invoice.

invoke (invoking, invoked; invocation) ❑ If someone **invokes** something like a law, they make use of it to get what they want. This is called an **invocation** of the law. ◇ If someone **invokes** something like a saying or idea, they mention it to justify their actions, or to persuade people to do something. *The President, once again invoking 'people power', is asking for a referendum to overrule the Senate.*

❑ If something **invokes** a feeling or memory, it makes you experience it. *German history was aggressive and nationalistic and invoked fear in all its neighbours.* Similarly, something can **invoke** a reaction. *This would inevitably invoke protests from Brussels.*

❑ If someone **invokes** a god, they appeal to him or her for help. An appeal like this is called an **invocation.**

involuntary (involuntarily) If you make an **involuntary** movement, you do it suddenly and unintentionally, because you are unable to control yourself. *His right hand clenched involuntarily.* ◇ **Involuntary** is also used to describe things people are made to do or be against their will. *Refugees found to be economic migrants will be involuntarily repatriated... De Gaulle was an involuntary exile, dependent on British hospitality.*

involve (involving, involved; involvement) ❑ When you talk about what something **involves,** you are talking about what it is concerned with, what it is about, or what it consists of. *...a property scandal involving the sale of holiday homes in Spain... This year's season involves 94 performances.* ◇ The things **involved** in taking on a job or responsibility are the things which go along with it, and which cannot be ignored or neglected. *He was too young to accept the responsibilities that rearing children involved... ...the labour costs involved in tearing out the old material.*

❑ The people or things **involved** in an event are the ones taking part in it or affected by it. *...demonstrations involving hundreds of thousands of people... ...incidents involving French vessels.*

❑ If you **involve** yourself in something which is happening or get **involved** in it, you take part in it. *The plan envisages the active involvement of the United Nations in the peace process.* You can also **involve** someone else in something. *He doesn't involve me in things I hate.*

❑ If you are **involved** with someone or have an in**volvement** with them, you have some sort of relationship with them, especially one in which you are trying to achieve something together. *In 1983 I was involved with the composer Dennis King in an adaptation of The Admirable Bashville.* ◇ You also say someone is **involved** with someone else when they are having an affair with them.

❑ If a situation or activity is **involved,** it is very complicated.

invulnerable (invulnerability) If someone or something is **invulnerable,** they cannot be harmed or damaged. *One day we may have genes built into our cells which will make our bodies invulnerable to attack by viruses... ...the proven accuracy and invulnerability of laser-guided bombs.*

inward (inwards, inwardly) ❑ Your **inward** thoughts or feelings are ones which you do not express or show to other people. *Inwardly seething, he went back into the changing room.*

❑ If something moves or faces **inward** or **inwards,** it moves or faces towards the inside or centre of something.

❑ **Inward-looking** people or countries are more interested in themselves than in developing relations with other people or countries.

iodine (*pron: eye-oh-deen*) is a dark-coloured substance used in medicine and photography.

ion (*pron: eye-on*) **Ions** are electrically charged atoms.

ionize (ionizing, ionized; ionization) (*can be spelled with an 's' instead of a 'z'*) If a substance **ionizes** or is **ionized,** the atoms it consists of are changed into ions. This process is called **ionization.**

ionizer (*or ioniser*) An **ionizer** is a device which sends out negative ions. Some people keep an ionizer in a room, believing it makes the air more healthy.

ionosphere The **ionosphere** is an area of ionized air in the Earth's upper atmosphere which reflects radio waves.

iota (*pron: eye-oh-ta*) An **iota** of something is an extremely small amount of it. **Iota** is often used in sentences with 'not' in them, for emphasis. *The allies have confirmed that they will not budge one iota from the commitments they have undertaken.*

IOU An **IOU** is a written note promising to pay back some money which is owed. IOU is short for 'I owe you'.

ipso facto means 'by that very fact'. You use it to say something automatically follows from the thing you have just mentioned. *A law whose operations cannot be scrutinised by any court is, ipso facto, bad law.*

IQ Your **IQ** or **intelligence quotient** is your level of intelligence, measured by a special test.

IRA The **IRA** or **Irish Republican Army** is an organization of Irish nationalists who are committed to a united independent Ireland, and have at various times been prepared to use violence to achieve this.

irascible An **irascible** person becomes angry very easily.

irate If you are **irate,** you are very angry.

ire is anger.

iridescent If something is **iridescent,** it has many bright colours which seem to keep changing.

iridium (*pron: eye-rid-ee-um*) is a very hard yellowish-white metallic element which occurs in platinum ores. It is used in alloys.

iris (irises) The **iris** is the round coloured part of your eye. ◇ **Irises** are flowers with long pointed leaves and large purple, blue, yellow, or white petals.

Irish is used to talk about people and things in or from Ireland. *...Irish affairs.* ◇ The **Irish** are the Irish people. ◇ **Irish** is a language spoken in Ireland.

Irishman (Irishwoman) An **Irishman** or **Irishwoman** is a person who comes from Ireland.

irk (irksome) If something **irks** you, it irritates or annoys you. You say something like this is **irksome**.

iron (ironing, ironed) ❑ **Iron** is a strong hard metallic element found mainly in rocks. It is widely used in making tools, building, and engineering. It is also an important component of blood.

❑ **Iron** is used to describe the behaviour of people who show great determination and self-control in difficult situations. *...his followers' iron discipline.* ◇ **Iron** is also used to talk about people in power exercising rigid control over the people under them, especially when they do it in a harsh or cruel way. *Hoxha ruled Albania with an iron grip... ...the iron-fist methods employed by the security forces.*

❑ An **iron** is an electrical device with a heated flat metal base which is rubbed over clothes to make them smooth. If you **iron** clothes, you remove the creases from them using an iron. ◇ If you **iron out** minor difficulties or problems, you succeed in getting rid of them.

❑ An **iron** is also one of a set of nine golf clubs with angled heads for making different kinds of strokes.

❑ **Irons** are chains put round prisoners' ankles to stop them escaping.

Iron Age The **Iron Age** was the phase of human history which followed the Bronze Age. It began in the Middle East about 1500BC and arrived in Britain about 700BC. It was the period when iron tools and weapons were first made.

Iron Curtain The border between the former USSR and its allies and Western Europe used to be called the **Iron Curtain**. People talked about things happening **behind the Iron Curtain**.

iron-grey hair is dark grey.

ironic (ironical, ironically) See **irony**.

ironing board An **ironing board** is a long narrow cloth-covered board for ironing clothes on.

ironmonger (ironmongery) An **ironmonger** or **ironmonger's** is a shop selling tools, nails, pans, and other things for doing jobs around the house or garden. **Ironmongery** is the things sold in an ironmonger's.

ironwork is iron objects like gates and balconies made in a skilful and attractive way.

ironworks An **ironworks** is a factory where iron is smelted or cast.

irony (*pron:* eye-ron-nee) (ironies; ironic, ironical, ironically) ❑ **Irony** is a form of humour, or an indirect way of conveying meaning, in which you say something in such a way that people realize you are joking, or really mean the opposite of what you say. You call remarks like this **ironic** or **ironical**.

❑ An **irony** is a situation involving two factors which contrast in an unexpected or amusing way. You talk about the **irony** of a situation like this, or say it is **ironic** or **ironical**. *He has been making a killing in the marriage bureau business, which is mildly ironic seeing that his dearest wish is to get married himself and produce an heir.* You say **ironically** when you are mentioning a situation like this. *Ironically, Hendrix's hard guitar-work won him almost instant fame in Britain and France, rather than in his own country.*

irradiate (irradiating, irradiated; irradiation) If you are **irradiated**, you are exposed to a large amount of radiation. ◇ If food is **irradiated**, it is exposed to radiation to kill bacteria and make it safe to eat for a longer period of time. This process is called **irradiation**.

irrational (irrationally, irrationality) If you call something **irrational** or talk about its **irrationality**, you mean it has not been thought out in a logical way. *Central planning has left many enterprises irrationally organised.*

irreconcilable If two opinions are **irreconcilable**, nobody could have both of them at the same time. Similarly, if two objectives are **irreconcilable**, they cannot both be achieved. *It was often said that democratic government and universal suffrage were irreconcilable.* ◇ An **irreconcilable** disagreement is so serious it cannot be settled.

irrecoverable If a bad situation is **irrecoverable**, it cannot be put right.

irredeemable (irredeemably) An **irredeemable** fault cannot be corrected. *...an irredeemably corrupt society.*

irredentism (*pron:* i-ri-dent-iz-um) (irredentist) **Irredentism** is a country's policy of regaining territory which once belonged to it, or is thought to have belonged to it. **Irredentist** is used to describe things to do with this policy.

irreducible If something is **irreducible**, it cannot be modified or made simpler. *...the irreducible complexity of human life.*

irrefutable If something is **irrefutable**, it cannot be denied or disproved. *...irrefutable arguments.*

irregular (irregularly; irregularity, irregularities) ❑ If something is **irregular**, it is not smooth or straight, or does not form a regular pattern. ◇ **Irregular** is also used to describe things which do not happen at regular intervals. *Pay comes irregularly to soldiers serving in areas remote from the capital.*

❑ **Irregular** is used to describe acts which break accepted rules or procedures. Acts like these can also be called **irregularities**. *The court was told that irregular payments were part of soccer routine... About half the results were cancelled because of electoral irregularities.*

❑ **Irregulars** are soldiers who fight in a war but do not belong to an official national army.

irrelevant (irrelevance; irrelevancy, irrelevancies) If something is **irrelevant** to what is being discussed or dealt with, it is not connected with it, or does not make any real difference to it. You can say something like this is an **irrelevance** or an **irrelevancy**. *He either ignored questions or gave irrelevant answers... The cabinet are splitting over irrelevancies.* ◇ You also say something is **irrelevant** when it might as well not exist, for all the difference it makes to what happens. Something like this can also be called an **irrelevance** or an **irrelevancy**. *His party's landslide victory in the elections makes a multi-party system something of an irrelevance.*

irreligious People who do not have a religion are sometimes called **irreligious**.

irremediable (*pron:* i-ri-mee-di-a-bl) (irremediably) If a situation is **irremediable**, it cannot be put right. *The party is irremediably corrupted.*

irreparable (*pron:* ir-rep-ir-a-bl) (irreparably) **Irreparable** damage cannot be put right. *The bank's reputation is* *irreparably tainted.*

irreplaceable If someone or something is **irreplaceable**, they are so special they cannot be replaced if they are lost or destroyed.

irrepressible (irrepressibly) **Irrepressible** people are lively and energetic, and never let things get them down. ...*an irrepressibly sprightly man.*

irreproachable (irreproachably) If you say someone's behaviour or character is **irreproachable**, you mean there is nothing anyone could find wrong with it. *He has done his job irreproachably.*

irresistible (irresistibly) ❑ You say someone or something is **irresistible** when you find them very attractive, entertaining, or amusing. *She found him irresistibly attractive.*
    ❑ If you have an **irresistible** urge to do something, you want to do it so much you cannot stop yourself. ◇ An **irresistible** force cannot be stopped or prevented. *The pressure on Olympic athletes to use drugs is becoming irresistible.*

irresolute (irresolution) If you are **irresolute**, you cannot decide what to do. Behaviour like this is called **irresolution.**

irrespective **Irrespective of** is used to say something is not taken into account when imposing a rule or deciding about something. *You pay the same fare irrespective of the length of the vehicle.*

irresponsible (irresponsibly, irresponsibility) If you call someone **irresponsible**, you mean they say or do things without considering their possible consequences. You can also call the things they say or do **irresponsible**. ...*irresponsible remarks... The owners resent the implication that they have behaved irresponsibly... He has been accused of incompetence and irresponsibility.*

irretrievable (irretrievably) If a situation or damage is **irretrievable**, it is so bad it cannot be put right. ...*an accusation that has irretrievably damaged his reputation.*

irreverent (irreverence) If someone is **irreverent**, they do not show the same respect for someone or something that other people do. *His irreverence for authority marks him out as a troublemaker.*

irreversible (irreversibly, irreversibility) If a decision or process is **irreversible**, it cannot be changed or stopped. *He went on to say that Romania was irreversibly set on the road to democracy... ...the irreversibility of the changes.* ◇ If damage or a bad situation is **irreversible**, it cannot be put right.

irrevocable (*pron:* ir-rev-oke-a-bl) (irrevocably) If something **irrevocable** happens or is done, you cannot afterwards change things back to the way they were before. *The union recognized that things had changed irrevocably.*

irrigate (irrigating, irrigated; irrigation) When land is **irrigated**, a system of ditches or pipes is introduced to make sure water reaches all parts of it. ...*an irrigation canal.*

irritable (irritably, irritability) Someone who is **irritable** is easily annoyed. *She shrugged irritably... He noted a marked increase in her irritability and aggression.*

irritant An **irritant** is something which keeps annoying someone. *For weeks the students blocked the main thoroughfare and were an extreme irritant to the government.* ◇ An **irritant** is also a substance which makes part of your body itch or feel sore.

irritate (irritating, irritated; irritatingly, irritation) If something **irritates** you or you feel **irritated** by it, it keeps annoying you. *He has an irritating habit of sweeping into meetings late... Computers remain irritatingly hard to connect with other brands.* You can talk about your **irritation** with something, or call it an **irritation**. *The proposal that strike ballots should be conducted by post is an irritation for the unions.* ◇ If something **irritates** part of your body, it makes it itch or feel sore.

is See **be**.

ISBN Every edition of a book printed in recent times has its own **ISBN** or **International Standard Book Number**. The ISBN is printed on the outside of the book, or inside near the front.

Islam (Islamic, Islamist) **Islam** is the Muslim religion, which teaches that Allah is the only God and that Mohammed is his prophet. **Islamic** is used to talk about things to do with Islam. ...*the teaching of Islamic history and culture.* ◇ An **Islamic** state is run on traditional Islamic principles, with religious leaders playing an important part in its affairs. **Islamic** movements are generally aimed at creating states like this. An **Islamist** is someone who is in favour of this kind of government.

island (islander) ❑ An **island** is a piece of land completely surrounded by water. Someone who lives on an island can be called an **islander**. ...*Faroe Islanders.* ◇ Any place can be called an **island** when it differs in some way from the area surrounding it. ...*proposals to create islands of heavily armed security in wealthier areas.*
    ❑ An **island** or **traffic island** is a raised area in the middle of a busy road where you can wait while crossing.

isle An **isle** is an island. Isle is used in the names of some islands. ...*Fair Isle.*

islet An **islet** is a very small island.

isobar An **isobar** is a line on a map joining points of equal atmospheric pressure.

isolate (isolating, isolated; isolation) ❑ If something **isolates** you or you **isolate** yourself, you become physically or socially separated from other people. *To counter isolation, workers are provided with special video screens enabling them to chat with co-workers.* ◇ If you are kept **in isolation**, you are kept away from other people.
    ❑ If you **isolate** people by your behaviour, you make them stop liking you or supporting you, because they do not approve of what you are doing.
    ❑ When a country or government is **isolated**, it is cut off politically from other countries or governments. ...*Albania's self-imposed isolation.*
    ❑ An **isolated** place is a long way away from any town or village.
    ❑ If a scientist **isolates** something, he or she separates it from other things, so it can be examined in detail. *They have been able to isolate the virus in laboratory conditions.*
    ❑ An **isolated** example or incident comes on its own and is not part of a general pattern. *They want to reassure people that it is an isolated mistake rather than a design fault... This was not an isolated case of racism.* ◇ If you do something **in isolation**, you do it on your own, rather than with other people.

isolationism (isolationist) **Isolationism** is a country's policy when it avoids becoming involved in relationships with other countries. **Isolationist** is used to talk about things to do with this policy; someone who favours isolationism is called an **isolationist**.

isosceles triangle (*pron:* ice-soss-ill-eez) An **isosceles tri-angle** has two sides of the same length.

isotherm An **isotherm** is a line on a map joining points of equal average temperature.

isotope Isotopes are forms of the same atom which have some different properties because they do not have the same number of neutrons.

issue (issuing, issued) ❑ An **issue** is something important which people are discussing or arguing about. *...the nuclear issue... ...the issue of women priests.* ◇ If you talk about what is at **issue**, you are saying what it is that needs to be discussed and settled. *The Home Secretary insisted that the problems of immigration were not the question at issue.* Similarly, you can say something is **the issue**. ◇ If you say someone is **making an issue** of something, you mean they are making a fuss about it.
   ❑ If you **take issue** with someone or **take issue** with what they say, you disagree with them.
   ❑ If someone **issues** a statement or warning, they make it formally or publicly. *The Peruvian government has issued a decree making such strikes illegal.* ◇ When something like a document is **issued,** it is officially produced and made available. You talk about the **issue** of something like this. *...a special issue of postage stamps.*
   ❑ An **issue** is an edition of a newspaper or magazine.
   ❑ If you are **issued** with something or it is **issued** to you, it is officially given to you. *Steel helmets were first issued to British troops on the Western Front.*
   ❑ If something **issues** from a place, it comes out of it. *A chorus of yells and cat calls issued from the audience.*
   ❑ If someone dies **without issue,** they have no living children, grandchildren, or other descendants at the time of their death.

isthmus (*pron:* iss-muss) (isthmuses) An **isthmus** is a strip of land with sea on either side, joining two large areas of land.

it is used to talk about an object, animal, or other thing which has already been mentioned. *Meat is cooked over a wood fire and potatoes are baked in it.* ◇ It is used to talk about a child whose sex is unknown, or to talk about any child, male or female. *You can usually see that the baby is responding when you play the sound to it.*
   ❑ It is used to talk about a situation you have just described or are about to describe. *The windows are traversed by a broad bar which makes it extremely awkward to see out.* ◇ It is used to talk about a statement which has just been mentioned. *The last time the Government said he was ill there was good reason to doubt it.*
   ❑ It is used to talk about things like the weather or the time. *It was raining hard... It is nine o'clock in the evening.*

IT See information technology.

it's is short for 'it is' or 'it has'. See also **its.**

Italian is used to talk about people and things in or from Italy. *...the Italian countryside.* ◇ An **Italian** is someone who comes from Italy. ◇ **Italian** is the main language spoken in Italy.

italics (italic) **Italics** are letters printed or written sloping to the right. They are often used to emphasize a word or sentence. The examples in this dictionary are printed in italics. **Italic** is used to describe writing like this. *...italic type.*

itch (itches, itching, itched; itchy) If you **itch** or a part of your body **itches,** you have an unpleasant feeling on your skin which makes you want to scratch. You can also say you are **itchy** or have an **itch.** ◇ If you are **itching** to do something or have an **itch** to do it, you are impatient to do it.

item An **item** is one of a collection or list of objects, for example one you are buying or selling. *There are 15 items up for sale.* ◇ An **item** is also one of a number of matters to be dealt with. *One of the main items on the agenda was independence for the province.* ◇ An **item** in a newspaper or magazine is a report or article.

itemize (itemizing, itemized) (*can be spelled with an 's' instead of a 'z'*) If you **itemize** something, you make a list of the things included in it. *...a fully itemized bill.*

iteration An **iteration** of something is a repetition of it.

itinerant (*pron:* eye-tin-er-ant) people travel around, living and working for short periods in different places. *...an itinerant preacher.*

itinerary (itineraries) An **itinerary** is a plan of a journey, showing the route and the places to be visited.

its is used to talk about something to do with an object, animal, child, or something else. *We liked the house and its position... As the child ages, its wishes must be taken into account... The touring company has never before included this particular ballet in its repertoire.* Note that when you use **its** like this, you do not write 'it's'. 'It's' is short for 'it is' or 'it has'.

itself ❑ You use **itself** to say something done by an object or substance affects that same object or substance. *For fertilisation to begin, a sperm has to attach itself to the outside of an egg cell.* You use **itself** in a similar way to talk about a baby, an animal, an organization, or anything else which can be referred to using 'it'. *The company has been marketing itself more vigorously lately.*
   ❑ You use **itself** after a word or phrase to make it clear that you are talking about the thing the word or phrase refers to. *In Athens itself, the decision was greeted with scenes of disbelief.*
   ❑ If you say something has a quality or effect **in itself,** you mean it has it on its own, without taking into account other things. *Getting the four parties to sit around the same table is being regarded as a worthwhile achievement in itself.*

ITV or **Independent Television** is a group of TV companies funded by advertising.

IUD An **IUD** or **intra-uterine device** is a contraceptive device, consisting of a piece of plastic or metal put inside a woman's womb. It is also known as the **coil.**

IVF or **in vitro fertilization** (*pron:* vee-troh) is a process in which an egg is taken from a woman, fertilized with a man's sperm in a laboratory, then returned to her body.

ivory is the valuable creamy-white bone which elephants' tusks are made of. It is often used to make ornaments. ◇ **Ivory** is also a creamy-white colour.
   ❑ When people talk about intellectuals living in an **ivory tower,** they mean they spend their lives cut off from reality and the problems of everyday life.

ivy is an evergreen plant which grows up trees and walls or along the ground.

Ivy League In the US, the **Ivy League** is a group of eight prestigious universities in the east of the country, including Yale and Harvard.

J j

jab (jabbing, jabbed) ❑ If you **jab** a pointed object somewhere, you push it there with a quick sudden movement. *Alan jabbed a finger at me.* ◇ If a boxer **jabs** his opponent, he hits him with a quick short punch. A punch like this is called a **jab.**

❑ A **jab** is also an injection. *...a flu jab.*

jabber (jabbering, jabbered) If you say someone is **jabbering,** you mean they are talking a lot, in an irritating way.

jack A **jack** is a device for lifting a heavy object off the ground. ◇ The **jack** in a pack of cards is the lowest-ranking picture card. ◇ In a game of bowls, the **jack** is the small white ball the players aim at.

jack-knife If a lorry **jack-knifes,** the trailer swings round at a sharp angle to the cab, and the vehicle goes out of control. ◇ A **jack-knife** is a large knife with a blade which can be folded into the handle.

jack-of-all-trades If you call someone a **jack-of-all-trades,** you mean they are able to do many kinds of work.

jackal Jackals are wild dog-like animals in parts of Africa and Southern Asia. They hunt in packs, and also eat carrion. ◇ People who take advantage of other people's misfortunes are sometimes called **jackals.**

jackboot Jackboots are knee-length leather boots worn by some soldiers. ◇ If people are **under the jackboot,** they are ruled by a harsh regime and not allowed any freedom.

jackdaw Jackdaws are grey birds with black faces. They are members of the crow family.

jacket (-jacketed) A **jacket** is a short coat. You can add **-jacketed** to a word to say what kind of jacket someone is wearing. *...the leather-jacketed security guard.* ◇ A potato baked in its skin is often called a **jacket** potato. ◇ The **jacket** of a book is the paper cover which protects it.

jackpot The **jackpot** is the biggest prize you can win in a competition. ◇ You say someone **hits the jackpot** when something they are involved in suddenly brings them a lot of money or other advantages.

Jacobean (*pron:* jak-o-bee-an) The **Jacobean** period was from 1603 to 1625. **Jacobean** is used to describe buildings, furniture, and other work dating from that time.

Jacquard (*pron:* jak-ard) fabric has the design woven into it, rather than printed or dyed on.

Jacuzzi (*pron:* jak-oo-zee) A **Jacuzzi** is a large circular bath fitted with a device which makes the water swirl. 'Jacuzzi' is a trademark.

jade is a semiprecious green or white stone which is carved to make jewellery and ornaments. Jade ornaments are sometimes called **jades.**

jaded is used to describe people who have been doing something so long they have lost their enthusiasm or become physically worn-out. *The players could be a bit jaded by November.*

Jaffa Jaffas are large oranges with thick skins. 'Jaffa' is a trademark.

jagged (*pron:* jag-gid) A **jagged** object has a lot of sharp projecting points.

jaguar (*pron:* jag-yoo-ar) Jaguars are the largest American wild-cats. They have spotted fur and live mainly in the forests of South America.

jail (jailing, jailed) (*or* gaol, gaoling, gaoled) **Jail** is another word for prison. If someone is **jailed,** they are sent to prison.

jailer (*or* gaoler) A **jailer** is someone in charge of a prisoner or prisoners in a jail. This word is no longer used to talk about people in charge of prisoners in Britain. See **prison officer.**

jam (jamming, jammed) ❑ **Jam** is a sweet food you spread on bread or toast. It is made by boiling fruit and sugar.

❑ If you **jam** something somewhere, you push it there firmly. *He jammed his hat back on.* ◇ If you **jam on** the brakes of a vehicle, you put your foot on the pedal hard, to stop the vehicle quickly.

❑ If something **jams,** it gets stuck in one position, and cannot move freely or work properly. *The lift was jammed between the fifth and sixth floors.* ◇ If a lot of people or things are **jammed** somewhere, they are packed tightly together and can hardly move. ◇ If something is **jam-packed,** it is so full of people or things there is no room for any more. ◇ If there is a **traffic jam,** the traffic on a road cannot move, because of the number of vehicles using it.

❑ If someone is in a **jam,** they are in a difficult situation.

❑ When people **jam** a radio or electronic signal, they interfere with it, and prevent it being received clearly. ◇ You say a telephone switchboard becomes **jammed** when so many people ring in that nobody else can get through.

❑ When musicians **jam** or have a **jam session,** they play jazz or rock music informally, often adapting the tune as they play.

jamb (*pron:* jam) A **jamb** is the upright part of a door frame or window frame.

jamboree A **jamboree** is a large party or celebration.

jangle (jangling, jangled) When loosely-held metal objects hit against each other noisily, you can say they **jangle.** ◇ If something **jangles** your nerves or makes them **jangle,** it makes you nervous and upset.

janitor A **janitor** is a person paid to look after a building.

Japanese is used to talk about people and things in or from Japan. *...the Japanese government... ...Japanese cameras.* ◇ A **Japanese** is someone who comes from Japan. ◇ **Japanese** is the main language spoken in Japan.

jar (jarring, jarred) ❑ A **jar** is a container with a lid, for storing food.

❑ If something **jars** you, (a) it shakes your whole body. *The defender put in three jarring tackles.* (b) it gives you a shock, or upsets you. *Foreign governments have been jarred by the depth of the disaster.* ◇ If a part of your body is **jarred,** it is shaken by the force of a collision, often causing an injury. *The tackle jarred Hirst's knee.*

❑ If something **jars on** you, you find it unpleasant or annoying. *There is a laziness about the writing that becomes* *jarring after a while.* ◇ If something **jars** with things around it, it looks out of place. ◇ If you say two ideas or statements **jar**, you mean they cannot both be right. *The report jars with the government figures.*

jargon is the specialist language of a subject or group of people. *...cricketing jargon.*

jasmine is a shrub with sweet-smelling yellow or white flowers. The flowers are used in making perfume and for flavouring tea.

jaundice is a blood condition in which a person's skin and the whites of their eyes turn yellow. It can be caused by diseases like hepatitis.

jaundiced If someone takes a **jaundiced** view of something, they see only the bad side of it.

jaunt A **jaunt** is a short trip taken for pleasure.

jaunty (jauntily, jauntiness) **Jaunty** behaviour is bright and cheerful. *He jauntily raised a hand to wave... The book is written with a jauntiness worthy of its subject.*

javelin The **javelin** is a field event in athletics. Competitors throw a kind of spear (the **javelin**) as far as they can.

jaw (jawing, jawed) ❑ When people talk about a person's jaw, they usually mean the lower edge of their face, including the chin and the parts between the chin and the ears. In biology, the **jaw** is the part of the skull a person's or animal's teeth are attached to. It is formed by two bones, the **upper jaw** and the **lower jaw**. ◇ If an animal has something in its **jaws**, it is holding it between its teeth.
❑ If you say people are **jawing**, you mean they are doing a lot of talking. ◇ People sometimes talk about **jaw-jaw**, meaning negotiations, as distinct from 'war-war', meaning fighting.
❑ If you **snatch victory from the jaws of defeat**, you are losing and then suddenly win.

jawbone A person's or animal's **jawbone** is their lower jaw.

jay Jays are pinkish-brown birds with blue-and-black wings and black-and-white crests. They are members of the crow family.

jaywalking (jaywalker) **Jaywalking** is walking across a road in a careless or dangerous way. Someone who does this is called a **jaywalker**.

jazz (jazzes, jazzing, jazzed) **Jazz** is a syncopated type of music which began in New Orleans. It is typically played on instruments like the trumpet, trombone, clarinet, and saxophone, with piano, guitar, drums, and bass accompaniment. It is often partly improvised. There are many types of jazz, including **traditional jazz** and **modern jazz**. ◇ If music is **jazzed-up**, it is played in a faster and more syncopated way than usual. ◇ If you **jazz up** a place or thing, you make it more colourful or exciting.

jazzy (jazzier, jazziest) **Jazzy** clothing is very bright and eye-catching. *...a jazzy green pin-stripe.* ◇ **Jazzy** music sounds like jazz.

JCB A **JCB** is a construction vehicle for digging earth. 'JCB' is a trademark.

jealous (jealously; jealousy, jealousies) ❑ If you are **jealous** of someone, you envy them because they have something you would like to have yourself. This feeling is called **jealousy**. You can talk about several people's **jealousies**. *A key task will be to overcome professional and po-*litical jealousies and persuade people to cooperate.
❑ You also say people are **jealous** when they worry about losing someone or something to someone else, and become possessive. *He has an insanely jealous girlfriend.*
❑ If people are **jealous** of something like a right, freedom, or privilege, they value it and are not willing to give it up. *In America, the right to jury trial is jealously guarded in civil cases.*

jeans are casual trousers, usually made of denim.

Jeep Jeeps are small four-wheeled vehicles which can travel over rough ground. 'Jeep' is a trademark.

jeer (jeering, jeered) If people **jeer** at someone, they shout out rude things about them. *Booing and jeering engulfed the stadium.*

Jehovah is another name for God.

Jehovah's Witness The Jehovah's Witnesses are a Christian fundamentalist sect who believe there will soon be a great battle between God and Satan, after which the Kingdom of Heaven will be created on Earth.

jello is the usual American word for jelly.

jelly (jellies, jellied) ❑ **Jelly** is (a) a fruit-flavoured dessert which shakes when you touch or move it. (b) a type of clear jam. ◇ **Jelly** is also a clear substance added to savoury food to preserve it and keep its flavour. **Jellied** food is prepared and served in this substance. *...jellied eels... ...jellied beef.* ◇ Some other jelly-like substances are also called **jelly**. *...royal jelly.*
❑ If you say your arms or legs feel like **jelly**, you mean they seem to have lost their strength, because you are frightened or exhausted.

jellyfish (*or* jelly-fish) (*plural:* jellyfish) **Jellyfish** are sea creatures with soft transparent bodies and stinging cells for paralysing their prey.

jemmy (jemmies) A **jemmy** is a short crowbar used by criminals.

jeopardize (*pron:* jep-pa-dize) (jeopardizing, jeopardized) (*can be spelled with an 's' instead of a 'z'*) If something could **jeopardize** something else, it could make it less likely to happen, continue, or succeed. *Union leaders told the striking miners to call off their action, because it could jeopardize wage negotiations.*

jeopardy (*pron:* jep-pa-dy) If something is **in jeopardy**, it is in danger of not continuing or not happening. *The move would put 800 jobs in jeopardy.*

jerk ❑ A **jerk** is a short quick movement. If you **jerk** something, you make it move like this. *...jerking the steering-wheel 360 degrees.*
❑ If something **jerks** you out of a way of thinking, it gives you a shock which makes you more alert.

jerky (jerkily) If something moves in a **jerky** way, it moves in short quick bursts. *When fish panic, they swim around very fast and jerkily.*

jerry-built You say a building or machine is **jerry-built** when it has been built quickly, cheaply, and carelessly.

jerry can A **jerry can** is a flat-sided can used for carrying petrol.

jersey is a stretchable material used to make clothing. ◇ A **jersey** is (a) a jumper. (b) a football shirt.

jest A **jest** is a joke. If you say something **in jest**, you say it as a joke.

jester Jesters were clowns who had the job of entertaining kings and queens in the past.

Jesuit (*pron:* jez-yoo-it) Jesuits are members of a Roman Catholic order called the Society of Jesus. They do missionary and educational work.

Jesus or **Jesus Christ** is the man who Christians believe is the Son of God. Jesus's teachings are the basis of Christianity.

jet (jetting, jetted) ❑ A jet engine propels a plane or other vehicle by shooting out a stream of hot gas. This method of propelling a vehicle is called **jet propulsion.** Vehicles with jet engines are said to be **jet-propelled.** ◇ A jet is a plane with a jet engine. ◇ If you **jet** somewhere, you fly by jet. *They spend a great deal of time jetting around the world.*
❑ A jet of liquid or gas is a thin fast powerful stream forced out through a small opening. ◇ A jet on something like an engine or gas cooker is a nozzle through which petrol or gas is forced before it burns.
❑ Jet is a hard black stone used in jewellery.

jet-black If you say something is **jet-black,** you are emphasizing that it is completely black, and not, say, dark brown or grey.

jet lag (*or* jetlag) (jet-lagged) Jet lag is a feeling of tiredness and confusion which people get after a long flight through different time zones. You say someone like this is **jet-lagged.**

jet set (jet-setting, jet-setted; jet-setter) Rich and fashionable people who live glamorous lives are sometimes called the **jet set.** An individual person like this can be called a **jet-setter.** ◇ People who **jet-set** fly to glamorous places around the world, for pleasure or important business. *...jet-setting businessmen.*

jet ski (jet-skier, jet-skiing) A jet ski is a small sea-going vehicle which looks like a motor-bike with skis instead of wheels. Someone riding a vehicle like this is called a **jet-skier;** what they do is called **jet-skiing.**

jet stream A jet stream is a trail of white vapour left in the sky by a jet plane. ◇ The jet stream is a stream of air which moves over the earth at a great height and speed, affecting the weather.

jetlag See jet lag.

jetsam is things thrown from a ship, which float on the sea or get washed onto the shore. See also flotsam. ◇ Jetsam is also used to describe rubbish in general.

jettison (jettisoning, jettisoned) When a ship jettisons something, it gets rid of it, to lighten its load. ◇ When people **jettison** something like an idea, plan, or policy, they decide to do without it. *Vickers has jettisoned plans to sell its ailing Rolls-Royces cars subsidiary.*

jetty (jetties) A jetty is a wide stone wall or wooden platform sticking out into the sea, a lake, or a river. Jetties are for boats to pull up against, so people can get on and off.

Jew A Jew is a person who practises the religion of Judaism, or is descended from the ancient Israelites.

jewel (jewelled) (*American spelling:* jeweled) ❑ A jewel is a precious stone, often in something like a ring or necklace. If something is **jewelled,** it has jewels in it. *...a jewelled cigarette case.* ◇ A person's jewels are the things they have with jewels in them, like rings and necklaces.
❑ If you call something a **jewel,** you mean it stands out from the things around it because it is so attractive. *On the other side is Portbraddan, a little jewel of a village.* ◇ If some-

thing is **the jewel in the crown** of a person, group, or place, it is the thing they are most proud of.

jeweller (*American spelling:* jeweler) A jeweller is a person who makes, sells, and repairs jewellery and watches. ◇ A shop which sells and repairs jewellery and watches is sometimes called a **jeweller** or **jeweller's.**

jewellery (*American spelling:* jewelry) is rings, necklaces, and other valuables which people wear.

Jewish A Jewish person is a Jew. *...a Jewish writer.* **Jewish** is used to talk about things to do with Jewish people. *...Jewish schools.*

Jewry is all the people who are Jewish, through religion or ancestry.

jib (jibbing, jibbed) ❑ If a horse or donkey jibs, it stops suddenly and refuses to go any further. ◇ If people **jib at** something, they object to it. *The countries expected to foot the bill jibbed at the astronomical sums being talked about.*
❑ The jib of a crane or derrick is its projecting arm. ◇ A sailing boat's jib is the triangular sail in front of the mainmast.

jibe (*or* gibe) A jibe is a rude or insulting remark.

jiffy A jiffy is a very short period of time. People say, for example, they will 'do something in a jiffy' or 'be back in a jiffy'.

jig (jigging, jigged) ❑ A jig is a lively traditional dance in which people make small kicks and leaps. ◇ A jig is also a lively tune people can dance to, usually played on the violin. ◇ When someone does a little dance to show they are pleased about something, this is often called a jig.
❑ A jig is also a device for holding things steady while they are being cut or drilled, and for guiding the tool to the correct place.

jiggery-pokery If you say there is **jiggery-pokery,** you mean something dishonest is going on. *...rules framed to prevent jiggery-pokery.*

jiggle (jiggling, jiggled) If something jiggles or is jiggled, it shakes up and down or from side to side.

jigsaw ❑ A jigsaw or jigsaw puzzle is a picture on cardboard or wood, cut into small interlocking pieces and sold in a box, so people can amuse themselves by putting the picture together again. ◇ Jigsaw is sometimes used to talk about a complicated situation involving many people or issues, all of which have to be taken into consideration before a solution can be found. If something is **a piece in the jigsaw,** it is one part of a complicated situation. If something is **the last piece in the jigsaw,** it is the only thing left to be sorted out before a problem can be solved.
❑ A jigsaw is also a mechanical saw with a thin steel blade for cutting curves in sheets of material.

jihad (*pron:* ji-had) A jihad is a holy war which Islam allows Muslims to fight against its enemies.

jilt If someone jilts the person they are having a relationship with, they end the relationship without warning.

jingle (jingling, jingled) When something jingles or is jingled, it makes a gentle ringing noise, like the sound of tiny bells. You call a noise like this a **jingle.** ◇ A jingle is also a short catchy song with easy-to-remember words, used in advertisements so people will remember the name of the product being advertised.

jingoism (jingoistic) When people publicly claim that

their country is better than all others, especially at the outbreak of a war, you call this **jingoism**. You use **jingoistic** to describe people like this, and their behaviour.

jink When a person or animal **jinks**, they make a sudden turn to left or right, usually to avoid an obstacle. ◇ You say there are **high jinks** when people do things for fun or pleasure which are not generally approved of. *...accusations of sexual high jinks with teenage girls.*

jinx (jinxes, jinxed) If you say someone has a **jinx** or is **jinxed**, you mean something seems to keep going wrong for them. If eventually things go right, you can say they have **broken** or **beaten the jinx**.

jitters (jittery) If someone gets the **jitters** just before doing something or receiving some important news, they become very nervous. You say someone in this state is **jittery**.

jiujitsu See jujitsu.

jive (jiving, jived) The **jive** is a lively dance, performed by couples to rock and roll music. Dancing like this is called **jiving**.

Jnr See junior.

job ❑ A **job** is paid work available for one person to do. ◇ If you talk about **jobs for the boys**, you mean people are unfairly giving jobs to their friends, or to influential people in return for their support.
　❑ A person's **job** is their regular paid occupation. ◇ If you learn a skill **on the job**, you learn it while you are actually working, rather than at a school or college.
　❑ A task is often called a **job**. *There are plenty of jobs to be done around here.* ◇ If you say it is someone's **job** to do something, you mean it is their duty or responsibility.

job centre See jobcentre.

job club A **job club** is a place where people who have been unemployed for some time are given help to find a job. Advice, newspapers, writing material, and the use of a phone are available free to job club members.

job lot A **job lot** is an assortment of things, sold together. *The frames were bought as part of a job lot.*

job market When people talk about the **job market**, they are talking about the jobs available at any particular time. When someone enters the **job market**, they start looking for a job.

job sharing is an arrangement in which one full-time job is split between two people who each work part-time.

jobber A **jobber** or **stockjobber** is a person who arranges the buying and selling of commodities between stockbrokers.

jobbing A **jobbing** worker does not have a regular employer, but is hired by people to do individual jobs. *...a jobbing builder.*

jobcentre (or **job centre**) A **jobcentre** is a government office which displays information about job vacancies, gives advice, and arranges job interviews for unemployed people.

jobless (joblessness) A **jobless** person is unemployed. Unemployed people are often called **the jobless**. *...better training for the jobless.* **Joblessness** is unemployment.

jockey (jockeying, jockeyed) ❑ **Jockeys** are people who ride racehorses for a living.
　❑ If people who are after the same thing **jockey for position**, they try to get an advantage over each other. *His two vice-presidents seem to be jockeying for position to replace*

him.

jockstrap A **jockstrap** is a piece of clothing, worn by sportsmen under their shorts, to support their genitals.

jocose (*pron:* joke-**kohss**) A **jocose** person is cheerful and always making jokes.

jocular (jocularity) A **jocular** remark is made as a joke. When someone is making jokes, you can say they are being **jocular** or talk about their **jocularity**.

jodhpurs are close fitting trousers, worn by horse riders.

jog (jogging, jogged; jogger) ❑ A **jog** is a gentle run. ◇ When someone **jogs**, they run at a gentle pace, usually for exercise. This kind of exercise is called **jogging**; the people who do it are called **joggers**.
　❑ If you **jog** someone or something, you give them a slight push or bump. ◇ If something **jogs your memory**, it reminds you of something you wanted to remember.

joie de vivre (*pron:* jwah de **veev**-ra) is enjoyment at being alive. *He found her joie de vivre infectious.*

join (joining, joined) ❑ If you **join** someone or are **joined** by them, you meet them somewhere, and spend time together. ◇ If you **join** someone who lives in a different place, you travel there to be with them.
　❑ If you **join** an organization, you become a member of it. ◇ If you **join** something which is already happening or **join in**, you become involved and take part in it. *Local residents joined the march.* You can also say you **join** a group of people. ◇ When people **join up**, they enlist in the armed services.
　❑ When someone or something is the latest one in a series to do something, you can say they **join the list** of people or things doing it. *Last month Jorge Carol, the painter, joined the long list of Cubans seeking asylum in Spain.*
　❑ If two roads or rivers **join**, or if one **joins** the other, they come together somewhere. ◇ If something **joins** two places together, it connects them. *...a narrow strip of land which joins the Jaffna peninsula to the rest of the island.*
　❑ If you **join** two things together, you attach them to each other. The place where they are attached is called a **join**. ◇ If people **join hands**, they take hold of each other's hands. ◇ If you **join** two points on a piece of paper, you draw a straight line between them.
　❑ **join forces:** see **force**.

joiner (joinery) A **joiner** is a person who makes wooden fixtures, such as window frames, door frames, and doors. The work a joiner does is called **joinery**. See also **carpenter**.

joint (jointly, jointed) ❑ **Joint** is used to talk about something shared by two or more people or groups. *...a joint press conference... It is operated jointly by the police and the army.*
　❑ A person's or animal's **joints** are the structures where certain bones meet. Joints act like hinges, making it possible for people to do things like clench their fists or bend their knees. ◇ If a structure is **jointed**, it can bend at certain places like human limbs.
　❑ A **joint** is also a place where two things, such as pieces of pipe, are fixed together. ◇ In woodwork, a **joint** is a join, formed by two interlocking pieces of wood, which are slotted together for extra strength.
　❑ A **joint** of meat is a large piece, suitable for roasting.
　❑ Americans call a disreputable bar or nightclub a **joint**.
　❑ A **joint** is also a marijuana cigarette.

❑ If someone's **nose has been put out of joint**, something has happened to make them feel insulted and angry. ◇ If you say things are **out of joint**, you mean they do not seem quite right. ◇ If a bone has been **put out of joint**, it has been dislocated.

joint-stock company A **joint-stock company** is a business whose shares can be bought by members of the public.

jointure is property which a husband legally arranges for his wife to receive if he dies before her.

joist Joists are long thick beams of wood, metal, or concrete, used in buildings to support floors, roofs, and ceilings.

jojoba (*pron:* hoe-hoe-ba) is an American shrub. Its seeds contain an oil used in cosmetics.

joke (joking, joked; jokingly) ❑ If you tell a **joke**, you tell a funny story. ◇ If you make a **joke**, you make a funny remark. When someone does this, you say they are **joking**. ◇ **running joke:** see run.

❑ If you say something **jokingly**, you mean it as a joke. If you say something **half-jokingly**, you are not being entirely serious.

❑ If you **play a joke** on someone, you do something to mislead them and make them look foolish. See also **practical joke**.

❑ If you say someone or something is a **joke**, you mean you cannot take them seriously. *Music lovers often dismiss heavy metal as a joke.* ◇ When something is very unpleasant or difficult to deal with, people sometimes say it is **no joke or beyond a joke.**

joker ❑ A **joker** is someone who likes telling or playing jokes.

❑ In a pack of playing cards, the **joker** is an extra card, usually with a picture of a jester. The joker is used in some card games as the highest ranking card, or as a substitute for any other card. There are two jokers in a pack. ◇ When people say someone or something is the **joker in the pack,** they mean they are unpredictable and could cause problems.

jokey (or **joky**) things are not meant to be taken seriously. *...jokey essays on bachelor housekeeping.*

jollity is cheerful behaviour.

jolly (jollier, jolliest; jollies, jollying, jollied) ❑ A **jolly** person is happy and cheerful. ◇ **Jolly** things are amusing or attractive, and tend to make you feel cheerful. ◇ A **jolly** event is lively and enjoyable.

❑ When people say something is **jolly good**, they mean it is very good. If they say something is done **jolly well**, they mean it is done very well. ◇ People also use **jolly well** to emphasize what they are saying, especially when they are annoyed or upset. *She was jolly well not going to let them get away with it.* ◇ **Jolly** is used in front of other words to make a point more strongly. *It all sounds jolly exciting.*

❑ If you **jolly** someone **along**, you keep them in a good mood.

jolt If something is **jolted** or given a **jolt**, it is shaken by a sudden bump or tremor. ◇ If something which happens **jolts** you or gives you a **jolt**, it gives you a nasty surprise or shock. *This threat has clearly jolted Britain into taking a more active role.*

jostle (jostling, jostled) When people in a crowd **jostle**, they push, knock, and elbow each other for space, or a good position. If someone is roughly treated like this, you can say they are **jostled**. ◇ When people or businesses **jostle** for something they all want, they compete for it in an aggressive way.

jot (jotting, jotted) ❑ A **jot** is a very small amount. You say, for example, someone does not care a **jot**.

❑ If you **jot** something **down** on a piece of paper, you write it in the form of a short note, so you will not forget it. ◇ **Jottings** are ideas and thoughts, written down as short notes.

jotter A **jotter** is a pad or notebook.

joule (*pron:* jool) In physics, energy is expressed in **joules**. A joule is the work done when a force of 1 newton is moved 1 metre in the direction of the force. 'Joules' is usually written 'J'.

journal A **journal** is a magazine which covers a subject or area of interest. *...a medical journal... ...a political journal.* ◇ **Journal** is also an old word for a diary.

journalese is a kind of lazy writing used by some journalists, which makes use of a lot of clichés.

journalism (journalist, journalistic) **Journalism** is the writing of news and features for newspapers, magazines, TV, or radio. *His first job was in journalism.* The news and features themselves are also called **journalism**. *...the best piece of journalism I have read in a long time.* A **journalist** is someone who writes journalism. **Journalistic** is used to talk about things to do with journalism and journalists. *...journalistic independence.*

journey If you **make a journey**, you travel somewhere. ◇ If you **journey** to a distant place, you travel there.

journeyman (journeymen) A **journeyman** is a qualified craftsman who works for someone else. ◇ **Journeyman** is also used to say someone is competent at their job, but not outstanding at it. *...a journeyman boxer.*

joust (*pron:* jowst) (jousting, jousted) In medieval times, a **joust** was a contest between two knights who tried to knock each other off their horses, using lances; this was called **jousting**. ◇ Nowadays, any contest in which one person tries to demonstrate their superiority over another can be called a **joust**. You can talk about people **jousting** with each other.

jovial (jovially; joviality) **Jovial** people are cheerful and good-humoured. You say their behaviour is **jovial** or talk about their **joviality**. *'Hello, there,' he said jovially.*

jowl (jowly) Flabby cheeks are called **jowls**. **Jowly** is used to describe people with flabby cheeks.

joy is a feeling of great happiness. ◇ If you say something is a **joy**, you mean it gives you a lot of pleasure. You can praise the appearance of something by saying it is a **joy to behold.**

❑ **Joy** is sometimes used to mean 'success'. For example, if you are trying to achieve something, you can say you have **no joy** or **little joy**. *They can expect little joy in their demands for increased help.*

joy-ride See joyride.

joyful (joyfully) A **joyful** occasion is one where people are very happy and enjoy themselves. You can say people are **joyful** on occasions like these; you can also say they are in a **joyful** mood or there is a **joyful** atmosphere. *They responded by joyfully pulling down statues of communism's founding fathers.*

joyless activities have no pleasure in them, or give no pleasure. *Shopping was as joyless as ever.*

joyous means the same as 'joyful'.

joyride (*or* **joy-ride**) (joyriding, joyrider) When people joyride, they steal a car, and drive it recklessly at high speed. People who do this are called **joyriders**; what they do is called **joyriding**.

joystick A joystick is (a) the lever a pilot uses to steer a plane. (b) a lever connected to a computer, which lets people control the movements of characters in a computer game.

JP A JP is a local magistrate. JP stands for 'Justice of the Peace'.

Jr See junior.

jubilant (jubilantly; jubilation) If someone is **jubilant**, they are happy and triumphant, because they have had a great victory or success. You can talk about the **jubilation** of people like this. *Troops drove jubilantly through the streets.*

jubilee A jubilee is a special anniversary of an important occasion, such as the time a king or queen came to the throne. A 25th anniversary is called a **silver jubilee**, a 50th anniversary a **golden jubilee**, and a 60th anniversary a **diamond jubilee**.

Judaism (Judaic) Judaism (*pron:* joo-day-iz-um) is the religion of the Jewish people, based on the teachings of the Old Testament of the Bible, and the Talmud. **Judaic** (*pron:* joo-day-ik) is used to talk about things to do with Judaism. *...Judaic law.*

Judas was the disciple who betrayed Jesus Christ. If you call someone a **Judas**, you mean they have betrayed a friend in this way.

judder (juddering, juddered) A **judder** is a violent vibration. When something **judders**, it shakes and vibrates in a violent way.

judge (judging, judged) ❑ A **judge** is a public official who tries cases and passes sentence in a court of law. ◇ You say someone acts as **judge and jury** when they decide someone has done something wrong and should be punished, without taking account of anyone else's views.

❑ A **judge** is also a person who decides the winner of a contest; you say he or she **judges** the contest.

❑ If you **judge** a situation, you come to a decision about its state or nature. If you **judge** a person, you come to a decision about their character. ◇ If you **judge** something which has been done or produced, you decide whether it is good or bad. *The experiment was judged a success.* ◇ If you say someone is a **good judge** of something, you mean their opinion can be relied on.

❑ You can say something is **well-judged** when it is done or said in just the right way. *...a well-judged performance.* You can also say something is **badly-judged** or **ill-judged**.

❑ You use expressions like **to judge by** and **judging from** when you are saying why you think something is true. *Judging from opinion polls, voters have not been impressed.*

❑ If you **judge** something like a time, distance, or speed, you make a sensible guess about what it is likely to be.

judgment (*or* **judgement**) ❑ **Judgment** is the ability to make sensible guesses about a situation and sensible decisions about what to do. ◇ If you do something **against your better judgment,** you do it although you think it is probably a mistake.

❑ **Judgment** is also the ability to decide what someone or something is like. *In my judgment, he is highly dangerous.* A decision like this is called a **judgment.** ◇ If you **pass judgment** on someone or something, you decide how good or bad they are. ◇ If you **reserve judgment**, you decide not to give an opinion about something until you know more about it.

❑ When people **sit in judgment** on someone, they decide whether they are guilty of doing something wrong. ◇ A **judgment** is a ruling by someone like a judge on a legal matter.

❑ In Judaism, Christianity, and Islam, **Judgment Day** is the day of God's final judgment on the world.

judgmental (*or* **judgemental**) If someone gives an opinion about something, rather than making neutral comments, you can say they are being **judgmental.** *I don't want to sound judgmental, but it really was a big mistake.*

judicial (*pron:* joo-**dish**-al) (judicially) **Judicial** is used to talk about things involving the law. *...a judicial review... Publication of the paper may be judicially suspended.*

judiciary (*pron:* joo-**dish**-ar-y) (judiciaries) A country's **judiciary** is its legal system, and the people who operate it. ◇ Judges are sometimes called the **judiciary.**

judicious (*pron:* joo-**dish**-us) (judiciously) **Judicious** is used to describe things being done in a sensible well-judged way. *Modern fertilizers should be used judiciously.*

Judo is a modern Japanese martial art, based on jujitsu. It is also a sport.

jug A jug is a container for liquids, with a handle and a small spout.

juggernaut A juggernaut is a very large lorry. ◇ A very large organization or system can also be called a **juggernaut.**

juggle (juggling, juggled; juggler) ❑ If you **juggle** objects like small balls or clubs, you keep several of them in the air at the same time, without dropping them; this activity is called **juggling.** Someone who juggles for a living is called a **juggler.**

❑ If you **juggle** things around, you arrange and rearrange them, to fit your needs. ◇ If you **juggle** facts or figures, you manipulate them, to give a false or misleading picture. ◇ If you **juggle** two or more activities, you manage to deal with them at the same time. *Her career involved constant juggling of home and work.* When someone does something like this, you can say they are performing a **juggling act.**

jugular The **jugular veins** are three veins in your neck which carry blood from your head back to your heart. People talk about these veins as if they were one vein, called the **jugular.** ◇ If someone **goes for the jugular,** they ruthlessly attack an opponent's weak points.

juice is the liquid in fruit and vegetables, which is often drunk or used for flavouring food. *...lemon juice.* ◇ The **juice** of a piece of meat is the liquid which seeps out while it is cooking. ◇ The **digestive juices** in a person's stomach are the fluids which help them digest food.

juicy (juicier, juiciest) A **juicy** fruit, vegetable, or piece of meat is full of juice, and good to eat. ◇ A **juicy** story is scandalous and exciting. *...more juicy rumours... ...juicy* headlines. ◇ You say other things are **juicy** when they are attractive and tempting. *...a juicy part for an actor.*

jujitsu (*or* **jiujitsu**) is an ancient and very violent Japanese martial art. Holds, throws, and locks are used to cause pain in an opponent's limbs, or to dislocate or break them. See also **Judo**.

jukebox A **jukebox** is an automatic coin-operated record player, usually found in pubs and bars.

jumble (jumbling, jumbled) ❑ A **jumble** of things is a confused mixture of them.

❑ A **jumble sale** is a sale of cheap second-hand goods donated by the public, to raise money for something such as a charity. The goods donated are called **jumble**.

❑ If things are **jumbled** or **jumbled up**, they are mixed together in a confusing way. *The events of his life are jumbled up in a series of flash-backs.*

jumbo A **jumbo** or **jumbo jet** is a large wide-bodied jet plane. ◇ **Jumbo** is used to describe things which are very large. *...jumbo steaks.*

jump (jumping, jumped) ❑ When you **jump,** you use the strength in your legs to propel yourself off the ground into the air. ◇ If you **jump into** a vehicle or **jump out** of it, you get in or out in a hurry. ◇ If you **jump up** or **jump to your feet**, you stand up quickly.

❑ If something **makes you jump,** it gives you a shock.

❑ If you **jump at** an offer or opportunity, you accept it eagerly, as soon as it is offered to you.

❑ In a steeplechase or equestrian event, the **jumps** are obstacles, such as hedges or fences, which the runners or horses have to jump over.

❑ If a figure, price, or level **jumps,** it rises sharply. A sudden rise like this is called a **jump**. *The unemployment rate jumped to 10.2%.*

❑ If someone **jumps** from one subject to another, they suddenly start talking about it.

❑ If someone **jumps the queue** for something, they get treatment or attention before it is their turn.

❑ If you are **one jump ahead** of other people, you do things before they do, or guess what they are going to do before they do it.

❑ **jump the gun:** see **gun**. ◇ **jump to conclusions:** see **conclusion**.

jump jet A **jump jet** is a jet plane which can take off and land vertically.

jump leads are a pair of thick electrical cables with clips at each end, for starting a vehicle with a flat battery. The battery is connected by the leads to the battery of another vehicle, to provide enough power to start the engine.

jump-off In a showjumping contest, a **jump-off** is an extra round, to decide which horse is the winner, if two or more horses are in joint first place.

jump-start If you **jump-start** a vehicle, you get the engine to start, either by connecting the battery to the battery of another vehicle, or by pushing or rolling the car while releasing the clutch. Either of these methods can be called a **jump start**. ◇ If someone **jump-starts** a country's economy, they do something to get it going again, such as borrowing money from other countries for building and investment programmes.

jumped-up is used to describe people who think they are more important than they really are. *Some jumped-up arrogant official was trying to tell me what to do.*

jumper ❑ A **jumper** is a sweater or pullover.

❑ A **jumper** is also an athlete who takes part in the high jump or long jump.

jumpsuit A **jumpsuit** is a one-piece garment, combining trousers and top.

jumpy (jumpier, jumpiest) You say someone is **jumpy** when they are nervous or worried about something, and are easily unsettled or alarmed.

junction A **junction** is a place where things meet, join, or cross each other, especially roads or railway lines. ◇ A **junction** is also a point where traffic can leave or enter a motorway. *...Junction 11 of the M25.*

junction box A **junction box** is a box where electrical wires or cables meet, and are joined together.

juncture If something happens at a particular **juncture**, it happens at an important point in time, within a period of change. *They know they take over the EU leadership at a crucial juncture.*

jungle A **jungle** is a dense tropical forest, where tall trees and other plants grow close together. ◇ You say something is a **jungle** when there is a lot of it and you cannot find what you want. *...a jungle of complex rules.* ◇ You call an environment a **jungle** when people there behave in a ruthless way. *...the political jungle.*

junior ❑ If someone has a **junior** position in a department, organization, profession, or partnership, they are of lesser rank or importance than other people in it. *...a junior minister in the Foreign Office.* Someone with a very low position in an organization can be called a **junior**. *...an office junior.*

❑ If you are someone's **junior**, you are younger than they are. *She married a man 29 years her junior.* ◇ British schoolchildren aged 7 to 11 are sometimes called **juniors**. ◇ In some sports, a **junior** is someone under 21 years of age.

❑ When a father and son have the same name, **Junior** is sometimes used after the son's name, to avoid confusion. In Britain, this is usually shortened to 'Jnr' or 'Jr'. *...John Hammond Jnr.*

junior school A **junior school** is one for children aged 7 to 11.

juniper is an evergreen shrub with purple berries. The berries are used in cooking, and for flavouring gin.

junk is discarded objects of little or no value. ◇ If you **junk** something, you throw it away, because it is no longer any use.

❑ A **junk shop** sells an assortment of cheap secondhand goods, often in poor condition.

❑ **Junk food** is snack food which is not very nutritious, like crisps and cakes. ◇ **junk mail:** see **direct mail**. ◇ **Junk** is used to describe things of poor quality. *...junk books... ...junk radio.*

❑ A **junk** is a Chinese sailing boat with a flat bottom and square sails.

junket A **junket** is a trip taken for pleasure and paid for by someone else, especially one taken by public officials and paid for from public funds. ◇ A **junket** is also a blancmange-like pudding, made with sweetened milk and rennet.

junketing **Junketings** are expensive events, put on to celebrate something or for the benefit of important visitors.

junkie A junkie is a drug addict. ◇ Someone who is obsessively interested in something can be called a **junkie**. ...*a computer junkie*... ...*news junkies*.

junta A junta is a small group of powerful people, usually military officers, who rule a country, having taken control of it by force. ·

Jurassic The Jurassic Age began about 200 million years ago and ended about 140 million years ago. The Jurassic Age was the period when many life forms evolved and dinosaurs existed.

juridical (*pron*: joor-rid-ik-al) is used to talk about things connected with the law and the administration of justice. *All this activity must take place within a strong juridical framework.*

jurisdiction The jurisdiction of a court is the power or authority it has to deal with a particular matter. *He claimed that the High Court had no jurisdiction to review the decision.* You can say something comes **within the jurisdiction** of a court. ◇ If a territory come under the **jurisdiction** of a country, that country's laws apply there.

jurisprudence is the study of law, especially the principles on which laws are based.

jurist A jurist is an expert on jurisprudence.

juror A juror is a member of a jury.

jury (juries) ❑ A **jury** is a panel of 12 members of the public, summoned to a court to listen to the facts about a crime, then give a verdict on whether the accused person is innocent or guilty.

❑ If you say **the jury is still out** on something which is being discussed or investigated, you mean no conclusion has yet been reached about it.

❑ The panel of judges in a competition is called the **jury**.

jury box The jury box is the place in a court where the jury sits.

just (justly) ❑ **Just** is used to emphasize how small an amount is, how short a length of time or distance is, or how young a person is. *The latest ceasefire lasted just 90 minutes... He was just 15 at the time.* ◇ **Just** is used to emphasize that something is not important, or that it is only a small part of a bigger thing. *Cutting down on fat is just one aspect of changing to a healthier lifestyle.*

❑ **Just** is used to say something happened a short time ago, or at the same moment as something else. *She put the telephone down just as the doorbell rang.*

❑ **Just** means exactly, or precisely. For example, if you say something is **just** what is required, you mean it is exactly what is required. *It may be just what the place needs.* ◇ People use **just** to emphasize what they are saying, especially when they have strong feelings about something. *This type of experiment is just not acceptable.* ◇ **Just** and **only just** are used to say something is successful, but only by a narrow margin. *The company is just breaking even.* ◇ **Just** is used with 'as' to emphasize that something has as much of a quality as something else. *A woman can be just as competitive as a man.*

❑ In a **just** social system, people are treated fairly and impartially. ◇ **Just** is used to say an action or belief is morally right. ...*a just war*... ...*a just cause*. ◇ A **just** reward or punishment is well-deserved. ◇ **Justly** is used to say that something deserves its reputation, or that a description of

something is particularly appropriate. *Elvis Presley can justly be called the King of Rock and Roll.*

justice ❑ If people want **justice**, they want fair treatment, especially when they have been treated unfairly in the past. *We are not seeking special favours, we are seeking justice.* ◇ **Justice** is also the principle that someone accused of a crime should get a fair hearing, and, if found guilty, should receive the right punishment for their crime. If a criminal is **brought to justice**, they are caught and punished. ◇ **rough justice**: see **rough**.

❑ A **justice** is a judge or magistrate. **Justice** in front of someone's name means they are a judge. ...*Lord Justice Bingham.* ◇ A country's **justice** system is its system for dealing with legal cases.

❑ When people talk about the **justice** of something they are trying to achieve, they mean its moral rightness. *They were confident in the justice of their cause.* ◇ If you say there is **justice** in what someone says, you mean there is a lot of truth in it. *Spain complains, with some justice, that present arrangements give it a raw deal.*

❑ If you **do justice** to something, you deal with it in a way which shows a full appreciation of it. *The official statement hardly does justice to the feelings of outrage here.*

Justice of the Peace See JP.

justifiable (justifiably) You say something like anger is **justifiable** when there are good reasons for it. *His reaction was justifiably bitter.*

justify (justifies, justifying, justified; justification) ❑ If something **justifies** an action or point of view, it provides a good or sufficient reason for it. *A reduction in inflation justifies a small reduction in interest rates.* When there is a good reason for an action or point of view, you say it is **justified** or there is **justification** for it. *There is no justification for the steep rise in prices.*

❑ If someone **justifies** something they do which seems to be wrong, they give their reasons for doing it. *She justifies the deception by saying that otherwise she would not have been selected.*

❑ If a printer **justifies** text, he or she adjusts it to make it fit a space exactly.

jut (jutting, jutted) If something like a rock **juts** out, it sticks out sharply.

jute is a fibre, used to make rope and sacks. It comes from a plant, also called **jute**, which grows mainly in Asia.

juvenile ❑ A **juvenile** is a young person or child. ◇ **Juvenile** is used to talk about young people, or things connected with young people, rather than adults. ...*juvenile offenders*... ...*a juvenile court*. ◇ **Juvenile** behaviour is silly and immature.

❑ A **juvenile** animal is not fully mature. ...*juvenile fish*. An animal like this can also be called a **juvenile**.

juvenile delinquent (juvenile delinquency) A **juvenile delinquent** is a young person who takes part in antisocial or criminal behaviour. Their behaviour is called **juvenile delinquency**.

juvenilia is work produced by an author in his or her youth. ...*an extensive collection of juvenilia*.

juxtapose (juxtaposing, juxtaposed; juxtaposition) If you **juxtapose** two things or ideas, you put them side by side, usually for a special effect. ...*the juxtaposition of two reports on the front page*.

K k

kaftan See caftan.

kalashnikov (*pron:* kal-lash-ni-koff) A **kalashnikov** is a type of automatic rifle made in Russia.

kale is a cabbage-like vegetable with curly green leaves.

kaleidoscope (*pron:* kal-lie-de-scope) A **kaleidoscope** is a toy in the shape of a tube which you hold in your hand. When you look through one end and turn or shake the tube, you see a changing pattern of colours. ◇ Any pattern of colours which keeps changing can be called a **kaleidoscope**. ◇ A constantly changing situation can also be called a **kaleidoscope**. ...*the revolutions which shook the kaleidoscope of East and Central Europe.*

kaleidoscopic (*pron:* kal-lie-de-**scop**-ik) is used to talk about things which keep changing their form, with the different parts being reassembled in different ways. ...*the traditional parties whose kaleidoscopic coalitions have formed 50 governments in the past 45 years.*

kamikaze (*pron:* kam-mee-**kah**-zee) In the Second World War, some Japanese pilots deliberately crashed their planes, loaded with explosives, into targets, killing themselves. These pilots were called **kamikaze** pilots. ◇ **Kamikaze** is used to talk about actions in which someone sacrifices their life or career, or risks injury, in order to achieve something. *He might have scored, but was thwarted by a kamikaze dive to his feet by Roberts.*

kangaroo **Kangaroos** are large animals in Australia. They move by jumping on their powerful back legs. Female kangaroos have a pouch on the front of their bodies for holding a baby. ◇ A **kangaroo court** is an unofficial trial of a member of a group or organization who is accused of having broken its rules.

kaolin (*pron:* kay-oh-lin) is a type of fine white clay used to make bone china and in some medicines.

karaoke (*pron:* ka-ree-oh-kee) is a form of entertainment in some bars and clubs. Customers take turns to sing well-known songs to a pre-recorded backing tape, reading the words from a TV screen.

karat See carat.

karate (*pron:* ka-**rah**-tee) is a sport and martial art in which two people fight each other using their hands, elbows, feet, and legs.

karma In the Buddhist and Hindu religions, **karma** is the belief that a person's actions in one life have an effect on all their later lives.

kasbah (*or* casbah) In many north African cities, the **kasbah** is the oldest part, surrounding a castle or citadel.

kayak (*pron:* kie-ak) A **kayak** is a type of canoe, covered except for the place where the canoeist sits. Kayaks are used by Inuits (eskimos), and also in the sport of canoeing.

kebab (*pron:* ke-bab) A **kebab** consists of grilled meat prepared in one of two ways. A **shish kebab** is pieces of grilled meat or vegetable stuck on a stick. A **doner kebab** is slices of grilled meat served with salad in a pitta bread.

keel (keeling, keeled) ❏ The **keel** of a boat is a long piece of shaped wood or metal along its bottom. It is there to strengthen the boat and keep it steady. ◇ If something is **on an even keel,** it is working or progressing smoothly and satisfactorily.

❏ If someone or something **keels over,** they fall over sideways.

keen (keener, keenest; keenly, keenness) ❏ If someone is **keen** to do something, they are anxious or eager to do it. *There has never been any doubt about Gower's keenness to play for England.* You can also say someone is **keen** for something to happen. *Both sides were keen that the mines should keep working.* ◇ **Keen** is used to say someone enjoys doing something and does it a lot. *Boys are as keen on cooking as girls are.*

❏ If someone takes a **keen** interest in something, they are very interested in it. Similarly, you can say someone has a **keen** wish or desire for something. *I was keenly interested in outdoor activities... ...their keen wish for military intervention.* ◇ If people are watching something **keenly,** they are paying a lot of attention to it, and waiting to see what happens.

❏ If someone has a **keen** eye for something, they are good at recognizing it when it appears. Similarly, you can say someone has a **keen** understanding or appreciation of something.

❏ In a **keen** contest or competition, the competitors take part in a very determined way. ...*a keenly contested football match.*

keep (keeping, kept) ❏ If you **keep** in a place or position, you stay there. *They kept away from the forest.* ◇ If someone **keeps** you somewhere, they do not let you go. *Anyone who challenged them was kept in jail for years.*

❏ If you **keep** something you need in a particular place, you have it there, so you can find it when you want it. ◇ You also say someone **keeps** something somewhere when they let it stay there, rather than removing it. *She kept her arm around her husband as she spoke.*

❏ If someone or something **keeps** or is **kept** in a particular state, they remain in that state. *They had been kept awake by nightingales.*

❏ **Keep** is used to say someone continues to do or have something. *The two navies now keep in touch by radio... The question is whether the Democrats can keep hold of this advantage.* ◇ If someone **keeps** doing something or **keeps on** doing it, they do it repeatedly or without stopping. *They kept on walking.*

❏ If you decide to **keep** something, you hold on to it, rather than giving it away or throwing it away. ◇ If you **keep** part of something **back,** you do not use it all or give it all away, so you have some for a later time. *Remember to keep back enough cream to make the topping.*

❏ If you **keep** something from someone, you do not tell them about it.

❏ If someone or something **keeps** you from doing something, they stop you doing it. *She had to hold the boy tight, to keep him from falling.*

❏ If you **keep** something **off** or **keep** it **away,** you stop it reaching you. *They built a bamboo shelter to keep the rain off.*

❏ If you **keep** a number or amount **down**, you stop it increasing. *The French are very concerned to keep costs down.* ◇ If something is **kept** to a particular amount, it is limited to that amount.

❏ If you **keep** something like a promise or appointment, you do what you said you would do. ◇ If you **keep** to a rule, plan, or agreement, you do what is required.

❏ If you **keep** a record of something, you write things down as they happen. Similarly, you can **keep** a list or a diary.

❏ People who **keep** animals own them and take care of them.

❏ If you **keep up** with a moving person or thing, you stay with them by going at the same speed. Similarly, you say something **keeps up** with something else when it increases at the same rate. *Pensions were increased to keep up with the rise in prices.* ◇ If you **keep up** with what is going on, you make sure you know about it.

❏ If someone **keeps on** about something, they talk about it repeatedly or without stopping, especially in a boring or irritating way. ◇ If someone **keeps on** at you, they repeatedly ask you or tell you to do something, especially in an irritating way.

❏ If something **keeps** you, or **keeps** you from something, it stops you from going somewhere at the time you are supposed to, and makes you arrive late. *What kept you?... Am I keeping you from your party?*

❏ A person's **keep** is the cost of food and other things they need each day.

❏ The **keep** of a castle is its main tower.

❏ **keep** someone **guessing**: see **guess**. ◇ **keep your head**: see **head**.

❏ See also **keeping**.

keep-fit is keeping your body in good condition by doing regular exercise.

keeper A **keeper** is someone who looks after something or is in charge of it. *...bee keepers.* ◇ Gamekeepers are often called **keepers**.

keeping If something is in **keeping** with a requirement or policy, it fits in with it. *In keeping with the government policy of non-interference, they refused to take any action.* ◇ You say something is in **keeping** when it is appropriate in a particular situation. If it is inappropriate, you say it is out of **keeping**. *Her costume was quite out of keeping with the character she was supposed to be playing.*

keg A **keg** is a small barrel for storing alcoholic drinks. ◇ **Keg** or **keg beer** is a type of beer kept under pressure in a metal barrel.

kennel A **kennel** is a small hut for a dog to sleep in. ◇ **Kennels** are a place where a large number of dogs are kept and looked after, for example while their owners are on holiday.

kept See **keep**.

kerb (*usual American spelling:* **curb**) The **kerb** is the edge of the pavement, next to the road.

kerb-crawling is the illegal activity of driving slowly next to a pavement to try and hire a prostitute.

kerfuffle You say there is a **kerfuffle** when there is a disagreement or argument about something.

kernel The **kernel** of a nut is the part inside the shell. ◇ The **kernel** of what a person says or does is its most important part.

kerosene is the usual American word for paraffin.

kestrel The **kestrel** is a small brown and grey falcon which hovers high above the ground when it is looking for its prey.

ketch (ketches) A **ketch** is a type of sailing ship with two masts.

ketchup is a thick cold sauce made from tomatoes or other vegetables. In the US, it is usually called **catsup**.

kettle A **kettle** is a covered container with a handle and a spout, for boiling water in.

key ❏ A **key** is a shaped piece of metal which fits into a lock and opens it.

❏ If you say something is the **key** to something desirable, you mean it is the way to get it. *Education became the key to progress.*

❏ The **key** to a map, diagram, or technical book is an explanation of the symbols or abbreviations used in it. ◇ The **key** to something strange or puzzling is something which explains it. *Only an inner group had the key to this mystery.*

❏ The **key** things or people in a group are the most important ones. *...military bases and other key installations.*

❏ The **keys** on a typewriter, computer keyboard, or cash register are the buttons you press to make it work. ◇ When someone uses a computer keyboard, you say they **key** information into the computer or **key** an instruction.

❏ The **keys** on a piano or organ are the horizontal black and white bars you press to play it. ◇ The **keys** on a woodwind instrument are the buttons you press to close the holes, to get different notes. ◇ If a piece of music is in a particular **key**, it is based on a particular scale of notes. For example, a piece in the key of G major is based on the notes G, A, B, C, D, E, F♯, G.

❏ If someone is **keyed up**, they are excited and nervous about something which is going to happen.

key-ring See **keyring**.

keyboard The **keyboard** of something like a typewriter or computer is the set of keys you press to make it work. ◇ The **keyboard** of an instrument like a piano or organ is the set of black and white keys you press to play it.

keyhole A **keyhole** is the hole you put a key in to operate a lock. ◇ **Keyhole** surgery involves operating on someone through a very small cut in their body.

keynote A **keynote** speech at a conference is a very important one, dealing with fundamental issues. ◇ If you say something is the **keynote**, you mean that is how people are expected to behave on a particular occasion. *Refinement and gentility were the keynote.*

keyring (*or* **key-ring**) A **keyring** is a ring for keeping keys on.

keystone A **keystone** is a stone at the top of an arch which keeps the other stones in place by its weight and position. ◇ The **keystone** of something like a system is the most important part, on which all the rest depends.

kg See **kilogram**.

KGB The **KGB** was the government organization in the USSR which dealt with the country's internal security. It also tried to obtain secret information about the political and military affairs of other countries.

khaki is a yellowish-brown colour. Soldiers' uniforms are often this colour.

kHz See kilohertz.

kibbutz (*plural:* kibbutzim *or* kibbutzes) A **kibbutz** is a place of work in Israel, for example a farm or factory, where the workers live together and share all the duties.

kick ❑ If you **kick** something or give it a **kick**, you hit it sharply with your foot. ◇ A sudden movement with your foot, for example when you are swimming or dancing, can also be called a **kick**.
    ❑ If you **kick** a habit, you succeed in giving it up.
    ❑ If someone is **kicked out** of a place, they are made to leave. ◇ If someone **kicks up** a fuss, they complain strongly about something.
    ❑ When a football match **kicks off**, it starts. The time it starts is called the **kick-off**. ◇ If an event **kicks off** with something, it starts with it. You can also say the people involved **kick off** with something. *We kicked off with a slap-up dinner.*
    ❑ If you get a **kick** from something, you find it exciting.

kick-off See kick.

kick-start If you **kick-start** something or give it a **kick-start**, you start it working, after which it continues working on its own. *The market needs a kick-start from the government.*

kickback A **kickback** is a sum of money paid for illegally helping someone make a profit.

kid (kidding, kidded) ❑ A **kid** is a child. A person's **kids** are their children. ◇ Young people who are no longer children are also sometimes called **kids**. *...college kids.* ◇ Someone's **kid brother** or **kid sister** is their younger brother or sister.
    ❑ A **kid** is a young goat, less than a year old. Kid is soft leather made from a young goat's skin. ◇ If you handle someone **with kid gloves**, you are careful not to annoy or upset them.
    ❑ If you **kid** yourself, you let yourself believe something which is not true. ◇ If you **kid** someone else, you tease them or try to make them believe something which is not true, as a joke.

kiddie Kiddies are very young children.

kidnap (kidnapping, kidnapped; kidnapper) If someone is **kidnapped**, they are taken away by force, usually to get money from their family, employer, or government. Kidnap is the crime of kidnapping someone. A **kidnapper** is someone who does it.

kidney A person's or animal's **kidneys** are the two organs which filter waste matter from their bloodstream and send it out of their body in their urine. ◇ Kidney is the cooked kidneys of an animal.

kidney bean Kidney beans are reddish-brown kidney-shaped beans.

kidney machine A **kidney machine** is a machine which does the work of a kidney for someone whose own kidneys do not work properly. See dialysis.

kill ❑ If someone or something **kills** a person or animal, they cause them to die. ◇ When there is a **kill**, a wild animal is killed by hunters or by another animal. *The female lions make the majority of kills.*
    ❑ If you **kill** something which has been going on, you bring it to an end. *His behaviour outraged me and killed our friendship.* ◇ If something is **killed off**, it is destroyed completely. *A penalty goal killed off Bath's last hope of retaining their League title.*
    ❑ If you do something to **kill time**, you do it while you are waiting for something else to happen.

killer ❑ A **killer** is someone or something that has killed several people. *Heart disease is the major killer of our time.* ◇ Someone's **killer** is the person who killed them.
    ❑ If someone has the **killer instinct**, they are very determined to defeat their opponents or rivals, and are more likely to win because of this.

killer whale The **killer whale** is a black and white whale which eats large fish and seals. Killer whales usually hunt in groups.

killing When there is a **killing**, someone deliberately kills someone else. ◇ If someone has **made a killing**, they have made a large profit quickly and easily.

killjoy A **killjoy** is someone who tries to stop people enjoying themselves.

kiln A **kiln** is a type of oven for baking things like bricks or pottery.

kilo (kilos) A **kilo** is the same as a kilogram.

kilogram (*or* kilogramme) Weight is often expressed in **kilograms**. A kilogram is 1,000 grams (about 2.2 pounds). 'Kilograms' is usually written 'kg'.

kilohertz (*plural:* kilohertz) The frequency of radio waves is often expressed in **kilohertz**. A kilohertz is equal to 1,000 cycles per second. 'Kilohertz' is usually written 'kHz'.

kilometre (*American spelling:* **kilometer**) Distance is often expressed in **kilometres**. A kilometre is 1,000 metres (about 0.62 miles). 'Kilometres' is usually written 'km'.

kilowatt Power is often measured in **kilowatts**. A kilowatt is 1,000 watts. 'Kilowatts' is usually written 'kW'.

kilowatt hour Energy is often measured in **kilowatt hours**. One kilowatt hour is the energy generated by 1,000 watts in one hour. 'Kilowatt hours' is usually written 'kWh'.

kilt A **kilt** is a short pleated tartan skirt. Kilts are worn, especially by men, as part of Scottish Highland dress.

kilter If a system is **out of kilter**, it is not working properly. ◇ If something is **out of kilter** with something else, it does not fit in with it. *It was an over-the-top piece of acting, wholly out of kilter with the rest of the cast.*

kimono (*pron:* kim-moan-no) (kimonos) A **kimono** is a long loose garment with wide sleeves and a sash, worn in Japan.

kin Your **kin** are your relatives. See also **next of kin**, **kith and kin**.

kind ❑ A particular **kind** of thing is a sort or type of that thing. ◇ You use **of a kind** to say something is a particular kind of thing, but not a very good example of it. *A solution of a kind has been found.* ◇ You use **a kind of** when you are giving a rough description of something. *He wore a kind of outsize smoking jacket.*
    ❑ A **kind** person is caring, gentle, and helpful. See also kindly, kindness.
    ❑ If you pay someone **in kind**, you pay them with goods or services rather than money. ◇ If you react to someone's action by doing something **in kind**, you do the same thing to them. *Our troops would retaliate in kind if attacked with chemical agents.*

kind-hearted people are caring, loving, and gentle.

kindergarten A **kindergarten** is the same as a nursery school.

kindle (kindling, kindled) If something **kindles** a feeling, it brings it on. *The war kindled his enthusiasm for politics.* ◇ If you **kindle** a fire, you start it by lighting wood or paper. The wood or paper you use is called **kindling**.

kindly (kindlier, kindliest; kindliness) ❑ **Kindly** people are gentle and caring. You talk about the **kindliness** of people like these. ◇ If you say someone **kindly** did something, you mean they helped you in some way and you are grateful for it.

❑ If you say someone does not **take kindly** to something, you mean they are not willing to accept it. ◇ If you say someone will **look kindly** on something, you mean they will be sympathetic towards it.

kindness (kindnesses) **Kindness** is kind behaviour. A **kindness** is a kind act.

kindred If you call someone a **kindred spirit**, you mean they have the same view of life as yourself.

kinetic (*pron*: kin-net-tik) ❑ In physics, **kinetic energy** is the energy an object has when it is moving. ◇ **Kinetics** is a branch of mechanics dealing with moving objects.

❑ **Kinetic art** consists of works of art with moving parts, or with parts which seem to move as you walk past.

king ❑ The **king** of a country is the male member of its royal family who is the head of state. ◇ A man is sometimes called the **king** of something when people think he is better at it than anyone else. *...Donald McGill, the King of the Saucy Postcard.* ◇ If you say something is **king** somewhere, you mean it is the most important or popular thing there. *...a place where cricket is king.*

❑ The **king** is a piece in chess. Each player has just one king; to win, you have to capture your opponent's king. ◇ A **king** is also a playing card with a picture of a king on it.

king-size or king-sized things are larger than the normal size. *...a king-sized bed.*

kingdom A **kingdom** is a country or region ruled by a king or queen. ◇ The **animal kingdom** is all animals, including birds, insects, and fish. The **plant kingdom** is all plants.

kingfisher The **kingfisher** is a small brightly-coloured bird which lives near fresh water and catches fish there.

kingpin The **kingpin** of an organization, especially a criminal one, is the most important person in it.

kink A **kink** is a twist or curve in something which is otherwise straight. ◇ A **kink** is also an interruption in the smooth progress of something.

kinky is used to describe strange sexual practices and the people who take part in them.

kinship is the connection between people who are related to each other. *...a people connected by geography, economics, and ties of kinship.* ◇ If you have a feeling of **kinship** with someone, you recognize similarities in their ideas or feelings and feel close to them because of it.

kinsman (kinsmen) A person's **kinsmen** are their relations, or people from the same ethnic group.

kiosk A **kiosk** is a small hut-like building where things like sandwiches or newspapers are sold. ◇ A telephone **kiosk** is the same as a telephone box.

kip If you have a **kip**, you sleep for a short time.

kipper A **kipper** is a smoked herring.

kirk is a Scottish word for a church. ◇ In Scotland, the

Kirk is the Church of Scotland.

kirsch (*pron*: key-ersh) is a brandy made from cherries.

kiss (kisses, kissing, kissed) ❑ If you **kiss** someone or give them a **kiss**, you touch or caress them with your lips, to show affection or for sexual pleasure.

❑ If you give the **kiss of life** to someone whose breathing has stopped, you put your mouth over theirs and breathe into their lungs, to start them breathing again. ◇ If you give something which is failing the **kiss of life**, you make it start to succeed again. *...his recent efforts to give the kiss of life to the peace process.*

❑ If something is the **kiss of death** to something like a plan or organization, it is guaranteed to make it go wrong or fail completely.

kit (kitting, kitted) ❑ A **kit** is a piece of equipment or group of items kept together and used for a particular purpose. *...the pregnancy predictor kit.* ◇ A **kit** is also a set of parts which you put together to make something.

❑ If you say someone is **kitted out** in a certain way, you are describing the clothes they are wearing. *...kitted out in smart new overalls.* ◇ Someone's **kit** is the clothes they wear for a particular activity, especially a sport. ◇ When a building or room is **kitted out**, it is furnished or equipped in some way.

kitbag A **kitbag** is a large cylindrical bag used, especially by people in the armed forces, for carrying clothes and personal possessions.

kitchen A **kitchen** is a room used for cooking and washing up.

kitchen garden A **kitchen garden** is the part of a large garden where vegetables, herbs, and fruit are grown, but not flowers.

kite ❑ A **kite** is a lightweight object made to float in the air on the end of a long string. It consists of a frame covered with paper or cloth. ◇ If you say someone is **kite-flying** or **flying a kite**, you mean they are putting forward an idea to see how people will react to it.

❑ The **kite** is a type of hawk with long narrow wings and a forked tail.

kitemark The **kitemark** is an official mark on certain articles. It shows they have been approved by the British Standards Institute as having reached a certain standard.

kith and kin Your **kith and kin** are your friends and relatives.

kitsch You use **kitsch** to describe things which are meant to be appealing, but which you think are vulgar or sentimental. *...kitsch decor... ...that pinnacle of 1970s kitsch 'Don't Cry For Me Argentina'.*

kitten A **kitten** is a very young cat.

kitty (kitties) A **kitty** is an amount of money which several people contribute to and which is kept for spending on things they can all use. ◇ In other situations, when people talk about the amount of money **in the kitty**, they mean the amount available for spending.

kiwi The **kiwi** is the national bird of New Zealand. It has short thick legs and a long beak. It cannot fly. ◇ People from New Zealand are sometimes called **kiwis**.

kiwi fruit (*plural*: kiwi fruit *or* kiwi fruits) **Kiwi fruit** are fruit with brown hairy skins and green flesh. They originally come from Asia, but are now also grown in New Zealand.

Kleenex (*plural*: Kleenexes *or* Kleenex) **Kleenex** is soft tissue paper used as a handkerchief. A **Kleenex** is a single tissue of this kind. 'Kleenex' is a trademark.

kleptomania (kleptomaniac) **Kleptomania** is a form of mental illness which makes people want to keep stealing things. A **kleptomaniac** is someone with this illness.

km See kilometre.

knack If you have the **knack** of doing something, you are able to do it, though other people may find it difficult.

knacker A **knacker** is a person who kills horses or farm animals which are useless or diseased and sells their bodies and those of other animals for profit.

knackered If you say you are **knackered,** you mean you feel very tired.

knapsack A **knapsack** is a canvas or leather bag you carry strapped over your back or slung over your shoulder.

knave A man who behaves in a dishonest way is sometimes called a **knave.**

knead (kneading, kneaded) If you **knead** something like dough, you press and squeeze it to make it smooth.

knee (kneeing, kneed) ❑ Your **knees** are the joints where your legs bend. ◇ If you have someone or something on your **knee,** you are supporting them on the upper part of your legs while you are sitting down. ◇ If someone **knees** you, they bring their knee up hard into your body.
❑ If someone is on their **knees,** they are kneeling. ◇ You say a person, organization, or country is **on their knees** when they are in a very bad state.

knee-deep If you are **knee-deep** in something like water or mud, it is as high as your knees.

knee-high If something like grass is **knee-high,** it is as high as a person's knees.

knee-jerk is used to describe someone's behaviour when they react to something in an automatic way, without thinking. ...*their knee-jerk hostility to the reforms.*

kneecap (kneecapped, kneecapping) Your **kneecaps** are the flat bones at the front of your knees. ◇ If a person or criminal organization **kneecaps** someone, they shoot them in the kneecaps, usually as a punishment. When this happens, you say there has been a **kneecapping.**

kneel (kneeling, knelt *or* kneeled) If someone **kneels** or **kneels down,** they bend their legs and lower their body until their knees are on the ground, supporting the rest of their body. When they are in this position, you say they are **kneeling.**

knell See death.

knelt See kneel.

knew See know.

knickerbockers are loose trousers fastened with a band at the knee or above the ankle. They used to be worn by men for golf, fishing, and shooting.

knickers are a piece of underwear worn by women and girls with holes for the legs and elastic around the waist to keep them up.

knife (knifing, knifed) A **knife** (*plural:* knives) is a tool with a handle and a blade, for cutting things. ◇ If one person **knifes** another, they attack and injure them with a knife. When this happens, you say there has been a **knifing.**

knife-edge If you say something like a game or an election is on a **knife-edge,** you mean things are very equal and the result could go either way. You can also say the result is on a **knife-edge.** ◇ If you say people are on a **knife-edge,** you mean they are anxiously waiting for the outcome of something.

knight (knighthood) ❑ If a man is **knighted,** he is given an honour called a **knighthood** by the king or queen for outstanding achievements or services to his country. A man who has this honour is called a **knight** and puts the title 'Sir' in front of his name.
❑ In historical times, a **knight** was a man of noble birth who served his king or queen in battle on horseback. ◇ These days, a man is sometimes called a **white knight** when he helps someone out of a difficult situation. This expression is often applied to someone who puts up the money to prevent a business being taken over in a way which would destroy its identity.
❑ A **knight** is also a piece in chess. Each player has two knights.

knit (knitting, knitted) ❑ If you **knit** something, you make it from wool, using knitting needles or a machine. A person's **knitting** is something they are making in this way.
❑ If you **knit** things together, you get them to fit together closely. You can also **knit** something into something else. *The agreement was designed to knit Quebec into the Canadian federation.* ◇ Knit is used after 'tightly', 'closely', or 'loosely' to say how strong the connection is between the people or countries in a group. ...*a tightly knit community.* -knit can be added to 'tight', 'close', and 'loose' with the same meaning. ...*a loose-knit confederation.*

knitting needle Knitting needles are long pointed plastic or metal rods for knitting with.

knitwear is clothing which has been knitted.

knives See knife.

knob A **knob** is (a) a round handle on a door or drawer. (b) a round projecting part of a device, which you press or turn to adjust the device or get it to perform a particular function. ◇ A **knob** is also a rounded lump of something. ...*a knob of butter.*

knobbly things have lumps on them. ...*knobbly tomatoes.*

knock ❑ If you **knock** on a door or window, you hit it, usually a few times, to attract someone's attention. When you hear someone do this, you say there is a **knock** at the door or window. ◇ If you **knock** a ball somewhere or give it a **knock,** you hit it with something like a bat or a golf club. ◇ If you **knock** against something, you collide with it. If you **knock** it **over,** it falls over.
❑ **Knock** is used to say someone hits someone else. For example, you can say someone **knocks** a person down. ◇ If someone **knocks** you **out,** they hit you so hard you become unconscious. Similarly, you can say a drug **knocks** someone **out.** ◇ If someone has been **knocked about** or **knocked around,** they have been hit several times.
❑ If a vehicle **knocks** someone **down,** it hits them and kills or injures them. ◇ If a building is **knocked down,** it is deliberately destroyed, usually because it is in bad condition or the site is needed for something else. ◇ In war, if something is **knocked out** by enemy action, it is destroyed.
❑ If a person or team is **knocked out** of a competition, they lose in a match or race and can take no further part in

the competition.

❑ If you **knock** a person or thing, you criticize them.

❑ If you **knock off** a series of things, you produce them quickly and easily. *Enid Blyton knocked off 600 books in all.*

❑ If an amount is **knocked off** the price of something, the price is reduced by that amount.

❑ If someone **knocks back** a drink, they drink it up quickly.

knock-down See knockdown.

knock-on If something you do has a **knock-on** effect, it makes something else happen, often something you do not intend.

knockabout is used to describe a type of comedy in which there is a lot of physical action. ...*knockabout farce.*

knockdown (*or* knock-down) If something is sold at a **knockdown** price, it is sold for much less than usual.

knocker A **knocker** is a piece of metal attached to the door of a building. You bang it on the door to attract the attention of the people inside.

knockout In boxing, you say there is a **knockout** when one of the boxers falls after being hit and cannot get up before a count of ten. ◇ In a **knockout** competition, the winner of each match or race goes on to the next round until one competitor or team is the overall winner.

knoll A **knoll** is a small hill.

knot (knotting, knotted) ❑ If you tie a **knot** in something like a rope, you make a loop in it and pass one end through, pulling the rope tight. You usually do this to make something more secure; you can also fasten two ropes together using a knot. If you **knot** something, you tie a knot in it.

❑ A **knot** of people is a group of them standing close together.

❑ The speed of ships and aircraft is usually expressed in **knots.** A knot is one nautical mile per hour (about 1.85kph or 1.15mph). Wind speed is also sometimes expressed in knots.

knotty A **knotty** problem is difficult to solve.

know (knowing, knew, have known) ❑ If you **know** something, you are aware of it. *I knew that she had recently graduated from law school.* ◇ If you **know** something like a person's name, you can say what it is. ◇ If you **know** of something or **know** about it, you have heard about it. ◇ If you **let** someone **know** about something, you tell them about it.

❑ If you **know** a language, you can understand it and speak it. ◇ If you **know** about a subject, you have studied it and could mention a lot of facts about it. ◇ If you **know** a place or thing, you are familiar with it. *He knew London well.* ◇ If you **know** a person, you are familiar with them because you have met them and talked to them. ◇ If you **get to know** someone, you find out what they are like, as a result of spending time with them. Similarly, you can **get to know** a place or thing.

❑ **Known as** is used to say what someone or something is usually called. ...*a professional caddie known as Big Brian.*

❑ If someone **lets it be known** that something is true, they make sure people know about it, but without telling them directly.

❑ When only a small number of people know about something, you can call them the people **in the know.** ◇ If you think someone has a mistaken belief, you can say

you **know better.** *The experts, who knew better, laughed at the idea.* ◇ If you say someone should **know better,** you mean they ought to behave in a more sensible and acceptable way. ◇ If you say someone **knows best,** you mean they are always right about what should be done.

❑ See also knowing, well-known.

know-how You say someone has the **know-how** when they have some kind of specialized knowledge. *They now had the facilities and know-how to produce advanced weapons.*

knowing (knowingly) If someone gives you a **knowing** look, they show they are aware of something even though it has not been mentioned directly. *The girls looked knowingly at each other.* ◇ If someone **knowingly** does something wrong, they are aware it is wrong when they do it. *He denied yesterday that he had knowingly put patients at risk.*

knowledge is things people know. Your **knowledge** of something is what you know about it. ...*advances in scientific knowledge... ...a knowledge of income-tax legislation.* ◇ If you say something is true **to the best of your knowledge,** you mean it is true as far as you know, but you are not completely sure.

knowledgeable (knowledgeably) (*can be spelled without an 'e' after the 'g'*) A **knowledgeable** person knows a lot about a subject, or about many different things. ...*the small group of people who write novels and discuss them knowledgeably in the Sunday papers.*

knuckle (knuckling, knuckled) ❑ A person's **knuckles** are the rounded pieces of bone where their fingers bend. ◇ If you **rap** someone's **knuckles** or give them a **rap on the knuckles,** you give them a warning or tell them off for something they have done.

❑ **White knuckle** is used to describe things like fairground rides which people enjoy because they are thrilling or frightening.

❑ If someone **knuckles down** to something, they begin to work or study very hard. ◇ If you say someone **knuckles under,** you mean they give way to pressure and do what someone else tells them to.

koala The **koala** or **koala bear** is an Australian animal which looks like a small bear with grey fur and tufted ears. Koalas live in trees and eat leaves.

kookaburra The **kookaburra** is a large Australian bird of the kingfisher family. It makes a loud noise like a person laughing, and is sometimes called the 'laughing jackass'.

kopeck (*or* kopek) The **kopeck** is a unit of money in Russia and in other countries formerly in the USSR. There are 100 kopecks in a rouble.

Koran (*pron:* kor-rahn) (Koranic) The **Koran** (or **Qur'an**) is the sacred book on which the religion of Islam is based. **Koranic** is used to talk about things connected with the Koran. ...*Koranic manuscripts... ...Koranic law.*

Korean is used to talk about things to do with North or South Korea or their people. ...*a shy Korean girl.* ◇ **Korean** is the main language spoken in Korea. ◇ A **Korean** is a person from North or South Korea.

kosher (*pron:* koh-sher) **Kosher** food is made in a way approved by the laws of the Jewish religion.

kow-tow (*or* kowtow) If you say a person **kow-tows** to someone else, you mean they behave in a very humble or respectful way, usually because they hope to get something out of them.

kph stands for 'kilometres per hour'. It is written after a number to give the speed at which something is moving. 100kph is about 62mph.

kraal A **kraal** is a village in southern Africa surrounded by a wooden fence.

Kremlin The **Kremlin** is a group of buildings in the centre of Moscow, now used as the government offices of the Russian Republic. In the past, **the Kremlin** was used to talk about the central government of the Soviet Union. *This change was welcomed by the Kremlin.*

krill (*plural:* krill) A **krill** is a small shellfish like a shrimp.

krona (*pron:* kroh-na) (*plural:* kronor) The **krona** is the main unit of currency in Sweden.

krone (*pron:* kroh-na) (*plural:* kroner) The **krone** is the main unit of currency in Norway and Denmark.

Ku Klux Klan The **Ku Klux Klan** is a secret organization of white Protestant Americans who use violence against African Americans, Jewish people, and members of other minority groups.

kudos (*pron:* kyew-doss) is fame or admiration someone gets because of something they have done.

kulak Kulaks were rich independent peasants in Russia before the 1917 revolution.

Kung Fu is a traditional Chinese way of fighting. In most kinds of kung fu, the fighters use only their hands and feet.

kW See kilowatt.

kWh See kilowatt hour.

L l

L-plate L-plates are small signs with an 'L' on them which you have to attach to your car when you are learning to drive.

lab A **lab** is a laboratory.

label (labelling, labelled) (*American spelling:* labeling, labeled) ❏ A **label** is a piece of paper, cloth, or plastic attached to an object, with information written on it about the object. If you **label** something, you attach a label to it. ◇ If a product is marketed under a particular **label**, it has a name on it which people can recognize when deciding whether to buy it. *Ott is the best known label among the Côtes-de-Provence wines.*

❏ A **label** is also a word or phrase people use to describe a person or thing. *...ex-Communists who have adopted the Socialist label.* ◇ If someone is **labelled** as a particular kind of person, people say they are that kind of person, although this may not be true. *They have found themselves labelled 'subversive'.*

labor See labour.

laboratory (laboratories) A **laboratory** is a building or room where scientific experiments and research are carried out. ◇ A **laboratory** at a school is a room with scientific equipment, where students learn science subjects like chemistry.

laborious (laboriously) A **laborious** task takes a lot of time and effort. *...laboriously hand-written books.*

labour (labouring, laboured) (*American spelling:* labor, *etc*) ❏ **Labour** is used to talk about the Labour Party. *Mr Hurd's decision has been attacked by Labour.*

❏ **Labour** is hard work. Someone's **labours** are the hard work they do. *...a pleasant distraction from his political labours.* ◇ If you **labour** at something, you work hard at it. ◇ If you do something as a **labour of love**, you do it because you really want to, although it may involve hard work and you may not get any pay or other reward.

❏ **Labour** is used to talk about the people available to do work in a place or industry. *...the city's supply of cheap labour.* A country's **labour force** is all the people there

who are able to work. The **labour market** is all the people who want to work and all the work which is available for them. *A million young people enter the labour market each year.* ◇ **Labour** is also used to talk about the work a group of workers does. *They are threatening a withdrawal of labour.*

❏ If you say someone is **labouring** under a misapprehension, you mean they believe something which is not true. *Local chefs are labouring under the delusion that they have invented a whole new cuisine.*

❏ If someone **labours** a point or argument, they talk about it in great detail and more than is necessary.

❏ If a woman is **in labour**, she is in the last stage of pregnancy, with the baby gradually being pushed out of her womb.

labour camp A **labour camp** is a prison camp where the prisoners have to do hard physical labour as part of their punishment.

labour-intensive industries or activities need or use a lot of workers.

Labour Party The **Labour Party** is the main left-of-centre party in the United Kingdom. It has strong links with the trade unions and believes in social justice within a market economy and properly funded public services.

labour-saving A **labour-saving** device or method saves people a lot of hard work or effort.

labourer A **labourer** is a person who does a job involving hard physical work.

labrador Labradors are fairly large dogs with black or pale gold coats. They are a type of retriever.

laburnum The **laburnum** is a small tree with long stems of yellow flowers. It is often planted in gardens.

labyrinth (*pron:* lab-er-inth) (labyrinthine) You call a complicated series of paths or passages a **labyrinth** when it is difficult to find your way through them. You can say paths or passages like these are **labyrinthine**. *...labyrinthine corridors.* ◇ You can call something you have to deal with a **labyrinth** when it is complicated and difficult to understand. *...a labyrinth of paperwork... ...the labyrinthine complexity of the case.*

lace (lacing, laced) ❏ Lace is a kind of delicate cloth with a pattern of holes in it.

❏ Laces are pieces of cord or string which are put through the holes along the two edges of something, pulled tight, then tied to fasten the edges together. If you lace something up, you fasten it with a lace or laces.

❏ If you lace food or drink, you put a small amount of alcohol or a drug in it. ◇ If something has a feature to a small extent, you can say it is laced with it. *The excitement of inheriting money is often laced with anxiety about what to do with it.*

lacerate (*pron:* lass-er-ate) (lacerating, lacerated; laceration) If someone lacerates something or makes a lacerating attack on it, they criticize it in a fierce and bitter way. *Mr Seguin has toured the country lacerating the text of the treaty.* ◇ If something lacerates a part of your body, it cuts the skin deeply. A laceration is a deep cut in someone's skin.

lachrymose (*pron:* lack-ree-moass) A lachrymose person cries often and easily.

lack If there is a lack of something, there is not enough of it, or none at all. *...the lack of affordable housing... ...his lack of tact.* You can also say something is lacking. *Vital information is still lacking.* ◇ If you lack something, you do not have it, or do not have enough of it. *The party has some good policies but its leaders lack conviction.* You can say someone is lacking in something. *The banks have been notably lacking in enthusiasm.* ◇ If you say there is no lack of something, you mean there is a lot of it.

lackadaisical A lackadaisical person is careless and not sufficiently interested in what they are doing. *Their attitude to safety was, to say the least, lackadaisical.*

lackey If you say someone is another person's lackey, you mean they do whatever that person tells them, as if they were their servant.

lacklustre (*American spelling:* lackluster) If you say something is lacklustre, you mean it has no brightness or liveliness. *...lacklustre performances.*

laconic (laconically) A laconic person uses very few words to say something. You can also call what they say laconic. *'Only the truth,'* it said laconically above his signature.

lacquer (lacquered) Lacquer is a special type of paint put on wood or metal to protect it and make it shiny. Lacquered wood or metal has been covered with this paint. ◇ Lacquer is also a liquid some people spray on their hair to hold it in place.

lacrosse (*pron:* lak-kross) is an outdoor game played by two teams who try to score goals. The players use long sticks with a net at one end to catch, throw, and carry the ball.

lactation is the production of milk by women and female mammals.

lactic acid is a type of acid found in sour milk. It is also produced by people's muscles when they have been exercising hard.

lactose is a type of sugar found in milk.

lacuna (*plural:* lacunae *or* lacunas) A lacuna is a missing part in something like a piece of writing.

lacy clothes are made from lace or have pieces of lace attached to them.

lad (laddish) Lad is an old or dialect word for a boy or young man. ◇ A young man is sometimes described as a lad when he behaves in a rowdy way, especially in the company of other young men. A young man like this is often called laddish.

ladder (laddering, laddered) ❏ A ladder is a piece of equipment for climbing up something like a wall or tree. It is made of two parallel pieces of wood, metal, or rope with steps fixed between them.

❏ Ladder is also used to talk about someone's career. For example, if you say someone has reached the top of the ladder, you mean they have reached a very high position in their job or profession. *...women with a foot on the career ladder.*

❏ A ladder in a woman's tights or stockings is a torn part where some of the vertical threads have broken, leaving only horizontal threads. When this happens, you say the woman has laddered her tights or stockings.

laddish See lad.

laden If a person, animal, or vehicle is laden with heavy things, they are holding or carrying a lot of them. ◇ You also use laden to say someone has an unusually large amount of something. *He returned laden with honours.* You often say people are laden with undesirable things; you say, for example, that a country is laden with debt.

ladies' man If you say a man is a ladies' man, you mean he likes to spend time with women and enjoys flirting with them in a way they also enjoy.

ladle (ladling, ladled) A ladle is a large round deep spoon with a long handle, for serving soup or stew. If someone ladles food, they serve it using a ladle.

lady (ladies) ❏ Lady is a title used in front of a woman's name, either because she is a member of the aristocracy or the House of Lords, or because she is married to a man who has been knighted. *...Lady Antonia Fraser.* ◇ People sometimes say a woman is a lady when she behaves in a polite and dignified way. ◇ Lady can also be used to talk about any woman. *She's an amazing lady.* ◇ You can use ladies to talk to a group of women. *Ladies, could I have your attention, please?*

❏ A ladies is a public toilet for women.

lady-in-waiting (ladies-in-waiting) A lady-in-waiting is a woman from the upper classes who acts as a companion to a female member of the royal family.

ladybird Ladybirds are small round beetles. Most kinds are red with black spots.

ladybug is the usual American word for a ladybird.

ladylike If you say a woman or girl is ladylike, you mean she behaves in a polite dignified way.

Ladyship When a woman has the title 'Lady', people use Ladyship when talking to her or about her. *Her Ladyship did not agree with the judge.*

lag (lagging, lagged) ❏ If you lag behind someone when you are going somewhere, you fail to keep up with them. ◇ If something lags behind something which is changing, it fails to keep up with it. *Statistics lag a long way behind what's happening in the real economy.*

❏ If something like trade or investment lags, it slows down or there is less of it than there was before.

❏ A time lag is a period of time between the ending of one thing and the beginning of another. ◇ See also jet lag.

❏ If you **lag** something like a hot water pipe or the inside of a roof, you cover it with a special material to stop heat escaping.

lager is a kind of light beer.

lager lout Lager louts are young men who behave in a noisy and violent way because they are drunk.

laggard (laggardly) If you call someone a **laggard**, you mean they are slow at dealing with something. You can also say they are **laggardly**.

lagoon A lagoon is an area of calm sea water separated from the ocean by reefs or sandbanks.

laid See **lay**.

laid-back people behave in a calm relaxed way, as if nothing ever worries them.

lain See **lie**.

lair A wild animal's **lair** is the place where it lives. A lair is usually underground or well-hidden. ◇ A person's lair is the place where they live or spend a lot of their time, especially if they are in hiding or want to be on their own.

laird A laird is a landowner in Scotland who owns a large area of land.

laissez-faire (pron: lay-say-fair) is a policy based on the idea that government should not interfere with the workings of business.

laity (pron: layi-tee) The **laity** are all the people involved in the work of a church who are not clergy, monks, or nuns.

lake A lake is a large area of fresh water, surrounded by land.

lakeside The lakeside is the area round the edge of a lake.

lama (pron: lah-ma) A lama is a Buddhist priest or monk in Tibet or Mongolia.

lamb (lambing) A **lamb** is a young sheep. ◇ **Lambing** is one of several times in a year when a large number of lambs are born on a farm. ◇ Lamb is the meat of a sheep or lamb.

lambast (lambasting) If someone **lambasts** a person or organization, they criticize them severely.

lambswool is the soft hair of young sheep, used mainly in knitwear.

lame (lamely, lameness) ❏ If a person or animal is **lame**, they cannot walk or run properly because of a leg injury. *Top Song was withdrawn at the start due to lameness.*
❏ If you say a person or organization is a **lame** duck, you mean they are not successful, and need help from other people or organizations.
❏ If you say something like an excuse or remark is **lame**, you mean it very poor or weak. *He explained lamely that 'there was simply not enough time.'*

lamé (pron: lah-may) is cloth with threads of gold or silver woven into it. *...a gold lamé shirt.*

lament (pron: la-ment) If someone **laments** something, they say how sad they are about it, or how much they regret it. You call what they say a **lament**. *He lamented the decline in participation in sports.* ◇ Originally, a lament was a poem or song written to show sadness about someone's death.

lamentable (lamentably) If you say something is **lamentable**, you mean it is very unfortunate or disappointing.

...lamentably infrequent opportunities.

lamentation You say there is **lamentation** when people express grief or great disappointment. Lamentations are expressions of grief or disappointment.

laminated (laminate) A **laminated** substance or material is made from two or more thin sheets or layers stuck together. A substance like this is called a **laminate**. ◇ If a product is **laminated**, it is covered with a thin sheet of clear plastic to protect it.

lamp A lamp is a light which works by electricity or by burning something like gas or oil.

lamp-post A lamp-post is a tall metal or concrete pole beside a road with a light on top.

lamplight is the light produced by a lamp.

lampoon (lampooning, lampooned) If you **lampoon** a person or thing, you write something or put on a performance which makes fun of them, as a way of criticizing them. A performance or piece of writing like this is called a **lampoon**.

lamprey The lamprey is an eel-like fish with a round sucking mouth.

lampshade A lampshade is a decorative cover over an electric light bulb which makes the light softer.

lance (lancing, lanced) If a doctor **lances** something like a boil, he or she pierces it with a sharp instrument to let the pus drain out. ◇ A **lance** is a long spear for killing whales or hunting. At one time, lances were used as weapons by soldiers on horseback.

lance-corporal A lance-corporal is an NCO of the lowest rank in the British army and the Royal Marines.

lancet A lancet is a small knife with a sharp point and two sharp edges, used by surgeons.

land (landed) ❏ You use **land** to talk about an area of ground. A person's land is the area they own. Landed people own large areas of land. *...the landed gentry.*
❏ Land is also used to talk about solid ground, as distinct from the sea or air. *We turned away from land and headed out to sea.* ◇ If something which has been moving through the air **lands** somewhere, it comes down onto the ground or an area of water. ◇ If a ship calls at a place so people can get off, you say it **lands** them there. You can also say a ship **lands** goods.
❏ Land is sometimes used to mean 'country'. *Australia is a land of opportunities.* ◇ When people talk about **the land**, they mean farming and the way of life in farming areas.
❏ If you **land** a desirable job, you succeed in getting it.
❏ If you **land up** in a place or situation, you get there after a long journey or a long series of events. ◇ If something **lands** you in an unpleasant situation, it causes you to be in it. *The trip landed them both in trouble.* ◇ If someone **lands** you with something difficult or unpleasant, they put you in a situation where you have to deal with it.

land mass A land mass is a very large area of land, such as a continent.

land reform is a change in the system of land ownership, especially one which involves the transfer of land from rich landowners to the people who farm it.

land registry A land registry is a government office where records are kept about each piece of land in a country or region, for example its size, where it is, and who owns it.

landfall is the first sighting of land after a long sea voyage. ...*four more days without landfall.*

landfill A **landfill** or **landfill site** is a place where large amounts of waste are disposed of by burying them in a large deep hole. Disposing of waste like this is called **landfill**.

landing ❑ In a house or other building, a **landing** is an area at the top of a staircase with rooms leading off it.
   ❑ If the pilot of an aircraft makes a **landing**, he or she brings the aircraft down to the ground. ◇ A **landing** is also the arrival of people by boat from the sea.

landing craft A **landing craft** is a boat or ship designed to land soldiers and military equipment on a beach.

landing gear The **landing gear** of a plane is the part, including the wheels, which supports the plane when it is on the ground.

landing stage A **landing stage** is a wooden platform for landing goods and passengers from a boat.

landing strip A **landing strip** is a long flat piece of land where aircraft can take off and land, especially one used by private or military aircraft.

landlady (landladies) A **landlady** is a woman who owns a house, flat, or room which she lets other people live in, in return for rent. ◇ The **landlady** of a pub is the woman who owns or runs it.

landless is used to describe people who do not own the land they farm, usually because they are prevented from doing so by large landowners or the economic system of their country. ...*landless labourers.*

landlocked A **landlocked** country is surrounded by other countries and has no sea coast.

landlord A **landlord** is a man who owns a house, flat, or room which he lets other people live in, in return for rent. ◇ The **landlord** of a pub is the man who owns or runs it.

landlubber People who are not used to travelling by boat or ship and know very little about the sea are sometimes humorously called **landlubbers**.

landmark A **landmark** is something like a building or hill which you can see from a lot of places and which can help you work out where you are. ◇ A **landmark** is also an important stage in the development of something.

landmine A **landmine** is an explosive device put on or under the ground which explodes when a person or vehicle touches it.

landowning (landowner) **Landowning** people are people who own a lot of land. People like these are also called **landowners**.

landscape (landscaping, landscaped) ❑ The **landscape** is everything you can see when you look across an area of land, including hills, rivers, buildings, and trees. ◇ A **landscape** is a painting of the countryside. ◇ If someone **landscapes** an area of land, they alter it to try and make it look attractive, for example by having different levels and planting trees and bushes. A person who designs schemes of this kind is called a **landscape gardener**; large-scale schemes are designed by a **landscape architect**.
   ❑ The **landscape** of a situation is its background and everything to do with it which affects it. ...*the bewildering political landscape of post-communist Russia.*

landslide If someone wins a general election by a land-slide, they win by a very large number of votes. ...*a landslide victory.* ◇ A **landslide** is also a large amount of earth and rocks which becomes loose and falls down the side of a mountain.

landslip A **landslip** is a small movement of earth and rocks down a hill or other slope.

landward The **landward** side of something on a coast is the side which faces away from the sea or is furthest from the sea.

lane A **lane** is a narrow road in the country. ◇ Roads, race courses, and swimming pools are sometimes divided into **lanes**. These are parallel strips separated from each other by lines or ropes. ◇ You also use **lane** to talk about a well-defined route used by ships or aircraft, which smaller or privately owned craft may not use. ...*the vital sea lanes... ...Europe's overcrowded air lanes.*

language ❑ A **language** is a system of sounds and written symbols used by the people of a country, area, or tribe to communicate with each other. ◇ **Language** is the use of words to communicate with other people. *This research helps teachers to understand how children acquire language.* ◇ **Language** is also used to talk about other means or systems of communication, for example sign language or a computer language.
   ❑ The **language** of a subject is the special words and phrases used to talk about it. ...*the language of sociology.* ◇ **Language** is also used to talk about the style in which something is written or spoken. *The Prince spoke in not particularly graceful language about the decline of English in schools.*

language laboratory A **language laboratory** is a room in a college or school where people can learn to speak languages or improve their knowledge of them by listening to recordings, recording their own voices, and having their mistakes corrected.

languid (languidly) If you say someone is **languid** or does something in a **languid** way, you mean they behave as though they have no energy or little interest in what they are doing. *The cat stretched himself languidly.*

languish (languishes, languishing, languished) If someone is forced to remain in a place where they are suffering or unhappy, you can say they are **languishing** there. ◇ You can also say someone is **languishing** when they are failing to escape from a bad situation. *His team has languished at the foot of the table for most of the season.*

languor (*pron:* lang-or) (languorous) **Languor** is a pleasant feeling of being relaxed and not having much energy or interest in anything. If you feel like this, you can say you feel **languorous**; you can also use **languorous** to describe something which gives you this feeling. ...*the languorous hot summer.*

lank hair is long and greasy and lies or hangs in a dull unattractive way.

lanky people are very tall and thin.

lantern A **lantern** is a lamp in a metal frame with glass sides.

lap (lapping, lapped) ❑ In a race, if you have completed a **lap**, you have gone round the course once. If you **lap** someone else, you pass them while they are still on the previous lap.
   ❑ A person's **lap** is the flat area formed by their thighs when they are sitting down.

❑ If water **laps** against something, it touches it gently and makes a soft slapping sound.

❑ If an animal **laps** a drink, it uses its tongue to flick the liquid into its mouth. ◇ If someone **laps up** something like attention, they accept it eagerly.

lap of honour (laps of honour) If the winner of a race does a **lap of honour**, they run or drive slowly round the track to receive the applause of the crowd.

lap-top A **laptop** computer is small enough to be carried around and used without a desk.

lapdog A **lapdog** is a small quiet well-behaved pet dog. ◇ If you say someone is a person's or organization's **lapdog**, you mean they do whatever that person or organization wants them to do.

lapel (pron: lap-pel) The **lapels** of a jacket are the two parts at the front which are folded back on each side and join the collar.

lapis lazuli (pron: lap-iss lazz-yoo-lie) is a bright blue semi-precious stone, which is used especially in making jewellery.

lapse (lapsing, lapsed) ❑ The **lapse** of time between two events is the period between them. ◇ If a period of time **lapses**, it passes.

❑ If something like a legal contract **lapses**, it is not renewed and becomes invalid.

❑ If someone has a **lapse** of some kind, they fail to do something or do not do it as well as they normally would. For example, if you have a **lapse** of memory, you forget about something. ◇ If someone starts behaving in a way you do not approve of, you can say they **lapse** into this behaviour. A **lapse** is a piece of bad behaviour by someone who normally behaves well.

lapwing The **lapwing** or **peewit** is a bird with a crest and black, white, and dark green feathers. Lapwings feed in fields, on moorland, and on coastal marshes.

larceny is the crime of theft.

larch (larches) The **larch** is a tree which produces cones and has needle-shaped leaves.

lard is soft white fat from a pig. It is used for cooking.

❑ If you say someone's speech or writing is **larded** with certain words or ideas, you mean they use them a lot, and they are unnecessary or unconvincing.

larder A **larder** is a room or cupboard where food is kept.

large (larger, largest) ❑ **Large** is used to say something is of great size, or to talk about a lot of things or people. ...*a large cloud*... ...*a large number of casualties*.

❑ **By and large** is used to say something is generally true, but not completely true. *By and large, they were free to do as they wished.*

❑ **At large** is used to talk about all the people in a country or community, as distinct from one group. *This anxiety is felt not only by MPs but by the people at large.* ◇ If a dangerous person or animal is **at large**, they are moving around freely and have not been captured.

large-scale is used to describe things which happen or exist over a wide area, or involve a lot of people or things. ...*a large-scale refugee problem*... *The country is forcibly resettling its citizens on a large scale.* ◇ A **large-scale** map or diagram is drawn to a larger scale than usual, and shows an area or object in greater detail.

largely is used to say something is true about most of something, or about most of the things or people in a group. *The radio's casualty figures were largely confirmed by hospitals.* ◇ **Largely** is also used when giving the main reason for something. *The crisis has arisen largely because of the refusal of three provinces to ratify the agreement.*

largesse (pron: lar-zhess; the 'zh' sounds like 's' in 'pleasure') If someone gives a very generous amount of money to someone or something, you can talk about their **largesse.**

largish things are fairly large.

lark ❑ The **lark** or **skylark** is a small brown bird which rises high in the sky singing a pleasant song.

❑ If you say someone is **larking about**, you mean they are enjoying themselves doing silly or mischievous things. A **lark** is a silly or mischievous piece of behaviour.

larva (larval) A **larva** (plural: larvae) is an insect at the stage before it becomes an adult. It looks like a short fat worm. **Larval** is used to talk about things to do with insect larvae. ...*larval wasps*.

laryngitis is a throat infection in which a person's larynx becomes swollen and painful, making it difficult for them to talk.

larynx (plural: larynxes or larynges) A person's **larynx** is the top part of the passage from their throat to their lungs. It contains their vocal cords.

lasagne is (a) a type of pasta made in wide flat sheets. (b) a cooked dish made from this pasta together with meat or vegetables.

lascivious If someone is **lascivious**, they are eager for sex.

laser A **laser** is a narrow beam of concentrated light. Lasers are used in surgery, and for cutting very hard materials. They are also used in CD players. ◇ A **laser** is also a machine which produces laser beams. ◇ A **laser printer** is a printer connected to a computer which produces very clear print or pictures using laser light.

LaserDisc or LD is a system similar to video but using 12-inch discs called **LaserDiscs**. 'LaserDisc' is a trademark.

lash (lashes, lashing, lashed) ❑ If someone **lashes** a person or animal or gives them a **lashing**, they hit them with a whip. **Lashes** are blows with a whip, especially blows on someone's back given as a punishment. ◇ If someone **lashes out**, they suddenly try to hit someone else with their hands or feet or a weapon. ◇ You also say someone **lashes out** or **lashes** another person when they attack them fiercely in speech or writing. ◇ If the rain or wind **lashes** something, it hits it violently.

❑ If you **lash** an object to something, you tie it there tightly, to prevent it being blown or swept away.

❑ A person's **lashes** are the hairs growing on the edge of their eyelids.

❑ **Lashings** of something means a lot of it. ...*hot-dogs served with lashings of mustard*.

lass (lasses) A **lass** is a girl or young woman.

lassie In Scotland, a **lassie** is a girl or young woman.

lassitude When people are too tired or too lazy to do anything or do not show much interest in anything, you can talk about their **lassitude**.

lasso (pron: lass-soo) (lassoes, lassoing, lassoed) A **lasso** is a long rope with a noose at one end, for catching cattle or horses. It is thrown so the noose lands round the animal's neck and pulls tight to stop it escaping. If someone **lassoes** an animal, they catch it using a lasso.

last is used to talk about the most recent period or event of a certain type. ...*last December*... ...*the last two months*... ...*the last general election*. ◇ If something **last** happened on a particular occasion, it has not happened since then. *They last saw their homeland nine years ago.* ◇ **The last** is used to say something did not happen or exist again after a particular time. *That was the last I ever saw of Northcliffe.*

❏ If something finally happens when you have been waiting for it for a long time, you can say it happens **at last** or **at long last**. *The government has acted at last.*

❏ The **last thing** of a particular kind is the one which comes at the end, after all the others. *He missed the last bus.* ◇ **The last** of something or the **last** parts of it are the remaining parts. *She removed the last traces of make-up.*

❏ If you want to emphasize that something is not wanted, needed, or expected, you can say it is **the last thing** someone wants, needs, or expects. *The last thing anyone expects is burglary in broad daylight.* Similarly, you can say someone would be **the last person** to do something. *I would be the last to suggest that.*

❏ **the last word**: see **word**. ◇ **the last straw**: see **straw**. ◇ **the last laugh**: see **laugh**.

❏ **Last** is used to say how long something continues. *His speech lasted for exactly fourteen minutes.* ◇ **Last** is also used to say (a) how long something will stay in good condition. *A fresh pepper lasts about three weeks.* (b) how long it will be before a quantity of something runs out. *He had only £8 left to last him till he reached Bury.* ◇ **Lasting** is used to describe something like peace or happiness when it goes on indefinitely, rather than coming to an end after a short time. ...*a plan to bring lasting peace to the Middle East.*

last-ditch is used to talk about a final attempt to prevent something bad happening. ...*a last ditch appeal for peace.*

Last Judgement For Christians, the **Last Judgement** is the end of the world, when God will judge everyone.

last-minute is used to describe things which happen just before something is due to begin. *He appealed for last-minute talks to avert war.*

last post The **last post** is an army bugle-call played at sunset and military funerals.

last rites If a Christian priest gives the **last rites** to a dying person, he holds a special religious ceremony for them; this can include confession, forgiveness, anointing, and communion.

lasting See **last**.

lastly You use **lastly** when you are making a final point, asking a final question, or mentioning a final item in a list. *Lastly, there is the vexed question of the ownership of guns.* ◇ You also use **lastly** when you are mentioning the last of a series of things to happen. *Lastly, he hit the bull's eye lying on his back on the ground.*

latch (latches, latching, latched) ❏ A **latch** is a fastening on a door or gate. It consists of a metal bar which slots into a catch. You lift the latch to open the door.

❏ If you **latch onto** something like an idea, you make use of it as a way of dealing with something.

latchkey child A **latchkey child** has to have a key to their house because their parent or parents are at work when they get home from school.

late (later, latest; lately, lateness) ❏ **Late** is used to talk about something happening towards the end of a period of time or the end of a person's life. ...*late September*... ...*Picasso's late work.* ◇ If something happens to someone in **later life**, it happens towards the end of their life. ◇ **As late as** is used to say something still existed or was still happening at a more recent time than might be expected. *Even as late as 1950 coal provided over 90% of our energy.*

❏ If you are **late** for something or arrive somewhere **late**, you should have been there earlier. *Her boss became infuriated with her lateness.* ◇ If it is **too late** to do something, it is no longer possible to do it. If you say something happens **too late**, you mean it happens after the time when it would have been useful. *I realized my mistake too late.* ◇ **Late** is also used to say someone does something after the time they normally do it. *We had a late lunch.*

❏ **Lately** and **of late** are used to talk about things which have happened recently. *Business has not been so good lately.* ◇ **The late** in front of someone's name means they have died recently. ...*the late Robert Maxwell.* ◇ **The latest** thing of a particular kind is the most recent one. ...*the latest news*... ...*her latest book.*

❏ You use **later** or **later on** to talk about a time coming fairly soon. *Later on, we shall have some music.* ◇ You also use **later** to talk about a time coming after the one you have been talking about. *I returned four weeks later.*

❏ You use **at the latest** to say something must be done at or before a particular time. *Changes will become necessary by the autumn at the latest.*

latecomer People who arrive late for an organized event are called **latecomers**. Similarly, people who join an organization later than other people can be called **latecomers**. *The Spaniards argue that as latecomers to the Community they get a raw deal.*

latent If someone has **latent** qualities or abilities, these qualities or abilities have not yet shown themselves, but may do so in the future. Similarly, you can talk about someone having **latent** feelings.

lateral movement is sideways, rather than upwards or forward. ◇ **Lateral thinking** is a way of solving problems in an imaginative way, rather than by using logic or accepted ways of thinking.

latex is a whitish fluid which occurs in many plants. Latex from the rubber tree is used to make rubber.

lath is strips of thin wood which you put onto the inside walls of buildings before covering them with plaster.

lathe A **lathe** is a device for shaping pieces of wood or metal. The pieces are rotated against a blade, which cuts them into a regular shape.

lather is a mass of bubbles produced when soap or washing powder is mixed with water.

Latin is the language of the ancient Romans.

❏ **Latin** is sometimes used to describe dark-haired, dark-eyed people who come from countries where French, Italian, Spanish, or Portuguese are spoken. ...*the sultry Latin lover.*

Latin America (Latin American) The countries of South and Central America where Spanish or Portuguese is spoken are called **Latin America**. **Latin American** is used to describe people and things from these countries. A **Latin American** is a person from Latin America.

latitude ❏ The **latitude** of a place is how far north or south it is from the equator, measured in degrees.

❏ **Latitude** is also the amount of freedom people have in choosing how to do things. *Actors say he allows them great latitude in interpreting his characters.*

latrine (*pron:* la-**treen**) **Latrines** are toilets, especially temporary ones or the ones in a camp or barracks.

latter is used to talk about the second of two people or things that have already been mentioned. *The novel was made into a film in 1943 and again in 1967: I prefer the latter version.* ◇ The **latter** half of something is the second half. *...the latter half of the century.*

latter-day things or people are the modern equivalents of things or people in the past. *...a latter-day Don Juan.*

latterly is used to say something has happened recently. *Latterly, he has been too ill to be involved.*

lattice A **lattice** is a structure made of strips of wood or some other material crossing each other diagonally.

laud (**lauding, lauded**) If someone **lauds** a person or **lauds** something they have done, they praise them.

laudable (**laudably**) If you call someone or something **laudable**, you mean they ought to be praised and admired. You use **laudably** to show you approve of what someone says or does. *Mr Walesa says, laudably, that Jews ought to be proud of their heritage.*

laudatory A **laudatory** speech or piece of writing is full of praise for someone or something.

laugh ❏ When someone **laughs** or gives a **laugh**, they make a noise which shows they are happy or amused.

❏ If people refuse to take something seriously, you can say they **laugh at** it. ◇ If you **laugh off** something like a danger, you say it is not important and you are not worried about it.

❏ If you do something **for a laugh,** you do it as a joke or for fun. ◇ If you **have the last laugh,** you get the better of someone in the end, having previously appeared to be defeated.

laughable (**laughably**) If you say something like an idea or statement is **laughable,** you mean it is ridiculous, because it is so unlikely or so obviously untrue. *Any pretence that athletics is still an amateur sport is laughable.* ◇ You say other things are **laughable** when they make you want to laugh. *They appear almost laughably pompous.*

laughing stock If someone or something has become a **laughing stock,** they have been made to appear ridiculous.

laughter is the act of laughing, or the sound of people laughing.

launch (**launches, launching, launched**) ❏ If someone **launches** something like a political movement, they start it. You can talk about the **launch** of something like this. ◇ When a company **launches** a new product, it makes it available for the first time. You call this the **launch** of the product. A **launch** is also a social event, held to publicize a new product.

❏ If someone **launches into** a speech, fight, or something else, they start doing it with a lot of energy and enthusiasm.

❏ When a ship is **launched,** it is put into water for the first time. ◇ When a rocket, missile, or satellite is **launched,** it is sent out into the air or space. You call this its **launch.**

❏ A **launch** is also a large motorboat.

launch pad A **launch pad** is the same as a launching pad.

launcher A **launcher** is (a) a device for holding a rocket, missile, or satellite before it is launched into the air or space. (b) a rocket from which a satellite is released into orbit.

launching pad A **launching pad** is a platform from which rockets, missiles, or satellites are launched. ◇ If you say something is a **launching pad** for something else, you mean people use it as a means of going on to something better or more important. *For most of them the college was a launching pad to a lucrative career.*

launder (**laundering, laundered; launderer**) When things like clothes and sheets are **laundered,** they are washed and ironed. ◇ If someone **launders** money they have got illegally, they invest it in legitimate businesses or send it to foreign banks, so the money they get back seems respectable and nobody knows it was originally obtained through crime. Someone who invests money like this for people is called a **money launderer.**

launderette A **launderette** is a place with washing machines and dryers which people can pay to use.

laundry (**laundries**) A person's **laundry** consists of things like clothes, sheets, and towels which need to be washed, or have just been washed. ◇ A **laundry** is a firm people pay to wash and iron their clothes, sheets, and towels. ◇ The **laundry** in a place like a hospital is a room where clothes, sheets, and towels are washed.

laureate (*pron:* **lor**-ee-at) A **laureate** is someone who has been honoured with an award for their work in art or science. See also **poet laureate.**

laurel is the name of several shrubs, including common laurel, which is used for hedges, and bay laurel, whose leaves are used as a herb in cooking. ◇ If you say someone is **resting on their laurels,** you mean they are satisfied with what they have already achieved and are not making any more effort.

lava (*pron:* **lah**-va) is hot liquid rock which comes out of a volcano and becomes solid as it cools.

lavatory (**lavatories**) A **lavatory** is the same as a toilet. ◇ In the US, a **lavatory** is a washbasin.

lavender is a garden plant with sweet-smelling bluish-purple flowers.

lavish (**lavishes, lavishing, lavished; lavishly**) ❏ A **lavish** amount of something is a great deal of it. *...lavish press coverage.* ◇ **Lavish** is also used to describe events which are very expensive to put on. *Rich merchants lavishly entertained travelling tradesmen.*

❏ If someone **lavishes** something like affection on another person, they give them a lot of it. ◇ If someone **lavishes** money on something, they spend a lot of it.

law ❏ The **law** is a system of rules for dealing with crime and its punishment, and also with things like property ownership and business agreements. Each rule is called a **law.** See also **criminal law, civil law.** ◇ **Law** is used to talk about a part of the law. For example, company law deals with the way companies are allowed to operate and do business.

❏ Rules of behaviour are sometimes called **laws.** *Children soon accept social laws.*

❏ If someone **lays down the law,** they order people about, because they think they know what is best.

❏ In science, a **law** is a general rule which says something will always happen in certain conditions.

law-abiding people obey the law. *People wanted a decent law-abiding society.*

law and order If you say there is **law and order** in a country, you mean the laws there are generally accepted and obeyed.

law-breaking (law-breaker) **Law-breaking** is doing something illegal. People who do illegal things are called **law-breakers**.

law court A **law court** is a place where legal matters are decided by a magistrate, or by a judge and jury.

law-enforcement is the methods used in a country to make sure its laws are obeyed.

Law Lord The **Law Lords** are the Lord Chancellor and other members of the House of Lords who belong to the legal profession. They act as the highest court of appeal in the country.

lawful (lawfully) If something like an activity or organization is **lawful**, it is allowed by law. *...the obligation on administrations to act lawfully.*

lawless (lawlessness) You say people are **lawless** when they regularly break the law, or do not accept any laws. *...lawless military dictatorships... ...acts of violence and lawlessness.*

lawmaker A country's **lawmakers** are the people, for example MPs, who decide about new laws.

lawn A **lawn** is an area of grass which is kept cut short, usually as part of a garden or park.

lawn tennis is tennis played on grass, rather than on clay or hard courts. Sometimes people use **lawn tennis** to talk about the game of tennis generally.

lawnmower A **lawnmower** is a machine for cutting the grass on a lawn.

lawsuit A **lawsuit** is a court case brought by one person or organization against another.

lawyer A **lawyer** is a person qualified to advise people about the law and represent them in court. See also **barrister, solicitor, attorney, advocate.**

lax (laxity) If you say a system is **lax**, you mean the rules are not being obeyed or standards are not being maintained. You can also say the people involved are **lax**, or talk about their **laxity**.

laxative A **laxative** is a medicine for curing constipation.

laxity See **lax.**

lay (laying, laid) ❑ See **lie.**
   ❑ If you **lay** something somewhere, you place it there. *She laid the baby gently down on its bed... She laid a hand on his shoulder.* ◇ If you **lay** the table, you put out the knives, forks, plates, etc before a meal. ◇ If you **lay out** a group of things, you spread them out and arrange them. *Chairs were laid out neatly in rows.* ◇ If you **lay** a carpet, you put it on the floor in the correct position. ◇ If someone **lays** a cable, they put it in the ground in the correct position.
   ❑ When a bird **lays** an egg, the egg comes out of its body.
   ❑ If someone **lays on** food, entertainment, or a service, they provide it. *Buses are laid on to take people to the mosques.*
   ❑ If someone **lays out** a garden or a new development, they plan or design it.
   ❑ If someone **lays** the basis or foundation for something, they do something which prepares the way for it.

❑ If someone **lays out** ideas or information, they express or present them clearly and thoroughly. You can also say someone **lays** an idea or proposal **before** someone, to obtain their approval or advice. *The proposed treaty will be laid before the conference on Tuesday.* ◇ If someone **lays down** something like a requirement, they say something must be done. ◇ **lay down the law: see law.**
   ❑ If soldiers **lay down** their arms or weapons, they stop fighting.
   ❑ If workers are **laid off**, they are told to leave their jobs, usually because there is no more work for them. When this happens, you say there is a **lay-off** or **layoff.** ◇ A **lay-off** is also a period of time when someone does not take part in something. *Pat Cash is at last finding form after a lengthy lay-off through injury.*
   ❑ If a charge is **laid against** someone, they are charged with committing an offence. ◇ If you **lay** yourself **open** to something like a criticism, you make it likely to happen to you. *They had laid themselves open to blackmail threats.*
   ❑ **Lay** is used to describe people involved with the Christian church who are not members of the clergy, or monks or nuns. *...a lay preacher.* ◇ **Lay** is also used to describe someone who is involved in something without being trained or qualified for it. *...a lay magistrate.*
   ❑ **lay a trap** for someone: see **trap.** ◇ **lay claim to** something: see **claim.** ◇ **lay** something **bare: see bare.** ◇ **lay** something **to rest: see rest.** ◇ **lay** something **at** someone's **door: see door.**

lay-by A **lay-by** is a short strip of road by the side of a main road, where vehicles can stop for a while.

lay-off See **lay.**

layabout If you call someone a **layabout**, you mean they spend a lot of time doing nothing, because they are lazy.

layer (layering, layered) ❑ A **layer** of something like paint is a quantity of it evenly covering a surface.
   ❑ If something consists of **layers**, it is made up of thin flat pieces, one on top of the other. You say something like this is **layered.** *...a layered structure.*
   ❑ The different levels of staff within an organization can be called **layers.** *Companies are sweeping away layers of management.*
   ❑ If you talk about something having **layers** of meaning, you mean it has several meanings besides the most obvious one.

layman (laymen) A **layman** is someone who has no specialized knowledge of a subject. *There are basically two types called, in layman's terms, blue and white asbestos.*

layoff See **lay.**

layout The **layout** of something is the way its different parts are arranged.

laze (lazing, lazed) If someone **lazes**, they sit or lie around and do nothing which involves effort.

lazy (lazier, laziest; lazily, laziness) You say people are **lazy** when they try to avoid doing any work, or cannot be bothered to do something. *Employment laws will be changed to reward effort and punish laziness.* ◇ **Lazy** actions are done slowly, without much effort. *He drew lazily on his cigarette.*

lb See **pound.**

lbw In cricket, if you are given out **lbw**, you are out because the ball has hit your leg and this has stopped it hitting the wicket. 'lbw' stands for 'leg before wicket'.

LCD An LCD or liquid crystal display is a display of information on a screen. It uses liquid crystals which become visible when electricity is passed through them.

LD See LaserDisc.

LEA See local education authority.

leach (leaches, leaching, leached) If something leaches from a substance, it is washed out by water passing through it or over it. *...the pesticides that leach into rivers.*

lead (leading, led) ❑ If someone is leading in a race or contest, they are in front, or doing better than their opponents. You also say they are in the lead. *Only twice before has Labour had a lead of over 20%.*

❑ If you lead someone somewhere, you take them there, or go in front of them. If you lead the way, you go in front of someone to show them where to go. ◇ If something like a road or pipe leads somewhere, it goes there. *The steps lead down to his basement.* ◇ If a door or gate leads to a place, you get there by going through it.

❑ If someone leads a group or organization, they are officially in charge of it. *A senior Foreign Ministry official has been flown over to lead the Iraqi delegation.* ◇ If someone leads an action involving several people, they start it, and get the rest to follow their example. *The rioting was led by students.*

❑ If someone takes the lead or leads the way, they start doing something before other people. You then say other people follow their lead. ◇ If you say someone is giving a lead, you mean they are setting a good example for other people to follow. ◇ The person who leads off is the first one to do something, for example in a game or meeting. *The chairman led off with a financial statement.*

❑ If one thing leads to another, the second thing happens as a result of the first. ◇ The things which lead up to something are all the things which happen before it, and which are responsible for it happening. *...the chain of events that led up to her death.* ◇ If something leads you to do something, you do it because of it. Similarly, something can lead you to feel or believe something.

❑ If you lead up to something in a conversation, you gradually guide the conversation towards it, so you can talk about it.

❑ The lead in a play or film is the most important acting role. ◇ The lead singer in a pop group is the main singer. ◇ The lead story in a newspaper is the piece of news thought to be most important and given the most space.

❑ If you say someone leads a particular type of life, you mean they live that way. *By all accounts he leads a life of considerable luxury.*

❑ A dog's lead is a chain or strip of leather attached to its collar, to keep it under control.

❑ Lead (*pron:* led) is a soft grey heavy metal. It is used in alloys and paints. ◇ The lead in a pencil is the part in the middle which makes a mark when you write.

lead-free petrol is the same as unleaded petrol.

lead-in A lead-in is an introduction to something like a talk or a TV report.

lead-up The lead-up to a public event is the time before it, when preparations are being made for it.

leaded petrol has had a small amount of lead added to it. This helps to make engines more efficient, but also increases air pollution. ◇ Leaded windows are made of small pieces of glass held together in a pattern by strips of lead between them.

leaden (*pron:* led-en) If you say conversation or writing is leaden, you mean it is very dull. ◇ If your movements are leaden, you are moving slowly and heavily, because you are very tired. You can also say your legs are leaden. ◇ A leaden sky or sea is dark grey, with very little movement in the clouds or waves.

leader ❑ The leader of a country, organization, or group of people is the person in charge. ◇ The leader in a race or contest is the person who is in front or doing better than the others. ◇ The leader in a commercial activity is the firm which is most successful at it. *...the world leader in audio alarm verification.*

❑ The leaders or leading articles in a newspaper are a small group of articles, often written by the editor, expressing views on the main news of the day.

leadership The people in charge of a country or organization are often called the leadership. ◇ Leadership is also used to talk about the position of being leader, or to comment on a leader's methods or performance. *Opponents grumble about her hard-nosed style of leadership.*

leading is used to talk about the most important or successful people of a particular kind. *...a leading Albanian intellectual.* ◇ The leading role in a play or film is the main one. The main male and female actors in a play are sometimes called the leading man and leading lady. ◇ If someone plays a leading role in getting something done, they have a lot to do with it. ◇ leading light: see light.

leading article See leader.

leaf (plural: leaves) (leafs, leafing, leafed) ❑ The leaves of a tree or other plant are the thin flat parts growing on its branches or stalks; they are usually green. If a tree or plant is in leaf, it has leaves growing on it.

❑ If you say someone has turned over a new leaf, you mean they have decided to try and behave better in some way. ◇ If you take a leaf out of someone's book, you copy something they have done, because you think it was a good idea.

❑ If you leaf through a book, you turn the pages quickly, without looking at anything carefully.

leaflet (leafleting, leafleted) A leaflet is a piece of paper or booklet giving information or advertising something. If you leaflet a place, you distribute leaflets there.

leafy trees and plants have a lot of leaves. ◇ Leafy places have a lot of trees and plants. *...leafy lanes.*

league ❑ A league is a group of people, organizations, or countries that have joined together for a common purpose, or because they share a common interest. *...the National League for Democracy.* ◇ A league is also a group of sports clubs which play the same sport in competition with each other, to see which club is best.

❑ If you say someone is in league with someone else, you mean they are secretly working together. *They are in league with the police.*

league table A league table is a list of people, teams, or organizations arranged with the most successful one at the top and the least successful one at the bottom.

leak (leaking, leaked) ❑ If a container or other object leaks or has a leak, it has a small hole or crack which lets liquid or gas through. You can also say the liquid or gas leaks through the hole or crack.

❑ If someone **leaks** a piece of information which is supposed to be confidential, they let other people know about it. When this happens, you say there is a **leak**.

leakage If there is a **leakage** of something like liquid or gas, some of it escapes from a pipe or container through a hole or crack. ◇ If there is a **leakage** of secret information, it is passed on to someone who is not supposed to know about it. ◇ If there is a **leakage** of funds, money is secretly taken and used for an unauthorized purpose.

leaky things have holes or cracks which let liquids in or out.

lean (leaning, leaned or leant; leaner, leanest) ❑ If you **lean** in a particular direction, you bend your body that way. ◇ If you **lean** on something, you rest your body against it and it partly supports you. Similarly, you can **lean** an object against something. *He leaned the bike against a nearby railing.*

❑ If someone **leans on** you, they try to get you to do something, by threatening you in some way. ◇ You also say one person **leans on** another when they depend on them. *They lean heavily upon each other for support.*

❑ If you **lean towards** a particular view of things, you tend to sympathize with it or agree with it. You can also say someone has **leanings** towards a particular view. *Her socialist leanings were not to the liking of her family.* ◇ If you are **leaning towards** a course of action, you are likely to adopt it. *The French government appears to be leaning towards the phasing out of its long-range nuclear missiles.*

❑ **Lean** people are thin, but also look fit and healthy. ◇ **Lean** meat has very little fat on it. ◇ **Lean** is used to describe organizations which have exactly the amount of staff and equipment they need. *...the struggle to turn the company into a lean commercial outfit.* ◇ In a **lean** period, people do not have much food, money, or success.

leap (leaping, leapt or leaped; both pron: lept) ❑ If you **leap**, you jump a long way. *Some of them suffered fractures when they leaped from the upper floor.* A jump like this is called a **leap**. ◇ You also say someone **leaps** somewhere when they move there quickly and suddenly. *She leapt into a taxi.*

❑ If something **leaps**, it suddenly increases by a large amount. You can talk about a **leap** in something. *...a leap in oil prices.* ◇ If something changes by **leaps and bounds**, it changes very quickly. *Since 1982, the organization has grown in leaps and bounds.* ◇ A **leap** is also a sudden change in someone's way of thinking. *...a leap of faith... ...that leap of understanding that would have made him a great ruler.*

❑ If you **leap at** a chance, you accept it quickly and eagerly.

leap year A **leap year** has 366 days. There is a leap year once every four years.

leapfrog (leapfrogging, leapfrogged) ❑ If something **leapfrogs** something else, it overtakes it and gets ahead of it. *That let Hitachi leapfrog IBM-Japan into the number two spot in mainframes, behind Fujitsu.*

❑ **Leapfrog** is a game for children in which some of them bend over and others jump over their backs.

leapt See **leap**.

learn (learning, learnt or learned; learner) ❑ If you **learn** something, you gain knowledge or a skill, especially by studying or training. ◇ A **learner** is someone who is studying a subject, or learning how to do something.

❑ **Learning** is knowledge gained through studying. ◇ **Learned** people (pron: ler-nid) have studied a lot and gained a lot of knowledge. The books and papers they write can also be called **learned**.

❑ If you **learn** of something, you hear about it or read about it. *He has since learned that NASA bought the land to build a satellite launching station.* ◇ If you **learn** to do something, you gradually start doing it, because you realize it needs to be done. *The Russian economy cannot be changed until citizens learn to embrace new economic thinking.*

lease (leasing, leased; lessor, lessee) ❑ If you **lease** a building or other property, you make a legal agreement with the owner and pay to be allowed to use it for a period of time. The agreement is called a **lease;** the owner is called the **lessor;** you are called the **lessee.** You can also say the owner **leases** you the building or property.

❑ If someone or something is given a new **lease of life,** they become useful or successful again, after it had seemed they would no longer be wanted or needed. *After a career as a comedian, he found a new lease of life as an actor.*

leasehold (leaseholder) A **leasehold** property is one which can be leased. If you lease property from someone, you are called the **leaseholder.** See also **freehold**.

leash (leashes) A dog's **leash** is a chain or strip of leather attached to its collar, to keep it under control. ◇ The control people have over other people is sometimes called a **leash.** For example, you say someone is being kept on a **short leash,** meaning they are allowed very little freedom of action. If someone is no longer under someone else's control, you say they have been **let off the leash.**

least ❑ You use **least** when comparing several things to say some of them have less of a feature or quality than others. *...the thinner animals, who had the least muscle over their bones... ...one of the least powerful of the African states.* ◇ You use **the least** to say something applies less to some people or things than others. *They're the ones who need it the least.* ◇ You also use **the least** to say something is less important or serious than other things of the same kind. *That was the least of her worries.* ◇ You use **least** to say something is less true at a particular time than at other times. *He came out when I least expected it.*

❑ If something is **at least** a number or amount, it cannot be less than that number or amount, and is probably more. *At least 32 people were injured... I must have slept twelve hours at least.* ◇ You also use **at least** to say something is the minimum a person ought to do, although they should really do more. *At the very least they could make donations.* Similarly, you can say something is **the least** someone should do. *The least they should do is to give full compensation to the relatives.*

❑ You also use **at least** to draw attention to a good point in something. *The process looks rather laborious but at least it's not dangerous.* ◇ You use **at least** to correct something you have just said. *A couple of days ago I spotted my ex-wife – at least I thought I did.*

❑ If something is not true **in the least,** it is not true at all. Similarly, you can say something is not **in the least bit** true. *He was not in the least bit downhearted.*

❑ **Not least** is used to mean 'especially', when you are giving an example of something, or a reason for it. *I hap-*

pen to be a fan of hers, not least because she has the courage to hold steadfastly to her belief. Similarly, **least of all** is used to mean 'especially not'. *Nobody seemed amused, least of all Jenny.*

❑ You use **to say the least** to suggest something is actually worse than the way you are describing it. *Some members of the public can be a bit abusive to say the least.*

leather is animal skin which has been treated to make it tough and strong so it can be used to make things like shoes, clothes, and bags.

leathery things have a tough texture like leather.

leave (leaving, left) ❑ If you **leave** a place, you go away from it. ◇ If you **leave** an organization or institution, you end your connection with it, usually for good. *The Vatican gave her permission to leave her convent.* ◇ If you **leave** your husband or wife or the person you are living with, you end your relationship with them and move out.

❑ If you **leave** something somewhere or **leave** it behind, you do not take it with you when you go. *I had left my raincoat in the restaurant.* Similarly, you can **leave** a person **behind**. *Many refugees have been forced to leave their families behind.* ◇ If you **leave behind** something like a way of life, you give it up completely, and behave as if it had never happened. *Together, our nations have a responsibility to leave behind not only the Cold War but also the conflicts that preceded it.*

❑ If you **leave** someone to do something, you let them get on with it on their own. Similarly, you can **leave** something to develop on its own. *Cover the mixture and leave it to stand for 12 hours.* ◇ If you **leave** a decision to someone, you let them make it. *Parliament sets out the broad principles, but leaves the details to the broadcasters.*

❑ If something **leaves** you in a particular state, you are in that state as a result of it. *This has left everyone dissatisfied.* ◇ If someone or something **leaves** something like a mark or impression, it is there as a result of what they have done. *The explosion left a crater as wide as the road.*

❑ If you **leave** something until a particular time, you wait until then before dealing with it. ◇ If you **leave** a subject, you stop talking about it and start talking about something else. ◇ If you continue with something from where you **left off**, you start again from the point where you stopped.

❑ If you **leave** an amount of something, you do not use it. If an amount is **left** or **left over**, it is still there after the rest has gone or been used.

❑ If someone **leaves** you money or other property, you get it when they die.

❑ If someone is **left out** of something, they are not included in it. *Both players were left out because of their poor performances.* Similarly, someone or something can be **left off** a list.

❑ If someone in authority gives you **leave** to do something, they give you permission. *He has been refused leave to appeal against his £5 million fine.* ◇ If you are given **leave of absence**, you are given permission to stay away from work for a time. ◇ **Leave** is a period when you are on holiday from your job or allowed to be absent for some other reason.

leaven (pron: lev-en) (leavening, leavened) If you say someone **leavens** the group of people they belong to, you

mean they are different from the other people in the group, and make it seem less dull or less extreme. *...one of those delinquent upper-class Bohemians who leaven the English class system.* You can also say someone like this provides a **leavening**. *Their activities are moderated by a leavening of external members and nominated outsiders.*

lecherous (lecher, lechery) If you say someone is **lecherous** or a **lecher**, you mean they are greedy for sex. You call their behaviour or inclinations **lechery**.

lectern A **lectern** is a high sloping desk for putting a book or notes on when you are standing up and reading or talking to an audience.

lecture (lecturing, lectured) ❑ A **lecture** is a talk given to an audience, to inform or teach them about something. If someone **lectures** on a subject, they give a lecture or series of lectures on it.

❑ If someone **lectures** you or gives you a **lecture**, they tell you off, or tell you how to behave.

lecturer (lectureship) A **lecturer** is a teacher at a university or college. His or her post is called a **lectureship**.

led See **lead**.

ledge A **ledge** is (a) a narrow flat area on the side of a cliff or mountain. (b) a narrow shelf along the bottom edge of a window.

ledger A **ledger** is a book in which an organization keeps a record of the amounts of money it receives and spends.

leech (leeches) **Leeches** are small worm-like animals which live in or near water and feed by attaching themselves to other animals and sucking their blood. ◇ If you call someone a **leech**, you mean they live off other people.

leek The **leek** is a vegetable which consists of a white part with a cluster of straight green leaves growing out of it. Its taste is like an onion's, but less strong.

leer (leering, leered) If someone **leers** at you, they smile in an unpleasant way; a smile like this is called a **leer**. If a man **leers** at a woman, it usually means he is sexually interested in her.

leery If someone is **leery** of something, they are suspicious or worried about it, or afraid it may happen. *Many businesses are leery of a recession and are not hiring.*

leeway is used to talk about the amount of freedom or flexibility someone has in dealing with something. *This would give Mr Major more leeway to cut bank interest rates.*

left ❑ See **leave**.

❑ **Left** is one of two opposite sides or directions. If you turn to the left, you turn quarter of a circle in an anticlockwise direction.

❑ The **left** are people who support socialism rather than capitalism.

left-hand The **left-hand** side of something is the side towards the left.

left-handed (left-hander) **Left-handed** people use their left hand rather than their right for things like writing or throwing a ball. In sport, people like these are called **left-handers**.

left-luggage office A **left-luggage office** is a place at a station or airport where you can pay to leave your luggage.

left-of-centre people or organizations have moderate political views which are closer to socialism than to conservatism or capitalism.

left-wing (left-winger) Left-wing people have socialist ideas and opinions. People like these are sometimes called **left-wingers**. ◇ The **left wing** of a party consists of the members whose beliefs are closest to socialism.

leftist A person with socialist or communist views is sometimes called **leftist** or a **leftist**. ...*leftist rebels*... *The government depends on the leftists for its survival.*

leftover The **leftovers** from a meal are the food which has not been eaten. ◇ If you say a thing or person is a **leftover** from an earlier time, you mean they were important or useful then, but are not so any more. *The General is a leftover from the old Communist regime.*

leftward (or **leftwards**) When a politician or party becomes more left-wing, you can talk about a **leftward** change in their views, or say they have moved **leftwards**.

lefty (or **leftie**) (*plural for both:* lefties) People who do not like left-wing people sometimes call them **lefties**. ◇ Americans call left-handed sportsmen and women **lefties**.

leg (-legged) ❑ A person's **legs** are the parts of their body between their hips and their feet. The **legs** of an animal, bird, or insect are the parts it uses to stand on or move across the ground. ◇ **-legged** is used to describe a person's or animal's legs, or to say how many legs they have. ...*a spindly-legged foal*... ...*a one-legged man*. ◇ If you say someone is **pulling your leg**, you mean they are telling you something untrue as a joke.

    ❑ A **leg** of lamb is a piece from the leg of a sheep or lamb. Similarly, a **leg** of pork is a piece from the leg of a pig. ◇ The **legs** of a table or chair are the thin vertical parts which support it. ◇ If you say something is **on its last legs**, you mean it is in bad condition and likely to stop working, break, or fall to pieces.

    ❑ A **leg** of something like a tour, journey, or visit is one part of it. *The Prime Minister has just arrived in Egypt on the first leg of a Middle East tour.* Similarly, a **leg** of a race or competition is one stage or part of it.

legacy (legacies) A **legacy** is money or property which someone leaves you in their will when they die. ◇ Anything left over from an earlier time which people have to put up with or deal with can be called a **legacy**. *The equivalent of $320,000 million would be needed to cope with the Chernobyl legacy.*

legal (legally) ❑ **Legal** is used to talk about things to do with the law. *The change may have legal implications.*

    ❑ If something is **legal**, it is allowed by law. ...*legal abortion*... *It was all done legally and properly.* ◇ If a coin or note is **legal tender**, it is officially a part of a country's currency and can be used to buy things there.

legal aid is financial help given by the government to people who cannot afford a lawyer.

legalise See **legalize**.

legalistic If you say something like a statement or argument is **legalistic**, you mean it concentrates too much on the legal side of things and is therefore not very helpful.

legality (legalities) If you talk about the **legality** of something, you are talking about whether it is legal or not. *Miss Bhutto has said she plans to challenge the tribunal's legality.* ◇ The **legalities** of something are its legal as-

pects. *Once both laws are passed, they will be able to sort out all the legalities of their investments in one go.*

legalize (legalizing, legalized; legalization) (*can be spelled with an 's' instead of a 'z'*) When something is **legalized**, it is made legal. *We believe that legalization of drugs would lead to an increased number of addicts.*

legation A **legation** is a group of government officials and diplomats who work in a foreign country as representatives of their government. The place where they work is also called a **legation**.

legend (legendary) A **legend** is a very old story which may be based on real events. ...*the Faust legend*. **Legendary** is used to talk about people and things in legends. ...*the legendary British chieftain, King Arthur*. ◇ You call a living person **legendary** or a **legend** when they are very famous and much admired. ...*the legendary Tina Turner*... *He is also modest, as befits a living legend.*

leggings are (a) skintight trousers, often made with stretchy material. (b) an outer covering worn over a normal pair of trousers to protect them.

leggy A **leggy** woman has very long legs.

legible writing is clear enough to be read.

legion ❑ A **legion** was a military unit in the Roman army, consisting of both cavalry and infantry, and numbering from 4,000 to 6,000 men. ◇ **Legion** appears in the names of some modern military forces. ...*the Libyan Islamic Legion*... ...*the French Foreign Legion.*

    ❑ A **legion** of people or things is a large number of them. *His sense of humour won him a legion of friends.* ◇ If you say things are **legion**, you mean there are a lot of them. *The examples of anti-social behaviour today are legion.*

legionnaire Legionnaires are soldiers who are members of a legion.

Legionnaires' disease is a serious lung infection.

legislate (legislating, legislated; legislation) When a government or other governing body **legislates**, it passes new laws. Laws passed by a government are called **legislation**.

legislative A **legislative** council or assembly is one which has the authority to make laws. ◇ **Legislative** is used to talk about things to do with making laws. ...*the Government's legislative programme.*

legislator A **legislator** is a person involved in making or passing laws, for example an MP.

legislature A **legislature** is a group of people with the authority to make laws.

legitimate (legitimately, legitimacy) ❑ If something is **legitimate**, it is allowed by law. You talk about the **legitimacy** of something like this. *Many legal experts have questioned the legitimacy of this move.*

    ❑ If you say something like a claim or argument is **legitimate**, you mean it is reasonable or justified. *The ITC can legitimately claim to have remade the face of commercial television.*

    ❑ If a child is **legitimate**, it was born to parents who were legally married at the time.

legitimize (legitimizing, legitimized) (*can be spelled with an 's' instead of a 'z'*) If something is **legitimized**, it is made legal.

legless If a person or animal is **legless**, they have no legs. ◇ You can also say someone is **legless** when they are extremely drunk.

Lego is a children's toy consisting of small coloured plastic blocks which can be fitted together to build things. 'Lego' is a trademark.

legumes (*pron:* leg-yooms) (leguminous) **Legumes** are a group of plants, including clover, peas, and beans, whose seeds grow in pods. **Leguminous** plants are members of this group.

leisure (leisured) ❑ Your **leisure** time is the time when you do not have to work and can do things you enjoy. The things people do for enjoyment in their leisure time are called **leisure** activities. ◇ **Leisured** is used to describe people who have so much money they never need to work. ...*the leisured classes.*

❑ If you are allowed to do something **at leisure** or at **your leisure**, you can do it when you want to, rather than having to do it immediately.

leisure centre A **leisure centre** is a large building with facilities for leisure activities, for example a sports hall, swimming pool, and meeting rooms.

leisurely is used to say something is done in a relaxed and unhurried way. *A tour of Oxford is best conducted at a leisurely pace over two days.*

leitmotif (*or* leitmotiv) (*pron:* lite-mote-eef) A **leitmotif** is a musical phrase which occurs many times in a piece of music, especially an opera, and represents a particular person or idea. Similarly, an object can be used as a leitmotif in a novel or film.

lemming The **lemming** is an animal which looks like a rat with thick fur. Lemmings sometimes migrate in large groups and there is a popular belief that these groups sometimes rush over the edges of cliffs and die. If you say people are behaving like **lemmings**, you mean they are behaving as a mindless group in a stupid or self-destructive way.

lemon Lemons are yellow citrus fruit with sour juice.

lemon curd is a sweet paste made from sugar, butter, eggs, and lemons. It is used as a spread on bread and as a filling in tarts.

lemonade is (a) a clear sweet fizzy drink. (b) a drink made from fresh lemons with water and sugar.

lemur Lemurs are monkey-like animals from Madagascar. They have large eyes, thick fur, and long tails.

lend (lending, lent) ❑ If you **lend** someone something you own, you let them have it or use it for a time. ◇ When organizations like banks **lend** money, they give it to someone who agrees to pay it back, often in several smaller amounts over a period of time and with interest added on.

❑ If you **lend** your support to someone, you show you agree with them and support them. You can also **lend** your support to a proposal or idea.

❑ If something **lends** a quality to something else, it gives it that quality. *The decorations for the games have lent a splash of colour to an otherwise drab city.*

❑ If something **lends** itself to being dealt with in a certain way, it has features which make it easy to deal with in that way. *Puccini's opera does not lend itself easily to concert performance.*

lender Lenders are people or institutions like banks that lend money to people.

length ❑ The **length** of something is the distance from one end to the other. ◇ If something happens or exists along the **length** of something, it happens or exists all the way along it.

❑ In a horse or boat race, a **length** is the distance from the front to the back of a horse or boat. *Pat Eddery guided the five-to-four favourite to a victory by half a length.* ◇ If someone swims a **length** in a swimming pool, they swim from one end to the other.

❑ A **length** of something is a piece of it ...*a short length of steel chain.*

❑ The **length** of a book or other piece of writing is the number of pages or the amount of writing in it.

❑ **Length** is used to talk about how long something lasts. ...*the length of time people have to wait for operations.* ◇ If you discuss something **at length,** you discuss it for a long time or in great detail. ◇ **At length** is also used to say something is done or happens eventually, after a long time. *At length, his obsessive desire destroyed his marriage.*

❑ If you **go to great lengths** to achieve something, you try very hard and do things you would not normally do to achieve it.

lengthen (lengthening, lengthened) If something **lengthens** or is **lengthened**, it becomes longer. *The list of exceptions has been steadily lengthening.*

lengthways means the same as lengthwise.

lengthwise If you cut something **lengthwise**, you cut it along its length rather than across its width.

lengthy If something is **lengthy**, it takes a long time.

lenient (leniently, leniency) If someone in authority is **lenient** or treats wrongdoers in a **lenient** way, they are not as strict or severe as they might be. Behaviour like this is called **leniency**. *Prisoners who show a good attitude will be treated more leniently.*

lens (lenses) A **lens** is a thin curved piece of glass or plastic which makes things look bigger, smaller, or clearer when you look through it. Lenses are used in cameras, telescopes, and spectacles.

lent ❑ See lend.

❑ **Lent** is the period of 40 days before Easter when many Christians give up something they enjoy.

lentil Lentils are small round brown or orange seeds from a bean-like plant. They are dried then boiled and eaten in curries and soups.

leopard The **leopard** is a large member of the cat family. It has yellow fur and black spots. Leopards live in Africa and Asia.

leotard A **leotard** is a tight-fitting piece of female clothing made of thin stretchy material, like a one-piece swimming costume. Some women wear leotards when they are doing things like aerobics.

leper Lepers are people who suffer from leprosy. ◇ If someone is treated as a **leper**, people avoid them or are unfriendly towards them, because they have done something shocking or offensive.

leprechaun (*pron:* lep-rik-kawn) In Irish folk tales, **leprechauns** are tiny people with magical powers who play tricks on people.

leprosy is a serious infectious disease which severely damages and disfigures the skin and can lead to fingers and toes dropping off.

leprous is used to describe a part of someone's body when it is affected by leprosy. ...*a pair of leprous hands.*

lesbian (lesbianism) **Lesbians** are women who are sexually attracted to other women rather than men. **Lesbianism** is sexual attraction and sexual activity between women.

lèse-majesté (*pron:* lezz-maj-est-ee) is behaviour likely to cause offence to someone like a president or king.

lesion A lesion is an injury or wound, or a change in a part of the body caused by an illness.

less is used to say an amount is below a certain level. *We had less than three miles to go.* Less is also used to say an amount is lower than it was before, or lower than another amount. *A shower uses less water than a bath.* ◇ Less is also used to say something does not have a quality as much as it used to, or does not have it as much as something else. *The future looks less secure... Carbon dioxide dissolves less easily in warm water.* ◇ **Less and less** is used to say an amount keeps decreasing. *The extended family is less and less common in British society.*

❏ Less is used to talk about one number or amount being subtracted from another. *He earns £53,200 a week, less tax.*

❏ **Less than** is used in front of words like 'fair', 'favourable', and 'perfect' to say something is not fair, favourable, or perfect. *The president's international image is less than favourable.*

❏ **No less** is used when mentioning someone important who is surprisingly involved in something. *The prime minister and Emperor Akihito, no less, apologised for Japan's occupation of the Korean peninsula from 1910 to 1945.* ◇ **No less than** is used when mentioning a surprisingly large amount of something. *By 1880, there were no less than fifty-six coal mines.*

❏ **Nothing less than** is used to emphasize that something really is a particular thing. *What passed as suicide was nothing less than murder.* ◇ If you say you want **nothing** less than a certain thing, you mean you will be satisfied with that thing and nothing else.

❏ **more or less:** see **more.** ◇ **no more no less:** see **more.**

lessee See **lease.**

lessen (lessening, lessened; lessening) If something **lessens** or is **lessened**, there is less of it than there was before. *The withdrawal of naval forces has lessened tensions in the region.*

lesser is used to say something is not as large, not as serious, or not as good as something else. *He has tried to reform the economy and, to a lesser extent, the political system... ...a new exam that did not exclude children of lesser ability.* ◇ **lesser of two evils:** see **evil.**

lesson ❏ A lesson is a short period of time when children are taught a subject at school.

❏ If you learn a lesson from something that happens, it acts as a warning or example from which you learn something. ◇ If you **teach** someone **a lesson**, you do something to punish them for what they have done and to make sure they do not do it again.

lessor See **lease.**

lest is used to give reasons for someone's feelings or behaviour when they are anxious to prevent something happening. *The police had been given orders to move the homeless from around the stadium lest the visitors see them.*

let (letting, let) ❏ If you let something happen, you allow it to happen. If you let someone do something, you allow them to do it. ◇ If you **let** someone or something **into** a place, you allow them to go in. *Police won't let in*

food and medical supplies. Similarly, you can let someone or something out of a place, or through a place.

❏ If something **lets in** water or air, it has a hole or crack which allows water or air to get in. Similarly, something can **let** water or air **out**. ◇ If you **let down** something filled with air, you do something which allows the air to escape. *My tyres had been let down.*

❏ If someone **lets** you **down**, they break their promise to you, or fail to do what you expect of them.

❏ If you **let** someone **in on** a secret or let them **into** it, you tell them about it. ◇ If you do not **let on**, you do not tell someone what they want to know.

❏ If someone is **let off**, they are not punished for something they have done. You can also say someone is **let off with** a lighter punishment than is normal or expected. ◇ If you are **let off** something like a task or duty, you are told you do not have to do it.

❏ If something does not **let up**, it continues at the same level or intensity. *The heat did not let up.* You can also say there is no **let-up** in something.

❏ If you **let go** of someone or something, you stop holding them.

❏ If you **let out** a sound, you utter it. *Students let out a loud cheer.* ◇ If you **let off** something like a gun or a bomb, you fire it or make it explode.

❏ **Let** and **let us** are used to make suggestions. *Let us give them the benefit of the doubt.*

❏ If you wonder what you have **let** yourself **in for**, you begin to think you may be getting involved in something difficult or unpleasant.

❏ You use **let alone** when you have said something is difficult or unlikely and you want to mention something else which is even more difficult or unlikely. *Most families consider themselves lucky to be able to afford one car, let alone two.*

❏ If you **let** your house or land to someone, you allow them to use it in exchange for regular payments.

let-down If you say something you have been looking forward to is a **let-down**, you mean it is disappointing.

let-up See **let.**

let's is short for 'let us' when you are making a suggestion. See **let.**

lethal (lethally) If something is **lethal**, it causes death. *...the use of lethal force... The shell would explode lethally in the air above its target.*

lethargic (*pron:* lith-ar-jick) (lethargy) If someone is **lethargic**, they have no energy or enthusiasm. This condition is called **lethargy** (*pron:* leth-ar-jee).

letter ❏ A letter is a message you write and send to someone, usually through the post.

❏ **Letters** are the written symbols which stand for the sounds of a language.

❏ If you keep to the **letter** of an agreement, you do nothing which goes against what is actually written, although you may go against its general principles. Similarly, you can say someone keeps to the **letter of the law.**

❏ A male writer is sometimes called a **man of letters** when he has a wide knowledge of literature and has done several different kinds of writing.

letter bomb A letter bomb is a small bomb made to look like a letter and sent to someone through the post.

letterbox (letterboxes) A **letterbox** is (a) a rectangular hole in a door which letters and small parcels are delivered through. (b) a large metal box in the street or at a post office with a rectangular hole for letters to be posted in.

letterhead A letterhead is the name, address, and sometimes the symbol of a person or organization printed at the top of their writing paper.

lettering is writing, especially when the letters are in a particular style or colour. *...the grey cloth spine with its gilt lettering.*

lettuce Lettuces are vegetables with large green leaves, used in salads.

leukaemia (*or* leukemia) (*pron:* loo-kee-mee-a) Leukaemia is a type of cancer which results in abnormal white blood cells being produced, causing weakness and sometimes death.

levee (*pron:* lev-vee) In the US, a levee is a ridge or bank built next to a river, to hold back water and stop floods.

level (levelling, levelled) (*American spelling:* leveling, leveled)
❏ A level is a point on a scale. *The FT-SE 100 index once again dipped below the 2,400 level.*
❏ A level is also one of the stages in a hierarchy. *...top-level meetings... ...talks at ministerial level.*
❏ The floors in a building are sometimes called levels.
❏ Level is used to talk about the height at which something happens or exists. *...dive-bombing at low level... ...a ground-level plaza.* ◇ The level of something like a lake or river is how high its surface is compared to normal.
❏ The noise level in a place is the volume of noise there.
❏ Someone's level of intelligence is how intelligent they are. Similarly, you can talk about someone's ability level.
❏ When people talk about the different levels of something like a story or film, they mean the different ways of thinking about it or understanding it. *On one level it's a comic romp, and on another it's a strong psychological story.*
❏ If something is level, it is flat and no part is higher than the rest. If an area of land is levelled, it is made flat.
❏ If something which has been increasing or decreasing levels off or levels out, it stops increasing or decreasing. *Inflation is finally levelling out at around 11% a month.*
❏ If two amounts are level, they are equal. If they are levelled, someone makes them equal. *Nilsen levelled the scores two minutes from time.* ◇ If you draw level with someone, you move towards them from behind until you are side by side with them.
❏ When someone is criticized or accused, you can say criticisms or accusations are levelled at them.
❏ See also A level, O level.

level crossing A level crossing is a place where a railway line and a road cross each other at the same level. There are usually gates to block off the road when a train is passing.

level-headed If you say someone is level-headed, you mean they behave in a calm and sensible way, even in difficult situations.

lever (levering, levered) ❏ A lever is a bar or handle you pull or push to make a piece of machinery work.
❏ A lever is also a bar, one end of which is pushed under a heavy object so that when you push down on the other end you can move the object. If you lever something, you move it in this way. *...levering open the window.*

❏ You can also call something a lever when you use it as a way of getting someone to do what you want. *Hostages remain a significant lever in influencing policy and drawing international attention.*
❏ If a person or political group holds the levers of power in a country, they are in control.

leverage If you have leverage over someone, you have the power or influence to make them do what you want, for example because you have control over something they need.

leveret (*pron:* lev-er-it) A leveret is a young hare, especially one less than a year old.

leviathan (*pron:* lev-vie-ath-an) In the Bible, the leviathan is a sea monster, sometimes thought to be a whale and sometimes a crocodile. ◇ Other things which seem very large and powerful, for example international companies, can be called leviathans.

Levis are a type of jeans. 'Levis' is a trademark.

levitate (levitating, levitated; levitation) Some people are supposed to be able to levitate objects. This means making them rise up in the air, with nothing holding or supporting them. Some people are also supposed to be able to levitate, which means making their own bodies rise up into the air. Making anything rise up like this is called levitation.

levity is treating serious matters in a light-hearted way.

levy (levies, levying, levied) When a government levies a tax or charge, it introduces it and collects it. The tax or charge can be called a levy.

lewd is used to describe people's behaviour when they talk about sex in a crude unpleasant way. Pictures which hint at sex in a crude way can also be called lewd.

lexicographer (lexicography) A lexicographer is someone whose job involves writing and editing dictionaries. This kind of work is called lexicography.

lexicon A lexicon is an alphabetical list of the words of a language, or of words used in connection with a subject. ◇ The words a group of people use among themselves can also be called a lexicon. *A more recent addition to the lexicon of upper-class slang is 'brill'.*

liability (liabilities) ❏ Liability for something like a debt or accident is being legally responsible for it. *Costs were awarded against the car driver who admitted liability.* ◇ A liability is a debt. *...her personal tax liabilities.*
❏ If someone or something is a liability, they cause problems or embarrassment rather than being a help.

liable ❏ If someone is liable for something like a debt or an accident, they are legally responsible for it. *...a tenant's agreement that makes the owner liable for upkeep of items such as lifts and gardens.* ◇ If someone who breaks a law is liable to a certain punishment, the authorities are entitled to punish them that way. *Such offenders will be liable to a seven-year prison term and a fine.*
❏ If someone or something is liable to do something, they are likely to do it. *Great men are at least as liable to behave badly when they are struck by love as other men.* ◇ If you are liable to something unpleasant, it is likely to happen to you. *Some people don't get enough of these vitamins... this makes them liable to life-threatening diseases... Any vehicles moving during curfew are liable to be attacked by the air force.*

liaise (*pron:* lee-aze) (liaising, liaised) If people or groups liaise with each other, they keep each other informed about what they are doing. If someone **liaises** between people or groups, they act as the means by which they can communicate with each other.

liaison (lee-aze-on) **Liaison** is communication between people or groups, in which they keep each other informed about what they are doing. ◇ A **liaison** is a sexual relationship, especially a secret one which involves someone being unfaithful to someone else.

liar A **liar** is a person who tells lies.

Lib Dem A **Lib Dem** is a member of the Liberal Democrat party.

libel (libelling, libelled; libellous) (*American spelling:* libeling, libeled, *etc*) If someone **libels** you, they write something untrue which damages your reputation and is therefore against the law. This offence is called **libel.** You can say a piece of writing is **libellous.**

liberal (liberalism, liberally) ❑ In the UK, **Liberals** were members or supporters of the former Liberal Party. **Liberal** was used to talk about things to do with this party. *...Liberal campaign strategists.*
❑ A **liberal** is a person who believes in individual freedom, is tolerant of other people's ideas and beliefs, and is ready to accept change and progress. **Liberal** is used to describe behaviour and ideas which reflect this attitude. *...liberal-minded free-marketeers... Traditionalists regularly condemn the more liberal approach to teaching.* Liberal behaviour and attitudes are called **liberalism.**
❑ **Liberal** is used to say something is used or given freely in large amounts. *She makes liberal use of the word 'feel'... Carmel soon persuaded us to use the rich colours liberally on our canvasses.*

Liberal Democrat The **Liberal Democrats** are the third largest political party in the UK and the main centre party. A **Liberal Democrat** is a member of this party. The party's official name is the Social and Liberal Democratic Party.

Liberal Party In Britain, the **Liberal Party** was a political party which was formerly very powerful, but became the country's third largest party with the rise of the Labour Party. In 1988, the Liberal Party merged with the Social Democratic Party to form the Liberal Democrats. Canada, Australia, and some other countries have Liberal Parties.

liberalize (liberalizing, liberalized; liberalization) (*can be spelled with an 's' instead of a 'z'*) If a country or organization **liberalizes** its laws or attitudes, it makes them less strict and lets people have more freedom. *...economic liberalization.*

liberate (liberating, liberated; liberation) ❑ If a place is **liberated,** it is freed from the control of another country or from a repressive government. ◇ If people are **liberated,** they are freed from captivity or from a situation in which they are cruelly or unjustly treated. *...the liberation of the hostages.*
❑ If you say someone is **liberated,** you mean their attitude to things like sexual behaviour and the roles of men and women is more tolerant and less restricted than that of most of the people where they live.

liberation theology is a belief held by some religious people in Latin America that they should try to change bad or oppressive social conditions by taking part in politics.

liberator Someone is called a **liberator** when they have done something to free people from oppression or foreign occupation.

libertarian A **libertarian** is someone who believes people should be free to think and behave as they want. **Libertarian** is used to describe behaviour and ideas which reflect this belief.

libertine (*pron:* lib-er-teen) A man is sometimes called a **libertine** when it is thought that he leads an immoral life, especially in his sexual behaviour.

liberty (liberties) ❑ **Liberty** is the freedom to live as you want or do things as you want without interference from other people. **Liberties** are the freedom to do particular things. *...religious liberties... ...political liberties.* See also civil liberties.
❑ **Liberty** is also the freedom to go where you want, rather than being imprisoned somewhere. If someone like a criminal is **at liberty,** he or she has escaped or has not yet been caught.
❑ If you say you are not **at liberty** to do something, you mean you are not allowed to do it.
❑ If you say someone is **taking liberties,** you mean they are being cheeky, or doing something they are not entitled to do.

libidinous A **libidinous** person has strong sexual feelings.

libido (*pron:* lib-ee-doe) (libidos) A person's **libido** is their sexual urges or desires.

librarian A **librarian** is a person who is in charge of a library, or has been trained to do responsible work in one.

library (libraries) A **library** is a place where a collection of books and other publications is kept for people to read, study, use, or borrow. The collection is also called a **library.** ◇ A **library** is also a collection of other objects, such as films or records. ◇ The **library** in a large house is a room where books are kept and where the people who live there can read them.

libretto (*plural:* librettos *or* libretti) (librettist) The **libretto** of an opera is the words sung and spoken in it. The person who wrote the libretto is called the **librettist.**

lice See louse.

licence (*American spelling:* license) ❑ A **licence** is an official document giving you permission to have, do, or use something. ◇ If you do something **under licence,** you do it using someone else's patent, trademark, or copyright, and have their permission to do so.
❑ If you call something like a law a **licence** to do something bad or immoral, you mean it makes people think they can behave badly and get away with it. *Amnesty International described the Act as a licence to kill with impunity.*
❑ If you talk about **poetic licence,** you mean a writer is doing something which would normally be unacceptable, such as using bad grammar or misrepresenting the truth, but it does not matter because the result is artistically satisfying. You use **artistic licence** in a similar way when you are talking about art.

license (licensing, licensed) ❑ When someone is **licensed** to do or have something, they are given official permission to do it or have it. *...licensed package tour operators.* ◇ If something like a drug is **licensed,** official permission has been given for it to be available. ◇ If something like a restaurant, pub, or hotel is **licensed,** it has permission to sell alcoholic drinks.

❑ See also **licence.**

license plate In the US, a vehicle's number plate is called its **license plate.**

licensee A **licensee** is someone who holds a licence, especially a licence to sell alcoholic drinks.

licensing hours are the times of day when a person with a licence to sell alcoholic drinks is allowed to sell them.

licensing laws are the laws which control the sale of alcoholic drinks.

licentious (*pron:* lice-sen-shuss) (licentiousness) **Licentious** behaviour or **licentiousness** is sexual behaviour which is considered to be shocking and immoral.

lichen (*pron:* lie-ken) is a spreading crusty or moss-like plant which grows on rocks, walls, or tree trunks. It can be a variety of colours, but is usually green or yellow.

lick ❑ When you **lick** something, you stroke your tongue across its surface.

❑ If someone is **licking their wounds,** they are recovering from a defeat or humiliation. ◇ When people are **licked into shape,** they are made to train or practise hard, so they will be able to do something well.

❑ If you **lick** a problem or difficulty, you overcome it.

❑ When people talk about a **lick of paint,** they are talking about a building or room being decorated. For example, they say a building 'needs a lick of paint'.

licorice See **liquorice.**

lid ❑ A **lid** is a cover for a container.

❑ If you **keep a lid on** something, you restrict it or stop it happening. *The soldiers' presence seemed to keep a lid on the violence.* ◇ If you **keep the lid** on a secret, you prevent people finding out about it. If you **lift the lid on** it or **take the lid off** it, you reveal it to other people.

❑ A person's **lids** are their eyelids.

lido A **lido** is an outdoor swimming pool, or part of a beach used for swimming, sunbathing, or water sports.

lie (lying, lay, have lain; lying, lied) (*If you are talking about the past, you say, for example, 'She lay on the beach' but 'She lied to the police.'*) ❑ If you **lie** somewhere or **lie down,** you place yourself in a horizontal position; you then say you are **lying** or **lying down.** ◇ If you **lie around,** you spend time relaxing and being lazy. ◇ **lie low:** see **low.**

❑ If you say someone will not **take** something **lying down,** you mean they will not accept it without putting up a fight. Similarly, if someone refuses to **lie down,** they refuse to accept that they are beaten.

❑ You say an object is **lying** somewhere when it is on the ground or on some other horizontal surface.

❑ You use **lie** when you are saying something about the state of a building or piece of land. For example, you say land is 'lying fallow' or a house is 'lying empty'.

❑ You use **lie** when you are saying where something is situated. *...stars that lie within 100 light years of our solar system.* ◇ You use **lie** when you are mentioning the position of a sports team in a competition or league table. *Britain, lying third overnight, dropped to seventh after tense performances from Laura Fry and Carol Parsons.*

❑ **Lie** is used to talk about things happening in the future. *...the political bargaining that lies ahead... I might not have gone had I thought what lay beyond.*

❑ **Lie** is used (a) when mentioning the cause of a problem. *It is this repression that lies at the heart of the latest unrest.* (b) when saying where the answer to a problem can be found. *The key may lie in dental records held by Scotland Yard.* ◇ If you say the blame or responsibility for something **lies with** someone, you mean they are to blame or responsible for it.

❑ If someone **lies** about something or tells a **lie,** they deliberately say something which is not true. ◇ If something **gives the lie to** something else, it shows it is not true. *This gives the lie to the common complaint that youngsters are devoid of civic virtues.*

lie-in If you have a **lie-in,** you stay in bed later than usual.

lieu (*pron:* lyew *or* loo) If you are given something **in lieu of** the thing you are expecting, you are given it instead of it.

lieutenant ❑ A **lieutenant** is a junior officer in the British army and in some other armed forces. In the British army, the rank below lieutenant is **second lieutenant.** ◇ A **lieutenant** is also a middle-ranking officer in the Royal Navy; the rank below lieutenant is **sub-lieutenant.** ◇ See also **flight lieutenant.**

❑ Someone who works closely with an important person, often acting as their assistant, can be called their **lieutenant.** *Mr Takeshita placed in the job one of his most faithful lieutenants, Keizo Obuchi.*

life (lives) ❑ A person's **life** is the time when they are alive, from their birth to their death. ◇ A **life** of a famous person is a book telling the story of their life.

❑ **For life** is used to say something lasts for the rest of a person's life. *The accident left her scarred for life.* ◇ If you have a job **for life,** you have it until you retire. ◇ If a person is jailed for **life,** they are sent to prison for a very long but unspecified time. You can also say they are given a **life sentence** or are sentenced to **life imprisonment.**

❑ A person's **life** is also their circumstances and the way they spend each day. *Her life changed dramatically... For those above the poverty line, life is more congenial than it was.* ◇ **Life** is also used to talk about one part of someone's activities. *...his professional life... ...his sex-life.* ◇ See also **walk of life, way of life.** ◇ **quality of life:** see **quality.**

❑ If you say something is a person's **life,** you mean it is what they care about most. *Dancing is their whole life.* ◇ If you talk about the man or woman **in** someone's **life,** you mean the person who matters to them most from a romantic or sexual point of view.

❑ **Real life** is the actual experiences people have, rather than what happens in their imagination or in books or films. ◇ If a story is **taken from life** or **drawn from life,** it is based on real people or events.

❑ If you say a portrait of someone is that person **to the life,** you mean it looks exactly like them.

❑ If you call someone the **life and soul of the party,** you mean they are the liveliest and most entertaining person in a group or place. ◇ If you say someone is **larger than life,** you mean everything about them seems exaggerated in some way.

❑ If someone **loses their life,** they are killed. You can also talk about **lives** being **lost** in an accident or disaster, or say it **claims** a certain number of **lives.**

❑ An attempt on someone's **life** is an attempt to kill

them. If someone **takes** someone else's **life**, they kill them. You can also say someone **takes** their own **life**.

❑ If someone or something **saves** your **life**, they prevent you being killed. ◇ If you have to run, jump, or swim **for your life**, you have to do it to avoid being killed.

❑ If you do something **for dear life**, you do it to try to save yourself when you are in a bad or dangerous situation. *The Pakistan bowling is so devastatingly superior that England are hanging on for dear life.*

❑ If you **risk life and limb** to do something, you put yourself in a lot of danger to do it.

❑ A **life and death** issue or struggle is an extremely serious or dangerous one. ◇ If you say something is **a matter of life and death**, you mean it must be given serious and urgent attention, because someone's life is in danger.

❑ If there is **life** somewhere, there are living things or creatures there.

❑ The **life** in a place is everything that goes on there. *In the capital, life is returning to normal.* ◇ If a place **comes to life**, it becomes active and busy. You can say a busy place is **full of life**.

❑ If a book, play, or film **comes to life** at a certain point, it becomes much more lively and interesting. ◇ If **new life** is **breathed** into something, it is made lively, active, or useful again.

❑ The **life** of something like a piece of machinery is the length of time it can be used before it needs to be replaced or scrapped.

❑ If something takes on a **life of its own**, it becomes independent of something else and becomes active and important in its own right. *They have turned the Front into a real political organization with a life of its own.*

❑ **fact of life**: see **fact**. ◇ **facts of life**: see **fact**. ◇ **time of your life**: see **time**. ◇ See also **still life**, **shelf-life**.

life assurance See **assurance**.

life cycle The **life cycle** of an animal is the stages of development it goes through from birth to death.

life expectancy The **life expectancy** of a person or other living thing is the length of time they can normally be expected to live. Similarly, the **life expectancy** of an object is the length of time it can be expected to survive, function, or remain useful.

life form A **life form** is any kind of living thing.

life insurance is a common name for life assurance.

life jacket (*or* lifejacket) A **life jacket** is a sleeveless jacket which you wear to keep you afloat in water and stop you drowning.

life peer (life peerage) A **life peer** is a person who has been awarded the title of 'Lord' or 'Lady' for the duration of their life. They cannot pass this title on when they die. When someone is awarded a title like this, you say they are given a **life peerage**.

life raft A **life raft** is an inflatable boat carried on a ship or aircraft for use in an emergency.

life-saver See **lifesaver**.

life science The **life sciences** are sciences like zoology, biology, and botany, which deal with living things.

life-size (life-sized) **Life-size** or **life-sized** paintings or models are the same size as the people or things they represent.

life span See **lifespan**.

life support A **life support** machine or system is used to keep a sick or seriously injured person alive when they are in danger of dying.

lifebelt A **lifebelt** is a large ring thrown to people to keep them afloat when they are in danger of drowning.

lifeblood If you say something is the **lifeblood** of a person, group, or organization, you mean their happiness, success, or survival depends on it.

lifeboat A **lifeboat** is (a) a boat kept on shore, which is sent out to rescue people in danger at sea. (b) a boat kept on a ship, which can be launched if the ship is in danger of sinking, or in some other emergency.

lifeguard A **lifeguard** is a person at a beach or swimming pool whose job is to rescue people who are in danger of drowning.

lifejacket See **life jacket**.

lifeless If you say something is **lifeless**, you mean it lacks excitement, liveliness, or interest. *...a dull, lifeless performance.* ◇ You can also say a dead body is **lifeless**.

lifelike You say a portrait or statue is **lifelike** when (a) it is so like a real person that it almost seems to be alive. (b) it is extremely like the person it represents.

lifeline If you call something a **lifeline**, you mean it provides a link needed for someone's survival or well-being. *Renewed fighting severed the fragile lifeline of relief flights linking the capital to the outside world.* ◇ If you **throw** someone a **lifeline**, you help them out of a difficult situation.

lifelong is used to describe something which lasts for the rest of your life. *The two women became lifelong friends... ...a vaccine which will give lifelong protection.* ◇ A **lifelong** ambition is one you have had since you were a child.

lifer A **lifer** is a criminal who has been sent to prison for the rest of his or her life.

lifesaver (*or* life-saver) Something which saves people's lives can be called a **lifesaver**. *Airbags have proved to be real lifesavers.*

lifespan (*or* life span) The **lifespan** of a person or other living thing is the length of time they live for. ◇ The **lifespan** of a product is the length of time it is in use, before it is replaced or thrown away.

lifestyle Your **lifestyle** is the way you live.

lifetime ❑ A person's **lifetime** is the period during which they are alive. ◇ **Lifetime** is used to describe things which last for the rest of your life. *Visiting the zoo became a lifetime habit.*

❑ If something happens extremely rarely, you can say it happens **once in a lifetime**.

❑ The **lifetime** of a parliament or government is the period of time it lasts for.

lift ❑ If you **lift** something or **lift** it **up**, you take it in your hand or hands and move it upwards to another position. ◇ If you **lift** your eyes or head, you look up.

❑ When a rocket **lifts off**, it leaves its launch pad at the beginning of its journey. The moment when this happens is called **lift-off**.

❑ A **lift** is a box-like device for carrying people or goods from one floor of a building to another.

❑ If something is given a **lift**, something is added to it which makes it more interesting, exciting, or lively. ◇ If something **lifts** your spirits or gives you a **lift**, it makes you more cheerful and confident.

❑ If you **lift** yourself out of a bad situation, you get out of it by your own efforts.

❏ If a restriction is **lifted**, it is removed.

❏ If something like an idea is **lifted** from someone else's work, it is copied and used as if it were the copier's own. *His analysis is, after all, lifted from Jung.*

❏ If fog or mist **lifts**, it goes away.

❏ If you **lift** root vegetables, you dig them up.

❏ If you give someone a **lift**, you take them with you in your car, so they get somewhere they want to go.

❏ If you **lift** something like a cup or trophy in a contest, you win it.

lift-off See lift.

ligament Ligaments are the bands of strong tissue which connect bones at the joints.

light (lighting, lit *or* lighted; lightly, lightness) ❏ **Light** is brightness which allows you to see things, and which comes from the sun, the moon, or something like a lamp or torch. ◇ **first light:** see first.

❏ If something **lights up** an area, it makes it bright with light. ◇ If something is **lit** in a particular way, that is how it gets its light. *...a gas-lit passage.*

❏ A **light** room or building has a lot of natural light, because it has large windows or many windows.

❏ If something **comes to light** or is **brought to light**, people find out about it. ◇ If something **sees the light of day**, people get the chance to see it or hear about it. *It's highly unlikely that any of this proof will ever see the light of day.* ◇ If a discovery **sheds, casts,** or **throws new light on** something, it helps people to understand it better.

❏ If you **see the light**, you suddenly understand something. People who have had a religious conversion often say they have **seen the light**.

❏ If someone or something is seen in a particular **light**, that is how people tend to regard them. Similarly, someone or something can be shown in a particular **light**. *Each of the republics wants to show itself in the best possible light.*

❏ If you say there is **light at the end of the tunnel**, you mean it is now possible to see when a period of difficulty will come to an end.

❏ A **light** is anything which provides artificial light. *...street lights... ...a warning light.* The **lighting** in a place is the lights there. ◇ Traffic lights are often just called **lights**. ◇ **bright lights:** see bright.

❏ If something **lights up**, it becomes illuminated. ◇ If someone's face or eyes **light up**, they look very pleased and happy about something.

❏ If someone is a **leading light** in an organization or campaign, they are one of the most important people in it. A **lesser light** is someone who is not quite as important.

❏ **In the light of** is used to mention circumstances which might affect a choice or decision. *He believes that in the light of recent reforms the time has come to relax sanctions.*

❏ If you **light** something like a fire or candle, you start it burning. ◇ If you **set light to** something, you start it burning in order to destroy it.

❏ If someone **lights** a cigarette, they start it burning so they can smoke it. You can also say they **light up**. If someone asks you for a **light**, they are asking for something like a match so they can light their cigarette.

❏ **Light** colours are pale, rather than bright or vivid. *...a light blue shirt.*

❏ **Light** is used to describe people or things that do not

weigh much. ◇ **Light** clothes are made of a thin fabric and are worn in warm weather. ◇ **Light** equipment and machines are small and easily moved. ◇ If you travel **light**, you do not take much luggage.

❏ **Light** is used to say there is not much of something. *Traffic was relatively light... ...lightly populated regions.*

❏ A **light** meal is a small one. ◇ **Light** pastry and cakes contain a lot of air, have a delicate flavour, and are easy to digest. ◇ If you cook something **lightly**, you do not cook it for long. ◇ A **light** wine has a relatively low alcohol content.

❏ A **light** wind is not strong.

❏ A **light** injury is not serious. ◇ A **light** punishment is not severe. ◇ If someone suffers less as a result of something than might be expected, you can say they **get off lightly**.

❏ **Light** entertainment is not serious, and does not require much attention or thought. ◇ If a writer has a **light touch**, he or she writes about a serious subject in a readable and humorous way. *Gifford writes with a lightness of touch that makes this essay easy and enjoyable reading.*

❏ If you **make light of** something, you pretend you do not think it is important. You can also say someone **speaks lightly** of something or **takes** it **lightly**. ◇ If you say something should not be done **lightly**, you mean people should think carefully before doing it.

❏ If you **light on** someone or something, (a) you find them unexpectedly. (b) you choose them. *Mr Bush could not have lighted on a better man than Tom Pickering.*

light aircraft A **light aircraft** is a small plane.

light-hearted (light-heartedly) **Light-hearted** behaviour is not at all serious. *Julian Critchley will take a light-hearted look at Westminster... There are stories that she light-heartedly tipped him off his surfboard.*

light industry is manufacture which does not involve heavy or dirty raw materials. See also **heavy industry**.

light pen A **light pen** is a device for electronically reading bar codes on items you buy in a shop.

light year Very long distances in space are measured in **light years**. One light year is the distance light travels in a year. ◇ If you talk about things being **light years** apart, you are saying how different they are from each other. *Thermal treatments, sea spray showers, mud baths – it all seems light years away from the traditional two weeks on the beach with a deckchair.*

lighten (lightening, lightened) ❏ If the sky **lightens**, it becomes less dark. ◇ If something like a mood or a situation **lightens**, it becomes less serious. ◇ If a person **lightens up**, they become less serious and more cheerful.

❏ If something like a burden is **lightened**, it is reduced. *They have seen their workload lightened by computers.*

lighter ❏ A **lighter** or **cigarette lighter** is a small device for lighting cigarettes.

❏ A **lighter** is also a kind of barge.

lighthouse A **lighthouse** is a tower by the sea or on a rock in the sea, which has a powerful light at its top for guiding ships or warning them of danger.

lighting See light.

lightly See light.

lightning is the bright flashes of light you see in the sky during a thunderstorm.

□ **Lightning** is used to describe things which happen very quickly or last for a very short time. *With another lightning forehand, Agassi reached match point.* Similarly, if something moves **like lightning**, it moves very quickly.

□ If workers go on a **lightning strike**, they stop working suddenly without any warning, to protest against something. ◇ A **lightning strike** is also a sudden attack by a military force, which depends on surprise for its success.

lightning conductor A **lightning conductor** is a metal device which sticks up from the highest point of a tall building and runs all the way down its side. It guides lightning safely to the ground and prevents the building being damaged.

lightweight A **lightweight** object or material weighs less than things of its type usually do. *...lightweight camcorders.* ◇ A **lightweight** book or play is for entertainment only, and is not meant to be serious. ◇ If you call someone a **lightweight**, you mean they are not capable of thinking deeply, or do not have much power or influence.

lignite is a brown mineral with a woody texture. It is burned as a fuel.

likable See likeable.

like (liking, liked) □ If you **like** someone or something, you find them pleasant or attractive, or you approve of them. ◇ A person's **likes** are the things they enjoy or find pleasant. ◇ If you **like** to do something in a certain way, you prefer to do it that way. *Big Japanese firms like to recruit graduates straight from university.*

□ If you want something, you can say you **would like** it. *Both countries would like a closer relationship.* Similarly, you can say you **would like** to do or be something. ◇ **Like** is also used with 'would' (a) to make polite suggestions, offers, requests, or invitations. *Would you like to tell us about that?* (b) to give instructions or orders. *I'd like you to wait here.*

□ You say **if you like** when you have just expressed something in an unusual or alternative way. *This is a down payment – or a deposit, if you like.*

□ **Like it or not** is used to say something is true and has to be accepted, even if you would prefer it not to be true. *Like it or not, a European central bank already exists.*

□ If one person or thing is **like** another, they have similar characteristics or behave in similar ways. You can also say one person or thing looks or sounds **like** another. *The ostrich looks like an overgrown chicken.* You can also say someone does something **like** someone else. ◇ You also use **like** to say someone is in a similar situation to someone else. *She had to defect in order to dance in the West, like Nureyev and Baryshnikov.*

□ You also use **like** to say someone is treated as if they were a particular kind of person. *He was wooed like visiting royalty by airlines competing to run routes to his country.*

□ If you talk about comparing **like with like**, you are talking about useful comparisons being made between things of the same kind, as distinct from unhelpful comparisons between things which are quite different.

□ **Like** can be used to give an example of something. *...big-spending countries like Holland and Canada.* ◇ You say **the likes of** when you are mentioning someone as an example of a type of person. *...the suggestion that Rangers can be put in the same category as the likes of AC Milan and Barce-*

lona. ◇ You add **and the like** after a list to indicate that there are other things which could be included in it. *The castles have a variety of new careers as hotels, museums, offices, old people's homes and the like.* ◇ You say **the like of which** when you are emphasizing how unusual something is. *...scenes of rejoicing the like of which Silverstone has never seen.*

□ **Like this** and **like that** are used when describing how something is done. *Eels and river fish are cooked like this.* ◇ **Like** can be used to mean 'in the same way that'. *The firm cannot afford to miss out like they did last year.*

□ **Nothing like** is used instead of 'not' for emphasis. *The gap is nothing like as wide as it was during Mrs Thatcher's final months.* ◇ If you say there is **nothing like** a particular thing, you mean there is nothing else as good or as effective as it is. ◇ **Something like** means 'approximately'. *The average British cow produces something like 6,000 litres a year.*

-like is added to a word to say someone or something is like the thing described by the word. *...his fortress-like Swiss villa... ...Scrooge-like tendencies.*

like-minded people have similar ideas or opinions.

likeable (*usual American spelling:* likable) If you say someone or something is **likeable**, you mean they are pleasant and easy to like.

likelihood If you talk about the **likelihood** of something, you are talking about the chances of it happening or being true. *The likelihood that it was the work of hooligans is remote.* If you say something will happen **in all likelihood**, you mean it will probably happen. You can also say something is true **in all likelihood**. *...pillars which archaeologists say in all likelihood were part of a temple.*

likely (likelier, likeliest) **Likely**, **very likely**, and **most likely** are used to say something will probably happen. *Very likely, there will be a price war.* ◇ **Likely** is used to describe people or things that will probably have a particular role or function in the future. *He is seen as a likely successor to the Chinese leader.*

liken (likening, likened) If you **liken** one person or thing to another, you say they are like them.

likeness (likenesses) If you talk about someone's **likeness** to another person, you mean they look like them. ◇ A **likeness** of someone is a painting or statue of them.

likewise means 'in the same way'. *These countries have now produced surpluses, which they can sell to other countries. Likewise other countries grow very good crops of sorghum and they in turn can sell this.* ◇ If you do something and another person does **likewise**, they do the same thing as you.

liking □ See like.

□ If you have a **liking** for something, you enjoy it or find it pleasant. ◇ If something is **to your liking**, (a) it is the way you like it. *Cook for about 8-10 minutes until the fish is to your liking.* (b) you are pleased about it. *Mrs Parsons' early socialist leanings were not to the liking of her family.* ◇ If something is, for example, too big **for your liking**, you would prefer it to be smaller.

lilac is a tree with large clusters of sweet-smelling white or mauve flowers. ◇ **Lilac** is also a pale mauve colour.

Lilo (Lilos) A **Lilo** is a long plastic mattress which you fill with air and use for lying on, especially out of doors. 'Lilo' is a trademark.

lilt (lilting) The **lilt** of a voice or tune is a pleasant rise and fall in the way it sounds. **Lilting** words, songs, or voices have a rise and fall like this.

lily (lilies) The **lily** is a plant which produces large trumpet-shaped flowers which can be white, pink, yellow, or orange.

lily of the valley (lilies of the valley) The **lily of the valley** is a small plant with large leaves and clusters of small fragrant bell-shaped white flowers.

limb (-limbed) ❏ A person's **limbs** are their arms and legs. You can add **-limbed** to a word to describe someone's limbs. ...*long-limbed ballerinas.* ◇ **life and limb:** see **life.**
❏ The **limbs** of a tree are its branches. ◇ If you are **out on a limb,** you have isolated yourself from other people by taking a different stance on something.

limber (limbering, limbered) If you **limber up** for something, especially a sport or some kind of physical activity, you prepare for it in some way.

limbo If you are **in limbo,** you are in a situation where you do not know what will happen next and you have no control over things. ◇ The **limbo** is a West Indian dance in which the dancers pass under a low bar while leaning backwards. The bar is lowered each time they do it.

lime ❏ The **lime** is a large European tree with pale green leaves, often planted in parks. ◇ Another kind of tree is also called a **lime.** This is a small Asian tree which has small green citrus fruit called **limes.** These fruit are edible and are rather like lemons. Their juice is often made into a drink.
❏ **Lime** or **lime-green** is a pale yellowish-green colour.
❏ **Lime** is also a white powder used in cement and whitewash, and as a fertilizer.

limelight If someone or something is in the **limelight,** they are getting a lot of attention.

limerick A **limerick** is a humorous poem which has five lines and a special rhythm and way of rhyming. One limerick goes: 'There was a young lady of Ryde – Who ate some green apples and died – The apples fermented – Inside the lamented – And made cider inside her inside.'

limestone is a white rock which is a form of calcium carbonate. It is used for building and making cement.

limit (limiting, limited) ❏ A **limit** is the greatest amount, extent, or degree of something which is allowed or possible. ...*a speed limit of 75mph.*
❏ If you talk about the **limits** of a situation, you are talking about the factors which prevent people having complete freedom to do what they want. *Authorities will be obliged, within limits, to respond to parents' wishes.*
❏ If something is **limited,** restrictions are put on it. ...*agreement to limit greenhouse gases.* ◇ If something is **limited** to certain people, they are the only ones allowed to have it or use it. ◇ See also **age limit.** ◇ If something is **limited** to a certain place, it is not allowed to happen anywhere else.
❏ If you **limit** yourself to a range of things, you keep within that range.
❏ If you say **the sky is the limit** for someone, you mean there is nothing to prevent them being very successful.
❏ The **limits** of an area are its boundaries or edges.

limitation ❏ **Limitations** on something are restrictions on how much someone is allowed to have. ...*limitations on royal power... ...arms limitation agreements.*

❏ A person's **limitations** are the limits of what they are capable of doing. You can also talk about the **limitations** of a method or a machine. *The engineers have become cleverer at hiding their computers' limitations.*

limited ❏ If there is a **limited** amount of something, there is only a certain amount and no more. ◇ **Limited** is also used to say something is restricted to certain things. ...*limited air strikes.*
❏ A **limited edition** of something like a book, engraving, or set of coins has been produced in very small numbers, and because of this may be valuable in the future.
❏ A **limited** company is a legally registered business. If it becomes insolvent, its shareholders are legally responsible for its debts and losses to a limited extent. A limited company always has 'Limited' or 'Ltd' as part of its name.

limitless You say something is **limitless** when there seems to be no limit to it.

limo (limos) A **limo** is the same as a limousine.

limousine (*pron:* lim-o-zeen) A **limousine** is a large luxurious car, usually driven by a chauffeur. Limousines are often hired for special occasions like weddings.

limp ❏ If someone **limps,** they walk in an uneven way, because they have injured their foot or leg. You can also say they have a **limp** or walk with a **limp.** ◇ You also say someone or something **limps** when they make slow progress, because of the poor state they are in. *America limped out of recession in the second quarter.*
❏ A **limp** object is soft and lacks stiffness or firmness. *The flags hung limply around the velodrome.* ◇ If someone goes **limp,** their body relaxes or hangs loosely, for example because they are unconscious. You can also say a part of someone's body is **limp.** ◇ You also use **limp** to describe things which are lacking in life or imagination. *Great Britain gave a limp performance last night.*

limpet **Limpets** are shellfish with circular shells which attach themselves very firmly to rocks.

limpet mine A **limpet mine** is a device containing explosives which is attached to its target by a magnet or adhesive and is very difficult to remove.

limpid If the water in a lake or the sea is **limpid,** it is so clear you can see to the bottom. ◇ If you describe writing as **limpid,** you mean it is easy to follow, because everything is expressed in a clear way.

linchpin (*or* lynchpin) The **linchpin** of an organization or process is the most important person or thing in it.

linctus (linctuses) A **linctus** is a thick syrupy medicine taken for a sore throat or cough.

linden The **linden** or **linden tree** is the same as the European lime tree.

line (lining, lined) ❏ A **line** is a long thin mark on a surface. ◇ In various sports, the **line** is a line painted on a court, pitch, or track, for example the goal line in football or the finishing line in a race.
❏ Your **line of sight** is an imaginary line stretching between your eye and the object you are looking at.
❏ The **lines** on a person's face are the wrinkles or creases there. A **lined** face has a lot of lines.
❏ A **line** of things is a row of them. A **line** of people is a queue or row. If people **line up** or are **lined up,** they form a queue or row. *Millions of Kenyans lined up to cast their votes.* ◇ If people or cars are **in line,** they are forming a queue. ◇ If people or things **line** something like a road,

they are present in large numbers along its edges. *The road was lined by thousands of Albanians... ...a book-lined corridor.*

❏ When people **line up** with other people or **line up** behind them, they support them or form an alliance with them. *It remains unclear how many Thatcher loyalists will line up behind Mr Hurd.* Similarly, people can **line up** against someone.

❏ If someone is **in line** for something, they are likely to get it. *32,000 Ford workers are in line for a pay rise.* ◇ The person who is **next in line** for a throne is the one who will become king or queen when the present king or queen dies. You can also talk about someone being **second in line**, **third in line**, and so on.

❏ If something is **in line** with a decision or recommendation, it is in accordance with it. ◇ If something is kept **in line** with something else, it is made to correspond to it. *Their liabilities for repayments will be adjusted annually in line with inflation.* If something is **out of line** with something else, it fails to correspond to it.

❏ If someone **steps out of line**, they do something different from other people, when they are supposed to be doing the same thing. If they are made to behave like the others, you can say they are brought **into line**. ◇ If someone falls **into line** with other people, they start to act the same way.

❏ A **line** is a company which provides services for transporting people or goods by sea, air, bus, or rail. *...the Cunard shipping line.*

❏ If you say something is the latest in a **line** of things, you mean there have been several similar things before. *...the latest in a long line of books on child rearing.*

❏ When two armies are fighting a battle, the formations of troops confronting each other are called the battle **lines**. *Civilians were recruited for spying and sabotage behind enemy lines.* ◇ **front line:** see front. ◇ If you are **in the line of fire**, you are in the direct path of bullets or shells, and therefore in great danger. ◇ **firing line:** see fire.

❏ If you say someone is **holding the line** against someone or something, you mean they are standing fast against them and refusing to give way.

❏ A length of string, wire, or cable used for a particular purpose can be called a **line**, for example a fishing line or a telephone line. ◇ If you say someone is **on the line**, you mean they are on the other end of a telephone line. See also **hot line**.

❏ A railway line is often just called a **line**.

❏ The outline or shape of something can be called its **lines**.

❏ Imaginary boundaries between groups of people or things are sometimes called **lines**. *Many children live below the poverty line... The dividing line between civil servants and local authority officials is now less clear.*

❏ The rows of words in a piece of writing are called **lines**. ◇ The words an actor learns are called his or her **lines**. ◇ If a school pupil is given **lines**, he or she has to write out a certain number of rows of writing as a punishment.

❏ If you **read between the lines**, you work out what someone really means, feels, or intends to do.

❏ The **line** someone takes on an issue or problem is the attitude or policy they adopt towards it. ◇ A **line** is also a way of setting about a problem or task. *This line of inquiry had reached its end.* ◇ If you say something like a policy is

on the right lines, you mean it is generally correct and likely to succeed.

❏ You can describe the way something develops by saying it develops along particular **lines**. *Community workers say that gangs are forming along racial lines.*

❏ Your **line** of work or business is the kind you do.

❏ A **line** is a type of product made by a particular company. *...its long-awaited new line of cheap personal computers.*

❏ **On the lines of** and **along the lines of** are used to talk about something having a general similarity to something else. *Most Japanese do not want to see their sport turned into an entertainment on the lines of professional wrestling.*

❏ If you say you **draw the line** at something, you mean it is unacceptable and goes beyond what you are prepared to do.

❏ If your job is **on the line**, you are in danger of losing it. Similarly, if something like your reputation is **on the line**, it is in danger of being harmed.

❏ If something happens at some point during a process or activity, you can say it happens somewhere **along the line**. Similarly, if you are talking about the future, you can say something will happen **further down the line**.

❏ If you **line** someone or something **up**, you arrange for them to be available. *The organisers are trying to line up a replacement.*

❏ If you **line** a container, you cover its inside surface with paper or some other material. Similarly, a piece of clothing can be **lined** with a fabric. ◇ **line your pockets:** see pocket.

❏ **toe the line:** see toe. ◇ See also **party line**.

line drawing A line drawing is a drawing made up entirely of lines. Darker and lighter areas are shown by the spacing and thickness of the lines.

line printer A line printer is a printer attached to a computer which prints a line at a time rather than a character at a time.

line-up (line-ups) A **line-up** is a group of people brought together to be members of a team or to take part in an event together. *...the Prime Minister's new cabinet line-up.* ◇ A **line-up** is also a series of things brought together for an activity or event. *The Leeds Film Festival showcases an impressive line-up of previously banned work.*

lineage (*pron:* lin-ee-ij) A person's **lineage** is the line of people they are descended from through one of their parents, going back to one ancestor.

linear ❏ A **linear** process is one where things happen one after another, each developing from the previous one. *The history of culture does not proceed in a linear way.*

❏ **Linear** is also used to describe things which form a long line or are in a long narrow shape. *...a linear archipelago... ...a linear city.*

linen is a fabric made from flax and used for making clothes, tablecloths, and sheets. Things like tablecloths and sheets are often called **linen**. ◇ If you talk about someone having their **dirty linen washed in public**, you mean unpleasant aspects of their private life have been revealed and are being discussed by other people.

liner ❏ A **liner** is a large passenger ship on which people travel long distances or take holiday cruises.

❏ A **bin liner** is a plastic bag which you put inside a waste bin or dustbin.

linesman (linesmen) A **linesman** is an official in a game like football who indicates when the ball goes over the boundary line or when a rule is broken.

linger (lingering, lingered) If something **lingers**, it stays around for a long time. *...the lingering effects of radiation.* ◇ If you **linger** somewhere, you stay longer than is necessary, usually because you are enjoying yourself. ◇ If you **linger on** something, you spend a long time doing it or thinking about it.

lingerie (*pron:* lan-zher-ee; *the 'zh' sounds like 's' in 'pleasure'*) **Lingerie** is women's lightweight underwear and nightclothes.

lingo (lingos) People sometimes call a foreign language a **lingo**. ◇ The **lingo** of a group of people is the special language they use. *...the quaint lingo of fast-talking advertising executives.*

lingua franca (*pron:* ling-wa frang-ka) A **lingua franca** is a language which is widely used as a means of communication between people who cannot speak each other's first language. For example, Swahili is a lingua franca in many parts of Africa.

linguist A **linguist** is (a) someone who speaks several languages. (b) someone who studies or teaches linguistics.

linguistic (linguistically; linguistics) ❑ **Linguistic** is used to talk about things to do with languages. *...an attempt to prevent the break-up of Canada along linguistic lines.* ◇ If someone has **linguistic** ability, they are good at learning languages. *...a linguistically proficient foreign correspondent.* ❑ **Linguistics** is the scientific study of the way language works.

liniment A **liniment** is a medicated liquid you rub into your skin to reduce pain or stiffness.

lining The **lining** of a hollow part of your body is a layer on its inner surface. *...the lining of the stomach.* Other hollow objects can also have a **lining**. *The wheel arches are given a plastic lining.* ◇ The **lining** of a piece of clothing is material attached to its inside, to make it warmer or more comfortable. ◇ **silver lining: see silver.**

link (-linked) ❑ If two things are **linked**, they are connected in some way. For example, if two organizations are **linked**, their work is connected. When a connection is made between two organizations or other things, you can say there is a **link-up** between them, or one thing is **linked up** to the other.

❑ You often say two things are **linked** or there is a **link** between them when one causes the other, or makes it more likely to happen. *...radiation-linked diseases.* ◇ You also say things are **linked** when it has been arranged that changes to one affect the other. *...linked European exchange rates.* ◇ If you **link** something with something else, you associate it with it. *Nagano's name has become closely linked with contemporary music.*

❑ If there are **links** between two groups of people, they have a friendly relationship with each other.

❑ If two objects are **linked**, they are joined together, or connected by something like a power cable. When a connection like this is made, you can say there is a **link-up** between the objects, or one object is **linked up** to the other.

❑ If two places are **linked** by a road or railway, the road or railway runs between them. You can talk about road or rail **links** between places. Similarly, you can talk about telephone or postal **links**.

❑ A **link** of a chain is one of the rings in it. ◇ The parts of a process or a series of events leading to something happening can be called the **links in a chain.** *Italy's action thus became an important link in the chain of events that led up to the outbreak of the First World War.* ◇ If part of something is less good than the other parts and prevents the whole thing from being effective, you can call it the **weak link** or the **weak link in the chain.**

❑ If several people link hands, they form a chain, each person holding the next person's hand. Similarly, people can **link arms.**

❑ A golf **links** is a golf course, especially one close to the sea.

link-up See link.

linkage If you say there is **linkage** between two things, you mean they are connected in some way. ◇ **Linkage** is also the deliberate connecting of two separate issues, so that someone agrees to do one thing only if something else is done. *Just how explicit the linkage was between the return of the aircraft and the hostages being freed will probably never be known.*

linnet The **linnet** is a small songbird of the finch family. The male has a red breast and forehead.

lino is the same as **linoleum.**

linoleum is a stiff old-fashioned floor covering made from hessian or jute with a shiny coating of powdered cork.

Linotype A **Linotype** is an old-fashioned typesetting machine operated by a keyboard. It casts each line on a piece of metal called a slug. 'Linotype' is a trademark.

linseed is the seed of the flax plant.

linseed oil is an oil made from linseed. It is used to make paints, varnishes, and inks. In the past, people rubbed it into wooden surfaces to protect them.

lint is a soft cotton or linen fabric used for dressing cuts and wounds.

lintel A **lintel** is a piece of stone or wood over a door or window. It supports the bricks or stones above it.

lion Lions are large wild members of the cat family. They have yellowish fur; the male has a long shaggy mane. Lions live mainly in Africa. ◇ If you get the **lion's share** of something, you get most of it.

lioness (lionesses) A **lioness** is a female lion.

lionize (lionizing, lionized) (*can be spelled with an 's' instead of a 'z'*) If someone is **lionized**, they are treated as a celebrity.

lip ❑ A person's **lips** are the top and bottom fleshy edges of their mouth.

❑ If you say someone is keeping a **stiff upper lip**, you mean they are hiding their emotions even though this may be difficult for them. ◇ If you say someone's **lips are sealed**, you mean they are refusing to reveal a secret.

❑ If a word or phrase is **on everyone's lips**, you keep hearing it everywhere, because people are interested in what it stands for. Similarly, you can say someone's name is **on everyone's lips**. If you say a question is **on everyone's lips**, you mean people keep asking it.

❑ **Lip-reading** is understanding what someone is saying by watching the position and movement of their lips. ◇ If you say to someone **'read my lips'**, you mean they should pay close attention to what you are going to say next.

❑ If you **curl your lip** at something, you sneer at it and show your contempt for it.

❏ If someone **pays lip service** to an idea, they pretend they approve of it, but in fact do nothing to support it.

lipid Lipids are substances like fats and oils which are insoluble in water but soluble in alcohol and ether. They are important structural materials in living things.

liposuction is a way of removing excess fat from under a person's skin. The skin is cut and the fat is sucked out by a machine.

lipstick is a coloured substance women put on their lips. It comes in the form of a small stick.

liquefaction is the process of making something liquid.

liquefied (*or* liquified) A liquefied substance is one which is normally solid or a gas, but has been changed to liquid form. ...*liquefied natural gas.*

liqueur (*pron:* lik-cure) Liqueurs are strong, usually sweet, alcoholic drinks. They are often drunk after a meal.

liquid ❏ A liquid is any substance which is not a solid or a gas and which can be poured. ❏ Liquid is used to describe things, especially assets, which can be quickly turned into cash if necessary.

liquid crystal A liquid crystal is a liquid which has some of the qualities of crystals, for example reflecting light from different directions in different ways. ◇ **liquid crystal display:** see LCD.

liquidate (liquidating, liquidated; liquidation, liquidator) ❏ When a company which fails is liquidated, it is closed down by a procedure called liquidation, in which its assets are sold off to help repay its debts. A liquidator is someone brought in from outside to supervise this procedure. ◇ You can also say someone liquidates their assets when they sell off property such as buildings or machinery, to get money. ❏ If someone liquidates something like a system, they destroy it. ◇ If someone liquidates another person, they get rid of them by killing them.

liquidity is having enough cash or liquid assets to pay any debts or cover any emergencies.

liquidize (liquidizing, liquidized; liquidizer) (*can be spelled with an 's' instead of a 'z'*) When you liquidize food, you blend it in an electrical machine called a liquidizer, to make it into a pulp or liquid.

liquified See liquefied.

liquor is strong alcoholic drink, especially spirits.

liquorice (*or* licorice) (*usual pron:* lik-ker-ish) Liquorice is a firm black substance with a strong flavour. It is used for making sweets.

lira (*plural:* lire) The lira is the unit of currency in Italy. Turkey and Syria also have a unit of currency called a lira.

lisp If someone lisps or has a lisp, they pronounce 's' and 'z' as 'th'. For example, they say 'thaw' instead of 'saw'.

lissom A lissom person is slim and graceful.

list (listing) ❏ A list is a series of things or names written one below the other. When a document contains a list, you can say it lists a number of things or people. ◇ If something is listed, it is included as an item on a list, especially an official list. The items in a list are sometimes called listings. ◇ A listed building is included in a list of buildings of architectural or historic interest which are protected by law from being demolished or altered. ❏ If a person lists something, they mention a series of

things or names. *She was asked to list her engagements.* ❏ A listed company is one whose shares have been approved and quoted for trading on a stock market. When this happens, you say the company is given a listing. ❏ The list price of something is the price suggested by the manufacturers in their catalogue, price list, or advertisements. You say something is listed at a particular price. ❏ If a ship lists, it leans over to one side, usually because it is damaged or sinking.

listen (listening, listened) ❏ If you listen to someone who is talking, you pay attention to what they are saying. Similarly, you can listen to music or other sounds. ◇ If you listen for a sound, you stay alert so you will hear it when it comes. ❏ You also say someone listens to someone else when they take account of what they say. *The commission has listened to its critics.* ❏ If you listen in on something like a discussion, you are there while it is taking place and pay attention to what is being said, but do not take part in it yourself. ◇ If someone listens in to a phone conversation or some other private conversation, they listen without the people concerned knowing about it.

listener People who listen to the radio are often called listeners. ◇ Anyone who listens to something can be called a listener. If you say someone is a good listener, you mean they listen patiently and sympathetically when someone talks to them.

listeria is a kind of bacteria. It can cause severe food poisoning, which is sometimes fatal.

listing See list.

listless (listlessly, listlessness) If someone is listless, they are weary and lacking in energy or enthusiasm. *They sit listlessly on the steps of their houses... All three began displaying signs of listlessness.*

lit See light.

litany (litanies) The litany is part of a church service in which the priest says a set group of prayers and the congregation replies with set responses. ◇ A litany is also any long or tedious speech or list of things.

liter See litre.

literacy is (a) the ability to read and write. (b) the ability to spell properly and use correct grammar. ...*a worrying decline in standards of literacy.*

literal (literally) ❏ The literal meaning of a word is its most basic meaning. People often use literal or literally to emphasize that they are using a word with its most basic meaning, although this may be surprising. *It could be said that Venice is literally sinking under the weight of visitors.* ◇ Some people use literal or literally when they are quite clearly not using a word with its literal meaning. For example, a football fan might say 'Arsenal literally massacred Standard Liège'. *'These jackets are literally walking out of the store,' a spokeswoman said.* This use is quite common in conversation, but is thought by many people to be wrong or silly. ❏ A literal translation of a phrase or sentence is based on the literal meaning of each word, although what is really meant could be quite different. ❏ If you have a literal belief in something, you believe it is exactly as it is described somewhere. For example, someone might have a **literal** belief in the story of Noah's ark. ◇ People who lack imagination and tend to take things at face value are sometimes called **literal-minded**.

literary people and things are connected in some way with literature. *...a prominent literary critic.* ◇ **Literary** words and expressions are used in novels and poems, but are not usually used in conversation, except in a humorous way. 'Steed' and 'resplendent' are literary words.

literate people can read and write. People who are highly **literate** have read a great deal and can express themselves well. You can also describe a well-written piece of writing as **literate**. *...Waller's literate financial thriller.* ◇ **-literate** can be added to words to describe other kinds of abilities. *...computer-literate film makers and animators.* You can also describe someone's abilities by using **literate** after a word ending in '-ly'. *...the conscientious, financially literate, top manager of those years.*

literati are well-educated people who are interested in literature.

literature is novels, plays, poetry, and other kinds of creative writing which are thought to be of a high standard.
❑ Books and articles about a subject can be called the **literature** of that subject. *A search of the scientific literature revealed that this theory had not been suggested before.* ◇ **Literature** is also any kind of printed information, usually in leaflet form, about a subject. *The opposition parties had difficulty in distributing campaign literature.*

lithe people move and bend their bodies easily and gracefully.

lithium is the lightest known metal. It is used in batteries and medicines, and in the manufacture of other metals.

lithography (lithograph, lithographic) **Lithography** is a method of printing and print making in which a piece of metal or plastic is specially treated so that ink sticks to some parts and not to others. When magazines or other publications are printed in this way, the process is called **offset lithography** or **offset printing**. **Lithographic** is used to describe the processes and equipment used in lithography. *...lithographic plates.* A **lithograph** is a printed picture made by this method.

litigant Litigants are the people, other than the lawyers, who are fighting or defending a civil law case.

litigate (litigating, litigated; litigation, litigator) If someone **litigates**, they take a dispute to a civil court for a decision. The process of taking a dispute to court and the legal proceedings which follow are called **litigation**. A **litigator** is a lawyer who fights or defends civil lawsuits.

litigious (*pron:* li-tij-uss) people are always taking issues to court for a decision.

litmus is a purple chemical which is turned red by acids and blue by alkalis. **Litmus** paper is a paper containing litmus which can be used to test whether something is acidic or alkaline.
❑ Any simple but effective way of determining something can be called a **litmus test**. *Mr Weld's status within his party may prove a good litmus test of its electoral chances.*

litre (*American spelling:* liter) The volume of liquids and gases is often expressed in **litres**. A litre is 1,000 cubic centimetres (about 1.76 pints).

litter (littering, littered) ❑ **Litter** is small pieces of rubbish, for example bits of paper, left lying around in a public place. You can say rubbish **litters** a place or the place is **littered** with it. *The streets are littered with broken glass.* ◇ You can say a place is **littered** with other things when it is full of them. *The nation's bathroom cabinets are littered with unwanted medicines.*
❑ A **litter** is a group of baby animals born at the same time to the same mother.

litter bin A litter bin is a container in a public place, for people to put their litter in.

little is used to describe things which are smaller in size than usual. ◇ **Little** is also used to describe things which do not extend far, or do not last long. *...a little walk... ...a little chat.* ◇ **Little** is also used to describe things which are unimportant or trivial. *He complained a lot about little things.*
❑ A **little** child is very young. ◇ Your **little** sister or brother is your younger sister or brother.
❑ A **little** means a short time. *If that difference persists, a little after 2010 China will have the world's biggest economy.*
❑ A **little** of something is a small amount or quantity of it. *I know a little French... Beat the egg yolk with a little of the sauce.* ◇ **A little** and **a little bit** mean to a small extent or degree. *He tapped again a little harder.*
❑ If something happens **little by little**, it happens very gradually.
❑ **Little** is also used to say there is not much of something. *Mr Baker has shown little interest in Mexico.* ◇ If someone does **little** or says **little**, they do not do or say much. You can use **little** after other words like this. *He cared little for social advancement... ...someone about whom you know little.* ◇ If you say something is **little** different from something else, you mean it is not much different.
❑ If you say **little** does someone know something, you mean they do not know it, and you are wondering what they would think or say if they did. *Little did she know that she bore within her the seeds of the future Miss Jean Brodie.*

little finger Your little finger is your shortest finger, the one furthest from your thumb.

little-known A little-known person or thing is not known to many people.

littoral The area along a sea coast is sometimes called a littoral.

liturgical is used to talk about things connected with religious services. *...liturgical music.*

liturgy (liturgies) A **liturgy** is a traditional form of service in some churches.

live (living, lived) ❑ If you **live** in a place, it is your home. *She lived in Hollywood for 48 years.* You can also say someone **lives** in a type of accommodation. *Much of the population lives in rudimentary camps.* ◇ If you **live** in a particular kind of society, that is the society you belong to. ◇ If an animal or bird **lives** in an area or type of country, that is its natural habitat.
❑ If you **live** for a certain length of time, you are alive for that time. ◇ If someone **lived** in a particular century or from one date to another, they were alive then. *Grandpa lived from 1871 to 1923.* ◇ If someone **lives through** a period or event in history, they experience it and survive it. *Maria Gregoriavna lived through Stalin's purges.* ◇ If you **live out** your life in a place or in particular circumstances, you stay in that place or remain in those circumstances

until you die.

❑ The way you **live** is the kind of lifestyle you have, or the circumstances of your daily life. *He and his mother returned to Solihull to live an average single-parent, middle-class family life.*

❑ The money you **live on** is the money you have for buying everyday things that you need. *He asked how anyone could live on the 1,300 roubles he now receives.* ◇ If you **live off** a source of income, you get the money you need from it. *They lived off their pensions and interest from savings.*

❑ If you **live off** the land, you eat food which you grow or hunt yourself, rather than buying it. ◇ If you **live off** a kind of food or **live on** it, it is the only kind you eat.

❑ If you **live with** someone, you share a home with them and have a sexual relationship with them but are not married to them. You can also say you and the other person are **living together**.

❑ If you **live by** a set of standards or rules, you behave the way they say you should. ◇ If you do not **live up to** something, you fail to do what is expected of you. *Many more children could be saved if governments lived up to their responsibilities.*

❑ If you have to **live with** an unpleasant decision or situation, you have to accept it and carry on with your life or work. *The inadequacy of funding is a problem theatre companies have learnt to live with.* ◇ If you are trying to **live down** something embarrassing which has happened to you, you are hoping people will forget about it.

❑ If you say someone will **live to** regret something they have done, you mean they will eventually be sorry they did it, whatever they feel now.

❑ If you **live for** something, it is the most important thing in your life. *Being the US Open champion is what I've lived for.*

❑ If you **live it up**, you have a good time, for example by going to parties.

❑ If you say **live and let live**, you mean people should be allowed to behave the way they want to and should not be criticized for being different.

❑ You can say something **lives on** when it no longer exists but people go on remembering it. *Elvis continues to live on in our hearts.*

❑ If a TV or radio programme is **live**, what you see or hear is happening now, and has not been recorded beforehand. *A deal is in the offing to broadcast live opera from major houses around the world.* ◇ A **live** performance takes place in front of an audience. *Much of today's best acting is to be found on the small screen, not in live theatre.*

❑ A **live** animal is one which is alive in circumstances where you would expect it to be dead. *One applicant sent us a box containing a live locust.*

❑ **Live** ammunition contains explosive and is intended to kill. ◇ If something electrical is **live**, it is directly connected to a source of electricity, and will give you a shock if you touch it.

livelihood Your **livelihood** is your job, or whatever provides you with an income.

lively (livelier, liveliest; liveliness) A **lively** person is active, enthusiastic, and cheerful. ◇ If people have a **lively** discussion, they discuss things in an enthusiastic way, because they are strongly interested in the thing they are talking about.

liven (livening, livened) If something **livens up** a place or event, it makes it more interesting and exciting.

liver Your **liver** is a large organ in your body. Its functions include regulating chemicals in your blood. ◇ **Liver** is the liver of some animals, which is cooked and eaten.

livery (liveries) A company's **livery** is a design or set of colours associated with it, appearing, for example, on its products or vehicles. ◇ A servant's **livery** is the uniform he or she wears, especially a uniform worn only by the servants of one person or family.

livestock is animals like cattle and sheep which are kept on a farm.

livid If someone is **livid**, they are extremely angry. ◇ If something is **livid**, it is an unpleasant dark purple or bluish-grey colour. *...a livid scar.*

living ❑ A **living** person is someone who is alive now. *Octavio Paz is considered by many to be Latin America's finest living poet.*

❑ If you earn your **living** in a particular way, you get the money you live on by doing a particular kind of work. ◇ If you are paid a **living wage**, you are paid just enough money to buy food, clothing, and other necessary things.

❑ **Living** is used to talk about places where people live, especially when they are attached to their workplace. *The extra money will be spent on improving living quarters.* ◇ **Living** is also used to talk about a particular way of life. *...the stresses of urban living.* ◇ When you talk about **living standards**, you mean the level of comfort in which people live, which usually depends on how much money they have.

living room The **living room** in a house is the room where people sit and relax.

lizard Lizards are reptiles with short legs, dry scaly skin, and long tails. They live mainly in hot countries.

llama The **llama** is a South American pack animal with thick hair. It looks like a small camel without a hump.

LLB after someone's name means they have a university degree in law. LLB stands for 'Bachelor of Laws'.

lo People sometimes say **lo** or **lo and behold** when they are mentioning something surprising. *Last Thursday I blinked and, lo, interest rates had changed again.*

load (loading, loaded) ❑ When people **load** a vehicle or container, they put things into it. *...lorries loaded with sheep.* ◇ A **load** of something is a quantity of it being carried somewhere. *The first plane-load of canned meat has already left Bologna.*

❑ If you **load** a weapon, you put ammunition into it, so it is ready to be fired. *...a loaded gun.* ◇ If you **load** a camera, you put film into it. Similarly, you can **load** a tape or disk into a cassette player or computer.

❑ A **loaded** remark or question has more meaning than it appears to have. A **loaded** question is usually intended to get someone to say something they do not want to say.

❑ If something is **loaded** in favour of someone, it gives them a better chance of success. Similarly, something can be **loaded** against someone. You can also say the **dice are loaded** in favour of someone or against them.

❑ A **load** of things or people means a lot of them. *The system seems to have bred a whole load of thugs who cannot add up.* **Loads** of something means a lot of it. *...loads of money.*

❑ If you say someone is **loaded**, you mean they have a

lot of money. ◇ You can also say someone is **loaded** when they are drunk.

loaf (loafing, loafed) ❏ A **loaf** (*plural:* loaves) is bread baked in a large regular shape which can be sliced.

❏ If you **loaf** about, you spend time not working, or not doing things you are supposed to.

loafer Loafers are a type of casual shoe, a bit like moccasins. ◇ If you call a person a **loafer**, you mean they spend their time lazing around and not working.

loan (loaning, loaned) ❏ A **loan** is an amount of money you borrow, for example from a bank, and have to pay back with interest, usually in instalments over a period of time. ◇ A **loan shark** is someone who lends people money at very high rates of interest and sometimes uses threats or violence to get it back.

❏ If you **loan** something to someone, you lend it to them. If you offer someone the **loan** of something, you offer to lend it to them. If a book or picture is **on loan**, it has been lent to someone.

loath (*or* loth) If you are **loath** to do something, you are unwilling to do it.

loathe (loathing, loathed) If you **loathe** someone or something, you dislike them intensely. **Loathing** is a feeling of great dislike.

loathsome If you say someone or something is **loathsome**, you mean they are very unattractive or unpleasant.

lob (lobbing, lobbed) If you **lob** something somewhere, you get it to land there by throwing it high in the air. *Police lobbed tear gas shells into the house.* ◇ If you **lob** the ball in tennis, you hit it high in the air so it lands behind your opponent. This kind of shot is called a **lob**.

lobby (lobbies, lobbying, lobbied; lobbyist) ❏ A **lobby** is a group of people who try to persuade a government or organization to do something or prevent something. *The farm lobby still has considerable clout in France.* ◇ If you **lobby** people like government ministers or local councillors, you try to get them to do something. *He lobbied loudly and constantly for passage of the Civil Rights Act.* People who lobby are called **lobbyists**.

❏ The **lobby** of a large building is the main entrance area, with corridors and staircases leading off it.

lobe The **lobe** of your ear is the soft fleshy part at the bottom. ◇ Rounded parts of some other parts of the body are also called **lobes**, for example parts of the brain, the lungs, and the liver.

lobelia The **lobelia** is a popular bedding plant covered with small flowers which are often blue.

lobster The **lobster** is a sea creature with a hard shell, two front claws, and eight legs. ◇ A **lobster pot** is a basket-like trap for catching lobsters.

local (locally) ❏ **Local government** is the organization and administration of public services on a local rather than a national basis. The **local authority** in an area is the council responsible for running the services there. **Local** is used to talk about things connected with local government. *...a member of the local council.*

❏ You use **local** to talk about things in the area where you live or work. *...a local restaurant... These schemes will employ 5,500, of whom about a quarter will be recruited locally.* ◇ You can call the people who live in an area the **locals**. ◇ Your **local** is a pub near where you live, where you of-

ten go for a drink.

❏ **Local colour** is the features of a place or period in history which are special to that place or period. *On his way to the opening, Mr Sottile took in some local colour with a visit to the statue of Thomas Telford.*

local anaesthetic A local anaesthetic stops the feeling in only one part of your body, and does not make you unconscious. See also general anaesthetic.

local authority See local.

local education authority In England and Wales, a **local education authority** or LEA is a local authority which deals with the provision of education at primary and secondary level, and the allocation of student grants. The corresponding authorities in Scotland are known as 'regional education authorities', and the ones in Northern Ireland are called 'education and library boards'.

local government See local.

local time is the time in a particular region or country, when it is different from a standard time such as GMT.

locale (*pron:* loh-**kahl**) The **locale** for something is the place chosen for it.

locality (localities) If you talk about something happening **in the locality,** you mean it happens in the general area you have been talking about.

localized (*or* localised) things are limited to a small area. *It must have been a fairly localized explosion because it did not seem to have done much damage elsewhere.*

locate (locating, located) If you **locate** someone or something, you succeed in finding them. ◇ If something is **located** somewhere, that is where it is. *His house is located in a leafy residential area of south London.* ◇ If people **locate** something somewhere, they build it there. *...plans to locate a radar station in an area of natural beauty.* ◇ If an organization **locates** somewhere, it moves its business there.

location The **location** of something is the place where it is. *...a map marking the location of the hoard.* ◇ If a film or TV programme is made **on location,** it is made in real surroundings away from the studio.

loch In Scotland, a **loch** is a large area of water completely or almost completely surrounded by land. In Ireland, an area of water like this is called a **lough.**

lock ❏ The **lock** on a door is the device you turn a key in, to fasten the door and prevent it being opened by anyone who does not have a key. If you **lock** a door, you fasten it like this. ◇ If you **lock** something **in** a cupboard, drawer, or safe or **lock** it **away** there, you put it there and lock the door. ◇ If something is **under lock and key,** it is in a locked room or container.

❏ If someone is **locked in** a room or other place, the door is locked and they cannot get out. If someone is kept somewhere like this as a prisoner, you say they are **locked up.**

❏ If you **lock up,** you close and lock all the outside doors of a building, to keep burglars out. ◇ If someone is **locked out,** they are prevented from getting into a place by the doors being locked. ◇ If you **lock** yourself **out** of a place, you cannot get in because the door is locked and you have left your keys inside. ◇ If the management of a factory or other workplace **locks out** the workers, it closes the factory and prevents the workers from coming in, because they refuse to accept the management's proposals or conditions of work. A situation like this is called a **lock-out** or **lockout**.

❏ If you are **locked** in a situation, you are unable to get out of it. *The London stock market seems locked in a terminal dive.* ◇ If people are **locked** in a fight or argument, they are fighting or arguing fiercely, and determined not to give in to their opponent.

❏ A **lock** on a canal is a short stretch of water between two barriers, where the water level can be raised or lowered to allow boats to move between higher and lower sections of the canal.

❏ A **lock** of hair is a small bunch of someone's hair, which they cut off and give to you so you will remember them. ◇ A person's hair can be called their **locks**.

lock-up garage A **lock-up garage** is not within the boundaries of your house, but is in a block of garages somewhere nearby.

locker A **locker** is a small cupboard with a lock, where you put your personal belongings temporarily, for example at a sports club or your workplace. ◇ A **locker room** is a room in a sports club where people change their clothes and store their belongings in lockers.

locket A **locket** is a piece of jewellery containing something like a picture, which you wear on a chain round your neck.

lockout See lock.

locksmith A **locksmith** is someone who makes and repairs locks as their job.

locomotion is moving from one place to another. *She dances with an ease that make the dance seem the only natural means of locomotion.*

locomotive A **locomotive** is a railway engine.

locum A **locum** is a doctor or priest who temporarily takes over the work of another doctor or priest while he or she is ill or on holiday.

locust Locusts are insects like large grasshoppers. They live in hot countries and usually travel in swarms, eating all the crops they land on.

lodge (lodging, lodged; lodger, lodgings) ❏ If you **lodge** something like a complaint or protest, you make it in a formal way. *They have been refused refugee status but have lodged appeals.*

❏ If you **lodge** money or other valuables somewhere like a bank, you leave them there.

❏ If something **lodges** somewhere or is **lodged** there, it becomes stuck. *These clots travel around in the blood system and can become lodged in the brain where they cause strokes.*

❏ If someone **lodges** in your house, they live there for a time, usually paying rent. You refer to them as your **lodger**; they call your house their **lodging** or **lodgings**. ◇ If your employers **lodge** you somewhere, they find accommodation for you.

❏ A **lodge** is a small house at the entrance to the grounds of a large one. ◇ A **lodge** is also a building where people stay on holiday, especially when they are taking part in sports like hunting or fishing.

❏ Some organizations have local branches or meeting places called **lodges**. *...a masonic lodge... He was master of his local Orange lodge.*

loft A **loft** is the space inside the roof of a house, often used for storing things.

lofty (loftier, loftiest; loftily) ❏ A **lofty** building is very high.

❏ **Lofty** ideas, motives, or aims are noble and admirable. *America needed a loftier view of its world mission.*

❏ If you say someone is **lofty**, you mean they speak or behave in a proud and rather unpleasant way. *...politicians who loftily insist, from the comfort of Westminster, that electors are interested only in mortgage rates.*

log (logging, logged; logger) ❏ A **log** is a piece of wood cut from a thick branch or from the trunk of a tree. ◇ If an area of forest is **logged**, some or all of the trees are cut down for timber. A **logger** is a person whose job is cutting down trees in a forest.

❏ A **log** is also an official written record of something, for example what happens each day on board a ship. If you **log** something, you record it officially in writing or on computer.

❏ If you **log into** a computer system, you gain access to it, usually by typing in your name or identity code and a password. You can also say you **log in** or **log on**. If you **log off** or **log out**, you finish using the system by typing in a command.

log book A **log book** is a book in which you record details and events over a period of time, especially ones to do with travel or transport.

log-jam (or logjam) If you say there is a **log-jam**, you mean many things are waiting to be dealt with, because they have been appearing at a faster rate than people can deal with them.

loganberry (loganberries) **Loganberries** are small purplish-red fruit, similar to large raspberries.

logger See log.

loggerheads You say people are at **loggerheads** when they disagree strongly about something.

logic is a way of reasoning which involves a progression of statements, each of which must be true if the statement before it is true. Mathematical logic uses symbols instead of words. ◇ The **logic** which leads to a conclusion is the reasoning behind it. *The logic is that this will be a decade of low economic growth, and shares, therefore, will perform less well.* ◇ Different kinds of **logic** are different ways of thinking and reasoning. *Leninist logic encouraged the belief that somehow the Soviet Union could ignore the laws of economics.*

logical (logically) You say an argument is **logical** when each step follows from the one before. If you say something is the **logical** conclusion of something else, you mean it seems to follow from it. *If property losses become tax-allowable, gains, logically, should be taxable.* ◇ A **logical** course of action seems reasonable or sensible in the circumstances. *It seemed logical to employ part-timers during the busy periods rather than employ full-time workers to do very little for a lot of the time.*

logician A **logician** is a specialist in logic, especially mathematical logic.

logistics (logistic, logistical, logistically) In the armed forces, **logistics** is the organization of transport, supplies, and maintenance for troops and equipment. **Logistic** and **logistical** are used to talk about things connected with logistics. *The American contribution is expected to include logistical support.* ◇ **Logistics, logistic**, and **logistical** are also used to talk about other things which need careful organization. *For logistical simplicity, the Americans want these negotiations to stay in Madrid.*

logjam See log-jam.

logo (logos) The **logo** of a company or other organization is the unique design it puts on its products, possessions, and publicity material.

loin is a piece of meat from the back or sides of an animal. *...boned loin of lamb.* ◇ A person's **loins** are the front part of their body between their waist and thighs, especially their genitals. ◇ If you **gird your loins** or **gird up your loins,** you prepare to do something difficult or dangerous.

loincloth A **loincloth** is a piece of cloth sometimes worn by men to cover their genitals, especially in countries where it is too hot to wear anything else.

loiter (loitering, loitered) If you **loiter** somewhere, you hang around with no real purpose.

loll If you **loll** somewhere, you sit or lie in a very relaxed way. If you **loll about** or **loll around,** you spend a lot of time sitting or lying like this, doing nothing in particular. ◇ If your head or tongue **lolls,** it hangs loosely.

lollipop A **lollipop** is a sweet on the end of a stick.

lollipop lady (lollipop man) A **lollipop lady** or **lollipop man** is a person whose job is to help children cross a busy road at a particular point. The official name for a lollipop lady or lollipop man is a 'school crossing patrol'.

lolly (lollies) ❑ A **lolly** is (a) a piece of flavoured ice or ice cream on a stick. (b) a lollipop.
   ❑ **Lolly** is money.

lone A **lone** person or thing is the only one of their kind, or the only one in a particular place. *Britain has often been perceived as a lone voice against a single European currency.*

lonely (lonelier, loneliest; loneliness) ❑ If someone is **lonely,** they are unhappy because they are alone or do not have any friends. This feeling is called **loneliness.** A **lonely** time is one when you are on your own like this.
   ❑ A **lonely** place is one where few people go.

lonely hearts The **lonely hearts** section of a newspaper or magazine consists of adverts placed there by people who want to find a friend or lover. A **lonely hearts** club is one people join for the same purpose. Single people who are thought to be on the lookout for a friend or lover are sometimes called **lonely hearts.**

loner A **loner** is a person who likes being on their own.

lonesome is the usual American word for 'lonely'.

long is used to talk about something lasting for a great deal of time. *...a long period of low interest rates... It was about two minutes before they made contact, but it seemed much longer.*
   ❑ **Long** is used to say how much time something lasts for. *'Don Carlos' is well over five hours long.* ◇ **Long** is used with 'how' to ask how much time something lasts for. *For how long should a simplified single benefit continue to be paid?*
   ❑ When people talk about **long** hours, days, or years, they are emphasizing the amount of time something lasts for, especially when it causes hardship or worry. *Long days of bargaining still lie ahead.* ◇ **Long** is used with 'all' to say something continues throughout a period of time. *The foreman shouted at me all day long.* ◇ If something happened **long** before something else or **long** after it, a great deal of time passed between the two things.
   ❑ If you say something will happen **before long,** you mean it will happen soon. ◇ If you say something will not

continue **for long** or not continue **much longer,** you mean it will soon be over. ◇ If something **no longer** happens or does **not** happen **any longer,** it used to happen but does not happen now.
   ❑ If something is true **as long as** something else is true, the first thing is true only if the second one is. *The tax advantages apply only so long as the money remains invested.*
   ❑ If you say **long live** something, you mean you are in favour of it and want it to continue. *Long live the Cuban revolution!... Long live democracy.*
   ❑ If something is **long,** it measures a large distance from one end to the other. *...a long corridor... ...a long black gown.* ◇ **Long** is used when mentioning the length of something. *...a tunnel of ice 1,340 metres long.* **Long** is used with 'how' to ask about the length of something. *How long is the capillary tube itself?*
   ❑ A **long** book or other piece of writing contains a great many words. A **long** sentence has a lot of words in it; a **long** word consists of a lot of letters.
   ❑ If you say someone has a **long face,** you mean they are disappointed or worried about something.
   ❑ If you **long** for something, you want it very much.

long- is added to words to describe things which last for a long time or have been going on for a long time. *...a long-drawn-out power struggle... ...the firm's long-awaited stockmarket flotation.*

long-distance is used to describe things to do with long journeys, or things connecting places which are far apart. *...long-distance pipelines... ...long-distance running.*

long division is a method of dividing one number by another which involves writing out each stage in the calculation.

long johns are warm underpants with long legs.

long jump The **long jump** is an event in athletics. Competitors run very fast up to a marker, then jump as far as they can.

long-lasting things last for a long time.

long-life things are made or treated so that they last longer than other things of the same kind. *...long-life milk.*

long-lived If people of a particular kind are **long-lived,** they tend to live longer than most other people.

long-lost is used to describe people, especially friends and relatives, who have not been seen for a very long time. *...a long-lost uncle.*

long-range is used to describe things, especially weapons, which operate over long distances. *...long-range missiles... The aircraft must have the ability to operate at long range against an opponent.* ◇ A **long-range** forecast or plan covers a period extending well into the future.

long-running is used to describe things which have been going on for a long time. *The BBC says this episode will be the last in the long-running series.*

long-sighted (long-sightedness) If you are **long-sighted,** you cannot see things near you clearly, and may need to wear glasses for reading.

long-standing A **long-standing** situation has existed for a long time. *...a long-standing row... I have a long-standing engagement in Hamburg.*

long-suffering is used to describe people who patiently put up with continual trouble or bad treatment. *When it comes to the weather, Britons like to see themselves as long-*

suffering but good-humoured victims.

long-term is used to talk about things happening at some time in the future, rather than immediately. *...a choice between short-term relief and long-term benefit.*

long-time is used to describe people and things that have had a role or function for a very long time. *...a long-time critic of the leadership.*

long wave is used to talk about the range of radio waves from 1,000 metres upwards.

long-winded If something someone says or writes is **long-winded**, it is boring because it is much longer than necessary.

longboat A **longboat** was a narrow uncovered boat powered by oars and sails, used by the Vikings.

longbow The **longbow** was a weapon for firing arrows used by English and Welsh medieval archers.

longed-for A **longed-for** thing or event is one someone wants very much.

longevity (pron: lon-**jev**-it-ee) is long life. *What makes his longevity more remarkable is that he worked in a coal mine for much of his life.*

longhand If you write something in **longhand**, you write it by hand using complete words and normal letters, rather than typing it or using shortened forms or special symbols.

longing A **longing** is a rather sad feeling of wanting something, especially something you know you are unlikely to get.

longingly If you look **longingly** at something, you look at it and want it. *They looked longingly at the hamburger stalls.* You can also think **longingly** about something.

longitude The **longitude** of a place is how far east or west it is from a north-south line passing through Greenwich, measured in degrees.

longitudinal A **longitudinal** measurement, axis, or cross-section runs from one end of a thing to the other, rather than across it from side to side. *Cut each walnut into six longitudinal wedges.*

loo Some people call the toilet the **loo.**

look (looking, looked) ❑ If you **look** in a certain direction, you direct your eyes that way, to see what is there. ◇ If a window, room, or building **looks** in a certain direction, it faces that way and has a view of whatever is there.

❑ If you **look** at something which is happening, you watch it. ◇ If you **look on** while something happens, you watch it and do nothing about it.

❑ If you **look** at an object, you examine it. You can also say you take a **look** at it or have a **look** at it. ◇ If you **look** at something like a plan or situation, you examine it and consider it carefully. You can also say you take a **look** at it. *It was only a matter of time before training bodies had another look at their teaching methods.*

❑ If you **look** at something from a particular point of view, you judge it from that point of view. *Looked at this way, it seems doubtful that the government has got public spending as firmly under its thumb as it claims.*

❑ **Look** is used to say how someone or something appears. *His blue bri-nylon anorak gave him the look of a warehouse foreman.* ◇ You also use **look** to describe someone's expression. *Mr Stephens looked puzzled... He wore a look of baffled disappointment.* ◇ When you talk about someone's

looks or **good looks,** you are talking about how beautiful or handsome they are.

❑ A particular **look** is a style in something like clothes, hairstyles, or furniture. *...the new look for winter.*

❑ If you **look** at someone in a particular way or give them a particular **look,** you indicate to them by your expression what you are thinking. *Morris gave Jack Bond a look of reproach.*

❑ If you **look up to** someone, you respect and admire them. ◇ If you **look down on** someone, you think they are inferior to you. ◇ **look down your nose** at something: see **nose.** ◇ If you say you can **look** someone **in the face** or **look** them **in the eye,** you mean you can meet them without feeling ashamed or embarrassed.

❑ If you **look on** something as a certain thing, you think of it as that thing. *It is very important that they are looked upon as security personnel and not as troops or soldiers.*

❑ If something **looks like** happening, it seems likely to happen.

❑ If you **look back,** you think about things in the past. ◇ If you say someone did something and never **looked back,** you mean they did it and then went on to be very successful. ◇ **look forward to:** see **forward.**

❑ If a situation is **looking up,** it is improving.

❑ If you **look after** someone or something, you take care of them. ◇ You also say someone **looks after** something when they are responsible for it. *The federation council will look after provincial affairs.* ◇ If you tell someone to **look to** something, you mean they should take care of it and make sure it is not harmed. *The ITV companies must look to the interests of their shareholders.*

❑ If you **look round** a place, you walk round it and look at its various parts.

❑ If you **look for** someone or something, you try to find them. ◇ If you **look into** something, you try to find out more about it. ◇ If you **look** something **up,** you consult a book to find out what you want to know. ◇ If you **look through** something or a series of things, you examine them to find something you want.

❑ If you tell someone to **look out** for something, you mean they should pay attention to their surroundings, to make sure they notice it. *Along the coastal path, look out for wild fennel.*

❑ If you **look** someone **up,** you call on them after you have not seen them for a long time. ◇ If you **look in** on a person or place, you visit them for a short time.

❑ If you **look to** someone for help or advice, you expect or hope they will provide it.

❑ If you **look to** the future, you think about it or plan for it.

look-in If you do not get a **look-in,** you do not get a chance to do something, because so many other people are doing it.

look-out See **lookout.**

lookalike Someone's **lookalike** is a person who looks very like them. *...a Marlene Dietrich lookalike.*

-looking You add **-looking** to a word to say how someone or something appears. *...an athletic-looking man... ...a dreary-looking place near Euston Station.* ◇ You also add **-looking** to a word to describe someone's attitudes. *Opportunity 2000 may have an effect on companies who have not been as forward-looking as Cadbury's.*

looking glass A looking glass is the same as a mirror.

lookout (or look-out) If you are **on the lookout** for something or **keeping a lookout** for it, you are watching out for it. *Hoare Govett remains on the lookout for quality staff.* ◇ A **lookout** is (a) a place from which you can see clearly in all directions. (b) a person sent to a place to watch out for something which might appear.

loom (looming, loomed) ❑ If you talk about something unpleasant **looming**, you mean it is going to happen soon. *...as the threat of another recession looms.* ◇ If you say something **looms large** in a situation, you mean it is a significant factor in it. *The continuing disagreement over farm subsidies will loom large at the summit in Rome today.*

❑ If you talk about an object **looming**, you mean it appears as a tall, unclear, and often frightening shape. *Great rectangular pillars of hard rock loom above the clifftop.*

❑ A **loom** is a device for weaving thread into cloth.

loony (loonies) If you call an idea or plan **loony**, you mean it is extremely silly. You say someone is a **loony** when you think their ideas and behaviour are very silly.

loop (looping, looped) ❑ A **loop** in something like a rope is a part where it has been bent until it crosses over itself. ◇ If you **loop** a piece of rope or string round something, you tie it in a circle round it.

❑ If something like a road **loops**, it goes round in a circle. *The 108 riders will race on a course looping the city.*

loophole A **loophole** in the law is a small mistake or omission which allows you to do something the law was meant to prevent.

loopy If you say someone is **loopy**, you mean they are mad or highly eccentric.

loose (looser, loosest; loosely, looseness; loosing, loosed) ❑ If something is **loose**, it is not firmly held or fixed in place. *Mansell dominated most of the race until a loose wheel-nut forced him to a pit-stop.* ◇ If something breaks **loose**, it becomes detached from the thing it is normally attached to. You use **loose** to describe things which are not attached to anything else. *Archaeologists have unearthed a loose piece of parchment.*

❑ **Loose** clothes do not fit your body closely. *The designers allowed the idea of looseness to creep into their collections.*

❑ A **loose** grouping or arrangement is not rigidly controlled or organized. *...a loose consortium of institutions... ...a loosely organised group.* ◇ If something is **loosely** based on something else, it takes its main idea from it, but is different in many details.

❑ If you **loose** an animal or let it **loose**, you release it so it can run around freely. ◇ If a dangerous person is **on the loose**, they have escaped from prison and have not yet been recaptured.

❑ If you **cut loose**, you break free from the influence or authority of other people.

❑ If someone **looses off** a weapon, they fire it. ◇ If you **let loose** something like a sigh, you utter it.

❑ The **loose ends** are the parts of a crime, situation, or story which have not been explained or resolved. *The legal loose ends have still to be tied up.* ◇ If you are **at a loose end**, you have nothing to do and are bored.

❑ **loose cannon: see cannon.**

loosen (loosening, loosened) ❑ If the authorities **loosen** laws or restrictions or **loosen** them **up**, they make them less strict or severe. ◇ If something **loosens** links between people, it makes them less close.

❑ If something **loosens** or is **loosened**, it becomes less firm or less tightly held in place. ◇ If you **loosen** something which is tied or fastened, you undo it slightly. *Loosen clothing around his neck, chest and waist.*

❑ If you **loosen up**, you become calmer and less worried.

loot (looting, looted; looter) When people **loot** shops or houses, they steal things from them during a riot, battle, or other disturbance. People who do this are called **looters**. ◇ **Loot** is money or goods stolen in a robbery.

lop (lopping, lopped) If you **lop** something **off**, you cut it off in a quick movement or series of movements. *She lopped off her famous auburn curls.* ◇ If you **lop** a certain amount **off** something, you reduce it by that amount. *Nationwide announced on Friday that it was lopping an average of 0.4% gross off its savings accounts.*

lop-sided See lopsided.

lope (loping, loped) When people or animals **lope**, they run in a relaxed way with long strides.

lopsided (or lop-sided) If an object is **lopsided**, it looks odd, because one side is bigger or higher than the other. ◇ If a system or policy is **lopsided**, it is unbalanced because too much emphasis is given to one thing. *The party was on a lopsided course: strong on individual values, weak on communal values.*

loquacious (loquacity) If you say someone is **loquacious** or talk about their **loquacity**, you mean they talk a lot.

lord is a title used in front of the name of a male member of the aristocracy or House of Lords, or a senior male judge. *...Lord Melchett... ...Lord Justice Woolf.* ◇ A **lord** is a man with a high rank in the British nobility.

❑ People who have a great deal of power are sometimes called **lords**. *...press lords... ...the drug lords.* ◇ If someone **lords it over** you, they use their power to order you around.

❑ When Christians talk about **the Lord**, they mean God. In their prayers, they often address God as **Lord**.

Lord's Prayer The **Lord's Prayer** is the most important Christian prayer. According to the Bible, Jesus Christ taught it to his disciples.

lordly is used in a humorous way to talk about things to do with lords. *Lordly eyebrows have been raised in the Upper Chamber.* ◇ **Lordly** is also used to describe something done in an impressive and confident way. *The book contains several passages of lordly brilliance.*

Lordship is used when talking respectfully to a lord, bishop, or senior male judge, or when talking about him in a formal way. *Their Lordships sat in apparent bafflement.*

lore The lore of a region or nation is its traditional stories and customs. ◇ When stories are told about an unusual person or event, you can say they become part of a particular **lore**. *The story has passed into stockbroking lore and is dragged out each year at the same dinner.*

lorry (lorries) A **lorry** is a large motor vehicle for transporting goods by road.

lose (losing, lost) ❑ If you have **lost** an object, you cannot find it, because you have dropped it without realizing it or cannot remember where you put it. ◇ You talk about **losing** other things when they are taken away from you or destroyed. For example, you can **lose** your job or **lose** your home in a fire.

❑ If you **lose** something like hope or interest, you no longer have it. *There is a widespread feeling that the US could be losing interest in the problem.* ◇ If you **lose** the ability to do something, you can no longer do it.

❑ If you **lose** something like a game or contest, you are defeated in it. ◇ If something **loses** you a game or contest, it is the reason you are defeated. *Many Tory MPs fear this could lose them the next election.*

❑ If a clock or watch **loses**, the hands move round slightly too slowly, and it shows the wrong time.

❑ If you **lose** time, you are interrupted in what you are doing, and get behind with it. *Classes will have to be extended on weekdays to make up for lost time.* ◇ If you say someone **loses no time** in doing something, you mean they do it straight away, without any delay.

❑ If you **lose** a chance or opportunity, you fail to take advantage of it.

❑ If you **lose** weight, your weight decreases, as a result of slimming, exercise, or illness. ◇ If you **lose** blood, some of the blood drains out of your body as the result of an injury, so there is less than there should be. ◇ If you **lose** a part of your body, it is cut or blown off in an accident or battle, or removed in an operation.

❑ If someone **loses their life,** they are killed in combat or an accident. ◇ The people **lost** in an accident or disaster are the ones who died in it. *Five men were lost at sea after a trawler sank in the English Channel.* ◇ If you **lose** a relative or friend, they die.

❑ If a business **loses** money, it earns less than it spends.

❑ If you **lose your way,** you get lost when you are trying to go somewhere. ◇ You also say someone **loses their way** when they are no longer sure what their aims are or how to achieve them.

❑ If you say you have **nothing to lose** by doing something, you mean you might as well do it, because it cannot put you in a worse situation. On the other hand, if you have **everything to lose** by doing something, there is no point in doing it, because it might lose you all the advantages you already have.

❑ **lose sight** of something: see **sight.**

loser ❑ The **loser** of a game or contest is the person who is defeated. ◇ If you say someone is a **bad loser,** you mean they refuse to accept that they have been defeated fairly, and keep complaining or criticizing the winner.

❑ If you are the **loser** as a result of something, you are worse off because of it.

loss (losses) ❑ When something is destroyed or ceases to exist, you can talk about its **loss.** *...the loss of bird habitats... ...the loss of 500 jobs.*

❑ If a company makes a **loss,** it earns less money than it spends. ◇ If a business or a shop sells something **at a loss,** they sell it for less than it cost to make, or less than the price they paid for it.

❑ When people die in an accident, you talk about the **loss** of a certain number of lives. *Two of the boats capsized, resulting in the loss of ten lives.* ◇ The **loss** of a relative or friend is their death.

❑ If you are **at a loss,** you do not know what to do or say. *Officials were at a loss to explain the acceleration in the rate of job losses.*

❑ If you **cut your losses,** you stop doing something which is unsuccessful, to prevent a bad situation becoming worse.

loss leader A **loss leader** is a product which is sold at much lower than cost price, to attract customers. The idea is that they will then go on to buy other normally priced goods in the same shop.

lost ❑ See **lose.**

❑ If you are **lost,** you do not know where you are, or you are unable to find your way.

❑ If something is **lost,** you cannot find it.

❑ **Lost** is used to describe things which people used to have but which they no longer have. *East Germans are beginning to seek their lost traditions.* ◇ You can also say things are **lost** when they are stolen or destroyed. *Each year ten per cent of the crop is lost to a pest called corn rootworm.*

❑ If you say you would be **lost** without someone or something, you mean you would be unhappy or unable to do something properly without them.

❑ If you say something is **lost** on someone, you mean they do not understand it. *Some of the baseball imagery is lost on British audiences.*

❑ If you tell someone to **get lost,** you are rudely telling them to go away.

❑ If you say something is a **lost cause,** you mean it has no chance of succeeding.

lost property is things people have accidentally left behind in a public place, which is kept for a time in case they claim it.

lot ❑ A **lot** of something or **lots** of it means a large amount of it. ◇ A **lot** in front of words like 'better' and 'sooner' means 'much'. *No airline is going to go bust, but some will do a lot worse than others this year.* ◇ If you do something **a lot,** you do it often.

❑ You can use **lot** to talk about (a) a group of people with something in common. *You've got the married couples, the divorced lot, and people who live together.* (b) a group of things of the same kind. *Another lot of seeds can be programmed to be watered every 20 seconds.* ◇ **The lot** means all of the thing you have just mentioned. *He once lent £17m to a man without references who later bolted with the lot.*

❑ At an auction, a **lot** is one of the items being sold. A lot can be an object or a group of objects. ◇ A **lot** is also one of the parts of an area of land, each of which is being sold separately.

❑ A person's **lot** is the kind of life they are forced to lead, and the kind of experiences they can expect to have. *Disappointment is the perennial lot of the middle-aged.* ◇ If you **throw in your lot** with someone, you decide to join them in what they are doing and stay with them from that time onwards.

❑ If people **draw lots** to decide who shall do something or be something, they use a method which involves chance, such as picking a name out of a hat.

loth See **loath.**

lotion A **lotion** is a liquid you use on your skin or hair to clean, protect, or improve it.

lottery (lotteries) A **lottery** is a type of gambling game in which large numbers of people buy numbered tickets. Several numbers are chosen by a random method, and the people with those numbers on their tickets win a prize. ◇ If you say something is a **lottery,** you mean there is no way of predicting what you are going to get.

Neighbours are a lottery... Medium-priced claret is a lottery.

lotus (lotuses) The **lotus** is a type of water-lily in Africa, Asia, and America.

louche (*pron:* **loosh**) is used to describe people who are seedy or disreputable. *No well-bred young lady would even contemplate behaviour so louche.*

loud (louder, loudest; loudly, loudness) ❏ A **loud** noise is one in which the volume of sound is very high. *You play a series of sounds, increasing in loudness, and observe what the baby does.*
❏ If you are **loud** in your support or condemnation of something, you express your opinion in a forceful way. *The loudest protests so far have come from the opposition party.*
❏ If you say something **out loud**, you say it aloud so people can hear it, rather than just thinking it.
❏ If you call a piece of clothing **loud**, you mean it has very bright colours or a striking pattern, and you find this vulgar.

loudhailer (*or* **loud-hailer**) A **loudhailer** is a hand-held cone-shaped device which you use to make your voice heard over a long distance.

loudmouth (loud-mouthed) If you call someone a **loudmouth** or describe them as **loud-mouthed**, you mean they talk a lot in an unpleasant, offensive, or stupid way.

loudspeaker A **loudspeaker** is a device which turns electrical signals into sound, so that words spoken into a microphone or the sound from a radio or record player can be heard.

lough See **loch**.

lounge (lounging, lounged) ❏ The **lounge** in a house or hotel is a room where people can sit and relax. ◇ The **lounge** or **lounge bar** in a pub is a comfortably furnished bar. ◇ The **departure lounge** at an airport is a large room where passengers wait for their flights.
❏ If you **lounge** somewhere, you sit, lie, or stand around in a relaxed way. If you **lounge about** or **lounge around**, you spend your time in a lazy way, avoiding doing anything which requires any effort.

lounge suit A **lounge suit** is an ordinary man's suit worn at work or on fairly formal occasions.

louse (*plural:* **lice**) **Lice** are small insects which live on the bodies of people or animals.

lousy (lousier, lousiest) If you say something is **lousy**, you mean it is very bad. *Inner-city children are trapped in lousy schools.* ◇ You can also say someone or something is **lousy** when they are covered in lice.

lout (loutish) A **lout** is a man who behaves in a rude or aggressive way. **Loutish** behaviour is rude and aggressive.

louvred (*pron:* **loo-vud**) A **louvred** surface is made up of flat overlapping sections attached to a frame. *...louvred windows.*

lovable (*or* **loveable**) If you say someone is **lovable**, you mean they have attractive qualities and are easy to like.

love (loving, loved) ❏ **Love** is a very strong feeling of affection for someone you are romantically and sexually attracted to. If you **love** someone, you feel like this about them. ◇ The person someone loves can be called their **love**. *At Cambridge he met his first and only love.* ◇ If you are **in love** with someone, especially someone you have met recently, you are romantically and sexually attracted to them, and think about them a lot when they are not there. If you **fall in love** with someone, you start to

feel like this about them.
❏ When two people **make love,** they have sex.
❏ **Love** is also caring deeply about someone like a member of your family, and showing this in your behaviour towards them. You can say you **love** someone like this. Your **loved ones** are the members of your family and other people you care about. ◇ If someone **loves** their country, they care deeply about it. You can talk about someone's **love** for their country.
❏ If you **love** something, you like it very much, or you enjoy doing it. You can talk about someone's **love** of something. *He loves a good row... There must be one or two politicians with a genuine love of such a silly sport.* ◇ If someone has an interest or hobby which they are very enthusiastic about, you can call it their **love**. *Mr Sparrow's great love was poetry.*
❏ If there is something you want to do but you do not have the opportunity to do it, you can say you would **love** to do it. *I would love to design someone else's house, if they would let me.* Similarly, you can say you would **love to** have something.
❏ In tennis, **love** is a score of zero. *He won the set six-love.*

love affair A **love affair** is a sexual or romantic relationship between two people who are not married to each other. ◇ When a person or group of people involve themselves enthusiastically with something for a period of time, you can say they have a **love affair** with it. *...his love affair with Venice.*

love child A **love child** is someone who was born to parents who were not married to each other.

love-hate If you have a **love-hate** relationship with someone or something, your attitude to them keeps changing, so that sometimes you like them or approve of them, and at other times you dislike them or disapprove of them.

love letter A **love letter** is a letter you write to someone to tell them you love them.

love life A person's **love life** is their romantic and sexual relationships.

love-making (*or* **lovemaking**) is the sexual activities which take place between two people.

love nest A **love nest** is a place where a couple meet, often secretly, to carry on a love affair.

love story A **love story** is a novel, short story, or film about a love affair.

loveable See **lovable**.

loveless You say a relationship is **loveless** when there is no love between the people involved. *...a loveless marriage.*

lovelorn If someone is **lovelorn**, they are miserable because the person they love does not love them.

lovely (lovelier, loveliest) You use **lovely** to describe people and things that are beautifully formed and therefore very pleasing to look at. *They set about restoring some lovely old buildings.* Music which is pleasing and attractive can also be called **lovely**. ◇ You can also use **lovely** to describe other things which give you pleasure. *The meal was lovely... ...a lovely summer evening.* ◇ You can say a person is **lovely** when they have qualities you admire, such as kindness, friendliness, or generosity. *They are a lovely family.*

lovemaking See **love-making**.

lover Someone's **lover** is a person they are having an affair with. When people are having an affair, you say they are **lovers**. ◇ You say someone is a **lover** of something when they like it very much and take great pleasure in it. *...lovers of good food.*

loving (lovingly) ❑ A **loving** person feels and shows love for someone, or for people generally. You can also say their behaviour is **loving**. *...his loving concern for abandoned children... She looked at her husband lovingly.*
❑ You also describe someone's behaviour as **loving** when they do something very carefully or thoroughly, because they enjoy doing it. *...car enthusiasts who labour away lovingly to bring a treasured roadster back up to speed.*

low ❑ If an amount of something is **low**, there is not much of it. *Pay is so low that many cannot survive without a second job... ...an EU attempt to boost low fish stocks.*
❑ A **low** temperature is below what is normal. **Low** can be used to talk about other things which are towards the bottom of a scale. *...low pressure... Housing starts have fallen to the lowest level for two years.* ◇ A **low** is the lowest point or level something reaches. *The pound crashed to a post-war low... Relations between the two countries sank to an all-time low last year.*
❑ In meteorology, a **low** is an area of low atmospheric pressure or a depression.
❑ **Low** is sometimes used to give an approximate amount. For example, if a number is in the low twenties, it is more than twenty but less than twenty-five. *The British eight had to go out at 11am, in temperatures in the low 40s.*
❑ If the quality or standard of something is **low**, it is below what it should be.
❑ If something is **low**, it measures a short distance from the bottom to the top, or from the ground to the top. *...a low wall... ...low hills.* ◇ **Low** is also used to say something is close to the ground, or close to the bottom of something else. *The helicopter swooped low... ...low cloud... Taps should be low on the butt so that all the water can be drained.* ◇ If the sun or moon is **low**, it is close to the horizon.
❑ A **low** note in music is close to the bottom of a singer's or instrument's range. ◇ If you speak in a **low** voice, you speak quietly or softly.
❑ A **low** position at work is less important than that of other people. *The early part of his career was in the lower echelons of the civil service.*
❑ If you have a **low** opinion of someone or hold them in **low** esteem, you disapprove of them or dislike them. Similarly, if someone's reputation is **low**, people no longer trust them or respect them.
❑ If you are feeling **low**, you are unhappy.
❑ If a light is **low**, it is dim, rather than bright or strong.
❑ If someone is **lying low**, they are in hiding, or keeping out of sight. ◇ If you are **laid low** by something like a disease or injury, it makes you weak or ill.
❑ **Low season** is the time of year when holiday resorts and attractions are least busy.

Low Church The **Low Church** group within the Church of England is opposed to excessive ceremony and ritual, and holds evangelical beliefs.

low-cut A **low-cut** dress or blouse leaves a woman's neck, shoulders, and the top of her chest bare.

low-key If an event is **low-key**, things are done in a restrained way, without much publicity.

low-life A city's **low-life** is the people who are involved in crime and vice there.

low-lying land is at, near, or below sea level.

low-paid workers earn only a small amount of money. These people are often called the **low-paid**.

low profile If someone has or keeps a **low profile**, they avoid publicity.

low-rise buildings are of normal height, as distinct from tower blocks. See also **high-rise**.

low-tech designs, systems, or practices do not make use of the most up-to-date methods or equipment.

low tide is the time when the sea is at its lowest level on the coast. This usually occurs twice a day.

low water is the same as low tide.

lowbrow entertainment, art, or music is simple and easy to understand, and does not have any deep meaning.

lower (lowering, lowered) ❑ See **low**.
❑ **Lower** is used to talk about (a) the bottom part of something. *...the lower part of the slope... The injury affects the lower part of the hamstring.* (b) the bottom one of a pair of things. *...the lower lip... ...a lower berth.*
❑ **Lower** is also used to talk about an institution whose status is below that of a similar institution. *It upheld a ruling by a lower court.* ◇ When a parliament consists of two parts meeting separately, one of them is usually called the **lower house** or **lower chamber**. In Britain, the **lower house** is the House of Commons.
❑ If you **lower** an amount, value, or quantity, you make it less. *The Japanese are expert at lowering manufacturing costs.*
❑ If you **lower** an object, you move it slowly downwards. *Flags were lowered... A message on a string was lowered to prison officers below.*
❑ If you **lower** your voice, you speak more quietly.
❑ **Lowering** (pron: lour-ing) clouds or skies are dark and unpleasant, and suggest there will be rain or snow soon.

lower case letters are small letters, rather than capitals.

lower class (lower classes) People whose social status is thought to be lower than that of other people are sometimes called the **lower classes**. **Lower-class** is used to describe things thought to be typical of this group of people. *Horse-racing was once considered vulgar and lower-class in Japan.*

lowest common denominator The **lowest common denominator** in an argument or negotiation is the set of things all the people involved agree about. ◇ The **lowest common denominator** of a group of fractions is the smallest number all their denominators can go into.

lowish If something is **lowish**, it is fairly low.

lowland The **lowlands** of a country are the parts which are flat or hilly rather than mountainous. **Lowland** is used to describe areas like these and the things in them. *...lowland bogs.*

lowly (lowlier, lowliest) You call someone or something **lowly** when they are low in rank, status, or importance. *The lowliest recruits earn as little as $45 a month.*

loyal (loyally) If you are **loyal** to someone or something, you remain firm in your friendship or support for them. *She remained loyally supportive of her daughter-in-law.*

loyalist In Northern Ireland, a **loyalist** is someone who wants to keep Northern Ireland as part of the United Kingdom and is opposed to the unification of Ireland.

◇ Other kinds of people can be called **loyalists** when they are firm in their support for their government, party, or ruler.

loyalty (loyalties) ❑ **Loyalty** is being firm in your friendship or support for someone or something. *He quickly won the loyalty of Labour supporters.*

❑ **Loyalties** are feelings of friendship, support, or duty. *The nation state is capable of inspiring deep loyalties.* ◇ If your **loyalties lie** with a particular person or organization, you support them rather than anyone else.

lozenge A **lozenge** is a medicated tablet which you suck, for example when you have a sore throat.

LP An **LP** is a record with about 25 minutes of music or speech on each side. LP is short for 'long player'.

LSD is a powerful illegal drug which causes hallucinations. It is also known as 'acid'. LSD is short for 'lysergic acid diethylamide'.

Ltd after a company's name means 'Limited'.

lubricate (lubricating, lubricated; lubrication, lubricant) If you **lubricate** something, you put a substance like oil on its moving parts, to make sure they operate smoothly. *...low-friction bearings needing no lubrication.* A substance used for this purpose is called a **lubricant**.

lucerne See **alfalfa**.

lucid (lucidly, lucidity) **Lucid** writing or speech is clear and easy to understand. *They had the ability to present complex matters lucidly and interestingly... ...prose of exceptional lucidity and grace.* ◇ If a sick person is **lucid**, their mind is unaffected by their illness and they are able to think clearly and logically.

luck is used to talk about things happening to you which are not the result of your own efforts, or not your fault. If you have **luck** or **good luck**, the things which happen are good or desirable. If you have **bad luck**, the things which happen are bad or unpleasant.

❑ If you are **in luck**, you get what you are hoping for on a particular occasion. If you are **out of luck** or **have no luck**, you do not get what you are hoping for.

❑ If someone is **down on their luck**, they have had a lot of misfortunes. This phrase is especially used about people who have lost all their money or income and cannot support themselves.

❑ If you **try your luck** at something you have not done before, you attempt it.

❑ If you say someone is **pushing their luck**, you mean they are taking a risk and may suffer as a result.

❑ You say **with luck** to express a hope that a particular thing will happen. *With luck, the Supreme Court will hear the case, and force California to back down.*

luckily You add **luckily** to a statement to say it is fortunate something happened or is the case. *Luckily I have a housekeeper to look after the children.*

luckless is used, often humorously, to describe people who have been unlucky in some way. *...the luckless weather-reader who said there wasn't much chance of storms, hours before the hurricane struck.*

lucky (luckier, luckiest) ❑ You say someone is **lucky** when they have something desirable or are in a desirable situation. *I was lucky enough to be one of the first customers.* You also say someone is **lucky** when something goes well for them, or they are not harmed in a dangerous situation. *We were lucky to come out of it alive.* You can

call something which happens to someone **lucky**. *...a lucky break... ...a lucky escape.* ◇ You also say someone is **lucky** when they always seem to have good luck.

❑ **Lucky** is used to describe things which people believe bring them luck. *Seven is his lucky number... ...a lucky rabbit's foot.*

❑ If you say someone **will be lucky** to do or get something, you mean you think it is unlikely they will do it or get it. ◇ If you say a situation is a **lucky dip**, you mean the result depends on chance rather than on any plan you might have.

lucrative A **lucrative** business or activity earns someone a lot of money.

lucre (*pron:* loo-ker) is another word for money. People call money **filthy lucre** when they do not approve of the way it has been acquired.

ludicrous (ludicrously) If you say something is **ludicrous**, you mean it is totally silly, unreasonable, or unsuitable. *Critics of this idea say it would be ludicrously expensive.*

lug (lugging, lugged) If you **lug** something heavy from one place to another, you carry or take it there with difficulty. *Women and children lug stones from miles around and lay them across the fields.*

luge (*pron:* loozh; *the 'zh' sounds like 's' in 'pleasure'*) A **luge** is a kind of toboggan used for racing. The rider lies on his or her back on the luge and goes down the course feet first.

luggage Your **luggage** is the suitcases and bags you take with you when you travel.

lugubrious (*pron:* loo-goo-bree-uss) (lugubriously) You say someone is **lugubrious** when they behave in a sad or gloomy way. *Godwin reappeared in the doorway, lugubriously shaking his head.*

lukewarm ❑ If someone's attitude or response to something is **lukewarm**, they do not show much enthusiasm for it or interest in it.

❑ If something is **lukewarm**, it is only slightly warm.

lull A **lull** is a period of quiet or little activity. *The upsurge of fighting follows a lull of several weeks.* ◇ If you are **lulled** into feeling calm or safe, someone or something makes you feel that way.

lullaby (lullabies) A **lullaby** is a quiet song which you sing to help a child go to sleep.

lumbar is used to talk about things to do with the lower part of the back. *...the lumbar vertebrae... ...orthopaedic seats with lumbar supports.*

lumber (lumbering, lumbered) ❑ If someone or something **lumbers** somewhere, they move slowly and clumsily. *Dixon lumbered about the field.* ◇ You can also say someone or something **lumbers** when they make slow progress, because of poor organization or inefficiency.

❑ If you are **lumbered with** something you do not want, you have to have it or deal with it. *They do not care to be lumbered with a building that they cannot sell.*

❑ **Lumber** is wood which has been roughly cut up.

lumberjack A **lumberjack** is a person whose job is to cut down trees.

luminary (luminaries) A **luminary** is a famous person, or an expert in a particular field.

luminosity is bright light.

luminous ❑ If something is **luminous**, (a) it shines or glows in the dark. *...a luminous watch.* (b) it gives out a very bright light. *Many of these 'active galaxies' spurt out jets of luminous matter.*

❑ If you say writing or speech is **luminous,** you mean it makes things very vivid and clear. *...a rich, luminous and original novel... ...luminous descriptive passages.*

lump ❑ A **lump** of something solid is an irregularly-shaped piece of it. ◇ A **lump** of sugar is a small cube of it. ◇ A **lump** in or on someone's body is a small hard swelling caused by injury or illness.

❑ If you have a **lump in your throat,** you have a tight feeling there and feel as if you are going to cry, because of a strong emotion like sorrow or gratitude.

❑ If you **lump** people or things together, you treat them as a group, ignoring any differences between them.

❑ If you say someone will have to **lump it,** you mean they will have to accept a situation or decision whether they like it or not.

lump sum A **lump sum** is a large amount of money which is paid all at once, rather than in instalments.

lumpy (lumpiness) If something is **lumpy,** it is full of lumps or covered in lumps. *This lumpiness seems to be a result of the way the body reacts to its own hormones.*

lunacy If you say a proposal or something someone does is **lunacy,** you mean it is stupid, unrealistic, or dangerous. ◇ In the past, severe mental illness was sometimes called **lunacy.**

lunar is used to talk about things to do with the moon, or things which remind you of the moon. *...a lunar eclipse... ...a ghostly lunar landscape.* ◇ A **lunar month** is the length of time it takes the moon to go round the earth once (about 29½ days). The **lunar calendar** is a calendar based on lunar months.

lunatic ❑ When a person behaves in a stupid or dangerous way, people sometimes call them a **lunatic** or describe their behaviour as **lunatic.** *There is even a lunatic lobby supporting legalisation of drugs.* ◇ A group of people with odd or extreme ideas is sometimes called the **lunatic fringe.**

❑ In the past, mentally ill people were called **lunatics.**

lunatic asylum In the past, a **lunatic asylum** was a place where mentally disturbed people were locked up.

lunch (lunches, lunching, lunched) **Lunch** is a meal in the middle of the day. When people **lunch,** they have this meal. **Lunch** or **lunchtime** is the time when people have lunch.

lunch break Your **lunch break** is the period in the middle of the day when you stop work to have lunch.

lunch hour Your **lunch hour** is the same as your lunch break.

lunchbox (lunchboxes) A **lunchbox** is a container for taking cold food to school or work to eat for lunch.

luncheon is a formal meal in the middle of the day.

luncheon voucher Luncheon **vouchers** are vouchers which some companies give their employees. They can be exchanged for food in certain restaurants.

lunchtime See lunch.

lung Your **lungs** are the two organs inside your chest which you use for breathing.

lunge (lunging, lunged) If you **lunge** or make a **lunge,** you make a sudden violent movement towards something.

lupin Lupins are a type of garden plant with tall spikes of brightly coloured flowers.

lurch (lurches, lurching, lurched) ❑ A **lurch** is a sudden forward or sideways movement. If someone **lurches** somewhere, they move suddenly like this. ◇ A sudden change in something like the economy can be called a **lurch.** ◇ If someone or something **lurches** from one thing to another, they move on to the second thing suddenly and in an uncontrolled way. *He has often lurched from one expedient to the next, apparently without thinking through all the implications.*

❑ If someone **leaves you in the lurch,** they suddenly withdraw their help or support at a time when you are depending on it.

lure (luring, lured) If you are **lured** somewhere, you are persuaded to go there by the promise of something attractive. *More of the country's best academics could be lured abroad by promises of higher salaries.* Similarly, you can be **lured** into doing something. A **lure** is something which attracts you in one of these ways.

lurid (luridly) **Lurid** is used to talk about things which attract a lot of attention because they involve sex or violent death. *...the most lurid sex scandal since the Profumo affair.* ◇ **Lurid** colours are unpleasantly bright and vivid. *...three women, luridly dressed in pink, lime and raspberry.*

lurk If you talk about a danger **lurking** somewhere, you mean it is present, but people are not yet completely aware of it. Similarly, you can talk about feelings **lurking** in people's minds. *Lurking behind the tolerance of Western liberals lies an insulting racism.* ◇ If someone **lurks** somewhere, they wait there secretly. *The sinister men lurking at the airport were black market agents.*

luscious People use **luscious** to describe someone or something they find very attractive and desirable. *...a luscious blonde... ...luscious gems.* ◇ **Luscious** fruit is juicy and delicious.

lush (lushness) ❑ **Lush** fields or gardens have a lot of healthy grass or plants.

❑ **Lush** is also used to describe things which are very luxurious. *Lush cruise trains will take rich Americans and Japanese through the cultural centres of Europe.*

lust is a strong feeling of sexual desire. When someone has this feeling, you can say they **lust after** someone or **lust for** them. ◇ A **lust** for something like power or money is a strong desire to get hold of it. You can say someone **lusts after** something like this or **lusts for** it. *The private sector lusted after a Tory victory and paid handsomely to get one.*

luster See lustre.

lustful people are always wanting sex. You can also call their behaviour or thoughts **lustful.** *...lustful desires.*

lustre (American spelling: **luster**) (lustrous) ❑ **Lustre** is a gentle shining light reflected from a smooth or polished surface. You say a surface like this is **lustrous.**

❑ If you say something lacks **lustre,** you mean it is not interesting or exciting. Similarly, you can say something has **lost its lustre.**

lusty (lustily) **Lusty** is used to talk about people doing things with a lot of physical strength or vocal power. *He was lustily cheered when he gave a slogan to the rally.* ◇ **Lusty** also means lustful. *...lusty executives leering at secretaries.*

lute A **lute** is an old-fashioned musical instrument with strings, played like a guitar.

Lutheran A Lutheran is a member of the Lutheran Church, a Protestant church founded in the 16th century by Martin Luther, the German leader of the Reformation.

luxuriant (luxuriantly) Luxuriant plants, gardens, or trees are healthy and growing well. *Lichens spread luxuriantly across their surfaces*. ◇ Luxuriant is also used to talk about hair which is growing thickly. *...a luxuriant moustache.*

luxuriate (luxuriating, luxuriated) If you luxuriate in something, you relax and enjoy it thoroughly. *Pemberton lay luxuriating in a bath.*

luxurious (luxuriously) Luxurious is used to describe buildings and other things which are very comfortable and expensive. *The offices were luxuriously refitted.*

luxury (luxuries) ❑ Luxury is great comfort among attractive and expensive surroundings. *...a life of luxury.*
   ❑ Luxury things are more expensive and comfortable than other things of the same kind. *...luxury saloons... ...a luxury hotel.* ◇ A luxury is something quite expensive which is not necessary but gives you pleasure. *Few people now have the money for luxuries.* Unnecessary articles which people buy for pleasure are called luxury goods.
   ❑ You can call an advantage a luxury when few people have it, or it does not come to you very often. *Without the luxury of selecting the brightest pupils, the north London comprehensive still managed to take first place in the results table.*

lychee Lychees are Chinese fruit with soft white flesh.

Lycra is a man-made elasticated fibre, or the fabric made from this fibre. It is used in sportswear and in women's underclothes. 'Lycra' is a trademark.

lymph is a colourless fluid which contains white blood cells and transports them round the body, defending it against infection.

lymph gland The lymph glands are small masses of tissue in various parts of the body. They contain large cells which absorb harmful matter and dead tissue.

lymph node is the medical term for a lymph gland.

lymphatic system The lymphatic system is the network of capillaries which transports lymph into the bloodstream.

lymphoma A lymphoma is a tumour which grows in the lymph glands.

lynch (lynches, lynching, lynched) If someone is lynched, they are attacked and killed by an angry crowd who think they have committed a crime. A killing like this is called a lynching; the people who carry it out are called a lynch mob.

lynchpin (or lynch-pin) See linchpin.

lynx (lynxes) The lynx is a wild animal like a large cat, with a short tail and very keen eyesight.

lyric ❑ The lyrics of a song are its words.
   ❑ Lyric poetry is written in a simple and direct style, usually expressing personal emotions such as love. A lyric is a poem written in this style.

lyrical (lyrically) Lyrical and lyrically are used to talk about things being expressed in a poetic way. *...the author's lyrical exposition of the world he has created... Each dish is lyrically described.* ◇ If you wax lyrical about something, you speak very enthusiastically about it.

lyricism is gentle and romantic emotion expressed in poetry, writing, or music.

lyricist A lyricist is someone who writes the words for songs or musicals.

M m

m See metre, million, mile.

M.A. An M.A. is a higher degree in a subject such as languages, literature, history, or social science. M.A. stands for 'Master of Arts'.

ma'am People sometimes say ma'am when speaking to the Queen or to some other female member of the royal family.

mac A mac is the same as a mackintosh.

macabre (pron: mak-kahb-ra) is used to describe things which are very strange and horrible. *...macabre stories... ...the macabre killing of a former communist prime minister.*

macaroni is a kind of pasta made in the shape of short hollow tubes. It is used in both sweet and savoury dishes.

macaroon A macaroon is a sweet biscuit flavoured with ground almonds.

mace A mace is an ornamental stick carried by an official or placed somewhere as a symbol of authority.

Mach (pron: mak) is a unit of measurement for very high speeds. Mach 1 at a particular height above the ground is the speed of sound at that height.

machete (pron: mash-ett-ee) A machete is a large knife with a broad blade.

Machiavellian (pron: mak-ee-a-vel-yan) is used to describe cunning and deceitful methods used by some people to get what they want. People who use these methods can also be called Machiavellian. *...Machiavellian schemes... ...Machiavellian republicans plotting to destabilise the throne.*

machinations (pron: mak-in-nay-shunz) are secret and complicated plans to gain power or harm someone. *...innocent people caught up in their machinations.*

machine (machining, machined) ❑ A machine is a piece of equipment which uses electricity or an engine to do a particular kind of work. If you machine something, you make it or work on it using a machine.
   ❑ A well-controlled system or organization can also be called a machine.

machine gun A machine gun is a gun which fires a lot of bullets very quickly one after the other.

machine tool A machine tool is a power-driven piece of equipment which cuts, shapes, or finishes metal or other materials.

machinery is machines in general. The machinery in a place is all the machines there. ◇ The machinery of a piece of equipment is the parts which move when it is working.

❏ The machinery of a government or other organization is the system it uses to deal with things. *The appendix sets out the proposed new policy-making machinery.*

machinist A machinist is a person whose job is to operate a machine, especially in a factory.

machismo (*pron:* mak-izz-moh) is aggressively masculine behaviour or attitudes. ◇ Attempts by politicians to appear strong, especially in their dealings with other politicians or governments, are also sometimes called **machismo**.

macho (*pron:* match-oh) You call a man **macho** if he behaves in an aggressively masculine way.

mackerel (*plural:* mackerel *or* mackerels) Mackerel are a kind of green-blue sea fish.

mackintosh (mackintoshes) A mackintosh is a raincoat.

macro- is added to some scientific and technical words to form other words. Words beginning with **macro-** describe things which are much larger in scope than usual. *...macropolitical issues... Investments will succeed only if the macroeconomy is stable.* See also **micro-**.

macroeconomics (macroeconomic) Macroeconomics is the study of the economic systems of countries or groups of countries, rather than those of companies or industries. Macroeconomic is used to talk about things connected with the economy of a country or group of countries. See also **microeconomics**.

mad (madder, maddest; madly, madness) ❏ If someone is mad, they behave in a strange or dangerous way because they are mentally ill. *Talking to yourself, it is said, is the first sign of madness.* ◇ You also say someone is mad when they do or say things which you think are very silly. *...a mad decision... To allow the lira to fall again would be madness.* ◇ Mad is also used to describe wild uncontrolled behaviour. *He ran madly around.*

❏ You say someone is mad or hopping mad when they are very angry about something.

❏ If someone is mad about something, they like it very much and spend a lot of time on it. *They are mad about cars.* You can add -mad to words to describe people like this. *...a horse-mad girl... ...these rugby-mad countries.* ◇ If you are madly in love with someone, you are very much in love with them.

❏ Some people use madly instead of 'very'. *Many people like opera only because it is very posh and madly expensive.*

mad cow disease is a fatal brain disease which affects cattle. It is also known as 'bovine spongiform encephalopathy', or BSE.

madam Some people call a woman Madam when they are being very polite. ◇ Madam is also used when addressing a woman in a position of authority. *...Madam Chairman... ...Madam Speaker.* ◇ A madam is a woman in charge of a brothel.

madcap A madcap plan or scheme is very silly and not likely to succeed.

madden (maddening, maddened; maddeningly) If something maddens you, it irritates you or makes you angry. You say something like this is **maddening**. *Politicians can find scientists maddeningly unhelpful.*

made See make.

madhouse People used to call a mental hospital a madhouse. ◇ If you say a place or situation is a madhouse, you mean it is full of noise and confusion.

madman (madmen) If you call a man a madman, you mean he is insane.

Madonna The Madonna is Mary, the mother of Jesus. ◇ A Madonna is a painting or sculpture of Mary.

maelstrom (*pron:* male-strom) A maelstrom is a confused situation in which things happen very quickly and it is difficult to make out what is going on. *...the maelstrom of Middle Eastern politics.*

maestro (*pron:* my-stroh) (maestros) People call a man a maestro when he is very skilful at something, especially conducting or playing music.

mafia (mafioso, mafiosi) The Mafia is a secret criminal organization which started in Sicily and organizes many illegal activities in the US. A member of this organization is called a **mafioso** (*plural:* mafiosi). ◇ Other criminal organizations which operate in a similar way are also called **mafias**. ◇ When a group of people with something in common seem to dominate an organization or activity, people sometimes jokingly call them a **mafia**.

mag A mag is a magazine.

magazine ❏ A magazine is a regular publication, usually weekly or monthly, which carries articles, stories, photographs, and advertisements. ◇ A radio or television **magazine** is a regular programme containing items about people, issues, or things in the news.

❏ The magazine in a gun is a metal case which holds several cartridges.

magenta (*pron:* maj-jen-ta) is a dark reddish-purple colour.

maggot Maggots are tiny creatures which look like very small worms and turn into flies.

magic (magical, magically) ❏ Magic is a special power which comes into children's stories and which some people believe exists. It can make apparently impossible things happen. Magic and **magical** are used to talk about things connected with magic. *...a wise woman with magical powers.* ◇ If something happens like magic or as if by magic, it happens unexpectedly and without any apparent explanation. Similarly, you can say something happens **magically**. *Stimulating architecture can almost magically change the texture of inner-city life.*

❏ Magic is also the art of performing tricks to entertain people, for example making things seem to appear and disappear.

❏ The magic of something is a special quality which makes it seem wonderful and exciting. *At first the city has a certain magic.* You call things which have this quality **magical**. *The hotel is set on the edge of a bay, backed by magical countryside.*

magic carpet In children's stories, a magic carpet is a carpet which can carry people through the air.

magic lantern A magic lantern was an old-fashioned type of projector which used large pieces of glass as slides to project a picture onto a screen.

magician A magician is a person who performs tricks as

a form of entertainment. ◇ In stories, a **magician** is a man with magic powers.

magisterial (*pron:* maj-is-**teer**-rial) If someone's behaviour or manner is **magisterial**, they act or speak in an impressive way, and seem to be in complete control of things.

magistrate A **magistrate** is an official who acts as a judge in a law court dealing with minor crimes or disputes.

magma is molten rock below the earth's crust.

magnanimous (magnanimously, magnanimity) If you are **magnanimous** or show **magnanimity**, you are generous or forgiving to someone, especially after you have beaten them in a fight or contest.

magnate A **magnate** is a person with a lot of power, especially in business.

magnesium is a light silvery-white metallic element which burns with an intense white flame. It is used in flashbulbs, flares, and fireworks.

magnet (magnetic, magnetism) ❑ A **magnet** is a piece of iron which attracts iron or steel towards itself. The area surrounding it where it has this effect is called its **magnetic field**. Its power to attract things is called **magnetism**; a **magnetic** object is one which has this power.

  ❑ If something attracts people because it is interesting or unusual, you can say it is **magnetic** or a **magnet**. *Hollywood has been a magnet for film-makers from across the globe.* ◇ If a person is **magnetic** or has **magnetism,** they have qualities which people find very attractive.

magnetic north is the direction in which a compass needle points.

magnetic tape is narrow plastic tape covered in a magnetic substance. It is used to record sound or video signals, or to store information in computers.

magnetise See magnetize.

magnetism See magnet.

magnetize (magnetizing, magnetized) (*can be spelled with an 's' instead of a 'z'*) If a substance or object is **magnetized**, it is made magnetic.

magnificent (magnificently, magnificence) Something which is **magnificent** is very beautiful and impressive. *...a magnificently reconstructed building... ...the magnificence of his surroundings.*

magnify (magnifies, magnifying, magnified; magnification) ❑ If an object is **magnified**, it is made to appear bigger than it really is, for example because you are looking at it through a microscope. *This tiny creature, visible only under magnification, lives on our discarded skin.* The **magnification** of a microscope, telescope, or pair of binoculars is the degree to which it can magnify things.

  ❑ If a feeling is **magnified**, it is made greater or more intense. If a problem is **magnified**, it is made worse. *The density of population and industry in the region merely magnifies the current troubles.*

magnifying glass A **magnifying glass** is a hand-held object with a lens which makes things appear bigger when you look through it.

magnitude The **magnitude** of something is how big it is. *No industry in history has suffered a decline of that magnitude.*

magnolia The **magnolia** is a type of oriental tree with large white or pink flowers. ◇ **Magnolia** is a very pale pink colour.

magnum A **magnum** is a wine bottle which holds the equivalent of two normal bottles (about 1.5 litres).

magnum opus The **magnum opus** of a writer, painter, or composer is their greatest or most important single work.

magpie The **magpie** is a black and white bird with a long tail. It is a member of the crow family.

maharaja (*or* maharajah) A **maharaja** is the head of one of the royal families which used to rule parts of India.

mahogany is the dark reddish-brown wood of several kinds of tropical trees. It is used to make furniture.

maid A **maid** is a female servant. ◇ In the past, a young unmarried woman was sometimes called a **maid**.

maiden ❑ In the past, a **maiden** was a young unmarried woman. ◇ A married woman's **maiden name** is the surname she had before she was married. ◇ Someone's **maiden aunt** is an aunt who has never married.

  ❑ The **maiden** voyage or flight of a ship or plane is its first official journey. ◇ A politician's **maiden** speech is the first speech he or she makes in the House of Commons or House of Lords.

  ❑ In cricket, a **maiden over** is one in which no runs are scored.

mail (mailing, mailed) The **mail** is the system by which the post office collects and delivers letters and parcels. The letters and parcels are called **mail**. If you **mail** something, you send it through the mail.

mail order If you buy things by **mail order**, you choose them from a catalogue or advertisement and they are delivered to your address.

mailbag A **mailbag** is a large bag used by the post office for carrying letters and parcels.

mailbox (mailboxes) In the US, a **mailbox** is (a) a box outside a house, where letters are delivered. (b) a post-box.

mailing list A **mailing list** is a list of names and addresses which is kept by an organization so it can send people information or advertising material.

mailshot When an organization sends out a **mailshot**, it sends advertising material or information to a large number of selected people at the same time.

maim (maiming, maimed) If someone is **maimed,** they are so badly injured that part of their body is permanently damaged.

main (mainly) ❑ The **main** thing in any situation is the most important one. *Establishing diplomatic relations with China is one of his country's main aims... ...the main opposition parties.*

  ❑ **Mainly** is used to say a statement is true in most cases or to a large extent. *The disease is carried mainly by foxes and by dogs.* ◇ If something is true **in the main,** it is generally true, although there may be exceptions.

  ❑ The **mains** are the pipes which supply gas or water to buildings, or take sewage from them. The cables which supply electricity are also called **mains**.

main line (mainline) A **main line** is an important route on a railway network, usually linking one large city with another. A **mainline** station is on a main line.

mainframe A **mainframe** is a large computer which can do very large or complicated tasks. It is usually connected to a number of terminals and can be used by many people at the same time.

mainland The **mainland** is the major part of a country or continent, in contrast to the islands which are part of it and lie off its shores.

mainline See main line.

mainly See main.

mainstay The **mainstay** of something like an organization is the part which gives it most of its strength or effectiveness. *Orange trees, the mainstay of local agriculture, are withering away for lack of irrigation... There are growing worries that the mainstay of the former Communist regimes, the secret police, may still be alive and kicking.*

mainstream is used to describe people who have the most orthodox ideas or methods. Their ideas and methods can also be called **mainstream**. *...mainstream theatre.*

maintain (maintaining, maintained; maintenance) ❏ If you **maintain** something, you keep it up, and do not let it stop or grow weaker. The **maintenance** of something is keeping it up like this. *Both the United States and Britain called for the maintenance of sanctions against Iraq.* ◇ If you **maintain** something at a particular rate or level, you keep it at that rate or level. *Many countries have shown a reluctance to maintain their budgeted level of financial contributions to the UN.*

❏ If you **maintain** someone, you provide them with money to pay for the things they need. Money paid like this is called **maintenance**. ◇ When people **maintain** a building, vehicle, road, or machine, they keep it in good condition.

❏ If you **maintain** something is true, you state firmly that it is so. *Police sources maintain that the situation is now under control.*

maisonette A **maisonette** is a flat on two floors of a larger building.

maître d'hôtel (*pron:* met-ra doh-tell) In some restaurants, the head waiter or restaurant manager is called the **maître d'hôtel**.

maize is a tall cereal plant which produces sweetcorn.

majestic (majestically) **Majestic** is used to describe things which are beautiful, dignified, and impressive. *...the hills of the Emerald Isle sweeping majestically down to the sea.*

majesty (majesties) ❏ When you begin talking to a king or queen, you are supposed to say **Your Majesty**. If you are talking about a king or queen in a formal way, you say **His Majesty**, **Her Majesty**, or **Their Majesties**. *Her Majesty unveiled a commemorative plaque.*

❏ When you talk about the **majesty** of something, you mean it is beautiful, impressive, and dignified. *The artist's impression of how Delphi must once have looked is mind-blowing in its majesty.*

major (majoring, majored) ❏ You use **major** to talk about something which is more important, serious, or significant than other things of its kind. *It has become a major social problem.*

❏ A **major** is a middle-ranking officer in the British army and in some other armed forces.

❏ In the US, if someone **majors** in a subject, they study it as their main subject at university.

major-general A **major-general** is a senior officer in the army, one rank above a brigadier.

majorette Majorettes or drum **majorettes** are girls or young women who march in front of a band or perform with it. They wear a uniform and carry batons which they twirl in their fingers and sometimes throw up into the air and catch.

majority (majorities) The **majority** of a group of people or things is more than half of it. If a group is **in the majority** or **in a majority**, they form more than half of a larger group. *Women students are in a majority in universities and colleges in all parts of Britain except Scotland.* ◇ In an election or vote, a **majority** is the difference between the number of votes gained by the winner and the number gained by the loser or losers. In Parliament, the government's **majority** is the difference between the number of seats it holds and the number held by the opposition parties together. ◇ **absolute majority**: see **absolute**. ◇ **overall majority**: see **overall**. ◇ **simple majority**: see **simple**. ◇ When people talk about **majority rule**, they usually mean a system in which a government is seen as representing the majority of people, rather than a minority. Originally, **majority rule** meant a system in which no action could be taken unless it had the consent of the majority of the people involved.

make (making, made) ❏ **Make** is used to say someone performs an action. For example, if you **make** a change, you change something. *The prime minister made the offer at a meeting of Solidarity activists.* ◇ If you **make** a visit, trip, or journey, you go somewhere. ◇ **Make** is used in phrases like 'make a move' or 'make a start' to talk about beginning to do something.

❏ If you **make it** to a place, you succeed in getting there, often with difficulty. ◇ If you **make for** a place, you go to it, or towards it. ◇ If you **make your way** somewhere, you go there. ◇ If you **make off**, you leave somewhere as quickly as possible, often to escape. *Police say they are looking for two men who made off on a motor-cycle.* If you **make off with** something, you steal it and take it away with you.

❏ **Make** is used to say someone or something is caused to be in a particular state, or to become a particular thing. *He says the charges have made him ill... These skills have helped make California the eighth-biggest economy in the world.*

❏ If something **makes** you do something, it causes you to do it. *...a series of misadventures that always made the reader laugh.* ◇ If a person **makes** you do something, they force you to do it. *The aim is to make the companies provide better service.*

❏ If you **make** something, you create it or produce it. *During the Second World War, Jaguar made components for warplanes.* Something which is **in the making** is in the process of being created. *The film took so long in the making that Clarke said they would have to retitle it 2002.* ◇ **Make** is also used to say something is turned into something else, or reproduced in a different form. *Many of his novels were made into films.* ◇ If you **make** something **up**, you prepare it according to a set of instructions. *Sunglasses can be made up by an optician to an individual prescription.*

❏ If something is **made of** a particular substance or material, it is formed or constructed from it. *...rafts made of car tyres.* ◇ If a number of things **make up** something, they are what it consists of. *The armies fighting the Saracens were no longer made up simply of Christians.*

❏ If a situation is of your **making**, you are responsible for it. *Some feel that the government's crisis is entirely of its own making.*

❏ If you **make** money, you get it by earning or winning it. Someone who is **on the make** is trying to get a lot of money or power, often by unfair means.

❏ If you **make yourself heard** or **understood**, you manage to get people to hear you or understand you. ◇ If you ask someone what they **make of** something, you want to know what they think about it. ◇ If you can **make** something **out,** (a) you can manage with difficulty to see it or hear it. *It's virtually impossible to make out the figures, unless you step up fairly close.* (b) you can identify it or understand it. *I don't think there were any injuries, as far as I can make out.*

❏ If you **make out** that something is true, you try to persuade people to believe it. *...criminal elements who make themselves out to be champions of democracy.*

❏ If you **make out** something like a cheque or will, you write all the necessary information on it.

❏ **Make** is used to say someone is appointed to a job, role, or position. *He was made editor of the New Statesman.* ◇ If you **make** something like a team or a shortlist, you succeed in getting yourself included in it. ◇ If you **make it** in a particular field or profession, you are successful in it. ◇ **make a go of**: see **go.** ◇ **make good**: see **good.** ◇ If something **is the making** of you, it changes you into a better or more successful person.

❏ You use **make** to say someone or something is suitable for a particular task or role. For example, if you say someone would **make** a good manager, you mean they have the right qualities for that job. ◇ If you say something has the **makings** of a particular thing, you mean it is likely to become it. *This dispute is not yet a war but has the makings of one.* ◇ If certain features **make for** a particular thing, they are responsible for something being that thing. *This and other candid confessions make for a hugely enjoyable autobiography.*

❏ You use **make** when you are talking about the result of a calculation. *Two and two makes four.* ◇ If you **make** an amount **up,** you add something to it to bring it to the required figure. *The balance was made up from investment income.* ◇ In cricket, if someone **makes** a particular score, they score that number of runs. *Hampshire made 446 for eight to overcome Gloucestershire.*

❏ The **make** of something like a car or TV set is the name of the company that made it.

❏ If you have to **make do with** something, you have to manage with it because you cannot have what you really want.

❏ If you **make** something **over** to someone, such as a piece of land or property, you legally transfer the ownership or control of it to them.

❏ If you **make up** something like a story, you invent it.

❏ If two people **make up,** they become friends again after a disagreement or a quarrel.

❏ If you **make** someone **up** or **make** yourself **up,** you apply cosmetics. See also **make-up.**

❏ **make up your mind**: see **mind.**

make-believe is pretending things are better or more exciting than they really are.

make-up is things like lipstick and powder which people put on themselves to try to be more attractive.

❏ A person's **make-up** is the combination of qualities in their character. *There was a lot of the hippy in her make-up.*

◇ The **make-up** of something is the combination of its various parts and the way they are arranged.

maker The **maker** of something is the person or company that makes it.

makeshift things are temporary and usually of poor quality.

maladjusted You say people are **maladjusted** when they have psychological problems and behave in socially unacceptable ways.

maladministration is inefficient or dishonest administration.

maladroit (*pron:* mal-a-**droyt**) is used to describe things which are done in a clumsy, awkward, or tactless way. *The Independent criticizes the government's maladroit handling of the issue.*

malady (*pron:* **mal**-a-dee) (maladies) A **malady** is an illness.

malaise (*pron:* mal-**laze**) is a vague feeling of ill-health, often indicating the beginning of a more serious illness. ◇ **Malaise** is also a state in which people feel dissatisfied or unhappy but do not know exactly what is wrong.

malapropism If someone says a word which is similar to the one they mean to say but has completely the wrong meaning, you call this a **malapropism.** For example, an old lady once went into an optician's and asked for 'a pair of bisexual glasses'.

malaria (malarial) **Malaria** is a serious disease carried by mosquitoes. It causes periods of fever and intense shivering. **Malarial** is used to talk about things to do with malaria. *...malarial areas... ...anti-malarial drugs.*

malcontent People who criticize the way society is run are sometimes called **malcontents** by people who think everything is all right.

male (maleness) A **male** is a person or animal belonging to the sex which cannot have babies or lay eggs. **Maleness** is being a male, rather than a female. ◇ **Male** is used to talk about (a) things to do with men. *...male attitudes.* (b) men of a particular kind. *...male athletes.*

male bonding See **bond.**

male chauvinism (male chauvinist) See **chauvinism.**

malevolent (*pron:* mal-**lev**-o-lent) (malevolently, malevolence) A **malevolent** person or animal wants or intends to cause harm. *He saw a huge bull glaring malevolently at him... Schlitter would arrest them, out of sheer malevolence, when they left the hospital.*

malformed (malformation) If something is **malformed** or has a **malformation,** it does not have its normal or correct shape.

malfunction (malfunctioning, malfunctioned) If something **malfunctions,** it fails to work properly. When this happens, you say there is a **malfunction.**

malice (*pron:* **mal**-liss) (malicious, maliciously) **Malice** is a desire to harm people. If an action is **malicious,** it is meant to cause harm. *...malicious damage... Anyone who claimed this was maliciously distorting the facts.*

malign (*pron:* mal-**line**) If someone **maligns** you, they say or do something to harm your reputation. ◇ **Malign** behaviour is intended to harm someone. *...malign policies... ...allegations of malign intent.* ◇ If something has **malign** effects, it is harmful.

malignant (*pron:* mal-**lig**-nant) (malignancy) ❏ **Malignant** behaviour is cruel and intended to cause harm. *Racist jokes of a malignant kind were a commonplace in some* *magazines.*

❑ A **malignant** disease spreads rapidly and is likely to cause death unless quickly treated. *Tissue that is removed during the operation is checked for signs of malignancy.*

mall (*pron:* **mawl** *or* **mal**) A **mall** is a shopping area, usually a large area surrounded by shops and open to pedestrians only.

mallard The **mallard** is a very common kind of wild duck. The male has a bright green head. Most kinds of domestic duck are descended from the mallard.

malleable (*pron:* **mal**-lee-a-bl) (**malleability**) ❑ **Malleable** people are easily influenced or controlled by other people. You talk about the **malleability** of people like these.

❑ If a substance is **malleable,** it can easily be changed into a new shape.

mallet A **mallet** is a wooden hammer with a square head.

malnourished (**malnutrition**) If someone is **malnourished** or suffering from **malnutrition,** they are physically weak because they have not eaten enough food or have been eating unhealthy food.

malodorous (*pron:* **mal-lode**-or-uss) If something is **malodorous,** it smells nasty.

malpractice You say someone is guilty of **malpractice** when they break the law or the rules of their profession for personal advantage.

malt is a substance used in making alcoholic drinks like beer and whisky. It is made from grain, usually barley, which has been soaked in water and allowed to germinate, then dried in a kiln. This process is known as **malt**ing the grain. ◇ A **malt** is a malt whisky.

malt whisky Malt **whisky** is made by distilling malted barley, rather than unmalted barley or other grain. Single malt whisky comes from one distillery only and is not blended with other whiskies.

malted milk is a drink made from milk and a powder containing malt.

maltreat (**maltreating, maltreated; maltreatment**) If people or animals are **maltreated,** they are treated badly, sometimes by being physically injured. *There have been allegations of serious maltreatment.*

mammal (**mammalian**) **Mammals** are animals whose females generally give birth to live young rather than eggs, and feed their young with milk. Humans, lions, mice, and whales are all mammals. **Mammalian** is used to talk about things to do with mammals. *Mammalian body temperature is controlled by processes in the brain.*

Mammon is used to talk about wealth and the pursuit of it. *...socialists sacrificing their convictions to Mammon... No one can successfully serve both God and Mammon at the same time.*

mammoth is used to describe things which are extremely large. *She has the mammoth task of trying to reconstruct the Nicaraguan economy.*

❑ **Mammoths** were very large elephant-like animals which became extinct a long time ago. They had long curling tusks. Some of them had long hair.

man (*plural:* **men**) (**manning, manned**) ❑ A **man** is an adult male human being. ◇ A **man-to-man** conversation involves two men talking openly and treating each other as equals. ◇ **the man in the street: see street.**

❑ **Man** is sometimes used to talk about human beings

in general. *Man is exterminating too many species for zoos to be much help.*

❑ When people **man** a position or machine, they look after it or operate it. *In busy periods they man the production lines... ...a special information centre manned by knowledgable advisors.* ◇ A **manned** vehicle has people inside it operating the controls. ◇ If you say something is, for example, a **two-man** operation, you mean it involves that number of people. *In May, he set up a three-man panel to advise him.*

❑ In the armed forces, the **men** are the ordinary soldiers, sailors, and airmen, rather than the officers.

man-hour A **man-hour** is the amount of work one person can do in an hour. You say a job will take a certain number of **man-hours.** From this you can work out how long the job will take, or how many people will be needed to do it in a certain time.

man-made things are constructed by people rather than formed naturally.

manacle (*pron:* **man-a-kl**) (**manacling, manacled**) **Manacles** are metal devices fastened round prisoners' wrists or ankles to stop them moving easily or escaping. **Manacled** prisoners are immobilized in this way.

manage (**managing, managed**) ❑ If you **manage** a business, you are responsible for running it.

❑ If you **manage** to do something, you succeed in doing it. *A few companies still manage to make healthy profits out of personal computers.* ◇ If you say someone **manages,** you mean they succeed in living or doing something on limited resources. *The government says that most students appear to be managing satisfactorily on their grants.*

manageable If something is **manageable,** it can be dealt with, because it is not too big or complicated.

management The running of a place or organization is called **management.** *...forest management... ...the management of schools.* **Management** is often used to say something is well or badly run. *These losses have arisen partly out of bad management.* ◇ The people who run an organization are called the **management.** *They have been holding talks with management and unions for some months.* ◇ When a company is going out of business or about to be taken over by another company, its managers sometimes buy it to run it themselves; this is called a **management buy-out.**

manager A **manager** is a man or woman responsible for running a business or a section of an organization. ◇ The **manager** of a pop star or other entertainer is the person who looks after their business interests. ◇ The **manager** of a sports team is the person responsible for organizing and training it.

manageress (**manageresses**) A **manageress** is a woman who runs a business such as a shop or a restaurant.

managerial is used to talk about things to do with the work of a manager or manageress. *...managerial jobs... ...managerial incompetence.*

managing director The **managing director** of a company is the director responsible for its day-to-day running.

mandarin ❑ A **mandarin** is a small orange which is easy to peel.

❑ Important civil servants are sometimes called **mandarins.** *...Treasury mandarins.* ◇ Originally, a **mandarin** was an important government official in China.

Mandarin Chinese is the official language of China.

mandate (mandating, mandated; mandatory) A government's mandate is the authority it has to carry out policies or tasks as a result of winning an election. ◇ When someone is **mandated** to do something or given a **mandate** to do it, they are given the authority to do it, or are instructed to do it. ◇ If something is **mandated**, the law states that it must be done. When this happens, it becomes **mandatory**. *Extended re-tests will be mandatory for drivers convicted of serious offences.*

mandolin A **mandolin** is a musical instrument like a small guitar with four pairs of strings. It is played with a plectrum.

mane The **mane** of an animal like a horse or lion is the long thick hair growing from its neck.

maneuver (maneuvring, maneuvred; maneuvrable) See **manoeuvre**.

manfully If you do something **manfully**, you do it in a very determined way.

manganese is a greyish-white metal used in making steel.

manger (*pron:* **mane**-jer) A **manger** is a feeding box for horses or cattle in a stable or barn.

mangetout (*pron:* **mawnzh**-too; *the 'zh' sounds like 's' in 'pleasure'*) **Mangetout** are a variety of pea with an edible pod.

mangle (mangling, mangled) If something is **mangled**, it is crushed and twisted. *...mangled heaps of iron that were once cars.* ◇ A **mangle** is a device for wringing water out of laundry. You pass the clothes between two heavy rollers in a metal frame.

mango (mangoes *or* mangos) **Mangoes** are large sweet yellowish fruit. They grow in tropical countries.

mangrove The **mangrove** is a tree which grows in tropical countries. Mangroves grow close together along coasts or riverbanks. Their roots grow above the water.

mangy (*pron:* **main**-ji) A **mangy** animal has lost a lot of its hair through disease.

manhandle (manhandling, manhandled) If someone **manhandles** you, they treat you very roughly.

manhole A **manhole** is a covered hole in the ground leading to a drain or sewer.

manhood is the state of being a man rather than a boy, or the period of a man's adult life. *...the training boys receive for manhood... His handwriting, from earliest manhood, was flowing and graceful.*

manhunt A **manhunt** is a search for someone who has escaped or disappeared.

mania A **mania** is a very strong interest in something, especially one shared by a lot of people. *...Gazza mania... ...the mania for plant collecting.* ◇ Some kinds of mental illness are also called **manias**. *...persecution mania.*

maniac (maniacal) A **maniac** is a psychologically disturbed person who is violent and dangerous. **Maniacal** behaviour (*pron:* man-**eye**-ak-l) is violent, uncontrolled, and dangerous.

manic (*pron:* man-**ik**) behaviour is very energetic because the person concerned is highly excited or anxious. *East Berliners have become manic shoppers... ...the manic hilarity of Woody Allen at his best.*

manic depression (manic depressive) **Manic depression** is a mental illness which makes people over-excited and confident some of the time and very depressed at other times. A person who has this illness is called a **manic de-**pressive.

manicure (manicuring, manicured; manicurist) If you have a **manicure**, the skin on your hands is moisturized and your nails are cut and varnished. A person who does this for a living is called a **manicurist**. You can say someone's nails are **manicured**. ◇ If you say something like a lawn is **manicured**, you mean it has been neatly trimmed in a rather fussy way.

manifest (manifesting, manifested; manifestly) If something is **manifest**, it is obvious to everyone. *It was manifest that the investigation was damaging to the applicant... All the performers were manifestly at home with their parts.* ◇ If you **manifest** something, you make people aware of it. If something **manifests** itself, it becomes apparent. *In all sufferers, a high level of insecurity often manifested itself as a fear of growing up.*

manifestation A **manifestation** of something is a sign that it is happening or exists. *Football hooliganism has become the most striking manifestation of this new wave of violence.*

manifesto (manifestos *or* manifestoes) A **manifesto** is a written statement in which a political party sets out its aims and policies.

manifold things are of many different kinds. *...the manifold effects of the war... The problems are manifold.*

manipulate (manipulating, manipulated; manipulation, manipulative, manipulator) ❏ If someone **manipulates** people, they control them and make them do what they want them to. *...a manipulation of innocent people's lives.* ◇ If you **manipulate** a situation or system, you control it to your own advantage. *...a campaign by the government to manipulate press coverage of the failed coup... His managers had manipulated the accounts to pay themselves big bonuses.* ◇ If you say someone is **manipulative** or a **manipulator**, you mean they try to control people or situations to their own advantage.

❏ If you **manipulate** a piece of equipment, you control it in a skilful way.

mankind is the whole human race.

manly (manliness) **Manly** is used to describe behaviour which is thought to be typical of a man, rather than a woman or a child. *He also began hunting regularly, an expression of manliness to which he became addicted.*

manna If something appears like **manna** or **manna from heaven**, it appears suddenly as if by a miracle and helps people out of a difficult situation.

mannequin A **mannequin** is a life-sized model of a person, used to display clothes, especially in a shop window. ◇ A **mannequin** is also a woman who models clothes, especially in a fashion show or in fashion photographs.

manner ❏ The **manner** in which you do something is the way you do it. *The move was intended to reassure boat people that they would be treated in a fair and safe manner on their return.* ◇ If you say a piece of art or writing is **in the manner of** someone, you mean it is done in a style typical of them.

❏ A person's **manner** is the way they behave and talk. *She claimed that officers investigating the case adopted an aggressive and unsympathetic manner towards her.* ◇ If someone has good **manners** or is **well-mannered**, they behave and speak politely. You can also say someone has bad manners or is **bad-mannered** or **ill-mannered**.

mannered If someone's speech or writing is **mannered**, it seems artificial, as though they were trying to impress someone.

mannerism A **mannerism** is a gesture or way of speaking which is characteristic of a person.

manning The level of **manning** in a company or operation is the number of workers employed.

manoeuvre (manoeuvring, manoeuvred; manoeuvrable) (*American spelling:* maneuver, maneuvring, *etc*) ❑ If you **manoeuvre** an object into or out of an awkward position, you move it there skilfully. If something is easily **manoeuvrable**, it is easy to move about.
❑ A **manoeuvre** is also something clever you do to turn a situation to your own advantage. *His offer is being seen as a political manoeuvre to weaken his opponents.* ◇ If you have **room for manoeuvre**, you have the opportunity to change your plans if it becomes necessary or desirable.
❑ Military **manoeuvres** are training exercises over large areas of countryside.

manor (manorial) A **manor** is a large country house and the land belonging to it, usually one where the original house was built in the Middle Ages. The house is called the **manor house**. **Manorial** is used to talk about things connected with a manor.

manpower People sometimes call workers **manpower**. *It will take the private sector many years before it has the skills and manpower to run existing jails.*

manqué (*pron:* man-kay) is used to talk about someone's failure to become something. For example, an actor or writer **manqué** is a person who wanted to be an actor or a writer, or who in your opinion could have been one, but who never succeeded in becoming one.

manse A **manse** is a house provided for the minister in certain Christian churches.

manservant A **manservant** is a man who works as a servant in a private house.

mansion A **mansion** is a very large house.

manslaughter is the crime of killing someone when this is not legally considered to be murder.

mantelpiece (*or* mantlepiece) A **mantelpiece** is a shelf over a fireplace.

mantle ❑ A **mantle** is a sleeveless piece of clothing worn over other clothes. ◇ If you take on the **mantle** of something, you take on its responsibilities and duties. *She might attempt to take on her husband's mantle and run for President.*
❑ A **mantle** is a layer of something covering a surface. *Future generations may have to live under a depleted ozone mantle.* ◇ The Earth's **mantle** is the part between the crust and the core.

mantlepiece See mantelpiece.

mantra In Hinduism or Buddhism, a **mantra** is a sacred word or sound which is repeated continually to aid religious contemplation. Any word or phrase which is repeated over and over again can be called a **mantra**. *Western politicians repeated, mantra-like, that reunification was 'not on the agenda'.*

manual (manually) **Manual** work involves using physical strength rather than mental skills. ◇ **Manual** is also used to describe things which are operated by hand, rather than by electricity or a motor. *Buyers have the alter-* native *of a six-speed manual gearbox... Previously, data had been typed manually into a computer terminal.* ◇ A **manual** is a book which tells you how to do something.

manufacture (manufacturing, manufactured; manufacturer) ❑ **Manufactured** things are made in a factory. You can talk about the **manufacture** of things in a factory. *...the manufacture of aircraft.* A **manufacturer** is a person or business that manufactures things.
❑ If someone **manufactures** information, they invent it. *They believe the allegations against them were manufactured out of bad feeling.*

manure is animal dung spread on the ground to improve the growth of plants.

manuscript A **manuscript** is the author's typed or handwritten version of a book before it is printed. ◇ A **manuscript** is also an old document which was written by hand before the printing press was invented.

Manx is used to talk about people and things in or from the Isle of Man. *...the Manx government.* ◇ The **Manx** are the Manx people. ◇ **Manx** is the language formerly spoken in the Isle of Man.

many is used to talk about a lot of people or things. *Many casualties were inflicted... Many feel they have little choice but to invest more money.*
❑ **How many** is used to ask about a number of people or things. *How many of the Smiths wore glasses?* ◇ **How many** is also used to talk about an unknown number of people or things. *Nobody knows how many spiders there are in Britain.*

many-sided If something is **many-sided**, it is made up of many different parts or aspects. *The problem of sickness and ill-health is many-sided.*

map (mapping, mapped) A **map** is a detailed representation of an area as it would appear if you saw it from above. When an area is **mapped**, a map is made of it. ◇ If you **map out** a route, you plan how to get somewhere using a map. ◇ If you **map out** a strategy or system, you work out how you will do it.

maple The **maple** is a tree with large colourful leaves which are usually five-pointed. Its wood is often used to make furniture and flooring. The maple leaf appears on the Canadian flag.

maple syrup is a very sweet syrup made from the sap of a type of maple tree.

mar (marring, marred) If you **mar** something, you spoil it. *Another major sporting event has been marred by problems with drugs.*

maraca (*pron:* mar-rak-a) A **maraca** is a percussion instrument, usually one of a pair. Maracas are traditionally made from hollow gourds filled with pebbles or beans.

marathon A **marathon** is a race in which people run about 26.2 miles (42.2 km), usually along roads. ◇ A **marathon** task takes a long time to complete. *Emerging from the marathon farm negotiations last night, the Minister was doubtful that a settlement would be reached.*

marauding (marauder) **Marauding** people or animals are looking for something to steal or kill. *A previous temple was destroyed by marauding Moguls in the sixteenth century.* People and animals like these can be called **marauders**.

marble (marbled) ❑ **Marble** is a very hard rock used to make statues, fireplaces, and floors. It often has a pattern of irregular lines and patches of colour. **Marbled** is used to describe rooms and buildings where many of the surfaces are marble. ...*the marbled elegance of Beijing's Palace Hotel.*

❑ **Marbles** is a children's game played with small balls called **marbles** which are usually made of glass. ◇ If you say someone has **lost their marbles,** you mean they have gone mad.

march (marches, marching, marched; marcher) ❑ When soldiers **march,** they walk with regular steps as a group. This way of walking is called a **march.** ◇ A **march** is also a piece of music written for soldiers to march to, or a piece with a similar beat.

❑ When a large group of people **march** or go on a **march,** they walk together somewhere, usually to protest about something. People doing this are called **marchers.**

❑ If you **march** somewhere, you walk there quickly and purposefully. ◇ If you **march** someone else somewhere, you force them to walk there by holding their arm.

❑ The **march** of something is its steady development or progress. ...*the march of science.*

❑ If you **steal a march** on someone, you start doing something before they do, to get an advantage over them.

❑ If you give someone their **marching orders,** you tell them to leave.

marchioness (*pron:* marsh-on-ness) (marchionesses) A **marchioness** is the wife of a marquess, or a woman who holds the rank of a marquess. She ranks below a duchess and above a countess.

mare A **mare** is an adult female horse.

margarine is a butter-like substance made from vegetable oil or animal fat or both.

marge is the same as margarine.

margin ❑ If you say someone won a race or an election by a particular **margin,** you are saying how close the result was. For example, you can say someone won by 'a narrow margin'. ◇ The **margin of error** is the extent to which you can afford to go wrong in something you are doing.

❑ On a written or printed page, the **margins** are the blank spaces down each side.

❑ The **margins** of a place or area are its edges. ...*a shallow lake with an island and gently sloping margins.* ◇ If you are **on the margin** of a group or situation, you are only just included in it. *The UN has long been kept on the margins of the peace process.*

marginal is used to describe things which are small and not very important. *The King would have only marginal influence in appointments to the upper house.* ◇ **Marginal** is also used to describe people who are not involved in the main part of something. *It is likely to be the more marginal religious groups that will put money into religious advertising.* ◇ In politics, a **marginal** seat is held by only a small majority.

❑ **Marginal** land is on the edge of a fertile area and is less suitable for growing food.

marginalize (marginalizing, marginalized; marginalization) (*can be spelled with an 's' instead of a 'z'*) If people or things are **marginalized,** they are made to seem unimportant. *The growth of crime has been attributed to the marginalization of some elements of our society.*

marginally means to only a small extent. *There seems to be marginally more snow in Colorado than in the Alps.*

marigold The **marigold** is a yellow or orange garden flower.

marijuana (*pron:* mar-ri-**wah**-na) is an illegal drug made from the dried flowers and leaves of the hemp plant. It can be smoked in cigarettes.

marimba The **marimba** is a percussion instrument which looks like a large xylophone.

marina A **marina** is a small harbour for pleasure boats and yachts.

marinade A **marinade** is a mixture of oil, wine, vinegar, herbs, and spices. You soak meat or fish in a marinade before cooking it, to add flavour to it or to make it more tender.

marinate (marinating, marinated) If you **marinate** meat or fish or leave it to **marinate,** you soak it in a marinade before cooking it.

marine A **marine** is a soldier in the Royal Navy or the Marine Corps. ◇ **Marine** is also used to talk about things to do with the sea. ...*marine life... Plankton are best known for being the lowest link in the marine food chain.*

Marine Corps The **Marine Corps** is a corps of soldiers which is part of the US Navy.

mariner A **mariner** is a sailor.

marionette A **marionette** is a puppet controlled by strings or wires.

marital is used to talk about things to do with a marriage. ...*marital difficulties... ...the marital home.* Your **marital status** is whether you are single, married, widowed, or divorced.

maritime is used to talk about things to do with the sea and ships. ...*maritime disputes... ...the National Maritime Museum.*

marjoram is a herb of the mint family. It is used in cooking as a flavouring.

mark ❑ A **mark** is a small stain or damaged area on a surface. If something **marks** a surface, it damages it or leaves a stain.

❑ A **mark** is also a number or letter indicating someone's score in a test or examination. When a teacher **marks** a student's work, he or she decides how good it is and writes comments or a mark on it.

❑ A **mark** is also a written or printed symbol, for example a short line or a letter of the alphabet. ◇ If you **mark** something, you put a written symbol or words on it. *My letter was returned, marked 'gone away'.* ◇ If you **mark off** an item on a list, you put a mark on the list to show it has been dealt with.

❑ If something reaches a particular **mark,** it reaches a significant stage. *Forecasts suggest that the number will swell this winter and touch the three million mark.*

❑ If someone sets a **mark,** they set a standard for people to aim at. *Jeff Rouse lowered his own 100 metres backstroke mark in the first leg of the relay in 53.86sec.* ◇ If something is not **up to the mark,** it is not satisfactory.

❑ If something **marks** a place or position, it shows where something is or was. *Now all that is left to mark the site is a few piles of rubble and a white concrete memorial.* ◇ If something **marks** an important occasion or change, it shows it is taking place. *Sunday's elections are meant to mark a return to the old traditions.*

❑ A **mark** of something is a sign or typical feature of it. *The ultimate mark of respect for a new dish is the interest* shown in it by other chefs. ◇ If something **marks** you or marks you out as a certain type of person, it shows you are that type of person. ◇ If a particular quality **marks** a person's life or career, they show that quality often during their life or career. *Briggs demonstrated the fighting spirit which has marked her career.*

❑ If you **make your mark** on something or **leave your mark** on it, you have an important influence on it.

❑ If you are **slow off the mark**, you respond to a situation slowly. If you are **quick off the mark**, you respond quickly. ◇ If something is **wide of the mark**, it is a long way from being correct.

❑ If you are **marking time**, you are doing something boring or unimportant while you wait for something else to happen.

❑ When prices are **marked up**, they are increased. When they are **marked down**, they are reduced. You can talk about a **mark-up** or a **mark-down** in prices.

❑ **Mark** is used in front of a number (a) to indicate the temperature level in a gas oven. *...gas mark 4.* (b) to talk about a particular version or model of something. *...the Harrier GR Mark 5.*

❑ The **mark** is the unit of currency in Germany. Some other countries, for example Finland, also have a unit of currency called a **mark**.

❑ See also **marked**, **marking**.

mark-down See **mark**.

mark-up See **mark**.

marked (markedly) (*pron*: markt, mark-id-ly) A **marked** quality or change is very obvious. *The results are markedly worse than those of a previous survey.*

marker ❑ A **marker** is an object which is placed somewhere to show the position of something. ◇ If a person or organization **puts down a marker**, they do something which is intended as a clear sign of what they want to happen or intend to do.

❑ A **marker** or **marker pen** is a pen with a thick felt tip for drawing and colouring things.

market (marketing, marketed) ❑ A **market** is a place, often in the open air, where people sell goods such as food and household items from stalls.

❑ A **market** for a product is a part of the world where it can be sold. *The British market is still the company's biggest source of profits.* ◇ The **market** for a product is the number of people who want to buy it. *The banks and building societies have been engaged in a fierce fight for mortgage lending business in a declining market.* ◇ When a company **markets** a product, they organize its sale by deciding on its price, the shops and areas it should be supplied to, and how it should be advertised. This process is called **marketing**.

❑ When people talk about **the market**, they mean a situation where the price of everything is decided by how much there is of it, and how many people want to buy it. *...a system based on market forces... Other goods will rise to their true market values.* If a country has a **market economy**, it has an economic system based on this kind of market, and the government does not regulate prices.

❑ See also **black market**, **job market**.

market garden (market gardening; market gardener) A **market garden** is an area like a small farm where fruit, vegetables, and sometimes flowers are grown for sale. Run-

ning a **market garden** is called **market gardening**; a **market gardener** is someone who does it.

market place When people talk about the **market place**, they are talking about the demand for products and their availability. *The Japanese have read the demands of the marketplace better than their British counterparts.* ◇ A **market place** is a small area in a town where a market is held, or used to be held in the past.

market research (market researcher) **Market research** is research into what people want, need, and buy. A **market researcher** is a person who does this kind of research.

marketable If something is **marketable**, it can be sold, because people want to buy it. ◇ **Marketable** skills are ones which are useful to an employer, and are therefore likely to get you a job.

marking **Markings** are shapes, patterns, or designs on the surface of something.

marksman (marksmen; marksmanship) A **marksman** is a person who can shoot very accurately. **Marksmanship** is the ability to shoot accurately.

marmalade is a jam-like food made from citrus fruits such as oranges or lemons.

marmoset **Marmosets** are very small South American monkeys with claws on their fingers and toes.

maroon (marooning, marooned) ❑ If you are **marooned** somewhere, you are stuck there and cannot get away. *Scores of people are marooned in remote parts of Northern England and weather conditions are deteriorating.*

❑ **Maroon** is a dark reddish-purple colour.

marque (*pron*: mark) A **marque** is a particular make of a product. *Pic's own marque of champagne accompanied the meal.*

marquee (*pron*: mar-kee) A **marquee** is a large tent used at outdoor events.

marquess (*pron*: mark-wiss) (marquesses) A **marquess** is a British nobleman ranking below a duke and above an earl.

marquetry (*pron*: mark-it-ry) is the technique of decorating furniture with a pattern of inlaid pieces of wood, ivory, or other substances.

marquis (marquises) In Britain, a **marquis** (*pron*: mark-wiss) is the same as a marquess. In some other countries, a **marquis** (*pron*: mar-kee) is a nobleman with the same rank as a British marquess.

marriage ❑ When a **marriage** takes place, two people get married. A **marriage** is also the relationship between a husband and wife. **Marriage** is the state of being married.

❑ When two skills or methods are combined to produce something, you can call this a **marriage** of skills or methods.

marriage of convenience (marriages of convenience) If someone marries another person for social, financial, or political reasons rather than for love, you call this a **marriage of convenience**. ◇ When two organizations or political parties who are normally opposed to each other join forces to gain some advantage, this can also be called a **marriage of convenience**.

marriageable If someone is of a **marriageable** age, they are old enough to get married. ◇ If someone is regarded as **marriageable**, people think they would be a good prospect as a husband or wife.

married If you are **married**, you have a husband or wife. ◇ If you **get married**, you marry someone. ◇ **Married** is used to talk about things to do with marriage. *...married life... ...married bliss... ...her married name.*

marrow or **bone marrow** is the fatty substance at the centre of human and animal bones.
❑ **Marrows** are long thick green vegetables with pale flesh.

marry (marries, marrying, married) When a man and a woman **marry**, they become husband and wife during a special ceremony. You also say the person who conducts the ceremony **marries** the couple.

marsh (marshes) A **marsh** is a very wet muddy area of land.

marshal (marshalling, marshalled) (*usual American spelling:* marshaling, marshaled) ❑ If you **marshal** things or people, you gather them together and organize them. A **marshal** is a person who helps organize a public event.
❑ A **marshal of the RAF** is an officer of the highest rank in the RAF. The ranks below this are **air chief marshal**, **air marshal**, and **air vice marshal**.
❑ In the US, a **marshal** is (a) a police officer in a small town with the same powers and duties as a sheriff. (b) a federal officer appointed to carry out court orders.

marshalling yard A **marshalling yard** is a place where railway rolling stock is kept and made up into trains.

marshland is land consisting mainly of marshes.

marshmallow is a soft spongy sweet food. Marshmallows are sweets made from marshmallow.

marshy land consists mainly of marshes.

marsupial (*pron:* mar-soop-ee-al) **Marsupials** are animals which carry their young in a pouch on their bodies. Kangaroos, koalas, and wombats are marsupials.

martial is used to describe things to do with war or soldiers. *...martial music... ...the martial regime of General Ershad.* See also **court martial**.

martial arts The **martial arts** are the techniques of self-defence from the Far East, such as judo and karate.

martial law If a place is under **martial law**, it is controlled by the armed forces, rather than civilians.

Martian is used to talk about things to do with the planet Mars. *A major purpose of the mission is to make detailed observations of Martian weather.* ◇ A **Martian** is an imaginary creature from the planet Mars.

martin See **house martin**.

martinet (*pron:* mar-tin-net) You call someone a **martinet** when they believe in strict discipline and expect all their orders to be obeyed.

martini A **martini** is a cocktail made from gin and vermouth, sometimes with a dash of bitters. 'Martini' is a trademark for a brand of vermouth.

martyr (martyred; martyrdom) When someone is killed for their religious or political beliefs, people call them a **martyr** or say they are **martyred**; they also talk about their **martyrdom**. *It was Ali's martyrdom that led to the great schism in Islam.* ◇ People who suffer in a lesser way for a cause can also be called **martyrs**. *Sherriden went to prison and Militant had its first martyr.* ◇ If someone plays the **martyr**, they exaggerate their sufferings as a way of getting sympathy, praise, or support.

marvel (marvelling, marvelled) (*usual American spelling:* marveling, marveled) If you **marvel** at something, it fills you with amazement or admiration. Something which has this effect on people can be called a **marvel**.

marvellous (marvellously) (*usual American spelling:* marvelous, marvelously) You use **marvellous** to describe things you think are very impressive or enjoyable. *The last chapter is marvellously chilling.*

Marxism (Marxist) **Marxism** is a political philosophy based on the writings of Karl Marx. Marx's view was that society would develop towards communism through the struggle between different social classes. **Marxist** is used to describe things connected with Marxism. *...Marxist ideas... ...a Marxist regime.* A **Marxist** is a person who believes in Marxism.

marzipan is a paste made of ground almonds, sugar, and egg. It is mainly used in cakes.

mascara is a substance used to colour and thicken eyelashes.

mascot A **mascot** is a person, animal, or toy thought to bring good luck.

masculine is used to talk about (a) things to do with men. *...the masculine mind.* (b) things thought to be typical of men rather than women. *He radiates a particularly masculine air of authority and decisiveness.*

masculinity If you talk about a man's **masculinity**, you mean the qualities he has which are thought to be typical of a man rather than a woman.

mash (mashes, mashing, mashed) If you **mash** vegetables, you crush them after cooking them. *...mashed potato.*

mask A **mask** is something you wear over your face as a protection or disguise. A **masked** person is wearing a mask. ◇ If something **masks** the true nature of something else, it hides it. You can call something which does this a **mask**. *Her literary flourishes mask an inability to face stark truths... There is little of substance behind their mask of authority.*

masking tape is plastic or paper tape which is sticky on one side. You use it when you are painting something to cover the parts you do not want to get paint on.

masochism (*pron:* mass-oh-kiz-m) (masochist, masochistic) **Masochism** is getting pleasure from your own mental or physical suffering. A **masochist** is someone who gets pleasure this way. If someone's behaviour is **masochistic**, they suffer mental or physical pain on purpose to get pleasure from their own suffering.

mason A **mason** is a person who is skilled at building things out of stone. ◇ A **Mason** is a Freemason.

masonic is used to talk about things to do with Freemasons. *...masonic symbols... ...masonic influences.* A **masonic lodge** is a local branch of the Freemasons.

masonry is the bricks or stones in a wall or building.

masquerade (*pron:* mask-er-aid) (masquerading, masqueraded) In the past, a **masquerade** was a costume ball or party where masks were worn. ◇ If you say something is a **masquerade**, you mean it is a show got up to deceive people. *He told a news conference that the elections would be a masquerade.* ◇ If you **masquerade** as something, you pretend to be that thing. *The van was ambushed by IRA members masquerading as soldiers.*

mass (masses, massing, massed) ❑ A **mass** of things is a very large number of them. ◇ A **mass** of a substance is a large amount of it. *...a mass of broken glass.* ◇ **Masses** of something means a great deal of it.

❑ **Mass** is used to talk about something involving a very large number of people. *...a mass airlift.* ◇ If people or animals **mass**, they gather to form a large crowd. *Shortly after the workers went on strike, police began to mass at the shipyard.* ◇ A **massed** group of people consists of several smaller groups. *...a massed band.* ◇ The **masses** are ordinary people. *The coming week will see a concerted media drive to explain privatization to the masses.*

❑ In science, the **mass** of an object is how much physical matter there is in it.

❑ In the Roman Catholic church and some Protestant churches, **Mass** is a ceremony in which bread and wine are consecrated and eaten by the congregation in remembrance of Christ's death and resurrection. The special words used in this ceremony are called the **Mass**. A **Mass** is a piece of music written to these words. *...Mozart's Mass in C Minor.*

mass-market products are designed to appeal to large numbers of people.

mass media The **mass media** are TV, radio, and popular newspapers.

mass produce (mass production) When people **mass produce** something, they manufacture it in large quantities by repeating the same process many times. **Mass production** is manufacturing things in this way.

massacre (massacring, massacred) If there is a **massacre**, a large number of people are deliberately killed. When this happens, you say the people are **massacred**.

massage (massaging, massaged) ❑ If you **massage** someone or give them a **massage**, you rub their body to make them relax or to stop their muscles hurting.

❑ If someone **massages** statistics or evidence, they alter them to deceive people.

masse See en masse.

massed See mass.

masseur (*pron:* mass-sur) A **masseur** is a person whose job is to give people massages.

masseuse A **masseuse** is a female masseur.

massif (*pron:* mass-eef) A **massif** is a group of mountains or a high plateau.

massive (massively) If something is **massive**, it is extremely large. *The demand for these plants has grown massively in recent years.*

mast The **masts** of a boat are the tall upright poles which support its sails. ◇ A radio or TV **mast** is a very tall pole used as an aerial to transmit sound or TV pictures.

mastectomy A **mastectomy** is a surgical operation to remove a woman's breast.

master (mastering, mastered) ❑ If you **master** a situation, you succeed in taking control of it. You then say you are **master** of it. *The President is making another attempt to show that he is master of the economy.*

❑ If you **master** something like a skill, you learn it. ◇ **Master** is used to describe someone who is very skilled at a job or technique. *The Georgian leader is a master tactician.* ◇ If you say someone is the **master** of something, you mean they are very good at it, or the best in their field. *Evans had become the master of the single telling phrase.*

❑ A **master plan** is a comprehensive plan produced by people in authority.

❑ In the past, a man who owned someone like a servant or slave was called his or her **master**. ◇ A **master** is also a

male teacher. ◇ The captain of a merchant ship is called the **master**.

master bedroom In a large house, the **master bedroom** is the largest bedroom.

master key A **master key** can be used to open several locks, for example all the locks in a building.

Master of Arts See M.A.

master of ceremonies At a formal event like a banquet, the **master of ceremonies** is the person who makes announcements. 'Master of Ceremonies' is often shortened to 'MC'. ◇ The **master of ceremonies** at a variety show is the person who announces the acts.

Master of Sciences See M.Sc.

Master of the Rolls The **Master of the Rolls** is the President of the Court of Appeal, the senior civil judge in the country, and the Keeper of the Records at the Public Records Office.

master's degree A **master's degree** is a higher degree, such as an M.A. or M.Sc.

masterclass (masterclasses) A **masterclass** is a class for trained musicians given by a famous musician.

masterful (masterfully) A **masterful** person behaves in a powerful and dominating way. ◇ If something is done in a **masterful** way, it is done with great skill. *His grandson has masterfully steered a course of survival for three and a half decades.*

masterly is used to describe things done in a very skilful way. *The book gives a masterly analysis of the environmental issues surrounding the motor industry.*

mastermind (masterminding, masterminded) If someone **masterminds** a complicated activity, they plan it in detail and make sure it is carried out successfully. You say someone like this is the **mastermind** behind the activity. *He was suspected of being the mastermind behind the Gandhi assassination.*

masterpiece If you call something like a work of art a **masterpiece**, you mean it is outstandingly good and one of the greatest of its kind. ◇ An artist's **masterpiece** is the greatest of his or her works.

masterstroke A **masterstroke** is a very clever move which helps you to achieve what you want.

mastery If you achieve **mastery** of something, you become an expert at it. *In a bruising parliamentary performance he demonstrated his mastery of political manoeuvring.* ◇ **Mastery** is also complete power or control over something. *...the mastery of space.*

masthead The **masthead** of a ship is the highest part of its mast. ◇ The **masthead** of a newspaper is its name as it appears in big letters at the top of the front page.

mastitis is an infection which causes inflammation of a woman's breast or the udder of an animal.

mastodon Mastodons were large elephant-like animals which became extinct during the Stone Age. ◇ If you call an organization a **mastodon**, you mean it is very large, cumbersome, and out-of-date. *...the state enterprises, these mastodons of the Communist era.*

masturbate (masturbating, masturbated; masturbation) If someone **masturbates**, they rub or stroke their own genitals to get sexual pleasure. This is called **masturbation**.

mat A **mat** is a piece of carpet or other thick material which you put on the floor to protect it or make the room more attractive. Some types of mats are used by people to exercise on, or for sports like judo. ◇ A **mat** is also a small piece of cloth, card, or plastic which you stand a plate or glass on to protect the surface of a table.

matador In a bullfight, the **matador** is the person who faces the bull and tries to kill it with a sword.

match (matches, matching, matched) ❑ A **match** is an organized game of football, cricket, chess, or some other sport.

❑ A **match** is also a little wooden stick which produces a flame when you strike it on a rough surface.

❑ If one thing **matches** another, it is the same or very similar. *The volume of cars handled during the first six months matched 1991 record levels.* ◇ You also say one thing **matches** another when they are the same colour or design, and therefore go well together. *...a skirt that matched the jacket.* You can say things like these are a **match**.

❑ If you **match** things or **match** them **up**, you choose ones which correspond to each other. *...the traditional way of teaching children to read through matching sounds to letters.*

❑ If two people are well **matched**, they are suited to each other and likely to have a successful relationship. You say people like these are a good **match**.

❑ If two people or teams are **matched** against each other, they have to play each other in a contest or competition. If they are evenly **matched**, they are of equal strength or ability. ◇ If you **meet your match**, you find you are competing against someone you cannot beat.

❑ If you **match** something which someone else has done, you do the same thing, or something else as good. ◇ If one thing **matches up** to another, it reaches the same standard. *In spite of her talents, her career never quite matched up to its promise.* ◇ If something is **no match for** something else, it is inferior to it and cannot compete successfully against it.

match point is a situation in a game like tennis in which the player in the lead can win the match if he or she wins the next point.

matchbox (matchboxes) A **matchbox** is a small box sold with matches in it.

matchless If you say something is **matchless**, you are praising it highly and saying nothing else is as good.

matchmaking (matchmaker) **Matchmaking** is encouraging people you know to form a relationship or get married. Someone who does this is called a **matchmaker**.

matchstick A **matchstick** is the wooden part of a match.

mate (mating, mated) ❑ Some people call their friends their **mates**.

❑ **-mate** is added to a word to talk about someone who has something in common with you. For example, your 'team-mate' belongs to the same team as you, and your 'room-mate' is someone you share a room with. See also **running mate, soulmate**.

❑ The **mate** or **first mate** of a merchant ship is the officer next-in-command to the captain.

❑ An animal's **mate** is its sexual partner. ◇ When a male and female animal **mate**, they have sex. If you **mate** captive or domestic animals, you bring them together so they will breed.

material (materially) ❑ A **material** is a solid substance. *Explosive material was found on beaches in Kent and Hampshire... The composted material would be used as fertiliser.*

◇ Cloth is often called **material**.

❑ **Materials** are the equipment and other things you need to do something or make something. ◇ People can also be called **material**. For example, if you say someone is officer **material** or management **material**, you mean they have the potential to be a good officer or manager.

❑ If someone is collecting **material** for a book or film, they are gathering information they can use in it.

❑ **Material** is used to describe things in the real world which have a physical form, as distinct from things to do with the mind or spirit. *Music, she says, is a kind of bridge between the material and the spiritual world.* ◇ **Material** is also used to describe things to do with possessions and wealth. *...the ban on any material reward being gained through rugby... They are well off materially.*

❑ In law, if something is **material** to a case, it is relevant to it. ◇ A **material** change or difference is a substantial or significant one. *Their position would not be materially worsened by the merger.*

materialise See materialize.

materialism (materialist, materialistic) **Materialism** is regarding money and possessions as more important than other things. People who have this view of life are called **materialists**. You say their attitude or behaviour is **materialistic**.

materialize (materializing, materialized) *(can be spelled with an 's' instead of a 'z')* If someone you are expecting to come does not **materialize**, they do not turn up. Similarly, if an expected event fails to **materialize**, it does not happen. *The expected post-election spending bounce never materialized.*

maternal is used to talk about things to do with being a mother. *...the importance of maternal education in raising standards of family health.* ◇ **Maternal** feelings are the kind a mother has about her child. Similarly, **maternal** behaviour is the kind a mother would show to her child. ◇ Your **maternal** grandparents are your mother's parents.

maternity is used to talk about things to do with pregnancy and birth. *...maternity leave... ...maternity units.* ◇ **Maternity** is also the state of being a mother.

matey If someone is being **matey**, they are behaving in a friendly way.

mathematical (mathematically) **Mathematical** is used to describe things involving numbers and calculations. *...a mathematical puzzle... Mathematically speaking, the poems represent 5 per cent of Shakespeare's output.*

mathematics (mathematician) **Mathematics** is the study of numbers, quantities, and shapes. A **mathematician** is someone who has studied this subject to an advanced level.

maths is the same as mathematics.

matinee (*or* matinée) *(pron: mat-in-nay)* A **matinee** is an afternoon performance of a play, or a morning or afternoon showing of a film.

matins is an Anglican religious service held in the morning. It is also known as **morning prayer**.

matriarch *(pron: mate-ree-ark)* (matriarchal, matriarchy) The **matriarch** of a family is an oldish female member who exerts power over all the other members. A woman like this can be described as **matriarchal**. ◇ A **matriarchal** society or **matriarchy** is one where the women exert a lot of power in their families.

matriculate (matriculating, matriculated; matriculation) Matriculation was an exam which English, Welsh, and Northern Irish schoolchildren used to take. It was replaced by GCE 'O' Level. In some countries, for example South Africa, **matriculation** is the exams a student takes at the end of high school. If the student passes, he or she is said to **matriculate**.

matrimonial is used to talk about things to do with marriage. ...*matrimonial difficulties*... ...*the matrimonial home*.

matrimony is the state of being married.

matrix (*pron:* may-triks) (*plural:* matrices, *pron:* may-triss-eez*) A **matrix** is the environment or framework within which something develops. ◇ In maths, a **matrix** is a rectangular arrangement of numbers, symbols, or letters, written in rows and columns and used in solving certain problems.

matron (matronly) ❑ The **matron** is the senior nurse in a hospital or nursing home. Hospital matrons are now usually called **chief nursing officers**. ◇ At a boarding school, the **matron** is a woman who looks after the health and welfare of the pupils.

❑ A **matron** is also a dignified middle-aged married woman, especially one with children. You describe a woman like this as **matronly**.

matt (*or* matte) A **matt** surface is dull, rather than shiny.

matted You say something is **matted** when it is twisted and sticks together untidily. ...*matted hair*... ...*thickly matted vegetation*.

matter (mattering, mattered) ❑ A **matter** is a situation which has to be dealt with. *This is a matter for Parliament.* ◇ **Matters** means the situation you are talking about. *The summit leaders ducked their toughest challenge, but at least they did not make matters worse.*

❑ If you do something **as a matter** of principle or policy, you do it for that reason. ◇ If something needs to be done **as a matter** of urgency or priority, it needs to be done as soon as possible. ◇ **as a matter of course**: see **course**.

❑ If you say something is just **a matter** of doing something, you mean it can be achieved just by doing that thing. *It is just a matter of working through these systematically until you hit upon something.* ◇ If you say something is only **a matter of time**, you mean it is certain to happen at some time in the future. ◇ If you talk about something being done in **a matter** of days or weeks, you are emphasizing how quickly it is done. *Americans, used to interminable campaigning, cannot believe that a top politician could be deposed in a matter of days.*

❑ If you say something is **a matter of opinion**, you mean it is not necessarily true; you are also implying that you do not agree with it. *Whether this amounts to a concession is a matter of opinion.*

❑ You say **for that matter** when you are saying that something applies equally to another situation or person. *There is nothing terminally sick about sterling or for that matter about the lira or the peseta.*

❑ **as a matter of fact**: see **fact**.

❑ If something **matters**, it is important. You often say something **matters** more or **matters** less than something else. *Often in these cases, the truth probably matters less than what people believe.* If something does not **matter**, it is not

important, because it has no effect on the situation you are talking about.

❑ **No matter** is used in front of words like 'how' and 'what' to say something happens or is true in all circumstances. *There was always fresh drinking water, no matter how dry it had been in recent months.* ◇ If you say you will do something **no matter what**, you mean you will do it regardless of what happens.

❑ If you say something is **no easy matter**, you mean it is not easy. If you say something is **no laughing matter**, you mean it is serious. You can use 'no' and 'matter' with other words like this. *Recession in America is no small matter for many of Japan's big manufacturers... It can be no light matter for the Home Office that so many young prisoners have wanted to kill or injure themselves.*

❑ **Matter** is physical substances generally. You can also talk about different kinds of **matter**. ...*solid matter*... ...*living matter*.

❑ Books and magazines are often called **reading matter**. ◇ The **subject matter** of a book or film is the topic it deals with.

matter-of-fact (matter-of-factly) If someone is being **matter-of-fact**, they are being very casual about something, often when you would not expect it. *'We played better football than they did,' Reilly said matter-of-factly.*

matting is a thick material used as a floor covering. It is usually woven from coarse fibre like rope or coir.

mattress (mattresses) A **mattress** is a rectangular object put on a bed to make it comfortable to sleep on. It consists of a thick layer of padding inside a fabric cover. Often there are also springs inside.

mature (maturing, matured; maturity, maturation) ❑ When a child or young animal **matures** or reaches **maturity**, it becomes an adult.

❑ You say people are **mature** when they behave in a sensible and responsible way. You can also call people's attitudes and behaviour **mature**. ◇ Calling a woman **mature** can be a polite way of saying she is no longer young.

❑ A **mature** plant or tree is fully grown. ◇ If something like a garden is **mature**, it is well-established and stable.

❑ When something like cheese or wine is **matured**, it is left for a time to allow its full flavour or strength to develop. This process is called **maturation**.

❑ When an investment or insurance policy **matures**, it becomes due for repayment.

mature student At a British college or university, a **mature student** is someone who starts their first degree when they are over 21.

maudlin If someone becomes **maudlin**, they start being sad and sentimental about their life, especially if they have been drinking.

maul (mauling, mauled) If someone is **mauled** by a person or animal, they are attacked and badly injured. ◇ You also say someone is **mauled** or given a **mauling** when they are heavily criticized or defeated.

mausoleum (*pron:* maw-so-lee-um) A **mausoleum** is a building containing the grave of someone rich or famous.

mauve is a pale purple colour.

maverick A **maverick** is someone who thinks and acts in a very independent way.

maw You call something a **maw** when it appears to

swallow things up like a giant mouth. *The hard currency gained by oil sales disappeared down the Soviet maw.*

mawkish (mawkishness) If you describe something like a scene in a film as **mawkish**, you mean it overdoes the emotion and seems awkward and silly. *...a tearful reconciliation of truly brazen mawkishness.*

maxim A **maxim** is a short saying recommending a particular form of behaviour.

maximize (maximizing, maximized) (*can be spelled with an 's' instead of a 'z'*) If you **maximize** something, you make it as large or extensive as you can. *Industry can no longer maximize its profits by polluting the environment.*

maximum The **maximum** amount of something is the largest amount possible.

may ❏ You use **may** to say something is possible. *He may even be asked to become their candidate for president.* ◇ You also use **may** to say something is allowed. *They may stay as long as they wish.*

❏ You use **may** when saying that, although one thing is true, another contrasting thing is also true. *The setting and exterior may be rural, but the business is a thriving international affair.*

❏ **May** is sometimes used to express a wish that something will happen. *May we have many more projects of this quality.*

May Day is May 1st. It is celebrated as a festival in many countries.

maybe You use **maybe** to say something is possible but you are not certain about it. *Maybe it will happen one day, but not today.* ◇ You also use **maybe** to say that though a comment is possibly true, there is another side to be considered as well. *Maybe the number of medals is not quite what we expected, but there are more countries getting among the medals now.* ◇ You also use **maybe** when you are making a guess at a number or quantity. *Once, maybe 100,000 people would watch a race. Now it's millions.*

mayday A **mayday** message or signal is a radio signal which a ship or plane sends out as a call for help when it is in serious difficulty.

mayhem is an uncontrolled and confused situation.

mayonnaise is a thick creamy dressing made from raw egg yolks, vinegar, and oil. It is usually eaten with salads.

mayor (mayoress, mayoresses; mayoral) The **mayor** of a town is a person elected for a year to lead and represent it. If the mayor is a man, his wife is called the **mayoress**. If the mayor is a woman, she can call herself either the **mayor** or the **mayoress**. **Mayoral** is used to talk about things to do with a mayor or mayoress. *He has pledged to serve out his mayoral term.*

maypole A **maypole** was a tall painted pole which people used to dance around on May Day.

maze A **maze** is a complicated system of paths or passages constructed for people's amusement. It is designed to make it difficult for them to find their way through. ◇ Any network of streets or paths which is difficult to find your way through can be called a **maze**. ◇ A complicated network of ideas or theories can also be called a **maze**.

MBE An MBE is an honour granted by the monarch for a special achievement. MBE stands for 'Member of the Order of the British Empire'.

MC See **Military Cross, Master of Ceremonies.**

McCoy If you describe something as the real **McCoy**, you mean it is the genuine article and not an imitation.

MD ❏ A doctor who has obtained a higher degree in medicine can put MD after his or her name. MD stands for 'Doctor of Medicine'.

❏ The MD of a company is its managing director.

ME is a medical condition involving chronic fatigue and muscular pain. ME stands for 'myalgic encephalomyelitis'. This condition is also called **post-viral syndrome.**

me A speaker or writer uses **me** to talk about himself or herself. *They agree with me.*

mead is an alcoholic drink made of honey, spices, and water.

meadow A **meadow** is a field with grass in it, often used for hay or grazing animals.

meagre (*American spelling:* **meager**) If something is **meagre,** there is very little of it.

meal ❏ A **meal** is (a) an occasion when people eat. (b) the food they eat on that occasion.

❏ **Meal** is the edible part of any grain or pulse which has been ground to a coarse powder.

meals-on-wheels is a service which provides hot meals to old or sick people in their own homes. It is usually organized by the local authority or by the WRVS.

mealtimes are the times when people in a house or institution eat their meals together.

mealy-mouthed If you say someone is being **mealy-mouthed,** you mean they are avoiding talking about something directly, for example because they find it unpleasant.

mean (meaning, meant; meaner, meanest; meanness) ❏ If you talk about the **meaning** of a word or phrase or what it **means,** you are talking about what it refers to or stands for. Similarly, you can talk about the **meaning** of a gesture or signal, or what it **means.** ◇ What a person **means** is what they are trying to tell you when they say or write something.

❏ If something **means** something else is true, the second thing must be true because of the first. *His inability to trust his fellow politicians means that he has never really understood what politics is about.* ◇ If doing something **means** something will happen, it will have that effect. *Taking ingredients from the same source means the beers stay the same.* Similarly, something like a new law can **mean** something will happen. *The ruling means the big stores can no longer break the law with impunity.*

❏ If you **mean** to do something, you intend to do it. ◇ If something is **meant** for a particular purpose, it is intended to be used for that purpose. ◇ If something is **meant** to be a particular thing, it is intended to be that thing. *The film was meant to be a big event comparable with Dr Zhivago.* ◇ You also say something is **meant** to be a particular thing when you are describing its reputation. *Ireland is meant to be a poor country.*

❏ If you **mean** what you say, you are serious about it.

❏ If something has **meaning** for you, it seems to be worthwhile and to have real purpose. Similarly, if something **means** a lot to you, it is very important to you.

❏ A **mean** person is unwilling to spend money on anything. *They were famous for their meanness.*

❏ If someone is **mean** to you, they are cruel or unkind.

❏ **Mean** streets are poor and dirty.

❏ If you say, for example, someone is **no mean** sprinter or **no mean** pianist, you mean they are very good at sprinting or playing the piano. You can also say, for example, that something is **no mean** achievement.

❏ In maths, the **mean** or **arithmetic mean** is the average of a set of numbers. For example, the mean of 5, 9, and 19 is 11.

❏ See also **means**.

meander (*pron:* me-and-er) (meandering, meandered) If a river or road **meanders**, it has a lot of bends. ◇ If you meander through a district, you wander around, not heading for anywhere in particular. ◇ Anything which proceeds without much purpose can be called **meandering**. *...the film's meandering plot.*

meaning See mean.

meaningful (meaningfully) ❏ You say something is **meaningful** when it conveys real information or has a definite meaning. *Gooch spoke meaningfully about the need for radical improvement.* ◇ You call something that happens **meaningful** when it shows there has been a real change, or something has really been achieved. *There was no meaningful progress towards political reform.*

❏ If you give someone a **meaningful** look, you look at them in a way which shows what you feel. **Meaningful** can be used to describe other ways of showing your feelings. *There was a meaningful silence... They winced meaningfully.*

meaningless (meaninglessly) If you say something is **meaningless**, you mean there is no way of understanding it. *...meaningless statements... The figures seem to me to be pretty meaningless.* ◇ You also use **meaningless** to say something is pointless, because it will not achieve anything. *He had been trying to spin the talks meaninglessly out for as long as possible.*

means is used to talk about the amount of money you have for spending on things. For example, if you have **limited means**, you have very little money. If something is **within your means**, you can afford it. If it is **beyond your means**, you cannot afford it. If you are **living beyond your means**, you are spending more money than you can afford, and are running up debts. If, on the other hand, you are **living within your means**, you are spending only the money you actually have, or less.

❏ If you have **the means** to do something, you have the equipment or other things needed for it. ◇ If you do something **by means of** a particular method or object, you do it using that method or object. ◇ If something is a **means to an end**, it is a way of achieving something, rather than something you do for its own sake.

❏ You say **by no means** to emphasize that something is not true. *It is by no means a poor restaurant.* ◇ You say **by all means** to emphasize that it is all right for someone to do something. *By all means let him have his way.*

means test (means-tested) A **means test** is a test in which your income is assessed to see if it is low enough for you to be eligible for certain state grants or benefits. *...means-tested income support.*

meant See mean.

meantime ❏ In the **meantime** means between now and the future event you have just mentioned. *They must get their supporters behind them at the negotiating table, whatev-er outrages occur in the meantime.* ◇ When you are talking about the past, **in the meantime** means in between the events you have just mentioned. *In the meantime, Caitlin had started at secondary school.*

❏ If you say something will do for **the meantime**, you mean it will do till you get something better.

meanwhile is used to say something is happening at the same time as something else. *His efforts to rally his allies are foundering and several of his ministers and advisers have resigned. The public, meanwhile, are lapping up the scandal.* ◇ **Meanwhile** can also mean in the meantime. *One day a new owner or a new use may arrive, but meanwhile Donadea looks reasonably secure.*

measles is an infectious illness which gives you red spots.

measly A **measly** amount of something is very small and inadequate.

measurable If something is **measurable**, it can be measured.

measure (measuring, measured) ❏ If you **measure** something, you find out exactly how big it is or how much of it there is, using an instrument of some kind. ◇ You can say how big something is by saying it **measures** a certain amount. *The Skomer vole measures 170mm from nose to tail.* ◇ If you talk about something like progress being **measured**, you are talking about ways of assessing how good or bad it is. *Performance should be measured over periods of three or even five years.*

❏ If you say something is a **measure** of a certain thing, you mean it is an indication of the extent to which it exists. *This was procedural anarchy, and was a measure of the shambles in the Community's current way of doing business.*

❏ If you get or take the **measure** of someone, you assess their abilities or intentions.

❏ If something **measures up** to people's expectations, it is as good as they were expecting. If something **measures up** to a certain standard, it reaches it.

❏ A **measure** of something is a certain amount or degree of it. *The idea still has a measure of support in the VAT office.* ◇ A **measure** of a drink like brandy or whisky is a standard amount poured into a glass.

❏ **For good measure** means in addition to the things which have already been mentioned. *It needs to become an all-out box office hit, possibly with a few Oscars thrown in for good measure.*

❏ **Measures** are actions taken by people in authority to try to achieve something. *Aggressive cost-cutting measures are also in the pipeline.*

measured behaviour or speech is careful and restrained.

measurement is measuring something. *...the measurement of pollution.* ◇ **Measurements** are the numbers you get when you measure something. ◇ A person's **measurements** are the size of their chest, waist, hips, and other parts of their body.

meat is the flesh of an animal which has been killed so people can cook it and eat it.

meaty (meatier, meatiest) If you say something like a book is **meaty**, you mean it is full of genuinely interesting or useful things. ◇ If you say a part of someone's body is **meaty**, you mean it has a lot of flesh on it. ◇ A **meaty** meal has a lot of meat in it.

Mecca is a city in Saudi Arabia. It is the holiest place in Islam, because the Prophet Mohammed was born there.

❑ If you say a place is a **mecca** for a certain group of people, you mean they go there in large numbers, because there is something which interests or attracts them. *Oahu is the mecca for surfers from the four corners of the earth.*

Meccano is a type of miniature construction set for children. It consists of metal or plastic parts with holes in them, also wheels, nuts, bolts, and other parts. 'Meccano' is a trademark.

mechanic (mechanics) ❑ A **mechanic** is someone whose job is to repair and maintain machines and engines.

❑ If you talk about the **mechanics** of something, you are talking about how it works or is done. *...the mechanics of implementing the agreement.*

❑ **Mechanics** is the branch of science which deals with forces acting on moving or stationary objects.

mechanical (mechanically) ❑ A **mechanical** device is one which has moving parts and uses power from an engine or electricity to do a particular job. ◇ If someone has a **mechanical** mind, they understand how machines work.

❑ A **mechanical** action is done automatically, without thinking about it. *The criteria should not be applied mechanically.*

mechanise See mechanize.

mechanism ❑ A **mechanism** is a part of a machine which does a specific task. *...the locking mechanism.*

❑ A **mechanism** is also a procedure for getting something done. *The party has no mechanism by which to appoint a new leader.*

❑ A **mechanism** is also an instinct in animals and humans which makes them always respond in a certain way to something that happens. *Humans have a huge capacity to shut off the unpleasant as a primitive survival mechanism.*

mechanistic A **mechanistic** view is one which tries to explain all human behaviour in terms of biological and physical causes.

mechanize (mechanizing, mechanized; mechanization) *(can be spelled with an 's' instead of a 'z')* When a type of work is **mechanized**, machines are introduced to do things previously done by hand. *Can African farmers increase production without mechanization?*

medal A **medal** is a small metal disc given as an award for bravery or as a prize in a sporting event.

medalist See medallist.

medallion A **medallion** is a round metal disc worn as an ornament on a chain round someone's neck.

medallist (*or* medalist) A **medallist** is a person who has won a medal in a sporting event.

meddle (meddling, meddled; meddler, meddlesome) If someone **meddles** in something, they try to influence or change it without being asked to. You call someone who behaves like this a **meddler** or say they are being **meddlesome**.

media ❑ Television, radio, and newspapers are often called the **media**. A **media** event is one specially staged for the media.

❑ See also medium.

mediaeval See medieval.

median The **median** value of a set of values is the middle one when they are arranged in order.

mediate (mediating, mediated; mediation, mediator) If someone **mediates** between two people or groups, they try to help them settle a dispute. Trying to help in this way is called **mediation;** a person who does it is called a **mediator**.

medic A **medic** is a doctor or a medical student.

Medicaid is a government scheme in the US which provides health care for people on low incomes.

medical (medically) **Medical** is used to describe things connected with the treatment of illness or injury. *...medical equipment... The water has medically attested curative powers.* ◇ A **medical** is a thorough examination of your body by a doctor.

medicament A **medicament** is a medicine or ointment.

Medicare In the US, **Medicare** is a government scheme which provides health insurance for the over-65s. In Canada and Australia, **Medicare** is a similar scheme for all citizens.

medication is the medicine someone takes or is given.

medicinal If something has **medicinal** properties, it can be used to treat illness.

medicine is the treatment of illness and injury by doctors and nurses. *He gave up medicine and retired to the country.* ◇ A **medicine** is a substance you drink or swallow to cure an illness.

medieval (*or* mediaeval) (*pron:* med-ee-eve-al) The **medieval** period in European history began with the end of the Western Roman Empire in 476 AD and ended about 1500 AD. **Medieval** is used to talk about things to do with this period. *Bristol evolved gradually from its medieval origins.*

mediocre (*pron:* mee-dee-oak-er *or* mee-dee-oak-er) (mediocrity, mediocrities) If you call something **mediocre** or talk about its **mediocrity** (*pron:* mee-dee-ok-rit-ee), you mean it is not particularly good. ◇ A **mediocre** person has no outstanding qualities or skills. People like this are sometimes called **mediocrities**.

meditate (meditating, meditated; meditation) ❑ If you **meditate** on something, you think about it carefully and deeply for a long time. A **meditation** on something is a piece of writing which examines it in a careful and thoughtful way.

❑ If you **meditate**, you stay in a calm silent state of concentration for a period of time, especially as part of religious training or practice. Being in this state is called **meditation**.

meditative is used to describe things to do with meditation. *...the Chinese meditative practice of taichi.*

❑ If someone is **meditative**, they are thinking deeply about something. **Meditative** is also used to describe things people say or write as a result of deep thought. *...meditative poetry.*

Mediterranean The **Mediterranean** is the area surrounding the Mediterranean Sea, the sea between Europe and North Africa. ◇ **Mediterranean** is used to describe things thought to be typical of this area. *...Mediterranean flamboyance... The man is said to be of Mediterranean appearance.*

medium is used to describe things which are about halfway between two extremes. For example, if something is medium-sized, it is neither large nor small. ◇ If you talk about what happens in the **medium term**, you are talking about what happens in the next few months or years, in contrast to what will happen immediately or in the distant future.

❑ A **medium** (*plural:* media) is a means of communicating, expressing, or teaching something. *In the National University of Singapore, English was the medium of instruction.* See also **media.**

❑ A **medium** (*plural:* mediums) is a person who claims to be able to communicate with people who have died.

medium wave is used to talk about the range of radio waves from 100 to 1,000 metres.

medley ❑ A **medley** is a selection of tunes or songs played one after another as a continuous piece of music.

❑ A **medley** is also a swimming race in which each competitor must use the four main strokes one after another. In a **medley relay,** different swimmers do the different strokes.

❑ Any assortment of different things can be called a **medley,** especially when they produce an odd or interesting effect together. *The port city is a raucous medley of sights and sounds.*

meek (meekly) A **meek** person is gentle and quiet and usually does what other people tell them to. *They are no longer willing meekly to surrender to more powerful opponents.*

meet (meeting, met) ❑ If you **meet** someone, either a stranger or someone you already know, you happen to be in the same place and start talking to them. ◇ If you arrange to **meet** someone, you arrange to be in the same place at the same time, so you can do something together. ◇ When people have a meeting, you can say they **meet.** ◇ In sport, when two players or teams **meet,** they compete against each other. ◇ If you **meet** someone who is arriving from somewhere or **meet** their train, plane, or bus, you go to the station, airport, or bus stop to be there when they arrive.

❑ If something **meets** a need, it is what is wanted. If it **meets** a requirement, it is good enough or large enough to be acceptable. *56 per cent of France's sea-water bathing spots met EU standards.* ◇ If you **meet** a problem or a challenge, you deal with it satisfactorily. ◇ If you **meet** the cost of something, you pay for it.

❑ If something **meets** or **meets with** a particular reaction, that is how people react to it. ◇ If you **meet with** something like an accident or setback, it happens to you. ◇ If someone **meets** their death or fate, they die.

❑ The place where two things **meet** is the place where they join or come into contact.

❑ If your eyes **meet** someone else's, you happen to look at each other at the same time.

❑ If there is more to something than **meets the eye,** it is not as simple or straightforward as it seems.

❑ **make ends meet:** see **end.**

meeting ❑ A **meeting** is an occasion when people get together to discuss things and make decisions. The people at a meeting can be called the **meeting.** *He advised the meeting not to pay any attention to negative media coverage.*

❑ A **meeting** is also an occasion when you meet someone, such as a friend. A **meeting place** is somewhere where people meet each other regularly.

mega- at the beginning of a unit of measurement means it is a million times greater than another unit. For example, a megawatt is 1,000,000 watts. ◇ **Mega-** is added to other words to say something is very large or important. *Valium became the drug industry's first mega-hit.*

megabyte Computer memory is often expressed in **megabytes.** A megabyte is 1,048,576 bytes. 'Megabytes' is usually written 'Mb'.

megahertz (*plural:* megahertz) The frequency of radio waves is often expressed in **megahertz.** One megahertz is 1,000,000 cycles per second. 'Megahertz' is usually written 'MHz'.

megalith (megalithic) A **megalith** is a very large upright stone or group of stones, thought to have been placed in its present position in prehistoric times. **Megalithic** is used to talk about things connected with stones like these. *...the megalithic site of Lagatjar.*

megalomaniac (megalomania) If you call someone a **megalomaniac** or talk about their **megalomania,** you mean they do things just because of the feeling of power it gives them. ◇ **Megalomania** is also a form of mental illness in which someone believes they are much more powerful than they really are.

megaphone A **megaphone** is a cone-shaped device for making your voice sound louder in the open air.

megaton The explosive power of a nuclear weapon is often expressed in **megatons.** One megaton is equal to the explosive power of 1,000,000 tons of TNT.

megawatt Power is often expressed in **megawatts.** A megawatt is 1,000,000 watts. 'Megawatts' is usually written 'MW'.

melancholy (melancholic) **Melancholy** is an intense feeling of sadness. If you are **melancholy** or **melancholic,** you feel like this. ◇ You say something like a story is **melancholy** or **melancholic** when it deals with sad things.

mélange (*pron:* may-lanzh; *the 'zh' sounds like 's' in pleasure*) A **mélange** is a mixture of people or things. *The libretto is a mysterious mélange of folk tales and magic motifs.*

melanoma (*pron:* mel-a-**nome**-a) is a malignant form of skin cancer. The tumour is marked by an irregular dark blotch on the skin.

meld If you **meld** a number of things together, you unite or combine them.

mêlée (*pron:* mel-lay) A **mêlée** is a crowd of people rushing about in different directions doing different things. ◇ A **mêlée** is also a riot or fight.

mellifluous A **mellifluous** voice or sound is very pleasant to listen to.

mellow colours are soft and gentle. ◇ **Mellow** stone or wood has an attractive soft colour, because it is old. ◇ **Mellow** music is smooth and pleasant to listen to.

❑ If someone **mellows** or if something **mellows** them, they become gentler and more relaxed, or less extreme in their opinions.

melodious A **melodious** sound is pleasant to listen to.

melodrama (melodramatic, melodramatically) A **melodrama** is a story or play in which a lot of dramatic and sensational things happen and people behave in an exaggerated and emotional way. Anything in fiction or real life which has features like this can be called **melodramatic.** *...a melodramatic tale... ...his early death, in melodramatic circumstances.* ◇ If you are being **melodramatic** about something, you are treating it as much more serious or dangerous than it really is. *He talked melodramatically about the need to combat an American plot.*

melody (melodies; melodic) A **melody** is a tune. **Melodic** is used to talk about things to do with writing tunes.

...*melodic invention*... ...*melodic ideas.* A **melodic** piece of music has a definite tune or tunes in it.

melon Melons are large juicy fruit with yellow or green skins and a lot of seeds.

melt ❑ When a solid substance **melts** or is **melted**, it changes to a liquid, because it has been heated. ◇ If you **melt down** a metal or glass object, you heat it until it becomes liquid.
  ❑ If something **melts** or **melts away**, it gradually disappears. *The crowd melted away.*

meltdown If there is a **meltdown**, the core of a nuclear reactor overheats until it melts, sometimes causing the supporting base to melt too. ◇ Any sudden dramatic collapse in a system can be called a **meltdown**. *Germany and Britain appeared to be heading towards meltdown in their deteriorating relations.*

melting pot A **melting pot** is a place or situation where people, cultures, and ideas of different kinds get mixed together. *Central Asia was the great melting pot of the world in ancient times.*

member ❑ A **member** of a group is one of the people or things belonging to it. ◇ If you become a **member** of an organization, you join it. ◇ The states or countries which have joined an international organization are called the **member** states or countries.
  ❑ The **member** for a place is its MP.

Member of Parliament See **MP**.

membership of an organization is belonging to it. *He was stripped of his party membership.* ◇ The **membership** of an organization is (a) the people who belong to it. *Documents were distributed to the entire membership.* (b) the number of people who belong to it. *In a year, membership has grown to 34.*

membrane A **membrane** is a thin piece of skin which covers or connects parts of a person's or animal's body.

memento (mementoes *or* mementos) A **memento** is an object you keep to remind you of a person or special occasion.

memento mori (*pron:* more-ee) A **memento mori** is something which reminds you of death or mortality.

memo (memos) A **memo** is an official note someone sends to a person, or to several people, within the same organization. 'Memo' is short for 'memorandum'.

memoir A person's **memoirs** are a book they have written about people they have known and events they remember. ◇ A **memoir** is a book or article about a well-known person written by someone who knew them well.

memorabilia are things you collect because they are connected with a person, organization, or event that interests you. *The wall is covered in Presley memorabilia.*

memorable (memorably) **Memorable** things are likely to be remembered because they are special or unusual. *The National Theatre's production is memorably staged.*

memorandum (*plural:* memoranda *or* memorandums) A **memorandum** is (a) a written report prepared for a person or committee. (b) an informal diplomatic communication from one government to another. ◇ See also **memo**.

memorial A **memorial** is a structure built to remind people of a famous person or event, or of people who have died in a war or disaster. ◇ A **memorial** event is held in honour of someone who has died. ...*a memorial Requiem Mass.* ◇ If something someone achieved continues to be remembered after their death, you can say it is a **memorial** to them.

Memorial Day In the US, **Memorial Day** is a public holiday, usually at the end of May, when Americans who have been killed in wars are remembered.

memorize (memorizing, memorized) (*can be spelled with an 's' instead of a 'z'*) If you **memorize** a piece of writing, you learn it by heart, so you can remember it without having to look at it again.

memory (memories) ❑ Your **memory** is your ability to remember things. If you **lose your memory**, you forget things you used to know. ◇ If you repeat something like a poem **from memory**, you do it without looking at anything written or printed.
  ❑ A **memory** is something you remember from the past. ◇ If something has happened **in living memory**, there are still people alive who remember it.
  ❑ If you do something **in memory** of someone who has died, you do it to show you remember them.
  ❑ A computer's **memory** is its capacity to store information.

men See **man**.

menace (menacing, menaced; menacingly) ❑ If you call something a **menace**, you mean it is likely to cause serious harm. *Excessive drinking is a social menace.*
  ❑ If someone **menaces** you, they threaten to harm you. You can call their behaviour **menacing**. *He dropped menacing hints about 'retaliatory measures'... A group of men suddenly emerged from a doorway and moved menacingly forward.* ◇ **Menace** is something in a person's behaviour or the atmosphere of a place which seems dangerous or threatening. *There is a real feeling of menace on the streets.*
  ❑ You also call someone or something a **menace** when they are a nuisance.

ménage (*pron:* may-nazh; *the 'zh' sounds like 's' in pleasure*) A **ménage** is a group of people living together in one house.

ménage à trois (*pron:* may-nazh ah twah) You call three people a **ménage à trois** when they live together and one of them is having a sexual relationship with both the others.

menagerie (*pron:* min-naj-er-ee) A **menagerie** is a collection of wild animals.

mend ❑ If you **mend** something which is damaged or broken, you repair it.
  ❑ If you are **on the mend**, you are recovering after an illness or injury. If a situation is **on the mend**, it is improving after a difficult period. *Relations with Moscow are on the mend.*
  ❑ If someone who has been behaving badly **mends their ways**, they start to behave better.
  ❑ If you try to **mend fences** with someone, you try to restore a friendly relationship after a dispute or quarrel.

mendacious (mendacity) A **mendacious** statement or remark is not truthful. **Mendacity** is telling lies.

menfolk When women talk about their **menfolk**, they mean the men in their family or community.

menial work is boring and tiring, and is regarded as having low status.

meningitis is a serious infectious illness which causes

inflammation of the membranes surrounding the brain and the spinal cord. It can be caused by a virus or by bacteria.

menopause (menopausal) The **menopause** is the time when a woman stops having periods, usually when she is about fifty. **Menopausal** is used to talk about things to do with this time. *Spinal fractures are one of the main symptoms of osteoporosis in post-menopausal women.*

menstruate (menstruating, menstruated; menstrual, menstruation) When a woman **menstruates**, blood comes from her womb. Women who are fertile menstruate once a month unless they are pregnant. **Menstrual** is used to talk about things to do with menstruation. *The length of menstrual cycles can be affected by stress, jet-lag, and illness.*

menswear is men's clothing.

mental (mentally) ❑ **Mental** is used to talk about things to do with the mind and the process of thinking. *He is a man of mental as well as physical courage.* ◇ **Mental** is also used to talk about the health of a person's mind. *...mental illness... ...mentally disturbed prisoners.*

❑ If you are **mentally** performing an action, you are not actually doing it but are having the kind of thoughts associated with it. *...mentally rubbing their hands at the prospect of fortunes.*

mental hospital A **mental hospital** is a hospital for people suffering from mental illness.

mentality (mentalities) A person's **mentality** is their attitudes or ways of thinking.

menthol is a substance which smells like peppermint. It is used in cough and cold medicines and in cigarettes.

mention (mentioning, mentioned) ❑ If you **mention** something, you say something about it, usually briefly. ◇ A **mention** is a reference to someone or something. *Economic pundits tremble at the mere mention of his name.*

❑ You use **not to mention** when adding something which makes what you are saying even more emphatic. *He has shown both insensitivity and poor judgement, not to mention ignorance.*

mentor Your **mentor** is someone who teaches you and gives you advice.

menu A **menu** is a list of the food you can order in a restaurant.

MEP An **MEP** is a person who has been elected to the European Parliament. MEP stands for 'Member of the European Parliament'.

mercantile is used to talk about things to do with merchants and trading. *...the mercantile system... ...mercantile wealth.*

mercenary (mercenaries) **Mercenaries** are soldiers paid to fight for a country or group they do not belong to. ◇ If you say someone is **mercenary**, you mean they will only do something if they are paid to do it.

merchandise is goods which are bought, sold, or traded.

merchandizing is (a) producing a range of goods closely connected with someone or something famous, for example a popular film. (b) promoting sales generally.

merchant A **merchant** is someone who buys or sells goods in large quantities, especially someone who imports and exports goods.

merchant bank A **merchant bank** is a bank which deals mainly with businesses and investment.

merchant navy A country's **merchant navy** consists of its

merchant ships and the people who man them.

merchant ship A **merchant ship** is a ship which carries cargo and sometimes passengers.

merciful (mercifully) ❑ A **merciful** person is kind and forgiving to people in their power.

❑ You say something that happens is **merciful** when it puts an end to suffering. For example, death is sometimes described as **merciful** when it happens to someone who is incurably ill and in great pain.

❑ **Mercifully** is used to express pleasure or relief that something unpleasant does not exist, or has been stopped or avoided. *Crime is mercifully rare here.*

merciless (mercilessly) A **merciless** person is cruel and shows no pity. *He mercilessly exploited the government's handling of the sterling crisis.*

mercurial If you say someone is **mercurial**, you mean they change their mind or mood often and without warning.

mercury is a heavy silvery-white liquid metal which is highly toxic. It is used in thermometers, barometers, and dental work.

mercy (mercies) ❑ If someone shows **mercy**, they show kindness and forgiveness and do not punish someone as severely as they could. ◇ If you **throw** yourself **on** someone's **mercy**, you appeal to them to help you or show forgiveness, when there are good reasons why they should not do so. ◇ If you are at someone's **mercy**, they have complete power over you.

❑ If you say someone who has had a misfortune should be **thankful for small mercies,** you mean they are lucky not to be in an even worse situation.

mercy killing is painlessly killing someone who is very ill to stop them suffering any more.

mercy mission If someone goes on a **mercy mission**, they try to rescue hostages or help people who are trapped in a war zone.

mere (merest) **Mere** is used to emphasize how small or unimportant something is, or how few of something there are. *The beach failed a mere three tests... This time there was not the merest hint of dissent.* **Mere** is often used to say something small or unimportant has a surprisingly strong effect. *She was so close to the edge that the merest pressure was enough to send her over.*

merely You use **merely** to emphasize that something is only what you say, and not something bigger, better, or more important. *The time difference between the drivers is merely a tenth of a second.* You say something is not **merely** a certain thing before going on to say it is really something more serious or important. *Recurrent or perpetual noise is not merely an inconvenience, but a nightmare.*

meretricious If something is **meretricious**, it seems attractive on the surface but has little real value.

merge (merging, merged; merger) When one organization is **merged** with another one, they are joined together to form a single organization. You call this a **merger** of the two organizations. ◇ If things which are next to each other **merge**, they are so similar you cannot distinguish one from the other.

meringue (*pron:* mer-rang) A **meringue** is a type of crisp sweet food made with sugar and whipped egg white.

merit (meriting, merited) ❑ If something has **merit**, it is good or worthwhile. ◇ The **merits** of something are its advantages or good qualities. If you judge something **on its merits**, you judge it according to its own qualities, and ignore any other factors.

❑ If something **merits** particular treatment, it is good enough or important enough to be treated that way. ◇ If someone **merits** a prize or position, they deserve it.

meritocracy (meritocracies; meritocratic) A **meritocracy** is a social system in which people have power or prestige because of their intelligence and abilities, rather than because of their wealth or social status. You say a system like this is **meritocratic.**

meritorious If something is **meritorious**, it has qualities which make it good or worthwhile.

mermaid In stories and legends, a **mermaid** is a woman with a fish's tail instead of legs, who lives in the sea.

merrily See merry.

merriment If something causes **merriment**, it makes people laugh.

merry (merrier, merriest; merrily) ❑ **Merry** is used to describe things which are happy and cheerful. *...merry reminiscences... He always laughs merrily over the documentary.* ◇ **Merry** can also mean slightly drunk. *He became merrier as the evening advanced.*

❑ **Merrily** is used to say something is done without people thinking properly about it or about the problems involved. *Government spending has gone on merrily unchecked, driving inflation well into four digits.*

merry-go-round A **merry-go-round** is a large revolving platform with models of animals or vehicles on it, which children can ride on. ◇ If you call a situation a **merry-go-round**, you mean a lot of things are happening and procedures are being followed, but nothing very much is being achieved.

merry-making is enjoying yourself in a happy way with other people, by doing such things as singing, dancing, or drinking.

mesh (meshes, meshing, meshed) ❑ **Mesh** is a net-like material made from wire, thread, or plastic.

❑ You say things like gears **mesh** when they operate by fitting precisely into each other. ◇ You talk about other things **meshing** when they correspond exactly. *This story never quite meshed with the facts.*

❑ If people **mesh** two systems or organizations, they get them to combine and operate as a single one.

mesmeric If something is **mesmeric**, it holds your attention as if you were being hypnotised.

mesmerize (mesmerizing, mesmerized) (*can be spelled with an 's' instead of a 'z'*) If you are **mesmerized** by something, you are so fascinated by it that your judgement is affected. *The Chancellor appealed to Britain's EU partners not to be mesmerized by the notion of a single currency.* ◇ If something is **mesmerizing**, it is so fascinating that it holds your attention completely.

Mesolithic (*pron: mess-o-lith-ik*) The **Mesolithic** period was the middle period of the Stone Age. In Europe, it began about 8000BC. In this period, people were hunters and fishermen and first began using boats. See also **Palaeolithic, Neolithic.**

mess (messes, messing, messed) ❑ A **mess** is dirt or stains or a lot of things left lying around in an untidy way. ◇ If a place is very untidy, dirty, or disorganized, it can be called a **mess.** ◇ If you call a situation a **mess**, you

mean things have gone badly wrong and it is difficult to see how they can be put right.

❑ If you **mess about** or **mess around**, you do things without any particular aim, and without achieving anything. ◇ If you **mess with** something or **mess about** with it, you interfere with it and make it worse than it was before. ◇ If you **mess** something **up**, you spoil it.

❑ If you **mess** someone **around** or **mess** them **about**, you treat them badly, for example by not being honest with them, or by continually changing plans which affect them.

❑ A **mess** is also a room or building where members of the armed forces eat.

message ❑ A **message** is a piece of information or a request which you send to someone, or leave for them.

❑ The **message** in a speech or piece of writing is what the speaker or writer is trying to convey. ◇ If a set of facts suggest that something is true, this can also be called a **message.** *The Community should heed the message of this survey.*

messenger A **messenger** is a person who takes a message to someone, or delivers messages as their job.

messiah ❑ For Jews, the **Messiah** is a king or leader promised in their holy writings, by God. ◇ For Christians, the **Messiah** is Jesus Christ.

❑ Someone who promises to rescue, or succeeds in rescuing, people from a difficult or dangerous situation can be called a **messiah.** *They were not now sure if he would be the messiah to take them out of their economic woes.*

messianic is used to describe things connected with the belief that a divine being has been born, or will be born, who will change the world. *Jesus' appreciation of his messianic task is repeatedly found in the gospels.* ◇ **Messianic** is also used to describe beliefs that something is destined to happen to a nation or group of people. *He instilled a messianic Maoist vision in his followers.*

Messrs (*pron: mess-erz*) is used before the names of two or more men, often as part of the name of a business. *...Messrs Lindt & Sprungli.*

messy (messily) ❑ **Messy** things are dirty or untidy. *Custard slopped messily onto the cloth.* ◇ A **messy** person or activity makes things dirty or untidy.

❑ A **messy** situation is confused or complicated and makes trouble for people.

met See meet.

Met See Metropolitan Police.

metabolise See metabolize.

metabolism (*pron: met-tab-oh-liz-zum*) (metabolic) Your **metabolism** is the chemical process in your body which causes food to be absorbed and used for growth and energy. **Metabolic** (*pron: met-tab-bol-lik*) is used to talk about things to do with this process. *This explains why cold-water creatures have such a low metabolic rate.*

metabolize (metabolizing, metabolized) (*can be spelled with an 's' instead of a 'z'*) When you **metabolize** a substance you have eaten, your body breaks it down chemically so it can be used for growth and energy.

metacarpal The **metacarpals** are the five bones connecting the wrist to the fingers.

metal is a substance which has special properties, such as being a good conductor of heat and electricity. Some metals are chemical elements, for example iron, steel, copper, and lead; others are alloys, such as steel and brass.

metal fatigue If something suffers from **metal fatigue**, the metal has been weakened by repeated movement and might break.

metallic things are made of metal. ◇ A **metallic** sound is like one piece of metal hitting another. ◇ **Metallic** colours shine like metal.

metallurgy (metallurgical, metallurgist) **Metallurgy** is the science and technology of extracting metals from their ores and preparing them for use. A **metallurgist** is an expert on this. **Metallurgical** is used to describe things connected with the refining of metals. ...*metallurgical research...* ...*metallurgical industries.*

metalwork is making things out of metal as a craft or hobby. **Metalwork** is also things made out of metal in this way. *The Armenian pottery and metalwork sold well.*

metamorphose (metamorphosing, metamorphosed; metamorphosis) When something **metamorphoses** or is **metamorphosed,** it changes to something completely different. A change like this is called a **metamorphosis** (*plural:* metamorphoses). *The building's metamorphosis into a visitors' centre could scarcely have been more successful.*

metaphor (metaphorical, metaphorically) A **metaphor** is a way of describing something by calling it something else which has a well-known quality or characteristic. For example, if you have to deal with something which is full of hidden problems and dangers, you can call it a minefield. This is called a **metaphorical** use of language. Sometimes when people are using a metaphor, they add **metaphorical** or **metaphorically** to what they are saying. *The aging Queen Mary may be heading for the metaphorical rocks unless a buyer can be found... Metaphorically speaking, the tide appears to be turning against the SRU.*

metaphysics (metaphysical) **Metaphysics** is the part of philosophy which deals with theories about what exists and how we know it exists. **Metaphysical** is used to talk about things connected with these theories. ...*metaphysical ideas about life.*

mete (meting, meted) The kind of punishment or treatment **meted out** to someone is the kind they receive.

meteor A **meteor** is a piece of rock or metal which burns very brightly when it enters the Earth's atmosphere from space and is seen from Earth as a bright star travelling very fast across the sky. Meteors are often called 'shooting stars'.

meteoric A **meteoric** success or rise to power happens very quickly.

meteorite A **meteorite** is a piece of rock or metal which lands on Earth from space. Meteorites have to be large enough to survive burning as they pass through the Earth's atmosphere.

meteorology (meteorologist, meteorological) **Meteorology** is the study of the processes in the Earth's atmosphere which cause weather conditions. A **meteorologist** is someone who studies and interprets these processes. **Meteorological** is used to describe things connected with the weather and weather forecasting. ...*meteorological conditions.*

meter (metering, metered) ❑ A **meter** is a device which measures and records something such as the amount of gas or electricity you use. When something is measured

and recorded in this way, you say it is **metered**.
  ❑ See also **metre**.

methane is a colourless flammable gas which has no smell. Natural gas consists mainly of methane.

methanol is a colourless flammable poisonous liquid. It is used as an antifreeze, a solvent, and a fuel.

method A **method** is a particular way of doing something.

methodical (methodically) A **methodical** person does things carefully and in a logical order. *At every stage he was given a complicated task which he tackled methodically.*

Methodist (Methodism) **Methodists** are Protestants who follow the teachings of John Wesley. They have their own branch of the Christian church and their own form of worship. Their beliefs and practices are called **Methodism**. **Methodist** is used to describe things connected with this Church. ...*Methodist publications.*

methodology A **methodology** is a system of methods and principles for doing something, for example for teaching or carrying out research.

meths is the same as methylated spirit.

methylated spirit is a poisonous liquid made from alcohol and other chemicals. It is used as a solvent and a fuel.

meticulous (meticulously) A **meticulous** person does things very carefully and with great attention to detail. *The details of every stag and hind culled have been meticulously recorded.*

métier (*pron:* met-ee-ay) Your **métier** is the type of work for which you have a natural talent or ability.

metre (*American spelling:* meter) ❑ Distance is often expressed in **metres**. A metre is 100 centimetres (about 39.4 inches). 'Metres' is usually written 'm'.
  ❑ In poetry, **metre** is the regular and rhythmic arrangement of words and syllables.

metric The **metric** system is the system which uses metres, centimetres, kilograms, and litres. These units are called **metric** units. See also imperial.

metric ton Heavy weights are sometimes expressed in **metric tons**. A metric ton is 1,000 kilograms (about 2,200 pounds). Metric tons are also called **tonnes**.

metrication is the process of changing from measuring things in imperial units to measuring them in metric units.

metro Some cities, for example Paris, Moscow, and Newcastle, have an underground railway system called the **metro**.

metronome A **metronome** is a device sometimes used by musicians to help them play a piece at the right speed. It has an arm which swings from side to side, making a regular clicking sound. The arm can be adjusted to swing at different speeds.

metropolis (metropolises) A **metropolis** is a very large city, especially a country's capital city.

metropolitan is used to talk about things relating to a large busy city. *He will be responsible for investigating fraud in the metropolitan area.*

Metropolitan Police The **Metropolitan Police** is the part of the British police force which operates in London (except in the City, which has its own police force). The Metropolitan Police is often called 'the Met'.

mettle is used to talk about people being made to show how good they are at handling something. You say, for example that something 'tests their mettle' or 'puts them on their mettle'. If someone shows they are capable of handling something well, you can say they 'show their mettle' or 'prove their mettle'.

mews A mews is a yard or street surrounded by houses which were originally built as stables.

mezzanine (*pron:* mez-zan-neen) A **mezzanine** floor is a partial floor built between two storeys in a building.

mezzo-soprano (*pron:* met-so) A **mezzo-soprano** or **mezzo** is a female singer who sings with a higher range than a contralto but a lower range than a soprano.

MFN See most-favoured-nation.

mg See milligrams.

Mgr in front of a priest's name stands for 'Monsignor' or 'Monseigneur'.

MHz See megahertz.

MI5 is a British government organization which is concerned with protecting important secrets and frustrating the activities of foreign agents. Its official title is 'The Security Service'.

MI6 is a British government organization which tries to obtain secret information about the political and military affairs of other countries. Its official title is 'The Secret Intelligence Service'.

miasma (*pron:* mee-az-ma) A **miasma** is an unpleasant or unhealthy atmosphere caused by decaying things.

mica (*pron:* my-kah) is a hard mineral which can be split into thin sheets. It has a great resistance to heat and electricity.

mice See mouse.

Michaelmas (*pron:* mik-kl-mass) is a Christian festival celebrated on the 29th of September in honour of the archangel Michael.

mickey If you **take the mickey** out of someone, you make fun of them.

micro A micro is the same as a microcomputer.

micro- is used at the beginning of words to talk about very small versions of things. ...*micro-nutrients.*

microbe (microbial) Microbes are very small living things like bacteria and viruses, which you can only see with a microscope. Microbial is used to talk about things to do with microbes. ...*microbial contamination.*

microbiology (microbiologist, microbiological) Microbiology is the study of microbes and their effects on other forms of life. A microbiologist is an expert on this. Microbiological is used to talk about things to do with this subject. ...*the Microbiological Research Centre.*

microchip A microchip is a small piece of silicon inside a computer with electronic circuits printed on it.

microcomputer A microcomputer is a small computer, usually used by one person in a small business, a school, or the home.

microcosm If you say a place or event is a microcosm of a larger one, you mean it has all the main features of the larger one and seems like a smaller version of it.

microeconomics (microeconomic) Microeconomics is the study of the economics of a small-scale system, for example a family, a small business, or a single industry. Microeconomic theories or policies are concerned with small-scale systems like these. See also macroeconomics.

microelectronics (microelectronic) Microelectronics is the branch of electronics which deals with very small circuits and components. Microelectronic devices are made up of these very small components.

microfiche (*pron:* my-kro-feesh) A microfiche is a small sheet of film on which information is stored in very small print. Microfiches are read on special machines which magnify them.

microfilm is film used for photographing information and storing it on reels in a reduced form. It can then be read on a machine which magnifies it. If you microfilm maps or documents, you reproduce them on microfilm.

micrometre (*American spelling:* micrometer) A micrometre is the same as a micron.

micron Very small distances are often expressed in microns. A micron is one millionth of a metre.

microorganism A microorganism is the same as a microbe.

microphone A microphone is a device for picking up sounds so that they can be amplified or recorded.

microprocessor A microprocessor is a microchip which can be programmed to do a large number of tasks or calculations, for example in a digital watch or a calculator.

microscope A microscope is an instrument which magnifies very small objects so they can be studied.

microscopic (microscopically) If something is microscopic, it is very small and can usually only be seen through a microscope. ...*a microscopically thin layer of tissue.* ◇ A microscopic examination of something is very detailed.

microsurgery is intricate surgery using a microscope and very small instruments.

microwave (microwaving, microwaved) ❑ A microwave or microwave oven is a cooker which cooks food very quickly using short-wave radiation rather than heat. If you microwave food, you cook it in this kind of oven.
  ❑ Microwaves are a type of electromagnetic radiation within the wavelength range 0.3 to 0.001 metres. Microwaves are used in telecommunications, in radar, and in cooking.

mid is used to talk about the middle part of a region or period of time. ...*mid-Wales.... ...mid September.*

mid-air If something happens in mid-air, it happens in the air rather than on the ground.

mid-life The mid-life crisis is a crisis of self-confidence which sometimes affects people who have just reached middle age and are worried about getting old.

mid-point See midpoint.

mid-term If something happens mid-term, it happens in the middle of a fixed period such as a school term or a political term of office.

mid-town See midtown.

Mid-west (Mid-western) (or Midwest, Midwestern) The Midwest is the northern central part of the US. Midwestern is used to talk about things to do with the Mid-West. ...*the Mid-Western state of Minnesota.*

mid-winter (or midwinter) is the period in the middle of the winter.

midday is the same as noon. ◇ Midday is used to describe things which happen at noon or in the middle part of the day. ...*midday meals*.

middle ❑ The **middle** of something is the part farthest from its edges, ends, or outside surface. ◇ The **middle** thing in a row or series is the one with an equal number of things on each side of it, or an equal number before it and after it. ◇ Your **middle** is the front part of your body at your waist.

❑ The **middle** of an event or period of time comes between the early part and the final part. ◇ If you are **in the middle** of doing something, you are busy doing it.

❑ If you take a **middle** course, you choose a moderate course of action which lies between two extremes.

❑ Someone's **middle name** is the name between their first name and surname. ◇ If you say a quality is someone's **middle name**, you mean it is a major part of their character. *Discretion is my middle name*.

middle age (middle-aged) **Middle age** is the middle part of a person's life, when they are neither old nor young. **Middle-aged** people are this age.

Middle Ages In European history, the **Middle Ages** was the period between the end of the Western Roman Empire in 476 AD and about 1500 AD.

middle-brow (*or* middlebrow) people are educated but have limited or conventional tastes. **Middle-brow** programmes and newspapers are aimed at people like these.

middle-class (middle classes) The **middle classes** are people who are neither working class nor upper class, for example managers, doctors, and lawyers. **Middle-class** attitudes are thought to be typical of people like these.

middle distance In athletics, **middle-distance** races are races like the 800 metres, the 1,500 metres, and the mile. ◇ The **middle distance** in a view or painting is the area between the foreground and the distance.

Middle East The **Middle East** consists of Iran and the countries in Asia to the west and south-west of Iran. **Middle Eastern** is used to talk about things to do with these countries. ...*Middle Eastern oil*.

middle-of-the-road political views are moderate, rather than extreme.

middle school A **middle school** is for children from the age of 8 or 9 to the age of 12 or 13.

middlebrow See middle-brow.

middleman (middlemen) A **middleman** is someone who buys things from the people who produce them and re-sells them at a profit. ◇ A **middleman** is also someone who acts as an intermediary between the parties in a dispute.

middling things are of average level or quality.

midfield (midfielder) In football, the **midfield** is the part of the pitch about halfway between the two goalmouths. A **midfielder** or **midfield** player is a player who normally plays in this part of the pitch.

midge Midges are very small flying insects which bite.

midget A **midget** is a very small person. ◇ **Midget** is used to describe other things which are very small. ...*a midget submarine*.

midi system A **midi system** is a small hi-fi system made in a single unit, rather than as a number of separate pieces.

midnight is 12 o'clock in the middle of the night. **Midnight** is used to describe things which happen at mid-

night or in the middle of the night. ...*midnight phone calls*.

midpoint (*or* mid-point) The **midpoint** of a line is the point which is an equal distance from each end. You can also talk about the **midpoint** of a scale. ◇ The **midpoint** of an event or period of time is the point halfway between the beginning and the end.

midriff Your **midriff** is the middle of your body, particularly your waist and the area just above it.

midshipman (midshipmen) A **midshipman** is an officer of the lowest rank in the Royal Navy.

midst If you are **in the midst** of doing something, you have started doing it and have not yet finished. ◇ If something happens **in the midst** of an event, it happens during it. ◇ If you are **in the midst** of a group of people, you are among them or surrounded by them.

midstream is the middle of a river, where the current is strongest. ◇ If you say someone is **changing horses in midstream**, you mean they are changing to a different objective from the one they have had up to now.

midsummer is the period in the middle of the summer.

Midsummer's Day is the 24th of June.

midtown (*or* mid-town) is the central part of a city. ...*the midtown financial district*.

midway If something is **midway** between two places, it is between them and roughly the same distance from each. ◇ If something happens **midway** through an event or period of time, it happens during the middle part of it.

midweek is used to talk about things happening in the middle of a week. *A midweek Gallup poll found a majority wanted him to resign*.

Midwest (Midwestern) See Mid-west.

midwife (midwives; midwifery) A **midwife** is a specially qualified nurse who advises pregnant women and helps them give birth. **Midwifery** (*pron:* mid-wiff-er-ree) is the work of a midwife and the skills it involves.

midwinter See mid-winter.

mien (*pron:* mean) Someone's **mien** is their general appearance and manner, especially the expression on their face which shows what they are thinking or feeling. *His mien at conference was that of a nervous best man*.

miffed If you are **miffed**, you are slightly annoyed and hurt because of something someone has said or done.

might ❑ You use **might** to say something is possible. *I think he might be a bit nervous*. ◇ If you say something **might have** happened, you mean (a) it is possible that it happened. (b) it was possible for it to have happened, but it did not actually happen. *Outside intervention might have prevented the fighting*.

❑ You use **might** when you are making suggestions. *You might try to put that extra bit in*. ◇ You also use **might** in polite requests. *I wonder if I might add a word... Might I trouble you for a drop more tea?*

❑ **Might** is power or strength. *The might of the army could prove a decisive factor*.

mightily means to a large extent or degree. *The team manager has been mightily impressed by their style of play*.

mighty (mightier, mightiest) ❑ **Mighty** is used to describe people and organizations that are very powerful. ...*the once mighty intelligence chiefs of East Berlin*.

❑ **Mighty** can be used in front of some words to emphasize them. *In this profession it is mighty irritating always to be in the hands of other people.*

migraine A **migraine** is a severe headache which makes you feel very ill.

migrant A **migrant** is someone who moves from one place to another, usually to find work. ◇ **Migrant** birds or animals go to a different area for part of the year to find food or breed.

migrate (migrating, migrated; migration, migratory) When people **migrate**, they move from one place to another, often looking for work. **Migratory** is used to describe people who move around like this. *...migratory industrial labour.* ◇ **Migratory** birds and animals make a journey to a different area at the same time each year, to find food or breed. When they make this journey, you say they **migrate.** *...the migration of young sea trout.*

mike A **mike** is a microphone.

mild (mildly, mildness) ❑ If something is **mild,** it is not strong and does not have any powerful effects. *...a mild stomach complaint... ...a mild sedative.* ◇ **Mild** weather is not as cold as might be expected. *The flowering period will vary with the severity or mildness of the winter.*

❑ **Mild** people are gentle and do not get angry easily.

❑ **Mild** also means not very great or extreme. *He wrote a novel that turned into a mildly successful film.*

❑ You say **to put it mildly** to indicate that what you are saying is an understatement and that things are actually much worse or more extreme than the way you are describing them. *The results have often been disappointing, to put it mildly.*

mild-mannered people are gentle and polite, and avoid using strong language.

mildew is various types of powdery fungus which grow in warm damp places on things like plants, books, and cloth.

mile Distance is often expressed in **miles.** A mile is 1,760 yards (about 1.6 km). 'Miles' is sometimes written 'm'.

mileage The **mileage** someone covers is the distance they travel in miles. ◇ The **mileage** you get out of something is what you gain from it, for example in terms of popularity. *Traditionally there has been little political mileage to be gained by pressing for prison reforms.*

mileometer A vehicle's **mileometer** is a device which shows how many miles it has travelled.

milestone If you say something is a **milestone,** you mean it represents an important stage in the history or development of something. ◇ A **milestone** is also a stone by the side of a road showing the distances to different places.

milieu (*plural:* milieux) (*both pron:* meel-yer) The **milieu** you live or work in is your surroundings and the people you live or work with.

militancy (militant, militantly) **Militancy** is the behaviour and attitudes of people who try to bring about political or social change using forceful methods which other people find unacceptable. You call methods like these **militant;** you say the people who use them are **militants.**

militarise See militarize.

militarism (militarist, militaristic) **Militarism** is a country's policy of having powerful armed forces and using them to threaten other countries. People in favour of a policy like this are called **militarists;** you say their ideas are **militarist** or **militaristic.**

militarize (militarizing, militarized; militarization) (*can be spelled with an 's' instead of a 'z'*) When a place is **militarized,** it is filled with military forces and their equipment. ◇ When an organization is **militarized,** it is run on military lines and the civilian staff are replaced by soldiers. *...the militarization of the Tunisian diplomatic corps.*

military (militarily) **Military** is used to talk about things to do with a country's armed forces. *Dangerous toxins are still being produced under military supervision... The administration is adamant that America will not intervene militarily.* ◇ The **military** are the armed forces of a country, especially the officers of high rank. *No violent reaction from the military is expected.* ◇ **Military service** is a period of compulsory service in a country's armed forces.

Military Cross The **Military Cross** is a medal awarded to army officers for bravery, and also to officers of the RAF for gallant service on the ground. After a person's name, 'Military Cross' is shortened to 'MC'. *...Ralph Cecil Vickers, MC.*

military police The **military police** are the part of an army, navy, or air force which acts as its internal police force.

militate (militating, militated) If something **militates against** something else, it makes it less likely to happen or succeed. *Male attitudes and patronage were perceived by trainees to militate against surgical careers for women.*

militia (militiaman, militiamen) The **militia** in a place is an armed force made up of people who live there and who can be called on to fight if necessary. Its members are called **militiamen.**

milk (milky) ❑ **Milk** is the white liquid produced by cows, goats, and ewes, which people drink and make into butter, cheese, and yoghurt. If you **milk** an animal, you get milk from it by pulling its udders. ◇ **Milky** food or drink contains a lot of milk. ◇ **Milk** is also the white liquid from a woman's breasts which babies drink.

❑ If something is **milky,** it is the colour of milk.

❑ If someone **milks** a situation, they try to get as much benefit from it as they can. ◇ If someone **milks** an organization, they regularly take money out of it for their own use.

milk float A **milk float** is a small van with a roof and no sides for delivering milk to people's houses. Milk floats usually have an electric motor.

milk round A **milk round** is the houses a milkman delivers milk to each day. ◇ The **milk round** is the series of interviews conducted on various university campuses each year by large companies who wish to recruit graduates.

milk shake See milkshake.

milk tooth Your **milk teeth** are your first set of teeth. After about the age of six, they come loose and are replaced by a second set.

milkman (milkmen) A **milkman** is a person who delivers milk to people's houses.

milkshake (*or* milk shake) A **milkshake** is a cold drink made by mixing milk with flavouring and sometimes with ice-cream, then whisking it.

Milky Way The **Milky Way** is the pale strip of light made up of many stars which you can see stretched across the sky at night.

mill ❏ A mill is a building where grain is crushed to make flour. ◇ Various kinds of factories are called **mills**, for example steel mills, woollen mills, and cotton mills.

❏ A **coffee mill** is a small device for grinding coffee beans into a powder. A **pepper mill** is a similar device for grinding pepper. When you use one of these devices, you say you **mill** the coffee or the pepper. *...freshly milled black pepper.*

❏ When a crowd of people **mill around** or **mill about**, they move around in an aimless or disorganized way.

millenarian Millenarians believe in a future period of peace and happiness in the world. Christian millenarians believe this will come about as a result of the second coming of Christ.

millennium (*plural:* millennia *or* millenniums) A **millennium** is a period of one thousand years. ◇ People sometimes call the year 2000 the **millennium**.

miller A miller is a person or firm that makes flour in a mill or mills.

millet is a tall grass cultivated for its edible seeds or for hay.

milli- at the beginning of a unit of measurement means it is one thousandth of a larger unit. For example, a millisecond is one thousandth of a second.

millibar Atmospheric pressure is usually expressed in millibars. A millibar is one thousandth of a bar (or 100 newtons per square metre). 'Millibars' is usually written 'mb'.

milligram (*or* milligramme) Very small weights are often expressed in milligrams. A milligram is one thousandth of a gram (about 0.000035 oz). 'Milligrams' is usually written 'mg'.

millilitre (*American spelling:* milliliter) Volume is sometimes expressed in millilitres. A millilitre is one thousandth of a litre, and is the same as a cubic centimetre. 'Millilitres' is usually written 'ml'.

millimetre (*American spelling:* millimeter) Small lengths are often expressed in millimetres. A millimetre is one thousandth of a metre (about 0.039 inches). 'Millimetres' is usually written 'mm'.

milliner (millinery) A **milliner** is a person whose job is making or selling women's hats. **Millinery** is making hats, or the hats made or sold by a milliner.

million (millionth) A **million** is the number 1,000,000.

millionaire (millionairess, millionairesses) A **millionaire** is a person who has money, investments, or property worth at least a million pounds or dollars. A woman who has this amount is sometimes called a **millionairess**.

millipede A millipede is a small creature with a long narrow body made of many small segments, each segment with two pairs of legs.

millstone ❏ A **millstone** is a problem or responsibility which makes it difficult for you to do the things you want to. *They are both eager for reconciliation and this has made the hostage issue a millstone round their necks.*

❏ Originally, **millstones** were two large flat round stones used to grind grain into flour.

mime (miming, mimed) **Mime** is the use of movements and gestures to express something or tell a story without using speech. ◇ If you **mime** something, you describe or express it using movements and gestures. ◇ You also say people **mime** when they pretend to be singing or playing a musical instrument, when the music is in fact coming from a recording.

mimic (mimicking, mimicked; mimicry) If you **mimic** someone's actions or voice, you imitate them in an amusing or entertaining way. Imitating people like this is called **mimicry**. Someone who does it well is called a **mimic**. ◇ If something **mimics** something else, it has the same characteristics and behaves in the same way. *...an all-purpose computer that could, in effect, mimic the processes of human thought.*

min is short for 'minute' or 'minutes'. *Let this simmer gently for 10 min.*

minaret (*pron:* min-ar-ret) A **minaret** is a tall slender tower which is part of a mosque.

mince (mincer; mincing, minced) ❏ **Mince** is meat cut into very small pieces by a device called a **mincer**. If you **mince** meat, you cut it up using a mincer.

❏ If someone **minces** somewhere, they walk with small quick steps in an affected or effeminate way.

❏ If you **do not mince your words**, you say something in a plain straightforward way, without trying to be polite or worrying about upsetting people.

mince pie A **mince pie** is a small pie containing mincemeat. Mince pies are especially eaten at Christmas.

mincemeat is a sticky mixture of dried fruit, apples, sugar, and suet. It is cooked in pastry to make mince pies. ◇ When Americans talk about **mincemeat**, they usually mean minced meat.

❏ If you **make mincemeat** of someone, you defeat them easily and completely in an argument or contest.

mind ❏ Your **mind** is your ability to think, reason, and imagine things. ◇ Your **state of mind** is your mental state at a particular time. ◇ If your **mind is on** something, you are thinking about it. ◇ If something is **on your mind**, you are worried about it and think about it a lot.

❏ If you are **in two minds** about something, you cannot come to a decision about it. ◇ If you **make up your mind**, you decide which of a number of things you will have or do. ◇ If you **change your mind**, you alter a decision you have made.

❏ If you talk about what someone has **in mind**, you mean the thing they are thinking about when they say or decide something. *Perhaps he had in mind an expansion of the Law Courts.* ◇ If you do something with a particular thing **in mind**, you do it for that reason or purpose. *He abandoned his usual indoor season and spent eight weeks training in Australia, with only the Olympic gold medal in mind.*

❏ If something **comes to mind**, you think of it when a particular subject is mentioned. *Vietnam is not the first country which comes to mind when booking a holiday.* If something makes you think of something else, you can say it **calls it to mind** or **brings it to mind**. ◇ If something is **at the back of your mind**, you are always aware of it, even when you are thinking about other things. ◇ If you say someone should **bear** or **keep** something **in mind**, you mean they should remember it when they are considering something.

❏ If you see something in your **mind's eye**, you imagine it and have a clear picture of it in your mind.

❏ You say **to my mind** when you are giving an opinion. *To my mind it is easily the best buy among Scottish country-house visits.* ◇ If you **speak your mind**, you say exactly what you think, even if it annoys or embarrasses people. ◇ keep an **open mind**: see **open**.

❏ If you **put your mind** to a problem, you set about solving it. ◇ If something **takes your mind off** a problem or disappointment, it makes you forget it for a while.

❏ If you do not **mind** something, you do not object to it. ◇ If you say you **wouldn't mind** something, you mean you would like it. *After four years in the same job, he wouldn't mind a change of scene.*

❏ You say **never mind** to indicate that something is not important. *Never mind, it's only money.* ◇ You also say **never mind** when you have talked about something not being achieved and you are going on to mention something even harder to achieve. *He did not even look like a genuine heavyweight, never mind a world class one.*

❏ If you **mind** something for someone, you look after it for them.

mind- is used with various words to say something is so extreme it is difficult to imagine or take in. *...mind-bending statistics... ...the car's mind-blowing 178 mph maximum speed... ...a mind-boggling bonanza of salary schemes.*

mind-numbing See **numb**.

mind-set If you talk about someone's **mind-set**, you mean their way of looking at things, which is fixed and unlikely to change.

minded ❏ **-minded** is added to words ending in '-ly' to describe a person's attitudes and outlook. *...commercially-minded operators... ...academically-minded pupils.*

❏ If you are **minded** to do something, you intend to do it.

minder A **minder** is someone who looks after a person who cannot look after himself or herself, for example an old person. ◇ A **minder** is also someone whose job is to protect an important person or public figure.

mindful If you are **mindful** of something, you are aware of it and take account of it when you do something.

mindless You say a destructive action is **mindless** when there seems to be no reason for it. *...mindless vandalism.* ◇ A **mindless** job or activity is so simple or repetitive it does not require any thought.

mine (mining, mined; miner) ❏ You use **mine** to talk about things to do with yourself, or things belonging to you. *...a friend of mine... It'll be their decision, not mine.*

❏ A **mine** is a place where people dig deep holes or tunnels to get coal, diamonds, or other minerals out of the ground. When minerals are **mined**, they are got out in this way; the industry concerned is called **mining**. A **miner** is a person who works down a mine.

❏ A **mine** is also a bomb hidden in the ground or floating on water, which goes off when something touches it. If a road or area is **mined**, mines are planted in it.

minefield ❏ A **minefield** is an area of land or water where mines have been laid.

❏ If you say a situation is a **minefield**, you mean it is full of hidden dangers or problems.

mineral Minerals are substances like lead, salt, diamonds, and coal, which are formed naturally in rocks and in the ground. ◇ The **minerals** you get in foods are substances like iron and sodium, which your body needs in order to function properly.

mineral water is untreated water which comes out of the ground containing dissolved mineral salts. It is often considered healthy to drink.

mineralogy (mineralogist) **Mineralogy** is the scientific study of minerals. A **mineralogist** is an expert on this.

minestrone is a soup made from stock and containing small pieces of vegetables and pasta.

minesweeper A **minesweeper** is a ship used to clear away mines in the sea.

mingle (mingling, mingled) If things like sounds or smells **mingle**, you get several of them in the same place together. Similarly, you talk about feelings being **mingled** when you feel more than one at the same time. ◇ If you **mingle**, you move around in a group of people, especially at a party when you chat to people you do not know.

mini See **miniskirt**.

mini- at the beginning of a word means it is a small version of something. *...a mini-submarine... ...a mini-zoo.*

mini-bus See **minibus**.

mini-series A **mini-series** is a TV drama in three or four parts which is shown on consecutive days or weeks.

mini-skirt See **miniskirt**.

miniature (miniaturist) ❏ A **miniature** version of something is much smaller than usual. ◇ If you say one thing is another thing **in miniature**, you mean it is exactly like the other thing, only much smaller. *The conference hotel is like Westminster in miniature.*

❏ A **miniature** is a very small detailed painting, often of a person. An artist who paints very small paintings is called a **miniaturist**.

miniaturize (miniaturizing, miniaturized; miniaturization) *(can be spelled with an 's' instead of a 'z')* When a product is **miniaturized**, very small versions of it are made. *Miniaturization could take computers out of the lap and into the pocket.*

minibus (minibuses) *(or mini-bus, mini-buses)* A **minibus** is a van with seats in the back, used as a small bus.

minicab A **minicab** is a car which is used as a taxi although it was not designed as one. Minicabs cannot be hailed in the street, but have to be ordered by phone or from the company's offices.

minicomputer A **minicomputer** is a computer which is smaller than a mainframe but more powerful than a microcomputer.

minim A **minim** is a musical note with the same time value as two crotchets.

minimal (minimally) A **minimal** amount of something is very small indeed. ◇ **Minimal** also means as little as possible. *America is likely to insist that UN interference should be minimal... The book has been minimally edited and updated.*

minimalism (minimalist) **Minimalism** is an artistic movement which aims to show everything in as simple a form as possible. Art, music, and other things produced in this way are called **minimalist**. The artists and musicians who produce them are called **minimalists**.

minimize (minimizing, minimized) *(can be spelled with a 's' instead of a 'z')* If you **minimize** something, you reduce it to the lowest level possible, or keep it at that level.

The unions have called on all except essential workers to stay at home in order to minimize the chances of clashes with police. ◇ You also say you **minimize** something when you make it seem smaller or less important than it really is. *It would be in their interests to minimize their differences.*

minimum The **minimum** of something is the smallest amount possible or necessary. *The three main networks have cut coverage to a minimum.*

minimum lending rate From 1972 to 1981, the **minimum lending rate** or **MLR** was the minimum rate of interest at which the Bank of England would lend money to other banks. The government has the right to reintroduce the MLR whenever it feels it is necessary to control the money supply.

mining See mine.

minion If you talk about a person's **minions**, you mean people with low status who carry out their orders for them.

miniskirt (or **mini-skirt**) A **miniskirt** or **mini** is a very short skirt.

minister (ministering, ministered) ❑ A **minister** is a person in charge of a government department.
    ❑ A **minister** is also a member of the clergy in a Non-conformist church.
    ❑ If a member of the clergy **ministers** to a community or congregation, he or she conducts religious services for them. ◇ If you **minister** to someone or their needs, you make sure they have everything they need or want.

ministerial is used to talk about things to do with a government minister or ministry. *...ministerial approval... Ministerial resignations cannot be ruled out.*

ministrations A person's **ministrations** are the things they do to help someone, especially a sick person.

ministry (ministries) ❑ A **ministry** is a government department. *...the Ministry of Transport.*
    ❑ The **ministry** of a religious person is the work they do as a result of their religious beliefs. ◇ Members of the clergy in some Christian churches are called the **ministry**.

mink (plural: mink or minks) **Mink** are small furry animals. Their fur, which is also called **mink**, is used to make coats and other articles of clothing. Coats made from mink are sometimes called **minks**.

minnow ❑ **Minnows** are very small freshwater fish.
    ❑ If you call something a **minnow**, you mean it is much smaller than other things of the same kind. *Malta will be the smallest addition to the community, tinier even than the current minnow of the European family, Luxembourg.*

minor things are not as important, serious, or significant as other things of the same kind. *There were a few minor alterations to the cast.* ◇ A **minor** is a person who is still legally a child. In Britain, young people are minors until they reach the age of 18.

minority (minorities) ❑ If you talk about a **minority** of the people or things in a group, you mean less than half the whole group. If a group is **in the minority** or **in a minority**, they form less than half of a larger group.
    ❑ A **minority** is also a group of people of a particular race or religion who live in a place where most of the people are of another race or religion. *...the country's white minority.*

minster A **minster** is a large church or cathedral, often one which was originally connected to a monastery.

minstrel In medieval times, a **minstrel** was a singer and musician who used to travel round performing for noble families. Some noble families had their own minstrels.

mint is a type of herb used in cooking, especially in mint sauce.
    ❑ A **mint** is a sweet with a peppermint flavour.
    ❑ The place where a country's coins are made is called a **mint**. When coins or medals are **minted**, they are made in a mint. ◇ A **mint** is also a large amount of money. *I talked to a man with six dogs, whacking great animals that cost a mint to feed.*
    ❑ If something is in **mint** condition, it is in very good condition, as if it was new.

mint sauce is a sauce made from vinegar, mint leaves, and sugar. It is often eaten with lamb.

minus (minuses) ❑ You use **minus** to show one number is being subtracted from another, for example, 'five minus three' means three is being subtracted from five. You represent this in figures as '5 – 3'. The sign between the 5 and 3 is called a **minus sign**. ◇ You also use **minus** to talk about money being reduced by a certain amount. *The government could reclaim the money, minus the interest, when it had made the necessary budget cuts.*
    ❑ **Minus** is also used to show a number is less than zero. *The temperature often falls to minus 20.*
    ❑ You also use **minus** to talk about the absence of something. *A neighbour who swapped his GTI for a diesel swears he gets there just as quickly, minus the stress.*

minuscule If something is **minuscule**, it is very small indeed.

minute (minutely) ❑ A **minute** is one of the sixty equal parts of an hour. ◇ A **minute** also means a short time. *She paused for a minute.*
    ❑ The **minutes** of a meeting are the written records of what is said and decided.
    ❑ If something is **minute** (pron: my-**newt**), it is extremely small. *In most cases the benefit of an X-ray far outweighs the minutely increased risk of cancer.* ◇ In a **minute** examination or study, great attention is paid to every detail. *The Americans will scrutinize this proposal minutely.*

minutiae (pron: my-**new**-shee-eye) The **minutiae** of something like a system are its small details. *...his boredom with the minutiae of police procedures.*

miracle (miraculous, miraculously) If something very surprising and fortunate happens, you can call it a **miracle** or say it is **miraculous**. *Martin Donelly miraculously escaped a 140mph crash.* ◇ When people with strong religious beliefs talk about a **miracle**, they mean a surprising and wonderful event caused by God.

mirage A **mirage** is an image which you see in the distance in very hot weather. With some kinds of mirage, the thing you see does not exist, as for example when people see water in the desert. With other kinds of mirage, the thing you see really exists, but is a long way from the place where it seems be. ◇ If something good seems about to happen and someone says it is a **mirage**, they mean people are misreading the signs and it will not really happen at all.

mire (mired) You call an unpleasant situation a **mire** when any attempt to get out of it seems to fail or make things worse. You can talk about people being **mired** in an unpleasant situation.

mirror (mirroring, mirrored) ❏ A **mirror** is a piece of glass with a metallic backing. You look in the glass and you see your reflection. ◇ If something is **mirrored** in water or a shiny surface, you see it reflected in it.

❏ If something is a **mirror image** of something else, it is identical to it, but the other way round. ◇ If something like an organization is a **mirror image** of another one, it has all the same features, although it may have quite different objectives.

❏ If something **mirrors** something else, it reproduces many of its features, and seems like a copy of it. *This religious divide has for decades been mirrored in everyday political life in Nigeria.*

mirth is amusement or laughter. *The idea that Californians might lack self-esteem was greeted with much mirth by the rest of the world.*

mis- is used to form words which describe things being done badly or wrongly. *...a serious misallocation of resources... Tests showed the device was misaligned.*

misadventure A **misadventure** is something unfortunate which happens to someone, like losing all their money or having an accident.

misandry (misandrist) **Misandry** is hatred of men. A **misandrist** is a woman who hates men.

misanthrope (misanthropic, misanthropy) A **misanthrope** is someone who does not like other people. You talk about the **misanthropy** of someone like this or say they are **misanthropic**.

misanthropist A **misanthropist** is the same as a **misanthrope**.

misapply (misapplies, misapplying, misapplied; misapplication) If you **misapply** something, you use it in a way it is not meant to be used. *The report accused the President and General Secretary of misapplication of funds.*

misapprehension If you are under a **misapprehension** about something, you have a wrong idea or impression about it.

misappropriate (misappropriating, misappropriated; misappropriation) If someone **misappropriates** money or other valuable things, they take them and use them for their own purposes. *The promotions director has been charged with misappropriation of funds.*

misbehave (misbehaving, misbehaved) If someone, especially a child, **misbehaves**, they behave in an unacceptable way.

misbehaviour (*American spelling:* **misbehavior**) is behaviour which is regarded as unacceptable.

miscalculate (miscalculating, miscalculated; miscalculation) If you **miscalculate** or make a **miscalculation**, you make a mistake in judging a situation.

miscarriage ❏ If a woman has a **miscarriage**, she gives birth to a foetus before it is properly formed and it dies.

❏ If there is a **miscarriage of justice**, a wrong decision is given by a court, with the result that an innocent person is punished.

miscarry (miscarries, miscarrying, miscarried) If a woman **miscarries**, she has a miscarriage.

miscast If you say an actor or actress is **miscast**, you mean they are playing a role which is not suitable for them.

miscellaneous (*pron:* miss-sell-**lane**-ee-uss) A **miscella-**neous group is made up of people or things of different kinds.

miscellany (*pron:* miss-**sell**-a-nee) A **miscellany** is a collection of things which are different from each other.

mischievous (mischievously; mischief) ❏ If you call something a person does **mischievous**, you mean it is intended to cause trouble. Causing trouble like this is called **mischief**; the trouble caused is also called **mischief**. Someone who tries to cause trouble between people is called a **mischief-maker**.

❏ You also say someone is **mischievous** when they are eager to have fun, especially by embarrassing people or playing harmless tricks. *Mischievously I asked her if the bill of fare included owl.* Eagerness to have fun can be called **mischief**. *She is rarely still, her eyes perpetually dancing with mischief.* ◇ A **mischievous** child is naughty, but does not do any real harm. You call a naughty child's behaviour **mischief**. *Keep young hands out of mischief on rainy days with this colourful kit.*

misconceived A **misconceived** plan or action is based on a mistake or misunderstanding and is not likely to succeed.

misconception A **misconception** is a wrong idea about something.

misconduct is bad or unacceptable behaviour, especially by a professional person.

misconstrue (misconstruing, misconstrued) If you **misconstrue** something which happens or is said, you interpret it wrongly.

miscreant (*pron:* miss-**kree**-ant) A **miscreant** is someone who has done something wrong, especially a criminal.

misdeed A **misdeed** is a bad or evil act.

misdemeanour (*American spelling:* **misdemeanor**) A **misdemeanour** is an act people consider to be shocking or unacceptable. ◇ In countries where the legal system distinguishes between very serious crimes and less serious ones, a **misdemeanour** is a less serious one.

misdirect (misdirection) ❏ If you say someone's qualities or energies are **misdirected**, you mean they are used wrongly or inappropriately. Similarly, public money or other resources can be **misdirected**. *The fertiliser subsidy is perhaps the clearest example of waste and misdirection, but there are many others.*

❏ If something is **misdirected**, it is sent to the wrong place. ◇ In sport, if you **misdirect** a kick or a shot, you send it in the wrong direction.

miser A **miser** is someone who enjoys saving money and hates spending it.

miserable (miserably) ❏ If you are **miserable**, you are unhappy or depressed. You also call something which makes you feel like this **miserable**. *They appealed for international help to ease their miserable conditions.* ◇ **Miserable** weather is wet, cold, and depressing.

❏ You also say someone is **miserable** when they are bad-tempered or unfriendly.

❏ A **miserable** failure is a particularly bad one. *They failed miserably to spot a series of financial irregularities.* ◇ **Miserable** is used to describe things which are disappointingly bad. *He crashed and stumbled his way through to finish a miserable seventh in the 110 metres hurdles.*

miserly (miserliness) A **miserly** person enjoys saving money and hates spending it. *The charge of miserliness infuri-*

ates GCC governments. ◇ A **miserly** amount of something is very small. *Being a student today, with miserly grants and diminishing career prospects, is not much fun.*

misery (miseries) ❑ Misery is great unhappiness. Miseries are unhappy experiences. ◇ If someone **makes your life a misery**, they keep behaving in an unpleasant way towards you and make you very unhappy.

❑ If you **put an animal out of its misery**, you kill it because it is fatally ill or injured. ◇ If you **put a person out of their misery**, you tell them something they are very anxious to know.

misfire (misfiring, misfired) If a plan **misfires**, it goes wrong. ◇ If a gun **misfires**, it fails to go off when expected. ◇ If a vehicle's engine **misfires**, the fuel does not ignite when it is started.

misfit A misfit is a person who is not easily accepted by other people, because their behaviour or beliefs are different from everyone else's.

misfortune A misfortune is something bad which happens to you. Misfortune is having bad things happen to you.

misgiving If you have **misgivings** about something, or view it with **misgiving** or **misgivings**, you are worried or unhappy about it.

misgovernment You say there is **misgovernment** when a country is run in a bad or corrupt way.

misguided If you say someone's behaviour is **misguided**, you mean they are doing the wrong thing, because they have not understood the situation they are dealing with. *...a misguided economic policy.*

mish-mash (*or* mishmash) A mish-mash is a confused mixture of things.

mishandle (mishandling, mishandled) If you **mishandle** something, you deal with it badly or inefficiently. *The Koreans felt the referee had mishandled the whole match.*

mishap A mishap is an unfortunate but not very serious accident.

mishmash See mish-mash.

misinform (misinformation) If you are **misinformed** about something, you are given wrong information about it, either accidentally or deliberately. Wrong information is called **misinformation**. See also disinformation.

misinterpret (misinterpreting, misinterpreted; misinterpretation) If you **misinterpret** something, you understand it wrongly. *The message left no room for misinterpretation.*

misjudge (misjudging, misjudged; misjudgement *or* misjudgment) If you **misjudge** someone or something, you form an inaccurate idea or opinion of them, and often make a wrong decision as a result. Getting something wrong like this is called a **misjudgement**. *Treasury officials who made gross misjudgements should be held responsible for their mistakes.*

mislay (mislaying, mislaid) If you have **mislaid** something, you cannot remember where you have left it.

mislead (misleading, misled; misleadingly) If you **mislead** someone, you get them to believe something which is not true. *The figures were misleading... Some data had been presented misleadingly.*

mismanage (mismanaging, mismanaged; mismanagement) If a system or organization is **mismanaged**, it is managed dishonestly or inefficiently. *Its development has been crippled by instability and economic mismanagement.*

mismatched (mismatch) If two things are **mismatched** or if there is a **mismatch** between them, they do not go together or do not correspond to each other.

misnamed If you say something is **misnamed**, you mean its name describes it badly or incorrectly.

misnomer A misnomer is a word or phrase which describes someone or something badly or incorrectly.

misogyny (*pron:* miss-soj-i-nee) (misogynist, misogynistic) Misogyny is hatred of women. A **misogynist** is a man who hates women. You say men like this are misogynistic.

misplaced A misplaced feeling or action is inappropriate, or directed towards the wrong person or thing. *Unbridled optimism about the economy is misplaced.*

misprint A misprint is a mistake in the way something has been printed, for example a spelling mistake.

misquote (misquoting, misquoted; misquotation) If you **misquote** what someone has said or written, you repeat it inaccurately. An inaccurate repetition of something is called a **misquotation**.

misread (misreading, misread) If you **misread** a situation or a person's behaviour, you do not understand it properly and often make a wrong decision as a result. A wrong understanding of a situation can be called a **misreading** of it. ◇ If you **misread** a piece of writing, you think it says something which it does not say.

misreport If the media **misreport** something, they report it wrongly or inaccurately.

misrepresent (misrepresentation) If someone **misrepresents** you or **misrepresents** what you say, they give a misleading or inaccurate account of what you say. An account like this is called a **misrepresentation**.

misrule (misruling, misruled) If a country is **misruled**, it is badly or inefficiently governed. Misrule is bad or inefficient government. *The former leaders are being forced to face the consequences of their years of misrule.*

miss (misses, missing, missed) ❑ If you **miss** something you are trying to hit, you fail to hit it. ◇ If a footballer **misses** a goal, he fails to score when he has an opportunity to do so. His failure to score is called a **miss**.

❑ If you **miss** a bus, train, or plane, you fail to catch it.

❑ If you **miss** a chance, you fail to take advantage of it. ◇ If you **miss out** on something worth having, you do not get it when other people do.

❑ If you **miss** something, you fail to notice it. *He claimed the referee missed a blatant penalty.* ◇ If you **miss the point** of something, you fail to understand its meaning or importance.

❑ If you **miss** something **out**, you do not include it in what you say or do.

❑ If you **miss** something you once had, you feel sad because you no longer have it. Similarly, if you **miss** a person, you feel sad because they are no longer with you. ◇ You also say you **miss** someone when you notice they are not where you expect them to be. *No-one had missed us yet at home.*

❑ If you **miss** something like a meeting or a match, you do not go, often because you are not able to. If you **give** something like a meeting or match **a miss**, you deliberately do not go.

❑ **near miss**: see near. ◇ See also missing.

❑ Miss is used in front of a girl's or unmarried woman's

name. ...*Miss Benning...* ...*Misses Elizabeth and Merci Nelson.*

misshapen If something is **misshapen**, it is an unusual and unattractive shape.

missile A **missile** is a weapon which travels long distances and explodes when it reaches its target. ◇ Anything thrown as a weapon can be called a **missile**. *There was a constant shower of stones, bricks, and other missiles.*

missing ❑ If part of something is **missing**, it is not there. Similarly, if something does not have a quality or feature you would expect it to have, you can say the quality or feature is **missing**.
❑ You also say something is **missing** when nobody has been able to find it. *Where do missing golf balls get to?* ◇ A **missing** person has disappeared completely and nobody knows where they are. ◇ If a member of the armed forces is **missing in action**, they have not returned from battle, their body has not been found, and they are not thought to have been captured.
❑ When people talk about the **missing link**, they mean something which needs to be added to something else to make it complete, for example a newly-discovered fact which, when added to what is already known, would provide a complete explanation of something. ◇ The **missing link** is also a theoretical creature, half-ape and half-human, whose existence is necessary to support the theory of evolution.

mission ❑ A **mission** is an important task someone is given to do, especially one which involves travelling abroad. A group of people given a task like this can also be called a **mission**. *A trade mission will visit Britain in September.* ◇ A **mission** is also a journey made by a military aircraft or space rocket for a particular purpose.
❑ If you have a **mission**, you have a task which you feel it is your duty to carry out. *The head gardener has made it his mission to show how wide a variety of plants can be grown in the region.* ◇ A **mission** is also the activities of a group of Christians who have been sent to a place to teach people about Christianity. The building or buildings they live and work in can also be called a **mission**.

missionary (missionaries) A **missionary** is someone who has been sent to a foreign country to tell people about his or her religion, and to try to convert them. Some missionaries also run clinics and schools.

missive A **missive** is a letter or other written message.

misspell (misspelling, misspelled *or* misspelt) If you **misspell** a word, you spell it wrongly.

misspend (misspending, misspent) If money is **misspent**, it is wasted, or used to buy things it was not meant for. ◇ You say someone's time is **misspent** when you think they could be spending it in a better or more productive way.

mist is tiny drops of water suspended in the air. ◇ If a piece of glass **mists over** or **mists up**, it becomes covered in drops of moisture so you cannot see through it easily.

mistake (mistaking, mistook, have mistaken) ❑ If you make a **mistake**, you do something you did not intend to, or something which produces a result you did not want. You can say something is done **by mistake**. *Government forces opened fire on the French troops by mistake.*

❑ If you **mistake** one person or thing for another, you wrongly think they are the other person or thing. *The USA nearly declared nuclear war when its computer mistook the rising moon for a missile attack.* ◇ If you **mistake** something like a name or address, you get it wrong. ◇ If you say there is **no mistaking** something, you mean you cannot fail to recognize it or understand it. *There is no mistaking the force of his personality.*

mistaken (mistakenly) If you are **mistaken** about something, you are wrong. A **mistaken** belief or decision is an incorrect one. *The plane crashed after being fired at by police, who mistakenly believed it was being used to smuggle drugs.* ◇ If someone thinks they recognize a person they are looking for or someone they know, but it turns out to be a different person, you call this a case of **mistaken identity**.

mister See Mr.

mistime (mistiming, mistimed) If you **mistime** something, you do it at the wrong time and it does not have the effect you want.

mistletoe is an evergreen plant which grows as a parasite on several types of trees. It has white berries and is traditionally used in Britain as a Christmas decoration.

mistral The **mistral** is a strong cold dry wind which blows through France down the Rhône valley towards the Mediterranean coast.

mistreat (mistreating, mistreated; mistreatment) If someone **mistreats** a person or animal, they treat them badly, especially by hitting them. *They were protesting against alleged mistreatment of Palestinians held in Israeli jails.*

mistress (mistresses) A married man's **mistress** is a woman who is not his wife and who he is having a sexual relationship with.

mistrial A **mistrial** is a trial which has been declared void because of some error in procedure.

mistrust (mistrustful) If you **mistrust** someone or something or are **mistrustful** of them, you do not trust them. **Mistrust** is the feeling you have about someone you do not trust.

misty If it is **misty**, there is a lot of mist in the air.

misty-eyed If you say someone is **misty-eyed**, you mean they are very emotional about something, and seem about to cry.

misunderstand (misunderstanding, misunderstood) If you **misunderstand** something someone says or does, you do not understand it properly. A **misunderstanding** is a failure to understand something properly. ◇ If two people have a **misunderstanding**, they have a minor disagreement or argument.

misuse (misusing, misused) If you **misuse** something (*pron:* miss-yewz), you use it incorrectly, carelessly, or dishonestly. When something is wrongly used, you talk about its **misuse** (*pron:* miss-yewss). ...*the misuse of power.*

mite ❑ A **mite** in front of another word means 'a bit' or 'rather'. For example, if you say someone is a **mite** extravagant, you mean they are rather extravagant.
❑ **Mites** are very tiny creatures which live in many different places, for example on the fur of animals, in food, in dust, or on plants.

miter See mitre.

mitigate (mitigating, mitigated; mitigation) ❑ If the bad effects of something are **mitigated**, they are made less unpleasant, serious, or painful.

❏ **Mitigating** circumstances are circumstances which partly explain why a crime was committed. They are told to the court in the hope that the person who committed the crime will get a lighter punishment. You say things like these are told to the court in **mitigation**.

mitre (*American spelling:* **miter**) A **mitre** is a tall headdress worn by bishops and archbishops on ceremonial occasions.

mitten Mittens are gloves which have one section for all your fingers and another for your thumb.

mix (mixes, mixing, mixed) ❏ When two or more things are **mixed** or **mixed up**, they are combined together. *Designers are mixing loose and tight clothing in new ways.* A **mix** is a combination of two or more things.

❏ **Mixed** is used to talk about a combination of good and bad things. *The two newcomers had mixed fortunes... My feelings on this matter are rather mixed.* ◇ If you say something is a **mixed blessing,** you mean it has disadvantages as well as advantages. ◇ If you say something is a **mixed bag,** you mean there are both good and bad things in it.

❏ If you **mix** two or more substances, you stir or shake them together. ◇ If you **mix** a drink, you prepare it by combining other drinks. ◇ A **mix** is a specially prepared powder which can be turned into something eatable by adding liquid. *...cheese sauce mix... ...cake mix.*

❏ **Mixed** is used to describe something which is made up of different things of the same general kind. *In the woods, mixed flocks of birds are forming.*

❏ **Mixed** means involving two or more races or religions. *In 1945 one-tenth of its marriages were mixed; now it is one in three.* ◇ **Mixed** also means involving both males and females. *He found himself playing against a mixed students' soccer eleven.* ◇ In a sport like tennis or badminton, **mixed doubles** is a match in which a man and a woman play as partners against another man and woman.

❏ In a **mixed ability** teaching system, pupils of different abilities are taught together in one class.

❏ In a **mixed economy,** some companies are owned privately and some by the state.

❏ A **mixed** farm is one where animals are kept and crops are grown.

❏ If you **mix** with other people, you meet them socially and talk to them. ◇ If you say someone is **mixed up** with a group of people, you mean they are spending a lot of time with them, and you do not think it is good for them. ◇ If someone is **mixed up** in a crime or scandal, they are involved in it in some way.

❏ If you **mix up** two things or people, you confuse them and think one is the other. ◇ If someone is **mixed up,** they are confused. ◇ If things get **mixed up,** they get out of order.

❏ When people **mix** a recording, they adjust the balance of sound, and sometimes add different sounds. ◇ A **mix** of a recording is a particular production of it.

mix-up A **mix-up** is a mistake which happens because of a misunderstanding or bad organization.

mixer A **mixer** is a machine for mixing things together. *...a food mixer... ...a concrete mixer.* ◇ A **mixer** is also a soft drink such as tonic, used to dilute an alcoholic drink.

mixture A **mixture** of different things is several of them

together. *Supporters greeted the decision with a mixture of disappointment and renewed hope... United Airlines is unusual in having a mixture of European and American cabin crew.* ◇ A **mixture** is also a substance made up of other substances shaken or stirred together.

ml See millilitre.

mm See millimetre.

mnemonic (*pron:* ni-mon-ik) A **mnemonic** is a word, phrase, or rhyme which helps you remember something like a scientific law or spelling rule. For example, 'i before e except after c' is a mnemonic to help people remember how to spell words like 'believe' and 'receive'.

MO An **MO** is a doctor who works in the armed forces. MO stands for 'medical officer'.

moan (moaning, moaned; moaner) When people **moan** about something, they complain about it. You call their complaints **moans.** Someone who complains a lot can be called a **moaner.** ◇ A **moan** is also a low miserable sound made by someone who is unhappy or in pain. If someone **moans,** they make a sound like this.

moat (moated) A **moat** is a deep wide ditch dug round a fort or castle for protection, and often filled with water. A **moated** tower or castle has a moat round it.

mob (mobbing, mobbed) ❏ A **mob** is a large, disorganized, often violent group of people.

❏ If a crowd **mobs** someone, they gather round them, because they are eager to see them or because they want to express their feelings about something.

❏ Any group of people who have something in common can be called a **mob.** *The East Yorkshiremen were a serious bunch, while the Westerners were a happy-go-lucky mob.*

❏ In the US, the **mob** is the Mafia.

mobile (mobility) ❏ You use **mobile** when you are talking about someone's ability to move around. *The Pakistani was much more mobile than his opponent... A thigh injury increasingly hampered her mobility.* ◇ **Mobile** is also used to talk about someone's freedom to move around to different parts of the country, for example to find work. *The young are often more mobile and more inclined to take temporary jobs.* ◇ See also **upwardly mobile.**

❏ **Mobile** is also used to describe facilities like hospitals or libraries when they are based in a van or caravan which can be driven around from place to place.

❏ If you say someone has a **mobile** face, you mean their expression changes quickly as their feelings change.

❏ A **mobile** is a light structure which hangs from the ceiling as a decoration and moves gently in the air.

mobile home A **mobile home** is a large caravan for people to live in. It can be towed around, but usually remains in one place.

mobile phone A **mobile phone** is a portable phone which uses radio waves to transmit signals instead of wires.

mobilize (mobilizing, mobilized; mobilization) (*can be spelled with an 's' instead of a 'z'*) ❏ If you **mobilize** a group of people, you get them organized, so they can start doing something which needs doing. *Special emergency health brigades were being mobilized to try and prevent the spreading of the disease.* ◇ If you **mobilize** support, you get people to support something in an active way. Similarly, you can **mobilize** public opinion. *The conference will try to mobilize the international community to impose harsher* *political and economic sanctions.* ◇ If you **mobilize** resources, you make them available for a particular task or project.

❏ When a country **mobilizes,** it prepares for war. *The parliament had decreed a general mobilization.*

mobster In the US, a **mobster** is a member of a violent criminal organization.

moccasin Moccasins are soft leather shoes with low heels and a raised seam round the top.

mock (mocking, mockingly; mockery) ❏ If you **mock** someone, you make fun of them in an unkind way. This sort of behaviour is called **mockery.** *McGuiness saluted mockingly... Although he will face open mockery from his critics, he will also have the chance to show his decisiveness.* ◇ If you say someone is **making a mockery** of something like a law or a system, you mean they are doing something which makes it appear worthless.

❏ **Mock** is also used to describe things which are an imitation or pretence, rather than the real thing. *...mock Gothic... ...a mock execution.* .

mock-up A mock-up of a structure or machine is a model of it made for a special purpose, such as to perform tests.

mod ❏ In the 1960s and 1970s, **mods** were young people who wore smart clothes, rode motor-scooters, and liked a particular type of music.

❏ In Scotland, a **mod** is an annual Highland Gaelic meeting, with musical and literary competitions.

MOD The MOD or **Ministry of Defence** is the government department which deals with things connected with the defence of the United Kingdom.

mod cons If a house has all **mod cons,** it has all the facilities such as hot water and heating which make a house pleasant and comfortable to live in.

mode ❏ A **mode** is a particular way of doing something. *The bike is the traditional mode of transport for students in the town.*

❏ If a machine or device is in a particular **mode,** it is ready to operate in a particular way. *The display switched to the weapons-aiming mode... ...a switch which puts the car into electric-only mode.*

❏ A **mode** is also a style, for example in art, literature, or fashion. *...a building in Byzantine mode.*

model (modelling, modelled) (*American spelling:* modeling, modeled) ❏ A **model** is a three-dimensional copy of something. It is usually smaller than the object it represents, and shows what it looks like or how it works.

❏ If you **model** shapes or figures, you make them out of a substance like clay or plasticine.

❏ A **model** of a system or process is a theoretical representation which helps you understand how it works, or predicts its effects. When someone creates a representation like this, you say they **model** the system or process. *Geophysicists are modelling in the lab what actually happens in an earthquake.*

❏ If a system is a **model** for other systems, the other systems are copied from it or based on it; you can also say they **modelled** on it. *...a national health service modelled on the German or Canadian systems.*

❏ If you **model** yourself or your behaviour on someone else, you copy the way they do things, because you admire them and want to be like them. ◇ **role model:** see role.

❏ If you say something is a **model** of a particular quality, you mean it has that quality to a high degree. *His approach has been a model of caution and diplomacy.* ◇ **Model** is used to say someone or something is a perfect example of their kind. For example, if you say someone is a **model** teacher, you mean they are a perfect example of what a teacher ought to be. ◇ A **model** farm or **model** prison has been designed to demonstrate the best way of running a farm or prison.

❏ A **model** is someone who poses for an artist or photographer. You say someone like this **models** for the artist or photographer. ◇ A **model** is also someone whose job is to display clothes by wearing them. You say he or she **models** clothes.

❏ A **model** of something like a car or washing machine is a particular version of it.

modem (*pron:* moe-dem) A **modem** is an electronic device which allows data to be sent from one computer to another using telephone lines.

moderate (moderating, moderated; moderately) ❏ **Moderate** political opinions or policies are not extreme. **Moderate** politicians hold views which are not extreme. Politicians like these are called **moderates.** ◇ Other kinds of non-extreme behaviour can also be called **moderate.** *People who drink moderately have less heart disease.* ◇ If something **moderates** (*pron:* mod-er-ates) or is **moderated,** it becomes less extreme.

❏ A **moderate** amount of something is neither large nor small. *...the moderately experienced hill-walker.* ◇ A **moderate** change is not very great. *The American economy was moving forward moderately but the recovery was uneven.*

moderation is self-control and restraint. *The Israelis are likely to respond with diplomatic moderation.* ◇ If you do something **in moderation,** you do not do it too much. *Exercise is good for all of us in moderation.*

moderator In some Protestant churches, a **moderator** is a member of the clergy who is appointed on a yearly basis to preside at important church meetings. ◇ A **moderator** is also someone who helps settle disputes between groups of people.

modern (modernity) **Modern** is used to describe things which exist or happen now, rather than in the past. *These rules are outdated and irrelevant to modern industrial relations.* ◇ **Modern** is also used to describe things which make use of the latest ideas or technology. *France is endowed with an excellent modern railway system.* You talk about the **modernity** of things like these. *Kenworthy was amazed at the modernity of Dr Aubin's consulting-room.* ◇ People are sometimes called **modern** when they have opinions which are ahead of those of other people. *His views are distinctly modern... ...a modern vicar.*

modern-day is used to talk about something as it is now, as distinct from the way it was in the past. *...modern-day photography... ...modern-day France.* ◇ **Modern-day** is also used to talk about something in the present which is similar to something which existed or happened in the past. *...a modern-day gold rush.*

modern languages When university students read **modern languages,** they study European languages which are in use today, such as French and German, rather than languages from the past like Latin and Greek.

modernise See modernize.

modernism (modernist) Modernism was a late 19th and early 20th-century movement in art, literature, and music. It rejected accepted ideas and techniques and introduced many new ones, some of which have taken hold. These new ideas and techniques are called **modernist.** The artists, writers, and composers who introduced them are called **modernists.**

modernity See modern.

modernize (modernizing, modernized; modernization) *(can be spelled with an 's' instead of a 'z')* When something like a system or factory is **modernized,** new methods or equipment are introduced into it. ...*the modernization of British industry.*

modest (modestly, modesty) ❏ If something is **modest,** it is quite small. ...*a modest improvement.*

❏ If someone is **modest,** they do not talk much about their abilities, achievements, or possessions. *He confessed modestly to having won a few prizes.* You talk about the **modesty** of someone like this.

modicum A modicum of something is a small amount of it.

modify (modifies, modifying, modified; modification.) If you **modify** something, you make a slight change to it, to improve it. The change is called a **modification.**

modish *(pron:* moe-dish) If something is **modish,** it is fashionable to have it or do it.

modular See module.

modulate (modulating, modulated; modulation) If you **modulate** your voice, you vary the way it sounds, for example its loudness, pitch, or tone, according to the effect you want to create. ...*vocal modulation.* ◇ If you **modulate** an activity or process, you alter it or adjust it, to make it more suitable to a particular set of circumstances.

module (modular) ❏ A **module** is one of a number of standard parts fitted together to form a building or other structure. A **modular** structure is put together in this way. ◇ A **module** is also (a) part of a machine or system, which performs a particular function. (b) part of a spacecraft which can operate independently from the other parts, often away from the spacecraft.

❏ Some university or college courses consist of separate units called **modules.** A **modular** course is made up of units like these.

modus operandi *(pron:* mode-uss op-per-and-die) A **modus operandi** is a way of doing something.

modus vivendi *(pron:* mode-uss vie-ven-die) If people with very different beliefs or attitudes have a **modus vivendi,** they have found a way of living or working together.

mogul The Moguls were Muslim rulers in India in the 16th to 18th centuries. ◇ Nowadays, a **mogul** is an important, rich, and famous businessman or businesswoman, especially one in the film or TV industry.

mohair is a kind of very soft fabric or yarn made from the wool of Angora goats.

moist If something is **moist,** it is slightly wet.

moisten (moistening, moistened) If you **moisten** something, you make it slightly wet.

moisture consists of tiny drops of water in the air or on a surface.

moisturize (moisturizing, moisturized; moisturizer) *(can be spelled with an 's' instead of a 'z')* If you **moisturize** your skin, you put a cream or lotion called a **moisturizer** on it, to restore moisture to it and soften it.

molar Your **molars** are the large teeth at the back of your mouth for chewing food.

molasses is a sweet thick dark brown syrup. It is produced when sugar is refined, and is used in cooking.

mold See mould.

molder See moulder.

mole ❏ A **mole** is a natural dark spot on someone's skin.

❏ The **mole** is a small black furry animal which digs tunnels and lives underground.

❏ A member of an organization who secretly reveals information to the press or to a rival organization can be called a **mole.**

molecule *(pron:* moll-lik-yule) (molecular) A **molecule** is the smallest amount of a chemical substance which can exist without breaking apart into other substances. **Molecular** *(pron:* moll-lek-you-lar) is used to talk about things to do with molecules. ...*the molecular basis of life... ...tackling the problem at a molecular level.*

molehill A **molehill** is a small pile of earth left by a mole digging a tunnel. ◇ If you say someone is **making a mountain out of a molehill,** you mean they are treating something unimportant as if it were very serious.

molest (molestation, molester) If someone **molests** women or children, they touch them in a sexual way against their will. Behaviour like this is called **molestation;** a person who does it is called a **molester.** ◇ You also say someone **molests** people when they physically interfere with them or prevent them from doing something.

moll A gangster's **moll** is a woman who lives with him and has a sexual relationship with him.

mollify (mollifies, mollifying, mollified) If you **mollify** someone, you make them less upset or angry.

mollusc A **mollusc** is an animal like a snail, slug, clam, or octopus, which has a soft body and no backbone. Many molluscs have hard shells to protect them.

Molotov cocktail A **Molotov cocktail** is the same as a petrol bomb.

molt See moult.

molten rock or metal has been heated to a very high temperature and has become a hot thick sticky liquid.

molybdenum *(pron:* mol-lib-din-um) is a very hard silvery-white metallic element. It is used in alloys, especially to harden and strengthen steel.

moment ❏ A **moment** is a very short period of time. *They emerge to look around them for a moment, then disappear into cover again.* ◇ If you say something will happen **in a moment,** you mean it will happen very soon.

❏ If something is happening **at the moment,** it is happening now. ◇ If you say a problem has been dealt with **for the moment,** you mean it has been dealt with temporarily, but will probably reappear later.

❏ If you do something **at the last moment,** you do it at the latest possible time at which it can be done. ◇ If something happens **the moment** something else happens, it happens as soon as the other thing does.

❏ A **moment of truth** is an important time when something which had been uncertain suddenly becomes very clear.

momentarily If something happens **momentarily,** it happens for only a short time. *The popping flashbulbs fooled us momentarily into thinking that there might be someone worth photographing in the room.* ◇ In the US, **momentarily** is used to say something will happen very soon. *We are expecting a statement from the presidential spokesman momentarily.*

momentary If something is **momentary**, it lasts for only a short time. *The explosion caused momentary panic.*

momentous A **momentous** event is very important or significant.

momentum is used to talk about things being active. For example, if you say something **gains momentum**, you mean it becomes more active. *The speculation surrounding the princess has gathered momentum.* ◇ The **momentum** of a moving object is its ability to keep moving because of the speed it already has. In physics, this is equal to its mass multiplied by its velocity.

monarch (monarchical) A **monarch** is a reigning queen or king. **Monarchical** is used to talk about things to do with a monarch. *...a reduction of monarchical powers.*

monarchist A **monarchist** is a person who thinks their country should have a monarch.

monarchy (monarchies) When people talk about **the monarchy**, they mean (a) their country's system of having a king or queen. *The Italian monarchy was ended by referendum in 1946.* (b) their country's royal family. ◇ A **monarchy** is a country which has a king or queen.

monastery (monasteries) A **monastery** is a building or group of buildings where a community of monks live.

monastic (monasticism) **Monastic** is used to talk about things to do with monks or monasteries. *...a monastic community.* **Monasticism** is the system of having monasteries.

monetarism (monetarist) **Monetarism** is the control of a country's economy by regulating the total amount of money which is available and in use. A **monetarist** is someone who favours this policy. **Monetarist** is used to talk about things to do with monetarism. *There is a major hole in the monetarist argument.*

monetary is used to talk about things to do with money, especially the finances of a country or group of countries. *...monetary policy... The French wanted an automatic move to full monetary union at least by 1999.*

money (monies) ❑ **Money** is coins and bank notes, and also funds such as savings held in a bank or building society. ◇ **make money:** see **make**.
   ❑ If you get your **money's worth**, you get good value for the money you spend on something.
   ❑ **Monies** is sometimes used to talk about separate sums of money forming part of a larger amount. *It would mean a substantial reduction in monies available for other services.*

money-box A **money-box** is a small box with an opening at the top, for putting coins in as a way of saving.

money changer A **money changer** is a person who converts money from one currency to another, often illegally.

money-lender See **moneylender**.

money market A country's **money market** consists of its commercial banks and all other institutions including the government which deal with short-term loans and foreign exchange.

money men See **moneymen**.

money order In Canada and the US, a **money order** is like a postal order, but is available from banks as well as post offices.

money-spinner (money-spinning) If something is a **money-spinner**, it makes a lot of money for someone. *...money-spinning opportunities.*

moneyed people have a lot of money.

moneylender (*or* money-lender) A **moneylender** is a person who lends money to people and charges a high rate of interest.

moneymen (*or* money men) People who work with finance, for example accountants, bankers, and stockbrokers, are sometimes called **moneymen**.

mongoose Mongooses are small furry animals with long tails. They live in hot countries and kill snakes.

mongrel A **mongrel** is a dog with parents of different breeds.

monies See **money**.

monitor (monitoring, monitored) ❑ If you **monitor** something, you regularly check its condition or development. ◇ If you **monitor** sounds or signals, you listen to them or record them to get information.
   ❑ A **monitor** is a machine used to check or record things, for example, a person's heartbeat or the picture and sound quality of a TV broadcast. ◇ The visual display unit of a computer is sometimes called a **monitor**.
   ❑ A **monitor** is also a person who checks that something is done fairly or correctly.

monk A **monk** is a member of a male religious community.

monkey Monkeys are long-tailed tree-climbing animals. They live mainly in hot countries.

monkey nut Monkey nuts are the same as peanuts.

mono is used to describe a record or a system of playing music in which all the sound is directed through one speaker.

monochrome A **monochrome** painting is done using one colour in various shades. ◇ **Monochrome** film, photography, and TV use black, white, and shades of grey but no other colours.

monocle A **monocle** is a lens which people used to wear in front of one eye to improve their vision in that eye.

monoculture A **monoculture** is an agricultural system in which only one type of crop is grown.

monogamy (*pron:* mon-nog-a-mee) (monogamous) **Monogamy** is being married to only one person at a time. See also **polygamy**. ◇ **Monogamy** is also sticking to one sexual partner. *Aids makes infidelity more dangerous and monogamy more appealing.* A **monogamous** person or animal has only one sexual partner at a time.

monogram (monogrammed) A **monogram** is a design based on someone's initials which is used to mark the things they own. A **monogrammed** object has a monogram on it.

monograph A **monograph** is a book or essay which is a detailed study of one subject.

monolith A **monolith** is a very large tall block of stone, set upright in the ground in ancient times.

monolithic A **monolithic** building is very tall, like a monolith. ◇ A **monolithic** organization or system is very large and very similar throughout.

monologue A monologue is a long speech by one person.

monomania is an obsession with one thing.

monopolise See monopolize.

monopolist (monopolistic) A **monopolist** controls or tries to control as much of an industry as he or she can. Similarly, a **monopolistic** firm tries to control as much of the market for its product or service as possible.

monopolize (monopolizing, monopolized) (*can be spelled with an 's' instead of a 'z'*) If you accuse someone of **monopolizing** something, you mean they are trying to control it completely and prevent other people from having a share in it.

monopoly (monopolies) ❑ If a person or a firm has a **monopoly** on something, they are in complete control or possession of it. *The board has held a monopoly on milk supplies in England and Wales for 59 years.*
    ❑ **Monopoly** is a board game played using dice. The players try to buy land and buildings, charge rent for them, and build new property on the land. The winner is the one who makes all the other players bankrupt. 'Monopoly' is a trademark.

monorail A **monorail** is a system of transport in which trains travel along a single rail, usually high above the ground.

monosodium glutamate is a white crystalline substance which is added to food, especially some restaurant and take-away food, to make the flavours stronger.

monosyllable (monosyllabic) A **monosyllable** is a word with only one syllable, for example 'yes' or 'no'. If someone is **monosyllabic**, they tend to talk in monosyllables. If you give **monosyllabic** answers, you answer a series of questions by saying 'yes' or 'no', usually because you do not want to give too much away.

monotheism (monotheistic) **Monotheism** is the belief that only one God exists. A **monotheistic** religion is founded on the idea that there is only one God.

monotone A **monotone** is a sound or a way of speaking which does not vary at all and is boring to listen to.

monotonous (monotonously, monotony) If you call something **monotonous**, you mean it has no variety and is boring. *The rain dripped monotonously from the trees.* You talk about the **monotony** of something like this.

Monsignor is the title of a priest of high rank in the Catholic Church.

monsoon The **monsoon** is the season of very heavy rain in Southern Asia.

monster ❑ A **monster** is a large frightening imaginary creature. ◇ People sometimes call a cruel, frightening, or evil person a **monster**.
    ❑ **Monster** is also used to describe things which are extremely large. *...monster sharks... ...a monster gun.*

monstrosity (monstrosities) You call something a **monstrosity** when it is large and very ugly. *Most of the older buildings have been torn down and replaced by modern monstrosities.*

monstrous (monstrously) A **monstrous** act is very cruel and shocking. ◇ You also say something is **monstrous** when you think it is disgraceful and ought not to have been allowed. *Concorde was a monstrously uneconomic project.* ◇ If you say an object is **monstrous**, you mean it is

very large and ugly.

montage (*pron:* mon-**tazh**; *the 'zh' sounds like 's' in 'pleasure'*) A **montage** is a picture, film, or piece of music made up of several different elements, often in an unusual combination or sequence.

month A **month** or **calendar month** is one of the twelve periods a year is divided into, for example January or February. ◇ **lunar month:** see lunar.

monthly (monthlies) **Monthly** is used to describe (a) something which happens every month. *...monthly broadcasts.* (b) something paid or received every month. *...monthly pay cheques.* ◇ A **monthly** is a magazine published once a month.

monument A **monument** is a large structure, often of stone, put up to remind people of a famous person or an event in history. ◇ A **monument** is also something like a castle or bridge which was built a long time ago and is thought to be important because of its historical interest. ◇ If you say something is a **monument** to something else, you mean it shows how important and powerful that thing is. *The average American supermarket is a monument to the power of consumer choice.*

monumental (monumentally) ❑ A **monumental** building or work of art is very large and impressive.
    ❑ A **monumental** mistake is a particularly bad one. ◇ **Monumental** can be used to describe other things which are particularly bad or unfortunate. *The debts of East German enterprises are monumental... ...teenagers getting monumentally plastered.*

mooch (mooches, mooching, mooched) If you **mooch about** or **mooch around,** you wander around aimlessly.

mood Your **mood** is the way you feel at a particular time. *Gilligan was in a boisterous mood.* ◇ If you are **in the mood** for something, you feel like doing it or experiencing it. ◇ The **mood** of a group of people is their general feeling or attitude to something which is happening. *My family's reaction mirrored exactly the mood of the nation.*

moody (moodily) You say a person is **moody** (a) when their mood changes quickly and unpredictably. (b) when they are gloomy, depressed, and unwilling to talk to people. *He was sitting moodily in his leather swivel chair.*

moon (mooning, mooned) ❑ The **moon** is the object in space which orbits the Earth about every four weeks, and which you see in the night sky as a circle or part of a circle. Other planets have objects orbiting them called **moons.**
    ❑ If you are **over the moon** about something, you are very pleased about it.
    ❑ If you say someone is **mooning** over another person, you mean they are thinking about them a lot, because they are in love with them.

moonbeam A **moonbeam** is a ray of light from the moon.

moonless A **moonless** night is one when no moon can be seen, and it is dark.

moonlight (moonlit) ❑ **Moonlight** is the light which reaches the Earth from the moon at night. If something is **moonlit,** it is lit by moonlight.
    ❑ If someone is **moonlighting,** they have a second job, often without informing their main employer or the tax office.

moonscape A **moonscape** is a desolate area of land

which looks like the surface of the moon.

moonshine is illegally distilled spirits.

❏ **Moonshine** is also foolish talk and ideas which have little to do with reality.

Moor (Moorish) The **Moors** were a Muslim people who established a civilization in North Africa and Spain between the 8th and 15th centuries. **Moorish** is used to describe things connected with these people and their culture. ...*a Moorish temple.*

moor (mooring, moored) ❏ A **moor** is an area of high open ground covered mainly with rough grass and heather.

❏ If a boat is **moored**, it is floating and tied up to something on land. A place where a boat can be tied up is called a **mooring**.

moorhen The **moorhen** is a black bird with a red bill which lives in and near water.

mooring See moor.

Moorish See Moor.

moorland is high open land, usually covered in rough grass and heather.

moose (*plural:* moose) is the North American name for an elk.

moot (mooting, mooted) If you say something is moot or a **moot point**, you mean it is doubtful or open to argument. *Whether the transfer of power was entirely peaceful is a moot point.* ◇ If an idea is **mooted**, it is suggested or introduced as a subject for people to discuss.

mop (mopping, mopped) ❏ A **mop** is a tool for washing floors. It has a long handle and a head made of sponge or many pieces of string. If you **mop** a floor, you clean it with a wet mop. ◇ If you **mop** a surface or **mop up** liquid from it, you wipe it with a dry cloth to remove the liquid.

❏ If a winning army **mops up** resistance, it deals with any people on the other side who are still fighting.

❏ If you talk about someone's **mop** of hair, you mean they have a lot of it and it is loose and untidy.

mope (moping, moped) If you **mope** or **mope about**, you feel miserable and are not interested in anything.

moped A **moped** is a type of lightweight motorbike with a small engine.

moral (morally) ❏ **Moral** is used to talk about things connected with right behaviour. *For genuinely held moral considerations they felt compelled to disobey their legal duty... Such behaviour is morally indefensible.* ◇ If you do something because it is your **moral** duty or **moral** responsibility, you do it because you believe it is right, rather than because you are legally obliged to do it. ◇ A **moral** person has moral principles and tries to stick to them. Principles like these are called **morals**. ◇ If you talk about someone's **moral fibre**, you mean they are determined to do what they think is right at all costs.

❏ If you give someone **moral support**, you give them encouragement, rather than practical help. ◇ If the loser of a dispute or contest claims to have won a **moral victory**, they mean they have shown they were in the right or superior to their opponent, in spite of the result.

❏ The **moral** of a story or situation is what it teaches you about what you should or should not do.

morale (*pron:* mor-**rahl**) When you talk about the **morale** of a group of people, you mean the amount of confidence and optimism they have in what they are doing. *Morale within the Party is low.*

moralise See moralize.

moralist (moralistic) A **moralist** is someone with strong ideas about right and wrong, which they try to get other people to accept. You say someone who behaves like this is **moralistic**.

morality is the belief that some behaviour is right and acceptable and other behaviour is wrong. *She was a woman whose personal morality would not countenance an affair with a married man.* ◇ The **morality** of something is how right or acceptable it is. *The Churches have been relatively quiet about the morality of military action.*

moralize (moralizing, moralized) (*can be spelled with an 's' instead of a 'z'*) If you **moralize** about something, you draw conclusions about the rights and wrongs of it.

morass (*pron:* mor-**rass**) (morasses) A **morass** is a complicated and confused situation which it is difficult to get out of.

moratorium (*plural:* moratoriums *or* moratoria) If there is a **moratorium** on some kind of activity, people or governments agree that they will stop doing it for a certain period. *Britain will firmly oppose any proposal to lift the moratorium on commercial whaling.*

morbid (morbidly, morbidity) ❏ If you say something like a book or conversation is **morbid**, you mean it is too concerned with unpleasant things, especially death. You can talk about the **morbidity** of something like this.

❏ **Morbidity** is also used to talk about disease, for example the number of cases of a particular disease. *Large scale drug therapy will reduce infection in communities and hopefully bring down the morbidity.*

mordant humour or wit is sarcastic and sharply critical.

more ❏ If there is **more** of one thing than another, or **more** of something than there was before, there is a greater amount of it. ◇ You also use **more** when you are talking about an additional thing or amount. *After two days in a local hospital and two more in Delhi, Venables was flown home to Britain... Add a little more olive oil.*

❏ **More** means to a greater extent. *Under her guidance the event has become more closely connected with the city.* ◇ You use **more and more** to say something happens to an increasing extent. *It looked as if Britons would continue drinking more and more lager.*

❏ You use **more** when you are comparing things, for example when you say one thing is more important than another. ◇ You can say how large a number or amount is by saying it is **more than** a certain figure or measurement. *The ruling could have implications for more than a million people.* Similarly, you can say how small a number or amount is by saying it is **no more than** a certain figure or measurement. *In the pole vault Bubka could clear no more than 5.70 metres.*

❏ You use **more** to talk about something continuing to happen. *We shall have to investigate this a bit more.* ◇ You use **no more** or **not any more** to say something has stopped happening or is no longer true. *In five years, this ancient culture won't exist any more... Let me hear no more about it.* ◇ If something is **no more**, it no longer exists.

❏ You use **no more than** or **nothing more than** to say something is only a particular thing, and not something bigger, better, or more important. *This plan will turn the BBC into nothing more than a retailer of goods manufactured* *by suppliers.*

❑ **More than** is used to say something not only reaches a certain standard, but goes beyond it. For example, if you say something is 'more than satisfactory', you mean it is not just satisfactory but very good.

❑ You use **more or less** to say something is true in a general way, rather than completely true. *The small Florida town of Verity is inhabited more or less entirely by divorced women.* ◇ If you say something is a particular thing **no more no less**, you mean it is exactly that thing.

❑ You say **what is more** when you are adding some information or making a further point. *He will know how to take orders and, what is more, how to execute them.*

❑ **all the more**: see **all**.

moreover You say **moreover** when you are adding more information or making a further point. *It must have been a real boneshaking ride, because in those days pneumatic tyres had not yet been heard of and the roads, moreover, were appalling.*

mores (pron: more-rayz) The **mores** of a place are the customs and habits there.

morgue In some countries, for example France and the US, a **morgue** is a place where unidentified bodies or the bodies of murder victims are kept until they are identified or released for burial.

moribund If something is **moribund**, it is about to come to an end because it no longer has any useful function.

Mormon The **Mormons** are a Christian group founded in the US in the 19th century. Their beliefs are based on the visions of their founder, Joseph Smith. Their church is called the Church of Jesus Christ of Latter-day Saints.

morning When people talk about the **morning**, they usually mean the time between sunrise and the middle of the day. However, a particular time **in the morning** means a time between midnight and noon. *I stayed up till 4.30 in the morning.* ◇ **Morning sickness** is the feeling of sickness some women have in the mornings during the first few months of pregnancy.

moron (moronic) If you call someone a **moron** or say they are **moronic**, you mean they are very stupid.

morose (morosely) If someone is **morose**, they are miserable, bad-tempered, and unwilling to talk. *Alberg waited, looking down morosely at his sodden shoes.*

morphine is a drug manufactured from opium poppies. It is a powerful painkiller and relaxes the body, but is also addictive.

morphology (morphological) **Morphology** is used to talk about the structure or formation of various things. For example, in biology, **morphology** is the study of the physical structure of plants and animals. The **morphology** of a language is the form and structure of the words in it. In geography, the **morphology** of a town or landscape is its physical development. You use **morphological** to talk about things connected with any of these kinds of morphology. *Identification of these flies up until now has been at the morphological level.*

morris dancing (morris dancer) **Morris dancing** is a type of old English country dancing, traditionally performed by men with handkerchiefs, sticks, and bells. The people who perform these dances are called **morris dancers**.

Morse or **morse code** is an international code for sending messages. It uses a system of written dots and dashes or short and long sounds to represent the letters of the alphabet.

morsel A **morsel** is a small piece of something, especially food.

mortal (mortally) ❑ Anything that dies is said to be **mortal**.

❑ When you are talking in a sarcastic way about someone who is supposed to be very important or clever, you can call other people **mere mortals** or **lesser mortals**. *Much of this was pure snobbishness, a means of putting lesser mortals in their proper place.*

❑ A **mortal** wound or injury causes death. *He was mortally wounded in an exchange of fire with police.* ◇ If someone is your **mortal** enemy, they are trying to kill you. ◇ If you are in **mortal** danger, you are in danger of being killed.

❑ In the Catholic Church, a **mortal sin** is a very serious and deliberate one which will result in the person being damned if he or she does not confess and fully repent.

mortality is the fact that everyone has to die sometime and nobody lives forever. *No president likes contemplating his own mortality, or suggesting to the electorate that he may die in office.* ◇ **Mortality** is also used to talk about the numbers of people who die at a particular age or from a particular cause. *India has been fighting battles against poverty, illiteracy and child mortality... Married people have lower mortality rates.*

mortar ❑ A **mortar** is a short cannon which fires shells high into the air for a short distance. Shells fired from a mortar can also be called **mortars**.

❑ **Mortar** is a mixture of sand, water, and cement used to hold bricks firmly together.

❑ A **mortar** is also a bowl in which you crush dried grains or spices with a tool called a pestle.

mortarboard (or mortar board) A **mortarboard** is a stiff black cap with a flat square top and a tassel hanging from it. Mortarboards are sometimes worn on formal occasions by university students and teachers.

mortgage (pron: more-gij) (mortgagor, mortgagee; mortgaging, mortgaged) A **mortgage** is a loan you get from a bank or building society to enable you to buy a house. In an arrangement like this, you are called the **mortgagor** and the bank or building society is called the **mortgagee**. ◇ If you **mortgage** your house or land, you use it as a guarantee to a company so they will lend you money. If you do not repay the money, they can repossess the property.

mortice (or mortise) A **mortice** is a slot cut in a piece of wood or stone. Another piece, called a **tenon**, fits into the slot.

mortify (mortifies, mortifying, mortified: mortification) If you are **mortified**, you feel very offended, ashamed, or embarrassed. *He will face the mortification of seeing the shop close prematurely.*

mortise A **mortise lock** is a type of lock which fits into a hole cut in the edge of a door rather than being fixed to one side of it. The lock cannot be seen or unscrewed when the door is closed. ◇ See also **mortice**.

mortuary (mortuaries) A **mortuary** is a place where dead bodies are kept before they are buried or cremated.

mosaic A **mosaic** is a design made up of small pieces of coloured stone or glass set in concrete or plaster. ◇ You can call something else a **mosaic** if it is made up of many different things of the same general type. *Firms face a mosaic of rules and standards that makes the cost of doing business anywhere prohibitively expensive.*

Moslem See **Muslim**.

mosque A **mosque** is a building where Muslims go to worship.

mosquito (mosquitoes *or* mosquitos) **Mosquitoes** are small flying insects which live in damp areas. They bite people and animals and suck their blood. One type of mosquito carries malaria.

mosquito net A **mosquito net** is a curtain made of very fine material which is hung round a bed to protect the person sleeping there from mosquitoes and other insects.

moss (mosses; mossy) **Moss** is a soft green covering on damp soil, wood, or stone. It is made up of dense clusters of a tiny plant. A **mossy** stone or lawn has moss growing on it.

most ❑ You use **most** to talk about the majority of a group of people or things, or the largest part of something. *A politician spends most of his time trying to justify his last six mistakes... This advice holds good for most bottles of red wine.* ◇ If something is true **for the most part**, it is generally true, or true about the largest part of something. *For the most part, the theatre in Germany is not about entertainment but about serious issues.* ◇ **The most** means the largest amount. *Austria charges the most for a soft drink and Bahrain the least.*

❑ You use **most** to say someone or something has more of a quality than anyone or anything else, as, for example, when you talk about the **most popular** person in a place or the **most expensive** hotel.

❑ If you talk about what happens **most** or **most of all**, you mean what happens more than anything else. You also use **most** when you are talking about something happening more to one person or thing than any other. *A league table of the colour of cars most involved in accidents shows clearly that black is worst.* ◇ You also use **most** or **most of all** to talk about something having more of an effect than other things. *What seems to irk the Moldavians most of all is the apparent unexpectedness of the Gagauz demands.* ◇ **Most of all** is also used to say what matters more than anything else in a situation. *Such change requires time, commitment and, most of all, planning.*

❑ **Most** can be used with some words to mean 'very'. *The authorities had been most careful to note down details of his family and address.*

❑ You say **at most** or **at the most** when you are mentioning the maximum amount something could be or should be. *Mr Axon believes there are, at most, 40 professional cheesemakers in Britain.*

❑ If you **make the most** of something, you get the maximum use or advantage from it.

most-favoured-nation If there is a **most-favoured-nation** agreement between two countries, they have agreed to apply their lowest tariff rates when they import each other's goods. You can also talk about one country granting **most-favoured-nation** status to another country.

mostly is used to say something is generally true, for example true of the majority of a group of people, or true most of the time. *Malaria mosquitoes bite mostly at dusk and through the night... 29 youths appeared in court, mostly on public order offences.*

MOT In Britain, an **MOT** or **MOT test** is a test carried out annually on all road vehicles three or more years old, to make sure they are safe to drive. MOT stands for 'Ministry of Transport'.

motel A **motel** is a type of hotel designed especially for people travelling by car. It usually has space to park cars near the rooms.

motet A **motet** is a piece of choral music usually based on a religious text. It is sung by a number of people but is not accompanied by instruments.

moth Moths are insects with large wings like butterflies. They fly about mostly at night and are attracted to bright lights.

moth-eaten things look very old and tattered.

mothball ❑ If a project is **mothballed** or **put in mothballs,** work on it is postponed for a time.

❑ **Mothballs** are small white balls of a substance such as naphthalene. You put them among clothes or blankets to keep moths away.

mother (mothering, mothered) ❑ Your **mother** is your female parent. ◇ If a woman **mothers** someone, she treats them with great care and affection, and often spoils them. ◇ If a woman is a **mother figure** to you, you think of her as someone you can turn to for help, advice, and support.

❑ **Mother** is sometimes used to describe the original thing of a certain kind, from which other things have developed. *It was Moscow that broke from the Kievan mother church in the 15th century.*

❑ A person's **mother country** is the country where they were born or where their ancestors came from, and which they feel emotionally linked to. ◇ Your **mother tongue** is the language you learned from your parents when you were a child.

❑ The **mother ship** of a group of ships is a larger one from which they are launched or provided with supplies.

❑ If you describe something like a battle as **the mother of all** battles, you mean it is the biggest or most important battle ever. *...the mother of all cock-ups.*

mother-in-law (mothers-in-law) Your **mother-in-law** is the mother of your husband or wife.

Mother Nature is another name for nature, especially when it is thought of as a force controlling things and people.

mother-of-pearl objects such as buttons or jewellery are made from certain types of shells which have a rainbow-coloured pearly lining.

Mother Superior The **Mother Superior** of a convent is the nun in charge.

mother-to-be (mothers-to-be) A **mother-to-be** is a pregnant woman.

Mother's Day is a special day when children give cards and gifts to their mothers. In Britain, Mother's Day was originally called **Mothering Sunday,** and is the fourth Sunday in Lent.

motherhood is the state of being a mother.

motherland When people talk about their **motherland,** they mean the country where they or their ancestors were born.

motherly You say a woman is **motherly** when she is

warm, kind, and protective.

motif (*pron:* mo-teef) In literature and music, a **motif** is an idea or musical phrase which is repeated and expanded. ◇ A **motif** is also a shape which is repeated in a design or pattern. *...a navy carpet with a light-blue star motif.*

motion (motioning, motioned) ❑ In a meeting or debate, a **motion** is a proposal which is discussed and voted on.

❑ **Motion** is movement. If something is **in motion**, it is moving. ◇ A **motion** is an action, gesture, or movement. If you **motion** someone to do something, you make a gesture which shows you want them to do it.

❑ If you **set** a process **in motion**, you do whatever is necessary to start it.

❑ If you **go through the motions** of doing something, you do it because you have to, but without any real interest or sincerity.

motion picture A **motion picture** is the same as a film.

motionless If something is **motionless**, it is not moving.

motivate (motivating, motivated; motivation) ❑ The thing which **motivates** you is the thing which makes you behave the way you do. *The member states have entirely different economic conditions and political motivation.*

❑ If you **motivate** someone to do something, you give them the incentive to do it. ◇ If someone is **motivated**, they are willing to work hard to achieve something. *Teacher morale and motivation are not as high as they should be.*

motive Your **motive** for doing something is your reason for doing it.

motley A **motley** collection or group consists of people or things that are all different, so that the group seems rather odd.

motocross is a type of motorcycle racing done over a rough cross-country course.

motor (motoring, motored) ❑ The **motor** of a car or other vehicle is its engine. ◇ **Motor** is used to talk about things to do with cars and other powered vehicles. *...a motor mechanic... ...the Birmingham International Motor Show.* ◇ **Motoring** is driving in a car. If you **motor** somewhere, you drive there in a car.

❑ The **motor** of a machine is the part which provides the power which makes it work.

motor boat A **motor boat** is a boat driven by an engine.

motor car A **motor car** is the same as a car.

motor cycle See **motorcycle**.

motor scooter A **motor scooter** is a two-wheeled motor vehicle. It is like a motorcycle, but has much smaller wheels and an enclosed engine.

motorbike A **motorbike** is the same as a motorcycle.

motorcade A **motorcade** is a procession of motor vehicles, usually cars.

motorcycle (motorcyclist, motorcycling) (*or* **motor cycle**, *etc*) A **motorcycle** is a two-wheeled vehicle powered by an engine. **Motorcycling** is riding a motorcycle; a **motorcyclist** is someone who does this.

motorist A **motorist** is someone who drives a car.

motorized (*or* **motorised**) If something is **motorized**, it is powered by a motor.

motorway A **motorway** is a wide road which has been specially built, often where there was no road before, to allow uninterrupted fast travel over long distances.

mottled If something is **mottled**, it is covered in irregular patches of different colours.

motto (mottoes *or* mottos) A **motto** is a short sentence or phrase which gives a rule for good or sensible behaviour.

mould (moulding, moulded) (*American spelling:* mold, molding, *etc*) ❑ You say someone **moulds** something when they are responsible for it having a particular form. *The Supreme Court has a decisive role in moulding all aspects of United States society.* ◇ The things that **mould** a person are the various influences that make them the kind of person they are. *...the generation of politicians moulded by the Second World War.* ◇ You can describe a person by saying they are in a certain **mould**. *He demonstrated that Britain could produce mega-stars in the mould of Elvis Presley.*

❑ If you **mould** a substance like clay or plasticine, you make it into a particular shape. ◇ A **mould** is a container for making substances into a particular shape. You put the substance into the mould and allow it to set; when it is removed, it has the shape you want. ◇ **break the mould:** see **break**.

❑ **Mould** is a soft grey, green, or blue substance which sometimes grows on old food or damp walls.

moulder (mouldering, mouldered) (*American spelling:* molder, moldering, *etc*) If something is **mouldering**, it is crumbling and decaying.

mouldy (*American spelling:* moldy) If something is **mouldy**, it has mould growing on it.

moult (*American spelling:* molt) When an animal or bird **moults**, it loses its coat or feathers so that a new coat or feathers can grow.

mound ❑ A **mound** is a pile of earth, often with grass growing over it, like a very small hill.

❑ A **mound** of something is a large quantity of it. *Civil servants produce mounds of paper on the national curriculum.*

mount ❑ If someone **mounts a challenge** to someone's leadership, they try to take over from them as leader, especially by beating them in an election. ◇ If someone **mounts a challenge** to a legal decision, they try to get it reversed.

❑ When someone **mounts** something like an exhibition or a performance, they organize it and present it.

❑ If something **mounts**, it increases. *Pressure has been mounting among MPs for a commitment to abolish county councils.* **Mounting** is used to describe things which are increasing. *...mounting crime.* ◇ If something **mounts up**, it gets bigger because more and more is being added to it. *Legal costs could mount up if a solicitor handled the affair.*

❑ If you **mount** a horse, you get onto its back. A **mounted** person is on horseback. The horse someone is riding can be called their **mount**.

❑ If something is **mounted** somewhere, it is fixed there. *Instead of a steering wheel, there is a joystick mounted in the centre of the dashboard.*

❑ Some mountains have **Mount** as part of their name. *...Mount Everest.*

mountain A **mountain** is a high area like a very large hill with steep sides. ◇ A **mountain** of something is a very large amount of it. *We were munching our way through a mountain of poppadoms.*

mountain bike A **mountain bike** is a type of bicycle designed to be used over rough ground. Mountain bikes have strong frames, heavy tyres, and at least 16 gears to help the cyclist ride up steep hills.

mountain lion The **mountain lion** is the same as the puma.

mountaineer (mountaineering) A **mountaineer** is someone who climbs mountains as a hobby or sport. **Mountaineering** is the activity of climbing mountains.

mountainous A **mountainous** country or area has a lot of mountains.

mountainside A **mountainside** is one of the steep slopes of a mountain.

Mountie The **Mounties** is the popular name for the Royal Canadian Mounted Police.

mourn If you **mourn** someone who has died or **mourn** their death, you express your sadness about their death. ◇ If someone is in **mourning**, they are wearing special clothes or behaving in a certain way, because someone in their family has died: ◇ If you **mourn** the loss of something, you are sad because it is no longer there.

mourner The people attending a funeral are called the **mourners**.

mournful (mournfully) If someone has a **mournful** expression, they look very sad. ◇ A **mournful** noise sounds sad.

mouse ❑ **Mice** are small furry mammals with long tails and whiskers.
❑ A **mouse** (*plural: mice or mouses*) is a hand-held electronic device used with a computer system. By moving it over a flat surface and pressing its buttons, you can move the cursor around the screen and perform certain operations without using the keyboard.

mousetrap A **mousetrap** is a small device for catching or killing mice.

mousse (*pron: moose*) is (a) a type of light frothy food made from whisked egg white with some sweet or savoury ingredients. (b) a light frothy substance used for keeping your hair in a particular style.

moustache (moustached) (*or mustache, mustached*) A man's **moustache** is the hair he has allowed to grow on his upper lip. A **moustached** man has a moustache.

mouth ❑ Your **mouth** is your lips, or the space behind your lips where your teeth and tongue are. ◇ If you **mouth** something, you form the words in an exaggerated way with your lips, without making any sound. You do this, for example, to say something to someone when it is too noisy for them to hear your voice. ◇ If someone **mouths** something like a slogan, they say it because they have to, and not because they really believe it.
❑ If you **put your money where your mouth is**, you show your commitment to a scheme or idea by investing your money in it.
❑ The **mouth** of a harbour or a river is the place where it opens into the sea. ◇ The **mouth** of a cave, hole, or bottle is its entrance or opening.

mouth organ A **mouth organ** is the same as a harmonica.

mouth-watering food looks or smells delicious. ◇ You describe other things as **mouth-watering** when the idea of having them is very attractive. *The associated rewards of owning a baseball franchise can also be mouth-watering.*

mouthful A **mouthful** of food or drink is the amount you can get in your mouth at any one time. ◇ If you say a word or phrase is a **mouthful,** you mean it is long and difficult to say.

mouthpiece ❑ The **mouthpiece** of a government or organization is the person who presents their opinions and policies to the outside world. A newspaper or radio station can also function as a mouthpiece.
❑ The **mouthpiece** of a musical instrument is the part you blow into. ◇ The **mouthpiece** of a telephone is the part you speak into.

mouthwash is a liquid you rinse your mouth with to freshen your breath.

movable (*or* **moveable**) If something is **movable**, it can be moved from one place or position to another.

move (moving, moved; movingly, mover) ❑ If someone or something **moves** or is **moved,** they change their position. ◇ In a game like chess or draughts, each change of position of a piece or counter is called a **move**.
❑ If you **move** or **move house,** you go to live in a different house, taking all your belongings with you. Going to live in another house is called a **move**. ◇ When you move your possessions into a house and start living there, you can say you **move in.** When you leave, taking your possessions with you, you say you **move out.** If you **move away,** you go to live in a different town or area. ◇ When an organization transfers to a different place or building, this can also be called a **move**.
❑ If you **move** to a different job, you go somewhere else to take it up. A change like this is called a **move**. When someone changes to a different job or position within the same organization, you can say they **move over.** *Mr Joxe, who moves over from the interior ministry, is unlikely to have any hesitation in carrying out his master's commands.* ◇ If you **move in** on a project or activity, you become involved in it.
❑ If you talk about someone's ability to **move about** or **move around,** you are talking about their ability to get from one place to another. *Visitors with disabilities can get into the home and move around easily.* ◇ You also say someone **moves about** or **moves around** when they keep changing their job or the place where they live. ◇ If you say someone **moves** in particular circles, you are talking about the people they spend a lot of their time with.
❑ If troops or police **move in,** they approach a place to attack the people there or restore order. ◇ When vehicles or people **move off,** they start moving away from a place. When this happens, you can say they are **on the move.** ◇ If the police **move you on,** they get you to leave a place and go somewhere else.
❑ When a situation is developing very rapidly, you can talk about things **moving** fast. Similarly, you can talk about things **moving** slowly.
❑ If people are **moving** towards a new system, they are gradually preparing to introduce it. Each step they take can be called a **move**. *The proposals coincide with moves to reform the training of primary teachers.* You can also talk about people **moving over** to a new system.
❑ If something **moves** you, it makes you feel sadness or sympathy. Something which has this effect on people can be called **moving.** *He spoke movingly about how his friend's resilience had helped them through the difficult times.* ◇ If something **moves** you to do something, it makes you

decide to do it.

❑ If you **move** a motion or an amendment at a meeting, you propose it so people can vote for or against it. ...*the mover of the resolution, Mr. T. J. Gray.*

❑ If you tell someone to **get a move on**, you are telling them to hurry up.

❑ If a proposed event is **moved** to a different date, the date when it will take place is changed.

moveable See movable.

movement ❑ When a large number of people in different places have the same general aims, this is called a **movement**. ...*the Civil Rights movement*... ...*the trade union movement.*

❑ **Movement** is the process by which something changes position. A **movement** is a change of position. ◇ Changes in the position of parts of an army are called **movements**, especially when they are preparing to attack.

❑ When numbers of people travel regularly between two places, you call this the **movement** of people between the places. *Article 8a of the Treaty stipulates the right of free movement of people, goods, services and capital across borders.* ◇ Your **movements** are everything you do during a certain period. *The former champion was questioned about his movements by police shortly after his arrest.*

❑ If there is **movement** or a **movement** in people's attitudes or opinions, there are signs that they are beginning to change. *There's a movement away from the notion of a regimented culture.* Similarly, if there is **movement** in something like negotiations, there are signs that progress is being made.

❑ A **movement** is also one of the sections of a piece of classical music.

mover The most powerful and influential people in an industry are sometimes called its **movers and shakers**.

movie A movie is a film. In Canada and the US, a **movie theater** or **movie house** is a cinema; when people there are going to the cinema, they say they are going to the **movies**.

moving (movingly) See move.

moving picture In the past, films were sometimes called **moving pictures**.

mow (mowing, mowed, have mowed *or* have mown) If you mow a lawn, you cut the grass. Similarly, you talk about a crop such as wheat being **mown**. ◇ If a group of people are **mown down**, they are killed at the same time, for example by machine-gun fire.

mower A mower is a machine for cutting grass, corn, or wheat.

mozzarella (*pron:* mot-sa-rel-la) is a type of soft white Italian cheese. It was originally made using buffalo milk, but outside Italy it is now usually made from cows' milk.

MP An MP or **Member of Parliament** is a person who has been elected to represent people in their country's parliament.

mpg is short for 'miles per gallon'. It is used to say how far a vehicle can travel for each gallon of fuel it uses.

mph Speed is often expressed in **mph** or 'miles per hour'.

Mr is used in front of a man's name. It is short for 'Mister'.

Mrs is used in front of a married woman's name.

MS See multiple sclerosis.

Ms is used in front of a woman's name when it is not known whether she is married, or when she does not want to be identified as married or single. ...*Ms Ann Morrison.*

M.Sc. An M.Sc. is a higher degree in a scientific subject. M.Sc. stands for 'Master of Science'.

much ❑ **Very much** is used to say something is true to a great extent. *It depends very much on the individual... We very much welcome any move to clear the cowboys out of our business.* ◇ **Much** is used with words ending in '-ed' to say something is very true of something or someone. *They do not play the counter-attacking game much favoured by Forest.* ◇ In sentences with words like 'not' in them, **much** is used to say something is true only to a small extent. *He speaks English, but not very much.*

❑ When you are comparing two things, you use **much** to emphasize the difference between them. *Britain's failure rate is much higher than some southern European states.*

❑ **How much** is used to ask about a quantity. *How much flexibility will the individual operator have over fares?* ◇ **How much** is also used to talk about an unknown quantity. *The more powerful republics are happy to play the president off against parliament to see how much autonomy they can win.*

❑ **Much** of something means a lot of it. *Much of the blame lies with the Americans... Neither company expects to make much money under such conditions.* ◇ **Nothing much** means very little. *Nothing much will happen before the new year.*

❑ If you say **so much for** a particular thing, you are commenting on how useless or meaningless it has turned out to be. *Of the committee's 57 members, 27 will be Chinese officials. So much for the promise made by China's leader, that Hong Kong's people would rule Hong Kong.* ◇ You also say **so much for** something to show you have finished talking about it. *So much for the policy goal; what about the ends for achieving it?*

❑ If something is **too much** for you, you cannot cope with it.

❑ People say something is a **bit much** when they are annoyed about it.

❑ If you say someone or something is **not much** of a certain type of thing, you mean they are a poor example of it. *She is a forceful and intense woman, but not much of a thinker about economics.*

muchness If you say a number of things are **much of a muchness**, you mean there is not much difference between them.

muck is dirt, sewage, or manure. ◇ If you **muck out** a stable, pigsty, or cowshed, you clean it.

❑ If you **muck** something **up**, you do it very badly. ◇ If you say someone is **mucking about**, you mean they are behaving stupidly and wasting time.

muck-raking is finding out details about the personal lives of public figures, and spreading scandal about them.

mucky If something is **mucky**, it is very dirty or muddy.

mucus (*or* mucous) (*pron:* mjew-kus) is a slimy liquid produced in some parts of the body. For example, it is produced in the stomach to protect it from the acid which digests food there, and in the throat to aid swallowing.

mud is a sticky mixture of earth and water.

mud-slinging is trying to damage someone's reputation

by accusing them of immoral or dishonest behaviour.

muddle (muddling, muddled) ❑ If something is in a **muddle**, it is in a confused state.

❑ If someone is **muddled**, they are not thinking clearly and are confusing different things. You can also say their behaviour is **muddled**. ...*the muddled reaction of the authorities.* ◇ If you **muddle** things or **muddle** them **up**, you mix them up or get them in the wrong order.

❑ If you **muddle through**, you manage to do something even though you do not really know how to do it properly. ◇ If you **muddle along**, you live or exist without a proper plan or purpose.

muddy (muddier, muddiest; muddies, muddying, muddied) ❑ If something is **muddy**, it is full of mud, or covered with mud. ◇ A **muddy** colour is dull and brownish.

❑ If something **muddies** a situation, it makes it more difficult to understand or sort out. You can also talk about something **muddying the waters**.

mudflat Mudflats are flat boggy or muddy areas of coastal land which are covered by sea when the tide is in.

mudguard The **mudguards** on a bicycle or other vehicle are metal or plastic flaps above the wheels which stop the rider or vehicle getting splashed with mud.

muesli (*pron:* mews-lee) is a mixture of grains such as oats, dried fruit, and sometimes nuts, which people eat for breakfast with milk or yoghurt.

muezzin (*pron:* moo-ez-in) The **muezzin** is the official in a mosque who calls the faithful to prayer five times a day.

muff If you are given the opportunity to do something and you do it badly, you can say you **muff** it or **muff your chances**.

muffin A **muffin** is (a) a small American-style cake, usually with fruit or some other flavouring in it. (b) a small flat round bread roll, which you eat toasted with butter.

muffle (muffling, muffled) If you **muffle** a sound, you make it quieter. A **muffled** sound is quiet and indistinct. ◇ If you **muffle** your feelings, you suppress them. ...*muffled desires.*

muffler A **muffler** is the same as a scarf.

mug (mugging, mugged; mugger) ❑ A **mug** is a large deep cup with straight sides.

❑ A person's face is sometimes humorously called their **mug**. ◇ If someone **mugs** at a camera, they smile at it continually.

❑ If you say someone would be a **mug** to do something, you mean they would be very foolish to do it. Similarly, if you say something is a **mug's game**, you mean anyone who gets involved in it is bound to come off badly.

❑ If you are **mugged**, you are attacked in a public place and your money is stolen. A robbery of this kind is called a **mugging**; the person who does it is called a **mugger**.

❑ If you **mug up** on something, you learn as much as you can about it.

muggy If the weather is **muggy**, the air is unpleasantly warm and damp.

mugshot A **mugshot** is (a) a photograph taken by the police of someone who has been charged with a crime. (b) any photograph of a person's head and shoulders.

mulberry (mulberries) The **mulberry** is a tree which bears purple or white berries, also called **mulberries**. The

leaves of one kind of mulberry tree are used to feed silkworms.

mulch (mulches, mulching, mulched) **Mulch** is a mixture of rotting plant material put round the roots of plants to protect and feed them. If you **mulch** plants, you put mulch around them.

mule A **mule** is the sterile offspring of a female horse and a male donkey. In the past, mules were commonly used as work animals.

mulish If someone is **mulish**, they are unco-operative and obstinate.

mull ❑ If you **mull** something **over**, you think about it for a long time, before deciding what to do.

❑ **Mulled** wine is served hot with sugar and spices added to it.

mullah A **mullah** is a Muslim who has studied Islamic religion and laws.

mullioned windows are divided into panes by vertical strips of material such as wood or stone.

multi- is added to words to indicate that something involves several people or things. ...*multi-candidate elections*... ...*a multi-faith society.*

multi-coloured (*or* multicoloured) is used to describe things which have many different colours. ...*multi-coloured balloons.*

multi-cultural (*or* multicultural) is used to describe things which combine or involve several different cultures. ...*a multi-cultural society.*

multi-ethnic A **multi-ethnic** country or society has people from several different ethnic backgrounds living in it.

multi-lingual (*or* multilingual) If someone is **multi-lingual**, they can speak several languages. A **multi-lingual** book or magazine is written in several languages.

multi-millionaire If someone is a **multi-millionaire**, they have money or property worth several million pounds or dollars.

multi-national See multinational.

multi-party If a country has a **multi-party** electoral system, it has regular elections contested by a number of parties.

multi-racial is used to describe something which involves people of several races or ethnic groups. ...*a multi-racial society.*

multi-storey A **multi-storey** building or car-park has several floors.

multicoloured See multi-coloured.

multicultural See multi-cultural.

multifarious things are of many different kinds. *Mr Patten has to perform multifarious ceremonial duties.*

multilateral is used to describe things which involve several countries or groups. ...*multilateral aid*... ...*a multilateral approach to arms talks.*

multilingual See multi-lingual.

multimedia A **multimedia** computer system combines text, graphics, animation, video, music, and sometimes voice synthesis.

multinational (*or* multi-national) **Multinational** is used to talk about things which involve several countries. *One of the issues raised was command and control of the* *multinational force in the event of military action.* ◇ A **multinational** company owns smaller companies in several countries. Multinational companies are often called **multinationals**.

multiple is used to say something involves many things or people. *...multiple injuries... ...her multiple affairs... Research suggests most diseases have multiple causes.* ◇ If a number is a **multiple** of a smaller number, the smaller one can be divided into the larger one an exact number of times. For example, 24 is a multiple of 6.

multiple choice In a **multiple choice** test, you are given a number of possible answers to each question, and you have to choose the correct one.

multiple sclerosis or **MS** is a serious disease of the nervous system which can eventually lead to partial or total paralysis and can also affect a person's speech and vision.

multiplex (multiplexes) A **multiplex** is a cinema complex which has several screens and usually also contains bars, restaurants, and small shops.

multiplication See multiply.

multiplication sign A **multiplication sign** is the sign × which is put between two numbers to show they are being multiplied.

multiplication table When children learn their **multiplication table**, they learn by heart all possible multiplications of numbers between 1 and 12.

multiplicity A **multiplicity** of things is a large number or variety of them.

multiply (multiplies, multiplying, multiplied; multiplication) ❑ You say things of a certain kind **multiply** when the number of them keeps increasing. *The multiplication of these cells is suppressed by chemotherapy.* ◇ When animals **multiply**, they produce large numbers of young.

❑ If you **multiply** one number by another, you calculate the total you would get if you added the first number to itself a certain number of times. For example, 2 multiplied by 3 is 2 plus 2 plus 2 which equals 6. Multiplying numbers is called **multiplication**.

multitude A **multitude** of people or things is a very large number of them.

mum If you **keep mum** about something, you do not tell anyone about it.

mumble (mumbling, mumbled) If you **mumble** something, you say it quietly and indistinctly.

mumbo-jumbo If something is **mumbo-jumbo** to you, it does not make any sense.

mummify (mummifies, mummifying, mummified; mummification) When a dead body is **mummified**, it is preserved, usually by embalming it or drying it and wrapping it in cloth. This process is called **mummification**.

mummy (mummies) A **mummy** is a mummified dead body, usually preserved in a painted coffin which looks like a person.

mumps is an infectious disease which causes a mild fever and painful swelling of the glands in the neck and jaw.

munch (munches, munching, munched) If you **munch** food, you chew it steadily and thoroughly.

mundane things are ordinary and not particularly interesting. *...mundane tasks.*

municipal is used to talk about things connected with the local government of a city or town. *...municipal*

taxes... ...municipal elections.

municipality (municipalities) A **municipality** is a city or town which has a local council and local officials to administer its internal affairs.

munificent (munificence) A **munificent** gift is a very generous one. When someone gives a gift like this, you can talk about their **munificence**.

munitions are military equipment or supplies, especially weapons and ammunition. *...a munitions depot.*

mural A **mural** is a large picture painted directly onto a wall.

murder (murdering, murdered; murderer) ❑ **Murder** is the crime of deliberately killing someone. If someone **murders** someone else or commits a **murder**, they kill someone deliberately. A person who has murdered someone is called a **murderer**.

❑ If you say someone is **getting away with murder**, you mean they are doing something they should not be doing, and nobody is stopping them or punishing them. ◇ You say something is **murder** when you want to emphasize how difficult, dangerous, or unpleasant it is. *To work with a bad sub-editor, of course, was murder.*

murderous (murderously) If you say someone is **murderous**, you mean they have murdered someone, or are likely to. *He went murderously insane.* ◇ If you call something **murderous**, you mean it has caused death, or is capable of it. *...a murderous gun battle.*

murk is darkness or thick mist which you cannot see through. *The cast, candles in hand, lead us through the murk into the old empty Corn Exchange.* ◇ **Murk** is also something which confuses or obscures a situation. *In the murk of war things are seldom what they seem.*

murky (murkier, murkiest) ❑ **Murky** water is so dark or dirty you cannot see through it. ◇ **Murky** places are dark and unpleasant.

❑ You also use **murky** to describe something which you suspect is dishonest or morally wrong. *He spent most of this spring dodging questions about a murky state election he won six years ago.*

murmur (murmuring, murmured) If you **murmur** something, you say it very quietly. The sound of people speaking quietly can be called a **murmur**. *There was a murmur at the back.* ◇ You say there are **murmurs** when people discuss something quietly among themselves, rather than speaking out openly about it. *...backbench murmurs of a possible challenge to his leadership.*

muscle (muscling, muscled) ❑ A **muscle** is a piece of tissue inside your body which is able to get bigger and smaller to enable your body to move.

❑ If you talk about someone having **muscle**, you mean they have the power to achieve what they want. *The Kremlin may now be preparing to use its economic and political muscle to break the current deadlock.*

❑ If you talk about someone **muscling in** on something, you mean they are intervening without being asked to. *An attempt by the EU to muscle in on space research is likely to meet stiff resistance.*

muscular is used to talk about things involving or affecting the muscles. *...muscular diseases.* ◇ A **muscular** person has strong firm muscles.

muscular dystrophy is a serious hereditary disease which makes a person's muscles gradually get weaker.

muse (musing, mused) ❏ If you **muse** about something, you think about it and wonder about it.
  ❏ When writers talk about their **muse**, they mean an imaginary force, often thought of as a woman, which is supposed to give them their inspiration and creative ideas.

museum A **museum** is a building where old, interesting, or valuable objects are kept on display, so the public can look at them. ◇ If you call something a **museum piece**, you mean it is old and out of date.

mush You call a substance a **mush** when it is like a thick soft paste.

mushroom (mushrooming, mushroomed) A **mushroom** is a fungus, usually with a short stem and a round top. You can eat some types of mushrooms, but others are poisonous. ◇ If something **mushrooms**, it grows very rapidly. *During the 1980s the number of radio stations mushroomed to more than 11,000.*

mushy You say food is **mushy** when it is too soft and has lost its shape or texture. ◇ A **mushy** book or film is very sentimental.

music is the pattern of sounds created by people singing or playing instruments. When music is written down, the symbols representing sounds are also called **music**.

music hall In the past, a **music hall** was a theatre where you could see shows consisting of performances by comedians, singers, and dancers. This type of entertainment was called **music hall**.

musical (musically) ❏ **Musical** is used to talk about things to do with music. *...a musical recital... He continued to develop musically* ◇ If someone is **musical**, they have a natural ability and interest in music. ◇ If you call a musician's performance **musical**, you mean it shows deep understanding of the music and is very satisfying. You can also call the musician **musical**.
  ❏ A **musical** sound is pleasant to listen to. *He was a superb public speaker with a musical voice.*
  ❏ A **musical** is a play or film which uses singing and dancing in the story.

musical chairs is a game small children play in which they run round a row of chairs while music is played and try to sit down when it stops. One chair is taken away each time, and anyone who cannot sit down has to drop out. The child who sits on the last seat is the winner. ◇ You can say people like cabinet ministers are playing **musical chairs** when they keep changing jobs or positions.

musical instrument See **instrument**.

musician A **musician** is someone who plays a musical instrument, especially someone who does it as their job.

musicianship is the skill involved in playing a musical instrument.

musicology (musicologist) **Musicology** is the scientific and historical study of music. A **musicologist** is an expert in this field.

musk is a substance with a strong persistent smell which is used to make perfume.

musket (musketeer) A **musket** is a gun with a long barrel which was used before rifles were invented. A **musketeer** was a soldier armed with a musket.

muskrat The **muskrat** is a large rat-like North American animal with brown fur which lives near water. Its fur, usually called **musquash**, is sometimes used to make coats.

musky If something is **musky**, it smells like musk.

Muslim (or **Moslem**) A **Muslim** is a person who believes in Islam and lives by its rules. ◇ **Muslim** is used to talk about people or things connected with Islam. *...Muslim fundamentalists.*

muslin is a soft loosely-woven cotton material.

musquash (musquashes) See **muskrat**.

mussel Mussels are a kind of edible shellfish. They live in black shells.

must ❏ If you say something **must** happen or **must** be done, you mean it is very important or necessary that it happens or is done. ◇ If you say something is a **must**, you mean it is absolutely necessary to have it or do it. *A meal in the Stables restaurant is a must.*
  ❏ You use **must** to make suggestions, or to say you intend to do something. *You must come and have dinner with me... I must come back here one day.*
  ❏ If you say something **must** have happened or **must** be true, you mean you feel sure it happened or is true. *The snow must have softened the impact... This must be the reason for his erratic driving.*

mustache See **moustache**.

mustang Mustangs are small wild horses in North America. They are descended from escaped Spanish ponies.

mustard is a yellow or brown spicy paste or powder made from the seeds of the mustard plant. It is used to flavour food.
  ❏ **Mustard** is also a brownish-yellow colour.
  ❏ If you say someone is **keen as mustard**, you mean they are very enthusiastic about doing something.

mustard gas is a very poisonous substance used in the First World War as a chemical weapon. Its vapour causes severe blistering and lung damage when inhaled.

muster (mustering, mustered) ❏ If you **muster** something such as strength or support, you gather as much of it as you can, in order to do something. *The next generation of leaders will gain legitimacy only if they can muster popular support.* ◇ If someone **musters** a group of people, especially soldiers, they gather as many as they can in one place. *Official journalists claim thousands attended the demonstrations, but opposition supporters insist the Communists could only muster a few hundred.*
  ❏ If you say someone or something **passes muster**, you mean they are good enough for what they are needed for.

musty If something is **musty** or has a **musty** smell, it smells stale and damp.

mutable (mutability) If something is **mutable**, it is capable of changing, or likely to change. You talk about the **mutability** of something like this.

mutant A **mutant** animal or plant is physically different from the rest of its species, because of a change in its genetic structure. An animal or plant like this is called a **mutant**.

mutate (mutating, mutated; mutation) If an animal or plant **mutates**, it develops different characteristics as a result of a genetic change. A change like this is called a **mutation**.

mute (mutely; muting, muted) ❏ If someone is **mute** on a particular occasion, they do not say anything. If you do something **mutely**, you do it without saying anything.

❑ If you **mute** a sound or noise, you make it quieter. ◇ A **mute** is a device fitted into a wind instrument, or onto a stringed instrument like a violin, to make it play more quietly.

❑ A **muted** reaction or emotion is not strong. ◇ A **muted** colour is soft and gentle, rather than bright and garish.

mutilate (mutilating, mutilated; mutilation) If someone is **mutilated**, their body is severely and permanently damaged. Damaging someone's body is called **mutilation**; the damaged part is called a **mutilation**. ◇ If someone **mutilates** something like a building or a statue, they damage it and spoil its appearance.

mutiny (mutinies; mutinous, mutineer) A **mutiny** is a rebellion by a group of people, especially members of the armed forces, against the people in authority over them. You say people who rebel like this are **mutinous**; you can also call them **mutineers**.

mutter (muttering, muttered) If someone **mutters** or speaks in a **mutter**, they speak very quietly so other people can hardly hear them. People sometimes do this when they are complaining about something or talking to themselves. ◇ If there are **mutterings** about something, people are talking about it, but not openly.

mutton is meat from an adult sheep.

mutual is used to describe something involving two or more people or groups, in which they do the same thing to each other, or have the same feeling about each other. *His relations with the press are full of mutual fear and loathing.* ◇ **Mutual** is also used to describe something which is shared by two or more people or groups. *Lithuania and Moscow have a mutual interest in peaceful compromise... ...our mutual friend.*

mutually is used to talk about something which affects two or more people in the same way. *Both sides said they wanted to maintain their existing mutually beneficial relationship.* ◇ If two things are **mutually exclusive** or **mutually contradictory**, they cannot both happen or be true at the same time.

Muzak is recorded music played as background music in places like supermarkets, restaurants, and shopping centres. 'Muzak' is a trademark.

muzzle (muzzling, muzzled) ❑ An animal's **muzzle** is its nose and mouth. ◇ If you **muzzle** a dog, you put a device called a **muzzle** over its nose and mouth, to stop it biting. ◇ If a person or group of people is **muzzled**, they are prevented from speaking out about something.

❑ The **muzzle** of a gun barrel is the end where the bullets come out.

MW is short for (a) 'medium wave'. (b) 'megawatts'.

my You use **my** when you are talking about something belonging to or connected with yourself. *I was there with my husband.*

mycology (pron: my-kol-o-jee) (mycologist) **Mycology** is the study of fungi. A **mycologist** is an expert on fungi.

myopia (myopic) **Myopia** is the medical term for shortsightedness. You say someone is **myopic** when they cannot see things beyond a certain distance without glasses. ◇ You say someone is being **myopic** when they think only about immediate problems and fail to look ahead to the future.

myriad If you talk about **myriad** things of a particular kind, you mean there are very many of them. *...the*

myriad peoples and cultures of South Africa.

myrrh (pron: **murr**) is an aromatic resin used in incense and perfume. It comes from several types of tropical shrubs.

myself You use **myself** to say something you do affects you rather than anyone else. *I restrained myself from giving it a good kick... I made a fool of myself.* ◇ You also use **myself** to emphasize that a statement really does apply to you. *I myself am going to Moscow in a week's time... I can't say I fancy it myself.* ◇ You also use **myself** to emphasize that you do something without help from anyone else. *If I need a new fence, I have to pay for it myself.*

mysterious (mysteriously) If something is **mysterious**, it is strange and not easily explained or understood. *Two-thirds of the ducks have mysteriously disappeared.* ◇ If you say someone is being **mysterious**, you mean they are indicating that they have some secret knowledge of something and are not going to reveal it.

mystery (mysteries) If you say something is a **mystery**, you mean it cannot be explained or understood. You can also say something is **surrounded by mystery.** ◇ A **mystery** person or thing is one whose identity or nature is not known. *The wife's mystery lover turns out to be her husband in disguise.* ◇ A **mystery** is a story in which strange things happen which are not explained until the end.

mystery play A **mystery play** is a medieval play based on incidents in the Bible, especially the life, death, and resurrection of Jesus.

mystic (mystical, mysticism) ❑ **Mystic** and **mystical** are used to talk about experiences people claim to have which do not come to them through their senses and cannot be understood by reasoning. *...mystical visions.*

❑ **Mysticism** is a religious practice in which people search intensely for truth, knowledge, and union with their God through meditation and prayer. A **mystic** is someone who practises mysticism. Mystics sometimes claim to see visions.

mystify (mystifies, mystifying, mystified; mystification) If something **mystifies** you, you cannot understand it. *The claimant is still mystified about why he has lost his benefits... The AA insurance was looked on with mystification by the garage.*

mystique (pron: miss-**teek**) The **mystique** of something is the atmosphere of mystery and secrecy associated with it. *Traditionalists are complaining that the wedding's publicity threatens the imperial mystique.*

myth (mythical) ❑ If you say something which is widely believed is **mythical** or a **myth,** you mean it is untrue. *Electricity privatisation exploded the myth of cheap nuclear power.*

❑ A **myth** is a story which has been made up in the past to explain natural events or justify religious beliefs. **Mythical** is used to describe people, creatures, and other things in myths. *The sky dragon is the mythical ruler of the empire.*

mythic is used to describe people and things that are like something in a myth, because they are fantastic or extreme. *Struggles between film-makers and studio bosses have, at times, escalated to mythic proportions.*

mythological is used to talk about things to do with myths, or things which remind you of myths. *...mytho-*

logical creatures... Her father was a drinker and liar of mythological proportions.

mythologize (mythologizing, mythologized) (*can be spelled with an 's' instead of a 'z'*) If someone or something is **mythologized**, myths are created about them.

mythology is stories made up in the past to explain natural events or justify religious beliefs. ◇ The **mythology** of an activity is the stories and beliefs connected with it, many of which may not be true. *...British food mythology.*

myxomatosis is an infectious disease which affects rabbits and usually kills them.

N n

n/a (*or* N.A.) You write **n/a** on a form to show that a question or category does not apply to you. **n/a** stands for 'not applicable'.

nab (nabbing, nabbed) If the police **nab** someone, they catch them doing something wrong, or they arrest them.

nadir (*pron:* nay-dear) If something reaches its **nadir**, it reaches its lowest point. If a person reaches their **nadir**, they reach the lowest point of their life or career.

naff If you say something is **naff**, you mean it is inappropriate or in bad taste, because it is showy, old-fashioned, or of poor quality. *...naff little flowers in naff little vases.*

nag (nagging, nagged) ❑ If something like a problem **nags** at you, it keeps troubling you. You use **nagging** to describe things like this. *...a nagging doubt... ...nagging injuries.* ◇ If someone **nags** you, they keep complaining or asking you to do something.

❑ A **nag** is a horse, especially an old one.

nail (nailing, nailed) ❑ A **nail** is a small sharp piece of metal which you hammer through something, to fasten it to something else. If you **nail** something to a surface, you fix it there with a nail or nails. If you **nail** something **down**, you fix it firmly with nails so it cannot move. ◇ If you **nail down** something like an agreement, you get people to agree to something definite. *The US wants to nail down a resolution before the end of the month.*

❑ If something you say or write **hits the nail on the head**, it makes exactly the right point. ◇ If someone **nails their colours to the mast**, they make their intentions clear and show they do not intend to change their mind. If you want to indicate what someone's intentions relate to, you can talk about them **nailing other things to the mast**. *Britain's chancellor nails interest rates to the mast.*

❑ If you **nail** something wrong or illegal, you reveal it or expose it. *A commission of inquiry will nail the ill-gotten gains of 25 members of their government.* You can also **nail** the person responsible for something. ◇ If you **nail** something someone has said or written, you show it is a lie. *This grotesque libel can be nailed once and for all.*

❑ If you call a job or responsibility a **bed of nails**, you mean it is unpleasant and difficult. ◇ a **nail in someone's coffin**: see **coffin.**

❑ A person's **nails** are the thin hard areas covering the ends of their fingers and toes. ◇ **fight tooth and nail**: see **tooth.**

nail-biting is used to describe situations in which people are anxiously waiting for something to happen or finish. *...the nail-biting wait for the final whistle.*

nail brush A **nail brush** is a small brush for cleaning your nails.

nail file A **nail file** is a small strip of rough metal which you rub on the ends of your nails to make them smooth and give them a rounded shape.

nail polish is the same as nail varnish.

nail scissors are small scissors for cutting your nails.

nail varnish is a thick, usually coloured, liquid which women paint on their nails.

naive (naively) (*pron:* nye-eev) ❑ If you say someone is being **naive**, you mean they are talking or behaving as if a situation was simpler than it really is, or as if people were nicer or more co-operative than they really are. *He naively assumed that the Americans would move in overnight to replace the Russians.* A **naive** person tends to behave like this all the time, because of lack of experience.

❑ **Naive** art involves the use of unsophisticated or primitive techniques. *...naive sculptures.*

naivety (*pron:* nye-eev-i-tee) **Naivety** is behaviour which shows simple and naive beliefs and a lack of knowledge or experience of life.

naked (nakedly, nakedness) ❑ If someone is **naked**, they are not wearing any clothes. *...the nakedness of Adam and Eve.* ◇ You use **naked** to describe other things which have no covering. *...naked light bulbs.* ◇ If you can see something with the **naked eye**, you can see it without something such as a telescope or microscope.

❑ You use **naked** to describe actions, emotions, or behaviour which are open and not disguised in any way. *...naked aggression... He was a nakedly ambitious man.*

namby-pamby You say people are **namby-pamby** when they are weak and timid and unwilling to expose themselves to risk or danger.

name (naming, named) ❑ The **name** of a person, animal, place, or thing is the word or words used to identify them. ◇ You use **named** or **by the name of** when mentioning someone's or something's name. *...a Japanese nightclub singer named Naoko Nemoto... ...an obscure young painter by the name of Hockney.* ◇ If you mention someone or something **by name**, you say their name, rather than referring to them in some other way. ◇ If you do something **under** a certain **name**, you do it using that name, which may not be your real one. *She began her career as an actress under the name of Beverly Brooks.* ◇ If something is registered or recorded in someone's **name**, it officially belongs to them or is reserved for them.

...hotel bedrooms booked in the name of John Smith. ◇ See also **Christian name, first name, given name.**

❑ When a child is **named,** it is given a name. If it is **named after** someone, it is given that person's name. Similarly, something like a ship or railway engine can be **named after** someone or something. Note that Americans say someone or something is **named for** a person or thing.

❑ If you **name** something like a team, you say who will be in it. *India's new Prime Minister is expected to name his Cabinet today.* ◇ If you **name** the person responsible for something bad, you say who did it. If several people are responsible, you can say you **name names.** ◇ If you **name** the source of a piece of information, you say who gave it you, or where you got it from. ◇ If you **name** something like a date, you say when something will take place. *They asked him to name a time and a place for the meeting.*

❑ You use **to name but** or **to name only** when you have mentioned an example or examples of something, and you want to suggest there are many others of the same kind. *Ireland has produced many great writers – Yeats, Wilde, Shaw, Goldsmith, Joyce, to name only a few.*

❑ The **name** of a person or thing is also their reputation. *The two teams had 'sullied the good name' of football... ...the kind of behaviour that gives English girls a bad name abroad.* ◇ **clear your name:** see **clear.** ◇ **blacken** someone's **name:** see **blacken.** ◇ If you **make a name for yourself** in a particular field, you become well-known and admired for what you do. ◇ **a big name:** see **big.**

❑ If you **call** someone **names,** you use unpleasant words to describe them.

❑ If you say something is a certain thing **in all but name,** you mean it has all the features of that thing, but is not supposed to be it. *It is now a political party in all but name.* If you say something is a certain thing **in name only,** you mean it is supposed to be that thing, but has none of the features it should have. *The present leadership is a leadership in name only.*

❑ If something is done **in the name of** an organization, it is done by people claiming to represent its wishes. *Action was taken in the name of the United Nations.* Similarly, you can say something is done **in the name of** a religion or ideal. *They called for sacrifice in the name of the revolution.*

❑ When people say something is **the name of the game,** they mean it is what matters most in the situation they are talking about. *Ratings are the name of the game in television.*

name-dropping is the habit of talking about famous people as though they were your friends, to impress people.

nameless is used to describe (a) people or things whose name is not known. *...a dead, nameless body.* (b) things which have not yet been given a name.

❑ If you say someone will remain **nameless,** you mean you will not mention their name, even though you know it, because you do not want to embarrass them.

namely You use **namely** to say more exactly what you mean, when you have just mentioned something in an indirect way. *The conference is far from achieving its aim, namely to break the deadlock.*

nameplate A **nameplate** is a small sign, usually on or next to the door of a room or a building, showing the name of the person or organization that uses it.

namesake Your **namesake** is someone who has the same name as you.

nanny (nannies) A **nanny** is a woman who is paid by parents to look after their children and sometimes lives in the family home. ◇ When people talk about a **nanny** state or society, they mean one where people are overprotected by the authorities and never have to think and make decisions for themselves.

nanny goat A **nanny goat** is a female goat.

nano- is used in words like 'nanotechnology' and 'nanocomputer' to indicate extreme smallness. ◇ **Nano-** is also used in measurement words to represent a thousandth of a millionth part of something. *...12.5 nanograms... ...357 nanometres.*

nap (napping, napped) ❑ A **nap** is a short sleep, especially one taken during the day. If you **nap,** you have a sleep like this. ◇ If you are caught **napping,** something happens to you when you are not prepared for it.

❑ In horse-racing, a **nap** is a tip given by a tipster for an almost certain winner.

napalm (*pron:* nay-parm) is a substance which is mixed with petrol to make bombs which burn and destroy people and plants.

nape A person's **nape** is the back of their neck.

naphtha (*pron:* naf-tha *or* nap-tha) is (a) a liquid mixture distilled from coal tar, used as a solvent. (b) a similar mixture distilled from petroleum, used as a solvent and in petrol.

naphthalene is a strong-smelling solid substance used in mothballs and dyes.

napkin A **napkin** is a small piece of cloth or paper used to protect your clothes when you are eating, or to wipe your face and hands.

nappy (nappies) A **nappy** is a piece of soft thick cloth or padded paper fastened round a baby's bottom to soak up urine and faeces.

narcissi See **narcissus.**

narcissistic (*pron:* nar-siss-siss-tik) (narcissism) If someone is **narcissistic,** they behave in a self-admiring way. Behaviour like this is called **narcissism** (*pron:* nar-si-siz-um).

narcissus (*plural:* narcissi) The **narcissus** is a type of daffodil, often white, with a short trumpet. **Narcissus** is also the scientific name for the whole daffodil family.

narco- is used to indicate a connection with narcotic drugs. *...narco-terrorist drug lords.*

narcotic Narcotics are addictive drugs like opium and morphine which make you sleepy and unable to feel pain. ◇ **Narcotic** is used to talk about substances having this effect or being used to obtain it. *Some salads possess interesting narcotic properties... Any narcotic use is to be discouraged.*

nark A **nark** is an informer or spy, especially one working for the police.

narrate (narrating, narrated; narration, narrator) If a story is **narrated** by someone, they tell it; they are called the story's **narrator.** ◇ If something like a film or TV documentary is **narrated,** someone gives a spoken commentary, to explain and accompany the pictures. This commentary is called the **narration.**

narrative A **narrative** is a story, or an account of events or experiences. ◇ The **narrative** in a novel is the way the events are presented. *The narrative is well handled, but the author has a weakness for corny jokes.* ◇ **Narrative** is also used to describe songs or poems which tell a story. *...Masefield's narrative verse.*

narrow (narrowly, narrowness) ❏ If something is **narrow**, the distance between its sides is very small. *...the narrow streets of the Old City.* ◇ If something **narrows**, it becomes less wide. *The road now narrows to a single track.*

❏ If the difference or gap between two things **narrows**, it becomes smaller. *The poll suggests a narrowing of the gap in popularity between the two main parties.* ◇ If you **narrow down** a range of choices or possibilities, you reduce it by getting rid of some of them.

❏ If you have a **narrow** victory or defeat, you only just win or lose. *The Conservatives narrowly won in the border state of Chihuahua... Their leaders have been encouraged by the narrowness of Sunday night's result.* ◇ If you have a **narrow** escape, you only just miss having something unpleasant happen to you. *Five firemen narrowly escaped death when a staircase collapsed beneath their feet.*

❏ If you say someone's ideas or views are **narrow**, you mean they are concerned with only a few aspects of a situation, and ignore others.

narrow boat A **narrow boat** is a long narrow barge-like boat, used on canals.

narrow-minded If you say someone is **narrow-minded**, you mean they are unwilling to consider new ideas or other people's opinions.

NASA is an American government organization concerned with research and development in the field of aeronautics and space flight. NASA stands for 'National Aeronautics and Space Administration'.

nasal (*pron:* **nay**-zal) is used to talk about things to do with the nose. *...nasal ulcers... ...nasal sprays.* Nasal sounds are produced by air passing through your nose as well as your mouth when you speak.

nascent (*pron:* **nass**-sent *or* **nace**-sent) Nascent things or processes are just beginning, and are expected to grow stronger or bigger. *...a nascent but ambitious aerospace company.*

nasturtium (*pron:* **nas-tur**-shum) Nasturtiums are garden plants with round leaves and red, orange, or yellow flowers.

nasty (nastier, nastiest; nastily, nastiness; nasties) ❏ If you say something is **nasty**, you mean it is unpleasant to smell, taste, see, or experience. ◇ You also use **nasty** to describe things which you find unattractive or in bad taste. *...his nasty, vulgar, show-off books.* ◇ A **nasty** problem or question is difficult to deal with.

❏ If you say a person's behaviour is **nasty**, you mean they act in an unpleasant or unkind way. *As the years went by his nastiness began to grate on his readers.* ◇ **Nasty** is used to describe things which could be harmful or dangerous. *...nasty petrochemicals... The occasional ball lifted nastily.* ◇ A **nasty** injury, illness, or disease is particularly unpleasant. ◇ **Nasties** are things, people, or creatures which are unpleasant in some way. *It contains some stimulants and other nasties linked with cancer.* ◇ See also **video nasty**.

natal is used to talk about things to do with birth. Prenatal and ante-natal both mean 'before birth'; postnatal means 'after birth'. *...an ante-natal clinic... ...postnatal depression.*

nation (national, nationally) ❏ A **nation** is a country, together with its social and political structures. **National** is used to talk about things involving one country, rather than several countries. *...national and international competitions.* **National** is also used to talk about things to do with the whole of a country, rather than part of it. *Americans vote in national and local elections on November 6... ...a regional beer which has become known nationally.* ◇ The **nation** is the people who live in a country. ◇ A country's **nationals** are its citizens.

❏ A **nation** is also a group of people with the same origins, history, customs, and language. They may live in one country, or in several countries. *Straddling five countries, the 20 million or so Kurds are a nation without a state.* **National** is used to talk about things connected with a group of people like these. *...national costumes.*

nation state A **nation state** is an independent state inhabited by people from the same national group.

national anthem A country's **national anthem** is its official song.

national debt A country's **national debt** is the money owed by its central government.

national government A **national government** is a coalition government, especially one formed during a crisis.

national grid The **national grid** is a network of high-voltage power lines connecting major power stations.

National Health Service See **NHS**.

national insurance is the system by which a government collects money regularly from employers and employees. This money is then paid to people who are ill, unemployed, or retired. 'National insurance' is sometimes shortened to 'NI'. *...NI contributions.*

national park A **national park** is a large area of land protected by the government of a country because of its natural beauty, plants, or wildlife.

national service is a period of compulsory service in a country's armed forces.

nationalise See **nationalize**.

nationalism (nationalist, nationalistic) **Nationalism** is a love for your country and a belief in its importance, often accompanied by a belief that it is better than other countries. Beliefs of this kind are called **nationalist** or **nationalistic**. *The conductor was unhappy about playing 'Land of Hope and Glory' – he was worried it would encourage nationalistic feeling.* ◇ **Nationalism** is also the desire for political independence by a group of people with the same language, religion, or culture. Anything connected with this desire can be called **nationalist**. *...a growing nationalist movement.* A **nationalist** is someone with nationalist beliefs.

nationality (nationalities) **Nationality** is used to say what country a person legally belongs to. For example you can say someone's nationality is Irish, or that they have Irish nationality. ◇ A **nationality** is a group of people who have the same racial origins, especially a group which does not have a country of its own. *The republic is a melting pot of different nationalities.*

nationalize (nationalizing, nationalized; nationalization) (*can be spelled with an 's' instead of a 'z'*) If a government **nationalizes** an industry, institution, or resource, it takes it out of private hands and places it under the control of the state. *...the nationalization of the coal industry.*

nationhood is a country's status as a nation. *This brought Canada to independent nationhood.*

nationwide is used to describe things which happen or exist throughout a country. *...a nationwide general strike.*

native ❑ Your **native** country is the one you were born in. You can also talk about someone's **native** town or village. You can also say someone is a **native** of a country or other place. *I am a native of Stornoway in Lewis.* ◇ Your **native** language is the one you learned as a child. ◇ A **native** plant or animal has existed in a place from earliest times, and was not introduced by man. *The Scots pine is a much loved native species.*

❑ A **native** ability or quality is one you possess naturally without having to learn it. *...conversation which revealed much native wit and shrewdness.*

❑ The descendants of the people who lived in a country before it was settled and colonized are sometimes called the **natives**. This use of 'native' is offensive and old-fashioned. ◇ If a visitor to a country **goes native**, he or she begins to act and live like the people who live there.

Native American See **American Indian**.

native speaker A **native speaker** of a language has it as their first language, rather than having learned it as a foreign language.

Nativity The **Nativity** is the birth of Jesus, celebrated by Christians at Christmas.

NATO is an international organization which was founded to provide joint defence for its members. These are the US, Canada, the UK, and other European countries. NATO stands for 'North Atlantic Treaty Organization'.

natty (nattier, nattiest) If you call clothes **natty**, you mean they are smart or fashionable; you can also call the people who wear them **natty**. *...the natty American Secretary of State.* Other smart fashionable things can be called **natty**. *...the natty airport of Phoenix.*

natural (naturally, naturalness) ❑ If you say something is **natural**, you mean it is normal and to be expected. *It is far more natural to fear a mouse than a nuclear explosion... We were nervous about the prospect of a war, naturally.*

❑ Someone with a **natural** ability was born with it and did not have to learn it. *I had natural ability as a footballer... ...a naturally gifted singer.* You can also say someone is a **natural**. *He's a natural with any kind of engine.* If something comes **naturally** to you, you can do it easily.

❑ **Natural** is used to talk about things which exist in nature, rather than being made or caused by man. *...a natural amphitheatre.*

❑ If someone's behaviour is **natural**, they are relaxed and do not behave in an affected or artificial way. *Everyone was enchanted by his complete naturalness and friendliness.*

❑ A person's **natural** parents are their real parents, rather than people who have adopted them.

❑ If someone has died of **natural causes**, they have died because they were ill, and not as a result of an accident, suicide, or murder. ◇ If something **dies a natural death**, it comes to an end because it is no longer useful, or because it is inappropriate or no longer up-to-date.

❑ In music, **natural** is used to say a note is not sharp or flat. 'Natural' is usually written ♮.

natural gas is gas, mainly methane, which is found underground or under the sea. It is collected and stored, then piped into people's houses to be used for cooking and heating.

natural history is the study of plants and animals. ◇ The **natural history** of a place is the plants and animals there.

natural justice is a fair and reasonable settlement of a legal matter, which may be different from what is actually decided in a court of law.

natural resources are things like land, forests, minerals, and sources of energy, which occur naturally and can be used by people.

natural science is the study of the whole physical world, including biology, chemistry, and physics. These sciences are sometimes called the **natural sciences**.

natural selection is the process by which plants and animals which are best adapted to their environment survive and reproduce, while those which are less well adapted die out.

natural wastage If a company or other organization reduces its workforce by **natural wastage**, it does it by not replacing employees who leave or retire, rather than by sacking people.

naturalise See **naturalize**.

naturalism (naturalistic) **Naturalism** is a movement in literature and art which aims to show people and objects as they really are, rather than in an idealistic or unnatural way. A **naturalistic** novel or painting shows people or things in this way.

naturalist A **naturalist** is a person who studies plants and animals.

naturalize (naturalizing, naturalized; naturalization) (*can be spelled with an 's' instead of a 'z'*) If someone is **naturalized**, they legally become a citizen of a country they were not born in. *He became French by naturalization.*

nature (-natured) ❑ **Nature** is all living things, and all events and processes not caused by man. ◇ When people talk about getting **back to nature**, they mean leaving the city or town and going to a fairly remote area of countryside, either for a holiday or to start a new life.

❑ The **nature** of something is its basic character. *This experiment raises important questions about the nature of the disease.* ◇ If you say something has a certain feature **by its nature** or **by its very nature**, you mean this feature is an essential part of being what it is. *One could argue that smoking, by its very nature, is addictive and therefore people are not entirely free to give it up.*

❑ You can describe something by saying it is of a particular **nature**. For example, you can say something is of a religious **nature**. Similarly, you can say something is religious **in nature**. *He will claim that charges against him are political in nature.* You can also say something is **in the nature** of a particular thing. *This is in the nature of a pilot study.*

❑ A person's **nature** is their character, which shows in the way they behave. *...Nicholas's gentle nature.* ◇ **-natured** is added to words to describe a person's character. *Some ill-natured fools will call this egotism.* ◇ If a way of behaving is **in** someone's **nature**, they cannot help it. *Henry does not lie because it is in his interest – he lies because it is in his nature.* ◇ **human nature:** see **human**. ◇ **the nature of the beast:** see **beast**. ◇ If something is **second nature** to you, you can do it easily, because you are used to doing it.

nature reserve A **nature reserve** is an area of land where animals, birds, and plants are officially protected.

nature trail A **nature trail** is a route through an area of countryside with signposts indicating interesting features like trees, plants, or rocks.

naturism (naturist) **Naturism** is the practice of going about without any clothes, which some people do in special areas, believing it is good for their health or for other reasons. A **naturist** is a person who does this.

naught see nought.

naughty (naughtier, naughtiest; naughtiness) A **naughty** child is badly behaved or disobedient. *Rewards for good behaviour usually work better than punishments for naughtiness.* ◇ **Naughty** is also used to describe things which are slightly rude or indecent. *...naughty lingerie... ...the artist famed for her cheerfully plump naughty ladies.*

nausea is a feeling of sickness as though you are going to vomit.

nauseam See ad nauseam.

nauseate (nauseating, nauseated; nauseous) If you are **nauseated** by something or it makes you **nauseous**, it gives you the feeling of wanting to vomit. ◇ You also say you are **nauseated** by something when it disgusts you or you dislike it intensely. You say something like this is **nauseating**. *He accused them of nauseating hypocrisy.*

nautical is used to talk about things to do with ships and the sea. *...his nautical background... ...their nautical adventures.*

nautical mile At sea, distances are usually expressed in **nautical miles**. A **nautical mile** is about 1852 metres or 2025 yards.

naval See navy.

nave The **nave** of a church or cathedral is the long central part where the congregation sits.

navel A person's **navel** is the small hollow in the middle of their abdomen where the umbilical cord was attached. ◇ If people spend time **navel-gazing** or **navel-contemplating**, they spend a lot of time examining their own thoughts, feelings, and ideas.

navigable A **navigable** river or waterway is wide enough or deep enough for a boat to travel along.

navigate (navigating, navigated; navigation, navigational) ❑ When someone on board a ship or aircraft **navigates**, they make sure it goes in the right direction, using such things as the sun and stars, maps, and compasses. *For the seamen, the stars and moon were the only means of navigation.* **Navigational** is used to talk about things to do with navigating ships or aircraft. *...navigational aids.* ❑ If you **navigate** your way somewhere, you get there with difficulty, because you have to take an indirect route, or because there are things in the way. *You may have to navigate your way round roadblocks.* ◇ If you **navigate** your way through difficulties, you deal with them skilfully.

navigator A **navigator** is someone in a car, ship, or aircraft who works out which way it should go.

navvy (navvies) A **navvy** is a person employed to do hard physical work, for example building roads.

navy (navies; naval) ❑ A country's **navy** is the part of its armed forces which is trained to fight at sea. **Naval** is used to describe people or things connected with a navy. *He was born into a naval family.* ❑ **Navy** or **navy blue** is a dark blue colour.

nay is an old or dialect word for 'no'. ◇ Some people say **nay** when they are improving on a word or phrase they have just used. *Hundreds, nay thousands, are said to apply for every job on offer.*

nay-sayer People who oppose something are sometimes called **nay-sayers**. *The nay-sayers choose as their central theme the importance of Westminster's power remaining unscathed.*

Nazi (Nazism) The **Nazis** were members of the National Socialist Party, which seized power in Germany in 1933 under Adolf Hitler. These people believed in **Nazism**, which meant especially state control of the economy, the racial supremacy of the German people, and the expansion of Germany's borders. Today, groups of people with strong racist views in Germany and other parts of the world are sometimes called **neo-Nazis**.

NB You write **NB** to draw people's attention to what follows. NB stands for 'nota bene', which is Latin for 'note well'. *The cooking time depends upon the age and type of the pulse. NB Red kidney beans must be boiled for a minimum of 10 min before simmering.*

NCO An **NCO** is a member of the armed forces who has a higher rank than a private, seaman, or aircraftsman, but does not have a commission. NCO stands for 'non-commissioned officer'.

Neanderthal (*pron:* nee-ann-der-tahl) **Neanderthal** man was an early type of man living in Europe about 35,000 to 70,000 years ago.

near (nearer, nearest; nearing, neared) ❑ If something is **near** a place or thing, it is a short distance away from it. ◇ If you **near** a place, you get near to it. ◇ If you say someone does not go **near** a place, you are emphasizing that they never go there. *As a neurotic claustrophobic I wouldn't go near the Channel Tunnel.*

❑ In front of a number, **near** means 'almost'. *We achieved near 100 per cent participation in this study.*

❑ If someone or something **nears** a point, state, or level, they get close to it. *The tournament neared its climax... Building neared completion... Unemployment rates are nearing 70 per cent.* You can also say someone or something is **near** a point, state, or level.

❑ If an event or time **nears**, it gets closer. If it is **near**, it will happen soon. *New alliances may form as the election nears... It was drawing near to Christmas.* ◇ If you say something will happen **in the near future**, you mean it will happen quite soon.

❑ In a competition, your **nearest** rival or challenger is the person who has the best chance of beating you.

❑ **Near-** and **as near as** are used to say someone or something is very close to being a particular thing. *...Intel's near-monopoly of the PC microprocessor market... Peter Rice is as near an artistic genius as the world of engineering has produced in half a century.* ◇ If you say someone or something is the **nearest** thing to a type of person or thing, you mean they are as close as possible to it without actually being it. *Mr Massoud is the nearest thing there is to an Afghan popular hero.* ◇ **Something near** is used to say something is close to a particular standard. *...proposals to restore Sherwood Forest to something near its ancient splendour.* ◇ **Nowhere near** and **anywhere near** are used to say something is a long way from a particular standard. *The reforms are nowhere near radical enough... I don't think it gives anywhere near the true measure of a school's worth.*

◇ **Nowhere near** is also used to say something is a long way from being achieved. *The guerrillas are nowhere near victory.*

❑ A **near miss** is (a) an attempt to do something which almost succeeds. (b) an incident in which there is almost an accident or disaster.

Near East The Near East is the same as the Middle East.

nearby things are only a short distance away. *...a nearby table... ...close friends living nearby.*

nearly If someone or something is **nearly** a particular thing, they are close to being that thing. If they are **not nearly** a particular thing, they are a long way from being it. *Her extravagant father was nearly bankrupt... The food they receive each month is not nearly enough.* ◇ **Nearly** an amount or number means slightly less than that amount or number. *The book has sold nearly 20,000 copies.* ◇ If something **nearly** happens, it comes close to happening.

nearside The **nearside** of a vehicle is the side normally nearest to the edge of the road. See also **offside**.

neat (neater, neatest; neatly, neatness) ❑ **Neat** is used to describe things which are tidy and well-organized. *...neat handwriting... ...fields of neatly sown potatoes.* ◇ You say a person is **neat** when their appearance is smart and tidy. *He was neatly dressed in a brown suit.* ◇ You also say someone is **neat** when they do things in a tidy way. *I regret to say neatness has never been one of my virtues.* ◇ A **neat** way of doing something is simple, clever, and efficient. *The book neatly exposes certain attitudes to art.*

❑ A **neat** alcoholic drink has nothing added to it.

nebula (*plural:* nebulas *or* nebulae) A **nebula** is an area of gas and dust in space. You see it as a patch of pale light in the night sky.

nebulous things are vague and not precise. *He mentioned some nebulous ailment.*

NEC The **NEC** is the committee which decides on the policies to be adopted by the British Labour Party. NEC stands for 'National Executive Committee'.

necessarily If you say something is **not necessarily** true, you mean it is not always true. *Economic progress does not necessarily solve human problems.*

necessary ❑ If something is **necessary**, you must have it, or it must be done. *None of the passengers carried the necessary travel documents... It was necessary to introduce blood testing.* ◇ If something is **necessary** to achieve a certain result, you must have it to get that result. *They failed to win the support necessary to bring the government down.*

❑ A **necessary** result or consequence is one which cannot fail to happen. *No one can say if this is a necessary side-effect of galaxy formation.* ◇ If you say something is a **necessary evil,** you mean you do not like it, but you accept that you have to put up with it, if something worthwhile is to be achieved.

necessitate (necessitating, necessitated) If something **necessitates** an action, it makes it necessary.

necessity (necessities) ❑ If there is a **necessity** for something, it must be done, provided, or obtained. *...the necessity for an exit visa.* ◇ **Necessities** are the things you must have in order to do something. When people talk about the **bare necessities** or the **basic necessities**, they usually mean things like food and clothing which people need in order to survive.

❑ **Of necessity** is used to say something must happen in particular circumstances, or someone has no choice but to do something. *The motorist's concentration must of necessity be less at these times... Smith is, of necessity, trimming down the scale of his ideas.*

neck (-necked) ❑ A person's or animal's **neck** is the part of their body which joins their head to the rest of their body. -necked is added to a word to say what kind of neck someone or something has. *...a long-necked dinosaur.* ◇ The **neck** of a piece of clothing is the part round your neck or just below it. -necked is added to words to describe various kinds of necks on clothing. *...polo-necked sweaters... ...an open-necked shirt.*

❑ If a racehorse wins **by a neck**, it wins by the length of its head and neck. ◇ In a race or contest, if two people are **neck and neck,** they are level and seem to have an equal chance of winning.

❑ If someone is **breathing down your neck,** they are watching you and checking what you do very carefully. ◇ If you are **up to your neck** in problems, you are deeply involved in them. You can also talk about problems being **round your neck.**

❑ If you **stick your neck out,** you do or say something which makes it likely you will be criticized or harmed. ◇ If you **risk your neck** to do something, you put yourself in danger in order to do it.

❑ **pain in the neck:** see pain.

❑ The **neck** of something like a bottle or musical instrument is the long narrow part at the top. ◇ The **neck** of the womb is the same as the cervix.

neckerchief A **neckerchief** is a piece of cloth folded and worn round the neck.

necklace A **necklace** is something worn round a person's neck as a decoration, for example jewellery or a string of beads.

neckline The **neckline** of a dress or blouse is the top edge at the front.

necktie In the US, a man's tie is often called a **necktie.**

necromancy is black magic or witchcraft.

necrophilia (necrophiliac) **Necrophilia** is sexual attraction towards dead bodies. Someone who feels this attraction is called a **necrophiliac.**

necropolis (*pron:* neck-rop-pol-liss) (necropolises) A **necropolis** is a burial site or cemetery.

nectar is a sweet liquid produced by flowers, which bees and other insects collect.

nectarine A **nectarine** is a type of smooth-skinned peach.

née is used to mention what a woman's surname was before she got married. *...Anne Heseltine, née Williams.*

need (needing, needed) ❑ If you say something **needs** doing or **needs** to be done, you mean some action should be taken. You can also say there is a **need** for something. *There is a need for us to develop different models.* You can also say something **needs** to happen. *The production of rice needs to rise by 45 percent.* ◇ If there is **no need** to do something or **no need** for it, it is unnecessary.

❑ If something is **needed,** it is required for people's survival, for the good of a community, or for people to have a better way of life. You can say something like this is **much-needed** or **badly needed.** *We need more hotels in London, preferably in the middle price range... ...much-needed aid... ...a badly needed library.* ◇ People's **needs** are things necessary for their survival or for them to live a healthy life. ...*the basic needs of life.* ◇ People who are **in need** are very poor or require help of some kind. ◇ A person's **hour of need** is a time when they are in a bad situation and require help or support.

❑ If something is done **as needed,** it is done when required. *We will take appropriate actions as needed to achieve sustained growth.* ◇ If something can be done **if need be,** it can be done if it becomes necessary. *This means a landlord can get rid of a tenant after six months, if need be.*

❑ If you **need** something, you must have it, for the sake of your health or appearance, or in order to achieve something. *She needs a new hair-do... Labour needs to win 51 seats to deny the Conservatives a clear majority.* You can also talk about your **need** for something, or say you are **in need of** something. ...*her desperate need to be liked... ...hikers in need of refreshment.* Your **needs** are the things you need. ...*customers' needs.* ◇ If you **need** to do something, you feel you must do it. You can talk about your **need** to do something. ...*her husband's need to dominate.* ◇ If you have **no need** of something, you can manage without it.

❑ If something like a machine **needs** something, it must have it, if it is to work properly. *It doesn't need a lot of maintenance.* If a machine or building is in a bad state, you can say it is **in need of** repair or decoration. ◇ If you say something **needs** to be done in a certain way, you mean it must be done that way to get the right result. *Tortillas need to be cooked over a proper fire.* You can also say something **needs** to have a certain quality or feature. *To convince people, an argument needs to be reasonably plausible.*

❑ If you say something **need not** have certain consequences, you mean they are not bound to happen as a result of it. *This need not lead to inflation.* ◇ If you say someone **need not** worry about something, you mean the thing they are concerned about is unlikely to be true, or unlikely to happen. *Lady Warnock need not despair about the future of the teaching profession.* ◇ You say '**it need hardly be said...**' when you are saying something obvious or predictable. *The batsman, it need hardly be added, was Ian Botham.*

needle (needling, needled) ❑ A **needle** is a small thin piece of metal with a hole at one end, for sewing. ◇ **needle in a haystack: see haystack.** ◇ See also **pins and needles, knitting needle.**

❑ A **needle** is also a sharp piece of hollow metal attached to a syringe, for giving injections. ◇ On a measuring instrument, the **needle** is the thin piece of metal or plastic which moves backwards and forwards on the dial. ◇ The **needle** on a record player is the stylus.

❑ The **needles** on a conifer are its thin hard pointed leaves.

❑ If someone or something **needles** you, they annoy you by constantly criticizing you. ◇ In sport, a **needle** match is one where there is hostility between the two sides or competitors, because there has already been a quarrel or dispute between them.

needlepoint is embroidery done on canvas, often using the same stitch throughout, to create a tapestry-like effect.

needless (needlessly) **Needless** is used to say something bad is completely unnecessary. ...*needless deaths... Tens of thousands more jobs and businesses will be needlessly lost.*

◇ People say '**needless to say...**' when they are saying something obvious or unsurprising. *Needless to say, he scored a graceful century.*

needlework is sewing or embroidering by hand. A person's **needlework** is a piece of work of this kind.

needy (needier, neediest) **Needy** people are very poor and do not have enough food or clothing or decent housing. People like these are often called **the needy.**

nefarious people are wicked and immoral. The things they do can also be called **nefarious.** *Sport has often been used by politicians for nefarious ends.*

negate (negating, negated; negation) ❑ If you **negate** something, you cancel it out. For example, if you negate the good effects of something, you cancel them out by doing something which has the opposite effect.

❑ If someone in authority **negates** something like a principle, they behave in a way which goes completely against it. *He described the President's rule as a negation of the principles for which he and others had fought.*

negative (negatively) ❑ If you give a **negative** response, you say 'no', or something which means no. *She answered negatively when pressed further on the question.*

❑ **Negative** is used to describe something which concentrates on the bad aspects of something and ignores its good side. *All too often it is only the negative images of Ireland that are portrayed... The audit should not be seen negatively, as a hindrance to the development of small companies.* When a person concentrates on the bad aspects of something, you can say they are being **negative** or talk about their **negative** attitude.

❑ If a medical or other scientific test is **negative,** it shows something like a disease or substance is not present.

❑ A **negative** is the image first produced when you take a photograph and which the final photograph is developed from.

❑ A **negative** number is less than zero. ◇ A **negative** electric charge is one of two opposite kinds of charge, the other one being a positive charge.

neglect (neglectful) If you **neglect** someone or something, you do not look after them properly. **Neglect** is failing to look after someone or something. You say someone who behaves like this is **neglectful.** ...*a neglectful parent.* ◇ If you **neglect** to do something, you fail to do it. ◇ If you say someone like a writer or composer is **neglected,** you mean their work does not get the attention you think it deserves. You can also say their work is **neglected.** ...*a neglected classic of the First World War.*

negligee (or **negligée**) (pron: neg-lee-zhay, the 'zh' sounds like 's' in 'pleasure') A **negligee** is a woman's dressing gown made of very thin material.

negligent (negligently, negligence) If someone is **negligent,** they fail to do something which it is their duty or responsibility to do. You talk about the **negligence** of someone like this. ...*evidence that the Council had acted negligently... Ramblers accuse local authorities of negligence.*

negligible Something which is **negligible** is so small or unimportant that it is not worth bothering about. *The damage is negligible... Television was still of negligible importance.*

negotiable If something is **negotiable,** it can be discussed, with the possibility of it being changed or done away with. *The conference insisted that human rights are not negotiable.*

negotiate (negotiating, negotiated; negotiation, negotiator) ❑ When people **negotiate**, they get together and talk about a problem or situation on which they have different standpoints, to try to find a solution. Talks like these are called **negotiations**; the people taking part are called **negotiators**. ◇ If something is **negotiated**, it is brought about by negotiating. *...a negotiated settlement... ...readiness to negotiate an exchange of prisoners.* If something is **negotiated away**, it is got rid of by negotiating. *The Americans are still trying to negotiate away the remaining obstacles.* ◇ When people, especially people who have been fighting, get round **the negotiating table**, they have serious discussions, to try and resolve their differences.

❑ If you **negotiate** an obstacle, you succeed in getting through it or round it. *She would have to negotiate a stream, a muddy bank and a cobbled road.*

Negro (Negroes) (*or* negro, negroes) A **Negro** is a person with black skin.

neigh When a horse **neighs**, it makes a loud quavering high-pitched noise. This noise is called a **neigh**.

neighbour (neighbouring) (*American spelling:* neighbor, neighboring) ❑ Your **neighbours** are the people who live near you, especially the ones next door. ◇ You can also call the person standing or sitting next to you your **neighbour**.

❑ Your country's **neighbours** are the countries next to it or nearest to it. They can also be referred to as **neighbouring** countries. You can call the people in a neighbouring country your **neighbours**. *Large numbers of Austrians are crossing the border to buy cheap food and drink from their neighbours.*

❑ A **neighbouring** piece of land is immediately next to the one you are talking about. Similarly, you can talk about a **neighbouring** building. *...the neighbouring baker's shop.* ◇ **Neighbouring** objects are side-by-side among a group of objects. You can also call them **neighbours**. *...neighbouring brain cells... Make a knot between each bulb to prevent it pressing on its neighbour.*

neighbourhood (*American spelling:* **neighborhood**) ❑ A **neighbourhood** is one of the parts of a town where people live. *...well-off neighbourhoods... ...complaints about neighbourhood noise.* ◇ A **Neighbourhood Watch** scheme involves getting residents to co-operate with each other and with the police, to try to reduce crime in their area.

❑ If something is **in the neighbourhood** of a place or object, it is not far away. *...material in the general neighbourhood of the exploded star.* ◇ If something is **in the neighbourhood of** an amount or rate, it is close to it. *Its speed is probably in the neighbourhood of 380 mph.*

neighbourly (neighbourliness) (*American spelling:* neighborly, neighborliness) **Neighbourly** is used to talk about things involving neighbours. *...neighbourly quarrels.* ◇ If someone living near you behaves in a **neighbourly** way, they are friendly and willing to give you help when you need it. *...the neighbourliness of the old urban communities.* You can also talk about countries behaving in a **neighbourly** way. *...a treaty aimed at guaranteeing good neighbourliness and co-operation.*

neither is used with 'nor' to say something is not true of two or more people, things, or groups. *Neither the people nor the state would tolerate such acts... Neither Britain, nor the European Community, nor the UN can impose peace from outside.* ◇ **Neither** is also used without 'nor' to say something is not true of the two people, things, or groups you have just mentioned. *Neither was badly injured... Neither case is quite that simple, of course.* ◇ If you have made a statement using a word like 'not' or 'never', you can make it apply to someone or something else by using **neither**. *You will not be getting everything you want. Neither will we... The teams wouldn't like that; and neither would the sponsors.*

❑ If you say something is **neither here nor there**, you mean it is unimportant because it has no relevance to what you are discussing.

nemesis (*pron:* nem-miss-iss) The **nemesis** of a person or group of people is someone or something that brings about their downfall or defeat.

neo- is used to form words which refer to modern versions of earlier beliefs and styles. *...neo-fascists... ...a neo-Georgian front door.*

neo-classical architecture and art is based on the architecture and art of the ancient Greeks and Romans. *...a neo-classical mansion.*

neo-colonialism is domination by a powerful country of another country which is supposed to be independent, by controlling its businesses or financial institutions.

Neolithic The Neolithic period or **New Stone Age** was the last period of the Stone Age. In Europe, it began about 4000BC. In this period, the earliest kind of farming began, and people used polished flint tools and weapons. See also **Palaeolithic, Mesolithic**.

neologism (*pron:* nee-ol-a-jiz-zum) A **neologism** is a new word or expression, or a familiar one being used with a new meaning.

neon is a colourless odourless gas which is used in glass tubes to make bright lights and signs.

neonate (neonatal) A **neonate** is a new-born baby. **Neonatal** is used to talk about things to do with new-born babies. *...a neonatal unit.*

neophyte A **neophyte** is someone who is new to an activity. *...Eastern Europe's neophyte bankers.*

nephew Your **nephew** is the son of your sister or brother, or the son of your husband's or wife's sister or brother.

nepotism If you accuse someone of **nepotism**, you mean they have used their power or influence to get jobs or other benefits for members of their family.

nerd If you call someone a **nerd**, you mean they are stupid.

nerve ❑ A **nerve** is one of the fibres which carry messages between your brain and the rest of your body.

❑ If you talk about someone's **nerves**, you mean their ability to stay calm, which may fail them when unpleasant things are happening around them. *Mortar explosions shatter the nerves of those who have to stay.*

❑ **Nerve** is the courage to do something difficult or dangerous. *Does the party have the nerve and will to grasp the opportunity?* ◇ If someone becomes afraid in the middle of doing something, you can say they **lose their nerve** or their **nerve fails**. *...a collective failure of nerve.*

❏ People say someone has a **nerve** when they behave in a disrespectful way, or behave as if everything is normal when they have done something wrong.

❏ If something **gets on your nerves,** it annoys or irritates you. ◇ If something like a remark **touches a raw nerve,** it upsets you because it concerns something you are sensitive about.

❏ **war of nerves: see war.**

nerve centre The **nerve centre** of an organization is the place its activities are controlled from.

nerve gas is a poisonous gas which has sometimes been used in war. It affects people's nervous systems, paralysing them and eventually killing them.

nerve-wracking (*or* nerve-racking) A **nerve-wracking** experience is worrying and upsetting, because it is full of uncertainty and danger.

nervous (nervously; nervousness) ❏ If you are **nervous,** you are anxious and frightened, and this shows in your behaviour. *The students laughed nervously... ...signs of nervousness.* ◇ If you are **nervous** about something, you are afraid to do it, or afraid to become involved with it. *He was clearly nervous about identifying his attackers... ...nervousness about new technology.* ◇ **Nervous** people are easily frightened or upset.

❏ Your **nervous system** is all the nerves in your body, together with your brain and spinal cord.

❏ A **nervous** illness or condition is one which affects a person's mental state. *...nervous exhaustion.* ◇ If someone has a **nervous breakdown,** they suddenly become mentally ill and need medical treatment.

❏ If financial markets become **nervous,** they start to behave in an unpredictable way. *Stock markets around the world have been reacting nervously to events in the Gulf... There is increasing nervousness in the oil markets.*

nervy people are tense, anxious, and easily upset.

nest A bird's **nest** is a structure it builds to lay its eggs in. Some insects also build nests, and some animals build them as a place to sleep in or give birth to their young in. When a bird **nests** somewhere, it builds a nest there. ◇ **hornets' nest: see hornet.** ◇ See also **love nest.**

nest-egg A **nest-egg** is a sum of money someone is saving for a particular purpose.

nestle (nestling, nestled) When a village or house has been built in a hollow or valley or some other sheltered position, you can say it **nestles** there.

net (netting, netted) ❏ **Net** or **netting** is material made of long pieces of string, wire, or thread, woven together in a criss-cross pattern with spaces you can see through. *...net curtains... ...plastic netting.* ◇ A **net** is a piece of this material used, for example, to catch fish. If you **net** a fish, you catch it in a net.

❏ If you **net** an amount of something, you obtain it as a result of something you do. *...a bank robbery which netted some £25,000.*

❏ If someone or something **slips through the net,** they avoid capture. ◇ If you talk about someone **casting their net wider,** you mean they are trying a greater variety of things, in the hope of achieving what they want.

❏ The **net** in a game like tennis is a long piece of netting dividing the two halves of the court. ◇ In football, the **net** is the back of the goal. When a footballer scores, you can say he **nets** the ball. ◇ In cricket, the **nets** are the areas enclosed by netting where the cricketers practise.

❏ See also **safety net.**

❏ A **net** amount is the final amount after all deductions have been made. *The three-year bond will pay 8.2 per cent net... ...a net profit margin of more than 2%.* See also **gross.** ◇ The **net** weight of something is its weight without its container or wrapping. See also **gross.** ◇ The **net** result of a series of events is the final result when some effects have cancelled each other out.

netball is a game played by two teams of seven players. The teams try to score goals by throwing a ball through a net on top of a pole at their opponents' end of the court.

nether means 'lower'. The lower part of a person's torso, including their buttocks, is sometimes humorously called their **nether regions.**

❏ **Nether** is also used to talk about ways of life which are not considered respectable. *...a nether world of drugs and sexual promiscuity.*

nett has the same meaning as 'net' when talking about an amount or weight.

nettle (nettling, nettled) ❏ A **nettle** is a wild plant covered with little hairs which sting. ◇ If you **grasp the nettle,** you deal with something unpleasant or difficult in a determined way.

❏ If someone is **nettled,** they are annoyed or offended.

network (networking, networked) ❏ A **network** is a number of people or organizations in different places working together as a system. *A car factory is part of a much wider network of manufacturers, deliverers, suppliers and designers... ...a network of secret police informers.* Similarly, a number of things can form a **network.** *...a telephone network... ...the country's road network.*

❏ A TV **network** is a company or group of companies which broadcasts the same programmes at the same time in different parts of the country. You say programmes broadcast like this are **networked.** *...four-and-a-half hours of live networked television.* ◇ When a computer is **networked,** it is connected to other computers so they can exchange information and work together as a system.

❏ When a group of professional people try to help each other out in their careers, this is called **networking.** If they went to the same public school, or knew each other at Oxford or Cambridge, you can say they are operating **the old-boy network.**

neural (*pron:* nyoor-ral) is used to talk about things relating to nerves or the nervous system.

neuralgia (*pron:* nyoor-ral-ja) is severe pain along the whole length of a nerve.

neuro- at the beginning of a word means it has something to do with nerves or the nervous system. *...the neuro-surgical ward... ...a neuro-psychiatrist.*

neurology (neurological; neurologist) **Neurology** is the medical study of the structure, function, and diseases of the nervous system. **Neurological** is used to talk about things to do with the nervous system. *...neurological disorders.* A person who specializes in neurology is called a **neurologist.**

neuron (*or* neurone) A **neuron** is a cell which is part of the nervous system and carries messages from one part of the body to another.

neuroscience (neuroscientist) **Neuroscience** is the

scientific study of the structure and function of the nervous system. An expert in this field is called a **neuroscientist.**

neurosis (*pron:* nyoor-**roh**-siss) (neuroses; neurotic, neurotically) Neurosis is a mental disorder which causes people to be depressed and obsessive, and to have continual and unreasonable fears and worries. **Neurotic** is used to describe a person suffering from this disorder, or to talk about behaviour connected with it. *...a neurotic delusion.* A **neurotic** is a person suffering from neurosis. ◇ Neurotic is also used to describe people who are not actually ill but show a lot of unreasonable anxiety about something. *Record companies have become neurotic about investing in anything not already tried and tested... The party has been less neurotically secretive in its relations with the outer world.*

neurosurgery (neurosurgeon) Neurosurgery is the branch of surgery concerned with the brain and spinal cord. A person who carries out this type of surgery is called a **neurosurgeon.**

neurotransmitter A neurotransmitter is a chemical by which a nerve cell communicates with another nerve cell or with a muscle.

neuter (neutering, neutered) When an animal is **neutered**, its reproductive organs are removed. ◇ If an organization or system is **neutered**, something is done to it which reduces its effectiveness. *Labour would neuter the power of the courts to punish unions that break the law.*

neutral (neutrality, neutralism) ❑ In a war, a **neutral** country does not support either side. Similarly, in a dispute or election, a **neutral** person is not involved with any of the people taking part. *...neutral observers.* Neutral countries and people can also be called **neutrals.** *The French were entitled to be regarded as neutrals.* Not supporting either side in a war or dispute is called **neutrality.** When this is the deliberate policy of a government, it is also called **neutralism.** ◇ A **neutral** zone is an area of land, usually between two countries or armies who are fighting each other, where it has been agreed that no fighting shall take place. ◇ If a meeting between opponents takes place on **neutral** ground, it happens in a place which does not belong to any of the people involved in the conflict. *...a peace conference on neutral territory.*
    ❑ Neutral is used to describe things which do not show any bias, preference, or opinion. *...the neutrality of the interview form.* ◇ In sport, a **neutral** umpire or referee is from a different country to either of the two sides.
    ❑ A **neutral** colour is a colour like grey or brown which is not bright and which harmonizes with most other colours. Neutral colours are sometimes called **neutrals.**
    ❑ Neutral is the position between the gears of a vehicle, in which the gears are not connected to the engine.

neutralize (neutralizing, neutralized; neutralization) (*can be spelled with an 's' instead of a 'z'*) If you **neutralize** something, you prevent it from having any effect or from working properly. *The devices are neutralized by a card key... ...an installation for the destruction, neutralization, and disposal of toxic waste.*

neutron A neutron is an atomic particle which has no electrical charge.

neutron bomb The neutron bomb is a nuclear weapon designed to kill all living things within a certain area without a large explosion and without long-lasting radioactive contamination. This bomb has never been used so far.

neutron star A neutron star is a star which is thought to have collapsed under its own gravity so that its matter is extremely dense. It is composed entirely of neutrons. See also **black hole.**

never means at no time in the past or future. *This feat has never before been attempted.* ◇ Never is also used to mean 'not in any circumstances'. *Destroying life could never be justified.* ◇ never mind: see mind.

never-ending is used to describe something which lasts for a long time and seems as if it will never end. *...a never-ending flow of new recruits.*

never-never land When people talk about a **never-never land**, they mean an imaginary place where everything is nice and pleasant.

nevertheless means in spite of what has just been said. *The Plaza is now dominated mainly by tourist shops, but nevertheless the town has a welcoming feel to it.*

new (newly, newness) ❑ New is used to describe things which have been recently made or created, or are in the process of being made or created. *...a new 10 per cent tax on luxuries... The new building dwarfs the monastery... ...the newness of the team.* ◇ New is also used to describe things you obtain which have never been used or owned by anyone else. For example, you talk about a new car, as distinct from a used car. ◇ New is also used to describe things which are different from things which came before, or which replace them. *...a new approach to music teaching... A new date has been announced for talks.*
    ❑ New, new-, and newly are used to talk about things which have just come into existence, just happened, or just been done. *...a new baby... ...the smell of new-cut hay... ...the newly-appointed Minister of State.* ◇ A new period of time is just beginning or about to begin. *It marks the start of a new age in astronomy... ...a new era of cheaper air travel.*
    ❑ If an activity is new to you or you are new to it, you have never done it before. You say other things are new to you when you have never experienced or come across them before. *...a young actor who is new to me.*
    ❑ New is also used to describe something which has recently been discovered. *...a new planet.*
    ❑ New potatoes or carrots have been produced early in the season, and are usually small with a delicate flavour.

New Age is used to describe groups of people who reject the idea that money and possessions are all-important and often travel around in groups, living in caravans and other vehicles. *...New Age travellers.*

new-fangled Some people use **new-fangled** to describe new ideas or new inventions which they do not like or do not trust.

new-found is used to describe things like interests or beliefs which someone has recently acquired. *...her new-found enthusiasm for sailing.*

New Man When people talk about the **New Man**, they mean men who are interested in spending time with their families and sharing the childcare and housework with their partners, rather than making money and doing well in their careers.

new moon The moon is called a **new moon** when it is seen as a thin crescent shape, after being invisible the previous night.

New Testament The New Testament is the part of the Bible which deals with the life of Jesus and with Christianity in the early Church.

new town A new town is a town which has been planned and built as a whole, rather than developing gradually in an unplanned way. New towns are usually built to relieve overcrowding in large cities.

new wave A new wave is a movement in art, music, or film which introduces many new ideas.

New World The New World is the whole of the American continent.

New Year or the New Year is the time when people celebrate the start of a year. ◇ When people say something will happen in the new year, they mean it will happen during the first few days or weeks of the coming year. *All important pay negotiations would take place early in the new year.*

New Year's Day is the first day of the year, which in Western countries is January 1st.

New Year's Eve is the last day of the year.

newborn A newborn baby has been born very recently.

newcomer A newcomer is someone who has just started a new job, or recently come to live in a place. ◇ If you are a newcomer to something, you have only become involved in it recently. *...a newcomer to politics.*

newel A newel or newel post is the thick post at the top or bottom of a staircase which supports the hand rail.

newly See new.

newlywed (*or* newly-wed) A couple who have just got married are often called newlyweds.

news is information about a recent event or a recently changed situation. *He is wondering how he can face his friends with the news.*

❑ News is also the information about recent events given in newspapers and on TV and radio. A regular news programme is often called the news.

news agency A news agency is an organization which collects news stories from all over the world and sells them to newspapers and TV and radio stations.

news conference A news conference is a meeting held by a famous or important person or someone in the news, to answer questions put to them by journalists.

news-stand (*or* newsstand) A news-stand is a moveable stand or stall in the street or at a railway station, which you can buy newspapers from.

newsagent A newsagent or newsagent's is a shop which sells newspapers, magazines, sweets, and cigarettes. The person who runs this type of shop can also be called a newsagent.

newscast (newscaster) A newscast is a TV or radio programme which gives news about recent events in the world. The person who reads the news on a newscast is called a newscaster.

newsflash (newsflashes) A newsflash is an interruption in the middle of a TV or radio programme, to announce an important piece of news.

newshound A newshound is a very eager newspaper reporter, who is always looking for new stories.

newsletter A newsletter is a printed sheet or small magazine containing information about an organization.

It is sent out regularly to people, especially members of the organization.

newsman (newsmen) A newsman is a reporter for a newspaper or a TV or radio programme.

newspaper ❑ A newspaper consists of news, articles, adverts, and other items printed on several large sheets of folded paper and sold to the public. Newspapers are produced either every day from Monday to Saturday, or once a week. ◇ The organization which produces a newspaper is also called a newspaper. *A short time later, a man called a newspaper.*

❑ Newspaper is old newspapers, especially when they are used for another purpose such as wrapping things up.

newspaperman (newspapermen) A newspaperman is a reporter or photographer who works for a newspaper.

newsprint is (a) the cheap paper on which newspapers are printed. (b) the ink used to print newspapers. (c) the text printed in newspapers. *The papers are still devoting pages of newsprint to the crisis.*

newsreader A newsreader is a person who reads the news on TV or radio.

newsreel In the past, newsreels were short films, made especially for showing in cinemas, which showed events which had recently happened.

newsroom A newsroom is (a) a TV or radio studio where news reports are prepared and broadcast. (b) a newspaper office where news reports are written and edited before they are printed.

newsstand See news-stand

newsworthy If you say something which has happened is newsworthy, you mean it is interesting or important enough to be in the news on TV, radio, or in the newspapers.

newt The newt is a small lizard-like creature with a moist skin, short legs, and a long tail. Newts can live on land or in water.

next is used to talk about a period of time coming after the present one, or a period of time starting now. *...next week... ...in the next 20 years.*

❑ You say next when you are mentioning what happened after the thing you have just described. *Next, the government introduced a green belt one kilometre wide along the Indian border.* ◇ The next thing is used to say something happened immediately after something else. *The next thing, there was pandemonium.*

❑ The next thing of a particular kind means the first one after the present one, or the first one since the last one. *...the next problem... ...her next book.* ◇ What you do next is what you do when you have finished what you are doing now. *I'd like to work in porcelain next.*

❑ The next time something happens will be the first time it has happened since the last time. *The next time competitors see land will be Cape Town.*

❑ If you are among a group of people or things, the next person or thing is the one nearest to you. *...in the next room... ...a man in the next row.* Similarly, you say one person or thing is next to another one. ◇ If a house or flat is next door to yours, there are no other houses or flats in between. ◇ If a town or district is next door to something, it is adjacent to it. *...the town of Paisley, next door to Scotland's largest city, Glasgow.*

❑ People sometimes say the next man, meaning the average person in the street. *He does not like what he sees any more than the next man.*

❏ The **next** best thing of a particular kind is better than all the others except the best one.

❏ **Next to nothing** means hardly anything. *They say next to nothing about real women.*

next of kin Your **next of kin** are your closest relatives.

nexus (*plural:* nexus) A **nexus** is a connection or system of connections linking things closely together. *...the nexus of money and politics.*

NHS In Britain, the **NHS** or **National Health Service** is a publicly-funded system which provides free or inexpensive medical care for everyone.

nib The **nib** of a fountain pen is the small pointed piece of metal at the end which releases ink onto the paper when you write.

nibble (nibbling, nibbled) ❏ A **nibble** is a quick snack or light meal which you have when you are not very hungry. ◇ If a person or animal **nibbles** something or **nibbles at** it, they take small repeated bites out of it.

❏ If something is **nibbled** away, it is slowly reduced, a bit at a time. *Competitors have nibbled away at their market share in PCs.*

nice (nicer, nicest; nicely, niceness) ❏ If you say something is **nice**, you mean it is enjoyable, pleasant, welcome, or reassuring. *...a nice cup of tea... It's nice to know that you can speak to an expert if you get stuck.* ◇ **Nice** can also be used to say something looks neat and attractive. *...nice clothes... The tables are nicely laid.*

❏ If you say someone is **nice**, you mean they are friendly, pleasant, and polite. *He has a reputation for decency and niceness.* ◇ If someone is **nice** to you, they are kind and thoughtful.

❏ If something is working **nicely**, it is working in a satisfactory way. ◇ If something will do **nicely**, it is just what you want.

nicety (niceties) **Niceties** are the small details of something, especially the finer points of polite behaviour.

niche (*pron:* **neesh**) A **niche** is a hollow area in a wall, or a natural hollow in a rock. ◇ If you find a **niche**, you find a job or position which is exactly right for you. *She has carved a niche for herself as a roly-poly comic actor.*

nick ❏ If someone **nicks** something, they steal it. ◇ If the police **nick** someone, they arrest them. ◇ Prison is sometimes called the **nick**.

❏ If you **nick** something, especially your skin, you make a small cut in it. A **nick** is a small cut in something.

❏ If something is **in good nick**, it is in good condition.

❏ If something happens **in the nick of time**, it happens just in time for something bad to be prevented.

nickel is a silvery-white metal which is resistant to corrosion. It is used in alloys and in electroplating. ◇ A **nickel** is an American or Canadian coin worth five cents.

nickname (nicknamed) A **nickname** is a name given to someone or something, which is used instead of their real name. It usually comes from something noticeable about their appearance or behaviour. You can say someone or something is **nicknamed** a particular thing. *...a secret policeman nicknamed 'the gorilla'.*

nicotine is a poisonous addictive substance in tobacco.

niece Your **niece** is the daughter of your sister or brother, or the daughter of your husband's or wife's sister or brother.

nifty If something is done in a **nifty** way, it is done cleverly or skilfully. ◇ A **nifty** device or gadget is cleverly designed to make something easy for you.

niggardly If someone is **niggardly**, they are not generous with something, especially money.

nigger is an offensive word for a black person.

niggle (niggling, niggled) A **niggle** is a minor problem which keeps worrying you. You can say a problem like this **niggles** you. *The question niggled me... Niggling doubts remain.*

nigh ❏ If you say something is **nigh**, you mean it is going to happen soon. *...his forecasts that the end of the recession was nigh.*

❏ **Nigh** is used in front of words like 'impossible' to mean 'almost'. *His family is finding it nigh impossible to sell his mansion.* **Well-nigh** and **nigh on** are used in a similar way. *His behaviour has become well-nigh intolerable... It renders any vehicle nigh on impossible to steal.*

night ❏ The **night** is the period each twenty-four hours when it is dark.

❏ If something happens **night and day**, it goes on all the time.

❏ If you have an **early night**, you get to bed early. If you have a **late night**, you do not get to bed until late.

❏ **Night** is also used to mean 'evening'. *...Khalid Skah, winner of the 10,000 metres on Monday night.* **Last night** means yesterday evening. *...last night's Italian football win.* ◇ The **first night** or **opening night** of a theatrical production is its first public performance.

night school is an institution where adults can go to take educational courses in the evenings.

night-time is used to talk about things connected with the period between sunset and sunrise. *...night-time visibility... ...night-time temperatures.*

night watchman See nightwatchman.

nightcap A **nightcap** is a drink, usually alcoholic, which you have just before going to bed. ◇ In the past, a **nightcap** was a kind of hat people wore in bed.

nightclothes are the clothes you wear in bed, such as pyjamas or a nightdress.

nightclub A **nightclub** is a place people go to late in the evening to drink and dance or see a show.

nightdress (nightdresses) A **nightdress** is a piece of clothing a woman or girl wears in bed.

nightfall is the time of day when it starts to get dark.

nightgown In the US, a nightdress is usually called a **nightgown**.

nightie A **nightie** is the same as a nightdress.

nightingale The **nightingale** is a small brown European bird. The male bird is famous for singing beautifully, especially in the evening.

nightlife The **nightlife** in a town or city is the entertainment available at night, such as nightclubs, theatres, and bars.

nightlight A **nightlight** is a very dim light which is left on at night, especially in a small child's bedroom.

nightly A **nightly** event happens every night or every evening. *...performing nightly in front of local audiences... A new and younger crowd filled the bar nightly.*

nightmare (nightmarish) ❏ A **nightmare** is a frightening

dream. A **nightmarish** situation is like a nightmare. *Clouds of tear gas cleared to reveal a truly nightmarish scene.*
❏ A **nightmare** is also a frightening or unpleasant experience. *Since then our lives have been a nightmare.* ◇ If you say something is someone's **nightmare,** you mean it is the thing they are most afraid of happening. *His nightmare was not being able to complete the 3-mile run we set for each volunteer.*

nightshirt A **nightshirt** is a long loose shirt some men and boys wear in bed.

nightspot A **nightspot** is the same as a nightclub.

nightwatchman (nightwatchmen) (*or* **night watchman**) A **nightwatchman** is a man who guards buildings at night as his job.

nightwear is clothing worn in bed, such as pyjamas and nightdresses.

nihilism (*pron:* **nye-ill-liz-zum**) (nihilistic; nihilist) ❏ **Nihilism** is the belief that there is no justification for any existing authorities or institutions, and that they should all be rejected or destroyed. Someone who takes this view is called a **nihilist;** you say his or her opinions are **nihilistic.**
❏ **Nihilism** is also the belief that nothing has any value or meaning. You say a novel or film which expresses this idea is **nihilistic.**

Nikkei (*pron:* nik-kay) The **Nikkei index** or **Nikkei average** is an index of share prices based on the average price of shares in 225 Japanese companies on the Japanese Stock Exchange. It is used by shareholders and investors to check general changes in share prices.

nil In a game like football, **nil** means a score of nought. *Fulham and Cambridge drew nil-nil.* ◇ If an amount of something is **nil,** there is none of it. *Unemployment has risen from close to nil to a level where it makes more sense to count those with jobs than those without.*

nimble (nimbler, nimblest; nimbly, nimbleness) A **nimble** person is quick and agile. *...one of the nimblest players on the field... For a large man he moved quickly, almost nimbly... He combines bulk with almost dainty nimbleness.* ◇ Someone who has a **nimble** mind is able to take things in quickly and make rapid decisions and judgements.

nimby (*or* NIMBY) stands for 'Not In My Back Yard'. It is used to talk about people who object to something (for example a probation hostel) being sited near their home, even though they may approve of such things in principle. *Local MPs have met with a barrage of NIMBY fury.*

nine (ninth) **Nine** is the number 9.

ninepin **Ninepins** is another name for the game of skittles. Each skittle can be called a **ninepin.** ◇ If you say people or things are going down like **ninepins,** you mean they are being injured or destroyed one after the other. *There was a time when Liverpool players never seemed to get injured, but now they are going down like ninepins.*

nineteen (nineteenth) **Nineteen** is the number 19.

ninety (ninetieth) (nineties) **Ninety** is the number 90. ◇ The **nineties** is the period from 1990 to 1999. ◇ If someone is in their **nineties,** they are aged 90 to 99.

ninny (ninnies) If you call someone a **ninny,** you mean they are rather silly.

nip (nipping, nipped) ❏ If an animal or insect **nips** you or gives you a **nip,** it takes a small bite at you. ◇ **nip** something **in the bud:** see bud.
❏ If you **nip** somewhere, you go there quickly or briefly, to do something or get something. *She nipped out for extra supplies of milk.* ◇ If you **nip** into a space, you move there quickly. *Halfway round the opening lap, he stormed past, nipped in front of me and tried to draw away.*

nipple A person's **nipples** are the two round pieces of slightly hard, dark-coloured flesh on their chest. Babies suck milk through their mother's nipples.

nippy A **nippy** person or vehicle moves around quickly among other people or vehicles. *...a nippy winger.*

nirvana (*pron:* near-vah-na) (nirvanas) For Buddhists and Hindus, **nirvana** is the highest state of spiritual enlightenment which can be achieved. ◇ When people talk about a **nirvana,** they are talking about some other perfect state of things, which someone would like to bring about. *Achieving that 4 – 5% nirvana is the task for both monetary and fiscal policy.*

nit **Nits** are the tiny eggs of a louse which have been laid in someone's hair, or the larvae which have hatched from these eggs.

nit-picking If you say someone is **nit-picking,** you mean they keep finding fault with something by concentrating on small and unimportant details.

nitrate **Nitrates** are chemical compounds consisting of nitrogen, oxygen, and some other element or elements. They are used as fertilisers.

nitrogen is a colourless gas with no smell. It forms about 78% of the earth's atmosphere.

nitroglycerine is a powerful liquid explosive. It is thick and pale yellow in colour.

nitrous oxide is a colourless gas used as a mild anaesthetic. It is also called 'laughing gas'.

nitty-gritty If you get down to the **nitty-gritty** of something, you deal with the most important and basic part of it.

no (noes) ❏ **No** is used to give a negative answer to a question, to refuse an offer, or to refuse permission for something. ◇ If someone **will not take no for an answer,** they keep asking for something and are not put off when they do not get it immediately.
❏ In Parliament, the **noes** are the people who vote against a motion. The people who vote in favour are called the 'ayes'.
❏ **No** is used to say there is nothing of a particular kind. *Hitler had no education beyond elementary school... Mrs Brown, a widow, had no children.*
❏ **No** is often used with 'more' and with words ending in '-er'. For example, if you say something is **no** bigger than something else, you mean it is the same size or smaller. *The risks are no greater than for any other new treatment... He said chemical weapons were no more dangerous than nuclear weapons.*
❏ You also use **no** to say someone does not have a particular skill or ability. *In truth, he was no politician either.*
❏ **No** is used on notices to say something is forbidden. *NO SMOKING.* ◇ If you say **there's no** doing a particular thing, you mean it is impossible to do it. *There's no concealing the delight with which developments in Moscow have been greeted within his administration... There's no going back to the old days.*

No. (Nos.) No. is short for 'number'. *...Brahms Symphonies Nos. 3 and 4.*

no-ball In cricket, if a bowler bowls a **no-ball**, he or she bowls in a way which is against the rules. When this happens, one run is awarded to the other side. If the batsman hits the ball, he or she can score runs in the usual way.

no-claims A **no-claims bonus** is a reduction in an insurance premium if no claims have been made within a certain period.

no-go A **no-go area** is a place controlled by people who prevent certain other people from getting into it, often by force.

no-nonsense people are firm, straightforward, and efficient.

no one means the same as 'nobody'.

nob Upper-class people are sometimes called **nobs**.

nobble (nobbling, nobbled) If a racehorse is **nobbled**, it is prevented from winning, often by giving it a drug. ◇ If you say a person has been **nobbled**, you mean they have been prevented from carrying out their duties properly, by threatening them or bribing them. *A second trial was stopped after allegations of attempts to nobble the jury.*

Nobel Prize (Nobel prizewinner) **Nobel Prizes** are international awards which originated in the will of Alfred Nobel, the Swedish chemist who invented dynamite. They are awarded yearly for the most important achievements in various fields, and are the most respected prizes in the world. A **Nobel prizewinner** is someone who has won a Nobel Prize.

noble (nobler, noblest; nobly, nobility) ❑ **Noble** behaviour is honest, brave, and unselfish. *...a noble gesture... In their efforts they were nobly supported by the crew of the other trawler.*

❑ A **noble** is someone of high social class who has a title; especially a peer. You also say someone like this belongs to the **nobility** or comes from a **noble** family.

❑ **Noble** is sometimes used to describe things which are very grand and impressive. *Hasell added a noble Georgian facade and flanking terrace to the house.*

nobleman (noblemen) A **nobleman** is a male member of the nobility.

noblesse oblige (*pron:* no-bless oh-**bleezh**; *the 'zh' sound is like 's' in 'pleasure'*) When people say **noblesse oblige**, they are referring to the traditional idea that members of the nobility are supposed to behave in an honourable and generous way.

noblewoman (noblewomen) A **noblewoman** is a female member of the nobility.

nobody (nobodies) **Nobody** or **no one** means not a single person. *Nobody wants a dump or an incinerator next door.* ◇ A **nobody** is someone who is not considered to be important.

nocturnal is used to talk about things which happen during the night. *...nocturnal noise.* ◇ A **nocturnal** animal is one which is active at night, rather than during the day.

nod (nodding, nodded) ❑ If you **nod** or give a **nod**, you move your head up and down quickly, as a way of saying 'yes'. ◇ If something gets the **nod** or is **given the nod**, permission is given for it to be done. You can also say a person gets the **nod** to do something.

❑ If something like a treaty goes through **on the nod** or is **nodded through**, it is accepted without being questioned or argued about. ◇ If something is done on a **nod and a wink**, it is done unofficially and with very little being said, because everyone understands the situation. *Now that formal tenure has given way to informal tenure, decisions are even more likely to be made on a nod and a wink.*

❑ If you **nod off**, you fall asleep.

❑ If a footballer **nods** the ball, he gives it a gentle tap with his head, to send it in a particular direction. ◇ If you **nod** towards something, you indicate where it is by making a quick movement of your head.

❑ **nodding acquaintance**: see **acquaintance**.

node ❑ On a plant, a **node** is one of the places on the stem which a leaf grows from.

❑ A **node** in someone's body is a swelling or roundish lump. *...the lymph nodes.*

nodule A **nodule** is a small round lump on something.

Noel is another word for Christmas.

noise ❑ A **noise** is a sound, especially an unpleasant one. *...the noise of typewriters... ...the noise of the city.*

❑ If you **make a noise** about something you think is wrong, you make a lot of fuss, to draw attention to it. ◇ If you say someone is making **noises** of a certain kind, you mean they are indicating their intentions. *John Major has been making noises about making government more open... Conservationists are astonished by the noises coming out of Beijing.* ◇ If you say someone is **making the right noises**, you mean they are responding to something in the way people hoped they would.

noiseless is used to describe things which do not make a noise, or things which happen without any noise being made. *The ride proved to be smooth and noiseless.*

noisy (noisier, noisiest; noisily) You say someone or something is **noisy** when they make a lot of noise. *...noisy bell-ringers... Dozens of protesters drove their motorbikes noisily around the streets.* A **noisy** place is one where there is a lot of noise. *...noisy amusement arcades.* ◇ You also call someone's actions **noisy** when they make a lot of fuss to draw attention to something they feel strongly about. *...a noisy campaign to save the Museum of English Naive Art from closure.*

nom de guerre (*plural:* noms de guerre) (*both pron:* nom duh **gair**) A **nom de guerre** is a false name someone uses for something they do.

nom de plume (*plural:* noms de plume) (*both pron:* nom duh **ploom**) A **nom de plume** is the same as a pen name.

nomad (nomadic) A **nomad** is a member of a tribe which travels from place to place, rather than living in one place all the time. **Nomadic** is used to describe people like these and their way of life. *...the great nomadic tribes of the Western Sahara... This sort of nomadic, pastoral lifestyle is unique in Mongolia.*

nomenclature (*pron:* no-men-**klatch**-er) A **nomenclature** is a system of naming a particular set of things. *Using traditional Scottish nomenclature, sea vegetables are sold under names such as slabhagan, dabberlocks and grockle... ...the Working Group on Planetary Nomenclature.*

nominal (nominally) **Nominal** is used to talk about a characteristic someone or something is supposed to have, but which they may not have in reality. *The two states* *are nominal allies... In these areas, nominally under UN control, fearful things are happening.* ◇ A **nominal** charge is a very small charge, usually made because a sum of money is expected to change hands, rather than to cover the cost of something.

nominate (nominating, nominated; nomination, nominee) ❏ If someone is **nominated** for a position or job, either they are officially appointed to do it, or their name is put forward as a candidate. In either case, you say they are a **nominee** for the position or job. *Leadership nominations close at noon next Thursday.*

❏ If someone or something is **nominated** for something like an award, their name is put forward as one of the people or things to be considered for it. You say they are a **nominee** for the award. *It was his first significant film role and won him an Oscar nomination.* ◇ If someone is **nominated** to receive a sum of money which is going to become available, they are chosen to get it.

non- is added to a word to say someone or something does not have the quality or characteristic described by the word. *...a non-cancerous condition... ...a non-custodial sentence.* ◇ **Non-** is also added to words to say someone does not do something. *...non-payers... ...the non-attendance of the two men.*

non-aggression A **non-aggression** pact is an agreement between countries that they will not attack or harm each other.

non-alcoholic drinks do not contain any alcohol.

non-aligned (non-alignment) A **non-aligned** country does not belong to any politically linked group of countries. You say a country like this is following a policy of **non-alignment.**

non-co-operation is a refusal to co-operate with someone. This term is especially used to talk about a type of industrial action in which employees refuse to do anything which is not part of their official duties.

non-combatant In a war, **non-combatants** are people who are in an area where there is fighting but are not fighting themselves, for example civilians or people like army doctors and chaplains.

non-commissioned officer See NCO.

non-committal If someone is being **non-committal,** they are not expressing a definite opinion, or not revealing any details about something.

non-conformist (non-conformity) (*or* nonconformist, nonconformity) ❏ **Non-conformists** are British Protestants who do not belong to the Church of England. Methodists, Baptists, and Quakers are all non-conformists. **Non-conformist** is used to talk about things connected with their beliefs and worship. *...non-conformist churches.*

❏ A **non-conformist** is also someone who holds unorthodox opinions or does not behave in the way people are normally expected to behave. You talk about the **non-conformity** of someone like this.

non-event If you say something was a **non-event,** you mean it turned out to be not as exciting or significant as people were expecting.

non-existent (non-existence) If you say something is **non-existent** or talk about its **non-existence,** you mean it does not exist.

non-ferrous metals do not contain iron.

non-fiction is writing which provides information or describes real events, rather than telling a story.

non-interference is the same as non-intervention.

non-intervention (non-interventionist) If a country has a policy of **non-intervention,** it purposely does not become involved in wars or disputes between other countries. People, especially politicians, who favour a policy like this are called **non-interventionists.**

non-nuclear means not involving nuclear weapons or nuclear power. *...a non-nuclear war.* A **non-nuclear** country is one which does not have nuclear weapons.

non-partisan is used to describe people and organizations that do not support any particular political party. *...a non-partisan head of state.* A **non-partisan** approach to a problem involves co-operation between political parties who would normally be opposing each other.

non-payment is failure to pay money which is owed. *The rate of disconnections following non-payment of water charges is rising.*

non-person If someone becomes a **non-person,** they are rejected by their countrymen or former colleagues, because they have done something wrong or fallen out of favour with the authorities.

non-profit-making A **non-profit-making** organization exists to raise money for a cause or charity, rather than to make a profit for shareholders.

non-proliferation A **non-proliferation** treaty is one in which countries agree to limit the production and spread of nuclear weapons.

non-resident Non-residents are people who use a building like a hotel, for example by having a drink or a meal, but do not stay overnight.

non-sectarian organizations are not connected with any particular religion.

non-sequitur (*pron:* non **sek**-wit-tur) If you say a statement or conclusion is a **non-sequitur,** you mean it does not follow logically from what was said before.

non-smoking (non-smoker) A **non-smoking** person or **non-smoker** does not smoke tobacco in any form. ◇ A **non-smoking** area is one where smoking is not allowed. *...a non-smoking compartment.*

non-standard objects are not of a usual or accepted type. *...non-standard window shapes.*

non-starter If you say something is a **non-starter,** you mean it has no chance of being accepted or succeeding.

non-stick A **non-stick** pan is coated with a substance which prevents food sticking to it.

non-stop is used to describe things which continue without any breaks or pauses. *The non-stop flight will take nine hours... ...non-stop criticism and arm-twisting.*

non-toxic things are not poisonous. *...non-toxic crayons.*

non-union workers are people who do not belong to a trade union.

non-verbal communication does not involve the use of words. *...a non-verbal joke.*

non-violent (non-violence) A **non-violent** way of achieving something does not involve attacking people or causing damage. *...a non-violent campaign.* Trying to achieve things in this way is called **non-violence.**

non-voting members of an organization do not have the right to vote at meetings.

non-white is sometimes used to describe people who

have black, brown, or yellow skin, rather than the white skin people of European descent have. *Non-white sportsmen and women are still severely disadvantaged in the sporting arena.*

nonagenarian (*pron:* no-nej-jin-**nair**-ee-an) A **nonagenarian** is a person in their nineties.

nonchalant (*pron:* non-**shall**-ant) (nonchalantly, nonchalance) You say someone is **nonchalant** when they are very calm and seem not to worry or care about things. *...sitting nonchalantly on a rock surrounded by agitated crabs.* You talk about the **nonchalance** of someone like this.

nonconformist (nonconformity) See **non-conformist**.

nondescript people and things are dull and uninteresting.

none means not a single person or thing, or not even a small amount of something. *None of these concerns should be dismissed... There was none of the drama and relief of a hostage release.* ◇ **second to none**: see **second**.

❑ **None too** is used in front of words like 'sure' and 'easily'. If you say someone is 'none too sure' about something, you mean they are not sure about it at all. *The City is none too keen on tycoons at present... The visit to Washington comes none too soon.*

❑ If someone will **have none of** something, they will not accept it or tolerate it. *He wanted to become an actor, but his father would have none of it and put him to work in a bank.*

❑ If you are **none the wiser** for an experience, you have not learned anything useful from it. ◇ If you are **none the worse** for an unpleasant experience, it has not done you any real harm. ◇ **none the less**: see **nonetheless**.

nonentity (nonentities) If you call someone a **nonentity**, you mean they are not special or important in any way.

nonetheless (*or* none the less) means the same as nevertheless.

nonplussed If you are **nonplussed** by something, you do not know what to do or say.

nonsense (nonsensical) ❑ If you say something is **nonsense** or **a nonsense**, you mean it is untrue or silly. *It is a nonsense to say we have untrained staff dealing with emergencies.* You can also say something like this is **nonsensical**.

❑ If something **makes nonsense of** a statement or set of figures, it makes it seem worthless or pointless. Similarly, something can **make nonsense of** a rule or a law.

❑ If you say someone in authority will stand **no nonsense**, you mean they will not tolerate any indiscipline or awkward behaviour.

❑ **Nonsense** is also a kind of humorous writing, especially for children. It deals with imaginary creatures or impossible situations.

noodle Noodles are long thin pieces of pasta which are cooked in soup or boiling water.

nook If you talk about every **nook and cranny** in a place, you mean every part of it. *...motorists allowed to penetrate every nook and cranny of the Lake District.*

nooky (*or* nookie) is a humorous word for sexual intercourse.

noon is twelve o'clock in the middle of the day.

noonday is used to talk about things happening in the middle of the day. *...the noonday sun.*

noose A noose is a loop at the end of a piece of rope, especially one used to hang someone. ◇ If you say someone is **tightening the noose**, you mean they are putting pressure on someone to force them to agree to something.

nor ❑ See neither.

❑ **Nor** is used to link two negative statements which have something in common. For example, instead of saying 'I have never been to Eurodisney. I do not want to go,' you can say 'I have never been to Eurodisney, nor do I want to go.' *We have certainly not lost a battle, nor do we plan to do so in the future.*

Nordic People are sometimes described as **Nordic** when they are fairly tall and have blond or fair hair, blue eyes, and a fair skin.

norm ❑ If you say something is the **norm**, you mean it is what usually happens. *In the industrialised nations, it's the norm to have cataracts if you reach the age of eighty.*

❑ A **norm** is an official standard or level which people are supposed to achieve or conform to. *...a national pay norm.* ◇ **Norms** are rules of behaviour which are considered normal in a society or group.

normal (normally) If you talk about what is **normal**, you are talking about the usual state of things, or what usually happens. *Life in the city was beginning to return to normal... ...altitude sickness, which normally occurs above 14,000ft... ...a hospital apparently functioning normally.* ◇ **Normal** things are the usual or standard ones. *All the normal baby clothes were far too large.* ◇ **Normal** people behave in an ordinary and expected way. ◇ **Normal** is also used to talk about people who were not born with anything wrong with them, mentally or physically. This use can be offensive to people who have a mental or physical handicap. *Sufferers have smaller brains than normal people.*

normalcy is the same as normality.

normalise See normalize.

normality is a situation where everything is normal. *Life was returning to somewhere near normality.*

normalize (normalizing, normalized; normalization) (*can be spelled with an 's' instead of a 'z'*) If a country **normalizes** relations with another country, it restores them to the way they were before they had a quarrel or conflict. This is called a **normalization** of relations. Other things can be **normalized** in a similar way. *...the normalization of sport in South Africa.*

Norman The **Normans** were a people from northern France who successfully invaded England in 1066. **Norman** is used to describe things relating to these people, especially the style of architecture developed in England during their rule. *...a twelfth-century Norman cathedral.*

normative is used to describe things which impose a standard for people to follow. *...normative guidelines.*

Norse The **Norse** people were the people who lived in Scandinavia in ancient and medieval times. **Norse** is used to talk about things to do with these people. *...the Norse myths.*

north is one of the four main points of the compass. ◇ The **north** is the direction on your left when you look towards the place where the sun rises. If you go in that direction, you go **north**; a place in that direction is **north** of the place where you are now. ◇ The **north** part of a place is the part north of its centre. *...North Yorkshire... ...the north of England.*

❏ A **north** wind blows from the north.

North Atlantic Treaty Organization See NATO.

north-east (*or* northeast) The **north-east** is the direction halfway between north and east. ◇ The **north-east** part of a place is the part north-east of its centre. *...in the north-east of England... ...north-east China.*

north-easterly A **north-easterly** wind blows from the north-east. ◇ If you travel in a **north-easterly** direction, you travel towards the north-east.

north-eastern (*or* northeastern) The **north-eastern** part of a place is the part north-east of its centre. *...north-eastern Australia.*

north-west (*or* northwest) The **north-west** is the direction halfway between north and west. ◇ The **north-west** of a place is the part north-west of its centre. *...north-west Afghanistan... ...the north-west of England.*

north-westerly A **north-westerly** wind blows from the north-west. ◇ If you travel in a **north-westerly** direction, you travel towards the north-west.

north-western (*or* northwestern) The **north-western** part of a place is the part north-west of its centre. *...north-western Spain.*

northbound traffic is heading towards the north.

northeast See north-east.

northeastern See north-eastern.

northerly ❏ A **northerly** wind blows from the north. ◇ If you travel in a **northerly** direction, you travel towards the north. Similarly, if you face in a **northerly** direction, you face towards the north.

❏ The most **northerly** part of a place is the part furthest to the north. Similarly, the most **northerly** place of a group of places is the one furthest to the north. *...the world's most northerly capital.*

northern The **northern** part of a place is the part north of its centre. *...northern England.* ◇ **Northern** also means to the north of a country or region. *...Turkey, Iraq's northern neighbour.*

northerner A **northerner** is a person who was born in or lives in the northern part of a country or region.

northernmost The **northernmost** part of a place is the part furthest to the north. Similarly, the **northernmost** place of a group of places is the one furthest to the north. *...the northernmost republic.*

northwards (northward) If you go **northwards** or **northward**, you go towards the north. You can also say you go in a **northward** direction.

northwest See north-west.

northwestern See north-western.

Norwegian is used to talk about people and things in or from Norway. *...a Norwegian economist.* ◇ A **Norwegian** is someone who comes from Norway. ◇ **Norwegian** is the main language spoken in Norway.

Nos. See No.

nose (nosing, nosed) ❏ A person's or animal's **nose** is the organ which enables them to smell things.

❏ If you hold something **under** someone's **nose**, you hold it close to them, where they can see it. ◇ If you say something is going on **under** someone's **nose**, you mean it is happening where they are, and they ought to be aware of it.

❏ If you **look down your nose** at something, you have

a low opinion of it. ◇ If you **turn up your nose** at something, you reject it because you think it is not good enough for you. ◇ If you do something **holding your nose**, you do it reluctantly because it involves you in something you dislike or disapprove of. ◇ If someone or something **gets up your nose**, they annoy you.

❏ If you **keep your nose clean**, you behave well and stay out of trouble.

❏ If you **thumb your nose** at someone, you do something which shows you have no respect for them. ◇ If you **rub** someone's **nose** in something like a past mistake, you keep reminding them about it. ◇ **put** someone's **nose out of joint**: see joint.

❏ If you have to **pay through the nose** for something, you have to pay a very high price for it.

❏ If you **nose around**, you search for something. ◇ If you **follow your nose**, you act in an instinctive way rather than following any thought-out plan or idea. ◇ If you have a **nose** for something, you have an instinctive ability to find it or recognize it. ◇ If you say someone is **poking their nose** into something, you mean they are interfering.

❏ The **nose** of a wine is its smell.

❏ The **nose** of a plane is the part at the front.

nose-dive See nosedive.

nosebag A **nosebag** is a bag containing food for a horse, hung over the horse's head.

nosebleed If you have a **nosebleed**, blood runs out of the inside of your nose, often because you have been hit.

nosedive (nosediving, nosedived) (*or* nose-dive, *etc*) ❏ If a plane **nosedives** or goes into a **nosedive**, it dives steeply, nose first, towards the ground.

❏ If something like a share price **nosedives** or goes into a **nosedive**, it falls suddenly and rapidly. ◇ If a situation **nosedives**, it takes a sudden bad turn.

nosey See nosy.

nostalgic (nostalgically, nostalgia) If you are **nostalgic** for something in the past or feel **nostalgia** for it, you think of it with pleasure and affection. *They talk nostalgically of the great television plays of the past... ...a wave of nostalgia for wartime romance.*

nostril A person's **nostrils** are the two openings at the lower end of their nose.

nostrum A **nostrum** is a simple remedy for dealing with a problem or situation, especially one which can be summed up in a few words.

nosy (*or* nosey) (nosier, nosiest) If you say someone is being **nosy**, you mean they are trying to find out about something which is none of their business.

not is used to give a sentence its opposite meaning. *It is not like that in real life... Secrecy must not become a habit.* After words like 'is' and 'have', **not** is often shortened to **'nt**. *It didn't make any difference... I'm beginning to wish I hadn't painted my house in such bright colours.*

❏ **Not** is used with 'a' or 'an' to emphasize that there is nothing of a particular kind. *There was not a tiara in sight.*

❏ **Not** is used with 'all', 'every', or 'always' to say there are exceptions to something which is generally true. *The news is not all bad... Not every Australian shirt is an outsize fitting.*

❏ **Not** is used with words like 'only' and 'just' at the beginning of a two-part statement; the second part begins with 'but' or 'but also', and usually mentions something more important than the first part. *These men stand to lose not just their jobs but all their health benefits as well... They lost a battle not only for themselves but also for press freedom.*

❏ **not for nothing:** see **nothing.** ◇ **not least:** see **least.**

notable is used to describe things which are important, remarkable, or especially interesting. *...a notable collection of clocks.* ◇ **Notables** are people who have an important position of some kind. *...the local notables.*

notably is used (a) when mentioning the most important or typical example of the thing you are talking about. *Foreign visitors, notably from Japan, regularly make their way to the site.* (b) when mentioning an important characteristic which someone or something has. *She is a notably gregarious woman.*

notary (notaries) A **notary** or **notary public** is a person, usually a lawyer, who has legal authority to witness the signing of documents so they are legally valid, especially for use overseas.

notation A **notation** is a set of written symbols used in something like maths, music, or chess.

notch (notches, notching, notched) ❏ A **notch** is a small cut, usually V-shaped, in the surface or edge of something. Making notches can be a way of keeping count of something. ◇ If something is raised or lowered a **notch,** it is raised or lowered by a small amount. *Her game has slipped a notch... I wanted to go under 47 seconds and take the record down a couple of notches.*

❏ If you **notch** a victory or **notch** it **up,** you achieve it. *The United Nations notched up a triumph this month.*

❏ See also **top-notch.**

note (noting, noted) ❏ A **note** is a short letter.

❏ A **note** in a book or other document is a short piece of additional information.

❏ If you **make a note** of something or **note it down,** you write it down, so you have the information when you need it. ◇ If you **make a mental note** of something, you try to make sure you remember it, without writing anything down.

❏ If you **note** something, you become aware of it. *I noted pride among residents in their town.* ◇ If you **take note of** something, you pay attention to it because you think it is important. *A reviewer remains duty bound to take note of the flaws in the book.*

❏ If you **compare notes** with someone, you talk to them to find out whether you have the same information, opinions, or experiences.

❏ A person or thing **of note** is important, worth mentioning, or well-known. *...a translator of note... ...two other performances of note.* ◇ If someone is **noted** for something, they are well-known for it. *...a noted embezzler... ...a highly respected priest who is noted for his work with the poor.*

❏ In music, a **note** is a sound with a particular pitch, or a written symbol representing this sound.

❏ You can describe the beginning or ending of something by saying it begins or ends on a particular **note.** *The meeting was opened on an optimistic note... The stock market closed on a high note.* ◇ You can describe what someone says by saying they **strike** or **sound** a particular **note.** *The Secretary-General sounded a note of caution.* ◇ If you say there is a particular **note** in someone's voice, you are talking about the way it shows their feelings. *There is in this woman's voice a note of despair.*

❏ A **note** is also a banknote.

notebook A **notebook** is a small book for writing notes in. ◇ A **notebook** computer is a portable computer, the size of a small book.

notepad A **notepad** is a small pad of paper for writing notes on. ◇ A **notepad** computer is a small portable computer and personal organizer.

notepaper is paper for writing letters on.

noteworthy is used to describe things which are unusual or remarkable in some way. *A lengthy thundery spell included several noteworthy storms.*

nothing means 'not anything'. *Nothing is being done... There is nothing sentimental about his work.*

❏ **Nothing** is used in front of 'more' and words ending '-er'. For example, if you say there is 'nothing nicer' than a certain thing, you mean it is the nicest thing of its kind. Similarly, you can say there is 'nothing so nice' as that thing. *I think there is nothing better than English roast beef.*

❏ **Nothing** is used to say there is none of something. *This has brought unemployment up from virtually nothing in December to 300,000 today.*

❏ If you do something **for nothing,** you do it without expecting to be paid. *Most of them work for nothing.* ◇ If you get **something for nothing,** you get something without giving anything in return.

❏ If you say something came **to nothing,** you mean it did not achieve anything. Similarly, you can say something turned out to have been **for nothing.**

❏ If you say **not for nothing** did something happen, you mean there was a very good reason why it happened. *Not for nothing did she have a radio play written about her.*

❏ **Nothing but** a particular thing means only that thing. *He insists that all he wrote is nothing but the truth... I feel nothing but admiration.* ◇ **Nothing if not** is used to emphasize that someone or something has a certain quality. For example, if you say someone is 'nothing if not frank', you mean they are very frank.

❏ If you say something that has happened is **nothing,** you mean it is not serious or important. *What they do to each other is nothing compared to the damage they inflict on the management.* ◇ If you say something is **nothing of the sort** or **nothing of the kind,** you are saying emphatically that it is not a certain thing. *As taught, economics is presented as a science. It is nothing of the kind.* ◇ You say **to say nothing of...** when adding something which makes your statement even more emphatic. *There are 1.5 million cars in Budapest, to say nothing of trolley buses and trams.*

❏ **nothing less than:** see **less.** ◇ **nothing more than:** see **more.** ◇ **nothing short of:** see **short.** ◇ **nothing like:** see **like.** ◇ **nothing much:** see **much.**

nothingness is complete non-existence. For example, people who do not believe in life after death believe that after death there is nothingness. ◇ **Nothingness** is also a total lack of anything. Some people believe there was a time in the past, before there was any matter, when there was nothingness.

notice (noticing, noticed) ❏ A **notice** is a written sign, placed where people can read it.

❏ A **notice** is also an official warning that something is going to happen. *...a notice of dismissal.* ◇ If someone has, say, an hour's **notice,** they receive one hour's warning that something is going to happen.

❑ If you **give notice** of something, you warn people how you intend to act in the future. *Referees gave notice that they would respond harshly to so-called professional fouls.* Similarly, you can **serve notice** that something is going to happen.

❑ If something is done **at short notice** or **at a moment's notice**, it is done with very little advance warning.

❑ If an employer **gives** someone their **notice**, he or she warns them they have a specified period of time before they have to leave their job. Similarly, an employee can **hand in their notice** by saying they will be leaving their job after a certain period of time.

❑ If you say a situation will exist **until further notice**, you mean it will exist until a decision is made to change it. *France says it's banning until further notice all imports of British cattle and beef.*

❑ If you **notice** someone or something, you become aware of them. You can also say someone or something comes or is brought **to your notice**. If someone or something **escapes your notice**, you fail to notice them.

❑ If you **take notice of** someone or something, you pay attention to them. If you **take no notice of** them, you pay no attention to them.

❑ If a performance or book gets good **notices**, it is liked by the critics and they write approving things about it.

notice board See noticeboard.

noticeable (noticeably) If something is **noticeable**, it is obvious and easily noticed. *Tension in the capital has eased noticeably.*

noticeboard (or **notice board**) A **notice board** is a board on a wall where people pin notices.

notifiable A **notifiable** disease is one which must be reported to the authorities whenever it occurs, because it is dangerous or can spread rapidly.

notify (notifies, notifying, notified; notification) If you **notify** someone of something you are going to do or give them **notification** of it, you officially inform them of it. *...a requirement of prior notification by any holder of waste.*

notion A **notion** is an idea or belief. *Most creative people object to the notion that the work they do comes easily.*

notional (notionally) **Notional** is used to describe something which exists for theoretical purposes only, and which may be very different from what really exists. *...an average notional family of four, whose semi-detached house and garden is displayed in rather improbable perfection... Both committees are notionally chaired by the president, but the effective chairman is always the attorney-general.*

notorious (notoriously; notoriety) If someone or something is **notorious** for something bad, they are well-known for it. *...Dodge City, once notorious for its gunfights... ...notorious womanisers... ...the notoriously fussy eating habits of infants and children.* Being well-known for something bad is called **notoriety**. *Michael Fagan achieved national notoriety by breaking into the Queen's bedroom.*

notwithstanding If you say something is the case **notwithstanding** something else, you mean it is so in spite of it. *Circulation figures notwithstanding, I detect that the public which the tabloids pretend to serve is beginning to be sickened by the reams of royal surmise and sexual fantasies they contain.*

nougat (pron: noo-gah or nug-gut) is a kind of firm chewy sweet, usually white, with nuts in it.

nought is the number zero.

❑ If you say something **came to nought**, you mean it did not achieve anything.

noughts and crosses is a game played on paper by two people. A square is divided into nine smaller ones, and the players take turns at filling these in, one putting Os in the squares and the other Xs. The winner is the player who succeeds in getting three Os or three Xs in a line.

noun **Nouns** are names and other words you use to refer to people, places, and things. 'James', 'engineer', 'Edinburgh', 'house', and 'love' are all **nouns**.

nourish (nourishes, nourishing, nourished; nourishment) You say food **nourishes** people or animals or provides **nourishment** for them when it keeps them alive and healthy. **Nourishing** food is particularly good at this. You say people are **well-nourished** when they have been eating plenty of healthy food. ◇ If something **nourishes** your mind or imagination, it keeps it active.

nous (rhymes with 'house') **Nous** is common sense and good judgement in practical matters. You can say someone has a particular kind of **nous**. *...diplomatic nous... ...commercial nous.*

nouveau riche (plural: nouveaux riches) (both pron: noo-voh reesh) When people talk about the **nouveaux riches**, they mean people who have made a lot of money and are spending it on expensive things without showing much taste or judgement.

nouvelle cuisine (pron: noo-vell kwi-zeen) is a style of French cooking, developed in the 1970s. It is known for its light sauces, fresh ingredients, textures, colours, and small portions. There is a special emphasis on the way the food is presented.

novel (novelist, novelistic) ❑ A **novel** is a long book which tells a story. A person who writes novels is called a **novelist**. **Novelistic** is used to talk about things to do with novels, or things which remind you of a novel. *...a novelistic device... ...the novelistic quality of his life.*

❑ If you say something is **novel**, you mean it is new, fresh, or original. *...a novel attempt to attract customers to high culture.*

novelette A **novelette** is a short novel intended for light reading.

novella A **novella** is a short novel.

novelty (novelties) A **novelty** is something which is interesting because it is new. *...the days when a motor car was a novelty.* ◇ If something has **novelty**, it is interesting because it has new or unusual features. *Though it fell short of being a classic final, it was refreshing, full of character and novelty.* ◇ **Novelty** objects are designed to appeal to people because they are curious and original. *...a novelty telephone shaped like a Jaguar car.* Objects like these are sometimes called **novelties**.

novice (pron: nov-viss) ❑ A **novice** is someone who is new to an activity. *...a figure-skating novice... ...a novice parachutist.*

❑ In a monastery or convent, a **novice** is a person preparing to be a monk or nun.

now is used to talk about a situation in the present, usually in contrast to one in the past. *He's now one min-*

ute and 23 seconds behind Auriol... The couple now have three children. ◇ **Now** and **now that** are used to give the reason for a situation which exists at present. In the former Soviet Union, few mines look viable now that the state no longer pays their bills.

❑ **Just now** is used to talk about something which happened a very short time ago. You were showing it me just now on a computer terminal.

❑ If something happens **now and then** or **every now and then**, it happens occasionally, but not regularly. **Now and again** and **every now and again** are used in the same way. Every now and again people get immensely excited about the appearance of a new object in the night sky.

❑ If you say something will happen **any day now** or **any time now**, you mean it will happen very soon. Voting finished about three hours ago, and the results are expected any time now.

❑ If you say it is **now or never**, you mean if something is to be done, it must be done immediately, as there will not be another chance in the future. Even the officials could see that it was now or never for reform.

❑ You use **now** in a story or account when you are mentioning the latest development in a situation. By now it was six o'clock in the evening.

nowadays is used to talk about the present, in contrast to the past. Kids nowadays know how babies are born.

nowhere means 'no place at all'. There was nowhere to sit... Nowhere in Dorset now is truly remote.

❑ If something is in the **middle of nowhere**, it is far away from other places and is usually difficult to get to.

❑ If you say someone or something came **from nowhere**, you mean they appeared suddenly and unexpectedly. ◇ If you say someone or something is **getting nowhere**, you mean they are not achieving anything. Similarly, you can talk about something **going nowhere** or **leading nowhere**. This time however diplomatic efforts led nowhere.

❑ **nowhere near**: see **near**.

noxious gases or substances are poisonous or harmful. ...noxious chemicals. ◇ You can call other unpleasant things and people **noxious**. ...a noxious smell.

nozzle A **nozzle** is a narrow piece on the end of something like a hose or pipe, which controls the flow of whatever goes into it or out of it.

nuance (pron: new-ahnss) (nuanced) The **nuances** in something someone says or writes are its finer shades of meaning. Similarly, the **nuances** in a musical or dramatic performance are small points of expression or interpretation which can make the performance more effective. **Nuanced** is used to describe things which are full of nuances. ...his delicately nuanced performance.

nub The **nub** of a problem or argument is its most basic and central part.

nubile (pron: new-bile) women are young, physically mature, and sexually attractive.

nuclear is used to talk about things to do with the nuclei of atoms, or with the energy produced when they are split or combined. ...nuclear energy... ...nuclear power stations. ◇ A **nuclear reaction** is a process in which the nuclei of atoms are changed, releasing energy. ◇ A **nuclear reactor** is a device which uses a nuclear reaction to produce nuclear energy.

❑ **Nuclear fission** is a way of producing massive amounts of energy by splitting the nuclei of atoms of certain materials such as uranium. Similarly, **nuclear fusion** produces massive amounts of energy by combining pairs of atoms of a substance such as tritium. ◇ A **nuclear weapon** produces an explosion by nuclear fission or fusion. ...nuclear missiles. ◇ **Nuclear** is used to talk about things involving nuclear weapons. ...nuclear war... ...the nuclear arms race. ◇ A country which has nuclear weapons is called a **nuclear power**.

nuclear family A **nuclear family** consists of a father and mother and their children.

nuclear-free zones are areas where the manufacture and transport of nuclear weapons are forbidden, as are nuclear reactors and the disposal of nuclear waste.

nuclear physics (nuclear physicist) **Nuclear physics** is a branch of physics which deals with the structure and behaviour of the nuclei of atoms and the particles they consist of. A **nuclear physicist** is a scientist who studies these things.

nuclear winter is a possible after-effect of a nuclear war or large nuclear explosion. It is thought that dust in the atmosphere could shut out the sunlight, and this would result in very low temperatures everywhere for a long period.

nucleus (pron: **nyoo**-klee-uss) (plural: nuclei) The **nucleus** of a cell or atom is its central part, consisting of protons and neutrons. ◇ The **nucleus** of something else is its central or most important part. This collection formed the nucleus of the British Library.

nude (nudity) If someone is **nude** or **in the nude**, they are not wearing any clothes. **Nudity** is being somewhere without any clothes. ◇ A **nude** is a picture or statue of someone not wearing clothes.

nudge (nudging, nudged) ❑ If something is **nudged** or given a **nudge**, people try gently to get it to change in a certain way. China has spent nearly a dozen years trying to nudge its economy towards the market-place.

❑ If you **nudge** someone or give them a **nudge**, you give them a gentle push with your elbow, usually to draw their attention to something. ◇ People say **nudge nudge wink wink** when they are mentioning something which is known to involve sex or illegal practices and which is thought to be amusing because of this.

❑ If something is **nudging** a level or figure, it is getting close to it. The temperature was nudging 80 degrees.

nudist A **nudist** is the same as a naturist.

nudity See **nude**.

nugatory (pron: new-gat-tree) things are without value. If the Secretary of State's powers were limited in this way, they would be wholly nugatory.

nugget A **nugget** is a small rough lump of something, especially gold. ◇ A **nugget** of information is a small piece of it which is especially interesting or valuable.

nuisance If you say someone or something is a **nuisance**, you mean they are annoying you and causing you problems.

nuke (nuking, nuked) If one country **nukes** another, it attacks it with nuclear weapons. A nuclear weapon is sometimes called a **nuke**.

null If something is declared **null and void**, it is officially decided that it is not legally valid.

nullify (nullifies, nullifying, nullified) If one thing **nullifies** another, it makes it lose its effect. *Policy-makers will no longer see their carefully calculated decisions nullified by unexpected crises.* ◇ If something like a contract is **nullified**, it is made no longer valid.

numb (numbing, numbingly, numbness) ❑ If part of your body is **numb**, you have no feeling there. *...numbness of the legs.*

❑ If an experience **numbs** you or leaves you feeling **numb**, you are so shocked or upset by it that you cannot feel any emotion or respond to things in a normal way.

❑ If you say something is **numbing** or **mind-numbing**, you mean it is very dull and uninteresting. *Programmes of study were laid down in mind-numbing detail... His life was numbingly bourgeois.*

number (numbering, numbered) ❑ A **number** is the thing represented by a figure like '17' or '43rd' or a word like 'three' or 'sixteenth'. Numbers are used for counting or calculating. They are also used to identify things. *...Room Number 118.* When 'number' is used to identify something, it is often represented by No. *...the No.6 bus to Hackney Wick.* **Numbered** is used to say what number something has. *...a row of beach huts numbered 13-16.*

❑ People say where someone is ranked in a sport or competition by calling them, say, the **number one** or **number two**. *...the world number one tennis player Boris Becker.* **Number one** is used to describe other things which are the best, most important, or most popular of their kind. *...its number-one brew... ...the number one priority.*

❑ The **number** of people or things involved in a situation is how many there are. *The casualties include an unknown number of foreigners... Their numbers have fallen by 900 since 1977.* You can say people or things **number** or are **numbered** a particular amount. *You could easily believe that his personal friends are numbered in the tens of thousands.*

❑ If you talk about **a number of** people or things, you mean several of them. *There have been a number of complaints.* ◇ **Any number of** people or things means a lot of them. *The trappings were familiar from any number of other hotels.*

❑ If you say someone or something **is numbered** among a particular group, you mean they belong to it. *She is still to be numbered among the best vocalists in jazz.* ◇ **One of their number** means one of the group of people you are talking about. *The remaining inmates are clearly angry and frustrated at losing one of their number.*

❑ When people say there is **safety in numbers**, they mean something you do is more likely to be successful if a lot of other people are doing the same thing.

❑ If you say something's **days are numbered**, you mean it will not be long before it is replaced by something else. Similarly, if a person's **days are numbered**, it will not be long before they are unable to continue with their job or type of business.

❑ If you say someone is playing the **numbers game**, you mean they are dealing with something by weighing up the probabilities.

❑ A **number** of a magazine or periodical is one edition of it. ◇ A **number** is also (a) a song or other short piece of music. (b) a smart piece of clothing, especially a woman's dress. *...a little satin-edged velvet number.*

❑ **opposite number**: see **opposite**.

number-crunching is doing large numbers of calculations, one after another. *...the number-crunching power of computers.*

number-plate A vehicle's **number-plates** are the signs on its front and back showing its registration number.

Number Ten is 10 Downing Street, London, the official address of the Prime Minister. **Number Ten** is often used to talk about the position of Prime Minister. *A candidate surrounded by such people is hardly fit for Number Ten.*

numeral A **numeral** is a symbol or group of symbols used to represent a number. Symbols like 3 and 7 are called Arabic numerals. Symbols like V and XII are called Roman numerals.

numerate (*pron:* nyoo-mer-rit) (numeracy) A **numerate** person is able to do arithmetic. **Numeracy** is having this ability. *...numeracy skills... ...an alarming decline in literacy and numeracy.*

numerical (numerically) ❑ **Numerical** and **numerically** are used to talk about the size of something in terms of the number of people or things in it. For example, you can say one army is **numerically** superior to another one, or talk about its **numerical** superiority. *I want to encourage the Church of England to grow numerically as well as in it's understanding of the Christian faith.*

❑ **Numerical** is also used to talk about things which involve using numbers. *...numerical puzzles.*

numerous is used to say there are a lot of things of a certain kind. *In the quieter streets there are numerous perfume shops... The pitfalls of working abroad are numerous.*

numinous is used to describe things which are holy, awe-inspiring, and mysterious. *Scottish folk culture provided a deep and rich source of numinous symbols from a mythological system with roots in the Celtic past.*

numismatics (numismatic) **Numismatics** is studying or collecting coins and medals. **Numismatic** is used to talk about things to do with these activities. *...numismatic dealers.*

nun A **nun** is a female member of a religious order.

nuncio (nuncios) A **nuncio** is a high-ranking member of the Roman Catholic church who works in a foreign country and acts as an ambassador for the Vatican.

nunnery (nunneries) **Nunnery** is an old word for a convent.

nuptial (nuptials) A person's **nuptials** are their wedding celebrations. ◇ **Nuptial** is used to talk about things to do with weddings, brides, or bridegrooms. *...the nuptial contract... ...her nuptial bedroom.*

nurse (nursing, nursed) ❑ A **nurse** is a person whose job is to look after sick people, usually in a hospital. ◇ If you **nurse** a sick person or animal, you look after them while they are ill. ◇ If you **nurse** an injury you have received, you try to protect if from further harm while it gets better. *He spent more than five hours in the pavilion nursing his badly bruised arm.*

❑ If someone is **nursing** a baby, they are cradling it gently and fondly. ◇ You also say a mother is **nursing** her baby when she is breast-feeding it.

❑ If someone has something which will be valuable to them in the future, you can say they are **nursing** it. *Most companies are busy nursing marketing or research agreements with Japanese computer firms.* ◇ If someone is **nursing** an ambition, they have it and are waiting for an opportunity to fulfil it. ◇ If someone is **nursing** a feeling like hatred, they still have it, although there may no longer be any reason for it.

nursemaid In the past, a **nursemaid** was a girl or woman who was paid to look after young children.

nursery (nurseries) ❑ A **nursery** is a place where very young children can be looked after, usually while their parents are at work. ◇ A **nursery** is also a room in a house where young children sleep or play.
❑ **Nursery** education is education at a nursery school.
❑ A place where many successful people started their careers is sometimes called a **nursery** of people of their kind. *From the very beginning, the company has been the nursery of choreographers.*
❑ A **nursery** is also a place where flowers, shrubs, and other plants are grown to be sold.

nursery nurse A **nursery nurse** is a person who has been trained to look after very young children.

nursery rhyme A **nursery rhyme** is a poem or song for young children, especially one which has been well-known for a long time.

nursery school A **nursery school** is a school for young children aged about 3 to 4, who usually go for part of the day only. Nursery schools prepare children for primary school.

nursery slope A **nursery slope** is a gentle slope on a mountain used by people learning to ski.

nurseryman (nurserymen) A **nurseryman** is a person who grows plants for sale.

nursing is the activity or profession of looking after people who are sick or need medical care. *He will need 24-hour-a-day nursing... ...a college of nursing.*

nursing home A **nursing home** is an institution, usually a private one, where people who are sick or need medical care are looked after. Most nursing homes are for old people who need more medical care than an ordinary rest home can provide.

nursing officer A **nursing officer** is a senior nurse in a hospital who is mainly concerned with management and administration.

nurture (nurturing, nurtured) ❑ **Nurture** is encouraging, caring for, and helping a child to develop while it is growing. When someone does this, you say they are **nurturing** the child. ◇ If you **nurture** something like a young person's talents or imagination, you encourage and develop them.
❑ If you **nurture** a plant, you care for it and make sure it grows properly.

nut ❑ **Nuts** are small objects which grow on trees. They have a hard shell and a firm inside which can usually be eaten. There are many different kinds of nuts.

❑ If you call someone a **hard nut** or a **tough nut**, you mean they are obstinate or difficult to deal with. ◇ If you say someone or something will be a **hard** or **tough nut to crack**, you mean they will be difficult to deal with or overcome. *Waterloo are a tough nut to crack on their own pitch.*

❑ If you say someone is **nuts** or call them a **nut**, you mean they are mad, or behave in a very strange way. ◇ If you say someone is, for example, a sports car **nut**, you mean they are extremely enthusiastic about sports cars.

❑ A **nut** is also a small piece of metal with a threaded hole which you screw a bolt into. ◇ If you talk about the **nuts and bolts** of something, you mean its practical aspects.

nutcase If you call someone a **nutcase**, you mean they are mad, or do extremely silly things.

nutcracker A **nutcracker** is a tool for cracking nuts open, so you can get to the edible part inside.

nutmeg **Nutmegs** are the nut-like seeds of a tropical tree called a **nutmeg**. The seeds are ground and used as a spice called **nutmeg**.

nutrient (*pron:* new-tree-ent) **Nutrients** are substances which are necessary for plants and animals to grow and be healthy.

nutrition (*pron:* new-trish-shun) (nutritional; nutritionist) **Nutrition** is the process by which nutrients from food are absorbed into the body. ◇ **Nutrition** is also obtaining nourishing food, or providing other people with it. *...better housing and nutrition for the poor.* **Nutritional** is used to talk about things to do with nutrition. *...nutritional experts... ...nutritional deprivation.* A person who studies different foods and gives advice about what you should eat to stay healthy is called a **nutritionist**.

nutritious foods contain substances, such as vitamins and minerals, which help you grow and keep you healthy.

nutshell You say **in a nutshell** when you are summing something up in a few words. *In a nutshell, the City is saying the recession is over.*

nutter If you call someone a **nutter**, you mean they are mad or very foolish.

nutty ❑ If you call a plan or proposal **nutty**, you mean it is very foolish or impracticable.
❑ If a food or a drink has a **nutty** flavour, it tastes of nuts.

nylon is a strong man-made material which can be made into many different things, such as clothes, rope, and carpets.

nymph In Greek and Roman mythology, a **nymph** was a spirit of nature who took the form of a young woman.

nymphomaniac A woman who keeps wanting to have sex with many different men is sometimes called a **nymphomaniac**.

O o

O-Level O-levels were the exams English, Welsh, and Northern Irish school students used to take at 15 or 16 before GCSEs were introduced in 1988. 'O-level' stands for 'Ordinary Level'.

o'clock is used to say what time it is. *...six o'clock.*

oaf (oafish) An **oaf** is a stupid or loutish person. You say someone like this is **oafish.**

oak The **oak** is a large deciduous tree which produces acorns. Its wood is hard and is used to make furniture.

OAP An **OAP** or **old-age pensioner** is a man over the age of 65 or a woman over the age of 60.

oar Oars are long poles for rowing a boat. They have flattened ends called blades.

oarsman (oarswoman) Someone rowing a boat, especially a racing boat, can be called an **oarsman** or **oarswoman.**

oasis (*pron:* oh-ay-siss) (*plural:* oases, *pron:* oh-ay-seez) An oasis is a small area with water and trees in the middle of a desert. ◇ Any place which is pleasantly different from the area around it can be called an **oasis.** *The country has had a reputation as one of the continent's few oases of political stability.*

oast-house An **oast-house** is a building which contains large ovens for drying hops. It usually has a conical-shaped roof.

oatcake Oatcakes are thin flat biscuits made from oat meal.

oath If you take an **oath,** you make a formal promise to do something, usually in front of witnesses. ◇ When someone **takes the oath** in court, they promise to tell the truth by swearing on the New Testament or the holy book of some non-Christian religion. After this, they are **under oath.**

oatmeal is a coarse flour made by grinding oats. It is used for making things like porridge and oatcakes.

oats are a kind of tall cereal grass.

OAU The **OAU** is an organization to promote co-operation and unity among African countries. OAU stands for 'Organization of African Unity'.

obdurate (*pron:* ob-joor-it) (obduracy) If someone is **obdurate,** they are determined not to change their mind about something. You talk about the **obduracy** of someone like this.

OBE An **OBE** is an honour granted by the monarch for a special achievement or service to the community. OBE stands for 'Officer of the Order of the British Empire'. *...Charles Abell, OBE.*

obedient (obediently, obedience) If someone is **obedient,** they do what they are told. *The boy walked obediently beside his mother... Many studies of child-rearing in Africa stress the importance placed on obedience to elders.*

obeisance (*pron:* ob-bay-sanss) **Obeisance** is holding someone in great respect and being prepared to carry out all their orders or commands. ◇ If someone makes **obeisance** to an important person, they make a gesture of respect, such as a bow.

obelisk (*pron:* ob-bill-isk) An **obelisk** is a tall tapering four-sided pillar, often with a pyramid-shaped point at the top. Obelisks are usually put up in honour of a person or an important event.

obese (*pron:* oh-beess) (obesity) If someone is **obese,** they are very fat. **Obesity** is being very fat.

obey If you **obey** a person or order, you do what you are told.

obfuscate (*pron:* ob-fuss-kate) (obfuscating, obfuscated; obfuscation) If someone **obfuscates** something, they make it more difficult to understand, for example by expressing it in a complicated or long-winded way. *The organization is dedicated to fighting bureaucratic obfuscation.*

obituary (obituaries) An **obituary** is a short article in a newspaper or magazine about someone who has just died. It gives an account of their life and achievements.

object ❏ An **object** is anything solid which you can touch and see, and which is not alive.
   ❏ The **object** of something you do is its aim or purpose.
   ❏ If something is the **object** of your attention, you are paying attention to it. ◇ If you are the **object** of certain feelings, someone has those feelings about you. *Bad guys began to look more like objects of pity than of fear.* Similarly, you can be the **object** of a certain kind of behaviour. *It's not really for the person who is the object of an attack to solve the problem.*
   ❏ If you say money is **no object,** you mean someone can spend as much as they like, because they do not have to worry about where the money comes from.
   ❏ An **object lesson** in something is an example of the best way to do it. *It was an object lesson for me on just how to conduct oneself on such an occasion.* ◇ You also say something is an **object lesson** when it brings home the truth about something. *Each piece of flotsam in the North Sea is an object lesson in how we mistreat our coastline.*
   ❏ If you **object** (*pron:* ob-ject) to something which is being done or being proposed, you show you dislike it or disapprove of it.

objection If you have an **objection** to something, you have reasons for disliking it or disapproving of it. *There is considerable objection in the village to these plans.* ◇ If you make an **objection** to something, you say you dislike it or disapprove of it.

objectionable If you say someone or something is **objectionable,** you mean they are unpleasant and offensive.

objective (objectively; objectivity) ❏ Someone's **objective** is what they are trying to achieve.
   ❏ If you are being **objective,** you are deciding about something purely by considering the facts, and are not letting your feelings influence you in any way. When someone makes a decision in this way, you can talk about their **objectivity.** *The jury was asked to look at every bit of the evidence fairly and objectively.* ◇ **Objective** information or evidence is based on facts, rather than on someone's opinions.

objector People who openly object to something which is being done or being proposed are called **objectors.** *Construction was delayed for years by environmental objectors.* See also **conscientious objector.**

objet d'art (plural: objets d'art) (both pron: ob-jay dar) An objet d'art is an ornament or other small decorative object made of precious materials which is of interest to collectors.

obligation If you have an **obligation** to do something, you are required to do it. *Water companies have a legal obligation to supply their consumers... Customers are free to try on the wide range of clothes with no obligation to buy.*

obligatory (pron: ob-lig-a-tree) ❏ If something is **obligatory**, there is a law or rule stating that it must be done.

❏ You also use **obligatory** to describe things you expect a certain type of person to wear or do, or expect to see in a certain place, because they are normal or fashionable. *They forgot to take the obligatory snapshots... ...an adolescent who wore jeans and T-shirt as an obligatory uniform.*

oblige (obliging, obliged; obligingly) ❏ If something **obliges** you to do something, it makes it necessary for you to do it. *Government spokesmen say this decree obliges unions to delay strikes.*

❏ If you **oblige** someone who has asked you to do something, you do it. An **obliging** person is always willing to do things for people. *The spectator obligingly moved further back.*

oblique (pron: oh-**bleak**) If something like a line is **oblique**, it is sloping or diagonal rather than straight. ◇ An **oblique** comment or remark expresses something in an indirect way. *From time to time, he makes oblique but pointed criticisms of the Prime Minister... He referred obliquely to his nation's worries about Germany.*

obliterate (obliterating, obliterated; obliteration) If something is **obliterated**, it is completely destroyed. *...the virtual obliteration of a once prosperous mining industry.*

oblivion If someone or something goes into **oblivion**, they become forgotten or ignored. *Other feasts and holidays held in old times have now passed into oblivion.* ◇ You say someone is in **oblivion** when they are unaware of what is happening around them, for example because they are asleep or unconscious.

oblivious (obliviously) If someone is **oblivious** to what is happening around them, they are not aware of it. *The couple were oblivious to stares from other shoppers... McCorkindale was still snoozing obliviously.*

oblong An **oblong** is a shape with two long sides, two short ones, and four right angles. **Oblong** objects have this shape. *...an oblong table.*

obnoxious If you call someone or something **obnoxious**, you mean they are extremely unpleasant.

oboe (oboist) An **oboe** is a woodwind instrument with a double reed. An **oboe** player is called an **oboist**.

obscene (pron: ob-seen) (obscenity, obscenities) ❏ If you say something is **obscene**, you mean it is indecent or pornographic. *...an obscene telephone call... ...an obscene gesture.* **Obscenity** (pron: ob-sen-it-tee) is indecent language or behaviour. An **obscenity** is an obscene word or action. *They screamed obscenities at each other.*

❏ You also say something is **obscene** when you feel it is utterly wrong that it should happen or exist. You talk about the **obscenity** of something like this. *For a company to be raking in profits of £95 a second is obscene in the middle of a recession... ...the obscenity of 40,000 children dying every day, mainly from preventable diseases.*

obscurantism (pron: obs-cure-**ran**-tiz-um) (obscurantist)

Obscurantism is deliberately making something vague and difficult to understand, especially to prevent people finding out the truth. You say someone who behaves like this is being **obscurantist**.

obscure (obscuring, obscured; obscurity) ❏ **Obscure** is used to describe people and places that are not well known. *...an obscure little town on the Kansas plains... ...the man who rose from obscurity to fame within a few months.*

❏ **Obscure** is also used to describe things which are puzzling or unclear. *Their political objectives still remain obscure.*

❏ If something is **obscured** by something else, you cannot see it because the other thing is in the way. *A plantation of poplars obscured the view.*

obsequious (pron: ob-seek-wee-uss) people are always trying to please people they think are important, by doing small favours for them or agreeing with everything they say.

observable If something is **observable**, it can be seen or noticed. *The drug was being given in doses too low to have an observable effect.*

observance See observe.

observant An **observant** person pays close attention to everything and notices things which other people might miss.

observation is keeping a close watch on someone or something, or examining them closely, to find out more about them. *He was taken to hospital for observation.*

❏ **Observation** is also noticing details of people's behaviour and describing or imitating them accurately. *Their anarchic humour is executed with subtlety and observation.*

❏ An **observation** is a comment or remark. ◇ Someone's **observations** are their written or spoken comments on something.

observatory (observatories) An **observatory** is (a) a building equipped with large telescopes to observe the sun, moon, and stars. (b) a building equipped to observe and record weather conditions.

observe (observing, observed; observance) ❏ If you **observe** something, you watch it carefully. *They spent months living in the bush observing the animals and birds.* ◇ You can also say you **observe** something when you notice it. *The breakthrough came when the group observed a distinctive pattern of atoms on a silicon crystal.*

❏ If you **observe** something like a law or custom, you obey it or follow it. *...the observance of a minute's silence.*

❏ If you **observe** that something is the case, you say it. *He observed that a week is a long time in politics.*

observer An **observer** is someone who watches something. *Nothing makes much sense to the casual observer.* ◇ People who watch and analyse the development of certain types of situations are also called **observers**. *...City observers... ...political observers.* ◇ An **observer** is also a member of a group sent to a country by an official organization, to monitor something like an election or ceasefire and make sure it is carried out fairly.

obsessed (obsession, obsessional, obsessive) If you are **obsessed** by something, you think about it all the time and find it difficult to think of anything else. When someone feels like this about something, you can say they have an **obsession** with it; you can also describe their behaviour as **obsessional** or **obsessive**.

obsolescent (obsolescence) If something is **obsolescent**, it is becoming obsolete. *The end of the Cold War has seemed to spell the obsolescence of the spy novel.*

obsolete If something is **obsolete**, it is out of date and no longer in use. *...obsolete equipment.*

obstacle Something like a fence or ditch which hinders you when you are making your way across an area of land can be called an **obstacle**. ◇ A problem which has to be dealt with and which slows down the progress of something can also be called an **obstacle**. *There are still obstacles blocking progress towards the resumption of diplomatic relations.*

obstetrics (obstetric; obstetrician) **Obstetrics** is the branch of medicine concerned with pregnancy and childbirth. **Obstetric** is used to describe things to do with obstetrics. *...hospitals specializing in obstetric care.* A doctor who specializes in obstetrics is called an **obstetrician**.

obstinate (obstinacy) If someone is being **obstinate**, they are determined to do something, or determined not to do something, and cannot be persuaded to change their mind. You talk about the **obstinacy** of someone like this. *Her patient remained obstinately uncooperative.*

obstreperous people are noisy and difficult to control.

obstruct (obstruction; obstructive) ❑ If something **obstructs** a road or path, it blocks it so people or vehicles cannot get past. You call something like this an **obstruction**. ◇ An **obstruction** is also a blockage in part of someone's body. *...an obstruction of the coronary arteries.*

❑ If someone or something **obstructs** a process, they make it difficult for it to take place. *The war is obstructing distribution of famine relief.* When someone deliberately obstructs the progress of something, you say they are being **obstructive**.

obstructionism (obstructionist) **Obstructionism** is deliberately delaying or preventing legal, business, or parliamentary matters. *The government was faced with increasing obstructionism from the opposition.* You say someone who behaves like this is being **obstructionist**.

obtain (obtaining, obtained; obtainable) ❑ If you **obtain** something you want, you succeed in getting it. *He obtained an engineering degree at Bristol.* If something is **obtainable**, it can be obtained. *Many of the best-value wines are obtainable in the high street.*

❑ The system or situation which **obtains** at a particular time is the one existing at that time. *The grants should be interpreted in the light of the specific circumstances which obtained at the time they were made.*

obtrusive If something is **obtrusive**, it stands out in an unpleasant way. *Ornate chandeliers have been replaced with far less obtrusive wrought-iron candelabra... A radio commentator should fill in the background without being too obtrusive.*

obtuse (obtuseness) ❑ If someone is **obtuse**, they have difficulty understanding things. ◇ If you say someone is being **obtuse**, you mean they are making no effort to understand something. *I was irritated by his obtuseness in this matter.*

❑ An **obtuse** angle is any angle between 90 degrees and 180 degrees. See also **acute**, **reflex**.

obverse The **obverse** of something like a situation or argument is its other side, which contrasts with it. *The ob-verse of rising unemployment is continued gains in productivity.* ◇ The **obverse** of a coin or medal is the side which has the main design. On most coins and medals, this is the side which shows a head. See also **reverse**.

obviate (obviating, obviated) If something **obviates** the need for something else, it makes it unnecessary. *The adoption of the resolution would obviate the need for force.*

obvious (obviously) If something is **obvious**, you can easily see it or understand it. *Obviously a monk's life has to be centred on God and the search for God.* ◇ If you have to choose between several things, the **obvious** choice is the one it seems most natural or sensible to go for. *They have no obvious candidate to replace him.*

occasion ❑ An **occasion** is a time when something happens. *They had to settle for a bronze medal on this occasion.* ◇ An **occasion** for doing something is an opportunity to do it. *The Lord Mayor's Banquet is always an important occasion for setting out government policy.* ◇ If someone **rises to the occasion**, they deal with a situation well, because they have the right qualities for it.

❑ An **occasion** is also an important event, ceremony, or celebration. *The European Cup is a big occasion.*

❑ If something happens **on occasion**, it happens sometimes but not often. *Opposition politicians may on occasion be invited to join the government.*

occasional (occasionally) **Occasional** is used to describe something which happens sometimes but not regularly or often. *Celebrities make occasional appearances... The occasional gold coin is still found in the sands... I occasionally have a drink.*

occidental (*pron:* ok-sid-**dent**-al) is used to talk about European and American people and customs, as distinct from those of the Far East. *...occidental approaches to land use.* See also **orient**.

occult People who are interested in the **occult** are interested in supernatural forces and happenings and magical powers.

occupancy is used to talk about the number of people living or staying in a building. *...an average occupancy of two people per dwelling.*

occupant ❑ The **occupants** of a house or other building are the people who live or work there.

❑ The **occupants** of something like a vehicle are the people who happen to be in it at a particular time. *Officials check each car and its occupants.*

occupation ❑ A person's **occupation** is their job or profession.

❑ An **occupation** is also something you do for pleasure or as part of your daily life. *The city's inhabitants remain addicted to their favourite occupations: eating and making money.*

❑ If you talk about the **occupation** of a building, you are talking about the people who live or work there. *The property must be a private dwelling for owner occupation.*

❑ The **occupation** of a country is its invasion and control by a foreign power. *...the wartime occupation of France.* Similarly, you talk about the **occupation** of a building when a group of people take control of it and refuse to leave, usually to protest about something.

occupational is used to talk about things to do with someone's work or profession. *...occupational stress... ...an occupational pension.* ◇ An **occupational hazard** is something unpleasant or dangerous you may suffer or experience as a result of having a particular job.

occupational therapy (occupational therapist) Occupational therapy is treatment which helps people recovering from a serious illness to cope independently with everyday life. The treatment involves helping them to re-learn basic skills, like getting dressed and making tea, and may also include creative activities like pottery. A person qualified to help people in this way is called an **occupational therapist**.

occupy (occupies, occupying, occupied; occupier) ❏ The people who **occupy** a building are the ones who live or work there. They can also be called its **occupiers**.

❏ When an army or foreign power **occupies** a place, it takes control of it by force. Similarly, people like demonstrators can **occupy** a building.

❏ If an area or space is **occupied** by certain things, it is taken up by them. *Every inch of floor space is occupied by albums, books and posters.* ◇ If something like a seat is **occupied**, it is in use and is not free for someone else to use.

❏ If someone **occupies** a certain job or position, they have it. *Many of these students now occupy senior positions in industry.*

❏ If a period of time is **occupied** in a certain way, it is spent that way. *Each day a considerable time was occupied in refuelling and inspection.* ◇ If you **occupy** yourself in doing something, you keep yourself busy by doing it. ◇ If you are **occupied** with someone or something, they are taking up your attention or time.

occur (occurs, occurring, occurred; occurrence) ❏ When something **occurs**, it happens. You talk about the **occurrence** of something. *The hope is that by preventing this type of infection we will be able to prevent the later occurrence of cancer.* An **occurrence** is something that happens. *Food queues have become a daily occurrence.*

❏ If something like a plant **occurs** in a place, it is present there. *...the tiny floating fern azolla, which occurs in parts of Asia.*

❏ If something **occurs** to you, you suddenly think of it. *It occurred to me that a flagpole might sit well in my own backyard.*

ocean (oceanic) ❏ An **ocean** is a very large stretch of sea, especially one of the five large areas of sea between the continents. **Oceanic** (*pron:* oh-shee-an-ik) is used to describe things to do with oceans. *...an oceanic navigator.* **Ocean-going** ships or boats are especially suited to travel on the open sea.

❏ **Oceans** of something means a huge amount of it. *I've got oceans of loyal fans out there.*

oceanography (oceanographer; oceanographic) Oceanography is the scientific study of oceans and their plant and animal life. A person who carries out this kind of study is called an **oceanographer**. **Oceanographic** (*pron:* oh-shun-oh-**graff**-ik) is used to talk about things to do with oceanography. *...oceanographic research.*

ocelot (*pron:* oss-il-lot) The **ocelot** is a wild cat with a spotted body and a striped head and neck. Ocelots live in the forests of Central and South America.

ochre (*pron:* oh-kur) is (a) a yellowish or reddish-brown earth used for making paints and dyes. (b) a golden-yellow colour.

octagon (octagonal) An **octagon** is a geometric shape with eight straight sides. Something with this shape is called **octagonal**.

octane is a chemical substance in petrol. ◇ -octane is used to describe the quality of petrol; the best quality is **high-octane**. ◇ **High-octane** is also used to describe things which are done with great energy and enthusiasm. *...high-octane tennis... He is renowned for his high-octane lifestyle.*

octave An **octave** is a musical interval equal to 12 semitones. A note an octave higher than another note has twice its frequency, and this means the two notes can be played together without harmony or dissonance, and sound almost like one note.

octet An **octet** is (a) a piece of music for eight instruments. (b) a group of eight people who sing or play music together.

octogenarian (*pron:* ok-toe-jin-**nair**-ee-an) An **octogenarian** is a person in their eighties.

octopus (octopuses) The **octopus** is a sea creature with eight long tentacles which it uses to catch its food.

odd (oddly, odds) ❏ **Odd** and **oddly** are used to describe things which are strange or unusual. *It seemed odd that he said so little... ...oddly dressed people... Oddly, the match's two main stars had been expecting to leave Test cricket.*

❏ **Odd** numbers are numbers like 7 and 53 which cannot be divided exactly by 2.

❏ You use **odd** after a round number like 40 or 100, to show you are talking about something which is a few more than that number, but less than the next round number. For example, 40-odd is a few more than 40 but less than 50. *I travel 60-odd miles every day.*

❏ You also use **odd** to talk about things which are random or unimportant. *She hoards odd bits of string for future use... The odd wrong telephone number is inevitable.* ◇ **Odds and ends** are assorted items or objects.

❏ You use **odd** to describe something like a sock when you do not have another one to match it. ◇ If someone or something is the **odd one out**, they are the only one that does not fit in among a group of people or things.

❏ In gambling, the **odds** show how much money you are likely to win compared with the amount you bet. For example, if you win a bet at odds of 100 to 1, you win 100 times as much as you put on, plus the amount of your bet. ◇ If you say someone or something is **odds on** to win something or **odds-on** favourite, you mean they are much more likely to win than any of the other competitors.

❏ If you say the **odds are...** you are saying something is very likely to happen. You can also say the **odds** are in favour of something happening. *The odds are that he will get his money... The odds are in favour of the conference taking place.* If the **odds** are against something happening, it is very unlikely to happen. ◇ If the **odds** shorten on something, it becomes increasingly likely that it will happen. If the **odds** lengthen, it becomes less likely that it will happen.

❏ If you pay **over the odds** for something, you pay more than it is worth.

❏ If you are **at odds** with someone, you are having a disagreement with them about something. ◇ If two descriptions or accounts are **at odds**, they contradict each other.

odd-job man An odd-job man is a man employed to do manual jobs like domestic repairs or maintenance.

oddball people or things are unusual or peculiar. ...*oddball humour.* Someone who behaves in an unusual way can be called an **oddball**.

oddity (oddities) A strange or unusual person or thing can be called an **oddity**. ...*the oddities of her behaviour.*

oddments are objects which do not seem to belong to any particular set or group.

odds See odd.

ode An ode is a poem written in praise of someone or something.

odious is used to describe people or things that are extremely unpleasant. *His political views will strike most people now as odious.*

odium is having people dislike you for something you have done. *The complainant has been exposed to public odium.*

odour (*American spelling:* **odor**) An odour is a smell, especially a strong one.

odourless (*American spelling:* **odorless**) If something is **odourless**, it has no smell.

odyssey (*pron:* od-i-see) An odyssey is a long and eventful journey. ...*a 6,000-mile odyssey across India.* You can also say something like a long-term project is an **odyssey**. ...*a six-year odyssey of reform.*

OECD The OECD is an association of 24 nations set up in 1961 to promote trade and economic growth and aid to developing countries. OECD stands for 'Organization for Economic Co-operation and Development'.

oedema (*plural:* oedemata) (*American spelling:* edema, edemata) An oedema (*pron:* id-eem-ah) is an abnormal swelling of part or all of a person's body, caused by the body retaining too much water.

oesophagus (oesophaguses) (*American spelling:* esophagus, esophaguses) A person's oesophagus (*pron:* ee-soff-ag-uss) is the tube which carries food from their throat to their stomach.

oestrogen (*American spelling:* estrogen) Oestrogen (*pron:* ee-stra-jen) is a hormone produced in the ovaries of female humans and animals. It controls female sexual development and the reproductive cycle. Synthetic oestrogen is used in most contraceptive pills.

of is used to show who or what a person or thing is connected with or belongs to. ...*the director of the Imperial War Museum... ...the commercial section of the British Embassy.*
  □ When someone's body is injured or diseased, you use of to say which part is affected. ...*cancer of the colon.*
  □ Of is used to say what a feeling or thought relates to. ...*fears of an economic slump... I was reminded of the train ride out to Venice.*
  □ Of is used when talking about amounts and quantities. ...*the amount of carbon dioxide in the atmosphere.*
  □ Of is used to talk about a characteristic or quality that someone has. ...*a man of the highest principles.* ◇ Of is used to mention someone's age. ...*a boy of nine.* ◇ Of is used to mention where someone lives. *George Lewis, of Wolverhampton, will seek compensation for his years in prison.*
  □ Of is used in dates. ...*the 2nd of July.*

of course See course.

off is used to say someone moves away from something or out of something. *She had wandered off absent-mindedly... They had just stepped off the plane.* ◇ If you are off to a place, you are about to go there.
  □ Off is used to talk about something being removed. *Take off your shoes.* ◇ Off is also used to say the price of something has been reduced. *Travellers in groups of 25 or more get 30% off the standard fare.*
  □ Off is used to say something is a little way from something like a road or shore. ...*off the coast of Newfoundland.* ◇ Off is also used to say how far away something is. *It ought to be spotted a mile off.* ◇ Off is used to say something is separated from other things. *The entire city centre is ringed off.*
  □ Off is used to say how long it will be before something happens. *Local elections are now less than two months off.* ◇ Off is used to say how close someone or something is to a certain stage or level. *He's still second, four points off the lead.*
  □ If you have time off, you have a break from your job or usual routine. If someone is away from work because of illness, you say they are off work or off sick.
  □ If you have gone off something, you do not like it any more. ◇ When food or drink goes off, it goes bad. You then say it is off.
  □ If an electrical or mechanical device is off, it is not switched on.
  □ If an event is off, it has been cancelled or postponed.

off-balance See balance.

off-beat (*or* offbeat) is used to describe entertainment which is different from what you normally expect. ...*an offbeat comedy.*

off-centre If something is off-centre, it is not exactly in the middle of a space or surface. *He hit the target off-centre.*

off-chance If you do something on the off-chance, you do it hoping things will go the way you want, although this may be unlikely.

off-colour If you say someone is off-colour, you mean they are slightly ill.

off-day If you have an off-day, you do not do something as well as usual.

off-guard If someone is caught off-guard, they are taken by surprise.

off-hand See offhand.

off-key If music is off-key, it is not in tune.

off-licence An off-licence is a shop which sells alcohol for people to take away and drink off the premises.

off-limits If a place is off-limits to certain people, they are not allowed to go there.

off-load See offload.

off-peak things are available at times when there is less demand, and are cheaper than usual. ...*off-peak travel.*

off-putting If you say something is off-putting, you mean it makes you feel uncomfortable or distracts you from what you are doing.

off-stage (*or* offstage) is used to describe things which take place behind the stage during the performance of a play and which the audience cannot see. ...*off-stage sound effects.*

off-the-cuff An off-the-cuff comment has not been planned or practised in advance. *He is good at talking off the cuff.*

off-the-peg clothing is ready-made, rather than made specially for you.

off-the-record statements and remarks are made unofficially, and are not intended to be made public.

off-white things are not pure white, but slightly yellow or grey.

offal The liver, kidneys, and other internal organs of an animal are called **offal** when they are used for food.

offbeat See **off-beat**.

offence (*American spelling:* **offense**) ❑ When someone commits an **offence**, they break a law or rule. ...*two men suspected of terrorist offences... This was clearly a sending-off offence under the new guidelines.*
❑ If someone **takes offence**, they are upset or annoyed because they think something is meant as a criticism of them. ◇ If something **gives offence**, it upsets or annoys people because they think it is indecent or it deals with something they care about in a way they find unacceptable.

offend (offending) If something **offends** people, it upsets or embarrasses them. ◇ If a person **offends**, they break a law or rule. *There is no evidence that offending by young people has gone up... She wanted the offending players punished.*

offender An **offender** is a person who has committed a crime. ...*a prison for young offenders.* ◇ People who behave badly in other ways are sometimes called **offenders**. *Some of the worst offenders of the tabloid press continue to invade people's personal lives in an unacceptable way.*

offense See **offence**.

offensive (offensively) ❑ If someone's behaviour is **offensive**, it is rude and unpleasant. ...*an offensively one-sided account of her son's marriage.*
❑ In war, an **offensive** is a strong determined attack. ◇ **Offensive** weapons are used for attack, rather than defence. ...*offensive nuclear missiles.*
❑ A positive attempt to take the initiative in a situation can also be called an **offensive**. *The Security Council stepped up the diplomatic peace offensive.*

offer (offering, offered) ❑ If you **offer** something to someone or make them an **offer** of it, you say they can have it if they want it. *The government had offered them compensation... He had been lured to London with the offer of a job.* ◇ When the management of a company proposes a new rate of pay for its workers, this is called a **pay offer**.
❑ If you **offer** something like advice or information, you provide it. ◇ If you **offer** to do something, you say you are willing to do it.
❑ If something is **on offer**, it is available to be bought, won, or used. ◇ A **special offer** is something available in a shop at a specially low price, or something extra you get if you buy something.
❑ If you make an **offer** for something, you say you will pay a certain sum of money for it.
❑ If something **offers** an advantage of some kind, it provides it. *New diesel engines will offer outstanding fuel economy and less pollution.*

offering ❑ An **offering** is something someone produces and makes available. *The company's products will provide important differences from mass-produced offerings... Critics see the movie as another offering from a film-maker who likes to play it safe.*

❑ An **offering** is also a gift or sacrifice to a god.

offhand (*or* off-hand) If someone behaves in an **offhand** way, they are careless in the way they behave towards people and make no attempt to be friendly or helpful.

office ❑ An **office** is a room or part of a building where people work sitting at desks. ◇ An **office** is also a small building or room where people go for things like information, tickets, or a service. ...*the local tourist office.*
❑ **Office** appears in the names of some government departments and other government organizations. ...*the Foreign Office... ...the Office of Fair Trading.*
❑ Someone who holds **office** has an important position in a government or other organization. A person like this can be called an **office-holder**. *The Prime Minister took office three weeks ago... His introduction to public life came as an office-holder in a trade union.*

Office of Fair Trading The **Office of Fair Trading** or **OFT** is a government organization which aims to ensure that the public are protected against unfair business practice.

officer ❑ An **officer** in the armed forces is a person who holds a commission and has authority over other ranks.
❑ People who work in local government are called local government **officers**. **Officer** appears in the names of some local government jobs. ...*the Chief Medical Officer of Health.*
❑ Members of the police force are sometimes called **officers**. ...*an officer from Scotland Yard.*

official (officially) ❑ **Official** is used to describe things published or approved by the government or by someone else in authority. *Official figures show that increases in average earnings have fallen to their lowest level for 25 years... There's been no official statement yet from the Pope.* ◇ **Official** is also used to describe things done or used by people in authority as part of their job or position. ...*the President's official residence... ...an official visit... The Queen has officially opened a new session of Parliament.*
❑ If you talk about the **official** reason for something, you mean a false reason people have been given in the hope they will believe it, often because the real reason is embarrassing. *The official reason given for the President's absence was sickness, but many observers will see it as a diplomatic way out of a difficult situation.*
❑ An **official** is a person who holds a position of authority in an organization. ...*a Foreign Office official.*

Official Receiver The **Official Receiver** is an officer appointed by the Department of Trade and Industry to manage the affairs of a bankrupt or a company which is being wound up.

officialdom is used to talk about government officials, usually in a disapproving way. *He does not welcome visits from officialdom.*

officiate (officiating, officiated) When someone **officiates** at something like a ceremony, they are in charge and perform the main part of it. *I was able to officiate at the wedding of my niece.* ◇ When someone **officiates** in a game, they are there to make sure the rules are followed.

officious (officiously) If you say someone is being **officious**, you mean they are being bossy and interfering. ...*officious interference... At the airport, they officiously told me that no hotel now offers free parking for security reasons.*

offing If something is **in the offing**, it is likely to happen soon.

offload (*or* **off-load**) When goods are **offloaded** from a container or vehicle, they are removed from it. ◇ If someone **offloads** something they cannot sell or do not want, they get rid of it by selling it off cheaply or giving it away.

offset (offsetting, offset *not 'offsetted'*) ❏ You say two things **offset** each other when the effects of one are balanced out by the effects of the other. *Temperatures in tropical areas could fall, offsetting the effects of global warming.*

❏ See also **lithography**.

offshoot If something is an **offshoot** of something else, it has developed from it. *The Historic Royal Palaces Agency is an offshoot of the Department of the Environment.*

offshore is used to describe things which take place or are situated in the sea near to a coast. *...offshore races... ...offshore oil rigs... ...offshore islands.*

❏ **Offshore** is also used to describe things which are based or operate abroad in places where the tax system is more advantageous than in the home country. *...offshore companies... ...an offshore banking haven.*

offside ❏ The **offside** of a vehicle is the side normally furthest from the edge of the road. See also **nearside**.

❏ Several games played by two teams on a pitch have an **offside** rule. A footballer is given **offside** when the ball is being played towards his opponents' goal and he is nearer to this goal than any of their defenders, except the goalkeeper. When this happens, the other side is awarded a free kick.

offspring (*plural:* offspring) A person's **offspring** are their children. You can also talk about the **offspring** of animals and birds.

offstage See **off-stage**.

Ofgas (*or* **OFGAS**) is a government organization set up to regulate prices and working practices in the gas industry when it was privatized in 1986. 'Ofgas' stands for 'Office of Gas Supply'.

Ofsted (*or* **OFSTED**) is a government organization responsible for inspecting schools and maintaining educational standards. 'Ofsted' stands for 'Office for Standards in Education'. It replaced Her Majesty's Inspectors of Schools in 1992.

OFT See **Office of Fair Trading**.

oft- is added to words to say something has happened often. *...his oft-repeated statement... ...our oft-stated aim.*

Oftel (*or* **OFTEL**) is a government organization set up to regulate prices and working practices in the telecommunications industry when it was privatized in 1984. 'Oftel' stands for 'Office of Telecommunications'.

often If something happens **often**, it happens many times. ◇ If you ask **how often** something happens, you are asking how long the intervals are between the times it happens. *How often do you brush your teeth?* ◇ If something happens **every so often**, it happens occasionally.

Ofwat (*or* **OFWAT**) is a government organization set up to regulate prices and working practices in the water supply industry when it was privatized in 1989. 'Ofwat' stands for 'Office of Water Services'.

ogle (ogling, ogled) When a man **ogles** a woman, he stares at her, in a way which shows sexual interest.

ogre An **ogre** is a cruel frightening giant in a fairy story.

ohm Electrical resistance is expressed in **ohms**. When there is a resistance of one ohm, each volt of electrical force produces one amp of current.

O.H.M.S. (*or* **OHMS**) is printed on stationery used for official government business. It stands for 'On Her Majesty's Service'.

oil (oiling, oiled) ❏ **Oil** is a smooth thick sticky liquid found underground and used as a fuel or to lubricate machinery. If you **oil** something like a machine, you put oil on it to make it work more smoothly. ◇ If someone **oils the wheels** of something like a system or organization, they make sure it runs smoothly. You can talk about a system or organization being **well-oiled**.

❏ If you **pour oil on troubled waters**, you do something to calm people down when they have been quarrelling.

❏ **Oil** is also the name given to various thick greasy liquids produced by plants and animals and used in cooking or cosmetic products. *...olive oil... ...whale oils... ...moisturizing oil.*

❏ Oil paints and oil paintings are often called **oils**. *He paints in oils... His modern pictures included oils by Monet and Roger Fry.*

oil-fired systems use oil as a fuel.

oil paint (oil painting) **Oil paint** is a thick paint made from coloured powder mixed with linseed oil. An **oil painting** is a picture painted with oil paints.

oil platform An **oil platform** is a structure built up from the sea bed or floating on the sea and used to support an offshore oil rig.

oil rig An **oil rig** is a structure on land or in the sea which is used as a base when drilling for oil.

oil slick An **oil slick** is a layer of oil floating on the sea, caused by oil tankers being wrecked or damaged, or being careless with waste oil.

oil tanker An **oil tanker** is large ship used for transporting oil in bulk. Lorries and special rail vehicles used for this purpose are also called **oil tankers**.

oil well An **oil well** is a hole bored into the earth or seabed to extract oil.

oilfield An **oilfield** is an area under the earth or seabed where oil is found and extracted.

oilman (oilmen) **Oilmen** are either the owners and senior staff of oil companies, or the workers who do the actual drilling.

oilseed rape See **rape**.

oilskins are a waterproof coat, trousers, and hat, worn by people like sailors as protective clothing.

oily is used to describe things which are covered in oil, or feel or look like oil. ◇ If you call a person **oily**, you mean you do not like them, because they keep flattering people or behaving in an exaggeratedly polite way.

ointment is a smooth thick medicated substance put on the skin to heal it or protect it.

okay (*or* **OK**) If you say something is **okay**, you mean it is all right.

okra (*pron:* oh-kra) is a tropical plant with long green edible pods.

old ❏ An **old** person has lived a long time. Old people are sometimes called **the old**. ◇ **Old** is also used to describe things which have existed or been in use for a long time. ...*one of the old British trading firms in Hong Kong...* ...*the old custom of reading aloud.* ◇ **Old** is also used to talk about the age of someone or something. ...*a 13-year-old girl*... *This bone is 12,000 years old.*

❑ **Old** is used to describe things which are no longer used or have been replaced by something else. *The old economic system has disintegrated... She still receives post from her old address.*

❑ If someone is an **old** friend, they have been your friend for a long time.

❑ **Old** is used, sometimes insincerely, to show pity or affection for someone or something. *The poor old taxman is, it seems, universally unpopular.*

❑ When people talk about **the old days**, they are talking about things which happened or existed in the past. *People have forgotten that in the old days everybody paid bank charges.* ◇ **Of old** is also used to talk about things which existed in the past. ...*the cartoon heroes of old.*

❑ You use **of the old school** to describe someone who has been doing something for a long time and does it in an older way which you think is better than more recent ways. ...*a professional diplomat of the old school.*

old-age pensioner See OAP.

old boy An **old boy** of a school or college is a man who used to be a pupil there. ◇ Old men are sometimes called **old boys**. *The old boy confessed that his early religious training had left him too scared of women to marry.*

old-fashioned is used to describe things which were common in the past, but have now been replaced by something else. ...*an old-fashioned rocking horse.* ◇ If you say a person is **old-fashioned,** you mean they behave in a way people behaved in the past, or they believe in things most people no longer believe in.

old girl An **old girl** of a school or college is a woman who used to be a pupil there.

old master The great European painters of the period 1500 to 1800 are called **old masters.** Their paintings are also called **old masters.**

old school tie When people talk about the **old school tie,** they mean the unofficial system by which men who have been to the same public school or university use their positions of influence to help each other.

old-style means the same as old-fashioned. ...*old-style phone kiosks*... ...*an old-style politician.*

Old Testament The **Old Testament** is the first part of the Christian Bible. It is also the holy book of the Jewish religion and contains writings relating to the history of the Jews.

old timer You say someone is an **old timer** when they have been in the same place, job, or way of life for a long time. ◇ In the US, an **old timer** is any old man.

old wives' tale If you call a popular belief an **old wives' tale,** you mean it is based on ignorance or superstition and has no truth in it.

Old World The **Old World** is the continents of Europe, Asia, and Africa, as opposed to America.

oldie An **oldie** is (a) an old person. (b) an old record or film.

olfactory is used to talk about things to do with the sense of smell. ...*the olfactory nerves.*

oligarchy (*pron:* ol-ig-gar-kee) (oligarchies; oligarch) An oligarchy is a small group of people who control and run a country or state. This system of government is called **oligarchy.** A member of an oligarchy is called an **oligarch.**

olive ❑ **Olives** are the small green or black fruit of a Mediterranean tree called an **olive tree.** They are used in cooking and salads. ◇ If someone offers you an **olive branch,** they say or do something to show they want to end a disagreement or quarrel.

❑ **Olive** is a dark yellowish-green colour.

olive oil is an oil obtained by pressing olives. It is used as a salad dressing or for cooking food in.

Olympiad Each staging of the modern Olympic Games is called an **Olympiad.** ◇ An international contest in a game like chess or bridge is also called an **Olympiad.**

Olympian ❑ Athletes who take part in the Olympic Games are sometimes called **Olympians.**

❑ **Olympian** is also used to describe things which are very large. ...*an understatement of Olympian proportions.*

Olympic The **Olympic Games** or **Olympics** are a series of international sports competitions which takes place every four years, each time in a different country. **Olympic** is used to describe things to do with the Olympic Games. ...*the Olympic movement*... ...*the International Olympic Committee.*

OM An **OM** is an honour awarded to people for special achievements in a particular field. OM stands for 'Order of Merit'.

ombudsman (ombudsmen) An **ombudsman** is an independent official who investigates complaints by the public. There are several ombudsmen. One deals with complaints against government departments, another with complaints against the NHS, and so on.

omega is Ω or ω the last letter of the Greek alphabet.

omelette (*American spelling:* omelet) An **omelette** is a pancake-shaped food made by whisking eggs and then cooking them with butter in a flat pan.

omen An **omen** is something thought to be a sign of what may happen in the future. *In Hollywood, past success is often an omen of future disaster... The omens for an amicable agreement look worse.*

ominous (ominously) If something is **ominous,** it is worrying or frightening, because it suggests that something unpleasant or dangerous is going to happen. ...*ominous black clouds... The West Indies were in ominously good form a week before the Test.*

omit (omits, omitting, omitted; omission) If something is **omitted** from a broadcast or piece of writing, it is left out of it. The part which is left out is called an **omission.** ◇ If you **omit** to do something, you do not do it.

omni-directional If something like a radio is **omni-directional,** it can send and receive radio signals equally in any direction.

omnibus (omnibuses) ❑ An **omnibus** is a collection of stories or articles, often by the same person or about the same subject. ...*the Sherlock Holmes omnibus.* ◇ An **omnibus** edition of a TV or radio programme contains two or more episodes or programmes which had previously been broadcast separately.

❑ **Omnibus** is also an old word for a bus.

omnipotent (*pron:* om-nip-o-tent) (omnipotence) If someone is **omnipotent,** they have unlimited power. ...*the omnipotence of God.*

omnipresent (*pron:* om-ni-**prez**-ent) (omnipresence) If someone or something is **omnipresent,** they are everywhere, or seem to be. *Conservation grants are available to woodland owners to keep out the omnipresent red deer... ...the omnipresence of tiny shops in Japan.*

omniscient (*pron:* om-**niss**-ee-ent) (omniscience) If you say someone is **omniscient** or talk about their **omniscience,** you mean they know everything, or seem to.

omnivorous If a person or animal is **omnivorous,** they eat all kinds of food, including meat and plants. ◇ You also say someone is **omnivorous** when they absorb or take an interest in a wide variety of subjects.

on is used to say where someone or something is, where something is put, or where something happens. *...posters on his bedroom wall... He hung his jacket on a hook... They must be prepared to play on the same pitch.* ◇ **On** is also used to say where something is written. *He drew two circles on a blackboard.*
  ❑ **On** is used to say someone is travelling somewhere by bus, train, or plane. *Within a week Yul was on a plane to Hollywood.*
  ❑ When you put your clothes **on,** you get dressed. If someone has a piece of clothing **on,** they are wearing it. ◇ If you have something **on** you, you are carrying it in your pocket or bag.
  ❑ You say something happens **on** a certain day or date.
  ❑ If a programme is **on** TV or the radio, it is being broadcast. You also say something like a play or a film is **on** when it is being shown or performed.
  ❑ If someone is **on** a medicine or drug, they are taking it regularly.
  ❑ If something like a report, speech, or book is **on** a certain subject, that is what it is about. You can also say someone writes or speaks **on** a subject.
  ❑ You say something has an effect **on** someone or something else. *Falling prices have had no effect on sales.*
  ❑ If something is done **on** a type of machine or instrument, it is done using it.
  ❑ If you are **on** something like a council or committee, you are a member of it.
  ❑ If something like a machine or light is **on,** it is functioning.
  ❑ **On** is used to say someone or something keeps doing something. *Prices kept on rising... We drove on to the border.*
  ❑ If you are very busy, you can say you have a lot **on.**
  ❑ If you say something is **not on,** you mean it is not possible or not acceptable.

on-line is used to talk about things being connected to the central processing unit of a computer, and to describe services or facilities which are available as a result. *...an on-line service offering news and information.*

on-screen is used to talk about things displayed on the screen of a computer or word-processor. *...on-screen graphics... Help and advice are available on-screen.*

on-the-job training is given while you are doing the job you are being trained for. You can also say someone gets **on-the-job** experience.

on-the-spot is used to describe things done or provided as an immediate response to something. *...on-the-spot fines.* ◇ **On-the-spot** investigations are carried out in the place where something is actually happening, rather than from somewhere else.

ONC The ONC and OND were qualifications in technical subjects. They have now been replaced by BTEC First and National certificates.

once ❑ If something happens **once,** it happens just one time. If it happens, for example, **once** a year, it happens one time each year. ◇ If you say something **never once** happened, you are emphasizing that it never happened. *He never once complained.*
  ❑ **Once** is used to say something used to be true, but is no longer true. *Bristol was once England's most important provincial city.*
  ❑ If something happens **once** something else has happened, it happens as soon as the other thing has happened. *Once they have money in their hands, they spend it quickly.*
  ❑ If you do something **at once,** you do it immediately. If something is needed **at once,** it is needed urgently.
  ❑ When several things happen at the same time, you can say they happen **at once** or **all at once.** *He regularly held three jobs at once.*
  ❑ If something has happened **once or twice,** it has happened occasionally. *I've been to his office once or twice.* Similarly, you can say something happens **once in a while.**
  ❑ **For once** is used to say something has happened which is very different from what normally happens. *For once, the weather has smiled on the thousands of holidaymakers heading for the coast.*
  ❑ **once and for all:** see **all.**
  ❑ **Once again** and **once more** are used to talk about something happening which has happened many times before. *The upheaval could end once more in disaster... Press freedom is once again under threat.*

oncoming is used to describe something which is moving towards you. *...oncoming traffic.*

OND See **ONC.**

one is the number 1.
  ❑ You use **one** when you are saying something about an individual person or thing belonging to a group of people or things. *One woman said she was ashamed to be British.*
  ❑ **One day** means at some unspecified time in the future or past. *Lasers can be very powerful, and may one day make formidable weapons... One day a blonde woman walked into the shop.* When you are talking about the past, you can also say, for example, something happened **one morning** or **one afternoon.** *Late one night the phone rang in the publisher's office.*
  ❑ **One or two** means a few. *There are one or two remaining questions.*
  ❑ If you say someone or something is **one in a million,** you mean they are very special or remarkable in some way.
  ❑ If a group of people act **as one,** they all do the same thing at the same time.
  ❑ If you are **at one** with someone, you are in complete agreement with them. ◇ If you are **at one** with something like the environment, you have a sense of belonging with it.
  ❑ **One by one** is used to talk about (a) each of a number of people doing the same thing in turn. *Ministers went in to see the Prime Minister one by one.* (b) one person doing a series of things in turn. *I enjoy the process of sewing on beads one by one.*

❑ If you are **one up** on someone, you have gained an advantage over them.

❑ **One** is sometimes used to mean people in general. *One does not cure this problem by throwing money around.* ◇ Some people use **one** to talk about themselves. *One knows that one is growing older.*

one-armed bandit A one-armed bandit is a gambling machine operated by putting coins in a slot and pulling down a lever at the side.

one-horse If you say something like an election or contest is a **one-horse race**, you mean only one contender has a realistic chance of winning.

One-hundred Share Index The One-hundred Share Index is the same as the FTSE.

one-liner A one-liner is a short joke or witty remark.

one-man is used to describe (a) things done by one person, especially a man. ...*a one-man show.* (b) things intended for one person. ...*a one-man submarine.*

❑ A **one-man band** is a street entertainer who has a lot of musical instruments fastened to him and plays them all at the same time. ◇ If all the decisions in an organization are taken by one person, you can call it a **one-man band** or **one-man show.**

one-night stand A one-night stand is something like a concert or play performed at a place on one evening only, rather than on several evenings. ◇ A **one-night stand** is also a brief sexual relationship, usually consisting of two people having sex with each other on one occasion only.

one-off is used to describe (a) things which happen only once. ...*a one-off fee of £95.* (b) items made individually as required and not as part of a production-line process. *Special one-off items will be ordered direct from the manufacturers.*

one-parent A one-parent family consists of a child or children living with just one of their parents.

one-piece is used to describe something made in one complete piece instead of two or more separate parts. *The one-piece tyre made from hard-wearing polyurethane has no inner tube or valve.*

one-sided You say a game or contest is **one-sided** when one of the players or teams is much stronger or better than the other. ◇ You also use **one-sided** to describe something involving two people in which one person takes a more active part than the other. ...*a one-sided conversation.* ◇ A **one-sided** account of a situation shows things from one point of view only.

one-time is used when mentioning something that a person or place used to be in the past. ...*a one-time actress...* ...*a one-time cemetery.*

one-to-one In a **one-to-one** relationship or situation, you deal with only one other person. ...*one-to-one tuition...* He *later held one-to-one talks with the president.*

one-upmanship is trying to appear better than someone else, for example by owning something unusual they have not got, or by having visited places they have not been to.

one-way ❑ In a **one-way** street, vehicles can travel in one direction only. When a system like this is operating, you say there is **one-way** traffic.

❑ A **one-way** ticket enables you to travel to a place, but not to come back again. ◇ If you make a **one-way** trip somewhere, you go there and do not come back.

❑ A **one-way** communications device, for example a pager or satellite, can either send signals or receive them, but not both.

one-woman is used to describe something done by just one woman. ...*Eleanor Bron's one-woman show.*

oneness is a sense of unity with other people or creatures. *Celebrities clambered onto a stage to express their oneness with whales.*

onerous (pron: ohn-er-uss) If something is **onerous**, it involves very hard work or heavy responsibilities. *Has the burden of the job become too onerous?*

oneself A speaker or writer uses **oneself** to talk about himself or herself in a formal way. *One can only speak for oneself.*

ongoing is used to describe things which continue to happen, rather than coming to a halt. ...*ongoing talks...* ...*an ongoing programme of maintenance and inspection.*

onion Onions are round strong-tasting vegetables with brown papery outer skin and layers of white flesh.

onlooker An onlooker is a person who watches something happening without taking part.

only is used to talk about something being limited to one person, thing, or group. *He is now the only potential owner... There was only a single diesel pump... Land like this should only be used for forestry.* ◇ If you are an **only** child, you have no brothers or sisters.

❑ You use **only** to emphasize that something is fairly small or unimportant. *It is only a bruise... This is only a village.*

❑ **Only too** is used to emphasize certain words, and often to express regret at a situation. *Young people are only too well aware of the dangers of AIDS... The effects for exports, industry and employment are only too obvious.*

❑ You use **only** to emphasize how small an amount or number is, or how short a length of time is. *Only a tiny fraction of the revenues from tourism filter down to rural people... It only lasted 10 seconds.* ◇ You also use **only** to emphasize (a) how recently something has happened. *He arrived at Bristol only last week.* (b) how rarely something happens. *The opportunity to send a spacecraft to the planet comes only once every 26 months.*

❑ You use **only** to express a wish or hope which is unlikely to be fulfilled. *I only wish he could tell me how he hits some of his shots.*

❑ You use **only** for emphasis when you are saying something is right, fair, or reasonable. *It is only right that the court should decide whether the needs of the press outweigh those of the police.*

❑ If you say something will happen **only if** something else happens, you mean it will not happen unless that thing happens. *Reducing accidents can be achieved only if there is a change in public attitude towards the way cars are driven.* ◇ **if only:** see **if.**

❑ If you say someone **has only** to do one thing in order to achieve something, you mean that is all they have to do to achieve it. *Mackay had only to pick up the loose ball to score.*

❑ You use **only** to say one thing followed another, and was a disappointment or anti-climax. *Hopes of recovery have come before, only to be dashed.*

❑ You use **only** when you are pointing out the difference between two things of the same kind. *Leaders of the two main parties also have big cars, only theirs are provided by the state.*

❏ **only just:** see **just**.

onomatopoeic (*pron:* on-o-mat-o-**pee**-ick) (onomatopoeia) Onomatopoeic words sound like the noise they are describing or referring to; for example, 'hiss' and 'buzz' are onomatopoeic. This feature is called **onomatopoeia**.

onrush If there is an **onrush** of something, it develops or increases suddenly and quickly. *...the onrush of new members.*

onrushing is used to describe someone or something that is moving quickly towards you. *...flicking the ball past the onrushing goalkeeper.*

onset The **onset** of something, especially something unpleasant, is its beginning. *...the onset of war... ...the onset of the rainy season.*

onshore is used to describe things which are on land, rather than out at sea. *...onshore jobs in the oil industry.* ◇ An **onshore** wind reaches the land from the sea.

onslaught An **onslaught** is a concentrated attack by an army or some other armed or violent group. ◇ Strong and repeated criticism can also be called an **onslaught**. *He kept up Labour's onslaught on the government's handling of the economy.*

onstage is used to talk about things happening on the stage in a theatre. *Onstage tonight are Paul McCartney and Pink Floyd... Her onstage antics have caused a fair amount of controversy.*

onstream When an oil well comes **onstream**, it starts producing oil.

onto ❏ If you go **onto** something, you change your position so you are standing on it or perched on it. *Eleven prisoners have climbed onto the roof... Crowds poured onto the streets.* Similarly, an object can fall **onto** something. ◇ When you get **onto** something like a bus or plane, you go inside it.
    ❏ **Onto** is used to say something is attached somewhere. *Those last sequins are being sewn onto the costumes.* ◇ **Onto** is also used to say something like a light is directed somewhere. *The image is projected onto a television-sized screen.*

onus (*pron:* **own**-uss) If the **onus** is on you to do something, it is your duty or responsibility to do it.

onward (onwards) ❏ **Onward** and **onwards** are used to talk about the continuation of a journey. *...a flight to Frankfurt with an onward flight to New York... Rivers carry the effluent to the Mississippi and onwards out to sea.*
    ❏ **Onward** is used with words like 'march' to talk about the development or progress of something. *...the onward march of technology... ...the onward surge of corruption.* ◇ If something moves **onwards and upwards**, it develops and improves. *In the meantime, helped by a series of sunny vintages, English wine moves onwards and upwards.*
    ❏ If something happens from a certain time **onwards**, it starts at that time and goes on happening.

onyx (*pron:* **on**-iks) is a semiprecious stone with layers of different colours, used for making ornaments and jewellery.

oodles of something means a lot of it. *...oodles of money.*

oomph If you say someone or something has **oomph**, you mean they create an impression of liveliness and

vigour. *Backbenchers are depressed by their leader's lack of oomph.*

ooze (oozing, oozed) ❏ If a thick sticky liquid **oozes** out of something, it flows out of it slowly. You can also say something **oozes** a liquid. *...a handful of cars oozing oil.*
    ❏ **Ooze** is a soft thin mud-like substance found at the bottom of the sea.
    ❏ If you say a person **oozes** a quality, you mean they are full of it. *They ooze vitality... He is oozing confidence.*

op An **op** is (a) a surgical operation. *...breast cancer ops.* (b) a military operation. *...night fighter ops from British bases.*

op. cit. (*pron:* **op** sit) When a book is mentioned more than once in a piece of writing, **op. cit.** is used after the author's name on each occasion apart from the first. This saves repeating the title every time the book is mentioned. *...Bancroft, op. cit., p. 47.*

opacity See **opaque**.

opal **Opals** are gemstones used for making jewellery. They are usually milky white, with flashes of many colours.

opaque (*pron:* oh-**pake**) (opacity) If something is **opaque**, you cannot see through it. *...opaque glass.* You talk about the **opacity** (*pron:* ope-**ass**-it-tee) of something like this. ◇ If you say something like a piece of writing is **opaque**, you mean it is difficult to understand.

OPEC (*pron:* **oh**-pek) is an organization of oil-producing countries, mainly in the Middle East, which aims to develop a common policy and system of pricing. OPEC stands for 'Organization of Petroleum-Exporting Countries'.

open (opening, opened; openly) ❏ If you **open** something like a door or window, you change its position, so it no longer fills or covers the opening it is designed to fit. When you have done this, you say the door or window is **open**. ◇ If you say a door **opens onto** an area, you mean the area is just outside the door. *...French windows which open onto a terrace.* You can also say a room **opens onto** something.
    ❏ When you **open** your mouth, you move your lips and teeth apart; your mouth is then **open**. When you **open** your eyes, you move your eyelids upwards, so you can see; your eyes are then **open**.
    ❏ If you **open** something like a letter or parcel, you remove the outer covering, so you can take out what is inside. ◇ If you **open** a book, you move the covers apart, so you can read the pages or write on them.
    ❏ **Open** things are not covered or enclosed. *...an open fireplace... ...an open-topped bus.*
    ❏ When a flower **opens**, it comes into bloom and its petals spread out.
    ❏ When something like a shop or public building **opens**, work or business starts for the day; you then say the shop or building is **open**. ◇ When a building is **opened up**, it is unlocked, so people can get in.
    ❏ When something like a new factory, public building, or road **opens**, it starts being used. *A huge convention centre is due to open in the spring.* ◇ When an event or activity **opens**, it starts. *The exhibition opens in London today.* ◇ When someone important **opens** a building, institution, or event, they officially declare it is ready to be used or to start.
    ❏ When someone **opens** something like a process, they

start it by being the first one to contribute to it. *Gynn opened the scoring for Coventry in the thirteenth minute.*

❑ When a country **opens** its borders or frontiers, it starts to allow people to move freely between it and other countries. When this happens, you say the country is **opened up.**

❑ If someone is **open** with you, they are frank and do not try to hide anything. ◇ If something is done **openly,** it is done without any secrecy. ◇ When people talk about **open** government, they mean a system in which a government keeps people informed about what it is doing, rather than keeping things secret. ◇ If something is brought **into the open,** people are told about it and it is no longer a secret. ◇ If something is an **open secret,** it is supposed to be a secret but everybody knows about it.

❑ When people talk about an **open** society, they mean one where people are free to discuss things and criticize their leaders.

❑ If someone is **open** to suggestions or new ideas, they are willing to consider them. ◇ If you are keeping an **open mind** on something or being **open-minded,** you are not making a decision or judgement until you know all the facts.

❑ If a course of action is **open** to you, you can go ahead with it, if you want to. ◇ If an opportunity **opens up,** it is there for you to take advantage of. ◇ If someone or something makes something possible, you can say they **open the door** to it; you then say **the door is open** to it. *The Americans say their door is open to the re-establishment of diplomatic relations.*

❑ **Open** is used to describe something like a meeting or competition which anyone can take part in. In some sports, an **open** tournament or championship is one which both amateurs and professionals can compete in.

❑ If you lay yourself **open** to something bad, your behaviour makes it likely to happen to you. *They have formed associations which lay them open to blackmail.* ◇ If something is **open** to being used in a certain way, something like that could happen to it. *Such a huge store of information is an invasion of privacy, and open to abuse.*

❑ If a situation is left **open,** no final decision is made about it. *We will keep our options open until the last moment.*

❑ If someone keeps **open house,** friends and visitors are welcome at their house at any time without needing invitations.

❑ An **open** area of land is not obstructed by things like buildings or trees.

❑ The **open** sea is the parts of the sea which are not close to land.

❑ If you do something **in the open** or **in the open air,** you do it out of doors. **Open-air** things are situated or take place out of doors. *...open-air rock concerts.*

❑ If something like a street or river **opens out,** it gradually gets wider.

❑ If you **open** an account with a bank, you start to use their services by depositing some of your money with them.

❑ When something like a share **opens** at a certain value, it has that value at the start of the day's trading.

❑ If something is for sale on the **open market,** it is advertised and sold publicly rather than privately.

open-air See open.

open-and-shut An open-and-shut case is something like a problem or a legal matter which is easily decided or solved because the facts are very clear.

open-cast In an open-cast mine, the coal or mineral deposits are near the surface, and can be dug out without tunnelling underground.

open college Open colleges are colleges which organize correspondence courses. They are called open colleges because you do not need any entry qualifications to enrol for their courses.

open day An open day is a special day when something like a school, university, or other institution is open for the public to visit.

open-ended is used to describe something like an agreement which you enter into without placing any limits on what you are prepared to do. *The Prime Minister has made an astonishingly open-ended commitment to provide 'substantial public funding'... ...the dangers of open-ended military involvement.*

open-heart surgery is performed on the heart while the circulation of the blood is maintained by a machine.

open learning is a system in which people with few or no qualifications can study by taking correspondence courses with an open college.

open letter An open letter is a letter, especially a protest, addressed to an important person or an organization but also made public, for example in a newspaper.

open-minded See open.

open-mouthed If you say someone is open-mouthed, you mean they are amazed at something which has happened.

open-necked An open-necked shirt or blouse is not buttoned at the collar and is worn without a tie.

open-plan buildings have only a few interior walls to divide up the living or working space. The rooms inside them are also called open-plan. *...open-plan classrooms.*

open prison An open prison has a more relaxed regime than a conventional prison and is used for prisoners who are not considered to be a security risk.

open season ❑ In hunting, fishing, and shooting, the open season is the time of the year when certain birds, animals, and fish can legally be killed.

❑ If you say it is **open season** on someone, you mean a lot of people are criticizing them or making fun of them.

Open University The Open University is a university founded in 1969. It runs degree courses for students wishing to study part-time mainly at home. Lectures are broadcast on TV and radio, and students send their work by post to their tutors.

open verdict At an inquest, an open verdict is recorded when the cause of death has not been established.

opener ❑ An opener is a device used for opening things like tins or bottles.

❑ In cricket, the batsman who goes in first to play for his or her team is called an **opener.**

opening ❑ The opening one of a series of things is the first one. *...the opening day of the baseball season.* ◇ The opening of a book or film is the beginning.

❑ An **opening** is a hole or space which things can pass through.

❑ An **opening** is also an opportunity to do something. *Anderson created the openings for the first three goals.*

opening hours The opening hours of something like a shop, pub, or bank are the times when it is open for business.

opening night The opening night of a new play or show is its first public performance.

opening time is the time when a pub opens for business.

opera (operatic) An opera is a musical work performed in a theatre. It is acted like a play, but most or all of the words are sung. This kind of music is called opera. Operatic is used to talk about things to do with opera. ...*an operatic aria*. Companies which perform opera often have Opera as part of their name. ...*the Welsh National Opera*.

operate (operating, operated) ❑ When you operate something like a machine, you make it work. The way it operates is the way it works. ...*a battery-powered grass trimmer, which operates on the strimmer principle*.

❑ If you operate something like a business, you run it. Operating is used to talk about things to do with running a business. *Half the company's operating income comes from its foreign operations*. You say a business or system operates in a particular way or in a particular place. *His company would continue to operate as an independent business*.

❑ When a surgeon operates, he or she cuts open a patient's body to remove or treat a damaged part.

operating system The operating system of a computer is the software program which controls things like the function of the keyboard, screen, printer, and disks. The computer will not run without an operating system.

operating theatre An operating theatre is a specially equipped room in a hospital where surgeons carry out operations.

operation (operational, operationally) ❑ An operation is a complex event or action which needs careful planning. ...*military operations*... ...*relief operations*. Operational is used to talk about things to do with operations like these. ...*operational patrols*... *The rocket has never been used operationally*.

❑ If something is in operation or operational, it is working or being used. ...*parts of London where driver-only trains are in operation*... *The overnight curfew remains in operation*... ...*a fully operational weapons system*.

❑ Businesses or companies can be called operations.

❑ An operation is also medical treatment in which a surgeon cuts open a patient's body to remove or treat a damaged part.

operative ❑ If something like a system or machine is operative, it is working. ◇ If you say a word you have just used is the operative word, you mean it sums up the most important aspect of a situation. *Japanese troops would be allowed to join any peace-keeping force, but 'peace' is the operative word*.

❑ Operative is also used to talk about things to do with surgical operations. ...*post-operative recovery*.

❑ An operative is a person who works for a secret service or a detective agency. ...*a former CIA operative*.

operator ❑ A person who controls or operates a machine is called an operator. ...*computer operators*. ◇ A switchboard operator is a person who works at a telephone exchange or on the switchboard of an office or hotel.

❑ Someone who runs a business can also be called an operator. ...*ferry operators*... ...*new-style pub operators*. ◇ If

you say someone is, for example, a clever operator, you mean they are skilled at getting what they want. ...*a formidable political operator*... ...*one of the few smart operators in the business*.

operetta An operetta is a light-hearted type of opera, often comic. It usually has more spoken dialogue than serious opera.

ophthalmic (*pron:* off-thal-mik) Ophthalmic is used to talk about things to do with the medical care of your eyes. ◇ ophthalmic optician: see optician.

ophthalmology (*pron:* off-thal-moll-o-gee) (ophthalmologist) Ophthalmology is the branch of medicine concerned with the eye and its diseases. A doctor who specializes in this is called an ophthalmologist.

opiate (*pron:* oh-pee-ate) An opiate is a drug containing opium. Opiates can reduce pain or make you sleep.

opine (opining, opined) When you opine something, you give your opinion about it. *The foreign minister opined that peace negotiations could be at a decisive stage*.

opinion ❑ An opinion is a personal belief or judgement about something. ◇ If you have a difference of opinion with someone, you disagree with them about something. ◇ Opinion is also used to talk about the beliefs or views held by many people. *Never before had world opinion been so united against aggression*.

❑ An opinion from an expert is their advice or judgement on something relating to their subject. *A Swiss judge will give a preliminary opinion and invite the two sides to negotiate a settlement*.

opinion poll An opinion poll is a way of finding out what people think about something. It involves getting the views of a representative sample.

opinionated If you call someone opinionated, you mean they have strong opinions and are fond of expressing them. *Listening to him is a bit like getting trapped with the more opinionated sort of cab driver*.

opium is a drug made from the seed pods of a type of poppy called the opium poppy. It is used in medicines to relieve pain or to help people sleep. Its use for non-medical purposes is illegal in many countries.

opossum The opossum is a small long-tailed animal which carries its young in a pouch on its body. Types of opossum are found in North and South America and in Australia.

opponent Your opponent is the person you are trying to beat in an argument, contest, or game. ◇ If you are an opponent of something, you disagree with it, and are trying to stop it or get rid of it.

opportune If something is opportune, it comes at just the right time. *The visit is seen as particularly opportune*. You can also say something comes at an opportune time. *The scandal has broken at an opportune moment*.

opportunist (opportunistic, opportunism) ❑ You say someone is opportunist or opportunistic when they take advantage of something which happens. *Some opportunist homeowners sold out in the 1980s to developers*. Opportunist is also used to describe things which are achieved in this way. *They knocked in three opportunist goals in the second half*. ◇ You also say someone is opportunistic or an opportunist when they are prepared to take advantage of any opportunity which comes along, to get money or power. This kind of behaviour is called opportunism.

❏ An **opportunistic** infection is caused by germs which are harmless to a healthy person but which affect someone whose immune system is weakened by disease or drug treatment.

opportunity (opportunities) If there is an **opportunity** for you to do something, a situation arises when you can do it. ◇ If there is **opportunity** for something in a place, it is possible to achieve it there. If there is **equal opportunity**, nobody is put at a disadvantage because of things like their sex or race.

oppose (opposing, opposed) ❏ If you **oppose** something or are **opposed** to it, you disagree with it and try to prevent it.

❏ **Opposed** or **opposing** ideas are totally different and conflict with each other. *Two ex-Cabinet ministers have been setting out widely opposing views on the future of Europe.*

❏ **Opposing** is used to describe groups of people who are fighting, arguing with, or competing against each other. *The sisters play in opposing teams.*

❏ You say **as opposed to** when you are distinguishing something from something else. *What about fiction, as opposed to fairy tales?... ...interim results as opposed to the final figures.*

opposite ❏ If things face in **opposite** directions, they face completely the other way to each other. Similarly, you can talk about people going in **opposite** directions. ◇ You use **opposite** to talk about two things being on either side of the same thing and facing each other. *...two high arches on opposite sides of the hall... ...an abandoned office in the building opposite... I was sitting opposite him.* ◇ You also use **opposite** to describe the part of something which is farthest away from you. *...the opposite end of the street.*

❏ When there are two possible opinions on something and they conflict with each other completely, you can say one is the **opposite** of the other. *Daniel Johnson, in The Times, presented the opposite view.* ◇ If something has the **opposite** effect from what you intend, it makes a situation worse, rather than resolving it or improving it.

❏ You say things of the same kind are **opposites** when they are unlike each other in every way. *Puttsborough Sands is the complete opposite of Blackpool.*

❏ When two actors perform **opposite** each other, they have the leading male and female roles in a play or film.

❏ Your **opposite number** is someone who has the same position as you in a different place or organization. *The British Foreign Secretary telephoned his German opposite number.* In sport, a player's **opposite number** is the person who plays at the same position in the other team.

❏ If you are a man, **the opposite sex** means women and girls. If you are a woman, it means men and boys.

opposition ❏ If there is **opposition** to something, a number of people disagree with it and are trying to prevent it.

❏ In parliament, the **opposition** are the politicians who do not belong to the government.

❏ In business or sport, the person or group you are competing against can be called the **opposition**. *When it comes to marketing, we lag behind the opposition.*

oppress (oppresses, oppressing, oppressed; oppression, oppressor) ❏ When people are **oppressed,** they are treated cruelly and unfairly by their rulers. People treated like this can be called the **oppressed**; their rulers are called their **oppressors.** *Diplomats have spoken out against the government's oppression... ...the rights of the oppressed... They could organize no defence against their oppressors.*

❏ If something **oppresses** you, it makes you feel depressed and uncomfortable. This feeling can be called **oppression.**

oppressive (oppressively) ❏ An **oppressive** government treats its people in a cruel and unfair way. You also call its methods **oppressive.**

❏ When the weather is hot and humid, you can say it is **oppressive.** *...oppressively hot temperatures.*

❏ An **oppressive** situation makes you feel depressed and uncomfortable.

oppressor See oppress.

opprobrium (*pron:* op-pro-bree-um) is strong public disapproval or dislike, brought on someone by their own actions.

opt ❏ If you **opt** for something, you choose it. Similarly, if you **opt** to do something, you choose to do it. *Voters opted for independence by a massive majority... They have opted to make the long journey by road.*

❏ If you **opt out** of something like a system, you choose not to be involved in it. An **opt-out** is something which allows you to opt out.

optic (optics) ❏ **Optic** is used to talk about things to do with the eyes. *...the optic nerve.* ◇ **Optics** is the branch of physics and engineering concerned with the properties of light. See also **fibre optics.**

❏ An **Optic** is a device attached to an upside-down bottle for dispensing a measured amount of a liquid like whisky or gin. Optics are used especially in pubs and hotels. 'Optic' is a trademark.

optical is used to talk about things to do with vision, light, and images. *...optical instruments.* ◇ **optical illusion:** see illusion.

optical fibre is a telecommunications cable consisting of a thin flexible glass fibre in a protective coating. Optical fibres transfer messages using light flashed by lasers.

optician An **optician** is a person who supplies glasses. A **dispensing optician** supplies and fits glasses and contact lenses, but is not qualified to prescribe them. An **ophthalmic optician** is qualified to examine eyes and prescribe and supply glasses and contact lenses.

optimal means the same as optimum.

optimise See optimize.

optimist (optimism; optimistic, optimistically) An **optimist** is a person who looks on the bright side of life and is hopeful about the future. You can talk about the **optimism** of someone like this or describe their behaviour as **optimistic.** *He optimistically predicts his business will still thrive.* ◇ If you say someone is **cautiously optimistic,** you mean they are fairly hopeful about something, but aware it may not happen or succeed.

optimize (optimizing, optimized) (*can be spelled with an 's' instead of a 'z'*) If you **optimize** something, you make the best use of it or develop it to the highest possible standard. *We need to put a lot of emphasis on understanding the disease better, and on optimizing the treatment.*

optimum The **optimum** one of a number of alternatives is the best one, or the one most likely to succeed. *Perhaps there is an optimum size for a village for it to be viable* *and have a secure future.*

option (optional) ❏ An **option** is one of a number of available choices. *Western aid still looks the best option for those worst hit by sanctions.*

❏ If you say someone has the **option** of doing something, you mean they can do it if they want to. *The government has the option of reintroducing the Bill next year.* ◇ If someone has **no option** but to do something, they have no choice but to do it.

❏ If something is **optional,** you can choose whether or not to have it or do it. ◇ If something is supplied as an **optional extra,** you can have it as an additional feature when you buy something, but you do not have to.

❏ An **option** is an agreement or contract which gives someone the right to buy or sell something at a fixed price within a certain period.

opulent (*pron:* op-yool-nt) (opulence) If you call something **opulent** or talk about its **opulence,** you mean it is luxurious or expensive-looking. *...an opulent mansion.*

opus (*pron:* oh-puss) (opuses) ❏ The published works of a classical composer are often given **opus** numbers. These show the order in which the works were published. So, for example, a composer's first published work is usually called his or her Opus 1. 'Opus' is often shortened to **Op.** *...Berg's Three Orchestral Pieces, Op 6.*

❏ A book or film on a large scale is sometimes called an **opus.** ◇ See also **magnum opus.**

or ❏ You use **or** when you are mentioning alternatives. *...national, regional or local authorities... It doesn't matter whether this is true or false.* See also **either, whether.** ◇ You use **or** between numbers when you are giving an approximate amount. *...two or three days.*

❏ You use **or** to say what will happen if something is not done. *We must resist aggression, or it will destroy our freedoms.* ◇ You use **or** to say why you think something is true. *The myths have an astonishing appeal, or they would not have lasted so long.*

❏ You use **or** when you are correcting something you have just said. *I did the illustrations, or at least some of them.*

oracle In ancient Greece, an **oracle** was a prediction about the future, revealed by a priest or priestess at the shrine of a god. The priest or priestess was also called an **oracle,** and so was the shrine. ◇ Anyone who has a reputation for predicting future events accurately can be called an **oracle.**

oral (orally) ❏ **Oral** is used to describe things to do with the mouth, or things taken through the mouth. *...oral hygiene... She could not have taken these massive doses orally.*

❏ **Oral** is also used to describe things which are spoken rather than written. *...oral evidence... No one warned him, either orally or in writing, of the risks involved.* ◇ An **oral exam** or **oral** is a spoken rather than written test of someone's knowledge or ability.

orang-utan (*or* orang-outang) **Orang-utans** are large apes with long reddish-brown hair. They live in the forests of Borneo and Sumatra.

orange is a reddish-yellow colour.

❏ **Oranges** are large round juicy citrus fruit with thick orange-coloured peel. They grow on trees called **orange trees.** ◇ **Orange blossom** is the white sweet-scented flowers of the orange tree or of a tree called the mock-orange tree.

Orangeman (Orangemen) An **Orangeman** is a member of a society founded in Ireland in 1795 to uphold the Protestant religion and cause.

orangey If something is **orangey,** it is slightly orange in colour.

oration An **oration** is a formal speech.

orator (*pron:* or-rat-tor) (oratory, oratorical) If someone is good at making powerful speeches, you can call them an **orator** or talk about their **oratory. Oratorical** is used to talk about someone's ability to make speeches. *...a vivid oratorical style.*

oratorio (*pron:* or-rat-tor-ee-oh) (oratorios) An **oratorio** is a piece of religious music for solo singers, a choir, and an orchestra.

orb An **orb** is a small ornamental sphere with a cross on top, carried by a king or queen as a symbol of their power.

orbit (orbiting, orbited) ❏ When an object in space **orbits** a planet, a moon, or the sun, it goes round and round it. You say an object like this is **in orbit.** Its curved path is called an **orbit.**

❏ If you are in someone's or something's **orbit,** you are under their influence. *The Marshall Plan had drawn Western Europe into the foreign policy orbit of the United States.*

orbital is used to talk about things to do with an orbit. *The comet moves in its orbital path roughly between Saturn and Uranus.* ◇ An **orbital** road goes all the way round a large city.

orchard An **orchard** is a piece of land where fruit trees are grown.

orchestra (orchestral) An **orchestra** is a large group of musicians who play a variety of musical instruments together. **Orchestral** is used to talk about things to do with orchestras. *...orchestral music.* ◇ In a theatre, the **orchestra pit** is a space reserved for musicians, immediately in front of or below the stage.

orchestrate (orchestrating, orchestrated; orchestration) ❏ If you say something a crowd does is **orchestrated,** you mean it is meant to look spontaneous, but has in fact been carefully organized in advance. *...a well-orchestrated demonstration.*

❏ When someone **orchestrates** a piece of music, they rewrite it so it can be played by an orchestra. This new version is called an **orchestration.**

orchid **Orchids** are plants with colourful and unusually shaped flowers.

ordain (ordaining, ordained; ordination) ❏ When someone is **ordained,** they are made a member of the clergy during a religious ceremony. This is called their **ordination.**

❏ If someone in authority **ordains** something, they order that it shall happen. *No painting was to be moved from where he had ordained it should hang.*

ordeal An **ordeal** is a difficult and extremely unpleasant experience.

order (ordering, ordered) ❏ If a person in authority **orders** you to do something, they tell you to do it. You can also say they give you an **order.** ◇ If you are **under orders** to do something, you have been told to do it.

❏ When you **order** goods from somewhere like a shop, you ask for them to be sent to you or obtained for you. Your request is called an **order;** the goods themselves are also called an **order**. When you are waiting for the goods, you say they are **on order**. ◇ If you **order** food in a restaurant, you ask for it to be brought to you; the food you ask for is called your **order**.

❏ If something is made or done **to order,** it is made or done to suit someone's requirements. *...fresh fish cooked to order.*

❏ If a set of things is arranged or done in a certain **order**, they are arranged or done according to a system or pattern. *...lists of words in alphabetical order... Voters number candidates in order of preference from 1 to 5.* ◇ If everything is in its correct place according to a system or pattern, you say things are **in order.**

❏ If you say someone should **put their house in order,** you mean they should sort out their own problems rather than become involved with other people's.

❏ You say there is **order** in a place when people are going about their business normally and there is no fighting or other trouble. *The army was helping to maintain order.* See also **law and order.** ◇ In an **ordered** society or system, things are properly planned or controlled.

❏ When one social or political system takes the place of another, you can call the old one the **old order** and the new one the **new order.**

❏ If a machine is **in working order,** it is able to do what it is supposed to. If it is broken and will not work, you say it is **out of order.** Similarly, you can describe the state of something by saying it is in **good order** or **bad order.**

❏ If you say something is **of a high order,** you mean it is very good.

❏ If you say a kind of behaviour is **the order of the day,** you mean that is the way people are tending to behave. *Restraint has become the order of the day.*

❏ You say **of the order of** when you are mentioning the approximate size or range of something. *The temperature range is typically of the order of 10 to 30 degrees above absolute zero.*

❏ A religious **order** is a group of monks or nuns who live according to certain rules, often in a religious community. *...the Franciscan order.* ◇ **holy orders:** see **holy.**

❏ Some honours are called **Orders.** *...the Order of the Garter.*

❏ If you do something **in order to** achieve something else, you do it for that reason. *Building societies had threatened to raise their mortgage rates in order to be able to pay more to borrowers.*

Order of Merit See **OM.**

orderly (orderliness; orderlies) ❏ **Orderly** things are well organized or arranged. *...an orderly transfer of power... Advocates of the presidential system argue it introduces a decent orderliness in political life.*

❏ In the past, hospital attendants who carried out routine non-nursing tasks were called **orderlies.**

ordinal number An ordinal number is a number like 'third' or '17th' which tells you what position something has in a group or series. See also **cardinal number.**

ordinance An **ordinance** is an official rule or order.

ordinand An **ordinand** is a person training to be a priest.

ordinary (ordinarily; ordinariness) **Ordinary** people or things are not special in any way. **Ordinary** is sometimes used to say something is dull and disappointing. *Six admirably taken goals could not conceal the ordinariness of what hap-*

pened in between. ◇ **Ordinary** is also used to talk about a normal situation where nothing unusual happens. *...an ordinary working week... The boys are ordinarily used to severe hardships.* ◇ If something is **out of the ordinary,** it is unusual.

ordination See **ordain.**

ordnance is military supplies, especially weapons and ammunition.

Ordnance Survey The Ordnance Survey is the official organization which produces detailed maps of Britain and Ireland.

ordure (*pron:* ord-yoor) is excrement.

ore is rock or earth from which metal can be extracted, for example iron ore.

oregano is a herb used in cooking. It is a type of wild marjoram.

organ (organist) ❏ An **organ** is a part of the body with a particular purpose or function, for example the heart or the lungs.

❏ The **organ** is a large musical instrument with a keyboard or keyboards and pipes of different lengths through which air is forced when the keys are pressed. A person who plays the organ is called an **organist.**

❏ The newspaper or journal of an organization or profession can be called its **organ.** *...the British Medical Journal, the organ of the British medical establishment.*

organdie (*American spelling:* **organdy**) **Organdie** is a sheer, slightly stiff cotton fabric used for making women's or children's clothes.

organic (organically) ❏ **Organic** is used to describe things produced by or found in plants or animals. *The Viking craft that landed on Mars reported that there was no organic material there.*

❏ **Organic** methods of farming and gardening use only natural animal and plant products as fertilizers or pesticides. *The basis of any organic system is compost... ...organically produced food and wine.* Food produced by these methods is also called **organic.** *...organic vegetables.*

❏ You say something is **organic** when it develops naturally without any outside help. *A more buoyant economy will generate tax revenues organically.* ◇ In an **organic** system, all the separate parts fit together in a logical way. *...the organic unity of British society and the state.* When something is an essential part of a system like this, you say it is an **organic** part of it.

organisation (organisational) See **organization.**

organise See **organize.**

organiser See **organizer.**

organism An **organism** is any living animal or plant. Organisms include very small things like bacteria and viruses.

organist See **organ.**

organization (organizational) (*can be spelled with an 's' instead of a 'z'*) ❏ An **organization** is an organized group of people who do something together, for example a business, a charity, or a society.

❏ The **organization** of a system is the way it is planned and run. *...the organization of our schools.* **Organizational** is used to talk about things to do with the organization of a system. *...the party's organizational structure.* ◇ When someone is good at organizing things, you can talk about their **organizational** ability.

❑ The **organization** of something like an activity or public event is the planning and making of arrangements.

organize (organizing, organized) (*can be spelled with an 's' instead of a 'z'*) ❑ If you **organize** an event, you plan it and make all the arrangements. ◇ **Organized** activities are planned and controlled on a large scale and involve a lot of people. *...organized crime.* ◇ **Organized** is also used to describe the way something is run. For example, you say something is 'well-organized' or 'badly-organized'.

❑ When employees **organize**, they form an organization like a union in order to have more power. *...organized labour.*

❑ If you **organize** a number of people or objects, you arrange them into some kind of order or system. *The employees were organized into teams.*

organizer (*or* organiser) ❑ The **organizer** of an activity or event is the person who organizes it.

❑ See also **personal organizer**.

organza is a sheer stiff fabric, made from cotton and silk or cotton and nylon. It is used to make evening dresses.

orgasm An **orgasm** is the moment of greatest pleasure and excitement during sexual activity.

orgy (*pron:* or-jee) (orgies) An **orgy** is a wild uncontrolled party involving a lot of drinking and sexual activity. ◇ If there is an **orgy** of something, people indulge in a lot of it. *...an orgy of lawmaking... ...an orgy of destruction.*

oriel (*pron:* aw-ree-ul) An **oriel** window projects from an upper wall of a building, and is supported by something like a bracket.

orient (oriental; oriented) ❑ The **Orient** is eastern and south-eastern Asia. **Oriental** is used to talk about things to do with the Orient. *...oriental practices such as Zen Buddhism.*

❑ If you **orient** yourself to a new situation, you adjust to it and become familiar with it.

❑ **Oriented** is used to say what a policy or activity is concerned with or directed towards. *...American policies oriented towards maintaining the status quo in Latin America.* ◇ **-oriented** is added to words to show who or what something is designed for. *...adult-oriented films.*

orientalist (orientalism) An **orientalist** is a person from the West who is very interested in things to do with the Orient and knows a lot about them. Interest in the Orient is called **orientalism.**

orientated You use **orientated** to show what someone is interested in or concerned with. *In Argentina, everybody's football orientated.* ◇ **-orientated** is added to words to show who or what something is designed for or directed towards. *...work-orientated courses for schoolchildren.*

orientation ❑ If you talk about a person's **orientation**, you are talking about some aspect of their beliefs or desires. For example, a person's religious orientation is the religion they believe in and practise; their sexual orientation is whether they are attracted to people of their own sex or the opposite sex. Similarly, you can talk about the **orientation** of an organization. *NATO's orientation is becoming less military and more political.*

❑ The **orientation** of something like a building is its position in relation to the points of the compass.

orienteering is a competitive sport in which people run from one place to another across country, using a map

and compass to guide them between checkpoints.

orifice (*pron:* or-if-iss) An **orifice** is an opening or hole, especially one in the body.

origami (*pron:* or-rig-gah-mee) is the Japanese art of folding paper to make it into shapes, for example animals or birds.

origin ❑ If you talk about the **origin** or **origins** of something, you mean the way it started, or what first caused it. *The origins of her defeat went back a long way.*

❑ If you talk about a person's **origin** or **origins**, you mean their family background. *Peruvians are mostly of Indian origin... ...a man of humble origins.*

original (originally, originality) ❑ **Original** is used to talk about the first version of something, which afterwards has to be changed or revised. *His original idea was to use it as his company headquarters... ...the number of planes they originally planned to buy.*

❑ The **original** of something like a document is the first version, rather than a copy.

❑ If you say someone's work or ideas are **original,** you mean they are unlike anything there has been before. You talk about the **originality** of work or ideas like these. Someone who keeps having original ideas can be called an **original.** *Feynman was an original, looking at the world in ways his colleagues could often hardly fathom.* ◇ An **original** is also someone whose behaviour or way of life is very strange and unlike anyone else's.

❑ For Christians, **original sin** is the state of human imperfection everyone is born with as a result of Adam's and Eve's disobedience to God.

originate (originating, originated; originator) ❑ If something **originated** in a place, that is where it started or came from.

❑ If someone **originates** a new idea or invention, they think it up. You say they are the **originator** of the idea or invention. *...Sir Rowland Hill, originator of the penny post.*

ormolu (*pron:* or-mul-oo) is a gold-coloured alloy of copper, tin, or zinc. It is used to add fancy decoration to furniture, picture frames, and clocks.

ornament (ornamented, ornamental, ornamentation) An **ornament** is a small attractive object you display in your home. You can also call a piece of jewellery an **ornament.** ◇ If something is **ornamented**, it is decorated to make it look more attractive. *...heavily ornamented clothes... In the 1920s and 1930s typeface designers dispensed with ornamentation.* ◇ **Ornamental** things are chosen or designed to be attractive rather than useful.

ornate buildings and other objects are highly decorated. *...an incredibly ornate altar.*

ornithology (ornithological, ornithologist) **Ornithology** is the study of birds. **Ornithological** is used to talk about things to do with this study. *...ornithological reference works.* An **ornithologist** is someone who studies birds.

orphan (orphaned) An **orphan** is a child whose parents are dead. You say a child is **orphaned** when its parents die. *He was orphaned at an early age.*

orphanage An **orphanage** is a place where orphans are looked after.

orthodontic (orthodontist) **Orthodontics** is the branch of dentistry concerned with straightening and correcting crooked or irregular teeth. A dentist who specializes in this is called an **orthodontist. Orthodontic** is used to talk about things to do with orthodontics. *...orthodontic care.*

orthodox (orthodoxy, orthodoxies) ❏ **Orthodox** beliefs or methods are ones which most people have or use and which are considered standard. An **orthodoxy** is an accepted view about something. *Another recent orthodoxy is that modern music should be part of normal everyday life.*
❏ The **orthodox** form of a religion or ideology is the older, more traditional form. **Orthodoxy** is traditional and accepted beliefs. ◇ The **Orthodox** Church is the part of the Christian Church which separated from the western European church in the eleventh century. It is the main church in Greece, the former USSR, and some other countries.

orthography (*pron:* or-**thog**-graff-ee) is spelling, especially the spelling system of a particular language.

orthopaedic (*American spelling:* orthopedic) (*pron:* orth-op-**pee**-dik) **Orthopaedic** is used to talk about things to do with the medical care of bones and muscles, especially the treatment or prevention of injuries or defects. *...an orthopaedic surgeon... ...orthopaedic shoes.*

Orwellian You use **Orwellian** to talk about things which remind you of the kind of totalitarian society described in George Orwell's novel '1984'. *There is something grim and Orwellian in the spectacle of kids clocking in to school.*

oryx (*plural:* oryx *or* oryxes) The **oryx** is an African antelope with very long horns.

OS is short for 'Ordnance Survey'.

Oscar An **Oscar** is a gold-plated statuette given as an award for an outstanding performance or achievement in films. Oscars are also called Academy Awards.

oscillate (*pron:* **oss**-ill-late) (oscillating, oscillated; oscillation) ❏ If something **oscillates**, it repeatedly moves backwards and forwards or from side to side. *...an oscillating sprinkler.* ◇ If someone **oscillates** between two moods, they keep changing from one to the other. *...oscillation between despair and distracted joy.*
❏ An **oscillating** electric current changes in the direction of its flow at rapid regular intervals.

osier (*pron:* **oh**-zee-er) The **osier** is a kind of willow tree. Its twigs are used for making baskets.

osmosis (*pron:* oz-**moh**-siss) ❏ **Osmosis** is a process by which a liquid passes through the thin outer layer of something and is soaked up by what is on the other side, for example the way moisture is soaked up through the roots of a plant.
❏ When someone seems to pick up knowledge about something without apparently learning it in the normal way, people sometimes say they acquire it by **osmosis**.

osprey (*usual pron:* **oss**-pray) The **osprey** is a large bird of prey which feeds on fish. It swoops down and catches the fish with its talons.

ossified If a soft object **ossifies**, it gradually becomes hard like bone. ◇ If you talk about other things **ossifying**, you mean they become fixed and difficult to change. *The time had come to reform Britain's ossified medical education system.*

ostensible (ostensibly) The **ostensible** purpose of something is the official or apparent purpose, which may not be the real one. Similarly, you can talk about the **ostensible** reason for something. *The ostensible reason for his party wanting to get rid of him is that he is in poor health... The pass has recently been closed, ostensibly because of landslides.*

ostentatious (ostentatiously; ostentation) **Ostentatious** things are expensive and showy, and intended to impress people. *...ostentatiously fake fur, dyed in bright colours.* ◇ You say people are **ostentatious** when they show off their wealth. *...an ostentatious elite.* Showing off wealth is called **ostentation.** ◇ If you do something in an **ostentatious** way, you do it in an exaggerated way, to make sure someone notices it. *We were ostentatiously followed in cars, to remind us who held the real power.*

osteopath (*pron:* oss-tee-oh-**path**) (osteopathy) An **osteopath** is a person who carries out a method of medical treatment based on the manipulation of joints, especially in the spine. This kind of treatment is called **osteopathy** (*pron:* oss-tee-**op**-path-ee).

osteoporosis (*pron:* oss-tee-oh-pore-**roh**-siss) is a condition in which the bones become very brittle. It particularly affects older women.

ostracize (ostracizing, ostracized; ostracism) (*can be spelled with an 's' instead of a 'z'*) If someone is **ostracized**, people deliberately behave in an unfriendly way towards them and do not let them join in things. Behaving like this towards someone is called **ostracism.**

ostrich (ostriches) The **ostrich** is a fast-running flightless African bird with a long bare neck, long legs, and two toes on each foot. It is the largest living bird. ◇ If you say someone is like an **ostrich**, you mean they refuse to accept the truth about something, just as an ostrich is supposed to bury its head in the sand when there is danger.

other ❏ If you have mentioned one of a pair of things or people, you call the second one **the other.** ◇ If you have mentioned some of the things or people in a group, you use **other** or **others** to talk about some or all of the remaining ones. *Some defendants were given bail, while others were remanded in custody... The other 343 seats on the plane remained empty.*
❏ You use **or other** after words like 'some' or 'something' to show you are not sure of the identity of something or someone. *...appearing in some play or other... He was playing the Sibelius concerto with someone or other.* ◇ **One or other** of a group of things or people means any of them, rather than one in particular. *Some areas still come under frequent shelling from one or other of the four warring factions.* ◇ **each other:** see **each.**
❏ If you say something happened the **other day** or the **other week**, you mean it happened recently. ◇ If something happens **every other day**, it happens on alternate days. *The election is held every other year.*
❏ You say **among other things** to show the thing you are mentioning is only one of several things. *They insist, among other things, that efficiency must be combined with fairness.*
❏ You use **other than** to introduce an exception to what you have just mentioned. *The latest round of talks made little progress, other than to set a date for another meeting.*

otherwise ❏ You use **otherwise** to say what will happen if something is not done. *Local authorities will have to stay within spending limits, otherwise they will be capped.*

❑ You use **otherwise** to talk about the opposite possibility from the one you have just mentioned. *He may be right, but history suggests otherwise... The children of unconventional families, single-parent or otherwise, should not be penalised.*

❑ You also use **otherwise** to say something would have a quality completely, if it were not for the thing you have just mentioned. *Hundreds of looters attacked shops during an otherwise peaceful march... The tourists were tired and dusty but otherwise unharmed.*

otherworldly You say something is **otherworldly** when it seems to belong to a world of ghosts or fairies, rather than the real world. *...otherworldly music.*

otiose (*pron:* oh-tee-oze) If you say something is **otiose**, you mean it is meaningless or pointless. *In my view, any more discussion as to whether global warming is taking place is simply otiose.*

otter The **otter** is a small animal with thick smooth dark-brown fur, a long tail, and webbed feet. Otters are extremely good swimmers and feed on fish.

ottoman ❑ An **ottoman** is a long low upholstered seat. Some ottomans have a storage space under the seat.

❑ The **Ottoman Empire** was the Turkish empire in parts of Europe, Asia, and Africa which lasted from the 13th century to the end of World War I. **Ottoman** is used to talk about things to do with this empire. *...Ottoman architecture.*

ought ❑ If you say something **ought to** happen, you mean you think it is right or a good idea. *If he's done wrong, he ought to be punished.* ◇ You also say something **ought to** happen when you are expecting it to happen. *She ought to win.*

❑ If you say something **ought to have** happened, you mean it would have been right or a good thing if it had happened, but it did not in fact happen. *I ought to have been a footballer.*

Ouija (*pron:* wee-ja) A **Ouija board** is a board marked with the letters of the alphabet. Some people think messages from the dead can be spelled out by a pointer moving around the board from one letter to another. 'Ouija' is a trademark.

ounce Weight is often expressed in **ounces**. An ounce is about 28.35 grams. There are sixteen ounces in a pound. 'Ounces' is usually shortened to 'oz.' ◇ An **ounce** of something is a very small amount of it. *If only my father had possessed an ounce of business sense.*

our (ours) You use **our** or **ours** when you are talking about something belonging to or connected with two or more people including yourself. *...our two children... Many carriages were empty, but ours was packed.*

ourselves You use **ourselves** to say something which is done by you and other people affects only you and those people. *We committed ourselves to this decision a long time ago.* ◇ You also use **ourselves** to emphasize that your statement really does apply to you and the other people you have been talking about. *Change would only be possible if we ourselves wanted it.*

oust If someone is **ousted** from a job or place, they are forced to leave.

out ❑ When you go **out** of a place or get **out** of a vehicle, you move so you are no longer in it.

❑ If you are **out**, you are not in your home or your usual place of work. ◇ If you are **out and about,** you are going to places and meeting people, rather than staying at home. ◇ If you have a day **out** or an evening **out,** you spend that period away from your home or work, usually enjoying yourself in some way.

❑ **Out** is used to talk about someone leaving an institution. *Life is going to be very difficult for him when he comes out of prison.*

❑ **Out** is used to talk about an object being removed from an enclosed space. *He takes an apple out of his pocket.* ◇ **Out** is used to talk about other things being removed from the place where they are normally kept. *Depositors would yank their money out of the bank at the first opportunity.*

❑ If you see something **out** of a window, you see it through the window from the inside of a building or vehicle.

❑ **Out** is used to talk about going to a distant place. *He went out to West Africa.* ◇ **Out** is used to say how far a place is from a town or city. *...three miles out of Stratford-on-Avon.* ◇ **Out** is used to talk about a number of things being sent to several places. *Invitations to the conference have gone out to government ministers.*

❑ If someone or something is kept **out** of a place, they are prevented from getting in.

❑ You say something is **out** when it is made available for people to buy or see. *His book is now out in paperback.* ◇ When a secret is revealed, you can say it is **out.**

❑ If a light is **out,** it is not shining. ◇ If a fire is **out,** it is not burning.

❑ You say flowers are **out** when their petals have opened.

❑ If workers are **out,** they are on strike.

❑ In sport, if someone is **out** of a competition, they have been eliminated. ◇ In cricket, if a batsman is **out,** the opposing team has put an end to his or her innings, in one of various ways.

❑ If a calculation or measurement is **out,** it is incorrect. ◇ If you say something like a proposal or suggestion is **out,** you mean it is unacceptable or will not be considered. ◇ When something is no longer fashionable, you can say it is **out.**

❑ **Out** is used to talk about a period of time coming to an end. *Those numbers could double before the week is out.*

❑ If someone is **out** to do something, they intend to do it.

❑ If you are **out of** something, you no longer have any of it.

❑ If something is made **out of** a certain material, it is made from it.

❑ **Out of** is used to express proportions. *Leicester had lost seven out of eight matches.*

❑ **Out of** is used to say why someone does something. *She must have deprived him of it out of sheer spite.*

❑ If something gives you pleasure, you can say you get pleasure **out of** it. Similarly, you can get satisfaction or a thrill **out of** something.

❑ If someone is **outed,** especially someone famous, their homosexuality is made public knowledge against their wishes, usually by someone who is also homosexual.

out- is put at the beginning of some words to form new words. Words formed like this describe someone doing something better than someone else and beating them at it. *Foreman outboxed Joe Frazier to become the world heavyweight champion... The bank outperformed its rivals with a record pre-tax profit.*

out-and-out is used to say someone or something has all the characteristics of a certain type of person or thing. *He is an out-and-out winner... It's out-and-out criminal damage.*

out-of-court See court.

out-of-date See date.

out-of-doors See door.

out-of-the-way places are remote and seldom visited.

out-of-touch See touch.

out-of-work See work.

out-patient An **out-patient** is a person who receives treatment in hospital but does not stay overnight.

out-take An **out-take** is a piece of film or part of a recorded TV programme which is cut out and not included in the final version, usually because it contains mistakes.

outback The remote areas of Australia are called the **outback**.

outbid (outbidding, outbid *not 'outbidded'*) If you **outbid** someone, you offer more than them for something you both want to buy. ◇ You can also say someone **outbids** someone else when they make a more attractive promise or offer. *Banks are trying to outbid each other's interest rates.*

outboard motor An **outboard motor** is a portable motor with a propeller, for attaching to a small boat.

outbox See out-.

outbreak An **outbreak** of something unpleasant is a sudden widespread occurrence of it. *...an outbreak of violence... ...cholera outbreaks.*

outbuilding An **outbuilding** is a building like a garage or barn which belongs to a house but is not part of the main living area.

outburst An **outburst** is a sudden strong expression of anger or some other emotion. *...an outburst of fury.* ◇ If there is an **outburst** of an activity, there is suddenly a lot of it. *...a sudden outburst of price-cutting.*

outcast You say someone is an **outcast** when people in their community or people they work with refuse to have anything to do with them. *The senator was a virtual outcast among his fellow Republicans.*

outclass (outclasses, outclassing, outclassed) If you **outclass** someone, you do something much better than they do.

outcome The **outcome** of something is its result.

outcrop An **outcrop** is a large area of rock sticking up out of the ground.

outcry (outcries) If there is an **outcry** about something, a lot of people get angry about it.

outdated If something is **outdated**, it is old-fashioned and no longer useful. *...outdated industries.*

outdistance (outdistancing, outdistanced) If you **outdistance** someone, you progress faster or more successfully than they do and leave them behind. *He has managed to outdistance his colleagues and critics to emerge as one of the most respected directors working in Hollywood.*

outdo (outdoes, outdoing, outdid, have outdone) If you **outdo** someone, you are more successful at something than they are. ◇ You say **not to be outdone...** when describing how someone responds to another person's actions by trying to do something better. *Not to be outdone, France exported vodka to Russia.*

outdoor (outdoors) **Outdoor** is used to describe things which take place or are used in the open air, rather than in a building. *...outdoor festivals... ...outdoor shoes.* ◇ If something happens or is located **outdoors**, it happens or is located in the open air. ◇ The **outdoors** is the open air. *She loved the outdoors and had a sense of adventure.*

outer The **outer** one of two things is the one which is outside the other. *...the prison's outer wall.* ◇ The **outer** parts of something are the parts furthest from its centre. *...the rundown areas between the city centre and the outer suburbs.*

outer space is any region of space beyond the Earth's atmosphere.

outermost The **outermost** of several things is the one furthest from the centre of something. *...Saturn's outermost ring.*

outfall An **outfall** is the end of a drain, where water pours out.

outfit An **outfit** is (a) a set of clothes. *His outfit consisted of a T-shirt and trousers.* (b) an organization or group of people. *...a retail and merchant-banking outfit.*

outfitter A gentlemen's **outfitter** or **outfitters** is a shop which sells men's clothes. Other kinds of shops selling clothes are also called **outfitters**. *...sports outfitters.*

outflank If an army **outflanks** another one, it manages to get round its side, to make an attack. ◇ If you **outflank** someone, for example in an argument, you get into a position where you can defeat them. *Labour has to outflank the Conservatives with a new strategy if it is to shake hard-core Conservative support.*

outflow ❑ When there is an **outflow** of something like money or resources, large amounts are transferred from one place or organization to another. *The group expected a cash outflow of £350m over the next four months.*

❑ The movement of large numbers of people out of a place can also be called an **outflow**. *...a massive outflow of emigrants towards Western Europe.*

outfox (outfoxes, outfoxing, outfoxed) If you **outfox** someone, you manage to beat them by being more clever or cunning.

outgoing is used to describe someone who will shortly be leaving their job or position. *...the outgoing chairman.*

❑ **Outgoing** is also used to describe something which is going out of a place. *The system allows only outgoing calls.*

❑ A person's or organization's **outgoings** are the amounts of money they spend or pay out.

❑ An **outgoing** person is friendly and enjoys meeting people.

outgrow (outgrowing, outgrew, have outgrown) ❑ If you **outgrow** an item of clothing, you get bigger and can no longer wear it. ◇ When people **outgrow** a place, the size of their family or business increases and there is no longer enough room for them.

❑ If you **outgrow** something like a type of behaviour or a way of life, you become more mature and no longer behave or live in that way. *She outgrew her little-girl awkwardness.*

outgrowth If something is an **outgrowth** of something else, it begins by being part of it, then gradually develops into a separate thing. *The Actors' Studio was an out-*

growth of the Group Theatre.

outgun (outgunning, outgunned) In war, if an army is **outgunned**, their opponents have a greater number of guns, or use them more effectively. ◇ If someone is **outgunned** in a sporting contest, they are beaten, because their opponents have greater strength, speed, or ability.

outhouse An **outhouse** is a small building attached to a house or in its garden.

outing ❑ An **outing** is a pleasure trip or excursion. ❑ When a sportsperson or team takes part in an event, this is sometimes called an **outing**. *He had a very hard race on his previous outing.*

outjump See out-.

outlandish (outlandishly) If you say something is **outlandish**, you mean it is strikingly unusual or strange. *Many of the clothes looked outlandish... ...his outlandish political views.*

outlast If something **outlasts** something else, it is still there when the other thing has gone.

outlaw When something is **outlawed**, it is made illegal. *...an international convention outlawing the possession of chemical weapons... ...outlawed paramilitary groups.* ◇ In the past, a criminal on the run was called an **outlaw**.

outlay An **outlay** is an amount of money spent on something by a company or other organization.

outlet ❑ An **outlet** is a means of releasing or expressing something like feelings or creative impulses. *Out-of-work engineers and scientists should be able to find plenty of creative outlets for their energy.* ❑ An **outlet** is also (a) a market for a product or service. *BSB will provide another outlet for Granada to sell programmes to.* (b) a shop or commercial organization selling goods made by a particular manufacturer. ❑ Something which provides a way out of a place can be called an **outlet**. *For years Assab has been Ethiopia's main outlet to the sea.* ◇ An **outlet** is also something like a hole or pipe which water or air can flow out of. *...a sewage outlet.*

outline (outlining, outlined) ❑ If you **outline** an idea or plan, you explain it in a general way without going into details. A general explanation can be called an **outline**. ◇ If something is given **outline** approval, it is approved in principle, with the details to be agreed later. ❑ If you can see the **outline** of something, you can see its general shape or silhouette, but no other details. You can also talk about seeing something **outlined** against something else. *...a tall, slender figure in black, sharply outlined against the white marble.*

outlive (outliving, outlived) ❑ If you **outlive** someone, you live longer than them. ❑ If something **outlives** something else, it is still there when the other thing has finished. *It is likely that widespread Sunday trading will outlive the festive season.* ◇ If something has **outlived its usefulness**, it is still around but is no longer useful or necessary.

outlook ❑ A person's **outlook** is their general attitude towards life. ◇ The **outlook** in a situation is the way things seem likely to develop. *The economic outlook is one of rising unemployment and sagging investment.* ❑ The **outlook** from a room or building is the view.

outlying The **outlying** parts of a place are the parts a long way from its centre. *...one of Hong Kong's outlying islands... ...refugees who have come into the town from the outlying countryside.*

outmanoeuvre (outmanoeuvring, outmanoeuvred) (*American spelling:* outmaneuver, outmaneuvring, *etc*) If you **outmanoeuvre** someone, you gain an advantage over them by being more clever or more skilful.

outmatch (outmatches, outmatching, outmatched) If you **outmatch** someone or **outmatch** what they do, you are more successful than they are at something.

outmoded things are old-fashioned and no longer useful.

outnumber (outnumbering, outnumbered) If one group **outnumbers** another, it has more people or things in it.

outpace (outpacing, outpaced) If you **outpace** someone, you go faster than they do. *Travelling at speeds of up to 35 knots, these hovercraft can easily outpace most boats.* ◇ If something **outpaces** something else, it grows at a faster rate. *The Japanese economy will continue to outpace its foreign rivals for years to come.*

outperform See out-.

outplacement firms offer counselling and careers advice to redundant executive or professional staff, or advice to businesses dealing with redundancy. ◇ Redundancy itself is sometimes called **outplacement**.

outplay See out-.

outpoll (*pron:* out-pole) If someone **outpolls** someone else in an election, they get more votes than the other person.

outpost An **outpost** is a small settlement a long way from a main centre, usually set up as a branch of a large organization. *...isolated government outposts... ...an army outpost.*

outpouring You say there is an **outpouring** of something when a large amount of it is produced suddenly and rapidly. *...an outpouring of editorials and television programmes.* ◇ When people express strong feelings in an uncontrolled way, you can talk about an **outpouring** of these feelings. *...public outpourings of grief.*

output The **output** of something is the amount which is made or produced. *Manufacturing output rose strongly... ...a loss of oil output from North Sea oil rigs.* ◇ The **output** from a TV or radio channel is the programmes it broadcasts. ◇ The **output** of a computer is the information it sorts and produces as a result of a program or operation. See also **input**.

outrage (outraging, outraged; outrageous, outrageously) ❑ If you are **outraged** at something which has happened, you are very shocked and angry about it. You say something like this is **outrageous** or an **outrage**; you can also call your feelings about it **outrage**. *This is an outrageous miscarriage of justice... ...outrageously racist insults... The proposals have caused outrage in the German press.* ❑ You also say someone's behaviour is **outrageous** when it goes beyond what is normally acceptable. *She flirted with him outrageously.*

outran See outrun.

outrank In organizations like the armed forces or the police, if one person **outranks** another, they have a higher rank. ◇ You also say a person or organization **outranks** another one when they have reached a higher level of success or power. *Renault now outranks Fiat and Nissan as Germany's top supplier of foreign cars.*

outré (*pron:* oo-tray) is used to describe things which are very unusual and rather shocking. *He cut an outré figure in his three-piece electric-blue suit.*

outreach is a system in which an organization deliberately sets out to make its services or facilities known and available to people who may otherwise be unaware of what it has to offer.

outrider An **outrider** is a member of the armed forces or police who rides on a motorbike or horse alongside or in front of an official vehicle to protect and escort the people in it.

outright is used to describe something which is complete and absolute. *...an outright victory... Neither man won an outright majority... They view their student leaders with suspicion, if not outright distrust.*
  ❑ If you come out with something **outright**, you say it in an open and direct way, rather than just hinting at it. *He is too skilful a politician to ask outright for an end to sanctions.*
  ❑ If someone is **killed outright**, they are killed at once, rather than being injured and dying slowly.

outrun (outrunning, outran) If you **outrun** someone, you run faster than they do. ◇ If something **outruns** something else, it develops at a faster rate. *...the extent to which spending could outrun the capacity of businesses to produce the goods.*

outsell (outselling, outsold) If one product **outsells** another, it is sold in larger quantities.

outset The **outset** of something is its very beginning. You say something happens **at the outset** of an event or is done **from** its **outset**. *The company has been concerned from the outset to ensure that the design has the necessary adaptability and economy.*

outshine (outshining, outshone) If you **outshine** someone at something, you are better at it than them.

outside ❑ The **outside** of something like a building or container is the part which faces outwards. ◇ If you are **outside** a building, you are close to its outside. *A few students demonstrated outside parliament.*
  ❑ If something happens **outside** a country, it happens somewhere else. *He said he would be forced to work outside Britain.*
  ❑ If a place is cut off from other places, you can call the other places **the outside world**. *Tibet remains as isolated from the outside world as it ever was.*
  ❑ If someone is **outside** an organization, they do not belong to it. *A third of these men have been appointed from outside the civil service... Products were bought in from outside suppliers.*
  ❑ If someone operates **outside** the law, they achieve what they want by illegal means. ◇ If something is **outside** your control or authority, you have no control or authority over it.
  ❑ If something happens **outside** certain hours, it happens at some other time. *Emergency cover will be provided outside surgery hours.*
  ❑ If something you do is just **outside** a record, you just fail to beat the record. *Jackson was only the tiniest of fractions outside his Commonwealth and European record.*
  ❑ If you say there is an **outside chance** of something happening, you mean there is a remote possibility it might happen.

outside broadcast An **outside broadcast** is a TV or radio programme which is not filmed or recorded in a studio.

outsider Someone who does not belong to a particular group can be called an **outsider**. *The job should not go to an outsider.* ◇ A horse which is considered unlikely to win a race is also called an **outsider**.

outsize or **outsized** things are much larger than the usual size. *...her outsized lumberjack shirt... ...an outsize desk.*

outskirts The **outskirts** of a city or town are the parts you come to first when you enter it.

outsmart If you **outsmart** someone, you get the better of them.

outspoken (outspokenness) If someone is **outspoken**, they tend to say what they think, even if it shocks or offends people. *He was taken aback by the visitor's outspokenness.*

outstanding (outstandingly) ❑ You say someone is **outstanding** when they are extremely good at something. *...one of England's outstanding players.* You also say what they do or achieve is **outstanding**. *All his novels were outstandingly well written.* ◇ An **outstanding** example of something is a particularly good or admirable one. *The Body Shop is an outstanding example of a small business that grew into a big one.*
  ❑ An **outstanding** issue or problem has not yet been resolved. ◇ If a debt is **outstanding**, it has not been paid off.

outstay ❑ If someone **outstays** the period they are supposed to be in a place, they are still there when they should have gone. ◇ If someone has **outstayed their welcome**, people are annoyed or irritated by them and wish they would go away.
  ❑ If someone **outstays** someone else, they are still in their place or position when the other person has gone.

outstretched is used to describe someone's hand, arm, foot, etc when they have stretched it out as far as it will go. *Walker deflected the ball around the post with his outstretched leg.*

outstrip (outstripping, outstripped) If something **outstrips** something else, it becomes greater. *Demand is outstripping supply.* ◇ If you **outstrip** someone else, you are more successful than they are. *He outstrips his rival in all the opinion polls.*

outvote (outvoting, outvoted) If someone is **outvoted**, they are defeated because their opponents get more votes than they do.

outward (outwardly, outwards) ❑ If something moves or faces **outward** or **outwards**, it moves or faces away from the inside or centre of something. ◇ If you go to a place and come back, your **outward** journey is your journey there.
  ❑ **Outward-looking** people are interested in other people and things and want to develop relations with them.
  ❑ **Outward** and **outwardly** are used to talk about the way people and things appear, which may be different from the way they really are. *There are no outward signs of political discontent... Outwardly it's an old-fashioned club in a smart street off Piccadilly.*

outward bound courses provide training in adventurous outdoor pursuits, usually for young people.

outweigh If the bad things in a situation **outweigh** the good ones, there are more bad things than good ones.

outwit (outwitting, outwitted) If you **outwit** someone, you cleverly defeat them or gain an advantage over them.

outworn beliefs or customs are old-fashioned and no

longer have any meaning or usefulness.

ouzo (*pron:* ooze-oh) is a strong aniseed-flavoured spirit from Greece.

ova See ovum.

oval An oval is a round two-dimensional shape, like a circle but wider in one direction than the other.

ovary (*pron:* oh-var-ree) (ovaries; ovarian) A woman's ovaries are the two small organs in her body which produce eggs. Ovarian (*pron:* oh-vair-ee-an) is used to talk about things to do with the ovaries. *...ovarian cancer.*

ovation An ovation is a long and enthusiastic round of applause from an audience. If someone receives a **standing ovation**, the audience all stand up and applaud them, to show extreme approval or pleasure.

oven An oven is the box-shaped part of a cooker with a door at the front, which food can be heated up or cooked in.

oven-proof dishes are made from special materials which prevent them being damaged by heat in an oven.

oven-ready foods are bought already prepared for cooking in an oven.

over ❑ If something is over something else, it is on top of it or directly above it. ◇ If you go over something, you cross from one side to the other. Similarly, if you look over something, you look from one side to the other. *Elderly couples sat on benches looking over the bay.* ◇ Over is used to say something is on the other side of something like a road or boundary. *...just over the border from Hong Kong's new territories.*
❑ If you go over to a place, you make your way there. ◇ In broadcasting, announcers say over to when they are introducing a speaker in a different place. *Now it's over to the sports desk.*
❑ Over is used to talk about the extent of something. *Crops have been damaged over a wide area.* ◇ All over a place means in every part of it.
❑ If something is over a limit, it is beyond it. *...driving while over the alcohol limit.* ◇ Over in front of a number means 'more than'. *Over two hundred people were arrested.* ◇ If you are over a certain age, you are older than that age.
❑ Over and above means 'in addition to'. *...a pay award over and above the 4.5% cost of living rise.*
❑ If you hear something over other noise, you hear it in spite of it.
❑ If something happens over a period of time, it happens during that time. If you do something over a meal, you do it while having the meal.
❑ Over is used to talk about ways of sending or receiving a message. *...talking over a digital telephone link.*
❑ You can use over to say how many times something has happened. *He was world champion three times over.* ◇ If you do something over and over or over and over again, you do it many times.
❑ If something is over, it is finished. ◇ If something is left over, it is still there when other things have been removed.
❑ Over is used to say what is being dealt with or discussed. *The ministers were trying to reach a compromise over a plan put forward by the EU Commission.* ◇ Over is also used to say why something is done to someone. *He came in for a lot of criticism over his decision to abstain on the crucial vote.*

❑ In cricket, an over is six consecutive balls bowled from the same end of the pitch.

over- ❑ Some words beginning with 'over' can be spelled with a hyphen after the 'r'. See, for example, entries at **overestimate, overreach.**
❑ over- is used to form words which say there is too much of something, or that something is done to too great an extent. *...over-production of cereals... ...over-ambitious plans for expansion... ...Arsenal's over-confidence.*

over-emphasis If you say there is over-emphasis on a certain thing, you mean it is given more importance than it deserves.

over-emphasize (*can be spelled with an 's' instead of a 'z'*) If you over-emphasize something, you give it too much importance.

over-react (over-reaction) If you over-react to something, you react in a more extreme way than is normal or necessary. *There should be an inquiry into whether police over-reaction made matters worse.*

overact If you say an actor is overacting, you mean he or she is playing a part in an exaggerated and unconvincing way.

overall ❑ You use overall when you are talking about the whole of something, rather than just parts of it. *...an overall increase in economic growth... He was still in overall charge.* ◇ If a political party wins an overall majority in an election, they win more votes or seats than the total number gained by all their opponents put together.
❑ An overall is a loose lightweight coat, with or without sleeves, which you wear over your clothes to protect them while you are working. ◇ Overalls are a single item of clothing consisting of a top and loose trousers joined together and worn over ordinary clothes to protect them.

overarm If you throw or hit a ball overarm, your arm is raised above your shoulder and moves forward and down.

overawe (overawing, overawed) If you are overawed by someone or something, you are very impressed by them and a little afraid of them.

overbalance (overbalancing, overbalanced) If you overbalance, you fall over or nearly fall over, because you have got into an unstable position.

overbearing An overbearing person is unpleasant and domineering.

overblown If you say something is overblown, you mean it is exaggerated or excessive. *Warnings of disaster may be overblown.* ◇ You say flowers are overblown when they are open wide and the petals are about to fall off.

overboard If you fall overboard, you fall over the side of a ship into the water.

overburdened If you are overburdened with something like work or problems, you have more than you can cope with.

overcame See overcome.

overcast If the sky is overcast, there are a lot of clouds.

overcharge (overcharging, overcharged) If someone overcharges you, they charge you too much for something.

overcoat An overcoat is a thick warm coat.

overcome (overcoming, overcame, have overcome) ❑ If you overcome someone, for example in a fight or struggle, you get control of them. ◇ If you overcome a problem, you deal with it successfully. ◇ If you overcome a feeling, you succeed in controlling it.

❑ If you are **overcome** by a feeling, you feel it very strongly. *She was overcome by horror.* ◇ If you are **overcome** by something like heat or smoke, you are seriously affected by it, so that, for example, you collapse or become unconscious.

overcrowded (overcrowding) If a place is **overcrowded**, there are too many people or things there. *...overcrowding on London's commuter rail links.*

overdo (overdoes, overdoing, overdid, have overdone) ❑ If you **overdo** something, you do it in an exaggerated way, or you do it too much. *While an occasional drink can be pleasant, overdoing it depresses the central nervous system.* ◇ You also say someone **overdoes** things when they try to do more than they can physically manage.

❑ You say food is **overdone** when it has been cooked for too long.

overdose (overdosing, overdosed) If someone **overdoses** or takes an **overdose**, they take more of a drug than is safe, and may lose consciousness and die.

overdraft If someone has an **overdraft**, their bank allows them to draw out more money than they have in their account, up to a certain amount and at a fixed rate of interest.

overdrawn If a person is **overdrawn**, they have drawn more money out of the bank than they have in their account. You also say their account is **overdrawn**.

overdressed If you say someone is **overdressed**, you mean they are dressed too elaborately or formally.

overdrive If something goes into **overdrive**, it operates in an unusually rapid or intense way. *His imagination went into overdrive... The government propaganda machine spun into overdrive.* ◇ **Overdrive** in a motor vehicle is an extra higher gear used at high speeds to reduce engine wear and save petrol.

overdue If you say something is **overdue**, you mean it should have happened sooner. *I'll go and pay an overdue visit to my mother.* ◇ If someone or something is late in arriving, you can say they are **overdue**. *...a long-overdue train.* ◇ If something like a payment is **overdue**, it is past the time when it should have been paid.

overeat (overeating, overate, have overeaten) If you **overeat**, you eat more than you need or more than is healthy.

overestimate (overestimating, overestimated) (*or* **overestimate**, *etc*) If you **overestimate** someone or something, you think they are bigger, better, or more important than they really are.

overflow ❑ When a liquid **overflows**, it flows over the edges of the container it is in. Similarly, you say a river or stream **overflows** when it flows over the edge of its banks. ◇ An **overflow** is a hole or pipe through which liquid can flow out of a container when it gets too full.

❑ If something is **overflowing** with things, it is full of them. *The street stalls are overflowing with fresh fruit and vegetables.* ◇ If someone is **overflowing** with a feeling, they are full of it and this shows in their behaviour. *She was overflowing with optimism.*

overfly (overflies, overflying, overflew, have overflown; overflight) When an aircraft **overflies** an area, it flies over it without landing. This is called an **overflight**.

overgrown You say an area is **overgrown** when it is covered with plants which have become too large or too thick. ◇ You also use **overgrown** to describe an adult who behaves in a childish way. *...an overgrown schoolboy.*

overhang (overhanging, overhung) ❑ If something **overhangs** something else, it sticks out above it from a higher place. *There are shady trees overhanging the garden.* The part of something which sticks out above something else can be called an **overhang**. *...red roofs with overhangs to carry snow safely away.*

❑ If something unpleasant **overhangs** a situation, it is there in the background and may spoil things. *This is the dispute that overhangs prospects for success... ...their huge overhang of foreign debt.*

overhaul (overhauling, overhauled) ❑ If you **overhaul** a piece of equipment or give it an **overhaul**, you clean and check it thoroughly and repair it if necessary. Similarly, if a system is **overhauled** or given an **overhaul**, it is examined carefully and changes may be made to it.

❑ If you **overhaul** someone who is moving in the same direction, you pass them, because you are moving faster. ◇ You can also say one person or organization **overhauls** another one when they become more successful or profitable.

overhead ❑ If something is **overhead**, it is above you, or above the place you are talking about. *A helicopter circled overhead... ...overhead luggage racks.*

❑ The **overheads** of a business are its regular essential expenses, for example wages and salaries, rent, and telephone bills.

overhear (overhearing, overheard) If you **overhear** a conversation, you hear what the people are saying.

overheat (overheating, overheated) ❑ If something **overheats**, it gets too hot.

❑ If a country's economy **overheats**, inflation increases rapidly, often because of excessive growth in demand.

overjoyed If you are **overjoyed**, you are extremely pleased about something.

overkill You say there is **overkill** when something is spoiled by being done too much.

overland is used to talk about journeys made across land rather than on water or by air.

overlap (overlapping, overlapped) If two things **overlap**, part of one covers part of the other. When this happens, you say there is an **overlap**. ◇ If two ideas or activities **overlap**, they involve some of the same subjects, people, or periods of time. *...the overlap between civil and military technology.*

overlay (overlaying, overlaid) If something is **overlaid** with something else, the second thing forms a cover over the first one. An **overlay** is something which forms a cover over something else. *She peeled back the overlay to reveal the illustration beneath.* ◇ If you talk about one characteristic in a book or film being **overlaid** with another, you mean both are present at the same time. *...bitter humour overlaying stark tragedy.*

overleaf is used to say something is on the next page. *Look at chart 22 overleaf.*

overload (overloading, overloaded) When a vehicle is **overloaded**, there are too many people or things in it. Similarly, you can talk about a place being **overloaded**. *The city is already overloaded with visitors.* ◇ If a person or organization is **overloaded** with work or problems, they have more than they can manage. You can talk about an overload of work or problems. ◇ If an electrical system is **overloaded,** too many electrical appliances are being used, and the system is likely to be damaged.

overlook (overlooking, overlooked) ❑ If a building **overlooks** a place, you get a view of the place from it. *...fisherman's cottages overlooking the beach.*

❑ If you **overlook** a feature of something or a fact about it, you ignore it, do not notice it, or do not realize its importance. *The official figures overlook considerable concealed unemployment.* ◇ If you **overlook** someone's faults or bad behaviour, you decide to ignore them.

❑ You say a person is **overlooked** when they are not chosen for a job or position.

overlord In the past, an **overlord** was a person who had power over many people.

overly is used to talk about the strength of someone's feelings. For example, if you say someone is **overly** excited, you mean they are too excited; if you say they are not **overly** pleased about something, you mean they are not very pleased about it.

overmanning (overmanned) If there is **overmanning** in a workplace or if it is **overmanned,** there are too many workers there.

overmuch means the same as 'too much'. *It did not really matter overmuch.*

overnight is used to describe (a) things which last all night. *...an overnight curfew.* (b) things which happen during the night. *...overnight rain.* ◇ An **overnight** bag is big enough to contain your clothes and belongings when you stay somewhere for one or two nights.

❑ **Overnight** is also used to describe something which happens suddenly. *...an overnight success... You can't expect the habits of centuries to disappear overnight.*

overpay (overpaying, overpaid) If you say someone is **overpaid,** you mean they are paid too much for the work they do.

overplay If you **overplay** something, you make it seem more important than it really is. ◇ If you **overplay your hand,** you act too confidently because you think you are in a stronger position than you really are.

overpopulated (overpopulation) An **overpopulated** city or country has too many people living in it. *Along with overpopulation, the country faces overwhelming poverty and high unemployment.*

overpower (overpowering, overpowered) ❑ If you **overpower** someone in a fight or struggle, you get control of them, because you are stronger than they are. ◇ If one sportsperson or team **overpowers** another, they play better and manage to defeat them.

❑ You say something is **overpowering** when it affects you very strongly. *The scent from lilies is almost overpowering... His urge to write was an overpowering one.*

overpriced things cost more than they are worth.

overran See overrun.

overrated If you say something is **overrated,** you mean people think it is better or more important than it really is.

overreach (overreaches, overreaching, overreached) (*or* **overreach,** *etc*) If you **overreach** yourself, you fail to achieve something because you try to be too clever or try to do more than you can.

override (overriding, overrode, have overridden) ❑ If some-

thing **overrides** other things, it is regarded as more important than them. *The Chancellor's concern to avoid a mortgage rate increase overrides all other considerations... The overriding need was to find a leader who could unite the party.*

❑ If someone **overrides** an order or decision made by someone else, they cancel or change it. You can also say they **override** the person who gave the order or made the decision.

❑ If you **override** a device which is normally automatic, you operate it by hand.

overrule (overruling, overruled) If a decision is **overruled,** someone in authority officially decides it is incorrect or invalid.

overrun (overrunning, overran, have overrun) ❑ If an army **overruns** a place, it captures every part of it. ◇ You can say a place is **overrun** by people or things when there are too many of them there. *Britain has never been so overrun with big outdoor rock concerts as it is this summer.*

❑ If an event **overruns,** it goes on longer than it was intended to.

❑ If a project turns out to be more expensive than was originally planned or expected, you can say there is a **cost overrun.**

oversaw See oversee.

overseas is used to talk about things and people connected with countries across the sea. *...overseas branches of banks... ...overseas aid... ...overseas visitors.*

oversee (overseeing, oversaw, have overseen; overseer) When someone **oversees** something, they watch it being done, to make sure it is done properly. You also say they **oversee** the people doing it. A person or organization that oversees something can be called an **overseer.** *The Bank of England would have to act as an official overseer.*

oversell (overselling, oversold) If you **oversell** something, you exaggerate its quality or importance.

overshadow ❑ If something is **overshadowed** by something else, people are less aware of it because of the other thing. *Her distinguished stage career has been overshadowed by her TV comedy role as Hyacinth Bucket.*

❑ If something unpleasant **overshadows** a situation or event, it makes it less enjoyable or successful.

❑ If a mountain or tall building **overshadows** a place, it is close to it or in the middle of it and is very noticeable.

overshoot (overshooting, overshot) If something **overshoots** a target or a place where it is supposed to stop, it goes beyond it. *The plane overshot the runway after landing.* ◇ When an organization **overshoots** its estimated budget, the amount it spends goes beyond its original estimate. When this happens, you say there is an **overshoot.** *...a £67m overshoot in 1989-90 expenditure.*

oversight An **oversight** is a mistake or omission, especially one made because someone failed to notice something.

oversimplify (oversimplifies, oversimplifying, oversimplified; oversimplification) If you **oversimplify** something, you make it seem simpler than it really is. *It would be an oversimplification to describe Radio 3 and Classic FM as direct competitors.*

oversized things are too big, or bigger than usual. *...oversized clothes... The pommelo is like an oversized grapefruit.*

oversleep (oversleeping, overslept) If you **oversleep,** you sleep longer than you meant to and are late getting up.

overspend (overspending, overspent) If an organization **overspends**, it spends more money than it has available, or more than it can afford. You can talk about an **overspend** of money. *Efforts are underway to avoid an £8000 overspend.*

overspill is used to talk about people from crowded cities who have been rehoused in smaller towns.

overstaffed (overstaffing) If an organization is **overstaffed**, there are too many people working there.

overstate (overstating, overstated; overstatement) If you **overstate** something, you make it out to be greater or more important than it really is. Making a claim like this is called **overstatement**; the claim you make is called an **overstatement**.

overstay means the same as 'outstay'.

overstep (overstepping, overstepped) If someone **oversteps** something like the rules of a system, they go beyond what is allowed or acceptable. *He said the EU Commission had overstepped its powers.* ◇ When someone behaves in an unacceptable way, you can say they **overstep the mark**.

overstretch (overstretches, overstretching, overstretched) If an organization or system is **overstretched**, it has been forced to take on more commitments than it can cope with. Similarly, you say a person is **overstretched** when they have to cope with too much work. *Casualty department consultants were often overstretched.*

oversubscribed If an event or educational course is **oversubscribed**, there are not enough places for the number of people who want to attend. ◇ Similarly, if a sale of shares in a company is **oversubscribed**, too many people want to buy them.

oversupply (oversupplies, oversupplying, oversupplied) If there is an **oversupply** of something, more of it is available than is needed. When this happens, you say the market for it is **oversupplied**.

overt (overtly) **Overt** attitudes and intentions are open and obvious. *...overt ambition... ...overt hostility... ...an overtly military role.*

overtake (overtaking, overtook, have overtaken) ❑ If you **overtake** a vehicle or person moving in the same direction as yourself, you pass them because you are moving faster than they are. ◇ You also say someone **overtakes** someone else when they are more successful than them. *A report predicted that Eastern Europe would overtake North America as a market for EU exports by the end of the century.* Similarly, one thing can **overtake** another when it becomes greater or more important. *Computer fraud has now overtaken burglary as a source of company loss.*
❑ If you are **overtaken** by something which happens, it happens unexpectedly or suddenly, before you are ready to deal with it. You can also say someone is **overtaken by events**. *The biggest sex scandal for years was about to overtake the government.*

overtax (overtaxes, overtaxing, overtaxed) If someone or something is **overtaxed**, they have too great a strain placed on them. ◇ If a government **overtaxes** people, it makes them pay too much tax.

overthrow (overthrowing, overthrew, have overthrown) If a government or leader is **overthrown**, they are removed from power by force. You call this their **overthrow**.

◇ If something like an idea, system, or rule is **overthrown**, it is replaced by something else. *...the overthrow of communism.*

overtime is time someone spends working in addition to their normal working hours. People who work overtime are paid extra for it, usually at a higher hourly rate. ◇ If you say someone is **working overtime** to achieve something, you mean they are putting a lot of effort, energy, or enthusiasm into it.

overtone If you say something has certain **overtones**, you mean there are further aspects to it apart from the obvious ones. *...a new financial scandal with political overtones.*

overtook See overtake.

overture ❑ An **overture** is a piece of music played as the introduction to an opera or play.
❑ If you **make overtures** to someone, you try to start a friendly, romantic, or business relationship with them.

overturn ❑ If something **overturns** or is **overturned**, it turns upside down or on its side.
❑ If someone in authority **overturns** a decision, they cancel it. ◇ If something **overturns** a belief, it shows it is wrong.
❑ In an election, when someone wins a seat which had previously been held by a different party, you can say they **overturn** that party's majority.

overvalued If you say something is **overvalued**, you mean it is not worth as much as people think it is.

overview If you have an **overview** of a situation, you have a good general understanding of it. Similarly, if you give someone an **overview** of something, you give a good general description of it.

overweening is used to say someone or something has too much of something. *...a handsome man full of overweening pride... ...the overweening power of television.*

overweight If someone is **overweight**, they weigh more than is good for their health.

overwhelm (overwhelming, overwhelmingly) ❑ If one person or group **overwhelms** another, they defeat them completely, usually by superior strength or ability. *The force has to be big enough to overwhelm the gunmen... They were eventually overwhelmed by four goals to one... His party was overwhelmingly defeated in the May elections.*
❑ If you are **overwhelmed** with something, you have more of it than you can cope with. *They're overwhelmed with paperwork... Officials fear the spread of diseases that could overwhelm the hospitals and clinics.* ◇ You can say someone is **overwhelmed** by something when it affects every aspect of their life. *...people overwhelmed by poverty.*
❑ **Overwhelming** is used to describe things which are much greater or more powerful than other things of their kind. *My overwhelming feeling has become one of anger... The House of Commons voted overwhelmingly in favour of the Bill.*

overwork If you **overwork**, you work too hard. Working too hard is called **overwork**. *...a heart attack brought on by overwork.* ◇ If people are **overworked**, they are given too much to do.

overwrought (*pron:* over-rawt) An **overwrought** person is nervous, worried, and upset. ◇ **Overwrought** is also used to describe things which are extremely elaborate and fussy. *...overwrought decorative schemes.*

ovulate (*pron:* ov-yew-late) (ovulating, ovulated; ovulation)

When a woman or female animal **ovulates**, she produces eggs from her ovary. This process is called **ovulation**.

ovum (*pron:* oh-vum) (*plural:* ova) The eggs produced in the ovaries of a woman or female animal are called **ova**.

owe (owing, owed) ❑ If someone **owes** you money, they have not paid back money they have borrowed from you.
❑ If you **owe** some advantage to someone or something, it is because of them that you have it. *She owed her long life to healthy eating.* ◇ If you say you **owe** gratitude, respect, or loyalty to someone, you mean they deserve it from you or have a right to expect it. *I owe a debt of thanks to a great many people.*
❑ **Owing to** means 'because of'. *They are facing higher costs owing to rising inflation.*

owl Owls are birds of prey which hunt at night. They have large eyes, short hooked beaks, and strong sharp claws.

owlish An **owlish** person looks very serious and studious.

own ❑ You use **own** to emphasize that something belongs to a certain person or thing. *...her own grandmother... My private affairs are no one's business but my own.* ◇ You also use **own** to talk about someone doing something without help. *We make our own decisions... His republic cannot survive on its own.* ◇ If someone is on their **own**, they are alone. ◇ **hold your own:** see **hold**.
❑ If you **get your own back** on someone, you pay them back for something unpleasant they have done to you.
❑ If you **own** something, it is your property. You add **-owning** to a word to say what someone owns. *...landowning farmers... ...home-owning voters.* You add **-owned** to a word to show who something belongs to. *...state-owned airlines... ...Britain's largest privately-owned bus company.*
❑ If you **own up** to something wrong you have done, you admit you did it.

own-brand See **brand**.

own goal In sport, if someone scores an **own goal**, they accidentally send the ball into their own goal. ◇ You also say someone scores an **own goal** when they do something unwise which turns out badly for them.

owner (ownership) The **owner** of something is the person it belongs to. **Ownership** is owning something. *...the private ownership of land... ...the trend towards increased car ownership.*

owner-driver An **owner-driver** is a person who owns and personally operates a vehicle for commercial purposes.

owner-occupier An **owner-occupier** is someone who owns the house they live in, rather than renting it.

ox (*plural:* oxen) An **ox** is a castrated bull. Oxen are very strong and are used in some parts of the world to pull carts and ploughs.

Oxbridge is the universities of Oxford and Cambridge, as distinct from other British universities. You talk, for example, about someone having an Oxbridge education.

oxidation See **oxidize**.

oxide An **oxide** is a compound of oxygen and another chemical element.

oxidize (oxidizing, oxidized; oxidation) (*can be spelled with an 's' instead of a 'z'*) When a substance **oxidizes**, it reacts chemically with another substance to form an oxide. This process is called **oxidation**.

oxtail is a cow's or bullock's tail when it is used in soups and stews.

oxyacetylene is a mixture of oxygen and acetylene which burns with a very hot, bright flame; it is used for cutting or welding metals at high temperatures.

oxygen is a chemical element which occurs on its own as a colourless gas, and also in many compounds. All animals and plants need oxygen to live, and things cannot burn without it.

oxygen mask An **oxygen mask** is a mask connected to an oxygen container. It is placed over the nose and mouth of a person to help them breathe more easily, for example if they are ill or working at high altitudes.

oxygen tent An **oxygen tent** is a clear plastic tent placed over a very ill patient in hospital and filled with pure oxygen to help them breathe more easily.

oxygenate (oxygenating, oxygenated) If something is **oxygenated**, oxygen is added to it.

oxymoron An **oxymoron** is a combination of words which appear to contradict each other, for example 'strangely familiar'.

oyster Oysters are large flat shellfish. Some types of oyster can be eaten; others produce pearls. ◇ If you say **the world is your oyster**, you mean you can go anywhere or do anything you want. *If a girl is well qualified and prepared to do her homework, then the world is her oyster.*

oystercatcher Oystercatchers are large black-and-white wading birds with long red bills which they use to catch shellfish and worms.

oz. See **ounce**.

ozone is a form of oxygen which is poisonous and has a strong smell. The **ozone layer** is a layer of ozone in the upper part of the Earth's atmosphere which protects living things from the harmful radiation of the sun.

P p

p See pence.

p. (pp.) p. is short for 'page'. pp. is short for 'pages'. ...*see pp. 209-14.*

p.a. See per annum.

PA Someone's PA is their personal assistant. ◇ PA also stands for 'public address system'.

pace (pacing, paced) ❑ A **pace** is a single step, or the length of a step. *His father followed a few paces behind.* ◇ If you **pace** a place or **pace** up and down, you walk up and down continually, because you are anxious or impatient.

❑ Your **pace** is the speed you walk or run at. *We all went at a leisurely pace.* ◇ Your **pace** is also the speed at which you do something. If you do something **at your own pace,** you do it at a speed which is comfortable for you. ◇ If you **set the pace** of something, you set the speed or standard other people have to reach. People who set a standard for other people are called **pace-setters.**

❑ The **pace** of something is the speed at which it happens. ...*the pace of reform.* ◇ If you **keep pace** with something, you do not get behind with it.

❑ If you **put** someone or something **through their paces,** you test their ability.

pace-setter See pace.

pacemaker (pacemaking) ❑ A **pacemaker** is a device attached to a person's heart to make it beat normally.

❑ In athletics, a **pacemaker** is a runner who keeps ahead of the other competitors for the first part of a race and sets the pace for them. This is called **pacemaking.**

pacey See pacy.

pacific A **pacific** person or country likes to have good relations with other people or countries, and tries not to quarrel with them.

pacifier ❑ In Canada and the US, a **pacifier** is a child's dummy.

❑ A person or organization that tries to settle differences between people can also be called a **pacifier.**

pacifism (pacifist) **Pacifism** is the belief that war and violence are always wrong. People who believe this are called **pacifists;** because of their beliefs, they often refuse to fight in wars or to do military service. **Pacifist** is used to describe people like this and their views. ...*a pacifist couple.*

pacify (pacifies, pacifying, pacified; pacification) If you **pacify** someone who is angry or upset, you calm them down. ◇ If an army **pacifies** people, it puts down a disturbance or uprising. This is called **pacification.**

pack (packer) ❑ A **pack** of things is a set of them sold together. ...*a six-pack of lager.* ◇ A **pack** is also a set of documents put together to provide information about something. ...*a study pack.* ◇ A **pack** of playing cards is a complete set.

❑ A **pack** is also a packet, especially a packet of cigarettes.

❑ A **pack** is also a rucksack.

❑ A **pack** of animals is a group of them which hunt together, especially dogs or wolves. ◇ Similarly, a group of people who go around together can be called a **pack.** ...*a pack of journalists.* ◇ A rugby team's **pack** is its forward players.

❑ If you call something a **pack** of lies, you mean it is all lies.

❑ When you **pack** or do your **packing,** you put clothes and other things into a bag or suitcase, because you are going away somewhere.

❑ When goods are **packed,** they are put into crates or boxes for transporting. Material put around them to protect them is called **packing.** A **packer** is a person or company whose job or business is packing goods.

❑ If someone is **packed** off somewhere, they are sent there. ◇ If someone is **sent packing,** they are told firmly to leave.

❑ When people **pack** a place or **pack into** it, they fill it until it becomes crowded. When this happens, you say the place is **packed.** ...*a packed hall.* If a place is **packed out,** it is completely full of people. ◇ If someone **packs** a meeting or assembly, they fill it with their supporters, to make sure things go the way they want. *He packed the Senate to get his goods-and-services tax through.*

❑ If something is **packed** with things, it is full of them. *Their catalogue is packed full of attractive gift ideas.*

❑ If you **pack** something **in,** you stop doing it.

❑ If someone **packs** a gun, they carry it around with them.

❑ If you say something **packs a punch,** you mean it has a powerful effect.

pack animal A **pack animal** is an animal like a horse or donkey, which is used to carry loads on its back.

pack ice is large masses of ice floating in the sea.

package ❑ A **package** is a small parcel.

❑ A **package** or **package deal** is a set of proposals or arrangements which are offered together, or have to be taken together. ◇ A **package holiday** or **package tour** is a holiday in which everything is arranged by one company, for a fixed price.

packaging A product's **packaging** is the wrapping or container it is sold in.

packet ❑ A **packet** is a small box, bag, or envelope in which something is sold. A **packet** of something can mean the packet and its contents, or just the contents. ...*a packet of cigarettes... I could eat four packets of biscuits in one sitting.* ◇ A **packet** is also a small parcel.

❑ If something costs a **packet,** it costs a lot of money.

packing case A **packing case** is a large wooden box in which things are stored or taken somewhere.

pact A **pact** is a formal agreement or treaty between two or more governments, organizations, or people, to do a particular thing or help each other.

pacy (or **pacey**) If you call a sportsperson **pacy,** you mean they move around at a fast pace. Similarly, if a book or film is **pacy,** the plot moves at a fast pace.

pad (padding, padded) ❑ A **pad** is a thick soft piece of material such as gauze, cotton wool, or foam rubber. Some kinds of pads are worn for protection or to fill out a shape; others are used to soak up, remove, or apply fluids. ...*knee pads*... ...*incontinence pads*. ◇ **Padding** is thick soft material placed or worn inside something to make it more comfortable, fill out a shape, or give protection. If something contains padding, you say it is **padded**.

❑ If you **pad** a piece of writing or **pad** it **out**, you put in unnecessary extra information, to get it up to a certain length. The extra material you put in is called **padding**.

❑ A **pad** is a number of sheets of paper fastened together at one end, for writing on.

❑ A landing **pad** is an area of flat hard ground where helicopters can land and take off. ◇ See also **launch pad**, **launching pad**.

❑ The **pads** of an animal like a cat or dog are the soft fleshy parts on the bottom of its paws. ◇ If you **pad** somewhere, you walk there with soft steps.

❑ A lily **pad** is the large floating leaf of a water lily.

❑ Someone's **pad** is their home.

padded cell A **padded cell** or a **padded room** is a small room with padded walls in a psychiatric hospital, where patients are put when it is thought they are in danger of harming themselves.

paddle (paddling, paddled) ❑ A **paddle** is a short pole with a wide flat part at one or both ends, for propelling a canoe through water. When you **paddle** a canoe, you propel it like this. ◇ When a bird or animal **paddles**, it swims by using its legs or feet to propel itself.

❑ When people **paddle** or have a **paddle**, they walk, stand, or splash around with bare feet in shallow water.

paddle steamer A **paddle steamer** is a steam-powered ship propelled by a large wheel at the back, or by large wheels at each side. These wheels, which have boards or paddles round their rims, are called **paddle wheels**.

paddock A **paddock** is a small field where horses are kept. ◇ At a racecourse, the **paddock** is an area where horses walk around before a race. ◇ In motor racing, the **paddock** is an area where the cars assemble before a race.

paddy (paddies) A **paddy** or **paddy field** is a flooded field where rice is grown.

padlock (padlocked) A **padlock** is a removable lock with a hinged U-shaped bar which clicks shut. Once it is shut, it can only be released with a key. If something is **padlocked**, it is locked with a padlock.

padre (*pron: pah*-dray) A **padre** is a chaplain in one of the armed forces.

paean (*pron: pee*-an) A **paean** to someone or something is something spoken, sung, or written in praise of them.

paediatrician (*American spelling:* **pediatrician**) A **paediatrician** (*pron:* peed-ya-trish-un) is a doctor who specializes in treating sick children.

paediatrics (paediatric) (*American spelling:* pediatrics, pediatric) **Paediatrics** (*pron:* pee-dee-ya-triks) is the branch of medicine which deals with children's diseases. **Paediatric** is used to talk about things connected with these diseases and their treatment. ...*a paediatric surgeon.*

paedophile (paedophilia) (*American spelling:* pedophile, pedophilia) A **paedophile** (*pron:* pee-do-file) is an adult who is sexually attracted to children. This kind of attraction is called **paedophilia** (*pron:* pee-do-fill-ya).

paella (*pron:* pie-ell-a) is a Spanish dish of rice, chicken, shellfish, and vegetables.

pagan (paganism) **Pagan** is used in a disapproving way to describe religious beliefs and practices which are not connected with any of the world's main religions. People involved in these practices are sometimes called **pagans**; their beliefs and worship are called **paganism**.

page (paging, paged) ❑ A **page** is one of the sheets in a book, newspaper, or magazine, or a side of one of these sheets.

❑ If you **turn the page** on an unhappy incident in your past, you decide to forget about it.

❑ If you **page** someone, you summon them over a loudspeaker or through a pager to come and receive a message or help someone.

❑ A **page** or **pageboy** is a small boy who attends a bride at her wedding.

page three A **page three** girl is a topless model whose photograph appears on the third page of a tabloid newspaper.

pageant A **pageant** is a show or parade, especially one with a historical theme. ◇ A **beauty pageant** is the same as a beauty contest.

pageantry is the elaborate and colourful ceremonies you get at certain state occasions.

pageboy ❑ See **page**.

❑ A **pageboy** is a medium-length hairstyle, in which all the hair is smooth and the ends are curled under, framing the face.

pager A **pager** is a small portable electronic device which relays messages to you on a small screen. It tells you there is a message by making a loud bleeping noise.

pagoda A **pagoda** is a tall ornately decorated tower where Buddhists worship, or a non-religious building in this style.

paid See **pay**.

paid-up If you are a **paid-up** member of an organization, you have paid the money required for membership.

pail A **pail** is a bucket, especially a metal or wooden one.

pain (paining, pained) ❑ **Pain** or a **pain** is an unpleasant feeling in part of your body caused by an illness or injury. ◇ **Pain** is also the unhappiness you feel when something upsetting happens. ...*the pain of divorce.* ◇ If something **pains** you, it hurts or upsets you.

❑ If you **take pains** to do something, you are very careful to do it. ◇ If someone is told they do something **on pain of** a certain punishment, they are being warned they will suffer that punishment if they do it.

❑ If you say someone or something is a **pain** or a **pain in the neck**, you mean they are very annoying or irritating.

painful (painfully) If something is **painful**, it causes you physical pain. *He jabbed him painfully in the back.* ◇ If a part of your body is **painful**, it hurts. ◇ A **painful** experience is upsetting and difficult to cope with.

painkilling (painkiller) A **painkilling** pill or drug reduces pain. Pills and drugs like these are called **painkillers**.

painless If a medical treatment or examination is **painless**, it does not cause you physical pain. ◇ You also say something is **painless** when it is managed without trouble or difficulty. *All this growth seems to have happened painlessly.*

painstaking (painstakingly) **Painstaking** work is very careful and thorough. ...*painstakingly piecing the aircraft back together.*

paint (painting) ❑ Paint is a coloured liquid which dries when it has been spread over a surface. When you **paint** something, you spread paint over it with a brush or roller, to protect or decorate it. ◇ You also say you **paint** something when you spread some other substance over it with a brush. For example, you say someone **paints** their fingernails.

❑ Paint is also a coloured liquid or thick paste which an artist uses to create a picture. You say an artist **paints** a picture; the picture is called a **painting**. **Painting** is creating pictures using paint.

❑ When someone describes a situation, you can say they **paint a picture of a certain kind.** *The report paints an alarming picture.*

paint stripper is a substance, usually a thick liquid, for removing old paint from woodwork.

paintbox (paintboxes) A **paintbox** is a flat box containing small blocks of dry paint for painting pictures.

paintbrush (paintbrushes) A **paintbrush** is a brush for painting surfaces.

painter (painterly) ❑ A **painter** is an artist who paints pictures. **Painterly** is used to talk about things to do with painters. *Lawrence had painterly ambitions.*

❑ A **painter** is also someone whose job is painting the insides or outsides of buildings.

painting See paint.

paintwork The paintwork of a building or vehicle is the paint on it.

pair (pairing, paired) ❑ A **pair** is a set of two matching things. *...a pair of gloves.* ◇ A **pair** is also two people, either a couple or two people who happen to be together at a particular time. Similarly, a **pair** can be two animals, either a mated male and female or just two animals together.

❑ When two people or things are **paired,** they are put together or made to do something together. They are then called a **pairing.** ◇ If you **pair up** with someone, you join with them to do something.

❑ When people **pair off,** they split up into pairs.

❑ Pair is used to talk about objects made up of two matching parts. *...a pair of jeans.*

❑ See also au pair.

paisley is a pattern of curving shapes rather like large commas, used especially in fabrics.

pajamas See pyjamas.

Pakistani is used to talk about things to do with Pakistan and its people. *...the Pakistani city of Karachi.* ◇ A **Pakistani** is someone who comes from Pakistan.

pal Your pals are your friends.

palace A palace is a very large and grand house, especially the home of a king, queen, or president.

Palaeolithic (*American spelling:* Paleolithic) The **Palaeolithic** period was the earliest period of the Stone Age. In this period, man began to walk upright and to use speech. The use of fire was discovered, and the first tools were made. See also Mesolithic, Neolithic.

palaeontology (*pron:* pal-ee-on-tol-a-jee) (palaeontologist) (*American spelling:* paleontology, paleontologist) Palaeontology is the study of the fossils of extinct animals and plants. A scientist who studies these fossils is called a palaeontologist.

palatable You say food or drink is **palatable** when it is pleasant to eat or drink. ◇ You say other things are **palatable** when they are easy to accept. *The licence fee can be made more palatable by being made payable in instalments.*

palate ❑ Your palate is the roof of your mouth.

❑ Your **palate** is also your ability to judge and appreciate good wine or food. *He has a very good palate.* ◇ A wine's **palate** is its taste, and the impression it gives when you hold it in your mouth before swallowing it.

palatial A palatial building or room is very large and grand.

palaver (*pron:* pah-lah-ver) is unnecessary fuss.

palazzo (*pron:* pal-lats-so) (*plural:* palazzi) A **palazzo** is a very large and grand Italian house.

pale (paler, palest; paleness; paling, paled) ❑ Pale colours are not strong or bright.

❑ If someone is **pale,** their face looks whiter than usual, because they are ill, frightened, or shocked. When someone's face becomes this colour, you say they **pale** or **turn pale.**

❑ If something **pales** when compared to something else, it seems less important or exciting. ◇ If something is a **pale imitation** of something else, it is a poor copy of it.

❑ If something is **beyond the pale,** it goes beyond what is acceptable.

Paleolithic See Palaeolithic.

paleontology See palaeontology.

palette A palette is a flat wooden or plastic board on which an artist mixes paints.

palette knife A palette knife is a knife with a long broad flat flexible blade, used in cookery and oil painting.

palimony In the US, palimony is money a person claims through a court from someone they have been living with, when the relationship has ended.

palindrome A palindrome is a word, phrase, or number which is the same whether you read it forwards or backwards, for example 'eye' or '1991'.

palings are a fence made up of a row of narrow upright posts.

palisade In the past, a palisade was a fence made of wooden posts, put up to protect people from attack.

pall (*pron:* pawl) ❑ If you say there is a **pall** over things, you mean people are full of gloom, because of something which has happened. ◇ A **pall** of smoke is a thick cloud of it hanging over a place.

❑ A **pall** is a cloth covering a coffin. Sometimes the coffin itself is called a **pall.**

❑ If something **palls,** it becomes less interesting, amusing, or exciting.

pallbearer The pallbearers at a funeral are the people who carry the coffin or walk beside it.

pallet A pallet is a wooden platform on which goods are stacked, so they can be lifted and moved using a fork-lift truck.

palliative (*pron:* pal-lee-a-tiv) Palliative is used to describe things which relieve pain or suffering, without treating its cause. *...palliative care... ...palliative treatment.* A **palliative** is a drug or medical treatment which has this effect. ◇ A **palliative** is also something done to relieve a problem, without tackling its cause.

pallid If someone is pallid, they are extremely pale. ◇ **Pallid** is also used to describe people and things that have little power or vigour.

pallor Someone's **pallor** is an unhealthy paleness in their face.

palm ❑ A **palm** or **palm tree** is a tropical tree with a long straight trunk, long fringed leaves at the top, and no branches.
   ❑ The **palm** of your hand is the flat part which your fingers bend towards.
   ❑ If you **palm** someone **off** with something, you give it to them, just to get rid of them. ◇ If you **palm** something **off** on someone, you get them to take it, to get rid of it.

palm oil is a thick yellow oil from the fruit of a tree called the oil palm tree. It is used in the manufacture of some foods and cosmetics.

Palm Sunday is the Sunday before Easter.

palmistry (palmist) **Palmistry** is telling people's fortunes by examining their palm. Someone who does this for a living is called a **palmist.**

palmtop A **palmtop** computer is a very small one. You can operate it with one hand while resting it on the palm of the other.

palomino (palominos) A **palomino** is a golden-coloured horse with a white or cream mane and tail.

palpable (palpably) **Palpable** is used to say something is very obvious. *This is palpable nonsense... He was palpably mistaken.* ◇ If you say something like the atmosphere in a place is **palpable**, you mean you are so aware of it you feel you could reach out and touch it.

palpitation (palpitations) If someone has **palpitations**, they feel their heart beating very fast or with an irregular beat.

palsied (*pron:* **pol**-zɪd) If someone is **palsied**, they are unable to control their muscles because of illness, and often their limbs shake uncontrollably as a result.

palsy (*pron:* **pol**-zee) is paralysis, or an illness which causes paralysis. See also **cerebral palsy.**

paltry If something, especially a sum of money, is **paltry**, it is disappointingly small.

pampas The **pampas** is a large area of flat grassy treeless land in South America.

pampas grass is a kind of tall grass with long feathery plumes.

pamper (pampering, pampered) If you **pamper** a person or animal, you do everything for them, and give them everything they want.

pamphlet (pamphleteer) A **pamphlet** is a thin book with a paper cover, giving information about something. Someone who writes pamphlets, especially political ones, is called a **pamphleteer.**

pan (panning, panned) ❑ A **pan** is a round metal container with a long handle, used for cooking things on top of a cooker. ◇ When people **pan** for gold, they search for it in a river by washing mud or sand in a shallow metal dish, to see if there is gold in it.
   ❑ If a critic **pans** something, he or she criticizes it severely.
   ❑ When a film camera **pans**, it follows a moving object, or turns slowly to take in a whole scene.

pan- at the beginning of a word means it refers to the whole of something, or every one of the things in a group. *...a pan-European ad campaign... ...a pan-Islamic movement.*

pan-pipes are a musical instrument made of wooden pipes of different lengths tied together. You play it by blowing across the tops of the pipes.

panacea (*pron:* pan-a-see-a) A **panacea** is something which is supposed to be a remedy for all problems.

panache (*pron:* pan-**ash**) If you do something with **panache**, you do it with style and confidence.

panama A **panama** or **panama hat** is a straw hat with a rounded crown and a fairly wide brim.

pancake **Pancakes** are flat thin circular pieces of fried batter. They are usually folded and eaten hot with a sweet or savoury filling.

Pancake Day See **Shrove Tuesday.**

pancreas (*pron:* **pan**-kree-ass) (pancreases, pancreatic) Your **pancreas** is a large gland behind your stomach, which produces insulin and helps with digestion. **Pancreatic** is used to talk about things to do with the pancreas. *...pancreatic cancer.*

panda The **panda** or **giant panda** is a large bear-like animal with black and white fur, which lives in the bamboo forests of China and Tibet.

panda car A **panda car** is a small police patrol car.

pandemic A **pandemic** is an illness or disease which affects people over a very large area or all round the world.

pandemonium is noisy confusion.

pander (pandering, pandered) If you **pander** to someone, you give them what they want, often to get their loyalty or support.

Pandora's box If you say someone has opened a **Pandora's box**, you mean they have started something which will bring a lot of trouble.

pane A **pane** is a flat sheet of glass in a window or door.

panegyric (*pron:* pan-i-**jir**-ik) A **panegyric** is a formal speech or piece of writing in praise of someone or something.

panel ❑ A **panel** is a flat rectangular piece of wood or other material, which forms part of a larger object, such as a door. ◇ A control or instrument **panel** is a board or surface containing switches and controls.
   ❑ A **panel** is also a small group of people who have been chosen to do something such as carry out an investigation or answer questions on TV or radio.

panelling (panelled) (*American spelling:* paneling, paneled) **Panelling** is rectangular pieces of wood covering a building's inside walls. A **panelled** room has walls like this.

panellist (*American spelling:* panelist) A **panellist** is a member of a panel, especially one which answers questions on TV or radio.

pang A **pang** of something like hunger or guilt is a sudden feeling of it.

panga A **panga** is an African knife, similar to a machete.

panic (panics, panicking, panicked) ❑ **Panic** is a sudden feeling of fear or anxiety, which makes someone act without thinking sensibly. When someone behaves like this, you say they **panic** or are **panicked**; if a lot of people do it, you say there is a **panic**.
   ❑ A **panic button** is a button you press in an emergency, which rings an alarm. When someone takes sudden emergency measures, you can say they hit, press, or push the **panic button**. ◇ If there is **panic buying**, people start

buying things in large quantities, because they think there are going to be shortages.

panic-stricken If someone is **panic-stricken,** they are so anxious or afraid they are unable to act sensibly.

panicky is used to describe people who are panicking, or things they do when they panic. *...panicky decisions.*

pannier A **pannier** is a bag, box, or basket, especially one of a pair on either side of a bicycle or pack animal.

panoply If you talk about a **panoply** of things, you mean there are a lot of them, of different kinds.

panorama (panoramic) A **panorama** is a view over a wide area. You say a view like this is **panoramic.** ◇ A **panorama** is also a detailed and wide-ranging description of something.

pansy (pansies) **Pansies** are small garden flowers with large round velvety petals. ◇ **Pansy** is also an offensive word for an effeminate or homosexual man.

pant ❑ **Pants** are a piece of underwear with holes you put your legs through and an elasticated waist. ◇ In the US and some parts of Britain, trousers are called **pants.**
❑ When you **pant,** you breathe quickly and loudly, because you have been doing something energetic. ◇ If you **pant** something, you say it with difficulty, because you are out of breath. *'Which way to Times Square?' I panted.*

pantaloons Various kinds of trousers have been called **pantaloons** at different times. Originally, **pantaloons** were men's tight-fitting trousers fastening under the instep.

pantheism (pantheist, pantheistic) **Pantheism** is the belief that God is present in everything in nature and the universe. Someone who believes this is called a **pantheist;** you say their beliefs are **pantheistic.**

pantheon A **pantheon** is a building or monument commemorating a nation's dead heroes. ◇ In ancient Greece and Rome, a **pantheon** was a temple to all the gods. ◇ People sometimes use **pantheon** to mean the best people ever in a particular field. They talk about someone joining this **pantheon.** *Agassi's name had joined the pantheon of the greats.*

panther A **panther** is a leopard with black fur.

panties are pants worn by women and girls.

pantile **Pantiles** are roofing tiles with an S-shaped cross-section.

pantomime A **pantomime** or **panto** is a type of traditional musical play for children, performed at Christmas.

pantry (pantries) A **pantry** is a room or cupboard for storing food.

pantyhose are women's tights.

pap is soft or mushy food, especially food for babies or sick people. ◇ If you call something **pap,** you mean it has no worth or value.

papacy (*pron:* **pay**-pa-see) The **papacy** is the position of being Pope.

papal (*pron:* **pay**-pal) is used to describe things connected with the Pope. *...a papal visit.*

paparazzi (*pron:* pap-a-**rat**-see) The **paparazzi** are the photographers who follow celebrities around, trying to get their pictures.

papaya (*pron:* pa-**pie**-ya) **Papayas** are West Indian fruit with yellowish skins, sweet yellow flesh, and small black seeds. They are also called 'pawpaws'.

paper (papering, papered) ❑ **Paper** is a material made from wood pulp, which people write or draw on, or wrap things up in.
❑ If you get something down **on paper,** you write it down. ◇ **On paper** also means in theory, as opposed to fact. *On paper, the congress's powers are superior to Mr Yeltsin's.*
❑ **Papers** are sheets of paper with information on them. ◇ Your **papers** are your identification documents, such as your passport.
❑ A **paper** is (a) one part of a written examination. (b) an article or essay on an academic or scientific subject.
❑ A **paper** is also a newspaper. ◇ A **paper boy** or **girl** is a young person who delivers newspapers to people's homes. The job of delivering papers along a certain route is called a **paper round.** ◇ A **paper shop** is a newsagent's.
❑ If you **paper** a wall, you put wallpaper on it. ◇ If you **paper over** a difficulty, you try to hide it by giving the impression that things are going well.
❑ If you call someone or something a **paper tiger,** you mean they are not as powerful as their reputation suggests.

paper clip A **paper clip** is a small piece of bent wire, used to fasten sheets of paper together.

paper knife A **paper knife** is a blunt knife for opening envelopes.

paper money is money in the form of banknotes.

paperback A **paperback** is a book with a thin cardboard cover. If a book is available **in paperback,** you can buy a paperback copy of it.

paperweight A **paperweight** is a small heavy object, placed on top of loose papers to stop them blowing away.

paperwork is things like letters, records, and reports which have to be dealt with as part of a job.

papery If something is **papery,** it is thin and dry like paper.

papier-mâché (*pron:* **pap**-yay **mash**-ay) is a mixture of pieces of paper and paste which hardens when it dries. It is used to make things like bowls, models, and ornaments.

papist (*pron:* **pape**-ist) is an offensive word for a Roman Catholic.

paprika is a mild red pepper made from capsicums.

papyrus (*pron:* pap-**ire**-uss) (papyruses) **Papyrus** is a tall reed-like African water plant. A type of paper made from its stems is also called **papyrus;** it was used in ancient Egypt, Rome, and Greece. A **papyrus** is an ancient document written on papyrus.

par is the normal standard of something. *His performance was not up to par.* ◇ If something is **on a par** with something else, it is of a similar standard or at a similar level.
❑ On a golf course, **par** is the number of strokes it is calculated a good golfer would take to complete a particular hole or the whole course.

par excellence (*pron:* par ek-sel-**lons**) is used to say someone or something is the best possible example of a kind of thing. *He is a travel writer par excellence.*

para See **paratroop.**

parable A **parable** is a story which makes a moral or religious point.

parabola (*pron:* pa-**rab**-bol-a) (parabolic) A **parabola** is a curve like the path of an object thrown forward and upward into the air and then coming down to earth again. If something is **parabolic**, it has a curve or curves like this.

paracetamol is a mild pain-relieving drug.

parachute (parachuting, parachuted; parachutist) A **parachute** is an apparatus which enables a person or package to float safely to the ground from an aircraft. It consists of a large umbrella-shaped piece of fabric, which is attached to the person or package by long cords. **Parachuting** is jumping from an aircraft, using a parachute. Someone who does this regularly is called a **parachutist**. If you **parachute** somewhere or are **parachuted** there, you jump from an aircraft and float down using a parachute.

parade (parading, paraded) ❑ A **parade** is a procession of people or things, to celebrate a special event. ◇ A **parade** is also an occasion when members of the armed forces assemble so they can be inspected by an officer or important person. ◇ When soldiers or other people **parade** somewhere, they march or walk together in a group.

❑ If you **parade** something, you display it in public. *She has paraded her naked body three times in magazines.* ◇ When someone, especially a prisoner, is **paraded** in front of people, they are put on display.

❑ A **parade** is also a promenade or street of shops.

parade ground A **parade ground** is an area where soldiers practise marching and assemble for parades.

paradigm (*pron:* **par-a-dime**) (paradigmatic) A **paradigm** is a model or example of something. If someone or something is **paradigmatic** (*pron:* par-a-dig-**mat**-tik), they serve as a model or example.

paradise is another name for heaven. ◇ Any place which seems perfect can be called **paradise**. *For anyone who loves being outdoors, Snowdonia is paradise.*

paradox (paradoxes; paradoxical, paradoxically) A **paradox** is a situation which is puzzling, because it seems to involve a contradiction. You say something like this is **paradoxical**. *Paradoxically, the rapid decline in the number of farmers makes them a more effective lobby.*

paraffin is a strong-smelling flammable liquid, used as fuel in heaters, lamps, and engines.

paragliding (paraglider) **Paragliding** is the sport of cross-country gliding using a specially designed rectangular parachute. Someone who takes part in this sport is called a **paraglider**.

paragon If you say someone is a **paragon** of a particular quality, you mean they are a perfect example of it. *Her fans see her as a paragon of female integrity and determination.*

paragraph A **paragraph** is one of the sections a piece of writing is divided into. Each paragraph begins on a new line.

parakeet A **parakeet** is a small long-tailed parrot.

parallel (paralleling, paralleled) ❑ If there are **parallels** between two things, there are similarities between them. You can say one thing **parallels** another. *The arguments of naval officers closely paralleled those of the Party.* ◇ If you draw a **parallel** between two things, you say they are similar.

❑ A **parallel** event is similar to one you have just mentioned, and is happening at the same time. *Parallel talks will open shortly between North and South Korea.* Similarly, a **parallel** system exists at the same time as another one and does the same thing.

❑ If two lines are **parallel**, they are the same distance apart along the whole of their length. ◇ A **parallel** is any of the lines of latitude which circle the earth parallel to the equator.

parallelogram A **parallelogram** is a four-sided shape in which each side is parallel to the one opposite to it.

paralyse (paralysing, paralysed; paralysis) (*American spelling:* paralyze, *etc*) If something, especially an illness or accident, **paralyses** you, it causes loss of movement in your body and usually loss of feeling. This condition is called **paralysis**. ◇ If something **paralyses** a process, place, or organization, it brings it to a standstill. *The strike paralysed the country.*

paralytic ❑ A **paralytic** disease or condition causes paralysis.

❑ If someone is **paralytic**, they are extremely drunk.

paramedical (paramedic) **Paramedical** staff or **paramedics** are hospital medical support staff, especially the crews of some emergency ambulances who have been trained to use life-saving equipment.

parameter (*pron:* par-am-it-er) The **parameters** affecting something are the factors limiting how it can be done, made, or operated. *...the safety parameters of nuclear power stations.*

paramilitary (paramilitaries) A **paramilitary** organization is an armed group, legal or illegal, which is organized on military lines, but is not part of a country's armed forces. Members of a group like this are called **paramilitaries**.

paramount (paramountcy) If something is **paramount** or of **paramount** importance, it is more important than anything else. You talk about the **paramountcy** of something like this. *...the paramountcy of the patient's needs.*

paramour (*pron:* par-a-moo-er) Someone's **paramour** is their lover.

paranoia (paranoid, paranoiac) ❑ **Paranoia** is a mental illness which makes an otherwise normal person have strange delusions, for example that other people are trying to harm them, or that they are much more important than they really are.

❑ **Paranoia** is also a tendency to suspect or mistrust other people. You say people who have this tendency are **paranoid** or **paranoiac**.

paranormal The **paranormal** is various things which happen or are believed to happen and for which there is at present no scientific explanation. Examples of the paranormal are telepathy, clairvoyance, memories of past lives, and the appearance of ghosts and poltergeists.

parapet A **parapet** is a low wall along the edge of a bridge, roof, or balcony.

paraphernalia is (a) bits of equipment. *...kitchen paraphernalia.* (b) souvenirs or mementoes of someone or something. *...posters, photographs, and other paraphernalia of the performing arts.*

paraphrase (paraphrasing, paraphrased) If you **paraphrase** what someone has said or written, you express it in a different, usually shorter, way. What you say or write is called a **paraphrase**.

paraplegic (*pron:* par-a-**pleej**-ik) (paraplegia) If someone is paraplegic or a **paraplegic**, they are paralysed from somewhere in the region of their waist downwards, usually as a result of an injury to their spine. This condition is called **paraplegia**. See also **quadriplegic**.

parapsychology is the study of mental abilities beyond normal explanation, such as ESP.

parasite (parasitic, parasitical, parasitism) ❑ A **parasite** is an animal, plant, or organism which lives on or inside a larger one and gets its food from it. You say an animal, plant, or organism like this is **parasitic. Parasitic** diseases are caused by parasites.
    ❑ If you call someone a **parasite**, you mean they live off other people without doing anything in return. You say people like this are **parasitic** or **parasitical**. You call their behaviour **parasitism**.

parasol A **parasol** is a light umbrella for providing shade from the sun.

paratroop (paratroops; paratrooper, para) **Paratroops** are soldiers trained to drop into battle by parachute. An individual soldier of this kind is called a **paratrooper** or **para**.

parboil (parboiling, parboiled) If you **parboil** vegetables, you boil them until they are partly cooked.

parcel (parcelling, parcelled) (*American spelling:* parceling, parceled) ❑ A **parcel** is something wrapped up in paper and secured with string or tape. If you **parcel** something **up**, you make it into a parcel.
    ❑ A **parcel** of land is a piece of it with definite boundaries.
    ❑ If you **parcel** something **out**, you divide it among several people or groups.
    ❑ **part and parcel:** see **part**.

parcel bomb A **parcel bomb** is a small bomb sent in a parcel through the post. It is designed to explode when the parcel is opened.

parched If the ground is **parched**, it is very dry, because the sun has been hot and there has been no rain. ◇ If you are **parched**, you are very thirsty.

parchment In the past, **parchment** was a type of paper made from goat or sheep skin. **Parchments** are writings on parchment. ◇ A modern type of stiff paper is also called **parchment**.

pardon (pardoning, pardoned) When a monarch, president, or government **pardons** someone, they free them from prosecution or a death sentence, or release them from prison. The order requiring this to be done is called a **pardon**. ◇ If you say someone could be **pardoned** for doing something, you mean you would not blame them if they did it.

pardonable If you say something like a mistake is **pardonable**, you mean it can be excused in the circumstances.

pare (paring, pared) When you **pare** something, you trim it or peel it. ◇ A **paring** is a thin piece cut off something, such as a fingernail. ◇ If you **pare** something **back** or **pare** it **down**, you reduce it to a minimum. *The federal government has pared back its spending on staff.*

parent (parental) Your **parents** are your mother and father. A **parent** is someone who has a child or children. **Parental** is used to talk about things to do with parents. *...parental responsibilities.*

parent company A company's **parent company** is a larger company which owns it or holds over half of its shares.

parentage If you talk about someone's **parentage**, you are talking about who their parents are or were. You can also say, for example, that someone is of German parentage.

parental See **parent**.

parenthesis (parentheses) (*pron:* par-en-thiss-iss, par-en-thiss-eez) A **parenthesis** is a word or phrase inserted into a sentence inside brackets, dashes, or commas. ◇ Brackets are themselves sometimes called **parentheses**. ◇ If you say something **in parenthesis**, you interrupt yourself to say it, then go on with what you were saying before.

parenthood is being a parent.

parenting is bringing up children.

pariah (*pron:* par-**rye**-a) You say a person or country is a **pariah** when other people or countries will have nothing to do with them, because of something they have done.

parish (parishes) A **parish** is (a) the area served by an Anglican or Catholic church. (b) one of the small areas a district council is divided into. Parishes have their own councils, with limited powers.

parishioner A priest's **parishioners** are the people who live in his or her parish and attend the church there.

parity (parities) If there is **parity** between two things, they have equal power, status, or value. ◇ In finance, a currency's **parity** is its exchange-rate value.

park ❑ A **park** is an area of public land with grass and trees. ◇ A **park** is also an area of private land with grass and trees, surrounding a large country house. ◇ Various areas used for a particular purpose are called **parks**, for example business parks, science parks, or theme parks. ◇ See also **national park**.
    ❑ When you **park** a vehicle, you drive it into a position where it can be left.

parka A **parka** is a warm jacket or coat with a quilted lining and a hood.

parking lot In the US, a **parking lot** is an outdoor car park.

parking meter A **parking meter** is a device standing next to a place where you can park your car. You put money in it if you want to park there.

parking ticket A **parking ticket** is a piece of paper with instructions to pay a fine, which a traffic warden puts on your car if you have parked somewhere illegally.

Parkinson's disease is a brain disease, which causes a person's hands to tremble uncontrollably, and makes walking difficult.

Parkinson's Law is the idea that work expands to fill the amount of time you have to do it in.

Parkinsonism is Parkinson's disease, or one of several other disorders which have similar effects.

parkland is land with grass and trees, especially around a country house.

parlance If you say something in a particular **parlance**, you use a word or phrase which is special to a trade or group of people. *The album went on to sell over 3 million copies worldwide, which in music business parlance means it went triple-platinum.*

parley When people **parley** or have a **parley**, they have a discussion, usually to try to settle a dispute.

parliament A country's **parliament** is an assembly of representatives which makes its laws. In Britain, **Parliament** consists of the House of Commons and the House of Lords.

parliamentarian ❑ A **parliamentarian** is an MP. ◇ **Parliamentarian** is used to talk about someone's skill at debating in Parliament. You say, for example, that someone is a 'brilliant parliamentarian'.
❑ In the English Civil War, the **Parliamentarians** were the people who supported Parliament and opposed the King.

parliamentary is used to talk about things to do with a parliament. ...*parliamentary elections*.

parlour (*American spelling:* **parlor**) ❑ **Parlour** is an old word for a living room.
❑ **Parlour** is used in the names of some types of shops and other establishments which provide a service. ...*pizza parlours*... ...*funeral parlours*. ◇ A building equipped for milking cows is called a **milking parlour**.

parlour game A **parlour game** is a game played indoors by families or at parties, for example a guessing game or a word game.

parlourmaid (*or* **parlour maid**) In the past, a **parlourmaid** was a female servant whose job was to do light housework and wait at table during meals.

parlous If something is in a **parlous** state, it is in a very poor state indeed.

Parmesan is a hard Italian cheese, usually served grated over food.

parochial (**parochially, parochialism**) ❑ If you call someone **parochial** or talk about their **parochialism**, you mean they take too narrow a view of things and are only interested in their own country or area. *There had been a temptation to think parochially*.
❑ **Parochial** is also used to talk about things relating to a priest's parish. ...*his parochial duties*.

parody (**parodies, parodying, parodied**) ❑ A **parody** is an exaggerated and amusing imitation of someone or something. If you **parody** someone or something, you imitate them like this.
❑ If something fails badly to be the thing it is supposed to be, you can say it is a **parody** of it. ...*a parody of justice*.

parole (**paroling, paroled**) When prisoners are **paroled** or let out **on parole**, they are released early on condition that they behave well.

paroxysm If someone goes into **paroxysms** of rage, they get so angry they lose control. ◇ **Paroxysms** are also spasms or convulsions.

parquet (*pron:* par-kay) A **parquet** floor is made of small rectangular blocks of wood, fitted together in a pattern.

parrot (**parroting, parroted**) ❑ A **parrot** is a tropical or subtropical bird with a short curved beak and brightly-coloured or grey feathers. Some parrots can imitate what people say.
❑ If you **parrot** something you have heard or read, you repeat it without really understanding it. Similarly, if you repeat something **parrot fashion**, you get the words right, but have not really understood what they mean.

parry (**parries, parrying, parried**) If you **parry** a question, you cleverly avoid answering it.

parsimonious (**parsimony**) If you say someone is **parsimonious** or talk about their **parsimony**, you mean they are reluctant to spend money.

parsley is a herb with curly leaves, used to flavour and decorate food.

parsnip Parsnips are long thick cream-coloured root vegetables.

parson A **parson** is a member of the clergy, especially a Church of England vicar.

parsonage A parsonage is a parson's house.

part or a **part** of something is (a) a certain amount of it. *Local government will have to bear part of the cost*. (b) one of the pieces or elements it consists of. *The lower part of the slope was less steep*.
❑ The **best part** or **better part** of something is most of it. *It will probably take them the best part of a week*. ◇ **For the most part** means mostly. *For the most part, the demonstration passed off quietly*. ◇ **In part** means partly. *In part, lower profits were due to the rapid growth in the number of banks fighting for business*. ◇ If something happens **part way** or **part of the way** through an event or period of time, it happens at some time during it.
❑ In cooking, you use **part** when you are talking about the proportions of substances in a mixture. *Use one part vinegar to three parts warm water*.
❑ If you say something is **part and parcel** of something else, you mean it is an essential part of it.
❑ A **part** in a play or film is one of the roles in it.
❑ Behaviour **on someone's part** is behaviour by that person. *He said that the delay was caused by the need to modify legislation, not by a lack of political will on his part*.
❑ If you **take part** in something, you become involved in it. ◇ If you play a **part** in something, you are one of the people involved in it. *She was jailed for seven years for her part in the conspiracy*.
❑ When things which are touching **part** or are **parted**, they move away from each other. *Her lips parted*... *She parted the curtains*. ◇ If you **part with** something, especially something you would rather keep, you give it or sell it to someone else.
❑ When people **part**, they leave each other. ◇ If people are **parted**, they are prevented from being together. ◇ **part company**: see **company**.
❑ If your hair is **parted**, it is combed in two different directions, so that a line of scalp is left showing between. This line is called a **parting**. In the US, it is called a **part**.

part-exchange If an item is taken in **part-exchange** for something else, it is taken as part of the payment towards it.

part-time (**part-timer**) If someone is a **part-time** worker or has a **part-time** job, they work for only a part of each day or week. Someone like this can be called a **part-timer**.

partake (**partaking, partook, have partaken**) If you **partake** of food or drink, you eat it or drink it. ◇ If you **partake** in an activity, you take part in it.

partial (**partially; partiality**) ❑ **Partial** means not complete or total. ...*partial deafness*... *The old house has been partially restored*.
❑ If you are **partial** to something, especially a kind of food or drink, you enjoy it very much.
❑ If you accuse someone of being **partial** in a dispute,

you mean they are showing favouritism towards one side; you also say they are showing **partiality**.

participant The **participants** in an activity are the people taking part.

participate (participating, participated; participation) If you **participate** in something, you take part in it.

participatory A **participatory** activity is one you take part in yourself, rather than just watching. *Fishing is the most popular participatory sport in the United Kingdom.*

particle ❏ A **particle** of something is a very small piece or amount of it.

❏ In physics, a **particle** is a piece of matter smaller than an atom, for example a proton, a neutron, or an electron. **Particle physics** is the study of the properties of particles. A **particle accelerator** is an apparatus used to speed up the movement of electrically-charged particles.

particular ❏ You use **particular** to emphasize that you are talking about just one thing, and not others of the same kind. *In this particular case, the bank did in fact refund the money.*

❏ If you talk about the **particular** qualities someone or something has, you mean qualities which are special to them, and which may not be shared by other people or things. *It turns out that cotton has a particular advantage.*

❏ If something is of **particular** interest or concern, people are especially interested in it or concerned about it.

❏ **In particular** means particularly or especially. *Britain, in particular, is opposed to the idea.*

❏ **Particulars** are details about something. *Once you have registered your particulars, the process begins.*

❏ If someone is **particular** about something, they like it to be a certain way, and are not satisfied with anything else.

particularise See particularize.

particularity (particularities) **Particularity** is setting something out in a detailed way. *The main complaint was that the reports lacked particularity.* The **particularities** of something are its details.

particularize (particularizing, particularized) (*can be spelled with an 's' instead of a 'z'*) If you **particularize** about something, you go into details.

particularly You use **particularly** to indicate that what you are saying applies more to one person, thing, or aspect of a situation than others. *There was a need for more relief supplies, particularly blankets... Conscripts resent having to do military service, particularly if they are sent far from home.* ◇ **Particularly** also means more than usually. *Her Wimbledon chances are particularly good this year.*

partisan (partisanship) ❏ If you say someone is being **partisan**, you mean they are prejudiced in favour of one side in a dispute or game. Showing prejudice like this is called **partisanship**.

❏ If you are a **partisan** of something, you support it. *She was never a partisan of the view that 'the end justifies the means'.*

❏ A **partisan** is a member of a resistance movement, especially one which fought occupying German troops during the Second World War.

partition (partitioning, partitioned) ❏ A **partition** is a thin wall or screen dividing one part of a room from another. If part of a room is **partitioned off**, it is separated

from the rest of the room by a partition or partitions.

❏ When a country is **partitioned**, it is divided into two or more independent countries.

partly means to some extent, but not completely. *There were delays at the main airports, partly due to action by air traffic controllers.*

partner (partnering, partnered; partnership) ❏ Your **partner** is the person you are married to or having a relationship with.

❏ When an activity involves people doing something in pairs, you call the person you do it with your **partner**. You also say you **partner** the other person.

❏ If you do something in **partnership** with someone else, you do it together.

❏ A country's **partners** are other countries which it has an alliance or agreement with. *...Britain's trading partners.*

❏ The **partners** in a business are its joint owners. Being one of the owners of a business is called a **partnership**.

partridge **Partridges** are wild or specially reared birds with round bodies and short tails, shot for their meat.

party (parties, partying, partied) ❏ A **party** is a social gathering with food and drink, usually held to celebrate something. When people **party**, they have a party or go to a party.

❏ A political **party** is an organization of people with similar political views, who try to win power in central and local government.

❏ A **party** of people is a group of them doing something together. *...a party of French tourists.*

❏ The **parties** in an agreement or dispute are the people, companies, or sides involved in it. ◇ If you are a **party** to something, you are involved in it. *He said that he had not been a party to the attacks.* ◇ See also **third party**.

party-goer (*or* partygoer) A **party-goer** is (a) one of the people at a party. *No-one was killed but many party-goers were injured.* (b) someone who goes to a lot of parties.

party line ❏ The **party line** is the official view on something taken by a political party.

❏ A **party line** is a telephone line shared by two or more subscribers.

party piece Someone's **party piece** is something they often do to entertain people, especially at parties.

party political activities are aimed at getting people to support a particular political party.

party politics If you say a political party is indulging in **party politics**, you mean it is doing something to get an advantage over other parties, rather than for the benefit of the country.

party pooper A **party pooper** is someone whose attitude or behaviour spoils a party.

party wall A **party wall** is the wall between two adjoining houses.

partygoer See party-goer.

parvenu (*pron:* par-ven-new) People who have recently become rich or important but are not very cultured or well-educated are sometimes called **parvenus**.

pas de deux (*plural:* pas de deux) (*pron:* pah duh duh) In a ballet, a **pas de deux** is a dance for two people.

pass (passes, passing, passed) ❏ If you **pass** someone or something, you go past them. ◇ If you **pass** through a place, you go through it. You can also say a road or river passes through a place.

❑ When something which is increasing **passes** a certain level, it goes beyond it. *The film quickly passed the $100m mark at the US box office.*

❑ If something **passes** someone **by**, they are not affected by it. *Even the comparatively wealthy South East, which the last recession mainly passed by, is badly hit this time.* ◇ If someone or something is **passed over**, they are ignored or disregarded. *She claims she was repeatedly passed over for promotion.* ◇ If something **passes** unnoticed or **passes** without comment, nobody notices it or comments on it.

❑ If you **pass** something to someone, you hand it to them. ◇ If a group of people **pass** something **round**, they each look at it or use it, then hand it on to the next person.

❑ If you **pass** something you have obtained to someone who wants it or needs it, you hand it over to them. You can also say you **pass** it **on** to them or **pass** it **along** to them. ◇ If you **pass on** a message to someone, you give it to them on someone else's behalf.

❑ If a company **passes on** an increase in its costs to its customers, it raises its prices or charges, to pay for the increase.

❑ If something is **passed down** in a family, each generation gives it or teaches it to the next one. *The recipe was passed down from mother to daughter.* ◇ When something **passes** to someone, it legally becomes theirs. *The estate passed to her son.*

❑ In sport, if you **pass** to someone, you hit, kick, or throw the ball in their direction. This is called a **pass**.

❑ You say a period of time **passes**. *Months passed... The time passed surprisingly quickly.* ◇ If you **pass** a period of time in a certain way, you spend it that way. *To pass the time the four sang songs and played cards.* ◇ If an event **passes off** in a particular way, it happens that way. *The demonstration passed off peacefully.* ◇ When something **passes**, it comes to an end. *The crisis passed.*

❑ When someone **passes away**, they die.

❑ **Passing** is used to describe things which do not last very long. *This awareness about the environment might be a passing phenomenon.* ◇ If you mention something **in passing**, you mention it briefly while talking or writing about something else.

❑ What **passes** between two people on a particular occasion is what they say to each other.

❑ If you **pass** a test or exam, you are successful at it. A successful exam result is called a **pass**. ◇ If something **passes** a test or is **passed**, it is officially judged to have reached a required standard.

❑ When a government **passes** a new law, it formally approves it.

❑ When a judge **passes sentence** on someone, he or she says what their punishment will be. ◇ **pass judgment**: see **judgment**.

❑ If someone makes a **pass** at you, they make sexual advances towards you.

❑ If you say someone or something could **pass for** a certain thing, you mean people could believe they were that thing. ◇ If you **pass** something **off** as something else, you convince people it is that thing.

❑ If you **pass out**, you faint.

❑ When members of the armed forces **pass out**, they formally complete their training. This is marked by a ceremony called a **passing out parade**.

❑ If you **pass up** an opportunity, you do not take advantage of it.

❑ A **pass** is an official document which allows you to do something.

❑ A **pass** is also a narrow route between mountains.

❑ When you **pass water**, you urinate.

passable (passably) ❑ If something is **passable**, it is of an acceptable standard. *Most Austrian resorts are passably well equipped.*

❑ If a road is **passable**, it is possible to get along it.

passage ❑ A **passage** is a narrow corridor or space connecting one room or place with another. ◇ In the body, **passages** are tubes or long narrow holes for air or liquid to pass along. *...the nasal passages.*

❑ A **passage** is also a way through something. *Using his horn sharply, he cleared a passage for himself through the crowded streets.* ◇ When something passes through something else, you call this its **passage** through it. *The development of fatty lumps in the walls of arteries impedes the passage of blood within.* You can also talk about people's **passage** through a place. *They negotiated the safe passage of 300 people from Bosnia.*

❑ A **passage** is also a journey, especially by ship.

❑ A **passage** in a book, speech, or piece of music is a short section of it.

passageway A **passageway** is a narrow corridor or space connecting one room or place with another.

passé (*pron:* pas-say) If you say something is **passé**, you mean it is no longer fashionable.

passenger A **passenger** is a person travelling in a vehicle, aircraft, or ship.

passer-by (passers-by) A **passer-by** is a person who happens to be walking past when something happens. *A passer-by alerted the police.*

passim is used to indicate that something is referred to throughout a book or other piece of writing. *...Fox, pp. 16-17 and passim.*

passion is a very strong feeling, especially anger or sexual desire. *Passions are running high... ...a night of passion.*

❑ If you have a **passion** for something, you have a great liking for it. *His passions were cricket and birdwatching.*

❑ For Christians, Jesus Christ's **Passion** is his suffering from his arrest until his death on the Cross. A **passion play** is a play about Christ's Passion and Resurrection. Some musical works dealing with Christ's Passion have **Passion** as part of their title. *...Bach's St Matthew Passion.*

passion fruit (*plural:* passion fruit) **Passion fruit** are the small egg-shaped fruit of some kinds of tropical flowering plants.

passionate (passionately) ❑ If someone is **passionate** about something, they have very strong feelings about it. *The French feel passionately about their native tongue.* You call something like a speech **passionate** when it expresses strong feelings. *...a passionate debate.*

❑ You call people's sexual behaviour **passionate** when it is full of desire. *She kissed him passionately.*

passive (passively, passivity) You say someone is being **passive** when they accept what is said or done to them without complaining. *Even the tanks had failed to rouse the Russians out of their passivity.* ◇ You also say someone is **passive** when they do not take an active part in something, or do not intervene in something which is happening. *He said that the international community could not* *passively allow the genocide to go on.*

passive resistance is showing resistance to something you believe is wrong by non-violent methods, such as fasting, demonstrating peacefully, or refusing to co-operate.

passive smoking is breathing in other people's tobacco smoke.

Passover is a Jewish festival lasting seven or eight days in late March or early April. It commemorates the sparing of the Jewish first-born when the first-born of Egypt were slain by the Angel of Death.

passport ❑ Your **passport** is an official document issued by the government, containing your name, photograph, and personal details. You take your passport with you when you go abroad, and show it when you enter or leave a country.
❑ If something is a **passport** to something you want, it enables you to get it. *Divorce may not be a passport to happiness.* You can also say something is a **passport** to an organization or institution. *A-levels are the traditional passport to university.*

passport-holder A **passport-holder** of a country is someone who has a passport issued by that country.

password A password is a secret word or phrase which enables you to enter a place or use a computer system.

past ❑ When people talk about the **past**, they mean a period of time before the present. The **past** is also things which happened in the past. *...coming to terms with the past.* ◇ **Past** is used to describe things which existed or happened in the past. *...past governments... ...past attempts at reform.* ◇ **Past** is also used to talk about a period of time leading up to the present. *In the past eight days, at least 170 people have been killed.*
❑ A person's **past** is the earlier part of their life. ◇ If you say someone has a **past**, you mean there is something in their past they would rather keep hidden.
❑ If something is **past**, it is over. *The days are past when the rich and powerful saw a fine orchestra as a way of putting their city on the map.*
❑ You use **past** when you are telling the time. *...quarter-past-eight.*
❑ If you go **past** something, you go up to it and beyond it. ◇ If you say something is **past** something else, you mean it is beyond it. *Past the stables there is a beautiful little chapel.*
❑ If you are **past** a particular stage, you are no longer at it. *The hotel was long past its prime.* ◇ If you say someone is **past it**, you mean they no longer have the strength or energy to do something.
❑ If you are a **past master** at something, you are very skilful at it because you have had a lot of experience of it.

pasta is a type of food made from flour, eggs, and water. It is produced in different shapes. Spaghetti and macaroni are types of pasta.

paste (pasting, pasted) ❑ A **paste** is a soft mixture which spreads easily. Some kinds of food which spread easily are called **paste**. *...fish paste.* ◇ Some substances for sticking paper to things are also called **paste**. *...wallpaper paste.* If you **paste** something to a surface, you stick it there with paste or glue.
❑ Is someone is given a **pasting**, (a) they are beaten soundly in a game or fight. (b) they suffer badly as a result

of something which happens. *Merchant banks took a terrible pasting during the recession.*

pastel colours are pale and soft. Colours like these are sometimes called **pastels**. *...clapboard houses painted in faded pastels.* ◇ **Pastels** are also small coloured sticks of chalk-like crayon, used for drawing. A drawing made with pastels is also called a **pastel**.

pasteurized (*or* pasteurised) milk or cheese has been treated in a special heating process to kill bacteria.

pastiche (*pron:* pass-**teesh**) In the arts, **pastiche** is combining several elements, or copying something else, usually for humorous effect. A **pastiche** is something produced like this. *The sleeve design was a pastiche of a Velvet Underground album.*

pastime A **pastime** is something you do for pleasure.

pastor In some Protestant churches, a **pastor** is a person in charge of a congregation.

pastoral is used to describe things relating to members of the clergy and their duties in their parishes. *...pastoral work.* ◇ **Pastoral** is also used to describe things to do with a peaceful country life. *...pastoral tranquillity.*

pastoral letter A **pastoral letter** is an open letter from a bishop to the people in his diocese.

pastrami (*pron:* pass-**trah**-mee) is strongly seasoned smoked beef.

pastry (pastries) **Pastry** is a dough made of flour, fat, and water. It is rolled flat and used to make pies and flans. ◇ A **pastry** is a small cake made of pastry.

pasture is grassy land for farm animals to graze on.
❑ If you move to **pastures new**, you move to a different place or type of work, looking for fresh opportunities.

pasty (pasties) ❑ A **pasty** (*pron:* past-**tee**) is a pie made of pastry folded around a savoury filling.
❑ If someone looks **pasty** (*pron:* **pay**-stee), their face looks pale and unhealthy.

pat (patting, patted) ❑ If you **pat** something or give it a **pat**, you tap it lightly with the flat of your hand.
❑ A **pat** of butter is a small mass of it.
❑ If you call what someone says **pat**, you mean it comes a little too easily and may not be true or sincere. ◇ If you have something **off pat**, you have memorized it and can repeat it exactly.

patch (patches, patching, patched) ❑ A **patch** is a piece of material used to cover a hole. If you **patch** something, you mend it with a patch.
❑ If you **patch** something **up**, you repair it in a makeshift way.
❑ If you **patch up** a relationship which is in difficulties, you make it work again. ◇ If you **patch up** a quarrel or difference with someone, you settle whatever is wrong and become on good terms with them again.
❑ When people who are negotiating **patch up** an agreement, they work out a compromise which is acceptable to everyone. You can also say they **patch** something **together**.
❑ An eye **patch** is a small piece of cloth worn over an injured or missing eye, to protect or conceal it.
❑ A nicotine **patch** is a small piece of material like a sticking plaster, which you stick on a part of your body to help you stop smoking. The patch releases nicotine into your bloodstream, and this is supposed to reduce your craving for cigarettes.

❑ A fog or mist **patch** is a small dense area of it.

❑ A **patch** is also a small part of a surface which looks different from the rest.

❑ A **patch** of land is a small piece of it, especially one for growing things. ...*a vegetable patch.* ◇ Someone's **patch** is their territory, or their area of responsibility. ◇ A police officer's **patch** is the area he or she covers.

❑ A bad **patch** is a period of difficulties or problems.

❑ If you say something is **not a patch** on something else, you mean it is nothing like as good as it.

patchwork ❑ If you call something a **patchwork**, you mean it is a clumsy or illogical arrangement of many different things. ...*a patchwork of rules and regulations.*

❑ A **patchwork** quilt or garment is made from many small pieces of material sewn together.

patchy (patchily) If you say something is **patchy**, you mean it is better in some parts than others. *The existing scheme operates only patchily.* ◇ If information about something is **patchy**, it is incomplete. You can also say someone's knowledge of something is **patchy**.

pate Your **pate** is your head, especially the top part.

pâté (*pron:* pat-ay) is a savoury paste, usually made from meat or fish.

patella The **patella** is the small flat bone which protects the human knee joint. It is commonly known as the kneecap.

patent (patently) ❑ If someone **patents** a new product or process or obtains the **patent** on it, they obtain the official right to be the only person or company to make and sell it for a certain period.

❑ If something is **patent**, it is obvious. ...*his patent decency... His traumas have patently left him a changed man.*

patent leather is leather with a very shiny surface.

paternal feelings are the kind a father has about his children. **Paternal** behaviour is the kind a father would show to his children. ◇ Your **paternal** grandparents are your father's parents.

paternalist (paternalistic, paternalism) You say a government or company is **paternalist** or **paternalistic** when it looks after its people's or employees' needs without giving them any say in how things are managed. Treating people like this is called **paternalism**.

paternity is used to talk about things connected with being a father. ...*a paternity test.* ◇ **Paternity leave** is time allowed off work for a man whose wife or partner has just had a baby. ◇ A **paternity suit** is a lawsuit brought by a woman to establish that a man is the father of her child, often so she can claim financial support from him.

path ❑ A **path** is a way across a piece of land, for people to walk along. ◇ If you clear a **path** for someone or something, you make it possible for them to get through a crowded or dangerous area. ◇ If something is in your **path** when you are walking or driving somewhere, it is directly in front of you.

❑ The **path** of a moving object is the line it travels along.

❑ A course of action can be called a **path**. *He would no doubt argue that the path he has chosen is the only one available.*

pathetic (pathetically) ❑ You say someone or something is **pathetic** when they bring out feelings of sadness and pity in you. *The shops have pathetically little on offer.*

❑ You also say something is **pathetic** when it is hopelessly unsatisfactory. *The choice of wines is pathetic.*

pathfinder You call someone a **pathfinder** when they find a new way of doing something which other people copy.

pathogen (pathogenic) **Pathogens** are very small organisms which cause disease. You say organisms like these are **pathogenic**.

pathologist A **pathologist** is a person who works in a medical laboratory testing such things as blood and tissue samples. Some pathologists also carry out post mortems.

pathology (pathological) ❑ **Pathology** is the study of the way diseases and illnesses begin and develop. **Pathological** is used to talk about things to do with this study.

❑ **Pathological** is also used to describe behaviour which is extreme and uncontrollable. ...*pathological gambling... He was a pathological liar.*

pathos (*pron:* pay-thoss) If you talk about the **pathos** of a situation, you mean you feel sadness and pity for the person or people involved.

pathway ❑ A **pathway** is the same as a path.

❑ A **pathway** is also a route which something travels along, for example in your body. ...*nerve pathways.*

patient (patiently, patience) ❑ A **patient** is someone who is receiving medical care from a doctor, dentist, or hospital.

❑ If you are **patient**, you stay calm in a difficult or irritating situation. **Patience** is the ability to stay like this. ◇ **try your patience:** see try.

❑ You also say someone is **patient** when they wait calmly for something for a long time, even when there is no sign of anything happening. *Around 30,000 fans waited patiently in the rain.*

❑ **Patience** is also a card game for one player.

patina A **patina** is (a) a fine layer of something on a surface. ...*a patina of 24 carat gold.* (b) a soft shine which something develops with age.

patio (patios) A **patio** is a paved area at the back of a house, where you can sit and relax.

patisserie (*pron:* pat-tiss-er-ee) is pastries. A **patisserie** is a shop selling fancy cakes and pastries.

patois (*pron:* pat-wah) (*plural:* patois) A **patois** is a form of a language spoken by the people in a particular area.

patriarch The **patriarch** of a family or tribe is the man who is its head. ◇ A **patriarch** is also a high-ranking bishop, especially the head of one of the Orthodox Churches.

patriarchal (patriarchy) A **patriarchal** society or system is one where men have all the power. A society or system like this can also be called a **patriarchy**.

patrician people come from a family with high social rank.

patrimony Someone's **patrimony** is the property or goods they have inherited from their father or ancestors. ◇ If you talk about a country's **patrimony**, you mean valuable things left over from an earlier time, such as its historic buildings.

patriotic (patriot, patriotism) If someone is **patriotic** or a **patriot**, they love their country and feel loyal towards it. You talk about the **patriotism** of someone like this. **Patriotic** is also used to describe things which express feelings of patriotism. ...*patriotic songs*.

patrol (patrolling, patrolled) When soldiers, police, or guards **patrol** a place or carry out a **patrol**, they make regular circuits, to make sure there is no trouble. A **patrol** is a group of people or vehicles doing this.

patrol boat A **patrol boat** is a small vessel used by the navy for patrolling the coast or a river, or for small operations.

patrol car A **patrol car** is a police car used for patrolling streets and motorways.

patrolman (patrolmen) A **patrolman** is a person employed by a motorists' association to assist members when their cars break down. ◇ In the US, a **patrolman** is a uniformed policeman who patrols a particular area.

patron ❑ A **patron** is a firm or wealthy person that supports artists, writers, or musicians by giving them money. ◇ The **patron** of a charity, group, or campaign is a public figure who supports it and allows their name to be used in its publicity.
  ❑ The **patron** of a restaurant is its owner.
  ❑ The **patrons** of a shop, pub, or place of entertainment are its customers.

patron saint The **patron saint** of a place or group of people is a saint who is believed to give them special help and protection. ...*St Vincent, patron saint of winemakers*.

patronage is the support given by a patron. ◇ **Patronage** is also the power someone has to appoint people to important jobs, regardless of whether they are suitable or not. ...*a system riddled with patronage*.

patroness (patronesses) A **patroness** is a female patron.

patronize (patronizing, patronized; patronizingly) (*can be spelled with an 's' instead of a 'z'*) ❑ If someone **patronizes** you, they treat you as if you are inferior to them or less intelligent. *It was often said, patronizingly, that he had 'the best untrained mind in politics'.*
  ❑ If you **patronize** a shop, pub, or place of entertainment, you are one of its customers.
  ❑ When a public figure **patronizes** a charity, group, or campaign, they support it and allow their name to be used in its publicity.

patter (pattering, pattered) ❑ If something **patters** on a surface, it makes light tapping sounds as it hits it. You talk about the **patter** of something on a surface. ...*the patter of the rain on the roof*.
  ❑ Someone's **patter** is something they have learned to say and which they can repeat at any time, to entertain people or persuade them to buy something.

pattern (patterned) ❑ A **pattern** is a decorative design of repeated lines, shapes, or colours. If something is **patterned**, it has a pattern on it.
  ❑ If something fits a particular **pattern**, it has features like something which has occurred before. *The killings fit the pattern of random attacks apparently designed to stir up further violence.*
  ❑ Behaviour **patterns** are regular ways of behaving.
  ❑ A **pattern** is also a set of instructions and diagrams for making something, for example a knitting pattern.

patterning is the manipulation of limbs which are not working properly, to get them to work on their own.
  ❑ The **patterning** on something is its pattern.

patty (patties) A **patty** is (a) a small pie. (b) a small flat cake of minced food.

paucity (*pron:* **paw-si-tee**) If there is a **paucity** of something, there is very little of it. Similarly, if there is a **paucity** of things or people of a certain kind, there are very few of them.

paunch (paunches; paunchy) If a man has a **paunch**, he has a fat stomach. You say a man like this is **paunchy**.

pauper A **pauper** is someone who is very poor.

pauperize (pauperizing, pauperized) (*can be spelled with an 's' instead of a 'z'*) If something **pauperizes** people, it makes them poor.

pause (pausing, paused) If you **pause** while you are speaking or doing something, you stop for a short time. This stop is called a **pause**. ◇ If you **pause** before doing something, you hesitate for a moment before doing it. ◇ If something **gives** you **pause**, it makes you stop and think carefully about what you were intending to do.

pave (paving, paved) ❑ When an area of ground is **paved** or **paved over**, it is covered with blocks of stone, bricks, or concrete. **Paving** is a paved area or surface.
  ❑ If something **paves the way** for something else, it makes it possible. *The new deal paves the way for a reduction in charges.* ◇ In parliament, a **paving** bill, debate, or motion prepares the way for new legislation.

pavement A **pavement** is a paved path for pedestrians along the side of a road.

pavement artist A **pavement artist** is a person who draws pictures on the pavement with coloured chalks, to get money from passers-by.

pavilion A **pavilion** is (a) a building at the edge of a sports ground, where players can wash and change. (b) a building, especially a temporary one, put up to house an exhibition.

paving stone **Paving stones** are flat square or rectangular pieces of stone or concrete, used to pave surfaces.

Pavlovian You say someone's behaviour is **Pavlovian** when they respond in an automatic way to something each time it happens.

paw The **paws** of a dog, cat, or bear are its feet, which have claws for gripping things and soft pads for walking and running. ◇ If an animal **paws** something, it scrapes it with its paw or hoof.

pawn ❑ A **pawn** is a piece in chess. Each player has eight **pawns**. They are the least valuable pieces. ◇ You say someone is a **pawn** when they are not one of the main people involved in an activity, and are being used by other people rather than making their own decisions.
  ❑ If you **pawn** something, you leave it with a person called a **pawnbroker** in return for a loan. If you do not pay back the loan within a certain time, the pawnbroker sells the item to someone else. A pawnbroker's premises are sometimes called a **pawnshop**.

pawnbroker See pawn.

pawpaw See papaya.

pay (paying, paid *not 'payed'*) ❑ When you **pay** for goods or a service, you give money to the person selling the goods or providing the service. ◇ If you **pay back** some money you have borrowed, you return it. ◇ If you **pay up**, you give someone the money you owe them. Similarly, you can **pay off** a debt.
  ❑ When your employers **pay** you, they give you your wages or salary. Your **pay** is what they give you. You can say your job is **well-paid** or **badly-paid**; you can also say it

pays a certain amount. *....a nanny's job paying £3.50 an hour.* Similarly, you can say an investment **pays** a certain amount. *The issue paid 7% tax-free.*

❑ If you have **paid** leave, you receive your pay while you are on holiday.

❑ If you say someone is **in the pay** of someone else, especially someone bad or crooked, you mean they are working for them.

❑ When an organization **pays out** a large sum of money, it gives it to someone, because it is required to. *British Airways paid out £610,000 in damages to Mr Branson and his airline.* A sum of money given like this is called a **payout.**

❑ If you **pay your way,** you manage without financial help from anyone else.

❑ If it **pays** to do something, it is to your benefit or advantage. *It pays to shop around.* ◇ If something **pays off,** it results in success. *Her determination paid off.*

❑ If you **pay** for something, you suffer because of it. *Throughout his life, he was made to pay for his political convictions.* ◇ If you **pay** someone **back** for some harm they have done you, you make them suffer in return.

❑ If something **puts paid** to someone's hopes or plans, it prevents them being fulfilled.

❑ If you **pay** someone a visit or a call, you visit them.

❑ **pay attention:** see **attention.** ◇ **pay a compliment:** see **compliment.** ◇ **pay your respects:** see **respect.**

pay award A **pay award** is an increase in pay for a group of people, especially people employed by the government or by local authorities.

pay-day (*or* **payday**) is the day when you are paid your salary or wages.

pay-off See **payoff.**

pay packet Your **pay packet** is the envelope containing your wages. The amount you earn can also be called your **pay packet.**

pay slip A **pay slip** is a piece of paper given to an employee at the end of each week or month, saying how much money they have earned, and how much has been deducted for things like income tax and national insurance.

payable ❑ If an amount of money is **payable,** it has to be paid. *The death duties payable on the estate could top £4 million.* ◇ If money is **payable** in a certain way, you can pay it that way. *The money is payable in three instalments.*

❑ If a cheque is made **payable** to you, it is made out to you.

payback A **payback** is a return on an investment.

paybed **Paybeds** are beds for private patients in an NHS hospital.

payday See **pay-day.**

PAYE is a system of paying income tax used in the UK, in which your employer deducts income tax from your wages, and pays it directly to the government. PAYE stands for 'pay as you earn'.

payee The **payee** of a sum of money is the person you are paying it to. ◇ The **payee** of a cheque or banker's order is the person it is made out to.

payer The **payer** of a sum of money is the person paying it. *...tax payers.*

paying guest A **paying guest** is a person who pays to stay in someone's home for a time.

paying-in A **paying-in** slip is a form you fill in when you pay cash or cheques into a bank account. A **paying-in** book is a book of paying-in slips.

payload An aircraft's **payload** is its cargo. The passengers are also sometimes called the **payload.** ◇ A missile's **payload** is the amount of explosives it carries. ◇ A spacecraft's **payload** is the main thing it is carrying, for example instruments or astronauts.

paymaster Someone's **paymaster** is the person or organization that pays their wages.

payment is paying money for something. *Payment must be made by cheque.* A **payment** is an amount of money paid for something.

payoff (*or* **pay-off**) ❑ The **payoff** from an action is the advantage or benefit you get from it.

❑ A **payoff** is a payment, especially a payment made to an executive who leaves or loses their job.

payola is another name for bribery or a bribe.

payout See **pay.**

payphone A **payphone** is a coin-operated telephone.

payroll An organization's **payroll** is (a) its list of paid employees. (b) the amount it spends paying its employees.

PC See (a) **police constable.** (b) **personal computer.** (c) **politically correct.**

PCB PCBs are chemical compounds, formerly used widely in industry. They are extremely poisonous, and, unless disposed of very carefully, can harm the environment and be a hazard to health. PCB stands for 'polychlorinated biphenyl'.

PE is a school lesson in which pupils do physical exercises, or take part in games or sports. PE stands for 'physical education'.

pea Peas are round green seeds which grow in pods and are eaten as a vegetable.

pea-green is a light-green colour.

peace is a state of undisturbed calm and quiet.

❑ **Peace** is also a time of not being at war. When a country or region is **at peace,** it is not involved in a war. A **peace treaty** is a treaty ending a war.

❑ **Peace** is also harmony between people. *For the sake of peace, she had never complained.* ◇ If you **make peace** with someone, or **make your peace** with them, you settle your differences with them. ◇ A **peace offering** is something given or said to someone as a way of apologizing to them or ending a quarrel with them.

❑ **The peace** is sometimes used to mean public order. *...behaviour likely to cause a breach of the peace.*

❑ **Peace of mind** is freedom from anxiety.

Peace Corps The **Peace Corps** is an American organization which sends volunteers to work in developing countries.

peace dividend When people talk about the **peace dividend,** they mean the money saved on defence since the end of the Cold War.

peace-keeping (**peace-keeper**) See **peacekeeping.**

peace-loving (**peace-lover**) A **peace-loving** person, group, or country avoids using violence to solve problems or to get what they want. People and countries like these are called **peace-lovers.**

peace-making (**peace-maker**) See **peacemaking.**

peaceable (**peaceably**) ❑ A **peaceable** person, group, or country tries to avoid quarrelling or fighting.

❑ A **peaceable** event or process takes place without any trouble or violence. *Matters would have been far more peaceably resolved if the authorities had stepped in earlier.*

peaceful (peacefully, peacefulness) ❑ A **peaceful** place is quiet and free from disturbance. *...the peacefulness of the gardens.* You can talk about having a **peaceful** time in a place like this. *He lives peacefully in Hampshire.* ◇ If you feel **peaceful**, you feel free from worry or anxiety. *That night I slept peacefully.*

❑ If an election, demonstration, or protest is **peaceful**, there is no trouble or violence.

❑ You also say something is **peaceful** when it does not involve war. *...a peaceful transition to civilian rule.*

❑ A **peaceful** person, group, or country is not violent, and tries to avoid quarrelling or fighting.

peacekeeping (peacekeeper) (*or* peace-keeping, peace-keeper) Peacekeeping is attempts to prevent further violence in a country or region where there is war or fighting. An organization which organizes attempts like these is called a **peacekeeper**. Troops sent to a place to prevent violence are called **peacekeepers** or a **peacekeeping** force.

peacemaking (peacemaker) (*or* peace-making, peace-maker) Peacemaking is trying to restore peace between groups of people who are fighting or quarrelling. A person who tries to do this is called a **peacemaker**.

peacetime is a period during which a country is not at war.

peach (peaches, peachy) ❑ **Peaches** are soft round juicy fruit with fuzzy yellow and red skins, yellow flesh, and a large stone. If something is **peachy**, it has the colour or flavour of peaches.

❑ **Peach** is a pinky-orange colour.

❑ If you say something is a **peach**, you mean it is excellent. *...a peach of a goal.* ◇ If you are delighted with something you can say it is **peachy**. *The weather was glorious and the snow just peachy.*

peaches-and-cream If you say a woman has a **peaches-and-cream** complexion, you mean she has fair healthy unblemished skin.

peacock (peahen, peafowl) **Peacocks** are large birds with shiny blue and green feathers. Male peacocks have long tail feathers which they spread out in a fan shape. Female peacocks are called **peahens**. Male and female peacocks together can be called **peafowl**.

peak (peaking, peaked) ❑ When something **peaks** or reaches its **peak**, it reaches its highest point. *Unemployment reached 3.2 million at its peak in 1986.*

❑ **Peak** periods are periods when demand for something, or the level of something, is at its highest. *The peak years of deforestation came in 1983-87.* ◇ In broadcasting, **peak time** is the same as prime time.

❑ When a person **peaks** or reaches their **peak**, they reach the height of their powers.

❑ A **peak** is a mountain, or the top of a mountain.

❑ The **peak** of a cap is the part at the front which sticks out over your eyes. You say a cap with a peak is **peaked**.

peaky If you say someone looks **peaky**, you mean they look pale and ill.

peal (pealing, pealed) ❑ When church bells ring, you can say they **peal**. You can talk about a **peal** of bells.

❑ A **peal** of laughter is a loud burst of it. Similarly, you can talk about a **peal** of thunder.

peanut ❑ **Peanuts** are small nuts eaten as a snack, usually after they have been roasted and salted. They are also used as an ingredient in other foods.

❑ You can call a very small amount of money **peanuts**.

peanut butter is a paste made from ground roasted peanuts.

peanut oil is an oil extracted from peanuts. It is used in cooking and the manufacture of soap.

pear **Pears** are a fruit with white flesh and yellow or green skins. They are narrow at the top and wider and rounded at the bottom.

pearl ❑ **Pearls** are hard shiny objects which grow in the shells of some molluscs, especially oysters. They are used in jewellery. See also **mother-of-pearl**.

❑ You can call a small thing of immense value a **pearl**. *...pearls of wisdom.*

pearl barley is barley grains with the husks removed. It is used in soups and stews.

pearl-grey is a light bluish-grey.

pearly is used to describe things which remind you of pearls, especially a person's teeth. *...pearly smiles.*

peasant (peasantry) In some countries, small farmers and people who work as agricultural labourers are called **peasants**. A country's peasants can also be called its **peasantry**.

peat is a kind of rich dark earth found in boggy areas. In some places, it is dried and used as a household fuel. Dried peat is also sometimes used in compost.

peaty soil, land, or water contains a lot of peat. ◇ **Peaty** whiskies taste slightly of peat.

pebble A **pebble** is a small smooth round stone.

pebble-dash (pebble-dashed) **Pebble-dash** is a coating for the outside walls of a house, made of small stones set in plaster. A **pebble-dashed** house has its outside walls coated in pebble-dash.

pebbly A **pebbly** beach or river bed is covered in pebbles.

pecan (*pron*: pee-kan) **Pecans** or **pecan** nuts are edible nuts similar to walnuts but with oval reddish shells. They grow on a type of hickory tree in the southern United States.

peccadillo (peccadillos *or* peccadilloes) A **peccadillo** is a small misdeed of no importance.

peck ❑ When a bird **pecks** something or **pecks** at it, it takes a bite at it with a sudden forward movement of its beak. A bite like this is called a **peck**.

❑ If you **peck** someone or give them a **peck**, you give them a quick light kiss, usually on the cheek.

❑ If you talk about the **pecking order** in an organization, you mean the order of seniority or power within it.

peckish If you feel **peckish**, you feel hungry.

pecs See **pectoral**.

pectin is a substance which helps jam to set. It occurs naturally in some fruit, such as plums. When other fruit such as strawberries are made into jam, pectin has to be added.

pectoral Your **pectorals** are the large chest muscles which help you move your shoulders and arms. 'Pectorals' is often shortened to 'pecs'. ◇ **Pectoral** is used to describe things to do with the chest, or objects worn on a person's chest. *...a pectoral cross.*

peculiar (peculiarly) ❑ If something is **peculiar**, it is strange or puzzling. *One of the eggs was peculiarly marked.* ❑ You also say something is **peculiar** if it is special in some way. *The peculiar difficulty of the operation must be realized... The inhabitants seem to be peculiarly susceptible to alcoholism.* ◇ If something is **peculiar** to a person, place, or thing, it applies only to them. *The problem is by no means peculiar to Jamaica... Such prejudice is a peculiarly British thing.*

peculiarity (peculiarities) A **peculiarity** is a characteristic or habit, especially an unusual one. *One of his distinguishing peculiarities is his extreme fairness.*

pecuniary is used to talk about things to do with money. *He was jailed for 12 months after admitting obtaining a pecuniary advantage by deception.*

pedagogue (pedagogy, pedagogic, pedagogical) **Pedagogue** (*pron:* **ped**-a-gog) is an old word for a teacher. **Pedagogy** is the principles and methods of teaching. **Pedagogic** (*pron:* ped-a-**goj**-ik) or **pedagogical** means related to teaching. *...immense pedagogic experience.*

pedal (pedalling, pedalled) (*American spelling:* pedaling, pedaled) ❑ The **pedals** on a bicycle are the two parts you push with your feet to make it move. When you **pedal** a bicycle, you make it move in this way.
❑ Various kinds of levers which you push with your foot are called **pedals,** for example the brake pedal in a car or the loud and soft pedals on a piano.

pedal bin A **pedal bin** is a waste bin with a lid which is raised and lowered by a pedal.

pedalo (pedalos *or* pedaloes) A **pedalo** is a small pleasure boat, driven by paddle wheels which you operate by pedals.

pedant (pedantic, pedantry) If you call someone a **pedant** or describe them as **pedantic**, you mean they are too concerned with small details and want everything done in the correct way. You can talk about the **pedantry** of someone like this.

peddle (peddling, peddled; peddler) If someone **peddles** something, especially something illegal or of poor value, they sell it. *Street vendors peddle fake designer watches to foreign tourists... ...drug peddling.* ◇ A **peddler** or **pedlar** is a person who sells things from place to place, or door-to-door. ◇ If someone **peddles** silly ideas or unreliable pieces of information, they try to interest people in them. *...peddlers of malicious gossip.*

pederasty (pederast) **Pederasty** is sexual relations, especially anal intercourse, between a man and a boy. Men who have sexual relations with boys are called **pederasts.**

pedestal ❑ The **pedestal** of a statue or column is the base it stands on.
❑ If you **put** someone **on a pedestal**, you admire them greatly and cannot accept that they have any faults. If someone is **knocked off their pedestal**, people no longer admire and respect them, because they have been shown to be dishonest or immoral.

pedestrian ❑ A **pedestrian** is a person who is walking somewhere, especially along a street.
❑ If you call something **pedestrian**, you mean it is dull and rather ordinary. *....a pedestrian performance.*

pedestrian crossing A **pedestrian crossing** is a place on a road where motorists have to stop when pedestrians want to cross. In Britain, pedestrian crossings are indi-cated by black and white stripes painted across a section of the road, or by special traffic lights operated by pedestrians pressing a control button.

pedestrian precinct A **pedestrian precinct** is a shopping area only open to pedestrians.

pedestrianize (pedestrianizing, pedestrianized; pedestrianization) (*can be spelled with an 's' instead of a 'z'*) If a street or part of a town is **pedestrianized**, it is closed to traffic so only pedestrians can use it. *Retailers have been pushing for pedestrianization of Oxford Street.*

pediatrician See paediatrician.

pediatrics See paediatrics.

pedicure is care or treatment of your feet, especially by a chiropodist or beautician.

pedigree A **pedigree** animal is descended only from animals of the same breed, and so is considered to be of high quality. ◇ An animal's **pedigree** is the list of its ancestors. ◇ A person's **pedigree** is their background or ancestry.

pediment A **pediment** is a piece of stone or wood, usually triangular, built over a door or window as a decoration.

pedlar See peddle.

pedometer (*pron:* pid-**dom**-it-er) A **pedometer** is a device you take with you when you are walking somewhere. It gives a rough measurement of the distance you walk, based on the number of paces you take.

pedophile (pedophilia) See paedophile.

pee (peeing, peed) **Pee** is urine. When someone **pees** or has a **pee**, they urinate.

peek (peeking, peeked) If you **peek** at something or take a **peek** at it, you have a quick look at it.

peel (peeling, peeled) ❑ The **peel** of a fruit like an orange or apple is its skin. When you **peel** a fruit or vegetable, you remove its peel with a knife. **Peelings** are strips of peel removed from a fruit or vegetable.
❑ If the paint is **peeling** off a surface, it is coming off in flakes. Similarly, if your skin **peels**, it comes off in flakes.
❑ If you **peel** something **off** a surface, you pull it off gently in one piece. *Peel off the backing paper.* ◇ If you **peel off** an item of clothing, you take it off by rolling it up over your head, or down over your arms or legs.

peep (peeping, peeped) ❑ If you **peep** at something or take a **peep** at it, you have a quick look at it.
❑ If something **peeps** out from somewhere, it just becomes visible. *I saw the moon peeping through a cloud.*
❑ If you say there is not a **peep** from someone, you mean they let something happen without objecting or making any comment.

peep-hole A **peep-hole** is a small hole in a door or wall through which you can spy on people on the other side.

Peeping Tom A **Peeping Tom** is a man who spies on women getting undressed, or couples having sex.

peer (peering, peered) ❑ If you **peer** at something, you look very hard at it, because it is difficult to see clearly.
❑ A **peer** or **peer of the realm** is a member of the nobility: a duke, marquis, earl, viscount, or baron. See also life peer.
❑ Your **peers** are people of the same age or status as yourself. You can also call people the same age as yourself your **peer group.**

peerage A **peerage** is the rank or position of a peer. *He* received his *peerage* in 1965. The system of having peers is also called the **peerage**. *There is a case for abolishing the peerage.*

peeress (peeresses) A **peeress** is a female peer.

peerless If you say someone is **peerless**, you mean they are better at something than anyone else. Similarly, if you say something is **peerless**, you mean it is better than anything else of the same kind.

peeved If you are **peeved** about something, you are annoyed about it.

peevish (peevishly) If someone is **peevish**, they are bad-tempered and irritable. *She frowned peevishly.*

peewit A **peewit** is the same as a lapwing.

peg (pegging, pegged) ❏ A **peg** is a small hook or knob for hanging something on. ◇ If you say something is a **peg** on which to hang something else, you mean it provides a chance or excuse for something you want to do.
❏ A **peg** is also a metal or wooden pin for securing something in place, for example a tent peg. See also **clothes peg**.
❏ If something is **pegged** at a certain level or value, it is fixed at that level or value. *BT has agreed to peg telephone price increases to 7.5% below inflation.*
❏ If someone is brought **down a peg**, they are made to realize they are not as important as they think.
❏ When someone **pegs out**, they die.

pejorative (*pron:* pij-jor-a-tiv) A **pejorative** word or phrase shows disapproval of the person or thing you are talking about.

Peke A **Peke** is the same as a Pekinese.

Pekinese (*usual plural:* Pekinese) **Pekinese** are small dogs with long hair, short legs, and short flat noses.

pelargonium **Pelargoniums** are a type of pot or bedding plant with frilly petals. The red flowers usually called geraniums are another type of pelargonium.

pelican **Pelicans** are large water birds, usually white, with short legs and huge pouches beneath their long bills. They use these pouches to scoop up water and filter out fish.

pelican crossing A **pelican crossing** is a place where pedestrians can cross a road safely by pressing a button which operates traffic lights to stop the traffic.

pell-mell is used to describe things which happen very quickly in an uncontrolled way. *...pell-mell expansion.*

pellagra is a disease caused by lack of vitamin B. The symptoms are tiredness, weight loss, and disorders of the skin and digestive system.

pellet A **pellet** is a small ball of something.

pellucid If something is **pellucid**, it is extremely clear. *...the pellucid waters of Long Beach harbour.*

pelmet A **pelmet** is a long narrow piece of wood or fabric fixed at the top of a window for decoration and to hide the curtain rail.

pelt ❏ If you are **pelted** with stones or other objects, people throw them at you.
❏ If you go somewhere **full pelt**, you go as fast as you can. *He drove his car through the gates at full pelt.*
❏ A **pelt** is the skin and fur of a dead animal which has been removed in one piece but has not yet been treated.

pelvis (pelvises; pelvic) The **pelvis** or **pelvic girdle** is the large bone structure between the rib cage and the top of the legs. It includes the hip bones and the sacrum. Pel-

vic is used to talk about things to do with the pelvis. *...pelvic bones... ...pelvic pain.*

pen (penning, penned) ❏ A **pen** is an instrument for writing in ink. ◇ If you **pen** something, you write it. *She penned a short memo to the prince's private secretary.*
❏ If you put **pen to paper**, you write or sign something. ◇ If you say something is **from the pen** of someone, you mean it is written by them.
❏ A **pen** is also a small fenced area where animals are kept. If animals are **penned** or **penned in**, they are kept in a pen. ◇ If people are **penned in** a small area, they are unable to get out, because their way is blocked in all directions. You can also talk about people being **penned behind** something. ◇ At a football ground, a **pen** is an area surrounded by a fence, where fans can watch the game without being able to get onto the pitch or reach other spectators.
❏ A **pen** is also a female swan.

pen computer A **pen computer** is a computer which you enter commands into by writing on the screen with a special pen.

pen-friend A **pen-friend** is someone, often in a foreign country, who you write to regularly and get to know through your letters.

pen name A **pen name** is a name used by an author instead of their real name.

pen-pal A **pen-pal** is the same as a pen-friend.

pen-pusher People who sit behind a desk all day doing paperwork are sometimes called **pen-pushers**.

penal (*pron:* pee-nal) **Penal** is used to talk about things to do with the punishment of criminals. *...penal practices.* ◇ A country's **penal code** is its system of laws for dealing with crime and punishment. ◇ You say something like a tax is **penal** when it is very severe.

penalize (penalizing, penalized) (*can be spelled with an 's' instead of a 'z'*) If someone is **penalized** for breaking a law or rule, they are punished for it. ◇ You also say someone is **penalized** when something places them at a disadvantage. *The tests, concentrating on areas such as comprehension and use of language, penalized black and Asian staff for whom English was not a first language.*

penalty (penalties) ❏ A **penalty** is a punishment for breaking a law or rule. ◇ **death penalty**: see **death**.
❏ If you **pay the penalty** for an action or decision, you suffer the consequences of it.
❏ In sports like football, hockey, and rugby, a **penalty** is a free kick or hit at goal, given to the attacking team if the defending team commit a foul near their own goal. In football, only the goalkeeper is allowed to stop or divert the penalty. ◇ In football, if a game ending in a draw is decided on **penalties**, each team takes five penalties, and the team scoring most goals wins. This way of deciding a game is called a **penalty shoot-out**.

penalty area The **penalty area** is a rectangular area on a football pitch in front of the goal. Inside this area, the goalkeeper is allowed to handle the ball, and a penalty is given if a foul is committed by the defending team.

penalty box In football, the **penalty box** is the same as the penalty area. ◇ In ice hockey, the **penalty box** or **penalty bench** is the area where players who have been sent off sit until they are allowed back onto the ice.

penalty clause A **penalty clause** is a clause in a contract stating the penalty for breaking the agreement.

penalty spot In football, the **penalty spot** is the place in front of the goal which penalties are taken from.

penance or a **penance** is something you do willingly as a punishment to show you are sorry for some wrong you have done. *He spent the past two years at a remote Buddhist monastery in a gesture of penance for official abuses committed during his eight years in power.*

❑ In the Roman Catholic Church, **penance** is obtaining forgiveness by performing a certain act to show repentance before confessing your sin to a priest.

pence The pound sterling is divided into 100 **pence.** 'Pence' is usually shortened to 'p'.

penchant (*pron:* **pon**-shon) If you have a **penchant** for something, you have a special liking for it, or a tendency to do it. *He had never previously shown any penchant for violence.*

pencil (pencilling, pencilled) (*American spelling:* penciling, penciled) ❑ A **pencil** is a thin wooden object used for writing and drawing. It has a strip of graphite down the centre which is exposed and sharpened at one end. If you **pencil** something, you write or draw it in pencil. *...a pencilled note.* ◇ Cosmetics shaped like pencils are also called **pencils.** *...eyebrow pencils... ...lip pencils.*

❑ If a proposal is **pencilled in**, it is agreed but not yet confirmed.

pendant A **pendant** is an ornament on a chain you wear round your neck.

pending ❑ If something is **pending**, it is going to happen soon. *...the pending court case.*

❑ You also say something is **pending** when it is waiting to be decided or settled.

❑ If something is done **pending** a future event, it is done until that event happens or is over. *The pool has been closed pending an investigation.*

pendulous is used to describe things which hang downwards swinging freely. *...pendulous breasts.*

pendulum ❑ In physics, a **pendulum** is a weight suspended from thin wire or thread so it swings freely. The swings of a pendulum always take the same amount of time, regardless of the distance of the swing. ◇ The **pendulum** in a clock is a rod which swings from side to side, helping to regulate the clock's movement.

❑ Something which keeps changing one way then changing back again can be called a **pendulum.** *...the pendulum of opinion.*

penetrate (penetrating, penetrated; penetration) ❑ If something like a bullet **penetrates** an object, it passes into it or through it. ◇ If something **penetrates** an enemy's defences, it passes through them. ◇ If an army **penetrates** an area, it succeeds in advancing some way into it.

❑ If someone **penetrates** an enemy organization, they succeed in joining it to gather information about it.

❑ If a company **penetrates** a market or area, it succeeds in selling its products there.

❑ If someone has failed to understand something people are trying to tell you, you can say the message has not **penetrated.** ◇ A **penetrating** remark or piece of writing shows deep understanding of something.

❑ A **penetrating** look makes you feel uncomfortable, because you feel the person looking at you can see into your mind.

❑ A **penetrating** sound is loud and very noticeable.

penetrative sexual intercourse involves a man inserting his penis into the vagina or anus of his sexual partner.

penguin Penguins are flightless black and white seabirds with webbed feet and flipper-like wings, mainly found in the Antarctic.

penicillin is an antibiotic used to treat a variety of infections and diseases.

penile See **penis.**

peninsula (peninsular) A **peninsula** is a large area of land surrounded by water on three sides. **Peninsular** is used to talk about things on or relating to a peninsula. *...a 43-acre peninsular farm.*

penis (penises; penile) A man's or male animal's **penis** is the part of the body used for urinating and having sex. **Penile** is used to talk about things involving the penis. *...penile surgery.*

penitent (penitence, penitential) If someone is **penitent**, they are very sorry for something wrong they have done. When someone is very sorry like this, you can talk about their **penitence** or call them a **penitent.** If someone's behaviour is **penitential**, it shows sincere regret for something wrong they have done.

penitentiary (penitentiaries) In the US, some prisons are called **penitentiaries.**

penknife (penknives) A **penknife** is a small knife with a blade or blades which fold back into the handle.

pennant A **pennant** is a long narrow flag

penniless If someone is **penniless**, they have no money.

penny (pennies) ❑ A **penny** is a coin worth 1p or one hundredth of a pound. See also **pence.** ◇ Before the change to decimal currency in 1971, a **penny** was a coin worth one twelfth of a shilling (about 0.4p). ◇ In the US, a **penny** is a cent coin.

❑ If you say **the penny has dropped**, you mean someone has just realized the truth about something.

penny-farthing The **penny-farthing** was an old-fashioned bicycle with a very large front wheel and a small back one.

penny-pinching is unwillingness to spend money on anything not considered essential.

penny whistle A **penny whistle** is a simple wind instrument consisting of a straight metal tube with holes in it and a mouthpiece.

pennyworth If you add your **pennyworth** to a discussion, you give your opinion.

pension (pensioning, pensioned) ❑ A **pension** is a sum of money paid regularly to someone who is old, retired, widowed, or disabled. ◇ If someone is **pensioned off**, they are made to retire and given a pension.

❑ A **pension** (*pron:* **pon**-see-on) is a boarding house in France and some other countries.

pension book A **pension book** is a small booklet issued to pensioners by the government, containing payment slips which can be exchanged for money at a post office each week.

pension fund A **pension fund** is a fund paid into by employers and employees. The money is invested to provide pensions for the employees.

pension scheme A **pension scheme** or **pension plan** is a scheme which provides you with a pension after you have contributed to it for a certain period.

pensionable If you are of **pensionable** age, you are at an age at which you are entitled to a pension from the state. ◇ **Pensionable** employment provides you with a works pension when you retire.

pensioner A **pensioner** is a person who is entitled to a state pension.

pensive (pensively) If someone is **pensive**, they are deep in thought. *He stroked his chin pensively.*

pent-up emotions have been held back for a long time. *...pent-up anger.*

pentacle A **pentacle** is a five-pointed star.

pentagon (pentagonal) ❑ A **pentagon** is a geometric shape with five straight sides. If something is **pentagonal**, it is shaped like a pentagon.
  ❑ The **Pentagon** is the headquarters of the US Defense Department in Washington. The Defense Department is itself often called the **Pentagon**. *The Pentagon is urging caution.*

pentamidine (*pron:* pen-**tam**-i-deen) is a drug used to treat a type of pneumonia suffered by people with HIV or AIDS.

pentathlon A **pentathlon** is an athletics contest in which competitors take part in five different events.

Pentecost ❑ In the Jewish religion, **Pentecost** is a festival held 50 days after Passover, to celebrate the harvest and the giving of the law to Moses.
  ❑ In the Christian religion, **Pentecost** is a festival held on the seventh Sunday after Easter, to celebrate the sending of the Holy Spirit to Jesus's disciples. This festival is also called 'Whit Sunday'.

Pentecostal (Pentecostalist, Pentecostalism) **Pentecostal** Christians or **Pentecostalists** believe strongly in the power of the Holy Spirit and in a literal interpretation of the Bible. They also believe Christ will return to the earth in the near future. Their beliefs and practices are called **Pentecostalism.**

penthouse A **penthouse** or **penthouse** apartment is a flat or maisonette built onto the top floor or roof of a building.

penultimate The **penultimate** thing in a series is the last but one. *...the penultimate lap.*

penumbra (*plural:* penumbras *or* penumbrae) A **penumbra** is a partial shadow.

penury (penurious) **Penury** is extreme poverty. **Penurious** people are extremely poor.

peony (peonies) **Peonies** are garden plants with large red, pink, or white flowers.

people (peopled) ❑ **People** is the usual plural of 'person'.
  ❑ A **people** is a race or nation. *...India's many peoples... ...the English-speaking peoples of the world.* ◇ The **people** are the ordinary men and women of a country. *British politicians like to think they are in touch with the people.*
  ❑ You use **peopled** to say what kind of people live in a place. *...a Caribbean island peopled by Americans.*

pep (pepping, pepped) ❑ **Pep** is energy and enthusiasm. *...a woman with more pep inside her than many writers half her age.* ◇ A **pep** talk is designed to give people encouragement.
  ❑ If you **pep** something **up**, you make it more lively or interesting. ◇ If you take something to **pep** you **up**, you take it to give you more energy. A **pep** pill is a pill which is

supposed to do this.

PEP A **PEP** is a way of investing in the stock market without paying income tax or capital gains tax. PEP is short for 'Personal Equity Plan'.

pepper (peppering, peppered) ❑ **Pepper** is a hot-tasting powder used to season food.
  ❑ **Peppers** are a kind of hollow green, red, or yellow vegetable.
  ❑ If soldiers **pepper** a building or area, they fire many bullets or shells into it.
  ❑ If something is **peppered** with a lot of small things, there are a lot of them all over it. *Its leaves are peppered with tiny umbrella-shaped hairs.* ◇ If a speech or piece of writing is **peppered** with something like jokes, it contains a lot of them.

peppercorn ❑ **Peppercorns** are the small dried berries which pepper is made from.
  ❑ A **peppercorn** rent is a very low one.

peppermint is a plant grown for its oil, which is used in medicine and as a flavouring. This oil is also called **peppermint.**
  ❑ A **peppermint** is a peppermint-flavoured sweet.

pepperoni is a kind of spicy sausage, usually eaten sliced on top of a pizza.

peppery If something is **peppery**, it tastes strongly of pepper. ◇ A **peppery** person is bad-tempered and irritable.

peppy If someone or something is **peppy**, they are full of energy and enthusiasm.

peptic ulcer A **peptic ulcer** is an ulcer in the stomach, the duodenum, or the lower end of the oesophagus.

peptide Peptides are small protein molecules.

per is used to mean 'each' when giving rates and ratios. *The membership fee is £650 per year... ...four ounces of dried pasta per person.*

per annum A particular amount **per annum** means that amount each year. 'Per annum' is often shortened to 'p.a.'. *...a service charge of £50 per annum.*

per capita A **per capita** amount is the amount, on average, for each head of population. *In 1990 we spent £582 per capita on health.*

per cent You use **per cent** to talk about amounts as a proportion of a hundred. For example, if an amount is 10 per cent of a larger amount, it is equal to 10 hundredths of the larger amount. 'Per cent' is usually written % .

per head means on average, for each person. *Their income per head, at $6,000 a year, is the highest in Latin America.*

per se (*pron:* per say) You use **per se** after mentioning something to say you are talking about that thing in itself, regardless of anything else. *Violence in art and entertainment is neither good nor bad per se.*

perambulate (perambulating, perambulated; perambulation) If you **perambulate**, you walk around different parts of a place. A **perambulation** is a walk like this.

perceive (perceiving, perceived) If you **perceive** something, you see, notice, or realize it. *They could perceive no sign of life below... Politicians perceived that lower tax rates were something which voters wanted.* ◇ If something is **perceived** as a certain thing, that is how people regard it. *Yacht racing is perceived as an elitist sport.*

percentage is used to say roughly how large or small an

amount is as a proportion of a whole. For example, you say an amount is 'a large percentage' or 'a small percentage' of a whole. *The percentage of girls in engineering has increased substantially in the past few years.*
❑ A **percentage point** is one per cent. *Their share of the vote dropped by five percentage points.*

perceptible (perceptibly) If something is **perceptible**, it is large enough to be seen or noticed. *The mood was perceptibly lightened by the announcement.*

perception is recognizing things by means of your senses, especially your sight. *...visual perception.*
❑ Your **perception** of something is your understanding or opinion of it.

perceptive (perceptively; perceptiveness) You say a remark or piece of writing is **perceptive** when it shows a real understanding of something. *The author writes perceptively about the tender relationship between young and old... His account is admirable for its clarity and perceptiveness.*

perceptual is used to talk about people's ability to recognize things through their senses, especially their sight. *...perceptual skills.*

perch (perches, perching, perched) ❑ If you **perch** on something, you sit on the edge of it. You can call the place where you sit your **perch**. ◇ If something is **perched** on something else, it is on top of it or on the edge of it. *The castle is perched on cliffs overlooking the Bristol Channel.*
❑ When a bird **perches** somewhere, it stands there, usually for a short time. ◇ A **perch** is a place for a bird to stand, especially a short horizontal rod in a pet bird's cage.
❑ The **perch** (*plural*: perch) is an edible freshwater fish.

perchance is an old word meaning 'perhaps'.

percolate (percolating, percolated) ❑ If a liquid **percolates** somewhere, it makes its way there slowly through small holes or gaps.
❑ If you **percolate** coffee, you make it in a percolator.
❑ If you talk about an idea or some information **percolating** to people, you mean it reaches them eventually.

percolator A **percolator** is a pot used to make and serve coffee, in which boiling water is passed repeatedly through ground coffee beans.

percussion (percussionist) **Percussion** instruments are musical instruments you hit, such as drums and cymbals. A person who plays percussion instruments in an orchestra is called a **percussionist**.

percussive sounds are the sounds you get when one object hits against another.

perdition is the state of never-ending punishment after death which some Christians believe sinners are condemned to.

peregrination A **peregrination** is a long rambling journey.

peregrine The **peregrine** or **peregrine falcon** is a large powerfully-built falcon with dark upper parts, a light underside, and long pointed wings. It is the falcon most often used in falconry.

peremptory (peremptorily) If someone says something in a **peremptory** way, they show they expect to be obeyed. *...peremptory demands... He called me in peremptorily.*

perennial is used to describe things which keep happening or seem to go on for ever. *...the perennial conflict between men and women.*
❑ **Perennial** plants live for several years. Plants like

these are called **perennials**.

perestroika was the policy of economic and political reform introduced by President Gorbachov in the former Soviet Union.

perfect (perfectly, perfection) ❑ If something is **perfect**, it is as good as it could possibly be. *The plan worked perfectly.* You talk about the **perfection** of something like this. *Others vouch for the perfection of the marriage.* ◇ If you **perfect** something (*pron*: per-fekt), you make it as good as it could possibly be. *She went to Paris to perfect her French.*
❑ You also use **perfect** to emphasize that something really is a particular thing. *She was a perfect stranger.*

perfect pitch If someone has **perfect pitch**, they can identify any musical note when they hear it, or sing any note when asked to.

perfectible (perfectibility) If something is **perfectible**, it can be made perfect. *...the illusion of human perfectibility.*

perfection See perfect.

perfectionist (perfectionism) If you say someone is a **perfectionist**, you mean they are never satisfied with what they do and are always trying to improve it. *...the dangers of excessive perfectionism.*

perfidious (perfidy) **Perfidious** people are treacherous and untrustworthy. **Perfidy** is treachery.

perforate (perforating, perforated; perforation) If something is **perforated**, small holes are made in it. These holes are called **perforations**.

perforce is used to say something happens because it cannot be avoided, rather than because it is intended or desired. *...the sort of withdrawn life led voluntarily by JD Salinger and perforce by Salman Rushdie.*

perform (performance) ❑ If you **perform** a task or action, you do it or carry it out. Similarly, you can say someone or something **performs** a service or function. You can talk about the **performance** of any of these things. *...the performance of his public duties.*
❑ You can use **perform** to say how well someone or something does a task or job. *Women pilots often perform better than men.* Similarly, you can talk about someone's **performance** of something. *Her performance suffered.*
❑ When musicians **perform** a piece of music, they sing or play it to an audience or make a recording of it. Similarly, you can talk about actors **performing** a play. A **performance** of a play or piece of music is an occasion when it is performed.

performer A **performer** is a person who does something to entertain an audience, for example acting, singing, or playing an instrument.

performing arts The **performing arts** are dance, drama, music, and other forms of entertainment usually performed live to an audience.

perfume (perfumed) **Perfume** is a pleasant-smelling liquid you put on your body. ◇ A **perfume** is a pleasant smell. If something is **perfumed**, it has a pleasant smell. *...the perfume of roses... ...perfumed soaps.*

perfunctory (perfunctorily) If something is **perfunctory**, it is done in a careless or half-hearted way, because it is expected rather than because the person wants to do it. *The applause was perfunctory... The sentry looked perfunctorily at their gate passes.*

pergola (*pron*: per-go-la) A **pergola** is an arched frame for climbing plants to grow on.

perhaps is used to say something may be the case. *He was perhaps the second most powerful man in the country.*

peril is great danger. *The whole package is now in peril... ...the perils of nicotine.* ◇ If you do something **at your peril**, you do it at great danger to yourself. *Those who underestimate him do so at their peril.*

perilous (perilously) Perilous is used to describe things which put people in danger. *...a perilous mountain trek.* ◇ If you come **perilously** close to something unpleasant, it almost happens to you. *The talks are perilously close to collapse.*

perimeter (pron: per-rim-it-er) The **perimeter** of an area of land is its outer edge or boundary.

perinatal means in the period shortly before or after birth. *...perinatal deaths.*

period ❑ A **period** is a length of time. *...a period of two years... The two lived together for a period.*
❑ A **period** is also a particular time. *...the Edwardian period.* ◇ Period costumes, objects, and buildings were made at an earlier time in history, or are in the style of that time.
❑ A woman's **period** is the monthly bleeding from her womb.
❑ In the US, a full stop is called a **period.**

periodic events or occurrences take place at regular intervals. *...periodic elections... There were periodic calls for it to be disbanded.*

periodical (periodically) ❑ **Periodical** means the same as periodic. *...the jets which fly over periodically.*
❑ A **periodical** is a magazine.

peripatetic (pron: per-rip-a-tet-ik) workers have jobs which involve them travelling from place to place. *...peripatetic teachers.* Similarly, someone can have a **peripatetic** life. *The family led a peripatetic existence.*

peripheral (pron: per-if-er-al) (peripherally) ❑ **Peripheral** means on or relating to the edge of something. *Thousands are fleeing from peripheral areas of Croatia... His peripheral vision was slightly impaired.*
❑ If something is **peripheral,** it is not very important compared to something else.
❑ **Peripherals** or **peripheral** devices are extra devices that can be attached to or put in a computer, such as printers and modems.

periphery (pron: per-if-er-ee) (peripheries) ❑ The **periphery** of something is its edge. *...the city's periphery.*
❑ The **periphery** of a field of activity is the parts which are not as important or basic as the other parts. *...those working on the peripheries of the paranormal.*

periscope A submarine's **periscope** is a vertical tube which can be raised so that the people inside can see above the surface of the water.

perish (perishes, perishing, perished) ❑ If people or animals **perish,** they die as a result of hard conditions, or they are deliberately killed.
❑ If fabric or a material **perishes,** it rots and falls apart.
◇ If food **perishes,** it goes bad.
❑ If a business **perishes,** it ceases to exist, because it is unable to make a profit.
❑ If you say **perish the thought,** you mean you hope the thing you are describing is not true or will not happen. *It may be that he is too carefree or – perish the thought – it may*

be that he needs a heavy dose of coaching.

perishable Perishable food goes bad quite quickly.

peritonitis (pron: per-rit-tone-ite-iss) is a painful and serious inflammation of the membrane lining the abdomen, often following a burst appendix.

periwinkle ❑ Periwinkles are evergreen plants with trailing stems and blue flowers.
❑ Winkles are also sometimes called **periwinkles.**

perjure (perjuring, perjured; perjury) If you **perjure** yourself or commit **perjury,** you commit an offence by deliberately telling lies in court while under oath.

perk ❑ A **perk** is something extra you get in addition to your salary or wages, for example a car or free living accommodation.
❑ If someone or something **perks up,** they become more cheerful or lively.

perky (perkier, perkiest; perkily, perkiness) If someone is **perky,** they are cheerful and lively. *'So what are we going to try next?' asked Trevor perkily... ...her natural perkiness.*

perm If you have a **perm** or have your hair **permed,** your hair is treated with chemicals and then curled so the curls last for several months.

permafrost is land, ice, and rock in the Arctic, which is permanently frozen to a great depth, although the surface may thaw in summer.

permanent (permanently, permanence) ❑ If something is **permanent,** it lasts forever. *Every year, 10,000 children are permanently disabled in accidents.* You talk about the **permanence** of something like this.
❑ You also say something is **permanent** (a) when it is there all the time. *The tired and perplexed expression on the president's face is now almost permanent.* (b) when it is not expected to change. *He didn't have a permanent address.*

permeable (permeability) If something is **permeable,** it is possible for something like light or liquid to pass through it. *...the permeability of the membrane of the cell.*

permeate (permeating, permeated) ❑ If something like an idea or attitude **permeates** a place or institution, everyone is affected by it. *Excessive respect for authority still permeates Japan's institutions.*
❑ If a liquid, smell, or flavour **permeates** a place, it spreads throughout it.

permissible If something is **permissible,** it is allowed.

permission If you give someone **permission** to do something, you allow them to do it.

permissive (permissiveness) You talk about people being **permissive** when they allow other people a great deal of freedom in the way they behave, especially in sexual matters. *...permissive parents... ...sexual permissiveness.* A period when this happens a lot can also be called **permissive.** *...the permissive Sixties.*

permit (permitting, permitted) If you are **permitted** to do something, you are allowed to do it. ◇ A **permit** (pron: per-mit) is an official document allowing you to do something. *...work permits.* ◇ If circumstances **permit** something, they make it possible. *As soon as the weather permits, his men will try to board the stricken vessel.*

permutation A **permutation** is one of the possible ways in which a number of things can be ordered or arranged. *Free insurance, extended warranties and special-rate finance are available in various permutations on various models.*

pernicious If you call something like an idea or policy **pernicious**, you mean it is very harmful.

pernicious anaemia is a type of anaemia caused by lack of vitamin B12.

pernickety If you call someone **pernickety**, you mean they are too concerned with small unimportant details.

peroration A **peroration** is (a) a speech. (b) the summing-up at the end of a speech.

peroxide or **hydrogen peroxide** is a chemical used for bleaching hair. It is also used as an antiseptic.

perpendicular If something is **perpendicular**, it stands or rises straight up from the ground. ...*a virtually perpendicular slope.* ◇ If something is **perpendicular** to a line or surface, it is at right angles to it.

perpetrate (perpetrating, perpetrated; perpetration, perpetrator) If someone **perpetrates** a crime or some other wrong or harmful act, they commit it. You say they are the **perpetrator** of the crime or act. ...*the perpetration of fraud... ...the perpetrators of the attack.*

perpetual is used to describe (a) things which never end. ...*perpetual motion.* (b) things which seem to be there all the time, or to be happening all the time. ...*perpetual fear... Nearly a quarter of women are perpetually on a diet.*

perpetuate (perpetuating, perpetuated; perpetuation) If someone or something **perpetuates** a situation, they cause it to continue. Similarly, someone or something can **perpetuate** a belief. ...*the perpetuation of negative stereotypes.*

perpetuity If something is meant to last **in perpetuity**, it is meant to last for ever. ...*an extraordinary contract which gave the publisher full rights in perpetuity.*

perplex (perplexes, perplexing, perplexed; perplexity, perplexingly) If you are **perplexed** by something or find it **perplexing**, you are confused and puzzled by it. *Most of the audience left in perplexity... That, perplexingly, is the kind of comparison he often evokes.*

perquisite A **perquisite** is the same as a perk.

perry is an alcoholic drink made from fermented pears.

persecute (persecuting, persecuted; persecution) If someone persecutes you, they treat you cruelly and unfairly over a long period. You call someone like this your **persecutor**. Treating people cruelly and unfairly is called **persecution**.

persevere (persevering, persevered; perseverance) If you persevere with something difficult, you continue doing it and do not give up. *Her perseverance has paid off.*

Persian is used to talk about things to do with ancient Persia or modern Iran. ...*Persian antiques.* A **Persian** is a person from ancient Persia or modern Iran. ◇ **Persian** is the main language spoken in Iran. It is also called **Farsi**.
❑ **Persian** carpets and rugs are from Persia or Iran. They have intricate patterns in rich colours, and are made by hand from silk or wool.

Persian cat Persian cats are a breed of long-haired cats with round flat faces.

persimmon Persimmons are a sweet orange-coloured fruit, grown in the US and the Far East.

persist (persistent, persistently, persistence) ❑ If something, especially a feeling or idea, **persists**, it continues to exist. You can also say something like this is persistent or talk about its **persistence**. ...*persistent rumours... ...persistently wet weather... ...the persistence of anti-Jewish sentiment.*
❑ If you **persist** in doing something, you keep doing it in spite of opposition or difficulty. You say someone who behaves like this is **persistent**. ...*persistent offenders... The government persistently refuses to legislate against age discrimination... Eventually her persistence paid off.*

person (*plural:* people *or* persons) ❑ A **person** is a man, woman, or child.
❑ Your **person** is your body. *Commoners were discouraged from looking directly at any part of his person other than his feet.* ◇ If you do something **in person**, you do it yourself, rather than getting someone else to do it for you.

persona (*pron:* per-soh-na) (*plural:* personae *or* personas) Your **persona** is the image of yourself that you present to other people. *Her persona was one of endearing cluelessness... ...his stage persona.*

persona non grata If someone is **persona non grata**, they are not welcome somewhere.

personable A **personable** person has a pleasant appearance and character.

personage A **personage** is a person, especially an important or distinguished one. ...*no less a personage than Henry the Eighth.*

personal ❑ A **personal** opinion, quality, or achievement belongs or relates to a particular person. *It was his personal view that workers had little need for unions... ...the Prime Minister's personal authority.* ◇ Your **personal** possessions are things which belong to you and are not shared with anyone else.
❑ If you give something your **personal** attention, you do it yourself, rather than getting someone else to do it. Similarly, you can make a **personal** appearance or visit.
❑ **Personal** is used to describe things connected with a person's health, feelings, and relationships. *He had to return to the United States for personal reasons.* ◇ **Personal** comments refer to someone's appearance or character in a critical or offensive way. ...*personal remarks.*

personal assistant Someone's **personal assistant** or PA is a person in charge of their secretarial and administrative work.

personal column The **personal column** of a newspaper is a column containing personal messages and advertisements.

personal computer A personal computer or PC is a small computer used by one person.

personal organizer (*or* personal organiser) A **personal organizer** is a personal filing system. It can be either a small ring-bound book like a Filofax or a personal computer or pocket-sized microcomputer.

personal stereo A personal stereo is a small portable cassette player with headphones.

personalise See **personalize**.

personality (personalities) Your **personality** is your character and nature as a whole. ◇ A **personality** is a famous person in sport, entertainment, or broadcasting.

personalize (personalizing, personalized; personalization) (*can be spelled with an 's' instead of a 'z'*) ❑ If you **personalize** a campaign, issue, or argument, you focus it on a particular person. ...*an acrimonious and personalized election campaign... ...personalization of the issues.*
❑ **Personalized** is used to describe (a) something designed to a particular person's requirements. ...*personalized number plates.* (b) something with a person's name or initials on it. ...*personalized envelopes.*

personally ❑ You use **personally** to emphasize that what you are saying is your own opinion. *Personally, I think she's gone too far.*
❑ If you do something **personally**, you do it yourself, rather than getting someone else to do it. Similarly, you can be **personally** responsible for something.
❑ If you take something, especially a remark or criticism, **personally**, you take it as referring to yourself.
❑ If you know someone **personally**, you have met them several times, and have not just heard about them from other people.

personify (personifies, personifying, personified; personification) If you say someone **personifies** a particular quality, you mean they are a perfect example of it. *He can be charm personified... She was the personification of kindness.*

personnel An organization's **personnel** are the people who work for it.

perspective In art, **perspective** is drawing objects as they appear to the human eye, so that things which are further away appear smaller than things which are close. ◇ A person's **perspective** is the way they view a situation. ◇ If you get something into **perspective**, you view it in proper relation to other things. *The incident needs to be kept in perspective.*

Perspex is a strong clear plastic material sometimes used instead of glass. 'Perspex' is a trademark.

perspicacious (perspicacity) If you say someone is **perspicacious** or talk about their **perspicacity**, you mean they notice, realize, or understand things quickly.

perspire (perspiring, perspired; perspiration) When you **perspire**, you sweat. **Perspiration** is sweat.

persuade (persuading, persuaded; persuasion, persuader) ❑ If you **persuade** someone to do something, you get them to do it, either by coaxing them or by getting them to see that it is a good idea. **Persuasion** is persuading someone to do something. *It took a lot of persuasion.* A **persuader** is someone or something that persuades people to do something. *...hidden persuaders.* ◇ If you **persuade** someone of something, you convince them that it exists or is true. *...a campaign to persuade people of the benefits of gas.*
❑ A **persuasion** is a belief. *...politicians of all political persuasions.*

persuasive (persuasively; persuasiveness) If someone or something is **persuasive**, they make you believe something is true or a good idea. *...persuasive evidence... He argued persuasively... ...the sheer persuasiveness of the account.*

pert A young woman is sometimes described as **pert** when she is lively and cheeky.

pertain (pertaining, pertained) ❑ If something **pertains** to something else, it belongs to it or is connected with it. *...vital military secrets pertaining to the Gulf War.*
❑ The situation that **pertains** at a particular time or in a particular place is the one that exists at that time or in that place. *...the circumstances that pertained at the year end.* You can also talk about something like a policy or rule **pertaining** at a particular time or in a particular place.

pertinent (pertinently, pertinence) If something is **pertinent**, it is important and relevant. *...pertinent questions... Botha pertinently points out that the South African tennis players were the ones who performed well at the Olympic Games... The number of complaints this year could have more pertinence than usual.*

perturb (perturbation) If something **perturbs** you, it worries you. **Perturbation** is worry and anxiety.

peruse (perusing, perused; perusal) If you **peruse** something, you read it. Reading something can be called a **perusal** of it. *I enclose a copy of our brochure for your perusal.*

pervade (pervading, pervaded; pervasive, pervasiveness) If something like a smell **pervades** a place, you can smell it everywhere. Similarly, you can talk about a feeling or attitude **pervading** among a group of people. *Despite the pervading pessimism, the championship is still within reach.* You call something like this **pervasive**. *...pervasive corruption... ...the global pervasiveness of American culture.*

perverse (perversely; perversity) ❑ If you say someone is being **perverse** or talk about their **perversity**, you mean they are deliberately being unreasonable. A **perverse** decision is an unreasonable one.
❑ You say **perversely** when you are talking about something working out the opposite way to what is intended or expected. *Perversely, such efforts to make amends for the past may actually widen New Zealand's racial division.*

pervert (perversion) ❑ If someone **perverts** something (*pron:* per-**verts**), they interfere with it so it is not what it should be. *...the perversion of justice.*
❑ People with abnormal sexual desires are sometimes called **perverts** (*pron:* per-**verts**); their behaviour is described as **perverted**. A **perversion** is an abnormal sexual act or desire.

peseta (*pron:* pe-say-ta) The **peseta** is the unit of money in Spain. There are 100 céntimos in a peseta.

pesky is used to describe people or things that are troublesome or a nuisance. *...a pesky tourist.*

peso (*pron:* pay-so) (pesos) The **peso** is the unit of money in a number of countries including Argentina, Cuba, Mexico, and the Philippines.

pessary (pessaries) A **pessary** is an object which a woman inserts into her vagina, where it melts. Some pessaries are for medication; others are contraceptives. ◇ A **pessary** is also a device placed in the vagina to support the womb.

pessimistic (pessimist; pessimism, pessimistically) If someone is **pessimistic** about a situation, they do not expect things to turn out well. You can talk about the **pessimism** of someone like this. *...pessimistic forecasts... He spoke pessimistically... He is not alone in his pessimism.* A **pessimist** is someone who always expects things to turn out badly.

pest (pestilential) A **pest** is an insect or small animal which damages plants or food supplies, harms livestock, or is a hazard to health. Insects and animals like these can be described as **pestilential**. *...the pestilential grey squirrel.* ◇ You can also call an annoying person a **pest**.

pester (pestering, pestered) If someone **pesters** you, they keep bothering or annoying you.

pesticide Pesticides are chemicals for killing insect pests.

pestilence A serious disease can be called a **pestilence** when it spreads quickly, killing a lot of people.

pestilential See pest.

pestle A **pestle** is a tool like a small club, used for grinding things to powder in a bowl called a mortar.

pet (petting, petted) ❑ **Pets** are animals people keep for pleasure and companionship. ◇ If you **pet** an animal, you pat or stroke it affectionately.

❑ You can call someone's favourite their **pet**. ...*teacher's pet*. ◇ Your **pet name** is the name people close to you call you instead of your real name.

❑ Someone's **pet** project or theory is one they particularly support or favour. Similarly, you can talk about someone's **pet** subject or their **pet** concerns or hates.

❑ **Petting** is used to describe a couple kissing and caressing each other.

petal (-petalled) A flower's **petals** are the coloured outer parts of its head. **-petalled** is used to describe a flower's petals. ...*the coppery red-petalled Nymphaea Graziella*.

petard If you have planned to harm someone and are **hoist with your own petard**, your plan backfires and you only succeed in harming yourself.

peter (petering, petered) If something **peters out**, it gradually comes to an end. *The letters started arriving in March and petered out in April*.

pethidine (*pron*: peth-i-deen) is a pain reliever given to women in labour.

petit four (*pron*: pet-ee for) (*plural*: petit fours *or* petits fours) **Petits fours** are very small fancy cakes and sweets, often made of marzipan.

petite A **petite** woman is small and dainty.

petition (petitioning, petitioned; petitioner) ❑ A **petition** is a document signed by many people, demanding that a particular action be taken. The people who sign it are called **petitioners**. ...*a petition calling on the Government to ban hunting*.

❑ A **petition** is also a formal application to a court of law for permission to do something. The person who makes the application is called a **petitioner**. ...*a divorce petition*. ◇ If you **petition** someone in authority, you make a formal request to them. *His brother has petitioned the President for a pardon*.

petrel **Petrels** are a group of seabirds which spend most of their lives at sea, returning to land only to breed.

petri dish (petri dishes) **Petri dishes** are flat shallow dishes used in laboratories, especially for growing cultures.

petrify (petrifies, petrifying, petrified) If you are **petrified**, you are very frightened. ◇ When an object **petrifies**, it turns to stone. ...*petrified tree trunks*.

petrochemical (*or* petro-chemical) **Petrochemicals** are chemicals obtained from petroleum or natural gas.

petrodollar (*or* petro-dollar) **Petrodollars** are the dollars a country earns from its oil exports.

petrol is a flammable liquid obtained from petroleum and used as fuel.

petrol bomb A **petrol bomb** is a simple bomb made from a bottle filled with petrol with a piece of cloth stuffed into its neck. If something is **petrol-bombed**, petrol bombs are thrown at it.

petrol station A **petrol station** is a garage by the side of the road where you can fill up your vehicle with petrol.

petroleum is the oil, located underground, which petrol and paraffin are obtained from.

petroleum jelly is a clear greasy substance obtained from petroleum, used in ointments and as a lubricant.

petticoat A **petticoat** is an item of women's underwear similar to a thin skirt, worn under a dress or skirt.

pettifogging A **pettifogging** person is too concerned with small details.

petty (pettiness) ❑ **Petty** is used to describe minor criminals and offences. ...*petty thieves*... ...*petty crime*.

❑ **Petty** matters are small and unimportant. ◇ If you say someone's behaviour is **petty**, you mean they behave in a mean or selfish way over some small matter. ...*petty jealousy*... *He was instantly sorry for his pettiness*.

petty cash is money kept in an office to make small payments.

petty officer A **petty officer** is an NCO in the Royal Navy. The highest-ranking NCO is **fleet chief petty officer**, followed by **chief petty officer** and **petty officer**.

petulant (petulantly, petulance) You say someone's behaviour is **petulant** when they are childishly bad-tempered or irritable. *He petulantly threatened to quit tennis... He has a reputation for petulance when things go wrong*.

petunia **Petunias** are garden plants with large pink, white, or purple trumpet-shaped flowers.

pew **Pews** are the long wooden benches people sit on in church.

pewter is a grey metal made by mixing tin and lead. In the past, things like plates and tankards were often made of pewter.

pfennig (*pron*: fen-ig) The **pfennig** is a unit of money in Germany. There are 100 pfennigs in one Deutschmark.

PGCE The **PGCE** is a teaching qualification for graduates. PGCE stands for 'Postgraduate Certificate in Education'.

pH The **pH** of a solution indicates how acidic or alkaline it is. Acid solutions have a pH less than 7, alkaline solutions a pH greater than 7.

phalanx ❑ A **phalanx** is any of the bones in the fingers or toes.

❑ A **phalanx** of soldiers or police is a group of them standing or marching close together. ◇ Any group of people of the same kind gathered together can be called a **phalanx**. *He was greeted at Heathrow by a phalanx of photographers*.

phallic If you describe something as **phallic**, you mean it is shaped like a penis or is meant to represent one. ...*a phallic symbol*.

phallus (phalluses) A **phallus** is a penis or a representation of one.

phantasmagoria A **phantasmagoria** is a series of confused images of real or imaginary things.

phantasy is an older spelling of 'fantasy'.

phantom ❑ A **phantom** is a ghost.

❑ **Phantom** is used to describe things which are thought to exist for a time, but turn out not to exist. ...*phantom pregnancies*... ...*phantom companies*.

pharaoh (*pron*: fare-oh) The **pharaohs** were the kings of ancient Egypt.

Pharisee The **Pharisees** were an ancient Jewish sect who believed in strictly obeying the laws of Judaism.

pharmaceutical is used to talk about things connected with the production of medicines and medical products. ...*pharmaceutical companies*... ...*the pharmaceutical trade*. **Pharmaceuticals** are medicines.

pharmacist A **pharmacist** is a person qualified to prepare and sell medicines and to give advice on medicines which do not need a doctor's prescription.

pharmacology (pharmacological, pharmacologist) **Pharmacology** is the study of medical drugs and their effects on the body. **Pharmacological** means connected with drugs or the study of drugs. **Pharmacologists** are researchers who test the effects of drugs, especially new ones.

pharmacy (pharmacies) **Pharmacy** is the preparation and giving out of drugs and medicines. ◇ A **pharmacy** is a shop where medicines are sold, or a hospital department where they are prepared or kept.

pharyngitis (pron: far-rin-jite-iss) is inflammation of the pharynx.

pharynx (pron: far-rinks) (plural: pharynges or pharynxes) The **pharynx** is the throat, from the back of the mouth down to the place where it divides into the air passage and the food passage.

phase (phasing, phased) A **phase** is a stage in a process or in the development of something. Chinese officials say this marks the start of a new phase in the winding-up of British rule. ◇ If something is **phased**, it is carried out in stages. ...plans for the phased release of all political prisoners. ◇ If something is **phased in**, it is introduced gradually. Similarly, something can be **phased out**. Sweden has pledged to phase out nuclear power. You can talk about the **phase-in** or **phase-out** of something.

PhD A **PhD** is a degree awarded to someone who has done advanced postgraduate research in a subject. 'PhD' is short for 'Doctor of Philosophy'.

pheasant Pheasants are large birds with long tails, shot for sport and food.

phenobarbitone is a drug used to treat epilepsy.

phenol is another name for carbolic acid.

phenomenal (phenomenally) **Phenomenal** is used to say something is extremely good or extremely successful. The results have been phenomenal... He did phenomenally well.

phenomenon (plural: phenomena) ❏ A **phenomenon** is something which happens or exists naturally, especially something unusual and interesting.
 ❏ A person who is very remarkable in some way is sometimes called a **phenomenon**.

phial A **phial** is a small tube-shaped glass bottle, often used for medicine.

philandering (philanderer) A **philandering** man has casual love affairs with many women. You call a man like this a **philanderer**.

philanthropic (philanthropy; philanthropist) A **philanthropic** person or organization helps less well-off people, especially by giving them money. You talk about the **philanthropy** of a person or organization like this. A person who helps less well-off people is called a **philanthropist**. ...philanthropic institutions... ...a millionaire who became known for his philanthropy.

philately (pron: fill-lat-a-lee) (philatelist, philatelic) **Philately** is stamp collecting. A **philatelist** is a stamp collector. **Philatelic** is used to talk about things to do with stamps and stamp collecting. ...the philatelic demand in those countries.

philippic A **philippic** is a speech or piece of writing attacking someone or something.

philistine (philistinism) If you call someone a **philistine** or talk about their **philistinism**, you mean they have no appreciation of art, literature, or music.

philology (philologist) **Philology** is the study of languages and their development. A **philologist** is an expert on

this. Philology is now usually known as 'historical linguistics'.

philosopher See philosophy.

philosophic means the same as philosophical.

philosophical (philosophically) ❏ **Philosophical** is used to talk about things to do with philosophy. ...philosophical conversations... ...the philosophical issues raised.
 ❏ If you are **philosophical** or takes things **philosophically**, you accept difficulties or disappointments calmly. They developed a philosophical attitude to life's twists and turns.

philosophize (philosophizing, philosophized) (can be spelled with an 's' instead of a 'z') When someone **philosophizes**, they talk about things to do with life generally. She loved all the sitting around at table and philosophizing.

philosophy (philosophies; philosopher) **Philosophy** is the study or creation of theories about the nature of existence, knowledge, beliefs, or behaviour. A person who creates theories like these is called a **philosopher**. A set of theories of this kind is called a **philosophy**.

phlegm (pron: flem) is the thick yellowish substance that develops in your throat when you have a cold.

phlegmatic (pron: fleg-mat-ik) (phlegmatically) If someone is **phlegmatic**, they stay calm even when something exciting or upsetting is happening. Not everyone is likely to react so phlegmatically.

phlox is a garden plant with clusters of sweet-smelling white, pink, or mauve flowers.

phobia (phobic) A **phobia** is an irrational fear or hatred of something. He had a phobia about flying. You say someone who has an irrational feeling like this is **phobic** or a **phobic**. You can also call their behaviour **phobic**.

phoenix (phoenixes) The **phoenix** was a legendary Arabian bird, said to live for 500 years. At the end of this time, it set fire to itself on a funeral pyre from which it rose again with renewed youth and vigour.

phone (phoning, phoned) ❏ **Phone** is short for 'telephone'. ◇ If you **phone** someone or **phone** them **up**, you telephone them.
 ❏ If someone is **on the phone**, they are speaking to someone else by telephone. ◇ You also say someone is **on the phone** when they have a telephone in their home.

phone card See phonecard.

phone-in A **phone-in** is a live radio or TV programme in which people telephone in with their questions or opinions.

phonecard (or phone card) A **phonecard** is a plastic card you can use to make telephone calls from certain public telephones.

phonetic (phonetically) **Phonetics** is the study of speech sounds. **Phonetic** is used to describe things connected with this study. ...phonetic training. ◇ **Phonetic** systems of spelling use special symbols to represent each sound. ...the phonetic alphabet... The words will be in the original language, spelled out phonetically.

phoney (or phony) If something is **phoney**, it is fake or false. ...a phoney American accent. ◇ If you say a person is **phoney** or a **phoney**, you mean they are insincere.

phonics (phonic) **Phonics** is a way of teaching children to read by matching sounds to letters or groups of letters. **Phonic** is used to talk about things connected with this method. Not all teachers rely on a phonic approach to teach *reading.*

phonograph In the US, a record player is sometimes called a **phonograph.**

phony (phonies) See **phoney.**

phosphate Phosphates are chemical compounds containing phosphorus, which are essential for the growth of plants and animals. They are often used in fertilizers.

phosphorescent (phosphorescence) If something is phosphorescent, it glows faintly. This glow is called phosphorescence.

phosphorus is a colourless substance which glows faintly in the dark. It burns in contact with the air, giving off white fumes.

photo (photos) A **photo** is a photograph.

photo-call A **photo-call** is a session arranged for someone to be photographed by the press.

photo-finish If there is a **photo-finish** at the end of a race, the finish is so close that the result can only be decided by studying a photograph taken of the winners crossing the finishing line.

photo-journalism (photo-journalist) **Photo-journalism** is reporting the news mainly in photographs. A photographer who does this kind of reporting is called a **photojournalist.**

photo-opportunity A **photo-opportunity** is a session arranged for someone famous to be photographed by the press or filmed by TV.

photochromic materials change colour when you shine light on them.

photocopier A **photocopier** is a machine which quickly copies documents by photographing them.

photocopy (photocopies, photocopying, photocopied) If you **photocopy** a document, you make a copy of it using a photocopier. A copy made like this is called a **photocopy.**

photofit A **photofit** is a picture of someone's face, especially someone wanted by the police, made up from photographs of different facial features. 'Photofit' is a trademark.

photogenic If you say someone is **photogenic,** you mean they look good in photographs.

photograph A **photograph** is a single picture taken with a camera. When you **photograph** someone or something, you take a picture or pictures of them.

photographer A **photographer** is someone who takes photographs, especially for a living.

photographic is used to talk about things to do with photography. *...photographic equipment.* ◇ If you have a photographic memory, you can remember things in great detail after seeing or hearing them once.

photography is the art of taking photographs.

photometer (*pron:* foe-tom-it-er) A **photometer** is a device for measuring light.

photomontage is creating a picture by sticking together bits of different photographs. A picture created like this is called a **photomontage.**

photon Photons are particles of light and all other forms of electromagnetic radiation.

photosensitive things are sensitive to light. *...photosensitive detectors.*

photostat A **photostat** is a special type of photocopy.

'Photostat' is a trademark.

photosynthesize (photosynthesizing, photosynthesized; photosynthesis) (*can be spelled with an 's' instead of a 'z'*) When a plant **photosynthesizes,** it uses sunlight to convert carbon dioxide and water into the sugars it needs for energy. This process is called **photosynthesis.**

photosynthetic plants obtain their energy by photosynthesis.

photovoltaic cells convert sunlight into electricity.

phrase (phrasing, phrased) A **phrase** is a group of words which are often used together, and whose meaning is not always obvious from the individual words. *They decided the phrase 'man in the street' must now become 'people in general'.* ◇ The way you **phrase** something is the way you express it in words. *He said later that the phrasing of the letter was a mistake.* ◇ If you say someone has a nice turn of phrase, you mean they are good at expressing things in a vivid or amusing way.

phrase book A **phrase book** is a book for travellers to a foreign country, containing useful words and expressions, with translations.

phraseology Your **phraseology** is the words you use to express something.

phylum (*plural:* phyla) A **phylum** is a group of species.

physical (physically) ❑ **Physical** qualities, actions, or experiences are to do with a person's body, rather than their mind. *...physical pain... Physically, they could not have been more different.*
    ❑ **Physical** is also used to describe things you can see or touch. *...physical evidence... ...a room physically separated from the dwelling portion of the house.*
    ❑ **Physical** is also used to talk about things connected with physics. *...basic physical laws.*

physical education See **PE.**

physical geography is the branch of geography dealing with the natural features of the earth's surface, such as mountains, lakes, and rivers.

physical science The **physical sciences** are sciences like physics, chemistry, astronomy, and geology, which deal with non-living things and natural forces.

physical training is the same as **PE.**

physicality Someone's or something's **physicality** is their physical nature or appearance.

physician A **physician** is a person legally qualified to practise medicine.

physics (physicist) **Physics** is the scientific study of forces and qualities such as heat, light, sound, pressure, gravity, and electricity. A **physicist** is a scientist who studies physics.

physio See **physiotherapy.**

physiognomy (*pron:* fiz-ee-on-om-ee) (physiognomies) A person's **physiognomy** is their face.

physiological (physiologically) **Physiological** is used to talk about things to do with the body. *...physiological changes... It can affect you physiologically.*

physiology (physiologist) **Physiology** is the scientific study of how the bodies of living things work. A **physiologist** is a scientist who studies this. ◇ Your **physiology** is the way your body works.

physiotherapy (physiotherapist) **Physiotherapy** is the treatment of disease or injury using methods such as exercise, heat treatment, or massage. A person who treats disease or injury in these ways is called a **physio-therapist**. 'Physiotherapy' and 'physiotherapist' are both often shortened to 'physio'. *I have been for some physio...* *...the Arsenal physio.*

physique Your **physique** is your body's build and muscular development.

pi is π, the sixteenth letter of the Greek alphabet. π is used as a mathematical symbol for the ratio of the circumference of a circle to its diameter, approx 3.14159.

pianistic is used to describe things connected with piano playing. *...his pianistic skills.*

piano (pianos; pianist) A **piano** is a large musical instrument with a row of black and white keys, which you play by pressing the keys with your fingers. A person who plays the piano is called a **pianist**.

pianoforte A **pianoforte** is the same as a piano.

pianola A **pianola** is a mechanical piano. 'Pianola' is a trademark.

piazza (*pron:* pee-ats-a) A **piazza** is a public square, especially in Italy.

pic See picture.

picaresque A **picaresque** novel is one in which a dishonest but likeable hero travels around having lots of exciting adventures.

piccolo (piccolos) A **piccolo** is a musical instrument like a very small flute. It can produce some very high notes.

pick ❏ If you **pick** someone or something, you choose them. Your **pick** is your choice. ◇ The **pick** of a group of things or people is the best of them.
❏ If you **pick out** someone or something, you identify them among a group of similar people or things.
❏ If you **pick** an object **up**, you lift it off the ground or some other surface. ◇ If you **pick yourself up** after you have fallen or been knocked down, you get back on your feet.
❏ If you **pick** something from a place, you remove it with your fingers. *She picked a leaf from her hair.* ◇ If you **pick** flowers, fruit, or leaves, you break them off the plant and collect them.
❏ If you **pick** your teeth, you remove bits of food from between them using your fingernail or a pointed object. ◇ If you **pick at** some food which is in front of you, you eat only small amounts of it.
❏ If someone **picks** a fight or quarrel with you, they deliberately start it. ◇ If someone **picks on** you, they single you out for criticism or harassment.
❏ If someone with a gun **picks off** people, he or she shoots them one by one.
❏ If you **pick** a lock, you open it without a key, for example using a piece of wire.
❏ If you **pick your way** across something, you walk carefully, avoiding any obstacles.
❏ If you go somewhere to **pick** someone or something **up**, you go there to collect them. *She was picking up her children from school.* ◇ If you **pick up** someone you have not met before, you speak to them and start a casual sexual relationship with them. Someone you become involved with like this can be called a **pick-up**. ◇ If someone is **picked up** by the police or security forces, they are arrested.
❏ If you **pick up** an object, for example in a sale, you ac-

quire it. ◇ If you **pick up** a skill, you acquire it gradually.
❏ If a piece of equipment **picks up** a signal or sound, it receives it or detects it. ◇ The **pick-up** on something like an electric guitar is a device which turns vibrations into sound.
❏ If something, especially trade or the economy, **picks up**, it improves or increases. ◇ If a vehicle **picks up** speed, it goes faster.
❏ If you **pick up the pieces** after things have gone badly wrong, you do what you can to get the situation back to normal again.
❏ **pick** someone's **brain**: See brain. ◇ **pick holes in** something: See hole. ◇ **pick** someone's **pocket**: See pocket. ◇ See also **picker**, **pickings**.
❏ A **pick** is the same as a pickaxe.

pick-me-up A **pick-me-up** is something which restores your energy, especially a drink.

pick-up See pick.

pickaxe (*American spelling:* pickax) A **pickaxe** is a tool for breaking up rocks or the ground. It consists of a curved iron bar, pointed at both ends, attached in the middle to a long wooden handle.

picker People paid to pick crops are called **pickers**. *...cotton pickers.*

picket (picketing, picketed) ❏ When strikers **picket** a place of work during industrial action, they stand outside and try to persuade other workers not to go in. This is called **picketing**. The people doing it are called a **picket** or a **picket line**. An individual member of a picket is also called a **picket**.
❏ A **picket** is also a position defended by a soldier or soldiers.
❏ **Pickets** are also pointed wooden stakes used to make fences.

pickings You can describe the money made from an activity, especially an illegal one, as the **pickings**.

pickle (pickling, pickled) ❏ When food is **pickled**, it is put into vinegar or salt water, to preserve it. **Pickles** are vegetables or fruit preserved in this way.
❏ An awkward situation can be called a **pickle**. *This put the British government in a pickle.*

pickpocket (pickpocketing) **Pickpockets** are thieves who steal things from people's pockets or bags. Stealing things in this way is called **pickpocketing**.

pickup A **pickup** or **pickup** truck is a truck with low sides. ◇ See also **pick**.

picky You say someone is **picky** when they are difficult to please and only like a small range of things. *...picky eaters.*

picnic (picnicking, picnicked; picnicker) When people **picnic** or have a **picnic**, they have an informal meal in the open air. People doing this are called **picnickers**.

Pict The **Picts** were a race of people who lived in northern Britain in ancient times.

pictorial (pictorially) **Pictorial** is used to talk about things involving or using pictures. *...a pictorial record of city life down the ages... Each section is explained pictorially.*

picture (picturing, pictured) ❏ A **picture** is a drawing or painting.
❏ If you take a **picture**, you take a photograph. 'Picture' is sometimes shortened to 'pic'. *The pic was taken by a remote controlled camera.* ◇ When someone is **pictured** do-

ing something, they are shown doing it in a photograph. *The two were pictured hand in hand.* ◇ You also call the image you see on a TV screen the **picture**.

❑ The cinema is often called the **pictures**. A cinema film can be called a **picture** or a **pic**. *...a night at the pictures... ...a baseball pic set in the 1940s.*

❑ If you **picture** something or have a **picture** of it, you have a mental image of it. *She pictured herself working with animals, perhaps in the veterinary field.*

❑ If you give or paint a **picture** of something, you describe it. *They gave a graphic picture of the hardships being faced by their two colleagues.* ◇ If you **put someone in the picture**, you fill them in on a situation. ◇ When you talk about **the picture**, you mean the general situation in a place. *The economic picture is now grim.*

❑ If you are a **picture** of something, you are a perfect example of it. *She was the picture of health.*

picture window A **picture window** is a large window consisting of a single pane of glass.

picturesque (picturesquely) A **picturesque** place is very attractive and unspoilt. *...the shanty-towns, perched picturesquely on the hillsides.*

piddling means small or unimportant. *...piddling amounts of money.*

pidgin A **pidgin** or **pidgin** language is a mixture of two or more languages, used by people who speak different languages to communicate with each other. *...pidgin English.*

pie A **pie** is a dish of meat, fruit, or vegetables baked in pastry.

pie chart A **pie chart** is a circular diagram divided into sections to show proportional amounts of something.

piebald A **piebald** horse or other animal is partly white and partly a dark colour, especially white.

piece (piecing, pieced) ❑ A **piece** of an object or substance is a portion, part, or section of it. *...a piece of the Berlin Wall. ...a piece of paper.*

❑ A **piece** is also something written or created, such as an article or musical composition. *...his piece in the New York Times... ...a piece by Tchaikovsky.*

❑ A **piece** is also a coin. *...a 50p piece.*

❑ In a board game, the **pieces** are the objects you move around the board.

❑ If you say someone or something is **in one piece**, you mean they are not damaged or hurt.

❑ If you **go to pieces**, you lose control of yourself because you are nervous or upset.

❑ If you **piece together** something which is broken, you put it together again. Similarly, if you **piece together** information about something which has happened, you try to work out the actual sequence of events. *The aim is to piece together the movements of known drug traffickers.*

❑ **piece of cake**: See **cake**.

pièce de résistance (*pron:* pyess de ray-ziss-tonss) The **pièce de résistance** is the most impressive thing in a series or collection of things.

piecemeal A **piecemeal** process happens a bit at a time. *...piecemeal privatisation.*

piecework is work you are paid for according to how much you do, rather than how long you work.

pied Some birds whose feathers are in two contrasting colours, especially black and white, have **pied** as part of

their name, for example the pied wagtail and the pied flycatcher.

pied-à-terre (pieds-à-terre) (*both pron:* pyayd-da-**tair**) A pied-à-terre is a small flat or house for occasional use.

pier A **pier** is a large platform sticking out into the sea, along which people can walk.

pierce (piercing, pierced; piercingly) ❑ If a sharp object **pierces** something, it goes through it, making a hole. You say something is **pierced** when it has had a hole made in it like this.

❑ If you **pierce** someone's defences or security, you succeed in getting through them.

❑ A **piercing** sound is shrill and high-pitched.

❑ If you talk about someone's **piercing** eyes, you mean they have eyes which seem to look at you very intensely. *He looked at her piercingly.*

pierrot (*pron:* pier-roe) A **pierrot** is a clown or entertainer who wears a white costume and whose face is covered with white make-up.

pietà (*pron:* pee-et-ah) A **pietà** is a painting, drawing, or sculpture of the Virgin Mary holding the dead body of Jesus and mourning over it.

piety is strong religious belief.

piffle If you say something is **piffle**, you mean it is nonsense.

piffling means small or unimportant. *...a piffling achievement.*

pig A **pig** is a farm animal with a snout and a bristle-covered skin, bred for its meat.

pig-headed If you call someone **pig-headed**, you mean they are stubborn or obstinate.

pig-iron is crude iron produced in a blast furnace.

pigeon Pigeons are birds with deep chests, small heads, and short legs, often seen in towns.

pigeon-hole (pigeon-holing, pigeon-holed) (*or* **pigeonhole**, *etc*) ❑ A **pigeon-hole** is one of several sections in a frame on a wall, where letters and messages can be left.

❑ If you **pigeon-hole** someone, you regard them as a particular type of person, rather than thinking of them as an individual. *He resisted being pigeon-holed as either a serious or popular composer.*

pigeon-toed If someone is **pigeon-toed**, their feet or toes turn inwards.

piggery (piggeries) A **piggery** is a place where pigs are kept and bred.

piggy-back (*or* **piggyback**) If you give someone a **piggy-back**, you carry them high on your back, supporting them under their knees.

piggy bank A **piggy bank** is a child's money box, usually shaped like a pig.

piglet A **piglet** is a young pig.

pigment or a **pigment** is the substance which gives something its colour.

pigmentation Someone's or something's **pigmentation** is their natural colour.

pigmy See **pygmy**.

pigpen A **pigpen** is the same as a pigsty.

pigskin is a kind of leather made from the skin of a pig.

pigsty (pigsties) A **pigsty** is a hut with a yard where pigs are kept. ◇ If you call a place a **pigsty**, you mean it is very dirty or untidy.

pigtail A pigtail is a length of hair which has been divided into three and then plaited.

pike ❑ The pike (plural: pike) is a large freshwater fish with a long narrow snout. Pike hunt other fish.
❑ In the past, a pike (plural: pikes) was a weapon consisting of a pointed metal blade attached to a long pole.

pilaster A pilaster is a rectangular column set into a wall.

pilchard Pilchards are small edible sea fish.

pile (piling, piled) ❑ A pile of things is a quantity of them lying one on top of another. If you pile things somewhere, you put them one on top of another in a pile. ◇ If something is piled with things or piled high with them, it is covered with piles of them. ...*tables piled high with leaflets waiting to be stuffed into envelopes.* You can also say things are piled up somewhere. *The books were piled up on either side of the stairs.*
❑ If people pile into or out of a place, they all go in or out in a disorganized way.
❑ If things pile up, more and more of them keep arriving or happening. *Throughout the day the phone calls start to pile up.* ◇ A pile of something is a large amount of it. *Boxing has made him a pile of money.*
❑ A large building is sometimes called a pile. ...*St Donat's Castle, a thirteenth-century pile.*
❑ The pile of a carpet is its soft surface, consisting of many small threads standing on end.
❑ See also **haemorrhoids**.

pile-up A pile-up is a road accident involving several vehicles.

pilfer (pilfering, pilfered) If someone pilfers things, they steal them.

pilgrim Pilgrims are people making a journey to a holy place for religious reasons.

pilgrimage If someone goes on a pilgrimage, they make a journey to a holy place for religious reasons. ◇ You also talk about someone going on a pilgrimage when they make a journey to a place connected with someone or something they are especially interested in. *The faithful dressed up in 10-gallon hats and rhinestones and made the pilgrimage to Nashville.*

pill ❑ Pills are small solid round masses of medicine or vitamins which you swallow without chewing. ◇ If a woman is on the pill, she regularly takes a special pill which prevents her becoming pregnant.
❑ You can say something like a failure or humiliation is a bitter pill. *The Swedes were forced to swallow the bitter pill of defeat by the unseeded Americans.* ◇ If someone does something to sugar the pill or sweeten the pill, they do it to make unpleasant news or an unpleasant measure more acceptable.

pill box See **pillbox**.

pillage (pillaging, pillaged) If people like soldiers pillage a place, they steal property from it using force and violence. Stealing things like this is called pillage. ◇ You can also say money is pillaged when it is dishonestly and unfairly taken from its owners. *£400 million has been pillaged from their pension funds.*

pillar (pillared) ❑ A pillar is a tall solid post used in building as a support or decoration. If a building or part of a building is pillared, it has pillars round it, or it is supported by pillars.
❑ If you say something is a pillar of an organization or system, you mean it is one of the features which make it strong or successful. *The pillar of her economic policy was keeping tight control over money supply.* ◇ If you say someone is a pillar of the community or a pillar of society, you mean they play an active, important, and respected role in society.

pillar box A pillar box is an upright red cylinder in the street with a narrow hole where you post letters.

pillbox (pillboxes) (or pill box, pill boxes) ❑ A pillbox is a small tin or box for keeping pills in.
❑ A pillbox is also a small, usually circular concrete shelter with narrow slits from which guns can be fired. Pillboxes are used as defensive positions during wartime.

pillion If you ride pillion on a motorbike or are a pillion passenger, you sit behind the person controlling it.

pillory (pillories, pillorying, pilloried) In the past, the pillory was a wooden frame with holes for the neck and wrists. People convicted of minor crimes were sometimes pilloried, which meant being locked in the pillory in a public place as a punishment. ◇ Nowadays, you say someone is pilloried when they are publicly ridiculed and criticized, especially in the newspapers or on TV.

pillow Pillows are the rectangular cushions you rest your head on in bed. ◇ Pillow talk is intimate conversation between people who are in bed together, especially conversation about secret subjects. *Official secrets are at risk through careless pillow talk.*

pillowcase A pillowcase is a cover for a pillow.

pillowslip A pillowslip is the same as a pillowcase.

pilot (piloting, piloted) ❑ A pilot is a person trained to fly an aircraft. When someone pilots an aircraft, they fly it.
❑ A pilot is also a person who steers a ship through a difficult stretch of water, for example the entrance to a harbour. *He regularly piloted ships through Rhode Island Sound.*
❑ If a government minister pilots a new bill through parliament, he or she makes sure it is approved.
❑ A pilot scheme or project is one used to test an idea before deciding whether to introduce it on a larger scale. ◇ A pilot or pilot episode is a single TV programme shown to find out whether a series is likely to be popular.

pilot light A pilot light is a very small gas flame in a cooker, boiler, or fire. It burns all the time and lights the main flame when the gas is turned fully on.

pilot officer A pilot officer is an officer of the lowest rank in the RAF.

pimp A pimp is a man who gets clients for prostitutes and takes a large part of the money they earn.

pimple (pimply) Pimples are small red spots, usually on the face, which most commonly appear during adolescence. If you call someone pimply, you mean they have pimples, and you are using this as a way of saying they are very young. ...*a book written while he was a pimply student at Leeds University.*

pin (pinning, pinned) ❑ Pins are small thin pieces of metal with a point at one end. They are used in needlework to fasten pieces of material together.
❑ Various other long narrow pieces of metal or wood are called pins, especially when they are used to fasten things together. ...*the 18-inch steel pin holding his left leg together... ...a two-pin continental adaptor.* ◇ In the US, a brooch is called a pin. ◇ The pin on a hand grenade is the

clip which prevents it from exploding and which you pull out when you want it to explode.

❏ If you **pin** something on something else, you attach it with a pin, a drawing pin, or a safety pin.

❏ If you **pin** your hopes on something, you rely on it as your best or only chance of getting what you want. *Many firms are pinning their hopes on government help.* ◇ If someone **pins** the blame on you for something, they say it is your fault.

❏ If you **pin** someone **down**, you force them to make a definite statement. *She couldn't pin him down to a date.* ◇ You also say someone is **pinned down** (a) when they are unable to move because there is something heavy on top of them. (b) when they are unable to leave a place because there are people shooting at them. *Government troops were pinned down around the presidential mansion.*

❏ If something is difficult to **pin down**, it is difficult to say exactly what it is or what it is like. *The unique quality of Fonteyn's dancing has never been easy to pin down.*

❏ **Pin money** is small amounts of extra money you earn to buy things you want but do not really need.

❏ Someone's **PIN** or **PIN number** is the secret number they use with their switchcard or bank card to withdraw money from a cash machine. PIN stands for 'personal identification number'.

pin-up A pin-up is an attractive man or woman who appears on posters or in photographs in newspapers, usually wearing very few clothes or none at all.

pinafore A pinafore is an apron, especially one with a bib. ◇ A **pinafore dress** is a sleeveless dress usually worn over a blouse or sweater.

pinball is an electronic game in which you press buttons to flick a ball up a slope so that it hits objects, lights lights, and rings bells to score points. You have to keep flicking the ball when it comes down again to prevent it falling down the hole at the bottom of the slope.

pince-nez (*pron: panss-nay*) were an old-fashioned kind of spectacles. They consisted of a pair of lenses which fitted tightly onto the top of the nose, with no side pieces to fit over the ears.

pincer ❏ Pincers are a tool for gripping things or pulling things out. They consist of two pieces of metal hinged in the middle. ◇ The **pincers** of an animal like a crab or lobster are its front claws, which it uses for gripping, squeezing, and tearing.

❏ A **pincer movement** is a move by an army in which they divide into two columns as they approach an enemy, to try to surround them.

pinch (pinches, pinching, pinched) ❏ If you **pinch** someone, you take a piece of their skin between your thumb and first finger and give it a short squeeze. ◇ A **pinch** of something is the amount you can hold between your thumb and first finger. *...a pinch of salt.*

❏ If something is possible **at a pinch**, it can be done if it is really necessary, although it will not be easy or comfortable. *The Primera will accommodate four people, five at a pinch, and a mountain of luggage.*

❏ If people are **feeling the pinch**, they do not have as much money as they used to, and cannot buy the things they would like to buy.

❏ If someone **pinches** something, they steal it.

❏ If you say someone's face is **pinched**, you mean it

looks pale or thin because of hunger, illness, or cold.

pincushion A pincushion is a small padded object you stick pins and needles into so you can get them easily when you need them.

pine (pining, pined) ❏ **Pines** are various kinds of tall trees which produce cones and have needle-shaped leaves. **Pine** or **pinewood** is the pale-coloured wood from these trees. It is often used for making furniture.

❏ If you are **pining** for someone or something, you feel very sad because you no longer have them with you. If you are **pining** for a place, you are sad because you are no longer there.

pine marten The pine marten is a weasel-like animal with dark brown fur and a creamy-yellow patch on its throat. Pine martens live in coniferous woods in northern Europe and Asia.

pineapple Pineapples are large oval fruit which grow in hot countries. They are sweet, juicy, and yellow inside and have a thick, tough, lumpy, pale brown skin.

pinewood A pinewood is a wood which consists mainly of pine trees. ◇ See also **pine**.

ping If something **pings** or goes ping, it makes a short, high-pitched, metallic sound.

ping-pong is the same as table tennis.

pinhead A pinhead is the small metal or plastic ball-shaped part at the top of a pin.

pinion (pinioning, pinioned) If someone is **pinioned**, they are tied or held firmly by their arms, so that they cannot move.

pink is the colour between red and white.

❏ **Pinks** are small fragrant garden flowers with pink or white petals and narrow leaves.

pinking shears are special scissors whose blades have V-shaped teeth which give a zig-zag edge to anything they cut.

pinkish If something is **pinkish**, it is slightly pink.

pinnacle A pinnacle is (a) a sharp rock pointing upwards, high up a mountain. (b) a cone-shaped stone high up on a building. ◇ If someone has reached the **pinnacle** of their career, they have reached its highest point.

pinny (pinnies) A pinny is an apron, especially one worn when doing housework.

pinpoint If you **pinpoint** something, you discover or show exactly what it is or where it is. *It was almost impossible to pinpoint the cause of death.*

pinprick A pinprick is something small which is meant to annoy someone, or which has the effect of annoying them. *...the pinprick of annoyance he feels every morning.* ◇ A **pinprick** of blood is a very small amount, taken as a sample.

pins and needles When you get pins and needles, you feel sharp tingling pains for a while, for example in your fingers, toes, or legs, because you have been in an awkward or uncomfortable position. This tingling is caused by the return of normal blood circulation.

pinstriped (pinstripes) Pinstriped suits or trousers are dark with very narrow vertical stripes. Pinstriped suits and trousers are sometimes called **pinstripes**.

pint The volume of an amount of liquid can be expressed in **pints**. A British pint is one eighth of an imperial gallon (about 568 cubic centimetres). An American pint is one eighth of an American gallon (about 473 cubic centimetres). ◇ A **pint** is also a pint of beer.

pint-sized A **pint-sized** person or thing is very small.

pioneer (pioneering, pioneered) ❑ In the past, **pioneers** were people who left their own country and went to settle in a part of the world which had not been settled before.

❑ If someone **pioneered** something or was a **pioneer** of it, they were one of the first people to be involved with it and develop it.

pious (piously) ❑ A **pious** person is very religious and moral. ◇ People are sometimes described as **pious** when they pretend to act in a very moral way without being sincere. *The party has been piously vowing for decades to reduce these disparities.*

❑ You can call a statement **pious** when it is full of good intentions but is unlikely to lead to anything useful being done. *All the pious declarations in the world will not bring peace without a practical mechanism for peace.* ◇ **Pious** hopes are unlikely to be fulfilled.

pip (pipping, pipped) ❑ **Pips** are the small hard seeds in a fruit like an apple, orange, or pear.

❑ If someone is **pipped** in a race or competition, they are beaten by a narrow margin.

❑ On the radio, the **pips** are a series of short high-pitched sounds which are used as a time signal. Similarly, when you make a call from a public phone, you hear a series of **pips** which are a signal to put more money in.

pipe (piping, piped; piper) ❑ A **pipe** is a long round hollow object, usually made of metal or plastic, for liquid or gas to flow through. ◇ If liquid or gas is **piped** somewhere, it is transferred from one place to another through a pipe. *...a piped water-supply.*

❑ **Piped** music is quiet background music played through speakers in public places like shops and restaurants.

❑ A **pipe** is an object for smoking tobacco, consisting of a cup-shaped part at the end of a narrow tube. You put the tobacco into the cup-shaped part, light it, and breathe in the smoke through the tube.

❑ The **pipes** of an organ are the long hollow tubes in which air vibrates, producing different musical notes. ◇ Small simple wind instruments such as penny whistles are sometimes called **pipes**. ◇ Bagpipes are often called **pipes**. A person who plays the bagpipes is called a **piper**.

❑ If someone who has been talking too much is told to **pipe down**, they are told to be quiet. ◇ If someone who has been silent for a while **pipes up**, they say something.

pipe cleaner A **pipe cleaner** is a piece of wire covered with a soft woolly substance which a pipe smoker uses to clean his pipe.

pipe-dream If you call a hope or plan a **pipe-dream**, you mean it has no chance of ever becoming a reality.

pipeline ❑ A **pipeline** is a large pipe used for carrying oil or gas over a long distance, often underground.

❑ If you say something is **in the pipeline**, you mean it has already been planned or begun.

piper See pipe.

pipette A **pipette** is a thin glass tube used in chemistry for measuring and dispensing small amounts of liquid.

pipework is pipes generally, or the pipes in a particular machine or other construction. *Pipework attached to the steam-generators began to crack.*

piping is (a) lengths of pipe. *...bits of metal piping.* (b) cloth made into a narrow tube and used to decorate the edges of things like clothing and cushions. *...a fawn anorak with red piping.*

pipit Pipits are small songbirds with brownish speckled feathers and long tails. There are several species of pipits.

piquant (*pron:* **pee**-kant) (piquancy) If food is **piquant**, it has a pleasantly spicy taste. ◇ You say other things are **piquant** when they are interesting and curious. *There may well have been a piquant novelty about her books when they came out.* When something brings this quality to something else, you can say it adds **piquancy** to it.

pique (*pron:* **peek**) (piqued) If someone does something out of **pique**, they do it because their pride has been hurt, rather than for any sensible reason. *In a fit of pique he stuck his hand through the dressing-room door and lacerated his arm.* ◇ If someone is **piqued** at something, they are angry and resentful, because their pride has been hurt.

piracy See pirate.

piranha (*pron:* pir-**rah**-nah) **Piranhas** are small fierce fish with sharp teeth. They live in rivers in South America.

pirate (pirating, pirated; piracy) **Pirates** are sailors who attack and rob other ships. This practice is called **piracy**. ◇ Someone who **pirates** things like video cassettes or computer software makes and sells illegal copies of them.

pirate radio is the illegal broadcasting of radio programmes.

piratical (*pron:* pire-**rat**-i-kl) is used to describe a person who looks like a pirate. *...Cash's piratical appearance... ...a weird housewife with a piratical eye-patch.*

pirouette (*pron:* pir-roo-**et**) (pirouetting, pirouetted) When a ballet dancer **pirouettes** or does a **pirouette**, he or she balances on one foot and spins round.

pistachio (*pron:* pis-**tash**-ee-oh) nuts come from a Mediterranean and Middle Eastern tree. They have greenish kernels and smooth pale-brown shells.

piste (*pron:* **peest**) A **piste** is a route through snow which has been flattened to make it suitable for skiing.

pistol A **pistol** is a handgun with a short barrel.

piston In a machine, a **piston** is a part which is made to move backwards and forwards as a result of fuel burning or gases expanding. It is connected to the crankshaft by a connecting rod.

pit (pitting, pitted) ❑ A **pit** is a large hole dug in the ground. ◇ If a surface is **pitted**, it is covered with holes.

❑ A **pit** is also a coal mine.

❑ In the US, the stones in fruit are called **pits**. If you **pit** a fruit, you remove its stone.

❑ In motor-racing, the **pits** are the areas at the side of the track where drivers stop to get more fuel and repair their cars during races.

❑ If you are **pitted** against someone, you are competing against them or in conflict with them. ◇ If you **pit your wits** against someone, you compete with them in a situation which tests your knowledge or intelligence.

pit bull terrier The **pit bull terrier** is a dog like a Staffordshire bull terrier but larger. It is well-known for its strength and ferocity, and was originally developed for dog-fighting.

pitch (pitches, pitching, pitched) ❑ A **pitch** is an area of ground marked out and used for playing a game like football, cricket, or hockey.

❑ If you **pitch** something somewhere, you throw it with a lot of force. ◇ In baseball or rounders, when you **pitch** the ball, you throw it to the batter, who tries to hit it.

❑ A **pitched** roof is sloping rather than flat.

❑ If a boat **pitches**, it moves violently up and down with the movement of the waves.

❑ If you are **pitched** into a new situation, you are suddenly forced into it.

❑ The **pitch** of a sound is how high or low it is.

❑ If you talk about something reaching a particular **pitch**, you mean it reaches that level or intensity. *The conflict reached its highest pitch so far.* ◇ **fever pitch**: see **fever**.

❑ If something is **pitched** at a certain level, it is set at that level. *The issue is expected to be competitively pitched at around £2.50 a share.*

❑ A **sales pitch** is an advertising campaign, or the things someone says to try to persuade you to buy a product. *Cigarette companies are aiming their sales pitches increasingly at developing countries.* ◇ If someone is **pitching** for something or making a **pitch** for it, they are trying to persuade people to agree to it or give it to them. *The president gave a near-hysterical pitch for lower interest rates.*

❑ When people **pitch in**, they join in and help with something.

❑ When people fight a **pitched battle**, they have a fierce and violent fight.

❑ When you **pitch** a tent, you put it up.

❑ **Pitch** is a black substance which is sticky when hot but very hard when it cools down. It is used on the bottoms of boats and the roofs of houses to stop water getting in. ◇ If a place is **pitch black**, it is completely dark.

pitcher ❑ In the US, a **pitcher** is a jug. ◇ A **pitcher** is also a large container made of clay. Pitchers are usually round with a narrow neck and two handles shaped like ears.

❑ In baseball, the **pitcher** is the person who throws the ball to the batter, who tries to hit it.

pitchfork A **pitchfork** is a large fork with a long handle and two prongs. It is used for lifting hay or grass.

piteous (piteously) You call something you see or hear **piteous** when it involves suffering and makes you feel pity. *...a piteous wailing... 'I can't bear to face anyone,' she said piteously.*

pitfall The **pitfalls** of doing something are the things which may go wrong or cause problems. *...the legal pitfalls of opening a racecourse on Sunday.*

pith The **pith** of an orange, lemon, or other citrus fruit is the white substance between the peel and the inside of the fruit.

pithead At a coal mine, the **pithead** is all the above-ground buildings and machinery.

pithy (pithily) A **pithy** comment or piece of writing is short, direct, and memorable. *Louis Armstrong defined jazz pithily as 'what I play for a living'.*

pitiable You call someone **pitiable** when they are in such a sad or weak state that you feel sorry for them. *Thirty years of civil war left Ethiopia in a pitiable condition.*

pitiful (pitifully) You call someone **pitiful** when they are in such a sad or weak state that you feel sorry for them. *...a pitiful queue of prisoners seeking help... Injured horses neighed pitifully.* ◇ You can also use **pitiful** to describe (a) things that are completely inadequate. *...pitiful wages.* (b) things which are of very poor quality. *...a pitiful batting performance.*

pitiless (pitilessly) If someone is **pitiless**, they show no feelings of pity or mercy. *The guerillas have laid many villages in ruins and pitilessly massacred the inhabitants.* A war in which people behave like this can also be called **pitiless**.

piton (*pron:* **peet**-on) **Pitons** are metal spikes used by climbers. They are driven into rock crevices or ice and used to secure ropes.

pitta bread is flat ovals of slightly leavened bread, originally from the Middle East, with a hollow inside like a pocket, which can be filled with food.

pittance If you say someone is paid a **pittance**, you mean they are paid only a very small amount of money.

pitted See **pit**.

pituitary (pituitaries) The **pituitary** or **pituitary gland** is a gland attached to the base of the brain. It produces hormones which affect growth, sexual development, and other functions of the body.

pity (pities, pitying, pitied) ❑ If you **pity** someone or feel **pity** for them, you feel sorry for them. If you **take pity** on someone, you help them because you are sorry for them. ◇ A **pitying** look or gesture shows pity, often mingled with contempt. *...a pitying shake of the head.*

❑ You say '**It's a pity...**' when you are expressing disappointment or regret about something. *It is a great pity that all pupils in the city cannot have the same chances.*

pivot (pivoting, pivoted) ❑ A **pivot** is the pin or central point on which something balances or turns. You can say something is **pivoted** on a particular point.

❑ The **pivot** in a situation or the thing it **pivots** on is the most important person or thing in it, which everything else is based on or arranged around. *The production pivots on Ron Cook's Odysseus.*

pivotal If a person or thing plays a **pivotal** role in something, they are extremely important to it and affect its success.

pixel A **pixel** is the smallest size of spot making up the image on a computer screen.

pixie In children's stories, **pixies** are little creatures a bit like fairies. They have pointed ears and wear pointed hats.

pizza A **pizza** is a flat round piece of dough covered with tomatoes, cheese, or other food, and then baked in an oven.

pizzazz (*or* pzazz) is an attractive combination of energy, style, vitality, and glamour. *She started up two catering businesses, to which she brought enviable gifts of salesmanship and pizzazz.*

pizzicato (*pron:* pit-see-kah-toe) If a stringed instrument is played **pizzicato**, it is played by plucking the strings with the fingers rather than using the bow.

placard A **placard** is a large notice carried in a march or demonstration or displayed in a public place.

placate (placating, placated; placatory) If you **placate** someone, you stop them feeling angry or resentful by doing or saying things which please them. The things you do or say can be described as **placatory**. *...placatory words.*

place ❑ A place is any point, building, town, country, etc.

❑ In the US, **any place** means 'anywhere'. Similarly, **no place** and **some place** mean 'nowhere' and 'somewhere'.

❑ Your place is the house or flat where you live.

❑ A place is a seat or position which is available for someone to occupy. *I found a place right at the back.*

❑ You call the position where something belongs its place. *The lieutenant returned the album to its place on the shelf.* If something is **in place**, it is in its correct or usual position. *Specimens are held in place by two magnetic clips.* ◇ You also say things are **in place** when they are set up and operating. *Sanctions are in place.* ◇ If someone or something is **out of place**, they do not fit in with their surroundings.

❑ If you have a place on a course, you have been accepted for it. *She won a place at Oxford to read environmental chemistry.*

❑ If someone is on a committee, you can talk about their place on it. *Mr Foote lost his place on the board.* ◇ If you talk about a person's place in a system or organization, you mean their position or role in it. *He says that it is not his place to comment on government commitment to further funds.* ◇ If you **put someone in their place**, you show them they are not as clever or important as they think they are.

❑ If you are **placed** with an organization, it is arranged for you to work with them. Similarly, if a child is **placed** with a family, arrangements are made for it to live with that family.

❑ Your place in a race or competition is your position at the end of it; you say, for example, you finished in fourth place. You can also say you were **placed** fourth. The **placings** in a race are the official positions of all the competitors.

❑ If something **takes second place** to something else, it is considered to be less important and less attention is given to it.

❑ Your place in a book or speech is the point you have reached in it.

❑ If you **place** something somewhere, you put it there carefully.

❑ If you are **placed** in a certain situation, you are put in that situation. *Security forces have been placed on a state of high alert.*

❑ If you **place** great importance on something, you regard it as very important. Similarly, you can **place** emphasis or reliance on something. ◇ If you **place** the blame on someone for something, you blame them for it.

❑ If someone is **well-placed** to do something, they are in a good position to do it. ◇ If a town or building is **well-placed** for something, it makes a suitable base for it. *St Malo is well-placed for exploring Brittany by rail.*

❑ If you **place** an order for something like goods or a meal, you ask for them to be sent or brought to you, usually paying for them after they have arrived. ◇ If you **place** an advert in a newspaper, you arrange for it to appear there. ◇ If you **place** a bet, you bet on something.

❑ If you **place** someone or something in a class or group, you classify them in that way. *...St George's Hall, which the Prince of Wales placed among the greatest buildings in Europe.* ◇ If you say you cannot **place** someone or something, you mean you recognize them but cannot remember exactly who or what they are, or where you have come across them before.

❑ When something **takes place**, it happens. *The meeting will take place at St Catherine's College, Cambridge.*

❑ You say **in the first place...** when you are mentioning the main purpose of something. *He had been appointed, in the first place, to teach and to do research work, not to write memoranda.*

❑ If something is brought in to **take the place** of something else, it is brought in as a replacement for it. You can also say it is brought in **in its place**.

❑ If things **fall into place**, they happen naturally to produce the situation you want. *The elements of a ceasefire were falling into place.* ◇ If you have been trying to understand something and everything **falls into place**, you suddenly understand how different pieces of information are connected and everything becomes clearer.

❑ If you say someone has found their **place in the sun**, you mean they are in a job or a situation where they will be happy, well-off, and have everything they want.

place setting A place setting at a table is an arrangement of knives, forks, spoons, and glasses laid out for the use of one person.

placebo (*pron:* plas-see-bo) (placebos) If a doctor gives you a placebo, he or she gives you a harmless inactive substance instead of an effective drug. Placebos are used when testing new drugs or to establish whether a patient has imagined their illness. The **placebo effect** is the fact that some patients' health improves after taking what they believe is an effective drug but which is in fact only a placebo.

placeman (placemen) If you call a public official a **placeman**, you mean he uses his position for personal benefit, or has been given it by people who knew they could rely on him for political support.

placement When someone is found a job, home, or school, this is sometimes called their **placement**. ◇ When someone who is being trained gets a **placement**, they get a temporary job intended to give them experience in the work they are training for.

placenta (placental) The **placenta** is the mass of blood vessels and tissue inside the womb of a pregnant woman or animal, which the foetus is attached to. **Placental** is used to describe things to do with the placenta. *...the placental barrier.*

placid ❑ A placid person is calm and does not easily get excited, angry, or upset.

❑ A placid stretch of water is calm and still.

plagiarize (*pron:* play-jer-ize) (plagiarizing, plagiarized; plagiarism) (*can be spelled with an 's' instead of a 'z'*) If someone **plagiarizes** another person's idea or work, they use it or copy it and pretend they thought of it or created it. You say someone who does this is a **plagiarist** or is guilty of **plagiarism**.

plague (plaguing, plagued) ❑ A **plague** is an infectious disease which spreads quickly and kills large numbers of people. ◇ When people talk about **the plague**, they usually mean the **bubonic plague**, a disease of rats which spreads to humans when they are bitten by a flea which has previously bitten an infected rat. This disease used to occur periodically in European history; people who suffered from it had a severe fever and swellings on their body and usually died.

❏ If you want to emphasize how eager you are to avoid something, you can say you **avoid it like the plague.**

❏ If there is a **plague** of unpleasant things, a large number of them arrive or happen at the same time. *Last year there was a plague of robbery, housebreaking and rape.* ◇ If you are **plagued** by unpleasant things, they continually cause you a lot of trouble or suffering. *The city has been plagued by strikes and stoppages for the past two years.*

plaice *(plural: plaice)* **Plaice** are a type of edible sea fish. They have flat spotted bodies which are brown on top and white underneath.

plaid *(usual pron: plad)* is material with a tartan or other check design on it. The design itself is also called **plaid.** *...a plaid flannel shirt.* If you are wearing **plaids,** you are wearing plaid clothes. ◇ A **plaid** is a long piece of tartan material worn over the shoulder as part of Scottish Highland national dress.

Plaid Cymru *(pron: plide kum-ri)* is the Welsh Nationalist Party, set up in 1925 to try to achieve Welsh home rule. 'Plaid Cymru' is Welsh for 'Party of Wales'.

plain *(plainer, plainest; plainly, plainness)* ❏ A **plain** object, surface, or fabric is entirely in one colour and has no pattern, design, or writing on it. *...a plain brown envelope.*

❏ If something is **plain,** it is simple in style and rather dull. *I was surprised at the plainness of the room.* ◇ In knitting, **plain** is the most basic type of stitch. ◇ A person is sometimes described as **plain** when they are not good-looking in any way.

❏ You say something is **plain** when you think it is obvious and people cannot fail to be aware of it. *The reason is plain... The judge's conclusion was plainly wrong... Plainly, he needed professional help.* ◇ A **plain** statement is very clear and cannot be misunderstood. *Mr Heath could hardly have put it more plainly.*

❏ **Plain speaking** is saying exactly what you think, even when it may not please other people. A **plain-speaking** person is someone who tends to speak like this.

❏ If you say something is **plain sailing,** you mean it does not present any difficulties or problems.

❏ **Plain** is used in front of some words to emphasize them. *To say that poverty or unemployment causes riots is plain silly.*

❏ A **plain** is a large flat area of land with very few trees.

plain clothed *(plain clothes)* *(or plainclothed, plainclothes)* **Plain clothed** or **plain clothes** police officers are wearing ordinary clothes, so they will not be recognized as police.

plain flour is flour which does not make cakes and biscuits rise when they are baked, because it has not had the required chemicals added.

plainsong is a type of church music in which a group of people sing one tune together with no harmony and without musical instruments. Plainsong originated in medieval times.

plaintiff In court, a **plaintiff** is someone who has brought a legal case against someone else.

plaintive *(plaintively)* A **plaintive** sound or voice is sad or mournful. *...a plaintive wail... 'What's going on here?' asked an official plaintively.*

plait *(pron: plat)* *(plaiting, plaited)* If you **plait** three or more lengths of hair, rope, or other material together,

you twist them over and under each other to make one thick length. **Plaits** are plaited lengths of hair.

plan *(planning, planned)* ❏ A **plan** is a method of achieving something which has been worked out in advance. *...an ambitious peace plan.* If you **plan** something, you work out a method like this. *The trip needs careful planning.*

❏ If you are **planning** to do something or are **planning** on doing it, you are intending to do it.

❏ When you **plan** something you are going to make, build, or create, you decide what the main parts will be and how they will be arranged. This often involves drawing a diagram called a **plan.**

❏ In a **planned economy,** prices and business activities are controlled by the government, rather than by individual businesses.

plane *(planing, planed)* ❏ A **plane** is an aircraft with wings and one or more engines.

❏ In science and geometry, a **plane** is a real or imagined flat surface at any angle.

❏ A **plane** is a tool which has a flat bottom with a sharp blade in it. You move the plane over a piece of wood to remove thin pieces of its surface and make it smaller or smoother. This is called **planing** the wood.

plane tree Plane trees are large trees with broad leaves which often grow in towns.

planeload A **planeload** of people or things is a quantity of them carried in a plane.

planet A **planet** is a large object in space which orbits around a star. The earth is one of the nine planets which orbit round the sun.

planetarium *(plural: planetariums or planetaria)* A **planetarium** is a building where lights are shone on a curved ceiling to represent the planets and the stars and to show how they appear to move.

planetary is used to talk about things to do with planets. *...planetary exploration... ...planetary systems.*

plangent *(pron: plan-jent)* A **plangent** sound is deep, loud, resonant, and slightly mournful. *...loud, plangent calls... ...plangent violins.*

plank ❏ A **plank** is a long thin rectangular piece of wood.

❏ The central **plank** of something like a policy is its main principle or aim. *Both governments have made a strong exchange-rate a central plank of their strategies to fight inflation.*

plankton consists of a mass of microscopic animals and plants living in the surface layer of the sea.

planner Planners are people whose job is to make decisions about what is going to be done in the future. For example, town planners decide how land should be used and what new buildings should be built.

planning permission is official permission from the local authority which is required before you can put up a new building or extend an existing one.

plant ❏ Plants are living things which typically grow in the earth and have a stem, leaves, and roots. Flowers, vegetables, cereal crops, and trees are all plants. ◇ When you **plant** seeds, garden plants, or young trees, you put them into the ground so they will grow there. You can also talk about **planting** land with crops, garden plants, or trees.

❏ If you **plant** something somewhere, you put it there firmly. *With her free hand planted on my chest she tilted me* *back*. ◇ If you **plant** a kiss on someone, you give them a kiss.

❑ If you **plant** an idea in someone's mind, you give them the idea, usually in a subtle way so they think it was their own.

❑ If someone **plants** a bomb, they hide it somewhere, set to explode.

❑ If someone **plants** something like an illegal drug or a weapon on you, they put it amongst your belongings without you realizing it, to get you into trouble.

❑ If an organization **plants** an informer or a spy somewhere, they send that person there so they can do something secretly. A person like this is sometimes called a **plant**.

❑ A **plant** is a factory, or a place where power is generated. *...a car assembly plant... ...the Sellafield nuclear plant.* ◇ **Plant** is large industrial or construction machinery.

plant pot A **plant pot** is a round container, usually made of clay or plastic, which you fill with earth and grow plants in.

plantain Plantains are large green banana-like fruit. The tree they grow on is also called a **plantain**. ◇ **Plantains** are also a type of wild plant with broad leaves and a small head of tiny green flowers on a long stem.

plantation A **plantation** is a large piece of land, especially in a tropical country, where a crop such as rubber, coffee, tea, or sugar is grown. ◇ A **plantation** is also a large number of trees which have been planted together. *...conifer plantations.*

planter ❑ Planters are people who own or manage plantations in tropical countries.

❑ A **planter** is a decorative pot or tub for house plants.

plaque A **plaque** is a flat piece of metal, wood, or stone, fixed to a wall in memory of a famous person or event. ◇ **Plaque** is a substance which forms on the surface of your teeth. It consists of saliva, bacteria, and food. Plaque can damage your gums and teeth.

plasma is the clear fluid part of blood which the blood cells are suspended in.

plaster (plastering, plastered) ❑ **Plaster** is a smooth paste usually made of sand, gypsum, and water, which dries and forms a hard layer. It is used to cover walls and ceilings, and in older buildings was often formed into elaborate and beautiful patterns. It is also used to make sculptures. ◇ If you **plaster** a wall or ceiling, you cover it with a layer of plaster.

❑ If a surface has things like posters or writing all over it, you can say it is **plastered** with them.

❑ A **plaster** is a strip of sticky material used for covering small cuts or sores on your body.

❑ If you have your leg or arm **in plaster**, you have a cast made of plaster of Paris around it to protect a broken bone and allow it to mend. The cast is called a **plaster cast**. Plaster casts are also used as moulds for sculptures.

plaster of Paris is a type of quick-drying plaster made from white powder and water.

plasterboard is thin rectangular sheets of board made from sheets of cardboard held together with plaster. It is used for covering walls and ceilings as an alternative to plaster.

plasterer A **plasterer** is a person whose job is plastering walls and ceilings.

plasterwork is a covering of plaster on a wall or ceiling, especially when it has been formed into elaborate patterns.

plastic is a strong lightweight material produced by a chemical process and used to make many objects. When hot, plastic is soft and can be moulded. ◇ If you pay for something using **plastic**, you pay by credit card.

plastic bullet Plastic bullets are a type of bullet made from a solid PVC. They are intended to injure people rather than kill them, and are typically fired by police or soldiers to control crowds during a riot.

plastic explosive is an explosive substance used to make small bombs. It is soft and can be shaped by hand.

plastic surgery (plastic surgeon) Plastic surgery is carrying out operations to repair or replace damaged skin and tissues, or to improve a person's appearance. A doctor who performs plastic surgery is called a **plastic surgeon**.

Plasticine is a soft coloured clay-like substance which children use for making small models. 'Plasticine' is a trademark.

plate (plating, plated) ❑ A **plate** is a round or oval flat dish, used to hold food.

❑ **Plate** is dishes, bowls, and cups made of silver or gold. Other silver or gold items can be called **plate**, for example church ornaments.

❑ **-plated** is used to say something made of metal is covered with a thin layer of another metal. For example, a **gold-plated** watch is made of a metal like steel covered with a thin layer of gold. The process of adding the layer of metal is called **plating**.

❑ A **plate** is also a flat piece of metal, for example one on the wall of a building with someone's name on.

❑ A **plate** in a book is a picture or photograph which takes up a whole page and is usually printed on better quality paper than the rest of the book.

❑ A dental **plate** is a piece of plastic shaped to fit inside a person's mouth, with a set of false teeth attached to it.

❑ In geology, **plates** are large pieces of the earth's surface, perhaps as large as a continent, which are believed to be drifting extremely slowly on the molten rock beneath.

❑ If you have too many things to deal with and cannot take on anything else, you can say you have **enough on your plate** or **too much on your plate**.

❑ If something is **handed to you on a plate**, you get it very easily, without having to work for it.

plate glass is thick, highly polished glass made in large flat pieces.

plate tectonics See **tectonic**.

plateau (*plural:* plateaus *or* plateaux) A **plateau** is an area of flat high-lying land. ◇ If something which has been increasing reaches a **plateau**, it stops increasing and stays at the same level. *Prices remain on the plateau reached during the last period of high inflation.*

platelet Platelets are a type of blood cell involved in the formation of clots.

platform ❑ A **platform** is a flat raised structure, especially one people stand on to give speeches.

❑ When people talk about the **platform** of a political party, they mean the basic policies and principles it presents to the people during its election campaign. ◇ If someone has a **platform**, they have an opportunity to get their views across to large numbers of people. *The law and* *order debate was a platform for the old style hardliners.*

❏ A **platform** at a railway station is an area next to the rails, where you get on or off a train.

❏ A **platform** is also a structure built over the sea for people to work and live on while they are drilling for or extracting oil or gas.

plating See **plate**.

platinum is a valuable silvery-white metal which is very resistant to heat and other chemicals. It is used for making jewellery, precision tools, and electrical equipment.

❏ A **platinum** record is one which has sold over 300,000 or 600,000 copies in Britain, or over one million copies in the US.

❏ A **platinum** blonde is a woman whose hair is so fair it has a silvery appearance.

platitude A **platitude** is an almost meaningless statement, resembling many statements which have been made before, which someone makes without really thinking about it.

platonic relationships and feelings do not involve sex.

platoon A **platoon** is a small group of soldiers commanded by a lieutenant.

platter A **platter** is a large flat plate for serving food.

platypus (platypuses) The **platypus** or **duck-billed platypus** is an Australian mammal which lives beside streams and can swim. It has brown fur, webbed feet, and a snout like a duck's bill. Although it is a mammal, it lays eggs.

plaudit If you receive **plaudits** for something you do, you are praised for it.

plausible (plausibly, plausibility) If a statement, explanation, or theory is **plausible**, it seems convincing and is likely to be true or correct. *After 40 years of Communist dictatorship, few people can plausibly claim to be morally clean... David Whitehouse assesses the plausibility of the theory that the pipes could be used to launch a satellite.* ◇ If you say a person is **plausible**, you mean the things they say sound convincing but are probably not true.

play ❏ When children **play**, they do things they enjoy, such as taking part in games or doing things with toys.

❏ When you **play** a sport, game, or match, you take part in it. ◇ When a person or team **plays** another one, they compete against them in a sport or game. You can also say they **play against** them. ◇ The time during which a game takes place is called **play**. *He beat Chinook after 5 hours 12 minutes of play... Rain stopped play.* ◇ In sport, when someone hits the ball during a game or match, you can say they **play** it. You can also say they **play** a shot or stroke. *Hall played a clever lob to Townsend.*

❏ When something **comes into play** or is **brought into play**, it begins to be used or to have an effect. *Other factors come into play... The theatre's high-tech stage mechanics were brought into play to enable taxis to drive on stage.* ◇ If you talk about something being **played out** somewhere, you mean it is happening there. *...the battle now being played out in the foreign exchanges.*

❏ If you **play** a musical instrument, you produce music from it. ◇ If you **play** a record, you put it on the record-player and listen to it. Similarly, you can **play** a tape or CD.

❏ A **play** is a piece of writing intended to be performed in a theatre, or on radio or TV. ◇ If an actor **plays** a char-

acter in a play or film, he or she performs that part.

❏ **Play** is used to describe someone's behaviour when they try to create a certain impression, especially a false one. For example, if someone **plays** the innocent, they pretend to be innocent; if someone **plays** dead, they pretend they are dead. ◇ You can describe how someone deals with a situation by saying they **play it** in a certain way. For example, if they **play it cool**, they keep calm and do not show much emotion.

❏ If you **play** a role or part in the way something develops, you are involved in it and have an effect on it. *...a family which played a major role in Kashmir's politics.*

❏ If someone **plays** a joke or trick on you, they deceive you or give you a surprise in a way they think is funny, but which may annoy or inconvenience you.

❏ If you **play along** with someone, you do what they suggest and let them think you agree with them, although you may disagree or have plans of your own. ◇ If you **play** people **off against** each other, you make them compete or argue, to gain some advantage for yourself. ◇ If you **play on** people's fears, you keep reminding them of the thing they are afraid of, to persuade them that something needs to be done. *The campaign played on white voters' fears by claiming the democrats would introduce job quotas for black and white workers.* ◇ If you are **playing for time**, you are delaying doing something, to give yourself a chance to think how best to deal with it.

❏ If you **play** something **down**, you try to make people believe it is not important. *Western diplomats have played down the significance of the reports.* ◇ If you **play** something **up**, you try to make people believe it is greater or more important than it really is. *This increase in crime is definitely being played up by the media.*

❏ If you **play around** with a problem or scheme, you try different ways of organizing it, to find the best solution or arrangement.

❏ A **play on words** is the same as a pun.

play-acting If you say someone is **play-acting**, you mean they are pretending to have attitudes or feelings they do not really have.

play-off A **play-off** is an extra game to decide the result of a competition when two competitors have finished on the same score.

playbill A **playbill** is a notice telling the public when and where a play will be performed.

playboy A **playboy** is a rich man who lives a life of expensive pleasure.

player ❏ The **players** in a sport or game are the people taking part. ◇ Some musicians can be called **players**. For example, a tuba player is someone who plays the tuba. ◇ Actors are sometimes called **players**.

❏ The people, organizations, or countries involved in some type of activity can be called the **players** in it. *The three big players in the video game magazine sector are Emap Images, Future and Europress.*

playful (playfully, playfulness) **Playful** behaviour is lively and mischievous, without meaning any real harm. *He aimed a playful punch at Gutteridge... She pushed him away playfully... Her playfulness after such a shock surprised me.* ◇ A **playful** animal is lively and eager to play.

playground A **playground** is a piece of land where children can play, for example at a school or in a public park. ◇ If you describe a place as a **playground** for a certain group of people, you mean they like to enjoy themselves there or go on holiday there. *This is the Riviera, a holiday playground for the rich and famous.*

playgroup A **playgroup** is a kind of nursery where young children learn things by playing. Playgroups are usually run by parents or other volunteers.

playing card See card.

playing field A **playing field** is a large area of grass where people play sports.

playmate A child's **playmate** is another child who often plays with him or her.

playpen A **playpen** is a small structure designed for a baby or young child to play safely in. It has bars or a net round the sides and is open at the top.

playroom A **playroom** is a room in a house for children to play in.

playschool A **playschool** is the same as a playgroup.

plaything A **plaything** is a toy, or any object a child plays with. ◇ You can say something is the **plaything** of a group of people when they use it for their enjoyment or advantage. *He was an unfaithful husband who treated women as playthings.*

playtime is what young children call the period of time between school lessons when they can play outside.

playwright A **playwright** is a person who writes plays.

plaza A **plaza** is an open square in a city.

plc stands for 'public limited company', meaning a company whose shares can be bought on the Stock Exchange. Companies which fall into this category must have 'plc' at the end of their official names. *...Barclays Bank plc.*

plea ❑ A **plea** is an appeal or request for something, made in an intense or emotional way. *...a plea for help.* ❑ In court, a **plea** is the answer given by the person accused of a crime as to whether they are guilty or not guilty. *They entered a plea of not guilty.* ◇ A **plea** is also someone's excuse for doing something or not doing something. *...his plea that he'd been provoked into killing his wife by her drunken, nagging behaviour.*

plead (pleading, pleaded) If you **plead** for something, you ask for it in an intense emotional way. *He pleaded for patience.* The things you say are called **pleadings**. ◇ If you **plead** someone's case or cause, you speak out in their support or defence. ◇ In court, when someone charged with a crime **pleads** guilty or not guilty, they make an official statement saying they are guilty or not guilty. ◇ If you **plead** something as the reason for doing or not doing something, you give it as your excuse. *They avoided death sentences by pleading insanity.*

pleasant (pleasantly) You say something is **pleasant** when it is likeable, enjoyable, or pleasing. *He was pleasantly surprised by the price of the meal.*

pleasantry (pleasantries) **Pleasantries** are friendly remarks people make to be polite. *He exchanged pleasantries about his hotel and the weather.*

please (pleasing, pleased) ❑ You say **please** when you are asking for something or inviting someone to do something. *Can we have the bill please?... Please come in.* You say 'Yes, please' when you are accepting an offer. ❑ If you are **pleased** with something, it makes you happy or satisfied, because it is what you want. ◇ If some-

thing **pleases** you or you find it **pleasing**, you enjoy it. *...a pleasing sight... ...pleasingly unpretentious lyrics.*

❑ **Please** is used in phrases like **as they please** to indicate people can do or have whatever they want. *People are free to come and go as they please... He has stashed away a personal fortune that will allow him to go where he pleases.*

pleasurable (pleasurably) **Pleasurable** experiences or sensations are pleasant and enjoyable. *Few recent films have been so pleasurable to watch... This will pass an evening quite pleasurably.*

pleasure ❑ If something gives you **pleasure**, you get a feeling of happiness, satisfaction, or enjoyment from it. If something makes you feel like this, you can say it is a **pleasure**. *Mr Frankland's book is a pleasure to read.* ❑ You use **pleasure** to talk about things people do for enjoyment, rather than because it is their work or duty. *...mixing business and pleasure... ...a pleasure trip.* ◇ **Pleasure** boats are boats people take trips on for relaxation and enjoyment.

pleat (pleated) A **pleat** is a permanent fold in a piece of clothing, made by folding one part over the other and sewing across the top end of the fold. If a piece of clothing is **pleated**, it has folds in it like this. *...a pleated skirt.*

plebeian (*pron:* pleb-ee-an) In the past, people of a low social class and things associated with them were sometimes described as **plebeian**. *...a man with a cockney accent and a plebeian manner.*

plebiscite (*usual pron:* pleb-iss-it) A **plebiscite** is a vote by all the electorate of a country or region on a particular issue, for example whether a region should become an independent state.

plectrum A **plectrum** is a small thin piece of material such as plastic or metal which is held between the fingers and used to pluck or strum certain stringed instruments, for example a guitar or mandolin.

pledge (pledging, pledged) ❑ If you make a **pledge**, you promise to do something. You can also **pledge** to do something. ◇ If you **pledge** something, you promise to provide it. *The World Wide Fund for Nature pledged £160,000 in emergency aid for the black rhino.* ❑ If you **pledge** yourself to something like a cause or aim, you commit yourself to supporting it or achieving it. ❑ If you **pledge** something valuable, you leave it with someone as a guarantee that you will repay money you have borrowed.

plenary (*usual pron:* pleen-na-ree) A **plenary** session or meeting is one attended by everyone who has the right to attend.

plenipotentiary (plenipotentiaries) A **plenipotentiary** is a person who has full power to make decisions or take action on behalf of their government, especially in a foreign country.

plentiful (plentifully) If something is **plentiful**, there is more than enough of it for people's wants or needs. *The rivers and lakes are plentifully stored with fish.*

plenty If there is **plenty** of something, there is a lot of it, or more than enough to satisfy people's wants or needs. *Every passenger gets plenty of leg-room.* You can also say things exist **in plenty**. *There were thrills in plenty on Saturday at Terrassa, where Germany won the gold medal.*

plenum (*pron:* plee-num) A **plenum** is a meeting which all the members of a committee or political assembly are expected to attend.

plethora (*pron:* pleth-or-a) If there is a **plethora** of things of a certain kind, there are far more than you need, want, or can cope with. *...the bewildering plethora of new products.*

pleurisy (*pron:* ploor-ris-see) is a painful inflammation of the lungs, often connected with pneumonia.

pliable If something is **pliable,** it bends easily without cracking or breaking. *...a pliable metal.* ◇ A **pliable** person is easily influenced and controlled by other people.

pliant A **pliant** person is easily influenced and controlled by other people.

pliers are a small tool made of two crossed pieces of metal with long flat jaws at one end. They are used to hold small things or to bend and cut wire.

plight If you talk about someone's **plight,** you mean the difficult or distressing situation they are in. *...the country's economic plight... Moved by the plight of the refugees, they have set up a fund.*

plimsoll Plimsolls are canvas shoes with flat rubber soles, worn for playing games and sports.

Plimsoll line Plimsoll lines are a series of markings on the outside of a ship which show the maximum load the ship can safely take in different sea conditions. When the appropriate Plimsoll line is level with the water, no more cargo can be taken on board.

plinth A **plinth** is a rectangular block of stone on which a statue or pillar stands.

plod (plodding, plodded) If someone **plods** somewhere, they walk slowly and heavily. A long tiring walk can be called a **plod.** *...the long plod down the hill.* ◇ If you **plod on** with something, you keep doing it, although you are making very slow progress. Slow progress towards something can be called a **plod.** *...the country's plod to modernity.*

plodder If you call someone a **plodder,** you mean they work slowly and steadily at something.

plonk ❏ If you **plonk** something somewhere, you put it or drop it there heavily and carelessly. *She plonked the beer on the counter and sat down.*
❏ **Plonk** is cheap or poor quality wine.

plop (plopping, plopped) If something **plops** somewhere, it drops there with a soft gentle sound.

plot (plotting, plotted; plotter) ❏ If people **plot** together, they secretly plan to do something wrong or illegal. Their plan is called a **plot.** They are called **plotters.** *The security forces have uncovered a plot to overthrow the government.*
❏ When people **plot** a strategy or a course of action, they carefully plan each step of it. *His way of dealing with challenges has been to plot a clear course and stick to it.*
❏ The **plot** of a novel, play, or film is the connected series of events which make up the story.
❏ If you **plot** a line on a graph, you mark a series of points then join them up. ◇ When someone **plots** the position or course of a plane or ship, they mark it on a map using instruments to obtain accurate information.
❏ A **plot** of land is a small piece of land, especially one marked out for a special purpose, such as building a house or growing vegetables.

plough (*American spelling:* **plow**) ❏ A **plough** is a large farming implement with sharp blades which is attached to a tractor or an animal such as a horse or ox. The plough is pulled across the soil to turn it over, usually before seeds are planted. ◇ When fields are **ploughed,** the soil is turned over using a plough. ◇ If land is **under the plough,** it is used for growing crops.
❏ If a vehicle **ploughs into** something, it crashes into it, out of control.
❏ If money is **ploughed into** something like a business or a service, a large amount is invested in it or spent on improving it. ◇ When profits are **ploughed back,** they are spent on improving or expanding the business which generated them.
❏ If you **plough on** with something, you continue doing it even though it may be difficult or unwise to do so.
❏ The **Plough** is a group of seven bright stars in the northern hemisphere which are thought to look like a plough.

ploughman (ploughmen) (*American spelling:* plowman, plowmen) A **ploughman** is a man whose job it is to guide a plough, especially a plough pulled by an animal rather than a tractor. ◇ A **ploughman's lunch** or **ploughman's** is a simple midday meal often served in pubs. It consists of bread, cheese, pickle, and sometimes onion and salad.

ploughshare (*American spelling:* **plowshare**) If you say **swords are being turned into ploughshares,** you mean a period of conflict has been replaced by a period of peace, so that resources spent on the war effort can now be put to practical peacetime uses. ◇ A **ploughshare** is the blade on a plough.

plover (*rhymes with 'cover'*) **Plovers** are various kinds of long-winged wading birds that live by the seashore or in marshland.

plow See **plough.**

ploy If you call something someone does a **ploy,** you mean it is a cunning way of getting something they want.

pluck (plucky) ❏ If you **pluck** something, you take it between your fingers and pull it sharply away from the place where it is. ◇ If you **pluck** a chicken or other dead bird, you pull its feathers out to prepare it for cooking.
❏ If you **pluck at** something like a person's sleeve, you give it a gentle tug.
❏ If you **pluck** the strings of a guitar or other stringed instrument, you pull them and release them with your fingers, to get them to vibrate and produce sounds.
❏ If someone is removed from an unpleasant or dangerous situation, you can say they are **plucked** from it. *He capsized halfway through his heat and had to be plucked out of the water by a rescue launch.* ◇ If someone unknown is given an important job or role and quickly becomes famous, you can say they were **plucked** from their former position. *Wilmot, the goalkeeper they plucked from Arsenal's reserves, saved fearlessly at Fashanu's feet.*
❏ If you say someone **plucks** something like a number or an answer **out of the air,** you mean they come up with it without thinking about it or working it out beforehand.
❏ **Pluck** is courage. If you admire someone's courage or determination, you can call them **plucky.** *By the 24th minute the contest appeared to be over, despite Oldham's plucky resistance.* ◇ If you **pluck up courage** to do something, you make an effort to be brave enough to do it.

plug (plugging, plugged) ❏ The **plug** on a piece of electrical equipment is a small plastic object with two or three metal pins which fit into the holes of an electric socket. The socket itself is sometimes called a **plug**. ◇ If you **plug in** a piece of electrical equipment, you connect it to the mains or to another piece of electrical equipment, by pushing its plug into a socket.

❏ If you **plug into** a computer system, you get access to the information in it.

❏ If you are **plugged into** what is being discussed or what is going on, you have a good knowledge and understanding of it. *The Centre for European Policy Studies is plugged into the thinking of the people who matter.*

❏ The **plug** in a bath or sink is a thick circular piece of rubber or plastic used to block the hole in the bath or sink when it is filled with water. ◇ If someone **pulls the plug** on something like a project, they put a stop to it, for example by withdrawing their financial support.

❏ If you **plug** a hole, gap, or leak, you block or stop it with something. Something blocking a hole like this is called a **plug**.

❏ **Plugs** are small hollow plastic cylinders designed to hold screws in masonry.

❏ If someone **plugs** a new product like a film or book, they give it publicity by mentioning it or praising it, especially on TV or the radio. You also say they give it a **plug**.

❏ If you **plug away** at something, you keep trying hard to make it succeed.

plughole (*or* **plug hole**) The **plughole** in a bath or sink is a small hole which allows the water to flow away. You block it with a plug. ◇ If you say something has gone **down the plughole**, you mean it has failed or has been lost or wasted. *The economy is going down the plughole.*

plum ❏ **Plums** are small sweet fruit with a smooth yellow or reddish-purple skin and a stone in the middle.

❏ A **plum** job, role, or deal is a very good one which a lot of people would like.

plum pudding is an old name for a Christmas pudding.

plum tomato Plum tomatoes are long egg-shaped tomatoes.

plumage A bird's **plumage** is its feathers.

plumb (**plumbing, plumber**) ❏ When someone **plumbs in** a device like a washing machine, toilet, or bath, they connect it to the water and drainage pipes in a building. ◇ The **plumbing** in a building consists of its water and drainage pipes, baths, and toilets. The work of connecting and repairing things like these is also called **plumbing**. A person who does it is called a **plumber**.

❏ A **plumb line** is a piece of string with a weight attached to the end. It is used to check that something like a wall is vertical. In the past, plumb lines were used to check the depth of the water in rivers, lakes, or the sea.

❏ If you talk about someone **plumbing the depths**, you mean they have reached a very low level in their life or in something they are involved in. For example, if you say someone has **plumbed the depths** of loneliness, you mean they have been extremely lonely. If you say something like a TV programme **plumbs new depths** of tastelessness, you mean it is even more tasteless than things shown in the past.

plume ❏ A **plume** of smoke, dust, or water is a large quantity of it rising into the air in a column.

❏ A **plume** is also (a) a large soft feather. (b) a bunch of long thin strands of material, tied at one end and flowing loosely at the other. ◇ If something is **plumed**, it is decorated with a plume or plumes.

plummet (**plummeting, plummeted**) If something **plummets down**, it falls suddenly and swiftly. *Daily the mortars plummet down.* ◇ If something like a rate or price **plummets**, it decreases rapidly by a large amount. *Producers are worried by plummeting sales... The president's popularity plummeted.*

plummy If you say someone has a **plummy** voice or accent, you mean they speak in a rather old-fashioned upper-class English way.

plump is used, usually in an affectionate or appreciative way, to say someone or something is rather fat or rounded. *...a plump, homely woman... ...plump, juicy olives.* ◇ If you **plump** a pillow or cushion, you shake it and pat it to get it back in a rounded shape.

❏ If you **plump for** someone or something, you choose them, often after some hesitation and uncertainty.

plunder (**plundering, plundered**) If someone **plunders** a place or **plunders** things from it, they steal things from it. Stealing things like this is called **plunder**. *...the systematic plunder of Egypt's ancient treasures.* The stolen property is also called **plunder**. *They cannot hoard their plunder indefinitely.* ◇ You also say people **plunder** a place when they make heavy use of its resources. *He said the country was suffering from the irrational plunder of natural resources such as forests and mineral deposits.*

plunge (**plunging, plunged**) ❏ If you **plunge** into something, you fall, rush, or throw yourself into it. *He plunged into the crowd... Twenty people were killed when a bus plunged into a canal.* ◇ If you **plunge** something like a knife into something, you push it in quickly and violently.

❏ If an amount, rate, or level **plunges** or there is a **plunge** in it, it decreases suddenly and rapidly. *Business confidence is plunging... ...a plunge in living standards.*

❏ If you say someone or something **plunges** or is **plunged** into an unpleasant or alarming situation, you mean they are suddenly put into it. *Ethnic conflicts could plunge the country into chaos.*

❏ If you **plunge** into an activity or take a **plunge** into it, you suddenly get involved in it. *In 1986 the company took a plunge into the American market when it bought Doubleday and Dell.* ◇ If you **take the plunge**, you decide to go ahead with a course of action.

❏ A dress or blouse with a **plunging** neckline is cut in a very low V-shape at the front.

plunger A **plunger** is a device for unblocking pipes and sinks. It consists of a rubber cup on the end of a stick. You press it up and down over the pipe or plughole and the suction moves the blockage.

plural ❏ The **plural** form of a word is the form used when referring to more than one person or thing. For example, the plural of 'dog' is 'dogs' and the plural of 'woman' is 'women'.

❏ A **plural** society is the same as a pluralist society.

pluralist (**pluralistic, pluralism**) A **pluralist** or **pluralistic** society is one where people of different races, religions, and cultures exist together and are allowed to have their own practices and customs. Having a society like this is called **pluralism**.

plurality A **plurality** of things means several of them, as opposed to just one. *The alliance now represents a plurality of views.* ◇ **Plurality** is a situation where more than one political group is allowed to exist. *He believes in a mixed economy and political plurality.*

plus (*plural:* pluses *or* plusses) ❏ You use **plus** to say one number is being added to another. *It will cost at least $100 million to repair the facilities, plus $5 million in annual maintenance.* In maths, 'plus' is indicated by the sign +. ◇ **Plus** is used to say a number is greater than zero. *The aircraft was subjected to temperatures of minus 65 degrees and plus 120 degrees.*

❏ You use **plus** to say that an additional item or factor is involved in the thing you are talking about. *The strength of Mr Papandreou's support, plus the rise in the ecologists' popularity, are expected to result in Greece's third hung parliament in less than a year.*

❏ You use **plus** after a number to show you are referring to this number or any number greater than it. *For sums of £20,000-plus, the rate is 10.6% gross.* ◇ You also use **plus** after a number to show you cannot be exact about an amount but it is greater than the number you have mentioned. *...seventy thousand-plus spectators.*

❏ A **plus** is an advantage or benefit. *Deregulation has some pluses: passengers say staff are more helpful.*

plus-fours are short baggy trousers fastened below the knees which men used to wear when shooting game or playing golf.

plush If you describe something as **plush,** you mean it is smart and luxurious. *...a plush hotel.* ◇ **Plush** fabrics and carpets have a thick soft texture similar to velvet.

plutocrat If you describe someone as a **plutocrat,** you mean they are powerful because they are very rich.

plutonium is a radioactive element used especially in nuclear weapons and as a fuel in nuclear power stations.

ply (plies, plying, plied) ❏ If someone **plies** you with food or drink, they keep offering you more of it.

❏ If you **ply** a trade, you do a particular kind of work regularly as your job, especially one which involves selling goods or services to passers-by. *Market traders plied their wares in the dusk.* ◇ If a ship, aircraft, or road vehicle **plies** a route, it makes regular journeys along it. *...the big trucks that ply Europe's long-distance routes... The ferries will ply back and forth to Albania.*

❏ **Ply** is used to say how many layers there are in a piece of fabric or wood or how many strands there are in knitting wool. *...a two-ply cashmere sweater.*

plywood is a kind of board made up of thin layers of wood stuck together.

PM The PM is the Prime Minister.

p.m. is used when stating a time between noon and midnight. For example, 7 p.m. means 7 o'clock in the evening. **p.m.** stands for 'post meridiem', which is Latin for 'after noon'.

PMS See premenstrual syndrome.

PMT See premenstrual tension.

pneumatic (*pron:* new-**mat**-ik) (pneumatically) If something is **pneumatic,** it is operated by or filled with compressed air. *...a pneumatic drill... The device is pneumatically driven.*

pneumonia (*pron:* new-**moan**-ee-ah) is a serious disease which affects the lungs and makes breathing difficult.

PO Box is used before a number as a kind of address. The Post Office keeps letters addressed to a PO Box until

they are collected by the person who has paid for the service. *...PO Box 737, Chelmsford, Essex.*

po-faced If you think someone is being unnecessarily serious about something, you can describe them as **po-faced.**

poach (poaches, poaching, poached; poacher) ❏ If someone **poaches** animals, birds, or fish, they catch or shoot them without permission on private land or on land where wildlife is protected. A person who does this is called a **poacher.**

❏ If an organization **poaches** members or customers from other organizations, it persuades them, often in a secret or dishonest way, to join them or become their customer instead.

❏ If you **poach** an egg, you cook it gently without its shell in boiling water or in a special pan called a **poacher.** ◇ If you **poach** food such as fish, you cook it gently in boiling water, milk, or some other liquid.

pocked means the same as 'pockmarked'.

pocket (pocketing, pocketed) ❏ A **pocket** is a kind of small flat bag which forms part of a piece of clothing, and which is used for carrying small things like money or a handkerchief. ◇ If you **pocket** something, you put it in your pocket.

❏ **Pocket** is used to describe something which is small enough to fit in your pocket, especially something which is a smaller version of something else. *...Collins Pocket English Dictionary... ...a pocket calculator.*

❏ You can use **pocket** in a lot of different ways to refer to the money people have, get, or spend. For example, if someone gives or pays a lot of money, you can say that they **dig deep into their pockets.** If you think a product is cheap, you can say it **suits people's pockets.** *...with property on the market to suit all pockets... 50,000 shopworkers could be hit in the pocket... Jack Woolley is so incensed he has actually put his hand in his pocket.*

❏ If you talk about someone **pocketing** money, you mean they obtain or keep it, often dishonestly, unfairly, or without having to do much work. *Dishonest importers would be able to pocket the VAT collected from customers.* Similarly, you can talk about someone **lining their pockets.** *In return for public works contracts, firms pay over the odds to the governing politicians, who then use the money to line their own pockets and those of their parties.*

❏ If you are **out of pocket,** you have less money than you should have or less than you intended, for example because you have spent too much or because of a mistake.

❏ If you say you have someone **in your pocket,** you mean they will do as you tell them, because you are paying them.

❏ If someone **picks your pocket,** they steal something from your pocket, usually without you noticing.

❏ A **pocket** of something is a small area where it exists. *The government forces are still putting down isolated pockets of resistance.*

pocket handkerchief Handkerchiefs used to be called **pocket handkerchiefs.**

pocket knife A pocket-knife is the same as a penknife.

pocket money is a small amount of money which someone is given regularly to spend on things they want.

pocket-size (pocket-sized) If something is **pocket-size** or **pocket-sized,** it is small enough to fit in your pocket.

pocketbook In the US, a **pocketbook** is a small folding wallet used for carrying money and papers.

pockmarked If a surface is **pockmarked**, it is covered with shallow holes and dents.

pod ❑ The **pods** of plants like peas and beans are their long narrow seed containers. ◇ A **pod** is also a strong container attached to something like a plane or a ship. Jet engines are often contained in pods.
  ❑ Small groups of whales or seals are called **pods**.

podgy people are rather short and fat.

podium A **podium** is a small platform on which someone stands to give a lecture, conduct an orchestra, or receive an award.

poem A **poem** is a piece of writing in which the words are chosen mainly for their sound and are carefully arranged, often in short lines which rhyme.

poesy is an old-fashioned word for poetry or the art of writing poetry.

poet A **poet** is a person who writes poetry.

poet laureate A country's **poet laureate** is an officially appointed poet who often writes poems for special national occasions. In Britain, the poet laureate is a member of the Royal Household and is appointed for the rest of his or her lifetime. In the US, the poet laureate is appointed for a fixed term.

poetess (poetesses) Female poets are sometimes called **poetesses**, although they usually prefer to be called 'poets'.

poetic (poetical, poetically) ❑ If you describe something like a film or novel as **poetic** or **poetical**, you mean it is beautiful, expressive, and sensitive. ...*a poetic portrait of contemporary Dublin... Ravens' Brood is fine, smooth and poetically nostalgic.*
  ❑ **Poetic** and **poetical** are also used to talk about things connected with poetry. ...*poetic conventions... ...the Poetical Works of Gerald Griffin.*
  ❑ If you say something bad which happens to someone is **poetic justice,** you mean it is exactly what they deserve, because of the things they have done in the past.

poetry is poems generally, or a collection of poems. ...*his first volume of poetry.*
  ❑ If you talk about the **poetry** of something, you mean the things about it which are beautiful and evoke powerful feelings. ...*the poetry of the Russian countryside.*

pogo stick A **pogo stick** is a pole with a step for your feet and a spring at the bottom. You hold the top, stand on the step, and bounce up and down for fun.

pogrom A **pogrom** is an organized official persecution for racial or religious reasons, often involving the mass killing of a group of people.

poignant (poignancy) If something is **poignant**, it affects you deeply and makes you feel sad or emotional. *The exhibition ends poignantly on the sound of electric saws in action in a tropical rainforest.* You can talk about the **poignancy** of something like this.

point ❑ A **point** is a fact, idea, or opinion which someone introduces into a conversation or discussion. *You've raised a very interesting point.* ◇ If you say someone **has a point**, you mean what they have said is important and worth thinking about.
  ❑ When people talk about the **point**, they mean the most important aspect of the thing being discussed. *This*

criticism misses the point. ◇ If what someone says is **to the point**, it is relevant to the subject being discussed and is expressed neatly without wasting words. *Levy had been frank and to the point.* ◇ If what someone says is **beside the point,** it is not relevant to the subject being discussed.
  ❑ When you **come to the point** or **get to the point,** you come to the main thing you want to talk about. ◇ If you **make your point** or **prove your point,** you do something which proves that what you have said is true.
  ❑ If you **make a point** of doing something, you do it in a deliberate or obvious way. *He made a point of praising his old boss.*
  ❑ **Point** is used in phrases like 'what is the point...?' and 'there is no point...' to say something has no purpose or would not be useful. *I don't see the point of worrying until I have to.*
  ❑ A **point** is a place or position. *There have been reports of fighting at several points along the road north of the capital.*
  ❑ A **point** is also a time when something happens, or a stage in the progress or development of something. *The civil war has reached a point where the very survival of the country is at stake.* ◇ **point of no return:** see return.
  ❑ If you are **on the point** of doing something, you are just about to do it.
  ❑ If you **point to** something or **point at** it, you hold out your finger towards it, to direct someone's attention to it or show where it is. ◇ Similarly, if you **point out** an object or place, you draw people's attention to it, though not necessarily using your finger. *He pointed out the house from which the men had emerged.* ◇ If you **point** something at a person or thing, you aim the tip or end of it towards them. *The guns are pointed at the nearby hills.*
  ❑ If you **point to** something which is happening, you draw attention to it, or use it as proof or evidence of something else. *He pointed to the rise in the street price of cocaine as evidence that the interception of drugs is restricting supply.* ◇ If a circumstance **points to** something happening, it suggests it will happen, or is already happening. *All the signals pointed to price inflation slowing down.*
  ❑ If you **point out** a fact, you tell people about it or draw their attention to it. *Lord Taylor has pointed out that the proposals would have the effect of raising the average retiring age rather than lowering it.*
  ❑ If you say something is true **up to a point,** you mean it is partly but not completely true.
  ❑ If you say something is a **point of honour** with someone, you mean they feel obliged to behave in a certain way to defend their principles or their good name.
  ❑ If you use something as a **point of reference,** you use it as a standard to compare other things with.
  ❑ The **point** of something like a pin or a knife is its thin sharp end.
  ❑ The **point** in a decimal number is the dot or mark which separates the whole number from the fraction.
  ❑ In many sports, games, and competitions, **points** are the units in which competitors' scores are measured. *Bristol City are still four points clear at the top of the table.*
  ❑ The **points** of a compass are the marks on it which show the different directions, such as North and South.
  ❑ On a railway line, the **points** are the levers and rails at a place where two tracks join or separate. They enable a train to move from one track to another.
  ❑ A **point** or **power point** is an electric socket.

❏ When builders **point** a wall, they use mortar or cement to finish or repair the joints in brickwork. The mortar or cement in the joints is called **pointing**.

point-blank ❏ If someone is shot **point-blank** or at **point-blank range**, the gun is touching them or extremely close to them when it is fired.

❏ If someone refuses **point-blank** to do something, they refuse firmly and will not discuss it any further.

point of order (points of order) A **point of order** is a question raised during a meeting or debate as to whether the rules governing procedures are being broken.

point of view (points of view) ❏ A person's **point of view** is how a situation seems to them, especially how they will be affected by it. *...the situation in Eastern Europe seen from the banker's point of view.* ◇ If you consider something from a particular **point of view**, you are considering one aspect of it, especially one kind of effect it will have. *The average man doing hard physical work has the best record, from the point of view of heart disease.*

❏ **Points of view** are also opinions about something.

point-to-point A **point-to-point** is a horse race across country over fences and hedges, organized by a recognized hunt or other body, and usually restricted to amateur jockeys and horses regularly used for hunting.

pointed (pointedly) ❏ If something is **pointed**, it has a point at one end. *...a pointed hat.*

❏ A **pointed** comment expresses disapproval or criticism in an obvious way. *...pointed remarks.* Similarly, behaviour can be **pointed**. *37 left-wing MPs pointedly refused to support him.*

pointer ❏ If something is a **pointer** to something else, it helps you understand it or gives an indication of how it will develop. *Sunday's elections should be a pointer to the public mood.*

❏ A **pointer** is a long thin stick used to point at something like a chart on a wall. ◇ The **pointer** on a measuring instrument is the thin piece of metal which points to the numbers.

❏ A **pointer** is also a dog used on shooting expeditions. When a bird has been shot, the dog points to it with its nose, body, and tail in a straight line.

pointless (pointlessly, pointlessness) If you say something is **pointless**, you mean it has no sense or purpose. *The treatment would pointlessly prolong the death process... ...the ghastly pointlessness of my existence.*

pointy means the same as pointed. *...pointy hats.*

poise If someone has **poise**, they are calm, dignified, and self-controlled. ◇ You can also say someone has **poise** when their movements and posture are controlled and graceful. *Ballet classes are important for poise and grace.*

poised ❏ If you are **poised**, you are completely still but ready to move at any moment. *The manager stood poised in the entrance.* ◇ If you are **poised** to do something, you are ready to do it at any moment. *The rebels are poised to attack the airport.*

❏ If a situation is **poised**, it is delicate, and the slightest change in circumstances could have a dramatic effect. *...the delicately poised negotiations between the government and the rebels.*

❏ If someone is **poised**, they are calm, dignified, and self-controlled.

poison (poisoning, poisoned; poisoner) ❏ **Poison** is a substance which harms or kills people or animals if they swallow or absorb it. If someone **poisons** a person or animal, they kill them or make them ill by giving them poison. A person who has killed someone using poison can be called a **poisoner**.

❏ If food, drink, or a weapon is **poisoned**, it has had poison added to it. ◇ If you are **poisoned** by a substance, it makes you very ill or kills you. *...aluminium poisoning.* See also food poisoning, blood poisoning.

❏ If water, land, or air is **poisoned**, it has been damaged by chemicals or other harmful substances.

❏ If something **poisons** a situation or relationship, it spoils it by making the people concerned violently disagree or quarrel with each other. *The old problem of Kashmir has poisoned the budding friendship between India and Pakistan.*

poison gas is a name given to a number of chemical agents which have been used at various times to execute criminals, as a weapon of war, and to kill harmful insects.

poison-pen letter A **poison-pen letter** is an anonymous letter sent to upset someone or cause trouble, saying unpleasant things about the person or about someone close to them.

poisonous substances make you very ill or kill you if you swallow or absorb them. ◇ A **poisonous** snake or other creature produces a poison which can kill you if it bites you.

❏ If something spoils a situation or relationship by making people quarrel or disagree, you can describe it as **poisonous**. *...the poisonous argument over the siting of new EU institutions.*

poke (poking, poked) ❏ If you **poke** someone or something, you push them with your finger or a sharp object. Similarly, you can **poke** an object into something.

❏ If something **pokes** out of something else, it projects from it. ◇ If you **poke** your head through an opening, you push it through, to see something more clearly.

❏ If you **poke about** or **poke around**, you search for something, often moving objects to try to find it.

❏ **poke fun** at someone: see fun. ◇ **poke your nose** into something: see nose.

poker is a card game usually played for money.

❏ A **poker** is a metal stick used to move coal or wood on a fire so that it burns better.

poker-faced If someone is **poker-faced**, their face does not show any emotion.

poky A **poky** house or room is uncomfortably small.

polar is used to talk about the areas around the North and South Poles. *...the polar regions.*

polar bear The **polar bear** is a large white bear which lives in the area around the North Pole.

polarise See polarize.

polarity (polarities) You say there is **polarity** when people or things are drawn towards opposite extremes. These extremes can be called **polarities**. *...the bitter polarity of the Spanish Civil War... He became fascinated by the polarities of good and evil.*

polarize (polarizing, polarized; polarization) (can be spelled with an 's' instead of a 'z') ❏ If people **polarize** or are **polarized**, they split into two separate groups holding opposite positions or opinions. A split like this can be called a **polarization**.

❑ If light is **polarized**, the light waves are made to vibrate in one direction only. This process, which is called **polarization**, is used in microscopes and sunglasses, and in photography.

Polaroid A **Polaroid camera** is a small camera which can take, develop, and print photos in a few seconds. A **Polaroid** is a photo taken with a Polaroid camera. 'Polaroid' is a trademark.

pole ❑ A **pole** is a long cylindrical piece of wood or metal, used for supporting things. ...*flag poles...* ...*bean poles*.

❑ A planet's **poles** are the two opposite ends of its axis. ◇ A magnet's **poles** are its two ends, where opposite magnetic forces are concentrated.

❑ Opposite beliefs, opinions, or qualities can be called opposite **poles**. ...*a gamut of reactions whose poles are near-adoration and near-contempt*. If you say two people are **poles apart**, you mean they have completely different beliefs or opinions.

❑ In motor racing, **pole position** is the front position at the start of a race. In other competitive situations, if someone is in **pole position**, they have an advantage over their competitors.

pole vault (pole vaulter) The **pole vault** is an athletics event in which contestants jump over a high bar using a long flexible pole to lift themselves into the air. A **pole vaulter** is an athlete who takes part in this event.

poleaxe (poleaxing, poleaxed) If you **poleaxe** a person or animal, you hit them so hard they become unconscious.

polecat Polecats are a type of large weasel. They have a very unpleasant smell.

polemic (*pron:* pole-lem-ik) (polemical, polemicist) A **polemic** is a strongly worded criticism or defence of a point of view. You say a book which contains writing of this kind is **polemical**. A speech can also be **polemical**. A **polemicist** (*pron:* pole-lem-iss-ist) is someone who produces writing or makes speeches of this kind.

police (policing, policed) ❑ The **police** are the official organization responsible for making sure people obey the law and for arresting criminals.

❑ If you talk about a place being **policed**, you mean the police or another organization, for example the army, keep law and order there. **Policing** is the system and methods used to keep law and order in a place. ◇ If a system is **policed**, someone makes sure laws or rules are not broken. *Such deals are policed by the country's national merger authorities*.

❑ See also **military police, secret police**.

police constable A **police constable** is a police officer of the lowest rank.

police dog A **police dog** is a specially trained dog used by the police, for example to find drugs or to track criminals.

police force A **police force** is the police organization in a particular country or area.

police officer A **police officer** is a policeman or policewoman.

police state If you say a country is a **police state**, you mean the government controls people's freedom by means of the police, especially secret police.

police station A **police station** is a building where local police are stationed.

policeman (policewoman) A **policeman** or **policewoman** is a member of the police force.

policing See **police**.

policy (policies) ❑ A **policy** is a set of ideas or plans used as a basis for making decisions, especially in politics, economics, or management. ...*monetary policy...* ...*a policy document*. In politics, the process of deciding new policies is called **policy-making**; the people who make the decisions are called **policy-makers**.

❑ An insurance **policy** is a document showing the agreement you have made with an insurance company. Someone who has an insurance policy is called a **policyholder**.

polio is a serious infectious disease which sometimes causes paralysis.

poliomyelitis is the same as polio.

polish (polishes, polishing, polished) ❑ If you **polish** something, you rub a substance called **polish** onto it, to clean it and make it shine. You can also say you **polish** something when you rub it with a cloth.

❑ If you call something like a performance **polished**, you mean it is sophisticated and of a high standard. ◇ If you say a person is **polished**, you mean they are confident and sophisticated. ◇ If you **polish** something to do with your public image or **polish** it **up**, you improve it by working at it. *The authorities are taking more positive steps to try to polish up their public relations*.

❑ If you **polish off** some food or drink, you eat or drink it all. ◇ If you **polish off** something like a job, you finish it quickly.

Politburo In a communist country or party, the **Politburo** is the highest committee, which makes all the policies and decisions.

polite (politely, politeness) A **polite** person has good manners and shows consideration for other people. *He listened politely... Some people mistake politeness for weakness*. ◇ If you talk about **polite society** or **polite company**, you mean well-educated people who have an accepted understanding of what counts as good manners. You say, for example, that a kind of behaviour is not acceptable 'in polite society'.

politic If you decide it is **politic** to do something, you decide it is a good idea to do it, to avoid trouble or keep someone happy.

political (politically) **Political** is used to talk about things to do with politics. ...*political parties...* *The police are treating the murders as politically motivated*.

political asylum is protection given by a government to people who have been forced to leave their own country for political reasons.

political correctness See **politically correct**.

political prisoner A **political prisoner** is someone who has been imprisoned for expressing views which are different from those of his or her government.

political science (political scientist) **Political science** is the study of politics and different kinds of government. An expert on this subject is called a **political scientist**.

politically correct (political correctness) If you say something is **politically correct** or talk about its **political correctness**, you mean it conforms with liberal opinions, especially those promoting equal opportunities for minorities and disadvantaged groups of people. 'Politically correct' and 'political correctness' are often shortened to 'PC'.

politician A politician is someone whose job is in politics, especially an MP.

politicize (politicizing, politicized; politicization) (can be spelled with an 's' instead of a 'z') You say people are **politicized** when they are made aware of political issues. ◇ If an activity is **politicized**, political considerations are introduced into the way it is run. ...*the politicization of New York policing*.

politicking is political activity and manoeuvring by politicians, especially to gain an advantage over their rivals or opponents.

politico (politicos) Politicians are sometimes referred to as **politicos**.

politico- is added to words to describe something which is partly political and partly something else. ...*another politico-financial scandal*.

politics is all the things politicians do to try to achieve or hold onto power or make sure it is used in a certain way. ◇ **Politics** is also the things people do to achieve or hold onto power in other situations. ...*office politics*.

❑ **Politics** is also the study of the ways political power is achieved and how countries are governed.

❑ Your **politics** are your beliefs about how a country should be governed.

polity (polities) A **polity** is a system of government, or a country with a particular political system. *The new Germany is seen as a stable and democratic polity.*

polka The **polka** is a fast lively dance in which couples dance together in circles around a room.

polka dot A polka dot pattern consists of regularly-spaced spots on a plain background. ...*a polka-dot tie.*

poll (pron: pole) ❑ A **poll** is the same as an opinion poll. If a group of people are **polled**, they are asked their opinions about something as part of an opinion poll. See also exit poll, straw poll.

❑ An election is often called the **polls**. When people vote in an election, you say they **go to the polls**. **Polling** is voting in an election. *The capital was reported calm during the polling.* ◇ If a political party or candidate **polls** a certain number of votes, they get that number.

poll tax A poll tax is a tax which every adult in a country must pay. ◇ The Poll Tax was the Community Charge.

pollen is a fine yellow powder produced by flowers. Each grain contains a male reproductive cell which can fertilize other flowers of the same species. The **pollen count** is a measurement of the amount of pollen in the air at a particular time.

pollinate (pollinating, pollinated; pollination) When a plant is **pollinated**, it is fertilized with pollen.

polling See poll.

polling booth A polling booth is a small cubicle at a polling station where you vote in private.

polling day is the day when people vote in an election.

polling station A polling station is a place like a school or church hall where people go to vote in an election.

pollster Pollsters are people or organizations that carry out opinion polls and try to make predictions from their results.

pollute (polluting, polluted; pollution, pollutant, polluter) If a substance **pollutes** the air, water, or the environment, it makes it dirty and dangerous to use or live in. Substances like these are called **pollutants**. When they are present, you say there is **pollution**. A **polluter** is a company or factory which causes pollution.

polo is a game played on horseback by two teams of players who try to score goals by hitting a small wooden ball with long-handled wooden hammers.

polo-necked (polo-neck) A **polo-necked** sweater has a thick fold of material at the top covering most of your neck. Sweaters like these are sometimes referred to as polo-necks.

polo shirt A polo shirt is a short-sleeved shirt made of knitted cotton material with a collar and three buttons at the neck.

poltergeist (pron: pol-ter-guyst) A **poltergeist** is an invisible force believed to move furniture or throw objects around. Poltergeists are often thought of as a type of ghost.

poly (polys) A **poly** was the same as a polytechnic.

polyandry is a custom in some places in which a woman can be married to more than one man at the same time. See also polygamy, polygyny.

polychrome (polychromatic) If something is **polychrome** or **polychromatic**, it has many colours.

polyester is a man-made fibre which is often blended with natural fibres to make clothes and bedclothes.

polyethylene is another name for polythene, especially in the US.

polygamy (pron: pol-lig-gam-ee) (polygamous) **Polygamy** is a custom in some places in which people can be married to more than one person at the same time, especially the custom of a man having more than one wife. **Polygamous** is used to talk about things to do with this custom. ...*a polygamous country*. See also polyandry, polygyny.

polyglot A **polyglot** is a person who speaks several different languages. You say a group of people are **polyglot** when they speak several different languages between them. ...*a polyglot UN force*.

polygon A **polygon** is any two-dimensional shape with three or more straight sides, for example a triangle or a pentagon.

polygyny (pron: pol-lidj-in-ee) is a custom in some places in which a man can have more than one wife at the same time. See also polyandry, polygamy.

polymath A **polymath** is someone who knows a lot about many different subjects.

polymer A **polymer** is a type of chemical compound consisting of large molecules made up of smaller ones.

polyp (pron: pol-lip) A **polyp** is a tiny sea creature with a hollow cylindrical body and tentacles around its mouth. Coral is made up of the skeletons of polyps. ◇ **Polyps** are also small unhealthy growths on a surface inside the body, especially the nose. They are not usually dangerous, but may sometimes become malignant.

polyphony (polyphonic) **Polyphony** (pron: pol-lif-fon-nee) is the singing or playing of several different melodies at the same time in a piece of music. You say music like this is **polyphonic** (pron: pol-lee-fon-nik).

polypropylene is a tough heavy-duty plastic used to make things like bottles and pipes. It is also used in fibres for ropes and carpets.

polystyrene is a very light plastic substance, used as packaging or insulating material.

polytechnic Some universities, especially ones where you can study for vocational qualifications, used to be called **polytechnics**.

polythene is a type of plastic which is made into thin sheets or bags.

polyunsaturated fats are fats which are thought to be healthier than saturated fats because they are less likely to be converted into cholesterol in the body. They are mostly found in vegetable and fish oils.

polyurethane is a plastic material used to make water-resistant paints and varnishes and also foams for upholstery and insulation.

Pom Australians sometimes call English people **Poms**.

pom-pom A pom-pom is a ball of woollen threads used as a decoration, for example on a hat.

pomegranate Pomegranates are round apple-sized fruit with thick gold-red skins. They contain a lot of small seeds, each one surrounded by a red juicy pulp.

pommel The **pommel** of a sword is the knob on the end of the handle. ◇ The **pommel** of a saddle is the part which rises up at the front.

pomp or **pomp and circumstance** is the use of ceremony, fine clothes, and decorations on special occasions.

pompous (pompously, pomposity) If someone is **pompous**, they behave in a serious and self-important way. You talk about the **pomposity** of someone like this. *He solemnly and pompously proclaimed that his newspapers would serve the Labour movement.*

poncho (ponchos) A **poncho** is a piece of clothing consisting of a long piece of material with a hole cut in the middle to put your head through.

pond A pond is a small, usually man-made, area of water. ◇ In the US, a **pond** is a lake.

ponder (pondering, pondered) If you **ponder** something, you think about it carefully.

ponderous (ponderously) ❑ If you say someone or something is **ponderous**, you mean they move slowly and with difficulty, because they are very big or heavy. You also call their movements **ponderous**. ◇ If you call something like an organization **ponderous**, you mean it tends to operate slowly, because of its size.
  ❑ If you say a speech or piece of writing is **ponderous**, you mean it uses long words and sentences to express something fairly simple. *...the rather ponderously titled 'Recommendation for National Reconciliation and Salvation'.*

pong A pong is an unpleasant smell.

pontiff The pontiff is the Pope.

pontificate (pontificating, pontificated) If someone **pontificates**, they state their opinions in a pompous way.

pontoon ❑ A pontoon is a floating platform, often used to support a bridge.
  ❑ **Pontoon** is a card game in which players try to collect a set of cards which add up to twenty-one. Pontoon is also called **blackjack** or **vingt-et-un**.

pony (ponies) A pony is a type of small horse.

pony trekking is the pastime of riding ponies cross-country.

ponytail (ponytailed) (*or* pony-tail, pony-tailed) If someone has their hair in a **ponytail**, it is tied at the back of their head. *...a pony-tailed American Indian.*

pooch (pooches) Dogs are sometimes called **pooches**.

poodle Poodles are a type of dog with thick curly hair.

pooh-pooh If you **pooh-pooh** an idea or suggestion, you show contempt for it.

pool (pooling, pooled) ❑ A **pool** is a small area of still water. ◇ A **pool** of liquid is a puddle of it. *...a pool of blood.* ◇ A swimming pool is often just called a **pool**.
  ❑ A **pool** of light is a small area of it.
  ❑ If a group of people **pool** their money, knowledge, or equipment, they allow it to be used or shared by everyone in the group. ◇ A **pool** of people, money, or things is a supply of them used or shared by several people or organizations.
  ❑ If you do the **pools**, you take part in a gambling competition in which people try to win money by guessing the results of several football matches.
  ❑ **Pool** is a game similar to billiards but played on a smaller table called a **pool table**. The players hit a white ball towards coloured balls with numbers on them. The idea is to get the coloured balls into the six pockets round the edge of the table.

poolside is used to talk about things situated or happening next to a swimming pool. *...poolside frolics.*

poop The poop of an old-fashioned sailing ship was the raised deck at the back.

pooper-scooper A **pooper-scooper** or **poop-scoop** is a small device like a shovel used by dog owners to pick up their dogs' excrement from a public path or pavement.

poor (poorer, poorest; poorly) ❑ If you are **poor**, you have very little money and few possessions. The **poor** are poor people. A **poor** country or area is inhabited by poor people.
  ❑ If a place is **poor** in something, it has very little of it. *The country was desperately poor in natural resources.* Similarly, you can talk about soil being **poor** in a substance. *If soil is poor in nitrogen, plants cannot grow and thrive.*
  ❑ **Poor** and **poorly** are used to describe things which are of low standard or quality. *He suffered from poor eyesight... ...a poorly educated workforce.* ◇ **Poor** and **poorly** are also used to talk about amounts or numbers being disappointingly low. *...the poor turn-out... ...poorly-attended press conferences.* ◇ **Poor** is also used to describe things which are unlikely to have a favourable outcome. *...the poor economic outlook.*
  ❑ If you are **poorly** or in **poor** health, you are ill.
  ❑ If you are **poor** at something, you are not very good at it. ◇ If you do something **poorly**, you do it badly.
  ❑ People use **poor** to show sympathy for someone. *The poor chap died at the age of 25.*
  ❑ If you say something is a **poor relation** to something else, you mean people see the first thing as inferior to the second. *Although usually a poor relation to oils, watercolours came into their own in Britain in the late 18th century.* ◇ If you say something is the **poor man's** version of something else, you mean it is a cheap substitute for it.

poorhouse In the past, a **poorhouse** was an institution where very poor people were housed if they could not support themselves.

poorly See poor.

pop (popping, popped) ❑ **Pop** is modern music written

mainly for young people. It features electric and electronic instruments, and has a strong rhythmic beat.

❑ If something **pops**, it makes a short sharp sound, like the sound of a cork being pulled out of a bottle. A noise like this is called a **pop**.

❑ If you talk about someone's eyes **popping**, you mean they are very surprised or excited. *I read this section of the book with my eyes popping out of my head.*

❑ If you **pop** something somewhere, you put it there. *Pop the mushrooms straight into hot fat.* ◇ If you **pop** somewhere, you go there for a short time. *I popped in to see if she was all right.* ◇ If someone or something **pops** out from a place where they could not be seen, they suddenly appear. *Suddenly, from behind a pile of rocks, up popped a man in a black raincoat.*

❑ Flavoured fizzy drinks are sometimes called **pop**.

❑ If you **pop** pills, you take them regularly. You call someone who does this a **pill-popper**.

pop art is a style of modern art which became well-known in the 1960s. It uses bright colours, copies styles of drawing from advertising and comics, and features everyday objects like Coca-Cola bottles.

pop group A **pop group** is a number of musicians who perform pop music.

pop song A **pop song** is a song, usually quite simple and with a strong beat, performed by a pop musician or group.

pop star A **pop star** is a famous pop musician.

pop-up A **pop-up** book has pictures which stand up when it is opened.

popcorn is the grains of a type of maize, which have been heated until they have burst and become large and light.

Pope The **Pope** is the head of the Roman Catholic Church.

poplar The **poplar** is a tall thin tree with triangular leaves.

poppadom (*or* **poppadum**) **Poppadoms** are large thin crisp pieces of Indian bread fried in oil.

poppy (poppies) The **poppy** is a flower with large delicate petals, usually red, and a hairy stem. ◇ A **poppy** is also an artificial red poppy worn in Britain on Remembrance Day in memory of those who died in the two World Wars. Remembrance Day is sometimes called **Poppy Day**.

poppycock If you say something is **poppycock**, you mean it is nonsense.

populace The **populace** of a town or country are the people who live there.

popular (popularly, popularity) ❑ If you are **popular**, you are liked by many people. *Her personal popularity has improved by 6 percent over the month.* Similarly, if something is **popular**, it is liked or enjoyed by many people. *Blackpool remains the most popular British seaside holiday resort.*

❑ **Popular** is used to describe ideas or attitudes held by large numbers of people. *...popular support for independence.* ◇ **Popularly** is used to show that an idea is believed by many people, although it may not be true. *The Great Wall of China is longer than popularly thought.* Similarly, **popularly** is used to show that a name is used by many people, although it is not the official one. *Popularly, dyslexia is known as 'word blindness'.*

❑ Newspapers aimed at the widest possible audience are sometimes called the **popular** press.

popular music is a type of music which appeals to a wide audience, and which often has romantic and sentimental melodies.

popularize (popularizing, popularized; popularization, popularizer) (*can be spelled with an 's' instead of a 'z'*) If something is **popularized**, a lot of people become interested in it and start to enjoy it. *...the popularization of sport through television.* ◇ If someone **popularizes** an academic or scientific subject, they make it more easily understandable to ordinary people. You call someone who does this a **popularizer**.

populate (populating, populated) If a place is **populated** by a certain kind of people or animals, they live there. You also use **populated** to say there are very few people living in a place, or very many. *...a densely populated island.* ◇ When a government **populates** an area, it gets people to live there.

population The **population** of a place is (a) the people living there. *...the safety of the local population.* (b) the number of people living there. *...a country with a population of 1.2 billion.* ◇ You also use **population** to talk about one section of the people or animals living in a place. *Over one-quarter of the world's adult population are not fully literate... Small increases in temperature can cause insect populations to grow dramatically.*

populist (populism) A **populist** is a politician who claims to represent the interests of ordinary people and who tries to get their support, often by deliberately trading on their fears and prejudices. This kind of politics is called **populism**.

populous A **populous** country or area has a lot of people living there.

porcelain is delicate, high quality china used especially for making tea services and ornaments. **Porcelain** is also things made of porcelain.

porch (porches) A **porch** is a sheltered area at the entrance to a building. ◇ In the US, a **porch** is a verandah.

porcine (*pron:* por-seen) is used to talk about (a) something to do with pigs. *Too many porcine imports suffered from foot and mouth disease.* (b) something which reminds you of a pig. *...porcine wrinkles of flesh.*

porcupine The **porcupine** is a large rodent with long spines on its back. There are many kinds of porcupines in different parts of the world.

pore (poring, pored) ❑ **Pores** are (a) very small holes in your skin or the surface of a plant, which allow moisture to pass through. (b) tiny gaps or cracks in rocks and soil.

❑ If you **pore over** a piece of writing, you study it very carefully.

pork is meat from a pig.

pork pie A **pork pie** is a deep round pie with cooked pork inside.

porker A **porker** is a pig raised or fattened for its meat.

porky (porkies) If you call someone **porky**, you mean they are fat. ◇ If you say someone is telling a **porky**, you mean they are telling a lie.

porn is the same as pornography.

porno means the same as pornographic. *...porno films.*

pornography (pornographic; pornographer) **Pornography** is magazines, pictures, or films designed to cause sexual excitement by showing naked people and sexual acts. You say things like these are **pornographic**. Someone who writes or produces pornographic material is called a **pornographer**.

porous (porosity) If something is **porous**, it has many small holes in it, which air and water can pass through. You talk about the **porosity** of something like this.

porpoise Porpoises are sea mammals related to dolphins. They have short rounded snouts.

porridge is a thick sticky food made from oats cooked in water or milk.

port ❑ A **port** is (a) a town which has a harbour or docks. (b) a harbour area where ships load and unload goods or passengers. ◇ A **port of call** is a place where a ship stops during a journey. You can call any place a **port of call** when you stop there for a short time, especially when you are visiting several places or people.

❑ The **port** side of a ship is the left side when you are facing the front.

❑ **Port** is a type of sweet fortified red wine.

portable (portability) A **portable** machine or device is designed to be easily carried. You talk about the **portability** of something like this.

portal A **portal** is a large impressive entrance or door to a building.

portcullis (portcullises) A **portcullis** is a strong metal gate above an entrance to a castle, which was lowered to keep out enemies.

portend (portent) If something **portends** something else or is a **portent** of it, it shows it is likely to happen. *Signs of recession in Germany portend trouble... The rise in unemployment is clearly a portent of worse things to come.*

portentous (*pron:* por-tent-uss) (portentously, portentousness) If something is **portentous**, it shows something is about to to happen. *The timing of President Mitterrand's visit could be portentous... The first heavy raindrops splashed portentously on the sill.* ◇ If someone is **portentous**, they try to impress people by doing or saying things in a very important or serious way. *...glossy record sleeves with portentous notes... There's an element of portentousness about his work.*

porter A **porter** is someone whose job is to carry things. ◇ A **porter** is also the person in charge of the entrance of a building like a hotel.

portfolio (portfolios) ❑ A cabinet minister's **portfolio** is the area of government he or she has responsibility for. A minister **without portfolio** does not have responsibility for any one area of government.

❑ In investment, a **portfolio** is a collection of stocks and shares in different businesses owned by a person or company.

❑ A **portfolio** is also a thin flat case for carrying large papers or drawings. ◇ An artist's **portfolio** is a selection of his or her work, used, for example, to show a prospective employer.

porthole A **porthole** is a small round window in the side of a ship or aircraft.

portico (porticoes *or* porticos) A **portico** is a large covered area at the entrance to a building, with pillars supporting its roof.

portion (portioning, portioned) A **portion** of something is a part of it. *The contractor removed a portion of the roof.* ◇ A

portion of food is the amount given to one person at a meal. *...a portion of chips.* ◇ If you **portion** something **out**, you give a share of it to each person in a group.

portly (portlier, portliest) A **portly** person is quite fat.

portmanteau (*plural:* portmanteaux) (*both pron:* portman-toe) A **portmanteau** is a large old-fashioned travelling case which opens into two compartments. ◇ **Portmanteau** is used to describe something which combines several things or features. *...portmanteau leisure departments.*

portrait (portraitist) A **portrait** is a painting, drawing, or photograph of a person, often showing only their face. An artist who specializes in portraits is called a **portraitist**. See also **self-portrait**. ◇ A **portrait** is also a piece of writing or film which shows what someone or something is like. *...a fascinating, and often rather comical, portrait of the East End underworld.*

portraiture is the art of painting or drawing portraits.

portray (portrayal) ❑ When an actor or actress **portrays** someone, he or she plays that person in a film or play. You talk about their **portrayal** of the person. *She gave an endearing portrayal of Cinderella.* ◇ If a writer **portrays** a person or thing, he or she shows what they are like. This is called a **portrayal** of the person or thing. You can also talk about a book, play, or film **portraying** someone or something. *Although the film inevitably fails to portray the true horror of the ghetto, it does its best to conjure up the atmosphere.*

❑ If you **portray** someone or something in a particular way, you make them appear to be a certain kind of person or thing. *The government has portrayed him as a traitor.*

Portuguese is used to talk about people and things in or from Portugal. *...the Portuguese president.* ◇ A **Portuguese** is someone who comes from Portugal. ◇ **Portuguese** is the main language spoken in Portugal, and also in Brazil.

pose (posing, posed; poseur) ❑ If something **poses** a problem or danger, the problem or danger exists because of it. *...the difficulties posed by heavily trafficked trunk roads.*

❑ If you **pose** a question, you ask it.

❑ If you **pose** as someone, you pretend to be them, to deceive people.

❑ If you call someone's behaviour a **pose**, you mean they are trying to create an impression which is different from their real character. *Her speech has been attacked as a hollow pose by opposition MPs.* You say someone who behaves like this is a **poseur**.

❑ If you **pose** for a photograph or painting, you stay in one position, so someone can photograph or paint you. Your position is called a **pose**.

poser A **poser** is a puzzling question or problem.

poseur See pose.

posh things and places are smart, fashionable, and expensive. ◇ You say people are **posh** when they come from a high social class.

posit (*pron:* pozz-it) (positing, posited) If you **posit** something, you put it forward as a possible way of dealing with a problem or difficult situation. *The IMF are positing a new austerity regime.*

position (positioning, positioned; positional) ❑ The **position** of something is the place where it is in relation to other things. ◇ If you **position** something somewhere, you put it in the place where it is meant to be. You then say it is **in position**.

❏ In a war or battle, the **positions** of the armies are the places where their soldiers and weapons are. *Air force helicopters bombed rebel positions around the fort.*

❏ If you are in a particular **position**, you are sitting, standing, or lying in a particular way. *She was forced to crouch in a sitting position.*

❏ Your **position** is the situation you are in at a particular time. *Norway is in a difficult position over Lithuania.* ◇ If you are **in a position** to do something, your present circumstances make it possible for you to do it. *He is now in a position to form a new coalition government.* You can also say someone is **well positioned** to do something.

❏ Your **position** among a group of people is your status among them. *...the once privileged position of the Russians.* ◇ Your **position** in a company or organization is the job you have with them. *...middle to upper management positions.*

❏ In a competition, your **position** is your place in a table compared to other competitors. *The side slipped from third position to fifth in the table.* ◇ In games like football and hockey, a player's **position** is the part of the field where he or she is based. **Positional** is sometimes used when talking about players' positions. *England make six changes, two positional, from the side that played Argentina.*

❏ Your **position** on an issue is your attitude towards it. *The United States has changed its position on moves to protect the Antarctic.*

positive (positively) ❏ **Positive** is used to describe something which concentrates on the good aspects of something. *...positive thinking... ...positive images of old age.* ◇ You say people are **positive** when they are hopeful and confident. *Government officials have spoken positively about the idea.*

❏ If you give a **positive** response, you say 'yes', or something which means yes. *A positive answer could result in a peace conference by October.*

❏ If you take **positive** action, you do something which is likely to have real effects on a situation. *A major demand was for positive moves on reducing the high budget deficit.*

❏ If you are **positive** about something, you are completely sure about it. ◇ **Positive** evidence gives definite proof of something. ◇ If a medical or scientific test is **positive**, it shows something like a disease or substance is present. *Three competitors have been positively tested for banned drugs.* ◇ **HIV positive:** see **HIV**.

❏ **Positive** is used to say something is true, where you might expect the opposite. *His youth may be a positive advantage... Regulations positively encourage the black economy.*

❏ A **positive** number is greater than zero. ◇ A **positive** electric charge is one of two opposite kinds of charge, the other being a negative charge.

positive discrimination is the policy of deliberately treating one group of people better than others, because it is thought they are often treated unfairly.

positive vetting is the checking of the character and background of someone who has applied for a civil service job which involves dealing with secret material.

positron A positron is a tiny particle of matter. It is like an electron, but has a positive electrical charge.

posse (*pron:* poss-ee) In the American West, a posse was a group of men brought together by a sheriff to help chase and capture a criminal. ◇ Any group of people arriving somewhere to do something together can be called a **posse**. *...a posse of reporters.*

possess (possesses, possessing, possessed; possession) ❏ If you **possess** something, you have it or own it. You can also say you **have possession of** something, or it is **in your possession**. Your **possessions** are things you have or own. ◇ **Possession** is the crime of having or owning something illegally. *A total of 111 people have been arrested, mainly for drug dealing and possession.*

❏ If you **possess** a quality or ability, you have it. You can also say someone is **possessed of** a quality. *She is still possessed of the same defiant energy.*

❏ If you are **possessed** by something, you are very interested in it and keep thinking about it. *The young Russell was so possessed by theories that he had little time for anything else.* ◇ If you ask **what possessed** someone to do something, you are expressing surprise because they have done something silly or dangerous. *One wonders what would possess a young man, bursting with life, health and appetite to swallow pills that he knows might kill him.* ◇ If someone is **possessed**, their mind and body are supposed to be controlled by an evil spirit or the devil.

❏ In a sport like football, if a team has **possession**, they have control of the ball.

possessive (possessiveness) ❏ You say someone is **possessive** when they want all of another person's love and attention. *I tried to overcome my possessiveness.* ◇ You also say someone is **possessive** when they do not like other people using their things.

❏ **Possessive adjectives** or **determiners** are words like 'my' and 'your'. **Possessive pronouns** are words like 'mine' and 'yours'.

possessor The possessor of something is the person who has it or owns it.

possible (possibly; possibility, possibilities) ❏ If it is **possible** to do something, it can be done. ◇ You use **possibly** with 'cannot' or 'could not' to emphasize that something cannot happen or cannot be done. *I couldn't possibly comment on this matter.* ◇ A **possibility** is something you are able to do and might do. *One possibility being considered is to cut the defence budget by 25%.*

❏ If you do something, for example, **as soon as possible** or **as fast as possible**, you do it as soon as you can, or as fast as you can. *Most refugees will want to stay as close to home as possible... There are signs that the Assembly intends to delay the procedure for as long as it possibly can.* ◇ If you do something **wherever possible** or **whenever possible**, you do it on every occasion when you have the opportunity.

❏ **Possible** is used to say something might be true or correct, or might happen. *The army was prepared for all possible developments... ...a difficult and possibly dangerous time.* A **possibility** is something which might be true or correct, or might happen. *I would not rule out the possibility of his returning... ...a contract to cover all possibilities.*

❏ **Possible** is used to emphasize that something has more or less of a quality than anything else of its kind. *These events have come at the worst possible moment... ...a world in which security is ensured by the lowest possible level of armaments.*

❏ A **possible** is one of several people or things that

could be chosen for a job or purpose. *He had been on the Nobel committee's list of possibles.*

❑ If you say something has **possibilities,** you mean it could be developed into something useful or profitable in the future.

❑ You say **if possible** when making a request, to show you realize you may not be able to have the thing you want. *We are keen that the castle and its contents should be kept together if at all possible.*

❑ You add **possibly** to what you are saying to show you are surprised or puzzled. *What could this possibly mean?... How could anything so artificial possibly work?*

possum In Australia and New Zealand, a **possum** is a long-tailed furry animal which lives in trees and carries its young in a pouch on its body. ◇ In the US, a **possum** is the same as an opossum.

post (postal, posting) ❑ The **post** is the public service by which letters and parcels are collected and delivered. The letters and parcels are called **post.** *...a pile of post.* **Postal** is used to talk about things to do with the post. *...postal deliveries... ...a postal ballot.* If you **post** something, you send it through the post.

❑ A **post** is an upright pole fixed into the ground. ◇ In games like football and hockey, the **posts** are the goalposts.

❑ A **post** is a job or official position. *...the newly-created post of vice president.*

❑ A **post** is also a place where someone like a soldier is commanded to be to do their job. You talk about a soldier being **posted** somewhere. ◇ If you are **posted** to another town or country, you are sent there by your organization to work. The place you are sent to is called a **posting.**

❑ If you **post** a notice, sign, or other piece of written information somewhere, you fix it to a wall or noticeboard where everyone can see it.

❑ If a company **posts** a profit or loss, it announces that it has made one and says what it is.

post- is used to form words which describe something taking place after a particular time or event. *...Hong Kong's post-1997 constitution... ...life in post-apartheid South Africa.*

post box A **post box** is a large metal container with a hole in it which you put letters into for collection.

post-dated If you write a **post-dated** cheque, you put a date on it which is later than when you write it, so it cannot be cashed before a certain time.

Post-Impressionism (Post-Impressionist) **Post-Impressionism** is a style of painting which was developed in France at the end of the 19th century as a reaction against Impressionism. Artists wanted to show more of their own emotions and individuality in the way they portrayed their subjects. **Post-Impressionist** is used to talk about things to do with Post-Impressionism.

post-industrial is used to describe the present state of many Western countries, especially the move from heavy industry to service industries, and the change in people's lifestyles, for example increased leisure time and higher disposable incomes.

post-modernism (post-modern, post-modernist) **Post-modernism** is a late 20th century style in art, literature, and architecture which rejects the rules of modernism and mixes old and new influences in unusual ways.

Post-modern and **post-modernist** are used to talk about things to do with post-modernism. *...a post-modern shopping arcade... ...post-modernist designs.* An artist, writer, or architect who uses this style is called a **post-modernist.**

post-mortem A **post-mortem** is the same as an autopsy. ◇ A **post-mortem** is also an attempt to discover why something has gone badly wrong for someone. *...the election post-mortem.*

post-natal (*or* postnatal) is used to talk about something that happens soon after the birth of a baby. *...post-natal depression.*

post office The Post Office is the national organization responsible for postal services. ◇ A **post office** is a place where you can buy stamps, post letters and parcels, and use other services provided by the Post Office.

post-operative is used to talk about something which happens or exists after a surgical operation. *...post-operative pain.*

post-prandial is used to talk about things which follow a meal, especially dinner. *...a post-prandial cigar.*

post-production is the work carried out on a film or TV programme after the filming has been done, for example the editing or dubbing.

post-war is used to describe something which happens or exists in the period after a war, especially the Second World War. *...the post-war boom years.*

postage is the money you pay for sending letters and parcels through the post.

postage stamp A **postage stamp** is a small piece of paper you buy and stick on an envelope or parcel before posting it.

postal See post.

postal order A **postal order** is a piece of paper representing a sum of money, which you buy at a post office and send to someone by post. The person who receives it can cash it at a post office or pay it into his or her bank account.

postbag A **postbag** is a bag in which a postman or postwoman carries letters and parcels. ◇ The **postbag** of an important person or organization is the letters they get from the general public.

postcard A **postcard** is a piece of card, often with a picture on one side, which you write on and then post to someone.

postcode Your **postcode** is a short series of letters and numbers at the end of your address. Postcodes make it quicker and easier for post to be sorted and delivered.

poste restante is a service by which post sent to you is kept at a particular post office until you collect it.

poster A **poster** is a large picture, notice, or advertisement which you stick on a wall or noticeboard.

poster paint is a type of thick brightly-coloured watercolour paint, usually sold in small pots.

posterior Your **posterior** is your buttocks.

posterity is used to talk about future generations of people, especially when you are saying how they will be affected by things happening or existing now. *Rich patrons are happy to leave their art collections to posterity.*

postgraduate work or research is done by a student who has a first degree and is studying or doing research at a more advanced level. A student like this is called a **post-**

graduate student or a **postgraduate**.

posthumous (*pron:* **poss-tume-uss**) (posthumously) **Posthumous** is used to describe something which happens after someone's death and relates to their life or achievements. *...a posthumous tribute... There is a campaign for him to be posthumously acquitted.*

posting See **post**.

postman (postmen) A **postman** is a man who collects and delivers the post.

postmark A **postmark** is a mark printed on letters and parcels at a post office. It shows the time, date, and place at which the letter or parcel is sorted.

postmaster (postmistress) A **postmaster** or **postmistress** is a person in charge of a post office.

postnatal See **post-natal**.

postpone (postponing, postponed; postponement) If you **postpone** an event, you arrange for it to take place later than was originally planned. *...the postponement of the elections.*

postscript A **postscript** is a message written at the end of a letter after you have signed it. You write 'PS' in front of it. ◇ An extra piece of information at the end of a piece of writing is sometimes called a **postscript**.

postulate (postulating, postulated) If you **postulate** something, you assume it exists or is true. *His theory postulated the existence of a lost manuscript of Wittgenstein's belonging to the year 1919.*

posture (posturing, postured) ❏ Your **posture** is the way you hold your body when you are standing or sitting. *...a stooped posture.*

❏ Your **posture** is also the attitude you adopt towards a particular issue. *A large number of parents have been offended by the anti-Christian posture of some teachers.* ◇ If you say someone is **posturing**, you mean they are pretending to have attitudes or views they do not really have, in order to get attention or support. You can talk about someone's **posturing** or **posturings**. *Much of his rhetoric is simply posturing... ...nationalist posturings.*

postwoman (postwomen) A **postwoman** is a woman who collects and delivers the post.

posy (posies) A **posy** is a small bunch of flowers.

pot (potting, potted) ❏ A **pot** is (a) a deep round container for cooking. (b) a container for paint, jam, or some other thick liquid. ◇ **Potted** meat or fish has been cooked and put into a small sealed container.

❏ A **pot** of tea is a teapot full of freshly made tea. Similarly, a **pot** of coffee is a coffee pot full of coffee.

❏ If you **pot** a plant, you put it into a flower pot filled with earth. A **potted** plant has been put into a flower pot and is growing there.

❏ A **potted** biography or history contains the main facts about someone or something in a short simplified form.

❏ In games like snooker, when you **pot** a ball, you hit it into one of the pockets.

❏ If you **pot** a small animal like a rabbit, you shoot and kill it, usually so it can be cooked and eaten.

❏ If you say someone has **pots** of money, you mean they have a lot of it.

❏ If you say something has **gone to pot**, you mean it has deteriorated and is in a very poor state.

❏ If you have to take **pot luck** on something, you have to take whatever is available, rather than being able to

choose.

❏ **Pot** is cannabis.

pot belly (pot-bellied) If someone has a **pot belly** or is **pot-bellied**, their stomach sticks out in a noticeable way.

pot plant A **pot plant** is a plant suitable for growing indoors in a flowerpot.

pot pourri (*pron:* **po poo-ree**) **Pot pourri** is a mixture of dried petals and leaves in a bowl. You put it in a room, to make the room smell pleasant. ◇ A **pot pourri** is also a collection of things which were not originally intended to go together. *Their arms are a pot-pourri of weapons from the Soviet Union, China and France.*

pot roast A **pot roast** is a piece of meat cooked very slowly with a small amount of liquid in a covered pot.

pot-shot If you take a **pot-shot** at someone or something, you shoot at them without taking aim carefully.

potash is a name used for various potassium compounds, some of which are used as fertilizers and others for making soap, detergents, and glass.

potassium is a soft silvery-white metal which reacts violently with water. Various compounds of potassium are used as fertilizers or for making soap, detergents, or glass.

potato (potatoes) **Potatoes** are round white root vegetables with a brown or red skin. ◇ If you say a problem or issue is a **hot potato**, you mean it is very controversial and nobody wants to get involved with it.

potato chip In the US, crisps are called **potato chips**.

potboiler If you call a piece of writing or music a **potboiler**, you mean it has been created to earn money quickly, rather than as a work of artistic merit.

potent (potently, potency) If something is **potent**, it is effective and powerful. You talk about the **potency** of something like this. *...a potent anti-cancer drug... ...the spell Iona has cast so potently for 1500 years... ...the extraordinary potency of his personality.* ◇ If a man is **potent**, he is able to have an erection and keep it during sex. The ability to do this is called **potency**.

potentate A **potentate** is a ruler who has great power over their people.

potential (potentially; potentiality, potentialities) ❏ **Potential** is used to describe things which are likely to occur in the future. *...the potential benefits of this scheme.* ◇ If there is **potential** for something, it is capable of happening. *...the potential for vegetation growth in the desert.* ◇ **Potentially** is used to say something is capable of becoming a particular thing. *...potentially dangerous dogs.*

❏ If something has **potential** or **potentiality**, it is capable of being useful or successful in the future. You can also talk about its **potentialities**. *All of these are quite useful breeds whose potentiality has not been realised.* ◇ If you have the **potential** to do something, you are capable of doing it. *The former prime minister gave ministers a taste of her potential to cause trouble in the Lords.* ◇ Your **potential** is the things you are capable of doing. *He never achieved his potential as writer, actor or even musician.*

pothole (potholing, potholer) A **pothole** is a large hole in the surface of a road. ◇ A **pothole** is also a deep hole in the ground in a limestone area, often leading to a network of underground caves and tunnels. **Potholing** is going down potholes to explore caves; a person who does this is called a **potholer**.

potion A **potion** is a drink which is supposed to have a certain effect on you, for example curing an illness or making you fall in love.

potted See **pot**.

potter (pottering, pottered) ❑ A **potter** is someone who makes pottery. ◇ A **potter's wheel** is a piece of equipment for making pottery. It consists of a flat disc which spins round. The potter puts soft clay onto the disc and shapes it into a pot.
❑ If you **potter about**, you pass the time in an unhurried way, doing pleasant but unimportant things.

pottery (potteries) **Pottery** is pots, dishes, and other objects made from clay. The craft of making things like these is called **pottery**. ◇ A **pottery** is a factory or workshop where pottery is made.

potting compost is a specially prepared mixture of substances such as peat, loam, and sand, for growing young plants in.

potting shed A **potting shed** is a garden shed for keeping things like seeds and tools in.

potty (potties) ❑ A **potty** is a deep bowl a small child uses as a toilet. **Potty-training** is teaching a child to use a potty.
❑ If you say someone is **potty**, you mean they are mad or very silly.

pouch (pouches) A **pouch** is a flexible container like a small bag. Pipe tobacco is often kept in a pouch. ◇ A **pouch** is also a fur-covered pocket of skin on an animal. Kangaroos and other marsupials have pouches on their stomachs in which their babies grow. Rodents like hamsters have pouches in their cheeks to carry food in.

pouffe (*pron:* poof) A **pouffe** is a piece of furniture for sitting or resting your feet on. It is like a low stool with feet rather than legs, and is made of some soft material.

poultice (*pron:* pole-tiss) A **poultice** is a pad with heated ointments in it which is put over a swollen or painful part of the body.

poultry is birds like chickens and ducks kept for their eggs and meat.

pounce (pouncing, pounced) When an animal or bird **pounces** on something, it leaps on it and grabs it to eat it. ◇ If you **pounce** on someone, you move towards them quickly and grab hold of them. ◇ If you **pounce** on something like a mistake someone has made, you notice it and quickly take advantage of it in some way. *Labour MPs have pounced on his allegations as proof that the intelligence agencies are out of control.*

pound (-pounder, pounding) ❑ The **pound** or **pound sterling** is the unit of currency in Britain. There are 100 pence in a pound. Pounds are usually represented by the symbol £. Some other countries, for example Cyprus and Egypt, have a unit of currency called a **pound**.
❑ Weight is often expressed in **pounds**. A pound is 16 ounces (about 0.454 kilograms). 'Pounds' is usually written 'lbs'. ◇ **-pounder** is used to describe (a) a fish weighing a certain number of pounds. *...a 27-pounder.* (b) a gun which fires a shell weighing a certain number of pounds. *...a 32-pounder cannon.*
❑ If something is **pounded** by something else, it is hit by it repeatedly. *The ship was pounded by huge waves.* ◇ If you **pound** something, you crush it into a paste or powder.

◇ If you talk about someone getting a **pounding**, you mean they suffer a heavy attack or severe criticism.
❑ When your heart or some other part of your body **pounds**, it beats or throbs with a strong fast rhythm. Similarly, you can talk about music **pounding**.
❑ If you **pound** somewhere, you run there with heavy noisy steps.

pour (pouring, poured) ❑ If you **pour** a liquid or some other substance, you make it flow out of a container by holding the container at an angle. ◇ If you **pour** someone a drink, you fill a cup or glass with it.
❑ If a liquid or some other substance **pours** somewhere, it flows quickly and in large quantities. *One man was taken away with blood pouring down his face.* ◇ When it **pours**, or **pours with rain**, it rains heavily.
❑ If people **pour** into a place, they go there in large numbers. ◇ If something like mail **pours** into a place, a lot of it is received. *Foreign offers of financial help are pouring in.* ◇ If someone **pours** money into an activity or organization, they keep spending money on it.
❑ **pour scorn**: see **scorn**. ◇ **pour cold water** on something: see **water**. ◇ **pour oil on troubled waters**: see **oil**.

pout (pouting, pouted) If someone **pouts**, they stick their lips out, because they are annoyed or because they want to look sexually attractive. An expression like this is called a **pout**.

poverty is being very poor. You say an area where there are many poor people is **poverty-stricken**. ◇ If a person or family lives below the **poverty line**, their income is less than the minimum considered necessary for a decent standard of living. ◇ If you say someone is caught in the **poverty trap**, you mean they are in a situation where they cannot increase their income by getting a job, because the extra money they earn will result in their state benefits being cut, and they will be no better off, or even worse off, than before.
❑ If you talk about the **poverty** of something, you mean there is not much of it, or what there is is not very good. *He became acutely aware of the poverty of truly American music.*

POW (*or* **pow**) (*pronounce each letter separately*) A **POW** is a prisoner of war.

pow-wow People sometimes call a meeting or conference a **pow-wow**.

powder (powdering, powdered) ❑ **Powder** is tiny particles of a solid substance. A **powdered** substance comes in the form of a powder. *...powdered milk.* ◇ If you **powder** yourself, you put talcum powder on your face or body. Similarly, you can **powder** a baby.
❑ If you call a situation or place a **powder keg**, you mean things could become violent at any time.

powder room A **powder room** is a women's toilet in a place like a department store.

powdery If something is **powdery**, it looks or feels like powder.

power (powering, powered) ❑ If someone has **power**, they have control over other people and their activities. ◇ If someone in authority has the **power** to do something, they have the legal right to do it. *The new constitution removes his power to declare an emergency... The police and intelligence service now get greater powers.* ◇ If you talk about **the powers that be** in a place, you are referring to the people in authority there.

❏ The person **in power** in a country is the person who has control there. You can also talk about someone gaining or losing **power**.

❏ A **power** is a very rich or important country, or one with strong military forces. *...a major conspiracy in which the big powers were involved.*

❏ A country's **air power** is its military aircraft. Similarly, its **naval power** is its warships.

❏ Your **power** to do something is your ability to do it. If something is **within your power**, you can do it. If you do **everything in your power** to achieve something, you try as hard as you can to achieve it.

❏ **Power** is energy obtained, for example, by burning fuel or by using the sun or wind. ◇ If a machine is **powered** in a certain way, that is how it gets the fuel or energy it needs to work. *...a wind-powered generator.*

❏ Electricity is often referred to as **power**. If there is a **power failure**, the electricity supply to a building or area is interrupted, for example because of damage to cables. If the supply is interrupted deliberately, you say there is a **power cut**. ◇ A **power** tool, device, or system is electrically operated. *...power drills.*

❏ The **power** of something is its physical strength. *...the power of the sea.* ◇ The **power** of something like the media is its ability to influence people's thoughts and behaviour. *...the power of television.*

❏ If you **power** somewhere, you go there quickly and powerfully.

power base A politician's **power base** is the supporters who provide him or her with power and influence.

power-broker A **power-broker** is someone who can influence people in political power, for example by promising or withdrawing their support.

power dressing was a style of women's dressing introduced in the 1980s. It included masculine tailoring and shoulder pads, and was intended to give an impression of power, confidence, and efficiency.

power line A **power line** is a cable, especially an overhead one, supplying power to a building or area.

power of attorney In law or business, **power of attorney** is the right to appoint someone, for example a solicitor, to perform certain acts on your behalf.

power plant A **power plant** is a place where power, for example electricity, is produced.

power point A **power point** is an electrical socket in a wall.

power-sharing is a system in which political power is shared by different groups.

power station A **power station** is a place where electricity is generated.

power steering or **power-assisted steering** is a way of making steering lighter and easier by using power from the vehicle's engine.

power worker A **power worker** is someone who works in a power station.

powerboat A **powerboat** is a fast powerful motorboat.

powered See **power**.

powerful (powerfully) ❏ A **powerful** person or organization has a lot of power.

❏ A **powerful** machine, device, or substance is very effective. *...a powerful laser... ...powerful medicines.*

❏ A **powerful** explosion is one where a very large amount of energy is released.

❏ If your body is **powerful**, it is physically strong. *He was very powerfully built.* ◇ A **powerful** voice is strong and easily heard. ◇ A **powerful** smell or flavour is strong and very noticeable.

❏ You say something like a book is **powerful** when it has a strong effect on people. *...a powerful and original first novel... ...the powerful influence of fashion.*

powerhouse If you call an industrial area the **powerhouse** of a region, you mean it is the part which creates the region's wealth.

powerless (powerlessly, powerlessness) If you are **powerless**, you are unable to control or influence events. *He watched powerlessly as rescue boats passed by without noticing his boat... For many people in rural areas, the feelings of powerlessness are as deep as any felt in the inner city.* ◇ If you are **powerless** to do something, you are unable to do it. *Allied soldiers looked on, powerless to intervene.*

pox The **pox** is syphilis.

pp You write **pp** in front of someone's name at the end of a letter to show you have signed it for them. **pp** means 'for and on behalf of'. ◇ See also **p**.

PR See (a) **public relations**. (b) **proportional representation**.

practicable (practicability) If a course of action is **practicable**, it can be carried out successfully. *We discussed the practicability of the idea over a cup of coffee.*

practical (practically; practicality, practicalities) ❏ **Practical** is used to talk about problems and situations which actually arise, and ways of dealing with them. *There's no possible practical use for a church capable of accommodating fifty thousand people in a small country town... As soon as is practically possible, the place will be shut down.* The practical aspects of something can be called **practicalities**. ◇ If you call a plan or method **practical** or talk about its **practicality**, you mean it is capable of being carried out successfully. *They have doubts about the practicality of the timetable adopted at the Rome Summit.*

❏ **Practical** skills are ones which involve doing things with your hands. ◇ **Practical** exams or lessons are ones in which students make things or do experiments, rather than just doing theoretical work. *...practical subjects.*

❏ A **practical** person deals with problems in a sensible and effective way.

❏ **Practical** clothes or household objects are useful rather than fashionable or attractive.

❏ **Practically** means almost. *I've lived here practically all my life.*

practical joke (practical joker) A **practical joke** is a trick played on someone to make them look silly. Someone who plays tricks like this is called a **practical joker**.

practically (practicality) See **practical**.

practice ❏ A **practice** is something people do regularly. *The general denied that the practice of selling weapons and uniforms to supplement low pay was widespread.* ◇ If something is normal or standard **practice**, it is the normal or accepted way of doing something. *The use of public relations companies is becoming increasingly common practice for businessmen and governments.*

❏ The **practices** of a religious group are the things they do regularly as part of their religion.

❏ **Practice** is regular training or exercise in something.

...piano practice.

❑ A doctor's or lawyer's **practice** is their business, often shared with other doctors or lawyers.

❑ What happens **in practice** is what actually happens, as distinct from what is supposed to happen. *Many states have not abolished the death penalty, but don't in practice carry it out.* ◇ If you put an idea or method **into practice**, you carry it out.

❑ In the US, 'practise' is spelled **practice**. *Freyberg had practiced dentistry in San Francisco.*

practise (practising, practised) (*American spelling:* **practice**, *etc*) ❑ If you **practise** something, you keep doing it regularly to improve your skill at it. If you are **practised** at something, you are good at it, because you have had a lot of experience of it. *...a practised politician.*

❑ **Practise** is used to talk about something being done in a certain way. *The Chief Medical Officer said it was vital for people to practise safe sex.* ◇ If you say someone **practises what they preach,** you mean they do what they encourage other people to do.

❑ If someone **practises** medicine, they work as a doctor. People can also **practise** other professions. *...a practising engineer.* ◇ When people **practise** something like a custom or religion, they take part in the activities associated with it. *...practising Catholics.*

practitioner People in some professions, for example medicine or the law, can be called **practitioners**. *...a dental practitioner.* ◇ **general practitioner**: see **general practice**. ◇ A **practitioner** of something involving skill is someone who does it regularly. *...judo practitioners.*

praesidium See **presidium**.

pragmatic (pragmatically; pragmatism, pragmatist) You say people are being **pragmatic** when they disregard theories or ideologies and do what they think is best in a situation. You call this behaviour **pragmatism**; someone who regularly behaves like this is called a **pragmatist**. *In employment, these firms respond pragmatically to local conditions.*

prairie A **prairie** is a large area of flat grassy land in North America.

praise (praising, praised) If you **praise** someone or something, you speak highly of their achievements or qualities. What you say is called **praise**. *Brazil's economic reform programme has won praise abroad but is running into trouble at home.* ◇ If you **sing** someone's **praises,** you praise them in an enthusiastic way.

praiseworthy If you say something is **praiseworthy**, you mean it is very good and deserves to be praised.

pram A **pram** is a vehicle for pushing a small baby around. It is like a cot on four large wheels.

prance (prancing, pranced) If someone **prances** around, they move around with exaggerated movements. ◇ If a horse **prances**, it moves with quick high steps.

prank (prankster) **Pranks** are childish tricks. You call someone who plays tricks like these a **prankster**.

prat If you say someone is a **prat**, you mean they are very stupid.

prattle (prattling, prattled) If you say someone is **prattling** on about something, you mean they are talking a lot without saying anything important.

prawn **Prawns** are small shellfish. They are similar to shrimps, but larger.

pray When people **pray**, they speak to the God they believe in, giving thanks to him or asking for help. ◇ If you **pray** that something will happen, you hope very much it will happen, because something important depends on it. *Investors pray that the Bank of Japan will lift the market from its doldrums by cutting interest rates.*

prayer is the practice of praying. A **prayer** is the words someone says when they pray, or a set form of words spoken during a religious service. A **prayer book** is a book containing the prayers used in church or at home. ◇ A short religious service can be called **prayers**. *...evening prayers.*

❑ If you say someone **hasn't got a prayer,** you mean they have no hope of succeeding in what they are trying to do.

pre- is used to form words which describe something as taking place before a particular date or event. *...pre-1900 literature... ...pre-Olympic trials.*

❑ **Pre-** is also used to form words which describe something being done in advance. For example, you say something is 'pre-planned' or 'pre-arranged'. Some words beginning with 'pre' can be spelled with or without a hyphen after the 'e'. For example, 'predate' can be spelled 'pre-date'. See entries at **precondition**, **predate**, **predetermined**, **prenatal**.

pre-arranged is used to say something was arranged in advance, and did not happen by chance. *...a pre-arranged meeting.*

pre-cooked food has been prepared and cooked in advance, so that you only need to heat it up before eating it.

pre-eminent (pre-eminently, pre-eminence) If someone is **pre-eminent** in a group, they are more important, powerful, or capable than other people in the group. *Despite his pre-eminence in the sport, it is only the second time he has won the title.* ◇ **Pre-eminently** is used to say something is more true of one person or thing in a group than others. *America is the pre-eminently religious nation of the West.*

pre-empt (pre-emptive, pre-emptively) If you **pre-empt** something, you stop it happening by doing something in advance which makes it pointless or impossible. *He resigned from the Communist party last week, pre-empting a decision to expel him.* **Pre-emptive** is used to describe actions done in advance like this. *...pre-emptive strikes against terrorists... If ever there was a case for deploying United Nations peacekeepers pre-emptively, Macedonia is it.*

pre-existing is used to describe something which already existed before the time you are talking about. *In some athletes the training may trigger a pre-existing condition.*

pre-industrial is used to talk about the time in a country's history before there was large-scale industry. *...pre-industrial technology.*

pre-let (pre-letting, pre-let *not* 'pre-letted') If you **pre-let** a building which is still being built, you have an agreement with someone that you will let it to them once it is completed.

pre-marital is used to talk about things which happen before marriage, especially things to do with sex. *...a pre-marital affair.*

pre-natal See **prenatal**.

pre-ordained (*or* preordained) When people talk about

something being **pre-ordained**, they mean it has been decided in advance that it will happen, for example by God or fate.

pre-packaged goods are packed or wrapped before they are sent to the shop where they are going to be sold.

pre-paid (pre-payment) (or prepaid, prepayment) Pre-paid items are paid for in advance. A **pre-payment** is money paid in advance for something.

pre-planned is used to say something was planned in advance, and did not just happen spontaneously or by chance. ...a pre-planned riot.

pre-prandial is used to describe things which happen before a meal, especially dinner. ...pre-prandial drinks.

pre-pubescent girls or boys are at the age just before puberty.

Pre-Raphaelite The Pre-Raphaelites were a group of 19th century English artists and writers. They typically based their work on themes from medieval literature, Shakespeare, and the Bible.

pre-recorded If something is **pre-recorded**, it has been recorded in advance, so it can be broadcast or played at a particular time. ...a pre-recorded interview. ◇ Pre-recorded cassettes already have music on them, rather than being blank for you to record on them yourself.

pre-school is used to talk about things to do with the care and education of children before they reach school age. ...pre-school nurseries.

pre-set is used to describe (a) things which have been decided on in advance. ...a pre-set rate of return. (b) equipment whose controls have been set in advance. ...pre-set radio stations.

pre-tax is used to talk about a company's profits or a person's earnings before tax has been deducted.

pre-term A pre-term baby is born prematurely.

pre-war is used to describe something which happened or existed in the period just before a war, especially the Second World War. ...pre-war Romania... ...the pre-war years.

preach (preaches, preaching, preached) When someone, especially a member of the clergy, **preaches**, they give a talk on a religious or moral subject as part of a church service. ◇ If you **preach** a set of ideas or beliefs, you try to persuade people to accept them. The industrial countries have been preaching free trade to the third world for years. ◇ If you say someone is **preaching to the converted**, you mean they are explaining their ideas or beliefs to people who already accept them. ◇ If you **preach at** someone, you give them unwanted advice in a moralizing way. ◇ **practise what you preach**: see practise.

preacher Members of the clergy are sometimes called preachers.

preamble (pron: pree-am-bl) The **preamble** of a speech or piece of writing is an introductory part at the beginning.

prebendary (pron: preb-en-der-ee) (prebendaries) A **prebendary** is a member of the clergy on the staff of a cathedral.

precarious (precariously, precariousness) If a situation is **precarious**, things could go badly wrong at any time. This has left the talks precariously close to collapse... ...the precariousness of the economy. ◇ **Precarious** is also used to talk about situations in which someone or something is likely

to fall because they are not well-balanced or secure. They perch precariously on tiny fold-up stools.

precaution (precautionary) If you do something as a **precaution**, you do it to try and prevent yourself or someone else being harmed. You call an action like this **precautionary**. The local administration says the curfew is a precautionary measure.

precede (preceding, preceded) ❑ If something **precedes** something else, it happens before it. The rise over the preceding six months was only 3.3%. ◇ The person who **preceded** you in your job was the one who had it before you.

❑ If you **precede** someone somewhere, you go in front of them. Now and again through the crowd would rush a runner, preceded by a torch-bearer.

precedence (pron: press-ee-denss) If something takes **precedence** over something else, the first thing is seen as more important than the second. Not offending one of the world's major powers usually takes precedence over the wishes of a small nation.

precedent (pron: press-ee-dent) ❑ You say something sets a **precedent** when the fact that it has happened once makes it likely that it will happen again, perhaps several times. Some would say that the airport affair has set a dangerous precedent for the future. ◇ If there has been a **precedent** for something, something similar has happened before. There are precedents for meetings at short notice at times of international tension.

❑ **Precedent** is used to talk about the way something has always been done, which is therefore considered to be correct. He has broken with precedent by refusing to go to the long, elaborate and often boozy lunches.

preceding See precede.

precentor (pron: pree-sen-ter) In some cathedrals and churches, the **precentor** is a member of clergy responsible for the music sung there.

precept (pron: pree-sept) A **precept** is a general rule which helps you decide how you should behave in particular circumstances.

precinct A shopping **precinct** or pedestrian **precinct** is a shopping area in which cars are not allowed. ◇ The **precincts** of a property are the land and buildings within its boundaries. ◇ In the US, a **precinct** is a division of a city for police purposes, or a subdivision of a county or ward for electoral purposes.

precious ❑ If a resource is **precious**, it is valuable and not to be wasted. Precious time has been wasted. ◇ If something you own is **precious** to you, it is important to you and you would not want to part with it.

❑ **Precious** objects and materials are worth a lot of money, because they are rare. ◇ **Precious metals** are valuable metals like gold and silver. ◇ **Precious stones** are valuable gemstones like diamonds and rubies. See also semi-precious.

❑ If there is **precious little** of something, there is very little of it.

❑ If you say a person is **precious**, you mean they behave in a formal and unnatural way.

precipice (pron: press-sip-iss) A **precipice** is a very steep rock face. ◇ If you say someone is close to a **precipice**, you mean they are in a dangerous situation where disaster or failure could easily happen. The prime minister said *this measure would draw the country back from a financial precipice.*

precipitate (precipitating, precipitated; precipitately) If something **precipitates** (*pron:* pris-**sip**-i-tates) a happening or change, it makes it happen sooner than expected. *Her resignation was precipitated by her failure to win a decisive majority in the first round of voting.* ◇ **Precipitate** (*pron:* pris-**sip**-i-tet) is used to describe things which happen suddenly and rapidly. *...a precipitate rush towards economic and monetary union... Her personal rating has fallen as precipitately as it rose in September.*

precipitation In meteorology, **precipitation** is rain, snow, or hail.

precipitous (precipitously) A **precipitous** slope is very steep. ◇ **Precipitous** events happen suddenly and rapidly. *The 1980s saw a precipitous decline in government investment... Living standards are falling precipitously.*

précis (*pron:* **pray**-see) (*plural:* précis) A **précis** is a short piece of writing summarizing the main points of a book or report.

precise (precisely) ❏ **Precise** is used to talk about something happening exactly at a particular time. *At this precise moment he has 11 buildings fully designed and ready to be built... The precise timing of the closure has yet to be confirmed.*

   ❏ **Precisely** is used to emphasize that something is a particular thing in every detail. *That is precisely what she has done.* ◇ If something like a measurement is **precise**, it is exact rather than approximate.

   ❏ You say '**to be precise**' when you are giving more exact information about something you have just mentioned. *By late yesterday, the pound was worth less than the Irish punt, changing hands at 99 Irish pence to be precise.*

precision If something is done with **precision**, it is done very accurately. ◇ **Precision** equipment is very accurate. *...high-precision radar.*

preclude (precluding, precluded) If something **precludes** something happening, it makes it impossible for it to happen. ◇ If circumstances **preclude** you from doing something, they make it impossible for you to do it. *His age might preclude him from selection for an England tour.*

precocious (precociously; precocity) If you call a child **precocious** or talk about its **precocity** (pree-**koss**-it-tee), you mean it does or says things which are very advanced for its age. *He had precociously mastered more than a dozen instruments.*

preconception (preconceived) If you say someone has **preconceptions** about something or **preconceived** ideas about it, you mean they have already made up their mind about it before they have had enough information or experience to form a fair opinion.

precondition (*or* pre-condition) If something is a **precondition** of something else, the first thing must happen or be done before the second thing can happen. *Both sides are expected to lay down preconditions before more substantial negotiations can take place.*

precursor If something is a **precursor** of something else, it happens before the other thing and acts as a signal or warning that it is going to happen. *The deal should not be seen as a precursor to a merger.*

predate (predating, predated) (*or* pre-date, *etc*) If something **predates** something else, it was made before it. Similarly,

something can **predate** an event. *The monument predates the arrival of the druids in Britain.*

predator (predatory; predation) A **predator** is an animal which kills and eats other animals. You say an animal like this is **predatory. Predation** is killing and eating other animals. ◇ You say a person or organization is **predatory** or call them a **predator** when they are eager to gain something out of someone else's weakness or suffering.

predecease (predeceasing, predeceased) If you **predecease** someone, you die before them.

predecessor Your **predecessor** is the person who had your job before you. ◇ The **predecessor** of something like a machine is the one it developed from or replaced. *The coin will have the same design as its predecessor, but will be smaller and lighter.*

predestined (predestination) If you say something was **predestined** to happen, you mean it could not have been prevented, because it had already been decided by God or some other supernatural power. People who believe in **predestination** believe events are controlled in this way.

predetermined (*or* pre-determined) If something is **predetermined**, it is decided on beforehand.

predicament A **predicament** is an unpleasant situation which is difficult to get out of.

predicate (predicating, predicated) If something is **predicated** on something else, it is based on the assumption that the other thing will happen or exist. *The whole process of unification is predicated on this hope of economic growth.*

predict (prediction, predictor) If you **predict** that something will happen, you say you believe it will happen, or will happen in a certain way. This is called making a **prediction**. A **predictor** is something which enables you to make a prediction. *The most reliable predictor of voting is education and age.*

predictable (predictably, predictability) You say something is **predictable** when you can tell in advance what is going to happen. *The power shortage has had predictably grave consequences for economic growth... Only eight seeds have survived to the last 16, undermining accusations of predictability in the women's game.*

prediction See predict.

predictive is used to talk about making predictions. *...a computer which can carry out predictive calculations.*

predictor See predict.

predilection (*pron:* pree-dil-**lek**-shn) If you have a **predilection** for something, you like having it or using it. *...his predilection for fast cars.*

predispose (predisposing, predisposed; predisposition) If you are **predisposed** to a medical condition or have a **predisposition** to it, you are likely to be affected by it. You can also say something **predisposes** someone to a medical condition. *US scientists have discovered a gene that predisposes people to alcoholism.* ◇ If something **predisposes** you to behave in a certain way, it makes it likely you will behave that way. You can talk about people having a **predisposition** to behave in a certain way.

predominant (predominantly, predominance) ❏ If certain things are **predominant** or there is a **predominance** of them, there are more of them, or they are more noticeable, than other things. *There is a predominance of civilian* *employees here.* ◇ You also say someone or something is **predominant** or has **predominance** when they are more powerful or important than other people or things.

❑ **Predominantly** means 'mainly'. *Pakistan is a predominantly agricultural country.*

predominate (predominating, predominated) If one type of person or thing **predominates** in a group, there are more of that type than any other. *US and European cyclists predominate and usually lead the field.* ◇ If a particular feature or quality **predominates**, it is the most important or noticeable one. *Three issues predominate: regional security, reconstruction and the Arab-Israeli conflict.*

preen (preening, preened) When a bird **preens** itself, it cleans and arranges its feathers. ◇ If you talk about people **preening** themselves, you mean (a) they spend a lot of time making themselves look neat and attractive. (b) they behave in a smug proud way,

prefab A **prefab** is a prefabricated building, especially a house.

prefabricated buildings are built from ready-made sections which are easily put together.

preface (*pron:* pref-fiss) (prefacing, prefaced) A **preface** is an introduction at the beginning of a book, explaining what the book is about or why it was written. ◇ If you **preface** an action or speech with something else, you do or say the other thing first.

prefect (prefecture) In some countries, a **prefect** is the chief administrator of a government department or region. The area a prefect deals with is called a **prefecture.** ◇ In some schools, a **prefect** is an older pupil who has been given special duties.

prefer (preferring, preferred) ❑ If you **prefer** one thing to another, you like the first thing better, and are more likely to choose it if there is a choice.

❑ If the police **prefer** charges against someone, they make a formal accusation against them which has then to be decided in court.

preferable (*pron:* pref-fer-a-bl) (preferably) If you say one thing is **preferable** to another, you mean it is more worthwhile or desirable. *Allow to stand at least 20 minutes, preferably an hour, to let the flavours blend.*

preference (*pron:* pref-fer-enss) If you have a **preference** for something, you would like to do it or have it rather than something else. ◇ If you give **preference** to someone, you choose them rather than someone else.

preference share Preference shares pay a fixed dividend and are safer than ordinary shares.

preferential If you get **preferential** treatment, you are deliberately treated better than other people, and therefore have an advantage.

preferment is promotion to a better and more influential job. *...backbenchers passed over for preferment.*

preferred See prefer.

prefigure (prefiguring, prefigured) If something **prefigures** something else, it shows or suggests that the second thing will happen. *That day the wall through Berlin was finally ruptured, prefiguring the complete disintegration of East Germany.*

prefix (prefixes, prefixing, prefixed) A **prefix** is a group of letters added at the beginning of a word to make a new word with a different meaning. 'semi-', 'pre-', and 'un-' are prefixes. ◇ If one word or number is **prefixed** by

another one, the second one is in front of the first one. *All telephone numbers should be prefixed by 010 33.*

pregnant (pregnancy) ❑ If a woman or female animal is **pregnant,** a baby is developing in her womb. A woman's **pregnancy** is the time during which she is pregnant.

❑ If you say there is a **pregnant** pause or silence, you mean nothing is said for a while, but this in itself seems to convey a special meaning.

preheat (preheating, preheated) If you **preheat** an oven, you switch it on and allow it to reach a certain temperature before putting food in.

prehistoric (prehistory) **Prehistoric** is used to describe things which happened or existed a long time ago in the past, before writing was invented. This time is called **prehistory.**

prejudge (prejudging, prejudged) If you **prejudge** a situation, you form an opinion about it before you know all the facts.

prejudice (prejudicing, prejudiced) ❑ **Prejudice** is an unreasonable dislike for someone or something, especially a group of people. *...the growing prejudice against gays and lesbians.* You say people who have unreasonable dislikes are **prejudiced.** ◇ If you say someone is **prejudiced in favour** of someone or something, you mean they unreasonably prefer them to other people or things.

❑ If something **prejudices** the chances of something succeeding, it makes it less likely to succeed.

prejudicial If something is **prejudicial** to something like a person's good reputation, it is harmful to it. ◇ **Prejudicial** is used to describe things which could unfairly influence people's opinions or decisions. *...the prejudicial effect of admitting previous convictions as evidence.* ◇ **Prejudicial** also means showing prejudice. *The Press Council received a complaint that the papers had reported the man's colour in a prejudicial way which had no relevance to the story.*

prelate (*pron:* prel-it) A **prelate** is a high-ranking member of the clergy, for example a bishop or an archbishop.

preliminary (preliminaries) **Preliminary** is used to describe things which are the first of their kind and serve as a preparation for others which are to follow. Things like these are also called **preliminaries.** *...a preliminary agreement on fishing rights... The Japanese went straight onto the offensive without lengthy preliminaries.* ◇ A **preliminary** is also the first part of a competition, which decides who will go on to the main competition.

prelude (*pron:* prel-yewd) ❑ If you say something is a **prelude** to something else, you mean it comes before it and serves as an introduction to it. *The interest-rate cut is a prelude to other economy-boosting measures.*

❑ A **prelude** is a short piece of music, usually for piano or organ.

premature (prematurely) **Premature** is used to describe things which happen earlier than usual, or earlier than expected. *...premature arthritis... ...prematurely white hair.* ◇ A **premature** baby weighs less than 2,500 grams (about 5½ lb) when it is born and is usually born earlier than expected. ◇ If you say something someone has done is **premature,** you mean they have done it too soon, at an inappropriate time. *The ANC described the United States decision as premature.*

premeditated (premeditation) A **premeditated** action, especially a crime, is planned or thought about beforehand. *The court should be strongly influenced by the considerable premeditation and planning that went into this attack.*

premenstrual syndrome If a woman suffers from **premenstrual syndrome** or PMS, changes in her hormone levels in the days before her periods start make her feel irritable and unwell. Premenstrual syndrome can strongly affect some women's behaviour.

premenstrual tension Premenstrual syndrome is sometimes called **premenstrual tension** or PMT.

premier (*pron:* **prem**-ee-er) ❑ A country's prime minister is sometimes called its **premier.**
❑ **Premier** is sometimes used to describe the most important thing of a particular kind. ...*the FA Premier League...* ...*the premier power in Central Asia.*

premiere (*pron:* **prem**-mee-air) (premiering, premiered) The **premiere** of something like a new play or film is its first public performance. When this performance takes place, you say the play or film is **premiered.**

premiership The **premiership** is the job or position of being prime minister. A person's **premiership** is the time during which they are prime minister.

premise (*pron:* **prem**-iss) ❑ The **premises** of a business are all the buildings and land it occupies.
❑ A **premise** or **premiss** is something which you suppose is true and which you use as a basis for something else. *The premise of the London peace conference is that this sinister practice can be stopped and reversed.*

premiss (premisses) See **premise.**

premium ❑ A **premium** is an extra sum of money paid in addition to the normal cost of something. ◇ A **premium** is also a sum of money you pay regularly to an insurance company when you have taken out a policy with them.
❑ If something is **at a premium**, it is hard to get because it is in short supply. *Parking space is at a premium.* ◇ If something is sold **at a premium**, it is sold at a high price because it is in short supply. Similarly, **premium** prices are higher than usual.
❑ **Premium** is sometimes used to describe things which are of high quality. ...*premium Scotch whisky.*
❑ If you put or place a **premium** on something, you consider it to be especially important. *Islam has always placed a high premium on education for both boys and girls.*

premium bond Premium bonds are numbered bonds sold by the government at post offices. You do not earn interest on them, but every month there is a draw for cash prizes.

premonition If you have a **premonition,** you have a feeling that something is going to happen, often something unpleasant.

prenatal (*or* pre-natal) is used to talk about things to do with the medical care of pregnant women. ...*pre-natal screening.*

preoccupy (preoccupies, preoccupying, preoccupied; preoccupation) If something **preoccupies** you or you are **preoccupied** with it, you pay a lot of attention to it. ...*Moscow's preoccupation with its economic crisis.* ◇ A **preoccupation** is something you think about a lot because it is important to you. *One of the central preoccupations of the trades unions has been to strike a deal with the Labour Party.*

preordained See **pre-ordained.**

prep school A **prep school** is a private school for children up to 11 or 13. ◇ In the US, a **prep school** is a secondary school, usually private, to prepare students to enter college.

prepaid See **pre-paid.**

preparation See **prepare.**

preparatory is used to describe things which are done in preparation for something. ...*a preparatory meeting before an Arab summit.* ◇ If you do something **preparatory to** something else, you do it before the other thing happens. *Today he flies to London to see John Major, preparatory to the peace conference to be held next month.*

preparatory school A **preparatory school** is the same as a prep school.

prepare (preparing, prepared; preparation) ❑ If you **prepare** something, you get it ready, or put it together. *The site is being prepared for a rock concert.* ◇ **Preparations** are all the things done and arrangements made for a forthcoming event.
❑ If you **prepare** for an event, action, or situation, you get ready to deal with it. ◇ If you **prepare** someone else for something, you make sure they are able to deal with it when it happens. *The system failed to prepare students for the harsh realities of being a working architect.* ◇ If you **prepare** something like a report, you write it, putting in everything that is needed. *The draft television bill has been in preparation for years.*
❑ When you **prepare** food, you get it ready. ◇ A **preparation** is a mixture prepared for use as a food, medicine, or cosmetic. ...*Chinese herbal preparations.*

prepared (preparedness) If you are **prepared** to do something, you are willing to do it. ◇ If you are **prepared** for something which may happen, you are ready to deal with it when it happens. *The police were criticized for their lack of preparedness.* ◇ **Prepared** is used to describe things which have been done or made in advance. ...*a prepared statement.*

prepayment See **pre-paid.**

preponderance (preponderant) If there is a **preponderance** of one type of person or thing in a group or if they are **preponderant,** there are more of them than other types, or they are more important or powerful. *Japan has a marked preponderance of smaller firms.*

preposition Prepositions are words like 'by', 'for', 'into', and 'with'.

preposterous (preposterously) If you call something **preposterous,** you mean it is extremely unlikely or unreasonable. *A spokeswoman described the allegations as preposterous and completely untrue... Some prices are preposterously high.*

preppy (*or* preppie) (preppies) In the US, a **preppy** is a student or former student of an expensive private school. Preppies are well known for wearing expensive conservative clothes.

prerequisite If one thing is a **prerequisite** of another, the first thing must happen or exist before the second thing is possible. *Party membership was an essential prerequisite of a successful career.*

prerogative If something is a **prerogative** of a particular person or group, it is a privilege or right which only they have.

presage (*pron:* **press**-ij) (presaging, presaged) If something **presages** a situation or event, it is seen as a sign or warning that it is about to happen. *The fact that he has been removed from office is very significant, and it has presaged several changes at the top.*

Presbyterian The **Presbyterian** Church is a Protestant church based on Calvinism. Its members are called **Presbyterians**. The Church is governed by a group of clerical and lay people of equal rank called 'elders' or 'presbyters'. The Presbyterian Church is especially strong in Scotland and Northern Ireland; the English Presbyterian Church combined with the Congregational Church in 1972 to form the United Reformed Church.

presbytery (presbyteries) In the Presbyterian Church, a **presbytery** is a local church court composed of ministers and elders. ◇ A **presbytery** is also the house in which a Roman Catholic priest lives.

prescient (*pron:* **press**-ee-ent) (prescience) If someone is **prescient**, they foresee what is going to happen in the future. You talk about the **prescience** of someone like this.

prescribe (prescribing, prescribed; prescription) ❑ If a doctor **prescribes** treatment or a medicine, he or she decides what treatment or medicine you should have, and arranges for the treatment or writes out an order for the medicine. The medicine a doctor prescribes is called a **prescription**; the form it is ordered on is also called a **prescription**. If a medicine is available only **on prescription**, you can only get it from a chemist if you have a prescription for it. Medicines like these are called **prescription drugs**.
❑ If someone in authority **prescribes** something, they give instructions that it shall be done. *They fear fines for having more than the prescribed one child per family.*

prescriptive If something is **prescriptive**, it sets down rules about what should be done. *A prescriptive approach would be neither workable nor desirable.*

presence ❑ Your **presence** somewhere is the fact that you are there. ◇ If you are **in** someone's **presence**, you are in the same place as them. ◇ If you **make your presence felt**, you do something which makes people pay attention to you. ◇ If a country has a military **presence** somewhere, it has soldiers stationed there. *...the American and European presence in the Gulf.*
❑ If you say someone has **presence**, you mean they have an impressive appearance and manner.
❑ **Presence of mind** is the ability to act quickly and sensibly in a difficult situation.

present (presentation, presenter) ❑ The **present** is the period of time taking place now. If something is happening **at present** or **at the present time**, it is happening now. ◇ If something exists **for the present**, it exists now and will continue until something happens to stop or change it. *For the present, the logging continues.* ◇ **Present** is used to describe people and things that exist now, rather than in the past or future. *...the present government... ...Hungary's present difficulties.* ◇ The **present day** is the period of history taking place now. **Present-day** is used to describe things which happen or exist now, in contrast to similar things in the past. *Present-day conferences are better organised than the early meetings.*
❑ If someone or something is **present** in a place, they are there. *Only a quarter of the officers present had any riot control training... This gene is present in all of us.*
❑ A **present** is something you give to someone, for example on their birthday. ◇ If someone is **presented** (*pron:* pri-**zent**-id) with something like an award, they are formally given it. The event or ceremony at which they are given it is called a **presentation**.
❑ If you **present** someone with something like information, you give it to them in a formal way. *...the presentation of the budget.*
❑ When people **present** something like a performance, they put it on, so the public can come and see it. *...a presentation of Handel's Messiah.*
❑ If you talk about the **presentation** of a piece of work, you are talking about the way it looks or is set out, and the impression it gives. *Standards of presentation, spelling and handwriting appeared to have fallen since the previous year.*
❑ If you **present** yourself somewhere, you arrive there, for example to keep an appointment. *The traditional system has been that people present themselves to employment agencies for placement.*
❑ If something **presents** a difficulty, challenge, or opportunity, it causes or provides it. ◇ If you **present** yourself as a particular thing, you try to get people to believe you are that thing. *He presents himself as a man of the people.*
❑ When someone **presents** a TV or radio programme, they introduce each part of it or each person on it. Someone who does this is called a **presenter**.

present-day See present.

presentable If you talk about someone or something being **presentable**, you mean they are suitable for people to see. *She had regularly raided her friends' wardrobes so she would have a presentable outfit to go out in.*

presentation (presenter) See present.

presently is used to say something is happening now. *Amnesty International is presently organizing a worldwide protest.*

preservation See preserve.

preservative A **preservative** is a chemical which prevents things from decaying. Some preservatives are added to food; others are used to treat wood or metal.

preserve (preserving, preserved; preserver; preservation, preservationist) ❑ If you **preserve** something, you take action to save it or protect it from damage, loss, or decay. *...proposals for preserving fish stocks in community waters... ...the International Council for Bird Preservation.* People involved in preserving things are called **preservationists**. ◇ A **preserve** is an area of land or water where animals are protected.
❑ If you **preserve** a desirable situation, you make sure it stays as it is. *The pact was vital for preserving peace and stability in Asia... ...the preservation of law and order.* You can say someone is a **preserver** of a desirable situation. *...NATO's role as the preserver of peace in Europe.*
❑ If you **preserve** food, you treat it in a way which prevents it from decaying, for example by freezing it or using sugar or salt. ◇ **Preserves** are foods such as bottled fruit, jams, marmalades, and chutneys.
❑ If something is the **preserve** of a group of people, it is restricted to that group. *Currently the preserve of jet-setting businessmen, supersonic flight could become a routine form of travel in the 21st century.*

preside (presiding, presided) The person who **presides** over a meeting is the person in charge of it. ◇ If someone **presides** over something which is taking place, they are responsible for it and in control of it. *The new cabinet would preside over the reconstruction of the country.*

presidency (presidencies) The **presidency** is the job or position of being a president. A person's **presidency** is the time during which they are president.

president The **president** of a country which is not a monarchy is the head of state there. In the US and some other countries, the president is also the person with the highest political position. ◇ The **president** of an organization is the person with the highest position in it.

president-elect The **president-elect** is the person who has been elected as the next president, but who has not yet taken up the post.

presidential is used to talk about things to do with a country's president. *...presidential elections.*

presidium (*or* **praesidium**) In communist countries, the **presidium** is a committee or other body which takes policy decisions on behalf of a larger group, for example a parliament.

press (presses, pressing, pressed) ❑ If you **press** a button or switch, you push it with your finger. You can also press something with your hand or foot. *When I pressed the accelerator there was nothing there.* ◇ If you **press** one thing against another, you push the first thing against the second. ◇ If you **press** clothes, you iron them. ◇ **press the flesh**: see **flesh**.

❑ A **press** is a machine or device which puts pressure on something, for example to squeeze liquid from it. *...garlic presses.*

❑ If you **press** for something, you try hard to get it introduced or brought into being. *We're determined to press for international protection for dolphins.* ◇ If you **press** someone to do something, you try hard to get them to do it.

❑ If you **press** charges against someone, you make an official accusation which has to be settled in court.

❑ Newspapers and journalists are often referred to as the **press**. *...the popular press... The Bill of Rights guarantees a free press.* ◇ If someone or something has a bad **press**, people get a bad impression of them because of what they read in the papers, or see or hear on TV or the radio.

❑ A printing **press** is a machine for printing books and papers. ◇ When a newspaper **goes to press**, the latest edition starts being printed.

❑ If you **press ahead** with an activity, you start doing it, or continue doing it, in a determined way. ◇ If you **press on**, you continue doing something in spite of difficulties.

❑ **press into service**: see **service**.

press box A **press box** is a room at a sports ground reserved for journalists.

Press Complaints Commission The **Press Complaints Commission** is an organization which tries to make sure the press works professionally and ethically, and deals with complaints about the press. It replaced the Press Council in 1991.

press conference A **press conference** is the same as a news conference.

press corps (*pron:* **kor**) The **press corps** is a group of reporters from different papers all working in the same place.

Press Council The **Press Council** was an organization set up to defend the freedom of the press and to deal with complaints about the press. It was replaced by the Press Complaints Commission in 1991.

press cutting A **press cutting** is an article you cut out of a paper and keep, usually because it is about you.

press-gang In the past, when someone was **press-ganged** into the navy, they were captured and forced to join it. The group of people who did the capturing were called a **press gang**. These days, if someone is **press-ganged** into doing something, they are made to do it, although they do not really want to.

press office The **press office** of a large organization or government department is the section which gives information about its activities to the press.

press officer A **press officer** is someone employed by an organization to give information about it to the press.

press release A **press release** is a written statement about a matter of public interest given to journalists by the organization involved in it.

press secretary A **press secretary** is the same as a press officer.

press stud A **press stud** is a small device in two pieces for fastening clothes. One piece has a knob which snaps into a hole on the other piece.

press-up **Press-ups** are exercises for strengthening the arm and chest muscles. They are done by lying with your face towards the floor and pushing with your hands until your arms are straight.

pressing ❑ See **press**.

❑ If something is **pressing**, it needs to be dealt with immediately. *...pressing economic problems.*

❑ A **pressing** is a batch of CDs or LPs made from a master recording.

pressman (pressmen) A **pressman** is a journalist, especially a man, who works for a newspaper or magazine.

pressure (pressuring, pressured) ❑ **Pressure** is the force of something pushing on something else. *Apply pressure on the middle of the backbone with your fist.* ◇ **Pressure** is also the force that a quantity of gas or liquid exerts on a surface when it touches it. It is measured by the amount of force over an area like a square metre or a square foot. See also **blood pressure**.

❑ If someone **pressures** you or puts **pressure** on you, they try to persuade you to do something. ◇ If you **bring pressure to bear** on someone, you use your influence to try and make them do something they do not want to, but which you think they should.

❑ **Pressure** is also the tension and stress you feel as a result of being in a difficult situation or because of the demands of work. You can also talk about the **pressures** of a job or situation.

pressure cooker A **pressure cooker** is a large saucepan with an air-tight lid in which you can cook food quickly using steam at high pressure.

pressure group A **pressure group** is an organization which campaigns to get a government or other authority to take a particular course of action.

pressurize (pressurizing, pressurized) (*can be spelled with an 's' instead of a 'z'*) ❑ If you are **pressurized** to do something, people try hard to persuade or force you to do it.

Women had been pressurized to have babies.

❏ If a container or area is **pressurized**, the pressure inside it is different from the pressure outside. *...a pressurized diving chamber.*

prestige (prestigious) If someone has **prestige**, people admire and respect them, because they are important or successful. Similarly, something like an event or project can have **prestige**; you can also say something like this is **prestigious**. *...the world's most prestigious cycle race.* **Prestige** is used to describe things which have prestige. *...prestige projects.*

presto See hey presto.

presumably You use **presumably** to say you think something is true, although you cannot be certain of it. *People in Yorkshire eat the most fish, and presumably chips.*

presume (presuming, presumed; presumption, presumptuous)
❏ If something is **presumed** to be true, people suppose it is true or behave as if it is true, although they have no proof and cannot be certain about it. You can also say there is a **presumption** that something is true.

❏ If you talk about someone **presuming** to do something, you mean they do it even though they have no right to. *They're resentful that outsiders presume to meddle in their affairs.* You say someone who behaves like this is **presumptuous**; you call their behaviour **presumption**.

❏ If a proposal **presumes** that something will happen, it takes it for granted that it will happen, and relies on it happening. *The governor is committed to an 'executive-led government', which presumes a more active Executive Council.*

presuppose (presupposing, presupposed) If something **presupposes** a certain thing, it can only happen or be true if that thing happens or is true. *It might be an option for other companies to take over British Steel's Scottish plants, but that presupposes there are buyers for them.*

pretend (pretence) (American spelling: pretense) ❏ If you **pretend** something is true, you try to make people believe it is true. Behaviour like this is called a **pretence**. *She would pretend to faint in class to get attention... The unions were persuaded to accept more free time instead of more pay, on the pretence that it would improve the quality of life.* ◇ If you do something **under false pretences**, you do it by pretending to be someone else, or by pretending to have different motives from your real ones. *Journalists, he says, got in to see him under false pretences.*

❏ If a child **pretends** to do something, they behave as if they are doing it, often as part of a game. **Pretend** things are imaginary or a substitute for the real thing. *...pretend tattoos... To a child a pretend playmate is for real.*

❏ If you say you do not **pretend** to be something, you mean you do not claim to be that thing. *He does not pretend to be a paragon of virtue.* Similarly, you can say you do not **pretend** to be able to do something. *I do not pretend to have any answer to this dilemma.*

pretender A **pretender** to a throne or title is someone who claims the right to it, but whose claim is disputed in some way.

pretense See pretend.

pretension (pretentious, pretentiously, pretentiousness) **Pretension** is trying to make people believe you are very important or sophisticated. When someone behaves like this, you say they are being **pretentious**. You can also call something like a play or book **pretentious**. *...preten-*

tiously titled volumes... There has been a pretentiousness about the work on show this year.* ◇ If someone has **pretensions** to something, they claim to be able to do it or be it. *Our own increasing economic weakness undermines our pretensions to 'lead Europe in more sensible directions'... ...Madrid's pretension to the title of cultural capital of Europe.*

preternaturally is used to say something is so unusual or exceptional that it seems unnatural. *The stars were preternaturally bright and clear.*

pretext If you use something as a **pretext** for doing something you want or intend to do, you use it as an excuse for doing it.

prettify (prettifies, prettifying, prettified) If you **prettify** something like a room, you try to make it look pretty, for example by adding ornaments or decorations.

pretty (prettier, prettiest; prettily, prettiness) ❏ A **pretty** woman or girl is attractive in a delicate way. ◇ A **pretty** place or building has many attractive features, and is pleasant to look at. *...the prettiest village in England... ...prettily restored old buildings... The house oozes charm and prettiness.*

❏ **Pretty** is used to mean 'quite' or 'rather'. *The situation is pretty bad in Bolivia.* ◇ **Pretty much** means 'more or less' or 'to a great extent'. *This party has for the past year had things pretty much its own way at the ballot box.* ◇ **Pretty well** means 'almost'. *He has been disliked, it seems, by pretty well everybody close to him.*

❏ If you say someone is **sitting pretty**, you mean they are in a safe or comfortable position while other people are still suffering or having to work hard.

❏ If you say things have come to a **pretty pass**, you mean a situation has become really bad.

pretzel A **pretzel** is a type of brittle salted biscuit made in the shape of a loose knot.

prevail (prevailing, prevailed) ❏ If a belief or feeling **prevails**, it is normal or generally accepted. *She went against the prevailing mood over cot deaths.* ◇ If something like a principle **prevails**, it emerges as the strongest factor in a dispute or argument. *We hoped that common sense would prevail in the need to come to an agreement.* Similarly, you say a person **prevails** if their ideas are accepted.

❏ If you **prevail upon** someone to do something, you persuade them to do it.

❏ If you talk about the **prevailing** wind in a place, you are saying which direction the wind usually blows from.

prevalent (prevalence) If something is **prevalent**, it exists or happens very commonly. *The authorities admit that torture is prevalent throughout the country... Distress is being caused to residents by the prevalence of jet-skis.*

prevaricate (prevaricating, prevaricated) If you **prevaricate**, you avoid doing something you should do, or you avoid giving a direct answer or making a firm decision. Behaviour like this is called **prevarication**.

prevent (prevention) If you **prevent** someone from doing something, you make it impossible for them to do it. Similarly, if you **prevent** something happening, you make sure it does not happen. *...the prevention of lung cancer.*

preventable If something is **preventable**, it can be prevented from happening.

preventative means the same as preventive.

prevention See prevent.

preventive actions are intended to stop something unpleasant like a disease from happening. ...*a book about preventive dentistry.*

preview If there is a **preview** of something like a film or exhibition, a limited number of people are allowed to see it before it opens to the general public. When this happens, you say the film or exhibition is **previewed.**

previous (previously) ❑ A **previous** event of a particular kind was one which took place before the one you are talking about. *England had won 12 of their previous 13 encounters with Scotland.* ◇ The **previous** day or week is the one immediately before the events you are talking about. *Iraq had been warned the previous weekend not to operate any aircraft or helicopters.*

❑ If you mention what happened **previously,** you are describing the situation up to the time you are talking about. *A spokesman said the find was very important, because few coins had previously been found from the reign of King Stephen.* ◇ **Previously** is also used to say how much earlier one event was than another. *Two years previously, when he joined the company, it had lost £189.9 million.*

prey ❑ An animal's or bird's **prey** are the creatures it hunts and eats. You say it **preys on** those creatures.

❑ If someone **preys on** someone else, they get money from them by tricking them or taking advantage of their weaknesses. *At the airport, visitors are regularly preyed on by greedy taxi drivers.* ◇ If you are **prey** to something unpleasant or **fall prey to** it, you are affected by it. *An ever increasing number of motorists are falling prey to vehicle thieves.*

priapic (*pron:* pry-ap-pik) is used to talk about things to do with male sexual powers. ...*the dangerous myth that all men naturally change into priapic beasts the minute they see a woman they fancy.*

price (pricing, priced) ❑ The **price** of something is the amount you have to pay to buy it. You can also say something is **priced** at a particular amount. *Everything is priced at between £100 and £1,500.* ◇ If you **price** something you are going to sell, you decide how much you will charge for it. ◇ If you **price yourself out of the market,** you offer goods or services at such a high price that nobody will buy them, especially when similar things can be bought more cheaply elsewhere. Similarly, you say people **price themselves out of their job** if they demand wages which are too high.

❑ If you have to **pay the price** for something, you suffer because of your own or someone else's actions. *He said patients were paying the price for the government's changes to the National Health Service.* Similarly, you can talk about something being achieved **at a price.** ...*the growing realisation that fame comes at a price.* ◇ If you want something **at any price,** you are determined to get it, whatever the consequences. Similarly, you can try to avoid something **at any price.**

priceless If something is **priceless,** it is so valuable it is impossible to say how much it is worth. ◇ Some people use **priceless** to say they find something very amusing. ...*a priceless remark.*

pricey If something is **pricey,** it is expensive.

prick ❑ If you **prick** something, you make a small hole in it with a sharp object like a pin. ◇ If something sharp **pricks** you or gives you a **prick,** it scratches or pierces your skin.

❑ If someone **pricks the bubble,** they put a stop to something which had been growing rapidly. *With land values rising a record 13.7 percent last year, the Japanese government has been desperately searching for a way to prick the bubble.*

❑ If something **pricks** your feelings of pride or confidence, it makes them suddenly less certain or less strong. ◇ If something **pricks** your conscience, it makes you feel guilty.

❑ If you **prick up** your ears, you listen eagerly when you hear something interesting or important.

prickle (prickling, prickled) ❑ **Prickles** are sharp points on the leaves or stalks of plants.

❑ If your skin **prickles,** it tingles, because you are feeling a strong emotion like fear or excitement.

prickly (prickliness) ❑ A **prickly** plant has a lot of prickles on it.

❑ A **prickly** person loses their temper easily. *There are fears that his personal prickliness could undermine the work of the government.* ◇ If a problem or issue is **prickly,** it is difficult to deal with.

❑ **Prickly heat** is a condition caused by very hot weather, in which your sweat ducts are blocked and your skin comes up in a hot and itchy rash.

pride (priding, prided) ❑ **Pride** is a feeling of satisfaction because you have done something well. ◇ If you **take pride in** something you have or in something you have done, you feel pleased and happy about it. ◇ If you **pride yourself** on a quality or skill, you are proud of having it, and usually make sure other people know about it too. ◇ If something you have is your **pride** or your **pride and joy,** you are very pleased with it and it is important to you.

❑ **Pride** is also (a) a feeling of dignity and self-respect. *Bristol felt a loss of civic pride when it lost control of local services.* (b) a feeling of being superior to other people. ◇ If you **swallow your pride,** you do something that you find humiliating, in order to get something you want or need.

❑ If something has **pride of place,** it is treated as the most important thing in a group of things.

❑ A **pride** of lions is a group of them.

priest (priestess, priestesses) A **priest** is a member of the clergy in the Catholic and Orthodox churches, and in some Protestant churches. ◇ In some non-Christian religions, a **priest** is a man with special duties and responsibilities in a place where people worship. A **priestess** is a woman with similar duties and responsibilities.

priesthood The **priesthood** is the position and office of being a priest. *He thought of going into the priesthood.* ◇ The **priesthood** is also all the members of the Christian clergy, especially in a particular Church. ...*the Roman Catholic priesthood.*

priestly is used to talk about things to do with a priest. ...*priestly duties.*

prig (priggish) If you call someone a **prig** or say they are **priggish,** you mean that they are irritating because they behave very correctly and disapprove of other people's behaviour.

prim (primly) A **prim** person is easily shocked by anything rude or improper. *His parents are primly respectable people.* ◇ If something is **prim,** it is very neat and tidy. ...*prim* *white blouses.*

prima ballerina (*pron:* pree-ma) In a ballet or ballet company, the **prima ballerina** is the most important female dancer.

prima donna A **prima donna** is a famous female opera singer. ◇ If you call someone a **prima donna**, you mean they are temperamental and difficult to deal with.

prima facie (*pron:* prime-a fay-shee) is used to describe something which seems to be true when you consider it for the first time. 'Prima facie' is Latin for 'as it seems at first'. ...*a prima facie case of libel.*

primacy (*pron:* prime-a-see) If something has **primacy** in a certain situation, it is the most important or powerful thing involved in it. ...*the growing primacy of television in broadcasting.*

primaeval See primeval.

primal is used to talk about something to do with the most basic causes or origins of things. ...*primal fears and urges.*

primarily is used to say what is the most important aspect of something. *Miró was primarily a painter... Their advice is aimed primarily at medium-sized companies.*

primary (primaries) ❑ The **primary** thing in a situation is the main one. *The primary aim of economic policy, the government says, is to reduce inflation.*
❑ **Primary** is used to talk about the first stage of a process. ...*the primary treatment of sewerage.* ◇ **Primary** education is for children aged between 4 or 5 and 11.
❑ In the US, various kinds of preliminary elections and selection procedures are called **primaries**. Their purpose is to choose convention delegates and candidates for political office.

primary colour The **primary colours** in light are red, green, and blue, which combine to produce all other colours, including white but not black. ◇ In art, the **primary colours** are red, yellow, and blue, which can be mixed to make other colours.

primary health care is the treatment or advice you get from a GP, district nurse, or health visitor, as distinct from hospital treatment.

primary school A **primary school** is for children aged between 4 or 5 and 11.

primate ❑ A **primate** is a member of the group of mammals which includes humans, monkeys, and apes.
❑ A **primate** is also an archbishop.

prime (priming, primed) ❑ The **prime** thing in any situation is the most important one. ...*the prime reason for their journey.* ◇ **Prime** is also used to describe things which are of the best possible quality. ...*prime cuts of venison.* ◇ A **prime** example of something is a very good example of it.
❑ If someone or something is a **prime mover** in a plan, idea, or situation, they have an important influence in starting it. *He is the prime mover behind a package of far-reaching economic reforms.*
❑ Your **prime** is the stage in your life when you are most active or successful. *In winning the world championship, she had already demonstrated she was in her prime.*
❑ If you **prime** someone, you prepare them for something by giving them information about it. ◇ If someone or something is **primed** to do something, they are ready to do it. *Cruise stands stripped to the waist, muscles primed for boxing.*

❑ If a government **primes the pump**, it puts money into an industry to encourage economic growth. This is called **pump-priming**.

Prime Minister (prime ministerial) The leader of the government in the UK and many other countries is called the **Prime Minister**. **Prime ministerial** is used to talk about things to do with being a prime minister. ...*the Party's prime ministerial candidate.*

prime number A **prime number** is a whole number greater than 1 which cannot be divided exactly by any whole number except itself and 1. So, for example, 2, 3, 7, and 11 are prime numbers.

prime time is the period in the evening when more people are watching TV than at any other time.

primer is a type of paint put onto a surface to prepare it for the main layer of paint.
❑ A **primer** is a book containing basic facts on a subject, used by someone beginning to study that subject.

primeval (*or* primaeval) (*pron:* prime-ee-val) is used to talk about things connected with a very early period in history. ...*a primeval oak.*

primitive In **primitive** social systems, people live in a simple way, usually without industries or a writing system. ◇ A **primitive** version of something is one made at an early stage of its development. ...*a kind of primitive bagpipe.* ◇ You also say something is **primitive** when it is very basic or old-fashioned. ...*the country's still primitive communications network.*

primly See prim.

primogeniture is a system in which the eldest son or eldest child inherits all their parents' property.

primordial is used to talk about things which have existed from a very early period of time or since the beginning of the world. ...*primordial forest.*

primrose ❑ **Primroses** are small, pale yellow wild flowers which come out in the Spring.
❑ **Primrose** is a pale yellow colour.

prince A **prince** is a male member of a royal family, especially the son of a king or queen. ◇ A **prince** is also a male royal ruler of a small country or state.

Prince of Wales The **Prince of Wales** is the title given to the eldest son of the British monarch.

princeling In the past, rulers of very small territories were sometimes called **princelings**.

princely is used to talk about things to do with a prince. ...*princely power.* ◇ A **princely** sum is a very large sum of money.

princess (princesses) A **princess** is a female member of a royal family, especially a daughter of a king or queen, or the wife of a prince. ◇ A **princess** is also a female royal ruler of a small country or state.

Princess of Wales The **Princess of Wales** is the wife of the Prince of Wales.

Princess Royal is a title sometimes given to the eldest daughter of the British monarch.

principal The **principal** person or thing in any situation is the main or most important one. ...*principal conductor of the BBC Symphony Orchestra... Rubber became the small country's principal cash crop.* ◇ The **principal** of a school or college is the person in charge of it.

principal boy In pantomime, the **principal boy** is the main male character, traditionally played by a woman.

principality (principalities) A **principality** is a country ruled by a prince or princess, for example Monaco.

principally is used when mentioning the main thing to which something applies. *There is extensive Chinese investment here, principally in the construction industry.*

principle (principled) ❑ A person's **principles** are their beliefs about the way they should behave. **Principled** behaviour is based on moral beliefs. *He has dared to take unpopular, but principled, stands at times.* ◇ If you do something **on principle**, you do it because of a moral belief you have.

❑ A **principle** is also a general rule which provides a basis for people's actions or for the way society is organized. *...the fundamental principle of one-person-one-vote.*

❑ If you agree to something **in principle**, you agree to the idea of it, but may be unable or unwilling to support it in practice.

❑ A **principle** is also a scientific law explaining how something happens or works. *...the mathematical principle of chaos.* ◇ If something is possible **in principle**, there is no known scientific reason why it should not happen, although it may not have happened so far.

print ❑ When something like a book, newspaper, or money is **printed**, it is produced in large quantities by a mechanical process. ◇ When something like a speech or piece of writing is **printed**, it is included in a paper, magazine, or book. When this happens, you say it appears **in print**. ◇ If a book is **in print**, it is available from a publisher; if it is **out of print**, it is no longer available. ◇ When people talk about the **printed word**, they mean information appearing in something like a book or newspaper. *It is also hard to compare the influence of television with the printed word.*

❑ The **print** on the page of a book, newspaper, or other document is all the letters and numbers appearing there. ◇ If you talk about the **small print** or **fine print** on a legal document, you mean the detailed parts, which people do not always read, though they may contain something important.

❑ If a government **prints money**, it tries to solve economic problems, for example increased prices, by producing a large supply of money. ◇ If you say something is a **licence to print money**, you mean it cannot fail to earn someone a very large amount of money.

❑ When information from a computer is **printed out**, it is reproduced on paper. This paper, with the information on it, is called **print-out**.

❑ When a pattern is **printed** on cloth, it is reproduced on the cloth using dye and special equipment. **Print** cloth has a pattern printed on it; the pattern is called a **print**.

❑ A **print** is a picture copied from a painting by photography or produced by contact with an engraved surface. Usually several copies are made at the same time. ◇ A **print** is also one of the photographs from a developed film.

❑ A **print** is also a mark or outline made by something pressing onto a surface. *...a bloody palm print found at the murder scene.*

❑ If you **print**, you write in letters which are not joined together.

print-out See **print**.

print run A **print run** is all the copies of something produced by a printing press at one time.

printable If something someone says is not **printable**, it is likely to offend people, and therefore not suitable to put in a paper or magazine.

printed circuit board A **printed circuit board** is a circuit in an electronic device which, instead of wire, uses lines of copper on a fibreglass base to conduct electricity.

printer A **printer** is (a) a person or firm that prints books or newspapers. (b) a machine for printing information from a computer.

printing press A **printing press** is a machine for printing books and papers.

prior ❑ If something happens **prior** to a time or event, it happens before it. *There has been a lot of fear prior to these elections.* ◇ **Prior** is used to describe something which has happened or been provided before the time you are talking about. *Demonstrations are illegal without prior permission from the police.*

❑ A **prior** claim or duty is more important than other claims or duties.

❑ A **prior** is a monk in charge of a priory, or one who is an abbot's deputy in a monastery.

prioress (prioresses) A **prioress** is a nun in charge of a priory, or one who is an abbess's deputy.

prioritize (prioritizing, prioritized) (*can be spelled with an 's' instead of a 'z'*) If you **prioritize**, you decide how important several things are compared to each other, then deal with them in order, starting with the most important one.

priority (priorities) ❑ If something is a **priority**, it must be done or dealt with as soon as possible. ◇ If you **give priority** to something, you treat it as more important than other things. ◇ If something **has** or **takes priority** over other things, it is considered to be more important than them, and is dealt with first.

❑ Your **priorities** are the things you consider to be most important.

priory (priories) A **priory** is a place where a small group of monks or nuns live.

prise (prising, prised) (*can be spelled with a 'z' instead of an 's'*) If you **prise** one thing away from another, you use force to remove it from the other thing. Similarly, you can **prise** something **open**. *The dog's jaws remained locked and had to be prised apart.* ◇ If you **prise** something like information out of someone, you get them to give it to you, although they do not want to.

prism In maths, a **prism** is a solid shape with two identical parallel ends and the same cross-section throughout. ◇ A **prism** is also an object made of clear glass with many flat sides. It separates light passing through it into the colours of the rainbow.

prison A **prison** is a building where criminals serving jail sentences are kept.

prison camp A **prison camp** is a guarded camp where prisoners of war or political prisoners are kept.

prison officer A **prison officer** is someone who supervises the prisoners in a prison.

prisoner ❑ A **prisoner** is (a) someone kept in a prison because they have committed a crime or are waiting to be tried for one. (b) someone captured by an enemy in a war. ◇ If someone is **taken prisoner**, they are captured. If they are **held prisoner**, they are guarded so that they cannot escape.

❑ If you describe yourself as a **prisoner** of a situation, you mean you feel trapped by it. *Public life is a goldfish bowl in which top people are the prisoners of what others think about them.*

prisoner of conscience (prisoners of conscience) A **prisoner of conscience** is someone imprisoned by a government for their political views, or for their religion or race, rather than because they have committed a crime.

prisoner of war (prisoners of war) A **prisoner of war** or **POW** is a member of the armed forces who has been captured by the enemy during a war and is kept as a prisoner until the end of the war.

prissy If you say someone is **prissy,** you mean they behave very correctly in a fussy way, and are easily shocked by anything rude or improper.

pristine If you call something **pristine,** you mean it is or seems completely new, clean, and unused.

privacy (*usual pron:* **priv**-a-see) is being alone, so you can do things without being seen or disturbed.

private (privately) ❑ **Private** is used to describe things or places which are for the use of one person or group, rather than the general public. *...a private jet.*

❑ **Private** is also used to describe services or industries which are owned and controlled by an individual person or group, rather than by the state. *...private medicine... ...privately-built toll roads.*

❑ **Private** discussions take place between a small group of people and are kept secret from others. *...a private meeting.* ◇ If you say something **privately** or **in private,** you say it to one person or group rather than the general public, because you do not want it to be generally known. You can also talk about things being done **privately** or **in private.** *Evidence will be heard in private.*

❑ Your **private** activities are connected with your personal life rather than with your work or business. *...a private telephone call.* ◇ Your **private** thoughts and feelings are personal and you do not discuss them with other people. ◇ If you describe someone as a **private** person, you mean they are very quiet and do not share their thoughts and feelings with other people.

❑ A **private** is a soldier of the lowest rank in the British army.

private company A **private company** is a limited company which does not issue shares to the public.

private detective A **private detective** is a detective who works alone rather than in the police force and who can be hired to carry out investigations.

private enterprise is industry and businesses owned by individual people or groups and not supported financially by the state.

private eye A **private eye** is another name for a private detective.

private member's bill A **private member's bill** is a law proposed by a backbench MP acting as an individual rather than as a member of his or her political party.

private parts Someone's **private parts** are their outer sex organs.

private school A **private school** is a school which is not supported financially by the government and charges fees. Private schools are now usually called 'independent schools'.

private secretary (private secretaries) A **private secretary** is a secretary working for just one person, especially an important person.

private sector The **private sector** is the part of a country's economy which is not controlled or supported financially by the state.

privation If you suffer **privation** or **privations,** you are deprived of the basic things you need to live a normal life. *The privations of the coming winter will be great.*

privatize (privatizing, privatized; privatization) (*can be spelled with an 's' instead of a 'z'*) If a state-owned organization is **privatized,** the government sells it by offering shares in it to private individuals or groups. This practice is called **privatization.**

privet (*pron:* **priv**-it) is an evergreen shrub, often used to make hedges.

privilege (privileged) ❑ A **privilege** is a special right or advantage which puts one person or group in a better position than others. **Privileged** is used to describe a right or advantage like this. *Unification is expected to give Germany privileged access to Central European markets.* ◇ **Privilege** is the power and advantages belonging to a small group of people, usually because of their wealth or social class. You say people like these are **privileged.** *...the new privileged classes.*

❑ If you say something involving yourself is a **privilege,** you mean you recognize that you have been given an advantage or opportunity which not many people have, and you are pleased and grateful about it. *It's been a tremendous privilege to serve this country as Prime Minister.*

privy (privies) ❑ If you are **privy** to something secret, you are allowed to know about it.

❑ In the past, a **privy** was a toilet, especially an outside one.

Privy Council In Britain, the **Privy Council** is a group of people appointed to advise the king or queen on political affairs.

prize (prizing, prized) ❑ A **prize** is something of value, for example money or a trophy, given to the winner of a game or contest, or as a reward for doing good work. ◇ If you say there are **no prizes for guessing** something, you mean it is extremely obvious and not difficult to guess. ◇ **Prize** is used to describe something which is of such high quality that it has won prizes, or deserves to. *...prize leeks.*

❑ You can call something a **prize** when it is very desirable and very hard to achieve. *The prize of permanently low inflation was within their grasp.* ◇ If you **prize** something, you consider it to be very valuable and important. *She prizes honour and honesty above all things.*

❑ See also **prise.**

prize-fighter (prize fight) A **prize-fighter** is a boxer who fights to win money. The matches he takes part in are called **prize fights.**

prize-giving A **prize-giving** is a ceremony where people are given prizes.

prize-money is the money paid to the winner of a competition.

prize-winning (prize-winner) **Prize-winning** is used to describe someone or something that has won a prize. *...a prize-winning poet.* A **prize-winner** is someone who has won a prize.

pro ❑ A pro is someone who does something, especially sport, professionally. ...*a pro baseball team.*

 ❑ The **pros** and **cons** of something are its advantages and disadvantages.

 ❑ If you are **pro** a plan or belief, you agree with it or support it. *He is pro choice on abortion.*

pro- is used to form words which say who or what someone supports. ...*a pro-democracy movement*... ...*the local pro-government press.*

pro-active See proactive.

pro rata If someone is paid **pro rata** for something they do, they are paid a proportionate amount. For example, if the wage for a job is £300 for a 40-hour week, and someone is paid **pro rata** for working a 30-hour week, they receive £225.

proactive (*or* pro-active) policies and actions involve taking the initiative and making things happen, rather than simply reacting to things.

probable (probably; probability, probabilities) ❑ If you say something is **probable** or talk about its **probability**, you mean it is likely to be true or correct, or likely to happen. *The final results will probably not be published until Thursday... He welcomed the probability that blood samples will be analysed for banned substances.* ◇ You say **in all probability** when you are confident that something is true or correct, or likely to happen. *In all probability there would be little reduction in oil supplies.*

 ❑ A **probability** is a mathematical measurement of how likely it is that something will happen.

probate In law, **probate** is the process of proving that a will is valid and can be carried out.

probation (probationary) **Probation** is a period of time during which a convicted person is not sent to prison but has to fulfil certain conditions and is supervised by a probation officer. During this time, you say the person is **on probation**. ◇ **Probation** is also a period of time during which someone's work is assessed before they are given a permanent job. This period is called a **probationary** period. **Probationary** is also used to describe the person being assessed. ...*probationary teachers.*

probation officer A **probation officer** is someone who supervises and helps people on probation and prepares reports on an offender's social background for use in court.

probationary See probation.

probe (probing, probed) ❑ If you **probe** something, especially something people want to keep secret, you investigate it. An investigation like this is called a **probe**. ...*a 1991 probe into corruption.*

 ❑ A **probe** is a thin metal object used by a surgeon to examine a patient's body during an operation.

 ❑ See also **space probe**.

probity is honest and trustworthy behaviour. *The bank has fought hard to recover its reputation for financial probity.*

problem ❑ A **problem** is an unsatisfactory situation which causes difficulties. ◇ **Problem** children continually cause difficulties for themselves and other people, often because they have had unhappy experiences.

 ❑ A **problem** is also a puzzle for people to solve.

problematic (problematical) If something is **problematic** or **problematical**, it involves problems and difficulties.

proboscis (*pron:* pro-boss-iss) (proboscises) A **proboscis** is a long flexible tube which some insects use as a mouth. ◇ An elephant's trunk can be called its **proboscis**. ◇ People sometimes humorously call a person's nose their **proboscis**, especially when it is very large.

procedure (procedural) A **procedure** is a way of doing something, especially the accepted or correct way. ...*a breakdown in safety procedures.* **Procedural** is used to describe something which involves a procedure or procedures. *The talks became bogged down in procedural problems.*

proceed (proceeding, proceeded) ❑ If you **proceed** to do something, you go on to do it after doing something else. *He then proceeded to tell us everything we needed to know.* ◇ If you **proceed** with a course of action, you go ahead with it, or continue with it. *He announced he would not proceed with his candidacy.* ◇ If an activity, event, or process **proceeds**, it continues as planned. *The auction of state firms has proceeded with few hitches.*

 ❑ When you are talking about a series of events, especially organized ones, you can refer to them as the **proceedings**. *There were about twenty violent incidents for which police blamed radicals trying to disrupt the proceedings.*

 ❑ Legal **proceedings** are legal actions taken against someone. ...*bankruptcy proceedings.*

 ❑ If you **proceed** in a certain direction, you go in that direction. *They proceeded towards the Croatian border.*

 ❑ The **proceeds** (*pron:* pro-seeds) of an event or activity are the money obtained from it.

process (processes, processing, processed) ❑ A **process** is a series of actions or events aimed at achieving a particular result. ...*the Middle East peace process.* ◇ If you are doing one thing and you do something else **in the process**, you do the second thing as a result of doing the first. *The farmers argue that the land reform policy will result in massive ecological damage and in the process ruin a viable agricultural industry.* ◇ If you are **in the process of** doing something, you are in the middle of doing it.

 ❑ When raw materials are **processed**, they are treated industrially to make them suitable for a particular purpose. ◇ When natural foods are **processed**, they are treated chemically, for example by adding colouring and preservative, before being sold.

 ❑ If you **process** information, you deal with it using a regular system. ◇ When a computer **processes** information, it runs programs to deal with it.

procession (processional) A **procession** is a line of people or vehicles moving together, for example as part of a ceremony. **Processional** is used to talk about things to do with processions. ...*the processional routes to Buckingham Palace.* ◇ A **procession** of things is a long series of them. ...*a seemingly endless procession of corruption cases.*

processor ❑ A **processor** is a company which processes something. ...*a cocoa processor.*

 ❑ In computing, a **processor** is the same as a central processing unit. ◇ See also **word processor**.

proclaim (proclaiming, proclaimed; proclamation) If someone **proclaims** something or makes a **proclamation**, they make an important public announcement. See also **self-proclaimed**.

proclivity (proclivities) If you talk about someone's **proclivities**, you mean their tendency to behave in certain ways. ...*a candidate's sexual proclivities.*

procrastinate (procrastinating, procrastinated; procrastination) If you **procrastinate**, you keep leaving something until later. *Further procrastination is unacceptable.*

procreate (procreating, procreated; procreation, procreative) When animals or people **procreate**, they produce offspring. *Early marriage and procreation are no longer discouraged.* **Procreative** is used to talk about things to do with procreating. *...women's procreative powers.*

procurator In the Roman Empire, a **procurator** was an official responsible for the finances of a province. Sometimes he was also an administrator. Some present-day countries have senior legal officials or administrators called **procurators**.

procurator fiscal In Scotland, the **procurator fiscal** is a legal officer who performs the functions of a public prosecutor in a particular district, and also acts as the coroner.

procure (procuring, procured; procurer) If you **procure** something, especially something difficult to get, you obtain it. ◇ Someone who **procures** introduces prostitutes to clients. A person who does this is called a **procurer**.

procurement is buying or obtaining something, especially supplies for a large organization like the army. *...changes in defence procurement.*

prod (prodding, prodded) ❑ If you **prod** someone or something or give them a **prod**, you push them quickly with your finger or a pointed object. ◇ A **prod** or **cattle prod** is a long pointed metal stick, often electrified, used to poke animals to make them move along.
❑ If you **prod** someone into doing something, you get them to do it by continually reminding them about it or urging them to do it.

prodigal If someone behaves in a **prodigal** way, they spend a lot of money carelessly and are wasteful, without thinking about the consequences. ◇ You call someone a **prodigal** or a **prodigal son** when they have gone away or done something wrong, but are now sorry for it and have been welcomed back or forgiven.

prodigious (prodigiously) If something is **prodigious**, it is amazingly large or extensive. *...her prodigious memory... ...the prodigiously gifted Chinese tenor Ya Lin Zhang.*

prodigy (prodigies) A **prodigy** or **child prodigy** is someone who shows an extraordinary natural ability for something at an early age.

produce (producing, produced) ❑ If something **produces** something else, it causes it to happen or exist. *The Gulf crisis has produced a new refugee problem.* You often talk about things being **produced** as a result of a biological process. For example, you say people or animals **produce** offspring. *...chemicals produced by the body's immune system.*
❑ When things like foodstuffs or goods are **produced**, they are grown or manufactured on a large scale. ◇ **Produce** (*pron:* **prod**-juice) is food grown or produced by farming. *There was almost no fresh produce in the shops.* ◇ A **producer** of a food or material is a company or country which grows or provides a large amount of it. *...the world's largest steel producer.*
❑ If you **produce** something like a book, you write it or publish it. ◇ If you **produce** something like evidence or proof, you provide it. *He produced a letter as evidence of secretive internal politics.* ◇ If you **produce** an object from

somewhere, you bring it out so it can be seen. *The assailant produced a knife and snatched the briefcase.*
❑ If someone **produces** a play, film, or record, they organize it and decide how it should be done. A person who does this is called a **producer**.

product ❑ A **product** is something a company makes and sells, often in large quantities. ◇ A **product** is also something formed naturally in a living thing. *...human waste products.* ◇ **dairy products:** see **dairy**.
❑ If someone is the **product** of something like a type of education, they get their attitudes and behaviour as a result of it. *He speaks and acts as if he is the product of a Victorian rather than a 20th-century upbringing.* ◇ If something like a book is a **product** of someone's experiences, it is based on those experiences.
❑ In maths, the **product** of two or more numbers is the result of multiplying them together.

production is growing or manufacturing something in large quantities. *...the production and export of cocaine.* **Production** is also the amount of goods grown or manufactured. *Industrial production in Britain rose last month.*
❑ When something is created as a result of a natural process, you can talk about its **production**. *These proteins stimulate the production of blood cells.* Similarly, you can talk about the **production** of something when it is created accidentally as a result of an industrial process. *Production of CFC's in the EU is to be ended completely by the middle of 1997.*
❑ **Production** is the organization and preparation of a play, film, TV programme, or record. *This film went very wrong during production.* ◇ A **production** is a performed version of a play or opera. *...the London production of 'Phantom of the Opera'.*

production line A **production line** is a system in a factory in which individual machines make one part of a product before passing it on to the next machine.

productive (productively) If you say someone or something is **productive**, you mean they produce a lot of goods or do a lot of work. *Sick people cannot work productively.* ◇ If something like a meeting is **productive**, useful things come out of it.

productivity is the rate at which goods are produced, and how efficiently they are produced. *...a reorganisation to boost productivity by 60% among clerical staff.*

Prof in front of someone's name means 'Professor'. *...Prof Michael Dummett.*

profane (profanity) If you call someone's actions **profane**, you mean they show disrespect for religion and are sinful. Showing disrespect for religion is called **profanity**. ◇ **Profane** is also used to talk about non-religious things, as opposed to religious ones. *...the sacred and profane pleasures of Kathmandu.*

profess (professes, professing, professed) If someone **professes** to be something, they claim they are that thing, although they may not be. You can also say someone **professes** to have certain feelings, beliefs, or principles. *...the President's professed belief in less intrusive government.* ◇ You also say someone **professes** something when they openly express it. *He openly professed his ambition to become Prime Minister... ...a professed liberal.* ◇ If you **profess** a particular religion, that is your religion.

profession ❑ A **profession** is a job requiring advanced education or training and which has a fairly high status. ◇ **Profession** is used to talk about all the people who have a particular profession. For example, you talk about the legal profession or the medical profession.

❑ When someone claims to have certain beliefs or feelings, you can talk about their **professions** of these beliefs or feelings. *The demonstrators reject his professions of sincerity about his democratic convictions.*

professional (professionally, professionalism) ❑ **Professional** is used to talk about things to do with professions. *...professional qualifications.* A **professional** person is someone who has a profession. ◇ **Professional** is also used to talk about things to do with people's work, as distinct from their private lives. *He spent the whole of his professional life working as a librarian... Professionally and personally, East German teachers have been left demoralised and depressed.*

❑ **Professional** is used to describe people who do something as a job which many people do as a hobby. *...a professional actress.* You can say a person like this is a **professional.** **Professional** is also used to describe their activities. *...professional tennis.* If someone, especially a sportsman or woman **turns professional,** they start to do an activity to earn money, rather than as a hobby. ◇ **Professional** is also used to praise things which are done skilfully or to a very high standard. *The coalition appeared to run a highly professional campaign.* You can talk about the **professionalism** of things like these.

professionalize (professionalizing, professionalized; professionalization) *(can be spelled with an 's' instead of a 'z')* If an activity is **professionalized,** people start to earn money from doing it, rather than doing it as a hobby. *...the professionalization of Paralympic sport.*

professionally See professional.

professor In a British university, a **professor** is a person with the highest academic rank, especially a person in charge of a department. ◇ In an American university or college, a **professor** is a teacher.

professorial is used to describe someone who looks or behaves like a professor. *He cuts an unlikely, almost professorial, figure.* ◇ **Professorial** is also used to talk about things to do with the work of a professor. *...professorial departments.*

professorship A **professorship** is the post of professor in a university.

proffer (proffering, proffered) If you **proffer** something to someone, you hold it towards them so they can take it. ◇ If you **proffer** something like advice, you offer it.

proficient (proficiency) If you are **proficient** at something, you are very good at it. **Proficiency** is the ability to do something well. *Many universities would only accept students who had some proficiency in Latin.*

profile (profiling, profiled) ❑ Your **profile** is the outline of your face seen from the side. If someone or something is seen **in profile,** they are seen from the side.

❑ A person's or thing's **profile** is their public image and how much they are noticed by people. If someone or something has a **high profile,** they are well known and noticed by the public. *...high-profile sporting contests.* **Low-profile** is used to describe things which are not noticed very much. ◇ If you **keep a low profile,** you deliberately avoid attracting attention to yourself.

❑ If someone like a reporter **profiles** someone, he or

she writes a short description of their life and character. This description is called a **profile.**

profit (profiting, profited) ❑ If you make a **profit,** you sell something for more than you paid for it, or more than it cost you to make. **Profit-making** is used to describe products and organizations which make a profit. *...a profit-making factory.* If an organization is not run for the purpose of making a profit, you say it is **non-profit-making.**

❑ If you **profit** from something, you gain an advantage or benefit from it. *If the talks do break down there is little doubt that the hard-liners on both sides will profit.*

profit margin A profit **margin** is how much greater the selling price of a product is than the cost of producing or marketing it. Profit margins are expressed as a percentage.

profit-sharing is a system by which all the people who work in a company have a share in its profits.

profitable (profitably, profitability) A **profitable** organization makes a profit. *It's difficult to run a wholly organic farm profitably... It appears that to maximise profitability, clubs should sell footballers when they become popular.* ◇ If something you do is **profitable,** it results in some advantage or benefit. *...a very profitable discussion... I fill my days profitably, never an idle moment.*

profiteering (profiteer) **Profiteering** is making large profits by charging high prices for goods which are hard to get. People who make money like this are called **profiteers.**

profligate (profligately, profligacy) If you call someone **profligate** or talk about their **profligacy,** you mean they are extravagant and wasteful. *Higher charges would also encourage consumers to use water and power less profligately.*

profound (profoundly; profundity) ❑ **Profound** and **profoundly** are used to emphasize how great or intense something is. *The discovery has caused profound embarrassment to the air force... ...profoundly deaf people.*

❑ If you say something is **profound** or talk about its **profundity,** you mean it shows great intellectual depth and understanding. *The Tempest is considered a profound play... This is not an ordinary book, and the profundity of its message easily eludes the reader.*

profuse *(pron: pro-fyooss)* (profusely, profusion) If something is **profuse,** there is a lot of it. *...profuse apologies... He was still alive, bleeding profusely.* You can also say something occurs in **profusion** or there is a **profusion** of it. *Viewers will soon be choosing from a profusion of channels... Orchids bloom in profusion.*

progenitor Your **progenitors** are your direct ancestors. ◇ The **progenitor** of an idea is the person who first thought of it.

progeny *(pron: proj-in-ee)* The **progeny** of people or animals are their offspring.

progesterone *(pron: pro-jest-er-ohn)* is a hormone secreted in the ovaries of female mammals, which prepares the uterus for pregnancy. It is also used in the birth control pill.

prognosis *(plural: prognoses)* A **prognosis** is a prediction about what will happen, especially a prediction about what course an illness or disease will take.

prognostication A **prognostication** is a prediction about something.

program (programming, programmed; programmer) ❏ If you **program** a computer, you give it a set of instructions called a **program**. A person who writes programs is called a computer **programmer**.

❏ **Program** is also the usual American spelling of 'programme'.

programme (*American spelling:* **program**) (programming, programmed) ❏ A **programme** is a detailed, large-scale plan devised for a particular purpose, for example to provide a service or to deal with a problem. *...a road-building programme... ...a programme to combat AIDS.* ◇ A **programme** is also a series of events which are planned to take place. ◇ If something has been **programmed** to happen, it has been planned in advance.

❏ A TV or radio **programme** is something like a play, show, or talk which is broadcast on TV or radio. **Programming** is choosing and organizing what is going to be broadcast on TV or radio. *A number of delegates criticised what they said was political bias in BBC programming.*

❏ The **programme** for a concert or show is the pieces of music or acts to be performed in it. A **programme** is also a booklet or sheet of paper giving information about the play or concert you are attending.

❏ If you **programme** a machine or system, you set its controls so it will work in a particular way. *The device can be programmed to water each plant as often and as long as required.* ◇ If you talk about people being **programmed** to behave in a certain way, you mean they are likely to behave like that, either because of something in their genes or because of the effect of their upbringing.

programmer See program.

progress (progresses, progressing, progressed) ❏ If you **pro-gress** (*pron:* pro-gress), you get better at something. You can also say you **progress** to a more advanced form of what you are doing. *She started by singing in church and then progressed to session singing.*

❏ **Progress** (*pron:* pro-gress) is gradually getting nearer to achieving something or completing something. You can also talk about something **progressing**. *Their talks made little progress... While the construction work progressed, another difficulty cropped up.* ◇ **Progress** is also new developments and changes made in a social system, to improve conditions or create a more advanced way of life. *The discovery has been described as a landmark in scientific progress.*

❏ When you talk about the **progress** of something or the way it **progresses,** you are talking about the way it develops. *...a progress report... As the match progressed, it became clear that Liverpool were doomed to drop their first points of the season.* ◇ If something is **in progress**, it is happening.

❏ When someone or something is moving in a certain direction, you can talk about their **progress** in that direction. *Each year in early June the summer monsoon arrives, its progress northwards marked by celebrations and festivals.*

progression A **progression** is a gradual development from one thing to another. *Unless there is a prospect of a career progression with reasonable salary levels, it is not possible to recruit well-motivated professionally qualified people.*

progressive (progressively) If someone is **progressive** or has **progressive** ideas, they have modern opinions and ideas and are eager to change the way things are done. Someone like this is called a **progressive**. ◇ A progres-

sive change happens gradually or in stages. *...a progressive eye disease... Anti-smoking laws have been progressively toughened in France since 1976.* ◇ Under a **progressive** taxation system, the more you earn, the higher the rate of tax you pay.

prohibit (prohibiting, prohibited; prohibition) If a law or rule **prohibits** people from doing something, it says they must not do it. *Fishing is prohibited... ...a prohibition of nuclear testing.* ◇ In the US, **Prohibition** was the period from 1920 to 1933 when the manufacture, sale, and transport of alcohol was banned.

prohibitive (prohibitively) If the cost of something is **prohibitive**, it is so high people can hardly afford it. *Food and firewood are prohibitively expensive.*

project (projection) ❏ A **project** (*pron:* pro-jekt) is a planned scheme to do something over a period of time. *...a rehabilitation project for young offenders... ...road construction projects.* **Projected** (*pron:* pro-jekt-id) is used to describe something someone is planning to do. *She was making notes for a projected autobiography.* ◇ A **project** is also a detailed study done by a student at a school or college. *...projects on women in Shakespeare.*

❏ If you **project** a figure, you estimate what it is likely to be, based on information you already have. An estimate like this is called a **projection**. *The finance ministry had projected a 3% increase for the year... On present projections, the number of tourists this year is likely to fall by around 1 million.*

❏ If you **project** a film or slide onto a screen or other surface, you make it appear there.

❏ If you **project** your voice, you speak loudly and clearly so you can be heard at a distance. *She's getting lessons in voice projection.*

❏ If you **project** something or someone in a certain way, you try to give people a particular impression of them. *His first job will be to project Glasgow as a friendly city which takes pride in itself.*

❏ If you **project** your feelings on other people, you imagine they have the same feelings as you. *She tends to be over-anxious and project her fears onto strangers.*

❏ If something **projects**, it sticks out beyond a surface or edge. A **projection** is something which sticks out like this. *...projecting roofs.*

projectile A **projectile** is an object fired from a weapon like a gun.

projection See project.

projectionist A **projectionist** is someone whose job is to operate a projector in a cinema.

projector A **projector** is a machine which projects films or slides onto a screen or other surface.

prolapse is a medical condition in which an inner organ slips down from its proper position. *...uterine prolapse.*

prole A **prole** is a member of the proletariat.

proletariat (*pron:* pro-lit-air-ee-at) (proletarian) Working-class people, especially industrial workers, are sometimes called the **proletariat**. **Proletarian** is used to talk about things to do with the proletariat. *In America, Levi jeans are still seen as a product with strong proletarian roots.*

proliferate (proliferating, proliferated; proliferation) You say things **proliferate** when the number of them increases rapidly. *Israel can no longer control the pace of nuclear proliferation in the area.*

prolific A prolific writer, artist, or composer produces a very large number of works. ◇ An animal or person that produces a large number of offspring can also be called **prolific**.

prolix If a piece of writing is **prolix**, it is longer than necessary and this makes it boring.

prologue A **prologue** is a piece of text at the beginning of a book, or a speech spoken at the beginning of a play.

prolong (prolonged; prolongation) If you **prolong** something, you make it last longer. *...the prolongation of healthy life.* ◇ A **prolonged** event or situation continues for a long time, or for longer than expected. You can also say something happens over a **prolonged** period of time. *...prolonged applause... ...a prolonged period of high interest rates.*

prom ❏ A **prom** is one of a series of promenade concerts, especially the ones held in the Royal Albert Hall in London.
❏ In the US, a **prom** is a formal dance held for students at a high school or college.
❏ In a seaside town, the **prom** is the promenade.

promenade (promenading, promenaded) In a seaside town, a **promenade** is a road or pedestrian way next to the sea. ◇ If you **promenade**, you go for a slow walk, especially in a public place. A walk like this can be called a **promenade**. ◇ A **promenade** concert is one at which some of the audience stand rather than sit.

prominent (prominently, prominence) ❏ A **prominent** person is important and well-known. *He swiftly achieved prominence for his violent opinions.* ◇ If something is **prominent**, it is very noticeable, or it is an important part of something. *There was a prominent army presence... Trade will figure prominently in the second day of talks... America will continue to occupy the place of greatest prominence on the world stage.* ◇ If something is **given prominence**, a lot of attention is paid to it. *Schools are starting to give as much prominence to Egypt as to Greece and Rome in their history courses.*
❏ You say an object is **prominent** when it sticks out. *...prominent teeth.*

promiscuous (promiscuity) If someone is **promiscuous**, they have sex with many different people. Behaviour like this is called **promiscuity**.

promise (promising, promised) ❏ If you **promise** to do something, you say you will definitely do it. This is called making a **promise**. If you **promise** something to someone, you guarantee that they will get it. *Everybody who has been promised a place will get one.*
❏ If something **promises** to be a particular thing or to have a particular quality, it shows signs that it will be that thing or have that quality. *The hearings promise to be lively and informative.* ◇ If someone or something shows **promise** or looks **promising**, they seem likely to be very good or successful. *...a future professional dancer of immense promise... ...a promising political career.*

promo (*pron:* **proe**-moe) (promos) A **promo** is a short video made to promote a pop record.

promontory (promontories) A **promontory** is a high part of the coast which juts out into the sea.

promote (promoting, promoted; promotion, promoter) ❏ If you **promote** something, you help or encourage it to develop or succeed. You can call someone who promotes something a **promoter** of it. *...the promotion of world peace... ...a promoter of animal welfare.* ◇ If a company **promotes** a product, it tries to increase its sales and popularity, for example by advertising. *...a book promotion tour.* ◇ If someone **promotes** a public event like a sports contest or a concert, they organize and finance it. Someone who does this is called a **promoter**.
❏ If you are **promoted** or given a **promotion**, you are given a more important and better-paid job. ◇ When a football team is **promoted**, it goes up into a higher division, because it is one of the teams which scored most points during a season.

promotional events or ideas are designed to increase the sales of a product or service. *...a promotional video.*

prompt (promptly, promptness, prompter) ❏ If something **prompts** an event or action, it causes it to happen. *The campaign prompted a 69% increase in sales.* ◇ If something **prompts** you to do something, it makes you decide to do it. *The results have prompted the President to say he may contest the next Presidential election.* ◇ If you **prompt** someone to do something, you urge them to do it.
❏ If you **prompt** an actor, you remind them of the next words they are supposed to say. The person who does this during a performance is called the **prompt** or **prompter**.
❏ A **prompt** action is taken without delay. *...a prompt decision... The shooting was carried out by a single attacker who was promptly arrested... The country has been well regarded by foreign suppliers because of its promptness in settling its debts.* ◇ If you do something **promptly**, you do it at exactly the time you are supposed to. *Make sure you arrive in plenty of time and start promptly.*

promulgate (promulgating, promulgated; promulgation) When something like a new law is **promulgated**, it is announced publicly. *...the promulgation of tough new security measures.*

pron is short for 'pronounced'.

prone ❏ If someone or something is **prone** to something, they have a tendency to be affected by it. *The area is prone to earthquakes.* -**prone** is added to words to say someone or something has a tendency to be affected by something, especially something bad. *...an accident-prone family... ...storm-prone areas.*
❏ If you are lying **prone**, you are lying flat on your stomach. See also **supine**.

prong (-pronged) The **prongs** of a fork are the thin pointed parts. ◇ -**prong** and -**pronged** are used to say an action is divided into a number of separate parts. *...a two-prong strategy for tackling poverty... ...a three-pronged ground attack from the south.*

pronoun A **pronoun** is a word you use instead of a noun. 'She', 'them', and 'something' are pronouns.

pronounce (pronouncing, pronounced; pronunciation) ❏ The way you **pronounce** a word or sound is the way you say it. *Feng shui (pronounced fung schway) is the ancient Chinese art of placing things.* The **pronunciation** of a word or sound is the way it is pronounced.
❏ If something is **pronounced** to be a particular thing, it is formally stated that it is that thing. *A team of observers pronounced the election free and fair... A specialist has now pronounced him fully fit.* ◇ If someone **pronounces** on something, they give their opinion on it, especially when they are an expert on it. ◇ When a decision or verdict is **pro-**

nounced, it is formally stated. *As sentence was pronounced, about 200 people in the courtroom jeered and shouted insults at the judge.*

❑ If something is **pronounced**, it is noticeable. *Attitudes are changing now, as nationalism becomes more pronounced.*

pronouncement A **pronouncement** is a public or official statement on an important topic.

pronunciation See pronounce.

proof of something is a piece of evidence which shows it is true or exists. *The figures were clear proof that the recession was biting deep... Driving licences are regularly demanded as proof of identity.* ◇ If you say something is **proof positive** of something else, you mean it provides definite evidence that it is true or exists. ◇ If you talk about the **proof of the pudding**, you are mentioning something which will show whether something like a plan or policy has worked or not.

❑ If someone or something is **proof** against something, they cannot be harmed or affected by it. *The fortress was proof against the techniques of attack then in use.*

❑ A **proof** is a first printed copy of a text. It is produced so that mistakes can be corrected before more copies are printed.

❑ **Proof** is a measure of the alcoholic strength of drinks like whisky and brandy. *While other gins have reduced their strength, Beefeater stands firm at 40% proof.*

-proof (-proofing, -proofed) **-proof**, **-proofed**, and **-proofing** are added to words to describe things which have been specially designed to prevent something harmful passing through them. *...bullet-proof vests... ...sound-proofed walls... ...draught-proofing.* See also fire-proof, oven-proof.

proof-reading (proof-reader) **Proof-reading** is reading a text which is going to be printed, to check for any mistakes which need to be corrected by the printer. Someone who does this as their job is called a **proof-reader**.

prop (propping, propped) ❑ If you **prop** an object on or against something, you put it in a position where it is supported by that thing. *The lunch menu board had been propped on the counter.* You can also say something is **propped up** by something else. ◇ A **prop** is a stick or some other object used to support something. *...a clothes prop.*

❑ If a government **props up** something like a system, it supports it and helps it to survive. *...emergency measures to prop up the housing market.* Something that helps keep a system or organization going can be called a **prop**.

❑ If you say someone is **propping up the bar** in a pub, you mean they are spending a lot of time there drinking.

❑ The **props** or **properties** in a play are the objects used in it, excluding the furniture and costumes.

❑ In rugby union, a **prop** or **prop forward** is one of two players in a team who stand at either end of the front row of a scrum.

❑ The **prop** on a plane or boat is its propeller.

propaganda (propagandist) **Propaganda** is information, often inaccurate or biased, which is published or broadcast by an organization to influence people. Someone who produces propaganda is called a **propagandist**.

propagate (propagating, propagated; propagation) ❑ If people **propagate** an idea or information, they spread it so that it will influence other people.

❑ If you **propagate** plants, you grow more of them

from the original ones, for example by taking cuttings or sowing seeds. This process is called **propagation**.

propane is a gas found in natural gas and petroleum. It is used as a fuel for cooking and heating and in some cigarette lighters.

propel (propelling, propelled) ❑ If something is **propelled**, it is made to move forward. *...a rocket-propelled grenade.*

❑ If something **propels** someone to victory, it makes them the winner in a competition or contest. *Mrs Thatcher's success on the first ballot propelled her to victory.* Similarly, something can **propel** someone to a position of power. *...the revolution which propelled the National Salvation Front to power.* ◇ If something **propels** you to do something, it makes you do it. *A mixture of ambition and concern for the country's future is propelling him to bid for the presidency.*

propellant A **propellant** is (a) a substance burned in a rocket motor, which gives the rocket its thrust. (b) an explosive in a gun which forces out the ammunition.

propeller A **propeller** on a boat or aircraft is a device with blades mounted on a shaft. It is made to rotate by the engine, causing the boat or aircraft to move.

propelling pencil A **propelling pencil** is a type of hollow pencil. You draw the lead back into the pencil when you are not using it, usually by turning the end of the pencil.

propensity (propensities) If you have a **propensity** to behave in a certain way, you have a natural tendency to behave that way.

proper is used to describe things which are of an acceptable standard, as opposed to similar things which are below this standard. *No proper investigation had been carried out.*

❑ **Proper** is used to emphasize that you are talking about a particular thing, and not about something similar connected with it. *The election proper is not until April.*

❑ **Proper** is also used to mean 'correct'. For example, the **proper** way of doing something is the correct way. *Its proper place is in a museum.* ◇ **Proper** behaviour is behaviour which is generally accepted as correct in a particular situation. *It would not be proper for a British prime minister to agree a treaty and then disown it.*

proper noun A **proper noun** or **proper name** is the name of a person, place, or individual thing, for example 'Tony Blair', 'Berwick', or 'the Statue of Liberty'.

properly If something is done **properly**, it is done correctly and satisfactorily. *...a properly conducted trial.* ◇ If you behave **properly**, you behave in a way which is considered acceptable and not rude or shocking.

property (properties) ❑ Your **property** is all the things you own. If something is your **property**, it belongs to you. ◇ **Stolen property** consists of articles which have been stolen from someone. See also lost property.

❑ **Property** is also buildings and land. *...a tax on residential property... ...the London property market.* A **property** is a building and the land that goes with it.

❑ The **properties** of a substance or object are its characteristics or qualities, especially how it behaves when various things are done to it. *...a light-weight plastic foam with good insulating properties.*

prophesy (prophesies, prophesying, prophesied; prophecy, prophecies) If you **prophesy** (*pron:* prof-iss-eye) something, you say it will happen. A **prophecy** (*pron:* prof-iss-see) is a statement saying something will happen.

prophet A prophet is a person believed to have been chosen by God to pass on the things God wants to tell people. ◇ A **prophet** is also (a) someone who predicts that a particular thing will happen. *The climate prophets are now predicting that this could cause global warming.* (b) someone who strongly and actively supports a particular idea. *...one of the prophets of Thatcherism.*

prophetic (prophetically) You say something was **prophetic** when it correctly described what happened afterwards. *...prophetic dreams... He does not know how prophetically correct those words will turn out to be.*

prophylactic A prophylactic drug or type of treatment is concerned with preventing disease, rather than curing it.

propitious If something is **propitious**, it is likely to lead to success. *They should wait for the most propitious moment between now and the next election.*

proponent A proponent of an idea or course of action is someone who actively supports it.

proportion (proportioned) ❏ **Proportion** is used to say roughly how large or small a part of something is when it is compared to the whole thing. For example, you talk about something being 'a large proportion' or 'a small proportion' of a certain thing. *A high proportion of Americans in Germany are there as members of the forces.* ◇ The **proportion** of one part of a group to another part is how much bigger or smaller it is. *In 1965 the proportion of European to non-European immigrants was nine to one.*
❏ If something increases or decreases **in proportion** to something else, it goes up or down at the same rate, so that the two things always have the same relationship to each other.
❏ If you talk about the **proportions** of an object, you mean the size of its parts in relation to each other.
❏ If you talk about something being of certain **proportions**, you are saying how big it is. *Farming subsidies have reached absurd proportions.*
❏ **In proportion** is used to compare two things. For example, if you say something is large **in proportion** to a certain thing, you mean it is large when compared with that thing.
❏ If you say something is **out of all proportion** to what is required, you mean it is far greater than is necessary or appropriate.
❏ If you say someone is getting things **out of proportion**, you mean they are behaving as if something is more important or worrying than it really is. On the other hand, if you say someone is keeping things **in proportion**, you mean they are behaving sensibly and not exaggerating the importance of anything. You say someone who behaves like this has a **sense of proportion**.

proportional (proportionally) ❏ **Proportional** and **proportionally** are used to say how large or small something is when it is compared to something else. *In the past Sweden has taken a proportionally higher number of refugees than any other country.*
❏ If something is **proportional** to something else, it remains the same size in comparison with it.

proportional representation or PR is a system of voting in elections in which each party, including the small ones, is represented in parliament according to the number of votes it wins. See also **first-past-the-post**.

proportionate (proportionately) **Proportionate** means the same as 'proportional'. *Each member pays a share of Community running costs and each claims a proportionate share of all top jobs... New Zealand has proportionately more burglaries than any of 20 industrialised countries.*

propose (proposing, proposed; proposal, proposer) ❏ If you **propose** something like a course of action, you suggest that it should be done. A **proposal** is a suggested course of action. *...the proposed cut in public expenditure.*
❏ If you **propose** to do something, you intend to do it.
❏ If you **propose** someone in an election or vote, you suggest them as a candidate. You are called a **proposer** of the person.
❏ If you **propose** a motion in a debate, you introduce it and say why people should agree with it. You are called the **proposer** of the motion. ◇ If you **propose** a toast to someone or something, you ask people to drink a toast to them.
❏ If you **propose** to someone, you ask them to marry you. This is called a marriage **proposal**.

proposition (propositioning, propositioned) ❏ A **proposition** is a statement put forward for discussion.
❏ If you make a **proposition** to someone, you make an offer or suggest an arrangement which you think might interest them. ◇ You use **proposition** to say whether you think something is likely to succeed or not. For example, you say something is 'a good proposition' or 'a bad proposition'. *Standing seventy years of Communist rule on its head was always going to be a risky proposition.*
❏ If someone **propositions** someone who they are not already having a sexual relationship with, they ask them to have sex with them.

propound If you **propound** an argument, idea, or opinion, you put it forward for people to consider.

proprietary products can only be made and sold by a certain person or group of people.

proprietor (proprietorial) The **proprietor** of a business is its owner. **Proprietorial** is used to talk about things to do with the ownership of a business. *The IBA's consent is needed for any proprietorial transfer of direct broadcasting satellite frequencies.* ◇ If your behaviour is **proprietorial**, you behave in a way which shows you are, or think you are, the owner of something.

propriety (proprieties) **Propriety** is behaviour which is socially or morally acceptable. The **proprieties** are ways of behaving which most people consider to be correct. *He is no respecter of proprieties.* ◇ **Propriety** is also suitability or rightness. *...notions of architectural propriety.*

propulsion is the power which moves something, especially a vehicle, in a forward direction. *...jet propulsion.*

prorogue (proroguing, prorogued; prorogation) If parliament is **prorogued**, it is suspended for a period of time, but not dissolved. This is called the **prorogation** of parliament.

prosaic (pron: pro-**zay**-ik) (prosaically) If you say something is **prosaic**, you mean it is dull and unimaginative. *The real vision that people cherish is, more prosaically, of living in a country where things work, or work better than they do in Britain.*

proscenium (pron: pro-**seen**-i-um) (plural: prosceniums or proscenia) The **proscenium** or **proscenium arch** in a theatre is the arch which separates the stage from the audience.

proscribe (proscribing, proscribed; proscription) If people in authority **proscribe** something, they ban it. If something is **proscribed**, it is forbidden. When something is forbidden, you can talk about its **proscription**.

prose is anything spoken or written which is not poetry. Prose is used especially to talk about writing of high literary quality.

prosecute (prosecuting, prosecuted; prosecution) If someone is **prosecuted** or a **prosecution** is brought against them, criminal charges are brought against them and they go on trial. *He was the highest ranking figure to face prosecution.* ◇ In court, the lawyer who **prosecutes** is the one who tries to prove that the accused person is guilty. This lawyer and his or her assistants are also called the **prosecution**. *...a key prosecution witness.*

prosecuting attorney In the US, a **prosecuting attorney** is an official who conducts criminal prosecutions on behalf of the state and people.

prosecution See prosecute.

prosecutor A **prosecutor** is a lawyer or official who brings charges against someone and tries to prove they are guilty in a trial, especially a criminal one.

proselytize (*pron:* **pross-ill-it-ize**) (proselytizing, proselytized) (*can be spelled with an 's' instead of a 'z'*) If you **proselytize**, you try to persuade people to leave their religious faith or political party and join yours.

prospect (prospector) ❏ If there is a **prospect** of something happening, there is a possibility it will happen. *The recent resumption of diplomatic relations may have improved prospects for hostage releases.* ◇ A **prospect** is something you expect or know is going to happen. *Americans are more and more worried by the prospect of a recession.*

❏ Your **prospects** are your chances of being successful in your career. *People were afraid they would damage their employment prospects.*

❏ If someone **prospects** (*pron:* **pross-pekts**) for a valuable substance like oil or gold, they look for it in a particular place. A person who does this is called a **prospector**.

prospective is used to describe a person who intends to be a particular thing or is likely to become one. *The Labour Party has four prospective candidates... Telephone calls from prospective customers are returned immediately.* ◇ **Prospective** is also used to describe things which are expected to happen. *...prospective earnings.*

prospector See prospect.

prospectus (prospectuses) A **prospectus** is a booklet produced by a university, school, or company giving details about it.

prosper (prospering, prospered; prosperous, prosperity) When people or businesses **prosper**, they are successful and do well financially. When this happens, you say they are **prosperous** or talk about their **prosperity**. Similarly, you can describe a country or region as **prosperous** or talk about its **prosperity**.

prostate The **prostate** or **prostate gland** is an organ situated just below the bladder in male mammals. It produces a liquid which forms part of the semen.

prosthesis (*pron:* **pross-theess-siss**) (prosthetic) A **prosthesis** (*plural:* prostheses) is an artificial body part, for example a limb or a breast. A part like this can also be called a **prosthetic** part (*pron:* **pross-thet-tik**). *...prosthetic limbs.*

prostitute (prostituting, prostituted; prostitution) A **prostitute** is a person, especially a woman, who has sex with men in exchange for money. This practice is called **prostitution**. ◇ If you **prostitute** yourself or **prostitute** your talents, you behave in a way which is unworthy of you, or use your talents for unworthy purposes.

prostrate (prostrating, prostrated) If you **prostrate** yourself (*pron:* pross-**strate**), you lie flat on the ground with your face downwards, especially as an act of worship or submission. If you are in this position, you say you are **prostrate** (*pron:* **pross**-strate).

protagonist The **protagonists** in a play or novel are the main characters. ◇ A **protagonist** of an idea or movement is a supporter of it. *...Labour's anti-EU protagonists.*

protean (*pron:* **pro-tee-an**) If something is **protean**, it has the ability to keep changing its nature, appearance, or behaviour. *...a protean virus.*

protect (protection; protectionism, protectionist) ❏ If you **protect** someone or something or give them **protection**, you keep them safe from harm or damage.

❏ A **protected** species of animal, bird, or plant is one you are not allowed to kill or interfere with, because it is in danger of becoming extinct.

❏ If criminals extort **protection money** from people like shopkeepers, they demand money and in return promise not to hurt them or damage their property.

❏ If a government **protects** an industry, it helps it by limiting imports or by putting a heavy tax on imported goods. Helping industries in this way is called **protectionism**. **Protectionist** is used to talk about things to do with protectionism; a **protectionist** is someone who favours a policy like this.

protective (protectively, protectiveness) A **protective** object or action is intended to protect someone or something from harm. *...protective clothing... Some people have mounted protective all-night vigils outside foreigners' apartment blocks.* ◇ If someone is **protective** towards you, they show a strong desire to keep you safe from things which could hurt or frighten you. Behaviour like this is called **protectiveness**. *Protectively, she cradled the hand of her friend.*

protector A **protector** of someone or something is someone who protects them. ◇ Various kinds of device which protect you from physical harm are also called **protectors**. *...ear protectors.*

protectorate A **protectorate** is a country controlled and protected by a more powerful country.

protégé (protégée) (*both pron:* **pro-ti-zhay**; *the 'zh' sounds like 's' in 'pleasure'*) If someone helps and guides a young man, especially in his career, you say the young man is the person's **protégé**. If it is a young woman who is being helped, you say she is the person's **protégée**.

protein (*pron:* **pro-teen**) A **protein** is a large compound consisting of complex amino acid chains. Proteins are found in many foods, for example meat, eggs, and beans. They are essential for all living things.

protest (protester, protestor) ❏ If you **protest** about something (*pron:* pro-**test**), you say or show publicly that you do not approve of it. A **protest** (*pron:* **pro**-test) is a demonstration or statement like this. A **protester** or **protestor** is someone who protests publicly about something, especially by taking part in a demonstration.

❑ If you **protest** when someone says or does something, you interrupt them to say you disagree with them or object to what they are doing. What you say is called a **protest**. *Despite his protests, six plainclothes officers searched the office and took away some documents.* ◇ If you **protest** that something is the case, you insist it is, especially when you are being accused of something. *He strenuously protested his innocence.*

Protestant (Protestantism) **Protestants** are Christians who are not Roman Catholics or members of one of the Orthodox churches.

protestation A **protestation** is a strong declaration that something is true or not true. *Protestations of peaceful intention on both sides are becoming louder.*

protester (protestor) See **protest**.

proto- is used to form words which describe things as being the first of their type. *...proto-galaxies... ...a proto-feminist pioneer.*

protocol is a system of rules about the correct way to act on important formal occasions, for example at meetings between governments of different countries. ◇ A **protocol** is the written record of a treaty or agreement.

proton A **proton** is a particle which forms part of the nucleus of an atom and has a positive electrical charge.

prototype The **prototype** of something like a new machine or vehicle is the first of its kind to be produced.

protozoan (*pron:* pro-toe-**zoe**-an) (*plural:* protozoa) A **protozoan** is a microscopic one-celled creature.

protract If something is **protracted**, it lasts longer than is usual or expected. *...a protracted civil war.*

protractor A **protractor** is a flat semicircular piece of plastic, wood, or metal used for measuring angles.

protrude (protruding, protruded; protrusion) If something **protrudes** from somewhere, it sticks out. *...protruding front teeth.* Something which sticks out can be called a **protrusion**.

proud (prouder, proudest; proudly) ❑ If you are **proud** of something you own or have done, it gives you a feeling of pleasure and satisfaction, and you show this in the way you behave. *The company proudly claims to have made a profit every month since December.* You can also be **proud** of something someone close to you has done. ◇ If someone **does you proud,** they do something very well, so you can feel proud of them.

❑ You say people are **proud** when they have great dignity and self-respect. *...a great, proud and noble people.* ◇ You also say people are **proud** when they believe they are superior to other people.

provable If statements or theories are **provable**, they can be proved to be true or correct.

prove (proving, proved, have proved *or* have proven) ❑ If you **prove** something is true, you show conclusively that it is true.

❑ In a Scottish court, a jury can return a verdict of **not proven** if there is not enough evidence to convict someone accused of a crime.

❑ If someone or something **proves** to have a certain quality, it becomes clear that they have it. *The first half of the course proved difficult.* ◇ **Proven** is used to say someone or something has been definitely shown to have a quality or ability. *...young musicians of proven talent.*

provenance The **provenance** of something, especially a

work of art, is the place it originally came from.

proverb (proverbial, proverbially) ❑ A **proverb** is a short well-known saying which is supposed to sum up some important truth about life. 'A stitch in time saves nine' is a typical proverb. ◇ **Proverbial** is used when mentioning a proverb or some other well-known expression. *The great hurricane of October 1987 was the proverbial ill wind that blew no good... ...the proverbial man-in-the-street.*

❑ If something is **proverbial**, it is well known or widely believed. *His generosity is proverbial... Proverbially, the British will suffer such daily stresses patiently.*

provide (providing, provided; provider) ❑ If you **provide** someone with something they need or want, you give it to them or make it available to them. ◇ If you **provide** for someone, you give them the things they need. *They found that the scheme rarely provides for children from disadvantaged backgrounds.* ◇ A **provider** of something is someone who gives people the things they need or want. *...Japan, China's biggest provider of foreign aid.*

❑ If something **provides** a useful or desirable feature or quality, it has it or gives it. *The war provided him with extraordinary opportunities... Condoms provide the best defence against catching the HIV virus.*

❑ If you **provide** for a possible future event, you take it into account when you plan or do something. *Charges may have to rise to provide for differing levels of water purity.*

❑ If a law or decision **provides** that something will happen, it states that it will happen. *The new scheme provided that, by December 31st 1994, the four countries would share a common external tariff, with free movement of goods and services among themselves.*

❑ If you say something will happen **provided** or **provided that** something else happens, you mean the first thing will happen only if the second one does. *The government has said they'll be allowed to take out Hungarian citizenship provided they're prepared to invest money in the country.* Similarly, you can say something will happen **providing** or **providing that** something else does. *The other proposal was to promise to cut income taxes, providing that spending was cut by an equal amount.*

providence (*or* Providence) is God, or a force believed to control the things which happen to people, especially in a positive way.

providential (providentially) If you say something which happens is **providential**, you mean it is very lucky. *Though some of us had our clothing torn by bullets, we providentially gained the sand hill.*

providing (provider) See **provide**.

province ❑ A **province** is a large section of a country with its own administration. ◇ The **provinces** are the parts of a country away from its capital.

❑ If a subject or activity is someone's **province**, they have a special interest in it or responsibility for it. *Running a school is a complex business, which should be the province of highly trained professionals.*

provincial (provincialism) **Provincial** is used to talk about things connected with the parts of a country which are away from its capital. *...provincial theatres.* ◇ People who live in a country's capital sometimes call people from other parts of the country **provincials**, implying that they are unsophisticated and perhaps narrow-minded. They may also talk about their **provincialism**.

provision (provisioning, provisioned) ❏ When something is provided for people, you talk about its **provision**. ...*the provision of sites for gypsies... ...childcare provision.* ◇ If you **make provision** for a future need, you make arrangements to deal with it.

❏ A **provision** in an agreement or law is a condition which must be fulfilled.

❏ **Provisions** are supplies of food. If you are **provisioned** with food or something else you need, you are supplied with it.

provisional (provisionally) **Provisional** is used to describe things which are created for a temporary period only. ...*a provisional licence... ...a provisional government.* ◇ A **provisional** arrangement is one which is not fixed and may be changed. *The deadlocked negotiations are provisionally scheduled to restart in Rome before the end of next month.*

proviso (*pron:* pro-vize-oh) (provisos) A **proviso** is a condition included in a legal or formal document. *All Germany became part of NATO with the proviso that no NATO troops will be stationed in former East Germany.*

provocateur A **provocateur** is the same as an agent provocateur.

provocative (provocatively, provocation) When people call an action **provocative** or a **provocation**, they mean it is deliberately done to provoke an angry reaction. *The troops fired shots in the air after the demonstrators behaved provocatively.* ◇ If you call something like a newspaper article as **provocative**, you mean it is likely to cause a lot of argument and discussion. ◇ Certain things can be described as **provocative** when they produce feelings of sexual desire. ...*sexually provocative advertising.*

provoke (provoking, provoked) If you **provoke** someone, you deliberately annoy them and try to make them react in an aggressive way. ◇ If something **provokes** a violent or unpleasant reaction, it causes it. *News of his death provoked widespread anger and demonstrations.*

provost Some colleges have a head called a **provost**, for example the university colleges at Oxford and Cambridge. ◇ In Scotland, a **provost** is the chairman and civic head of a district council. ◇ In the Catholic and Anglican Churches, a **provost** is the person in charge of the administration of a cathedral or collegiate church.

prow The **prow** of a ship or boat is its front part.

prowess If you talk about someone's **prowess**, you mean their ability to do something extremely well. ...*East Germany's sporting prowess.*

prowl When an animal **prowls**, it moves around quietly, trying not to be noticed, usually because it is hunting. You can also say a person **prowls** when they move around very quietly. If someone is **on the prowl**, they are looking for something and trying not to be noticed.

prowler A **prowler** is someone who creeps around houses at night, usually intending to harm someone or commit a robbery.

proximate The **proximate** cause of something is the last of a series of things which have been leading up to it and which finally makes it happen.

proximity to a place is nearness to it. *One of the reasons the Lyneham base was chosen was because of its close proximity to the military hospital at Wroughton.*

proxy (proxies) **Proxy** is authority given to someone to act or make decisions on your behalf when you are not present, for example at an election or meeting. If you do something **by proxy**, you arrange for someone to act on your behalf like this; the person who does it is called your **proxy**. ◇ **Proxy** is used to describe other things carried out by someone on someone else's behalf. *Many observers have seen the Cambodian conflict as a proxy war between China and Vietnam.*

prude See prudish.

prudent (prudently, prudence) If you are **prudent**, you are sensible and careful. *Reformers are repeatedly forced to choose between making changes quickly and making them prudently... ...the need for caution and prudence.*

prudish (prude, prudishness, prudery) If you say someone is **prudish** or call them a **prude**, you mean they are easily shocked by things to do with nudity and sex. You talk about the **prudishness** or **prudery** of someone like this.

prune (pruning, pruned) ❏ A **prune** is a dried plum.

❏ When you **prune** a tree or bush, you trim back some of its branches to make it look neater, or to get it to produce better fruit or flowers.

❏ If an organization is **pruned**, it is made smaller, for example by reducing its staff or the amount of money it spends. You can also say its staff or expenditure is **pruned**. ◇ If you **prune** something like a piece of writing, you make it shorter by removing parts of it.

prurient (pruriently, prurience) If someone or something is **prurient**, they are excessively interested in things to do with sex. You talk about the **prurience** of someone like this *His biographer writes so pruriently about his sexual fantasies.*

prussic acid or **hydrocyanic acid** is an extremely poisonous substance which is used as an insecticide and has also been used for executing criminals.

pry (pries, prying, pried) If you accuse someone of **prying**, you mean they keep trying to find out about other people's private affairs.

PS is written before a message which has been added at the end of a letter. PS stands for 'postscript'.

psalm (*pron:* sahm) The **psalms** are the 150 songs, poems, and prayers which form the Book of Psalms in the Bible.

psalter (*pron:* sawl-ter) A **psalter** is a book containing a collection of psalms, for use in church services.

PSBR See public sector.

psephology (*pron:* sif-fol-loj-ee) (psephologist, psephological) **Psephology** is the study of elections and how people vote in them. A **psephologist** is an expert on this. **Psephological** is used to talk about things connected with psephology. ...*psephological research.*

pseud (*pron:* syood) If you say someone is a **pseud**, you mean they pretend to be very wise, knowledgeable, or artistic, when in fact they are not.

pseudo- is put at the beginning of a word to describe something which is not what it is claimed to be. ...*pseudo-scientific theories... ...pseudo-designer spectacles.*

pseudonym (*pron:* syoo-doe-nim) A **pseudonym** is a name used by someone, especially a writer, instead of his or her real name.

psoriasis (*pron:* so-rye-a-siss) is a skin disease which produces red patches covered with silvery scales.

psych (*pron:* sike) If you **psych** yourself **up** to do something or **psych** yourself **into** doing something, you prepare yourself mentally, especially by telling yourself you can succeed.

psyche (*pron:* **sigh**-kee) Your **psyche** is your mind and your deepest feelings and attitudes.

psychedelic (*pron:* sigh-ked-**del**-lik) (psychedelia) Psychedelic drugs are drugs like LSD, which affect your mind and make you hallucinate. ◇ **Psychedelic** clothing or art is brightly coloured and strangely patterned in a way associated with the effects of psychedelic drugs. Clothing and art like this can also be called **psychedelia** (*pron:* sigh-ked-**dee**-lee-a).

psychiatry (psychiatric, psychiatrically, psychiatrist) Psychiatry is the branch of medicine concerned with the treatment of mental illness. **Psychiatric** is used to talk about things to do with psychiatry. ...*a psychiatric hospital*... *They refused to accept that he was psychiatrically ill.* A **psychiatrist** is a doctor who treats people suffering from mental illness.

psychic ❑ A **psychic** is someone who claims to have unusual mental powers, such as being able to read the minds of other people, to communicate with the spirits of dead people, or to see into the future.

❑ **Psychic** is used to talk about things to do with the mind rather than the body. ...*psychic power.*

psycho (psychos) A **psycho** is the same as a psychopath.

psycho- is used to form words which describe things to do with the mind or mental processes. ...*a psycho-thriller.*

psychoactive drugs are drugs like LSD which affect your mind or behaviour.

psychoanalyse (psychoanalysing, psychoanalysed) (*American spelling:* **psychoanalyze,** *etc*) When a psychiatrist or psychotherapist **psychoanalyses** someone, they examine or treat them using psychoanalysis.

psychoanalysis (psychoanalyst; psychoanalytic, psychoanalytical) Psychoanalysis is a method of treating someone who is disturbed or mentally ill by asking them about their feelings and past in order to discover the cause of their problem. Someone who is trained to do this is called a **psychoanalyst. Psychoanalytic** and **psychoanalytical** are used to talk about things to do with psychoanalysis. ...*a psychoanalytical investigation.*

psychoanalyze See psychoanalyse.

psychobabble Some people call the words and expressions used in psychology, especially in psychotherapy, **psychobabble.**

psychological (psychologically) ❑ **Psychological** is used to talk about things to do with people's minds and thoughts. ...*psychological problems*... *The experience has destroyed me psychologically.*

❑ **Psychological** is also used to talk about things to do with psychology. ...*the British Psychological Society.*

❑ **Psychological warfare** is the use of propaganda to weaken an enemy's morale.

psychology (psychologist) ❑ **Psychology** is the scientific study of the mind and of the reasons for people's behaviour. An expert in this field is called a **psychologist.**

❑ Your **psychology** is the kind of mind you have and the way you think.

psychometric tests are designed to assess things like your personality, abilities, and suitability for certain kinds of work.

psychopath (psychopathic) A **psychopath** is someone with a severe personality disorder who does violent and anti-social things. You say someone like this is **psychopathic.** ...*psychopathic killers.*

psychosis (psychotic) A **psychosis** (*plural:* psychoses) is a severe mental illness. You say a person with an illness like this is **psychotic** or a **psychotic;** you also call their behaviour **psychotic.**

psychosomatic A **psychosomatic** illness is a physical condition brought on by a person's mental or emotional problems.

psychotherapy (psychotherapist) **Psychotherapy** is using psychological methods to treat mentally ill people, rather than physical methods such as drugs. A person who treats people in this way is called a **psychotherapist.**

psychotic See psychosis.

psychotropic (*pron:* sigh-ko-**trope**-ik) drugs are drugs such as sedatives, anti-depressants, and stimulants which affect people's mental states.

PTA A **PTA** or **parent-teacher association** is a school organization run jointly by teachers and parents to discuss school matters and try to improve school facilities.

pterodactyl (*pron:* terr-roe-**dak**-til) Pterodactyls were various kinds of flying reptiles with bat-like wings in prehistoric times.

PTO is short for 'please turn over'. It is written at the bottom of a page to show that the writing continues on the other side.

pub A **pub** is a building with a bar or bars licensed to sell alcoholic drinks, where people go to meet friends and relax. ◇ If you go on a **pub crawl,** you go from one pub to another, having a drink in each one.

puberty (*pron:* **pew**-ber-tee) is the stage in your life when your body changes from that of a child to that of an adult.

pubescent A **pubescent** girl or boy has reached puberty.

pubic is used to talk about things to do with the area just above the genitals. ...*pubic hair.*

public (publicly) ❑ The **public** is people in general, or the people in a particular place. ...*members of the public*... ...*the American public.* **Public** is used to talk about the feelings and behaviour of people in general. ...*public enthusiasm for environmental issues.*

❑ **Public** is used to talk about money provided by a government for the benefit of the people in their country. ...*public spending*... ...*the publicly-funded British Film Institute.* ◇ **Public** is also used to talk about things like buildings and services which are provided for everyone to use. ...*public lavatories*... ...*public libraries.* ◇ A **public** place is one where everyone is allowed to go. ...*a public square.*

❑ **Public** is used to talk about all the people who enjoy a particular kind of entertainment. ...*the television-viewing public*... ...*the reading public.*

❑ A **public** figure is someone who is well-known, for example because they are often mentioned in the media. You say someone like this is **in the public eye.** ◇ If you talk about someone entering **public life,** you mean they start doing a kind of work, especially in politics, which may result in them becoming well-known. ◇ If someone holds **public office,** they have been elected or appointed to an important position in central or local government.

❑ **Public** is used to talk about things being said or done in such a way that everyone can hear them or see them.

The treasures will go on public display tomorrow... The police chief publicly apologised for the corruption case. ◇ If you say or do something **in public,** you do it when other people are present. *In public, she wore dark glasses.*

❑ If something is **made public,** everyone is made aware of it and it is no longer a secret. You can also say someone **goes public** on something which had previously been a secret.

❑ If a company **goes public,** it starts selling shares to the public.

public address system The public address system or PA in a place is electrical equipment, including a microphone, amplifier, and loudspeakers, which enables a speaker or music to be heard by a large number of people.

public bar A public bar is a room in a pub where the furniture is plain and the drinks are cheaper than in the other bars.

public convenience A public convenience is a toilet in a public place for anyone to use.

public domain If you talk about a piece of news entering the public domain, you mean everyone gets to know about it. ◇ If something like a piece of music or an invention is in the public domain, it is not the property of the composer or inventor, and can be used by anyone without permission. When the copyright on something expires, you say it enters the public domain.

public holiday A public holiday is a day which is a holiday for everyone in the whole country.

public house A public house is the same as a pub.

public limited company See plc.

public nuisance If someone causes a public nuisance, they disturb or annoy members of the public and in doing so break the law.

public opinion is what people in general think about a particular matter. *The mood of American public opinion is definitely anti-war.*

public order is a situation in which people are going about their business normally and there is no fighting or other trouble. *Displays of Islamic fervour which were regarded as a threat to public order were cracked down upon.*

public prosecutor In some countries, a public prosecutor is an official who carries out criminal prosecutions on behalf of the government and people.

public relations or PR is the work of presenting a good image of an organization or well-known person to the public. A person employed to do this is called a **public relations officer.** ◇ The relationship between an organization and the public is also called **public relations.** *The authorities are taking slightly more positive steps to try to polish up their public relations.* If you say something is a **public relations exercise,** you mean it is done to create a good impression, rather than for any practical reason.

public school (public schoolboy) In England and Wales, a public school is a private school, usually a boarding school, providing secondary education. A **public schoolboy** is a male pupil at a school like this, or a former pupil. Public schools are now usually called 'independent schools'. ◇ In some countries, for example the US, Australia, and Scotland, a **public school** is a free local school supported financially by the government.

public sector ❑ The public sector is the part of a

country's economy which is controlled or supported financially by the government or local authorities.

❑ In Britain, the **public sector borrowing requirement** or **PSBR** is the difference between the money the government collects, for example through taxation, and the money it spends.

public service (public servant) A public service is a service provided for the community, for example transport. ◇ If you work in public service, you work for the government or a local authority. A **public servant** is a civil servant or local government officer.

public-spirited (public-spiritedness) If you say someone is **public-spirited** or talk about their **public-spiritedness,** you mean they try to help other people or the community they belong to.

public transport is transport like buses and trains for the general public to use.

public works are things like buildings and roads which are built by the government for use by the public.

publican A publican is someone who owns or manages a pub.

publication When a book, magazine, or newspaper is printed and made available, this is called its **publication.** A publication is a book, magazine, or newspaper.

publicise See publicize.

publicist A publicist is someone who publicizes things, especially as part of a job in advertising or journalism.

publicity is advertising, information, or actions intended to attract the public's attention to someone or something. *...a publicity campaign.* ◇ Publicity is also the attention paid to someone or something by the media. *The meat industry has had to contend with a lot of bad publicity lately.*

publicize (publicizing, publicized) *(can be spelled with an 's' instead of a 'z')* If you **publicize** something, you make it widely known to the public. *...a much-publicized meeting.*

publish (publishes, publishing, published; publisher) When a company **publishes** a book, magazine, or newspaper, it prints copies of it, which are then sent to shops and sold. ◇ **Publishing** is the business of publishing books. A **publishing house** is a company that publishes books. A **publisher** is a person or company that publishes books. ◇ When a piece of writing is **published** in a newspaper or magazine, it appears in it. ◇ If facts are **published,** they are made available to the public.

puce is a dark reddish-purple colour.

puck In ice hockey, the puck is the small rubber disc used instead of a ball.

puckered If someone's face is **puckered,** it is wrinkled or creased.

puckish A puckish person is mischievous and enjoys playing tricks on people.

pudding A pudding is a hot sweet cooked food, usually boiled or baked. Pudding is also the dessert course of a meal. ◇ Some boiled savoury dishes are also called **puddings.** *...steak and kidney pudding.* ◇ **proof of the pudding:** see proof.

pudding basin A pudding basin is a deep round bowl used especially for cooking puddings. The pudding mixture is put into the basin, which is then put in boiling water.

puddle A puddle is a small shallow pool of liquid on the ground.

pudgy A pudgy person is fairly fat.

puerile (*pron:* pyoo-rile) If you say something is **puerile**, you mean it is silly and childish. *...puerile humour.*

puff ❏ If you **puff** a cigarette or pipe or **puff** on it, you smoke it. ◇ A **puff** of smoke is a small amount of it. Similarly, you can talk about a **puff** of air or wind. ◇ If you are **puffing**, you are breathing loudly and quickly because you are out of breath. You can also say you are **out of puff**.
❏ If something **puffs out** or **puffs up**, it swells and becomes larger. ◇ If you say a person is **puffed up**, you mean they are proud and self-important.
❏ A **puff** is a type of cake made of hollow puff pastry filled with cream, fruit, or jam. *...a cream puff.*

puff pastry is a type of very light pastry which consists of many thin layers.

puffin Puffins are black and white seabirds with large brightly-coloured striped beaks.

puffy If something is **puffy**, it is round and swollen.

pug Pugs are small short-haired dogs with flat noses.

pugilism (*pron:* pew-jil-iz-zum) (pugilist) Boxing is sometimes called **pugilism**. A **pugilist** is a boxer.

pugnacious (pugnacity) If someone is **pugnacious**, they are always ready to quarrel or start a fight. You can talk about the **pugnacity** of someone like this.

puke (puking, puked) If you **puke**, you vomit.

pukka Things are sometimes described as **pukka** when they are rather superior and posh. *He speaks in the pukka tones of the ruling class.*

pull ❏ If you **pull** something or **pull at** it, you hold it firmly and move it towards you.
❏ If you **pull** something like a cart, you move forward holding on to it, so that it moves along behind you. Similarly, an animal or vehicle can be attached to something and **pull** it.
❏ If you **pull** yourself into a particular position, you hold onto something and use your strength to get yourself into that position.
❏ If you **pull** a muscle, you injure it by stretching it too much or too suddenly.
❏ If you **pull on** your clothes, you get dressed quickly.
❏ When you **pull** a curtain or a blind, you move it across a window, to cover or uncover it.
❏ If you **pull** something **out**, you take it out of the place where you were keeping it, for example your pocket. ◇ If someone **pulls** a gun on you, they produce it and threaten you with it.
❏ If a building is **pulled down**, it is deliberately destroyed, often to make room for something else.
❏ If something like a show or a festival **pulls** people **in**, it attracts them in large numbers. *The 1937 World Fair pulled in nearly 40 million visitors... The pulling power of the royal family as a tourist attraction may be beginning to falter.* ◇ If you talk about the **pull** of something, you are talking about its ability to attract people.
❏ The **pull** of something like a magnet is the force it exerts which draws things towards it. *...the earth's gravitational pull.* ◇ If you talk about how well a vehicle's engine **pulls**, you are talking about its ability to make the vehicle move. *The car's pulling power seemed as good as new.*
❏ **Pull** is used to talk about the movements of a vehicle.

For example, when a vehicle starts moving forward, you can say it **pulls away**. If it moves into a faster lane, you say it **pulls out**. If it **pulls up**, it stops. ◇ When a train **pulls in** to a station, it arrives there. When it **pulls out**, it leaves.
❏ If an army **pulls out** of a place which it has occupied, it leaves it. You can talk about a **pull-out** of troops. You can also say an army **pulls back** from a place it has occupied or from a position it has reached.
❏ If you **pull out** of something you are involved in, you withdraw from it. *Jahangir was the top seed for the championship, but pulled out because of ill health.*
❏ If someone has succeeded in something, you can say they have **pulled** it **off**. ◇ If you **pull through** a difficult situation, you manage to survive it. ◇ If you **pull back** from a difficult or losing position, you manage to improve your position or go on to succeed. ◇ If you are seriously ill and then you **pull through**, you recover.
❏ If people **pull together**, they co-operate in a difficult situation. ◇ If you **pull yourself together** when you are upset, you get your feelings under control and are able to behave calmly and sensibly again.
❏ If you **pull ahead** or **pull away** from other people in a contest, you take the lead.
❏ If something which has been planned is **pulled**, it is suddenly cancelled. *The government asked the BBC to pull a programme on Northern Ireland.*
❏ If someone **pulls** a trick on you, they deceive or trick you. You can also say they **pull a fast one** on you. ◇ **pull someone's leg:** see **leg**.
❏ **pull punches:** see **punch**. ◇ **pull rank:** see **rank**. ◇ **pull strings:** see **string**. ◇ **pull your weight:** see **weight**.

pull-out A pull-out is a section of a magazine which can easily remove and keep. ◇ See also **pull**.

pullet A pullet is a young hen.

pulley (pulleys) A **pulley** is a device for lifting heavy weights. It consists of one or more wheels which a rope is passed over.

Pullman In the past, a **Pullman** was a type of railway carriage which was very comfortable and luxurious. A **Pullman** train was made up of carriages like this.

pullover A **pullover** is a knitted piece of men's clothing which covers the upper part of the body and sometimes the arms.

pulmonary is used to talk about things to do with the lungs. *...pulmonary TB.*

pulp ❏ If something is **pulped** or turned into a **pulp**, it is crushed or beaten until it is soft, smooth, and moist.
❏ **Pulp** is a substance made from crushed wood, rags, and other fibres which is used to make paper. ◇ People sometimes use **pulp** to describe books and magazines considered to be of poor quality, because they are written in a sensational or predictable way. *...pulp fiction.*

pulpit The **pulpit** in a church is a small raised platform with a rail or barrier around it, where a member of the clergy stands to preach. ◇ If you say something like a job is a **pulpit** for someone, you mean it gives them the opportunity to express their views publicly. *His pulpit was a local radio station, the only one to denounce human rights violations.*

pulsar Pulsars are small, very dense stars which give out regular bursts of radio waves. They are thought to be the remains of larger stars which have exploded.

pulsate (pulsating, pulsated; pulsation) If something **pulsates,** it moves in and out or beats or shakes with strong regular movements. A movement like this is called a **pulsation.**

pulse (pulsing, pulsed) ❏ Your **pulse** is the regular beating of blood through your body which you can feel, for example, at your wrists and neck. When someone takes your **pulse,** they find out the speed of your heartbeat by feeling the pulse in your wrist. ◇ If something **sets your pulse racing,** it makes you feel excited.

❏ If you say someone has **their finger on the pulse,** you mean they know all about the latest news and developments in a particular field.

❏ Other kinds of regular beat can also be called a **pulse,** for example the beat in a piece of music. ◇ If something **pulses,** it beats or shakes with strong regular movements.

❏ **Pulses** are the dried edible seeds of certain plants. Lentils and dried and split peas are pulses.

pulverize (pulverizing, pulverized) (can be spelled with an 's' instead of a 'z') ❏ If something is **pulverized,** it is crushed into a powder. ◇ If a place is **pulverized,** it is badly damaged or destroyed by bombs or gunfire.

❏ If someone is **pulverized** in a contest, they are beaten by a large margin.

puma The **puma** is a large American wild cat. It is also called a 'cougar' or 'mountain lion'.

pumice (pron: **pum**-iss) is a lightweight grey stone which can be used to remove areas of hard skin.

pummel (pummelling, pummelled) (American spelling: pummeling, pummeled) If you **pummel** someone or something, you beat them with your fists. ◇ You can say a place is **pummelled** when it is repeatedly bombed or shelled. ...the American-led pummelling of Iraq.

pump ❏ If liquid or gas is **pumped** in a certain direction, it is forced in that direction using a machine or device called a **pump.** ◇ You also say water, oil, or gas is **pumped** when a supply of it is got from below the ground, also using a device called a **pump.** ◇ If you **pump** something like a tyre or **pump** it **up,** you fill it with air using a **pump.** ◇ A petrol **pump** is a machine with a hose attached, for putting fuel into a car.

❏ If you talk about money or energy being **pumped** into something, you mean a lot of money or energy is put into it. ◇ **prime the pump:** see prime.

❏ If you talk about something being **pumped out,** you mean it is produced or supplied continually in large amounts. ...the 300 hours of storytelling pumped out annually by Radio 4.

❏ In the past, **pumps** were a type of lightweight men's shoe used for dancing. ◇ Plimsolls are also sometimes called **pumps.**

pump-priming See prime.

pumpernickel is a kind of dark brown bread made from rye.

pumping station A **pumping station** is a place with pumps, where a substance like water, sewage, or oil is pumped away to another area.

pumpkin Pumpkins are large round orange-coloured vegetables.

pun (punning, punned) A **pun** is a clever and amusing use of words which have more than one meaning. If you **pun,** you make a pun. Colin Scarsi has come up with the world's first, pardon the pun, recyclable bicycle tyre.

punch (punches, punching, punched) ❏ If you **punch** someone or give them a **punch,** you hit them hard with your fist. If you **throw a punch,** you try to punch someone. ◇ If you do not **pull punches** when you criticize someone, you say exactly what you think, without softening your criticism. ◇ **pack a punch:** see pack.

❏ If you **punch** holes in something, you make holes in it using something sharp. A **punch** is a special tool or machine for doing this.

❏ **Punch** is a drink made from a mixture of fruit juice and alcohol, often served hot.

Punch and Judy show A Punch and Judy show is a comic puppet show for children, usually performed in a small booth at a fair or the seaside.

punch-drunk If a boxer is **punch-drunk,** he shows signs of brain damage, for example unsteadiness and inability to think clearly, because he has had too many blows to the head. ◇ You can also say someone is **punch-drunk** when they are dazed and confused, because they have been severely criticized by someone.

punch line The **punch line** of a joke or story is the part at the end which makes it funny.

punch-up A **punch-up** is a fight in which people hit each other.

punchbag A **punchbag** is a heavy leather bag stuffed with something like horsehair. It hangs from a rope and is punched by boxers for training and exercise.

punchball A **punchball** is a large leather ball fixed on a spring which is punched by boxers for training and exercise.

punchbowl A **punchbowl** is a large bowl in which punch or some other drink is mixed and served.

punchy (punchier, punchiest) If you call something like a piece of writing **punchy,** you mean it is effective and forceful, because the author makes his or her points clearly, briefly, and decisively.

punctilious You say people are **punctilious** when they are very careful to behave correctly.

punctual (punctually, punctuality) If an air or rail service is **punctual,** the planes or trains arrive and leave at the right time. Punctually at 7.45, the express left Singapore station... When booking a flight, passengers should check the airline's record for punctuality. Similarly, if a person is **punctual,** they arrive at the right time for an appointment or meeting.

punctuate (punctuating, punctuated) If an activity is **punctuated** by something, it is regularly interrupted by it. Their opening game was punctuated by disputes involving umpires and scorers.

punctuation The marks in writing such as commas, full stops, and question marks are called **punctuation** or **punctuation marks.**

puncture (puncturing, punctured) ❏ A **puncture** is a small hole in a tyre made by a sharp object. ◇ If you **puncture** something, you make a small hole in it.

❏ If something **punctures** someone's cheerful feelings, it puts an end to them. Similarly, something can **puncture** a belief.

pundit (punditry) A **pundit** is someone who knows a lot about a subject and is asked to give information or an opinion about it. **Punditry** is the things pundits say.

pungent (pungently, pungency) If something is **pungent**, it has a strong bitter smell or taste. ◇ **Pungent** speech or writing is direct, powerful, and critical. You talk about the **pungency** of speech or writing like this. *The director Christopher Much has his own ideas, expressed pungently in this award-winning film.*

punish (punishes, punishing, punished; punishingly, punishable) ❏ If someone is **punished**, they are made to suffer because they have done something wrong. ◇ If a crime or offence is **punished** in a certain way, people who commit it are made to suffer that way. You can also say a crime or offence is **punishable** in a certain way. *...a felony punishable by four years in prison.*

❏ **Punishing** is used to describe things which make you very weak and tired. *Mr Mandela has set himself a punishing schedule... ...punishingly hard work.*

punishment ❏ A **punishment** is a particular way of punishing someone. See also capital punishment, corporal punishment.

❏ Severe treatment of any kind can be called **punishment**. *Voters inflicted heavy punishment on the ruling party.*

punitive (*pron:* **pew**-nit-iv) (punitively) **Punitive** actions are intended to punish people. *...a punitive crackdown by the security forces.* ◇ You can say other things which make people suffer are **punitive**. *...punitive economic measures... Interest rates are still punitively high.*

punk or **punk rock** is a type of aggressive rock music which began in the late 1970s as a protest against conventional ideas and behaviour. A **punk** is a follower of punk rock. Punks usually dress in ripped clothes, decorate themselves with chains, and have brightly coloured spiked hair.

punnet A **punnet** is a small light box or basket which soft fruits like strawberries are sold in.

punt ❏ A **punt** is a long shallow flat-bottomed boat, square at both ends. You move it along by standing in it and pushing a long pole against the bottom of the river.

❏ The **punt** is the unit of currency in the Republic of Ireland.

punter ❏ A **punter** is someone who bets money, especially on horse races.

❏ Some people call their customers or clients **punters**.

puny (punier, puniest) If someone or something is **puny**, they are small and weak. *...a puny youth... ...the Bank of England's puny efforts to defend the pound.*

pup ❏ A **pup** is a young dog. ◇ The young of some other animals, for example seals, are also called **pups**.

❏ If you are **sold a pup**, you are persuaded to buy or agree to something which turns out to be worthless.

pupa (*pron:* **pew**-pa) (*plural:* pupae) A **pupa** is an insect at the stage of development between a larva and a fully developed adult.

pupil ❏ The **pupils** at a school are the children there. ◇ A **pupil** of a painter, musician, or other expert is someone who studies with them.

❏ The **pupils** of your eyes are the black parts at the centre.

puppet (puppetry) A **puppet** is a doll or toy animal which performs actions when you pull strings attached to it or put your hand inside it. **Puppetry** is the art of making puppets or operating them. ◇ **Puppet** is used to describe countries which are controlled by other more powerful ones. *...a puppet state.*

puppy (puppies) A **puppy** is a young dog. ◇ **Puppy fat** is fat which children have on their bodies when they are young but which disappears when they get older and taller.

purchase (purchasing, purchased; purchaser) ❏ When you **purchase** something, you buy it. A **purchase** is something you buy; **purchase** is buying it. A **purchaser** is a person who buys something. ◇ Your **purchasing power** is the amount of money you have available to buy things with. *Inflationary pressures are still threatening the purchasing power of wage earners.* ◇ The **purchasing power** of a currency is its value in terms of how much can be bought with it at any one time.

❏ If you get or gain **purchase** somewhere, you find something you can hold on to firmly. *He pushed his hand down the side of the settee to gain a better purchase.*

purdah In some Muslim societies, **purdah** is the custom by which women conceal themselves from public view, for example by staying in a special part of the house or by keeping their faces and bodies covered.

pure (purity) ❏ If something is **pure**, it is not mixed with anything else. You talk about the **purity** of something like this. *...pure gold... ...Germany's ancient law on beer purity.* ◇ You also say something is **pure** when it is clean and healthy and does not contain any harmful substances. *...pure mountain air... The sea here meets EU regulations on purity.*

❏ A **pure** sound is clear and pleasant to hear.

❏ **Pure** is used to talk about a form of art produced or done exactly according to an accepted standard, form, or pattern. *...pure classical dance.*

❏ You say someone is **pure** when they have never done anything bad or sinful. *...the use of choirboys as symbols of purity and innocence.*

❏ **Pure** science or research is concerned only with increasing knowledge and not with how things can be put to practical use.

❏ **Pure** is also used to mean 'complete and total'. *We found out about these changes by pure accident... ...the school's pursuit of pure academic excellence.*

puree (*or* purée) (*pron:* **pure**-ray) A **puree** is food which has been sieved or liquidized so that it forms a thick smooth pulp. *...tomato puree.*

purely is used to emphasize that something is limited or restricted in some way. *The UN troops' role will be purely defensive.*

purgative A **purgative** is a medicine which helps to clear the bowels.

purgatory is the place where Roman Catholics believe the spirits of some dead people are sent, to suffer for their sins before they can go to heaven. ◇ Any unpleasant experience which people have to suffer can be called **purgatory**. *The Guardian suggests Britain could see four or five years of economic purgatory, with strikes, low wages and rising unemployment.*

purge (purging, purged) If an organization is **purged** of unacceptable members, they are removed from it. This is called a **purge** of the members. *...demands for the army to be purged of corrupt officers.* ◇ If you **purge** something of undesirable things, you get rid of them. *...a technique in which the white blood cells are removed and purged of cancer* *cells before being replaced in patients.*

purify (purifies, purifying, purified; purification) When a substance is **purified**, it is made pure by removing any harmful, dirty, or inferior substances. *...water purification.*

purist (purism) A **purist** is someone who believes in sticking strictly to the correct way of doing something. You can talk about the **purism** of someone like this. *...jazz purists... ...Communist purism.*

puritan (puritanical, puritanism) The **Puritans** were a group of English Protestants who tried to get rid of all Roman Catholic influences in English churches in the 16th and 17th centuries. ◇ If you say someone is a **puritan**, you mean they live according to strict moral or religious principles, especially by avoiding physical pleasures. **Puritanical** is used to describe people like this and their behaviour. You can also talk about their **puritanism**.

purity See pure.

purl is a knitting stitch in which you put the needle into the back rather than the front of the stitch on the other needle.

purlieus (*pron:* **per**-lyooz) The **purlieus** of a place are the areas immediately surrounding it.

purloin (purloining, purloined) If you **purloin** something, you steal it or borrow it without asking permission.

purple is a dark reddish-blue colour.

purplish If something is **purplish**, it is slightly purple.

purport (purported, purportedly) If you say something **purports** to be a particular thing, you mean it is claimed to be that thing. *...a photograph purporting to show three American pilots, missing since the Vietnam war... He was given a letter purportedly signed by the Deputy Assistant Commissioner.*

purpose ❏ The **purpose** of something is the reason why it is made or created. *Abuse of drugs designed for medical purposes has long been widespread.* Similarly, the **purpose** of an action is the reason why it is done. *...the purpose of his visit.* ◇ If something **serves a purpose**, it is useful and can help you achieve a particular aim.
❏ **Purpose** is having a definite aim which you are determined to achieve. ◇ Your **purpose** is the thing you want to achieve. ◇ If you do something **on purpose**, you do it deliberately.
❏ **For all practical purposes** is used to suggest a situation is not exactly as you describe it but the effect is the same. *For all practical purposes the Warsaw Pact has already ceased to exist.* ◇ **to all intents and purposes:** see intent.

purpose-built If something is **purpose-built**, it has been specially designed and built for a particular use. *...the first purpose-built Olympic stadium.*

purposeful (purposefully) You say someone is **purposeful** when they have a definite aim and a strong desire to achieve it. *He strode purposefully into his final round.* Similarly, you say an action is **purposeful** when it is done to achieve a definite aim. *He said he hoped the talks would be comprehensive, purposeful and instrumental in contributing to an elimination of the real cause of tension.*

purposeless If you say something is **purposeless**, you mean it does not seem to have a sensible purpose.

purposely If you do something **purposely**, you do it deliberately.

purr When a cat **purrs**, it makes a low vibrating sound in its throat. ◇ If you talk about a person **purring**, you mean they speak in a soft gentle voice because they are pleased about something. ◇ When an engine or machine **purrs**, it makes a quiet continuous vibrating sound.

purse (pursing, pursed) ❏ A **purse** is an object like a very small bag used, especially by women, to keep money in.
❏ When people talk about the **public purse**, they mean the amount of money a country has available for spending. *The economy was thriving and the public purse appeared bottomless.*
❏ The person who controls the **purse strings** in a particular situation is the one who decides how much money is spent and what it is spent on. If you talk about someone **loosening the purse strings**, you mean they make more money available for spending. Similarly, you can talk about someone **tightening the purse strings**.
❏ The **purse** in a competition or contest, especially a boxing match, is the prize money.
❏ In the US, a handbag is called a **purse**.
❏ If you **purse** your lips, you draw them together to make a small rounded shape.

purser The **purser** on a ship is an officer who deals with the accounts and official papers. On a passenger ship, the **purser** is also responsible for the welfare of the passengers, and is in charge of the stewards.

pursuance of something is attempting to achieve it. If you do something in **pursuance** of a particular aim, you do it as part of attempting to achieve it. *In pursuance of this political goal, great concessions and allowances were made for their relative economic weakness.*

pursuant If something is done **pursuant to** a law or rule, it is done in accordance with it. *The Authority was found guilty of carrying out operations on a Site of Special Scientific Interest without having given notice pursuant to Section 28(5).*

pursue (pursuing, pursued; pursuer, pursuit) ❏ If someone **pursues** you, they follow you, to try to catch you. If people are chasing you or searching for you, you can talk about their **pursuit** of you; you can also call them your **pursuers**. If they are in **hot pursuit**, they are chasing after you in a very determined way.
❏ In cycling, a **pursuit** race is one where the riders set off at intervals along the track and try to overtake each other.
❏ If you **pursue** something, you try to achieve it. You can talk about your **pursuit** of something. *Mexico is eagerly pursuing a free-trade agreement with the United States and Canada... Electricity workers have voted for industrial action in pursuit of a pay claim.* ◇ If you **pursue** something like a plan, you go ahead with it. *The committee is to pursue its enquiry into the Maxwell pension funds.* ◇ When someone stays in the same kind of work, gaining experience and being given more responsibility, you can say they **pursue** a career.
❏ Your **pursuits** are the activities you take part in, especially the ones you do for enjoyment. *Music is often seen as a middle-class pursuit.*
❏ If you **pursue** a topic, you try to find out more about it by asking questions. *The Democrats vowed to pursue the matter when the President returns from his trip.*

purvey (*pron:* **per**-vay) (purveyor) If you **purvey** something like information, you pass it on to people. Someone who does this is called a **purveyor** of information. *He saw the writer as an onlooker and not a purveyor of opinions.* ◇ If someone **purveys** goods or services, they provide them. A **purveyor** of goods or services is a person or company that supplies them.

purview The **purview** of an organization or law is the range of things it deals with. *His abduction was beyond the purview of the court; it was a diplomatic matter.*

pus is a thick yellowish liquid which forms in abscesses and wounds when they are infected.

push (pushes, pushing, pushed; pusher) ❑ If you **push** someone or something or give them a **push**, you press your hand or hands hard against them, to get them to move. ◇ If you **push through** things blocking your way or **push your way** through them, you use force to get through them or past them.

❑ If an army **pushes** into a country it is invading or makes a **push**, it moves further into it. If it is **pushed back**, it is forced to retreat.

❑ If a group of people are **pushed out** of a place, they are forced to leave. Similarly, when someone is forced to leave an organization, you can say they are **pushed out** or **given the push.**

❑ If a value or amount is **pushed** up or down, something causes it to increase or decrease.

❑ If you **push** someone to do something or **push** them into doing it, you urge or force them to do it. *...a mass rally in order to push the government towards faster democratisation.* ◇ If you **push** someone **around,** you give them orders in a bossy way. ◇ If someone or something is **pushed** into a certain situation, they are forced into it. *The recession has pushed many small businesses into liquidation.*

❑ If you **push** for something, you try hard to achieve it, by persuading other people that it is a good idea. *The five permanent members of the UN Security Council have been pushing hard for a Cambodian settlement.* ◇ If you **push** an idea or belief, you try to make people agree with you or support you. ◇ When manufacturers **push** a product, they try to increase its popularity by making it more attractive to people. An attempt like this can be called a **push.** *An autumn marketing push will begin this week.*

❑ If someone **pushes** drugs, they sell them illegally. A person who does this is called a drug **pusher.**

❑ If you **push ahead** with something you are intending to do, you start doing it. If you **push on** with it, you continue with it. *The government pushed on with its health reforms.* ◇ When a government **pushes through** a proposal, it succeeds in getting it accepted, often with difficulty.

❑ If you **push on** in a particular direction, you keep going in that direction. *The rebels say they will push on to the capital.*

❑ You say 'if **push comes to shove...**' when you are describing how people would behave if a situation became really serious. *They know that, should push come to shove, they could destroy the city at an even faster rate.*

❑ **push your luck:** see **luck.**

❑ If you are **pushing** a particular age, you are nearly that age. *I'm pushing forty.*

push bike People sometimes call a bicycle a **push bike.**

push-button A **push-button** machine or process is worked by buttons or switches. *...push-button phones.*

pushchair A **pushchair** is a chair on wheels in which a small child can sit and be wheeled around.

pusher See **push.**

pushiness See **pushy.**

pushover If you say something is a **pushover,** you mean it is easy to do or easy to get. ◇ If you say someone is a **pushover,** you mean they are easy to influence or defeat.

pushy (pushiness) You say someone is **pushy** when they are very forceful about getting what they want, often at other people's expense. *He quickly established himself, as much through pushiness as talent.*

pusillanimous You say someone is **pusillanimous** when they are too timid and scared to take risks.

pussy (pussies) People often call cats **pussies** or **pussy cats.** ◇ If you call a person a **pussy cat,** you mean they are kind and gentle, and could not harm anyone.

pussyfoot (pussyfooting, pussyfooted) If you accuse people of **pussyfooting,** you mean they are behaving too cautiously and are afraid to commit themselves to a course of action.

pustule A **pustule** is a pimple or blister containing pus.

put (putting, put, have put) ❑ If you **put** something in a particular place or position, you move it there. *They put a paper in front of me and told me to sign.* ◇ If you **put** something **away,** you put it into the place where it is normally kept. ◇ If you **put** something **aside,** you keep it to be dealt with or used at a later time.

❑ If you **put on** a piece of clothing, you place it on your body in order to wear it.

❑ If you **put on** something like a television or a light, you turn on the electricity that makes it work. You can also **put off** a device to stop it working.

❑ If you **put on** a CD, record, or tape, you place it on a CD or record player or in a tape machine so you can listen to it. Similarly, if you **put on** a video, you place it in a video player so you can watch it.

❑ If you **put up** a poster or notice, you fix it to a wall or board.

❑ If someone is **put** somewhere, they are made to go there. *The officer was put in jail.*

❑ **stay put:** see **stay.**

❑ If something is **put together,** its different parts are joined to each other to make it whole. *Jaguars are virtually put together by hand.* ◇ If a wall or building is **put up,** it is built.

❑ If the price of something is **put up,** it increases. *The government should put up interest rates.*

❑ If you **put on** weight, you become heavier.

❑ If you **put on** a way of behaving, you behave in a way which is not natural to you or which does not express your real feelings.

❑ If you **put through** a phone call, you make the connection, allowing the caller to speak to the person they are phoning. You also say you **put through** the caller.

❑ If you **put** money or effort **into** something, you spend it that way. *The Vatican demanded that more of the country's money be put into health and education.* ◇ If you **put** money **into** a business or project, you invest in it. ◇ If someone **puts up** the money for something, they provide the money needed to pay for it.

❑ If you **put in** a certain number of hours, that is the

number of hours you work. *British and American workers put in around 1,900 hours a year.*

❑ If a firm **puts out** work, it gives it to other firms or offers it to them. *More companies will put work out to subcontractors.*

❑ If you **put** something **forward,** you ask for it to be considered or chosen for a particular purpose. *Mr Ryzhkov put his name forward for the presidency... He said he would take into account the various views put forward.*

❑ If you **put** a question or suggestion to someone, you ask them the question or make the suggestion to them. ◇ If you **put** your case or point of view, you give your reasons for doing or thinking something. *Many people are refused entry before they can put their case.*

❑ If you **put in** a request for something, you make it in a formal way. ◇ If you **put in** for something, you apply for it. *We'd put in for a rebate.*

❑ When you **put** a remark or idea in a particular way, you express it in that way. *He said a visit to Tokyo could – as he put it – clear the air... The local police, to put it politely, failed to cope.*

❑ If you succeed in **putting** something **across** or **putting** it **over,** you succeed in describing or explaining it to someone. *We have stepped up our presentation a bit, to put over what we offer in a better way.*

❑ If something **puts** you in a particular state or situation, it causes you to be in that state or situation. *...an economic policy that put 1.9 million people out of work... The failure of the share offer has put the company under a severe cashflow strain.* ◇ If you are **put through** an experience, you are made to experience it. *He put me through a series of rigorous exercises to improve my car control.*

❑ If you **put up with** something, you tolerate or accept it, even though you are unhappy about it.

❑ If something **puts** you **off** something, it makes you dislike it. ◇ If you are **put out** by something, you are upset by it.

❑ If you **put** yourself **out** for someone, you do something for them even though it requires a lot of effort or causes you problems. ◇ If you are **put upon,** you are treated badly and advantage is taken of your willingness to help.

❑ If you **put** something **together,** you organize it or arrange it. *Having put together a coalition, the President is now obliged to listen to its views.* ◇ When someone **puts on** a show, exhibition, or service, they perform it, arrange it, or organize it. *I can't understand why British Rail doesn't put on a shuttle service for commuters.*

❑ If you **put out** an announcement, you make it known to a lot of people. *The company is hoping to put out a statement on the loan.*

❑ If someone **puts** you **down,** they criticize you or make you appear silly. A **put-down** is a remark which makes someone appear silly.

❑ If you **put** something **down to** a particular thing, you believe it is caused by that thing. *I thought the sound was muddy and muffled but put it down to the rain.*

❑ If the cost, age, or value of something is **put at** a particular amount, it is estimated to be that amount. *Newspapers put the figure at around 600 million dollars.*

❑ If something is **put back,** it is delayed or postponed. Similarly, if you **put** something **off,** you delay it or postpone it. *Consumers have put off major purchases such as cook-*

ers and refrigerators.

❑ If you **put** a problem **aside,** you deliberately do not think about it and try to forget about it.

❑ If you **put** an end or a stop to something, you prevent it from continuing.

❑ If people **put up** opposition or resistance to something, they oppose it or resist it.

❑ If soldiers, police, or the government **put down** a riot or rebellion, they stop it by using force.

❑ If an animal is **put down,** it is killed humanely because it is very ill or injured.

❑ If you say something is bigger than a number of things **put together,** you mean it is bigger on its own than they are as a group. *The 36 windows are said to contain as much stained glass as all the churches of France put together.*

❑ If you **put out** a fire or cigarette, you make it stop burning.

❑ In sport, if a player or team **puts** another player or team **out** of a contest or tournament, they beat them, and the beaten player or team can no longer take part.

❑ When a ship begins a voyage, you can say it **puts to** sea.

put-down See put.

put-upon See put.

putative (*pron:* **pew**-tat-iv) is used to say someone or something is thought to be a particular thing, but is not definitely that thing. *...putative fathers.*

putrefy (*pron:* **pew**-tri-fie) (putrefies, putrefying, putrefied) If something **putrefies,** it rots and produces a disgusting smell. *...putrefying corpses.*

putrid (*pron:* **pew**-trid) If something is **putrid,** it is rotten and smells disgusting.

putsch A **putsch** is a violent or illegal attempt to overthrow a government.

putt In golf, if you **putt** the ball, you hit it gently when it is near the hole. A stroke like this is called a **putt.**

putter (puttering, puttered) ❑ A **putter** is a type of golf club for putting the ball.

❑ In the US, **puttering about** means the same as pottering about.

putting green A **putting green** is a small golf course on which the grass is kept short, and where there are no obstacles.

putty is a stiff paste used to fix glass panes into frames and to fill cracks or holes in woodwork.

puzzle (puzzling, puzzled; puzzlingly, puzzlement) ❑ If something **puzzles** you or you find it **puzzling,** you do not understand it. You can talk about your **puzzlement** at something like this. *...the puzzlingly weak growth in the service sector... Independent observers have expressed puzzlement over the wide swing in the vote in some constituencies.* ◇ A **puzzle** is something which is hard to understand. *New data from Voyager II has presented astronomers with a puzzle about why our outermost planet exists.*

❑ A **puzzle** is also a question, game, or toy which involves solving a problem of some kind. *...crossword puzzles... ...a jigsaw puzzle.*

❑ If you **puzzle over** something, you try to think of the answer or explanation for it. If you **puzzle** it **out,** you succeed in finding the answer.

PVC is a plastic material used for making things such as clothing, pipes, and tiles. PVC is short for 'polyvinyl chloride'.

pygmy (pygmies) (*or* pigmy, pigmies) Pygmy is used to describe the smallest of a group of related things. ...*pygmy chimpanzees.* ◇ A **pygmy** is a very small person, especially one who belongs to a racial group in which all the people are small.

pyjamas (*American spelling:* pajamas) Pyjamas are loose trousers and a jacket or top worn in bed, especially by men.

pylon A pylon is a tall metal structure for carrying overhead electric cables.

pyramid (pyramidal) ❑ A **pyramid** is a three-dimensional shape with a flat bottom and flat triangular sides sloping upwards to a point. ◇ The Pyramids are ancient pyramid-shaped stone structures built over the tombs of Egyptian kings and queens.

❑ **Pyramid** is used to talk about a system which is arranged in layers, with lower-ranking people or things at the bottom and higher-ranking people or things above. The higher layers get progressively smaller, ending up with the person in charge or the most important thing at the top. **Pyramidal** is used to describe a system like this. *He joined the organization only ten years ago, and has climbed the party pyramid with startling speed.*

❑ **Pyramid** selling is a dishonest method of selling goods which is illegal in the UK. Manufacturers sell their goods to distributors, who then sell batches of these goods at an increased price to further distributors. The process continues until the final distributors are left with stock they can only sell at a loss.

pyre A pyre is a high pile of wood for ceremonially burning dead bodies or a religious offering. ...*a funeral pyre.*

Pyrex is a type of glass which can withstand oven temperatures and is used for making dishes. 'Pyrex' is a trademark.

pyromaniac (pyromania) A **pyromaniac** is someone who gets uncontrollable urges to set fire to things. This condition is called **pyromania.**

pyrotechnics (pyrotechnic) Pyrotechnics is the making or display of fireworks. **Pyrotechnic** is used to talk about things to do with fireworks. ◇ **Pyrotechnics** is sometimes used to talk about a brilliant display of skill. *She does not go in for vocal pyrotechnics.*

Pyrrhic If you call a result a Pyrrhic victory, you mean that, although someone has won or gained something, it was not worth the losses they have suffered or the sacrifices they have made.

python Pythons are snakes which kill their prey by squeezing it. Most pythons live in trees. Some of them are very large.

pzazz See pizzazz.

Q q

QC A QC is a senior British barrister. QC stands for 'Queen's Counsel'. ...*Barbara Mills, QC.*

QED In maths, you write QED at the end of a proof. People sometimes say 'QED' when they think they have just shown logically that something must be true.

quack ❑ A quack is the sound a duck makes. When it makes this noise, you say it **quacks.**

❑ A **quack** or **quack doctor** is someone who claims dishonestly to be able to cure people of their illnesses.

quad See (a) quadrangle. (b) quadruplet.

quadrangle A quadrangle or quad is a courtyard with buildings all round it, especially at a school or college.

quadrant A quadrant is a quarter of a circle.

quadrilateral A quadrilateral is any shape with four straight sides.

quadrille (*pron:* kwod-reel) The quadrille was a dance for four couples, popular in the 18th and 19th centuries.

quadripartite A quadripartite organization or agreement involves four people or groups.

quadriplegic (*pron:* kwod-ri-pleej-ik) (quadriplegia) If someone is **quadriplegic** or a **quadriplegic**, they are paralysed in their body and in their arms and legs, usually because they have broken their neck. This condition is called **quadriplegia.** See also **paraplegic.**

quadruped A quadruped is any animal with four legs.

quadruple (quadrupling, quadrupled) When an amount or number **quadruples**, it becomes four times as large.

quadruplet Quadruplets or quads are four children born to the same mother at the same time.

quaff (*pron:* kwoff) If someone regularly drinks the same alcoholic drink, you can talk about them **quaffing** it. *He would quaff pints with colleagues.*

quagmire A quagmire is a soft wet area of land which you sink into if you try to walk on it. ◇ A **quagmire** is also a complicated situation which it is difficult to get out of.

quail (quailing, quailed) ❑ Quails are small game birds with round bodies and short tails.

❑ If someone **quails**, they are alarmed at something they hear.

quaint (quaintly; quaintness) If you say something is **quaint**, you mean it is attractively old-fashioned or unusual. *Here are bookshops and what are quaintly termed 'gents outfitters'... ...the quaintness of the rural north.*

quake (quaking, quaked) ❑ An earthquake is sometimes called a **quake.**

❑ If you talk about a person **quaking**, you mean they are very frightened or concerned about something which may happen to them.

Quaker Quakers are members of a Christian group, the Religious Society of Friends. They have 'meetings' rather than services, and they do not have priests or use prayer books. Their meetings are mainly silent, though anyone can speak if they feel inspired to. Quakers are pacifists.

qualify (qualifies, qualifying, qualified; qualification, qualifier) ❑ When someone **qualifies**, they pass the exams they need for a particular job. *...a qualified teacher... Even after qualification, jobs were hard to find.* An examination pass which helps you in your career is called a **qualification**.

❑ If you are **qualified** to do something, you have the qualities, knowledge, or skills necessary for it.

❑ If you **qualify** for something like a grant, you are entitled to it.

❑ If you **qualify** in a competition, you are successful in an early round and go on to the next one. People or teams who do this are called **qualifiers**. *The women's eight missed qualification by a length.* The early rounds of a competition are sometimes called **qualifying** rounds or **qualifiers**.

❑ If you **qualify** something you have said, you add something which makes it less strong or less general.

❑ **Qualified** is used to say something is not complete. For example, if you give **qualified** agreement to something, you agree to it, but make some exceptions or conditions. If something is a **qualified** success, it is not a complete success.

qualitative is used to talk about things to do with quality. For example, if you talk about a **qualitative** change in something, you mean its quality has improved or declined.

quality (qualities) ❑ The **quality** of something is how good or bad it is. *The singing was of extremely high quality.* ◇ **Quality** goods and services are of a high standard. High standards in general are sometimes called **quality**. *The 1980s were the decade of quality.*

❑ **Quality control** in a factory is a process in which products are checked, to make sure they are satisfactory before they are sent out to be sold.

❑ Your **quality of life** is the extent to which you are able to enjoy yourself and do interesting things in healthy surroundings.

❑ A person's or thing's **qualities** are their good characteristics.

❑ The **quality** press or **qualities** are the larger, more serious newspapers.

qualm If you have **qualms** about what you are doing, you are worried that it may not be right or safe.

quandary (quandaries) If you are in a **quandary**, you cannot decide what to do.

quango (quangos) A **quango** is any partly independent official organization or committee set up by the government.

quantifiable If something is **quantifiable**, it can be expressed as a number or amount.

quantify (quantifies; quantifying, quantified) If you **quantify** something, you express it as a number or amount. *They required the Forest Service to quantify the water needs of Colorado's current wilderness areas.*

quantitative is used to talk about the size or amount of something. For example, if you say there has been a **quantitative** change in something, you mean there is more of it, or less. *From next week quantitative limits on imports are to be removed.*

quantity (quantities) ❑ A **quantity** of something is an amount of it. *...a small quantity of explosives.* ◇ The **quantity** of something is the amount there is. *The qual-*

ity of investment matters more than the quantity. ◇ If something is present **in quantity**, there is a lot of it.

❑ If you say someone or something is an **unknown quantity**, you mean you do not know much about them or how they will behave.

quantity surveyor A **quantity surveyor** is someone whose job is to estimate how much new building works will cost.

quantum ❑ A **quantum leap** is a very great advance or increase. *...a quantum leap in the rate of prison suicide.*

❑ **Quantum** is used to talk about things to do with the properties and behaviour of atomic particles. *...quantum mechanics... ...quantum theory.*

quarantine (quarantining, quarantined) If a person or animal is **quarantined** or kept in **quarantine**, they are kept separate from other people or animals, in case they have an infectious disease.

quark Quarks are very tiny particles which neutrons and protons are thought to consist of. Each neutron or proton is thought to consist of three quarks.

quarrel (quarrelling, quarrelled) (*American spelling:* quarreling, quarreled) ❑ If you **quarrel** with someone you know well or have a **quarrel** with them, you have an angry argument with them and are on bad terms with them for some time.

❑ If you say you have **no quarrel** with what someone is doing, you mean you do not object to it.

quarrelsome people are always quarrelling.

quarry (quarries, quarrying, quarried) ❑ When stone is **quarried**, it is dug or blasted out of the ground in large quantities. A **quarry** is a place where this is done.

❑ If someone is hunting an animal or group of animals, you can say the animal or group is their **quarry**. Similarly, if someone like a police officer is trying to find and catch someone, you can say the person they are looking for is their **quarry**.

quart The amount of liquid in a container is sometimes expressed in **quarts**. In Britain, a quart is two pints (about 1.136 litres). A US quart is about 0.946 litres. 'Quarts' is usually written 'qt'.

quarter (quarterly) ❑ A **quarter** is one of four equal parts of something. ◇ A **quarter** or **one quarter** is also the fraction $\frac{1}{4}$.

❑ A **quarter** is also a period of three months. If something happens **quarterly**, it happens every three months.

❑ In the US, a **quarter** is a coin worth 25 cents.

❑ In a city, a **quarter** is an area where a particular group of people live or work. *...the mainly Christian quarter of East Jerusalem.*

❑ A soldier's or servant's **quarters** is the house or set of rooms where he or she lives.

❑ If you talk about feelings or reactions from a certain **quarter**, you mean the feelings or reactions of a group of people. *The team selection had been greeted by mirth in some quarters.*

❑ If you see someone or something **at close quarters**, you are close enough to see them very clearly.

quarter-final (quarter-finalist) A **quarter-final** is one of the four games, matches, or races in a competition which decide who will take part in the semi-finals. The people or teams taking part in a quarter-final are called **quarter-finalists**.

quarterback In American football, a **quarterback** is a player who tells the other players in his team how and where to direct their attack.

quartermaster In the army, a **quartermaster** is an officer responsible for housing, food, and equipment.

quartet Music written for four musicians is called a **quartet**. A **quartet** is also a group of four people who do things together, especially four people who sing or play music together.

quartz is a hard shiny mineral. It is usually colourless. Its crystals are used in making electronic equipment and clocks and watches.

quasar (*pron*: **kway**-zar) **Quasars** are star-like objects in distant outer space which produce very bright light and other forms of energy.

quash (quashes, quashing, quashed) If a decision or criminal conviction is **quashed**, it is overturned and made no longer legally valid. ◇ If you **quash** something like a rumour, you put an end to it. ◇ If something like an uprising is **quashed**, it is put down by force.

quasi- (*pron*: **kwaze**-eye) is used in front of a word to say something has many of the features of the thing described by that word. ...*quasi-military rule*... *Georgia has about 100 parties or quasi-parties.*

quaver (quavering, quavered) ❏ A **quaver** is a musical note with the same time value as two semiquavers or half a crotchet.
❏ If your voice **quavers**, it is unsteady, because you feel nervous or emotional.

quay (*pron*: **kee**) A **quay** is a long platform built beside the sea or a river, where boats can tie up and be loaded and unloaded.

quayside The **quayside** is the area next to a quay.

queasy (queasier, queasiest; queasiness) If you feel **queasy**, (a) you feel as though you are going to be sick. (b) you are uneasy and worried about something. ...*a gamble needing firm leadership and no queasiness.*

queen ❏ The **queen** of a country is the female member of its royal family who is the head of state. ◇ The wife or widow of a king is also called a **queen.**
❏ A woman is sometimes called the **queen** of something when she is better or more successful at it than any other woman. ...*the undisputed queen of archery.*
❏ A **queen** bee or ant is a very large female. She is the only one in the hive or nest who can lay eggs.
❏ The **queen** is a piece in chess. Each player has just one queen. The queen is a valuable piece to capture, because it can move in any direction.
❏ A **queen** is also a playing card with a picture of a queen on it.

Queen's Counsel See QC.

Queen's Speech The **Queen's Speech** is a speech which the Queen reads at the beginning of a session of Parliament. It is written by the government and gives a summary of their policies and the Bills they propose to introduce.

queer (queerest) ❏ If you say something is **queer**, you mean it is strange or peculiar.
❏ If you say a man is **queer**, you mean he is homosexual. A **queer** is a homosexual man. This use of 'queer' is generally considered to be offensive, but some homosexual men use it to talk about themselves.

quell If someone in power **quells** opposition or an uprising, they put an end to it using force. ◇ If someone **quells** something harmful, they succeed in stopping it.

quench (quenches, quenching, quenched) If you **quench** your thirst, you drink something and no longer feel thirsty. ◇ If you **quench** a fire, you put it out. ◇ If something **quenches** people's feelings, it makes them disappear. *Nothing can quench the high spirits of the cast.*

querulous (*pron*: **kwer**-yoo-luss) A **querulous** person is always complaining.

query (queries, querying, queried) A **query** is a question about a particular aspect of something. *He has agreed to answer all your queries on the legal problems which will arise.* ◇ If you **query** something, you ask if it is correct or you express doubt about it. ◇ **Query** is sometimes used to say someone asks a question. '*Gascoigne is a very well-known footballer,*' *he replied. The judge queried:* '*Rugby or association football?*'

quest (questing) A **quest** is a long and difficult search for something. If you are **in quest of** something, you are trying to find it or achieve it. ◇ **Questing** is used to describe people who are searching for something, especially something like wisdom or understanding. ...*a questing young intellectual.*

question (questioning, questioned; questioner) ❏ If you ask a **question**, you ask someone to tell you something you want to know. The person who is asking a question can be called the **questioner**. ◇ If you **question** someone, you try to get some information from them by asking them questions. ◇ In an exam, a **question** is a problem set to test your knowledge or ability.
❏ **Question** is used to talk about what really counts in a situation. *What's at stake here is a question of power.*
❏ The person or thing **in question** is the one you have just mentioned.
❏ If you **question** something, you express doubts about whether it is genuine, reasonable, or worthwhile. *The Community has questioned the commitment of the United States to international trade agreements.* Similarly, if you **call** something **into question**, you express serious doubts about it.
❏ If you talk about something being **in question**, you mean there is doubt about whether it will happen or continue. *Italy's participation is also in question.* ◇ If you say something **comes into question** or is **brought into question**, you mean doubts are raised about its value or usefulness. *His leadership is increasingly coming into question.*
❏ If you say something is **open to question**, you mean it is not certain and people may disagree about it. ◇ If you say there is **no question** about something, you mean it is obvious and cannot be doubted. Similarly, you can say something is **beyond question** or is true **without question**. *Ours is without question the best league in the world.*
❏ If you say there is **no question** of something happening, you are saying emphatically that it will not happen. *There was no question of him resigning, he said.* Similarly, you can say something is **out of the question.**
❏ If you say a statement **begs the question**, you mean it assumes something is true, when there are no real grounds for assuming it is true at all.
❏ If you obey an instruction **without question**, you do

it without arguing about it or asking whether it is necessary.

❑ If you say something is **another question**, you mean it is a separate matter from the one you have been talking about.

question mark ❑ A **question mark** is the punctuation mark ? which you write after a question.

❑ If you say there is a **question mark** over something, you mean there is some doubt or uncertainty about it.

question time is a period of time in both Houses of Parliament when ministers, especially the Prime Minister, answer members' questions.

questionable If you say something is **questionable**, you mean it is not at all certain that it is true or correct. ◇ You also use **questionable** to describe things people do which may be improper or illegal. *He has been dogged by allegations of questionable business practices.*

questionnaire A **questionnaire** is a written list of questions you are asked to answer, to provide information for a report or survey.

queue (queuing *or* queueing, queued) ❑ A **queue** is a line of people or vehicles, one behind the other, waiting for something. When people form a line like this, you say they are **queuing** or **queuing up**.

❑ If you say people are **queuing up** to do something, you mean there are a lot of them eagerly waiting to do it. *Chinese banks were queuing to join the scheme.*

quibble (quibbling, quibbled) A **quibble** is a small objection to something. If someone keeps making small objections, you say they are **quibbling**.

quiche (*pron:* keesh) A **quiche** is a pastry case filled with a savoury mixture of eggs and things like cheese or onion. Quiches can be eaten hot or cold.

quick (quickly, quickness) ❑ **Quick** is used to describe things which take or last a very short time. *...a quick drink after work... Bank machines quickly ran out of money.* ◇ **Quick** is also used to describe (a) people and things that move at speed. *...a car which was not as quick as Prost's Ferrari... ...games aimed at developing quickness and skill.* (b) things being done at speed. *The women worked quickly... He is so quick with his fingers.* ◇ If you say someone is **quick** to do something, you mean they do it very soon after something else, and in response to it. *Readers have been quick to write in with their opinions on the revived Swansea to Cork ferry service.*

❑ The **quick** on your fingernails or toenails is the area around the edge where the nail joins the finger or toe.

quick-fire is used to describe something which involves several things happening quickly, one after another. *...his quick-fire repartee.*

quick-fix A **quick-fix** solution to a problem works in the short term but is unlikely to last for long.

quick-tempered people get angry very easily.

quick-witted people are able to think quickly and do the right thing in difficult or dangerous situations.

quicken (quickening, quickened) If something **quickens**, it gets quicker. *...the recent quickening of the peace process.*

quicksand is deep wet sand you sink into when you try and walk on it.

quicksilver is used to describe people who are very quick and agile. *...the quicksilver young forward.*

❑ **Quicksilver** is also an old word for mercury.

quid (*plural:* quid) A pound is sometimes called a **quid**. *...twenty quid.*

quid pro quo A **quid pro quo** is something you agree to give someone, to get them to do what you want. *It isn't clear what quid pro quo the kidnappers want.*

quiescent (*pron:* kwee-ess-ent) (quiescence) You say people are **quiescent** when they calmly go about their business without demanding changes or causing problems for anyone in authority. *They marvelled at their low labour costs and the quiescence of the workforces.*

quiet (quieter, quietest; quietly, quietness) ❑ **Quiet** people or things make very little noise. *Mr Zardari sat quietly and uneasily in the courtroom.* ◇ A **quiet** place is one where there is very little noise. *...the quietness of the countryside.* ◇ **Quiet** is also used to say there is not much activity in a place. *The high streets have been quiet this year.*

❑ A **quiet** life is a peaceful one, with nothing to upset or disturb you. *For five years he lived quietly in Eberswalde.*

❑ If an event passes off **quietly**, there are no interruptions or disturbances.

❑ If you **keep quiet** about something you have seen or heard, you do not tell anyone about it.

❑ **Quiet** is used to describe feelings people have but keep to themselves. *The British government is quietly furious at Washington's veto.* ◇ **Quiet** is also used to describe things which are done without attention being drawn to them. *He worked quietly away at measures to revive Scottish industry.* ◇ If someone does something **on the quiet**, they do it secretly.

quieten (quietening, quietened) ❑ If you **quieten** someone's fears, you do something to make them less worried or afraid. ◇ If you **quieten** someone's protests or complaints, you provide them with something which stops them protesting or complaining.

❑ If a place **quietens** or **quietens down**, things become quiet after there has been a lot of noise or trouble.

quietist A **quietist** approach to life involves calmly accepting what happens and not trying to change things.

quiff If a man has a **quiff**, he has long hair at the front which crosses his forehead in a curve.

quill A bird's **quills** are the large stiff feathers on its wings and tail. A **quill** is a pen made from one of these feathers. ◇ A porcupine's or hedgehog's **quills** are the long sharp spines on its back.

quilt A **quilt** is a bed covering filled with feathers or some other warm soft material.

quilted clothes or coverings are made up of two layers of fabric with a layer of soft thick material between them. The layers are held together and decorated by lines of stitching. *...a quilted jacket.*

quin See quintuplet.

quince Quinces are sour-tasting fruit used for making jam and marmalade.

quinine (*pron:* kwin-neen) is a drug sometimes used to treat leg cramps and malaria.

quintessential (quintessentially, quintessence) Quintessential is used to describe someone or something that seems to sum up what is most typical of a place, or of a kind of person or thing. *For many people, computers were the quintessential industry of tomorrow... Mars bars are one of the few things that are quintessentially British, like HP Sauce and Birds Eye.* You say someone or something like this is the **quintessence** of the place, person, or thing.

quintet Music written for five musicians is called a **quintet**. A **quintet** is also a group of five people who do things together, especially five people who sing or play music together.

quintuple (quintupling, quintupled) When an amount or number **quintuples**, it becomes five times as large.

quintuplet **Quintuplets** or **quins** are five children born to the same mother at the same time.

quip (quipping, quipped) If someone **quips** or makes a **quip**, they make a clever amusing remark.

quirk A **quirk** is something strange that happens by chance. *By a tantalising quirk of fate, the pair have been drawn to meet in the first round of the Cup.* ◇ A **quirk** is also an odd or unusual habit or characteristic. *Every hotel has been briefed on the fads and quirks of its distinguished guests.*

quirky (quirkier, quirkiest; quirkily, quirkiness) If you call something or someone **quirky**, you mean their behaviour, character, or appearance is odd or unusual. *...a quirkily brilliant play... You will probably notice an element of quirkiness in his behaviour.*

quisling A **quisling** is a traitor who helps an enemy that is occupying his or her country.

quit (quitting, quit *not* 'quitted') If you **quit** your job or **quit**, you resign. ◇ If you **quit** doing something, you stop doing it. ◇ If you **quit** a place, you leave it.

quite is used to say someone or something has a quality or characteristic to some extent. *Bangor is quite small... In the United States small specialised bookshops survive quite well.* ◇ In front of words like 'certain' and 'different', **quite** means 'completely'. *I am quite sure that there's absolutely no truth in it.* **Not quite** means 'not completely'. *I am not quite ready.* ◇ **Not quite** is also used to express polite disagreement. *Actually, that is not quite true.*

❏ **Quite** is used with 'a' or 'an' to emphasize how big something is. *It was quite a blunder.* ◇ If you say something is **quite something**, you mean you are very impressed by it. *To build your way out of the worst housing market for 50 years at a profit is quite something.*

❏ **Quite** is used in front of words like 'how' and 'who' to mean 'exactly'. *Quite how popular Latin could become is an interesting question.*

quitter You call someone a **quitter** when you think they are giving up too easily.

quiver (quivering, quivered) ❏ A **quiver** is a slight trembling movement. When something **quivers**, it moves like this. ◇ If a person **quivers**, they tremble slightly, because they are experiencing a strong emotion. You can also say a part of someone's body **quivers**. *His lower lip quivered.* ◇ If you say someone is **quivering** with anger or rage, you mean they are very angry indeed.

❏ A **quiver** is a container for carrying arrows.

quixotic (*pron:* kwik-sot-ik) You call someone's behaviour **quixotic** when they keep trying to achieve something good or worthwhile without any serious hope of success.

quiz (quizzes, quizzing, quizzed) A **quiz** is a game or competition in which people are asked questions which test their knowledge. ◇ If you are **quizzed** about something, you are asked questions about it.

quizzical If someone's expression is **quizzical**, it is slightly mocking and suggests they know more about something than has actually been mentioned. You can also say someone gives you a **quizzical** look.

quoits (*pron:* koyts) is a game in which people try to throw rings over a small post.

quorum A **quorum** is the minimum number of members of an organization, group, or committee that must be present before a meeting can begin.

quota A **quota** is the number or quantity of people or things allowed or required in a particular situation. *His company has benefited from import quotas for cane sugar from poor countries.*

quotable A **quotable** phrase in a speech or piece of writing is one which can be quoted afterwards. *His speeches will contain carefully designed six-second quotable slogans.*

quotation ❏ A **quotation** is a passage or phrase from a book, poem, or play, especially one used to support a point or argument.

❏ If someone gives you a **quotation**, they tell you their price for doing a piece of work or some kind of service.

quotation marks are the punctuation marks ' ' or " " used to show where speech or a quotation begins and ends.

quote (quoting, quoted) ❏ A **quote** from a book, poem, play, or speech is a passage or phrase from it.

❏ If you **quote** someone or **quote** what they have said or written, you repeat the exact words they used.

❏ If you **quote** something like an example or a fact, you mention it, because it supports what you are saying.

❏ If someone **quotes** you for a piece of work or gives you a **quote** for it, they tell you how much they will charge you for it. Similarly, if a stock market trader **quotes** a price or gives you a **quote**, he or she tells you the current value of something like a share.

❏ A **quoted** company is one whose shares can be bought and sold on the stock market.

quotient (*pron:* kwoh-shent) is used to say how much of something a person or thing has. *The bullshit quotient of the summit communique was high even by the usual standards.* ◇ In arithmetic, a **quotient** is the number you get when you divide one number into another.

Qur'an (Qur'anic) The **Qur'an** is the Koran. **Qur'anic** means 'Koranic'.

R r

R See three Rs.

RA after an artist's name means he or she is a member of the Royal Academy of Arts. RA stands for 'Royal Academician'.

rabbi (*pron:* **rab**-bye) (rabbinic, rabbinical) A **rabbi** is a Jewish religious teacher, often the leader of a congregation. **Rabbinic** (*pron:* rab-**bin**-ik) and **rabbinical** are used to talk about things involving rabbis. *...the rabbinic tradition... ...a rabbinical court.*

rabbit Rabbits are small furry animals with long ears. They are kept as pets or live in the wild in burrows.

rabble A crowd of noisy disorderly people can be called a rabble.

rabble-rouser (rabble-rousing) If you call a speaker a **rabble-rouser,** you mean he or she is good at stirring up anger or violence. *...Mr Le Pen's rabble-rousing methods.*

rabid (*pron:* **rab**-bid *or* **ray**-bid) (rabidly) A **rabid** animal is infected with rabies. ◇ **Rabid** is also used to describe people whose views or behaviour are considered to be extreme and unreasonable. *He wrote on history and politics in a rabidly reactionary manner.*

rabies (*pron:* **ray**-beez) is a serious infectious disease which causes people and animals to go mad and die. It is usually caused by a bite from an infected animal.

RAC The **RAC** is a British motoring organization which helps members when their cars break down. RAC stands for 'Royal Automobile Club'.

raccoon (*or* racoon) The **raccoon** is a small animal in North and South America. Raccoons have long grey fur, patches round their eyes, and long striped tails. They eat meat and fish.

race (racing, raced) ❑ A **race** is one of the groups which humans are sometimes divided into according to physical characteristics like skin colour. *The Olympic charter outlaws discrimination on the grounds of race, religion or politics.* ◇ See also **human race.**
❑ A **race** is also a competition to see who is the fastest at something such as running or driving. When you **race,** you take part in a competition like this. ◇ Any situation in which people are competing eagerly for something can be called a **race.** *...the race for the party leadership.*
❑ If you **race** somewhere, you go there very quickly. *Ambulances raced down the streets carrying the injured to hospitals.* ◇ If something is **racing** ahead, it is going ahead very quickly. *The tunnel-building is now racing ahead.* ◇ A **race against time** is a situation in which you have to work very hard to get something done before a certain time.

race meeting A **race meeting** is an occasion when a series of horse races are held at the same racecourse, often over a period of several days.

racecourse A **racecourse** is a track where horses race.

racegoer People who go to a racecourse to watch horseracing are called **racegoers.**

racehorse A **racehorse** is a horse bred and trained to be ridden in races.

racer Anyone who takes part in races can be called a **racer.** *...a famous Welsh motorcycle racer.* ◇ A **racer** is also a

bicycle, car, or boat designed for racing.

racetrack A **racetrack** is a track for races, especially car or cycle races. In the US, a racecourse is usually called a racetrack.

racial (racially) **Racial** is used to talk about things involving race. *...racial segregation... ...racially motivated attacks.*

racialism (racialist) **Racialism** is the same as racism. A **racialist** is a racist.

racism (racist) **Racism** is believing that people of some races are inferior to others, and treating them differently because of this. **Racist** is used to describe beliefs and behaviour like this. *...racist attacks.* A **racist** is a person who holds racist beliefs.

rack ❑ A **rack** is a piece of equipment, usually with bars, hooks, or pegs, for holding things or hanging things on. *...a wine rack.*
❑ The **rack** was a piece of equipment used in the past to torture people. The victim's wrists and ankles were tied to it, then pulled in opposite directions, stretching them and causing great pain. ◇ Nowadays, when people say someone is **on the rack,** they mean they are in a very worrying or unhappy situation. ◇ If someone is **racked** or **wracked** by something unpleasant, they are suffering or in great pain because of it. *Angola is a nation that has been racked by war for the last three decades.*
❑ If you **rack up** a large amount of something, you build it up over a period of time. *They racked up losses of over $1 billion.*

racket ❑ A **racket** or **racquet** is a bat consisting of nylon strings stretched across a frame with a handle. Rackets of various kinds are used in games like tennis, badminton, and squash.
❑ An illegal way of making money can be called a **racket.** *...a protection racket... ...a drugs racket.*
❑ A loud unpleasant noise can also be called a **racket.**

racketball (*or* racquetball) is a fast indoor game similar to handball but using short-handled rackets.

racketeer (racketeering) A **racketeer** is someone who makes money illegally, especially by running operations involving extortion, smuggling, or drugs. Making money like this is called **racketeering.**

raconteur (*pron:* rak-on-**tur**) If you say someone is a good **raconteur,** you mean they can tell stories and anecdotes in an interesting or amusing way.

racoon See raccoon.

racquet See racket.

racquetball See racketball.

racy (racier, raciest) If you say something is **racy,** you mean it is lively, exciting, and slightly shocking. *...racy bestsellers.*

radar is a system by which radio signals are used to track the position and speed of objects like ships and aircraft when they cannot be seen. 'Radar' stands for 'radio detecting and ranging'.

raddled If you describe someone as **raddled,** you mean they have lost their good looks as a result of old age and leading a debauched life.

radial is used to describe things which form a pattern like straight lines spreading out from the centre of a circle.

radiant (radiantly, radiance) ❏ If someone is **radiant**, they look bright and happy. ...*a radiant smile*... ...*an intensely lovable man, generous, natural and radiantly vital.* You can talk about the **radiance** of someone like this.
    ❏ A **radiant** light shines brightly.

radiate (radiating, radiated) ❏ If things **radiate** from a place, they form a pattern like straight lines spreading outwards from the centre of a circle.
    ❏ If something **radiates** heat or light, it gives it off.
    ❏ If someone **radiates** a quality, they have it in a very obvious way. *She radiated love, warmth and generosity.*

radiation is particles of radioactive material. ...*the risk of developing a fatal cancer from radiation exposure.* ◇ **Radiation** is also the giving off of energy in the form of electromagnetic waves such as X-rays, infra-red rays, or ultra-violet rays.

radiation sickness is an illness caused by exposure to high levels of radiation. In the most severe cases, the person affected can die within a few days. Less severe cases can result in cancers and birth defects. Low doses can cause nausea and loss of appetite.

radiator A **radiator** is a hollow metal device for heating a room. It is connected to a central heating system, and gives out heat when hot water or steam passes through it. ◇ The **radiator** in a car is a device for cooling the engine.

radical (radicalism, radically) A **radical** or someone with **radical** beliefs is a person who thinks there should be major changes in a political or social system, and tries to bring these changes about. **Radicalism** is the beliefs and behaviour of someone like this. ...*radical feminism.* ◇ **Radical** is used to describe things which involve the most basic aspects of something. ...*a radical change in the law*... ...*radically different opinions.*

radicalize (radicalizing, radicalized) (*can be spelled with an 's' instead of a 'z'*) If a group of people are **radicalized**, they start to have radical opinions.

radii See **radius**.

radio (radios, radioing, radioed) **Radio** is the broadcasting of programmes for the public to listen to by sending out signals from a transmitter. A **radio** is a device for listening to these signals. ◇ **Radio** is used to talk about other systems which involve transmitting sound using electrical signals. ...*police radio messages.* A **radio** is a device which sends and receives these signals. If you **radio** someone, you contact them using a radio.

radio-controlled If something is **radio-controlled**, it is operated from a distance using radio signals. ...*a radio-controlled model boat.*

radio telephone A **radio telephone** is a telephone which sends out and picks up sound using radio signals rather than wires. Radio telephones are often used in cars.

radio telescope A **radio telescope** is a huge dish-shaped device which receives radio waves from space, enabling it to find the positions of stars and other objects.

radioactive (radioactivity) If something is **radioactive**, it contains a substance which produces energy in the form of rays or particles which are harmful in high doses, although they can be used to medical benefit in controlled conditions. This energy is called **radioactivity**.

radiocarbon dating is the same as carbon dating.

radiographer (*pron: ray-dee-og-raf-fer*) A **radiographer** is a person trained to take X-rays.

radiology (*pron: ray-dee-ol-a-jee*) (radiologist) is the branch of medical science which uses X-rays and other forms of radiation. A **radiologist** is a doctor trained in radiology.

radiotherapy is the treatment of diseases, especially cancer, using radiation.

radish (radishes) **Radishes** are small red and white root vegetables which are eaten raw in salads.

radium is a highly radioactive element, formerly used in the treatment of cancer.

radius (*plural:* radii) ❏ The **radius** of a circle is the distance from its centre to its outside edge. ◇ If you talk about the area within a certain **radius** of a place, you mean all the area which is not more than that distance from it.
    ❏ The **radius** is the slightly shorter of the two bones in the human forearm, extending from the elbow to the wrist.

radon is a radioactive gas formed by the disintegration of radium.

RAF The **RAF** or **Royal Air Force** is the air force of the UK.

raffia is a strawlike fibre made from palm leaves. It is used to make mats and baskets.

raffish If you describe someone as **raffish**, you mean their appearance and behaviour are not conventional or respectable, but you find them rather stylish and likeable.

raffle A **raffle** is a competition in which you buy numbered tickets. A few tickets are randomly chosen and if one of them is yours, you win a prize.

raft (rafting) A **raft** is a floating platform, usually made of wood, used as a boat or a landing place for swimmers. ◇ A **raft** is also a fairly large inflatable boat. If you go **rafting**, you travel down a river on a boat like this.

rafters are the sloping pieces of wood which support a roof.

rag ❏ A **rag** is a piece of old cloth which you can use, for example, to clean or wipe things. ◇ If someone is dressed in **rags**, their clothes are old and torn.
    ❏ When people are talking about a newspaper which they do not like, they sometimes call it a **rag**.
    ❏ If something is a **red rag** to you, it makes you angry.

rag-and-bone man A **rag-and-bone man** is a man who goes from street to street with a lorry, van, or horse and cart asking for things like old clothes and furniture and makes money by selling them.

rag doll A **rag doll** is a soft doll made from pieces of cloth.

rag trade The business of making and selling clothes is sometimes called the **rag trade**.

ragbag A **ragbag** is an unusual collection of things which do not have much in common. *The opposition is a ragbag of right-wing liberals, Flemish nationalists and greens.*

rage (raging, raged) ❏ **Rage** is a strong feeling of anger which is difficult to control. If you **rage** about something, you speak angrily about it. ◇ **Raging** is used to describe unpleasant feelings which are persistent and powerful. ...*raging disaffection*... ...*a raging hangover.*
    ❏ If something like a storm, a fire, or an argument **rages**, it goes on with great force or violence.

❑ If something is **all the rage,** it is popular or fashionable.

ragga is a type of pop music originating in Jamaica which combines aspects of reggae and rap.

ragged (*pron:* rag-gid) If you say a performance by a group of people is **ragged,** you mean the performers do not always keep together. ◇ If someone is **ragged,** their clothes are torn and dirty.

ragout (*pron:* rag-goo) is a richly seasoned stew.

rags-to-riches A **rags-to-riches** story involves someone starting life in poverty and then going on to becoming rich and successful.

ragtime is a type of music which was popular in the 1920s. It was usually played on a solo piano. 'The Entertainer' by Scott Joplin is a famous ragtime piece.

raid (raiding, raided) When soldiers, police, or criminals **raid** a place, they make a sudden quick attack on it, or enter it by force to look for someone or something. An attack or search like this is called a **raid.**

raider ❑ A **raider** is someone who takes part in a raid. *Armed raiders have shot and killed a sub-postmaster in East London.*

❑ A **raider** is also a person or organization that suddenly buys a large number of shares in a company, before making a takeover bid.

rail (railing, railed) ❑ **Rail** is used to talk about transport by train. *...rail traffic... More goods went by water than by rail.* The steel bars which trains run on are called **rails.**

❑ If you say something is **on the rails,** you mean it is going as planned. *The ANC is keen to get the negotiating process back on the rails.* If something is **off the rails,** it is going wrong, or it is no longer going ahead. ◇ If someone goes **off the rails,** they start behaving in a foolish or unacceptable way.

❑ A **rail** is a horizontal bar used as part of a fence, as a support, or for hanging things on.

❑ If you **rail** against someone or something, you complain loudly and bitterly about them.

railcard A **railcard** is an identity card which allows its owner to buy train tickets at a lower price than usual.

railing A fence made from metal bars can be called **railings** or a **railing.**

railroad (railroading, railroaded) **Railroad** is the usual American word for a railway. ◇ If someone is **railroaded** into something, they are hurried into doing it using unfair pressure. ◇ If a law or plan is **railroaded** through, it is passed or carried out quickly without proper discussion and in spite of strong opposition.

railway A **railway** or **railway line** is a route along which trains travel. The steel rails on which the trains run can be called **railway tracks** or **railway lines.**

railwayman (railwaymen) **Railwaymen** are people such as engine drivers, guards, and signalmen who work on a railway.

rain (raining, rained) ❑ **Rain** is water which falls from the clouds in drops. When rain falls, you say it is **raining.** ◇ In countries where rain tends to fall only during certain seasons, this rain is called **the rains.** ◇ If an event is **rained off,** it is cancelled because of rain.

❑ If things **rain** down on a place, they fall in large quantities. *The heaviest mortar and artillery fire in more than a month rained into Sarajevo that night.*

rainbow A **rainbow** is an arch of different colours you sometimes see in the sky when it is raining and the sun is shining at the same time. ◇ A **rainbow** coalition or alliance is a political group made up of several smaller groups with a wide range of different principles who have joined together to compete against larger groups.

raincoat A **raincoat** is a long waterproof coat.

raindrop A **raindrop** is a single drop of rain.

rainfall The **rainfall** in a place is the amount of rain which falls during a certain period.

rainforest A **rainforest** is a thick forest of tall trees in a place where the climate is very warm and wet.

rainstorm A **rainstorm** is a heavy fall of rain.

rainswept You say a place is **rainswept** when it is very windy and it is raining hard.

rainwater is water which has fallen as rain.

rainy A **rainy** period is one when it rains a lot.

raise (raising, raised) ❑ If you **raise** something, you move it to a higher position. *He defiantly raised a clenched fist.* ◇ A **raised** area or structure is higher than the area surrounding it. *...a raised platform.*

❑ If something is **raised** to a higher rate or level, it is put up to that rate or level. *He raised interest rates from 10% to 12%.* Similarly, something can be **raised** to a higher standard.

❑ If you **raise** your voice, you speak louder.

❑ If you **raise** money for a charity or cause, you organize an event which results in money being received for the charity or cause.

❑ When someone **raises** a child, they care for it while it is growing up, and teach it how to behave. *He was born and raised in Berlin.* ◇ When people **raise** animals, they breed them, usually so they can be slaughtered and eaten.

❑ If you **raise** a subject, you introduce it into a discussion. ◇ If you **raise** an objection, you object to something which is being proposed.

❑ If you say something **raises** a particular question or issue, you mean it forces people to think about it. *This research raises questions about the wisdom of closures.*

raisin Raisins are dried grapes, used in cooking and baking.

raison d'être (*pron:* ray-zon det-ra) The **raison d'être** of something is the reason for its existence.

Raj (*pron:* rahj) The Raj was the period of British rule in India before 1947.

rajah A **rajah** is an Indian king or prince.

rake (raking, raked) ❑ A **rake** is a garden tool consisting of a row of metal or wooden teeth on the end of a long handle. You use it, for example, to scrape leaves into a pile. When you use a rake to do something like this, you say you are **raking** the leaves or **raking** the garden.

❑ If you say someone is **raking in** money, you mean they are earning a lot of it quickly and easily.

❑ If you **rake up** something unpleasant or embarrassing from the past, you talk about it and remind people of it. ◇ If something is **raked over,** it is investigated by people looking for faults or embarrassing pieces of information.

❑ If you call a man a **rake,** you mean he lives an immoral irresponsible life.

rake-off A **rake-off** is a share in profits taken by someone who has helped to arrange a business deal. Rake-offs are sometimes illegal.

rakish (rakishly) If someone wears a hat at a **rakish** angle, they wear it pulled down at one side in a way intended to seem casual and confident. ...*a trilby hat cocked rakishly over one eye.* ◇ If someone is **rakish**, they give the impression of being immoral and irresponsible. *The man holds a cigar rakishly between his teeth.*

rally (rallies, rallying, rallied) ❑ A **rally** is a large public meeting held, for example, in protest at something or in support of a political party.

❑ If people **rally** to a cause, they unite to support it. If someone **rallies** support for a cause, they get people to support it. ...*a co-ordinated European campaign to rally support for the deal.* If something is a **rallying cry** or a **rallying call**, it inspires people to unite in support of a cause.

❑ A **rallying point** is a place where people gather at the start or finish of a political demonstration. You can also call someone or something a **rallying point** when they symbolize a political cause and inspire people to unite in support of it.

❑ When people **rally round** a person, they support them in a time of difficulty.

❑ If a sick person **rallies**, they start to get better. Similarly, you can say a sportsperson **rallies** when they have been losing and start to win. ◇ If prices **rally**, they start increasing after a fall. An increase like this is called a **rally**.

❑ A **rally** is also a competition in which vehicles are driven in timed stages over roads. Taking part in competitions like this is called **rallying**.

❑ In racket games like tennis and squash, a **rally** is a continuous series of shots.

ram (ramming, rammed) ❑ If one vehicle **rams** another, it is driven into it with great force, usually deliberately. ◇ If you **ram** something somewhere, you push it there with great force.

❑ If a law is **rammed** through, the government succeeds in getting it approved quickly, despite strong opposition. ◇ If a fact is **rammed home**, people are made aware of it in a forceful way. *The polls ram home the depth of public unease about the economy.*

❑ A **ram** is an uncastrated adult male sheep.

ram-raid (ram-raiding, ram-raider) A **ram-raid** is a robbery which involves people driving a stolen car through a shop front, loading it up with goods, and driving off again. Committing robberies like this is called **ram-raiding**. The people who do it are called **ram-raiders**.

Ramadan is the ninth month of the Muslim year. In this month, Muslims must go without food and drink from sunrise to sunset.

ramble (rambling, rambled; rambler) ❑ A **ramble** is a long walk in the countryside. If you go **rambling**, you go for walks like this. People who do it regularly are called **ramblers**, especially when they go in organized groups.

❑ A **rambling** building is large and old with an irregular shape.

❑ If someone **rambles** or **rambles on**, they speak or write about something for a long time in a tedious way and do not make much sense. You can call the things they say or write their **ramblings**.

ramekin (*pron:* ram-ik-in) A **ramekin** is a savoury dish for one person baked in a small fire-proof container. The container is also called a **ramekin**.

ramifications The **ramifications** of a situation are all its consequences and effects, especially ones which are not obvious at first.

ramp A **ramp** is a sloping surface between two places which are at different levels. ◇ A **ramp** is also a short section of road which has been deliberately made higher than the rest, to slow the traffic down.

rampage (rampaging, rampaged) When people or animals **rampage** through a place or **go on the rampage**, they rush about in a wild or violent way, causing damage and destruction.

rampant If something undesirable is **rampant**, it is growing and spreading rapidly. *Drug and alcohol abuse were rampant...* ...*rampant inflation.*

ramparts are mounds of earth, usually with walls along the top, which used to be built round towns and castles to protect them from attack.

ramrod is used to describe people who are holding their bodies straight and stiff. *The general stood ramrod straight.*

ramshackle A **ramshackle** building is in a very bad state of repair. ◇ You describe other things as **ramshackle** when they are very badly organized. ...*a ramshackle economy.*

ran See run.

ranch (ranches; ranching, rancher) In the western US and Canada, a **ranch** is a large farm on which sheep, cattle, or horses are bred. Running a ranch is called **ranching**. A person who owns, manages, or works on a ranch is called a **rancher**.

rancid If fatty foods like butter or bacon go **rancid**, they go bad and taste unpleasant.

rancour (*American spelling:* rancor) (rancorous) **Rancour** is a deep bitter feeling of anger. If something is **rancorous**, it involves people having feelings like this. ...*a rancorous quarrel.*

rand (*plural:* rand *or* rands) The **rand** is the unit of currency in South Africa.

random (randomly, randomness) **Random** is used to say that people or things affected by something are not chosen according to any plan or pattern. *Three people were killed by shots fired at random from a minibus... Researchers interviewed people in randomly selected homes... ...the seeming randomness of their crimes.*

randy If someone is **randy**, they are eager to have sex.

rang See ring.

range (ranging, ranged) ❑ The **range** of something like a gun is the greatest distance at which it can be used effectively. If something it is aimed at is **within range**, it is less than this distance away. If it is **out of range**, it is beyond this distance.

❑ The **range** of a singer or musical instrument is all the notes they are capable of producing, from the lowest one to the highest one.

❑ A **range** of things is a number of different ones of the same general kind. *The new prime minister has reimposed price controls on a range of basic goods like bread, meat and milk.* ◇ A **range** of products is a number of them of the same general kind produced or sold by the same firm. *Mazda is to launch a new range of luxury cars.* ◇ If you want to show how varied a group of things is, you can say they **range** from one thing to another. *Reactions ranged from amusement to horror.*

❑ If you talk about things in a particular **range**, you are talking about all the things between two points on a scale. *...cars in the price range £15,500 to £19,499.*

❑ If a large number of people are **ranged** against you, they are all attacking you or criticizing you together.

❑ A **range** of hills or mountains is a group of them together.

❑ A **range** is also a place where people can practice shooting or where rockets are tested. *...a rifle range.*

rangefinder A **rangefinder** is an instrument which tells you how far away something is when you want to shoot it or photograph it.

ranger A **ranger** is a person whose job is to look after a forest.

rangy If you call a person or animal **rangy**, you mean they have long slender limbs.

rank ❑ A person's **rank** is their position or grade in an organization. **-ranking** is used after a word like 'high' to describe someone's rank. *...high-ranking government officials.* ◇ If someone **pulls rank**, they use the fact that they have a higher rank to make someone do something.

❑ The **ranks** are the ordinary members of an organization, rather than its officers or leaders.

❑ If you become a member of a large group of people, you can say you **join its ranks**. *He soon joined the ranks of the unemployed.*

❑ If people **close ranks**, they respond to a difficult situation by supporting each other, to protect themselves from attack or criticism. ◇ If someone **breaks ranks**, they are disloyal or fail to support a group of which they are a member.

❑ When you say where someone or something **ranks** or is **ranked**, you are describing their position on a scale. A position like this can be called a **ranking**. *The victory gave him the overall lead in the world rankings.*

❑ A **rank** smell is strong and unpleasant.

❑ A **rank outsider** in a competition or vote is someone who is not expected to win.

rank and file The **rank and file** are the ordinary members of an organization rather than its leaders.

rankle (rankling, rankled) If something **rankles**, it makes you feel bitter and angry. *The fact that the Queen paid no taxes had long rankled with many voters.*

ransack If you **ransack** a building or room, you disturb a lot of the things in it and leave it in a mess because you are looking for something.

ransom (ransoming, ransomed) A **ransom** is an amount of money demanded for the return of someone who has been kidnapped. When someone is kidnapped and money is demanded, you can say they are **ransomed** or **held to ransom**. ◇ You can say a government or other group of people is **held to ransom** when they are forced to agree to the demands of people who have something they need.

rant (ranter) If someone talks about something in a loud angry way and you think this is silly or unnecessary, you can say they are **ranting** or having a **rant**. If they make a habit of doing it, you can call them a **ranter**; you call what they say their **rantings**.

rap (rapping, rapped; rapper) ❑ If you **rap** on something or give it a **rap**, you hit it quickly and firmly. *There was a sharp rap on my hotel door.*

❑ If you say someone has had their knuckles **rapped**, you mean they have been told off or given a small punishment. ◇ If you **take the rap** for something, you are blamed and punished for it.

❑ **Rap** is a style of pop music which involves talking rhythmically rather than singing. A person who performs rap is called a **rapper**.

rapacious (rapacity) If you call someone **rapacious** or talk about their **rapacity**, you mean they are extremely greedy for something, especially money.

rape (raping, raped; rapist) ❑ **Rape** is the crime of forcing sexual intercourse upon someone against their will. When this is done to someone, you say they have been **raped** or there has been a **rape**. A **rapist** is someone who has committed a rape.

❑ **Rape** or **oilseed rape** is a plant with bright yellow flowers, grown on farms. Its seeds are crushed to make lubricants or oil for cooking. Its leaves are used as fodder.

rapid (rapidly, rapidity) ❑ If something is **rapid**, it moves or happens quickly. *...the rapid growth of private businesses... ...a rapidly changing world.* You can talk about the **rapidity** with which something happens. *He disappeared with the same rapidity and ease as he had arrived.*

❑ **Rapids** are parts of a river where it is rocky and the water is very fast-moving.

rapid eye movement See REM.

rapier (*pron:* ray-pyer) A **rapier** is a thin pointed sword.

rapist See rape.

rapper See rap.

rapport (*pron:* rap-pore) If you have a **rapport** with someone, you get on well and you feel you understand each other.

rapporteur (*pron:* ra-pore-tur) A **rapporteur** is a person appointed by an investigating committee to prepare reports for the organization which the committee is part of. *...the United Nations special rapporteur on torture.*

rapprochement (*pron:* ra-prosh-mong) If there is a **rapprochement** between two countries, the relationship between their governments becomes friendly, after a period when it had been hostile.

rapt is used to say people are fascinated by something they are watching and are concentrating all their attention on it. *Delegates sat in rapt silence as Mrs Fisher spoke.*

rapture is an intense feeling of delight.

rapturous (rapturously) A **rapturous** response to something shows great joy and enthusiasm. *They were rapturously applauded.*

rare If something is **rare**, it is very uncommon. *In certain rare circumstances it might be necessary to break the law... ...one of Britain's rarest birds.* ◇ **Rare** meat is only slightly cooked.

rarebit See Welsh rarebit.

rarefied (*pron:* rare-if-ide) is used to describe things which seem far removed from everyday life. *...the rarefied atmosphere of a chamber recital.*

rarely If something **rarely** happens, it hardly ever happens.

raring If you say someone is **raring to go**, you mean they are excited and eager to start doing something.

rarity (rarities) A **rarity** is something which is very uncommon. You can talk about the **rarity** of something like this. *The extreme rarity of the plants made the treatment* *prohibitively expensive.*

rascal If you call a child a **rascal**, you mean they have done something naughty but you are amused rather than cross about it.

rash (rashes, rashly, rashness) ❏ You say someone is being **rash** when they do or say something without thinking properly what the consequences might be. *...rash promises... She rashly ignored the warning signals... ...the rashness of youth.*

❏ If you have a **rash**, an area of your body is covered in small red spots, as a result of illness or an allergy.

❏ When a lot of the same kind of things happen in a short time, you can say there is a **rash** of them. *....a rash of revelations about the rich and famous.*

rasher A slice of bacon is called a **rasher**.

rasp If something **rasps**, it makes a low dry harsh sound. A sound like this can be called a **rasp**.

raspberry (raspberries) **Raspberries** are soft red fruit made up of a mass of small red balls. They grow on spiky bushes. ◇ If you **blow a raspberry**, you make a noise like a fart by putting out your tongue and blowing. People do this to insult someone or make fun of them.

Rasta is short for 'Rastafarian'. *...the Rasta faith.*

Rastafarian **Rastafarians** are people who follow a religious faith which originated in Jamaica. They regard Africa, especially Ethiopia, as their spiritual home. Rastafarian men usually wear their hair in long dreadlocks.

rat **Rats** are long-tailed animals which look like large mice. ◇ If you say you **smell a rat**, you mean you suspect someone is up to no good. ◇ The **rat race** is the everyday struggle of daily life in a town or city, especially when this involves trying to succeed in a job in the business world.

ratchet (ratcheting, ratcheted) A **ratchet** is a wheel or bar with sloping teeth which is only able to move in one direction because a piece of metal prevents the teeth from moving backwards. ◇ If the level of something **ratchets up** or **ratchets down**, something causes it to rise or fall. When this cause is removed, the thing does not return to its previous level but stays where it is.

rate (rating, rated) ❏ The **rate** at which something happens is the speed or frequency with which it happens. *Tropical forests are disappearing at the rate of between 40 and 50 million acres a year.* ◇ The **rate** of something is its level expressed as a percentage. *...a national unemployment rate of over 10%.* See also **exchange rate**.

❏ In Britain until 1990, **rates** were local taxes paid by people who owned buildings or paid rent on unfurnished buildings.

❏ **Rate** is used when talking about someone's opinion or assessment of something. For example, you can **rate** one thing as better than another. **-rated** is added to a word to describe someone's assessment or classification of something. *...Craig Short, the highly-rated Notts County central defender... ...X-rated films.* ◇ A politician's or political party's **rating** is an assessment of their popularity according to the opinion polls. ◇ The **ratings** are statistics published weekly in Britain which give the estimated numbers of people who watch each TV programme.

❏ **At this rate** is used to say what will happen if a situation remains unchanged. *At this rate, the case will turn out to be the longest in Sri Lanka's legal history.* ◇ You say at any **rate** (a) when you are correcting something you have just said, because it was too general or an exaggeration. *Western democracy has bested, or at any rate outlasted, its rival system.* (b) when you are mentioning something which is definitely true, after talking about things which you were not sure about. *At any rate, they had failed to work as they should have done.*

rateable value In the past, the **rateable value** of a house was a value assigned to it, based on its size and facilities. Rateable values were used to calculate how much owners had to pay in rates.

ratepayer **Ratepayers** were people who had to pay rates, before they were abolished in 1990.

rates See **rate**.

rather means 'to some extent'. *I think it's rather sad.* ◇ When you are praising something or speaking positively about something, **rather** means 'to quite a large extent'. *...a rather clever idea... Prospects do sound rather good.*

❏ You use **rather than** to say something is one thing and not something else. *The scandal was greeted with hilarity rather than indignation.* ◇ If you **would rather** do one thing than another, you would prefer to do the first thing.

ratify (ratifies, ratifying, ratified; ratification) When a government or organization **ratifies** an agreement or proposal, it formally approves and adopts it. *They were determined to press ahead with the ratification of the Maastricht treaty.*

ratings See **rate**.

ratio (ratios) A **ratio** is a measurement of the relationship between two numbers which shows how many times greater one is than the other. For example, if there are 6 girls and 2 boys in a room, the ratio of girls to boys is 3 to 1. *The Commons backed the War Crimes Bill by a ratio of four-to-one.*

ration (rationing, rationed) ❏ If something is **rationed**, each person is only allowed a limited amount of it, because it is scarce. The amount each person gets is called their **ration**. The system of allowing people to have only certain amounts of things is called **rationing**.

❏ **Rations** are amounts of food supplied each day to someone such as a soldier or a member of an expedition.

rational (rationally, rationality) **Rational** behaviour is based on reason rather than the emotions. *He was not thinking clearly and rationally at the time.* Basing behaviour on reason is called **rationality**. ◇ If there is a **rational** explanation for something, there is an explanation which does not involve anything such as supernatural forces.

rationale (*pron: rash-a-nahl*) The **rationale** for a decision or policy is the reason or motive which leads to it being taken or adopted.

rationalise See **rationalize**.

rationalism (rationalist) **Rationalism** is the belief that reason should be valued above emotion or religious belief. A **rationalist** is someone who believes this.

rationalize (rationalizing, rationalized; rationalization) (*can be spelled with an 's' instead of a 'z'*) ❏ If you **rationalize** something you feel unsure or unhappy about, you think of reasons to justify or explain it. *Mr Kesri said he was not trying to rationalize or justify the violence.*

❏ If a company or other organization is **rationalized**, it is made more efficient, for example by laying off some of the staff. A change like this is called a **rationalization**.

rattan (*pron: ra-tan*) is the tough thin stems of various climbing palms, used to make wickerwork.

rattle (rattling, rattled) ❑ When something **rattles** or is **rattled**, it makes a rapid series of short regular knocking sounds, for example because it is being shaken or is hitting against something hard. This sound is called a **rattle**. ◇ A **rattle** is a baby's toy. It consists of a container with loose bits inside which make a noise when the container is shaken.
❑ If something **rattles** you, it gives you a shock or makes you feel nervous and uneasy.
❑ If you **rattle** something **off**, you do or say it quickly and without much effort.
❑ An exciting and enjoyable book is sometimes called a **rattling** good book.

rattlesnake The **rattlesnake** is a poisonous American snake with a series of horny segments on the end of its tail which rattle when it shakes them.

raucous You say people are **raucous** when they behave in a noisy way, for example by shouting, laughing, or singing. ◇ A **raucous** voice is loud and rough.

raunchy is used to describe people whose behaviour is intended to be sexually exciting. *...the Chippendales' raunchy performance.* Similarly, a book or film can be called **raunchy**. *...a raunchy paperback thriller.*

ravage (ravaging, ravaged) If people or places are **ravaged**, they are severely harmed or damaged. *...the recession-ravaged east coast.* ◇ The **ravages** of something like war, pollution, or time are its damaging effects. *He devoted much of his life to trying to protect his native island from the ravages of mass tourism.*

rave (raving, raved; raver) ❑ If you **rave** about something, you speak or write about it excitedly and enthusiastically. ◇ A **rave** review is a very enthusiastic one.
❑ If someone **raves**, they talk loudly about something without making much sense, because they are very angry or worked up. You can call what they say their **ravings**.
❑ A **rave** is a party held somewhere like a warehouse in which very loud dance music is played. People who go to these parties are called **ravers**.

raven The **raven** is a large black bird with a deep harsh call. Ravens are members of the crow family.

ravening is used to describe animals which are fierce and hungry. *...ravening wolves.*

ravenous If you are **ravenous**, you are very hungry. ◇ If you are **ravenous** for something, you want or need it badly. *...his school's ravenous demands for cash.*

raver See rave.

ravine (*pron: rav-veen*) A **ravine** is a deep narrow steep-sided valley, especially one formed by a river.

ravioli (*pron: rav-ee-oh-lee*) is small squares of pasta filled with meat and served in a sauce.

ravish (ravishes, ravishing, ravished; ravishingly) ❑ If you describe a place as **ravished** by war, famine, or disease, you mean it has been severely harmed by it.
❑ If you say you are **ravished** by something, you mean you are amazed and delighted by its beauty. *He decided to go for a walk in the city and was ravished by it.* ◇ If someone or something is **ravishing**, they are extremely beautiful. *...a ravishing pale pink and blue dress... She looked ravishingly beautiful.*

raw food is uncooked. ◇ **Raw** is used to describe other things which are in their natural state and have not yet been treated or processed. *...raw sewage... ...raw data.* If something is **in the raw**, it is in its typical natural state. *He wanted to see Bangladesh in the raw.*
❑ **Raw** emotions are natural, basic, and uncontrolled. ◇ If something is achieved by **raw** power, it is achieved by power alone, rather than by skill.
❑ You can call people **raw** when they are untrained and inexperienced. *...raw recruits.*
❑ If you say someone has had a **raw deal**, you mean they have been treated unfairly.
❑ **raw nerve**: see nerve.

raw material Raw materials are the natural substances used to make things, for example in an industrial process. ◇ **Raw** materials are also the basic things you need for something. *That the raw material of an outstanding international team is available is not in doubt.*

ray A **ray** is a beam of light or heat. *...the sun's rays... ...harmful ultra violet rays.* ◇ If something provides a **ray of hope**, it suggests that a bad situation may eventually improve.

rayon is a smooth fabric made from synthetic fibres.

raze (razing, razed) If a building or town is **razed** or **razed to the ground**, it is completely destroyed.

razor A **razor** is a tool for shaving.

razor blade A **razor blade** is a small thin piece of metal with sharp edges which you fix to a razor and use for shaving.

razor wire is strong wire with sharp-edged pieces of metal on it. It is used to make fences or barriers which are difficult to cross without hurting yourself.

RC stands for 'Roman Catholic'.

RE stands for 'Religious Education'.

re is used, especially in business letters, to say what something applies to. *There have recently been several complaints lodged against him re the lax discipline on A Wing.*

re- re- at the beginning of a word indicates that something is being done again. *The books look as if they have been read and re-read by their owners... A warrant for his re-arrest has been issued.* ◇ Some words beginning with 're' can be spelled with a hyphen after the 'e'. For example, 'readmit' can be spelled 're-admit'. See entries at readmit, recreation, reroute, rerun, reuse.

re-educate When an authoritarian government re-educates people, it tries to force them to adopt new attitudes and beliefs.

re-elect (re-election) When someone who has been elected to a post is **re-elected**, they win a further election and are able to continue in the post.

re-enact (re-enactment) If people **re-enact** an incident, they act out what happened. *...a spectacular re-enactment of the Battle of Waterloo.*

re-entry ❑ When people return to something like a country, an organization, or a field of activity after being away from it for a while, you can talk about their **re-entry** into it. *...Britain's re-entry into the ERM.*
❑ **Re-entry** is also the moment when a spacecraft comes back into the Earth's atmosphere after being in space.

re-examine (re-examination) If you **re-examine** something like your opinions or plans, you think about them carefully, because you are no longer sure they are correct or appropriate. *The shock galvanized decision-makers into a re-examination of their priorities.*

reach (reaches, reaching, reached) ❑ When you **reach** a place, you arrive there.

❑ If you **reach** for something, you stretch out your arm so you can get it or touch it.

❑ If you **reach** someone who is in a different place, you manage to contact them. *The announcement was delayed while the academy tried to reach Markowitz, who was visiting Japan.*

❑ If something **reaches** a certain point or level, it gets to that point or level. *Profit margins reached 20%.*

❑ If people **reach** a decision, agreement, or result, they succeed in achieving it.

❑ If something is **within reach**, you can get it or achieve it. If it is **out of reach**, it is impossible for you to get it or achieve it. *Success seemed within reach... The ceiling on housing benefit has put private rented accommodation out of reach of many poorer people.* ◇ If you are **within reach** of a place, it is close enough for you to get to it. *There are 15 beaches within easy reach of the main population centres.*

❑ The upper **reaches** of something are its upper parts. *...the upper reaches of government.* Similarly, you can talk about the lower **reaches** or further **reaches** of something. *...the furthest reaches of the solar system.*

react ❑ If you **react** to something in a particular way, you feel or behave like that because of it. *France and Italy reacted angrily to the decision.* ◇ If you **react** against the way other people do things, you deliberately do things in a different way.

❑ When substances **react**, they change chemically when they come into contact with each other, and new substances are formed.

reactant A **reactant** is any substance taking part in a chemical reaction, especially a substance present at the start of the reaction.

reaction ❑ Your **reaction** to something is what you feel, say, or do as a result of it. ◇ If there is a **reaction** against something, people express their disapproval of it. *Nowhere in the West has the popular reaction against the coup been stronger than in Germany.*

❑ Your **reactions** are your ability to move quickly in response to something. *Table tennis requires faster reactions than almost any other sport.*

❑ A chemical **reaction** takes place when substances change chemically as a result of coming into contact with each other.

❑ A **reaction** is also an unintended harmful or unpleasant effect which something like a drug can have on your body.

reactionary (reactionaries) You call someone a **reactionary** when they are stubbornly opposed to political or social change. You can also call their behaviour **reactionary**. *...reactionary propaganda.*

reactivate (reactivating, reactivated) If something is **reactivated**, it is started up again. *Top of the agenda will be a plan to reactivate the Central American Common Market.*

reactive A **reactive** chemical is one which easily reacts with other chemicals. ◇ If you call a person's behaviour **reactive**, you mean they behave in response to what happens, rather than deciding in advance what to do.

reactor See nuclear.

read (reading, read *pron:* red) ❑ When you **read** something, you look at it and understand the words written in it or on it. ◇ If you **read** a piece of writing to someone or **read** it **out**, you say the words aloud. ◇ A **reading** is an event at which poetry or extracts from books are read to an audience.

❑ **Read** is used to comment on the qualities of a book or other piece of writing. For example, if you say a book is a good **read**, you mean it is interesting and enjoyable. *Falcone's memoirs are a compelling read.* ◇ When people talk about the way a piece of writing **reads**, they are talking about its style or the impression it gives. *Most of the book reads like office gossip.*

❑ **Read** is also used to say what is written somewhere. For example, if a sign **reads** 'exit', the word 'exit' is written on it.

❑ If you **read** someone's mood or mind, you work out how they feel or what they are thinking without them telling you. ◇ **read** someone's **lips:** see lip.

❑ The way you **read** a situation is the way you interpret or understand it. *He said it would be unwise to read too much into next week's expected fall in inflation.* ◇ **read between the lines:** see line.

❑ If you **take** something **as read**, you take it for granted or accept it as true or right, and do not feel it needs to be discussed or proved.

❑ If you can **read** music, you can understand the symbols used in written music.

❑ When you **read** a meter or gauge, you look at the figure or measurement on it. You can also say you take a **reading.** ◇ If a measuring device **reads** a particular amount, it shows that amount. *The fuel gauge reads below zero.*

❑ If you **read** a subject at university, you study it.

readable If you describe a book or article as **readable,** you mean it is possible to read it and understand it without getting bored. If a book is **highly readable,** it is enjoyable as well as giving you information.

reader ❑ The **readers** of a newspaper or magazine are the people who read it regularly. *...Guardian readers.* ◇ People who read books regularly can also be called **readers.** *Attracting younger readers should be the industry's top priority.* ◇ If you talk about **the reader** of a book, you mean anyone who happens to read it. *Much is left to the reader's imagination.*

❑ At a British university, a **reader** is a senior lecturer just below the rank of professor.

readership The **readership** of a magazine, newspaper, or book is all the people who read it.

readily If you do something **readily,** you do it willingly or eagerly. ◇ **Readily** is also used to say something is easily obtained or easily understood. *Once food is readily available on the market, the economy will revive.*

readiness If you do something **in readiness** for something happening, you do it to be prepared for it. *Security has been tightened in readiness for a general strike tomorrow.* ◇ Your **readiness** to do something is your willingness or eagerness to do it. *Albania has declared its readiness to accept the Helsinki agreements on human rights.*

reading lamp A **reading lamp** is a small adjustable lamp kept on a desk or table to give you light when you are reading.

reading room A **reading room** is a quiet room in a library or museum where you can read and study.

readjust (readjustment) If you **readjust**, you learn to cope with a change in your circumstances. *The next few weeks will be a period of readjustment and will not be easy.* ◇ If you **readjust** your attitude or approach to something, you alter it to make it more effective or appropriate.

readmit (readmitting, readmitted; readmittance, readmission) (*or* **re-admit**, *etc*) When people are **readmitted** to an organization or group, they are allowed to join it again or take part in its activities again, after a period when they have been excluded. When this happens, you can talk about their **readmittance** or **readmission** to the organization or group.

ready (readier, readiest; readies, readying, readied) ❑ If you are **ready**, you are prepared for something which is going to happen. If you are **ready** to do something, you have made all necessary preparations and are about to do it. ◇ You also say someone is **ready** to do something when they are willing to do it. *No one was more ready to help any student in need.*

❑ If something is **ready**, it has reached the stage where it can be used. If you **ready** something, you get it ready for use.

❑ If there is a **ready** supply of something, people can get it quickly and easily. You can also talk about the **ready availability** of something. ◇ If you have **ready access** to something, you can get to it or use it whenever you need to. ◇ **Ready money** or **ready cash** is money immediately available for spending. ◇ If you have something **at the ready**, you have it in a position where it can be used quickly and easily. *The army is patrolling with guns at the ready.*

❑ **Ready-made** is used to describe something which is available and can be used immediately to solve a problem. *Neither Moscow nor Washington had a ready-made solution to achieve a settlement.* ◇ If you buy something **ready-made**, you can use it immediately, because the work you would normally have to do to it has already been done. *All the parts are delivered ready-made to the site.* **Ready-** is used in a similar way with words like 'mixed' and 'cooked'. *...ready-mixed concrete... ...ready-prepared meals.*

❑ If someone has a **ready** smile, they tend to smile in a cheerful friendly way, whatever the situation.

reaffirm (reaffirmation) If you **reaffirm** something, you state it again clearly and firmly. *...a reaffirmation of the importance of the relations between the two countries.*

reafforestation is the same as reforestation.

reagent (*pron:* ree-age-ent) Any substance used in a chemical reaction can be called a **reagent**, especially when the reaction is used to produce or analyze other substances.

real ❑ You use **real** when you are talking about the thing that counts most in a situation. *The real question is whether to take military action... The real drama was still to unfold.* ◇ You also use **real** when you are saying what something actually is, as distinct from what it appears to be. *The firm's real aim may be to grab Hong Kong's commercial-television market.*

❑ If something is **real**, it actually exists and is not imagined, invented, or theoretical. ◇ You also say something is **real** when it is genuine rather than artificial or an imita-

tion. *...a real diamond bracelet.*

❑ If you say something is **for real**, you mean it is genuine, rather than a joke, an imitation, or a rehearsal. ◇ If you compare something to **the real thing**, you are comparing it to something which is genuine or actually exists. *An exaggerated fear of crime is almost as damaging as the real thing.*

❑ **Real** is used to emphasize that something like a problem or possibility exists and is serious. *The right-wing coup was a real threat... They were at a very real risk of being swept away by an avalanche.* ◇ **Real** is used for emphasis when describing something. *It's a real thrill.*

❑ **Real** is used to say the effect of inflation has been deducted from an amount. *The duty on whisky has now fallen by 23% in real terms since 1980.*

real ale is traditionally brewed beer which is stored in a barrel and pumped from it without the use of any carbon dioxide.

real estate In the US, property in the form of land and buildings is called **real estate**.

real time If something is done in **real time**, there is no noticeable delay between the action and its effect or consequences. ◇ **Real-time** is used to describe computer systems or programs which process and respond to information as soon as it is received.

real world When people talk about the **real world**, they are talking about what actually exists and the true nature of things, as distinct from what someone imagines things to be like or wants them to be like. *With inflation running at 9.4%, the revised offer had to take account of what was happening in the real world.*

realign (realignment) When people **realign** their ideas, policies, or plans, they alter them to take account of new circumstances. ◇ If a country's currency is **realigned**, changes are made to the upper and lower exchange-rate levels between which it is supposed to be kept. *...a declaration ruling out realignment of currencies.*

realisable See realizable.

realise See realize.

realistic (realistically; realism, realist) ❑ If you are **realistic** about a situation, you recognize and accept its true nature, and try to deal with it in a practical way. This is called showing **realism**. Someone who regularly behaves like this can be called a **realist**. *More realistically, Friends of the Earth argues that the British may not have much choice about water standards.* ◇ If something you are hoping to achieve is **realistic**, you can reasonably expect to achieve it.

❑ In painting, novels, and films, **realism** is representing people and things in a way which is like real life. A **realist** painter, writer, or director tries to do this. If he or she is successful, you call the result **realistic**. ◇ If a fake or imitation of something is **realistic**, it looks like the real thing.

reality (realities) **Reality** is the real nature of things. If someone's ideas do not correspond with this, you can say they are **out of touch with reality**. *M. Artaud assumed that the officer had lost touch with reality... The TUC must face up to reality.* ◇ The **realities** of a situation are the facts about it, especially when they are unpleasant or difficult to deal with. *People must begin to accept the realities of modern life.* ◇ If something you have imagined or wanted to happen becomes a **reality**, it actually happens. ◇ In **reality** is used to say what is actually true, in contrast with what is supposed to be true or what seems to be true. *On paper the farmers still owned their smallholdings, but in reality they lost all control over the land.*

realizable (*or* realisable) ❏ If assets are **realizable**, they can be sold or turned into cash quickly and easily. The **realizable** value of something is the amount you can sell it for.

❏ If your aims or goals are **realizable**, you can reasonably expect to achieve them.

realize (realizing, realized; realization) (*can be spelled with an 's' instead of a 'z'*) ❏ If you **realize** something, you know it or you become aware of it. *Many parents don't realise that measles can kill.* When people become aware of something, you can say there is a **realization** of it. *There is now a growing realization that things cannot go on like this for much longer.*

❏ If your hopes or fears are **realized**, they come true. *The project represents the realization of a European dream.* ◇ If you **realize** an idea or design, you make or organize something based on it. *He needs at least two years to realize these plans.*

❏ If a business **realizes** its assets, it turns them into cash by selling them. When this happens, you can say a certain amount of cash is **realized** from the sale.

reallocate (reallocating, reallocated; reallocation) If something is **reallocated**, it is given to different people from those who had it before, or from those who were originally meant to have it. *...the reallocation of powers and duties.*

really ❏ People use **really** to emphasize what they are saying. *We really ought to get another car... It was really good.*

❏ You use **really** when you are talking about the facts of a situation, in contrast to what people may mistakenly believe. *There's always been a sense of mystery about what really happened.* ◇ Similarly, when you are correcting a mistaken belief or wrong impression, you can say something is **not really** true. *Hitler did not really want or expect war at this stage.*

realm Any area of activity, interest, or thought can be called a **realm**. *...the economic realm.* ◇ A **realm** is also a kingdom. *...the ruler of a subterranean realm.*

realpolitik (*pron:* ray-arl-pol-i-teek *or* ray-arl-pol-i-teek) In politics, **realpolitik** means dealing with issues in a practical realistic way, especially by recognizing who is powerful and who is not powerful, rather than trying to do what is morally right.

realtor In the US, estate agents are sometimes known as **realtors.**

reams If you talk about **reams** of something, especially paper or writing, you mean very large amounts of it. *Manufacturers churn out reams of gloomy figures.*

reap (reaping, reaped) ❏ When people **reap** a crop like corn, they cut and gather it.

❏ If you get a benefit from something you have done, you can say you **reap** the benefit. *Manufacturers can reap healthy profits on finished products.*

reaper A **reaper** is (a) a machine used to cut and gather crops. (b) a person who cuts and gathers crops by hand.

reappear (reappearing, reappeared; reappearance) When someone or something **reappears,** you see them again, or they come into existence again, after a period when they have not been present. *Unless goods and foodstuffs start to reappear soon in the shops, the country could lose all hope... ...the reappearance of hyper-inflation.*

reappoint (reappointment) When someone who has been appointed to a post is **reappointed,** they are appointed again and are able to continue in the post. *...his re-appointment as Prime Minister.*

reappraise (reappraising, reappraised; reappraisal) If you re-**appraise** your approach to something or your opinions on something, you carefully reconsider them. A reconsideration of things like these is called a **reappraisal.**

rear (rearing, reared) ❏ The **rear** of something like a building or vehicle is its back part. A **rear** window or door is at the back of a building or vehicle.

❏ If you are **bringing up the rear,** you are at the back of a moving line of people or vehicles.

❏ When people **rear** children, they bring them up. ◇ People who **rear** animals keep and look after them until they are old enough to be used for work or food, or until they can look after themselves.

❏ If a horse **rears** or **rears up,** it raises the front part of its body, so that its front legs are high in the air and it is standing on its hind legs.

❏ If something unpleasant **rears its head,** it happens or appears. *The threat of strikes has reared its head again this summer.*

rear admiral See admiral.

rear-view A **rear-view** mirror is a mirror inside a car which lets you see the traffic behind you.

rearguard You say someone is fighting a **rearguard** action when they are trying to stop something they disapprove of from happening and they have little chance of success. *Cigarette manufacturers are having to fight rearguard actions against anti-smoking laws.*

rearm (rearmament) When a country **rearms,** it starts to build up a stock of military weapons again, after a period when it has not been doing so. *Mrs Thatcher was President Reagan's staunchest supporter in the Western rearmament of the early 1980s.*

rearrange (rearranging, rearranged; rearrangement) If you re-**arrange** something, you organize or arrange it in a different way. *No rearrangement of responsibilities within the boardroom can guarantee business success.*

reason (reasoning, reasoned) ❏ The **reason** for something is the fact or situation which explains why it happens or exists. *An increase in Soviet exports is one reason why the prices of metals have recently tumbled.* ◇ If you say you **have reason to** believe or feel something, you mean there are facts or circumstances which justify what you believe or feel. *We have reason to believe that additional villages will be attacked.* ◇ If one thing happens or is true **by reason of** another, the first thing happens or is true because of the second. *He could plead not guilty by reason of insanity.*

❏ **Reason** is the ability to think logically and sensibly. ◇ **Reasoned** is used to describe things which involve the use of logical thought. *They are capable of reasoned judgment.*

❏ If you **reason with** someone, you try to convince them of something using logical arguments. ◇ If you get someone to **listen to reason,** you persuade them to listen to sensible arguments and be influenced by them.

❏ **Reasoning** is the process of reaching conclusions by considering things in a logical way. ◇ If you **reason** that something is true, you decide it must be true after thinking about all the facts. *I reasoned that changing my diet would lower my cholesterol level.* ◇ A person's reasons for doing something can be called their **reasoning.**

❏ If you can do anything **within reason,** you can do anything you like so long as it is sensible and not too extreme. *Weather permitting, and within reason, you can travel just about anywhere.*

reasonable (reasonably, reasonableness) ❏ If you say what someone decides or does is **reasonable,** you mean it is fair and sensible. *If claims of this sort are made, it is reasonable to ask for evidence to support them... ...a perfectly reasonable decision.* ◇ You say a person is **reasonable** when they talk in a sensible way. *Great Aunt Bertha spoke with calm reasonableness.*

❏ If the price of something is **reasonable,** it is not at all expensive. *Housing is plentiful and reasonably priced.*

❏ A **reasonable** amount of something is a fairly large amount. *The discriminating viewer should be able to find a reasonable number of watchable programmes.*

❏ **Reasonably** is used to say something is true to a fair extent. *It worked reasonably well.*

reassemble (reassembling, reassembled) If something which has been taken apart is **reassembled,** it is put together again. ◇ If a group which has split up **reassembles,** they get together again.

reassert (reassertion) ❏ When people **reassert** themselves or **reassert** their authority or control, they make it clear they are still in charge, by issuing strict orders and making sure they are carried out. *The end of the Suharto era may herald a reassertion of military authority.* ◇ If you **reassert** a claim or demand, you make it again, firmly and forcefully. *A military spokesman reasserted that troops had moved south into the town of Kilinochchi.*

❏ If an idea or custom **reasserts** itself, it becomes significant or dominant again. *Tribalism seems to be reasserting itself.*

reassess (reassesses, reassessing, reassessment) If you **reassess** something or make a **reassessment** of it, you reconsider it carefully. *The bank is now reassessing its criteria for lending money to forestry projects.*

reassign If people are **reassigned** to new jobs, they are given them in place of their old ones.

reassure (reassuring, reassured; reassurance, reassuringly) If you **reassure** someone, you say things to make them less worried. The things you say are called **reassurances.** ◇ If you are **reassured** by something or find it **reassuring,** it makes you less worried. *The numbers involved seem to be reassuringly low.*

reawaken (reawakening, reawakened) If feelings or principles are **reawakened,** they come into existence again. You can talk about a **reawakening** of things like these. *...the reawakening of democracy after years of war.*

rebarbative If you describe something as **rebarbative,** you mean it is extremely unattractive and repellent. *The invention will soon be marketed under the rebarbative name of Gotta Bite.*

rebate If you get a **rebate,** some of the money you have paid for something is returned to you.

rebel (rebelling, rebelled; rebellion) ❏ **Rebels** are people who are fighting against their own country's army, to try to bring about a change in the political system. You say people like these are **rebelling** (*pron:* re-bel-ing). You call their actions a **rebellion.**

❏ Politicians who oppose some of their own party's policies are often called **rebels.** You say they are **rebelling** against their party. Their action can be called a **rebellion.** ◇ You also call someone a **rebel** or say they are **rebelling** when they refuse to conform to other people's ideas about normal acceptable behaviour.

rebellious (rebelliousness) You call a group of people **rebellious** when they are involved in a rebellion, or likely to start one. *It's not clear whether he will be able to impose his will on the increasingly rebellious republics.* ◇ You also call people **rebellious** when they reject the values of other people around them and behave differently from them. *She has a strong rebellious streak... ...social conformists whose sole gesture at rebelliousness involves a half-hearted commitment to green issues.*

reborn (rebirth) If you say something has been **reborn** or talk about its **rebirth,** you mean it has appeared again after being absent, or has changed into something better. *...Spain's rebirth as a modern state after the long years of backwardness.*

rebound If something **rebounds** from a solid surface, it bounces back after hitting it. ◇ If something someone does **rebounds** on them, it has unexpected unpleasant effects for them.

rebuff If you are **rebuffed** when you propose something or ask for something, your proposal or request is turned down. You then say you have received a **rebuff.**

rebuild (rebuilding, rebuilt) ❏ If people **rebuild** a town or building, they build it again after it has been damaged or destroyed. ◇ When surgeons **rebuild** a part of someone's body after it has been severely damaged and disfigured, they use plastic surgery to try and make it look the way it did before.

❏ When people **rebuild** something like an institution, a system, or an aspect of their lives, they take action to restore it to its previous condition. *The Prime Minister will not easily rebuild his power and authority.*

rebuke (rebuking, rebuked) If you **rebuke** someone or give them a **rebuke,** you speak sternly to them, because they have done something you disapprove of.

rebut (rebutting, rebutted; rebuttal) If someone **rebuts** a charge or criticism made against them, they give reasons why it is untrue or unjustified. You call what they say a **rebuttal** of the charge or criticism.

recalcitrant (recalcitrance) If you call someone **recalcitrant** or talk about their **recalcitrance,** you mean they stubbornly refuse to conform or obey orders. People who behave like this are sometimes called **recalcitrants.**

recall ❏ If you **recall** something, you remember it.

❏ If you are **recalled** to a place, you are ordered to return there. ◇ If a player is **recalled** to a team, he or she is included in the team again after being left out for a while. *Ruud Gullit has been recalled to the Holland squad for next week's qualifying match in Malta.*

❏ If something is lost or harmed **beyond recall,** it is no longer possible to recreate it or return it to the condition it was once in. *He appeals desperately for a Zulu unity which now looks lost beyond recall.*

recant If someone **recants**, they publicly declare they have rejected beliefs they used to hold.

recap People say 'to recap...' when they are about to go over the main points of something like a story or discussion again.

recapitulate (recapitulating, recapitulated; recapitulation) If something is **recapitulated**, it is repeated, either in full or in a summarized form. *...a recapitulation of the headlines.*

recapture (recapturing, recaptured) ❑ When an army **recaptures** territory which it had lost in an earlier engagement, it captures it back again. Similarly, you can talk about a sports team **recapturing** something like a sporting trophy. ◇ When prisoners are **recaptured**, they are captured again after escaping.
❑ If you **recapture** the ability to do something, you are able to do it again.

recast (recasting, recast *not* 'recasted') ❑ If something like a system or policy is **recast**, it is organized in a different way. *The Labour Party has recast many of its ideas.*
❑ If a play or film is **recast**, parts in it are given to different actors.

recede (receding, receded) ❑ If an object is **receding**, it is moving away from you into the distance.
❑ If something like a storm or dispute **recedes**, it becomes less and gradually dies away.
❑ If a man's hair or hairline is **receding**, he is losing his hair at the front of his head, above his forehead.

receipt ❑ A **receipt** is a piece of paper which confirms that money or goods have been received. ◇ If you have received something, you can talk about your **receipt** of it. *All those acknowledging receipt of the letters have said they will co-operate.*
❑ The money taken in a place like a shop or theatre is often called the **receipts**.

receive (receiving, received) ❑ When someone gives you something, you say you **receive** it. *The quarter-finalists could receive up to £3.13 million each.* ◇ If you **receive** something which has been sent to you, you get it. ◇ **Receiving** stolen goods is the crime of buying or accepting them, knowing they have been stolen.
❑ When you **receive** a visitor or guest, you greet them. *Dr Boutros Ghali has been received warmly in Moscow by President Yeltsin.*
❑ If you say something is **received** in a particular way, you mean people react to it in that way. *The idea has been received coolly by the British Prime Minister.*
❑ You can use **receive** to say certain things happen to someone or are directed at them. For example, when someone is injured, you can say they **receive** an injury. *Cuba has received strong criticism for its human rights record.* ◇ If you are **on the receiving end** or **at the receiving end** of something unpleasant, it is directed at you. *He has been on the receiving end of abuse from business associates.*
❑ A **received** opinion is one which is generally accepted as correct. *The received wisdom has it that the main culprit is ABC.*

Received Pronunciation or **RP** is a way of pronouncing English which is often considered to be the standard English accent. This accent is most common in the south-east of England.

receiver (receivership) ❑ A telephone's **receiver** is the part you hold to your ear and speak into. ◇ The **receiver** of a radio or TV set is the part which picks up incoming signals and converts them into sound or pictures.
❑ When a business is in severe financial difficulty, the people it owes money to can officially appoint a person called a **receiver**, whose job is to take over the business and recover the money which is owed. If a business is in **receivership**, it has been taken over by the receiver. You call businesses in this situation **receiverships**.

recent (recently) A **recent** event took place only a short time ago. *...recently opened jails.* **Recent** is also used to describe things which were written or published only a short time ago. *...a recent survey.* Similarly, you can talk about things happening **in recent times** or **in recent years**.

receptacle A **receptacle** is any object you put or keep things in.

reception ❑ The **reception** in a hotel, office, or doctor's surgery is the part of the building where people are received and their reservations, appointments, or enquiries are dealt with.
❑ A **reception** is a formal party given to welcome someone or celebrate a special event. *...a wedding reception.* ◇ When a well-known person arrives somewhere, you can describe the way they are greeted by saying they get a particular kind of **reception**. *Mr De Klerk got a warm reception in Athens and Paris.* ◇ Similarly, you can say something like a proposal gets a particular kind of **reception**. *MPs can hardly be surprised at the hostile reception their decision has met.*
❑ You use **reception** to talk about the quality of a TV picture or the quality of the sound on your radio. *Locals complain that the building of Canary Wharf interfered with their television reception.*

reception centre A **reception centre** is a place which provides temporary accommodation for people like refugees or the homeless.

reception class In an infant school, the **reception class** is the first class children go into when they start school.

reception room A **reception room** is a room in a house where people can sit, for example a living room or a dining room. Estate-agents often say that a house has a certain number of **reception rooms**.

receptionist In a hotel, office, or doctor's surgery, the **receptionist** is the person whose job is to deal with people when they first arrive, answer the telephone, and arrange reservations or appointments.

receptive If someone is **receptive** to new ideas, they are willing to consider them.

receptor **Receptors** are nerve endings in the body which detect changes in conditions and cause the body to respond accordingly.

recess (recesses) ❑ A **recess** is a break between the sessions of work of an official body such as a committee, court, or parliament. When a parliament has a break like this, you say it is **in recess**.
❑ In a room, a **recess** is part of a wall built further back than the rest. ◇ The **recesses** of a place are the remote or hidden parts of it. *...the darkest recesses of the jungle.* ◇ You can also use **recesses** to talk about the mysterious or se-

cret aspects of something like a person's mind or an organization. ...*the Conservative Party's darkest recesses.*

recession (recessionary) A **recession** is a period when a country's economy is doing badly, for example because industry is producing less and unemployment is increasing. **Recessionary** is used to describe things connected with recession. ...*recessionary gloom.*

recharge (recharging, recharged; recharger) If you **recharge** a battery, you put an electrical charge back into it by connecting it to a machine called a **recharger** which draws power from another source of electricity such as the mains. Similarly, you can **recharge** a device containing rechargeable batteries.

rechargeable batteries can be recharged and used again.

recherché (*pron:* rish-**air**-shay) If you call something like a book or film **recherché,** you mean it is exotic, strange, and likely to be appreciated or understood by only a few people.

recidivist (*pron:* ris-**sid**-iv-ist) (recidivism) A **recidivist** is someone who repeatedly commits crimes even though they are caught and punished for them. Behaviour like this is called **recidivism.**

recipe (*pron:* **res**-sip-ee) A **recipe** is a list of ingredients and a set of instructions telling you how to cook something. ◇ If you say something is a **recipe** for success, you mean it is a sure way of achieving it. *This is hardly a recipe for a booming economy.* ◇ If you say something is a **recipe** for failure or disaster, you mean it is very likely to result in it.

recipient The **recipient** of something is the person who receives it. ...*recipients of blood transfusions.*

reciprocal (*pron:* ris-**sip**-pro-kal) (reciprocally) A **reciprocal** action or agreement involves two people or groups doing the same thing to each other or agreeing to help each other in a similar way. *Both sides would cooperate in designing doctrines which would be reciprocally recognized as purely defensive.*

reciprocate (reciprocating, reciprocated; reciprocation) If your feelings or actions towards someone are **reciprocated,** the other person feels or behaves in the same way towards you. *What they will be looking for is some reciprocation from countries like Britain and the United States.*

reciprocity (*pron:* ress-i-**pross**-i-tee) If there is **reciprocity** between two people or groups, each does something for the other or behaves in the same way towards the other. *The kidnappers want some reciprocity for these releases.*

recital A **recital** is a performance of music or poetry, usually given by one person. ◇ When someone repeats something which has been heard many times before, you can call this a **recital** of it.

recitative (*pron:* ress-it-at-**teev**) is speech-like singing which continues the story of an opera between songs.

recite (reciting, recited; recitation) If you **recite** a piece of writing, you read or say it aloud. What you say is called a **recitation.** ◇ When someone is talking and they give a list of things, you can say they **recite** the list. *They recited their litany of demands and complaints.*

reckless (recklessly, recklessness) If you call someone's behaviour **reckless,** you mean they foolishly do things without thinking about the dangers involved or the consequences of their actions. *He has been accused of recklessly jeopardizing relations with the United States... ...wanton*

financial recklessness.

reckon (reckoning, reckoned) ❑ If you say you **reckon** something is true, you mean you think it is true. *I reckon we are all on a below-average wage.*

❑ If you say someone **reckons** to do something, you mean they expect to do it. *The chef reckons to get through about two kilograms of sea vegetables in a season.* ◇ If you **reckon on** something, you expect it and take it into consideration when making your plans. *When we laid out the car parks, we reckoned on one car per four families.* ◇ If you say you had not **reckoned with** something or had **reckoned without** it, you mean you had not expected it and so were not prepared for it.

❑ If you have to **reckon with** a difficult person or situation, you have to deal with them. *They may well have to reckon with a small encampment of peace protesters.* ◇ If you say someone is a **force** or **power to be reckoned with,** you mean they are formidable and difficult to deal with.

❑ When an amount is **reckoned,** it is calculated or estimated. *Forbes magazine reckoned his personal wealth at $2.1 billion.* ◇ You use **in my reckoning** or **by my reckoning** when you are saying what you have estimated an amount to be, especially when it is only a rough estimate. *There were a lot of them, a thousand or so in my reckoning.*

❑ Someone's **day of reckoning** or **moment of reckoning** is a time when they have to face the consequences of what they have done in the past.

reclaim (reclaiming, reclaimed; reclamation) ❑ If you **reclaim** some lost property of yours which has been found, you go to the place where it is being kept and get it back. ◇ If you **reclaim** some money you have spent or some tax you have paid, you succeed in getting that amount paid back to you.

❑ When people **reclaim** land, they make it suitable for purposes like farming or building, for example by draining it. ...*a land reclamation project.*

reclassify (reclassifies, reclassifying, reclassified; reclassification) If something is **reclassified,** it is officially given a different classification from the one it had before. *Mr Lamont said he would not accept the reclassification of cider as a wine.*

recline (reclining, reclined) If you **recline,** you relax in a position between sitting and lying with the upper part of your body supported at an angle. A **reclining** chair or seat has a back which can be adjusted so you can recline on it.

recluse (reclusive) A **recluse** is a person who lives alone and deliberately avoids other people. You say someone like this is **reclusive.**

recognisable See recognizable.

recognise See recognize.

recognition ❑ If there is **recognition** of something, people acknowledge that it exists or is true.

❑ When someone receives **recognition** for something they have done, people acknowledge the significance of their achievements. *Mr Specter's strong record on human rights has not received the recognition it deserves.* If something is done to show official appreciation for what someone has done, you say it is done **in recognition** of their achievements.

❑ If something is granted **recognition,** it is officially accepted as legal or valid. ...*recognition of professional teaching* *qualifications.* ◇ When a new country is granted **recognition,** other countries officially accept it to be an independent country rather than part of a larger country.

recognizable (recognizably) *(can be spelled with an 's' instead of a 'z')* If something is **recognizable,** it can be easily recognized or identified as a certain type of thing. *...a recognizably capitalist tax system.*

recognize (recognizing, recognized) *(can be spelled with an 's' instead of a 'z')* If you **recognize** someone or something, you know who or what they are, because you have come across them before, because you have seen a picture of them, or because they have been described to you. ◇ If you **recognize** that something is true, you can see that it is true. *Most managers recognized that expanding a business also involves new costs.* ◇ **Recognized** is used to say something is acknowledged to be a particular thing. *The Baltic republics became the first former Soviet republics to be recognized as fully sovereign states.*

recoil (recoiling, recoiled) If you **recoil** from something, you view it with fear or disgust, and do not want to be near it or associated with it. ◇ **Recoil** is a sudden backward movement, especially of a gun when it is fired.

recollect (recollection) If you **recollect** something or have a **recollection** of it, you remember it.

recommence (recommencing, recommenced) If you **recommence** something, you begin doing it again.

recommend (recommendation) If you **recommend** something, you tell people it is enjoyable, useful, or good value. *She chose the school after a recommendation from relatives.* ◇ If you **recommend** a course of action, you say it would be the best thing to do.

recompense (recompensing, recompensed) If you are **recompensed,** you get money or something else which makes up for some harm that has been done to you. You say the thing you get is a **recompense** for the harm that has been done.

reconcile (reconciling, reconciled; reconciliation) ❑ If you **reconcile** two beliefs, facts, or demands which seem to be opposed or completely different, you find a way in which they can both be true or both be fulfilled. *He could not reconcile the idea of a loving Creator with the doctrines of original sin and damnation.*

❑ If you are **reconciled** with someone after a quarrel, you become friends or partners again. *This will put paid to any hope of a reconciliation between the duke and duchess.*

❑ If you are **reconciled** to an unpleasant situation or have **reconciled** yourself to it, you accept that it cannot be changed or avoided and are prepared to make the best of it.

recondite *(pron: rek-kon-dite)* If you call a fact or area of knowledge **recondite,** you mean it is not at all well-known, or of interest only to experts. *...the most recondite areas of modern science.*

recondition (reconditioning, reconditioned) If a machine is **reconditioned,** its worn or damaged parts are replaced or repaired, often so it can be sold as a cheaper alternative to a new machine.

reconnaissance *(pron: rik-kon-iss-anss)* is the process of obtaining military information about the size and positioning of an enemy army or the geographical features of an area using soldiers, planes, or satellites. *...reconnaissance aircraft... ...a reconnaissance mission.*

reconnoitre (reconnoitring, reconnoitred) *(American spelling: reconnoiter, reconnoitering, reconnoitered)* When people **reconnoitre** an area, they explore it to obtain information about its geographical features or the size and positioning of armies stationed there.

reconsider (reconsidering, reconsidered; reconsideration) If you **reconsider** a decision or opinion, you think about it and try to decide whether it should be changed. *Mr Shevardnadze's departure led to a reconsideration of Soviet policy.*

reconstitute (reconstituting, reconstituted) ❑ If an organization is **reconstituted,** it begins to operate in a new way, with different principles or a different structure.

❑ When things like dried foods or building materials are **reconstituted,** they are returned to their original form by adding water to them. *...reconstituted milk powder.*

reconstruct (reconstruction) ❑ If you **reconstruct** something which has been badly damaged, destroyed, or taken apart, you rebuild it and get it going again. *...the reconstruction of Kuwait's oil industry.*

❑ If you **reconstruct** something which happened in the past, you try to get a complete picture of it, by piecing together all the information available. ◇ A **reconstruction** of a crime is an attempt to act out what happened, in the hope that people will remember details they had forgotten about.

reconstructive surgery is the same as plastic surgery.

reconvene (reconvening, reconvened) If a parliament, court, or conference **reconvenes** or is **reconvened,** it meets again after a break.

record ❑ If you keep a **record** *(pron: rek-ord)* of something, you keep a written account of it, or store information about it on a computer. ◇ When you **record** *(pron: ri-kord)* information, you write it down, film it, or enter it on a computer, so people can look it up in the future. When something has been recorded in any of these ways, you say it is **on record.**

❑ Your **record** is everything that is known about your achievements or character. ◇ If someone has a **criminal record,** they have been found guilty of crimes in the past.

❑ When music or other sounds are **recorded,** they are preserved in a process called **recording,** which makes it possible for them to be played back later. ◇ A **record** is a round flat piece of plastic on which sound, especially music, is recorded. ◇ A **recording** of something is a record or tape of it.

❑ A **record** is the best result ever achieved in a sporting or other activity, for example the fastest time, the furthest distance, or the greatest number of victories. ◇ **Record** is used to describe something which is higher, lower, better, or worse than it has ever been before. *Water levels are at a record low.*

❑ You say **for the record** when you are giving people an extra piece of information which is not very important, or not relevant to what you are talking about. *Mr Chao, for the record, was wearing black slacks and a red linen jacket.*

❑ If someone speaks **off the record,** they do not intend what they say to be taken as official, or they do not want it published with their name attached to it. If, on the other hand, they go **on the record** or speak **on the record,** they say something officially and publicly. ◇ If someone is **on record** as saying or doing something, they have publicly said or done it, and it has been noted and remembered.

❏ If you **set** or **put the record straight**, you reveal the truth about something and show that what was believed before was wrong.

record player A **record player** is a machine which plays records.

recorded delivery is a Post Office service which gives you an official record of a letter or parcel being posted and delivered.

recorder ❏ A **recorder** is a machine which records sound or TV pictures, for example a tape recorder or a video recorder.

❏ Anyone or anything that records information can be called a **recorder**. *The paper sees itself as an enthusiastic recorder of great events in the 1990s... A data recorder is being tested on Intercity 125s.*

❏ In England and Wales, a **recorder** is someone who has been a barrister or solicitor for at least 10 years and has been appointed to sit as a part-time judge in a crown court.

❏ The **recorder** is a hollow wooden or plastic musical instrument. You play it by blowing down one end and covering a series of holes with your fingers.

recount ❏ If you **recount** (*pron:* ri-**count**) a story, you tell it. *...an audio-visual exhibition recounting the history of the lace industry.*

❏ If there is a **recount** (*pron:* ree-count) in an election, the votes are counted again. This happens when the result is very close.

recoup (*pron:* ri-**koop**) (recouping, recouped) If you **recoup** a sum of money you have spent or lost, you get it back.

recourse If you have **recourse** to something, you use it to help you in a difficult situation. *Is it possible to challenge discrimination without recourse to the law?*

recover (recovering, recovered) ❏ When you **recover** from an illness or injury, you get better. ◇ If you **recover** from an unpleasant experience, you get over it. *...a tragedy from which he never fully recovered.* ◇ If something **recovers** from a period of weakness or difficulty, it improves or gets stronger again. *...when the economy recovers from the recession.*

❏ If you **recover** something which has been lost or stolen, you find it or get it back.

recoverable ❏ If debts, costs, or expenses are **recoverable**, you are entitled to claim your money back. *Only nominal damages of a few hundred pounds would be recoverable by the plaintiff.*

❏ If natural resources are **recoverable**, it is possible and financially worthwhile to get them out of the ground.

recovery (recoveries) ❏ If a sick person makes a **recovery**, they become well again. ◇ If something makes a **recovery** after a period of difficulty or weakness, it improves or becomes stronger again. *...an economic recovery... ...a recovery of confidence.*

❏ You talk about the **recovery** of something when you get it back after it has been lost or stolen. *A substantial reward is being offered for the recovery of a painting by Turner which was stolen on Thursday.*

recreate (recreating, recreated) (*or* re-create, *etc*) ❏ If you **recreate** something, you make it happen or exist again. *It's not possible to recreate the conditions in the laboratory.*

❏ If you **recreate** something someone once did, you do

the same thing. *Devotees of Arthur Ransome are planning to recreate their hero's voyage from Helsinki to Riga in 1922.*

recreation ❏ **Recreation** (*pron:* rek-kree-ay-shun) is the various activities people take part in, for enjoyment or interest, during their spare time.

❏ A **recreation** (*pron:* ree-kree-ay-shun) of something from the past is a new version of it, made to look or operate just like the original. *The Shakespeare Globe project is building a faithful recreation of the original Elizabethan theatre on London's Bankside.* ◇ The **recreation** of something is the process of bringing it into existence again. *He urges the recreation of local councils.* For this meaning 'recreation' can be spelled 're-creation'.

recreation ground A **recreation ground** is a piece of public land, usually in a town or village, where people can go to play sport and games.

recreational is used to describe things to do with recreation. *His chief recreational interest was horticulture... ...recreational facilities.* ◇ **Recreational** drugs are drugs people use for pleasure rather than as medicines, especially illegal drugs like marijuana and cocaine.

recrimination You say there is **recrimination** when people or groups make angry accusations about each other. These accusations are called **recriminations**.

recruit (recruiting, recruited; recruitment, recruiter) When people are **recruited** for an organization, they are selected for it and persuaded to join it or work for it. *...an army recruiting office... Recruitment and training will start next year.* People or organizations that recruit people are sometimes called **recruiters**. *...the Association of Graduate Recruiters.* ◇ **Recruits** are people who have recently joined one of the armed forces, or some other similar organization.

rectal See rectum.

rectangle (rectangular) A **rectangle** is any four-sided shape in which all the angles are right angles, especially one where two sides are longer than the other two. If something is **rectangular**, it is shaped like a rectangle.

rectify (rectifies, rectifying, rectified; rectification) If you **rectify** something which is wrong or unacceptable, you put it right. *...the rectification of an injustice.*

rectitude is moral correctness and honesty of character. *Janet Fry's faith in her daughter's moral rectitude remained unshaken during the trial.*

rector A **rector** is a Church of England priest in charge of a parish. ◇ In some universities, a **rector** is a high-ranking official.

rectory (rectories) A **rectory** is a house in which a rector and his family live.

rectum (rectal) A person's **rectum** is the last part of the tube down which waste material passes from their body. **Rectal** is used to talk about things which involve the rectum. *...rectal examinations... ...rectal bleeding.*

recumbent If you are **recumbent**, you are lying down.

recuperate (recuperating, recuperated; recuperation) When you **recuperate**, you recover your health or strength after an illness, an injury, or an exhausting experience. *John Sheridan nursed Paul Gascoigne through his prolonged recuperation.*

recur (recurring, recurred; recurrence, recurrent) If something **recurs** or there is a **recurrence** of it, it happens again. *Troops and police are out in force to prevent a recurrence of* the violence that forced the cancellation of elections in 1987. ◇ You also say something **recurs** when it happens over and over again. *Violent disputes over mosques and religious processions have recurred with monotonous frequency.* You use **recurring** or **recurrent** to describe things which keep happening over and over again. *...a recurring nightmare... He suffered from recurrent bouts of psychotic illness.*

recyclable If something is **recyclable**, it can be recycled. *...recyclable waste.*

recycle (recycling, recycled) If you **recycle** things which have already been used, you process them so they can be used again. *...recycled materials... ...an efficient bottle recycling programme.*

red (redder, reddest) ❑ **Red** is the colour of blood or a ripe tomato. ◇ **Red** hair is between red and brown in colour. ◇ If you say someone's face is **red**, you mean it is redder than usual, because they are embarrassed, angry, or out of breath. ◇ If you say there are **red faces**, you mean people are very embarrassed about something.
❑ Communists, socialists, and other people with left-wing ideas are sometimes called **reds** by people who disapprove of them.
❑ If you **see red**, you become very angry.
❑ If you are **in the red**, your bank account is overdrawn.
❑ If you think a subject someone has raised is irrelevant and merely distracts people's attention from what is important, you can call it a **red herring**.

red alert If an organization is on **red alert**, it is ready to deal with an emergency.

red-blooded People sometimes call a man **red-blooded** when he has what people think of as typical male characteristics, for example strength, courage, and aggression. *...old-fashioned red-blooded Englishmen.*

red card In football, if the referee shows a player the **red card**, he holds up a red card and sends the player off the pitch.

red carpet The **red carpet** is a strip of red carpet laid out for an important or honoured visitor to walk on. When someone is given a special ceremonial welcome, you can say they are given the **red carpet** treatment.

Red Crescent The **Red Crescent** is an organization in Muslim countries with the same functions as the Red Cross.

Red Cross The **Red Cross** is an international organization which helps people who are suffering because of war, famine, or natural disaster.

Red Ensign The **Red Ensign** is the flag of the British Merchant Navy. It is red with the Union Jack in the top left corner.

red-handed If someone is caught **red-handed**, they are caught in the act of doing something wrong.

red-headed See redhead.

red-hot If metal is **red hot**, it is so hot it is glowing red. Similarly, you can talk about **red hot** coals or cinders. ◇ Food which is very hot can be called **red hot**. *...red-hot curry.* ◇ **Red-hot** is used to emphasize the strength of someone's enthusiasm or commitment. *...red-hot socialists.*

Red Indian See American Indian.

red light A **red light** is a traffic signal which indicates that traffic must stop. ◇ The **red light** district of a city is the

part where prostitutes operate.

red meat When people talk about **red meat**, they mean meat like lamb and beef which is dark brown in colour after it has been cooked.

red shift is the lengthening of the wavelengths of light given off by galaxies, which is thought to show they are moving away from the Earth. This supports the theory that the universe is expanding.

red tape When people talk about **red tape**, they mean official rules and procedures which waste time when you want to get something done.

redbrick British universities built in industrial cities in the Victorian and Edwardian periods are sometimes called redbrick universities.

redcurrant **Redcurrants** are small red edible berries which grow in bunches on bushes.

redden (reddening, reddened) If someone's face **reddens**, it turns pink or red, for example because they are hot or embarrassed.

reddish If something is **reddish**, it is slightly red.

redecorate (redecorating, redecorated; redecoration) If you **redecorate** a room or a building, you put new paint or wallpaper on it. *The house needs some interior redecoration.*

redeem (redeeming, redeemed) ❑ If you **redeem** yourself or **redeem** your reputation, you do something which gives people a good opinion of you again after you have behaved badly. ◇ If something **redeems** something which is of poor quality, it helps make up for the bad things about it. *I could not find a single redeeming feature in this book.*
❑ If you **redeem** a loan, you finish paying back the money you owe.

redeemable If something is **redeemable**, it can be exchanged for a certain sum of money or for goods worth a certain sum. *...electricity vouchers redeemable against bills.* ◇ If a company issues shares which are **redeemable**, it has the right to buy them back.

redeemer In Christianity, the **Redeemer** is Jesus Christ, who is believed to have saved people from the consequences of sin and evil.

redefine (redefining, redefined; redefinition) If you **redefine** something, you change it or make people consider it in a new way. *He has redefined the concept of a public museum.* A change like this is called a **redefinition**. *...a redefinition of the role of the LEA.*

redemption (redemptive) ❑ The **redemption** of a loan is the repayment of the money owed.
❑ **Redemption** is freedom from the consequences of sin and evil, which Christians believe was made possible by Christ's death. **Redemptive** is used to describe things connected with this idea. *...the redemptive power of love.* ◇ If you say something is **beyond redemption**, you mean it is so bad that nothing can put it right again.

redeploy (redeployment) If military forces or equipment are **redeployed**, they are moved to different positions where they will be more useful. Similarly, if the people who work for an organization are **redeployed**, they are moved to different jobs. *...the redeployment of skilled workers.*

redesign If something is **redesigned**, plans are drawn up to rebuild or change it with the intention of improving it.

redevelop (redeveloping, redeveloped; redevelopment) When an area is **redeveloped**, existing buildings and roads are removed and new ones are built in their place. ...*a big redevelopment project*.

redhead (red-headed) A **redhead** is a person whose hair colour is between red and brown. You say someone like this is **red-headed**.

redirect (redirection) ❏ If you **redirect** your actions or plans, you begin trying to achieve something different. *Mr Shevardnadze was responsible for the redirection of Soviet policy in Europe in the late 1980s.*
❏ If something like traffic is **redirected**, it is sent in a different direction. ◇ If you **redirect** something you receive in the post, you send it on somewhere else, because it is addressed to someone who no longer lives in your house.

rediscover (rediscovering, rediscovered) If you **rediscover** a quality or ability you used to have, you have it again. *PSV need to rediscover their goal-scoring form.*

redistribute (redistributing, redistributed; redistribution, redistributive) If money or property is **redistributed**, it is shared out in a different way. *Some ANC supporters see nationalization as an essential tool for the redistribution of wealth.* **Redistributive** is used to talk about methods for achieving this. *...Labour's much-criticized redistributive tax plans.*

redneck When Americans talk about **rednecks**, they mean men in country areas who are uneducated and typically have narrow-minded views, especially sexist and racist ones.

redolent is used to say something conveys strong feelings or reminds you of things from the past. *...a display of guts redolent of the best boys' adventure stories.* ◇ **Redolent** is also used to say a place or thing smells strongly of something. *...a spartan room with sink, rags and bare walls, all redolent of turps.*

redouble (redoubling, redoubled) If you **redouble** your efforts, you try much harder to achieve something.

redoubt A **redoubt** is a temporary defence work built inside a fortification as a last defensive position. ◇ You can also call something like an organization, a situation, or a set of ideas a **redoubt** when it represents all that is left of something which was once widespread and dominant. *The organization is the last redoubt of white power in the city.*

redoubtable If you call someone **redoubtable**, you mean they are bold and have a strong character, and people tend to respect or fear them.

redound If something you do **redounds** to your advantage, it has an advantageous effect for you. *Politicians have the opportunity to plant stories which redound to their credit and discomfit their enemies.*

redraft If something like a law or plan is **redrafted**, a new version of it is produced.

redraw (redrawing, redrew, have redrawn) If the borders or boundaries of a country or region are **redrawn**, they are changed so the country or region covers a slightly different area. ◇ If things like plans or rules are **redrawn**, they are altered to take account of changing circumstances.

redress (redresses, redressing, redressed) If you **redress** something such as a wrong or a grievance, you do something to put it right. *...laws designed to redress racial inequality.* ◇ **Redress** is compensation for a wrong done to someone. *Under present English law, it is only possible to gain financial redress for an injury if it can be proved that someone else was responsible.* ◇ If you do something to **redress the balance**, you try to put right something which is unfair or unequal.

redskin In the past, Native Americans in North America were sometimes called **redskins**.

reduce (reducing, reduced; reduction) ❏ If something is **reduced** or there is a **reduction** in it, it is made smaller or there is less of it. *He called for measures to reduce unemployment... There are signs of reduced tension in the Middle East... ...a nuclear arms reduction treaty.* ◇ In a shop, **reduced** goods are for sale at a reduced price.
❏ If people or things are **reduced** to an unpleasant condition or state, they are put in that condition or state. *Thousands of Mozambicans have been reduced to extreme poverty... The town of Baidoa has been reduced to rubble.* ◇ If circumstances force you to do something humiliating or unpleasant, you can say you are **reduced** to doing it. *The North is reduced to pleading with China for enough food and heating oil to get it through the coming winter.*

reductio ad absurdum The **reductio ad absurdum** of something like a principle is the absurd result you get if you take it to its extreme.

reduction See reduce.

redundant (redundancy, redundancies) ❏ If you are made **redundant**, you lose your job, because your employer can no longer afford to pay you, or because the work you have been doing is no longer necessary. **Redundancy** is losing your job like this. When several people are dismissed in this way, you say there are **redundancies**.
❏ If something is **redundant**, it is no longer needed, because it is not serving any useful purpose or has been replaced by something else. ◇ If something you do is **redundant**, it is pointless, because it cannot achieve anything. *The conference called to bring the warring parties together looks like a redundant exercise.*

redwood **Redwoods** are trees which grow in forests in California and Oregon. They are extremely tall, often reaching a height of over 80 metres.

reed **Reeds** are tall grasslike plants which grow in large groups in shallow water or marshy ground. They have strong stems which can be used for making things like mats and baskets. ◇ A **reed** is a small piece of cane inserted into the mouthpiece of a woodwind instrument like a clarinet or an oboe. The reed vibrates when you blow through it and makes a sound.

reedbed **Reedbeds** are areas of shallow water or marshy ground where reeds are growing.

reef A **reef** is a narrow line of sand, rocks, or coral, the top of which is just above or just below the surface of the sea.

reef knot A **reef knot** is a type of double knot for tying two pieces of rope or string firmly together.

reefer A **reefer** is (a) a home-made cigarette in which marijuana is mixed with tobacco. (b) a thick double-breasted jacket or short coat.

reek (reeking, reeked) If someone or something **reeks**, they have a strong unpleasant smell. A **reek** is a smell like this. *...the reek of floor polish.* ◇ You can criticize someone's behaviour by saying it **reeks** of something unpleasant. *The clamour to draw a veil over the minister's extra-marital activities reeks of hypocrisy.*

reel (reeling, reeled) ❑ A **reel** is a cylindrical object designed to have something like film, fishing line, or cotton thread wound around it. ◇ Sections of cinema film are sometimes called **reels**.

❑ If you **reel off** information, you repeat it from memory quickly and easily.

❑ If someone is **reeling**, they are moving around unsteadily as if they are about to fall. *...reeling drunks.* ◇ If you are **reeling** from an unpleasant experience, you are in a state of shock and are confused or upset.

❑ A **reel** is a fast traditional Scottish dance.

reel-to-reel magnetic tape goes from one reel of a tape recorder or computer to another and is not enclosed in a cassette.

ref In a football or boxing match, the referee is often called the **ref**.

refashion (refashioning, refashioned) If you **refashion** something, you change it significantly to take account of changing circumstances or to suit your own requirements.

refectory (refectories) In a university or a monastery, the **refectory** is the dining hall.

refectory table A **refectory table** is a long narrow dining table supported on two trestles.

refer (referring, referred) ❑ If you **refer** to something, you mention it or talk about it. *He did not refer to the controversy in his speech.* ◇ If you **refer** to people or things by a particular name, that is what you call them. *...a group of men referred to as 'the technocrats'.*

❑ **Refer** is used to say what something relates to. *The figures in the survey refer only to the published prices.*

❑ If you **refer** to a source of information such as a book, you look at it to find something out.

❑ If a task or problem is **referred** to a person or organization, they are asked to deal with it. *The ambassador referred the matter to the commander of the US navy task force.* ◇ If someone is **referred** to a person or organization, they are sent to them for the help they need. *Sometimes the client will be referred to a planning or environmental consultant.*

referee (refereeing, refereed) A **referee** is an official who controls something like a football match or a boxing match. You say this person **referees** the match. ◇ A **referee** is also someone who gives you a reference, for example when you are applying for a job.

reference ❑ If you make a **reference** to someone or something, you mention them. ◇ If something you say is taken as a **reference** to a particular thing, people think that is what you are talking about, although you have not mentioned it directly. *In an apparent reference to reports that he would be made a scapegoat for the defeat, Mr Hamrouche declared that he had no intention of resigning.* ◇ **With reference to** is used to say what something relates to. *Sir, with reference to the article on buying goods from America (Weekend Money, August 8) may I urge caution?*

❑ **Reference** books are books you consult when you need information, for example dictionaries and encyclopedias.

❑ A **reference** or **reference number** is a series of letters or numbers which identifies something.

❑ A **reference** is a letter written by someone who knows you which describes your character and abilities. Employers usually ask for references if you apply for a job.

reference library A **reference library** is a library containing reference books which you can look at on the premises but cannot take away.

referendum (*plural:* referendums *or* referenda) A **referendum** is a vote in which all the people in a country are asked whether they agree or disagree with a proposal or policy.

referral is sending someone to a person or authority that is authorized or better qualified to deal with them. A **referral** is an occasion when this is done. *He talks of unnecessary referrals to hospital consultants.*

refill If you **refill** something, you fill it again after it has been emptied.

refinance (refinancing, refinanced) If a person, organization, or country **refinances** a debt, it creates a new debt by borrowing money to pay the old one.

refine (refining, refined; refinement, refiner) ❑ When a substance is **refined**, it is made pure by having other substances removed from it. *...refined cocaine... ...the refinement of crude oil into aviation fuel.* A **refiner** is a firm or organization which refines a substance like oil or sugar in order to sell it.

❑ If something like an idea or process is **refined**, slight alterations or improvements are made to it, to make it more effective or efficient. These alterations or improvements are called **refinements**.

❑ If you call something **refined** or talk about its **refinement**, you mean it is elegant and tasteful. *...a refined, civilized play... British food is not as refined as French food.* ◇ **Refined** people have good taste and good manners.

refinery (refineries) A **refinery** is a factory where a substance like oil or sugar is refined.

refit (refitting, refitted) When a ship, train, or building is **refitted** or given a **refit**, it is made ready for further use, for example by repairs being done to it or new machinery being installed.

reflate (reflating, reflated; reflation, reflationary) If a government **reflates** its country's economy, it increases the amount of money available for spending, for example by cutting interest rates, to stimulate demand for goods and create more jobs. *...a US-style reflation strategy.* A **reflationary** policy is one which tries to achieve this.

reflect (reflection) ❑ If something **reflects** an attitude or desire, it shows people have it. *These innovations reflect the public's desire to have some choice in the education of their children.* You can say something is a **reflection** of an attitude or desire.

❑ If something **reflects** badly on someone, it gives a bad impression of them. You can also say something is a **reflection** on someone. *The library is unique and its break-up would be a sad reflection on the value we place on our heritage.*

❑ When light or heat **reflects** off a surface or is **reflected** off it, it bounces back from it rather than passing through it. This phenomenon is called **reflection**. ◇ When something is **reflected** in a mirror or water, you can see its image there. The image is called a **reflection**.

❑ When you **reflect**, you think carefully about something. *...a brief period of calm reflection.* If you change your mind about something **on reflection,** you change your mind after thinking about it carefully. ◇ If you **reflect** that something is true, you think about it and come to the conclusion that it is true. *He reflected that for once old Harold had been right.*

❑ People's comments or writings on a subject are sometimes called their **reflections.** *...a collection of prose-poems and reflections on Mexican culture by Octavio Paz.*

reflective ❑ If a material or surface is **reflective,** light or heat bounces off it rather than being absorbed by it or passing through it. *...reflective glass offices.*

❑ If you are **reflective,** you are thinking deeply about something. *...a sombre and reflective mood.*

reflector A **reflector** is a small piece of specially patterned glass or plastic which glows when light shines on it. Reflectors are often fitted to the backs of bicycles and cars. ◇ A **reflector** is also a type of telescope which contains a concave mirror.

reflex (reflexes) ❑ A **reflex** is a movement of part of your body which happens automatically in response to something else, and is not controlled by your mind. Blinking when something is brought close to your face is a type of reflex. ◇ If someone has quick **reflexes,** they are able to react quickly when something unexpected happens, for example when playing football or driving a car.

❑ If someone responds to something in an automatic way out of habit, you can call this response a **reflex** or a **reflex action.**

❑ A **reflex** angle is any angle between 180 degrees and 360 degrees. See also **acute, obtuse.**

reflexive If something you do is **reflexive,** you do it immediately and without thinking about it, as a habit or as a reaction to something. *The speed of the denial suggests more a reflexive attempt at damage control than a considered response.*

reflexive pronoun A **reflexive pronoun** is a pronoun which refers back to the subject of the sentence. For example, in the sentence 'She washed herself', 'herself' is a reflexive pronoun.

reflexology is a type of alternative medicine which involves massaging certain parts of the feet in the belief that this can help with seemingly unconnected medical problems.

refloat (refloating, refloated; reflotation) If a company is re**floated,** shares in it are offered for sale to the public again after a period when it has been controlled by a small number of private owners. This is called the **reflotation** of the company. ◇ If a ship is **refloated,** it is made to float again after it has run aground.

reforestation is planting trees on large areas of open land where there had been woodland in the past.

reform (reformer, reformist) ❑ **Reform** is used to talk about significant changes and improvements being made in the way a country, organization, or system is run. Each change can be called a **reform.** *...radical economic reforms.* When a system or organization is being changed and improved, you can say it is being **reformed.** A person who tries to bring about reforms is called a **reformer;** you call their behaviour and ideas **reformist.** *...a strongly reformist speech.*

❑ If someone **reforms,** they stop doing something socially unacceptable, such as drinking or committing crimes, and start to live a better life. *...a reformed cocaine trafficker.*

Reformation (*pron:* ref-for-**may**-shun) The **Reformation** was the movement to reform the Catholic Church begun by Martin Luther in the sixteenth century. It led to the Protestant Church being formed.

reformer (reformist) See **reform.**

refract (refraction) When rays of light are **refracted,** their direction is changed as a result of leaving one substance and entering another, for example when they move from air to water. This process is called **refraction;** it is responsible, for example, for a straight stick looking bent when you put one end in water.

refractory (refractories) ❑ You say someone is **refractory** when they are stubborn or unmanageable.

❑ **Refractories** are materials like fireclay and alumina which can withstand high temperatures and are used to line things like furnaces and kilns.

refrain (refraining, refrained) ❑ If you **refrain** from doing something, you deliberately do not do it. *President Havel has refrained from taking sides.*

❑ A **refrain** is a short simple part of a song which is repeated after each verse. ◇ When someone keeps saying the same thing, you can call what they say a **refrain.** *The stress on the importance of stability has been a constant refrain of the Chinese media this year.*

refresh (refreshes, refreshing, refreshed; refreshingly) ❑ If something **refreshes** you when you have become tired, hot, or thirsty, it cools you or makes you more energetic again. *...a refreshing drink.* ◇ You can call something **refreshing** when it is pleasantly different from what you are used to. *He was refreshingly honest.*

❑ If something **refreshes** your memory, it reminds you of things you had forgotten.

refresher course A **refresher course** is a training course intended to improve people's knowledge or skills and bring them up to date with new developments.

refreshment Refreshments are drinks and snacks. ◇ Food and drink, especially alcoholic drink, is sometimes called **refreshment.** *They took refreshment at an ancient pub.*

refrigerate (refrigerating, refrigerated; refrigeration) A **refrigerated** building or vehicle is one whose inside is kept at a low temperature, to preserve food being stored or transported in it. ◇ When food or drink is **refrigerated,** it is kept cool in a refrigerated building or a refrigerator. This process is called **refrigeration.**

refrigerator See **fridge.**

refuel (refuelling, refuelled) (*American spelling:* refueling, refueled) When an aircraft or other vehicle **refuels** or is **refuelled,** it is filled with more fuel so it can continue its journey.

refuge ❑ If you take **refuge,** you go to a place where you can get protection, for example from physical attack. A place like this is called a **refuge.**

❑ If you take **refuge** in a certain kind of behaviour, you try to protect yourself from unhappiness or unpleasantness by behaving in that way. ◇ If you take **refuge** in something like an argument or law, you use it to defend yourself against criticism or legal action. *Mr Aznar has repeatedly taken refuge in claims that the Socialists are hiding the true figures.*

❏ If you call a place the **last refuge** of a doctrine or attitude, you mean it is the only place where it still exists, although it used to be very common. *The golf club and the Garrick now seem to be the last refuges of the male chauvinist.*

refugee Refugees are people who have been forced to leave their homes or their country because of war or because of their political or religious beliefs.

refund A refund (*pron: ree-fund*) is a sum of money which is returned to you, for example because you have paid too much for something or because you have returned goods to a shop. When this happens, you say your money is **refunded** (*pron: re-fund-id*).

refundable A refundable deposit or charge will be paid back in certain circumstances. *...a refundable full-fare economy ticket.*

refurbish (refurbishes, refurbishing, refurbished; refurbishment) If something like a building or aircraft is **refurbished,** it is cleaned and redecorated and new equipment or furnishings are installed. *Inmate accommodation was in need of urgent and extensive refurbishment.* ◇ If people try to **refurbish** the image of an organization or regime, they try to make it respected or popular again.

refuse (refusing, refused; refusal) ❏ If you **refuse** to do something, you deliberately do not do it, or you say firmly that you will not do it. You talk about someone's **refusal** to do something. *...the government's refusal to negotiate.* ◇ If someone **refuses** you something, they do not give it to you, or do not allow you to have it. *The United States has refused him a visa.*

❏ If you **refuse** something which is offered to you, you do not accept it. ◇ If you have **first refusal** on something, it is offered to you before it is offered to anyone else.

❏ **Refuse** (*pron: ref-yoos*) is the rubbish and other unwanted things in a house, shop, or factory which are regularly thrown away.

refute (refuting, refuted; refutation) ❏ If you **refute** an allegation or theory or make a **refutation** of it, you prove it is wrong or untrue. *His work can legitimately be read as a refutation of Marxist categories and methodologies.*

❏ If you say you **refute** something you are accused of, you mean you strongly deny it. Similarly, if you say you **refute** a suggestion, you mean you reject it completely. Some people think these uses of 'refute' are wrong.

regain (regaining, regained) If you **regain** something you have lost, you get it back. *The Peronists have regained control of the western province of San Juan.*

regal (regally) If you describe something as **regal,** you mean it is typical of a king or queen, or suitable for one. *...a long black gown, very Renaissance-looking and rather regal... She waved regally.*

regale (regaling, regaled) If someone **regales** you with stories or jokes, they keep telling you them, one after another.

regalia The **regalia** of someone like a monarch or soldier is their traditional clothing and other objects they wear or carry on formal occasions. *Election posters still portray him in full military regalia... ...a couple dressed in wedding regalia.*

regally See regal.

regard ❏ If you **regard** someone or something in a certain way, that is how you think of them or feel about them. *Sir Ralph was regarded with suspicion in the City...*

China has long regarded human rights as an internal issue.

❏ If you have a **regard** for someone, you respect and admire them. You can also have a **regard** for what they say or do. *I have high regard for the work of the World Council of Christians.*

❏ If you do something without **regard** for a particular thing, you fail to take it into consideration. *Some doctors treat patients with little regard for the effect of their actions.*

❏ You use **regarding** to show what you are referring to. *The verdict regarding the arms charges is expected at 1130 GMT.* **In regard to, with regard to,** and **as regards** are used in a similar way. *As regards the campaign, he said it was unnecessarily loud and contradictory.*

❏ If you send someone your **regards,** you are expressing friendly greetings to them.

regardless If something happens **regardless** of something else, it is not affected or influenced by it. *Humanitarian missions should include everyone regardless of nationality or creed.* ◇ If you say someone carries on **regardless,** you mean they carry on doing something even though circumstances make it difficult or unwise to do so.

regatta A **regatta** is a sporting event at which sailing or rowing races are held.

Regency The **Regency** was the period of British history between 1811 and 1820, when the Prince Regent acted as king, because of his father's madness. **Regency** is used to describe the art, architecture, and furniture popular during this period and for a decade or so afterwards. *...a grand old Regency hotel.*

regenerate (*pron: ree-jen-er-ate*) (regenerating, regenerated; regeneration) ❏ If something like an area or an industry is **regenerated,** it is developed and improved to make it more active and successful, usually after a period of decline. *...the regeneration of British manufacturing.*

❏ If living things or parts of living things **regenerate,** they grow back again after they have been lost or damaged. *...the regeneration of hair-cells... ...forest regeneration.*

regenerative powers cause something to heal or become active again after it has declined or been damaged. *...the regenerative power of nature.*

regent A **regent** is a person who rules a country when the king or queen is unable to rule, for example because they are too young or too ill.

reggae (*pron: regg-ay*) is a type of music which originated in Jamaica. Songs are sung to a steady four-beat accompaniment with a strong bass line.

regicide is the crime of killing a king or queen.

regime (*pron: ray-zheem; the 'zh' sounds like 's' in 'pleasure'*) The rulers of a country are sometimes called a **regime,** especially when they are not democratically elected and run the country in a harsh restrictive way. Their system of ruling the country can also be called a **regime.** *...General Pinochet's military regime.* ◇ The people who run an organization or industry are sometimes called a **regime.** ◇ A **regime** is also a strict set of rules and requirements.

regimen A **regimen** is a strict programme or procedure, especially one involving medical treatment, diet, or exercise.

regiment (regimental) A **regiment** is a large group of soldiers commanded by a colonel. **Regimental** is used to describe people or things belonging to or connected with a regiment. *...regimental colonels... ...the regimental badge.* ◇ A **regiment** of people is a very large number of them. *A regiment of farm workers and their wives and children made hay in the summer.*

regimented (regimentation) If something is **regimented**, everything about it is strictly controlled. You call this control **regimentation**. *Such scenes of order and discipline are common to Pyongyang, one of the most regimented cities in the world.*

region ❑ A **region** is a large area, especially a part of a country or of the world which is distinguished from the rest by geographical features or the type of people living there. *...the remote, semi-desert region of the Northern Cape... ...the Gulf region... ...the Muslim region of western China.* ◇ The parts of a country which are away from its capital are sometimes called the **regions**. *48 staff have been moved from London to the regions.*

❑ Some areas of the body are called **regions**. *...the lumbar region... ...a region of the brain called the substantia negra.*

❑ You use **in the region of** when you are giving an approximate figure. *...an annual running cost in the region of £25m.*

regional (regionally) **Regional** is used to talk about things to do with geographical regions. *...regional issues... ...a regionally-elected senate.*

regionalism (regionalist) **Regionalism** is a strong feeling of pride or loyalty which people have for the region they live in, often including a desire to govern themselves. **Regionalist** is used to describe people like these and their organizations and activities. *...the proudly regionalist Christian Social Union.*

register (registering, registered) ❑ A **register** is an official record in the form of a list. *...registers of births, deaths and marriages.* See also **electoral register**.

❑ If you **register** for something, you put your name down for it. *Many women do not register for benefit if they lose their jobs.* ◇ If something is **registered**, it is accepted officially and placed on a register. *Britain has more than ten thousand registered fishing vessels.*

❑ A **registered** letter or parcel is sent by a special postal service, for which you pay extra money to insure it in case it is lost. Registered letters and parcels have to be signed for on delivery.

❑ If something **registers** a particular figure on a measuring instrument, that is the reading the instrument gives when it is measured. Similarly, you can talk about something **registering** a figure on a scale. *The earthquake registered 7.5 on the Richter scale.*

❑ If you **register** your feelings of disapproval about something, you tell people about them, or do something which makes them clear. ◇ If someone's face **registers** a feeling, their expression shows they have that feeling. *Christie's face registered blazing aggression.*

❑ If a piece of information does not **register** with you, you fail to take it in.

register office A **register office** is a place where births, marriages, and deaths are officially recorded, and where people can get married without a religious ceremony.

registrar A **registrar** is a person whose job is to keep official records, especially of births, marriages, and deaths. ◇ At a university, a **registrar** is a senior administrative official.

registration The **registration** of something like a person's name or the details of an event is its inclusion on an official record. *...the registration of births... ...a national dog registration scheme.* ◇ The **registration number** or **registration** of a road vehicle is the sequence of letters and numbers displayed on plates at the front and back. The plates are called **registration plates** or **number plates**.

registry (registries) A **registry** is a collection of official records or a place where records like these are kept. *They agreed to set up a central registry of arms sales.*

registry office A **registry office** is the same as a register office.

regress (regresses, regressing, regressed; regression, regressive) ❑ When people **regress**, they return to an earlier, less advanced stage of development. When this happens, you call their behaviour **regressive**. *...the teacher's regression to small-boy fury and helplessness.*

❑ In a **regressive** taxation system, the rate of taxation becomes lower as the amount to be taxed increases.

regret (regretting, regretted) If you **regret** something you have done or feel **regret** about it, you wish you had not done it. ◇ You also say you **regret** something when you feel sad and disappointed that it has happened. *My only regret is that Mal Reilly is unable to fit Jonathan Davies into the team.* ◇ People say I **regret...** when they are apologizing for something, or breaking bad news. *We regret no personal replies can be given.*

regretful (regretfully) **Regretful** is used to describe someone's behaviour when it shows they are sad and disappointed. *Mr Griffin gave a regretful smile.* ◇ People sometimes use **regretful** and **regretfully** to say something is unfortunate and undesirable. *He added that regretfully the extremist wing had made no peace offer.* Some people think this use is incorrect. Instead, they say you should say 'regrettable' and 'regrettably'.

regrettable (regrettably) If you describe something as **regrettable**, you mean it is unfortunate and undesirable. *Regrettably, it has not been possible to settle the contractual disputes.*

regroup (regrouping, regrouped) When soldiers **regroup**, they form an organized group again, ready to continue fighting. ◇ When an organization comes to an end, you can say its members **regroup** to form a new organization.

regular (regularly, regularity) ❑ **Regular** is used to describe things which happen repeatedly with the same time gap between each occasion, for example things which happen at the same time each week. *The European Commission will assemble for its regular weekly meeting on Wednesday... They'll have to report regularly at police stations.* ◇ **Regular** is also used to describe things which happen often. *These tests are regularly used in selecting people for jobs.* You can also say something happens with **regularity**. *Closures and job losses are again being announced with monotonous regularity.*

❑ **Regular** is used to say a person often does something. For example, instead of saying someone 'regularly visits Egypt', you can say they are 'a regular visitor to Egypt'. *He was a regular attender at opera first nights in London.* ◇ People who often do something, for example drink in a certain pub, are called the **regulars**.

❏ **Regular** is used to describe professional soldiers who are a permanent part of an official national army. ...*regular troops... ...a regular army.*

❏ **Regular** is used, especially in the US, to say something is the standard size. ...*a large or regular soft drink of your choice.*

❏ **Regular** is also used to describe something which has a symmetrical or orderly appearance, because it consists of similar things all arranged the same way or with equal spaces between them. ...*a bookcase with regularly spaced shelves.* This characteristic is called **regularity.**

regularize (regularizing, regularized) (*can be spelled with an 's' instead of a 'z'*) If something is **regularized**, it becomes legal and official by being made to conform to certain rules and requirements. ◇ If something like an area of business is **regularized**, a single set of rules and standards are created to govern it. *The first necessity is to regularize accounting practices.*

regulate (regulating, regulated; regulation) ❏ If something is **regulated**, it is controlled by a set of rules. *Britain is moving towards statutory regulation of financial services.* These rules are called **regulations.**

❏ If you **regulate** the amount of something, you control it, for example by means of a mechanical device.

regulator A **regulator** is a person or organization that controls the activities of companies and other organizations, usually by means of rules. Regulators are usually appointed by governments. ◇ A **regulator** is also a device which automatically controls something, for example a temperature regulator.

regulatory organizations, powers, and measures are intended to control the activities of companies and other organizations, usually by means of rules.

regurgitate (*pron:* rig-**gur**-jit-tate) (regurgitating, regurgitated) If someone **regurgitates** information, they repeat it without thinking about it or understanding it properly. ◇ If a person or animal **regurgitates** food, they bring it back up from their stomach.

rehabilitate (rehabilitating, rehabilitated; rehabilitation) ❏ When people are **rehabilitated**, they gradually return to living normal lives as part of the community, for example after they have been in prison, addicted to drugs, or ill. ...*the rehabilitation of young offenders.*

❏ You say someone who has been in disgrace is **rehabilitated** when people no longer condemn them but begin to accept them or think well of them. You can also say someone's reputation is **rehabilitated.**

❏ If something like a building or area of land is **rehabilitated**, it is improved so it can be used again.

rehash (rehashes, rehashing, rehashed) If you **rehash** old ideas, you use them again, often rearranging them to try to make them appear new. You call something produced like this a **rehash.** *The 'new' models promised by car makers turned out to be little more than rehashes of existing products.*

rehearse (rehearsing, rehearsed; rehearsal) ❏ When people like actors, dancers, and musicians **rehearse**, they practise for a public performance. Each occasion when they practise is called a **rehearsal.** See also **dress rehearsal.**

◇ You can say other people **rehearse** things when they practise them, to make sure they get them right before doing them properly. *Surgeons are now able to rehearse*

complicated operations on life-size dummies.

❏ You can also say something is a **rehearsal** for a later event when it is similar to it, but is less important or on a smaller scale.

rehouse (rehousing, rehoused) If someone is **rehoused**, their local council or another authority provides them with a different place to live.

rehydrate (rehydrating, rehydrated; rehydration) When someone who is suffering from lack of water is **rehydrated**, they are given liquid to drink, or liquid is put back into their body through a tube. *The primary treatment for cholera is still early rehydration with intravenous or oral fluids.*

reign ❏ When a king or queen **reigns**, they rule a country. The period when they are king or queen is called their **reign.** *The Civil List came into being in the reign of King George III.* ◇ The period when someone is in charge of an organization is sometimes humorously called their **reign.** ...*Mr Akers's reign at IBM.*

❏ The **reign** of a sporting champion is the period when they are champion. ◇ The **reigning** champion of a sport is the person who is champion at the moment.

❏ If you say confusion **reigns**, you mean everyone is very confused about what is happening. You can talk about other things **reigning** in a similar way. *Panic reigned in Annaba after the assassination.*

reimburse (reimbursing, reimbursed; reimbursement) If you are **reimbursed** for money you have spent or lost, you are paid back. *You should get the object repaired and claim in writing for reimbursement.*

rein (reining, reined) ❏ **Reins** are the thin leather straps attached to a horse's bridle which are used to control the horse. ◇ If you talk about someone holding the **reins** or holding the **reins of power**, you mean they are in control of a country or organization.

❏ If someone is given **free rein** or **full rein**, they are allowed to do something without any controls or restrictions being imposed on them. ...*economic and social policies which allow free rein to market forces.* ◇ If you keep a **tight rein** on someone or something, you keep them firmly under your control. ◇ If you **rein** something **in** or **rein** it **back**, you reduce it or get it back under strict control. *His administration's economic policy would focus on reining in inflation.*

reincarnated (reincarnation) ❏ Hindus, Buddhists, and followers of some other religions believe that people are **reincarnated**, that is, they are born again after their death in the body of another person or living thing. Being born again like this is called **reincarnation**; you say someone is the **reincarnation** of a person or animal. ...*a man claiming to be a reincarnation of Leo Tolstoy.*

❏ If something like an organization is **reincarnated**, it is recreated in a different form or with a different name. *The first demonstration was held by the Socialists, the reincarnation of the former Communist Party.*

reindeer (*plural:* reindeer) The **reindeer** is a type of large deer which is different from other deer in that both sexes have branched antlers. Reindeer live in northern areas of Europe, Asia, and North America. In North America, they are called **caribou.**

reinforce (reinforcing, reinforced; reinforcement) ❏ If an army or a group of police is **reinforced**, it is made stronger by increasing its size or providing it with more weapons.

◇ **Reinforcements** are soldiers or police sent to join an army or group of police to strengthen it. ◇ If a place is **reinforced**, it is made stronger and better able to withstand an attack, by sending in more soldiers or weapons.

❑ If someone's power is **reinforced**, they are made more powerful. ...*the reinforcement of presidential powers.*

❑ If something **reinforces** an idea or a belief, it provides more evidence or support for it. *Recent events reinforced Britain's conviction that the problems of the region could be solved only by negotiation.* ◇ If something **reinforces** a feeling, it makes it stronger.

❑ A **reinforced** material has been made stronger or harder, by putting another material into it. For example, reinforced concrete has steel bars or mesh inside it.

reinstate (reinstating, reinstated; reinstatement) ❑ If someone is **reinstated**, they are given their job or position back. *Workers have gone on strike, demanding the reinstatement of 33 dismissed union leaders.*

❑ If something like a law or a system is **reinstated**, it is brought back again. *In 1972, the Supreme Court voted to ban the death penalty, but by 1976 it had been reinstated.*

reinterpret (reinterpreting, reinterpreted; reinterpretation) If you **reinterpret** something, you interpret it in a new way. The new interpretation is called a **reinterpretation**. *The bill reinterprets Japan's constitution to allow its soldiers to take part in UN peace-keeping operations.*

reinvent (reinvention) If something is **reinvented**, it is reorganized in such a way that it seems like something fresh and new. *The Bush Administration promoted the reinvention of the high school by setting up a national competition for new types of schools.*

reinvest (reinvestment) When a company **reinvests**, it spends its profits on improving itself in some way. This is called **reinvestment**.

reissue (reissuing, reissued) If something like a book or record is **reissued**, it is published or produced again when it has not been available for some time. The new version is called a **reissue**.

reiterate (*pron:* ree-it-er-ate) (reiterating, reiterated; reiteration) If you **reiterate** something which has already been said, you repeat it. ...*her reiteration of her opposition to a single European currency.*

reject (rejection) ❑ If you **reject** something like a proposal, a request, or an offer, you do not accept it or do not agree to it. ◇ If you **reject** what someone says, you say it is untrue or unjustified. ...*a rejection of the allegations levelled against him.* ◇ If you **reject** something like a belief or a set of values, you do not accept it. ◇ If you **reject** a type of activity, you refuse to take part in it or support it. ...*a civil rights leader renowned for his rejection of violence.*

❑ If you are **rejected** by someone, they show they do not want to have anything to do with you.

❑ If you are **rejected** for a job or a place on a course, you are not accepted for it.

❑ If someone's body **rejects** something like a new heart after a transplant, their own immune system starts attacking and destroying it.

❑ A **reject** (*pron:* ree-ject) is a product which is sold cheaply or not sold at all, because it does not meet the standards required by the manufacturer.

rejectionist A **rejectionist** is someone who is strongly opposed to a change which is being proposed to a system. *Several popular rejectionist factions may attempt to disrupt the process.*

rejig (rejigging, rejigged) If you **rejig** something, you alter it or reorganize it in a crude or clumsy way. *The promoter hastily rejigged the running order.*

rejoice (rejoicing, rejoiced) ❑ If you **rejoice**, you are extremely pleased about something. *The French government rejoiced at the happy outcome to events.* ◇ **Rejoicing** is behaviour in which people show their delight, usually in a noisy way. *The result was greeted with scenes of rejoicing in the Slovene capital.*

❑ If you say someone or something **rejoices** in a certain name, you are drawing attention to how unusual or amusing their name is. ...*George Galloway, the Labour MP who rejoices in the nickname of 'Gorgeous George'.*

rejoinder A **rejoinder** is a quick, witty, or critical reply to what someone has just said.

rejuvenate (*pron:* ree-joov-en-ate) (rejuvenating, rejuvenated; rejuvenation) If something **rejuvenates** you, it makes you feel young and energetic again. ◇ If something **rejuvenates** an organization or activity, it makes it more lively or successful. *The railway extension is widely seen as the key to the rejuvenation of east London.*

rekindle (rekindling, rekindled) If things like feelings or problems are **rekindled**, something starts them up again. *The disintegration of the Soviet empire is rekindling old national and ethnic tensions.*

relapse (relapsing, relapsed) If a sick person suffers a **relapse**, their health suddenly gets worse after it has been improving. ◇ If someone or something **relapses**, they go back to behaving in an undesirable way. You call this a **relapse**. *It is by no means clear that the financial markets will not relapse into panic.*

relate (relating, related) ❑ If something **relates** to a subject, it concerns that subject. *The corrections relate to chapter 20...* ...*the laws relating to inheritance.*

❑ If things are **related** or one is **related** to the other, there is a connection between them. ...*closely related issues...* ...*drug-related crimes.*

❑ People who are **related** belong to the same family. ◇ You say things like animals or languages are **related** when they have evolved or developed from the same animal or language. ...*an extinct South African animal related to the horse... The Gagauz speak a language related to Turkish.*

❑ If you can **relate** to someone or something, you have an understanding of them which helps you deal with them or makes you sympathetic to them. ...*the need for leaders who can relate to ordinary people.*

❑ If you **relate** a story, you tell it.

relation ❑ **Relations** between people, groups, or countries are the contacts between them and the way they feel and behave towards each other. *Boston experimented with closer relations between schools and local business.*

❑ The **relation** of one thing to another is the connection between them. ...*the relation of fiction to life.*

❑ Your **relations** are the members of your family.

❑ **In relation to** is used to say what something concerns. *Colonel Herrera is the sixth person to be arrested in relation to the alleged coup plot.* ◇ **In relation to** is also used to compare two things. For example, if you say something is large **in relation to** something else, you mean the first thing is large when compared to the second. *The corporation is selling coal at prices that are absurdly low in relation to its costs.*

relationship ❑ The **relationship** between two people or groups is the way they feel and behave towards each other. *His country's relationship with France is now very cordial.*
❑ A **relationship** is a close friendship between two people, especially one involving romantic or sexual feelings.
❑ If there is a **relationship** between two things, they are connected in some way.

relative (relatively) ❑ Your **relatives** are the members of your family. ◇ If you talk about one type of animal being a **relative** of another, you mean both types evolved from the same animal. *The quagga was a very close relative to the zebra.*
❑ You use **relative** and **relatively** to indicate that the accuracy of your description is based on a comparison with other things. *Thousands of residents fled to the relative safety of underground shelters... Land Rover markets a range of relatively highly-priced vehicles.* ◇ The **relative** advantages and disadvantages of two things are their advantages and disadvantages compared to each other. *...the relative costs of gas and coal.* ◇ If you say something is **relative**, you mean it needs to be considered and judged in relation to other things. *Failure, like success, is relative.*
❑ **Relative to** means (a) 'in comparison with'. *Academic salaries have fallen, relative to those in other professions.* (b) 'in proportion to'. *A formula now restricts weight relative to bat length.*

relativism or **ethical relativism** is the view that there are no absolute standards of right and wrong and that there is only what an individual or society thinks is right or wrong.

relativity The theory of **relativity** is Einstein's theory concerning space, time, motion, mass, and gravitation.

relaunch (relaunches, relaunching, relaunched) If something like a product or a political campaign is **relaunched**, it is promoted in a new way in an attempt to increase its popularity. *In 1985 Penguin relaunched their classics in smart, black colour-coded jackets.*

relax (relaxes, relaxing, relaxed; relaxation) ❑ If you **relax**, you allow yourself to feel calm, rather than worried or tense. When you are in this state, you say you are **relaxed**. If something is **relaxing**, it makes you feel like this. ◇ If a discussion or meeting is **relaxed**, it is calm, unhurried, and informal. You can also say it takes place in a **relaxed** atmosphere.
❑ You also say you **relax** when you spend time in a pleasant or restful way. **Relaxation** is spending time like this. *His favoured form of relaxation was walking on the local moors.*
❑ When your body or a part of your body **relaxes**, it becomes less stiff, firm, or tense.
❑ If rules or controls are **relaxed**, they are made less strict or severe. *A further relaxation of fiscal policy would risk overstimulating the economy.* ◇ If you are **relaxed** about something, you are not worried about it. *Eurotunnel is taking a relaxed attitude towards the apparent stock market cold shoulder.*
❑ If you **relax your grip** on something, you hold it less tightly. ◇ If someone who is in control of a country or or-

ganization **relaxes their grip**, they no longer keep it under such tight control.

relay ❑ A **relay** or **relay race** is a race between a certain number of teams, for example runners or swimmers. Each member of the team runs or swims one section of the race. There are usually four sections.
❑ When radio or TV signals or programmes are **relayed**, they are transmitted, or received and retransmitted. *The first pictures should be relayed to earth in about a week.* A transmission like this is called a **relay**. **Relay satellites** and **relay stations** are used in transmissions like these.
❑ When you **relay** information, you pass it on to other people.

release (releasing, released) ❑ If a prisoner or captive animal is **released**, they are set free. You call this their **release**. ◇ If someone is **released** from hospital, they are allowed to go home.
❑ If you **release** something you are holding, you let go of it.
❑ When energy or a substance is **released** from something, it escapes from it. *Efficient lights and appliances release less heat.*
❑ If you **release** a vehicle's brakes, you take your foot off the brake pedal or move a control, so that the brakes are no longer slowing the vehicle down or preventing it moving.
❑ When information or documents are **released**, they are made available to the public or the press. ◇ When something like a new record or film is **released** or **goes on release**, it is made available for the public to buy or see. New records and films are sometimes called **releases**.
❑ If you are **released** from something like a duty, you no longer have to perform it.
❑ If you **release** a strong feeling, you express it in some way. *President Nixon said they were merely releasing pent-up anger.*

relegate (relegating, relegated; relegation) If a team is **relegated**, it is moved to a lower division because it finished at or near the bottom of its division at the end of a season. *Gall scored 14 goals in 29 appearances, but failed to save Brighton from relegation.* ◇ If someone or something is **relegated** to a less important position or role, they are moved to that position or role.

relent If you **relent**, you give in over something you had previously been opposed to or insisting on. *Unless the unions relent on wage rises, productivity will slump.*

relentless (relentlessly, relentlessness) You say someone's behaviour is **relentless** when they keep doing something and refuse to stop or give in. *They have relentlessly tortured those bold enough to criticize the government.* ◇ If something is **relentless**, it shows no sign of stopping or slowing down. *...a relentless downpour... Inflation and interest rates increased relentlessly... ...the relentlessness with which misfortune follows misfortune.*

relevant (relevance) ❑ If something is **relevant** to what is being described or discussed, it has some real bearing on it. You talk about the **relevance** of something like this. *They reported the man's colour in a prejudicial way which had no relevance to the story.* ◇ You also say something is **relevant** when it has some real importance or significance for people. *With the removal of repression in most* former communist states, anti-Communist songs have lost their relevance and popularity.

❏ The **relevant** thing or person in a particular situation is the appropriate one. *They called for action to be taken by the relevant authorities.*

reliable (reliably, reliability) If you say someone or something is **reliable,** you mean they can be depended on to work well or behave in the way you want. This characteristic is called **reliability.** ◇ **Reliable** information is highly likely to be correct, because you can trust the source it comes from. *They are owned, I am reliably informed, by crack dealers.*

reliant (reliance) If you are **reliant** on someone or something, you need them and cannot do without them. You can talk about your **reliance** on someone or something.

relic ❏ If you call something a **relic** of something bad in the past, you mean it came about because of it, and is still around. *The division between amateur and professional is a relic of England's Victorian class structure.*

❏ **Relics** are things made or used a long time ago and kept for their historical importance. *...a collection of historical relics.* ◇ A **relic** is also an object kept in a church or chapel which people believe is part of the body of a saint or something connected with a saint, and which they consider to be holy.

relief is a feeling of gladness and release from worry, because something unpleasant has not happened or a problem has been solved. When something gives you this feeling, you can say it is a **relief.** *For many it was a relief to be back at work.* ◇ If something provides **relief** from pain, it eases it.

❏ **Relief** is also money, food, or clothing provided for people who are very poor or hungry, or who have been affected by war or a natural disaster.

❏ **Relief** is used to describe people who step in to do a job when the person who normally does it is not available. *No relief drivers were available.*

❏ If one thing **throws** another **into relief,** it emphasizes it and exposes its characteristics or faults. *...private affluence thrown into relief by public squalor.*

❏ A **relief** is a sculpture carved so that it stands out of a vertical surface. See also **bas-relief.**

relieve (relieving, relieved) ❏ If you are **relieved,** you feel glad and released from worry, because something unpleasant has not happened or a problem has been solved.

❏ If something **relieves** an unpleasant situation or feeling, it eases it or stops it. *The road should relieve city centre congestion considerably... ...pain-relieving drugs.*

❏ If you are **relieved** of something, it is taken away from you. ◇ If someone is **relieved** of their post or duties, they are discharged or sacked.

❏ If you **relieve** someone, you take over from them and continue doing what they were doing, so they can leave. *At seven o'clock the night nurse came in to relieve her.*

❏ If an army **relieves** a town or other place which has been besieged, it frees it.

❏ When people or animals **relieve** themselves, they urinate or defecate.

religion is belief in a god or gods, and the activities connected with this belief, such as prayer or worship. A **religion** is a particular set of beliefs and activities of this kind.

religiosity If you talk about someone's **religiosity,** you are talking about what you see as their extreme and perhaps insincere religious beliefs and practices.

religious (religiously) ❏ **Religious** is used to describe things connected with religion. *...a religious service... India has always been one of the most religiously diverse countries in the world.* ◇ If someone is **religious,** they have a strong belief in a god or gods.

❏ If you do something **religiously,** you do it conscientiously and exactly. *By sticking religiously to the rules of the system, they destroy it in the process.*

relinquish (relinquishes, relinquishing, relinquished; relinquishment) If you **relinquish** something, you give it up. *The Rt Hon Neil Kinnock, MP was received by The Queen on the relinquishment of his post as Leader of the Opposition.*

reliquary (*pron:* rel-lik-wer-ee) (reliquaries) A **reliquary** is a container in which a religious relic is kept.

relish (relishes, relishing, relished) ❏ If you **relish** something, you get a lot of enjoyment from it. You can talk about someone's **relish** for something. *Cantona still displays a wonderful relish for the game.* ◇ If you **relish** the prospect or idea of something, you look forward to it eagerly. *Many are still in refugee camps, and cannot be relishing the prospect of another harsh winter.*

❏ **Relish** is a sauce or pickle you add to food after it has been served, to give it more flavour.

relive (reliving, relived) If you **relive** something from your past, you imagine you are going through it again, or you have a similar experience which reminds you of it.

relocate (relocating, relocated; relocation) If people or businesses **relocate** or are **relocated,** they move to a different place. *Texaco yesterday announced that it was delaying the relocation of 1,000 staff to Westferry Circus.*

reluctant (reluctantly, reluctance) If you are **reluctant** to do something, you are unwilling to do it. You talk about someone's **reluctance** to do something. *Senior officers have made no secret of their reluctance to use force.* ◇ If you do something **reluctantly,** you do it, but are not happy about doing it.

rely (relies, relying, relied) If you **rely on** someone or something, you need them, often to the extent that you cannot do without them. ◇ If you say someone or something can be **relied on,** you mean they can be depended on to work well or behave in the way you want. ◇ If you are **relying on** something happening, you are expecting it to happen, so something can be achieved. *They are relying on emigration to relieve the country's job crisis.*

REM or **rapid eye movement** is a darting movement of the eyes beneath closed lids, which occurs when you are dreaming.

remade See remake.

remain (remaining, remained) ❏ If someone or something **remains** in a certain state or condition, they stay like that. *Residential property costs remain high.* ◇ If you **remain** in a place, you stay there.

❏ You also say something **remains** when it still exists. *It's hoped that the remaining obstacles will be resolved within a few weeks.*

❏ If something **remains** to be done, it has not yet been done. ◇ If you say it **remains to be seen** whether something will happen, you mean there is no way of knowing whether it will happen or not.

❑ You use expressions like **the fact remains** and **the question remains** to emphasize that an important point or problem still exists. *Whatever the unsatisfactory structure of the poll tax, the fact remains that lawbreaking was allowed to triumph.*

❑ The **remains** of something are what is left of it after most of it has been destroyed or removed. *...dismantling the remains of apartheid.* ◇ The **remains** of a person or animal are the parts of their body left after they have died, especially when they have been dead for a long time. *Excavators have found mass graves containing the remains of about 12,500 people.* ◇ **Remains** are also things like parts of buildings and pieces of pottery which have survived from an earlier period of history, usually buried in the ground.

remainder (remaindering, remaindered) ❑ The **remainder** of something like a period of time is the part which is still to come. *...the remainder of his two-year term as prime minister.* ◇ The **remainder** of something like a task is the part which has still to be dealt with. ◇ The **remainder** of something is also the part which is left after some of it has been taken away.

❑ If a book is **remaindered**, it is sold at a reduced price because it has not been selling well and the publishers have decided not to produce any more copies of it.

remake (remaking, remade) If an old film is **remade,** a new film is made with a similar story and often with the same title as the old film. The new film is called a **remake.** ◇ If something like an organization or a country is **remade,** it is changed into a different form. *The peaceful revolution in Czechoslovakia was a key event in the remaking of Europe.*

remand If someone who is accused of a crime is **remanded on bail** by a judge or magistrate, they are freed and ordered to come back for trial at a later date. You say this person is **on remand.** If someone is **remanded in custody,** they have to stay in prison or a remand centre until their trial. A person like this is called a **remand prisoner.**

remand centre A **remand centre** is an institution where young people who are accused of crimes are sent until their trial begins or until a decision about their punishment has been made.

remark If you **remark** on something or make a **remark** about it, you say something about it, often in a casual way. *Murov remarked that Castro's mood was optimistic... He has been criticized recently for making racist remarks.*

remarkable (remarkably) If you say someone or something is **remarkable,** you mean they are impressive or extraordinary. *The most remarkable thing about his village is that it has escaped the war... Kate Adie is a remarkably courageous reporter.*

remarry (remarries, remarrying, remarried; remarriage) If someone **remarries** after divorce or the death of their spouse, they marry someone else. You call this their **remarriage.**

remaster (remastering, remastered) If an item of recorded music is **remastered,** a new and better master copy is made, from which new copies can then be produced.

rematch (rematches) In sport, especially boxing, a **rematch** is a second match between the same two competitors. Rematches are often arranged because there is a dispute about some aspect of the first match.

remedial action is intended to correct something which has been unsuccessful or has gone wrong. *...tough remedial measures.* ◇ **Remedial** education involves special teaching for young people who find it difficult to learn as quickly as most others. *...remedial reading lessons.*

remedy (remedies, remedying, remedied) ❑ A **remedy** is a successful way of dealing with a problem. If you **remedy** a problem, you deal with it successfully. *The shortage can be remedied only by action on the part of developers.*

❑ A **remedy** is also something intended to cure illness or stop pain.

remember (remembering, remembered) ❑ If you **remember** people or things from your past, your mind still has an impression of them and you are able to think about them. ◇ If you **remember** how to do something, you know how to do it because you learned it in the past and have not forgotten it. Similarly, you can **remember** facts you learned in the past.

❑ If you **remember** to do something you intended to do, you think of it and do it at the right time. *He remembered to switch on his answering-machine.*

❑ If you say someone will be **remembered** for something, you mean they will continue to be associated with it in people's minds. *Mr Kohl will always be remembered as the chancellor who made the two Germanies legally one.*

❑ When people **remember** a person or an event, they hold a ceremony in honour of them.

❑ If an occasion is particularly exciting or enjoyable, you can call it an occasion **to remember.**

remembrance If something is done in **remembrance** of people who have died, it is done to show respect for them.

Remembrance Day is the Sunday nearest to November 11th when people in Britain show their respect for British and Commonwealth citizens killed in recent wars, especially the two World Wars.

remind ❑ If someone **reminds** you about something, they get you to remember it, by bringing your attention to it.

❑ If you are **reminded** of a fact, something makes you aware of it again, when you had not been thinking about it. *There was now a chill in the evening that reminded him that he was fifteen hundred feet above sea-level.*

❑ If someone or something **reminds** you of another person or thing, they are similar to them and make you think of them. *The landscape reminded him of Kenya.*

reminder ❑ If something is a **reminder** of another thing, it makes you remember it or think about it. *The government decided to leave the building in ruins as a reminder of the follies of war.*

❑ A **reminder** is also a letter or note sent to remind you to do something, especially something you should have done already.

reminisce (*pron:* rem-in-iss) (reminiscing, reminisced; reminiscence) If you **reminisce,** you remember things which have happened to you in the past and write or talk about them, usually with pleasure. The things you write or say are called **reminiscences.**

reminiscent If something is **reminiscent** of a certain thing, it reminds you of it. *...a spectacular operation reminiscent of a spy film.*

remiss If you say someone has been **remiss**, you mean they have not done something they ought to have done.

remission If a prisoner gets **remission**, their prison sentence is reduced, because they have behaved well in prison. ◇ If a person with a serious illness has a **remission**, their symptoms are less severe for a time.

remit (remitting, remitted) ❏ The **remit** of a person or organization is the group of things they are authorized to deal with. *Traditionally, defence matters have been outside the Community's remit.*

❏ If you **remit** money to someone, you send it to them as payment for something.

remittance A **remittance** is a sum of money sent to someone.

remix (remixes, remixing, remixed) When a pop record is **remixed**, a new version is produced using a computer to adjust the balance of sound, usually to emphasize the rhythm section and make it more suitable for playing in nightclubs. The new version is called a **remix**.

remnant The **remnants** of something are small parts of it left over when the main part has disappeared or been destroyed. *The remnants of the force were fleeing in total disarray.*

remodel (remodelling, remodelled) (*American spelling:* remodeling, remodeled) ❏ If a building or room is **remodelled**, it is redesigned and its shape is altered.

❏ If an organization is **remodelled**, its structure and the way it operates are changed significantly.

remonstrate (remonstrating, remonstrated) If you **remonstrate** with someone, you protest to them about something they have done or are doing.

remorse is a strong feeling of regret and guilt.

remorseless (remorselessly) You call someone's behaviour **remorseless** when they keep on doing something without showing any pity for the people harmed by it. *They remorselessly beat up anyone they suspected of supporting the opposition.* ◇ You say something undesirable is **remorseless** when it goes on happening. *...the remorseless rise in budget deficits.*

remote (remoteness) ❏ **Remote** places are far away from large centres of population and are often difficult to get to. *Pay comes irregularly to soldiers serving in areas remote from the capital... ...the remoteness of that calm lake.*

❏ If something is **remote** from what people want or need, it has little or no connection with it. *The precise point of dispute is rather remote from the concerns of the ordinary European citizen.* ◇ If a political leader is **remote** from what is happening in their country, they are cut off from it and unaware of it.

❏ If you call someone **remote**, you mean they are not friendly and they do not get closely involved with other people.

❏ If you say there is only a **remote** possibility that something will happen, you are emphasizing that there is very little chance of it happening. *The disease poses only a remote risk to humans.* ◇ See also **remotely**.

remote control (remote-controlled) **Remote control** is the control of something like a machine or vehicle from a distance, for example by radio signals. *The bomb was detonated by remote control.* The device used to transmit the signals is called a **remote control**. *...the TV remote-control.* A **remote-controlled** machine or vehicle is controlled in this way.

remotely is used to emphasize that something is not true or not the case. *I have never said anything remotely like that... Nobody was remotely interested.*

❏ If something is done **remotely**, it is done by remote control. *The mine was detonated remotely from a distance of nearly half a mile.*

remould (*American spelling:* remold) ❏ If something is **remoulded** (*pron:* ree-mold-id), it is changed and reorganized completely. *The post-war constitution had the aim of remoulding Japanese society into a peaceful democracy.*

❏ A **remould** (*pron:* ree-mold) is an old tyre with a new tread moulded on it so it can be used again.

remount When you **remount** a horse or a bicycle, you get back on it after getting off or falling off.

removable If something is **removable**, it can be removed easily. *...a removable sticker.*

removal When someone or something is removed, you can talk about their **removal**. *...the removal of an appendix.* ◇ A **removal** company transports furniture from one building to another, for example when people move house. The vehicles the company uses to transport the furniture are called **removal vans**.

remove (removing, removed) ❏ When you **remove** something, you take it off, take it out, or take it away. *He removed his hat... Remove the loaf from the oven.*

❏ If you **remove** something undesirable, you get rid of it. *Economists said the vote had not removed the threat of further currency chaos.*

❏ If someone is **removed** from their position, for example, as ruler of a country or head of an organization, they lose that position, usually against their will.

❏ If you say one thing is **far removed** from another thing, you mean it is very different from it or has no connection with it. *The racing cars, bicycles, and boats of today are far removed from the sporting vehicles of the past.*

remover A **remover** is a substance used to remove things like make-up or stains. *...nail polish remover.*

remunerate (*pron:* rim-yoo-ner-ate) (remunerating, remunerated; remuneration) If you are **remunerated** for doing something, you are paid for it. The money you receive is called **remuneration**.

remunerative (*pron:* rim-yoo-ner-at-ive) If something is **remunerative**, it is well-paid or profitable. *...a highly remunerative investment.*

renaissance (*pron:* ren-nay-sonss) ❏ The **Renaissance** was the period in Europe during the 14th, 15th, and 16th centuries when there was a great revival of interest in art, literature, and learning.

❏ If something experiences a **renaissance**, it becomes popular or successful again. *Marketing has long been seen as one of the better commercial careers, but manufacturing management is experiencing a renaissance too... The changes could signal a renaissance in English football.*

❏ If you call someone a **renaissance woman** or a **renaissance man**, you mean they have interests and skills in many subjects, especially in both the arts and the sciences.

renal (*pron:* ree-nal) is used to talk about things involving the kidneys. *...renal failure... ...renal dialysis.*

rename (renaming, renamed) If something is **renamed**, it is given a new name.

render (rendering, rendered) ❏ **Render** is used to say someone's or something's condition, state, or significance is changed or weakened. For example, if something is **rendered** harmless, it is made harmless. *She had been rendered unconscious by her attacker... Such a move would render the entire election meaningless.*

❏ If someone describes something in writing, you can say they **render** a description of it. *Ann Cameron renders a moving account of life among the women of an Indian society in western Canada.* ◇ If a piece of writing is **rendered** into another language, it is translated into it. ◇ A **rendering** of a song or a piece of music is a performance of it.

❏ If you **render** assistance to someone, you help them. ◇ When people talk about **services rendered**, they mean services which have already been performed.

❏ When a wall is **rendered**, it is covered with a layer of plaster or cement in order to protect it. This layer is called **rendering**.

rendezvous (*pron:* **ron**-day-voo) If you have a **rendezvous** with someone, you meet them by arrangement at a certain time and place. The place where you meet can also be called a **rendezvous**. *The pub became a popular rendezvous for colleagues in the industry.*

rendition A **rendition** of a play, poem, or piece of music is a performance of it.

renegade A **renegade** is a person who abandons his or her former group, and joins or forms a different or opposing group. *...a renegade general.*

renege (*pron:* rin-**nayg**) (reneging, reneged) If someone **reneges** on a promise or agreement, they break it.

renegotiate (renegotiating, renegotiated; renegotiation) If something like a treaty or a contract is **renegotiated**, a new agreement with new terms and conditions is drawn up. *A meeting will be held in January to discuss renegotiation of debt repayments.*

renew (renewal) ❏ If you **renew** something, you begin it again. *Rescue workers are renewing their efforts to free survivors... The meeting comes at a time of renewed fighting in north-east Somalia.* When something is begun again, you can talk about its **renewal**. *...the renewal of US military action.*

❏ If something like a licence or contract is **renewed**, the period for which it is valid is extended.

❏ You can also say something is **renewed** when it is modernized or replaced with something new. *The hopelessly outdated equipment is being renewed.* ◇ **Urban renewal** is the replacing of old buildings in towns and cities with new housing and facilities and the encouragement of investment there.

renewable A **renewable** source of energy is one which does not run out. For example, wind power is renewable, coal is not. Renewable resources are sometimes called **renewables**. *...solar power and other renewables.* ◇ If a contract is **renewable**, it can be extended when it reaches the end of the period it is valid for.

renewal See **renew**.

rennet is a substance from the stomachs of cows which causes milk to become thick and sour and is used in making cheese.

renounce (renouncing, renounced; renunciation) If you **renounce** a belief, a claim, or an intention, you say you are giving it up, usually in a formal public announcement. An announcement like this is called a **renuncia-**

tion. *...the PLO's formal renunciation of terrorism.*

renovate (renovating, renovated; renovation) If you **renovate** a building, you repair it to get it back into good condition. The repairs you do are called **renovations**. ◇ If a struggling economy is **renovated**, action is taken to get it working satisfactorily again.

renown If someone gains **renown**, they become famous, as a result of their achievements. *...architects of international renown.*

renowned If someone is **renowned** for something, they are well-known for it.

rent If you **rent** something, you regularly pay its owner for the use of it. *Miss Morgan rented a shop in Welshpool... ...rented property.* The money you pay is called **rent**. ◇ If someone **rents out** property, they allow people to use it in exchange for rent.

rent boy Young male prostitutes are sometimes called **rent boys**.

rent-free If you live **rent-free** in a house, you live there without having to pay rent.

rent strike When people take part in a **rent strike**, they refuse to pay their rent as a form of protest.

rental is used to talk about things to do with renting out goods or property. *...video-rental stores.* ◇ **Rental** is money you pay regularly to the owner of something like an office, a car, or a television you are using. *21,000 sq ft at Royalmead has been let to the Inland Revenue at an annual rental of £393,000.*

renunciation See **renounce**.

reoffend If someone who has been in prison **reoffends**, they commit more crimes after their release.

reopen (reopening, reopened) ❏ If something like a shop or a restaurant **reopens** or is **reopened**, it opens again after it has been closed for some time. ◇ If a border or a route is **reopened**, people are allowed to cross it or go along it again after a period when it has been closed.

❏ If someone **reopens** something like a discussion or a legal case, they start it again after it has stopped or been closed.

❏ If a wound **reopens** or is **reopened**, it breaks open again after the skin has begun to heal. ◇ You also say wounds are **reopened** when old arguments or disagreements start again after it seemed they were over.

reorder (reordering, reordered) If you **reorder** things, you arrange them in a different order. A change like this is called a **reordering**.

reorganize (reorganizing, reorganized; reorganization) (*can be spelled with an 's' instead of a 'z'*) If you **reorganize** something, you organize it in a different way. A change like this is called a **reorganization**.

reorient (reorientation) If you **reorient** something, you alter it to fit in with changing circumstances, objectives, and priorities. *Mr Dumas predicted a reorientation of Britain's European policy.*

rep ❏ A **rep** is a person whose job is to sell a company's products or services, usually by travelling round and visiting other companies and organizations. ◇ A **rep** is also a person who acts as a representative for a group of people, usually a group of colleagues.

❏ In the theatre, **rep** is short for 'repertory'.

repackage (repackaging, repackaged) If someone or something is **repackaged**, they are presented in a different way or given a new image.

repaid See **repay**.

repair (repairing, repaired) If you **repair** something which is damaged or carry out **repairs** to it, you mend it. ◇ If something like a building is in **good repair**, it is in good condition. ◇ If you **repair** a bad situation, you improve it or put it right. *The cash will help repair the company's financial position.*

reparation If you make **reparation** for a wrong you have done to someone, you do something to make up for it, such as giving them money. ◇ **Reparations** are sums of money paid after a war by a defeated nation for the damage and suffering caused.

repartee (*pron:* rep-part-tee) is an exchange of witty remarks between two people or groups.

repatriate (repatriating, repatriated; repatriation) If someone is **repatriated**, they are sent back to their own country. *The government favours the forced repatriation of people it does not regard as genuine refugees.*

repay (repaying, repaid; repayment) ❑ If you **repay** money, you give it back to the person you borrowed it from. **Repayment** is giving money back; if you give it back in instalments, each one is called a **repayment**.
    ❑ If you **repay** a favour, you do something in return for it. ◇ If you **repay** someone for some harm they have done you, you get your own back.

repayable If a loan is **repayable** over a certain period, it must be paid back during that period.

repeal (repealing, repealed) If a law is **repealed**, it is abolished. You call this the **repeal** of the law.

repeat (repeating, repeated; repeatedly) ❑ If you **repeat** something, you say or write it again. ◇ If you **repeat** something someone else has said or written, you say or write the same thing. *Daniel was probably only repeating what he had heard his parents say at home.*
    ❑ If you **repeat** yourself, you say things you have said before. ◇ When people say **history repeats itself**, they mean the same kinds of things keep happening in much the same way.
    ❑ If something is **repeated** or there is a **repeat** of it, it happens or is done again. *Can this small victory for the United Nations be repeated on a much larger scale?* ◇ If there is a **repeat performance** of something, especially something undesirable, it happens again. *Britons are preparing for a repeat performance of the storms that devastated much of southern England in October 1987.*
    ❑ **Repeated** is also used to say something happens or is done many times. *Serbia has repeatedly denied the accusations of genocide.*
    ❑ If a TV or radio programme is **repeated**, it is broadcast again. You call this additional broadcast a **repeat**.

repeater A **repeater** is a device which amplifies or improves incoming electrical signals and retransmits them.

repel (repelling, repelled) ❑ When soldiers or police **repel** an attack or invasion, they succeed in driving back the people who are attacking or invading. ◇ If something such as a chemical **repels** insects or other creatures, it keeps them away.
    ❑ If something **repels** you, (a) you thoroughly disapprove of it. *He is known to be repelled by the idea of monetary union.* (b) you find it horrible and disgusting. *He is repelled by the seediness of London's streets.*

repellent ❑ A **repellent** is a substance used to keep insects or other creatures away. *...mosquito repellent.*
    ❑ If you find something **repellent**, you find it horrible and disgusting.

repent (repentant, repentance) If someone **repents**, they show they are sorry for bad things they have done. When someone behaves like this, you say they are **repentant** or talk about their **repentance**. *Both men showed no signs of repentance during their trials.*

repercussions If something has **repercussions**, other things happen as a result of it, especially undesirable things. *One politician warned that the detentions would have serious repercussions.*

repertoire (*pron:* rep-et-twar) ❑ An actor's **repertoire** is all the parts they have learned and can perform. Similarly, you can talk about a musician's **repertoire**. ◇ Plays or pieces of music of a particular kind can also be called a **repertoire**. *...the late-19th and early 20th-century post-romantic repertoire.*
    ❑ Someone's **repertoire** is all the things of a particular kind they are capable of making or doing. *Boiled bacon is still very much part of Ireland's culinary repertoire.*

repertory (repertories) ❑ A **repertory** company is a group of actors who perform plays for short runs of a few weeks. The plays are often performed in **repertory theatres**. When an actor is a member of a repertory company, you say they are in **repertory**. *After experience in repertory at Croydon and Eastbourne, she joined the Stratford company in 1949.*
    ❑ A musician's **repertory** is the pieces of music they have learned and are able to perform. Similarly, you can talk about an actor's **repertory**. ◇ Plays or pieces of music of a particular kind can also be called a **repertory**. *...the operatic repertory.*

repetition If there is a **repetition** of something which has happened before, it happens again. *A four-mile exclusion zone is in force to prevent a repetition of the violence seen in past years.* ◇ If there is **repetition** in something like a book or speech, the same things are written or said more than once.

repetitious means the same as 'repetitive'.

repetitive If something is **repetitive**, it involves doing the same things again and again or the same things happening again and again, and therefore tends to be boring. *...the drudgery of menial, repetitive tasks.*

repetitive strain injury People who suffer from **repetitive strain injury** or RSI have pains in their muscles or joints caused by performing the same movements over and over again every day, usually as part of their job.

rephrase (rephrasing, rephrased) If you **rephrase** something you have said, you say it again using different words, for example because the words you used the first time could be misunderstood.

replace (replacing, replaced; replacement) ❑ If you **replace** something with something else, you get rid of the first thing and use the second thing instead. *...the replacement of propeller aircraft with jets.* When something takes the place of something else, you say it is a **replacement** for it.
    ❑ If you **replace** something, you put it back where it was before. *Replace the caps on the bottles.*

replay ❑ On TV, a **replay** (*pron:* ree-play) is the same as an action replay. ◇ If you **replay** (*pron:* ree-**play**) something you have recorded on tape or film, you play it back.

❑ If there is a **replay** of something which happened in the past, something happens which is very similar in some way. *The debate over the aircraft is unlikely to be a replay of the Westland row of 1985-86.*

❑ In sport, when competitors **replay** a match, they play it again, for example because the first match was a draw. The second match is called a **replay.**

replenish (replenishes, replenishing, replenished; replenishment) If you **replenish** something which has run out, you get in fresh stocks. *US warships could once again use Cam Ranh Bay for replenishment and repairs.* Similarly, if you **replenish** someone's empty glass, you fill it up again.

replete If something is **replete** with things, it is full of them. *The play is replete with Glasgow humour and local references.*

replica A **replica** of something is an exact copy of it.

replicate (replicating, replicated; replication) ❑ When organisms or molecules **replicate**, they multiply by creating exact copies of themselves.

❑ If you **replicate** someone's work, you do the same work yourself in exactly the same way.

reply (replies, replying, replied) ❑ If you **reply** to something someone says or give them a **reply,** you say something back to them. You can also **reply** to something someone has written. *He had asked the Prime Minister to release the report but had not yet received a reply.* You can say something is said or written **in reply to** something else.

❑ You say someone **replies** in a certain way when they do something in response to something someone else has done. *The army replied with a mortar attack.*

repo (*pron:* ree-po) is short for 'repossession'. A **repo man** is a man whose job involves repossessing property, especially cars, which the owners are unable to finish paying for.

report ❑ If you **report** something which has happened, you tell people about it. *Thirteen people were reported killed.* ◇ A **report** is an account of something which has happened, especially in a newspaper or on a news programme. ◇ If you say there are **reports** of something, you mean people say it has happened, but you cannot be sure about it. *There are reports of heavy fighting around Gabiro military barracks.* You use **reported** to describe things you have heard about, which you cannot be sure really exist or are really true. *...America's reported willingness to supply helicopter gunships.*

❑ **Reporting** is the presenting of news in newspapers and on TV and radio. *The paper has achieved a reputation for honest and impartial political reporting.*

❑ If you **report** on something you have been asked to look into, you tell people what you have found out about it. Similarly, you can **report back** on something to someone. ◇ A **report** is an official document issued by a person or group of people in which they say what they have found out about a subject.

❑ A school **report** is a written account of a pupil's progress at school, sent to their parents at the end of each term. In the US, school reports are called 'report cards'.

❑ If you **report** a person, you tell people in authority about something wrong the person has done.

❑ If you **report** to a place, you go there to start work or to be told what to do. You can also **report** to a person. ◇ You also say you **report** to someone when they are responsible for supervising your work.

❑ A **report** is a sudden loud noise made, for example, by a gun being fired or an explosion.

reportage (*pron:* rep-pore-tahzh; *the 'zh' sounds like 's' in 'pleasure'*) **Reportage** is the reporting of current events by the media.

reported speech is a way of repeating things people have said. When reported speech is written down, quotation marks are not used. Here are some examples of reported speech. *He said he wanted to wait... Caroline replied that she would come for Christmas.*

reportedly If you say something is **reportedly** true, you mean people have said it, but you cannot be sure about it. *The princess was reportedly furious.*

reporter A **reporter** is someone who writes news articles or broadcasts news reports.

repose is a state in which you are resting and feeling calm.

reposition (repositioning, repositioned) If you **reposition** something, you change its position. *...Iraq's repositioning of anti-aircraft batteries.* ◇ If a product is **repositioned,** its producers try to get a different type of person to buy it, for example by changing its packaging.

repository (repositories) ❑ A **repository** is a place where something is kept safely.

❑ If you call a place a **repository** of something useful or valuable, you mean a great deal of it is kept there. *The Bank and the Fund are unrivalled repositories of information and expertise on third-world economies.*

❑ If you say a place is the last **repository** of a certain type of person or thing, you mean it is the only place left where that type of person or thing still exists. *The army was left as the last repository of orthodox Communists in the country.*

repossess (repossesses, repossessing, repossessed; repossession) If your house or car is **repossessed,** the people who supplied it or lent you the money for it take it back, usually because you are unable to finish paying for it. *The rises in unemployment and mortgage repossessions threaten hopes of a quick, strong economic recovery.*

repot (repotting, repotted) If you **repot** a plant, you take it out of its pot and plant it in a larger one.

reprehensible If you say someone's behaviour is **reprehensible,** you mean it is very bad and morally wrong.

represent ❑ If someone **represents** an organization or another person, they act on their behalf. *The caller claimed to represent the Animal Liberation Front.* ◇ If you **represent** your country in a competition, you take part on its behalf.

❑ If a group is well **represented** in an event, a lot of its members are taking part. Similarly, a group can be well **represented** in an organization. You can also say that a group is poorly **represented** in an event or organization. *Women are always under-represented in parliament in comparison with their overall proportion in the population.*

❑ If you say something **represents** a victory for someone, you mean it amounts to a victory for them. **Represent** can be used in a similar way with other words.

Today's announcement represents a triumph for Chancellor Kohl... The inclusion of a written paper will represent a change of policy for the government.

❑ If someone or something is **represented** as a certain type of person or thing, people are led to believe they are that thing. *The United States were represented as the chief enemy.*

❑ If a sign or symbol **represents** something, it stands for it. ◇ If you say something **represents** a particular thing for people, you mean they see it as standing for that thing. *The Berlin Wall represented everything East Germans hated about their regime.*

representation ❑ If a group or person has **representation** in court, in parliament, or on a committee, they have someone there who will speak, vote, or make decisions on their behalf.

❑ A picture of someone or something can be called a **representation** of them. *...a representation of the face of Christ.* ◇ The way someone or something is described can also be called a **representation** of them. *The lack of consultation resulted in an inaccurate and misleading representation of our work and role.*

❑ If you make **representations** to a government or other official group, you make a formal complaint or request to them.

representational art is intended to show people and things exactly as they look in real life. *...representational paintings.*

❑ If an organization has a **representational** role, it acts on behalf of a group of people.

representative ❑ A **representative** is a person who has been chosen to act or make decisions on behalf of another person or a group. When a group does this on behalf of a larger group, you call them a **representative** group.

❑ A **representative** is also someone whose job is to sell a company's products or services, usually by travelling round and visiting other companies and organizations.

❑ If a person or thing is a good example of their type, you can say they are **representative** of it. *Shancarrig is representative of a thousand small-town communities.* ◇ If a sample is **representative**, it is large and broad enough to provide useful information about the larger group it is taken from.

repress (represses, repressing, repressed; repression) ❑ If you **repress** a feeling, you make a deliberate effort not to show it or give way to it. ◇ You also say someone is **repressing** something like a feeling or a memory when they are not consciously aware of experiencing it although it probably affects their behaviour. *...repressed homosexual fantasies.* ◇ **Repressed** people do not allow themselves to have natural feelings and desires, especially sexual ones.

❑ You also say people are **repressed** when their freedom is restricted and their activities are controlled by force. *...reports of continuing repression.*

repressive (repressively) A **repressive** government is one which uses force to control people and restrict their freedom. *The country had been repressively ruled for ten years.*

reprieve (reprieving, reprieved) If someone who has been sentenced in a court is **reprieved** or given a **reprieve**, their punishment is officially postponed or cancelled. ◇ If something is **reprieved** or wins a **reprieve**, it is prevented from being destroyed or coming to an end. *Lord Carrington's latest attempt to bring peace won a reprieve last night when it was announced that the talks would continue for a third day.*

reprimand If someone is **reprimanded** by someone in authority or given a **reprimand**, they are told off for something they have done.

reprint If a book is **reprinted**, additional copies are printed, because it is selling well or all existing copies have been sold. A **reprint** is an occasion when a book is reprinted. *The book has already sold 30,000 copies and is in its fourth reprint.* The additional copies of the book are called **reprints**. ◇ If an article which has appeared in print before is **reprinted**, it is printed again.

reprisal Reprisals are violent or unpleasant actions carried out against people or countries that have caused harm. *New precautions have been taken to prevent reprisal attacks.*

reprise (pron: ri-**preez**) (reprising, reprised) If an actor **reprises** a role, he or she plays the same character or a similar character to one they have played before. This repeat performance is called a **reprise**. *Hoskins is rather wasted in what amounts to a reprise of his Roger Rabbit part.* ◇ If there is a **reprise** of something, it happens again. *Aston Villa's victory over Internazionale provided a reprise of England's World Cup euphoria.* ◇ In music, if there is a **reprise**, an earlier track or section of music is repeated.

reproach (reproaches, reproaching, reproached) ❑ If you **reproach** someone or express **reproach**, you indicate that you are disappointed, upset, or angry because they have done something wrong. *Unhappy at the decision, Morris gave Jack Bond a look of reproach.*

❑ If you say someone or something is a **reproach** to other people or things, you mean their high standards show up the low standards of the others. *The grandeur of the 18th and 19th century is a standing reproach to the shoddiness of the 20th.*

❑ If you say someone's character or behaviour is **beyond reproach**, you mean it is so good it cannot be criticized in any way.

reproachful (reproachfully) If someone's behaviour is **reproachful**, they show you they are disappointed, upset, or angry because you have done something wrong. *He pointed reproachfully at us.*

reprobate (pron: **rep**-roh-bate) A man who behaves in an immoral way is sometimes called a **reprobate**.

reprocess (reprocesses, reprocessing, reprocessed) When materials such as toxic waste are **reprocessed**, they are treated to make them safe or ready to be used again. *...the Sellafield nuclear reprocessing plant.*

reproduce (reproducing, reproduced; reproduction, reproductive) ❑ If you **reproduce** something, you make a copy or copies of it. A **reproduction** is a copy of something like a painting or an antique. *...a reproduction Rembrandt... ...reproduction furniture.* ◇ Sound **reproduction** is the recording of sound onto things like cassettes, records, and films so it can be heard by a large number of people.

❑ If you **reproduce** an achievement, you repeat it. *Milan were unable to reproduce the tremendous football which* *swept aside Steaua Bucharest.*

❏ When living things **reproduce**, they produce more of their own species. This process is called **reproduction**. **Reproductive** is used to talk about things to do with reproduction. *...reproductive organs... ...the male reproductive system.*

reproof is telling someone you disapprove of something they have done. *The father utters no word of reproof.*

reprove (reproving, reproved) If you **reprove** someone, you tell them off.

reptile Reptiles are a group of scaly-skinned creatures which lay eggs. Unlike birds and mammals, they do not keep their bodies at a constant temperature. Lizards, snakes, crocodiles, and tortoises are all reptiles.

reptilian (*pron:* rep-till-ian) is used to describe (a) things to do with reptiles. *The creature has an odd mixture of reptilian and mammalian features.* (b) things which remind you of a reptile. *He has a mean, reptilian twinkle in his eye.*

republic (republican, republicanism) ❏ A **republic** is a country which does not have a monarch and which has a government chosen to represent the people. A system of government like this is called a **republican** system. People who favour such a system are called **republicans**; their beliefs are called **republicanism**.

❏ In Northern Ireland, a **Republican** is someone who believes Northern Ireland should not be ruled by Britain but should be part of the Republic of Ireland. Support for this idea is called **Republicanism.**

❏ In the US, a **Republican** is a person who belongs to or supports the Republican Party.

repudiate (*pron:* rip-pew-dee-ate) (repudiating, repudiated; repudiation) If you **repudiate** someone or something, you show you strongly disagree with them and do not want to be connected with them. *The speech was a repudiation of her as a person and her style of government.*

repugnant (repugnance) If you find something **repugnant**, you think it is horrible and disgusting. You can talk about your **repugnance** at something like this.

repulse (repulsing, repulsed) When soldiers **repulse** an enemy that is attacking them, they successfully defend themselves and drive the enemy back.

repulsive (repulsion) If you find something **repulsive**, you find it horrible and disgusting. You call the feeling it gives you **repulsion.**

reputable (*pron:* rep-yoo-tab-bl) A **reputable** person or company is known to be reliable and trustworthy.

reputation Your **reputation** is the opinion people have of you. If you have a good reputation, people have a high opinion of you. *The trial has severely damaged her reputation.* ◇ If you have a **reputation** for something, you are well-known for it.

repute A person or organization of **repute** is respected and highly thought of. *...an engineer of international repute.* ◇ A person's **repute** is their reputation, especially when it is a good one. *Under his stewardship, the UN's repute has risen immeasurably.*

reputed (reputedly) If you say something is **reputed** to be true, you mean people say it is true but you cannot be certain about it. *He is paid a reputed £5.25 million per year... The loan was reputedly arranged over a cup of tea.*

request If you **request** something or make a **request** for it, you ask for it. If you do something at someone's request, you do it because they ask you to. ◇ If something is done on request, it will be done if someone asks for it. *Maid service is available on request.*

requiem (*pron:* rek-wee-em) A **requiem** or **requiem mass** is a Catholic church service held in memory of someone who has recently died. ◇ A **requiem** is also a piece of music for singers and musicians which can be performed either as part of a requiem mass or in a concert.

require (requiring, required) If something is **required**, it is needed or necessary. *The injury is expected to require surgery... Neither candidate obtained the required level of support.* ◇ If you are **required** to do something, for example by law, you have to do it. *New EU regulations require companies to replace ancient equipment.*

requirement A **requirement** is something like a quality you must have or a standard you must reach before you are allowed to do something. *The selection procedures include a minimum height requirement.* ◇ Your **requirements** are your needs.

requisite (*pron:* rek-wizz-it) is used to describe things which are needed for a certain purpose. *Neither bloc has the requisite two-thirds support.* Something which is needed like this can be called a **requisite**. *Miraculous powers are normally a requisite for sainthood.*

requisition (requisitioning, requisitioned) If something like a car or a building is **requisitioned**, it is taken from its owners by people like soldiers or the government to use for their own purposes.

requite (requiting, requited) If someone's love is **requited**, the person they love responds and loves them back.

reredos (*usual pron:* rear-doss) (reredoses) A **reredos** is a decorated wood or stone screen or partition wall behind the altar in a church.

reroute (rerouting, rerouted) (*or re-route, etc*) If vehicles are **rerouted**, they are sent along a different route, because the usual one cannot be used.

rerun (rerunning, reran, have rerun) (*or re-run, etc*) ❏ If something like an election is **rerun**, it is held again, for example because the correct procedures were not followed. You can talk about a **rerun** of something like this. *A rerun of the contest is almost certain.*

❏ If a play, film, or TV series is **rerun**, it is put on again. This additional showing is called a **rerun**. *Bill Cosby will earn millions from reruns of the show.*

❏ If you say something is a **rerun** of something which happened previously, you mean it is very similar to it. *Residents were concerned that the festival would become a rerun of the rave in May in Castlemorton.*

resale When someone buys goods then sells them again, you call this the **resale** of the goods. *...attempts to stop the resale of tickets... The Bucharest government imposed a ban on travellers exporting goods for resale.*

reschedule (rescheduling, rescheduled) ❏ If an event is **rescheduled**, arrangements are made for it to take place at a different time. *The talks have been rescheduled for May 2nd.*

❏ If a debt is **rescheduled**, the country or bank which lent the money agrees that it can be paid back over a longer period.

rescind (*pron:* ris-sind) If a law, agreement, or decision is **rescinded**, it is withdrawn and no longer applies.

rescue (rescuing, rescued; rescuer) If you **rescue** someone or come to their **rescue**, you get them out of a dangerous or difficult situation. Someone who rescues someone else can be called their **rescuer**.

research (researches, researching, researched; researcher) If you **research** a subject, you study it and try to discover facts about it. Work like this is called **research**. A person who does research is called a **researcher**.

resell (reselling, resold) If you **resell** something you have bought, you sell it again.

resemble (resembling, resembled; resemblance) If something **resembles** something else or bears a **resemblance** to it, it is similar to it.

resent (resentment; resentful, resentfully) If you **resent** something, you feel bitter and annoyed about it. This feeling is called **resentment**. *There is resentment against the newcomers from all sides.* If you are **resentful**, you feel like this. *Resentful locals regard them as living on state handouts... They are muttering resentfully among themselves.*

reservation ❏ If you have **reservations** about something which is proposed, you have serious doubts about it. *NATO generals voiced reservations about making air strikes.*
❏ If you make a **reservation**, you arrange for something like a table in a restaurant or a room in a hotel to be kept for you.

reserve (reserving, reserved) ❏ If something is reserved for certain people, it is kept for them and cannot be used by anyone else. *Thirty parliamentary seats will be reserved for women.* Similarly, you can say something is reserved for a particular purpose. *...airspace reserved for military use.*
❏ A **reserve** is an extra supply of something kept in case it is needed. You say you keep something like this in **reserve**. *The country had only four days of oil and petrol supplies in reserve.*
❏ **Reserve** soldiers or police are people who only act as soldiers or police if they are needed in an emergency. ◇ In sport, a **reserve** is an extra person who is kept ready to take the place of a team member who cannot take part or who is injured or withdrawn during a match.
❏ If you call someone **reserved**, you mean they keep their feelings well hidden. You talk about the **reserve** of someone like this.
❏ **reserve judgment**: see **judgment**.
❏ See also **nature reserve**.

reserve price When something is sold by auction, the reserve price is the lowest price the owner will accept for it. If the reserve price is not reached, the owner has the right to withdraw the article from sale.

reservist Reservists are reserve soldiers or police.

reservoir A reservoir is a place where liquid is stored, especially an artificial lake used to supply an area with water.

reset (resetting, reset *not 'resetted'*) ❏ When a doctor **resets** a broken bone, he or she moves it back into its correct position.
❏ If you **reset** a machine or device, you adjust it so it is ready to work again or ready to do something different. *Reset the timer for another five minutes.*

resettle (resettling, resettled) If people like refugees are resettled by a government or other organization, they are found somewhere else to live. This process is called resettlement.

reshape (reshaping, reshaped) If something is reshaped, it is altered or adapted to fit changing circumstances. *New technology is reshaping the way people use their banks.*

reshuffle (reshuffling, reshuffled) If a government or the management of a company is **reshuffled**, people's jobs or responsibilities are changed around, usually with some people losing their jobs in the process. This is called a **reshuffle**.

reside (*pron:* riz-zide) (residing, resided) If someone **resides** somewhere, they are living there at present. *...European workers residing in Iraq.* ◇ **Reside** is also used to say what it is that gives something a particular quality. *...those stretches of coastline whose magic resides in their loneliness and wild desolation.*

residence ❏ A **residence** is a place where people live, for example a house or a flat.
❏ Your country of **residence** is the country where you live. ◇ If you obtain **residence** in a country, you are officially allowed to live there. ◇ If you **take up residence** somewhere, you start living there. If you are **in residence** somewhere, you are living there.
❏ An artist or writer **in residence** teaches or works in an institution like a university. *...the orchestra's composer-in-residence.*

residency (residencies) If you obtain **residency** in a country, you are officially allowed to live there. ◇ When an organization is based at a place, you can talk about its **residency** there. *The London Philharmonic began its South Bank residency last week.*

resident The **residents** of an area are the people who live there. ◇ If you are **resident** in a town or country, you live there. ◇ **Resident** is used to describe people who live in the place where they work. *...the resident caretaker.* ◇ **Resident** is also used to describe someone who is employed by a company for their special knowledge or skill. *...the company's resident choreographer.*

residential is used to describe buildings and areas where people live, as distinct from places used for some other purpose such as business or industry. *...a smart residential district.* ◇ **Residential** is used to describe places where people can live and be looked after by professional staff. *...the care of old and disabled people in residential homes.* **Residential care** involves people being looked after in places like these.

residue (residual) A **residue** is a small amount of something which is left over after most of it has gone. You call an amount like this a **residual** amount. *The malt residues left behind after mashing are known as brewers' grains... A small residual staff will be retained.*

resign (resignation) ❏ If someone **resigns** from a job or position, they formally announce that they are leaving it. This announcement is called their **resignation**.
❏ If you have **resigned** yourself to an unpleasant fact or situation, or if you are **resigned** to it, you accept it because you believe you cannot change it. *Many smile with resignation at the hopelessness of their case.*

resilient (resilience) If you say someone is **resilient** or talk about their **resilience**, you mean they have the ability to recover quickly from unpleasant experiences. ◇ If an object or substance is **resilient**, it is strong and does not damage easily. *The paint dries to a hard-wearing, resilient finish.*

resin (*pron:* rezz-in) is (a) a sticky substance produced by some trees. (b) a similar substance produced industrially and used to make plastics.

resist (resistance) ❑ If someone **resists** something, they fight against it or refuse to accept it. When this happens, you talk about their **resistance** to it. *...China's resistance to political reform.*
❑ When soldiers **resist** an attack, they fight back. *Addis fell with little resistance.* ◇ When people talk about the Resistance, they mean one of various groups which fought against the Nazi occupation of their countries during the Second World War.
❑ If you **resist** the temptation to do something, you do not give in to it. ◇ If you cannot **resist** doing something, you are unable to stop yourself doing it, although you know you should not.
❑ If an object or substance **resists** something harmful or damaging, it is not affected by it. *Aircraft engineers use the alloy because of its high strength and resistance to wear.*
❑ **Resistance** is any force which slows down a moving object or vehicle. ◇ In physics and electrical engineering, **resistance** is the ability of a substance or an electrical circuit to obstruct the flow of an electrical current through it.

resistant If something is **resistant** to something else, it is unlikely to be harmed or damaged by it. *The bricks have to be very resistant to abrasion... ...weather-resistant tents.* ◇ If people are **resistant** to something, they are opposed to it and want to prevent it. *Hardline communists were strongly resistant to any change.*

resister People who refuse to accept something or refuse to take part in something are sometimes called **resisters**. *...the resisters of change... ...war resisters.*

resistor A **resistor** is a device which obstructs the flow of electric current within a circuit.

resit (resitting, resat) If someone **resits** an examination, they take it again, usually because they failed the first time. This additional examination is called a **resit**.

resold See resell.

resolute (resolutely) If someone is **resolute**, they are determined to do something or determined not to do something, and they will not change their mind. *He resolutely refused to give interviews.*

resolution ❑ A **resolution** is a formal decision taken at a meeting by means of a vote. *Pakistan's national assembly has passed a resolution demanding a total ban on alcohol.*
❑ **Resolution** is determination not to give in or change your mind. *They show no signs of weakness or lack of resolution.* ◇ If you make a **resolution** to do something, you promise yourself you will do it. *My new resolution was to spend 20 minutes or so every morning learning a poem.*
❑ When a problem or a disagreement is sorted out, you can talk about its **resolution**. *China has consistently stressed it wants to see a peaceful resolution to the crisis.*

resolve (resolving, resolved) ❑ If a problem or a disagreement is **resolved**, it is sorted out. *There will be urgent talks today to try to resolve the bitter dispute over agriculture subsidies.*
❑ If you **resolve** to do something, you make a firm decision to do it. ◇ If you are **resolved** to do something, you are determined to do it. You can talk about people's resolve to do something. *He said sanctions would not weaken the resolve of the Lithuanian people.*

resonate (resonating, resonated; resonant, resonance) ❑ If something **resonates**, it vibrates and produces a deep strong sound. ◇ A **resonant** sound is loud and echoing. You talk about the **resonance** of a sound like this.
❑ **Resonant** is also used to describe things which have a special meaning for people or are particularly important to them, often because they remind them of something else. You can say things like these **resonate** or have a particular **resonance**. *...names resonant with tradition... The disappearance of the old 10p, the former florin, has a certain historic resonance, for it marks the end of the old pre-decimal coinage.*

resort ❑ If you **resort** to doing something humiliating or morally wrong, you do it in order to survive, or because you can see no other way of achieving what you want. *Some people have resorted to begging for food.* ◇ If you do something as a **last resort**, you do it when you have tried every other way of solving a problem, and this seems to be the only way left. *Mr McAvoy has warned that strike action must be a last resort.*
❑ You say **in the last resort** when stating an important underlying fact which will remain true whatever else happens. *The British will in the last resort support the Americans whatever they do.*
❑ A **resort** is a place where many people spend their holidays.

resound (*pron:* riz-**zownd**) (resoundingly) ❑ If something **resounds**, it makes a loud echoing noise. You say a place **resounds** when it is full of noises like this. *The streets again resounded with the sound of teargas being fired.*
❑ **Resounding** is used to describe a result which is powerful and definite. *Their campaign has been a resounding success... The election was won resoundingly by Dr Mahathir's UMNO-led coalition.*

resource (resourcing, resourced) The **resources** of a country, organization, or person are the things available for their use, for example money, materials, and staff. *Mongolia has considerable untapped resources of oil and minerals.* The provision of resources, especially money, is called **resourcing**. *Desperately deprived and needy localities compete for major government resourcing.* If an organization does not have enough resources, you can say it is **under-resourced**.

resourceful (resourcefulness) **Resourceful** people are good at finding ways of dealing with problems. *The authorities were impressed by his resourcefulness.*

respect ❑ If you **respect** someone or something or have **respect** for them, you have a high opinion of them and admire them. You say someone is **respected** when a lot of people feel like this about them. *...a controversial but widely-respected scientist.* ◇ If you **respect** the law, you do not break it. Similarly, if you **respect** people's wishes, rights, or beliefs, you do not interfere with them or go against them.
❑ If you **pay your respects** to someone, you speak to them or call on them out of politeness. ◇ If you **pay your respects** or **your last respects** to someone who has died, you express your respect or affection for them, for example by going to their funeral.
❑ People say **with respect** when they are politely disagreeing with someone or criticizing them. *With respect, I suggest the editor is missing the point.*

❏ You use phrases like **with respect to** and **in respect of** to indicate what you are referring to. *We share a common purpose with respect to the problems in the Gulf.* ◇ You say **in this respect** to indicate that what you are saying applies to the feature you have just mentioned. *The children are not unintelligent – in fact, they seem quite normal in this respect.* ◇ You say **in some respects** or **in many respects** to indicate that what you are saying applies in more than one way. *Japan has a different way of organising business life, in some respects a more efficient way than America's.*

respectable (respectably, respectability) You say a person or organization is **respectable** when they live or operate in a way which most people approve of and think is morally correct. *...respectable middle-class parents... Her appointment will boost the tobacco industry's respectability.* ◇ **Respectable** is also used to describe things which are adequate or acceptable. *He batted respectably.*

respecter If you say something harmful is **no respecter** of boundaries or of distinctions between people, you mean it takes no account of these things, but affects everyone equally. *Pollution is no respecter of international borders.*

respectful (respectfully) If you are **respectful**, you show respect for someone. *They sat around him in a respectful silence... He bowed his head respectfully.*

respective means relating separately to each of the people or things you have just mentioned. *The two prime ministers hold little executive power in their respective countries.*

respectively means in the order you have just mentioned. *...Stephen Hendry and John Parrott, respectively first and third in the world rankings.*

respiration is the process by which living things take in the oxygen they need to create energy, and send out carbon dioxide. Humans and other mammals achieve this by breathing.

respirator A **respirator** is a machine which helps you to breathe when you are having difficulty breathing naturally, for example because you are ill or have been injured. It is also called a 'ventilator'. ◇ A **respirator** is also a device you wear over your mouth and nose to breathe when you are surrounded by smoke, poisonous gas, or some other harmful substance.

respiratory is used to describe things connected with respiration. *...respiratory infections... ...the respiratory system.*

respite (*pron:* ress-pit *or* ress-pite) A **respite** is a short period of rest or escape from something unpleasant. *An adjournment brought a brief respite from the mayhem.*

resplendent If you talk about people being **resplendent** in particular clothes, you mean their clothes are bright, impressive, or expensive-looking. ◇ If you say other things are **resplendent,** you mean they are glorious or impressive. *...the most resplendent of his 1915 paintings.*

respond (response) ❏ When you **respond** to something someone has said or done or give a **response** to it, you react by saying or doing something yourself. *He responded angrily to Western criticism... America says it has received a positive response from Syria to its proposals.* You can also say something is done **in response** to something else. *In response to a request by France, it has been announced that EU Foreign Ministers are to meet during the coming week.* ❏ If you **respond** to a change or problem, you take the

necessary action to deal with it. *Insects respond faster than any other organism to climate changes... ...America's response to the crisis.* ❏ If a patient **responds** to treatment, the treatment works and they get better.

respondent The **respondents** to a survey or questionnaire are the people who answer the questions. ◇ In court, a **respondent** is someone who defends a lawsuit, especially a divorce suit.

response See **respond.**

responsibility (responsibilities) ❏ If you have **responsibility** for someone or something, or they are your **responsibility,** it is your job or duty to deal with them and to take decisions relating to them. *He now has responsibility for the day-to-day running of party affairs.* ◇ If you say someone has a **responsibility** to do something, you mean it is their duty to do it. *The government has a responsibility to protect the weakest in society.* ❏ Your **responsibilities** are your duties, especially ones which come with your job or position. ◇ If someone is given **responsibility,** they are given the right or opportunity to make important decisions or to take action without asking permission. ❏ If you claim **responsibility** for something which has happened, you say you caused it. *No one has claimed responsibility for the blast.* ◇ If you accept **responsibility** for something which has failed or gone wrong, you say it is your fault.

responsible (responsibly) ❏ If you are **responsible** for something, it is your job or duty to deal with it and make decisions relating to it. *...the cabinet minister responsible for environmental matters.* ◇ If you are **responsible** to a person or group, they have authority over you and you have to report to them about what you do. ❏ If you are **responsible** for something happening, it happens as a result of what you have done. *Alison was 95 per cent responsible for our success.* ◇ If you are **held responsible** for something bad which has happened, you are blamed for it. ❏ **Responsible** behaviour is sensible and does not create problems for other people. *He urged everyone to act responsibly.* ◇ **Responsible** jobs involve making important decisions or carrying out important tasks.

responsive (responsiveness) If you are **responsive** to something, you are quick to react to it and show interest or concern about it. *...responsiveness to change.*

rest ❏ The **rest** of something is the other parts of it. *...the rest of your life... China's system of trade, like the rest of its economy, has been considerably reformed.* ❏ If you **rest** or have a **rest,** you do not do anything active for a time. ◇ In sport, if a team **rests** a player, he or she is left out for one match, for example because of a minor injury. ❏ If you **rest** something somewhere, you put it on top of something else. If something is on top of something else, you can say it is **resting** there. *The ship rested on the sea-bed.* ◇ A **rest** is an object used to support a part of your body, for example a headrest or armrest. ❏ If something like a theory or a person's success **rests** on something, it depends on it. *All hope now rests on Friday's 10,000 metres.* ❏ If responsibility for something **rests** with you, you are responsible for it. Similarly, if a decision about something rests with you, you are the person who makes it. *The power to dismiss staff rests with the governors.*

❑ If you say someone can rest **assured** that something is true, you mean they can be certain it is true and do not need to worry. You can also tell them to rest **easy.** ◇ If you **put** or **set** someone's **mind at rest,** you tell them something which stops them worrying.

❑ If you **lay** something like a fear or a rumour **to rest,** you succeed in showing that it is unfounded.

❑ If someone does **not let** a subject **rest,** they refuse to to let people forget about it by continually raising it. *He has urged the government to let the matter rest.*

❑ When an object which has been moving **comes to rest,** it stops.

❑ The place where a dead person is buried is sometimes called their **resting place.**

rest home A rest home is an institution where old people are cared for.

rest room In the US, the toilets in a public place like a restaurant or theatre are called the **rest room.**

restate (restating, restated; restatement) If you **restate** something, you say it again, sometimes in a different way, to emphasize it or make it clear. You call this a re-**statement** of what you first said.

restaurant A **restaurant** is a place where you have a meal which you pay for.

restaurant car The part of a train where you sit down to have a meal is sometimes called the **restaurant car.**

restaurateur (*pron:* rest-er-a-tur) A **restaurateur** is a person who owns and manages a restaurant.

restful If something makes you calm and relaxed, you can say it is **restful.**

restitution If you demand the **restitution** of something which has been taken away from you, you demand to have it back.

restive When people are **restive,** they are impatient and dissatisfied.

restless (restlessly, restlessness) If you are **restless,** you are bored and dissatisfied, and want to leave or do something else. *From the audience came increasing sounds of rest-lessness.* ◇ You also say someone is **restless** when they find it difficult to keep still. *He paces about restlessly.* ◇ If you have a **restless** night, you do not sleep properly and toss and turn a lot.

restock If someone **restocks** a shop or warehouse, they fill it with goods to replace the ones they have sold. Similarly, you can **restock** something like a shelf or a fridge.

restoration See restore.

restorative (*pron:* rest-or-a-tiv) If something is **restorative** or a **restorative,** it makes you feel livelier, stronger, or more cheerful after you have been feeling tired, weak, or miserable. *...the restorative powers of evening primrose oil... ...the pub's role as a restorative for travellers.*

restore (restoring, restored; restoration, restorer) ❑ If something like a practice or state of affairs is **restored,** it is brought back into existence. *Britain and Argentina re-stored diplomatic relations... ...the restoration of the death penalty.* ◇ If someone or something is **restored** to their previous condition or position, they are returned to it. *He will return to his duties when he is restored to health...*

Within two years Bridgestone had restored the La Vergne plant to full-scale output.

❑ When someone **restores** something like an old building, a painting, or a piece of furniture, they repair and clean it, so it looks as it did when it was new. *More than £200,000 must be found for restoration work.* A person who restores things as their job is called a **restorer.**

❑ If something which was lost or stolen is **restored** to its owner, it is returned to them.

❑ The **Restoration** period was the period following the crowning of Charles II in 1660 after a time when there had been no King or Queen. **Restoration** is used to talk about the drama, architecture, and furniture of this period. *...Restoration plays.*

restrain (restraining, restrained) ❑ If you **restrain** someone, you stop them doing what they intend to do or want to do, often by using physical strength. *The security forces must be restrained from inflicting atrocities on the people.* ◇ If you **restrain** yourself from doing something, you stop yourself doing it. *He could not restrain himself from applauding.* ◇ If you **restrain** an emotion, you stop yourself showing it. *Grahame would do well to restrain his enthusiasm.*

❑ If you **restrain** something which is likely to get out of hand, you keep firm control over it. *...a government dedicated to restraining expenditure.*

❑ If someone behaves in a **restrained** way, they do not show any strong feelings. *The leadership was very restrained in its public reaction to this week's developments.*

restraint ❑ Laws or rules which prevent people doing something can be called **restraints.** *The Government will place no restraints on coal imports... The British press is currently under threat of legal restraint.*

❑ **Restraint** is calm, controlled, and unemotional behaviour. *The police need to exercise restraint in handling disturbances of this nature.*

restrict ❑ If you **restrict** something, you put a limit on it to reduce it or prevent it becoming too great. *He should have restricted the number of prisoners attending services.*

❑ If people are unable to move or behave as they want, you can say their movements or behaviour are **restricted.** *The legislation will restrict press freedom.* ◇ If someone is re-**stricted** to something, they can only use, do, or deal with that thing. *He said the central government should restrict itself to activities such as defence and foreign policy.*

❑ If a document is **restricted,** only people with special permission are allowed to see it or use it. Similarly, a re-**stricted** area can only be entered by people with special permission. ◇ If something is **restricted** to a group of people, nobody else can have it, do it, or use it. *The discount scheme was restricted to new customers.* ◇ If something is **restricted** to a certain place or activity, it only exists in that place or activity. *Such difficulties are not restricted to desk-top publishing.*

❑ If something is **restricted,** there is only a limited amount of it. *...restricted space.*

restriction A restriction is a rule which limits what you can do or limits the amount or size of something. *Villagers want noise restrictions imposed on Alton Towers.* ◇ Other things which limit what you can do can also be called **restrictions.** *The second restriction upon the president's power is the limited time at his disposal.*

restrictive If something is **restrictive**, it limits what people can do. *Britain is to adopt a more restrictive policy on arms sales.* ◇ If people talk about **restrictive practices**, they mean ways in which the people involved in an industry, trade, or profession protect their own interests, rather than having a system which is fair to the public, employers, or other workers.

restructure (restructuring, restructured) If an organization or system is **restructured**, the way it is organized is changed, and often some employees are laid off, to try to make it more efficient.

result ❑ If something **results** from something else or is a **result** of it, it happens because of it. *The suspension resulted from complaints by banking clients.* ◇ If something **results in** something else, it causes it. *Two of the boats capsized, resulting in the loss of ten lives.*

❑ The number you get when you do a calculation is called a **result**. ◇ A **result** is also the outcome of something like a contest or an experiment. *...the results of a detailed survey.* ◇ A company's **results** are the figures representing its income and expenditure as shown in its accounts. ◇ When you take an exam, your **results** are the marks or grades you get. ◇ In football, getting a **result** means winning a match, rather than just drawing.

resultant is used to say something is caused by the thing you have just mentioned. *More than a quarter of a million people have died in the fighting and resultant famines.*

resume (resuming, resumed) If you **resume** something, you start doing it again. *Mr Mandela will be taking a short break before resuming his schedule of meetings.* ◇ If you **resume** your place or position, you take it up again. *He can resume his seat in the Commons once released.*

résumé (*pron:* rez-yoo-may) A **résumé** is a short account of something which has happened or of something someone has said or written. *Before Mr Kinnock made his speech, the Press was given a résumé of its contents.*

resumption If there is a **resumption** of something, it begins again. *General Nambiar ordered the resumption of relief flights into Sarajevo.*

resupply (resupplies, resupplying, resupplied) When an army is **resupplied**, it is provided with things like food, equipment, and ammunition to replace the items which have been used.

resurface (resurfacing, resurfaced) ❑ If something like an idea or problem **resurfaces**, it becomes important or prominent again. *One of Europe's most intractable problems – the century-old Macedonian question – has resurfaced in recent months.* ◇ If someone who has not been seen or heard about for a long time **resurfaces**, they suddenly reappear or return to the public eye.

❑ If something which has been underwater **resurfaces**, it comes back to the surface again.

❑ When something like a road is **resurfaced**, it is given a new surface.

resurgence (resurgent) If there is a **resurgence** of something, it starts to grow in strength or popularity after a period of decline. You can say something like this is re-**surgent**. *The Conservatives may be pushed to hold on to second place against the resurgent Liberal Democrats.*

resurrect (resurrection) ❑ If something is **resurrected**, it is brought back into existence when it seemed to have finished or disappeared forever. *...the resurrection of the Scot-*

tish parliament.

❑ When people talk about a dead person being **resurrected**, they are talking about a miraculous event in which the person is supposedly brought back to life. *...a belief in the resurrection of the dead.* ◇ When Christians talk about the **Resurrection,** they mean the event when Jesus Christ is supposed to have come back to life on the third day after his execution.

resuscitate (*pron:* ris-suss-it-tate) (resuscitating, resuscitated; resuscitation) If you **resuscitate** someone, you get their heart and breathing to start again after they have stopped. *...mouth-to-mouth resuscitation.* ◇ If you **resuscitate** something, you make it become active or successful again. *The economy needs vigorous resuscitation.*

retail (retailing, retailed) ❑ **Retail** is the business of selling goods to the public, usually in fairly small quantities. Retail goods are sold in ordinary shops direct to the public. *...retail jewellery.* ◇ If you say something **retails** at a particular price, you mean that is how much it usually costs in the shops.

❑ If someone **retails** a story or account they have heard, they tell it to someone else.

retail price index In Britain, the **retail price index** or RPI is a monthly list of prices of typical goods and services. It shows how much the cost of living and inflation change from one month to the next.

retailer A **retailer** is a person or business that sells goods to the public.

retain (retaining, retained) If you **retain** something, you keep it. ◇ If someone **retains** a lawyer, they pay the lawyer a fee to make sure he or she will represent them if their case comes before court.

retainer ❑ If you pay someone a **retainer**, you pay them a fee to make sure they will be available to work for you if you need them.

❑ A servant who has been with one family for a long time is sometimes called a **retainer**.

retake (retaking, retook, have retaken) ❑ If a military force **retakes** a place which it has lost to the enemy, it captures it again.

❑ In film-making, if there is a **retake** of a scene, the scene is filmed again because it needs to be changed or improved.

❑ If you **retake** an exam, you take it again, usually because you failed the first time.

retaliate (retaliating, retaliated; retaliation) If you **retaliate** or do something **in retaliation** when someone has harmed or upset you, you do something similar to them in return. *A taxi driver was shot dead by paramilitary forces in retaliation for a gun attack by the separatists on Monday.*

retaliatory is used to say something is done in retaliation. *...a retaliatory strike.*

retard (retardation) ❑ If something **retards** the development or progress of something, it slows it down.

❑ Someone who is **retarded** is much less advanced mentally than most people of their age. This condition is called mental **retardation**.

retch (retches, retching, retched) If you **retch**, you vomit or your stomach muscles move as if you are vomiting.

retd is short for 'retired'. It is written after someone's name to show they have retired from the army, navy, or air force. *...Squadron Leader W. B. Wells, RAF (retd).*

retell (retelling, retold) If a story is **retold**, it is told again, often in a different way. *...this briskly attractive retelling of the Biblical creation story.*

retention When something is kept somewhere, you can talk about its **retention**. *The case challenges MI5's indefinite retention of files... The drug helps protein retention.*

retentive If you have a **retentive** memory, you are good at remembering things.

rethink (rethinking, rethought) If you **rethink** something like a plan or policy, you look closely at it to consider what changes could be made. This is called having a **rethink**.

reticent (reticence) If someone is **reticent** about something or shows **reticence**, they are unwilling to talk about it.

retina (retinal) The **retina** is the light-sensitive membrane at the back of the eye. It receives images and sends them to the brain. **Retinal** is used to talk about things to do with the retina. *...retinal damage.*

retinue An important person's **retinue** is the group of servants, friends, or assistants who go with them and look after their needs.

retire (retiring, retired; retirement) ❑ When older people **retire**, they leave their job and usually stop working altogether. *He announced his retirement... Two out of three retired people own their own homes.* Similarly, when sports players **retire**, they stop playing competitively. ◇ A person's **retirement** is the period in their life after they have retired from their work.

❑ When a sports player **retires** from a race or a match, they stop taking part, usually because of injury.

❑ When you **retire**, you go to bed. ◇ If you **retire** to another room or place, you go there. *I retired to my room.* ◇ When a jury **retires**, its members leave the courtroom to decide their verdict.

❑ **Retiring** people do not like being the centre of attention.

retiree Retired people are sometimes called **retirees**.

retold See retell.

retook See retake.

retool (retooling, retooled) If a factory **retools** or is **retooled**, its machinery or equipment is replaced or changed so it can perform new tasks.

retort If someone **retorts**, they quickly reply to what someone else has said, often in an angry way. A **retort** is a reply like this.

retouch (retouches, retouching, retouched) If a photograph is **retouched**, it is altered by painting over parts of it, often to improve the appearance of a person in the photograph.

retrace (retracing, retraced) If you **retrace** your steps, you return to the place you started from by going back along the same route. ◇ If you **retrace** another person's route, you follow the same route yourself.

retract ❑ If you **retract** something you have said or written, you take it back. *She appeared to implicate her father in the killing, but later retracted the remarks.* Taking something back like this is called a **retraction**.

❑ If part of something is **retracted**, it is pulled back into the main part. *Fire spread to the rest of the aircraft when the wheels were retracted.*

retractable If a part of something is **retractable**, it can be

pulled inwards or backwards. *...a 20,000-seat arena with a retractable roof.*

retrain (retraining, retrained) If you **retrain** or are **retrained**, you learn new skills, usually so you will be able to start a fresh career.

retreat (retreating, retreated) ❑ If you **retreat**, you move away from someone or something. *He retreated from the public eye.* ◇ If an army is **retreating** or in **retreat**, it is moving away from enemy forces to avoid fighting them. ◇ If you **beat a retreat**, you leave a place quickly or end your involvement in something, to avoid an unpleasant situation.

❑ If something is in **retreat**, it is declining. *Inflation is already in retreat.*

❑ If you **retreat** from something like a plan, you back down from it. *He's already retreated from radical privatisation plans towards the cautious programme favoured by his government.* ◇ If you **retreat** into something, you occupy yourself with it, rather than face up to other things. *People responded by retreating into their private lives, their own circle of intimate friends.*

❑ A **retreat** is a quiet secluded place where people go, for example to rest or to concentrate on their religion.

retrench (retrenches, retrenching, retrenched; retrenchment) If an organization **retrenches**, it reduces its costs. *A deeper need for industrial retrenchment and restructuring will remain for years.*

retrial See retry.

retribution is punishment. *He warned of very severe retribution if Baghdad resorted to chemical weapons.*

retried See retry.

retrieve (retrieving, retrieved; retrieval) If you **retrieve** something, you get it back. Getting something back is called its **retrieval**. *The intensity of the fighting has prevented the retrieval of bodies from the battle zone.* ◇ When you **retrieve** information stored on computer files, you print it out or bring it up on the screen.

retriever Retrievers are large dogs often used by people who go shooting to bring back birds and animals they have shot.

retro clothes, music, and objects are based on styles of the past. *...retro-rock acts.*

retroactive (retroactively) **Retroactive** laws and decisions take effect from an earlier date than when they are officially approved. *The Act does not apply retroactively.*

retrograde When something has been improving, a **retrograde** action puts it back to the way it was before. *The Prime Minister described transferring education to central government funding as a retrograde step.*

retrogressive If you call an action or idea **retrogressive**, you mean it returns to old ideas or beliefs and does not take advantage of recent progress.

retrospect The way things seem in **retrospect** is the way they seem some time afterwards, when you may have a better understanding of them. *The film's producer, furious at the time, sees things differently in retrospect... In retrospect, though, it's clear that the leadership was right to be worried.*

retrospective (retrospectively) ❑ A **retrospective** is an exhibition or showing of work done by an artist or film director over many years.

❑ **Retrospective** laws and decisions take effect from an

earlier date than when they are approved. *The nil-rate band for inheritance tax is retrospectively effective from March 10.*

❑ **Retrospective** feelings or opinions concern things which happened some time ago. *...Yeats's retrospective views of his early years... Retrospectively, it seems as if they probably were negligent.*

retry (retries, retrying, retried; retrial) If someone is **retried** or given a **retrial**, they are tried again for the same offence, either because the jury at the first trial could not reach a decision or because the first trial was not carried out properly.

retsina (*pron:* ret-see-na) is a Greek wine flavoured with resin.

return ❑ If you **return** to a place, you go back there. When you go back to a place, this is called your **return**.

❑ If you **return** something, you give it back or put it back. *The main demand of the Indians is for the return of one-and-a-half-million acres of forest to their communities.*

❑ If you **return** a favour, you do something to help someone who has previously helped you. You say you are helping them **in return for** what they have done. ◇ You can also **return** something unpleasant that someone does to you. *The Indian troops returned the fire.*

❑ If you make a **return visit**, you visit someone who has already visited you, or you go back to a place where you have already been.

❑ A **return** match is the second of two matches between the same two sports teams.

❑ If you **return** someone's feelings about you, you feel the same way about them. *She returns his affection.*

❑ If a feeling or situation **returns**, it comes back or happens again. *The pain returned... Official reports suggest that calm is returning to the country.* ◇ If you **return** to a state you were in before, you go back to that state. *The opposition fears a return to martial rule.*

❑ If you **return** to something you were doing before, you start doing it again. *He seems to be returning to his old ways.* ◇ If you **return** to a subject you have mentioned before, you start talking or writing about it again. *The power of the Church is one theme all these writers return to.*

❑ When a judge or jury **returns** a verdict, they announce whether they think the person on trial is guilty or not.

❑ A **return** or **return ticket** is a ticket for a journey to a place then back again. ◇ The **return** trip or journey is the part of a journey which takes you back to where you first started from.

❑ The **return** on an investment is the profit you get from it.

❑ A tax **return** is an official form on which you declare your income, so the authorities can decide how much tax you must pay.

❑ **Returns** are the results of votes counted in various places as part of an election or ballot. *Early returns show Bulgaria's opposition party may have won the country's parliamentary elections held yesterday.*

❑ If you reach **the point of no return**, you reach a stage in something when it is too late to change or go back.

returnee People who return to the country where they were born after living abroad are sometimes called **returnees**.

returning officer The **returning officer** is the official responsible for supervising an election in a town or district. He or she also announces the result.

reunify (reunifies, reunifying, reunified; reunification) If a country is **reunified**, it becomes one country again, after being split into two or more separately controlled parts. This is called the **reunification** of the country.

reunion A **reunion** is a party attended by members of the same family, school, or other group who have not seen each other for a long time. ◇ A **reunion** is also an occasion when close friends or family members meet each other after being separated for some time. *After a joyful reunion with his mother, Wallace turned himself in to the authorities.*

reunite (reuniting, reunited) If close friends or family members are **reunited**, they meet each other again after being separated for some time. ◇ If a divided country is **reunited**, it becomes a single country again. *...a reunited Germany.* ◇ If a political party is **reunited**, the disputes and disagreements within it are resolved.

reusable If something is **reusable**, it can be used again or used more than once. *...a fully reusable spacecraft.*

reuse (reusing, reused) (*or* re-use, *etc*) When you **reuse** something, you use it again instead of getting rid of it. You call talk about the **reuse** (*pron:* ree-yooss) of something. *...the reuse of rubbish.*

rev (revving, revved) ❑ Engine speed is measured in revs. Revs are revolutions per minute. ◇ If you **rev** a car engine or **rev it up**, you increase its speed by pressing the accelerator. ◇ If you **rev** something else up, you get it to operate more quickly. *Its rivals are having to spend heavily to rev up production.*

❑ **Rev** in front of someone's name stands for 'Reverend'. *...the Rev George Glover.*

revalue (revaluing, revalued; revaluation) ❑ If a country's currency is **revalued**, its value is increased so it is worth more foreign currency than it was before.

❑ If a business **revalues** some of its property, it increases its value as shown in the accounts, usually because its market value is now higher.

revamp If you **revamp** something or give it a **revamp** (*pron:* ree-vamp), you make changes to it to improve it, modernize it, or give it a fresh image. *...Poland's revamped local government system... ...Labour's thorough revamp of policies and image.*

revanchist When people call a government **revanchist**, they mean its foreign policy is based on a desire for revenge or a wish to recover lost territories.

reveal (revealing, revealed; revealingly) ❑ If you **reveal** something, you make people aware of it. *He prefers not to reveal the exact terms of the deal.* ◇ If you call something like a book or statement **revealing**, you mean it provides interesting new information, not always intentionally. *She talks revealingly about her new-found fame in a recent magazine interview.*

❑ If you **reveal** something which has been out of sight, you uncover it so people can see it. *Curtains were drawn back to reveal the 56-year-old Emperor and his wife.* ◇ You can call someone's clothes **revealing** when they allow more of their body to be seen than is usual.

revel (revelling, revelled) (*American spelling:* reveling, reveled) If you **revel in** a situation or experience, you enjoy it very much. *Opposition leaders are revelling in the govern-*

ment's misfortune. ◇ Revels are noisy and often drunken celebrations.

revelation (revelatory) When people are made aware of important facts, you talk about the **revelation** of these facts or say there are **revelations**. *Several papers lead on the latest revelations in the BCCI affair.* ◇ If something you experience is unexpectedly good or reveals unexpected qualities, you can call it a **revelation** or describe it as **revelatory**. *The Allegri Quartet gave a revelatory performance.*

reveller (*American spelling:* **reveler**) Revellers are people enjoying themselves in a noisy drunken way.

revelry (revelries) Revelry is noisy and often drunken enjoyment. *...Trafalgar Square, a traditional scene of New Year revelries.*

revenge (revenging, revenged) If you **revenge** yourself or get your **revenge**, you harm someone because they have harmed you. You can also say something is done **in revenge.**

revenue is money received by a company, organization, or government as a result of such things as sales, subscriptions, or taxes. *...the company's advertising revenues.* See also **Inland Revenue.**

reverberate (reverberating, reverberated; reverberation) ❑ When a loud sound **reverberates** in a place, it echoes there. *Gunfire reverberated in the city every night.*

  ❑ You can say events or ideas **reverberate** when they have a powerful and long-lasting effect. You call these effects **reverberations**. *The reverberations of last Friday's surprise announcement continue to occupy all the papers.*

revere (revering, revered) If you **revere** someone or something, you respect and admire them greatly. *...an ancient and highly-revered tradition.*

reverence (reverent, reverently) If people show great respect for someone or something, you can talk about their **reverence** for the person or thing, or describe their behaviour as **reverent**. *...the reverent hush of a rapt audience... Reverently, the husband and wife led me to the front to worship the gods.*

Reverend is a title used before the name of an officially appointed religious leader. *...the Reverend Lou Sheldon.*

reverent See reverence.

reverential (reverentially) You call people's behaviour **reverential** when they show great respect, admiration, and awe for someone or something. *The parliament rises reverentially to its feet whenever a message from the president is read out to it.*

reverie A reverie is a pleasant daydream.

reverse (reversing, reversed; reversal) ❑ When something like a decision, policy, or trend is **reversed**, it is changed to its opposite. You call this its **reversal**. *The move represents a complete reversal of previous US policy.*

  ❑ If the positions or roles of two things are **reversed**, they are changed so each has the position or role the other had.

  ❑ If things are arranged in **reverse order**, the last goes first, the next-to-last second, and so on.

  ❑ **The reverse** is used to say something is the opposite to what has just been described. *The changes in international finance have not made the crisis any less likely. In some ways, quite the reverse.*

  ❑ When a vehicle **reverses** or is **reversed**, it is driven

backwards. If it is **in reverse**, it is in the gear used to drive it backwards. This gear is called the **reverse** gear.

  ❑ A **reverse** is a serious failure or setback.

  ❑ You can call the other side, or the less important side, of a flat object the **reverse** side or just the **reverse**. *On the reverse side of the donor card there was a little 'delete as appropriate' section.*

  ❑ If you **reverse the charges** when you make a phone call, the person you are phoning pays for the call.

reversible ❑ If a process is **reversible**, its effects can be reversed so the original situation is restored. *...reversible vasectomies.*

  ❑ **Reversible** clothes are designed so people can also turn them inside out and wear them with the other side showing. *...a reversible waistcoat.*

reversing light A vehicle's **reversing lights** are the lights at the back which come on when it is in reverse gear.

revert (reversion) If someone or something **reverts** to their previous behaviour or form, they change back to it. A change like this is called a **reversion**. *His most recent Test record shows a reversion to his early days of underachievement.* ◇ In law, if land, property, rights, or money **reverts** to someone, it becomes theirs again after someone else has had it for a time. *The estate should revert to the Crown.*

review ❑ When people **review** a situation or system or carry out a **review** of it, they study it carefully, to decide whether it should be changed or improved.

  ❑ A **review** is a report, for example in a newspaper or on TV, in which someone gives their opinion of something like a new book or film. When someone gives a report like this on something, you say they **review** it. A person who does this regularly is called a **reviewer**.

  ❑ When a military or political leader **reviews** troops, he or she inspects the troops or watches them in a military parade.

reviewable If something is **reviewable**, it will be reconsidered, usually after a certain period, and changed if necessary. *...a rent of £15 per sq ft reviewable after five years.*

reviewer See review.

revile (reviling, reviled) If someone or something is **reviled**, people hate them intensely or show hatred of them. *Niku Ceauşescu was just as feared and reviled as his tyrannical parents.*

revise (revising, revised; revision) ❑ If you **revise** something, you alter it to improve it or make it more suitable or accurate. A **revision** is an alteration like this. *...a radical revision of the parliamentary system.*

  ❑ When you **revise** or do **revision** for an exam, you prepare for it by going over what you have already studied, to improve your understanding and refresh your memory.

revisionism (revisionist) Revisionism is the challenging of traditionally accepted political or historical beliefs. People who challenge beliefs in this way are called **revisionists**; you say they have **revisionist** ideas.

revisit (revisiting, revisited) ❑ If you **revisit** a place, you return there for a visit after you have been away for a long time.

  ❑ If you **revisit** something like an earlier experience, you experience something like it again. *The audience won't* *be going so much to see the man, as to revisit the image of forty years ago.*

revitalize (revitalizing, revitalized; revitalization) *(can be spelled with an 's' instead of a 'z')* If someone or something is **revitalized**, they are made active, successful, and healthy again. *...the revitalization of the Labour party.*

revival See revive.

revivalism (revivalist) Religious **revivalism** is activity aimed at producing conversion to a religion on a large scale, especially at mass meetings. A **revivalist** is someone involved in this kind of activity.

revive (reviving, revived; revival) ❑ If something **revives** or is **revived**, it becomes active, popular, or successful again. When this happens, you talk about its **revival**. *...the revival of nationalism.*

❑ When something like a play, opera, or ballet is **revived**, a new production of it is presented after it has not been performed for some time. *...John Clements' revival of Chekhov's The Seagull.*

❑ If someone is **revived**, they are brought back to consciousness after they have fainted or stopped breathing.

revivify (revivifies, revivifying, revivified) If something is **revivified**, it becomes active and successful again. *...ways of revivifying the world economy.*

revoke (revoking, revoked; revocation) If something like a declaration, law, or licence is **revoked**, it is officially cancelled. When this happens, you talk about its **revocation**.

revolt ❑ When people **revolt**, they rise up against the rulers of their country and try to overthrow them by force. When this happens, you can say there is a **revolt**. ◇ You can call any rejection of authority a **revolt**. *The prime minister is facing a revolt by Conservative party activists over his refusal to hold a referendum.*

❑ If you are **revolted** by something or find it **revolting**, you find it horrible and disgusting.

revolution ❑ If there is a **revolution** in a country, a large group of its people rises up and changes the country's political system by force.

❑ You can also call any great change a **revolution**, especially a change for the better. *The Prime Minister promised that his Citizen's Charter would be a revolution.*

revolutionary (revolutionaries) ❑ **Revolutionary** organizations are involved in trying to bring about a political revolution. People belonging to these organizations are called **revolutionaries**; their activities are also called **revolutionary**. *They are involved in armed revolutionary struggle.*

❑ If something like an idea or a development causes great changes, especially changes for the better, you can describe it as **revolutionary**. *...revolutionary new drugs for the treatment of asthma.*

revolutionize (revolutionizing, revolutionized) *(can be spelled with an 's' instead of a 'z')* If something is **revolutionized**, it is dramatically changed, usually for the better, as a result of a new discovery or invention.

revolve (revolving, revolved) ❑ When something **revolves**, it turns round and round. *...a revolving stage.* ◇ If one object **revolves around** another, it moves in a circle around it. *The satellite revolves around the Earth once every 100 minutes.*

❑ If you say a book or conversation **revolves around** a particular thing, you mean that thing is its main feature or focus. *The debate revolves around specific accounting techniques.*

revolver A **revolver** is a type of hand gun. Its bullets are kept in a revolving cylinder behind the barrel of the gun.

revolving door A **revolving door** consists of four glass doors which turn together around a vertical post.

revue A **revue** is a light theatrical show, usually with songs, dances, and jokes about recent events.

revulsion is a feeling of disgust and strong disapproval.

reward ❑ If someone **rewards** you or gives you a **reward**, they give you something in recognition of your hard work or good behaviour. ◇ A **reward** is a sum of money offered to anyone who can give information about lost or stolen property or about someone wanted by the police.

❑ If you are **rewarded** by something happening, it happens as a result of what you do. *Make the extra effort to impress the buyer and you will be rewarded with a quicker sale at a better price.* ◇ If something is **rewarding**, it brings satisfaction or other benefits. *She has found the work rewarding.*

rewind (rewinding, rewound) When you **rewind** a tape, you make it go backwards so it can be played again.

rewire (rewiring, rewired) If something like a building or an electrical appliance is **rewired**, a new system of electrical wiring is put into it.

reword If something like a speech or part of a law is **reworded**, it is written again in a different way, usually to avoid some problem arising from the way it was originally written.

rework If you **rework** something like an idea or a piece of writing, you reorganize it and make changes to improve it or bring it up to date. The new version is referred to as a **reworking**.

rewound See rewind.

rewrite (rewriting, rewrote, have rewritten) ❑ If someone **rewrites** something like a book or a law, they write it again to try to improve it. *The Americans want us to rewrite the Common Agriculture Policy.* ◇ In the film industry, a **rewrite** (*pron:* ree-rite) involves writing parts of a script again to try to improve it.

❑ If you accuse someone of **rewriting** history, you mean they have selected and presented historical events to suit their own purposes rather than to reflect the truth.

❑ When journalists say someone has **rewritten** the record books, they mean they have broken a record or several records.

rhapsodic is used to describe language or writing which expresses great delight in something. *...a rhapsodic love poem.*

rhapsodize (rhapsodizing, rhapsodized) *(can be spelled with an 's' instead of a 'z')* If you **rhapsodize** about something, you express great delight or enthusiasm about it.

rhapsody (rhapsodies) A **rhapsody** is a piece of music which has an irregular form and is full of feeling. *...George Gershwin's Rhapsody In Blue.*

rhea (*pron:* ree-a) The **rhea** is a flightless South American bird which looks like a small ostrich.

rhesus ❑ The **rhesus** or **rhesus monkey** is a short-tailed monkey from Southern Asia, often used in medical and psychological research.

❏ The **rhesus factor** is an antigen often present in blood. Blood containing this factor is called **rhesus positive** and blood without it is called **rhesus negative.**

rhetoric (*pron:* ret-o-rik) is fine-sounding speech or writing which is meant to convince and impress people but may lack sincerity or honesty. *Some suggest the party's attachment to socialism is no more than empty rhetoric.*

rhetorical (*pron:* rit-tor-ik-kal) (rhetorically) **Rhetorical** language is intended to seem grand and impressive. ◇ A **rhetorical question** is used for effect and does not require an answer. You say a question like this is asked **rhetorically.**

rheumatic diseases are caused by rheumatism.

rheumatic fever is a serious disease which causes fever, a sore throat, and swelling and pain in the joints.

rheumatism (*pron:* room-at-izm) is an illness which makes the joints or muscles stiff and painful. It is most common among older people.

rheumatoid arthritis is a long-lasting disease which causes the joints, for example the hands, wrists, or knees, to swell up and become painful.

rheumatology (rheumatologist) **Rheumatology** is the branch of medicine concerned with diseases of the joints and muscles. A specialist in rheumatology is called a **rheumatologist.**

rheumy If someone has **rheumy** eyes, their eyes are moist and watery, usually because they are very ill or old.

rhinestone Rhinestones are shiny glass jewels made to look like diamonds. They are used in cheap jewellery and to decorate clothes.

rhino (rhinos) A **rhino** is the same as a rhinoceros.

rhinoceros (rhinoceroses) The **rhinoceros** is a large plant-eating African or Asian animal with thick grey skin and either one or two horns on its nose.

rhizome (*pron:* rye-zome) A **rhizome** is a thick underground stem, whose buds develop into new plants. Plants such as mint and irises develop from rhizomes.

rhodium (*pron:* rode-ee-um) is a rare hard silvery-white metal similar to platinum. It does not corrode easily, and is used in alloys and to make reflecting surfaces for optical instruments.

rhododendron The **rhododendron** is an evergreen bush with large clusters of bell-shaped flowers.

rhombus (*plural:* rhombuses or rhombi) A **rhombus** is a shape with four equal sides and no right angles. The diamond shape on a playing card is a type of rhombus.

rhubarb is a plant with large leaves and long red stems. The stems can be cooked with sugar to make jam and puddings.

rhyme (rhyming, rhymed) ❏ If one word **rhymes** with another or if two words **rhyme**, they sound very similar, except that they begin with a different sound. For example, 'might' rhymes with 'bite'. Poems often make use of words which rhyme. ◇ **Rhyme** is the use of rhyming words as a technique in poetry.

❏ If you say something was done **without rhyme or reason**, you mean there seems to be no sensible reason why it was done the way it was.

rhyming slang is a form of language in which you do not use the normal word for something, but say a word or phrase which rhymes with it instead. For example, in rhyming slang, 'apples and pears' means 'stairs'.

rhythm A **rhythm** is a regular pattern of sounds or movements. *...disco rhythm... The obstruction causes an immediate disturbance of the heart's rhythm.* ◇ A **rhythm** is also a regular pattern of changes, for example changes in the body, in the seasons, or in the tides.

rhythm and blues is a style of popular music developed in the 1940s from blues music, but using electrically amplified instruments.

rhythm method The **rhythm method** is a form of contraception in which a couple try to prevent pregnancy by having sex only at times during the woman's monthly cycle when she is unlikely to become pregnant.

rhythm section The **rhythm section** of a band is the group of musicians whose main job is to supply the rhythm. It usually consists of keyboard instruments, double bass, and drums.

rhythmic (rhythmical, rhythmically) A **rhythmic** movement or sound is repeated at regular intervals, forming a regular pattern or beat. *The girls began to clap rhythmically.*

rib (ribbing, ribbed) ❏ The **ribs** are the 24 bones which curve round from the spine to form the **rib cage** in the human chest. The rib cage protects the lungs and other organs. ◇ A **rib** of beef, pork, or veal is a piece of meat which has been cut to include one or more ribs.

❏ You can call a series of long thin supports ribs. *...the ribs of a whaling boat... ...the ribs of an umbrella.* ◇ A **ribbed** surface, material, or garment has a raised pattern of parallel lines on it. *...ribbed leaves... ...cotton-ribbed sweaters.*

❏ If you **rib** someone, you tease them in a friendly way.

ribald (*pron:* rib-ald) You call songs, jokes, and remarks **ribald** when they mention sex in a humorous, rather rude way. *...the Gallic tradition of ribald humour.*

ribbon A **ribbon** is a strip of cloth, usually thin and shiny like silk. You use it for tying things together or as a decoration. ◇ A typewriter **ribbon** is a long narrow strip of cloth on a spool containing a special ink. You put it in a typewriter and, when you press the keys, the arm hits the ribbon and presses the ink onto the paper.

riboflavin (*pron:* rye-boe-flay-vin) is a vitamin found mainly in milk, cheese, eggs, and liver.

rice is the edible grains of a tall grass, also called **rice**, which is grown mainly in warm countries on wet ground.

rice paper is very thin paper made from a tree grown in the Far East. Cakes can be baked on rice paper and it can also be eaten.

rice pudding is a food made by baking rice in milk and sugar. It is usually eaten as a dessert.

rich (richly, richness) ❏ A **rich** person has a lot of money or valuable possessions. Rich people are sometimes called **the rich.** ◇ **Rich** countries have a strong economy and produce a lot of wealth. Many of their inhabitants have a high standard of living.

❏ If a place is **rich** in something, it contains a lot of it. *...a swampland rich in wildlife.* You can also say something is a **rich** source of a certain kind of thing. *Repossessions provide a rich source of bargains.*

❏ A **rich** deposit of a mineral or other substance consists of a very large amount of it. *...Mongolia's rich coal deposits.* ◇ If you **strike** or **tap a rich vein** of something, you find and make use of a very large supply of it. *Southampton* *had struck a rich vein of teenage talent.*

❑ **Rich** food contains a lot of sweet or fatty ingredients. *...a rich dark fruitcake.* ◇ **Rich** soil contains plenty of the substances required to grow crops or flowers.

❑ You can call colours, smells, or sounds **rich** when they are pleasantly deep or strong. *...rich vanilla aromas... ...his rich baritone voice.* ◇ If something is **richly** decorated, it is lavishly or expensively decorated. *...a fireplace richly adorned with carved salamanders.*

❑ You can describe something as **rich** when it covers a wide and interesting variety of different things. *...richly varied countryside... ...the richness of human experience.*

❑ If you are **richly** rewarded for something, you are rewarded very well for it. ◇ If you want to emphasize how much someone deserves something, you can say they **richly** deserve it.

riches are valuable possessions or large amounts of money. ◇ People also use **riches** to refer to resources like coal and oil which exist naturally in large quantities and which are useful and valuable. *...the prospect of mining riches from the sea.*

❑ The **riches** of something are the wonderful things it has to offer. *I would like to conserve the riches of our culture.*

Richter Scale The **Richter Scale** is a scale used to measure how severe an earthquake is.

rickets is a condition people, especially children, get when their food does not contain enough Vitamin D. It makes children's bones remain soft, causing deformities.

rickety If something is **rickety**, it is not very strong and seems about to collapse, because it is old or badly made. *...a rickety wooden table.* ◇ You can describe a business or organization as **rickety** when it has a lot of problems, especially financial ones, and seems likely to collapse.

rickshaw A **rickshaw** is a small two-wheeled carriage, usually pulled by a person rather than an animal, and used most commonly in Asia as a sort of taxi.

ricochet (*pron:* rik-osh-ay) (ricocheting, ricocheted) When a fast-moving object like a bullet or ball **ricochets**, it hits a surface and bounces away from it.

rid (ridding, rid *not 'ridded'*) If you **get rid of** someone or something you do not want, you remove them or do something so you no longer have them. *They want to get rid of the monarchy.* Similarly, you can say you **rid yourself** of something or someone. *The party has rid itself of the men associated with two decades of repression.* You can also **rid** a place of something. ◇ When you are no longer troubled by someone or something, you can say you are **rid** of them.

riddance You say **good riddance** to show you are glad someone or something has gone.

ridden See **ride**.

riddle A **riddle** is a puzzle or joke in which you ask a question which seems to be nonsense but which has a clever or amusing answer. ◇ You can call something a **riddle** when people have been trying to understand or explain it but have so far failed to do so. *The book will solve the riddle of why he quit the presidential race.*

riddled If something is **riddled** with bullets, it has had a lot of bullets fired into it. ◇ You can also say something is **riddled** with damaging or undesirable things when it contains a lot of them. *The recent report is riddled with inaccuracies.*

ride (riding, rode, have ridden) ❑ If you **ride** something like a horse or a bicycle, you sit on it and control it. ◇ If you **ride** in or on a vehicle, you travel in it. ◇ A **ride** is a journey on a horse or bicycle, or in a vehicle. *...a seven-hundred mile bus ride.*

❑ **Riding** is the sport or pastime of riding horses.

❑ If something is **riding on** something else, it is dependent on it happening. *I have £100 riding on the result.*

❑ If a garment **rides up**, it moves upwards, out of its proper position.

❑ If you say someone is **riding high,** you mean they are doing very well. *British architects are now riding high in world esteem.*

❑ When people talk about the sort of **ride** someone gets, they mean the extent to which people criticize them and make things difficult for them. *So far the Labour Party has given Mr Waldegrave a remarkably easy ride.*

❑ If someone **rides out** a storm or a crisis, they manage to get through a difficult period without suffering serious harm. *The ruling Liberal Democratic Party think they can ride out the political storm.*

❑ If you say someone has been **taken for a ride,** you mean they have been deceived or cheated.

rider A person riding a horse, bicycle, or motorcycle is called its **rider.**

ridge A **ridge** is a long strip of land which is higher than the land on each side of it. ◇ A **ridge** is also a raised line on a flat surface.

ridicule (ridiculing, ridiculed) If people **ridicule** someone or something, they make fun of them in an unkind way. When someone is treated like this, you can say they are made an object of **ridicule** or are held up to **ridicule.**

ridiculous (ridiculously) If you say something is **ridiculous,** you mean it is very silly. *We have been leasing out some land for ridiculously low rents.*

rife When something is extremely common, you can say it is **rife.** *Corruption is rife.* You can also say a place is **rife** with something. *Dhaka is rife with rumours.*

riff In jazz and rock music, a **riff** is a short repeated tune or sequence of chords, especially a memorable one which forms the basis of a song or piece.

riff-raff If someone calls a group of people **riff-raff,** they are showing their disapproval of them, because they think they are not respectable or of low social standing.

riffle (riffling, riffled) If you **riffle** through papers or the pages of a book, you turn them quickly and have a look at them without reading everything.

rifle (rifling, rifled) ❑ A **rifle** is a gun with a long barrel, which can be fired accurately over a long range.

❑ If you **rifle** through something, you make a quick search through it. *Thieves had rifled through his suitcase.*

rifle range A **rifle range** is a place where people practise rifle shooting.

rift A **rift** is a large crack in the ground. ◇ A **rift** between people or countries is a serious quarrel. *...a diplomatic rift.*

rift valley A **rift valley** is a valley with steep sides and a flat bottom, formed when the land between two faults sinks.

rig (rigging, rigged) ❑ If someone **rigs** something like an election or a game, they dishonestly arrange it to get the result they want, or to give someone an unfair advantage.

❑ If you **rig up** a device or structure, you make it and fix it in place using any available materials. *One of his guards had managed to rig up a makeshift radio.*

❑ You can use **rig** to refer to a set of special or unusual clothes and any extras which go with them. *He was decked out in full highland rig with dirk, pistols and powder horn.*

❑ The ropes which support a ship's masts and sails are called the **rigging**.

❑ See also **oil rig**.

rigger A **rigger** is (a) a person skilled at using things like pulleys, lifting gear, and cranes. (b) a person who works on oil-rigs.

rigging See **rig**.

right (rightly, rightness) ❑ If you say something is **right**, you mean it is correct and in accordance with the facts. *That's absolutely right... ...the right answer... She attended one meeting only, if I remember rightly.* You also say a person is **right** about something.

❑ If you say a choice, action, or decision is the **right** one, you mean it is the best one. *They decided the time was right for their escape.* ◇ If an object is the **right** one, it is the one you are looking for or the one you want. *They have computerized systems to ensure delivery of the right pizza to the right place.*

❑ You also say something is **right** when it is as it should be. *Ratatouille doesn't taste right with any other oil.*

❑ If you say an action is **right**, you mean it is justified or morally correct. *An American minority is now questioning the rightness of a blockade.* ◇ When people talk about **right and wrong**, they are distinguishing between morally correct and morally incorrect behaviour. *School children should be taught the difference between right and wrong.* ◇ If you say someone is **in the right,** you mean they have behaved in a morally correct way.

❑ People or things that are fashionable or socially correct are sometimes called the **right** people or things. *Through his father he had met all the right people.*

❑ If you **right** something which has fallen over, you bring it back to its normal upright position. *He held on tight as his son righted the yacht.* ◇ If you **right** something which has got into a bad state, you correct it or get it back to the way it should be. You can also talking about putting something **right**. *Sometimes the more obvious flaws are the cheapest to put right.* ◇ If you talk about someone **righting** a wrong, you mean they are doing something to make up for an injustice.

❑ **Right** is one of two opposite sides or directions. If you turn to the right, you turn quarter of a circle in a clockwise direction.

❑ If someone works closely with an important person and assists and advises them, you can say they are **at the** person's **right hand.** You can also call them the person's **right-hand man** or **right-hand woman.**

❑ The **right** are people who support capitalism rather than socialism.

❑ **Right** is used to emphasize the exactness of a position or time. *The lamp-post was right in front of a hospital... His resignation came right in the middle of a two-day holiday for EU officials.* ◇ **Right** is used to emphasize how far something moves or extends or how long it continues. *She was kept very busy right up to the moment of her departure.* ◇ If

you do something **right away,** you do it immediately.

❑ **Right** is used to emphasize how bad or severe something is. *He gave them a right telling off... England's European Championship plans are in a right mess.*

❑ Your **rights** are the things you are morally entitled to do or have. *The measures will give part-time workers the same rights as normal staff.* If you have a **right** to something, you are morally entitled to it. *Constituents have a right to know how their MPs vote.* If you are **within your rights** to do something, you are entitled to do it.

❑ **By rights** is used to indicate what should be happening, in contrast to what is actually happening. *So banks hang on to business that they should by rights lose.*

❑ If someone is a successful or respected person **in their own right**, they are so because of their own efforts and talents rather than those of the people they are closely connected with.

❑ **Right** is used in some British titles. It indicates high rank or status. *...The Right Reverend John Baker... ...the Right Honourable David Mellor MP.*

right angle A **right angle** is an angle of 90°. If two things are **at right angles** or one is **at right angles** to the other, they form an angle of 90° where they touch or cross each other.

right-hand The **right-hand** side of something is the side towards the right.

right-hand man See **right**.

right-handed (right-hander) **Right-handed** people use their right hand rather than their left for things like writing or throwing a ball. In sport, people like these are called **right-handers.**

right-of-centre people or organizations have political opinions closer to conservatism and capitalism than to socialism.

right of way (rights of way) A **right of way** is a public path across private land. ◇ When a car or other vehicle has **right of way** at a junction or roundabout, traffic approaching from other directions must stop for it.

right-thinking If you talk about **right-thinking** people, you mean people with sensible opinions and beliefs – in other words, people with the same opinions and beliefs as your own. *Every right-thinking American would be proud of them.*

right-wing (right-winger) **Right-wing** people have capitalist and conservative ideas and opinions. People like these are sometimes called **right-wingers.** ◇ The **right wing** of a party consists of the members whose beliefs are closest to capitalism and conservatism.

righteous (righteously, righteousness) **Righteous** behaviour is morally good. *What matters in waging a war is not righteousness but victory.* ◇ If someone feels **righteous** anger at something, they are angry because they think it is unfair or unjust. *People get righteously angry and want to vent their anger.*

rightful (rightfully) The **rightful** owner of something is the person who should have it, because it belongs to them. *The NUM maintained that the money was rightfully theirs.* Similarly, the **rightful** ruler of a place is its legitimate ruler, rather than someone who has illegally seized power. If someone takes their **rightful** place somewhere, they take the place they should have, which they have not been able to take until now. *South*

Africa was poised to take its rightful place in the international community.

rightist People who have capitalist and conservative ideas and opinions are sometimes called **rightists**.

rightward (*or* **rightwards**) When a politician or party becomes more right-wing, you can talk about a **rightward** change in their views, or say they have moved **rightwards**.

rigid (**rigidly**, **rigidity**) ❑ If something is **rigid**, it is stiff and does not bend or stretch easily. You talk about the **rigidity** of something like this. *Thomsen's disease causes spasms and rigidity in certain muscles when any attempt is made to move.* ◇ If you are very frightened by something, you can say it scares you **rigid**.

❑ If you call a person **rigid**, you mean they are unwilling to change their way of thinking or behaving. ◇ If a law or system is **rigid**, it cannot be changed or departed from. *...the rigidity of the British class system.*

rigmarole You can call a complicated procedure a **rigmarole**.

rigor See **rigour**.

rigor mortis is stiffness in the joints and muscles of a body soon after death as a result of chemical changes in the tissues. ◇ If a system seems unable to change or develop, you can say it is suffering from **rigor mortis**. *Rigor mortis still grips the housing market.*

rigorous (**rigorously**) **Rigorous** is used to describe procedures which are carried out thoroughly. *He called for the licensing laws to be rigorously enforced.*

rigour (*American spelling.* **rigor**) ❑ If something is done with **rigour**, it is carried out strictly and thoroughly. *Trouble makers will be treated with the full rigour of the law.*

❑ When something makes life difficult and unpleasant, you can talk about its **rigours**. *One of the first countries to suffer directly from the rigours of economic sanctions was Sri Lanka.*

rile (**riling**, **riled**) If someone or something **riles** you, they make you angry.

rim (**rimmed**) The **rim** of something like a cup or a glass is its top edge. ◇ The **rim** of a wheel is its outside edge. The outside edge of an area can also be called its **rim**. *...the ex-republics around Russia's rim.* ◇ If there is a **rim** of dirt round something like the inside of a bath, there is a dirty mark round it. ◇ If something is **rimmed** with a substance or colour, it has that substance or colour around its border. *...pink-rimmed specs.*

rind The **rind** of a fruit such as a lemon or orange is its thick outer skin. ◇ The **rind** of cheese or bacon is the hard outer part, which you do not usually eat.

ring (**ringing**, **rang**, **have rung**) ❑ When a telephone **rings**, it makes a sound which lets you know someone is phoning you. ◇ When you **ring** someone, **ring** them **up**, or **give** them **a ring**, you phone them.

❑ When a bell **rings** or you **ring** it, it makes a metallic sound. This sound is called a **ring**. ◇ If something **rings out**, it can be heard loudly and clearly. *Shots rang out across the city.* ◇ If you say a place is **ringing** with a sound, you mean it is filled with it.

❑ If someone has said something to you recently and you still have a vivid memory of it, you can say it is **ringing in your ears**. *They left with warnings ringing in their ears.*

❑ A **ringing** statement or declaration is made forcefully and is intended to make a powerful impression. ◇ You can use **ring** to say something like a statement or an argument has a certain quality. For example, if a statement seems plausible, you can say it has a 'plausible ring'. *Much of what Mr Kryuchkov had to say had a familiar ring to it.* ◇ If you get the impression that something someone says is not true or not genuine, you can say it **rings hollow** or does not **ring true**. *His offer did not ring true.*

❑ If you **ring the changes**, you make alterations to something, usually for the sake of variety.

❑ A **ring** is a small circle of metal you wear on your finger as an ornament or to show you are engaged or married. ◇ If you **ring** an animal, you attach a small metal or plastic ring to it, so it can be easily identified and its movements and habits studied. (*Note that, when you use 'ring' like this, you say 'ringed', not 'rang' or 'rung'.*)

❑ Some other things shaped like circles are also called **rings**. *...a single electric cooking ring... ...smoke rings.* ◇ If people or things are arranged in a circle, you can say they form a **ring**. You can also say something is **ringed** by people or things. *Kabul is ringed by mountains.*

❑ An organized group of people involved in an illegal activity is sometimes called a **ring**. *...the Cambridge spy ring.*

❑ A **ring** is an enclosed space with seats around it where, for example, a boxing match or circus performance takes place.

❑ If someone **runs rings round** you, they are much better or quicker at something than you are.

ring binder A **ring binder** is a hard file, often plastic-covered, which you can insert pages into. The pages are held in place by metal rings attached to a bar inside the file.

ring road A **ring road** is a road which goes all the way round the edge of a town, so traffic can avoid the centre.

ringleader The **ringleaders** in a disturbance or illegal activity are the people who start it or cause most of the trouble.

ringlet **Ringlets** are long curls of hair.

ringmaster The **ringmaster** in a circus is the person who introduces the acts.

ringside The **ringside** is the area immediately around the edge of a circus ring, boxing ring, or show jumping ring. ◇ If you are close to something and can follow exactly what is going on, you can say you have a **ringside seat**.

ringworm is a skin disease caused by a fungus. It produces itchy red patches on a person's or animal's skin, especially on their scalp or trunk. It is most common in children.

rink A **rink** is a large area for ice-skating or roller-skating.

rinse (**rinsing**, **rinsed**) ❑ When you **rinse** something or give it a **rinse**, you wash it without using soap. ◇ You also say **rinse** something when you dip it in water or run water over it to remove soap from it. ◇ If you **rinse** your mouth, you wash it with a mouthful of water or an antiseptic mouthwash.

❑ A hair **rinse** is a hair dye which is not permanent but gradually fades after you have washed your hair a number of times.

riot (**rioting**, **rioted**; **rioter**) ❑ When crowds of people **riot** or **run riot**, they behave violently in a public place, for example by fighting, throwing stones, or damaging buildings and vehicles. An outbreak of behaviour like this is called a **riot**; the people who take part in it are called **rioters**.

❑ A **riot** of something means a lot of different kinds of it mingled together in a striking way. *With Indian cuisine, you expect a riot of tastes and spices.*

❑ If something **runs riot**, it gets out of control. *Joanna's imagination had run riot.*

❑ If someone **reads the riot act**, they give people a stern warning.

riot gear is the special clothing and equipment worn and carried by police when they are trying to control violent crowds.

riot police are police officers specially trained to deal with rioters.

riot shield Riot shields are see-through shields used by police officers to control crowds and protect themselves from attack.

rioter See riot.

riotous ❑ When people are rioting, you can describe them as **riotous**. *...a riotous crowd.*

❑ You can describe a party or someone's behaviour as **riotous** when it is noisy, lively, and rather uncontrolled.

RIP is short for the Latin expression 'requiescat in pace'. It is written on gravestones and expresses the hope that the person buried there may rest in peace.

rip (ripping, ripped) ❑ If you **rip** something, you tear it. A **rip** is a tear.

❑ If something **rips through** a place, it passes through it violently, causing damage and destruction. *Hurricane Andrew ripped through Florida and Louisiana.* ◇ **Rip** is used to describe the violent effects of something like a wind or an explosion. *The first explosion ripped open one of the gas tanks.*

❑ If you **let rip**, you do something forcefully and without restraint.

❑ If someone **rips** you **off**, they cheat you, for example by charging you too much for something or selling you something which is faulty. An unfair deal like this is called a **rip-off**.

rip-roaring A **rip-roaring** film or story is full of action and excitement.

ripcord The cord used to open a parachute is called the **ripcord**.

ripe (ripeness) ❑ **Ripe** fruit or grain is fully grown and ready to be harvested or eaten. *...the ripeness of the grapes.*

❑ If someone lives to be very old, you can say they reach a **ripe old age**.

❑ If you say something is **ripe** for a change of some kind, you mean it is ready for it. *...offices ripe for conversion.* ◇ If you say **the time is ripe** for something, you mean a suitable time has arrived for doing it.

ripen (ripening, ripened) When fruit or grain **ripens**, it becomes ripe.

riposte (*pron:* rip-**posst**) (riposting, reposted) A **riposte** is a quick reply, especially a clever, witty, or angry one. When someone **ripostes**, they give a reply like this. *'It's tough at the top,' he said. 'It's tougher at the bottom,' riposted the billionaire.* ◇ An action taken in response to something can also be called a **riposte**. *The operation is being*

seen as a riposte to the killing of a senior army commander yesterday.

ripple (rippling, rippled) ❑ **Ripples** are little waves on the surface of water caused by something like the wind. When water **ripples** or is **rippled**, waves like these appear on its surface.

❑ When emotions pass among a group of people, you can say they **ripple** through the people. *When it was Jackson's turn, you could sense a ripple of anticipation.* ◇ A **ripple** of something like laughter or applause is a short, fairly quiet burst of it.

rise (rising, rose, have risen) ❑ If something **rises**, it moves upwards. *The powdery dust rose in a cloud around him.* ◇ If something like the water level of a river **rises**, it becomes higher. ◇ When the sun or moon **rises**, it appears above the horizon. ◇ If you **rise,** (a) you stand up. (b) you get out of bed. *He rose at 6.30.*

❑ You can also say something **rises** or **rises up** when it appears as a large tall shape. *Huge grey-barked trees rose up from a carpet of bluebells.*

❑ If land **rises**, it slopes upwards. ◇ A **rise** is a small hill.

❑ If an amount **rises**, it increases. You can talk about a **rise** in an amount. *...a rise in interest rates.* ◇ If you get a **rise**, you get an increase in your salary or wages. ◇ If there is more of something than there was before, you can talk about a **rise** in it. *...the rise in crime.*

❑ If a sound **rises**, it becomes louder or higher. *His voice rose almost to a scream.* ◇ When feelings **rise**, they become more intense. *...rising public anger.*

❑ When people **rise** or **rise up**, they rebel against the people who have authority over them and start fighting them. A rebellion like this is called a **rising**.

❑ If someone **rises** to a higher position or status, they become more powerful or successful. When this happens, you can talk about their **rise**. *Haig's rise was fuelled by an all-consuming sense of patriotic duty.* ◇ If you call someone a **rising star**, you mean they are extremely good at their job and likely to become successful and well-known in the future.

❑ If you **rise above** something, you do not let it affect you. *Politicians lack the capacity to rise above short-term concerns.*

❑ If one thing **gives rise to** another, it causes it. *Low levels of choline in the body can give rise to high blood-pressure.*

riser ❑ Early **risers** are people who get up early. Late **risers** are people who get up late.

❑ The flat vertical part of a step or stair is called a **riser**.

risible (*pron:* riz-zib-bl) (risibly) If you think something is ridiculous and does not deserve to be taken seriously, you can describe it as **risible**. *The idea has proved risibly wrong.*

rising damp If a building has **rising damp**, moisture which has entered the brickwork from the ground has moved upwards above floor level, causing damage to the walls.

risk ❑ If there is a **risk** of something undesirable, there is a possibility it will happen. *If economic reform doesn't succeed, there is a risk of a return to dictatorship.* ◇ If you **risk** something undesirable or **run the risk** of it, you do something which might result in it. *...a brave reporter who had risked death to bring the story to the world.* You can also say you do something **at the risk of** something undesirable. *73 per cent of Hong Kong people believed Mr Patten should try to speed up the pace of democracy, even at the risk of confronting China.*

❑ If you **risk** doing something, you do it, even though you know it might have undesirable consequences. When you do something like this, you can say you **take a risk**. You can also say the thing you do is a **risk**. ◇ If something is a good **risk**, the chances of it going wrong are very small. ◇ If you **risk** something or **put it at risk**, you do something which might result in it being damaged or lost. *He condemned the Home Office for putting the lives of his officers at risk.* ◇ If people are **at risk**, they are in danger.

❑ If you tell someone they do something **at their own risk,** you mean it will be their own responsibility if they are harmed or suffer some kind of loss.

risky (riskier, riskiest; riskily, riskiness) If something you do is **risky**, there is a chance it will fail or have undesirable consequences. *They had borrowed riskily without telling the shareholders... ...the riskiness of making predictions.*

risotto is an Italian dish of rice cooked in stock with vegetables and sometimes meat or seafood.

risqué (*pron:* risk-ay) A **risqué** joke or performance is one which might offend some people because of its sexual content.

rissole Rissoles are pieces of chopped meat or vegetables pressed into a flat round shape and fried.

rite A **rite** is a traditional ceremony. *...initiation rites... ...marriage rites.* ◇ A **rite of passage** is an event which seems to represent a change from one stage of your life to another, especially a change from childhood to adulthood. For example, a young man's first pint in a pub could be regarded as a rite of passage. ◇ See also **last rites.**

ritual (ritually; ritualistic, ritualized *or* ritualised) ❑ A **ritual** is a religious service or some other kind of ceremony which involves a series of actions performed in a fixed order. **Ritual** and **ritualistic** are used to describe activities performed as part of a ritual. *...ritual sacrifices... ...allegations of ritualistic Satanic abuse... Afterwards they feasted on buffalo, ritually slaughtered and cooked all day in a pit.*

❑ If something is always done in the same way, you can call it a **ritual**. *After the usual lengthy legal ritual, the case finally arrived in the High Court.* ◇ A **ritual** response to a situation is one you always get when that situation occurs. You can say a response like this is **ritualized.**

ritzy (ritzier, ritziest) **Ritzy** is used to describe things which are fashionable, glamorous, and expensive. *...Washington's ritzier hotels.*

rival (rivalling, rivalled; rivalry, rivalries) (*American spelling:* rivaling, rivaled) ❑ You call people or groups **rivals** when they are competing against each other, or have similar aims but are hostile to each other. *...clashes between rival groups of students.* You can talk about the **rivalry** between people or groups. *...a city torn apart by deep ethnic rivalries.*

❑ If you say something **rivals** something else, you mean it is of a similar standard. *...a health service whose standards rivalled the best in the world.* ◇ If you say something has no **rival**, you mean nothing else is as good.

riven If a country or organization is **riven** by something, its people are divided into groups because of it, and it is

weakened as a result. *...a nation riven by inter-clan hatreds.*

river A **river** is a large amount of fresh water flowing continuously towards the sea across land. ◇ A long line of moving things or people can also be called a **river**. *The slow-moving river of mourners followed the flower-decked lorries.* ◇ A continuous supply of something can also be called a **river**. *...the river of money and technology flowing into Eastern Europe and Asia.*

river blindness is a serious disease caused by a parasitic worm in parts of Africa and tropical America. It often results in whole communities becoming blind.

riverbank The edge of a river is sometimes called the **riverbank**.

riverboat A **riverboat** is a large boat which carries passengers along a river.

riverbus (riverbuses) A **riverbus** is a large boat which operates like a bus carrying passengers along a river.

riverside The area of land next to a river is called the **riverside**.

rivet (*pron:* riv-vit) (riveting, riveted; rivetingly) ❑ **Rivets** are short metal pins with flat heads, used to fasten flat pieces of metal together. If pieces of metal are **riveted,** they are joined together using rivets.

❑ If you are **riveted** by something or find it **riveting,** you are fascinated by it and it holds your attention completely. *...a riveting book... ...his ability to make the familiar seem rivetingly strange.*

rivulet A **rivulet** is a small stream.

RN after a person's name stands for 'Royal Navy'. *...Captain Neil Blair, RN.*

roach The **roach** (*usual plural:* roach) is a European freshwater fish. ◇ In the US, a **roach** (*plural:* roaches) is a cockroach.

road A **road** is a long strip of hard material built across land for cars and other vehicles to travel along.

❑ You can call a means of achieving something a **road** to it. *Regional agreements are the slow road to free trade.* If you are **on the road** to something, you are going about things in a way which will achieve it. *His priority is to put France's economy on the road to recovery.*

road block When the police or army set up a **road block,** they stop all traffic at a certain place on a road, and search the vehicles or question their occupants. This is usually because they are looking for a criminal.

road hog If you think someone's driving is selfish and reckless, you can call them a **road hog.**

road test A **road test** is a test of a vehicle on public roads to see if it is fit to be driven. ◇ If a motoring journalist takes a car for a **road test,** he or she takes the car for a drive and then writes a review expressing opinions on its performance.

roadholding A car's **roadholding** is its ability to grip the road and not slide or skid when turning corners.

roadie Roadies are people hired by rock musicians to transport, maintain, and erect equipment for their stage shows.

roadshow A **roadshow** is a travelling show organized by something like a radio station.

roadside The area next to a road is called the **roadside**. *...a roadside restaurant.*

roadster A **roadster** is a two-seater sports car with no roof.

roadway The roadway is the part of a road which is used by traffic.

roadworks are repairs or improvements being carried out to a road.

roam (roaming, roamed) If you **roam** an area or **roam** around it, you wander around it, not heading for anywhere in particular.

roan A **roan** is a horse which has black or brown hair with some white hair among it.

roar (roaring, roared) ❑ When a lion **roars** or lets out a **roar**, it makes a loud threatening noise in its throat. Some other large animals can also **roar**. ◇ If a crowd **roars**, all the people shout together, producing a loud noise. They do this to show approval, or because they are angry. *Several thousands of opposition supporters roared their approval as they heard the announcement.* ◇ If someone **roars** with laughter, they laugh in a very noisy way.

❑ If something **roars**, it makes a long loud noise. *The volcano roared... ...a roar of engines.*

❑ If something is a **roaring** success, it is very successful indeed. ◇ If someone is **doing a roaring trade**, they are selling a lot of goods or services very quickly.

roast When you **roast** meat or other food, you smear it with oil or fat and cook it in an oven. **Roast** is used to describe meat and vegetables cooked this way. *...roast beef... ...roast potatoes.* ◇ A **roast** is a large roasted piece of meat. ◇ If someone is given a **roasting**, they are told off or criticized severely.

rob (robbing, robbed; robbery, robberies; robber) ❑ If you are **robbed**, money or valuables are stolen from you, often by means of force or threats. You can also talk about a building being **robbed**. *He was convicted of robbing a bank.* When money or valuables are stolen like this, you say there has been a **robbery**. The person who steals them is called a **robber**.

❑ If someone is **robbed** of something they deserve or need, it is taken away from them. *Tenants could be robbed of their compensation rights.*

robber baron A person who makes a lot of money in business by acting in a dishonest way is sometimes called a **robber baron**.

robe A **robe** is a loose piece of clothing which covers your whole body and reaches to the ground. Robes are worn on ceremonial occasions. ◇ A **robe** is also a bathrobe.

robin The **robin** is a small brown bird, often seen in gardens. Adult robins have orangey-red faces and breasts.

robot (robotic, robotics) A **robot** is a machine which is programmed to move and perform certain tasks automatically. **Robotic** is used to describe machines like these and the tasks they perform. *...robotic roving vehicles... ...robotic surgery.* ◇ **Robotics** is the science of designing and building robots. ◇ You call a person **robotic** when they move in a jerky way like a robot, or think in a logical unemotional way.

robust (robustly) ❑ A **robust** person is strong and healthy. *They were very robustly built people compared with us.* ◇ You say something like a machine or tool is **robust** when it is strong and durable. *The robustness of diesels is another attractive quality.*

❑ If your speech or manner is **robust**, you express yourself in a forceful way. *Mr Rocard robustly defended French nuclear testing in the Pacific... He countered with characteristic robustness.* ◇ **Robust** humour is rather coarse.

rock is the hard substance which the Earth is made of. ◇ If something is **rock hard**, it is very hard, like rock.

❑ A **rock** is a large piece of rock, for example a piece sticking up out of the ground or the sea, or a piece which has broken away from a mountain or a cliff. ◇ In the US, a **rock** is also a stone. *Rocks were hurled at the police lines.*

❑ If something **rocks** or is **rocked**, it moves slowly and regularly backwards and forwards or from side to side. ◇ If an explosion or earthquake **rocks** a building or area, it makes it shake violently. ◇ If people are **rocked** by something that happens, they are shocked and upset by it.

❑ **Rock** or **rock music** is loud music with a strong beat, usually played and sung by a small group of people using a variety of instruments including electric guitars and drums.

❑ **Rock** is a sweet made in long hard sticks. It is often sold in seaside towns.

❑ If you have a drink like whisky **on the rocks**, you have it with ice cubes in it.

❑ If something like a marriage or a business is **on the rocks**, it is in serious trouble and not likely to last. *The economy is on the rocks.*

❑ If you have to decide between two equally unpleasant options, you can say you are **between a rock and a hard place**.

❑ When things are as bad as they are likely to get, you can say they are at **rock bottom**. Similarly, **rock bottom** prices are as low as they can get.

❑ **rock the boat**: see boat.

rock and roll (or **rock'n'roll**) is a type of pop music which developed in the late 1950s. It has a heavily accented beat and simple repeated phrases.

rock cake A **rock cake** is a small cake containing dried fruit. It has a rough surface supposed to make it look like a rock.

rock climbing (rock climber) **Rock climbing** is climbing cliffs or rock faces as a hobby or sport. People who do this are called **rock climbers**.

rock garden A **rock garden** is part of a garden in which rocks are arranged with small plants growing among them.

rock-like A **rock-like** person is strong, firm, and unlikely to change.

rock pool A **rock pool** is a small pool left between rocks on the seashore when the tide goes out.

rock salt is layers of hard salt formed in the ground in places where the sea or some other salt water evaporated a long time ago. Rock salt is often removed by mining and is also called 'halite'.

rockabilly is a type of pop music which combines aspects of rock and roll and hillbilly country music.

rocker ❑ People who perform or enjoy rock music are sometimes called **rockers**.

❑ In the US, rocking chairs are called **rockers**.

rockery (rockeries) A **rockery** is a raised part of a garden, built of small rocks and soil, in which small plants are grown.

rocket (rocketing, rocketed) ❑ A **rocket** is a gas-powered missile. ◇ A space **rocket** is a tube-shaped vehicle which is launched into space. ◇ A **rocket** is also a firework which shoots high into the air.

❑ When something increases suddenly and rapidly, you can say it **rockets**. *Unemployment rocketed as firms stopped paying their bills.*

rocket launcher A **rocket launcher** is a portable tube-shaped device used by soldiers for firing rockets.

rocketry is the science of designing and launching rockets.

rockfall A **rockfall** is a mass of falling or fallen rocks.

rocking chair A **rocking chair** is a chair built on two curved pieces of wood so you can rock yourself backwards and forwards when you are sitting in it.

rocking horse A **rocking horse** is a toy horse built on two curved pieces of wood so a child can sit on it and rock backwards and forwards.

rocky (rockier, rockiest) A **rocky** place is covered with rocks or consists of large areas of bare rock.

rococo (*pron:* rok-koe-koe) is a style of art and design which was popular in Europe in the eighteenth century. Its main features were complicated curly decoration and delicate colours.

rod A **rod** is a long thin metal or wooden bar.

rode See ride.

rodent **Rodents** are small mammals with sharp front teeth for gnawing. Rats, mice, and squirrels are rodents.

rodeo (rodeos) In the US, a **rodeo** is a show in which cowboys demonstrate their skills or compete against each other in events which include riding wild horses and catching calves with ropes.

roe is fish eggs or sperm which people eat.

roe deer The **roe deer** is a small graceful deer with a brown coat and a stumpy tail. The male has short antlers. **Roe deer** live in parts of Europe and Asia.

rogue ❑ When someone behaves in a dishonest, immoral, or criminal way, people sometimes call them a **rogue**. A group of people like this can be called a **rogues' gallery.** ◇ People also call someone a **rogue** when they cannot help liking them, although they disapprove of their behaviour.

❑ **Rogue** is also used to describe people and things that behave differently from others of their kind, especially when this results in harm or damage. *...rogue cops... ...a rogue elephant.*

roguish If someone behaves in a mischievous but rather likeable way, you can describe their behaviour as **roguish.**

role ❑ Your **role** is your position and function in a given situation. *Mr Rabin was last in Egypt in 1989 in his role as defence minister.* Similarly, you can talk about the **role** of an organization, institution, or means of communication. *...the role of television in modern society.*

❑ A **role** in a film, play, or opera is one of the characters in it. ◇ **Role playing** is acting out the behaviour of people in a particular situation, for example as a training exercise to promote understanding and improve relationships.

❑ You say someone is a **role model** when their behaviour is admired by a group of people, especially young people, who try to behave in the same way.

roll ❑ If a round object **rolls** or is **rolled**, it moves along, turning over and over. ◇ If you are lying down and you **roll over**, you move so a different part of you is facing

upwards. ◇ When a moving car **rolls over**, it falls to one side and lands on its roof.

❑ You say a vehicle **rolls** somewhere when it moves at a slow steady pace. *...when the tanks rolled into Prague.* ◇ If drops of liquid **roll** down a surface, they run down it. *The tears were rolling down my face.*

❑ If you **roll** something into a sausage shape or a ball, you form it into this shape by wrapping it several times around itself or turning it over again and again. You can also say you **roll** it **up.** *...rolled-up newspaper.* ◇ A **roll** of paper, plastic, cloth, or wire is a long piece wrapped many times around itself or around a tube.

❑ If you **roll** a cigarette, you make one by wrapping a cigarette paper around some tobacco.

❑ When you **roll** or **roll out** pastry, you spread it out into a flat shape using a rolling pin.

❑ When you **roll up** something like a car window or **roll** it **down,** you move it upwards or downwards, usually by turning a handle. ◇ If you **roll up** your sleeves or trouser legs, you fold the ends back several times, exposing your forearms or calves. ◇ People also say they are **rolling up their sleeves** when they are preparing themselves for a difficult or demanding task.

❑ If a machine is **rolling,** it is operating.

❑ If you **roll** your eyes, you turn them upwards briefly, as a way of showing annoyance or disapproval.

❑ If you say **roll on** something, you mean you want it to happen soon and you are looking forward to it. *Roll on the day someone develops an effective vaccine against malaria.*

❑ If someone repeatedly achieves success and it seems they will continue to do so, you can say they are **on a roll.**

❑ If you **roll back** new developments or changes, you reverse them. *The hardliners failed to roll back the reforms.*

❑ If something like money is **rolling in,** it is being received in large amounts.

❑ When people **roll up** somewhere, they arrive in large numbers, to see something interesting.

❑ **Rolling** hills are gently sloping ones which extend a long way into the distance. *...the rolling Perthshire countryside.*

❑ A **roll** is a piece of bread like a very small loaf for eating as a snack or side dish by one person. Rolls are usually broken open and spread with butter or other fillings.

❑ A **roll** is an official list of people's names.

roll-call If someone takes a **roll-call,** they check which members of a group are present by reading their names out. ◇ A **roll-call** is also an imaginary list of the best people or things of a particular kind. *Her list of pupils read like a roll-call of the great and good.*

roll of honour A **roll of honour** is a list of the names of people who have achieved great success in some field, for example in a sport.

roll-on/roll-off A **roll-on/roll-off** ship is designed so cars and lorries can drive on at one end before the ship sails, then drive off at the other end after the voyage.

roll up A **roll up** is a cigarette you make yourself by wrapping a cigarette paper around some tobacco.

roller A **roller** is a revolving cylinder in a machine or device. ◇ **Rollers** are hollow tubes used to make people's hair curly. The hair is wrapped around the rollers when it is wet, and they are left there while it dries.

roller-coaster (*or* rollercoaster) A **roller-coaster** is a ride at a fairground in a long train-like vehicle travelling up and down steep slopes, and sometimes doing loops, at high speed. ◇ If you call an experience a **roller-coaster**, you mean it involves many dramatic changes in a short space of time. ...*a week of roller coaster emotions for traders and savers alike.*

roller-skate Roller-skates are shoes with four small wheels on the bottom, two at the front and two at the back. If you **roller-skate**, you move over a flat surface on roller-skates, for enjoyment.

rollerblade Rollerblades are similar to roller-skates except that the narrow wheels on the bottom are arranged in a single line from front to back.

rollercoaster See **roller-coaster**.

rollicking books and films are fast-moving, entertaining, and enjoyable.

rolling mill A rolling mill is a machine or factory which uses rollers to flatten metal into sheets or bars.

rolling news A rolling news network, service, or programme broadcasts news and news commentaries continuously.

rolling pin A rolling pin is a cylinder you roll over pastry to flatten it out.

rolling stock is railway engines, carriages, and wagons.

roly-poly people are fat and round.

Roman is used to describe things related to or connected with ancient Rome and its empire. ...*the remains of a Roman town*... ...*the third-century Roman historian Dio Cassius.* The **Romans** were citizens of ancient Rome.
  ❑ **Roman** is also used to describe things to do with present-day Rome. ...*a Roman hotel room*. A **Roman** is someone who lives in or comes from Rome. ...*soccer-mad Romans.*

Roman alphabet The Roman alphabet is the alphabet used by the Romans in ancient times and still used for writing in most European languages, including English.

Roman Catholic means the same as Catholic. A **Roman Catholic** is a Catholic.

Roman Catholicism is the same as Catholicism.

Roman numerals are the letters used by the Romans in ancient times to represent numbers. For example I, IV, VIII, and XL represented the numbers 1, 4, 8, and 40. Roman numerals are still sometimes used today.

romance ❑ A romance is a relationship between two people who are in love with each other. ...*a holiday romance.* ◇ A **romance** is also a story or film about a love affair.
  ❑ You can talk about the **romance** of something when it is exciting and strange or glamorous. ...*the romance of the desert.*
  ❑ **Romance** is also stories from the medieval period involving knights, battles, and adventures.
  ❑ The **Romance** languages are languages like French, Spanish, and Italian, which developed from Latin.

Romanesque is a style of architecture which was common on the mainland of western Europe from about the 9th to the 12th century. It is characterized by rounded arches and thick pillars. ...*the magnificent Romanesque church of St Fidelis.*

romantic (romantically, romanticism) ❑ If someone is romantic or does romantic things, they say and do things which make their partner feel special and loved. ◇ **Romantic** is used to describe things involving sexual

love. ...*a romantic meeting... I wanted to be romantically involved with him.* ◇ A **romantic** play, film, or story deals with a love affair.
  ❑ **Romantic** is also used to describe things which are beautiful or exciting in a way which strongly affects your feelings. ...*a wild romantic landscape*... ...*a romantically dark-skinned hero.* ◇ If you call someone a **romantic** or say they have **romantic** ideas, you mean they tend to see things as better or more exciting than they really are. You talk about the **romanticism** of someone like this.
  ❑ The **Romantic** movement was an artistic movement which began in the late 18th century. It was concerned with emotion rather than reason, and imagination rather than order. The artists, writers, and composers who were part of this movement are often called the **Romantics**. The movement itself is sometimes called **Romanticism**.

romanticize (romanticizing, romanticized) (*can be spelled with an 's' instead of a 'z'*) If someone **romanticizes** something, they think about it or show it in an unrealistic way which makes it seem better or more exciting than it really is.

Romany (Romanies) A **Romany** is a gypsy. Many gypsies call themselves Romanies rather than gypsies. ◇ **Romany** is a language spoken by gypsies.

romp ❑ When people or animals **romp**, they play and move around in a noisy happy way. ...*two energetic spaniels romping around the patio.* ◇ When newspapers talk about people **romping**, they usually mean they are taking part in sexual activities.
  ❑ You can call something like a book, film, or play a **romp** when it is funny, light-hearted, and full of action.
  ❑ When horses or people **romp** home or **romp** to victory, they win a race or competition easily.

romper A romper or romper suit is a one-piece garment for babies combining a top and a short trouser-like bottom.

rondo (rondos) A **rondo** is a piece of classical music in which the main tune is repeated several times. A rondo is usually the last part of a longer work like a sonata or concerto.

roof (roofs, roofed) ❑ A roof is the covering on top of a building. Similarly, you can talk about the roof of a vehicle. ◇ **Roofed** is used to say a building has a roof, or to describe its roof. ...*a roofed stadium*... ...*a square central courtyard which is roofed with clear plastic.*
  ❑ If someone is not homeless, you can say they have a **roof over their head.** ◇ If a number of people or things are **under one roof** or **under the same roof**, they are in the same building.
  ❑ If the level of something increases very rapidly and seems to be out of control, you can say it **goes through the roof.** *Prices for Korean art have gone through the roof.*
  ❑ The **roof** of your mouth is its upper surface. Similarly, you can talk about the roof of a cave.

roof rack A roof rack is a frame fixed on top of a car for carrying things.

roofer A roofer is a person whose job is repairing roofs or putting new roofs on buildings.

roofing is (a) material used for making or covering roofs. (b) the work of repairing roofs or putting new roofs on buildings.

rooftop ❑ The rooftop of a building is the outside part of its roof. ◇ **Rooftop** is used to describe things on the roof of a building. *...the rooftop helipad... A group of prisoners have staged a rooftop demonstration.*

❑ If you tell a lot of people about something you are angry or excited about, you can say you **shout it from the rooftops.**

rook ❑ The **rook** is a large black bird, a member of the crow family.

❑ In chess, a **rook** is the same as a castle.

rookery (rookeries) A **rookery** is a place, usually a group of trees, where a lot of rooks nest and breed. ◇ The breeding grounds of certain sea creatures, such as penguins and seals, are also called **rookeries.**

rookie In the US, a **rookie** is a new recruit without much experience, especially a recruit in the army or police force.

room (-roomed) ❑ A **room** is one of the sections of a building, separated from the rest by a wall or walls. ◇ **-roomed** is used to say how many rooms a building or part of a building has. *...a three-roomed flat.*

❑ If there is **room** for something, there is enough space for it. *With room for 15 guests, here is a house to laze in.*

❑ If you think some kind of change or development is possible, you can say there is **room** for it. *There is still plenty of room for improvement at most banks.*

room-mate Your **room-mate** is someone you share a rented room with, for example when you are a student.

room service is a service in a hotel in which meals or drinks are brought up to guests in their rooms.

roomful When there are a lot of people or things in a room, you can say there is a **roomful** of them. *...a roomful of executives.*

roomy (roomier, roomiest) If a place is **roomy**, it is large and spacious.

roost ❑ When birds or bats **roost** somewhere, they rest or sleep there. The place where they rest or sleep is called their **roost.**

❑ If someone is beginning to suffer the consequences of bad or unfortunate things they have done in the past, you can say these things **have come home to roost,** or the **chickens have come home to roost.** *The debts they had run up came home to roost as interest rates went higher and higher.*

❑ If you say someone **rules the roost,** you mean they are the most important or powerful person in a group.

rooster A **rooster** is the same as a cockerel.

root (rooting, rooted) ❑ The **roots** of a plant are the parts which usually grow underground. They support the plant, draw water and minerals from the soil, and in some plants are used to store food. ◇ If you **root** a plant or cutting or if it **roots,** roots form on it and it starts to grow. ◇ Plants which have large edible roots, such as carrots and potatoes, are called **root vegetables** or **root crops.**

❑ The **root** of a hair or tooth is the part beneath the skin.

❑ When you talk about a person's **roots,** you mean the place or culture they originate from. *He deliberately returned to his Catholic Polish roots as a source of richer spiritual sustenance.* Similarly, you can talk about the **roots** of a political or religious movement.

❑ If someone **puts down roots** in a place, they stay for a fairly long time and make it their home, for example by making friends and developing a social life there. ◇ If ideas **take root** in a place, they become established and accepted there. ◇ If something is **rooted** in people's minds, it is firmly established there. *The idea of staking a claim to a piece of land is deeply rooted in the American psyche.*

❑ The **root** of a problem is its main cause.

❑ If you **root around** for something, you look for it, moving things as you search. ◇ If the authorities **root out** people who are doing wrong, they search for them, and put a stop to the things they are doing.

❑ If something has been completely destroyed or changed, you can say it has been destroyed or changed **root and branch.**

❑ If you **root** for someone, you give them support and encouragement while they are competing against other people.

root crop See root.

rootless (rootlessness) You say people are **rootless** when they have no permanent home or job, or feel they do not have a place or purpose in society. *The theme of rootlessness runs through many of his poems.*

rope (roping, roped) ❑ A **rope** is a thick cord or wire, made by twisting together several thin cords or wires. If you **rope** one thing to another, you tie the two things together with a rope. ◇ If an area is **roped off,** ropes are tied between posts around it, to stop people entering without permission.

❑ In boxing, the **ropes** are the ropes surrounding the ring. ◇ If you say someone is **on the ropes,** you mean they are in severe difficulty and close to giving up.

❑ If you are **learning the ropes,** you are learning how to do something.

❑ If someone is **roped in** to do something, they are persuaded to help with it. *Visitors were roped in for potato picking and harvesting.*

rope ladder A **rope ladder** is a ladder which consists of two long ropes connected by short pieces of rope, wood, or metal.

ropey (ropier, ropiest) If you say something is **ropey,** you mean it is of poor quality.

roro is another name for roll on/roll off.

rosary (rosaries) A **rosary** is a string of beads which members of certain religions, especially Catholics, use for counting the prayers they have said. A series of prayers counted in this way is also called a **rosary.**

rose ❑ The **rose** is a large garden flower with many petals and a pleasant smell. Roses grow on bushes with thorny stems. ◇ You say something is not a **bed of roses** when you want to emphasize that not everything about it is pleasant.

❑ A young Englishwoman is sometimes described as an **English rose** when she is pretty and has fair smooth skin, blue eyes, and rosy cheeks.

❑ **Rose** is a reddish-pink colour. ◇ If you say someone is looking at a situation through **rose-tinted** or **rose-coloured spectacles,** you mean they believe it is better or more pleasant than it really is.

❑ A **rose** is a device with very small holes in it which fits onto the end of a hose or the spout of a watering can. The water comes out of the rose in a fine spray suitable for watering plants.

❑ See also **rise.**

rose window A rose window is a large round stained-glass window, especially one in a church.

rosé (*pron:* roe-zay) is pink wine made either by removing the skins of red grapes after only a little colour has been extracted or by mixing red and white wines.

rosemary is a herb with thin spiky greyish-green leaves, used for flavouring in cooking, especially with lamb.

rosette A rosette is a large circular badge made from coloured ribbons, worn to show support for a political party or sports team, or given as a prize in a competition. ◇ A rosette is also a decoration or design which looks like a rosette.

rosewood is a hard dark-coloured wood used for making furniture. Rosewood comes from various tropical trees.

roster A roster is a list giving details of the order in which different people have to do a regular task, or the people available to do a job when necessary.

rostrum A rostrum is a raised platform on which someone stands when they are speaking to an audience, receiving a prize, or conducting an orchestra.

rosy (rosier, rosiest) ❑ If something is rosy, it is a reddish-pink colour. *...a rosy-cheeked woman.*
❑ If you say the situation looks rosy, you mean things look good for the future. *As the meeting ended, the picture looked much rosier.*

rot (rotting, rotted) ❑ When food, wood, or some other substance rots, it decays and falls apart. If it rots away, it decays until there is nothing left. ◇ When a substance, especially wood, begins to rot, you say there is rot in it.
❑ You say other things rot when they deteriorate. When something like a system is deteriorating, you can say the rot is setting in. If someone manages to prevent this happening, you can say they stop the rot.
❑ If someone is left to spend their life in an undesirable situation, for example in prison or unemployment, you can say they are left to rot.

rota A rota is a list giving details of the order in which people take turns to do something. *...cleaning rotas.*

rotarian A rotarian is a member of a Rotary Club.

rotary is used to describe things which turn with a circular movement or have parts which turn like this. *...the old rotary dial telephones... ...a turbo-charged rotary engine.*

Rotary Club A Rotary Club is a club for business and professional people in a town. Its members work together for the good of the town, often by raising money for the poor and sick. Rotary Clubs are all part of Rotary International, an organization started in the US in 1905.

rotate (rotating, rotated; rotation) ❑ When something rotates or is rotated, it turns with a circular movement. A movement like this is called a rotation. *...a rotating chair... ...the rotation of the Earth.*
❑ When people take turns to do a job, you can say they rotate or do the job in rotation. You can also say the job rotates among them.
❑ When farmers rotate their crops, they use fields for different crops each year. They do this because a single crop would attract more and more pests or would result in minerals in the soil being used up. *...crop rotation.*

rote If you learn something by rote, you learn it by memorizing it, but without thinking about it or trying to understand it. This way of learning things is called rote-learning.

rotor The rotor blades of a helicopter are the long strips of metal which rotate and lift it off the ground. The blades together are called the rotor.

rotten ❑ If a substance like food or wood is rotten, it has decayed and is no longer usable. ◇ If you call a political system rotten, you mean it is so bad that it cannot be put right and needs to be replaced altogether. *...the corrupt and rotten Communist regimes of Eastern Europe.*
❑ Rotten is also used to say someone has been very unlucky, or has been treated very badly. *Most Canadians acknowledge that the aboriginal people have had a rotten deal.*

rotter In the past, a person who behaved in an unkind or selfish way was sometimes called a rotter. Nowadays, this word is only used humorously.

Rottweiler (*pron:* rot-vile-er) Rottweilers are large strong dogs with stocky bodies, short black fur, and tan face markings. They can be aggressive and are often used as guard dogs.

rotund (*pron:* roe-tund) A rotund person is round and fat.

rotunda A rotunda is a round building or room, especially one with a dome.

rouble (*pron:* roo-bl) The rouble is the unit of currency in Russia and some other republics of the former Soviet Union.

rouge (*pron:* roozh; *the 'z' sounds like 's' in 'pleasure'*) Rouge is a pink or red cosmetic which women and actors sometimes put on their cheeks to give them more colour.

rough (roughly, roughness) ❑ If a surface is rough, it is not smooth or even. *A fine sand is needed to remove any roughness in the grain.* ◇ On a golf course, the rough is the uneven ground with longer grass around the edges of the fairway.
❑ If the sea is rough, there are big waves on it.
❑ Rough and roughly are used to say something is approximate. *Travis puts a rough figure of £25,000 on the cost of making and marketing one single... They all follow roughly the same training programmes.*
❑ If something is rough and ready, it is simple and unsophisticated but works fairly well. *The Economist's Big Mac index is a rough-and-ready guide to whether a currency is under or over-valued.*
❑ Rough behaviour involves using physical force against someone. *Hockey is a far rougher game than football... He was roughly handled.* ◇ If someone is roughed up, they are attacked, beaten, or hit.
❑ A rough area of a town or city is unpleasant and dangerous because it is run down and there is a lot of violence or crime there. *...one of Athens' roughest suburbs.*
❑ If someone has a rough ride or a rough time, they have some unpleasant experiences, especially in the way they are treated by other people. *He does believe that teachers have been given a rough time.* ◇ If someone is treated harshly and unfairly by the law, or by people who have taken the law into their own hands, you can say they have received rough justice.
❑ When people sleep rough, they sleep out of doors, usually because they have no home. ◇ If you have to rough it, you have to live without the possessions and comforts you are used to.
❑ If you talk about the rough and tumble of something,

you mean it is exciting because it involves people competing hard against each other. *He is enjoying his return to political rough and tumble.*

rough-hewn wood or stone has been cut into a shape but has not yet been smoothed or finished off. ◇ You can also call other things **rough-hewn** when they are not done with great care or precision but are still fairly powerful and effective. *The glossy conventions of Hollywood were spurned in favour of a rough-hewn cinematic style.*

roughage If food contains **roughage**, it contains substances like bran or fibre which help your bowels work properly.

roughen (roughening, roughened) If something is **roughened**, it is made rough.

roughneck Men who work on oil rigs or oil wells are sometimes called **roughnecks**, especially in the US. ◇ Other people can be called **roughnecks** when they are not gentle or polite. *He is regarded as something of a political roughneck.*

roughshod If you say someone **rides roughshod over** another person, you mean they use their power and authority to get what they want and completely ignore the other person's wishes.

roulette is a gambling game in which a ball is dropped onto a revolving wheel with numbered holes in it. The players bet on which hole the ball will be in when the wheel stops spinning.

round (roundness) ❑ You use **round** or **around** when talking about the area surrounding something, or the area along its edge. *...eight seats arranged around a table.* ❑ If you go **round** something like an obstacle, you move in a curve until you reach the other side. Similarly, you can **round** a corner, or a ship can **round** a headland. ◇ If you go **round** to someone's house, you visit them. ❑ If you turn **round** or turn **around**, you turn so you are facing the opposite direction. Similarly, you can look **round** or **around**. ◇ If something is spinning or moving in circles, you say it is going **round** or **round and round**. ◇ If something is passed or handed **round**, it is passed from person to person in a group. ❑ **All round** is used to say something applies to all parts of a situation or all the members of a group. *It ought to make life much easier all round.* ◇ If something happens all year **round**, it happens throughout the year. ❑ If something is built **round** an idea, it is based on it. *...a design built round an existing American engine.* ❑ If someone changes their mind and begins to agree with you, you can say they have **come round** or you have **won** them **round**. ❑ **Round** is used in phrases like 'the first time round' when describing something which has happened before or which happens regularly. *...the man many expect to run for President next time round.* ❑ In sport, a **round** is a series of games in a competition. The winners go on to play in the next round, and so on until only one player or team is left. ◇ In a boxing or wrestling match, a **round** is one of the periods the boxers or wrestlers fight. ◇ If you play a **round** of golf, you play all 18 holes of the course. ❑ A **round** of meetings or talks is a series of them, especially one which comes before or after a similar series. *...the latest round of negotiations.*

❑ A **round trip** is a journey to a place and back again.

❑ A **round** is a regular delivery routine. For example, if someone does a paper **round**, they deliver newspapers to the same houses every morning or every week. ◇ When people like doctors go on their **rounds**, they make a series of visits as part of their job.

❑ If a story, idea, or joke is **doing the rounds** or **going the rounds**, a lot of people are hearing it and passing it on.

❑ If you buy a **round** of drinks, you buy a drink for everyone present. If you say it is your **round**, you mean it is your turn to do this.

❑ A **round** of ammunition is the bullets released when a gun is fired.

❑ When people clap, you say there is a **round** of applause.

❑ A **round** is also a simple song sung by several people. People start the song at different times, so different parts are being sung at the same time.

❑ If something is **round**, it is shaped like a circle or ball. *She had a flat, round face... ...large round loaves.* ◇ If something is **rounded**, it is curved in shape, without any points or sharp edges.

❑ If you say a book or article gives a **rounded** picture, you mean it is fair and balanced and shows all sides of a subject.

❑ If a play is performed **in the round**, it is performed on a stage which is surrounded by the audience.

❑ If you give an amount as a **round** number, you give it to the nearest multiple of 10, 100, 1000, etc. *The money goes into the team pool, which this summer, in round figures, has now reached £78,000.* ◇ If you **round** an amount up or down, you change it to the nearest whole number or nearest multiple of a number.

❑ **Round about** is used to say a time or amount is approximate. *In the first five years, we will be employing round about 3000 ex-servicemen.*

❑ If you **round off** an enjoyable or successful experience, you end it in a pleasing or satisfying way.

❑ If someone **rounds on** you, they suddenly criticize you aggressively.

❑ If the police or army **round** people **up**, they arrest or capture them. ◇ When animals like sheep or cattle are **rounded up**, they are driven close together into a group.

round robin A round robin tournament is a sports competition in which each player or team plays every other player or team.

round table In a round table discussion, all the participants meet on equal terms.

round-the-clock See clock.

roundabout ❑ A **roundabout** is a circular structure at a place where two or more roads meet. You drive round it until you come to the road you want.

❑ In a playground, a **roundabout** is a revolving structure which children can push round and ride on. ◇ A merry-go-round is also sometimes called a **roundabout**.

❑ If you go somewhere by a **roundabout** route, you go by a route which is not the shortest and quickest one. ◇ If you do something in a **roundabout** way, you do it in a long and indirect way. Similarly, you can say something in a **roundabout** way.

rounders is a British ball game, similar to baseball, in which a player hits a ball and then runs round the edge of a square area. Rounders is usually played by children.

roundly If someone is **roundly** condemned, they are strongly condemned for something they have done. ◇ If someone is **roundly** defeated in a competition or contest, they are defeated by a clear margin.

roundup On TV or radio, a **roundup** is a summary of the main items in the news.

rouse (rousing, roused) If someone **rouses** you, they wake you up. ◇ You can also say someone or something **rouses** people when it makes them very emotional or excited. *...a rousing speech.* If something **rouses** a feeling in you, it gives you that feeling. *He used the civil rights legislation of 1964 and 1965 to rouse the fears of white voters.*

rout (routing, routed) If an army **routs** another army, it defeats them completely. Similarly, a sports team can **rout** its opponents. A defeat like this is called a **rout**.

route (routing, routed) ❑ A **route** is a way from one place to another. ◇ A bus, air, or shipping **route** is a way between two places along which buses, planes, or ships travel as part of a regular service. ◇ When people or vehicles are **routed** a particular way, they are told which route to take to get somewhere. ◇ See also **en route**.

❑ You can call a way of achieving something a **route** to it. *His scheme is a better and swifter route to monetary co-operation and eventual union.*

routine (routinely) ❑ **Routine** is doing things regularly in a fixed order. *He sees himself as the embodiment of genius and talent over training and routine.* ◇ A **routine** is a series of things done at certain times or in certain situations. *...a basic training routine.* ◇ **Routine** is used to describe things which are done as a normal part of a job or process, rather than for special reasons. *The California Highway Patrol routinely tests the exhausts of lorries coming into America.* ◇ **Routine** is also used to describe things which are standard and not interesting or exciting. *We had to sit through routine speeches from two party hacks.*

❑ In entertainment, a **routine** is a short sequence of jokes, remarks, actions, or movements forming part of a longer performance. *...a dance routine.*

roving is used to describe people who travel around as part of their job. *...our roving reporter Peter Beer.*

row ❑ If people **row** or have a **row**, they quarrel or have a serious argument or disagreement. *(For this and the following meaning, 'row' rhymes with 'cow'.)*

❑ If someone is making a **row**, they are making a loud unpleasant noise.

❑ A **row** of people or things is a number of them arranged in a line. *(For this and the remaining meanings, 'row' rhymes with 'go'.)* *...a row of glass jars.* ◇ In a theatre or cinema, each side-by-side line of seats is called a **row**.

❑ If something happens several times in a **row**, it happens that number of times, one after another. *He lost five games in a row.*

❑ When you **row** a boat, you move it through the water using oars. ◇ **Rowing** is a sport in which people or teams race against each other in special rowing boats.

rowan The **rowan** is a tree with red berries and small leaves which grow in pairs. It is also called the 'mountain ash'.

rowboat In the US, a rowing boat is usually called a **rowboat**.

rowdy (rowdier, rowdiest; rowdies, rowdiness) If people are rowdy, they are noisy, rough, and try to cause trouble. People like these are sometimes called **rowdies**; their behaviour is called **rowdiness**.

rower A **rower** is someone who takes part in rowing races. You can also call anyone who is rowing a **rower**.

rowing boat A **rowing boat** is a small boat you move through the water using oars.

rowlock Rowlocks are the U-shaped pieces of metal on the sides of a rowing boat. They hold the oars in position while you row.

royal A **royal** person is a king, queen, or emperor, or a member of their family. People like these are sometimes called **royals**. *Her clients include several Norwegian royals.* **Royal** is used to indicate that something is connected with a king, queen, or emperor, or their family. *...the royal wedding.* ◇ **Royal** is used in the names of institutions or organizations which are officially appointed or supported by a member of a royal family. *...the Royal Navy... ...the Royal National Institute for the Blind.*

royal blue is a deep blue colour.

royal jelly is a substance made by bees and fed to their larvae.

royalist A **royalist** is someone who supports their country's royal family, or believes their country should have a king or queen.

royally If something is done **royally**, it is done grandly and impressively. *Cockburn was royally received by Henry Lorimer.* ◇ You can also use **royally** to add emphasis to your description of something. *They got royally drunk.*

royalty (royalties) ❑ The members of royal families are sometimes referred to as **royalty**. *The estate lies in an area favoured by pop stars and royalty.*

❑ **Royalties** are payments made to authors and musicians when their work is sold or performed. They usually receive a fixed percentage of the profits. ◇ Payments made to someone whose invention, idea, or property is used by a commercial company are also called **royalties**.

RP See Received Pronunciation.

RPI See retail price index.

rpm is a measure of how many times per minute something goes round in a circle. It is most commonly used to indicate record playing speeds. LPs are usually played at 33rpm and singles at 45rpm. 'rpm' stands for 'revolutions per minute'.

RSI See repetitive strain injury.

RSVP stands for 'répondez s'il vous plaît', which is French for 'please reply'. It is written at the bottom of invitations.

Rt Hon is a short way of writing 'Right Honourable'. It is part of a formal title used, for example, by some members of the Privy Council and some judges. *...the Rt Hon Kenneth Clarke, MP.*

rub (rubbing, rubbed) ❑ If you **rub** something or give it a **rub**, you move your hand or a cloth backwards and forwards on it, pressing it firmly. For example, you might rub a surface with a cloth to clean it. ◇ If you **rub** a substance **into something**, you press it in by continuously moving it over its surface. ◇ If you **rub out** something you have written on paper or a blackboard, you remove it by rubbing it with a rubber or a cloth.

❑ A **rubbing** is a picture you create by putting a piece of paper over a carved surface and rubbing crayon, charcoal, or chalk over the paper.

❑ If someone keeps reminding you of something you would rather forget, you can say they are **rubbing it in**.

❑ If two or more people **rub along**, they manage to live or work together in a fairly friendly way.

❑ If someone's qualities or habits **rub off** on you, you develop some of them yourself as a result of spending time with them.

rubber is a strong waterproof elastic substance made from the sap of a tropical tree or produced chemically. It is used for making things like tyres and boots. **Rubber** things are made from rubber. *...rubber gloves.* ◇ A **rubber** is a small piece of rubber or other material used to rub out mistakes made while writing, drawing, or typing.

❑ In the US, a **rubber** is also a condom.

❑ In cricket, bridge, and some other games, a **rubber** is a series of matches played between the same two people or teams.

rubber band A **rubber band** is the same as an elastic band.

rubber bullet A **rubber bullet** is a bullet made of hard rubber. Rubber bullets are intended to injure people rather than kill them, and are fired by police or soldiers to control crowds during a riot.

rubber stamp A **rubber stamp** is a small device with something like a name or date on it. You press it onto an ink pad and then onto a document, to show the document has been officially dealt with. ◇ When something like a proposal is officially approved, you can say it is **rubber-stamped**, especially when the approval is merely a formality and the person who approves it barely looks at it.

rubbery If something is **rubbery**, it is soft and stretchable like rubber.

rubbish (rubbishes, rubbishing, rubbished) ❑ **Rubbish** is unwanted things or waste material.

❑ If you think an idea or statement is foolish or wrong, you can say it is **rubbish**. *All these allegations are absolute rubbish.* ◇ If you **rubbish** a person, you say their ideas or work are of little value. You can also **rubbish** an idea or suggestion. *In Westminster last week sources rubbished the idea that the formula would be abandoned.*

rubble When a building is destroyed, the bits of brick, stone, or other materials which remain on the site are called **rubble**.

rubella See **German measles**.

rubric (*pron:* roo-brik) A **rubric** is a set of rules or instructions, for example the rules and instructions at the beginning of an examination paper. ◇ A **rubric** is also a title or heading under which something is considered. *The other problem falls under the general rubric of nationalism.*

ruby (rubies) A **ruby** is a clear red jewel. ◇ **Ruby** is a dark red colour.

ruby wedding A **ruby wedding** is a 40th wedding anniversary.

ruched (*pron:* rooshd) curtains or clothes are trimmed or gathered to produce a frilled effect. *...billowing ruched skirts.*

ruck A **ruck** is a situation where a group of people are fighting or struggling. *There'll be a huge ruck with the cops*

as they try to take photographs. ◇ In rugby union, a **ruck** is a situation where a group of players are struggling for possession of the ball.

rucksack A **rucksack** is a bag with straps which go over your shoulders so you can carry things on your back, for example when you are walking or climbing.

ruction If someone or something causes **ructions**, they cause strong protests, quarrels, or other trouble.

rudder A **rudder** is a vertical wooden or metal blade at the back of a boat. It is made to turn left or right, to steer the boat. Similarly a plane has a **rudder**.

rudderless If you say an organization or country is **rudderless**, you mean it does not have a good leader to follow or a clear aim to pursue.

ruddy If someone's face is **ruddy**, it is a reddish colour. *...a ruddy-cheeked Irishman.*

rude (rudely, rudeness) ❑ When people are **rude**, they behave impolitely. *He pushed past her rudely... Thais think it is the height of rudeness to show anger.*

❑ You say things are **rude** when they refer to sex or bodily functions in a way which is meant to amuse or titillate people. *...rude jokes.*

❑ If someone receives a **rude** shock, something unpleasant happens to them unexpectedly. *Opposition hopes were rudely shattered last month.* ◇ **rude awakening**: see awaken.

❑ If you say someone is in **rude health**, you mean they are strong and healthy.

rudimentary things are simple, basic, and undeveloped. *...students with a rudimentary grasp of English... He was able to provide rudimentary medical care to his fellow inmates.*

rudiments The **rudiments** of something are its simplest or most essential parts. *There would be at least the rudiments of a common defence policy.*

rue (ruing, rued) If you **rue** something you have done, you regret it and wish you had not done it. You can also say you **rue the day** you did it.

rueful (ruefully) If someone is **rueful**, they show or express regret or disappointment about something which has happened to them. *He resigned as prime minister, saying ruefully: 'I have accepted the verdict of the people.'*

ruff A **ruff** was a starched finely-pleated white collar shaped like a wheel, worn in Europe in the 16th century. ◇ A **ruff** is also a thick band of feathers or fur round the neck of a bird or animal.

ruffian Men who behave in a bad-mannered or violent way are sometimes called **ruffians**.

ruffle (ruffling, ruffled) ❑ If something **ruffles** you, it makes you lose your composure.

❑ When a bird **ruffles** its feathers, it makes them stand out from its body. Birds do this when they are cleaning themselves or when they are frightened. ◇ If something **ruffles** a person's **feathers**, it upsets them or makes them angry.

❑ When the wind **ruffles** something like grass or the surface of the sea, it makes it move gently with a wave-like motion.

❑ **Ruffles** are small decorative frills, especially on clothes.

rug ❑ A **rug** is a piece of thick material you put on a floor. It is like a carpet but covers a smaller area. ◇ A rug is also a small blanket you use to cover your shoulders or knees.

❏ If someone **pulls the rug from under you**, they make it impossible for you to do what you were intending to do.

rugby or **rugby football** is a game played by two teams using an oval ball. Players try to score points by putting the ball down at their opponents' end of the pitch, or by kicking it over a bar fixed between two goalposts. There are two types of rugby: **Rugby League** is played by teams of thirteen players, **Rugby Union** by teams of fifteen players.

rugged (pron: rug-gid) (ruggedness) ❏ A **rugged** area of land is rocky, rough, and impressive. ...a rugged coastline... ...the ruggedness of the terrain.

❏ A **rugged** man is strong, tough, and rather handsome. ◇ You also say people are **rugged** when they are determined and resilient. Rugged individualism forged America's frontier society.

rugger is another word for rugby.

ruin (ruining, ruined) ❏ If you **ruin** something or bring about its **ruin**, you spoil it or severely damage it. Several British smokers are preparing to demand compensation for their ruined health.

❏ If someone is **ruined**, they lose all their money. Thousands of small businesses face ruin in what's been called the world's biggest banking scandal.

❏ A **ruined** building is in a very bad state, for example with no windows or roof. ◇ The **ruins** of a building are the parts which remain after the rest has fallen down or been destroyed.

❏ You can talk about the **ruins** of other things which have been destroyed, for example civilizations or political systems. The Pope said he hoped a united Christian Europe could be built from the ruins of Communism.

ruinous (ruinously) If something is **ruinous**, it has a disastrous effect, especially financially or economically. Cleaning up eastern Germany's disastrous pollution could prove ruinously expensive.

rule (ruling, ruled) ❏ **Rules** are a set of statements which tell you what is allowed and what is not. ...trading rules... ...the rules of the competition. ◇ **bend the rules**: see bend. ◇ **rule of thumb**: see thumb. ◇ **golden rule**: see golden. ◇ The set of rules or principles governing something like a game or an organization are sometimes called its **rule book**. ...one of the most serious offences mentioned in the Party rule-book.

❏ If someone in authority **rules** on a matter or gives a **ruling**, they give an official decision. They continued to defy federal rulings on lowering petrol prices.

❏ The people who **rule** a country are the ones who run its affairs. ...Japan's ruling party.

❏ When people say something **rules**, they mean it is regarded as the most important thing in a situation. That is the necessity in every country where capitalism rules.

❏ When people talk about the **rule of law**, they mean a situation in which people respect and obey the law, enabling society to function properly.

❏ When workers **work to rule**, they protest about something by refusing to do any extra work and just doing the minimum required by their contracts. A protest like this is called a **work-to-rule**.

❏ If something is the **rule**, it is the normal state of affairs. The trauma of the 1980s was the exception, not the rule. ◇ If something happens as a **rule**, it normally happens. Industrialised countries as a rule can afford to spend more on their education.

❏ If you **rule out** something like an idea or a solution, you decide it is impossible or unsuitable. ◇ If something **rules out** something else, it prevents it from happening or being possible. He bought a small farm, but a serious car accident in 1986 ruled out a permanent future in farming.

❏ If you **rule** a straight line, you draw it using something like a ruler. ◇ **Ruled** paper has thin straight lines printed across it.

ruler ❏ A country's **rulers** are its government. A monarch or dictator is sometimes called a **ruler**.

❏ A **ruler** is a long flat piece of wood, metal, or plastic with straight edges marked in centimetres or inches. Rulers are used to measure things and to draw straight lines.

rum is a strong alcoholic drink made from sugar cane juice.

❏ If you say something is **rum**, you mean it is rather odd. It is a rum old industry, British life assurance.

rumba The **rumba** is a ballroom dance from Cuba.

rumble (rumbling, rumbled) ❏ A **rumble** is a low continuous throbbing sound. When something **rumbles**, it makes a sound like this. The thunder of heavy artillery rumbles round the mountains.

❏ If something like an argument or a dispute **rumbles on**, it goes on without any sign of a settlement.

❏ You use **rumble** to talk about people expressing feelings of dissatisfaction. For example, you can say there are **rumbles** or **rumblings** of discontent. There were rumblings of revolt from the left of the party.

❏ If someone is **rumbled**, the truth about them or their actions is discovered.

rumbustious A **rumbustious** person is energetic, cheerful, and noisy.

ruminant Ruminants are animals which chew the cud and have a stomach divided into four compartments. Deer, cattle, sheep, and goats are all ruminants.

ruminate (ruminating, ruminated; rumination) ❏ If you **ruminate** on something, you think about it slowly and carefully. Thoughts like these are called **ruminations**.

❏ When animals like cattle and deer **ruminate**, they bring food back from their stomach into their mouth and chew it again.

rummage (rummaging, rummaged) If you **rummage** through something or **rummage** around in it, you search for something in it by moving things around in a careless or hurried way.

rummy is a card game in which players try to collect cards of the same value or cards in a sequence in the same suit.

rumour (rumoured) (American spelling: rumor, rumored) A **rumour** is a piece of information circulating among people which may or may not be true. You can say something is **rumoured** to be true. He is rumoured to have at least 53 yachts of differing sizes.

rump ❏ An animal's **rump** is its rear end. ◇ **Rump** or **rump steak** is meat cut from the rear part of a cow's back.

❏ The **rump** of a group or organization is what is left when most of it has gone or been removed. Similarly, you talk about the **rump** of a country when most of it has broken away and become independent. ...*the prime minister of rump Yugoslavia.*

rumpled clothes or bedclothes are creased and disordered. Disordered hair can also be called **rumpled**. If you say a person is **rumpled,** you mean their clothes and hair look like this. ...*fashionably rumpled lecturers.*

rumpus (rumpuses) If someone or something causes a **rumpus,** they cause a lot of noise, fuss, and argument.

run (running, ran, have run) ❑ When you **run,** you make your way quickly on foot, losing contact with the ground during each stride. If you go for a **run,** you do this over a long distance, for training or exercise. **Running** is training like this and taking part in races in which people try to run faster than each other.

❑ In games like cricket and baseball, a **run** is a score of one, which is made by players running between marked places on the pitch after hitting the ball. ◇ In cricket, if a batsman is **run out,** a fielder gets him out by hitting the stumps with the ball before the batsman has completed his run.

❑ If you **run** someone somewhere in a car, you drive them there.

❑ You say something like a road **runs** somewhere when you are describing its course or position. ...*the wall which runs beside the Palace gardens to Hyde Park Corner.* ◇ If trains or buses **run** from one place to another, they regularly travel between them.

❑ If you **run** something like a cable between two places, you position it between them and connect it up.

❑ In sports like skiing, a **run** is a course or route.

❑ If liquid **runs** somewhere, it flows there. ◇ If you **run** a tap, you turn it on and let water flow from it. Similarly, you can talk about **running** a bath. If a tap is **running,** water is flowing from it. ◇ If someone's nose is **running,** mucus is dribbling out of it.

❑ If the colour in a piece of clothing **runs,** it comes out in the wash and often stains other clothing.

❑ If you **run** your hand **over** or **through** something, you move your hand over or through it.

❑ If you **run** something through a process such as a series of tests, you put it through that process. You can also say you **run** the process. ◇ If you **run** a computer program, you get the computer to carry out the instructions in the program.

❑ If a machine is **running** or being **run,** it is switched on and operating. If it **runs on** or **runs off** a source of energy, that source of energy is used to make it work. ...*vehicles that run on petrol or diesel.*

❑ The person who **runs** an organization is the person in charge.

❑ If someone **runs** for office, they take part in an election for a post or position.

❑ If a show or TV programme **runs** for a certain length of time or a certain number of performances, that is how long it continues before it is taken off. This length of time or number of performances is called its **run.** ...*the long running soap opera Dallas.*

❑ **Running** and **long-running** are used to describe things which continue or keep occurring over a period of time. ...*running jokes... ...long-running investigations.* ◇ If two groups fight a **running battle,** there is violence and

fighting between them over a fairly long period of time.

❑ If a feeling **runs** through a group of people, it spreads among them. *Ripples of excitement ran through the group's ranks.* ◇ You say feelings are **running high** when people are very angry, concerned, or excited.

❑ When a newspaper or magazine **runs** an item or story, it prints it.

❑ You say an amount is **running** at a certain level when it is at that level. *Inflation is running at 10.6 per cent.*

❑ If something is taking more time than was planned, you can say it is **running late.**

❑ A **run** of successes or failures is a series of them.

❑ A **run** of a product is the amount a company or factory decides to produce at one time. *It's a popular magazine, with a weekly print run of over four million copies.*

❑ If there is a **run** on something, there is a sudden increase in the number of people buying it. *The easing of tension in the Gulf caused a run on the dollar.*

❑ If you talk about what will happen in the **long run,** you mean what will happen over a long period of time in the future. *Deep cuts in spending may bring short-term budget relief, but will cripple us in the long run.* Similarly, the **short run** is used to talk about the immediate future.

❑ If a team scores **against the run of play,** they score even though the other team had been playing better.

❑ If a criminal is **on the run,** he or she has escaped from prison or is trying to avoid capture by the police. ◇ You can also say someone is **on the run** when they look like being defeated in something like a game or election.

❑ If you are **running low** on something or **running short** of it, you do not have much left. ◇ If something **runs out,** there is none of it left. *The government ran out of money.* Similarly, if a source of water **runs dry,** there is no longer any water there.

❑ When a legal document or agreement **runs out,** it expires.

❑ If someone **runs away** from home, they leave without permission or without telling people beforehand. ◇ If someone **runs off** with someone else, they go away with them to live with them or marry them.

❑ If you **run away** from something, you try to avoid dealing with it or facing up to it. *Let's not run away from the issue.*

❑ If someone **runs away** with a competition or prize, they win it easily. *Villa were running away with the game.*

❑ If you let your imagination or emotions **run away with** you, you fail to control them and cannot think sensibly.

❑ If an industry or organization is being **run down,** its size or activities are being deliberately reduced. You can talk about the **run-down** (or **rundown**) of an industry or organization. ◇ If the amount of something is **run down,** it is reduced or allowed to decrease. *Production costs are being cut by running down stocks as fast as possible.*

❑ If you **run into** someone, you meet them unexpectedly. ◇ If you **run into** something when you are driving, you accidentally hit it. ◇ If someone is **run down** or **run over** by a vehicle, they are knocked down by it.

❑ If you **run into** or **run up against** problems or difficulties, you experience them.

❑ You use **run to** or **run into** when emphasizing how great an amount or cost is. *The tuition fees could run into thousands of pounds.*

❏ If you **run through** a number of items of information, you read or mention all of them quickly. ◇ When actors **run through** a play or give it a **run-through,** they read through it quickly before starting to rehearse it properly.

❏ If a theme or feature **runs through** something like a book, it keeps occurring in it. *The theme of rootlessness runs through many of his poems.*

❏ If someone **runs up** large debts or losses, they accumulate them.

❏ If you say a person or group is **running scared,** you mean they are very worried and are trying to avoid something unpleasant happening to them.

run-down ❏ If someone is **run-down,** they are tired or slightly ill, often because they are under a lot of stress or have been working too hard.

❏ A **run-down** building or area is in very poor condition because it has not been properly maintained. *...a run-down inner-city estate.*

❏ See also **run.**

run-in ❏ If you have a **run-in** with someone, you have a dispute, argument, or fight with them.

❏ The **run-in** to an event is the period leading up to it. *Both campaigned for a confederation during the run-in to their elections.*

run-of-the-mill A **run-of-the-mill** person or thing is very ordinary, with no special or interesting features. *...run-of-the-mill politicians... ...a run-of-the-mill school.*

run-off ❏ A **run-off** is an extra vote or contest held to decide the winner of an election or competition when nobody has yet clearly won.

❏ **Run-off** is rainwater which is not absorbed by the ground and forms a stream.

runabout A **runabout** is a small car used mainly for short journeys.

runaway ❏ A **runaway** is someone who leaves home without telling anyone or without permission.

❏ **Runaway** is used to describe things which suddenly increase rapidly and cannot be controlled. *...runaway inflation... ...the runaway success of the NLD.*

rune Runes are letters from an ancient alphabet which were carved in wood or stone by people in Northern Europe from the third century AD to the Middle Ages. They were believed to have magical properties.

rung ❏ See **ring.**

❏ The **rungs** of a ladder are the wooden or metal bars which form the steps. ◇ You can talk about someone being on a particular **rung** when you are mentioning their position in an organization or the stage they have reached in their career. *...the bottom rung of the managerial ladder.*

runner ❏ A **runner** is someone who runs for sport or pleasure.

❏ A drug **runner** or gun **runner** is someone who illegally gets drugs or guns into a country.

❏ A **runner** is also someone employed to take messages, collect money, or do other small errands.

❏ **Runners** are long shoots which grow out from a plant's main stem, put down roots, and become new plants.

❏ The **runners** on something like a sledge are thin strips of wood or metal underneath it which enable it to move smoothly.

runner bean Runner beans are the long green pods of a climbing plant. They are eaten as a vegetable.

runner-up (runners-up) The **runner-up** is someone who finishes second in a race or competition.

running commentary If someone gives a **running commentary** on something that is happening, they continuously describe and comment on it as it happens.

running costs An organization's **running costs** are the amounts of money it spends on day-to-day requirements, rather than on things like expansion or development.

running mate In an American election campaign, a candidate's **running mate** is the person they have chosen to have the next-ranking political office if they win.

running order The **running order** of the items in a broadcast, concert, or show is the order in which they are due to be presented.

runny If someone has a **runny** nose, mucus is dribbling out of it, usually because they have a cold.

runt The **runt** is the smallest and weakest of a group of animals born to the same mother at the same time.

runway A **runway** is a long strip of ground with a hard surface for planes to land on and take off from.

rupee The **rupee** is the unit of currency in India, Pakistan, and some other countries.

rupture (rupturing, ruptured) If something **ruptures** or there is a **rupture** in it, it tears or bursts open. *...a ruptured liver... ...a pipeline rupture.* See also **hernia.**

❏ If relations between people or groups are **ruptured,** something happens which spoils them or puts an end to them. *The UN runs the risk of rupturing the unity of the Council... Mexico restored diplomatic relations with the Vatican, after a rupture of more than 130 years.*

rural is used to describe things to do with country areas as opposed to large towns. *...rural communities.*

rural dean A **rural dean** is a member of the clergy who has authority over a group of Church of England parishes.

ruse A **ruse** is a clever trick or plan intended to deceive someone.

rush (rushes, rushing, rushed) ❏ If you **rush** somewhere, you go there as quickly as you can. ◇ If you **rush** someone else somewhere, you take them there as quickly as you can. *He was rushed to hospital for emergency brain surgery.* ◇ If people **rush** to do something, they do it as soon as they can, because they are eager to do it. You can also say there is a **rush** to do something. *...a headlong rush towards privatisation.*

❏ If you are in a **rush,** you need to go somewhere or do something quickly. ◇ If you are **rushed off your feet,** you are extremely busy. ◇ If a place like a shop has a regular busy period, this period is often called the **rush.** *...the evening rush... ...the Christmas rush.*

❏ If you **rush** something, you do it in a hurry, often too quickly and without much care. ◇ If you **rush** into something or are **rushed** into it, you do it without taking time to think about it properly.

❏ If something is **rushed out,** it is produced very quickly. ◇ If something is **rushed through,** it is dealt with very quickly. *The supplementary budget was rushed through ahead of schedule.*

❏ If police or soldiers **rush** a place or group of people, they move quickly towards them, to attack or capture them.

❏ If something like air, water, or blood **rushes** or there is a **rush** of it, it moves rapidly. *Air rushing past the fuselage causes it to vibrate.*

❏ If you experience a sudden powerful feeling, you can say you have a **rush** of it. *I felt a rush of pure joy.*

❏ **Rushes** are plants with long thin stems which grow near water. **Rush** mats and baskets are woven from their stems.

❏ The **rushes** of a film are the parts which have been filmed but have not yet been edited.

rush hour The **rush hour** is a period during the day when roads and railways are particularly busy because most people are travelling to or from work.

rusk Rusks are hard dry biscuits fed to babies and small children.

russet is a reddish-brown colour.

Russian roulette When someone plays **Russian roulette**, they put a bullet in one of the chambers of a gun, spin the chambers, then fire the gun at their own head, not knowing whether it will go off or not.

rust is a reddish-brown coating of an oxide formed on iron or steel when it is in continual contact with water or water vapour. When a metal **rusts**, rust forms on it. ◇ **Rust** is also a reddish-brown colour.

rust belt A **rust belt** is a part of a country which used to be a centre of industrial activity but is now suffering economically because its industries have declined.

rustic is used to describe things which are simple and homely in a way considered typical of the countryside. *...rustic charm... ...rustic traditions.* ◇ Simple unsophisticated country people used to be called **rustics**.

rustle (rustling, rustled; rustler) ❏ If something **rustles**, it makes soft whispering sounds as it moves. Sounds like these are called **rustlings**. *...the rustlings of the poplar on windy nights.*

❏ If you **rustle** something **up**, you make, prepare, or get hold of it quickly, with little time to plan or arrange it. *See if somebody can rustle up a cup of coffee.*

❏ **Rustling** is stealing farm animals, especially cattle. People who do this are called **rustlers**.

rusty ❏ If a metal object is **rusty**, rust has formed on it. ◇ You can also say something is **rusty** when it is a reddish-brown colour. *...rusty hair.*

❏ If you are **rusty**, you are not as good at something as you used to be, because you are out of practice.

rut (rutting, rutted) ❏ If a road or track is **rutted** or has **ruts** in it, its surface has deep narrow grooves, made by the wheels of vehicles.

❏ If you say someone or something is **stuck in a rut**, you mean they carry on in the same way without changing or adapting, and so are unable to progress or provide satisfaction. *His career remained stuck in a rut.*

❏ The **rut** is the period of the year when some animals, especially deer, are sexually active, and males fight each other before mating with the females. During this period, you say the males are **rutting**.

ruthless (ruthlessly, ruthlessness) A **ruthless** person will do anything necessary to achieve what they want. *The demonstration was ruthlessly crushed by the authorities... He was renowned for his toughness and ruthlessness.*

rye is a cereal grown in colder countries. Its grains can be used to make flour, bread, and other foods.

rye bread is dark brown bread made with rye or with a mixture of rye and flour.

rye whiskey is American whiskey made from rye.

S s

Sabbath The **Sabbath** is the day of the week which Jews and Christians devote to religious worship. Jews celebrate the Sabbath on Saturdays and Christians celebrate it on Sundays.

sabbatical When someone, especially a university lecturer, takes a **sabbatical**, they take time off from their normal work, to study, travel, or rest. They often receive their normal pay during this period.

sable The **sable** is a small weasel-like animal which lives in northern Europe and northern Asia. **Sable** is the very expensive brown fur of these animals.

sabotage (*pron:* sab-ot-ahzh; *the 'zh' sounds like 's' in 'pleasure'*) (sabotaging, sabotaged; saboteur) If someone **sabotages** something like a piece of machinery, they damage or destroy it, for some political or military purpose. Damaging and destroying things like this is called **sabotage**; someone who does it is called a **saboteur**. ◇ If someone **sabotages** a government's policy or something like talks or negotiations, they prevent them from being successful. Similarly, people can **sabotage** an activity like a hunt. *...hunt saboteurs.*

sabre A **sabre** is (a) a heavy sword with a curved blade, formerly used by soldiers on horseback. (b) a light sword used in fencing.

sabre-rattling is an aggressive show of force by a country or government, intended to intimidate other countries.

sac A **sac** is a part inside a person's or an animal's body shaped like a small bag and containing something like air or fluid.

saccharine (*or* saccharin) (*both pron:* sak-er-rin) is a sweet chemical substance. It is used in drinks instead of sugar by people who want to lose weight. ◇ If you call something **saccharine** (*pron:* sak-er-reen), you mean it is too sweet or sentimental.

sachet (*pron:* sash-ay) A **sachet** is a small sealed plastic or paper packet, containing a small quantity of something.

sack ❏ A **sack** is a large bag made of rough material, for carrying or storing things.

❏ If you are **sacked** or given the **sack**, you are dismissed from your job.

❏ If an army **sacks** a place, they destroy it and take away anything of value.

sackcloth is rough woven material used to make sacks. ◇ When people talk about **sackcloth and ashes,** they are referring, usually humorously, to someone's public display of regret or sorrow for something they have done badly or failed to do.

sackful A **sackful** of something is the amount you can get into one sack.

sackload When something is normally delivered in sacks, you can talk about receiving **sackloads** of it, meaning a great deal of it.

sacrament (sacramental) A **sacrament** is an important Christian religious ceremony such as communion, baptism, or marriage. **Sacramental** is used to talk about things to do with the sacraments. *...sacramental wine.*

sacred (*pron:* say-krid) ❏ **Sacred** objects, places, or people are believed to be holy. ◇ **Sacred** is used to describe other things connected with religion or used in religious ceremonies. *...sacred music.*

❏ **Sacred** is also used to describe things which are considered to be too important to be changed or interfered with. *...the once sacred notions of socialism and anti-fascism.*

❏ If you call something like a custom or an institution a **sacred cow,** you mean people regard it as something which cannot be criticized or questioned.

sacrifice (sacrificing, sacrificed; sacrificial) ❏ If you **sacrifice** something or someone that is important to you, you give them up for something worthwhile or for another person's sake. You call this making a **sacrifice.** *He warned that citizens may have to sacrifice food and health services to help the authorities end the civil war.*

❏ In the past, if a person or animal was **sacrificed,** they were killed as an offering to a god or gods. This was called making a **sacrifice. Sacrificial** is used to talk about things to do with making sacrifices. *...sacrificial victims.*

sacrilege (*pron:* sak-ril-ij) (sacrilegious) **Sacrilege** is disrespectful behaviour towards something holy. Behaviour like this can be called **sacrilegious.** ◇ Other kinds of behaviour are sometimes humorously called **sacrilege** when they show disrespect for something which people think is very important and should not be interfered with.

sacrosanct (*pron:* sak-roe-sangkt) is used to describe things which are considered so important or special that they must not be criticized or changed in any way. *The weekend rest days were considered sacrosanct by staff.*

sacrum The **sacrum** is the triangular bone at the bottom of the spine between the hip bones.

SAD or **Seasonal Affective Disorder** is a depressive condition which some people suffer from during the winter. It is thought to be caused by a lack of sunlight.

sad (sadder, saddest; sadness, sadly) ❏ If you are **sad,** you are unhappy, especially about something which has recently happened. *I am not alone in feeling sadness at the changes that have come about.* ◇ If you say something like a story is **sad,** you mean it makes you feel sad.

❏ **Sad** and **sadly** are also used to say something is regrettable. *It is sad that his knowledge of English is poor... Britain's motorways are sadly lacking in loos.*

sadden (saddening, saddened) If you are **saddened** by

something, it makes you feel sad.

saddle (saddling, saddled) ❏ If you **saddle** a horse, you fasten a leather seat called a **saddle** on its back, so you can ride it. ◇ If you talk about someone being **in the saddle,** you mean (a) they are riding a horse. (b) they are in control of something or in power. ◇ The seat on a bicycle or motorbike is also called a **saddle.**

❏ A **saddle** is also a large cut of meat, especially mutton, from the middle part of an animal's back.

❏ If you are **saddled with** something unpleasant or difficult, you have to put up with it or are prevented by it from doing things you would like to do.

saddlebag A **saddlebag** is a bag attached to the saddle of a horse, bicycle, or motorbike.

sadism (sadist; sadistic, sadistically) **Sadism** is getting pleasure from inflicting physical or mental cruelty on someone. A **sadist** is someone who gets pleasure this way. **Sadistic** is used to describe people like this and their behaviour. *...sadistic beatings... Perhaps he had acted deliberately, to enjoy sadistically the misery he had created.*

sado-masochism (sado-masochistic, sado-masochist) **Sado-masochism** is sexual behaviour between two people in which one of them has a sadistic role and the other a masochistic one. **Sado-masochistic** is used to talk about things connected with sado-masochism. *...the classic sado-masochistic novel.* A **sado-masochist** is someone who gets pleasure from inflicting suffering or receiving it or both.

sae (*pronounce each letter separately*) An **sae** is an envelope which you stamp and address to yourself. You send it to someone so they do not have to pay for postage or stationery when they reply. 'sae' stands for 'stamped addressed envelope'.

safari A **safari** is an expedition for hunting or observing animals, especially in Africa.

safari park A **safari park** is a large enclosed area of land where wild animals live and move around freely. People pay to drive their cars through these parks to watch the animals.

safe (safer, safest; safely) ❏ If you are **safe,** you are unharmed or not in danger. ◇ You can emphasize that someone is unhurt by saying they are **safe and sound.** ◇ If you have had a **safe** journey, you have arrived somewhere without being harmed on the way. You can also talk about your **safe** arrival. *The two envoys have now arrived safely in Baghdad.* Similarly, you can say a plane has had a **safe** landing.

❏ If it is **safe** to do something, you can do it without any risk. ◇ A **safe** way of doing something is one which carries no risk. ◇ If you **play safe** or **play it safe,** you do not take unnecessary risks. ◇ If you do something **to be on the safe side,** you do it as a precaution even though it may be unnecessary or excessive. ◇ If you think no risk was involved in what someone has said or done, you can say they were **on safe ground** in saying or doing it. ◇ If you say it is **safe** to say something, you mean it can be said with little chance of being wrong. *We can safely say that the UK retail turnaround is under way.*

❏ If you are at a **safe distance** from something, you are far enough away not to be harmed by any danger connected with it. Similarly, you can do something from a **safe distance.**

❏ A **safe** place is one where someone or something will not be harmed. ◇ You can call a place a **safe haven** when people or animals are protected from danger there. *The 2.2m acre national park is a safe haven for 30,000 elk.*

❏ If you say someone or something will be **in safe hands**, you mean they will be looked after properly by a reliable person. ◇ If you call someone a **safe pair of hands**, you mean they can be trusted to do the job they were chosen to do.

❏ If you say something is a **safe bet**, you mean things will almost certainly turn out in the way you are describing.

❏ A **safe** is a strong metal cupboard with special locks for keeping money, jewellery, and other valuable things in.

safe conduct If someone or something has been given **safe conduct**, they have been given official permission to travel through a place, especially enemy territory, with a promise that they will not be harmed in any way.

safe deposit boxes are containers, usually in a special room at a bank, in which people keep money, jewellery, and other valuable things.

safe house A **safe house** is a place where someone like a spy or a hunted criminal can hide and be protected from danger.

safe passage If someone is guaranteed **safe passage**, they are given a promise that they can pass from one place to another without any risk of harm.

safe seat You call a parliamentary seat a **safe seat** when it has been held by the same party with a large majority for a long time and is unlikely to be won by any other party.

safe sex or **safer sex** is having sex in a responsible way, for example using a condom, to prevent the spread of sexually transmitted diseases, especially AIDS.

safeguard If you **safeguard** something, you protect it from harm. Something which is introduced to give protection from harm can be called a **safeguard**.

safekeeping If something is given to someone for **safekeeping**, it is handed over so it will be protected and kept safe from harm.

safer sex See **safe sex**.

safety is being safe and secure, and protected from harm or danger.

❏ If you are concerned about the **safety** of something like a nuclear installation, you are concerned about how dangerous it might be. ◇ **Safety** measures and equipment are intended to make something less dangerous.

safety belt A **safety belt** is the same as a seat belt.

safety catch A **safety catch** is a device on a gun which is there to prevent the gun being fired accidentally. It has to be released before the gun can be fired.

safety net A **safety net** is a large net spread out as a precaution beneath a person trying to do a difficult stunt high up in the air. ◇ A **safety net** is also part of a system which is there to prevent serious harm being done if something goes wrong.

safety pin A **safety pin** is a bent metal pin, used to fasten things together. The point of the pin has a cover over it when closed, to stop it doing any harm and prevent it becoming accidentally unfastened.

safety valve A **safety valve** is a piece of equipment in something like a boiler which allows steam to escape when too much pressure has built up. ◇ You also call something a **safety valve** when it acts as a release for built-up emotions or energy without harming other people. *Sport can be a social safety valve, a substitute for shooting one another.*

saffron is a yellowish-orange spice from a type of crocus. It is used to colour and flavour food. ◇ **Saffron** is also a yellowish-orange colour.

sag (sagging, sagged) ❏ If part of a person's body **sags**, it hangs down loosely and heavily because of its weight or lack of support. ◇ If something like a bed **sags**, it dips in the middle.

❏ If you say a person's reputation is **sagging**, you mean people do not think as highly of them as they used to. You can also say there is a **sag** in their reputation. ◇ If something like a level **sags**, it goes down. *By the time he left the paper in 1973 its circulation had sagged to barely 15,000.*

saga (*pron*: sah-ga) The **sagas** were medieval Icelandic and Norwegian legends. They were often very long and usually told the story of a Norse king or hero or a family. ◇ Nowadays, any long story, novel, TV series, or film telling the story of a family over several generations can be called a **saga**. ◇ A long-running sequence of events described in the media can also be called a **saga**. *The saga of a hostile takeover that backfired took another turn yesterday.*

sagacious (*pron*: sag-gay-shuss) (sagacity) If you call someone **sagacious** or talk about their **sagacity**, you mean they behave in a wise and intelligent way. A wise action can also be called **sagacious**.

sage (sagely) ❏ **Sage** is a herb with long greyish-green leaves. It has a strong flavour, and is used in cooking. In Britain, its most common use is in sage and onion stuffing.

❏ A **sage** is a person who is regarded as being wise. ◇ **Sage** people are wise and knowledgeable. You can also call a remark or piece of advice **sage**.

sago (*pron*: say-go) The **sago** is a type of palm tree whose trunk produces an edible starch, also called **sago**. This starch is used for making puddings and for thickening sauces.

said See **say**.

sail (sailing, sailed) ❏ When a ship **sails** somewhere, it goes there. You can also say someone **sails** on it. When a ship starts its journey, you can say it **sets sail**. You can also say the people in it **set sail**. ◇ A **sailing** is a regular voyage made by a ship from one place to another. The departure of a ship can also be called a **sailing**.

❏ A **sail** is a large piece of material fastened to the mast of a boat or ship, which catches the wind and makes the vessel move. ◇ **take the wind out of** someone's **sails**: see **wind**.

❏ A **sailing ship** is a ship with sails, especially one which used to carry passengers and cargo in the past. A **sailing boat** is a smaller vessel with a sail or sails. ◇ **Sailing** is the activity of going out in sailing boats, for sport or pleasure.

❏ If someone **sails through** a difficult situation or experience, they get through it successfully and without difficulty. ◇ If you say something is **plain sailing**, you mean it is uncomplicated and easy to achieve.

❏ The **sails** on a windmill are the flat parts which are

turned by the wind.

sailboard A sailboard is a flat board with a sail attached to it, used for windsurfing.

sailing See sail.

sailor A sailor is a person whose job involves working on ships as part of the crew.

saint A saint is a dead person who has been officially recognized and honoured by the Christian Church because of their holy life. 'Saint' is often shortened to 'St'; 'Saints' is shortened to 'SS'. ◇ People sometimes call someone a saint when their behaviour is unusually kind, patient, and unselfish.

sainthood When someone becomes a saint, you can say they achieve sainthood.

saintly people behave in a very good or holy way. Saintly is also used to describe things connected with people like these. ...a saintly reputation.

sake ❏ If something is done for someone's sake, it is done for their benefit. ◇ If something is done for the sake of a certain thing, it is done so that thing can happen or continue. The Free Democrats are arguing for a coalition for the sake of stability. ◇ Sake is used in several phrases which explain why something is done. Let's assume for the sake of argument that we manage to build a satisfactory database... ...for old time's sake.
❏ If you do something for its own sake, you do it because you enjoy it, and not for any other reason.
❏ Some people say things like for God's sake and for goodness sake to express annoyance or impatience, or to add emphasis to a question or request.
❏ Sake (pron: sah-kee) is a Japanese alcoholic drink made from fermented rice.

salacious If you call something like a story, picture, or song salacious, you mean it is too concerned with sex or deals with sexual matters in an unnecessarily detailed way.

salad ❏ A salad is a mixture of raw or cooked vegetables which are eaten cold. Salad is often served as an accompaniment to a main meal. ◇ Salad leaves are leaves such as various types of lettuce which can be used to make up a salad. ◇ See also fruit salad.
❏ If you talk about someone's salad days, you mean the period in their life when they were young and inexperienced.

salamander The salamander is a lizard-like amphibian in many parts of Asia, Europe, and North America.

salami (pron: sal-lah-mee) is a type of sausage made from chopped meat and spices.

salary (salaries; salaried) A salary is the fixed payment someone is paid for their job, usually each month, especially when they have a professional job. A salaried person is someone who receives a salary. You also say their job is salaried.

sale ❏ When something is sold, you talk about its sale. ◇ If something is for sale or up for sale, its owner is trying to sell it. ◇ If something is on sale, it is available to be bought, for example in a shop or showroom.
❏ When people talk about the sales of a product, they mean the number that have been sold. ...the drop in sports-car sales. ◇ Sales is used to talk about the part of a company which deals with selling its products. ...sales staff. A company's sales force is a group of people specially trained to sell its products.
❏ A sale is an occasion when a shop sells goods at lower than normal prices. ◇ A sale is also an auction. ◇ jumble sale: see jumble.

saleable things can be sold easily or are suitable for being sold.

saleroom A saleroom is a place where things are sold by auction.

sales clerk In the US, shop assistants are called sales clerks.

salesman (salesmen) A salesman is a man whose job is to sell things, either in a shop or directly to customers.

salesmanship is the skill of persuading people to buy things.

salesperson (salespeople) A salesperson is a person whose job is to sell things, either in a shop or directly to customers.

saleswoman (saleswomen) A saleswoman is a woman whose job is to sell things, especially in a shop.

salient (pron: say-lee-ent) The salient features of something are its most prominent, noticeable, or striking ones.

saline (pron: say-line) (salinity) Saline things contain salt. ...a saline drip. Salinity (pron: sal-lin-it-ee) is used to talk about the amount of salt in something. Irrigated land deteriorates as its salinity rises.

saliva (pron: sal-lie-va) (salivary) Saliva is the clear liquid produced in a person's mouth by glands called the salivary glands. Saliva helps in the swallowing and digesting of food.

salivate (salivating, salivated) When a person or animal salivates, they start to produce extra saliva, often as a result of seeing or smelling food. ◇ You can also say someone salivates at something when they get very excited at the thought of seeing it or having it.

sallow If you describe something, especially skin, as sallow, you mean it is an unhealthy pale or yellowish colour.

sally (sallies, sallying, sallied) ❏ When someone sets out in an energetic way to do something, you can say they sally forth to do it.
❏ A sally is a clever and amusing remark.

salmon (usual plural: salmon) ❏ Salmon are large silver-coloured fish with edible pink or reddish flesh. Their flesh is also called salmon.
❏ Salmon pink is an orangey-pink colour.

salmonella is a kind of bacteria which can cause severe food poisoning.

salon ❏ A hairdresser's or beautician's salon is a place where they carry out their business.
❏ In the past, a salon was an elegant room in which guests were received. ◇ A salon was also a gathering of people in a fashionable household, usually the most important literary, political, or artistic figures of society.
❏ A salon is also an exhibition of works of art, particularly those by living artists, or the hall where these works are displayed.

saloon ❏ A saloon is a car with a fixed roof and seats for four or more people.
❏ In Britain, the saloon or saloon bar in a pub or hotel is a comfortable bar where the drinks are more expensive than in the other bars. ◇ In the Wild West, a saloon was a

place where alcoholic drinks were sold and drunk.

salsa is (a) a type of Puerto Rican big-band dance music. (b) a spicy tomato-based sauce.

SALT stands for 'Strategic Arms Limitation Talks'. These were a series of discussions between the US and the former Soviet Union on how to limit the number of nuclear weapons they possessed.

salt is a substance in crystal form which is used to improve the flavour of food or preserve it. Salt occurs naturally in sea water and is also mined from the earth. If you **salt** food, you add salt to it. ...*salted peanuts.*

❑ If you say something should be **taken with a pinch of salt,** you mean it is probably not completely true.

❑ If you say someone is **rubbing salt into the wound,** you mean they are making an unpleasant situation worse for someone.

❑ People use **salt** with 'worth' to say something would not be acceptable to a competent person of a certain kind. For example, they say 'No employer **worth his salt** would put up with work of this sort.'

❑ **Salt** water is seawater, as distinct from fresh water.

❑ In chemistry, a **salt** is a compound formed from an acid. ◇ **Salts** are also certain minerals used for medicinal purposes.

❑ If someone **salts away** something valuable, especially money, they store it away somewhere for safekeeping.

salt cellar A **salt cellar** is a small container for salt which is put on the table at mealtimes.

salt flat A **salt flat** is a flat area covered with salt left behind when an area of salt water has completely evaporated.

salty things taste of salt or contain salt. ◇ **Salty** stories and songs are humorous and a little rude.

salubrious (*pron:* sal-**loo**-bree-uss) If you say a place is not **salubrious,** you mean it is unpleasant or unhealthy.

salutary If you call an experience **salutary,** you mean it is good for you or you learn something from it, although it is unpleasant or difficult at the time.

salutation A **salutation** is a greeting.

salute (saluting, saluted) ❑ If you **salute** someone, you greet them or show respect, usually by raising the fingers of your right hand to the side of your forehead. A sign like this is called a **salute.** ◇ When a head of state or military leader **takes the salute** at a military parade, they watch as the troops passing by salute them. Often they salute back. ◇ On some ceremonial occasions, cannons or other large guns are fired into the air; this is also called a **salute.**

❑ If you say you **salute** a person or their achievements, you mean you want to express your admiration for them. *I salute the restraint of Western leaders, when fierce words could have made a peaceful solution less and less possible.*

salvage (salvaging, salvaged) ❑ If something is **salvaged** from a sunken ship or the wreckage of a plane or building, it is removed, because it can give information or can be used again. Items removed from sunken ships or destroyed buildings so they can be used again are called **salvage.**

❑ If you **salvage** something from a disastrous situation, you manage to get something useful out of it.

❑ If someone **salvages** a company which is in serious difficulties, they rescue it.

salvation ❑ In Christianity, **salvation** is being saved by belief in Jesus Christ from the power of sin and punishment for your sins.

❑ When someone or something is rescued from a very serious situation, you can call this their **salvation.**

Salvation Army The **Salvation Army** is a Christian evangelical organization, structured like an army, which helps people in need.

salve (salving, salved) ❑ If you **salve your conscience** by doing something, it makes you feel less guilty.

❑ A **salve** is a substance you put on your skin or lips to prevent soreness or dryness.

salvo (salvoes) When several guns are fired at the same time, for example as part of a ceremony, this is called a **salvo.** ◇ In a dispute, a **salvo** is a sudden strong action taken by one side against the other.

Samaritan If someone generously helps you out when you are in difficulty, you can call them a **good Samaritan.** ◇ The **Samaritans** is a voluntary organization which tries to help people who are suicidal or in despair, especially by talking to them on the phone.

samba The **samba** is a lively Brazilian dance.

same ❑ You use **the same** to say two or more things are exactly alike in some way. *I want my son to look like everybody else at the school and wear the same clothes... The rich pay the same as those on average incomes.*

❑ You use **the same** to indicate that you are talking about only one person, thing, place, or time, rather than different ones. *The bank corrected the mistake the same day... The same area was struck by a bigger earthquake in May.* For emphasis, you can say **one and the same.** *When shareholder, supervisor and the boss's patron are one and the same, vital checks and balances are missing.* ◇ You also use **the same** to indicate that you are talking about the person or thing you have just mentioned. *Now there are day tours from Morecambe to those same towns.*

❑ If something is still **the same,** it has not changed. *The GCSEs are the same from year to year and neither get easier nor harder.*

❑ **All the same** or **just the same** means in spite of what has just been said. *He speaks almost no English and may not want the job. All the same, he is the sort of man that is needed.*

sameness If you talk about the **sameness** of something, you mean it lacks variety.

samizdat In the former Soviet bloc, **samizdat** was a system in which banned literature or writing criticizing the state was secretly printed and distributed.

samovar In Russia and some other countries, a **samovar** is a large decorated metal container used for boiling water to make tea.

sample (sampling, sampled) ❑ A **sample** of a product or substance is a single item or a small amount of it, provided so you can see what it is like. ◇ If you **sample** something, you try it or experience it to see what it is like. ◇ A **sample** of something like blood or urine is a small amount which you provide so it can be examined and analysed scientifically. Taking samples like these is called **sampling.**

❑ A **sample** of people or things is a number of them chosen from a larger group, so they can be used in tests or to provide information about the whole group. *Mori interviewed a representative sample of 1,868 adults aged 18 and* *over.*

sampler ❏ A **sampler** is a collection of samples of things, for example a tape or CD containing music by different artists.
❏ In the past, a **sampler** was a piece of embroidery sewn by a young girl to show her skill at needlework.

samurai (*plural:* samurai) A **samurai** was a member of a warrior caste which formed the administrative and fighting aristocracy in Japan from the 12th to the 19th century.

sanatorium (*plural:* sanatoriums *or* sanatoria) A **sanatorium** is an institution where people who are suffering from long-term illnesses are sent for medical treatment and rest.

sanctify (sanctifies, sanctifying, sanctified) ❏ If a priest **sanctifies** something, he blesses it to make it holy.
❏ If you talk about something like an informal arrangement being **sanctified,** you mean it is officially accepted or approved.

sanctimonious (sanctimoniousness) If you accuse someone of being **sanctimonious,** you mean they are making a great show of being more virtuous than other people. You talk about the **sanctimoniousness** of someone like this.

sanction (sanctioning, sanctioned) ❏ If someone in authority **sanctions** something, they give it their official approval. *...a sanctioning of the use of force.* You can say something has the **sanction** of someone in authority.
❏ **Sanctions** are measures one country takes against another, to try to persuade them to do something or stop doing something. *...trade sanctions.* Illegal attempts to get round sanctions are called **sanctions-busting.**
◇ **Sanctions** are also a severe or tough course of action taken against a group of people, to try to make them obey the law or comply with accepted standards.

sanctity If you talk about the **sanctity** of a place, you mean it should be respected because it is holy. *Cardinal Daly called for the sanctity of Church property to be preserved.* ◇ You can talk about the **sanctity** of other things which you think are very important and should be respected or preserved. *...the sanctity of marriage.*

sanctuary (sanctuaries) A **sanctuary** is a place of safety where a person can be sure of protection. If you give someone **sanctuary,** you provide them with a place like this. ◇ A wildlife **sanctuary** is a place where birds or animals are protected and can live freely.

sanctum A **sanctum** or **inner sanctum** of a religious building is a part which is regarded as especially holy. ◇ If you talk about the **inner sanctum** of some other building, you mean a part which is supposed to be very private and used by only a few people.

sand is a very fine powder-like substance consisting of tiny rock or mineral grains. Deserts and beaches are made up mainly of sand. Sand is used in making cement and glass. ◇ Large areas of sand are sometimes called **sands.** *...the desert sands.*
❏ If you talk about the **shifting sands** of something, you mean it is constantly changing.
❏ If you talk about something **running into the sand,** you mean it has gone wrong or got into difficulties.
❏ If you **sand** an object, you rub sandpaper over it to make it smooth or clean.

sandal Sandals are light open shoes with straps which are usually worn in the summer.

sandalwood is a sweet-smelling wood from a tree called the sandalwood tree. **Sandalwood** is also an oil extracted from sandalwood and used to make perfume.

sandbag (sandbagged) **Sandbags** are sacks filled with sand which are used to form barriers, for example against floods or explosions. **Sandbagged** positions or places have had sandbags piled around them for protection or to strengthen them.

sandbank A **sandbank** is a raised area of sand just below the surface of the sea or a river which may be uncovered at low tide.

sandblast If you **sandblast** something like a building, you clean it with a jet of sand or grit blown from a nozzle under air or steam pressure.

sandcastle A **sandcastle** is a model castle made of sand, built on a beach by or for a child.

sandpaper is a piece of strong paper with a covering of sand on it which you rub over a surface to make it smooth or clean.

sandpit A **sandpit** is a shallow hole in the ground or a box filled with sand, for children to play in.

sandstone is a type of rock which contains a lot of sand and is often used in building.

sandstorm A **sandstorm** is a strong wind in the desert which creates large moving clouds of sand.

sandwich (sandwiches, sandwiching, sandwiched) ❏ A **sandwich** is two slices of bread with a filling between them.
❏ If something is **sandwiched** between two other things, it occupies a small or narrow space between them. ◇ If something is **sandwiched** between two events, it takes place in the very short space of time between them.

sandwich board A **sandwich board** consists of two connected boards covered with advertisements or other messages, hung over a person's shoulders so that it hangs down over their front and back. The person walks around the streets wearing it to display the advertisements.

sandwich course A **sandwich course** is an educational course in which you spend periods working in industry or business in between periods of full-time study.

sandy is used to describe something which contains a lot of sand. *...sandy soils.*

sane (saner, sanest) You say someone is **sane** when they are not mentally ill. ◇ If you say something like a policy or idea is **sane,** you mean it is sensible and reasonable.

sang See **sing.**

sang-froid (*pron:* sahng-frwah) If you talk about someone's **sang-froid,** you mean their ability to stay calm in a dangerous or difficult situation.

sanguine (*pron:* sang-gwin) If you say someone is **sanguine** about something, you mean they are cheerful and confident that things will turn out as they want them to.

sanitary is used to talk about things connected with hygiene and cleanliness. *...appalling sanitary conditions.*

sanitary towel A **sanitary towel** is a pad of soft absorbent material which some women wear to absorb blood when they have their period.

sanitation is the practice of keeping places clean and hygienic, especially by providing a sewage system and clean water supply.

sanitize (sanitizing, sanitized) (*can be spelled with an 's' instead of a 'z'*) If someone **sanitizes** something unpleasant, they deal with it in a way which makes it more acceptable.

sanity If you have doubts about someone's **sanity**, you are not sure they are completely sane. ◇ If someone brings **sanity** to a situation, they make it sensible and reasonable again after a period of confusion and worry.

sank see sink.

sans is an old word meaning 'without'.

Sanskrit is an ancient language of India. Although it is now only used for religious purposes, it is still one of the official languages of India.

Santa Claus is the legendary patron saint of Christmas, usually identified with Saint Nicholas. Santa Claus is supposed to bring presents for children at Christmas. He is also called 'Father Christmas'.

sap (sapping, sapped) ❑ **Sap** is a liquid in trees and plants. It contains things like mineral salts and sugar.
❑ If something **saps** your strength, it slowly weakens you. You can also talk about something **sapping** your confidence, energy, or enthusiasm.

sapling A **sapling** is a young tree.

sapper A **sapper** is a soldier of the lowest rank in the Royal Engineers. ◇ A **sapper** is also any soldier whose job is to dig trenches and prepare minefields.

sapphire A **sapphire** is a precious stone which is usually blue. ◇ **Sapphire** is a bright blue colour.

sarcastic (sarcastically, sarcasm) You say someone is being **sarcastic** when they mock someone else in an unpleasant way, usually by saying something good about them when it is obvious that the opposite is true. Mocking someone like this is called **sarcasm**. *He sarcastically thanked the president for all he had done for the federation.*

sarcophagus (*pron:* sar-kof-fag-uss) (*plural:* sarcophagi *or* sarcophaguses) A **sarcophagus** is a large coffin, often decorated and usually made of stone.

sardine Sardines are any small sea fish belonging to the herring family, especially small pilchards. They are usually sold tightly packed in tins.

sardonic (sardonically) If a speaker or writer is being **sardonic**, they are being mocking or scornful. *He looked at me sardonically.*

sari (*pron:* sah-ree) (saris) A **sari** is a traditional piece of clothing worn by Indian women. It consists of a long piece of thin material, which is elaborately wrapped around the body.

sarong (*pron:* sar-rong) A **sarong** is a traditional piece of clothing worn by men and women in places like Malaysia and the Pacific islands. It consists of a piece of material tied around the waist like a skirt or under the armpits like a dress.

sartorial is used to talk about the clothes someone wears. *Eton's last concession to sartorial modernity was to do away with top hats.*

SAS The SAS is a team of highly trained British soldiers who work on secret or very difficult military operations. SAS stands for 'Special Air Service'.

sash (sashes) A **sash** is a long piece of material which a person wears round their waist or over one shoulder, usually at official or formal ceremonies.

sash window A **sash window** is a window consisting of two frames placed one above the other in such a way that the lower one can be raised or the upper one lowered.

Sassenach Scottish people sometimes call English people **Sassenachs**. They do this to be humorous or insulting.

sassy When Americans call someone **sassy**, they mean they are cheeky and full of life.

sat See sit.

Satan (Satanic, Satanism, Satanist) **Satan** is the name given to the Devil in the Jewish, Christian, and Muslim religions. **Satanic** is used to describe things connected with or influenced by the Devil. ...*satanic forces.* **Satanists** are people who worship the Devil. This practice is called **Satanism**.

satchel A **satchel** is a bag made of leather or cloth with a long shoulder strap.

sate (sating, sated) If you talk about someone's appetite or demand for something being **sated**, you mean it is fully satisfied. ◇ If you are **sated** with something, you have more than you want or need.

satellite ❑ A **satellite** is a man-made device sent into space to send back information or as part of a communications system. Satellites move continually round the earth or other planets. ◇ A planet's or star's **satellite** is a natural object which moves round it.
❑ If you talk about a country's **satellites**, you mean other countries which it controls, and which have very little power of their own. ◇ **Satellite** is used describe other things which depend on something larger and more powerful. ...*satellite towns.*

satiate (*pron:* say-she-ate) (satiating, satiated) If something **satiates** someone's appetite or need, it satisfies it fully.

satin is a smooth shiny type of cloth, like thick silk.

satire (satirical, satirist) **Satire** is writing or entertainment which uses humour and exaggeration to ridicule something, especially something to do with present-day life. A **satire** is a book or play like this. Anything which uses humour like this can be called **satirical**. ...*a satirical poem.* A person who uses satire in their writing is called a **satirist**.

satirize (satirizing, satirized) (*can be spelled with an 's' instead of a 'z'*) When a writer **satirizes** someone or something, he or she uses satire to criticize or mock them.

satisfaction is the feeling of pleasure or contentment you get when you have achieved something you wanted. ◇ **Satisfaction** is also being satisfied with something you have bought or with a service which has been provided. If something is to **your satisfaction**, you are satisfied with it.
❑ If you **get satisfaction** from someone, they give you an apology or make amends in some other way for some harm they have caused you.

satisfactory (satisfactorily) If you say something is **satisfactory**, you mean it is good enough for what is needed. ...*the parts of the system which are working satisfactorily.* If you say something is **highly satisfactory**, you mean you are very pleased with it.

satisfy (satisfies, satisfying, satisfied) ❑ If you **satisfy** someone, you make them happy or contented, by giving them what they want. You can also say you **satisfy** someone's needs or desires. ◇ If you are **satisfied** with something, you find it acceptable. If you are **highly**

satisfied with something, you are very pleased with it.

❏ If something **satisfies** certain requirements, it fulfils them.

❏ If someone or something **satisfies** you that something is true, they persuade you of it. Similarly, by making a thorough examination, you can **satisfy yourself** that something is true. When either of these things happens, you can say you are **satisfied** that something is the case.

satisfying (satisfyingly) If something is **satisfying**, it gives you a feeling of pleasure, contentment, or fulfilment. *Agassi completed victory, satisfyingly, with a crisp forehand volley.*

satsuma (*pron:* sat-soo-ma) A **satsuma** is a type of small seedless orange, originally from Japan.

saturate (saturating, saturated; saturation) ❏ If someone or something is **saturated**, they are extremely wet.

❏ If you say a place or system is **saturated** with something, you mean it is so full of it it cannot take any more. When this happens, you say the place or system has reached **saturation point**. *British radio is saturated with news and snippets of information.*

❏ **Saturated fats** include butter and lard. Too much saturated fat is thought to be a cause of heart disease and cancer. See also **unsaturated**.

saturnine people are gloomy and unfriendly.

sauce A **sauce** is a liquid served with food to add to its flavour.

saucepan A **saucepan** is a deep cooking pot, usually made of metal and often with a long handle and lid.

saucer A **saucer** is a small round dish which you stand a cup on.

saucy (saucier, sauciest; saucily) **Saucy** is used to describe people and things that are rude or cheeky in an entertaining way. *...a saucily raised eyebrow.*

sauerkraut (*pron:* zow-er-krowt) is cabbage cut into very small slices and pickled. It is very popular in Germany.

sauna (*pron:* saw-na) A **sauna** is a hot steam bath. The room or building where you have a bath like this is also called a **sauna**.

saunter (sauntering, sauntered) If you **saunter** somewhere, you walk there in a slow casual way.

sausage A **sausage** is a mixture of finely minced meat, bread, and seasonings wrapped in a skin in a long thin shape. The contents are called **sausage meat**. A **sausage roll** is a small amount of sausage meat wrapped in pastry.

sauté (*pron:* so-tay) (sautés, sautéing, sautéed *or* sautéd) If you **sauté** food, you fry it quickly in a little oil or butter.

savage (savaging, savaged; savagely, savagery) ❏ **Savage** behaviour is violent and cruel. *Isolated groups of people were attacked and savagely beaten.* Behaviour like this is also called **savagery**.

❏ Fierce criticism of someone or something can also be called **savage**. When someone criticizes someone else in a fierce way, you can say they **savage** them. ◇ Other actions which are likely to cause suffering can also be called **savage**. *...savage cuts in public spending.*

❏ In the past, people thought to be primitive and uncivilized were often called **savages**.

❏ A **savage** animal is dangerous, because it is likely to attack people or other animals. ◇ If an animal like a dog **savages** someone, it attacks them and bites them, causing

injury. ◇ You can talk about other things being **savaged** when they are harmed or damaged severely. *The lira has been savaged by Italy's political troubles lately.*

savannah (*or* savanna) A **savannah** is an open flat stretch of grassland with occasional trees, especially in Africa.

save (saving, saved) ❏ If you **save** someone, you prevent them from being harmed, or get them out of an unpleasant situation. *Sixteen years ago he saved Olivetti from bankruptcy.* ◇ **save someone's life:** see **life**.

❏ If you **save** something which is in danger, you prevent it from being lost or destroyed. *The government has been urged to save the jobs of thousands of civilian staff.*

❏ When Christians talk about someone being **saved**, they are talking about them being delivered from sin and from punishment for their sins as a result of believing in Jesus Christ.

❏ If something **saves** you having to do something, it makes it unnecessary for you to do it. ◇ If you **save** yourself some inconvenience, you find a way of avoiding it.

❏ If you do something to **save** money, time, space, or energy, you do it to avoid wasting it. **-saving** is added to words to describe something which helps you avoid wasting something. *...energy-saving equipment.*

❏ If you **save** something or **save** it **up**, you keep it or set it aside for later use. ◇ If you **save** money, you gradually collect it over a period of time. If you do this so you can buy something, you say you **save up** for it.

❏ When a goalkeeper **saves** a shot or makes a **save**, he stops the ball going into the goal.

❏ **Save** and **save for** are sometimes used when mentioning an exception to something. *The streets are completely empty save for the presence of the soldiers.*

❏ **save face:** see **face**. ◇ **save the day:** see **day**.

saver People who save money by putting it aside, especially in a bank or building society, are called **savers**. *The rates for savers will follow lending rates downwards.*

saving ❏ A **saving** is a reduction in the cost of something, or in the amount of money spent or needed. *Commercial companies claim they could do the job for 2p an item – a saving of nearly £10m sterling a year.* Similarly, you can talk about a **saving** in time or energy. *The saving in fuel would be more like 700,000 gallons.*

❏ A person's **savings** are the money they have saved, especially in a bank or building society.

❏ If you talk about someone's or something's **saving grace**, you mean their one good quality, which prevents them being completely bad or worthless.

saviour ❏ If you call someone or something your **saviour**, you mean they have saved you from a difficult or dangerous situation.

❏ In Christianity, the **Saviour** is Jesus Christ.

savoir-faire (*pron:* sav-wahr-fair) If you talk about someone's **savoir-faire**, you mean they have the confidence and ability to behave in the right way in any situation.

savour (savouring, savoured) (*American spelling:* savor, etc) ❏ If you **savour** something, you take great pleasure and delight in it.

❏ If you **savour** food or drink, you eat or drink it slowly to fully appreciate its flavour. ◇ The special taste or smell of a kind of food or drink can be called its **savour**.

savoury (savouries) (*American spelling:* savory, savories)

❑ **Savoury** food has a salty or meaty flavour, rather than a sweet one. ◇ **Savouries** are small savoury titbits.

❑ If you say something is not too **savoury**, you mean it is rather unpleasant or not very respectable.

savvy If you say someone has a certain kind of **savvy**, you mean they have practical knowledge or skill in that field. *The corporate-finance bankers lacked political savvy.* ◇ **Savvy** is also used to describe people who are shrewd or well-informed.

saw (sawing, sawed, have sawn) ❑ See **see**.

❑ A **saw** is a tool for cutting through wood or other things. It has a blade with sharp teeth along one edge. If you **saw** through something, you cut through it with a saw. If you **saw** wood or **saw** it **up**, you cut it into pieces using a saw.

❑ A **saw** is a well-known short saying or proverb.

sawdust is the very fine pieces of wood produced as a waste product when wood is sawn.

sawmill A **sawmill** is a factory where wood is sawn into planks using a power-driven saw.

sawn see **saw**.

sawn-off A **sawn-off** shotgun has had its barrel sawn off to make it shorter and easier to handle.

sax (saxes) A **sax** is the same as a saxophone.

saxophone (saxophonist) A **saxophone** is a metal wind instrument with keys and a single reed. There are several sizes of saxophone. Most of them are made in a curved shape. They are played especially in jazz and rock bands and in military bands. A saxophone player is called a **saxophonist**.

say (saying, said) ❑ When you **say** something, you make a comment or statement or ask a question. ◇ If you **say** something you have learned, you recite it aloud. ◇ If you **say** something **to yourself**, you think it without actually speaking.

❑ You use **say** when you are mentioning another person's statement or opinion. *Large shareholders say that if the dividend is cut, boardroom jobs will come under threat.* You use expressions like 'It is said...' and 'They say...' when you are mentioning an opinion which many people hold. *They say that when you achieve a goal you have long sought, the immediate feeling is one of anti-climax.*

❑ If you talk about a letter, book, or other document **saying** something, you are quoting from it or mentioning what is in it. *The letter said their appeal was inspired by a sincere wish for a peaceful settlement of the crisis.*

❑ If you **have a say** in something, you have the right to give your opinion and influence decisions. ◇ If you **have your say**, you give your opinion on something.

❑ If you say something **says** something about a person, situation, or thing, you mean it reveals something about them. *In many ways, the book says more about America than it does about Mrs Bush.*

❑ You can use **say** to introduce an example of something or to provide an estimate of something. *This raises the option of catching a train to, say, Bordeaux, then hiring a car... My opinion is that between, say, five and ten years from now, we will have a device which will operate in a very reliable fashion.*

❑ You say 'that is to say...' when you are adding something to explain what you have just said. *One of the book's attractive features is that it unfolds within living memory (that is to say, the last 10 years).*

❑ If you say **there is a lot to be said for** something or **there is something to be said for** something, you mean it is a good idea. ◇ If you say something **goes without saying**, you mean it is obvious.

❑ **needless to say**: see **needless**.

say-so If something needs a certain person's **say-so**, it can only be done with their permission.

saying A **saying** is something like a proverb which is often repeated and which is supposed to be a wise comment on some aspect of life.

scab A **scab** is a hard dry crusty covering which forms on a wound or sore. ◇ If someone on strike calls another person a **scab**, he or she is accusing that person of breaking the strike by working.

scabbard A **scabbard** is a holder for a sword or knife, especially one which hangs from a belt.

scabies (*pron:* skay-beez) is an infectious skin condition which causes severe itching. It is caused by mites.

scabrous (*pron:* skay-bruss) When people call something **scabrous**, they mean it is indecent.

scaffold (scaffolding) ❑ A **scaffold** or **scaffolding** is a temporary structure, usually of wood and metal, for supporting people and their materials while they are erecting, repairing, or decorating a building. The materials **scaffolds** are built from are also called **scaffolding**.

❑ In the past, a **scaffold** was a raised platform on which people were executed.

scald If you are **scalded** or **scald** part of your body, you burn yourself with boiling liquid or steam. ◇ If you say something is **scalding** or **scalding hot**, you mean it is very hot. ◇ **Scalding** is also used to describe very strong emotions, especially anger. *...scalding indignation.*

scale (scaling, scaled) ❑ If you talk about the **scale** of something, you mean its size or extent, especially when it is very large. *AIDS in Africa is already frightening in its scale.* ◇ You use **scale** in expressions like 'on a small scale' when you are comparing the size, extent, or degree of something to other similar things. *The Sydney researchers plan to conduct clinical trials on a larger scale.* See also **time scale**.

❑ If a company or organization makes **economies of scale**, they produce things in larger numbers, so the average cost of each item is less.

❑ **Scales** are equipment for weighing things. ◇ **tip the scales**: see **tip**.

❑ A **scale** is a graded set of levels or figures. *...a new ten-point pay scale for teachers.* ◇ A **scale** is also (a) a series of marks along the edge of something, for taking measurements. (b) a wooden or plastic ruler.

❑ In music, a **scale** is a sequence of notes played or sung in a rising or falling order.

❑ The **scale** of a map, plan, or model is the length of any part of it compared with the length of the thing it represents. For example, if a plan of a piece of land has a scale of 1:500, 1cm on the plan represents 500cm (5 metres) on the land. ◇ A **scale** or **scaled-down** model is smaller than the original but has the same proportions.

❑ If something is **scaled down**, it is made smaller. Similarly, something can be **scaled up**. ◇ If something is **scaled back**, it is reduced. *...an amendment scaling back the defence cuts by $60 billion over five years.*

❏ A fish's or reptile's **scales** are the small overlapping pieces of skin-like substance covering its body.

◇ If you **scale** something like a wall or cliff, you climb it. ◇ If you talk about someone **scaling the heights,** you mean they have reached a successful and desirable place or position.

❏ **Scale** is (a) a hard substance made from calcium which forms on the teeth. (b) a hard layer of a substance such as calcium which forms on the inside of kettles and hot water pipes.

scallion A scallion is the same as a spring onion.

scallop Scallops are edible shellfish. They have two fan-shaped shells which open and close together.

scalp A person's **scalp** is the skin on top of their head, which their hair is attached to. ◇ If someone **is scalped,** their scalp is removed from their head, for example in an accident. People also jokily say someone has been **scalped** when their hair has been cut very short. ◇ If you claim or gain someone's **scalp,** you win a victory over them.

scalpel A scalpel is an instrument with a short, thin, extremely sharp blade, used by surgeons in operations.

scaly A **scaly** animal is covered in scales. ◇ If you say a person's skin is **scaly,** you mean it is covered in stiff flaking patches.

scam A scam is an illegal or dishonest scheme for making money.

scamper (scampering, scampered) If a small animal **scampers** somewhere, it moves with small quick bouncing steps. ◇ When people **scamper** somewhere, they make their way there as quickly as they can. You can call a rush like this a **scamper.**

scampi is a dish of large prawns dipped in batter or crumbs and fried.

scan (scanning, scanned) ❏ If you **scan** written material, you glance through it quickly, to pick out important or interesting information.

❏ If a machine **scans** something, it examines it quickly, for example by moving X-rays or a beam of light over it. An examination of a person's body carried out in this way is called a **scan.** ...*a brain scan.* ◇ If a machine **scans** something like an image or text, it passes a beam of light over it to produce a copy of it in a computer. ◇ If a machine **scans** an area or region, it examines or searches it by sending radar or sonar beams over it.

❏ If you **scan** an area, you look towards all parts of it, because you are hoping to see something.

scandal (scandalous, scandalously) ❏ A **scandal** is something which happens, usually involving money or sex, which people talk about a lot and which is thought to be shocking and immoral. You say something like this is **scandalous. Scandal** is scandals generally. *On Monday there was more scandal.* ◇ **Scandal** is also the spreading of stories about scandals. Spreading stories like this, often with exaggerations, is also called **scandal-mongering.** A person or newspaper that does it is called a **scandal-monger.**

❏ You also say something is **scandalous** or a **scandal** when you think it is very wrong or unfair. *The Ukraine also issues border visas, but they are scandalously expensive.*

scandalize (scandalizing, scandalized) (*can be spelled with an 's' instead of a 'z'*) If you are **scandalized** by something,

you are very shocked by it.

scandalous See scandal.

Scandinavia (Scandinavian) Scandinavia is usually taken to mean Norway, Sweden, and Denmark. Finland, Iceland, and the Faroe Islands are also sometimes considered to be part of Scandinavia. **Scandinavian** is used to talk about people and things in or from Scandinavia. ...*Scandinavian art.* People from Scandinavia are sometimes called **Scandinavians.**

scanner A **scanner** is a machine used to examine people's bodies, for example by moving X-rays or ultra-sound waves over them. ◇ A **scanner** is also (a) an electronic device which can read things like the bar-codes on groceries and transfer this information into a computer. (b) an aerial or similar device used to send out and receive radio or radar signals.

scant If you pay **scant** attention to something, you pay very little attention to it. **Scant** is used in a similar way with words like 'respect', 'regard', and 'evidence'. *Wall Street is notorious for having scant regard for the future and even less for the past.*

scanty (scantier, scantiest; scantily) If you describe something as **scanty,** you mean there is very little of it. ...*scanty evidence...* ...*a scantily-furnished villa.*

scapegoat (scapegoating) If someone is made a **scapegoat,** they are blamed or punished for something which has gone wrong, although it may not have been their fault. **Scapegoating** is making someone a scapegoat.

scapula The **scapula** is the bone in the shoulder usually called the shoulder blade.

scar (scarring, scarred) ❏ A **scar** is a mark left on your body as a result of a wound. If a part of your body is **scarred,** it has a mark or marks like this.

❏ If something like a building or piece of land is **scarred,** its exterior or surface has been damaged as a result of war or industry, leaving ugly marks.

❏ If a bad experience has **scarred** someone's mind or conscience, it has had a permanent effect on it. ...*the psychological scars left by what the victims suffered.*

scarce (scarcity, scarcities) If something is **scarce,** there is very little of it. Similarly, if certain things are **scarce,** there are very few of them. You can talk about the **scarcity** of things like these. *Because it was wartime there were great scarcities of everything.*

scarcely is used to say someone or something is only just a certain thing. *He was scarcely a toddler at the time.* ◇ If there is **scarcely any** of something, there is almost none of it.

❏ **Scarcely** is also used in an ironic way to say something is definitely not the case. For example, if you say someone is **scarcely** a Pavarotti, you mean he is not really a very good singer.

❏ If you say **scarcely** had one thing happened when something else happened, you mean the second thing happened immediately after the first.

scarcity See scarce.

scare (scaring, scared) ❏ If something **scares** you or gives you a **scare,** it frightens or worries you. ◇ If there is a **scare** about something, many people are frightened or worried by it.

❏ If you call something people are saying a **scare story,** you mean it is not true, and has been invented by someone to frighten people. ◇ If you say someone is using **scare tactics**, you mean they are trying to frighten people, to get them to do something. ◇ If something **scares** you **into** doing something, it makes you do it, because you are worried about what is happening.

❑ If you **scare off** a person or animal or **scare** them **away**, you make them go away by frightening them. ◇ If something **scares** you **off** or **scares** you **away**, it worries you so much that you do not do something you were intending to do.

scarecrow A **scarecrow** is an object shaped like a human figure, made of things like straw and old clothes and placed in a field to scare birds away from crops.

scared If you are **scared** of someone or something, you are frightened of them. If you are **scared** that something unpleasant will happen, you are worried or nervous about it. ◇ **scared to death**: see **death**. ◇ **running scared**: see **run**.

scaremongering (scaremonger) If you call someone a **scaremonger** or accuse them of **scaremongering**, you mean they are deliberately trying to frighten people by spreading worrying stories which may not be true.

scarf (scarves) A **scarf** is a piece of cloth or other material which you wear around your neck, head, or sometimes your shoulders, to keep yourself warm, to cover yourself up, or for decoration.

scarlet is a bright red colour.

scarlet fever is an infectious disease which gives you a sore throat, a high temperature, and a red rash. Its medical name is **scarlatina**.

scary (scarier, scariest; scarily) If you say something is **scary**, you mean it is frightening. *As always in his books, vulnerability is scarily conveyed.*

scathing (scathingly) If you are **scathing** about something, you criticize it in a scornful way. *In a major anniversary speech, President Castro was scathingly critical of Spain.*

scatological (scatology) If you call a book or song **scatological** or talk about the **scatology** in it, you mean it is full of references to things like sex or excrement.

scatter (scattering, scattered) ❑ If you **scatter** things around an area, you drop or throw them over the whole area so they fall in an irregular pattern. If things or people are **scattered** over an area, they are spread around it. You can talk about a **scatter** or **scattering** of things or people.

❑ If a group of people or animals **scatter**, they suddenly move off in different directions.

❑ **Scattered** is also used to describe things which happen only occasionally. *Last year's scattered complaints have become a general howl.*

scatty If you call someone **scatty**, you mean they are absent-minded and unreliable.

scavenge (scavenging, scavenged; scavenger) When someone **scavenges** for something, especially food, they search for it among waste products, often rubbish. A person who does this is called a **scavenger**. ◇ If a bird or an animal **scavenges**, it obtains food by searching for and eating the flesh of dead creatures and other waste material. Birds and animals like these are also known as **scavengers**.

SCE stands for 'Scottish Certificate of Education' which covers the two Scottish public exams – the Standard Grades and the Higher Grades (or 'Highers').

scenario (*pron:* sin-nar-ee-oh) (scenarios) ❑ If you talk about a likely or possible **scenario**, you are talking about a sequence of events which might develop. *I tend to think the least likely scenario is a military takeover.*

❑ The **scenario** of a film or play is a summary of the plot and a description of the characters.

scene ❑ A **scene** in a film, play, opera, or book is one part of it, in which all the action happens in one place.

❑ What you see when you look around you can be called a **scene**. *...a scene of incredible beauty.*

❑ The **scene** of an incident, especially an accident or a disaster, is the place where it happened. ◇ If you say someone appears **on the scene**, you mean they arrive at the place you are talking about. Similarly, you can talk about someone leaving **the scene**.

❑ You say there are **scenes** of a particular kind when a crowd of people behaves in an extreme way. *There were scenes of violence as police and soldiers tried to distribute food.* ◇ If someone **makes a scene**, they publicly show their anger or distress about something.

❑ You can refer to an area of activity as a **scene** of a particular kind. *...the British political scene.* ◇ When someone arrives **on the scene**, they become important or well-known in a particular field. Similarly, you can talk about someone departing **from the scene**.

❑ If you say something is being done **behind the scenes**, you mean it is happening without the general public being aware of it.

❑ If someone or something **sets the scene** for a certain event, they create the conditions which make it likely to happen. ◇ When a TV or newspaper reporter **sets the scene**, he or she provides background information at the beginning of a report or programme.

❑ Any event or situation can be called a **scene**. *It could be a scene from any time in the past 45 years.*

scenery ❑ The **scenery** is everything you see around you when you are in the open air, especially when you are in the countryside.

❑ In the theatre, the **scenery** is the backcloth and other things used to represent where the action is taking place.

scenic (scenically) **Scenic** is used to describe roads and other routes which give you attractive views of the countryside. *...an arduous, but scenically rewarding, trip.*

scent (-scented) ❑ A **scent** is a pleasant smell. **-scented** is used to describe smells, especially pleasant ones. *...delicately-scented freesias.* ◇ **Scent** is perfume.

❑ A creature's **scent** is its special smell which allows another creature to identify it or hunt it.

❑ If you are **on the scent** of something you are looking for, you are getting close to finding it. If something **puts you off the scent**, it misleads you and makes it less likely that you will find what you want. ◇ If you **scent** something like an opportunity, you feel it is going to come your way soon. *The left had now scented victory.* ◇ If you **scent blood**, you feel you are about to triumph over your enemy or opponent.

scepter See **sceptre**.

sceptical (sceptically, sceptic, scepticism) (*American spelling:* **skeptical**, *etc*) If you are **sceptical** about something, you have doubts about it. *All these ideas have been considered sceptically by NATO commanders.* **Scepticism** is doubt about something. A person who has doubts about things which other people believe in is called a **sceptic.**

sceptre (*American spelling:* **scepter**) (*both pron:* sep-ter) A **sceptre** is an ornamental rod which a monarch carries on some ceremonial occasions as a symbol of his or her power.

Schadenfreude (*pron:* shah-den-froid-eh) is delight in someone else's misfortune.

schedule (*pron:* shed-yool *or* sked-yool) (scheduling, scheduled) ❑ A **schedule** is a plan which lists events or tasks and the times when each of them should happen or be done. ◇ If something is **scheduled** to happen at a certain time, it is due to happen then. ◇ A **scheduled** flight is part of a regular service, rather than one chartered for a special purpose or a group of people. Airlines which operate these flights are called **scheduled** airlines.

❑ If something happens **on schedule,** it happens at the planned time. If it happens **ahead of schedule,** it happens earlier than planned. If it is **behind schedule,** it is running late. ◇ If it goes **according to schedule,** everything happens at the right time and in the right way.

❑ A **schedule** is also a timetable for buses, trains, boats, or planes.

❑ A **schedule** is also a written list of things, for example a list of prices or conditions. If something is **scheduled,** it is on a list of this type. *The main area has been scheduled as an ancient monument.*

schematic A **schematic** representation of something is a drawing or diagram showing how it works in a simplified way.

scheme (scheming, schemed; schemer) ❑ A **scheme** is someone's plan for achieving something. ◇ A **scheme** is also a large-scale plan produced by a government, an organization, or someone in authority. *...company pension schemes.*

❑ When people **scheme,** they make secret plans. *...scheming politicians.* You can call a person who schemes a lot a **schemer.**

❑ If you talk about the **the scheme of things,** you mean the way everything in the world or in a particular situation seems to be organized.

❑ See also **colour scheme.**

schilling The **schilling** is the unit of currency in Austria.

schism (*pron:* skizz-um *or* sizz-um) (schismatic) When **schism** or a **schism** occurs, a group or organization divides into two groups as a result of differences in thinking and beliefs. **Schism** is used especially to talk about an Established Church splitting into two separate Churches. **Schismatic** is used to talk about things connected with a schism. *...schismatic wars.*

schizophrenia (*pron:* skit-soe-free-nee-a) (schizophrenic) ❑ **Schizophrenia** is a serious mental disorder which makes people have delusions and lose touch with the world around them. You say someone who suffers from this disorder is **schizophrenic** or a **schizophrenic.**

❑ **Schizophrenia** is also used to describe people's behaviour when they act in a contradictory way. You say people who behave like this are **schizophrenic.**

schmaltz (*pron:* shmalts) is excessive sentimentality.

schmooze (schmoozing, schmoozed) When people **schmooze,** they chat or gossip.

schnapps (*pron:* shnaps) is a strong alcoholic spirit from

Germany.

scholar A **scholar** is (a) someone who studies a subject deeply and knows a lot about it. (b) a pupil or student who holds a scholarship.

scholarly A **scholarly** person enjoys studying and knows a lot about academic subjects. ◇ A **scholarly** piece of writing is carefully researched, detailed, and displays a lot of knowledge.

scholarship If you win a **scholarship** to a school or university, you receive money or a free place to study there. ◇ **Scholarship** is academic achievement or learning.

scholastic is used to talk about things to do with schools and schoolwork. *...scholastic examinations.*

school (schooling, schooled) ❑ **School** or a **school** is a place where children are educated. ◇ In the US, someone's **schooling** is the education they get while they are at school.

❑ University departments, colleges, and institutions for specialized subjects are sometimes called **schools.** *...business schools... ...the city's university medical school.* ◇ In the US, universities and colleges are often called **schools.** *...Chicago's Graduate School of Business.*

❑ If you talk about someone being of the **old school,** you mean they have qualities or opinions which are no longer common. ◇ When people talk about **the old school tie,** they mean the assistance, especially in business, which ex-pupils of the same public school sometimes give to each other.

❑ A **school** of artists, writers, or thinkers is a group of them with similar ideas, opinions, or theories. ◇ If you talk about a **school of thought,** you mean a group of people who share an opinion or idea; sometimes **school of thought** refers to the opinion or idea itself.

❑ If you **school** a horse, you train it. ◇ If you say someone has been **schooled** in something, you mean they have been trained in a particular way.

❑ A **school** of whales, dolphins, or fish is a large group of them.

school age children are between the ages when they must legally go to school.

school-leaver School-leavers are young people who are about to leave school or who have just left.

school teacher (*or* schoolteacher) A **school teacher** is a person who teaches in a school.

schoolboy A **schoolboy** is a boy who goes to school. ◇ **Schoolboy** behaviour by adults is childish and immature.

schoolchild (schoolchildren) **Schoolchildren** are children who go to school.

schooldays Your **schooldays** are the period of your life when you are at school.

schoolfriend Your **schoolfriends** are the friends you have while you are at school.

schoolgirl A **schoolgirl** is a girl who goes to school.

schoolhouse In the US, Australia, and some other countries, a **schoolhouse** is a building used as a school, especially in a village.

schoolmaster A **schoolmaster** is a male schoolteacher, especially in an independent school.

schoolmate Your **schoolmates** are your schoolfriends.

schoolmistress (schoolmistresses) In the past, female

schoolteachers were called **schoolmistresses**.

schoolroom A schoolroom is the same as a classroom.

schoolteacher See school teacher.

schoolwork is the work a pupil does while at school or as homework.

schoolyard A schoolyard is a school playground.

schooner ❑ A schooner is a sailing ship or yacht with at least two masts.
❑ A schooner is also a large sherry glass.

sci-fi (*pron:* sie fie) is short for 'science fiction'.

sciatica (*pron:* sigh-at-tik-ka) is a severe pain in a nerve called the **sciatic nerve** in your buttock and thigh.

science is the study of the nature and behaviour of everything in the universe using observation and experiments, and trying to arrange the results into a system of laws. A science is a particular branch of science, for example biology or physics. See also **political science, life science, social science**.
❑ Anything which is studied in a systematic way can be called a science. *Property appraisal has always been the most inexact of sciences in Japan.*

science fiction is stories, films, and other forms of entertainment which describe events taking place in the future or in other parts of the universe. Science fiction often uses real science as its basis.

science park A science park is an area where several companies carry out scientific research and commercial development, often in co-operation with a nearby university.

scientific (scientifically) Scientific is used to talk about things to do with science. *...scientific research... Cauliflowers, cabbages, sprouts and kale all belong to the same class of plants known scientifically as Brassicae.* ◇ If you do something in a scientific way, you do it systematically, using experiments or observations. *There is no scientific way to study intelligence in animals.*

scientist A scientist is a person who studies or does work in one of the sciences.

scimitar (*pron:* sim-mit-ar) A scimitar is a short curved oriental sword.

scintilla (*pron:* sin-til-a) A scintilla of something is a tiny amount of it.

scintillating (*pron:* sin-til-late-ing) is used to describe things which are lively, sparkling, and amusing.

scion (*pron:* sigh-on) A scion of a famous or aristocratic family is an heir, descendant, or young member of it.

scissors are a tool for cutting things. They consist of two sharp blades hinged together.

sclerosis (sclerotic) ❑ Sclerosis is a disease in which the tissue in part of a person's body becomes abnormally hard or thick. See also **multiple sclerosis**.
❑ If you talk about a system suffering from sclerosis, you mean it has seized up and is not making any headway. You can also call a system like this **sclerotic**.

scoff If you scoff at someone or something, you mock them or speak about them with contempt. ◇ When someone scoffs food, they eat it in a greedy way.

scold If you scold someone or give them a scolding, you tell them off for something they have done.

scone (*pron:* skon *or* skone) Scones are small plain cakes made from flour and fat. They are usually eaten with butter.

scoop (scooping, scooped) ❑ If you scoop something or scoop it up, you lift it up with a shovelling motion, using your hands or a tool of some kind.
❑ A scoop is a device consisting of a handle and a hollow part for scooping up food such as ice-cream.
❑ If you scoop a lot of something desirable or scoop it up, you obtain it, as a result of luck or skill. *In the election of October 5th he scooped 54% of the votes.*
❑ A scoop is an exciting news story which a newspaper gets hold of and prints before other papers. When this happens, you say it scoops the other papers.

scoot (scooting, scooted) If you scoot somewhere, you go there quickly.

scooter ❑ A scooter is the same as a motor scooter.
❑ A scooter is also a child's toy consisting of a narrow platform on two wheels, one behind the other, with a raised part with handlebars on it. The child holds the handlebars and moves the scooter along by pushing backwards against the ground with one foot while keeping the other foot on the platform.

scope If there is scope for a certain kind of behaviour, there is opportunity for it. *There is some scope for a reduction in interest rates below present levels.* ◇ The scope of something is the range of things it deals with or includes. *...the scope of the survey.*

scorch (scorches, scorching, scorched) ❑ If something such as fire or the sun scorches something, it burns it slightly and damages it. ◇ Scorching weather is extremely hot.
❑ A scorched earth policy is the deliberate burning, destruction, and removal of everything in an area which could be useful to an enemy.

score (scoring, scored; scorer) ❑ If a player, team, or competitor scores in a game, they get a goal, run, or point. The person who gets a goal in a football match is called the **scorer**. ◇ The total numbers of goals, runs, or points obtained in a game is called the score. You say each side or competitor scores a certain number of goals, runs, or points.
❑ You can also talk about someone's score in a test or exam. ◇ If you give people marks or points for something they do, you can say you score them.
❑ If you score a success, you succeed at something. Similarly, you can score a victory or hit. *The company scored a hit with its elegantly designed laptop computers.* ◇ If you score a point over someone, you gain an advantage over them or defeat them in some way. *Labour has scored a propaganda point.*
❑ In the past, twenty was sometimes called a score. ◇ Scores of things or people means a large number of them. You can also talk about things existing or happening **by the score**. *Restaurants are opening by the score.*
❑ The score of a piece of music is the written version of it. If a piece of music is scored for certain instruments, it is written to be played on those instruments.
❑ If you say someone **knows the score**, you mean they know all the facts about a situation.
❑ If someone gets revenge for something done to them in the past, you can say they **settle a score** or **settle old scores**.
❑ On this score and on that score means in relation to the thing just mentioned. *Japan has responded well to*

international pressure to open its markets. European complaints on this score have largely ceased.

❏ If you **score** something with a sharp object, you cut lines into it.

score sheet If you say someone gets their name on the score sheet, you mean they have scored a goal or been successful in a sport.

scoreboard The **scoreboard** is a large board which shows the current score in a match or competition.

scorecard A **scorecard** is a printed card which tells you who is playing or taking part in a match or race, and on which you can record the scores. ◇ A **scorecard** is also a card on which players keep a record of the scores they achieve in various games or competitions.

scoreline The **scoreline** is the score or final result of a game or match.

scorer See **score**.

scorn is a strong feeling of contempt for someone or something, which you show in the way you talk about them. When someone talks about someone or something with contempt, you can say they **scorn** them or **pour scorn** on them.

❏ If you **scorn** something, you reject it because you do not consider it to be good enough or suitable for you.

scornful (scornfully) If you are **scornful** of someone or something, you show contempt for them. *One minister scornfully referred to the cabinet as a 'discussion-free zone'.*

scorpion The **scorpion** is a small tropical creature. It has a long tail which bends upwards and has a poisonous sting at its end.

Scot A **Scot** is someone who comes from Scotland.

scot-free If you say someone has got off **scot-free**, you mean they have not been punished at all for something wrong they have done.

scotch (scotches, scotching, scotched) ❏ **Scotch** is an old-fashioned word for 'Scottish'. ◇ **Scotch** or **scotch whisky** is whisky made in Scotland. A **scotch** is a glass of scotch.

❏ If you **scotch** something like a rumour or plan, you put an end to it.

Scotch egg A **Scotch egg** is a hard-boiled egg which has been covered with sausage meat and breadcrumbs and then fried in oil.

Scotland Yard is the headquarters of the London Metropolitan Police Force, which is controlled directly by the Home Office and has certain national responsibilities. This police force is itself sometimes called **Scotland Yard** or **the Yard**, especially the department dealing with serious crime.

Scots is used to talk about people and things in or from Scotland. *...the Scots climate.* ◇ **Scots** is the dialect of English spoken in Scotland.

Scotsman (Scotswoman) A **Scotsman** or **Scotswoman** is a person who comes from Scotland.

Scottish (Scottishness) **Scottish** is used to talk about people and things in or from Scotland. *...the Scottish west coast... His son inherited his father's fierce pride in his Scottishness.* ◇ The dialect of English spoken in Scotland is sometimes called **Scottish**.

scoundrel You call someone a **scoundrel** when they cheat and deceive people in an unscrupulous way.

scour (scouring, scoured; scourer) ❏ If you **scour** a place or a collection of writing, you make a thorough search of it, to try to find something.

❏ If you **scour** something like a saucepan, you clean it with a rough pad called a **scourer**.

scourge (*rhymes with 'urge'*) If you call something a **scourge**, you mean it causes a lot of trouble or suffering. *Disease, drugs and crime are the scourges of daily life here.*

scout (scouting, scouted) ❏ A **Scout** or **Boy Scout** is a member of the Scout Association, which aims to develop the character and responsibility of older boys by teaching them such things as practical and outdoor skills. See also **girl scout**.

❏ A **scout** is also a person sent out to discover the position of an enemy army. ◇ If you **scout** around for people or things of a certain kind, you look in several places to try to find them. ◇ A **scout** is also a talent scout.

scowl If someone **scowls**, they frown, because they are angry or disapprove of something or someone. You call an expression like this a **scowl**.

scrabble (scrabbling, scrabbled) ❏ If you **scrabble** for something, you move your fingers and hands about, trying to find it or get hold of it. ◇ You also say people **scrabble** for something when they struggle to obtain it for themselves, often in an undignified way.

❏ **Scrabble** is a word game. People take turns to make up words by putting letter tiles on a special board. Each tile put down gets a score. The game finishes when all the tiles are used up; the winner is the player with the highest score. 'Scrabble' is a trademark.

scramble (scrambling, scrambled; scrambler) ❏ If you **scramble** somewhere in an emergency, you get there quickly, often in a clumsy and undignified way. When a lot of people move somewhere like this, you can say there is a **scramble**. ◇ If you **scramble** over rough or difficult territory, you move over it with difficulty, sometimes using your hands to help you.

❏ If you **scramble** for something or are involved in a **scramble** for it, you are one of several people competing for it in a disorganized way. You can also talk about people **scrambling** to find something or **scrambling** to achieve something.

❏ If you **scramble** a radio, telephone, or other transmitted message, you interfere with the sound using an electronic device called a **scrambler**; the message can then only be understood by someone with special equipment.

❏ When fighter planes **scramble** or are **scrambled**, they take off immediately.

❏ A **scramble** is also a motorbike rally in which riders race across very rough ground. This activity is called **scrambling.**

scrambled egg or **scrambled eggs** is a dish made of eggs beaten up with milk and then cooked for a short time in a little butter while stirring.

scrap (scrapping, scrapped) ❏ A **scrap** of something is a very small amount or piece of it. ◇ **Scraps** are pieces of unwanted food which are thrown away or given to animals.

❏ If something is **scrapped**, it is got rid of or cancelled, because it is no longer needed.

❏ **Scrap** or **scrap metal** is metal from old machinery or vehicles which is reprocessed so it can be used again. If something is **scrapped**, especially a car, it is turned into scrap. ◇ If you say something is heading for the **scrap heap** or **scrapheap**, you mean it is no longer required, because it is no longer suitable or useful.

❑ If people **scrap** or have a **scrap**, they have a quarrel or fight.

scrapbook A **scrapbook** is a book with blank pages in which people stick things such as pictures or newspaper cuttings.

scrape (scraping, scraped) ❑ If you **scrape** something from a surface or **scrape** it **off**, you remove it by rubbing something sharp against it. ◇ If something **scrapes** against something else or **scrapes** it, it rubs against it, damaging it or making a harsh noise.

❑ If you **scrape a living**, you make just enough money to survive. Similarly, if you **scrape by**, you manage to survive on very little money.

❑ If you **scrape** something **together**, you manage to arrange or complete it with difficulty.

❑ If you **scrape through** in something like an exam, you just manage to pass. Similarly, if someone **scrapes** a victory, they just manage to win. You can also say someone **scrapes home**.

❑ If you are in a **scrape**, you are in a difficult situation which you have caused yourself.

scrapheap See **scrap**.

scrapie is a fatal viral disease of sheep and goats which destroys their central nervous system and may be related to a similar disease in cows called BSE or 'mad cow disease'.

scrappy (scrappier, scrappiest) If you say something is **scrappy**, you mean it is uneven, untidy, and not well organized.

scrapyard A **scrapyard** is a place where scrap, especially from old vehicles, is collected and often reprocessed.

scratch (scratches, scratching, scratched) ❑ If you **scratch** something, you make a small mark or cut on it with your fingernail or some other sharp object. The mark or cut is called a **scratch**. ◇ If you **scratch** yourself or **scratch**, you scrape your fingernails over your skin because it is itching.

❑ A **scratch** is a small injury caused by something sharp catching against your skin. ◇ If someone emerges from a dangerous or difficult situation **without a scratch**, they are uninjured or unharmed by it.

❑ If you talk about two people **scratching each other's back**, you mean they do things to help each other in a competitive situation. Behaviour like this is called **back-scratching**.

❑ If you say something barely **scratches the surface** of a problem, you mean it only goes a small way towards dealing with it.

❑ If you talk about people **scratching their heads** over a problem, you mean they are trying to think of a way of solving it.

❑ If you **scratch around** for something you need, you try hard to find it. ◇ If you **scratch a living**, you make just enough money to survive.

❑ **Scratch** is used to describe things which are put together in a hurry. ...*a scratch supper*. ◇ If you make something **from scratch**, you make it from its basic components. *It uses less energy to melt old glass than to make new*

glass from scratch.

❑ If you say something is **not up to scratch** or does not **come up to scratch**, you mean it does not meet a required standard or is not good enough.

scratchy ❑ If you say someone is **scratchy**, you mean they are irritable.

❑ If something you are listening to is **scratchy**, it is interfered with by noises like something being scratched.

scrawl If you **scrawl** something, you write it in a careless untidy way. Writing like this can be called a **scrawl**.

scrawny (scrawnier, scrawniest) A **scrawny** person is thin and bony.

scream (screaming, screamed) ❑ If someone **screams** or lets out a **scream**, they make a loud piercing sound because they are very afraid, in pain, or very excited.

❑ If someone shouts something in a high-pitched voice, you can say they **scream** it. ◇ If a newspaper has a sensational headline, you can say it **screams** it. *'First AIDS case in India', screamed the headlines.*

❑ When something like a machine makes a loud high-pitched noise, you can say it **screams**.

scree is a mass of loose stones on the side of a mountain or lying at its foot.

screech (screeches, screeching, screeched) ❑ If a person or animal **screeches** or lets out a **screech**, they give a loud unpleasant high-pitched cry.

❑ If something **screeches**, it makes a loud high-pitched unpleasant sound. You call a noise like this a **screech**.

❑ If a vehicle **screeches** somewhere, it moves quickly, making a loud high-pitched unpleasant noise from its tyres or brakes. When it pulls up sharply, you can say it **screeches to a halt**. ◇ You can talk about other things **screeching to a halt** when they come to a sudden end. *High rates at first failed to slow the economy, then brought it to a screeching halt.*

screen (screening, screened) ❑ The **screen** of something like a TV set or computer is the flat vertical surface on which you see the display or picture. ◇ In a cinema, the **screen** is the surface on which films are shown. ◇ **Screen** is used to talk about films or the film industry. ...*a screen actress*. ◇ When a programme or a film is **screened** or given a **screening**, it is broadcast on TV or shown at the cinema. ◇ See also **small screen**.

❑ A **screen** is also a vertical panel or frame used to divide an area, or to hide or protect something.

❑ If you are **screened** from something harmful, something else is in the way and prevents it reaching you. *Residents will be screened from noise pollution.* ◇ When people are **screened** for a disease or condition, they are examined to see if they have it.

❑ You also talk about people being **screened** when they are tested or checked to see if they are suitable for something. ...*the question of whether to screen candidates to see if they had contact with the former secret police.*

screen-printing is the same as silk-screen printing.

screenplay The script of a film or a TV play is called the screenplay.

screenwriter (screenwriting) A **screenwriter** is a person who writes screenplays. Writing screenplays is called **screenwriting**.

screw ❑ A **screw** is a small sharp piece of metal with a spiral groove used to fix one thing firmly to another. If

an object has been **screwed** somewhere, it has been fixed there by a screw or screws.
❏ If you **tighten the screw** on someone, you increase the pressure you are putting on them, to get them to do what you want.
❏ If someone **screws** someone else, (a) they have sex with them. (b) they cheat them or take advantage of them. ◇ If someone **screws** something, especially money, out of you, they force it from you or get you to give it to them by using strong persuasion. ◇ If you **screw** something **up,** you make it go badly wrong. Similarly, something can be **screwed up** by events.
❏ If you **screw up** the courage to do something, you force yourself to be brave so that you can do it.

screwball comedy is zany and odd.

screwdriver A screwdriver is a tool for fixing screws into place.

scribble (scribbling, scribbled; scribbler) ❏ If you **scribble** something, you write it quickly and untidily and it may be difficult to read. Something written like this can be called a **scribble.**
❏ Writers are sometimes said to **scribble.** They are also called **scribblers** and their work is referred to as their **scribblings.**

scribe In the past, a **scribe** was a person who made copies of things like books or letters by hand, especially before printing was invented. ◇ Authors and journalists are sometimes humorously called **scribes.**

scrimp If you **scrimp,** you live cheaply and spend as little money as possible, often because you are saving up for something.

script (scripted) ❏ The **script** for a film, play, or TV programme is the written version of it. If a writer **scripts** a film or TV programme, he or she writes the script.
❏ A **scripted** speech or lecture has been written in advance, although the speaker may try to make it appear spontaneous.
❏ **Script** is used to talk about different systems of writing. *...Latin script.* ◇ **Script** is also handwriting.

scripture (scriptural) The sacred writings of a religion are called its **scriptures.** ◇ When Christians talk about **Scripture** or the **Scriptures,** they mean the Bible. **Scriptural** is sometimes used to talk about things connected with the Bible. *...scriptural accounts of the process of salvation.*

scriptwriter A scriptwriter is a person who writes scripts for films, plays, or TV programmes.

scroll ❏ A **scroll** is a long roll of parchment, paper, or other material with writing on it. ◇ A **scroll** is also an ornamental carving in stone or wood, made to look like a scroll.
❏ When you are using a computer and you **scroll** something like data, you get it to move across the screen from left to right or up and down, so you can read more of it than can be fitted on the screen at one time.

Scrooge If you call someone a **Scrooge,** you mean they are very mean with their money.

scrotum (*plural:* scrotums *or* scrota) A man's **scrotum** is the bag of skin which contains his testicles.

scrounge (scrounging, scrounged; scrounger) If you **scrounge** something, you ask people for it, rather than buying it or earning it. People who regularly scrounge things are called **scroungers.**

scrub (scrubbing, scrubbed) ❏ If you **scrub** something, you rub it with water and something rough like a stiff brush to make it clean. ◇ If you **scrub** something like dirt off something, you remove it by rubbing hard.
❏ If you **scrub** something you were thinking of doing, you cancel it.
❏ **Scrub** is stunted trees and bushes in a very dry area. The area itself can also be called **scrub.**

scrubland is land covered in scrub.

scruff The **scruff** of an animal's neck is the loose skin at the back. ◇ If you take something **by the scruff of its neck,** you deal with it in a direct and forceful way.

scruffy (scruffier, scruffiest) **Scruffy** people are untidy and badly dressed. You can also say their clothes are **scruffy.** ◇ If a place is **scruffy,** it is shabby and rather dirty.

scrum In rugby, a **scrum** is a formation in which players from both sides form a tight group and push against each other with their heads down to try to get the ball after it has been thrown into their midst. A scrum takes place to re-start a game after one of the rules has been broken. ◇ Any tightly packed crowd of people can be called a **scrum.**

scrum-half (scrum-halves) In rugby, the **scrum-half** is the player who puts the ball into a scrum.

scrummage (scrummaging) A **scrummage** is the same as a scrum. **Scrummaging** is used to talk about things to do with scrums. *...the new scrummaging rules.*

scrumptious If you say food is **scrumptious,** you mean it is delicious. People call other things **scrumptious** when they are very pleased with them. *...scrumptious fabric prints.*

scruple Scruples are moral principles which make people unwilling to do something which seems wrong.

scrupulous (scrupulously) **Scrupulous** is used to say (a) something is done in a fair, honest, and morally correct way. *He is being noticeably scrupulous in his conduct of the affair.* (b) something is done in an accurate, exact, and thorough way. *The institute was kept scrupulously clean.*

scrutineer A **scrutineer** is an official who scrutinizes something to make sure it is being done correctly.

scrutinize (scrutinizing, scrutinized) (*can be spelled with an 's' instead of a 'z'*) If a person, especially someone with specialized knowledge, **scrutinizes** something, they examine it very carefully.

scrutiny If something comes under **scrutiny,** it is observed or examined very carefully.

scuba diving is swimming underwater using cylinders containing compressed air which are strapped to the swimmer's back and attached to a face mask.

scud (scudding, scudded) If clouds **scud** across the sky, they move very quickly, because there is a strong wind.

scuffed is used to talk about things, especially shoes, which have marks or patches on them caused by rubbing against something.

scuffle (scuffling, scuffled) If people **scuffle** or have a **scuffle,** they have a short fight or struggle.

scull (sculling) A **scull** is a lightweight boat propelled by one or more people, each person using two short oars, also called **sculls. Sculling** is rowing in boats like these. **Sculls** is a race between sculls.

scullery (sculleries) In some houses, a **scullery** is a small room next to the kitchen where washing up is done and the preparation of vegetables takes place.

sculpt If you **sculpt** something, you carve and cut it out of a material such as stone, marble, or wood.

sculptor (sculptress, sculptresses) A **sculptor** is a person who makes sculptures. Female sculptors are sometimes called **sculptresses**, although they usually prefer to be called 'sculptors'.

sculpture (sculptured, sculptural) A **sculpture** is a work of art created by carving or shaping stone, marble, wood, or some other material. **Sculptured** is used to describe things which have been made in this way. **Sculpture** is the art of creating sculptures. **Sculptural** is used to talk about things to do with sculpture, or things which remind you of sculpture.

scum is a layer of an unpleasant-looking substance on the surface of a liquid.
❑ People whose behaviour is regarded as heartless or disgusting are sometimes called **scum**.

scupper (scuppering, scuppered) If someone **scuppers** something like a plan or a treaty, they do something which prevents it going through.

scurrilous is used to describe things people say or write about other people which are untrue or greatly exaggerated and could damage the reputation of the people concerned. Newspapers and magazines which publish things of this sort are themselves often described as **scurrilous**.

scurry (scurries, scurrying, scurried) If a person or small animal **scurries** somewhere, they run there very quickly.

scurvy is a disease caused by a lack of Vitamin C. People get it when they do not eat enough fresh fruit and vegetables. Scurvy results in bleeding gums and extreme weakness.

scuttle (scuttling, scuttled) ❑ If a person or animal **scuttles** somewhere, they run with short quick steps.
❑ When a ship is **scuttled**, it is deliberately sunk by making holes in its bottom or opening up valves.
❑ You say an activity is **scuttled** when something prevents it continuing or succeeding.

scythe A **scythe** is a tool with a handle and a long curved blade for cutting grass or grain.

SDI stands for 'Strategic Defense Initiative'. SDI was a defence system developed by the US during the 1980s. It consisted of satellites armed with lasers which could destroy enemy missiles in space. This system, popularly known as 'Star Wars', was abandoned in 1993.

SDLP The SDLP or **Social Democrat and Labour Party** is a political party formed in Northern Ireland in 1970. Its supporters are mainly Catholic. It aims to unite Ireland by peaceful and democratic means.

sea ❑ The **sea** is the area of salty water which covers most of the earth's surface. Some parts of this area have **Sea** as part of their name. ...the Irish Sea. Some very large inland areas of water also have **Sea** as part of their name. ...the Red Sea.
❑ If you travel somewhere **by sea**, you go in a ship. ◇ If something happens **at sea**, it happens on a ship sailing on the sea. If it happens **on the high seas**, it happens on a part of the sea which is beyond the control of any country. ◇ **open sea**: see **open**.
❑ You can describe the state of the sea by talking, for

example, about calm **seas** or rough **seas**.
❑ **Sea** is sometimes used to talk about the life or career of a sailor. He ran away to sea as a child.
❑ A **sea** of people is a large number of them moving along together. ◇ A large area of something is sometimes called a **sea**. For example, you talk about a 'sea of mud'.
❑ If you say someone is **at sea** or **all at sea**, you mean they are confused.

sea anemone A **sea anemone** is a sea animal which lives attached to a rock and looks like a flower. It has tentacles which trap food.

sea bird (or **seabird**) **Sea birds** are birds like seagulls and albatrosses which live on or near the sea and get their food from it.

sea breeze A **sea breeze** is a wind blowing from the sea.

sea-change A **sea-change** is an important change which makes something quite different from what it was before.

sea-going (or **seagoing**) boats and ships are designed for travelling on the sea. ◇ **Sea-going** is used to talk about things connected with sea travel. This three-masted schooner was the last word in Victorian sea-going comfort.

sea level is the height of the sea's surface. If something is at **sea level**, it is the same height as the sea's surface. You also talk about things being a certain distance above or below **sea level**. The island stands less than three metres above sea level.

sea lift A **sea lift** is the transportation by sea of people, troops, or goods, especially during wartime.

sea lion **Sea lions** are large seals in the north Pacific.

sea urchin The **sea urchin** is a small sea animal with a round hard spiny shell.

sea wall A **sea wall** is a defence like an embankment built against the sea, for example to stop it eroding the land or to act as a breakwater.

seabed The **seabed** is the bottom of the sea.

seabird See **sea bird**.

seaboard The **seaboard** of a country is the part which borders the sea.

seaborne is used to talk about actions carried out from ships, or things transported by ships. ...a seaborne landing exercise... ...seaborne trade.

seafarer Sailors who makes long sea voyages are sometimes called **seafarers**.

seafaring people are sailors. A **seafaring** country or community is one which many sailors come from.

seafood consists of various types of sea creatures which you can eat, especially shellfish.

seafront The **seafront** of a port or seaside resort is the part next to the sea.

seagoing See **sea-going**.

seagull A **seagull** is the same as a gull.

seahorse The **seahorse** is a type of small fish with a plated body, a long curling tail, and a head which looks like a horse's head.

seal (sealing, sealed) ❑ When a place is **sealed** or **sealed off**, all the entrances are blocked and nobody can get in or out. ◇ When a country's borders are **sealed**, people are prevented from passing through them, and nobody can enter or leave the country.
❑ If you **seal** something, you close or fasten it in some

way, often to make it airtight or watertight. You can also **seal** something inside something else. ◇ A **seal** is (a) a substance or device for closing or fastening something tightly. (b) a substance or device fixed to the opening of something like a container or letter, which must be broken to get at the container's or letter's contents. ◇ If you **seal** an envelope, you stick down the flap.

❑ If something **seals** someone's **fate**, it makes it certain that something unpleasant will happen to them.

❑ If you **seal** something like a victory or achievement or **put the seal** on it, you make it complete. *He sealed his 5-1 victory with a break of 104.*

❑ If a person in authority **seals** an important document, they put an official mark on it called a **seal**, to show it is genuine. ◇ When people in authority officially authorize something or show they approve of it, you can say they give it their **seal of approval**.

❑ **Seals** are large mammals with flippers. They eat fish and live partly on land and partly in the sea.

sealant A **sealant** is a substance used to fill in or cover a gap of some kind, usually to make it waterproof.

sealskin is the skin or fur of a seal.

seam ❑ A **seam** is a straight line of stitching joining two pieces of material together. ◇ If you say a system is **coming apart** or **falling apart at the seams,** you mean things have started to go wrong and it is no longer working effectively. ◇ **bursting at the seams: see burst.**

❑ A **seam** is also a long narrow underground layer of a mineral such as coal. ◇ When there is something useful which can continue to be exploited, you can say there is a **rich seam** of it. *...a rich seam of talent.*

seaman (seamen) A **seaman** is a sailor. ◇ A **leading seaman** is a sailor in the Royal Navy, ranking just below petty officer. The next rank down is **able seaman,** followed by **ordinary seaman** and **junior seaman.**

seamanship is the skill of being able to navigate, look after, and handle a vessel at sea.

seamless (seamlessly) ❑ A **seamless** piece of clothing has no seams. ◇ You say other objects are **seamless** when their covering or casing has no obvious joins.

❑ You call the way something is done or presented **seamless** when you cannot see where the different parts join together. *Archive footage of the actual disaster was seamlessly woven into the film, heightening the sense of reality.*

seamstress (seamstresses) In the past, a **seamstress** was a woman whose job was sewing and making clothes.

seamy (seamier, seamiest) You say something is **seamy** when it is connected with things like crime, pornography, or violence.

séance (*or* seance) (*pron:* say-anss) A **séance** is an occasion when a group of people attempt to communicate with spirits of the dead, usually through a person called a medium.

seaplane A **seaplane** is a type of plane which is able to land and take off on water.

seaport A **seaport** is a town or city with docks or a large harbour which sea-going ships can use.

sear (searing, seared; searingly) ❑ If you say someone has been **seared** by a bad experience, you mean it has had a lasting harmful effect on them.

❑ **Searing** is used to describe intense heat, or other things which are very intense. *...searing determination...*

...a searingly powerful first novel. ◇ A **searing** piece of writing or speech uses forceful language and is very critical.

search (searches, searching, searched; searcher) ❑ If you **search** for someone or something, you try to find them. You can also **go in search** of someone or something. People who are looking for someone or something can be called **searchers.** If you **search** a place, you examine it in the hope of finding someone or something. Looking for something is called a **search.** ◇ If you **search** something **out,** you keep looking for it until you find it.

❑ If someone in authority **searches** you, they examine your clothing for hidden objects.

❑ **Searching** questions are intended to get people to reveal the truth, especially when they are trying to hide it. You can also talk about a **searching** investigation or interview.

search party A **search party** is a group of people taking part in an organized search for someone, especially someone who is lost or wanted by the police.

search warrant A **search warrant** is an official document which entitles the police to enter a building to search for things connected with criminal activities, for example stolen goods.

searchlight A **searchlight** is a light with a large powerful beam which can be turned in any direction to shine on someone or something.

seascape A **seascape** is the scenery of the sea, or a painting of it.

seashell A **seashell** is the empty shell of a small sea creature.

seashore The **seashore** is sand, shingle, or rocks next to the sea.

seasick (seasickness) If someone in a boat or ship is **seasick,** they feel nauseous because of the vessel's movements, and may vomit. *He was very prone to seasickness.*

seaside The **seaside** is parts of the land next to the sea, especially parts where people spend their holidays.

season (seasoning, seasoned) ❑ The **seasons** are spring, summer, autumn, and winter, the four periods into which the year is divided. ◇ A **season** is also a period of the year when a particular activity takes place. *...the tourist season.* ◇ If shellfish, fruit, or vegetables are **in season,** it is the time of the year when they are naturally available. At other times, they are **out of season.** ◇ If fish or game are **in season,** it is the time when you are officially allowed to hunt or catch them. ◇ If you visit a resort **out of season,** you go outside the usual holiday period.

❑ A **season** of films, plays, or concerts is a series of them with something in common. *...a Mozart season.*

❑ If you **season** food, you add salt, pepper, or spices to it, to give it extra flavour. Things added to food like this are called **seasoning.**

❑ See also **seasoned.**

season ticket A **season ticket** is a ticket which you can use as many times as you like over a certain period, for example a ticket to a football ground or one for use on public transport.

seasonal (seasonally) **Seasonal** is used to talk about something connected with a particular season or time of the year. *...the seasonal rainfall... Seasonally adjusted unemployment has risen for seven consecutive months.*

Seasonal Affective Disorder See SAD.

seasoned is used to describe people who have had a lot of experience of something and so are well prepared for it or know what to expect. *...seasoned rock climbers.*

seat (seating, seated) ❑ A **seat** is an object you can sit on, for example a chair. ◇ The part of a chair you sit on is called the **seat.**

❑ If you **seat** yourself somewhere, you sit down. If you are **seated** somewhere, you are sitting there.

❑ If a building or vehicle **seats** a certain number of people, it has seats for that number. You can also say a building has **seating** for a certain number of people. If a table **seats** a certain number of people, that number can sit round it to eat a meal.

❑ If someone has a **seat** in parliament, they have been elected there as an MP. Similarly, someone can have a seat on a council or committee.

❑ If something **takes a back seat,** it is treated as less important than other things.

❑ The **seat** of an organization is the place where it has its base. ◇ The **seat** of an activity is the place where it happens. ◇ The **seat** of an aristocratic family is their most important residence.

❑ The **seat** of a pair of trousers is the part which covers your bottom. ◇ If a pilot **flies by the seat of his pants,** he does it by relying on his instinct and experience, rather than using sophisticated equipment or following a carefully prepared plan. You can talk about other people **flying by the seat of their pants** when they rely on instinct and experience to see them through something, rather than making careful preparations.

seat belt A **seat belt** is a strap you fasten around your body in a vehicle or plane to reduce the chances of your being injured in an accident or crash.

-seater is used to say how many people something like a vehicle, restaurant, or stadium can hold. *...a new 105-seater twin-engined jet.*

seaweed is a plant which grows on the seabed or on the seashore below the level of high tide.

seaworthy If a boat or ship is **seaworthy,** it is in a fit state to travel on the sea.

secateurs (*pron:* sek-at-**turz**) are a gardening tool like a pair of scissors with short powerful blades. They are used for cutting flowers and pruning.

secede (*pron:* siss-**seed**) (seceding, seceded; secession) If a region **secedes** from a country, it breaks away and becomes an independent country. Similarly, a group of people can **secede** from an organization. Breaking away from a country or organization is called **secession.**

secessionist (secessionism) People who want their region to secede from a country are called **secessionists;** their aims or policies are called **secessionism.**

secluded (seclusion) A **secluded** place is quiet, private, and undisturbed. You talk about the **seclusion** of a place like this. ◇ If someone is **in seclusion,** they are living apart from other people.

second (seconding, seconded; secondly, seconder) ❑ A **second** is one of the sixty parts a minute is divided into. ◇ People use a **second** or **seconds** to mean a very short period of time. *He looks genuinely stunned for a second.*

❑ The **second** item or person in a series is the one that comes after the first one. *...the second week in January.*

❑ The **second** best thing of a particular kind is not as good as the best one, but better than all others. Similarly, something can be the **second** biggest, **second** fastest, etc. ◇ If you say something is **second only to** something else in importance, you mean nothing else is more important except that other thing. ◇ If you say someone or something is **second to none,** you mean they are better than anyone or anything else of their kind.

❑ You say **second** or **secondly** when you are mentioning the second in a series of points or items. *Second, the annual return of 20.55% is dependent on investors getting their tax back in February.*

❑ If something happens, for example, **every second** month, it happens on alternate months. *Regular summits will be held every second year.*

❑ If you have **second thoughts** about a decision you have made, you begin to have doubts about it and to wonder whether it was wise. ◇ You say 'on **second thoughts...**' when you are changing your mind about something you have just said. *Any exotic car will do so long as it isn't a clapped out Ford Cortina, although on second thoughts that's probably a classic now.*

❑ **second nature:** see **nature.** ◇ **second wind:** see **wind.**

❑ **Seconds** are goods sold at a cheaper price because they are slightly imperfect.

❑ If you **second** a proposal or motion in a meeting or debate, you indicate formally that you support it, or you make a speech in support of it. You are called the **seconder** of the proposal or motion. ◇ If you **second** something someone says, you show you agree with it or support it.

❑ A boxer's **seconds** are people who assist him before and after a match and in between rounds.

❑ If someone is **seconded** (*pron:* si-**kond**-id) somewhere, they are moved there temporarily to carry out special duties.

second-best See **second.**

second-class ❑ If people are treated as **second-class** citizens, they are not given the same rights as other people. You can also say things provided for them are **second-class.** *...a second-class education.*

❑ If you travel **second-class** on a train or ship, you use standard accommodation rather than first-class. ◇ If you send a letter **second class,** it costs less than first-class mail and may take longer to get to its destination.

second cousin Your **second cousins** are the children of your parents' cousins.

second-guess If you try to **second-guess** someone, you try to anticipate what they will say or do. Similarly, you can try to **second-guess** what will happen in a situation.

second-hand (*or* secondhand) ❑ A **second-hand** object has already been owned by someone else. ◇ A **second-hand** shop sells second-hand goods.

❑ If you experience something **at second-hand,** you experience it indirectly, as a result of hearing or reading about it. Similarly, if you receive news or information **at second-hand,** you get it from someone who has heard it from someone else.

second-in-command See **command.**

second language Someone's **second language** is a language which is not their own language but which they use for certain purposes, for example for work or school, or for communicating with other people in a country where several languages are spoken.

second-rate If you call someone or something second-rate, you mean they are of poor quality or ability.

secondary (secondarily) ❏ Secondary is used to describe things which are less important than something else in a particular situation. *Mr Major has presented ratification as a mark of Britain keeping its word, and only secondarily in terms of influence on European developments.*
❏ Secondary education is for pupils from the age of 11 until they leave school.
❏ Secondary is used to describe things which come after something else, or which result or develop from something which has already happened. *The secondary effects on the miners' health are considerable.*

secondary modern In the past, a secondary modern school was a school for pupils aged over 11 which concentrated on teaching practical skills and taught fewer academic subjects than grammar schools.

secondary school A secondary school is a school for pupils aged 11 to 18.

seconder See second.

secondhand See second-hand.

secondment (*pron:* sik-**kond**-ment) If someone is on secondment, they have been sent somewhere temporarily to do a job or carry out special duties.

secrecy is keeping things secret.

secret (secretly) ❏ If something is secret or a secret, only a few people know about it and they are careful not to tell anyone else. *The POWs were secretly tunnelling to freedom.* You can also say something is done in secret. If you keep a secret, you do not tell it to anyone else.
❏ Secret is also used to describe people who have opinions or take part in activities which they do not tell anyone else about. *...a secret anarchist.*
❏ The secret of achieving something is what you need to do to achieve it. *Staying one jump ahead of the pack is the secret of successful property-buying.*
❏ If you **make no secret** of something about yourself, you do not try to hide it. ◇ an **open secret**: see open.
❏ A secret is also a mystery which has never been explained or understood. *...the secrets of human genetic diseases.*

secret agent A secret agent is a person employed to discover the secrets of governments or organizations which threaten their country, or to carry out secret work against them.

secret police In some non-democratic countries, the secret police is a police force which operates secretly against people opposed to the government.

secret service A country's secret service is a government department responsible for the country's security, whose job is to find out enemy secrets and prevent other governments from discovering their own country's secrets. ◇ In the US, the Secret Service is a government agency responsible for protecting the President, preventing counterfeiting activities, and certain other police activities.

secretarial See secretary.

secretariat A secretariat is a department or office responsible for the administration of an international organization.

secretary (secretaries; secretarial, secretaryship) ❏ A secre-

tary is someone whose job is to type letters, answer phone calls, and carry out other office work. Secretarial is used to talk about things connected with this work and the people who do it. *...secretarial staff.*
❏ 'Secretary of State' is sometimes shortened to Secretary. ◇ Some MPs and senior civil servants who act as assistants to government ministers have Secretary as part of their title. ◇ In the US, heads of government departments have Secretary as part of their title. *...the United States Treasury Secretary.* ◇ When 'Secretary' is part of a title, the post that goes with the title is often called the secretaryship.
❏ The secretary of a club or other organization is the person whose job is to keep records and write letters.

Secretary General (Secretaries General) The Secretary General of an international political organization is the person in charge of its administration.

Secretary of State (Secretaries of State) In Britain, a Secretary of State is a senior government minister who is usually also a cabinet minister. ◇ In the US, the Secretary of State is the foreign minister.

secretaryship See secretary.

secrete (secreting, secreted) ❏ If part of an animal or plant secretes a fluid, it produces it. For example, glands in the stomach secrete juices which help in digesting food. Producing fluids like this is called secretion; a secretion is a substance which has been secreted.
❏ If you secrete something somewhere, you hide it there.

secretive (secretiveness) A secretive person tries to keep their feelings, intentions, or actions hidden from other people. You can also talk about organizations and governments being secretive. *...the secretiveness of government in Britain.*

sect A sect is a religious group which has broken away from a larger group and has its own beliefs and practices.

sectarian is used to talk about things connected with the differences between sects. In Northern Ireland, sectarian is used to talk about things based on the differences between the Protestant and Roman Catholic communities. *...sectarian killings.*

sectarianism is strong, often narrow-minded support for a sect or faction.

section ❏ A section of something is a part of it which can be considered separately from the rest. *...large sections of Africa.* ◇ A section of an official document is one of the parts it is divided into. ◇ A section of something like a fence is one of the parts it consists of. ◇ A section of an organization is one of its branches or divisions.
❏ A section is also a cross-section.

sectional interests are the interests of a particular group within a country or community.

sector (sectoral) ❏ A sector of something is a part of it, for example part of a country's economy. *...the service sector.* Sectoral is used to talk about things to do with a sector or sectors. *...sectoral strikes.* See also private sector, public sector.
❏ A sector is also one of the areas a place is divided into, often for military reasons.
❏ A sector of a circle is one of the two parts you divide it into when you draw two straight lines from its centre to

its edge.

secular is used to describe things which are not based on religion. ...*a secular state.*

secularise See **secularize**.

secularism (secularist) **Secularism** is the belief that religion should not have any influence on such things as a country's political or educational system. A **secularist** is someone who believes this.

secularize (secularizing, secularized; secularization) (*can be spelled with an 's' instead of a 'z'*) If something is **secularized**, it is changed so that it no longer has any religious connection. ...*the secularization of daily life.*

secure (securing, secured; securely) ❑ If you **secure** something, you obtain it. *They secured 80 seats in the first round.*
❑ You say something is **secure** when it can be relied on to continue. ...*secure jobs.* If you **secure** something, you make it secure. *Cheap labour alone will not secure Indonesia's economic future.*
❑ If you feel **secure**, you feel safe and happy because you have nothing to worry about or be afraid of.
❑ When a place is **secured** or made **secure**, it is made safe from attack. Similarly, you say a building is made **secure** when it is made safe from burglary. ◇ A **secure** prison is one which it is impossible to escape from.
❑ If you **secure** something to something else, you fix or fasten it firmly. You then say it is **secure**. You can also say something is **securely** fixed or fastened.
❑ If you **secure** a loan, you promise to give something valuable to the person lending you the money if you are not able to repay it.

security (securities) ❑ **Security** is the measures and precautions taken to protect someone or something, for example from terrorist attacks. *Amid tight security, leaders of the world's seven richest nations have begun their annual summit.* ◇ If you say someone or something is a **security risk**, you mean they may be a threat to the safety of a country or organization.
❑ **Security** is also a situation in which you feel safe and do not need to worry about the future. ...*the security of a happy home life.*
❑ A **security** is something valuable you promise to give someone if you fail to repay a loan.
❑ **Securities** are shares, stocks, or bonds, or certificates showing that you own them.
❑ See also **social security**.

Security Council The **Security Council** is a permanent body of the United Nations whose purpose is to maintain world peace. It is made up of five permanent and ten elected member countries.

sedan In the US, a saloon car is called a **sedan**.

sedan chair In the 17th and 18th centuries, a **sedan chair** was an enclosed chair for one person which was carried on two poles by two men, one behind and one in front.

sedate (sedately; sedating, sedated; sedation, sedative) ❑ If you go somewhere at a **sedate** pace, you go slowly, not hurrying at all. *We proceeded sedately on our way.* ◇ A **sedate** person is calm, serene, and dignified.
❑ If a person or animal is **sedated**, they are given a drug called a **sedative** to calm them or make them sleep. When someone has been given a sedative, you say they are under **sedation**.

sedentary A **sedentary** occupation or way of life involves a lot of sitting down and not much exercise.

sediment is small grains of solid material which settle at the bottom of a liquid.

sedimentary rocks are rocks formed when layers of clay, sand, or shells, which were once underwater, become compressed. Sandstone and limestone are sedimentary rocks.

sedition (seditious) If someone is charged with **sedition**, they are charged with encouraging people in their country to rebel against the government. The things they have written or said are described as **seditious**.

seduce (seducing, seduced; seduction, seducer; seductress, seductresses) ❑ If someone **seduces** another person, they persuade them to have sex with them. Seducing someone is called **seduction**. A person who does it is called a **seducer**; a woman who seduces someone can be called a **seductress**.
❑ If you are **seduced** into doing something, someone persuades you to do it, by making it seem very attractive.

seductive (seductively) A **seductive** person is sexually attractive. You can also call someone's behaviour **seductive**. ...*Marlene Dietrich rasping seductively in The Blue Angel.* ◇ You can say something like an idea or offer is **seductive** when it is tempting and attractive.

seductress See **seduce**.

see (seeing, saw, have seen) ❑ When you **see** something, you are aware of it through your eyes. ◇ If you **see** something like a film or TV programme, you watch it. ◇ If you **see** something in the papers, you read it there.
❑ If you **see** someone, you meet them, by arrangement or accident. If you go to **see** someone, you visit them. ◇ If you **see** someone **off**, you go with them to the place where they are catching a train, plane, or ship, and say goodbye to them there. ◇ You also say you **see** someone off when you force them to leave a place.
❑ If you **see** something exists or is true, you realize it. *They should have seen that drink was contributing to many deaths.* ◇ If you can **see** why something happens or exists, you can understand the reason for it. Similarly, if you can **see** what someone means, you can understand the point they are making.
❑ If you **see** a quality in someone or something, you form the opinion that they have it. ◇ If you **see** a situation or someone's behaviour in a certain way, you regard it that way. *In Brussels many people see this move as a change of policy.*
❑ If you **see to** something that needs doing, you do it. ◇ If you say you will **see if** you can do something, you mean you will try to do it. ◇ If you **see** something is done or **see to** it that it is done, you make sure it is done. ◇ If you **see about** something, you try to arrange it, provide it, or sort it out. *I went to the local employment bureau in Ladbroke Grove to see about a job.* ◇ If you **see** something **through**, you make sure it is done or completed.
❑ If you **see** if something is true, you try to find out about it. *The Highway Patrol routinely tests the exhausts of lorries to see if they are too smoky.*
❑ If you say a period of time **sees** something happening, you mean it happens during that time. *The last year has seen a spate of neighbourhood watch schemes spring up.* Similarly, you can talk about a place **seeing** something

happening. ◇ If something happens which concerns or affects you, you can say you see it happen. *One airline has seen its tourist bookings for this summer fall 75% short of the bookings made by this time last year.* Similarly, if you say you would like to **see** something happen, you mean you would like it to happen.

❑ 'You see...' is sometimes used to say something exists or is happening. *There's a new kind of city poverty. You see it in Britain, in Paris and the United States.*

❑ If you **see** something happening in the future, you expect it or predict it. ◇ **remains to be seen**: see remain. ◇ **wait and see**: see wait.

❑ If you **see through** someone, you realize what their intentions are, even though they are trying to hide them. You can also say you **see through** their behaviour.

❑ If you **see off** a challenge or threat, you deal with it successfully by defeating the person who challenged or threatened you.

❑ **See** is used in a book or other publication to say where the reader should look for some information. *...the increase in the proportion of children born out of wedlock (see chart on previous page).*

❑ **Seeing that** is used to mention the reason for something. *Few people bother to put any effort into their work, seeing that it is so poorly rewarded.*

❑ A bishop's **see** is the city where his cathedral is, or his diocese.

see-saw (see-sawing, see-sawed) (*or* seesaw, *etc*) A **seesaw** is a device for children to play on. It consists of a long plank which balances on a fixed point in the middle. Children sit on opposite ends and each in turn pushes off against the ground to make the ends of the plank move up and down. ◇ If you talk about something **see-sawing** from one opposite state to another, you mean it keeps changing between the two states. *Over the last two months the crisis has see-sawed between hopes of peace and fears of war.*

see-through materials or objects are transparent.

seed (seeding, seeded) ❑ A **seed** is the fertilized grain of a plant, from which a new plant can grow. **Seed** is a quantity of seeds of a particular kind. *...a packet of cabbage seed.*

❑ The **seeds** of something are its origins or beginnings. *The agreement to talk contains the seeds of a more serious problem still.*

❑ In some sports tournaments, the best players or teams are **seeded,** which means they are ranked according to their playing ability. These players are called **seeds.** They do not usually meet each other in the early rounds or stages of the tournament.

seed-bed (*or* seedbed) If you say a situation is a **seed-bed** for something like a political movement, you mean it provides a good opportunity for it to develop.

seed money or **seed capital** is money provided for setting up some kind of enterprise.

seedling A **seedling** is a young plant grown from a seed.

seedy (seediness) A **seedy** place or person is shabby, untidy, and unpleasant. *...the seediness of London's streets.*

seek (seeking, sought) ❑ If you **seek** something, you try to obtain it. *France is expected to seek support for its demands.*

❑ If you **seek** something **out,** you keep looking for it until you find it or obtain it.

❑ If you are **seeking** to achieve something, you are trying to achieve it.

❑ If you go somewhere to **seek your fortune,** you go there to try to become rich and successful.

-seeker is added to words to describe people who are looking for something or trying to obtain something. *...sun-seekers... ...peace-seekers.*

seem ❑ If you say something **seems** to be true, you mean you get the impression that it is true. *Sanctions, it seemed, had failed.* ◇ You also use **seem** to describe the impression you have of a person or thing. *He seemed like a nice bloke.*

❑ If you say you cannot **seem** to do something, you mean you have tried doing it without success.

seeming (seemingly) **Seeming** is used to say something appears to exist or be true. For example, if someone appears to be unwilling to do something, you can talk about their **seeming** unwillingness to do it. *...a seemingly impossible task.*

seemly is used to describe things like behaviour or dress which are considered to be decent or appropriate in particular circumstances. *She felt it would not be seemly for her to attend the wedding.*

seen See see.

seep (seeping, seeped) ❑ If a liquid or gas **seeps** into or out of something, it slowly leaks in or out.

❑ If news or information **seeps** out of a place, it comes out very slowly, a bit at a time. ◇ If someone's power or confidence **seeps** away, it slowly disappears.

seepage ❑ When a liquid or gas slowly leaks out of something, you can say there is a **seepage.**

❑ When small quantities of something are gradually and secretly transferred from one place to another, you can say there is a **seepage** of those things.

seer People who make predictions about what will happen in the future are sometimes called **seers.** ◇ In ancient times, a **seer** was a person who supposedly had supernatural powers and could see into the future.

seesaw See see-saw.

seethe (seething, seethed) If someone is **seething** with anger, they are very angry indeed. ◇ If a place is **seething** with people, there are a lot of them there moving around constantly.

segment (segmentation) ❑ A **segment** of something is a part which can be considered separately from the rest. *Three-to-five day cruises are the fastest-growing segment of the market.* ◇ If an area of activity is **segmented,** it is split up into parts or sections. *Many agree that such segmentation would miss the point of basic research.*

❑ A **segment** of a fruit like an orange or grapefruit is one of the sections it is easily divided into.

❑ A **segment** of a circle is one of the two parts you divide it into when you draw a straight line across it, cutting the edge at two points.

segregate (segregating, segregated; segregation, segregationist) If hostile groups are **segregated,** they are kept apart. *...the police policy of strict segregation of the supporters.* ◇ You also say people are **segregated** when they are kept apart for other reasons, for example because of their race. *Men and women had been segregated.* **Segregated** is used to describe places where people are kept apart because of their race. *...a segregated night club.* A

segregated system is one which keeps people apart because of their race. People who are in favour of this kind of segregation are called **segregationists**.

seismic (*pron: size-mik*) ❏ **Seismic** is used to talk about things to do with earthquakes. *...seismic activity.* ◇ **Seismic waves** are shock waves in the earth caused by earthquakes or large explosions.

    ❏ **Seismic** is also used to talk about major divisions occurring in something. *...the possibility of a seismic rift in the Scottish Labour Party.*

seismograph A **seismograph** is an instrument which registers and records the strength of earthquakes or large explosions.

seismology (*seismologist, seismological*) **Seismology** is the scientific study of earthquakes. **Seismological** is used to talk about things to do with this study. A person who studies seismology is called a **seismologist**.

seismometer A **seismometer** is an instrument similar to a seismograph.

seize (*seizing, seized; seizure*) ❏ If you **seize** someone or something, you take hold of them quickly and firmly.

    ❏ You also say someone is **seized** when they are captured or arrested. Similarly, illegal drugs or weapons can be **seized** by the police. You can talk about a **seizure** of drugs or weapons.

    ❏ When a place is **seized**, it is captured. You can also say a group of people **seize control** of a place. When vehicles or weapons are **seized**, they are captured. You can talk about a **seizure** of any of these things. *...the seizure of Kuwait.* ◇ If someone **seizes** power, they take control of a place quickly and suddenly, using force.

    ❏ If you **seize control** of a situation, you put yourself in charge of it. *Mr Csurka's effort to seize control of Hungary's agenda suffered a setback at the congress.* ◇ If you **seize** an opportunity, you quickly take advantage of it. When someone does this, you can also say they **seize the moment**. ◇ If you **seize on** something, you make use of it for your own purposes. *Labour seized on the speech as a damning indictment of government economic policy.*

    ❏ If an engine **seizes up**, it stops working. Similarly, a system can **seize up**.

    ❏ A **seizure** is a sudden violent attack of illness, especially a stroke or epileptic fit.

    ❏ If you are **seized** by a desire or an emotion, you feel it strongly.

seldom If something **seldom** happens, it hardly ever happens.

select (*selection*) ❏ If you **select** someone or something, you choose them. A **selection** of people or things is a group of them chosen from among others. *Paul McCartney played a selection of Beatles songs.* ◇ If you say there is a **selection** of things, you mean you have several to choose from.

    ❏ A **select** group of people or things is a small one of special merit or quality.

    ❏ A **select committee** is a small committee of MPs or lords set up to investigate a topic and report back to Parliament with their findings.

selective (*selectively, selectivity*) A **selective** process is one in which some people or things are carefully chosen for a particular purpose in preference to others. *Cutting trees is done selectively... ...a move towards selectivity.* ◇ If you

say a person is **selective**, you mean they choose things very carefully, for example which people they spend time with or what products they buy.

selector The **selectors** are the people who choose the members of a sports team for a particular match.

self (*selves*) Your **self** is your basic personality or nature. *Hateley has shown his true self in the past two games.*

self- is used at the beginning of a word to describe something a person does to himself or herself. *...self-destructive behaviour... ...self-mocking efforts.*

self-addressed A **self-addressed** envelope has your own address and usually a stamp on it. You send it to another person so they can send something back to you.

self-appointed If you call someone a **self-appointed** leader, you mean they have taken on their position of leader without anyone appointing them or asking them to do it. You can also talk about someone doing a **self-appointed** task.

self-assertion (*self-assertive*) **Self-assertion** is putting forward your ideas or opinions, or demanding your rights, in a bold and confident way. When someone behaves like this, you say they are being **self-assertive**.

self-assured (*self-assurance*) **Self-assured** people show confidence in their own abilities. You talk about the **self-assurance** of people like these.

self-catering If you stay in **self-catering** accommodation, you provide your own meals.

self-centred **self-centred** people think only about themselves and their own desires and needs.

self-confessed is used to describe someone who openly admits to being something, or to having done something. *...a self-confessed railway fanatic.*

self-confident (*self-confidence*) **Self-confident** people behave confidently because they believe in themselves and their own abilities. You talk about the **self-confidence** of people like these.

self-conscious (*self-consciously, self-consciousness*) A **self-conscious** person is shy and easily embarrassed, and feels everyone is looking at them and judging them. *He laughed self-consciously... Blushing usually starts at about the age of nine, when self-consciousness sets in.*

self-contained A **self-contained** unit of accommodation, for example a flat, has all its own facilities, including a bathroom and kitchen. ◇ If you say something like a village is **self-contained**, you mean it is able to supply all its own needs, and requires no help from outside. ◇ If you say a person is **self-contained**, you mean they do not need the company of other people.

self-control If you exercise **self-control**, you control your emotions and keep calm, even though you are angry or afraid.

self-declared is used to say someone has adopted a name or title without getting anyone else's agreement to it. *...their self-declared state, the Bosnian Serb Republic.*

self-defeating If you say a plan or course of action is **self-defeating**, you mean it is bound to fail, because it would spoil its own chances of success.

self-defence (*American spelling: self-defense*) ❏ **Self-defence** is using violence or special physical skills to protect yourself when attacked by another person.

    ❏ If someone says or writes something **in self-defence**, they do it in response to criticism, to try to justify their actions.

self-denial If you practise self-denial, you do not allow yourself to have things you like or do things you enjoy.

self-deprecating (self-deprecation) Self-deprecating people make jokes about their own faults. You call this behaviour self-deprecation.

self-determination If you talk about the right to self-determination, you mean people's right to choose whether their country should be independent or be part of another country.

self-discipline (self-disciplined) See discipline.

self-drive cars are cars which people hire to drive themselves, as opposed to cars hired with a driver.

self-educated people have educated themselves rather than having had a formal education in a school.

self-effacing people are modest and do not draw attention to themselves or their achievements.

self-employed (self-employment) A self-employed person is their own boss and organizes their own work, pay, tax, and national insurance payments. ...the rapid growth in self-employment.

self-esteem If you have self-esteem, you have a good opinion of yourself and believe you deserve to be respected.

self-evident (self-evidently) If you say something is self-evident, you mean it is so obvious it does not need to be proved or explained. From football to the business of running an economy, British is no longer self-evidently best.

self-explanatory If you say something is self-explanatory, you mean it is clear and easy to understand and does not require an explanation.

self-expression is expressing your personality and feelings through a creative activity such as painting.

self-financing If something is self-financing, it provides enough money to pay its own costs and needs no outside financial support.

self-governing (self-government) A self-governing country or region is administered by its own people, rather than by another country or central authority. ...the right to self-government. Similarly, a self-governing organization is run by its own members.

self-help is used to talk about people helping themselves, rather than relying on the authorities or other organizations. ...a self-help group which organizes AIDS sufferers to fight for their civil rights.

self-important (self-importance) If you call someone self-important, you mean they have an exaggerated idea of their own importance. You can also say they are full of self-importance.

self-imposed If something someone does is self-imposed, it was their own idea to do it and it was not forced on them by someone else.

self-indulgent (self-indulgently, self-indulgence) If you are self-indulgent, you let yourself do things you enjoy doing. This is called self-indulgence.

self-inflicted When people injure themselves, you say their injuries are self-inflicted. Similarly, when people bring trouble on themselves, you can say their troubles are self-inflicted.

self-interest (self-interested) Self-interest is showing concern only for what benefits you. You say people who

behave like this are self-interested. ...a succession of self-interested decisions.

self-made A self-made person has become successful and rich through their own efforts. You can also talk about a person's wealth being self-made.

self-perpetuating If you say something is self-perpetuating, you mean it is organized or structured in such a way that it will continue indefinitely.

self-pity (self-pitying) Self-pity is feeling sorry for yourself. You can call someone's behaviour self-pitying. ...the self-pitying ramblings of a lunchtime drunk.

self-portrait A self-portrait is a portrait of an artist painted by himself or herself. A person's written description of himself or herself can also be called a self-portrait.

self-possessed (self-possession) A self-possessed person is calm, confident, and in control of their emotions. You talk about the self-possession of someone like this.

self-preservation is making sure you are not harmed in a dangerous situation.

self-proclaimed is used to say someone has adopted a name or title without getting anyone else's agreement to it. ...the self-proclaimed provisional government.

self-raising flour is flour containing baking powder. When you use it to bake cakes, it makes them rise.

self-regulation (self-regulatory) Self-regulation is making sure yourself that certain standards are met in what you do, rather than having someone else do it for you. A system which allows people to do this is called a self-regulatory system.

self-reliant (self-reliance) Self-reliant people and organizations are able to look after themselves. ...activities designed to develop youngsters' self-reliance.

self-respect (self-respecting) ❑ Self-respect is a feeling of pride in your own abilities and worth. You say people who have this feeling are self-respecting.

❑ Self-respecting is also used humorously to mention something a particular kind of person would never do. Air conditioning is standard, automatic transmission – which no self-respecting Ferrari enthusiast would touch – is optional.

self-restraint If you show self-restraint, you manage to control your feelings or desires.

self-righteous (self-righteously, self-righteousness) You call someone's behaviour self-righteous when they are confident that what they are doing is morally right. Her mother self-righteously informed her of her husband's infidelities... ...a slight feeling of self-righteousness.

self-rule is the same as self-government.

self-sacrifice is sacrificing yourself or something important to you, to achieve something worthwhile or to help other people.

self-same means the same one or ones you have just mentioned. In the USA and England, political parties are calling for a return to traditional methods, while in France the government wants to move away from these self-same traditions.

self-satisfied (self-satisfaction) You call people self-satisfied when you think they are much too pleased with themselves and with what they have achieved. You talk about the self-satisfaction of people like these.

self-seeking You say people are self-seeking when they are only interested in doing things which serve their own interests.

self-service restaurants, petrol stations, etc are ones where you serve yourself rather than being served by someone else.

self-serving people do a certain kind of work only because it serves their own interests.

self-styled names or descriptions are ones which people have chosen for themselves.

self-sufficient (self-sufficiency) A **self-sufficient** person does not need other people's help or company. Similarly, a **self-sufficient** country is not dependent on other countries. You can talk about the **self-sufficiency** of a person or country.

self-supporting You say people or organizations are **self-supporting** when they earn enough to support themselves financially.

self-taught people have educated themselves or have taught themselves a skill, rather than being taught by someone else.

self-willed If you say someone, especially a child, is **self-willed**, you mean they are obstinate, determined to do what they want, and not prepared to listen to other people's advice.

selfish (selfishly, selfishness) **Selfish** people are only concerned about themselves and what suits them, and do not consider other people. *The landowners are selfishly keeping vast acres of land to themselves... He had repaid her love and loyalty with selfishness and unkindness.*

selfless (selflessly, selfishness) A **selfless** person considers other people's needs rather than their own. *The reassurance she so badly needed had been given selflessly... It would take unusual courage and selflessness for MPs to give up their seats and challenge the government in this way.*

sell (selling, sold) ❑ If you **sell** something, you give it to someone in exchange for money.

❑ If a shop **sells** a certain product, it normally has it available for sale. If it **sells out** of it, it sells all its stock of it, and there is none left. When this happens, you say the product has **sold out.** ◇ If a concert, show, or film **sells out,** all the tickets are sold. When this happens, you say the concert, show, or film is a **sell-out.**

❑ If something **sells** at a certain price, it is for sale at that price. If it **sells** well, a lot of people buy it. ◇ If you say a certain thing **sells** a product, you mean it makes people buy it. You call something like this a **selling point.**

❑ When people **sell** something **off,** they get rid of it by selling it, often at a reduced price, because they need the money, because they cannot afford to keep it any longer, or because it is no longer useful. ◇ If a person or company **sells up,** they sell all their property, because they need the money. ◇ If the owners of a company **sell out to** another company, they sell their company to them.

❑ If you **sell yourself,** you present yourself in a way which gives people confidence in you and your abilities. Similarly, you can talk about an organization or place **selling itself.** *Birmingham really needs to sell itself as a major international city.* ◇ If you try to **sell** something like an idea, you try to convince people it is worthwhile. ◇ If someone is very keen on an idea, you can say they are **sold** on it.

❑ If you say someone has **sold** something like their principles, you mean they have given them up, to gain some personal advantage. ◇ If you say someone has **sold** someone else **out** or **sold** them **down the river,** you mean

they have betrayed them or let them down. You can call behaviour like this a **sell-out.** ◇ **sell someone short:** see **short.** ◇ See also **hard sell, soft sell.**

sell-by The **sell-by** date of a food is the date it must be sold by to be sure it is fresh and safe to eat. This date is printed on the packaging. ◇ If you say something or someone is past their **sell-by** date, you mean they are old, or no longer interesting, important, or useful. .

sell-out See **sell.**

sellable If you say a product is **sellable,** you mean people will buy it. ◇ If you say something like an idea is **sellable,** you mean people will accept it.

seller The **seller** of something is the person or company selling it. ◇ If you say a product is a big or top **seller,** you mean a lot of it is sold. See also **best-seller.**

Sellotape is a thin transparent sticky tape sold in rolls. 'Sellotape' is a trademark.

selves See **self.**

semantic (semantics) **Semantic** is used to talk about things to do with the meaning of words. *...a semantic error.* **Semantics** is the study of the meaning of words.

semaphore is a system of sending messages using two flags. One flag is held in each hand and the arms are moved to various positions representing different letters of the alphabet.

semblance If you achieve a **semblance** of something, you achieve something like it, although it may not be the real thing. *Can Europe maintain a semblance of unity?*

semen (pron: see-men) is the liquid containing sperm produced by the sex organs of men and male animals.

semi (semis) A **semi** is a semi-detached house.

semi- is combined with words like 'darkness' or 'naked' to talk about someone or something being almost but not completely in a particular state. *...semi-independent states.*

semi-automatic A **semi-automatic** weapon reloads itself but has to have its trigger pulled each time to make it fire.

semi-circle (semi-circular) (or semicircle, semicircular) A **semi-circle** is half a circle or something with this shape. Things with this shape are described as **semi-circular.**

semi-colon A **semi-colon** is the mark ; used in writing to separate parts of a sentence or to indicate a pause.

semi-conscious If a person is **semi-conscious,** they are in a state between consciousness and unconsciousness.

semi-detached A **semi-detached** house is attached to the neighbouring house on one side by a shared wall.

semi-final (semi-finalist) A **semi-final** is one of two games, matches, or races in a competition which decide who will take part in the final. The people or teams taking part in a semi-final are called **semi-finalists.**

semi-precious stones are stones like agates and turquoises which are used in jewellery and are less valuable than precious stones like diamonds and rubies.

semi-skilled workers are partly trained but are not able to do the most specialized work. The work they do is also described as **semi-skilled.**

semi-skimmed milk has had about half of its fat removed.

semi-staged A **semi-staged** production of a play or opera is one in which no costumes, scenery, or props are used.

semibreve A semibreve is a musical note with the same time value as four crotchets.

semicircle (semicircular) See **semi-circle**.

semiconductor A semiconductor is a substance such as silicon which conducts a small amount of electricity and is suitable for tiny electronic parts such as microchips.

seminal If you describe someone as a seminal figure in a particular field, you mean they have had very great influence in that field. Similarly, you can call a book a seminal work on a subject.

seminar A seminar is a class at a university in which a tutor and a small group of students discuss a topic. ◇ A seminar is also any meeting where a topic or problem is discussed or where information about a subject is passed on.

seminary (seminaries; seminarian) A seminary is a college where priests or other ministers of religion are trained. A person who attends a seminary is called a seminarian. ◇ In the past, a seminary was also a private school, usually for girls.

semiotics is the study of signs and symbols and their function and meaning in communication.

semiquaver A semiquaver is a musical note with a time value equal to a quarter of a crotchet.

semitone A semitone is the smallest interval between two notes in Western music. An octave consists of 12 semitones.

semolina is tiny particles of wheat used for making pasta. It is also used to make a sweet milky pudding called semolina.

Semtex is an odourless plastic explosive often used by terrorists.

senate The Senate is one of the two law-making bodies in some countries, for example the US. ◇ A senate is also the governing body in some universities.

senator (senatorial) A senator is a member of the US Senate. Senatorial is used to talk about things to do with senators or with being a senator. ...the conservative senatorial candidate.

send (sending, sent) ❏ If you send something to someone, you have it delivered to them, for example by post. ◇ If you send in something like a report, you post it to a place where it will be officially dealt with. ◇ If you send something off, you post it. ◇ If you send off for something, you write and ask for it to be delivered to you. ◇ If you send out information, you distribute it to people by post.

❏ If someone sends for you, they send a message asking you to come and see them.

❏ If someone sends you somewhere, they tell you to go there, or make arrangements for you to go there. You can also talk about someone being sent off to a place.

❏ If something sends you somewhere, it causes you to go there. The charges, if proven, are enough to send him to prison. Similarly, if something sends you into a certain state, it puts you into that state. This sent him positively wild.

❏ If a player is sent off in football, he is made to leave the pitch, because he has seriously broken the rules. You call an incident like this a sending-off.

❏ If a machine sends out sound or light, it transmits it in a particular direction. If an electronic message or signal is sent somewhere, it is transmitted by radio waves or some other electronic system.

❏ If a writer sends something up, he or she makes fun of it in a novel or play. Similarly, a film or comedy sketch can send something up. Anything which makes fun of something like this can be called a send-up.

send-off If someone who is going away is given a send-off, people gather to say goodbye to them.

send-up See send.

sender The sender of a letter, message, or other communication is the person who sent it.

sending-off See send.

senile (senility) Senile people are old and mentally confused and unable to look after themselves. Their condition is called senility.

senile dementia is an illness affecting old people in which the person's mind deteriorates.

senior ❏ The senior members of an organization are the ones with the highest and most important jobs. You can call people at your workplace who have a more important job than you your seniors.

❏ If someone is your senior, they are older than you.

❏ When a father and son have the same name, Senior is sometimes used after the father's name, to avoid confusion. In Britain, this is usually shortened to 'Snr' or 'Sr'.

senior citizen A senior citizen is a person who is old enough to receive an old-age pension.

seniority is being older than other people, or more experienced or higher in rank.

sensation is the ability to feel things physically. A sensation is a physical feeling.

❏ The emotional effect of an experience can also be called a sensation. *It was a slightly jarring sensation having spent three hours with someone, only to discover they are someone else.*

❏ Someone or something that causes great interest and excitement can be called a sensation.

sensational (sensationally) ❏ If you say something is sensational, you mean it is remarkable and causes great interest and excitement. *Douglas is not the man he was when taking the title sensationally from Mike Tyson.*

❏ If you call a TV or newspaper report sensational, you mean it presents facts in a way intended to produce strong feelings of shock, anger, or excitement.

❏ If you are extremely impressed by something, you can say it is sensational.

sensationalise See sensationalize.

sensationalism (sensationalist) If you accuse someone of sensationalism or of being sensationalist, you mean they are presenting facts in a way which makes them seem worse and more shocking than they really are.

sensationalize (sensationalizing, sensationalized) (can be spelled with an 's' instead of a 'z') If someone, especially a journalist or TV reporter, sensationalizes a situation, they present the facts in a way which makes them seem worse and more shocking than they really are.

sense (sensing, sensed) ❏ Your five senses are your ability to see, smell, hear, touch, and taste.

❏ A sense is also a feeling of something being the case. *There is the comforting sense of being in the hands of a benign, sympathetic narrator.* Sense can also be used to say several people have a feeling. *There is no sense of urgency on either side.*

❏ If you **sense** something such as danger, you are aware of it although you cannot see or hear anything. ◇ If a machine or instrument **senses** something, it detects it.

❏ A **sense** is also a natural ability or talent. *...their dress sense.* ◇ **sense of humour:** see **humour.** ◇ If someone has a **sense** of something like duty or justice, they recognize it and believe in its importance.

❏ **Sense** is the ability to make good judgements and behave sensibly. *One activist praised him for having the sense to stand back once the charity could run without him.* See also **common sense.** ◇ If you say someone **talks sense,** you mean what they say is sensible.

❏ If you say something like a proposal **makes sense,** you mean it seems sensible. ◇ If you say there is **no sense** in doing something, you mean there is nothing useful to be gained by it.

❏ If you can **make sense** of something, you can understand it.

❏ If you say someone has **taken leave of their senses,** you mean they are behaving as if they have gone mad. ◇ If you talk about someone **coming to their senses,** you mean they are acting in a reasonable and sensible way after behaving rather foolishly. You can also say someone is **brought to their senses.**

❏ A **sense** of a word or expression is one of its meanings. *He was a big man in all senses of the phrase.*

❏ **In a sense** is used to say something is partly true or is true from a certain point of view. *All cathedrals should try to offer the best in music and art, to be, in a sense, a patron of the arts.* **In no sense** is used to say something is not true at all. *He is in no sense a snob.* ◇ **In a very real sense** is used, often in a rather meaningless way, to emphasize that something is so. *And when I married Ronald the following year, I did so from my father's house but then, in a very real sense, I'd never left it.*

senseless (senselessness) ❏ If you describe something as **senseless,** you mean it serves no purpose. *...the senselessness of the guerrillas' struggle.*

❏ If someone has been beaten **senseless,** they have been hit until they are unconscious.

sensibility (sensibilities) ❏ If something upsets people's **sensibilities,** it shocks or offends them.

❏ If you talk about the **sensibility** of someone like a writer or an artist, you mean their ability to experience and express deep feelings.

sensible (sensibly) ❏ A **sensible** person is able to make good decisions and judgements based on reason rather than emotion. Similarly, a **sensible** action or decision is reasonable and well thought out. *Individuals are sensibly using any spare cash they have to reduce debt.*

❏ **Sensible** things, especially clothes, are practical, rather than fashionable and attractive.

sensitise See **sensitize.**

sensitive (sensitively; sensitivity, sensitivities) ❏ If you are **sensitive** to other people's problems or feelings, you are aware of them and try to take account of them in what you do. *They're appalled by what they see as their neighbours' lack of sensitivity.* You can also say someone is **sensitive** to the good qualities of something they are dealing with. *The house has been sensitively restored over the last ten years with the help of grants from English Heritage.*

❏ **Sensitive** people are easily offended or hurt by other people's behaviour. ◇ A **sensitive** issue needs to be handled carefully, because it is likely to upset people or cause a dispute. ◇ If you talk about people's **sensitivities,** you mean things which are likely to upset them. ◇ A **sensitive** time is one when things have to be handled carefully.

❏ **Sensitivity** is also delicacy of feeling or style. *All the company danced with fine sensitivity.*

❏ If something is **sensitive** to something else, it is easily affected or harmed by it. *...light-sensitive plastic.* Similarly, people can be **sensitive** to certain substances or conditions. ◇ A **sensitive** piece of equipment responds to tiny changes or differences in things.

sensitize (sensitizing, sensitized) (*can be spelled with an 's' instead of a 'z'*) If you are **sensitized** to something like an allergen or an insect sting, you experience it and as a result suffer a more powerful reaction when it happens to you again.

sensor A **sensor** is an instrument which reacts to certain physical conditions and which can provide information or give a warning of danger. *...a blood-pressure sensor.*

sensory is used to talk about things to do with the physical senses. *...sensory loss... ...sensory pleasures.*

sensual (sensuality) **Sensual** pleasures are ones in which you indulge your physical appetites. If something arouses one of these appetites, you can describe it as **sensual** or talk about its **sensuality.** *...sensual dance rhythms.* ◇ A **sensual** person shows a fondness for physical pleasures, especially sexual ones. You can talk about the **sensuality** of someone like this.

sensuous (sensuously) You say something is **sensuous** when it is pleasing to the senses. *Pink gauze curtains billow sensuously in a boudoir full of white light.*

sent See **send.**

sentence (sentencing, sentenced) ❏ A **sentence** is the punishment a criminal receives after being found guilty in a court of law. You say the criminal is **sentenced** to a particular punishment. ◇ **pass sentence:** see **pass.** ◇ **death sentence:** see **death.** ◇ **life sentence:** see **life.**

❏ A **sentence** is one of the groups of words a piece of writing or speech is divided into. In writing, each sentence begins with a capital letter and ends with a full stop, a question mark, or an exclamation mark.

sententious (sententiously) If you say someone is being **sententious,** you mean they are trying to make wise remarks but just sound pompous. You also call the things they say **sententious.** *A new corporate era has dawned. Or to put it a little less sententiously, last week saw the beginning of two interesting trends.*

sentient (*pron:* **sen-tee-ent**) creatures have senses through which they can experience physical sensations. If you talk about the **sentient** life in a place, you mean all the creatures there that are capable of having these sensations.

sentiment ❏ If people have strong feelings about something, you can say there is **sentiment** of a particular kind. *...anti-war sentiment.* ◇ A person's **sentiments** are their opinions about something.

❏ **Sentiment** is also gentle feelings such as tenderness or sadness expressed in what someone says or writes.

sentimental (sentimentally, sentimentality; sentimentalist) ❏ You say a person is **sentimental** when they show exaggerated feelings of tenderness, affection, or sadness. You call a book, film, or song **sentimental** when it is too full of feelings of this sort. *The main weakness of his play is sentimentality.*

❑ If something you own is of **sentimental** value, it is valuable to you because of its associations with someone or something in the past, rather than because it is useful or worth a lot of money. Similarly, you can talk about something being done for **sentimental** reasons. *...theatre programmes sentimentally cherished for the occasions they recall.* People who keep things because of their associations with the past are called **sentimentalists**.

sentimentalize (sentimentalizing, sentimentalized) *(can be spelled with an 's' instead of a 'z')* When people **sentimentalize** something, they think or talk about it in a very sentimental way, overlooking all the unattractive features which it has.

sentinel is an old word for a sentry. Someone or something standing on their own like a sentry can be called a **sentinel**.

sentry (sentries) A **sentry** is a soldier who stands outside a place, guarding it.

sentry-box A **sentry-box** is a narrow shelter with an open front which can be used by a sentry on duty.

separate (separating, separated; separately, separation, separateness) ❑ If you talk about a number of **separate** things, you are emphasizing that there really are that number and that each one is individual and distinct from the others. *He has examined 650 separate American beaches... The giant mirror is being built of 36 separate 2 metre mirrors.*

❑ If things or people **separate** or are **separated**, they move apart. ◇ If one thing is **separate** from another, the two things are apart and are not connected. *The Quebecois have long upheld their cultural separateness from the English speakers in North America.*

❑ If something like an obstacle **separates** people, it prevents them reaching each other or having contact with each other. *Fans of the two teams broke through the fences that separated them... ...her wartime separation from her parents.*

❑ If people do something **separately**, they do not do it together. ◇ If two things which have been operating together are **separated**, they are made to operate separately. *...the separation of Church and State.*

❑ If a married couple **separate**, they start to live apart.

❑ If you **separate** different ideas, you distinguish between them. ◇ If some feature **separates** one person or thing from another, it shows they are different.

❑ **Separates** are individual items of women's clothing, such as skirts, tops, or trousers, which are not part of a matching outfit.

separatism (separatist) **Separatism** is a movement in which an ethnic or cultural group within a country tries to achieve independence with the object of having its own territory and government instead of being ruled by the country's government. Supporters of a movement like this are called **separatists**.

sepia *(pron: see-pee-a)* things are reddish brown, the colour of old photographs.

septic If a wound is **septic**, it has become infected.

septic tank A **septic tank** is a tank, usually underground, where sewage is broken down by bacteria.

septicaemia *(pron: sep-tis-see-mee-a)* is blood poisoning.

septuagenarian *(pron: sept-yoo-a-jin-nair-ee-an)* A **septuagenarian** is a person in their seventies.

sepulchral *(pron: sip-pulk-ral)* things are gloomy and solemn.

sepulchre *(pron: sep-pull-ker)* A **sepulchre** is a tomb or vault where dead people are buried.

sequel The **sequel** to a book or film is another one which continues the story or has the same characters. ◇ The **sequel** to an event is something else which happens after it or as a result of it.

sequence ❑ A **sequence** of things or events is a series of them coming one after the other. ◇ If things happen or are arranged in a particular **sequence**, they happen or are arranged in that order.

❑ In a film or TV programme, a **sequence** is a single uninterrupted episode. *...a chase sequence.*

sequential (sequentially) **Sequential** is used to talk about things happening or being done in a definite order or sequence. *Anthologies are things to be browsed through at leisure, rather than read sequentially.*

sequestrate (sequestrating, sequestrated; sequestration) When property is **sequestrated**, it is taken away from its owner by court authority, either because its ownership is in question or because the owner owes money or has disobeyed the court. The property is returned when the matter is settled.

sequin (sequinned *or* sequined) **Sequins** are small shiny discs sewn onto clothes as a decoration. **Sequinned** clothes are decorated with sequins.

serenade (serenading, serenaded) A **serenade** is a piece of music in several movements, usually for a small orchestra. ◇ Originally, a **serenade** was a song or piece of music performed in the evening, especially by a man under the window of the woman he loved. If a man **serenaded** a woman, he sang or played a serenade to her.

serendipity (serendipitous) **Serendipity** is a natural talent for making interesting or valuable discoveries by accident. You say a discovery made like this is **serendipitous**.

serene (serenely, serenity) ❑ If you call a place **serene** or talk about its **serenity**, you mean it is calm and peaceful. You can also say life in a place like this is **serene**.

❑ A **serene** person is quiet and calm. You can also call someone's expression **serene**. *...a serenely satisfied smile.*

serf (serfdom) In medieval Europe, **serfs** were people who worked on their master's land and could not leave it. **Serfdom** was the state of being a serf.

serge is a type of strong woollen cloth used to make coats, suits, trousers, and other clothes.

sergeant ❑ A **sergeant** is a middle-ranking NCO in the British army, the RAF, and some other armed forces. In the British army, the rank above sergeant is **staff sergeant**; in the RAF, it is **flight sergeant**.

❑ A police **sergeant** is a police officer between constable and inspector in rank.

sergeant major A **sergeant major** is a high-ranking NCO in several armed forces.

serial ❑ A **serial** is a story which is broadcast or published in several parts, usually at regular times, over a period of time.

❑ **Serial** is used to talk about someone doing a series of things of the same kind. A **serial** killer is someone who has committed a series of murders.

❏ A product's **serial number** is a special number which identifies it. Similarly, a member of the armed forces has a **serial number** which is unique to them.

serialize (serializing, serialized; serialization) *(can be spelled with an 's' instead of a 'z')* If a book is **serialized**, it is broadcast or published in a number of parts, usually at regular times, over a period of time. *The type of books chosen for serialization vary enormously.*

series ❏ A **series** of people, things, or occurrences is a number of them coming one after the other.

❏ A **series** of books is a set of them with the same format and similar subject matter, published by the same publisher. ◇ A TV or radio **series** is a set of related programmes with the same title, often with the same characters or about the same subject. ◇ A **series** of lectures or concerts is several of them given over a period of time and related to each other in some way.

serious (seriously, seriousness) ❏ A **serious** problem or situation is very bad and causes concern. *Rail traffic was seriously affected... ...the seriousness of his injuries.* ◇ When people are very concerned about something, you can say it causes **serious** concern. *The city authorities are seriously concerned at the possibility of social unrest.* ◇ If you have **serious** doubts about something, you are not at all sure it is a good idea.

❏ **Serious** is also used to describe things which require careful consideration. *...the serious business of managing a modern industrial economy.* ◇ A **serious** book or play requires thought and concentration and is not just for entertainment. You say someone who writes books or plays like this is a **serious** writer. ◇ **Serious** is used to describe other people who try to do well at something or to be an expert at something. *His work is for the serious collector.*

❏ A **serious** person is thoughtful, quiet, and rather solemn.

❏ If you are **seriously** thinking of doing something, you are considering it as a real possibility and may well do it. ◇ If you genuinely try to do something, you can say you make a **serious** attempt to do it.

❏ If you are **serious** about something, you mean what you say and are not joking. ◇ If you are taking something **seriously**, you are regarding it as important and are taking steps to deal with it. *The threat to the leadership is being treated with high seriousness by Number 10, as well as by the media.* ◇ If a person is taken **seriously**, they are regarded as important and treated with respect.

sermon A **sermon** is a talk on a religious or moral subject given during a religious service. ◇ Any speech in which someone tells you how you ought to behave can be called a **sermon.**

serpent is an old word for a snake.

serpentine is used to describe (a) animals which look like snakes. *...a long serpentine creature with a small horse-like head.* (b) things which have a curved winding shape like a snake. *...serpentine Ullswater.*

SERPS stands for 'State Earnings-Related Pension Scheme'. SERPS is a government-run scheme which pays out pensions in addition to the normal state pension. The additional amount is based on the person's earnings since entering the scheme.

serrated A **serrated** object has an edge with teeth-like points or saw-like notches along it.

serried things or people are closely packed together in a regular arrangement.

serum *(pron: seer-um)* is the clear watery part of the blood without clotting agents. A **serum** is this part of the blood taken from a person or animal that has immunity to a disease. It is injected into a person's blood to protect them from the disease. Some serums are also used as antidotes to poisons. *...snake-bite serum.*

servant ❏ A **servant** is someone employed to work in someone else's house, for example as a cleaner or a gardener.

❏ If you want to emphasize that someone's job is to help a group of people, you can say they are the **servant** of those people. *...the idea that a police officer is the servant of the community.* You can also say someone is the **servant** of something like an ideal or a cause. *...a servant of peace.*

serve (server) ❏ If something **serves** as a particular thing, it has that use or function. You can also say something **serves** a particular purpose. *...a cinema serving as a makeshift opera house.* ◇ If something **serves to** produce a particular result, it has that result.

❏ If you talk about someone **serving** their country, you mean they contribute in some way to its safety, stability, or prosperity. *...long-serving heads of African states.* ◇ If someone is a member of one of the armed forces, you say they **serve** in it. You also say a member of the armed forces **serves** in a particular place.

❏ If something **serves** an area or a community, it provides the people there with something they need or with something useful. *The temple was built to serve a mainly Thai immigrant community.*

❏ If someone in a shop **serves** you, they provide you with what you want to buy. ◇ If someone **serves** you in a restaurant, they bring the food to your table. ◇ If a restaurant **serves** particular food, they provide it for their customers to eat.

❏ If you **serve** food or **serve** it **up,** you put it on plates and present it to people. ◇ A **serving** of food is an amount given to one person at a meal. ◇ A **serving** dish or spoon is used for serving food. ◇ If a recipe or meal **serves** a certain number of people, it provides enough food for that many people.

❏ If a legal document like a writ or summons is **served** on someone or they are **served** with it, it is officially delivered or presented to them.

❏ If someone is **serving** a prison sentence, they are spending a period in jail for a crime they have committed.

❏ If you **serve out** a period of service, you continue with it until you get to the end.

❏ You can describe the treatment someone or something has received by saying they have been **served** in a particular way. *The reader has been well served by the likes of Penguin Classics, World's Classics, and Everyman Paperbacks.*

❏ If you say it **serves** someone **right** when something unpleasant happens to them, you mean they deserve it and you have no sympathy for them.

❏ If it is your **serve** in tennis or badminton, it is your turn to start play by hitting the ball or shuttlecock towards your opponent's half of the court. When you do this, you say you **serve** or are the **server.**

service (servicing, serviced) ❑ A **service** is an organization or system which provides something for the public. *...the postal and telephone services.* ◇ Some government organizations are called **services**. *...the West's intelligence services... ...the prison service.*

❑ The **services** are the army, navy, and air force.

❑ A **service** consists of journeys regularly made by planes, ships, or other vehicles between two places, taking passengers or goods.

❑ A **service** is also a type of work you pay someone to do for you.

❑ If you **do** someone a **service**, you do something which helps or benefits them. ◇ If you offer your **services**, you offer to help someone, usually by doing something you are good at. ◇ If you put yourself **at** someone's **service**, you offer to help them in some way. Similarly, you can put something you own **at** someone's **service**.

❑ If you **press** someone **into service**, you get them to do something for you. ◇ If a building or vehicle is **pressed into service**, it is taken over so it can be used for a particular purpose. ◇ If a vehicle or machine is **in service**, it is working or it can be used. Similarly, you can talk about a vehicle or machine being **out of service**.

❑ **Services** or **service areas** are places on motorways where you can stop for a rest, buy refreshments or petrol, or go to the toilet.

❑ If something **services** a group of people, it provides them with something they need. *Refuse collection can be designed and planned to service a specific area.*

❑ If someone **services** a machine, especially a vehicle, they examine it and maintain it. This type of examination and maintenance is called a **service**.

❑ **Service** is being served in a shop or restaurant.

❑ Your **service** with an organization is the period of time you have spent working for them. Similarly, the time someone spends in the armed forces is called their **service**. You can also talk about their **service** in a place or conflict.

❑ A dinner or tea **service** is a complete set of crockery for dinner or tea.

❑ A **service** is also a religious ceremony, especially a Christian or Jewish one.

❑ If you **service** a debt, you pay interest and capital repayments on it.

❑ In tennis and badminton, a person's **service** is the same as their serve.

service charge A **service charge** is (a) an amount added to your restaurant bill for the services of your waiter or waitress. (b) an amount payable to the landlord of flats for the maintenance of common areas.

service industry A **service industry** is one which provides services, such as transport or entertainment, rather than goods.

service station A **service station** is a garage which carries out repairs and maintenance and often sells petrol and oil. ◇ On a motorway, a **service station** is a place where you can rest, go to the toilet, shop, or buy refreshments and petrol.

serviceable If something is **serviceable**, it is in a good enough state to be used. ◇ You also say something is **serviceable** when it is adequate, but not especially good.

serviceman (servicewoman) A **serviceman** or **service-** **woman** is a person in the army, navy, or air force.

serviette A **serviette** is a square of cloth or paper for protecting your clothes when you are eating, and for wiping your mouth and fingers.

servile (servility) You say someone is **servile** or talk about their **servility** when they are too eager to obey someone or to do things for them.

serving See **serve**.

servitude is the condition of being a slave or of being completely under the control of another person.

sesame (*pron:* sess-am-ee) ❑ **Sesame** seeds are the seeds of a tropical plant. They are used for their edible oil, and sometimes sprinkled on the tops of loaves and rolls.

❑ If you say something is an **open sesame**, you mean it gives you access to something desirable.

session ❑ A **session** is a series of meetings of a law court or parliament. When meetings like these are taking place, you say the court or parliament is **in session**. ◇ A **session** is also a university year or one of the terms it is divided into.

❑ A **session** of an activity is a period when you do it. *...a training session.*

session musician A **session musician** is a professional musician who is not a member of a particular band, but plays for different performers, especially in a recording studio.

set (setting, set *not 'setted'*) ❑ A **set** of things or people is a number of them that belong together or have been grouped together. *...a boxed set of CDs... ...a member of her social set.*

❑ **Set** is used to say something is put into a certain state. *The birds were to be set free in the woods.* ◇ **set fire to**: see **fire**. ◇ **set light to**: see **light**.

❑ If you **set** something somewhere, you put it there in a careful or deliberate way. ◇ If you **set the table**, you place all the objects on it which you need for a meal, such as plates, cutlery, or glasses. ◇ If you **set things out**, you arrange them in a certain way for particular purposes. ◇ **set out your stall**: see **stall**.

❑ You say a building is **set** somewhere when you are describing its position. *...a studio set back from the sea.*

❑ If something is **set** into a surface, it is fixed there and does not stick out.

❑ If someone **sets** you some work or a task, they require you to do it. Similarly, someone can **set** you a target or goal.

❑ **Set** is used to describe something which is fixed and cannot be varied. *The enquiry will also examine whether set procedures were followed.* ◇ **set in your ways**: see **way**. ◇ A **set** book or text is one a schoolchild or student is expected to read for a particular course.

❑ If something is **set** to happen, it seems likely to happen. ◇ If you are **set on** a particular goal, you are determined to achieve it.

❑ When glue, jelly, or cement **sets**, it becomes hard or firm.

❑ When the sun **sets**, it goes down below the horizon.

❑ If a story or poem is **set** to music, someone writes music for it or arranges someone else's music to go with it.

❑ If you **set** a device or piece of machinery, you adjust it so that it operates in a particular way. ◇ **set a trap**: see trap.

❏ If you **set** a precedent, standard, fashion, or example, you establish it for other people to copy or try to achieve.

❏ If you **set** a time for something, you arrange for it to happen at that time. *...the setting of a deadline.* Similarly, things like prices and levels can be **set**.

❏ If you **set about** something, you begin doing it in a purposeful way. ◇ If you **set out** to do something or be something, you start trying to do it or be it.

❏ If you **set up** somewhere, you start something such as a business or professional practice. Similarly, you can **set** someone else **up**. ◇ If you **set up house** somewhere, you start a home of your own. ◇ If you **set yourself up** for something, you prepare yourself for it.

❏ If you **set** something **up**, you make the necessary preparations for it to start up or be used, or for it to work. ◇ If a structure of some kind is **set up**, it is erected somewhere.

❏ If someone **sets** you **up**, they deliberately get you into trouble by making it appear that you have done something wrong.

❏ If something **sets** people **against** each other, it makes them enemies or rivals.

❏ If something like a fact or argument is **set against** an opposite one, it is weighed up against it or compared with it.

❏ If an expense is **set against** tax, it is deducted from your income before calculating how much tax you must pay.

❏ If a characteristic **sets** someone or something **apart** from other people or things, it makes them noticeably different from them.

❏ If a play, film, or story is **set** in a particular place or period, that is where or when the action happens. ◇ The **set** for a play or a film scene is the scenery and furniture used on the stage or in the studio. ◇ **set the stage for:** see **stage**.

❏ A television **set** is a box-like object with a screen, for receiving television signals.

❏ If you **set** something **aside**, you reserve it for a special purpose or use. ◇ If a farmer **sets aside** a piece of land, he or she does not use it and receives a special payment from the government for not doing so. This practice is called **set-aside**. The land is also called **set-aside**.

❏ If you **set** something like a feeling or difficulty **aside**, you make sure it does not influence you.

❏ If something **sets** you **back** a certain amount, especially a large amount, that is how much it costs you.

❏ If something is **set back** a certain period of time, it is delayed for that period.

❏ If you **set** something **out**, you present it in a clear and organized way. *He has written a letter to The Times setting out his views.* ◇ If you **set forth** something such as principles or facts, you present them in speech or writing in a clear and organized way. ◇ If you **set down** something such as your memories, you write them down.

❏ If someone **sets down** certain rules or requirements, they say these rules or requirements must be followed.

❏ If something unpleasant **sets in**, it starts and seems likely to continue or develop.

❏ When you **set off** or **set out**, you start a journey. ◇ **set sail:** see **sail**.

❏ If something is **set off** by something else, the second thing provides a contrast to the first and makes it seem more attractive than it would have been without it. *Shocking pink satin was set off against violet and rich gold.*

❏ If something **sets off** another thing or a series of things, it causes them to begin. *The food price rises set off violent demonstrations.* ◇ If someone **sets off** a bomb or other explosive device, they detonate it.

❏ In a tennis match, a **set** is one of the groups of six or more games which make up the match.

❏ **set your face against:** see **face**. ◇ **set foot on:** see **foot**. ◇ **set your heart on:** see **heart**. ◇ **set great store by:** see **store**.

❏ See also **setting**.

set-piece In a game like football, a **set-piece** is a move like a corner kick which has been carefully rehearsed and which begins with a player taking a kick from a certain position after a break in play. In other situations, you can call an action a **set-piece** when it has been carefully planned in a similar way. ◇ In a novel or film, a **set-piece** is an episode or scene which seems complete in itself, and is often not an essential part of the story.

set square A **set square** is a flat piece of plastic or metal in the shape of a right-angled triangle which is used for drawing angles and lines.

set-to If people have a **set-to**, they have an argument or fight.

set-up A system or way of organizing things can be called a **set-up**. *Bulgaria may still face difficulties because of its unstable political set-up.*

setback If you suffer a **setback** when you are trying to achieve something, something happens which delays your progress.

sett A badger's **sett** is its burrow.

settee A **settee** is the same as a sofa.

setter A **setter** is a breed of gun dog with a silky coat and a plumed tail.

-setter is added to words to describe people who set a standard or trend. *...fashion-setters.*

setting ❏ The **setting** for something is the surroundings in which it takes place.

❏ A **setting** is one of the positions or levels which the controls of a machine can be adjusted to.

❏ See also **place setting**.

settle (settling, settled; settlement) ❏ If you **settle** in a place, you arrive there and make it your home. You can also talk about the authorities **settling** people in a place. *The settlement of civilians near such facilities is of a deliberate nature.* ◇ A **settlement** is a place where people have arrived and built their homes.

❏ If you **settle** somewhere or **settle in**, you make yourself comfortable. ◇ If you **settle down** to something, you make yourself comfortable so you can concentrate on it.

❏ You also say someone **settles down** when they begin to lead an orderly routine life and behave in a responsible way. Settling down often involves getting married and having children, or taking on a permanent steady job. If someone continues to live like this, you say they have a **settled** way of life.

❏ If a situation **settles down**, it becomes calmer and more stable. ◇ If something **settles** you or **settles** your nerves, it makes you calmer after you have been upset or nervous.

❏ **Settled** is used to describe something which does not

change very much. *...the forecasts of sunny, settled spells.*

❑ If you **settle** a bill, you pay it. *Some firms give a discount for early settlement.* ◇ If you **settle** a debt, you repay the money you owe.

❑ If you **settle for** something, you accept it although it is not what you really want.

❑ If you **settle on** something or someone, you choose them after considering other alternatives.

❑ If something is **settled**, it has all been decided and arranged.

❑ If you **settle** a problem, you succeed in sorting it out.

❑ When people **settle** an argument or conflict, they solve it by reaching an agreement. ◇ A **settlement** is an official agreement to end a conflict.

❑ If a legal dispute is **settled** out of court, it is ended without having to go to court, for example by one side agreeing to accept money or an apology from the other.

❑ If something **settles** at a certain level, it stabilizes at that level after a period of going up and down.

❑ If something like dust **settles**, it falls or sinks slowly and forms a covering over something.

❑ If an insect **settles** on something, it lands there.

❑ If a mood or a feeling **settles** over a place, it strongly affects the people there.

❑ A **settle** is a long wooden seat with sides and a high back.

settler Settlers are people who go to live in a place where nobody has lived before, or which other people have been driven out of.

seven is the number 7. ◇ **at sixes and sevens:** see **six**.

seventeen (seventeenth) Seventeen is the number 17.

seventh ❑ The **seventh** item in a series is the one counted as number 7. ◇ A **seventh** or one **seventh** is the fraction ⅐.

❑ **seventh heaven:** see **heaven**.

seventy (seventieth, seventies) Seventy is the number 70. ◇ The **seventies** was the period from 1970 to 1979. ◇ If someone is in their **seventies**, they are aged 70 to 79.

sever (severing, severed; severance) ❑ If you **sever** a connection with someone, you end it. This is called the **severing** or **severance** of the connection. *Parliament ordered the immediate severing of all ties with Serbia.*

❑ If a part of someone's body is **severed**, it is cut off. You can talk about other things being **severed** like this. *French fishermen allegedly used wirecutters to sever the nets.*

❑ If one group of people is **severed** from another, they are separated completely and are unable to reach each other. Similarly, you can talk about a piece of land being severed from another piece.

❑ **Severance** is also the process of getting rid of employees who are no longer needed, for example because their work has been taken over by machinery. A **severance** payment is money paid to someone who is got rid of like this.

several is used in an imprecise way to talk about a number of things or people, when the number is more than two but not large. *...several hundred pounds of explosives.*

❑ Several is also used to mean separate or different. *They were both as militant as ever in their several ways.*

severance See **sever**.

severe (severer, severest; severely, severity) ❑ Severe is used to emphasize how bad or serious something is. You talk

about the **severity** of something like this. *More than 100,000 homes were severely damaged or destroyed.*

❑ A **severe** person is strict or harsh. A punishment can also be **severe**. *Panda hunters and traders are punished with extreme severity.* Criticism can also be **severe**.

sew (sewing, sewed, have sewn) ❑ If you **sew**, you join things together, usually pieces of cloth, using a needle and thread or a sewing machine. If you **sew** something such as clothes, you make them in this way. A person's **sewing** is something they are making. If you **sew** something onto something else, you attach it using a needle and thread.

❑ If you have something **sewn up**, you have arranged things so you are certain of success.

sewage is water containing waste matter from homes and industries and also water from drains, all of which is carried away along sewers to be treated at a sewage works.

sewage works A **sewage works** or **sewage treatment works** is a place where sewage is treated so it can be disposed of safely.

sewer A **sewer** is a large channel, usually underground, which carries away sewage from homes, drains, and industries.

sewerage is the system of pipes and sewers used to take sewage away from homes, drains, and industries. ◇ Sewage is sometimes called **sewerage**.

sewing machine A **sewing machine** is a machine which sews by means of a needle driven by an electric motor. Old-fashioned sewing machines were operated by pedals or by turning a handle.

sewn See **sew**.

sex (sexes) ❑ Sex is a physical activity involving two people whose aim is sexual pleasure, and sometimes the production of children. When people talk about **sex**, they usually mean an act which involves a man's penis entering a woman's vagina. When a man and a woman perform an act like this, you say they **have sex**. ◇ Sex is used to talk about various things to do with sex. *...a sex scandal.* See also **safe sex**.

❑ Sex is also the division of human beings and other living things into male and female. *What actually determines sex?* ◇ The **sex** of a person or other living thing is whether they are male or female. *...young Europeans of both sexes.* ◇ If a person has a **sex change**, they undergo medical treatment and an operation which changes their body's sexual characteristics to that of the opposite sex.

sex appeal If you say someone has **sex appeal**, you mean they are sexually attractive.

sex education is teaching children about sex and matters connected with it such as contraception and protection against disease.

sex object If a woman is treated as a **sex object**, she is treated as though she is important only for her sexual attractiveness and not for other reasons such as her intelligence or skills.

sex shop A **sex shop** is a shop which sells things connected with sexual pleasure such as pornographic magazines, videos, and special clothing and equipment.

sex symbol A **sex symbol** is someone such as a film star who is very attractive to the opposite sex.

sexagenarian (*pron:* sex-a-jin-**nair**-ee-an) A **sexagenarian**

is a person in their sixties.

sexiness See sexy.

sexism (sexist) **Sexism** is prejudice and discrimination against members of one sex, especially women. **Sexist** is used to describe people and things that show prejudice of this sort. ...*a sexist joke.*

sextant A **sextant** is an instrument for navigating, especially at sea. It consists of a small telescope for locating a heavenly body like the sun, and protractors for measuring the angle between this body and the horizon.

sextet A **sextet** is (a) a piece of music for six instruments or singers. (b) a group of six people who sing or play music together.

sexton In the past, a **sexton** was a person employed by the church authorities whose main job was to dig the graves in a churchyard.

sextuplet Sextuplets are six children born to the same mother at the same time.

sexual (sexually) ❏ **Sexual** activities and feelings are connected with the act of sex or with desire for sex. ...*sexual desire*... ...*sexually abused children.* ◇ If a person has **sexual relations** with someone, they have sex.

❏ **Sexual** is used to talk about the biological process by which people, animals, and plants produce young. ...*sexual reproduction.* ◇ **Sexual** is also used to talk about things connected with the differences between men and women. ...*sexual equality.*

sexual harassment is persistent unwelcome behaviour of a sexual nature, especially in the workplace. It can consist of touching a person's body, looking at them in a sexual way, or making indecent remarks.

sexual intercourse See intercourse.

sexuality A person's **sexuality** is their ability to experience sexual feelings, or their sexual orientation.

sexually transmitted disease A sexually transmitted disease is a disease such as syphilis or AIDS which is mainly passed on through sexual contact. 'Sexually transmitted disease' is sometimes shortened to 'STD'.

sexy (sexier, sexiest; sexiness) ❏ If you say someone is **sexy**, you mean they are sexually attractive. ...*her fears about losing her sexiness.* ◇ Things which excite people sexually can also be called **sexy**. *The clothes are classic but sexy and well-cut.* ◇ A **sexy** film or novel has a lot of sex in it.

❏ Non-sexual things are sometimes described as **sexy** when people find them exciting and stimulating. ...*the less sexy bits of the business such as distribution and licensing.*

shabby (shabbier, shabbiest; shabbily, shabbiness) ❏ If you say a person's clothes are **shabby**, you mean they are worn and scruffy. You can also call the person wearing them **shabby**. ◇ If you say something like a building is **shabby**, you mean it has deteriorated and is in a bad condition. ...*the shabbiness of the room.*

❏ You say someone's behaviour is **shabby** when they behave in an unfair or dishonest way. *He has been treated shabbily by his party.*

shack A **shack** is a small makeshift dwelling built from pieces of things like wood and metal.

shackle (shackling, shackled) ❏ **Shackles** are two metal rings joined by a chain which are fastened around a person's wrists or ankles to prevent them from moving or escaping. ◇ If a person is **shackled**, they are unable to move or escape because they have shackles or some

sort of chains restraining them.

❏ You also say someone is **shackled** when they are prevented by laws or other restrictions from doing something they want to. ◇ **Shackles** are restrictions which prevent you doing what you want to. ◇ If you are **shackled** to someone or something, you are closely linked with them in some way and cannot break free from them.

shade (shading, shaded) ❏ **Shade** is an area which is cooler and darker than other parts because the sun does not reach it. ◇ If something is **shaded** by something like a tree, it is protected by it from the heat or glare of the sun. ◇ A **shade** is something which partly covers an electric light and prevents it shining too brightly in your eyes. ◇ **Shades** are sunglasses. ◇ In the US, **shades** are also blinds.

❏ If something puts something else **in the shade,** it is so impressive it makes the other thing seem unimportant by comparison.

❏ A **shade** of a colour is one variation of it. For example, navy blue is a shade of blue.

❏ The **shades** of something are its different aspects, especially when there is only a slight difference between them. *Political parties of any shade may register.*

❏ A **shade** means a very small amount. *He sounded a shade defensive.*

❏ A person's **shade** is their ghost.

❏ If you say **shades of** someone or something, you mean the thing you have just mentioned reminds you of that person or thing. *The debate had been brought forward by a week, in an effort to avert the protest planned by the students' leaders – shades of 1968, perhaps?*

❏ If one thing **shades** into another, it gradually changes into it, little by little.

shadiness See shady.

shadow ❏ A **shadow** is a dark shape on a surface caused by something standing between a light and the surface. ◇ The **shadows** are the dark parts of a place which the light does not reach.

❏ If someone **shadows** you, they follow you very closely, to see what you are doing, to stop you doing something, or to protect you.

❏ If you **shadow** what someone else does, you do the same thing.

❏ In Britain, the **shadow cabinet** consists of members of the main opposition party. There is a shadow cabinet member for each member of the official cabinet and they speak for their party on the same things as that person. ...*the shadow Secretary of State for Wales.*

❏ If something casts a **shadow** over something else, it prevents it being completely happy or successful. ◇ If someone lives **in the shadow** of a famous person, they are known only because of their connection with that person, rather than because of their own achievements or talents.

❏ If you say there is not a **shadow of a doubt** about something, you mean there is no doubt whatever that it is true.

❏ If you say someone is a **shadow of their former self,** you mean they are nothing like as vigorous or lively as they used to be, for example because they are ill.

shadow-boxing You say someone is **shadow-boxing** when they threaten to do something just to test people's reactions, rather than because they really mean to do it.

shadowy is used to describe people and activities that very little is known about. *...the shadowy world of spies.*

❏ Shadowy places are dark and full of shadows. Things which can just be seen in places like these are also called **shadowy**.

shady (shadier, shadiest; shadiness) ❏ **Shady** activities are dishonest or illegal. You can also call the people involved in them **shady**. *...shady deals... Their involvement with a man of Scarpia's known shadiness is inexplicable.*

❏ **Shady** places are cool because there is a lot of shade there.

shaft ❏ A **shaft** is a vertical passageway in a building or mine for a lift to travel up and down.

❏ The **shaft** of something like a spear, tool, or golf club is the straight part which you hold.

❏ A **shaft** is also a revolving rod which transfers motion or power from one part of a machine to another. *...the transmission shaft.*

❏ A **shaft** of light is a narrow beam of light.

❏ A **shaft** of humour or wit is a humorous or witty remark, especially one made as an attack on someone or something.

shaggy animals have a lot of long hair or fur hanging down in an untidy way.

Shah In the past, the ruler of Iran was called the **Shah**. Some other Asian countries, including Afghanistan, have also had rulers called **Shahs**.

shake (shaking, shook, have shaken) ❏ If something **shakes**, it moves quickly backwards and forwards or up and down. If you **shake** something or give it a **shake**, you make it move like this. ◇ If someone is **shaking**, they are trembling violently and unable to control their movements because they are nervous, afraid, or ill.

❏ If something unpleasant or unexpected **shakes** you, it shocks, upsets, or disturbs you. ◇ If something **shakes** your ideas or beliefs, it makes you less certain about them. Similarly, if something **shakes** your confidence or determination, it makes you less confident or determined.

❏ If you **shake hands** with someone, you grasp their right hand with your own. Typically, you do this to greet someone, to say goodbye, or to congratulate someone on something they have achieved.

❏ If you **shake your head**, you move it from side to side repeatedly. You do this as a way of saying 'no' or of expressing a feeling such as disbelief or wonder.

❏ If you **shake your fist** at someone, you hold it up and wave it at them vigorously to show you are angry with them.

❏ If you **shake off** something which is troubling you, you succeed in getting rid of it.

❏ If someone or something **shakes** you out of a feeling such as complacency or apathy, they do something which rouses you into action of some kind. ◇ If someone **shakes up** an organization, system, or profession, they make major changes to it. The changes are called a **shake-up**.

❏ If you say something is **no great shakes**, you mean it is not very good or effective.

shake-out If there is a **shake-out** of an organization or an industry, the workforce is reduced.

shake-up See shake.

shaky (shakier, shakiest) ❏ You say things are **shaky** when they seem unlikely to succeed or last.

❏ If an object is **shaky**, it is unsteady and shakes about.

❏ If a person is **shaky**, their body shakes or their hands shake, because they are nervous, ill, or very old. You can also say a person's hands are **shaky**.

shale is smooth soft rock which breaks easily into thin layers.

shall ❏ You use **shall** when you are talking about something you are going to do, or something you and someone else are going to do. You also use **shall** when you are talking about something which is going to happen to you, or to you and someone else. *Soon we shall know the name of the novel that has won the Booker prize.*

❏ **Shall** is used to say something must happen or be done, especially in official or legal documents. *The state shall regulate all domestic and foreign trade... No picture shall be produced which will lower moral standards.*

❏ You use **shall** in questions where you are asking for advice. *How shall we spend the money?*

shallot (pron: shal-lot) **Shallots** are vegetables similar to small onions. They are eaten cooked or pickled.

shallow (shallows, shallowness) ❏ **Shallow** is used to describe something which is not deep. *...a shallow baking dish.* ◇ The parts of an area of water which are not very deep are sometimes called the **shallows**.

❏ If you say someone is **shallow**, you mean they are not capable of thinking deeply about things. *He is impatient of intellectual shallowness or pretension.*

sham If you say something is **sham** or a **sham**, you mean it is not what it is supposed to be. *...sham marriages... The students believe the forthcoming elections will be a sham.*

shaman (pron: sham-an) A **shaman** is a priest in some religions who is thought to be able to influence and control good and evil spirits.

shamble (shambling, shambled) ❏ If you say something, for example an organization or a place, is a **shambles**, you mean it is in disorder or confusion.

❏ A large slow clumsy person is sometimes described as **shambling**. You describe the way someone like this moves by saying they **shamble** along or **shamble** around.

shambolic is used to describe things which are disorganized and chaotic. *...shambolic public services.*

shame (shaming, shamed) ❏ **Shame** is an uncomfortable feeling of regret and guilt you have when you have done something wrong. You can also feel **shame** when someone close to you does something wrong, or when your country behaves towards another country in a way you think is wrong.

❏ If you say something **shames** someone, you mean it makes them ashamed, or you think it ought to. *It has been a bad week for Bosnia's Muslims and a shaming one for the outside world.* ◇ If you are mentioning a situation which you think someone should be ashamed of, you can say it is **to their shame**. *Britain, to our shame, is in no position to lecture its allies.* ◇ If you **shame** someone **into** doing something, you get them to do it by making them feel ashamed that they have not done it already.

❏ If you say something is a **shame**, you mean it is regrettable. *It would clearly be a great shame if work like this were not carried out.*

❏ If you say something **shames** something else or **puts it to shame**, you mean it is so much better that it makes the other thing look unimpressive by comparison.

shamefaced If someone is **shamefaced,** they are ashamed or embarrassed about something they have said or done.

shameful (shamefully) If you say someone's behaviour is **shameful,** you mean they ought to be ashamed of it. *He was treated shamefully.* ◇ **Shameful** is used to describe something which makes people feel ashamed, although it may not actually be their fault. *Getting into debt was considered a shameful failure.*

shameless (shamelessly) If you say someone's behaviour is **shameless,** you mean they do wrong or immoral things without feeling ashamed. *Delegates responded well to a shamelessly manipulative pro-European speech.*

shammy A **shammy** is the same as a chamois leather.

shampoo A **shampoo** is a liquid soap or detergent which lathers and which you use to wash things, for example carpets or your hair.

shamrock The **shamrock** is a plant with three small leaves on each stem which is the national emblem of Ireland. There is no actual species of plant called a shamrock, and the name is used to talk about several similar plants, including some types of clover.

shandy (shandies) **Shandy** is a drink made of beer or lager mixed with lemonade.

Shangri-La If you call a remote place a **Shangri-la,** you mean everything seems so wonderful there that it seems like paradise.

shanty (shanties) ❑ A **shanty** is a small rough dwelling made of bits and pieces of flimsy material such as tin or wood. A place where many dwellings of this kind have been built is called a **shanty town.**

❑ A **shanty** is also a song sailors used to sing at sea while doing work such as pulling in ropes.

shape (shaping, shaped) ❑ The **shape** of something is its form or outline, for example whether it is round or square. You use **-shaped** when you are describing something's shape. *...a heart-shaped silver balloon.*

❑ You can call a person, animal, or object a **shape** when you cannot see them clearly, because it is too dark or because they are too far away.

❑ Things like circles, squares, and triangles can be called **shapes.**

❑ If you **shape** a material, you give it a particular shape.

❑ When people **shape** something like a new organization, they help it to develop in a certain way. ◇ The **shape** of something, for example an organization or system, is the way it is organized or structured.

❑ If you say something is **taking shape,** you mean it is beginning to develop and take on a definite structure or form. ◇ If you say something is **shaping up,** you mean it is developing the way you want it to.

❑ If something is **shaped** by events or circumstances, it has a certain form because of them. *Munro's stories are shaped by life in rural Ontario.*

❑ You can describe the general state or condition of something by saying it is **in good shape** or **in bad shape.** If you get something **in shape** or **into shape,** you get it into a satisfactory condition. ◇ If you say a person is **in shape** or **in good shape,** you mean they are healthy and fit. If they are **out of shape,** they are unfit.

❑ You use **in the shape of** when you are saying precisely what you mean after describing something in a general way. *The Voyager has a European rival in the shape of the Renault Espace.*

❑ If you say something is **the shape of things to come,** you mean it is an early example of something which will become common in the future.

shapeless If you say something is **shapeless,** you mean it does not have a definite shape, or its shape is unattractive.

shapely If you say something is **shapely,** you mean it has an attractive shape.

shard A **shard** is a fragment of broken pottery or glass.

share (sharing, shared) ❑ If you **share** something with someone else, you both use it.

❑ If something like an amount of money is **shared** between people or **shared out,** they each get some of it. The amount each person gets is called their **share.** Similarly, people can **share** something like power. You can talk about a **share-out** of money or power.

❑ If people **share** a task, they each do some of it. You say each person does their **share** of a task. People can also **share** duties or responsibilities.

❑ If something goes wrong and it is the fault of more than one person, you can talk about people **sharing** the responsibility or blame.

❑ If you say someone has had their **share** of misfortunes, you mean they have had a lot of them. You can also say someone has had **more than their fair share** of misfortunes.

❑ If people **share** a feeling, characteristic, or opinion, each of them has it.

❑ If you **share** something like a piece of news or information, you tell someone else about it.

❑ In a competition, if two people or teams **share** the lead, they have the same number of points and are ahead of everyone else.

❑ A company's **shares** are the equal parts its capital stock is divided into. People buy shares for investment purposes because they may rise in value and also because ownership of shares carries a right to a part of the company's profits.

shareholder (shareholding) People who own shares in a company are called its **shareholders.** You say each person has a **shareholding** in the company.

shark ❑ **Sharks** are large powerful fish with long bodies and several rows of sharp teeth. Some species of shark attack people.

❑ If you call a person a **shark,** you mean they try to swindle people out of their money, for example by getting them to spend too much on something, or by buying things from them at too low a price. ◇ **loan shark:** see **loan.**

sharp (sharply, sharpness) ❑ A **sharp** object has a very thin edge or a pointed end and can cut or pierce things easily. ◇ **Sharp** is used to describe other things which are pointed rather than rounded. *...a sharp collar.*

❑ A **sharp** bend in a road is a place where it changes direction very suddenly. Similarly, you can talk about a vehicle making a **sharp** turn.

❑ A **sharp** change in something is a significant one which happens suddenly. *Theft from farms has risen sharply this year.*

❏ If something is **in sharp contrast** to something else, it is noticeably different from it.

❏ If you say someone is **sharp**, you mean they are clever and think quickly. *At first, he lacked the sharpness he had shown against Chang.* You can also say someone has a **sharp** brain or **sharp** intelligence.

❏ If you call something someone does **sharp practice,** you mean it is cunning and dishonest.

❏ **Sharp** is also used to describe things people say or write which are harshly critical of someone or something. *Sharp words were exchanged between Spain and Cuba.*

❏ You say there are **sharp** differences between people when they disagree strongly about something.

❏ A **sharp** action is sudden and abrupt. *She braked sharply.* ◇ In sport, **sharp** is used to describe actions which are skilful and accurate. *His volleys were sharp and decisive.*

❏ If an image is **sharp**, it is very clear and distinct. *Scientists said they were amazed at the sharpness of the first picture.* ◇ If something is brought **into sharp focus** or **sharp relief**, it is made more obvious.

❏ If you call someone's clothes **sharp**, you mean they are smart and fashionable.

❏ A **sharp** pain is sudden and very painful. ◇ If someone is **at the sharp end of** something difficult or unpleasant, they suffer or experience the worst aspects of it.

❏ **short sharp shock: see shock.**

❏ If something has a **sharp** taste, it tastes bitter and acid.

❏ **Sharp** after a time means precisely at that time. *They always kick you out at 2.30pm sharp.*

❏ In music, **sharp** is used to talk about a note a semitone higher than another note. For example, F sharp is a semitone higher than F. 'Sharp' is usually written ♯. ◇ If a note is played or sung **sharp**, it is slightly higher than it should be.

sharp-eyed If someone is **sharp-eyed**, they are quick to see or notice things.

sharp-suited men wear very smart elegant suits.

sharpen (sharpening, sharpened; sharpener) ❏ If you **sharpen** something like a knife or a pencil, you make its edge or point sharper. A **sharpener** is a device for sharpening something. ◇ If you say people are **sharpening their knives**, you mean they are preparing to criticize someone severely or to harm them in some way.

❏ If you **sharpen** something or **sharpen** it **up**, you make it more effective. ◇ If you **sharpen** your ability to do something, you improve it by practice. Similarly, you can **sharpen** other people's abilities by training them.

❏ If a bad situation **sharpens** or is **sharpened**, it gets worse.

sharpish If you do something **sharpish**, you do it quickly and without delay.

sharpshooter A **sharpshooter** is an expert marksman, especially with a rifle.

shatter (shattering, shattered) ❏ If something **shatters** or is **shattered**, it is broken into a lot of small pieces.

❏ If something like a belief or hope is **shattered**, it is destroyed completely. ◇ You can also say the peace in a place is **shattered** when violence breaks out there.

❏ If someone **shatters** a record, they break it by a large margin.

❏ If you are **shattered** by something that happens, you are extremely shocked and upset by it. *...the shattering ef-*

fect of his suicide on his favourite daughter. ◇ People also say they are **shattered** when they are exhausted.

shave (shaving, shaved) ❏ When a man **shaves** or has a **shave**, he removes the hair from his face with a razor. People also remove hair from other parts of their body in this way. **Shaving** is used to describe equipment used for shaving. *...shaving foam.* ◇ **close shave: see close.**

❏ If a price or rate is reduced by a very small amount, you can say it is **shaved** by that amount. Similarly, an athlete can **shave** a very small amount off a record.

❏ **Shavings** are very thin pieces of something cut from a larger piece. *...wood shavings.*

shaven is used to describe a person's head when it has been shaved. *...shaven-headed youths.* See also **clean-shaven.**

shaver A **shaver** is an electric device for shaving hair.

shawl A **shawl** is a large soft piece of cloth or knitting for wrapping around a person's shoulders or around a baby, to keep them warm.

she ❏ You use **she** to talk about a woman or girl you have already mentioned.

❏ **She** is sometimes used to talk about a nation. *Between 1803 and 1805 Britain came the closest she ever came before 1916 to being a nation in arms.* ◇ **She** is also used to talk about a ship, car, or other vehicle. *Hoverspeed Great Britain will now go to Portsmouth where she'll sail regular services across the Channel.*

sheaf (sheaves) ❏ A **sheaf** of papers is a bundle of them.

❏ A **sheaf** of corn is a bundle of ripe corn plants tied together.

shear (shearing, sheared, have shorn *or* have sheared) ❏ **Shears** are a garden tool like a large pair of scissors with long blades, used especially for trimming hedges.

❏ When people **shear** animals, especially sheep, they cut off their wool. See also **shorn.**

sheath A **sheath** is a close-fitting covering for something like a sword or knife. ◇ A **sheath** is also a condom.

sheath knife A **sheath knife** is a knife with a heavy handle and a blade which is sharp on one side.

sheathe (sheathing, sheathed) You say something is **sheathed** in a covering of some sort when the covering fits very closely to it. ◇ If you **sheathe** a sword or a knife, you put it back into its sheath.

sheaves See **sheaf.**

shed (shedding, shed *not 'shedded'*) ❏ A **shed** is a small building for storing things, for example garden tools. ◇ A **shed** is also a large building used as a store or workshop.

❏ If someone **sheds** their clothes, they take them off. Similarly, snakes and some other creatures can **shed** their skins. ◇ If a lorry **sheds** its load, the load falls off into the road. ◇ If you **shed** weight, you lose it as a result of dieting or exercise. ◇ If a company or other organization **sheds** some of its employees, it makes them redundant.

❏ If someone **sheds light on** something, they increase people's knowledge or understanding of it.

❏ If someone **sheds blood,** they kill or wound someone else. ◇ If someone is prepared to **shed** their own **blood,** they are willing to die to achieve something important.

❏ If you **shed a tear** or **tears,** you cry. ◇ If you say someone will **shed few tears** over something, you mean they will not be sorry about it at all.

sheen ❑ If a surface has a **sheen**, it is smooth and shiny.

❑ If something loses its **sheen**, it seems less impressive or admirable.

sheep (*plural*: sheep) ❑ **Sheep** are animals with thick woolly coats kept for their meat or wool. ◇ If you say people behave **like sheep**, you mean if one person does something, all the others do it.

❑ If something **separates the sheep from the goats**, it enables you to see which people are better at something than others.

❑ **black sheep**: see **black**.

sheepdog A **sheepdog** is any dog trained to control sheep, or any breed of dog originally used for this task.

sheepish (sheepishly) If someone looks **sheepish**, they look embarrassed because they have done or said something silly. *They grinned sheepishly on realizing what they had done.*

sheepskin A **sheepskin** is the wool-covered skin from a dead sheep. Sheepskins are often made into rugs or coats.

sheer is used to say something is being experienced to its fullest extent. *...the sheer beauty of the sound... Obviously, my immediate reaction is sheer delight.* ◇ If you say something is **sheer** luck, you mean it is the result of luck rather than anything else.

❑ A **sheer** cliff or drop is vertical or nearly vertical.

❑ **Sheer** fabrics are very fine and therefore transparent.

sheet ❑ A **sheet** is a thin covering for a bed.

❑ A **sheet** of something like metal, glass, or wood is a flat thin piece cut in a regular shape.

❑ A **sheet** of paper is a rectangular piece of it. A piece of paper containing information is often called a **sheet**. *...a song sheet.*

❑ An **ice sheet** is a thick layer of ice covering a very large area.

❑ If it is raining in **sheets**, it is raining so heavily it is difficult to see anything.

❑ If you say someone has a **clean sheet**, you mean they have a good record and have never done anything wrong or dishonest, or made a bad mistake.

sheet music is music printed on single sheets of paper or on sheets fastened together without a hard cover.

sheeting is a material such as plastic, cloth, or metal, used as a covering.

sheikh (*or* sheik) (*usual pron*: shake) A **sheikh** is an Arab chief or ruler. ◇ A **sheikh** is also a Muslim religious leader.

shekel The **shekel** is the unit of currency in Israel.

shelf (shelves) ❑ A **shelf** is a ledge for keeping things on, typically made of wood, metal, or glass. Shelves are attached to a wall or are part of a piece of furniture.

❑ If you buy something **off the shelf**, you get it ready-made, usually from existing stock.

❑ A **shelf** is also a natural ledge of ice or rock.

shelf-life The **shelf-life** of a product, especially food, is the length of time it is usable or can exist without deteriorating. ◇ The **shelf-life** of something else is how long it can be expected to last or survive.

shell (shelling) ❑ A **shell** is an explosive device fired from a large gun over long distances. If a place is **shelled**, shells are fired at it.

❑ The **shell** of an egg or nut is its hard outer casing. If

you **shell** an egg or nut, you remove its shell. Similarly, if you **shell** peas, you remove them from their pods.

❑ The **shell** of a sea creature such as a winkle is its hard outer protective covering. ◇ The **shell** of a tortoise or snail is the hard covering on its back.

❑ If someone **comes out of their shell**, they are no longer quiet, shy, and reserved.

❑ The **shell** of something like a building or car is its frame, around which the rest of it is built.

❑ If you **shell out** for something, you pay a lot of money for it.

shell-shock (shell-shocked) **Shell-shock** is a mental illness affecting people who have had horrific experiences in battle and have been close to many explosions. You say people suffering from this illness are **shell-shocked**. ◇ You also say people are **shell-shocked** when they have had a bad experience or some bad news and are unable to think clearly or do very much because of it.

shell suit A **shell suit** is a loose casual lined garment in bright colours consisting of trousers and a top, made of a lightweight, slightly shiny material. Shell suits are worn by men and women.

shellfire is the firing of shells during a battle or conflict.

shellfish (*plural*: shellfish) are sea creatures such as mussels, lobsters, and oysters which have a hard outer protective shell around them.

shelter (sheltering, sheltered) ❑ A **shelter** is a building or covered place providing protection from bad weather or danger. If something **shelters** you or provides **shelter**, it gives protection of this kind. ◇ If you **shelter** somewhere or **take shelter**, you go somewhere where you are protected from bad weather or other harm. ◇ A **sheltered** place is protected from bad weather.

❑ If something is **sheltered** from something which could harm it, it is protected from it.

❑ If someone has had a **sheltered** upbringing, they have been protected from experiences which could harm or upset them and are therefore rather gullible and innocent.

❑ **Sheltered** accommodation consists of small dwelling units supervised by a warden. It is designed for elderly people or for other people who want homes of their own but need some kind of supervision or help.

shelve (shelving, shelved) ❑ If a problem or proposal is **shelved**, it is put on one side, to be dealt with later.

❑ **Shelves** is the plural of 'shelf'. ◇ If you **shelve** objects, especially books, you put them on shelves. ◇ **Shelving** is a set or system of shelves.

shenanigans Various kinds of irregular behaviour which other people find shocking or amusing are called **shenanigans**. Sometimes the word refers to sexual behaviour, sometimes to acts of trickery or deception involving money.

shepherd (shepherdess, shepherdesses) ❑ A **shepherd** is a person whose job is to look after a herd of sheep. In the past, a female shepherd was called a **shepherdess**.

❑ If you **shepherd** a group of people somewhere, you guide them to make sure they reach the right place.

shepherd's pie is a dish consisting of minced meat, especially lamb, covered with a layer of mashed potato.

sherbet is a sweet dry powder which tastes fizzy and is eaten as a sweet or used to make a drink.

sheriff ❑ In the US, a **sheriff** is a person who is elected to make sure the law is obeyed in a particular county.

❑ In Scotland, a **sheriff** is a legal officer whose chief duty is to act as judge in a Sheriff Court. These courts deal with all but the most serious crimes and with most civil actions.

❑ The **sheriff** of an English or Welsh county is a person appointed by the monarch to carry out ceremonial duties.

sherpa Sherpas are a group of people who live on the slopes of the Himalayas in Nepal. They are well known for their abilities as mountain guides.

sherry (sherries) Sherry is a fortified white wine originally from the Jerez region of southern Spain.

Shetland pony A Shetland pony is a very small strong pony with long shaggy hair.

shibboleth A shibboleth is a principle or practice, especially one which is thought of as old-fashioned and no longer appropriate.

shield ❑ A shield is a large piece of a strong material such as metal or plastic, carried for protection by someone likely to be involved in fighting. ◇ If someone or something **shields** you, they protect you from harm or danger by being between you and the danger.

❑ Other things which provide protection of some kind are called **shields**. *Greenpeace intends to form a human shield to protect the whales.* When people or things are protected from harm or danger, you can say they are **shielded** from it.

❑ A shield is also a sports trophy.

shift ❑ If you **shift** something somewhere, you move it there. If something **shifts**, it moves slightly. *...shifting sand dunes.*

❑ A **shift** in a situation or in something like a policy is a change in it. When something like this changes, you can say it **shifts**.

❑ When a responsibility or duty is transferred to a different person, you can say it is **shifted** to them. Similarly, you can talk about blame being **shifted** from one person to another.

❑ When a kind of work goes on continuously, people often work set periods called **shifts**. The people who work a particular shift are themselves called a **shift**. *Most of the morning shift at the shipyard stopped work.*

❑ A shift is also a loose-fitting dress or petticoat.

❑ shifting sands: see sand. ◇ See also **red shift**.

shift key A shift key on a typewriter or computer keyboard is the button you press to make the next letter you type a capital or to make it print the symbols or punctuation marks appearing on the top row of some keys.

shifty (shiftiness) Shifty is used to describe people who behave in a cunning and deceitful way. *He had begun to develop a reputation for shiftiness and hypocrisy.*

shilling Before the change to decimal currency in 1971, the shilling was a British coin worth 5p. ◇ Kenya has a unit of currency called a **shilling**, and so do Somalia, Tanzania, and Uganda.

shilly-shally (shilly-shallies, shilly-shallying, shilly-shallied) If you say someone is **shilly-shallying**, you mean they keep putting off making a decision about something.

shimmer (shimmering, shimmered) If something **shimmers**, it shines with a faint unsteady light, like the moon does when reflected in water. ◇ You also say something

shimmers when you see it in the distance in hot conditions and it seems to tremble slightly in the heat.

shin (shinning, shinned) ❑ A person's **shin** is the front part of their leg between their knee and their ankle. The bone in this part of the leg is called the **shin bone** or tibia.

❑ If you **shin up** something, you climb it quickly and easily.

shine (shining, shone) ❑ When the sun, a star, or something like a torch **shines**, it gives off a bright light. ◇ If you **shine** a torch or searchlight on something, you direct its light there.

❑ If something like metal **shines**, it gleams because light is reflected off it. If you **shine** something, you make it gleam by rubbing or polishing it.

❑ If you put a **shine** on something, you improve the impression it makes. ◇ If something loses its **shine**, it is no longer as impressive or important as it once was. ◇ If something **takes the shine off** something such as a victory or success, it makes it less impressive.

❑ If you **shine** at an activity or skill, you are particularly good at it. ◇ If something like a feeling or a quality **shines** from someone, it is very obvious that they have it. ◇ **Shining** is used to talk about behaviour and personal qualities which are outstandingly good and much admired. *...a shining reputation.*

shingle is small pieces of stone you find on the sea shore or the edge of a river.

shingles is a disease, mainly affecting elderly people, which causes a rash of painful red spots, usually on just one side of the body. Shingles is caused by the same virus as chicken pox.

Shinto is the main religion of Japan. Its followers worship many gods, who they believe live in places like rivers, mountains, and trees.

shiny (shinier, shiniest) Shiny things have a gleaming surface and reflect light.

ship (shipping, shipped) ❑ A **ship** is a large boat which carries passengers or cargo. ◇ **Shipping** is used to talk about ships in general. *All shipping in the vicinity was directed to the scene... ...shipping forecasts.*

❑ If things or people are **shipped** somewhere, they are taken there by ship or some other means of transport.

shipboard is used to talk about (a) objects used on a ship. *...shipboard winches.* (b) things which happen on a ship. *...shipboard romances.*

shipbuilding (shipbuilder) Shipbuilding is the activity or industry of building ships. A **shipbuilder** is a person or business that builds ships.

shipload A shipload of something is a large amount being carried by ship. Similarly, a **shipload** of people is a large number of them being taken somewhere by ship.

shipment A shipment of something is a large amount being transported somewhere by sea, land, or air. ◇ When something is being transported somewhere, you call this the **shipment** of it.

shipowner A shipowner is a person who owns or has shares in a ship or ships.

shipping See ship.

shipshape If you say something is shipshape, you mean it is neat, tidy, and in good order.

shipwreck If there is a shipwreck, a ship is sunk or destroyed in an accident at sea. After the accident, what remains of the ship is also called a **shipwreck**. ◇ If you have been **shipwrecked,** the ship you were sailing in has sunk or been destroyed but you have managed to survive.

shipyard A **shipyard** is a place where ships are built or repaired.

shire is an old-fashioned word for a county. ...*northern shires.* ◇ The **shires** or **shire counties** are the counties in the central part of England which are mainly rural.

shire horse A **shire horse** is a large strong heavy horse used for pulling loads.

shirk (shirker) If someone **shirks** something difficult or unpleasant that needs to be done, they avoid dealing with it. Similarly, you can talk about someone **shirking** their responsibilities. A person who behaves like this or who avoids work is called a **shirker.**

shirt (-shirted) ❏ A **shirt** is a piece of clothing worn on the upper part of the body. **-shirted** is used to describe the kind of shirt someone is wearing. ...*black-shirted militiamen.*
❏ If you **lose your shirt,** you lose most or all of your money, for example as a result of a business venture.
❏ **stuffed shirt**: see **stuff.**

shirt-sleeved (shirt sleeves) If a man is **shirt-sleeved** or **in shirtsleeves,** he is wearing a shirt but not a jacket, usually because it is hot.

shish kebab See **kebab.**

shit is a rude word for faeces.
❏ Some people describe things as **shit** when they have a poor opinion of them. *That experiment is a bunch of shit.*
◇ Some people call a person they do not like a **shit.**

shiver (shivering, shivered) ❏ If you **shiver,** you shake or tremble uncontrollably, because you are cold, frightened, or ill.
❏ If something **sends a shiver** through a group of people, it makes them alarmed or uneasy. You can also say something **sends a shiver down** someone's **spine.**

shoal A **shoal** of fish is a large group of them swimming together. ◇ You can also call a large number of things or people a **shoal.**

shock (shocking, shockingly) ❏ **Shock** is the feeling of distress you get when something unpleasant happens to you or when you get some bad news. **Shock** is used to describe things which give you this feeling. ...*yesterday's shock announcement.*
❏ If you are **shocked** by something, it gives you a feeling of horror, disgust, or dismay. You say something like this is **shocking.** *The film was considered shockingly violent.*
◇ If you use **shock tactics,** you expose people to something horrific, as a way of getting them to take some action.
❏ A **short sharp shock** is a way of solving a problem which involves people being first made to suffer for a short time. Solving a problem like this can also be called **shock treatment** or **shock therapy.**
❏ You also say something is **shocking** when it upsets or offends people because they think it is rude.
❏ **Shock** is also a serious medical condition which can affect people who have been involved in a bad accident or have had a very frightening or upsetting experience. The person collapses or nearly collapses because their blood is not circulating properly or because of loss of blood.
❏ A **shock** is a slight movement in something like a building when it is hit by something else or when there is an explosion or earthquake.
❏ A **shock** is also an electric shock.
❏ A **shock** of hair is a thick mass of it.
❏ **Shocking** pink is a vivid pink colour.

shock absorber A **shock absorber** is a device designed to reduce the effect of a force or shock, especially a device fitted to a vehicle to give it a smoother ride.

shock-horror headlines and stories are meant to shock people but are usually exaggerated.

shock wave ❏ A **shock wave** is a wave of intense pressure moving through air, earth, or water. Shock waves can be caused by earthquakes, explosions, or by a plane flying faster than the speed of sound.
❏ You say a serious incident produces a **shock wave** when its effects are felt for some time afterwards.

shocker A **shocker** is (a) a story or film which is meant to shock or frighten people. (b) a piece of news which shocks or upsets someone.

shod See **shoe.**

shoddy (shoddier, shoddiest; shoddiness) **Shoddy** is used to describe things which have been done or made badly or carelessly, or are of poor quality. *The grandeur of the 18th and 19th century is a standing reproach to the shoddiness of the 20th.*

shoe (shod) ❏ **Shoes** are matching objects worn on your feet, usually over socks, tights, or stockings. Shoes usually cover most of your foot but end at your ankle. ◇ You can describe what someone is wearing on their feet by saying they are **shod** in a particular way. ...*workers shod in carpet slippers.*
❏ If you **step into** someone's **shoes** or **fill their shoes,** you take their place and take over the activities they were doing. ◇ If you talk about putting yourself **in** someone else's **shoes,** you mean you are trying to imagine what you would do or how you would feel in their situation.

shoehorn A **shoehorn** is a slightly curved piece of metal or plastic which you place at the back of your shoe and slide your heel down so you can put the shoe on more easily.

shoelace **Shoelaces** are the long narrow cords used to fasten some kinds of shoes.

shoemaker A **shoemaker** is a person whose job is making and repairing shoes and boots.

shoestring If you do something **on a shoestring,** you do it with very little money.

shone See **shine.**

shoo If you **shoo** an animal somewhere, you make it go there by waving your arms or hands at it and possibly shouting 'shoo' while you do it. ◇ If you **shoo** people away when they are being a nuisance, you tell them to go somewhere else.

shook See **shake.**

shoot (shooting, shot) ❏ If you **shoot** at someone or something, you fire a gun at them. ◇ If a person or animal is **shot,** they are killed or injured by a person firing a gun at them. When there is a **shooting,** someone is killed or injured by being shot with a gun. If someone is **shot down,** they are hit by gunfire and fall to the ground.
❏ **Shooting** is killing birds or animals for sport by firing

a gun at them. A **shoot** is a session or meeting in which people do this. ◇ **Shooting** is also firing a rifle or some other type of gun at a target as a sport.

❏ If an aircraft is **shot down**, it is hit by a missile and falls to the ground. You can also say the pilot is **shot down**. ◇ If armed people **shoot up** a building, they fire a lot of shots into it.

❏ When people talk about a **shooting war**, they mean a real war fought with weapons, rather than just an angry argument between countries.

❏ If you **shoot** an arrow, you fire it from a bow.

❏ If something **shoots** somewhere, it moves there suddenly and quickly. Similarly, you can talk about a person **shooting** somewhere. *Jackson shot out of his blocks towards the first hurdle.*

❏ If you **shoot** someone a glance, you look at them quickly and briefly.

❏ When a film is being made, you say it is being **shot**.

❏ When someone **shoots** in football, they try to score by suddenly kicking the ball towards the goal.

❏ A **shoot** is a plant which is just beginning to grow above the soil, or a new part growing from a plant or tree.

❏ If something **shoots up**, it increases or grows very quickly.

❏ See also **shot**.

shoot-out A **shoot-out** is a fight in which people shoot at each other with guns until one side wins. ◇ **penalty shoot-out**: see **penalty**.

shooting star A **shooting star** is the same as a meteor.

shop (shopping, shopped) ❏ A **shop** is a place, especially part of a building, where things are sold. ◇ When you **shop** or **go shopping**, you go to the shops to buy things. Your **shopping** is the things you have bought when you have been shopping.

❏ A **shopping list** is a written list of items you want to buy from the shops. ◇ A **shopping list** is also a number of things a government or organization wants to obtain or buy, or a number of actions they want to be carried out.

❏ If you **shop around**, you go to different shops or businesses to compare prices and quality before buying something.

❏ A **shop** is also a part of a factory where a certain kind of work is carried out. *...the machine shop.*

❏ If you **set up shop**, you start a business. ◇ If a business or organization **shuts up shop**, it closes earlier than expected, or stops doing business altogether.

❏ See also **closed shop**.

shop assistant A **shop assistant** is a person who works in a shop, especially one who serves customers.

shop floor The **shop floor** is the area in a factory where the workers do their work. The **shop floor** is also used to talk about the workers themselves, as distinct from the management. *Managers may have to face up to losing authoritarian power, devolving decisions to the shop floor.*

shop-front (*or* shopfront) A **shop-front** is the outside part of a shop which faces the street, including the door and window.

shop-soiled goods are slightly dirty or damaged, and are sold at a cheaper price.

shop steward A **shop steward** is a trade union member, especially in a factory, who has been elected to represent other members.

shopfront See **shop-front**.

shopkeeper A **shopkeeper** is a person who owns a small shop.

shoplifting (shoplifter) **Shoplifting** is stealing things from shops by walking round the shop and hiding items in shopping bags or clothes. A person who does this is called a **shoplifter**.

shopper A **shopper** is a person who is shopping.

shopping See **shop**.

shopping centre A **shopping centre** is an area or special complex in a town where a lot of shops have been built close together.

shopping mall A **shopping mall** is a special indoor complex made up of lots of shops, usually on different levels, and sometimes including cinemas and restaurants.

shore (shoring, shored) ❏ The **shore** of a sea, lake, or wide river is the land along its edge. ◇ If someone is **on shore**, they are on the land rather than on a ship.

❏ **Shores** is used in various ways when talking about a country which has a coastline. You say, for example, something happened **beyond** a country's **shores**.

❏ If you **shore up** something which is weak or about to fail, you support it or strengthen it in some way. ◇ If you **shore up** something like a wall or building, you put strong supports against it or under it to stop it falling down.

shore leave When a sailor or naval officer is given **shore leave**, he or she is given permission to leave the ship for a certain period.

shoreline The **shoreline** is the place where the sea, a lake, or a wide river meets the land.

shorn If you are **shorn** of something, it is taken away from you. ◇ If an animal is **shorn**, its hair or wool is cut off close to its skin. Similarly, you can talk about a person's head being **shorn**. See also **shear**.

short is used to describe things which do not last for a long time. *He died on August 21 after a short illness.* ◇ If you want to emphasize how recently something happened, you can say, for example, that it happened only a few **short** weeks ago. Similarly, you can say something will happen in only a few **short** weeks.

❏ A **short** distance or journey is not long, so you can, for example, easily walk or drive it.

❏ A **short** person is of less than average height. ◇ A **short** object measures less than usual from one end to the other. ◇ **Short** speeches, letters, or books do not have very many words or pages in them. ◇ A **short** is a short film, often shown before the main film in a cinema.

❏ If something is **short** or **in short supply**, very little of it is available. ◇ If you are **short** of something, you do not have enough of it. If you are **running short** of something, you will soon have used up your supply of it.

❏ If you say something is **short on** some desirable quality or feature, you mean it does not have enough of it.

❏ If you say something is **nothing short of** a particular thing, you mean it really is that thing. *The economic situation is nothing short of catastrophic.* ◇ If you say a situation calls for **nothing short of** a particular thing, you mean that thing is necessary and nothing less will do.

❏ If something is **cut short**, it is forced to stop before it would normally end. ◇ If something **pulls** or **brings you up short**, it surprises or startles you, and makes you suddenly stop what you were doing.

❏ If you **sell** someone or something **short,** you make them appear to be worth less than they really are.

❏ If you **stop short** of an action, you come close to doing it, but do not actually do it. ◇ If something **falls short** of a standard or amount, it does not reach it.

❏ If you **make short work of** someone or something, you deal with them or defeat them very quickly.

❏ If you have a **short** temper, you get angry easily.

❏ You say **in short** when you are summing up what you have just said. *He's relaxed, charming – in short, a regular guy.*

❏ If a name is **short for** another name, it is a short version of it. You can also say someone or something is called a particular name **for short.**

❏ You use **short of** to say you are not including something in the thing you are talking about. *Short of a single currency, the existing European monetary system has already achieved as much as can be done on that score.*

❏ A **short** is a small measure of a drink such as whisky, brandy, or vodka.

❏ **Shorts** are trousers with short legs. ◇ In the US, **shorts** are men's short underpants.

short-change If someone **short-changes** you, they behave badly or unfairly towards you, especially by giving you less of something than they should. ◇ If someone **short-changes** you when you pay for something, they cheat you by not giving you enough change.

short-circuit (short-circuiting, short-circuited) If there is a **short-circuit** in an electrical device, there is a wrong connection or damaged wire, so that the electricity travels along the wrong path and damages the device. When this happens, you say the device has **short-circuited.** ◇ If you **short-circuit** a procedure, you find a quicker way of doing something which misses out some parts of the procedure.

short cut A **short cut** is a way of achieving something which is quicker than the usual way. ◇ A **short cut** is also a way of getting somewhere which is shorter than the usual route.

short-haul See haul.

short-list See shortlist.

short-lived is used to describe things which do not last very long, or people who do not last long in a particular job. *...the short-lived emergency committee.*

short-range is used to describe things which reach or cover only a short distance. *...a new short-range passenger aircraft.*

short-sighted (short-sightedness) If you are **short-sighted,** you cannot see distant things clearly. ◇ If you say someone is being **short-sighted,** you mean they are failing to take account of the way things may develop in the future. *Their continuing opposition to the new airport shows the short-sightedness of the government's approach.*

short story A **short story** is a short piece of fiction. Short stories are often first published in magazines.

short-tempered people get angry easily.

short-term effects and developments will happen soon, rather than more gradually over a longer period. ◇ **Short-term** problems, solutions, or arrangements last for only a short time.

short-time If workers in a factory or business are on **short-time,** they are working fewer hours than they would normally work in a week, usually to avoid people being made redundant.

short wave is used to talk about the range of radio waves up to 100 metres.

shortage If there is a **shortage** of something, there is not enough of it.

shortbread is a kind of biscuit made from flour, sugar, and butter.

shortcoming A person's or thing's **shortcomings** are their faults or defects.

shorten (shortening, shortened) If something is **shortened,** it is made to last for a shorter period. *There was talk of shortening the seven-year presidential term to five years.* ◇ If something like an object or route is **shortened,** it is reduced in length. ◇ **shorten the odds:** see odd.

shortfall If there is a **shortfall** of something, there is not enough of it, or less than was expected.

shorthand is a quick way of writing which uses signs to represent words and syllables.

❏ If you say a word or phrase is **shorthand** for something, you mean it is a short way of referring to something which has a long name.

shortlist (*or* short-list) If you are **shortlisted** or put on a **shortlist,** you are included in a small number of people being considered for a job or prize. A winner is later chosen from the people on the shortlist.

shortly If something is going to happen **shortly,** it is going to happen soon. ◇ If something happens **shortly** before or after something else, it happens just before it or just after it.

shot ❏ See shoot.

❏ If you fire a **shot,** you fire a gun once. ◇ If someone is a good **shot,** they are able to shoot very accurately.

❏ In sport, a **shot** is hitting or kicking the ball in an attempt to score.

❏ A **shot** of something is a photograph of it. ◇ A **shot** is also a single picture or uninterrupted sequence in a film. *...the opening shots.*

❏ An injection of a drug is often called a **shot.** ◇ If you say something is a **shot in the arm,** you mean it provides help and encouragement, and is likely to produce an improvement.

❏ If you **have a shot** at something, you try to do it. ◇ If you say a course of action is a **long shot,** you mean it is unlikely to succeed but is worth trying anyway.

❏ If you talk about the person who is **calling the shots,** you mean the one who is controlling what happens.

❏ If you do something **like a shot,** you do it without any delay.

❏ If you want to **get shot of** something or **be shot of** it, you want to get rid of it.

❏ If you say something is **shot through** with a particular quality or element, you mean it is full of it.

❏ A **shot** of a strong alcoholic drink is a small measure of it.

❏ See also shot put.

shot put (shot putter) In athletics, the **shot put** or **shot** is a competition in which contestants throw a heavy metal ball called the **shot** as far as possible. A **shot putter** is someone who competes in the shot put.

shotgun A **shotgun** is a gun designed for shooting birds and animals. It fires a lot of small metal balls at one time.

should ❑ If you say something **should** happen, you mean you think it is right or a good idea. *The President should resign... Some think that all the foundation money should be put solely into football.* ◇ You can also say something **should** happen when you are expecting it to happen. *The inspectors' report, which should be published next week, will bring the controversy to a head.*

❑ If you say something **should have** happened, you mean it did not happen because something like a rule or procedure was not observed. *It seems the director who received your letters, and should have replied, was under extreme business pressure at the time.* ◇ You also say something **should** have happened when it was expected to happen but did not. *For one reason or another, he did not win as many grand slam events as he should have.*

❑ You say 'I **should** think...' or 'I **should** imagine...' when you are saying you think something is probably true. ◇ You say 'I **should** like...' when you are expressing a wish.

❑ You use **should** in questions when you are asking for advice, permission, or information. *Should I give him the benefit of the doubt?... Why should I take out an endowment mortgage?* ◇ You also use **should** when you are giving advice. *I should press for a rematch, if I were you.*

❑ **Should** is sometimes used at the beginning of a sentence or group of words when mentioning the effect something might have if it happened. *Should the lobbying succeed, then changes could occur over here as well.*

shoulder (shouldering, shouldered) ❑ A person's **shoulders** are the parts of their body between their neck and the tops of their arms. ◇ If you **shoulder** something heavy, you put it across one or both of your shoulders to carry it.

❑ If you **shoulder** something like a responsibility, you accept that it is your responsibility, and behave accordingly. ◇ If you **shoulder** something like a debt, you agree to pay it. ◇ You can also talk about a person's problems or responsibilities being **on their shoulders**.

❑ If you **look over your shoulder,** you look behind you by turning your neck. ◇ You can also say someone is **looking over their shoulder** when they are worried by a possible challenge or threat. ◇ If someone else **looks over your shoulder,** they stand behind you and look at what you are doing or at what is in front of you.

❑ If you **rub shoulders** with people, especially famous people, you meet them and talk to them. ◇ If you talk about different things or styles **rubbing shoulders,** you mean they are mixed up together.

❑ If people are **shoulder to shoulder,** they are side by side, close together. ◇ If you talk about a group of people standing **shoulder to shoulder,** you mean they are supporting each other in trying to achieve a common aim.

❑ If you say someone or something is **head and shoulders** above other people or things, you mean they are a lot better than them.

❑ A **shoulder** is also a joint of meat from the upper part of the front leg of an animal.

shoulder bag A **shoulder bag** is a bag which you carry on a long strap over your shoulder.

shoulder blade Your **shoulder blades** are the two large flat triangular bones in the upper part of your back. In biology, they are called the **scapulas** or **scapulae**.

shoulder-length hair is long enough to reach the shoulders.

shout (shouting, shouted) ❑ If you **shout,** you raise your voice when you speak, so you can be heard a long way away. ◇ If you **shout at** someone, you talk angrily to them in a loud voice. ◇ If you **shout** someone **down,** you prevent them from being heard by shouting at them. ◇ A **shouting match** is a loud angry argument between two or more people.

❑ A **shout** is a loud call or cry.

shove (shoving, shoved) ❑ If you **shove** someone or something or give them a **shove,** you push them hard. ◇ You also say people give someone or something a **shove** when they take some strong action to get something done. *The temptation for the victors to give one more shove and get rid of the tyrant himself is growing stronger.*

❑ If you **shove** something somewhere, you push it there quickly and carelessly.

❑ if **push comes to shove**: see push.

shovel (shovelling, shovelled) (*American spelling:* shoveling, shoveled) A **shovel** is a tool like a spade, for lifting and moving things like earth, coal, or snow. If you **shovel** something somewhere, you move it there using a shovel. ◇ If you **shovel** something into a container, you push a lot of it in quickly.

show (showing, showed, have shown) ❑ If something **shows** that something is the case, it proves it or makes people aware of it. *Plaster fragments show that the walls were decorated with figurative and geometric murals.* ◇ If you say something **goes to show** that something is true, you mean it proves it.

❑ If an instrument **shows** something such as a change, it indicates it.

❑ If something **shows,** it is obvious or visible. *Although the government has begun a series of economic reforms, the benefits won't show for some time yet.*

❑ If someone **shows** a quality or characteristic, people can see they have it by the way they behave. Similarly, someone can **show** an attitude to something. *In the past he has shown reluctance to intercede.*

❑ What a picture or diagram **shows** is what you see when you look at it, or what it represents.

❑ If you **show** something to someone, you give it to them, take them to it, or point it out, so they can see it. ◇ If you **show** someone how to do something, you do it while they are there, so they can watch you and learn how to do it.

❑ If you **show** someone to a room or a seat, you take them to it. ◇ If you **show** someone **round** a place, you take them round it, pointing out its interesting features.

❑ If you make a **show** of doing something, you pretend to do it. ◇ If you do something **for show,** you do it just to make a good impression.

❑ If someone **shows off,** they try to impress people. If they do it a lot, you can call them a **show-off.** ◇ If you **show off** something you have and are proud of, you show it to a lot of people. ◇ If something **shows** something else **off,** it makes it look especially effective or attractive, because it emphasizes its good qualities or features.

❑ A **show** is (a) an entertainment in the theatre, especially a musical. (b) an entertainment on TV or radio.

◇ When a film or TV programme is **shown**, it appears in a cinema or is broadcast.

❏ A **show** is also an exhibition of things, often involving a competition to judge which of them is best. *...the Chelsea Flower Show.* ◇ If something like a collection of paintings is **shown** or **on show**, it appears in an exhibition or in some place where it can be seen by the public.

❏ If someone **steals the show**, they get more attention and praise than anyone else.

❏ If you **show up** somewhere, you arrive there.

❏ A **show of hands** is a way of voting in which people raise their hands to indicate their support for something.

❏ If you **have** something **to show** for your efforts, you have achieved something definite as a result of them.

show business (*or* **showbusiness**) is the entertainment industry, including films, theatre, and television.

show jumping (*or* **showjumping**) is a sport in which horses are ridden in competitions to demonstrate their skill in jumping over walls and fences.

show-off See show.

show trial A **show trial** is a public trial held mainly for propaganda purposes. Often the evidence has been rigged, or the person on trial has been tortured into making a false confession.

showbiz is another name for show business.

showbusiness See show business.

showcase (showcasing, showcased) ❏ A **showcase** is a situation or setting in which something is shown off to its best advantage. *This non-profit-making show has proved an effective showcase for young British talent over the past six years.* When something is placed in a situation or setting like this, you can say it is **showcased**.

❏ A **showcase** is also a glass container used to display things which are valuable, interesting, or important.

showdown A **showdown** is a big argument or conflict which is intended to settle a dispute once and for all.

shower (showering, showered) ❏ A **shower** is a device which sprays water on you so you can wash yourself. If you **shower** or have a **shower**, you wash yourself by standing under a shower.

❏ A **shower** is also a short period of rain or snow.

❏ A lot of small objects falling can be called a **shower**. If you are **showered** with small objects, a lot of them fall on you from above.

❏ If you **shower** someone with something, you give them a lot of it.

showery If the weather is **showery**, it keeps raining on and off.

showily See showy.

showing ❏ See show.

❏ If you talk about someone's **showing**, you are talking about how well or badly they have done in a contest or competition. *...their strong showing in the local elections.*

❏ A **showing** of a film is a presentation of it somewhere so that people can see it.

showjumping See show jumping.

showman (showmen; showmanship) If you call a man a **showman**, you mean he keeps trying to impress people by presenting things in a dramatic or entertaining way. You can talk about the **showmanship** of someone like this.

shown See show.

showpiece You call something like a piece of music a **showpiece** when it can be used to show a performer's skill. ◇ A **showpiece** is also something which is meant to be admired, because it is supposed to be the best possible example of a certain type of thing. *Betws drift mine, opened in 1978 as a showpiece pit, is now reduced to a mere 95 miners.*

showroom A **showroom** is a shop where goods such as cars, furniture, or electrical goods are displayed for sale.

showy (showily) If you call something **showy**, you mean it is large or expensive-looking and is meant to impress people.

shrank See shrink.

shrapnel is small pieces of metal scattered from exploding bombs and shells.

shred (shredding, shredded; shredder) ❏ If you **shred** something, you cut or tear it into very small pieces. A **shredder** is a machine which cuts things like paper or scrap metal into tiny pieces. ◇ A **shred** of a material is a small piece cut or torn from a larger piece.

❏ If you say there is not a **shred** of something, you are emphasizing that there is none of it.

shrew ❏ The **shrew** is a small mouse-like animal with a long pointed nose.

❏ A bad-tempered woman is sometimes called a **shrew**.

shrewd (shrewdly, shrewdness) A **shrewd** person is able to understand and judge a situation quickly and use this understanding to their own advantage. You call an action **shrewd** when it shows this ability. *He shrewdly bought and traded oil properties far below their real values... His natural shrewdness tells him what is needed to succeed.*

shriek (shrieking, shrieked) If someone **shrieks** or lets out a **shriek**, they give a loud scream, because they are in pain or suddenly frightened. Sometimes people **shriek** with laughter when they find something extremely funny. ◇ If you **shriek** something, you shout it in a loud high-pitched voice.

shrift If someone or something is given **short shrift**, they are dealt with quickly and unsympathetically.

shrill (shrilly) A **shrill** sound is high-pitched, piercing, and unpleasant to listen to. *She began to sing shrilly.*

shrimp Shrimps are small shellfish with long tails and a lot of legs. There are many types of shrimp, some of which can be eaten.

shrine A **shrine** is a place people believe to be holy, because it is associated with a sacred person or object. ◇ A **shrine** is also a place which people visit and treat with respect because it is associated with a famous person or event.

shrink (shrinking, shrank, have shrunk) ❏ If something **shrinks** or you **shrink** it, it gets smaller.

❏ If you **shrink** from doing something, you are reluctant to do it because you find it unpleasant.

❏ **Shrink** is also a humorous word for a psychiatrist.

shrinkage is a decrease in the size or amount of something.

shrivel (shrivelling, shrivelled) (*American spelling:* shriveling, shriveled) ❏ If something like a plant **shrivels** or **shrivels up**, it becomes dry and wrinkled.

❏ You also say something **shrivels** when it gets smaller in size, amount, or influence.

shroud (shrouding, shrouded) ❏ If something is **shrouded in**

secrecy or mystery, very little is known about it. ◇ If a place is **shrouded** in darkness, cloud, or fog, it is hidden by it.

❑ A **shroud** is the cloth a dead body is wrapped in before it is buried.

Shrove Tuesday is the day before the beginning of Lent. It is also known as Pancake Day because people traditionally make pancakes on this day.

shrub A **shrub** is a plant like a small tree with several woody stems instead of a trunk.

shrubbery (shrubberies) A **shrubbery** is an area where shrubs are grown. ◇ **Shrubbery** is shrubs in general. *...clumps of exotic shrubbery.*

shrug (shrugging, shrugged) If you **shrug** your shoulders or give a **shrug**, you raise and lower your shoulders to show you are not interested in something, or do not know or care about it. ◇ If you **shrug** something **off**, you treat it as trivial or unimportant.

shrunk See **shrink**.

shrunken If something is **shrunken**, it has become gradually smaller.

shudder (shuddering, shuddered) ❑ If you **shudder** or give a **shudder**, your body gives a brief violent movement, because you are afraid, horrified, or disgusted. ◇ If you say someone **shudders** at something, you mean they are shocked or disgusted by it. *He notes with a shudder that the average American lives in a country where shopping malls outnumber high schools.*

❑ If something like a machine **shudders**, it shakes violently.

shuffle (shuffling, shuffled) ❑ If you **shuffle** somewhere, you walk without lifting your feet properly. ◇ If you **shuffle** your feet, you move them about when you are standing or sitting somewhere, because you are uncomfortable or embarrassed.

❑ If you **shuffle** things, you move them around or change their order. ◇ If you **shuffle** cards, you mix them up before a game, to make sure they are dealt in a random order.

shun (shunning, shunned) If you **shun** someone or something, you deliberately avoid them.

shunt If someone or something is **shunted** about, they are moved from one place to another. ◇ When railway engines **shunt**, they push or pull carriages or wagons from one railway line to another.

shut (shutting, shut) ❑ If you **shut** a door, window, or lid, you move it so it fills or covers the opening it is designed to fit.

❑ If a shop or other business **shuts** or **shuts down**, work stops there. When this happens, you say there is a **shutdown**.

❑ If you **shut down** something like an engine or a power supply or **shut** it **off**, you turn it off to stop it working.

❑ If someone **shuts off** the supply of a commodity or type of goods, they stop sending the commodity or goods to the people who normally use them.

❑ If someone **shuts** something **away**, they store it somewhere where people cannot see it. ◇ If a person is **shut up** or **shut away**, they are kept in a prison or other institution. ◇ If you are **shut in** a room, you are kept in it and not allowed to leave. If you **shut** yourself **in**, you close the door to keep other people out.

❑ If people are **shut out** of a place, they are prevented from getting in. ◇ If someone is **shut out** of something like a competition or a deal, they are prevented from taking part in it.

❑ If you **keep your mouth shut** about something, you do not tell anyone about it. ◇ If you tell someone to **shut up**, you are telling them rudely to stop talking. If you **shut** someone **up**, you stop them talking.

shutdown See **shut**.

shutter (shuttering, shuttered) ❑ **Shutters** are a pair of hinged wooden or metal objects which can be closed to cover a window. **Shuttered** windows or doors have their shutters closed. The **shutters** on a shop are metal covers which can be pulled down to cover the windows and doors.

❑ The **shutter** in a camera is the part which opens to allow light through when a photograph is taken.

shuttle (shuttling, shuttled) ❑ A **shuttle** service is an air, bus, or train service which makes frequent journeys between two places. A service like this is sometimes just called a **shuttle**. See also **space shuttle**.

❑ If someone or something **shuttles** between two or more places, they move frequently between them. ◇ **Shuttle diplomacy** is the movement of a diplomat between countries in order to mediate between leaders who refuse to talk directly to each other.

shuttlecock A **shuttlecock** is the object you hit over the net in a game of badminton. It is cone-shaped and has real or artificial feathers stuck in it.

shy (shyly, shyness; shies, shying, shied) ❑ A **shy** person is nervous and uncomfortable with other people. *...children peering shyly out... Despite his shyness, there is no doubt he holds a high opinion of his own abilities.* ◇ You say a wild animal is **shy** when it avoids people and is therefore rarely seen.

❑ If you are **shy of** doing something, you do not want to do it, because you are afraid of the consequences. ◇ If you **fight shy** of something, you try to avoid it. ◇ If you **shy away** from something, you avoid becoming involved in it.

❑ If a figure is **shy of** a particular amount, it does not quite reach it.

❑ If a horse **shies**, it makes a sudden violent movement, because it is frightened.

shyster A **shyster** is a dishonest or unscrupulous person, especially a politician or a lawyer.

SI The SI system is an international system of metric units. There are seven basic SI units, including the metre, kilogram, second, and amp. SI is short for 'Système International d'Unités'.

Siamese cat The **Siamese cat** is a type of cat with short cream or brown fur, blue eyes, and dark brown ears and tail.

Siamese twins are twins who are born joined to each other by part of their bodies.

sibilant Sibilants are speech sounds like 's' or 'z' which produce a hissing effect. You can call a language **sibilant** when it has a lot of sounds like these.

sibling Your siblings are your brothers and sisters.

sic When you are reproducing a piece of writing, you write **sic** in brackets after a mistake to show it is the author's mistake, not your own. *The school advertises a* *'wide rnage (sic) of 6th form courses'.*

sick (sickness, sicknesses) ❑ If you are **sick,** you have a disease or illness. **Sickness** is being ill. A **sickness** is a disease or illness. People who are ill are sometimes called **the sick.** ◇ If you are **off sick,** you are absent from work or school because of illness.

❑ If you feel **sick,** you feel as if you are going to bring up food from your stomach. If you are **sick,** the food comes up from your stomach and out through your mouth.

❑ If you are **sick** of something, you are annoyed or bored by it and want it to stop. If you are very annoyed with something, you can say you are **sick and tired** of it.

❑ A **sick** story or joke deals with death, cruelty, or suffering in a frivolous or tasteless way.

sick bay A **sick bay** is an area, for example on a ship, where people can be given medical treatment and care.

sick bed Your **sick bed** is the bed you are lying in while you are ill.

sick building syndrome is a name given to a collection of symptoms, including tiredness and depression, experienced by some people who work in air-conditioned and artificially-lit office buildings.

sick leave If you are on **sick leave,** you are officially allowed to spend time away from work because of illness or injury.

sick pay or **statutory sick pay** is money you can sometimes get from your employer if you are ill and unable to work.

sicken (sickening, sickened; sickeningly) If something **sickens** you, it makes you feel disgusted and horrified. You say something like this is **sickening.** *The violence is sickeningly graphic.*

sickle A **sickle** is a tool with a short handle and a curved blade, used in the past for cutting long grass or grain crops.

sickle cell anaemia is a hereditary disease occurring mainly in black people, in which the red blood cells become sickle-shaped, causing attacks of pain and fever.

sickly (sicklier, sickliest) A **sickly** person is weak and often ill. ◇ **Sickly** things are unpleasant to smell, taste, or look at.

sickness benefit is money you can sometimes get from the government or an insurance company if you are unable to work because of illness.

side (siding, sided) ❑ The two **sides** in a game such as football are the two teams who are playing each other. Similarly, the two **sides** in a battle are the armies fighting each other. The two **sides** in a debate are the two groups involved in it who have opposing points of view.

❑ If you **take sides** or **take** someone's **side** in an argument or conflict, you support one position or point of view. You can also **side with** someone in an argument or conflict. If you are **on** someone's **side,** you are supporting them in an argument or dispute.

❑ If someone stays **at your side** or **by your side,** they stay near you and support you or comfort you.

❑ If you have something **on your side,** it gives you an advantage in what you are trying to do. *She has the constitution on her side as it mandates her staying in office until May and prohibits the holding of an election before then.*

❑ If you stay **on the right side** of someone, you succeed in pleasing them and avoid annoying them. If you get **on**

the wrong side of someone, you annoy them and make them dislike you.

❑ A particular **side** of something is one aspect of it.

❑ If something is at the **side** of something else, it is in a position to its right or left. ◇ If something is on one **side** of a boundary or barrier, it is in one of the two areas the boundary or barrier separates.

❑ If two people or things are **side by side,** they are next to each other. ◇ If someone or something moves **from side to side,** they move repeatedly to the left and right.

❑ The **sides** of an area or surface are its edges. *The room is lined on three sides by sofas.* ◇ The **sides** of an object are its outside surfaces, excluding the top and bottom. ◇ The **sides** of something like a piece of paper are its front and back.

❑ The **sides** of a road or street are (a) its two halves, which vehicles drive along in opposite directions. *The pursuing car was on the wrong side of the road.* (b) its edges. *The convoy forced other motorists to the side of the road.*

❑ The **sides** of a hill or valley are the sloping parts between its top and bottom. ◇ The **sides** of a river or stream are its banks.

❑ A **side** road or **side** street is a less important road leading off an important one.

❑ Your **sides** are the parts of your body from your armpits down to your hips.

❑ The two **sides** of your family are your mother's family and your father's family.

❑ You can use **side** to give your opinion of something. For example, if you think something is too large, you can say it is 'on the large side'.

❑ If you **put** something **to one side,** you keep it separate from other things, so you can deal with it later. ◇ Similarly, if you **put** something like a plan **to one side,** you disregard it for the time being, so you can concentrate on something else.

❑ If you do some work **on the side,** you do it in addition to your main job.

side effect The **side effects** of a drug or medicine are any additional effects it has, especially bad ones, besides the ones it is intended to have. ◇ Similarly, the **side effects** of an action or situation are other things which happen in addition to its main consequences.

side issue A **side issue** is an issue or subject which is not considered to be as important as the main one.

side-saddle If you ride a horse **side-saddle,** you sit with both your legs on one side, rather than with one leg on each side.

sideboard A **sideboard** is a long low cupboard, in which plates and glasses are kept.

sideburns A man's **sideburns** are the hair he has allowed to grow down the side of his cheeks, in front of his ears.

sidecar A **sidecar** is a small structure attached to the side of a motorbike for carrying a passenger. It has an additional wheel at the side, making the motorbike into a three-wheeled vehicle.

sidekick If you talk about a powerful person's **sidekicks,** you mean their assistants.

sideline (sidelining, sidelined) ❑ A **sideline** is an extra job you do in addition to your main one.

❑ If you are **on the sidelines** when something is happening, you are not actively involved in it. ◇ If you are

sidelined, you are not included in what other people are doing, and are made to seem unimportant.

sideshow If you call an event or issue a **sideshow**, you mean it is less important or less significant than other things happening at the same time. ◇ The **sideshows** at a fairground are the stalls where you do things like shooting and throwing darts.

sidestep (sidestepping, sidestepped) If you **sidestep** a problem or question, you avoid dealing with it. ◇ If you **sidestep** something like a punch, you avoid it by taking a pace sideways.

sideswipe If you take a **sideswipe** at something, you make an unexpected attack on it while discussing something else.

sidetrack If you are **sidetracked** by something, you forget what you are supposed to be doing and start doing something else.

sidewalk is the usual American word for a pavement.

sideways ❑ If you move **sideways**, you move to your left or right. ◇ If a vehicle moves **sideways**, it moves with its side in front, because it is out of control.
  ❑ If you say something like your career is moving **sideways**, you mean it is making no progress but simply staying at the same level.
  ❑ If something **knocks you sideways**, it amazes you, because it was totally unexpected.

siding A railway **siding** is a short stretch of track beside the main tracks where engines, trucks, or carriages can stand when they are not being used.

sidle (sidling, sidled) If someone **sidles** up to you, they come up to you cautiously, because they do not want to be noticed.

SIDS is the sudden death of a young baby in sleep, which doctors cannot account for. The letters stand for 'sudden infant death syndrome'. SIDS is also known as 'cot death'.

siege ❑ A **siege** is a military operation in which an army tries to capture a town or other place by attacking it from all sides and preventing food or other help from reaching its inhabitants. You say the army is **laying siege** to the town; you can also say the town is **under siege**. ◇ A **siege** is also any situation where a place is surrounded for a long period, for example by the police, in an attempt to force the people inside to come out.
  ❑ If a government or other authority declares a **state of siege**, it puts restrictions on the movement of people into and out of a place.
  ❑ You can say someone or something is **under siege** when they are constantly under pressure or attack.
  ❑ If a country has a **siege economy**, its economic system is designed to be as self-sufficient as possible, so that it does not have to import many goods or services. ◇ If a person or organization has a **siege mentality**, they refuse to compromise or co-operate because they think other people are constantly trying to harm or defeat them.

sierra A **sierra** is a range of mountains with jagged peaks, especially in Spain or America.

siesta In hot countries, when people have a **siesta**, they have a short sleep early in the afternoon.

sieve (sieving, sieved) A **sieve** is an implement consisting of a metal or plastic ring with a wire or plastic net underneath. You pass substances through the net when you want to separate solids from liquids, or larger pieces of something from smaller pieces. ◇ If you **sieve** a liquid, you put it through a sieve to remove any solids from it. Similarly, you can **sieve** a powdery substance to remove large lumps.

sift ❑ If you **sift** something such as evidence or **sift through** it, you examine it carefully and thoroughly, to separate what is important or useful from what is not.
  ❑ If you **sift** a powdery substance such as flour or sand, you put it through a sieve to remove large lumps.

sigh If you **sigh** or let out a **sigh**, you let out a deep breath which is loud enough to be heard. Sighs express feelings such as disappointment, tiredness, relief, or pleasure. ◇ If you **sigh** something, you say it in a voice which expresses disappointment or sadness.

sight (sighted, sighting) ❑ **Sight** is the ability to see. A **sighted** person has this ability. **-sighted** is added to some words to describe the extent to which someone can see. *...a near-sighted person.*
  ❑ The **sight** of something is seeing it. *The sight of blood made him sick.* ◇ If something is **in sight**, you can see it, because it is not too far away or because you have a clear view of it. Similarly, something can be **out of sight**. ◇ If you are **within sight** of a place, you can see it from where you are.
  ❑ When something unusual is **sighted**, someone notices it. An occasion like this is called a **sighting**. ◇ If you do something **on sight**, you do it as soon as you notice someone or something. *Police were given the legal right to fire on sight at suspects.*
  ❑ If you **catch sight of** something, you suddenly see it or notice it. If you **lose sight of** it, it moves to a position where you cannot see it. ◇ If you **lose sight of** an aim or objective, you become confused or distracted by other issues and forget the point of what you are doing.
  ❑ If something appears a certain way **at first sight**, that is how it appears when you first see it or consider it, although it may appear differently later.
  ❑ If something like a result or decision is **in sight**, it is likely to happen soon. *His supporters claimed that a breakthrough was in sight.*
  ❑ A **sight** is something you see. *Basking sharks, once a rare sight off British shores, are now commonly spotted.* ◇ The **sights** are the places, especially in a city, which are interesting to see and are often visited by tourists.
  ❑ The **sight** or **sights** of a gun are the part or parts you look through, to help you aim more accurately.
  ❑ If you have someone or something **in your sights**, you are concentrating on them, because they may be the person or thing you are looking for. ◇ You can also say you have something **in your sights** when you want to achieve it and you think you have a good chance of doing so. ◇ If you **set your sights on** something, you decide you want it, and try hard to get it.
  ❑ If you say something is **a sight** better or **a sight** worse than something else, you mean it is very much better or very much worse.

sight-read Musicians who can **sight-read** can play or sing music from the printed sheet the first time they see it, without practising beforehand.

sighted See **sight**.

sighting See **sight**.

sightscreen In cricket, the **sightscreens** are the tall white wooden screens which are placed behind the bowler so that the batsman can see the ball clearly.

sightseeing (sightseer) If you go **sightseeing**, you travel around, usually in a city, looking at the interesting places tourists usually visit. People who do this are called **sightseers.**

sign (signing) ❑ If you **sign** a document, you write your signature on it. You do this to show, for example, that you wrote the document, that you agree with what is in it, or that you were present on a particular occasion.

❑ If you **sign on**, you officially state you are unemployed so you can receive money from the government to live on. ◇ If you **sign for** something, you officially state you have received or accepted it by signing a form.

❑ If a sports team **signs** a player, they get the player to sign a document saying he or she will play for them. A player who has just joined a team in this way is called a **signing.** ◇ If a firm **signs** you **up**, they get you to sign a contract saying you will work for them. ◇ If you **sign up** for something like a course, you sign a form to say you will do it. You can also **sign on** for a course.

❑ If you **sign off** from a job or activity, you give it up. ◇ If you **sign** something **away**, you sign official documents saying you no longer own it or have any right to it.

❑ If you say something is **signed and sealed**, you mean it is absolutely definite because everyone involved has signed the legal documents.

❑ A **sign** of something is evidence that it exists or is happening. *...signs of infection.* ◇ If you say something is a **sign of the times**, you mean it indicates something about present-day life.

❑ A **sign** is also a mark or shape with a particular meaning, for example in maths or music.

❑ If you make a **sign,** you move your hand or hands in a way which conveys a special meaning.

❑ A **sign** is also a piece of wood, metal, or plastic with words and sometimes a picture on it, giving information or instructions.

sign language is a way of communicating used especially by people who are deaf or unable to speak. It involves special movements of the hands and arms combined with facial expressions to represent words and ideas.

signal (signalling, signalled; signally) (*American spelling:* signaling, signaled) ❑ If an event or action **signals** something or is a **signal** of it, it suggests it exists or is going to happen. *Pundits were divided over whether the budget signalled a June election.*

❑ If you **signal** something, you indicate it by means of a gesture. *The referee signalled that the fight was over.* ◇ You can also say you **signal** something or send someone a **signal** when you indicate something in an indirect way.

❑ A **signal** is a series of sound or light waves which carry information.

❑ A **signal** is also a piece of equipment beside a railway track which tells train drivers if it is safe to go on or if they should stop.

❑ A **signal** success or failure is a particularly significant and noticeable one. *...the measures that have so signally failed since 1990.*

signal box A **signal box** is a building next to a railway track which houses the switches and buttons controlling

the signals and points on that stretch of the track.

signalman (signalmen) A **signalman** is a person whose job is to control the signals and points on a stretch of railway track.

signatory (*pron:* sig-na-tree) (signatories) The **signatories** of an official document are the people who have signed it.

signature ❑ Your **signature** is your name as you write it yourself, for example on a cheque. ◇ The signing of a document is called its **signature.**

❑ The **signature tune** of a regular TV or radio programme is the tune played at the beginning or end of it.

signboard A **signboard** is a piece of wood with information written or printed on it.

signet ring A **signet ring** is a ring with a small panel in the middle engraved with an initial or some other pattern.

significant (significantly, significance) If something is **significant**, it is important. *The legislation was of immense significance.* ◇ A **significant** amount is a large amount. *Britain's negotiating position has been significantly weakened.*

signify (signifies, signifying, signified) If you talk about what something **signifies**, you are talking about what it means. *Their help signified a silent protest against the government.*

signpost ❑ A **signpost** is a sign at a road junction showing where the different roads go to and how far it is to the nearest towns and villages. Signposts are also placed on footpaths. ◇ If a route is **signposted**, it has signposts beside the road or path showing the way.

❑ If something **signposts** something else or is a **signpost** for it, it is a good indication of it. *The work signposts hope one day for a cure.*

Sikh (Sikhism) **Sikhism** is an Indian religion which separated from Hinduism in the 16th century and which teaches that there is only one God. Someone who practises this religion is called a **Sikh.**

silage (*pron:* sile-ij) is a crop such as grass which is harvested when it is green and then partially fermented in a silo to make fodder for animals.

silence (silencing, silenced) ❑ If there is **silence**, there is no noise at all. ◇ If something is **silenced**, it is prevented from making a noise.

❑ If you say there is **silence** on an issue, you mean nothing is being said about it. ◇ If someone is **silenced**, they are prevented from speaking. ◇ If someone **breaks their silence**, they speak out about something they had earlier refused to discuss.

silencer A **silencer** is a device on a car or motorbike exhaust, or on a gun, which makes it quieter.

silent (silently) ❑ If you are **silent**, you are not speaking or not making any noise. ◇ A **silent** person does not talk much. ◇ If you are **silent** about a particular matter, you are not saying anything about it.

❑ You call an action **silent** when it takes place without any words being spoken. *...silent prayer.*

❑ A **silent** film has no sound or speech.

silhouette (silhouetted) A **silhouette** is the outline of a dark shape against a bright light or a pale background. When you see a person or object like this, you say you see them **silhouetted** against the light or background;

you also say you see them in silhouette.

silica is a substance which is the main ingredient of sand, quartz, and flint. It is used to make glass.

silicon is an element used to make parts of computers and other electronic equipment.

silicon chip A silicon chip is a tiny square of silicon with electronic components on it. Silicon chips are used as part of a circuit in computers and electronic equipment.

silicone is a tough artificial substance made from silicon. It is used in paints and non-stick surfaces and in cosmetic surgery.

silk is a substance produced by silkworms to make their cocoons. It is made into smooth fine cloth or sewing thread. The cloth and thread are also known as silk.
  ❑ When a barrister takes silk, he or she becomes a Queen's Counsel or QC. QCs are sometimes called silks.

silk-screen (silk-screening) Silk-screen printing or silk-screening is a method of printing patterns onto paper or cloth by forcing ink through a patterned mesh, usually of silk.

silken things are smooth and soft. ◇ Silken material is made of silk.

silkworm Silkworms are a type of caterpillar. They are reared to obtain silk from their cocoons.

silky things are smooth, soft, and shiny like silk.

sill A sill is a ledge at the bottom of a window.

silly (sillier, silliest; silliness) ❑ If you say someone is being silly, you mean they are behaving in a foolish or childish way. You can also call their behaviour silly. *She looked round to make sure there was no giggling or silliness.*
  ❑ In Britain, the silly season is the period in the summer when Parliament and the law courts are not sitting, and the newspapers often run trivial or silly stories because they have little serious news to report.

silo (silos) A silo is (a) a tall round metal tower on a farm in which silage is made or grain is stored. (b) a specially built place underground where missiles are kept ready to be launched.

silt is fine sand, soil, or mud carried along by a river. If a river, lake, or harbour silts up, it becomes blocked with silt which has settled at the bottom.

silver is a valuable greyish-white metal used for making jewellery and ornaments. ◇ In a house, the silver is the things made of silver, such as cutlery or dishes. ◇ Silver is also coins such as 10p and 5p pieces, which look like silver. ◇ Silver is also used to describe other things which look like silver or have a similar colour. *...a silver trout.*
  ❑ The runner-up in a race or competition often gets a silver medal, made either of silver or a silver-coloured metal.
  ❑ If you say there is a silver lining, you mean there are reasons for thinking that a bad situation will not continue.
  ❑ If you say someone was born with a silver spoon in their mouth, you mean they were born into a rich or aristocratic family.
  ❑ The cinema is sometimes called the silver screen.
  ❑ If you celebrate the silver jubilee of something, you are celebrating the fact that it has been going for 25 years. ◇ A silver wedding is a 25th wedding anniversary.

silver birch The silver birch is a tree with greyish-white bark which looks as if it is peeling off.

silver paper is thin paper covered with silver-coloured foil.

silver-plated objects are covered in a thin layer of silver.

silver-tongued If you call someone silver-tongued, you mean they are very persuasive.

silversmith A silversmith is a person whose job is making things out of silver.

silverware is cutlery and dishes made of silver or of a metal which looks like silver.

silvery is used to describe things which look like silver.

simian is used to talk about things to do with monkeys and apes. *...our simian ancestors.* ◇ Simian is also used to describe people whose features remind you of a monkey.

similar (similarity, similarities) If things are similar, they have features in common and are quite like each other. You can also say there is a similarity between them. ◇ Similarities are features things have in common. *The two books show remarkable similarities in their plots.*

similarly You use similarly to say one situation is very like another one. *He learned his English mainly from comic books. Similarly, I owe most of my oral French to Tintin and Asterix.* ◇ You also use similarly to talk about two things being like each other in a particular respect. *Paris has shown how full use of the river can be combined with activities other than industry. Our report argues for a similarly imaginative approach in London.*

simile (pron: sim-ill-lee) A simile is a way of describing something by saying it is like something else.

simmer (simmering, simmered) When you simmer food, you cook it by keeping it just below boiling point. ◇ If a violent situation or quarrel is simmering, it is not openly expressed, but is liable to break out at any time.

simper (simpering, simpered) If someone simpers, they smile in a silly self-conscious way.

simple (simpler, simplest; simplicity) ❑ If something is simple, it is easy to understand. You can talk about the simplicity of something like this. ◇ A simple task or action is easy to do.
  ❑ Simple things are plain and not elaborate in style. ◇ A simple way of life is uncomplicated and fairly basic.
  ❑ A simple plant or organism is not very advanced biologically.
  ❑ Simple is also used to emphasize that one particular thing is responsible for something happening. *The simple addition of a new bonnet grille has changed the car's whole character.*
  ❑ If you need a simple majority to win a vote, you only need to gain more than half of the votes, rather than any higher percentage.

simple interest is interest calculated only on the amount of money you originally invest, and not on any interest added to it later. See also compound interest.

simple-minded If someone is simple-minded, they interpret everything in a way which is too simple, because they do not understand how complicated things really are.

simpleton In the past, a person of very low intelligence was sometimes called a simpleton.

simplicity See simple.

simplification is the process of making something simpler. A simplification is the thing you produce when you make something simpler.

simplify (simplifies, simplifying, simplified) If you **simplify** something, you make it easier to understand or easier to do.

simplistic (simplistically) A **simplistic** view or interpretation of something is misleading because it makes it seem less complicated than it really is. *The dispute is simplistically seen as the poor against the rich.*

simply ❑ You use **simply** to emphasize that something is only one thing, happens for only one reason, or is done in only one way. *I am simply a science reporter... They were simply overwhelmed by the power and determination of the Australians.* ◇ You also use **simply** to emphasize what you are saying. *We simply must find a better way to do it.*

❑ If you do something **simply**, you do it in an uncomplicated way, without adding any unnecessary elements. *The flat was painted very simply in white throughout.*

simulate (simulating, simulated; simulation) If you **simulate** something, you imitate it or produce an artificial version of it. *Training includes realistic simulation of casualty procedures.*

simulator A **simulator** is a device designed to reproduce actual conditions, for example to train pilots or test new cars.

simulcast If a programme is **simulcast,** it is broadcast on two or more TV channels at the same time, or on TV and radio at the same time. A **simulcast** is a programme broadcast in this way. 'Simulcast' is short for 'simultaneous broadcast'.

simultaneous (simultaneously) **Simultaneous** things happen or exist at the same time. *Five of his productions are running on Broadway and in the West End simultaneously.*

sin (sinning, sinned; sinner) In many religions, **sin** is breaking God's laws by doing something very bad or immoral. A person who behaves like this is called a **sinner.** A particular kind of bad or immoral behaviour is called a **sin.** If you **sin,** you commit a sin.

sin-bin In some team sports such as ice hockey and rugby league, the **sin-bin** is the place where players sit when they have been temporarily sent off.

since ❑ If something has been happening **since** a particular time, it has been happening from that time until now. ◇ **Since** is also used to say something happened at some point between a time in the past and the present. *He died in 1984 and has since been named as a key member in the so-called Oxford spy ring.*

❑ **Since** is also used to say something happened a certain length of time ago. *It is 250 years since the wolf became extinct in Britain.* ◇ If something has **long since** ceased to happen, it has not happened for a very long time.

sincere (sincerely, sincerity) ❑ If someone is **sincere,** they genuinely mean the things they say. You talk about the **sincerity** of someone like this. *He sincerely believed that there were reasonable solutions which could serve the interest of all the countries involved.*

❑ You write **Yours sincerely** followed by your signature at the end of a formal letter when you have addressed it to someone by their name. For example, if you begin a letter 'Dear Mrs Smith' you end it 'Yours sincerely'.

sine die (*pron:* sign-ee die-ee) If something is postponed **sine die,** it is postponed indefinitely. Similarly in sport, a

player can be suspended **sine die.**

sine qua non (*pron:* sign-ee kwa non) If something is a **sine qua non,** it is essential if you want to achieve something or take part in something.

sinecure (*pron:* sign-i-cure) If you call a job a **sinecure,** you mean it is well-paid but does not involve much work or responsibility.

sinew A **sinew** is a cord which connects a muscle to a bone.

sinewy A **sinewy** person has a lean body with strong muscles.

sinful When religious people talk about behaviour being **sinful,** they mean it is wicked or immoral.

sing (singing, sang, have sung) If you **sing,** you use your voice to produce a tune and the words that go with it. ◇ When birds or insects **sing,** they make pleasant musical sounds. ◇ If you **sing** someone's **praises,** you praise them very enthusiastically.

sing-song ❑ A **sing-song** is an occasion when a group of people sing songs together for pleasure.

❑ A **sing-song** voice rises and falls in pitch.

singe (singeing, singed) If something is **singed,** it is burned slightly so that it changes colour but does not catch fire.

singer A **singer** is someone who sings, especially as their job.

single (singling, singled) ❑ A **single** thing is just one thing and not more. *He left behind a single book on the subject of climbing.* ◇ If you talk about each **single** thing, you mean each one taken individually. *Everyone believed it was the right way forward for Europe but not everyone liked every single point.* ◇ The **single** thing which matters most in a situation is the one which matters most when they are all considered individually. *Television is the single most important source of information for the majority of our population.*

❑ If you are **single,** you are not married. ◇ **Singles** activities and organizations are aimed at unmarried people.

❑ A **single** parent is someone who is bringing up their child on their own, because the other parent is not living with them.

❑ **Singles** is a game between two players in tennis, badminton, and several other sports.

❑ A **single** bed or room is intended for one person.

❑ A **single** ticket is for a journey from one place to another but not back again.

❑ A **single** is a recording of one or two short pieces of music on a small record, CD, or cassette.

❑ You use **single** to describe something which has only one part or feature, rather than two or more. *...single yellow lines.*

❑ If a number is in **single figures,** it is less than 10.

❑ If you **single** someone or something **out,** you choose them from a group for special treatment.

❑ **single file:** see file.

single-breasted A **single-breasted** coat, suit, or jacket meets in the middle of the chest and has only one set of buttons.

single cream is thin cream with less fat than most other types.

single-decker A **single-decker** bus does not have an upstairs area.

single-handed (single-handedly) If you do something

single-handed or single-handedly, you do it without help from anyone else.

single-minded If someone is **single-minded**, they have one aim or purpose and are determined to achieve it.

single sex schools, clubs, or other organizations accept people of only one sex.

singlet A **singlet** is a sleeveless T-shirt shaped like a vest.

singly If things happen **singly**, they happen one at a time.

singular (singularity) ❑ If you call something **singular** or talk about its **singularity**, you mean it is unusual and remarkable.

❑ A **singular** noun or pronoun is used to talk about just one person, thing, or group.

singularly means to a remarkable or extraordinary degree. *The property market, in particular, is singularly depressed.*

sinister is used to describe people or things that seem evil or threatening.

sink (sinking, sank, have sunk) ❑ A **sink** is a basin with taps, especially one in a kitchen.

❑ If something **sinks**, it moves slowly downwards and disappears behind something or below the surface of water. *...the sinking sun.* ◇ If a ship is **sunk**, it is attacked with bombs, torpedoes, or other weapons and made to sink. *...the sinking of the Belgrano.*

❑ If you say someone is **abandoning a sinking ship**, you mean they are leaving an organization or project which is in difficulties before it fails completely. ◇ If someone is left to **sink or swim**, they are left to cope on their own without help or support.

❑ If something like a building is **sinking**, it is gradually moving down to a lower level. ◇ If a person **sinks** somewhere, they move or fall into a lower position. *We sank into deep, squashy sofas... He sank to his knees.*

❑ If a value or amount **sinks**, it becomes lower or less.

❑ If something **sinks** into an undesirable or less active state, it passes gradually into it. *The American economy sank into recession in 1990.*

❑ In golf, if you **sink** a putt, you succeed in hitting the ball into the hole from somewhere on the green. Similarly, billiards and snooker players talk about **sinking** a ball. ◇ If you **sink** an alcoholic drink, you drink it.

❑ If your **heart sinks**, you feel dismayed or depressed.

sinner See sin.

Sino- is used to talk about something involving China and another country. *...the Sino-Russian border.*

sinuous is used to describe (a) things which are full of turns or curves. *It's a great drive, a sinuous meander through redwoods.* (b) people and animals that are supple and graceful. *...a tall man with long, sinuous arms.*

sinus (sinuses) Your **sinuses** are the spaces in the bones around your nose.

sinusitis is a painful inflammation of the sinuses.

sip (sipping, sipped) If you **sip** a drink, you drink a small amount at a time. Each mouthful can be called a **sip**.

siphon (siphoning, siphoned) (*or* syphon, *etc*) If someone siphons money or **siphons** it **off**, they use it for a purpose it was not intended for. ◇ If you **siphon** a liquid or siphon it **off**, you draw it out of a container through a tube using atmospheric pressure.

sir ❑ A man is sometimes addressed as **sir**. Official letters often begin 'Dear Sir'.

❑ **Sir** is used in front of the name of a knight or baronet. *...Sir Charles Chadwyck-Healey.*

sire (siring, sired) A horse's **sire** is its father. You talk about a male horse **siring** a foal. ◇ People sometimes say a man **sires** a child.

siren ❑ A **siren** is a warning device which makes a long loud wailing sound.

❑ **Siren** is used to talk about ideas which are attractive and tempting, but which are likely to lead to disaster. You can talk about the **siren song** or **siren call** of ideas like these. ◇ A woman is sometimes called a **siren** when she is attractive and dangerous to men.

sirloin A **sirloin** is a piece of beef cut from the lower part of the animal's back.

sisal (*pron:* sigh-sal) is a plant which is cultivated so that the fibre from its leaves can be used to make rope. It is grown in the West Indies, South America, and Africa.

sissy (sissies) (*or* cissy, cissies) When children call someone a **sissy**, they mean they are cowardly and physically weak.

sister ❑ Your **sister** is a girl or woman who has the same parents as you. See also half-sister. ◇ A **sister** is a member of a female religious community. ◇ In a hospital, a **sister** is a female senior nurse who supervises a ward. ◇ If you talk about a woman's **sisters**, you mean other women she has something in common with. *The score for American women managers is also strikingly lower than the 8% reached by their British sisters.*

❑ **Sister** is used to describe something of the same kind as the thing you have just mentioned, when they are both owned or run by the same company. *The launch of an upmarket sister newspaper to The Voice had been on the cards for a couple of years.*

sister-in-law (sisters-in-law) Your **sister-in-law** is the sister of your wife or husband, or your brother's wife.

sisterhood is affection and loyalty between women who have something in common, especially women who support feminism. ◇ A **sisterhood** is a female religious community.

sisterly is used to describe the feelings sisters have for each other, and the ways they typically behave to each other. *She continued to babysit on the odd occasion and tried to maintain some sisterly contact.* ◇ **Sisterly** is also used to describe feelings of affection and loyalty between women, especially women who support feminism.

sit (sitting, sat) ❑ When you are **sitting** somewhere, your body weight is resting on your buttocks rather than your feet. When you **sit** or **sit down**, you lower your body until you are sitting on something. When you **sit up**, you bring yourself into a sitting position after you have been lying down or leaning back. ◇ If you **sit around** or **sit about**, you spend a lot of time doing nothing except sitting.

❑ If you **sit through** something like a film or lecture, you stay until it is finished even though you are not enjoying it. ◇ If you **sit tight** or **sit** something **out**, you wait for it to finish without taking any action. ◇ If you **sit back** while something is happening, you do not become involved with it. *Tory MPs in the South cannot sit back complacently as they have during other recessions.*

❑ If you **sit up** all night, you do not go to bed. ◇ If something makes you **sit up**, it makes you pay attention.

❑ If you **sit** an examination, you take it.

❑ If you **sit** for an artist, you stay in one position while he or she paints you.

❑ If you **sit** on something like a board or committee, you are a member of it. ◇ If you **sit in on** something like a meeting, you are present but do not take part.

❑ When a parliament, law court, or other official body **sits,** it assembles officially to carry out its work. Each time it does this is called a **sitting.**

❑ The **sitting** member for a parliamentary constituency is its current MP, rather than a past or future one. ◇ A **sitting** tenant is a person who rents a house or flat as their home and is often legally entitled to stay there if the owner sells the property.

❑ If you say someone is **sitting on** something, you mean they are avoiding dealing with it. ◇ **sitting pretty:** see **pretty.**

❑ If you say someone is a **sitting duck,** you mean they are very easy to attack or harm.

sit-down In a **sit-down** strike or protest, the strikers or protestors refuse to move until they get what they are asking for. ◇ A **sit-down** meal is served to people sitting down at tables.

sit-in A **sit-in** is a protest in which people sit in a public place and refuse to be moved.

sitar The **sitar** is a type of Indian stringed musical instrument with a long neck.

sitcom A **sitcom** is a TV comedy series which shows the same set of characters each time becoming involved in amusing situations which are similar to everyday life. 'Sitcom' is short for 'situation comedy'.

site (siting, sited) ❑ A **site** is a piece of ground which is being used or will be used for a particular purpose. ...*a building site... Disney were slow to put hotels on the Florida site.* ◇ If something is **sited** in a particular place or position, it is put there or built there. *Member states will also decide on the siting of the central bank.*

❑ The **site** of something which is no longer there is the place where it used to be. *Make a detour via the Grassmarket, site of the old gallows.* ◇ The **site** of something like a battle is the place where it happened.

sitter A **sitter** is (a) someone who sits for an artist. (b) a baby-sitter.

sitting See **sit.**

sitting room A **sitting room** is a room in a house where people sit and relax.

situated The place where something like a building is **situated** is the place where it is. *Situated on the banks of the Thames, the Centre is engineered for energy efficiency.* You can describe the location of a building by saying, for example, that it is pleasantly **situated** or conveniently **situated.**

situation ❑ When you talk about the **situation,** you are talking generally about what is happening in a particular place at a particular time. *The UN withdrew its relief personnel because it judged the situation too dangerous.* ◇ You also use **situation** to talk about a particular aspect of what is happening. ...*the current financial situation... ...the military situation.*

❑ Your **situation** is your circumstances and the things which are happening to you. *I do what many others would do in my situation.*

❑ The **situation** of something like a building or town is the place where it is, for example its surroundings or its distance from other buildings or towns. *With moated castle and riverside situation, this is an excellent base for exploring the lower part of the Blavet valley.*

situation comedy See **sitcom.**

six is the number 6. ◇ If people are **at sixes and sevens,** they are in a state of confusion.

six-pack A **six-pack** is a set of six cans or bottles of a drink, especially beer.

sixpence The **sixpence** was a small silver coin which was used in Britain until the 1970s. It was worth six old pence (2½p).

sixteen is the number 16.

sixteenth The **sixteenth** item in a series is the one counted as number 16. ◇ A **sixteenth** or **one sixteenth** is the fraction $\frac{1}{16}$.

sixth ❑ The **sixth** item in a series is the one counted as number 6. ◇ A **sixth** or **one sixth** is the fraction $\frac{1}{6}$.

❑ If you say someone has a **sixth sense,** you mean they know things, or seem to know them, without having any direct evidence of them. *His sixth sense in locating the fish was uncanny.*

sixth form (sixth former) In English, Welsh, and Northern Irish schools, the **sixth form** is the class pupils go into at sixteen to study for 'A'-levels. Pupils normally spend two years in this form. Sixth form pupils are called **sixth-formers.**

sixty (sixties, sixtieth) **Sixty** is the number 60. ◇ The **sixties** was the period from 1960 to 1969. ◇ If someone is in their **sixties,** they are aged 60 to 69.

sizable See **sizeable.**

size (sizing, sized) ❑ The **size** of something is how big or small it is. *The departure lounge is now twice its original size.* ◇ The **size** of something is also the fact that it is very large. *More details are emerging of the sheer size of the disaster... The only private-sector industry of any size is tourism.*

❑ A **size** is one of a series of graded measurements, especially for things like clothes and shoes. ...*size 12 feet... ...size 2 eggs.*

❑ If someone is **cut down to size,** they are made to realize that they are not as important or powerful as they thought they were.

❑ If you **size** someone or something **up,** you look at them or think about them carefully, so you can decide how to deal with them.

sizeable (or sizable) If you say something is **sizeable,** you mean it is fairly large.

-sized (or -size) You add **-sized** or **-size** to a word to describe the size of something. ...*medium-sized companies.*

sizzle (sizzling, sizzled) ❑ When food which is being fried or roasted **sizzles,** it makes a hissing sound.

❑ In sport, **sizzling** is used to describe things which are exciting and involve a lot of energy or skill. ...*a sizzling effort by McMahon.*

skate (skating, skated) ❑ A **skate** is an ice-skate or roller-skate. If you **skate,** you move about on ice wearing ice-skates, or on a flat surface wearing roller-skates.

❑ If you **skate over** a difficult subject, you avoid dealing with it fully. ◇ If someone is **skating on thin ice,** they are doing something risky which may get them into trouble.

❏ The **skate** (*plural:* skate) is a flat sea fish which has two large fins like wings.

skateboard (skateboarding, skateboarder) A **skateboard** is a narrow board on wheels which some young people stand on and ride for pleasure. **Skateboarding** is riding on a skateboard; young people who do it are called **skateboarders**.

skater A **skater** is someone who ice-skates or roller-skates, especially in races or competitions.

skein (*pron:* skane) A **skein** is a loosely coiled length of thread, especially wool or embroidery cotton.

skeletal is used to talk about things to do with skeletons. *At least one skeletal fragment is thought to be of a female.* ◇ If a person is **skeletal**, they are so thin you can see the shape of their bones through their skin.

skeleton ❏ The **skeleton** of a person or animal is the framework of bones which supports and protects the muscles and organs of their body. ◇ If someone has a **skeleton in the cupboard** or **in the closet**, they are keeping secret something from their past which is scandalous or embarrassing.

❏ The **skeleton** of a building or other structure is its basic framework. ◇ The **skeleton** of a plan or scheme is its basic outline, to which details may be added later.

❏ If an organization operates with a **skeleton** staff, it keeps going with the smallest possible number of staff.

skeptical (skeptic, skepticism) See **sceptical**.

sketch (sketches, sketching, sketched) ❏ A **sketch** is a quick rough drawing without a lot of detail. If you **sketch** something, you make a quick drawing of it.

❏ If you **sketch** something or **sketch** it **out**, you give a brief description of it without many details. A brief description can be called a **sketch**. ◇ If you **sketch in** details about something, you add them.

❏ A **sketch** is also a short funny piece of acting, usually part of a comedy show. *...Monty Python sketches.*

sketchbook A **sketchbook** is a book of blank pages for drawing on.

sketchpad A **sketchpad** is the same as a sketchbook.

sketchy (sketchily) **Sketchy** reports or accounts are brief and incomplete. You can also say your knowledge of something is **sketchy**. *After Chernobyl, the authorities began to reveal a catalogue of nuclear disasters which had been known about only sketchily or not at all.*

skew ❏ If something is **skewed**, it is altered or distorted so people do not get an accurate picture of a situation.

❏ If something **skews**, it turns aside sharply from the direction it should be going in.

skewer (skewering, skewered) A **skewer** is a long sharp metal pin for holding food together during cooking. ◇ If you **skewer** something, you push a long thin pointed object through it.

ski (skiing, skied) **Skis** are long flat narrow pieces of wood, metal, or plastic which you fasten to boots so you can move easily over snow or slide down snow-covered slopes. When people **ski,** they slide down slopes on skis. ◇ **Ski** is used to talk about various things to do with skiing. *...ski instructors... ...ski boots.*

ski jump A **ski jump** is a specially-built steep slope covered in snow. People ski down it to gather speed, then jump into the air at the end. The **ski jump** is a sporting event in which people ski down a slope like this then try to jump as far as possible.

ski-lift A **ski-lift** is a machine for taking people to the top of a ski slope. It usually consists of a series of seats hanging down from a moving cable.

skid (skidding, skidded) ❏ If a vehicle **skids** or goes into a **skid**, it slides sideways while moving, for example on a wet or icy road.

❏ If you say something like a plan or someone's career is **on the skids**, you mean it is going badly wrong and is about to fail.

skier A **skier** is someone who skis.

skiff A **skiff** is a small light boat.

skiffle A **skiffle** band plays music on guitars and improvised instruments made from household objects.

skilful (skilfully) (*American spelling:* skillful, skillfully) If you are **skilful** at something, you do it very well, often because you have had a lot of experience of it. A **skilful** action is done very cleverly. *The Dutch have skilfully amended their earlier draft to pacify potential opponents.*

skill is the knowledge and ability which enables you to do something well. ◇ A **skill** is a type of work or craft which requires special training and knowledge.

skilled If someone is **skilled**, they have the knowledge and ability to do something well. *...a skilled fisherman.* ◇ **Skilled** work can only be done by people who have been trained to do it. People like these are called **skilled** workers.

skillful See **skilful**.

skim (skimming, skimmed) ❏ If you **skim** something from the surface of a liquid, you remove it. ◇ If something **skims** a surface or **skims over** it, it moves quickly and lightly over the top of it.

❏ If you **skim** a piece of writing or **skim through** it, you read it quickly without looking at all the details.

❏ If someone **skims off** money or some other resource, they take some of it for their own use.

skimmed milk (*or* skim milk) is milk with the cream removed.

skimp If you **skimp** on something, you spend less time or money on it than you should or you use inferior materials, with unsatisfactory or dangerous results.

skimpy (skimpier, skimpiest) If something is **skimpy**, there is very little of it. *...the skimpiest of data.*

skin (skinning, skinned) ❏ A person's or animal's **skin** is the thin outer covering of their body. You use **-skinned** to describe someone's or something's skin. *...fair-skinned people.* ◇ A **skin** is the natural covering of an animal's body, together with its fur or hair, taken from the dead animal to make something like a coat or rug. *...tiger skins.* If you **skin** a dead animal, you remove its skin. ◇ If you describe a person or animal as **skin and bone**, you mean they are very thin.

❏ If you say someone **gets under your skin**, you mean they irritate you.

❏ If you try to **save your own skin**, you selfishly try to get yourself out of a difficult or dangerous situation, often putting other people at risk in the process.

❏ If you do something **by the skin of your teeth**, you only just succeed in doing it.

❏ If you say something is only **skin deep**, you mean it is not as well-established as it seems.

❏ The **skin** of a fruit or vegetable is its outer covering. If you **skin** a fruit or vegetable, you remove its skin.

skin-tight clothes fit very tightly.

skinflint A skinflint is a very mean person who hates spending money.

skinhead A skinhead is a young man whose hair is shaved or cut very short. Some skinheads go round in groups and are thought of as violent and aggressive.

skinny A skinny person is unattractively thin.

skint If you are skint, you have no money.

skip (skipping, skipped) ❑ If you skip something you usually do or are supposed to do, you deliberately do not do it. ◇ If you skip something such as a section of a book you are reading, you miss it out.

❑ If you skip somewhere, you move along with a series of little jumps from one foot to the other. Lambs and other small animals can also skip.

❑ If you skip, you hold the ends of a rope one in each hand and keep turning the rope so it passes over your head and you have to jump over it as it goes under your feet. Sometimes when children skip, the ends of a long rope are held by two children and other children jump over it while it is turned.

❑ A skip is a large metal container for holding rubbish, usually from building work.

skipper (skippering, skippered) The skipper of a boat or ship is its captain. The captain of a sports team is also sometimes called the skipper. You can say someone skippers a boat or team.

skipping-rope A skipping-rope is a rope for skipping, usually with a handle at each end.

skirmish (skirmishes, skirmishing, skirmished) A skirmish is a short battle which is not part of a planned war strategy. If two armed groups skirmish, they have a short battle like this. ◇ A skirmish is also a short sharp argument or dispute. If you skirmish with someone, you have a dispute with them.

skirt ❑ A skirt is a piece of clothing worn by women and girls. It fastens at the waist and hangs down around the legs. ◇ The skirt of a dress or coat is the part which hangs down below the waist.

❑ If you skirt something or skirt round it, you go round the edge of it. You can also talk about a road or path skirting an area.

❑ If you skirt a problem or a question, you avoid dealing with it, because it is difficult or controversial.

skirting board A skirting board is a narrow length of wood which goes round the bottom edge of a wall in a room.

skit A skit is a short performance in which actors make fun of people, events, or types of literature by imitating them.

skitter (skittering, skittered) If an animal skitters somewhere, it moves very quickly and lightly.

skittish If you call someone skittish, you mean they are lively and do not concentrate on anything for very long or take life very seriously. ◇ If an animal is skittish, it is nervous and easily frightened.

skittle Skittles is a game in which players throw a ball at a group of nine wooden objects called skittles. The idea is to knock down as many as possible.

skive (skiving, skived) If you skive, you avoid working, especially by staying away from the place where you

should be working.

skulduggery is behaviour in which someone acts secretly in a dishonest way to achieve their aim.

skulk If someone skulks somewhere, they stay there quietly because they do not want to be seen.

skull The skull is the structure of bones which form the head. ◇ A skull and crossbones is a picture of a human skull above a pair of crossed bones, used to warn of death or danger. It used to appear on the flags flown by pirate ships and is now sometimes found on containers holding poisonous or toxic substances.

skunk The skunk is a small black and white American animal which gives off an unpleasant smell when it is frightened.

sky (skies) ❑ The sky is the space around the earth, which appears white or pale blue in the daytime and black at night. ◇ The air or space above a country or region is sometimes called its skies, especially when talking about aircraft passing through it. ...fighters patrolling the skies over southern Iraq.

❑ the sky is the limit: see limit.

sky-blue is a very pale blue colour.

sky-diving is the sport of jumping out of an aircraft and falling freely through the air for a time before opening your parachute.

sky-high If prices or wages are sky-high, they have reached an exceptionally high level.

skylight A skylight is a small window set in a flat or sloping roof.

skyline The skyline is the outline of buildings, hills, or mountains seen against the sky.

skyscraper A skyscraper is a very tall building with many storeys.

skyward (skywards) If you look skyward or skywards, you look up towards the sky. Similarly, you can talk about something moving skyward or skywards. ◇ If you talk about the price or value of something going skyward or skywards, you mean it is going up very rapidly.

slab A slab of something such as meat, concrete, or ice is a thick flat piece of it.

slack (slackness) ❑ A slack period is one when there is not much activity, especially in business.

❑ If you say someone is slacking, you mean they are being lazy or careless and not doing their job properly. You say people like this are slack or talk about their slackness.

❑ If a rope between two places is slack, it is hanging loosely rather than tightly stretched.

❑ If there is slack in a country's economy, it has resources which are not being fully employed. ◇ If an employer takes up the slack, they regulate their company so that activity and production increase.

❑ Casual trousers are sometimes called slacks.

slacken (slackening, slackened) ❑ If something slackens or slackens off, it becomes slower, less active, or less intense. The protests show no sign of slackening.

❑ If you slacken your grip on something, you hold it less tightly. ◇ You also say someone slackens their grip on something when they control it less firmly, or show signs of being prepared to give it up. Likud was unable to countenance any slackening of the grip on the occupied territories.

slacker A slacker is someone who is lazy and does less

work than they should.

slag (slagging, slagged) ❑ Slag is waste material such as rock left over from mining or waste products from blast furnaces. A **slag heap** is a hill made from large amounts of this material.

❑ If you **slag** someone **off**, you criticize them in an unpleasant way.

slain See slay.

slake (slaking, slaked) If you **slake** your thirst, you drink something to take your thirst away.

slalom (*pron:* slah-lom) The **slalom** is a race, on skis or in canoes, in which competitors follow a twisting difficult course.

slam (slamming, slammed) ❑ If a door or window **slams** or is **slammed**, someone shuts it noisily and with great force. ◇ If you **slam** something somewhere, you put it there quickly and noisily.

❑ If a reviewer **slams** something like a new play or film, he or she criticizes it very severely.

slammer Prison is sometimes called the **slammer**.

slander (slandering, slandered; slanderous) If you **slander** someone, you make untrue spoken statements about them, with the intention of damaging their reputation. The things you say are called **slanders**. Statements of this kind can also be described as **slanderous**. ◇ **Slander** is the offence of making untrue spoken statements about someone with the intention of damaging their reputation. You can be sued for this in a court of law.

slang (slangy) ❑ A **slang** word is an informal one which you would normally only use in conversation. **Slangy** speech or writing has a lot of slang in it.

❑ When people have a **slanging match**, they quarrel and insult each other.

slant ❑ If news or information is **slanted**, it is presented in a way which is biased towards a particular group or opinion. ◇ A **slant** on a subject is a way of looking at it or describing it.

❑ If a surface is **slanting**, it is sloping rather than horizontal or vertical. If something is on a slanting surface, you can say it is **on a slant** or **at a slant**.

slap (slapping, slapped) ❑ If you **slap** someone or give them a **slap**, you hit them with the palm of your hand. ◇ If you **slap** someone on the back, you hit them on their back in a friendly way. Hearty friendly behaviour is sometimes called **back-slapping**.

❑ If you call someone's behaviour towards you a **slap in the face**, you mean you are shocked and upset by it, because you feel it is not justified and it seems like a betrayal. ◇ A **slap on the wrist** is a gentle warning or mild punishment.

❑ If you **slap** something onto a surface, you put it down quickly, carelessly, and noisily. ◇ If something like a tax is **slapped** on something, it is imposed suddenly and unexpectedly.

❑ If someone **slaps down** an idea or suggestion, they dismiss it. ◇ If someone **slaps** someone else **down**, they defeat them quickly and effectively in a dispute or fight.

❑ If you walk or drive **slap bang** into something, you collide with it violently, because you failed to see it. ◇ If you say something is **slap bang** in the middle of a place, you are emphasizing that that is where it is.

slap-up A **slap-up** meal is a large enjoyable one.

slapdash If something is done in a **slapdash** way, it is done quickly and carelessly without much thought or planning.

slapstick is a simple type of comedy in which actors or clowns try to make people laugh by behaving in a silly way, for example by falling over and throwing things at each other.

slash (slashes, slashing, slashed) ❑ If the amount of money spent on something is **slashed**, it is reduced by a large amount. Other things can be **slashed** in a similar way. *Yale is contemplating slashing its academic staff by 11%.*

❑ If you **slash** something with a knife, you make a long deep cut in it.

❑ A **slash** is the symbol / which is used when giving alternatives. *A person can get married at the age of 16, that's two years before he/she can vote.*

slash and burn is a method of tropical farming which involves clearing new land for cultivation by cutting down and burning the natural vegetation on it.

slat (slatted) **Slats** are flat narrow pieces of wood, metal, or plastic set in things such as Venetian blinds or cupboard doors. If something is **slatted**, it is made with slats.

slate (slating, slated) ❑ **Slate** is a dark grey rock which can easily be split into thin layers. **Slates** are small flat pieces of slate used for covering roofs. ◇ In the past, a **slate** was a small piece of slate in a wooden frame which schoolchildren used to write on.

❑ If you **wipe the slate clean** or **start with a clean slate,** you decide to forget previous failures, mistakes, or debts and make a fresh start.

❑ If you **slate** someone or something, you criticize them severely.

❑ If something is **slated** to happen, it is planned or expected to happen.

❑ A **slate** is a short list of people for a political post, from which a parliamentary candidate is chosen.

slaughter (slaughtering, slaughtered) ❑ If a large number of people are deliberately killed, you can say they are **slaughtered** or describe their killing as **slaughter**. ◇ When animals like cows and pigs are **slaughtered**, they are killed for their meat. You can talk about the **slaughter** of farm animals.

❑ If you **slaughter** someone in a competition or contest, you beat them easily and by a large margin.

slaughterhouse A **slaughterhouse** is a place where animals are killed for their meat.

Slav (*pron:* slahv) The **Slavs** are a group of peoples who speak similar languages, mainly in Eastern Europe. Russians, Poles, Czechs, and Bulgarians are all Slavs. **Slav** is used to talk about things to do with Slavs and their countries. *...the first Slav Pope in history.*

slave (slaving, slaved; slavery) ❑ A **slave** is someone who is owned by someone else and has to work for them without pay. The practice of having slaves, which has disappeared in most parts of the world, is called **slavery.** ◇ The **slave trade** was the buying and selling of slaves, especially the transport of black Africans to America and the Caribbean from the 16th century to the early 1800s.

❑ If work is done by **slave labour,** it is done using slaves or very badly-paid workers working long hours in very unpleasant conditions.

❑ If you **slave** or **slave away** at something, you work very hard at it. ◇ If you are a **slave** to something, you allow yourself to be influenced or controlled by it.

slaver (slavering, slavered) If a person or animal **slavers**, saliva drips from their mouth.

slavery See **slave**.

slavish (*pron:* slave-ish) (slavishly) You use **slavish** to describe things which copy or imitate something exactly, without any attempt to be original. *Bulgaria was the East European state which most slavishly followed Moscow lines.*

slay (slaying, slew, have slain) If someone **slays** a person or animal, they kill them.

sleazy (sleazier, sleaziest; sleaze) If you call an activity **sleazy,** you mean it is dishonest or immoral. **Sleaze** is immoral activities, and the reporting of them in some newspapers.

sled A sled is the same as a sledge.

sledge A sledge is a vehicle designed to travel over snow. It consists of a frame mounted on narrow wooden or metal strips called runners which slide over the snow.

sledgehammer A sledgehammer is a large heavy hammer with a long handle.

sleek (sleeker, sleekest) A **sleek** person looks stylish and smart. ◇ A **sleek** vehicle has a smooth graceful shape. ◇ **Sleek** hair or fur is smooth and glossy.

sleep (sleeping, slept) ❑ **Sleep** is the natural state of rest in which your eyes are closed and your mind and body are inactive and unconscious. When you **sleep**, you are in this state. If you have a **sleep**, you sleep for a short time.

❑ If you **sleep through** a noise or disturbance, it does not wake you up. ◇ If you **sleep** something **off,** such as the effects of too much food or alcohol, you recover from it by sleeping.

❑ If you say you are not **losing any sleep** over something, you mean you are not worrying too much about it.

❑ If you say a house, hotel room, or caravan **sleeps** a certain number of people, you mean it has beds or sleeping space for that number of people.

❑ If you **sleep with** someone, especially someone you are not married to or living with, you have sex with them. When two people are doing this regularly, you say they are **sleeping together.** ◇ If someone **sleeps around,** they have sex with several different people.

sleeper ❑ A **sleeper** is an overnight train some of whose carriages have beds for passengers. These beds are in compartments, also called **sleepers.**

❑ On a railway track, the **sleepers** are the large heavy beams, usually of wood or concrete, which support the rails.

❑ You can use **sleeper** to describe the way someone sleeps. For example, if someone is a sound sleeper, they are not likely to be woken up by anything while they are asleep.

sleeping bag A sleeping bag is a large warm bag made of padded fabric, which you use for sleeping in, especially when you are camping.

sleeping car A sleeping car is a railway carriage with beds for passengers to sleep in.

sleeping pill A sleeping pill or sleeping tablet is a pill you take to help you sleep.

sleeping sickness is a serious disease carried by certain types of insects in Africa, which eventually causes a deep coma. The medical name for sleeping sickness is 'trypanosomiasis'.

sleepless (sleeplessness) If you have a **sleepless** night, you are unable to sleep, usually because you are worrying about something. If you suffer from **sleeplessness,** you are often unable to sleep.

sleepwalk If someone **sleepwalks,** they get up and walk around while they are still asleep.

sleepy (sleepier, sleepiest; sleepily, sleepiness) If you are **sleepy,** you feel tired and ready to go to sleep. When someone is in this state, you can talk about their **sleepiness** or say they do something **sleepily.** ◇ A **sleepy** place is quiet and does not have much activity or excitement.

sleet is a mixture of falling snow and rain.

sleeve (-sleeved) ❑ The **sleeves** of a garment are the parts which cover your arms. You use **-sleeved** to describe the sleeves on a garment. *...a short-sleeved shirt.* ◇ If you have something **up your sleeve,** you have an idea or plan you have not told anyone about.

❑ The **sleeve** of a gramophone record is the stiff envelope it is kept in. Some other kinds of protective coverings are also called **sleeves.**

sleeveless A sleeveless garment has no sleeves.

sleigh (*pron:* slay) A sleigh is the same as a sledge.

sleight (*pron:* slite) If something is done by **sleight of hand,** it is done using a skilful piece of deception.

slender ❑ A **slender** person is thin in an attractive way.

❑ **Slender** is also used to say something is quite small. For example, you can say the chances of something happening are **slender.** A **slender** amount is a small amount.

slept See **sleep**.

sleuth (sleuthing) A **sleuth** is a detective. The work a detective does is sometimes called **sleuthing.**

slew (slewed) ❑ See **slay**.

❑ A **slew** of people or things is a lot of them.

❑ If a vehicle **slews,** it slides or skids to one side.

slice (slicing, sliced) ❑ A **slice** is a piece of food cut from a larger piece. ◇ If you **slice** food, you cut it into thin pieces or wedges of about the same size.

❑ If you talk about someone obtaining a **slice** of something, you mean they obtain a part of it. *...a prime slice of Britain's defence industry.* ◇ If a certain amount is **sliced off** something, it is reduced by that amount.

❑ If something **slices through** air or water, it cuts through it like a knife.

❑ If you **slice** the ball in tennis, golf, or cricket, you hit its edge rather than its centre, so it travels away from you at an angle.

slick (slickly, slickness) ❑ A **slick** is the same as an oil slick.

❑ A **slick** person is persuasive and speaks easily, but may not be sincere. Similarly, you say something like a book or film is **slick** when it is well-made but lacks depth or sincerity.

❑ You can call an action or performance **slick** when it appears quick, easy, and effortless. *...a highly accomplished, slickly staged show... They brought a new sophistication and slickness to modern theatre.*

❑ If you **slick back** your hair, you smooth it close to your head and make it shiny by putting something like hair oil or gel on it.

slide (sliding, slid) ❑ When something **slides** or when you slide it, it moves smoothly over or against a surface. ◇ In a children's playground, a **slide** is a structure which has a steep slope for the children to slide down. ◇ If there is a mud **slide** or a rock **slide**, a large amount of rock or mud comes loose and falls down a hill.

❏ If something like the economy **slides** or goes into a **slide**, it gradually gets worse. *His political ratings are sliding.* ◇ If you let something **slide**, you allow it to get worse by not attending to it.

❏ If a country **slides** towards a new situation or a different type of political system, it gradually gets closer to it. *The slide towards federalism started in 1968.*

❏ If you say someone **slides** somewhere, you mean they move there smoothly and quietly.

❏ A **slide** is a small piece of photographic film mounted in a frame. You project light through the slide to display the picture on a screen. ◇ A **slide** is also a piece of glass which you put something on when you want to examine it under a microscope.

❏ A **slide** is also the same as a hair slide.

slide rule A **slide rule** is an instrument you can use for making calculations. It looks like a ruler and has a middle part which slides backwards and forwards. Slide rules have now been replaced by calculators.

sliding scale A **sliding scale** is a system for calculating something like taxes or wages, in which the amounts paid vary as other things vary.

slight (slightly) ❏ If something is **slight**, it is quite small. *...a slight increase.* ◇ **Slightly** is used to say something has a quality to a small extent. *He poured the coffee with a slightly shaky hand.* ◇ You use **in the slightest** to emphasize that something is not so. *I don't feel guilty about it in the slightest.*

❏ A **slight** person is small and slim. *...a slightly built man with a moustache.*

❏ If you call a book or play **slight**, you mean there is nothing in it of real interest or importance.

❏ If someone **slights** you, they insult you by ignoring you or treating you as if you were unimportant. You call behaviour like this a **slight.**

slim (slimmer, slimmest; slimming, slimmed) ❏ A **slim** person has a thin attractive well-shaped body. ◇ If you **slim,** you try to lose weight by eating less or by eating healthier food. People who try to lose weight are called **slimmers.**

❏ A **slim** object is smaller or thinner than usual. *He published only three slim volumes of verse.*

❏ If you **slim** something or **slim** it **down,** you reduce it.

❏ If you say the chances of something happening are **slim,** you mean it is unlikely to happen.

slime (slimy, slimier, slimiest) You call a substance **slime** when it is thick and slippery and looks or smells unpleasant. ◇ **Slime** is also a thick sticky substance which comes from the bodies of slugs, snails, fish, and some other creatures. ◇ If something is **slimy,** it is covered in slime. ◇ If you call a person **slimy,** you mean they flatter people and behave in a friendly way towards them, but only so they can get something out of them.

slimline objects are thinner than other objects of their kind. *...a slimline storage heater.*

slimmer See slim.

slimy See slime.

sling (slinging, slung) ❏ If you **sling** something over your shoulder or on your back, you hang it there so you can carry it. ◇ If something is **slung** between two points, it is attached to them and hangs loosely between them.

❏ If you **sling** something somewhere, you throw it there carelessly.

❏ A **sling** is (a) a device made of ropes or straps, for lifting and carrying heavy loads. (b) a piece of cloth hung round your neck to support a broken or injured arm. (c) a device for carrying a baby on your back or across the front of your body.

slingshot A slingshot is the same as a catapult.

slink (slinking, slunk *not 'slinked'*) If you **slink** somewhere, you move there in a slow secretive way because you do not want to be seen.

slinky clothes fit closely to a woman's body in a sexually attractive way.

slip (slipping, slipped) ❏ If something like the price of a commodity **slips,** it falls to a lower level. A fall like this can be called a **slip.** ◇ If someone or something **slips** into a certain state, they gradually worsen until they are in that state. *The little boy was slipping into a coma.*

❏ If you **slip,** your feet start to slide and you lose your balance. You can also talk about objects **slipping** when they slide out of place or out of your hands.

❏ If you **slip** somewhere, you go there quickly and quietly, usually trying to avoid being seen. ◇ If you **slip** something somewhere, you put it there quickly in a way which does not attract attention. ◇ If you **slip** someone something, you give it to them secretly.

❏ If you **slip up** or make a **slip,** you make a mistake. A **slip-up** is a small mistake. ◇ If you let something **slip,** you accidentally tell someone about it when you had intended to keep it secret. ◇ If something **slips your mind,** you forget about it.

❏ If you **slip into** clothes or **slip** them **on,** you put them on quickly and easily. Similarly, you can **slip out of** clothes or **slip** them **off.**

❏ A **slip** is also a small piece of paper, for example one which records the details of a payment in a bank or shop.

❏ A **slip** is also a petticoat.

❏ **slip a disc:** see disc.

slip-on shoes have no laces and can be put on and taken off easily.

slip road A **slip road** is a road leading off or onto a motorway or other main road.

slip-up See slip.

slippage is failure to maintain a steady level or to meet a deadline. *...a substantial slippage in the value of sterling.*

slipper Slippers are soft comfortable shoes for wearing indoors.

slippery (slipperiness) ❏ If something is **slippery,** it is smooth, wet, or greasy, and is difficult to keep hold of or walk on. *...the slipperiness of the surface.*

❏ A **slippery** person is dishonest and cannot be trusted.

❏ You can also say something is **slippery** when it is hard to pin down or define. *Anti-Americanism is a slippery concept.*

❏ When people talk about a **slippery slope,** they are suggesting that something could start an unstoppable process which would have very serious consequences for everyone, especially by restricting people's freedom.

Speed limits, they declare, are the first step down tyranny's slippery slope.

slipshod If something is done in a **slipshod** way, it is not done carefully or thoroughly.

slipstream The **slipstream** of a fast-moving object, especially a car or plane, is the flow of air directly behind it.

slipway A **slipway** is a large platform sloping down into water on which ships are built or repaired and from which they are launched.

slit (slitting, slit *not 'slitted'*) If you **slit** something or make a **slit** in it, you make a long narrow cut in it. ◇ A **slit** is also a long narrow opening in something.

slither (slithering, slithered) If something **slithers**, it slides along in an uneven way. *After overturning, the coach slithered for about sixty yards.*

slithery If something is **slithery**, it is wet and slippery and moves in a twisting way, like a snake.

sliver A **sliver** is a very small thin piece of something.

Sloane A **Sloane** or **Sloane Ranger** is a young upper-class person, especially a woman, who wears expensive but informal clothes and comes from the area of London around Sloane Square.

slob (slobbish) If you call someone a **slob** or describe them as **slobbish,** you mean they are very dirty and untidy.

slobber (slobbering, slobbered) If someone **slobbers**, they let saliva fall from their mouth, like a baby.

sloe **Sloes** are small sour fruit which have a dark purple skin and are often used to make alcoholic drinks.

slog (slogging, slogged) ❏ If you say a piece of work is a **slog,** you mean it is difficult and needs a lot of effort. ◇ If you **slog** at something, you work hard and steadily at it.

❏ A **slog** is also a long and difficult journey on foot. If you **slog** somewhere, you make your way there on foot.

❏ If two people **slog it out,** they fight, compete, or argue over something.

slogan **Slogans** are short easily-remembered phrases used in advertising or by politicians.

sloganeer (sloganeering, sloganeered) If you accuse someone of **sloganeering,** you mean they are using slogans rather than reasoned arguments to try to get people's support.

sloganize (sloganizing, sloganized) (*can be spelled with an 's' instead of a 'z'*) **Sloganizing** is the same as sloganeering.

sloop A **sloop** is a yacht or small sailing ship with a mast and two sails.

slop (slopping, slopped) ❏ If you **slop** liquid somewhere, you spill it messily over the edge of its container.

❏ **Slop** or **slops** is a mixture of food waste and liquid which is fed to animals.

slope (sloping, sloped) ❏ A **slope** is a side of a hill, mountain, or valley. ◇ A **slope** is also a flat surface which is at an angle, so that one end is higher than the other. You say a surface like this **slopes.** The **slope** of something is the angle at which it slopes.

❏ If you **slope off,** you go away quickly and quietly, often because you are trying to escape or avoid something.

sloppy (sloppily, sloppiness) ❏ If you call a piece of work **sloppy,** you mean it has been carelessly done. *The experiment had been sloppily performed... He ranted against what he saw as sloppiness on the job.*

❏ A **sloppy** substance is soft and almost liquid.

slosh (sloshes, sloshing, sloshed) If a liquid **sloshes** or if you **slosh** it **around,** it splashes or moves around messily. ◇ When people make their way on foot through water or mud, you can say they **slosh** through it.

slot (slotting, slotted) ❏ A **slot** is a narrow opening in a machine or container, for example a hole you put coins through to make a machine work. ◇ If something **slots** into something else or is **slotted** into it, it fits into it exactly.

❏ A **slot** is also a place in a schedule or scheme, especially a place kept for a particular purpose. *BBC Scotland will be providing programmes for the Late Show slot every month.* ◇ If you **slot** someone or something into a schedule or scheme, you find a place for them in it.

slot machine A **slot machine** is a machine for gambling, operated by putting coins into a slot. Slot machines are found in places like amusement arcades and casinos.

sloth (*rhymes with 'both'*) ❏ **Sloth** is laziness.

❏ The **sloth** is an animal found mainly in Central and South America. Sloths move very slowly and live in trees, hanging upside down from the branches.

slothful If someone is **slothful,** they are lazy and unwilling to work.

slouch (slouches, slouching, slouched) If you **slouch,** you sit or walk in a lazy or tired way with your shoulders and head drooping downwards. ◇ If you say someone is **no slouch** at something, you mean they are skilful at it or know a lot about it.

slough ❏ If you **slough off** something you no longer need, you get rid of it. (*For this meaning, 'slough' rhymes with 'rough'.*)

❏ If someone is in a **slough** of despair or self-pity, they are in a bad emotional state which they cannot get rid of. (*For this meaning, 'slough' rhymes with 'now'.*)

slovenly A **slovenly** person is untidy in their appearance or careless in their work.

slow (slowly, slowness) ❏ **Slow** is used to describe things which move or happen without much speed. *...a slow train... The gas built up slowly in the cabin.* ◇ If you say someone is **slow** to do something, you mean they do not respond as quickly as they should.

❏ If something **slows** or is **slowed,** it starts to move or happen less quickly. You can also say something is **slowed up** or **slowed down.** ◇ If you talk about a person **slowing down,** you mean they are becoming less active, because they are getting old.

❏ If you say someone is **slow,** you mean they take a long time to understand something. *We sighed at the slowness of our classmates.*

❏ If a clock is **slow,** it is showing a time earlier than the real time.

❏ If you say something like business is **slow,** you mean there is very little activity.

slow motion If a film is shown in **slow motion,** it is shown at a slower speed than its correct speed.

slow-witted If you say someone is **slow-witted,** you mean they are not very clever or take a long time to understand things.

slowdown A **slowdown** in an activity is a reduction in it.

sludge is a mixture of liquid and solids, for example thick mud or sewage.

slug (slugging, slugged) ❏ The **slug** is a small slow-moving creature with a long slimy body, like a snail without a shell.

❏ If you take a **slug** of a drink, you take a large mouthful of it.

❏ If two people **slug it out**, they fight each other or argue angrily about something.

sluggard A **sluggard** is a lazy person.

sluggish (sluggishly, sluggishness) You say something is **sluggish** when it is moving or operating at a very slow rate. ...*traffic moving sluggishly north...* ...*the continued sluggishness of the economy.*

sluice (sluicing, sluiced) A **sluice** is a passage which carries a current of water. It has an opening called a **sluice gate**, which can be opened and closed to control the flow. ◇ If you **sluice** something, you wash it with a stream of water or some other liquid.

slum (slumming, slummed) A **slum** is an area of a city where poor people live and where houses are overcrowded and badly in need of repair. ◇ If someone says they are **slumming it**, they mean they are doing something more cheaply than usual, such as staying in a cheaper hotel or eating in a cheaper restaurant.

slumber (slumbering, slumbered) **Slumber** is sleep. If someone is **slumbering**, they are asleep.

slump ❏ If there is a **slump** in something such as demand or if it **slumps**, it falls suddenly and sharply. *Porsche sales have slumped badly.* ◇ A **slump** is a period when a country's industry or economy slows down, causing high unemployment and poverty.

❏ If you **slump** somewhere, you sit down heavily, because you are very tired.

slung See sling.

slunk See slink.

slur (slurring, slurred) ❏ A **slur** is an insulting remark which could damage someone's reputation.

❏ If someone **slurs** their speech, their words are indistinct and tend to run into each other. People who are drunk often slur their speech.

slurp If someone **slurps** a liquid, they drink it noisily.

slurry is a watery mixture of something such as mud, cement, or manure.

slush (slushy) **Slush** is snow which has begun to melt and is very wet and dirty. You say snow like this is **slushy**. ◇ A **slushy** story or novel is very romantic and sentimental.

slush fund A **slush fund** is money put aside to finance an illegal activity or to pay bribes, especially in politics or business.

slut A woman is sometimes called a **slut** when people think her sexual behaviour is immoral.

sly (slyly) A **sly** look or remark shows you know something other people do not. ◇ A **sly** person is secretive and clever at deceiving people. ◇ If something is done **on the sly**, it is done without many people knowing about it, because they might object if they did.

smack ❏ If you **smack** someone, you hit them sharply with the flat of your hand.

❏ If you say something **smacks** of a particular thing, you mean it suggests that thing is present or happening. *The announcement smacked of panic.*

❏ If you say something is **smack** in a particular place, you mean it is exactly in that place. ...*the Keats-Shelley Me-*

morial House, smack by the Spanish Steps.

❏ **Smack** is heroin.

small is used to describe things which are not as large in size as usual. ...*a small garden.* ◇ A **small** child is a very young child. ◇ **Small** is also used to describe amounts and numbers which are not large. *They were the work of a small group of architects.* ◇ **Small** is also used to describe things which are not significant or great in degree. *It's now becoming clear that Vietnam is content to play a smaller role in Cambodia.*

❏ If you talk about the **small fry**, you mean the less important people of a particular kind.

small ad The **small ads** in a newspaper are the short advertisements, often for things people want to sell or buy privately, or for rooms they want to let.

small arms are lightweight guns such as rifles and pistols, as opposed to artillery.

small business A **small business** is a company or firm which does not have many employees and does not belong to a larger company. A **small businessman** or **businesswoman** owns or runs a business like this.

small change is coins of low value. ◇ If you say an amount of money is **small change** to someone, you mean it is not a large amount to them, because they are very rich.

small-minded (small-mindedness) If you say someone is **small-minded** or talk about their **small-mindedness**, you mean they have fixed opinions and are unwilling to change them or to think about a wider range of subjects.

small-scale activities or organizations are small in size and limited in scope.

small screen The **small screen** is television.

small talk is polite conversation at social occasions, usually about fairly trivial things.

small-time businesses or crooks are not considered very important because they do not operate on a large scale.

small-town things exist in small towns as opposed to cities. ...*small-town courts.* ◇ **Small-town** is also used to describe attitudes thought to be typical of people living in small towns.

smallholding (smallholder) A **smallholding** is a piece of agricultural land run like a very small farm. A person who runs a smallholding is called a **smallholder**.

smallish means fairly small.

smallpox was a serious infectious disease which caused a high fever and a rash that scarred the skin badly. Smallpox used to be common in some parts of the world, but now appears to have been wiped out.

smarmy If you call someone **smarmy**, you mean they are unpleasantly over-polite and flattering.

smart (smartly) ❏ A **smart** person is well-dressed and tidy in appearance. **Smart** clothes are clean, neat, and usually fashionable. ◇ A **smart** place or event is connected with rich and fashionable people.

❏ **Smart** also means clever.

❏ A **smart** movement or action is sharp and quick. ...*a smartly taken goal.*

❏ If a part of your body **smarts**, you feel a sharp stinging pain there. ◇ If you are **smarting** from something which has happened to you, you are upset about it, because you feel you have been humiliated or unfairly treated.

smart-alec (*or* smart-aleck) If you call someone a smart-alec, you mean they keep trying to appear cleverer than other people.

smart card A smart card is a small plastic card containing a microchip. Smart cards have a number of uses. For example, at some checkouts you can use a smart card to pay for goods directly from your bank account.

smarten (smartening, smartened) If you smarten something or smarten it up, you make it look neater, tidier, and more appealing.

smash (smashes, smashing, smashed) ❑ If you smash something, you hit it, throw it, or drop it so that it breaks into a lot of pieces. When something breaks into pieces like this, you say it smashes. ◇ If you smash something up, you deliberately destroy it by hitting it so that it is crushed or breaks into many pieces. ◇ If you smash down a door or barrier, you hit it very hard so that it breaks and falls down. ◇ If you smash through something or smash your way through it, you hit it hard enough to break through it. ◇ If something smashes into something else, it hits it with great force. ◇ A car crash is sometimes called a smash.

❑ If someone smashes something like an organization, they succeed in destroying it. You can also talk about someone smashing something like a person's career.

❑ If a song, play, or film is a smash or a smash hit, it is very successful and popular.

❑ In tennis, a smash is a stroke in which a player hits the ball downwards very hard.

smash-and-grab In a smash-and-grab robbery, a thief smashes a shop window, seizes the goods which are on display, and runs off with them.

smashing If you call something smashing, you mean you like it or admire it very much.

smattering A smattering of something is a small amount of it. A smattering of people or things is a small number of them.

smear (smearing, smeared) ❑ A smear is an unpleasant and untrue rumour or accusation. If you say there is a smear campaign against someone, you mean people are trying to damage their reputation by circulating unpleasant and untrue rumours about them. This can also be called smearing the person.

❑ If you smear a surface with a substance, you spread it over the surface. You can also say you smear the substance onto the surface. ◇ A smear is a dirty or greasy mark on a surface, caused by something coming into contact with it. If something smears a surface, it leaves a dirty or greasy mark.

❑ A smear or a smear test is a medical test in which a few cells from a woman's cervix are removed and analysed to detect any early signs of cervical cancer.

smell (smelling, smelled *or* smelt) ❑ If you smell something, you become aware of it through your nose. The quality you become aware of is called its smell. If something has a strong smell, especially an unpleasant one, you say it smells. ◇ -smelling is used to describe something's smell. ...*sweet-smelling shrubs.* ◇ You also say you smell something when you put your nose near to it and breathe in to discover its smell.

❑ If you say you smell something like danger or trouble, you mean you feel it is present or likely to happen.

◇ If you smell a rat, you become suspicious that something is wrong.

smelly (smellier, smelliest) If you call something smelly, you mean it has an unpleasant smell.

smelt (smelter) ❑ See smell.

❑ When an ore is smelted, it is heated in a furnace called a smelter until it melts, so that the metal can be extracted.

smidgeon (*or* smidgen *or* smidgin) A smidgeon is a very small amount. *I have a smidgeon of sympathy for Gatting.*

smile (smiling, smiled; smilingly) ❑ When you smile, the corners of your mouth curve outwards and slightly upwards, because you are pleased or amused. An expression like this is called a smile. ◇ Smile is used to say someone is smiling when they say something. *Mr Kantor smilingly announced that America would go along with its original plan.*

❑ If you say luck or fate has smiled on you, you mean you have been very lucky in some way. Similarly, if you get the right weather for what you want, you can say the weather has smiled on you.

smirk If someone smirks, they smile in an unpleasant and smug way, because they have gained an advantage over you, or know something you do not know. You call their expression a smirk.

smite (smiting, smote, have smitten) ❑ If you smite something, you hit it hard. ◇ If you say someone smote something or smote another person, you are saying in a humorous way that they attacked them or criticized them.

❑ If you are smitten by something, you are very impressed with it and enthusiastic about it. ◇ If you are smitten with another person, you are strongly attracted to them or in love with them.

smith A smith is the same as a blacksmith.

smithereens If something is smashed to smithereens, it is smashed into a lot of tiny pieces and is completely destroyed.

smithy (smithies) A smithy is a place where a blacksmith works.

smitten See smite.

smock A smock is (a) a loose garment, rather like a long blouse, worn especially by women. (b) a loose garment worn over other clothes to protect them.

smog (smoggy) Smog is a mixture of smoke and fog which occurs in some industrial cities. You call a city like this smoggy or describe the air there as smoggy.

smoke (smoking, smoked; smoker) ❑ Smoke consists of gas and particles of solid material sent into the air when something burns. If something is smoking, it is sending smoke into the air. ◇ If people smoke someone out, they force them to come out of a place by filling it with smoke.

❑ When someone smokes a cigarette, cigar, or pipe, they breathe in smoke from it, then blow it out again. If someone smokes or is a smoker, they do this regularly. ◇ A smoking section or compartment of a vehicle is for people who want to smoke.

❑ When meat or fish is smoked, it is hung over burning wood so the smoke will preserve it and give it flavour.

❑ If something goes up in smoke, it is completely destroyed by fire. ◇ You also say something goes up in smoke when it fails or ends without anything being achieved.

smokeless fuel burns without producing any smoke.

smoker See smoke.

smokescreen If you call what someone does or says a smokescreen, you mean it is intended to hide the truth about their actions or intentions.

smokestack A smokestack is a tall chimney used in heavy industry to carry smoke away from a factory. ◇ Smokestack industry is old-fashioned coal-powered industry which tends to cause pollution.

smoky You say a place is smoky when there is a lot of smoke there. ◇ Smoky food tastes or smells of smoke.

smolder See smoulder.

smooch (smooches, smooching, smooched; smoochy) When people smooch, they kiss and hold each other closely. ◇ You also say people smooch when they dance very slowly with their arms round each other. Smoochy songs and music are slow and suitable for this sort of dancing.

smooth (smoothly; smoothie or smoothy) ❑ A smooth surface or object has no roughness, lumps, or holes. ◇ If you smooth something or smooth it out, you remove the creases or roughness from it and make it flat.

❑ A smooth liquid or mixture has been mixed well and has no lumps in it.

❑ A smooth movement or process is steady and even, with no sudden changes or breaks. ◇ If you have a smooth ride or flight, it is comfortable because there are no sudden bumps or jolts.

❑ Smooth is used to say something goes well and is free of problems or trouble. *Whether things continue to go smoothly depends mainly on the reaction of the United States.*

❑ If you smooth the path or smooth the way for something, you make it easier or more likely to happen. ◇ If you smooth over a problem or difficulty, you make it seem less serious and easier to deal with.

❑ If you call a man smooth or a smoothie, you mean he is confident and polite, but probably not sincere. You say someone is smooth-talking when they talk in a persuasive way but you do not trust them.

smorgasbord is a type of Scandinavian buffet with a wide choice of savoury dishes.

smote See smite.

smother (smothering, smothered) If something is smothered in things, it is completely covered with them. ◇ If you smother a fire, you cover it with something to put it out. ◇ If someone smothers someone else, they kill them by covering their face to stop them breathing. ◇ If an activity or process is smothered, it is prevented from continuing or developing.

smoulder (smouldering, smouldered) (*American spelling:* smolder, *etc*) If something smoulders, it burns slowly, producing smoke but not flames. ◇ If a feeling such as anger or hatred smoulders, people keep it inside themselves and do not express it.

smudge (smudging, smudged; smudgy) ❑ A smudge is a dirty mark. If you smudge a surface, you make dirty marks on it. ◇ If you smudge writing, you rub it and make it blurred so that its outline or details are no longer clear.

❑ If something like a photograph is smudgy, it is blurred. ◇ If something in the distance appears as a

smudge, you see it as an unclear or blurred shape.

smug (smugly, smugness) If you call someone smug, you mean they are too pleased with their behaviour or achievements. *...smugly congratulating themselves on a victory... His smugness was getting me down.*

smuggle (smuggling, smuggled; smuggler) If you smuggle things or people into or out of a place, you get them in or out illegally or secretly. A person who smuggles goods into or out of a country is called a smuggler.

smut (smutty) Smut is stories, films, and pictures which deal with sex or nudity in a crude way, to entertain and titillate people. You call this sort of thing smutty. *...a smutty sex film.* ◇ Smut or smuts is dirt in the air, especially soot, which leaves dark marks on things.

snack A snack is a light quick meal. ◇ Snacks are small light things to eat, often served with drinks. If you snack, you eat things like these instead of main meals, or in between main meals.

snack bar A snack bar is a place where you can buy light meals and drinks.

snaffle (snaffling, snaffled) If you snaffle something or snaffle it up, you take it quickly for yourself.

snag (snagging, snagged) ❑ A snag is a small difficulty, disadvantage, or problem.

❑ If something like clothing or a rope snags on a rough or sharp object, it gets caught on it.

snail The snail is a small slow-moving creature with a slimy body and a spiral-shaped shell on its back. ◇ If you say something is done at a snail's pace, you mean it is done very slowly.

snake (snaking, snaked) Snakes are long thin scaly reptiles with flexible bodies and no legs. ◇ If something snakes, it goes along in a series of curves. *...a queue of more than sixty people snaked its way down the pavement.*

snakes and ladders is a children's game played with dice on a board which has squares, some of which are connected with drawings of snakes and ladders. You move up the board if you reach the bottom of a ladder and move down it if you get to the top of a snake. The first player who gets to the finishing square at the top of the board is the winner.

snap (snapping, snapped) ❑ If someone snaps at you, they speak in a sharp unfriendly way. ◇ If an animal snaps at you, it shuts its jaws suddenly as if it was going to bite you.

❑ If you snap or your patience snaps, you stop being calm and become angry, because you cannot put up with someone's behaviour any longer.

❑ A snap decision or action is made suddenly, often without careful thought. ◇ If a government holds a snap election, it announces it suddenly and tries to get it over with as quickly as possible, because it thinks it is in a good position to win.

❑ If an object snaps or is snapped, it breaks suddenly with a short loud sound. ◇ If something is snapped into position, it is moved there suddenly with a clicking sound. *The Queen snapped shut her spectacle-case and folded away her speech.* ◇ If you snap your fingers, you make a clicking sound by moving one of your middle fingers sharply across your thumb.

❑ A snap is a photograph taken quickly and casually. If you snap someone or something, you take a photograph of them.

❏ If you **snap** something **up,** you buy it quickly because it is a bargain or because it is exactly what you want.

❏ A **cold snap** is a sudden short period of cold and frosty weather.

snapdragon The **snapdragon** is a common garden plant with small colourful flowers which can be opened and shut like a mouth.

snappy (snappier, snappiest; snappily) ❏ If you call something like a show **snappy,** you mean it is lively, energetic, and well performed. ◇ A **snappy** slogan or advert is brief and to the point.

❏ A **snappy** dresser wears smart stylish clothes. *The Brodskys are certainly Britain's most snappily dressed string quartet.*

❏ If someone is **snappy,** they answer in a sharp unfriendly way when you speak to them.

snapshot A **snapshot** is a photograph taken quickly and casually. ◇ If something gives you a good indication of what a situation is like, you can call it a **snapshot** of the situation. *A balance sheet is a snapshot of a company's value.*

snare (snaring, snared) ❏ A **snare** is a trap used to catch birds or small animals. If a bird or animal is **snared,** it is caught in a trap like this. ◇ If someone **snares** an opponent or enemy, they get them into a dangerous or difficult situation by deceiving them.

❏ If someone **snares** something like a prize, they win it. Similarly, you can say a company **snares** a certain share of the market or a certain amount of new business.

snarl ❏ When an animal **snarls,** it makes a fierce growling sound and shows its teeth. ◇ If you **snarl** something, you say it in a fierce angry way.

❏ If a process is **snarled up,** it is slowed down or brought to a standstill by something that is happening. You call a situation like this a **snarl-up.**

snatch (snatches, snatching, snatched) ❏ If you **snatch** something, you quickly take it from a person or place. ◇ You also say someone **snatches** something when they steal it.

❏ If you **snatch** an opportunity, you quickly make use of it to do what you want. If you **snatch** some sleep, you take advantage of an opportunity to sleep for a short time. ◇ If you **snatch** victory in a competition or contest, you defeat your opponent by winning a vital goal or point at the last minute.

❏ If you hear a **snatch** of a conversation or song, you hear a very small part of it.

snazzy (snazzier, snazziest) If you say something is **snazzy,** you mean it is stylish and attractive, sometimes in a rather showy way.

sneak (sneaking, sneaked) ❏ If you **sneak** somewhere, you go there quietly, trying not to be seen or heard. Similarly, if you **sneak** something somewhere, you put it there secretly.

❏ If you **sneak** a look at something, you look at it when you think nobody is watching. ◇ **Sneak** is used to describe other things people do which they hope will not be noticed. *Earlier this year senators had sneaked through a pay rise for themselves.*

❏ If you get a **sneak preview** of something like a film or exhibition, you get to see it before its official opening.

❏ If you have a **sneaking** feeling that something is true, you suspect it is true, although you are not sure why. ◇ **Sneaking** is used to describe other feelings you have which you cannot explain and which you are not too willing to admit to. *I even have a sneaking fondness for the architecture of Sizewell A.*

sneaker **Sneakers** are light casual shoes, usually made of canvas, with rubber soles.

sneaky (sneakily) If you call an action **sneaky,** you mean it is done secretly, in the hope that people will not notice. *I was sneakily reading a Len Deighton thriller instead of the edition of The Tempest my wife had packed.*

sneer (sneering, sneered) If someone **sneers** at something, they show by their remarks or manner that they think it is stupid or inferior. ◇ A **sneer** is an expression on someone's face which shows they think something is stupid or inferior. A remark can also be called a **sneer.**

sneeze (sneezing, sneezed) When you **sneeze,** you suddenly and involuntarily gasp in air then blow it down your nose explosively. This is called a **sneeze.** ◇ If you say something is **not to be sneezed at,** you mean it is quite important or worth having, and should not be rejected without thinking about it.

snicker (snickering, snickered) If someone **snickers,** they laugh quietly in a disrespectful way.

snide If someone makes a **snide** remark or comment, they criticize someone or something in an unpleasant but indirect way.

sniff ❏ When you **sniff,** you breathe in air noisily through your nose, for example because you have a cold, or are trying not to cry. ◇ If you **sniff** something, you smell it by breathing in through your nose. ◇ If someone **sniffs** a substance like glue, they deliberately breathe it in to get its effects as a drug.

❏ You can use **sniff** to say someone says something in a superior or contemptuous way. *'You can't have peacekeepers if there's no peace to keep,' a British minister sniffed.* ◇ If you **sniff** at something, you reject or ignore it because you think it is stupid or inferior.

❏ If you say something is **not to be sniffed at,** you mean it is well worth having.

❏ If you **sniff** something **out,** you eventually find it after looking for it.

sniffer dog A **sniffer dog** is a dog used by the police, customs officers, or the army to find drugs or explosives by sniffing their scent.

sniffle (sniffling, sniffled) If you **sniffle,** you sniff repeatedly, because you have a cold or have been crying.

sniffy (sniffier, sniffiest; sniffily) If someone is **sniffy,** they are scornful or contemptuous about something. *The Morris Minor was the runabout that Lord Nuffield sniffily described as a 'poached egg'.*

snigger (sniggering, sniggered) If you **snigger,** you laugh quietly in a disrespectful way. A laugh like this is called a **snigger.**

snip (snipping, snipped) ❏ If you say something which is for sale is a **snip,** you mean it is cheap and good value.

❏ If you **snip** something or **snip** through it, you cut it with a pair of scissors.

snipe (sniping, sniped; sniper) ❏ If someone **snipes** at you, they keep criticizing you. ◇ You also say someone **snipes** at you when they shoot at you from a hidden position. A person who does this is called a **sniper**.

❑ The **snipe** is a bird with a very long beak which normally lives in marshy areas.

snippet A **snippet** of news or information is a small piece of it.

snivel (snivelling, snivelled) (*American spelling:* sniveling, sniveled) If someone **snivels**, they keep crying or sniffing in an irritating way.

snob (snobbish, snobbishly, snobbishness, snobbery) ❑ Upper-class people who look down on the lower classes are sometimes called **snobs**. Their behaviour is called **snobbish**. ◇ You say other people are **snobs** when they admire and respect upper-class people and try to behave like them.

❑ You also say someone is **snobbish** or a **snob** when they think they have better taste than other people.

❑ The attitudes of any kind of snob can be called **snobbishness** or **snobbery**.

snook If you **cock a snook** at someone in authority, you do something cheeky which they cannot punish you for, and which shows your contempt for them.

snooker is a game played by two people on a large table covered in smooth green cloth with six pockets at the edges. The players use long sticks called cues to hit a white ball so that it knocks coloured balls into the pockets.

snoop (snooping, snooped; snooper) You say someone is **snooping** when they are secretly trying to find out things about a person's private or business affairs. You call someone like this a **snooper**.

snooty (snootier, snootiest; snootily, snootiness) If you say someone is **snooty** or talk about their **snootiness**, you mean they behave as if they are superior to other people. *Many West Berliners snootily complain of the Easterners who came over to shop.*

snooze (snoozing, snoozed) If you **snooze** or have a **snooze**, you have a short light sleep.

snore (snoring, snored) If someone **snores** when they are asleep, they make a loud noise when they breathe. This noise is called a **snore**.

snorkel (snorkelling, snorkelled) (*American spelling:* snorkeling, snorkeled) A **snorkel** is a short tube used by someone swimming face down on the surface of the sea. One end of the snorkel stays just above the surface, so the swimmer can breathe. If you **snorkel**, you swim like this using a snorkel.

snort If you **snort** or let out a **snort**, you blow air out noisily through your nose. ◇ If someone **snorts** a drug like cocaine, they breathe it in quickly through one nostril.

snout An animal's **snout** is its nose.

snow is the soft white pieces of frozen water that sometimes float from the sky in cold weather. When snow falls, you say it is **snowing**. ◇ If you are **snowed in** or **snowed up**, you cannot leave your house or go anywhere because there is so much snow on the ground.

❑ If you are **snowed under**, you have a great deal of work to deal with, especially paperwork.

snow-capped A **snow-capped** mountain is covered with snow at the top.

snow-white If something is **snow-white**, it is a pure white colour.

snowball ❑ A **snowball** is snow pressed into a ball. Children throw snowballs at each other for fun.

❑ If a situation **snowballs**, it gets out of hand and rapidly becomes more serious.

snowboard (snowboarding, snowboarder) A **snowboard** is a narrow board like a skateboard without wheels, which some people use for travelling over snow instead of skis. Riding a snowboard is called **snowboarding**; a person doing it is called a **snowboarder**.

snowbound If a road is **snowbound**, it is blocked by snow. If a place is **snowbound**, you cannot get to it because of deep snow on the ground.

snowdrift A **snowdrift** is a high bank of snow which the wind has blown into one place.

snowdrop The **snowdrop** is a small white flower which appears in early spring.

snowfall A **snowfall** is a shower of snow which settles on the ground and covers it. ◇ The **snowfall** in an area or country is the amount of snow which falls there over a certain period.

snowflake A **snowflake** is one of the soft white bits of frozen water which float to the ground as snow.

snowline The **snowline** is the height on a mountain or group of mountains above which there is snow all year round.

snowman (snowmen) A **snowman** is a mass of snow which has been pressed together to look roughly like a person.

snowplough (*American spelling:* snowplow) A **snowplough** is a vehicle used to clear snow off roads, airport runways, or railway lines.

snowstorm A **snowstorm** is a very heavy fall of snow, usually with a strong wind.

snowy A **snowy** place is covered in snow. ◇ You also say something is **snowy** when it is white like snow.

SNP The **SNP** is the Scottish National Party. The SNP contests parliamentary seats in Scotland and campaigns for Scottish independence from the United Kingdom.

Snr See **senior**.

snub (snubbing, snubbed) If someone **snubs** you, they insult you by ignoring you or behaving rudely to you. ◇ A **snub** is a deliberately insulting remark or piece of behaviour.

snuff ❑ If someone in power **snuffs out** something like a rebellion, they put a stop to it quickly and forcefully. ◇ If you **snuff** a flame or **snuff** it **out**, you put it out, usually by covering it with something.

❑ A **snuff** movie is a pornographic film in which one of the actors is actually killed at the end.

❑ **Snuff** is powdered tobacco which people take by sniffing it up one nostril.

snuffle (snuffling, snuffled) If people or animals **snuffle**, they make sniffing noises.

snug (snugly) ❑ If you are **snug**, you feel warm and comfortable. ◇ A **snug** place is small, warm, and comfortable. ◇ If something like a piece of clothing is **snug**, it fits closely or tightly. *The tennis shoes fitted snugly.*

❑ A **snug** or **snug bar** is a small room in a pub.

snuggle (snuggling, snuggled) If you **snuggle** somewhere, you settle yourself into a warm comfortable position, especially by moving closer to another person.

so ❑ You use **so** when you are mentioning something for a second time, to avoid repeating yourself. *One driver in* *three admitted leaving a car unlocked at some time, one in ten did so often.* ◇ You also use **so** when you are saying that something which has just been said about one person or thing is also true of another one. *The price of present economic policy is high, but then so is the goal.*

❑ You use **so** or **so that** when you are mentioning the result of something. *Waves have further eroded the limestone, so that each island is wider above the high-tide mark than it is at water-level.* ◇ You also use **so that** when you are mentioning the reason for doing something. *It can be wired in several ways so that thieves cannot easily learn how to override the system.*

❑ You use **so** to emphasize the degree or extent of something. *No other country is so devoted to good food... Neither had expected to reach an Olympic final so soon in life.*

❑ You use **so** with words like 'much' and 'many' to indicate that there is a limit to something. *You can only go so far by car before you have to walk.* ◇ You also use **so many** when you are saying what a group of things reminds you of. *...those unblinking television cameras hanging over them like so many black spiders.*

❑ You use **or so** when you are giving an approximate number. *If this continues, the native squirrel will be extinct in ten years or so in England and Wales.* ◇ You use **and so on** or **and so forth** at the end of a list to show there are other items you could also mention. *Hospitals, universities, airports and so forth require a great deal of maintenance.*

❑ If you say something **is so**, you mean it is as just described. *This suggests that the disease might be passed on from cow to calf. If that is so, BSE will persist for many years to come.* ◇ You use **so called** to explain how something gets its name. *Another species invading Britain is the American crazy ant, so called because of its erratic movements.*

❑ You use 'as' or 'just as' with **so** to say two events or situations are alike in some way. *Just as the old Communist Party had to go, so too must the old Union.* ◇ You use **not so much** and **not so much...as** to say something is one kind of thing rather than another. *Newbridge is not so much a village, more a pair of pubs.*

❑ You use **so much as** after words like 'no' and 'not' to say something does not happen or exist even in the smallest amount or degree. *No piece of paper exists, the advisers say, that so much as mentions a two-speed Europe.*

so-and-so You use **so-and-so** to stand for any person or thing. *You may have noticed that the words 'so-and-so is on holiday' have been cropping up under regular opinion columns recently.*

so-called ❑ You use **so-called** in front of the name of something when you think it is an unsuitable name for the thing you are talking about. *On Wednesday the so-called rush hour lasted until well after midnight for some commuters.*

❑ **so called**: see **so**.

soak (soaking, soaked) ❑ If you **soak** something or leave it to **soak**, you put it into a liquid and leave it there for a period of time. ◇ When a liquid **soaks** something, it makes it very wet. If you say someone or something is **soaked, soaking,** or **soaking wet**, you mean they are very wet. ◇ If a liquid **soaks** through something, it passes through it. ◇ If a substance **soaks up** a liquid or a gas, it absorbs it.

❑ If someone **soaks** you, they take a lot of money from

you, for example by getting you to buy something very expensive or by making you pay heavy taxes.

❑ A **soak** is a person who drinks too much alcohol and is often drunk.

soap (soaping, soaped) ❑ **Soap** is a substance used with water for washing.

❑ A **soap** or **soap opera** is a TV drama serial about the daily lives of a group of people. Soap operas are often shown daily or several times a week at a regular time and do not have a fixed number of episodes.

soapbox (soapboxes) A **soapbox** is a small temporary platform which a person stands on when making a speech outdoors to passers-by.

soapy If something is **soapy**, it is full of soap or covered with soap.

soar (soaring, soared) ❑ If an amount **soars**, it increases rapidly.

❑ If something **soars** into the air, it moves quickly upwards. ◇ **Soaring** is used to describe things like trees or buildings when they are unusually tall or high. *...a soaring vaulted roof.*

sob (sobbing, sobbed) ❑ When someone **sobs,** they cry in a noisy way, taking short gasping breaths. The noises they make are called **sobs.** ◇ If you **sob** something, you say it at the same time as you are crying.

❑ If someone tells you a **sob story**, they tell you about something bad which has happened to them, to make you feel sorry for them.

sober (sobering, sobered; soberly) ❑ If you are **sober,** you are not drunk. ◇ When someone **sobers up**, they become sober again after being drunk.

❑ A **sober** person is serious and thoughtful. You can also call someone's behaviour **sober.** ◇ You say things are **sobering** when they make you take a more serious view of something. You can also say they have a **sobering** effect.

❑ **Sober** clothes are plain and rather dull. *For court work they should be dressed suitably soberly.*

sobriety is serious and thoughtful behaviour. ◇ If you say someone is in a state of **sobriety,** you mean they are not drunk.

sobriquet (pron: so-brik-ay) (or **soubriquet**) A **sobriquet** is the same as a nickname.

soccer is the same as football.

sociable (sociability) **Sociable** people are friendly and enjoy meeting and talking to other people. You talk about the **sociability** of people like these.

social (socially) ❑ **Social** is used to talk about things to do with society and the way it is organized. *...social classes... The country has developed socially and economically in recent decades.* ◇ The **social order** in a place is the way society is organized there.

❑ **Social** occasions are organized so that people can meet other people. *The last great social event of the Scottish season is the Perth Ball.* ◇ A person's **social skills** are their manners and their ability to get on well with other people.

❑ **Social** animals live together in groups and co-operate regularly with other members of the group. *How do social insects like bees and ants successfully resist infections?*

social climber (social climbing) A **social climber** is someone who mixes with people of a higher social class, hoping they will be accepted as a member of that class.

Behaviour like this is called **social climbing**.

social democracy is a political system in which social justice and equality are maintained within the framework of a mixed economy. A **social democracy** is a country organized on these lines.

social democratic (social democrat) A **social democratic** party is a political party whose principles are based on social democracy. Its members and supporters are called **social democrats**.

social drinking is drinking alcohol on social occasions and with friends, rather than on your own.

social engineering consists of attempts by a government to change the way people behave in order to produce the type of society it wants.

social life (social lives) Your **social life** consists of the time you spend with your friends and acquaintances, for example at parties or in their homes. ◇ The **social life** of a country is the way relations between different social groups and classes are organized there.

social science (social scientist) **Social science** is the scientific study of society. A **social scientist** is a person who studies or teaches social science. ◇ The **social sciences** are the various branches of social science, including sociology, anthropology, economics, and politics.

social security In Britain, **social security** is the system by which the government pays money regularly to people who have no income or only a very small income, to help them pay for essentials such as food, clothes, and heating. ◇ In the US, **social security** is the system by which the government pays money regularly to people who have retired from work, to people who are disabled or unemployed, or to the family of a worker who has died.

social services are the services and facilities provided by a local authority to help people who have social and financial problems.

social studies is a subject taught in some British schools and colleges. It includes sociology, politics, and economics.

social work (social worker) **Social work** involves giving help and advice to people with serious personal, family, or financial problems. People who do this kind of work are called **social workers**.

socialise See socialize.

socialism (socialist) **Socialism** is a set of beliefs and principles whose general aim is to create a system in which everyone has an equal opportunity to benefit from the country's wealth. This is usually achieved by having all the country's main industries owned by the state. **Socialist** is used to talk about things connected with or based on socialism. *...socialist economies*. A **socialist** party is one which sets out to fulfil the aims of socialism. A **socialist** is a person who believes in socialism or is a member of a socialist party. A **socialist** country has a political system based on some kind of socialism, especially a Marxist kind.

socialite A **socialite** is a person who attends a lot of fashionable upper-class social events and who is well-known because of this.

socialize (socializing, socialized; socialization) *(can be spelled with an 's' instead of a 'z')* ❏ If you **socialize**, you meet other people socially, for example at parties.

❏ You say young people are **socialized** when they learn to behave in a way which is acceptable in their society or culture. This process is called **socialization**.

society (societies) ❏ **Society** is people in general, thought of as a large organized group. *...women's role in society*. You talk about the people in a country or region, or the people living in a certain period, as a particular kind of **society**. *We are now living in a multi-cultural society... ...Edwardian society*.

❏ A **society** is an organization for people who have the same interests or aims. *...the Geological Society of London*.

❏ **Society** is also the rich upper-class fashionable people in a place who meet at dinners, parties, and other entertainments.

socio- is added to some words to say something has two aspects, one of them being a social aspect. For example, socio-legal studies are concerned with how the law operates in a social system. *...socio-economic conditions... ...socio-political organizations*.

sociology (sociologist, sociological) **Sociology** is the study of human societies and of the relationships between groups in these societies. A **sociologist** is an expert on this subject. **Sociological** is used to talk about things to do with sociology. *...sociological analysis*.

sock Socks are pieces of clothing which cover the foot and ankle and are worn inside shoes. ◇ If you tell someone to **pull their socks up,** you mean they should make an effort to do better or work harder.

socket A **socket** is a device on a wall or on a piece of electrical equipment which you put something like a plug or bulb into. ◇ A **socket** is also a hollow part or opening which another part fits into, for example in the body. *...eye sockets... ...tooth sockets*.

sod A **sod** of earth is a chunk of the surface of the ground, together with the grass and roots growing in it.

soda In Britain, **soda** or **soda water** is fizzy water which people add to alcoholic drinks or fruit juice. ◇ In the US, **soda** is a sweet fizzy flavoured drink. *...cherry soda*.

sodden If something is **sodden,** it is very wet.

sodium is a silvery-white chemical element which combines with other chemicals. Salt is a compound of sodium.

sodomy is anal sexual intercourse, especially between males.

sofa A **sofa** is a long comfortable stuffed seat with a back and arms, which two or more people can sit on.

sofa-bed A **sofa-bed** is a sofa with a seat which folds out so it can be used as a bed.

soft (softly, softness) ❏ If something is **soft,** it changes shape easily when you press it and is not hard or stiff. *A sudden downpour of rain made the pitch soft*. ◇ You also say something is **soft** when it is very smooth and pleasant to touch. *...soft fur*.

❏ If you give something, for example, a **soft** kick, you kick it gently.

❏ A **soft** sound or voice is quiet and not harsh. *They replied softly in Hindi*. ◇ A **soft** light or colour is pleasant and restful rather than bright or glaring.

❏ If you take a **soft** line or approach to a problem, you are careful and diplomatic when dealing with it. ◇ If you choose the **soft** option in a certain situation, you take the course of action which will cause you the fewest immediate difficulties, although it may not be the best course in the long run.

❑ If you say someone is **soft on** something, you mean they are not strict or severe enough when dealing with it. *They believe the Home Secretary has gone soft on law and order.* ◇ If you say someone is a **soft touch**, you mean they are easily persuaded to do things or lend money.

❑ If you have a **soft spot** for someone or something, you are particularly fond of them.

❑ **Soft** drugs are drugs like marijuana, which are illegal but are not considered as strong or harmful as other addictive drugs.

❑ **Soft** water is the water obtained through the water supply in most parts of the country. It contains relatively small amounts of iron, calcium, and magnesium, and produces a lather fairly easily when soap is added. See also **hard**.

soft drink Soft drinks are cold drinks like lemonade or fruit juice, as opposed to alcoholic drinks.

soft-focus If something is filmed or photographed in soft-focus, it is deliberately filmed or photographed so the image is slightly blurred.

soft furnishings are things like cushions, curtains, and furniture covers.

soft-hearted people are kind and sympathetic.

soft-pedal If you **soft-pedal,** you reduce the amount of activity or pressure you have been using to get something done. *He clashed with the establishment when he refused to soft-pedal an investigation into the scandal.*

soft porn is pornography which shows or mentions sexual acts, but not in a very specific or violent way.

soft sell A **soft sell** is a method of selling or advertising which involves gentle persuasion rather than putting pressure on people.

soft-soap If you **soft-soap** someone, you flatter them to try to persuade them to do something.

soft-spoken If someone is **soft-spoken,** they have a quiet gentle voice.

soft target A **soft target** is one which can be easily attacked and destroyed because it is not a military target and is not defended.

softball is a game similar to baseball, but played with a larger softer ball and a smaller bat. The ball used in this game is called a **softball.**

soften (softening, softened) ❑ If something **softens** or is **softened,** it becomes less hard, stiff, or firm.

❑ If something **softens** the shock or the damaging effect of something, it reduces it and makes it less severe.

❑ If you **soften** towards someone or something, you become more sympathetic and less hostile towards them.

❑ If you **soften** someone **up,** you put them in a good mood or prepare them in some way, so they are more likely to agree with you or help you. ◇ When a military force **softens up** an opposing army, it attacks it from a distance to weaken it before approaching it and fighting it at close range.

softie See **softy.**

softly-softly If you have a **softly-softly** approach to something, you are cautious and patient and avoid force or confrontation.

software Computer programs are often referred to as software.

softwood is wood such as pine, which can be sawn easily.

softy (*or* softie) (softies) If you call someone in authority a **softy,** you mean they are weak, easily persuaded, and not strict enough. ◇ You can also call someone a **softy** if they are easily made to feel sympathy or sadness, for example by a sad film or story.

soggy If something is **soggy,** it is unpleasantly soft and wet.

soil (soiling, soiled) ❑ Soil is the top layer on the surface of the earth, which plants grow in. You can say an area has a particular **soil.** *...thin, dry sandy soils.*

❑ **Soil** is sometimes used to talk about the territory covered by a particular country. For example, you can talk about something happening 'on Irish soil'. *She became the first British sovereign to set foot on Spanish soil.*

❑ If something is **soiled,** it becomes dirty and stained.

soiree (*or* soirée) (*pron:* swah-ray) A **soiree** is a social gathering in the evening.

sojourn (*pron:* soj-urn) A **sojourn** is a short stay in a place which is not your home.

solace (*pron:* sol-iss) If you find **solace** in something, you get comfort from it when you are sad, upset, or disappointed.

solar is used to talk about things to do with the sun. *...solar radiation.* ◇ **Solar** is also used to describe things which use the sun's light and heat as a source of energy. *...solar powered fridges.*

solar cell A **solar cell** is a device which converts the sun's rays into electricity.

solar eclipse See **eclipse.**

solar panel A **solar panel** is a panel-shaped device for generating electricity, made up of solar cells.

solar plexus (solar plexuses) The **solar plexus** is the network of nerves at the back of the stomach, or the area between the navel and the breastbone.

solar system A **solar system** consists of a sun and all the planets, comets, and asteroids which go round it. When people talk about **the solar system,** they usually mean the system the Earth belongs to.

solar wind Solar winds are streams of ions and electrons which are constantly released by the sun and which travel at very high speeds.

solarium A **solarium** is a place equipped with sun-lamps, where you can go to get a suntan artificially. ◇ A **solarium** is also a room which is mostly made of glass, to allow as much sun in as possible.

sold See **sell.**

solder (soldering, soldered) If you **solder** two pieces of metal together, you join them by putting a piece of soft metal called **solder** between them and heating it up, so that when it cools down it holds them together. A **soldering iron** is a tool used for soldering things together.

soldier (soldiering, soldiered) ❑ A **soldier** is a person who serves in an army.

❑ If you **soldier on** with something, you keep working hard at it, although it is difficult or unpleasant.

soldiery is soldiers thought of as a group rather than as individuals. *...the local soldiery.*

sole (solely) ❑ The **sole** thing or person of a certain type is the only one. *...Dublin's sole remaining racecourse.* Similarly, the **sole** reason for doing something is the only one.

The decisions were made solely on medical grounds. ◇ Sole is also used to describe something which is not shared with anyone or anything else. *Local authorities will have sole responsibility for carrying out assessments... ...a museum devoted solely to his work.*

❑ The **sole** of your foot is the underneath part which you stand on. ◇ The **sole** of a shoe is the underneath part towards the front.

❑ **Sole** are a kind of flat sea fish you can eat.

solecism (*pron:* sol-iss-izz-um) A **solecism** is an embarrassing mistake.

solemn (solemnly, solemnity) **Solemn** behaviour is serious, rather than humorous or cheerful. *He paused and solemnly read them their rights.* When people behave like this, you can talk about their **solemnity**. *With great solemnity we assented.* ◇ A **solemn** promise or oath is made in a very formal way and cannot be broken.

solemnize (solemnizing, solemnized; solemnization) (*can be spelled with an 's' instead of a 'z'*) When a wedding ceremony is held in a place of worship, you say the marriage is **solemnized.** You can also say something like an agreement is **solemnized** when it is signed as part of a ceremony or in a very formal way.

solicit (soliciting, solicited) If you **solicit** something such as money from someone, you try to get them to give it to you. ◇ When a prostitute **solicits,** she or he approaches someone and offers to have sex with them for money. The offence of publicly offering sex for money is called **soliciting.**

solicitor A **solicitor** is a lawyer who gives legal advice and prepares legal documents and cases.

Solicitor General In England and Wales, the **Solicitor General** is the second most important law officer, next in rank to the Attorney General. Scotland also has a **Solicitor General,** who is next in rank to the Lord Advocate.

solicitous (solicitude) If someone is **solicitous,** they show a lot of concern for someone such as a visitor or guest, and are anxious that everything should be all right for them. You call behaviour like this **solicitude.**

solid (solidly, solidity) ❑ A **solid** substance or object is firm and does not change shape easily. Solid substances can be called **solids.**

❑ You also say an object is **solid** when it is not hollow. ◇ **Solid** is also used to say an object is made of the same substance all the way through. For example, you say an object is **solid** gold or **solid** oak.

❑ A **solid** structure is strong and not likely to collapse or fall over. You can talk about the **solidity** of a structure like this.

❑ **Solid** people are respectable and reliable.

❑ **Solid** facts are specific and definite, rather than vague.

❑ If support for someone is **solid,** everyone supports them and there is no opposition. *The Cabinet remained solidly behind her throughout the leadership campaign.*

❑ **Solid** is also used to say something takes place throughout a period of time. *After seven solid years of growth, imported cars accounted for 5% of the cars sold in Japan last year.*

solid fuel is any fuel which is not a liquid or a gas, for example coal, wood, or peat.

solid-state electronic equipment is made using transistors, silicon chips, or other semi-conductors instead of valves or mechanical parts.

solidarity If a group of people show **solidarity,** they show unity and agreement in their aims or actions.

solidify (solidifies, solidifying, solidified) When a liquid **solidifies** or is **solidified,** it changes into a solid. ◇ If something like a system **solidifies,** it becomes firmer or more definite and is less likely to change. Similarly, you can talk about someone's opinions **solidifying.**

soliloquy (soliloquies) A **soliloquy** is a speech in a play in which a character speaks to himself or herself, rather than to another character. ◇ If you talk to yourself, you can say you are conducting a **soliloquy.**

solitary ❑ If there is a **solitary** thing of a particular kind, there is just one. *He left a solitary fingerprint.*

❑ A **solitary** activity is one you do on your own. ◇ A **solitary** person or animal spends a lot of time alone. ◇ If a place is **solitary,** there are no people there.

solitary confinement If a prisoner is kept in **solitary confinement,** he or she is kept alone, away from other prisoners.

solitude is being on your own.

solo (solos; soloist) ❑ In an orchestral or choral work, an important part for an individual player or singer is called a **solo.** The person who plays it or sings it is called a **soloist.** ◇ A **solo** is also a piece of music played or sung by just one person.

❑ Any performance given by just one person can be called a **solo** performance. You can also talk about someone doing something **solo.** *She lost her life when flying solo in 1937.*

solstice The **solstices** are the two times in the year when the sun is farthest away from the equator. In the northern hemisphere, the summer solstice is on June 21 or 22, and the winter solstice is on December 21 or 22. In the southern hemisphere, the winter solstice is in June and the summer solstice is in December.

soluble A **soluble** substance will dissolve in a liquid. ◇ If a problem is **soluble,** it can be solved.

solution ❑ A **solution** to a problem or difficulty is a way of dealing with it or overcoming it. ◇ The **solution** to a question or puzzle is the answer or explanation.

❑ A **solution** is also a liquid in which a solid substance or a gas has been dissolved.

solve (solving, solved) If you **solve** a problem or a puzzle, you find a solution to it.

solvent (solvency) ❑ If a person or an organization is **solvent,** they have enough money to pay all their debts. Being in this position is called **solvency.**

❑ **Solvents** are liquids which dissolve other substances. ◇ **Solvent abuse** is the dangerous practice of inhaling the vapour from glue and other substances, to experience pleasant sensations.

sombre (sombrely) (*American spelling;* somber, somberly) If you say someone is **sombre** or their mood or view is **sombre,** you mean they are serious or pessimistic. ◇ **Sombre** colours are dark and dull.

sombrero (sombreros) A **sombrero** is a man's hat with a very wide brim. Sombreros are worn especially in Mexico.

some is used to talk about an amount of something or a

number of people or things. *I've managed to find some money... Some houses were damaged.*

❏ **Some of** is used to talk about a part of something, or part of a group of people or things. *Some of the money will be used to repay Panama's debts... Enterprising attempts have been made to release some of the captives.*

❏ **Some** is used to say a distance or period of time is fairly large. *He is likely to remain an officer for some years to come.*

❏ **Some** is used in front of a number to show it is approximate. *The next four years are expected to bring in some $3 billion worth of sponsorship.*

❏ **Some** is also used to talk about an individual person or thing vaguely, without saying exactly which one you mean. *The government was terrified of people getting into the country under some pretext and turning out to be spies.* **Some...or other** is used in a similar way. *Every day there's an column written by some economist or other saying let the dollar fall.*

❏ **Some day** or **someday** means at a date in the future which is unknown or has not yet been fixed. *Like the dinosaur, the human race could some day face extinction.*

somebody See someone.

someday See some.

somehow You use **somehow** to say you do not know how something was done or how it will be done. *I had somehow put on a grey jacket with a pair of trousers that didn't match... Somehow or other, Project Europe has to be re-launched.* ◇ You also use **somehow** to indicate that you do not know the reason for something. *The giants of the industry are somehow supposed to be different.*

someone (*or* **somebody**) You use **someone** or **somebody** to talk about a person without saying who. *The idea that somebody had to pay the bill never entered our heads.*

someplace In the US, **someplace** means somewhere. *He decided he would go someplace for a beer.*

somersault ❏ If you **somersault** or turn a **somersault**, you roll forward on the ground, so your body goes over your head. You also say a diver or acrobat turns a **somersault** when they turn over completely in mid-air.

❏ You can also say someone performs a **somersault** when they completely reverse their opinions or policies. *Germany's Social Democrats performed yet another somersault in announcing that they were, after all, prepared to enter a coalition with the conservatives.*

something ❏ You use **something** to talk about an action, event, object, or quality, without saying which one. *Something must be done to assist the repossessed families who have nowhere to go... Every traveller looks for something different from a guidebook.*

❏ If you say a person or thing is **something of** a particular thing, you mean they are that thing to a limited extent. *There was something of the hippy in Gordon... The portrait caused something of a scandal when it was first exhibited.*

❏ If you say there is **something in** what someone says, you mean it is at least partly true.

sometime means at a time in the future which is unknown or has not yet been fixed. *The drug will be launched in Europe sometime this year.*

❏ **Sometime** is also used to say someone had a particular job or role in the past. For example, the **sometime** Archbishop of Canterbury is someone who used to be Archbishop of Canterbury.

sometimes You use **sometimes** to say something happens on certain occasions or in certain cases rather than all the time or in every case. *Symptoms of malaria may sometimes not appear until a year after a traveller has returned.*

somewhat means to some extent. *Recently, the movement has appeared to recover somewhat, with its membership put at 100,000 by some commentators... Sales and profits were somewhat lower than the previous year.*

somewhere ❏ You use **somewhere** to talk about a place without saying where. *She wants the sculpture to be removed and put on permanent exhibition somewhere in London.*

❏ You also use **somewhere** when you are giving an approximate number, amount, or time. *I calculate that it will be somewhere around 2030 before we can expect to see the judiciary equally balanced between men and women.*

❏ If you say you are **getting somewhere**, you mean you are making progress.

somnolent If you feel **somnolent**, you are drowsy or sleepy.

son ❏ Someone's **son** is their male child.

❏ If you say a man is the **son** of a place, you mean that is where he comes from. *...New Orleans's most famous son, Louis Armstrong.*

son et lumière (*pron:* **sonn** eh **loo**-mee-air) is an entertainment held at night in an old building such as a castle. A person describes the history of the place while different parts of the building are brightly lit and music is played.

son-in-law (sons-in-law) Someone's **son-in-law** is their daughter's husband.

sonar is a device on a ship which uses sound waves to measure the depth of the sea or to find the position of underwater objects.

sonata (*pron:* **sonn**-nah-ta) A **sonata** is a piece of classical music, usually written for a solo instrument or for a piano and one other instrument. Most sonatas are in three or four movements.

song ❏ A **song** is a piece of music with words which are sung to the music. ◇ **Song** is used to talk about the act of singing. *You expect her and the rest of the cast to break into song at any minute.* ◇ A bird's **song** is the pleasant musical sounds it makes.

❏ If you buy something **for a song**, you buy it for much less than its real value.

song and dance A **song and dance** act is one in which a person or group of people both sing and dance. ◇ If you say someone is making a **song and dance** about something, you mean they are making an unnecessary fuss about it.

songbird A **songbird** is any bird which produces musical sounds which are like singing. Blackbirds and larks are songbirds.

sonic is used to talk about things to do with sound. *...sonic imaging... ...sonic scanning.*

❏ A **sonic boom** is the sudden loud noise heard when an aircraft reaches a speed faster than the speed of sound.

sonnet A **sonnet** is a poem with 14 lines in which some lines rhyme with others according to a fixed pattern.

sonorous (sonority, sonorities) ❏ A **sonorous** sound is deep and rich. You talk about the **sonority** of a sound like this. ◇ When people talk about the **sonorities** produced by an orchestra, they mean the range and quality of the different sounds.

❑ **Sonorous** words sound important and impressive.

soon (sooner, soonest) ❑ If something is going to happen **soon**, it will happen after a short time. If something happened **soon** after a particular time or event, it happened a short time after it.

❑ If you say you will do something **as soon as you can** or **as soon as possible**, you mean you will do it immediately it becomes possible.

❑ If you say something will happen **sooner or later**, you mean it will certainly happen, although you cannot be sure when.

❑ If you say **the sooner the better**, you mean something should be done as quickly as possible.

❑ If you say something happened **as soon as** something else happened, you mean it happened immediately after it. *As soon as Meryl dropped out, I lost interest.* ◇ Similarly, if you say **no sooner** did one thing happen **than** another thing happened, you mean the second thing happened immediately after the first. *No sooner had the justices had their say than a flurry of legislative activity began on Capitol Hill.*

❑ If you say you **would sooner** do something, you mean you would prefer to do it. *I would sooner live in an enterprising and changing society than in a stagnant one.*

soot (sooty) **Soot** is a black powder which rises in the smoke from a fire and collects on the insides of chimneys and other surfaces. A **sooty** place is covered in soot.

soothe (soothing, soothed; soothingly) If you **soothe** someone who is angry, worried, or upset, you make them feel calmer. *...soothing words... Certain of victory, Mr Albert is now soothingly talking of co-operation, not conquest.* ◇ If something like an ointment **soothes** pain, it makes it less severe.

soothsayer A **soothsayer** is someone who predicts the future.

sooty See **soot**.

sop A **sop** is something small or unimportant you offer to someone who is dissatisfied or discontented to prevent them from getting angry or causing trouble. *His title of Deputy Prime Minister was a sop awarded on his sacking as Foreign Secretary last year.*

sophisticated (sophistication, sophisticate) ❑ A **sophisticated** device, machine, or method is very advanced and complex. ◇ **Sophisticated** is used to describe people who have become knowledgeable in a particular field and are able to deal with fairly complicated matters in that field. *As users become more sophisticated, they are often happy to install the equipment themselves.*

❑ A **sophisticated** person knows about culture, fashion, and other matters considered to be socially important. People like these are sometimes called **sophisticates**. You can also talk about their **sophistication.**

sophistry (*pron:* **soff-iss-tree**) (sophistries) **Sophistry** is using clever arguments which sound convincing but are actually false. Arguments like these can be called **sophistries**.

soporific If something is **soporific**, it makes you feel sleepy.

sopping If something is **sopping** or **sopping** wet, it is very wet.

soppy If you say someone or something is **soppy**, you mean they are sentimental and silly.

soprano (sopranos) A **soprano** is a woman, girl, or boy with a high singing voice. In four-part choral singing, the highest part is called the **soprano** part.

sorbet (*pron:* **sor-bay**) is a dessert made from semi-frozen syrup of sugar and water flavoured with liqueurs or fruit.

sorcery (sorcerer; sorceress, sorceresses) In stories, **sorcery** is performing magic using the power of evil spirits. A person who does this is called a **sorcerer**. A female sorcerer is sometimes called a **sorceress**.

sordid behaviour is dishonest or immoral. *A series of new financial scandals has reminded ordinary folk of the sordid shenanigans going on among the rich and the powerful.* ◇ You can say a place is **sordid** when it is dirty, unpleasant, and depressing.

sore (sorely) ❑ If part of your body is **sore**, it is causing you pain and discomfort, for example because of a wound or infection. ◇ A **sore** is a painful place on someone's body where the skin is infected.

❑ If you are **sore** about something, you are angry and upset about it. ◇ If a subject is a **sore point** with you, you do not like to talk about it and are likely to become angry or upset if it is mentioned.

❑ If you are **in sore need** of something, you need it very badly. *...a sorely needed loan.* ◇ If something is **sorely** missed, people regret very much that they no longer have it or it is no longer available. *His talents are sorely missed in the current crisis.*

❑ If you say something **sticks out like a sore thumb**, you mean it does not fit in well with other things and is very noticeable.

sorghum is a tall cereal grass which looks similar to maize. It originally came from Africa and Asia, but is now mainly grown in the US.

sorrel is a leafy bitter-tasting herb used in salads and soups.

sorrow is a feeling of great sadness or regret. ◇ **Sorrows** are events or situations which cause great sadness. *The region can blame man, rather than God, for its sorrows.*

sorrowful (sorrowfully) If someone is **sorrowful**, they are very sad. *He shook his head sorrowfully.* ◇ **Sorrowful** things make you feel sad. *...a sorrowful tale.*

sorry (sorrier, sorriest) ❑ You say **sorry** when you are apologizing for something. ◇ You also say **sorry** when you are correcting something you have just said. *The seaweeds (sorry, sea vegetables) are then dried to maintain the absolute cleanliness, consistency and taste.*

❑ You say you are **sorry** when you are expressing regret about something. *He said Israel was sorry that the US had not used its power of veto... I'm sorry to say I found the piece totally unfunny.*

❑ If you feel **sorry** for someone who is unhappy or in an unpleasant situation, you feel sympathy for them.

❑ **Sorry** is also used to describe people or things that are in a bad state. *It is, of course, too simple to blame the Conservatives for the whole sorry situation.*

sort ❑ A particular **sort** of thing is a kind or type of that thing. ◇ You use **of sorts** or **of a sort** to say something is a particular kind of thing, but not a very good example of it. *Guests can always get a meal of sorts in the hotel restaurant.* ◇ You use **sort of** when you are giving a rough description of something. *I use the top floor of a barn as a sort of office.*

❏ If things are **sorted** or **sorted out**, they are arranged into groups according to some kind of system. *At the recycling plant the bags are automatically sorted by colour.*

❏ If you **sort out** a problem, you deal with it and find a solution to it.

❏ If you feel **out of sorts**, you are not your usual self, because you are feeling slightly unwell, annoyed, or discontented.

sortie If a military force makes a **sortie**, it makes an attack or raid by leaving its own position and going briefly into enemy territory. ◇ You can also say someone makes a **sortie** when they make a brief trip away from their home or base, especially a trip to an unfamiliar place.

sorting office A **sorting office** is a place where letters and parcels are taken after posting and are sorted according to their delivery address.

SOS An **SOS** is a distress signal which indicates to other people that you are in danger and need help quickly.

sotto voce (*pron:* sot-toe voe-chay) If you say something **sotto voce**, you say it very quietly.

soubriquet See **sobriquet**.

souffle (*or* **soufflé**) (*pron:* soo-flay) A **souffle** is a light fluffy food made from whisked egg whites and other ingredients and baked.

sought See **seek**.

sought-after If something is **sought-after**, it is in great demand, because it is rare or of very good quality.

souk (*pron:* sook) In Muslim countries, a **souk** is an open-air market.

soul ❏ A person's **soul** is the spiritual part of them which some people believe goes on existing after their body is dead. ◇ Your **soul** is also your mind, character, thoughts, and feelings. *Making a fool of oneself is probably the fear most deeply rooted in the British soul.*

❏ The **soul** of something like a nation or political movement is the special quality which is thought to represent its basic character.

❏ A person can be referred to as a particular kind of **soul**. *The banking industry will now be modernised by these entrepreneurial souls.* ◇ **Soul** is used with words like 'not' to mean 'nobody' or 'not a single person'. *He moved through rooms of sleeping couples without ever waking a soul.*

❏ **Soul** or **soul music** is a type of pop music performed mainly by black American musicians. It developed from jazz, gospel, and blues music and often expresses deep emotions.

soul-destroying work is boring and depressing.

soul-searching is long and careful examination of your thoughts, feelings, and motives, especially when you are trying to make a difficult decision.

soulful music expresses deep emotions.

soulless If you call a place where people live or work **soulless**, you mean it is dull and depressing.

soulmate If you call someone your **soulmate**, you mean they are very close to you and share your views or interests.

sound (soundings) ❏ A **sound** is something you hear. **Sound** is everything that can be heard. *...babies who respond to sound and light in the womb.*

❏ If something **sounds** or is **sounded**, it produces a noise. *The bell sounded to end the second round.*

❏ When you are describing a noise, you can talk about the way it **sounds**. *The noise he made must have sounded like a whale distress call.* ◇ The **sound** of a singer or band is the distinctive quality of their music. You can also talk about the **sound** of a kind of music.

❏ You can give your impression of something you have heard about by talking about the way it **sounds**. You can also say you like or do not like the **sound** of it. *To some observers that sounds like an anti-fundamentalist coalition... Hungarians seem to like the sound of such radicalism more and more.* ◇ If you talk about the way a person **sounds**, you are describing the impression you get of their state of mind when they are speaking. *He sounded relieved that the game was over.*

❏ If something is **sound**, it is in good condition, strong, or healthy. ◇ If a piece of advice is **sound**, it is reliable and sensible. ◇ **safe and sound:** see **safe**.

❏ If you **sound off** about something, you express your opinions loudly and strongly to everyone without being asked.

❏ If you **sound** someone **out** about something, you ask them questions to find out what their opinion is. If you **take soundings**, you ask several people's opinions. ◇ If you use someone as a **sounding board**, you discuss your ideas with them to help you develop them.

❏ **Soundings** are also measurements of the depth of something like a well or the sea, using sonar or a weighted line.

sound barrier The **sound barrier** is the sudden increase in the force of the air against an aircraft when it approaches the speed of sound.

sound effect **Sound effects** are sounds created artificially to make a play or film more realistic.

sound system A **sound system** is a set of electrical equipment used for playing amplified music, for example at a disco or rock concert.

soundbite A **soundbite** is a short report or statement included in a news bulletin on TV.

soundings See **sound**.

soundly If someone is **soundly** defeated, they are defeated thoroughly and convincingly. ◇ If you sleep **soundly**, you sleep deeply and peacefully.

soundproof (soundproofing, soundproofed) If a building or room is **soundproof**, no noise gets into it or out of it. If you **soundproof** a building or room, you make it soundproof.

soundtrack The **soundtrack** of a film is its sound, including speech, music, and sound effects.

soup (souping, souped) ❏ **Soup** is savoury liquid food, usually served hot.

❏ If a car is **souped up**, it is made more powerful.

soup kitchen A **soup kitchen** is a place which provides free food for people who are very poor or have become homeless.

soupy If you say something like a song is **soupy**, you mean it is too emotional and sentimental.

sour (souring, soured; sourly, sourness) ❏ **Sour** food has a sharp taste like the taste of a lemon or an unripe apple. ◇ **Sour** milk has an unpleasant taste because it is no longer fresh.

❑ **Sour** people are bad-tempered and unfriendly.

❑ If a relationship **sours** or is **soured**, it becomes less friendly. You can also talk about an occasion being **soured**. *The dispute has soured the atmosphere surrounding the summit.* You can also say things **turn sour** or **go sour**. *I used to be on the area sports council, but things went sour after a while and I had to leave.*

❑ You call someone's behaviour **sour grapes** when they fail to get what they want and then start telling everyone it is not worth having.

sour cream is cream used in cooking which has been artificially made sour.

source ❑ The **source** of something is the person, place, or thing it comes from. *Botanic gardens are an invaluable source of plant material for scientists.*

❑ The **source** of a difficulty or problem is the thing which caused it in the first place.

❑ A **source** is also a person who provides you with information. *One senior source said yesterday: 'He still seems to be fighting the leadership campaign.'* A book can also be called a **source**.

❑ The **source** of a river is the place where it begins.

south is one of the four main points of the compass. ◇ The **south** is the direction on your right when you look towards the place where the sun rises. If you go in that direction, you go **south**; a place in that direction is **south** of the place where you are now. ◇ The **south** part of a place is the part south of its centre. *...South London... ...the south of France.*

❑ A **south** wind blows from the south.

south-east (*or* southeast) The **south-east** is the direction halfway between south and east. ◇ The **south-east** part of a place is the part south-east of its centre. *...South-East Asia... ...the south-east side of Chicago.*

south-easterly A **south-easterly** wind blows from the south-east. ◇ If you travel in a **south-easterly** direction, you travel towards the south-east.

south-eastern (*or* southeastern) The **south-eastern** part of a place is the part south-east of its centre. *...south-eastern Europe.*

south-west (*or* southwest) The **south-west** is the direction halfway between south and west. ◇ The **south-west** of a place is the part south-west of its centre. *...South-West England... ...the south-west tip of Norway.*

south-westerly A **south-westerly** wind blows from the south-west. ◇ If you travel in a **south-westerly** direction, you travel towards the south-west.

south-western (*or* southwestern) The **south-western** part of a place is the part south-west of its centre. *...south-western Uganda.*

southbound traffic is heading towards the south.

southeast See **south-east**.

southeastern See **south-eastern**.

southerly ❑ A **southerly** wind blows from the south. ◇ If you travel in a **southerly** direction, you travel towards the south. Similarly, if you face in a **southerly** direction, you face towards the south.

❑ The most **southerly** part of a place is the part furthest to the south. Similarly, the most **southerly** place of a

group of places is the one furthest to the south. *...the most southerly harbour in England.*

southern The **southern** part of a place is the part south of its centre. *...southern England.* ◇ **Southern** also means to the south of a country or region. *...Belize's large southern neighbour, Guatemala.*

southerner A **southerner** is a person who was born or lives in the southern part of a country or region.

southernmost The **southernmost** part of a place is the part furthest to the south. Similarly, the **southernmost** place of a group of places is the one furthest to the south. *...South Australia's southernmost wine district.*

southpaw A **southpaw** is a boxer who leads with his left hand.

southwards (southward) If you go **southwards** or **southward**, you go towards the south. You can also say you go in a **southward** direction.

southwest See **south-west**.

southwestern See **south-western**.

souvenir A **souvenir** is something you buy or keep to remind you of a holiday, place, or event.

sovereign ❑ A **sovereign** is a king, queen, or other royal ruler.

❑ A **sovereign** state or country is independent and not under the authority of any other country. ◇ **Sovereign** is used to describe the person or organization that has supreme power in a country. *Sovereign power will continue to lie with the Supreme People's Assembly.*

❑ The **sovereign** was an old British coin worth one pound. Sovereigns are now only made to commemorate special occasions.

sovereignty is the power a country has to govern itself or to govern other territories. *Germany has already given up an important part of its economic sovereignty to the joint Community institutions.*

Soviet is used to talk about things to do with the former Soviet Union and its people. *...the Soviet ambassador... ...the Soviet space programme.* ◇ The **Soviets** were the people of the former Soviet Union, especially its leaders. *The Soviets pledged to remove their remaining forces.*

❑ A **soviet** was an elected local, regional, or national council in the former Soviet Union.

sow (sowing, sowed, have sown) ❑ If you **sow** seeds or **sow** an area of land with seeds, you plant the seeds in the ground.

❑ If you talk about someone **sowing** confusion or panic, you mean they are causing it on a large scale by telling people something unpleasant is about to happen.

❑ A **sow** (*rhymes with 'now'*) is an adult female pig.

soy sauce is a dark brown salty liquid made from soya beans. It is used as a flavouring, especially in Chinese cooking.

soya Soya beans are protein-rich beans which are eaten as a vegetable or used to make flour, oil, or soy sauce. Soya flour, butter, etc is made from soya beans.

sozzled If you say someone is **sozzled**, you mean they are drunk.

spa A **spa** is a place where water which is rich in minerals bubbles out of the ground. People sometimes drink the water or bathe in it to improve their health.

space (spacing, spaced) ❑ **Space** is the unoccupied parts of a place which are available to be used for a particular

purpose. *Rapid growth means a big demand for office space.*
◇ A **space** is a gap or an empty place in something. *Local papers sometimes appear with white spaces where stories should have been... The cooler has a double wall made of burnt clay bricks and the space in between is filled with sand.*
◇ A **space** on a form is a blank area for you to write something in.

❑ The **space** for an article or feature in a newspaper is the number of columns or lines available for it.

❑ The **space** you have in which to do something is the amount of freedom you have for it. *This leaves elected officials little space to make decisions.*

❑ A **space** of time is a certain period of time. *All of the centre's fifty terminals were infected by a virus in the space of a week.*

❑ **Space** is the area beyond the Earth's atmosphere which contains all the other planets and stars.

❑ If you **space** a series of things or **space** them **out**, you arrange them so they have gaps between them. Similarly, you can **space** or **space out** a series of actions. The **spacing** between a series of things or actions is the distance or amount of time between them. *The timing and spacing of births is changing – a gap of less than three years is increasingly popular.*

space age The **space age** is the present period in history, in which travel in space has become possible. ◇ **Space-age** is used to describe things which are very modern and high-tech. *...space-age yachts.*

space probe A **space probe** is a small unmanned computer-controlled spacecraft sent into space to transmit information back about space or other planets.

space shuttle A **space shuttle** is a spacecraft designed to travel into space and back several times; rather than just once.

space station A **space station** is an artificial satellite sent into orbit for research purposes. Space stations may eventually be used as bases by people travelling into space.

space suit (*or* spacesuit) A **space suit** is a special protective suit worn by an astronaut.

spacecraft (*plural:* spacecraft) A **spacecraft** is a rocket or other vehicle which can travel in space.

spaced-out If someone is **spaced-out**, they feel as if nothing around them is real, usually because they are on drugs.

spaceman (spacemen) A **spaceman** is the same as an astronaut.

spaceship A **spaceship** is the same as a spacecraft.

spacesuit See space suit.

spacing See space.

spacious (spaciousness) If a room or other place is **spacious**, it is large, with plenty of room to move around. *Inside the house there was an air of spaciousness.*

spade ❑ A **spade** is a tool for digging. It has a broad flat metal blade and a long wooden handle.

❑ **Spades** is one of the four suits in a pack of playing cards. All cards in this suit have the symbol ♠ on them.

spadework (*or* spade work) The **spadework** for a project or activity is the routine or uninteresting work which has to be done as a preparation.

spaghetti is a type of pasta formed into long thin strings. It is usually served with a sauce.

❑ A **spaghetti western** is a film about the Wild West made in Europe by an Italian director.

span (spanning, spanned) ❑ If something **spans** a period of time, it lasts for that time. *In a professional career spanning 11 years Scudamore has suffered few serious accidents.* You can talk about a **span** of time between two events. ◇ Your attention **span** or concentration **span** is the length of time you are able to concentrate on something or stay interested in it.

❑ If something **spans** a range of things, it includes all of them. A **span** of things is a range of them. *...his broad span of interests.*

❑ If something **spans** a certain distance, it measures that distance from one side to the other. Similarly, something can **span** a certain area. *The planned forest is on the site of the ancient Needwood and Charnwood forests, spanning parts of Leicestershire, Derbyshire, Staffordshire and Warwickshire.* The **span** of something is the distance from one side to the other. *We're building a big mechanical model of this insect with about a metre wing span.* ◇ If a bridge **spans** a river or a valley, it stretches right across it.

❑ See also **spick and span**.

spangle (spangled) **Spangles** are small pieces of metal or plastic which sparkle brightly and are used for decoration. If something is **spangled**, it is decorated with spangles. *...a spangled mini-dress.*

Spaniard A **Spaniard** is someone who comes from Spain.

spaniel **Spaniels** are a type of dog with long drooping ears and a silky coat.

Spanish is used to talk about people and things in or from Spain. *...the Spanish authorities.* ◇ The **Spanish** are the Spanish people. ◇ **Spanish** is the main language spoken in Spain. It is also the main language in most countries in South and Central America.

spank (spanking) ❑ If you **spank** a child or give it a **spanking**, you hit it on the bottom with your hand, usually several times, as a punishment.

❑ **Spanking** is used to describe things which are clean, bright, and in excellent condition. *...spanking new concert halls.*

spanner A **spanner** is a metal tool with a specially shaped end for loosening or tightening nuts. ◇ If someone **throws a spanner in the works**, they create a difficulty which prevents something happening in the way that was intended.

spar (sparring, sparred) ❑ If you **spar** with someone, you argue with them, but not in an unpleasant or serious way. ◇ If a boxer **spars** with someone, he punches fairly gently, for example when he is training or to test an opponent's reactions during a fight.

❑ The mast, boom, etc on a sailing ship are called **spars**.

spare (sparing, spared; sparingly) ❑ **Spare** objects are ones you keep handy in case they are needed to replace the ones in use at present. *...spare bulbs.* Objects you keep handy like this are called **spares**. *An extra fan belt is one of the spares that should always be in your car.*

❑ **Spare parts** are parts you can buy separately to replace old or broken parts in a piece of equipment, especially ones which are designed to be easily removed or replaced.

❑ **Spare** is used to describe things which are not being used at present and are therefore available. *He would like to* be able to lease out spare space to independent businesses. ◇ A **spare room** is a bedroom for guests to sleep in.

❑ If you can **spare** something, you can afford to part with it or make it available. *Nurses and students volunteered what time they could spare to supplement these efforts.*

❑ If you are **sparing** with something, you use it or give it away only in very small quantities. *There is still two to three weeks supply of petrol left if it is used sparingly.*

❑ Your **spare time** is time when you do not have to work and can do what you want.

❑ If you are **spared** something unpleasant, it does not happen to you. *They were spared the anxieties of previous generations whose children had to suffer the long-term consequences of these diseases.*

spare ribs are the ribs of a pig with most of the meat trimmed off, often cooked in a spicy source.

spark ❑ A **spark** is a tiny bright piece of burning material which flies up from a fire. ◇ A **spark** is also a flash of light caused by electricity.

❑ A **spark** of a feeling or a quality is a small but noticeable amount of it. *His phrasing lacked that vital spark of imagination.*

❑ If something **sparks** something else or **sparks** it **off**, it starts it happening. *Massive over-capacity has sparked a price war in Europe and America.*

❑ When people have a lively argument or heated discussion, you can say the **sparks fly.**

spark plug (*or* **sparking plug**) A **spark plug** is a device in the engine of a motor vehicle which produces an electric spark to ignite the fuel.

sparkle (sparkling, sparkled) ❑ If something **sparkles**, it shines with a lot of small points of flickering light. *...the sparkling sea.* ◇ If someone **sparkles**, they are lively and witty. *...sparkling wit.*

❑ **Sparkling** wine is slightly fizzy and is sold in bottles with the cork held in place by wire.

sparkler A **sparkler** is a small firework you hold in your hand. It looks like a piece of thick wire and burns with a lot of small bright sparks.

sparky is used to describe things which are lively and amusing. *Her first catwalk show will be a sparky, no-holds-barred affair.*

sparrow The **sparrow** or **house sparrow** is a very common small bird with brown and grey feathers.

sparrowhawk The **sparrowhawk** is a hawk which preys on smaller birds.

sparse (sparsely) If something is **sparse**, there is very little of it and it is spread out over a large area or a long period of time. *The area around Envigado is thick jungle, sparsely inhabited... Information from the region has been sparse.*

spartan A **spartan** way of life is very simple with no luxuries. *...spartan living conditions.*

spasm ❑ A **spasm** is a sudden uncontrollable tightening of the muscles in a part of your body.

❑ A **spasm** of something is a sudden short burst of it. *...spasms of terror... ...this latest spasm of union militancy.*

spasmodic (spasmodically) If something is **spasmodic**, it happens for short periods at irregular intervals. *The tremor was felt in Bucharest, where buildings trembled spasmodically for forty-five seconds or so.*

spastic People born with cerebral palsy used to be called

spastics.

spat ❑ See spit.

❑ A **spat** is a brief quarrel which is not very serious.

❑ **Spats** are specially shaped pieces of cloth or leather which button down one side. They used to be worn by men over their ankles and part of their shoes.

spate A **spate** of things is a lot of them happening or appearing within a short time. *...this spate of misfortunes.*

spatial is used to talk about things relating to size, area, or position, rather than, for example, to time. *...spatial information... ...a spatial relationship.* ◇ A child's **spatial** ability is its ability to see and understand the relationships between shapes, spaces, and areas.

spatter (spattering, spattered) If a liquid **spatters** a surface or is **spattered** over it, it covers it in small drops. You can also say the surface is **spattered** with the liquid. ◇ If a conversation or piece of writing is **spattered** with something, it is full of it. *She spattered her application form with jargon and spelling mistakes.*

spatula A **spatula** is (a) a tool used in cooking with a handle and a flexible blunt blade. (b) a similar smaller instrument used by doctors.

spawn ❑ If something **spawns** something else, it causes it to happen or be created. *The war's enduring significance is reflected in the mammoth literary industry which it has spawned.*

❑ When fish, frogs, and other amphibians **spawn**, they lay a large number of eggs. The eggs are called their **spawn.**

speak (speaking, spoke, have spoken) ❑ When you **speak**, you say words. ◇ If you **speak to** someone, you have a conversation with them. Americans say you **speak with** someone. *They prevented me speaking with civilians in the area.* ◇ If you **speak** to a group of people, you make a speech. ◇ If you **speak** for a group of people, you act as their spokesperson.

❑ If you **speak** about something or **speak** of it, you mention it. ◇ If you **speak** well or badly of someone, you say good or bad things about them.

❑ If you **speak** a foreign language, you know it and are able to have a conversation in it.

❑ If you **speak out** about something or **speak up** about it, you give your opinion about it publicly. ◇ If you **speak your mind**, you say exactly what you think about something.

❑ If you are **not speaking** to someone or **not on speaking terms** with them, the relationship between you has broken down, because you have had an argument or dispute.

❑ If you ask someone to **speak up**, you are asking them to speak louder.

❑ If you say something **speaks volumes**, you mean it tells you a lot about something in an indirect way.

❑ You use phrases like **generally speaking** and **strictly speaking** to indicate the way you are describing something. *Climatically speaking, the best time to visit is in autumn.* ◇ You say **so to speak** when you are describing something in a colourful non-literal way. *He was to be the man who would, so to speak, wring out the last of Tory wetness.*

❑ Nobody or nothing **to speak of** means hardly anyone or anything at all, or only unimportant people or things. *We don't have any storage space to speak of.*

-speak is added to the name of a person, group, or organization to describe words they are fond of using, or words they use in a different way from anyone else. *Radical is usually BBC-speak for job-cutting... ...his tendency to fall into football-speak.*

speaker ❑ In a parliamentary assembly, the **Speaker** acts as the chairperson and makes sure the assembly proceeds according to its constitution.

❑ A **speaker** at a conference or meeting is someone who makes a speech.

❑ A **speaker** of a language is someone who can speak it. *My parents were Gaelic speakers.*

❑ Anyone who is speaking at a particular time can be called the **speaker**. *This must be as boring to the speaker as it is to the listener.*

❑ A **speaker** is also a loudspeaker.

spear (spearing, speared) A **spear** is a weapon consisting of a long pole with a sharp tip. ◇ If you **spear** something, you push a pointed object such as a fork or pin into it. ◇ A **spear** of asparagus or broccoli is an individual stalk of it.

spearhead (spearheading, spearheaded) The person or group that **spearheads** a campaign or attack is the one that leads it. They can also be called its **spearhead**.

special ❑ If something is **special**, it is better or more important than other things of the same kind. *Two events during this week's debates seem of special significance.*

❑ **Special** also means unusual or different from normal. *...a special meeting of shareholders... For those staying a maximum of four nights abroad, a special return fare of £108 is available.* ◇ A **special** is something which is available only for a limited period or in limited numbers. *Bar meals include some specials, such as half a roast duckling in orange sauce.*

❑ **Special** is used to describe a person or group that has been officially appointed to carry out a task. *The UN special envoy arrives in Johannesburg today.*

❑ **Special** schools or other institutions are for people who have particular needs, for example people with physical handicaps or learning difficulties. You say people like these have **special needs**.

❑ **Special** is also used to talk about something to do with one particular person, group, or place. *The fashion industry is full of individualists with their own special recipe for success.*

❑ **Special** is also used to describe something designed and made for a particular purpose. *The batteries can be recharged in six minutes, but it requires special high-voltage circuits to do this.* ◇ In films and TV, **special effects** are unusual things you see on the screen or hear on the soundtrack which are achieved using special techniques.

Special Branch The **Special Branch** is the department of the British police force concerned with political security. It deals with problems such as terrorism and visits by foreign leaders.

special constable **Special constables** are unpaid volunteers who assist the police in various duties in their spare time.

special delivery is a service provided by the Post Office which guarantees to deliver letters or parcels the following morning. Special delivery is more expensive than the normal postal service.

specialise See specialize.

specialism Someone's **specialism** is something they have studied or practised a lot and which they are an expert at.

specialist ❑ A **specialist** is someone who studies a subject and knows a lot about it. ◇ A **specialist** is also someone who has practised a skill and is an expert at it. *...a runner who is a specialist at the distance.*

❑ A **specialist** company or organization deals in one type of product or area of work. *...a specialist comic shop.*

❑ A **specialist** is also a doctor or surgeon who specializes in one area of medicine.

speciality (specialities) Someone's **speciality** is the kind of work they do best or the subject they know most about. *Wine-making was his speciality.* ◇ If a product is the **speciality** of a place, it is always very well made there. *Green sage cheese is an old Derbyshire and Lancashire speciality.*

specialize (specializing, specialized; specialization) (*can be spelled with an 's' instead of a 'z'*) ❑ If you **specialize** in something, you concentrate most of your time and resources on it. *Many younger women solicitors now specialize in business affairs... To avoid premature specialization, pupils aged 16-18 will study for examinations in six subjects, with a mix of arts and sciences.*

❑ **Specialized** things have been developed for a particular purpose. *Specialized contact lenses may be supplied to those who have had cataract surgery.* Similarly, **specialized** people have been trained to do an unusual job.

specially is used to say something is done, made, or provided for a particular purpose. *246 English fans were subsequently rounded up and put on a specially chartered plane back to England.*

❑ **Specially** is also used to mean 'especially'. *Large families are specially popular in farming areas, where more hands mean more work done.*

specialty (specialties) A **specialty** is the same as a speciality.

species (*plural:* species) A **species** is a class of plants or animals whose members have the same main characteristics and are able to breed with each other and produce fertile young.

specific ❑ You use **specific** to emphasize that you are talking about one particular thing or subject. *No specific organisation has been linked with the document.* ◇ If something is **specific** to a particular thing, it relates to that thing and nothing else. *Many of the reasons for IBM's swift decline are specific to the computer industry.*

❑ If a statement is **specific**, it is precise and exact. *You can make much more specific predictions about what would happen if galaxies collided.* Similarly, a document can be **specific**. *A new treaty will need to be more specific.* ◇ The **specifics** of a subject are its details. *Although the leaders issued a communique covering a wide range of issues, it was somewhat short of specifics.*

specific gravity The **specific gravity** of a substance is the ratio of the density of the substance to the density of water.

specifically is used to say something is being given special attention and considered separately from other things. *One of the factors that the council will specifically address is that of its staff's attitude to the public.*

❑ **Specifically** is also used to say precisely what a

statement or question applies to. *When people were asked specifically about press intrusion into the lives of the royal family, 65 per cent said there was too much.*

❑ You also use **specifically** to emphasize that you are talking about one particular aspect of something. *NATO sees the need to reform itself and assume a more specifically political role as a stabilising factor.*

specification ❑ A **specification** for something like a new machine or building is a detailed description of the features in its design or composition. You say something is built to a particular **specification**.

❑ **Specifications** are also clearly stated requirements, for example about how something should be done or used.

specify (specifies, specifying, specified) ❑ If you **specify** something, you state or describe it precisely, so it is clear exactly what you mean. *The statement did not specify which countries would attend.*

❑ If you **specify** a particular requirement, you say exactly what is required. *Agencies are given targets specifying things like speed of delivery and productivity... One option would be to increase mortgage tax relief for first-time buyers to £60,000 for a specified period.*

specimen ❑ A **specimen** of something like a plant, animal, or rock is an example which is taken somewhere to be examined or analysed. ◇ A **specimen** is also a small quantity of someone's blood or urine taken for a special purpose, for example to discover if they are ill.

❑ If you say someone or something is a fine **specimen** of a type of thing, you mean they are a fine example of it. Similarly, you can say someone is a poor **specimen** of something.

specious (*pron:* spee-shuss) (speciously) A **specious** argument appears to be correct, but is in fact false. Other things which wrongly give the impression of being correct, true, or genuine can also be called **specious**. *...specious logic... ...a specious claim... They speciously argued that restrictions on the right to political asylum were necessary to stem the upsurge in far-right violence.*

speck A **speck** is a very small mark or shape. *An astronomer first spotted the asteroid as a fast-moving dark speck.* ◇ A **speck** of a substance is a very small amount of it.

speckled If something is **speckled**, it is covered in a pattern of small marks or spots of a different colour. *...speckled feathers... ...speckled wood.*

specs Someone's **specs** are their glasses.

spectacle (spectacles) ❑ Someone's **spectacles** are their glasses.

❑ You can describe something you see happening as a **spectacle** of a particular kind. *Insults have been freely hurled in this campaign, which has often been an unedifying spectacle.* ◇ A **spectacle** is also something like a large theatrical event which is very impressive and thrilling to watch.

spectacular (spectacularly) ❑ If something is **spectacular**, it is very impressive to see or watch. ◇ A **spectacular** is a grand impressive show or performance.

❑ A **spectacular** mistake is a particularly bad one. *The agency has been spectacularly wrong in its economic forecasts.*

spectate (spectating, spectated) If someone is **spectating** at an event, they are watching rather than taking part.

spectator A **spectator** is someone who is watching something, especially a sporting event. ◇ A **spectator sport** is

one which is enjoyable to watch and tends to interest people more as spectators than as participants.

spectral is used to describe (a) something to do with ghosts. (b) someone who looks like a ghost.

❑ **Spectral** is also used to talk about things to do with the wavelengths of different colours of light. *...spectral characteristics.*

spectre (*American spelling:* specter) ❑ A **spectre** is a ghost.

❑ A **spectre** is also something frightening or alarming which seems likely to happen. *...the spectre of higher taxes.* If someone warns of something like this, you can say they **raise the spectre** of it. *Dr Mahathir had raised the spectre of communal unrest if he failed to win a resounding majority.*

spectrograph A **spectrograph** is an instrument for photographing a spectrum. The photograph it takes is also called a **spectrograph**.

spectrometer A **spectrometer** is a device which splits light into a spectrum so that it can be studied.

spectrum (*plural:* spectra *or* spectrums) ❑ The **spectrum** is the range of different colours, arranged in order of their wavelengths, which is produced when light passes through something like a prism or a drop of water.

❑ A **spectrum** of things is a complete range of them, especially when one end of the range is in complete contrast to the other. *Her reviews at the Edinburgh Festival had covered the spectrum from reverent awe to disgust... Plum trees will grow in a wide spectrum of soils.*

speculate (speculating, speculated; speculation, speculator) ❑ If you **speculate** about something, you think about its possible nature or identity, or about what might happen. *Speculation about his fate is rife.*

❑ When people **speculate** financially, they buy property, stocks, or shares in the hope of selling them quickly at a profit. This is called **speculation.** People who do it are called **speculators.**

speculative (speculatively) ❑ **Speculative** statements are based on guesses rather than facts.

❑ **Speculative** investments involve taking a risk in the hope of making a quick profit. *...speculatively built commercial and industrial properties.*

speculator See **speculate.**

sped See **speed.**

speech (speeches) ❑ **Speech** is the ability to speak, or the act of speaking. ◇ **Speech** is also spoken language. *Deafness becomes evident at about two years through an infant's lack of response to speech.*

❑ A **speech** is (a) a formal talk given to an audience. (b) a set of lines from a play, spoken by an actor or actress.

❑ The **speech** of a place is the language or dialect spoken there. ◇ A person's **speech** is their characteristic way of speaking. *...the crisp, clipped speech of most BBC newsreaders.*

speech therapy (speech therapist) **Speech therapy** is the treatment of people who have difficulties with speech and language. A **speech therapist** is someone whose job is to help people overcome these difficulties.

speech-writer (*or* speechwriter) A **speech-writer** is a professional writer who helps write speeches for someone like a politician.

speechify (speechifies, speechifying, speechified) Making speeches is sometimes humorously called **speechifying**. *Once, the Tory wife's role was to be dutiful, smile beatifically* *at her husband as he speechified and perhaps dabble in her local NSPCC.*

speechless If you say someone is **speechless**, you mean they are so shocked or angry they cannot find words to express their feelings.

speechwriter See **speech-writer**.

speed (speeding, sped; speeded) (*If you are talking about the past, you say, for example, 'The car sped off' but 'The government speeded up its reforms.'*) ❑ The **speed** of something is the rate at which it moves or travels. ◇ **Speed** is fast movement. *Even Volvo, which has sold its cars on a safety ticket for years, cannot resist flirting with speed.*
❑ If you **speed** somewhere, you move or travel there quickly. *We sped down the back streets of Battersea.* ◇ If a motorist is **speeding,** he or she is driving faster than the legal speed limit.
❑ The **speed** of something is also the rate at which it happens or is done. *...the speed of economic reform.*
❑ If something **speeds up** or is **speeded up,** it moves, happens, or is done more quickly.
❑ See also **amphetamine**.

speed limit The **speed limit** on a stretch of road is the maximum speed at which you can legally drive along it.

speed trap A **speed trap** is a stretch of road on which the police are checking whether vehicles are travelling faster than the speed limit.

speedboat A **speedboat** is a lightweight boat with a powerful engine, which can travel at high speed.

speedometer (*pron:* speed-dom-it-er) A **speedometer** is an instrument in a vehicle which shows how fast it is going.

speedway is the sport of racing lightweight motorcycles without brakes on special tracks.

speedy (speedier, speediest; speedily) A **speedy** action happens or is done very quickly. *Soon after the first Wilson victory, he was created a life peer and speedily given office.* ◇ You also say someone or something is **speedy** when they move very quickly.

speleology (speleologist) **Speleology** is the study of caves. An expert on this is called a **speleologist**. ◇ **Speleology** is also exploring caves, for pleasure or interest.

spell (spelling, spelled *or* spelt) ❑ When you **spell** a word, you say or write the individual letters in their correct order. The **spelling** of a word is the correct order of the letters in it. ◇ If someone can **spell,** they can say or write the letters of most words in their correct order. **Spelling** is the ability to do this; you say for example, someone is 'good at spelling'.
❑ If you say something **spells** trouble or danger, you mean it is likely to lead to it.
❑ If you **spell** something **out,** you explain it in detail and as clearly as possible. *Britain has spelt out its policy of cutting off aid to Third World countries which violate human rights.*
❑ A **spell** of something is a short period of it. *...a spell of frantic activity.*
❑ In children's stories, a **spell** is a sequence of words used to perform magic. ◇ If you are **under** someone's **spell,** you are so fascinated by them you are prepared to believe anything they say or do anything they ask.

spellbound (spellbinding) If you are **spellbound** by something, you are fascinated by it and cannot think of any-

thing else while it is happening. You say something like this is **spellbinding.**

spelt See **spell**.

spend (spending, spent; spender) ❑ When you **spend** money, you use it to pay for things. ◇ You can say how much money someone spends by describing them as, for example, a big **spender**. *The UK remains one of the smallest spenders on health services in the developed world.*
❑ **Spending money** is money you can spend how you like, for example when you are on holiday.
❑ If you **spend** a period of time in a place, you are in that place during that time. Similarly, you can **spend** time doing something. *They have spent 40 years building easily adaptable networks.*
❑ See also **spent**.

spendthrift A **spendthrift** is someone who spends money in a wasteful or extravagant way.

spent ❑ See **spend**.
❑ If something is **spent,** it has already been used and cannot be used again. *...spent fuel.* ◇ If you say someone is a **spent force,** you mean they no longer have the power they once had.

sperm (*plural:* sperm *or* sperms) A **sperm** is a cell produced in the sex organs of a male animal. It can join a female's egg and fertilize it.

sperm whale The **sperm whale** is a large whale which has a cavity in its head containing a large amount of oil.

spermatozoon (*pron:* sper-mat-ta-zoe-on) (*plural:* spermatozoa) A **spermatozoon** is the same as a sperm.

spew If something **spews** things or **spews** them **out,** they flow out of it in large quantities. *Oil continued to spew from the Braer, the tanker wrecked on the Shetland Islands.*

sphere ❑ A **sphere** is a perfectly round three-dimensional object like a ball.
❑ When you talk about activities within a particular **sphere,** you mean activities of a particular kind. ◇ An organization's **sphere of activity** is all the activities it is officially supposed to be involved in.
❑ A country's **sphere of influence** is the area of the world where it is the dominant power.
❑ People of a certain social class are said to belong to a particular **sphere**. *...the lowest sphere of society.*

spherical If something is **spherical,** it is shaped like a sphere.

sphinx (sphinxes) ❑ In Egypt, the **sphinx** is a huge statue at Al Giza, with a lion's body and a human head. There are also some smaller sphinxes. They have a lion's body and the head of a man, ram, or hawk.
❑ In Greek mythology, the **sphinx** was a monster with a human head, wings, a serpent's tail, and the body of a lion. The sphinx stopped travellers and asked them a riddle. If they could not answer it, it ate them.

spice (spicing, spiced) ❑ **Spices** are the seeds, powdered roots, or bark of certain plants which are used in cooking to add flavour. ◇ If you **spice** food or **spice** it **up,** you add spices to it.
❑ If you **spice** something you do or say or **spice** it **up,** you do something extra to make it more lively or exciting. You can also say you add **spice** to it. *An increasing number of skiers are also trying out snowboards, to spice up their winter holiday.*

spick and span If you say something is **spick and span,**

you mean it is very clean and tidy.

spicy (spicier, spiciest; spiciness) Spicy food is strongly flavoured with spices. ...*the fragrant spiciness of Thai food.*

spider Spiders are small creatures with eight legs. Most spiders feed on insects which they catch by building webs.

spidery handwriting is very thin and angular and is difficult to read.

spiel (*pron:* shpeel) Someone's spiel is a speech they make, usually one they have made many times before and often one in which they try to persuade you to do something or buy something.

spike (spiking, spiked) ❑ A spike is a long piece of metal with a sharp point on one end. ◇ The spikes on sports shoes are pointed pieces of metal on the soles which help your feet grip the ground or track when you are running. Shoes with spikes on them are called spikes.
❑ Some plants have tall stems called spikes covered with flowers or buds.
❑ If someone spikes your drink, they put alcohol or a drug in it.
❑ If you spike someone's plans, you do something which stops them being carried out. This is also called spiking someone's guns.
❑ A spike is also a sudden increase in something. When something increases suddenly, you can say it spikes up. *The Nikkei could spike up to 16,000 within a month.*

spiky ❑ A spiky object has a sharp point or points. ...*spiky pinnacles and battlements.*
❑ A spiky person is bad-tempered and easily irritated.

spill (spilling, spilled *or* spilt) ❑ If a liquid spills or is spilled, it accidentally flows out of its container. Liquid spilled like this can be called a spill. ...*an oil spill.* ◇ If people or things spill out of a place, they come out of it in large numbers.
❑ If something in one place or situation spills over into another, it begins to happen or have an effect in the other one. *The rapid increase in wealth quickly spilled over into consumer spending and inflation... Fighting, if it comes, might spill over the borders of Hungary, Albania, perhaps even Greece.*
❑ If you spill the beans, you tell someone something which has been kept secret.
❑ If blood is spilt in a fight or battle, people are killed or seriously wounded.

spillage You say there is spillage or a spillage when something such as oil escapes from a ship into the sea.

spin (spinning, spun) ❑ If something spins or is spun, it turns quickly round its central point. ◇ If you put spin on a ball, you deliberately make it spin rapidly when you hit it, kick it, or throw it, to get it to travel through the air in a curve or bounce in a certain way.
❑ If your head is spinning, you feel dizzy and confused.
❑ When someone spins, they make thread by pulling out and twisting together strands of a natural fibre such as wool or cotton using a device or machine.
❑ If you spin something out, you make it last longer than it normally would.
❑ If you talk about someone spinning a story or spinning a yarn, you mean they are telling a story which is not true or only partly true.

spin doctor A spin doctor is someone skilled in public relations who advises political parties on how to present their candidates and policies in the best possible light.

spin-dry When you spin-dry clothes that have just been washed, you get most of the water out of them using a spin dryer or the spin cycle on a washing machine.

spin dryer (*or* spin drier) A spin dryer is a machine which gets most of the water out of washing by spinning it round at high speed.

spin-off ❑ A spin-off is something useful which happens as a result of trying to achieve something else. *The company expects more than 20,000 new jobs to be created as a spin-off from its investment in the area.*
❑ A spin-off is also a book, film, or TV series derived from something similar which has already been successful. ◇ Products you can buy which are based on a successful book, film, or TV programme are also called spin-offs.

spina bifida is a condition of the spine which some people are born with. It can cause paralysis in the legs.

spinach is a vegetable with large dark green leaves which are usually boiled.

spinal is used to talk about things to do with the spine. ...*a spinal injury... ...a spinal anaesthetic.*

spinal column The spinal column is the spine.

spinal cord The spinal cord is a rope-like structure of nerve tissue inside the spine. It connects the brain to nerves in all parts of the body.

spindle A spindle is a rod in a machine, around which another part of the machine turns.

spindly things are long, thin, and weak-looking.

spine (spiny) ❑ The spine is the row of bones down the middle of your back which supports your body and has your spinal cord inside it.
❑ The spine of a book is the stiff narrow part the pages and covers are attached to. The spine usually has the title and author's name printed on it.
❑ Spines are long sharp points on an animal's body or on a plant. A spiny animal or plant is covered in points like these.

spine-chilling If you say something is spine-chilling, you mean it is very frightening.

spineless If you say someone is spineless, you mean they are weak and cowardly.

spinnaker The spinnaker on a racing yacht is its large three-cornered sail.

spinner A spinner is a cricketer who makes the ball spin when he or she bowls so that it changes direction when it hits the ground.

spinney A spinney is a small wood.

spinster In the past, an older woman who had never married was sometimes called a spinster.

spiny See spine.

spiral (spiralling, spiralled) (*usual American spelling:* spiraling, spiraled) ❑ A spiral is a curved shape which winds round and round, with each curve above or outside the previous one. ◇ If something spirals, it moves up or down in a spiral curve.
❑ If an amount or level spirals, it rises quickly and at an increasing rate. ...*spiralling costs.* Similarly, an amount or level can spiral downwards. *Prices are spiralling down and public confidence is going the same way.* You can also say something rises or falls in a spiral.

spire The spire of a church or cathedral is a tall cone-shaped structure rising from a tower.

spirit (spiriting, spirited) ❑ When people talk about a person's **spirit**, they mean a part of them which is not physical and which involves their deepest thoughts and feelings. ◇ When some people talk about a person's **spirit**, they mean a non-physical part of them which continues to exist after they die. ◇ Some people believe in supernatural beings called **spirits**.

❑ The **spirit** in which you do something is the attitude you show when you do it. *They welcomed what they called the positive spirit displayed by the Warsaw Pact's declaration in Moscow.* ◇ **Spirit** is also used to talk about feelings of loyalty to a group which are shared by all the people in the group. *...team spirit... ...community spirit.*

❑ You use **spirits** when you are saying how you feel. For example, if you are in **good spirits** or in **high spirits**, you are happy. ◇ If someone shows **spirit**, they are enthusiastic, energetic, and self-confident. ◇ A **spirited** action shows courage and determination. *Australia held off a spirited challenge from Holland to win 3-2.*

❑ If you **enter into the spirit** of an event, you take part in it in an enthusiastic way.

❑ The **spirit** of a law or agreement is the way it was intended to be interpreted or applied. *The New Zealanders went to court, arguing that the use of a catamaran breached both the letter and the spirit of the rules.* See also **letter**.

❑ **Spirits** are strong alcoholic drinks such as whisky, gin, or vodka.

❑ If you **spirit** someone or something into or out of a place, you get them in or out quickly and secretly.

spirit level A **spirit level** is a device for testing a surface to see if it is horizontal. It consists of a piece of wood or metal containing a tube of liquid with a bubble of air in it. When the bubble is exactly in the middle of the tube, the surface is level.

spiritual (spiritually) **Spiritual** is used to talk about things connected with people's deepest thoughts and feelings, rather than their bodies or physical surroundings. *Leading the simple life is more spiritually refreshing.* ◇ **Spiritual** is also used to talk about things connected with people's religious beliefs. *...spiritual fulfilment... ...Tibet's exiled spiritual leader.*

spiritualism (spiritualist) **Spiritualism** is the belief that dead people can communicate with people who are still alive. Someone who believes this is called a **spiritualist**. Spiritualists have their own churches and their own forms of religious worship.

spirituality If you talk about a person's **spirituality**, you mean their dedication to God and to spiritual things.

spit (spitting, spat) ❑ If someone **spits**, they make a small amount of saliva shoot out of their mouth into the air. This is sometimes done to show contempt for someone. A person can also **spit out** a mouthful of food or drink.

❑ If you say someone is the **spitting image** of someone else, you mean they look just like them.

❑ A **spit** is a wooden or metal rod which is pushed through a piece of meat so the meat can be turned over an open fire and roasted.

❑ A **spit** is also a long flat narrow piece of land sticking out into the sea.

spite ❑ You use **in spite of** when you are mentioning something which might have prevented something hap-

pening, but which did not in fact prevent it. *In spite of overwhelming odds, they succeeded in conquering the world champions.*

❑ If someone does something out of **spite**, they do it deliberately to annoy or upset someone else, because they feel jealous or resentful. You can also say they do it to **spite** the other person.

spiteful If someone is **spiteful**, they deliberately try to annoy or upset people they dislike.

spittle is the watery liquid produced in your mouth.

spiv A **spiv** is someone who makes money, usually small amounts, in dishonest ways.

splash (splashes, splashing, splashed) ❑ When water **splashes** somewhere, it hits against something, sending up a lot of small drops. *At the far end, a waterfall splashed over artificial rocks.* ◇ A **splash** is the sound made when water hits something, or when something is dropped into water. ◇ If you **splash** about in water, you move about in it, making a noise as you disturb it.

❑ If you **splash** a liquid somewhere, you throw or spill it carelessly. ◇ A **splash** of something like water or whisky is a small amount added to another drink.

❑ A **splash** of bright colour is an area of it, which catches your attention. *Autumn-flowering gentians are creating brilliant splashes of blue throughout the show.*

❑ If you **make a splash**, you do something which draws everyone's attention to you.

❑ If a newspaper or magazine **splashes** a story, it prints it in a very noticeable way, usually on the front page. A story treated in this way is called a **splash**. *Germany's mass circulation Bild splashed the duchess's predicament on its Friday front page.*

❑ If you **splash out** on something, you buy it even though it costs a lot of money.

splashy is used to describe things which are intended to attract a lot of attention. *...a splashy new advertising campaign.*

splatter (splattering, splattered) If a surface is **splattered** with something like mud or paint, the mud or paint has been dropped or splashed on it leaving small amounts all over it.

splay If things **splay** out, their ends spread out away from each other. *Feet slightly splayed, he leaned forward and began to march.*

spleen ❑ Your **spleen** is an organ near your stomach which controls the quality of your blood.

❑ **Spleen** is violent and spiteful anger. *The angry Chancellor again vented his spleen on Bonn yesterday.*

splendid (splendidly) ❑ If you say something is **splendid**, you mean it is extremely good. *...a splendidly renovated park.* ◇ A **splendid** building or work of art is very beautiful and impressive. *Here the battlements rise splendidly, a reminder of the town's place in history.*

splendour is great beauty and magnificence. The **splendours** of a place are its beautiful and magnificent features.

splenetic A **splenetic** person is bad-tempered and irritable.

splice (splicing, spliced) If you **splice** two pieces of rope, film, or tape together, you join them neatly at the ends so they make one continuous piece.

splint A **splint** is a long piece of wood, metal, or some other stiff material which is fastened to a broken arm or leg to keep it straight and still.

splinter (splintering, splintered) ❑ A **splinter** is a thin sharp piece of wood, metal, or glass which has broken off from a larger piece. If something **splinters**, it breaks into splinters.

❑ If a group or organization **splinters**, some of its members break away to form groups of their own, because they no longer agree with the main group's views. The new groups are called **splinter groups**.

split (splitting, split not 'splitted') ❑ If an organization **splits** or is **split**, it divides into two or more organizations. You can also say part of an organization **splits away** from the main part or is **split off** from it. ◇ If there is a **split** in an organization, there is a serious disagreement, with some members taking one view and others a different one.

❑ If a group of people **split up**, they separate and go different ways. You can also say people are **split up** by something that happens. *Whole families have been split up by the fighting.* ◇ When a couple **split up**, they end their relationship or marriage. ◇ If you **split** something **up**, you divide it into a number of separate parts or sections.

❑ If something like wood **splits** or is **split**, a long crack appears in it. The crack is called a **split**.

❑ A **split second** is a very short period of time.

❑ If you say someone has a **split personality**, you mean their moods change so much they appear to have two separate personalities.

❑ If you **split the difference**, you agree on a figure half-way between two numbers which have already been mentioned.

❑ split infinitive: see **infinitive**.

splodge A **splodge** is a large uneven mark or stain, especially one caused by a liquid.

splurge (splurging, splurged) If you **splurge** or have a **splurge**, you spend a lot of money. ◇ A **splurge** of something is a lot of it happening in a short time. *There was a splurge of last-minute fighting.*

splutter (spluttering, spluttered) If you say someone **splutters**, you mean they have difficulty speaking clearly, because they are angry, embarrassed, or surprised. ◇ If something like an engine **splutters**, it makes a series of short spitting noises.

spoil (spoiling, spoiled or spoilt) ❑ If something **spoils** an occasion, it makes it less enjoyable, attractive, or interesting than it would otherwise have been. *Everyone seemed determined the rain would not spoil the event.* ◇ If people **spoil** something like the countryside, they damage it so that it loses part of its value, beauty, or usefulness. ◇ If food **spoils**, it becomes unfit to eat.

❑ If you **spoil** someone, especially a child, you give them everything they want, and they become badly-behaved as a result.

❑ If you are **spoiling for** something like trouble or a fight, you are eager for it to happen.

❑ **Spoils** are the things people get as a result of winning a battle or doing something else successfully. *At the end of next year, the horses will be sold and the spoils, if any, divided.*

❑ **Spoil** is waste material such as clay and rock removed from somewhere such as a pit or mine.

spoilsport If you say someone is a **spoilsport**, you mean

they behave in a way which ruins other people's pleasure or enjoyment.

spoke ❑ See **speak**.

❑ The **spokes** of a wheel are the bars which connect the outer ring to the centre.

spoken ❑ See **speak**.

❑ **Spoken** means produced by speaking. *Computers which recognise spoken commands are on the way.*

❑ See also **well-spoken**.

spokesman (spokesmen) A **spokesman** is a male spokesperson.

spokesperson (spokespersons or spokespeople) The **spokesperson** for a group or organization is the person who speaks as its representative, especially to the media.

spokeswoman (spokeswomen) A **spokeswoman** is a female spokesperson.

sponge (sponging, sponged; sponger) ❑ A **sponge** is a piece of a squashy absorbent substance with holes in it, used for cleaning or washing your body. Sponges can be natural or synthetic. If you **sponge** something, you wipe it with a wet sponge.

❑ A **sponge** or **sponge cake** is a very light cake made from flour, eggs, sugar, and sometimes fat. ◇ A **sponge** is also a light pudding.

❑ If someone **sponges off** you or **sponges on** you, they get money and other things from you without giving anything in return. A person who behaves like this is called a **sponger**.

spongy If something is **spongy**, it is soft and squashy.

sponsor (sponsoring, sponsored; sponsorship) ❑ If an organization **sponsors** something like an event or someone's training, they pay some or all of its costs, usually in return for publicity. An organization which sponsors something is called its **sponsor**. You talk about an organization's **sponsorship** of something. *From that date, sponsorship of sports and cultural events by tobacco companies will be prohibited.* **Sponsorship** is also financial support given by a sponsor. *This year's Tests are expected to have attracted over £3m in sponsorship.*

❑ If you **sponsor** someone who is doing something to raise money for charity, for example trying to walk or swim a certain distance, you agree to give them a certain amount of money if they succeed in doing it. People who sponsor someone like this are called the person's **sponsors**.

❑ If you **sponsor** a proposal or are its **sponsor**, you officially put it forward and support it.

❑ When an organization like the United Nations **sponsors** talks or negotiations, they arrange for them to take place and organize them. *...a UN-sponsored meeting.*

❑ If one country accuses another of **sponsoring** terrorism, they mean they encourage it and help the terrorists in some way.

spontaneous (spontaneously; spontaneity) ❑ You say something someone does is **spontaneous** when it happens because they feel like doing it, rather than because they planned it in advance. *...spontaneous standing ovations... The demonstrators claim that they are not organised by any political group and that they have gone to the square spontaneously.* Spontaneous behaviour is called **spontaneity**.

❑ **Spontaneous** is also used to describe something which happens because of processes within something, rather than being caused by things outside it. *...sponta-neous bleeding.*

spoof A spoof is something like an article or TV programme which seems to be about a serious matter but is actually a joke.

spook (spooking, spooked) ❑ A spook is a ghost. ◇ If something spooks you, it frightens you or makes you very nervous.

❑ A spook is also a spy.

spooky If something is spooky, it is strange and frightening. *The setting for the programme climax, a cemetery near Sherwood Forest at the dead of night, was suitably spooky.*

spool A spool is a round object which thread, film, or tape is wound onto.

spoon (spooning, spooned) A spoon is an object like a very small shallow bowl with a long handle. Spoons are used for eating, stirring, or serving food. ◇ If you spoon something somewhere, you put it there a small amount at a time, using a spoon.

spoonful (*plural:* spoonfuls *or* spoonsful) A spoonful of a substance is the amount one spoon can hold. *...a spoonful of olive oil.*

spoor The spoor of an animal is the visible trail it leaves as it moves along, especially its footprints.

sporadic (sporadically) If something is sporadic, it happens at irregular intervals. *Soldiers fired sporadically into the air.*

spore Spores are cells produced by non-flowering plants such as ferns, mosses, and fungi. They can develop into new plants.

sporran A sporran is a large purse, usually made of leather or fur, which Scotsmen wear on a belt round their waists when they are wearing a kilt.

sport (sporting) ❑ Sport is games like football and cricket and other competitive activities involving physical effort and skill. Each game or activity is called a sport. *She became involved in boxing when one of her sons took up the sport.* Sporting is used to talk about things to do with sport. *...sporting facilities... We'll have a full round-up of today's main sporting action.*

❑ If you sport something noticeable or unusual, you wear it. *He sported a dandyish little beard... A posse of bodyguards, sporting Raybans and dark suits, surrounded him as he swept in to his engagements.*

❑ If you have a sporting chance of achieving something, you might just succeed, if things happen to go your way.

sports car A sports car is a low fast car, usually with room for only two people.

sportsman (sportsmen) A sportsman is a man who takes part in a sport or sports.

sportsmanship is the behaviour and attitudes of someone who takes part in sport in a good-humoured way and does not take unfair advantage of their opponents.

sportsperson (*plural:* sportspeople) A sportsperson is a sportsman or sportswoman.

sportswear is any kind of special clothing worn for sports or informal leisure activities.

sportswoman (sportswomen) A sportswoman is a woman who takes part in sports.

sporty A sporty person likes playing sports.

spot (spotting, spotted) ❑ Spots are small coloured circles forming a pattern on something. You say something

with a pattern like this is spotted. *...a red and white spotted toadstool.* ◇ Spots are also small dirty marks or patches on a surface.

❑ Spots on a person's skin are small lumps or marks, sometimes caused by a disease or an infection.

❑ A spot of something is a small amount of it. *Adjust the seasoning, and add a spot of lemon juice.*

❑ A place where something happens or happened is often called a spot. *A stone memorial cross marks the spot where Lord Audley was killed... Few people had any way of knowing which bathing spots were safe.* ◇ A person on the spot is in the actual place where something is happening. *He had been told that nobody should attempt any action unless the UN officials on the spot were prepared to give their backing.*

❑ If something is done on the spot, it is done immediately. ◇ A spot check is a random inspection made without warning on one of a group of things.

❑ If you put someone on the spot, you put them in a position where they have to make a difficult decision or judgement. ◇ a tight spot: see tight.

❑ If you spot someone or something, you notice them. *Mistakes have been spotted at an early stage and put right.*

❑ A spot on a radio or TV show is a part which is regularly reserved for a particular performer or type of entertainment. *He has a weekly column in Elle magazine, and a spot on a national radio station.*

❑ If something is spot on, it is exactly right or accurate.

spotless (spotlessly) If something is spotless or spotlessly clean, it is perfectly clean. ◇ If someone's image or reputation is spotless, they are not known to have done anything bad or dishonest.

spotlight (spotlit) ❑ If someone or something is in the spotlight, a lot of attention is being paid to them, especially by the media. ◇ If something spotlights a situation or problem, it directs attention towards it. *The fighting over how to reduce the budget deficit has spotlighted weaknesses in the economy.*

❑ A spotlight is a very powerful light which can be directed so that it lights up a small area. Spotlights are often used in the theatre. If something is spotlit, it is lit up brightly by one or more spotlights.

spotty A spotty person has spots or pimples on their skin, especially their face. Calling someone spotty is often a way of saying they are very young. *Spotty youths mount the rostrum, clutching their speech-notes.*

spouse Someone's spouse is their husband or wife.

spout (spouting, spouted) ❑ If you talk about someone spouting something, you mean they are saying things they have learned or been told, without really thinking about what they are saying.

❑ When liquid or a flame spouts out of something, it comes out fast in a long stream.

❑ A spout is a specially shaped opening or tube which allows liquids to be poured easily out of a container.

sprain (spraining, sprained) If you sprain your ankle, knee, or wrist, you accidentally injure it by tearing the ligaments. An injury like this is called a sprain.

sprang See spring.

sprawl ❑ If you talk about something like a housing development sprawling, you mean it covers a large area. *...Wellcome's huge, sprawling research park.* ◇ When people talk about urban sprawl, they mean places where a city or town has expanded into the countryside in a seemingly uncontrolled way.

❏ If you **sprawl** somewhere or are **sprawled** there, you sit or lie with your arms and legs spread out in a careless way.

spray (sprayer) ❏ **Spray** is a lot of small drops of water being splashed or forced into the air. ◇ If you **spray** something with a liquid, you cover it with small drops of it, using something like a hose or an aerosol. ◇ A **spray** or **sprayer** is a device for spraying water or some other liquid. ◇ A **spray can** is a can containing liquid under pressure which can be forced out in a fine spray. ◇ A **spray** is also a liquid which you spray on something. *...nasal sprays... ...a fungal spray.*

❏ A **spray** of flowers or leaves is a number of them on a single stem.

❏ If gunmen **spray** something with bullets, they shoot a lot of bullets at it very rapidly.

spread (spreading, spread *not* 'spreaded') ❏ If you **spread** something or **spread** it **out**, you arrange it over a surface so all of it can be seen or used easily. ◇ If you **spread** your arms or legs, you stretch them as far apart as they will go. Similarly, you can **spread** your hands, often to indicate how large something is.

❏ If you **spread** a substance on a surface, you put a thin layer of it on it. ◇ A **spread** is a soft food which you spread on bread.

❏ If something like a liquid, a gas, or smoke **spreads**, it moves outwards, covering a larger and larger area. ◇ If a disease **spreads**, it affects more and more people. ◇ If something like news or an idea **spreads**, it reaches more and more people. ◇ When something involves more and more people, you can talk about its **spread**. *...the spread of nuclear weapons.*

❏ If people or things are **spread** or **spread out** over an area, they are far away from each other. *Electron's employees were spread out over 100 branches in the former Soviet Union and Eastern Europe.* ◇ If people **spread out**, they move away from each other. *It encouraged waves of emigrants to spread out across the union.*

❏ If something **spreads** or is **spread** over an unusually long period of time, it takes place over that period. *The election was spread over three days to enable security forces to move from one area to another.*

❏ A **spread** of ideas, interests, or other things is a range of them.

spreadeagled If someone is **spreadeagled**, they are lying with their arms and legs spread out.

spreadsheet A **spreadsheet** is a computer printout with columns of figures included. The computer program can also be called a **spreadsheet**. Spreadsheets are used especially for financial planning and budgeting.

spree When someone does a lot of something in a short time, you can say they have been on a **spree** of a certain kind. *High consumer debt will prevent a consumer-spending spree.*

sprig A **sprig** of a plant, especially a herb, is a small piece of stem with leaves on it.

sprightly If you say an old person is **sprightly**, you mean they are lively and active.

spring (springing, sprang, have sprung) ❏ **Spring** is the season between winter and summer. In the northern hemi-

sphere, this is between March and June.

❏ A **spring** is a coiled piece of wire which returns to its original shape after it has been pressed or pulled.

❏ A **spring** is also a place where water comes up naturally through the ground.

❏ When a person or animal **springs**, they jump upwards or forwards suddenly and quickly. *Martha sprang to her feet.*

❏ If something **springs** from something else, it is the result of it. *His interest in the subject sprang from work he carried out for the Rand Corporation in the 1950s.*

❏ If you **spring** some news on someone, you tell it to them without any warning. Similarly, you can **spring** a surprise on someone.

❏ If a boat **springs** a leak, a hole or crack appears in it and it starts leaking.

❏ **Spring** is used to say something happens very suddenly. For example, you say someone 'springs into action' or 'springs to life'. *One union chief sprang to Willis's defence.*

❏ If something **springs up**, it suddenly appears or comes into existence. *Second-hand shops have been springing up recently and have some wonderful 1930s clothes.*

❏ If something **springs to mind**, it is the first thing you think of when a subject is mentioned.

spring chicken If you say someone is no **spring chicken**, you are emphasizing that they are no longer young.

spring-clean When you **spring-clean** a house, you clean everything in it thoroughly, including things you do not clean very often.

spring onion **Spring onions** are small onions with long green leaves. They are often eaten raw in salads.

spring roll A **spring roll** is an Oriental pancake, filled with vegetables and sometimes meat, and then fried.

springboard A **springboard** is a flexible board you jump on before performing a dive or a gymnastic movement. ◇ If you use something as a **springboard**, you use it to help you advance further in your aims or ambitions. *Enlightened employers would like to see initial higher education providing a springboard for periods of specialised study.*

springbok The **springbok** is a small southern African antelope which leaps very high in the air when it is frightened.

springtime is the period of time when it is spring.

springy If something is **springy**, it returns quickly to its original shape after you press it.

sprinkle (sprinkling, sprinkled; sprinkler) ❏ If you **sprinkle** water or some other substance over something, you scatter it in small drops or pieces. ◇ A **sprinkler** is a device for spraying water. Sprinklers are used to water lawns and flowers or to put out fires.

❏ If you say something is **sprinkled** with things, you mean there are several of them on it or in it. *The grass was sprinkled with flowers... The text is sprinkled with errors.* ◇ A **sprinkling** of something is a small amount of it. *Most high Swiss resorts have had at least a sprinkling of snow.*

sprint (sprinter) A **sprint** is a short fast race, typically over 100 metres or 200 metres. A person who runs in sprints is called a **sprinter**. ◇ If you **sprint** somewhere, you run there as fast as you can.

sprite A **sprite** is a type of fairy. ◇ In computer graphics, a **sprite** is an object which can be moved round the computer screen.

spritzer A **spritzer** is a drink consisting of white wine and soda water.

sprout (sprouting, sprouted) ❑ When plants or vegetables **sprout**, they produce new shoots or leaves. ◇ If you talk about other things **sprouting**, you mean a lot of them are appearing suddenly and rapidly. *There are new hotels sprouting in Bratislava.*
   ❑ **Sprouts** or **Brussels sprouts** are vegetables which look like very small cabbages.

spruce (sprucing, spruced) ❑ The **spruce** (*usual plural:* spruce) is an evergreen tree with needle-like leaves and cones. Spruce are grown specially for their wood, which is used in making paper.
   ❑ If someone is **spruce**, they look very neat and smart. If you **spruce** yourself **up**, you make yourself look neater and smarter. Similarly, a building can be spruced up.

sprung See **spring**.

spry If you say an old person is **spry**, you mean they are lively and active.

spud A **spud** is a potato.

spun See **spin**.

spunk (spunky) **Spunk** is courage. You say someone is **spunky** when they show a lot of courage.

spur (spurring, spurred) ❑ If something **spurs** you to do something, it encourages you to do it. You can also say it acts as a **spur**. *The driver's concern for economy will act as an additional spur to purchase more fuel-efficient cars.* ◇ If something **spurs you on**, it makes you want to make progress or achieve something. ◇ If something **spurs** a change or event, it makes it happen faster or sooner. *The lowering of interest rates has done little to spur recovery.*
   ❑ If you do something **on the spur of the moment**, you do it suddenly, without thinking about it beforehand.
   ❑ **Spurs** are sharp metal points attached to the heels of a rider's boots. The rider presses them into the horse's sides to make it go faster. ◇ If you **win** or **earn** your **spurs**, you earn a certain right or status by doing something successfully.

spurious (spuriously) If something is **spurious**, it is not genuine. *...a spurious academic qualification.* ◇ A **spurious** argument or statement is based on faulty reasoning. *The Communist Party still claims, however spuriously, to represent the interests of the workers and peasants.*

spurn If you **spurn** something, you refuse to accept it or make use of it. *Until recently Albania spurned international diplomacy, breaking off diplomatic relations with all the superpowers.*

spurt ❑ A **spurt** of activity is a sudden brief period of it. *There appears to have been a sudden spurt of genuine progress in the search for an end to confrontation.* ◇ If something **spurts** or **puts on** a **spurt**, it begins to happen much faster.
   ❑ When a liquid or flame **spurts**, it shoots out quickly in a thin stream.

sputter (sputtering, sputtered) If something **sputters** or **sputters on**, it keeps going, but in a very unstable way, as though it might stop at any moment. *...a sputtering economic recovery.*

spy (spies, spying, spied) ❑ A **spy** is a person whose job is to find out secret information about another country or organization. This activity is called **spying**. You say the person **spies** for their own country or organization. ◇ A **spy satellite** is a small satellite equipped with video cameras and radar, which can be positioned over a place to send back detailed information about it. Spy satellites are used in war to monitor the movement of troops and weapons.
   ❑ If you **spy** on someone, you watch them secretly.
   ❑ If you **spy** someone or something, you notice them. *They spied heavy objects being heaved onto lorries.*

sq is short for 'square' in measurements of area. For example, 'sq ft' is short for 'square feet' and 'sq km' is short for 'square kilometres'.

squabble (squabbling, squabbled) When people **squabble** or have a **squabble**, they quarrel, usually about something unimportant.

squad A **squad** is a group of players or athletes chosen to take part in a sports competition, often to represent their country. ◇ A **squad** is also a unit of a police force responsible for dealing with a particular type of crime. *...the serious fraud squad.* ◇ A **squad** is also a small group of soldiers who work closely together.

squaddie Soldiers of the lowest ranks are sometimes called **squaddies**.

squadron A **squadron** is a section of one of the armed forces, especially the air force.

squadron leader A **squadron leader** is a middle-ranking officer in the RAF.

squalid (squalor) You say a place is **squalid** when it is dirty, untidy, and in bad condition. You talk about the **squalor** in a place like this. *Many were living in squalor on the streets.* ◇ You say activities are **squalid** when they are dishonest or immoral.

squall A **squall** is a brief spell of heavy rain or snow with a strong wind.

squalor See **squalid**.

squander (squandering, squandered) If you **squander** something, you waste it. *...squandered opportunities.*

square (squaring, squared) ❑ A **square** is a shape with four sides of the same length and four corners which are all right angles. ◇ If something is **square**, it has a shape similar to a square. *...a square courtyard.*
   ❑ In a town or city, a **square** is a flat open space, surrounded by buildings.
   ❑ **Square** is used in front of units of length to change them into units of area. *...square metres... ...square inches.* ◇ **Square** is also used to say how long each side of a square is. *...a piece of land measuring 50ft square.*
   ❑ If you **square** a number, you multiply it by itself. For example, 3 squared is 3×3, or 9. ◇ The **square** of a number is the number obtained by multiplying the first number by itself. For example, the square of 4 is 16. In maths, this is expressed as $4^2 = 16$.
   ❑ If you **square** something with something else, you find a way in which the two things can operate together or both be acceptable. *Protecting the victims of the recession has to be squared with economic pressures that favour spending on capital projects.* ◇ If you have to **square** something with another person, you have to make it acceptable to them. *He would like to see private wings in NHS hospitals closed, but realises that he will have to square this first with the leadership.*
   ❑ If you are **back to square one**, you have to start dealing with something from the beginning again.

❑ If you **square up to** a difficulty or a hostile person, you get ready to deal with them.

❑ If you say someone is trying to **square the circle**, you mean they are trying to do something impossible.

❑ In a competition, if you **square** things or make them **square**, you win a point, game, match, or round and bring your score up to your opponent's, so that you are equal. *Britain must win to square the series and keep interest alive for the third match.*

❑ If you say a person is **square**, you mean they are boring and unfashionable.

square root A **square root** of a number is another number which when multipled by itself produces the first number. For example, the square roots of 16 are 4 and -4. In maths, this is expressed as $\sqrt{16} = 4$ or -4.

squarely If you say something such as blame or responsibility lies **squarely** with someone, you mean it is their fault or responsibility and nobody else's. *Others put the blame for the problem squarely on the shoulders of the Conservative government.* ◇ If you face up to something **squarely**, you deal with it in a determined way, and do not try to avoid it.

squash (squashes, squashing, squashed) ❑ If you **squash** something, you press it or crush it so that it becomes flat or loses its shape.

❑ If someone **squashes** something which is causing them trouble, they put a stop to it, often using force. *The President and his security men will probably be successful in squashing the current wave of dissent.*

❑ **Squash** is a game between two players or two pairs of players in a court surrounded by walls. The players hit a small rubber ball against the walls using light long-handled rackets.

❑ A **squash** is a marrow or any vegetable belonging to the marrow family.

❑ **Squash** is a drink made from fruit, sugar, and water.

squashy If something is **squashy**, it is soft and can be squashed easily.

squat (squatting, squatted; squatter) ❑ When people **squat** in a disused building, they live there illegally without paying rent. A building used like this is called a **squat**. The people who live in it are called **squatters**. ◇ **Squatters** are also people who occupy unused land, either to farm it or build on it, without having a legal right to do so.

❑ If you **squat**, you crouch close to the ground, balancing on your feet with your legs bent.

❑ A **squat** person is unusually short and fat. Buildings and other things can be described as **squat** when they are wide and not very high.

squawk When a bird **squawks** or lets out a **squawk**, it makes a loud harsh noise.

squeak (squeaking, squeaked) ❑ If someone or something **squeaks** or gives a **squeak**, they make a short high-pitched sound.

❑ If someone succeeds in doing something by a narrow margin, you can say they **squeak through**. *Mr Isomura ought to squeak home, but it will be a close-run race.*

squeaky If something is **squeaky**, it makes squeaking noises. *...a squeaky toy.*

squeaky-clean If you say someone like a politician is **squeaky-clean**, you mean they are very honest and there is nothing in their personal life which could be used to embarrass them.

squeal (squealing, squealed) If someone or something **squeals** or lets out a **squeal**, they make a long high-pitched sound.

squeamish (squeamishness) If someone is **squeamish** about something, they are reluctant to do it, watch it, or have it done to them. *Some people are squeamish about having needles inserted into their veins... He had the scholar's squeamishness about making factual assertions unwarranted by the evidence.*

squeeze (squeezing, squeezes) ❑ If you **squeeze** something or give it a **squeeze**, you press it firmly from two sides, usually between your thumb and fingers. ◇ If you **squeeze** a substance **out** of something like a tube, you get it out by squeezing the tube.

❑ If you **squeeze through** a small space, you just manage to get through it. You can also **squeeze into** a small space. If it is only just possible to get people or things into a small space, you can say it is a **squeeze**.

❑ If you **squeeze** something out of someone, you get it by force or persuasion. *The bigger clubs would like to use this power to squeeze more money out of television and advertising.*

❑ If something to do with money is **squeezed**, it is restricted or reduced. *This would squeeze still further the disposable incomes of the poor... ...ferry companies which find their business squeezed as a result of the Channel Tunnel.* ◇ If someone is being **squeezed**, they are having problems, usually because of lack of money. *People on fixed incomes are being badly squeezed.* ◇ If a government imposes a **squeeze**, it cuts back on public spending and makes it difficult for people to borrow money, because it is trying to fight inflation.

❑ If you **squeeze** something into a small amount of time, you manage to fit it in. *Most of their extra-curricular activities have to be squeezed into the lunch hour.*

❑ If someone is **squeezed out** of something, they are prevented from being involved in it. *Private producers are being squeezed out of the credit markets.*

squelch (squelches, squelching, squelched) If something **squelches**, it makes a wet sucking sound, like someone walking across wet muddy land.

squib A **squib** is a small firework which makes a loud bang. ◇ If you say something was a **damp squib**, you mean it should have been interesting, exciting, or impressive, but it was not.

squid (usual plural: squid) The **squid** is an edible sea creature with a soft body and ten tentacles.

squidgy If something is **squidgy**, it is very soft and squashy.

squiggle A **squiggle** is a line which twists and curves in an irregular way.

squint If you **squint** at something, you look at it with your eyes partly closed, to try to see it better. ◇ A **squint** is a medical condition in which a person's eyes look in different directions.

squire In the past, the **squire** of an English village was the man who owned most of the land in and around it.

squirm If you **squirm**, you wriggle, because you are nervous or uncomfortable. ◇ You also say people **squirm** when they are embarrassed or ashamed. *Officials have squirmed in the face of such truthful reporting.*

squirrel (squirrelling, squirrelled) (*American spelling:* squirreling, squirreled) ❑ **Squirrels** are small furry animals with long bushy tails. Most species live in trees.

    ❑ If you **squirrel** things away, you collect them together and keep them in a safe place.

squirt If a liquid **squirts** or is **squirted**, it comes out of a narrow opening in a thin fast stream.

Sr See **senior**.

St (*plural:* SS) is short for 'Saint' in front of a saint's name. *...St George... ...SS Cyril and Methodius.*

    ❑ **St** is also short for 'Street'. *....Oxford St.*

stab (stabbing, stabbed) ❑ If someone **stabs** another person, they push a knife into their body. An injury caused like this is called a **stab** wound. A **stabbing** is an incident in which someone is stabbed.

    ❑ If someone **stabs you in the back,** they do something very harmful to you when you thought you could trust them. *Dr Mahathir denounced the defection as a stab in the back.*

    ❑ If you **stab** something or **stab** at it, you poke it sharply with your finger or with something you are holding.

    ❑ If you make a **stab** at something, you try to do it. *The government is now set to have a fresh stab at changing these laws.*

    ❑ A **stab** of something such as pain or fear is a sudden feeling of it. *He felt a stab of jealousy.*

stabilise See **stabilize**.

stabiliser See **stabilizer**.

stability See **stable**.

stabilize (stabilizing, stabilized; stabilization) (*can be spelled with an 's' instead of a 'z'*) If something **stabilizes** or is **stabilized**, it becomes stable. *The ministers indicated they wanted to see a stabilization of the Japanese yen.*

stabilizer (or **stabiliser**) A **stabilizer** is a device which helps a plane, ship, or racing car remain stable. ◇ A **stabilizer** is also something which helps to stabilize a system or situation. *...the role of taxes and public spending as automatic stabilizers in modern economies.*

stable (stabler, stablest; stability) ❑ If something is **stable**, it is not likely to change or come to an end suddenly. *Last night his condition was stable after an operation... The new government could provide the stability Poland has been lacking since the elections last October.*

    ❑ If an object is **stable**, it is not likely to move or fall over. *The pillars were bolted to the warehouse floors for stability and safety.*

    ❑ A **stable** or **stables** is (a) a building where horses are kept. (b) an organization which breeds and trains racehorses. ◇ A **stable lad** or **stable boy** is a person who works in a stable looking after the horses.

stablemate If two organizations, especially newspapers, are **stablemates**, they are owned by the same person or company. You can also say two people are **stablemates** when they work for the same company or belong to the same political party.

staccato (*pron:* stak-ah-toe) If a piece of music is played or sung **staccato**, the individual notes are played or sung very briefly with gaps in between them. ◇ A **staccato** noise consists of a series of short sharp separate sounds. *...a staccato laugh.*

stack ❑ A **stack** of things is a neat pile of them. If you **stack** things or **stack** them **up**, you arrange them in neat

piles. ◇ If a place or surface is **stacked** with objects, it is filled with piles of them.

    ❑ A **stack** of something is a very large amount of it. *The Supreme Court faces a stack of legal suits against the proposal... This brings in stacks of cash.*

    ❑ If you say the odds or the cards are **stacked against** someone, you mean they are unlikely to succeed in what they are doing because the conditions are not favourable.

stadium (*plural:* stadiums *or* stadia) A **stadium** is a large sports ground with tiers of seats all round it.

staff (staffing) ❑ The **staff** of an organization are the people who work for it. You can say an organization is **staffed** by certain people. *The college is staffed by Japanese teachers on three-year secondments from the Ministry of Education.* ◇ The **staffing** in a place is the number of people employed to work there. *Staffing and investment are being cut.*

    ❑ A **staff** is a strong stick or pole.

staff nurse A **staff nurse** is a hospital nurse whose rank is immediately below that of a sister or charge nurse.

staff room At a school or college, the **staff room** is a room where teachers can go to work or relax when they are not teaching.

staffer A **staffer** is a member of staff, especially in a government organization or on a newspaper.

staffing See **staff**.

stag ❑ A **stag** is an adult male deer.

    ❑ All-male parties and social evenings are sometimes called **stag nights** or **stag parties**. A man often has a **stag night** just before he gets married.

stage (staging, staged) ❑ A **stage** is a part of a process or activity, or a particular point during it. *The legal action was the last stage of the campaign... At one stage, not only his wife but two of his four children were in the business.*

    ❑ In a theatre, the **stage** is the raised platform where the actors or entertainers perform. ◇ The **stage** is also used to talk about acting in the theatre and the production of plays there. *Too mature to play romantic leads in front of the cameras, she returned to the stage.* ◇ If someone **stages** a play or other show, they present a performance of it.

    ❑ If someone **stages** an event, they organize it. *The Football League is staging a six-a-side competition in Manchester from 2-5 December.*

    ❑ If you **set the stage** for something, you make preparations for it to happen. *President Lee said the move would set the stage for eventual reunification.*

    ❑ If someone is involved in something which attracts a lot of public attention, you can talk about them appearing on a particular **stage**. *Most world leaders expressed regret at the departure of such an important player on the world stage.*

stage-coach (or **stagecoach**) A **stage-coach** was a large horse-drawn carriage which carried passengers and mail.

stage door The **stage door** of a theatre is the entrance used by the performers and theatre employees, rather than the public.

stage fright is the feeling of fear or nervousness some people have just before they appear in front of an audience.

stage hand In a theatre, the **stage hands** are the people whose job is to move the scenery and equipment on the stage.

stage-manage If something which happens is **stage-**

managed, it is carefully organized and controlled, rather than happening spontaneously.

stage manager In a theatre, the **stage manager** is the person responsible to the director for the scenery and the lights, and for making sure nothing goes wrong during a performance.

stagecoach See **stage-coach.**

stagger (staggering, staggered; staggeringly) ❑ If someone **staggers,** they walk very unsteadily, for example because they are ill or drunk.

❑ If something **staggers** you, you are very surprised or shocked by it. You say something like this is **staggering.** *...staggeringly expensive hotels.*

❑ When things like people's holidays or hours of work are **staggered,** they are arranged so they do not all happen at the same time.

staging post A **staging post** is a place where people or things stop on their way somewhere. *The aircraft will use Doha as a staging post as they fly up to the northern Gulf from their bases in Oman.*

stagnant If something like a business or economy is **stagnant,** there is very little activity or growth in it. *Stagnant for three years, property prices are beginning to move.* ◇ **Stagnant** water is not flowing or moving, and therefore is often dirty and smells unpleasant.

stagnate (stagnating, stagnated; stagnation) If something **stagnates,** it does not change or develop. *The gap between rich and poor grew, while living standards for those in the middle stagnated... This obsession with a 400-year-old playwright has become, for some, a sad reflection on what they see as Britain's cultural stagnation.*

staid people are serious, dull, and rather old-fashioned.

stain (staining, stained) If a substance **stains** something, it leaves marks called **stains** which are difficult to remove. *Soon the tablecloth was stained in strawberry juice.*

stained glass is pieces of coloured glass fixed together by lead strips to make decorative windows or other objects.

stainless steel is a type of metal made from steel, chromium, and often nickel. Stainless steel does not rust and is often used to make household items such as cutlery.

stair Stairs are a set of steps, usually inside a building.

staircase A **staircase** is a set of stairs inside a building.

stairway A **stairway** is a set of stairs inside or outside a building.

stairwell A **stairwell** is part of a building which contains a staircase.

stake (staking, staked) ❑ If something which is important to you is **at stake,** you are in danger of losing it as a result of something which is happening. *The credibility of both organisations is at stake.* ◇ If you **stake** something you value on achieving a result, you risk losing it if you do not achieve that result. *The United Nations is staking its reputation on its ability to ensure free and fair elections.* ◇ The **stakes** involved in a risky action are the things which can be gained or lost. If someone **raises the stakes,** they add to the things which can be gained or lost. *Russia raised the stakes by warning that it might revise its borders with any republic which left the union.*

❑ If you have a **stake** in something, its success matters to you, because you will gain in some way if it succeeds. ◇ If someone has a **stake** in a company, they own part of

it. *The German government agreed to sell its remaining 20% stake in Deutsche Airbus.*

❑ If you **stake a claim** to something, you say you have a right to it. ◇ If you **stake out** a claim, you say precisely what things you are claiming for yourself.

❑ When police officers **stake out** a building, they watch it secretly for evidence of criminal activity.

❑ A **stake** is a wooden post with a pointed end.

stakeholder The **stakeholders** in a business or enterprise are all the people who have an interest in its success, for example shareholders, creditors, and employees.

stalactite A **stalactite** is a piece of rock which looks like an enormous icicle and which hangs down from the roof of a cave. It is formed over many years by the constant dripping of water containing lime.

stalagmite A **stalagmite** is a candle-shaped piece of rock which sticks up from the floor of a cave. It is formed over many years by water containing lime dripping from the roof of the cave onto the same spot.

stale ❑ If something like food or tobacco is **stale,** it is old and no longer fresh or good to eat or use. ◇ **Stale** air has an unpleasant smell because it is no longer fresh.

❑ If you say something like an attitude or idea is **stale,** you mean it is old and dull.

stalemate (stalemated) ❑ If a situation reaches **stalemate** or is **stalemated,** it reaches a position where neither side can win and where no further progress seems possible.

❑ In chess, **stalemate** is a position in which a player cannot make any move which is permitted by the rules, so that the game ends in a draw.

stalk ❑ The **stalk** of a leaf, flower, or fruit is the thin part which joins it to the plant or tree.

❑ If you **stalk** a person or a wild animal, you follow them quietly and secretly, so you can kill them, capture them, or observe them carefully. ◇ If you talk about something unpleasant **stalking** a place, you mean it is present and threatens to cause destruction or disaster. *Hunger stalks Africa.*

❑ If someone **stalks** somewhere, they walk in a stiff way, because they are proud or angry. *She stalked into the editor's office and threatened to resign.*

stalking horse A **stalking horse** is something which is used to disguise someone's real intentions. In leadership contests, a stalking horse is a candidate who is not expected to win but who tests the feelings of the voters before the real challenger stands.

stall ❑ If a process **stalls** or is **stalled,** it stops but may start again later. *These negotiations have so far stalled over the Community's unwillingness to lift import tariffs and quotas... The West has complained that Moscow has been stalling the talks.* ◇ If you **stall,** you try to avoid doing something until later.

❑ If a motor vehicle **stalls** or is **stalled,** its engine stops suddenly.

❑ The **stalls** in a theatre or concert hall are the seats on the ground floor directly in front of the stage.

❑ A **stall** is a large table, for example at a market or exhibition, where people set out goods for sale or give information. ◇ If someone **sets out their stall,** they do something publicly which shows their intentions.

stallholder A **stallholder** is a person who sells goods on a market stall.

stallion A stallion is an adult male horse.

stalwart (*pron: stawl-wart*) You say someone is **stalwart** or a **stalwart** when they are loyal and reliable. *...the stalwart fidelity of the islanders... ...a policeman who is the stalwart of his local athletics club.*

stamen The **stamens** of a flower are the small delicate stalks which grow inside the blossom and produce the pollen.

stamina is the physical or mental energy needed to do a tiring activity for a long time.

stammer (stammering, stammered) If someone **stammers**, they speak with difficulty, hesitating and repeating words or sounds. Some people stammer when they are nervous, and a few people stammer most or all of the time because they have a speech defect. You say someone like this has a **stammer**.

stamp ❑ A **stamp** or **postage stamp** is a small piece of gummed paper which you stick on an envelope or parcel to show you have paid the correct fee before posting it.
  ❑ A **stamp** is also a small block of wood or metal with words or a design on it. You press it onto an inky pad and then onto a document or object, to make the words or design appear there; what appears is also called a **stamp**. You say you have **stamped** the document or object.
  ❑ If someone **puts their stamp** on something, they affect it in a way which makes it obvious they were involved in it. You then say it **bears their stamp.**
  ❑ If you **stamp** your foot, you bring it down very hard, because you are angry. ◇ If you **stamp** on something, you bring your foot down on it hard.
  ❑ If someone **stamps on** an activity they think is undesirable, they stop it happening or spreading. *The Treasury yesterday stamped on speculation about an early cut in bank base lending rates.* ◇ If someone **stamps** something **out**, they put an end to it or destroy it completely. *The Equal Opportunities Commission yesterday called for stringent new laws to stamp out sexual discrimination at work.*

stamp duty is a tax which has to be paid on certain legal documents, especially when buying property above a certain price.

stampede (stampeding, stampeded) ❑ When a group of large animals **stampede**, they run together in a wild uncontrolled way. This is called a **stampede**. A **stampede** is also an occasion when many people dash somewhere together. *Many pilgrims are reported to have died in a stampede in a crowded tunnel.*
  ❑ If someone **stampedes** you into doing something, they rush you into it without giving you time to think about it properly.

stamping ground Someone's **stamping ground** is a place where they spent a lot of time in the past or did something they were famous for. *He is returning to his old stamping ground as the new deputy governor of the Bank of England.*

stance ❑ Your **stance** on a particular matter is your attitude to it. *China needs the West for economic reasons, but is compelled for ideological reasons to adopt a hostile stance... Is Moscow hardening its stance on arms control issues?*
  ❑ Your **stance** is also the way you are standing. *Adopting the stance of a victorious pugilist, he denounced the treaty as a lie.*

stand (standing, stood) ❑ When you **stand** or **stand up**, you change your position so your body is upright, your legs are straight, and your weight is supported by your feet; you then say you are **standing** or **standing up**. ◇ If there is **standing room** somewhere, all the seats have been taken but there is room for people to stand.
  ❑ If you **stand** something somewhere, you put it there in an upright position. *He stood the bottle on the bench.* ◇ If something like a building or statue **stands** somewhere, it is situated there.
  ❑ You use **stand** when you are saying something about the state of a building, vehicle, or piece of land. You say, for example, that a vehicle is 'standing idle'. *Nearly six months later, very little work has been done and the flats still stand empty.*
  ❑ If you **stand up** to someone or something, you defend yourself against their attacks or demands. ◇ If you **stand up** for someone or something that is being criticized or threatened, you defend them. ◇ If you **stand out** for or against something, you continue to support or oppose it, even though this is an unpopular or difficult thing to do. ◇ If you say people should **stand up and be counted,** you mean they should say publicly whether they support or oppose something.
  ❑ If someone or something can **stand** a situation or a test, they are good enough or strong enough to cope with it.
  ❑ If something **stands up** to a lot of use, pressure, or wear, it remains unharmed or in good condition after being severely tested in this way. *New trees are far less able to stand up to the ravages of cyclones.*
  ❑ If you say something like a claim or piece of evidence **stands up**, you mean it can be accepted as true or satisfactory.
  ❑ If you **stand in** for someone, you take their place or do their job for a short time. Someone who does this is called a **stand-in.**
  ❑ If you **stand** in an election, you are a candidate in it.
  ❑ If someone **stands down** from an important position, they resign. ◇ If soldiers or police officers are **stood down,** they are sent off duty, rather than being ready for action.
  ❑ If someone or something **stands out,** they are very noticeable, because they are better or more important than other people or things of their kind. *A restaurant of this calibre would stand out anywhere.* ◇ You can also say something **stands out** when it can be seen very clearly.
  ❑ If you say something **stands to reason,** you mean it is obvious. *Their legal system differs; their education system differs; it stands to reason that their reading habits should be different as well.*
  ❑ If you **stand** something like an idea or argument **on its head,** you reverse it completely. *He stood his previous position on its head by indicating that he could now support higher income taxes on the super-rich in exchange for cuts in capital gains taxes.*
  ❑ If a group of letters **stand for** a name, they are a shortened version of it. *WPP stands for Wire and Plastic Products.*
  ❑ If you say someone or something **stands for** a particular idea or attitude, you mean they represent it. *The Lion was long seen as the unmistakable symbol of Venice, standing for strength, courage and political continuity.*
  ❑ If you are **standing by,** you are ready to provide help

or take action if necessary. *French radio says twelve Mirage-2000 fighters are standing by at the Orange airbase.* See also **standby**. ◇ If you **stand by** while something bad happens, you do not do anything to stop it. *The international community cannot stand by and allow innocent children, women and men to be starved to death.*

❑ If you **stand by** an earlier decision or agreement, you do not change it. ◇ If you **stand by** someone, you continue to give them help and support when they are in a difficult position.

❑ If you **stand back** from a situation, you avoid being closely involved in it for a time, so you can understand it better.

❑ If you cannot **stand** something, you are not able to bear it or put up with it. ◇ You also say you cannot **stand** someone or something if you dislike them very strongly. ◇ If you say someone will not **stand for** something, you mean they will not allow it to happen or continue. *He warned that China would not stand for any interference in its internal affairs.*

❑ If you make or take a **stand** on a question or issue, you publicly take up a particular position and stick to it. *He felt the need to make a stand against racism.*

❑ If you **stand to** gain something, you are in a position where you might gain it. Similarly, you can **stand to** lose something.

❑ If something **stands** at a particular level or value, that is its level or value at present. *The inflation rate now stands at 3.6 per cent.* ◇ When you are saying how tall someone is, you say they **stand** a particular height. *For a man who stands 6ft 2in and weighs 230lb, Jackson's speed is remarkable.*

❑ If something like a decision or offer still **stands**, it is still effective or valid.

❑ When someone **stands trial**, they are tried in a court of law.

❑ If you **stand** someone **up**, you fail to keep an arrangement to meet them.

❑ A **stand** is a small stall or shop at an exhibition or in the street. ◇ A **stand** is also a large structure at a sports ground, where the spectators sit or stand to watch what is going on.

❑ The **stand** is the place in a court of law where the witness sits or stands when he or she is giving evidence.

❑ See also **standing**.

stand-by See standby.

stand-in See stand.

stand-off ❑ In a **stand-off**, two opposing groups or forces each refuse to make a move until the other one does something.

❑ **Stand-off** missiles are designed to be released a long distance from a target.

stand-offish You say someone is being **stand-offish** when they behave in a rather formal and unfriendly way.

stand-up comedy is a form of entertainment in which a comedian stands up alone in front of an audience and tells jokes. Someone who does this is called a **stand-up** comedian.

standard ❑ A **standard** is a level of quality or achievement. *There's been a record number of complaints about the standard of service on Britain's railways.* ◇ A **standard** is also something which is used to judge the quality of

something else. *The festival is by any standard a popular success... Other firms are setting common standards to make it easier to do business together.*

❑ **Standards** are moral principles which govern people's behaviour. *...protests by some clergy against what they describe as falling moral standards.* ◇ See also **double standards**.

❑ Your **standard of living** is the level of comfort in which you live, which usually depends on how much money you have.

❑ The **standard** version of a product is the normal one. Similarly, you can obtain something in a **standard** size. ◇ **Standard class** travel is cheaper and less luxurious than first class.

❑ A **standard** work or text on a subject is one which is widely known and often recommended.

standard-bearer The **standard-bearer** of a group with a particular interest is a person who acts as their leader or public representative.

standard lamp A **standard lamp** is an electric light mounted on a pole, which stands on the floor in a living room.

standardize (standardizing, standardized; standardization) (*can be spelled with an 's' instead of a 'z'*) When things are **standardized**, they are made the same, or made to have the same features. *The committee wants to see a standardization of speed limits throughout the Community.*

standby (*or* **stand-by**) ❑ If someone or something is **on standby**, they are ready to be used when needed. *Riot police have been on standby... Its crew were rescued by a standby vessel.* ◇ Something which you keep ready for use can be called a **standby**. *Pasta and rice are two cheap, filling student standbys.*

❑ **Stand-by** tickets for the theatre are cheap tickets which sometimes become available just before the performance starts. Similarly, you can sometimes obtain a **stand-by** ticket for a plane flight.

standing is used to describe things which exist all the time, rather than being formed or made when necessary. *...a standing commission on human rights... Turkey has the second largest standing army in NATO.*

❑ Someone's **standing** is their status or reputation. *His standing has suffered as a result of the coup.* ◇ A politician's or party's **standing** in the polls is the number of percentage points they get compared to the number obtained by their opponents.

❑ If you say something is of a certain number of years' **standing**, you mean it has existed for that number of years. *...a party boss of 18 years' standing.* See also **long-standing**.

standing order ❑ A **standing order** is an instruction to your bank to pay someone a fixed amount at regular intervals.

❑ A **standing order** is also a rule or order which is permanently in force.

standing stone A **standing stone** is a very large upright stone. Many standing stones are thought to have been erected in ancient times.

standpipe A **standpipe** is a vertical pipe connected to a water supply which stands in a street or some other public place.

standpoint If you look at something from a particular

standpoint, you look at it in a particular way, depending, for example, on the kind or person you are. *Perhaps I listened from the jaded standpoint of one who has heard the work too often... The argument was always questionable from an economist's standpoint.*

standstill If movement or an activity comes to a standstill, it stops completely. *Industrial disputes have brought traffic to a virtual standstill.*

stank See stink.

stanza A stanza is a verse of a poem.

staple (stapling, stapled; stapler) ❑ A **staple** food is one which forms a basic part of someone's everyday diet. A food like this can be called a **staple**.

❑ **Staples** are small pieces of bent wire used for holding sheets of paper together. They are pushed through the paper using a special device called a **stapler**. If you **staple** something, you fix it in place using staples.

star (starring, starred; stardom) ❑ Famous actors, musicians, and sportspeople are often called **stars**. Being a star is called **stardom**. *From birth Perkins had been earmarked for stardom.* ◇ If an actor or actress **stars** in a film or play, he or she has one of the main parts in it. You can also say the film or play **stars** the actor or actress.

❑ A **star** is a large ball of burning gas in space. You see stars on clear nights as small points of light.

❑ A **star** is also a shape with four, five, or more points sticking out of it in a regular pattern. ◇ **Stars** are star-shaped marks printed against the name of something such as a hotel or a restaurant to indicate its quality. *...a three-star hotel.*

star-studded A **star-studded** show or film has a lot of famous people in it.

Star Wars See SDI.

starboard The **starboard** side of a ship is the right side when you are facing the front.

starch (starches; starched) **Starch** is a carbohydrate in foods like bread, potatoes, and rice. ◇ **Starch** is also a substance used for stiffening cloth. **Starched** clothes have been treated with starch to make them stiff.

starchy foods contain a lot of starch.

stardom See star.

stare (staring, stared) ❑ If you **stare** at something, you look at it for a long time. A **stare** is a long fixed look.

❑ If you say something unpleasant is **staring** someone **in the face**, you mean it seems likely to happen to them. *Bankruptcy stares every team in the face... The communists could be staring defeat in the face.* ◇ If you say the answer to a problem is **staring** someone **in the face**, you mean it is so obvious they should have noticed it.

starfish (*plural:* starfish) **Starfish** are flat star-shaped sea creatures with five arms.

stark (starkly) ❑ A **stark** statement is unpleasantly clear and simple. *He gave a stark warning about the dangers of complacency.* ◇ A **stark** choice is between two alternatives, both of which are unpleasant. ◇ A **stark** contrast is between something very unpleasant and something very good or desirable. *The refugees' poverty is in stark contrast to the potential wealth of the republic... The college's conclusions contrast starkly with assertions last week by Eric Caines.*

❑ If someone is **stark** naked, they are completely naked. ◇ **Stark** is also used to describe things which have a

very bare and plain appearance. *...stark landscapes... ...stark white walls.*

starlet A **starlet** is a young actress who might become a film star in the future.

starlight is light from the stars at night.

starling **Starlings** are very common European birds. They have greenish-black feathers and often gather together in large noisy flocks.

starry ❑ A **starry** night is a very clear one, when you can see many stars.

❑ A **starry** film or show has many famous people in it. You can also say it has a **starry** cast.

starry-eyed If someone is **starry-eyed**, they are so optimistic or idealistic they do not see things as they really are.

Stars and Stripes The Stars and Stripes is the American national flag.

start ❑ If you **start** doing something, you begin to do it. ◇ If you **start** something, you begin doing it, saying it, or dealing with it. *He started a conversation with his neighbour.* ◇ If you **start** by doing something or **start** with something, you do that thing first. Similarly, you can **start off** or **start out** by doing something. *They started out by looking at the computer screens which display the images.*

❑ If you **start on** something which needs to be done, you begin doing it. *The new government has started on a major liberalisation of the country's economy.*

❑ When something **starts**, it begins to happen. The **start** of something is its beginning. ◇ If something **starts** something else **off**, it causes it to start.

❑ If someone **starts** a business or organization, or **starts** it **up**, they create it or set it up.

❑ If you **start** a car or **start** it **up**, you get its engine running.

❑ If something **starts** as a certain thing, it is like that at first, before it becomes something else. *The museum at Beaulieu started as a three-car collection.* Similarly, a person can **start** or **start out** as a certain thing. *Mr Allen has spent 38 years in catering, having started out as a hotel cook.*

❑ If a commodity **starts** at a certain price, that is the cheapest price at which it is available. *Small unconverted stone cottages and barns in the area start from £15,000.*

❑ When you make a journey, your **starting point** is the place you start from. ◇ A **starting point** is also an idea, statement, or position which can be used to begin a conversation, argument, or process. *We're prepared to talk about anything, he said, and suggested the starting point might be an attempt to define what independence is supposed to mean.*

❑ You use **to start with** to talk about the earliest part of something, before it changes. *To start with, it may be expensive.* ◇ You say **to start with** or **for a start** when you are mentioning the first of a series of things. *For a start, it is not entirely certain who owns the building.*

❑ If you **start** or give a **start**, your body jerks because you are surprised or frightened.

❑ **in fits and starts**: see fit.

START stands for 'Strategic Arms Reduction Talks', the talks which led to a treaty being signed in 1991 between the US and the former USSR reducing the number of strategic nuclear weapons on each side.

starter ❑ A **starter** is a small amount of food served as the first course of a meal.

❏ The **starter** in a car is the device which starts the engine.

❏ The **starters** in a race are the people or animals who begin it, as distinct from the ones that finish. ◇ The **starter** of a race is the person who starts it, usually by firing a gun or waving a flag.

❏ You say **for starters** to indicate that there are other things of a particular kind, apart from the ones you are mentioning. *Dickens, Conan Doyle, P G Wodehouse and Virginia Woolf, just for starters, have given London an existence in the popular consciousness quite independent of the facts.*

startle (startling, startled; startlingly) If something **startles** you, it surprises you and slightly frightens or worries you. You say something like this is **startling**. *The men made some startling allegations... ...a startlingly intimate biography.*

starve (starving, starved; starvation) ❏ If people or animals are **starving**, they are suffering from lack of food and are likely to die. **Starvation** is death or extreme suffering caused by lack of food. ◇ If people are **starved** into doing something, they are deprived of food to make them do it.

❏ If you say you are **starving**, you mean you are very hungry.

❏ If people or organizations are **starved** of something they need, they are suffering because they are being deprived of it. *Education, so long starved of funds, has only now been moved to the top of the political agenda.*

stash (stashes, stashing, stashed) If you **stash** something valuable somewhere, you store it there to keep it safe. You call something hidden like this a **stash**. *A stash of ammunition and hand grenades was found in his room.*

state (stating, stated) ❏ Countries are sometimes called **states**. *...the Baltic states... All member states supported the idea except Britain.* ◇ Some countries are divided into areas called **states**, each with a certain amount of self-government. ◇ The US is sometimes called **the States**.

❏ The **state** is a country considered as a unit, as distinct from its individual citizens and non-government organizations. *...treason against the state.* ◇ **State** schools, industries, and other organizations are financed and controlled by the government, rather than by private companies.

❏ A **state** occasion is a formal one involving the head of a country. *...a state banquet.*

❏ In some countries, when an important person dies, their body is publicly displayed for a few days before the funeral. This is called their **lying in state**.

❏ If you **state** something, you say or write it in a definite and fairly formal way. *The King has publicly stated that he is ready to serve his country in any capacity.*

❏ Someone's or something's **state** is the condition they are in or what they are like at a particular time. *The property market in Tokyo was in a worse state than London's.* ◇ If you are **in a state**, you are upset and nervous. ◇ If you are **not in a fit state** to do something, you are too upset or ill to do it.

state- is added to words to describe something owned or controlled by the government. *...state-run universities... ...the sale of the state-owned British Nuclear Fuels.*

State Department The **State Department** is the US government department which deals with foreign affairs.

state of affairs A situation which you have just described can be called a **state of affairs**. *How did this extraordinary state of affairs come about?*

state of emergency (states of emergency) If a government declares a **state of emergency**, it gives itself much stronger powers, so that citizens have less freedom than usual. This can happen when there is rioting or fighting on a large scale. A government can also declare a state of emergency in all or part of a country when there has been a major disaster and it wants to use all available resources to help.

state of mind (states of mind) Your **state of mind** is your mood at a particular time, especially as this shows in the way you behave.

state-of-the-art is used to describe things which make use of the most up-to-date methods, materials, or ideas. *...state-of-the-art medical equipment... ...state-of-the-art conservation techniques.*

state room The **state rooms** in a palace or other building are large splendid rooms used on formal occasions. See also **stateroom**.

state-wide See **statewide**.

statehood When a territory achieves **statehood**, it becomes an independent state.

stateless If someone is **stateless**, they are not a citizen of any country.

stately things are dignified and impressive.

stately home A **stately home** is a large old house which has belonged to an aristocratic family for a long time and can now be visited by the public.

statement (statemented) ❏ A **statement** is an official or formal announcement which has been specially prepared for a particular occasion or situation.

❏ Anything you say in a definite way can be called a **statement**. ◇ If you make a **statement** to the police, you officially give your version of events after a crime or accident.

❏ Something a person does can be called a **statement** when it clearly shows their feelings about something. *The receiver said that the deal provided an unqualified statement of confidence in the Butlers Wharf estate.*

❏ A bank or building society **statement** is a printed document showing all the money put into and taken out of an account.

❏ When a child has learning difficulties, a **statement of special educational need** is a record of these difficulties. It obliges the LEA to provide appropriate education for the child. The child concerned is said to have been **statemented**.

stateroom Luxurious cabins in liners and other ships are sometimes called **staterooms**. See also **state room**.

Stateside means in, from, or to the United States. *This makes manufacturers more willing to take lower prices to get established Stateside... Poor weather is driving many of Britain's top women amateurs Stateside.*

statesman (statesmen; statesmanlike, statesmanship) A **statesman** is an experienced and respected senior politician. When politicians behave in a way which inspires respect, you can call their behaviour **statesmanlike**, or talk about their **statesmanship**. See also **elder statesman**.

statewide (or **state-wide**) In the US, if something is **statewide**, it covers the whole of a state. *...a statewide*

static

campaign... The governor now wants to copy the idea state-wide.

static ❑ If something remains **static**, it does not move or change. *The earnings of the middle classes had remained static.*

❑ **Static** or **static electricity** is electricity created by friction, which builds up in things like nylon carpets and metal objects. ◇ **Static** on the radio or TV is atmospheric interference which causes loud crackling noises or makes the picture break up.

station (stationing, stationed) ❑ A **station** is a place on a railway line where trains stop to pick up and set down passengers. ◇ A bus **station** or coach **station** is a place where a large number of buses or coaches start their journey.

❑ If you talk about a TV or radio **station,** you mean a TV or radio company and the programmes it broadcasts.

❑ If soldiers or officials are **stationed** somewhere, they are sent there to do a job or to work for a period of time.

station master A **station master** is the person in charge of a railway station.

station wagon In the US, Australia, and New Zealand, an estate car is usually called a **station wagon.**

stationary If something is **stationary**, it is not moving.

stationer A **stationer** is a person or firm that sells paper, envelopes, and writing equipment. A shop where these things are sold is called a **stationer** or **stationer's.**

stationery is paper, envelopes, and writing equipment.

statistic Statistics are facts which are expressed in numbers and which are obtained by gathering and analysing information. The branch of mathematics concerned with this type of analysis is also called **statistics.**

statistical (statistically) **Statistical** is used to talk about things which involve the use of statistics. *It is a curious statistical fact that the presidents of the United States have between them had 90 sons and 61 daughters... The average Taiwanese is statistically three times richer than the average Malaysian.*

statistician A **statistician** is a person who studies statistics or who works using statistics.

statuary The **statuary** in a place is the statues and other sculptures there.

statue A **statue** is a large stone or metal sculpture of a person or animal.

statuesque (*pron:* stat-yoo-esk) A **statuesque** woman is big and tall and has good posture.

statuette A **statuette** is a very small statue.

stature ❑ Someone's **stature** is their reputation and importance. *In 1991 his international stature was recognised by honorary membership of the American Dental Association.* ❑ Someone's **stature** is also their height and general size. *At 5ft 4in, Gregory has always made up for his lack of physical stature by a phenomenal work-rate and intuition.*

status ❑ Your **status** is your position in society. *They called for a review of the status of women.* ◇ **Status** is also prestige and importance. A **status symbol** is something people like to own because it gives the impression they are important or rich.

❑ The **status** of something is its position or importance compared to other similar things. *...the quality and status of technology.*

❑ **Status** of a particular kind is an official classification giving people certain rights or advantages. *...diplomatic status... ...grant-maintained status for schools and colleges.*

status quo When a place or organization has been run in the same way for a long time, you can refer to the established way of doing things as the **status quo**. *He has maintained the status quo... They fear that it will upset the status quo.* If someone restores the **status quo**, they return things to the way they were before something changed them.

statute A **statute** is a law passed by Parliament and formally written down. If a law is on the **statute book**, it is currently in force. ◇ The **statutes** of an institution or organization are its formal written rules.

statutory is used to describe things which are required by law. *...his statutory duty... ...statutory regulation of the press... ...a statutory right of privacy.*

staunch (staunchly; staunches, staunching, staunched) ❑ If you give someone your **staunch** support, you support them in a firm and loyal way. ◇ A **staunch** opponent of someone or something is firmly opposed to them. *...a plan which is staunchly opposed by the governors.*

❑ If you **staunch** the flow of something, you stop it or slow it down. *Increases in customs duties staunched the flow of imported cars.*

stave (staving, staved) ❑ If you **stave off** something unpleasant, you delay it or stop it happening. *...staving off defeat.*

❑ **Staves** are strips of wood, like the strips wooden barrels are made of.

❑ In music, a **stave** is the five parallel lines the notes are written on.

stay ❑ If you **stay** in a place or position, you do not move. If you refuse to move from a place, you can say you **stay put.** ◇ If you **stay behind** in a place, you remain after other people have gone.

❑ If you go to **stay** in a place, you visit it for a short period. You call this period your **stay** there. *...an overnight stay in Helsinki.* If you **stay on** in a place, you remain there longer than you had intended to. ◇ You also talk about someone **staying on** when they continue in their job. *...staying on as prime minister.*

❑ If you **stay away** from a place, you do not go there. ◇ If you **stay away** from something or **stay off** it, you avoid it. *Stay away from alcohol... They should stay off drugs and fighting.* ◇ If you **stay out** of a situation, you do not get involved in it. *He stayed out of trouble for years.*

❑ If someone or something **stays** in a certain state or condition, they continue to be like that. *The office stayed open until midnight.*

❑ If you say someone has **staying power,** you mean they have the ability to keep doing something for a long time. *The team simply did not have the staying power to reach the top.*

❑ If you **stay in,** you remain at home and do not go out. If you **stay out** late, you get home late after an evening out. ◇ If you **stay up,** you go to bed much later than usual.

❑ If you are granted a **stay of execution,** you are allowed to delay obeying a ruling which a court has passed on you.

STD See **sexually transmitted disease.**

stead ❑ If you say something will **stand you in good**

stead, you mean it will be useful to you in the future.

❏ If you do something in someone else's **stead**, you do it instead of them.

steadfast (steadfastly, steadfastness) If someone is steadfast, they hold on firmly to their beliefs or principles and refuse to alter them, because they are convinced they are right. *She remains steadfastly attached to these principles... ...the steadfastness of his resistance.*

steady (steadier, steadiest; steadies, steadying, steadied; steadily, steadiness) ❏ **Steady** is used to describe things which happen at the same pace, without any interruptions or sudden changes. *...steady progress... The rain came down steadily.* ◇ If someone has a **steady** job, they have a regular job which is likely to last for a long time.

❏ If you keep an object **steady**, you make sure it does not move about. Similarly, if you **steady** something, you bring it under control and stop it moving about.

❏ If you **steady** yourself, you control and calm yourself. ◇ **Steady** is used to describe things which are calm and controlled. *...a slow, steady voice... ...a steady gaze.* ◇ A **steady** person is sensible and reliable. *His steadiness was a source of great strength to the Government.*

steak A **steak** is a thick slice of meat or fish which is usually grilled or fried. *...gammon steak... ...a salmon steak.* When people talk about **steak** or a **steak**, they usually mean a beef steak. Various other cuts of beef are also called **steak**, for example braising steak and stewing steak.

steal (stealing, stole, have stolen) ❏ If someone **steals** something which does not belong to them, they take it without intending to return it.

❏ If you **steal** something like the attention of an audience, you draw it towards yourself and away from someone else. *Another old-timer stole the limelight at Wimbledon yesterday.* ◇ **steal the show**: see **show**. ◇ **steal a march**: see **march**. ◇ **steal someone's thunder**: see **thunder**.

❏ If you **steal** somewhere, you move there quietly and secretly.

stealth (stealthy, stealthily) ❏ If something is done by **stealth**, it is done secretly, in the hope that nobody will notice. *They are accused of using stealth to raise taxes.* You describe an action like this as **stealthy**. *...the stealthy partition of Bosnia.* ◇ Similarly, a **stealthy** movement is quiet and not intended to be heard or noticed. *He was moving stealthily, doing his best not to disturb the household.*

❏ **Stealth** bombers or fighters are types of military aircraft which use advanced technology to avoid enemy radar and infra-red detecting devices.

steam (steaming, steamed) ❏ **Steam** is the hot mist formed when water boils or when something hot is exposed to cooler air. When a window is covered in steam, you say it is **steamed up**. ◇ If something **steams**, it gives off steam. *...a steaming mug of tea.* ◇ If you **steam** food, you cook it in steam. *...steamed suet pudding.*

❏ **Steam** vehicles and machines are powered by steam. *...steam trains.* When a ship **steams** somewhere, it moves along by steam or some other form of power.

❏ If you build up a **head of steam**, you get together all the strength or support you can, in order to achieve something. ◇ If you do something **under your own steam**, you do it without help from anyone else.

❏ If you **run out of steam**, you have no more energy or

enthusiasm left to finish what you are doing. Similarly, you can say a process or system **runs out of steam** when it stops working or making progress. *The reforms of the 1980s were beginning to run out of steam.*

❏ If you **let off steam**, you get rid of your anger or stress by doing something noisy or energetic. ◇ If something **takes the steam out of** a situation, it calms it down. *The withdrawal of threatened trade sanctions took the steam out of the negotiations.*

steam engine A steam engine is any engine which uses steam to operate machinery.

steam iron A steam iron is an electric iron with a water compartment in it. The heat of the iron turns the water into steam, which passes through the base onto the material, making it easier to iron out creases.

steamboat Steamboats were steam-powered boats which travelled mainly on rivers and lakes.

steamer ❏ A steamer is a ship powered by steam.

❏ A **steamer** is also a container with small holes in the bottom which is placed over boiling water so food can be cooked in the steam.

steamroller (steamrollered) In the past, steamrollers were steam-powered vehicles with heavy rollers at the front and back. They were used for flattening the surface of new roads. ◇ If you are **steamrollered** into doing something, you are made to do it against your will.

steamship In the past, steamships were large ocean-going ships powered by steam.

steamy ❏ A steamy place is hot and humid.

❏ **Steamy** is also used to describe erotic films or novels. *...steamy sex scenes.*

steed The horse someone is riding can humorously be called their steed.

steel (steeling, steeled; steely) ❏ **Steel** is a strong metal made from iron and small quantities of other elements such as nickel.

❏ **Steel** and **steely** are used to describe firm determined behaviour. *...nerves of steel... ...a will of steel... They were impressed by his steely determination.*

❏ If you **steel** yourself, you prepare to do something difficult or unpleasant.

❏ **Steely** is used to describe things which are a hard greyish colour. *...the steely grey North Sea.*

steel band A steel band is a group of musicians who play special drums traditionally made from metal oil barrels. Steel bands originated in the West Indies.

steel wool is a mass of fine threads of steel, used for scouring things.

steelwork is the parts of a structure which are made from steel. *An entire Victorian wharf has been roofed over with glass and steelwork.*

steelworks (steelworker) A steelworks is a factory where steel is made. A person who works in a steelworks is called a **steelworker**.

steep (steeper, steepest; steeply, steepness; steeping, steeped) ❏ A steep slope rises sharply. *...a steeply sloping roof... He reached the hill crest, panting slightly from the steepness of the climb.* ◇ **Steep** is used to describe a sudden large change in the amount or rate of something. *...a steep rise in interest rates... Membership has been declining steeply in recent years.*

❏ If you **steep** something in a liquid, you leave it to soak in it. ◇ If you say people are **steeped** in something such as tradition, you mean they are strongly influenced by it.

steeple A **steeple** is a tall pointed structure on top of a church tower.

steeplechase (steeplechaser) A **steeplechase** is a long horse race in which the horses have to jump over obstacles like fences and ditches. Horses specially trained to run in these races are called **steeplechasers**. ◇ A **steeplechase** is also a long race on an athletics track in which the competitors jump over hurdles and a water jump. Athletes who take part in steeplechases are called **steeplechasers**.

steeplejack A **steeplejack** is someone whose job is to carry out maintenance or repairs on steeples or factory chimneys.

steer (steering, steered) ❏ When you **steer** a vehicle, you control it so it goes in the direction you want. The **steering** in a vehicle is the mechanical parts which make it possible to steer.

❏ If you **steer** someone towards a certain type of behaviour, you guide or persuade them in that direction. *These methods were much more likely to steer offenders away from crime.*

❏ If you **steer** a certain course, you take a particular line of action, being careful to avoid extremes. *...steering a middle course between Communism and democracy.* ◇ If you **steer clear** of someone or something, you manage to avoid them. *He was able to steer clear of trouble for most of the time.*

❏ A **steering committee** or **group** is a group of people who manage the early stages of a project, setting out guidelines and overseeing progress.

❏ A **steer** is a young castrated bull, raised for its meat.

steering wheel A vehicle's **steering wheel** is the wheel the driver uses to control its direction.

stellar is used to talk about things to do with the stars. *...stellar explosions... ...inter-stellar space.*

stem (stemming, stemmed) ❏ If you **stem** something undesirable which is continuing, spreading, or increasing, you put a stop to it. *The international relief effort may have stemmed the worst of the starvation.*

❏ If something like a condition or problem **stems from** a certain thing, that is what originally caused it. *The president's anger may stem from personal feelings.*

❏ The **stem** of a plant is the thin central part which the leaves and flowers grow out of. ◇ The **stem** of a glass or vase is the thin part connecting the bowl to the base. ◇ The **stem** of a pipe is the long hollow part which smoke is sucked through.

stench (stenches) A **stench** is a strong unpleasant smell. ◇ You talk about the **stench** of a type of bad behaviour when it is evident that it is taking place. *...a strong stench of hypocrisy... ...the stench of corruption.*

stencil (stencilled) (*American spelling:* stenciled) A **stencil** is a piece of card, metal, or plastic with a design, letters, or other symbols cut out of it. You rest the stencil on a surface and use paint, pencil, or ink to reproduce the cutout areas. **Stencilled** designs have been reproduced in this way.

stenography (stenographer) **Stenography** is writing in shorthand by hand or machine, especially taking verbatim notes of proceedings in court or at a meeting. A person who does this is called a **stenographer. Stenographer** is also the usual American word for a shorthand-typist.

stentorian A **stentorian** voice is extremely loud and strong.

step (stepping, stepped) ❏ A **step** is a movement which involves lifting the foot and putting it down again in a different place. In a dance, the different types of foot movements are called **steps**. ◇ If you **step** somewhere, you move in that direction. If you **step** on something, you tread on it.

❏ A **step** is a raised flat surface, often one of a series, which you use to walk up or down to a different level.

❏ A **step** is also one of a series of actions or stages necessary to achieve something. *It's another step towards privatisation... The meetings are a first step towards ending fifteen years of civil war.* ◇ If you do something **step by step**, you do it by progressing gradually from one stage to the next. *...the gradual lifting of sanctions step by step... ...a step-by-step guide to filling in a tax form.* ◇ If you **take steps** to achieve something, you take some positive action to achieve it. *...farmers who take steps to protect wildlife and the environment.*

❏ If you **step aside**, you allow someone else to take your place. *It's time for the politicians to step aside and make room for new leaders.* ◇ If someone **steps down**, they resign from an important job or position. *He might finally decide to step down as party leader.*

❏ If you **step back** from something you were intending to do, you decide not to do it. ◇ If you **step in** to help someone, you intervene to help them.

❏ If you **step up** an activity, you increase it. *The firm has plans to step up production this year.*

❏ If people march **in step**, their feet move forward at exactly the same time. If their feet move at different times, you say they are **out of step**. ◇ If you are **in step** with other people, you are setting about something in the same way. If someone is doing something differently from other people, you can say they are **out of step**. *In taking this extreme pro-car attitude, Britain is out of step with much of the rest of Europe.* ◇ You can also say two things are **in step**, for example when they are in agreement or making equal progress. *So far, politics and principle are in step... In normal countries, consumption and production move more or less in step.*

stepbrother Your **stepbrother** is a man or boy whose father or mother has married your mother or father.

stepchild (stepchildren) Someone's **stepchildren** are their stepsons or stepdaughters.

stepdaughter Your **stepdaughter** is the daughter of your husband or wife, but is not your own child.

stepfather Your **stepfather** is a man who has married your mother, but is not your natural father.

stepladder A **stepladder** is a ladder consisting of two parts hinged at the top so that it stands on its own when opened out.

stepmother Your **stepmother** is a woman who has married your father, but is not your natural mother.

steppe (*pron:* step) **Steppes** are large areas of land with grass but no trees, especially in the former USSR.

stepping stone **Stepping stones** are a line of stones which you walk on to cross a shallow stream or river.

◇ A **stepping stone** is something which enables you to make progress towards something else. *Many students now see university as a stepping stone to a good job.*

stepsister Your **stepsister** is a woman or girl whose father or mother has married your mother or father.

stepson Your **stepson** is the son of your husband or wife, but is not your own child.

stereo (stereos; stereophonic) **Stereo** and **stereophonic** are used to describe things which involve recorded sound being directed through two separate speakers, with the sound from one speaker being different from that coming out of the other. *...stereo televisions... ...a new loudspeaker system which gives a stereophonic effect.* A **stereo** is a piece of stereophonic equipment for playing records, tapes, or CDs.

stereoscopic is used to describe things which involve two images of the same object being seen from slightly different angles, creating a three-dimensional effect. *...stereoscopic observations of the solar environment.*

stereotype (stereotyping, stereotyped; stereotypical) A **stereotype** of a kind of person or thing is what people commonly think of when they think of that person or thing. Stereotypes are often formed by the way people and things are portrayed in plays, films, and cartoons. You can talk about someone or something being **stereotyped** in a certain way. *There is a persistent popular stereotype of feminists as curious beings, distinct from 'normal' women... This hamlet is the Hollywood stereotype of a sleepy little town... The film is guilty of racist stereotyping.* **Stereotypical** is used to describe people or things that are like their stereotypes. *...a stereotypical teenager.*

sterile (sterility) ❑ **Sterile** is used to describe things which are completely free from germs. *...sterile dressings... ...sterile needles and syringes.*

❑ **Sterile** people and animals are unable to produce babies. This condition is called **sterility.**

❑ If you call something **sterile** or talk about its **sterility,** you mean it is unproductive or unimaginative. *Too much time has been wasted in sterile debate.*

sterilize (sterilizing, sterilized; sterilization) (*can be spelled with an 's' instead of a 'z'*) ❑ If something is **sterilized,** it is made free from germs. *...sterilized orange juice.*

❑ If a person or animal is **sterilized,** they have an operation which makes it impossible for them to produce babies. Having this operation is called **sterilization.**

sterling is the money system of the United Kingdom. *Sterling continued to be seen as the second most important reserve currency.* ◇ **pound sterling:** see **pound.**

❑ **Sterling silver** is an alloy containing not less than 92.5% silver. The rest is usually copper.

❑ **Sterling** is used to say someone has an excellent character. *...a man of sterling reputation.* ◇ If you say someone has done a **sterling** job, you mean they have done something worthwhile and have done it very well. *She has done sterling work in the rehabilitation of the disabled poor... ...a sterling fighter for civil rights.*

stern (sternly, sternness) ❑ **Stern** behaviour is strict and severe. *...one of his sternest critics... I was told sternly to let her finish... The President has combined sternness with caution throughout the crisis.* ◇ **Stern** is also used to describe things which are very difficult. *...a stern task... Racing around Britain is one of the sterner yachting challenges.*

❑ If you say someone is **made of sterner stuff,** you mean they are tougher or more determined than they appear at first.

❑ The **stern** of a boat is the part at the back.

sternum The **sternum** is the long flat vertical bone in the middle of the chest, often called the breastbone. The collar bones and the first seven pairs of ribs are attached to it.

steroid **Steroids** are organic compounds which occur naturally in the body, for example as hormones, and can also be made artificially. They are sometimes prescribed by a doctor as a medical drug. See also **anabolic steroid.**

stet In a draft copy of a piece of writing, **stet** is written alongside something which has been deleted, to say it should be included after all. 'stet' is mainly used by people working in newspapers or publishing. It is Latin for 'let it stand'.

stethoscope The **stethoscope** is a medical instrument consisting of two earpieces connected to a hollow tube with a disc at the end. It is used to listen to the sounds of a patient's heart or breathing.

stetson A **stetson** is a tall-crowned broad-brimmed hat, traditionally worn by cowboys.

stevedore A **stevedore** is a dock worker who loads and unloads cargoes, especially in the US.

stew If you **stew** meat, you simmer it slowly in a liquid. Similarly, you can **stew** vegetables or fruit. *...stewed mushrooms.* ◇ A **stew** is meat and vegetables simmered slowly in stock.

steward ❑ A **steward** is a man who works on a ship or plane looking after passengers and serving meals.

❑ A **steward** is also an official who helps to organize and supervise a race, march, or other public event.

❑ Someone who has the responsibility of looking after another person's property or land is sometimes called a **steward.**

❑ See also **shop steward.**

stewardess (stewardesses) A **stewardess** is a woman who works on a ship or plane looking after passengers and serving meals.

stewardship is the responsibility of looking after something on behalf of someone else. *Under his stewardship, the UN's reputation has risen immeasurably.*

stick (sticking, stuck) ❑ A **stick** is a thin straight piece of wood. ◇ Some other thin straight objects are called **sticks.** *...a stick of celery... ...a stick of Brighton rock... ...sticks of dynamite.*

❑ If someone **gets hold of the wrong end of the stick,** they completely misunderstand a situation. ◇ If you use something as a **stick to beat** someone **with,** you use it as an excuse for criticizing them. *Reformers have been using the issue of corruption as a stick with which to beat the hard-line old guard.* ◇ **carrot and stick:** see **carrot.**

❑ If you **stick** something somewhere, you put it there in a casual or careless way. ◇ If you **stick up** something like a picture, you attach it to a wall or noticeboard so it can be seen.

❑ If you **stick** a long or pointed object into something, you push it in.

❑ If you **stick** one thing to another, you fix them together using something like glue. You can also **stick** something to a surface. ◇ When things **stick together,** they become attached to each other and are difficult to separate. Similarly, something can **stick** to something else.

❑ If something **sticks** in your mind, you remember it for a long time.

❑ If you **stick around**, you stay where you are, often because you are waiting for something.

❑ If something **sticks at** a certain point or amount, it stops there and does not change. *The latest economic figures show unemployment sticking at 7 per cent.*

❑ A **sticking point** in a discussion or negotiations is a point on which speakers cannot agree, and which may delay or stop the talks. *The question of land reform still remains a sticking point.*

❑ If you are **stuck** in a place or an unpleasant situation, you cannot get away from it. ◇ If you are **stuck with** something you do not want, you cannot get rid of it.

❑ You also say you are **stuck** when you cannot continue with something because you do not know how to do the next stage.

❑ If you **stick to** an agreement or principle or **stick by** it, you continue to abide by it. ◇ If you **stick to** something you have said, you do not withdraw it. ◇ If you **stick at** a task or job or **stick to** it, you carry on with it, even though it is difficult or unpleasant. Similarly, you can **stick out** a difficult or unpleasant situation.

❑ If you **stick up** for a person, principle, or belief, you support or defend them. ◇ If you **stick to** someone or **stick by** them, you continue to give them help and support, especially when they are in difficulty. Similarly, you can talk about people **sticking together**. *Both sides have an interest in sticking together while negotiations continue.*

❑ If you **stick with** someone, you continue your involvement or connection with them. ◇ If you **stick with** something or **stick to** it, you continue to use it or do it, and do not change to something else. *Some of the patients stuck to the diet rigorously.* ◇ If you **stick to** one subject during a speech or conversation, you talk only about that subject.

❑ If you **get stuck into** something, you start doing it or become involved in it with enthusiasm and determination.

❑ If something **sticks out** or **sticks up**, it extends beyond or above something else. *The rocks stick up out of the sea.* Similarly, you can **stick something out**. *He sticks out the tip of his tongue.* ◇ You can also say something **sticks out** when it is very noticeable.

stick-in-the-mud is used to describe people with little imagination or enthusiasm for new ideas.

stick insect Stick insects are insects with long thin bodies and legs. When a stick insect remains still on a tree or bush, it is difficult to see it because it looks like a twig, stick, or stem.

sticker A sticker is a small piece of paper or plastic with writing or a picture on it. It has adhesive on the back so you can stick it onto a surface.

sticking plaster is material which you can stick over a cut or sore to protect it.

stickler If someone is a **stickler** for a certain type of behaviour, they insist on people behaving that way. *They were sticklers for tidiness.*

sticky (stickier, stickiest; stickiness) ❑ A sticky substance

sticks to a surface when it comes into contact with it. You say an object is **sticky** when it is covered in a substance like this. ◇ Sticky paper or tape has glue on one side so you can stick it to something.

❑ **Sticky** weather is unpleasantly hot and humid.

❑ A **sticky** situation is difficult or embarrassing. *The stickiest moment for the speakers came over academic rates of pay.*

❑ If you say someone **came to a sticky end**, you mean they died in a particularly unpleasant way.

stiff (stiffness, stiffly) ❑ Stiff things are firm and rigid. ◇ If you feel **stiff**, your muscles or joints ache when you move. *I was crippled with stiffness.*

❑ **Stiff** behaviour is formal and not relaxed. ◇ **stiff upper lip**: see **lip**.

❑ **Stiff** is used to describe things which are very strong, difficult, or harsh. *The army has met some of the stiffest resistance in the area near the border... ...a stiffly enforced planning regime.* ◇ A **stiff** punishment is severe. *...stiffer penalties for drug criminals.*

❑ If you are charged a **stiff** price for something, you have to pay a lot for it.

❑ A **stiff** drink is a strong alcoholic drink, for example whisky.

❑ A **stiff** breeze blows strongly.

stiff-necked people are proud and stubborn.

stiffen (stiffening, stiffened) ❑ If your joints or muscles **stiffen**, they become difficult to bend or move. ◇ You say someone **stiffens** when they suddenly stop moving and their muscles become tense.

❑ If ideas or attitudes **stiffen**, they become fixed, or they change in a way which makes them tougher and less sympathetic. You can talk about a **stiffening** of ideas or attitudes.

❑ If fabric or material is **stiffened**, it is made firmer so it does not bend easily.

stifle (stifling, stifled) ❑ If something is **stifled**, it is prevented from happening or continuing. *She stifles discussion and imposes ready-made decisions... ...stifled laughter.*

❑ If you feel **stifled**, you feel as if you cannot breathe properly. *...the hall's stifling heat.*

stigma ❑ If something has a **stigma** attached to it, people think it is unacceptable or disgraceful. *Today, there's much less stigma attached to cosmetic surgery than there was a decade ago.*

❑ A **stigma** is a small scar or mark on the skin.

stigmata are marks which appear on a person's body and are like the wounds made on Christ when he was crucified. Some Christians believe these marks are a sign of holiness.

stigmatize (stigmatizing, stigmatized; stigmatization) (can be spelled with an 's' instead of a 'z') If someone or something is **stigmatized**, they are regarded as unacceptable or shameful. *Unjust laws and social stigmatization were hampering AIDS prevention efforts.*

stile A stile is a step or steps on either side of a fence or wall. It is put there so people can get across from one side to the other.

stiletto (stilettos) A stiletto is a small dagger with a narrow blade. ◇ **Stiletto** shoes or **stilettos** are women's shoes with very high narrow heels.

still (stillness) ❑ You use **still** to say that a situation which existed previously has continued and exists at the present time. *Summer flowers can still be found in bloom on the roadside... The fighting is still going on.*

❏ You use **still** to say something is better, larger, etc than something else which is itself very good or very large. *Worse still was the threat of nuclear pollution... Some may now leave, making the party smaller still.* ◇ You use **still less** when you have mentioned something which is not the case, and you are going on to mention something even less likely. *I can't compete with it, still less beat it.*

❏ You use **still** when you are saying what remains when part of something has gone or been dealt with. *There were still 12 hours of voting to go... That still leaves two big problems.*

❏ You use **still** when you are adding a hopeful or positive comment which contrasts with what you have just said. *It wasn't a perfect disguise, but still, I did escape.*

❏ If you stay **still**, you remain in the same position without moving. Similarly, you use **still** to say there is no movement or activity in a place. *...the still waters of the lake... ...the drowsy stillness of a hot summer day.*

❏ If you say something **does not stand still**, you mean it keeps progressing or changing. *Time does not stand still... Meanwhile, trade policy will not stand still.*

❏ If a noise is **stilled**, it is brought to an end. *Every now and then the laughter is stilled... These upheavals have not stilled debate over the right form of regulation.*

❏ A **still** is a photograph taken from a cinema film or video, often used for publicity purposes.

❏ A **still** is also an apparatus for distilling alcoholic drinks.

still life A still life is a painting or drawing of an arrangement of objects like flowers or fruit.

stillborn (stillbirth) A **stillborn** baby is born dead. The birth of a dead baby is called a **stillbirth**.

stilt Stilts are two long vertical poles with supports for the feet. Performers who walk around on stilts to entertain people are called **stilt-walkers**. ◇ In some parts of the world, buildings are supported on long wooden or metal poles called **stilts**.

stilted conversation or behaviour is very formal and seems awkward and unnatural.

stimulant Stimulants are medicines and other substances such as caffeine which make the body work faster, increasing the heart rate. Stimulants can make it difficult to sleep.

stimulate (stimulating, stimulated; stimulation) ❏ If something **stimulates** you, it encourages you to think and develop ideas. *...stimulating conversation... ...the mental stimulation of a challenging job.*

❏ If something is **stimulated**, it is made to grow or develop. *Interest in the book had been stimulated by press publicity... ...stimulation of the housing market.*

❏ If something **stimulates** a process in the body, it encourages it to operate. *Drinking stimulates the production of enzymes in the liver.*

stimulus (plural: stimuli) ❏ If something is a **stimulus** for something else, it encourages it to happen or develop. *The country's economic troubles are providing the latest stimulus for unrest.*

❏ If something gives you **stimulus**, it makes you feel energetic and enthusiastic. *To be a mother and still to have*

the stimulus of work would be superb.

❏ A **stimulus** is also something which produces a response in an organism or part of the body.

sting (stinging, stung) ❏ If an insect **stings** you or gives you a **sting**, it pricks your skin, leaving some poison behind and giving you a sharp pain. The part it uses to sting you with is called its **sting**. ◇ You say other things **sting** when they give you a sharp tingling pain in part of your body. *The teargas in the air was stinging their eyes.*

❏ If you are **stung** by someone's remarks or criticisms, you are upset by them.

❏ If something like a statement or joke has **a sting in the tail**, it has a surprisingly unpleasant ending. *He warned that the Budget came with a sting in its tail – future tax increases.* ◇ If something **takes the sting out** of a situation, it makes it less unpleasant.

❏ If you have had to pay an unreasonably large amount of money for something, you can say you have been **stung**.

❏ A **sting** is a carefully planned deception to gain an advantage over someone, especially one carried out by police to trap criminals.

stingy (pron: stin-jee) (stinginess) If you say someone is **stingy**, you mean they give or spend only small amounts of money, when they could easily afford more. *The company's stinginess has been a little disappointing.*

stink (stinking, stank, have stunk) ❏ If something **stinks**, it has a very unpleasant smell. A smell like this is called a **stink**. ◇ If you say someone's behaviour **stinks**, you mean it is disgraceful. *Even in an election year, such hypocrisy stinks.* ◇ If you say a situation **stinks** of some kind of bad behaviour, you mean it is obvious people have been behaving like that. *The whole thing stank of incompetence... ...the stink of dishonesty.*

❏ If you create a **stink** about something, you make a lot of fuss about it, so people have to take notice. *The tabloid press kicked up a stink about his visit.*

stint ❏ A **stint** is a period of time spent doing a certain job or activity. *She recently returned from a two year stint abroad... ...his second stint as the theatre's director.*

❏ If you say someone **does not stint** on something, you mean they do not hesitate to use or provide a lot of it. *The average British businessman doesn't stint on wining and dining.*

stipend (pron: sty-pend) (stipendiary) A **stipend** is a fixed or regular allowance or salary, especially one paid to a clergyman or magistrate. ◇ **Stipendiary** is used to describe a person who receives a stipend. *...a stipendiary magistrate.* **Non-stipendiary** is used to indicate that the person doing a job does not receive a stipend for it. *...non-stipendiary part-time priests.*

stippled things have the appearance of being covered with small dots or flecks. *...an expanse of sand, already stippled by the feet of thousands of sandpipers.*

stipulate (stipulating, stipulated; stipulation) ❏ If something is **stipulated** or is a **stipulation**, it is stated as an essential condition for an agreement or regulation. *...a law providing safeguards for shopworkers and stipulating limits on hours.*

❏ **Stipulated** is used to describe things which have to be done as part of an agreement or rule. *A chess clock is used to ensure that each player completes the stipulated number of* *moves in the allotted time.*

stir (stirring, stirred) ❑ When you **stir** a liquid, you mix it inside a container by moving something like a spoon around in it.

❑ When something **stirs** or is **stirred**, it moves slightly. *The boy stirred in his sleep... A gentle breeze stirred the flags.*

❑ If something **stirs** you, it arouses strong feelings in you. You say something like this is **stirring**. *...a stirring speech in defence of family values.* If something **stirs** you into doing something, it makes you do it. *The protesters had been stirred into action.* ◇ If someone **stirs up** trouble, they cause it by arousing strong feelings in people.

❑ If an event causes a **stir**, it causes great excitement, shock, or anger.

stir-fry If you **stir-fry** food, you fry small pieces of it very quickly over a high heat, stirring at the same time.

stirrup Stirrups are the two metal loops attached by leather straps to a horse's saddle and used to support the rider's feet.

stitch (stitches, stitching, stitched) ❑ When you **stitch** two pieces of material together, you use a needle and thread to join them. Similarly, you can **stitch** a design on a single piece of material. Each time the thread is pulled through the material, this is called a **stitch**. ◇ In knitting and crochet, you make a **stitch** by passing a loop of yarn round a knitting needle or crochet hook. ◇ A **stitch** is also a particular method of sewing or knitting, and the pattern this creates. For example, 'running stitch' and 'satin stitch' are types of sewing, and 'stocking stitch' and 'cable stitch' are types of knitting.

❑ When a wound is **stitched** by a doctor or nurse, a special needle and thread are used to fasten the edges of the skin together while it heals. You can talk about the number of **stitches** needed to close a wound. *One victim needed twenty stitches in a leg wound.*

❑ If something like a deal is **stitched up**, it is agreed on. *The promoters stitched up a film deal to prevent bankruptcy.* ◇ If you say something like a decision or result is **stitched up**, you mean it is arrived at in an unfair way. You can say something like this is a **stitch-up**. ◇ If you say someone has been **stitched up**, you mean they have been tricked or deceived. ◇ You also say someone has been **stitched up** when they have been set up to take the blame for something.

❑ If you say something like a plan is **stitched together**, you mean it is put together in a clumsy and hasty way.

❑ **Stitch** is a sharp pain under the ribs, which you can get when you run fast or laugh too much. ◇ If you say someone is **in stitches**, you mean they find something so funny that they cannot stop laughing.

stoat Stoats are small predatory mammals living in the wild in Europe, North America, and Asia. A stoat has a long body with brown fur on top and white below, and a black tip to its tail. See also **ermine**.

stock ❑ Stocks are investments, usually in the government or a local authority, on which a fixed amount of interest is paid. ◇ In the US, shares in a company are called **stocks**.

❑ If a shop **stocks** certain goods, it normally has a supply of them for sale. If it has some at a particular time, you say the goods are **in stock**. If it has run out of them, you say the goods are **out of stock**. ◇ All the goods for sale in a shop are called its **stock**. *The store imports most of its stock from Germany and Holland.*

❑ If you **stock** something like a cupboard, you fill it. *His fridge is stocked with German beer.* If you **stock up**, you buy a large supply of things. *Weathermen advised people to stock up with food and fuel.* ◇ A **stock** of things is a supply of them. *...stocks of food... ...a large stock of weapons.* ◇ You can say a place is **well stocked** with things when there are a lot of them there. *The lochs are well stocked with wild brown trout.*

❑ **Housing stock** is the supply of houses available for people to buy or rent.

❑ **Stock** is a liquid made by simmering meat, bones, or vegetables in water. It is used as a basis for soups and sauces.

❑ The **stock** a person or animal comes from is the type of people or animals they are descended from. *They were of German stock... ...the best pedigree stock.* ◇ Farm animals are often called **stock**. *Chicken farmers are having to slaughter their stock.*

❑ A **stock** expression or way of doing something is one which is commonly used. *The Chancellor issued a statement repeating the stock phrase that the government was prepared 'to take whatever measures are necessary'... Moves to co-education and a younger intake have become the stock response of the traditional public school struggling to fill its places.*

❑ If you **take stock** of a situation, you stop and think about it before deciding what to do next.

❑ You can refer to someone's reputation or status as their **stock**. *Their stock has never been lower.*

❑ The **stock** of a gun like a rifle is the part you hold against your shoulder.

❑ If someone stands **stock still**, they stand without any part of their body moving.

❑ See also **laughing stock**.

stock car A stock car is an old car, usually a saloon model, which has been strengthened and altered for a type of racing in which the cars often collide.

stock exchange A stock exchange is a place where people buy and sell stocks and shares.

stock-in-trade A person's **stock-in-trade** is a usual part of their behaviour or work. *Although television became his stock-in-trade, he has published seven novels... Understatement was not part of her stock-in-trade.*

stock market The organization and business involved in buying and selling stocks and shares is called the **stock market**. A stock market is also a stock exchange. *...the price of shares on the Tokyo stock market.*

stockade A stockade is a wall of high wooden posts built round an area to keep out enemies or wild animals.

stockbroker (stockbroking) A stockbroker is a person whose job is to buy and sell stocks and shares for other people. The work a stockbroker does is called stockbroking.

stockholder In the US, a stockholder is a shareholder.

stocking (stockinged) Stockings are two pieces of clothing which fit closely over a person's feet and legs. Some stockings cover a person's calves and thighs, others just the calves. ◇ If someone is in their **stockinged feet**, they are wearing socks, tights, or stockings, but no shoes.

stockist A stockist of a certain type of goods sells those goods in their shop. *...your local health food stockist.*

stockpile (stockpiling, stockpiled) If people **stockpile** things, they store large quantities for future use. A **stockpile** is a large store of something.

stockroom In a place like a shop or factory, the **stockroom** is a room where a stock of goods is kept.

stocktaking is (a) counting and checking all the goods in a shop or warehouse. (b) thinking about the present situation and considering what to do in the future. *Ambassadors to the General Agreement on Tariffs and Trade met for a stocktaking session yesterday.*

stocky people are fairly short, but look strong and solid.

stockyard A **stockyard** is a large yard with pens or covered buildings, where farm animals are herded together or sold in an auction.

stodgy food is extremely solid and makes you feel too full. ◇ You say other things are **stodgy** when they are dull and uninteresting. *...the firm's stodgy image... The party was a very stodgy affair.*

stoic (*pron:* stow-ik) (stoical, stoically, stoicism) If someone behaves in a **stoic** or **stoical** way, they accept difficulties and suffering without complaining or getting upset. *...stoic loyalty... ...stoical courage... A rain-drenched row of dignitaries sat stoically through a storm to hear Luciano Pavarotti sing in Hyde Park.* When someone behaves like this, you can call them a **stoic** or talk about their **stoicism** (*pron:* stow-iss-izz-um).

stoke (stoking, stoked) If you **stoke** a fire or **stoke** it **up**, you add fuel so it burns more fiercely. ◇ If something **stokes** certain feelings, it makes people feel them more intensely. You can also say something **stokes** or **stokes up** trouble of some kind. *Big pay rises will stoke inflation.*

stole ❑ See steal.
❑ A **stole** is a long scarf which a woman wears over her shoulders when she is in evening dress.

stolen See steal.

stolid (stolidly) **Stolid** people are unimaginative and do not easily get excited or show much interest in things. *He sat stolidly, drinking his coffee.*

stomach ❑ The **stomach** is the organ inside the body where food is digested. ◇ The front part of a person's body, below the waist, is often called their **stomach**.
❑ If you say someone **has no stomach** for something, you mean they are unable to face it, because they do not have the strength or courage. *They might not have the stomach to fight a war.* ◇ If you say you cannot **stomach** something, you mean you dislike it strongly and cannot accept it. You can also say something is hard to **stomach**.

stomp If someone **stomps** around, they tread or stamp heavily. *He stomped up the stairs to bed.*

stone (stoning, stoned) ❑ **Stone** is a hard solid substance found in the ground and often used for building. A **stone** is a small piece of stone. ◇ If people **stone** someone, they throw stones at them. Similarly, people can **stone** something like a building.
❑ If you say a place is a **stone's throw** away, you mean it is not far away. ◇ If you **kill two birds with one stone**, you achieve two things by a single action. ◇ If you **leave no stone unturned**, you try everything you can think of to achieve what you want.
❑ Jewels are sometimes called **stones**.
❑ The **stone** in a fruit like a peach or plum is the large

seed in the middle.
❑ Weight is often expressed in **stones**. A stone is 14 pounds (about 6.35 kilograms). The plural of 'stone' is either 'stone' or 'stones'. *She weighed 14 stone.*
❑ If someone is **stoned**, they are under the influence of drugs.

Stone Age The **Stone Age** was the period of human history in which stone tools were used, before metal ones were invented. It started about 2.5 million years ago, and continued in Europe until about 2000BC. It is usually divided into the Paleolithic, Mesolithic, and Neolithic periods.

stonewall You say someone **stonewalls** when they deliberately delay or prevent progress in something like a discussion or argument, for example by refusing to answer questions.

stoneware is a kind of hard pottery fired at a very high temperature.

stonework is objects or parts of a building which are made out of stone.

stony ground is rough and contains a lot of stones or rocks.
❑ If someone's behaviour or expression is **stony**, it shows no friendliness or sympathy.

stood See stand.

stooge If you call someone a **stooge**, you mean they are being used by someone else to carry out unpleasant or dishonest tasks. ◇ In a comedy act, a **stooge** is someone who is there to give a comedian the opportunity to make jokes at his or her expense.

stool ❑ A **stool** is a seat without a back or arms, for one person. ◇ If you say something **falls between two stools**, you mean it does not fit neatly into either of two categories, and ends up belonging to neither.
❑ A **stool** is also a piece of faeces.

stoop (stooping, stooped) ❑ If someone **stoops** or has a **stoop**, they walk or stand with their shoulders bent forwards. ◇ If someone **stoops** on a particular occasion, they bend forwards and down, for example to pick something up.
❑ If you talk about someone **stooping** to do something, you mean they are lowering their standards by doing it. *His Lordship does not stoop to giving interviews.*

stop (stopping, stopped) ❑ If you **stop** doing something, you no longer do it. ◇ If an activity or process **stops**, it comes to an end. *Bidding stopped at £74,000.*
❑ If you **stop** something, you prevent it happening or continuing. *Police have tried to stop people carrying such weapons.*
❑ If something like a machine **stops** or is **stopped**, its parts are no longer moving. Similarly, you say a vehicle **stops** when it comes to a halt.
❑ If you **stop** somewhere during a journey, you stay there for a short while before going on. You can also say you **stop off** or **stop over**. *The President is to stop over in London on his way to Holland.* You can also talk about making a **stop** somewhere. *His first stop is Spain.*
❑ If you **stop** a cheque, you instruct the bank not to pay it. Similarly, if someone's pay is **stopped**, the money is not paid to them.
❑ If someone **pulls out all the stops**, they do everything possible to make something happen or be successful.

❑ If you say someone will **stop at nothing**, you mean they are prepared to do anything to achieve what they want, even if it is morally wrong.

stop-go is used to describe a government's economic policies when they alternate between two different strategies. One strategy is imposing restraint when inflation is high, the other is trying to boost the economy when there is high unemployment. ◇ **Stop-go** is used to describe similar policies applied to other areas of government or management. *...the disastrous stop-go approach to community care.*

stop press The **stop press** is the latest news inserted into a special section of a newspaper after the rest has been printed.

stopcock A **stopcock** is a tap which controls or stops the flow of liquid through a pipe.

stopgap A **stopgap** is something which serves a purpose for a short time, but is replaced as soon as possible. *The grain was to serve as a stopgap before the November harvest... ...a stopgap solution.*

stopover A **stopover** is a short stay somewhere during a journey. *The passengers are due to make a brief stopover in London and then head for home.*

stoppage ❑ When there is a **stoppage**, people stop working because of a disagreement with their employers.

❑ If there is a **stoppage** in a game like football, play is held up briefly, for example because a player is injured. **Stoppage time** is time added on at the end of the match to make up for stoppages.

❑ **Stoppages** are also deductions made from pay, for example income tax or National Insurance contributions.

stopper A **stopper** is a piece of glass, plastic, or cork which fits into the top of a bottle or jar to seal it.

stopwatch (stopwatches) A **stopwatch** is a type of watch which can be started or stopped by pressing a button. It is used for timing things like sporting events.

storage of materials or other things is keeping them in a special place until they are needed. **Storage** is also space where things can be stored. See also **cold storage**. ◇ **Storage** is also storing data in a computer.

storage heater A **storage heater** is an electric heater which stores heat generated by off-peak electricity overnight and then gives out heat gradually during the day.

store (storing, stored) ❑ When you **store** things, you keep them somewhere until you need them. ◇ A **store** of something is a supply kept for future use. *...stores of spare parts.* ◇ A **store** is also a place where things are kept until they are needed. *...a grain store.*

❑ A shop can be called a **store**. *...the local video store.* In the US, **store** is the usual word for a shop.

❑ When you **store** information, you keep it in something like a file or on a computer. Similarly, you can **store** information in your brain.

❑ Something which is **in store** for someone is going to happen to them. *...the terrible fate that lies in store for them.*

❑ If you **set great store** by something or **put great store** on it, you think it is extremely important or necessary. *They place great store by education.*

❑ If you **store up** trouble for yourself, you behave in a way which will cause you problems in the future.

store card A **store card** is the same as a charge card.

storehouse A **storehouse** of things or ideas is a large collection of them. *...a vast storehouse of natural resources... ...a storehouse of knowledge.*

storekeeper A **storekeeper** is a person who owns or manages a shop.

storeroom A **storeroom** is a room where things are kept until they are needed.

storey (storeys) (*American spelling*: story, stories) The **storeys** of a building are its floors or levels.

stork Storks are large wading birds with long legs and long bills. In parts of Europe, the white stork sometimes nests on rooftops.

storm (stormy) ❑ When there is a **storm**, there is heavy rain, a strong wind, and often thunder and lightning. You say weather like this is **stormy**. ◇ **Storm clouds** are the dark clouds seen before a storm. If you say **storm clouds** are gathering, you mean there are signs that trouble or violence is going to break out.

❑ An outburst of angry or excited behaviour can be called a **storm**. *His comments provoked a storm of protest... ...a storm of bad publicity.* A **stormy** occasion is one where there is a lot of angry behaviour. *There had been twenty four hours of stormy debate.* ◇ If someone **storms** somewhere, they go there suddenly and angrily. *She stormed off through the crowd.* ◇ If you call something like a disagreement a **storm in a teacup**, you mean there has been a lot of fuss over something unimportant.

❑ If people **storm** a place, they suddenly attack it.

❑ If you say someone has **taken** a place **by storm**, you mean they have made a strong favourable impression there. *...the Brazilian pianist who has taken New York by storm.*

stormtrooper (or **storm-trooper**) Stormtroopers were members of a force of soldiers in Nazi Germany who were specially trained to be violent and ruthless. ◇ Other people who use bullying tactics sometimes get called stormtroopers.

story (stories) ❑ A **story** is a description of imaginary people and events written or told to entertain people.

❑ The **story** of something which has actually happened is an account of it. Similarly, a person's **story** is an account of their life, or of some particularly dramatic part of it. ◇ In newspapers, a **story** is a report of something which has happened. *...front-page news stories.*

❑ You say '**...but that's another story**' when you have just mentioned something, but do not propose to say any more about it.

❑ If you say something is **not the whole story**, you mean there are more details which need to be known before the situation can be understood properly. *Those figures do not tell the whole story.*

❑ See also **storey**.

storybook A **storybook** is a book of stories for small children. ◇ **Storybook** is used to describe real-life situations which seem like something in a fairy story. *...a storybook romance.*

storyline The **storyline** of something like a film, TV serial, or book is the plot.

storyteller (storytelling) A **storyteller** is a person who tells or writes stories. **Storytelling** is telling or writing stories.

stoup (*pron*: stoop) A **stoup** is a small stone basin for holy water in a church.

stout (stoutly) ❑ A stout person is quite fat.
❑ Stout objects are thick and strong. ...*a stout pair of shoes...* ...*a stoutly-fortified headquarters.*
❑ Stout resistance to something is strong and determined. *Growers are stoutly resisting any notion of a price cut.*
❑ Stout is a strong dark beer.

stove A stove is a piece of equipment which provides heat for a room or for cooking.

stow (stowaway) If you stow something, you put it into a space or container until it is needed. ◇ If a person stows away on a plane or ship, they hide on board so they can travel without paying and without anyone knowing they are there. Someone who does this is called a stowaway.

straddle (straddling, straddled) If someone straddles something, they sit or stand with one leg on either side of it. ◇ Similarly, if an area straddles something like a boundary or a river, it is on both sides of it. ...*an Indian reserve which straddles the border between the two countries.*

strafe (strafing, strafed) If an area is strafed, it is attacked by gunfire or bombs from low-flying enemy aircraft, or by enemy artillery.

straggle (straggling, straggled; straggler) You say people or vehicles are straggling when they are moving along slowly in irregular and disorganized groups. ...*straggling convoys of buses and vans.* You can talk about a straggle of people or vehicles. ...*a straggle of refugees.* ◇ Small numbers of people or vehicles following a larger group can be called stragglers.

straggly is used to describe things which grow or spread out in an untidy way. ...*a straggly beard.*

straight is used to describe things which continue in the same direction without curving or bending. ...*a straight line...* ...*looking straight ahead.* ◇ On a race track, the straight is a part of the track which does not curve or bend. The home straight or finishing straight is a straight part of a track where the last part of a race is run.
❑ Straight hair has no curls or waves in it.
❑ If you go straight to a place, you go there immediately and directly.
❑ Straight is used to say something happens immediately after something else. *He joined the company straight from the Army.* ◇ If you do something straight away (or straightaway), you do it immediately.
❑ Straight is used to talk about a number of things of the same kind happening one after the other. *Newcastle's defeat on Saturday ended a run of 11 straight wins.* ◇ In tennis, if you win a match in straight sets, you defeat your opponent without losing a set.
❑ A straight fight or choice involves only two people or things. *It is a straight fight between the National Party and the far-right Conservative Party.*
❑ If someone gives you a straight answer or tells you something straight, they are honest and frank and do not try to hide the truth. You say people who are honest and frank like this are straight.
❑ If you get things straight, you sort out a confused situation. ◇ If you put the record straight, you do or say something to remove any misunderstanding or confusion from a situation.
❑ If you keep a straight face, you manage to look seri-

ous while telling someone something untrue as a joke.
❑ Straight is used to describe heterosexual people as distinct from homosexuals.
❑ If a criminal goes straight, he or she gives up being involved in crime. ◇ If you say someone keeps on the straight and narrow, you mean they do not do anything criminal or immoral.
❑ When people talk about the straight theatre, they mean serious plays as distinct from comedies or musicals.

straightaway See straight.

straighten (straightening, straightened) ❑ If you straighten something, you make it straight. ◇ You can also say you straighten something when you arrange or adjust it so it is in its proper position or is neat and tidy. *He straightened his tie.*
❑ If you straighten or straighten up, you make your body straight and upright, after you have been bending or stooping.
❑ If you straighten out a confused situation, you deal with it and put it in order.

straightforward (straightforwardly) If something is straightforward, it is clear and simple without any special complications or difficulties. *I always try to present things straightforwardly.* ◇ A straightforward person is honest and frank and does not try to hide their feelings.

strain (straining, strained) ❑ If there is strain on an object, it is being pushed, pulled, or stretched tightly, and may bend or break. *Water rushed past the boat, putting intense strain on the mooring lines.*
❑ If there is strain on a system or if it is being strained, it is unable to cope with the demands being made on it, and may fail or collapse. ...*an economy already strained to its very limits.* Similarly, you can talk about strain being put on a person. ...*the strains of living on the street.* ◇ If you say someone looks strained, you mean they look worried and nervous.
❑ If you strain a muscle or some other part of your body, you injure it by using it suddenly and violently, or using it too much. An injury like this is called a strain. See also repetitive strain injury.
❑ If you strain to do something, you make a great effort to do it.
❑ When you strain food, you remove the liquid from it, by pouring it away.
❑ A strain of a plant or some other living thing is a variety or type of it.
❑ If you hear the strains of a piece of music, you hear it being played. ...*the familiar strains of Mozart's compositions.*

strainer A strainer is a device for separating liquids from solids. It has small holes which liquid can pass through, but solids cannot.

strait A narrow strip of sea joining two large areas of sea is sometimes called a strait or the straits. ...*the Dover Straits.* ◇ If you say someone or something is in dire straits, you mean they are in a very serious situation.

strait-laced people have a strict and serious attitude towards moral behaviour.

straitened is used to describe a situation where people do not have as much money as they used to have. *In these straitened times...* ...*in very straitened financial circumstances.*

straitjacket A straitjacket is a type of jacket with extra long sleeves which can be tied together. Straitjackets were formerly used to restrain violent patients in mental hospitals. ◇ Anything which restricts growth, development, or freedom can be called a **straitjacket.** *Doubts remain over whether the debt-laden company can extricate itself completely from its financial straitjacket.*

strand (stranded, stranding) ❑ A **strand** of something like thread or hair is a single piece of it. ◇ A **strand** of something like a situation is one aspect of it. *There is a growing strand of nationalist opinion in Romania.*

   ❑ If you are **stranded** somewhere, you are stuck there and cannot leave. *The occupants of five vehicles had to be rescued after they became stranded in blizzard conditions... ...a study of whale strandings around the British coast.*

   ❑ A **strand** is also a shore or beach.

strange (stranger, strangest; strangely, strangeness) ❑ **Strange** is used to describe things which are odd, unfamiliar, or unexpected. *Truth, as everyone knows, is stranger than fiction... ...the strangely named Pope Pippin the Short... He could not help being puzzled by the strangeness of the monument he had uncovered.*

   ❑ If you are in a **strange** place, you are somewhere you have never been before.

   ❑ You say **strangely** or **strangely enough** when you are making a statement which is surprising. *Strangely, there is not a lot to say.*

stranger ❑ A **stranger** is someone you have not met before. ◇ If you are a **stranger** to a place, you have not been there before.

   ❑ If you say someone is **no stranger** to something, you mean they have a lot of experience or knowledge of it. *She is no stranger to controversy.*

strangle (strangling, strangled; strangulation, strangler) ❑ If a person is **strangled**, someone squeezes their throat until they are dead. Killing someone like this is called **strangulation**; a criminal who has strangled several people is sometimes called a **strangler.**

   ❑ You talk about things being **strangled** when something prevents them from developing or succeeding and they are unable to survive. *The Federal Reserve's monetary policy is strangling the economy... The corporation needed to shut many of its 14 studios if it was to avoid strangulation by international rivals.*

   ❑ A **strangled** laugh or cry is muffled and unclear.

stranglehold If someone has a **stranglehold** on something, they have firm control of it. *He must not be allowed to gain a stranglehold over the world's oil supplies.*

strap (strapping, strapped) ❑ A **strap** is a narrow piece of leather or cloth. Some bags have straps for carrying them, and clothes sometimes have straps which go over the shoulders. Other kinds of straps are used to fasten things together. ◇ If you **strap** something in position, you fasten it there with a strap.

   ❑ **Strapping** is adhesive bandage applied to give support to a part of the body.

   ❑ A **strapping** person is tall, strong, and healthy-looking.

   ❑ If you say someone is **strapped for cash,** you mean they do not have much money.

strapless A **strapless** dress or bra does not have the usual straps over the shoulders.

strata See **stratum.**

stratagem A **stratagem** is a plan or tactic.

strategic (strategically) ❑ **Strategic** is used to talk about things being done or planned to put someone in a situation where they can achieve what they want, or gain an advantage over others. *...the strategic thinking of a chess player... Strategically placed ladders allowed visitors to inspect the aircraft cockpits.*

   ❑ **Strategic** is also used to talk about things to do with the distribution and positioning of armies and weapons for military advantage. *...the strategic thinking underlying a fundamental cut-back in Britain's armed forces... ...a strategically important town.* ◇ **Strategic** weapons are long-range weapons, especially nuclear ones, which are targeted to destroy an enemy's industry, economy, or military bases. ◇ **Strategic Defense Initiative:** see **SDI.**

strategy (strategies; strategist) ❑ A **strategy** is a plan you adopt to get something done, especially in business, economics, or politics. *We've worked out the company's marketing strategies.*

   ❑ **Strategy** is planning the best way to achieve something, especially in war. A **strategist** is an expert on strategy. *...a military strategist.*

stratified (stratification) **Stratified** rock is formed in layers of different materials. ◇ A **stratified** society is one where there are distinct social classes. *There may have been some changes in social stratification during wartime.*

stratosphere The **stratosphere** is the layer of the earth's atmosphere which is between 10 and 50 kilometres above the earth.

stratum (*plural:* strata) ❑ The **strata** in the earth's surface are the different layers of rock.

   ❑ The different social levels or classes in society can also be called **strata.** *...an underprivileged stratum of society.*

straw is the dried stalks of cereal crops like wheat, oats, or barley. It is used, for example, as bedding for animals, or for packaging. ◇ A **straw** is a thin tube of paper or plastic which you use to suck a drink into your mouth.

   ❑ If someone is **clutching at straws,** they are trying desperate or unusual methods to achieve something, because all their other attempts have failed.

   ❑ If you say something is **the last straw,** you mean it is the latest in a series of bad things, and it finally makes it impossible for you to continue with something. *Public spending cuts may prove the final straw for the electorate.*

   ❑ If you say you have **drawn the short straw,** you mean you have been chosen from a number of people to do a job which nobody wants to do.

   ❑ If you say an incident or piece of information is a **straw in the wind,** you mean it gives an indication of what might happen in the future.

straw poll A **straw poll** is a quick unofficial poll or vote taken to get an indication of people's opinion.

strawberry (strawberries) **Strawberries** are small soft red fruit which are eaten as a dessert or made into jam.

stray ❑ If an animal **strays,** it wanders away from the place where it is supposed to be. Animals which have wandered away and got lost are called **strays.** ◇ If you **stray** from the road or path you are travelling along, you leave it and go off in a different direction. Similarly, you can say someone **strays** from what they normally do. *The committee differ on how far to let banks and bank-owners stray from the business of banking.* ◇ You can also say someone **strays** when they are unfaithful to their partner.

❑ If your thoughts **stray**, you lose concentration and start thinking about something different.

❑ **Stray** is also used to describe something which has become separated from a group of similar things. *...stroking stray hairs across his bald patch.*

streak (streaking, streaked; streaky, streaker) ❑ A **streak** is a long narrow mark or stripe which contrasts with its surroundings because it is a different colour. *...streaks of faded paint.* When something has marks like this, you can say it is **streaked** or **streaky**. ◇ **Streaky bacon** has roughly equal amounts of fat and meat, giving it a striped appearance.

❑ You can describe an aspect of someone's character by saying they have a certain **streak**. *I never doubted he had the ruthless streak necessary to carry him into the Cabinet.*

❑ If someone or something **streaks** somewhere, they move there extremely quickly. ◇ If a person **streaks**, they run quickly through a public place without any clothes on. Someone who does this is called a **streaker**.

❑ A **lucky** or **winning streak** is a series of successes, especially in sport or gambling. Similarly, an **unlucky** or **losing streak**, is a series of failures.

stream (streaming, streamed) ❑ A **stream** is a small river.

❑ You can refer to a steady flow of something as a **stream**. *...a stream of hot air.* Similarly, if a number of things happen one after the other, you can say there is a **stream** of them. *...a continuous stream of phone calls.*

❑ If you say something is **streaming**, you mean it is flowing in large quantities. *Some left with tears streaming down their faces.* If you have a **streaming** cold, your nose keeps running and your eyes water.

❑ If people or things **stream** somewhere, they move in a long line or in large numbers. *If the fighting continues, refugees will stream into that country.*

❑ If something like a person's hair is **streaming** in the wind, it is blowing about freely.

❑ If there is **streaming** in a school, pupils of the same age are put into groups according to their ability. A group like this is called a **stream**.

streamer A **streamer** is a long narrow strip of coloured paper used for decoration.

streamline (streamlining, streamlined) ❑ If something is **streamlined**, it has a smooth shape and can move easily through air or water. The smooth shape of something like this can be called its **streamlining**.

❑ If something like a process is **streamlined**, it is altered to make it more efficient. *Many will lose their jobs as part of modernisation and streamlining of the economy.*

street ❑ A **street** is a road in a town or large village, usually with buildings along it.

❑ **Street** is used to talk about outdoor activities in a town and the people involved in them. *...street theatre... ...street traders.*

❑ If you say someone is **on the streets**, you mean they are homeless. ◇ You also say someone is **on the streets** when they are working as a prostitute. ◇ **On the street** is used to talk about unofficial or illegal activities. *The new craze on the street is for the 1960s hallucinogenic LSD.*

❑ If you talk about **the man in the street**, you mean ordinary people in general. *The man in the street readily dis-*

misses today's politicians as faceless wonders.

street cred If someone says you have **street cred** or **street credibility**, they mean ordinary young people would approve of you and consider you to be part of their culture, usually because you share their sense of fashion or their views. *Well-worn Levi 501s are still the ultimate street cred label.*

street value The **street value** of a drug is the price paid for it when it is sold illegally to drug users.

streetcar is the usual American word for a tram.

streetwalker is an old-fashioned word for a prostitute.

streetwise You use **streetwise** to describe people who know how to cope with rough people or dangerous situations, especially in big cities. *Young people today are much more streetwise than their parents were.* ◇ You can also use **streetwise** to describe people who are quick to size up a situation and take advantage of it. *England were beaten in the second round by the more streetwise Gala seven.*

strength ❑ Someone's **strength** is their physical ability to do things like lifting heavy objects. ◇ The **strength** of an object or material is its ability to stand up to rough treatment or heavy weights. *...high-strength, corrosion-resistant steel.* ◇ The **strength** of a relationship is the fact that it continues to hold in spite of problems and difficulties.

❑ **Strength of character** is courage and determination. ◇ If you say someone is a **tower of strength**, you mean they give reliable help and support in a difficult situation.

❑ Good qualities or features can be called **strengths**. *It is one of the great strengths of the British university system that the drop-out rate is very low.*

❑ **Strength** is also power and influence. *The opposition has grown in strength and confidence.* ◇ If someone or something **goes from strength to strength**, they become more and more successful.

❑ If something causes **strength** of feeling, people react strongly to it.

❑ When there are large numbers of people in a place, you can say they are there **in strength**. *The police are out in strength.* ◇ The **strength** of a group of people is the total number of people in it. *The regiment's strength is 650 men.* ◇ If a group of people is at **full strength**, all its members are present or available. *...a full-strength England team.*

❑ The **strength** of a currency is its stability or high value in relation to other currencies.

❑ If something is done **on the strength** of something else, the first thing provides the basis or reason for the second. *She was convicted on the strength of forensic evidence.*

strengthen (strengthening, strengthened) ❑ If an object or material is **strengthened**, it is made stronger and better able to withstand rough treatment or heavy weights. ◇ If something **strengthens** your body, it makes you stronger and fitter. *Regular exercise will strengthen joints and muscles.*

❑ If something **strengthens** your beliefs, it makes them stronger. Similarly, something can **strengthen** an argument or the case for doing something. *The net effect of the reforms would be to strengthen the case for certain rail investment schemes.* ◇ If something **strengthens** you, it gives you more courage and determination.

❑ If a relationship **strengthens** or is **strengthened**, it becomes closer and more likely to continue. *The President's* *visit is intended to strengthen ties between the two countries.*

❑ If someone's power or influence **strengthens**, it increases.

❑ If a currency **strengthens** or is **strengthened**, its value increases in relation to other currencies. *He welcomed yesterday's strengthening of the dollar against European currencies.*

strenuous (strenuously) ❑ If you make a **strenuous** effort or attempt to do something, you try very hard to do it. ❑ If someone **strenuously** denies something, they strongly deny it. ◇ A **strenuous** action or activity involves a lot of effort or energy. *...strenuous physical labour.*

streptococcus (*plural:* streptococci) (streptococcal) **Streptococci** (*pron:* strep-toe-**kok**-eye) are a group of bacteria responsible for infections called **streptococcal** infections. Scarlet fever and sore throats are caused by infections like these.

stress (stresses, stressing, stressed) ❑ **Stress** is worry and nervous tension. If someone is **stressed**, they are anxious or worried.

❑ **Stress** is also strong physical pressure or strain on an object. *This exercise puts too much stress on the lower back.*

❑ If you **stress** something, you emphasize it or draw attention to it, because you think it is important. *The report stresses the need to reduce military spending.* ◇ If you put **stress** on a certain aspect of something, you concentrate on it. *The company is putting more stress on design and style to win competitive advantage.*

❑ If you **stress** a word when you are saying something, you emphasize it, making it sound slightly louder than other words. Similarly, you can **stress** part of a word. The emphasis you put on a word or part of a word is called **stress**. *Eisteddfod (pron: eye-steth-fod – stress on second syllable) is a Welsh word meaning competitive festival.*

stressful situations cause a lot of anxiety and worry. *Buying a house is reckoned to be the most stressful experience in an individual's life, after marriage and divorce.*

stretch (stretches, stretching, stretched) ❑ When something soft or elastic **stretches** or is **stretched**, it is extended, or pulled until it is tight.

❑ When you **stretch**, you hold your arms or legs out as far as you can and tighten your muscles, often just after waking up. ◇ If you **stretch out** part of your body, you hold it out straight. *I crept along with my hands stretched out in front of me.* ◇ If you **stretch out**, you lie with your legs and body in a straight line.

❑ If you **stretch your legs**, you go for a short walk, often after you have been sitting for a long time.

❑ If something **stretches** over a period of time, it lasts that long. *...an unbroken home league record that had stretched back over 17 months.* ◇ A period of time can be called a **stretch**. *...his five-year stretch as commissioner.* If you do something for a certain length of time **at a stretch**, you do it for that length of time without stopping.

❑ If something **stretches** over a certain distance, it extends that far. *...a traffic jam that stretched for several miles.* Similarly, something can **stretch** from one place to another. *...huge stained glass windows stretching from floor to ceiling.* ◇ A **stretch** of land or water is a large area of it. *...a one-mile stretch of beach.*

❑ If someone's money or resources are **stretched**, they have hardly enough for their needs. *The city's public-sector*

services are stretched to breaking-point. ◇ If you talk about how far a sum of money will **stretch**, you are considering what you can afford to buy with it. *...wondering whether the company budget will stretch to a prestige car.*

❑ If a job or task **stretches** you, it makes you use all your energy and skill. If it has you **at full stretch**, you are only just managing to cope with it.

❑ If you say something is not true or possible **by any stretch of the imagination**, you mean it is completely untrue or absolutely impossible.

stretcher (stretchered) A **stretcher** is a device made of canvas stretched over a frame and carried between two people to transport a sick or injured person. When someone is carried off a sports field because of an injury, you say they are **stretchered off**. The people who carry a stretcher are called **stretcher-bearers**.

stretchy material becomes longer or wider when you pull it and returns to its normal shape when you let it go.

strew (strewing, strewed, have strewn) If an area is **strewn** with things or if they are **strewn** across it, a lot of them are scattered untidily across it. *The walkways into the underground are strewn with litter.* You add -strewn to a word like 'litter' or 'paper' to show that these things are scattered about in a place. *...rubbish-strewn streets.*

striated (*pron:* strie-ay-tid) (striation) If something is **striated**, it is marked with narrow bands of colour or with ridges or grooves. These marks or ridges are called **striations**. *...striated ridges of solid rock.*

stricken If someone or something is **stricken** by something unpleasant, they are badly affected by it. You add -stricken to a word to show that something has caused a bad effect on someone or something. *...grief-stricken mothers... ...drought-stricken areas.*

strict (strictly, strictness) ❑ A **strict** person controls other people very firmly. *The prison regime will be much stricter... She resented her parents' strictness.*

❑ A **strict** rule or order is very firm and must be obeyed absolutely. ◇ **Strict** is used to talk about rules and principles being firmly enforced or obeyed. *Security restrictions were being strictly enforced... ...a strict vegetarian.*

❑ **Strict** can be used to mean 'precise' or 'exact'. *...in strict alphabetical order... What you were told is not strictly accurate.* ◇ **Strictly** can be used to emphasize that someone or something is of a particular kind, rather than something else. *The parade had originally been planned as a strictly military affair.* ◇ If something is **strictly** for a particular thing or person, it is intended only for them. *...supplies intended strictly for medical purposes.*

❑ The **strict** sense of a word is its precise meaning. *It's not quite peace in the strictest sense of the word, rather the absence of war.* ◇ You say **strictly speaking** to correct a statement or add more precise information. *We cannot, strictly speaking, cure diabetes but we have some very effective treatments for treating the consequences.*

stricture When someone criticizes something severely, you can call what they say their **strictures**. *The campaign is justifying every stricture he has ever voiced about referendums.* ◇ **Strictures** are also limits or restrictions imposed on someone or something. *We whined and complained under our parents' strictures.*

stride (striding, strode) ❑ If you **stride** somewhere, you walk quickly with long steps. ◇ Each step you take when you walk or run can be called a **stride**.

❏ If you make **strides** towards something you are trying to achieve, you make progress towards it. *Our struggle for freedom has made great strides.*

❏ If you **get into your stride**, you settle to a regular pace or rate of progress in what you are doing. ◇ If something **puts you off your stride**, it distracts you or interrupts your progress. ◇ If you **take** something **in your stride**, you deal with it calmly and easily.

strident (*pron:* stry-dent) (stridently, stridency) ❏ You call someone's behaviour **strident** when they keep criticizing something strongly. *He has toned down his earlier stridently anti-Communist language.*

❏ **Strident** sounds are loud and harsh. You talk about the **stridency** of sounds like these.

strife is trouble and fighting. *Most asylum seekers come to escape strife-torn conditions in their own countries.*

strike (striking, struck; striker, strikingly) ❏ If there is a **strike**, workers stop working for a time, because of a disagreement with their employers, or as a protest about something. You also say people **strike** or **go on strike**; people taking part in a strike are called **strikers**. ◇ See also **hunger strike**.

❏ If something **strikes** something else, it hits it, often causing damage. *Houses were struck by lightning.* ◇ If you **strike** something, you hit it or kick it. ◇ In football, a **striker** is a player whose main function is to attack and score goals, rather than defend.

❏ If someone **strikes** you, they deliberately hit you.

❏ If you **strike back** at someone who has harmed you, you try to harm them in return.

❏ If something like an illness or disaster **strikes**, it suddenly happens. *A violent storm had struck the area.* ◇ You can say someone is **struck down** by an illness. ◇ If someone is **struck dumb**, they are suddenly unable to speak.

❏ If something like a blow **strikes home**, it hits the target exactly. ◇ You also say something **strikes home** when it achieves the effect you want. *The signs are that the message is striking home and that the public may be ready to listen.*

❏ When a military force **strikes**, it makes a sudden attack; the attack is called a **strike**.

❏ If you are **within striking distance** of something, you are very near to it and can easily reach it. *Rebels are reported to be within striking distance of the capital.* ◇ You also say you are **within striking distance** of something when you have nearly achieved what you set out to do. *The President is within striking distance of a strategic arms treaty.*

❏ If an idea or thought **strikes** you, you suddenly have it.

❏ If something **strikes fear** into someone, it makes them very frightened.

❏ If something **strikes** you in a certain way, it gives you that impression. *He never struck me as much of a rebel... The situation struck me as all but hopeless.* ◇ If something is **striking**, it is very noticeable. *The single most striking feature of successful schools is their clear sense of collective purpose.* ◇ If you are very impressed by something, you can say you are **struck by** it. *What struck me was the enormous commitment of the students.* ◇ If you say someone is **striking**, you mean they are especially noticeable because of their beauty.

❏ When a clock **strikes**, its bells chime to show what the time is.

❏ If you **strike a deal** or bargain with someone, you come to an agreement with them.

❏ If you **strike** a match, you scrape it against something to make it burst into flame.

❏ If someone **strikes** oil or gold, they discover it in the ground by mining or drilling.

❏ If you say someone **strikes it lucky**, you mean they have good luck. ◇ If someone **strikes it rich** or **strikes gold**, they suddenly become rich or successful.

❏ If you **strike a balance**, you reach a compromise between two extremes. *The act is meant to strike a balance between police powers and suspects' rights.*

❏ If a doctor or lawyer is **struck off**, their name is removed from the professional register and they are not allowed to carry on in their profession, because they have done something wrong.

❏ If you **strike out** in a certain direction, you set off in that direction. *He had struck out through the jungle until he found a stream that led him to the village.*

❏ If you **strike up** a conversation or friendship with someone, you begin it. ◇ When musicians begin to play, you can say they **strike up**. *The band strikes up the national anthem.*

❏ **strike a chord**: see **chord**.

strike-breaker (strike-breaking) A **strike-breaker** is a person who continues to work during a strike, or is brought in to do the work of someone who is on strike. Working during a strike like this is called **strike-breaking**.

string (stringing, strung) ❏ **String** is thin cord made of twisted threads.

❏ A **string** of things like beads or pearls is a number of them threaded onto a piece of thread or wire.

❏ If something is **strung** somewhere, it is suspended between two or more points high up in the air. *...a hammock strung between two coconut palms.*

❏ If things are **strung out** somewhere, they are spread out in a long line. *Anti-aircraft weapons are strung out on the quay in front of the cathedral.* Similarly, you can say things are **strung along** something like a road. *...the summer houses strung along the coast.*

❏ A series of similar events or things can be called a **string**. *...a string of attacks... ...a string of tiny islands off the south Florida coast.*

❏ If you **string** a number of things together, you get them to follow each other in an unbroken sequence. *If they cannot string half a dozen passes together, what are they doing in football?*

❏ The **strings** on a musical instrument are the tightly-stretched lengths of wire or nylon which vibrate to produce notes. A **stringed** instrument is one which has strings, for example a violin or a guitar. ◇ In an orchestra, the **strings** are the stringed instruments.

❏ If you say someone has **another string to their bow**, you mean they have another idea, job, or ability which they can use if the first one is not successful.

❏ **Second string** is used to describe people or things that are not the best of their kind but are kept in reserve in case the best ones are not available. *...her second-string horse.*

❏ If something is offered to you **with no strings attached**, it is offered without any conditions or restrictions.

❏ When someone **pulls strings**, they use their influence or power to get something which is difficult to obtain.

❏ If someone **strings you along**, they deceive you over a period of time by encouraging you to think they share your hopes or beliefs.

❏ If someone is **strung out**, they are addicted to a drug, or under the influence of drugs. You also say a drug addict is **strung out** when he or she is suffering or distressed because of the lack of a drug.

string beans are the same as runner beans.

string quartet A **string quartet** is a group of four musicians who play together. Their instruments are two violins, a viola, and a cello. A piece of music written for this combination is also called a **string quartet**.

stringent (*pron:* **strin**-jent) (**stringently; stringency**) Stringent laws or rules are very severe or are strictly controlled. You can talk about the **stringency** of laws or rules like these. *The standards were not applied very stringently.* ◇ **Stringency** is also spending very little money, or having very little available. *...a period of great stringency in public expenditure.*

stringer A **stringer** is a journalist employed part-time by a newspaper or news service to report on a certain area.

stringy food is tough and difficult to chew.

strip (**stripping, stripped**) ❏ A **strip** of something is a long narrow piece of it. *...a strip of land... ...a strip of brown paper.*

❏ If someone **strips**, they take off all their clothes. If they are **stripped**, their clothes are taken off by someone else. See also **strip-search**.

❏ If someone is **stripped** of something like their property or power, it is officially taken away from them.

❏ If you **strip** something like a building or an area of land, you take everything out of it. *He saw private apartments stripped bare by the occupying forces... Critics of the companies say they are rapidly stripping the forest of its mahogany trees.* ◇ If you **strip** something which is covering a surface, you remove it. Similarly, you can **strip out** parts of a building. *The interior fittings were stripped out 20 years ago.*

❏ If you **strip down** a piece of equipment, you take it to pieces to clean it or repair it. ◇ **Stripped-down** is used to describe something which is very basic or has only the bare essentials. *...a stripped-down theatre company.*

❏ A **strip cartoon** is a series of drawings which tell a story, with the words spoken by the characters printed in each drawing.

❏ In sport, especially football, a player's **strip** is the kit they wear to play in.

strip club A **strip club** is a club where striptease is performed.

strip lighting is a type of electric lighting which uses long tubes rather than light bulbs.

strip-search (**strip-searched**) If a person is **strip-searched**, someone such as a police officer makes them take off all their clothes and searches them, usually to see if they are carrying drugs or weapons.

stripe (**striped, stripy**) **Stripes** are long thin lines, usually of different colours. You use **striped** or **stripy** to describe things marked or patterned with stripes. *...red and black striped ribbon... ...a stripy T-shirt.* ◇ **Stripes** are also narrow bands of material sewn onto a uniform to indicate someone's rank. *...a soldier with a corporal's stripes on his arms.*

stripling A young man who is not fully grown is sometimes called a **stripling**.

stripper A **stripper** is a person who performs striptease.

striptease is an entertainment in which a performer takes off all their clothes in a sexually provocative way, usually to a musical accompaniment.

strive (**striving, strove** *or* **strived, have striven** *or* **have strived**) If you **strive** for something, you try hard to achieve it. ◇ Similarly, if you **strive** to do something, you try hard to do it. *They strove to play intelligent, passing football.*

strobe or **strobe lighting** is a moving beam of very bright flashing light, used to create special effects in places like discos.

strode See **stride**.

stroke (**stroking, stroked**) ❏ If you **stroke** something, you move your hand slowly and gently over it. ◇ The **strokes** of a brush are the movements or marks you make when you use it.

❏ A **stroke** is a sudden attack of illness caused by the rupture or blockage of a blood vessel in or near the brain. A stroke can result in brain damage, loss of speech, paralysis, and sometimes death.

❏ In rowing, a **stroke** is a single pull of the oar. ◇ In swimming, a **stroke** is a single movement of the arms and legs. Different styles of swimming are also called **strokes**. *...back stroke.* ◇ In sports like tennis, cricket, and golf, a **stroke** is one hit of the ball, or a particular way of hitting it. *He won the US Golf Open by two strokes... ...forehand strokes.*

❏ If you say, for example, that something happens **on the stroke of** seven, you mean it happens at exactly seven o'clock.

❏ If something is achieved **at a stroke**, it is achieved suddenly and completely by a single action. *At a stroke the prime minister had upset her three principal colleagues.* ◇ If something is achieved **at the stroke of a pen**, it is brought about as an immediate result of the signing of an agreement or law.

❏ A **stroke** of luck is a piece of good luck. ◇ A sudden brilliant idea can be called a **stroke** of genius.

❏ If you say someone does not do a **stroke of work**, you mean they are very lazy.

stroll If you **stroll** somewhere, you walk there in a slow relaxed way. A **stroll** is a slow pleasant walk.

strong (**strongly**) ❏ **Strong** people or animals have well-developed muscles and great physical ability so they can carry or move heavy objects or do hard physical work.

❏ If you say someone is a **strong** personality, you mean they are very determined and not easily influenced by other people. ◇ A person's **strong** points are their good qualities or the things they are good at. ◇ If someone is a **strong** candidate or contender in a competitive situation, they are likely to do well or win.

❏ If someone has a **strong** belief in something, they believe in it very firmly, and are not likely to change their mind. *...his strongly-held views.* Similarly, you can say someone is a **strong** believer or supporter of something.

❏ **Strong** action is firm and severe. *Sir William also*

called for stronger measures to protect key conservation sites. Criticism can also be **strong**. ◇ If someone uses **strong** language or **strong** words, they make their views known very forcefully. ...a strongly worded letter of protest. Swearing or obscene language is also called **strong** language.

❏ You use **strong** to describe things which have a lot of force. ...a strong, gusting wind.

❏ **Strong** objects are not easily damaged or broken.

❏ A **strong** relationship is close and likely to last.

❏ A **strong** economy is successful and stable. You can also say a currency is **strong**.

❏ If you say someone or something is **still going strong**, you mean they are still healthy or working well after a long time.

❏ If there is a **strong** case or argument for something, there are very good reasons for introducing it or going ahead with it.

❏ If something makes a **strong** impression on you, you remember it and think about it afterwards.

❏ A **strong** taste or smell is very noticeable and distinct.

❏ You say a drink like tea is **strong** when it contains a lot of tea in proportion to the amount of water in it. Similarly, a **strong** alcoholic drink contains a high proportion of alcohol.

❏ If someone has a **strong** accent, their accent is very noticeable and shows where they live or what their native language is.

❏ You can use **strong** to talk about the number of people in a group. For example, if a group is a hundred **strong**, it has a hundred people in it. ◇ If you talk about a **strong** force of police or soldiers, you mean a lot of them.

❏ **strong suit**: see **suit**.

strong-arm You say people use **strong-arm** tactics when they use threats or force to get what they want.

strong-minded people have firm opinions or attitudes and are not easily influenced by other people.

strong-willed people are very determined to get their own way.

stronghold ❏ A **stronghold** is a place which is held and defended by an army or other military force.

❏ If you say a place is a **stronghold** of a type of attitude or belief, you mean a lot of people have it there.

strongroom A **strongroom** in a bank is a reinforced fireproof room with a special security door, where money and valuable documents are kept.

strontium is a soft silvery-white metal used in making fireworks. **Strontium-90** is one of the most dangerous fallout products after a nuclear explosion.

stroppy If someone is **stroppy**, they are bad-tempered and difficult. ...a stroppy teenage son.

strove See **strive**.

struck See **strike**.

structural (structurally) **Structural** is used to talk about things to do with the structure of buildings. ...severe structural damage... ...structural engineers... Many of the properties are in high-rise, structurally unsound blocks. ◇ You can also use **structural** to talk about things to do with the structure of a system or organization. ...structural changes to the welfare system... Their economy was small and structurally weak.

structuralism (structuralist) **Structuralism** is an academic theory which suggests you can study subjects like litera-

ture, language, or society as if they were made up of structures, each structure consisting of smaller components or elements. A person who studies something in this way is called a **structuralist**. **Structuralist** is used to describe things to do with structuralism.

structure (structuring, structured) ❏ The **structure** of something like a building is the way it is constructed. The original structure of the freeway was preserved. ◇ A **structure** is anything which has been built or constructed, for example a building, a monument, or an oil-rig.

❏ The **structure** of something like a system is the way it is organized. ...the command structure of the army... ...the changing structures within the civil service. A system can itself be called a **structure**. ...security structures like NATO.

❏ If you **structure** something, you arrange it in an organized system. ...a new way of structuring the work force. When something has been arranged like this, you say it is **structured** or has **structure**. ...a carefully structured interview... He tries to give the story some kind of structure.

struggle (struggling, struggled) ❏ If you **struggle** to do something, you try hard to do it, even though it is difficult. Many miners' families struggled to make ends meet. ◇ When it is difficult to do something, you can say it is a **struggle** to do it. England face a hard struggle to save the Fourth Test against the West Indies. ◇ You use **struggling** to talk about a person or organization trying hard to do something but not having much success. He is struggling on his small income... ...the struggling Third Division club.

❏ If you talk about the **struggle** for something, you mean the efforts people make to achieve it. ...a struggle for power... ...the non-violent struggle for freedom and democracy. Similarly, you can talk about a **struggle** against something. ...the struggle against apartheid.

❏ If someone **struggles** when they are being held captive, they try hard to get free. ◇ If two people **struggle**, they fight each other. A fight can be called a **struggle**. He was stabbed in the struggle.

strum (strumming, strummed) If you **strum** a guitar, you play chords on it by moving your fingers or a plectrum across all the strings.

strung See **string**.

strut (strutting, strutted) ❏ If someone **struts**, they walk in a proud way with their head high and their chest out.

❏ If you say someone **struts their stuff**, you mean they show their talents or abilities off to their best advantage. The pick of 200 youth theatre companies strutted their stuff at the National Theatre.

❏ A **strut** is a piece of wood or metal which strengthens or supports a building or structure.

strychnine (pron: strik-neen) is a strong poison which can cause convulsions and death.

stub (stubbing, stubbed) ❏ The **stub** of a pencil or cigarette is the short piece left when the rest has been used. ◇ The **stub** of a cheque is the small part you keep as a record of what you have paid. Similarly, the **stub** of a ticket is the part you keep to prove you have paid for something.

❏ When someone **stubs out** a cigarette, they put it out by pressing it against something hard. ◇ If you **stub** your toe, you hurt it by accidentally kicking something hard.

stubble (stubbly) **Stubble** is the short stalks left in the ground after the harvesting of crops like wheat or oats.

◇ **Stubble** is also the very short coarse hairs on a man's chin when he has not shaved for a day or so. When a man's chin is like this, you can describe it as **stubbly**.

stubborn (stubbornly, stubbornness) ❑ **Stubborn** people are very determined to do what they want and are not easily put off. *They stubbornly refuse to surrender control... They never forgave him for his stubbornness.*
 ❑ **Stubborn** things are very difficult to deal with. *One of the most stubborn problems has been the percentage of weapons any one nation may hold.*

stubby things are short and thick. *...stubby fingers.*

stucco (stuccoed) **Stucco** is a mixture of cement, sand, and lime which people used to put on exterior walls as a hard-wearing finish. A **stuccoed** building has this kind of finish. *...stuccoed villas.* ◇ **Stucco** is also a type of plaster used for decorative work on interior walls, for example mouldings. *...stuccoed ceilings.*

stuck See **stick**.

stuck-up people are proud and conceited.

stud (studded) ❑ **Studs** are pieces of metal attached to a surface and sticking out of it. They are put there for decoration or protection. ◇ When an object is decorated with small hard objects, you can say it is **studded** with them. *...a cowboy hat studded with rhinestones... ...diamond-studded high-heeled shoes.* ◇ You can also say a surface is **studded** with objects when there are a lot of them scattered over it. *...rich dark soil studded with large boulders.*
 ❑ A **stud** is also (a) a small earring attached so it lies flat against the ear. (b) a similar ornament attached to the side of the nose.
 ❑ **Studs** are the small objects attached to the soles of some kinds of footwear, for example football boots, to give a better grip on the ground.
 ❑ Male animals, especially horses, which are kept for **stud** are kept for breeding purposes. A group of animals kept for this purpose is called a **stud**; the place where they are kept is also called a **stud** or a **stud farm**.

student A **student** is a person studying at a university or college. ◇ Senior school pupils are also sometimes called **students**. ◇ You say someone is a **student** of something when they take a great interest in it. *...a keen student of opinion polls.*

studentship A **studentship** is the same as a scholarship.

studied See **study**.

studio (studios) ❑ A **studio** is a room or building where TV or radio programmes, films, or records are made. The **studios** of a film, TV, radio, or record company are the buildings where its productions are made and its main offices are based.
 ❑ An artist's **studio** is a room where he or she paints; similarly, a photographer can have a **studio** to take photographs, especially of people. ◇ A **studio** is also a room used for practice or rehearsals by dancers or actors.
 ❑ A **studio theatre** is a small theatre, often in the same building as a larger theatre and used for performances of less well-known or experimental productions.
 ❑ A **studio** or **studio flat** is a small flat, usually with one room for living and sleeping, and a kitchen and bathroom.

studio audience A **studio audience** is a group of people watching, and sometimes taking part in, a TV or radio programme. Their laughter, applause, and talking are recorded and transmitted as part of the programme.

studious (studiously) A **studious** person spends a lot of time reading and studying. ◇ If someone **studiously** avoids doing something, they are careful not to do it. *Any discussion of contentious issues was studiously avoided.*

study (studies, studying, studied) ❑ If you **study** a subject, you spend time learning about it. Learning about a subject is called the **study** of it. *...the study of technology at A level.* ◇ **Study** is learning about a subject or subjects. *...the right environment for quiet study.* A person's **studies** is the studying they do. *We decided to get married once we had finished our studies.*
 ❑ You also say someone **studies** something when they conduct research into it. A **study** is a piece of research. *...well-publicised studies on the decline of spelling.*
 ❑ When someone looks at something carefully, you can say they **study** it. *...travellers studying maps.* ◇ If someone **studies** something like a proposal, they consider it carefully before making a decision.
 ❑ A **studied** action has been carefully planned and is not spontaneous. *Previous governments maintained a studied neutrality in most industrial disputes.*
 ❑ A **study** by an artist or photographer is a drawing or photograph done in preparation for other work. ◇ In music, a **study** is a piece of music for a single instrument written to show off the player's technical skill.
 ❑ A **study** is also a room for reading, writing, and studying.

stuff ❑ You call actions, objects, or other things **stuff** when you are talking about them in a general way. *I do a lot of dangerous stuff in my show... The Red Cross has been shipping stuff in for months.*
 ❑ If you say someone **knows their stuff**, you mean they know a lot about a subject.
 ❑ If you say something is **the stuff** or **the very stuff** of a certain thing, you mean it is a characteristic feature of it. *Such confrontations are the very stuff of parliamentary democracy.* ◇ **made of sterner stuff**: see **stern**.
 ❑ Strong alcoholic drinks, especially spirits, are sometimes called **the hard stuff**.
 ❑ If you **stuff** something somewhere, you push it there quickly and roughly. *...a plastic bag stuffed down a storm drain.* ◇ If a place or container is **stuffed** with things, it is full of them. *...cabinets stuffed full of expensive china.*
 ❑ If you **stuff** something like a chicken, you put other food inside it before cooking it. ◇ **Stuffing** is a mixture of chopped and seasoned ingredients which a piece of meat or poultry is stuffed with before cooking.
 ❑ **Stuffing** is also material used to fill things like furniture, cushions, or toys. ◇ If something **knocks the stuffing out** of something else, it seriously weakens it. *Fear of flying abroad since the Gulf War has knocked the stuffing out of overseas travel from Japan.*
 ❑ If a dead animal, bird, or fish is **stuffed**, it is carefully filled with special material and restored to the shape of the live creature so it can be preserved and displayed, for example in a museum.
 ❑ If you call someone a **stuffed shirt**, you mean they are extremely formal, old-fashioned, and pompous.

stuffy people are formal, old-fashioned, and dull.
 ❑ If a place is **stuffy**, it is unpleasantly warm and there is not enough fresh air.

stultify (stultifies, stultifying, stultified) If something stultifies a person's mind, it prevents them using it properly. *...the sort of corporate mentality that stultifies imagination and daring.* ◇ You say something is **stultifying** when it holds back progress. *...Spain's campaign to emancipate itself from the stultifying years of Franco's rule.*

stumble (stumbling, stumbled) ❑ If you **stumble** when you are walking or running, you trip and fall or almost fall.

❑ If you **stumble** when you are speaking, you hesitate or make a mistake. ◇ If you make a lot of mistakes when you are doing something, you can say you **stumble** through it.

❑ If you **stumble across** something or **stumble on** it, you discover it accidentally. *Scientists have accidentally stumbled across what may be the key to finding a cure for muscle and heart diseases.*

stumbling block A **stumbling block** is a problem which gets in the way and prevents you achieving something. *The role of the army has become the critical stumbling block to the full implementation of the peace plan.*

stump ❑ A **stump** is the base or lowest part of something, which remains when the rest has been broken off or removed. *...a tree stump... They had worn their teeth down to brown stumps.*

❑ In cricket, the **stumps** are the three upright wooden sticks which, together with the bails, form the wicket. When a batsman is **stumped,** the wicketkeeper gets him or her out by knocking the bails off.

❑ If a question or problem **stumps** you, you cannot think of a solution to it.

❑ You say someone **stumps** somewhere when they walk in a clumsy way. *He stumped into the office.*

❑ If you **stump up** an amount of money, you produce it to pay for something. *Buyers have to stump up deposits of at least 5%.*

❑ If a politician is **on the stump,** he or she is travelling around campaigning for support, especially in the run-up to an election.

stumpy things are short and thick. *...the mole's stumpy tail.*

stun (stunning, stunned; stunningly) ❑ If you are **stunned,** you are very shocked by something. *The election result was a stunning blow to the regime... ...a stunned silence.*

❑ If you say someone or something is **stunning,** you mean they are extremely beautiful or impressive. *...stunning views... ...a stunningly beautiful girl.*

❑ If a blow on the head **stuns** you, it knocks you out, or makes you confused and unsteady. ◇ A **stun** grenade or gun is designed to knock someone out, rather than kill them or injure them seriously.

stung See **sting**.

stunk See **stink**.

stunning (stunningly) See **stun**.

stunt ❑ A **stunt** is something someone does to get publicity. *The view seems to be that his visit is a propaganda stunt.*

❑ A **stunt** is also a skilful and dangerous trick in something like a car or plane, performed to entertain people. ◇ In film-making, a **stunt** is something dangerous someone does in front of the cameras, which is made to look like part of the action. Stunts are usually performed by **stunt men** or **stunt women,** whose job is to stand in for leading actors so they do not get injured.

❑ If something is **stunted,** it is prevented from growing or developing as it should. *...plants with stunted leaves... Their imaginations are being stunted.*

stupefy (stupefies, stupefying, stupefied; stupefaction) If you say someone is **stupefied** or in a state of **stupefaction,** you mean they are so tired or bored they cannot think properly. If you find something very boring, you can call it **stupefying.** *The report is couched in such stupefying jargon as to be barely comprehensible.* ◇ You can also say someone is **stupefied** when they are very surprised or shocked by something.

stupendous (stupendously) If something is extremely large or impressive, you can say it is **stupendous.** *...a stupendous meal... ...a stupendously wealthy businessman.*

stupid (stupidly; stupidity, stupidities) If you call an idea or action **stupid,** you mean it is not at all sensible. *We had stupidly been looking at the wrong column of figures.* If you call a person **stupid,** you mean they lack intelligence or keep doing silly things. When someone does something silly, you can talk about their **stupidity. Stupidities** are stupid actions. *I'd hate to see two innocent children suffer for my stupidities.*

stupor If you say someone is in a **stupor,** you mean they are almost unconscious, for example because they are drunk.

sturdy (sturdier, sturdiest; sturdily, sturdiness) ❑ A **sturdy** person is strong and healthy. ◇ **Sturdy** is also used to describe someone's behaviour when they are very strong in their support for someone or something. *His old pals sturdily rallied round to testify to the strength of his morals.*

❑ **Sturdy** objects are strongly made and not easily damaged. *...sturdy stone cottages... ...a craft much admired for its handling and sturdiness.*

sturgeon (*pron:* stur-jon) The **sturgeon** is a large edible fish. Its eggs are called caviar when they have been prepared as food.

stutter (stuttering, stuttered) If someone **stutters,** they find it difficult to say the first sound of a word and hesitate or repeat it two or three times. You say someone like this has a **stutter.** ◇ If something like a machine or a system **stutters,** it proceeds in a hesitant way. *...his stuttering economic reforms.*

sty (sties) ❑ A **sty** is the same as a pigsty.

❑ See also **stye**.

stye A **stye** or **sty** is a painful red swelling on a person's eyelid.

style (styling, styled) ❑ The **style** of something is the general way it is done or presented. *The biography is written in a straightforward yet lively style.* ◇ Your **style** of doing something is your way of doing it. *...Liverpool's style of play.* ◇ If you say something is **not your style,** you mean it is not the kind of thing you would do. *Bearing grudges is not my style.*

❑ The **style** of a product is its design, especially its shape and other features which make it look different from similar products.

❑ You add **-style** to a word to say someone or something is of a particular type. *...American-style cheerleaders... ...an old-style liberal.*

❑ The **style** of something like a painting or piece of music is its special features which make it recognizable as belonging to a particular type. *...architecture in the classical* *style.*

❑ **Style** is fashionable good taste. If you say someone or something has **style**, you mean they are smart, fashionable, or elegant in a distinctive way. *Teddy Tinling was the dress designer who put colour and style into tennis.*

❑ If you do something **in style** or **in fine style**, you do it in a grand way. *...celebrating his birthday in style.*

❑ If you **style** yourself in a certain way, you call yourself by a particular name or title. *Bryan Adams styles himself The Groover From Vancouver.* See also **self-styled.**

stylised (stylisation) See **stylized.**

stylish (stylishly, stylishness) A **stylish** person or object is smart and fashionable. *The three bedrooms are all stylishly decorated... ...modern Italian stylishness.* ◇ If you call something someone does **stylish**, you mean they do it in a neat efficient impressive way. *That was the most stylish performance I've seen from United this season.*

stylist ❑ Hairdressers are sometimes called **stylists.** ◇ A **stylist** is also someone like a designer who creates a certain image or effect. *...a fashion stylist.*

❑ If you call a writer a **stylist**, you mean he or she writes in an attractive and elegant way.

stylistic (stylistically) **Stylistic** is used to talk about the methods, techniques, and principles involved in creating a work of art or a piece of writing or music. *There is virtually no stylistic influence from the older to the younger artists... The films are stylistically very different.*

stylized (stylization) (or stylised, stylisation) **Stylized** is used to describe things which are made or presented according to a certain fixed style, and not in a realistic or natural way. *The trees are depicted on the new stamps in a distinctive stylized design... He gradually moved away from realism, towards an increasing degree of stylization.*

stylus (usual plural: styluses) The **stylus** on a record player is the small pointed object which picks up the sound signals on the records.

stymie (stymieing, stymied) If you are **stymied**, someone prevents you from doing something you want to do. *Every now and then he's suggested a reform; and, at each stage, he has been stymied by the hardliners.* Similarly, if something like a process is **stymied**, someone prevents it from proceeding or progressing.

styptic is a substance used to stop bleeding. A **styptic** pencil is a styptic substance in the form of a small stick, for dabbing on slight cuts.

suave (pron: swahv) (suavely, suavity) A **suave** person is smooth and sophisticated. *Shaw Taylor presided suavely over both programmes... ...gestures of unhurried suavity.*

sub ❑ A **sub** is a submarine.

❑ **Subs** are the fixed regular amounts of money which members of a club or society pay into its funds.

sub- is used to form words which describe something as being underneath something else. *...sub-sea vehicles... ...sub-surface structure.*

❑ **Sub-** is also used to form words which show that a job or rank is lower than another job or rank. *...a sub-manager.*

❑ **Sub-** is also used to talk about something being below a certain level or point on a scale. *I will have to run sub-19.9 sec to get a medal... ...sub-zero temperatures.*

❑ **Sub-** is used to form words which describe something as being part of a larger thing. *With its four sub-clauses, this paragraph is the longest section of the will... Management is de-*

volved: every sub-company has its own board of directors.

❑ Some words beginning with **sub-** can be spelled with or without a hyphen. For example, 'sub-contract' can be spelled 'subcontract'. See entries at **subcontinent, subcontract, sub-standard, sub-tropical.**

sub-aqua is used to talk about things to do with underwater diving or sport using an aqualung. *...sub-aqua gear... ...the British Sub Aqua Club.*

sub-atomic A **sub-atomic** particle is one which is part of an atom.

sub-committee A **sub-committee** is a small committee made up of some of the members of a larger committee. A sub-committee is usually formed to consider a subject in detail and report what they find to the main committee.

sub-editor A **sub-editor** is a person whose job is to check and correct articles in newspapers or magazines before they are published.

sub-group A **sub-group** is a group which is part of a larger one.

sub-human If someone is treated as **sub-human**, they are treated in a cruel or uncaring way, as if they were not really a human being.

sub judice (pron: sub joo-diss-ee) If something is **sub judice**, the media are not allowed to comment on it because it is the subject of a trial which is currently taking place.

sub-let (sub-letting, sub-let not 'sub-letted') If you **sub-let** a building or part of a building which you are renting, you allow someone else to use it and you take rent from them.

sub-lieutenant See **lieutenant.**

sub-machine gun A **sub-machine** gun is a portable machine gun with a short barrel.

sub-plot The **sub-plot** in a novel, play, or film is a connected series of events which are less important than the main plot.

sub-post office A **sub-post office** is a small branch post office run by a **sub-postmaster** or **sub-postmistress**, often as part of a shop.

sub-Saharan is used to refer to African countries south of the Sahara desert where people are mainly of African rather than Arab origin.

sub-section A **sub-section** of a document is one of the smaller parts which its main parts are divided into. *...Section 19, Sub-section 11.*

sub-species (plural: sub-species) A **sub-species** of a plant or animal is a group within the species which has characteristics distinguishing it from other members of the species.

sub-standard (or substandard) is used to describe things which are not up to a required standard and are therefore unacceptable. *The contractor may cut costs by using sub-standard materials.*

sub-station A **sub-station** is a place where high voltage electricity from power plants is converted to lower voltage electricity for homes or factories.

sub-tropical (or subtropical) is used to describe the parts of the world between the tropical and temperate regions, which have no cold season. *...sub-tropical Florida... ...a steamy, subtropical island.*

subconscious (subconsciously) If something is in a person's

subconscious, it is in their mind and can influence their behaviour, although they are not aware of it or not thinking about it. *Each relationship we pursue is a subconscious attempt to re-create a familiar pattern... I've tried not to allow the crisis to affect me but I suppose subconsciously it has.*

subcontinent (*or* sub-continent) When people talk about the Indian **subcontinent,** they mean the whole of the area which includes India, Pakistan, Bangladesh, and Sri Lanka.

subcontract (subcontractor) (*or* sub-contract, sub-contractor) If a firm which is contracted to do a piece of work **subcontracts** all or part of the work to another firm, it pays the other firm to do it. The second firm is called the **subcontractor.** An arrangement or agreement like this is called a **subcontract.**

subculture A **subculture** is the ideas, art, and way of life of a particular group within a larger society.

subcutaneous (*pron:* sub-cute-**ayn**-ee-uss) is used to talk about things which are located or applied immediately beneath the skin. *...subcutaneous fat... ...a subcutaneous injection.*

subdivide (subdividing, subdivided; subdivision) If an area is **subdivided,** it is split up into smaller areas, or it officially consists of smaller areas. The smaller areas are called **subdivisions.** *...the subdivision of pastoral farms into smallholdings.*

subdivide (subduing, subdued) ❏ If someone **subdues** a person or group that is causing trouble, they bring them under control, often using force. *50 police officers took an hour to subdue 30 youths fighting in the street.*

❏ If you call someone's behaviour **subdued,** you mean they are unusually quiet, because they are sad or worried. *The congregation was in a subdued mood.* When a lot of people behave like this, you can say the atmosphere is **subdued.** ◇ If things like lights, colours, or sounds are **subdued,** they are soft and muted, rather than bright or loud.

subject (subjection) ❏ The **subject** of something like a talk, conversation, or book is what it is about. ◇ The **subject** of something like a photograph, painting, or film is the main person or thing in it. ◇ **subject matter:** see **matter.**

❏ If someone **changes the subject** when they are talking, they deliberately start talking about something else, because they are embarrassed or uneasy about what is being said.

❏ A **subject** is an area of study, for example maths, biology, or English literature.

❏ The **subjects** of a king or queen are the people they rule. ◇ British **subjects** are people with British citizenship.

❏ **Subject** people or countries are controlled by the government of another country.

❏ If an activity is **subject** to something like a law or rule, the law or rule says how it should be carried out. *Newspaper mergers are subject to the Fair Trading Act 1973.*

❏ If you are **subject** to something unpleasant, you are affected by it. *Sarajevo's residents were subject to a constant barrage of firepower.* ◇ If someone **subjects** (*pron:* subjects) you to something unpleasant, they make you experience it. *Only they can ensure that prisoners are not subjected to degrading treatment or punishment.*

❏ If someone **subjects** someone else to their control, they take complete control of them. When someone is completely controlled by someone else, you can talk about their **subjection** to them. *He was subjected to her will... Hostages can be thrust into a dependent state because of their complete subjection to their captors.*

subjective (subjectively, subjectivity) If you say someone is being **subjective,** you mean they are allowing their personal feelings to influence them in what they say or write; you can also talk about their **subjectivity.** *I reacted not as an ordinary member of an audience but very subjectively as an appalled and outraged mother... Historical accuracy is limited by the availability of resources and the subjectivity of the historian.* You can also call what someone says **subjective.** *...a subjective response.* See also **objective.**

subjugate (*pron:* sub-joo-gate) (subjugating, subjugated; subjugation) If someone **subjugates** a group of people, they take complete control of them, usually by defeating them in a war. *...brutal subjugation of native tribes.* ◇ If someone's wishes are **subjugated** to someone or something else, they are treated as less important. *We must all subjugate ourselves to the rules of democracy.*

sublimate (sublimating, sublimated; sublimation) If you **sublimate** a strong desire or feeling, you express it in a different way, often a way which is more socially acceptable. *The erotic impulse is sublimated into art... I suppose my campaigning is a sublimation for missing out on having a family.*

sublime (sublimely) ❏ If you say something is **sublime,** you mean it is so wonderful or beautiful that it affects you emotionally. *...some of the most sublime scenery on earth.* ◇ If something changes from being extremely good or beautiful to being very silly or trivial, you can say it goes **from the sublime to the ridiculous.**

❏ **Sublime** is sometimes used to describe someone's behaviour when they do something very badly or show astonishing ignorance. *...the administration's sublime incompetence... The New Agers seem sublimely unaware of the possible danger.*

subliminal (subliminally) **Subliminal** is used to describe the use of images on a cinema or TV screen which are so brief or weak that you are not aware of them, although they can be used to influence your feelings or attitudes. *Flickering TV pictures could be used to subliminally convey changes in mood.* ◇ **Subliminal** is also used to talk about other ways of influencing people's minds without them being aware of it. *...the subliminal messages we all receive through the media, advertising and films.*

submarine A **submarine** is a ship which can travel either on or beneath the surface of the sea.

submerge (submerging, submerged) ❏ When something like a submarine or a whale **submerges,** it goes beneath the surface of the sea.

❏ If something is **submerged,** it is completely covered by water. ◇ If you are **submerged** by something that happens, you are overwhelmed by it. *The party would then be submerged by events over which it has already lost control.*

❏ If people **submerge** their differences, they reach agreement over something they had previously disagreed about. ◇ If you **submerge** yourself in something, you give all your time and attention to it. *Momma submerged herself in her social life again.*

submersible A **submersible** is a small submarine designed and equipped for underwater research at depths which a diver cannot reach. ◇ **Submersible** equipment is designed so that it can be used under water.

submission See **submit**.

submissive (submissively) If someone is **submissive**, they are quiet and obedient. *The manufacturers finally bowed submissively to the demands of the consumer.*

submit (submitting, submitted; submission) ❑ If you **submit** to something, you accept it because you are not powerful enough to resist it. You can talk about your **submission** to something. *Opponents have been terrified into submission.*

❑ If you **submit** something like a proposal or application to someone, you send it to them so they can decide what action to take. *The trustees would have to prepare detailed accounts for submission to the Department of Trade and Industry.*

subordinate (subordinating, subordinated; subordination) ❑ A person's **subordinates** are people in a lower position in the organization they work for. *He inspires limitless loyalty among his subordinates.* ◇ If someone is **subordinated** to someone else, they are brought under their authority or control. *The president wants the central administration to be directly subordinated to him.*

❑ If you **subordinate** something to something else, you treat it as less important. *...the subordination of economic goals to political ones.* ◇ **Subordinate** is used to describe something which is less important than something else. *...a subordinate role.*

suborn If someone is **suborned**, they are bribed or enticed to do something wrong. *Criminals have suborned the country's politicians.*

subpoena (pron: sub-pee-na) (subpoenaing, subpoenaed) A **subpoena** is a document ordering a person to attend a court as a witness or to make evidence available to the court. If someone is **subpoenaed**, they are issued with a subpoena. Similarly, something like evidence can be **subpoenaed**. *Already they have subpoenaed records from banking regulators.*

subscribe (subscribing, subscribed; subscriber, subscription) ❑ If you **subscribe** to a belief or opinion, you support it or agree with it. *The family still subscribes to the idea of arranged marriages.*

❑ If you **subscribe** to a magazine or newspaper or are one of its **subscribers**, you pay to receive it regularly. Similarly, you can **subscribe** to a service. *...cable telephone subscribers.* The amount of money you pay regularly for a magazine, newspaper, or service is called your **subscription**. ◇ If you **subscribe** to something like a charity or political party or are one of its **subscribers**, you support it by sending it money regularly; the money is called your **subscription**. ◇ Your **subscription** to a club or society is the money you pay regularly to be a member.

❑ When a company's shares are open for **subscription**, you can make an offer to buy them. Making an offer like this is called **subscribing** for shares.

subsequent (subsequently) You use **subsequent** to describe something which happens or comes into being later than something else. *The candidate got 82 votes, and subsequently became Mrs Thatcher's deputy.*

subservient (subservience) ❑ If someone is **subservient**, they do whatever someone else wants them to. When

someone behaves like this, you talk about their **subservience**.

❑ If something is **subservient** to something else, it is controlled or heavily influenced by it. *The game has become increasingly subservient to the demands of marketing and sponsorship.*

subside (subsiding, subsided; subsidence) If water **subsides**, it sinks to a lower level. *The flood waters have subsided.* ◇ If the ground **subsides**, parts of it sink. When this happens, you say there is **subsidence** (pron: sub-sid-dense). ◇ You talk about other kinds of things **subsiding** when they become less intense. *It took six hours before the pain subsided... The fighting subsided, but never stopped.*

subsidiarity In the EU, **subsidiarity** is the principle of allowing individual member states to make decisions on issues which specifically affect them, rather than leaving those decisions to the European Commission.

subsidiary (subsidiaries) ❑ A **subsidiary** or subsidiary company is part of a larger company.

❑ **Subsidiary** is used to describe something which is less important than something else it is connected with. *In addition to the principal crops, the tenants produced subsidiary crops which belonged entirely to them.*

subsidize (subsidizing, subsidized; subsidization) (can be spelled with an 's' instead of a 'z') If a government or other authority **subsidizes** a service, they make it cheaper for the public by paying part of the cost. *...subsidized housing.* ◇ If a government **subsidizes** an essential industry, it provides money to enable it to continue. Similarly, if a government **subsidizes** a certain area or a part of the community, it provides financial aid for it. *...the federal government's subsidization of poorer parts of the country.*

subsidy (subsidies) A **subsidy** is money paid by a government or other authority to help a company financially or to make something cheaper for the public.

subsist You say people **subsist** when they obtain just enough food to keep them alive. If they **subsist** on a certain kind of food, that is what keeps them alive. *Three-quarters of the islanders subsist on Madagascar's main crop, rice.* You can also say someone **subsists** on a certain income when they depend on it to obtain food and other necessities. *...subsisting on occasional freelance work.*

subsistence If someone lives at **subsistence** level, their income is barely enough to support them. ◇ **Subsistence** farms produce just enough food to support the people who live there, with no surplus left to sell.

subsoil The **subsoil** is a layer of rather infertile soil lying between the surface soil and the rock beneath.

subsonic speeds are very fast, but not as fast as the speed of sound. **Subsonic** aircraft fly at these speeds. See also **supersonic**.

substance ❑ Any solid, powder, liquid, or paste can be called a **substance**.

❑ If you say there is **substance** to what someone says, you mean they are saying something meaningful and important. *Persuading the public that the Citizen's Charter has real substance is high on the list of government priorities... There seems some substance to the opposition's grievance.* ◇ The **substance** of what someone says is the main point they are making.

❑ A person of **substance** is someone with a lot of money, power, and influence.

substandard See sub-standard.

substantial (substantially) A **substantial** amount or change is a very large one. *...a substantial increase in funding... ...substantial progress in talks to end the war... Supplies of gas have been substantially reduced.* ◇ **Substantial** is also used to describe things which are large and very solid or strong. *...a substantial meal... ...substantial Victorian houses.*

substantiate (substantiating, substantiated; substantiation) If you **substantiate** a statement or story, you provide evidence to prove it is true. *The advertisement was rebuked for claiming without substantiation that British drinking water meets World Health Organisation standards.*

substantive is used to describe things which have real importance or significance. *...substantive progress... Our goal has been to reach agreement on the major substantive issues by the time of the summit meeting.*

substitute (substituting, substituted; substitution) ❑ If you **substitute** one thing for another, you use it instead of the other thing. *...the substitution of machinery for human labour.* ◇ If you **substitute** one object for another, you remove the second object and put the first object in its place. ◇ A **substitute** is something you have or use instead of something you had previously, or instead of something you would prefer to have. *This oil could be used as a direct substitute for diesel.* ◇ If you say one thing is **no substitute** for another or is a **poor substitute** for it, you mean it cannot be used satisfactorily instead of it. *Trial and error is no substitute for thinking and planning.*

❑ In sport, a **substitute** is a player who comes on to replace another team member who is injured or withdrawn during a match. When this happens, you say the team makes a **substitution**.

substructure The substructure of a large structure like a bridge is its foundations or framework. ◇ A **substructure** is also part of some other kind of structure, for example part of a large organization.

subsume (subsuming, subsumed) If something is **subsumed** into something else, it becomes a part of it and is no longer a separate thing. *The two alliances might be subsumed into a new European security system.*

subterfuge is deceiving people to get something you want. A **subterfuge** is a trick or deception.

subterranean is used to talk about things under the ground. *...a subterranean labyrinth of rivers and caverns.*

subtext When people talk about the subtext of a piece of writing or a film, they are suggesting that it has an underlying subject or message. *There was always an erotic subtext to the Dracula films.*

subtitle (subtitling, subtitled) ❑ The subtitle of something like a book or film is a second title, which is often longer and explains more than the main title. When a book or film has a subtitle, you can say it is **subtitled** in a certain way. *Ken Hom's recent book, Fragrant Harbour Taste, is subtitled 'The New Chinese Cooking of Hong Kong'.*

❑ In the cinema, **subtitles** are a printed translation appearing at the bottom of the screen when a foreign film is shown. When a film is shown with subtitles, you say it is **subtitled**. ◇ **Subtitles** are also a printed display at the bot-

tom of a TV screen, shown for people with hearing difficulties. You say programmes which have this display are **subtitled**.

subtle (*pron:* sut-tl) (subtly; subtlety, subtleties) ❑ **Subtle** is used to describe changes or differences which are so slight they are not easy to notice, although they may be important or significant. *...subtle changes in the earth's environment... The unification of Germany changes the relationship subtly but unmistakably.* Changes and differences like these are sometimes called **subtleties**; the ability to recognize and deal with them is called **subtlety**. *The subtlety of the referee's decision was lost on the Leeds fans.*

❑ A **subtle** book is cleverly written and needs to be thought about to be appreciated properly. Similarly, you can talk about **subtle** humour or a **subtle** performance in the theatre. You can talk about the **subtlety** of any of these things. *French and Saunders' anarchic humour is executed with subtlety and observation.*

❑ You say a person is **subtle** or talk about their **subtlety** when they use clever indirect methods to achieve something. *The party has subtly exploited the workers' fear of private ownership.*

❑ **Subtle** is sometimes used to describe things which are delicate or faint. *...subtle oriental flavours... ...subtly-lit supermarkets.*

subtract (subtraction) If you **subtract** one number from another, you take the first one away from the second. For example, if you subtract 3 from 5, you get 2. Subtracting numbers is called **subtraction**.

subtropical See sub-tropical.

suburb (suburban, suburbanite) The **suburbs** of a town or city are residential areas which are close to its boundaries and away from its centre. **Suburban** is used to talk about things to do with a town's or city's suburbs. *...quiet suburban houses.* People who live in suburbs are sometimes called **suburbanites**.

suburbanization (*or* suburbanisation) is a process in which more and more housing is built in an area next to a town or city until the area gradually becomes one of the town's or city's suburbs.

suburbia A city's suburbs are sometimes called **suburbia**.

subvention or a **subvention** is a grant or subsidy from a government or other authority.

subversive (subversion) **Subversive** activities are aimed at weakening or destroying a political system or government. Activities like these are called **subversion**; the people taking part in them are sometimes called **subversives**.

subvert If someone **subverts** something, they undermine it or make it fail. *The president was subverting the national interest to ensure his own political survival.*

subway A subway is a passage for pedestrians underneath a busy road. ◇ In the US, a **subway** is an underground railway.

succeed ❑ If you **succeed** in doing something, you manage to do it. ◇ If something **succeeds**, it has the result you want, or it works in a satisfactory way. ◇ You can say someone **succeeds** when they do well in their life.

❑ If you **succeed** another person, you have their job after them. *He is being succeeded at the Welsh office by David Hunt.* ◇ When someone **succeeds** to the throne, they become the next monarch, following the death or abdication of the previous monarch.

❏ If one thing **succeeds** another, it comes after it. *A golden age of TV which began around 1960 has been succeeded by something less wholesome.*

success (successes) ❏ **Success** or a **success** is achieving something you have been trying to achieve. *They have stressed their commitment to the success of the talks... She has had many successes in minor tournaments.* ◇ If you are a **success** at something like your job, you do it very well.

❏ If something like an event or a new product is a **success**, it is very popular and makes a lot of money. You can also say something is a **success story**. *Warwick Castle has become one of the success stories of British 'heritage' tourism.*

successful (successfully) ❏ If you are **successful**, you achieve what you have set out to do. ◇ If an attempt to do something is **successful**, it succeeds. *Bone-marrow cells could be successfully transplanted.*

❏ If something like an event or a new product is **successful**, it is very popular and makes a lot of money.

❏ A **successful** person has had a good career, achieved an important position, or become famous or rich.

succession ❏ A **succession** of people or things is a number of them coming one after the other. *The country was ruled by a succession of military leaders.* ◇ If something happens, for example, for a number of weeks **in succession**, it happens each week for that number of weeks. *GCSE examination results have improved for the fifth year in succession.*

❏ When someone takes over a position according to some recognized procedure, you can call this their **succession** to it. *...James Callaghan's succession to the premiership.* ◇ When people talk about the **succession** to the throne, they mean the people who are entitled to succeed to it, in a particular order.

successive (successively) **Successive** is used to talk about people or things coming one after another. *During his 34 years with the company he served under ten successive chairmen... Macedonia was successively colonised by Greeks, Bulgarians and Serbs.*

successor Someone's **successor** is the person who takes over their job after them. ◇ The **successor** to something is the thing which replaces it. *Several leading aircraft manufacturers are examining the feasibility of a supersonic successor to Concorde.*

succinct (*pron:* suk-sinkt) (succinctly) If something like a statement or an order is **succinct**, it is expressed clearly and in very few words. *The sign by the rickety wooden jetty sums it up succinctly: Welcome To Isolation.*

succour (*American spelling:* succor) (*pron:* suk-kur) If you give **succour** to someone, you give them your help or support.

succulent food is juicy and delicious.

succumb If you **succumb** to something like persuasion or temptation, you give in to it. ◇ If you **succumb** to something like an illness or injury, you are badly affected by it. *He managed to bowl only two overs before succumbing to a groin injury.* You also say someone **succumbs** to an illness or disease when they die from it. *Two of them have succumbed to Aids.*

such ❏ You use **such** to talk about things of the kind you have just mentioned. *His members are voting on a strike.*

British Coal warned miners that such action would result in the loss of redundancy payments.

❏ You use **no such** to say something of a certain kind does not exist. *There are no such things as vampires.*

❏ You use **such as** when you are giving an example of something. *...contemporary painters, such as David Hockney.*

❏ You use **such** to emphasize your description of something. *It seemed such a good idea... It's all been such fun.*

❏ You use **such and such** to talk about a particular thing of a certain kind, without saying which one. *There was no information that between such and such a time, something was going to happen... He can find 25 reasons why such and such a proposal is rubbish.*

❏ You say **such as it is** to show you think something is not very good or not very significant. *His help, such as it was, won more American aid... The evils of science, such as they are, are considerably less than the evils of the alternatives.*

suchlike means other things like the ones just mentioned. *...mince, barbecue kebabs and suchlike.*

suck ❏ If you **suck** something, you draw liquid from it into your mouth. ◇ If you **suck** something like a sweet, you hold it in your mouth, taste it with your tongue, and let it dissolve without chewing it.

❏ If something is **sucked** somewhere, it is drawn there by a powerful force. *About 170 birds a year are sucked into aircraft engines.* ◇ If you are **sucked** into a situation, you are unable to stop yourself becoming involved in it. *The American people would not stand for being sucked into a civil conflict without an obvious end in sight.*

❏ If a person **sucks up** to someone in a position of authority, they try to please them by flattering them or doing things for them.

sucker ❏ If you call someone a **sucker**, you mean they are easily cheated, because they believe anything they are told. ◇ If you say you are a **sucker** for something, you mean you enjoy it very much and find it difficult to resist. *I'm a sucker for anything sung in either French or Japanese.*

❏ A **sucker** is a rubber device which can attach itself to a surface by suction. ◇ Some animals and insects have pads called **suckers** on their bodies which they use to cling to a surface.

suckle (suckling, suckled) When a mother **suckles** her baby, she feeds it with milk from her breast. All female mammals **suckle** their young with milk from their bodies. You can also say babies or young animals **suckle**. A **suckling** is a young animal still feeding on milk from its mother.

sucrose (*pron:* syoo-kroze) is sugar in crystalline form extracted from sugar cane or sugar beet.

suction is the force involved when a substance is drawn or sucked from one place to another. ◇ **Suction** is also the process by which two surfaces stick together when the air between them is removed.

sudden (suddenly, suddenness) You use **sudden** to describe things which happen quickly and unexpectedly. *...a sudden rise in house prices... When the war began, life suddenly became harsh... The car came to a halt with a suddenness that sent her jerking forward.* ◇ If something happens **all of a sudden**, it happens so quickly and unexpectedly that you are surprised by it.

sudden-death In sporting competitions, a **sudden-death**

play-off is an extra game between two people or teams who have finished with an equal score. In the play-off, the first person or team to take the lead is the winner.

sudden infant death syndrome See SIDS.

suds are the bubbles produced when soap is mixed with water.

sue (suing, sued) If you **sue** someone, you start a legal case against them, to claim money from them because they have harmed you in some way. ◇ If someone **sues** for something, they formally ask for it. *He may hope to fight for a while, then stop and sue for peace... He sued for custody of the three children.*

suede (*pron*: swade) is thin soft leather with a raised velvet-like surface.

suet is hard fat from around the kidneys and loins of an animal, grated and used in cooking.

suffer (suffering, suffered; sufferer) ❑ If someone **suffers** pain or an illness, they are affected by it. You can also say someone is a **sufferer** from pain or an illness. *...treatments which relieve suffering... ...cancer sufferers.* ◇ You can also talk about people **suffering** from other things, such as poverty or oppression.

  ❑ You say something **suffers** when it is badly affected by neglect or an unfavourable situation. *Sales to industry suffered because of recession.*

  ❑ If you say someone **does not suffer fools gladly**, you mean they have no patience with people who say or do unintelligent things.

sufferance If you let someone do something **on sufferance**, you let them do it although you would rather they did not.

suffice (sufficing, sufficed) ❑ If you say something will **suffice**, you mean it is enough for what you want.

  ❑ **Suffice it to say...** at the beginning of a statement means what you are saying is enough to explain your meaning or prove your argument, although you could say much more. *It would not be appropriate for me to make a statement at this point. Suffice it to say that my beliefs and principles have left me increasingly uneasy with certain recent political trends.*

sufficient (sufficiently; sufficiency) **Sufficient** is used to say there is enough of something. You can also say there is a **sufficiency** of it. *In many areas the facilities are not sufficient to meet demand... The video evidence is not sufficiently strong.*

suffix (suffixes) A **suffix** is a group of letters added at the end of a word to make a new word with a different meaning. For example, the suffix '-ist' can be added to 'sex' to form the word 'sexist'.

suffocate (suffocating, suffocates; suffocation) ❑ If someone **suffocates**, they die because they have too little air to breathe. You can also say they die of **suffocation**. ◇ You can say you are **suffocating** when you feel as if you cannot breathe properly, for example in a hot and crowded room. **Suffocating** is used to describe situations like this. *During the summer the heat was suffocating.*

  ❑ You also say people are **suffocated** when they are prevented from developing properly. *Suffocated by male prejudice, the women have no opportunity to fulfill their potential... They have just escaped from the suffocation of the English class system.*

suffragan (*pron*: suff-rag-gan) A **suffragan** or **suffragan**

bishop is a bishop appointed to assist an archbishop or another bishop.

suffrage is used to say which people have the right to vote for a government or national leader. For example, if there is male **suffrage**, only men have the right to vote. If there is universal **suffrage**, everyone has the right to vote.

suffragette A suffragette was a woman involved in the campaign to get women the right to vote.

suffuse (suffusing, suffused) If something is **suffused** with light or colour, the light or colour is spread over it or through it. Similarly, you can talk about an experience or piece of writing being **suffused** with a certain feeling. *The book is suffused with sadness.*

sugar (sugaring, sugared) Sugar is a substance, often in the form of white crystals, used to sweeten food and drink. If you **sugar** a drink, you add sugar to it. ◇ **sugar the pill**: see pill. ◇ The **sugar** in a person's blood is the glucose circulating in it. In medicine, it is called **blood sugar**. See also diabetes.

sugar beet is a plant with a large white parsnip-shaped root which sugar is obtained from.

sugar cane is a very tall tropical plant with thick stems. Sugar is obtained from its sap.

sugar daddy A sugar daddy is an older man who gives money and presents to a young woman, in return for her companionship or sexual favours.

sugar lump A sugar lump is a small cube of sugar, for putting in tea or coffee.

sugary food and drinks contain a lot of sugar.

  ❑ **Sugary** is also used to describe things which are unpleasantly sweet or sentimental. *...sugary images of women as happy housewives.*

suggest ❑ If you **suggest** a plan or idea to someone, you mention it as a possibility for them to consider.

  ❑ If something **suggests** something is true or will happen, it makes you think it is true or will happen. *Opinion polls are suggesting a close race between the leading contenders.*

suggestible (suggestibility) A **suggestible** person is easily influenced by what other people say. *People with exaggerated suggestibility or fear of authority are most likely to confess falsely.*

suggestion ❑ A **suggestion** is a plan or idea mentioned as a possibility for someone to consider.

  ❑ If you say there is a **suggestion** of something, you mean there is a slight indication or faint sign of it. *...suggestions of woodsmoke... There was no suggestion of yellowness in the blooms.*

suggestive (suggestively, suggestiveness) If one thing is **suggestive** of another, it makes you think of it. *The clink of ice in tall glasses is one of the happiest sounds of summer, suggestive of hot sunny days.* ◇ **Suggestive** remarks or gestures make people think about sex. *...pictures of a sexually suggestive nature... She winked suggestively... ...saucy suggestiveness.*

suicide (suicidal, suicidally) ❑ People who commit **suicide** deliberately kill themselves. If you say people are **suicidal**, you mean they want to kill themselves. ◇ **Suicidal** behaviour is so dangerous it is likely to result in death. *One eye-witness said that people have confronted the army in what he described as a suicidal way.* ◇ A **suicide** attack is made by someone who expects to die in their attempt to inflict death or destruction on an enemy.

❏ You can also say someone's behaviour is **suicide** or **suicidal** when they do something which is likely to ruin their career or bring about the end of their organization. *Accepting the conditions was political suicide... Foolish banks offered suicidally generous terms to risky borrowers.*

suit (suiting, suited) ❏ A man's **suit** is a matching jacket and trousers, sometimes with a matching waistcoat as well. A woman's **suit** is usually a matching jacket and skirt. A **trouser suit** is a matching jacket and trousers for a woman. ◇ Other sets of clothing worn for a particular purpose are called **suits**, for example a boiler suit or a space suit.

❏ If you say something **suits** you, you mean it is convenient, acceptable, or right for you. *The job couldn't have suited me better.* ◇ If you say a piece of clothing or a certain style or colour **suits** someone, you mean it makes them look attractive.

❏ If you say someone or something is **suited** for a certain thing, you mean they are right or appropriate for it. *The new tank is ideally suited to desert warfare.* ◇ If you say people are **suited** to each other, you mean they are likely to get on well because they have similar interests and personalities. *They appear a most ideally suited couple.*

❏ If you do something to **suit** yourself, you do it for your own benefit, without considering other people.

❏ A **suit** is also a legal action taken by one person against another.

❏ A **suit** is also one of the four types of card in a set of playing cards. The four suits are hearts, diamonds, clubs, and spades. If someone **follows suit** in a card game, they play a card of the same suit as the previous player.

❏ You also say someone **follows suit** when they do something which someone else has just done. *The Bank of England yesterday reduced interest rates to 11%. High street banks and building societies immediately followed suit.*

❏ A person's **strong suit** or **strongest suit** is the thing they are best at. *Logic is not always a politician's strongest suit.*

suitable (suitably, suitability) If someone or something is **suitable** for a certain purpose or occasion, they are just right or appropriate for it. *...suitably qualified people to fill the senior posts... ...assessing the suitability of accommodation for the needs of a homeless person.*

suitcase A **suitcase** is a portable rectangular case for carrying your clothes when you are travelling.

suite (pron: sweet) ❏ A **suite** is a set of rooms, for example in a hotel. See also **en suite.** ◇ A **suite** is also a set of matching furniture or bathroom fittings. *...three-piece suites.*

❏ A **suite** is also a piece of music, made up of several short pieces.

suitor In the past, a man who was courting a woman and hoped to marry her was called her **suitor.** ◇ Nowadays, a person or organization hoping to take over a company is sometimes called a **suitor.** *Other obvious suitors for STC include Northern Telecom and Siemens.*

sulfate See **sulphate.**

sulfur (sulfurous) See **sulphur.**

sulk (sulky, sulkily) If someone **sulks** or goes into a **sulk**, they are silent or bad-tempered for a while, because they are annoyed. When someone behaves like this,

you say they are being **sulky.** *Sulkily she did as she was told.*

sullen (sullenly) A **sullen** person is bad-tempered and does not speak much. *...staring sullenly from behind bars.*

sully (sullies, sullying, sullied) If someone **sullies** something, they spoil it or make it dirty. *The two teams had sullied the good name of football.*

sulphate (American spelling: **sulfate**) A **sulphate** is a chemical compound formed when sulphuric acid reacts with a metal.

sulphur (American spelling: **sulfur**) **Sulphur** is a chemical element which exists on its own in a yellow crystalline form and in various compounds.

sulphur dioxide is a colourless poisonous gas with a strong unpleasant smell. It is used as a preservative and in the manufacture of bleach, disinfectant, and sulphuric acid. Acid rain is caused by waste sulphur dioxide in the air.

sulphuric acid is a colourless oily highly corrosive acid.

sulphurous (American spelling: **sulfurous**) is used to describe things which contain sulphur or one of its compounds, especially things which have a strong unpleasant smell. *...black sulphurous smoke.*

sultan (sultanate) In some Muslim countries, the ruler is called a **sultan.** A country ruled by a sultan is called a **sultanate.** *...the Sultanate of Oman.*

sultana ❏ **Sultanas** are dried grapes.

❏ A **sultana** is also a female relative of a sultan, especially his wife.

sultanate See **sultan.**

sultry weather is unpleasantly hot and humid. ◇ A woman is described as **sultry** when she is attractive in a way which suggests hidden passion.

sum (summing, summed) ❏ A **sum** of money is an amount of it. *The country has already spent large sums on flood control... ...the sum of £20,000.*

❏ A **sum** is a simple calculation in arithmetic.

❏ If you talk about the **sum** of something, you mean all of it. *Liberalised divorce law has not, so far, resulted in a greater sum of human happiness.* ◇ The **sum total** of something is all its separate elements or parts added together or considered as a whole. ◇ See also **lump sum.**

❏ If you **sum** something **up,** you briefly describe its essential character. ◇ When a judge **sums up,** he or she makes a speech to the jury at the end of a trial, reminding them of the evidence and the main arguments they have heard. This is called the judge's **summing-up.**

summarize (summarizing, summarized) (can be spelled with an 's' instead of a 'z') If you **summarize** something, you give a brief description of its main points. *The survey will be summarized in a league table to be published early in the New Year.*

summary (summaries; summarily) ❏ A **summary** is a short account of something, giving the main points but not the details. *Here is a summary of the news.*

❏ A **summary** action is carried out without delay and without careful consideration. *...summary executions... His reform proposals had been summarily dismissed.*

summation ❏ A **summation** is the same as a summing-up. See **sum.**

❏ If you describe something you have produced as a **summation** of all your earlier work or experiences, you mean it is the result of everything you have learned from them. *Llosa's book is a summation of his career as a writer.*

summer is the season between spring and autumn. In the northern hemisphere, this is between June and September.

summer camp In the US, a **summer camp** is a place where children go on holiday together, usually without their parents, and take part in sporting activities.

summer school A **summer school** is an educational course on a particular subject run during the summer.

summer time is a period of time in the summer in some countries during which the clocks are put forward, so people can have extra daylight in the evening. See also BST.

summerhouse A **summerhouse** is a small building in a garden where you can sit in the shade.

summertime is the period of time when it is summer.

summery is used to describe things which are suitable for summer or typical of summer. *...a summery dish.*

summing-up See sum.

summit (summitry, summiteer) ❑ A **summit** is a meeting between the leaders of different countries. **Summitry** is conducting negotiations by meetings of this kind. The leaders taking part are sometimes called **summiteers.**
❑ The **summit** of a mountain is its top.

summon (summoning, summoned) ❑ If you are **summoned** somewhere, you are ordered to go there. ◇ If someone **summons** a meeting, they tell people to come to it.
❑ If you **summon** your strength or courage or **summon** it **up,** you make a great effort to be strong or brave.

summons (summonses, summonsed) A **summons** is an official order to appear in court. You say someone is **summonsed** to appear in court. ◇ A **summons** is also an order to go and see someone. *I received a summons to the Palace.*

sumo is a traditional Japanese style of wrestling, in which the contestants are very heavily built.

sump The **sump** is the place under an engine which holds the engine oil.

sumptuous (sumptuously, sumptuousness) **Sumptuous** is used to describe things which are splendid or luxurious and obviously expensive. *...a sumptuous buffet... ...a sumptuously comfortable car... ...the almost unbelievable sumptuousness of the luxury liners.*

sun (sunning, sunned) ❑ The **sun** is the star which the planet Earth revolves around. People often use **the sun** to talk about the heat and light from the sun. *...the bright Finnish sun and invigorating northern air.* ◇ If you **sun** yourself, you sit or lie where the sun shines on you.
❑ You say everything **under the sun** to emphasize that you are talking about a very large number of things. *I was accused of every crime under the sun.* ◇ **place in the sun:** see place.
❑ Any star which has planets revolving around it can be called a **sun.**

sun cream is the same as sunscreen.

sun-drenched places have a lot of hot sunny weather.

sun-kissed means the same as sun-drenched.

sun lamp (*or* sunlamp) A **sun lamp** is a lamp which produces ultraviolet rays, and which people use to make their skin look tanned. Some doctors think sun lamps are dangerous.

sun lounge A **sun lounge** is a room with walls made mostly of glass so that a lot of sunlight gets into the room.

sun lounger A **sun lounger** is a type of bed for sunbathing on.

sunbathe (sunbathing, sunbathed; sunbather) When people **sunbathe,** they lie in the sun to get a tan. A person who does this is called a **sunbather.**

sunbeam Sunbeams are rays of light from the sun.

sunbed A **sunbed** is (a) a sun lounger. (b) a bed-like structure with sun lamps above it which people lie on to get a tan.

Sunbelt The southern and south-western states of the US are sometimes called the **Sunbelt.**

sunblock is the same as sunscreen.

sunburn (sunburnt *or* sunburned) If you have **sunburn** or are **sunburnt,** your skin is red and sore because you have spent too much time in the sun. ◇ You also say someone is **sunburnt** when their skin has become permanently brown because they have spent a long period of their life in the sun.

sundae A **sundae** is a glass of ice cream with cream, nuts, a sweet sauce, and fruit on top.

Sunday school is a class organized by a church for children to go to on Sundays to learn about Christianity.

sundeck On a passenger ship, a **sundeck** is an open upper deck.

sundial A **sundial** is a device for telling the time. It consists of a fixed pointer in the middle of a flat base on which the hours of the day are marked. As the sun moves round, the shadow of the pointer also moves, indicating the time on the base.

sundown is an American word for sunset.

sundry things are of many different kinds. *...a small shop that supplied sundry items.* ◇ **All and sundry** means 'everyone'. *Contrary to popular belief, the business of banking is not open to all and sundry.*

sunflower Sunflowers are tall plants with very large daisy-like yellow flowers. The seeds are edible and are also used to make cooking oil.

sung See sing.

sunglasses are spectacles with dark lenses to protect your eyes from bright sunlight.

sunhat A **sunhat** is a hat which protects your head from the sun.

sunk See sink.

sunken is used to describe things which have sunk to the bottom of the sea, a lake, or a river. *...a sunken wreck.* ◇ **Sunken** is also used to describe things built below the level of the surrounding area. *...an old sunken garden.* ◇ If part of a person's face is **sunken,** it seems to sink or curve inwards and makes them look thin and unwell. *...his large, sunken eyes.*

sunlamp See sun lamp.

sunlight (sunlit) **Sunlight** is the light which reaches the Earth from the sun. If something is **sunlit,** it is brightly lit by the sun.

sunny (sunnier, sunniest) ❑ When it is **sunny,** the sun is shining. ◇ A **sunny** place is brightly lit by the sun.
❑ A **sunny** person is always cheerful.

sunrise is the time when the sun first appears above the horizon. A **sunrise** is the colours and light you see in the sky when this is happening.

sunroof A **sunroof** is a part of the roof of a car which you can open to let sunshine or air in.

sunscreen is a cream which helps stop you getting burned by the sun, by blocking out all or most of the ultraviolet rays.

sunset is the time when the sun goes down below the horizon. A **sunset** is the colours and light you see in the sky when this is happening.

sunshade A **sunshade** is a type of umbrella for protecting yourself from strong sunlight.

sunshine is the light and heat which comes from the sun.

sunspot Sunspots are temporary cooler areas which appear as dark patches on the sun's surface. They have a strong magnetic field.

sunstroke is an illness caused by spending too much time in very hot sunshine.

suntan (suntanned) If you have a **suntan** or are **suntanned**, the sun has turned your skin darker than usual. **Suntan** lotions, creams, and oils protect your skin from the sun and help you develop a suntan.

sup (supping, supped) If you **sup** something, you drink it.

super People say something is **super** when they are very pleased or excited by it. *There really are some super trains in India.*

super- is used to form words which describe something as having a quality to an unusually large degree. *...the super-cool world of rock journalism... ...a tiny super-rich state.* ◇ **Super-** is also used to form words which describe things as being bigger, more powerful, or more important than other things of their kind. *...super-computers... ...a centralised European super-state.*

superabundance If there is a **superabundance** of something, there is a very large amount of it, often more than is wanted or needed.

superannuated is used to describe people who no longer do the work they have done in the past, because they are too old for it. *...superannuated politicians.*

superannuation is money people pay regularly into a special fund so they will get a regular pension when they retire.

superb (superbly) If you say someone or something is **superb**, you mean they are very good indeed. *...superbly engineered cars.*

supercharged (supercharger) A **supercharged** engine has a device called a **supercharger** which increases the engine's power by forcing extra air in.

supercilious people are scornful of other people and think they are superior to them.

superconductor A **superconductor** is a substance which has almost no electrical resistance at temperatures close to absolute zero. Superconductors are used in making powerful electromagnets.

superficial (superficially, superficiality) ❑ If you describe something as **superficial** or talk about its **superficiality**, you mean it deals with only the most obvious or easily understood aspects of a subject. *We have seen a draft of the book and the analysis is very superficial.* ◇ **Superficial** people do not care very deeply about anything serious or important.

❑ **Superficial** is used to describe the first impression something gives, especially when this does not reflect what it is really like. *...the superficial appearance of calm... The situations in Angola and in Mozambique are superficially similar.*

❑ A **superficial** wound is not deep or severe.

superfluous (*pron:* soo-per-flew-uss) If something is **superfluous**, it is unnecessary or no longer needed.

supergrass (supergrasses) A **supergrass** is someone, especially a criminal, who gives the police a lot of information about the activities of terrorists or other criminals.

superhero (superheroes) A **superhero** is a comic strip character with superhuman abilities or magic powers who fights against evil.

superhighway In the US, a **superhighway** is a long-distance motorway which vehicles can travel along at high speeds. ◇ The **information superhighway** is the name given to the proposed worldwide communications network which will enable people to send and receive information by computer anywhere in the world, and to have access to a range of services via their TV sets.

superhuman is used to talk about a quality or ability someone has which is greater than that of ordinary people. *...his superhuman efficiency.*

superimpose (superimposing, superimposed) If one image is **superimposed** on another, the first one appears on top of the second.

superintend If you **superintend** an activity, you make sure it is carried out properly. You can also **superintend** the people doing it.

superintendent In the police force, a **superintendent** is an officer above the rank of inspector, but lower in rank than a **chief superintendent**. ◇ A **superintendent** is also someone who is officially responsible for an activity or department.

superior (superiority) ❑ **Superior** things are of higher quality than other things of their kind. *...a standard of education that is vastly superior to our own.* You talk about the **superiority** of things like these. ◇ **Superior** is also used to say one army is more powerful than another. *...the Warsaw Pact's hitherto massive superiority in conventional weaponry.*

❑ If someone is **superior** to you in an organization, they have a higher position than you. You call someone like this your **superior**.

❑ A **superior** person behaves in a way which shows that they believe they are better than other people. *...feelings of superiority.*

superlative (*pron:* soo-per-lat-iv) (superlatively) **Superlative** is used to describe things which are of the highest quality. *...superlative seafood... The Philharmonia played this difficult music superlatively well.* ◇ **Superlatives** are words which are used to say that a person or thing has more of a quality than anyone or anything else. For example, 'biggest', 'greatest', and 'most remarkable' are superlatives.

superman (supermen) If you call someone a **superman**, you mean they have extraordinary physical or mental powers.

supermarket A **supermarket** is a large shop selling many kinds of food and household goods.

supermodel Supermodels are highly-paid fashion models

who are very well-known to the public.

supernatural is used to describe things like ghosts which some people believe exist and which cannot be explained by normal scientific laws. *...supernatural powers.* Things like these are referred to as **the supernatural.**

supernova (*plural:* supernovae *or* supernovas) A **supernova** is a star which explodes and for a few days becomes much brighter than the sun.

superpower (superpowerdom) A **superpower** is a very powerful and influential country, especially one with nuclear weapons. **Superpowerdom** is being a superpower. *...a superpower summit... It is hard to imagine China achieving real nuclear superpowerdom until well into the next century.*

supersede (superseding, superseded) If one thing **supersedes** another, it replaces it, usually because it is better or more efficient.

supersonic aircraft can travel faster than the speed of sound.

superstar (superstardom) Very famous entertainers or sports players are sometimes called **superstars**. **Superstardom** is being a superstar. *The trio was on the brink of superstardom.*

superstition (superstitious) **Superstition** is belief in magic or in powers which bring good or bad luck. Beliefs like these are called **superstitions.** You say someone who has these beliefs is **superstitious.**

superstore A **superstore** is a very large supermarket, often selling things like clothes as well as household goods and food.

superstructure The **superstructure** of a ship is the part above the main deck.

supertanker A **supertanker** is a very large fast ship for transporting oil.

supervise (supervising, supervised; supervision) If you **supervise** an activity or the people doing it, you make sure it is done properly. *...internationally-supervised elections... A number of large financial firms are subject to supervision by two or more regulators.* If you do something **under supervision**, someone supervises you while you do it. A **supervisor** is someone who supervises activities or people, especially an employee who supervises workers or a tutor who supervises students.

supervisory is used to talk about things to do with supervising activities or people. *The inspectorate will retain only a supervisory role... ...the company's supervisory board.*

supine (*pron:* soo-pine) If you are **supine**, you are lying flat on your back. See also **prone.** ◇ **Supine** is also used to describe people who let things happen and do not try to influence them, because they are too lazy or afraid. *...their supine, order-taking mentality.*

supper is a meal eaten in the early part of the evening or just before going to bed.

supplant If one person or thing **supplants** another, they take their place. *Mixed forests of Douglas fir, cedar, spruce and oak are often supplanted by Douglas fir alone.*

supple (suppleness) A **supple** person moves and bends easily and gracefully. *The first exercises should aim at increasing the suppleness of the body.* ◇ If an object or material is **supple**, it is flexible and bends easily without cracking or breaking.

supplement (supplementary) ❑ If you **supplement** something, you add something else to it. The thing you add is called a **supplement**. *Lower-grade civil servants supplement their wages with other work... ...vitamin C supplements.* **Supplementary** things are added to other things. *...a supplementary budget.*

❑ A **supplement** is an extra amount of money you pay to get special facilities or services, for example when you are travelling or staying at a hotel. *...a high season supplement of £22 a person.*

❑ A newspaper or magazine **supplement** is a separate part which comes with a newspaper or magazine, often covering a particular range of subjects. See also **colour supplement.**

supplemental means the same as supplementary. *...supplemental legislation.*

supplementary See supplement.

supplementary benefit was an amount of money which people with a very low income or no income at all used to be able to claim from the government. It was replaced by income support in 1988.

supplication (supplicant) **Supplication** is humbly asking or pleading for something. A person who does this is called a **supplicant.**

supplier A **supplier** is a person, company, or country that supplies something. *The United Arab Emirates is Japan's main oil supplier.*

supply (supplies, supplying, supplied) ❑ If you **supply** someone with something, you provide them with it, by giving or selling it to them. *Moscow says it will supply no more weapons to Iraq... Three keys are supplied with each kit.* When something is being supplied, you call this the **supply** of it. *...a ban on the sale and supply of arms.* A **supply** of something is an amount which is being supplied. *Supplies of cheap oil and gas had been reduced... During a stroke the blood supply to the brain becomes disrupted.*

❑ **Supply** is the amount of a commodity which can be produced and made available for people to buy. *As lower interest rates boost demand for money, supply will increase.* ◇ If something is in **short supply**, it is hard to get because there is very little of it.

❑ **Supplies** are food, equipment, and other things needed by a group of people over a period of time, for example people going on an expedition.

supply-side economics is the economic theory that if taxation is reduced, the money people and businesses will save will be reinvested into industry and boost the economy.

supply teacher A **supply teacher** is a teacher who stands in for other teachers at different schools when they are absent.

support (supporting) ❑ If you **support** a political party, you want them to succeed, and you vote for them at elections. Similarly, you can **support** an individual in a contest for a political post. You can talk about people's **support** for a party or an individual. *Support for the Christian Democrats slumped.*

❑ If you **support** someone who is trying to do something or give them your **support**, you help them in a practical way. *The reservists will give medical support to the British forces.*

❑ If you give **support** to someone during a difficult time, you are kind to them and help them.

❑ If you **support** a sports team, you go regularly to

their games and cheer them on.

❑ In a play or film, the **supporting** actors and actresses are the ones who do not play the main parts.

❑ If something **supports** an object, it is underneath it and holding it up. Something which does this is called a **support**. *The structure of the roof is supported by tubular steel columns.* ◇ If you **support** yourself on something, you prevent yourself from falling by holding onto it. *I saw her at the door of her bungalow supporting herself on sticks.*

❑ If you **support** someone or something, you provide them with money or the things they need. *Fortunately my parents were still supporting me... The service will be free, but supported by advertising.* ◇ **Support** is money provided to enable a person to live, or an organization to continue. *He told ministers that selective support for the construction industry is vital to Britain's recovery from recession.*

❑ If the land in a place **supports** the people or wildlife there, it provides them with the food they need to live.

❑ If a fact **supports** a statement or theory, it helps to show it is true or correct. *Opposition leaders presented documents to support accusations of government corruption.*

support group A **support group** is (a) an organization formed to help and counsel people with a particular problem. *...an AIDS support group.* (b) a local organization formed to raise funds for a charity or political party.

supporter A **supporter** is someone who supports something, for example a political party or a sports team. *...a Leeds United supporter.*

supportive If you are **supportive,** you are kind and helpful to someone at a difficult time. ◇ If you are **support-ive** of someone or their aims, you show your support for them. *Washington and Tokyo both put out statements that were highly supportive of Baltic independence.*

suppose (supposing, supposed; supposedly) ❑ If you **suppose** something is true, you think it is true. *It is a fallacy to suppose that a single currency implies political union and loss of national identity.* ◇ If something is **supposed** to be true, people generally think it is true. *There are supposed to be large amounts of oil underneath the Gobi Desert.*

❑ **Supposed** and **supposedly** are used to show doubt about a way of describing someone or something, or about the truth of something. *Fewer and fewer of his supposed allies stick up for him in public... ...the supposed 'benefits' of higher interest rates... ...supposedly accidental deaths.*

❑ If something is **supposed** to be done, it should be done, because of a rule, instruction, or custom. *They've given us notice to quit – we're supposed to be out by 22nd March.* ◇ If something is **supposed** to happen, it is planned or intended to happen. *The first shipment of this fuel is supposed to be ready for sea transportation on Friday.* If you say something **was supposed** to happen, you mean it was planned or intended to happen, but did not in fact happen. *...a new truck factory which was supposed to have been built near Berlin.*

❑ You say **suppose** and **supposing** when you are considering a possible situation or action and trying to think what effects it would have. *Supposing, against the odds, that Mr Fujimori does win back his lost popularity, the November elections could produce an assembly strongly in his favour.*

supposition is taking certain things to be true, often without any real evidence. *Much of the report was based on supposition or inaccuracy.* A **supposition** is something which is taken to be true. *There's a popular supposition that we're publicly funded, but the bulk of our money comes from competitive contracts.*

suppository (suppositories) A **suppository** is a solid medicine inserted into the rectum or vagina, where it melts.

suppress (suppresses, suppressed; suppression, suppressor) ❑ If people in authority **suppress** an activity, they stop it continuing. *...the suppression of religious institutions.* ◇ If information is **suppressed,** people are prevented from hearing about it.

❑ If you **suppress** your feelings, you do not express them. *...suppressed jealousy.* ◇ If something like a drug **suppresses** a disease, it stops it developing. Drugs which have this effect are called **suppressor** drugs.

suppurate (suppurating, suppurated) When a wound **suppurates,** it produces pus.

supranational (supranationalism) (or supra-national, supra-nationalism) **Supranational** is used to describe things which cross national borders and involve more than one country. **Supranationalism** is the setting up of systems and organizations which involve more than one country. *...supranational institutions.*

supremacist A **supremacist** is someone who believes that a particular group of people should be more powerful and have more influence than other groups. *...white supremacists... ...Hindu supremacists.*

supremacy If one group of people has **supremacy** over another, they are more powerful and can therefore control or defeat them. ◇ If one law or instruction has **supremacy** over another, the first one must be obeyed rather than the second.

supreme is used in a title to show that a person or group is at the highest level of an organization. *...NATO's Supreme Allied Commander in Europe... ...the Supreme Court.*

❑ **Supreme** also means the greatest possible. *He showed supreme confidence... ...the supreme importance of education for creating a civilised society.*

supremely means 'extremely'. *...their supremely happy marriage.*

supremo (supremos) A **supremo** is someone who has overall charge of something. *...China's economic supremo.*

surcharge (surcharging, surcharged) A **surcharge** is an extra amount of money paid in addition to the usual payment for something. *...an import surcharge.* If you are **surcharged,** you have to pay a surcharge.

sure (surer, surest; sureness) ❑ If you are **sure** something is true, you are certain it is true and have no doubt about it. ◇ If you are **sure** about your feelings or wishes, you know exactly what you feel or want.

❑ If you are **sure** of getting something, you are certain to get it. ◇ If you say something is **sure** to happen, you mean it will definitely happen. ◇ If you say something is **for sure** or that you know it **for sure,** you mean it is definitely true or will definitely happen. *It's not known for sure why seals leave the water in great numbers.*

❑ If you **make sure** something happens or is done, you take action to see that it happens or is done.

❑ You say **sure enough** when you are saying something has happened which could be expected to happen in the circumstances you have described. *People are taping music for free. Sure enough, sales of recorded music per head in Japan are 50% lower than in America, where CD rental is illegal.*

❑ If you are **sure** of yourself, you are very confident about your abilities or opinions. ◇ **Sure** is used to talk about someone's ability to judge situations well and do things without making mistakes. *...his sure touch... ...the sureness and composure of Chelsea's performance.*

❑ A **sure** way of doing something can be relied on to succeed. ◇ If you say something is a **sure** sign of a certain thing, you mean it shows for certain that thing exists or is happening. *The Treasury claims that the figures are a sure sign of the government's policy of high-interest rates leading to a slowdown in spending.*

sure-fire is used to describe things which are certain to succeed. *...a sure-fire hit.*

sure-footed people or animals can move easily over steep or uneven ground without falling. Similarly, you can say someone is **sure-footed** when they handle a difficult situation well without making mistakes.

surely ❑ You say **surely** when you are making a point in an emphatic way and are expressing surprise that nobody has made the same point before or that anybody might take a different view. *Surely such weighty matters merit a higher level of debate?*

❑ If something is happening **slowly but surely**, it is only happening gradually but seems likely to continue.

surety (sureties) A **surety** is something valuable, especially money, given as a guarantee that you or someone else will do a particular thing.

surf (surfing, surfer) **Surf** is the white foam formed by waves as they break near the shore. ◇ **Surfing** is the sport of riding towards the shore on the crest of a wave by standing or lying on a long narrow board called a **surfboard**. If you **surf**, you ride on a board like this; people who surf are called **surfers.**

surface (surfacing, surfaced) ❑ The **surface** of an area of land or water is its top part. ◇ When something like a submarine **surfaces**, it comes up to the surface of the water.

❑ **Surface** is used to talk about methods of transport which involve travel across land or sea, rather than by air. *...surface mail.*

❑ A **surface** is a flat area, for example the top of a table, where you can work or do a particular job. ◇ The **surface** or **surfaces** of a solid object are its outside parts.

❑ The aspects of a situation which can easily be seen are called the **surface**. You talk, for example, about things being 'on the surface' or 'beneath the surface'. *Fear of political violence is never far from the surface in Turkey... The incident was a sign of the emotion, even hatred, that lies just below the surface in this campaign.*

❑ If information **surfaces** or **comes to the surface**, it becomes known. If feelings **surface** or **come to the surface**, people start to show them.

surface-to-air missiles are fired from the land or sea at aircraft or other missiles.

surface-to-surface missiles are fired from the land or sea at targets on the ground or at sea.

surfboard See **surf.**

surfeit (*pron:* sur-fit) If there is a **surfeit** of something, there is too much of it.

surfing (surfer) See **surf.**

surge (surging, surged) If something **surges** or there is a **surge** in it, there is a sudden large increase in it. *Car ex-ports have surged by 47% over the past year.* ◇ If people or vehicles **surge** somewhere, they move forward suddenly and powerfully in a mass. Similarly, if water **surges**, it moves forward suddenly and powerfully. ◇ If someone **surges ahead** in a contest, they quickly move into a leading position.

surgeon A **surgeon** is a doctor who performs surgery.

surgery (surgeries) ❑ **Surgery** is medical treatment which involves cutting open a person's body to repair or remove a diseased or damaged part. ◇ **cosmetic surgery:** see **cosmetic.** ◇ See also **plastic surgery.**

❑ A **surgery** is the room or building where a doctor or dentist works. ◇ A doctor's **surgery** is also the time each day when he or she sees patients at the surgery. Similarly, an MP's **surgery** is a regular time when constituents can visit him or her to discuss their problems.

surgical (surgically) ❑ **Surgical** is used to talk about things to do with surgery. *...new surgical techniques... Doctors can often surgically remove the primary tumour.*

❑ **Surgical** military actions are designed to attack or destroy a military target without harming civilians or damaging nearby buildings. *...surgical strikes to knock out the principal artillery positions.*

surgical spirit is a liquid made from methylated spirit and other chemicals. It is used for sterilizing and cleaning.

surly (surliness) If you say someone is **surly** or talk about their **surliness**, you mean they are rude and bad-tempered.

surmise (surmising, surmised) If you **surmise** that something is true, you decide it must be true because of other things you know.

surmount ❑ If you **surmount** a difficulty, you deal with it successfully.

❑ If one thing is **surmounted** by another, the second thing is on top of the first. *...a slim square tower surmounted by a cross.*

surname Your **surname** is the name you share with other members of your family.

surpass (surpasses, surpassing, surpassed) ❑ If someone or something **surpasses** another person or thing, they are better than them or have more of a particular quality. *In the late Eighties, the pharmaceutical industry became the UK's fastest growing high-technology industry, surpassing even electrical engineering.* ◇ If you **surpass** yourself, you do better at something than you have ever done before.

❑ If something **surpasses** expectations, it is even better than it was expected to be.

surplice A **surplice** is a loose white knee-length garment worn by some priests over a cassock. Church officials and choir members also wear surplices during services in some churches.

surplus (surpluses) ❑ If there is a **surplus** of something, there is more than is needed. **Surplus** is used to describe amounts of something which are left over because there is more than is needed. *The EU dumps surplus food on world markets.*

❑ If a country has a trade **surplus**, it exports more than it imports. ◇ If a government has a budget **surplus**, it received more in revenues than it has spent.

surprise (surprising, surprised; surprisingly) ❑ A **surprise** is an unexpected event. When something happens unexpectedly, you can say it **comes as a surprise.** ◇ **Surprise** is used to describe things which are unexpected. *Sri Lanka opened the tournament with a surprise victory over India.*

❑ **Surprise** is the feeling you have when something unexpected happens. You say something like this **surprises** you or **gives you a surprise.** You also say you are **surprised** by it. ◇ If something is **surprising,** it is unexpected or unusual and makes you feel surprised. *After just one night I was allowed home feeling surprisingly well.*

❑ If you **surprise** someone, you catch them doing something when they are not expecting it. ◇ If an army **surprises** another one, it launches an attack when the other army is not expecting it.

surreal If you say something is **surreal,** you mean it is very strange and dreamlike, because it involves connections between things which you would not expect to be connected in the real world.

surrealism (surrealist) **Surrealism** is a style in art and literature in which ideas, images, or objects are combined in a strange dreamlike way. **Surrealist** is used to talk about things to do with surrealism. A **surrealist** is an artist or writer whose work is based on the ideas of surrealism. *...surrealist cinema.*

surrealistic means the same as 'surreal'.

surrender (surrendering, surrendered) ❑ When people who have been losing a battle **surrender,** they stop fighting and accept that the other side has won. Doing this is called **surrender.**

❑ If you **surrender** something to someone, you give it up to them. *The process is scheduled to culminate in a complete surrender of weapons by June 10th.* ◇ If you **surrender** a ticket, your passport, or some other document, you give it to someone in authority when they ask for it.

❑ If you **surrender** to a force, temptation, or feeling, you allow it to gain control over you.

surreptitious (surreptitiously) A **surreptitious** action is done secretly. *He surreptitiously made an extra copy.*

surrogate (surrogacy) **Surrogate** is used to describe someone or something that acts as a substitute for someone or something else. *British Airways claims its staff are being forced to act as surrogate immigration officers.* You also say someone or something like this acts as a **surrogate.** ◇ A **surrogate mother** is a woman who has agreed to conceive and give birth to a baby for another woman who is unable to have children of her own. **Surrogacy** is conceiving and giving birth like this.

surround (surrounding, surroundings) ❑ If something **surrounds** a place, it is all the way round it. *...high-security compounds surrounded by electrified fences.* ◇ **Surrounding** is used to describe the area round a place. *...Leicester Square and the surrounding streets.* The area round a place can be called its **surroundings.**

❑ If a group of people **surround** a place, they position themselves all the way round it. Similarly, people can **surround** other people. *Riot police surrounded and handcuffed the protesters before driving them off in vans.*

❑ If you **surround** yourself with particular people or things, you make sure you have a lot of them near you all the time. ◇ Your **surroundings** are everything around you. *He was happiest in his home surroundings.*

❑ If you say something is **surrounded** by problems or dangers, you mean there are many problems or dangers

associated with it.

surtitles are brief translations of the text of an opera which are projected above the stage when the opera is being sung in a foreign language.

surveillance If someone is under **surveillance,** they are being closely watched.

survey ❑ A **survey** is an investigation in which a group of people are asked about their opinions or behaviour.

❑ If an area of land is **surveyed,** it is measured or photographed from the air so a map can be made of it. Measuring or photographing an area like this is called a **survey.** ◇ If a building is **surveyed,** it is examined for any structural problems, especially when someone is planning to buy it. An examination like this is called a **survey.**

❑ If you **survey** something, you look carefully at the whole of it. *Every day police aircraft have been surveying the region for signs of travellers amassing.*

surveyor A **surveyor** is someone whose job is to survey land or buildings.

survive (surviving, survived; survival) ❑ If you **survive,** you stay alive in spite of great danger, hardship, or serious illness. Staying alive in situations like these is called **survival.** *Life became a struggle for survival.*

❑ If you **survive on** a certain amount of money, you earn or receive just enough to buy the things you need to live. Similarly, if you **survive on** a certain kind of food, it is the only food you have and it just keeps you alive. *According to reports, most people are surviving on sweet potatoes.*

❑ When someone dies, you can say they are **survived** by certain close relatives who are still alive. *She is survived by two daughters from her first marriage.*

❑ If you **survive** a difficult experience, you are still in the same position at the end of it. *The Indian Prime Minister survived a challenge to his leadership... Now he is fighting for his political survival.*

❑ If something **survives,** it continues to exist. *Slavery may be dead in theory, but in practice it survives around the world... ...Europe's surviving computer makers... For some car firms, survival will depend on how successful they are at promoting teamwork throughout their organizations.* ◇ If something is a **survival** from an earlier time, it has continued to exist from that time. *The theatre is a glorious survival of the West End's mid-Victorian golden age.*

❑ **Survival of the fittest** is another name for natural selection. It is also used to talk about the idea that, in any situation, it is the strongest or cleverest people who come off best.

survivor ❑ A **survivor** of a disaster is someone involved in it who is still alive at the end of it.

❑ If you say someone is a **survivor,** you mean they seem able to carry on in their job or way of life in spite of difficult times.

susceptible (susceptibility, susceptibilities) ❑ If you are **susceptible** to something, you are easily influenced by it or easily become involved in it. *He is susceptible to flattery... ...the Tory susceptibility to sexual scandal.* ◇ If you are **susceptible** to a disease or injury, you are likely to suffer from it. *Susceptibility to diabetes is linked to inherited genetic factors.*

❑ Someone's **susceptibilities** are their feelings, especially if they are likely to be hurt. *The American electorate has perhaps acquired a way of noticing where its patriotic* *susceptibilities are being exploited for partisan purposes.*

sushi (*pron:* soo-shee) are rice balls, a kind of food eaten in Japan. They are often decorated with raw fish or pieces of omelette.

suspect ❑ If you **suspect** something is true, you have a feeling it is true. *The collector made her purchase in good faith, never suspecting that the painting was stolen.* ◇ If you **suspect** something bad or undesirable, you think it may exist. *They said they suspected a political motive for the explosion... He ended up with a suspected broken wrist.*

❑ If you **suspect** someone of a crime, you think they may be guilty of it. *...suspected terrorists.* A person thought to be guilty of a crime is called a **suspect** (*pron:* suss-pekt).

❑ If something is **suspect** (*pron:* suss-pekt), it cannot be trusted or regarded as genuine.

suspend (suspension) ❑ If something is **suspended** from a high place, it is hanging from it.

❑ If small bits of a substance are **suspended** in a liquid, they are mixed with it without dissolving in it. A **suspension** is a liquid mixture containing bits of an undissolved substance.

❑ A vehicle's **suspension** is the springs and shock absorbers which support its body and enable it to give a smooth ride.

❑ If something which has been happening is **suspended**, it is stopped for a while. When this happens, you talk about its **suspension**. *The hearing was suspended because of the protest... ...a mutual suspension of hostilities.*

❑ If someone is **suspended** from their job, they are not allowed to do it for a period of time, usually as a punishment. Similarly, a player can be **suspended** from a sports team or a pupil can be **suspended** from school. *...lists of party members who could face suspension.*

❑ If someone receives a **suspended** sentence as a punishment for a crime, they do not serve it unless they commit another crime within a specified period.

suspenders are fastenings for holding up stockings. They hang down from a belt called a **suspender belt**. ◇ In the US, braces for holding up trousers are called **suspenders**.

suspense is excitement or anxiety caused by not knowing what is going to happen next. ◇ If you **keep** someone **in suspense**, you delay telling them something they are eager to know about.

suspension See suspend.

suspension bridge A **suspension bridge** is a bridge supported from above by cables attached to towers.

suspicious (suspiciously, suspicion) ❑ If you are **suspicious** of someone, you feel they cannot be trusted. This feeling is called **suspicion**. *He looked me over suspiciously... Black victims of crime are still faced with insensitivity and suspicion.* ◇ If you describe something as **suspicious**, you mean it makes you think something is wrong in some way. *...suspiciously large sums of money.* You can also say something like this arouses your **suspicions**.

❑ If someone is arrested **on suspicion** of something, they are arrested because they are suspected of committing a crime. *Other people were detained on suspicion of involvement in the attack.* ◇ If someone is **under suspicion**, they are suspected of being guilty of a crime. ◇ If you say someone is **above suspicion**, you mean they could not possibly be guilty of something, because of their good

character.

❑ If you have a **suspicion** that something is true, you think it may be true.

suss (susses, sussing, sussed) If you **suss** someone **out**, you discover what their true character is. ◇ If you **suss** something **out**, you discover how it works or how to do it.

sustain (sustaining, sustained) ❑ If you **sustain** something you have achieved, you manage to hold on to it or keep it going. *They and other Nashville-based artists have found it difficult to sustain mainstream chart success... ...economies that are capable of sustained growth.* ◇ If something **sustains** someone, it keeps them alive. Similarly, if something **sustains** a system or organization, it keeps it going. *Soil is disappearing at such a rate that eventually there may not be enough left to sustain any agriculture at all.* ◇ If something **sustains** you through a difficult time, it stops you becoming depressed or giving up what you are doing.

❑ If you **sustain** something like a defeat, loss, or injury, it happens to you. *The pier has already sustained damage in the gales.*

sustainable (sustainably, sustainability) If a plan or system is **sustainable**, it can be made to continue or remain the same. *...a sustainable ceasefire... ...doubts about the sustainability of present ERM exchange rates.* ◇ **Sustainable** methods of farming ensure that natural resources remain available at a steady level and that no serious harm is done to the environment.

sustenance is food and drink which helps to keep a person, animal, or plant alive, strong, and healthy.

❑ If something gives you **sustenance**, it gives you help, strength, or encouragement when you are having difficulties. *Reading about a family's courage gives other people sustenance.*

suture (*pron:* soo-cher) **Sutures** are stitches used to sew up a wound.

svelte A **svelte** person is attractively slim, elegant, and stylish.

Svengali If you say someone is a **Svengali**, you mean they can control other people's minds and influence them, especially in a bad way.

swab A **swab** is a small piece of cotton wool, sometimes on a short stick, used to clean a wound or to take a sample, for example of body fluids. A sample taken like this is also called a **swab**.

swaddle (*pron:* swod-dl) (swaddling, swaddled) If a baby is **swaddled**, it is wrapped tightly in strips of cloth to keep it warm or prevent it from moving. ◇ If something is **swaddled** in rules or restrictions, they prevent it from developing. *...the controls in which the Indian economy had been swaddled.*

swag is stolen property.

swagger (swaggering, swaggered) If you **swagger**, or walk with a **swagger**, you walk in a proud way, holding your body upright and swinging your hips.

swallow ❑ If you **swallow** something, you make it go down from your mouth into your stomach. ◇ If you **swallow**, you make a movement in your throat as if you were swallowing something, because you are nervous or frightened.

❑ If you talk about someone **swallowing** a story or

statement, you mean they believe it completely.
◇ **swallow your pride: see pride.**

❏ If one thing is **swallowed up** by another, it becomes part of it and no longer has a separate identity of its own.

❏ If something **swallows up** money or resources, it uses them up at an unacceptable rate.

❏ The **swallow** is a bird with long pointed wings and a forked tail. Swallows migrate to Africa in the autumn and return in the spring.

swam See swim.

swamp (swampy) ❏ A **swamp** is an area of permanently waterlogged land. **Swampy** land consists mainly of swamps.

❏ If an area is **swamped,** it is filled with water, because there has been heavy rain or a flood. ◇ If you are **swamped** by things, there are more of them than you can deal with. *...action that will save our cities from being swamped by cars.*

swan (swanning, swanned) ❏ **Swans** are large water birds which are usually white. There are several kinds of swans. The one most commonly seen in Britain is called the **mute swan.**

❏ If you **swan** around, you move around without any real purpose.

❏ Someone's **swan song** is the last time they do something they are famous for.

swanky (swankier, swankiest) **Swanky** is used to describe things which are smart and fashionable. *...swanky sports facilities.*

swap (swapping, swapped) (*or* swop, *etc*) ❏ If you **swap** something, you give it in exchange for something else. An arrangement like this is called a **swap.** ◇ You also say you **swap** something when you replace it with something else. *He is swapping his job for a rather less exacting one.*

❏ If you **swap** stories or information with someone, you tell each other stories or give each other information.

❏ If someone **swaps** sides in a war, they decide to support the people they were previously fighting against.

swarm ❏ When bees or other insects **swarm,** they move or fly in a large group, usually to to find a new place to live. A group of insects like this is called a **swarm.**

❏ If people **swarm** somewhere, they move there in a large group. A group of people moving like this can be called a **swarm.** ◇ If a place is **swarming** with people or animals, there are a lot of them moving about there.

swarthy A **swarthy** person has a dark complexion.

swashbuckling (swashbuckler) **Swashbuckling** is used to describe characters in historical stories and films who behave in a swaggering daredevil way. People in real life who remind you of these characters can also be described as **swashbuckling;** you can also call them **swashbucklers.** *...a swashbuckling media proprietor.*

swastika The **swastika** is an ancient symbol which looks like a cross with the arms bent at right angles. It was adopted as the emblem of Nazi Germany.

swat (swatting, swatted) If you **swat** an insect, you hit it with something. ◇ If you **swat aside** someone who is trying to oppose you, you deal with them quickly and easily. *Briskly swatting aside party rivals, he plunged into the second great challenge of his political career.* Similarly, if you **swat aside** something like a suggestion, you dismiss

it. *Labour's demand for the recall of parliament was swatted aside with contempt.*

swathe (swathed) ❏ A **swathe** of land is a strip of it which has been altered in a way which makes it different from the land on either side. ◇ A **swathe** of something else is a large part of it which has been changed and made different from the rest. *Mexico has also privatized swathes of its economy.* ◇ If something **cuts a swathe** through something else, it destroys a large part of it. *The recession is cutting a swathe through America's managerial and professional elite.*

❏ A **swathe** is strip of cloth, especially one for wrapping around someone or something. If you are **swathed** in something, you are wrapped in it.

sway ❏ When people or things **sway,** they lean or swing from side to side.

❏ If you are **swayed** by something you hear or read, you are influenced by it. ◇ If you are **under the sway** of someone or something, they have a lot of influence over you. ◇ If someone or something **holds sway,** they have more power or influence than anyone or anything else. *Waitz will be the first to accept that she no longer holds sway in women's marathon running.*

swear (swearing, swore, have sworn) ❏ If someone **swears,** they use words considered to be rude or blasphemous. Words like these are called **swear words.**

❏ If you **swear** to do something, you formally promise to do it, sometimes by taking an oath. ◇ If you make a **sworn** statement or declaration, you swear on oath that it is true. ◇ When someone is **sworn in,** they take an oath and promise to fulfil certain duties. This is called their **swearing-in.**

❏ If you **swear** something is true, or **swear** to the truth of it, you say very firmly that it is true.

❏ If people are **sworn** enemies, they dislike each other very much and do not want to become friendly towards each other.

sweat (sweating, sweated) ❏ **Sweat** is the salty colourless liquid produced by the sweat glands when you are hot, ill, or afraid. When you **sweat,** sweat comes out through your skin. If something makes this happen, you say it **brings you out in a sweat.**

❏ If you say someone is **in a cold sweat,** you mean they are worried and alarmed about something which seems likely to happen. ◇ If you **sweat it out,** you endure something unpleasant in the hope that when it ends the situation will have improved.

sweat gland **Sweat glands** are the organs under the skin which produce sweat.

sweatband A **sweatband** is a strip of absorbent material worn round your head to keep sweat out of your eyes.

sweater A **sweater** is a woollen garment which covers the upper part of your body and your arms.

sweatshirt A **sweatshirt** is a garment made of thick cotton which covers the upper part of your body and your arms.

sweatshop You call a factory or workshop a **sweatshop** when the people there work long hours in poor conditions, often for low pay.

sweaty A **sweaty** place or activity makes you sweat. ◇ If your body or clothing is **sweaty,** it is covered with sweat.

swede ❑ Swedes are large round root vegetables with yellow flesh and a brownish-purple skin.
❑ A Swede is someone who comes from Sweden.

Swedish is used to talk about people and things in or from Sweden. ...*Swedish farmers.* ◇ Swedish is the main language spoken in Sweden. It is also spoken by many people in Finland.

sweep (sweeping, swept *not 'sweeped'*) ❑ If you sweep a floor or some other surface, you push dirt or rubbish off it with a brush. When you do this, you say you sweep up the dirt or rubbish. ◇ If you sweep something off a surface, you push it off with a quick movement of your arm.
❑ If something is swept somewhere by the wind or by moving water, it is carried along by it.
❑ If someone or something sweeps somewhere, they move along quickly and forcefully. *Periodically, convoys of black Mercedes cars sweep down the road to the city... A sandstorm is sweeping across parts of eastern Saudi Arabia.*
❑ If you talk about land sweeping somewhere, you mean it stretches out in a long wide curved shape. You can talk about the sweep of a stretch of land. ...*lawns that sweep down to the sea... ...breathtaking sweeps of heather.*
❑ If ideas, beliefs, or emotions sweep a place, they spread quickly there. *Panic swept the city.* You can also talk about people being swept along by an idea, belief, or emotion. *We were all swept along in the excitement of the race.*
❑ If something is swept away, it is removed completely. *The law will also sweep away the 20% limit on foreign investment in privatized firms... Right wing parties swept the communists from power.* ◇ Sweeping changes are wide-ranging and dramatic. ...*sweeping economic reforms.*
❑ When someone wins something easily, you can describe their win as a sweeping victory. ◇ When a political party wins an election easily, you can say they sweep the country or sweep the polls. ◇ If someone makes a clean sweep in a competition, they win everything. ◇ sweep the board: see board.
❑ A sweeping statement is a general one made without considering all the facts properly.
❑ If the police make a sweep of a place, they search it.
❑ A sweep is the same as a chimney sweep.

sweeper A sweeper is someone employed to sweep things like roads and factories. ◇ In football, a sweeper is a defender who does not have a fixed position, but operates in all parts of his team's defence area.

sweepstake A sweepstake is a method of gambling in which each person is given, for example, the name of a horse in a race and pays a small amount of money. The person who has the winning horse's name wins all the money.

sweet (sweeter, sweetest; sweetness, sweetly) ❑ Sweet food and drink contains a lot of sugar, or tastes as if it does. ◇ Sweets are small sweet things you eat, chew, or suck, for example toffees, chocolates, or mints. ◇ A sweet is a dessert served at the end of a meal. ◇ If you have a sweet tooth, you like sweet sugary foods.
❑ A sweet smell is pleasant and fragrant. ◇ A sweet sound is pleasant and gentle.
❑ A sweet feeling or experience gives you great pleasure and satisfaction. *Revenge is sweet... Gooch responded*

with one sweetly struck boundary.
❑ You can call someone's behaviour sweet when they are pleasant and kind. ◇ If you say someone is all sweetness and light, you mean they are behaving in a very pleasant way, although they do not usually behave like that. ◇ If you do something to keep someone sweet, you do it to please them and prevent them becoming annoyed or dissatisfied.

sweet-and-sour sauce includes sweet substances like sugar and fruit, and sharp ones like vinegar. It is served with savoury food.

sweet pea Sweet peas are climbing plants with delicate light-coloured fragrant flowers.

sweet potato Sweet potatoes are large root vegetables with pink skins and yellow flesh.

sweet-talk If you sweet-talk someone into doing something, you persuade them to do it by flattering them.

sweet william is a garden plant with round clusters of scented flowers.

sweetbread Sweetbreads are meat obtained from the pancreas or thymus gland of a calf or lamb.

sweetcorn is the yellow seeds of the maize plant, which are eaten as a vegetable.

sweeten (sweetening, sweetened; sweetener) ❑ If you sweeten food or drink, you add sugar, honey, or some other sweet substance to it. ◇ A sweetener is an artificial substance used instead of sugar to make things taste sweet. Sweeteners are usually low-calorie.
❑ If someone sweetens an offer or a business deal, they make it more attractive by improving it or raising the amount of money they are willing to pay. Something which makes an offer or deal more attractive is called a sweetener. ◇ If you sweeten someone, you give them a gift or do something nice for them, to prepare them for something unpleasant or to get them to do something you want. ◇ sweeten the pill: see pill.

sweetheart Someone's sweetheart is their boyfriend or girlfriend.

sweetie A sweetie is a sweet, for example a toffee, chocolate, or mint.

swell (swelling, swelled, have swollen *or* have swelled) ❑ If something swells or swells up, it becomes larger and rounder than normal. When this happens, you say it is swollen. ◇ A swelling is a raised curved patch on the body which appears as a result of an injury or infection.
❑ If a river is swollen, there is much more water in it than usual, because it has been raining heavily.
❑ If numbers or amounts swell, they increase as more and more is added to them. *The industry reckons it will see orders swell by 10% this year... The population of the capital has swollen to half-a-million.*
❑ If a sound swells, it suddenly gets louder.
❑ The swell of the sea is the regular up-and-down movement of the waves.

swelter (sweltering, sweltered) If you swelter or are sweltering, you are very uncomfortable because the weather is extremely hot. If the weather is sweltering, it is extremely hot.

swept See sweep.

swerve (swerving, swerved) If you swerve when you are running or driving a car, you suddenly change direction, usually to avoid colliding with someone or something.

A movement like this is called a **swerve**. ◇ In sport, if a ball **swerves**, it moves in a slight curve, usually because there is spin on it.

swift (swiftly, swiftness) ❑ A **swift** process or event happens very quickly. *The swiftness of the decision calmed investors.* ◇ If you are **swift** to do something, you do it quickly in response to something else. *Her remarks were swiftly attacked by opposition parties.*

❑ If something like an animal is **swift**, it moves very quickly.

❑ **Swifts** are small birds with crescent-shaped wings. They fly very quickly, often making a screaming noise. Swifts spend most of their time in flight. They migrate to Africa in the autumn and return in the spring.

swig (swigging, swigged) If you **swig** a drink, you drink it quickly and in large mouthfuls. If you **take a swig** at a drink, you drink one large mouthful quickly.

swill ❑ If you **swill** an alcoholic drink, you drink a lot of it. *...beer-swilling men.*

❑ If you **swill** something like a floor, you clean it by pouring water over it.

❑ **Swill** is a liquid mixture containing waste food like vegetable peelings, which is given to pigs to eat.

swim (swimming, swam, have swum) When you **swim**, you move through water by making movements with your arms and legs. If you go **swimming** or go for a **swim**, you spend some time swimming for pleasure. If you **swim** a stretch of water or a particular distance, you keep swimming until you have crossed the water or completed the distance. *Thieves have swum the moat at least 12 times.* ◇ When a fish **swims**, it moves through water by making movements with its tail and fins.

swimmer A **swimmer** is someone who swims regularly or takes part in swimming races.

swimming baths A **swimming baths** is a public swimming pool.

swimming costume A **swimming costume** is a tight-fitting piece of clothing a woman wears when she goes swimming.

swimming pool A **swimming pool** is a large hole which has been tiled and filled with water for people to swim in.

swimming trunks are shorts a man wears when he goes swimming.

swimmingly If something goes **swimmingly**, it goes well without any problems.

swimsuit A **swimsuit** is the same as a swimming costume.

swindle (swindling, swindled; swindler) If someone **swindles** you, they trick you to get money or something valuable from you. You call a trick like this a **swindle**. Someone who tricks people in this way is called a **swindler**.

swine (*plural:* swine) ❑ If you call someone a **swine**, you mean they are cruel or very selfish.

❑ **Swine** is an old word for a pig.

swing (swinging, swung) ❑ If something **swings** or if you **swing** it, it moves repeatedly backwards and forwards or from side to side, from a fixed point. A movement like this is called a **swing**. *A car swung from a nearby crane... ...a swing of the hips.*

❑ A child's **swing** is a seat hanging by two ropes or chains from a frame or tree. The child sits on it with its feet off the ground, and is pushed so it moves forwards and backwards through the air.

❑ **Swings and roundabouts** is used to talk about a situation in which there are both gains and losses.

❑ If someone or something **swings** in particular direction, they turn suddenly in that direction. *I swung around furiously.*

❑ If you **swing** at someone or take a **swing** at them, you try to hit them.

❑ If people's opinions or attitudes **swing** in a particular direction, they change significantly. A change like this is called a **swing**. *...the recent swing in American public opinion against military action.*

❑ If there is a **swing** in an amount or number, it suddenly increases or decreases. *...interest-rate swings.*

❑ If something is **in full swing**, it is operating fully and is no longer in its early stages.

❑ **Swing** was a style of big band dance music popular in the 1930s and 1940s.

swing door A **swing door** swings on a hinge so that it can open either towards you or away from you.

swing vote When the result of an election is likely to be close, the people who have the **swing vote** are the ones who might vote either way and whose vote could decide who wins.

swingeing (*pron:* swin-jing) is used to describe things which are very severe and cause serious harm or hardship. *...swingeing defence cuts... ...a swingeing attack on social workers.*

swipe (swiping, swiped) ❑ If you **swipe** at something, you try to hit it. ◇ If you take a **swipe** at someone or something, you strongly criticize them.

❑ If someone **swipes** something, they steal it.

swirl (swirling) If something **swirls**, it moves round and round. A movement like this can be called a **swirl**. *...swirling rain... Thousands of starlings fly around in mad swirls.* ◇ A **swirl** is also something shaped like a curl or spiral.

swish (swishes, swishing, swished) ❑ If something **swishes**, it moves quickly through the air, making a soft sound. *The cow swished her tail.*

❑ **Swish** things are smart and fashionable. *...a swish restaurant.*

Swiss is used to talk about people and things in or from Switzerland. *...Swiss hotels.* ◇ The **Swiss** are the Swiss people.

swiss roll A **swiss roll** is a flat oblong sponge cake spread with jam or cream then rolled into a cylindrical shape.

switch (switches, switching, switched) ❑ A **switch** is a small control for an electrical device which you use to operate the device. If you **switch on** a light or other electrical device, you make it work by pressing a switch. Similarly, you can **switch off** a light or other device.

❑ If you **switch off**, you stop paying attention to something or stop thinking about it.

❑ If you **switch** to something different, you change to it from what you were doing or using before. A change like this is called a **switch**. *Concerns over the environment are resulting in a switch away from coal-fired power stations.* ◇ If you **switch** two things, you replace one with the other. *The ballot boxes have been switched.*

switchback You call a mountain road a **switchback** when it rises and falls sharply many times or has many sharp bends.

switchblade A **switchblade** is the same as a flick knife.

switchboard The **switchboard** in an organization is a place where all the phone calls are received.

swivel (swivelling, swivelled) (*American spelling:* swiveling, swiveled) If something **swivels** or is **swivelled**, it turns around a central point so it is facing in a different direction. ◇ A **swivel** chair is mounted on a device called a swivel so that it can be turned in any direction without the base being moved. ◇ If you **swivel** in a particular direction, you suddenly turn in that direction.

swollen See **swell**.

swoon (swooning, swooned) If someone **swoons** or goes into a **swoon**, they almost faint as a result of a strong emotion or shock.

swoop (swooping, swooped) ❑ When a bird or plane **swoops**, it suddenly moves downwards in a smooth curving movement. ◇ If soldiers or police **swoop** on a place, they move towards it suddenly and quickly to attack it or arrest someone. An action like this is called a **swoop**.

❑ If you achieve something **in one fell swoop**, you do it on a single occasion or by a single action. ...*the only occasion when a prime minister of Britain dismissed seven ministers in one fell swoop.*

swop (swopping, swopped) See **swap**.

sword A **sword** is a weapon with a handle and a long blade. ◇ If you **cross swords** with someone, you disagree with them and argue about something.

swordfish (*usual plural:* swordfish) The **swordfish** is a large sea fish with a very long upper jaw.

swore (sworn) See **swear**.

swot (swotting, swotted) ❑ If you **swot**, you study very hard, especially when preparing for an exam. ◇ If you call someone a **swot**, you mean they study very hard and are not interested in other things.

❑ If you **swot up** on a subject, you read as much about it as you can.

swum See **swim**.

swung See **swing**.

sybarite (*pron:* sib-bar-ite) (sybaritic) A **sybarite** is someone who likes to lead a life of luxury. **Sybaritic** is used to describe people like this and the things they enjoy. ...*the sybaritic existence of the former Shah.*

sycamore The **sycamore** is a tree with large leaves which have five points. Its seed cases have two wings and spin as they fall.

sycophantic (*pron:* sik-o-fan-tic) (sycophant, sycophancy) You say people are **sycophantic** when they flatter an important person, to gain some advantage for themselves. You call people like these **sycophants** or describe their behaviour as **sycophancy**.

syllable A **syllable** is a part of a word which contains a single vowel sound, and is pronounced as a unit. For example, 'book' has one syllable and 'reading' has two.

syllabus (syllabuses) The subjects studied for a course or exam are called the **syllabus**.

sylvan is used to talk about things to do with trees and woods, or places surrounded by trees and woods. ...*a sylvan Surrey village.*

symbiosis (symbiotic) **Symbiosis** is a relationship between two creatures or organisms which benefits both of them. **Symbiotic** is used to describe relationships like this. ◇ **Symbiosis** is also any relationship between different things, people, or groups which benefits all the things or people concerned. *This symbiosis of a chatty president and a ravenous press is potent... ...the party's symbiotic relationship with the ANC.*

symbol ❑ A **symbol** is something, for example a shape or design, which is chosen to represent something else. *The new symbol of the Italian Communist Party is to be a sturdy oak tree.* ◇ A **symbol** is also something which is seen by people as representing a particular thing. *According to native American legend, rainbows are a symbol of union... The Queen is seen by many Quebec nationalists as a symbol of English Canada.* ◇ **status symbol**: see **status**. ◇ See also **sex symbol**.

❑ A **symbol** is also a number, letter, or shape used in maths, science, or music to represent something like a quantity, operation, or function. *Beryllium is a rare metal; its chemical symbol is Be.*

symbolic (symbolically; symbolism, symbolist) ❑ A **symbolic** action has a special meaning for a group of people and often represents a feeling or wish they all have. *In a symbolic gesture, the parliament passed a declaration praising the 1956 uprising... Last year he was symbolically reburied and today hundreds of people came to the cemetery to lay flowers on his tombstone.* You can talk about the **symbolism** of an action like this. ◇ **Symbolic** is also used to talk about things to do with symbols or involving symbols. **Symbolism** is the use of symbols.

❑ **Symbolism** was a late 19th-century movement in French literature and art in which words and images were used to express abstract and mystical ideas. **Symbolist** is used to talk about things to do with this movement. ...*a brilliant symbolist portrait.*

symbolize (symbolizing, symbolized) (*can be spelled with an 's' instead of a 'z'*) If a person or thing **symbolizes** something else, they are regarded as a symbol of it. *These dissidents symbolize an era most people would rather forget.*

symmetrical (symmetry, symmetries) ❑ If something is **symmetrical**, it has two halves which are the same except that one half is the mirror image of the other. You talk about the **symmetry** of something like this.

❑ You also say there is **symmetry** when there is balance and similarity between two groups of people who are opposed to each other. *In Europe, America's role can be trimmed without upsetting the symmetry.*

sympathetic (sympathetically) See **sympathy**.

sympathize (sympathizing, sympathized; sympathizer) (*can be spelled with an 's' instead of a 'z'*) ❑ If you **sympathize** with someone who has had a misfortune, you show you feel sorry for them. ◇ If you **sympathize** with someone's feelings, you understand them and are not critical of them.

❑ If you **sympathize** with a proposal, action, or cause, you approve of it and are willing to support it. People who support an organization or cause are called its **sympathizers**. ...*Communist party sympathizers.*

sympathy (sympathies; sympathetic, sympathetically) ❑ If you show **sympathy** for someone who has had a misfortune or are **sympathetic** to them, you show you feel sorry for them and understand their feelings. *I spoke to her quietly and sympathetically.*

❑ If you describe someone as **sympathetic**, you mean you like them and approve of the way they behave. *...a sympathetic character.*

❑ If you have **sympathy** with a proposal, action, or cause or are **sympathetic** to it, you agree with it. *The unions are not likely to be sympathetically disposed to a policy which will result in massive lay-offs.* Your **sympathies** are your feelings of approval or support for an organization, action, or cause. *...a priest with left-wing sympathies.*

❑ **Sympathy** is used to describe actions taken by one group of workers to show support for another group. You say the first group takes action **in sympathy** with the second group. *...sympathy strikes... Taxi drivers stopped work for several hours in sympathy with the lorry drivers' protest.*

symphony (symphonies; symphonic) ❑ A **symphony** is a large-scale piece of music for an orchestra, usually in four movements. **Symphonic** is used to describe orchestral pieces which have similar features to a symphony. *...Schumann's Symphonic Studies.*

❑ A pleasing arrangement of colours and shapes is sometimes called a **symphony**. *The amphitheatre is a symphony of honey-coloured columns.*

symphony orchestra A symphony orchestra is a large orchestra.

symposium (*plural:* symposia *or* symposiums) A **symposium** is a conference in which experts or scholars discuss a particular subject.

symptom (symptomatic) ❑ A **symptom** is something wrong with your body which is a sign of an illness. *...AIDS-like symptoms.*

❑ If you say something is a **symptom** of a bad situation or is **symptomatic** of it, you mean it shows it exists. *The dispute is symptomatic of wider tensions.*

synagogue A **synagogue** is a building where Jewish people meet to worship or to study their religion.

synapse (*pron:* sigh-naps) (synaptic) A **synapse** is the point where a nerve impulse is relayed from one nerve cell to another. **Synaptic** is used to talk about things to do with synapses. *...synaptic processes.*

sync (*or* synch) (*pron:* sink) If two things are **out of sync**, they are not synchronized with each other.

synchromesh In a gearbox, **synchromesh** is a system which allows a smooth gear change by making the gears spin at the same speed before engaging them.

synchronicity See **synchronous**.

synchronize (synchronizing, synchronized; synchronization) (*can be spelled with an 's' instead of a 'z'*) If things are **synchronized**, they are made to happen in the same way and at the same time. This is called **synchronization**. *...a union initiative which aims to synchronize all pay bargaining.* ◇ If people **synchronize** watches or clocks, they adjust them so they say exactly the same time. ◇ When a film is **synchronized**, the sound track and pictures are fitted together so the sound is heard at exactly the right time.

synchronized swimming is the art or sport of one or more swimmers moving in graceful patterns in the water in time to music.

synchronous (*pron:* sink-kro-nuss) (synchronicity) If two things are **synchronous**, they happen in the same way

and at the same time. You talk about the **synchronicity** of things like these.

syncopated (syncopation) If a piece of music is **syncopated**, the weak beats are stressed instead of the strong ones. You talk about the **syncopation** or **syncopations** of music like this.

syndicate (syndicating, syndicated; syndication) ❑ A **syndicate** is an association of people or organizations formed for business purposes or to carry out a project together. ◇ If a group or organization **syndicates** something, it produces it or agrees to it through a syndicate. *...syndicated loans.*

❑ If articles, cartoons, or programmes are **syndicated**, they are sold to several different organizations who then publish or broadcast them. *...the US syndication market.*

syndrome A **syndrome** is a medical condition which produces a particular set of symptoms. Syndromes are often called after the person who first discovered or described them, for example 'Down's syndrome'. ◇ A **syndrome** is also a pattern of behaviour which keeps occurring over and over again with different people.

synergy (*pron:* sin-er-gee) (synergies) **Synergy** is the successful result of two firms or other organizations merging. An instance of this happening is called a **synergy**.

synod A **synod** is a special council of members of a Church, which meets to discuss religious issues or make rulings.

synonym (synonymous) If two words or expressions are **synonyms**, they have the same meaning or a very similar meaning. You say words or expressions like these are **synonymous**. ◇ If two things are closely associated, you can say one is **synonymous** with the other. *...the 1980s, a decade that has become synonymous with greed and corporate excess.*

synopsis (*plural:* synopses) A **synopsis** of a book, play, or film is a summary of it.

syntax (syntaxes) The **syntax** of a language is its grammatical rules and the way its words are arranged.

synth A **synth** is the same as a synthesizer.

synthesis (syntheses) ❑ A **synthesis** of different ideas or styles is a mixture or combination of them.

❑ The **synthesis** of a substance is its production from other substances by means of a chemical or biological reaction.

synthesize (synthesizing, synthesized) (*can be spelled with an 's' instead of a 'z'*) When a substance is **synthesized**, it is produced from other substances by a chemical or biological reaction.

synthesizer A **synthesizer** is an electronic machine, usually with a keyboard, which produces music, speech, or other sounds from electronic signals of different frequencies.

synthetic (synthetically) **Synthetic** products are made from man-made substances rather than natural ones. *...synthetic diamonds... The best chance of getting penicillin in sufficient quantity for all purposes lay in making it synthetically.*

syphilis is a type of venereal disease.

syphon See **siphon**.

syringe (syringing, syringed) A **syringe** is a small tube with a plunger and a fine hollow needle used for injecting or extracting liquids.

syrup is a fairly thick sweet liquid made with sugar, water, and sometimes fruit juice. It is used, for example, to sweeten fruit. ◇ Various other thick sweet liquids containing sugar are also called **syrup**. ...*maple syrup*... ...*cough syrup*.

syrupy A **syrupy** liquid is sweet or thick like syrup. ◇ **Syrupy** is also used to describe things which are sentimental in an irritating way. ...*a syrupy tale*.

system ❑ A **system** is a way of organizing or doing something which involves following a fixed plan or set of rules. ...*the system of proportional representation*... ...*a system of bartering*. ◇ A **system** is also a way of counting or measuring things. ...*the metric system*.

❑ The way a profession or institution operates can be called a **system**. ...*the banking system*... ...*the Scottish education system*.

❑ The network of roads, railways, or canals in a place can be called a **system**. Similarly, a transport network can be called a **system**. *Most bus systems in Britain are now privately owned*. ◇ A set of equipment or parts, which work together to carry out a process, can also be called a **system**. ...*the central heating system*... ...*a car stereo system*.

❑ A **system** in your body is a set of organs or other parts which together perform a particular function. ...*the immune system*... ...*the digestive system*. ◇ The functioning of a person's body as a whole can be called their **system**. ...*the level of barbiturates found in her system*.

❑ If you get something **out of your system**, you do or say something you have been wanting to do or say for a long time.

systematic (systematically) You say something is **systematic** when it operates like a fully organized system. ...*the discovery of a massive and systematic fraud*... *Military intelligence has been systematically spying on prominent citizens*.

systematize (systematizing, systematized) (*can be spelled with an 's' instead of a 'z'*) If you **systematize** things, you arrange them in a well-organized pattern or system.

systemic (*pron:* siss-**team**-ik) If something is **systemic**, it affects the whole of an organization or system, rather than just one part of it. *Delays in settling large payments between clearing banks will be shortened to reduce systemic risks if a bank collapses*.

systems analyst A **systems analyst** is someone who designs computer systems to suit the individual needs of a business or other organization.

T t

T-shirt A **T-shirt** is a short-sleeved shirt with no collar or buttons.

TA See **Territorial Army**.

tab ❑ A **tab** is a small piece of cloth or paper attached to something, especially one used for identification.

❑ If you **pick up the tab,** you pay for something on behalf of a group of people.

❑ If you **keep tabs** on someone, you make sure you always know where they are and what they are doing.

Tabasco is a hot spicy sauce made from peppers. 'Tabasco' is a trademark.

tabby (tabbies) A **tabby** is a cat whose fur has dark stripes.

tabernacle A **tabernacle** is a building for worship in certain Christian churches. ◇ In a Roman Catholic church, the **tabernacle** is a decorated box in which the communion bread and wine are kept.

table (tabling, tabled) ❑ A **table** is a flat-topped piece of furniture which you put things on or sit at to eat a meal. ◇ If you talk about someone's **table manners**, you mean the way they behave when eating a meal and to what extent their behaviour is polite or socially acceptable.

❑ A **table** is also a written set of facts or figures arranged in columns or rows.

❑ In Britain, if a proposal is **tabled,** it is put forward for discussion at a meeting. ◇ In Canada and the US, if a proposal is **tabled,** it is set aside for consideration at a later date. ◇ If something has been proposed and is awaiting discussion, you can say it is **on the table**. *There are at least five proposals on the table*.

❑ If you **turn the tables** on someone who has been causing you problems, you succeed in reversing the situation so you cause problems for them instead.

table tennis is a game played on a special table by two or four people. They use small bats to hit a small hollow plastic ball backwards and forwards across a net. The idea is to hit the ball onto your opponent's half of the table, and to stop your opponent hitting it onto yours.

tableau (*pron:* tab-loh) (*plural:* tableaux *or* tableaus) A **tableau** is a scene from history or legend represented either by people standing on a stage wearing costumes or by a painting, sculpture, or photograph.

tablecloth A **tablecloth** is a cloth used to cover a table at mealtimes.

tablespoon A **tablespoon** is a large spoon for serving food. ◇ A **tablespoon** of something is the same as a tablespoonful.

tablespoonful (*plural:* tablespoonsful *or* tablespoonfuls) A **tablespoonful** of something is the amount contained in a tablespoon.

tablet A **tablet** is a large pill containing a dose of medicine. ◇ A **tablet** is also a flat piece of stone with words cut into it.

tableware consists of things like plates, glasses, and cutlery which are put on the table at mealtimes.

tabloid A **tabloid** is a newspaper printed on fairly small sheets of paper, measuring about 30cm by 40cm. Tabloids are usually less serious than other newspapers. See also **broadsheet**.

taboo ❏ A **taboo** is a religious or social rule forbidding people to do something.
❏ If a kind of behaviour is **taboo** in a place, it is not considered acceptable there. A **taboo** subject is one which it is not considered polite to discuss.

tabulate (tabulating, tabulated; tabulation) If you **tabulate** information, you arrange it in columns on a page. ...*the tabulation of results.*

tachograph (*pron:* tak-o-graf) A **tachograph** is a device which records things like a vehicle's speed and the distance it has travelled. In Britain, tachographs are legally required to be fitted to most heavy goods vehicles.

tacit (*pron:* tass-it) (tacitly) **Tacit** is used to say something is understood or implied without actually being stated. ...*tacit support... An uneasy truce was tacitly acknowledged.*

taciturn (*pron:* tass-it-turn) (taciturnity) If you say someone is **taciturn**, or talk about their **taciturnity**, you mean they do not talk very much.

tack ❏ A **tack** is a short nail with a broad flat head. If you **tack** something somewhere, you nail it there with tacks.
❏ If you **tack** pieces of material together, you sew them together with big loose stitches called **tacks** before sewing them properly.
❏ If you **tack** something **on** to something else, you add it as an afterthought. *Safety cannot be an optional extra to be tacked on at the end.*
❏ When a sailing boat **tacks**, it moves by a series of diagonal movements rather than in a straight line, because the wind direction will not allow a direct route.
❏ If you change **tack** or try a different **tack**, you try a different method or policy from the one you were using before.

tackle (tackling, tackled) ❏ If you **tackle** a problem, you make a determined attempt to deal with it.
❏ If you **tackle** someone in a game like football, you try to take the ball off them. In rugby, if you **tackle** someone or make a **tackle**, you grab them around the legs and try to bring them down.
❏ If you **tackle** someone on a matter, you start asking them questions about it. *Sue Lawley tackled him on the problem of home repossessions.*
❏ Fishing **tackle** is equipment for fishing. It includes things like rods, line, floats, and hooks.

tacky (tackier, tackiest; tackiness) If you say something is **tacky**, you mean it is of poor quality or rather showy and lacking in good taste. ...*the tackier tabloids... In the 1960s British popular music lost its provincial tackiness and became world class.*

tact (tactful, tactfully) If you behave with **tact** or are **tactful**, you are careful to avoid upsetting or offending people. *She excused herself tactfully and left.*

tactic Your **tactics** are the methods and strategies you use to get what you want.

tactical is used to describe actions and behaviour which form part of a strategy. *Coyne's brilliant tactical kicking has been the principal feature of the Sydney side's success... Tactically, he's improved a lot.*
❏ **Tactical** voting means voting for a party or candidate not because you agree with their policies, but because you hope to stop another party or candidate winning.
❏ **Tactical** weapons are used over fairly short distances. ...*a tactical air-launched missile.*

tactician If you say someone is a good **tactician**, you mean they are good at devising plans and strategies.

tactile is used to talk about things relating to the sense of touch. ...*tactile stimulation.* ◇ **Tactile** is also used to describe things which are pleasant or distinctive to touch. ...*a texture as rich and tactile as leather.*
❏ A **tactile** person likes touching and being touched by other people.

tactless If someone is **tactless**, their behaviour is likely to upset or offend people. ...*tactless remarks.*

tad A **tad** means to a small extent or degree. *It was a tad too far-fetched to be true.*

tadpole Tadpoles are the larvae of frogs and toads. They are dark-coloured with large round heads and long tails and live in water.

taffeta is a stiff shiny material made of silk or a man-made fibre. It is used mainly for making women's clothes.

tag (tagging, tagged) ❏ A **tag** is a label, especially one tied to an object. If something is **tagged**, it is marked for identification, often using a label like this.
❏ A **tag** or **electronic tag** is a device which is firmly attached to someone or something and sets off an alarm if that person or thing moves away or is removed. The practice of fitting devices like this is called **electronic tagging**.
❏ A **tag** is a nickname or description which comes to be associated with someone or something. *He has sought to shrug off the right wing Thatcherite tag.* You can also say the person or thing is **tagged** with the name or description. *The party is scared of being tagged federalist.* ◇ The **tag line** of something like an advert or joke is the phrase which comes at the end and which is meant to be memorable or amusing.
❏ If someone **tags along** with you when you go somewhere, they go with you because they want to, rather than because you need them or have asked them to.

tagliatelle (*pron:* tal-lee-a-**tel**-lee) is pasta made in narrow strips.

tai chi (*pron:* tie jee) or **tai chi chuan** (*pron:* tie jee chwahn) is a Chinese form of physical exercise which involves moving slowly to train the body and mind in balance and control.

tail (tailing, tailed) ❏ The **tail** of an animal, bird, or fish is the part which grows out of the rear end of its body. **-tailed** is used to describe the tails of some birds and animals. ...*the fan-tailed warbler... ...white-tailed deer.*
❏ The **tail** of a plane is the part at the back.
❏ If a man is **in tails**, he is wearing a formal evening jacket called a **tail coat**, which has two long pieces hanging down at the back.
❏ When someone like a detective **tails** a person, he or she follows them, to find out where they go and what they do.
❏ If you toss a coin and it comes down **tails**, the side facing upwards does not have a person's head on it.
❏ If something **tails off**, it gradually decreases. *The workload has now tailed off significantly.*
❏ If someone **turns tail**, they turn around and run away.
❏ If you say **the tail is wagging the dog**, you mean a small or unimportant part of something is becoming too important or controlling the whole thing.

❑ If you say someone who has been defeated has **their tail between their legs**, you mean they are ashamed and embarrassed.

tail light The **tail lights** on a road vehicle are the two red lights at the back.

tailback A **tailback** is a long queue of traffic moving very slowly or not at all.

tailgate The **tailgate** of a hatchback car or truck is the door at the back, which is hinged at the top so it opens upwards.

tailor (tailoring, tailored) ❑ A **tailor** is a person who makes clothes, especially clothes of high quality. The work of a tailor is sometimes called **tailoring**.

❑ **Tailored** women's suits are smart, formal, and follow the lines of the body fairly closely, rather than being loose-fitting.

❑ If something is **tailored** to particular requirements, it is specially designed, or carefully altered and adjusted, to fit those requirements.

tailor-made If something is **tailor-made** for a particular purpose, it has been specially designed for that purpose, or is particularly suitable for it. *...tailor-made holidays... His vocal style and larger-than-life personality are tailor-made to inspire loyalty.*

tailplane The **tailplane** of an aeroplane is the part at the rear, consisting of the rudder and the stabilizers.

tailspin A **tailspin** is an uncontrolled spinning dive by a plane, in which the tail spins in a wider circle than the nose. ◇ If you say something **goes into a tailspin,** you mean it begins a sudden and alarmingly rapid decline. *Share prices around the world went into a tailspin.*

tailwind A **tailwind** is a wind blowing in the direction you are travelling.

taint If water is **tainted**, impurities have got into it, and it may be dangerous to drink. ◇ You say a person is **tainted** when they are associated with something bad and this harms their reputation. *...politicians tainted by allegations of corruption.* Something which harms a person's reputation can be called a **taint**. *The taint of the bad old strike-happy days still hangs over British industry.*

take (taking, took, have taken) ❑ **Take** is used to say someone does something. For example, if you **take a look** at something, you look at it. *The woman took another step backwards... He took a photograph showing the officer examining the object.*

❑ If you **take** an attitude or view, you have that attitude or view. *The Community ministers clearly take the view that more urgent action is necessary.*

❑ The way you **take** something like a piece of news is the way you react to it. *New Yorkers took the news personally, and with great sadness.* ◇ If you are **taken aback**, you are surprised or shocked by something. ◇ The way you **take** what someone says is the way you interpret it. *He took the request as as a joke.*

❑ If you cannot **take** something, you cannot bear it. *Some wept during phone calls to their families and said they could not take much more.*

❑ If something **takes** a certain amount of time, that time will pass before it is completed. *The project will take eight years to complete.* ◇ If something **takes up** time, space, or effort, it requires it. *Large boats certainly take up more lock-space than small ones.* ◇ If something **takes** a

quality or skill, you need that quality or skill to do it. *It will take courage to take on so tough a job.*

❑ If you **take** something or **take hold** of it, you grasp it. *The constable took her arm.*

❑ If you **take** something from a place, you remove it. *The gag was taken from his mouth.* ◇ If you **take off** something you are wearing, you remove it from your body.

❑ If you **take down** a structure, you separate it into pieces and remove it. *He has been told to take down his new garden fence.*

❑ If you **take** something somewhere, you carry it there. *He took the coffee back to his office.* ◇ If you **take** someone somewhere, you drive them or lead them there. *Two people were taken to hospital... He took the children to school.* ◇ If you **take** someone **out**, you take them somewhere like a restaurant and treat them.

❑ If you **take** something which is offered to you, you accept it. ◇ If you **take** someone's advice, you follow it. ◇ If you **take** responsibility or blame for something, you accept it.

❑ If you **take** pills, medicines, or drugs, you swallow them.

❑ If someone **takes** your temperature or pulse, they measure it.

❑ If someone **takes** something of yours, they steal it, or remove it without your permission. You can also say something is **taken away** from you. *They are demanding the return of land taken away by the government.*

❑ If an army **takes** a place, it captures it.

❑ If someone **takes office** or **takes power**, they start being in control of a government or organization. *He took office as President of The Royal Society of Chemistry on July 16.*

❑ If you **take** a road or route, you travel along it. *Leave the motorway at junction 40 and take the A66 towards Keswick.* ◇ If you **take** a form of transport like a train or a taxi, you use it to travel somewhere.

❑ If you **take** a subject or course at school or university, you study it. *He decided to take a degree in political science at the University of Minnesota.* ◇ If you **take** an exam, you sit it.

❑ If you **take down** what someone is saying, you write it down.

❑ When living things **take in** air, drink, or food, they get it to enter their body, for example by breathing, drinking, or swallowing. *We take in vitamin A in our food.*

❑ If you **take in** information, you understand it when you hear it or read it. *The news seemed too much for them to take in.* ◇ If someone is **taken in,** they are deceived. *Few were taken in by his election pledge.*

❑ If a family, organization, or country **takes** people **in,** it accepts them and agrees to help them or look after them. *Germany has taken in more than 200,000 refugees.*

❑ If you **take in** something while on a trip, you include it in it. *The Ritz offers a weekend of wining, dining and dancing plus the chance to take in a West End show.*

❑ When an aircraft **takes off,** it leaves the ground. The moment when it leaves the ground is called **take-off.** *The plane caught fire on take-off.*

❑ If you **take on** a job or responsibility, you accept it. *I cannot take on any more commitments.* ◇ If an employer **takes** you **on,** they give you a job.

❑ If you **take up** a job or hobby, you start doing it. ◇ If you **take up** a post or position, you begin work in that post or position. *He was soon to take up an appointment as head of creative writing at Lancaster University.*

❑ If you **take over** a job which someone else has been doing, you start doing it in their place.

❑ If you **take to** doing something, you start doing it fairly often. *He took to criticising his ministers.* ◇ If you **take up** something which was interrupted, you continue it from the point where it stopped. *Valentine takes up the story of the rock star who disappeared at the end of the first book.*

❑ If you **take up** an offer or challenge, you accept it. ◇ If you **take** someone **on**, you fight them or compete against them. *Adidas also plans to take on Reebok and Nike in America.*

❑ If you **take it upon yourself** to do something, you do it even though it is not your duty or you have not been asked to do it.

❑ If something **takes on** a new character or meaning, it begins to have it. *The anniversary has taken on a special significance.* ◇ If you say something **takes off**, you mean it suddenly becomes successful. *She dropped out of art school when her modelling career took off.*

❑ If you **take to** someone or something, you like them immediately.

❑ If something **takes a lot out of** you, it uses up a lot of your energy.

❑ If you feel angry or upset and **take it out on** someone, you behave unpleasantly towards them, even though it is not their fault.

❑ If you **take back** something you have said, you admit you were wrong.

❑ If you **take after** someone in your family, you look or behave like them.

❑ If you **take** someone **to court,** you bring a legal case against them.

❑ If a boat is **taking in** water, water is getting into it, for example because there is a leak.

❑ **Take** is used to say someone or something is given the opportunity to show what they can do. *On Saturdays, Le Balejo comes alive with afternoon tea dances, when elderly Parisians take to the floor in real style.*

❑ You say **take** to introduce an example you want people to consider. *The city, however, is very far from quiet. Take, for example, the Trocadero fountains by the Eiffel Tower.*

take-home drinks are ones you buy to drink at home, rather than drinks bought in a pub or restaurant. *Guinness has captured a significant chunk of the take-home market.* ◇ Your **take-home pay** is the amount of your wages or salary which is left after things like tax and pension contributions have been deducted.

take-off See take.

takeaway A **takeaway** is a shop or restaurant which sells hot cooked food to be eaten elsewhere. A meal bought at a place like this is also called a **takeaway.**

taken See take.

takeover ❑ A **takeover** occurs when someone buys enough shares in a company to gain control of it. A **takeover bid** is an attempt to gain control of a company in this way.

❑ When someone takes control of a country by force, this can also be described as a **takeover.** *They believe they can achieve a classic Marxist takeover through mass action.*

taker ❑ If there are few **takers** for an offer or challenge,

hardly anyone is willing to accept it. *Existing shareholders are offered 17 new shares for every three held at the same price, but the board does not expect many takers.*

❑ **Taker** is also used to describe people who take things of various kinds. For example, a drug taker is someone who takes drugs.

takings The money something like a shop or theatre receives from selling goods or tickets is called its **takings.** *Box-office takings broke all records.*

talc is short for 'talcum powder'. **Talc** is also the mineral talcum powder is made from.

talcum powder is a soft perfumed powder which people put on their bodies after a bath or shower.

tale A **tale** is a story, especially one involving adventure. ◇ A **tale** is also an account of things which have really happened, especially an exciting or shocking one. *All families have dreadful tales of relations or neighbours who were abducted, abused or murdered.*

talent (talented) **Talent** is natural ability to do something well. A **talented** person has this ability. *...talented young journalists.*

talent scout A **talent scout** is someone whose job is to find new people who have talent, for example as footballers, models, or actors, and offer them work.

talisman A **talisman** is an object someone carries around with them because they believe it has magic powers to protect them or bring them luck. ◇ Anything people expect to bring them success or good luck can be called a **talisman.**

talk ❑ When you **talk,** you communicate using speech. If you have a **talk** with someone, you have a conversation or discussion with them. ◇ If you **talk** something **over** with someone, you discuss it with them. ◇ **Talks** are formal discussions, especially between two countries or two sides in a dispute. *...the Arab-Israeli peace talks.* ◇ When people **talk** politics or business, they discuss it. ◇ A **talking point** is something which is being discussed a lot.

❑ A **talk** is a speech or lecture, often a fairly informal one.

❑ If there is **talk** of something being done, people are considering doing it. *In the 1850s, there was talk of making adultery into a criminal misdemeanour.*

❑ If someone **talks down** to you, they talk in a way which shows they think they are cleverer or more important than you.

❑ If you **talk** something **down,** you try to make people think it is weaker or less important than it really is. *Mr Hurd was at pains to talk down his image as a son of the wealthy Tory establishment.* Similarly, if you **talk** something **up,** you try to make it seem greater or more important than it really is. *Politicians accuse the media of talking up the possibility of a riot.*

❑ If you **talk** someone **into** doing something, you persuade them to do it. Similarly, you can **talk** someone **out** of doing something. *His friends are trying to talk him out of another trip.*

❑ You say **talking of...** when you are starting a new topic which is suggested by something which has just been mentioned. *Talking of judgments, how do you assess Margaret Thatcher?*

talk show A **talk show** is the same as a chat show.

talkative If someone is **talkative**, they talk a lot.

talker is used to describe the way someone talks. *...an animated talker.*

talkie When cinema films with sound as well as pictures first came in, they were called **talkies**.

talking book A **talking book** is the same as an audio book.

talking shop If you say an organization is no more than a **talking shop**, you mean a lot of discussion takes place there but nothing useful is ever achieved.

tall ❑ If someone or something is **tall**, their height is above average. *...a tall dark man... ...tall chimneys.* ◇ **Tall** is used in questions and statements about height. *How tall are you?... She was over six feet tall.*
   ❑ If you say people can **walk tall**, you mean they can be proud of themselves and of what they are doing.
   ❑ If you say a task or job is a **tall order**, you mean it will be very difficult to achieve.
   ❑ If you call what someone says a **tall story**, you mean it is difficult to believe, because it seems so exaggerated or unlikely.

tallow is a hard animal fat used for making things like candles and soap.

tally (tallies, tallying, tallied) ❑ A **tally** is a total which keeps being added to. *Hick held three stunning catches to bring his tally to 31 for the season.*
   ❑ If two accounts of an event **tally**, they are the same, and so are probably both correct. Similarly, you can say two sets of figures **tally**.

Talmud (Talmudic) The **Talmud** is the written collection of ancient Jewish laws and traditions which governs the way of life of Orthodox Jews. **Talmudic** is used to talk about things to do with the Talmud. *...the Talmudic tradition... ...a noted Talmudic scholar.*

talon A bird of prey's **talons** are its sharp hooked claws.

tam-o'shanter A **tam-o'shanter** is a soft brimless woollen hat with a bobble on top.

tamarind The **tamarind** is a tropical tree. It has pod-like fruit called **tamarinds**, which are used in chutneys and curries.

tambourine The **tambourine** is a musical instrument which you shake or hit with your hand. It consists of a skin on a circular frame with pieces of metal around the edge which clash together.

tame (tamer, tamest; taming, tamed; tamely) ❑ A **tame** animal or bird belongs to a species which is normally wild, but has been trained or brought up to be someone's pet. *...a tame fox.* ◇ If someone **tames** a wild animal, they train it to be obedient and not to be afraid of people. A person who trains lions is called a lion **tamer**.
   ❑ When people do what they are told without questioning it, you can call their behaviour **tame**. *It is hard to imagine the great scientists of the past responding tamely to the dictates of committees.*
   ❑ If you **tame** people or things that are dangerous or likely to cause trouble, you bring them under control. *Belgium has been fairly successful at taming Flemish nationalism.*
   ❑ If you call something **tame**, you mean it is not in any way exciting or shocking. *Last night's episode of 'Casualty' proved to be a tame, rather restrained affair.*

Tampax (*plural*: Tampax) A **Tampax** is a tampon. 'Tampax' is a trademark.

tamper (tampering, tampered) If someone **tampers** with something, they interfere or meddle with it. *A preliminary investigation has found that the brakes of the train were tampered with.*

tampon A **tampon** is a firm, specially shaped piece of cotton wool which a woman places inside her vagina to absorb the blood during her period.

tan (tanning, tanned) If you **tan** or get a **tan**, your skin becomes darker as result of being exposed to the sun. *He was looking tanned and fit.* ◇ **Tan** is a pale brown colour.

tandem A **tandem** is a bicycle for two people to ride, with two saddles and two sets of pedals, one behind the other. ◇ If two people or groups work **in tandem**, they work together. Similarly, you can say two things happen **in tandem**. *The shares have fallen in tandem with the oil price for the past year.*

tandoori is an Indian method of cooking meat in a clay oven.

tang A **tang** is a strong sharp taste or smell. *...a salty tang... ...the tang of fish.* ◇ If something has some other quality which you are strongly aware of, you can say it has a particular **tang**. *Set in a town in the north of England, its language and its details have the tang of authenticity.*

tangent In geometry, a **tangent** is a straight line which touches a curve at one point but does not cross it. ◇ If someone **goes off at a tangent**, they start talking about something not directly connected with what they were talking about before.

tangential (tangentially) If there is a **tangential** relationship between two things, they are only slightly or indirectly connected. *The official figures bear only a tangential relationship to reality... The question of sovereignty will only be touched on tangentially.*

tangerine Tangerines are a type of small sweet orange with a loose skin. ◇ **Tangerine** is a reddish-orange colour.

tangible (tangibly) If something is **tangible**, it can be seen to exist or be happening. *He must make the reforms work in such a way as to improve people's lives tangibly.*

tangle (tangling, tangled) ❑ If something like hair or string is **tangled** or in a **tangle**, it is twisted together untidily. *...the tangled wreckage of the coach... Most of the fungus is a tangle of tentacles called the mycelium.* ◇ A **tangled** story or plot is extremely complicated.
   ❑ If you are **tangled** in something like rope or **tangled up** in it, you are caught or trapped in it. ◇ If you are involved in a complicated and difficult situation, you can say you are **tangled** or **tangled up** in it. You can call a situation like this a **tangle**. *The government and the opposition are tangled in a constitutional row... ...the complex tangle of claims and counter-claims.*
   ❑ If you **tangle with** someone, you get involved in a fight or dispute with them. *By obeying the Code, film makers could usually avoid tangling with censorship boards.*

tango (tangos) The **tango** is a South American dance for two people. When people **tango**, they dance the tango.

tangy If food is **tangy**, it has a strong sharp taste. *...a tangy tomato and thyme sauce.*

tank ❑ A **tank** is a large container for liquid or gas.
   ❑ A **tank** is also an armour-plated military vehicle which has caterpillar tracks instead of wheels and is equipped with guns or rockets.

tankard A tankard is a large metal beer mug.

tanker A tanker is a ship, lorry, or rail vehicle used for transporting large quantities of gas or liquid.

tankful A tankful of liquid or gas is the amount you can get in a tank.

tanned See tan.

tannery (tanneries) A tannery is a factory where animal skins are made into leather.

tannin is a yellow or brown chemical which occurs in the bark and leaves of many trees. It is used in the processing of leather and in dyeing.

Tannoy A Tannoy is a system of loudspeakers used to make public announcements, for example at a fete or a sports stadium. 'Tannoy' is a trademark.

tantalize (tantalizing, tantalized; tantalizingly) (can be spelled with an 's' instead of a 'z') If something tantalizes you, it gives you an exciting feeling of anticipation without actually giving you what you want. ...a tantalizing glimpse of leg... The prospect of agreement is tantalizingly close.

tantamount If you say something is tantamount to a certain thing, you mean it has the same effects or implications, and can be regarded as that thing. Mr Shapi said the raid was tantamount to a declaration of war.

tantrum A tantrum is a noisy childish outburst of bad temper.

Taoiseach (pron: tee-shak) The Taoiseach is the prime minister of the Republic of Ireland.

Taoism (pron: tow-iz-zum) is a Chinese religious philosophy according to which people should live a simple honest life and not seek to interfere with the natural course of events.

tap (tapping, tapped; tapper) ❑ A tap is a device you turn in order to control the flow of liquid or gas from a pipe or container.
   ❑ If you tap something or give it a tap, you hit it lightly with your fingers or with something like a hammer. You can also tap on something like a door. ◇ If you tap your fingers, you repeatedly hit them against a surface like a table. Similarly, you can tap your feet on the floor, especially in time to music.
   ❑ If your phone is tapped, a device is secretly connected to it, so someone can listen to your calls without you knowing.
   ❑ If someone taps a tree, especially a rubber tree, they get sap out of it by making a cut in its trunk. The sap of a rubber tree is called latex, and is used to make rubber. People who tap rubber trees as their job are called rubber tappers. ◇ If you tap a resource or situation, you make use of it. The opposition parties could succeed by tapping this anti-government feeling.

tap dance (tap dancer) When people tap dance, they do a rapid dance wearing special shoes with metal on the heels and toes which make clicking noises as their feet hit the floor. People who entertain audiences by doing this kind of dancing are called tap dancers.

tape (taping, taped) ❑ Tape is a narrow plastic strip covered with a magnetic substance. It is used to record sounds, pictures, and computer information. ◇ A tape is a cassette or spool with magnetic tape wound round it. ◇ If you tape something, you record it on a tape. ...a taped interview.
   ❑ Tape or sticky tape is thin strips of plastic coated with adhesive, used for sticking things together. If you tape one thing to another, you attach it using tape like this. ...a sign taped to the wall.

tape deck In a hi-fi system, the tape deck is a machine for playing tapes or for recording on them.

tape measure A tape measure is a strip of plastic, cloth, or thin flexible metal which is marked, usually in both centimetres and inches, so it can be used for measuring things.

tape recorder A tape recorder is machine for playing tapes or for recording on them.

taper (tapering, tapered) ❑ If something tapers or is tapered, it gradually becomes narrower at one end. ...tapering black candles... ...a tapered concrete channel.
   ❑ If something tapers off, it gradually decreases.
   ❑ A taper is a fast-burning strip of material, used, especially in the past, for lighting fires.

tapestry (tapestries) A tapestry is a piece of heavy cloth with a picture or pattern woven into it.

tapeworm Tapeworms are parasitic worms which live in the intestines of some animals, including humans.

tapioca (pron: tap-ee-oh-ka) is a starchy substance obtained from dried cassava root. It looks like tiny beads and is used with milk to make a pudding, also called tapioca.

tapir (pron: tape-er) Tapirs are large pig-like mammals in South and Central America and south-east Asia. They have long snouts and short legs.

tapper See tap.

tar (tarred) ❑ Tar is a thick black sticky substance obtained by distilling coal or wood. It is used especially in making road surfaces. If something is tarred, it is coated in tar. ◇ Tar is also one of the poisonous substances in tobacco.
   ❑ If someone's reputation is tarred, it has been seriously harmed. You can also say someone is tarred with something when they are blamed for it. ...the Front's tarred image... He will not want to be tarred with responsibility for throwing thousands out of work. ◇ If you talk about someone being tarred with the same brush as someone else, you mean they are considered to have the same faults.

taramasalata (pron: tar-ram-as-sal-lah-ta) is a pinkish Greek food made from smoked cod roe. It is usually served as a starter in the form of a dip.

tarantula (pron: ta-rant-yoo-la) Tarantulas are large hairy spiders from warm places such as South America and the tropics. They can give you a bite which is painful but not usually serious.

tardy (tardiness) If you say someone is tardy in doing something, you mean they are not doing it quickly enough. ...Washington's tardy response... He grew impatient with their tardiness.

target (targeting, targeted) ❑ A target is an object you fire bullets or arrows at when you are practising shooting or archery.
   ❑ In war, any place or object which a shell, bomb, or missile is aimed at can be called a target. You can also say a place or object is targeted. The government had rejected claims that there were civilian casualties, saying the rebel bases were targeted very carefully.
   ❑ If someone is threatened or criticized, you can say they are the target of threats or criticism. They are the

target of insult and abuse from local people.

❑ Your **target** is the thing you are trying to achieve. *The park has already fallen behind schedule for its annual target of 11 million visitors.* If you are **on target,** you are making good progress and likely to achieve the thing you want.

❑ If you **target** a particular group of people, you try to appeal to them or help them. *Games companies are targeting the young female market.*

tariff A **tariff** is a tax on imported goods. ◇ A **tariff** is also a scale of charges. *...electricity tariffs.*

Tarmac is a material for making road surfaces. It consists of crushed stones mixed with tar. 'Tarmac' is a trademark. ◇ You can refer to any area with a Tarmac surface as the **tarmac,** especially the parts of an airport where planes stand when they load or unload.

tarn A **tarn** is a small mountain lake or pool, especially in the north of England.

tarnish (tarnishes, tarnishing, tarnished) ❑ If a metal **tarnishes** or becomes **tarnished,** it becomes stained and loses its brightness. ❑ If something **tarnishes** someone's reputation, it spoils it. *Corruption scandals tarnished the party's image.*

tarot (*pron:* **tarr-oh**) The **tarot** is a set of special cards with pictures on them, used for telling the future.

tarpaulin A **tarpaulin** is a sheet of heavy waterproof material used as a protective cover.

tarragon is a herb with narrow green leaves used in cooking.

tarred See **tar.**

tarry (tarries, tarrying, tarried) If you **tarry** somewhere, you stay longer than you intended to.

tarsal (tarsus) The **tarsals** are the bones forming the ankle, heel, and upper foot. Together they are called the **tarsus.**

tart (tartly, tarty) ❑ A **tart** is a shallow pastry case with a sweet filling like fruit or jam. ❑ A **tart** remark is unpleasant and rather cruel. *'I thought one or two of our players were more interested in making war than playing football,' Taylor observed tartly.* ❑ Prostitutes are sometimes called **tarts.** ◇ Other women get called **tarts** when they dress or behave in a vulgar, sexually provocative way. Women like these are also described as **tarty.** *...tarty girls in miniskirts.* ❑ If you say something has been **tarted up,** you mean someone has tried to improve its appearance, but in a way you consider cheap and vulgar. *The pub has been tarted up with carriage lamps, horse brasses and so on.*

tartan is woollen cloth with a pattern of woven stripes of different widths and colours crossing each other at right angles. Each Scottish clan has its own design of tartan.

tartar is a hard yellowish substance which forms on teeth. It consists of mineral salts, food particles, and bacteria.

tartare sauce is a thick unheated sauce made of chopped onions, capers, and mayonnaise. It is usually eaten with fish.

tarty See **tart.**

task (tasked) ❑ A **task** is a job or piece of work. If someone is given an important job or responsibility, you can say they are **tasked** with it. *...international institutions tasked with keeping the peace.* ❑ A **task force** is a section of an army, navy, or air force

sent to carry out a military operation. ◇ A **task force** is also a group of people assembled to do a piece of work. *The bank recently set up an internal task force to deal with the robbery problem.*

taskmaster If you say someone is a hard **taskmaster,** you mean they make the people under them work very hard.

tassel (tasselled) (*American spelling:* tasseled) A **tassel** is a bunch of loose threads or cords bound at one end and hung as a decoration from something like a curtain or piece of clothing. If something is **tasselled,** it is decorated with a tassel or tassels. *...a red tasselled dressing table.*

taste (tasting, tasted) ❑ Your sense of **taste** is your ability to recognize the flavour of things with your tongue. ❑ The **taste** of something is its flavour. If you **taste** something, you become aware of its flavour. If it **tastes** good, it has a pleasant flavour. If it **tastes** of a particular thing, it has that flavour. *The Edradour tastes of mint, honey and nuts.* ◇ If you **taste** food, for example when you are cooking, you put a small amount in your mouth to see what it tastes like. Similarly, you can **taste** a wine to judge its quality or see if you like it. ❑ If you have a short experience of something, especially for the first time, you can say you have a **taste** of it. *India has had a taste of success as an exporter.* ◇ If you develop a **taste** for something, you get to like it. ❑ A person's **tastes** are the types of thing they enjoy or like to have around them. *Ferdinand was strongly influenced by the musical tastes of his father.* ◇ If you say a person has good **taste,** you mean they recognize and appreciate things of good quality. *She had impeccable taste in clothes.* ❑ If you say something is in bad **taste,** you mean it does not conform to what is proper or decent, and is offensive. *I wish to object in the strongest possible way to the poor taste of Heath's cartoon.* **Good taste** is conforming to what is proper and decent. *Hollywood needs to bring back decency and good taste.*

taste bud Your **taste buds** are the clusters of cells on the surface of your tongue which enable you to taste food and drink.

tasteful (tastefully) If you say something is **tasteful,** you mean it is attractive and elegant and shows good taste. *Her tasteful home was furnished with prints by Klee, Picasso, and Cartier-Bresson... ...this tastefully-packaged triple-album boxed set.*

tasteless (tastelessly, tastelessness) ❑ If you say something is **tasteless,** you mean it is vulgar and unattractive and shows poor taste. *...tasteless and excessive decorations.* ◇ A **tasteless** joke or remark does not conform to what is considered decent and is therefore offensive. *His book lost the Whitbread First Novel prize on an objection for tastelessness.* ❑ **Tasteless** food has very little taste and is therefore not pleasant.

taster ❑ A **taster** is someone whose job is tasting wines, teas, or other things to test their quality. ❑ A **taster** is also a small sample of something which gives an indication of what it is like. *I fear this is only a taster of what will happen when more services are privatised.*

tasty (tastier, tastiest) **Tasty** food has a strong pleasant flavour. **Tasty** is usually used to describe savoury rather than sweet food.

tat is used to talk about things which are tasteless, worthless, or of poor quality. *...shops selling an astounding variety of tat.*

tattered (tatters) A **tattered** piece of clothing is badly torn. You can also say it is **in tatters**. If you describe people as **tattered**, you mean their clothes are badly torn. *...tattered troops.* ◇ If something like a system, organization, or plan is **tattered** or **in tatters**, it is in a very bad state. *The country's economy is in tatters.*

tattoo (tattooist) ❑ If someone is **tattooed**, they have designs drawn on their skin by a process which involves pricking little holes and filling them with coloured dye. These designs are called **tattoos**. A person who tattoos people is called a **tattooist**.
❑ A military **tattoo** is a public display of parades, exercises, and music by the armed forces, usually at night.
❑ A **tattoo** is also a rapid and regular series of drumbeats or similar sounds. *Her fingers played a frantic tattoo on the back of her chair.*

tatty If something is **tatty**, it is shabby and untidy. *...a tatty briefcase.*

taught See **teach**.

taunt If someone **taunts** you, they speak offensively and mock you about your weaknesses or misfortunes, to upset or annoy you. The things they say are called **taunts**. *The prison governor has criticised his staff for taunting the inmates.*

taut (tautly) ❑ If something is **taut**, it is stretched very tight. *He pulled the rope taut.*
❑ If you call something like a book or film **taut**, you mean it is concentrated and controlled, with no unnecessary details. *...a taut thriller... ...tautly written stories.* ◇ If a situation is **taut**, it is full of tension and anxiety. *The atmosphere is taut.*

tautology (tautologies; tautological) A **tautology** is a phrase or statement which uses different words to say the same thing twice. For example, calling something a 'new novelty' would be a tautology. You say a phrase or statement like this is **tautological**.

tavern is an old word for a pub.

tawdry (tawdriness) ❑ **Tawdry** things are cheap, vulgar, and of poor quality. You can call entertainment **tawdry** when it is of poor quality and in bad taste. *The tawdriness of the show's perpetual phone-ins and insulting jokes have to be heard to be believed.* You say a place is **tawdry** when it is showy and vulgar and has shops selling cheap things. *...a tawdry seaside town.*
❑ If you say someone's actions are **tawdry**, you mean they are shameful and unpleasant, and perhaps dishonest or immoral. *...a tawdry series of affairs and free holidays.*

tawny If something is **tawny**, it is yellowish-brown.

tax (taxes, taxing, taxed) ❑ **Tax** is money people have to pay to the government. It is used to pay for things like defence, education, and health care. ◇ If a sum of money is **taxed**, the person who receives it must pay a proportion of it as tax. ◇ When goods are **taxed**, a proportion of their price must be paid to the government. *Whisky will be taxed at a minimum of £1 a bottle.* ◇ If a person or company is **taxed**, they have to pay a proportion of their income or profits to the government.
❑ **Tax evasion** is breaking the law by deliberately not paying any tax or not paying enough tax.

❑ **tax avoidance:** see **avoid**.
❑ A **tax haven** is a country where taxes are so low that wealthy people choose to live or register companies there, to save money on tax. Wealthy people who live in places like these are called **tax exiles**.
❑ If something **taxes** you, it requires a lot of physical or mental effort. You say something like this is **taxing**. *...his taxing four-day schedule.*

tax-deductible See **deductible**.

tax disc A **tax disc** is a small round piece of paper displayed on a car windscreen or in a special holder on a motorcycle, to show the owner has paid the annual road tax.

tax-free If things like payments, goods, or services are **tax-free**, you do not have to pay tax on them. *...a tax-free bonus.*

tax return See **return**.

tax year A **tax year** is a twelve-month period used by the government as a basis for calculating taxes and organizing its own finances and accounts. In Britain, the tax year begins on April 6th.

taxable If something is **taxable**, you have to pay tax on it.

taxation is the system by which a government collects money from people to spend on things like defence, education, and health care. **Taxation** is also the amount of money collected. *They will have to cut spending on services or increase local taxation.*

taxi (plural: taxis) (taxies, taxiing, taxied) ❑ A **taxi** is a car whose driver is paid by people to take them where they want to go.
❑ When an aircraft **taxies**, it moves slowly along the runway, for example to get into position for take-off or to return to the terminal after landing.

taxi rank A **taxi rank** is a place where taxis wait for passengers, for example at an airport or outside a station.

taxicab is an old name for a taxi.

taxidermy (taxidermist) **Taxidermy** is the craft of stuffing dead animals and birds so they look lifelike and can be displayed. A **taxidermist** is an expert at this.

taxing See **tax**.

taxman (taxmen) When people talk about the **taxman** or the **taxmen**, they mean the government department responsible for collecting taxes. In Britain, this department is the Inland Revenue.

taxonomy (taxonomist) **Taxonomy** is the naming of things like plants and animals and their classification in groups according to their similarities and differences. A **taxonomist** is a person who studies or specializes in taxonomy.

taxpayer **Taxpayers** are people who pay a proportion of their income to the government as tax.

TB See **tuberculosis**.

Te Deum (pron: tee dee-um) The **Te Deum** is an ancient Christian prayer, originally in Latin. There are many musical settings of the Te Deum, including some by famous composers.

tea is a drink made by pouring boiling water over the chopped dried leaves of a plant called the tea bush. The dried leaves are also called **tea**. ◇ Other drinks made by pouring hot water on dried leaves are also called **tea**, for example mint tea and camomile tea.
❑ **Tea** is also a meal. For some people, **tea** is a light

afternoon meal consisting of things like sandwiches and cakes; for others, it is the main meal of the day, eaten in the early evening.
❏ If you say something is **not your cup of tea**, you mean it is not the sort of thing that appeals to you.

tea bag Tea bags are small perforated paper bags with tea leaves in them. You put them in a cup or teapot and pour in hot water to make tea.

tea break If you have a **tea break**, you stop working and have a cup of tea or coffee.

tea caddy (tea caddies) A **tea caddy** is a small tin for storing tea.

tea chest A **tea chest** is a large wooden box in which tea is packed when it is exported. People sometimes use tea chests to pack things in, for example when moving house.

tea cosy (tea cosies) A **tea cosy** is a wool or cloth cover which you put over a teapot to keep the tea hot.

tea leaf Tea leaves are the small pieces of dried leaves left in a teapot or cup after you have drunk the tea.

tea party A **tea party** is a social gathering in the afternoon at which people have tea, sandwiches, and cakes.

tea room A **tea room** is a small restaurant or cafe where tea, coffee, cakes, and light meals are served.

tea service A **tea service** or **tea set** is a set of cups, saucers, and plates with a milk jug, sugar bowl, and teapot, used when tea is served.

tea shop A **tea shop** is the same as a tea room.

tea strainer A **tea strainer** is a metal or plastic object with small holes in it, used to stop tea leaves going into the cup when you are pouring tea.

teacake Teacakes are round flat sweet rolls, usually containing dried fruit. You eat them toasted and spread with butter.

teach (teaches, teaching, taught) ❏ If you **teach** someone something, you explain it to them, to help them learn about it or learn how to do it. ◇ If you **teach** as your job, you help students learn about something at a school, college, or university.
❏ If you have been **taught** to think or behave in a certain way, you have been brought up to believe that is the correct way to think or behave. *Youngsters growing up in the federal republic have been taught to be good Europeans.*
❏ The **teachings** of a religious faith or political doctrine are the ideas upheld and taught by its followers.

teach-in A **teach-in** is a meeting between students and teachers at which important and controversial subjects can be discussed. Teach-ins are not usually part of a formal academic course.

teacher A **teacher** is someone who teaches, especially at a school.

teaching hospital A **teaching hospital** is a hospital linked to a medical school, where medical students and newly qualified doctors receive practical training.

teacloth A **teacloth** is a cloth for drying dishes.

teacup A teacup is a cup you drink tea from. ◇ **storm in a teacup**: see storm.

teak is a hard wood from a South-East Asian tree. It is golden brown, resistant to decay, and often used to make high quality furniture.

teal (plural: teal) Teal are a kind of small wild duck. The male has a brightly coloured head.

team (teaming, teamed) ❏ A **team** is a group of people who play against another group in a sport or game. ◇ You can call any group of people who work together a **team**. *...the new management team... ...a team of auditors.* ◇ **Team spirit** is a feeling of pride, loyalty, and companionship which enables people in a team to work well together.
❏ If you **team up** with someone, you join with them to try to achieve something together.

team-mate A sportsperson's **team-mates** are other people in the same team.

teamster In the US and Canada, lorry drivers are sometimes called teamsters.

teamwork is the ability of a group of people to work together effectively.

teapot A **teapot** is a container with a lid, handle, and spout, used for making and serving tea.

tear (tearing, tore, have torn) ❏ Tears are the drops of liquid which come out of your eyes when you cry. If someone is **in tears**, they are crying.
❏ If you **tear** something like a piece of cloth or paper, you pull it so it starts to come apart or a long narrow hole appears in it. The hole is called a **tear**.
❏ If you **tear up** a piece of paper, you destroy it by pulling it into small pieces. ◇ If you talk about something like a contract being **torn up**, you mean it is abandoned or abolished. *...the Europhobes who would like the Treaty of Rome torn up.*
❏ If you **tear** your clothes **off**, you take them off quickly and roughly.
❏ If people **tear** something **down**, they quickly dismantle or destroy it. *The barbed-wire fence has been torn down.*
❏ **Tear** is used to describe the violent effects of something like a wind or an explosion. *The blast tore away a granite block at the base.*
❏ If a country or organization is **torn apart**, it is seriously harmed by fighting or disputes among its citizens or members. *Airbus now risks being torn apart by another dispute.* ◇ If a country or region is **war-torn**, it is suffering from the effects of a war. **-torn** can be added to other words which describe fighting or conflict. *...the riot-torn city... ...a highly unstable and strife-torn country.*
❏ If you say people are **torn**, you mean they cannot make up their minds about something, or they have desires or responsibilities which conflict. *Today's career woman is torn between family and work.*
❏ If you cannot **tear yourself away** from a place, you are very unwilling to leave, because you are enjoying yourself.
❏ If you say someone is **tearing their hair**, you mean they are full of anxiety or frustration.
❏ If you are **tearing along**, you are walking or driving very quickly.

tear gas is a gas which irritates the eyes and can cause severe coughing. It is sometimes used by police to control crowds.

tear-jerker (tear-jerking) If you call a play, film, or book a **tear-jerker**, you mean it tries to appeal to people by being very sad and sentimental. Things which try to appeal to people in this way can be called **tear-jerking**. *...a tear-jerking speech.*

tearaway A tearaway is a badly-behaved young person.

teardrop A teardrop is a single tear.

tearful (tearfully) If someone is **tearful,** they are crying, or on the verge of crying. ...*Mary Decker's tearful departure from the stadium... He tearfully asks forgiveness.*

tease (teasing, teased) ❑ If you **tease** someone, you say things to embarrass or provoke them, as a joke. ◇ You also say someone **teases** someone else when they offer them something and get them excited only to disappoint and frustrate them by not giving it to them. ...*keeping us in teasing suspense.*

❑ If you **tease out** information, you discover it by persistent questioning or investigation.

teaser A teaser is a difficult problem or puzzle.

teaspoon A teaspoon is a small spoon, often used to stir sugar in tea or coffee. ◇ A **teaspoon** of food or liquid is the same as a teaspoonful.

teaspoonful (*plural:* teaspoonsful *or* teaspoonfuls) A **teaspoonful** of food or liquid is the amount a teaspoon will hold.

teat A female animal's **teats** are the pointed parts on her body which her babies suck to get milk. ◇ A **teat** is also a piece of rubber shaped like a teat and fitted to a baby's feeding bottle.

teatime is the period of the day when people have their tea.

tech (*pron:* tek) A **tech** is the same as a technical college.

technical (technically) ❑ **Technical** is used to talk about such things as the working of machinery, industrial processes, transport, and communications. *Production has been troubled by delays and technical problems.*

❑ **Technical** is also used to talk about a person's ability to cope with practical things or with the practical aspects of something. *They had difficulty finding workers with the right technical skills... Few British jazz singers have ever been really convincing, technically or emotionally.*

❑ **Technical** language consists of special words, or familiar words used in a special way, in a subject like law, accountancy, or engineering. *Their information handouts use so many long technical words that I spend half my time looking them up in the dictionary.*

❑ If something is **technically** true, it is true according to a strict interpretation of the facts, laws, or rules, but may not be important or appropriate in the situation you are describing. *These states are still technically in a state of war with Israel.*

technical college A technical college is a college of further education which runs various courses, especially in work-related subjects.

technicality (technicalities) The **technicalities** of a process or subject are its practical details, especially those which only experts are likely to know about or understand. ◇ A **technicality** is a point based on a strict interpretation of a law or set of rules. *The three suspected IRA members may go free next week because of a legal technicality.*

technician A technician is someone whose job involves skilled practical work. ...*a laboratory technician.*

Technicolor is a system of colour photography used in making cinema films. 'Technicolor' is a trademark.

technique A technique is a way of doing something. ...*a manufacturing technique... ...a new surgical technique which involves 'patching' damaged heart tissue after a heart attack.*

◇ **Technique** is skill or ability developed through training and practice. *He went off to the Amsterdam Academy to improve his technique.*

techno is a form of dance music with a harsh repetitive thumping rhythm and usually no melody or lyrics.

techno- is used to create words which describe things involving technology, especially high technology. ...*sophisticated techno-thrillers... ...techno-parks full of computer companies.*

technocracy (technocracies; technocrat, technocratic) A **technocracy** is a system of government or management in which the important decisions are made by scientists, engineers, and other technical experts. A system like this can be called **technocratic**; the people in charge are called **technocrats.**

technology (technologies; technological, technologist) **Technology** is the practical application of scientific knowledge, especially in the form of advanced scientific methods and equipment. ...*the wonders of modern technology.* **Technological** is used to talk about things to do with technology. ...*technological advances... ...a technological breakthrough.* A specialist in some form of technology is called a **technologist.** ...*air-quality technologists.* ◇ Advanced scientific equipment is often called **technology.** *Big firms can afford to buy new technology.* ◇ A particular set of equipment or methods can be called a **technology.** *Both products claim to use fuzzy logic, a technology that tries to make computers copy humans.*

tectonic Tectonics or **plate tectonics** is the study of the earth's crust based on the theory that it is divided into large pieces called 'plates', which are drifting extremely slowly on the molten rock beneath. **Tectonic** is used to talk about things to do with this theory. ...*tectonic drift... ...the tectonic history of continents.*

teddy (teddies) A **teddy** or **teddy bear** is a soft toy which looks like a friendly bear.

Teddy boy Teddy boys were young men of the 1950s who wore long jackets, tight 'drainpipe' trousers, and soft thick-soled shoes. They brushed their hair back and had sideburns. Teddy boys were associated with early rock and roll music and were often thought of as violent and aggressive.

tedious (tediously, tedium) If something is **tedious,** it is dull and boring, because it is repetitive or seems to take a long time. *These introductory chapters are tediously repetitive and lacking in style.* You can talk about the **tedium** of something like this. *Gruber graphically depicts the grinding tedium of life in a penal colony.*

tee (teeing, teed) In golf, a **tee** is a small piece of plastic or wood which the golfer pushes into the ground and stands the ball on, ready for a shot. Tees are only used for the first shot of each hole. When a golfer plays this shot, you say he or she **tees off.** The area of ground where the golfers are allowed to tee off is also called a tee.

tee-shirt A tee-shirt is the same as a T-shirt.

teem (teeming, teemed) If a place is **teeming** with people or animals, there are very many of them moving around or going about their business. ...*a teeming city... The rivers of Connemara once teemed with sea trout.*

teen See teens.

teenager (teenaged, teenage) **Teenagers** are young people aged 13 to 19. **Teenaged** is used to describe young people of this age. *...teenaged car thieves.* **Teenage** is used to describe things to do with teenagers. *...teenage fashion... ...the problem of teenage pregnancy.*

teens (teen) A person's **teens** are the years of their life when they are a teenager. *...a girl in her late teens.* **Teen** is used to describe things involving or associated with teenagers. *He became the United States' first teen idol... Betsy Byars is one of the best American writers for the preteen and teen market.*

teeny means the same as 'tiny'. *...a teeny chair... It could be just a teeny bit embarrassing if the news gets out.*

teepee See tepee.

teeter (teetering, teetered) ❑ If someone is **teetering**, they are wobbling or moving about unsteadily. **Teetering** is used especially to describe a woman walking on very high heels.
   ❑ If something is **teetering** on the edge of some disaster, it is very close to it. *The corporation was teetering on the edge of collapse... ...the teetering economy.*

teeth See tooth.

teething ❑ If a baby is **teething**, its teeth are starting to appear. This can cause pain and make the baby irritable.
   ❑ If a project experiences a few problems at its start, you can say it has **teething problems** or **teething troubles**.

teetotal (teetotaller) (*American spelling:* teetotaler) If someone is **teetotal** or a **teetotaller**, they never drink alcohol.

TEFL is teaching English to people whose first language is not English. TEFL stands for 'teaching English as a foreign language'.

Teflon is a type of plastic used to coat non-stick pans. 'Teflon' is a trademark.

tele-conference (tele-conferencing) A **tele-conference** is a conference or discussion where the people involved are connected via television and telephone links rather than sitting in the same room. Having conferences of this sort is called **tele-conferencing**.

telecom is short for 'telecommunications'.

telecommunications is the science and technology of sending and receiving signals and messages over long distances using electronic equipment. Telecommunications includes the telephone, radio, television, and fax.

telecommute (telecommuting, telecommuted; telecommuter) People who **telecommute** work from home and are connected to their office by a computer link and a telephone or fax. People who work like this are called telecommuters.

telegenic If you say someone is **telegenic**, you mean they look good on TV.

telegram A **telegram** is a message sent by telegraph and then printed and delivered.

telegraph (telegraphic) **Telegraph** is a system of sending messages over long distances by electrical or radio signals. **Telegraphic** is used to talk about things to do with this system. *Some of the payments were telegraphic transfers and others went by mail.* If you **telegraph** someone, others send them a message by telegraph.

telegraph pole Telegraph poles are the tall poles used to hold up telephone wires.

telemetry (*pron:* til-lem-i-tree) is the use of things like radio waves and telephone cables to transmit the readings of measuring instruments over a long distance to a device where they are displayed or recorded.

telepathy (telepathic) **Telepathy** is direct mind-to-mind communication without words or visual signals which is thought to exist but which has not been explained scientifically. **Telepathic** is used to describe communication like this. *...telepathic messages.*

telephone (telephoning, telephoned; telephonic) The **telephone** is an electrical system you use to talk to someone in another place by dialling a number on a piece of equipment and speaking into it. The piece of equipment is called a **telephone**. When you **telephone** someone, you dial their number and speak to them by telephone. When you are speaking to someone like this, you say you are on the telephone. **Telephonic** is used to talk about things to do with the telephone. *...a telephonic conversation.*

telephone booth A telephone booth is (a) the same as a telephone box. (b) a small cubicle or screened-off area in a public building where there is a public telephone.

telephone box A telephone box is a small shelter in the street with a public telephone in it.

telephone directory A telephone directory is a book containing an alphabetical list of names, addresses, and telephone numbers of the people in a town or area.

telephone exchange A telephone exchange is a building where telephone calls are connected. Nowadays, most telephone exchanges are automatic.

telephone number Your telephone number is the number people dial when they telephone you.

telephonic See telephone.

telephonist (*pron:* tel-lef-o-nist) A **telephonist** is someone who works in a telephone exchange, or whose job is to answer the telephone for a business or other organization.

telephony (*pron:* tel-lef-o-nee) is telephone communication, either by wires or radio signals.

telephoto A **telephoto** lens is a lens you attach to a camera and adjust to make distant things appear larger and clearer on your photographs.

teleprinter A **teleprinter** is a telegraphic printer which prints out messages it receives from machines in other places, and can also be used to transmit messages.

telescope (telescoping, telescoped) ❑ A **telescope** is an instrument, usually long and tube-shaped, for looking at distant objects. Lenses in the telescope make the objects seem larger and nearer.
   ❑ If something is **telescoped**, it is made to last for a shorter period, by leaving some parts out.

telescopic instruments and lenses make things seem larger and nearer. *...a rifle with telescopic sights.*
   ❑ A **telescopic** device has sections which fit or slide into each other so its length can be adjusted.

teletext is a system of broadcasting pages of written information, for example news, weather, and sports reports, on TV.

telethon A **telethon** is a very long TV programme which is broadcast live to raise funds for a charitable cause.

televangelist Televangelists are evangelists, chiefly in the US, who preach on TV, often on their own cable networks.

televiewer People who watch TV are sometimes called

televiewers.

televise (televising, televised) If something is **televised**, it is shown on TV.

television or **TV** is the system of sending pictures and sounds by electrical signals over a distance so people can receive them in their homes. The device you receive them on, which has a glass screen where pictures appear, is called a **television** or a **television set**. ◇ Television is also the programmes people watch on these sets. *I watch television all the time.* ◇ The business of making and broadcasting TV programmes is also called **television**. *She is looking for a job in television.*

televisual is used to talk about things to do with television. *In many Olympic sports, televisual evidence is not accepted... ...a moment of televisual history.*

telex (telexes, telexing, telexed) **Telex** is an international system of sending written messages. The message is typed on a machine in one place and is immediately printed out by a machine in another place. These machines are called **telexes**. If you **telex** someone or send them a **telex**, you send them a message using this system.

tell (telling, told; tellingly) ❑ If someone **tells** you something, they speak or write to you, giving you information. *'Some guys thought they'd be here forever,' one worker told a reporter.*
❑ If something **tells** you something, you can draw conclusions from it. *The results tell us that it's a very effective treatment.* ◇ If you say something is **telling**, you mean it reveals the truth about a situation *The BBC Moscow correspondent said the result was a telling sign of Georgians' desire for independence... His list is tellingly short.*
❑ If you can **tell** what is happening or what is true, you are able to make correct judgements about it. *By then the audience couldn't tell the difference between reality and illusion.* ◇ If you cannot **tell** people or things **apart**, you cannot see the difference between them.
❑ If you **tell** someone to do something, you order, instruct, or advise them to do it.
❑ If you **tell** someone **off**, you speak crossly to them about something wrong they have done.
❑ If you **tell** a story or joke, you repeat it to someone.
❑ If an unpleasant or tiring experience begins to **tell**, it begins to have a serious effect on you. *His punishing schedule is beginning to tell on his health.*

teller ❑ If someone tells a lot of stories or jokes, you can say they are a **teller** of stories or jokes.
❑ A **teller** is a cashier, especially one in a bank.
❑ A **teller** is also someone appointed to count votes, for example at an election or in parliament.
❑ A **teller machine** or **automated teller machine** is the same as a cash dispenser.

telly (tellies) **Telly** is television. A **telly** is a television set.

temerity (*pron:* tim-**merr**-it-tee) If someone does something impudent or disrespectful, you can say they have the **temerity** to do it. *He had the temerity to flatly refuse a Government edict.*

temp A **temp** is a secretary employed by an agency to work for short periods for different organizations.

temper (tempering, tempered) ❑ If you say someone has a **temper** or a **bad temper**, you mean they become angry easily, and express their anger in a violent or emotional

way. You say someone who becomes angry easily is **quick-tempered**. When someone becomes angry on a particular occasion, you say they **lose their temper**. If a lot of people do it, you can describe the occasion as a **bad-tempered** or **ill-tempered** one. *Australia and Spain drew 1-1 in an ill-tempered match.*
❑ If you talk about the **temper** of a group of people, you mean their general mood or attitude to something. *The public temper is for stiff penalties and the locking up of offenders, not tender care.*
❑ When newly-made steel or a steel tool is **tempered,** it is re-heated at a lower temperature, to make it less hard and brittle.
❑ If something is **tempered** by something else, it is softened or made less severe or extreme. *Admiration of him is tempered by a sense that he is too aloof... He has been trying to temper his naturally aggressive style of play.*

temperament (temperamentally) Your **temperament** is your basic nature and outlook, which shows in the way you respond to various things that happen. You use **temperamentally** when you are talking about someone's temperament. *He was temperamentally unsuited to be president.*

temperamental people are emotional, excitable, and subject to sudden mood changes. ◇ If you say a machine or device is **temperamental**, you mean it is unreliable and often does not work properly.

temperance The **temperance** movement is a campaign to stop people drinking alcohol because it is thought to be dangerous or morally wrong. The temperance movement was powerful in the 19th and early 20th centuries.

temperate If a place is **temperate** or has a **temperate** climate, it never gets very hot or very cold there. **Temperate** plants grow best in temperate climates.

temperature ❑ The **temperature** is how hot or cold it is, usually expressed in degrees Celsius or Fahrenheit. ◇ Your **temperature** is the temperature of your body. If you **have a temperature**, your temperature is higher than normal, because you are ill. If someone **takes your temperature**, they use a thermometer to measure your temperature.
❑ If you talk about the **temperature** of a situation, you mean the level of excitement or emotion involved. *The political temperature was raised by a series of interventions from the Conservative backbenches.*

tempest ❑ A **tempest** is a violent storm.
❑ You can also call an angry outburst a **tempest**. *Sony's 1989 purchase of Columbia provoked a tempest of criticism.*

tempestuous If you call an event or relationship **tempestuous**, you mean the people involved keep having angry arguments or quarrels. *The only try of a tempestuous game was scored by full back Greg Martin.* ◇ You can also call stormy weather conditions **tempestuous**.

template A **template** is a thin board or plate cut into a special shape or pattern, used as a guide for cutting materials like metal, wood, or fabric. ◇ A **template** is also a model or example which people try to follow. *In terms of plot, Boam and Kamen have conformed to the perfect template of the cop movie.*

temple ❑ In some religions, a building of worship is called a **temple**. *...a Sikh temple.*
❑ A person's **temples** are the flat parts on each side of

their forehead.

tempo (plural: tempos or tempi) The **tempo** of a piece of music is the speed at which it is played. ◇ If you talk about the **tempo** of a situation, you mean the speed at which things are taking place. *Pressure from inside as well as outside is likely to speed up the tempo of change.*

temporal is used to talk about aspects of human life not directly concerned with religion or spirituality. *He is the spiritual and temporal leader of Iranian Islam.*

temporary (temporarily) If something is **temporary**, it is not permanent or only lasts a short time. *...a temporary ban... The airport was temporarily closed as a result of the attack.*

temporize (temporizing, temporized) (*can be spelled with an 's' instead of a 'z'*) If someone **temporizes**, they do or say unimportant things, to delay making a decision or giving an opinion.

tempt (temptation) ❑ If you **tempt** someone, you try to persuade them to do something by offering or promising them something. *Banks and building societies are using competitions to tempt customers to open savings accounts.* ◇ If you are **tempted** by something, you feel you want to do it or have it, although it may not be a good idea. You say something like this is **tempting**. The desire to have it or do it is called **temptation**. *Most people seem to be resisting the temptation to spend lots of money.*

❑ If you say someone is **tempting fate**, you mean they are taking too many risks. ◇ You also say someone is **tempting fate** if you have a superstitious feeling that by talking as if things will go right they are encouraging them to go wrong. *Ferguson had tempted fate on numerous occasions by openly discussing the possibility of United winning the championship.*

temptress (temptresses) A **temptress** is a woman who sets out to allure or seduce a man or several men.

ten is the number 10.

tenable If you say something like a plan or opinion is **tenable**, you mean it is reasonable and can be defended against criticism. *The claim is really not tenable.*

tenacious (tenaciously, tenacity) A **tenacious** person is very determined and does not give up easily. You talk about the **tenacity** of someone like this. *He has clung tenaciously to power... His tenacity saw him through 11 gruelling games.*

tenancy (tenancies) A **tenancy** is an arrangement in which someone pays rent to use another person's land or buildings for a period of time.

tenant (tenanted) A **tenant** is a person who pays rent for the place they live in, or for other land or buildings they use. ◇ If a pub is **tenanted**, the landlord or landlady rents it from the owner, usually a brewery.

tench (plural: tench) The **tench** is a dark-green thick-bodied freshwater fish.

tend ❑ If something **tends** to happen, it usually or often happens. *The glass tended to buckle and distort during the toughening process.*

❑ If you **tend** someone or something, you look after them carefully. *During his retirement he had time to tend his beautiful garden.*

tendency (tendencies) ❑ If you have a **tendency** to do something, you often do it. You can also say there is a **tendency** for something to happen. *Generally, if a farmer*

goes over to a completely organic system, there is a tendency for yields to fall.*

❑ A group of people with similar political views is sometimes called a **tendency**, especially a group within a larger political organization.

tendentious If you call what someone says **tendentious**, you mean it deliberately presents information or other people's views in a biased way.

tender (tenderly, tenderness; tendering, tendered) ❑ If someone is **tender**, they behave in a gentle caring way. *The man's arm is placed tenderly around the woman's shoulders... He is attracted by her maternal tenderness.*

❑ If someone is at a **tender** age, they are young and inexperienced. *McCormack first teed off at the tender age of six.*

❑ If food is **tender**, it is soft and easy to cut or chew.

❑ If a part of your body is **tender**, it hurts when you touch it.

❑ When someone **tenders** for a contract, they make a formal offer to supply goods or services. This offer is called a **tender**. ◇ If work is **tendered** or put **out to tender**, private companies or individuals are invited to make offers to do it, instead of it remaining the responsibility of the government or a local authority.

❑ If you **tender** your resignation, you formally resign.

❑ **legal tender**: see **legal**.

tendon A **tendon** is a strong cord of tissue which joins a muscle to a bone.

tendril **Tendrils** are thin curling stems which some plants put out to attach themselves to walls or other plants.

tenement A **tenement** is a large building divided into several flats.

tenet (*pron:* ten-nit) The **tenets** of a theory or belief are the principles it is based on. *...the basic tenets of Marxism.*

tenner A **tenner** is (a) ten pounds. (b) a ten-pound note.

tennis is a game played on a rectangular court by two or four players. They use rackets to hit a ball backwards and forwards across a net. The idea is to hit the ball onto your opponent's half of the court in such a way that he or she cannot hit it back onto yours.

tenon See **mortice**.

tenor A **tenor** is a man with a high singing voice. ◇ Several musical instruments have **tenor** as part of their name. They are often in the middle of a range of instruments of a particular type. *...a tenor saxophone.*

tenpin bowling is an indoor game in which you try to knock down ten bottle-shaped objects called **tenpins** by rolling a heavy ball at them.

tense (tensing, tensed; tensely) ❑ If you are **tense**, you are worried and nervous and cannot relax. You say a situation is **tense** when the people involved feel like this. *...tense negotiations... The soldiers wait tensely for an attack.*

❑ If you **tense** your muscles, you tighten and stiffen them. ◇ If you **tense**, your muscles tighten suddenly because you are afraid.

❑ The **tense** of a verb is its form, which shows whether you are talking about the past, present, or future. For example, the past tense of 'run' is 'ran'.

tensile The **tensile** strength of a material is a measurement of its strength, and is the maximum stress it can stand without breaking when it is stretched.

tension is a feeling of stress or fear, especially before something difficult, dangerous, or important happens. *The incident follows a weekend of tension and uncertainty in the Republic... In a tension-packed atmosphere at the Oval, England have taken their score to 135 for 5.* ◇ **Tension** is also hostility or bad feeling between two people or groups. *...the tension between Hindus and Muslims.*

❏ You can also talk about the **tension** between two things which have conflicting requirements. *...the growing tension between price and quality.*

❏ The **tension** in a rope or wire is how tightly it is stretched.

tent (tented) A **tent** is a canvas or nylon shelter held up by poles and ropes, which people sleep in when camping. A **tented** area has a tent or tents in it.

tentacle The **tentacles** of a creature like an octopus are the long thin flexible parts it uses to feel with and to hold things, catch food, and move around. ◇ When people talk about the **tentacles** of a group or organization, they are talking about the extent of its power or influence. *The Mafia is spreading its tentacles into the industrialised north.*

tentative (tentatively) If something you do is **tentative**, you act slowly or hesitantly because you are nervous or uncertain. *I tentatively suggested that we ought to start again.* ◇ **Tentative** arrangements are at an experimental or preparatory stage. *The Chancellor announced that tentative agreement had been reached.*

tented See tent.

tenterhooks If you are on **tenterhooks**, you are waiting to see what is going to happen and are nervous and excited about it.

tenth The **tenth** item in a series is the one counted as number 10. ◇ A **tenth** or **one tenth** is the fraction $\frac{1}{10}$.

tenuous (tenuously) If the connection between things is **tenuous**, it is very slight or weak. *My line to the throne is somewhat tenuous... The tales are tenuously linked.* ◇ If the evidence for something is **tenuous**, it is slight and unconvincing.

tenure is the legal right to rent land, a dwelling, or some other building for a period of time. *The 1988 Housing Act ended security of tenure and rent controls.*

❏ **Tenure** is also the period during which someone holds an important job. *...his brief and unremarkable tenure as prime minister.* ◇ If you have **tenure** in your job, you can hold it until you retire, without having to have a contract renewed.

tepee (*or* teepee) (*pron:* tee-pee) A **tepee** is a tall pointed tent, usually made from animal skins, the traditional dwelling of many Native Americans.

tepid If something is **tepid**, it is neither hot nor cold, and rather unpleasant as a result. *...a cup of tepid orange juice.* ◇ If you say a response or reaction is **tepid,** you mean it is not very enthusiastic. *He drew only tepid applause.* ◇ You can also describe something as **tepid** when it is not very lively or exciting. *...tepid political debates.*

tercentenary (tercentenaries) A **tercentenary** is a year when you celebrate something important which happened exactly 300 years earlier.

term ❏ A **term** is a word or phrase with a specific meaning, especially one used in a particular subject. For example, you can say a word is a 'medical term'. ◇ If something is **termed** a particular thing, that is what peo-

ple call it. *...the pollution of space by what has been popularly termed 'space junk'.*

❏ A **term** is one of the periods a school or college year is divided into. ◇ A **term** is also (a) the period in which someone holds an important position. *In the last half century, only one elected leader has managed to serve his full term.* (b) the period someone is required to spend in prison as a punishment. *The offence would normally carry a long prison term.* ◇ See also long-term, mid-term, short-term.

❏ The **terms** of an agreement or arrangement are the conditions which are part of it. *Under the terms of the new agreement, Fitch is expected to remain chairman.*

❏ You use **terms** to say which aspect of something you are talking about. *What this means in terms of human misery and hardship can neither be imagined nor described... In Conservative party terms, his first year in office has been a triumph.*

❏ If you are thinking or talking **in terms of** doing something, you are considering doing it. *The BBC should not be thinking in terms of competing with Classic FM.*

❏ If you **come to terms with** something difficult or unpleasant, you learn to accept it. *Almost 20 years later, many parents are still trying to come to terms with their loss.*

❏ If you are **on good terms** with someone or **on friendly terms** with them, you are friendly towards them. ◇ **on speaking terms:** see speak.

❏ If two people are treated **on the same terms** or **on equal terms**, they are treated in the same way and neither of them has an advantage over the other.

terminal (terminally) ❏ A **terminal** illness or disease causes death, often slowly, and is incurable. *...terminal lung cancer... ...patients who were terminally ill.*

❏ A **terminal** is a place where vehicles, passengers, or goods begin or end a journey. *...the ferry terminal... ...an airport cargo terminal.*

❏ A computer **terminal** is a piece of equipment consisting of a keyboard and a screen which is used for entering information on a computer or for getting information from it.

terminate (terminating, terminated; termination) ❏ If something **terminates** or is **terminated**, it ends completely. *Any recovery in the housing market will lead to many owners terminating tenancies so that they can put their properties up for sale... ...the termination of pregnancy.*

❏ If a train or a bus **terminates** at a place, it ends its journey there.

terminology (terminologies) The **terminology** of a subject is the set of special words and phrases used in connection with it. *Mr Nixon liked football terminology – gameplans, moving the ball downfield, playing tough defence and the like.*

terminus (terminuses) A **terminus** is a place where trains or buses begin or end their journeys.

termite **Termites** are small white insects which live in warm countries in large colonies and feed on wood.

tern **Terns** are a group of seabirds, all of which have long pointed bills, long wings, and forked tails.

terra firma is used to talk about the ground when you are contrasting it with the sea or the air, especially because it seems safer. *At last Bailey had his feet on terra firma.*

terrace (terracing, terraced) ❏ A **terrace** is a row of similar houses joined together by their side walls. A house in a row like this is called a **terraced** house.

❏ A **terrace** is also a flat area of stone or grass next to a building, where people can sit. *Shows were held on the terrace of the Excelsior Hotel.* ◇ If a hillside is **terraced,** it is built up into a series of flat areas of ground like steps where crops can be grown. These flat areas are called **terraces.** *...terraced hills.*

❏ The **terraces** at a football ground are the wide flat steps where some spectators stand.

terracotta is a brownish-red clay which has been baked but not glazed and is used for making things like flower pots, tiles, and small statues.

terrain The **terrain** in an area is the type of land there, for example whether it is hilly or flat or open or covered with trees. *It is known as the garden island because of its lush tropical terrain.*

terrapin Terrapins are a type of small turtle.

terrestrial means to do with the planet Earth. *...terrestrial motion.* ◇ **Terrestrial** TV or radio signals are sent over the earth's surface from a transmitter on land, rather than by satellite.

❏ A **terrestrial** animal lives on land or on the ground rather than in the sea, in trees, or in the air.

terrible (terribly) ❏ A **terrible** experience or situation is very serious and unpleasant. *When such waves hit the coasts, they can cause terrible destruction... There are some deeds which are so terrible that they cannot be forgotten.*

❏ If you say something is **terrible,** you mean it is very bad or of very poor quality. *They have included material from certain authors that unintentionally exposes what terrible writers they were.*

❏ You can also use **terrible** to emphasize how bad something is. *Pulling it down is a terrible waste of public resources... These injections are terribly painful.*

❏ If you say you feel **terrible,** you mean (a) you feel ill. (b) you feel embarrassed or guilty about a bad situation you have caused.

❏ Some people use **terribly** to emphasize certain words. *I work terribly hard... These tests are terribly important.*

terrier Several breeds of small dogs are called **terriers.**

terrific (terrifically) If you say something is **terrific,** you mean you are very pleased with it or you like it a lot. *The view is terrific... These are terrific stories for children of seven upwards.* ◇ You can also use **terrific** to say something is very great in amount, degree, or intensity. *The force of the explosion must have been terrific... She was terrifically supportive in those bleak, early days.*

terrify (terrifies, terrifying, terrified; terrifyingly) If someone or something **terrifies** you, they make you feel very frightened. You say someone or something like this is **terrifying.** *The dinosaurs appear terrifyingly real on screen.*

terrine (*pron:* terr-een) A **terrine** is a mixture of blended meat, vegetables, or fish, similar to pâté.

territorial is used to talk about things to do with the ownership of land. *...a territorial dispute.* ◇ A country's **territorial waters** are the parts of the sea around its coast which it considers to be under its control, especially with regard to fishing rights.

Territorial Army The Territorial Army or TA is a British armed force whose members are not professional soldiers but train in their spare time in case they are needed in a national emergency.

territory (territories) ❏ **Territory** is land controlled by a country or ruler. *Saudi Arabia faces a gigantic task in dealing with the many archaeological sites dotted around its vast territory.* ◇ Areas of land which are under a country's control are sometimes called its **territories.**

❏ An animal's **territory** is the area it regards as its own and tries to defend from other animals.

❏ **Territory** is also a particular type of land. *...Amazon rainforest territory.*

❏ **Territory** is also used to talk about an area of knowledge or experience. *Their negotiations led both AT&T and the General Physics Institute into unfamiliar territory.*

terror is great fear. A **terror** is something which makes you very frightened. *...the terrors of a difficult birth.*

❏ **Terror** is also violence or the threat of violence, especially when it is used for political purposes. *Shining Path has used terror as well as skilful exploitation of Peru's economic woes to organise a small but solid base of support.*

terrorise See terrorize.

terrorism (terrorist) **Terrorism** is the use of violence to achieve political aims. A **terrorist** is someone who commits violent acts for political reasons. **Terrorist** is used to talk about things to do with terrorism. *...a wave of terrorist attacks.*

terrorize (terrorizing, terrorized) (*can be spelled with an 's' instead of a 'z'*) If someone **terrorizes** you, they frighten you by using or threatening violence.

terse (tersely) A **terse** statement or comment is brief and says no more than is necessary. *...a terse note... The official Chinese press have reported the latest events tersely and without comment.*

tertiary means third in order, third in importance, or at a third stage of development. *A drug acting on one set of synapses can have secondary and tertiary effects.*

❏ **Tertiary** education is education at university or college level.

Terylene is a light strong man-made cloth used especially for making clothes. 'Terylene' is a trademark.

TESSA A TESSA is a type of bank or building society savings account which pays tax-free interest providing you leave your money in it for five years. TESSA stands for 'Tax-Exempt Special Savings Account'.

test ❏ If you **test** something, you try it out for a short time to see what condition it is in or if it works properly. A trial like this is called a **test.** ◇ When a car is taken for a **test** drive or an aircraft is taken for a **test** flight, it is given a practical trial by an expert driver or pilot to see how it operates under extreme conditions. ◇ If you **put** something like a suggestion **to the test,** you try it out to see how useful or effective it is.

❏ If you **test** someone, you ask them questions to see how much they know about something. A series of questions like this, either written or oral, is called a **test.**

❏ A medical **test** is an examination of part of your body or your body fluids to check the state of your health. *...a blood test.*

❏ If an event or situation **tests** a person or thing or is a **test** of them, it reveals their qualities or effectiveness. *The durability of the peace will soon be tested as the political parties choose their candidates for the general election.* ◇ If you say something will **stand the test of time,** you mean it is strong enough or effective enough to last a very long time.

❏ **Testing** problems or situations are very difficult to deal with.

test case A **test case** is a legal case which becomes an example for deciding other similar cases.

Test match A **Test match** is one of a series of cricket or rugby matches played between two countries.

test pilot A **test pilot** is a pilot who flies aircraft of a new design to test their performance.

test tube A **test tube** is a small glass container used in chemical experiments. ◇ A **test tube baby** is a baby born as a result of an egg being fertilized outside a woman's body and then replaced in her womb.

testable If something like a theory or claim is **testable**, it can be tested to see if it works or is true.

testament ❏ If one thing is a **testament** to another thing, it shows the other thing exists or is true. *The British bands which played at last weekend's festival are a testament to the healthy blues scene around the UK.*

❏ See also **Old Testament, New Testament**.

testator (testatrix) A **testator** is someone who makes a will. A female testator can be called a **testatrix**.

testes A man's **testes** are the same as his testicles.

testicle (testicular) A man's **testicles** are the two sex glands between his legs which produce sperm. **Testicular** is used to talk about things relating to a man's testicles. *...testicular cancer.*

testify (testifies, testifying, testified) ❏ When someone **testifies**, they make a formal statement in a court of law. *North testified that he'd kept the admiral informed of the details of arms sales to Iran.*

❏ If something **testifies** to something else, it shows it exists. *The fact that the film managed to make money testifies to Shakespeare's remarkable durability with the public.*

testimonial A **testimonial** is a statement from someone in authority saying how good something or someone is. ◇ A **testimonial** or **testimonial** match is a sports match specially arranged so that part of the profits can be given to a particular player, for example because the player is injured or is about to retire.

testimony (testimonies) Someone's **testimony** is a statement they make in court. ◇ If something is a **testimony** to something else, it shows it exists or is true. *The banks of empty seats bore silent testimony to the general lack of interest in this semi-final.*

testing See **test**.

testosterone (pron: tess-toss-ter-rone) is a hormone produced mainly in the testicles, although it is also present in small quantities in women. It can also be made synthetically or taken from animals. Testosterone is used in the treatment of some medical conditions. It is also used to manufacture anabolic steroids, which are sometimes used illegally to improve athletic performance.

testy (testily) If someone is **testy**, they are impatient and bad-tempered. *He testily told journalists that the protesters would be disciplined as his government saw fit.*

tetanus is a serious disease caused by germs getting into a wound. It causes muscle spasms and convulsions.

tetchy (tetchily) A **tetchy** person is irritable and gets angry suddenly for no obvious reason. *Sir Ivan tetchily said far too much time had been wasted.*

tête-à-tête (pron: tet ah tet) A **tête-à-tête** is a private meeting between two people.

tether (tethering, tethered) ❏ A **tether** is a rope or chain used to tie an animal up so it can only move within a small area. If you **tether** an animal, you tie it up like this.

❏ If you are **at the end of your tether**, you feel you cannot put up with an unpleasant situation any longer.

tetralogy (pron: tet-ral-o-jee) (tetralogies) A **tetralogy** is a series of four related works, for example four novels involving the same characters.

Teutonic is used to describe behaviour which is thought to be typical of German people. *Sophie plodded on with Teutonic thoroughness.*

text ❏ The **text** of a book is the main written part, rather than things like the introduction, notes, pictures, or index. ◇ The **text** of a speech, broadcast, or recording is the full written version of it. *The following is the text of a statement from the Israeli Foreign Ministry.*

❏ **Text** is any written material. *This move towards combining text and images is bringing multimedia into the debate.* ◇ A **text** is a book or other piece of writing, especially one connected with an academic subject. *His writings included a number of books which became standard texts.*

textbook A **textbook** is a book about a particular subject, for use by students or schoolchildren. ◇ If you say something is a **textbook** example of a certain thing, you mean it has been done or made exactly as it should be according to an accepted standard or set of rules. *The house next door is a textbook example of medieval domestic architecture.*

textile **Textiles** are cloths or fabrics, especially woven ones.

textual is used to talk about things to do with the study of the way literature is written. *...textual analysis.*

texture The **texture** of something is the way it feels when you touch it, for example how rough, smooth, or lumpy it is.

textured A **textured** surface is not smooth and has a particular feel.

Thalidomide is a drug which used to be prescribed as a tranquiliser and to pregnant women to prevent morning sickness. It was withdrawn in Britain after it was discovered that it caused babies to develop deformed limbs. 'Thalidomide' is a trademark.

than You use **than** when you are comparing two things. *She was 12 years older than me.* ◇ You also use **than** to emphasize how large or small something is by comparing it to a particular figure or level. *Some top independent schools cost more than £10,000 a year.*

thank ❏ When you **thank** someone or express your **thanks** to them, you express your gratitude for something they have given you or something they have done. You often do this by saying 'thanks' or 'thank you'. *At a news conference, Mr McCarthy thanked his well-wishers... She said that she wanted to give her special thanks to all her friends who helped in the Democracy Movement.*

❏ If you say something happens **thanks to** a certain thing, you mean it happens because of that thing. *Thanks to its well-separated highways with limited access, America has the lowest traffic accident rates in the world.*

thankful If you are **thankful** for something, you are

happy and relieved about it. *He was thankful that they were safe and well.*

thankfully ❑ You say **thankfully** to express pleasure or relief about the thing you are mentioning. *We ended up with two out of three riders in hospital, thankfully with nothing more serious than a damaged knee and a cut face.*

❑ If you do something **thankfully**, you do it feeling happy and relieved. *'The last two days have been fairly unpleasant,' Slade admitted after stepping thankfully back on to land at Cowes.*

thankless A **thankless** job or task involves a lot of difficulties or hard work and is not appreciated by other people.

Thanksgiving or **Thanksgiving Day** is a public holiday in the autumn in the US and Canada.

❑ A **thanksgiving** service is a special religious service held to thank God for something good which has happened.

thankyou A **thankyou** is something you say or do as a way of thanking someone. *....a thankyou letter.*

that ❑ **That** person or thing means the one you have just mentioned. *That evidence was not disputed.* **That** is also used on its own to refer to something you have just been talking about. *That is a view beginning to take hold in government ranks.*

❑ **That** is used after words like 'said' or 'explained' before saying what was said or explained. *He explained that the Scottish climate was ideal for wild mushrooms to flourish... I suggested that I take her to dine at the nearby Hilton Hotel.*

❑ You use **that** to say which thing or things you are talking about. *I reached the gate that opened onto the lake.*

❑ If you say, for example, something is **not that** good, you mean it is not really very good. *The outlook for the economy is still not that good... It isn't that difficult a job.*

❑ You say **that is...** or **that is to say...** when you are explaining something more fully. *Three-quarters of the French population are 'federalist' without knowing it – that is to say, they favour a common defence policy, foreign policy and currency, and a sharing of sovereignty.*

❑ You say **that's that** to indicate that there is nothing more you can do or say about a particular matter. *You are simply expected to be available when needed, and that's that.*

❑ **this and that: see this.**

thatch (thatches, thatching, thatched; thatcher) If someone **thatches** a house, they make a roof for it with straw or reeds. The straw or reeds they use are called **thatch**. You say the house has a **thatched** roof; you can also call it a **thatched** house. A **thatcher** is a person whose job is to thatch roofs.

Thatcherism is the name given to the policies and aims of the British government when Margaret Thatcher was Prime Minister (1979 - 1990), in particular privatization, monetarism, self-help, and reducing state intervention.

Thatcherite is used to talk about people, especially politicians, who believed in the principles of Thatcherism. *....a member of the Thatcherite No Turning Back group.*

thaw ❑ When ice or snow **thaws**, it melts because the temperature has risen. A **thaw** is a period of warmer weather when this happens. ◇ When you **thaw** frozen food, you take it out of the freezer so it can reach room temperature ready for use.

❑ If someone who has been unfriendly **thaws**, they

start to be more friendly. Similarly, you can say an unfriendly relationship **thaws**; you can also talk about a **thaw** in a relationship. *The thaw in relations between Moscow and Seoul has angered North Korea.*

the is called the 'definite article'. You use it when it is clear which person or thing you are talking about. *Heat the olive oil... ...the Secretary of State.*

❑ You use **the** in front of the name of a species to talk about the typical behaviour or characteristics of the whole species. *Other animals, such as the gazelle, get their speed and acceleration directly from their long hind legs.* ◇ You use **the** in front of a word like 'rich' or 'unemployed' to talk about all the people described by the word. *Under the social fund, the poor are entitled to apply for loans or grants to cover sudden emergencies.* ◇ You use **the** in front of the plural form of a surname to talk about a couple or family. *In later years the Winterbottoms became involved in the textile trade.*

❑ You use **the** in dates. *...the first of May.* ◇ You use **the** to talk about decades. *Much of the old town has hardly changed since the twenties.*

❑ You use **the** with words like 'more', 'longer', or 'easier' to show how one quality or amount changes in relation to another. *The more the tactic succeeds the more it will be used... The higher the contribution, the less impact expenses have on the return.*

theatre (*American spelling:* **theater**) ❑ A **theatre** is a building with a stage on which plays and other entertainments are performed. ◇ **Theatre** is used to talk about the performing of plays and the people involved in their performance. *Some of the best-loved names in theatre will gather there on July 26.*

❑ In the US, cinemas are often called **theaters** or **movie theaters**.

❑ In a hospital, an operating theatre is often called a **theatre**.

❑ A **theatre** of war or conflict is the area or region where it is happening. *The vast territory has become the theatre of extremely violent repression.*

theatregoer (*American spelling:* **theatergoer**) A **theatregoer** is someone who regularly goes to the theatre to see plays.

theatrical (theatrically, theatricality) ❑ **Theatrical** is used to talk about things to do with the theatre. *Her early career was in theatrical and operatic design... There are plans to film the theatrically successful Evita.* ◇ **Amateur theatricals** is the performing of plays by amateur actors.

❑ **Theatrical** behaviour is exaggerated, unnatural, and done for effect. You talk about the **theatricality** of behaviour like this. *She sighed theatrically.*

thee is an old-fashioned for 'you' when you are talking to one person. *'Thy own speech betrayeth thee,' as the girl said to St Peter.*

theft is the crime of stealing.

their (theirs) ❑ You use **their** or **theirs** when you are talking about something belonging to or connected with people or things that have just been mentioned. *Men do not always get their own way... But these rights are theirs as citizens, not as a group.* ◇ You also use **their** or **theirs** to talk about something belonging to or connected with a person whose sex is not known or not stated. *It's not fair to come round to someone's house and drink all their coffee.*

❏ You also use **their** when you are talking in a formal way about two or more royal or titled people. ...*their Royal Highnesses.*

them You use **them** to talk about people or things that have already been mentioned. *A few of them have got jobs, but not many... It should have been obvious to them.* ◇ You also use **them** to talk about an individual person whose sex is not known or not stated. *Two bowls of Unimix are given to each child every day and this provides them with 900 calories, enough to survive.*

thematic (thematically) If something is organized in a **thematic** way, it is divided up according to subjects or topics. *Its division into short, thematic sub-chapters means it will become a trusted reference book... The show is organised thematically.*

theme ❏ The **theme** of a discussion or lecture is its main subject. ◇ A **theme** in an artist's or writer's work is an idea which is developed or repeated in it.

❏ The **theme** of something like a concert is a common link between the different items in it. *This year's festival broke with tradition by basing itself not on a single composer but on the theme of A Midsummer Night's Dream.*

❏ In a piece of classical music, a **theme** is a short simple tune which is often repeated or developed. ◇ A **theme** or **theme tune** is (a) a piece of music played at the beginning and end of a TV or radio programme. (b) a piece of music played several times during a film or musical, which has become very well-known. ...*the theme from Dr Zhivago.*

theme park A **theme park** is a large outdoor area with fairground rides, amusement arcades, and other forms of entertainment, all of which have a common theme, for example space travel or the Wild West.

themselves You use **themselves** to say something which is done by two or more people affects those people. *Women are more likely than men to delude themselves about their drinking.* ◇ You also use **themselves** to emphasize that your statement really does apply to the people you are talking about. *The biggest costs are often met by the groups themselves.*

then ❏ You use **then** to talk about a time in the past or future. *She had, by then, married and divorced a pharmacist... Discovery will be back at the same time next week, so from me, Tony Durham, goodbye till then.* ◇ You use **then** to say one thing happens or comes after another. *I stared, frozen for a moment, then ran, then stopped... Like his father, he became a teacher and then headmaster of a secondary school.*

❏ You also use **then** to introduce a summary or conclusion to what you have just said, or to end a conversation. *There is, then, no general pattern of decline in the fortunes of Green parties... So much for the finish then.* ◇ You use **then** at the beginning of a sentence or after 'and' or 'but' to introduce an extra piece of information. *Then there is the little matter of electricity.*

❏ **now and then**: see now. ◇ **there and then**: see there.

thence is an old-fashioned word meaning 'from there'. *The mosaics found their way to Munich, and thence to Geneva.*

theocracy (theocratic) A **theocracy** or **theocratic** state is a society ruled by priests.

theodolite A **theodolite** is an instrument used in surveying for measuring angles.

theology (theologian; theological, theologically) **Theology** is the study of religion and ideas about God. A **theologian** is someone who studies these things. **Theological** is used to talk about things to do with religion. *The concept of animal rights is founded theologically on the belief that God has a right to have his creatures treated with respect.*

theorem A **theorem** is a mathematical statement which can be logically proved to be correct.

theoretical (theoretically) ❏ **Theoretical** is used to talk about the ideas and abstract principles of a subject, rather than its practical aspects. **Theoretical** is also used to describe scientists whose work involves theories and ideas, rather than experiments or research. ...*theoretical physicists.*

❏ A **theoretical** situation is supposed to exist, but in reality may not do so. *In the absence of a peace treaty, Japan may still theoretically be at war with Russia.*

theoretician A **theoretician** is the same as a theorist.

theorise See theorize.

theorist A **theorist** is someone who produces a theory to explain something. *Theorists had been unable to explain how an economy with a stable population could grow in the long term.*

theorize (theorizing, theorized) (*can be spelled with an 's' instead of a 'z'*) If you **theorize** about something, you develop ideas about it to try and explain it. *Northrop theorized that the conflict between East and West arose from their different values.*

theory (theories) ❏ A **theory** is an idea or set of ideas intended to explain something. *One theory is that depression affects the level of cortisol in the blood.*

❏ The principles or ideas on which a practice or skill is based are called its **theory.** *Anyone interested in the theory and practice of sustainable agriculture can now turn to a new book on the subject.*

❏ You use **in theory** to say although something is supposed to happen or be true, in reality it may not happen or be true. *The excesses of the last boom in house prices ought, in theory, to bring a return to older habits.*

therapeutic If something is **therapeutic**, it helps you to feel happier and more relaxed. ◇ **Therapeutic** medical treatment is given to treat a disease or improve a person's health, using drugs or other methods.

therapy (therapies; therapist) **Therapy** is the medical treatment of any disease or abnormal condition. A **therapist** is a person skilled in a particular type of therapy. ...*a speech therapist.*

there ❏ You use **there** with words like 'is', 'are', 'was', or 'were' to say something exists or does not exist. *There is an administration fee of £195... He said there was no quick solution to the war.* ◇ If you say something is **there**, you mean it exists. If you say what something is **there for**, you are saying why it exists. *The need for careful market research is still there... Elitism, seeking the best in scholarship and science, is what Oxford is there for.*

❏ You use **there** to talk about a place which has already been mentioned. *My school didn't have a drama club until I went there.* ◇ You say **there** to indicate a place you are pointing to or looking at. *Over there is where the pig is.*

❏ You use **there** to talk about a point someone has made in a conversation. *He is right there, you know.* ◇ You also use **there** to talk about a stage in an activity or in a process. *Its strategy is simply to pick the ending it likes best and work back from there.*

❑ If something is done **there and then,** it is done immediately.

❑ You say '**there you are**' when you are accepting a situation you cannot change. *It is very sad, but there you are.*

thereabouts You say **or thereabouts** after a number or date to show it is approximate. *They will hatch out in 17 days or thereabouts.*

thereafter means after the date or event you have just mentioned. *Reyes left school at 18 and married shortly thereafter.*

thereby means as a result of the thing you have just mentioned. *This increases our costs of manufacture, thereby making us less competitive.*

therefore You use **therefore** when you are mentioning the logical result or conclusion of what you have just described. *We budgeted for an increase in revenue which has not taken place, therefore we have to make cutbacks.*

therein means in the place you have just mentioned, or in the book or document you have just mentioned. *His life story is worth reading in itself, aside from the spiritual teachings contained therein.*

❑ If you say **therein lies** a problem, you mean the problem exists because of the thing you have just mentioned. *This argument goes down well with party activists – and therein lies the Democratic dilemma.*

thereof means of the thing just mentioned. *...accounting practices and the abuse thereof.*

thereupon means straight after an event and as a result of it. *This last point so needled the European Parliament that it blocked a routine package of aid. Morocco thereupon threatened not to renew a fishing agreement.*

therm Heat is sometimes expressed in **therms.** A therm is about 105.5 million joules.

thermal is used to talk about things to do with heat. *...the thermal efficiency of timber-frame homes... ...a thermal imaging camera.* ◇ **Thermal** clothing is specially designed to keep you warm. *...thermal vests.*

thermodynamics is the branch of physics which deals with the relationship between heat and other forms of energy.

thermometer A **thermometer** is an instrument for measuring temperature.

thermonuclear A **thermonuclear** weapon or device is detonated by the very high temperatures generated by nuclear fission.

thermoplastic materials are made of a kind of plastic which becomes soft when it is heated and hardens again when it cools.

Thermos (Thermoses) A **Thermos** or **Thermos flask** is a container used to keep hot or cold drinks at a constant temperature. 'Thermos' is a trademark.

thermostat A **thermostat** is a device which automatically maintains the temperature of something at a particular level.

thesaurus (thesauruses) A **thesaurus** is a reference book in which words which have similar meanings are grouped together.

these **These** people or things means the ones you have just mentioned. *These magnets are the largest part of the project's cost.* **These** can also be used on its own to refer

to people or things you have just been talking about. *There are many more where these came from.*

thesis (*plural:* theses) A **thesis** is an idea or theory expressed as a statement and discussed in a logical way. *My thesis is that game-shooting will gradually wither away and men and women will find other and better forms of sport.* ◇ A **thesis** is also a long piece of writing based on original research, done as part of a higher university degree.

thespian is used to talk about things to do with drama and the theatre. Actors and actresses are sometimes called **thespians.**

they ❑ You use **they** to talk about people or things that have already been mentioned. *15th-century sailors knew exactly how fast they were moving.*

❑ You also use **they** to talk about people in general, or a group of people whose identity is not actually stated. *It is, they say, the housing of the future.*

❑ You also use **they** to talk about an individual person whose sex is not known or not stated. *The patient is talked into a trance-like state, and once they are in a calmer state of mind, work may be carried out.*

thick (thickly, thickness) ❑ If something solid is **thick,** its opposite sides or surfaces are further apart than usual. *...a thick stone wall.* ◇ You also use **thick** when giving the distance between the opposite sides or surfaces of something. *The metal is only an eighth of an inch thick... The total thickness of the plastic skin is just one-third of a millimetre.*

❑ A **thick** liquid does not flow easily. *...thick cream.* ◇ **Thick** smoke or fog is difficult to see through.

❑ **Thick** is also used to describe something which consists of several things growing close together. *Pink snapdragon flowers grow in thick clumps on the roadsides... ...thick glossy hair.* ◇ If something is **thick with** something else, it is full of it or covered with it. *Shakespeare's texts were thick with spelling mistakes.*

❑ If things happen **thick and fast,** they happen quickly and in large numbers. *Redundancies are coming thick and fast.*

❑ If you keep doing something **through thick and thin,** you do it even when conditions or circumstances are very bad.

❑ If you are **in the thick of** an activity or situation, you are very involved in it. *As a politician, she has been in the thick of battles on difficult and sensitive questions.*

❑ If you say someone is **thick,** you mean they are unintelligent. ◇ If you say someone has a **thick skin** or is **thick-skinned,** you mean they are not easily hurt by what people say to them.

thicken (thickening, thickened) ❑ If a crowd **thickens,** it becomes more closely packed as more people join it. You can talk about other things **thickening** when they become more closely packed. *The man looked up at the clouds thickening above his rows of khaki tents.* ◇ When a liquid **thickens** or is **thickened,** it becomes stiffer and flows less easily.

❑ If you say **the plot thickens,** you mean the situation you are talking about is getting more and more complicated and mysterious.

thicket A **thicket** is a small group of trees or bushes growing closely together. ◇ A **thicket** of people or things is a dense group of them. *The linesman's view was* *obscured by a thicket of players.*

thief (thieves; thieving) A **thief** is a person who steals something. **Thieving** is stealing things.

thigh A person's **thighs** are the top parts of their legs between their knees and their hips.

thimble A **thimble** is a small metal or plastic object which protects the end of your finger when you are sewing.

thin (thinner, thinnest; thinly, thinness; thinning, thinned) ❑ If something is **thin**, the distance between its sides is quite small. *...a thin strip of land.* ◇ A **thin** person or animal has very little fat on their body. *He had good muscle tone despite his thinness.* ◇ **Thin** liquids flow very easily.

❑ If a crowd or audience is **thin**, there are fewer people in it than was expected or hoped for. ◇ If an area is **thinly** populated, there are very few people living there. ◇ If people or things are **thin on the ground**, there are not many of them. *Ideas are thin on the ground in the British film industry.* ◇ If someone's hair is **thinning**, they are beginning to go bald. ◇ If your patience or temper is **wearing thin**, you are becoming impatient or angry.

❑ If you **thin** something or **thin** it **out**, you make it less densely packed by removing certain items. *The heavy concentration of weaponry in central Europe must be thinned out.*

thin-skinned people are easily hurt by what other people say about them.

thine is an old-fashioned word for 'your' or 'yours' when you are talking to one person. *Trust in the Lord with all thine heart.*

thing ❑ You use **thing** instead of a more precise word when it is clear what you are talking about. *At Tory conferences you can do all manner of things so long as you do not openly attack the leader... Everybody thinks they know at least one thing about red wine.*

❑ A **thing** is a physical object. *He came into my father's house and started to smash things up.*

❑ You sometimes call a person or animal a **thing** when you are expressing your feelings about them. *They are doing their best, poor things.*

❑ **Things** is used to talk about a situation in general and the way it affects people. *Things are no better among retailers... The power vacuum created by his departure can only make things worse.*

❑ If something is a **thing of the past**, it no longer exists or no longer happens.

❑ If you **do your own thing**, you live or behave the way you want to, without paying attention to convention or to what other people think. ◇ the **done thing**: see **do**.

❑ If someone tries to be **all things to all men**, they try to please everyone.

❑ You say '**the thing is...**' when you are making a point about something which has just been said. *The thing is, he just proposes this, he doesn't actually have evidence to back it up.* ◇ You say '**for one thing**' when you are making a point and suggesting that you could make others of the same kind. *If there had been proper electoral reform, the poll tax for one thing would not have happened.*

❑ **one thing leads to another**: see **lead**. ◇ the **real thing**: see **real**.

think (thinking, thought) ❑ If you **think** about something, you consider it. *The judge said he had thought about the case over the weekend.* ◇ What you **think** about some-

thing is your opinion of it. *I think it's a lot of nonsense.* ◇ If you do not **think** much of someone or something, you have a low opinion of them. ◇ The opinions of a group of people can be called their **thinking**. *He believes the union and the TUC have moved closer together in their thinking.*

❑ If you **think** of something, you recall it. *I couldn't think of a single fact about Columbus that was in the least bit funny.* ◇ You also say you **think** of something when you create it in your mind, using your intelligence and imagination. *This is not an entirely new idea: the Scots thought of it first.* ◇ If you **think up** a clever scheme or idea, you create it in your mind. You can also **think up** something like an excuse.

❑ If you **think back** on something, you remember it.

❑ If you **think** of someone, you show consideration for them. *It was sweet of you to think of me.*

❑ If you are **thinking** of doing something, you are planning to do it. ◇ If you **think again** or **think twice** about doing something, you reconsider it, and may decide to do it differently or not at all. If you **think better** of something, you decide not to do it.

❑ If you **think nothing of** doing something other people might find strange or difficult, you do it without concerning yourself about it at all. *He is a tireless traveller and will think nothing of clocking up 20,000 miles in a week.*

❑ If you **think** something **over**, you consider it carefully before making a decision. ◇ If you **think** something **through**, you consider it thoroughly. *Some of the politicians are not thinking through the effects of their actions.*

❑ See also **thought**.

think-tank A **think-tank** is a group of experts appointed by the government or an organization to examine various issues and problems and consider possible solutions to them.

thinker You call someone a **thinker** when they spend a lot of time thinking about important issues and produce new ideas which influence other people. *Louis Althusser was one of the most important Marxist thinkers of the twentieth century.*

thinner ❑ See **thin**.

❑ **Thinner** is a liquid you add to another liquid such as paint to make it less thick and easier to use.

third (thirdly) The **third** item in a series is the one counted as number 3. ◇ A **third** or **one third** is the fraction ⅓. ◇ You say **third** or **thirdly** when you are mentioning the third in a series of points or items. *He will attack him first as a tax-and-spend liberal, secondly on his record as governor of Arkansas, and thirdly on the character issue.*

third class If people are treated as **third class** citizens, they are not given the same rights as other people.

third party ❑ A **third party** is someone who is not one of the two main people or groups involved in a dispute or argument, but who is brought in to help reach a settlement.

❑ If you have **third party** insurance and you cause an accident, your insurance company will pay money only to other people who are hurt or whose property is damaged and not to you.

third-rate If you describe something as **third-rate**, you mean it is of a very low quality or standard. *MPs are behaving like contestants in a third-rate game show.*

Third World The poorer countries of Africa, Asia, and South America are sometimes called the **Third World**.

thirst is not having enough to drink. *3.1 million people are in danger of dying of thirst or hunger as a result of the drought.*
❑ A **thirst** for something is a strong desire for it. If you **thirst** for something, you want it very much. *There is a desperate thirst for knowledge about the outside world.*

thirsty (thirstily) If you are **thirsty**, you feel the need to drink something. If you drink something **thirstily**, you drink it eagerly because you are thirsty.

thirteen (thirteenth) **Thirteen** is the number 13.

thirty (thirtieth, thirties) **Thirty** is the number 30. ◇ The **thirties** was the period from 1930 to 1939. ◇ If someone is in their **thirties**, they are aged 30 to 39.

this ❑ **This** person or thing means the one you have just mentioned. *We are satisfied that this woman is taking good care of the baby.* **This** is also used on its own to refer to something you have just been talking about. *This was to be his debut as a director.*
❑ You use **this** to talk about the place you are in at the moment. *Everyone eats out every night in this town.*
❑ You use **this** to talk about the current week, month, etc. You also use **this** to talk about the morning, afternoon, etc of the current day. *About 100 students gathered outside this morning.* ◇ You also use **this** to talk about the next occurrence in the future of a particular day, month, or season. *The grand prix season ends this Sunday.*
❑ **This and that** means a variety of things. *We chat about this and that.*

thistle The **thistle** is a wild plant with prickly leaves and purple flowers. It is the national emblem of Scotland.

thither is an old word meaning 'to that place'. *If a man is to go to the devil, he may as well go thither from the House of Lords as from any other place.* ◇ **hither and thither:** see **hither**.

thong A **thong** is a long thin strip of leather, rubber, or plastic.

thorax (thoraxes; thoracic) A person's **thorax** is the part of their body between their neck and their waist, including the organs inside such as the heart and lungs. **Thoracic** is used to talk about things to do with the thorax. *...the thoracic muscles.* ◇ An insect's **thorax** is the central part of its body between its head and its abdomen, which its legs and wings are attached to.

thorn **Thorns** are the sharp points on some plants and trees, for example on a rose bush. ◇ If you say someone or something is a **thorn in your side** or a **thorn in your flesh**, you mean they are a constant problem or annoyance to you. *She has been a thorn in government's side for most of her campaigning career.*

thorny (thornier, thorniest) A **thorny** plant or tree is covered in thorns. ◇ A **thorny** question or issue is difficult to deal with.

thorough (thoroughly, thoroughness) ❑ **Thorough** is used to describe things which are done very carefully and methodically so that nothing is overlooked. *The vehicle has to be thoroughly checked every two years.* ◇ If someone is **thorough**, they do things in a careful and methodical way. *Mrs Festing is an unusually thorough biographer... It is Scales's thoroughness that makes her characterisations so recognisable.*

❑ You can also use **thorough** to emphasize how bad something is. *Trevino had made a thorough hash of it... Quebec is thoroughly cheesed off.*

thoroughbred A **thoroughbred** is an animal, especially a racehorse, whose parents are both of the same high quality breed.

thoroughfare A **thoroughfare** is a main road in a town or city.

thoroughgoing is used to say something is complete in every way, or has all the qualities of a particular thing. *...a thoroughgoing programme of constitutional reform... ...a thoroughgoing conservative.*

those ❑ **Those** people or things means the ones you have just mentioned. *Most of those houses are for sale, and few of the homeless are in a position to buy.* **Those** is also used on its own to refer to people or things you have just been talking about. *Those are the things which really matter in local government.*
❑ **Those** is also used when you are saying which group of people you are talking about. *Those of you with pencils might now care to draw a beard on the photo above.*

thou is an old-fashioned word for 'you' when you are talking to one person. *Thou shalt not steal.*

though ❑ You use **though** when you are mentioning something which contrasts with the rest of what you are saying. *Though it fell short of being a classic final, it was refreshing, full of life and novelty... Marks & Spencer, too, has been frantically introducing wines, though not quite on the Gateway scale.* ◇ **even though:** see **even**.
❑ **Though** is also used to mean 'in spite of what has just been said'. *Nobody, though, could begrudge the Sussex girl her victory.*
❑ **as though:** see **as**.

thought ❑ See **think**.
❑ **Thought** is the activity of thinking. *The idea is to involve the audience and, by asking questions, provoke thought.* ◇ **school of thought:** see **school**.
❑ A **thought** is an idea in your mind. *He was consumed with only one thought, that of winning.* ◇ Your **thoughts** on a subject are your opinions on it.
❑ If you say something like a plan is well **thought out**, you mean it has been prepared carefully and sensibly. If you say it is badly **thought out**, you mean it has not been prepared carefully. *The coup attempt was amateurish and poorly thought out.*
❑ **second thoughts:** see **second**.

thought-provoking If you say something like a novel, play, or film is **thought-provoking**, you mean it makes you think about a subject in a different way.

thoughtful (thoughtfully, thoughfulness) ❑ A **thoughtful** speech or piece of writing has been carefully thought out.
❑ If you are **thoughtful**, you are quiet and serious, because you are thinking about something. *He paused and looked at me thoughtfully.* ◇ You also say someone is **thoughtful** when they are kind and helpful, and think about what other people want or need.

thoughtless (thoughtlessly, thoughtlessness) If you do something in a **thoughtless** way, you do it without thinking what you are doing. *It is possible that she just thoughtlessly stepped out onto the road.* ◇ You also say people are **thoughtless** when they forget or ignore what other people want, need, or feel. *Any lapse is due to thoughtlessness, not malice.*

thousand A thousand is the number 1,000. ◇ Thousands of things means a very large number of them. *Thousands of jobs will go at whichever yard loses the contract.*

thousandth The thousandth item in a series is the one counted as number 1,000. ◇ A thousandth or one thousandth is the fraction 1⁄1000.

thrall If you are in thrall to someone, you are completely in their power. *Many state legislatures were corrupt and incompetent, and state courts were in their thrall.*

thrash (thrashes, thrashing, thrashed) ❑ If you thrash someone in a game or contest or give them a thrashing, you defeat them by a large margin.

❑ When people thrash out something like a policy or strategy, they discuss it until they agree on a solution.

❑ If a fish or some other creature thrashes about, it twists and turns quickly and violently.

thread (threading, threaded) ❑ Thread or a thread is a long thin piece of cotton, silk, nylon, or wool. ◇ If you thread something like thread, ribbon, or tape through a hole or a space, you pass it through.

❑ If someone's life hangs by a thread, there is only a small chance they will survive. Similarly, if something like an arrangement hangs by a thread, there is only a small chance it will last or continue. *The ceasefire is hanging by a thread with as yet nobody to monitor or supervise it.*

❑ The thread on something like a screw or a screw-top container is the thin raised spiral line around it.

❑ If you thread your way through a group of people or things, you pass through the narrow gaps between them.

❑ The thread in an argument or story is the idea or theme which connects the different parts. *There were few scenes of pure dialogue and no narrative thread beyond a poorly worked out sense of flight and pursuit.*

threadbare If you say things like carpets or clothes are threadbare, you mean they are old and have become thin and nearly worn out. *He was wearing threadbare tweeds.* ◇ If you say something like an argument or method is threadbare, you mean it no longer has much force or effect, and people are not convinced by it.

threat ❑ If someone makes a threat, they say they will harm you if you do not do what they want.

❑ If someone or something is a threat to a person or thing, they may harm them. *Fishermen are incensed by this apparent threat to their livelihoods.* ◇ If there is a threat of something unpleasant, it is likely or possible it will happen. *Some see it all as a terrible waste of money, especially now the threat of nuclear war has diminished.*

threaten (threatening, threatened) ❑ If someone threatens to do something violent or harmful, they say they will do it unless they get what they want.

❑ You say something threatens people or things when it is likely to harm them or cause them problems. *The English countryside is threatened by a huge increase in traffic.* ◇ If something threatens to have a harmful effect, it seems likely to have it. *The very success of that policy now threatens to rebound upon the government.*

threatening (threateningly) If someone's behaviour is threatening, they say they will harm you unless you do what they want. *A number of other newspapers have since received threatening calls.* ◇ You say other things are

threatening when they seem likely to cause harm. *The United States and big business were portrayed as threateningly rich and powerful.*

three is the number 3.

three-dimensional A three-dimensional shape is a shape like a cube or cylinder which can be measured in three different directions, as distinct from a two-dimensional shape like a square or circle. ◇ A three-dimensional image or picture gives the impression of being deep or solid rather than flat.

three-line whip In Parliament, if a party imposes a three-line whip, it brings strong pressure to bear on its MPs to attend a debate and vote in a particular way.

three-quarters of something is half of it plus a quarter of it.

three Rs When people are talking about children's education, they call the basic skills of reading, writing, and arithmetic the three Rs.

threefold If a number or amount is increased threefold, it becomes three times as big. *Algeria's official trade union has called for a threefold increase in the national minimum wage.* ◇ If something such as the reasons for doing something are threefold, there are three of them. *The central lessons that the armed forces learned from Vietnam were threefold.*

threesome A threesome is a group of three people.

threnody (threnodies) A threnody is a lament for the dead.

thresh (threshes, threshing, threshed) When people thresh corn, wheat, or rice, they beat it to separate out the grains.

threshold ❑ A threshold is an amount, level, or limit at which something begins to happen or take effect. *Every applicant will have to meet a minimum quality threshold, set at roughly the quality of the existing ITV output.*

❑ If you are on the threshold of something exciting or new, you are about to experience it. *Hollingsworth, 26, is on the threshold of her first major victory.*

❑ The threshold of a building or room is the floor in the doorway, or the doorway itself.

threw See throw.

thrice is an old-fashioned word meaning 'three times'. *Arias was thrice elected president and deposed.*

thrifty (thrift) ❑ If someone is thrifty, they save money and do not waste things. You talk about the thrift of someone like this.

❑ In the US, building societies are called thrifts.

thrill ❑ If something thrills you or gives you a thrill, it gives you a feeling of excitement and pleasure. You can also say something like this is thrilling. *The performance was thrilling from start to finish.*

❑ If you are thrilled about something, you are pleased and excited about it.

thriller A thriller is a book, film, or play which tells an exciting story about dangerous, frightening, or mysterious events.

thrive (thriving, thrived or throve) When people or things thrive, they are healthy, happy, or successful. *The company had prided itself on its ability to thrive during a recession.*

throat ❑ A person's throat is the back of their mouth and the top part of the tubes which go down into their stomach and lungs. ◇ The front part of a person's neck is also sometimes called their **throat**.

❏ If two people or groups are **at each other's throats**, they are quarrelling or fighting. ◇ If you **force** or **ram** something **down** someone's **throat**, you make them accept it.

throaty If someone's voice or laugh is **throaty**, it sounds low and rather rough.

throb (throbbing, throbbed) If a part of your body **throbs**, you feel a series of strong painful beats there. *My head was throbbing.* ◇ You also say something **throbs** when it vibrates and makes a loud rhythmical noise. *You can hear the vehicle throb into action, making the sand vibrate beneath you.*

throes If you are busy doing something, especially something complicated, you can say you are **in the throes of** it. *Poland is in the throes of a painful economic reform.* ◇ **death throes**: see **death**.

thrombosis (*plural:* thromboses) A **thrombosis** is a serious condition caused by a clot of blood blocking a blood vessel. A **coronary thrombosis** is a heart attack caused by a clot in one of the arteries around the heart.

throne A **throne** is a special chair used by royalty on important formal occasions. ◇ **The throne** is often used to talk about the position of being a monarch. *The move was never publicly acknowledged until the Queen took the throne in 1952.*

throng A **throng** is a large crowd of people. If people **throng** somewhere, they go there in large numbers.

throttle (throttling, throttled) ❏ If someone **throttles** another person, they kill them by squeezing their throat so they cannot breathe. ◇ If someone **throttles** something like a process, they put an end to it by stopping the thing which helps it exist. *...attempts to throttle the criminal supply of drugs.*

❏ The **throttle** of a motor vehicle is the device which controls the engine's speed by regulating the flow of fuel entering it. ◇ If you do something **at full throttle**, you do it with great speed and eagerness.

through ❏ If something moves **through** an opening or hole, it passes from one side to the other. ◇ If you cut **through** something solid, you make a cut from one side to the other, so it is in two pieces.

❏ If you move **through** a place or area, you travel across it or within it.

❏ If you see something **through** a window, you are on one side of the window and the thing you see is on the other side. Similarly, you can hear something **through** a wall or feel something **through** a layer of material.

❏ If something happens **through** a period of time, it happens from the beginning to the end. ◇ If you go **through** an experience, it happens to you. *Allen has been through two divorces.*

❏ If you say you are **through** with someone or something, you mean you are determined not to have any more to do with them.

❏ If something happens **through** something else, it happens because of it. You can also say something is achieved **through** something else. *The Sandinistas were deposed, not through force, but through the ballot box.* ◇ If you do something **through** another person, they take the necessary action on your behalf. *Escobar has said through his lawyers that he is prepared to surrender under certain conditions.*

❏ **Through and through** means completely and to the greatest extent possible. *Mr Reich is a free-trader through and through... The system was rotten through and through.*

throughout If something happens **throughout** an event or period of time, it happens during all of it. ◇ If something happens or exists **throughout** a place or area, it happens or exists in every part.

throughput The **throughput** of an organization, company, or system is the amount of things it does or deals with in a particular period of time. *Steel throughput rarely met the target figures because of labour disputes.*

throve See **thrive**.

throw (throwing, threw, have thrown) ❏ If you **throw** an object you are holding, you move your hand quickly and let go of the object so it moves through the air. In sport, an action like this is called a **throw**.

❏ If you are **thrown** somewhere, for example in a collision, you fall there. *The motor-car was overturned and the occupants were thrown out.* ◇ If a horse which you are riding **throws** you, it makes you fall off, for example by rearing suddenly.

❏ If you **throw** your hands or arms in a certain direction, you move them there quickly and suddenly. *As Gunnell crossed the line, she threw her arms up high.*

❏ If you **throw** yourself into an activity, you take part in it actively and enthusiastically. *At Oxford he sang in choirs, threw himself into drama and got a First in English.*

❏ If something **throws** you into a situation or state, especially an unpleasant one, it causes you to be in it. *Mapanje's arrest threw him into such confusion that he began saying it was he who denounced his friend.* ◇ If something like a remark or action **throws** you, it makes you confused or bewildered, because it is unexpected or strange.

❏ If someone **throws** a fit or a tantrum, they have one.

❏ If someone **throws open** something which had previously not been available or accessible to people, they make it available to them. *The only possible solution will be to throw open the oil and gas fields to international oil firms.*

❏ If items cost a certain amount **a throw**, they cost that much each.

❏ If you **throw** a party or other social event, you organize it.

❏ If the authorities **throw** someone in jail, they send them there immediately and without trial.

❏ If you **throw** a switch, you turn it on or off.

❏ If you **throw away** something you do not want or **throw** it **out**, you get rid of it, for example by putting it in a bin. ◇ If you **throw away** an opportunity, you waste it. Similarly, you can **throw away** money on something which is not worth having.

❏ If something like a plan or proposal is **thrown out**, it is rejected. ◇ If something like a policy is **thrown overboard**, it is abandoned. ◇ If a court of law **throws out** a case, it decides not to try it, for example because there is not enough evidence, or because evidence has been illegally obtained.

❏ If a person who is selling you something **throws in** something else, they give you the extra thing free. *A glass of wine is thrown in with the ticket price.*

❏ If you **throw off** something which is restricting you, you free yourself from it. *The Socialists hope they can throw off the burden of their communist past.*

❑ If someone is **thrown out** of a place, they are forced to leave. Similarly, if someone is suddenly dismissed from their job, you can say they are **thrown out** of it.

❑ If you **throw up**, you vomit.

❑ If an event or situation **throws up** something, it reveals it or makes people notice it. *They recently had an environment week, which threw up lots of ideas.*

❑ If people **throw up** a building or some other structure, they build it hurriedly.

throw-in When there is a **throw-in** in football or rugby, a player throws the ball back onto the pitch after it has been kicked off by one of the other side.

throwaway A **throwaway** product is intended to be used for a short time and then thrown away. *...throwaway razors.* ◇ A **throwaway** remark is made in a casual way, but is meant to pass on information or to have a particular effect.

throwback If you say something like an idea or attitude is a **throwback** to an earlier time, you mean it is like something which existed at that time.

thrown See **throw**.

thru is short for 'through', especially in signs and advertisements. *...Woburn Wild Animal Kingdom drive-thru safari park.*

thrush (thrushes) ❑ The **thrush** or song **thrush** is a small brown songbird with a speckled chest. The mistle thrush is a similar larger bird which makes a loud rasping noise.

❑ **Thrush** is an infectious disease which mostly occurs in babies' mouths and women's vaginas.

thrust (thrusting, thrust *not* 'thrusted') ❑ If you **thrust** something somewhere, you push it or move it there quickly and forcefully. *As I was leaving, he thrust a fiver into my top pocket.* A **thrust** is a sudden forceful movement.

❑ **Thrust** is the power or force needed to make a plane, rocket, or other vehicle move.

❑ The **thrust** of an activity is what it is mainly concentrated on. *The major thrust of the US strategy has been to tackle the drugs problem at its source.* ◇ The **thrust** of what someone says is the main point they are making. *The thrust of his speech was that it was imperative to stick to the timetable already agreed for economic union.*

❑ When people talk about the **cut and thrust** of an area of activity, especially politics, they mean all the arguing and debating that goes on.

❑ If you **thrust** something **upon** someone, you force them to have it, whether they want it or not.

thud (thudding, thudded) A **thud** is a dull sound, usually made by a solid object hitting something soft. If something **thuds** against something else, it hits it making a noise like this.

thug (thuggish, thuggery) A **thug** is a rough violent man, especially a criminal. You say someone like this is **thuggish**; you call their behaviour **thuggery**.

thumb ❑ A person's **thumb** is the jointed part which is like a finger but shorter and nearer their wrist.

❑ If you are **under** someone's **thumb**, you are under their control or heavily influenced by them.

❑ A **rule of thumb** is a simple rule or principle you can follow when you have to make a choice or decision. *A rule of thumb says that if a new field produces less than 150 barrels of oil a day, it is not worth developing.*

❑ If you **thumb through** a book or magazine, you turn the pages quickly, because you are trying to find a particular page.

❑ **thumb your nose at** someone: see **nose**. ◇ **stick out like a sore thumb**: see **sore**. ◇ **twiddle your thumbs**: see **twiddle**. ◇ See also **well-thumbed**.

thumb tack In the US, drawing pins are called **thumb tacks**.

thumbnail Your **thumbnail** is the nail on your thumb. ◇ A **thumbnail** sketch or account is a very brief one.

thumbs-down If you give something like a plan, idea, or suggestion the **thumbs-down**, you indicate that you do not approve of it.

thumbs-up A **thumbs-up** is a sign you make with your hand to show you agree with someone or are happy with an idea or situation. ◇ If you give something like a plan, idea, or suggestion the **thumbs-up**, you indicate you approve of it or are willing to accept it.

thump ❑ If you **thump** something or give it a **thump**, you hit it with your fist. ◇ If your heart **thumps**, it beats very strongly and quickly.

❑ If something **thumps** against something else, it hits it making a loud dull sound. *A mortar shell thumped somewhere behind us.*

thumping (thumpingly) A **thumping** amount is very large. *...a thumping Conservative majority.* ◇ If something is **thumpingly** obvious, it is very obvious indeed.

thunder (thundering, thundered) ❑ **Thunder** is the loud noise you hear in the sky after a flash of lightning. ◇ If something **thunders**, it makes a loud deep continuous noise. You talk about the **thunder** of something like this. *...the thunder of heavy machine gun fire.*

❑ If someone **thunders** something, they say it very loudly and forcefully. *'Arrant nonsense!' thundered the Commissioner.*

❑ If you **steal** someone's **thunder**, you attract attention instead of them, often by saying or doing something they had intended to say or do.

thunderbolt A **thunderbolt** is a flash of lightning accompanied by thunder.

thunderclap A **thunderclap** is a short loud bang you hear just after a flash of lightning.

thunderous A **thunderous** noise is very loud and deep. *...thunderous applause.*

thunderstorm A **thunderstorm** is a storm in which there is thunder and lightning.

thunderstruck If you are **thunderstruck**, you are very surprised or shocked.

thundery If the weather is **thundery**, there is a lot of thunder, or there are heavy clouds which suggest there will be thunder soon.

thus ❑ You say **thus** when you are mentioning the consequences of an action or of something that happens. *Excessive litigation has inflated insurance premiums and thus the cost of goods and services.*

❑ You also say **thus** when you have described, or are about to describe, how something happened. *Thus was one of the crucial partnerships in the modern cinema formed.*

thwart If you **thwart** someone or **thwart** their plans, you prevent them from doing or getting what they want. *Wardens will be guarding the nests 24 hours a day to thwart* *egg collectors.*

thy is an old-fashioned word for 'your' when you are talking to one person. *Love thy neighbour as thyself.*

thyme is a low-growing plant with scented leaves which are used in cooking.

thyroid Your **thyroid** or **thyroid gland** is a gland in your neck which produces hormones to control the way your body grows and functions.

thyself is an old-fashioned word for 'yourself' when you are talking to one person. *Know thyself and thou shalt know God.*

tiara A **tiara** is a small crown worn by a woman of high social rank on formal occasions.

tibia The **tibia** is the inner and thicker of the two bones of the human leg below the knee, between the kneecap and the ankle. The tibia is often called the 'shinbone'.

tic If someone has a **tic**, a part of their face or body keeps twitching and they cannot control it.

tick ❑ A **tick** is a written mark in the shape of a V with the right side extended upwards. You use it to show something is correct, acceptable, or has been dealt with. If you **tick** something, you put a mark like this beside it. ◇ If you **tick off** an item on a list, you put a tick next to it to show it has been dealt with.

❑ When a clock or watch **ticks**, it makes a regular series of short sounds as it works. You call these sounds its **tick** or **ticking**. ◇ If you say the seconds, minutes, or hours are **ticking away** or **ticking by**, you are emphasizing that time is passing.

❑ If you talk about what makes someone **tick**, you are talking about why they behave or think the way they do.

❑ If you **tick** someone **off** or give them a **ticking-off**, you speak to them crossly because they have done something wrong.

❑ If an engine is **ticking over**, it is running at a low speed, for example when it is switched on and you are not actually using it. ◇ If a system or process is **ticking over**, it is working or operating at a low rate. *Engineers hope that a small amount of money can be found to keep the project ticking over.*

❑ **Ticks** are small creatures like fleas which live on the bodies of people and animals and suck their blood as food.

ticker-tape is long narrow strips of paper on which information such as stock exchange prices is printed. In the US, if a famous person is driven in a parade or procession through the streets, people sometimes throw ticker-tape from the windows of high buildings to welcome them.

ticket ❑ A **ticket** is an official piece of card or paper which shows you have paid for a journey or for entry to a place of entertainment or other building. ◇ When a motorist gets a **ticket**, they are given an official piece of paper stating they have committed a driving or parking offence.

❑ In an American election, a party's **ticket** is its list of candidates. *His presence on the Democratic ticket has done more than anything else to please organised labour.*

❑ If you say something is **just the ticket**, you mean it is just what is wanted.

❑ dream ticket: see dream. ◇ See also **season ticket**.

ticking-off See tick.

tickle (tickling, tickled) ❑ When you **tickle** someone, you move your fingers lightly over a part of their body, to make them laugh. ◇ If something **tickles**, it causes an irritating feeling by lightly touching part of your body.

❑ If something like a remark or situation **tickles** you, it amuses you. *They were tickled with the idea that a public schoolboy should adopt such an unorthodox way of life.* ◇ If you are **tickled pink**, you are delighted by something.

ticklish If someone is **ticklish**, it is easy to make them laugh by tickling them. ◇ A **ticklish** problem or situation is awkward or embarrassing and needs to be dealt with carefully.

tidal is used to talk about things to do with the movement of tides. *An attempt will be made to bring the seals ashore when tidal conditions are suitable.*

tidal wave A **tidal wave** is a very large wave which comes up from the sea and spreads over the land, causing damage and sometimes loss of life. Tidal waves are often caused by earthquakes. ◇ A **tidal wave** of people or things is a large number of them arriving or happening at the same time. *...a tidal wave of refugees... A tidal wave of sensational stories broke around them.*

tiddler A **tiddler** is a very small fish of any kind. ◇ Things which are very small compared to other things of the same kind can be called **tiddlers**. *Conde Nast's British division is a relative tiddler compared with the giant IPC, which has a turnover of £300 million a year.* ◇ People who are thought to be unimportant are sometimes called **tiddlers**. *...political tiddlers.*

tiddlywinks is a game played on a soft surface like a carpet in which players try to flick small plastic counters into a cup.

tide (tiding, tided) ❑ The **tide** is the regular change in the level of the sea on the shore, caused by the gravitational pull of the sun and moon. When it is at its highest level, you say the tide is in or it is **high tide**. When it is at its lowest level, you say the tide is out or it is **low tide**.

❑ The **tide of opinion** is what the majority of people think about an issue. *There are signs that the tide of opinion is turning.*

❑ A **tide** of something is an amount which is getting larger. *...a rising tide of violence... Growing tides of people took to the streets.*

❑ If you say something will **tide you over**, you mean it will help you to survive until something else becomes available. *The money was needed to tide Nicaragua over until US aid had been approved by Congress.*

tidily (tidiness) See tidy.

tidings are news. *They hope that next year will bring better tidings... ...dire tidings of shortages and harvest problems.*

tidy (tidies, tidying, tidied; tidier, tidiest; tidily, tidiness) ❑ When you **tidy** a place or **tidy** it **up**, you make it neat by putting things in their proper place. When you **tidy** things **away**, you put them where they belong, to make a place tidy. ◇ You say something is **tidy** when it is neat and arranged in an orderly way. *They had never seen the park looking tidier... I put the letters tidily away in a drawer.* ◇ A **tidy** person keeps things neat and arranged in an orderly way. *I used to be far more obsessive about tidiness.*

❑ If you **tidy up** something like a plan or a piece of work, you deal with the small unfinished or unsatisfactory parts, so it is completely ready or finished.

❑ A **tidy** amount of money is a fairly large amount. *The* *business made a tidy profit.*

tie (ties, tying, tied) ❑ If you **tie** something to something else, you fasten it using something like string or rope.

❑ If you **tie** something like a piece of string round something, you put the string round it and fasten the ends with a knot or bow. ◇ If you **tie** something or **tie** it **up**, you fasten string or rope round it to secure it. *...a box tied up with ribbon.* ◇ If someone **ties** you **up**, they fasten ropes around you so you cannot escape.

❑ When you **tie** your shoelaces, you fasten the ends together with a knot or bow.

❑ When you **tie up** an animal, you fasten it to a fixed object with a length of rope, so it cannot run away. Similarly, when you **tie up** a boat, you fasten it to something with a rope or chain, so it cannot float away.

❑ If something **ties** you **down**, it restricts your freedom by limiting the number of things you are able to do. *Is it really sensible to tie ourselves down now to specific commitments in the distant future?* ◇ When an army is **tied down**, an opposing force keeps it in one place for a while.

❑ You say something is **tied up** when it is used in such a way that it is not available for other people or other purposes. *More and more old people will also have capital tied up in a house.* ◇ If you are **tied up**, you are very busy and are not available to do something.

❑ If something is **tied to** something else or **tied up with** it, it is kept closely linked to it. *Their bonuses are tied to the company's profits... Economic assistance is to be tied up with progress towards democracy.*

❑ A **tied** pub is owned by a brewery and has to sell the brewery's beer. ◇ A **tied** cottage is owned by an employer, especially a farmer, and rented to a worker while they work for that employer.

❑ **Ties** are close links between people, organizations, or countries. *...family ties... The foreign ministers decided to open the way for diplomatic and economic ties with Vietnam.*

❑ If an idea or fact **ties in with** something else, it fits in with it or agrees with it. *There will be videos and illustrated talks to tie in with exhibitions on the subject.*

❑ In sport, a **tie** is a match played as part of a competition. The losers of the match are eliminated and the winners continue into the next round. *...an exciting Cup tie between First Division sides.* ◇ If you **tie** with someone in a competition or a game, you finish with the same number of points. A result is called a **tie** when two people or teams finish with the same number of points and with more points than anyone else.

❑ A **tie** is a long narrow piece of cloth worn under someone's shirt collar and tied in a knot at the front.

tie-break A **tie-break** is an extra game played in a tennis match when the score in a set is 6-6. The player who wins the tie-break wins the set.

tie-breaker In tennis, a **tie-breaker** is the same as a tie-break. ◇ A **tie-breaker** is also an extra question or round which decides the winner of a competition or game when two or more people have the same score at the end.

tie-dye When a garment is **tie-dyed**, parts of it are tied in knots before it is immersed in a dye. The knotted parts soak up less dye than the rest, and a coloured pattern appears on the garment.

tie-in A **tie-in** is a product like a toy, book, or record which is connected in some way to a new film or TV show and is put on sale at the same time.

tie-pin A **tie-pin** is an ornamental pin used to pin a person's tie to their shirt.

tie-up You say there is a **tie-up** between two companies or other organizations when they join together for a particular purpose. *The bill would block tie-ups between foreign banks and big American securities houses.*

tier (-tiered) A **tier** is a row or layer which has other rows or layers above it or below it. *Spectators sat watching from tiers of seats... ...a second-class sleeping carriage, lined with two tiers of beds.* You use **-tiered** to say how many tiers something has. *...a three-tiered silver chandelier.* ◇ A **tier** in an organization or system is one of the levels at which it operates. *...the existing two-tier structure of county and district councils.*

tiff A **tiff** is a small unimportant quarrel.

tiger Tigers are large carnivorous animals belonging to the cat family. They come from Asia and usually have an orange coat with black stripes.

tigerish behaviour is very fierce. *...the tigerish tackling of an inspired Britain team.*

tight (tightly, tightness) ❑ **Tight** clothes fit closely to the body. *...tight jeans... ...the tightness of her sweater.*

❑ If you hold something **tight**, you hold it very firmly. *The instinct when braking hard is to grip the steering wheel as tightly as possible.* ◇ You say something is **tight** when it is firmly fastened and difficult to move. If something is shut **tight**, it is shut very firmly.

❑ If something like skin, cloth, or string is stretched **tight**, it is stretched or pulled so it is smooth or straight.

❑ You use **tight** to describe things which are closely packed together in a small space. *Many animals travel in tightly packed lorries.* ◇ If you have a **tight** schedule, you have a lot of things to do in a short time and cannot afford to spend too long on any of them. ◇ If you are operating on a **tight** budget, you have very little money to spend on things. *Money is tight for students.*

❑ A **tight** bend in a road is a place where it changes direction very suddenly. Similarly, you can talk about a vehicle making a **tight** turn. *The aircraft turned tightly round a steep hill.* ◇ A **tight** angle is very narrow.

❑ You say your chest or stomach feels **tight** when it feels painful, because you are ill or anxious.

❑ **Tight** controls or rules are very strict. *The trial was held amid tight security... Tighter controls on vehicles entering the City are essential.* ◇ If a company or operation is **tightly** run, it is well organized and very efficient.

❑ A **tight** situation is a difficult or dangerous one. If you are in a dangerous situation, you can say you are in a **tight spot.** ◇ If a competition or sports match is **tight**, none of the competitors has a clear advantage, so it is difficult to say who will win.

❑ sit tight: see sit.

tight-fisted people are unwilling to spend their money.

tight-lipped If someone is **tight-lipped**, they are unwilling to give any information about something. *The authorities are tight-lipped about the attack.* ◇ You also say someone is **tight-lipped** when they have their lips pressed together, because they are angry.

tighten (tightening, tightened) ❑ If you **tighten** your hold on something, you hold it more firmly. You can also say your hold **tightens**. *My hands tightened on the steering wheel.* ◇ If an army **tightens** its grip on a place, it takes greater control of it.

❏ If you **tighten** something like a rope, chain, or strap, you stretch it or pull it until it is straight, or until it grips something firmly. ◇ If you **tighten up** a fastening, you move it so it is more firmly in place or holds something more firmly.

❏ When things like rules or conditions are **tightened** or **tightened up**, they are made stricter. *...new legislation to tighten up immigration law... The likelihood is that there will be a tightening of monetary policy.*

tightrope A **tightrope** is a tightly-stretched rope fixed high above the ground on which an acrobat balances and performs tricks. ◇ If you say someone is **on a tightrope** or **walking a tightrope**, you mean they are in a difficult or delicate situation and have to be careful about what they say or do.

tights are a piece of clothing, usually made of thin stretchy material like nylon, which fit closely over a person's feet, legs, and body up to their waist.

tigress (tigresses) A **tigress** is a female tiger.

tike See tyke.

tilde (*pron:* til-duh) The **tilde** is a symbol written over 'n' in Spanish to show it is pronounced like the first 'n' in 'onion' rather than the 'n' in 'money'. *...His Excellency Señor Antonio Espinoza.*

tile (tiling, tiled) **Tiles** are regularly-shaped pieces of baked clay, used as a roof or wall covering. When a roof or wall is **tiled**, it is covered with tiles. Floors can also be covered with flat regularly-shaped objects called **tiles.**

till means the same as 'until'. *I didn't meet Doris till many years later.*

❏ A **till** is a drawer or box where money is kept in a shop, usually as part of a cash register. ◇ If you say someone has **their hand in the till** or **their fingers in the till**, you mean they are stealing money from their company or organization.

❏ When people **till** the land, they prepare it for planting and growing crops.

tiller The **tiller** of a boat is a handle fixed to the rudder. It is used to turn the rudder and steer the boat.

tilt ❏ If something **tilts** or is **tilted**, it changes position so one end or side is higher than the other. You then say it has a **tilt**. ◇ If you say something like a proposal is **tilted** in a certain direction, you mean it shows a tendency towards policies of a certain kind. *The chairman criticised the plan for its tilt towards higher taxes.*

❏ If something is moving **at full tilt**, it is moving as fast as possible. Similarly, you can talk about something happening **at full tilt**. *Firms have kept production lines running at full tilt.*

❏ When someone makes an attempt to achieve something, you can say they have a **tilt** at it. *...a tilt at the world title.* ◇ If you say someone is **tilting at windmills**, you mean they are fighting imaginary enemies.

tilth is soil with a fine crumbly surface, which makes it good for sowing in. *Rake the soil to a fine tilth.*

timber (timbered) **Timber** is wood used for things like building houses or making furniture. ◇ The **timbers** of something like a house or ship are the large pieces of wood forming part of its basic structure. *...roof timbers.*

◇ A **timbered** building has a wooden frame or wooden beams showing on the outside.

timbre (*pron:* tam-bra) The **timbre** of a sound is a special quality which it has. *There is a timbre to his voice that can still sound awkwardly like a whine.*

time (timing, timed) ❏ **Time** is what we measure in units like hours, days, and years. ◇ **Time** is used to say how long something lasts or how long someone takes to do something. *The argument will go on for a long time... He went on to win in a time of 3hr 53min 37sec.* ◇ If you **time** something, you measure how long it takes or lasts.

❏ If something **takes time**, it cannot be done quickly. ◇ If you **take your time** doing something, you do it slowly, without hurrying.

❏ If you **make time** to do something, you give yourself an opportunity to do it. *You should make time to stroll around the park.* ◇ If you take **time out** to do something, you have a break in your normal activities so you can do it. *Employers are reluctant to let them take time out for training purposes.*

❏ If something happens **for a time** or **for some time**, it happens for a fairly long period. *He worked for a time in business in Paris... She had been with him for some time.*

❏ A particular **time** is a specific point in the day or night. *Meet me tomorrow afternoon at this same time... We like to know what time people will be arriving.* ◇ A **time** is also an occasion when something happens. *This time it's different... Sales were dropping for the first time in 22 years.* ◇ **Time** and **times** are also used to talk about a certain stage in someone's life or a period in history. *...about the time of World War One... ...the true history of Roman or medieval times.* ◇ **At one time** means at a certain stage in the past. *At one time they were living seven to a room.*

❏ If someone is **ahead of their time**, they have an idea long before other people start thinking in the same way. ◇ If you say someone is **behind the times**, you mean they are old-fashioned.

❏ If you are **in time** for something, you are not late. If you are **in good time**, you are early. ◇ If something happens **on time**, it happens at the expected or scheduled time.

❏ When you talk about how well a watch or clock **keeps time**, you are talking about how accurate it is. *A £10 digital watch may keep as good time as the most expensive Rolex.*

❏ If you **make good time** on a journey, you complete it quicker than you expected to.

❏ You use **times** to say how often something happens. *I was playing football four or five times a week.* ◇ If something happens **at times**, it happens occasionally. *At times the government has been forced to cut interest rates when it did not want to.* You can also say something happens **from time to time**. *Hibernating dormice wake up from time to time but only for a few hours.* ◇ If something happens **time after time** or **time and again**, it keeps happening. *Both countries have exceeded their quotas time and again in the past.*

❏ If something happens **all the time**, it goes on happening. *It rained all the time, from morning to night... I watch television all the time.* ◇ **At all times** means 'always' or 'on every occasion'. *They must carry their identity tags at all times... Players and team officials must at all times accept the umpire's decision.*

❏ You use **at the best of times** to say something is always bad even when circumstances are as favourable as possible. *Transport and communications are appalling at the best of times.*

❏ **Time** is used to say how soon something will happen. For example, you say something will happen 'in six weeks' time' or 'in two years' time'. ◇ If you say something will happen **in time**, you mean it will happen eventually. *Perhaps in time I'll acquire the skill to improvise.*

❏ If you say it is **time** for something to be done or to happen, you mean it ought to be done or happen now. *It is time for a change.* ◇ If you say it is **about time** something was done, you are saying firmly that it should be done. *It is about time the government gave young people something to do.* ◇ If you say it is **high time** something was done, you mean it should be done at once, and should really have been done before. Similarly, if you talk about something happening **not before time,** you mean it should have happened sooner. *It is back to basics, and not before time.*

❏ You say **for the time being** when you are talking about something which exists or is true now, but which will not necessarily continue to exist or be true in the future. *For the time being, the building process goes on.*

❏ If you say you **have no time for** someone or something, you mean you do not approve of them or cannot be bothered with them.

❏ If you say you have had **a good time** or **the time of your life,** you mean you have enjoyed yourself very much.

❏ If an event or action is **timed** for a certain time, it is planned to happen then. *The advertisements were timed to coincide with the end of the Proms.* Similarly, if something is **timed** to achieve a certain result, it is planned to happen at the best time to achieve that result. *His demands have been timed to achieve maximum impact.* ◇ If you **time** something right, you do it at the most effective or appropriate moment. Similarly, if you **time** something badly, you fail to do it when it would be effective.

❏ In music, **time** is used to talk about the number of beats in each bar, which gives a piece its rhythm. *...a poignant song in slow waltz time.* If you do something **in time** to a piece of music, you fit in exactly with its rhythm and speed. *She tapped her feet happily in time to the music.*

❏ If you say someone is **doing time,** you mean they are in prison.

❏ You use **at a time** to say how many things or people there are in each of a number of groups or sequences. *People ring us and order 500 at a time... We take these things one step at a time.*

❏ You use **at one time** or **at any one time** to talk about things happening or being done simultaneously. *...cinema complexes where two or three films would be showing at any one time.*

❏ You use **times** to say how much bigger one thing is than another. *...a country three times the size of France.* ◇ In arithmetic, you say **times** when you are multiplying one number by another.

❏ You say **at the same time** when you are mentioning something which contrasts with what you have just said. *...somewhere not too far from home, but at the same time remote.*

time bomb A **time bomb** is a bomb which is set to go off at a particular time. ◇ Something which is likely to have a devastating effect in the future can be called a **time bomb.** *'Tuberculosis is a time bomb waiting to go off',* warns Dr Sheldon... *The Government is sitting on a time-bomb with its forthcoming tax.*

time capsule See **capsule.**

time-consuming If something is **time-consuming,** it takes up a great deal of time.

time frame The **time frame** for something is a fixed period of time during which it must take place. *The move follows the refusal of the rebels to lay down their weapons within the time frame agreed last month.*

time-honoured A **time-honoured** way of doing something has been used for a long time. *In time-honoured fashion, the chairman set up a committee... ...a time-honoured tradition.*

time-keeping If you talk about someone's **time-keeping,** you are talking about how good or bad they are at getting to work on time, or working the correct number of hours. You also use **time-keeping** to talk about the punctuality of something like a transport service. *The report applauds British Rail for improved time-keeping.*

time lag The **time lag** between two events is the interval of time between them.

time limit If you set a **time limit** for something, you say it must be done before a certain time.

time scale The **time scale** for doing something is the length of time it is expected to take.

time-server If you say someone is a **time-server,** you mean they make very little effort in their job and are just passing the time until they retire.

time signature A **time signature** is a sign written at the beginning of a line of music. It is usually in the form of two numbers, showing the number of beats in each bar.

time switch A **time switch** is a device which makes a machine start or stop working at specific times.

time trial A **time trial** is a race, especially a cycle race, in which each competitor goes separately over a specified course. The winner is the person who completes the course in the fastest time.

time warp If you say someone is in a **time warp,** you mean they are living or behaving in a way which would have been acceptable many years ago, but now seems strange or inappropriate. *...stories about boarding schools isolated in the countryside in a 1920-ish time-warp.*

time-worn is used to describe things which have been used for a long time and have now lost their effect or usefulness. *...time-worn techniques... ...a time-worn cliché.*

time zone A **time zone** is one of the areas the world is divided into, where the time is taken as being a certain number of hours behind or ahead of Greenwich Mean Time.

timeless (**timelessness**) If you say something is **timeless,** you mean it is so good, beautiful, or perfect that it cannot be affected by the passing of time or changes in fashion. *Coco Chanel created designs of timeless elegance... The villages have an atmosphere of timelessness and permanency.*

timely (**timeliness**) If something is **timely,** it happens at just the right time. *The report is a timely reminder that neglect, oversight or tunnel vision could damage a buoyant section of the economy... The play was revived in 1989, and events since then have given it new timeliness.*

timepiece is an old-fashioned word for a clock or watch.

timer A timer is a device which measures time, especially one which is part of a machine and makes it start or stop at a specific time.

timeshare A timeshare is holiday accommodation in which several people buy a share. Each person then has the right to use the accommodation for a certain amount of time each year.

timetable (timetabling, timetabled) A timetable is a schedule of the times when events or tasks are due to take place or be done. If you timetable something, you prepare a timetable for it. ...*the timetabling of school option groups*. ◇ A timetable is also a list of the times when trains, boats, buses, or planes arrive and depart.

timid (timidly, timidity) A timid person or animal is shy and easily frightened. ◇ You also say someone's behaviour is timid when they are not very bold or adventurous. ...*one of a number of states moving timidly towards multi-party democracy... One reason for his timidity was the desire to scrape through an election without bad publicity*.

timing ❑ Someone's timing is their skill in judging the right moment at which to do something. *Her comic timing was equal to that of her fellow comedians*. ◇ The timing of an event is the time when it happens or is planned to happen. *Some head teachers expressed resentment over the timing of the announcement... ...the timing of the next election*.
❑ A timing device is a mechanism attached to a bomb or missile to make it explode at a particular time.

timorous people are very frightened and nervous.

timpani (*pron:* tim-pan-ee) (timpanist) Timpani are large drums shaped like half a sphere with the flat part uppermost. They can be tuned to a particular pitch and are the drums most commonly used in an orchestra. The person who plays the timpani in an orchestra is called the timpanist.

tin (tinned) ❑ Tin is a silvery-white metal. It is used in alloys, especially bronze and pewter, and as a non-corrosive coating for steel.
❑ A tin is a metal container which is filled with food and sealed to preserve the food. You say food preserved like this is tinned. ...*tinned salmon*. ◇ Various types of metal containers, with or without lids, can be called tins. ...*a biscuit tin... ...a roasting tin*.

tin opener A tin opener is a tool for opening tins of food.

Tin Pan Alley The popular music business is sometimes called Tin Pan Alley.

tincture (*pron:* tingt-chur) A tincture is an extract of a medicinal substance mixed with alcohol. ...*tincture of iodine*.

tinder is small pieces of something like dry wood or grass which burn easily and can be used for lighting a fire. If something is tinder dry, it is very dry and likely to catch fire easily.

tinderbox (tinderboxes) ❑ In the past, a tinderbox was a small metal box used to hold tinder and keep it dry. It often contained a flint and steel to light the tinder.
❑ If you say something is a tinderbox, you mean it is very dry and could catch fire and burn easily. *In a dry summer, heather moor is a tinder box*. ◇ You also say a place is a tinderbox when trouble or conflict could break out there very easily. *The region was once the tinderbox of Europe*.

tine The tines of something like a fork or a rake are its prongs.

tinge (tinged) A tinge of something like a feeling or a colour is a small amount of it. ...*a tinge of regret... ...a large green apple with a reddish tinge*. You can say one thing is tinged with another. *The celebrations were tinged with sadness... ...pink-tinged granite rocks*.

tingle (tingling, tingled) If part of your body tingles, you feel a slight prickling feeling there. You call this feeling a tingle. ◇ If you tingle with excitement or fear, you are very excited or frightened. This feeling can also be called a tingle. ...*a certain tingle of special anticipation*.

tinker (tinkering, tinkered) ❑ Tinkers are people who travel from place to place mending metal pots and pans or doing other small repair jobs.
❑ If you tinker with something, you make small adjustments to it, to repair or improve it. You often say someone is tinkering when they are making small changes and you think major ones are needed. *The government is tinkering with tax concessions*.

tinkle (tinkling, tinkled) If something tinkles, it makes a sound like a small bell ringing. This sound is called a tinkle. ...*the tinkle of teaspoons on bone china*.

tinned See tin.

tinnitus (*pron:* tin-nie-tuss) is a ringing, booming, or hissing sensation in the ear.

tinny If you say a sound is tinny, you mean it has an unpleasant high-pitched quality. ◇ If you say something like a car is tinny, you mean it is made of thin metal and is of poor quality.

tinpot People use tinpot to talk about countries and governments they regard as inferior and unimportant. ...*tinpot military dictators*.

tinsel is long threads with strips of metallic shiny paper attached, used as a decoration at Christmas.

Tinseltown is a humorous name for Hollywood.

tint (tinted) A tint is a small amount of a colour. Tinted things are slightly coloured. ...*fair thick hair, with a reddish-gold tint... ...cars with tinted windscreens*. ◇ If you tint something, you add a small amount of a colour to it. ◇ When someone tints their hair, they change its colour slightly using a type of dye called a tint.

tiny (tinier, tiniest) Tiny people or things are extremely small.

tip (tipping, tipped) ❑ The tip of something is the extreme end of it. ...*the northern tip of Japan... ...the tips of their fingers*. ◇ If an object is tipped with a certain colour or material, it has that colour or material at one end of it. ...*a white-tipped tail... ...a piece of wood tipped with metal*.
❑ If you say that a word or someone's name is on the tip of your tongue, you mean you cannot think of it just at that moment but feel sure you do actually know it.
❑ tip of the iceberg: see iceberg.
❑ If you tip an object, you move it so it is no longer flat or upright. ...*champagne glasses tipped upside down*. ◇ If you tip something somewhere, you pour it or dump it quickly and carelessly. *The rubble was tipped into the river*.
❑ A tip is a place where rubbish is dumped.
❑ If something tips into a certain state or situation, a small change or development puts it into that state or situation. *The economy tipped into recession*. ◇ If something tips the balance, it is sufficient to make a situation go one

way rather than another. ◇ If something **tips the scales** in someone's favour, it is just enough to give them an advantage over someone else.

❑ If a heavy person **tips the scales** at a certain weight, that is how much they weigh.

❑ A **tip** is a useful piece of advice or information. ◇ A **tip** is also a suggestion of the likely winner of a horse race. ◇ If someone is **tipped** for success or for a certain job, people in the know say they are likely to be successful or get the job.

❑ If you are **tipped off** about something, you are given some information or a warning, often privately or secretly. The information or warning is called a **tip-off**.

❑ If you **tip** someone like a taxi driver or a waiter, you give them money to show your appreciation of the service they have provided. The money you give them is called a **tip**.

tip-off See **tip**.

tip-top If you say something is **tip-top**, you mean it is as good as it could possibly be. *...in tip-top physical condition.*

tipple (tippler) A person's **tipple** is the alcoholic drink they usually drink. *My favourite tipple is a glass of port.* Someone who drinks alcohol regularly but in small quantities can be called a **tippler**.

tipster A **tipster** is a person who sells tips to people who bet on horses or greyhounds or speculate on the stock market.

tipsy If someone is **tipsy**, they are slightly drunk.

tiptoe (tiptoeing, tiptoed) ❑ If you walk or stand on **tiptoe**, you walk or stand on your toes. ◇ If you **tiptoe** somewhere, you walk there on your toes, to make as little noise as possible.

❑ You can also say someone **tiptoes** through or around a difficult situation when they deal with it very carefully or delicately. *...a campaign that tiptoed around the difficulties – acknowledging them without specifically mentioning them.*

tirade (*pron:* tie-rade) A **tirade** is a long angry speech, criticizing someone or something.

tire (tiring, tired; tiredness) ❑ If something **tires** you, it makes you use a lot of energy so you want to rest or sleep. *Training for distance running tends to be dull, repetitive and very tiring.* If something **tires** you **out**, it makes you exhausted. ◇ If you are **tired**, you feel the need to rest or sleep.

❑ If you **tire** of something or get **tired** of it, you become bored with it or irritated by it. *More Britons appear to be tiring of poolside package holidays to Spain.*

❑ You use **tired** to describe something which is no longer very interesting because people have heard it or seen it many times before. *...the commissioning of new dramas and comedies to replace tired hits on ITV.*

❑ See also **tyre**.

tireless (tirelessly) If you say someone is **tireless**, you mean they have a lot of energy and never seem to need a rest. *She campaigned tirelessly for his release.*

tiresome If you say someone or something is **tiresome**, you mean they make you feel irritated or bored.

tissue ❑ Animal or plant **tissue** consists of similar cells grouped together and usually performing a particular function. *...brain tissue... ...scar tissue.*

❑ **Tissue paper** is thin paper used for wrapping breakable objects. ◇ A **tissue** is a small piece of soft paper used as a handkerchief.

tit **Tits** are a common type of small bird. There are several species of tits, including blue tits, coal tits, and great tits.

tit-for-tat actions are harsh measures you take against someone in response to something similar they have done to you. *...tit-for-tat killings.*

titan (*pron:* tie-tan) (titanic) You call someone a **titan** when (a) they are very big and strong. (b) they are very important and powerful. *...the country's two richest business titans.* ◇ You use **titanic** to describe things which are very great or powerful. *...Brian Cox's titanic performance in King Lear... ...the titanic struggle which led to his first Senate victory.*

titanium (*usual pron:* ti-tane-i-um) is a strong silvery metal which is very resistant to corrosion. It is used in the manufacture of alloys which need to be strong and light, such as those used in aircraft parts.

titbit A **titbit** is a small tasty piece of food. ◇ A small piece of news or gossip can also be called a **titbit**.

tithe A **tithe** was a fixed part, originally one tenth, of a person's income or agricultural produce, paid as a tax to the church. A **tithe barn** is a very large barn where the agricultural tithe of a parish was stored.

titillate (titillating, titillated; titillation) If something **titillates** someone, it pleases and excites them, especially in a sexual way. *...titillating stories... The cover usually promises more titillation than the contents deliver.*

title (titled) ❑ The **title** of something like a book, play, or piece of music is its name. You say something is **titled** in a certain way. *...an album titled 'As Time Goes By'.* ◇ Books, magazines, and videos are sometimes called **titles**. *A further eight titles are due to be launched by the end of the year.*

❑ When an actor or singer plays the **title role** in a play, film, or opera, he or she plays the part of the character it is named after. *...her performance in the title role of The Marie Lloyd Story.* ◇ The **title track** of an album is the song or piece of music the album is named after.

❑ A person's **title** is a word like 'Lord', 'Mrs', or 'Doctor' which is used before their name to show their status or profession. ◇ A **titled** person has a title like 'Princess', 'Lord', 'Lady', or 'Sir' which shows their high social rank. *...a titled friend of the prince.*

❑ Someone's **title** is also the name of their job or status in an organization. *He has the title of chief executive.*

❑ In a sports competition, a **title** is the position of champion. *She won the Olympic title.* The present champion is called the **title holder**.

❑ The person who holds the **title** to some property or land is its legal owner. ◇ A **title deed** is a document proving a person's legal right to the ownership of property or land.

titter (tittering, tittered) If someone **titters** or gives a **titter**, they laugh quietly, either in a disrespectful way or because they are nervous.

tittle-tattle is gossip.

titular (*pron:* tit-yoo-lar) A **titular** job or position has a name which makes it seem important, although the person has no real power. *...the titular head of a new confederation.*

tizzy If someone is in a **tizzy**, they are excited, worried, or nervous, often over something unimportant.

TM is a short way of writing (a) 'trademark'. (b) 'transcendental meditation'.

TNT is a powerful explosive substance used in shells and bombs and for demolishing buildings. TNT stands for 'trinitrotoluene'.

to ❑ If you go **to** a place, you make your way there. You can also talk about going **to** an event. *I do hope you'll be able to come to the wedding.*

❑ To is used when talking about the position of something. For example, if something is **to** your left, it is nearer your left side than your right. ◇ **To** is used to say where a road, path, or staircase leads. *An external staircase leads to a downstairs room.*

❑ If one thing is attached or fixed **to** another, the two things are joined together.

❑ **To** is used when saying who or what an action or feeling is directed towards. *He gave instructions to his staff... The audience is broadly sympathetic to feminine aims... ...the problem of cruelty to children.*

❑ **To** is used when mentioning reactions. For example, something can happen **to** someone's surprise or relief.

❑ **To** is used when mentioning someone's opinion or point of view. *To me this seems unlikely.*

❑ **To** is used when saying what someone or something becomes. *Much of the area has been converted to farmland.*

❑ **To** is used when talking about a range of possibilities. *...everything from beds to hat stands.*

❑ **To** is used when saying when something finished. *He was Chancellor of the Exchequer from 1983 to 1989.*

❑ **To** is used when talking about something reaching a point or level. *Business confidence had fallen to its lowest level since 1974.*

❑ **To** is used when mentioning certain times of day. *...ten minutes to eight.*

❑ **To** is used when talking about ratios and rates. *The car gives a regular 40 miles to the gallon... ...a mixture of one part milk to two parts water.*

❑ **To** is used when indicating that two things happen at the same time. For example, if something happens **to** music, it happens when music is being played.

❑ **To** is very commonly used in the structures called 'infinitives'. See **infinitive**. For example, you use **to** when talking about the purpose or intention of an action. *...emergency programmes set up to save animals.* You also use **to** when commenting on what you are saying. *I'm disappointed, to be honest.*

❑ **To** is used when mentioning a forthcoming event. *A new national assembly is to be elected in April.*

❑ **to and fro**: see **fro**.

to-do When there is a **to-do**, there is a lot of fuss or excitement about something.

to-ing and fro-ing See **fro**.

toad Toads are small amphibious creatures which look like frogs, but have drier skin and live more on land than in water.

toadstool Toadstools are various types of poisonous mushrooms.

toady (toadies; toadying) A **toady** is someone who flatters or tries to please important or powerful people in the hope of being liked by them or getting some advantage

from them. Behaviour like this is called **toadying**.

toast (toaster) ❑ When you **toast** a slice of bread, you cook it at a high temperature under a grill or in an appliance called a **toaster**, so it becomes brown and crisp. Bread cooked like this is called **toast**.

❑ If you **toast** someone or drink a **toast** to them, you drink a glass of wine or some other drink in their honour. If you propose a **toast** to someone, you make a short speech and then invite everyone to drink a toast to them.

❑ If you say someone is the **toast** of a place or organization, you mean they are very popular and greatly admired there, because they have done something especially well.

toastmaster A **toastmaster** is a person who proposes the toasts and introduces the speakers at a formal reception or dinner.

tobacco is the dried leaves of a plant called the **tobacco** plant, which people smoke in cigarettes, cigars, and pipes.

tobacconist A **tobacconist** or **tobacconist's** is a shop selling tobacco, cigarettes, and cigars. The person who runs it is sometimes called a **tobacconist**.

toboggan (tobogganing, tobogganed) When you **toboggan**, you slide downhill over snow on a sledge without runners called a **toboggan**.

toby jug A **toby jug** is a beer mug or jug in the shape of a person, traditionally a fat man wearing a three-cornered hat and smoking a pipe.

today is (a) the day on which you are writing or speaking. *An announcement is expected later today.* (b) the present period of history. *Business is the most powerful force in society today.*

toddle (toddling, toddled) When a small child **toddles**, it walks unsteadily with short quick steps.

toddler A **toddler** is a young child aged between about one and three.

toe (toeing, toed) ❑ A person's **toes** are the five jointed parts at the end of each of their feet.

❑ If someone **toes the line**, they behave in the way people in authority expect them to.

toehold If you get a **toehold** in something like an area of business, you make a small start in it, which you hope will eventually lead to something better. *Mitsubishi was anxious to get a toehold in the European market.* ◇ A **toehold** is also a small crack or ledge on a cliff or rock face where climbers can place their feet when climbing.

toenail A person's **toenails** are the hard areas at the end of their toes.

toff Rich or upper-class people are sometimes called **toffs**.

toffee is a sticky chewy sweet made by boiling sugar and butter together with water.

toffee apple A **toffee apple** is a toffee-coated apple on a stick.

toffee-nosed If you say someone is **toffee-nosed**, you mean they are snobbish and look down on other people.

tofu (*pron:* toe-foo) is a soft food made from soya-bean curd.

tog (togged) ❑ A person's **togs** are their clothes. You say someone is **togged up** when they are wearing clothes designed for a particular purpose. *...togged up in wetsuits and gasmasks.*

❑ The **tog rating** of a quilt is an official measurement of how warm it is. ...*a snug 13.5-tog winter duvet.*

toga (*pron:* toe-ga) A **toga** was a long loose robe worn in public by citizens of ancient Rome.

together ❑ You say people get **together** or come **together** when they meet for a particular purpose. ◇ If people do something **together,** they do it in company with each other. ◇ If people are **together** on an issue, they have the same attitude about it.

❑ You say things or people are close **together** when they are very near to each other. ...*village houses clustered tightly together.*

❑ If things are joined or fixed **together,** they are joined or fixed to each other.

❑ If you say things go **together,** you mean they fit or suit each other or can both happen at the same time or in the same place without causing problems. *Creativity and commercialism can go together.*

❑ If you say something is bigger than a number of things **put together,** you mean it is bigger on its own than they are as a group.

❑ If two things happen **together,** they happen at the same time.

❑ You use **together with** when you are mentioning someone or something else, in addition to the person or thing you have just mentioned. *Britain, together with other nations, is committed not to supply weapons to those countries.*

togetherness is a feeling of affection and closeness among a group of people.

togged See **tog.**

toggle A **toggle** is a bar-shaped button which you fasten by pushing it through a loop or hole.

toil (toiling, toiled; toiler) You say people **toil** when they work very hard doing something unpleasant, difficult, or tiring. Work like this is called **toil.** ◇ The **toilers** in an organization are the people who do the hard routine work.

toilet A **toilet** is a large bowl, connected by a pipe to the drains, which you use for getting rid of urine or faeces from your body. A small room containing a toilet is also called a **toilet.**

toilet paper is thin soft paper you use to clean yourself after you have been to the toilet.

toilet roll A **toilet roll** is a long strip of toilet paper wound round a cardboard tube.

toilet soap is for people to wash themselves with, rather than for washing clothes or for household cleaning. It is often scented.

toilet water is a lightly scented and inexpensive perfume.

toiletries are things like soap, toothpaste, shampoo, and deodorant which people use to clean or perfume themselves with.

token (tokenism) ❑ A **token** is a piece of paper or card worth a certain amount of money, which can be exchanged for goods in a shop. ◇ **Tokens** are also flat round pieces of metal or plastic which are sometimes used instead of money.

❑ If you give someone a present as a **token** of your feelings, you give it as a way of showing your feelings for them. ◇ **Token** actions are small or unimportant in themselves but are symbols of someone's intentions or feelings. *Coal miners in Poland have staged a two-hour token*

stoppage.

❑ **Token** is also used to describe someone who is chosen for a post or position just to show that a particular group is being represented. Choosing someone for this reason is called **tokenism.** ...*female tokenism.*

❑ You use **by the same token** to say that if one thing is true, logically something else ought to be true too. *Until recently the Commission for Racial Equality was run by white men. By the same token, a minister for women could be male.*

told See **tell.**

tolerable (tolerably) If you say something is **tolerable,** you mean it is acceptable or bearable but not pleasant or good. *Their captors treated them tolerably well.* ◇ If you say something is not **tolerable,** you mean it is unacceptable and something should be done to stop it. *Violations of human rights and democracy are no longer tolerable.*

tolerance (tolerant, tolerantly) ❑ **Tolerance** is allowing other people to say and do what they like, even if you do not agree with them or approve of what they say or do. ...*a greater tolerance of differing opinions.* A **tolerant** person shows tolerance to others. ...*the need for blacks and whites to live tolerantly together.* ◇ **Tolerance** is also putting up with something undesirable. *Today's tolerance of unemployment would have astonished people in the 1960s.*

❑ If animals or plants have **tolerance** to something harmful, they have been exposed to it so often that it no longer has much effect on them. You can also talk about plants or animals being **tolerant** of something. ...*crops resistant to disease or tolerant of weedkillers.*

❑ **Tolerance** is also an amount of variation permitted in certain measurements, to allow for such things as slight changes in materials affected by heat or cold.

tolerate (tolerating, tolerated; toleration) If you **tolerate** things you do not agree with or do not approve of, you allow them to exist or happen. ...*tolerating the views of others...* ...*religious freedom and toleration.* ◇ If you can **tolerate** something unsatisfactory, unsuitable, or unpleasant, you can put up with it. *It's a question of how much more upheaval the populace can tolerate.*

toll ❑ The death **toll** in something like an accident or a war is the number of people killed.

❑ You talk about something **taking its toll** when it causes serious loss or damage. *The winds have already taken their toll of ships at sea.*

❑ If you have to pay a **toll** to use a road or bridge, you have to pay a sum of money to use it.

❑ When a bell is **tolled,** it is rung slowly and repeatedly, often as a sign that someone has died.

tom See **tomcat.**

tom-tom **Tom-toms** are drums, originally from Africa and Asia, played either with the hands or with sticks. The ones used in an orchestra can be tuned to different pitches.

tomahawk A **tomahawk** is a small lightweight axe used by North American Indians.

tomato (tomatoes) **Tomatoes** are small round red fruit with soft juicy flesh. They are often eaten raw in salads.

tomb A **tomb** is a vault or chamber in which a dead body is placed. ...*the tomb of Tutankhamen.* ◇ **Graves** are sometimes called **tombs.**

tombola is a lottery in which tickets are drawn from a revolving drum.

tomboy Young girls who behave or dress in a boyish way are sometimes called **tomboys**.

tombstone A **tombstone** is the same as a gravestone.

tomcat A **tomcat** or **tom** is a male cat.

tome A **tome** is a large heavy book.

tomfoolery is playful behaviour of a silly, noisy, or rough kind.

tomorrow is the day after today. ◇ You can also refer to the future as **tomorrow**. *Tomorrow's cars may be cleaner and more economical.*

ton (-tonner) ❑ Weight is sometimes expressed in **tons**. In Britain, a ton is 2,240 pounds (about 1,016 kilograms); in the US, it is 2,000 pounds (about 907 kilograms). See also **tonne**.
❑ **-tonner** is used to describe a boat or lorry weighing a certain number of tons. *I pulled in between a couple of 32-tonners.*
❑ If you have **tons** of something, you have a lot of it. *...tons of money.*

tonal is used to talk about the quality or pitch of music or other sounds. *...an orchestra of gongs and xylophones using its own unique tonal system.* ◇ **Tonal** is also used to talk about shades and tones of colours. *...a black and white print with a full tonal range.*

tone (toning, toned) ❑ The **tone** of a musical instrument or of someone's voice is the kind of sound it has. *...talking in quiet, deferential tones.*
❑ If you talk about someone's **tone**, you mean the manner they adopt when they are dealing with someone. *His tone was firm... The government was preparing to adopt a more conciliatory tone.* Similarly, you can talk about the **tone** of a speech or piece of writing.
❑ If you **tone down** something you have written or said, you make it less forceful, severe, or offensive. *Sex scenes have been toned down in the television version of Lady Chatterley's Lover.*
❑ In music, a **tone** is an interval between two notes, equal to two semitones.
❑ The **tones** of a colour are its lighter, darker, or brighter shades. *...two-tone shoes... ...tones of autumn brown.* ◇ If one thing **tones** with another, the two things create a pleasing effect together because they are similar in colour.
❑ If something **tones** your muscles or **tones** them **up**, it makes them firm and strong. **Tone** is used to talk about the quality of a person's muscles. *...poor muscle tone.*

toneless A **toneless** voice is dull and does not express any feeling.

tongs are a tool made of two long narrow pieces of metal or wood joined at one end by a hinge or pivot. You press the pieces together to grip an object and pick it up.

tongue ❑ A person's **tongue** is the soft movable part inside their mouth which they use for tasting, licking, and speaking.
❑ If you say someone has a sharp **tongue**, you mean they say unpleasant or critical things.
❑ If you **hold** your **tongue**, you do not say anything. Similarly, if you **bite** your **tongue**, you keep quiet about something although you really want to speak about it.
❑ A **slip of the tongue** is a small mistake you make when you are speaking.
❑ Languages are sometimes called **tongues**. *...the Gaelic tongue.* ◇ **mother tongue**: see **mother**.

❑ **Tongue** is the cooked tongue of an ox. It is usually eaten cold.

tongue-in-cheek A **tongue-in-cheek** remark is made as a joke and is not meant to be taken seriously.

tongue-tied If someone is **tongue-tied**, they cannot speak because they are shy or nervous.

tongue-twister A **tongue-twister** is an expression or group of words which is very difficult to say, especially if you try to say it quickly a number of times. An example is 'red lorry, yellow lorry'.

tonic or **tonic water** is a colourless fizzy drink with a slightly bitter flavour which is often mixed with alcoholic drinks.
❑ A **tonic** is a medicine which makes you feel stronger, healthier, and less tired. ◇ Anything which makes you feel stronger or more cheerful can be called a **tonic**. *His dry humour was a stimulating tonic.*

tonight is the evening or night which will come at the end of today.

tonnage (pron: tun-nij) The **tonnage** of a merchant ship is its capacity, or the weight of cargo it can carry. The **tonnage** of a fleet of ships is their total capacity. ◇ The **tonnage** of certain other things is their total weight, measured in tons. *...the tonnage of fish taken from the North Sea.*

tonne (pron: tun) Large weights are often expressed in **tonnes**. A tonne is 1,000 kilograms (about 2,204.6 pounds). Tonnes are sometimes called 'metric tons'.

tonsil A person's **tonsils** are the two small soft lumps in their throat at the back of their mouth.

tonsillectomy (tonsillectomies) A **tonsillectomy** is a surgical operation to remove a person's tonsils.

tonsillitis is a painful swelling of the tonsils caused by an infection.

tonsure (pron: ton-sher) A **tonsure** is a shaved area on the top of a man's head, leaving hair around the sides. Some monks have their heads shaved like this.

too means 'also' or 'as well'. *Hopefully they'll be happy here, and if they are, we will be, too.*
❑ **Too** is used to say an amount, distance, etc is greater than is desirable, necessary, or acceptable. *It was too far from London... Too many people are out of work.*
❑ You use **too** after words like 'not' to make what you are saying sound less forceful or more polite or cautious. *They are not too happy with the result.*

took See **take**.

tool ❑ A **tool** is any device or simple piece of equipment, for example a hammer or a knife, which you hold in your hand and use for a particular kind of work. See also **machine tool**.
❑ Other things used for a particular purpose can be called **tools**. *As a management tool, the information on levels of performance is vital.* ◇ Things considered necessary for a particular task or job can be called the **tools of the trade**. *The essential tools of the trade are good reference books, which will vary from journalist to journalist.*
❑ If you say someone or something is a person's **tool**, you mean they are controlled by them and used by them to do unpleasant or dishonest things. *...a legal system that was the willing tool of the old regime.*

tool box A **tool box** is a box containing tools for general purposes, for example house or car repairs.

tool kit A tool kit is a special set of tools kept together and used for a particular purpose.

toot (tooting, tooted) If you **toot** the horn of a car, you get it to make a short loud sound. You can talk about the **toot** of a horn or say the horn itself **toots**.

tooth (teeth) ❑ A person's or animal's **teeth** are the hard white objects in their mouth used for biting and chewing. ◇ The **teeth** of a comb, saw, or zip are the hard parts which stick out in a row.

❑ If you say an official body has **teeth**, you mean it is powerful and able to enforce its decisions.

❑ If you fight something **tooth and nail,** you fight very hard against it. If you fight **tooth and nail** for something, you do everything you can to achieve it or get it. *She intended to fight tooth and nail to stay in office.*

❑ If you say a type of activity is **red in tooth and claw,** you mean it is very fierce, ruthless, or savage.

❑ If someone is **armed to the teeth,** they are carrying a lot of weapons. Similarly, you can say a country or army is **armed to the teeth** when it has a lot of powerful weapons.

❑ If you **get your teeth into** something, you get very involved in it and put a lot of energy and concentration into it. ◇ If you do something **in the teeth of** difficulty or danger, you do it in spite of it. *...an employer trying to run a business in the teeth of the recession.*

❑ **grit your teeth:** see grit. ◇ **by the skin of your teeth:** see skin.

toothache is a pain in a tooth or teeth.

toothbrush (toothbrushes) A **toothbrush** is a small brush for cleaning your teeth.

toothless If someone is **toothless,** they have no teeth. ◇ If you say an organization is **toothless,** you mean it has no real power. *The Press Complaints Commission remains a toothless and ineffectual body.*

toothpaste is a thick paste you put on a toothbrush and use to clean your teeth.

toothpick A **toothpick** is a small pointed stick for removing food from between your teeth.

toothy If someone has a **toothy** smile, they show a lot of their teeth when they smile.

tootle (tootling, tootled) ❑ If you **tootle** somewhere, you go without hurrying. *...tootling around the West Country in a Morris Minor.*

❑ If you **tootle** on an instrument like a flute, you play it.

top (topping, topped) ❑ The **top** of something is its highest part, point, or surface. ◇ **-topped** is used to describe the top of something. *...a glass-topped coffee-table.*

❑ If something is **on top of** something else, it is on its highest part. You can also say the first thing is **topped by** the second one. *...a huge dome topped by a copper cross.*

❑ The **top** of something like a bottle, jar, or tube is its cap or lid.

❑ The **top** thing of a number of things is the highest one. *...the top floor of a factory... ...the top bunk.* ◇ If something is at the **top** of a list, it is the first item on it.

❑ The **top** of a street is one end of it.

❑ A **top** is a piece of clothing worn on the upper part of the body.

❑ The **top** of an organization is its highest or most important level. *The company is still in trouble, despite changes at the top... ...his dramatic rise to the top of the military hierarchy.* ◇ **top brass:** see brass.

❑ The **top** people of a certain kind are the most important or successful ones. *...two top officials from the Department of Foreign Affairs.*

❑ **Top** is used to talk about the highest point on a scale of measurement. *The top rate of tax will be 38%.* **Top** is also used to talk about people who reach a higher point on a scale than anyone else. *He is currently the Premier League's top scorer.*

❑ If someone comes **top** in a test or exam, they have the highest marks. Similarly, if a person or team comes **top** in a game or competition, they do better than anyone else. ◇ If someone or something is **top** of a league or table, they have the highest number of points. You can also say someone or something **tops** a league or table. *'Unchained Melody' topped the British charts for the whole of November.*

❑ If something **tops** an amount, it is greater than that amount. *Pre-tax profits in 1991 topped £3 million.*

❑ If you **top up** something like a glass or a fuel tank, you fill it again when it has been partly emptied. A refill like this is called a **top-up**. ◇ If a sum of money is **topped up,** an extra amount is added to it. *The erosion of state pensions is encouraging more and more people to provide a top-up from their own savings.*

❑ **On top of** means 'in addition to'. *The Ombudsman's report comes on top of a spate of other bad news for the industry.*

❑ If you are **on top of** a situation, you are in control of it and can cope with it. ◇ If something gets **on top of** you, it makes you feel depressed because you feel you cannot cope with it.

❑ If you say something is **over the top,** you mean it is unacceptable because it is too extreme.

❑ A **top** is a toy which spins on the floor when it is wound up or twisted sharply.

top-class is used to describe people who achieve the highest standards in what they do. *...top class athletes... ...top-class engineers.* ◇ **Top-class** is also used to describe things of the highest quality. *...top-class tennis... ...a top-class hotel.*

top-down In a **top-down** system, the people in charge make all the decisions, without involving anyone else.

top hat A **top hat** is a tall hat with a narrow brim, worn by men on some very formal occasions.

top-heavy If something is **top-heavy,** it is larger or heavier at the top than at the bottom, and this makes it unstable. ◇ If you say an organization is **top-heavy,** you mean it has too many senior people in relation to the total number of employees.

top-level discussions or activities involve people with the greatest amount of power and authority in an organization, group, or country. *...a top-level meeting of American generals.* ◇ **Top-level** sport involves the most skilful and successful players or athletes.

top-notch If you describe someone or something as **top-notch,** you mean they are of the highest standard or quality. *...top-notch candidates.*

top-of-the-range or top-of-the-line things are the most expensive and highly developed ones of their kind. *...a top-of-the-range Mercedes.*

top-ranking is used to describe the most important or successful people in a country, organization, or activity. *...the world's top-ranking woman tennis player.*

top secret is an official classification for government or military matters which must be kept absolutely secret.

top-up See top.

topaz is a yellowish-coloured gemstone.

topiary (*pron:* toe-pee-ar-ee) is cutting bushes and hedges into ornamental shapes.

topic A **topic** is a subject which is discussed or written about. *The weather is a constant topic of conversation in Britain.*

topical (topicality) If something is **topical**, it is connected with events which are happening at the time when you are speaking or writing. *The events which this novel brings to life have an urgent topicality.*

topless If a woman is **topless**, she is not wearing anything on the upper part of her body. *...topless sunbathing.*

topmost The **topmost** thing in a group of things is the highest one. *...the topmost levels in the government... ...the cones which grow on their topmost branches.*

topography (topographical) **Topography** is the study and description of the physical features of places, for example the hills, valleys, and rivers. ◇ The **topography** of a place is its physical features. **Topographical** is used to talk about a place's physical features. *...a topographical description.*

topping is food like cream or cheese which is put on top of other food to decorate it or add to its flavour.

topple (toppling, topples) If something **topples**, it becomes unsteady and falls over. ◇ If a government or leader is **toppled**, something happens which makes them lose power.

topsoil is the fertile layer of soil nearest the surface of the ground.

topsy-turvy is used to describe things which are in a state of confusion or disorder. *...a topsy-turvy house.*

tor A **tor** is a bare rocky hill.

Torah In the Jewish religion, the **Torah** is (a) the first five books of the Old Testament, and the scroll on which they are written, which is used in synagogue services. (b) the whole body of traditional Jewish teaching.

torch (torches, torching, torched) ❑ A **torch** is a small portable lamp, powered by batteries. ◇ A **torch** is also (a) a long stick with burning material at one end. (b) a device which produces a hot flame for tasks like welding and cutting metal. *...acetylene torches.*
  ❑ If a building is **torched**, someone sets fire to it deliberately.
  ❑ If you say someone **carries the torch** for a belief or policy, you mean they take over from someone else in making sure that it continues and develops. *Since his death in 1985 his widow has carried the torch of his Stalinist legacy.* ◇ If you say someone **carries a torch** for another person, you mean they are in love with them, although their love may not be returned.

torchlight is (a) light produced by an electric torch. *Surgeons are performing operations by torchlight.* (b) light produced by burning torches. *...a torchlight procession.*

tore See tear.

toreador (*pron:* tor-ee-a-dor) A **toreador** is a bullfighter.

torment (tormentor) **Torment** (*pron:* tor-ment) is extreme pain or unhappiness. *The continuing torment suffered by these people is harrowing.* ◇ If someone or something **torments** (*pron:* tor-ments) you, they cause you extreme pain or unhappiness. A person who deliberately makes

you suffer can be called your **tormentor**.

torn See tear.

tornado (tornadoes *or* tornados) A **tornado** is a violent storm with strong winds whirling round a funnel-shaped cloud.

torpedo (torpedoes, torpedoing, torpedoed) ❑ A **torpedo** is a tube-shaped underwater missile which can be launched from an aircraft, ship, or submarine. When a ship is **torpedoed**, it is hit by a torpedo, and usually sunk.
  ❑ If someone **torpedoes** something like a plan, they deliberately prevent it succeeding.

torpid (torpor) If someone is **torpid** or in a **torpor**, they are mentally or physically inactive, because they are lazy or sleepy. ◇ You call a place or system **torpid** when everything is very slow-moving. *...the torpid state of local government.*

torque (*pron:* talk) In engineering, **torque** is a force which tends to cause something to rotate around a central point.

torrent (torrential) ❑ A **torrent** is a fast-flowing stream or river. You often talk about a stream becoming a **torrent** when there has been very heavy rain. ◇ When it rains very heavily, you can talk about the rain falling in **torrents**. You describe rain like this as **torrential**.
  ❑ A **torrent** of something like criticism or abuse is a lot of it directed continuously at someone. ◇ You can call any series of bad things coming one after another a **torrent**. *...a torrent of job losses... ...a torrent of bad publicity.*

torrid weather is very hot and dry. ◇ If you call a situation **torrid**, you mean the people involved are highly emotional. *...torrid family squabbles... ...a torrid romance.*

torso (torsos) A **person's torso** is the main part of their body, excluding their head, neck, arms, and legs.

tort In law, a **tort** is a civil wrong or injury for which damages may be claimed by an individual, as distinct from a criminal act which is prosecuted by the state.

tortilla (*pron:* tor-tee-a) A **tortilla** is a thin Mexican pancake made from corn.

tortoise The **tortoise** is a slow-moving reptile with a hard shell over its body which it can pull its head and legs into for protection.

tortoiseshell is the hard brown and yellow shell of a type of sea turtle. In the past, it was often polished and used to make jewellery and ornaments. Nowadays, objects described as **tortoiseshell** are usually made of a similar-looking synthetic material.

tortuous A **tortuous** road or route is full of bends and twists. ◇ A **tortuous** process or piece of writing is long and complicated.

torture (torturing, tortured; torturer) ❑ If someone **tortures** another person, they deliberately cause them great pain, usually to punish them or get information from them. Making someone suffer like this is called **torture**; a person who tortures someone else is called a **torturer**.
  ❑ You can call any mental or physical suffering **torture**. *Waiting for the result was torture.* ◇ You can say something **tortures** you when it causes you mental suffering. *I haven't tortured myself with their problems.*

Tory (Tories; Toryism) A **Tory** is a member or supporter of the Conservative Party in Great Britain or Canada. Tory principles and beliefs are called **Toryism**.

tosh If you say something like a book or article is **tosh**, you mean it is rubbish.

toss (tosses, tossing, tossed) ❑ If you **toss** something somewhere, you throw it there in a careless way.

❑ If something **tosses** or is **tossed**, it is moved or jerked around from side to side or up and down. *Boats and yachts were tossed around as huge waves pounded into the bay.* ◇ If you **toss** food while you are preparing it, you shake it or turn it over quickly and lightly in something like oil or breadcrumbs.

❑ If you **toss** a coin or **toss up**, you decide something by throwing a coin up in the air and guessing which side will be facing upwards when it falls. You can say something is decided by the **toss** of a coin. In cricket, a coin is **tossed** at the beginning of a match. The team captain who guesses correctly which side of the coin will face upwards **wins the toss** and can choose whether to bat or field first. ◇ See also **toss-up**.

❑ If someone **tosses and turns** when they are in bed, they move their body around restlessly, because they cannot sleep.

❑ When someone **tosses** their head, they move it suddenly backwards, especially when they are angry or annoyed. You can say someone does something with a **toss** of their head. ◇ You say someone **tosses** their hair when they flick it back by a movement of the head.

toss-up If you call a situation a **toss-up**, you mean the outcome is uncertain. ◇ If you say it is a **toss-up** between two things, you mean either of them is equally likely or acceptable.

tot (totting, totted) ❑ A **tot** is a very young child.

❑ A **tot** of whisky, rum, or brandy is a small amount of it, equal to a single measure bought in a bar.

❑ If you **tot up** numbers, you add them up.

total (totalling, totalled; totally) (*American spelling:* totaling, totaled) ❑ The **total** number of things of a particular kind is how many there are altogether. Similarly, the **total** cost of something is how much it costs altogether. **Total** can be used with other words like this. *...the total value of goods on sale.* You can also say something **totals** a certain number, cost, weight, etc. *Official western sales of gold bullion last year totalled 105 tonnes.*

❑ When you **total** a set of numbers or objects, you add them all together. The result you get is called the **total**.

❑ **Total** means complete. *...a total ban on mining in Antarctica... Industry is a totally different matter.*

totalitarian (*pron:* toe-tal-it-tair-ee-an) (totalitarianism) In a **totalitarian** system, one political party controls everything and does not allow other parties to exist. Complete control by a single political party is called **totalitarianism**.

totality The **totality** of something is the whole of it. *An inspector who was a circuit judge would have the authority to comment on the totality of the court's performance.*

tote (toting, toted) ❑ The **tote** is an automated system of betting money on horses or greyhounds at a racetrack. 'Tote' is short for 'totalizator' or 'totalisator'.

❑ If someone **totes** something, especially a gun, they carry it or have it on them. *...gun-toting rebels.*

totem A **totem** is an object or person regarded as a symbol by a particular group of people, who treat them with great respect. *...pop singers, film directors and other totems of youth culture.* ◇ A **totem pole** is a tall wooden pole with symbols and images carved or painted on it. **Totem poles** are made by some North American Indians and erected in front of their houses.

totter (tottering, tottered) When someone **totters**, they walk in an unsteady way. ◇ If you say something like a system is **tottering**, you mean it is weak and unstable. *Today the country totters on the edge of economic disaster.*

toucan (*pron:* too-kan) The **toucan** is a large fruit-eating bird in the tropical forest areas of America. It has brightly coloured plumage and a very large beak.

touch (touches, touching, touched) ❑ If you **touch** something, you gently put your fingers or hand on it. If this is enough to make something happen, you say it happens at a **touch**. *Cupboards spring open at a touch.* ◇ Your sense of **touch** is your ability to tell how something feels when you touch it. *The wine should feel distinctly cold to the touch.*

❑ When things **touch**, their surfaces are in contact with each other.

❑ If you are **touched** by something, you are emotionally affected by it. *I am deeply touched by the decision to award me the Nobel Peace Prize.* ◇ If you find something **touching**, it makes you sad or sympathetic. *...a touching story of violence redeemed by love.*

❑ You can say something **touches** something else when it has an effect on it. *The reform programme was an extensive one, touching every area of economic and industrial life.*

❑ If you get **in touch** with someone, you contact them by writing to them, phoning them, or visiting them. If you keep **in touch**, you continue to see each other or write to each other. If you **lose touch**, you gradually stop writing to each other or visiting each other.

❑ If you are **in touch** with what is happening, you have all the latest information about it. ◇ If you are **out of touch** with something, your knowledge of it is out-of-date.

❑ When an aircraft **touches down**, it lands. The landing of an aircraft is called **touchdown**.

❑ If something **touches off** something else, it makes it happen or begin. *This latest wave of disturbances was touched off by a dispute over the distribution of land.*

❑ If you **touch on** a subject, you mention it briefly.

❑ If something **touches** a certain point or level, it just reaches it. *Most forecasts suggest that the unemployment number will touch the 3 million mark.*

❑ In games like football, rugby, and hockey, if the ball goes **into touch**, it goes over a line called the **touchline** which marks the side of the pitch. ◇ If you say something like a problem is **kicked into touch**, you mean it is put aside instead of being dealt with immediately.

❑ If you say someone will not **touch** something, you mean they will not handle it, deal with it, or get involved with it. Similarly, you can say someone will not **touch** a certain kind of food or drink. *High-caste Hindus do not touch alcohol.* ◇ If you say someone did not **touch** something on a certain occasion, you mean they left it alone. *The thieves did not touch the other paintings.*

❑ If you say something is **touch and go**, you mean it is uncertain whether it will happen or succeed.

❑ A **touch** is a detail added to something to improve it or complete it. *He is putting the final touches to his plans.*

❑ If you talk about a person's **touch**, you mean their

skill at dealing with something. *He'd been losing his touch as a publisher.* ◇ If a firm shows the **personal touch**, they treat you in a thoughtful and considerate way.

❑ A **touch** of something is a very small amount or hint of it. *...a touch of sadness... ...a touch of indigestion.* ◇ A **touch** means 'slightly' or 'rather'. *This seems a touch over-confident.*

touch paper The **touch paper** on a firework is a small piece of dark blue paper on one end. When you light it, it burns down slowly and sets off the firework.

touchdown See touch.

touching See touch.

touchline See touch.

touchstone A **touchstone** is a standard by which something is measured or judged.

touchy (touchier, touchiest) If someone is **touchy**, they are easily upset or offended. ◇ A **touchy** subject needs to be dealt with carefully because it might upset or offend people.

tough (toughness) ❑ **Tough** policies or actions are very strict and firm. *The tough line on wages will help to get inflation down... ...governors who are renowned for toughness on crime.*

❑ A **tough** person is strong and independent and can put up with a lot of pain, hardship, or difficulties.

❑ A **tough** substance is strong and difficult to break or tear.

❑ A **tough** problem or task is difficult to deal with.

toughen (toughening, toughened) ❑ If something is **toughened**, it is made stronger so it will not break easily. *...toughened glass.* ◇ If policies or actions are **toughened**, they are made stricter and firmer. *...the toughening of sentences in the courts.*

❑ If an experience **toughens** you, it makes you stronger and more independent.

toupee (*pron:* too-pay) A **toupee** is a small wig worn by a man to cover a bald patch.

tour (touring, toured) ❑ When politicians or royalty **tour** an area, they go on an organized trip, stopping at various places to meet and speak to people. A trip like this is called a **tour**. Similarly, entertainers or sports teams can **tour** an area, giving performances or playing matches. You can say a theatrical production or a sports team is **on tour**.

❑ A **tour** is a short trip round something like a city or a famous building, often with a guide to point out interesting features. ◇ **guided tour:** see guide.

❑ A **tour** is also a holiday in which you visit a number of places in an area. When you have a holiday like this, you say you **tour** the area. *...holidaymakers touring Europe.*

tour de force (*pron:* toor de forss) A **tour de force** is a brilliant and impressive display of someone's skill or ability.

tour operator A **tour operator** is a company which organizes holidays and sells them, usually through a travel agent.

tourism (tourist) ❑ **Tourism** is the industry which provides services like hotels, sightseeing trips, and leisure facilities for people on holiday. **Tourist** is used to talk about things to do with this industry. *...tourist attractions.* ◇ A **tourist** is a person visiting a place for pleasure and interest.

❑ When a sports team are on tour, they are sometimes called the **tourists**. *England reached 243 for five in their 55 overs. In reply, the tourists could do no better than 180.*

tourist office The **tourist office** or **tourist information office** in a place is an office providing information for visiting tourists.

tournament A **tournament** is a sports competition in which the winner of each match goes on to the next round until one competitor or team is the overall winner.

tourniquet (*pron:* toor-nik-kay) A **tourniquet** is a strip of cloth tied tightly round an injured arm or leg to stop the bleeding.

tousled hair is tangled and untidy.

tout (touting, touted) If someone **touts** for business or custom, they offer their services in a very direct way. *...an advertising agency touting for clients.* ◇ If someone **touts** something, they try to sell it or persuade people it is a good thing. *The energy tax has always been touted by the administration as a revenue-raiser rather than an environmental measure.* ◇ A **tout** is a person who unofficially sells tickets outside a sports ground or theatre, charging more than the official price.

tow ❑ If one vehicle or ship **tows** another or gives it a **tow**, it pulls it along behind it. Other things can also be **towed** like this. *In water-ski racing, the competitor is towed at unbelievable speeds across lakes, rivers and seas.* ◇ When a ship is being towed, you say it is **in tow** or **under tow**.

❑ If you have to take someone around with you when you go somewhere, you can say you have them **in tow**. *...a woman with a child in tow.* ◇ When an important person visits a place, you can say they have their followers or staff **in tow**. *When the President visits Tokyo, he will have several new advisers in tow.*

towards (*or* toward) ❑ If you move, look, or point **towards** someone or something, you move, look, or point in their direction.

❑ If there is progress **towards** something, it is made more likely to happen. *Progress towards peace is being made... There have been some moves towards a political settlement.*

❑ If you have a particular attitude **towards** someone or something, you feel like that about them. *This explains the loyalty and devotion felt towards him.*

❑ If you give money **towards** something, you help pay for it.

❑ **Towards** a certain time means just before it. *...towards the end of October.* Similarly, **towards** a place means in the area just before you get to it. *...a seat towards the back of the stalls... ...towards the bottom of the second page.*

towel ❑ A **towel** is a square or oblong piece of absorbent cloth for drying yourself.

❑ If you **throw in the towel**, you stop trying to do something because you realize you cannot succeed.

towelling is thick soft cloth used for making things like towels and bathrobes.

tower (towering, towered) ❑ A **tower** is a tall narrow building, sometimes forming part of a larger building like a castle or church. ◇ **tower of strength:** see strength.

❑ If something **towers** over something close to it, it is much higher or taller. *A monstrous gibbet towers over one half of the stage... ...towering cliffs.* ◇ If you say someone towers over other people, you mean they are much more successful, important, or impressive than the other people. *Polls indicate that he towers above the party's other potential candidates.*

tower block A **tower block** is a tall building divided into flats or offices.

town ❑ A **town** is an area where a lot of people live close together. It is generally larger than a village and smaller than a city. ◇ You can refer to a certain town or city simply as **town**. *...the best view in town.* ◇ **Town** is also the central part of a town or city where most of the shops and offices are. *We arranged to meet in town.*
❑ If you go **on the town** or have a **night on the town**, you go into the centre of a town or city in the evening and enjoy yourself at places like nightclubs or pubs.
❑ You say someone **goes to town** when they do something extremely thoroughly, or with a lot of enthusiasm or expense. *She had rather gone to town on her bridal outfit.*

town crier In the past, a **town crier** was a man who walked through the streets of a town shouting out news and official announcements.

town hall The **town hall** is a large building in a town or city owned and used by the council or corporation, often as its headquarters.

town house A **town house** is a tall narrow house built in a row of similar houses, usually in a city or town. ◇ The **town house** of a wealthy person is the house they own in a town or city, rather than the one they own in the country.

town planning is the planning, design, and development of things like new buildings, roads, and parks in towns and cities.

townie Country people sometimes call people who come from large towns and cities **townies**.

townscape A **townscape** is (a) everything you can see when you look across an area of a town or city. (b) a painting of a view of a town.

townsfolk are the same as townspeople.

township In South Africa, a **township** is an urban area where mainly black or coloured people live. Townships are usually on the outskirts of a city.

townspeople The **townspeople** of a town or city are people who live there

towpath A **towpath** is a path alongside a canal or river, originally for horses to walk along when they towed boats.

toxaemia (*pron:* tox-seem-ya) (*American spelling:* **toxemia**) Toxaemia is (a) blood poisoning. (b) a disease causing seriously high blood pressure in pregnancy.

toxic (toxicity) A **toxic** substance is poisonous. *...toxic waste... ...a cloud of highly toxic gas.* You can say how poisonous a substance is by saying it is of high or low **toxicity**.

toxicology (toxicologist) **Toxicology** is the scientific study of poisons. An expert in this field is called a **toxicologist**.

toxin A **toxin** is a poisonous substance produced by bacteria, which is harmful to people or other living things. Some poisonous substances produced by animals and plants are also called **toxins**.

toxoplasmosis is an infection spread by eating undercooked meat or by handling domestic cats. It is not generally dangerous to humans, but, if caught by a preg-

nant woman, can cause serious damage to her unborn child. It can also be dangerous to people with AIDS.

toy ❑ A **toy** is an object for children to play with.
❑ If you **toy** with an idea, you consider it casually without making any firm decisions about it.
❑ If you **toy** with an object, you fiddle with it aimlessly. ◇ If you **toy** with food, you fiddle with it but do not eat it, or eat very little of it.

toy boy A woman's **toy boy** is a much younger man who is her boyfriend or lover.

trace (tracing, traced) ❑ If you **trace** someone or something, you succeed in finding out where they are. *One of the suspects has been traced to Geneva.* ◇ If someone or something disappears **without trace**, there is no sign of where they have gone. You can also say there is **no trace** of them.
❑ A **trace** is a very small amount or hint of something. *No one would worry if a trace of onion got into the fish... He spoke without a trace of self-pity.* ◇ If you find **traces** of something in a place, you find things which show it has been there. *Workmen digging sewage trenches found traces of the building, which was probably demolished in the fourteenth century.*
❑ If you **trace** the development of something, you find out or describe how it developed. *Many companies can trace their history back centuries.* ◇ If you **trace** something to a person or place, you find out that it came from that person or place. *Only 20% of donations to the party could be traced to British companies.*
❑ If you **trace** something like a drawing or a map, you copy it by covering it with a piece of transparent paper called **tracing paper** and drawing over the lines underneath. Copies made in this way are called **tracings**.

trace element **Trace elements** are chemical elements which are necessary for normal animal and plant growth but are needed only in very small amounts.

traceable is used to describe people or things that can be traced. *More than 2 million calls are made each day from mobile phones, many of which may be traceable.* ◇ If it can be shown that something was caused by a particular thing, you can say it is **traceable** to that thing. *The numerous diseases suffered there are all traceable to malnutrition.*

tracer **Tracers** or **tracer bullets** are bullets which can be seen in flight because they contain a substance which burns brightly.

tracery is a decorative pattern of interlacing lines or bars, for example in the stonework towards the top of a stained glass window.

trachea (*pron:* trak-kee-a) A person's **trachea** is their windpipe.

tracheotomy (*pron:* trak-ee-ot-a-mee) A **tracheotomy** is a surgical operation to cut into the trachea, usually carried out when the upper air passage is blocked. A similar operation called a **tracheostomy** involves inserting a breathing tube into the trachea.

tracing paper See trace.

track ❑ A **track** is a narrow road or path. ◇ If a place is **off the beaten track**, it is in a quiet and isolated area.
❑ The rails which trains travel on are called **tracks** or **track**.
❑ A **track** or **running track** is an oval-shaped route

which athletes race round. Greyhounds also race round a track. ◇ In athletics, a **track** event is a race.

❑ **Tracks** are footprints or other marks left on the ground by a person or animal. ◇ If you **track** an animal or person, you follow their footprints or other signs they have left behind. ◇ You also say you **track** someone or something when you follow their movements using a special device. *The Britons' 17-hour journey was tracked by an American spy satellite.*

❑ If you **track** someone **down**, you search for them until you find them.

❑ If you **cover your tracks**, you are careful not to leave any signs or clues which could let people know what you have been doing.

❑ If you **keep track** of things or people, you pay attention to them so you know where they are or what is happening. If you **lose track** of them, you no longer know where they are or what is happening.

❑ If you say a person or organization is **on track**, you mean they are following the right course of action to succeed in what they are doing. Similarly, you can say something like a policy or process is **on track**. ◇ If you say someone is **on the right track**, you mean they are dealing with a situation or problem in the right way. Similarly, you can say someone is **on the wrong track**.

❑ If something which is progressing or developing is **stopped in its tracks**, it is stopped very suddenly.

❑ A **track** on a record or tape is one of the songs or pieces of music on it.

track record The **track record** of a person or company is how well or badly they have done at things they have attempted in the past. *...an obscure company with a poor track record.*

tracker A **tracker** is a person skilled at finding people or animals by following their footprints or other signs they have left behind. ◇ A device which follows the movement of people or things is also called a **tracker**. *...tracker radar.*

tracker dog Tracker dogs are dogs specially trained to search for people who are missing or for prisoners who have escaped.

tracking shot In film-making, a **tracking shot** is a camera shot in which the camera follows a certain person as they move around, or moves along a certain route to give the impression of travelling along it.

tracking station A **tracking station** is a building from which the movement of things like spacecraft and satellites can be followed by means of radar or radio.

tracksuit A **tracksuit** is a warm loose-fitting top and trousers, designed to be worn when taking exercise or training for sports.

tract ❑ A **tract** of land is a large area of it.

❑ A **tract** is a system of organs or tubes with a particular function in a person's or animal's body. *...the urinary tract... ...the digestive tract.*

❑ A **tract** is also a pamphlet expressing a strong opinion on a religious, moral, or political matter.

tractable people or problems are easily controlled or dealt with.

traction is pulling something using a particular type of power. *...steam traction.* ◇ A vehicle's **traction** is the grip its wheels have on the ground.

❑ **Traction** is also a form of medical treatment for an injured limb which involves a steady pull on the limb for long periods of time using a system of weights and pulleys.

traction engine A **traction engine** is a large heavy steam-powered vehicle used in the past for pulling heavy loads.

tractor A **tractor** is a farm vehicle with large rear wheels used for pulling machinery, trailers, and other heavy loads.

trad is traditional jazz. *...the Edinburgh trad scene.*

trade (trading, traded) ❑ **Trade** is the buying, selling, or exchanging of goods or services. When firms or countries **trade**, they buy, sell, or exchange things. *The syndicate stopped trading in 1991... ...changes in Sunday trading laws.* ◇ A country's **trade figures** are the value of its exports and imports over a period of time and the difference between them. ◇ If a country has a **trade gap**, the value of its imports is greater than the value of its exports.

❑ If you **trade in** a car or TV, you take it to the dealer when you buy a new one and get a small price reduction on the new one. A deal like this is called a **trade-in**.

❑ When people **trade up**, they buy more expensive things to replace the ones they have at present. If they **trade down**, they replace the things they have with cheaper ones.

❑ When people **trade** ideas, they exchange them. You can also talk about people **trading** compliments or insults.

❑ If you **trade off** one thing against another, you make a compromise, so that, for example, you accept less of one thing in order to have more of the other. A situation in which gaining something means losing something else is called a **trade-off**. *...the trade-off between quality and affordability.*

❑ If you **trade on** some advantage you have, you make use of it to get what you want.

❑ A person's **trade** is the kind of work they do, especially when it requires special training in practical skills.

trade fair A **trade fair** is an exhibition where manufacturers show products they want to sell to other firms, rather than to members of the public.

trade-in See trade.

trade name A **trade name** is a name a manufacturer gives to a product or to a range of products.

trade-off See trade.

trade secret If something like a process is a **trade secret**, the company which uses it does not give details of it to anyone else.

trade union (trade unionism, trade unionist) A **trade union** is an organization of workers which represents the interests of its members and tries to improve or maintain pay and working conditions. **Trade unionism** is the system, practices, and ideology of trade unions; a **trade unionist** is an active member of a trade union.

trademark ❑ A **trademark** is a name or symbol which a company uses on its products and which cannot legally be used by anyone else.

❑ A feature which is associated with a certain person or thing can be called their **trademark**. *The last time I saw Acker Bilk in action he was still wearing his trademark striped waistcoat.*

trader A **trader** is (a) a person or company that trades in goods or services. ...*a street trader*... ...*international oil traders.* (b) a person who buys and sells stocks and shares.

Trades Union Congress See TUC.

tradesman (tradesmen) A **tradesman** is a person who sells goods or services, especially someone who owns their own small business or is skilled in a certain trade.

trading estate A **trading estate** is the same as an industrial estate.

tradition ❑ A **tradition** is a custom or belief which a group of people have had for a long time. **Tradition** is all the customs of a country or group. *The wedding will be an occasion steeped in centuries-old tradition.* ◇ You can also say some other kind of behaviour is a **tradition** when it has existed in a place for a long time. *Farms in the Upper Vosges have a tradition of providing inexpensive meals and accommodation for tourists.*
❑ If someone's behaviour is like that of several people before them, you can say they are **in the tradition** of those people. ...*women travellers in the tradition of Isabella Bird.*

traditional (traditionally) ❑ **Traditional** beliefs or ways of behaviour have existed for a long time without changing. ...*traditional methods of teaching*... *Living away from home has traditionally been a central aspect of British degree courses.* **Traditional** is also used to describe other types of things which have existed for a long time. ...*traditional family structures.* ◇ A country's or organization's **traditional** allies or enemies are other countries or organizations which have often been its allies or enemies in the past.
❑ A **traditional** organization prefers old and established methods and ideas to modern ones.

traditionalist is used to describe people who support the established customs and beliefs of their society or group, and do not want them changed. ...*the traditionalist movement within the Church of England.* People like these can be called **traditionalists**.

traduce (traducing, traduced) If someone **traduces** you, they deliberately say things about you which are untrue and unpleasant.

traffic (traffics, trafficking, trafficked; trafficker) ❑ The vehicles moving along a road are called the **traffic**. *Rush-hour traffic came to a halt.* Aircraft, ships, and trains following regular routes are also called **traffic**. ...*cross-Channel traffic*... *Strikes disrupted air and rail traffic.* ◇ **Traffic** is also the transporting of people or goods from one place to another. *The east-coast route accounts for 57% of passenger traffic to and from Scotland.*
❑ If someone **traffics** in drugs or other goods, they buy and sell them illegally. A person who does this is called a **trafficker**. Illegal trade in something is called **traffic** in it. *Drug abuse and drug traffic are global problems.*

traffic jam You say there is a **traffic jam** when vehicles cannot move or can only move very slowly because there are so many of them coming from different directions.

traffic lights are the set of red, amber, and green lights at a road junction which control the traffic flow.

traffic warden A **traffic warden** is a person whose job is to make sure cars are parked legally. Traffic wardens also help the police direct traffic.

tragedy (tragedies) ❑ You can call a sad and terrible event a **tragedy**.
❑ **Tragedy** is a type of literature, especially drama, which is serious and sad and usually ends with the death of the main character. A **tragedy** is a play like this.

tragic (tragically) You say something is **tragic** when it is very sad because it involves death, suffering, or disaster. *He died tragically young.* ◇ **Tragic** is also used to talk about tragedy as a form of literature. ...*Shakespeare's greatest tragic hero.*

tragicomedy (tragicomedies; tragicomic) A **tragicomedy** is a film or play which is both tragic and funny. **Tragicomic** is used to describe films, plays, and real-life situations which are like this.

trail (trailing, trailed) ❑ A **trail** is a rough path, for example across open country or through forests. ◇ A **trail** is also a route along certain paths or roads, often specially planned for a particular purpose. *Dublin is a good city for walking, with heritage trails well signposted.* ◇ A politician's **campaign trail** is the route they follow when they tour a country or area trying to persuade people to vote for them in an election.
❑ The **trail** of a person, animal, or vehicle is the footprints, scent, or marks they leave behind them. ◇ If you **trail** someone or something, you follow them or chase them. When you do this, you say you are **on their trail**.
❑ You can say someone is on a certain **trail** when they take part in a series of events or competitions with the intention of achieving a particular aim. *We'll be back on the Championship trail this weekend.*
❑ If something leaves a **trail** of damage, it passes through a place causing a lot of damage on its way. *The storms have left a trail of devastation.*
❑ You say something **trails** when it drags along the ground behind something else. ...*a trailing velveteen skirt.* ◇ You can also say a plant **trails** when it hangs or droops over something.
❑ If a speaker's voice **trails away** or **trails off**, it gradually becomes quieter or more hesitant until it stops completely.
❑ If you say someone is **trailing** in a competitive situation, you mean they are a long way behind their rivals or opponents. *His party had been trailing in recent opinion polls.*

trailblazer A pioneer in a certain field of activity is sometimes called a **trailblazer**.

trailer ❑ A **trailer** is a small vehicle which can be loaded with things and pulled behind a car or van. ◇ A **trailer** is also the long rear section of an articulated lorry, in which the goods are carried. ◇ Caravans are also sometimes called **trailers**.
❑ A **trailer** for a film or TV programme is a series of short extracts from it, often with a commentary, shown or broadcast to advertise it.

train (training, trained) ❑ A **train** is a number of connected carriages or trucks pulled by a railway engine. ◇ You can also call a long moving line of people or animals a **train**. ...*a train of camels.*
❑ A series of events can be called a **train**. *The train of unsettling events continued.* ◇ A **train** of thought is a connected series of thoughts.
❑ If something is **in train**, it is happening or being done. *He praised the economic and political reforms set in train by the Vietnamese government.*

❏ The **train** on a formal dress or robe is a long part at the back which trails on the ground.

❏ If you **train** for a certain job, you learn how to do it. If someone **trains** you to do something, they teach you. **Trained** is used to describe someone who has been taught a skill or job. *...trained technicians... ...a team of trained negotiators.*

❏ If you **train** for a sporting activity, you prepare for it by doing exercises.

❏ If you **train** an animal or bird, you teach it to obey commands or perform tricks. ◇ If someone **trains** an animal like a racehorse, they get it fit and ready to run in races.

❏ If a gun or a camera is **trained** on you, it is aimed towards you and kept pointing at you.

train spotter A **train spotter** is a person whose hobby is collecting the numbers of railway engines.

trainee (traineeship) A **trainee** is someone being taught how to do a job. A **traineeship** is a job for a trainee in a company or organization. The period of time someone spends as a trainee is also called a **traineeship**.

trainer ❏ A **trainer** is (a) a person who trains people in a skill. (b) a person who trains animals.

❏ **Trainer** aircraft are used for training pilots.

❏ **Trainers** are special sports shoes for running or jogging. They are also worn as fashion items, especially by young people.

trainload A **trainload** of people or things is the number of them a train can carry.

traipse (traipsing, traipsed) If you **traipse** somewhere, you walk there slowly and wearily.

trait (*pron:* **trate** *or* **tray**) A **trait** is a tendency in someone's behaviour. *...personality traits... Not all the traits that have been bred into the pit-bull terrier are bad.*

traitor (traitorous) A **traitor** is someone who betrays their country or the group they belong to. A person like this is sometimes called **traitorous**. *Authorities say the plot was the work of a traitorous force within the government's inner ranks.*

trajectory (*pron:* traj-jek-tor-ee) (trajectories) The **trajectory** of an object thrown or launched into the air is the curving path it follows as it rises then comes down again. ◇ The way in which something is changing can be called a **trajectory**, especially when it is steadily improving or declining. *...the trajectory of the British economy... ...a turnround in the inflationary trajectory.*

tram A **tram** is a vehicle like a bus which travels through streets on rails called **tramlines**. Trams are powered by electricity, usually from an overhead wire.

tramcar A **tramcar** is the same as a tram.

tramp ❏ A **tramp** is a person with no permanent home or job who travels from place to place and gets money by begging or doing occasional work.

❏ If you **tramp** somewhere, you walk with regular heavy footsteps. ◇ If you go for a **tramp**, you go for a long walk.

trample (trampling, trampled) ❏ If people or animals **trample** on something, they tread heavily on it and damage or destroy it. ◇ If someone is **trampled** underfoot, they are injured or killed by being trodden on by animals or other people.

❏ If a government treats people in a cruel or unjust way, you can say it **tramples** on their rights or liberties.

trampoline (trampolining) A **trampoline** is a gymnastic apparatus made of a large piece of strong cloth held taut by springs in a large frame. People bounce up and down on it and also do acrobatic jumps and somersaults on it; this activity is called **trampolining**.

trance A **trance** is a mental state in which someone appears to be asleep, but can see and hear things and respond to commands. ◇ You can also say someone is in a **trance** when they are in a stunned or dazed state.

tranquil (tranquillity) (*American spelling:* tranquility) A **tranquil** person is calm and relaxed. ◇ A **tranquil** place is calm and peaceful. *...Dorset's rural tranquillity.*

tranquillize (tranquillizing, tranquillized; tranquillizer) (*can be spelled with an 's' instead of a 'z'*) (*American spelling:* tranquilize, tranquilizing, *etc*) If a person or animal is **tranquillized**, they are given a drug called a **tranquillizer** to make them calm, sleepy, or unconscious.

trans- is used to form words which describe things going or extending from one side of a place to another. *...the trans-Siberian railway... ...trans-European communications.*

transact (transaction) When you **transact** a payment or some business, you carry it out or negotiate it. A **transaction** is a piece of business like this. *Keep careful records of all financial transactions.*

transatlantic ❏ A **transatlantic** journey or communication involves travelling or communicating across the Atlantic. *...transatlantic flights... ...a transatlantic phone call.* ◇ **Transatlantic** is also used to talk about things involving countries or regions on both sides of the Atlantic. *...a transatlantic declaration between the EU and the democracies of North America.*

❏ **Transatlantic** is sometimes used to mean 'American'. *His films were too slow and talkative for transatlantic tastes.*

transcend (transcendence, transcendent) If you say something **transcends** something else, you mean it is not limited by it like other things are. You talk about the **transcendence** of something like this or say it is **transcendent**. *The best fiction transcends genre... ...the transcendence of God... ...an all-powerful, transcendent deity.*

transcendental things are beyond normal human experience or understanding. *...a transcendental event.*

transcendental meditation is a form of meditation in which you mentally relax by silently repeating a special word or sound.

transcontinental means extending across a continent. *...a transcontinental railway.*

transcribe (transcribing, transcribed; transcript, transcription) ❏ If you **transcribe** something like a taped message, you write it down in full. Similarly, if you **transcribe** a piece of writing, you copy it. Writing or copying something down is called **transcription**; what you write is called a **transcript** or a **transcription**. *...a transcript of a telephone conversation... Transcriptions of the text were available as early as 1960.*

❏ If someone **transcribes** a piece of music, they arrange it for different instruments. An arrangement like this is called a **transcription**. *Elgar's Cello Concerto is not often heard in its transcription for viola.*

transept The **transepts** of a church or cathedral are the parts which project north and south of the main building, giving it the shape of a cross.

transfer (transferring, transferred) ❏ If someone or something is **transferred** from one place to another, they are moved there. Similarly, someone can be **transferred** to a different part of the same organization. A move like this is called a **transfer.** *The authority offered him a transfer to community nursing.* ◇ If a sports player is **transferred,** he or she is sold to another team. *His transfer to Manchester United came a few months later.*

    ❏ If something is **transferred** from one group or organization to another, it is taken from the first one and given to the second one. *...the transfer of power from the minority to the majority.*

    ❏ A **transfer** is also a piece of paper with a design on one side, which can be ironed or pressed onto cloth, paper, or china.

transferable If something is **transferable,** it can be passed to another person or organization and used by them. *Membership cards are not transferable.*

transferee A person who has been moved from one job, place, or team to another is sometimes called a **transferee.**

transference is sometimes used instead of 'transfer' to talk about the transferring of something to a different person, place, or group. *...a transference of power with the minimum of bloodshed.*

transfigure (transfiguring, transfigured; transfiguration) If someone or something is **transfigured,** their appearance is completely changed. A change like this is called a **transfiguration.**

transfix (transfixes, transfixing, transfixed) If you are **transfixed** by something, you are so impressed, fascinated, or frightened by it that you cannot move.

transform (transformation) If something is **transformed,** it is changed completely. A change like this is called a **transformation.** *My life has been transformed... ...the transformation of the American economy.*

transformer A **transformer** is a piece of electrical equipment which changes the voltage of a current.

transfuse (transfusing, transfused; transfusion) When blood is **transfused,** it is fed into someone's circulation system by means of a drip. This is called a blood **transfusion.**

transgenic plants and animals have been genetically altered so that they contain one or more genes from another species. *...transgenic tomato plants... ...transgenic mice.*

transgress (transgresses, transgressing, transgressed; transgression, transgressor) If someone **transgresses** a rule or law, they break it. This is called a **transgression** of the rule or law; the person who breaks it is called a **transgressor.**

transient (transience) If something is **transient,** it does not last very long. *The effects are transient... ...the transience of fame.* ◇ **Transients** are people who only stay in a place for a short time.

transistor A **transistor** is a tiny electronic device used to control the flow of electric current in, for example, a TV or radio. ◇ A **transistor** or **transistor radio** is a small portable radio containing transistors.

transit is the carrying of goods or people by vehicle from one place to another. If goods or people are **in transit,** they are being taken from one place to another.

    ❏ A **transit** area or building is a place where people wait or goods are kept between different stages of a journey. *...a new transit camp for the refugees... ...a transit lounge at Moscow airport.*

transition A **transition** is a change from one state to another. *...the transition from being partners to parents... ...South Africa's transition to democracy.*

transitional A **transitional** period or stage is one when something changes from one state to another. **Transitional** is also used to describe something which happens or exists during a transitional period or stage. *...a transitional government.*

transitory If something is **transitory,** it lasts only a short time. *The effects tend to be transitory... ...transitory success.*

translate (translating, translated; translation) ❏ If you **translate** something someone has said or written, you say or write it in another language. *They had to take the letter to a Welsh-speaking neighbour for translation.* A **translation** is a piece of writing or speech translated into another language.

    ❏ When someone does something they have been talking about doing, you can say they **translate** words into action. *...the question of what it might take to translate Scottish sentiment for independence into votes in a general election.*

translator A **translator** is a person who translates speech or writing from one language into another.

transliterated (transliteration) If words or letters are **transliterated,** they are written in the alphabet of a different language. Something written in the alphabet of a different language is called a **transliteration.** *The American surnames had to be transliterated first into Vietnamese, and then into Russian.*

translucent If something is **translucent,** light passes through it, so that it seems to glow.

transmit (transmitting, transmitted; transmission) ❏ If something is **transmitted** from one person or thing to another, it is passed on to them. *...cheap condoms which help prevent the transmission of the AIDS virus.*

    ❏ When a programme is **transmitted,** it is broadcast on TV or radio. You talk about the **transmission** of a TV or radio programme. A **transmission** is a broadcast.

    ❏ When a message or electronic signal is **transmitted,** it is sent by radio waves. A message or signal sent like this is called a **transmission.**

    ❏ The **transmission** on a car or other vehicle is the system of gears and shafts by which the power from the engine reaches and turns the wheels.

transmitter A **transmitter** is a piece of equipment used for sending TV or radio signals.

transmogrify (transmogrifies, transmogrifying, transmogrified) If someone or something is **transmogrified,** they are completely transformed. *He was transmogrified from most hated man in Britain into vindicated folk hero.*

transmute (transmuting, transmuted; transmutation) If a substance is **transmuted** into something different, it is converted into it. *Alchemists never succeeded at transmuting these base metals into gold... ...the transmutation of food into energy.*

transnational is used to describe things which involve more than one country. *...transnational companies... ...transnational problems.*

transparent (transparently; transparency, transparencies) ❏ If something is **transparent,** you can see through it. You talk about the **transparency** of something like this. ...*transparent plastic sheeting*.

❑ If a feature or quality is **transparent**, it is very obvious that it exists. ...*his transparent sincerity*... *He was transparently uneasy with the decision*.

❑ If something like a dishonest statement or action is **transparent**, people are not deceived by it. ...*a transparent ploy to delay the transfer of power*.

❑ A **transparency** is a small piece of photographic film mounted in a frame, viewed using a projector.

transpire (transpiring, transpired) ❑ If something turns out to be the case, you can say it **transpires** that it is the case. *It transpired that his death was caused by lung cancer, not by the beating*.

❑ When something **transpires**, it happens. *Nothing is known as yet about what transpired at the meeting*.

transplant (transplantation) ❑ When surgeons **transplant** an organ or tissue, they take it from one person's body and put it into someone else's. Tissue can also be **transplanted** to a different part of the same person's body. Transferring organs and tissue is called **transplantation**; an operation in which this is done is called a **transplant**. ...*organ transplantation*... ...*liver transplants*.

❑ When people or organizations are **transplanted** to a different place, they are moved there. *He even suggested the transplanting of Russian arms factories to India*.

transponder ❑ A **transponder** is an electronic device which transmits a radio or radar signal when it receives a signal to do so.

❑ On a broadcasting or communications satellite, a **transponder** is a device which receives a signal, amplifies it, and returns it to earth at a different frequency. Most satellites have several transponders.

transport (transportation) When goods or people are **transported** from one place to another, they are moved there. **Transport** or **transportation** is the moving of goods or people from one place to another. *The major problem is the transportation of refugees from Kuwait to Jordan*. ◇ **Transport** is also cars, buses, and other vehicles which people travel in. *He said the authorities would provide transport to take them to Iraq*.

transport cafe A **transport cafe** is a cafe beside a main road, mainly used by lorry drivers.

transportable If something is **transportable**, it can be moved from place to place.

transporter A **transporter** is a large vehicle, used to transport people, vehicles, goods, or equipment. ...*troop transporters*... ...*car transporters*. ◇ Firms that transport things are also called **transporters**.

transpose (transposing, transposed; transposition) If you **transpose** something, you move it from one place to another. *He transposes the action from 16th century France to post-Civil War America*. ◇ If you **transpose** two things, you get them the wrong way round, or you deliberately swap them round. *Three quarters of the spelling mistakes involved the transposition of letters*.

transputer A **transputer** is a type of fast powerful microchip.

transsexual A **transsexual** is a man or woman who believes they were meant to be a member of the opposite sex, or someone who has had a sex-change operation.

transubstantiation is the doctrine that the bread and

wine consecrated in Communion change into the body and blood of Christ, although their appearance stays the same.

transverse is used to describe something which is at right angles to something else, or at right angles to the position you would normally expect it to be in. ...*the coupe's transverse 3-litre V-6 engine*.

transvestite (transvestism) A **transvestite** is a person, especially a man, who likes to dress in the clothing of the opposite sex. Dressing up like this is called **transvestism**.

trap (trapping, trapped) ❑ A **trap** is a device for catching an animal. If you **trap** an animal, you catch it in a trap.

❑ A **trap** is also a trick intended to catch or deceive someone. If you **set a trap** or **lay a trap** for someone, you prepare a trick like this. ◇ If you **trap** someone into saying or doing something, you get them to say or do it although they do not intend to.

❑ A **trap** is also a mistake which is easily made. *He largely succeeds in avoiding the trap of boring his reader with lengthy analysis of modern day Arab politics*.

❑ If you are **trapped** somewhere, you cannot move or escape because something is blocking your way or holding you down. *Rescue workers say many more people may be trapped in the rubble*. ◇ You can also say someone is **trapped** when they are in an unpleasant situation which it is difficult to escape from. A situation like this can be called a **trap**. *More than two million British women are trapped in unhappy marriages*... ...*the debt trap*.

❑ In the past, a **trap** was a light two-wheeled carriage drawn by one horse.

trapdoor A **trapdoor** is a small horizontal door in a floor, ceiling, or stage.

trapeze A **trapeze** is a horizontal wood or metal bar hanging from two ropes, on which acrobats and gymnasts swing and perform acrobatics. A **trapeze artist** is a circus performer who performs on the trapeze.

trapper A **trapper** is a person who traps animals, especially for their fur.

trappings The **trappings** of something like wealth or power are the external signs of it. ...*the trappings of presidential office*.

Trappist A **Trappist** or **Trapist** monk is a member of an order of Christian monks who observe strict silence.

trash (trashy; trashes, trashing, trashed) ❑ In the US, rubbish is called **trash**. A **trash can** is a dustbin.

❑ If you call a book or film **trash**, you mean it is of very poor quality. You can also describe it as **trashy**. ...*the sort of low-budget trash that is shown in sleazy cinemas in London's Soho*... ...*trashy novels*.

❑ If you **trash** a person, their work, or their ideas, you ridicule them.

❑ If someone **trashes** a place, they wreck it.

trattoria A **trattoria** is an Italian restaurant.

trauma (*pron:* traw-ma) (traumatic) ❑ A **trauma** is an extremely upsetting experience which can cause long-term psychological damage. You say an experience like this is **traumatic**. ...*childhood traumas such as rejection or sexual abuse*... *For a child, the death of a pet can be traumatic*.

❑ In medicine, a wound or injury is called a **trauma**.

traumatize (traumatizing, traumatized) (*can be spelled with an 's' instead of a 'z'*) If someone is **traumatized** by something that happens, they are extremely upset by it, and may suffer long-term psychological damage.

travail Someone's **travails** are the difficult things they have to do and the problems they have to cope with.

travel (travelling, travelled) (*American spelling:* traveling, traveled) ❑ When you **travel** between two places, you go from one to the other.

❑ If you **travel**, you visit several places. If you **travel** a country or region or **travel around** it, you visit several parts of it. ◇ **Travel** is the act of travelling. ◇ Someone's **travels** are the journeys they make to places a long way from their home. *He plans to sell his flat and use the money to fund his travels.*

❑ When something moves from one place to another, you can say it **travels** there. *Nothing travels faster than the speed of light... News soon travels.* ◇ If something **travels** at a particular speed, it moves at that speed. *The train was travelling at 25mph.*

travel agency (travel agent) A **travel agency** or **travel agent** is a business which makes arrangements for people's holidays and journeys. A **travel agent** is also someone who runs or works in a travel agency.

travel-sick (travel sickness) If someone is **travel-sick**, they feel sick as a result of travelling in a vehicle. This feeling is called **travel sickness**.

travelcard A **travelcard** is a pass which enables you to travel on buses or trains without having to buy a ticket.

traveller (*American spelling:* traveler) A **traveller** is a person going from one place to another. *...travellers on the London Underground.* ◇ A **traveller** is also (a) someone who travels a lot, for pleasure or to increase their knowledge of other countries. (b) someone who travels from place to place, often living in a van or some other vehicle.

traveller's cheque (*American spelling:* traveler's check) Traveller's cheques are special cheques you can exchange for foreign currency when you are abroad.

travelling expenses Your **travelling expenses** are the money you have to spend on travelling as part of your work.

travelling salesman (travelling salesmen) A **travelling salesman** is a salesman who travels around selling goods or taking customers' orders.

travelogue (*American spelling:* travelog) A **travelogue** is a book, film, or talk about travel to a place, or about a person's travels.

traverse (traversing, traversed) If you **traverse** something, you cross it.

travesty (travesties) If you call something a **travesty**, you mean it is not what it is supposed to be, but a very poor imitation of it. *The trial was a travesty... This is a travesty of justice.*

trawl ❑ When fishermen **trawl**, they drag a large bag-like net along the seabed behind their boat, to catch large numbers of fish. This net is called a **trawl** or a **trawl net**.

❑ If you **trawl** for things or people of a certain kind, you search among a large number of them, to find the best or most suitable ones. A search like this is called a **trawl**. *...the Emergency Beds Service, which trawls London for beds in emergency cases... The trawl for investors will continue.*

trawler A **trawler** is a fishing boat from which fish are caught using a trawl.

trawlerman (trawlermen) A **trawlerman** is a fisherman who works on a trawler.

tray A **tray** is a flat object with raised edges, used to put things on or carry things, especially food or drinks.

treacherous (treacherously) A **treacherous** person is likely to betray you. ◇ You say things are **treacherous** when they are unreliable and dangerous. *Rain made the ground treacherously slippery.*

treachery is betraying someone.

treacle is a thick sweet sticky liquid obtained as a by-product when sugar is refined. It is used in some cakes, puddings, and toffees.

treacly If something is **treacly**, it is thick and sticky like treacle.

tread (treading, trod, have trodden) ❑ If you **tread** on something, you step on it, or press your foot on it. *Holding my breath and attempting not to tread on any dry twigs, I crept up towards him... He trod on the accelerator.* ◇ If you **tread** something into the ground or into a carpet, you step on it and crush it in. ◇ Someone's **tread** is the sound their feet make when they walk.

❑ If you **tread** carefully, you behave cautiously. *Sensible investors will tread warily.*

❑ If you **tread water**, for example when you are in the sea, you stay afloat in an upright position by moving your legs slightly. ◇ In other situations, you say someone is **treading water** when they are doing just enough to survive. *The organisation's latest survey of its members revealed that 55 per cent were just about treading water.*

❑ The **tread** of a tyre or shoe is the pattern of ridges on it which stops it slipping.

❑ The flat part of a stair is called the **tread**.

treadle (*pron:* tred-dl) A **treadle** is a lever on something like a sewing machine, which you work with your foot to turn a wheel in the machine.

treadmill ❑ In the past, a **treadmill** was a large wheel, turned by people or animals walking on or inside it. ◇ Nowadays, a **treadmill** is an exercise machine. It has a moving belt which you run on.

❑ Any task or job which you must keep doing, even though it is unpleasant or tiring, can be called a **treadmill**.

treason (treasonable) **Treason** or **high treason** is the crime of betraying your country, for example by helping its enemies, or by trying to overthrow its government. You say activities of this kind are **treasonable**. *...a treasonable breach of the law.*

treasure (treasuring, treasured) ❑ **Treasure** is a collection of gold, silver, or jewels, especially one which has been hidden. ◇ **Treasures** are objects of great value, especially works of art.

❑ If you **treasure** something you have, you regard it as very valuable. *I treasure our friendship... ...one of my most treasured possessions.*

treasure trove is money or valuable objects which have been found, often buried, and whose ownership is not known. ◇ If you call a place a **treasure trove**, you mean a lot of valuable things can be found there.

treasurer The **treasurer** of an organization is the person in charge of its finances.

treasury (treasuries) In Britain and some other countries, the **Treasury** is the government department responsible for the country's finances. ◇ If you talk about a country's **treasury**, you mean the money it has available to spend on things. *Africa's wars are long-lasting conflicts which drain the money from already limited treasuries.*

treat (treating, treated) ❑ If you **treat** someone in a particular way, you behave that way towards them. *He treated her badly.* ◇ If you **treat** something as a particular thing, you behave as if it was that thing. *I treated it as a joke.*

❑ When a doctor **treats** a patient, he or she gives them medical care and attention. You can also talk about a doctor **treating** an illness.

❑ When something like wood or cloth is **treated**, a special substance is put on it to protect it or give it special properties. *The woodwork is treated with preservative.*

❑ If you **treat** someone or give them a **treat**, you buy or arrange something special for them which they will enjoy.

treatable If a disease or illness is **treatable**, it can be treated effectively. *Cerebral malaria is treatable if diagnosed in time.*

treatise (*pron:* treat-izz) A **treatise** is a long formal piece of writing on a particular subject. *...a treatise on accounting methods.*

treatment is medical attention given to a sick or injured person or animal. *Many of the injured are being taken to American military hospitals for treatment.* ◇ A **treatment** is a way of treating an illness or disease. *Deprenyl is sometimes used as a treatment for Parkinson's disease.*

❑ Your **treatment** of a person or thing is the way you behave towards them or deal with them. *His treatment of her was callous and cruel.*

treaty (treaties) A **treaty** is a written agreement between countries. *...the Maastricht Treaty.*

treble (trebling, trebled) ❑ If something **trebles** or is **trebled**, it becomes three times as big. You then say it is **treble** the number, size, or amount it was before. *Some owners are charging treble the normal price.*

❑ A **treble** is a boy singer, especially in a choir.

tree Trees are large plants with hard trunks, leaves, and usually branches.

tree house A **tree house** is a shed-like structure built in a tree for children to play in.

tree-lined streets or roads have trees on both sides of them.

tree surgeon (tree surgery) A **tree surgeon** is a person who repairs damaged trees. This kind of work is called **tree surgery**.

treeless A treeless area has no trees.

treeline The **treeline** in a mountainous area is the height above which trees do not grow. *The skiing is fairly limited, mostly on exposed slopes above the treeline.*

treetop The **treetops** are the highest parts of the trees around you.

trefoil (*pron:* tref-foil) is clover and other similar plants whose leaves divide into three smaller leaves.

trek (trekking, trekked; trekker) If you **trek** somewhere, you make a long and difficult journey, especially on foot. A journey like this can be called a **trek**. *Some of the refugees had trekked 200 miles to the frontier.* ◇ **Trekking** is making long journeys on foot over difficult terrain for pleasure. People who do this are called **trekkers**. See also **pony trekking**.

trellis (trellises) A **trellis** is a frame made of bars crossing each other, which supports climbing plants.

tremble (trembling, trembled) If you **tremble**, you shake slightly, because you are frightened. ◇ If a building or other object **trembles**, it shakes slightly.

tremendous (tremendously) **Tremendous** is used to say something is very large or very intense. *They faced tremendous problems... The heat was tremendous... The advice they get from schools varies tremendously.* ◇ You can also say something is **tremendous** if you think it is very good or impressive. *It was a tremendous performance.*

tremor ❑ A **tremor** is a shaking of your body or voice which you cannot control.

❑ A **tremor** is also a small earthquake.

tremulous (tremulously) If someone's voice is **tremulous**, it shakes slightly. *'Who is it?' she called tremulously.*

trench (trenches) A **trench** is a long narrow channel dug into the ground, usually so pipes can be laid or to provide drainage. ◇ **Trenches** are also similar channels dug to give soldiers protection from enemy fire. **Trench warfare** was the kind of warfare, common in the 1914-1918 war, in which soldiers on both sides sheltered in trenches, and fired weapons or launched attacks from them.

trench coat (or **trenchcoat**) A **trench coat** is a type of raincoat with pockets and a belt, especially one similar in design to a military coat.

trenchant (trenchantly) **Trenchant** means strong and to the point. *He wrote many trenchant articles... ...trenchantly held views.*

trenchcoat See **trench coat**.

trend A **trend** is a general change in a particular direction in something like people's behaviour or attitudes. *Spending in the High Street has shown a slight downward trend.*

trend-setter (trend-setting) A **trend-setter** is a person or thing that starts a new fashion or trend. **Trend-setting** is used to describe people and things like this. *...Madonna's trend-setting wardrobe.*

trendy (trendier, trendiest; trendily, trendiness; trendies) **Trendy** people or things are fashionable. *...one of Manhattan's trendiest restaurants... ...the trendiness of Oxfam gear.* ◇ **Trendies** are people who try to keep up with all the latest fashions, either in things like clothes or in ideas. *...left-wing trendies.*

trepidation is fear or anxiety about something you are going to do or experience.

trespass (trespasses, trespassing, trespassed; trespasser) If you **trespass** on someone's land or property, you go onto it without permission. People who do this are called **trespassers**; they are said to commit a **trespass**.

tress (tresses) A woman's **tresses** are her long flowing hair. *...her long blonde tresses.*

trestle Trestles are a pair of wooden or metal structures which you stand on the floor and put a long board on, to form a table. A table formed like this is called a **trestle table**.

trews are close-fitting tartan trousers.

triad ❑ A **triad** is a group of three similar things. *These can be roughly divided into a triad of mental, physical and chemical causes.*

❑ A **Triad** is a secret Chinese criminal organization.

trial ❑ A **trial** is a legal process in which a judge and jury listen to evidence and the jury decides whether an accused person is guilty of a crime. When this happens, you say the accused person is **on trial.**

❑ A **trial** is also an experiment in which something is tested for a period of time to see how well it works. When something is being tested like this, you say it is **on trial.** *About 30 AIDS vaccines are on trial around the world.*

❑ A **trial run** is a test to see if something works as it is intended to.

❑ If you do something by **trial and error,** you try different ways of doing it, until you find the best one.

❑ In a sport like cricket or football, a **trial** is a test to see whether someone is suitable for a place in a team. ◇ **Trials** are a sporting competition which tests a competitor's skill and ability. *...one-day horse trials.*

❑ If you talk about someone's **trials,** you mean the unpleasant things they experience. *Their trials began with a ban by Customs officials and ended with an earthquake.*

triangle ❑ A **triangle** is a shape with three straight sides.

❑ The **triangle** is a percussion instrument consisting of a thin steel bar bent in the shape of a triangle. The player hits it with a small steel rod.

triangular If something is **triangular,** it is shaped like a triangle. *...triangular panels.* ◇ A **triangular** relationship involves three people or three groups of people. *...a triangular love affair.*

tribal (tribally) **Tribal** is used to talk about things to do with a tribe or tribes. *...tribal conflicts... ...tribally motivated killings.*

tribalism (tribalist, tribalistic) **Tribalism** is a feeling of loyalty towards a tribe felt by its members, often involving hostility towards other tribes. ◇ **Tribalism** is also a similar feeling felt by people belonging to other groups, especially in a community where there are people of different religions or ethnic backgrounds. People who have feelings like these are sometimes described as **tribalist** or **tribalistic.**

tribe A **tribe** is a group of people of the same race who speak the same language, have the same customs, and live together in a community, often ruled by a chief.

tribesman (tribesmen) A **tribesman** is a man who belongs to a tribe.

tribespeople are the members of a tribe. *...the Dani tribespeople.*

tribulation is trouble or suffering. A person's **tribulations** are their troubles.

tribunal A **tribunal** is a special court or committee, appointed to pass judgement on a particular matter.

tributary (tributaries) A **tributary** of a river is a smaller river which flows into it.

tribute ❑ A **tribute** is something you say or do to show your admiration or respect for someone. ◇ If you **pay tribute** to someone or something, you express your admiration or respect for them.

❑ If you say something is a **tribute** to something else, you mean it came about as a result of it and shows how good it is. *The fact he is only the tenth United player to score 100 League goals is a tribute to his ability.*

trice If you deal with something **in a trice,** you deal with it very quickly.

triceps (plural: triceps) Your **triceps** is the long muscle at the back of your upper arm.

trick (trickery) ❑ If someone **tricks** you or plays a **trick** on you, they deceive you, usually to obtain something from you or to get you to do something. *He may have been tricked into carrying the bomb on board.* Tricking people is called **trickery.** *He accused the authorities of using trickery to disrupt communication in remoter areas.*

❑ Something natural which misleads you can also be called a **trick.** *...a trick of the light.*

❑ A **trick** is also a clever or skilful action done to entertain people. *...magic tricks.* ◇ **Trick** devices and methods are designed to create misleading effects, to amuse and entertain people. *...trick mirrors... ...trick photography.*

❑ A clever or effective way of doing something can be called a **trick.** *There is a trick to peeling them... The trick is to plan ahead for such emergencies.* ◇ If something **does the trick,** it achieves what you want.

❑ The cards played or won in a round of cards are also called a **trick.**

trick or treat is a custom, originally American, in which children in fancy dress go round to people's doors on Halloween and say 'Trick or treat.' If you do not give them a small gift, they play a practical joke on you.

trickle (trickling, trickled) ❑ When a liquid **trickles** somewhere, it flows in a thin stream. A **trickle** of liquid is a thin stream of it. *...a trickle of blood.*

❑ If people or things **trickle** somewhere, they go there gradually in small groups or numbers. You talk about a **trickle** of people or things going somewhere. *The results trickled in... ...the trickle of foreign money going into Russia's oil industry.*

trickster A **trickster** is a person who deceives people to obtain money or get some other advantage.

tricky (trickier, trickiest) If something is **tricky,** it is difficult and requires careful attention. *The next stage will be tricky... ...a tricky accounting problem.* ◇ A **tricky** person is crafty or deceitful.

tricolour (pron: trick-kol-lor) (American spelling: tricolor) A **tricolour** is a flag made up of three stripes of different colours. *...the French tricolour.*

tricycle A **tricycle** is a vehicle similar to a bicycle but with two wheels at the back and one at the front. 'Tricycle' is sometimes shortened to 'trike'.

trident A **trident** is a three-pronged spear.

triennial is used to describe something which happens once every three years. *...the triennial Commonwealth Law Conferences.*

trier You say someone is a **trier** when they try very hard to do something. *People love a trier.*

trifle (trifling, trifled) ❑ A **trifle** means 'slightly' or 'rather'. *He looked a trifle overwhelmed.* ◇ **Trifles** are objects of little value. *They survive by peddling trifles on the streets.* ◇ **Trifling** things are of little importance. *...a trifling matter.*

❑ **Trifle** or a **trifle** is a pudding made of sponge cake covered in layers of jelly, custard, and cream, and sometimes other ingredients.

❑ If you **trifle** with someone or something, you treat them in a frivolous or disrespectful way.

trigger (triggering, triggered) ❑ The **trigger** of a gun is the small lever you pull to fire it.

❑ If something **triggers** an event or **triggers** it **off,** it makes it happen. *The announcement triggered a brief rise in* *share prices.* The immediate cause of an event is sometimes called its **trigger**. *The trigger was the killing by the security forces of 13 Kurdish separatists.*

trigger-happy people are too ready to use violence and weapons, especially guns.

trigonometry is the branch of mathematics concerned with calculating the angles of triangles, or the lengths of their sides.

trike See **tricycle**.

trilateral is used to describe things like meetings which involve three people or groups. *...trilateral talks.*

trilby (trilbies) A **trilby** or **trilby hat** is a man's hat made of felt, with a dent along the top from front to back and a narrow brim.

trilingual If someone is **trilingual**, they can speak three languages.

trill ❑ A **trill** is two musical notes repeated one after the other several times, very quickly.

❑ When a bird **trills**, it sings with short high-pitched repeated notes. You can talk about the **trill** or **trilling** of a bird.

❑ If you talk about a woman **trilling**, you mean she talks or laughs in a high-pitched voice. *'How wonderful!' she trilled... ...the trill of women's voices.*

trillion (trillionth) A **trillion** is the number 1,000,000,000,000.

trilogy (*pron:* trill-a-jee) (trilogies) A **trilogy** is a series of three books, films, or plays with the same characters or subject. *...the Star Wars trilogy.*

trim (trimming, trimmed) ❑ If something is **trim**, it is neat and tidy. *...the trim garden.* ◇ **Trim** also means slim. *...her trim figure.* ◇ If a person or thing is **in trim**, they are in good condition.

❑ If you **trim** something or give it a **trim**, you cut off small amounts of it, to make it look neater. *His hair needed a trim.* ◇ If you **trim away** parts of something, or **trim them off**, you cut them off because they are not needed. *Trim away any excess fat.*

❑ You say other things are **trimmed** when they are reduced. *Student grants will be trimmed by 10 per cent.* You can also talk about things being **trimmed down** or **trimmed back**. *...the trimming back of the defence budget.*

❑ The **trim** of something you make or buy is a decoration along its edges which is a different colour from the rest or made of a different material. *...coats with fake-fur trim.* You can also say something is **trimmed** with a particular material. *...crimson gowns trimmed with ermine.*

❑ **Trimmings** are extra things added to accompany food when it is served. *...turkey and all the trimmings.*

trimaran (*pron:* trime-a-ran) A **trimaran** is a fast sailing boat similar to a catamaran, but with three hulls instead of two.

trimmer A **trimmer** is a device for trimming grass or hedges.

trimmings See **trim**.

trinity ❑ In the Christian religion, the **Trinity** is the union of Father, Son, and Holy Spirit in one God.

❑ A **trinity** is any group of three people or things. *...one of Germany's trinity of chemical giants.*

trinket Trinkets are cheap ornaments or pieces of jewellery.

trio (trios) A **trio** is a group of three people or things, es-

pecially a group of three musicians or singers. *...a jazz trio.* ◇ A piece of music for three performers is also called a **trio**. *...Ravel's Piano Trio.*

trip (tripping, tripped) ❑ A **trip** is a journey. *...a trip to London... ...a boat trip.*

❑ If you **trip**, **trip over** something, or **trip up**, you catch your foot on something and fall. If you **trip** someone else or **trip them up**, you make this happen to them, usually by sticking your own foot out in front of them.

❑ You can also say you **trip up** when you make a mistake. Similarly, you can **trip** someone else **up**. *He will do all he can to trip up the new government.*

❑ A **trip** is also a strange experience, often involving hallucinations, caused by drugs.

trip wire See **tripwire**.

tripartite is used to describe something which has three parts or involves three groups of people. *...a tripartite gala concert... ...tripartite talks.*

tripe is the white stomach lining of a cow or ox, which people cook and eat.

❑ If you call what someone says **tripe**, you mean it is nonsense. Similarly, you can call a book or film **tripe**.

triple (tripling, tripled) ❑ **Triple** means consisting of three parts or things. *...a triple bill... ...a triple album.*

❑ If something **triples** or is **tripled**, it becomes three times as big. You then say it is **triple** the number, size, or amount it was before.

triple jump The **triple jump** is an athletics event similar to the long jump except that the athlete lands first on one foot, then the other, and finally on both.

triplet Triplets are three children born at the same time to the same mother.

triplicate If something has been produced **in triplicate**, there are three copies of it.

tripod A **tripod** is a stand with three legs, used to support something like a camera or telescope.

tripper A **tripper** is a person on a trip or holiday somewhere. *...trippers from England... ...day-trippers.*

triptych (*pron:* trip-tick) A **triptych** is a painting or carving on three panels fixed or hinged side by side, especially an altarpiece in a church.

tripwire (or **trip wire**) A **tripwire** is a wire stretched just above the ground, which triggers a trap or explosion if someone touches it.

trite (tritely) If you say something like a phrase or idea is **trite**, you mean it is dull and unoriginal. *...trite lyrics... ...a new programme called, somewhat tritely, 'In Tune'.*

tritium (*pron:* trit-ee-um) is a radioactive form of hydrogen.

triumph ❑ A **triumph** is a great success or achievement. ◇ **Triumph** is a feeling of great satisfaction when you win or achieve something.

❑ If you **triumph**, you win a victory, or succeed in overcoming something. *West Ham triumphed 3-1 at Upton Park... She said terrorists must never be allowed to triumph.*

triumphal is used to describe things which are done or made to celebrate a victory or great success. *...triumphal May Day parades... ...a triumphal arch.*

triumphalism (triumphalist) Victory celebrations can be called **triumphalism**, especially when they are overdone or go on too long. You can also call people's behaviour **triumphalist** or talk about them being in a **triumphalist**

mood.

triumphant (triumphantly) If you are **triumphant**, you feel very happy because you have won a victory, or achieved something. ...*Mr Kohl's triumphant mood... He smiled triumphantly.*

triumvirate (*pron:* try-**um**-vir-rit) A **triumvirate** is a group of three people or things, especially a group of three people at the head of something. ...*Italy's triumvirate of top designers Armani, Valentino and Versace.*

trivia If you call things **trivia**, you mean they are of little value or importance.

trivial (triviality, trivialities) If you say something is **trivial**, you mean it is not important. ...*a trivial matter.* You can talk about the **triviality** of something like this. ◇ **Trivialities** are things of little importance. *Since the Assembly opened in July, its 400 members have bickered, often over trivialities.*

trivialize (trivializing, trivialized; trivialization) (*can be spelled with an 's' instead of a 'z'*) If you say someone is **trivializing** something, you mean they are making it seem less important than it is. *His family complained that the show was a trivialization of his life.*

trod (trodden) See **tread**.

troglodyte A **troglodyte** is someone who lives in a cave.

troika A **troika** is a group of three people, countries, or things, especially three people in charge of something. ◇ Originally, a **troika** was a Russian sledge drawn by three horses.

troll (*usual pron:* **trole**) In Scandinavian mythology, **trolls** are unpleasant creatures which live in caves and under bridges.

trolley ❑ A **trolley** is a small cart on wheels, used to carry things such as shopping or luggage. ◇ A hospital **trolley** is a table on wheels for moving patients around. ◇ In a house or restaurant, a **trolley** is a small table on wheels for carrying food and drinks.
❑ In the US, trams are called **trolleys**.

trolley bus A **trolley bus** is a bus powered by electricity from an overhead wire.

trombone (trombonist) The **trombone** is a brass instrument with a U-shaped slide. A musician who plays the trombone is called a **trombonist**.

troop (trooping, trooped) ❑ **Troops** are soldiers. ◇ A **troop** is a group of soldiers in a cavalry or armoured regiment. ◇ When soldiers **troop the colour**, they take part in a ceremony in which they parade their regimental flag.
❑ A **troop** is also a large group of Scouts.
❑ A **troop** of people or animals is a large group of them. ...*troops of tourists... ...a troop of baboons.* ◇ If people **troop** somewhere, they go there in a group. *We trooped back to the house.*

trooper ❑ A **trooper** is an ordinary soldier in the cavalry or in an armoured regiment.
❑ In the US, a state **trooper** is a member of a state police force.

trophy (trophies) A **trophy** is something like a cup or shield, given as a prize to the winner of a competition. ◇ A **trophy** is also something you keep to remember a success or victory. *They can keep the horn as a trophy.*

tropic (tropical) The **tropics** are the hottest parts of the earth, lying between two lines of latitude, the Tropic of Cancer, $23\frac{1}{2}°$ north of the equator, and the Tropic of Capricorn, $23\frac{1}{2}°$ south of the equator. **Tropical** is used to talk about things to do with the tropics. ...*tropical countries... ...tropical diseases.*

trot (trotting, trotted) ❑ When a horse **trots**, it moves fairly fast, lifting one front foot together with the opposite back foot at each step. This pace is called a **trot**.
❑ If a person **trots** or moves at a **trot**, they move fairly fast, with quick small steps.
❑ If things happen **on the trot**, they happen one after the other. *She lost five games on the trot.*
❑ If someone **trots** out something like an old idea, they repeat it. *He went on and on, trotting out exactly the same tedious arguments.*

trotter A pig's **trotters** are its feet, which can be cooked and eaten.

troubadour (*pron:* troo-bad-oor) In medieval times, a **troubadour** was a man who sang love songs which he had composed himself.

trouble (troubling, troubled) ❑ If something causes you **trouble**, it causes problems or difficulties. ◇ If you say **the trouble** is a certain thing, you are saying what is causing a problem. *The trouble is that there are just not enough places available at the moment.* ◇ Your **troubles** are your personal problems.
❑ If something **troubles** you, it makes you worried or anxious. You say a person who is worried or disturbed by something is **troubled**. ◇ You say a place or organization is **troubled** when it is experiencing problems, difficulties, or conflicts. ...*troubled firms... ...troubled regions.*
❑ You say there is **trouble** in a place when there is fighting there. *At least six people were killed in the trouble... There were no reports of trouble.* A place where there is a lot of fighting can be called a **trouble spot**. ◇ A long period of civil unrest or fighting in a place is sometimes called the **troubles**. ...*the troubles in Yugoslavia.*
❑ When someone suffers from an illness or injury, you can say it **troubles** them. You can also say they have **trouble** of a particular kind. ...*a viral complaint that has troubled him for some time... ...heart trouble.*
❑ If you say someone is **in trouble**, you mean (a) they are having serious problems. *The airline was in trouble, losing £150 million each year.* (b) they have been involved in something illegal and are likely to be punished for it. ...*children in trouble with the law.*
❑ If you **take the trouble** to do something, you do it, although it requires time and effort. *When Gary joined Barcelona, he took the trouble to learn Spanish.*

trouble-free You say something is **trouble-free** when it takes place without problems or difficulties. ...*a trouble-free pregnancy.*

troublemaker (troublemaking) If you call someone a **troublemaker**, you mean they are responsible for causing trouble in a place. Causing trouble is called **troublemaking**.

troubleshooter A **troubleshooter** is a person employed by a government or organization to sort out a problem.

troublesome people keep causing trouble. ...*troublesome pupils.* ◇ You can also call a painful injury **troublesome**. ...*a troublesome wrist injury.*

trough ❑ A **trough** is a long narrow container for animals to drink or feed from.
❑ At sea, a **trough** is a low point between two waves.

❏ In weather forecasting, a **trough** is a long narrow area of low pressure.

trounce (trouncing, trounced) In sport, if someone is **trounced**, they are thoroughly beaten.

troupe (*pron:* troop) A **troupe** is a group of performers who work together. ...*a troupe of actors...* ...*a dance troupe.*

trouper A **trouper** is a member of a troupe.

trouser suit A **trouser suit** is a woman's suit of jacket and trousers.

trousers (trousered) **Trousers** are a piece of clothing worn over the body from the waist down and covering each leg separately. **Trousered** is used to say someone is wearing trousers, or to describe the kind of trousers they are wearing. *It seems women have won the right to go trousered in their leisure time but not in the workplace... He slapped his leather-trousered thigh.*

trousseau (*pron:* troo-so) (*plural:* trousseaus or trousseaux) A bride's **trousseau** is the set of clothes she collects to wear for her wedding.

trout (*plural:* trout) **Trout** are spotted freshwater fish which are often caught and eaten.

trove See treasure trove.

trowel A **trowel** is (a) a small garden tool with a curved pointed blade. (b) a small tool with a flat diamond-shaped blade, for spreading mortar or cement.

troy weight is a system of weight for weighing gold, silver, platinum, and jewels. In troy weight, 1 pound equals 12 ounces or 5760 grains.

truant (truancy) When children **truant** or **play truant**, they stay away from school without permission. This is called **truancy**; the children who do it are called **truants**.

truce A **truce** is an agreement between two sides to stop fighting for a short time.

truck ❏ A **truck** is a lorry. If something is **trucked** somewhere, it is transported by truck. *Supplies will have to be trucked in.* ◇ A **truck** is also a wagon for carrying goods on a railway.

❏ If you say you will have **no truck** with someone or something, you mean you will have nothing to do with them.

trucker A **trucker** is a person whose job is driving a truck.

truckload A **truckload** of people or things is a truck full of them. ...*two truckloads of steel pipes.*

truculent (*pron:* truck-yew-lent) (truculently, truculence) If someone is **truculent**, they are bad-tempered and aggressive. ...*her customary truculence... He stared truculently at the Superintendent.*

trudge (trudging, trudged) If you **trudge** somewhere, you walk there with slow heavy steps. A long walk can be called a **trudge**.

true (truer, truest) ❏ If something is **true**, it is based on facts and not made up.

❏ **True** is also used to mean 'genuine'. *He was a true American hero...* ...*a first step on the road to true equality.* ◇ **True** feelings are genuine and sincere. *She will be remembered with true affection... True love never dies.*

❏ If you are **true** to something, you are faithful to it. *She remains true to her convictions... He was true to his word.* ◇ If you are **true** to yourself, you stick to your principles.

❏ If a dream **comes true**, the thing you dreamed actual-

ly happens. Similarly, you can talk about a wish or prediction **coming true**.

true-blue A **true-blue** person is completely loyal, especially to their country or the Conservative Party.

truffle ❏ A **truffle** is a soft round chocolate, sometimes flavoured with rum.

❏ A **truffle** is also a round mushroom-like fungus which grows underground, and is considered very good to eat.

truism A **truism** is a statement which is believed to be true and which is repeated so often it is no longer original. *It is a truism that charming people often have something to hide.*

truly means completely and genuinely. ...*one of the few truly amateur sports...* ...*a truly democratic society.*

❏ You can use **truly** to emphasize that what you are saying is true. *Truly, I've never enjoyed myself more.*

❏ **Truly** is also used to emphasize words. ...*a truly remarkable man... It was truly awful.*

❏ You can refer to yourself as **yours truly**. ...*insomniacs like yours truly.* ◇ Some people write **Yours truly** before their signature at the end of a formal letter.

trump ❏ In a game of cards, **trumps** is the suit with the highest value. A **trump** is a card belonging to this suit.

❏ Your **trump card** is the most powerful thing you can use or do to gain an advantage. *He sees his foreign policy experience as a possible trump card in the election.*

❏ If you **trump** someone, you beat them to something, or outdo them at it. *They did not want to be trumped, so they had to publish their findings quickly.*

❏ If a person or thing **comes up trumps** or **turns up trumps**, they do unexpectedly well at something.

trumped-up is used to describe things which are made up and not true. ...*trumped-up charges of treason...* ...*some trumped-up excuse.*

trumpet (trumpeter; trumpeting, trumpeted) ❏ The **trumpet** is a brass wind instrument with three valves. A musician who plays the trumpet is called a **trumpeter**.

❏ If you **trumpet** something, you announce it to everyone. ◇ If you say someone is **blowing their own trumpet**, you mean they are boasting.

truncate (truncating, truncated) If something is **truncated**, it is shortened. ...*a truncated version of its annual report.*

truncheon A **truncheon** is a short thick stick, used by the police as a weapon.

trundle (trundling, trundled) If a vehicle **trundles** somewhere, it moves there slowly. ◇ If you **trundle** something like a wheelbarrow, you push it along slowly.

trunk ❏ The **trunk** of a tree is the large main stem which the branches grow from.

❏ Your **trunk** is the main part of your body, excluding your head, neck, arms, and legs.

❏ An elephant's **trunk** is its long nose.

❏ A **trunk** is also a large strong case or box with a hinged lid, used for storing or transporting things such as clothes.

❏ In the US, the boot of a car is called the **trunk**.

❏ Swimming **trunks** are a man's swimming costume, similar to briefs.

trunk call A **trunk call** is a long-distance telephone call.

trunk road A **trunk road** is a main road, especially one suitable for heavy vehicles.

truss (trusses, trussing, trussed) ❏ A **truss** is a device worn to support a hernia.

❑ A **truss** is also a framework of steel bars, used to support something like a roof or a bridge.

❑ A **truss** is also a cluster of flowers or fruit. ...*trusses of pinkish-white flowers.*

❑ If you **truss** a bird, you prepare it for cooking by tying its legs and wings. ◇ If a person is **trussed** or **trussed up**, they are tied up so they cannot move.

trust (trusting, trustingly) ❑ If you **trust** someone, you believe they are honest and sincere, and will not deliberately do anything to harm you. You can talk about your **trust** in someone like this. ...*children's trust in adults.* ◇ A **trusting** person tends to believe all people are honest and sincere and will not harm them. *He'd offered to help, and she'd trustingly gone with him.*

❑ **Trust** is also responsibility for things which are secret or important. ...*details on anyone employed in a position of trust.* ◇ If you **trust** someone to do something, you have confidence in their ability to do it. *I knew I could trust him to meet a tight deadline.*

❑ If you **trust** someone with something precious, you give it to them to look after. Similarly, if you **trust** someone with a secret, you tell it to them, believing they will not tell anyone else.

❑ If you **trust** someone's judgement or advice, you believe it is sound and you are prepared to act on it. ◇ If you **take** something someone tells you **on trust**, you accept it as being true without checking it.

❑ If you say you **trust** something is the case, you mean you hope it is the case. *I trust you are well.*

❑ A **trust** or **trust fund** is a financial arrangement in which a group of people or an organization looks after and invests money for someone else. See also **unit trust**. ◇ A **charitable trust** is a fund-raising registered charity. ◇ If money or property is held **in trust**, it is looked after and invested for someone by a group of people or an organization. *The money will be put in trust until she is 18.*

❑ In the US, a **trust** is a group of companies which illegally join together to control the market for their product.

trustee (trusteeship) A **trustee** is a person who is legally in control of money or property which is being looked after or invested for someone else. The position of trustee is called a **trusteeship**.

trustworthy (trustworthiness) A **trustworthy** person is honest and reliable. ...*trustworthy advice... ...doubts about his trustworthiness.*

trusty (trusties) A **trusty** person or thing can be relied on. ...*his trusty lieutenant... ...my trusty camera.* ◇ A person's **trusties** are people they can rely on. *He surrounded himself with trusties and cronies.*

truth ❑ The **truth** is the facts about something, rather than things which are made up. ◇ If you talk about the **truth** of something, you mean the fact that it is true. *I am absolutely certain of the truth of every one of the allegations.* ◇ If you say there is **truth** in what someone has said or written, you mean it is true, or partly true.

❑ A **truth** is an idea or principle which is generally accepted to be true.

truthful (truthfully, truthfulness) A **truthful** person is honest and tells the truth. *I answered all their questions truthfully... Truthfulness and rudeness are not to be confused.*

◇ A **truthful** statement is true, rather than made up. *She could not give him a truthful answer.*

try (tries, trying, tried) ❑ If you **try** to do something, you attempt to do it or make an effort to do it. An attempt to do something is called a **try**. *We mean to go back for another try.* ◇ If you **try** your **hand** at something, you attempt it. *The Government is doing its best to encourage ordinary homeowners to try their hand at becoming landlords.* ◇ **try** your **luck**: see **luck**.

❑ If you **try for** something, you make an effort to get it or achieve it. *Many of them will try for higher education... He tried for the presidency in 1988.*

❑ If you **try** something or **try** it **out**, you use it or do it to find out how useful, effective, or enjoyable it is. You can also say you give it a **try** or a **try-out**. *You could try placing an ad in a newspaper... The scheme gets its first try-out in Dorset.* See also **well-tried**.

❑ If you **try on** a piece of clothing, you put it on to see if it suits you or fits you.

❑ If you **try** a person or place, you go to them because they may be able to provide you with what you want. *They suggested we try the hotel shop.*

❑ If someone or something **tries your patience**, they make you angry or frustrated and you find it difficult not to lose your temper. You say someone or something like this is **trying**. ...*a trying experience.*

❑ If you say someone is **trying it on**, you mean they are doing something they should not do, to see if they can get away with it.

❑ When a person is **tried**, they appear in court, and a jury or magistrate decides if they are guilty, after hearing the evidence.

❑ When a rugby player scores a **try**, he puts the ball on the ground behind the opposing team's goal-line. A try scores four points in Rugby Union, three points in Rugby League.

try-out See **try**.

tryst (*usual pron:* trist) A **tryst** is a secret meeting between lovers.

tsar (*pron:* zahr) (*also spelled:* czar *or* tzar) The **tsar** was the emperor of Russia in former times.

tsarist (*also spelled:* czarist *or* tzarist) is used to talk about things to do with Russia before 1917, when it was ruled by a tsar. ...*the tsarist empire... ...the tsarist period.*

tsetse (*pron:* tset-see) (*plural:* tsetse) **Tsetse** or **tsetse flies** are African flies which feed on the blood of people or animals. Their bite can cause sleeping sickness in humans.

tub A **tub** is a wide circular container. ...*a tub of margarine... ...flower tubs.* ◇ People sometimes call a bath a **tub**. *She lay back in the tub.*

tuba The **tuba** is a large brass wind instrument which can produce some very low notes.

tubby A **tubby** person is rather fat.

tube ❑ A **tube** is a long hollow cylinder, especially one which air or a liquid passes through.

❑ A **tube** is also a narrow flexible container with a cap at one end, for holding a substance such as toothpaste.

❑ The London Underground is often called the **Tube**.

❑ In the US, television is often called the **tube**. ...*eyes glazed from too many hours in front of the tube.*

tuber A **tuber** is the swollen and fleshy root of a plant such as a potato or a dahlia.

tubercular means suffering from or caused by tuberculosis. *...a tubercular child... ...a tubercular cough.*

tuberculosis is an infectious disease which affects the lungs. 'Tuberculosis' is often shortened to 'TB'.

tubing is a tube or tubes. *...rubber tubing.*

tubular If something is **tubular,** it is shaped like a tube. *...tubular steel columns.*

TUC The TUC is an association of British trade unions. TUC stands for 'Trades Union Congress'.

tuck ❑ A **tuck** is a fold stitched in a garment.
❑ If you **tuck** something in a place like a pocket, you put it there, to keep it safe. ◇ If you **tuck** money **away,** you save it, rather than spending it. *...a worker who has some savings tucked away in the bank.*
❑ If something is **tucked away,** it is in a place where it cannot easily be found. *Berliners queue to get into the club, tucked away in the back streets of the city.*
❑ If you **tuck in** something such as a shirt, you put the loose ends inside your trousers or skirt. Similarly, you can **tuck in** bedclothes. If you **tuck** someone **in,** you make them comfortable in bed by arranging the blankets, and pushing the loose ends under the mattress.
❑ If you **tuck into** food, you eat it with a lot of pleasure. *Everyone tucked in.*

Tudor The Tudor period was from 1485 to 1603. **Tudor** is used to describe people and things from that period. *...Tudor composers... ...Tudor houses.*

tuft (tufted) A **tuft** of something like hair or grass is a bunch of it growing closely together. You say something which grows in tufts is **tufted.** *...tufted grass.*

tug (tugging, tugged) ❑ If you **tug** something, **tug at** it, or give it a **tug,** you give it a quick hard pull. *I tugged her arm... I felt a tug at my sleeve.*
❑ A **tug** or **tugboat** is a small powerful boat used to pull large ships.

tug-of-love is used to describe a situation in which the parents of a child are divorced, and the parent without custody tries to get possession of the child, for example by kidnapping it.

tug-of-war A **tug-of-war** is a contest in which two teams test their strength by pulling against each other on opposite ends of a rope. ◇ You can call any situation in which two people or groups are trying hard to get an advantage over each other a **tug-of-war.** *...a diplomatic tug-of-war between China and Taiwan.*

tugboat See tug.

tuition is the teaching of a subject, especially to one person or a small group. *...individual tuition... ...tuition fees.*

tulip Tulips are brightly coloured cup-shaped flowers with long stems, which grow in spring.

tulle (*pron:* tewl) is a fine net-like material made of silk or nylon, used to make dresses and veils.

tum See tummy.

tumble (tumbling, tumbled) ❑ If you **tumble,** you fall. A **tumble** is a fall.
❑ If an amount or value **tumbles,** it falls rapidly. *The shares tumbled 12p to 67p within minutes of the news.*
❑ If water **tumbles,** it flows quickly over an uneven surface, splashing a lot.
❑ If you **tumble to** something, you suddenly understand it, or realize what is happening.

tumble dryer (*or* tumble drier) A **tumble dryer** is a machine in which washing is dried inside a rotating drum, heated by hot air.

tumbledown A **tumbledown** building is in very bad condition, and is partly falling down.

tumbler ❑ A **tumbler** is a drinking glass with straight sides.
❑ A **tumbler** is also an acrobat who performs on a flat surface such as a stage, often with other members of a group.

tumbril A **tumbril** is a farm cart, used during the French Revolution to transport prisoners to the guillotine.

tummy (tummies) A person's **tummy** or their **tum** is their stomach.

tumour (*American spelling:* tumor) A **tumour** is a mass of diseased or abnormal cells which has grown in a person's or animal's body. *...a brain tumour... ...a breast tumour.*

tumult (*pron:* tew-mult) A **tumult** is a lot of noise caused by a crowd of people. *Amid the tumult, she jumped into her car and fled.* ◇ A **tumult** is also a lot of discussion and argument about something in the news. *...the recent tumult over the behaviour of the young royals.*

tumultuous behaviour is very noisy, because people are happy, enthusiastic, or excited. *...tumultuous applause... He was given a tumultuous welcome.*
❑ A **tumultuous** time is one when a lot of exciting and confusing things are happening. *...the tumultuous years between 1965 and 1974.*

tumulus (*pron:* tew-mew-luss) (*plural:* tumuli) A **tumulus** is an ancient burial mound.

tuna (*plural:* tuna) **Tuna** or **tuna fish** are large edible sea fish.

tundra The **tundra** is a flat treeless Arctic region where the ground below the top layer of soil is always frozen.

tune (tuning, tuned) ❑ A **tune** is a series of musical notes arranged in a satisfying or memorable way.
❑ If you sing or play a piece of music **in tune,** you produce exactly the right notes. If you sing or play **out of tune,** some of the notes are wrong.
❑ If you **tune** an instrument like a guitar, you adjust the strings, so they have the correct pitch in relation to each other. Similarly, when musicians **tune** their instruments or **tune up,** they adjust their instruments so that each musician is producing the correct pitch in relation to the other musicians.
❑ If you **tune** an engine or machine, you adjust it so that it works as it is supposed to.
❑ If you **tune** to a TV or radio station or programme or **tune in** to it, you turn or press the controls on your TV or radio to receive it. *More than 6 million youngsters tune in to 'Blockbusters' every day.* If your TV or radio is **tuned** to a station or programme, the controls have been adjusted so you can receive it. *...a short-wave radio, tuned to the BBC World Service.*
❑ If a political leader is **in tune** with the feelings or thoughts of a group of people, he or she thinks in a similar way and is likely to do what they want.
❑ The person who **calls the tune** in a certain situation is the one who gives the orders.
❑ If you **change** your **tune,** you say or do something different from what you previously said or did.

❏ To the **tune of** a sum of money means amounting to that sum. ...*losses to the tune of almost $1 billion.*

tuneful (tunefulness) A **tuneful** piece of music is full of good tunes. ...*one of the few ballet scores able to match Tchaikovsky's for sheer tunefulness.*

tuneless music has no tunes in it. **Tuneless** singing is out of tune. *They broke into a tuneless rendition of 'Rule Britannia'.*

tuner ❏ A **tuner** is a piece of equipment you adjust to receive TV or radio signals.

❏ A piano **tuner** is a person whose job is tuning pianos.

tungsten is a greyish-white metal used to make light bulb filaments and to harden steel.

tunic In ancient Greece and Rome, a **tunic** was a loose-fitting sleeveless garment worn by men and women. ◇ Nowadays, a **tunic** or **tunic top** is a woman's loose-fitting blouse or jumper. ◇ A **tunic** is also a close-fitting jacket worn as part of a uniform.

tuning fork A **tuning fork** is a two-pronged steel fork used when tuning an instrument like a piano or harp. When you strike it, it produces a clear note of a fixed pitch.

tunnel (tunnelling, tunnelled) (*American spelling:* tunneling, tunneled) A **tunnel** is a long underground passage, especially one for trains or other vehicles to travel through. When people **tunnel** somewhere, they dig a tunnel. ◇ **light at the end of the tunnel:** see **light**.

tunnel vision is a condition in which you are unable to see things which are not straight in front of you.

❏ If you say someone has **tunnel vision,** you mean they have a narrow point of view, caused by concentrating on just one aspect of something. ...*the government, with its tunnel vision firmly locked upon the objective of low inflation.*

tunny (*plural:* tunnies *or* tunny) is an old name for tuna.

tuppence is two old pence.

Tupperware is a range of plastic containers used to store food. 'Tupperware' is a trademark.

turban (turbaned *or* turbanned) A **turban** is a traditional head-covering worn by some men in parts of Asia, North Africa, and the Middle East, often to show their religion or rank. It consists of a long piece of cloth wound round and round the head. If a man is **turbaned,** he is wearing a turban. ...*a turbaned Sikh.*

turbine A **turbine** is a machine or engine driven by water, wind, gas, or steam turning the blades of a wheel. ...*gas turbines.*

turbo (turbos) See **turbocharger.**

turbo-prop (*or* turboprop) A **turbo-prop** aircraft or **turbo-prop** has propellers driven by gas turbine engines called **turbo-prop** engines.

turbocharger (turbocharged) (*or* turbo-charger, turbo-charged) A **turbocharger** or **turbo** is a turbine-driven fan which increases an engine's power by blowing the fuel vapour into it at a higher pressure than usual. A **turbocharged** engine or vehicle is fitted with a turbocharger. Engines and vehicles like these are often just called **turbos.**

turbofan A **turbofan** or **turbofan** engine is an aircraft engine which sucks air in at the front and forces it out at the back, to increase the thrust.

turboprop See **turbo-prop.**

turbot (*plural:* turbot) **Turbot** are large flat edible sea-fish.

turbulent (turbulence) ❏ A **turbulent** period is one when there is a lot of change and confusion. You talk about the **turbulence** of a period like this. ...*the turbulent 1960s... ...the turbulence of the past four years.*

❏ **Turbulent** air or water contains strong currents which change direction suddenly. You talk about **turbulence** in air or water. ...*the turbulent seas off Iceland... His plane encountered severe turbulence.*

turd A **turd** is a lump of faeces.

tureen (*pron:* tyu-reen) A **tureen** is a large covered dish for serving soup or vegetables.

turf is short thick even grass.

❏ Your **turf** is your territory, or an area of activity which you think is exclusively yours. *Advertising companies saw their turf invaded by an agency with no experience in advertising.*

❏ If you **turf** someone **out,** you force them to leave a place.

turgid (*pron:* tur-jid) A **turgid** speech or piece of writing is long and boring.

Turk A **Turk** is someone who comes from Turkey.

turkey ❏ A **turkey** is a large bird bred for its meat. **Turkey** is the meat of a turkey.

❏ People say a a film or play is a **turkey** when it is an artistic or financial failure. ...*a box office turkey.*

❏ You call a contest a **turkey shoot** when it is very one-sided.

❏ See also **cold turkey.**

Turkish is used to talk about people and things in or from Turkey. ...*a Turkish businessman.* ◇ **Turkish** is the main language spoken in Turkey.

Turkish bath A **Turkish bath** is a health treatment which involves sitting in a hot dry room, then a steamy room, then having a wash, massage, and cold shower. A **Turkish bath** is also a place where you can have a Turkish bath.

Turkish delight is a jelly-like sweet coated in icing sugar.

turmeric is a mild yellow spice used in Indian cooking.

turmoil is a state of anxiety, confusion, and disorder. *Financial markets everywhere are in turmoil.*

turn ❏ If you **turn,** you move all or part of your body so you are facing in a different direction. ◇ If you **turn** your head, you look to the left or right. You call a movement like this a **turn** of the head. ◇ **turn** your **back:** see **back.**

❏ You also say you **turn** when you change the direction you are moving in. Similarly, a vehicle can **turn.** *Turn left at the traffic lights... The plane turned round and returned to Leningrad.* ◇ If you **turn off** a road, you start going along a different road leading from it. A **turning** is a road leading away from another road. A **turn-off** is a road leading away from a major road or a motorway. ...*the M20 turn-off.*

❏ When you **turn** a corner, you go round it. ◇ If you say someone or something has **turned the corner,** you mean their fortunes have started to improve after they had been getting worse.

❏ If you **turn back** when you are travelling somewhere, you stop and go back towards the place you came from. You can also say someone is **turned back** at something like a border.

❏ If you **turn** something, you move or rotate it so the front or top part is facing in a different direction. *He turned* the chair around... She turned the page.

❏ When you turn a knob, key, or handle or give it a turn, you twist it, to open something, lock something, or start something working. The engine started at the first turn of the key.

❏ If you turn something on or off, you switch it on or off. If you turn out a light, you switch it off. ◇ If you turn down something like a TV, radio, or heater, you reduce the amount of sound or heat coming out of it. You also say you turn down the sound or heat. Similarly, you can turn up any of these things.

❏ If you turn to something, you start becoming involved with it. More young people are turning to crime. ◇ If you turn your attention or thoughts to something, you start thinking about it.

❏ If you turn something over in your mind, you think carefully about it.

❏ If you turn to someone for help, advice, or support, you go to them for it.

❏ If you do someone a good turn, you do something to help them.

❏ When something turns or is turned into something else, it changes into it. The water turns to steam for the turbine... ...an academic turned journalist.

❏ If something turns a particular colour, it becomes that colour. The sky turned black.

❏ A turn is a change in the way something is happening or being done. Experts fear the bombing could mark a new turn in the campaign... ...a remarkable turn of events. ◇ If things take a turn for the better or take a turn for the worse, they get better or worse.

❏ When a group of people take turns to do something, they do it one after the other in a fixed order. You say each of them does it in turn. If it is someone's turn to do it, they are the next person in the group to do it. She directed the final question to each child in turn... It was my turn to look after Kate.

❏ When you turn a particular age, you pass that age. Similarly, if it turns a particular time, it passes that time. It had just turned twelve.

❏ The turn of the century is the very last part of one century and the beginning of the next one. Similarly, you can talk about the turn of the year.

❏ If you are turned on by someone or something, you are sexually aroused by them. You can say something which has this effect is a turn-on. While leather may be a turn-on for many men, it arouses few women. ◇ If you are turned off by someone or something, you do not find them attractive or appealing. You say something which is unattractive or unappealing is a turn-off. His enthusiasm for high taxes has proved a turn-off for the voters.

❏ If you turn against someone, you start to dislike or distrust them, or to treat them as an enemy. The Conservative press turned against him... She feared that she would turn her daughter against her. ◇ If someone turns on you, they suddenly attack you, or start criticizing you.

❏ If you turn down a request or offer, you refuse it or reject it. The district council agreed with the objectors and turned down the application. ◇ If you turn someone away, you refuse to let them enter a place. The top business schools turn away an average of three MBA applicants for every one they accept. ◇ If you are turned out of a place, you are forced to leave.

❏ You say someone turns up when they arrive somewhere. He turned up for his interview half an hour late. ◇ If something turns up, it is discovered somewhere. The four-foot high urns, valued at £10,000, turned up in a London antiques shop.

❏ If people turn out for an event or activity, they go and watch it or take part in it. Only a third of the electorate are expected to turn out to vote. See also turnout.

❏ If you turn in, you go to bed.

❏ If you turn something over to someone, you hand it to them. He threatened to turn the tapes over to the international news agencies. ◇ If you turn someone in, you give them up to the police or authorities.

❏ You can describe what happens in a situation by saying things turn out in a particular way. Everything turned out well. ◇ If someone or something turns out to be a particular thing, they are discovered to be that thing. It turned out to be a hoax... He turned out to be a middle-aged salesman.

❏ If a firm turns out a product, it produces it in large quantities. The factory turns out 380,000 fridges a year.

❏ You can describe what someone is wearing by saying they are turned out in a particular way. ...a cluster of residents turned out in their Sunday best.

❏ If you turn out your pockets, you empty them.

turn-off See turn.

turn-on See turn.

turn-up ❏ The turn-ups on a pair of trousers are the ends of the trouser legs, which are folded upwards on the outside.

❏ If you say something is a turn-up or a turn-up for the books, you mean it is very surprising.

turnabout See turnaround.

turnaround ❏ A turnaround or turnabout is a change in a politician's or government's attitude or policy. He praised Brazil's turnaround in attitudes towards conservation of the Amazon rainforests.

❏ A turnaround or turnround is a sudden change in a situation, either for better or for worse. We may be on the verge of a turnaround in the labour market.

turncoat You say someone is a turncoat when they leave your group or organization and join an opposing one.

turning point A turning point is a time when an important change takes place in something. This was to be a turning point in his career... The turning point for Sino-Soviet relations came in 1982.

turnip Turnips are round root vegetables with white or yellow skins.

turnout The turnout at an event is the number of people who come to it. Organisers said they were disappointed by the turnout. ◇ The turnout in an election is the number of people who vote. The turnout is expected to be high.

turnover The turnover of people in an organization is the rate at which people leave and are replaced. The turnover is particularly high among junior grades. ◇ The turnover of a business is the value of goods or services sold over a particular period. Annual turnover has grown from £17,000 to more than £250,000.

turnround See turnaround.

turnstile A turnstile is a revolving barrier which allows only one person at a time to pass through it.

turntable A turntable is a revolving circular platform, especially the flat round part of a record player which you put a record on.

turpentine is a strong-smelling colourless liquid used to clean paint off brushes. 'Turpentine' is often shortened to 'turps'.

turpitude is wicked or depraved behaviour.

turps See turpentine.

turquoise A turquoise is an opaque greenish-blue gemstone. ◇ Turquoise is a greenish-blue colour.

turret (turreted) ❏ A turret is a small tower on top of a building or wall. If a building or wall has turrets, you say it is turreted. ...a turreted castle.
❏ A turret is also a revolving structure on a tank or warship, on which a gun is mounted.

turtle Turtles are reptiles similar to tortoises, which live mainly in water. Some turtles are very large.

turtleneck A turtleneck sweater has a high round close-fitting neck, which you can roll down.

tusk The tusks of an elephant, wild boar, or walrus are its two very long pointed teeth.

tussle (tussling, tussled) ❏ A tussle is a fight involving several people. When people fight, you can say they tussle. *They made their displeasure known by ripping down perimeter fencing and tussling with security staff.*
❏ If you tussle with a difficult problem, you try hard to solve it.

tussock A tussock is a thick clump of grass.

tut (tutting, tutted) If you tut or tut-tut, you make a clicking sound with your tongue to show disapproval or sympathy. *The waitress tutted sympathetically... There is a lot of tut-tutting about how slack behaviour has become.*

tutelage (*pron:* tew-till-lij) is guidance or instruction. *Under his tutelage, Wales completed the Grand Slam twice.*

tutor (tutoring, tutored) A tutor is a teacher at a college or university. You say someone like this tutors a subject or a group of students. *Dr Howe was to have tutored in English literature.* ◇ A tutor is also a private teacher. You say someone like this tutors a particular pupil. *His father tutored Ganesh from the age of five.*

tutorial A tutorial is a teaching session involving a university tutor and a small group of students.

tutti frutti is ice cream containing small pieces of preserved fruit.

tutu (*pron:* too-too) A tutu is a short stiff skirt made of many layers of material, worn by a female ballet dancer.

tuxedo (tuxedos) In the US, a dinner jacket is called a tuxedo.

TV See television.

twaddle If you call what someone says twaddle, you mean it is nonsense.

twain is an old word meaning 'two'. *Never the twain shall meet.*

twang ❏ A twang is a sound like a wire being pulled then released. If you twang something, you pull it and release it to make a sound like this.
❏ A twang is also an accent. ...a gruff Glaswegian twang.

tweak (tweaking, tweaked) ❏ If you tweak something or give it a tweak, you hold it between your finger and thumb and twist or pull it. *She tweaked his ear.*
❏ If you tweak something like a plan or give it a tweak, you make a slight adjustment to it. ...*ways of tweaking conventional economic ideas to incorporate the occasional environ-*

mental constraint... ...tweaks to the Maastricht treaty.

twee If you say something is twee, you mean it is supposed to be pretty but you find it sentimental and in bad taste.

tweed is a type of thick woollen cloth used to make clothes. Tweeds are outdoor clothes, especially a suit, made of tweed. ...a rosy-cheeked lady in tweeds.

tweedy clothes are made of tweed. People who wear tweeds are sometimes called tweedy, especially upper-class people who live in the country.

tweet (tweeting, tweeted) When a bird tweets, it makes a series of high-pitched sounds.

tweezers are a small tool for pulling out hairs or picking up small objects.

twelve (twelfth) Twelve is the number 12.

twentieth The twentieth item in a series is the one counted as number 20. ◇ A twentieth or one twentieth is the fraction $\frac{1}{20}$.

twenty (twenties) Twenty is the number 20. ◇ The twenties was the period from 1920 to 1929. ◇ If someone is in their twenties, they are aged 20 to 29.

twice means two times. *He was married twice... ...an area twice the size of Paris.*

twiddle (twiddling, twiddled) ❏ If you twiddle something or twiddle with it, you twist or turn it with your fingers. *She twiddled a knob on the dashboard.*
❏ If you are twiddling your thumbs, you have nothing to do. *50,000 workers will be left twiddling their thumbs.*

twig (twigging, twigged) ❏ A twig is a very small branch of a tree or bush.
❏ If you twig something, you realize or understand it.

twilight is the period just before the sun rises, or just after it sets, when there is a soft light in the sky. This light can also be called twilight.
❏ The twilight of something is the period when it is coming to an end. *Both men are in the twilight of their careers... ...the twilight years of the Soviet Union.*

twill is cloth woven in a way which produces diagonal lines or ridges across it.

twin (twinning, twinned) ❏ Twins are two children born at the same time to the same mother.
❏ You can use twin to describe a pair of things. ...Wembley's twin towers... ...the twin objectives of full employment and stable prices.
❏ If a town is twinned with one in another country, the two towns have a friendly relationship and people from each town regularly visit the other one. A town's twin town is the town it is twinned with.

twin-set See twinset.

twin-tub A twin-tub is a washing machine which has one section for washing clothes and another for spin-drying them.

twine (twining, twined) ❏ Twine is strong smooth string.
❏ If you twine something round something else, you twist it or coil it round it. *She had a habit of twining a strand of hair around her finger.*

twinge A twinge is a sudden sharp feeling of pain or of an emotion. ...a twinge of loneliness.

twinkle (twinkling, twinkled) ❏ If something twinkles, it shines brightly with a small flickering light. A light like this is called a twinkle. ...twinkling stars.
❏ If you do something in the twinkling of an eye, you

do it very quickly.

twinset (*or* twin-set) A twinset is a woman's matching jumper and cardigan.

twirl If something twirls or is twirled, it turns round several times. *He twirled his bat.* ◇ If you twirl when you are dancing, you spin round.

twist ❏ If you twist something or give it a twist, you turn one end of it, while holding the other end still. ◇ If you twist part of your body, you turn it while keeping the rest of your body still. *He twisted his head to the right... She twisted round in the saddle.* ◇ If you twist your ankle or knee, you injure it by turning it too sharply in an unusual direction.

❏ If metal is twisted, it is bent out of shape, as a result of heat, an explosion, or a collision.

❏ A twist is a twisted piece of something. ...*a twist of silk ribbon.*

❏ If a road or river twists, it bends sharply. A sharp bend in a road or river can be called a twist. ...*a twisting mountain road... He had every twist of the river committed to memory.*

❏ If you say a person's mind or behaviour is twisted, you mean they think or behave in an unpleasant and unnatural way. ...*the workings of a twisted mind.*

❏ If someone twists what you say, they distort it. Similarly, you can talk about someone twisting facts or the truth. *Mr Farrakhan says his words were twisted by the media.*

❏ If someone twists your arm, they put pressure on you to do something. *After a good deal of White House arm-twisting, the bill was endorsed without debate.*

❏ A twist is also an unexpected development in a story or film.

twister A twister is a dishonest person who deliberately deceives people.

twisty A twisty road or river has many sharp bends.

twit (twitting, twitted) ❏ A twit is a silly person.

❏ If you twit someone, you make fun of them.

twitch (twitches, twitching, twitched) If someone twitches, they make little jerky movements which they cannot control. You say someone like this has a twitch. ◇ If you twitch something, you make it move slightly with a jerky motion. *He twitched his shoulders.*

twitcher Twitchers are bird-watchers who concentrate on spotting rare species, which they tick off on a list, like train-spotters.

twitchy (twitchiness) If you say someone is twitchy, you mean they are anxious or nervous. *Dealers are twitchy about the trading statement due out tomorrow... Some brokers were beginning to show twitchiness about placing business with the company.*

twitter (twittering, twittered) When birds twitter, they make short high-pitched noises. ◇ You can say people twitter when they speak in excited high-pitched voices.

two is the number 2.

❏ If you put two and two together, you work out the truth about something from what you see or hear, often when people are trying to conceal things.

two-bit People use two-bit to describe someone or something they think is of little importance. ...*some two-bit artist.*

two-dimensional ❏ A two-dimensional shape is a shape like a square or circle which can be measured in two di-rections only, as distinct from a three-dimensional shape like a cube or cylinder.

❏ If you say a character in a book or play is two-dimensional, you mean everything about them is too simple and obvious and they do not seem like a real person. Similarly, you can say an actor's performance is two-dimensional.

two-edged ❏ If something is two-edged, it has two opposite sides or aspects. ...*a two-edged argument.*

❏ If you call something a two-edged sword, you mean it has disadvantages as well as advantages. *Firepower proved a two-edged sword, as it destroyed the country US forces were pledged to protect.*

two-faced If you say someone is two-faced, you mean they are not sincere or honest in the things they do and say.

two-stroke engines deliver power in one up-and-down movement of a piston, rather than two.

two-way means moving or working in two opposite directions. ...*two-way traffic... ...a two-way radio.*

twofold If something is twofold, it has two parts. *The answer is twofold.* ◇ If there is a twofold increase in something, it doubles in size.

twosome A twosome is two people, especially a couple. *We hardly ever spent time together doing things as a twosome.*

tycoon A tycoon is a rich powerful businessman.

tyke (*or* tike) A tyke is a small mischievous child.

type (typing, typed) ❏ A type of something is one kind of it. ...*a series of leaflets covering different types of work... ...suitable for all skin types.*

❏ You can describe a person as a particular type. *He was a quiet type... ...intellectual types.* ◇ If you say someone is not your type, you mean they are not the sort of person you find interesting or attractive.

❏ If you type something, you write it using a typewriter or word processor. ◇ If you type up handwritten material, you produce a typed copy of it.

❏ If you type something into a computer or word processor, you put it in by pressing keys on the keyboard.

❏ Type is used to talk about the size or style of printing used in a book or newspaper. *The type is larger and there is more colour.*

typecast (typecasting) If an actor or actress is typecast, they keep being given the same kind of roles to play. *She is desperate to avoid typecasting.*

typeface The typeface in a book or newspaper is the style of printing in it.

typescript A typescript is a typed copy of a piece of writing.

typeset (typesetting, typeset *not* 'typesetted'; typesetter) When a piece of writing is typeset, it is arranged so it is ready for printing. Arranging a piece of writing for printing is called typesetting; the person or machine that does it is called a typesetter.

typewriter A typewriter is a machine with keys, which you press to produce print on a piece of paper.

typewritten If something is typewritten, it has been typed on a typewriter or word processor.

typhoid or typhoid fever is an infectious disease spread by contaminated food or water. It causes fever and diarrhoea, and can be fatal.

typhoon A **typhoon** is a violent tropical storm or hurricane in the China Seas or western Pacific.

typhus is an infectious disease spread by lice, fleas, or mites.

typical (typically) ❑ **Typical** and **typically** are used to say something shows the usual characteristics of a person or thing. *...a typical summer day... This is a typically brave and selfless decision by the Prime Minister.*

❑ **Typically** is also used to say what normally happens in particular circumstances. *Typically, the cause of death will be entered in the medical records as 'cardiac arrest'.*

typify (typifies, typifying, typified) If someone or something **typifies** a certain thing, they are a typical example of it. *He typified a certain kind of British comedy.*

typist A **typist** is a person whose job is typing.

typographical is used to talk about things to do with the way printed material is arranged or presented. *...a typographical error.*

typography (typographer) **Typography** is the arranging and preparing of printed material, ready for printing. A **typographer** is a person who does this kind of work.

tyrannical A **tyrannical** person or government acts cruelly and unjustly towards the people they have authority over.

tyrannize (tyrannizing, tyrannized) *(can be spelled with an 's' instead of a 'z')* If someone **tyrannizes** you, they treat you cruelly and unjustly.

tyranny (tyrannies) ❑ **Tyranny** is cruel and unjust rule by a person or government. A cruel unjust government can be called a **tyranny**.

❑ You can talk about the **tyranny** of something when it makes severe demands on people in their work or daily life. *...the tyranny of daily, if not hourly, deadlines.*

tyrant A **tyrant** is a person, especially a ruler, who treats the people he or she has authority over cruelly and unjustly.

tyre *(American spelling:* **tire***)* A **tyre** is a thick rubber ring filled with air, fitted round the wheel of a vehicle.

tyro (tyros) A **tyro** is someone who is just beginning to learn something. *...a tyro journalist.*

tzar See tsar.

tzarist See tsarist.

U u

U-boat U-boats were German submarines used in the two World Wars.

U-turn When a politician or government does a **U-turn**, they abandon a policy they had embarked on and start doing its opposite. ◇ When a vehicle performs a U-turn, it turns through a half-circle and goes off in the direction it has just come from.

UB40 A **UB40** is a registration card given to someone who is unemployed.

ubiquitous *(pron: yew-bik-wit-uss)* (ubiquity) You say things of a certain kind are **ubiquitous** when you seem to see them everywhere. *Fax machines existed for 30 years before a fall in their price and size made them ubiquitous.* You can talk about the **ubiquity** of things like these.

udder A cow's **udders** are the large bag-like parts of its body which hang down near its back legs and produce milk.

UDI *(pronounce each letter separately)* If a colony or other place declares **UDI**, the people there formally announce that they are an independent country and that they are no longer ruled by another country. UDI stands for 'Unilateral Declaration of Independence'.

UFO *(pronounce each letter separately)* UFOs are strange objects seen in the sky which some people think are spaceships from other planets. UFO stands for 'unidentified flying object'.

ugly (uglier, ugliest; ugliness) **Ugly** people and things are unattractive to look at. *These two buildings are the last word in concrete ugliness.* ◇ You call a situation **ugly** when it involves unpleasantness and violence.

UHT stands for 'ultra heat treated'. It is used to describe milk and other foods which have been treated at a very high temperature so they will keep for a long time if their container is not opened.

UK See United Kingdom.

ulcer An **ulcer** is a painful open sore on the skin or inside the body.

ulna The **ulna** is the inner and longer of the two bones in the human forearm. See also radius.

ulterior If you say someone has an **ulterior** motive for doing something, you mean they have a hidden reason for it.

ultimate ❑ The **ultimate** aim of a series of actions is what they are finally intended to achieve. The **ultimate** result of a series of events is what finally happens as a result of them.

❑ **Ultimate** is used to describe the best, most important, or most powerful thing of a particular kind. *It is the result of seven years of tinkering towards the ultimate bicycle... National will and moral courage are the ultimate means of defeating terrorism.*

ultimately is used to say something happens after a long series of events or after a long time. *A tightening of the monetary screw would ultimately lead to sharper base rate cuts.* ◇ You also use **ultimately** when you are mentioning the final or strongest effect of something. *When they get down to the business of storytelling, this is an engrossing and ultimately moving meditation on death.*

❑ You also use **ultimately** when you are mentioning something which is essential if something else is to succeed. *Future computing ultimately depends on hardware.*

ultimatum An **ultimatum** is a warning that unless someone does a certain thing, action will be taken against them.

ultra- is added to words to talk about an extreme form of something. ...*ultra-small computers*... *It is expected that he will attract support from the two ultra-orthodox groups.*

ultramarine is a very bright blue colour.

ultrasonic (ultrasound) Ultrasonic sounds have very high frequencies which human beings cannot hear. Ultrasonic sound waves are sometimes called **ultrasound**. They have various uses in medicine.

ultraviolet light or radiation is invisible to humans. It comes from the violet end of the spectrum, and is produced, for example, by the sun or by special kinds of lamps. It can harm the skin.

umbilical cord (*pron:* um-bill-ik-al) The **umbilical cord** is the tube connecting an unborn baby to its mother, through which it gets oxygen and food. ◇ You can call any system which provides a place or organization with the things it needs an **umbilical cord**. ...*the 15,000 lorries that make up the umbilical cord that nourishes the Jordanian economy*... *From January 1, Channel 4's umbilical cord to ITV will be cut.*

umbrage If someone takes **umbrage** at something you say or do, they feel upset, annoyed, or hurt by it.

umbrella ❑ An **umbrella** is a device consisting of a long stick with a folding cloth-covered frame at one end, which you take with you to protect you from the rain. ◇ An **umbrella** is also a similar, larger device which you sit or lie under and which provides shade from the sun.
❑ Any arrangement which provides protection for people can be called an **umbrella**. *What protection does exist is afforded under the umbrella of race legislation.*
❑ An **umbrella** organization exists to co-ordinate the work of all organizations of a certain type. ...*the umbrella body for the province's charities.*

umlaut (*pron:* um-lout) The **umlaut** is a two-dot symbol sometimes written over 'a', 'o', or 'u' in German and over certain letters in some other languages. It indicates a change in the pronunciation of the letter. *Honecker's favourite opera was Weber's Der Freischütz.*

umpire (umpiring, umpired) The **umpire** in a game like cricket or tennis is the person who supervises a match and makes sure the rules are not broken. You say this person **umpires** the match.

umpteen (umpteenth) **Umpteen** things means a very large number of them. *He has produced umpteen books, plays and television series.* ◇ If you say something happens for the **umpteenth** time, you mean it happens yet again, when it has happened many times before. Similarly, you can talk about something being the **umpteenth** thing in a series.

UN See United Nations.

unabashed If someone is **unabashed** about what they say, do, or feel, they are not at all ashamed or embarrassed by it.

unabated If something continues **unabated**, it goes on just as much as ever. *Amnesty says human rights abuses and torture continue unabated.*

unable If you are **unable** to do something, you cannot do it, for example because you do not have the skill or because something is preventing you.

unacceptable (unacceptably) If you say something is **unacceptable**, you mean you disapprove of it and feel it should not happen. *Inflation is unacceptably high.*

unaccompanied ❑ If you are **unaccompanied**, you have nobody with you. ◇ **Unaccompanied** luggage, goods, or other objects are being sent somewhere separately from the person who owns them.
❑ An **unaccompanied** piece of music is played by a single instrument or is sung by a singer or choir without any instruments playing with them.

unaccountable (unaccountably) ❑ If you say something is **unaccountable**, you mean there does not seem to be any explanation for it. *Pathe's shares unaccountably jumped one third in value in two days.*
❑ **Unaccountable** people or organizations do not have to explain or justify their actions to anyone else.

unaccounted If people or things are **unaccounted** for, it is not known where they are or what has happened to them.

unaccustomed If you are **unaccustomed** to something, you are not used to it. ◇ If someone behaves in an **unaccustomed** way, they behave in a way they do not usually behave.

unacknowledged ❑ If a fact or situation is **unacknowledged**, it is ignored or not accepted as true. ◇ If your qualities or achievements are **unacknowledged**, they are not officially recognized. You can also say, for example, that someone is an **unacknowledged** genius or an **unacknowledged** hero.
❑ If you are **unacknowledged** when you arrive somewhere, nobody seems to know you or recognize you.

unadorned If you describe something as **unadorned**, you mean it is simple and plain, rather than having extra things added to it to make it more attractive. ...*unadorned stone buildings.*

unadulterated is used to say something is in its pure form and has not been changed in any way. ...*unadulterated honey*... ...*Soviet communism, now surviving in its unadulterated form only in North Korea and Cuba* ◇ **Unadulterated** is also used to say how bad something is. ...*ninety minutes of pure unadulterated rubbish.*

unaffected If something is **unaffected** by something else, it is not affected by it.

unaided If you do something **unaided**, you do it without help from anyone else.

unalloyed feelings are not spoiled or made less intense by being mixed with other feelings. *The business world has greeted the interest rate cut with unalloyed relief.*

unalterable things cannot be changed.

unaltered If something is **unaltered**, it has not been changed.

unambiguous (unambiguously) An **unambiguous** statement has only one possible meaning. *He had failed to condemn the attack unambiguously.*

unambitious An **unambitious** person does not want to change their way of life or get a better job. ◇ You say something like a plan is **unambitious** when it does not set out to achieve very much.

unanimous (*pron:* yew-nan-im-uss) (unanimously, unanimity) If a group of people are **unanimous**, they all agree about something. When this happens, you say there is **unanimity** (*pron:* yew-nan-**nim**-it-ee) among them. *The resolution was passed unanimously.*

unannounced If you arrive somewhere **unannounced**, you do not tell anyone you are coming. *This was an* *unannounced visit.*

unanswerable An **unanswerable** question is one nobody can answer. ◇ If you say something like an argument is **unanswerable**, you mean it is so obviously correct that nobody could disagree with it.

unanswered questions or letters have not been answered.

unappealing If you say something is **unappealing**, you mean it creates such a poor impression that nobody will want to have it or be involved with it.

unappetizing (*or* **unappetising**) food is unpleasant to eat, or looks as though it might be.

unapproachable people are difficult to talk to and are not friendly.

unarguable (**unarguably**) If you say something is **unarguable**, you mean there can be no doubt about it. *This is unarguably wonderful music.*

unarmed people are not carrying any weapons.

unashamed (**unashamedly**) **Unashamed** is used to describe someone's behaviour when they do something openly which other people find shocking or unacceptable. *...the unashamed use of superior force to exterminate whole peoples... We unashamedly wooed the media.*

unasked An **unasked** question is one nobody has asked, although it may be in many people's minds. ◇ If you do something **unasked**, you do it without being asked to.

unassailable If some advantage you have gained is **unassailable**, it cannot be taken away from you. *Australia have an unassailable 3-1 lead over New Zealand.*

unassuming people are modest and quiet.

unattached If you say someone is **unattached**, you mean they are not married, do not have a regular partner, or are doing something on their own rather than as a member of a group.

unattended An **unattended** vehicle or piece of luggage has been left with nobody looking after it.

unattractive people are unpleasant to look at, or unpleasant in the way they behave. Similarly, an **unattractive** place is unpleasant to look at or be in. ❑ If you say something like an idea or plan is **unattractive**, you mean it does not appeal to you and you do not want to be involved with it.

unauthorized (*or* **unauthorised**) actions do not have official permission. *...unauthorized visits.* An **unauthorized** person does not have official permission to do something.

unavailable If something is **unavailable**, you cannot obtain it. ◇ If a person is **unavailable**, they are unable to meet you and talk to you. *Dwyer was unavailable for comment.*

unavailing An **unavailing** attempt to do something does not succeed.

unavoidable (**unavoidably**) If something is **unavoidable**, it cannot be avoided or prevented. *Mr Major acknowledged that Britain might be heading unavoidably into a recession.*

unaware If you are **unaware** of something, you do not know it exists or is happening.

unawares If something catches you **unawares**, it happens when you are not expecting it.

unbalance (**unbalancing**, **unbalanced**) ❑ If you say someone is **unbalanced**, you mean they are slightly mad.

❑ If you say something like a report is **unbalanced**, you mean it emphasizes some aspects of a situation and ignores others, and is therefore unfair or inaccurate. You can also say it gives an **unbalanced** view of a situation. ◇ If you say something like the membership of a committee is **unbalanced**, you mean there are too many people in it representing one point of view.

❑ If something **unbalances** a system, it upsets it and stops it working properly.

unbearable (**unbearably**) If you say something is **unbearable**, you mean it is so unpleasant, painful, or upsetting you cannot accept it or cope with it. *Pressure on young people is sometimes unbearably intense.*

unbeatable If a person or team is in an **unbeatable** position in a contest or competition, they are certain to win. ◇ If you say something is **unbeatable**, you mean it is the best thing of its kind. *As a farm dog, the border collie is unbeatable.*

unbeaten If a sportsperson or team is **unbeaten** in a certain number of games or matches or has had an **unbeaten** run, they have not been defeated. ◇ An **unbeaten** record is one which nobody has ever beaten.

unbecoming A person's behaviour is described as **unbecoming** when it is thought to be shocking and not the sort of behaviour expected from someone in their position.

unbeknown (*or* **unbeknownst**) If something happens **unbeknown** to you, you do not know anything about it.

unbelievable (**unbelievably**) **Unbelievable** is used to say something is amazingly large, or amazingly good or bad. *The bravery of the staff is unbelievable... When I remonstrated, he was unbelievably offensive.* ◇ If you say a story or report is **unbelievable**, you mean it is so unlikely you cannot believe it.

unbeliever When religious people talk about **unbelievers**, they mean people with a different religion from themselves, or people with no religion at all.

unbelieving is used to describe someone who does not believe something they have just been told. *He stared at me, dazed and unbelieving.*

unbending You say someone is **unbending** when they refuse to change their beliefs, attitudes, or ways. *...her unbending opposition to Communist rule.*

unbiased If you say something like an opinion or report is **unbiased**, you mean it does not show prejudice or favouritism. Similarly, you can say a person is **unbiased**.

unborn An **unborn** child has not yet been born and is still inside its mother's womb.

unbounded If you say something is **unbounded**, you mean there is no limit to it. *My admiration for him is unbounded.*

unbridled behaviour and feelings are not controlled or limited in any way. *...a tale of lust and unbridled passion.*

unbroken is used to say something goes on throughout a period of time without stopping. *...his 33 unbroken years as an MP.*

unburden (**unburdening**, **unburdened**) ❑ If you **unburden** yourself, you tell someone about something you have been secretly worried about.

❑ If you are **unburdened** by problems, you do not have any, and can get on with what you want to do. *These bursaries allow writers a period of time during which they can* *simply write unburdened by immediate financial pressures.*

unbutton (unbuttoning, unbuttoned) When you **unbutton** something, you unfasten the buttons on it.

uncanny (uncannily) If you say something is **uncanny**, you mean it is strange and hard to explain. *The horoscope has proved to be uncannily accurate.*

uncapped In some sports, an **uncapped** player is one who has not played for a national team before.

uncaring If you say someone is **uncaring**, you mean they have no sympathy for other people's suffering.

unceasing (unceasingly) If something is **unceasing**, it goes on without stopping. *He would sit on the edge of his chair, talking unceasingly.*

uncensored films and newspapers are released without any parts having been removed by an official censor.

unceremonious (unceremoniously) You say treatment of someone is **unceremonious** when it is carried out swiftly and shows no respect for them. *In 1988 General Tembo was unceremoniously recalled from West Germany to be charged with high treason.*

uncertain (uncertainly) ❑ If you are **uncertain** about something, you are not sure it is true, or not sure it is a good idea. ◇ If you are **uncertain** what to do, you do not know what to do. *The audience laughed uncertainly.*

❑ If the future is **uncertain**, nobody knows what will happen. ◇ If the cause of something is **uncertain**, nobody knows what caused it.

❑ If you tell someone something **in no uncertain terms**, you say it so firmly or clearly there can be no doubt about what you mean.

uncertainty (uncertainties) If there is **uncertainty**, people do not know what will happen or what they should do. ◇ **Uncertainties** are things, especially things that might happen in the future, which nobody is sure about.

unchallenged If something goes **unchallenged**, people accept it without questioning it or opposing it.

unchanged If something remains **unchanged**, it stays the same.

uncharacteristic (uncharacteristically) If you call someone's behaviour **uncharacteristic**, you mean it is not the way they normally behave. *Buckingham Palace has made two uncharacteristically firm denials of rumours surrounding the Princess.*

uncharitable If you say someone is being **uncharitable**, you mean they are being harsh in their judgement of someone else.

uncharted If you say you are moving into **uncharted** waters or territory, you mean you are dealing with something totally new. ◇ **Uncharted** areas of land or sea are not shown on any maps.

unchecked If you say something undesirable is left **unchecked**, you mean nothing is done to prevent it continuing or increasing.

uncivil behaviour is rude and impolite.

uncivilized (*or* uncivilised) If you call someone's behaviour **uncivilized**, you mean it is cruel, or shows no respect or consideration for other people.

unclaimed If something is **unclaimed**, nobody has claimed it or said it belongs to them.

uncle Your **uncle** is the brother of your mother or father, or the husband of your mother's or father's sister.

Uncle Sam When people talk about **Uncle Sam**, they mean the United States of America. In pictures, Uncle Sam is shown as a man wearing a top hat with stars on it, a tail-coat, and striped trousers.

unclean When people talk about something being **unclean**, they mean it goes against the teachings of their religion. In some religions, certain foods which people are forbidden to eat are described as **unclean**.

unclear If something is **unclear**, it is not obvious. *The extent to which they've been influenced by events in Eastern Europe remains unclear.* Similarly, if you are not certain about something, you can say you are **unclear** about it.

unclothed If someone is **unclothed**, they are not wearing any clothes.

uncomfortable (uncomfortably) ❑ If you are **uncomfortable**, you are unable to relax or unable to concentrate on something, because something is having an unpleasant effect on your body. For example, your clothes may not fit you well; you say clothes like these are **uncomfortable**. You can also say a chair or bed is **uncomfortable**. *He was squatting uncomfortably on a teeny chair.*

❑ If a situation makes you **uncomfortable**, it makes you slightly worried or embarrassed.

uncommitted people have not yet decided which side to support in a dispute or contest.

uncommon (uncommonly) **Uncommon** things do not happen often or are not often seen. ◇ If someone has an **uncommon** quality or ability, they have it to an unusual extent. *At the age of 13, Mary Whitehouse was uncommonly good at tennis.*

uncommunicative people are unwilling to talk to other people.

uncomplaining people do not complain when they have to do difficult things, or when they have to put up with something unpleasant.

uncomplicated things are simple and straightforward.

uncomprehending is used to describe people who do not understand what is happening or why. *This is of little comfort to people standing, uncomprehending, in queues for staple products.*

uncompromising (uncompromisingly) If you say someone is **uncompromising** or has an **uncompromising** attitude, you mean they are determined not to change their opinions or aims. *Dr Habash's tone was uncompromising throughout... Their work is bright, bold, and uncompromisingly modern.*

unconcealed You say people's feelings, beliefs, or wishes are **unconcealed** when they do not try to hide them.

unconcerned (unconcern) If someone is **unconcerned** about something which is happening, they are not interested in it, not worried by it, or have no sympathy for the people involved. You say someone like this behaves with **unconcern**. *...another demonstration of the terrorists' increasing unconcern about civilian casualties.*

unconditional (unconditionally) If you make an **unconditional** demand, you say something should be done without any conditions being attached to it. *Such aid should be granted unconditionally.*

unconfirmed If a report or rumour is **unconfirmed**, it has not yet been established whether it is true or not.

unconnected If something is **unconnected** with something else, it has no connection with it.

unconscionable (*pron:* un-con-shun-ab-l) (unconscionably) Unconscionable is used to say something is much more than it ought to be. *The police are taking an unconscionably long time arresting and charging the killers.*

unconscious (unconsciously, unconsciousness) ❑ If someone is **unconscious**, they are in a sleep-like state called **unconsciousness** in which they are unable to notice or react to things, for example because they have fainted or have had a blow to the head.

❑ If you are **unconscious** of something, you are not aware of it. ◇ Your **unconscious** feelings and attitudes are ones you are unaware of but which sometimes show in the way you behave. The part of your mind where these feelings and attitudes exist is called the **unconscious**. *Women whose fathers left home unconsciously expect to be betrayed by their own partners.*

unconstitutional (unconstitutionally) If something is **unconstitutional**, it goes against the constitution of a country or organization. *The country's Supreme Court ruled that the parliament was elected unconstitutionally.*

uncontrollable (uncontrollably) If something, especially something dangerous or unpleasant, is **uncontrollable**, there is nothing you can do to stop it or change it. *His leg muscles quivered uncontrollably.*

uncontrolled If you say something, especially a kind of behaviour, is **uncontrolled**, you mean no attempt is made to stop it or restrain it. *He accused the government of uncontrolled and irresponsible spending.*

unconventional (unconventionally) **Unconventional** people do not behave in the way most people do. If someone has an **unconventional** way of doing something, they do it differently to the way it is usually done. *Their married life started rather unconventionally with both of them continuing to live in neighbouring flats.*

unconvinced (unconvincing, unconvincingly) If you are **unconvinced** by something someone says, you find it difficult to believe. You can also say you find it **unconvincing**. *The president promised, unconvincingly, to offset tax cuts with spending cuts.* ◇ If you find a book, play, or film **unconvincing**, you cannot believe in the characters or the plot.

uncooked food has not yet been cooked.

uncooperative You say someone is being **uncooperative** when they do not try to help you with what you want.

uncoordinated If something a group of people do is **uncoordinated**, it is badly organized and their different tasks do not fit in with each other. ◇ **Uncoordinated** people do not have good control over the way they move, and their movements are not graceful or smooth.

uncork When you **uncork** a bottle, you open it by pulling out the cork.

uncounted is used to say a number of people or things is very large. *Uncounted numbers of civilians appear to have fled.*

uncouth people have bad manners and behave in a rude unpleasant way.

uncover (uncovering, uncovered) If people **uncover** something secret or illegal, they find out about it. ◇ If you **uncover** an object, you take off its cover.

uncritical (uncritically) If you say someone is **uncritical** or has **uncritical** attitudes, you mean they accept something or give it their approval without thinking about

whether it is good or bad. *Teaching methods are based uncritically on Western models.*

unctuous You say someone is **unctuous** when they pretend to be full of kindness, interest, or praise but are obviously insincere.

uncut precious stones have not yet been cut into a regular shape and polished. ◇ An **uncut** version of a film, book, or play has not been shortened or censored.

undaunted If you say someone is **undaunted** by something like a setback or disappointment, you mean they are not put off by it.

undecided If you are **undecided** about something, you have not yet made your mind up about it.

undeclared An **undeclared** war has never officially been declared. ◇ **Undeclared** is also used to describe people who have views or sympathies which they do not tell anyone about. *...undeclared supporters of the Front.* ◇ **Undeclared** sums of money have not been acknowledged to exist and have therefore not been taxed or officially approved.

undemanding things are not difficult to do, enjoy, or understand. *...undemanding jobs... ...the undemanding pleasures of pop music.* ◇ If you say someone you are looking after is **undemanding**, you mean they do not expect you to do a lot for them.

undemocratic You say a government is **undemocratic** when it has not been elected in a free and fair election. ◇ You say a decision is **undemocratic** when it is made unfairly by one person or a small group, rather than by all the people involved.

undemonstrative (*pron:* un-dim-**mon**-stra-tiv) people do not let their feelings show.

undeniable (undeniably) **Undeniable** is used to say something obviously exists or is obviously a particular thing. *...her undeniable intelligence... The countryside around Daventry is undeniably attractive.*

under ❑ If something is **under** something else, it is directly below it, or covered by it.

❑ **Under** is used to talk about the circumstances in which people live, or in which something is done. *The poll was held under tight security conditions.*

❑ If something happens **under** a person or organization, it happens while they are in power or have control. *The figures indicate that a higher number than originally thought were executed under Krushchev.*

❑ **Under** is used to talk about what is allowed or not allowed by a law or rule. *We believe an offence was committed under EU regulations.*

❑ If someone works or studies **under** a person, that person is their boss or teacher.

❑ **Under** is used to say something is less than an amount, rate, or level. *Johnson had run under 10.4sec only once.*

❑ If a book is written **under** an invented name, that name appears on it as the name of the author.

under-secretary An **under-secretary** is an MP who acts as an assistant to a government minister. Some very senior civil servants are also called **under-secretaries**.

underarm is used to talk about people's armpits. *...underarm odour.* ◇ If you throw or hit a ball **underarm**, you swing your arm upwards, keeping it below the level of your shoulder.

undercarriage An aircraft's **undercarriage** is its wheels and landing gear.

underclass An **underclass** is a group of people in a country who are much poorer than everyone else and who have little chance of improving their life.

underclothes Your **underclothes** are the clothes you wear next to your skin and under your other clothes, for example a vest, bra, or pants.

undercoat is a type of paint you use before putting on the top layer of paint.

undercover work is carried out secretly by the police or on behalf of the government, to obtain information about criminal or anti-state activities.

undercurrent If there is an **undercurrent** of a feeling, people do not express it openly, but show it in the way they behave.

undercut (undercutting, undercut not 'undercutted') If a company **undercuts** another one or **undercuts** its prices, it charges less than the other company for a product or service. ◇ If something **undercuts** your attempts to do something, it stops you succeeding.

underdeveloped countries and regions do not have modern industries or proper social organization and usually have a low standard of living.

underdog In a competitive situation, if you call a person, team, or organization the **underdog**, you mean they are the one least likely to win or be successful.

underemployed If you say someone is **underemployed**, you mean they do not have enough work to do.

underestimate (underestimating, underestimated) ❑ If you **underestimate** something, you fail to realise how large, difficult, or complicated it is. ◇ An **underestimate** is an estimate about how big something is which is wrong because it is too low.
    ❑ If you **underestimate** a person, you fail to realize what they are are capable of. You can also **underestimate** their talents or capabilities.

underfed You say people are **underfed** when they are unhealthy because they have not had enough to eat.

underfoot You use **underfoot** to talk about something you are walking or standing on. *It was still wet underfoot.* ◇ If you trample something **underfoot**, you destroy or damage it by treading on it.

underfunded If an organization is **underfunded**, it cannot work properly because not enough money is being spent on it.

undergo (undergoes, undergoing, underwent, undergone) If you **undergo** something unpleasant, it happens to you or is done to you.

undergraduate An **undergraduate** is a university student who is studying for his or her first degree.

underground things are below the surface of the ground. ◇ In London and Glasgow, the **Underground** is a railway system in which electric trains travel underground in tunnels.
    ❑ **Underground** organizations operate secretly against the government in countries where no opposition is allowed. If someone **goes underground**, they carry on what they are doing secretly, because they are in danger of being arrested for political reasons.

undergrowth is bushes and other plants growing close together under trees.

underhand If you call someone's behaviour **underhand**, you mean they secretly do things in an unfair or dishonest way.

underlay is a thick material you put on the floor before laying a carpet. Some carpets have a built-in underlay. ◇ See also **underlie**.

underlie (underlying, underlay, underlain) If you say something **underlies** something else, you mean it is the cause or basis of it. *Right and justice, he claims, underlie his continuing tiff with the chairman.* ◇ **Underlying** is used to describe the aspects of something which are not obvious but are the ones which really matter. *July's underlying inflation fell to 4.4 per cent... If the company's underlying business is sound, this loss will not harm its long term prospects.*

underline (underlining, underlined) ❑ If something **underlines** a problem, it shows how serious it is. *The gloomy outlook was underlined by figures that show money available for spending has slumped by 40% since 1989.* ◇ If something **underlines** the need for some kind of action, it shows how important it is. *The minister responsible for water said that this year's reduced rainfall underlines a need for a common strategy.*
    ❑ If you **underline** a word or sentence, you draw a line under it.

underling If you talk about a person's **underlings**, you mean people with lower rank or status who take orders from them.

underlying See underlie.

undermanned (undermanning) If a business or other organization is **undermanned**, it does not have as many people working for it as it needs. When this situation occurs, you say there is **undermanning**.

undermine (undermining, undermined) If someone **undermines** a person or **undermines** their position, they make it difficult for them to stay in power or continue with their work. Similarly, someone can **undermine** a system or **undermine** someone's efforts to do something.

underneath If something is **underneath** something else, it is directly below it, or covered by it. ◇ **Underneath** is also used to talk about feelings or qualities people have which they do do not normally show. *Underneath her public personality was a tremendous generosity of heart.*

undernourished people are weak and unhealthy because they have not been eating enough.

underpaid If you say someone is **underpaid**, you mean they are not paid enough for the work they do.

underpants are an item of male underwear with holes for the legs and elastic round the waist.

underpass (underpasses) An **underpass** is a place where a road or footpath goes underneath another road or a railway.

underpin (underpinning, underpinned) If something **underpins** something else, it supports or strengthens it and helps it to carry on or be successful. When something has this effect, you call it the other thing's **underpinning**. *The relative improvement in Britain's trade position might also help to underpin confidence in the pound.*

underplay If you **underplay** something, you make it seem less important than it really is.

underprivileged people have less money and opportunities than other people. People like these are often called the underprivileged.

underrated If you say a person or thing is underrated, you mean people do not realize how, clever, important, or good they are.

underscore (underscoring, underscored) ❏ If something underscores something else, it shows how important, serious, or extensive it is. *State Department officials say the visit underscores the importance that both sides place on the talks.*
❏ If you underscore a word or sentence, you draw a line under it, to draw attention to it or show how important it is.

undersea things are below the surface of the sea. *...undersea cables.*

underside The underside of something is the part which normally faces or touches the ground. ◇ The underside of an activity or job is its unpleasant side, which you do not normally hear about.

understaffed If a business or other organization is understaffed, it does not have as many people working for it as it needs.

understand (understanding, understood) ❏ If you understand a situation, you know why or how it happens, or what might happen as a result of it. ◇ If you understand a person, you know how they feel and why they behave the way they do.
❏ If you understand someone or understand what they say, you know what they mean or what they are trying to tell you. ◇ If you understand a language, you know what people are saying when they speak it.
❏ If you say you understand that something has happened or is true, you mean you have been told it. *I understand a consensus has been reached.*
❏ If you understand something a certain way, that is how you interpret it. *Courts usually understand a contract to be with the company that issued the confirmation invoice.*
❏ See also understanding.

understandable (understandably) If you say someone's behaviour or feelings are understandable, you mean they are what you would expect from someone in their situation. *Estate agents are understandably concerned about what they perceive to be a restriction of their trade.*

understanding ❏ If there is understanding or an understanding between people, they get on well together and trust each other. ◇ An understanding person is kind and forgiving.
❏ If someone has an understanding of something, they know how it works, what it means, or why it is the way it is. ◇ Your understanding of a situation is the way you interpret it.
❏ If you are allowed to do something on the understanding that you do something else, you are allowed to do the first thing only because you have agreed to do the second.

understate (understating, understated) If you understate something, you make it out to be smaller, less important, or less serious than it really is. ◇ If you say something in a painting or piece of writing is understated, you mean it is not made too obvious, and is more effective because of this.

understatement If you call what someone says an understatement, you mean it fails to describe how big

something is, or how serious or important it is.

understood See understand.

understudy (understudies) An actor's understudy is a person who has learned their part in a play and can stand in for them, for example if they are ill.

undertake (undertaking, undertook, have undertaken) ❏ If you undertake a task or job, you start doing it and accept responsibility for it. An undertaking is a job or task someone has agreed to do.
❏ If you undertake to do something, you promise to do it. An undertaking is a formal promise to do something.

undertaker An undertaker is a person whose job is to prepare bodies for burial and arrange funerals.

undertaking See undertake.

undertone ❏ If you say something has certain undertones, you mean it suggests ideas or attitudes which are not directly expressed.
❏ If you say something in an undertone, you say it very quietly.

undertook See undertake.

undervalue (undervaluing, undervalued) If someone undervalues something, they say it is worth less money than it really is. ◇ If you say someone or something is undervalued, you mean people do not realize how important or good they are.

underwater is used to describe things which exist or happen below the surface of the sea, a river, or a lake. *...underwater currents.*

underwear is the same as underclothes.

underwent See undergo.

underworld When people talk about the underworld, they mean criminals and their activities.

underwrite (underwriting, underwrote, have underwritten; underwriter) When an insurance company or other organization underwrites something like a business, it agrees, in return for a fee, to provide money if there are any losses or special expenses. An organization which does this is called an underwriter. ◇ An underwriter is also a person employed by an insurance company to work out the appropriate insurance charge for particular risks, such as a ship being lost at sea.

undeserved If you say something is undeserved, you mean the person who has it does not deserve it.

undesirable If you say something is undesirable, you mean it would be better if it did not happen or exist, because it is likely to have harmful effects. ◇ People arriving in a place are sometimes called undesirables when it is thought they might cause trouble.

undetected If something is undetected, nobody notices it or finds out about it.

undeveloped If you say something is undeveloped, you mean it has not been used, improved, or increased as much as it could be. ◇ An undeveloped country or region is the same as an underdeveloped one.

undid See undo.

undies Underwear is sometimes called undies.

undignified You say someone's behaviour is undignified when they do silly or embarrassing things which make people lose respect for them.

undiluted feelings or qualities are very strong and are not mixed with other feelings or qualities. *...a smile of* *undiluted pleasure.* ◇ An **undiluted** liquid is concentrated and has not been mixed with water to make it weaker.

undisciplined If you say someone's behaviour is **undisciplined**, you mean they behave badly, without much self-control.

undiscovered things have not yet been found or detected. *The area is still relatively undiscovered by British property buyers... ...an undiscovered computer fraud.*

undisguised feelings or wishes are shown openly and not hidden. *The withdrawal of troops was greeted with undisguised relief.*

undismayed If you are **undismayed** by something which goes wrong, you are not worried or upset by it.

undisputed If something is **undisputed**, everyone accepts that it exists or is true. ◇ If someone is the **undisputed** leader of a group, everyone in the group accepts them as leader.

undistinguished things are not particularly good or interesting. *His short and undistinguished career as an art student came to an end.*

undisturbed If you say something has remained **undisturbed**, you mean it has not been moved or changed in any way. *The ODP brought up samples of ooze which had lain undisturbed on the seabed since the end of the Palaeocene era.* ◇ If you do something **undisturbed**, you do it without anybody interfering with you or trying to stop you.

undivided If you give something your **undivided** attention, you give it all your attention and concentrate on it fully.

undo (undoes, undoing, undid, have undone) ❑ If something **undoes** someone's achievements, it cancels them out. *China's continuing population growth threatens to undo many of its social and economic achievements.* ◇ If you say something was someone's **undoing**, you mean it was the reason why they failed at something.
❑ If you **undo** something that is tied, fastened, or held together, you unfasten it or release it.

undocumented events have not been recorded by anyone. ◇ **Undocumented** is also used to describe people who live and work in a country without official permission.

undoing (undone) See **undo**.

undoubted (undoubtedly) **Undoubted** is used to describe things which definitely exist or are definitely true. *Despite his undoubted abilities, he has not always inspired trust... The organisation has undoubtedly become less secretive in its dealings with the press.*

undreamed of (*or* undreamt of) is used to say something is much better, much worse, or much more unusual than anyone thought possible. *The past three months have produced undreamt of changes in political systems fossilised for more than twenty years.*

undress (undresses, undressing, undressed) When you **undress**, you take off most or all of your clothes. When a small child or hospital patient is **undressed**, most or all of their clothes are taken off.

undue means more than is reasonable or acceptable. *Greeks blame the company for exercising undue influence over the Olympic Committee... No-one is expected to suffer undue hardship.*

undulate (undulating, undulated) If something **undulates**, it consists of gentle curves or slopes. *...undulating country-*

side.

unduly is used to talk about things being done or felt more than is necessary. *Dr Nolan said that patients should not be unduly alarmed by the report.*

undying is used to say something will last for ever. *Many lost their lives but won undying fame.*

unearned income is money obtained from things like investments and property rather than from doing work.

unearth If you **unearth** something hidden or secret, you discover it. *Dr Van Houts has unearthed evidence that suggests the poem was written in 1067.*

unearthly things are strange and unnatural. *An unearthly quiet descended on the city.* ◇ If you do something at an **unearthly** hour, you do it very early in the morning or very late at night.

uneasy (uneasily, unease, uneasiness) If you are **uneasy**, you feel something is wrong and are worried or tense about it. This feeling is called **unease** or **uneasiness**. *Patrolling soldiers and sullen residents rub shoulders uneasily.* ◇ **Uneasy** is also used to describe situations which seem likely to come to an end and are not at all stable or definite. *After three weeks of uneasy calm it's now clear that a new rebel offensive is underway... He welded together an uneasy coalition of two traditional conservative parties and his own liberal political movement.*

uneconomic (uneconomical, uneconomically) If you say something like a business is **uneconomic** or **uneconomical**, you mean it wastes money or is not earning enough to be worth carrying on with. *...an uneconomically large coal industry.*

uneducated people have not had much education.

unemotional people do not experience strong feelings, or do not show them.

unemployable If you say someone is **unemployable**, you mean they are not likely to get a job, because of the way they behave or because they do not have any skills or qualifications.

unemployed If someone is **unemployed**, they want to work but cannot get a job. People in this situation are often called **the unemployed**.

unemployment If there is **unemployment** in a place, many people are out of work and cannot get a job.

unemployment benefit is a payment some people get from the state when they are unemployed.

unending If you say something is **unending**, you mean it carries on for a very long time and looks as though it will never stop. *...the country's seemingly unending cycle of political violence.*

unenviable If you say someone is in an **unenviable** situation, you mean they are in a difficult or unpleasant situation nobody would like to be in.

unequal (unequally) If you call something like a system **unequal**, you mean it is unfair because it treats different people differently. *Proposers of the motion said the law allowing abortion was unequally implemented.* ◇ **Unequal** things are different in size or amount. *This system was ruled to be unconstitutional, because rich and poor counties spent such unequal amounts of money on education.*

unequalled is used to say something is bigger, better, or more extreme than anything else of its kind. *Andy Capp won the panel strip prize for five consecutive years – an unequalled achievement.*

unequivocal (*pron:* un-i-**kwiv**-o-cal) (**unequivocally**) If something you say or do is **unequivocal**, it is clear and definite and can only have one meaning or purpose. *He was unwilling to commit himself unequivocally.*

unerring (*pron:* un-**er**-ing) (**unerringly**) If you talk about someone's **unerring** ability to do something, you mean they always manage to do it. *...his unerring good judgement... ...South Africa's unerringly accurate fast bowler.*

UNESCO (*pron:* **yew**-ness-co) is part of the United Nations, set up to encourage worldwide education, science, and the arts. UNESCO stands for 'United Nations Educational, Scientific and Cultural Organization'.

unethical behaviour goes against accepted beliefs about what is right and wrong.

uneven (**unevenly**) An **uneven** surface is not smooth or flat. ◇ **Uneven** is also used to describe things which are not completely the same in all their parts. *Inspectors said that the quality of GCSE papers was uneven... Galaxies are distributed very unevenly in space.*

uneventful An **uneventful** occasion or period of time is one when nothing interesting or important happens.

unexceptionable If you say something is **unexceptionable**, you mean nobody is likely to disagree with it, object to it, or criticize it.

unexceptional things are not particularly good or bad, and not unusual in any way.

unexciting If you say something is **unexciting**, you mean it contains no surprises and is rather boring.

unexpected (**unexpectedly**) **Unexpected** things surprise you because you did not think they would happen. *The congress unexpectedly lasted into a second day.*

unfailing (**unfailingly**) **Unfailing** is used to describe a quality or ability which someone seems to have on all occasions. *...John's unfailing sense of humour... His tone is unfailingly reserved.*

unfair (**unfairly**, **unfairness**) If you say something is **unfair**, you mean it is not right or just, because it treats some people differently from others. *Branson says this policy unfairly discriminates against smaller independent airlines... ...the unfairness of the voting system.*

unfaithful (**unfaithfulness**) If someone is **unfaithful** to their wife, husband, or lover, they have a sexual relationship with someone else. *Confessing his unfaithfulness was one of the toughest things he has ever had to do.*

unfamiliar If something is **unfamiliar** to you, you have not seen it before, heard of it before, or been involved with it before. You can also say you are **unfamiliar** with it.

unfashionable (**unfashionably**) If something is **unfashionable**, it is not fashionable or popular at a particular time. *He chose unfashionably to write in Yiddish.*

unfasten (**unfastening**, **unfastened**) If you **unfasten** something, you undo the buttons, hooks, or straps which hold it together.

unfathomable things are very difficult to understand or explain. *...an unfathomable mystery.*

unfavourable (**unfavourably**) (*American spelling:* unfavorable, unfavorably) If you have an **unfavourable** opinion of something, you do not like it or do not think it is very good. *He commented unfavourably that only people in mourning wore black.* ◇ If something compares **unfavourably** with something else, it appears less good

when compared with it. ◇ **Unfavourable** circumstances make it less likely that something will succeed.

unfeeling If you say someone is **unfeeling**, you mean they are not sympathetic to people who are suffering or unhappy.

unfettered is used to say someone is not limited in what they are allowed to do. *...unfettered competition... Mr Yeltsin appears to be far from enjoying unfettered power.*

unfinished things have not yet been completed.

unfit ❑ If you are **unfit**, your body is not in good condition, because you have not been doing enough exercise.
    ❑ If someone or something is **unfit** for a particular purpose, they are not good enough for it.

unflagging (**unflaggingly**) **Unflagging** is used to say someone's positive feelings about something never change, or their ability to do something never gets any less. *Her unflagging energy and inventiveness overcame all problems... He was unflaggingly delighted with everyone and everything.*

unflappable If you say someone is **unflappable**, you mean they are always calm and never panic or get angry or upset.

unfocused (*or* **unfocussed**) If you say someone is **unfocused** in what they do, think, or want, you mean they do not seem to be very clear about it, or do not seem to have a definite aim. ◇ If someone's eyes are **unfocused**, they are open but not really looking at anything.

unfold ❑ When something like a situation **unfolds**, it develops in a certain way. *Much more will be at stake as the drama unfolds... As the film unfolds, the characters grow through their trials and tribulations until they emerge with the ability to survive.*
    ❑ If you **unfold** something which has been folded up, you open it out.

unforeseen things cannot be predicted.

unforgettable (**unforgettably**) If you say something is **unforgettable**, you mean you are not likely to forget it, because it is very good, very bad, or very unusual. *The enthusiasm of the crowd made it an unforgettably emotional moment.*

unforgivable (**unforgivably**) If you call someone's behaviour **unforgivable**, you mean it is so bad or unpleasant it can never be justified or accepted. *Leyland was a generous patron and Whistler insulted him unforgivably.*

unforgiven If someone's behaviour is **unforgiven**, people have not forgiven them for it.

unforgiving You say people are **unforgiving** when they are unwilling to forgive someone for some wrong they have done.

unformed things are at an early stage of development and are not yet fully formed. *...an unformed foetus... ...unformed ideas.*

unfortunate (**unfortunately**) ❑ If you say someone is **unfortunate**, you mean they are unlucky and do not deserve something unpleasant which has happened to them. ◇ If you say something is **unfortunate**, you mean it is a pity it happened, because of the trouble or embarrassment it has caused. *They are all victims of their governments' unfortunate decisions to back the wrong side.*
    ❑ You say **unfortunately** when you are mentioning something which you think is regrettable. *The President*

has unfortunately said he would veto such a bill.

unfounded If you say a statement is **unfounded**, you mean there are no facts or evidence to back it up and it should not have been made. Similarly, you can say people's hopes or fears are **unfounded**.

unfriendly ❑ If someone is **unfriendly**, they are not pleasant or welcoming and do not make you feel relaxed or comfortable. You can also talk about a place or system being **unfriendly**.
  ❑ An **unfriendly** takeover bid is an attempt by a company to take control of another one against its wishes.

unfruitful If an attempt to achieve something is **unfruitful**, it does not succeed.

unfulfilled If something like a hope or promise is **unfulfilled**, the thing that was hoped for or promised does not happen.

unfurl If you **unfurl** something like an umbrella or a flag, you unroll it or open it out.

unfurnished If you rent a house or flat **unfurnished**, you have to provide all your own furniture.

ungainly people move in an awkward or clumsy way.

ungodly ❑ If you say something happens at an **ungodly** hour, you mean it happens very early in the morning when most people are still in bed.
  ❑ Some people use **ungodly** to describe language or behaviour which they think is sinful or blasphemous.

ungovernable If you say a country or region is **ungovernable**, you mean it cannot be controlled or administered effectively. ◇ You can call other things which cannot be controlled **ungovernable**. *...ungovernable hatred... The game is being made to look ungovernable.*

ungracious (ungraciously) You say someone is **ungracious** when they are not polite or friendly, especially to someone who is trying to help them. *Melanie snatched the mug rather ungraciously from my hand.*

ungrateful If you say someone is **ungrateful**, you mean they do not show pleasure when someone helps them or gives them something. You also say someone is **ungrateful** when they behave badly towards someone who has helped them.

unguarded ❑ If someone makes an **unguarded** comment, they carelessly say something they did not want other people to know. You can also say someone says something in an **unguarded** moment.
  ❑ **Unguarded** buildings or other places do not have anyone guarding them.

unhampered If you do something **unhampered**, you do it without being restricted or interfered with.

unhappy (unhappier, unhappiest; unhappily, unhappiness) ❑ If someone is **unhappy**, they are sad or depressed. *She was unhappily married... There is no simple answer to human unhappiness.* ◇ An **unhappy** time for someone is one when things go badly for them.
  ❑ If you are **unhappy** about something, you are not at all pleased about it. ◇ An **unhappy** situation is unsatisfactory and needs to be put right.
  ❑ You say **unhappily** when you are mentioning something which you think is regrettable. *It was a match that unhappily had to be decided by the Appeals Committee.*

unharmed If a person is **unharmed** in an accident, attack, or some other bad experience, they are not injured at all. Similarly, you say a building is **unharmed** when it is not destroyed or damaged.

unhealthy (unhealthily) ❑ You talk about things being **unhealthy** when they are likely to cause illness or bad health. *Many refugees face years in crowded, uncomfortable and often unhealthy camps.* ◇ **Unhealthy** people are often ill. *Her skin was unhealthily pale.*
  ❑ You also say something is **unhealthy** when it is likely to have a bad effect on people's behaviour. *...an unhealthy fear of sex.*
  ❑ If you say someone's financial situation is **unhealthy**, you mean they are not earning enough to cover their costs or pay off their debts.

unheard ❑ If a noise goes **unheard**, nobody hears it or takes any notice.
  ❑ You use **unheard of** to describe situations which never happen, or which are very shocking or surprising when they do happen. *A professor gave a talk on Malcolm X and 300 youths turned up – that's totally unheard of.*

unheeded If something goes **unheeded**, it is ignored.

unhelpful (unhelpfully) If you say someone's comments or actions are **unhelpful**, you mean they do not help to solve a difficulty, and may make it worse. *Other companies unhelpfully suggest mixing two foundations together.* ◇ If something like a manual is **unhelpful**, it does not tell you what you want to know.

unheralded things happen unexpectedly and without any warning. *...an unheralded visit.* In sport or entertainment, a person is described as **unheralded** when they are suddenly successful and nobody has heard of them before. *LeMond was fifth behind an unheralded Pole, Zenus Jaskula.*

unhesitatingly If you do something **unhesitatingly**, you do it without hesitating, because you are sure it is the right thing to do.

unhinge (unhinged) If something **unhinges** you, it destroys your confidence and upsets your ability to do something well. ◇ If you say someone is **unhinged**, you mean they are mentally ill.

unholy A serious quarrel or dispute is sometimes called an **unholy row**. Similarly, a confused situation can be called an **unholy mess**. ◇ When two or more people or groups get together for a purpose you do not approve of, you can call them an **unholy alliance**.

unhook (unhooking, unhooked) If you **unhook** something which is fastened with a hook, you unfasten it.

unhurried is used to say something is done in a slow relaxed way. *He writes in a rich, unhurried style.*

unhurt If a person is **unhurt** in an accident, attack, or some other bad experience, they are not injured at all.

unhygienic things are dirty and are likely to cause infections and disease.

UNICEF (*pron:* yew-nee-sef) is part of the United Nations which was set up to help more children be educated in poorer countries, and also to help poor children and their mothers stay well and healthy. UNICEF stands for 'United Nations International Children's Emergency Fund'.

unicorn A **unicorn** is an imaginary animal in stories. It looks like a white horse with a single horn growing out of its forehead.

unidentifiable If someone or something is **unidentifiable**, it is not possible to say exactly who or what they are.

unidentified is used describe people whose identity is not known. *Unidentified attackers have ambushed a relief mission in north-eastern Somalia.*

unified (unification) See unify.

uniform (uniformed; uniformly, uniformity) ❑ A **uniform** is a set of clothes which identifies a person as belonging to a particular organization or group of people. A **uniformed** person is wearing a uniform.
❑ If something is **uniform**, it is the same in all its parts. You talk about the **uniformity** of something like this. *Progress has not been uniform... Codifying this information allows basic costs and values to be applied uniformly across branches.*

unify (unifies, unifying, unified; unification) ❑ A **unified** country has been created by two or more countries joining together. This process is called **unification**.
❑ If something **unifies** people, it gets them to join together or do something together. ◇ If countries or groups do something in a **unified** way, they do it together. *Colonel Gaddafi called for a unified Arab oil policy.*

unilateral (unilaterally) A **unilateral** action or decision is made by only one of the organizations or countries in a group, without the agreement or consent of the others. *...a unilateral ceasefire... Different republics have unilaterally announced their own price changes.*

unilateralism (unilateralist) **Unilateralism** is the belief that a country should get rid of its nuclear weapons without waiting for other countries to do the same. A person who believes this is called a **unilateralist**.

unimaginable (unimaginably) If you say something is **unimaginable**, you mean nobody can imagine it happening, or imagine what it is like. *Conditions in prisons there are unimaginably bad.*

unimaginative You say something like a decision is **unimaginative** when it takes into account only a small range of possibilities or options. ◇ You say a person is **unimaginative** when they lack imagination.

unimpeachable If you say someone's behaviour or character is **unimpeachable**, you mean nobody could find fault with it.

unimportant If you say something is **unimportant**, you mean it has very little significance or importance.

unimpressed If you are **unimpressed** by something, you do not think it is very good or very interesting.

unimpressive If you say someone or something is **unimpressive**, you mean they are not particularly good or interesting.

uninformed You say people are **uninformed** when they do not know much about a subject. You can also call their remarks or decisions **uninformed**.

uninhabitable places or buildings are impossible to live in.

uninhabited places or buildings do not have anyone living in them.

uninhibited (uninhibitedly) **Uninhibited** people behave freely and naturally and do not care what other people think about their behaviour. *Only one other dissident has spoken so uninhibitedly to the foreign media.*

uninitiated People who know very little about a subject are sometimes called the **uninitiated**.

uninspired If you say something is **uninspired**, you mean it is dull and very little imagination seems to have gone into it.

uninspiring If you say something is **uninspiring**, you mean it is dull and not likely to cause interest or excitement.

unintelligible If a remark or piece of writing is **unintelligible**, nobody can understand it.

unintended If something that happens is **unintended**, it was not planned or not meant to happen.

unintentional (unintentionally) If something that happens is **unintentional**, it was not meant to happen. *She might, albeit unintentionally, have inflicted serious damage.*

uninterested If someone is **uninterested** in something, they do not think it is particularly important or worthwhile and do not want to know any more about it.

uninteresting If you say something is **uninteresting**, you mean there is nothing interesting about it.

uninterrupted is used to describe things which carry on without any interruptions. *Work could proceed uninterrupted by bad weather.*

uninvited is used to describe things people do or say without being asked. *He had been answering an uninvited question from a reporter.* **Uninvited** is also used to describe people who do something without being asked, or come somewhere without being asked. *...uninvited car-window cleaners... ...uninvited guests.*

union ❑ A **union** is the same as a trade union.
❑ **Union** is the joining together of two or more things so they become one thing. For example, you can talk about the **union** of countries or political parties. *We want political union in Europe.* When two or more things are joined together like this, the result is called a **union**. *...an unbreakable union of free republics.*

Union Jack The **Union Jack** is the national flag of the United Kingdom of Great Britain and Northern Ireland.

unionise (unionisation) See unionize.

unionism (unionist) ❑ **Unionism** is the same as trade unionism. A **unionist** is a trade unionist.
❑ **Unionism** or **Ulster Unionism** is the belief that Northern Ireland should remain part of the United Kingdom. **Unionists** are people, especially Northern Irish people, who have this belief.

unionize (unionizing, unionized; unionization) *(can be spelled with an 's' instead of a 'z')* When the people in a workplace join a trade union or form one, you can say they **unionize** or are **unionized**. *...the unionization of women office workers... ...a heavily unionized workforce.*

unique *(pron: yew-neek)* (uniquely, uniqueness) ❑ A **unique** person or thing is the only one of their kind. *Uniquely among Europeans, the French have never emigrated to the United States in large numbers... ...the uniqueness of Beethoven's Fidelio.* ◇ If something is **unique** to a person or thing, they are the only person or thing that has it. *They have discovered a fragment of DNA which is unique to humans.* Similarly, you can say something is **unique** to a place or culture. *Having your baby sleep in a different room is almost unique to western society.*
❑ Sometimes, especially in conversation, people say someone or something is **unique**, meaning they are very unusual or special. *She was really a unique person... Her voice is so unique.*

unisex things can be used by either women or men. *...a unisex hair salon.*

unison If a group of people do something **in unison**, they all do it together at the same time. *When he asked if any of them wanted to disarm the combatants, all shouted in unison, no.* ◇ When people or groups act in unison, they do something together or act in the same way because they agree with each other or have the same aims.

unit ❑ Various kinds of things are called **units**. A unit is something which is thought of as a single complete thing, separate from other things. *...a floating accommodation unit... ...a digital display unit.*
   ❑ A unit is also a part of a large organization, or a group of people who do a specialized job. *...a specialist burns unit.*
   ❑ A unit of measurement is a standard length, amount, weight, etc. For example, the metre is a unit of length and the gram is a unit of weight. ◇ A unit of currency is a standard amount of money such as the pound, the dollar, or the yen.

unit trust A unit trust is an organization you can use to invest money. You buy a certain number of units from the organization, which invests the money in many different types of businesses; you then get a share in any profits.

Unitarian Unitarians are a group of Christians who have their own Church and their own form of worship. They believe God is one being and reject the idea of the Holy Trinity.

unitary If you talk about two or more countries being made into a **unitary** country, you mean they become one country and lose their separate identities. Similarly, you can talk about a group of local councils being made into a **unitary** council.

unite (uniting, united; unity) ❑ When people **unite**, they get together and act as a single group. ◇ If people are **united** about something, they agree about it, and often decide to act together in some way. When this happens, you say there is **unity** between them.
   ❑ If two or more countries **unite**, they join together to form a single country. A **united** country is one which has been formed in this way. *...a united Germany.*

United Kingdom The United Kingdom is England, Scotland, Wales, and Northern Ireland. 'United Kingdom' is often shortened to 'UK'.

United Nations The United Nations or UN is an international organization which tries to encourage peace, cooperation, and friendship between countries. See also UNESCO, UNICEF, World Health Organization.

unity See unite.

universal (universally) If something is **universal**, it involves all the people in a group, or everyone in the world. *Condemnation of his actions was universal... It was universally accepted that the Left would make life uncomfortable for a right-wing party leader.* ◇ **Universal** is also used to describe things which affect every part of a place. *...a universal parcel service.*

universality If you talk about the **universality** of something, especially something in art or literature, you mean it applies to all people, and not just the people of one place or culture.

universe The universe is everything physical that exists, including all matter, energy, and space.

university (universities) A university is an educational institution where students study for degrees and research is carried out.

unjust (unjustly) If you say something like a law is **unjust**, you mean it is wrong, because it treats people unfairly or more harshly then they deserve. Similarly, you can say a punishment is **unjust**. *The prisoners maintain that they were unjustly convicted by the former regime.*

unjustifiable (unjustifiably) If you say some strong action is **unjustifiable**, you mean it cannot be justified by what has gone before. *...this unjustifiable act of aggression... ...unjustifiably high levels of taxation.*

unjustified If you say someone's comments or actions are **unjustified**, you mean they are not deserved by the person they were aimed against.

unkempt You say someone is **unkempt** when they look scruffy and untidy. You can also say someone's hair or beard is **unkempt**. ◇ An **unkempt** garden or other place is very untidy, because it has been neglected.

unkind (unkindly, unkindness) You call a person **unkind** when they do or say unpleasant things to someone, or say unpleasant things about them. You also call the things they do or say **unkind**. *He had treated her unkindly... He repaid her love and loyalty with selfishness and unkindness.* ◇ If someone has had a lot of bad luck, you can say Fate has been **unkind** to them. You can also say a period of time has been an **unkind** one for someone. *The 1980s were an unkind decade for Africa, with war, recession and debt meaning especially severe economic hardship.*

unknowable If you say something is **unknowable**, you mean it is impossible to know much about it.

unknowing (unknowingly) You describe someone as **unknowing** when they are not aware of something important connected with what they are doing. *African governments had been victims and perhaps unknowing accomplices in the bank's activities... Some humans may unknowingly already have contracted the disease.*

unknown ❑ If something is **unknown**, people do not know, for example, what it is or how much it is. *What is still unknown is the Chinese point of view... Rich Gulf states have poured unknown billions into Egypt's central bank.* Something which nobody knows can be called an **unknown**. *Apart from the obvious unknown of oil prices, a lot depends on the size of the problems caused by the collapse of the economy.*
   ❑ The **unknown** is used to talk about all the things people do not know about, including things which might happen in the future. *...the fear of the unknown.*
   ❑ If someone is **unknown** to you, you do not know their name, or do not know anything about them. *...Maurice Greiffenhagen, a painter previously unknown to me.* ◇ **Unknown** is also used to describe people who are not well-known or famous. *Many of the artists are young and still unknown... ...a political unknown.*
   ❑ If you say a type of situation is **unknown**, you mean it never happens. *It's almost unknown for women to die during sporting exercise.* If you say something is **not unknown**, you mean it happens quite often. *Such debauchery was not unknown here.*

unlawful (unlawfully) Unlawful things are against the law. *The review will examine the councils' assertion that the government acted unlawfully.*

unleaded petrol has less lead in it than normal petrol. People use it to try and reduce the amount of pollution in the air.

unleash (unleashes, unleashing, unleashed) If you **unleash** something unpleasant or undesirable, you accidentally start it and then can do nothing to control it.

unleavened bread is made without yeast or any other substance which would make it rise.

unless ❑ If you say something will happen **unless** something else happens, you mean only the second thing can prevent the first one happening. *The company announced the closure of six of its factories unless buyers could be found.* ❑ If you say something will **not** happen **unless** something else happens, you mean the first thing will only happen if the second one does. *Mahokoe is refusing to take part in the trial unless a black judge presides.*

unlicensed If something is **unlicensed**, no licence has been issued for it. *...unlicensed handguns.* **Unlicensed** is also used to describe people who do something without a licence. *...tickets sold by unlicensed operators.*

unlike You use **unlike** when you are mentioning a difference between two people, things, or situations. *Unlike India, Burma had no intellectual elite.* ◇ If you say something is **unlike** anything else, you mean there is nothing else like it. *There is something about the Grand National that is quite unlike any other race.*

unlikely (unlikeliest; unlikelihood) If you say something is **unlikely** to happen or **unlikely** to be true, you mean it will probably not happen or is probably not true. You can talk about the **unlikelihood** of something happening or being true. ◇ **Unlikely** is also used to describe a strange or unexpected thing or occurrence, or a person who achieves something you would not expect them to achieve. *Agassi out-hit Ivanisevic to become the unlikeliest Wimbledon champion of all.*

unlimited If something is **unlimited**, there is no end to it, or nothing to stop it getting bigger or more extreme. *The decision means Italians can keep unlimited amounts of foreign currency in banks at home.*

unlit places are dark because there are no lights there. ◇ An **unlit** fire or cigarette has not yet been lit.

unload (unloading, unloaded) If you **unload** things from a vehicle, you take them out of it or off it. You can also say you **unload** the vehicle. ◇ You can also say you **unload** something when you get rid of it by selling it.

unlock ❑ If you **unlock** something, you open it using a key. ◇ An **unlocked** door has not been locked. You also say a house or vehicle is **unlocked** when its doors have not been locked. ❑ If you talk about knowledge being **unlocked**, you mean it becomes available to people for the first time. *We have an opportunity now to unlock the secrets of the universe.* ◇ You can say certain feelings are **unlocked** when someone experiences them for the first time. *They embark upon a passionate affair which finally unlocks her dormant sexual feelings.* ❑ If something **unlocks** a process which has come to a halt, it gets it going again.

unloved An **unloved** person is not loved by anyone.

unlovely If you say something is **unlovely**, you mean it is not pleasant or attractive.

unloving If you say someone is **unloving**, you mean they do not show love to other people, especially to their partner or members of their family.

unlucky (unluckier, unluckiest; unluckily) ❑ You say someone is **unlucky** when something unfortunate happens to them which is not their fault, or when they are in a bad situation which they could not avoid. *His only faults occurred at fence nine, when he unluckily lost his stirrup.* ❑ When people say it is **unlucky** to do something, they mean you should not do it, because it is supposed to bring bad luck.

unmade An **unmade** bed has not been made.

unmanageable If you say something is **unmanageable**, you mean people are unable to control it or cope with it. ◇ **Unmanageable** children are naughty and difficult to control.

unmanned spacecraft or other vehicles do not have anyone in them. ◇ **Unmanned** places and buildings do not have anyone working in them or in charge of them.

unmarked ❑ If something is **unmarked**, it shows no signs of damage or injury. ◇ You also say something is **unmarked** when there is nothing on it to identify it. *...an unmarked grave.* ❑ An **unmarked** player in a football or rugby match has nobody from the other side standing near them to stop them getting the ball. ❑ If an anniversary goes **unmarked**, nobody does anything to celebrate it.

unmarried An **unmarried** person is not married.

unmask If you **unmask** someone, you show who they really are, or what they are really like.

unmatched is used to say something is the best or most successful thing of its kind. *...an unmatched view of Lake Windermere.*

unmentionable things are too unpleasant or embarrassing to talk about.

unmerciful (unmercifully) **Unmerciful** is used to describe something unpleasant which keeps being done to someone. *The unpadded seat was giving his back an unmerciful battering... The members opposite were heckling Dame Jill unmercifully.*

unmistakeable (unmistakeably) (or unmistakable, unmistakably) If you say something is **unmistakeable**, you mean there can be no doubt about what it is or what it means. *The unification of Germany changes the situation subtly but unmistakeably.*

unmitigated means 'total' or 'absolute'. *...a series of unmitigated blunders... The programme proved an unmitigated pleasure.*

unmolested If you say someone does something **unmolested**, you mean they are allowed to do it without being stopped or interfered with.

unmoved If someone is **unmoved** by something, it does not affect the way they behave, think, or feel. ◇ If you say something is **unmoved**, you mean it stays in the same place or at the same level.

unnamed An **unnamed** person or thing is mentioned in a statement or report without their name being given.

unnatural (unnaturally) If you say something is **unnatural**, you mean you do not approve of it, because it does not fit in with your idea of how things ought to be. *...a somewhat unnatural state of affairs... Self-denial in the matter of sex has come to be thought unnatural.* ◇ If you say there is an **unnatural** calm or silence, you mean things are very calm or silent and you find this strange or worrying. *The water seemed unnaturally still.* ◇ If you say someone does something in an **unnatural** way, you mean that their way of doing it seems artificial and unconvincing.

unnecessary (unnecessarily) If you say something is **unnecessary**, you mean there is no need for it to happen or be done. *Mr Newall was treated in an unnecessarily harsh way.*

unnerve (unnerving, unnerved; unnervingly) If something **unnerves** you, it alarms and worries you. You say something like this is **unnerving**. *Daniel Illsley is unnervingly convincing as a budding psychopath.*

unnoticed If something happens **unnoticed**, nobody notices it or realizes it is happening.

unobserved If you do something **unobserved**, nobody notices you doing it.

unobtainable If something is **unobtainable**, it is impossible to obtain.

unobtrusive (unobtrusively) If someone or something is **unobtrusive**, they are not too obvious or do not attract too much attention. *The animals live happily while being unobtrusively observed by residents and visitors.*

unoccupied buildings or other places do not have anyone in them.

unofficial (unofficially) **Unofficial** is used to describe things which have not been officially authorized or recognized, or do not come from an official source. *In the final session, Wayne Rainey broke the unofficial lap record... Unofficial accounts say the sum involved may be as much as $400 million... When he was a child, Joffe had been unofficially adopted by Epstein's youngest daughter.* **Unofficial** is also used to describe people who are not officially recognized as being a particular thing. *...an unofficial guide.*

unopened An **unopened** package or container has not yet been opened.

unopposed If someone is **unopposed** in an election, nobody stands against them. ◇ If an application or proposal is **unopposed**, nobody objects to it.

unorthodox beliefs or ways of doing things are different from the usual or accepted ones.

unpack If you **unpack** something like a bag, suitcase, or box, you take everything out of it. You can also say you unpack the things in it.

unpaid ❏ If someone is **unpaid**, they are not paid for the work they do. *They run play schemes unpaid.* ◇ If you take **unpaid** leave, you do not get paid while you are away from work.
❏ If a bill is **unpaid**, the money that is owed has not been paid.

unpalatable truths are unpleasant and difficult to accept. ◇ **Unpalatable** food is unpleasant to eat.

unparalleled is used to describe people and things that are better than any others of their kind. *He was an unparalleled husband and father.* ◇ **Unparalleled** is also used to describe things which are bigger, better, or worse than anything there has been before. *It comes at a time of unparalleled shortages of bread and flour.*

unpardonable If you say someone's behaviour is **unpardonable**, you mean it is wrong or rude and cannot be excused.

unpick If you **unpick** something which someone else has done or organized, you change it completely.

unplanned An **unplanned** event happens by accident.

◇ You also say something is **unplanned** when it is allowed to happen without being properly organized. *...unplanned development.*

unpleasant (unpleasantly, unpleasantness) ❏ You say something is **unpleasant** when it upsets people or they react to it in some other unfavourable way. *...an unpleasant smell... This new nationalism could turn into something unpleasantly close to racism.*
❏ If you say a person is **unpleasant**, you mean they are unfriendly or rude. ◇ If there is **unpleasantness** between people, they disagree, argue, or fight with each other.

unpopular (unpopularity) If someone or something is **unpopular**, they are disliked by a lot of people. *...the growing unpopularity of the Government.*

unprecedented (unprecedentedly) If you say something is **unprecedented**, you mean there has never been anything like it before. *He has an unprecedentedly broad range of powers.*

unpredictable (unpredictably) If someone's behaviour is **unpredictable**, you never know what they are going to do next. You can say other things are **unpredictable** when you cannot tell how they will develop. *The circulation can switch suddenly and unpredictably between different patterns.* You can also say an action could have **unpredictable** results.

unprepared If you are **unprepared** for something, you are not ready for it.

unprepossessing If you say a person or thing is **unprepossessing**, you mean they do not look very attractive or impressive.

unpretentious people do not try to impress other people with their importance or wealth. Similarly, you say things are **unpretentious** when they have not been designed to impress people.

unprincipled If you say someone is **unprincipled**, you mean they have no moral principles and do not care whether what they do is right or wrong. You can also call their behaviour **unprincipled**.

unprintable If you say a remark is **unprintable**, you mean it cannot be repeated because it is very rude.

unproductive If something is **unproductive**, it does not produce anything useful. *...50,000 acres of unproductive grouse moor.* Similarly, an **unproductive** action does not have any useful results. *It would have been unproductive to send him to prison.* An **unproductive** time is one in which nothing useful is achieved.

unprofessional (unprofessionally) If you say someone's behaviour is **unprofessional**, you mean it is not the kind of behaviour expected of someone in their profession. *The inquiry accused the social work department of behaving unprofessionally.*

unprofitable things do not make a profit.

unprotected things or people are not protected from something that could harm them. *Victims of such abuse may be going unprotected because the police do not know that it is occurring.* ◇ **Unprotected** sex is performed without any precautions being taken, especially without a condom being worn to prevent the spread of sexual diseases like AIDS.

unprovoked You say an attack is **unprovoked** when someone attacks a person who has not harmed them in any way.

unpublished writings have never appeared in print. An **unpublished** writer is someone whose works have never appeared in print.

unpunished If a crime goes **unpunished**, the person responsible is never punished for it.

unqualified ❏ An **unqualified** person does not have the right qualifications for the job they are doing, or does not have any qualifications at all.
❏ **Unqualified** feelings are not limited in any way. *Hadlee has won unqualified admiration for his achievements.* Similarly, something can be an **unqualified** success, or you can give someone your **unqualified** apologies.

unquestionable (unquestionably) If you say something is **unquestionable**, you mean there can be no doubt it exists or is true. *...a man of unquestionable integrity... Thomas Hardy is unquestionably one of the great novelists.*

unquestioned If something is **unquestioned**, everyone accepts that it exists or is true. *The need for reform is unquestioned.* **Unquestioned** is also used to say someone or something is accepted as a particular thing. *...their unquestioned leader.*

unquestioning If someone has an **unquestioning** belief in something, they believe in it completely and do not consider that it might be wrong or mistaken. Similarly, someone can give a person or cause their **unquestioning** help or support.

unravel (unravelling, unravelled) (*American spelling:* unraveling, unraveled) If you **unravel** something woven or knitted, you take it apart, so that it returns to the material it was made from. ◇ If you **unravel** something like a problem or mystery, you work out the answer or find out the truth about it.

unread You say a piece of writing is **unread** when the person it is intended for does not read it, or when nobody reads it.

unreadable If you say a piece of writing is **unreadable**, you mean it is very difficult to read, or very boring.

unreal (unreality) If you say an experience is **unreal**, you mean it is so strange you find it difficult to believe it is really happening. You can talk about the **unreality** of an experience like this.

unrealistic (unrealistically) You say something is **unrealistic** when it shows a failure to recognize the truth about a situation. For example, if someone's hopes are **unrealistic**, there is little chance of them being fulfilled. ◇ If you say something is for sale at an **unrealistic** price, you mean nobody will buy it because it is too expensive. *Some enterprises will be priced so unrealistically that nobody will buy them.*

unreasonable (unreasonably) If you say someone is being **unreasonable**, you mean they are behaving unfairly or illogically and are difficult to deal with because of this. *The leadership had acted unreasonably and irresponsibly.* ◇ If you say something like a requirement is **unreasonable**, you mean it is difficult to justify, or is difficult to carry out.

unrecognizable (*or* unrecognisable) If you say someone or something is **unrecognizable**, you mean they have changed so much they cannot be recognized as the person or thing they were before.

unrecognized (*or* unrecognised) ❏ If a well-known person goes somewhere **unrecognized**, nobody recognizes them. ◇ You can say certain things are **unrecognized** when people are not aware of them. *Marital conflicts may be the cause of much unrecognized suffering.* ◇ If your achievements are **unrecognized**, people do not show their appreciation of them.
❏ **Unrecognized** organizations are not officially approved. Other things, for example qualifications, can also be **unrecognized**.

unreconstructed If you say something like a policy or system is **unreconstructed**, you mean it has not changed at all, although circumstances have changed since it was introduced. *...unreconstructed monetarism.* Unreconstructed is also used to describe people whose beliefs have not changed. *...an unreconstructed hardliner.*

unrefined substances have not been changed and are still in their natural state. *...unrefined oil.*

unrelated things are not connected with each other.

unrelenting is used to describe unpleasant things which carry on without stopping or becoming weaker. *...unrelenting violence... ...the unrelenting sun.* ◇ **Unrelenting** is also used to describe someone's behaviour when they carry on doing something in a very determined way. *Clint Eastwood's domination over his own work has been unrelenting.*

unreliable If you say someone or something is **unreliable**, you mean they cannot be trusted to do what they are supposed to do.

unrelieved is used to describe something unpleasant which goes on without stopping, or something bad which has no good features at all. *The picture is one of unrelieved pessimism.*

unremarkable If you say something is **unremarkable**, you mean it is not particularly interesting, exciting, or attractive.

unremarked If something goes **unremarked**, nobody pays any particular attention to it.

unremitting (unremittingly) **Unremitting** is used to describe something which continues without stopping, or something bad which has no good features. *...an unremitting stream of customers... It is a merciless read – short, brutal and unremittingly bleak.*

unrepentant If someone is **unrepentant**, they are not sorry about something they have said or done.

unrepresentative If you say a group is **unrepresentative**, you mean their ideas and beliefs are not typical of the people in the place they come from.

unrepresented If a person, group, or organization is **unrepresented** in something like a meeting, parliament, or court, there is nobody there to speak for them.

unrequited If someone's feelings or wishes are **unrequited**, they are not fulfilled or satisfied. *...unrequited love... ...his unrequited ambitions.*

unreserved (unreservedly) ❏ **Unreserved** is used to describe feelings which are not limited in any way. *Democrats greeted the confusion with unreserved glee... We have just found something we can unreservedly agree about.* Similarly, someone or something can receive **unreserved** praise.
❏ **Unreserved** seats in a theatre or concert hall are ones which cannot be booked in advance.

unresolved An **unresolved** problem has not yet been solved or dealt with satisfactorily. Similarly, you can talk about an argument or discussion being **unresolved.**

unresponsive If you are **unresponsive** to someone's ideas or suggestions, you do not change the way you work or behave because of them.

unrest You say there is **unrest** when people are angry and dissatisfied and cause trouble.

unrestrained behaviour is not controlled or limited in any way.

unrestricted If something is **unrestricted**, no restrictions are placed on it. *The Sunday Times was granted unrestricted access to the glass plates for research purposes.* ◇ If you have an **unrestricted** view of something, there is nothing in your way and you can see all of it.

unrewarding If something you do is **unrewarding**, you get very little enjoyment or satisfaction out of it.

unrivalled If you say something is **unrivalled**, you mean it is better than anything else of its kind. *...a company with an unrivalled reputation for class and quality.*

unroll If you **unroll** something which has been rolled up, you open it out.

unruffled If someone is **unruffled** in a difficult situation, they stay calm.

unruly If people behave in an **unruly** way, they do not keep to normal rules of good behaviour. *The debate so far has been ill-tempered and unruly.* ◇ **Unruly** hair is difficult to keep tidy.

unsafe If something is **unsafe**, it is dangerous and is likely to cause death, illness, or injury. ◇ **Unsafe** is also used to describe criminal convictions which are judged to be invalid because they were made on false evidence or not enough proof.

unsaid If something is left **unsaid**, it is not mentioned directly in what someone says or writes. *What Jane Austen and her characters leave unsaid is often more important than what they actually put into words.*

unsaleable (*American spelling:* **unsalable**) If you say something is **unsaleable**, you mean nobody will want to buy it.

unsatisfactory (unsatisfactorily) If you say something is **unsatisfactory**, you mean it is not good enough. *The play has an unsatisfactorily happy ending.*

unsatisfied If you are **unsatisfied**, you are disappointed because you have not got what you want. ◇ If a need is **unsatisfied**, the thing which is needed is not being provided. *...a great unsatisfied demand for fresh milk.*

unsaturated fats include most margarines. **Unsaturated** oils include most vegetable oils, for example olive oil and sunflower oil. Unsaturated fats and oils are thought by many people to be healthier than saturated ones.

unsavoury (*American spelling:* **unsavory**) You call activities **unsavoury** when you disapprove of them because you think they are morally wrong.

unscathed If you are **unscathed** after being involved in something like an accident, you have not been injured or harmed by it.

unscheduled (*pron:* un-shed-yoold *or* un-sked-yoold) If something is **unscheduled**, it was not planned in advance.

unscientific If you say something is **unscientific**, you mean that it is not based on scientific knowledge or methods.

unscrew If you **unscrew** something like a lid, you remove it by turning it.

unscripted If something like a speech is **unscripted**, it has not been composed or written down in advance. An **unscripted** action has not been planned in advance.

unscrupulous (unscrupulously) **Unscrupulous** people will do anything to get what they want, even if it is illegal or harms other people. *When you have a little power, it is tempting to use it unscrupulously.*

unseasonable (unseasonably) **Unseasonable** weather is unusual for the time of the year. *...such unseasonably high temperatures.*

unseat (unseating, unseated) If someone is **unseated**, they are removed from power, usually by being beaten in an election. ◇ If a horse you are riding **unseats** you, it throws you to the ground.

unseeded competitors in a sporting event, especially tennis, are not thought to have a good enough record to be given a special position in the draw.

unseemly If you say someone's behaviour is **unseemly**, you mean it is not appropriate for a particular place or occasion, because it is not polite or dignified.

unseen is used to describe people or things that cannot be seen from the place where you are. *...a prolonged firefight with unseen attackers in the hills.*
❑ If you say something which is happening is **unseen** since a certain time, you mean this is the first time it has happened since then. *...a propaganda onslaught unseen since the Cultural Revolution.* If you say something was **unseen** before a certain time, you mean it did not happen or was not around until then. *Unseen before, the cheery little Minis became the darlings of Japanese media types.*

unselfish (unselfishly, unselfishness) **Unselfish** people think about other people and their needs rather than about themselves. *She has unselfishly spent every day at her husband's side... The Mahayana Buddhist way of life is based on unselfishness and compassion for others.*

unsentimental (unsentimentally) If you are **unsentimental** about something, you do not let feelings of kindness or gentleness interfere with what you are doing. *Problem areas were reviewed unsentimentally.* ◇ If you say something like a book or film is **unsentimental**, you mean it deals with a subject in a realistic way and does not try to make things appear more attractive than they are.

unsettle (unsettling, unsettled) ❑ If something **unsettles** people, it makes them feel restless, dissatisfied, or worried. You say people in this state are **unsettled.** ◇ An **unsettled** situation is one where nothing is certain and things are liable to keep changing.
❑ An **unsettled** problem has not been resolved.

unshakeable (unshakeably) (*or* unshakable, unshakably) If you have an **unshakeable** belief in something, nothing can make you change your mind about it. *...a belief held more unshakably than at any time since 1945.*

unshaken If your beliefs are **unshaken** by something that happens, they are not changed by it.

unshaven If a man is **unshaven**, there are short hairs on his face and chin because he has not shaved recently.

unsightly If you say something is **unsightly**, you mean it is not very nice to look at.

unskilled workers have not been trained to do any particular job. **Unskilled** work is work which can be done by people like these.

unsociable people do not like talking to other people and sometimes behave in an unfriendly or aggressive way.

unsocial If you work **unsocial** hours, you work at times when few other people are working, for example at night or at weekends.

unsolicited is used to describe things people get or are given which they did not ask for. *A spokesman confirmed that a number of unsolicited inquiries had been received from potential buyers.*

unsolved problems and mysteries have not yet been solved.

unsophisticated people have simple tastes and ideas, often because they have had little experience of life outside their own community.

unsound ❑ If you say something like a decision or argument is **unsound,** you mean it is based on wrong information or faulty reasoning. ◇ If you say something to do with money is **unsound,** you mean it is not reliable. *Any fall in prices makes such loans unsound.*
  ❑ If someone is **of unsound mind,** they are mentally ill.

unspeakable (unspeakably) People use **unspeakable** to describe someone or something they dislike intensely. *...an act of unspeakable cruelty... She keeps saying how ghastly and unspeakably vile everything is.*

unspecified If you talk about an **unspecified** time, you mean one which has not yet been decided. *At some unspecified date this autumn, the BBC is showing a series of classic revivals.* Similarly, you can talk about an **unspecified** person or thing.

unspoilt (or **unspoiled**) If you say something, especially a place, is **unspoilt,** you mean it has not changed and is still as nice as it ever was.

unspoken thoughts, wishes, and feelings exist but are not talked about. Similarly, you can talk about an **unspoken** agreement or understanding between people. *The unspoken rules are still respected.*

unsporting If you say someone's behaviour is **unsporting,** you mean they use methods which are not acceptable and give them an unfair advantage over their opponents or competitors.

unstable ❑ If a situation is **unstable,** it is likely to change suddenly, causing problems for everyone. ◇ If a person is **unstable,** their feelings and behaviour change suddenly and often, because they are mentally disturbed.
  ❑ **Unstable** objects are likely to move or fall.

unstated If something is **unstated,** it is not spoken or written down. *Mr Hurd left unstated many of the questions this conference might eventually tackle.*

unsteady (unsteadily) ❑ If someone is **unsteady,** they find it difficult to stand or walk. *We rose unsteadily.* ◇ If someone's hands are **unsteady,** they have difficulty controlling them.
  ❑ If something like an arrangement is **unsteady,** it is kept going with difficulty and may not last.

unstinting help is given generously and is not limited in any way.

unstoppable If something is **unstoppable,** nobody can stop it happening or continuing.

unstructured If something people do is **unstructured,** it is not done according to a schedule or in any organized way. ◇ **Unstructured** clothing is not formal in style and

is loose and comfortable.

unstuck If something comes **unstuck,** it fails. *High expectations could make trouble if the talks come unstuck.* Similarly, a person trying to achieve something can come **unstuck.** ◇ If an object comes **unstuck,** it comes apart from the thing it is attached to.

unsubstantiated An **unsubstantiated** story, claim, or accusation has not been proved to be true.

unsuccessful (unsuccessfully) If something is **unsuccessful,** it fails. *Environmentalists tried unsuccessfully to get the bypass stopped.* ◇ **Unsuccessful** is also used to describe someone who has failed in their career. *...an unsuccessful lawyer.*

unsuitable If something is **unsuitable** for a particular purpose, it is not the right kind of thing for that purpose. Similarly, something can be **unsuitable** for a kind of person. *Endowment policies are unsuitable for many house purchasers.* You can also say a person is **unsuitable** for something, such as a job.

unsuited If something is **unsuited** to a person or thing, it is not suitable for them. Similarly, a person can be **unsuited** to a kind of work.

unsullied If you say something is **unsullied** by a certain thing, you mean it has not been spoiled by it. *She possessed an innocence unsullied by contact with the world.*

unsung If you call someone an **unsung hero,** you mean they are not appreciated or praised as much as they should be.

unsupported ❑ If something someone says is **unsupported,** there is nothing to show it is definitely true or right. *The guidelines are based on a view of healthy eating unsupported by scientific evidence.*
  ❑ If someone is **unsupported** in something they are trying to do, nobody is helping them. *...an attempt to walk to the North Pole unsupported by dogs, vehicles or air-dropped supplies.*
  ❑ If someone or something is **unsupported,** they are not being held up by someone or something else. *He was still too weak to walk unsupported.*

unsure ❑ If you are **unsure** about something, you are not certain about it. ◇ If something is **unsure,** it is not certain or definite. *It was always on the cards that the elections would be in December – only the actual date was unsure.*
  ❑ If you are **unsure** of yourself, you are not very confident.

unsurpassed is used to say something is better than anything else of its kind. *...the unsurpassed luxury of London's most famous hotel.*

unsuspected is used to describe something which nobody had previously guessed was there. *...a previously unsuspected link between radon gas and cancer.*

unsuspecting people do not realize what is happening or what is going to happen. *The policemen drank until 1am with unsuspecting regulars in a covert operation to expose 'lock-ins' at the pub.*

unswerving (unswervingly) **Unswerving** beliefs and attitudes are not affected by anything that happens. *German unity, said the statement, was unswervingly supported by the Community and its member states.*

unsympathetic If you say someone is **unsympathetic,** you mean they are not kind, helpful, or understanding.

untangle (untangling, untangled) If you **untangle** string or rope that is twisted or knotted, you straighten it out and undo the knots in it. ◇ If you **untangle** a complicated situation, you sort it out so people can understand it or agree about it.

untapped is used to describe things which have not yet been used or developed. *...untapped deposits of gold, silver and lithium... The trade fair is a rare opportunity to gain access to a largely untapped market.*

untenable If you say someone's position, for example as a government minister, is **untenable**, you mean they will not be able to continue in it for long, because of something they have done or said. ◇ If something like a proposal or policy is **untenable**, it cannot be made to work.

untested things have not been tried out, so people do not know how good or effective they are.

unthinkable If you say something is **unthinkable**, you mean it cannot be considered as a possible course of action. *Nuclear weapons make war absolutely unthinkable.* ◇ When people talk about **the unthinkable**, they mean something which nobody could imagine happening.

unthinking If someone behaves in an **unthinking** way, they do not consider what they are doing, and just take it for granted that it is the right thing to do.

untidy (untidily) ❑ If something is **untidy**, it is not neat or well-arranged. *...an untidily packed suitcase.* ◇ An **untidy** person leaves things in an untidy state.
❑ If a sporting or artistic performance is **untidy**, it is not as smooth or accurate as it should be, often because of carelessness. *The game began untidily.*

untie (untying, untied) If you **untie** something, you undo the rope or string which has been tied round it. ◇ If something like a person's shoelaces are **untied**, they have not been tied.

until If a situation continues **until** a particular time, it stops when that time occurs. *Mr Keys served as general secretary of SOGAT from 1971 until 1985... The resignation was kept secret until a successor had been found.* ◇ If something will not happen **until** a particular time, it will happen then but not before. *The brunt of the shutdown would not be felt until workers return to their jobs on Tuesday.*

untimely When someone dies before they reach old age, people say their death is **untimely**. ◇ You also say something is **untimely** when it happens at a particularly bad time.

unto is sometimes used instead of 'to' in old-fashioned English. *I will do unto others what they did to me.*

untold is used to talk about a very large amount of something, or a very large number of things or people. *...untold wealth... The President added that untold numbers of Germans had been expelled from their traditional homelands.*

untouchable ❑ An **untouchable** is someone who belongs to the lowest caste in India.
❑ If you say something is **untouchable**, you mean it cannot be challenged or changed in any way.

untouched If you say a person or place is **untouched** by something, you mean they have not been affected by it, especially in a harmful way. *It is difficult to find any corner of Bosnia untouched by the war.* ◇ If food is left **untouched**, none of it is eaten.

untoward (*pron:* un-to-ward) happenings are unexpected and out of the ordinary and usually mean trouble for someone. *One can never totally exclude the possibility of some untoward development occurring.*

untrained people have not been taught the skills they need to do their job.
❑ You use **untrained** with words like 'eye' and 'ear' to describe how something seems to someone who is not an expert. *The untrained nose is quickly bewildered and cannot tell mimosa from oilseed rape after ten minutes.*

untrammelled (*American spelling:* untrammeled) If you are **untrammelled** by something, you are not affected by it and can therefore get on with your work or some other activity.

untreated ❑ If an illness or injury is **untreated**, it has not received any medical treatment.
❑ **Untreated** foods such as milk or cheese have not been pasteurized and may make some people ill.
❑ **Untreated** is also used to talk about dirty or harmful things which have not been made clean or safe. *...untreated effluent.*

untried things have not yet been tested or tried out.

untroubled If you are **untroubled** by something, (a) you are not affected by it. *At this time he was untroubled by the burdens of office.* (b) it does not worry you. *Employers appear untroubled by this directive.*

untrue ❑ If a statement is **untrue**, it is not correct.
❑ If someone is **untrue** to their beliefs and principles, they do something which goes against them. ◇ If someone is **untrue** to a friend or lover, they betray them or let them down.

untrustworthy If you say someone or something is **untrustworthy**, you mean they cannot be trusted.

untruthful (untruth) If you say a statement is **untruthful** or an **untruth**, you mean it is a lie. If you say a person is **untruthful**, you mean they tell lies.

untutored If someone is **untutored** in a subject, they have not been taught about it.

unusable If something is **unusable**, it cannot be used because of its poor state.

unused If something is **unused**, it is not being used or has never been used. ◇ If you are **unused** to something, you are not familiar with it, or have not experienced it before.

unusual If something is **unusual**, there are not many other things like it. ◇ An **unusual** occurrence is one which does not happen very often.

unusually is used to say something is bigger, smaller, etc than usual. *...unusually heavy rain... ...an unusually blunt statement.* ◇ You say **unusually** when you are mentioning an unusual situation which has occurred. *Belgium, unusually, attracts wide press coverage today.*

unveil (unveiling, unveiled) When someone **unveils** a plan or proposal, they give details of it for the first time. ◇ When someone **unveils** something like a statue, they uncover it in a special ceremony, and the public see it for the first time.

unwanted things are not desired or wanted, either by a particular person or by people in general.

unwarranted If you say something is **unwarranted**, you mean it is not deserved or not needed. *...unwarranted criticism.*

unwary people are not cautious enough and are likely to be hurt or tricked in some way.

unwavering feelings, attitudes, and ways of behaving are strong and firm and do not change or weaken. ...*a man of unwavering integrity.*

unwelcome (unwelcoming) If something which happens is unwelcome to someone, they do not like it or are not happy about it. ◇ If you are **unwelcome** somewhere, the people there are not pleased to see you and would rather you stayed away. If they show this in the way they behave, you can call their behaviour **unwelcoming**.

unwell If someone is **unwell**, they are ill.

unwholesome If you say food is **unwholesome**, you mean it is not healthy or not very good for people. ◇ When people call someone's behaviour **unwholesome**, they mean it is unpleasant and unnatural.

unwieldy things are difficult to move or carry, because they are very big or heavy. ◇ If you say an organization or system is **unwieldy**, you mean it does not work well because it is too large or complicated.

unwilling (unwillingness, unwillingly) ❑ If you are **unwilling** to do something, you do not want to do it. ...*an unwillingness to dispose of property at depressed prices.*
   ❑ **Unwilling** and **unwillingly** are used to say someone does something or becomes something against their will. *Developers have defaulted, making banks the unwilling owners of chunks of city space... Japan has continued to support the economic embargo, albeit unwillingly.*

unwind (unwinding, unwound) ❑ When you **unwind**, you relax and rest, especially after working hard.
   ❑ If you unwind something that is wrapped round itself or round something else, you untangle it and straighten it out. ◇ If you **unwind** something which has failed, you sort it out or bring it to an end. *She may be forced to unwind some of her husband's transactions.*

unwise If you say it would be **unwise** to do something, you mean it would not be a good idea.

unwitting (unwittingly) **Unwitting** is used to describe people who have become involved in something without understanding what is really happening. *The agency believes that he may have been an unwitting courier for the bombers, and was tricked into carrying the explosives onto the plane... They have unwittingly done enormous damage.*

unwonted (*pron:* un-**woan**-tid) is used to describe things which do not often happen. *There was an unwonted pallor in her cheeks.*

unworkable If you say something like a plan or idea is **unworkable**, you mean it cannot be made to work.

unworldly If you describe someone as **unworldly**, you mean they are concerned with spiritual or intellectual things, rather than with things like making money or building a career. ◇ People are also sometimes described as **unworldly** when they have had very little experience of life.

unworthy If you say someone is **unworthy** of something, you mean they do not deserve to have it. ◇ If you say someone's behaviour is **unworthy** of someone in their position, you mean they should behave better. *His accusations are unworthy of a Prime Minister.*

unwound See unwind.

unwrap (unwrapping, unwrapped) If you **unwrap** something, you take off its covering.

unwritten rules and agreements have not been officially written down but are known about, understood, and accepted by everyone. ...*Britain's unwritten constitution.*

up (upping, upped) ❑ **Up** is used to talk about movement towards a higher place or position. *We climbed high up the mountain... Bill put up his hand... She scrambled up from the floor.*
   ❑ **Up to** is used to say someone moves towards something. *A man ran up and fired several shots.* ◇ If you go **up** a road, you go along it. If you go **up** a river, you go along it towards its source.
   ❑ If you move **up and down,** you keep moving first in one direction then the other. *We were forced to walk endlessly up and down a muddy towpath.* ◇ If you are **up,** you are not in bed.
   ❑ If an amount goes **up,** it increases. You can also say an amount is **upped.** *The US upped its offer of subsidy cuts from 70% to 75%.* ◇ **Up to** is used to talk about reaching a certain standard or level. *An enormous investment is going to be needed to bring this up to a reasonable level.* ◇ **Up to** is also used to emphasize how large a number is. *Up to 4,000 Liberians have fled the country as refugees.*
   ❑ If something happens **up to** or **up until** a particular time, it happens until then. ◇ If a period of time is **up,** it has ended. *When the six weeks were up, everyone was sad that she had to leave.*
   ❑ If a computer is **up,** it is working.
   ❑ If you say something is **up,** you mean something is wrong. *My family rang the coastguard to find out what was up.* ◇ If you say someone is **up to** something, you mean they are secretly doing something they should not do.
   ❑ If you say it is **up to** someone to do something, you mean it is their responsibility.
   ❑ If you are **up against** something, you have a difficult problem or situation to deal with. ◇ If you are not **up to** something, you do not feel well enough to deal with it.
   ❑ If you have your **ups and downs,** both good and bad things happen to you.

up-and-coming people are likely to be successful in the future. ...*an up-and-coming Irish actor.*

up-to-date If something is **up-to-date**, it is the newest thing of its kind. ◇ If you try to keep **up-to-date** with something, you try to make sure you always have the latest information about it.

up-to-the-minute information is the latest information available.

upbeat people are cheerful and positive about the future.

upbraid (upbraiding, upbraided) If you **upbraid** someone, you tell them off for something they have done.

upbringing Your **upbringing** is the way your parents treat you and the things they teach you to care about and believe in. *He had a strict Calvinist upbringing.*

upcoming things are about to happen soon.

update (updating, updated) If you **update** something like a system, you make it more modern, for example by using the latest ideas, materials, or information. ◇ An **update** is something like a report which gives the latest information on something.

upend If something like a box is **upended,** it is turned upside down.

upgrade (upgrading, upgraded) If you **upgrade** something, you improve it or give it more importance.

upheaval You say there is **upheaval** in a place or organization when a major change causes trouble and confusion. An **upheaval** is a change like this.

upheld See uphold.

uphill If you go **uphill**, you go up a slope. ◇ If you say someone has an **uphill** task, you mean they have a difficult task ahead and will need a lot of effort and determination to succeed.

uphold (upholding, upheld; upholder) If someone **upholds** something like a system or principle, they support it and try to make it work. *Both President Bush and Dan Quayle were campaigning vigorously as upholders of the traditional family unit.* ◇ If someone in authority **upholds** a decision, they officially decide it is correct and should stand.

upholstered (upholstery, upholsterer) **Upholstered** chairs and sofas have a soft covering which makes them comfortable to sit on. This covering is called **upholstery**. An **upholsterer** is someone who covers chairs and sofas as their job.

upkeep The **upkeep** of something like a building is everything that needs to be done to keep it in good condition and working properly. ◇ The **upkeep** of a family is everything that needs to be provided for them.

uplands (upland) **Uplands** are areas of high land. **Upland** is used to describe things situated in areas like these. *...upland farms.*

uplift ❏ If something **uplifts** you or gives you **uplift**, it makes you happier and helps you do something better or more successfully.
❏ If your arms are **uplifted**, you are holding them up high. ◇ If your face is **uplifted**, you are looking upwards.

upmarket products are aimed at well-off people, especially people with sophisticated tastes. **Upmarket** places are lived in or visited by people like these.

upon is used to say something lands or falls on top of something else, or is placed there. *A large dragonfly settled upon the bowl of artificial flowers.*
❏ You can say something has an effect **upon** someone or something else. *The fact that they're missing contacts with their families will have some effect upon these prisoners.*
❏ **Upon** is used to say one thing is immediately followed by another. *Upon release, he went into exile.* ◇ If something is **upon** you, it is just about to happen to you. *With the Easter holiday upon us, The Sun focuses on a strike by French air traffic controllers.*
❏ **Upon** is used to talk about several things occurring straight after each other. *...volunteers carrying out series upon series of exercises... Hogan would practise for hour upon hour.*

upper is used to talk about (a) the top part of something. *...the upper atmosphere.* (b) the higher ones of a series of things. *Nurses waved from upper windows.*
❏ When a parliament consists of two parts meeting separately, one of them is usually called the **upper house** or **upper chamber**. In Britain, the **upper house** is the House of Lords.
❏ If you have the **upper hand** in a situation, you are likely to get your own way or to control what happens.
❏ The **upper** of a shoe is the top part.

upper case letters are capitals.

upper class (upper classes) People of a high social status are sometimes called the **upper classes**. **Upper-class** is used to describe things relating to the upper classes.

...upper-class speech.

upper crust Upper class people are sometimes called the **upper crust**. *...upper crust Indians.*

upper lip Your **upper lip** is the part of your face between your mouth and your nose. ◇ **stiff upper lip**: see lip.

uppercut In boxing, an **uppercut** is a hard upward blow to an opponent's chin.

uppermost If something is **uppermost in your mind**, it is the main thing you are thinking about it. ◇ If something is **uppermost** in a situation, it is the most important thing in it. *The question of prisoners has been uppermost in both negotiations and intelligence gatherings.*

uppity If you call someone **uppity**, you mean they are behaving as if they are more important than they really are.

upright ❏ If you are **upright**, you are standing up, or you are sitting with your back straight rather than leaning back. Similarly, if an object is **upright**, it is standing up, rather than lying on its side. ◇ An **upright** chair has a straight back and no arms.
❏ You say people are **upright** when they behave in a moral way.

uprising If there is an **uprising** in a country, people start fighting against whoever is in power there.

uproar If there is **uproar**, there is a lot of shouting and noise, because people are angry about something. ◇ If something causes an **uproar**, it starts a lot of angry discussion and argument.

uproarious (uproariously) **Uproarious** laughter is very loud. You can say someone laughs **uproariously**. You can also say something like a play or film is **uproarious** when it is very funny.

uproot (uprooting, uprooted) If you are **uprooted** from a place where you have lived for a long time, you have to leave it. ◇ If something like a tree or a road sign is **uprooted**, it is torn out of the ground.

upset (upsetting, upset *not 'upsetted'*) ❏ If an experience **upsets** you, it makes you troubled and unhappy. When you are in this state, you say you are **upset**.
❏ If something **upsets** a plan or system, it makes it go wrong.
❏ If a sportsperson or team **upsets** another one that is supposed to be superior to them, they beat them. A win like this is called an **upset**. Similarly, an unexpected victory in an election can be called an **upset**.
❏ A stomach **upset** is a mild illness affecting a person's stomach, usually caused by something they have eaten.

upshot The **upshot** of a series of events is the final result.

upside The **upside** of something is its good parts or results, as distinct from its bad ones.

upside down If something is **upside down**, it has been turned over so the top or highest part is underneath the rest. ◇ If you turn a place **upside down**, you move everything around and make it untidy, because you are looking for something. ◇ If an organization or way of doing something is turned **upside down**, it is changed completely.

upstage (upstaging, upstaged) If you **upstage** someone, you behave in a way which takes everyone's attention away from them and onto yourself.

upstairs If something is **upstairs**, it is on one of the upper floors of a building, or on a higher floor than you.

If you go **upstairs**, you go up to a higher floor. ◇ An **upstairs** room or window is on an upper floor of a building.

upstanding people are very respectable and trustworthy.

upstart If you call someone an **upstart**, you mean they are behaving as if they are important, and are not showing respect for people who have been doing something longer than they have.

upstream If you go **upstream**, you go along a river in the opposite direction to its flow. If something is **upstream** of you, it is further along the river in this direction.

upsurge If there is an **upsurge** in something, it suddenly increases by a large amount.

upswing If there is an **upswing** in something, it suddenly increases or improves.

uptake The **uptake** of something is the amount which is used. *The drug increases the number of red cells in the blood, enhancing oxygen uptake by 10%.*

uptight If someone is **uptight**, they are very tense, because they are worried or annoyed about something.

uptown If you go **uptown**, you leave the centre of a city and make for one of its outer parts. If something is **uptown**, it is in a part of a city away from its centre.

upturn If there is an **upturn** in something, it increases or improves. *Mr Wylde does not expect signs of an upturn in the jobs market until the spring.*

upturned If something is **upturned**, (a) it is facing upwards. *He sat crosslegged, his palms upturned.* (b) it is upside down. *He slid off the road as he tried to avoid the upturned Toyota.*

upward (upwards) ❑ If you move or look **upward** or **upwards**, you move or look towards a higher place. ◇ If an amount or rate moves **upward** or **upwards**, it increases. *It's the third month running that the trend has been upward.*
❑ **Upwards** of a certain number means more than that number. *...pigs weighing from about 20 kilos upwards.*
❑ **upward mobility**: see **upwardly mobile**.

upwardly mobile people are becoming richer and are improving their social status. You talk about the **upward mobility** of people like these.

upwards See **upward**.

upwind If you move **upwind**, you move directly into the wind.

uranium is a radioactive metal used in nuclear weapons and to produce nuclear energy.

urban is used to talk about things to do with towns and cities. *...urban areas.*

urbane (urbanity) If you describe someone as **urbane** or talk about their **urbanity**, you mean they have very good manners and seem relaxed and comfortable when meeting and mixing with people.

urbanization (urbanized) (*or* urbanisation, urbanised) Urbanization is a process in which more and more towns are built in a country or region which had formerly been rural. When this happens to a place, you say it becomes **urbanized**. **Urbanized** people are accustomed to living in towns. *There is now a well-educated, urbanized Malay middle class.*

urchin Children are sometimes called **urchins** when they look dirty and are poorly dressed.

Urdu (*pron:* **oor**-doo) is the official language of Pakistan. It is also spoken by many people in India and Britain.

urethra (*pron:* yew-**reeth**-ra) A person's **urethra** is the tube which takes urine from their bladder out of their body. A man's sperm also passes down his urethra.

urge (urging, urged) An **urge** is a strong desire to do something. ◇ If you **urge** someone to do something, you try hard to persuade them to do it. ◇ If you **urge** someone **on**, you encourage them.

urgent (urgently, urgency) If you say something is **urgent**, you mean it needs to be dealt with as soon as possible. You talk about the **urgency** of something like this. *More telephone lines are needed urgently.* ◇ If someone speaks in an **urgent** way, they show in the way they speak that they are anxious or excited. *There was a note of urgency in his voice.*

urinal A **urinal** is a bowl or trough in a public lavatory for men to urinate in.

urinary is used to talk about things relating to urine and the parts of the body it flows through. *...the urinary tract.*

urinate (urinating, urinated) When someone **urinates**, urine passes out of their body.

urine is the liquid people get rid of from their body when they go to the toilet.

urn Urns are containers like large vases. Decorated urns are sometimes used to hold the ashes of people who have been cremated. ◇ A tea or coffee **urn** is a large metal container used for making a large amount of tea or coffee and keeping it warm.

US The US is the United States of America.

us is used to talk about a group of people which includes the person who is speaking or writing. *That is very good news for all of us.*

USA The USA is the United States of America.

usable things are in a good enough condition to be used.

usage is used to talk about the ways words are used. *Many of the words may not even be in modern usage... The exact usage of the term can cause problems for beginners.* ◇ Usage is also used to talk about the way other things are used, or the extent to which they are used. *...energy usage... ...rail usage.*

use (using, used) ❑ If you **use** something or make **use** of it, you do something with it, to do a job or achieve something. When something is used, you talk about its **use**. *The drug is safe for widespread use... Iraq denies that the cargo had any military use.* ◇ If something is **in use**, it is being used regularly. If it is **out of use**, it is no longer being used.
❑ If a supply of something is **used up**, all of it has been used and there is none left.
❑ If you find a **use** for something, you find a purpose for which it can be used. ◇ If something is **of use**, it is useful. If it is **no use**, there is nothing it can be used for.
❑ If you have the **use** of something, you are allowed to use it. ◇ If you lose the **use** of a part of your body, you are unable to use it, because of an accident or illness.
❑ If you buy a **used** car, you buy one which has already had at least one owner.
❑ When you **use** a word or phrase, you say it or write it. You talk about a word or phrase being **used** to mean a particular thing; this is called a **use** of the word or phrase. *His*

15 complaints include two about the use of 'poof'.

❏ If you say you are being **used**, you mean someone is getting you to do something for them, without caring about you or your feelings at all.

❏ If you say it's **no use** doing something, you mean it will not achieve anything.

❏ If something **used to** be true or **used to** be done, it was true or was done regularly in the past.

❏ If you are **used to** something, you have experienced it and know what it is like.

useful (usefully, usefulness) ❏ If something is **useful**, it can be used to do a task or to achieve something. *...a useful tool... The Argentine army has far more sergeants than it can usefully employ... ...an idea that has outlived its usefulness.* ◇ If something **comes in useful** on a particular occasion, you are able to use it and are glad you have it.

❏ **Useful** is sometimes used to say someone is good at a sport. *He is an accomplished basketball player and a useful cricketer.*

useless (uselessly, uselessness) ❏ If something is **useless**, it is no good for what you want, or cannot be used for anything at all. Similarly, if something you do is **useless**, it does not help to achieve anything or does not get the result you want. *They fired their machine guns uselessly into the sky... ...the uselessness of abstract theorising.*

❏ If you say someone is **useless** at something, you mean they are no good at it.

user The **users** of something are the people who use it. *Bleach and caustic sodas are fairly hazardous both to the user and to the environment.*

user-friendly things are easy to understand or use.

usher (ushering, ushered) ❏ If someone **ushers** you to a place where you are supposed to be, they go with you, to make sure you get there. ◇ An **usher** is someone who shows people where to go or sit, for example at a wedding or a concert.

❏ If a person or event **ushers in** an important change, they help make it happen. *...a collapse in world trade that would usher in an era of turmoil.*

usherette **Usherettes** are women who show people where to sit in a cinema or theatre and sometimes sell programmes and refreshments.

USSR The **USSR** was the former Soviet Union. USSR stood for 'Union of Soviet Socialist Republics', which was the country's official name.

usual (usually) **Usual** and **usually** are used to talk about what normally happens in a certain situation. *The usual cost-cutting and marketing drive is under way... As usual on such occasions, there were banners and slogans praising the achievements of socialism... Our father read aloud to us, usually after supper.* ◇ **More than usually** is used to say a

description of something applies even more than usual. *The government is likely to be even more than usually sensitive to criticism.*

usurp (*pron:* yewz-**zurp**) (usurpation, usurper) If you **usurp** someone's position or role, you take it over for yourself, without having any authority to do so. This is called a **usurpation** of their position or role. Someone who behaves like this is called a **usurper.**

usury (*pron:* yewz-yoor-ee) is an old word for lending people money, especially at high interest rates.

utensil **Utensils** are the tools and other things you use for making or preparing something.

uterus (*pron:* yew-ter-russ) (uterine) A woman's **uterus** is her womb. **Uterine** (*pron:* yew-ter-rine) is used to talk about things to do with the womb. *...uterine contractions.*

utilise See utilize.

utilitarian things are meant to be useful and practical rather than beautiful.

utilitarianism is the idea that all actions should be aimed at producing the greatest happiness for the greatest number of people.

utility (utilities) ❏ **Utility** is used to talk about how useful something is. *In one to two years we'll have a better idea about the real utility of this approach.*

❏ **Utilities** are important services such as water or electricity which are provided for the public to use.

utilize (utilizing, utilized; utilization) (*can be spelled with an 's' instead of a 'z'*) If you **utilize** something, you use it. *...the utilization of fossil fuels.*

utmost If you do your **utmost** to achieve something, you do the best you can or as much as you can. ◇ **The utmost** in front of a word means 'the greatest'. *Environmental considerations are of the utmost importance when considering new routes.*

utopia (utopian) A **utopia** is someone's idea of a perfect social system in which everyone is happy and all their needs are met. **Utopian** is used to describe ideas and systems like this. *...the utopian vision of one of France's neglected geniuses, Charles Fourier.*

utter (uttering, uttered; utterly) ❏ If you **utter** words, you say them. You can also **utter** other sounds in your throat, for example a grunt or a scream. You can also **utter** an idea or an opinion. *Many of the parents who utter such sentiments are perfectly sincere.*

❏ **Utter** and **utterly** are used to emphasize certain words. *...utter confusion... She was hopelessly, utterly besotted with him.*

utterance An **utterance** is something a person says. *His public utterances are becoming increasingly unpredictable.*

UV is short for 'ultraviolet'.

V v

v is used in writing to say two people or teams are competing against each other. 'v' is short for 'versus'. *Linford Christie v Carl Lewis, the race the athletics world wants to see.*

V-neck A V-neck is a V-shaped neckline on a piece of clothing.

V-sign In Britain, a V-sign is a rude gesture made by moving your hand quickly upwards with your palm facing toward you, and with your first and middle fingers pointing up and spread out like a V. ◇ A V-sign is also a sign meaning 'victory'. It involves the same gesture but with your palm facing away from you.

vacancy (vacancies) A vacancy is a job or position which has not been filled. ◇ If there are vacancies at a hotel or other building, some of the rooms are available for people to stay in or rent.

vacant (vacantly) ❑ If something is vacant, it is not being used. *...vacant office space.* ◇ If a job or position is vacant, it has not yet been filled. *Steve McCarthy won the vacant light-heavyweight title at Battersea on Thursday.*

❑ If you say someone looks vacant, you mean they do not seem to understand what is being said to them, or they show no sign of emotion or thought. *Hubert stared vacantly out into the June night.*

vacate (vacating, vacated) If you vacate a place or a job, you leave it and make it available for other people.

vacation The vacation is one of the periods each year when a university or college is officially closed. ◇ If you take a vacation, you have a holiday.

vaccinate (vaccinating, vaccinated; vaccination) When people or animals are vaccinated against a disease or have a vaccination, they are given a vaccine, usually by injection, to stop them getting the disease.

vaccine A vaccine is a substance containing the bacteria or viruses which normally cause a disease. When given to patients, the vaccine makes their bodies produce antibodies to fight the disease, so they are protected against the disease itself.

vacillate (*pron:* vass-ill-late) (vacillating, vacillated; vacillation) If you vacillate, you keep changing your mind. *He vacillated between republican and monarchist sentiments... ...a year of vacillation, indecision and lack of purpose.*

vacuous (vacuity) If you call something vacuous or talk about its vacuity, you mean it does not express any intelligent ideas. *...vacuous slogans... He fought a campaign notable for its intellectual vacuity and personal nastiness.* You can also call a person vacuous when they do not seem to have any intelligent ideas.

vacuum (vacuuming, vacuumed) ❑ A vacuum is a space containing no air, gases, or other matter.

❑ If you say someone or something has created a vacuum, you mean their absence has created a space which needs to be filled by another person or thing.

❑ If you vacuum a carpet, you clean it using a vacuum cleaner.

vacuum cleaner A vacuum cleaner is an electric machine which cleans by sucking up dust and dirt.

vacuum flask A vacuum flask is a container used to keep drinks hot or cold. It has two thin silvery glass walls with a vacuum between them.

vacuum-packed food has been preserved by being packed in a container or packet from which most of the air has been removed.

vagabond A vagabond is a person who moves from place to place and does not have a fixed home or job.

vagaries (*pron:* vaig-a-reez) The vagaries of something are the unexpected and unpredictable changes in it. *...the vagaries of the weather... ...the vagaries of fashion.*

vagina (*pron:* vaj-jine-a) (vaginal) A woman's or female animal's vagina is the passage connecting her outer sex organs to her womb. Vaginal is used to talk about things involving the vagina. *HIV is spread through penetrative sexual intercourse whether anal or vaginal.*

vagrant (*pron:* vaig-rant) (vagrancy) A vagrant is a person who moves from place to place and has no home or job, and so has to beg or steal to live. This way of life is called vagrancy.

vague (vaguer, vaguest; vaguely, vagueness) If something is vague, it is not clear, distinct, or definite. *She had a vague notion that she wanted to work with children... Both papers are vaguely leftish... ...the vagueness of the government's funding plans.* ◇ If someone is vague, they make statements which are not clear or precise, often because they want to avoid telling people all the facts. *Mr Landsbergis was vague about how long fuel supplies could hold out.*

vain (vainer, vainest; vainly) ❑ A vain action or attempt is unsuccessful. *He returned to the scene in a vain search for his son's body... The British had vainly tried to stem the German invasion.* You can also say an action or attempt was in vain. ◇ A vain hope is unlikely to come true.

❑ If someone is vain, they think a lot about their own beauty, intelligence, or other good points and are extremely proud of them.

vainglorious A vainglorious person is boastful and likes to show off. Things which are done or created to show off someone's power can also be called vainglorious. *...vainglorious public monuments.*

valance (*pron:* val-lenss) A valance is a decorative cover for the base of a bed, with a frill which hangs around the edge of the bed.

vale A vale is the same as a valley.

valediction (*pron:* val-lid-dik-shun) (valedictory) A valediction is something you say or do as a way of saying farewell. Valedictory is used to describe things said or done as a farewell. *...his valedictory speech.*

Valentine A Valentine or Valentine card is a card you send to someone you love on St Valentine's Day, February 14th.

valet (valeting, valeted) ❑ A valet (*pron:* val-lay) is a wealthy man's personal manservant, who does things like look after his clothes and cook his meals.

❑ If you have your car valeted (*pron:* val-it-id), the bodywork and fittings are cleaned and repaired, but no mechanical work is done.

valiant (valiantly) You call someone's behaviour **valiant** when they are brave and determined, despite being in a situation where they are unlikely to succeed or win. *The Poles fought valiantly before being overwhelmed.*

valid (validly, validity) ❏ If something is **valid**, it is based on sound reasoning. You talk about the **validity** of something like this. *Her article casts doubt on the validity of this interpretation.*

❏ If something like a document is **valid**, everything about it is correct and it can be used for the purpose it is required for. *Anyone caught travelling without a valid ticket will have to pay a penalty of ten pounds... Certain aspects of the design were not validly patented.*

validate (validating, validated; validation) If you **validate** something, you prove it is correct, or make it legitimate. *Auditors play a critical role in validating the information supplied to shareholders... It is crucial that validation is based on research, not on anecdotes and ideas.*

Valium is the potentially habit-forming drug diazepam, a tranquillizer and muscle-relaxant usually prescribed for the short-term relief of tension and anxiety. 'Valium' is a trademark.

valley A **valley** is an area of land between two lines of hills or mountains, often with a river running through it.

valour (*American spelling:* **valor**) is great bravery, especially in battle.

valuable ❏ If something is **valuable**, it is worth a lot of money. ◇ **Valuables** are small valuable items people wear or carry around.

❏ You also say things are **valuable** when they are very useful or helpful. *The tomb has provided valuable information about the Moche civilisation.*

value (valuing, valued; valuation) ❏ The **value** of something is how much it is worth. ◇ When experts **value** something, they judge how much it is worth. This is called making a **valuation**. ◇ If something is of **value**, it is valuable. ◇ If something is **good value** or **value for money**, it is worth the money you pay for it.

❏ The **value** of something is also its importance or usefulness. *They appreciate the value of higher education.* ◇ If you **value** something, you think it is important and you appreciate it. *He values his new-found privacy.*

❏ People's **values** are their moral principles.

❏ **Value** is used after words like 'novelty' and 'shock' to say something has a particular kind of importance or usefulness. *'Married Man Not Having Affair' will soon warrant front-page coverage because of its novelty value.*

❏ The **face value** of something like a ticket or a stamp is its value according to the price on it, rather than its actual market value. ◇ If you **take** something **at face value**, you interpret it in the most obvious way, rather than disbelieving it or considering what it might really mean.

value-added tax See **VAT**.

value judgement A **value judgement** is an opinion based on moral principles rather than facts which can be checked or proved.

valueless If something is **valueless**, it is not worth any money, or is not useful in any way.

valuer A **valuer** is a person whose job is to decide how much things are worth.

valve A **valve** is a device attached to a pipe or tube to control the flow of gas or liquid passing through. ◇ In your body, **valves** are small flaplike structures in the heart and veins. They control the flow of blood and stop it going in the wrong direction. ◇ In an instrument like a trumpet, the **valves** are the pieces you push or release to vary the length of the tube and produce different notes.

vamp A **vamp** is a woman, especially a character in a film, who uses her feminine charms to entice and exploit men.

vampire In horror stories, **vampires** are ghostly people who come out of their graves at night and suck the blood of living people.

vampire bat Vampire bats are tropical American bats which feed on the blood of live animals.

van A **van** is a vehicle for carrying goods, usually smaller than a lorry and with an enclosed box-shaped body.

vandalize (vandalizing, vandalized; vandalism, vandal) (*can be spelled with an 's' instead of a 'z'*) If someone **vandalizes** something, they deliberately damage it, for no special reason. Damaging things like this is called **vandalism**; the people who do it are called **vandals**.

vane A **vane** or **weather vane** is a metal object on top of a building which rotates to indicate which way the wind is blowing.

vanguard The **vanguard** of an army moving into battle is the group or part at the front. ◇ If you say people are in the **vanguard** of a new development, you mean they are involved in its most advanced part.

vanilla is a flavouring used in ice cream and other sweet food. It is taken from the dried pods of a tropical plant.

vanish (vanishes, vanishing, vanished) If something **vanishes**, it disappears suddenly or ceases to exist.

vanity (vanities) If you talk about someone's **vanity**, you mean they are too proud of their own appearance or other good points. Their **vanities** are ways in which they show this pride.

vanquish (vanquishes, vanquishing, vanquished) If someone is **vanquished** in a battle or competition, they lose it or are defeated.

vantage point A **vantage point** is a place, usually fairly high up, where you can get a good view of something. ◇ If someone's job allows them to know what is happening in their community or in the world, you can say they see things from a particular **vantage point**.

vapid (*rhymes with 'rapid'*) If you call something **vapid**, you mean it is dull and uninteresting, because it contains nothing stimulating or challenging. *Instead of the promised revelations, we get only vapid speculation about her emotional life.*

vapor See **vapour**.

vaporize (vaporizing, vaporized) (*can be spelled with an 's' instead of a 'z'*) If a liquid or solid **vaporizes** or is **vaporized**, it changes into vapour or gas.

vapour (*American spelling:* **vapor**) is a mass of tiny drops of water or other liquid in the air.

vapour trail A **vapour trail** is a white trail of water vapour left in the sky by a plane flying at high altitude.

variable (variability) ❏ If something is **variable**, it is liable to change. *...variable winds... ...variable-rate mortgages.* You can talk about the **variability** of something like this. ◇ The factors which can change in a situation are called variables.

❏ **Variable** is also used to talk about things which you can alter or adjust yourself. *...variable-speed turntables.*

❏ You also say something is **variable** when it is not always of good quality. *The cooking is variable.*

❏ In maths, a **variable** is a symbol, usually a letter, used to represent any number. In the equation $2(x + y) = 2x + 2y$, x and y are variables.

variance If something is **at variance** with something else, the two things seem to contradict each other. *The decision was at variance with the Brioni declaration.*

variant If one thing is a **variant** of another, it is the same type of thing, but different in various small ways. *Two thirds of the population still speak their own dialect, Elsassdutch, a sing-song variant of German.*

variation ❏ If there is **variation** in something, it exists in slightly different forms. Each form can be called a **variation**. ◇ If there is **variation** in a level or amount, it does not stay the same.

❏ If something is a **variation** on something else, it is the same thing but changed in some way. *'Memories of the Space Age' is a variation on two earlier stories.*

varicella (*pron:* va-ri-sell-a) is the scientific name for chicken pox.

varicose veins If someone has **varicose veins**, their veins have become swollen, twisted, and painful, especially in their legs.

varied See vary.

variegated leaves or plants have different coloured markings on them.

variety (varieties) ❏ If something has **variety**, it consists of different things, and is therefore more interesting than it would be otherwise.

❏ A **variety** of things is a number of different ones. *They are being released for a variety of reasons... The Inversnaid Centre provides a wide variety of courses for all levels.*

❏ A **variety** of something is a particular kind or type. *My local Safeway displays more than 80 varieties of beer.*

❏ **Variety** is a type of entertainment which includes many different kinds of acts in the same show.

various is used to say there are several different things of the type mentioned. *There are various ways to restore the balance... Various countries will be putting forward ideas.*

variously is used when mentioning the different ways in which something has been described, defined, or interpreted. *Last year's deficit has been variously estimated at between 15% and 18% of gross domestic product... The pollution has been blamed variously on poorly maintained septic tanks and broken sewer pipes.*

varnish (varnishes, varnishing, varnished) **Varnish** is an oily liquid which you paint onto wood, where it dries and hardens to give a clear shiny protective coating. When you **varnish** wood, you put varnish on it.

varsity is another word for 'university'. It is used especially when talking about sports matches between Oxford and Cambridge Universities.

vary (varies, varying, varied) If things **vary**, they are not all the same. *Prices may vary greatly... ...varying degrees of risk.* ◇ If something is **varied**, it consists of a lot of different things. *...a varied diet... These poems are remarkably varied in content and structure.* ◇ If you **vary** something you do, you keep changing the way you do it.

vascular is used to talk about things to do with the tubes or ducts which carry blood in animals and sap in plants. *...vascular medicine... ...the cardio-vascular system.*

vase A **vase** is a jar, usually of glass or pottery, used for holding cut flowers or as an ornament.

vasectomy (vasectomies) A **vasectomy** is a surgical operation to cut the two ducts which carry sperm to a man's penis. Men usually have **vasectomies** because they do not want to have any more children.

Vaseline is a clear greasy substance obtained from petroleum. It is used in ointments and as a lubricant. 'Vaseline' is a trademark.

vast (vastness, vastly) If something is **vast**, it is extremely large. *...the vastness of the Sinai desert.* ◇ **Vastly** means 'very much' or 'very'. *Ms Brown vastly increased the circulation of Vanity Fair... ...vastly enjoyable movies.*

VAT or **value-added tax** is a tax in Britain and many other European countries. It is added to the price of many goods and services, then paid to the government by the seller.

vat A **vat** is a large barrel or other container for holding liquids like whisky or dye, especially while they are being made.

Vatican **Vatican City** is a tiny separate state within the city of Rome. In it are St Peter's Church and the Vatican Palace where the Pope lives. **The Vatican** is sometimes used to talk about the Pope and his officials. *The Vatican said yesterday it was re-establishing diplomatic relations with Mexico.*

vaudeville (*pron:* vaw-de-vil) is a type of theatrical entertainment involving songs, jokes, and acts of skill. It was popular in the US from the late 1800s until the 1950s. Many famous comedians began their careers in vaudeville.

vault ❏ A **vault** is a secure room where money and other valuable things can be kept safely. ◇ A **vault** is also a burial chamber, especially one underneath a church or cemetery.

❏ A **vault** is also an arched structure which forms a roof or ceiling. You say a roof or ceiling like this is **vaulted**.

❏ In gymnastics, the **vault** is an event in which gymnasts jump over an apparatus called a **vaulting horse**, placing their hand or hands on top of it to support their weight. ◇ If you **vault** over something, you jump over it using your hands or a pole to support your weight. See also **pole vault**.

vaunted You use **vaunted** or **much-vaunted** to describe things which are praised or admired a lot, especially when you think the praise or admiration is not justified. *For all his vaunted sex appeal, he looks his age.*

VC See Victoria Cross.

VCR A **VCR** is the same as a video recorder. VCR stands for 'video cassette recorder'.

VD is the same as venereal disease. *...a VD clinic.*

VDU A **VDU** is a device with a screen which is used to display information from a computer. VDU stands for 'visual display unit'.

veal is meat from a calf.

vector ❏ In maths, a **vector** is a variable quantity, such as a force, which has magnitude and direction.

❏ In biology and medicine, a **vector** is an animal or organism which is a carrier of a disease-causing parasite.

Mosquitoes are a common kind of vector.

veer (veering, veered) ❑ If a person or thing is moving quickly and suddenly changes direction, you can say they **veer** in the new direction. *The hurricane veered off to the west... The car veered out of control and hit a bus queue.* ❑ If someone starts behaving in a different or more extreme way, you can talk about them **veering** into a certain kind of behaviour. *...fears that a stronger Germany might veer towards neutrality.* ◇ If something **veers** towards a certain quality, it comes quite close to having that quality. *Some of the pieces of furniture veer towards the ridiculous.*

veg is short for 'vegetables'. *...roast chicken and two veg.*

vegan (*pron:* vee-gan) A **vegan** is a person who does not eat meat or fish or any other animal products such as milk, butter, or cheese.

vegeburger Vegeburgers are flat round cakes of food which look like beefburgers and may even taste like them but are in fact made of vegetables and pulses.

vegetable ❑ Vegetables are edible plants and roots like cabbages, potatoes, and onions. They are usually eaten cooked. ❑ **Vegetable** matter comes from plants. ❑ People sometimes say a person has become a **vegetable** when they are so sick or brain-damaged that they are unable to move or think.

vegetarian (vegetarianism) A **vegetarian** is a person who does not eat meat or fish. **Vegetarian** food does not contain meat or fish. The practice of not eating meat or fish is called **vegetarianism**.

vegetation is plant life in general.

vehement (*pron:* vee-i-ment) (vehemently, vehemence) If someone is **vehement** about something, they have strong feelings or opinions about it and express them forcefully and passionately. You can talk about the **vehemence** of someone like this. *...Mrs Thatcher's vehement opposition to a single European currency... This 'conspiracy theory' has been vehemently denied.*

vehicle A **vehicle** is a means of transport, especially one with wheels. ◇ You can say something is a **vehicle** for something else when it is used to achieve it. *The proposed body has been dismissed by some as simply a vehicle for the government to dominate the press.*

vehicular is used to talk about things to do with vehicles. *...vehicular access.*

veil (veiling, veiled) ❑ A **veil** is a piece of thin soft cloth worn by a woman over her head or to cover her face. If a woman is **veiled**, she is wearing a veil. ◇ When people talk about **the veil**, they mean the traditional form of dress in some religions, especially Islam, which involves women covering all their body except their eyes whenever they go out. ❑ If there is a **veil** of secrecy or silence over a subject, no information is being made available about it. ❑ A **veiled** comment is expressed in a disguised form rather than directly and openly. *Mr Kaifu made only a veiled reference to concerns over human rights.*

vein (veined) ❑ Your **veins** are tubes which carry blood back to your heart after it has been pumped out to the other parts of your body. ❑ The **veins** of a leaf are the thin lines which run through it, often in a forked pattern. ❑ A **vein** of a metal or mineral is a thin layer of it which has filled a crack or fissure in a mass of rock. ❑ **Veined** is used to describe things which have veins in them, or a pattern which looks like veins. *...beautifully veined marble... ...a blue-veined cheese.* ❑ If you talk about a **vein** of something being present somewhere, you mean it exists there. *Funar has tapped a rich vein of support at the margins of Romanian society.* ❑ You can describe the style or mood of something by saying it is done in a particular **vein**. *The entire piece continued in the same comic vein.*

Velcro is a material for fastening things together. It consists of two strips of nylon fabric. One strip is covered in tiny hooked threads which attach to the coarse surface of the other when the two strips are pressed together. You can pull the two strips apart and re-attach them whenever you need to. 'Velcro' is a trademark.

veld (*or* veldt) (*both pron:* velt) A **veld** is a level area of open grassland in southern Africa.

vellum is fine parchment made from the skin of young sheep, goats, or cows. In the past, it was used as writing paper and also as bookbinding material. ◇ **Vellum** is also a name given to heavy fine-quality writing paper which looks like real vellum.

velocity (velocities) The **velocity** of a moving object is its speed in a particular direction.

velour (*pron:* vel-loor) is a cloth similar to velvet but thicker and cheaper. It is used to make things like curtains and upholstery.

velvet is a closely-woven material usually made of silk, nylon, or cotton, with a soft furry surface of short cut threads on one side.

velveteen is a cotton material similar to thin velvet.

velvety is used to describe things which make you think of velvet, because they have an attractive smooth quality. *...a velvety wine... ...her rich, dark velvety voice.*

venal (*pron:* vee-nal) (venality) If you call someone **venal** or talk about their **venality**, you mean they are corrupt and willing to take bribes.

vendetta If someone pursues a **vendetta** against you, they have a grudge against you and do everything they can to harm or upset you.

vending machine A **vending machine** is a machine from which you can buy things like cigarettes, coffee, or chocolate by putting money in a slot and pressing a button.

vendor A **vendor** is a person who sells things like newspapers, cigarettes, and hamburgers in the street from a cart or stall. ◇ In legal documents, the person who is selling something, especially a house or piece of land, is called the **vendor**.

veneer is a thin layer of wood, or plastic made to look like wood, on the outside of furniture. ❑ If someone behaves in a way which hides their true feelings or their true nature, you can call their behaviour a **veneer**.

venerable If you call someone **venerable**, you mean they are entitled to respect because they are old and wise. Similarly, you can call an old and respected organization **venerable**. *...a venerable City firm.*

venerate (venerating, venerated; veneration) If someone or something is **venerated**, they are greatly respected. *The statue seems to have a good chance of survival, though as an* *object of public ridicule rather than veneration.*

venereal disease (pron: ven-ear-ee-al) Venereal diseases are a group of diseases, including syphilis and gonorrhoea, which are passed on through sexual intercourse.

Venetian blind A Venetian blind is a window blind made of thin horizontal strips attached to strings. You pull the strings to raise, lower, and change the angle of the strips so they let in or shut out light.

vengeance is revenge, usually in the form of violence.
❏ You use with a vengeance to emphasize the extent to which something happens. *Back she came with a vengeance to break the Yugoslav's delivery... Finally, his luck changed with a vengeance.*

vengeful If someone is vengeful, they are eager for revenge.

venison is meat from a deer.

venom (venomous) ❏ The venom of a creature like a snake, scorpion, or spider is the poison it injects with its bite or sting. You say an animal which has a poisonous bite or sting is venomous.
❏ When someone criticizes someone else in an angry bitter way, you can talk about the venom of their attack or describe it as venomous.

vent ❏ A vent is an opening designed to allow gases, fumes, or liquid to escape. ◇ A vent is also the shaft of a volcano or a hole in the earth's crust through which lava and gases erupt.
❏ When people vent strong feelings, especially anger, they express them in an unrestrained and forceful way.
❏ A vent is also a narrow opening at the bottom of a jacket or other piece of clothing. A garment can have a vent at the back or vents at each side.

ventilate (ventilating, ventilated; ventilation) ❏ If a room or building is well ventilated, fresh air is allowed to get in. If it is badly ventilated, not enough fresh air gets in. A ventilation system is intended to ensure that plenty of fresh air gets into a building.
❏ If an issue is ventilated, it is discussed in public.

ventilator ❏ A ventilator is a machine which helps you to breathe when you are having difficulty breathing, for example because you are ill or have been injured. It is also called a 'respirator'.
❏ A ventilator is also a device in a room or building, for example a fan, which lets fresh air in and stale air out.

ventricle (ventricular) The ventricles are the two chambers of the heart which pump blood into the arteries. Ventricular is used to talk about things to do with the ventricles. *...the left ventricular muscle.* ◇ The cavities of the brain are also called ventricles.

ventriloquist (ventriloquism) A ventriloquist is an entertainer who holds a dummy and speaks without noticeable lip movements, so the words seem to be spoken by the dummy. This skill is called ventriloquism.

venture (venturing, ventured) ❏ A venture is something new which is being tried out. *...one of the most successful ventures in space astronomy.* ◇ A venture is also a business operation.
❏ If you venture into a subject you are not familiar with, you become involved in it or start discussing it. Similarly, you can venture into a new area of activity. *He enjoyed little success when he ventured into business.*
❏ If you venture somewhere, you go there. *Few foreign nationals are said to be venturing outside their homes.*

venture capital (venture capitalist, venture capitalism) Venture capital is money lent to start up a new business, especially a risky one, in the hope of securing a high return. A person who lends money for this purpose is called a venture capitalist; lending money like this is called venture capitalism.

venue The venue for an event is the place where it will happen. *Mr Fernandes said that UNITA would like Portugal as a venue for talks with the MPLA.* ◇ A building where concerts, shows, or sporting events are held can also be called a venue. *...the Roundhouse, the former theatre and concert venue in north London.*

veracity ❏ If you talk about someone's veracity or the veracity of what they are saying, you are talking about whether they are telling the truth or not. *She disputed Ms Perdue's veracity... Putnam was concerned about the veracity of the book's claims.*
❏ If you talk about the veracity of an actor's performance, you mean it is true to life. *Rula Lenska brings considerable emotional veracity to the role of Madam Ranyevskaya.*

veranda (*or* verandah) A veranda is an area adjoining a house which has a floor and a roof but no sides. Houses in hot countries often have verandas.

verb A verb is a word which describes an action or a state. In the sentences 'I ran down the road' and 'I am happy', 'ran' and 'am' are verbs.

verbal (verbally) Verbal is used to describe things which involve words rather than actions. *The West must back up its verbal support with substantial economic aid... A number of young women have been attacked verbally.* ◇ If something is verbal, it is spoken rather than written. *...a verbal agreement.*

verbatim (pron: ver-bait-im) If you repeat something verbatim, you use exactly the same words. *...verbatim transcripts of BBC Radio programmes.*

verbiage is using too many words and making things over-complicated and unclear.

verbose (pron: verb-bohss) If someone is verbose, they use more words than are necessary, and are therefore tedious or annoying.

verdant places are covered with grass, trees, or other green plants.

verdict The verdict of a jury is the decision it reaches. ◇ A verdict is also a decision or opinion, especially one reached after careful consideration. *Arthur Cox offered a succinct verdict on yesterday's match.*

verge (verging, verged) ❏ A verge is a narrow strip of ground by the side of a road, usually with grass or flowers growing on it.
❏ If you are on the verge of something, you are about to do it or it is about to happen to you. *He was constantly on the verge of bankruptcy.*
❏ If something is almost the same as something else, you can say it verges on it. *The congregation greeted him with admiration verging on awe.* ◇ If something is close to some extreme, you can say it verges on it. *...a move that verges on the ridiculous.*

verger The verger of a Church of England church is someone whose main job is to look after the church building, its contents, and sometimes the grounds.

verifiable If something is **verifiable**, it can be proved to be true or correct.

verify (verifies, verifying, verified; verification) If you **verify** something, you check or confirm that it is true or correct. ◇ If something like a treaty or agreement is **verified**, officials check that the people who signed it are conforming to it. *...the verification of arms treaties.*

verisimilitude If a story or film seems realistic and convincing, you can talk about its **verisimilitude**.

veritable You use **veritable** when you are exaggerating, often humorously, to emphasize a feature of something. *The lake is a veritable ark of rare and threatened wildlife... The ruling elites are enjoying a veritable orgy of self-satisfaction.*

verity (verities) **Verities** are general truths or principles.

vermicelli (*pron:* ver-me-**chell**-ee) is a kind of very thin spaghetti.

vermilion is a bright red colour.

vermin Animals which people regard as pests are often called **vermin**, especially rats and mice.

vermouth (*pron:* ver-muth *or* ver-**mooth**) is an alcoholic drink made from wine flavoured with herbs.

vernacular (*pron:* ver-**nak**-yew-lar) The **vernacular** in a place is the language or dialect spoken by the ordinary people there, as distinct from the official language or the language spoken by educated people.

verruca (*pron:* ver-**roo**-ka) A **verruca** is a wart, especially one on the sole of the foot.

versatile (versatility) If you say someone is **versatile** or talk about their **versatility**, you mean they have many different skills and abilities, and are therefore able to move easily from one task to another. ◇ If something like a vehicle or device is **versatile**, it can be used to do a variety of different jobs.

verse is writing arranged in lines which have a rhythm and often rhyme. ◇ The **verses** of a poem, song, or hymn are the parts it is divided into. Chapters of the Bible are also divided into **verses**.

versed If you are **versed** or **well-versed** in something, you know a lot about it.

version A **version** of something is one form of it. *...a screen version of Virginia Woolf's Orlando.* ◇ Someone's **version** of an event is their account or description of what happened.

versus is used to say two people, things, or groups are opposed to each other or competing against each other. *...the Leeds versus Liverpool match.*

vertebra (*plural:* vertebrae) (vertebral) The **vertebrae** are the bones which form the spinal column. The spinal column is also called the **vertebral column**.

vertebrate A **vertebrate** is a creature with a backbone and a skull, for example a fish, bird, or mammal.

vertical (vertically) If something is **vertical**, it stands or points straight up from a flat surface. Similarly, a **vertical** cliff or drop goes straight up or straight down. ◇ **Vertical** is also used to talk about movement straight up into the air, or straight down. *...a vertical take-off plane... You can move the cine camera both vertically and horizontally.*

vertiginous (vertiginously) You can say something is **vertiginous** when it is sheer or high up and makes you feel dizzy. *...vertiginously steep angles.*

vertigo is a dizzy feeling some people get when they look down from a high place. ◇ **Vertigo** is also the medical name for any severe dizziness.

verve If something is done with **verve**, it is done with energy and enthusiasm.

very is used to say someone or something has a characteristic to a great degree. *Stephen was very brave... ...a very unusual car.*
    ❑ **Very** is used to emphasize that you are talking about an extreme point in something. *I was to go to the very top floor of Bush House.* ◇ **Very** is also used to emphasize that you are talking about an exact time or place. *The first experiments are taking place in Washington at this very moment.* ◇ **Very** is also used to emphasize that you are talking about a particular person or thing. *Some patients may even kill themselves with the very same drugs that are intended to protect them from their illness.*
    ❑ If something is your **very own**, it belongs to you and to nobody else.

vessel ❑ A **vessel** is a ship or large boat.
    ❑ A **vessel** is also a container, usually for liquid.
    ❑ See also **blood vessel**.

vest A **vest** is a short, usually sleeveless piece of underwear worn on the top half of the body. ◇ In the US, a waistcoat is called a **vest**.

vested ❑ If something is **vested** in someone, it is given to them as a right or responsibility. *...a constitutional monarchy with sovereignty vested in the people.*
    ❑ If someone has a **vested interest** in something, it involves their own money, reputation, or power, and therefore they may act out of self-interest rather than for the general good. *A fifth of its members are directors of state enterprises, with a vested interest in blocking change.* People in this position are themselves sometimes referred to as **vested interests**.

vestibule A **vestibule** is an enclosed area between the outside door of a building and the inner door.

vestige (*pron:* vest-ij) (vestigial) The **vestiges** of something are the parts left over when most of it has gone. *The last vestiges of Communism have been destroyed.* **Vestigial** (*pron:* vest-tij-ee-al) is used to describe the remaining parts of something. *...the vestigial functions of the Crown.*

vestments are the robes worn by priests, church officials, and choir members during church ceremonies.

vestry (vestries) In a church, the **vestry** is the room used by the priest as an office and as a place to store vestments and change into them.

vet (vetting, vetted) ❑ A **vet** is a person qualified to treat sick or injured animals. 'Vet' is short for 'veterinary surgeon'. Vets are also sometimes called **veterinarians**.
    ❑ A **vet** is also a veteran. *...a Vietnam vet.*
    ❑ When people or things are **vetted**, they are carefully checked to make sure they are acceptable. *...the vetting of job applicants.*

vetch is a plant with flowers like small sweet peas. Some kinds of vetch are used to feed cattle.

veteran ❑ A **veteran** is someone who has served in their country's armed forces, especially during a war. *...a Falklands veteran.* ◇ **Veteran** is also used to describe someone who has been doing their job for a long time. *...a veteran columnist on the San Francisco Chronicle.*
    ❑ A **veteran** car is a very old one, sometimes reckoned

veterinarian See vet.

as one constructed before 1919 and sometimes as one constructed by 1905. See also vintage.

veterinarian See vet.

veterinary is used to talk about things to do with the treatment of sick or injured animals. ...*veterinary medicine*... ...*a veterinary laboratory*.

veterinary surgeon See vet.

veto (vetoes, vetoing, vetoed) If a member of a voting group has a **veto,** they have the right to stop a resolution being put into action, even if all the other members are in favour. If they exercise this right, you say they **veto** the resolution.

vex (vexes, vexing, vexed) If something **vexes** you, it annoys or troubles you. ◇ A **vexed** question or issue is very difficult and causes people a lot of trouble.

VHF is a range of radio frequencies which produce good sound quality. VHF stands for 'very high frequency'.

via ❏ If you go to one place **via** another, you pass through the second place on your way to the first.

❏ If something like a signal or message is sent using a particular method, you can say it is sent **via** that method. *The show will be broadcast to schools via satellite from the Continent.*

❏ If you achieve something **via** something else, you achieve it by means of it. *The obvious way to establish consent is via a referendum.*

viable (viability) If an idea is **viable,** it would probably work and is worth considering. Similarly, you can talk about a new product being **viable.** *British Aerospace reckon that the plane will be commercially viable if 400 - 500 can be sold.* You can talk about the **viability** of an idea or product.

viaduct A **viaduct** is a long high bridge carrying a road or railway across a valley, usually supported by a series of arches.

vial A **vial** is the same as a phial.

vibe ❏ When people talk about the **vibes** they get from a person or place, they mean the impression they have of them and the kind of feelings they arouse.

❏ The vibraphone is sometimes called the **vibes.**

vibrant (pron: vibe-rant) (vibrantly, vibrancy) ❏ If you describe someone as **vibrant** or talk about their **vibrancy,** you mean they are full of life, energy, and enthusiasm.

❏ You can describe certain things as **vibrant** when they involve a lot of activity. ...*the world's most vibrant economy.*

❏ **Vibrant** colours are bright and attractive. ...*vibrantly coloured rugs.*

vibraphone The **vibraphone** is an electronic musical instrument similar to a xylophone but with metal bars. When you hit the bars, they produce a lingering vibrating sound.

vibrate (vibrating, vibrated; vibration) When something **vibrates** or is **vibrated,** it makes rapidly repeated shaking movements. These movements are called **vibrations.**

vibrato (pron: vib-brah-toe) is a rapidly repeated slight variation in the pitch of a musical note, produced to improve the quality of the sound.

vibrator A **vibrator** is an electronic device which vibrates, used in massage or for sexual pleasure.

vicar A **vicar** is a parish priest in the Church of England.

vicarage A **vicarage** is a house a vicar lives in, especially one provided by the church.

vicarious (pron: vick-air-ee-uss) (vicariously) A **vicarious** experience or feeling is one you get by watching, listening to, or reading about other people doing something, rather than doing it yourself. *More than 300 people are due to attend the first Archers convention, to share reminiscences of a country life lived vicariously over the airwaves.*

vice at the beginning of someone's rank or title indicates that they are next in line to someone else. For example, an organization's vice-chairman is next in line to its chairman.

❏ **Vices** are faults or moral weaknesses in someone's character or behaviour. ◇ **Vice** is criminal activities, especially ones connected with pornography, prostitution, and gambling.

❏ A **vice** (*American spelling:* vise) is a tool used to hold an object tightly while you work on it. ◇ You can say you are caught in a **vice** when you are trapped in an undesirable situation.

vice admiral See admiral.

vice-chancellor The **vice-chancellor** is the head of administration in a British university.

vice squad The **vice squad** is the section of the police force which deals with crime connected with pornography, prostitution, and gambling.

vice versa (pron: vie-suh ver-sa or vice ver-sa) is used to indicate that the reverse of what you are saying also applies. For example, 'Women may bring their husbands, and vice versa' means men may also bring their wives.

viceroy In the past, a **viceroy** was a man who ruled a colony, province, or country on behalf of his king or queen.

vicinity (pron: viss-in-it-ee) If something is **in the vicinity** of a place, it is in the nearby area.

vicious (viciously, viciousness) A **vicious** attack is particularly unpleasant and violent. *She had been viciously attacked and beaten*... ...*the viciousness of these crimes.* Similarly, a **vicious** criticism is very harsh and unpleasant. ◇ A **vicious** person is cruel, spiteful, and eager to cause harm.

vicious circle If you say a situation is a **vicious circle,** you mean one problem causes another one, which in turn tends to make the first one worse, and so on.

vicissitudes (pron: viss-iss-it-yewds) are changes in circumstances at different times in someone's life.

victim The **victims** of something are the people who suffer because of it. ...*earthquake victims*... ...*victims of crime.* ◇ A person's **victims** are the people who have died or suffered as a result of their actions. ◇ If you **fall victim** to something or someone, you suffer because of them. *In the early 1960s, Blyton fell victim to Alzheimer's disease.*

victimize (victimizing, victimized; victimization) (can be spelled with an 's' instead of a 'z') If someone is **victimized,** they are deliberately treated unfairly or picked on. ...*the victimization of ethnic groups.*

victor The **victor** in a contest or battle is the person, team, or army that wins.

Victoria Cross The **Victoria Cross** or VC is the highest award for gallantry in the face of the enemy awarded in Britain and the Commonwealth.

Victorian is used to describe things which existed, were made, or are associated with the period of British history when Victoria was Queen, between 1837 and 1901. ...*Victorian commercial buildings*... ...*Margaret Thatcher's* *call for a return to Victorian values.*

Victoriana Objects made during the Victorian period are called **Victoriana.**

victorious If someone has won a victory, you can say they are **victorious.**

victory (victories) A **victory** is a win or success in a battle or contest.

vide (*pron: vie-dee*) is used in a book or other publication to advise the reader where to look for information, or where to look for evidence supporting the writer's argument. *They now know that within 45 minutes a full-sized village (vide attached photos) can be practically wiped out.*

video (videos) **Video** is the recording of events using a video camera, the recording of TV programmes using a video recorder, or the showing of videotape on a TV set using a video recorder. ◇ A **video** is a video recorder. ◇ A **video** is also a film or TV programme recorded on videotape for people to watch on their TV set. ◇ If you **video** an event, you record it on videotape, using a video camera. If you **video** a TV programme, you record it using a video recorder.

video camera A **video camera** is a camera which takes moving pictures and records them on videotape so they can be played back using a video recorder attached to a TV set.

video cassette A **video cassette** is a cassette containing videotape.

video cassette recorder A **video cassette recorder** is the same as a video recorder.

video conference (video conferencing) A **video conference** is a conference in which several people a long way away from each other communicate using audio and video equipment. Running conferences like this is called **video conferencing.**

video game **Video games** are games created by a computer program, in which you manipulate images on a screen using an electronic control.

video nasty (video nasties) A **video nasty** is a film on video showing a lot of violence and horrific special effects.

video recorder A **video recorder** is a machine you attach to a TV set and use to record programmes on a video cassette. You also use it to play video cassettes on the TV set.

videotape (videotaping, videotaped) (*or* **video-tape**, *etc*) **Videotape** is magnetic tape used to record pictures or films so they can be played back on a TV set. A **videotape** is a video cassette or a piece of film recorded on videotape. If you **videotape** something, you record it on videotape.

vie (vies, vying, vied) If people **vie** for something, they compete for it. *The various institutions vie for the best students... The two firms are vying to provide the best sales and service back-up.*

view ❑ Your **views** on a subject are your beliefs or opinions on it.
❑ Your **view** of something or the way you **view** it is the way you understand and think about it. *BBC Scotland was widely viewed as something of a backwater.* ◇ If you take a **dim view** of something, you disapprove of it.
❑ If you take the **long view**, you consider what is likely to happen in the future over a long period, rather than

thinking only about the immediate effects of something.
❑ The **view** from a place is everything you can see from it. If you have a **view** of something, you can see it. *I have a glorious view of Bantry Bay from my bedroom window.* ◇ You use **view** in phrases like 'comes into view' and 'in full view' to talk about being able to see something. *We cruised steadily until Sarajevo airport came into view.*
❑ If you **view** something, you watch it or look at it. ◇ If something is **on view**, it is exhibited in public for people to see or examine. *A hundred drawings by the German Romantics are now on view at the Fitzwilliam Museum.*
❑ If you say something is **in view**, you mean it will happen soon. *The end of the recession was not yet in view.*
❑ If your actions are directed towards achieving an aim, you can say you have that aim **in view.**
❑ If you do something **with a view to** doing something else, you do it hoping or expecting to do that thing. *Mr Mitterrand tried to maintain an independent policy, with a view to playing a mediating role.*
❑ You use **in view of** when mentioning the reason for an opinion, decision, or conclusion. *Some City institutions have been pressing for him to stand aside as chairman in view of the seriousness of the allegations.*

viewer ❑ People who watch TV are called **viewers.**
❑ When people talk about **the viewer**, they mean anyone who happens to be looking at the thing they are talking about. *These four pictures have retained their ability to discomfit the viewer.*
❑ A **viewer** is also a device for looking at transparent slides.

viewfinder The **viewfinder** on a camera is a small square of glass which you look through to see what you are going to photograph.

viewpoint ❑ A person's **viewpoint** of a situation is how it seems to them and how it affects them.
❑ A **viewpoint** is also a place from which you can get a good view of something.

vigil A **vigil** is a long period, especially at night, when people remain quietly in a place, for example to look after someone, to pray, or to make a political protest.

vigilant (vigilance) If you are **vigilant**, you are alert and on the lookout for danger or trouble. *The newspaper called for renewed vigilance against what it called a latent communist threat.*

vigilante (*pron: vij-ill-ant-ee*) **Vigilantes** are people who unofficially organize themselves into a group to protect their community and catch and punish people they see as criminals.

vignette (*pron: vin-yet*) A **vignette** is a short piece of creative writing, usually describing a character or scene. ◇ A **vignette** is also a painting, drawing, or photograph with shaded-off edges.

vigor See vigour.

vigorous (vigorously) **Vigorous** exercise uses a lot of energy. ◇ A **vigorous** person is healthy and full of energy and enthusiasm. ◇ **Vigorous** is used to describe things people do or say with a lot of energy and enthusiasm. *Sir Marcus vigorously defended the rule change.*

vigour (*American spelling:* **vigor**) is energy and enthusiasm.

Viking The **Vikings** were groups of seamen from Scandinavia who were explorers and also attacked villages in many parts of western Europe from the 8th to the 11th centuries. They often settled in the places they reached and started farms.

vile (vilely, vileness) If you describe something as **vile**, you mean it is very unpleasant or disgusting. *...vile weather... Any penal system can be vilely abused... ...the vileness of people like these.*

vilify (vilifies, vilifying, vilified; vilification) If someone is **vilified**, people say or write unpleasant or highly critical things about them. *He said he was being subjected to an intense media campaign of lies and vilification.*

villa A **villa** is a fairly large house, especially one used for holidays in a Mediterranean country.

village A **village** is a number of houses built close together in a country area, usually with a church, a shop, and a pub.

villager **Villagers** are people who live in a village.

villain (villainous) ❑ If you say someone is **the villain** or **the villain of the piece**, you mean they are the person seen as the cause of all the trouble in a situation.
  ❑ The **villain** in a novel, film, or play is the main bad character. A bad character in fiction is often described as **villainous**. ◇ Criminals or other people who deliberately harm other people are sometimes called **villains**.

villainy is bad, dishonest, or criminal behaviour.

vim is energy and vigour.

vinaigrette is a salad dressing made from oil and vinegar with seasonings. **Vinaigrette** is used in the names of dishes served with this dressing.

vindicate (vindicating, vindicated; vindication) If someone is **vindicated**, their ideas or actions are proved to be correct or worthwhile. You can also say their ideas or actions are **vindicated**. *The arrests may vindicate the president's strongarm tactics.* If something proves someone's ideas or actions to be correct or worthwhile, you can say it is a **vindication** of them.

vindictive (vindictiveness) If someone is **vindictive**, they are motivated by a desire to hurt other people. You can also say their actions are **vindictive**. *The prime minister is letting vindictiveness get in the way of his judgement.*

vine A **vine** is a climbing or trailing plant, especially one which produces grapes. ◇ If you say something is **withering on the vine**, you mean it is deteriorating or disappearing, because nothing is being done to save or maintain it. *...as UN officials contemplate their latest peace plans withering on the vine.*

vinegar (vinegary) **Vinegar** is a sharp tasting liquid, usually made from fermented wine, cider, or malt. It is used to preserve food and is sometimes added to food after it has been served, to give it more flavour. If food or drink is **vinegary**, it tastes of vinegar.

vineyard (*pron:* vinn-yard) A **vineyard** is a piece of land planted with vines.

vintage wine is good quality wine which has been stored for several years to improve its quality. If you talk about the **vintage** of a wine, you mean the year and place it was made in before being stored to improve it.
  ❑ A **vintage** car is a fairly old one, usually reckoned as one constructed between 1919 and 1930. See also **veteran**. ◇ **Vintage** is used to describe other things which are old but admired. *...vintage aircraft... ...vintage British comedy.*
  ❑ You can also use **vintage** to describe entertainment

or sport which is the best of its kind. *This was vintage cricket, immensely skilful and exciting.*

vintner A **vintner** is someone whose job is to buy and sell wines.

vinyl is a strong plastic used in some paints and for making things like wallpaper, floor coverings, and records. ◇ **Vinyl** is sometimes used to mean records rather than CDs or other forms of recorded music. *...recordings available on vinyl.*

viol (*pron:* vie-ol) **Viols** are a family of musical instruments similar to violins and cellos. They have a fretted fingerboard, a flat back, and usually six strings. They are held between the knees or on the lap and played using a curved bow. Viols were popular in the 16th and 17th centuries.

viola (*pron:* vee-oh-la) The **viola** is a musical instrument which looks like a violin but is slightly larger and has a lower range of notes.

violate (violating, violated; violation, violator) ❑ If someone **violates** something like an agreement or law, they ignore it and do something which goes against it. Similarly, someone can **violate** people's rights. You can say someone's actions are a **violation** of an agreement, a law, or people's rights. People who violate something are called **violators** of it. *...human rights violators.*
  ❑ If an army, ship, or aircraft **violates** another country's territory, it enters it without permission.
  ❑ If someone **violates** a special place, for example a tomb, they damage it or treat it with disrespect.
  ❑ If a woman is **violated**, she is raped.

violent (violently, violence) ❑ You say someone's behaviour is **violent** when they try to hurt, injure, or kill other people using weapons or physical force. *The anti-government demonstrations were violently suppressed.* Behaviour like this is called **violence**. ◇ You say something like a film is **violent** when it contains a lot of violence.
  ❑ **Violent** is used to describe things like explosions when they happen with great force. You can also call their effects **violent**. *...an extremely violent collision... The cabins vibrated violently.*
  ❑ A **violent** change is sudden and powerful. *...violent price-swings.* ◇ You also use **violent** to describe things which are felt or expressed powerfully. *...violent pain... Mr Kohl violently disagreed with the statement.*
  ❑ If someone is **violently sick** or **violently ill**, they suddenly vomit a lot.
  ❑ **Violent** weather is very stormy. *...violent thunderstorms.*

violet **Violets** are small perfumed flowers which bloom in spring. They are usually bluish-purple but are sometimes white. ◇ **Violet** is a bluish-purple colour.

violin (violinist) The **violin** is a wooden musical instrument with four strings. You play it by holding it under your chin and moving a bow across the strings. A **violinist** is a musician who plays the violin.

VIP A **VIP** is someone who is given better treatment than ordinary people because he or she is famous or important. VIP stands for 'very important person'.

viper **Vipers** are a group of poisonous snakes from Europe, Africa, and Asia. The adder is a kind of viper.

viral (*pron:* vie-ral) is used to describe things which are caused by or connected with viruses. ...*viral meningitis.*

virgin (virginity) ❏ A **virgin** is someone, especially a woman or girl, who has never had sex. You talk about the **virginity** of someone like this. *She was determined to preserve her virginity until they were married.* When someone loses their **virginity,** they have sex for the first time.
❏ **Virgin** is sometimes used to describe things which are new or have never been used or spoiled. *The script was based on the life of Billy the Kid, not exactly virgin territory as Western heroes go... ...the last of the world's virgin forests.*

Virgin Birth Christians who believe in the **Virgin Birth** believe that Mary conceived and gave birth to Jesus Christ through God's power rather than as a result of sexual intercourse.

virginal If you describe a young person as **virginal,** you mean they have had no experience of sex, or appear not to have had.

virginity See **virgin.**

virile (virility) ❏ If you describe a man as **virile,** you mean he has what are considered to be typical manly characteristics, especially energy and sex drive. You can talk about the **virility** of a man like this.
❏ You can use **virile** to describe other things which are healthy and active. ...*a virile national economy.*

virology (virologist) **Virology** is the branch of medicine concerned with the study of viruses and the diseases they cause. A specialist in this subject is referred to as a **virologist.**

virtual (virtually) ❏ **Virtual** is used to say something is so close to being a particular thing that for most purposes it can be regarded as that thing. *Industrial disputes have brought traffic to a virtual standstill... Today I am virtually bankrupt.*
❏ **Virtual** is also used to describe things to do with virtual reality. *Wearing a Dataglove you can use hand movements to do things in the virtual world... ...a virtual kitchen.*

virtual reality is the use of computers to generate an environment which people can interact with and which seems real to them. An environment like this is called a **virtual reality.**

virtue is thinking and doing what is right and avoiding what is wrong. ◇ A **virtue** is a good quality or way of behaving. ...*the traditional American virtues of sportsmanship and modesty.*
❏ You can call the advantages or benefits of something its **virtues.** *One virtue of the British system is its simplicity.*
❏ If you **make a virtue** of something, you turn a bad thing into a good thing or make it seem like a good thing.
❏ You use **by virtue of** to explain why something happens or is true. *What also had to go, Mr Mandela said, was the notion that some people were born superior to others by virtue of their skin colour.*
❏ In former times, a woman who was considered to be sexually immoral was sometimes called **a woman of easy virtue.**

virtuoso (*plural:* virtuosi *or* virtuosos) (virtuosity, virtuosic) A **virtuoso** is an exceptionally skilled musician, singer, or dancer. ...*the double bass virtuoso Paul Rogers.* People who are exceptionally skilled in other ways are sometimes called **virtuosi.** ...*knitwear virtuoso Kaffe Fassette.* When someone is skilled in any of these ways, you can talk about their **virtuosity.** *Lisa Cullum danced throughout*

with splendid **virtuosity.** ◇ A **virtuoso** or **virtuosic** performance shows exceptional skill.

virtuous (virtuously) **Virtuous** behaviour is moral and correct. ◇ **Virtuous** is sometimes used in a rather critical way to describe someone who is pleased with their own good behaviour or who pretends to act in a very moral way without being sincere. *They virtuously insist that they are opening markets for everyone, not just America.*

virulent (*pron:* vir-yew-lent) (virulently, virulence) **Virulent** feelings or actions are extremely bitter and hostile. *The talk was virulently hostile to the Labour leadership... Women were perplexed by the virulence of male opposition.* ◇ A **virulent** disease spreads very quickly and is extremely harmful.

virus (viruses) **Viruses** are living things which are smaller than bacteria and can only reproduce themselves within the cells of animals or plants. Many viruses cause infectious diseases. ◇ Computer **viruses** are programs which can damage computer systems by interfering with them, for example by destroying files or other programs. Viruses are deliberately introduced into computer systems and can then unintentionally be spread via infected disks.

vis-à-vis (*pron:* veez-ah-vee) is used to indicate what you are referring to or what you are comparing something with. *Moldova's position vis-à-vis the union treaty is unclear... The Socialists emerged from the elections stronger vis-à-vis their coalition partners.*

visa A **visa** is a document issued to you, or a special stamp on your passport, which you need to enter or leave certain countries.

visage (*pron:* viz-zij) Someone's **visage** is their face.

visceral (*pron:* viss-er-al) ideas and attitudes are based on powerful gut feelings rather than reason. ...*sheer visceral hatred.*

viscosity The **viscosity** of a liquid is how thick and sticky it is.

viscount (*pron:* vie-count) A **viscount** is a nobleman ranking below an earl and above a baron.

viscountess (viscountesses) A **viscountess** is the wife or widow of a viscount, or a female member of the nobility who holds the title in her own right. She ranks below a countess and above a baroness.

viscous A **viscous** liquid is thick, sticky, and does not flow easily.

vise See **vice.**

visibility (visibilities) ❏ The **visibility** in a place is how well or how far you can see, which depends on weather conditions or the amount of light. ◇ The **visibility** of something is how well it can be seen. *He criticized cockpit layout and the visibility of the instruments.*
❏ The **visibility** of something is also the extent to which people are aware of it. ...*the new visibility of gay-rights issues.*

visible (visibly) If something is **visible,** it can be seen. *The journalists were visibly shaken by their experience.*

vision is the ability to see. ◇ **field of vision:** see **field.**
❏ If someone says they have had a **vision,** they mean they have had a mysterious experience in which they saw something such as God or an angel.
❏ A **vision** of something is a mental picture of it. *Their very presence conjures up a vision of bleached bones and broken*

tusks.

❏ Someone's **vision** of something is the way they see it or represent it in a book or film. *...his gloomy vision of the world.* ◇ Someone's **vision** of something in the future is their idea of how it will be or should be. *The Prime Minister has set out his vision of Britain's new role in Europe.* ◇ If you say someone has **vision**, you mean they are good at foreseeing what will happen in the future and at making plans which are likely to succeed.

visionary (visionaries) ❏ A **visionary** is someone who is believed to have mysterious spiritual experiences during which things are revealed to them, for example by means of messages from God.

❏ You also say someone is a **visionary** when they have great and imaginative ideas or plans. You can also call their ideas or plans **visionary**.

visit (visiting, visited) If you **visit** someone or pay them a **visit**, you go to see them and spend some time with them. ◇ **Visiting hours** are the times when you are allowed to visit someone in a hospital, prison, or some other institution. ◇ If you **visit** a place, you go there.

visitation A **visitation** is an experience or vision thought to involve communication with God, an angel, or some other mysterious force.

visitor A **visitor** is someone who is visiting a person or place.

visor A **visor** is a piece of clear or tinted plastic, especially one attached to a helmet, used to protect someone's eyes or face.

vista ❏ A **vista** is a view. *...a gentle rolling vista of fields, hedges and spinneys.*

❏ A **vista** is also a range of ideas and possibilities which people are made aware of. *His scholarly output opened new vistas in the appreciation and understanding of art.*

visual (visually) ❏ **Visual** is used to talk about sight and things you can see. *...the way our brain processes visual information... ...visually impaired people... His style is slick and visually exciting.*

❏ **Visuals** are things like photographs, slides, diagrams, and film, used to illustrate or explain something or as an accompaniment to a musical performance.

visual aid Visual aids are things like films, models, maps, or slides, shown to help people understand or remember information, especially during a talk or lecture.

visual arts The **visual arts** are arts like painting, sculpture, and engraving, as opposed to literature, drama, and music.

visual display unit See **VDU**.

visualize (visualizing, visualized) *(can be spelled with an 's' instead of a 'z')* If you **visualize** something, you form a mental picture of it. ◇ You can also say you **visualize** something when you imagine it happening or expect it to happen. *It is not hard to visualize the difficulties confronting veterans and their families.*

vital (vitally, vitality) ❏ If you say something is **vital**, you mean it is absolutely essential. *It is vitally important that world production keeps pace with consumption this year.*

❏ If you call a person **vital** or talk about their **vitality**, you mean they are energetic and full of life. You can also call organizations and activities **vital**. *The first objective is to restore and enhance the city's economic vitality.*

vitamin Vitamins are substances found in small quan-

tities in certain foods. They are essential for growth and good health.

vitiate *(pron:* vish-ee-ate*)* (vitiating, vitiated) If something is **vitiated**, it is made less effective. *The content of the work is vitiated by exaggeration.*

vitriolic (vitriol) A **vitriolic** speech or piece of writing is extremely bitter and angry. Speech or writing like this can also be called **vitriol**. *The judge now has the task of unravelling the truth behind the vitriol.*

vituperation *(pron:* vite-tyew-per-ray-shun*)* (vituperative) **Vituperation** is bitter spiteful abuse. A **vituperative** attack on someone is bitter and spiteful.

vivacious (vivacity) If you say someone is **vivacious** or talk about their **vivacity**, you mean they are energetic and full of life.

vivid (vividly, vividness) **Vivid** colours are very bright or brilliant. ◇ You say things like memories and descriptions are **vivid** when they are powerful, clear, and detailed. *I vividly remember the 1974 premiere of the play... The descriptions of characters and locations possess an almost Dickensian vividness.*

vivisection is using live animals in scientific experiments.

vixen A **vixen** is an adult female fox.

viz You use **viz** in writing to say exactly what you mean, when you have just mentioned something in a general way. *She invented a style of historical biography that has never been bettered, viz Wellington: Years of the Sword (1969) and Pillar of State (1972).*

vocabulary (vocabularies) Your **vocabulary** is all the words you know. ◇ The **vocabulary** of a language is all the words in it. ◇ The **vocabulary** of a subject is the words typically used when discussing it. *...the vocabulary of environmentalism.*

vocal (vocally) ❏ **Vocal** is used to talk about things involving the voice, especially singing. *...the vocal talents of Jocelyn Brown.* ◇ When a pop song is being performed, the singing is sometimes called the **vocals**.

❏ You say someone is **vocal** when they speak loudly and forcefully about something. *An increasingly vocal minority of politicians wants a devaluation... Both these proposals were resisted, most vocally by the United States.*

vocal cords Your **vocal cords** are the parts in your throat which enable you to speak. They vibrate and produce sound when air is passed through them.

vocalist A **vocalist** is a singer with a band or pop group.

vocation If you have a **vocation**, you have a strong feeling that you are especially suitable to do a particular job or to fill a particular role in life. You can call your job a **vocation** if you feel like this about it.

vocational (vocationally) **Vocational** training is specialized training for particular jobs, rather than more general education. *...the vocationally oriented new universities.*

vociferous *(pron:* voh-sif-er-uss*)* (vociferously) You say someone is **vociferous** when they express their views loudly and forcefully. *Hard-pressed homeowners are certain to complain vociferously.*

vodka is a strong clear alcoholic drink distilled from grain or potatoes. It originally came from Russia and Poland.

vogue If something is **in vogue** or there is a **vogue** for it, it is popular and fashionable.

voguish If something is fashionable, you can call it **voguish**, especially when you are making fun of it.

voice (voicing, voiced) ❏ When someone speaks or sings, you hear their voice.

❏ If you lose your voice, you cannot speak for a while or your voice becomes faint, because you are ill or have been shouting too much. ◇ If you shout something at the top of your voice, you shout it as loudly as possible.

❏ If you voice something like an opinion or emotion or give voice to it, you say what you think or feel.

❏ If you have a voice in something, you have the right to express an opinion and to influence any decisions which are made. *Parents will have some voice in drawing up school districts.* ◇ If a person or organization provides a voice for a group of people, they speak or campaign on their behalf. *John Marsh was the recognised voice of British management.* ◇ If you say a group of people speak with one voice, you mean they show unity and agreement in what they say.

❏ If someone finds their voice, they start to speak or make their opinions known in spite of fear, shock, or other difficult circumstances. ◇ You can also say someone finds their voice when they find a way of getting their feelings, opinions, or ideas across effectively, for example through painting or poetry.

voice-over A voice-over is a commentary or explanation heard as part of a film or TV programme but spoken by someone who is not actually seen.

void ❏ A void is a large empty space.

❏ If something which is no longer there leaves a void, there is a need for something else to take its place. When this new thing appears, you say it fills the void.

vol-au-vent (*pron*: voll-oh-von) A vol-au-vent is a small light pastry case with a savoury filling.

volatile (volatility) ❏ A volatile situation could suddenly change at any moment, especially for the worse. You talk about the volatility of a situation like this. ◇ A volatile person is temperamental and easily gets angry.

❏ Volatile liquids and solids change easily into a gas.

volcano (volcanoes; volcanic) ❏ A volcano is an opening in the earth's crust from which hot molten rock, steam, and gas sometimes burst out. The rock and ash often form a mountain around the opening; this mountain is also called a volcano. Volcanic is used to talk about things to do with volcanoes. *...volcanic ash... ...volcanic activity.*

❏ You can describe other things as volcanic when they remind you of an erupting volcano, because they are powerful, exciting, unpredictable, or uncontrollable. *...a volcanic outburst of rage... Ferraro has a reputation for volcanic energy and determination.*

vole Voles are small animals similar to mice but with a shorter tail. They usually live in fields or near rivers.

volition If you do something of your own volition, you do it because you have chosen to, rather than because you have been forced to or told to.

volley ❏ A volley of gunfire is a lot of shots fired at the same time. Similarly, a volley of stones or other missiles is a number of them thrown at the same time. ◇ A volley of criticisms or accusations is a lot of them made against someone.

❏ In games like tennis and football, a volley is a shot in which the player hits or kicks the ball before it has touched the ground. When this happens, you say the player volleys the ball.

volleyball is a game, usually played on an indoor court, in which two teams hit a large ball backwards and forwards over a high net with their hands or arms. The idea is to get the ball to touch the floor in the opposing team's half of the court.

volt The force of an electric current is expressed in volts.

voltage The voltage of an electric current is its force in volts. ◇ People also use voltage when describing how powerful or exciting something is. *No speaker in America matches the Rev Jesse Jackson for voltage... Llanelli have indulged in some high-voltage rugby in the first three weeks of this season.*

volte-face (*pron*: volt-fass) If a government performs a volte-face, it reverses its policy on something, so that it has completely the opposite policy.

voluble (volubly) If someone is voluble, they have a lot to say, and they say it with energy and enthusiasm. *Bethan was talking volubly.*

volume ❏ The volume of something is the amount there is of it. *...the growing volume of traffic on country roads.* ◇ The volume of an object is the amount of space it contains or occupies. ◇ The volume of a sound, especially the sound from a TV, radio, or stereo, is how loud it is.

❏ A volume is a book. *He published his first volume of poetry while still a teenager.* ◇ A volume is also one book in a series of books. One video in a series is also called a volume. ◇ A volume is also a collection of several issues of a magazine or journal, for example all the issues for one year.

❏ If you say something speaks volumes, you mean it tells you a lot about someone or something. *Some items of clothing speak volumes about their owner... The episode speaks volumes about the current state of the country.*

voluminous If something is voluminous, it is large and bulky. *...voluminous skirts... ...a voluminous quantity of research notes.*

voluntary (voluntarily) ❏ Voluntary is used to describe things you do because you choose to do them, rather than because you have to. *...voluntary redundancy... He has been in voluntary exile for more than a year.* You can also say you do something voluntarily.

❏ Voluntary work is unpaid work which people do to help a good cause such as a charity. People who do work like this are called voluntary workers. The organizations they work for are called voluntary organizations.

volunteer (volunteering, volunteered) ❏ If someone volunteers to do something, they offer to do it. You call someone who does this a volunteer. *A Sydney family volunteered to allow a film crew unlimited access to their lives for six months.*

❏ A volunteer is also someone who does unpaid work, especially for a charity or some other good cause.

❏ A volunteer is also someone who chooses to join the armed forces, especially during wartime, as opposed to someone who is forced to join by law.

❏ If you volunteer information, you tell someone something without being asked.

voluptuous A woman is sometimes described as voluptuous when she has attractively large breasts and hips.

vomit (vomiting, vomited) If you vomit, partly-digested

food comes back up from your stomach and out through your mouth. This partly-digested food is called **vomit**.

voodoo is a form of religion involving animal sacrifices, magic, and belief in spirits, practised by some people in the West Indies, especially Haiti.

voracious (voraciously) **Voracious** is used to say someone is eager to have a lot of something. You can also say someone has a **voracious appetite** for something. *Shearing is a voracious reader... ...the Scots' voracious appetite for newspapers... He was voraciously hungry.*

vortex (*plural:* vortexes *or* vortices) ❑ A **vortex** is a mass of wind, water, or gas spinning round so fast that it pulls objects into its empty centre.
❑ If someone is becoming trapped in a nasty situation, you can call the situation a **vortex**. *He drifts into a self-destructive vortex of alcoholic binges and blackouts.*

vote (voting, voted) ❑ A **vote** is an occasion when a group of people make a decision by each one indicating his or her choice. The choice most people support is then accepted by the group. *Union leaders are preparing for a vote on industrial action.* When you **vote** or cast your **vote**, you indicate your choice, usually by raising your hand or by making a mark on a piece of paper. The **vote** is the total number of votes cast. *The Social Liberals looked like getting less than 20 per cent of the vote.* The result of the voting is called a **vote** of a particular kind. *He believes a 'yes' vote might cause equities and unit trust prices to go up.*
❑ If people have a legal right to vote in an election, you say they have **the vote**. *The Swiss confederation granted women the vote in 1971.*
❑ If a proposal is **voted down**, it is rejected when a vote is taken. ◇ If someone is **voted out** of office, they do not gain enough votes to retain their post. Similarly, someone can be **voted off** something like a committee.
❑ If you **vote with your feet**, you show you do not support something by going to a different place, or by staying away from a place. *Thousands are already voting with their feet, and leaving the country for the hope of a better life... People are expected to vote with their feet by staying at home to show that they regard the elections as futile.*

vote of confidence (votes of confidence) A **vote of confidence** is a vote in which members of a group are asked to indicate that they still support the person or group in power, usually the government.

vote of no confidence A **vote of no confidence** is a vote in which members of a group are asked to indicate that they do not support the person or group in power, usually the government.

vote of thanks (votes of thanks) A **vote of thanks** is an official speech in which the speaker formally thanks a person for doing something.

voter Voters are people who have the right to vote in an election.

vouch (vouches, vouching, vouched) If you say you can **vouch for** someone, you mean you can guarantee their good behaviour. ◇ If you say you can **vouch for** something, you mean you have evidence from your own experience that it is true, correct, or reliable.

voucher A **voucher** is a ticket or piece of paper which can be used instead of money to pay for something.

vouchsafe (vouchsafing, vouchsafed) If something such as a secret is **vouchsafed** to you, you are told about it.

vow If you **vow** to do something or make a **vow** to do it, you make a solemn promise to do it. *She has not broken her vow of silence.* ◇ You can also say you **vow** to do something when you decide very emphatically that you will do it. *He vowed never to play cricket again.*

vowel A **vowel** is a sound like 'ah', 'i', or 'oo', which you pronounce by letting the air flow freely through your mouth. All speech sounds are either vowels or consonants.

vox pop A **vox pop** is an inquiry carried out in the street by a TV, radio, or newspaper reporter who tries to find out people's opinions on a matter of public interest.

voyage (voyaging, voyaged; voyager) A **voyage** is a long journey by ship or spacecraft. If someone is **voyaging** somewhere, they are making a journey like this. People who make long journeys by ship or spacecraft are sometimes called **voyagers**.

voyeur (voyeuristic, voyeurism) A **voyeur** is a person who gets pleasure from watching other people's private or sexual activities. Watching people like this is called **voyeurism**. **Voyeuristic** is used to describe things to do with voyeurism. *...voyeuristic televised dating games.*

vs is sometimes used in writing to say two people or teams are competing against each other. 'vs' is short for 'versus'. *...Aston Villa vs Banik Ostrava.*

VSO is a British organization which sends skilled people to developing countries to work on projects helping the local community. VSO stands for 'Voluntary Service Overseas'.

vulgar (vulgarity, vulgarian) ❑ If you describe something as **vulgar** or talk about its **vulgarity**, you mean it is lacking in taste or of poor artistic quality.
❑ **Vulgar** pictures, gestures, or remarks refer to sex or bodily functions in a rude and distasteful way. *...vulgar jokes... Hanoi radio said the book had ridiculed the class struggle by resorting to vulgarity and pornography.*
❑ People are sometimes called **vulgar** when they are thought to be rude or lacking in taste. People like these are also called **vulgarians**. *He was a common, vulgar person who told dirty stories and picked his nose... ...the vulgar habits of jumped-up entrepreneurs.*

vulgarize (vulgarizing, vulgarized; vulgarization) (*can be spelled with an 's' instead of a 'z'*) If something is **vulgarized**, it is made vulgar. *He preached against the vulgarization of sex and the commercialization of American culture.*

vulnerable (vulnerably, vulnerability) ❑ If someone or something is **vulnerable**, they are weak and badly protected, and are open to attack, criticism, or misfortune. *...vulnerable coastal cities... ...the bravery of the bomber crews as they lumbered vulnerably through the flak... ...the vulnerability of being HIV-positive.*
❑ You can also say someone is **vulnerable** if they are easily influenced or led astray, because they are lacking in wisdom or experience.

vulture ❑ Vultures are large birds which live in hot countries and eat the flesh of dead or dying animals.
❑ If you call a person a **vulture**, you mean they are eager to take advantage of other people's misfortune. *The vultures of the press have been circling for some time.*

vulva (*plural:* vulvas *or* vulvae) The **vulva** is the outer part of a woman's sexual organs.

W w

wacky (or **whacky**) If you say someone is **wacky**, you mean they are eccentric, unusual, and a bit crazy.

wad A **wad** of banknotes is a thick bundle of them. ◇ A **wad** of something soft is a compressed ball of it. ...*a wad of chewing-gum.*

wadding is soft material used as stuffing or padding in things like clothes or soft furnishings, for example quilts.

waddle (waddling, waddled) If a creature like a penguin **waddles** somewhere, it walks with short steps, swaying slightly from side to side. Similarly, you can talk about a very fat person **waddling**.

wade (wading, waded) ❏ If you **wade** through water or mud, you walk through it slowly and with difficulty.

❏ If you **wade into** a dangerous or difficult situation, you become involved in it.

❏ If you **wade through** a lot of papers, you spend a lot of time reading them.

wader ❏ **Waders** are various kinds of long-legged birds which hunt for food in shallow water.

❏ **Waders** are also long waterproof rubber boots which cover your legs up to your thighs. People who fish for salmon and trout usually wear waders.

wadi (pron: wod-dee) A **wadi** is a narrow valley in a desert area which is dry except after a rainstorm, when a stream appears.

wafer A **wafer** is (a) a thin crisp biscuit, often eaten with ice cream. (b) a thin round piece of a special kind of bread which the priest gives the congregation to eat as part of the service of Holy Communion.

wafer-thin A **wafer-thin** piece of something is extremely thin. ◇ **Wafer-thin** is also used to say something is only just above a certain level. *It is hard for a prime minister to look good with a wafer-thin majority.*

waffle (pron: woff-l) (waffling, waffled; waffler) ❏ If you say someone is **waffling**, you mean they are talking or writing in a vague way, without saying anything important. You call what they say or write **waffle**. If someone often talks or writes like this, you can call them a **waffler.**

❏ **Waffles** are a type of food, usually made in oblong shapes with a raised or cut-out grid pattern on them. Waffles can be either sweet or savoury.

waft (pron: woft) If a smell **wafts** somewhere, it drifts gently through the air. Similarly, you can talk about a gentle sound **wafting** somewhere.

wag (wagging, wagged) ❏ When a dog **wags** its tail, it waves it vigorously from side to side, because it is pleased or excited. ◇ **tail wags the dog:** see tail.

❏ If you **wag your finger** at someone, especially a child, you point your finger at them and move it up and down, to warn them not to do something or to tell them off.

❏ If you say **tongues are wagging**, you mean people are gossiping about something.

❏ Someone who makes witty remarks can be called a **wag.**

wage (waging, waged) ❏ A person's **wages** or **wage** is the money they get, usually weekly, for the work they do, especially in a manual job. ◇ **living wage:** see living.

❏ If a country **wages war** against another country, it starts a war and continues fighting it. Similarly, if a person or organization **wages war** against something unpleasant, they keep trying to get rid of it. *Our movement is committed to wage war on poverty, illiteracy and under-development.*

wage packet A person's **wage packet** is their wages. If they are paid in cash, they usually receive the money in a packet called a **wage packet.**

wager (wagering, wagered) A **wager** is a bet. If you **wager** someone that something will happen, you make a bet on it.

waggle (waggling, waggled) If you **waggle** your fingers or toes, you move them backwards and forwards. Some people can also **waggle** their ears.

wagon (or **waggon**) ❏ A **wagon** is a strong four-wheeled vehicle for carrying heavy loads, pulled by a horse or tractor. ◇ Railway **wagons** are vehicles pulled by a railway engine and used for carrying freight.

❏ If someone is **on the wagon,** they have given up drinking alcohol.

wagtail **Wagtails** are small birds with long tails which flick up and down. There are several kinds of wagtails.

waif A child or young person is sometimes called a **waif** when they are very thin and look as if they are hungry and uncared for.

wail (wailing, wailed) If someone **wails**, they make a loud continuous high-pitched sound, usually because they are in great distress. You can also say a bagpipe or siren **wails**. Any of these sounds can be called a **wail.** ...*the relentless wail of police sirens.* ◇ If someone **wails** something, they say it in a miserable voice. ◇ If someone **wails** about something, they complain about it. A person's complaints can be called a **wail.** *The perennial wail of the accountancy profession is that 'no one understands us'.*

waist (-waisted) A person's **waist** is the middle part of their body above their hips. ◇ The **waist** of a piece of clothing is the part which fits around your waist. **-waisted** is used to describe the waist of a piece of clothing. ...*baggy-waisted trousers.*

waistband A **waistband** is a narrow piece of material sewn round the waist of a pair of trousers, skirt, or other garment to strengthen it.

waistcoat A **waistcoat** is a short sleeveless piece of clothing with buttons. It is usually worn over a shirt and under a jacket, especially as part of a three-piece suit.

waistline If you talk about a person's **waistline**, you mean the size of their waist.

wait (waiting, waited) ❑ If you have to **wait** for something you want or need, you do not get it immediately. You can also say you have a **wait** for something. *A-level students continued the long wait for their results.* ◇ If you **wait** or **wait around**, you spend some time in a place, usually doing very little, until someone arrives or something happens.

❑ If someone **lies in wait** for someone else, they wait for them, keeping out of sight, so they can attack them, rob them, or arrest them. ◇ You can also say someone **lies in wait** for someone else when they wait for the right moment to gain some advantage over them.

❑ If you **wait up** for someone, you do not go to bed until they come home.

❑ If something is **waiting** for you, it is ready for you to use or to take some action on. *There will be a great stack of letters waiting for them when they return.*

❑ If you say something **can wait**, you mean it can be dealt with later.

❑ If you say you **can't wait** for something, you mean you are very eager for it to happen. *I can't wait for Williams's next play.*

❑ If you **wait and see** what happens, you do not do anything until you know how a situation develops. *He said the rebels would wait and see what the new government could offer.* ◇ If you play a **waiting game**, you deal with a situation by deliberately not doing anything and waiting to see what the other person does before you decide how to act.

❑ If you say some disaster is **waiting** to happen, you mean the circumstances are right for it to happen at any time.

❑ If someone **waits on** you, they act as your servant, looking after your needs and bringing you things such as food.

waiter (waitress, waitresses) A **waiter** is a man whose job is to serve food and drink to people at their table in a restaurant. A woman who does this job is referred to as a **waitress**.

waiting list A **waiting list** is a list of people who want or need something which is not immediately available. As it gradually becomes available, the people highest on the list are the first ones to get it.

waiting room A **waiting room** is a room in a place like a doctor's surgery or a railway station where people can sit while they wait.

waitress See **waiter**.

waive (waiving, waived) ❑ If someone **waives** something they are entitled to have or do, they give up their right to have it or do it. *I noted that four of the directors waived their fees.*

❑ If someone **waives** something like a rule, they do not enforce it. A **waiver** is an official statement saying that a rule does not have to be enforced in a particular case.

wake (waking, woke, have woken) ❑ When you **wake** or **wake up**, you become conscious again after being asleep. You can also say someone or something **wakes** you or **wakes** you **up**. ◇ **Waking** is used to talk about the times when a person is awake rather than asleep. *...his waking hours.*

❑ If you **wake up** to a situation, you become aware of it. *British chemical firms are waking up to their environmental responsibilities.*

❑ The **wake** of a ship is the trail of white foaming water it leaves behind it. ◇ If something is left **in the wake** of something else, it is left as a result of it. *The Arctic conditions are now sweeping south, leaving a trail of damage in their wake.* Similarly, if something follows **in the wake** of something else, it happens after it and usually as a result of it. *In the wake of the doctors' strike last November, hundreds of people were arrested.*

❑ A **wake** is a gathering of people who watch over the body of a dead person on the night before the burial. A gathering after a funeral is also called a **wake** in some parts of Ireland.

waken (wakening, wakened) If you **waken** or are **wakened**, you wake up.

walk ❑ When you **walk**, you move forward at a steady pace, putting one foot after the other in front of you. When someone moves at this pace and does not run, you say they move at a **walk**. *I swung into a brisk walk.* ◇ A person's **walk** is the way they walk. *...his rolling walk.*

❑ If you go for a **walk**, you walk a certain distance for pleasure or exercise. **Walking** is going for walks in the country for pleasure. ◇ A **walk** is a route or path which people walk along for pleasure. *...the most spectacular coastal walk in the British Isles.*

❑ If you **walk** someone somewhere, you walk with them to keep them company or protect them. *He walked me all the way to the door of the bank.* ◇ If you **walk** your dog, you take it for a walk to give it exercise.

❑ If someone **walks out** of a meeting, organization, or situation, they leave it suddenly, to show their disapproval of something. When several people do this, you say there is a **walk-out** or **walkout**. ◇ If someone **walks away** from a difficult situation, they abandon it, instead of trying to deal with it. ◇ If someone **walks out on** someone else, especially someone who depends on them, they suddenly abandon them. ◇ If workers **walk out**, they go on strike. A strike can be called a **walk-out** or **walkout**.

❑ If someone **walks over** another person, they treat them very badly. ◇ You also say someone **walks over** another person when they easily defeat them in a contest or argument.

❑ If someone **walks away with** something like a prize, they obtain it easily. You can also say they **walk off with** it. ◇ If you **walk into** a job, you get it very easily.

❑ If you **walk into** a dangerous or difficult situation, you get into it without being aware of the dangers or difficulties beforehand.

❑ **Walking** is sometimes used to describe someone who has a special ability or noticeable feature. For example, if someone knows an extraordinary number of facts, you can say they are a 'walking encyclopaedia'.

❑ **walk tall**: see **tall**.

walk of life (walks of life) Your **walk of life** is your position in society and the kind of job you have. *These crews come from all walks of life.*

walk-on A **walk-on** part in a play is a very small one, often involving just one brief appearance on the stage.

walk-out See **walk**.

walkabout When an important person, especially a member of a royal family, goes on a **walkabout**, they go among the crowds in a public place and talk to people.

walker A walker is a person who walks, especially one who does it for pleasure or as a sport.

walkie-talkie A walkie-talkie is a small portable radio for talking to someone at a distance and receiving their replies.

walking stick A walking stick is a long strong stick with a curved or flattened end which a person uses to lean on while walking.

Walkman (Walkmans) A Walkman is a small portable cassette player, often with a radio, which you carry around and listen to through headphones while doing something else. 'Walkman' is a trademark.

walkout See walk.

walkover If you say something like a contest is a walkover, you mean it is won very easily.

walkway A walkway is a footbridge over a road, or a raised footpath by the side of one.

wall (walled) ❑ The walls of a building are the solid vertical parts which support its roof and upper floors and divide each floor into rooms. ◇ The walls of a room are its vertical sides.

❑ A wall is also a vertical structure, made of stone or brick, surrounding an area of land or separating one area from another. A walled area is surrounded by a wall. ...the old walled town of Aigues Mortes.

❑ A high dense mass of something can be called a wall. Survivors spoke of a wall of water up to twenty feet high smashing through the town. ◇ A line of people acting as a barrier can also be called a wall.

❑ If you say there is a wall of silence surrounding something, you mean you cannot find out anything about it, because nobody is willing to talk about it.

❑ If you have your back to the wall, you are in a very difficult situation.

❑ If you say the writing is on the wall for someone, you mean they are not likely to survive in their job or position. ◇ If people see the writing on the wall, they are aware of a danger to themselves, and take some action to avoid it.

❑ If a business goes to the wall, it is in such serious financial difficulties that it has to close down.

❑ The wall of something hollow is its outer covering. ...the walls of arteries.

wall-mounted A wall-mounted object is fixed or attached to a wall.

Wall Street is a street in New York where the Stock Exchange and the important banks are. Wall Street is often used to talk about the financial activities in Wall Street and the people who work there. Wall Street was overwhelmingly backing George Bush for a second term.

wall-to-wall carpeting completely covers the floor of a room. ◇ Wall-to-wall entertainment is available at all times on TV or radio. ...wall-to-wall football.

wallaby (wallabies) Wallabies are a kind of small kangaroo.

wallet A wallet is a small flat folding case, usually made of leather or plastic, which you keep in your pocket and use for carrying banknotes and bank and credit cards. ◇ If you talk about people's wallets, you mean the amount of money they earn and the amount they have to pay in taxes. It seems to Americans that both political parties are ignoring their opposition to further raids on their

wallets.

wallflower ❑ Wallflowers are garden plants with sweet-smelling yellow, red, orange, or purple flowers.

❑ Shy people who do not like to attract attention to themselves are sometimes called wallflowers.

wallop (walloping, walloped) If you wallop someone, you hit them hard with something like a stick.

wallow If you wallow in something, you enjoy it and try to make it last. Britain is currently wallowing in nostalgia.

wallpaper is thick plain or patterned paper which people paste onto the walls of their rooms.

wally (wallies) You call someone a wally when they do something silly or make a silly mistake.

walnut The walnut is a tree which produces edible nuts, also called walnuts. The nuts have a wrinkled appearance and a hard light-brown shell. The light-brown wood of the tree is also called walnut. It is used for making expensive furniture.

walrus (walruses) The walrus is sea creature which looks like a large seal with a tough skin, coarse whiskers, and two tusks. Walruses live mainly in the Arctic.

waltz (waltzes, waltzing, waltzed) The waltz is a dance performed by couples. It has a rhythm of three beats in each bar. When people waltz, they perform this dance.

wan (wanly) If you say someone looks wan, you mean they look pale and tired. She smiled wanly.

wand A wand is a thin rod which a magician pretends to use when he or she performs tricks. ◇ If you say a problem cannot be solved by waving a magic wand, you mean it cannot be solved easily. There is no magic wand which will reduce the rate at which Britain's pay settlements are rising.

wander (wandering, wandered; wanderer) ❑ If you wander somewhere, you go there in a casual unhurried way.

❑ Wandering people travel around rather than staying in one place. People like these are called wanderers. ◇ A person's wanderings are the journeys they make when they travel around.

❑ If your mind or attention wanders, you start thinking about something else rather than the thing you are supposed to be thinking about.

wanderlust is a strong urge to travel.

wane (waning, waned) ❑ If someone's power, influence, or popularity wanes, it gets weaker, often to the point of disappearing altogether. You can also talk about someone's interest or enthusiasm waning. ◇ If you say something is on the wane, you mean it is decreasing or getting weaker. The government had been expressing confidence that certain types of crime were on the wane.

❑ When the moon wanes, a smaller area of brightness can be seen each day as it changes in its cycle from full moon to new moon. See also wax.

wangle (wangling, wangled) If someone wangles something they want, they manage to get it by cleverness or persuasion.

wannabe (or wannabee) (both pron: wan-a-bee) A wannabe is someone who wants to be a particular kind of person. For example, a Madonna wannabe is someone who wants to be like Madonna.

want ❑ If you want something, you feel a desire for it or a need to have it.

❑ A want of something is a lack of it. This shows a want

of commitment on the part of the new minister. If you say something is **wanting** in a certain thing, you mean it does not have it. *...a performance seriously wanting in imagination, energy and tension.* ◇ If you say something is happening **for want of** a particular thing, you mean it is happening because that thing is not being provided. *Children are dying for want of medical care.*

❏ If someone or something is **found wanting**, they turn out not to have the qualities they are supposed to have.

❏ If someone is **wanted**, the police are looking for them, because they have committed a crime.

wanton is used to describe bad or cruel things which are done for no reason at all. *...the wanton destruction of schools and hospitals.*

war (warring) ❏ **War** or a **war** is a period of armed conflict between two or more countries. **War** is used to talk about things connected with a war. *...the war effort... ...a war zone.* ◇ **Warring** countries or groups are fighting against each other.

❏ If a country **goes to war**, it begins a period of conflict with another country or countries. If a person **goes to war**, they go off to fight in a war.

❏ If you say two countries or groups are fighting a **war of nerves**, you mean they are involved in a psychological battle, in which each side hopes the other will be weakened by the tension.

❏ Other kinds of conflict can be called **war**. *...the class war.* Commercial competition can also be called a **war**. For example, you can talk about a 'trade war' or a 'price war'. ◇ **Warring** is used to describe people who are in conflict with each other. *...the warring factions within the Tory party.*

❏ **war of words**: see **word**.

war crime (war criminal) **War crimes** are acts committed during a war in violation of the accepted rules of war, for example ill treatment of prisoners. People found guilty of acts like these are called **war criminals**.

war cry Someone's **war cry** is a slogan they use to try to get people to support them. *'Affordable housing' remains the war-cry of every local politician.* ◇ Originally, a **war cry** was a cry uttered by a soldier during a charge against the enemy.

war widow A **war widow** is a woman whose husband has been killed fighting in a war.

warble (warbling, warbled) If someone **warbles** a tune, they sing it.

warbler **Warblers** are small songbirds. There are several species, for example the garden warbler, the willow warbler, and the blackcap.

ward ❏ In a hospital, a **ward** is a large room with beds for patients.

❏ If you **ward off** a blow, you prevent it reaching the part of your body it was aimed at. ◇ If you **ward off** something else unpleasant, you prevent it reaching or harming you. *...urgent measures to ward off the real threat of starvation.*

❏ A **ward** is one of the districts a city or town is divided into for administration purposes. Each ward is represented by a councillor.

❏ A **ward** or **ward of court** is a person, usually a child, officially put in the care of a court of law or a guardian because they need protection.

warden A **warden** is an official whose job is to make sure certain laws or regulations are obeyed. ◇ The person in charge of a building or institution is sometimes called the **warden**. *...a youth hostel warden.* ◇ In the US, the person in charge of a prison is called the **warden**.

warder Prison officers used to be called **warders**.

wardrobe A **wardrobe** is a tall large wooden cabinet for keeping clothes in. ◇ Your **wardrobe** is the clothes you own. *She asked her friend for advice on building up her wardrobe.*

wardrobe mistress The **wardrobe mistress** is a woman in charge of the costumes in a theatre company.

ware Someone's **wares** are the goods or services they sell. ◇ **Ware** is used to talk about products made of a certain material, for example crystal ware, or made for a certain purpose, such as sanitary ware.

warehouse A **warehouse** is a very large building where things like raw materials or manufactured goods are stored.

warehouse club A **warehouse club** is a large cash-and-carry store which sells goods at reduced prices to people who pay an annual subscription.

warfare is carrying on a war with another country. ◇ Other kinds of fighting between groups are sometimes called **warfare**, for example gang warfare.

warhead A **warhead** is the front end of a missile, where the explosive is carried.

warhorse An old person is sometimes called a **warhorse** when they are still active in their profession. ◇ A play or piece of music which is often performed can also be called a **warhorse**. *...an outstanding young pianist who kicked some new life into an old warhorse.*

warlike is used to describe hostile and aggressive talk and actions. *The rhetoric from Washington has grown more warlike in recent days.*

warlock A **warlock** is a male witch.

warlord A **warlord** is a military leader of a country or part of a country, especially one who is not answerable to anyone else.

warm (warmly; warming) ❏ If something is **warm**, its temperature is fairly high. If you are **warm**, your body temperature is at a comfortable level and you are not cold. ◇ **Warm** clothes and blankets are thick and made of a material which helps to keep you warm.

❏ If the weather is **warm**, it is pleasant and neither cool nor hot.

❏ If something **warms** or is **warmed**, it gets hotter. You can also say something **warms up** or is **warmed up**. *Atmospheric pollution is causing the world climate to warm up gradually.* ◇ If you **warm up** an engine, you run it until it reaches a temperature at which it will operate well.

❏ When an athlete or a performer **warms up**, they prepare themselves for performing by doing mental or physical exercises or by practising. A preparation like this is called a **warm-up**.

❏ If people's behaviour is **warm**, they are friendly and welcoming. *The visiting team have been warmly welcomed by the crowds.* ◇ If relations between people **warm**, they improve and become more friendly. *...this warming of relations between former allies.*

❏ If you **warm to** a person, you get to like them. ◇ If you **warm to** an idea, you become more enthusiastic about it. You can also **warm to** something you use regularly. *After driving it for a year, I warmed to the Audi.*

◻ **Warming** is used to describe things which give you a feeling of pleasure. *...the warming effect of comradeship.*

warm-blooded A **warm-blooded** creature, for example a mammal or a bird, is one whose body temperature is kept at a constant warm level, regardless of the surrounding temperature. See also **cold-blooded**.

warm-hearted people are friendly, kind, and affectionate.

warm-up See **warm**.

warmonger (warmongering) If you accuse someone of being a **warmonger**, you mean they are trying to start a war. You can also say they are **warmongering**.

warmth is friendly or welcoming behaviour. *They were surprised by the warmth and hospitality they met with.* ◇ When people or groups have a friendly relationship, you can talk about the **warmth** of relations between them. *...the new warmth in superpower relations between Moscow and Washington.*

◻ **Warmth** is also moderate heat.

warn (warning) If you **warn** someone about something harmful or dangerous, you tell them about it. You can also say you give them a **warning**. ◇ If you **warn** someone to do something, you advise them to do it for their own safety. *Residents have been warned to stay inside their homes.* You can also **warn** someone not to do something. ◇ **Warning** is used to describe things which are said or done to warn people. *Police fired warning shots.* ◇ If you **warn** someone **off**, you tell them not to go somewhere.

warp ◻ If something **warps** something else, it has a harmful effect on it, making it unpleasant and unnatural. *Something has warped the president's thinking.* If you say something is **warped**, you mean it is unpleasant and unnatural. *...someone with a very warped sense of humour.*

◻ If wood **warps**, it becomes distorted, often because of the effect of heat or water.

◻ The **warp** in a piece of woven material is the threads which are stretched taut along the loom. See also **weft**.

◻ See also **time warp**.

warpath If you say someone is **on the warpath**, you mean they are preparing for a fight or argument.

warplane A **warplane** is any plane designed for use in warfare.

warrant ◻ A **warrant** is an official document signed by a judge or magistrate which allows the police to perform a certain action, for example to arrest someone or to seize papers. ◇ **death warrant**: see **death**.

◻ If you say something **warrants** a certain thing, you mean it justifies it or makes it necessary. *British officials say there is not yet enough information to warrant further action at the United Nations.*

warrant officer A **warrant officer** is an NCO of the highest rank in the British army and in some other armed forces.

warranty (warranties) A **warranty** is a written guarantee which enables you to get a product repaired or replaced free of charge within a certain period of time.

warren A **warren** is an underground system of holes connected by tunnels where rabbits live. ◇ You can call a place a **warren** when there are a lot of rooms or buildings with connecting passages where it would be easy to

get lost.

warring See **war**.

warrior In the past, a **warrior** was a brave soldier or an experienced fighter.

warship A **warship** is any ship designed to be used in warfare.

wart A **wart** is a small hard growth on someone's skin. ◇ If you describe someone or something **warts and all**, you mention their bad points as well as their good ones. *...a warts-and-all look at Edinburgh.*

warthog Warthogs are large wild pigs in Africa. They have tusks and wart-like bumps on their faces.

wartime is used to talk about a period of war, especially the Second World War. *She seldom spoke of her wartime life.*

wary (warier, wariest; warily, wariness) If you are **wary** of something, you are nervous or cautious about it, because you think it may be dangerous or cause you problems. *He stepped ashore warily... This may not be enough to overcome public wariness.*

was See **be**.

wash (washes, washing, washed) ◻ If you **wash** or have a **wash**, you clean yourself using soap and water. Similarly, you can **wash** clothes or other things. When someone washes clothes, you say they do their **washing**. You call the clothes being washed the **wash** or the **washing**. ◇ If you **wash up** or do the **washing-up**, you wash the crockery, pans, etc used for cooking and eating a meal.

◻ A **car wash** is a place where your car can be mechanically washed.

◻ If something is **washed away**, a powerful wave or other mass of water hits it and carries it away. You can also say something is **washed** to a particular place. *A car on the seafront was washed into the water.* ◇ If something is **washed up** on a coast, it is carried there by the sea and left there. You can also say something is **washed ashore**.

◻ If heavy rain **washes out** something like a sporting competition, the competition has to be stopped, because the weather is too bad for it to continue.

◻ The **wash** of a boat or ship is the wave it causes when it moves through the water.

◻ If you **wash down** food with a drink, you have the drink with it, to help digest it.

◻ If you say an argument or excuse will **not wash**, you mean it is not convincing.

◻ A **wash** is a thin covering or layer of a colour.

washable clothes or materials can be washed without suffering damage.

washbasin A **washbasin** is a large basin, usually with hot and cold taps, which you can fill with water so you can have a wash.

washed-out colours are very pale. ◇ If you feel **washed-out**, you feel very tired, because of illness or overwork.

washer A **washer** is a thin flat ring of metal, rubber, or plastic. Washers are used as a seal in something like a tap, or to make a tight connection with a nut and bolt.

washer-dryer (*or* **washer-drier**) A **washer-dryer** is an automatic machine which is both a washing machine and a tumble dryer.

washing See **wash**.

washing line A **washing line** is a cord stretched from one point to another, usually between two posts, on which you hang out washing to dry.

washing machine A **washing machine** is a machine for washing clothes and other things such as sheets and towels.

washing powder A **washing powder** is a detergent in powder form for washing clothes.

washing-up See **wash**.

washing-up liquid is a thick soapy liquid which you add to hot water to wash dirty crockery after a meal.

washroom A **washroom** is a room with toilets and washing facilities, especially one in a large building like an office block or factory.

wasp Wasps are insects which can sting. The most common kinds have yellow-and-black striped bodies.

waspish If you call someone **waspish**, you mean they get angry easily and say harsh things.

wastage If there is **wastage** of something valuable or useful, some of it is not used, or it is used wrongly or inefficiently. ◇ See also **natural wastage**.

waste (wasting, wasted) ❑ If you **waste** time, you spend it doing something unnecessary or unimportant, when something more important needs to be done. You can say the thing you do is a **waste** of time. *He stood there, glumly contemplating a wasted afternoon.* ◇ If money, energy, or some other resource is **wasted**, it is used unnecessarily or in a thoughtless or unsuitable way. You can talk about a **waste** of something like this. *...a waste of public money.* ◇ **-wasting** is added to words to describe things people do which result in time, money, etc being wasted. *...time-wasting travel... ...money-wasting projects.*

❑ If you **waste** an opportunity, you do not take advantage of it.

❑ If you **waste no time** in doing something, you do it straight away.

❑ **Waste** is material which has been used and is no longer wanted, or material which is left over from an industrial process. *...nuclear waste... ...waste paper.*

❑ If something **goes to waste**, it remains unused, goes bad, or is thrown away.

❑ If an army **lays waste** to a place, it destroys it.

❑ If someone is **wasting away**, they are slowly getting thinner and weaker. A **wasting** disease is one which has this effect.

❑ **Waste** land is land which is not used or looked after by anyone, and is covered by wild plants and often rubbish. ◇ **Wastes** are large areas of land where there are very few people, plants, or animals. *...the frozen wastes of Mongolia.*

❑ If you say something is **wasted** on someone, you mean it is too good, clever, or sophisticated for them to appreciate or understand.

wasteful (wastefully, wastefulness) If you call an organization or activity **wasteful**, you mean it uses money or resources extravagantly or in a careless or inefficient way. *...penalties on companies that use energy wastefully... Wastefulness is not only bad management, it is also theft from the taxpayer.*

wasteland A **wasteland** is an area of land which is infertile or desolate and not used for anything.

wastepaper basket A **wastepaper basket** is a basket for putting waste paper and other rubbish in.

wasting See **waste**.

watch (watches, watching, watched) ❑ A **watch** is a device like a small clock which you take around with you, usually wearing it on a strap on your wrist.

❑ If you **watch** something which is happening, you spend a period of time looking at it. Similarly, you can **watch** television. ◇ If someone like a detective **watches** someone, he or she spies on them, and often follows them secretly.

❑ If you **watch** a situation, you pay careful attention to what is happening. *The success of these reforms is being closely watched throughout Latin America.* ◇ You also say you **watch** something when you make sure it does not get out of control. *They need to be more careful in keeping weight down, watching their diet and taking adequate exercise.*

❑ If you **keep watch** on a place or activity, you watch what is happening, to make sure nothing undesirable happens. *A close watch has been kept for any signs of militaristic revival.* You can also be **on the watch** for something undesirable. *Environmentalists will be on the watch for damage to wildlife.* ◇ **Watch** comes in the names of some organizations set up to monitor a situation. *...Helsinki Watch, the human rights group.*

❑ If you tell someone to **watch out** for something, (a) you are warning them to beware of it. (b) you are telling them to look for it because it might be interesting or useful to them.

❑ If you **watch over** someone or something, you make sure no harm comes to them.

❑ If someone like a soldier is **on watch**, he or she is guarding a place and is there to warn other people of danger or an attack. Each period in which someone has this duty is called a **watch**.

watch strap A **watch strap** is a strip of leather, plastic, or metal which is attached to a watch so you can wear it on your wrist.

watchable If you say someone or something is **watchable**, you mean they are enjoyable to watch.

watchdog A **watchdog** is a person or a group of people responsible for making sure that organizations of a certain kind do not act irresponsibly or illegally.

watcher People who pay close attention to what is happening in a certain field are sometimes called **watchers**. *...the Daily Mirror's seasoned royal watcher, James Whitaker.* ◇ Similarly, people who spend a lot of time looking at something can be called **watchers**, for example television watchers.

watchful (watchfulness) If someone is **watchful**, they are attentive and careful to notice everything that is happening. *The task requires tact and watchfulness.*

watchman (watchmen) A **watchman** is a person whose job is to guard buildings or property, especially at night.

watchtower A **watchtower** is a tall tower from which a guard has a good view of the area he or she is guarding.

watchword If you say a word or phrase is the **watchword** for a group of people, you mean it sums up their attitude or what they are trying to achieve. *Luxury was the watchword of the Cunard fleet.*

water (watering, watered) ❑ **Water** is a clear colourless liquid which is necessary for the survival of all plants and animals.

❑ When you **water** plants, you pour water onto the soil around them, to help them grow.

❏ When people are talking about a large area of water, they sometimes call it the **water** or the **waters**. *...the long grass by the water's edge.* ◇ A country's **waters** are its territorial waters. *The French have been fishing in British waters for centuries.*

❏ If your eyes are **watering**, you have tears in them, for example because smoke is getting into them. ◇ If your mouth is **watering**, it is producing saliva, because you can smell or see some appetizing food. See also **mouth-watering.**

❏ If someone is in a difficult situation, you can say they are, for example, in **troubled waters**. *The Government may be in stormy economic waters.* ◇ If you are **keeping your head above water**, you are just managing to avoid getting into financial difficulties.

❏ If you **test the water** or **test the waters**, you test people's reactions to something before going ahead with it, usually by trying it out on a small scale.

❏ If you **pour cold water on** an idea or suggestion, you show you have a low opinion of it. ◇ If you say a theory or argument does not **hold water**, you mean it is based on faulty reasoning or does not fit in with the facts.

❏ If you **water** something **down**, you add water to it to make it weaker. ◇ If something like a plan or scheme is **watered down**, it is made less forceful or controversial.

water-borne diseases are passed on through the water people drink or wash in.

water buffalo Water buffaloes are large buffaloes from the swampy regions of south Asia. They are often used as work animals.

water cannon A water cannon is a machine which shoots out a powerful jet of water. It is used by the police to break up crowds.

water chestnut A water chestnut is the bulb of a Chinese plant. Water chestnuts are crunchy, have a mild taste and are used in Chinese cooking.

water main A water main is a large underground pipe which supplies water to houses or other buildings.

water pistol A water pistol is a toy gun which squirts water.

water polo is a game played in a swimming pool by two teams of seven players. Each team tries to throw or propel an inflated ball into the other team's goal.

water rates are charges made for the use of water from the public water supply.

water-ski (water-skiing) When someone **water-skis**, they ski on water while being pulled along by a boat. This activity is called **water-skiing.**

water softener A water softener is a device or substance for making hard water soft.

water-soluble If something is **water-soluble**, it dissolves in water.

water supply The water supply in an area is the water which is collected and passed through pipes to buildings for people to use.

water table The water table is the level under the ground below which rock is saturated with water.

water tower A water tower is a large tank of water mounted on a tower so water can be supplied at a steady pressure to surrounding buildings.

water wheel A water wheel is a large wheel which is turned by water flowing through it. In the past, water wheels were used to provide power to drive machinery.

waterbed A waterbed is a bed with a waterproof mattress filled with water.

watercolour (watercolourist) (*American spelling:* **watercolor,** *etc*) Watercolours are coloured paints for painting pictures, which you put on the paper with a wet brush or dissolve in water first. A **watercolour** is a picture painted with watercolours. A painter who paints with watercolours is called a **watercolourist.**

watercourse A watercourse is the channel a river or stream flows along.

watercress is a white-flowered plant which grows in freshwater streams and pools. Its leaves taste hot and are eaten raw in salads.

waterfall A waterfall is water flowing over the edge of a steep cliff and falling to the ground or water below.

waterfowl (*plural:* waterfowl) Waterfowl are birds which swim in water, especially ducks, geese, and swans.

waterfront A waterfront is a street or strip of land next to a harbour, dock, or the sea.

waterhole A waterhole is a pond or pool in a desert or other dry area where animals can find water to drink.

watering can A watering can is a container with a long spout, used to water plants.

watering hole A watering hole or watering place is a place where you can get a drink, especially a pub. ◇ Originally a **watering hole** or **watering place** was a town with a spa.

waterlily (waterlilies) Waterlilies are plants with large flat leaves and attractive flowers which float on the surface of a lake or pond.

waterline When a ship is afloat, the waterline is the part of its hull which is level with the surface of the water.

waterlogged ground is so wet it cannot absorb any more water, so rainwater tends to remain on the surface.

watermark A watermark is a design put into paper when it is made, which you can only see if you hold the paper up to the light. Bank notes have a watermark, to make them harder to forge.

watermelon Watermelons are large round fruit with green skin, pink flesh, and black seeds.

watermill A watermill is a mill powered by a water wheel.

waterproof (waterproofing, waterproofed) If something is **waterproof**, water cannot pass through it. If you **waterproof** something, you make it waterproof. ◇ Waterproof clothing is often called **waterproofs.**

watershed ❏ A watershed is a ridge or area of high ground which divides two or more river systems, so that water on one side of the watershed flows into one river and water on the other side flows into a different river.

❏ A **watershed** is also a point when one phase of something ends and another phase begins. *He has reached a watershed in his presidency.*

waterside is used to describe things which are situated or take place beside a lake, river, or some other stretch of water. *...waterside restaurants.*

watertight If a container is **watertight**, it does not let water in. ◇ If something like a theory or an argument is **watertight**, nobody can disprove it or find fault with it.

The police had a watertight case. ◇ If rules and regulations are **watertight**, there is no way round them.

waterway A **waterway** is a canal, river, or narrow channel of sea along which ships or boats travel.

waterworks *(plural:* waterworks*)* A **waterworks** is a place where water is stored and purified before being distributed to the public.

watery is used to describe something which contains, resembles, or involves water. *...dim, watery eyes... He is doomed to a watery grave.* ◇ If food or drink is **watery**, it contains a lot of water. ◇ You also say something is **watery** when it is pale or weak. *A watery light began to show through the branches... ...a dim, watery smile.*

watt *(pron:* wott*)* Electrical power is measured in **watts**. One watt is equal to one joule per second.

wattage The **wattage** of a piece of electrical equipment is the amount of electrical power, expressed in watts, which it uses or generates. *...low-wattage light bulbs.*

wattle *(pron:* wott-tl*)* is a type of construction in which twigs and small branches are woven over a strong wooden framework. Fences are sometimes made of wattle. In the past, house walls were sometimes made of **wattle and daub**, which was wattle plastered with clay or mud.

wave *(waving, waved)* ❏ When you **wave**, you raise your hand and move it up and down in the air, as a way of saying hello or goodbye. ◇ **Wave** is used to describe other gestures made with the hand. For example, if you **wave** someone **away**, you gesture to them to go away. If you **wave** someone **through**, you gesture to them to come past you. *The men had been waved through a checkpoint.*

❏ If you **wave** something, you hold it up and move it rapidly from side to side. ◇ When something like a flag **waves**, it moves gently up and down or from side to side.

❏ If you **wave aside** something like an idea or comment, you show you do not think it is worth any serious consideration.

❏ **Waves** are raised masses of water on the surface of the sea or a lake, caused by the wind or the tide.

❏ A **wave** is also the form in which some types of energy travel, for example light, sound, or radio signals. See also **shock wave**. ◇ **Wave** is used to talk about a range of radio waves. See **long wave, medium wave, short wave**.

❏ A **wave** of emotion is a powerful burst of it passing quickly among a group of people. *Fear of hijacking has sent a wave of panic through New York chauffeurs.* ◇ A **wave** of activity is a sudden increase in it. *...a fresh wave of violence.*

❏ A **wave** of people is a large group of them moving somewhere. *...a fresh wave of refugees.*

❏ If your hair has **waves**, it curves slightly instead of being straight.

waveband A **waveband** is a group of radio waves of similar frequency used for radio transmission.

wavelength ❏ A **wavelength** is the distance between the same point on consecutive cycles of a light wave, sound wave, or radio wave. It is this distance you are referring to when you say a radio station broadcasts on a particular **wavelength**.

❏ If two people are **on the same wavelength**, they share the same attitudes and get on well with each other.

waver *(wavering, wavered; waverer)* ❏ If you **waver** about

something, you are uncertain and indecisive about it. People who cannot make up their minds about something are called **waverers**. ◇ If something such as your confidence **wavers**, it becomes less strong than usual.

❏ If something like a sound **wavers**, it becomes unsteady.

wavy *(wavier, waviest)* If something is **wavy**, it has curves in it. *...a wavy line.*

wax *(waxes, waxing, waxed)* ❏ Various substances made from fat or oil are called **wax**, for example the substance candles are made from. ◇ If you **wax** a surface, you spread a type of wax on it, to polish or protect it. ◇ If a woman **waxes** her legs, she removes the hair from them by spreading wax on them, allowing it to dry, then pulling it off quickly. ◇ **Wax** is also the sticky yellow substance found in your ears.

❏ When the moon **waxes**, a larger area of brightness can be seen each night as it changes in its cycle from new moon to full moon. See also **wane**. ◇ If you talk about something **waxing and waning**, you mean it keeps getting greater then smaller. *Enthusiasm for croquet has waxed and waned over the years.*

❏ **wax lyrical**: see **lyrical**.

waxen is used to describe things which are very pale. *...a waxen-faced child.*

waxwork A **waxwork** is a model of a famous person, made out of wax. A **waxworks** *(plural:* waxworks*)* is a place where waxworks are on display.

way ❏ A **way** of doing something is a method by which it can be done. *Freezing isn't a bad way of preserving food.* ◇ If you do something **by way of** a particular method, you use that method to do it. *...those who choose to prosper by way of financial manipulation rather than hard work.*

❏ The **way** something is done is also the manner in which it is done. *She smiled in a friendly way.*

❏ The **way** you feel about something is your attitude to it or your opinion about it.

❏ You use **way** when talking about the impression something makes on you. *Foreign observers were impressed by the way that refugees had been able to vote.*

❏ You use **way** in phrases like 'in some ways' and 'in many ways' to say something is true to a certain extent. *It's quite comforting in a way.*

❏ You use **way** when talking about possible alternatives. *If I were you, I wouldn't reveal which way you voted.* ◇ You use **way** in phrases like 'the right way up' or 'the wrong way round' to say something is in one of two possible positions. *...a man wearing a baseball cap the wrong way round.* ◇ You use **way** to say in which direction someone or something is facing or moving. *A man coming the other way was shot dead.*

❏ The **way** to a place is the route you take to get there. *...the quickest way to the bank.* If you **make your way** somewhere, you walk or travel there. If you are **on your way** somewhere, you are going there.

❏ If you **lose your way**, you get lost. ◇ You also say someone has **lost their way** when they no longer have any good ideas or seem unsure about what to do.

❏ If someone or something is **in the way**, they are blocking your path or stopping you doing something properly. *He does not allow tradition and sentiment to stand in the way of hard-nosed commercial decisions.* ◇ If you **keep** out of someone's **way,** you avoid them, for example because they are in a bad mood.

❑ If you **make way** for someone else, you give up your position or post and allow them to take your place. Similarly, something can be removed or done away with to **make way** for something else. *She had no intention of abolishing the pound sterling to make way for a single currency.* ◇ If you say something is **on the way out,** you mean it is likely to disappear or be replaced soon. Similarly, a political leader can be **on the way out.**

❑ If something is **on the way,** it is due to happen or arrive soon. ◇ If you **clear the way, open the way,** or **prepare the way** for something, you create an opportunity for it to happen. *The constitution prepares the way for the introduction of a multi-party system of government.*

❑ If something is **under way,** it has started. ◇ If something happens **on the way** or **along the way,** it happens during the course of something.

❑ You use **way** in phrases like 'all the way' and 'half the way' to indicate the extent to which something is complete. *Snead is the leader at the half-way stage.*

❑ If you are **on your way** to achieving something, you are making good progress and are likely to achieve it. *I am now out of hospital and well on the way to recovery.* ◇ You use **way** to talk about someone's progress, or to say how far from achieving something they are. *A long term solution is still some way off.* ◇ You use **way** in phrases like 'work your way' or 'eat your way' when you are talking about someone's progress through something. *He is eating his way through a packet of cream crackers.*

❑ If you say something **goes a long way** towards achieving a result, you mean it greatly helps with achieving it.

❑ When something is over or has been dealt with, you can say it is **out of the way.** *With the election out of the way, Major reshuffled Central Office.*

❑ If you **go out of your way** to do something, you make a special effort to do it.

❑ **Way** is used when talking about distances. *Guntur is quite a way from the coast.*

❑ You use **way** to emphasize that something is a great distance away or very much below or above a certain level or amount. *These exam results are way above average.*

❑ If something is split a number of **ways,** it is divided into a number of parts or quantities, usually fairly equal in size. *There is a three-way split on the Conservative back benches over Europe.*

❑ If you talk about the **ways** of a person or group, you mean their customs or usual behaviour. If you say someone is **set in their ways,** you mean they have had the same habits and attitudes for some time and are unlikely to change.

❑ If you have a **way** with people or things of a particular type, you are skilful at handling them. *He has a way with crowds.* ◇ If someone or something **has a way** of doing a particular thing, they tend to do it. *Wars have a way of throwing up exceptional men and women.*

❑ If you **get your own way,** you get what you want. ◇ If you **go your own way,** you do what you want, rather than what is usual or expected. If people **go their separate ways,** their lives develop differently and they have less contact with each other.

❑ If something **comes your way,** you get it or receive it.

❑ You use **no way** to emphasize that a statement is not at all true. *There is no way we could afford it.*

❑ You use **in a big way** or **in a small way** to talk about scale or importance. *Our sponsorship will, we hope, contribute in a small way to the survival of the species.*

❑ If someone or something is **in a bad way,** they are in a poor state or condition.

❑ You say **by the way** when you are adding an extra piece of information. *It is, by the way, the largest show of Miro's sculpture ever staged.*

❑ You use **by way of** to explain someone's actions. For example, if someone does something by way of thanks, they do it to express their thanks. ◇ You use **in the way of** to say what kind of thing you are talking about. *Small companies are unlikely to offer a great deal in the way of child-care facilities.*

❑ **The other way round** means the opposite process or relationship to the one you have just described. *He said peace would come as a result of negotiations, not the other way round.*

❑ The **way in** is the entrance to a public building or area. The **way out** is the exit.

way of life (ways of life) The **way of life** of a group of people is their normal day-to-day activities. *...the American way of life.* ◇ If you say something is **a way of life** in a place, you mean it is an important feature of normal life there. *Smuggling is a way of life along this coastline.*

waylay (waylaying, waylaid) If you are **waylaid** when you are on your way somewhere, you are stopped by someone, for example because they want to ask you a question.

wayside things are by the side of a road, especially a country road. *...a wayside cafe.*

❑ If someone **falls by the wayside,** they are unable to survive or to continue with what they are doing. *About 126,000 small businesses fell by the wayside in April to June.* ◇ If plans or ideas **fall by the wayside,** they are discarded, ignored, or forgotten.

wayward people are undisciplined and rebellious, or behave in unpredictable ways.

WC A WC is a toilet. WC stands for 'water closet'.

we is used to talk about a group of people which includes the person who is speaking or writing. *We reached the summit at exactly 3pm.*

weak (weakly; weakness, weaknesses) ❑ If someone is **weak,** they do not have much strength or energy. *She leaned weakly against a wall... He was suffering from weakness and lack of co-ordination.*

❑ A **weak** person is not very confident or determined, and is easily influenced by other people. *The association is suffering from weak leadership.* ◇ You say a group of people are **weak** when they do not have much influence or power, and are easily defeated or exploited. People like these are sometimes called **the weak.**

❑ If something like a blow or kick is **weak,** it is not strong or powerful. ◇ If part of the structure of something is **weak,** it is not strong and is likely to break easily. *Swimming is helpful for bones that are porous and weak.*

❑ A **weak** argument is unconvincing and will not stand up to criticism. *...a weak excuse.*

❑ A **weak** economy is unsuccessful and unstable. A currency can also be **weak.**

❑ Your **weaknesses** or **weak points** are your faults or the things you are not very good at. Similarly, you can talk about the **weaknesses** or **weak points** of something like a system. You can also say someone or something is **weak on** a particular thing. *Short stories tend to be weak on plot.* ◇ If you have a **weakness** for something, you like it very much and find it hard to resist.

❑ You say a drink like tea is **weak** when it contains very little tea in proportion to the amount of water in it.

weak-kneed If you call someone **weak-kneed**, you mean they lack courage and determination.

weaken (weakening, weakened) ❑ If something **weakens** or is **weakened**, it becomes less strong or powerful. *There will be no weakening in Western solidarity.*

❑ If a person **weakens**, they become less able to resist something.

❑ If a currency **weakens** or is **weakened**, its value decreases in relation to other currencies.

weakling A man or boy who is physically weak is sometimes called a **weakling**. ◇ A person who gives in easily to other people can also be called a **weakling**.

weal A **weal** is a swelling on someone's skin caused by a blow, often from something like a cane or a whip.

wealth is possessing money, property, or other valuable things. ◇ If you talk about a rich person's **wealth**, you mean the total value of everything they own.

❑ If someone or something has a **wealth** of good features or qualities, they have a lot of them. *...such a wealth of experience.*

wealthy (wealthier, wealthiest) A wealthy person has a lot of money, property, or valuable possessions. Wealthy people are sometimes called **the wealthy**. ◇ A **wealthy** area has a lot of rich people living in it. ◇ A **wealthy** country has a large amount of financial and other resources, with a large proportion of its people enjoying a high standard of living.

wean (weaning, weaned) When you **wean** a baby, you gradually stop feeding it milk and move it onto solid food. ◇ If you **wean** someone **off** something, you help them gradually give it up, often by replacing it with something else. *People can be weaned off cigarettes with nicotine chewing gum.*

weapon A **weapon** is an object like a gun, knife, or missile, used to kill or hurt people in a fight or war. ◇ You can call something else a **weapon** when you can use it to protect yourself or get what you want in a difficult situation. *Phone tapping is acknowledged as an effective weapon against serious crime.*

weaponry If you talk about a country's or group's **weaponry**, you mean all the weapons they have available to them.

wear (wearing, wore, have worn) ❑ If you are **wearing** certain clothes, you have them on your body. You can also say, for example, someone is **wearing** glasses, a watch, or jewellery. ◇ **Wear** is used to describe clothes suitable for particular occasions or activities. *...evening wear.*

❑ The way you **wear** your hair is the way it is cut, styled, or arranged.

❑ You can say someone is **wearing** a particular expression. *Her face wore a slightly puzzled look.*

❑ If something **wears**, it gradually becomes thinner, weaker, or damaged as a result of being used. *The stone*

steps, dating back to 1855, are beginning to wear. You say something like this becomes **worn**. The damage is called **wear**. *...a large, well-upholstered armchair which showed signs of wear.* ◇ **Wear and tear** is damage and gradual deterioration as a result of regular use. ◇ You can say people suffer from **wear and tear** when they become tired or unfit as a result of constant stress or exertion.

❑ If something is **worn down**, it becomes flatter or smoother as a result of constantly rubbing against something else. ◇ If something is **worn away**, it becomes gradually thinner and eventually disappears, as a result of something like scraping or rubbing. ◇ If something **wears out**, it becomes too old, weak, or damaged to be used any more.

❑ If something is resistant to wear, you can say it **wears well**.

❑ If you **wear** a person **down**, you gradually weaken their resistance to something.

❑ If you find something **wearing**, it tires or irritates you. ◇ If you say someone looks **worn**, you mean they look old and tired. ◇ If you say someone is **the worse for wear**, you mean they are tired, ill, or in a bad state generally, often because they have been drinking too much. ◇ If something **wears** you **out**, it exhausts you.

❑ If your patience is **wearing thin**, you are finding it more difficult to be patient with someone. ◇ You say other things are **wearing thin** when people no longer find them funny or interesting. *Some of Wilson's eccentricities are beginning to wear thin.*

❑ If a feeling **wears off**, it disappears slowly until it no longer exists or no longer has any effect.

❑ You can talk about time **wearing on** when it seems to pass very slowly. *As Thursday morning wore on, the hotel foyer began to resemble a bazaar.*

wearable When fashion reporters call clothes **wearable**, they mean they are comfortable and practical.

wearer A **wearer** of something is a person who wears it. *There are more than two million contact-lens wearers in the UK.*

wearisome If you call something **wearisome**, you mean it is tiring, boring, or frustrating.

weary (wearier, weariest; wearily, weariness; wearies, wearying, wearied) ❑ If you are **weary**, you are very tired. *We trudged wearily away... ...the weariness of a Saturday supermarket shopper.*

❑ If people are **weary** of something, they have had enough of it and wish it would come to an end. You can also say people are **wearied** by something.

weasel ❑ **Weasels** are small wild animals with long slender bodies, tails, short legs, and reddish-brown fur. They hunt and eat creatures like mice and rabbits.

❑ If you talk about people, especially politicians, using **weasel words**, you mean they are deliberately expressing themselves in an unclear way, to hide the truth about something or to avoid committing themselves.

weather (weathering, weathered) ❑ The **weather** is the atmospheric conditions in a place, including the temperature and whether there is cloud, rain, or sunshine. ◇ If you do something **in all weathers**, you do it regularly, regardless of whether the weather is good or bad.

❑ If rock is **weathered**, it is worn down or broken up as a result of being exposed to things like hot sun, rain, or frost.

❏ If you **weather** a difficult time, you get through it and are able to continue normally after it. You can also say you **weather the storm.**

❏ If you say someone is making **heavy weather** of a task, you mean they are handling it in an inefficient manner and making it seem more difficult than it really is.

weather forecast A **weather forecast** is details of what the weather will be like in the near future, especially when presented as a report on TV or radio.

weather forecaster A **weather forecaster** is someone whose job is to study weather conditions and predict what the weather will be like.

weather station A **weather station** is one of a network of observation posts where weather data is recorded.

weather vane See vane.

weathercock A **weathercock** is a flat metal plate, often shaped like a cockerel, fixed to the roof of a tall building, where it rotates and shows which way the wind is blowing.

weatherman (weathermen) A **weatherman** is a man who gives weather forecasts at regular times on TV or radio.

weatherproof (weatherproofing, weatherproofed) If something like a roof is **weatherproof,** it keeps out the wind and rain. If you **weatherproof** something, you make it weatherproof.

weave (weaving, wove *or* weaved, have woven *or* have weaved) ❏ When people **weave** cloth or a carpet, they make it by crossing threads over and under each other using a machine called a loom. ◇ The **weave** of a cloth or carpet is the way the threads are arranged. ◇ If someone **weaves** something like a basket, they make it by crossing long plant stems or fibres over and under each other.

❏ If you **weave your way** somewhere, you move between and around things in order to get there. You can also say a road or river **weaves its way** somewhere.

❏ If one thing is **woven** into another, it is added to it or combined with it, often in a complicated or creative way. *...the ability of electronics to weave together images, sound and information.*

❏ You can say an author **weaves** a story.

weaver Weavers are people who weave cloth or carpets.

web ❏ A **web** is a thin net made by a spider from a sticky substance which it produces in its body. Insects stick to the web and are eaten by the spider.

❏ You can call a complicated pattern of connections or relationships a **web.** *He was at the centre of a web of 30 banks and advisers.*

webbed Birds and animals with **webbed** feet have pieces of skin between their toes which make swimming easier for them.

webbing is strong material woven in strips and used to make things like straps.

wed (wedding, wed *or* wedded) When two people **wed,** they get married. You can also say one person **weds** another. ◇ If you are **wedded** to something like an idea or principle, you are totally committed to it and unwilling to give it up.

wedding A **wedding** is a marriage ceremony and the party or special meal that follows it.

wedding ring A **wedding ring** is a plain ring you wear to show you are married.

wedge (wedging, wedged) ❏ If you **wedge** something like a door or window, you keep it firmly in position by pushing something between it and the surface next to it. ◇ A **wedge** is an object with one pointed edge and one thick one, which you use for wedging a door or window.

❏ If something is **wedged** somewhere, it is pushed there so it fits tightly.

❏ A **wedge** is a also piece of metal with a pointed edge. It is used to split stone, slate, or wood by hammering it into a crack.

❏ A **wedge** is also a type of golf club.

❏ A **wedge** of something is a piece which is thick at one end and thin at the other, for example a piece cut from a round cake. *....a wedge of cheese.*

❏ If something **drives a wedge** between people, it causes ill feeling between them and damages an otherwise good relationship.

❏ If you call something **the thin end of the wedge,** you mean that although it may not seem significant in itself, it could lead to something extremely damaging or harmful.

wedlock is the state of being married. If a baby is born **out of wedlock,** its parents are not married to each other at the time it is born.

wee is a dialect word meaning 'little'. *We've all been a wee bit hasty.*

weed (weeding, weeded) ❏ A **weed** is a wild plant growing where it is not wanted, for example in a garden. If you **weed** an area of ground, you remove the weeds from it.

❏ **Weed** is a flowerless plant which grows in water and usually forms a thick floating mass. There are many kinds of weed.

❏ Tobacco and marijuana are sometimes called **weed.**

❏ If you **weed out** unwanted people or things, you identify them and get rid of them.

weeder A **weeder** is a machine or tool for removing weeds.

weedkiller is a substance used to kill weeds. Many weedkillers are poisonous to humans.

weedy If you call a person **weedy,** you mean they are thin and weak.

week ❏ A **week** is a period of seven days, especially one starting on a Sunday or Monday. ◇ Your working **week** is the hours you spend at work each week. *The plant will continue to work a three-day week in October.*

❏ The **week** means the part of the week other than the weekend. *...looking after the children during the week.*

weekday A **weekday** is any day except Saturday and Sunday.

weekend The **weekend** is Saturday and Sunday.

weekender A **weekender** is someone who lives in a place only at weekends, especially a place they use as a second home in the country.

weekly (weeklies) **Weekly** is used to describe things which happen or appear once a week. *...a weekly column in The Guardian.* ◇ **Weekly** quantities or rates relate to a period of one week. *...a weekly income of £350.* ◇ A **weekly** is a newspaper or magazine which is published once a week.

weep (weeping, wept; weepy) If someone **weeps,** they cry. If they are **weepy,** they are sad and likely to cry at any moment. ◇ Sad stories and music are also sometimes called **weepy**.

weevil Weevils are small beetles and their grubs which feed on grain and seeds and destroy crops.

weft The **weft** of a piece of woven material is the threads which are passed sideways in and out of the threads held in the loom. See also **warp**.

weigh ❑ If you **weigh** an object, you measure how heavy it is. Similarly, you can **weigh** yourself. You say an object or person **weighs** a certain amount. ◇ You can say a very large or heavy person **weighs in** at a certain amount.

❑ If you **weigh** something **out**, you get a certain amount of it together, weighing it to make sure the amount is correct.

❑ If you **weigh** the facts about a situation or **weigh** them **up**, you consider them carefully before making a decision. ◇ If you **weigh** someone or something **up**, you consider them carefully and form an opinion about them.

❑ If a problem **weighs on** you, it troubles or upsets you.

❑ You can use **weigh** to say how important something is to someone. *Human life weighed more with him than purity of policy.*

❑ If you are carrying something very heavy, especially on your back, you can say you are **weighed down** by it. ◇ If you are **weighed down** by a difficulty, it is causing you great problems and preventing you from achieving your aims.

❑ If you **weigh in** in a debate or a competition, you join in in an enthusiastic way.

❑ **weigh anchor**: see **anchor**.

weigh-in The **weigh-in** before a boxing match or a horse race is a procedure in which the boxers or jockeys are weighed to check their weight.

weight (weighting) ❑ The **weight** of a person or thing is how heavy they are, expressed in units such as kilos, pounds, or tons. ◇ If someone **gains weight** or **puts on weight**, their weight increases. If they **lose weight**, their weight decreases.

❑ **Weights** are metal objects which weigh a known amount. They are used with scales to measure the weight of other things. ◇ **Weights** are also heavy objects designed for people to lift as a form of exercise to improve their muscle performance.

❑ You can call a heavy object a **weight**, especially when you have to lift it.

❑ If you **weight** something, you add something heavy to it. ◇ If you **weight** something **down**, you put something heavy on it to stop it moving.

❑ A system which is **weighted** in favour of a person or group is organized to give them an advantage. Similarly, something can be **weighted** against a person or group.

❑ A **weighting** is a value given to something according to how important or significant it is. ◇ A **weighting** is also an extra sum of money people receive on top of their salary if they work in a city where the cost of living is very high.

❑ The **weight** you give to something is the degree of importance you attach to it. *A Consumer Protection Commission would give more weight to environmental considerations.* ◇ If something lends or adds **weight** to what someone says, it makes it more likely to be true. *The figures add weight to criticism of irresponsible lending by the banks.* ◇ If a person's opinions **carry weight**, people respect them and are likely to be influenced by them.

❑ If you **pull your weight**, you work as hard as everyone else involved in the same task or activity.

❑ If you say someone is **throwing their weight about**, you mean they are using their strength or influence in a bullying way. ◇ If you **throw** or **put your weight behind** a plan or campaign, you use all your influence and do everything you can to support it.

weight training is physical exercise which involves lifting weights to improve muscle performance.

weightless (weightlessness) If something is **weightless**, it weighs nothing or seems to weigh nothing. You say people and objects are **weightless** when they are in space and the earth's gravity does not affect them, so they float around. *...the dizzying effects of weightlessness.*

weightlifting (weightlifter) **Weightlifting** is a sport in which people called **weightlifters** compete to see who can lift the heaviest weight.

weighty (weightier, weightiest) ❑ If you call a problem or issue **weighty**, you mean it is very important and serious. You can also call a statement or discussion **weighty**, especially when you think it is more serious than it needs to be. *...another weighty theological dialogue.*

❑ A **weighty** country or organization is powerful and influential.

❑ You can call a heavy object **weighty**.

weir A **weir** is a low dam built across a river to control or direct the flow of water.

weird (weirdly, weirdness) If you say something is **weird**, you mean it is very odd and unusual. *Like many film stars, he is weirdly proportioned.* ◇ If you say a person is **weird**, you mean they behave in a strange way. Similarly, you can say a place is **weird** when the people there behave in strange ways. *The weirdness of Hollywood suits him well.*

weirdo (*pron:* **weer**-doh) (weirdos *or* weirdoes) If you call someone a **weirdo**, you mean they behave in a strange way.

welcome (welcoming, welcomed) ❑ If you **welcome** someone or give them a **welcome**, you greet them in a friendly way when they arrive at the place where you are. ◇ If you **make** someone **welcome** when they arrive in a new place, you make sure they have what they want and show you are pleased to see them.

❑ If you say someone is **welcome** in a place, you mean they can go there and people will be pleased to see them. ◇ If you tell someone they are **welcome** to do something, you mean they can do it if they want to and you will be pleased if they do.

❑ If you **welcome** something new, you approve of it and support it. You say something like this is **welcome**. *Another fall in the oil price would be highly welcome.*

weld (welder) ❑ If you **weld** two pieces of metal together, you join them together using heat, pressure, or electricity. The join you make is called a **weld**. A **welder** is a person whose job is welding.

❑ If you **weld** people into a group, you form them into a united organization.

welfare ❑ If you talk about a person's **welfare**, you mean their health and their ability to lead a contented life. You can also talk about the **welfare** of animals. *...laws* *affecting animal welfare.*

❑ **Welfare** is used to talk about services provided to help with people's living conditions and financial problems. *...welfare agencies.* ◇ In the US, **welfare** is money paid by the government to people who are very poor. If someone is receiving money like this, you say they are **on welfare.**

welfare state A country's **welfare state** is the system in which its government uses money from taxes to provide things like health care, benefits, and pensions.

well ❑ If you do something **well,** you do it to a high standard. *He spoke English well.* ◇ **Well** means thoroughly or to a great extent. *The process is not well understood... We knew a lot of people in the fashion world quite well.* ◇ **Well-** is used with other words to say something is done to a high standard or to a great extent. *...a well-organized rebel force.*

❑ **Well** is used to say how successful or satisfactory something is. *He has done very well in these elections.* ◇ If you **do well out of** something, you gain money or some advantage as a result of it.

❑ If you say someone **would do well to** do a certain thing, you mean it would be a good idea if they did it, for their own sake.

❑ If you say it is **just as well** that a certain thing happens or exists, you mean it is fortunate that it happens or exists. *Fortunately, few cases are reported in the UK. This is just as well, since the condition cannot be cured.*

❑ If you think or speak **well** of someone, you think or say good things about them.

❑ **Well** is used to give emphasis. *Osborne House is well worth a visit.*

❑ If you say something **may well** happen, you mean there is a good chance it will happen. Similarly, you can say something **may well** exist or be true.

❑ **As well as** means 'in addition to'. *Leeds now face a stiff test of character as well as physical endurance.* ◇ **As well** means 'too' or 'also'. *Other countries have been seeking the release of their citizens as well.*

❑ If you say you **may as well** do something or you **might as well** do it, you mean it would make no difference to the end result if you did it. *People with money in banks and building societies may as well leave it there for the moment.*

❑ If you are **well,** you are in good health.

❑ A **well** is a hole in the ground from which a supply of water is extracted.

❑ If a liquid **wells up** somewhere, it comes to the surface and forms a pool. ◇ If a feeling **wells up** inside you, you start to feel it.

well-appointed A **well-appointed** room or building is equipped or furnished to a high standard.

well-balanced See **balance.**

well-behaved See **behave.**

well-being Your **well-being** is your health and happiness.

well-bred Upper-class people are sometimes described as **well-bred.**

well-built A **well-built** man is strong and muscular.

well-connected If you say someone is **well-connected,** you mean they have important or influential relatives or friends.

well-dressed A **well-dressed** person is wearing smart or elegant clothes.

well-earned See **earn.**

well-educated See **educate.**

well-established If something is **well-established,** it has existed for a long time and is successful.

well-fed If you say someone is **well-fed,** you mean they get plenty of healthy food.

well-founded See **found.**

well-groomed See **groom.**

well-grounded See **ground.**

well-heeled If you say someone is **well-heeled,** you mean they are wealthy.

well-informed If someone is **well-informed,** they know a lot about a subject or situation.

well-intentioned means the same as **well-meaning.**

well-known If you say a fact is **well-known,** you mean a lot of people know it. ◇ A **well-known** person is known to a lot of people, for example because they appear a lot on TV or are often in the news.

well-mannered See **manner.**

well-meaning (well-meant) You say someone is **well-meaning** when they try to be kind or helpful but things do not work out the way they intend. You can also say what they do is **well-meaning** or **well-meant.** *...the well-meant but disastrous 1974 Rent Act.*

well-nigh See **nigh.**

well-off If someone is **well-off,** they are wealthy.

well-placed See **place.**

well-preserved If something old is **well-preserved,** it does not show many signs of its age.

well-read A **well-read** person has read a lot of books and learned a lot from them.

well-received If something is **well-received,** people react favourably to it.

well-spoken A **well-spoken** person speaks in a polite correct way and with a standard accent.

well-thought-of If someone is **well-thought-of,** they are admired and respected, and have a good reputation.

well-thumbed A **well-thumbed** book or magazine is creased and marked because it has been read so often.

well-timed If something is **well-timed,** it happens or is done at the most suitable time.

well-to-do means the same as 'well-off'.

well-tried If something is **well-tried,** it has been used or done many times before and is known to work well or to be successful.

well-versed See **versed.**

well-wisher A **well-wisher** is someone who shows support for a person or cause.

well-worn A **well-worn** expression or remark has been used so often it has lost a lot of its meaning or impact. ◇ A **well-worn** object or piece of clothing has been used so much that it looks old and untidy.

wellington **Wellingtons** are the same as **wellies.**

welly (wellies) **Wellies** are long rubber boots you wear to keep your feet dry.

Welsh is used to talk about people and things in or from Wales. *...a small Welsh town.* ◇ **Welsh** is a language spoken by many people in Wales.

Welsh rarebit or **Welsh rabbit** is melted seasoned cheese on hot buttered toast.

Welshman (Welshwoman) A **Welshman** or **Welshwoman** is a person who comes from Wales.

welt ❑ A **welt** is a mark on someone's skin caused by a blow from something like a whip or stick.

❑ A **welt** is also a strengthened seam or edge sewn onto a garment for strength or decoration. ◇ The **welt** of a shoe is the leather strip between the sole and the upper part.

welter A **welter** of things is a large number of them jumbled together. *...the welter of conflicting reports coming out of Rwanda.*

wench (wenches) **Wench** is an old word for a lower-class girl, especially a servant or a prostitute.

wend If you **wend** your way somewhere, you go there slowly.

went See go.

wept See weep.

were See be.

werewolf (werewolves) In ancient folklore, a **werewolf** was a man who could turn himself into a wolf.

west is one of the four main points of the compass. ◇ The **west** is the direction where the sun sets. If you go in that direction, you go **west**; a place in that direction is **west** of the place where you are now. ◇ The **west** part of a place is the part west of its centre. *...the west of Scotland... ...the West Midlands.*

❑ A **west** wind blows from the west.

❑ The **West** is used to talk about the US, Canada, and Western and Southern Europe. *He wants the West to recognize his country.* ◇ See also Wild West.

❑ If you say that something has **gone west**, you mean it has been destroyed or is lost for good.

westbound traffic is heading towards the west.

westerly ❑ A **westerly** wind blows from the west. ◇ If you travel in a **westerly** direction, you travel towards the west. Similarly, if you face in a **westerly** direction, you face towards the west.

❑ The most **westerly** part of a place is the part furthest to the west. Similarly, the most **westerly** place of a group of places is the one furthest to the west. *...Foula, the most westerly of the Shetland isles.*

western ❑ The **western** part of a place is the part west of its centre. *...Western Australia.* ◇ **Western** also means to the west of a country or region. *...Uganda, Kenya's western neighbour.*

❑ **Western** things come from the US, Canada, and Western and Southern Europe. *...western technology.*

❑ A **western** is a book or film about life in the west of America in the the 19th century.

westerner A **westerner** is a person who was born in or lives in the western part of a country or region. ◇ A **westerner** is also a person who was born in or lives in the US, Canada, or Western or Southern Europe.

westernize (westernizing, westernized; westernization) (*can be spelled with an 's' instead of a 'z'*) If a country or system is **westernized**, ideas and behaviour common in the West are introduced there. *...the westernization of Poland's economy.*

westernmost The **westernmost** part of a place is the part furthest to the west. Similarly, the **westernmost** place of a group of places is the one furthest to the west.

Westminster is the area in London where the Houses of Parliament are. **Westminster** is often used to talk about parliament itself. *He has never been widely popular at Westminster.*

westward (westwards) If you go **westward** or **westwards**, you go towards the west. You can also say you go in a **westward** direction. *High winds are already blowing westwards across much of the country... ...a westward route.*

wet (wetter, wettest; wetness; wetting, wet *or* wetted) ❑ If a surface is **wet**, it is covered in a liquid. If something like a garment is **wet**, it has absorbed a liquid and has not yet dried out. ◇ If something like paint, ink, or cement is **wet**, it is not yet dry or solid. ◇ If you **wet** something, you pour or sprinkle liquid on it.

❑ If the weather is **wet**, it is raining. If you do something **in the wet**, you do it when it is raining. *The car was prone to skid when braking in the wet.*

❑ If people, especially children, **wet** their beds or clothes or **wet** themselves, they urinate in their beds or clothes because they cannot control their bladder.

❑ **Wet fish** is fresh fish, rather than salted or dried fish.

❑ If you say someone is **wet,** you mean they are weak and lack confidence, energy, or enthusiasm. ◇ In British politics, moderate Conservatives are sometimes called **wets.**

wet nurse In the past, a **wet nurse** was a woman who was paid to breast-feed another woman's baby.

wet suit A **wet suit** is a close-fitting rubber suit worn by people like divers to keep them warm in the water.

whack ❑ If you **whack** someone or something or give them a **whack,** you hit them hard.

❑ A **whack** of something is a share of it. *Governments ensure that consultants from their country win a fair whack of the contracts.*

whacky See wacky.

whale (whaling, whaler) **Whales** are very large sea mammals, sometimes hunted for their oil and flesh. Hunting whales is called **whaling.** It is done in special ships called **whalers;** the people who work on these ships are also called **whalers.**

whalebone is a hard substance taken from the mouth of a whale. It was used in the past for stiffening cloth, especially in corsets.

whammy See double whammy.

wharf (wharves) A **wharf** is a platform built by a river or the sea, where ships can be tied up for loading and unloading.

what ❑ You use **what** in various ways to refer to a specific thing. *I didn't know what to do... It is hard for journalists to find out what is going on.* You also use **what** to ask about a specific thing, or to mention a question of this kind. *What are you going to do next?... I asked him what he was waiting for.*

❑ You use **what** with 'for' to ask about the purpose of something. *Just what is a car for?*

❑ You say **what about...** when you are reminding someone of something, or drawing their attention to it. *It does seem as if the climate is changing, but what about carbon dioxide levels?* ◇ You say **what if...** when you are asking about the consequences of something. *What if the train breaks down?*

❑ You say **what** instead of 'the thing that', 'the amount that', etc. *They have negotiated what few would have believed* possible: *the merging of their private guerrilla armies under a unified command... Their assets are now worth less than what fund managers paid for them.*

❑ You can say **what** instead of 'whatever'. *He can do what he wants.*

❑ You use **what** in exclamations to express your opinion of something. *What a splendid idea... What a pity!*

whatever ❑ You use **whatever** to talk about anything or everything of a particular kind. *Western nations will continue to scramble for whatever crude oil is available... My job is to get whatever customers want.*

❑ You use **whatever** to talk about something you cannot be specific about. *She is the opposite of a pacifist, whatever that is.* ◇ You use **whatever** to say something is the case in all circumstances. *The ruling council has authority to proceed and will do so whatever the outcome of the voting.*

❑ You say **whatever** or **whatsoever** when you have used a word like 'no' or 'nothing', to emphasize what you are saying. *...medical information which the patient has no right whatever to see... There's been no sign that anybody has suffered any ill effects whatsoever.* ◇ You say **whatever** instead of 'what' when you are asking about something in an emphatic way. *Whatever happened to her?*

whatnot You use **and whatnot** after a list to show there are other things you have not mentioned. *Rabbits can soon damage your crops and your sugar beet and whatnot.*

whatsoever See **whatever**.

wheat is a cereal grown for its grain, which is used to make flour. ◇ **separate the wheat from the chaff**: see **chaff**.

wheatgerm is the middle part of a grain of wheat, which is rich in vitamins and is sometimes added to other food.

wheatmeal is a brown flour made from wheat grains, including some of the husks.

wheedle (wheedling, wheedled) If you **wheedle** someone into doing something, you gently and cleverly persuade them to do it. ◇ If you **wheedle** something out of someone, you persuade them to give it to you.

wheel (wheeling, wheeled) ❑ A **wheel** is a circular object, which turns on a rod in its centre. Wheels are fixed underneath vehicles so they can move along. **-wheeled** is used to say how many wheels a vehicle has. *...a four-wheeled buggy.* ◇ **-wheel** is used to say how a car is powered. For example, in a **front-wheel** drive car, the engine's power goes to the front wheels. See also **four-wheel drive**.

❑ The **wheel** of a car is its steering wheel. *She drove out of the grounds at the wheel of a Ford Granada.* ◇ The **wheel** of a ship is a vertical wheel used for steering.

❑ If you **wheel** something like a bike or cart, you push it along. Similarly, you can **wheel** an object in a cart or trolley, or **wheel** a person in something like a wheelchair.

❑ If you say someone or something is **wheeled out** for a particular purpose, you mean they appear and are used for that purpose. *Psychologists were wheeled out to pronounce on the dangers or otherwise of heavy metal.*

❑ You say birds **wheel** when they fly round in large circles. *...wheeling cormorants.*

❑ **Wheeling and dealing** is using cunning methods to get what you want, especially by making deals with people. A politician or businessman who behaves like this is called a **wheeler-dealer**.

wheel clamp (wheel clamping) A **wheel clamp** is a device fitted to one wheel of an illegally parked vehicle, which immobilizes it. The wheel clamp is removed only after a fine has been paid. Fitting a wheel clamp to a vehicle is called **wheel clamping**.

wheelbarrow A **wheelbarrow** is a small cart with handles and one wheel, used for moving small loads on a building site or in a garden.

wheelbase The **wheelbase** of a vehicle is the distance between its front and back axles.

wheelchair A **wheelchair** is a chair on wheels which sick or disabled people use to move about in.

wheeler-dealer See **wheel**.

wheelhouse The **wheelhouse** on a boat is a small room or shelter above the level of the deck, where the wheel for steering is situated.

wheelspin is what happens when a vehicle's wheels turn round but cannot get a grip on the road surface.

wheeze (wheezing, wheezed) ❑ If you **wheeze**, you breathe with difficulty, making a hissing or whistling sound.

❑ A **wheeze** is a cunning plan or trick.

whelk Whelks are snail-like shellfish with strong shells and soft edible bodies.

when ❑ You use **when** to ask about the time of something, or to mention a question of this kind. *When did you come back from Zambia?... Graf was asked when last she enjoyed playing tennis.* ◇ You also use **when** to mention the time at which something happens. *His mother had died when he was a baby.*

❑ You use **when** to indicate why you are making a statement or asking a question. *How can you enjoy conducting when it is such a responsibility?* ◇ You also use **when** to mean 'although'. *He was attempting to give the impression that there had been no change of policy, when in fact there had been.*

whence means 'from where'. *The disbanding of the York and Lancaster Regiment virtually halted recruitment in Sheffield, whence it used to draw most of its men.*

whenever You use **whenever** to say something always happens in certain circumstances. *The park is closed whenever shooting is in progress.* ◇ You also use **whenever** to talk about an unknown time. *The general election, whenever it comes, looks like being close.*

where ❑ You use **where** to ask about the location or destination of something, or about the place something comes from. *Where do you live?... Where is the money to come from?* You also use **where** when mentioning questions of this kind. *He asked her where she wanted to go.* You use **where** in various other ways to talk about the location, destination, or source of something. *Drains would be dug to divert flood water to areas where it could do no harm.*

❑ You also use **where** when you are talking about a situation, or a stage in something. *Asthma is increasing to a point where there will be three asthmatic children in every primary school class.*

❑ **Where** is sometimes used to mean 'whereas'. *Where Mr Perot has built real companies, Mr Riordan's career has mainly been spent as a wheeler-dealer.*

whereabouts A person's or thing's **whereabouts** is the place where they are. *There has been no word of his where-*

abouts. ◇ You use **whereabouts** to ask more precisely where someone or something is. *Whereabouts in Liverpool are you from?*

whereas You say **whereas** when you are mentioning two contrasting facts. *People tend to vote Labour in local elections, hoping for better services, whereas they vote Tory nationally, to keep taxes down.*

whereby means 'by which' when you are saying how something is achieved or made possible. *...a clandestine intelligence operation whereby the Americans obtained latest versions of Soviet-made weapons systems.*

wherefore see why.

wherein means 'in which'. *Mother rented lock-up shops wherein she sold fashions, knitting patterns, wool and stuff like that... ...a programme wherein children raise seedlings in the schools.*

whereupon is used to say something happened immediately after something else. *His enemies rejected his message, whereupon he tried again, offering to call off his war preparations in exchange for an amnesty for his supporters.*

wherever ❏ You use **wherever** to say something always happens or is always true in any place or situation. *Demonstrators howl abuse at the prime minister wherever he goes.* ◇ You also use **wherever** to say someone can do something in any place they want to. *All citizens who met the legal requirements were free to travel abroad and settle wherever they chose.* ◇ You also use **wherever** to show you do not know where a place or person is. *They have been sent back to Germany or Belgium or wherever they came from.*

❏ **Wherever** is used with 'possible' to mean the same as 'when' or 'whenever'. *They try to use local and free range produce wherever possible.*

wherewithal If you have the **wherewithal** to do something, you have the money or resources for it. *Japan has the financial wherewithal to provide much-needed assistance to Cambodia.*

whet (whetting, whetted) ❏ If something **whets** your appetite for something, it increases your desire for it.

❏ If you **whet** a knife or some other tool, you sharpen it.

whether You use **whether** when you are mentioning two or more alternatives. *He was unsure whether the others had been shot or arrested.* When the alternatives are opposites, you only need to mention one of them after **whether**. *He could not decide whether he wanted to move north.*

whetstone A **whetstone** is a stone for sharpening knives or other tools.

whey (*pron:* **way**) is the watery liquid which is separated from the curds in sour milk when cheese is made.

which ❏ You use **which** to ask questions when there are two or more possible answers or alternatives. *Which of these two long-time rivals has the upper hand?* You also use **which** when mentioning questions of this kind. *Frank was asked which paper he worked for.* **Which** is used in various other ways to talk about a choice between possible answers and alternatives. *...the passionate arguments about which regiments to keep and which to lose.*

❏ You use **which** when you are adding an extra piece of information. *The plans, which are opposed by many students, have led to disturbances across northern India.* ◇ You use

which to refer back to what you have just said. *The scan was clear, which is good news.*

whichever ❏ You use **whichever** to say something is unaffected by which of a number of possible things happens or is chosen. *Civil servants normally refuse to comment on government policy, whichever party is in power.*

❏ You also use **whichever** to talk about the most appropriate one of a number of possibilities. *Manufacturers had to leave the public to attach whichever plug suited their home.*

whiff A **whiff** of something is a slight sign or trace of it. *...a whiff of scandal.* ◇ A **whiff** is also a faint smell.

while (whiling, whiled) ❏ If something happens **while** or **whilst** something else is happening, it happens throughout the time the second thing is happening, or at some point during it. *Some residents have to move out while work is in progress... Events like Comic Relief allow people to have fun whilst filling the charity coffers.*

❏ A **while** is a period of time. *For a while we would go to the beach in a taxi... ...the first promising development in a long while.* ◇ **once in a while:** see **once.** ◇ If something happens **all the while,** it happens all the time, or throughout the time something else is happening.

❏ **While** and **whilst** are also used to mean 'whereas' or 'although'. *Whilst academic excellence is admirable, it is useless without maturity.*

❏ If you **while away** the time in a particular way, you spend it that way because you are waiting for something or because you have nothing to do.

❏ **worth your while:** see **worth.**

whilst See **while.**

whim A **whim** is a sudden desire to do or have something. *Lately, the president has been sacking and picking new ministers at whim.*

whimper (whimpering, whimpered) When children or animals **whimper**, they make little low unhappy sounds. You call these sounds **whimpers.** ◇ If someone **whimpers** something, they say it in an unhappy or frightened way. ◇ If something ends with a **whimper**, it ends in a quiet unnoticed way.

whimsical (whimsically, whimsy) If you call something like a piece of writing **whimsical**, you mean it is amusing in a quaint or playful way, and is not trying to make a serious point. Playful humour of this kind is called **whimsy.** *As he whimsically says, the mortgage and the bank manager can concentrate the mind wonderfully.*

whine (whining, whined) If something **whines**, it makes a long high-pitched noise. A noise like this is called a **whine.** ◇ If someone **whines** about something, they complain about it in an annoying way.

whinge (whingeing, whinged; whinger) If someone **whinges** about something, they complain about it in an irritating way. People who behave like this are called **whingers.**

whinny (whinnies, whinnying, whinnied) When a horse **whinnies**, it neighs softly.

whip (whipping, whipped) ❏ A **whip** is a piece of leather or rope attached to a handle and used for hitting people or animals. If someone **whips** a person or animal, they hit them with a whip.

❏ If you have the **whip hand** over someone, you have power over them or an advantage over them. ◇ If you get a **fair crack of the whip,** you are allowed a reasonable opportunity to do something.

❏ If you **whip** cream or eggs, you beat them quickly to make them thick and frothy.

❏ If something **whips** somewhere, it moves very quickly. ◇ If you **whip** something **out**, you take it out quickly and suddenly. Similarly, you can **whip** something **off**. *German tourists are renowned for whipping off all their clothes at the first sign of a sunny beach.*

❏ If someone **whips up** a strong emotion, they deliberately make people feel it. *...a campaign designed to whip up terror ahead of the elections.*

❏ When a political party suspends an MP, you say the MP loses the **whip** or has the **whip** withdrawn. ◇ In parliament, a **whip** is a member of a political party who is responsible for making sure members are there to vote on important issues. ◇ See also three-line whip.

whip-round If a group of people have a **whip-round**, money is collected from each person to buy something.

whiplash (whiplashes) A **whiplash** is a blow with a whip. ◇ A **whiplash injury** is a neck injury caused by someone's head suddenly jerking backwards and forwards, for example in a car accident.

whippet Whippets are thin dogs which look like small greyhounds.

whipping boy You say someone is made the **whipping boy** when they are blamed for something which has gone wrong, although it may not be their fault.

whipping cream is cream which becomes stiff when it is whipped.

whir See whirr.

whirl ❏ If something **whirls** or if you **whirl** it round, it turns round quickly.

❏ You can call a lot of intense activity a **whirl** of activity. *...the hectic whirl of interviews.*

❏ If you **give** something **a whirl**, you try it.

whirlpool ❏ A **whirlpool** is a small area in a river or the sea where the water moves quickly round and round, so that objects floating near it are pulled into its centre.

❏ A **whirlpool bath** is the same as a Jacuzzi.

whirlwind A **whirlwind** is a tall column of air which spins round and round very rapidly, moving across the land or sea. ◇ A situation in which there is a lot of frantic activity can be called a **whirlwind**. *...a whirlwind of deals.* ◇ A **whirlwind** event happens much more quickly than usual. *...a whirlwind romance.*

whirr (*or* **whir**) (whirring, whirred) If something **whirrs**, it makes a low buzzing sound, for example like a motor running. A noise like this is called a **whirr**.

whisk ❏ If you **whisk** someone or something somewhere, you take them there quickly.

❏ If you **whisk** eggs or cream, you stir air into them quickly with a device called a **whisk**.

whisker (whiskered, whiskery) ❏ The **whiskers** of an animal like a cat or mouse are the long stiff hairs growing near its mouth. ◇ You can call the hair on a man's face, especially on the sides of his face, his **whiskers**. If a man has hair like this, you can say he is **whiskered** or **whiskery**.

❏ A **whisker** is a very small amount. *The two firms are within a whisker of agreeing on a deal.*

whiskey is the usual Irish and American spelling of 'whisky'.

whisky (whiskies) **Whisky** is a strong alcoholic drink made from barley or rye.

whisper (whispering, whispered) ❏ If you **whisper** something or say it in a **whisper**, you say it very quietly, using only your breath and not your voice. When people talk like this, you say they speak **in whispers**. ◇ You also say people **whisper** when they talk about something secretly among themselves. A **whisper** is a rumour. *Ministers began to whisper that he would be sacked.* A **whispering campaign** is a deliberate attempt to discredit someone by spreading rumours about them.

❏ You say trees **whisper** when they make a low quiet sound as the wind passes through their branches.

whist is a card game in which two people play against two other people. A **whist drive** is a social event where whist is played by several people.

whistle (whistling, whistled) ❏ If you **whistle** or let out a **whistle**, you form a small 'o' with your lips and force your breath out, making a high-pitched sound. By adjusting your lips, you can **whistle** a tune. ◇ You also say you **whistle** when you make a high shrill sound by forcing your breath out between your teeth and two fingers, usually to show disapproval of something. A sound like this is also called a **whistle**.

❏ If you say someone is **whistling in the wind,** you mean they are saying or doing something which will have no effect on a situation.

❏ A **whistle** is a small metal tube you blow in to produce a loud sound and attract someone's attention. In sports like football, the **whistle** is the signal the referee gives when he blows his whistle to say the match is over. ◇ If you **blow the whistle** on someone, you tell someone in authority about something illegal or secret they are doing. A person who does this is called a **whistle-blower**.

❏ If something **whistles**, it makes a loud high sound. *...a wind that whistled through the building site.*

whistle-stop If a politician makes a **whistle-stop** tour, he or she travels around calling briefly at several places as part of a political campaign.

whit ❏ A **whit** is a very small amount. Whit is often used with 'not' to emphasize that something is not the case at all. *My strategy hasn't changed one whit.*

❏ **Whit** is the same as Whitsun.

white (whiter, whiteness) ❏ **White** is the colour of snow or milk. *...the whiteness of her teeth.* ◇ Someone who is white belongs to a race of people with pale skins. *...the white community.*

❏ **Whites** are white-coloured clothes worn for playing some sports, for example cricket or tennis. ◇ A **white wedding** is one where the bride wears white and the ceremony takes place in a church.

❏ A **white** Christmas is a Christmas when there is snow on the ground.

❏ **White** coffee or tea is drunk with milk or cream. ◇ **White wine** is a pale yellowish colour. ◇ **White meat** is meat like chicken breast or veal which is pale in colour after it has been cooked. ◇ The **white** of an egg is the transparent liquid surrounding the yolk, which turns white when the egg is cooked.

❏ A **white lie** is a harmless one, told to avoid hurting someone's feelings.

❏ If you say someone raises the **white flag**, you mean they admit they are defeated in an argument or conflict. In a battle, a white flag is displayed as a symbol of surrender or truce.

❑ **white elephant:** see **elephant.** ◇ **white knight:** see **knight.** ◇ **white knuckle:** see **knuckle.**

white-collar workers work in offices rather than doing manual work. See also **blue-collar.**

white goods are large domestic appliances like fridges and cookers.

white-hot If something is **white-hot,** it is extremely hot.

White House The White House is the official home of the US President. **The White House** is often used to mean the President and his staff. *The meeting is being sponsored by the White House.*

white light is colourless light, for example sunlight, containing all the wavelengths of visible light.

white noise is a sound with an equal amount of power at all its frequencies, for example the sound a radio makes when it is not tuned in.

white paper In Britain and some other countries, a **white paper** is an official report setting out the government's proposals on a matter which is to be considered by parliament.

white spirit is a colourless liquid made from petrol. It is used to make paint thinner or to clean surfaces or paintbrushes.

white water is a stretch of water with a broken foamy surface, for example rapids. **White-water** sports take place in or on water like this. *...white-water rafting.*

whitebait are very small young herrings or sprats, usually eaten fried.

Whitehall is a street in an area of London where there are many government offices. **Whitehall** is often used to talk about the Civil Service, or about the Government itself. *There is little enthusiasm in Whitehall for such wholesale reform.*

whiten (whitening, whitened) If something **whitens** or is **whitened,** it becomes whiter or paler.

whitewash (whitewashes, whitewashing, whitewashed) ❑ You say there is a **whitewash** when the full facts about something unpleasant are kept from the public and it is made to look as if things are not as bad as they really are. You can talk about something unpleasant being **whitewashed.** ❑ In a game or contest, if a team or player suffers a **whitewash,** they are thoroughly beaten and do not even manage to score. ❑ **Whitewash** is a mixture of water and lime or chalk, formerly used for painting walls white. A **whitewashed** wall has been painted with whitewash.

whither is an old-fashioned word meaning 'to which place'. *...Pakistan, whither many Meerut Muslims emigrated during and after partition in 1947.*

whiting (plural: whiting) **Whiting** are a kind of sea fish related to cod.

Whitsun is the seventh Sunday after Easter, and the week following it.

whittle (whittling, whittled) If something is **whittled down** or **whittled away,** it is slowly made smaller or less effective.

whizz (or **whiz**) (whizzes, whizzing, whizzed) If someone or something **whizzes** somewhere, they move there very quickly. ◇ If you are a **whizz** at something, you are very good at it. *...a whizz hairdresser.*

whizz-kid (or **whiz-kid** or **whizzkid**) A **whizz-kid** is someone who is outstandingly successful in their career at an early age.

WHO See **World Health Organization.**

who ❑ You use **who** to ask about someone's name or identity, or to mention a question of this kind. *Who is to blame for all this?... He asked her who she lived with.* You use **who** in various other ways to talk about someone's identity. *We know who he is.*
❑ You use **who** to say which person or people you are talking about, or to give more information about them. *She is waiting to join her family who have all emigrated to Canada.*

who's is short for 'who is' or 'who has'. See also **whose.**

whodunit (or **whodunnit**) A **whodunit** is a detective book, film, or play, usually about a murder.

whoever You use **whoever** to talk about any person or every person of a particular kind. *He can talk to whoever he wants.* **Whosoever** is sometimes used instead of 'whoever' *They can share the contract with whosoever they choose.* ◇ You also use **whoever** to talk about someone whose identity is not known. *Whoever did this will sooner or later be caught and will be punished.* ◇ You also use **whoever** to show that the actual identity of the person who does something will not affect a situation. *Whoever takes over the leadership will have little room for manoeuvre.*

whole (wholeness) ❑ You use **whole** to talk about all of something. *The whole ship started to shake violently... The whole of his working life was spent in government service.* ◇ If you talk about something **as a whole,** you are talking about all of it, rather than just a part of it. *In rural India as a whole, 80% of women are illiterate.*
❑ If several things together form a **whole,** they form one recognizable unit. *The group's various businesses do not yet form a coherent whole.* You talk about the **wholeness** of something when all its parts or elements seem to belong together. *...the wholeness of human experience.*
❑ **Whole** is also used to mean 'in one piece'. *The government decided that a key part of the new body should be transferred into the agency whole and not split up.*
❑ You say **on the whole** to show that what you are saying is true in general, but not in every detail. *We know that women are on the whole having their children much later.*
❑ You use **whole** to emphasize the variety or completeness of something. *A whole range of social activities is coordinated by the trust.*

whole-hearted See **wholehearted.**

whole number A **whole number** is a number such as 1, 7, or 24, rather than a fraction.

wholefood Wholefoods are foods which have been refined as little as possible, do not contain additives, and are eaten in their natural state.

wholehearted (wholeheartedly) (or whole-hearted, wholeheartedly) If you support something or agree to something in a **wholehearted** way, you do it enthusiastically and completely. *A poll showed that 87 per cent of the population agree with him wholeheartedly.*

wholemeal flour or bread is made from the complete grains of the wheat plant, including the husks.

wholesale (wholesaling, wholesaler) ❑ **Wholesale** is buying goods cheaply in large quantities and then selling them again, especially to shops. This is called **wholesaling;** a person or company that does it is called a **wholesaler**. *We buy fruit and vegetables wholesale.*

❑ **Wholesale** is also used to talk about something undesirable or unpleasant which is done or happens to an excessive extent. *...a wholesale collapse among small independent travel companies.*

wholesome (wholesomeness) You say something is **wholesome** when it is free of any kind of immorality. *...good wholesome entertainment.* Similarly, you can say a person is **wholesome** or talk about them leading a **wholesome** life. *...his all-American wholesomeness.* ◇ **Wholesome** food is good for you.

wholly means 'completely'. *Official procedures for dealing with asylum-seekers are still wholly inadequate.*

whom ❑ You use **whom** to ask about someone's name or identity, or to mention a question of this kind. *Whom do we blame?... They were asked whom they fear more, the drugs police or the thugs from the cartels.*

❑ You use **whom** to say which person or people you are talking about, or to give more information about them. *...a baby sister whom they all adored.*

whomever You use **whomever** to talk about any person or every person of a particular kind. *They insist that they have the right to appoint whomever they chose to be part of that delegation.*

whomsoever means the same as 'whomever'.

whoop (whooping, whooped) If you **whoop** or let out a **whoop**, you shout loudly in a happy or excited way.

whooping cough is a serious infectious disease which makes people cough and produce a loud noise when they breathe in. Whooping cough mostly affects children.

whoosh (whooshes, whooshing, whooshed) If something **whooshes** somewhere, it moves there quickly with a hissing or rushing sound. You call a noise like this a **whoosh**.

whopping (whopper) If you say something is **whopping** or a **whopper**, you mean it is unusually large. *...a whopping new tax... Deauville's beach is a whopper.* ◇ If someone tells a **whopper**, they tell a lie.

whore (*pron:* **hore**) A **whore** is a prostitute. ◇ A woman is sometimes called a **whore** when people think her sexual behaviour is immoral.

whorehouse A **whorehouse** is a brothel.

whose ❑ You use **whose** to say something belongs or relates to the person or thing you have just mentioned. *...a scientist whose judgment is well respected in diplomatic circles.* You also use **whose** to ask who something belongs or relates to. *Whose fault is it?* You use **whose** in various other ways to talk about something belonging or relating to someone. *It's not known on whose initiative this meeting was called.*

❑ See also **who's**.

whosoever See **whoever**.

why ❑ You use **why** to ask about the reason for something, or to mention a question of this kind. *Why do so few Britons play tennis?... I asked him why he wrote the book.* You use **why** in various other ways to talk about the reason for something. *That is why unemployment is still high... There seems no reason why the car should not give continued reliable service.*

❑ You say **why not...** when you are making a sugges-

tion. *Why not phase out export subsidies, the single largest distortion in world agricultural trade?*

❑ The **whys and wherefores** are the reasons why certain things happen or are done. *Even successful bosses need to be queried about the whys and wherefores of their actions.*

WI See **Women's Institute**.

wick The **wick** of a candle is the piece of string down its centre, which burns when it is lit. ◇ The **wick** of a paraffin lamp or cigarette lighter is the part which supplies the fuel to the flame when it is lit.

wicked (wickedness, wickedly) ❑ You say someone is **wicked** when they deliberately cause great suffering. You also say their actions are **wicked**. *...a crime of staggering wickedness.*

❑ **Wicked** is also used to describe things which are amusing in a rather cruel way. *...a wickedly funny novel.*

wicker or **wickerwork** objects are made from interwoven twigs or cane.

wicket In cricket, the **wicket** is one of the two sets of three upright wooden stumps with two bails on top, which the ball is bowled at. The area between the wickets is also called the **wicket**. ◇ When a batsman is given out, you say the bowler has taken his or her **wicket**.

wicketkeeper In cricket, the **wicketkeeper** is the player who stands behind the wicket to stop balls that the batsman misses and to catch some balls that the batsman hits.

wide (wider, widest; widely) ❑ If something is **wide**, it measures a large distance from one side to the other. *...a wide avenue.* ◇ **Wide** is also used when mentioning the width of something. *...8in-wide wheels... The tunnel is twenty metres wide.*

❑ If you open or spread something **wide**, you open or spread it as far as it will go. ◇ If your eyes are **wide** or **wide open**, they are more open than usual, because you are surprised or frightened.

❑ A **wide** variety, range, or selection of things is more extensive than usual. *The proposed changes would grant the President wider powers to rule by decree.*

❑ **Wide** is used to describe something which is believed, felt, or known about by many people. *The case has attracted wide publicity... ...widely-held fears.* ◇ **Wide** is also used to describe things which are located or available throughout a large area. *His work is now widely available in translation.* ◇ **-wide** is added to words to describe things which happen or exist throughout the whole of an area. *...a nation-wide strike... ...a world-wide ban on ivory.* ◇ **far and wide**: see **far**.

❑ A **wide** gap or difference is a large one. *Storage conditions can vary widely.*

❑ The **wider** aspects of something are the more general ones. *The arrests are part of a wider political power struggle being played out in Cambodia.*

❑ If something like a shot goes **wide**, it misses the desired point or mark. ◇ **wide of the mark**: see **mark**.

wide-angle A **wide-angle** lens is a camera lens which allows you to photograph a wider view than a normal lens.

wide-eyed If someone is **wide-eyed**, their eyes are wider open than usual. ◇ You also say someone is **wide-eyed** when they are innocent and inexperienced.

wide-ranging If something is **wide-ranging**, it includes or deals with a great variety of different things. ...*wide ranging economic and agricultural reforms.*

widen (widening, widened) If something **widens** or is widened, it gets wider. ...*the widening gap between rich and poor.* ◇ You also say something **widens** when it becomes greater in range, size, or variety, or affects a larger number of people or things. *The scope of the investigation continues to widen.*

widescreen is a type of film projection in which the picture is much wider than usual in proportion to its height. ...*widescreen versions of classic epics.*

widespread If something is **widespread**, it exists or happens over a large area or to a very great extent. ...*evidence of widespread fraud.*

widget People call a small device a **widget** when its real name is not known or has been forgotten. ◇ A **widget** is also a plastic disc in a can of beer used to make the beer taste like draught beer. 'Widget' is a trademark.

widow (widower, widowed) A **widow** is a woman whose husband has died and who has not remarried. A **widower** is a man whose wife has died and who has not remarried. A **widowed** person is someone whose husband or wife has died.

widowhood is the state of being a widow. The period of time when a woman is a widow can be called her **widowhood.**

width The **width** of something is the distance from one side to the other. ◇ If someone swims a **width** in a swimming pool, they swim from one side to the other.

wield If someone **wields** power or influence, they have it and are able to use it. ◇ If you **wield** something like a weapon or tool, you carry it or use it.

wife (wives; wifely) A man's **wife** is the woman he is married to. **Wifely** is used to talk about things to do with a woman's relationship with her husband. ...*wifely devotion.*

wig A **wig** is a false head of hair worn to cover someone's own hair, to hide baldness, or as part of the uniform of someone like a judge.

wiggle (wiggling, wiggled) If you **wiggle** something or make it **wiggle**, you make it move around with small quick movements. Movements like these are called **wiggles.**

wigwam A **wigwam** is a traditional dwelling of many Native Americans, consisting of bark, rushes, or animal skins spread over or enclosed by an arched or dome-shaped framework of poles.

wild (wildness, wildly) ❑ **Wild** animals and birds live in natural surroundings and are not kept as pets or as farm animals. ...*wild geese.* You say animals and birds like these live **in the wild.** ◇ **Wild** plants grow naturally and are not specially grown as crops.

❑ **Wild** land is natural and not cultivated. ...*the wildness of Utah.* ◇ Remote areas, far away from towns, are sometimes called **the wilds.** ...*the wilds of Canada.*

❑ **Wild** is used to describe the weather or the sea when it is very stormy. ...*a wild October night.*

❑ **Wild** behaviour is excited and uncontrolled. *The crowd went wild with anger... He swung his boot wildly at the ball.* ◇ If people **run wild,** they behave in an uncontrolled, often violent way.

❑ If you say someone's hair is **wild,** you mean it is long

and untidy.

❑ If you say a remark or statement is **wild,** you mean it is not based on reliable information or sound reasoning. *Rumours about payments are wildly exaggerated.* Similarly, you can say a guess or prediction is **wild.** ◇ If you say something is **beyond your wildest dreams,** you mean it is better than you had ever hoped for or believed possible.

❑ If things vary **wildly,** they are very different from each other. ...*two wildly different taxes.*

wild card In a sports contest, a **wild card** is a player or team allowed to take part although they have not qualified. ◇ A **wild card** is also an unpredictable person, organization, or situation.

wild-goose chase If you are sent on a **wild-goose chase,** you waste a lot of time searching for something which does not exist or which you have no chance of finding.

Wild West The **Wild West** was the western part of the US during the time when it was first settled by Europeans. Films and stories about this period are mainly about cowboys, American Indians, gunfights, and law-breaking.

wildcat (wildcatter) ❑ The **wildcat** is a type of cat which lives in mountains and forests and looks like a larger version of the domestic cat.

❑ **Wildcat** is used to talk about industrial action, especially strikes, arranged spontaneously and without the official approval of the union. ...*wildcat strikers... ...wildcat roadblocks.* ◇ **Wildcat** is also used to talk about mining or drilling for oil or gas in an area where there are no known reserves. People who do this are called **wildcatters.**

wildebeest (*plural:* wildebeest) (*pron:* wil-dee-beest) A **wildebeest** is the same as a gnu.

wilderness (wildernesses) A **wilderness** is an area of uncultivated natural land. ◇ If a politician spends some time **in the wilderness,** he or she is not in an influential position in politics for that time.

wildfire If something spreads like **wildfire,** it spreads very quickly.

wildfowl are birds like wild duck, pheasants, and quails which are hunted and shot.

wildlife Wild animals and plants are sometimes called **wildlife.**

wiles If you talk about someone's **wiles,** you mean the tricks they play to persuade people to do something.

wilful (wilfully, wilfulness) (*American spelling:* **willful** etc) **Wilful** is used to describe bad or harmful actions which are done deliberately. *Both countries are now wilfully antagonizing former Arab friends.* ◇ A **wilful** person is obstinate and determined to get what they want. You talk about the **wilfulness** of someone like this.

will ❑ If you say something **will** happen, you mean it is going to happen. ◇ If you say you **will** do something, you mean you intend to do it.

❑ You also use **will** to say you are assuming something is true. *Those of us who have observed his dedicated hours of training will know the man is a phenomenon.*

❑ You use **will** to say you are willing to do something. *We will accept personal or company cheques.* ◇ You also use **will** when you are asking someone to do something. *Will you marry me?*

❑ **Will** is the determination to do something. *He accused them of lacking the political will to overcome their differences.*

-willed is used to describe the extent of someone's determination. You say, for example, someone is **strong-willed** or **weak-willed**. When two very determined people are in conflict, you say there is a **battle of wills**.

❏ If something is the **will** of a person or group, they want it to happen. *I have to bow to the will of the people.* ◇ If you can do something **at will**, you can do it whenever you want to. ◇ If something is done **against your will**, it is done although you do not want it.

❏ If you do something **with a will**, you do it with a lot of enthusiasm and energy.

❏ If you **will** something to happen, you try to make it happen using mental effort. *I was amazed to find myself willing him to win.*

❏ A **will** is a legal document saying what you want to happen to your money and property when you die.

will-power See willpower.

willing (willingness, willingly) If you are **willing** to do something, you will do it if someone wants you to. *...a willingness to cooperate.* ◇ **Willing** and **willingly** are used to say someone does something eagerly and with enthusiasm, rather than because they are made to do it. *Most employees have gone east willingly.*

willow The **willow** is a tree with long thin branches and narrow leaves which often grows near water. Its wood is used for making baskets and cricket bats.

willowy A **willowy** person is tall and thin.

willpower (*or* **will-power**) is very strong determination to do something.

willy-nilly If something happens to you **willy-nilly**, it happens whether you like it or not.

wilt If a plant **wilts**, it gradually bends downwards and becomes weak, because it needs more water or is dying. ◇ If you **wilt**, you become weak or tired or lose confidence.

wily (wilier, wiliest) A **wily** person is clever and cunning.

wimp (wimpish, wimpishness) If you call someone a **wimp**, you mean they are feeble and timid. You can also say they are **wimpish** or talk about their **wimpishness**.

WIMP In computing, WIMP is used to talk about a user-friendly interface or screen display. WIMP stands for 'windows, icons, mouse (or menus), pointer'.

wimple A **wimple** is a cloth worn over a woman's hair and round her neck and chin, so only her face is showing. Wimples were worn in medieval times and are still worn by some nuns today.

win (winning, won) ❏ If you **win** a game or competition, you defeat the person or people you are competing against. You can also **win** an argument or a bet. Similarly, an army can **win** a battle, and a country can **win** a war. ◇ **win the day**: see day. ◇ A **win** is a victory in a game or competition.

❏ If you **win out** in a contest, you are the one who eventually wins. Similarly, you can say something like a course of action **wins out** when it is eventually chosen in preference to others.

❏ If you say you **can't win**, you mean you are bound to fail or suffer in some way whatever you do. *We can't win – people complained about how we used to farm the land; now they complain when we don't farm it.*

❏ If you **win** something like a medal or a prize, you are presented with it, because you are one of the most suc-

cessful people in a competition or in some other activity. *...an award-winning novelist.* You can also say an achievement **wins** you a medal or a prize. *His side's flying start won him the Manager of the Month award.* ◇ If you **win** praise for something you do, people praise you for it.

❏ If you **win** something you want, you succeed in getting it. *...the Roman Catholic Church's efforts to win converts in Africa.*

❏ If you **win** someone **over** or **win** them **round**, you persuade them to support you or agree with you.

wince (wincing, winced) If you **wince** or give a **wince**, the muscles in your face tighten suddenly, because you are in pain or have experienced something unpleasant or embarrassing.

winch (winches, winching, winched) A **winch** is a machine for lifting heavy objects. It consists of a cylinder which a rope or chain is wound around. If you **winch** an object or person somewhere, you lift them using a winch.

wind ❏ A **wind** is a current of air moving across the earth's surface.

❏ If you **get wind** of something, you get to hear about it. ◇ If something **takes the wind out of your sails**, it makes you much less confident in what you are doing or saying. ◇ If you say someone is **sailing close to the wind**, you mean they are taking a risk by doing or saying something which is only just legal or acceptable.

❏ If you say the **wind of change** is blowing through a place, you mean there are signs that very important political or social changes are beginning to take place.

❏ If you are **winded** by something like a punch, air is suddenly knocked out of your lungs and you have difficulty breathing. ◇ If you get a **second wind**, you get more energy to continue doing something after being tired or out of breath.

❏ **Wind** instruments are instruments you play using your breath, for example woodwind instruments like the flute and oboe or brass instruments like the trumpet and trombone. The wind instruments in an orchestra are sometimes called the **wind section** or just the **wind**.

❏ If a road or river **winds** somewhere, it has many bends or twists. (*When you use 'wind' like this, it rhymes with 'mind'. If you are talking about the past, you say 'wound' not 'wounded'.*) *The road inland wound along the Prabang river.* Similarly, you can talk about a line of people **winding** somewhere. *...the procession of floats winding its way through the crowded streets.*

❏ If you **wind up** a mechanical device, for example a watch or a clock, you turn a knob or key several times to make it operate. ◇ If you **wind down** a car window, you open it by turning a handle. If you **wind it up**, you close it.

❏ When a business is **wound up** or **wound down**, it stops trading and is closed down. ◇ If an activity is **wound down**, the amount of work done is gradually reduced until it stops completely.

❏ If you **wind up** in a certain place or situation, you find yourself in it, although you may not have expected it or intended it.

❏ If you are **wound up** about something, you are very tense or excited about it. ◇ If you **wind down**, you relax.

wind-assisted In athletics, if a runner's time or a jumper's distance is **wind-assisted**, the wind behind them is greater than a certain speed, and the time or distance does not count for record purposes.

wind farm A wind farm is a large group of wind-driven generators for supplying electricity.

wind tunnel A wind tunnel is a passage designed so air can be made to flow through it at controlled speeds. Wind tunnels are used to test equipment and machinery, especially cars and planes.

windbreak A windbreak is a barrier such as a line of trees or a fence which gives protection against the wind.

windcheater A windcheater is a warm jacket, usually with a close-fitting knitted neck, cuffs, and waistband. 'Windcheater' is a trademark.

windfall A windfall is a large sum of money you receive unexpectedly. ◇ Windfall profits are unexpectedly large.

windlass (windlasses) A windlass is the same as a winch.

windmill A windmill is machine for grinding grain or pumping water. It is driven by vanes or sails turned by the wind. ◇ tilt at windmills: see tilt.

window ❏ A window is a space with glass in it in a wall or roof or in the side of a vehicle. ◇ A shop window is a large glass window along the front of a shop, for displaying goods for sale. ◇ If you go window shopping, you spend time looking at goods in shop windows without intending to buy anything.
❏ In computing, a window is an area of the VDU display which can be manipulated separately from the rest of the area. Several windows can be displayed at the same time.

window box A window box is a long narrow container on a window sill for growing plants in.

window-dressing (window-dresser) Window-dressing is arranging goods attractively in a shop window. Someone who does this as their job is called a window-dresser. ◇ In other contexts, if you say an action is window-dressing, you mean it is done to create a good impression and to hide the real situation.

window frame A window frame is the frame round the edge of a window, which the glass is fixed into.

window pane A window pane is a piece of glass in a window.

windowsill A windowsill is a ledge along the bottom of a window, either inside or outside.

windpipe Your windpipe or trachea is the tube which carries air into your lungs when you breathe.

windscreen The windscreen of a car or other vehicle is the window at the front which the driver looks through.

windscreen wiper Windscreen wipers are electrically operated blades with rubber edges which wipe rain from a windscreen.

windshield is the usual American word for a windscreen.

windsock A windsock is a cone of material with the end cut off. It is flown from a mast, especially at an airport, to show the local wind direction.

windsurfing (windsurfer) Windsurfing is the sport of moving along the surface of the sea or a lake standing on a sailboard. A person who does this is called a windsurfer.

windswept A windswept place is exposed to high winds.

windward The windward side of something is the side facing the wind.

windy ❏ If it is windy, the wind is blowing a lot.
❏ Windy speech contains long and important-sounding words chosen to impress people rather than to express things clearly. ...windy phrases.

wine (wining, wined) ❏ Wine is an alcoholic drink made from grapes fermented with water and sugar. ◇ Some other alcoholic drinks have wine as part of their name. They are made in a similar way, but using other fruit or vegetables instead of grapes. ...damson wine.
❏ If someone wines and dines you, they give you a very good meal, usually at an expensive restaurant.

wine bar A wine bar is a place where you can buy and drink wine, and usually also obtain food.

winery (wineries) A winery is a place where wine is made.

wing ❏ The wings of a bird or insect are the parts it uses for flying. ◇ The wings of a plane are the long flat parts at each side which support it in the air. ◇ -winged is used to describe a bird's or plane's wings. ...blue-winged teal... ...the bat-winged American B2 Stealth bomber. ◇ Winged things have wings. ...winged dinosaurs.
❏ If something wings somewhere or wings its way there, it flies there, or goes there quickly as if it was flying.
❏ If you spread your wings, you start doing new activities or expand your activities into new areas. ◇ If someone clips your wings, they restrict your freedom.
❏ A wing of a building is a smaller part which sticks out from the main part or which has been added at a later date.
❏ The wings of a stage are the sides, which cannot be seen from the audience. ◇ If you say someone is waiting in the wings, you mean they are ready to take action if necessary.
❏ A wing of an organization is a group within it which has a particular function or particular beliefs. ...the party's more liberal wing. See also left-wing, right-wing.
❏ The wings of a car are the parts around and above the wheels.

wing commander A wing commander is a middle-ranking officer in the RAF.

winger In sports like football and hockey, a winger is an attacking player who plays mainly on the far left or far right of the pitch.

wingspan The wingspan of a bird, insect, or plane is the distance from the end of one of its wings to the end of the other.

wink ❏ If you wink or give a wink, you close one eye briefly, usually as a signal that something is a joke or a secret.
❏ If a light winks, it shines or reflects in short flashes.

winkle (winkling, winkled) ❏ Winkles are small edible sea snails.
❏ If you winkle information out of someone, you get them to give it to you, although they do not want to. ◇ If you winkle someone out of a place where they are hiding, you make them come out.

winner ❏ The winner of a prize, race, or competition is the person who wins it. ◇ Winner-takes-all is used to talk about a situation where the person who wins gets everything.
❏ In football, the goal which wins the match is often called the winner.
❏ If you say something like a new product is a winner,

you mean it is popular and successful.

winning ❏ See win.

❏ You call money you win in a competition or by gambling your **winnings**.

❏ **Winning** is used to describe actions and qualities which are charming and attractive. ...*her winning ways*.

winnow When people **winnow** grain, they separate the chaff from the rest by blowing a stream of air across it. ◇ If you **winnow out** things which are not needed, you separate them from things which are wanted or important.

wino (*pron:* wine-oh) (winos) A **wino** is a vagrant who is addicted to alcohol, especially wine.

winsome (winsomely) **Winsome** is used to describe people who are attractive and charming. ...*models smiling winsomely*.

winter (wintering, wintered) **Winter** is the season between autumn and spring. In the northern hemisphere, it is between December and March. ◇ If you **winter** somewhere, you spend the winter there.

winter sports are sports which take place on ice or snow, for example skating, skiing, or bobsleigh racing.

wintertime is the period when it is winter.

wintry If something is **wintry**, it has features typical of winter. ...*wintry landscapes*. ◇ If someone's expression or behaviour is **wintry**, they seem cold and unfriendly. *She smiled a characteristic wintry smile.*

wipe (wiping, wiped) ❏ When you **wipe** a surface, you rub it with something like a cloth or your hand to remove dirt or liquid from it. You can also say you **wipe** the dirt or liquid from the surface.

❏ If you **wipe** something like a video or audio tape or a computer disk, you remove the pictures, sounds, or information stored on it.

❏ If an army **wipes out** a place, it destroys it. ◇ You can talk about other things being **wiped out** when they are destroyed or got rid of. *That wiped out any prospect that the airline could pay its way on debts of around $2.8 billion.*

❏ If something **wipes the smile off** someone's face, it spoils their feeling of satisfaction or triumph.

❏ If an amount is **wiped off** the value of something, its value is reduced by that amount. *Billions of pounds were wiped off shares.*

wire (wiring, wired) ❏ **Wire** is metal made in a long very thin flexible strip and used, for example, for carrying electric current or for fastening things. A **wire** is a piece of wire. ◇ If you **wire** something **up**, you connect it to something else with electrical wires so electricity can pass between them. ◇ The **wiring** in a building or electrical appliance is the system of wires which carry electricity through it.

❏ In the US, a **wire** is a telegram. If you **wire** someone, you send them a telegram.

wire netting is a wide mesh made from wire, often used in fences.

wire service In the US, a **wire service** is the same as a news agency.

wire wool is very thin pieces of wire twisted together, often in the form of small pads. Wire wool is used to clean metal objects, especially saucepans and other kitchen equipment.

wireless (wirelesses) **Wireless** is an old word for radio. A

wireless or **wireless set** is a radio.

wiretapping (wiretap) **Wiretapping** is secretly making a connection to someone's telephone line so their conversations can be heard without them knowing about it. The connection is called a **wiretap**.

wiring See wire.

wiry A **wiry** person is thin but has strong muscles.

wisdom is having a great understanding of things, usually as a result of long experience, so you can make sensible decisions and judgements and give other people good advice. ◇ If you talk about the **wisdom** of an action or decision, you are talking about how sensible it is. *It was a tactic of dubious wisdom.* ◇ The **wisdom** of a group of people on a matter is their general opinion about it.

wisdom tooth A person's **wisdom teeth** are the four teeth at the back of their mouth, which usually grow much later than the rest. Some people do not have any wisdom teeth.

wise (wiser, wisest; wisely) ❏ **Wise** people are able to use their experience and knowledge to make sensible decisions and judgements. ◇ If you say a decision or action is **wise**, you mean it shows good sense. *Americans have wisely never looked to government to solve all their problems at a stroke.*

❏ If you **get wise** to something, you find out about it. ◇ If you say something was done and nobody was **any the wiser**, you mean nobody found out about it. ◇ If you say you are **none the wiser** after someone has explained something to you, you mean you do not understand it any better than you did before.

-wise is added to another word to indicate what aspect of something you are talking about. *At the top end of the market car-wise, Americans aspire not to Lincolns or Cadillacs but to the Lexus, made by Toyota.*

wisecrack (wisecracking) A **wisecrack** is a clever remark which is intended to be amusing, but is often rather unkind. A **wisecracking** person often makes remarks like this.

wish (wishes, wishing, wished) ❏ A **wish** is a desire for something. *A good journalist has the wish, if not the ability, to present both sides of an argument.* ◇ If you **wish** to do something, you want to do it.

❏ If you say you **wish** something would happen, you mean you want it to happen, and you are often expressing impatience or annoyance that it has not happened already. *I wish he'd stop throwing these rumours about.* ◇ If you say you **wish** something was true, you mean you would like it to be true, although you know it is impossible or unlikely.

❏ If you make a **wish**, you express a desire for something, usually silently as part of a custom or ritual.

❏ If you say you **wish** someone luck, you mean you hope they will be lucky in something new they are starting to do. Similarly, you can **wish** someone happiness or success. You can also offer someone your good **wishes**. ◇ If you say you **would not wish** something on someone, you mean it is so unpleasant you would not want that person to have to experience it or deal with it.

wishful If you say a hope or desire is **wishful thinking**, you mean it is unlikely to be fulfilled.

wishy-washy If you call someone's ideas **wishy-washy**, you mean they are vague and not at all clear. You can also call a person with ideas like these **wishy-washy**.

wisp (wispy) A **wisp** of hair is a thin untidy strand of it. If someone's hair is **wispy**, it grows in strands like this. ◇ A **wisp** of something like smoke or fog is a long thin amount of it.

wisteria is a climbing garden plant with clusters of mauve or white flowers.

wistful (wistfully, wistfulness) If you are **wistful**, you are sad because you want something which you cannot have. ...*a wistful glance... The campaigners hark back wistfully to the turn of the century.*

wit is the ability to talk or write using words or ideas in a clever and amusing way. A **wit** is someone who has this ability.
  ❏ If you talk about a person's **wits**, you mean their ability to think quickly in a difficult situation. *By now I had recovered my wits.* ◇ If you **have** your **wits about** you, you are alert and ready to act if a problem or danger arises.
  ❏ If something frightens you **out of your wits**, it frightens you very much indeed. ◇ If you are **at your wits' end**, you have so many problems or difficulties you do not know what to do next.

witch (witches) A **witch** is a person, usually a woman, who is believed to have magic powers.

witch-doctor A **witch-doctor** is a person in some societies, especially in Africa, who is thought to have magic powers and is believed to use them to heal people or sometimes to harm them.

witch hazel is a winter-flowering garden shrub. Its leaves and bark are sometimes used to make a liquid, also called **witch hazel**, which is put onto sore or bruised skin to heal it.

witch-hunt A **witch-hunt** is a determined attempt to find and punish people whose opinions or actions are considered harmful to society. Often the victims of witch-hunts are innocent people whose views are different from those of the authorities.

witchcraft is the use of magic powers by witches.

with ❏ If one thing or person is **with** another, they are together in the same place. If you do something **with** someone else, you do it together. ◇ **With** is used to talk about an arrangement or relationship between people or groups. ...*Egypt's peace treaty with Israel... ...his affair with his secretary.* ◇ **With** is also used to talk about a war, fight, or argument between people or groups. ...*the bitter row with the European Union over farm subsidies.*
  ❏ If you do something **with** a tool or some other object, you use it.
  ❏ **With** is used to mention a feature, characteristic, or possession that someone or something has. ...*a naturalist with a long white beard.* ◇ A person **with** an illness is suffering from it. *He had been in hospital with a liver complaint.*
  ❏ **With** is used to describe the feeling someone has when they do something. *His resignation had been accepted with great regret.* **With** is also used to describe a feeling which makes someone behave in a certain way. *My mum started crying with joy.*
  ❏ **With** is used to say what a statement relates to. *With most modern windows, a top or side opener can be left partially open and then locked.* ◇ **With** is also used to say something happens as a result of something else. *With growth slowing and consumer confidence falling, voters are worried that the*

fragile recovery is giving way to another downturn.

withdraw (withdrawing, withdrew, have withdrawn; withdrawal)
  ❏ If you **withdraw** something, you remove it or take it away. *Romania's provisional government has withdrawn his visa.* When something is removed, you call this its **withdrawal**. ◇ If you **withdraw** money from a bank account, you take it out so you can spend it or use it. The money you take out is called a **withdrawal**.
  ❏ When troops **withdraw** or are **withdrawn**, they leave the place where they have been fighting or where they are based. ...*a call for the withdrawal of Israeli forces from the occupied territories.* ◇ If you **withdraw** somewhere, for example to a quieter room, you go there.
  ❏ If you **withdraw** a remark or statement, you formally say it no longer represents your views and you want it to be disregarded.
  ❏ If you **withdraw** an offer, you say it no longer stands. ◇ If you **withdraw** your support from something, you stop supporting it. *The engineer heading the project confirmed that the company had decided to withdraw funding.*
  ❏ If you **withdraw** from an activity, you stop taking part in it. Similarly, if you **withdraw** from an organization, you stop being a member of it.
  ❏ A **withdrawn** person is quiet and shy.
  ❏ **Withdrawal symptoms** are the unpleasant physical and mental effects people experience when they stop taking a drug they are addicted to.

wither (withering, withered) ❏ If something **withers** or **withers away**, it becomes weaker until it no longer exists or is no longer effective. *If things go badly, support could wither.*
  ❏ If a plant **withers**, it shrinks, dries up, and dies. ◇ If a person's skin **withers**, it becomes wrinkled and dry. Old people are sometimes described as **withered** when their skin has become like this.
  ❏ A **withering** look or remark is intended to make the person it is directed at feel ashamed or stupid.

withhold (withholding, withheld) If you **withhold** something from someone, you do not let them have it.

within ❏ If something is **within** a place, it is inside it. Similarly, you say something is **within** a border or boundary. *Work will be carried out mainly within the present motorway boundaries.* ◇ If something is **within** a certain distance of something, it is less than that distance from it.
  ❏ If something happens **within** a certain length of time, it happens before that length of time has passed. *The policy explicitly stated that claims would be paid within 30 days.*
  ❏ If something happens **within** a society, organization, or system, it happens inside it, or to something which is part of it. *It has already led to angry outbursts from within the ruling Labour Party.*
  ❏ If something is **within** certain limits or restrictions, it does not go beyond them. *The deal was constructed within the confines of American law.*
  ❏ If you talk about an emotion **within** someone, you mean they are experiencing it. *His accomplished prose gave little hint of the turmoil that went on within him.*

without ❏ If you are **without** something, you do not have it. ◇ **do without**: see **do**. ◇ If you do something **without** someone else, you do not have them with you when you do it, or you do not have their help.

❑ If you do something **without** doing something else, you do not do the second thing when you do the first one. Similarly, you can do something **without** being aware of something else. *People sometimes jump to conclusions without knowing all the facts.* ◇ If you do something **without** a particular feeling, you do not have that feeling when you do it. *Young men discussed the assassination without anger.*

withstand (withstanding, withstood) ❑ If you **withstand** something that happens to you, you survive it or do not give in to it. *A woman of iron constitution, she withstood the pressures of the past two years better than her husband.*

❑ If a material can **withstand** certain extreme conditions, it is not harmed by them, or it can prevent other things being harmed by them. *...steel-reinforced concrete to withstand fires and earthquakes.* Similarly, a plant can **withstand** extreme conditions.

witless If you call something like a film or show **witless**, you mean it is very silly.

witness (witnesses, witnessing, witnessed) ❑ If you **witness** something or **are witness to** it, you see it happen. Someone who has seen something happen can be called a **witness**. ◇ A **witness** is also someone who appears in court or at an inquiry to say what they know about a crime or other matter.

❑ A **witness** is also someone who signs their name under your signature to confirm that the signature really is your own. You say this person **witnesses** your signature.

❑ If something **bears witness** to something else, it shows it existed or happened. *The range of portraits bears witness to the great popularity of the genre in 19th-century Russia.*

witness box In a court, the **witness box** or **witness stand** is the place where people stand or sit while they give evidence.

witter (wittering, wittered) If you say someone is **wittering**, you mean they are saying a lot of silly or unimportant things.

witticism A **witticism** is a witty remark.

wittingly If you do something **wittingly**, you are fully aware of what you are doing and what its consequences may be.

witty (wittier, wittiest; wittily) A **witty** remark or piece of writing is amusing in a clever way. *He talked wittily about his experiences.* You say a person is **witty** when they are clever and amusing like this.

wives See **wife**.

wizard In legends and fairy stories, a **wizard** is a man with magical powers. ◇ You can call someone a **wizard** when they are very good at something. *...a keyboard wizard.*

wizardry You can call a very clever piece of work **wizardry**, especially when you do not understand how it is done. *...computer wizardry.*

wizened A **wizened** person is old and has wrinkled skin.

woad was a blue vegetable dye used by the ancient Britons to paint their bodies.

wobble (wobbling, wobbled; wobbly) If something **wobbles** or is **wobbly**, it makes small movements from side to side, because it is loose or unsteady.

wodge A **wodge** of something is a large amount of it or a large piece of it.

woe is great unhappiness or sorrow. You can call someone's problems or misfortunes their **woes**. *To add to the woes of would-be divorcees, they are likely to spend up to £5,000 in legal costs.* ◇ **woe betide**: see **betide**.

woebegone If someone looks or feels **woebegone**, they look or feel very sad.

woeful (woefully) ❑ If someone is **woeful**, they are very sad. You can say a story is **woeful** when it describes sad events.

❑ You also say something is **woeful** when it is very bad. *Despite a constant battle with woefully inadequate funds, the festival has a record of launching new talent and new films.*

wok A **wok** is a large bowl-shaped pan for frying Chinese-style food.

woke (woken) See **wake**.

wolf (wolves) ❑ The **wolf** is a wild animal which looks like a large dog and preys on other animals.

❑ If someone **cries wolf**, they say there is a problem when there is not, with the result that people do not believe them when there really is a problem.

❑ If you **wolf down** food, you eat it very quickly and greedily.

wolf-whistle A **wolf-whistle** is a whistle consisting of a rising note followed by one which rises and falls. If someone **wolf-whistles**, they produce a whistle like this. A man sometimes wolf-whistles at an attractive woman who passes in the street, especially when he is with a group of other men.

wolfhound The **wolfhound** is a type of very large dog used in the past to hunt wolves.

wolves See **wolf**.

woman (women) A **woman** is an adult female human being. ◇ You can talk about women in general as **woman**. *They have rejected the most common image by which woman has been defined over centuries.*

womanhood is women in general. The **womanhood** of a country or community are its women. ◇ **Womanhood** is also the state of being a woman rather than a girl, or the period of a woman's adult life. *They all had begun their womanhood during these years of war.*

womanizer (womanizing) (*or* womaniser, womanising) If a man is a **womanizer**, he likes to flirt with women and often has short sexual relationships with them. This kind of behaviour is called **womanizing**.

womankind is women in general. *Child-care is seen by them as the essential concern of womankind.*

womb (*pron*: woom) A woman's **womb** is the organ inside her body where a baby grows during pregnancy.

wombat The **wombat** is a furry Australian animal with short legs and a pouch for carrying its young. Wombats eat plants.

women See **woman**.

Women's Institute The **Women's Institute** or **WI** is an organization for women. It has many branches, mostly in rural areas. Its members meet for social and cultural activities.

women's liberation or **women's lib** is a name given to the ideal that women should have the same social and economic rights and privileges as men.

women's movement The **women's movement** is a social and political movement which aims to achieve women's liberation by organizing groups and campaigns and by getting individual women and men to change their attitudes.

womenfolk The **womenfolk** of a community are its women.

womenswear is women's clothing.

won See win.

wonder (wondering, wondered) ❑ If you **wonder** about something, you think about it and try to guess or understand more about it. *Allen must now be wondering if things could possibly get worse.*

❑ If you **wonder** at something, you are amazed by it. **Wonder** is a feeling of amazement. *...shaking their heads in wonder.*

❑ If you say something is a **wonder**, you mean it is very surprising. *Six ropes are at full stretch, some under such strain it is a wonder they do not snap.* ◇ **No wonder** is used to say something is not at all surprising. *No wonder the voters are confused.* **Little wonder** and **small wonder** are also used like this. *Small wonder that first-time buyers are now returning: buying a home has rarely been cheaper.*

❑ A **wonder** is something remarkable which people admire. *...the wonders of modern technology.*

❑ If something **works wonders**, it produces amazing results.

wonderful You say an experience is **wonderful** when it makes you very happy and pleased. *It would be wonderful to finish with the gold medal.* ◇ You also use **wonderful** to show your admiration for someone or something. *...his wonderful sense of humour.*

wonderfully is used to emphasize how good something is. *Star of the meal was a wonderfully thick slab of marinated tuna.*

wonderland You can call a place a **wonderland** when it seems very strange or unusually beautiful. *At night, the melted snow and ice gleamed like diamonds, turning the forest around us into a jewelled wonderland.*

wonderment is a feeling of amazement and admiration. *She and her friend stared in wonderment.*

wondrous (wondrously) If you say something is **wondrous**, you mean it is amazing and impressive. *...rolls of silk that seemed wondrously beautiful.*

wonky If something is **wonky**, it is likely to wobble or not work properly, because it is not steady or not firmly in place.

wont (*pronounced the same as 'won't'*) If someone is **wont** to do something, they do it regularly as a habit. *Tolstoy was wont to consider his life a failure.*

woo (woos, wooing, wooed) If someone **woos** you, they try to get you to support them, or to do something for them. *Republicans are concentrating on wooing suburban voters.* ◇ When a man **woos** a woman, he tries to persuade her to marry him.

wood is the material which forms the trunks and branches of trees and which is used in building and to make furniture and paper.

❑ A **wood** is a large area of trees growing close together. When the area is very large, it is sometimes called the **woods**. *The birds were to be set free in the woods around the royal residence.*

❑ If you say someone is **not out of the woods** yet, you mean they are still involved in a difficult or dangerous situation. ◇ If you say someone **can't see the wood for the trees**, you mean they are so involved in the details of something that they are failing to recognize the importance of the thing as a whole.

❑ If someone talks about getting rid of the **dead wood** in an organization, they mean getting rid of people who have been there a long time but do not really contribute anything useful.

wood pulp is wood which has been reduced to fibres by grinding or a chemical process. It is used to make paper.

woodcock (*plural:* woodcock) The **woodcock** is a small brown bird with a long beak. Woodcock are sometimes shot for sport or food.

woodcut A **woodcut** is a print made by cutting an image into the surface of a block of wood and then dipping the cut surface in ink and pressing it onto paper.

wooded A **wooded** area is covered in trees.

wooden ❑ A **wooden** object is made of wood.

❑ If you say an actor is **wooden**, you mean his or her performance is dull and unconvincing.

wooden spoon A **wooden spoon** is a spoon made from wood, used in cooking. ◇ You say the person or team that finishes last in a race or competition gets **the wooden spoon**.

woodland is land covered with trees.

woodlouse (*plural:* woodlice) The **woodlouse** is a grey oval creature with scales, about the size of an insect. It has fourteen legs and lives in damp places.

woodpecker The **woodpecker** is a bird with a long sharp beak. Woodpeckers hammer with their beaks on tree trunks so they can get at the insects living under the bark.

woodwind In an orchestra, the **woodwind** or **woodwind section** consists of the flutes, oboes, clarinets, and bassoons and any other instruments related to them.

woodwork ❑ The **woodwork** in a building is the doors, skirting boards, window frames, and other parts made of wood. ◇ If you talk about people **crawling out of the woodwork**, you are criticizing them for suddenly appearing in public or revealing their opinions when previously they did not make themselves known.

❑ **Woodwork** is making things out of wood.

woodworm are the larvae of certain type of beetle which make holes in wood by feeding on it. You also call the damage they do **woodworm**.

woody plants have very hard stems.

❑ A **woody** area is covered in trees.

woof (woofing, woofed) When a large dog **woofs**, it barks.

wool is the hair of sheep, goats, and some other animals. The material spun from it is also called **wool**. It is knitted or woven and used to make clothes, blankets, and carpets.

❑ If someone **pulls the wool over your eyes**, they deliberately deceive you.

woollen clothes are made from wool.

woolly (woollies) ❑ A **woolly** garment is made from wool or from a mixture of wool and artificial fibres. ◇ A **woolly** is a woollen garment, especially a jumper.

❑ If you say someone is **woolly** or **woolly-minded**, you mean their ideas are vague or confused. You can also say their ideas are **woolly** or **woolly-minded**.

woozy If you are **woozy**, you feel weak and unsteady and cannot think clearly.

word ❑ A **word** is one of the units a piece of speech or writing is divided into. In English, words are separated by spaces when they are written down.

❑ If you have **a word** or **a few words** with someone, you have a short conversation with them. ◇ A **word** of advice is a short piece of advice. Similarly, a **word** of warning is a brief warning. *Carol Manning has a word of caution: increasing the glucose intake of old people can bring on a form of diabetes.*

❑ If you cannot hear **a word** of what someone is saying, you cannot hear it at all. Similarly, you can talk about not believing or not understanding **a word** of what someone says.

❑ If you get **word** of something happening, you hear news of it. *There has been no word of any renewed fighting.*

❑ If you **give your word**, you make a promise. If you **break your word**, you fail to keep a promise. ◇ If you say someone is **as good as their word**, you mean they do what they have promised to do.

❑ If you **word** something in a particular way, you express it that way. ◇ The **wording** of a piece of writing or a speech is the way it is expressed. *Diplomats have been working into the night on the final wording of the treaty.*

❑ If you repeat something **word for word**, you repeat it exactly as it was said or written, without changing anything. ◇ If you say something **in your own words**, you express it in your own way, without copying or repeating what someone else has said.

❑ You say **in a word** when you are summarizing what you have just been saying. *This vote has made it very clear that the Government is very deeply divided and incurably disabled. In a word, it isn't fit to rule.* ◇ You say **in other words** when you are expressing something in a simpler or clearer way. *These events can be held on up to 28 days a year without planning permission – in other words, every weekend during summer.* ◇ If someone has not said something **in so many words**, they have not said it, but have said other things which amount to the same thing.

❑ If news or information is passed **by word of mouth**, people tell it to each other directly, rather than reading it in the newspapers or hearing it on the radio or TV.

❑ If you **put in a word** for someone, you speak favourably about them to someone who may be able to help them in their career.

❑ If you have the **last word** in an argument, you say something which is so effective that it puts an end to the argument. ◇ You also say someone has the **last word** when they make the final decision about what is to be done. *The government is letting it be known that the Federal Bank doesn't have the last word, and that no final government decisions have yet been made.*

❑ A **war of words** is a fierce and bitter debate between two people or groups.

❑ If you **take someone at their word**, you accept what they say literally.

❑ A person **of few words** says very little.

❑ If you say someone has had to **eat their words**, you mean they have had to admit they were wrong about something they said earlier.

❑ If you say something is the **last word** in something like comfort or luxury, you mean it is the most comfortable or luxurious thing of its kind.

❑ If you want to emphasize for example, that someone is very stupid or stubborn, you can say they are too stupid

for words or too stubborn for words.

word-blindness is another name for dyslexia.

word-perfect If you are **word-perfect**, you are able to repeat from memory the exact words of something you have learned.

word processor (word processing) A **word processor** is a small computer which has a keyboard and a VDU. It is used as a typewriter to produce documents, letters, and other printed material. This kind of work is called **word processing**.

wording See word.

wordless is used to describe events which take place without any words being spoken. *...a simple and wordless ceremony.*

wordy If you say a piece of writing is **wordy**, you mean there are too many words in it, especially long ones.

wore See wear.

work ❑ If you **work**, you have a job which you are paid to do. ◇ If you have **work** or are **in work**, you have a job, rather than being unemployed. If you are **out of work**, you are unemployed.

❑ Your **work** is the tasks you do as part of your job. *Irresponsible action would only make the work of the police more difficult.* ◇ If you **work hard**, you put a lot of effort into your work. ◇ If you **work your way** to a higher position in an organization, you reach it gradually as a result of your efforts.

❑ **Work** is also something produced as a result of people's work or as a result of research. *...a skilful piece of work... This brought together previous work done by United States and Canadian army research agencies.*

❑ If you **get to work** on something, you start doing it. Similarly, you can **go to work** or **set to work** on something. ◇ If you are busy doing something, you can say you are **at work** doing it. *The BBC drama department is at work on several novel adaptations.*

❑ If you **work your way** through a piece of writing, you read it slowly and with difficulty.

❑ If you **put** someone or something **to work** or **set** them **to work**, you give them a job or task to do.

❑ If a machine or piece of equipment **works**, it is able to do what it is supposed to. *The lift doesn't work.* ◇ **in working order**: see order. ◇ If you **work** a machine or piece of equipment, you operate it.

❑ If part of a machine **works** itself into a particular position, it gradually moves into that position. Similarly, part of a machine can **work loose** or **work free**.

❑ If an idea, method, or system **works**, it is successful. Similarly, if a drug or medicine **works**, it produces the effect you want.

❑ You say something is **at work** when it is having an influence on the way people behave. *There is a kind of inverted snobbery at work here.* ◇ If something **works** in your favour, it helps you in some way. Similarly, if something **works** against you, it causes you problems.

❑ If you talk about the way a situation will **work out**, you are talking about its outcome. *Privately Japanese officials say they've no idea how the talks will work out.*

❑ If the cost of something **works out** at a particular amount, it comes to that amount.

❑ If you **work out** how to do something, you find a way of doing it. ◇ If you **work out** the solution to a problem, you solve it.

❏ If you **work on** an assumption or idea, you make decisions based on it.

❏ A writer's **works** are the books, poems, or plays he or she has written. Similarly, you can talk about an artist's or composer's **works**.

❏ If you **work** yourself **into** a state, you gradually get into that state. *...oratory in which he works himself up into a passion.* ◇ If you are **worked up** about something, you are upset or angry about it.

❏ If you **work up** something such as enthusiasm or an appetite, you gradually acquire it. ◇ If you **work off** a feeling, you get rid of it by doing something energetic or violent.

❏ If you **work out**, you do physical exercises to make your body fit and strong. A session like this is called a **workout**.

❏ A factory is often called a **works**. *...a cement works.* ◇ **Works** are activities such as digging or building on a large scale, especially to install pipes or wires, or to construct roads, bridges, or buildings.

❏ See also **worker, working**.

work of art (works of art) A **work of art** is a painting, drawing, or sculpture of high quality. ◇ High-quality novels, plays, and pieces of music can also be called **works of art**. ◇ You can say anything is a **work of art** when it is made or done with unusual skill. *Michael's riding over the final three fences was a work of art.*

work-shy If someone is **work-shy**, they are lazy and do not want to work.

work surface A **work surface** is a flat surface over a low cupboard or kitchen appliance which is easily cleaned and which you can prepare food on.

work-to-rule See **rule**.

workable If you say something like a plan is **workable**, you mean it can be put into operation.

workaday things are ordinary and not especially interesting or unusual.

workaholic A **workaholic** is someone who finds it difficult to stop working.

workbench (workbenches) A **workbench** is a heavy wooden table which you make or repair things on.

worker The **workers** in an industry or business are the ordinary employees, as distinct from the employers or managers. ◇ **Worker** is sometimes used to say what kind of work someone does. *...a railway worker.* ◇ You can also use **worker** to say how well or badly someone works. *...a hard worker.*

workforce A company or organization's **workforce** is all the people it employs. ◇ The **workforce** of a country or region is all the people who are physically able to work and are available to do a job.

workhorse You call someone a **workhorse** when they do a large amount of dull or routine work. Similarly, a much-used machine or vehicle can be called a **workhorse**. *...airlines flying the 737, the workhorse of most short-haul airlines.*

workhouse In the past, a **workhouse** was a place where very poor homeless people did unpleasant jobs in return for food and shelter.

working people have jobs which they are paid to do. *...working mothers.* ◇ Your **working life** is the period of your life when you have a job, or are available to do a job.

❏ **Working** is used to talk about the period people spend working each day or each week. *...flexible working hours... Germans have the shortest working week of the big economies.* ◇ **Working** is also used to talk about the conditions people work in. *...a strike in support of better working conditions.*

❏ A **working** lunch or dinner is arranged so people can discuss work matters informally over a meal.

❏ If you have a **working** knowledge of something like a foreign language, you have a reasonable knowledge of it and can use it effectively.

❏ A **working** relationship is a good relationship you have with someone at work. You can also have a **working** relationship with someone you have to meet and deal with regularly.

❏ If a government has a **working** majority in parliament, its majority is large enough for it to be able to carry out most of the measures it wants to.

❏ The **workings** of a piece of equipment, an organization, or a system are the ways in which it operates. *He has a wide knowledge of the workings of Whitehall.*

working capital A company's **working capital** is the money it has available for use immediately, rather than money invested in property or equipment.

working class (working classes) The **working class** or **working classes** are the people in a society who do not own much property and whose work involves physical and practical skills, rather than intellectual ones.

working party A **working party** is a group of people set up to look into a matter and to produce a report about what should be done.

workload Your **workload** is the amount of work you have to do.

workman (workmen) A **workman** is a man whose job involves working with his hands, for example building houses or plumbing.

workmanlike is used to describe something which is done skilfully and efficiently. *...a workmanlike performance.*

workmanship If you talk about the **workmanship** of something, you mean the skill with which it has been made or done. *In my opinion there is no other designer in the world whose standard of workmanship is as high.*

workmate Your **workmates** are people you work with and get on well with.

workout See **work**.

workplace Your **workplace** is the place where you work.

workshop ❏ A **workshop** is a room or building containing tools or machinery for making or repairing things.

❏ A **workshop** is also a period of discussion or practical work on a subject, in which a group of people learn about the subject by sharing their knowledge or experience. *...one-day workshops on vital business skills.*

workstation A **workstation** is a computer, including a keyboard and VDU, connected to a network of other computers, printers, and faxes. Workstations are used especially in offices.

world ❏ The **world** is the planet we live on. ◇ Other planets are sometimes called **worlds**. *We haven't yet come across life from other worlds.*

❑ **The world over** means throughout the world. *Astronomers the world over have been waiting for the Hubble Space Telescope for years.* ◇ **The world** is used to talk about people throughout the world, especially people who have power. *The world has chosen not to intervene to help the Kurds.* ◇ **World** is used to describe people and things that are among the best or most important in the world. *Rapid industrialisation had transformed a backward peasant society into a world power.*

❑ Some groups of countries are called a particular **world**, for example the 'Arab world' or the 'western world'. See also **Third World**. ◇ A period in history can also be called a **world**, for example the 'ancient world' or the 'modern world'.

❑ A group of living things is often called a **world**, for example the 'animal world', the 'plant world', or the 'insect world'.

❑ A **world** is also a field of activity and the people involved in it. *...the world of high finance.*

❑ A person's **world** is their way of life, the things they are involved in, and their relationships with other people. *Anthony Howard knew Crossman and his world intimately.* ◇ If you say someone is **in a world of their own**, you mean they seem not to notice other people or the things going on around them.

❑ When a baby is born, you can say its mother **brings it into the world.** You can also say the doctor or midwife **brings it into the world.** ◇ Religious people often use **this world** to talk about the state of being alive. They also talk about the **next world**, meaning a state of existence after death.

❑ If you call someone a **man of the world** or a **woman of the world,** you mean they know a lot about the immoral and dishonest things people get up to, and are not easily shocked.

❑ If you say someone has **the best of both worlds**, you mean they have all the benefits from two different situations without the disadvantages of either.

❑ If you **think the world of** someone or something, you admire them or care about them very much.

❑ If you say there is a **world of difference** between two things or people, you mean the difference between them is very great. ◇ You can also say two very different things or people are **worlds apart.**

❑ If someone does something **for all the world** as if a particular thing was true, they do it as if that thing were true, although it is not.

world-class A **world-class** sports player or musician is one of the best in the world.

world-famous If someone or something is **world-famous**, people know about them all over the world.

World Health Organization The **World Health Organization** or **WHO** is an international agency which is part of the United Nations. It is concerned with improving health standards and services throughout the world.

World Series In the US, the **World Series** is the annual series of games between the winners of the two major baseball leagues. It is held to decide which team is the overall champion.

world war A **world war** is a war involving countries from many parts of the world.

world-weary (world-weariness) A **world-weary** person no

longer feels excited or enthusiastic about anything. You talk about the **world-weariness** of someone like this.

worldly is used to talk about the ordinary things of life, especially things like possessions, rather than spiritual things. *...all his worldly goods... Whatever spiritual depths the novel may have, it has brought its creator worldly rewards beyond reckoning.* ◇ A **worldly** person is concerned with practical things, such as making money, rather than spiritual things.

worldly-wise If you say someone is **worldly-wise**, you mean they are experienced and knowledgeable about life, and are not easily shocked or impressed by anything.

worldwide means throughout the world. *There are now a billion speakers of English worldwide.*

worm ❑ **Worms** or **earthworms** are creatures which look like very small snakes and live in the soil. ◇ If an animal or person has **worms**, tiny worm-like creatures are living as parasites in their intestines.

❑ When a normally timid person stands up to someone who has been bullying them, you can say the **worm has turned.**

❑ If you call a situation a **can of worms**, you mean it is complicated, difficult, or unpleasant, and might be better left alone.

❑ If someone **worms their way** into a position of power or influence, they get there using patience and cunning.

worm-eaten If something is **worm-eaten**, it has been damaged by insects eating holes in it.

wormwood is a bitter-tasting plant used to make alcoholic drinks.

worn See **wear**.

worn-out things are too old or damaged to be used any more. ◇ If you are **worn-out**, you are very tired and feel no enthusiasm for anything. ◇ You can also use **worn-out** to describe ideas or attitudes which are out-of-date or which you have heard too many times before. *He said it was time to set aside worn-out arguments about sanctions.*

worried (worrier) See **worry**.

worrisome If you say something is **worrisome**, you mean it serious and people should be worried about it.

worry (worries, worrying, worried; worrier) ❑ If you **worry**, you keep thinking about a problem or about something unpleasant which might happen. You say you are **worried** about something like this; the feeling you have is called **worry**. *Worry over this new coalition is visible in both Labour and Liberal ranks.* Someone who worries a lot is called a **worrier**.

❑ If something **worries** you, it makes you worry. You say something like this is **worrying**. *The report goes on to provide worrying evidence of the speed and spread of the decline.* Things which make you worry are called **worries**.

worse ❑ If something is **worse** than something else, it is more unpleasant or undesirable or of poorer quality. *The unemployment figures were far worse than anyone expected... Even worse material is often dished up for TV series.* You can also say something is **worse** than it was before. *Shortages are worse than ever.* ◇ If a situation changes **for the worse**, it gets worse, rather than improving. ◇ If someone who is ill gets **worse**, they become more ill.

❑ If you are **worse off** as a result of something, you are in a worse situation than you were before. *55% of those questioned thought Britain would be worse off without the monarchy.*

❏ If someone is **the worse for** something like drink, their behaviour is badly affected by it. ◇ If someone is **none the worse for** something, they are not harmed by it.

worsen (worsening, worsened) If something **worsens** or is **worsened**, it becomes more difficult, unpleasant, or unacceptable. *Any reduction in meat supplies will worsen already desperate shortages... ...the worsening condition of school buildings.*

worship (worshipping, worshipped; worshipper) (*American spelling:* worshiping, worshiped, *etc*) ❏ When people **worship**, they show their respect, admiration, and love for a god or goddess, for example by saying prayers. Their behaviour is called **worship**. People who are worshipping, for example in a church or mosque, are called **worshippers**.

❏ If you **worship** a person, you love and admire them very much.

❏ Certain people in positions of authority can be addressed as **Your Worship**, for example mayors or magistrates.

worst ❏ The **worst** of several things is the one or ones which are most unpleasant, most undesirable, or of poorest quality. *...the worst railway line in Britain... ...one of the worst financial results in the industry's history.* ◇ **Worst-ever** is used to say something is worse than anything of its kind that has happened before. *...the country's worst ever floods.*

❏ If you say something is true or possible **at worst**, you mean it is true or possible when you consider a situation in the most unfavourable or pessimistic way. *At worst, the whole country could fall under the control of organised crime.* ◇ If you talk about what would happen **if the worst comes to the worst**, you are talking about things developing in the most unfavourable way possible.

worst-case The **worst-case** situation or scenario is the most unfavourable one of a number of possible outcomes to a situation.

worsted (*pron:* wuss-tid) is a type of woollen cloth used to make jackets, trousers, and skirts.

worth ❏ If something is **worth** a certain amount of money, it can be sold for that amount. *He has a mortgage of £60,000 on a house now worth only £50,000.* ◇ **Worth** is used to describe an amount of something in terms of how much it costs. *The tank holds barely a pound's worth of unleaded fuel.* Similarly, **worth** is used to describe damage in terms of the cost of putting it right. *The invasion resulted in two billion dollars' worth of damage to the country's economy.*

❏ **Worth** is also used to say how long something will last. For example, a week's **worth** of food will last you for a week. *That should provide at least a year's worth of vital spare parts for the military.*

❏ A person's **worth** is their value, usefulness, or importance. *She will have proved her worth both to her employer and her clients.*

❏ If you say something you have achieved was **worth** the trouble, you mean the results are good enough to justify the trouble you have taken. Similarly, you can say something is **worth** the money you have paid for it. *The prices are high but worth it for cooking of quite exceptional quality.* ◇ If it is **worth your while** to do something, it is to your advantage to do it.

❏ If you do something **for all you are worth** or **for all it is worth,** you do it as much as possible and for as long as you can get any benefit from it.

❏ You say **for what it's worth** when you are not sure that what you are saying is particularly valuable or helpful. *My guess, for what it's worth, is that it will go to a third ballot.*

worthless If something is **worthless**, it is of no real use or value.

worthwhile If you say something is **worthwhile**, you mean it is useful or helpful, and worth the time, money, or effort spent on it.

worthy (worthiness; worthies) ❏ If you say someone or something is **worthy** of respect, support, or admiration, you mean they deserve it because of their qualities or abilities. A **worthy** person or thing deserves respect, support, or admiration. *An eminent scientist looks at the work and assesses its worthiness in the light of his own skill and knowledge.*

❏ The important people in a place or organization are sometimes humorously called its **worthies.** *...the worthies of the London wine trade.*

would ❏ You use **would** when you are talking about the past and mentioning what someone said or believed was going to happen. *We had assumed that it would be a big helicopter.* ◇ You also use **would** when you are talking about the past and saying what used to happen. *We would talk a lot. I would suggest ideas, and many of them got into the film.*

❏ You use **would** not when you are saying someone was unwilling to do something, or refused to do it. *Scotland Yard would give no further details of the enquiries.*

❏ You use **would have** when you are talking about something which did not happen in the past, but which might have happened if things had turned out differently. *The eastern economy would have been characterised by high levels of employment at low wages, which would have risen in line with productivity.*

❏ You use **would** when you are talking about the result or effect of a possible situation. *Should he lose, it would take the edge off his Olympic achievement.*

❏ If you say someone **would** do something, especially something bad or foolish, you mean it is typical of them. *Of course, they would say that, wouldn't they?*

❏ **would like:** see like. ◇ **would you like...:** see like. ◇ **would rather:** see rather.

would-be is used to talk about what someone wants to do or become. For example, if you are a **would-be** artist, you want to become an artist.

wound (wounded) ❏ A **wound** is an injury to part of your body, especially a cut or hole caused by a weapon or sharp instrument. If someone has an injury like this, especially a fairly serious one, you say they are **wounded**. In a battle, the people who have been injured are called **the wounded.** ◇ If someone **wounds** you, they injure you using a gun, knife, or other sharp weapon.

❏ If you are **wounded** by what someone says or does, you are hurt and upset by it.

❏ See also **wind**.

wove (woven) See **weave**.

wow If you say something **wows** people, you mean it thrills or impresses them. *Olga wowed the world with her back somersault on the beam.*

WPC is used in front of the name of a female police officer of the lowest rank. WPC stands for 'woman police constable'.

wpm stands for 'words per minute'. It is used to talk about how fast someone can type or take shorthand. ...*a typing speed of 50wpm.*

wracked See **rack**.

wraith A **wraith** is a ghost.

wrangle (wrangling, wrangled) When people **wrangle**, they argue about something in a noisy or angry way. An argument like this is called a **wrangle**.

wrap (wrapping, wrapped) ❑ If you **wrap** an object or **wrap** it **up**, you fold paper or cloth tightly round it to cover it completely. You also say you **wrap** the paper or cloth round the object. ◇ If you **wrap** your arms or fingers around something, you put them tightly around it.
    ❑ If you **wrap up**, you put warm clothes on.
    ❑ If you are **wrapped up** in something, you are giving it a lot of attention.
    ❑ If you **wrap up** something like a job or an agreement, you complete it in a satisfactory way.
    ❑ If something like a plan is **kept under wraps**, it is kept secret until a suitable time for making it public.

wrapper A **wrapper** is a piece of foil, plastic, or paper used to cover or protect something. ...*sweet wrappers.*

wrapping is paper or plastic for covering or protecting something.

wrapping paper is special paper with a decorative design on it, for wrapping presents.

wrath is anger. *He has incurred the wrath of the accountancy profession.*

wreak (wreaking, wreaked *or* wrought) If something **wreaks** changes, it causes them. ...*the changes wrought by German unification.* Similarly, if something **wreaks** havoc or damage, it causes it. ◇ If someone **wreaks** vengeance on someone who has harmed them, they harm them in return.

wreath A **wreath** is a circle of flowers and leaves put on a grave or memorial as a sign of remembrance for the dead.

wreathe (wreathing, wreathed) If something is **wreathed** in mist or smoke, it is surrounded by it. ◇ If something is **wreathed** with flowers or leaves, it has a chain or circle of them around it. ◇ If someone is **wreathed in smiles**, they are smiling a lot.

wreck ❑ If something like a building is **wrecked**, it is very badly damaged.
    ❑ If a ship is **wrecked**, it sinks in a storm or as a result of damage, or is driven onto rocks where it breaks up. The remains of the ship are called a **wreck**. ◇ The remains of a plane, car, or other badly damaged vehicle can also be called a **wreck**.
    ❑ If you call a person a **wreck**, you mean they are in a very poor state mentally and physically.
    ❑ If something **wrecks** an organization or system, it destroys it completely. *Incompetence and corruption wrecked the fragile economy.*

wreckage The **wreckage** of a car, plane, or building is what remains of it after it has been badly damaged or destroyed.

wrecker A **wrecker** is someone who destroys or spoils something.

wren ❑ A **wren** is a very small brown songbird.
    ❑ Members of the former WRNS were often called **Wrens**.

wrench (wrenches, wrenching, wrenched) ❑ If you **wrench** something away from a place, you pull or twist it away violently. ◇ If you **wrench** a limb, a muscle, or one of your joints, you twist it and injure it.
    ❑ If you say leaving someone or something is a **wrench**, you mean it is difficult and you feel very sad about it. You can say something is **wrenching** when it makes you feel sad. ...*a wrenching tale.* ◇ **Wrenching** changes are very severe and can cause difficulty and hardship.
    ❑ A **wrench** is an adjustable metal tool for tightening or loosening a nut. ◇ In the US, a spanner is called a **wrench**.

wrest If you **wrest** something from someone who is holding it, you take it away from them by pulling hard at it or twisting it. ◇ If someone **wrests** power or control from someone else, they succeed in taking it from them.

wrestle (wrestling, wrestled; wrestler) ❑ If you **wrestle** someone or **wrestle** with them, you fight them by forcing them into painful positions or throwing them to the ground, rather than by hitting them. People who do this as a sport are called **wrestlers**; the sport is called **wrestling**.
    ❑ If you **wrestle** with a large or awkwardly-shaped object, you try to control it or arrange it in a particular way.
    ❑ If you **wrestle** with a problem or a difficult situation, you try to resolve it.

wretch (wretches) People sometimes call an unfortunate person a **wretch**. *Many of the wretches released from detention camps have nowhere to go.* ◇ A wicked person is also sometimes called a **wretch**.

wretched (wretchedly, wretchedness) ❑ You use **wretched** to talk about people you feel sorry for, because they have suffered unpleasant experiences or are in an unpleasant situation. *The country's 37 million people are wretchedly poor.* You can also call someone's situation **wretched**. *Workers cannot be enticed to the mines because living conditions are so wretched... ...the wretchedness of most people's lives.*
    ❑ You can also call a person **wretched** when you dislike them or are angry with them. *We are the victims of the short-sighted Philistines who run this wretched government.*

wriggle (wriggling, wriggled) ❑ If you **wriggle** a part of your body, you twist and turn it with quick movements.
    ❑ If you **wriggle out of** something you do not want to do, you manage to avoid doing it.

wring (wringing, wrung *not* 'wringed') ❑ If you **wring** a wet cloth or **wring it out**, you squeeze the water out of it by twisting it tightly. ◇ When someone **wrings** a bird's neck, they kill it by twisting its neck.
    ❑ If you **wring** something **out of** someone, you get them to give it to you when they do not want to.
    ❑ If you say someone is **wringing their hands**, you mean they are complaining bitterly about something which has happened to them.

wringer If someone is put **through the wringer**, they have to undergo a difficult stressful experience.

wrinkle (wrinkling, wrinkled) **Wrinkles** are lines which appear on your face as you get older. When someone's face has lines like these, you say their skin is **wrinkled**. ◇ If you **wrinkle** your nose, you tighten the muscles so that the skin folds. Similarly, you can **wrinkle** your forehead. ◇ If something **wrinkles** or is **wrinkled**, little folds or lines appear in it.

wrinkly (wrinklies) If something is **wrinkly**, it has uneven folds or lines in it. ◇ A **wrinkly** person has wrinkles as a result of getting older. Old people are sometimes humorously called **wrinklies**.

wrist A person's **wrist** is the part of their arm between their hand and their forearm.

wristwatch (wristwatches) A **wristwatch** is a watch with a strap which you wear round your wrist.

writ ❏ A **writ** is a legal document ordering a person to do something or not to do something.
❏ If you say something is something else **writ large**, you mean it is a larger or exaggerated version of the same thing. *The nation is often described by Lady Thatcher as a household writ large.* ◇ You also say something is **writ large** when it is very obvious. *The legacy of their past incompetence is writ large on their balance sheets.*

write (writing, wrote, have written) ❏ When you **write** something, you use a pen or pencil to produce words, letters, or numbers on a surface. ◇ If you **write** something **down**, you make a record of it by writing it somewhere. ◇ A **written** agreement, statement, rule, or law has been officially written down. *...written confirmation... They also want a written constitution and a Bill of Rights.*
❏ If you **write up** something like notes, you re-write them in a neat and complete form. ◇ If you **write out** a list, you write all the items on a piece of paper.
❏ If you **write** something like a book, poem, or piece of music, you create it on paper. When someone writes books, stories, or articles for a living, you can say they **write**. *He also had time to write for Granta.*
❏ If you **write** to someone, you write a letter and send it to them.
❏ If you **write** something like a cheque, receipt, or prescription or **write** it **out**, you put all the necessary information on it and sign it.
❏ A **written** test or piece of work involves writing rather than doing an experiment or giving spoken answers.
❏ The **written word** is written or printed language in contrast to speech.
❏ If a rule or condition is **written into** a contract or agreement, it is officially included when the contract or agreement is made.
❏ If you **write off** an amount of money you have lost, you accept that you will never get it back. When a bank or company does this, you call it a **write-off**. ◇ If you **write off** a plan or project, you accept that it will not be successful and you do not proceed any further with it. ◇ If you **write** a person **off**, you decide they are unimportant or cannot succeed at something. *Eighteen months ago the sixty-year-old Rhinelander had been written off as a failure.*
❏ If a company's assets are **written down**, their official value in the accounts is changed, because they are now worth less than they were originally valued at. A revalua-

tion like this is called a **write-down**.
❏ If a character is **written out** of a TV drama series, something like their death is included in the script, and they no longer appear in the series.
❏ See also **writing**.

write-down See **write**.

write-off If a vehicle involved in an accident is a **write-off**, it is so badly damaged it is not worth repairing. ◇ See also **write**.

write-up ❏ A **write-up** is an article in a newspaper or magazine in which someone describes something like a play, a new product, or a restaurant and says how good or bad they think it is.

writer A **writer** is someone who writes stories, books, or articles as their job. ◇ The **writer** of a piece of writing is the person who wrote it. *The writer of these words was a 13th-century friar.*

writer's cramp is an uncomfortable stiff feeling in your hand which you can get when you have been writing continuously for a long time.

writhe (writhing, writhed) If someone **writhes**, they twist and turn their body violently, usually because they are in great pain.

writing ❏ Anything written or printed can be called **writing**. *References are always taken up, normally in writing.* ◇ A person's handwriting is often called their **writing**.
❏ If you talk about the **writing** in a piece of written work, you mean the author's style. *Some passages go on too long, but the writing is always intriguing.* ◇ An author's **writings** are all the things they have written.

writing desk A **writing desk** is a piece of furniture with drawers and a surface you can rest your paper on while writing.

writing paper is good quality smooth paper for writing letters.

written See **write**.

WRNS The WRNS was the women's branch of the Royal Navy. It was disbanded in November 1993, the women becoming regular members of the Royal Navy. WRNS stood for 'Women's Royal Naval Service'.

wrong (wrongly) ❏ If you say there is something **wrong** with the thing you are talking about, you mean it is unsatisfactory in some way. *There was something wrong with the way the government made decisions.*
❏ If something like a measurement or answer is **wrong**, it is incorrect.
❏ If you are **wrong** about something, what you say or think is not correct. *Companies are not taking action to protect their workers because they believe, often wrongly, that it will cost too much.* ◇ If you **go wrong** or **get** something **wrong**, you make a mistake. *Where Sweden went wrong was in pushing unemployment below this rate.* ◇ If you choose the **wrong** thing or person, you make a mistake and do not choose the thing or person you really want or need. *Buying the wrong type of software can often turn out to be a costly error.*
❏ If something **goes wrong**, it stops working or is no longer successful. *Instead of pulling out when things went wrong, the bank increased its exposure in a vain effort to win the money back.*
❏ If you say an action is **wrong**, you mean it is bad or immoral. ◇ If someone is **in the wrong**, what they are

doing is not fair or just. ◇ **right and wrong: see right.**

❑ If someone **wrongs** you, they treat you in an unfair or unjust way. A **wrong** is an unjust action or situation.

wrong-foot (wrong-footing, wrong-footed) If you **wrong-foot** your opponent in a game like tennis, you throw them off-balance by playing your shot in an unexpected way. ◇ In other situations, if something **wrong-foots** someone, it catches them by surprise and puts them in an embarrassing or difficult position.

wrong-headed If you call an action or decision **wrong-headed**, you mean it is mistaken and based on bad judgement.

wrongdoer A **wrongdoer** is someone who does something illegal or immoral.

wrongdoing is illegal or immoral behaviour.

wrongful (wrongfully) **Wrongful** actions are immoral, il-legal, or unfair. *The companies are accused of wrongfully compensating privileged clients for losses they sustained in share dealing.*

wrote See write.

wrought ❑ See wreak.

❑ **Wrought** metal has been made into a particular shape, usually a decorative one. *...wrought gold.* ◇ **Wrought iron** is the purest from of iron available commercially. It is often formed into decorative shapes and used to make things like gates and railings.

wrung See wring.

wry (wryly) If someone has a **wry** expression, their face shows they find a bad or difficult situation slightly amusing. *James Dean's face is on each frame, smiling wryly.* ◇ A **wry** remark or piece of writing deals with a bad or difficult situation in an amusing or ironic way.

XYZ xyz

x In a mathematical equation, **x** is used to represent any number, or a number that is to be calculated. *Find a value of x that satisfies the equation 4 = 2x.* **y** is used to represent another number in the same equation. ◇ In conversation and writing, you use X and Y to talk about people or things, without saying which ones. *There is only X amount of leisure money for people to spend... The Treasury merely supplies the information that minister X needs to attack minister Y.*

X chromosome An **X chromosome** is one of an identical pair of chromosomes found in a woman's cells, or one of a non-identical pair found in a man's cells. X chromosomes are associated with female characteristics. See also **Y chromosome**.

X-rated (X-rating) If you describe a film, play, or book as **X-rated** or say it deserves an **X-rating**, you mean it involves a lot of sex or violence.

X-ray (X-raying, X-rayed) **X-rays** are a type of radiation which can pass through most solid materials. X-rays are produced by some stars, but can also be artificially produced by machines. ◇ If someone is **X-rayed**, a photograph or image of the inside of part of their body is produced using X-rays. The photograph or image is called an **X-ray**. Doctors use X-rays to check the condition of people's bones or organs. Security officers use them to search people and luggage for things like bombs or drugs.

xenophobia (*pron:* zen-oh-fobe-ee-a) (xenophobic) **Xenophobia** is unreasonable fear and dislike of people from other countries. You say people who have this feeling or attitude are **xenophobic**.

Xmas is a short way of writing 'Christmas'.

xylophone (*pron:* zile-oh-fone) The **xylophone** is a musical instrument consisting of wooden bars of different lengths arranged like a piano keyboard. You play the xylophone by hitting the bars with special hammers.

y See x.

Y chromosome A **Y chromosome** is a single chromosome which exists together with a single X chromosome in a man's cells. The Y chromosome is associated with male characteristics. See also **X chromosome**.

yacht (yachting) A **yacht** is a fairly large boat with sails or a motor, used for pleasure trips. Yachts with sails also take part in races. **Yachting** is going out in a yacht, for sport or pleasure.

yachtsman (yachtsmen) A **yachtsman** is a man who sails a yacht.

yachtswoman (yachtswomen) A **yachtswoman** is a woman who sails a yacht.

yak The **yak** is a type of long-haired long-horned ox found mainly in the mountains of Tibet. Yaks are kept as work animals or to provide meat and milk.

yam **Yams** are tropical root vegetables, similar in appearance and texture to potatoes. ◇ In the US, certain kinds of sweet potatoes are called **yams**.

yank ❑ If you **yank** something, you give it a sudden hard pull. ◇ **Yank** is also used to describe a strong sudden action taken to change a situation. *He yanked his party back from the wilder shores of religious enthusiasm.*

❑ People from the US are sometimes called **Yanks**.

Yankee People from the US are sometimes called **Yankees**. ◇ In the US, people from the southern states call people from the northern states **Yankees**.

yap (yapping, yapped) If a small dog **yaps**, it lets out high-pitched barks.

yard ❑ A **yard** is a flat area of concrete or stone next to a building, often with a wall around it. ◇ In the US, the back garden of a house is often called the **yard**. ◇ A **yard** is also a large area where a particular type of work is done. *...a ship repair yard.*

❑ Length is often expressed in **yards**. A yard is about 91.4 centimetres. There are 36 inches in a yard. 'Yards' is sometimes written 'yds'. *...a 50-yard dash... ...600 yds.*

yardstick If you use someone or something as a **yard-**

stick, you use them as a standard for comparison when judging other people or things.

yarmulke (*pron: yar-mull-ka*) A **yarmulke** is a skullcap worn by male orthodox Jews at all times, and by other male Jews during prayer.

yarn is thread used for knitting or making cloth.
❑ A **yarn** is a story, especially one involving adventure or fantastic events.

yashmak A **yashmak** is a veil some Muslim women wear to cover their faces in public.

yawn ❑ When you **yawn**, you open your mouth wide and breathe in more air than usual. People yawn when they are tired or bored.
❑ A **yawning** gap or opening is large and wide. *...a yawning 15ft wide pit.* ◇ You can emphasize how wide the difference is between two things by saying there is a **yawning gap** between them.

yd (yds) See yard.

ye is an old-fashioned word for 'you' when you are talking to more than one person. *Abandon hope all ye who enter here.* ◇ Ye is sometimes used in names instead of 'The'. This is because the old written form of 'The' looked like 'Ye'. *...Ye Olde King's Head.*

year ❑ A **year** or **calendar year** is a period of 365 or 366 days, beginning on the first day of January and ending on the last day of December. See also **financial year**, **tax year**. ◇ A school **year** is the period of time in each 12 months when schools are open and students are studying there. ◇ A **year** is also any period of twelve months. *It was a year ago today that the former Party leader, Hu Yaobang, died.*
❑ You use **-year-old** to say how old someone or something is. *...her 12-year-old sister.*
❑ If you talk about a person's **years**, you mean their age. *He was moving with surprising speed for a man of his years.*

year-end is used to talk about a situation at the end of a year, especially a financial year. *Year-end profit forecasts stood at £170 million.*

year-round is used to say something happens during all seasons of the year. *The Redstones believe in providing a year-round service... ...year-round all-weather racing.*

yearbook A **yearbook** is a book published once a year containing information on events and achievements connected with an organization or field of interest.

yearling A **yearling** is an animal between one and two years old.

yearly A **yearly** event happens once a year. *...the yearly meeting of SAARC.* ◇ **Yearly** is also used to say how much there is of something each year. *Demand for mineral water in the UK is growing at a yearly rate of 50 per cent.*

yearn (yearning) If you **yearn** for something or have a **yearning** for it, you want it very much.

yeast is a kind of fungus, used to make bread rise and, in alcohol production, to cause fermentation.

yell If you **yell** or let out a **yell**, you shout loudly, because you are excited, angry, or in pain.

yellow is the colour of lemons, butter, and the sun. When something **yellows**, it turns yellow. *...a yellowing photograph... ...yellowed parchment.*

yellow card In football, if the referee shows a player the **yellow card**, he holds up a yellow card and notes the

player's number in his book. If a player is shown the yellow card twice in one match, the referee holds up a red card and sends the player off.

yellow fever is a serious infectious disease transmitted by mosquitoes in tropical countries. Symptoms include fever, vomiting of blood, and jaundice.

Yellow Pages The **Yellow Pages** is a telephone directory in which companies and traders are grouped and listed according to the kind of business they are involved in. 'Yellow Pages' is a trademark.

yellowish If something is **yellowish**, it is slightly yellow.

yelp If a person or animal **yelps** or lets out a **yelp**, they let out a short loud cry, usually of excitement or pain.

yen ❑ The **yen** is the unit of currency in Japan.
❑ If you have a **yen** to do something, you have a strong desire to do it.

yeoman (yeomen; yeomanry) In the past, a **yeoman** was a man who owned a small farm and did not have to work for the local lord, although he had to do military service for him. Yeomen were referred to collectively as the **yeomanry**. The words **Yeoman** and **Yeomanry** are still used in the names of some military groups.

yes is used to give a positive answer to a question, to accept an offer, or to give permission for something.

yes-man (yes-men) If you call someone a **yes-man**, you mean they always agree with people who have authority over them.

yesterday is the day before today. ◇ You can also refer to the past, especially the recent past, as **yesterday**. *Yesterday's bogeymen are today's allies... The record companies are putting more effort into exploiting the tastes of yesterday.*

yesteryear is used to talk about a time in the past when things were different from the way they are now. *The indiscretions being reported today are as nothing to those of the royals of yesteryear.*

yet ❑ If something has not happened **yet**, it has not happened up to the present time. ◇ If something cannot be done **yet**, it must wait until later.
❑ **Yet** is used to say there is still a possibility something will happen. *A negotiated settlement might yet be possible.* ◇ **Yet** and **as yet** are used to say something has not happened so far, but may happen in the future. *Japan has yet to face a real recession... As yet there is no test which enables the virus to be detected.*
❑ **Yet** is used to say how much longer something is expected to continue. *The forecasters say the bad weather will continue for some days yet.*
❑ If something is the best or worst of its kind **yet**, it is the best or worst so far. ◇ **Yet** is used to say something is even bigger, better, worse, etc than before. *They fall in love, making Ross's life yet more complicated.*
❑ **Yet** is used when mentioning something which seems surprising after what has just been said. *How long ago it all seems, yet it was only in the spring.*

yeti The **yeti** is a large hairy ape-like animal which is supposed to live in the Himalayas. Its existence has never been proved. The yeti is also known as the 'Abominable Snowman'.

yew Yews or **yew trees** are coniferous trees with flattened needle-like leaves, fine-grained flexible wood, and cup-like red waxy cones which look like berries.

Yiddish is a language spoken by many Jewish people of

European origin. Yiddish developed mainly from German.

yield ❑ When a tax or investment **yields** an amount of money or profit, it produces it. This amount is called its **yield**.

❑ When a farm **yields** a certain amount of produce, that amount is successfully grown there. You call this the farm's **yield**. Similarly, you can talk about a mine **yielding** minerals. *The pits were no longer yielding enough coal to make mining profitable.*

❑ If something like a discussion, meeting, or investigation **yields** results, it produces them.

❑ If you **yield** to someone or something, you stop resisting them. *He yielded to pressure from some of his colleagues for tougher controls.* ◇ If you **yield** something to someone or **yield** it **up**, you give it to them. *There is little prospect that he will yield up the wanted men.*

❑ If something **yields**, it breaks or moves because of force or pressure on it.

YMCA The YMCA is an organization which encourages young men to adopt Christian moral values. YMCA stands for 'Young Men's Christian Association'. ◇ A YMCA is a hostel for men run by the YMCA.

yo-yo (yo-yos) A **yo-yo** is a toy made of a round piece of wood or plastic attached to a piece of string. You play with the yo-yo by getting it to wind itself up and down on the string.

yob (yobbery; yobbish, yobbishness) A **yob** is a man or youth who behaves in a noisy, aggressive, bad-mannered way. You say someone like this is **yobbish**; you call his behaviour **yobbishness** or **yobbery**.

yodel (yodelling, yodelled; yodeller) (*usual American spelling:* yodeling, yodeled, *etc*) When someone **yodels**, they sing normal notes with brief, much higher notes in between. A person who sings like this is called a **yodeller**.

yoga is a Hindu discipline aimed at training the consciousness for a state of perfect spiritual insight and union with the universal spirit. **Yoga** is also a name given to various types of exercise connected with this discipline. Some exercises involve moving the body into various positions, others concentrate on meditation.

yoghurt (*or* yogurt) is a thick slightly sour liquid food made from milk curdled by bacteria. It is often sweetened and flavoured with things like fruit or chocolate.

yogi A **yogi** is a person who has spent many years practising yoga, and is considered to have reached an advanced state of spiritual awareness.

yogurt See yoghurt.

yoke (yoking, yoked) ❑ A **yoke** is a long piece of wood tied across the necks of two oxen or other draught animals to make them walk close together when they are pulling a plough.

❑ If two things are kept closely linked, you can say they are **yoked** together. *Hong Kong's dollar has been yoked to America's at the rate of 7.8 to 1 since 1983.*

❑ When people are being oppressed by a cruel and unjust system, you can say they are **under the yoke** of that system. *People are still suffering under the yoke of slavery.*

yokel Country people are sometimes called **yokels**, especially by city people who see them as uneducated and simple.

yolk The **yolk** of an egg is the yellow part in the middle.

Yom Kippur or the **Day of Atonement** is the most sacred and important Jewish holy day, regarded as a day for fasting and prayers of repentance. It falls in September or October.

yon is an old-fashioned or dialect word for 'that' or 'those'. *Don't let yon dog nod off.*

yonder is an old-fashioned or dialect word meaning 'that' or 'over there'. *But, soft, what light through yonder window breaks?... Now look yonder, just beyond the wooden post there.*

yore You use **of yore** when you are talking about something which existed a long time ago. *...in days of yore.*

Yorkshire pudding Yorkshire puddings are savoury puddings made by baking a thick mixture of flour, milk, and eggs. They are often eaten with roast beef.

you A speaker or writer uses **you** to refer to the person or people they are speaking to. *I agree with you... Have you just moved in?* ◇ **You** is also used to refer to people in general, rather than to a particular person or group. *Renting gives you flexibility.*

young ❑ A **young** person, animal, or plant has not lived for very long and is not yet mature. ◇ Young people are often called **the young**. ◇ If you talk about a person's **young** days or **younger** days, you mean the time when they were young.

❑ An animal's **young** are its offspring.

youngish A **youngish** person is fairly young.

youngster Children and young people are sometimes called **youngsters**.

your ❑ You use **your** when you are talking about something belonging to or connected with the person or people you are speaking to. *I left your messages on your desk.*

❑ You also use **your** to talk about something relating to people in general, rather than a particular person. *Painkillers are very useful in small amounts to bring your temperature down.* ◇ You also use **your** with words like 'typical' and 'average' to say something is a standard example of its type. *He's your typical Japanese factory-floor company man.*

❑ **Your** is also used when addressing people with certain titles. *...Your Majesty... ...Your Highness.*

yours ❑ You use **yours** when you are talking about something belonging to or connected with the person you are speaking to. *I'll take my coat upstairs. Shall I take yours, Roberta?... I believe Paul was a friend of yours.*

❑ You write **Yours, Yours faithfully**, or **Yours sincerely** at the end of a letter, before you sign your name.

yourself (yourselves) ❑ You use **yourself** or **yourselves** when the action you are describing is done by the person or people you are speaking to and affects only them. *You've cut yourself... Did you set yourself goals?... Look after yourselves.* ◇ You also use **yourself** when talking about people in general, rather than a particular person or group. *You can lose yourself among giant bamboo thickets.*

❑ **Yourself** can be used to emphasize 'you'. *Who will look after you when you yourself are old?*

❑ If you do something **yourself** or **by yourself**, you do it personally or without help from anyone else.

❑ If you are **by yourself**, you are alone.

youth ❑ Your **youth** is the stage of your life before you are a fully mature adult. **Youth** is being at this stage, and therefore lacking experience. *...serving and volleying* *with the true confidence of youth.*

❑ Young men up to the age of about 20 are sometimes called **youths.**

❑ The **youth** of a place are the young people there. You can also talk about the **youth** of a particular time. *...the youth of today.*

youth club A **youth club** is a club where young people can go to meet each other and take part in various leisure activities. Youth clubs are often run by churches or local authorities.

youth hostel A **youth hostel** is a place where people can stay cheaply when they are travelling around, especially when they are walking or cycling in country areas. There are youth hostels in many countries all over the world.

youthful (youthfulness) **Youthful** is used to say someone is young for the kind of work they are doing, or to say someone looks young for their age. *...a woman of youthful appearance... His relative youthfulness clearly appealed.* **Youthful** is also used to describe behaviour which is typical of young people. *...youthful exuberance.*

yuan (*pron:* joo-an) (*plural:* yuan) The **yuan** is the unit of currency in the People's Republic of China.

yucca Yuccas are tropical plants, often with long pointed leaves on thick woody stems and large white flowers.

Yuletide is another name for Christmas.

yuppie A yuppie is a young person in a professional job with a high income who enjoys a fashionable and expensive lifestyle. Yuppie is short for 'young upwardly-mobile professional'.

YWCA The YWCA is an organization which encourages young women to adopt Christian moral values. YWCA stands for 'Young Women's Christian Association'. ◇ A YWCA is a hostel for women run by the YWCA.

zany (zanier, zaniest; zaniness) If you call someone or something zany, you mean they are amusingly strange or eccentric. *...the zany humour of Rowan Atkinson and Rik Mayall... ...his zaniest project yet... ...the zaniness of Barcelona's turn-of-the-century architecture.*

zap (zapping, zapped) If someone zaps a person or thing, they shoot them or fire something at them, usually a laser or some other electronic device.

zeal is great enthusiasm, especially in connection with work, religion, or politics. *Why this sudden outbreak of reforming zeal?... He brings to his task an almost missionary zeal.*

zealot (*pron:* zel-lot) (zealotry) A zealot is a single-minded fanatical supporter of a religion or political cause. You talk about the zealotry of someone like this.

zealous (*pron:* zel-luss) (zealously) If someone is zealous, they are fanatically keen and enthusiastic about something. *...a zealous Communist... ...over-zealous policing... Traditions are zealously upheld.*

zebra The zebra is a type of African wild horse with dark and whitish stripes on its head and body.

zebra crossing A zebra crossing is a place where the road is marked with black and white stripes. Vehicles must stop at zebra crossings to let people cross the road.

Zeitgeist (*pron:* zite-guyst) The Zeitgeist is the general spirit of a period of history, as represented by people's ideas and beliefs. *Swept along by the Zeitgeist of the 1980s, Berry ended up well out of his depth.*

Zen or **Zen Buddhism** is a Japanese form of Buddhism which concentrates on enlightenment through meditation rather than through studying religious writings.

zenith The zenith of something is the time when it is most successful or powerful. *His career is now at its zenith... The organisation reached its zenith in 1974.*

zephyr A zephyr is a gentle wind.

zeppelin Zeppelins were German airships used for passenger transport between 1910 and 1937 and for bombing during the First World War.

zero is the number 0. ◇ Zero is also 0°C, freezing point on the centigrade scale. *...sub-zero temperatures.* See also **absolute zero.**

❑ You can use **zero** to say there is none of something. *We can effectively regard the risk as zero... ...zero inflation.*

zest (zestful) ❑ Zest is keen enthusiasm and enjoyment. *He has a zest for life... He'd been working with tremendous zest.* Something which shows enthusiasm and enjoyment like this can be called **zestful.** *...this zestful new production of Les Fourberies De Scapin.*

❑ The **zest** of a lemon, orange, or lime is its peel when it is grated and used to give flavour to things like cakes or drinks.

zigzag (zigzagging, zigzagged) (*or* zig-zag, *etc*) A zigzag is a line with a series of angles in it, like a continuous series of 'W's. You say a line like this zigzags. *...studded leather straps zigzagging up the leg.* ◇ If someone or something zigzags, they move in a zigzag course. *Warren ran away from his attacker, zig-zagging to avoid being shot again.* ◇ You also say people zigzag when they keep contradicting themselves or changing their mind. *He distanced himself from the president's zigzagging.*

zillion When people talk about a zillion people or things, they mean a very large number of them.

zimmer A zimmer or zimmer frame is a portable metal frame for old or ill people to lean on when they are walking.

zinc is a bluish-white metal used in several alloys, especially brass and nickel-silver. It is also used in galvanising metals, die-casting, and battery electrodes.

zing If there is a zing about something, it is lively and exciting. *There is a special zing about the Olympics... His batting has lost its zing.*

Zionism (Zionist) Zionism is a movement which was originally concerned with establishing a political and religious state in Palestine for Jewish people, and is now concerned with the development of Israel. A Zionist is someone who is involved with or supports Zionism.

zip (zipping, zipped) ❑ A zip is a device used to open and close things like parts of clothes and bags. It consists of two rows of metal or plastic teeth which separate or fasten together as you pull a small tag along them. ◇ If you zip something or zip it up, you fasten it using its zip.

❑ If you **zip** somewhere, you go there very quickly. *The helicopter can zip along at about 150 kilometres an hour.* ◇ Zip is also used to say something happens or is done very quickly. *She zips through her repertoire... Half an hour zips by before you know it.*

❑ **Zip** is excitement, energy, and liveliness. *Showbiz stories add a little zip to a biography.*

zip code In the US, postcodes are called **zip codes.**

zipper In the US, zips are called **zippers**.

zither The **zither** is a musical instrument which consists of two sets of strings stretched over a flat box. You hold the zither flat on your lap and pluck the strings using your finger tips or a plectrum.

zloty (*plural:* zloty *or* zlotys) The **zloty** is the unit of currency in Poland.

zodiac The **zodiac** is a diagram used by astrologers to represent the positions of the planets and the stars. It is divided into 12 sections, each with a name and symbol, for example Cancer the crab and Leo the lion.

zombie In horror films, a **zombie** is a dead body which has been brought back to life.

zonal When an area is divided into zones, **zonal** is used to talk about people or things connected with a particular zone. ...*zonal commissioners*... *Hong Kong have taken a one-nil lead over Thailand in their Davis Cup zonal final.*

zone A **zone** is an area with special features and often distinct boundaries. *A large civilian population is still trapped in the war zone*... ...*the new eastern seaboard industrial zone*. See also **time zone**.

zoo A **zoo** is a park where live animals are kept in cages and enclosures so people can look at them. Zoos also help to preserve rare species.

zoology (zoological, zoologist) **Zoology** is the scientific study of animals. **Zoological** is used to talk about things to do with this subject. ...*zoological research*... ...*the Zoological Society of London*. A **zoologist** is an expert in zoology.

zoom (zooming, zoomed) ❑ If you **zoom** somewhere, you go there very quickly. ◇ If you **zoom** through something, you deal with it very quickly. *My aim was to write something that you could zoom through, rapidly turning the pages.*

❑ A **zoom** or **zoom lens** is a lens you attach to a camera, allowing you to make the image larger or smaller while keeping it in focus. ◇ If a camera **zooms** in on something, it gives a close-up of it.

zucchini (*plural:* zucchini) In the US, courgettes are called **zucchini**.